Col

LON

ESSENTIAL STREETFINDER

Contents

Key to map pages 2-3

Key to map symbols 4-5

Central London maps 6-37

Main London maps 38-207

Theatres and cinemas map 208

Shopping map 209

Heathrow map 210-211

Index to street names, place names,
and places of interest 212-376

Published by Collins
An imprint of HarperCollins Publishers
77-85 Fulham Palace Road, Hammersmith, London W6 8JB

www.collinsworld.com

Mapping generated from Collins Bartholomew digital databases

London Underground Map by permission of Transport Trading Limited
Registered User No. 09/1619/P

The grid on this map is the National Grid taken from the Ordnance Survey map with the permission of the Controller of Her Majesty's Stationery Office.

Printed in China by South China Printing Company Ltd.

Paperback ISBN 978 0 00 731787 5 XM12489
Spiral ISBN 978 0 00 731788 2 XM12490

Imp 001 NDN

e-mail: roadcheck@harpercollins.co.uk

Key to map pages

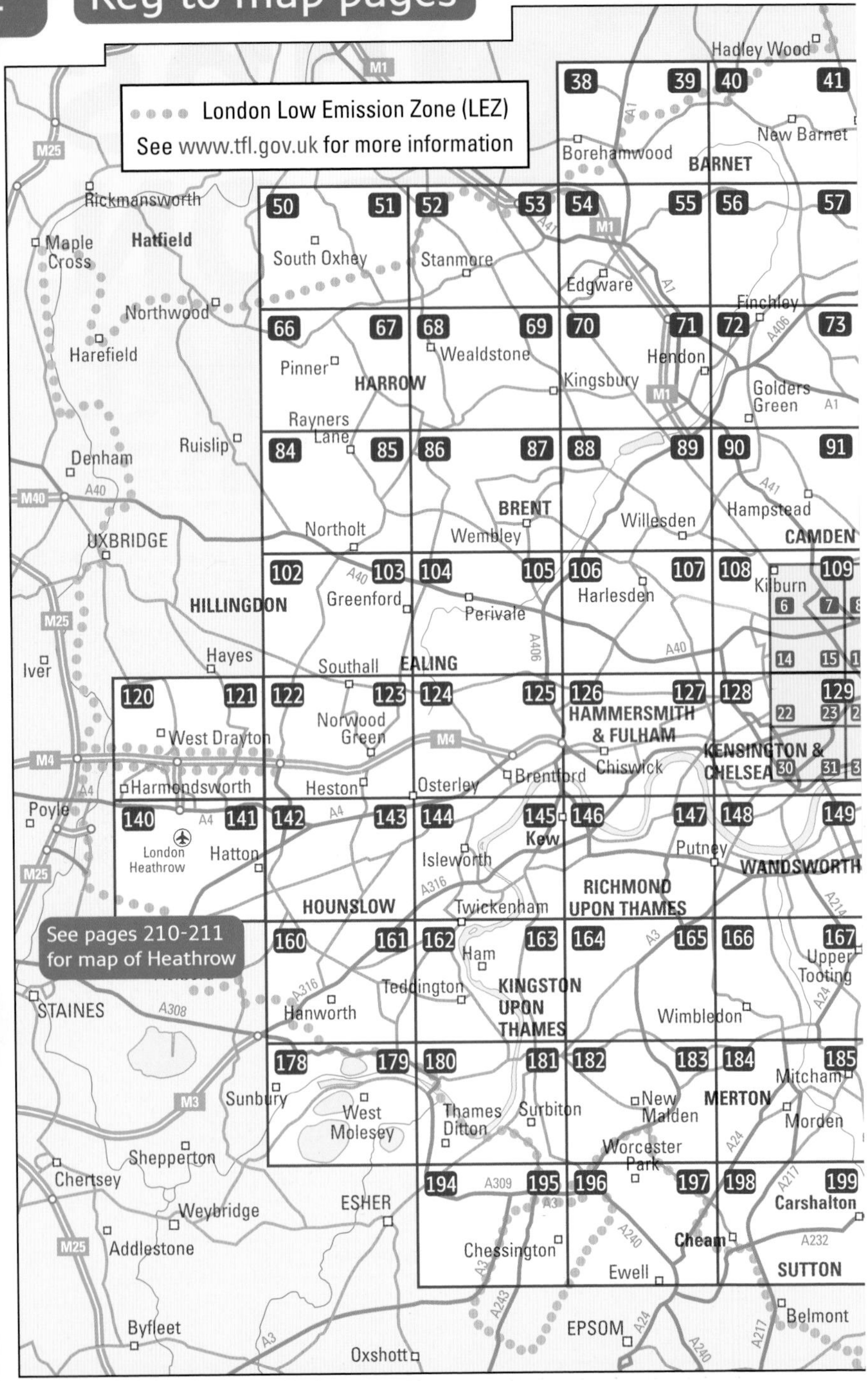

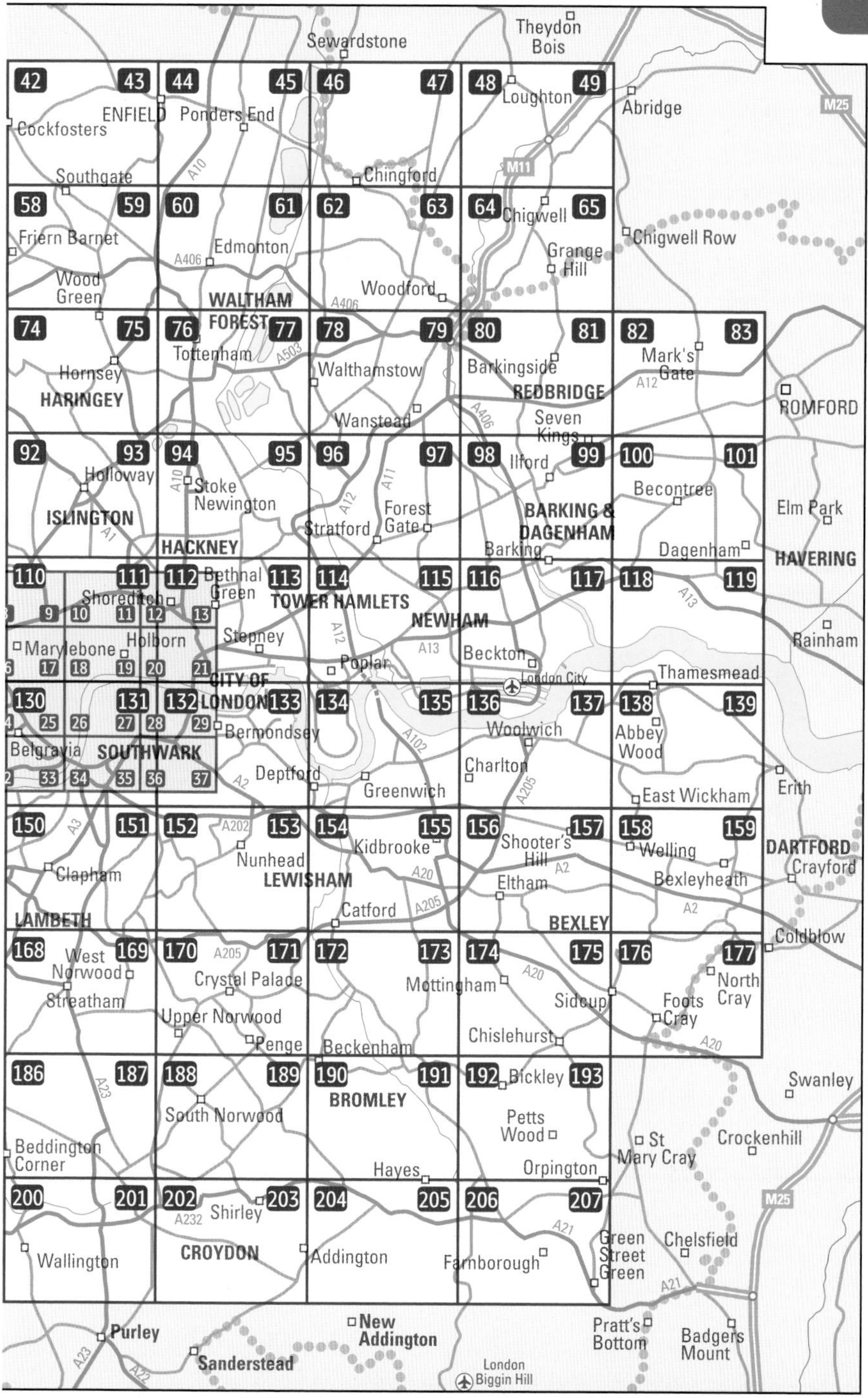
Sewardstone
Theydon Bois
ENFIELD
Cockfosters
Ponders End
Loughton
Abridge
M25
A10
Chingford
M11
Southgate
Friern Barnet
Edmonton
A406
Chigwell
Chigwell Row
Grange Hill
Wood Green
WALTHAM FOREST
Woodford
A406
Tottenham
A503
Walthamstow
Barkingside
Mark's Gate
A12
ROMFORD
Hornsey
HARINGEY
REDBRIDGE
Wanstead
A406
Seven Kings
Holloway
Stoke Newington
A10
A11
A12
Ilford
Becontree
Elm Park
ISLINGTON
A1
Forest Gate
Stratford
BARKING & DAGENHAM
HACKNEY
Barking
Dagenham
HAVERING
Bethnal Green
Shoreditch
TOWER HAMLETS
NEWHAM
A13
Stepney
Marylebone
Holborn
A12
A13
Beckton
Rainham
Poplar
Thamesmead
London City
CITY OF LONDON
Bermondsey
Woolwich
Abbey Wood
A102
Belgravia
SOUTHWARK
Charlton
Deptford
Greenwich
A2
A205
East Wickham
Erith
A3
A202
Nunhead
Kidbrooke
Shooter's Hill
Welling
DARTFORD
Crayford
Clapham
LEWISHAM
A20
A2
Eltham
Bexleyheath
A205
Catford
A2
LAMBETH
BEXLEY
Coldblow
West Norwood
A205
Crystal Palace
Mottingham
A20
North Cray
Streatham
Sidcup
Foots Cray
Upper Norwood
Chislehurst
Penge
Beckenham
A20
A23
Swanley
Bickley
BROMLEY
South Norwood
Petts Wood
Beddington Corner
St Mary Cray
Crockenhill
Hayes
Orpington
M25
Shirley
A232
A21
Wallington
CROYDON
Addington
Farnborough
Green Street Green
Chelsfield
A21
Purley
New Addington
Pratt's Bottom
Badgers Mount
A23
A22
Sanderstead
London Biggin Hill

Key to central map symbols

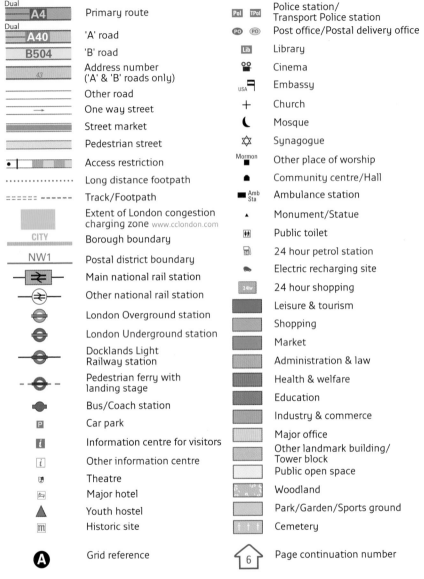

- Dual A4 — Primary route
- Dual A40 — 'A' road
- B504 — 'B' road
- 43 — Address number ('A' & 'B' roads only)
- Other road
- One way street
- Street market
- Pedestrian street
- Access restriction
- Long distance footpath
- Track/Footpath
- Extent of London congestion charging zone www.cclondon.com
- CITY — Borough boundary
- NW1 — Postal district boundary
- Main national rail station
- Other national rail station
- London Overground station
- London Underground station
- Docklands Light Railway station
- Pedestrian ferry with landing stage
- Bus/Coach station
- P — Car park
- i — Information centre for visitors
- i — Other information centre
- Theatre
- Major hotel
- Youth hostel
- m — Historic site
- A — Grid reference

- Pol TPol — Police station/Transport Police station
- PO PO — Post office/Postal delivery office
- Lib — Library
- Cinema
- USA — Embassy
- Church
- Mosque
- Synagogue
- Mormon — Other place of worship
- Community centre/Hall
- Amb Sta — Ambulance station
- Monument/Statue
- Public toilet
- 24 — 24 hour petrol station
- Electric recharging site
- 24hr — 24 hour shopping
- Leisure & tourism
- Shopping
- Market
- Administration & law
- Health & welfare
- Education
- Industry & commerce
- Major office
- Other landmark building/Tower block
- Public open space
- Woodland
- Park/Garden/Sports ground
- Cemetery
- 6 — Page continuation number

SCALE

1: 10,000 6.3 inches (16 cm) to 1 mile/10 cm to 1 km

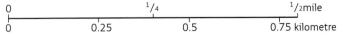

0 — 1/4 — 1/2 mile

0 — 0.25 — 0.5 — 0.75 kilometre

The reference grid on this atlas coincides with the Ordnance Survey National Grid system. The grid interval is 250 metres.

Key to main map symbols

M4	Motorway
Dual A4	Primary route
Dual A40	'A' road
B504	'B' road
	Other road/One way street
	Toll
	Street market
	Restricted access road
	Pedestrian street
	Cycle path
	Track/Footpath
THAMES PATH	Long distance footpath
LC	Level crossing
V P	Vehicle/Pedestrian ferry
	Extent of London congestion charging zone www.cclondon.com
	Low Emission zone
	County/Borough boundary
	Postal district boundary
	Main national rail station
	Other national rail station
	London Overground station
	London Underground station
	Docklands Light Railway station
	Tramlink station
	Pedestrian ferry landing stage
	Bus/Coach station
i	Information centre for visitors
i	Other information centre
A	Grid reference

P	Car park
	Youth hostel
m	Historic site
Pol	Police station
USA	Embassy
PO/Lib/ Fire Sta	Post Office/Library/Fire station
	Public toilet
H	Heliport
+	Church
	Mosque
	Synagogue
24	24 hour petrol station
	Electric recharging site
24hr	24 hour shopping
	Leisure & tourism
	Shopping
	Market
	Administration & law
	Health & welfare
	Education
	Industry & commerce
	Major office
	Other landmark building/ Tower block
	Cemetery
	Golf course
	Public open space/Allotments
	Park/Garden/Sports ground
	Wood/Forest
106	Page continuation number

35	OS National Grid kilometre square

SCALE

1:20,000 3.2 inches (8 cm) to 1 mile/5 cm to 1 km

0 — 1/4 — 1/2 mile

0 — 0.25 — 0.5 — 0.75 — 1 kilometre

The reference grid on this atlas coincides with the Ordnance Survey National Grid system. The grid interval is 500 metres.

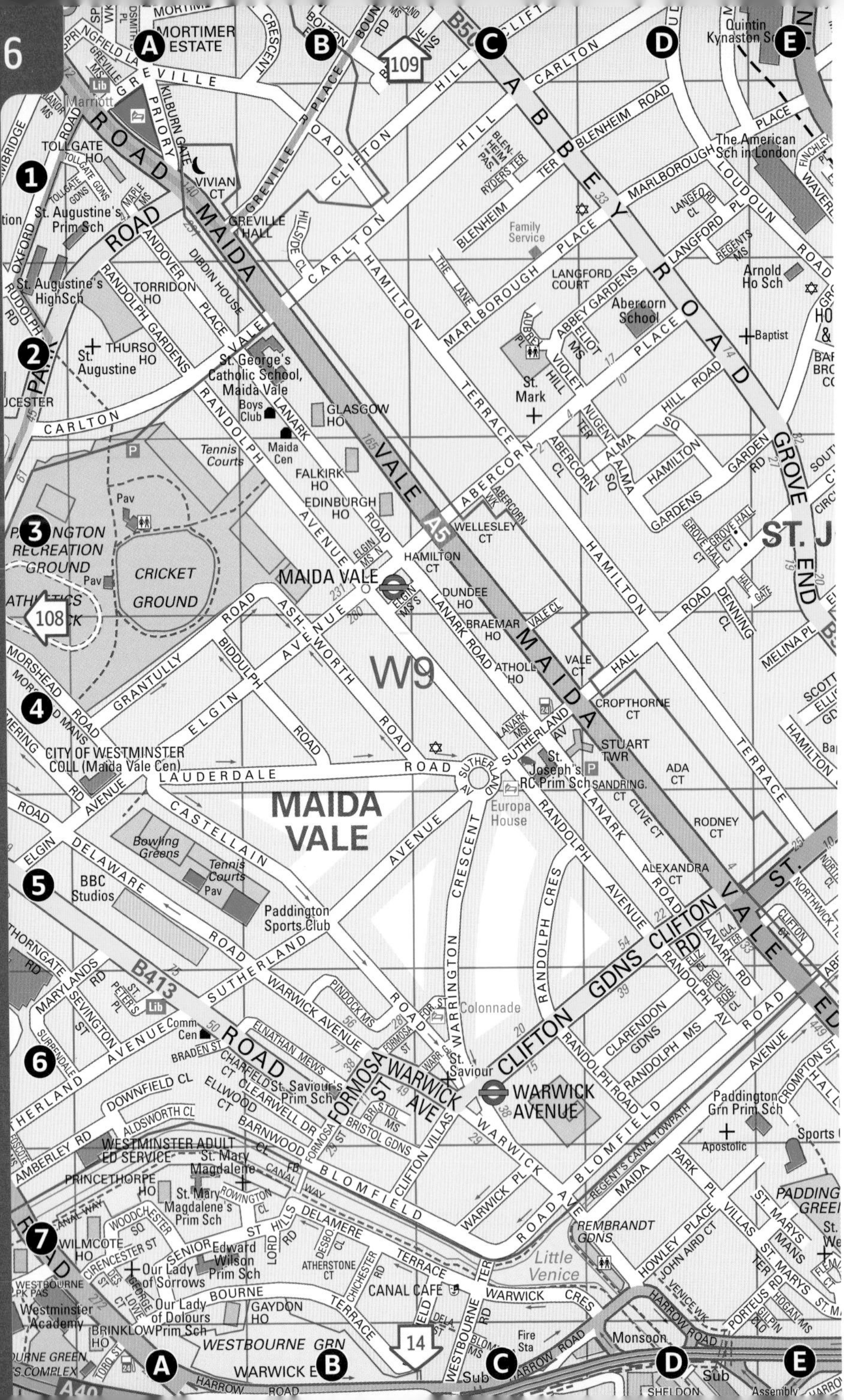
A
B
C
D
E
1
2
3
4
5
6
7
MORTIMER ESTATE
109
108
14
Quintin Kynaston Sch
GREVILLE
Lib
Marriott
KILBURN PRIORY
KILBURN GATE
TOLLGATE HO
TOLLGATE GDNS
MAPLE MS
VIVIAN CT
St. Augustine's Prim Sch
St. Augustine's HighSch
OXFORD RD
RUDOLPH RD
ROAD
MAIDA VALE
A5
B507
GREVILLE HALL
GREVILLE PLACE
GREVILLE ROAD
BOUNDARY ROAD
CLIFTON HILL
CARLTON HILL
HILLSIDE CL
CARLTON
HAMILTON TERRACE
BLENHEIM ROAD
BLENHEIM TER
BLENHEIM PAS
RYDERS TER
BLENHEIM
Family Service
THE LANE
MARLBOROUGH PLACE
MARLBOROUGH HILL
ABBEY ROAD
LANGFORD COURT
LANGFORD PL
LANGFORD CL
LANGFORD RD
REGENTS MS
LOUDOUN ROAD
The American Sch in London
FINCHLEY
WAVERLEY
Arnold Ho Sch
Baptist
ABBEY GARDENS
Abercorn School
ELIOT MS
AUBREY PL
VIOLET HILL
St. Mark
ABERCORN PLACE
ABERCORN CL
NUGENT TER
ALMA SQ
HILL ROAD
HAMILTON GARDENS
GARDEN RD
GROVE END ROAD
GROVE HALL CT
HALL GATE
ST. JOHN'S WOOD
HALL ROAD
DENNING CL
MELINA PL
TORRIDON HO
ANDOVER PLACE
DIBDIN HOUSE
RANDOLPH GARDENS
THURSO HO
St. Augustine
PARK
GLOUCESTER
VALE
St. George's Catholic School, Maida Vale
Boys Club
LANARK
Maida Cen
GLASGOW HO
FALKIRK HO
EDINBURGH HO
RANDOLPH AVENUE
Tennis Courts
P
Pav
PADDINGTON RECREATION GROUND
CRICKET GROUND
ATHLETICS TRACK
WELLESLEY CT
ABERCORN WK
HAMILTON CT
MAIDA VALE
ELGIN MS N
ELGIN MS S
DUNDEE HO
BRAEMAR HO
VALE CL
ATHOLL HO
VALE CT
LANARK ROAD
W9
CROPTHORNE CT
STUART TWR
ADA CT
SANDRING. CT
CLIVE CT
RODNEY CT
ALEXANDRA CT
ASHWORTH ROAD
ELGIN AVENUE
GRANTULLY ROAD
BIDDULPH ROAD
MORSHEAD ROAD
MORSHEAD MANS
CITY OF WESTMINSTER COLL (Maida Vale Cen)
LAUDERDALE ROAD
SUTHERLAND AV
LANARK MS
St. Joseph's RC Prim Sch
Europa House
MAIDA VALE
CASTELLAIN ROAD
Bowling Greens
Tennis Courts
BBC Studios
DELAWARE ROAD
ELGIN AVENUE
RANDOLPH CRES
Paddington Sports Club
SUTHERLAND AVENUE
WARRINGTON CRESCENT
CLIFTON GDNS
CLIFTON RD
ST. JOHN'S WOOD
NORTHWICK TER
CLIFTON CT
ELIZ CL
BRO. CL
ROB. CL
CLA. TER
THORNGATE RD
MARYLANDS RD
SEVINGTON ST
ST. PETER'S PL
B413
SURRENDALE PL
PINDOCK MS
WARWICK AVENUE
FORMOSA ST
Colonnade
CLARENDON GDNS
RANDOLPH MS
RANDOLPH ROAD
EDGWARE ROAD
Comm Cen
BRADEN ST
ELNATHAN MEWS
CHARFIELD CT
CLEARWELL DR
ELLWOOD CT
St. Saviour's Prim Sch
BRISTOL MS
BRISTOL GDNS
WARWICK AVE
St. Saviour
WARWICK AVENUE
CROMPTON ST
Paddington Grn Prim Sch
Apostolic
Sports Cen
DOWNFIELD CL
ALDSWORTH CL
AMBERLEY RD
WESTMINSTER ADULT ED SERVICE
BARNWOOD CL
BLOMFIELD ROAD
CLIFTON VILLAS
WARWICK PL
St. Mary Magdalene
CANAL WAY
ROWINGTON CL
PRINCETHORPE HO
St. Mary Magdalene's Prim Sch
WOODCHESTER SQ
ST HILLS
DELAMERE TERRACE
LORD HILLS RD
DESBOROUGH CL
REGENT'S CANAL TOWPATH
MAIDA AVE
PARK PL VILLAS
ST. MARYS MANS
ST. MARYS TER
PADDINGTON GREEN
REMBRANDT GDNS
Little Venice
HOWLEY PLACE
JOHN AIRD CT
WILMCOTE HO
CIRENCESTER ST
SENIOR ST
Edward Wilson Prim Sch
Our Lady of Sorrows
ATHERSTONE CT
CHICHESTER RD
CANAL CAFE
WESTBOURNE TER
WARWICK CRES
VENICE WK
HARROW ROAD
PORTEUS RD
HOGAN MS
GILPIN CL
WESTBOURNE PK PAS
Westminster Academy
Our Lady of Dolours Prim Sch
BOURNE TERRACE
GAYDON HO
BRINKLOW HO
WESTBOURNE GRN
WESTBOURNE GREEN SPORTS COMPLEX
TORO ST
A40
WARWICK EST
Fire Sta
Monsoon
Sub
SHELDON
Assembly

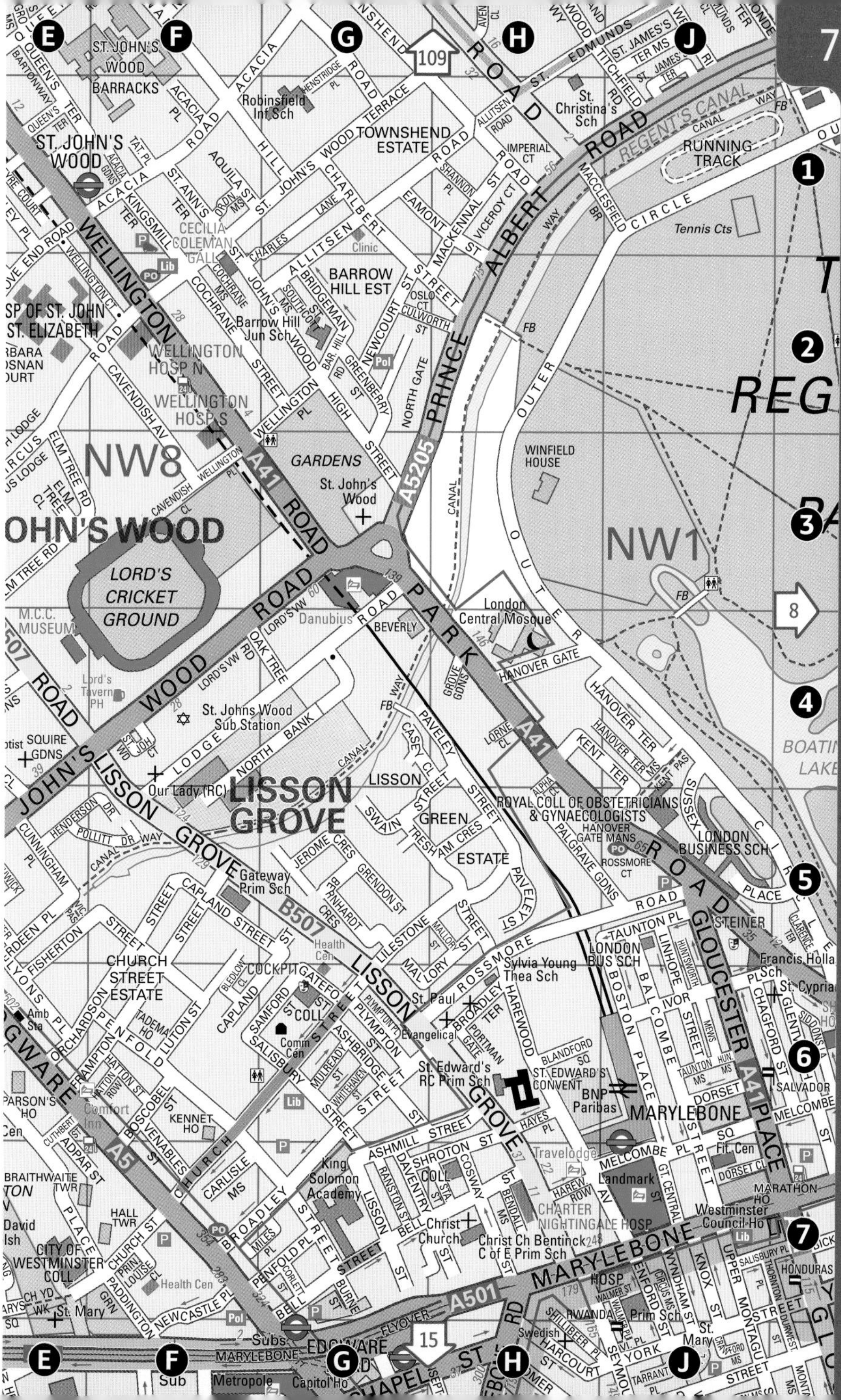
ST. JOHN'S WOOD BARRACKS
ST. JOHN'S WOOD
Robinsfield Inf Sch
TOWNSHEND ESTATE
St. Christina's Sch
REGENT'S CANAL
RUNNING TRACK
PRINCE ALBERT ROAD
CECILIA COLEMAN GALL
Clinic
BARROW HILL EST
Barrow Hill Jun Sch
WELLINGTON ROAD
WELLINGTON HOSP N
WELLINGTON HOSP S
Tennis Cts
OUTER CIRCLE
REG
NW8
GARDENS
St. John's Wood
WINFIELD HOUSE
NW1
ST. JOHN'S WOOD
LORD'S CRICKET GROUND
M.C.C. MUSEUM
Danubius
BEVERLY
PARK ROAD
London Central Mosque
HANOVER GATE
Lord's Tavern PH
St. Johns Wood Sub Station
Our Lady (RC)
LISSON GROVE
LISSON GREEN ESTATE
ROYAL COLL OF OBSTETRICIANS & GYNAECOLOGISTS
HANOVER GATE MANS
ROSSMORE CT
LONDON BUSINESS SCH
BOATING LAKE
Gateway Prim Sch
CHURCH STREET ESTATE
COCKPIT
Health Cen
COLL
Comm Cen
LONDON BUS SCH
Sylvia Young Thea Sch
St. Paul
Evangelical
St. Edward's RC Prim Sch
ST. EDWARD'S CONVENT
BNP Paribas
MARYLEBONE
Francis Holland Sch
St. Cyprian
SALVADOR
MELCOMBE
Fit. Cen
DORSET CL
MARATHON HO
Westminster Council Ho
Comfort Inn
KENNET HO
King Solomon Academy
Travelodge
Landmark
CHARTER NIGHTINGALE HOSP
Christ Church
Christ Ch Bentinck C of E Prim Sch
CITY OF WESTMINSTER COLL
Health Cen
St. Mary
MARYLEBONE ROAD
FLYOVER
EDGWARE ROAD
Prim Sch
HONDURAS
Swedish
Subs
Metropole
Capitol Ho
EDGWARE ROAD
LISSON GROVE
GLOUCESTER PLACE
A41
A5
A501
A5205
B507
109
8
15
E
F
G
H
J
1
2
3
4
5
6
7

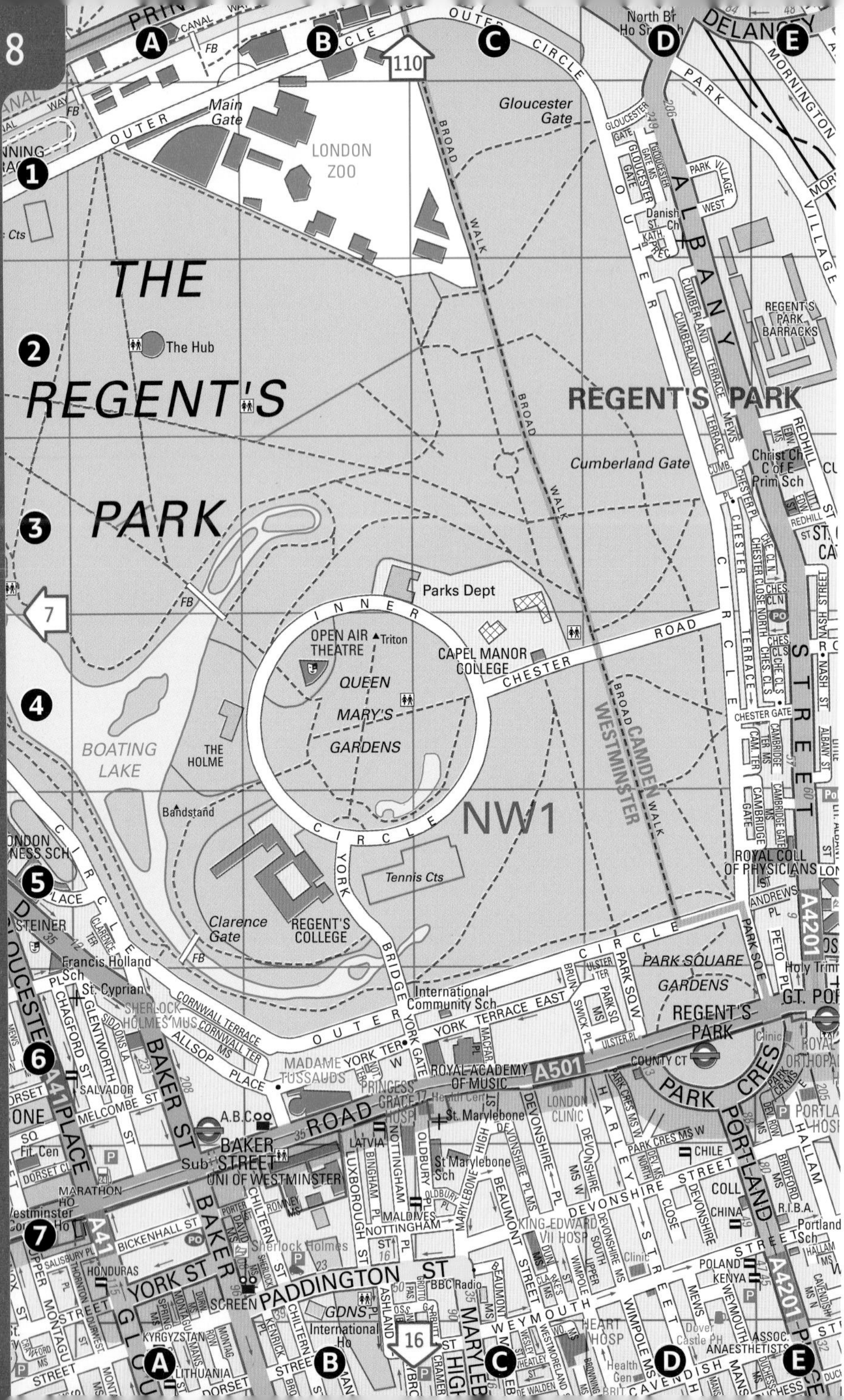
110
7
16
A
B
C
D
E
1
2
3
4
5
6
7
THE REGENT'S PARK
REGENT'S PARK
NW1
LONDON ZOO
Main Gate
OUTER CIRCLE
Gloucester Gate
BROAD WALK
The Hub
Cumberland Gate
Parks Dept
INNER CIRCLE
OPEN AIR THEATRE
Triton
QUEEN MARY'S GARDENS
CAPEL MANOR COLLEGE
CHESTER ROAD
BOATING LAKE
THE HOLME
Bandstand
Tennis Cts
Clarence Gate
REGENT'S COLLEGE
YORK BRIDGE
FB
CAMDEN
WESTMINSTER
ALBANY STREET
PARK VILLAGE WEST
REGENT'S PARK BARRACKS
Danish Ch
CUMBERLAND TERRACE
CHESTER TERRACE
CHESTER GATE
CAMBRIDGE GATE
Christ Ch C of E Prim Sch
REDHILL ST
NASH STREET
ROYAL COLL OF PHYSICIANS
PARK SQUARE GARDENS
PARK SQUARE EAST
PARK SQUARE WEST
ULSTER TER
International Community Sch
YORK TERRACE EAST
YORK GATE
ROYAL ACADEMY OF MUSIC
MADAME TUSSAUDS
PRINCESS GRACE HOSP
St Marylebone
LONDON CLINIC
PARK CRES
PORTLAND PLACE
A4201
A501
MARYLEBONE ROAD
BAKER STREET
BAKER ST
ALLSOP PLACE
CORNWALL TERRACE
SHERLOCK HOLMES MUS
Francis Holland Sch
St. Cyprian
GLOUCESTER PLACE
A41
CHAGFORD ST
GLENTWORTH
MELCOMBE ST
DORSET SQ
SALVADOR
A.B.C.
Sub
UNI OF WESTMINSTER
LATVIA
NOTTINGHAM
BINGHAM PL
LUXBOROUGH ST
OLDBURY PL
St Marylebone Sch
MARYLEBONE HIGH ST
BEAUMONT ST
DEVONSHIRE PL
DEVONSHIRE STREET
HARLEY STREET
KING EDWARD VII HOSP
MALDIVES
CHILE
CHINA
COLL
R.I.B.A.
Portland Sch
BICKENHALL ST
MARATHON HO
Westminster Ho
HONDURAS
YORK ST
Sherlock Holmes
PADDINGTON ST
PADDINGTON ST GDNS
SCREEN
International Ho
BBC Radio
WEYMOUTH ST
HEART HOSP
WIMPOLE ST
POLAND
KENYA
Dover Castle PH
ASSOC. ANAESTHETISTS
NEW CAVENDISH ST
KYRGYZSTAN
LITHUANIA
DORSET ST
MONTAGU
CHILTERN
ROYAL ORTHOPAEDIC
GT. PORTLAND ST
Holy Trinity
Health Gen
Clinic

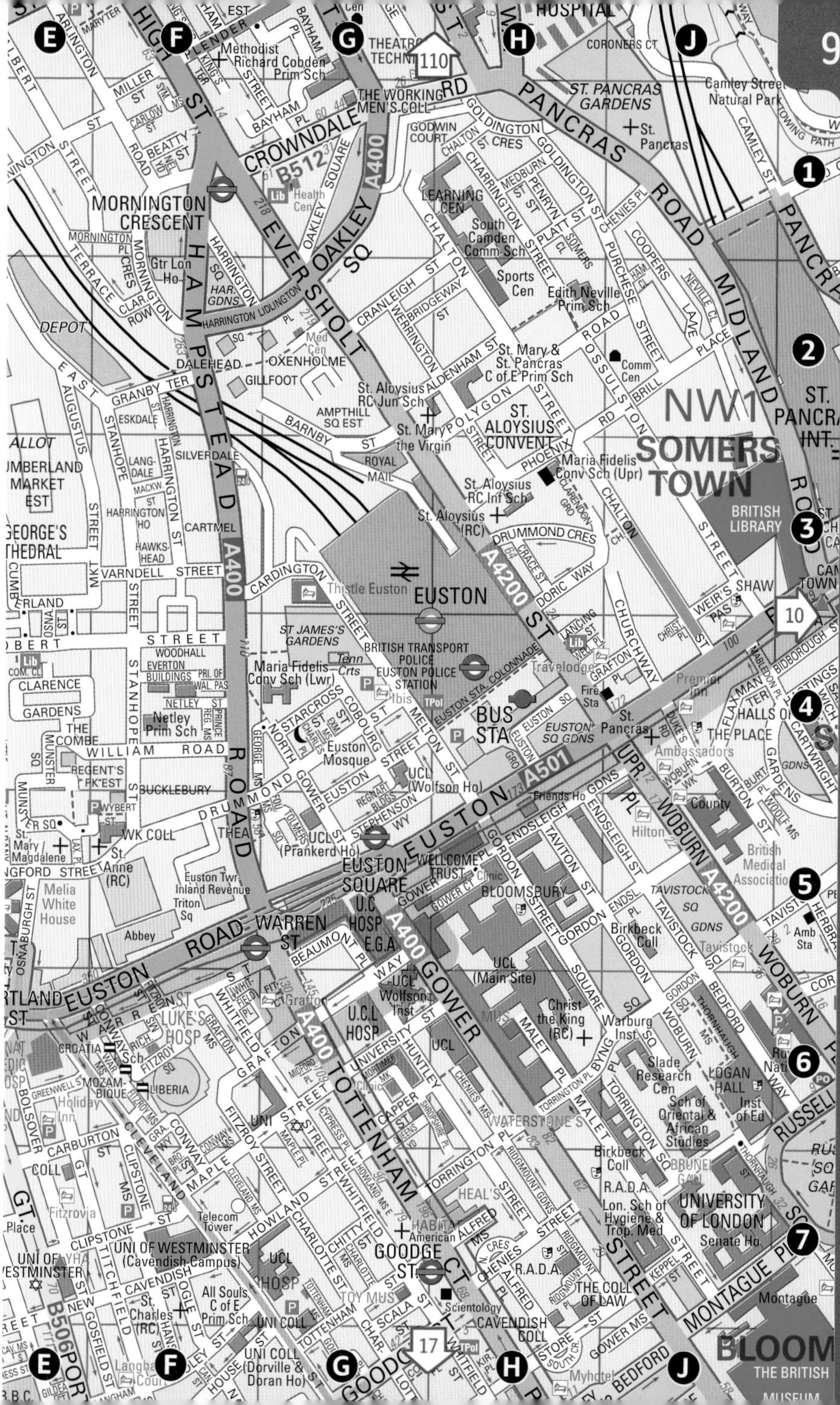
E
F
G
H
J
1
2
3
4
5
6
7
110
10
17
HOSPITAL
CORONERS CT
Camley Street Natural Park
ST. PANCRAS GARDENS
St. Pancras
PANCRAS ROAD
MIDLAND ROAD
Methodist
Richard Cobden Prim Sch
THEATRE TECHN
THE WORKING MEN'S COLL
CROWNDALE RD
B512
A400
OAKLEY SQ
Health Cen
MORNINGTON CRESCENT
Gtr Lon Ho
DEPOT
HAMPSTEAD ROAD
EVERSHOLT ST
LEARNING CEN
South Camden Comm Sch
Sports Cen
Edith Neville Prim Sch
St. Mary & St. Pancras C of E Prim Sch
Comm Cen
NW1
SOMERS TOWN
ST. PANCRAS INT.
BRITISH LIBRARY
St. Aloysius RC Jun Sch
St. Mary the Virgin
ST. ALOYSIUS CONVENT
Maria Fidelis Conv Sch (Upr)
St. Aloysius RC Inf Sch
St. Aloysius (RC)
ROYAL MAIL
DRUMMOND CRES
A4200
EUSTON
Thistle Euston
ST JAMES'S GARDENS
BRITISH TRANSPORT POLICE EUSTON POLICE STATION
Maria Fidelis Conv Sch (Lwr)
Ibis
Travelodge
Fire Sta
St. Pancras
BUS STA
EUSTON SQ GDNS
Premier Inn
THE PLACE
Ambassadors
County
Hilton
Euston Mosque
UCL (Wolfson Ho)
UCL (Prankerd Ho)
Friends Ho
A501
EUSTON ROAD
EUSTON SQUARE
WELLCOME TRUST
BLOOMSBURY
British Medical Association
TAVISTOCK SQ GDNS
Tavistock
Amb Sta
Birkbeck Coll
UCL (Main Site)
Christ the King (RC)
Warburg Inst.
Slade Research Cen
LOGAN HALL
Inst of Ed
Sch of Oriental & African Studies
Birkbeck Coll
R.A.D.A.
Lon. Sch of Hygiene & Trop. Med
UNIVERSITY OF LONDON
Senate Ho
RUSSELL
MONTAGUE PL
Montague
BLOOMSBURY
THE BRITISH MUSEUM
WARREN ST
U.C HOSP E.G.A
GOWER ST
UCL Wolfson Inst
U.C.L HOSP
UCL
TOTTENHAM CT RD
WATERSTONE'S
HEAL'S
Habitat
American
GOODGE ST
Scientology
CAVENDISH COLL
R.A.D.A.
THE COLL OF LAW
TOY MUS
UNI COLL
UNI COLL (Dorville & Doran Ho)
Telecom Tower
UNI OF WESTMINSTER (Cavendish Campus)
UCL HOSP
All Souls C of E Prim Sch
St. Charles (RC)
Fitzrovia
UNI OF WESTMINSTER
B506
Holiday Inn
LIBERIA
Melia White House
Abbey
Euston Twr Inland Revenue
Triton Sq
St. Mary Magdalene
St. Anne (RC)
WK COLL
REGENT'S PK EST
Netley Prim Sch
CLARENCE GARDENS
WILLIAM ROAD
CUMBERLAND MARKET EST
ALLOT
GEORGE'S CATHEDRAL

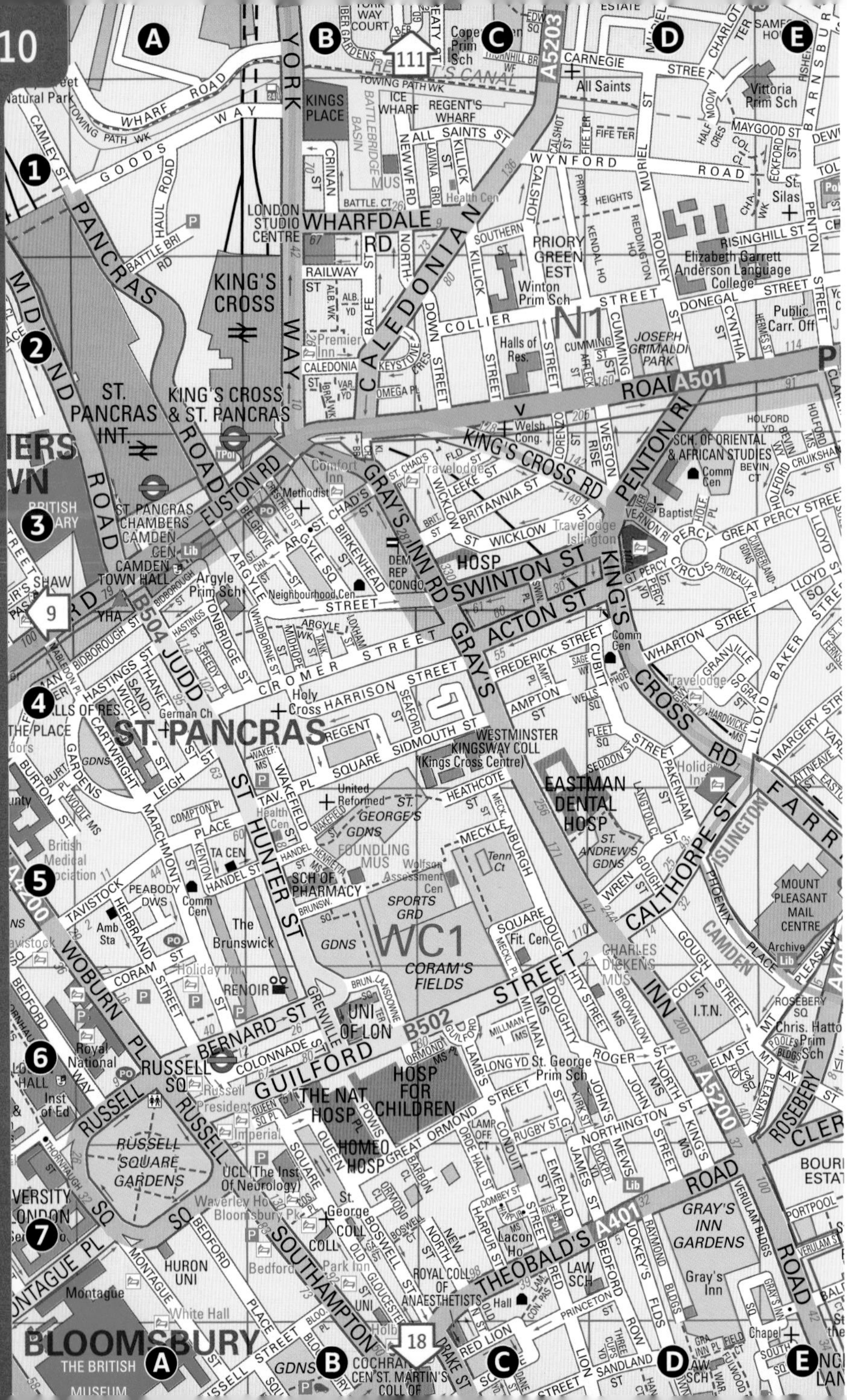
A
B
C
D
E
1
2
3
4
5
6
7
111
9
18
YORK WAY
REGENT'S CANAL
TOWING PATH WK
KINGS PLACE
ICE WHARF
REGENT'S WHARF
BATTLEBRIDGE BASIN
CARNEGIE STREET
All Saints
Vittoria Prim Sch
WHARF ROAD
GOODS WAY
CAMLEY ST
Natural Park
A5203
ALL SAINTS ST
KILLICK ST
WYNFORD ROAD
CALEDONIAN ROAD
WHARFDALE RD
LONDON STUDIO CENTRE
PANCRAS ROAD
MIDLAND ROAD
KING'S CROSS
ST. PANCRAS INT.
KING'S CROSS & ST. PANCRAS
RAILWAY ST
Premier Inn
CALEDONIA ST
PRIORY GREEN EST
Winton Prim Sch
COLLIER STREET
N1
Halls of Res.
CUMMING ST
JOSEPH GRIMALDI PARK
Elizabeth Garrett Anderson Language College
DONEGAL STREET
Public Carr. Off
PENTONVILLE ROAD
A501
PENTON RI
SCH. OF ORIENTAL & AFRICAN STUDIES
KING'S CROSS RD
Welsh Cong.
EUSTON RD
ST. PANCRAS CHAMBERS
CAMDEN TOWN HALL
Argyle Prim Sch
YHA
Travelodge
ST. CHAD'S ST
GRAY'S INN RD
BRITANNIA ST
WICKLOW ST
HOSP
SWINTON ST
ACTON ST
DEM REP CONGO
Neighbourhood Cen
ARGYLE ST
ARGYLE SQ
BIRKENHEAD ST
GREAT PERCY STREET
PERCY CIRCUS
LLOYD SQ
WHARTON STREET
GRANVILLE SQ
B504
JUDD ST
CROMER STREET
HARRISON STREET
FREDERICK STREET
AMPTON ST
Holy Cross
ST. PANCRAS
German Ch
REGENT SQUARE
SIDMOUTH ST
WESTMINSTER KINGSWAY COLL (Kings Cross Centre)
EASTMAN DENTAL HOSP
HEATHCOTE ST
MECKLENBURGH SQUARE
ST. ANDREW'S GDNS
CALTHORPE ST
FARRINGDON RD
MOUNT PLEASANT MAIL CENTRE
LEIGH ST
CARTWRIGHT GDNS
MARCHMONT ST
COMPTON PL
HUNTER ST
United Reformed
ST. GEORGE'S GDNS
FOUNDLING MUS
SCH OF PHARMACY
SPORTS GRD
WC1
CORAM'S FIELDS
TA CEN
HANDEL ST
British Medical Association
A4200
TAVISTOCK SQ
PEABODY DWS
Amb Sta
The Brunswick
CORAM STREET
RENOIR
WOBURN PL
BERNARD ST
GRENVILLE ST
UNI OF LON
GUILFORD STREET
B502
Royal National
RUSSELL SQ
COLONNADE
HOSP FOR CHILDREN
THE NAT HOSP
HOMEO HOSP
GREAT ORMOND STREET
CHARLES DICKENS MUS
DOUGHTY STREET
I.T.N.
ROSEBERY AVE
St. George Prim Sch
NORTHINGTON ST
RUSSELL SQUARE GARDENS
UCL (The Inst Of Neurology)
QUEEN SQUARE
Imperial
President
Waverley Ho
Bloomsbury Pk
St. George
THEOBALD'S ROAD
A401
GRAY'S INN GARDENS
Gray's Inn
A5200
GRAY'S INN ROAD
ROYAL COLL OF ANAESTHETISTS
LAW SCH
Lacon Ho
HURON UNI
MONTAGUE PL
Montague
White Hall
BEDFORD PLACE
SOUTHAMPTON ROW
BLOOMSBURY
THE BRITISH MUSEUM
RED LION ST
SANDLAND ST
Chapel
Bedford
Park Inn
COLL

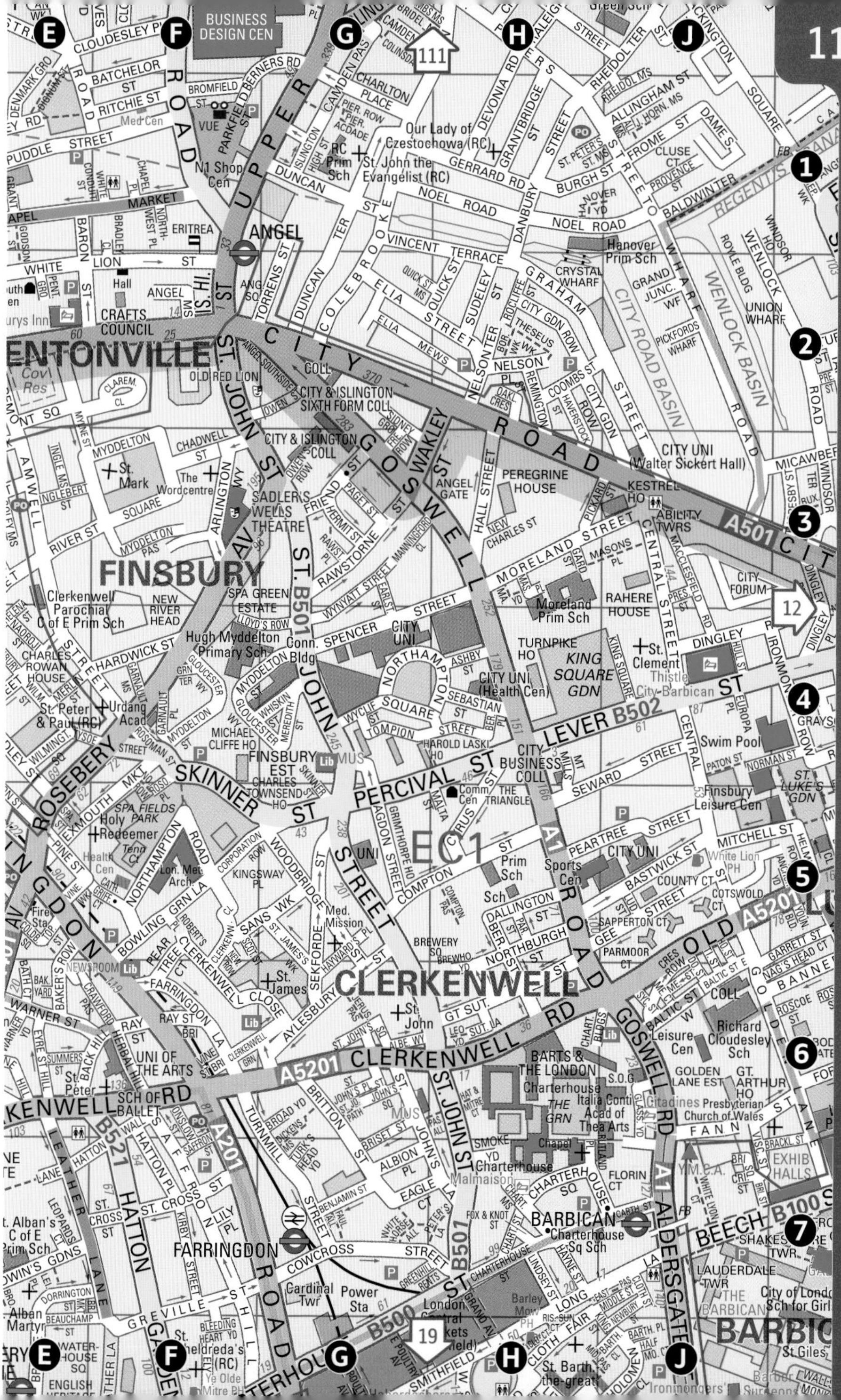

E
F
G
H
J
1
2
3
4
5
6
7
111
12
19
BUSINESS DESIGN CEN
CLOUDESLEY PL
BATCHELOR ST
RITCHIE ST
BROMFIELD ST
PARKFIELD ST
BERNERS RD
CAMDEN PAS
CHARLTON PLACE
UPPER ST
ROAD
VUE
Med Cen
N1 Shop Cen
PUDDLE STREET
MARKET
CHAPEL
ERITREA
WHITE LION ST
ANGEL
ANGEL MS
CRAFTS COUNCIL
Hall
PENTONVILLE
Covl Res
OLD RED LION
CLAREM. CL
DUNCAN ST
DUNCAN TER
TORRENS ST
ANG. SQ
ISLINGTON HIGH ST
PIER. ROW
RC Prim Sch
St. John the Evangelist (RC)
Our Lady of Czestochowa (RC)
GERRARD RD
DEVONIA RD
GRANTBRIDGE ST
NOEL ROAD
COLEBROOKE ROW
VINCENT TERRACE
QUICK ST
ELIA STREET
ELIA MEWS
SUDELEY ST
DANBURY STREET
RHEIDOL TER
RHEIDOL MS
ALLINGHAM ST
FROME ST
CLUSE CT
PROVENCE ST
BURGH ST
ST. PETER'S STREET
DAME ST
HANOVER YD
Hanover Prim Sch
BALDWINTER
REGENT'S CANAL
CRYSTAL WHARF
GRAHAM STREET
GRAND JUNC. WF
WHARF ROAD
WENLOCK BASIN
CITY ROAD BASIN
UNION WHARF
PICKFORDS WHARF
ROYLE BLDG
WENLOCK
WINDSOR HO
CITY ROAD
NELSON TER
NELSON PL
CITY GDN ROW
COOMBS ST
REMINGTON ST
HAVERSTOCK ST
COLL
CITY & ISLINGTON SIXTH FORM COLL
CITY & ISLINGTON COLL
GOSWELL ROAD
SIDNEY GRO
WAKLEY ST
ANGEL GATE
HALL STREET
PEREGRINE HOUSE
CITY UNI (Walter Sickert Hall)
KESTREL HO
ABILITY TWRS
A501 CITY
MICAWBER
ST. JOHN ST
OWEN ST
MYDDELTON SQUARE
CHADWELL ST
St. Mark
The Wordcentre
ARLINGTON WY
SADLER'S WELLS THEATRE
FRIEND ST
PAGET ST
HERMIT ST
RAWSTORNE
MANNINGFORD CL
FINSBURY
AMWELL ST
INGLEBERT ST
RIVER ST
MYDDELTON PAS
NEW CHARLES ST
MORELAND STREET
MASONS PL
GARD ST
CENTRAL STREET
MACCLESFIELD RD
CITY FORUM
DINGLEY
Clerkenwell Parochial C of E Prim Sch
NEW RIVER HEAD
SPA GREEN ESTATE
B501
WYNYATT STREET
STREET
Moreland Prim Sch
RAHERE HOUSE
LLOYD'S ROW
SPENCER ST
CITY UNI
Conn. Bldg
NORTHAMPTON SQUARE
Hugh Myddelton Primary Sch
HARDWICK ST
CHARLES ROWAN HOUSE
ASHBY ST
TURNPIKE HO
KING SQUARE GDN
St. Clement
Thistle City Barbican
DINGLEY PL
IRONMONGER
CITY UNI (Health Cen)
SEBASTIAN ST
WYCLIF ST
TOMPION
St. Peter & Paul (RC)
Urdang Acad
GLOUCESTER WY
MICHAEL CLIFFE HO
WHISKIN ST
LEVER B502 ST
Swim Pool
GRAYS
HAROLD LASKI HO
CITY BUSINESS COLL
SEWARD STREET
ROSEBERY AV
ROSOMAN ST
SKINNER ST
FINSBURY EST
CHARLES TOWNSEND HO
Lib
MUS
PERCIVAL ST
Comm Cen
THE TRIANGLE
MALTA ST
Finsbury Leisure Cen
ST. LUKE'S GDN
EXMOUTH MKT
SPA FIELDS PARK
Holy Redeemer
NORTHAMPTON ROAD
Lon. Met Arch.
Health Cen
CORPORATION ROW
KINGSWAY PL
WOODBRIDGE ST
AGDON STREET
EC1
CYRUS ST
COMPTON ST
Prim Sch
A1
Sports Cen
PEARTREE STREET
CITY UNI
BASTWICK ST
MITCHELL ST
White Lion PH
COUNTY CT
COTSWOLD CT
A5201
FARRINGDON
BOWLING GRN LA
Fire Sta
SANS WK
ST. JAMES'S WK
Med. Mission
BREWERY SQ
DALLINGTON ST
NORTHBURGH ST
SAPPERTON CT
GEE STREET
PARMOOR CT
OLD ST
GARRETT ST
NAG'S HEAD CT
BANNER
NEWSROOM Lib
CLERKENWELL CLOSE
St. James
AYLESBURY ST
CLERKENWELL
GT SUT.
St. John
BALTIC ST
COLL
WARNER ST
RAY ST
Leisure Cen
Richard Cloudesley Sch
SUMMERS
UNI OF THE ARTS
St. Peter
SCH OF BALLET
CLERKENWELL RD
A5201 CLERKENWELL RD
BARTS & THE LONDON
Charterhouse
THE GRN
Italia Conti Acad of Thea Arts
S.O.G.
GOLDEN LANE EST
GT. ARTHUR HO
Citadines
Presbyterian Church of Wales
FANN ST
EXHIB HALLS
B521
HATTON GARDEN
LEATHER LANE
SAFFRON HILL
A201
TURNMILL ST
BRITTON ST
ALBION PL
EAGLE CT
ST. JOHN ST
Malmaison
Charterhouse
CHARTERHOUSE SQ
FLORIN CT
Chapel
SMOKE YD
ST. CROSS ST
HATTON PL
LILY PL
BENJAMIN ST
Y.M.C.A.
A1 ALDERSGATE
BEECH ST
B100
St. Alban's C of E Prim Sch
FARRINGDON
COWCROSS STREET
BARBICAN
Charterhouse Sq Sch
SHAKESPEARE TWR.
LAUDERDALE TWR
THE BARBICAN
City of London Sch for Girls
BARBICAN
St. Alban Martyr
GREVILLE ST
FARRINGDON ROAD
Cardinal Twr
Power Sta
B500
London Central Markets (Smithfield)
CHARTERHOUSE ST
LONG LA
CLOTH FAIR
St. Barth. the-great
St. Etheldreda's (RC)
Ye Olde Mitre PH
WATERHOUSE SQ
ENGLISH
St. Giles
Barley Mow PH
FOX & KNOT ST
LINDSEY ST
HOLBORN

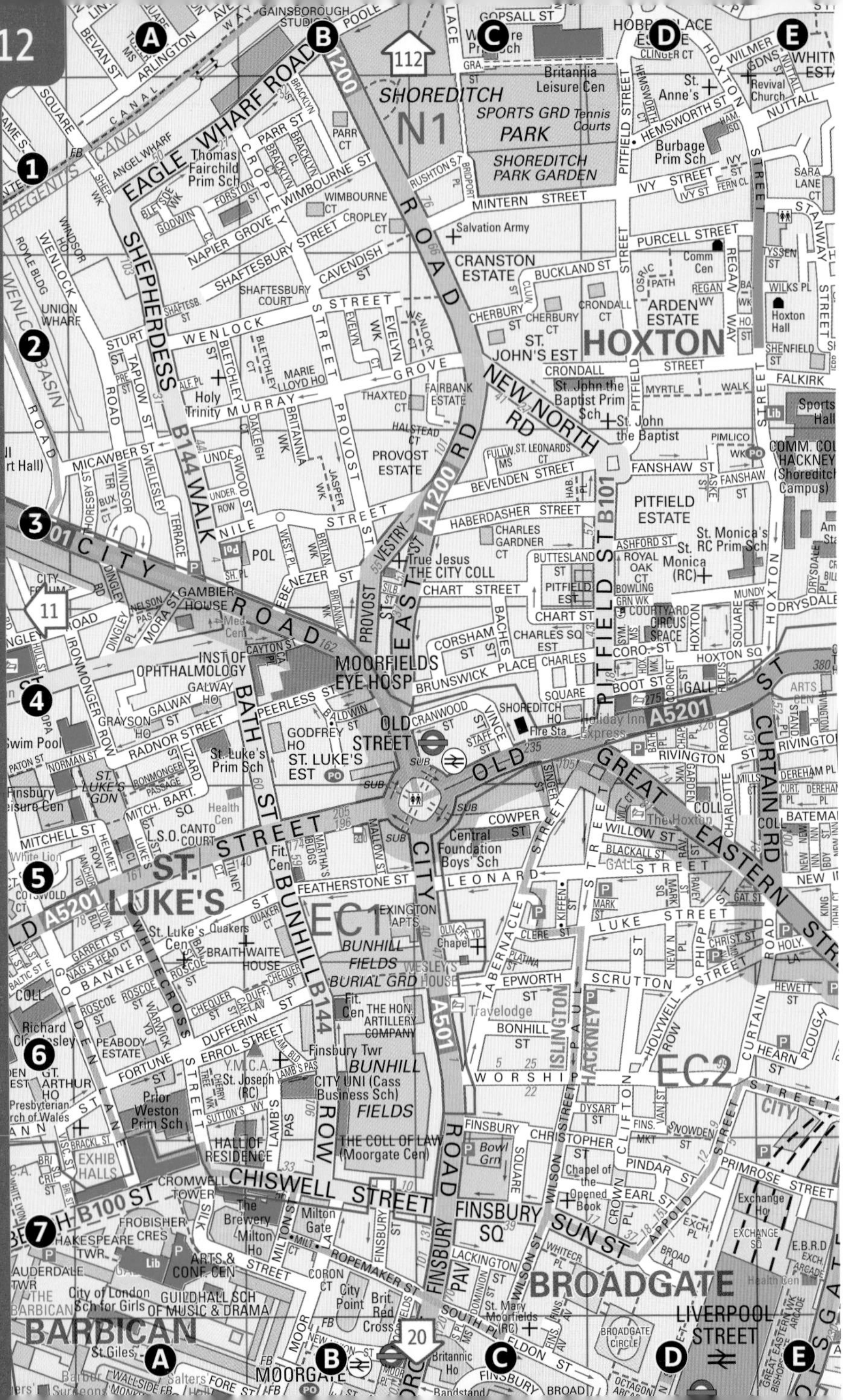
A
B
C
D
E
1
2
3
4
5
6
7
112
11
20
N1
EC1
EC2
SHOREDITCH
SPORTS GRD
PARK
Tennis Courts
SHOREDITCH PARK GARDEN
Britannia Leisure Cen
GOPSALL ST
HOBBS PLACE
CLINGER CT
St. Anne's
Revival Church
WILMER
NUTTALL
HEMSWORTH ST
Burbage Prim Sch
IVY STREET
SARA LANE CT
STANWAY
GAINSBOROUGH STUDIOS
POOLE
ARLINGTON
BEVAN ST
REGENT'S CANAL
ANGEL WHARF
EAGLE WHARF ROAD
Thomas Fairchild Prim Sch
PARR ST
PARR CT
BRACKLYN
CROPLEY
WIMBOURNE ST
WIMBOURNE CT
CROPLEY CT
NAPIER GROVE
SHAFTESBURY STREET
CAVENDISH ST
SHAFTESBURY COURT
SHEPHERDESS
B144 WALK
WENLOCK
WENLOCK BASIN
UNION WHARF
ROYLE BLDG
WINDSOR HO
RUSHTON ST
BRIDPORT PL
MINTERN STREET
Salvation Army
CRANSTON ESTATE
BUCKLAND ST
CHERBURY ST
CHERBURY CT
CRONDALL CT
ST. JOHN'S EST
PITFIELD STREET
PURCELL STREET
Comm Cen
ARDEN ESTATE
REGAN WY
HOXTON
TYSSEN ST
WILKS PL
Hoxton Hall
SHENFIELD ST
CRONDALL
STREET
MYRTLE WALK
FALKIRK
Sports Hall
St. John the Baptist Prim Sch
St. John the Baptist
NEW NORTH RD
WENLOCK STREET
STURT ST
TAPLOW ST
ROAD
Holy Trinity
MURRAY
GROVE
MARIE LLOYD HO
EVELYN WK
EVELYN CT
WENLOCK CT
THAXTED CT
FAIRBANK ESTATE
HALSTEAD CT
PROVOST ESTATE
PROVOST STREET
BRITANNIA WK
JASPER WK
FULLWOOD MS
ST. LEONARDS CT
BEVENDEN STREET
FANSHAW ST
PIMLICO WK
COMM. COLL HACKNEY (Shoreditch Campus)
PITFIELD ESTATE
MICAWBER ST
WINDSOR TER
WELLESLEY TERRACE
UNDERWOOD ST
UNDER. ROW
NILE STREET
HABERDASHER STREET
CHARLES GARDNER CT
ASHFORD ST
St. Monica's RC Prim Sch
St. Monica (RC)
ROYAL OAK CT
BUTTESLAND ST
PITFIELD EST
CITY ROAD
CITY FORUM
DINGLEY RD
GAMBIER HOUSE
POL
WEST PL
EBENEZER ST
VESTRY ST
True Jesus THE CITY COLL
CHART STREET
EAST RD
A1200
PROVOST ST
BOWLING GRN WK
COURTYARD
CIRCUS SPACE
HOXTON SQUARE
MUNDY ST
DRYSDALE
IRONMONGER ROW
NELSON PAS
MORA ST
Med Cen
CAYTON ST
INST OF OPHTHALMOLOGY
MOORFIELDS EYE HOSP
CORSHAM ST
BACHES ST
CHARLES SQ EST
CORONET ST
BRUNSWICK PLACE
CHARLES SQUARE
BOOT ST
GALWAY HO
GALWAY ST
PEERLESS ST
BALDWIN ST
GODFREY HO
GRAYSON HO
Swim Pool
RADNOR STREET
St. Luke's Prim Sch
ST. LUKE'S EST
OLD STREET
CRANWOOD ST
VINCE ST
SHOREDITCH HO
Fire Sta
Holiday Inn Express
A5201
GREAT EASTERN
RIVINGTON ST
CURTAIN RD
ARTS CEN
PATON ST
NORMAN ST
ST. LUKE'S GDN
BONMONGER PASSAGE
LIZARD ST
Finsbury Leisure Cen
MITCH. BART. SQ
Health Cen
SINGER ST
COWPER ST
Central Foundation Boys' Sch
The Hoxton
WILLOW ST
BLACKALL ST
CHARLOTTE RD
DEREHAM PL
BATEMAN
MITCHELL ST
HELMET ROW
L.S.O.
CANTO COURT
ST. LUKE'S
STREET
Fit. Cen
MARTHA'S BLDGS
MALLOW ST
LEONARD STREET
White Lion
COTSWOLD CT
TILNEY CT
FEATHERSTONE ST
BUNHILL ROW
EXINGTON APTS
OLIVERS YD
Chapel
TABERNACLE STREET
KIFFEN ST
MARK ST
LUKE STREET
NEW INN
St. Luke's Cen
Quakers
QUAKER CT
BRAITHWAITE HOUSE
BUNHILL FIELDS BURIAL GRD
WESLEY'S HOUSE
CLERE ST
PLATINA ST
EPWORTH ST
SCRUTTON STREET
HOLYWELL ROW
HEWETT ST
GARRETT ST
NAG'S HEAD CT
BANNER ST
ROSCOE ST
WHITECROSS STREET
CHEQUER ST
GOLDEN LANE
COLL
Richard Cloudesley
PEABODY ESTATE
WARWICK YD
DUFFERIN ST
Fit. Cen
THE HON. ARTILLERY COMPANY
A501
Travelodge
BONHILL ST
PAUL STREET
ISLINGTON
HACKNEY
CURTAIN ROAD
PLOUGH YD
HEARN ST
ERROL STREET
FORTUNE ST
GT. ARTHUR HO
Prior Weston Prim Sch
Y.M.C.A.
St. Joseph (RC)
LAMB'S PAS
Finsbury Twr
BUNHILL FIELDS
CITY UNI (Cass Business Sch)
WORSHIP STREET
Presbyterian Church of Wales
EXHIB HALLS
SUTTON'S WY
HALL OF RESIDENCE
THE COLL OF LAW (Moorgate Cen)
FINSBURY SQUARE
Bowl Grn
CHRISTOPHER ST
DYSART ST
CLIFTON ST
FINS. MKT
SNOWDEN ST
PINDAR ST
PRIMROSE STREET
CITY
B100 ST
CROMWELL TOWER
The Brewery
CHISWELL STREET
Milton Gate
FINSBURY SQ
Chapel of the Opened Book
EARL ST
CROWN PL
WILSON ST
SUN ST
APPOLD ST
EXCH. PL
Exchange Ho
EXCHANGE SQ
E.B.R.D.
FROBISHER CRES
SHAKESPEARE TWR
Lib
ARTS & CONF. CEN
MILTON ST
Milton Ho
MILT. CT
ROPEMAKER ST
CORON CT
FINSBURY PAV
LACKINGTON ST
DOMINION ST
BROADGATE
BROAD LA
Health Cen
LAUDERDALE TWR
THE BARBICAN
City of London Sch for Girls
GUILDHALL SCH OF MUSIC & DRAMA
City Point
Brit. Red Cross
St. Mary Moorfields (RC)
BROADGATE CIRCLE
LIVERPOOL STREET
GREAT EASTERN WK
BISHOPSGATE ARCADE
BARBICAN
St Giles
MOOR LA
NEW UNION ST
MOORGATE
Britannic Ho
SOUTH PL
ELDON ST
FINSBURY CIRCUS
BROAD
OCTAGON ARCADE
FORE ST
WALLSIDE
Salters
Bandstand
Barber Surgeons

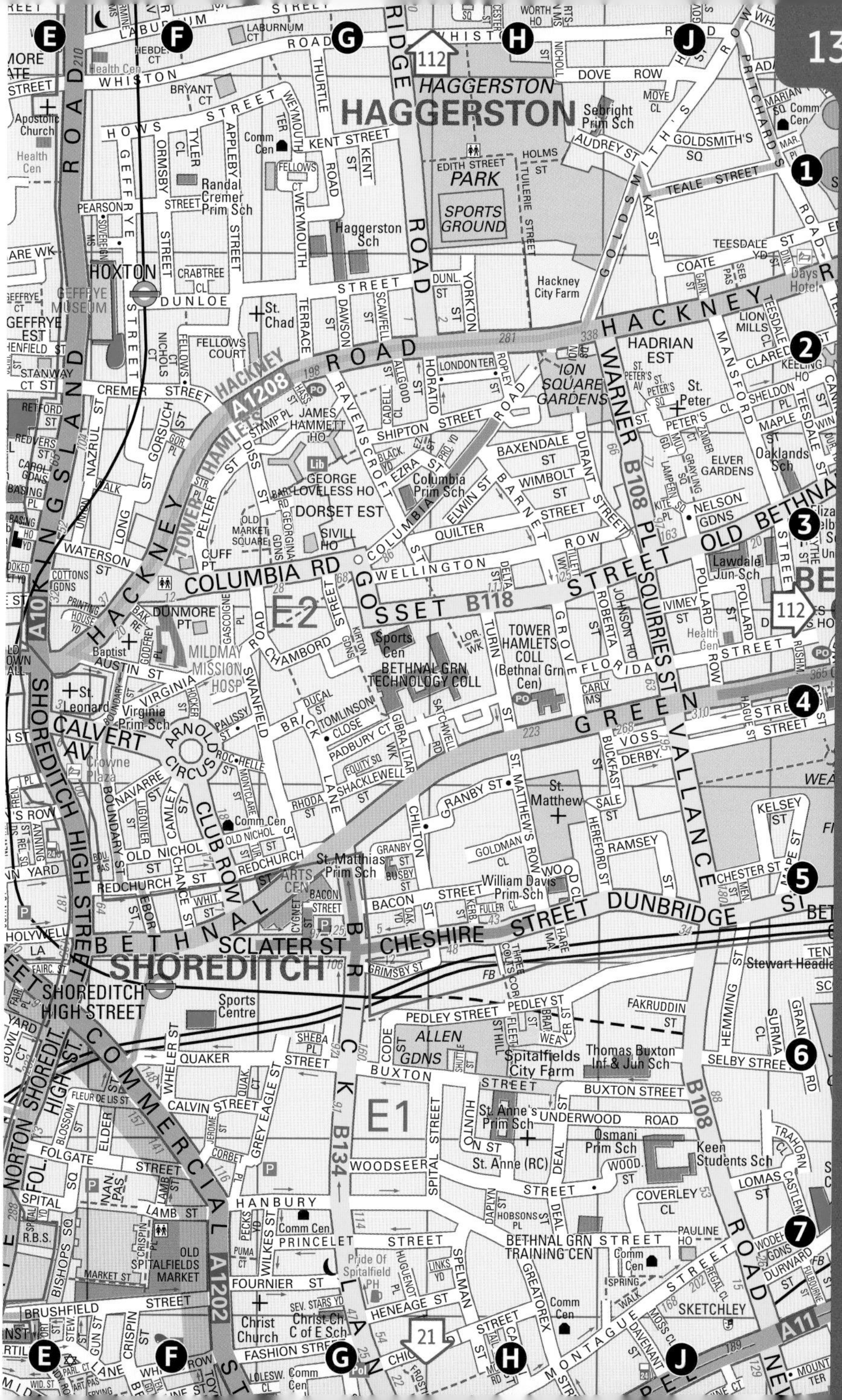
E
F
G
H
J
1
2
3
4
5
6
7
112
HAGGERSTON
HAGGERSTON
PARK
SPORTS GROUND
WHISTON ROAD
LABURNUM ST
DOVE ROW
HOWS STREET
KENT STREET
AUDREY ST
GOLDSMITH'S SQ
TEALE STREET
GOLDSMITH'S ROW
PRITCHARD'S ROAD
HAGGERSTON ROAD
KINGSLAND ROAD
A10
Apostolic Church
Health Cen
GEFFRYE ST
ORMSBY ST
TYLER CL
APPLEBY ST
Randal Cremer Prim Sch
Comm Cen
Haggerston Sch
WEYMOUTH TER
THURTLE ROAD
Sebright Prim Sch
EDITH STREET
HOLMS ST
TUILERIE STREET
COATE STREET
TEESDALE ST
Days Hotel
HOXTON
GEFFRYE MUSEUM
DUNLOE STREET
CRABTREE CL
St. Chad
DAWSON ST
SCAWFELL ST
YORKTON ST
Hackney City Farm
HACKNEY ROAD
A1208
HADRIAN EST
MANSFORD ST
LION MILLS
FELLOWS COURT
CREMER STREET
HACKNEY ROAD
TOWER HAMLETS
ION SQUARE GARDENS
WARNER PL
B108
St. Peter
ST. PETER'S CL
SHELDON PL
MAPLE ST
Oaklands Sch
ELVER GARDENS
NELSON GDNS
JAMES HAMMETT HO
RAVENSCROFT ST
SHIPTON STREET
COLUMBIA ROAD
BAXENDALE ST
WIMBOLT ST
DURANT STREET
GEORGE LOVELESS HO
DORSET EST
Columbia Prim Sch
SIVILL HO
CUFF PT
QUILTER ST
ROW
OLD BETHNAL GREEN ROAD
Lawdale Jun Sch
COLUMBIA RD
WELLINGTON
GOSSET STREET
B118
E2
WATERSON ST
COTTONS GDNS
DUNMORE PT
Baptist
MILDMAY MISSION HOSP
AUSTIN ST
St. Leonard
VIRGINIA RD
Virginia Prim Sch
CALVERT AV
ARNOLD CIRCUS
Crowne Plaza
SWANFIELD ST
CHAMBORD ST
Sports Cen
BETHNAL GRN TECHNOLOGY COLL
TOWER HAMLETS COLL (Bethnal Grn Cen)
FLORIDA STREET
SQUIRRIES ST
POLLARD ROW
IVIMEY ST
Health Cen
BRICK LANE
TOMLINSON CLOSE
PADBURY CT
GIBRALTAR WK
BETHNAL GREEN ROAD
VOSS ST
DERBY
VALLANCE ROAD
St. Matthew
GRANBY ST
ST. MATTHEW'S ROW
HEREFORD ST
RAMSEY ST
KELSEY ST
CHESTER ST
NAVARRE ST
CAMLET ST
CLUB ROW
Comm Cen
OLD NICHOL ST
BOUNDARY ST
REDCHURCH ST
St. Matthias Prim Sch
GOLDMAN CL
William Davis Prim Sch
BACON STREET
CHESHIRE STREET
DUNBRIDGE ST
SHOREDITCH HIGH STREET
SCLATER ST
SHOREDITCH
SHOREDITCH HIGH STREET
GRIMSBY ST
Stewart Headlam
Sports Centre
PEDLEY STREET
FAKRUDDIN ST
ALLEN GDNS
Spitalfields City Farm
Thomas Buxton Inf & Jun Sch
SELBY STREET
QUAKER STREET
BUXTON STREET
WHELER ST
CALVIN STREET
GREY EAGLE ST
E1
UNDERWOOD ROAD
St. Anne's Prim Sch
Osmani Prim Sch
Keen Students Sch
COMMERCIAL ST
NORTON FOLGATE
FOLGATE STREET
B134
WOODSEER
SPITAL STREET
St. Anne (RC)
WOOD ST
COVERLEY CL
LOMAS ST
LAMB ST
HANBURY ST
Comm Cen
OLD SPITALFIELDS MARKET
A1202
PRINCELET STREET
Pride Of Spitalfield PH
BETHNAL GRN TRAINING CEN
SPELMAN ST
GREATOREX ST
Comm Cen
PAULINE HO
FOURNIER ST
BRUSHFIELD STREET
Christ Church
Christ Ch C of E Sch
HENEAGE ST
21
FASHION STREET
SKETCHLEY
MONTAGUE STREET
A11
DURWARD ST

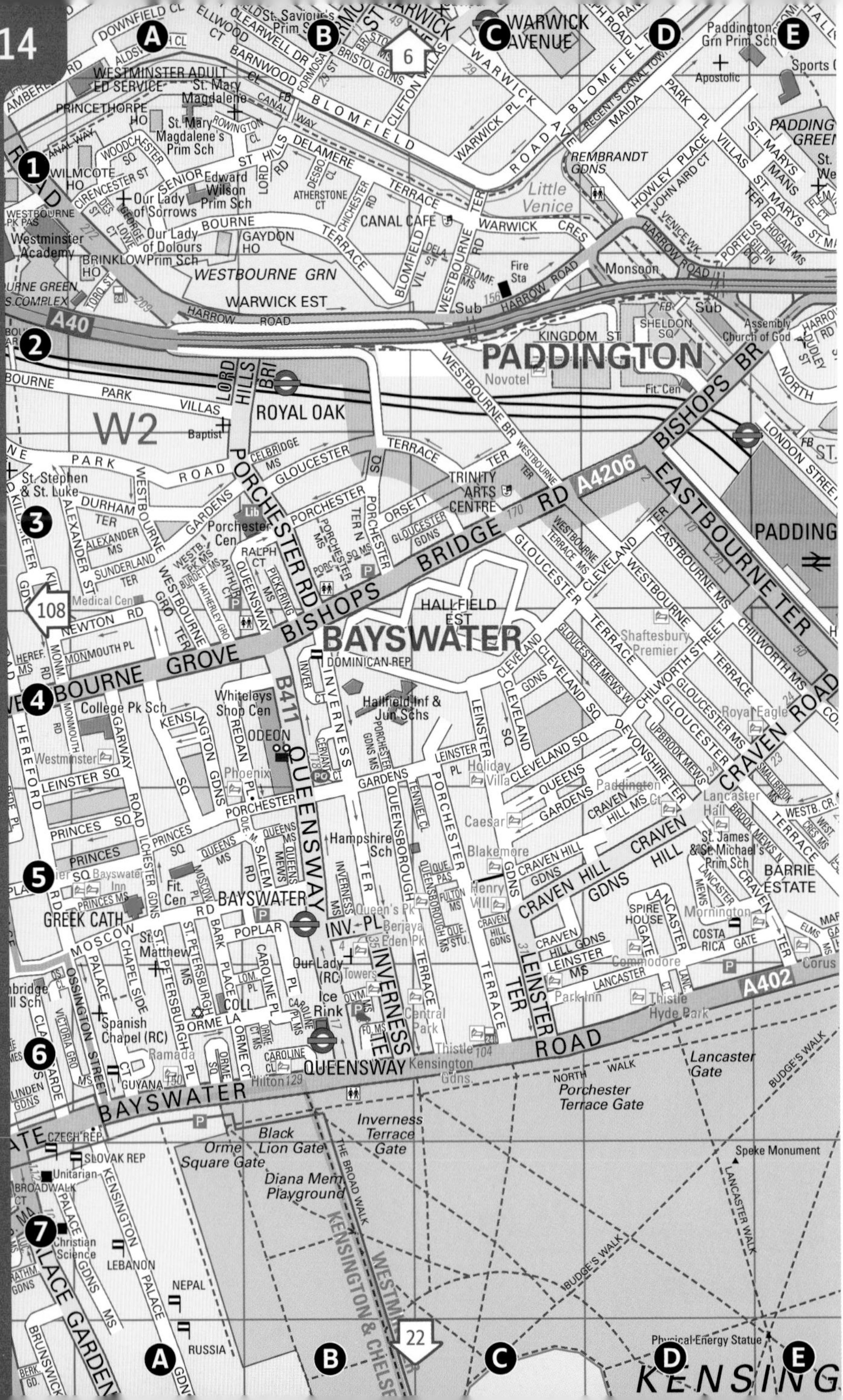
A
B
C
D
E
1
2
3
4
5
6
7
6
108
22
WARWICK AVENUE
Paddington Grn Prim Sch
Sports
Apostolic
PADDINGTON GREEN
WESTMINSTER ADULT ED SERVICE
St. Mary Magdalene
St. Mary Magdalene's Prim Sch
PRINCETHORPE HO
St. Saviour's Prim Sch
DOWNFIELD CL
ELLWOOD CT
CLEARWELL DR
BARNWOOD CL
FORMOSA ST
BRISTOL GDNS
CLIFTON VILLAS
BLOMFIELD RD
WARWICK PL
WARWICK AVE
BLOMFIELD RD
REGENT'S CANAL TOWPATH
MAIDA AVE
PARK PL VILLAS
ST. MARYS MANS
ST. MARYS TER
PORTEUS RD
HOGAN MS
GILPIN CL
HOWLEY PLACE
JOHN AIRD CT
VENICE WK
REMBRANDT GDNS
Little Venice
CANAL WAY
ROWINGTON CL
DELAMERE TERRACE
ST HILLS LORD RD
DESBOROUGH CL
ATHERSTONE CT
CHICHESTER RD
WOODCHESTER SQ
WILMCOTE HO
CIRENCESTER ST
SENIOR ST
Edward Wilson Prim Sch
Our Lady of Sorrows
Our Lady of Dolours Prim Sch
BOURNE TERRACE
GAYDON HO
CANAL CAFE
WARWICK CRES
WESTBOURNE PK PAS
Westminster Academy
BRINKLOW HO
WESTBOURNE GRN
WESTBOURNE GREEN SPORTS COMPLEX
TORO ST
WARWICK EST
BLOMFIELD VIL
DELAMERE ST
WESTBOURNE TER
BLOMF. MS
Fire Sta
Monsoon
HARROW ROAD
Sub
A40
KINGDOM ST
SHELDON SQ
FB
Assembly Church of God
PADDINGTON
Novotel
Fit. Cen
BISHOPS BR
NORTH WHARF RD
LONDON STREET
ST.
WESTBOURNE PARK VILLAS
LORD HILLS BRI
ROYAL OAK
W2
Baptist
WESTBOURNE PARK ROAD
St. Stephen & St. Luke
CELBRIDGE MS
GLOUCESTER TERRACE
PORCHESTER SQ
WESTBOURNE TER
TRINITY ARTS CENTRE
A4206
EASTBOURNE TER
PADDINGTON
DURHAM TER
ALEXANDER ST
ALEXANDER MS
SUNDERLAND TER
WESTBOURNE GARDENS
Lib
Porchester Cen
PORCHESTER RD
PORCHESTER TER N
ORSETT TER
GLOUCESTER GDNS
BISHOPS BRIDGE RD
WESTBOURNE TERRACE MS
GLOUCESTER TERRACE
CLEVELAND TER
EASTBOURNE MS
WESTBOURNE TER
RALPH CT
PICKERING MS
ARTHUR CT
QUEENSWAY
HALLFIELD EST
BAYSWATER
Shaftesbury Premier
CHILWORTH STREET
CHILWORTH MS
Medical Cen
NEWTON RD
MONMOUTH PL
WESTBOURNE GROVE
HEREFORD MS
DOMINICAN REP.
GLOUCESTER MEWS W
CLEVELAND GDNS
CLEVELAND SQ
INVERNESS CT
CRAVEN ROAD
Royal Eagle
Whiteleys Shop Cen
B411
Hallfield Inf & Jun Schs
College Pk Sch
MONMOUTH RD
GARWAY ROAD
KENSINGTON GDNS SQ
REDAN PL
ODEON
QUEENSWAY
LEINSTER PL
DEVONSHIRE TER
UPBROOK MEWS
GLOUCESTER MS
SMALLBROOK MS
Westminster
Phoenix
PO
CERVANTES CT
PORCHESTER GDNS MS
GARDENS
QUEENSBOROUGH TER
TENNIEL CL
PORCHESTER TER
Holiday Villa
CLEVELAND SQ
QUEENS GARDENS
Paddington Ct
CRAVEN HILL MS
Lancaster Hall
BROOK MEWS N
WESTB. CR.
LEINSTER SQ
HEREFORD RD
PORCHESTER PL
Caesar
CRAVEN HILL
St. James & St. Michael's Prim Sch
CRAVEN TER
BARRIE ESTATE
PRINCES SQ
PRINCES MS
ICHESTER GDNS
QUEENS MS
SALEM RD
QUEENS MEWS
Hampshire Sch
Blakemore
CRAVEN HILL GDNS
LANCASTER MEWS
Bayswater Inn
Fit. Cen
GREEK CATH
MOSCOW RD
BAYSWATER RD
P
INV. PL
Queen's Pk
Berjaya Eden Pk
Henry VIII
CRAVEN HILL GDNS
SPIRE HOUSE
LANCASTER GATE
COSTA RICA
Mornington
ELMS MS
St. Matthew
ST. PETERSBURGH MS
POPLAR PL
CAROLINE PL
INVERNESS TER
QUEENSBOROUGH TER
QUEENSBOROUGH MS
Our Lady (RC)
Towers
LEINSTER TER
LEINSTER MS
Commodore
LANCASTER MS
Corus
A402
OSSINGTON ST
PALACE CT
CHAPEL SIDE
COLL
Ice Rink
OLYMPIA MS
Central Park
Park Inn
Thistle Hyde Park
Spanish Chapel (RC)
ST. PETERSBURGH PL
ORME LA
ORME CT
CAROLINE PL MS
VICTORIA GRO
Ramada
GUYANA
Hilton
QUEENSWAY
Kensington Gdns
Thistle
BAYSWATER ROAD
LINDEN GDNS
CZECH REP
SLOVAK REP
Unitarian
BROADWALK CT
PALACE GDNS MS
KENSINGTON PALACE
Christian Science
LEBANON
NEPAL
RUSSIA
PALACE GARDEN
BRUNSWICK GDNS
BERK. GD.
NORTH WALK
Lancaster Gate
Porchester Terrace Gate
Inverness Terrace Gate
Black Lion Gate
Orme Square Gate
Diana Mem Playground
THE BROAD WALK
KENSINGTON & CHELSEA
WESTMINSTER
BUDGE'S WALK
LANCASTER WALK
Speke Monument
Physical Energy Statue
KENSINGTON

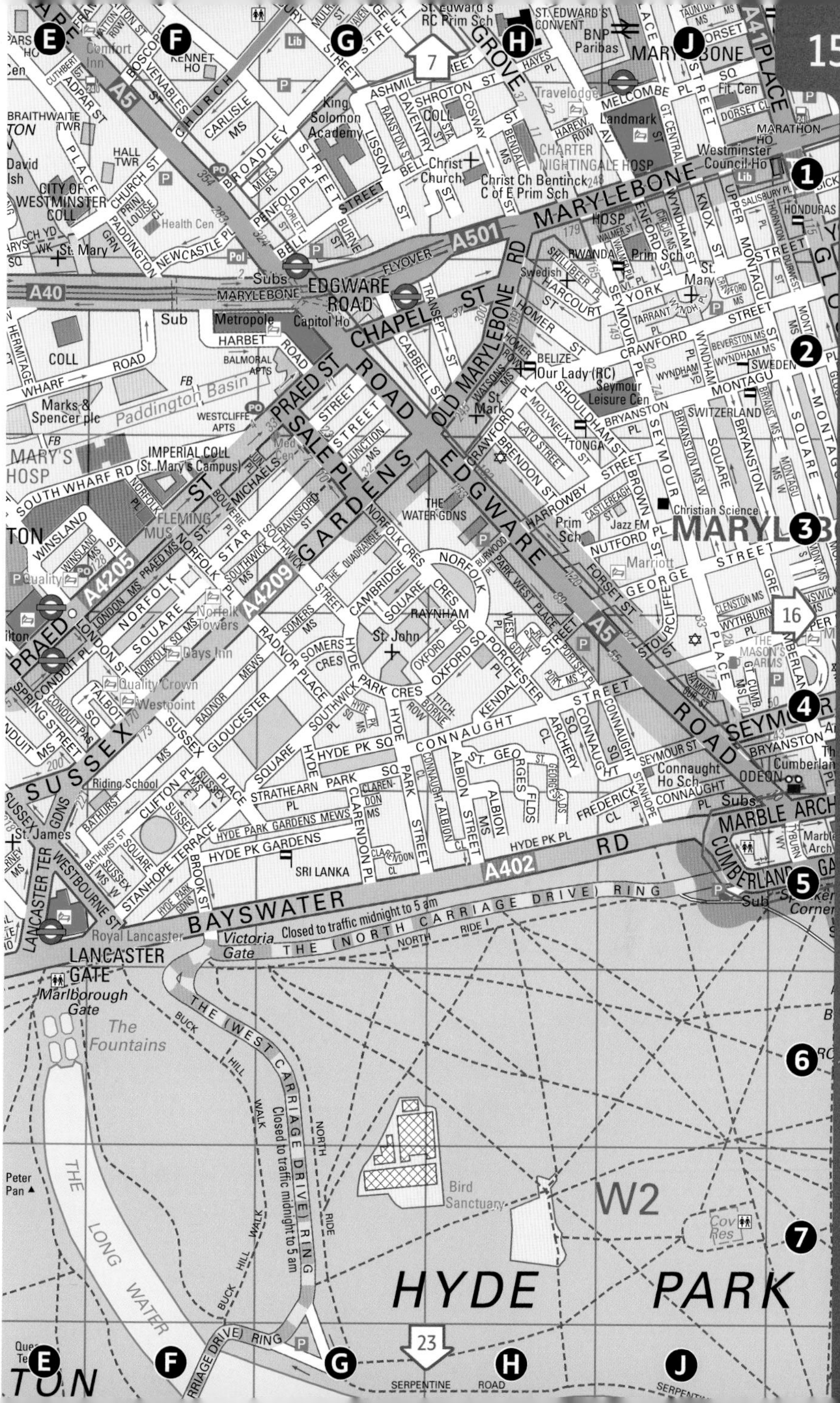
E
F
G
H
J
7
St. Edward's RC Prim Sch
ST. EDWARD'S CONVENT
BNP Paribas
MARYLEBONE
Comfort Inn
KENNET HO
Lib
GROVE
HAYES PL
TAUNTON MS
DORSET
A41 PLACE
SQ.
Fit. Cen
DORSET CL
MARATHON HO
Westminster Council Ho
BOSCOBEL
VENABLES ST
CHURCH
CARLISLE MS
King Solomon Academy
ASHMILL
DAVENTRY
SHROTON ST
COSWAY
COLL
Travelodge
MELCOMBE PL
GT. CENTRAL
Landmark
HAREW PL
CHARTER NIGHTINGALE HOSP
BENDALL MS
BRAITHWAITE TWR
CUTHBERT
ADPAR ST
A5
HALL TWR
PLACE
BROADLEY
MILES
LISSON
RANSDON ST
BELL
Christ Church
Christ Ch Bentinck C of E Prim Sch
David Ish
CITY OF WESTMINSTER COLL
CHURCH ST
PRIN LOUISE CL
PENFOLD PL
PENFOLD ST
STREET
BURNE ST
MARYLEBONE
HOSP
ENFORD ST
KNOX
UPPER MONTAGU
SALISBURY PL
THORNTON
HONDURAS
1
Health Cen
PADDINGTON GRN
NEWCASTLE PL
CORLETT
BELL ST
FLYOVER
A501
RD
RWANDA
Prim Sch
St. Mary
SHILLIBEER PL
HARCOURT ST
WALMER ST
CIRCUS MS
WYNDHAM ST
STREET
CH YD
WK
St. Mary
SQ
Pol
Subs
EDGWARE ROAD
A40
MARYLEBONE
TRANSEPT ST
CHAPEL ST
Swedish
HARCOURT
SEYMOUR PL
YORK
TARRANT PL
CRAWFORD
WYNDH PL
MS
STREET
MONT MS
Sub
Metropole
Capitol Ho
HARBET
ROAD
CABBELL ST
OLD MARYLEBONE
HOMER ST
HOMER ROW
BELIZE
Our Lady (RC)
Seymour Leisure Cen
WYNDHAM YD
BEVERSTON MS
WYNDHAM MS
SWEDEN
MONTAGU
2
HERMITAGE
COLL
WHARF
ROAD
FB
BALMORAL APTS
PRAED ST
ROAD
WATSONS MS
St. Mark
SHOULDHAM ST
BRYANSTON
SWITZERLAND
MONTAGU SQUARE
Marks & Spencer plc
Paddington Basin
WESTCLIFFE APTS
PO
STREET
SALE PL
JUNCTION MS
CRAWFORD PL
MOLYNEUX ST
CATO STREET
TONGA
BRYANSTON MS W
SQUARE
BRYANSTON ST
MONTAGU MS W
IMPERIAL COLL (St. Mary's Campus)
MARY'S HOSP
Med Cen
GARDENS
EDGWARE
BRENDON ST
SEYMOUR
BROWN
STREET
SOUTH WHARF RD
NORFOLK PL
ST
MICHAELS
BOUVERIE
RAINSFORD ST
HARROWBY
CASTLEREAGH
Christian Science
TON
FLEMING MUS
STAR
SOUTHWICK
THE WATER GDNS
Prim Sch
Jazz FM
MARYL
3
WINSLAND
WINSLAND MS
PRAED MS
NORFOLK CRES
NUTFORD PL
Marriott
STREET
MONT MS
Quality
A4205
NORFOLK
SOUTHWICK MS
THE QUADRANGLE
CAMBRIDGE
NORFOLK CRES
BURWOOD PL
PARK WEST PLACE
FORSET ST
GEORGE
CLENSTON MS
16
PRAED
LONDON MS
SQUARE
A4209
SOUTHWICK
STREET
SQUARE
CRES
RAYNHAM
WEST GDN PL
PA PK
A5
STOURCLIFFE ST
WYTHBURN PL
THE MASON'S ARMS
Hilton
LONDON ST
NORFOLK SQ MS
Norfolk Towers
RADNOR MS
SOMERS MS
St. John
OXFORD SQ
PORCHESTER PL
PORTSEA PL
PORT MS
PLACE
GT CUMB MS
HAMPDEN GUR ST
CONDUIT PL
Days Inn
SOMERS CRES
HYDE PARK CRES
STREET
ROAD
4
SPRING STREET
Quality Crown
TALBOT SQ
Westpoint
RADNOR PLACE
TITCHBORNE ROW
KENDAL
CONNAUGHT SQ
SEYMOUR
BRYANSTON
Cumberland
CONDUIT MS
CONDUIT PAS
SUSSEX
GLOUCESTER
SOUTHWICK PL
HYDE PK MS
HYDE
CONNAUGHT
ARCHERY CL
ST. GEORGES FLDS
SEYMOUR ST
Connaught Ho Sch
ODEON
200
SUSSEX
Riding School
SUSSEX PLACE
SQUARE
HYDE PK SQ
STRATHEARN PL
CLARENDON MS
CONNAUGHT CL
ALBION STREET
ALBION MS
FREDERICK CL
STANHOPE PL
CONNAUGHT
Subs
MARBLE ARCH
SUSSEX GDNS
St. James
BATHURST
CLIFTON PL
SUSSEX PL
HYDE PARK GARDENS MEWS
TYBURN WY
Marble Arch
WESTBOURNE ST
BATHURST ST
SUSSEX MS W
SQUARE
STANHOPE TERRACE
BROOK ST
HYDE PARK GDNS
HYDE PK GARDENS
SRI LANKA
CLARENDON PL
CLARENDON CL
HYDE PK PL
A402
RD
CUMBERLAND GA
5
LANCASTER TER
Royal Lancaster
BAYSWATER
Victoria Gate
Closed to traffic midnight to 5 am
THE (NORTH CARRIAGE DRIVE) RING
NORTH RIDE
Sub
Speakers' Corner
LANCASTER GATE
Marlborough Gate
The Fountains
THE (WEST CARRIAGE DRIVE) RING
Closed to traffic midnight to 5 am
BUCK HILL
6
BUCK HILL WALK
NORTH RIDE
THE LONG WATER
Peter Pan
Bird Sanctuary
W2
Cov Res
7
HYDE
PARK
23
Queens Ter
TON
SERPENTINE ROAD
SERPENTINE

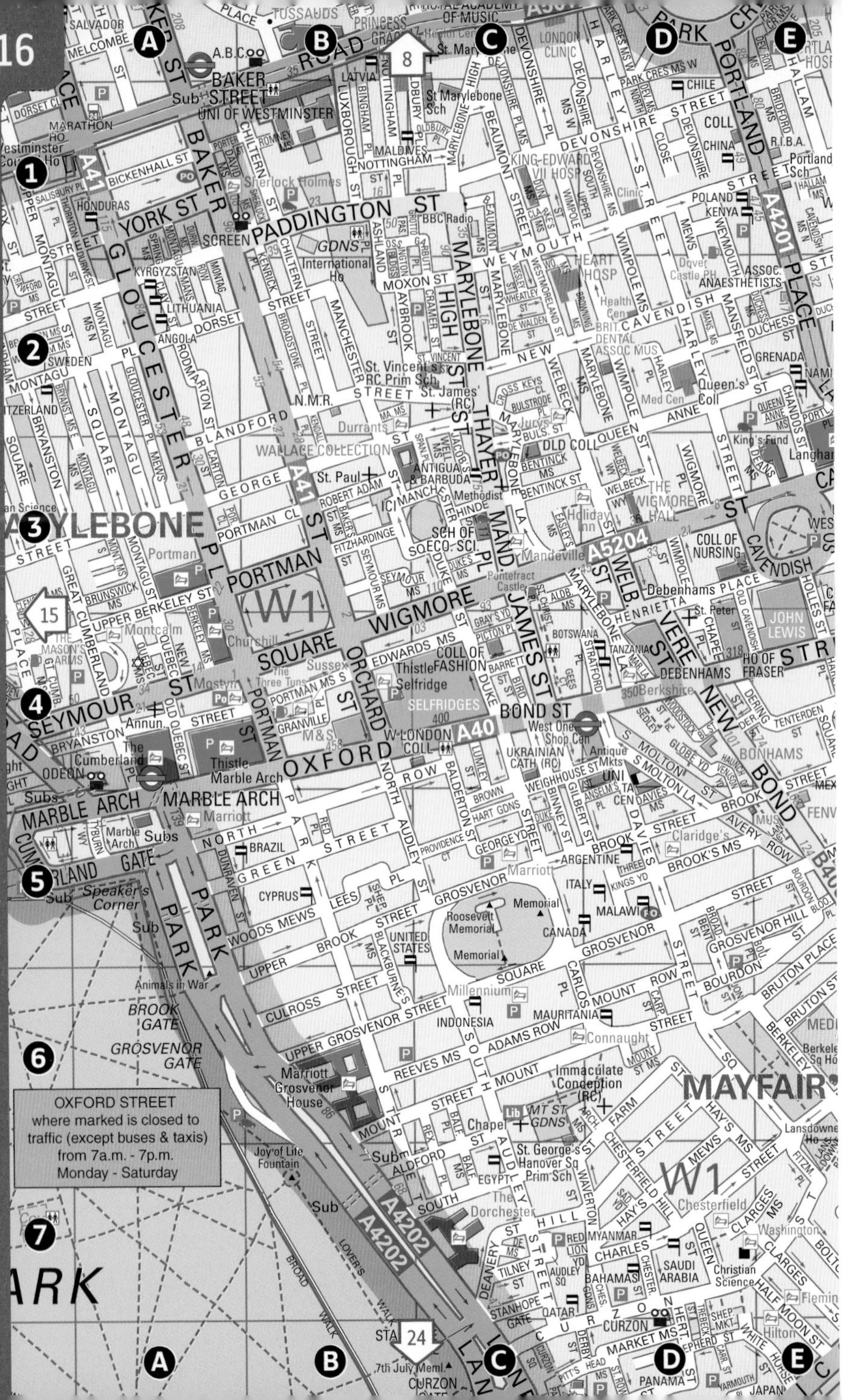

A
B
C
D
E
1
2
3
4
5
6
7
8
15
24
MARYLEBONE
MAYFAIR
W1
BAKER ST
BAKER STREET
PADDINGTON ST
YORK ST
GLOUCESTER PL
MARYLEBONE HIGH ST
PORTMAN SQUARE
WIGMORE ST
OXFORD STREET
MARBLE ARCH
PARK LANE
SEYMOUR ST
GROSVENOR SQUARE
NEW BOND ST
CAVENDISH SQUARE
PORTLAND PLACE
HARLEY STREET
WIMPOLE ST
WELBECK ST
DUKE ST
JAMES ST
NORTH AUDLEY ST
SOUTH AUDLEY ST
MOUNT ST
CURZON ST
UPPER BROOK ST
UPPER GROSVENOR ST
NORTH ROW
GREEN ST
PARK ST
SELFRIDGES
WALLACE COLLECTION
BOND ST
Speaker's Corner
Animals in War
BROOK GATE
GROSVENOR GATE
Joy of Life Fountain
Roosevelt Memorial
Memorial
7th July Meml.
A41
A40
A5204
A4201
A4202
OXFORD STREET
where marked is closed to
traffic (except buses & taxis)
from 7a.m. - 7p.m.
Monday - Saturday

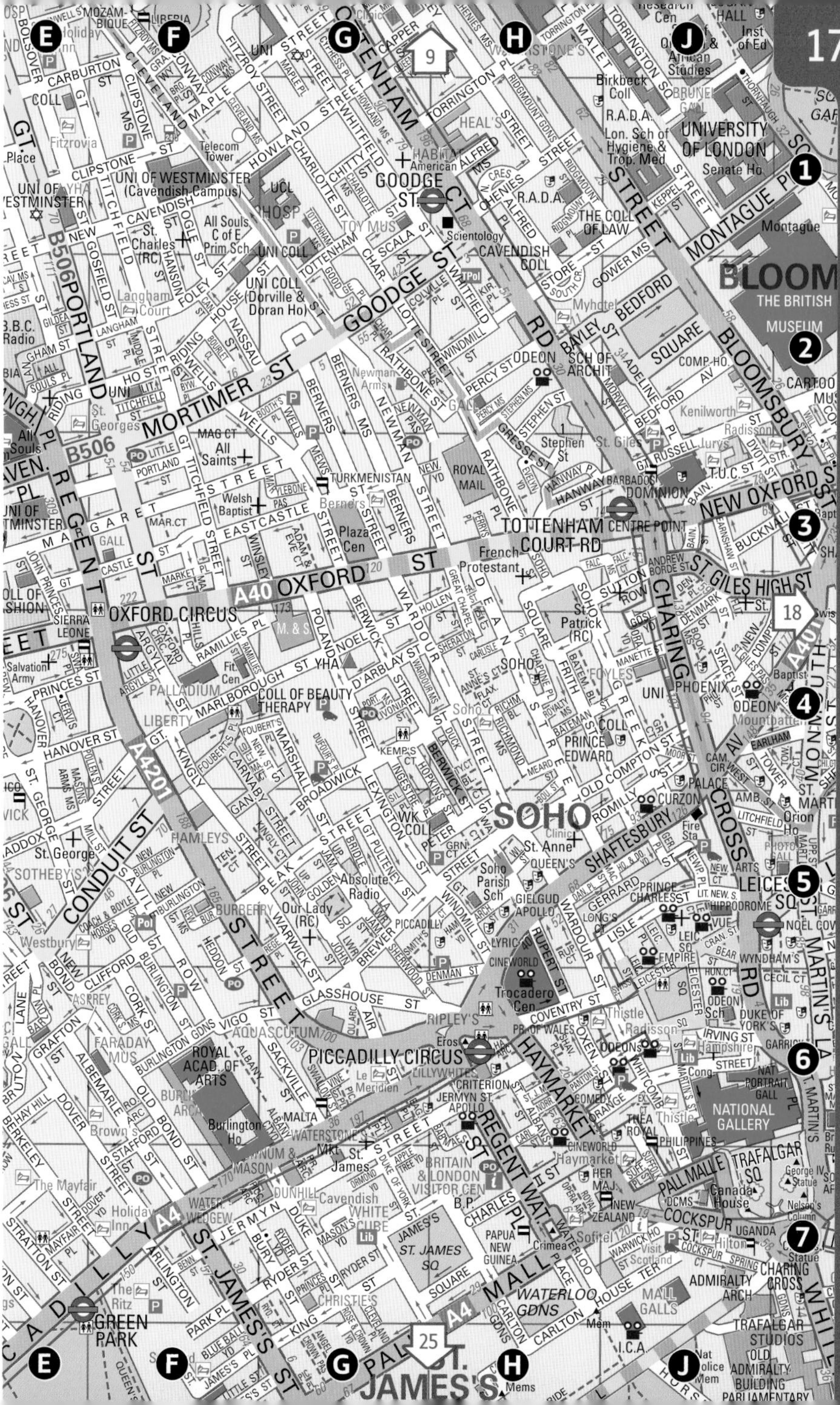
E
F
G
H
J
9
UNIVERSITY OF LONDON
Senate Ho.
Birkbeck Coll
R.A.D.A.
Lon. Sch of Hygiene & Trop. Med
GOODGE ST
Telecom Tower
UNI OF WESTMINSTER (Cavendish Campus)
UCL HOSP
TOY MUS
Scientology
UNI COLL (Dorville & Doran Ho)
GOODGE ST
TOTTENHAM CT RD
BLOOMSBURY ST
BLOOM
THE BRITISH MUSEUM
MONTAGUE PL
BEDFORD SQUARE
MORTIMER ST
PORTLAND PL
B506
REGENT ST
ROYAL MAIL
TOTTENHAM COURT RD
CENTRE POINT
NEW OXFORD ST
DOMINION
A40 OXFORD ST
OXFORD CIRCUS
SOHO SQUARE
ST. GILES HIGH ST
CHARING CROSS RD
18
PALLADIUM
LIBERTY
A4201
CONDUIT ST
HAMLEYS
SOHO
SHAFTESBURY AV
LEICESTER SQ
CARNABY ST
BROADWICK ST
OLD COMPTON ST
DEAN ST
WARDOUR ST
GREEK ST
ODEON
PHOENIX
SOTHEBY'S
NEW BOND ST
Trocadero Cen
PICCADILLY CIRCUS
HAYMARKET
ROYAL ACAD. OF ARTS
Burlington Ho
NATIONAL GALLERY
TRAFALGAR SQ
Nelson's Column
Canada House
PALL MALL
COCKSPUR ST
ST. JAMES'S SQ
WATERLOO PLACE
THE MALL
ADMIRALTY ARCH
I.C.A.
PICCADILLY
A4
GREEN PARK
The Ritz
ST. JAMES'S ST
JERMYN ST
25
ST. JAMES'S
1
2
3
4
5
6
7

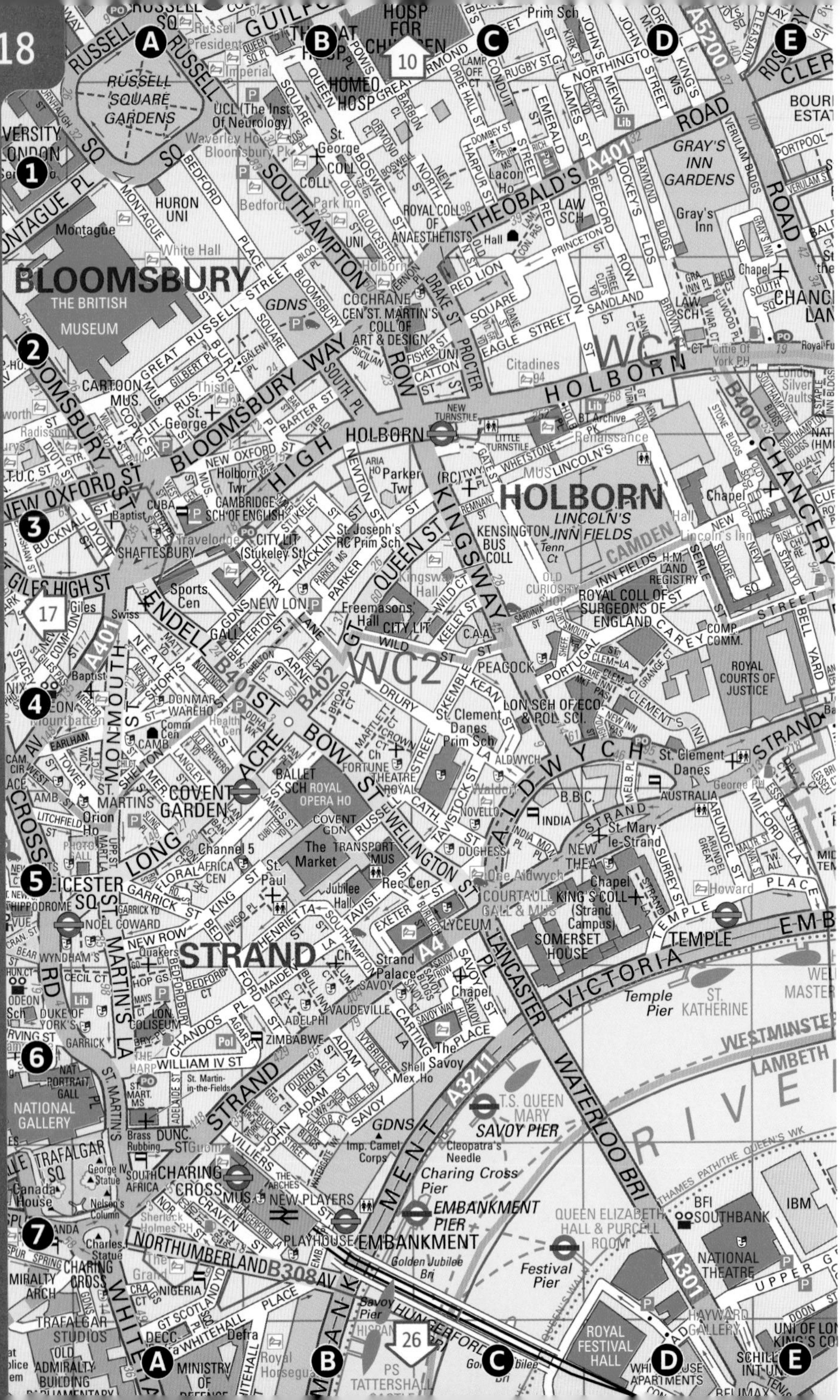
A
B
C
D
E
1
2
3
4
5
6
7
10
17
26
BLOOMSBURY
THE BRITISH MUSEUM
RUSSELL SQUARE GARDENS
RUSSELL SQ
SOUTHAMPTON ROW
THEOBALD'S ROAD
A401
GRAY'S INN GARDENS
Gray's Inn
WC1
HOLBORN
HOLBORN
LINCOLN'S INN FIELDS
CAMDEN
BLOOMSBURY WAY
NEW OXFORD ST
HIGH HOLBORN
KINGSWAY
CHANCERY LANE
ROYAL COLL OF SURGEONS OF ENGLAND
ROYAL COURTS OF JUSTICE
WC2
COVENT GARDEN
ROYAL OPERA HO
LONG ACRE
BOW ST
DRURY LANE
ALDWYCH
STRAND
STRAND
SOMERSET HOUSE
KING'S COLL (Strand Campus)
TEMPLE
VICTORIA EMBANKMENT
LEICESTER SQ
CHARING CROSS RD
ST. MARTIN'S LA
NATIONAL GALLERY
TRAFALGAR SQ
CHARING CROSS
EMBANKMENT
NORTHUMBERLAND AV
WHITEHALL
WATERLOO BRI
Temple Pier
Savoy Pier
Festival Pier
ROYAL FESTIVAL HALL
NATIONAL THEATRE
BFI SOUTHBANK
HAYWARD GALLERY
QUEEN ELIZABETH HALL & PURCELL ROOM
Cleopatra's Needle
RIVER
LAMBETH
WESTMINSTER
A3211
A4
A301
B400
B401
B402
B308
A5200
SHAFTESBURY
MONMOUTH ST
ENDELL ST
The Savoy
Strand Palace
LYCEUM
COURTAULD GALL & MUS
LON SCH OF ECO & POL SCI
St. Clement Danes
St. Mary-le-Strand
B.B.C.
AUSTRALIA
INDIA
ZIMBABWE
NIGERIA
SOUTH AFRICA
Canada House
MINISTRY OF DEFENCE
ADMIRALTY ARCH
TRAFALGAR STUDIOS
Sherlock Holmes PH
Golden Jubilee Bri
HUNGERFORD
IBM
UNI OF LON KING'S COLL

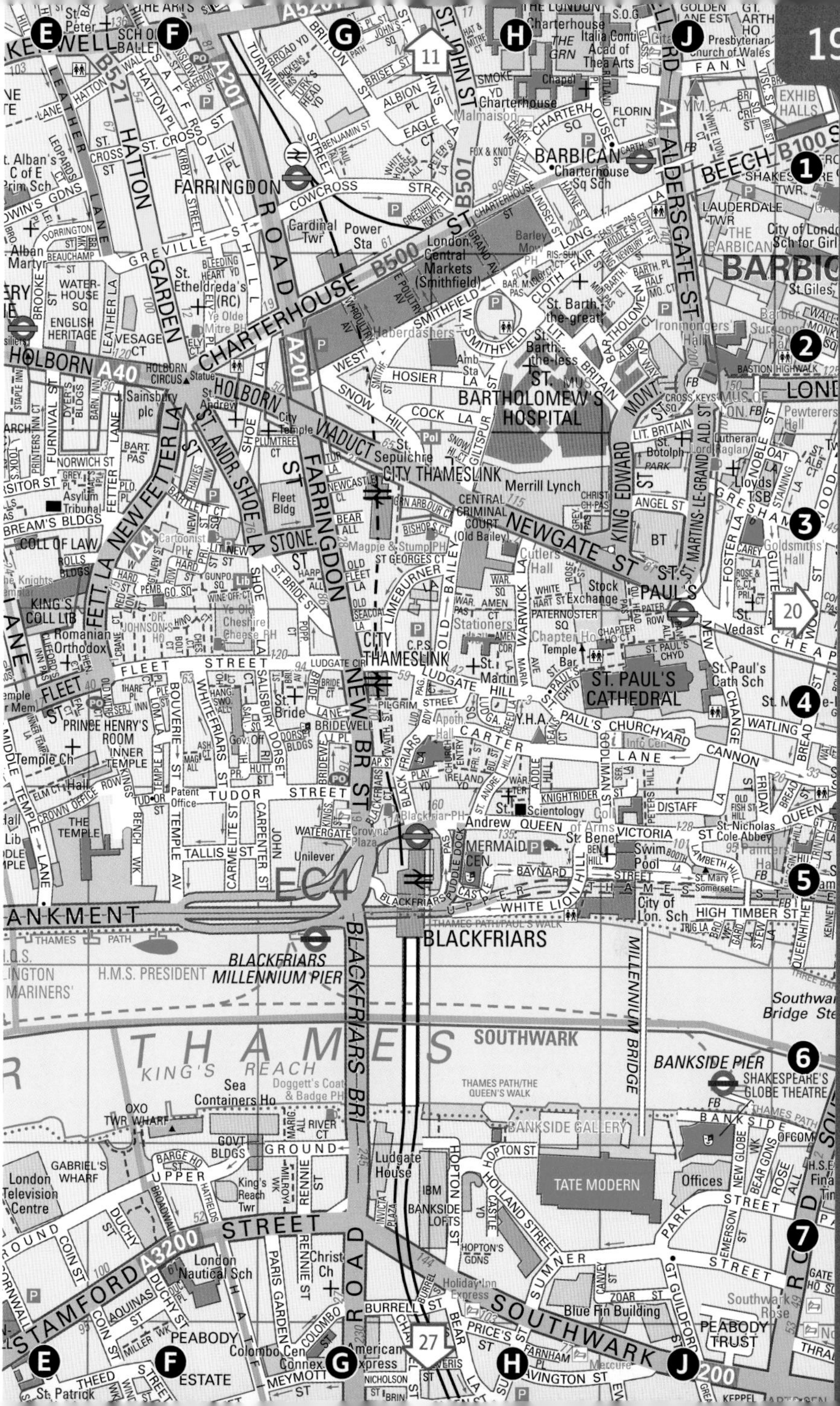

E
F
G
H
J
11
FARRINGDON
BARBICAN
Charterhouse
Charterhouse Sq Sch
HATTON GARDEN
ST. CROSS ST
COWCROSS STREET
CHARTERHOUSE ST
B500
London Central Markets (Smithfield)
St. Bartholomew-the-great
ST. BARTHOLOMEW'S HOSPITAL
ALDERSGATE ST
A1
BEECH ST
B100
1
2
3
4
5
6
7
LAUDERDALE TWR
City of London Sch for Girls
HOLBORN
A40
HOLBORN CIRCUS
HOLBORN VIADUCT
FARRINGDON ST
A201
J. Sainsbury plc
St. Andrew
City Temple
St. Sepulchre
CITY THAMESLINK
Merrill Lynch
CENTRAL CRIMINAL COURT (Old Bailey)
NEWGATE ST
KING EDWARD ST
ST. MARTINS-LE-GRAND
ST. PAUL'S
NEW FETTER LA
A4
COLL OF LAW
KING'S COLL LIB
Romanian Orthodox
Ye Olde Cheshire Cheese PH
FLEET STREET
FLEET ST
LUDGATE HILL
ST. PAUL'S CATHEDRAL
ST. PAUL'S CHURCHYARD
CANNON ST
20
Stock Exchange
Stationers' Hall
PRINCE HENRY'S ROOM
INNER TEMPLE
Temple Ch
THE TEMPLE
St. Bride
NEW BR ST
TUDOR STREET
QUEEN VICTORIA ST
Unilever
EC4
MERMAID CEN
UPPER THAMES ST
HIGH TIMBER ST
City of Lon. Sch
BLACKFRIARS
H.M.S. PRESIDENT
BLACKFRIARS MILLENNIUM PIER
THAMES
KING'S REACH
SOUTHWARK
MILLENNIUM BRIDGE
BANKSIDE PIER
SHAKESPEARE'S GLOBE THEATRE
Southwark Bridge
Sea Containers Ho
OXO TWR WHARF
BLACKFRIARS BRI
BANKSIDE GALLERY
TATE MODERN
Offices
London Television Centre
STAMFORD STREET
A3200
London Nautical Sch
Christ Ch
BANKSIDE LOFTS
IBM
Ludgate House
Holiday Inn Express
SOUTHWARK ST
Blue Fin Building
PEABODY TRUST
PEABODY ESTATE
SUMNER STREET
PARK STREET
American Express
27

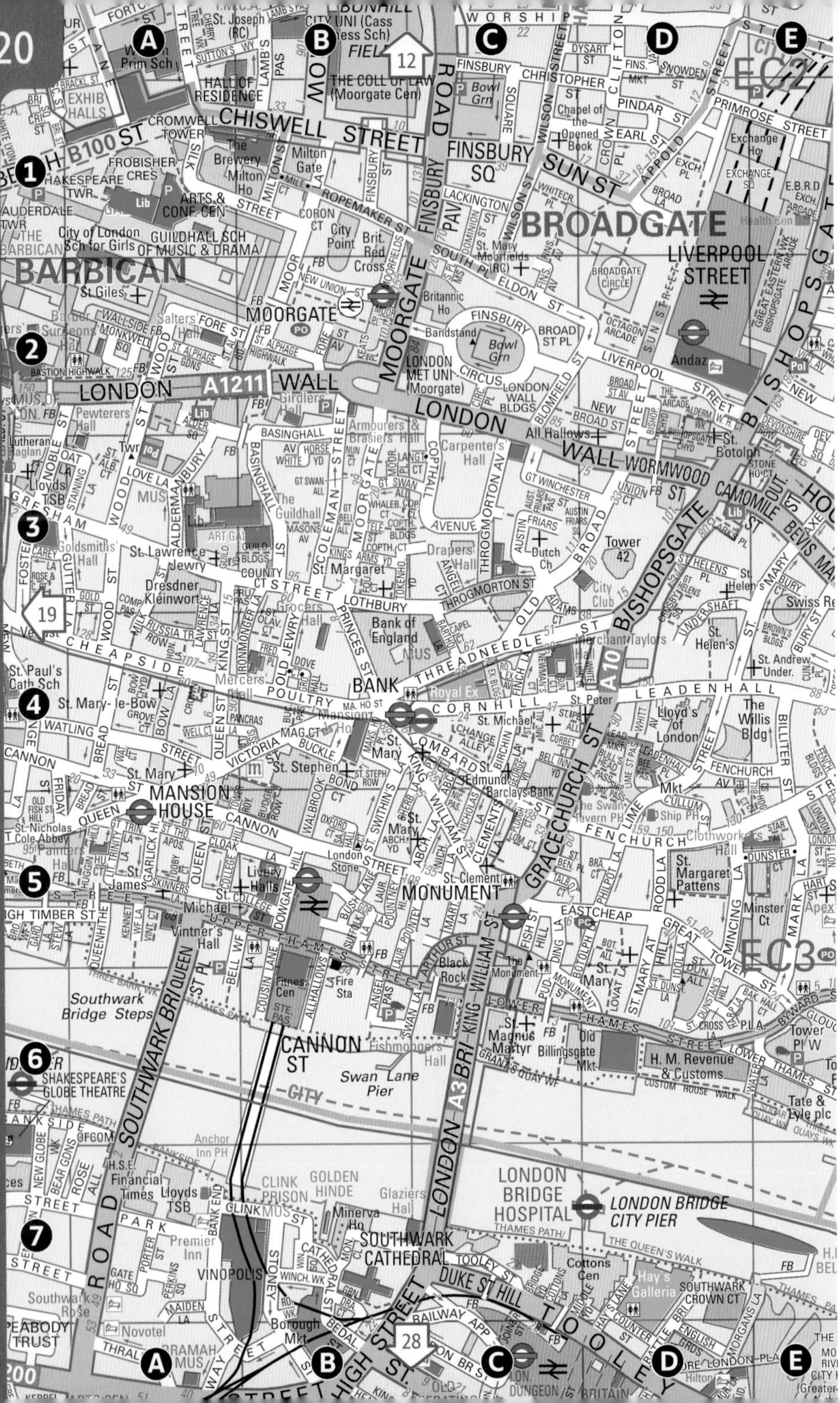
A
B
C
D
E
1
2
3
4
5
6
7
12
19
28
EC2
EC3
BARBICAN
BROADGATE
CHISWELL STREET
FINSBURY SQ
SUN ST
LIVERPOOL STREET
MOORGATE
LONDON WALL
A1211
BISHOPSGATE
A10
CHEAPSIDE
BANK
Bank of England
Royal Ex
THREADNEEDLE ST
CORNHILL
LEADENHALL
FENCHURCH
LOMBARD ST
KING WILLIAM ST
GRACECHURCH ST
CANNON ST
QUEEN VICTORIA ST
MANSION HOUSE
MONUMENT
EASTCHEAP
GREAT TOWER ST
UPPER THAMES STREET
LOWER THAMES STREET
CANNON ST
Swan Lane Pier
LONDON BRIDGE CITY PIER
A3
LONDON BRI
SOUTHWARK BRI
SOUTHWARK ROAD
SHAKESPEARE'S GLOBE THEATRE
BANKSIDE
CLINK PRISON
GOLDEN HINDE
VINOPOLIS
SOUTHWARK CATHEDRAL
Borough Mkt
LONDON BRIDGE HOSPITAL
Hay's Galleria
TOOLEY ST
DUKE ST HILL
BOROUGH HIGH STREET
THE COLL OF LAW (Moorgate Cen)
CITY UNI (Cass Business Sch)
City of London Sch for Girls
GUILDHALL SCH OF MUSIC & DRAMA
ARTS & CONF. CEN
The Guildhall
Tower 42
The Willis Bldg
Lloyd's of London
H. M. Revenue & Customs
Old Billingsgate Mkt
Tate & Lyle plc
Southwark Bridge Steps
Fishmongers' Hall
St. Magnus Martyr
Financial Times
Novotel
PEABODY TRUST
Southwark Rose
Premier Inn
Andaz
Barclays Bank
Dresdner Kleinwort
Mercers' Hall
Grocers' Hall
Goldsmiths' Hall
Pewterers' Hall
Girdlers' Hall
Armourers & Brasiers' Hall
Carpenters' Hall
Drapers' Hall
Merchant Taylors' Hall
Clothworkers' Hall
Vintner's Hall
Painters' Hall
St. Paul's Cath Sch
St. Mary-le-Bow
St. Lawrence Jewry
St. Margaret
St. Stephen
St. Mary
St. Michael
St. Edmund
St. Clement
St. Peter
St. Botolph
St. Helen's
St. Andrew Under.
St. Margaret Pattens
St. Giles
All Hallows
Dutch Ch
Britannic Ho
LONDON MET UNI (Moorgate)
Bandstand
FINSBURY CIRCUS
BROADGATE CIRCLE
EXCHANGE SQ
E.B.R.D.
Minster Ct
CITY

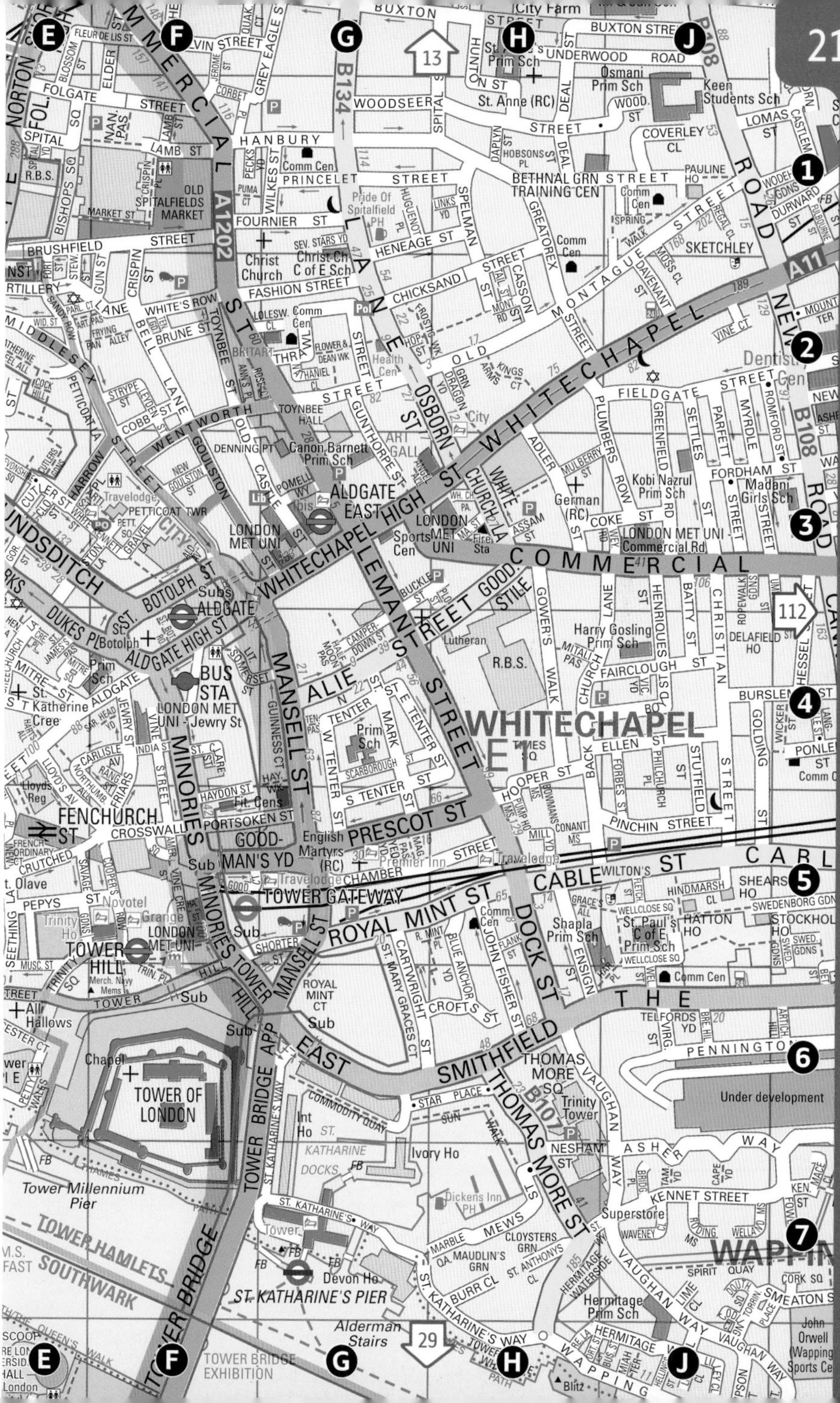

E
F
G
H
J
13
1
2
3
4
5
6
7
112
29
WHITECHAPEL
E1
WHITECHAPEL HIGH ST
COMMERCIAL
MANSELL ST
LEMAN STREET
ALIE STREET
PRESCOT ST
ROYAL MINT ST
CABLE ST
DOCK ST
EAST SMITHFIELD
THE HIGHWAY
THOMAS MORE ST
TOWER BRIDGE
TOWER BRIDGE APP
TOWER OF LONDON
Tower Millennium Pier
ST. KATHARINE'S PIER
ST KATHARINE DOCKS
TOWER HAMLETS
SOUTHWARK
MINORIES
ALDGATE
ALDGATE EAST
ALDGATE HIGH ST
TOWER GATEWAY
TOWER HILL
FENCHURCH ST
HOUNDSDITCH
OLD SPITALFIELDS MARKET
COMMERCIAL ST
A1202
A11
B134
B108
B107
HANBURY STREET
PRINCELET STREET
FOURNIER ST
BRUSHFIELD STREET
WENTWORTH STREET
OLD MONTAGUE STREET
FIELDGATE STREET
NEW ROAD
BUXTON STREET
UNDERWOOD ROAD
PETTICOAT LANE
MIDDLESEX STREET
GOODMAN'S YD
ROYAL MINT CT
WAPPING
Under development
TOWER BRIDGE EXHIBITION
Alderman Stairs
Harry Gosling Prim Sch
Canon Barnett Prim Sch
LONDON MET UNI
Travelodge
Premier Inn
Novotel
Christ Church
R.B.S.

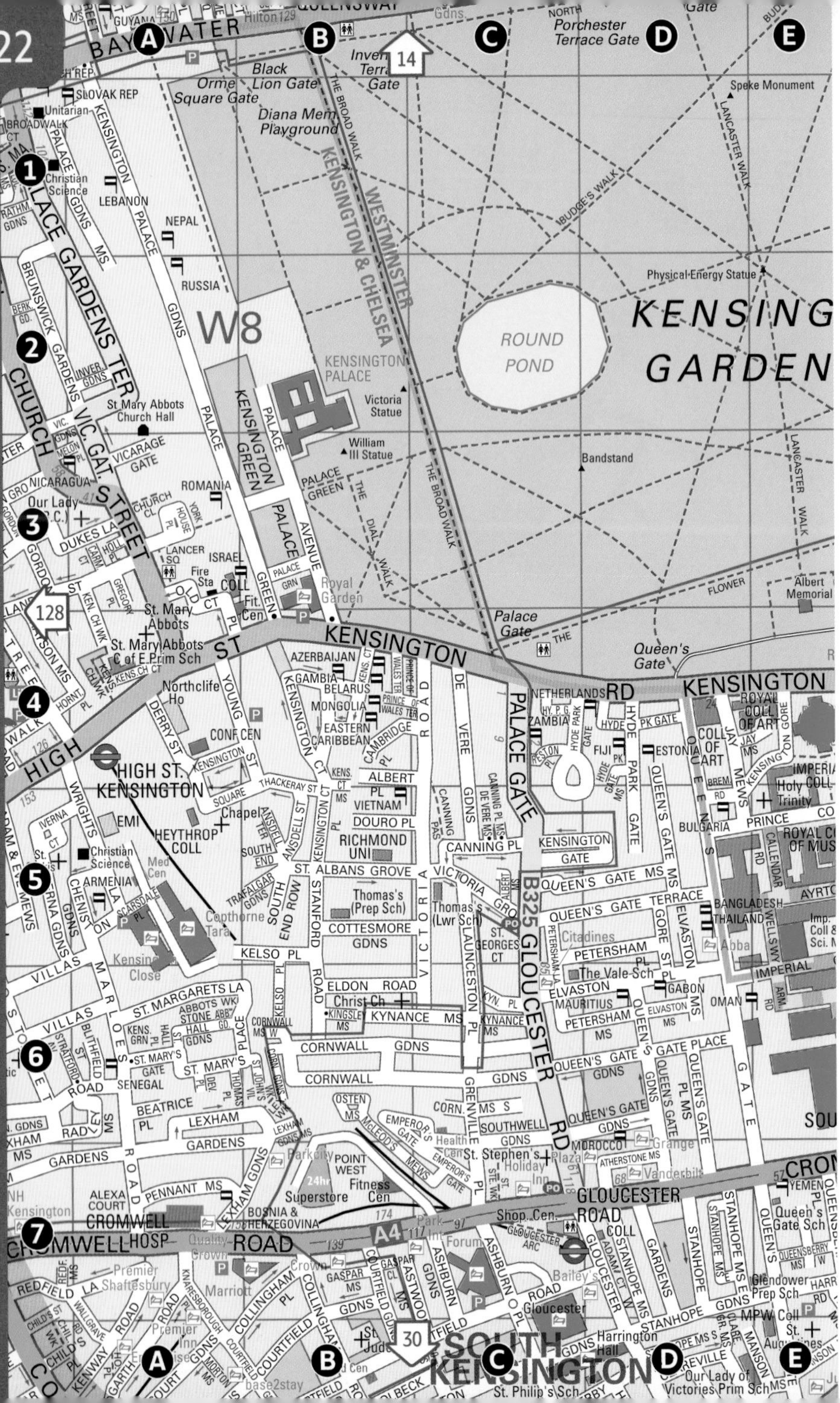
A
B
C
D
E
1
2
3
4
5
6
7
14
128
30
BAYSWATER
QUEENSWAY
North Porchester Terrace Gate
Speke Monument
Orme Square Gate
Black Lion Gate
Diana Mem Playground
Inverness Terrace Gate
THE BROAD WALK
KENSINGTON & CHELSEA
WESTMINSTER
LANCASTER WALK
BUDGE'S WALK
Physical Energy Statue
KENSINGTON GARDENS
ROUND POND
W8
KENSINGTON PALACE
Victoria Statue
William III Statue
Bandstand
LANCASTER WALK
THE DIAL WALK
PALACE GREEN
Royal Garden
Albert Memorial
FLOWER WALK
Palace Gate
Queen's Gate
KENSINGTON GARDENS
LEBANON
NEPAL
RUSSIA
SLOVAK REP
Unitarian
Christian Science
BRUNSWICK GARDENS
PALACE GARDENS TER
CHURCH STREET
VIC. GAT.
VICARAGE GATE
St Mary Abbots Church Hall
NICARAGUA
Our Lady (R.C.)
ROMANIA
YORK HOUSE PL
CHURCH CL
DUKES LA
LANCER SQ
ISRAEL
Fire Sta
COLL
Fit. Cen
St. Mary Abbots
St. Mary Abbots C of E Prim Sch
KENSINGTON HIGH ST
Northcliffe Ho
HIGH ST. KENSINGTON
KENSINGTON SQUARE
CONF CEN
THACKERAY ST
Chapel
HEYTHROP COLL
EMI
Christian Science
ARMENIA
Copthorne Tara
Kensington Close
KELSO PL
AZERBAIJAN
GAMBIA
BELARUS
MONGOLIA
EASTERN CARIBBEAN
CAMBRIDGE PL
ALBERT PL
VIETNAM
DOURO PL
RICHMOND UNI
ST. ALBANS GROVE
Thomas's (Prep Sch)
Thomas's (Lwr Sch)
COTTESMORE GDNS
ELDON ROAD
Christ Ch
KYNANCE MS
CORNWALL GDNS
VICTORIA ROAD
VICTORIA GRO
DE VERE GDNS
CANNING PL
LAUNCESTON PL
ST. GEORGES CT
NETHERLANDS
ZAMBIA
FIJI
ESTONIA
HYDE PARK GATE
KENSINGTON GATE
PALACE GATE
B325 GLOUCESTER RD
QUEEN'S GATE MS
QUEEN'S GATE TERRACE
PETERSHAM PL
PETERSHAM MS
Citadines
The Vale Sch
ELVASTON PL
MAURITIUS
GABON
OMAN
BULGARIA
Holy Trinity
ROYAL COLL OF ART
COLL OF ART
IMPERIAL COLL
ROYAL COLL OF MUSIC
PRINCE CONSORT RD
BANGLADESH
THAILAND
Abba
IMPERIAL COLL RD
Imp. Coll & Sci. Mus
QUEEN'S GATE
QUEEN'S GATE PLACE
GORE ST
ELVASTON MS
ST. MARGARETS LA
ABBOTS WK
STONE HALL GD.
ST. MARY'S GATE
ST. MARY'S PLACE
SENEGAL
MARLOES ROAD
STRATFORD ROAD
BEATRICE PL
LEXHAM GARDENS
LEXHAM GDNS
PENNANT MS
ALEXA COURT
BOSNIA & HERZEGOVINA
Parkcity
POINT WEST
Superstore
Fitness Cen
EMPEROR'S GATE
McLEOD'S MEWS
Health Cen
St. Stephen's
Holiday Inn
SOUTHWELL GDNS
GRENVILLE PL
CORN. MS S
MOROCCO
Grange
ATHERSTONE MS
Vanderbilt
GLOUCESTER ROAD
Shop. Cen.
GLOUCESTER ARC
COLL
CROMWELL ROAD
A4
CROMWELL HOSP
NH Kensington
Quality Crown
Crowne
Park Int
Forum
Marriott
Premier
Shaftesbury
Premier Inn
REDFIELD LA
COLLINGHAM PL
COLLINGHAM
COURTFIELD
GASPAR MS
ASHBURN PL
Bailey's
Gloucester
STANHOPE GDNS
STANHOPE MS
STANHOPE GARDENS
YEMEN
Queen's Gate Sch
Glendower Prep Sch
MPW Coll
St. Augustines
Harrington Hall
SOUTH KENSINGTON
Our Lady of Victories Prim Sch
St. Philip's Sch
St. Jude
base2stay
KENWAY RD
NH Kensington

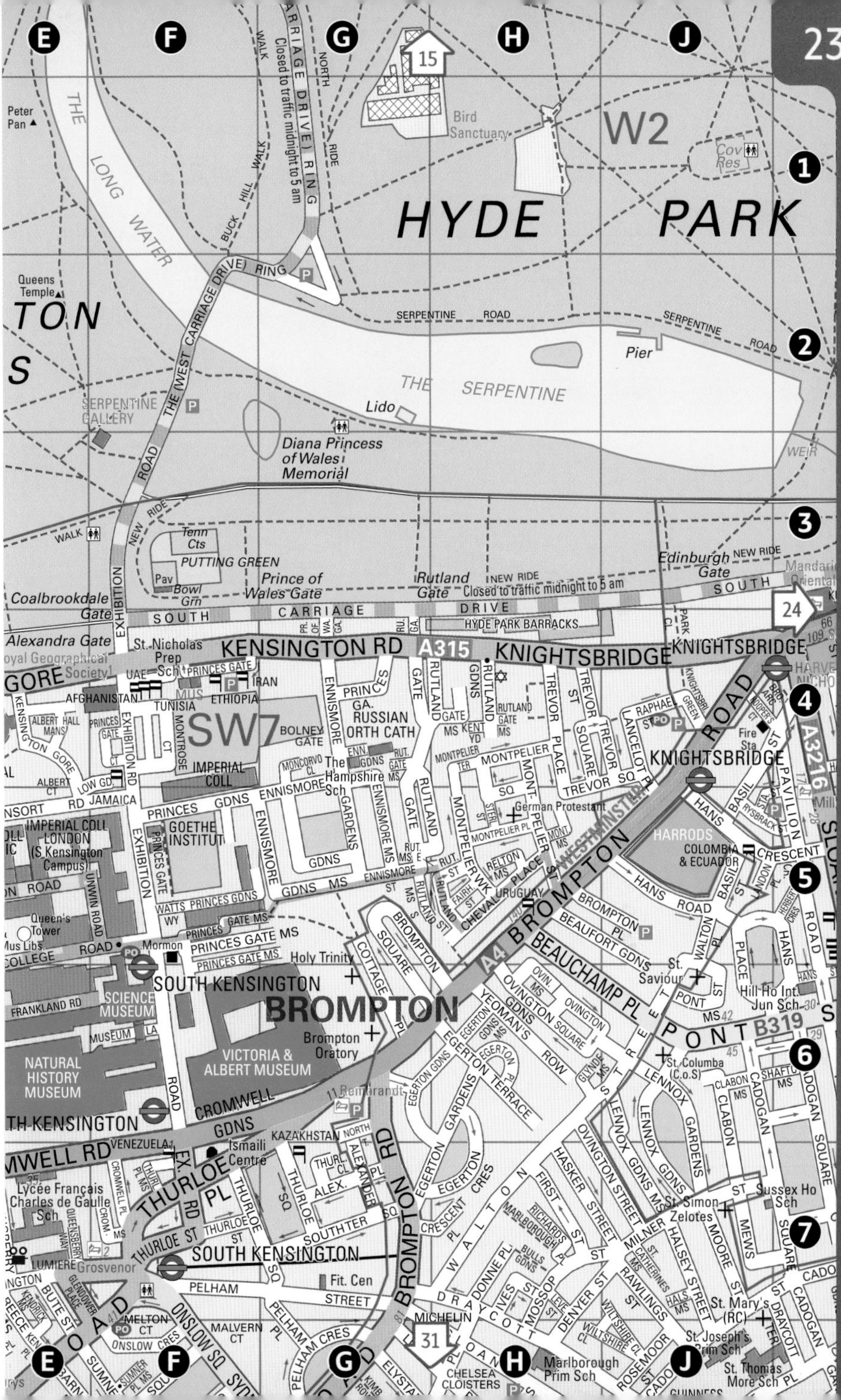
E
F
G
H
J
15
HYDE PARK
W2
Peter Pan
THE LONG WATER
BUCK HILL WALK
NORTH RIDE
(WEST CARRIAGE DRIVE) RING
Closed to traffic midnight to 5 am
Bird Sanctuary
Cov Res
Queens Temple
TON
S
SERPENTINE ROAD
Pier
THE SERPENTINE
Lido
SERPENTINE GALLERY
THE (WEST CARRIAGE DRIVE) RING
EXHIBITION ROAD
Diana Princess of Wales Memorial
WEIR
WALK
NEW RIDE
Tenn Cts
PUTTING GREEN
Pav
Bowl Grn
Prince of Wales Gate
Rutland Gate
Closed to traffic midnight to 5 am
Edinburgh Gate
Mandarin Oriental
SOUTH CARRIAGE DRIVE
Coalbrookdale Gate
Alexandra Gate
24
HYDE PARK BARRACKS
St. Nicholas Prep Sch
KENSINGTON RD
A315
KNIGHTSBRIDGE
Royal Geographical Society
GORE
UAE
PRINCES GATE
IRAN
AFGHANISTAN
ETHIOPIA
TUNISIA
MUS
SW7
ENNISMORE GARDENS
PRINCES GA.
RUSSIAN ORTH CATH
BOLNEY GATE
RUTLAND GATE
RUTLAND GDNS
TREVOR PLACE
TREVOR SQUARE
TREVOR ST
RAPHAEL ST
LANCELOT PL
KNIGHTSBRIDGE GREEN
Fire Sta
IMPERIAL COLL
The Hampshire Sch
MONTPELIER PLACE
MONTPELIER SQ
TREVOR SQ
KNIGHTSBRIDGE
BROMPTON ROAD
A3216
ALBERT CT
JAMAICA RD
PRINCES GDNS
German Protestant
HARRODS
COLOMBIA & ECUADOR
HANS CRESCENT
BASIL ST
PAVILION RD
SLOANE ST
IMPERIAL COLL LONDON (S.Kensington Campus)
GOETHE INSTITUT
EXHIBITION RD
UNWIN ROAD
MONTPELIER WK
RUTLAND ST
CHEVAL PLACE
URUGUAY
WESTMINSTER
HANS ROAD
BROMPTON PL
BEAUFORT GDNS
WALTON PL
HANS PLACE
Queen's Tower
Mus Libs
COLLEGE ROAD
Mormon
PRINCES GATE MS
Holy Trinity
COTTAGE PL
BROMPTON SQUARE
A4
BEAUCHAMP PL
St. Saviour
PONT ST
Hill Ho Int. Jun Sch
SOUTH KENSINGTON
FRANKLAND RD
SCIENCE MUSEUM
MUSEUM
BROMPTON
Brompton Oratory
VICTORIA & ALBERT MUSEUM
OVINGTON GDNS
OVINGTON SQUARE
YEOMAN'S ROW
EGERTON TERRACE
PONT
B319
St. Columba (C.o.S)
LENNOX GARDENS
CLABON MS
CADOGAN SQUARE
NATURAL HISTORY MUSEUM
ROAD
CROMWELL GDNS
11 Rembrandt
SOUTH KENSINGTON
CROMWELL RD
VENEZUELA
Ismaili Centre
KAZAKHSTAN
NORTH TERR.
ALEXANDER PL
BROMPTON RD
EGERTON GARDENS
EGERTON CRES
WALTON ST
HASKER STREET
OVINGTON STREET
LENNOX GDNS
St. Simon Zelotes
MOORE ST
Sussex Ho Sch
Lycee Français Charles de Gaulle Sch
THURLOE PL
THURLOE SQ
CROMWELL PL
THURLOE ST
SOUTH TER
SOUTH KENSINGTON
LUMIERE
Grosvenor
Fit. Cen
PELHAM STREET
FIRST ST
MILNER ST
HALSEY STREET
DRAYCOTT
DENYER ST
RAWLINGS ST
St. Mary's (RC)
CADOGAN ST
MELTON CT
ONSLOW SQ
ONSLOW CRES
MALVERN CT
PELHAM CRES
MICHELIN
31
SLOANE AVE
Marlborough Prim Sch
St. Joseph's Prim Sch
St. Thomas More Sch
CHELSEA CLOISTERS
1
2
3
4
5
6
7

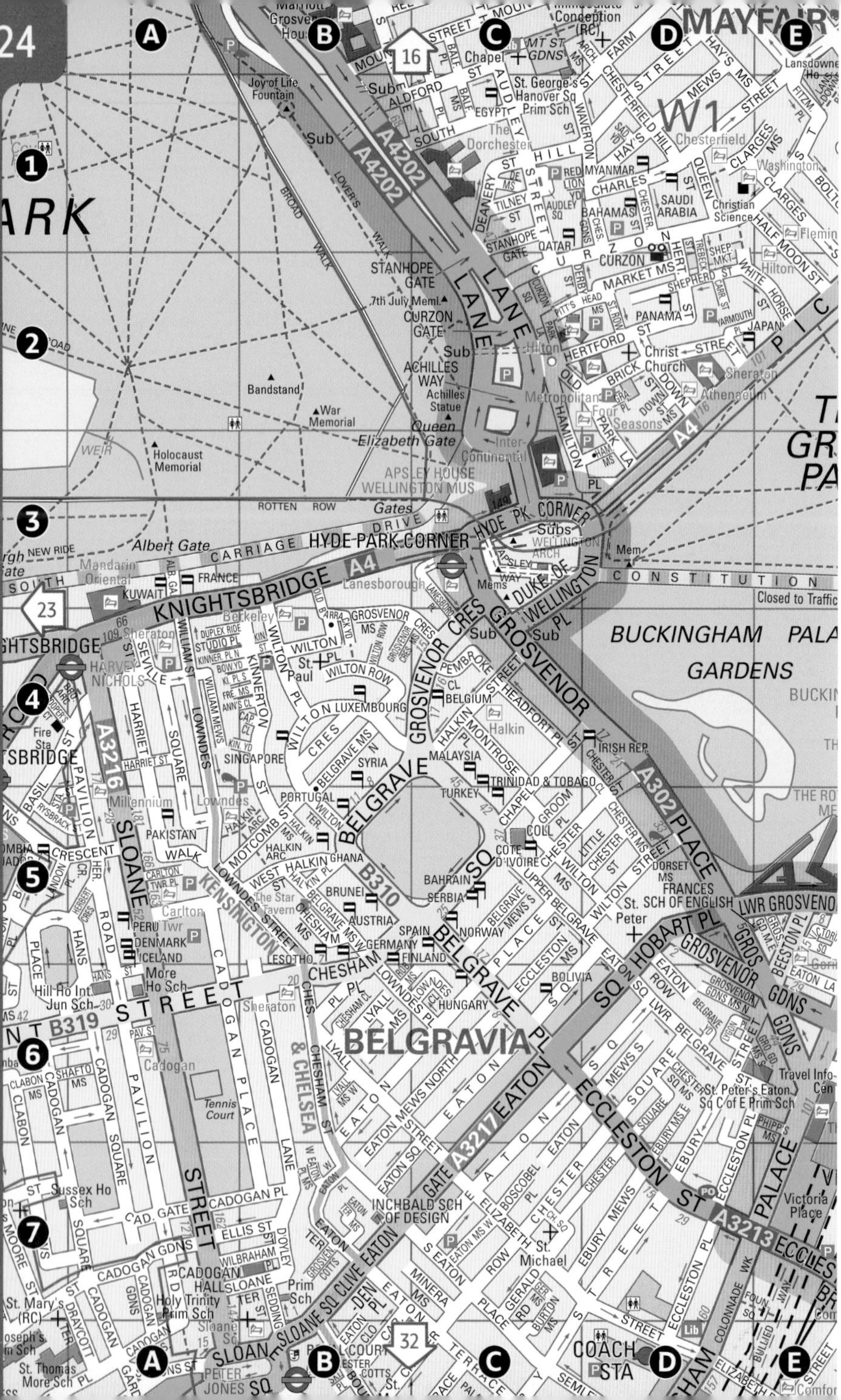
A
B
C
D
E
1
2
3
4
5
6
7
16
23
32
MAYFAIR
W1
ARK
BELGRAVIA
BUCKINGHAM PALA
GARDENS
HYDE PARK CORNER
KNIGHTSBRIDGE
A4202
A4
A3216
A3217
A3213
A302
B310
B319
Joy of Life Fountain
Sub
BROAD WALK
LOVER'S WALK
PARK LANE
STANHOPE GATE
7th July Meml.
CURZON GATE
ACHILLES WAY
Achilles Statue
Bandstand
War Memorial
Holocaust Memorial
WEIR
Queen Elizabeth Gate
Inter-Continental
APSLEY HOUSE
WELLINGTON MUS
ROTTEN ROW
Gates
CARRIAGE DRIVE
Albert Gate
NEW RIDE
Mandarin Oriental
KUWAIT
FRANCE
SOUTH
Lanesborough
Subs
WELLINGTON ARCH
APSLEY WAY
Mems
DUKE OF WELLINGTON PL
CONSTITUTION
Closed to Traffic
Mem
The Dorchester
Chapel
MT ST GDNS
St. George's Hanover Sq Prim Sch
Immaculate Conception (RC)
ALDFORD ST
SOUTH ST
MOUNT ST
FARM ST
HILL ST
DEANERY ST
TILNEY ST
STANHOPE GATE
CURZON ST
HERTFORD ST
Hilton
Metropolitan
Four Seasons
Christ Church
Sheraton
Athenaeum
Chesterfield
Washington
Christian Science
Hilton
MYANMAR
SAUDI ARABIA
BAHAMAS
QATAR
PANAMA
JAPAN
CHARLES ST
QUEEN ST
CLARGES ST
HALF MOON ST
WHITE HORSE ST
SHEPHERD MARKET
CHESTERFIELD HILL
HAY'S MEWS
Lansdowne Ho
Berkeley
Sheraton
HARVEY NICHOLS
GROSVENOR CRES
GROSVENOR PL
WILTON PL
WILTON ROW
WILTON CRES
KINNERTON ST
LOWNDES SQUARE
SLOANE ST
SEVILLE ST
WILLIAM ST
Halkin
HEADFORT PL
BELGIUM
IRISH REP.
MALAYSIA
TRINIDAD & TOBAGO
TURKEY
SINGAPORE
SYRIA
PORTUGAL
PAKISTAN
GHANA
BAHRAIN
SERBIA
NORWAY
BRUNEI
AUSTRIA
GERMANY
FINLAND
SPAIN
LESOTHO
HUNGARY
BOLIVIA
PERU
DENMARK
ICELAND
COTE D'IVOIRE
BELGRAVE SQ
CHAPEL ST
CHESTER ST
UPPER BELGRAVE ST
WILTON ST
HOBART PL
LWR GROSVENOR PL
St. Peter
Millennium
Lowndes
Carlton Twr
The Star Tavern
KENSINGTON & CHELSEA
CHESHAM ST
CHESHAM PL
LOWNDES ST
CADOGAN PLACE
CADOGAN SQUARE
PONT STREET
HANS PLACE
HANS CRES
BASIL ST
Fire Sta
Hill Ho Int. Jun Sch
More Ho Sch
Cadogan
Tennis Court
Sussex Ho Sch
CADOGAN PL
CADOGAN GATE
ELLIS ST
CADOGAN GDNS
WILBRAHAM PL
CADOGAN HALL
Holy Trinity Prim Sch
St. Mary's (RC)
St. Thomas More Sch
Sloane Sq
SLOANE SQ
PETER JONES
Prim Sch
INCHBALD SCH OF DESIGN
EATON PL
EATON SQ
EATON TER
EATON GATE
ELIZABETH ST
CHESTER SQ
St. Michael
EBURY MEWS
EBURY ST
ECCLESTON ST
ECCLESTON PL
St. Peter's Eaton Sq C of E Prim Sch
Travel Info Cen
Victoria Place
BUCKINGHAM PALACE RD
COACH STA
Lib
PO

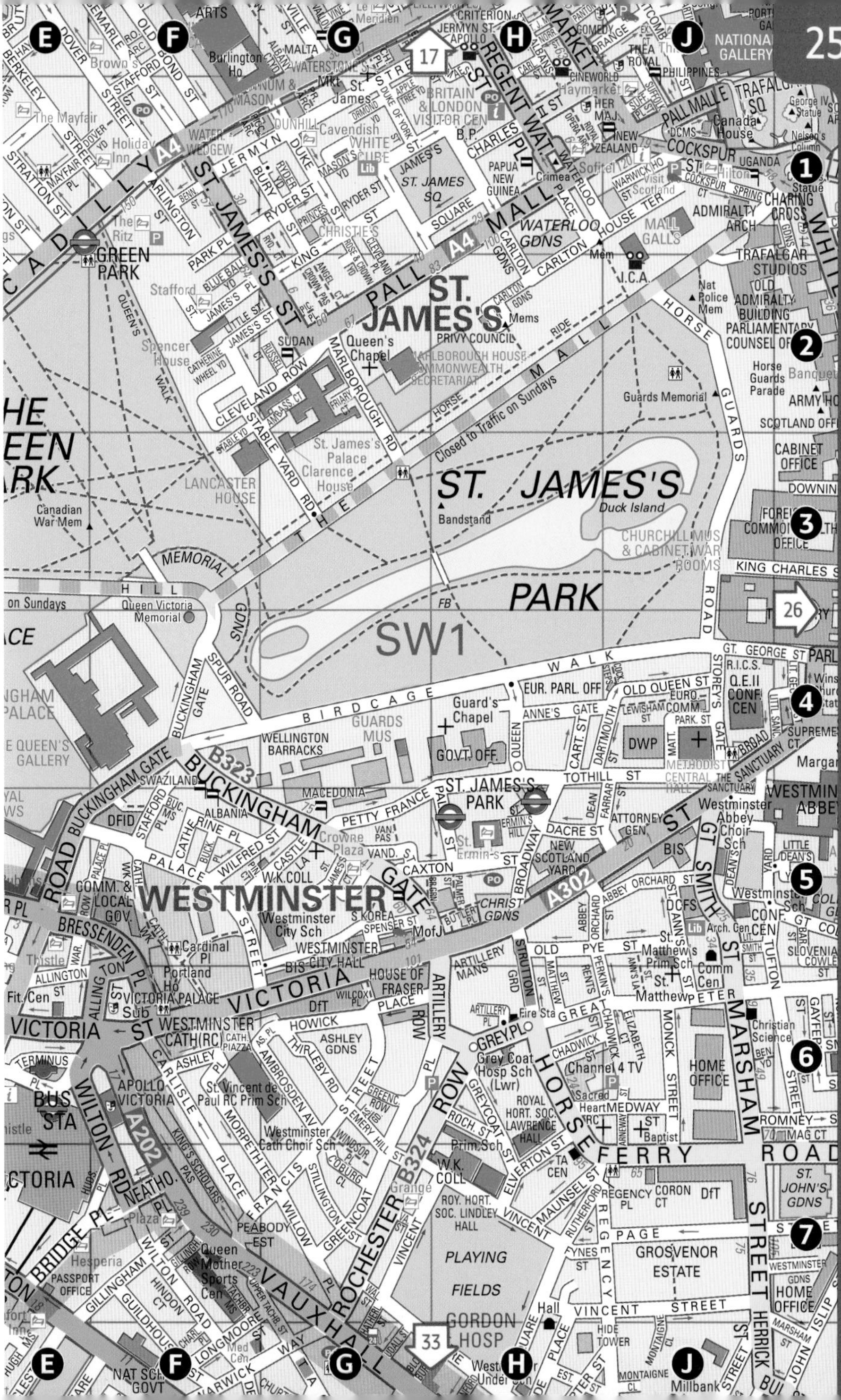
E
F
G
H
J
17
NATIONAL GALLERY
PICCADILLY
A4
Burlington Ho
ARTS
Brown's
The Mayfair
Holiday Inn
The Ritz
GREEN PARK
ST. JAMES'S ST
JERMYN ST
DUKE OF YORK ST
ST. JAMES'S SQUARE
REGENT ST
WATERLOO PLACE
HAYMARKET
PALL MALL
TRAFALGAR SQ
Canada House
COCKSPUR ST
CHARING CROSS
WHITEHALL
Nelson's Column
ADMIRALTY ARCH
THE MALL
ST. JAMES'S
PRIVY COUNCIL
Queen's Chapel
MARLBOROUGH HOUSE COMMONWEALTH SECRETARIAT
St. James's Palace
Clarence House
LANCASTER HOUSE
Spencer House
WATERLOO GDNS
CARLTON HOUSE TER
I.C.A.
MALL GALLS
HORSE GUARDS ROAD
Horse Guards Parade
Guards Memorial
Closed to Traffic on Sundays
THE GREEN PARK
Canadian War Mem
MEMORIAL
CONSTITUTION HILL
Queen Victoria Memorial
BUCKINGHAM PALACE
THE QUEEN'S GALLERY
ST. JAMES'S PARK
Duck Island
Bandstand
CHURCHILL MUS & CABINET WAR ROOMS
KING CHARLES ST
PARK
SW1
26
BIRDCAGE WALK
Guard's Chapel
WELLINGTON BARRACKS
GUARDS MUS
BUCKINGHAM GATE
B323
SPUR ROAD
PETTY FRANCE
St. James's Park
TOTHILL ST
BROADWAY
NEW SCOTLAND YARD
CAXTON ST
WESTMINSTER
WESTMINSTER ABBEY
THE SANCTUARY
A302
VICTORIA ST
WESTMINSTER CITY HALL
HOUSE OF FRASER
Portland Ho
VICTORIA PALACE
WESTMINSTER CATH (RC)
BRESSENDEN PL
VICTORIA
BUS STA
WILTON RD
A202
VAUXHALL BRIDGE ROAD
ROCHESTER ROW
B324
HORSEFERRY ROAD
MARSHAM STREET
HOME OFFICE
Channel 4 TV
GREAT PETER ST
GREAT SMITH ST
PAGE ST
GROSVENOR ESTATE
PLAYING FIELDS
GORDON HOSP
33
VINCENT SQUARE
Millbank

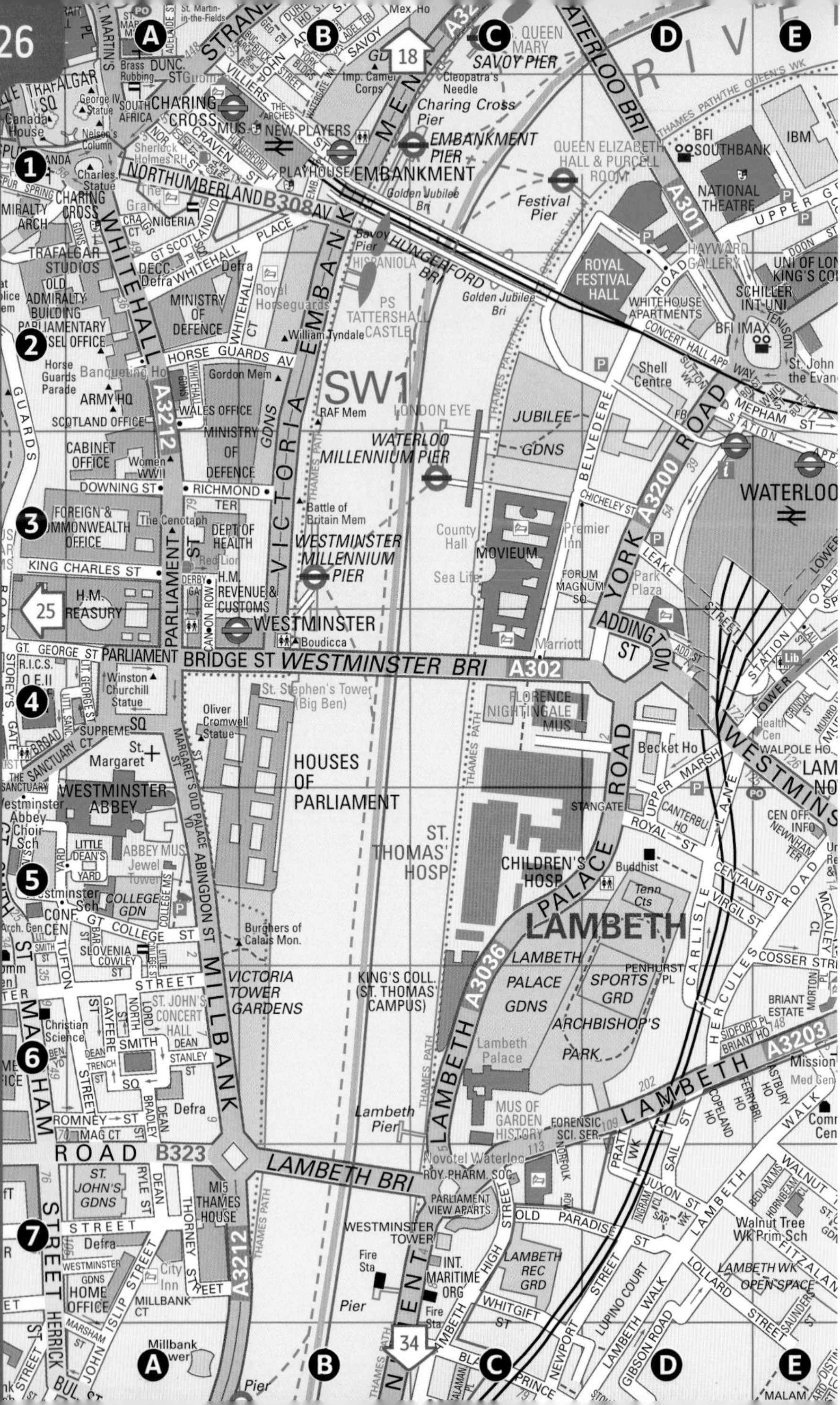
A
B
C
D
E
1
2
3
4
5
6
7
18
25
34
STRAND
TRAFALGAR SQ
Canada House
Nelson's Column
George IV Statue
Charles I Statue
CHARING CROSS
SOUTH AFRICA
Brass Rubbing
DUNC. ST
St. Martin-in-the-Fields
VILLIERS
JOHN ADAM ST
SAVOY
Imp. Camel Corps
Cleopatra's Needle
SAVOY PIER
QUEEN MARY
Charing Cross Pier
EMBANKMENT PIER
EMBANKMENT
MUS.
NEW PLAYERS
PLAYHOUSE
Sherlock Holmes PH
CRAVEN ST
NORTHUMBERLAND AV
B308
ADMIRALTY ARCH
The Grand
NIGERIA
WHITEHALL
GT SCOTLAND YD
WHITEHALL PLACE
Golden Jubilee Bri
HUNGERFORD BRI
Savoy Pier
HISPANIOLA
PS TATTERSHALL CASTLE
William Tyndale
TRAFALGAR STUDIOS
OLD ADMIRALTY BUILDING
PARLIAMENTARY COUNSEL OFFICE
DECC
Defra
MINISTRY OF DEFENCE
Royal Horseguards
WHITEHALL CT
HORSE GUARDS AV
Horse Guards Parade
Banqueting Ho
ARMY HQ
Gordon Mem
SCOTLAND OFFICE
WALES OFFICE
A3212
CABINET OFFICE
Women WWII
DOWNING ST
RICHMOND TER
FOREIGN & COMMONWEALTH OFFICE
The Cenotaph
DEPT OF HEALTH
KING CHARLES ST
H.M. TREASURY
Red Lion
DERBY GA
CANON ROW
H.M. REVENUE & CUSTOMS
WESTMINSTER
Boudicca
PARLIAMENT ST
GT. GEORGE ST
PARLIAMENT SQ
BRIDGE ST
WESTMINSTER BRI
A302
R.I.C.S.
Q.E.II
STOREY'S GATE
Winston Churchill Statue
LIT. GEORGE ST
BROAD SANC.
SUPREME CT
THE SANCTUARY
St. Margaret
WESTMINSTER ABBEY
Westminster Abbey Choir Sch
ABBEY MUS
Jewel Tower
LITTLE DEAN'S YARD
Westminster Sch
COLLEGE GDN
CONF. CEN
GT COLLEGE ST
TUFTON
SLOVENIA
COWLEY ST
St. Stephen's Tower (Big Ben)
Oliver Cromwell Statue
HOUSES OF PARLIAMENT
ST. MARGARET'S ST
OLD PALACE YD
ABINGDON ST
MILLBANK
Burghers of Calais Mon.
VICTORIA TOWER GARDENS
GREAT PETER STREET
MARSHAM ST
GAYFERE ST
LORD NORTH ST
ST. JOHN'S CONCERT HALL
Christian Science
SMITH SQ
DEAN STANLEY ST
DEAN TRENCH STREET
BRADLEY
Defra
ROMNEY ST
MAG CT
HORSEFERRY ROAD
B323
ST. JOHN'S GDNS
DEAN RYLE ST
MI5 THAMES HOUSE
THORNEY STREET
PAGE STREET
WESTMINSTER GDNS
HOME OFFICE
City Inn
JOHN ISLIP STREET
MILLBANK CT
Millbank Tower
HERRICK ST
THAMES PATH
Pier
SW1
VICTORIA EMBANKMENT
RAF Mem
LONDON EYE
WATERLOO MILLENNIUM PIER
Battle of Britain Mem
WESTMINSTER MILLENNIUM PIER
County Hall
Sea Life
JUBILEE GDNS
MOVIEUM
Premier Inn
FORUM MAGNUM SQ
Marriott
BELVEDERE RD
CHICHELEY ST
WATERLOO BRI
RIVER
QUEEN ELIZABETH HALL & PURCELL ROOM
Festival Pier
BFI SOUTHBANK
NATIONAL THEATRE
IBM
A301
THAMES PATH/THE QUEEN'S WK
UPPER GROUND
ROYAL FESTIVAL HALL
HAYWARD GALLERY
WHITEHOUSE APARTMENTS
BFI IMAX
UNI OF LONDON KING'S COLL
SCHILLER INT UNI
TENISON WAY
CONCERT HALL APP
Shell Centre
SUTTON WK
St. John the Evangelist
YORK ROAD
A3200
MEPHAM ST
STATION APP
WATERLOO
LEAKE ST
Park Plaza
ADDINGTON ST
LOWER MARSH
WESTMINSTER BRIDGE ROAD
FLORENCE NIGHTINGALE MUS
Becket Ho
WALPOLE HO
Health Cen
STANGATE
UPPER MARSH
CANTERBURY HO
CEN OFF INFO
NEWNHAM TER
ROYAL ST
ST. THOMAS' HOSP
CHILDREN'S HOSP
Buddhist
Tenn Cts
CENTAUR ST
VIRGIL ST
CARLISLE LANE
LAMBETH
LAMBETH PALACE RD
A3036
LAMBETH PALACE GDNS
SPORTS GRD
ARCHBISHOP'S PARK
PENHURST PL
COSSER STREET
HERCULES ROAD
MCAULEY CL
BRIANT ESTATE
SIDFORD PL
BRIANT HO
A3203
Mission
Med Cen
Lambeth Palace
KING'S COLL. (ST. THOMAS' CAMPUS)
Lambeth Pier
MUS OF GARDEN HISTORY
FORENSIC SCI. SER.
LAMBETH RD
LAMBETH BRI
Novotel Waterloo
ROY. PHARM. SOC.
PARLIAMENT VIEW APARTS.
WESTMINSTER TOWER
INT. MARITIME ORG
Fire Sta
ALBERT EMBANKMENT
LAMBETH HIGH STREET
NORFOLK ROW
OLD PARADISE ST
LAMBETH REC GRD
WHITGIFT ST
PRATT WK
SAIL ST
COPELAND HO
FERRYBRI. HO
ASTBURY HO
WALK
Comm Cen
JUXON ST
INGRAM CL
WALNUT TREE WALK
HORNBEAM CL
BEDLAM MS
Walnut Tree Wk Prim Sch
FITZALAN ST
LAMBETH WK OPEN SPACE
LOLLARD STREET
SAUNDERS
NEWPORT STREET
LUPINO COURT
LAMBETH WALK
GIBSON ROAD
BLACK PRINCE RD
MALAM

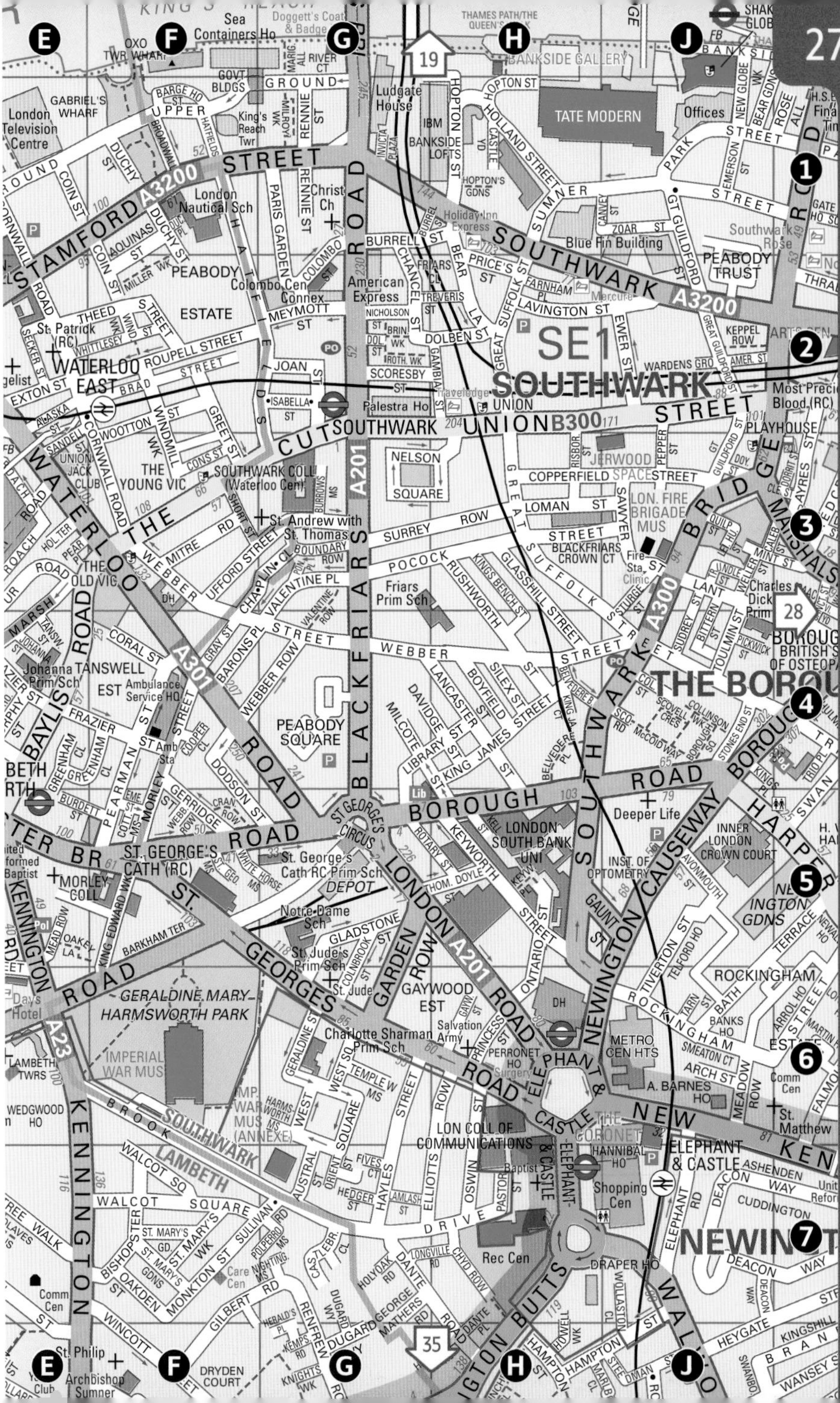
Sea Containers Ho
Doggett's Coat & Badge
THAMES PATH/THE QUEEN'S WALK
OXO TWR WHARF
GABRIEL'S WHARF
London Television Centre
GOVT BLDGS
King's Reach Twr
Ludgate House
IBM
BANKSIDE LOFTS
BANKSIDE GALLERY
TATE MODERN
Offices
HOPTON ST
HOLLAND STREET
SUMNER STREET
PARK STREET
STAMFORD STREET A3200
UPPER GROUND
London Nautical Sch
Christ Ch
PARIS GARDEN
RENNIE ST
BLACKFRIARS ROAD A201
HOPTON'S GDNS
Holiday Inn Express
SOUTHWARK STREET A3200
Blue Fin Building
PEABODY TRUST
Southwark Rose
PEABODY ESTATE
Colombo Cen
Connex
American Express
BURRELL ST
PRICE'S ST
FARNHAM PL
LAVINGTON ST
Mercure
St. Patrick (RC)
WATERLOO EAST
ROUPELL STREET
MEYMOTT ST
JOAN ST
SCORESBY ST
DOLBEN ST
SE1
SOUTHWARK
WARDENS GRO
Most Precious Blood (RC)
Travelodge
UNION STREET B300
Palestra Ho
THE CUT
SOUTHWARK
PLAYHOUSE
THE YOUNG VIC
SOUTHWARK COLL (Waterloo Cen)
NELSON SQUARE
JERWOOD SPACE
COPPERFIELD STREET
LONDON FIRE BRIGADE MUS
LOMAN ST
SURREY ROW
St. Andrew with St. Thomas
BOUNDARY ROW
POCOCK ST
BLACKFRIARS CROWN CT
Fire Sta. Clinic
MARSHALSEA ROAD
MINT ST
Charles Dickens Prim
28
THE OLD VIC
WATERLOO ROAD A301
WEBBER STREET
VALENTINE PL
Friars Prim Sch
RUSHWORTH
GLASSHILL STREET
GREAT SUFFOLK STREET
BOROUGH
BRITISH SCH OF OSTEOPATHY
THE BOROUGH
Johanna Prim Sch
TANSWELL EST
Ambulance Service HQ
BAYLIS ROAD
PEABODY SQUARE
KING JAMES STREET
SOUTHWARK BRIDGE ROAD A300
BOROUGH ROAD
BOROUGH HIGH STREET
Deeper Life
LAMBETH NORTH
Amb Sta
ST GEORGE'S CIRCUS
LONDON SOUTH BANK UNI
INNER LONDON CROWN COURT
HARPER ROAD
WESTMINSTER BR ROAD
ST. GEORGE'S CATH (RC)
St. George's Cath RC Prim Sch
DEPOT
MORLEY COLL
INST. OF OPTOMETRY
NEWINGTON CAUSEWAY
NEWINGTON GDNS
Notre Dame Sch
St. Jude's Prim Sch
St. Jude
LONDON ROAD A201
ROCKINGHAM
ROCKINGHAM ESTATE
GERALDINE MARY HARMSWORTH PARK
IMPERIAL WAR MUS
ST. GEORGES ROAD
GAYWOOD EST
Salvation Army
Charlotte Sharman Prim Sch
METRO CEN HTS
Days Hotel
A23
LAMBETH TWRS
IMP. WAR MUS (ANNEXE)
PERRONET HO
Surgery
ELEPHANT & CASTLE
A. BARNES HO
Comm Cen
St. Matthew
NEW KENT ROAD
WEDGWOOD HO
KENNINGTON ROAD
BROOK DRIVE
SOUTHWARK
LAMBETH
LON COLL OF COMMUNICATIONS
THE CORONET
HANNIBAL HO
ELEPHANT & CASTLE
Shopping Cen
Baptist
DEACON WAY
NEWINGTON
WALCOT SQUARE
ST. MARY'S GDNS
Care Cen
Rec Cen
DRAPER HO
Comm Cen
KENNINGTON
NEWINGTON BUTTS
WALWORTH
35
St. Philip
Archbishop Sumner
DRYDEN COURT
HEYGATE ST
WANSEY ST

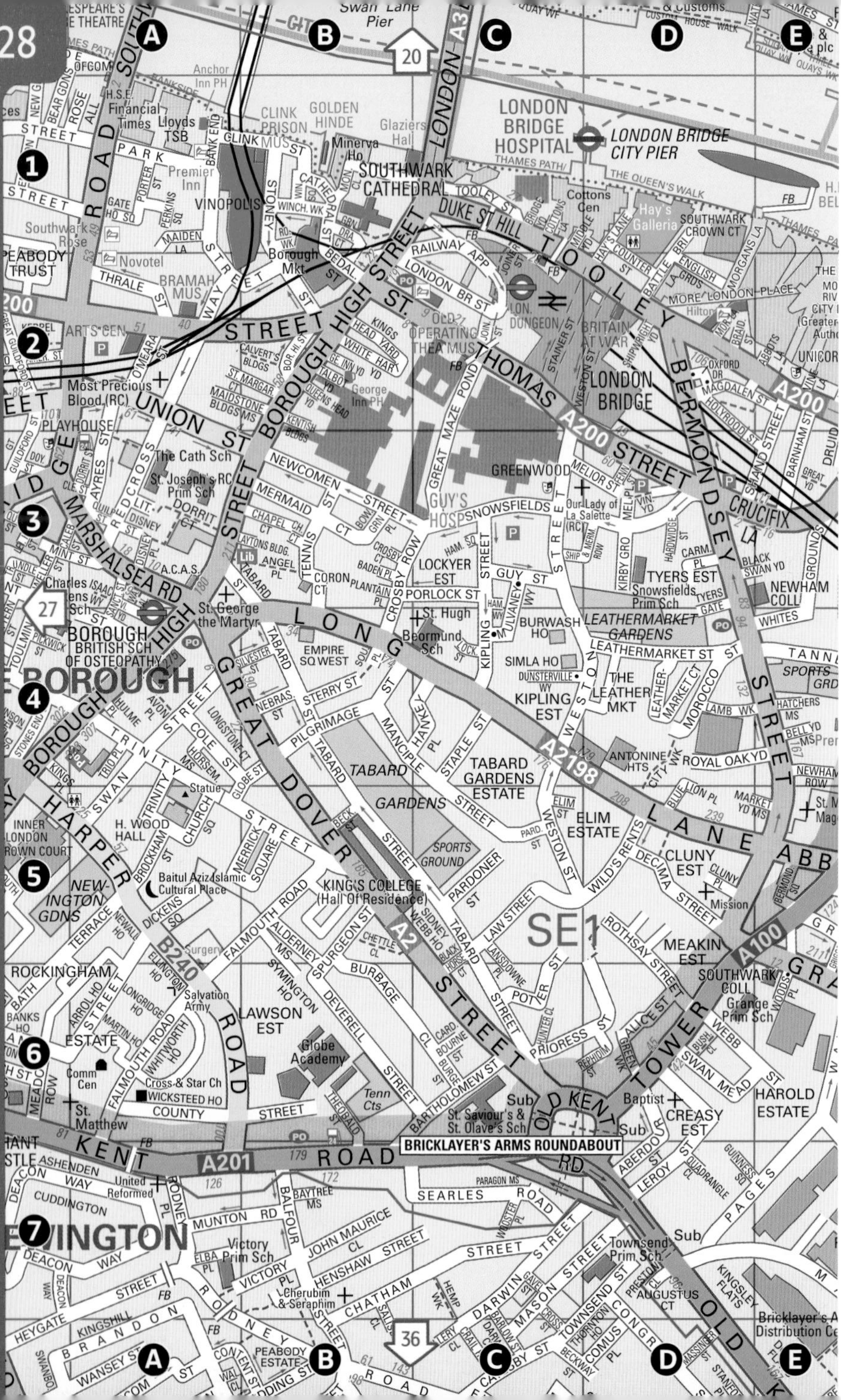
A
B
C
D
E
1
2
3
4
5
6
7
Swan Lane Pier
20
27
36
LONDON BRIDGE HOSPITAL
LONDON BRIDGE CITY PIER
THAMES PATH
THE QUEEN'S WALK
Anchor Inn PH
CLINK PRISON
GOLDEN HINDE
Glaziers Hall
Minerva Ho
SOUTHWARK CATHEDRAL
Financial Times
Lloyds TSB
H.S.E.
OFCOM
Premier Inn
VINOPOLIS
Southwark Rose
PEABODY TRUST
Novotel
BRAMAH MUS
Borough Mkt.
CLINK MUS
PARK ST
PORTER ST
PERKINS SQ
MAIDEN LA
THRALE ST
SOUTHWARK ST
STONEY ST
CATHEDRAL ST
BEDAL ST
WINCH. WK
Cottons Cen
Hay's Galleria
SOUTHWARK CROWN CT
TOOLEY ST
DUKE ST HILL
RAILWAY APP
LONDON BR ST
LON. DUNGEON
BRITAIN AT WAR
LONDON BRIDGE
STAINER ST
WESTON ST
MORE LONDON PLACE
Hilton
HAY'S LANE
COUNTER ST
BATTLE BRI. LA
ENGLISH GRDS
MORGANS LA
OXFORD DR
MAGDALEN ST
HOLYROOD ST
BERMONDSEY STREET
ABBOTS LA
A200
ARTS CEN
KEPPEL ROW
O'MEARA ST
Most Precious Blood (RC)
UNION ST
PLAYHOUSE
The Cath Sch
St. Joseph's RC Prim Sch
REDCROSS WAY
AYRES ST
DORRIT ST
LIT. DORRIT CT
DISNEY PL
MARSHALSEA RD
A.C.A.S.
Charles Dickens Sch
BOROUGH
BRITISH SCH OF OSTEOPATHY
BOROUGH HIGH STREET
KINGS HEAD YARD
WHITE HART YD
GEORGE INN YD
TALBOT YD
QUEENS HEAD YD
George Inn PH
CALVERT'S BLDGS
ST MARGARETS CT
MAIDSTONE BLDGS MS
KENTISH BLDGS
OLD OPERATING THEA MUS
ST THOMAS ST
GREAT MAZE POND
GUY'S HOSP
GREENWOOD
NEWCOMEN ST
MERMAID CT
CHAPEL CT
LAYTONS BLDG.
Lib
ANGEL PL
TENNIS ST
CORON CT
CROSBY ROW
PLANTAIN PL
PORLOCK ST
LOCKYER EST
SNOWSFIELDS
Our Lady of La Salette (RC)
MELIOR ST
KIRBY GRO
TYERS EST
Snowsfields Prim Sch
BLACK SWAN YD
NEWHAM COLL
WHITES GRDS
CRUCIFIX LA
GUY ST
KIPLING ST
St. Hugh
Beormund Sch
BURWASH HO
LEATHERMARKET GARDENS
LEATHERMARKET ST
SIMLA HO
DUNSTERVILLE WY
KIPLING EST
THE LEATHER MKT
MOROCCO ST
LAMB WK
HATCHERS MS
BELL YD MS
ROYAL OAK YD
TANNER ST
SPORTS GRD
St. George the Martyr
LONG LANE
A2198
TABARD ST
EMPIRE SQ WEST
STERRY ST
NEBRAS. ST
PILGRIMAGE ST
MANCIPLE ST
HANKEY PL
STAPLE ST
TABARD GARDENS ESTATE
TABARD GARDENS
SPORTS GROUND
ELIM ESTATE
ANTONINE HTS
CITY WK
LION PL
MARKET YD MS
BLUE
NEWHAM ROW
St. Mary Magdalen
BOROUGH RD
TRINITY ST
COLE ST
HORSEM. MS
LONGSTONE CT
GLOBE ST
Statue
TRINITY CHURCH SQ
H. WOOD HALL
BROCKHAM ST
SWAN ST
HARPER RD
INNER LONDON CROWN COURT
NEW-INGTON GDNS
Baitul Aziz Islamic Cultural Place
DICKENS SQ
MERRICK SQUARE
GREAT DOVER STREET
KING'S COLLEGE (Hall Of Residence)
PARDONER ST
WESTON ST
WILD'S RENTS
DECIMA STREET
CLUNY EST
CLUNY PL
Mission
SE1
ABBEY ST
LAW STREET
LANSDOWNE PL
POTIER ST
ROTHSAY STREET
MEAKIN EST
SOUTHWARK COLL
Grange Prim Sch
A100
TOWER BRIDGE RD
FALMOUTH ROAD
ALDERNEY MS
SPURGEON ST
CHETTLE CL
BURBAGE CL
DEVERELL STREET
SYMINGTON HO
LAWSON EST
Globe Academy
A2
SIDNEY WEBB HO
BLACK HORSE CT
PRIORESS ST
HUNTER CL
ALICE ST
GREEN WK
SWAN MEAD
WEBB ST
HAROLD ESTATE
TERRACE
NEWALL HO
B240
Surgery
ROCKINGHAM ESTATE
BATH TER
ARROL HO
BANKS HO
LONGRIDGE HO
ELLINGTON HO
MARTIN HO
Salvation Army
WHITWORTH HO
Comm Cen
St. Matthew
Cross & Star Ch
WICKSTEED HO
COUNTY STREET
MEADOW ROW
Tenn Cts
THEOBALD ST
BARTHOLOMEW ST
St. Saviour's & St. Olave's Sch
Sub
OLD KENT RD
Baptist
CREASY EST
BRICKLAYER'S ARMS ROUNDABOUT
A201
NEW KENT ROAD
ASHENDEN
DEACON WAY
United Reformed
CUDDINGTON
NEWINGTON
RODNEY PL
RODNEY RD
MUNTON RD
BALFOUR ST
BAYTREE MS
JOHN MAURICE CL
HENSHAW STREET
Victory Prim Sch
VICTORY PL
ELBA PL
PARAGON MS
SEARLES ROAD
WOOSTER PL
ABERDOUR ST
LEROY ST
QUADRANGLE CL
GUINNESS SQ
PAGES WK
Townsend Prim Sch
Sub
KINGSLEY FLATS
Bricklayer's Arms Distribution Cen
HEYGATE STREET
KINGSHILL
BRANDON
WANSEY ST
Cherubim & Seraphim
CHATHAM ST
HEMP WK
DARWIN ST
MASON STREET
TOWNSEND ST
PRESTON CL
AUGUSTUS CT
CONGREVE ST
COMUS PL
THORNTON HO
BECKWAY ST
MASSINGER ST
PEABODY ESTATE
CONTENT ST
BARLOW ST

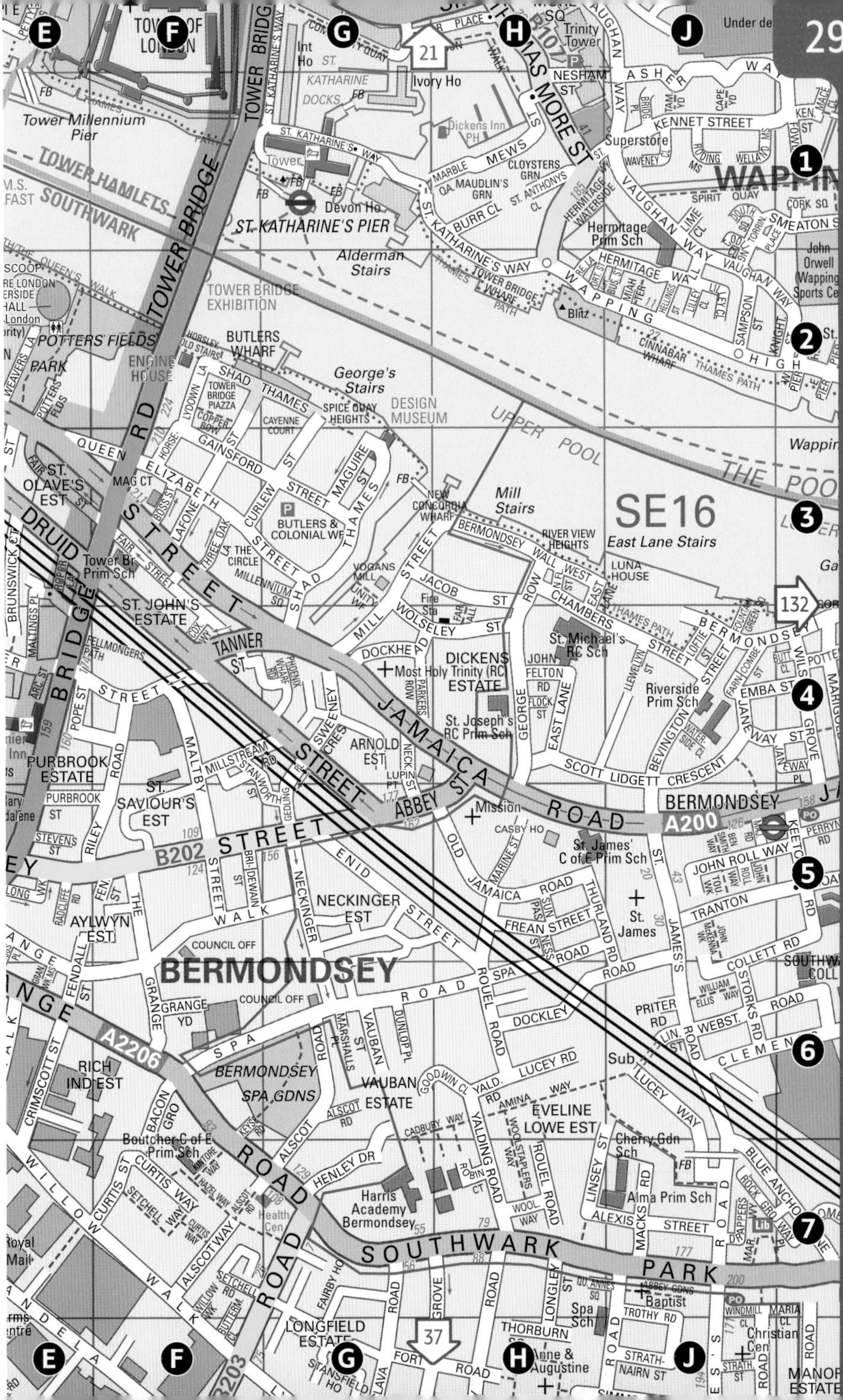
E
F
G
H
J
TOWER OF LONDON
Tower Millennium Pier
TOWER HAMLETS
SOUTHWARK
TOWER BRIDGE
TOWER BRIDGE RD
ST. KATHARINE DOCKS
ST. KATHARINE'S WAY
ST. KATHARINE'S PIER
Ivory Ho
Devon Ho
Dickens Inn PH
Alderman Stairs
TOWER BRIDGE EXHIBITION
THOMAS MORE ST
Trinity Tower
NESHAM ST
ASHER WAY
KENNET STREET
Superstore
WAPPING
HERMITAGE WATERSIDE
Hermitage Prim Sch
VAUGHAN WAY
SMEATON ST
John Orwell (Wapping) Sports Cen
WAPPING HIGH ST
CINNABAR WHARF
THAMES PATH
Blitz
POTTERS FIELDS PARK
BUTLERS WHARF
ENGINE HOUSE
George's Stairs
DESIGN MUSEUM
SHAD THAMES
UPPER POOL
THE POOL
Wapping
SE16
Mill Stairs
East Lane Stairs
BERMONDSEY WALL WEST
RIVER VIEW HEIGHTS
LUNA HOUSE
NEW CONCORDIA WHARF
BUTLERS & COLONIAL WF
GAINSFORD ST
QUEEN ELIZABETH ST
ST. OLAVE'S EST
DRUID ST
Tower Br Prim Sch
ST. JOHN'S ESTATE
TANNER ST
JACOB ST
Fire Sta
WOLSELEY ST
CHAMBERS ST
St. Michael's RC Sch
BERMONDSEY ST
Riverside Prim Sch
DICKENS ESTATE
Most Holy Trinity (RC)
St. Joseph's RC Prim Sch
JAMAICA ROAD
JAMAICA ST
SCOTT LIDGETT CRESCENT
BERMONDSEY
A200
Mission
St. James' C of E Prim Sch
ARNOLD EST
ABBEY ST
PURBROOK ESTATE
ST. SAVIOUR'S EST
B202
NECKINGER EST
ENID STREET
AYLWYN EST
BERMONDSEY
COUNCIL OFF
GRANGE YD
SPA ROAD
A2206
RICH IND EST
BERMONDSEY SPA GDNS
VAUBAN ESTATE
EVELINE LOWE EST
St. James
Boutcher C of E Prim Sch
Health Cen
Harris Academy Bermondsey
Cherry Gdn Sch
Alma Prim Sch
SOUTHWARK PARK ROAD
Spa Sch
Baptist
Christian Cen
LONGFIELD ESTATE
Anne & Augustine
MANOR ESTATE
Royal Mail
21
132
37
1
2
3
4
5
6
7

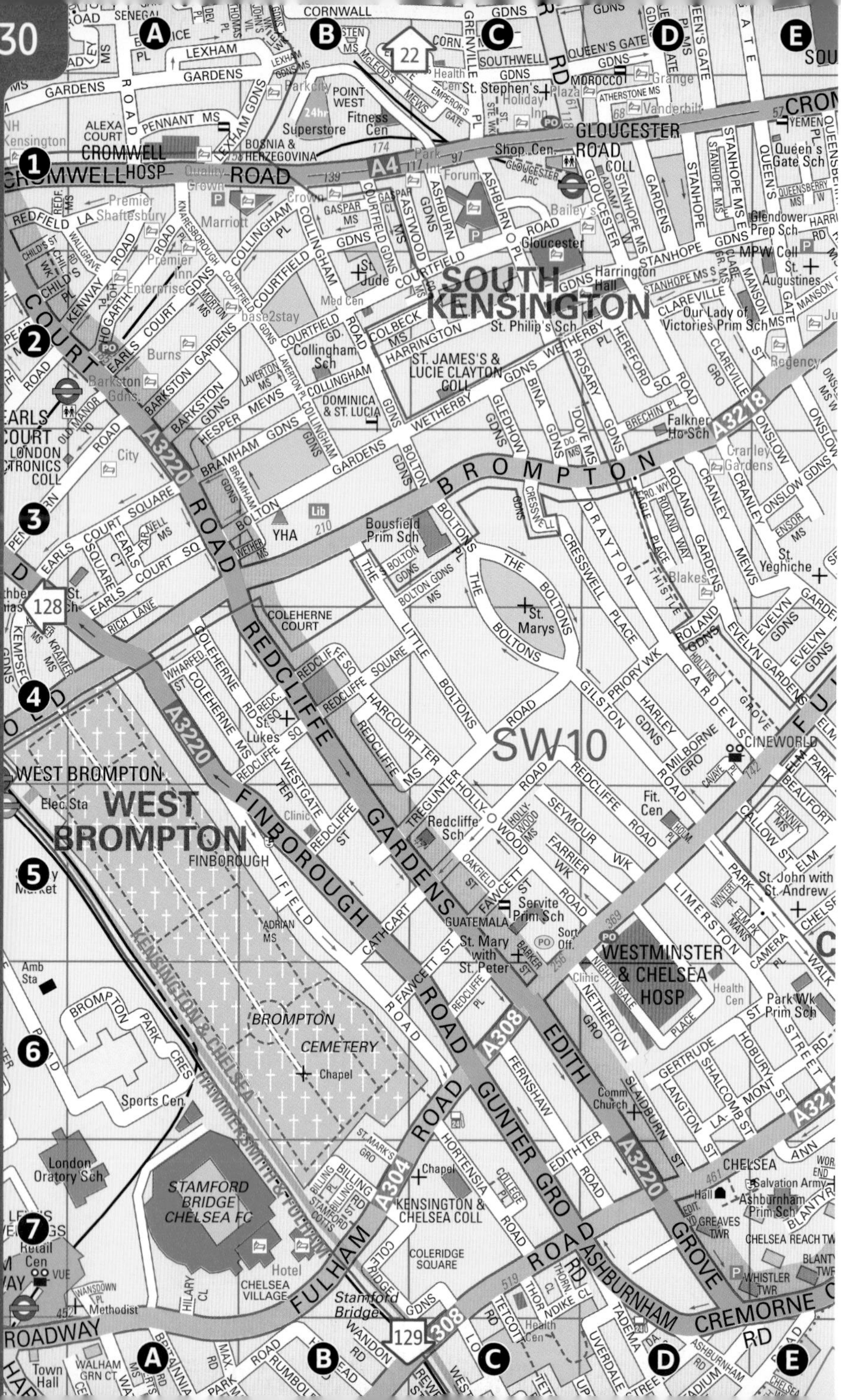
A
B
C
D
E
1
2
3
4
5
6
7
22
128
129
CORNWALL
LEXHAM
GARDENS
PENNANT MS
ALEXA COURT
CROMWELL HOSP
CROMWELL ROAD
BOSNIA & HERZEGOVINA
Superstore
Point West
Fitness Cen
A4
SOUTHWELL
QUEEN'S GATE
GLOUCESTER ROAD
Shop. Cen.
St. Stephen's
Holiday Inn
Forum
Morocco
Atherstone Ms
Vanderbilt
Grange
Queen's Gate Sch
YEMEN
COLL
STANHOPE
GARDENS
Glendower Prep Sch
MPW Coll
St. Augustines
REDFIELD LA
Premier Shaftesbury
Marriott
Premier Inn
Enterprise
KENWAY ROAD
HOGARTH
COLLINGHAM
COURTFIELD
GASPAR MS
ASHBURN
Bailey's
Gloucester
St. Jude
Med Cen
SOUTH KENSINGTON
Harrington Hall
St. Philip's Sch
CLAREVILLE
Our Lady of Victories Prim Sch
Regency
EARLS COURT
Burns
Barkston Gdns
BARKSTON GARDENS
HESPER MEWS
Collingham Sch
COLBECK MS
HARRINGTON
ST. JAMES'S & LUCIE CLAYTON COLL
DOMINICA & ST. LUCIA
WETHERBY
GLEDHOW
ROSARY
HEREFORD
BRECHIN PL
Falkner Ho Sch
A3218
ONSLOW
BRAMHAM GDNS
City
LONDON TRONICS COLL
A3220
BROMPTON
Cranley Gardens
CRANLEY
ONSLOW GDNS
Lib
210
YHA
BOLTON
EARLS COURT SQUARE
Bousfield Prim Sch
THE BOLTONS
St. Marys
DRAYTON
CRESSWELL PLACE
ROLAND GARDENS
Blakes
St. Yeghiche
EVELYN GARDENS
COLEHERNE COURT
LITTLE BOLTONS
REDCLIFFE SQUARE
REDCLIFFE
HARCOURT TER
SW10
GILSTON ROAD
PRIORY WK
CINEWORLD
WEST BROMPTON
Elec.Sta
WEST BROMPTON
FINBOROUGH
Clinic
Redcliffe Sch
SEYMOUR WK
Fit. Cen
BEAUFORT
St. John with St. Andrew
GUATEMALA
Servite Prim Sch
Sort Off.
St. Mary with St. Peter
WESTMINSTER & CHELSEA HOSP
Health Cen
Park Wk Prim Sch
Amb Sta
BROMPTON PARK CRES
KENSINGTON & CHELSEA
BROMPTON CEMETERY
Chapel
HAMMERSMITH & FULHAM
A308
EDITH GROVE
Sports Cen
London Oratory Sch
STAMFORD BRIDGE CHELSEA FC
Hotel
CHELSEA VILLAGE
A304
KENSINGTON & CHELSEA COLL
COLERIDGE SQUARE
Comm Church
CHELSEA
Salvation Army
Ashburnham Prim Sch
GREAVES TWR
CHELSEA REACH TWR
WHISTLER TWR
CREMORNE RD
ASHBURNHAM
FULHAM ROAD
Stamford Bridge
Methodist
ROADWAY
Town Hall
WALHAM GRN CT
Retail Cen
VUE
LILLIE ROAD

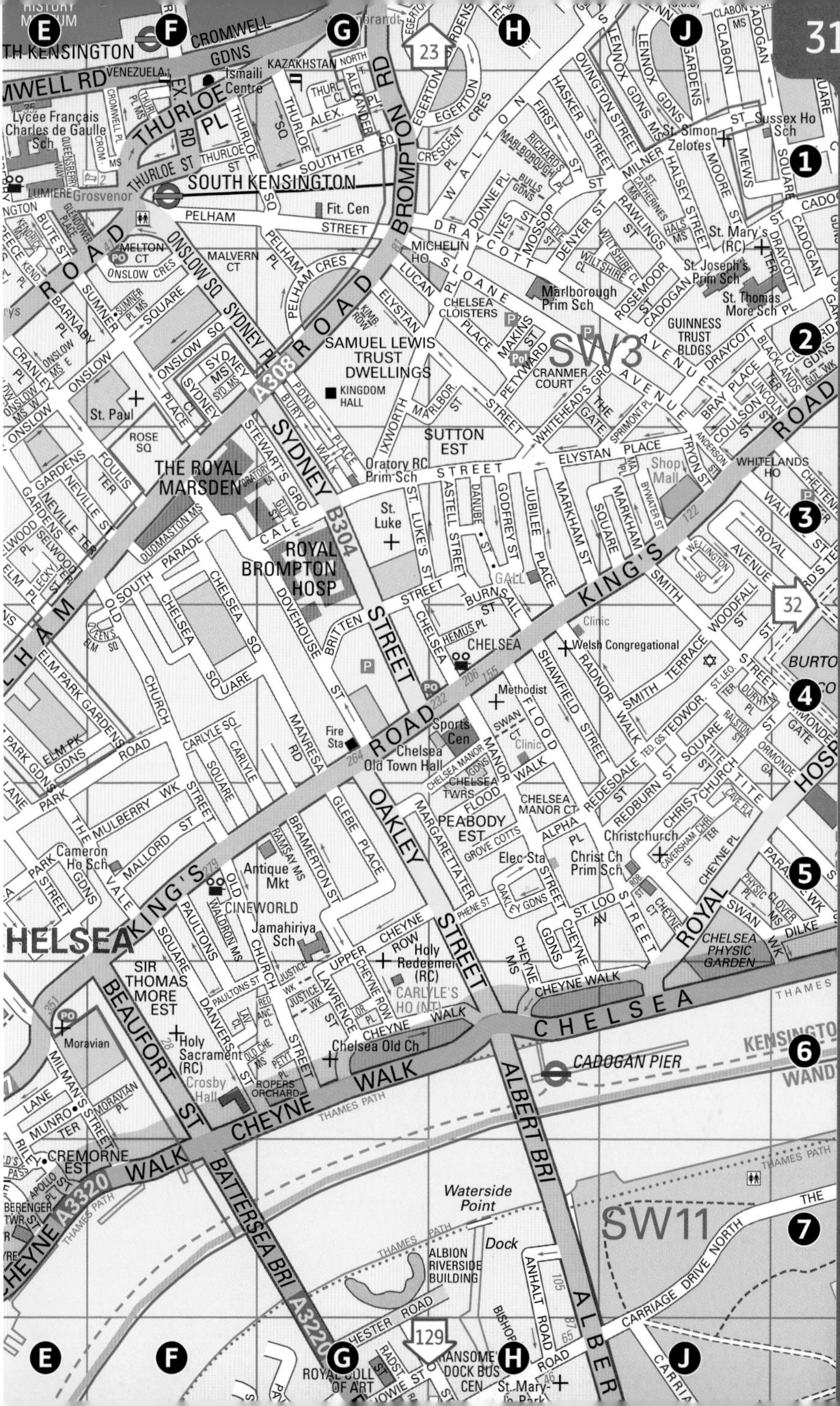
E
F
G
H
J
1
2
3
4
5
6
7
23
32
129
SOUTH KENSINGTON
CROMWELL GDNS
CROMWELL RD
VENEZUELA
Ismaili Centre
KAZAKHSTAN
Lycée Français Charles de Gaulle Sch
THURLOE PL
THURLOE ST
THURLOE SQ
ALEX. PL
ALEXANDER SQ
SOUTHTER
EGERTON GARDENS
EGERTON CRESCENT
EGERTON PL
BROMPTON RD
WALTON ST
LENNOX GDNS
LENNOX GDNS MS
OVINGTON STREET
HASKER STREET
FIRST ST
MILNER ST
HALSEY STREET
MOORE ST
CLABON MS
CADOGAN SQUARE
St. Simon Zelotes
Sussex Ho Sch
LUMIERE
Grosvenor
PELHAM STREET
Fit. Cen
MICHELIN HO
DRAYCOTT AVENUE
DONNE PL
IVES ST
MOSSOP ST
DENYER ST
RAWLINGS ST
St. Mary's (RC)
St. Joseph's Prim Sch
St. Thomas More Sch
CADOGAN ST
ROSEMOOR ST
Marlborough Prim Sch
GUINNESS TRUST BLDGS
SLOANE AVENUE
MELTON CT
ONSLOW CRES
ONSLOW SQ
MALVERN CT
PELHAM CRES
SUMNER PL
SUMNER PL MS
FULHAM ROAD
SYDNEY PL
SYDNEY ST
SYDNEY MS
LUCAN PL
ELYSTAN ST
CHELSEA CLOISTERS
MAKINS ST
PETYWARD
CRANMER COURT
SW3
SAMUEL LEWIS TRUST DWELLINGS
KINGDOM HALL
A308
ONSLOW GARDENS
St. Paul
ROSE SQ
FOULIS TER
IXWORTH PL
MARLBOR. ST
SUTTON EST
WHITEHEAD'S GRO
THE GATE
ELYSTAN PLACE
Shop Mall
TRYON ST
WHITELANDS HO
THE ROYAL MARSDEN
STEWART'S GRO
Oratory RC Prim Sch
ST. LUKE'S ST
ASTELL STREET
DANUBE ST
GODFREY ST
JUBILEE PLACE
MARKHAM ST
MARKHAM SQUARE
BYWATER ST
CALE ST
St. Luke
ROYAL BROMPTON HOSP
B304
DUDMASTON MS
ROYAL AVENUE
WELLINGTON SQ
SMITH ST
GALL
BURNSALL ST
KING'S ROAD
WOODFALL ST
CHELSEA SQUARE
DOVEHOUSE ST
BRITTEN ST
HEMUS PL
CHELSEA
Clinic
Welsh Congregational
RADNOR WALK
SHAWFIELD STREET
SMITH TERRACE
ELM PARK GARDENS
OLD CHURCH ST
MANRESA RD
Fire Sta
Methodist
FLOOD ST
Sports Cen
Chelsea Old Town Hall
TEDWORTH SQUARE
ROYAL HOSPITAL RD
CARLYLE SQ
ELM PK GDNS
MULBERRY WK
MALLORD ST
GLEBE PLACE
OAKLEY STREET
MARGARETTA TER
CHELSEA MANOR GDNS
CHELSEA TWRS
PEABODY EST
CHELSEA MANOR CT
REDESDALE ST
REDBURN ST
CHRISTCHURCH TER
Christchurch
Christ Ch Prim Sch
Elec Sta
ALPHA PL
GROVE COTTS
Cameron Ho Sch
Antique Mkt
RAMSAY MS
BRAMERTON ST
CINEWORLD
PAULTONS SQUARE
Jamahiriya Sch
Holy Redeemer (RC)
UPPER CHEYNE ROW
PHENE ST
ST. LOO AV
CHEYNE GDNS
CHEYNE PL
SWAN WK
PARADISE WK
DILKE ST
CHELSEA PHYSIC GARDEN
CHELSEA
SIR THOMAS MORE EST
LAWRENCE ST
CARLYLE'S HO (N.T.)
CHEYNE WALK
CHELSEA EMBANKMENT
THAMES
KENSINGTON
WANDSWORTH
Moravian
Holy Sacrament (RC)
Crosby Hall
ROPERS ORCHARD
Chelsea Old Ch
ALBERT BRI
CADOGAN PIER
BEAUFORT ST
MILMAN'S STREET
MORAVIAN PL
CREMORNE EST
THAMES PATH
A3320
BATTERSEA BRI
A3220
Waterside Point
Dock
SW11
CARRIAGE DRIVE NORTH
ALBION RIVERSIDE BUILDING
HESTER ROAD
ANHALT ROAD
ROYAL COLL OF ART
RANSOME'S DOCK BUS CEN
St. Mary-le-Park

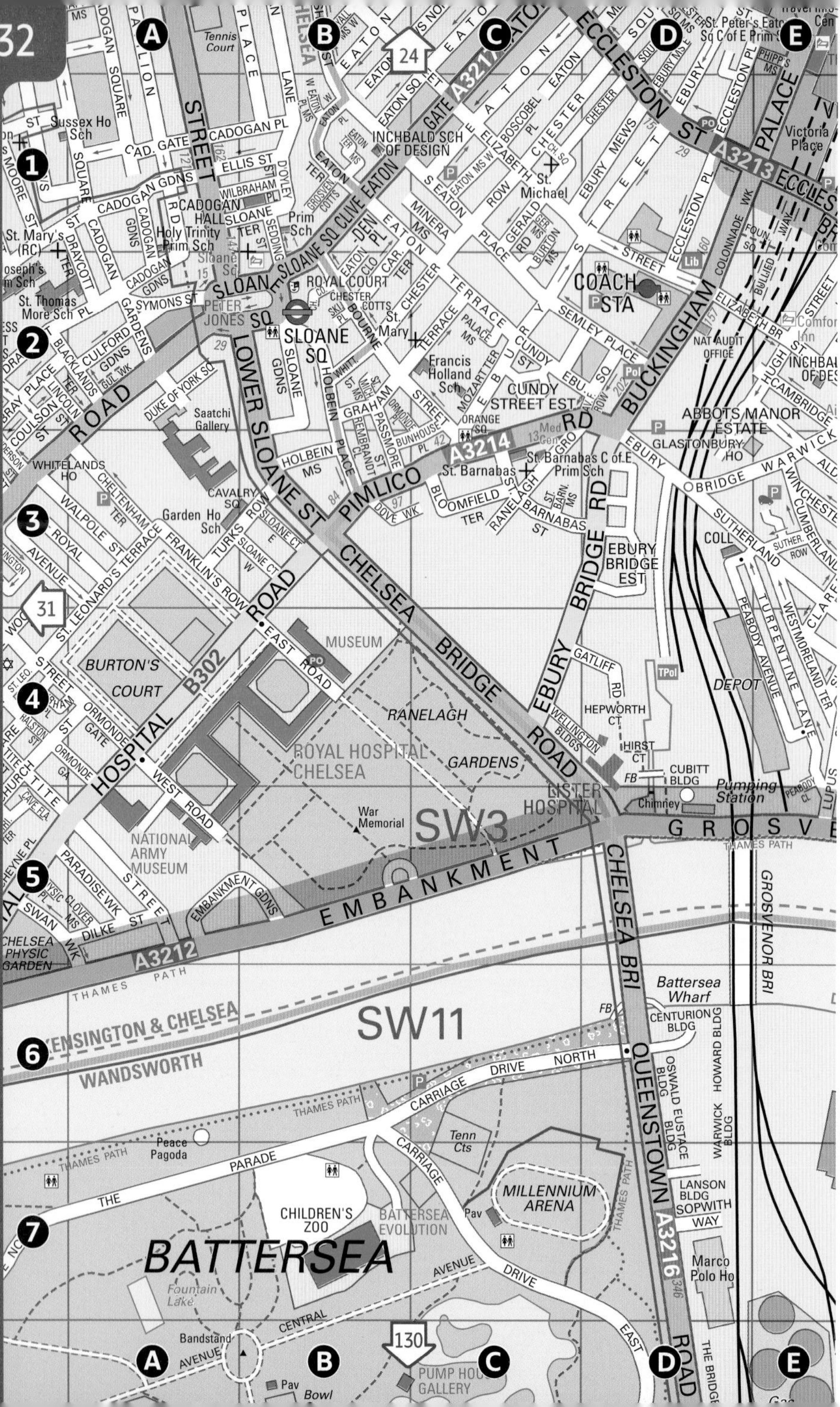
A
B
C
D
E
24
1
2
3
4
5
6
7
31
130
Tennis Court
Sussex Ho Sch
CADOGAN SQUARE
PAVILION RD
SLOANE STREET
CADOGAN PL
CAD. GATE
ELLIS ST
CADOGAN GDNS
WILBRAHAM PL
CADOGAN HALL
Holy Trinity Prim Sch
St. Mary's (RC)
St. Thomas More Sch
DRAYCOTT
SYMONS ST
SLOANE SQ
PETER JONES
CULFORD GDNS
BLACKLANDS TER
LINCOLN ST
COULSON ST
ROAD
KING'S ROAD
DUKE OF YORK SQ
Saatchi Gallery
WHITELANDS HO
WALPOLE ST
ROYAL AVENUE
CHELTENHAM TER
FRANKLIN'S ROW
ST. LEONARD'S TERRACE
Garden Ho Sch
CAVALRY SQ
TURKS ROW
SLOANE CT E
SLOANE CT W
BURTON'S COURT
ROYAL HOSPITAL ROAD
B302
MUSEUM
EAST ROAD
WEST ROAD
ROYAL HOSPITAL CHELSEA
RANELAGH GARDENS
War Memorial
NATIONAL ARMY MUSEUM
ORMONDE GATE
TITE ST
PARADISE WK
SWAN WK
DILKE ST
EMBANKMENT GDNS
CHELSEA PHYSIC GARDEN
A3212
CHELSEA EMBANKMENT
SW3
THAMES PATH
KENSINGTON & CHELSEA
WANDSWORTH
SW11
LOWER SLOANE ST
SLOANE GDNS
HOLBEIN PL
HOLBEIN MS
ROYAL COURT
CHESTER COTTS
BOURNE ST
St. Mary
Francis Holland Sch
GRAHAM TER
PASSMORE ST
BUNHOUSE PL
PIMLICO RD
A3214
ORANGE SQ
DOVE WK
BLOOMFIELD TER
CHELSEA BRIDGE ROAD
St. Barnabas
St. Barnabas C of E Prim Sch
RANELAGH GROVE
ST. BARNABAS ST
EBURY BRIDGE RD
EBURY BRIDGE EST
GATLIFF RD
HEPWORTH CT
HIRST CT
WELLINGTON BLDGS
LISTER HOSPITAL
CUBITT BLDG
Pumping Station
Chimney
GROSVENOR RD
CHELSEA BRI
GROSVENOR BRI
INCHBALD SCH OF DESIGN
EATON SQ
EATON GATE
A3217
EATON PL
EATON TER
ELIZABETH ST
CHESTER ROW
CHESTER SQ
St. Michael
S EATON PL
MINERA MS
ECCLESTON ST
EBURY ST
EBURY MEWS
GERALD RD
CUNDY ST
COACH STA
SEMLEY PLACE
CUNDY STREET EST
BUCKINGHAM PALACE RD
ECCLESTON PL
ECCLESTON BR
Victoria Place
St. Peter's Eaton Sq C of E Prim Sch
A3213
ELIZABETH BR
NAT AUDIT OFFICE
HUGH ST
CAMBRIDGE ST
ABBOTS MANOR ESTATE
GLASTONBURY HO
EBURY BRIDGE
WARWICK WAY
WINCHESTER ST
SUTHERLAND ST
PEABODY AVENUE
TURPENTINE LANE
WESTMORELAND TER
DEPOT
Battersea Wharf
CENTURION BLDG
OSWALD EUSTACE BLDG
HOWARD BLDG
WARWICK BLDG
LANSON BLDG
SOPWITH WAY
Marco Polo Ho
QUEENSTOWN ROAD
A3216
NORTH CARRIAGE DRIVE
Peace Pagoda
THE PARADE
CARRIAGE DRIVE
Tenn Cts
MILLENNIUM ARENA
CHILDREN'S ZOO
BATTERSEA EVOLUTION
Pav
BATTERSEA
Fountain Lake
CENTRAL AVENUE
EAST CARRIAGE DRIVE
Bandstand
Bowl
PUMP HOUSE GALLERY

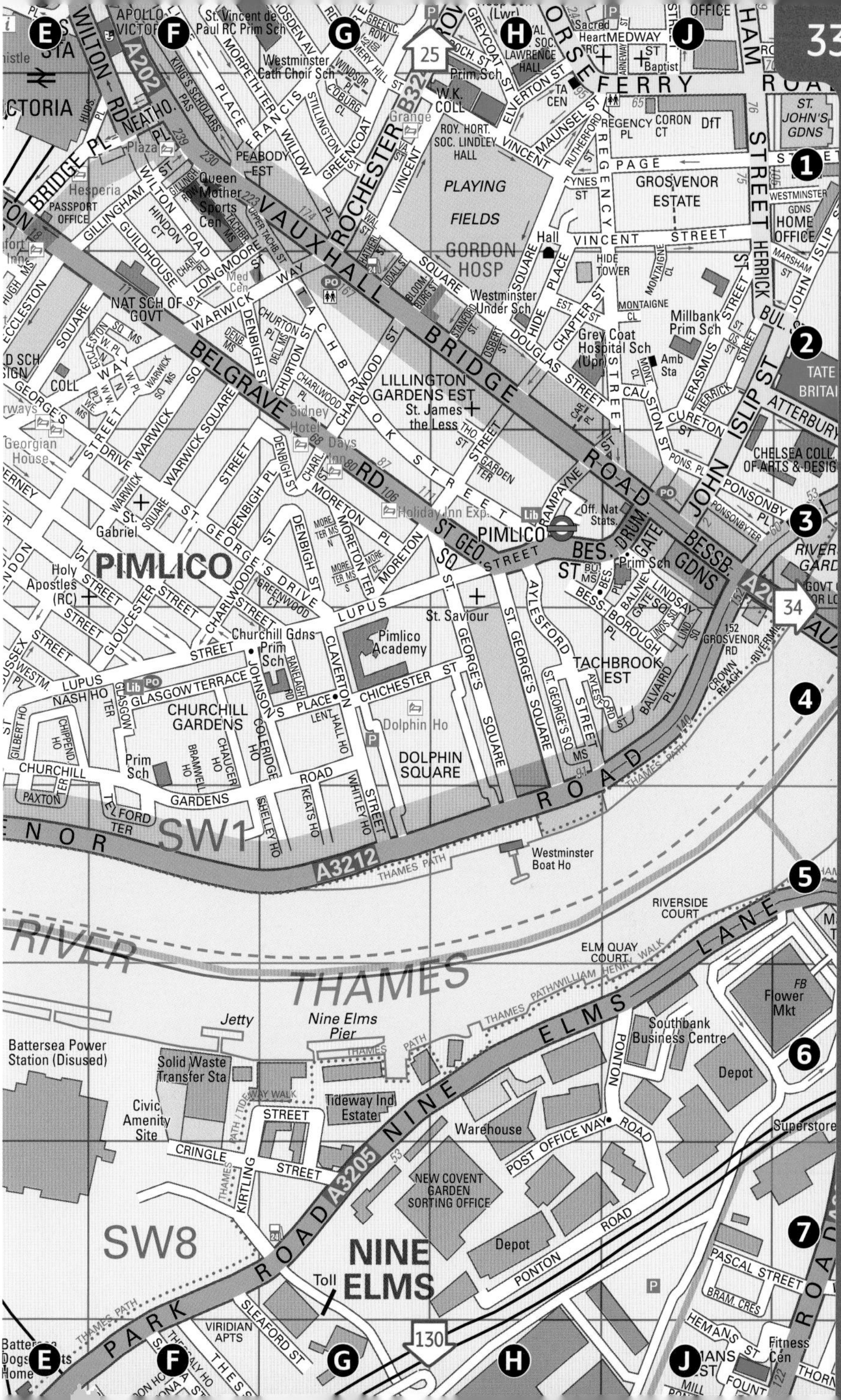
PIMLICO
SW1
RIVER
THAMES
SW8
NINE
ELMS
VAUXHALL BRIDGE ROAD
BELGRAVE RD
GROSVENOR ROAD
NINE ELMS LANE
PARK ROAD
A3212
A3205
A202
25
34
130
VICTORIA
PLAYING
FIELDS
GORDON HOSP
LILLINGTON
GARDENS EST
CHURCHILL
GARDENS
DOLPHIN
SQUARE
TACHBROOK
EST
Pimlico
Academy
St. Saviour
PIMLICO
GROSVENOR
ESTATE
TATE
BRITAIN
Westminster
Boat Ho
Battersea Power
Station (Disused)
Nine Elms
Pier
Jetty
NEW COVENT
GARDEN
SORTING OFFICE
Flower
Mkt
Southbank
Business Centre
Depot
Warehouse
Superstore
Tideway Ind
Estate
Solid Waste
Transfer Sta
Civic
Amenity
Site
RIVERSIDE
COURT
ELM QUAY
COURT
THAMES PATH
Toll

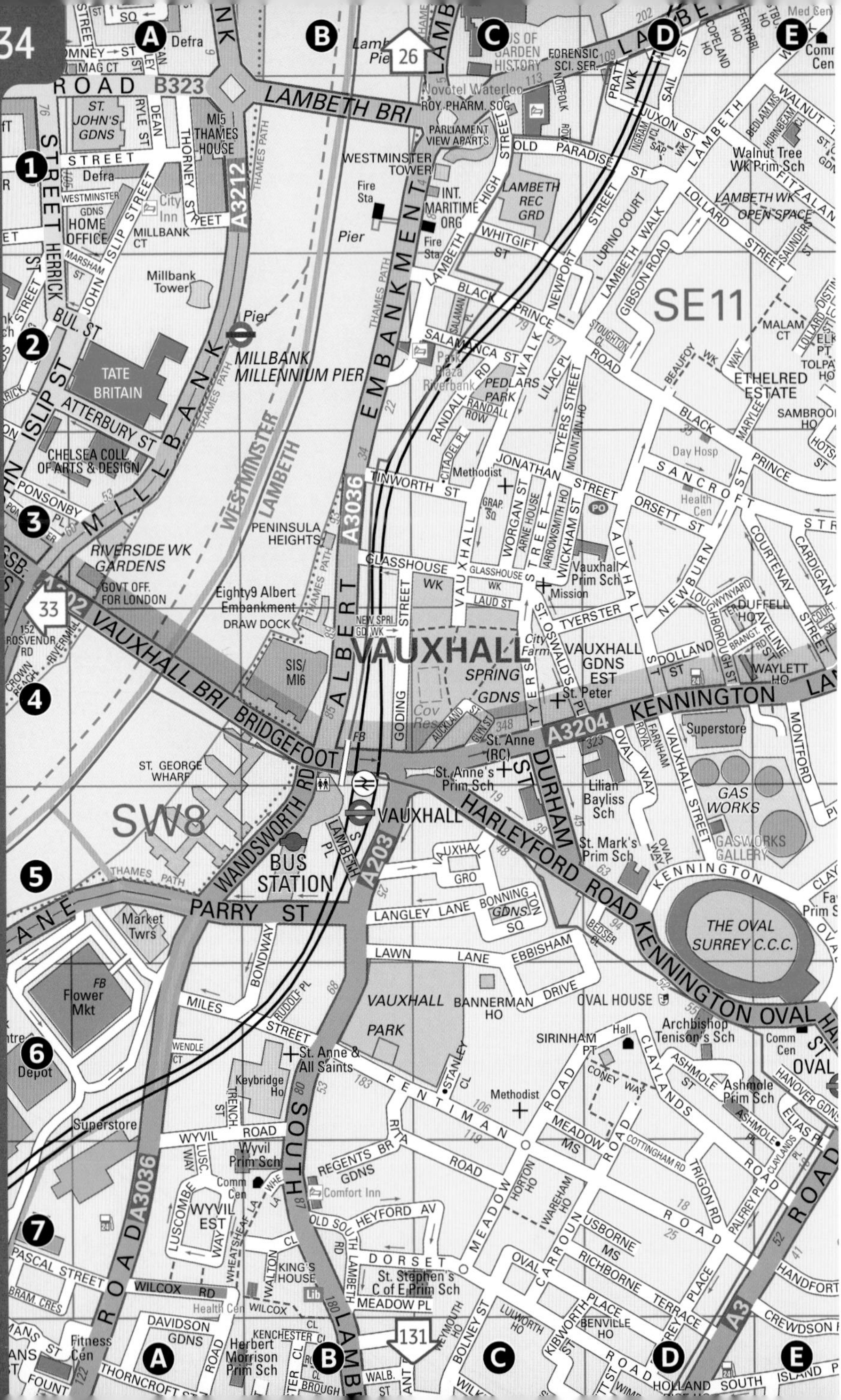
A
B
C
D
E
1
2
3
4
5
6
7
Defra
ROAD B323
LAMBETH BRI
ST. JOHN'S GDNS
RYLE ST
DEAN ST
MI5 THAMES HOUSE
THORNEY STREET
A3212
THAMES PATH
26
Lambeth Pier
LAMBETH
GARDEN HISTORY
FORENSIC SCI. SER.
Novotel Waterloo
ROY. PHARM. SOC.
PARLIAMENT VIEW APARTS.
WESTMINSTER TOWER
OLD PARADISE ST
PRATT WK
SAIL ST
JUXON ST
COPELAND HO
Walnut Tree Wk Prim Sch
WALNUT
LAMBETH
FITZALAN
LAMBETH WK OPEN SPACE
LOLLARD STREET
SAUNDERS ST
STREET
Defra
WESTMINSTER GDNS
HOME OFFICE
City Inn
MILLBANK CT
MARSHAM ST
JOHN ISLIP STREET
HERRICK ST
Millbank Tower
Fire Sta
INT. MARITIME ORG
Pier
EMBANKMENT
LAMBETH HIGH STREET
LAMBETH REC GRD
WHITGIFT ST
NEWPORT STREET
LUPINO COURT
LAMBETH WALK
GIBSON ROAD
SE11
BUL. ST
TATE BRITAIN
ISLIP ST
ATTERBURY ST
MILLBANK
MILLBANK MILLENNIUM PIER
BLACK PRINCE
SALAMANCA ST
Park Plaza Riverbank
PEDLARS PARK
RANDALL ROW
RANDALL RD
WALK
LILAC PL
TYERS STREET
MOUNTAIN HO
STOUGHTON CL
ROAD
MALAM CT
BEAUFOY WK
WAY
ETHELRED ESTATE
SAMBROOK HO
BLACK PRINCE
MARYLEE
CHELSEA COLL OF ARTS & DESIGN
WESTMINSTER
LAMBETH
A3036
TINWORTH ST
CITADEL PL
Methodist
JONATHAN STREET
Day Hosp
SANCROFT ST
Health Cen
ORSETT ST
PONSONBY PL
PENINSULA HEIGHTS
GRAP. SQ
WORGAN ST
ARNE HOUSE
ARROWSMITH HO
WICKHAM ST
PO
COURTENAY
CARDIGAN
RIVERSIDE WK GARDENS
GOVT OFF. FOR LONDON
GLASSHOUSE WK
GLASSHOUSE
VAUXHALL
STREET
Vauxhall Prim Sch
Mission
NEWBURN
LOUGHBOROUGH ST
DUFFELL HO
AVELINE
33
A202
VAUXHALL BRI
Eighty9 Albert Embankment
DRAW DOCK
THAMES PATH
NEW SPRI. GD. WK
LAUD ST
ST. OSWALD'S PL
TYERS TER
BRANGT.
WAYLETT HO
SIS/ MI6
ALBERT
VAUXHALL
City Farm
VAUXHALL GDNS EST
DOLLAND ST
SPRING GDNS
St. Peter
KENNINGTON LANE
BRIDGEFOOT
GODING STREET
Cov Res
AUCKLAND ST
GLYN ST
348
A3204
Superstore
MONTFORD
ST. GEORGE WHARF
FB
St. Anne (RC)
St. Anne's Prim Sch
DURHAM ST
Lilian Bayliss Sch
OVAL WAY
FARNHAM ROYAL
VAUXHALL STREET
GAS WORKS
SW8
WANDSWORTH RD
VAUXHALL
HARLEYFORD ROAD
St. Mark's Prim Sch
GASWORKS GALLERY
BUS STATION
LAMBETH PL
A203
VAUXHALL GRO
KENNINGTON
THAMES PATH
PARRY ST
LANGLEY LANE
BONNINGTON GDNS SQ
BEDSER CL
THE OVAL SURREY C.C.C.
LANE
Market Twrs
BONDWAY
LAWN LANE
EBBISHAM DRIVE
KENNINGTON OVAL
FB Flower Mkt
MILES
RUDOLF PL
VAUXHALL PARK
BANNERMAN HO
OVAL HOUSE
Archbishop Tenison's Sch
STREET
WENDLE CT
St. Anne & All Saints
STANLEY CL
SIRINHAM PT
Hall
CLAYLANDS
Comm Cen
OVAL
Depot
Keybridge Ho
TRENCH ST
FENTIMAN
CONEY WAY
ASHMOLE ST
Ashmole Prim Sch
Methodist
HANOVER GDNS
Superstore
WYVIL ROAD
Wyvil Prim Sch
SOUTH
RITA
ROAD
MEADOW MS
COTTINGHAM RD
TRIGON RD
ELIAS PL
LUSCOMBE WAY
Comm Cen
WHEATSHEAF LA
REGENTS BR GDNS
Comfort Inn
MEADOW
HORTON HO
WAREHAM HO
ROAD
PALFREY PL
CLAYLANDS PL
WYVIL EST
HEYFORD AV
OLD SOUTH LAMBETH RD
USBORNE MS
A3036
PASCAL STREET
WALTON
KING'S HOUSE
DORSET
St. Stephen's C of E Prim Sch
OVAL
CARROUN
RICHBORNE TERRACE
PLACE
HANDFORTH
BRAM. CRES
WILCOX RD
Health Cen
WILCOX
MEADOW PL
LAMBETH
131
WEYMOUTH HO
BOLNEY ST
LULWORTH HO
KIBWORTH ST
PLACE
BENVILLE HO
A3
CREWDSON
DAVIDSON GDNS
Fitness Cen
Herbert Morrison Prim Sch
KENCHESTER CL
THORNCROFT ST
FOUNT
WALB.
BROUGH
HOLLAND
SOUTH ISLAND

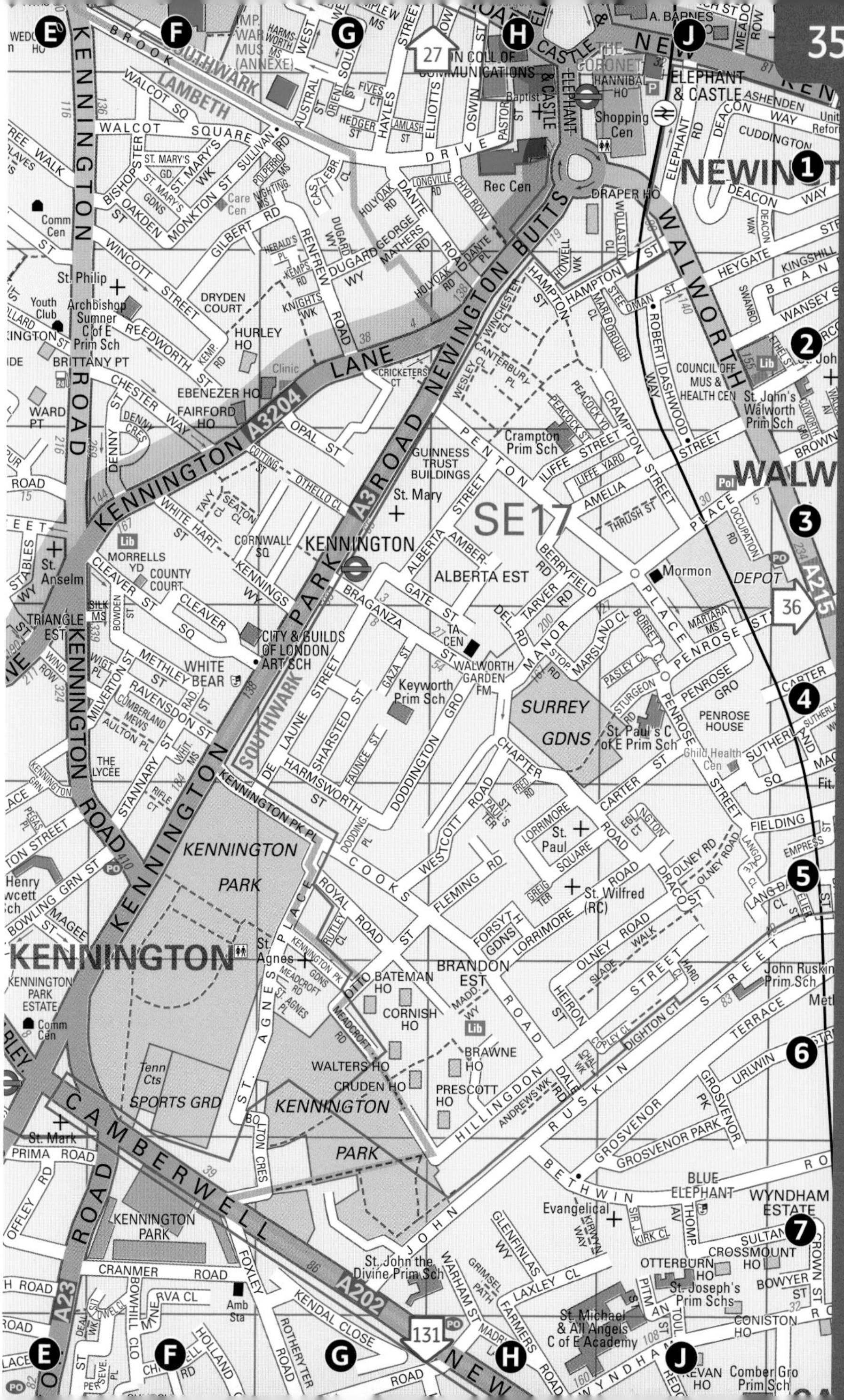
E
F
G
H
J
E
F
G
H
J
1
2
3
4
5
6
7
27
36
131
NEWINGTON
WALWORTH
KENNINGTON
SE17
KENNINGTON PARK
SPORTS GRD
Tenn Cts
SURREY GDNS
ELEPHANT & CASTLE
Shopping Cen
Rec Cen
LONDON COLL OF COMMUNICATIONS
HANNIBAL HO
DRAPER HO
THE CORONET
A. BARNES
IMP. WAR MUS (ANNEXE)
HARMSWORTH MS
LAMBETH
SOUTHWARK
BROOK
WALCOT SQ
WALCOT SQUARE
ST. MARY'S GDNS
ST. MARY'S WK
BISHOPS TER
OAKDEN ST
MONKTON ST
SULLIVAN RD
POLPERRO MS
NIGHTINGALE MS
Care Cen
Comm Cen
St. Philip
Youth Club
Archbishop Sumner C of E Prim Sch
WINCOTT STREET
REEDWORTH ST
BRITTANY PT
CHESTER WAY
DENNY CRES
DENNY ST
WARD PT
KENNINGTON ROAD
KENNINGTON LANE
A3204
DRYDEN COURT
HURLEY HO
Clinic
EBENEZER HO
FAIRFORD HO
OPAL ST
COTTINGTON ST
OTHELLO CL
TAVY CL
SEATON CL
WHITE HART ST
CORNWALL SQ
KENNINGS WY
GILBERT RD
RENFREW ROAD
DUGARD WY
GEORGE MATHERS RD
HOLYOAK RD
DANTE ROAD
DANTE PL
LONGVILLE RD
CHYDE ROW
KNIGHTS WK
CRICKETERS CT
NEWINGTON BUTTS
A3
KENNINGTON PARK ROAD
GUINNESS TRUST BUILDINGS
St. Mary
KENNINGTON
BRAGANZA ST
ALBERTA ST
ALBERTA EST
AMBERGATE ST
TA CEN
WALWORTH GARDEN FM
Keyworth Prim Sch
GAZA ST
DE LAUNE STREET
SHARSTED ST
FAUNCE ST
HARMSWORTH ST
DODDINGTON GRO
DODDINGTON PL
KENNINGTON PK PL
COOKS RD
ROYAL ROAD
RUTLEY CL
PENTON PL
WINCHESTER CL
CANTERBURY PL
WESLEY CL
HAMPTON ST
HOWELL WK
WOLLASTON CL
STEEDMAN ST
MARLBOROUGH CL
ROBERT DASHWOOD WAY
PEACOCK ST
PEACOCK YD
CRAMPTON STREET
Crampton Prim Sch
ILIFFE STREET
ILIFFE YARD
AMELIA ST
THRUSH ST
BERRYFIELD RD
TARVER RD
MANOR PL
DELVERTON RD
MARSLAND CL
BORRETT CL
PASLEY CL
STURGEON RD
PENROSE ST
PENROSE GRO
PENROSE HOUSE
St. Paul's C of E Prim Sch
Mormon
DEPOT
OCCUPATION RD
MARTARA MS
COUNCIL OFF MUS & HEALTH CEN
Lib
Pol
ELEPHANT RD
DEACON WAY
CUDDINGTON
ASHENDEN
HEYGATE ST
KINGSHILL
BRANDON
WANSEY ST
SWANBOURNE
St. John's Walworth Prim Sch
COLWORTH GRO
BROWNING
WALWORTH ROAD
A215
CARTER ST
SUTHERLAND SQ
Child Health Cen
FIELDING ST
EMPRESS
LANGDALE CL
CHAPTER RD
WESTCOTT ROAD
St. Paul
LORRIMORE SQUARE
LORRIMORE ROAD
EGLINTON CT
OLNEY RD
OLNEY ROAD
DRACO ST
St. Wilfred (RC)
FLEMING RD
FORSYTH GDNS
GREIG TER
SLADE WALK
HEIRON ST
BRANDON EST
BRANDON ROAD
MADDOCK WY
OTTO ST
BATEMAN HO
CORNISH HO
WALTERS HO
CRUDEN HO
BRAWNE HO
PRESCOTT HO
HILLINGDON ST
ANDREWS WK
DALE RD
COPLEY CL
DIGHTON CT
RUSKIN TERRACE
URLWIN ST
GROSVENOR PARK
GROSVENOR TER
BETHWIN ROAD
John Ruskin Prim Sch
BLUE ELEPHANT
WYNDHAM ESTATE
Evangelical
KIRKWOOD WAY
SIR JOHN KIRK CL
THOMPSON AV
SULTAN ST
CROSSMOUNT HO
OTTERBURN HO
St. Joseph's Prim Schs
BOWYER ST
CROWN ST
CONISTON HO
St. Michael & All Angels C of E Academy
PITMAN ST
WYNDHAM RD
KEVAN HO
Comber Gro Prim Sch
GLENFINLAS WY
LAXLEY CL
FARMERS ROAD
GRIMSEL PATH
WARHAM ST
MADRON ST
St. John the Divine Prim Sch
JOHN RUSKIN STREET
KENDAL CLOSE
ROTHERY TER
CAMBERWELL NEW ROAD
A202
FOXLEY RD
CRANMER ROAD
Amb Sta
BOLTON CRES
ST. AGNES PLACE
St. Agnes
KENNINGTON PK GDNS
MEADCROFT RD
ST. AGNES PL
KENNINGTON PARK ESTATE
KENNINGTON PARK
St. Mark
PRIMA ROAD
OFFLEY RD
CAMBERWELL ROAD
A23
HOLLAND
BOWHILL CL
HENRY FAWCETT
BOWLING GRN ST
MAGEE ST
KENNINGTON GRN
STANNARY ST
RIFLE CT
THE LYCEE
AULTON PL
CUMBERLAND MEWS
RAVENSDON ST
METHLEY ST
MILVERTON ST
WIGTON PL
WHITE BEAR
CITY & GUILDS OF LONDON ART SCH
CLEAVER SQ
CLEAVER ST
SILK MS
BOWDEN ST
COUNTY COURT
MORRELLS YD
TRIANGLE EST
St. Anselm
STABLES WY
WINDMILL ROW
PO

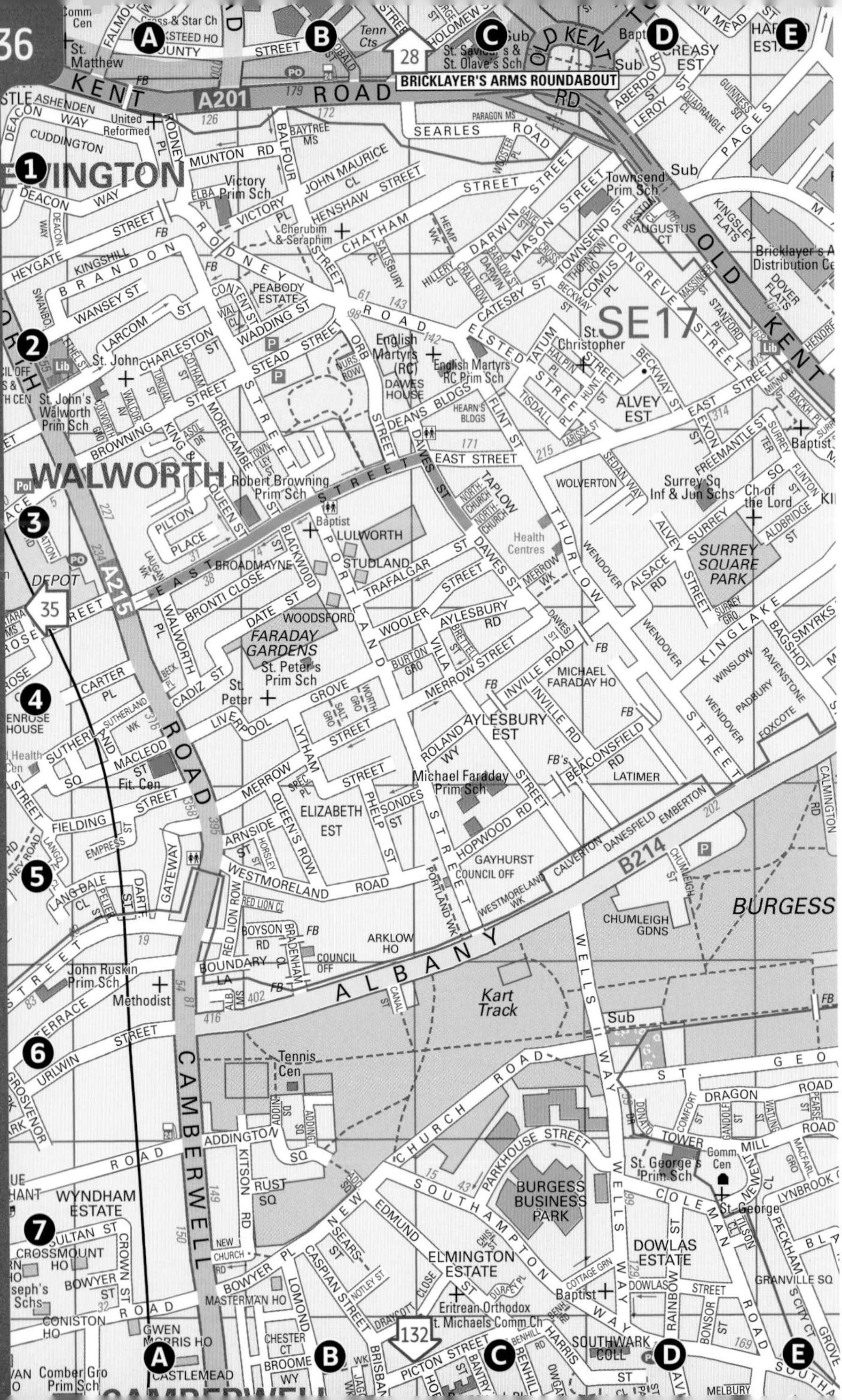
A
B
C
D
E
1
2
3
4
5
6
7
28
BRICKLAYER'S ARMS ROUNDABOUT
OLD KENT RD
KENT ROAD
A201
St. Matthew
Cross & Star Ch
St. Saviour's & St. Olave's Sch
Tenn Cts
CREASY EST
HARPER ESTATE
ASHENDEN
DEACON WAY
CUDDINGTON
United Reformed
RODNEY PL
MUNTON RD
BALFOUR
BAYTREE MS
SEARLES ROAD
PARAGON MS
ABERDOUR ST
LEROY ST
QUADRANGLE CL
GUINNESS SQ
PAGES
NEWINGTON
Victory Prim Sch
JOHN MAURICE CL
HENSHAW STREET
VICTORY PL
ELBA PL
Cherubim & Seraphim
CHATHAM
STREET
Townsend Prim Sch
Sub
KINGSLEY FLATS
AUGUSTUS CT
PRESTON CL
OLD KENT ROAD
Bricklayer's Arms Distribution Centre
DOVER FLATS
HEYGATE STREET
KINGSHILL
BRANDON
WANSEY ST
LARCOM ST
CONTENT ST
PEABODY ESTATE
WADDING ST
RODNEY ROAD
DARWIN
MASON STREET
TOWNSEND ST
CONGREVE
CATESBY ST
BECKWAY ST
COMUS PL
THORNTON HO
SE17
STANFORD PL
MASSINGER ST
St. Christopher
ELSTED
TATUM
HALPIN PL
BECKWAY ST
ALVEY EST
EAST STREET
EXON ST
Lib
St. John
St. John's Walworth Prim Sch
CHARLESTON ST
COTHAM ST
TURQUAND ST
WALCORD AV
MORECAMBE
BROWNING
KING & QUEEN ST
STEAD STREET
ORB STREET
English Martyrs (RC)
English Martyrs RC Prim Sch
DAWES HOUSE
DEANS BLDGS
HEARN'S BLDGS
FLINT ST
TISDALL PL
LARISSA ST
HUNT ST
WALWORTH
Robert Browning Prim Sch
EAST STREET
DAWES ST
TAPLOW
WOLVERTON
SEDAN WAY
Surrey Sq Inf & Jun Schs
Ch of the Lord
FREEMANTLE ST
SURREY TER
FLINTON ST
ALDBRIDGE ST
Baptist
Pol
PILTON PLACE
QUEENS ST
Baptist
LULWORTH
STUDLAND
BLACKWOOD ST
PORTLAND
TRAFALGAR ST
Health Centres
THURLOW
WENDOVER
ALSACE RD
ALVEY
SURREY
SURREY SQUARE PARK
DEPOT
35
A215
BROADMAYNE
BRONTI CLOSE
DATE ST
WOODSFORD
WOOLER STREET
AYLESBURY RD
MERROW WK
DAWES ST
KINGLAKE
BAGSHOT
SMYRKS
FARADAY GARDENS
St. Peter's Prim Sch
St. Peter
WALWORTH PL
CADIZ ST
BURTON GRO
VILLA ST
MERROW STREET
INVILLE ROAD
MICHAEL FARADAY HO
WINSLOW
RAVENSTONE
PADBURY
FOXCOTE
CARTER PL
GROVE
LIVERPOOL
SUTHERLAND WK
SUTHERLAND SQ
MACLEOD ST
Fit. Cen
ROAD
LYTHAM STREET
ROLAND WY
AYLESBURY EST
INVILLE RD
BEACONSFIELD RD
LATIMER
FIELDING STREET
EMPRESS ST
MERROW
QUEEN'S ROW
PHELP ST
SONDES ST
Michael Faraday Prim Sch
ELIZABETH EST
HOPWOOD RD
EMBERTON
DANESFIELD
CALVERTON
B214
CHUMLEIGH ST
CALMINGTON RD
GATEWAY
ARNSIDE ST
HORSLEY ST
GAYHURST
COUNCIL OFF
WESTMORELAND ROAD
WESTMORELAND WK
PORTLAND WK
BURGESS
LANGDALE CL
PELIER ST
DARTFORD ST
RED LION ROW
RED LION CL
BOYSON RD
BRADENHAM CL
ARKLOW HO
CHUMLEIGH GDNS
STREET
John Ruskin Prim Sch
BOUNDARY LA
COUNCIL OFF
ALBANY
WELLS WAY
Kart Track
TERRACE
Methodist
CANAL ST
Sub
URLWIN STREET
CAMBERWELL
Tennis Cen
ROAD
ST. GEORGE'S
DRAGON ROAD
COMFORT ST
GANDOLFI ST
WATLING ST
PEARSE ST
ROAD
GROSVENOR
ADDINGTON SQ
ADDINGTON SQ
CHURCH ROAD
PARKHOUSE STREET
TOWER MILL ROAD
MACFARLANE
ROAD
KITSON RD
RUST SQ
BURGESS BUSINESS PARK
St. George's Prim Sch
Comm Cen
St. George
COLEMAN
NEWENT CL
LYNBROOK
WYNDHAM ESTATE
SULTAN ST
CROWN ST
CROSSMOUNT HO
BOWYER ST
NEW CHURCH RD
BOWYER PL
SEARS ST
EDMUND
SOUTHAMPTON
ELMINGTON ESTATE
DOWLAS ESTATE
RAINBOW ST
PECKHAM ROAD
GRANVILLE SQ
MASTERMAN HO
LOMOND
CASPIAN STREET
NOTLEY ST
CLOSE
COTTAGE GRN
Baptist
DOWLAS STREET
BONSOR ST
CONISTON ROAD
HO
Eritrean Orthodox
St. Michaels Comm Ch
GWEN MORRIS HO
CHESTER CT
BROOME WY
132
PICTON STREET
SOUTHWARK COLL
ST
CASTLEMEAD
Comber Gro Prim Sch
MELBURY

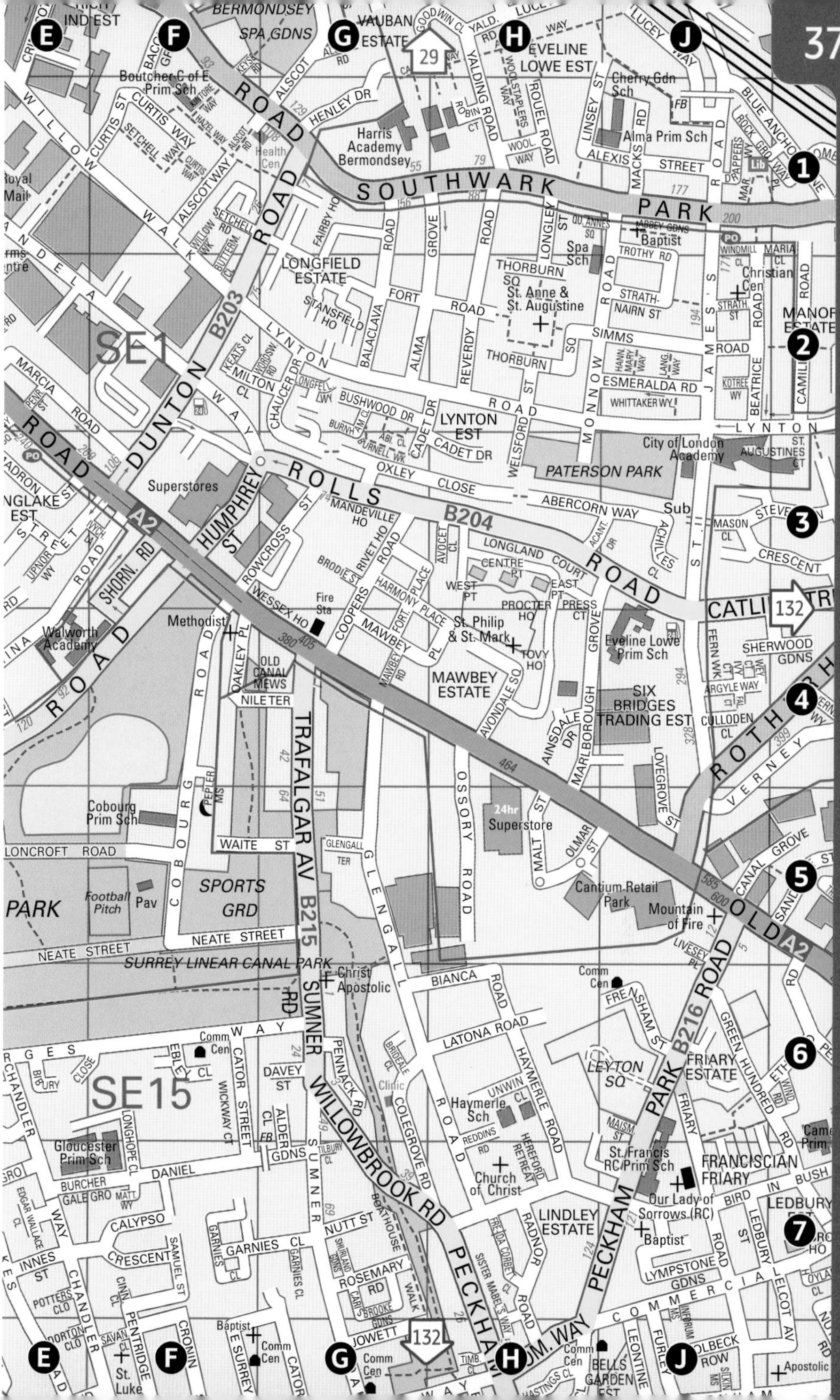
E
F
G
H
J
1
2
3
4
5
6
7
BERMONDSEY SPA GDNS
VAUBAN ESTATE
29
EVELINE LOWE EST
IND EST
Boutcher C of E Prim Sch
Cherry Gdn Sch
Alma Prim Sch
Harris Academy Bermondsey
Health Cen
SOUTHWARK PARK ROAD
HENLEY DR
ALSCOT RD
ALSCOT WAY
CURTIS ST
CURTIS WAY
SETCHELL WAY
YALDING ROAD
WOOLSTAPLERS WAY
ROUEL ROAD
LINSEY ST
MACKS RD
ALEXIS STREET
BLUE ANCHOR LANE
ROCK GRO WAY
Lib
WILLOW WALK
MANDELA WAY
Royal Mail
LONGFIELD ESTATE
STANSFIELD HO
BALACLAVA ROAD
ALMA GROVE
REVERDY ROAD
FORT ROAD
LONGLEY ST
Spa Sch
Baptist
TROTHY RD
THORBURN SQ
St. Anne & St. Augustine
STRATHNAIRN ST
Christian Cen
MANOR ESTATE
SIMMS ROAD
THORBURN SQ
ESMERALDA RD
WHITTAKER WY
KOTREE WY
BEATRICE ROAD
MONNOW ROAD
ST. JAMES'S ROAD
SE1
B203
DUNTON ROAD
LYNTON ROAD
KEATS CL
MILTON CL
CHAUCER DR
BUSHWOOD DR
LYNTON EST
CADET DR
WELSFORD ST
City of London Academy
AUGUSTINES CT
PATERSON PARK
MARCIA ROAD
OLD KENT ROAD
A2
Superstores
HUMPHREY ST
ROLLS ROAD
OXLEY CLOSE
ABERCORN WAY
B204
Sub
MASON CL
CRESCENT
CATLIN ST
132
MANDEVILLE HO
ROWCROSS ST
LONGLAND COURT
CENTRE PT
WEST PT
EAST PT
PROCTER HO
PRESS CT
SHORN. RD
UPNOR WAY
Walworth Academy
Methodist
WESSEX HO
Fire Sta
COOPERS ROAD
HARMONY PLACE
MAWBEY PL
St. Philip & St. Mark
TOVY HO
Eveline Lowe Prim Sch
SHERWOOD GDNS
FERN WK
ARGYLE WAY
CULLODEN CL
MAWBEY ESTATE
OAKLEY PL
OLD CANAL MEWS
NILE TER
SIX BRIDGES TRADING EST
AVONDALE SQ
AINSDALE DR
MARLBOROUGH GROVE
ROTHERHITHE
VERNEY
TRAFALGAR AV
B215
OSSORY ROAD
LOVEGROVE ST
Cobourg Prim Sch
COBOURG ROAD
PEPLER MS
WAITE ST
LONCROFT ROAD
24hr Superstore
MALT ST
OLMAR ST
CANAL GROVE
GLENGALL TER
GLENGALL ROAD
Football Pitch
Pav
SPORTS GRD
PARK
Cantium Retail Park
Mountain of Fire
NEATE STREET
SURREY LINEAR CANAL PARK
Christ Apostolic
BIANCA ROAD
Comm Cen
FRENSHAM ST
LIVESEY PL
PECKHAM PARK ROAD
B216
GREEN HUNDRED RD
SUMNER RD
LATONA ROAD
HAYMERLE ROAD
LEYTON SQ
FRIARY ESTATE
SE15
EBLEY CL
CATOR STREET
WICKWAY CT
DAVEY ST
PENNACK RD
WILLOWBROOK RD
Clinic
COLEGROVE RD
Haymerle Sch
UNWIN CL
REDDINS RD
HEREFORD RETREAT
MAISM. ST
St. Francis RC Prim Sch
FRANCISCIAN FRIARY
FRIARY ROAD
Gloucester Prim Sch
LONGHOPE CL
ALDER GDNS
TILBURY CL
Church of Christ
BIRD IN BUSH
LEDBURY EST
LEDBURY ST
DANIEL
BURCHER GALE GRO
CALYPSO CRESCENT
SAMUEL ST
NUTT ST
BOATHOUSE WALK
PECKHAM HILL ST
LINDLEY ESTATE
RADNOR ROAD
Our Lady of Sorrows (RC)
Baptist
LYMPSTONE GDNS
INNES ST
CHANDLER WAY
GARNIES CL
ROSEMARY RD
SISTER MABEL'S WAY
COMMERCIAL WAY
PECKHAM ROAD
FURLEY RD
MELCOT AV
POTTERS CLO
PENTRIDGE ST
CRONIN ST
Baptist
Comm Cen
JOWETT ST
St. Luke
BELLS GARDEN EST
LEONTINE CL
COLBECK ROW
Apostolic
HASTINGS CL
TIMB. CL

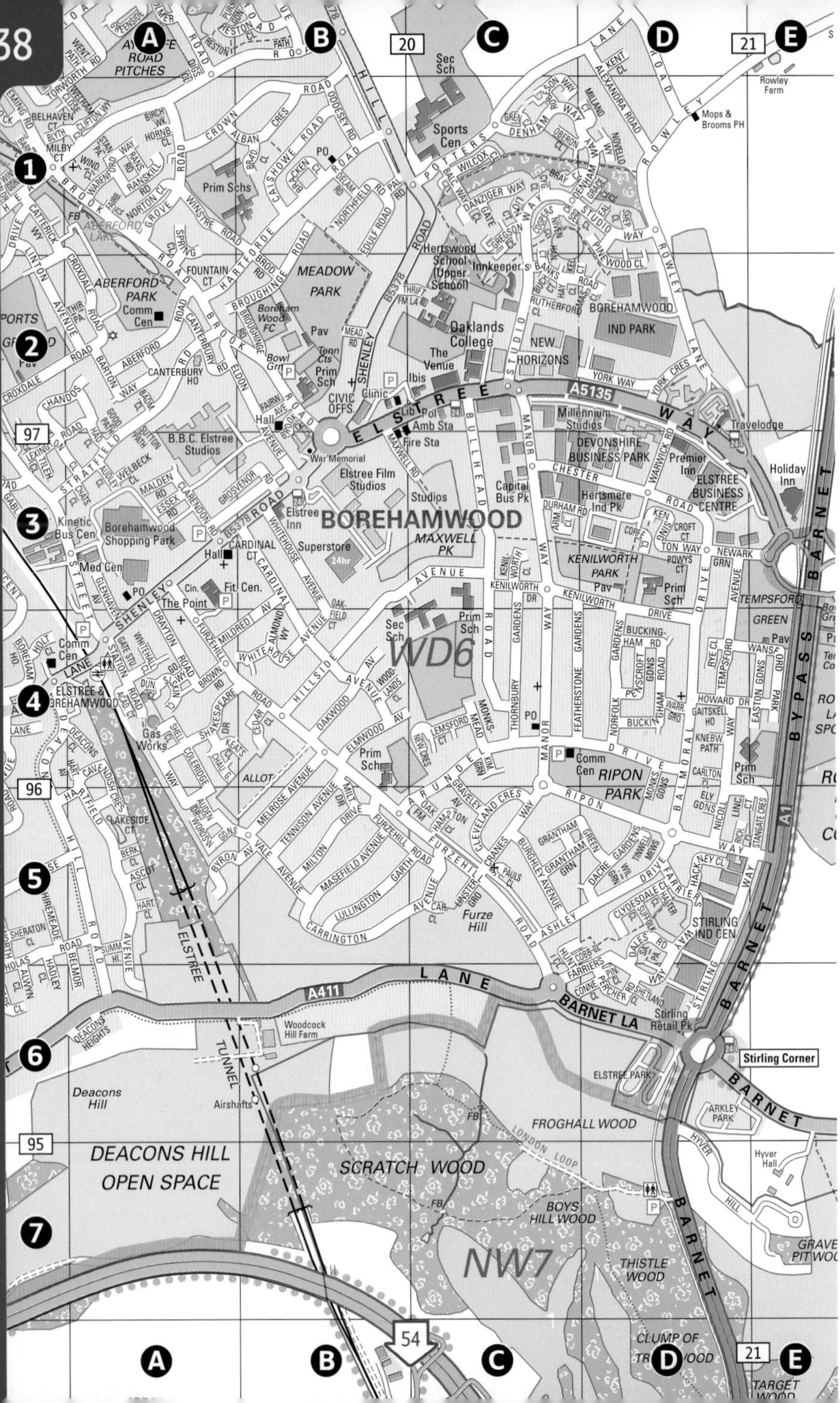
A
B
C
D
E
1
2
3
4
5
6
7
20
21
97
96
95
54
BOREHAMWOOD
WD6
NW7
ELSTREE WAY
A5135
A411
LANE
BARNET LA
BARNET BY PASS
A1
B5378
SHENLEY ROAD
ROWLEY LANE
POTTERS
ABERFORD PARK
ABERFORD LAKE
MEADOW PARK
Boreham Wood FC
Prim Schs
Sec Sch
Sports Cen
Hertswood School (Upper School)
Oaklands College
The Venue
Ibis
Clinic
Libr
Pol
Amb Sta
Fire Sta
CIVIC OFFS.
War Memorial
Elstree Film Studios
Studios
B.B.C. Elstree Studios
Borehamwood Shopping Park
Kinetic Bus Cen
Med Cen
Elstree Inn
Superstore
24hr
The Point
Fit. Cen.
MAXWELL PK
NEW HORIZONS
BOREHAMWOOD IND PARK
Millennium Studios
DEVONSHIRE BUSINESS PARK
Premier Inn
ELSTREE BUSINESS CENTRE
Hertsmere Ind Pk
Capital Bus Pk
Travelodge
Holiday Inn
Rowley Farm
Mops & Brooms PH
KENILWORTH PARK
TEMPSFORD GREEN
RIPON PARK
Comm Cen
ELSTREE & BOREHAMWOOD
Gas Works
ALLOT
Furze Hill
STIRLING IND CEN
Stirling Retail Pk
Stirling Corner
ELSTREE PARK
ARKLEY PARK
Hyver Hall
Woodcock Hill Farm
ELSTREE TUNNEL
Airshafts
Deacons Hill
DEACONS HILL OPEN SPACE
SCRATCH WOOD
FROGHALL WOOD
LONDON LOOP
BOYS HILL WOOD
THISTLE WOOD
CLUMP OF TREES WOOD
GRAVEL PIT WOOD
TARGET WOOD

E
F
22
G
H
23
J
THE S
LONDON
GOLF COURSE
ALLOTM
1
Fold Farm
FB
BYPASS
A1
FB
GALLEY LANE
Homestead Farm
POOR CLARE MONASTERY
HERTFORDSHIRE
BYNG
PLAYING FIELDS
2
ALLOT
DENIS BL
NATURE RESERVE
97
Barn
Elizabeth
R.F.C
HERTSMERE
BARNET
SPORTS GROUND
A1 DRIVING RANGE
Clubhouse
Woodlands Farm
Sec Sch
3
OLD FOLD VIEW
CAVENDISH ROAD
JENNINGS WY
GRIMSDYKE CRES
GRIMSDYKE CRESCENT
KINGS
40
Rowley Green Farm
ARKLEY OPEN SPACE
ARKLEY
Nursery
EN5
Three Elms Farm
WOOD
WHALEBONE PARK
4
ROWLEY
Pav
Rowley Green
ARKLEY GOLF COURSE
ARKLEY RISE ESTATE OPEN SPACE
ROWLEY LANE GOLF COURSE
OAKLANDS
FIELD END
GARDEN CL
KERRI CL
STONE CROFT
ELMBANK AV
WELLHOUSE
WELLSIDE CL
96
SPRING CL
ARKLEY VW
OAKLANDS LA
VYSE CL
DRIVE
BARNET ROAD
QUINTA
ARKLEY DRIVE
CARRINGTON CL
CHALET CL
CHENIES PLACE
HEDGEROW LA
HAZEL ME.
GARTHLAND
NORTH CL
ENDERSBY RD
TRINDER
PEPYS CRES
WELL APP
Arkley Manor Farm
SANDALW. CL
Clubhouse
COV RES
ROWLEY GREEN ROAD
War Memorial
SADDLERS CLOSE
RAYBARN GDNS
MALINS CL
DENTON CL
ESCOT WAY
AITKEN RD
HILL CL
ROAD
5
Water Tower
PO
WEST CL
RYECROFT CRESCENT
ST. PETER'S CL
HACKFORTH CL
FARM CL
BRETT ROAD
DRIVE
Prim Sch
WHITINGS ROAD
PALMER GDNS
DORMER CL
MINERAL CL
EDWYN CL
STANHOPE
DEXTER RD
COV RES
KATES CL
MEAD
LYNF. CL
LANE
GLEBE LA
Arkley
WHITINGS HILL OPEN SPACE
GREENLAND RD
NUPTON DRIVE
SHELF RD
MAYS
6
WINDMILL LA
DINGLE CL
ROCKWAYS
WYLO DR
Tennis Courts
Pavs.
BARNET GATE SPORTS GRD
BRICKFIELD LA
HAW. GRO
ROCKWAYS
BARNET
The Gate PH
Barnet Gate
PARTRIDGE CL
Whitings Hill Farm
SPORTS GROUND
Cottage Farm
FB
A411
WINIF. CL
HENDON
CHANTRY CL.
95
NEW RD
BARNET GATE WOOD
OLD ELIZABETHANS (BARNET) MEMORIAL PLAYING FIELDS
Pav
GATE
MAYS LANE
Dollis Brook
Brent Lodge Farm
AITHORP CL
FB
7
MOAT MOUNT OPEN SPACE
Dollis Brook
WOOD
B552
55
CHOLMELEIAN SPORTS GROUND
TOTTERIDGE
E
F
22
G
H
23
J

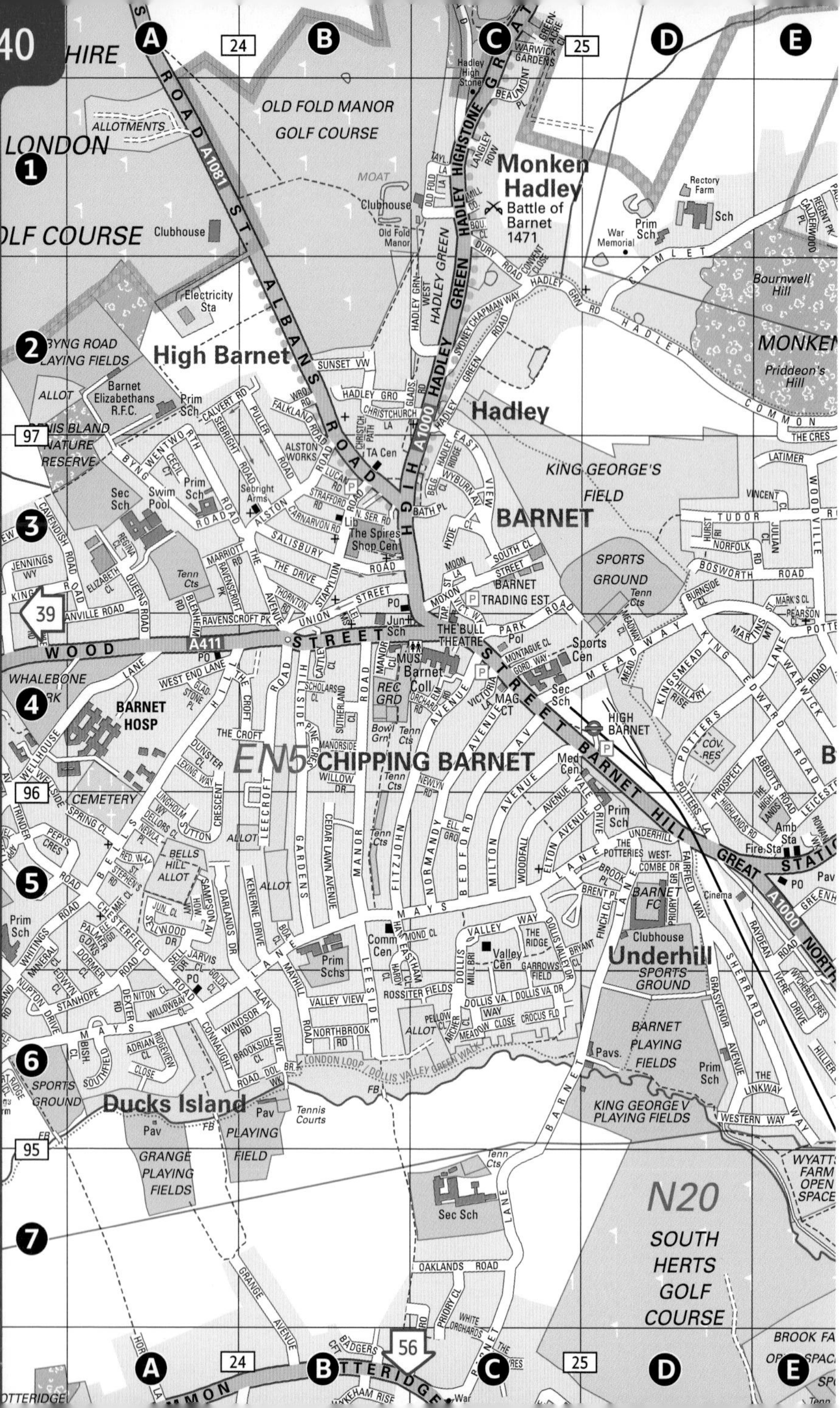
A
B
C
D
E
24
25
1
2
3
4
5
6
7
97
96
95
39
56
HIRE
LONDON
OLF COURSE
Clubhouse
ALLOTMENTS
OLD FOLD MANOR
GOLF COURSE
MOAT
Clubhouse
Old Fold Manor
Hadley High Stone
Monken Hadley
Battle of Barnet 1471
Rectory Farm
Sch
Prim Sch
War Memorial
CAMLET
Bournwell Hill
MONKEN
Priddeon's Hill
HADLEY COMMON
THE CRES
LATIMER
VINCENT CL
TUDOR RD
WOODVILLE
HURST RI
NORFOLK
JULIAN CL
BOSWORTH ROAD
ST. ALBANS ROAD
A1081
Electricity Sta
High Barnet
BYNG ROAD PLAYING FIELDS
ALLOT
Barnet Elizabethans R.F.C.
Prim Sch
DENIS BLAND NATURE RESERVE
SUNSET VW
HADLEY GRO
CHRISTCHURCH LA
WEST HADLEY GREEN
HADLEY GREEN
HADLEY HIGHSTONE
GREAT NORTH ROAD
SYDNEY CHAPMAN WAY
HADLEY GRN RD
DURY ROAD
CONVENT CLOSE
WARWICK GARDENS
BEAUMONT PL
GREEN-ACRE CL
LANGLEY ROW
Hadley
KING GEORGE'S FIELD
BARNET
SPORTS GROUND
Tenn Cts
A1000
HIGH ST
TA Cen
ALSTON WORKS
CALVERT RD
SEBRIGHT ROAD
PULLER ROAD
FALKLAND ROAD
WENTWORTH ROAD
CECIL CT
BYNG
Sec Sch
Swim Pool
Prim Sch
Sebright Arms
ALSTON ROAD
CARNARVON RD
STRAFFORD RD
LUCAN RD
SALISBURY ROAD
THE DRIVE
Lib
The Spires Shop Cen
N. SER. RD
BATH PL
HYDE CL
WYBURN AV
SOUTH CL
MOON LA
BARNET TRADING EST
MOXON ST
PARK ROAD
Pol
Sports Cen
MEADOWAY
MEADWAY
BURNSIDE CL
KINGSMEAD
HILLARY RISE
KING EDWARD ROAD
MARTINS MT
WARWICK ROAD
POTTERS ROAD
ST MARK'S CL
PEARSON CL
CAVENDISH ROAD
JENNINGS WY
KING
REGINA CL
ELIZABETH CL
QUEENS ROAD
MARRIOTT RD
RAVENSCROFT PK
BLENHEIM RD
THORNTON AVENUE
STAPYLTON
UNION STREET
PO
Jun Sch
THE BULL THEATRE
GRANVILLE ROAD
WOOD STREET
A411
WHALEBONE PARK
WEST END LANE
BARNET HOSP
LANE
THE CROFT
HILLSIDE GARDENS
SCHOLARS CL
SUTHERLAND CL
MANOR ROAD
MUS
REC GRD
Barnet Coll
Bowl Grn
Tenn Cts
ORCHARD RD
ELM
VICTORIA LA
MAG CT
AVENUE
HIGH STREET
Sec Sch
HIGH BARNET
MONTAGUE CL
COV. RES
PROSPECT
ABBOTTS ROAD
THE HIGHLANDS
HIGHLANDS RD
LEICESTER
EN5
CHIPPING BARNET
WELLHOUSE
WELLSIDE
CEMETERY
DUNSTER CL
LEXING WAY
MANORSIDE
WILLOW DR
NEWLYN RD
Med Cen
SPRING CL
LINGHOLM WY
DELLORS CL
SUTTON
CRESCENT
LEECROFT
ALLOT
CEDAR LAWN AVENUE
FITZJOHN
NORMANDY
BEDFORD
MILTON AVENUE
WOODFALL
ELTON AVENUE
VALE DRIVE
Prim Sch
BARNET HILL
UNDERHILL
POTTERS LA
Amb Sta
Fire Sta
GREAT NORTH ROAD
STATION
PO
Pav
TRINDER
PEPYS CRES
BELLS HILL
BELLS HILL ALLOT
SAMPSON AV
DARLANDS DR
KENERNE DRIVE
LANE
THE POTTERIES
WEST-COMBE DR
BROOK PL
BRENT PL
FAIRFIELD WAY
PRIORY GR
BARNET FC
Clubhouse
Cinema
RAYDEAN
Prim Sch
WHITINGS
CHESTERFIELD ROAD
PALMER GDNS
DORMER CL
MAYS LANE
SELLWOOD DR
JARVIS CL
PO
Comm Cen
HAMMOND CL
EASTHAM CL
VALLEY WAY
THE RIDGE
DOLLIS VALLEY DR
BRYANT CL
Valley Cen
FINCH CL
Underhill SPORTS GROUND
SHERRARDS
IVERE DRIVE
NUPTON DRIVE
STANHOPE
DEXTER RD
NITON CL
WILLOWBAY CL
CONNAUGHT
WINDSOR RD
ALAN DRIVE
MAYHILL ROAD
Prim Schs
VALLEY VIEW
LEESIDE
ROSSITER FIELDS
DOLLIS VA. WAY
DOLLIS VA. DR
GARROWS FIELD
NORTHBROOK RD
PELLOW CL
ARCHER CL
MEADOW CLOSE
CROCUS FLD
ALLOT
BARNET PLAYING FIELDS
GRASVENOR AVENUE
Prim Sch
BISH. CL
SOUTHFIELD
ADRIAN CL
RIDGEVIEW CLOSE
BROOKSIDE CL
ROAD
DOL WK
LONDON LOOP / DOLLIS VALLEY GREEN WALK
Pavs.
BARNET LANE
THE LINKWAY
WESTERN WAY
SPORTS GROUND
Ducks Island
Pav
Tennis Courts
PLAYING FIELD
Pav
FB
KING GEORGE V PLAYING FIELDS
GRANGE PLAYING FIELDS
Tenn Cts
Sec Sch
LANE
N20
WYATTS FARM OPEN SPACE
SOUTH HERTS GOLF COURSE
GRANGE AVENUE
OAKLANDS ROAD
PRIORY CL
WHITE ORCHARDS
BADGERS CFT
TOTTERIDGE
BROOK FARM OPEN SPACE
OTTERIDGE
WYKEHAM RISE
War

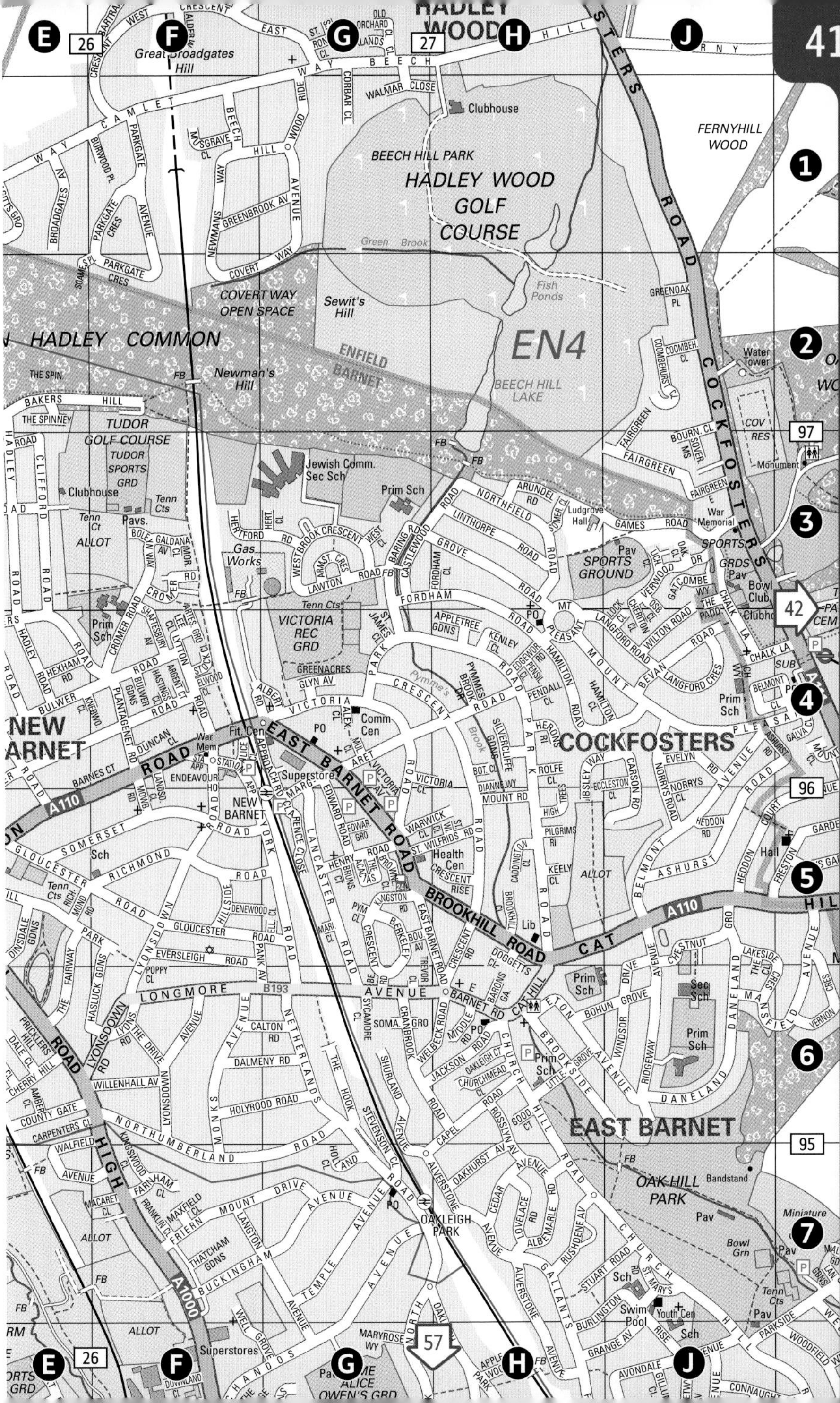
E
26
F
G
27
H
J
HADLEY WOOD
Great Broadgates Hill
BEECH HILL
CAMLET WAY
Clubhouse
FERNYHILL WOOD
BEECH HILL PARK
HADLEY WOOD GOLF COURSE
Green Brook
COCKFOSTERS ROAD
COVERT WAY
COVERT WAY OPEN SPACE
Sewit's Hill
Fish Ponds
EN4
HADLEY COMMON
ENFIELD
BARNET
Newman's Hill
BEECH HILL LAKE
Water Tower
BAKERS HILL
THE SPINNEY
TUDOR GOLF COURSE
TUDOR SPORTS GRD
Jewish Comm. Sec Sch
Prim Sch
COV RES
97
Monument
NORTHFIELD ROAD
GAMES ROAD
War Memorial
Gas Works
SPORTS GROUND
SPORTS GRDS
Bowl Club
42
VICTORIA REC GRD
LAWTON ROAD
FORDHAM ROAD
MOUNT PLEASANT
LANGFORD ROAD
CHALK LANE
GREENACRES
VICTORIA ROAD
PARK ROAD
NEW BARNET
EAST BARNET ROAD
Comm Cen
Superstore
COCKFOSTERS
96
A110
ROAD
SOMERSET ROAD
RICHMOND ROAD
GLOUCESTER ROAD
Health Cen
BROOKHILL ROAD
CAT HILL
Lib
ASHURST
5
LONGMORE AVENUE
B193
ALLOT
EAST BARNET
95
NORTHUMBERLAND ROAD
OAK HILL PARK
Bandstand
OAKLEIGH PARK
Miniature
7
A1000
HIGH ROAD
Superstores
57
ALICE OWEN'S GRD
1
2
3
4
6

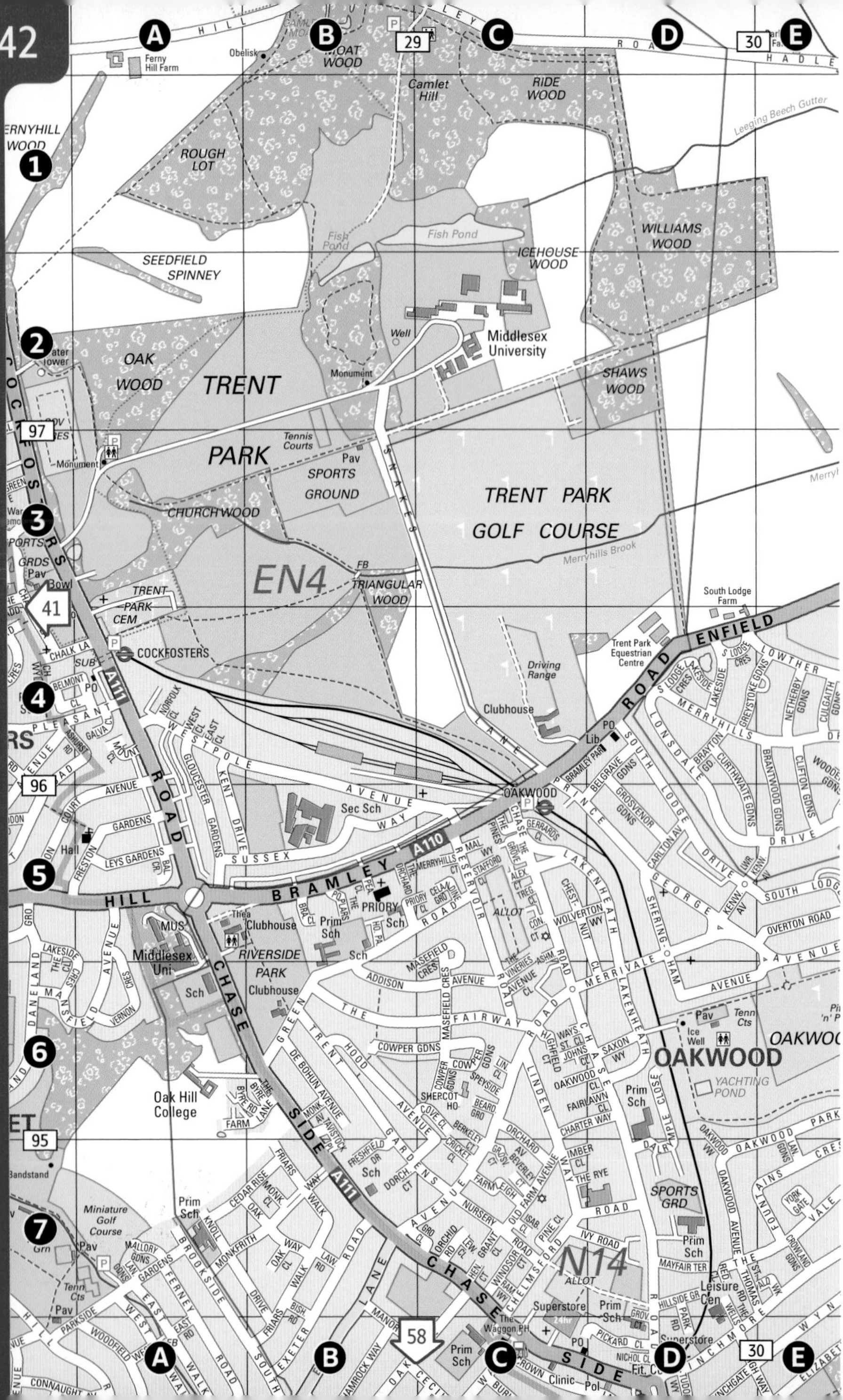
A
B
C
D
E
1
2
3
4
5
6
7
29
30
97
96
95
41
58
HILL
ROAD
HADLEY
Ferny Hill Farm
Obelisk
MOAT WOOD
Camlet Hill
RIDE WOOD
Leeging Beech Gutter
FERNYHILL WOOD
ROUGH LOT
Fish Pond
WILLIAMS WOOD
SEEDFIELD SPINNEY
ICEHOUSE WOOD
Well
Middlesex University
Water Tower
OAK WOOD
TRENT
Monument
SHAWS WOOD
Tennis Courts
PARK
Pav
SPORTS GROUND
TRENT PARK
GOLF COURSE
CHURCH WOOD
Merryhills Brook
SNAKES LANE
EN4
FB
TRIANGULAR WOOD
TRENT PARK CEM
South Lodge Farm
ENFIELD ROAD
Trent Park Equestrian Centre
Driving Range
COCKFOSTERS
CHALK LA
SUB
BELMONT CL
PO
A111
Clubhouse
PLEASANT
LOWTHER
MERRYHILLS
LONSDALE
BRAYTON GD
CURTHWAITE GDNS
BRANTWOOD GDNS
CLIFTON GDNS
NETHERBY GDNS
CULGAITH GDNS
GREYSTOKE GDNS
LAKESIDE
Lib
BELGRAVE GDNS
GROSVENOR GDNS
SOUTH LODGE DRIVE
COCKFOSTERS ROAD
GLOUCESTER GARDENS
KENT DRIVE
WESTPOLE AVENUE
Sec Sch
OAKWOOD
AVENUE
GARDENS
LEYS GARDENS
Hall
FRESTON
SUSSEX WAY
A110
BRAMLEY ROAD
HILL
MERRYHILLS CT
PRIORY
Prim Sch
Sch
RESERVOIR ROAD
ALLOT
LAKENHEATH
WOLVERTON WY
SHERINGHAM AVENUE
GEORGE
OVERTON ROAD
Thea
Clubhouse
MUS
Middlesex Uni
RIVERSIDE PARK
Clubhouse
LAKESIDE
DANELAND
MANSFIELD
VERNON CRES
ADDISON
MASEFIELD CRES
THE FAIRWAY
MERRIVALE
AVENUE
Pav
Tenn Cts
Ice Well
OAKWOOD
YACHTING POND
CHASE SIDE
GREEN
TRENT
HOOD
DE BOHUN AVENUE
COWPER GDNS
SAXON WY
OAKWOOD PARK
LINDEN
Oak Hill College
FARM
CHARTER WAY
DALRYMPLE CLOSE
Sch
FRESHFIELD DR
DORCH. CT
ORCHARD
OLD FARM AVENUE
THE RYE
OAKWOOD AVENUE
FOUNTAINS
YORK GATE
VALE
CROWLAND GDNS
Bandstand
Miniature Golf Course
Prim Sch
CEDAR RISE
MONK CL
FRIARS WALK
OAK WAY
NURSERY
IVY ROAD
SPORTS GRD
Prim Sch
Pav
KNOLL
MONKFRITH
BROOKSIDE
FERNEY ROAD
MALLORY GDNS
GARDENS
N14
ALLOT
MAYFAIR TER
Leisure Cen
Tenn Cts
Pav
PARKSIDE
WOODFIELD
EAST
WEST
Superstore
Prim Sch
HILLSIDE GR
WINCHMORE
The Waggon PH
FRIARS DRIVE
LANE
MANOR
Prim Sch
PO
PICKARD CL
NICHOL CL
Fit. Cen
Superstore
CROWN
Clinic
Pol
CONNAUGHT
EXETER
OAK
ELIZABETH

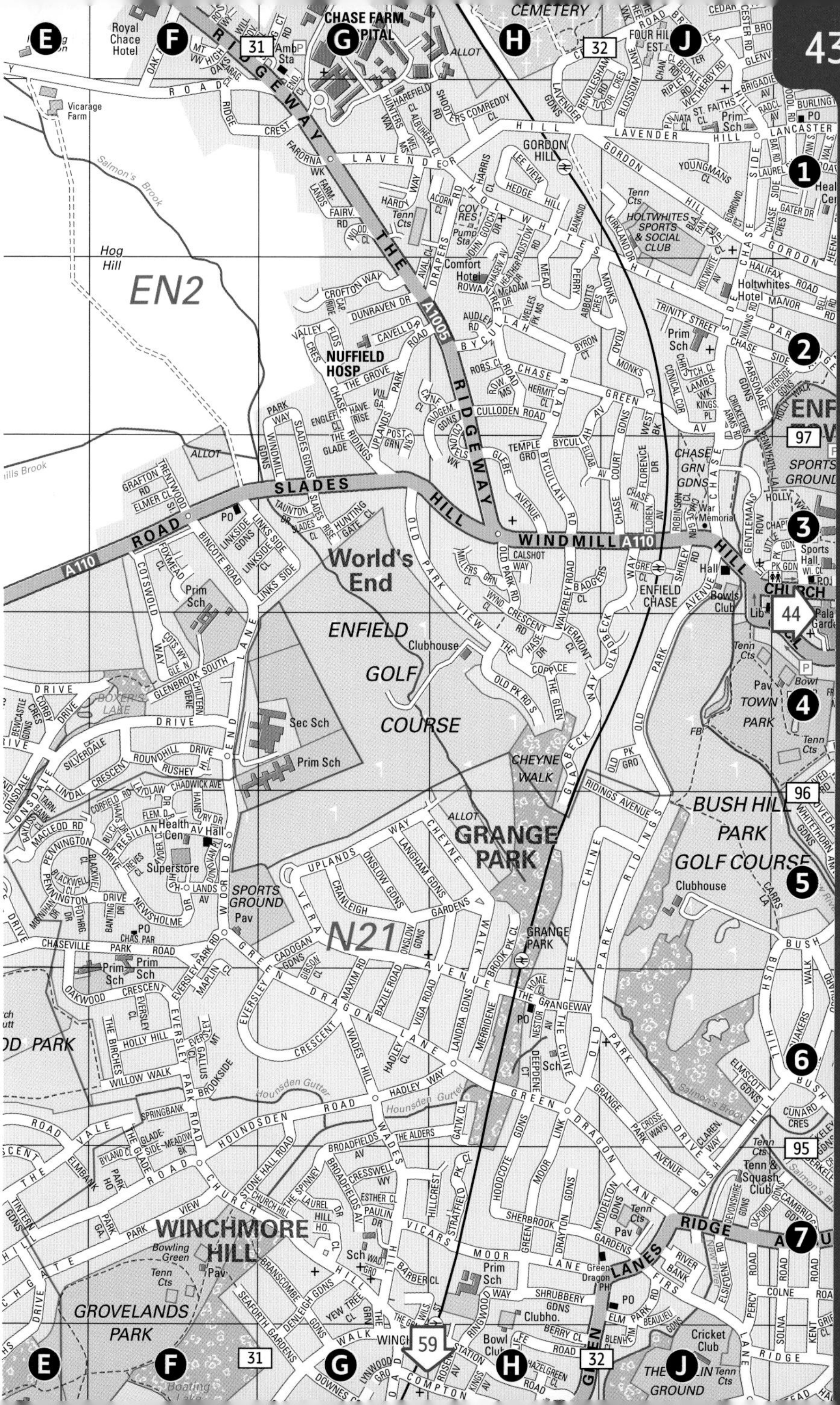
E
F
G
H
J
Royal Chace Hotel
CHASE FARM HOSPITAL
CEMETERY
31
32
Vicarage Farm
Salmon's Brook
Hog Hill
EN2
RIDGEWAY
THE RIDGEWAY
A1005
LAVENDER HILL
GORDON HILL
GORDON HILL
HOLTWHITES HILL
HOLTWHITES SPORTS & SOCIAL CLUB
Holtwhites Hotel
Comfort Hotel
NUFFIELD HOSP
CHASE SIDE
CHASE GREEN AV
CHASE GRN GDNS
BYCULLAH RD
SLADES HILL
A110
ROAD
WINDMILL HILL
ENFIELD CHASE
World's End
ENFIELD GOLF COURSE
Clubhouse
Sec Sch
Prim Sch
BOXER'S LAKE
CHEYNE WALK
GRANGE PARK
BUSH HILL PARK GOLF COURSE
TOWN PARK
CHURCH
44
97
96
95
SPORTS GROUND
N21
CHASEVILLE PARK ROAD
GREEN DRAGON LANE
HADLEY WAY
HOUNDSDEN ROAD
Hounsden Gutter
WINCHMORE HILL
GROVELANDS PARK
VICARS MOOR LANE
GREEN LANES
RIDGE AV
A105
OLD PARK RIDINGS
OLD PARK ROAD
THE CHINE
WORLDS END LANE
Cricket Club
59
1
2
3
4
5
6
7

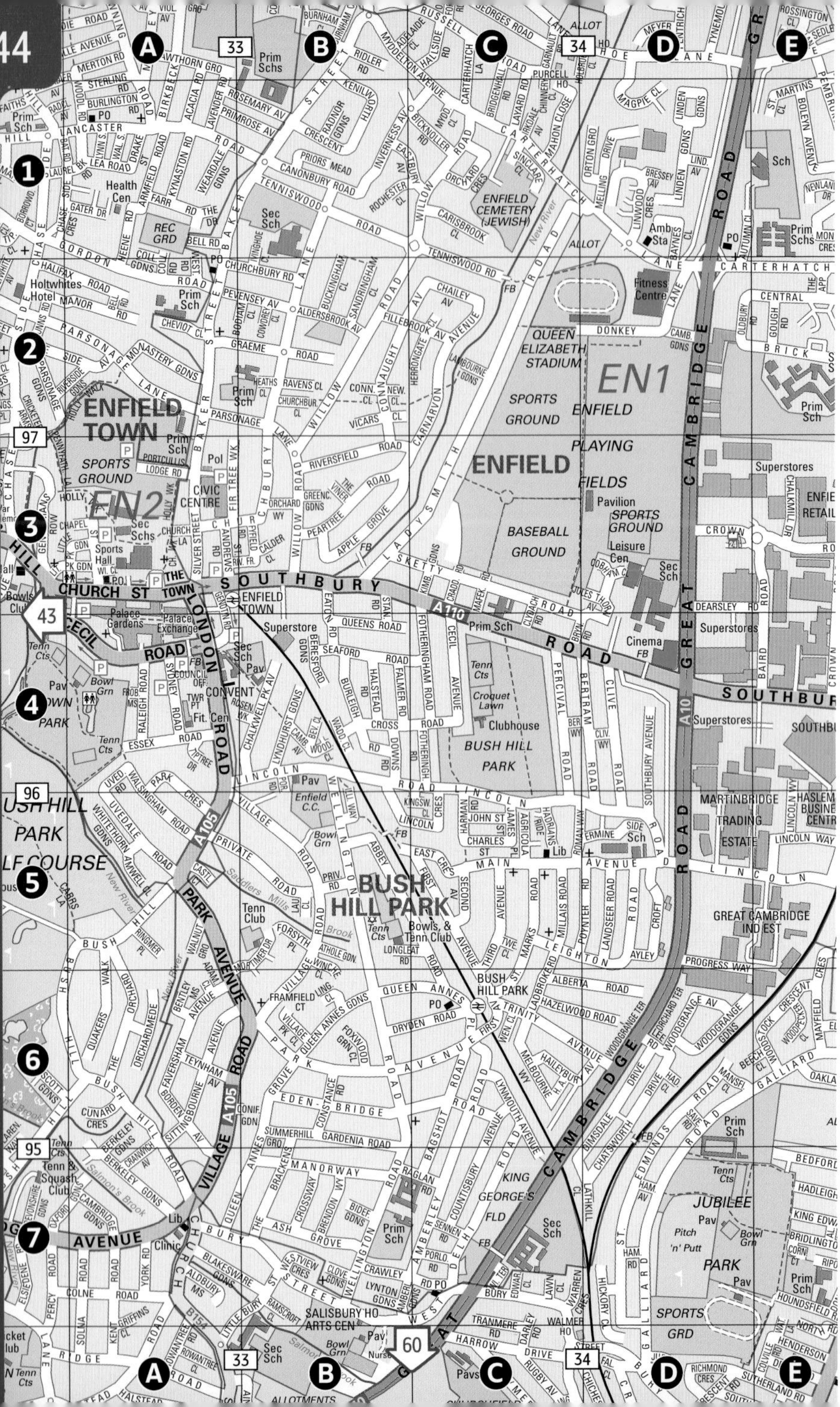
A
B
C
D
E
1
2
3
4
5
6
7
33
34
97
96
95
43
60
ENFIELD TOWN
EN2
EN1
ENFIELD
BUSH HILL PARK
SPORTS GROUND
CIVIC CENTRE
Pol
Sec Schs
Sports Hall
Prim Sch
Prim Schs
Health Cen
REC GRD
Holtwhites Hotel
PO
Palace Gardens
Palace Exchange
TOWN PARK
Tenn Cts
Bowl Grn
Pav
Bowls Club
CONVENT
Fit. Cen
ENFIELD TOWN
Superstore
ENFIELD CEMETERY (JEWISH)
New River
QUEEN ELIZABETH STADIUM
SPORTS GROUND
ENFIELD PLAYING FIELDS
Pavilion
SPORTS GROUND
BASEBALL GROUND
Leisure Cen
Sec Sch
Cinema
Fitness Centre
Amb Sta
Superstores
ENFIELD RETAIL
MARTINBRIDGE TRADING ESTATE
HASLEMERE BUSINESS CENTRE
GREAT CAMBRIDGE IND EST
Croquet Lawn
Clubhouse
BUSH HILL PARK
Enfield C.C.
Lib
BUSH HILL PARK GOLF COURSE
Tenn Club
Bowls, & Tenn Club
BUSH HILL PARK
KING GEORGE'S FLD
Tenn & Squash Club
Clinic
JUBILEE PARK
Pitch 'n' Putt
SPORTS GRD
SALISBURY HO ARTS CEN
Nurse
Pavs
ALLOTMENTS
Saddlers Mills
Salmon's Brook
GREAT CAMBRIDGE ROAD
A10
A105
A110
B154
SOUTHBURY ROAD
CHURCH ST
LONDON ROAD
CECIL ROAD
SILVER STREET
BAKER STREET
LANCASTER ROAD
GORDON ROAD
CHASE SIDE
PARSONAGE LANE
CHURCHBURY ROAD
CHURCHBURY LANE
TENNISWOOD ROAD
CARTERHATCH LANE
CARTERHATCH ROAD
LADYSMITH ROAD
WILLOW ROAD
QUEENS ROAD
LINCOLN ROAD
MAIN AVENUE
VILLAGE ROAD
PARK AVENUE
BUSH HILL
BURY STREET WEST
CHURCH STREET
RIDGE AVENUE
DONKEY LANE
CROWN ROAD
DEARSLEY RD
PROGRESS WAY
LINCOLN WAY
GALLIARD ROAD
HERTFORD ROAD

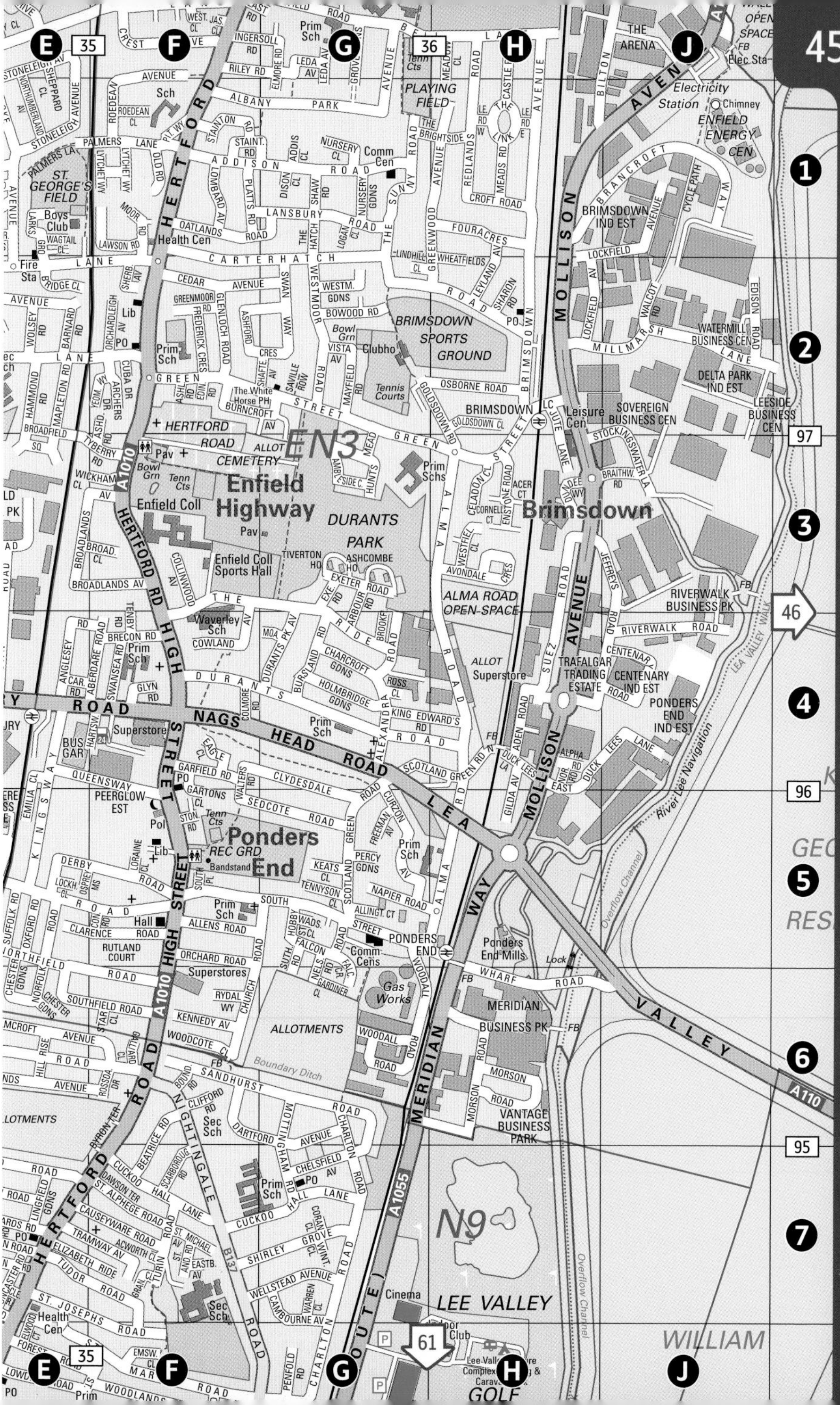
E
35
F
G
36
H
J
THE ARENA
OPEN SPACE
Elec Sta
Electricity Station
Chimney
ENFIELD ENERGY CEN
1
2
3
4
5
6
7
97
96
95
46
61
HERTFORD ROAD
HERTFORD RD
HIGH STREET
A1010
A1055
A110
MOLLISON AVENUE
MERIDIAN WAY
LEA VALLEY ROAD
NAGS HEAD ROAD
PLAYING FIELD
ST. GEORGE'S FIELD
Boys Club
Health Cen
CARTERHATCH LANE
BRIMSDOWN SPORTS GROUND
BRIMSDOWN IND EST
WATERMILL BUSINESS CEN
DELTA PARK IND EST
LEESIDE BUSINESS CEN
SOVEREIGN BUSINESS CEN
Leisure Cen
EN3
Enfield Highway
Brimsdown
HERTFORD ROAD CEMETERY
Enfield Coll
Enfield Coll Sports Hall
DURANTS PARK
ALMA ROAD OPEN SPACE
RIVERWALK BUSINESS PK
TRAFALGAR TRADING ESTATE
CENTENARY IND EST
PONDERS END IND EST
River Lee Navigation
LEA VALLEY WALK
Superstore
Ponders End
REC GRD
Bandstand
PONDERS END
Ponders End Mills
Gas Works
ALLOTMENTS
Boundary Ditch
MERIDIAN BUSINESS PK
VANTAGE BUSINESS PARK
Overflow Channel
N9
LEE VALLEY
Cinema
GOLF
WILLIAM
GEO
RES
Lock

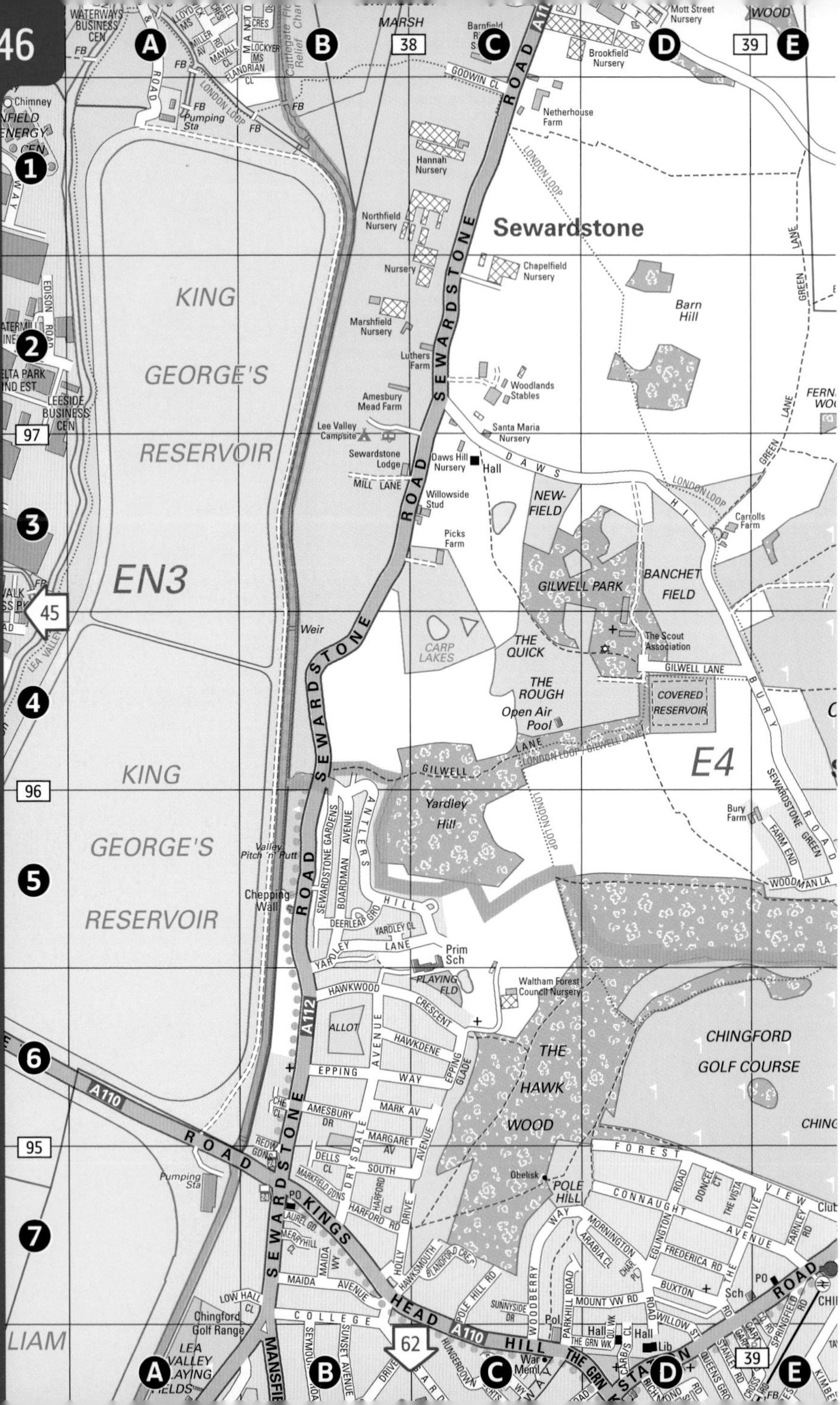
A
B
C
D
E
1
2
3
4
5
6
7
38
39
97
96
95
45
62
WATERWAYS BUSINESS CEN
LOYD MS
MILLER AV
MAYALL CL
FLANDRIAN CL
LOCKYER MS
CRES
MARSH
Barnfield
Mott Street Nursery
WOOD
Brookfield Nursery
GODWIN CL
Chimney
ENFIELD ENERGY CEN
Pumping Sta
LONDON LOOP
FB
Cattlegate Flood Relief Channel
Netherhouse Farm
Hannah Nursery
Northfield Nursery
Sewardstone
Nursery
Chapelfield Nursery
EDISON ROAD
KING GEORGE'S RESERVOIR
Barn Hill
GREEN LANE
Marshfield Nursery
Luthers Farm
LEESIDE BUSINESS CEN
Woodlands Stables
Amesbury Mead Farm
Lee Valley Campsite
Santa Maria Nursery
Sewardstone Lodge
Daws Hill Nursery
Hall
DAWS HILL
MILL LANE
Willowside Stud
NEW-FIELD
Carrolls Farm
Picks Farm
SEWARDSTONE ROAD
EN3
BANCHET FIELD
GILWELL PARK
Weir
CARP LAKES
THE QUICK
The Scout Association
GILWELL LANE
THE ROUGH
COVERED RESERVOIR
Open Air Pool
BURY ROAD
LEA VALLEY
GILWELL LANE
LONDON LOOP / GILWELL LANE
E4
Yardley Hill
ANTLERS
Bury Farm
SEWARDSTONE GREEN
FARM END
SEWARDSTONE GARDENS
BOARDMAN AVENUE
Valley Pitch 'n' Putt
WOODMAN LA
Chepping Wall
HILL
DEERLEAP GRO
YARDLEY CL
YARDLEY LANE
Prim Sch
PLAYING FLD
HAWKWOOD CRESCENT
Waltham Forest Council Nursery
A112
ALLOT
HAWKDENE
CHINGFORD GOLF COURSE
THE HAWK WOOD
EPPING WAY
EPPING GLADE
A110
MARK AV
AMESBURY DR
MARGARET AV
DRYSDALE AVENUE
FOREST VIEW
DELLS CL
SOUTH
Obelisk
POLE HILL
Pumping Sta
MARKFIELD GDNS
HARFORD RD
HARFORD CL
CONNAUGHT AVENUE
DONCEL CT
THE VISTA
DRIVE
Club
PO
KINGS HEAD HILL
LAUREL GD
HOLLY DRIVE
MORNINGTON
EGLINGTON ROAD
FREDERICA RD
FARNLEY RD
MERRYHILL CL
MAIDA WY
HAWKSMOUTH
BLANDFORD CRES
ARABIA CL
WOODBERRY
BUXTON
Sch
MAIDA AVENUE
POLE HILL RD
PARKHILL ROAD
MOUNT VW RD
WILLOW ST
STATION ROAD
LOW HALL CL
SUNNYSIDE DR
Pol
Hall
Lib
SPRINGFIELD RD
COLLEGE
Chingford Golf Range
SEYMOUR ROAD
SUNSET AVENUE
HUNGERDOWN
THE GRN WK
THE GRN
War Meml
RICHMOND
QUEENS GRO
STANLEY RD
KIMBERLEY
LEA VALLEY PLAYING FIELDS
WILLIAM
MANSFIELD
CHINGFORD
FERN WOOD

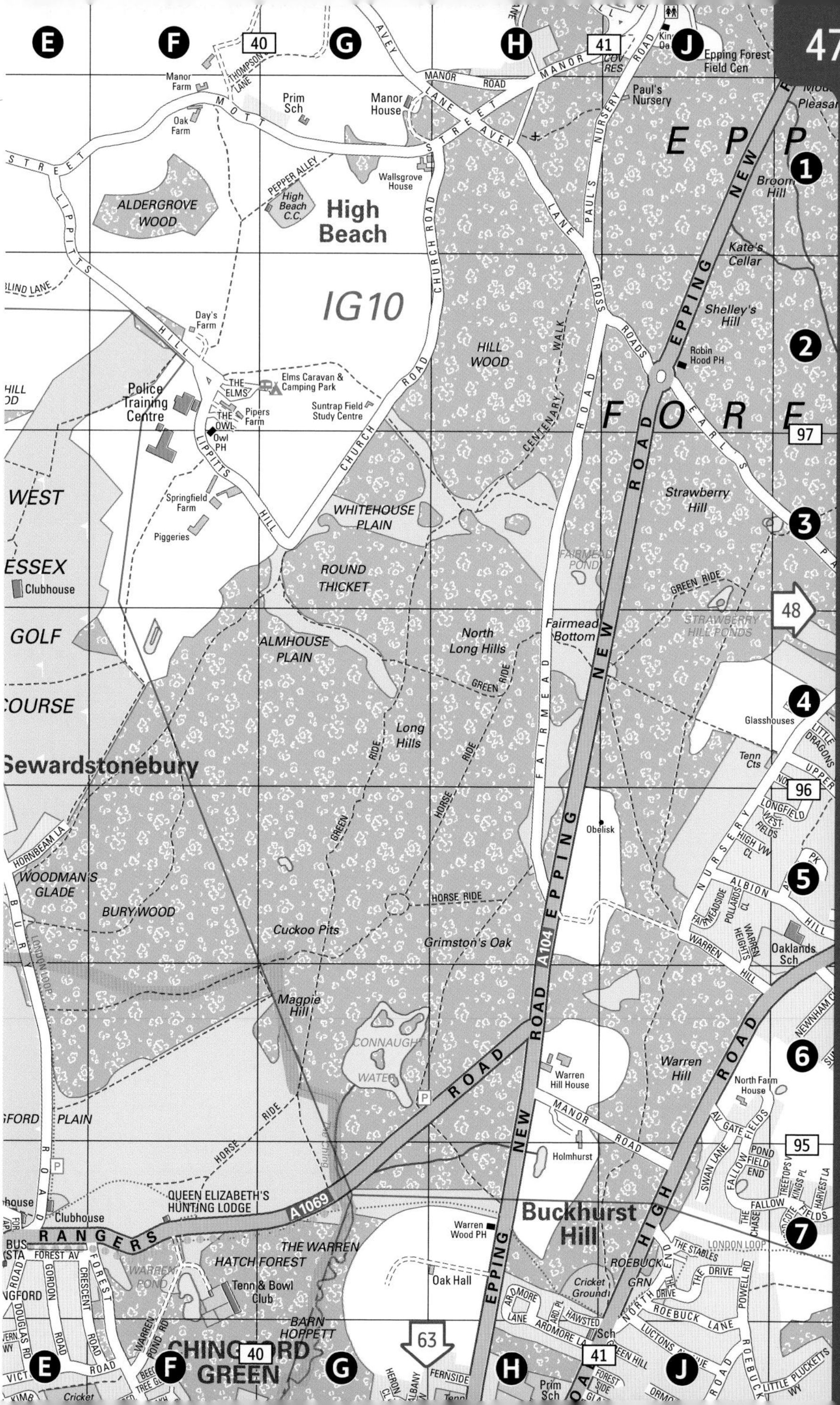
E
F
G
H
J
40
41
1
2
3
4
5
6
7
95
96
97
48
63
Manor Farm
Thompson Lane
Mott Street
Oak Farm
Prim Sch
Manor House
Manor Road
Manor Lane
Avey Lane
Cov Res
Nursery Road
Paul's Nursery
Epping Forest Field Cen
Street
Lippitts Hill
Aldergrove Wood
Pepper Alley
High Beach C.C.
High Beach
Wallsgrove House
Church Road
Paul's Lane
Cross Roads
Epping New Road
Broom Hill
Kate's Cellar
Shelley's Hill
Blind Lane
IG10
Day's Farm
Hill Wood
Centenary Walk
Robin Hood PH
Epping Forest
Earls Path
The Elms
Elms Caravan & Camping Park
Police Training Centre
The Owl
Pipers Farm
Owl PH
Suntrap Field Study Centre
Strawberry Hill
West Essex Golf Course
Springfield Farm
Whitehouse Plain
Piggeries
Fairmead Pond
Round Thicket
Green Ride
Clubhouse
Strawberry Hill Ponds
Fairmead Bottom
North Long Hills
Almhouse Plain
Fairmead Road
Glasshouses
Little Dragons
Long Hills
Horse Ride
Tenn Cts
Upper
Sewardstonebury
Longfield
West Fields
Obelisk
Nursery Road
High Vw Cl
Hornbeam La
Woodman's Glade
Albion Hill
Bury Wood
Fairmeadside
Pollards Cl
Warren Heights
Warren Hill
Cuckoo Pits
Grimston's Oak
Oaklands Sch
A104
London Loop
Bury Road
Magpie Hill
Newnham Cl
Connaught Water
Warren Hill House
Warren Hill
North Farm House
High Road
Plain
Manor Road
Gate Fields
Swan Lane
Pond Field End
Fallow Fields
Treetops
Kings Pl
Harvest La
Holmhurst
The Ching
Queen Elizabeth's Hunting Lodge
A1069
Clubhouse
Rangers Road
Buckhurst Hill
The Chase
Warren Wood PH
Bus Sta
Forest Av
The Warren
The Stables
Hatch Forest
Roebuck Grn
The Drive
Powell Rd
Gordon Road
Crescent Road
Forest Road
Warren Pond
Tenn & Bowl Club
Oak Hall
Ardmore Lane
Ard Pl
Hawsted
Cricket Ground
North End
Roebuck Lane
Douglas Rd
Warren Pond Rd
Barn Hoppett
Chingford Green
Sch
Luctons Avenue
Queen's Hill
Roebuck Road
Little Pluckets Wy
Heron Cl
Albany
Fernside
Forest Side
Prim Sch
Ormo
Vict
Cricket

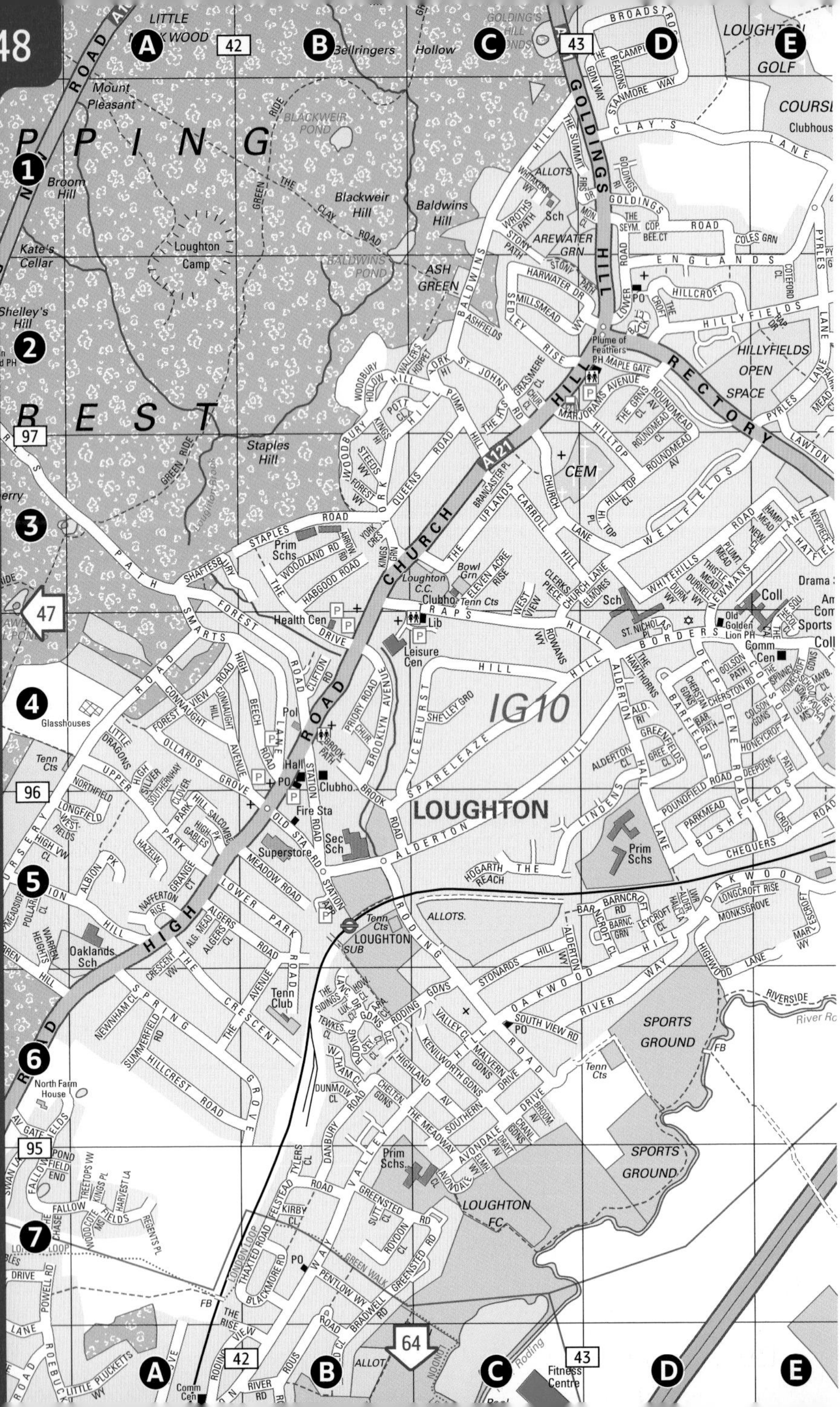
A
B
C
D
E
1
2
3
4
5
6
7
42
43
97
96
95
47
64
LITTLE
Bellringers
Hollow
GOLDING'S HILL PONDS
LOUGHTON GOLF COURSE
Clubhouse
EPPING FOREST
Mount Pleasant
Broom Hill
Kate's Cellar
Loughton Camp
Shelley's Hill
BLACKWEIR POND
Blackweir Hill
Baldwins Hill
BALDWINS POND
ASH GREEN
Staples Hill
Loughton Brook
GREEN RIDE
THE CLAY ROAD
GOLDINGS HILL
CLAY'S LANE
ENGLANDS LANE
HILLYFIELDS OPEN SPACE
RECTORY LANE
AREWATER GRN
Plume of Feathers PH
CHURCH HILL
A121
CEM
HIGH ROAD
STAPLES ROAD
Prim Schs
Loughton C.C.
Bowl Grn
Tenn Cts
Health Cen
Lib
Leisure Cen
TRAPS HILL
BORDERS LANE
Drama
Coll
Sports
Comm Cen
Old Golden Lion PH
IG10
LOUGHTON
SMARTS LANE
FOREST ROAD
Glasshouses
Pol
Hall
PO
Clubho.
Fire Sta
Superstore
Sec Sch
STATION ROAD
ALDERTON HILL
ALLOTS.
LOUGHTON SUB
Oaklands Sch
Tenn Club
RODING ROAD
OAKWOOD HILL
RIVER WAY
SPORTS GROUND
RIVERSIDE
River Roding
FB
North Farm House
LONDON LOOP
GREEN WALK
LOUGHTON FC
ALLOT
Roding
Fitness Centre
Comm Cen

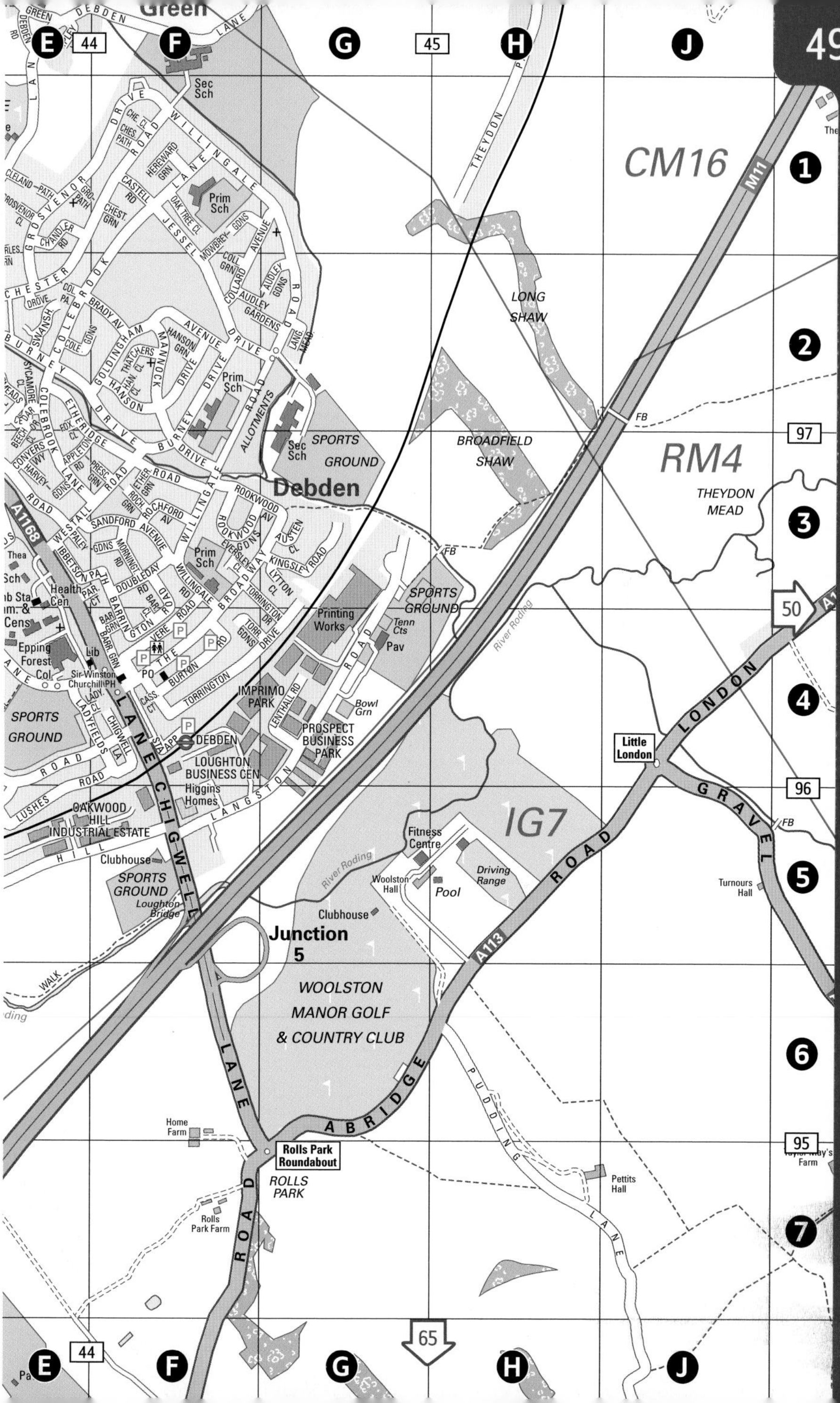
Green
DEBDEN
DEBDEN RD
LANE
E
44
F
G
45
H
J
Sec Sch
WILLINGALE
THEYDON
CM16
M11
1
CHE. CL
CHES. PATH
HEREWARD GRN
CASTELL RD
Prim Sch
CLELAND PATH
GROSVENOR
GRO. PATH
CHEST. GRN
OAK TREE CL
JESSEL
MOWBREY GDNS
AVENUE
CHANDLER RD
COLL GRN
COLLARD
AUDLEY GDNS
ROAD
AUDLEY GARDENS
CHESTER
COL. PA.
BRADY AV
DROVE
SWANSH.
COLEBROOK
BURNEY
COLE.
GDNS
GOLDINGHAM
HANSON GRN
MANNOCK
AVENUE
DRIVE
LANG. MEAD
LONG SHAW
2
THATCHERS
HAN. CL
HANSON
DRIVE
Prim Sch
ROAD
ALLOTMENTS
SYCAMORE
ETHERIDGE
FOX CL
BURNEY
FB
97
BROADFIELD SHAW
CONYERS WY
APPLETON RD
PRESC. GRN
Sec Sch
SPORTS GROUND
RM4
HARVEY GDNS
LANE
ROAD
ETHER. GRN
ROAD
THEYDON MEAD
Debden
ROCH. GRN
ROCHFORD AV
ROOKWOOD AV
A1168
WESTALL
SANDFORD AVENUE
ROOKWOOD GDNS
AUSTEN CL
3
Thea
Sch
PALEY GDNS
MORNINGT. RD
EVERSLEY CL
KINGSLEY ROAD
FB
Health Cen
IBBETSON PATH
DOUBLEDAY RD
WILLINGALE RD
BROADWAY
LYTTON CL
SPORTS GROUND
Amb Sta
Comm. & Cens
PAR. CT
BARR. RD
BARRINGTON
VERE
ROAD
TORRINGTON DR
Printing Works
River Roding
50
Epping Forest Col
Lib
BARR. GRN
THE
TORR. GDNS
DRIVE
ROAD
Tenn Cts
Pav
Sir Winston Churchill PH
PO
BURTON
TORRINGTON
LONDON
4
LADY. CL
CASS. CT
IMPRIMO PARK
LENTHALL RD
Bowl Grn
SPORTS GROUND
LADYFIELDS
CHIGWELL LA
STA. APP.
DEBDEN
PROSPECT BUSINESS PARK
Little London
ROAD
ROAD
LOUGHTON BUSINESS CEN
LUSHES
Higgins Homes
LANGSTON
GRAVEL
96
OAKWOOD HILL INDUSTRIAL ESTATE
IG7
FB
HILL
Clubhouse
CHIGWELL
LANE
Fitness Centre
ROAD
SPORTS GROUND
Loughton Bridge
River Roding
Woolston Hall
Pool
Driving Range
Turnours Hall
5
Clubhouse
Junction 5
A113
WALK
Roding
WOOLSTON MANOR GOLF & COUNTRY CLUB
6
LANE
PUDDING
ABRIDGE
Home Farm
Rolls Park Roundabout
95
Taylor May's Farm
ROLLS PARK
Pettits Hall
LANE
ROAD
Rolls Park Farm
7
65
E
44
F
G
H
J

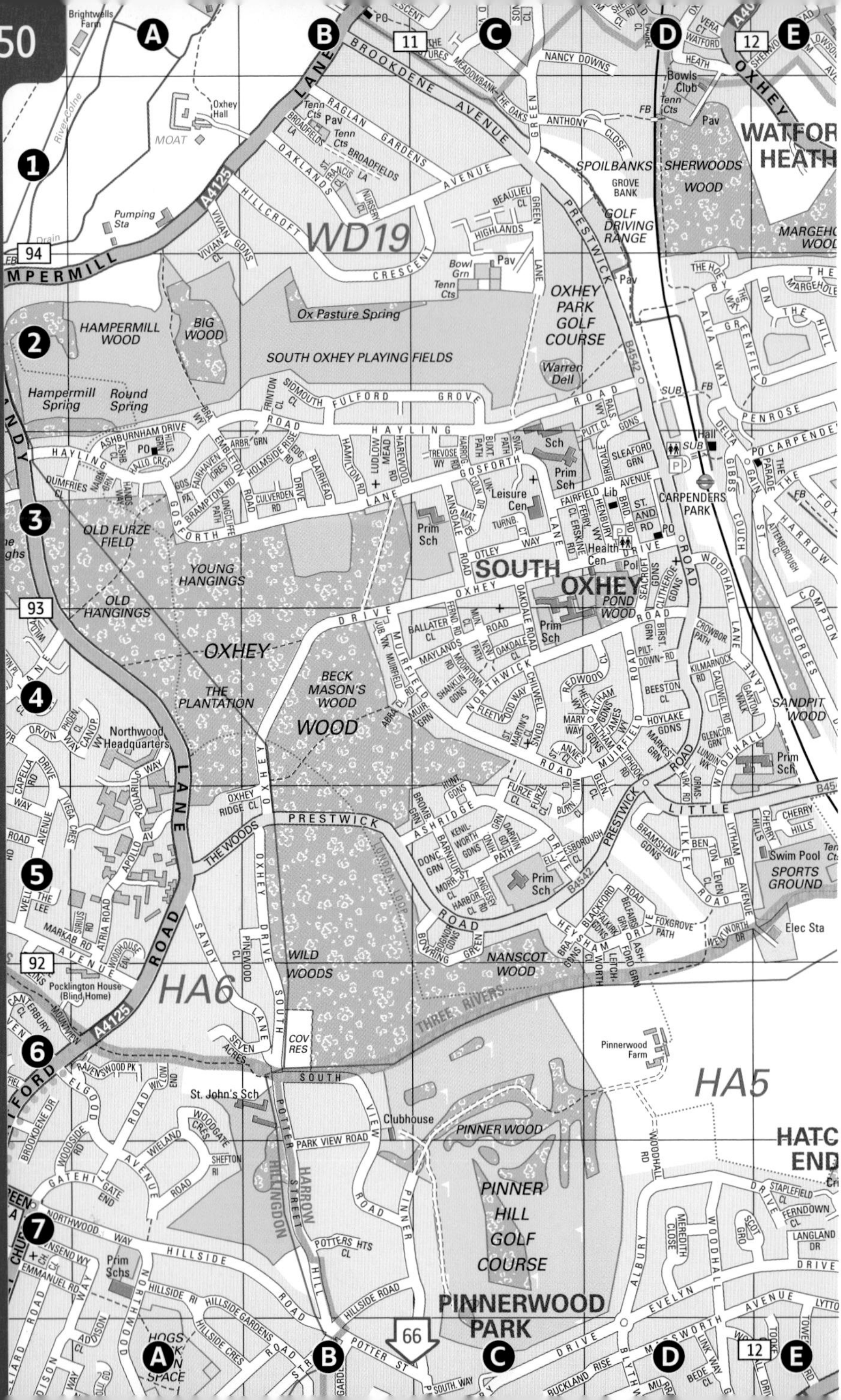

A
B
C
D
E
11
12
1
2
3
4
5
6
7
94
93
92
66
Brightwells Farm
Oxhey Hall
MOAT
River Colne
Pumping Sta
Drain
HAMPERMILL
LANE
A4125
BROOKDENE AVENUE
RAGLAN GARDENS
BROADFIELDS
OAKLANDS
HILLCROFT CRESCENT
Tenn Cts
Pav
NANCY DOWNS
MEADOWBANK
THE OAKS
GREEN LANE
ANTHONY CLOSE
Bowls Club
HEATH
WATFORD
VERA CT
SPOILBANKS
SHERWOODS WOOD
GROVE BANK
GOLF DRIVING RANGE
WATFORD HEATH
MARGEHOLES WOOD
OXHEY
WD19
BEAULIEU CL
HIGHLANDS
VIVIAN GDNS
VIVIAN CL
Bowl Grn
PRESTWICK
OXHEY PARK GOLF COURSE
Warren Dell
B4542
HAMPERMILL WOOD
BIG WOOD
Ox Pasture Spring
SOUTH OXHEY PLAYING FIELDS
Hampermill Spring
Round Spring
FULFORD GROVE
SIDMOUTH CL
FRINTON CL
HAYLING ROAD
ASHBURNHAM DRIVE
EMBLETON RD
HOLMSIDE RISE
HAMILTON RD
HAREWOOD RD
TREVOSE WY
GOSFORTH LANE
DUMFRIES CL
Sch
Prim Sch
Leisure Cen
Lib
Health Cen
Pol
PO
CARPENDERS PARK
SUB
FB
Hall
DELTA
PENROSE
CARPENDERS
GIBBS COUCH
PARADE
OLD FURZE FIELD
YOUNG HANGINGS
OLD HANGINGS
OXHEY
THE PLANTATION
BECK MASON'S WOOD
WOOD
SOUTH OXHEY
POND WOOD
OXHEY DRIVE
FAIRFIELD AVENUE
SLEAFORD GRN
BALLATER CL
MAYLANDS
OAKDALE ROAD
MUIRFIELD
NORTHWICK ROAD
CHILWELL GDNS
REDWOOD CL
BEESTON CL
HOYLAKE GDNS
WOODHALL LANE
KILMARNOCK RD
SANDPIT WOOD
ATTENBOROUGH CL
HARROW
COMPTON
ST. GEORGES
LITTLE OXHEY LANE
CHERRY HILLS
Swim Pool
SPORTS GROUND
Elec Sta
Northwood Headquarters
AQUARIUS WAY
APOLLO AV
CAPELLA RD
VEGA CRES
SANDY LANE
OXHEY RIDGE CL
THE WOODS
PRESTWICK ROAD
ASHRIDGE
ILKLEY
LYTHAM AVENUE
BRAMSHAW GDNS
ESBOROUGH
FOXGROVE PATH
WENTWORTH DR
HEYSHAM DRIVE
BLACKFORD ROAD
BOWRING GREEN
NANSCOT WOOD
WILD WOODS
PINEWOOD CL
SOUTH
MARKAB RD
ATRIA ROAD
SIRIUS RD
THE LEE
Pocklington House (Blind Home)
HA6
THREE RIVERS
LONDON LOOP
CANTERBURY
COV RES
SEVEN ACRES
Pinnerwood Farm
HA5
RAVENSWOOD PK
ELGOOD
WILLOW
St. John's Sch
POTTER STREET
HILLINGDON
HARROW
PARK VIEW ROAD
VIEW ROAD
PINNER
Clubhouse
PINNER WOOD
PINNER HILL GOLF COURSE
WOODHALL RD
HATCH END
STAPLEFIELD CL
FERNDOWN CL
LANGLAND DR
DRIVE
WOODSIDE RD
BROOKDENE DR
WIELAND
WOODGATE CRES
SHEFTON RI
GATEHILL ROAD
GATE END
NORTHWOOD WAY
HILLSIDE ROAD
HILLSIDE RI
HILLSIDE GARDENS
HILLSIDE CRES
POTTERS HTS CL
Prim Schs
EMMANUEL RD
TOWNSEND WY
ADDISON
NORTHWOOD
HOGS BACK OPEN SPACE
POTTER ST
SOUTH WAY
PINNERWOOD PARK
ALBURY DRIVE
MEREDITH CLOSE
SCOT GRO
EVELYN AVENUE
BUCKLAND RISE
BLYTH
MARSWORTH
LINK WAY
BEDE CL
LYTTON

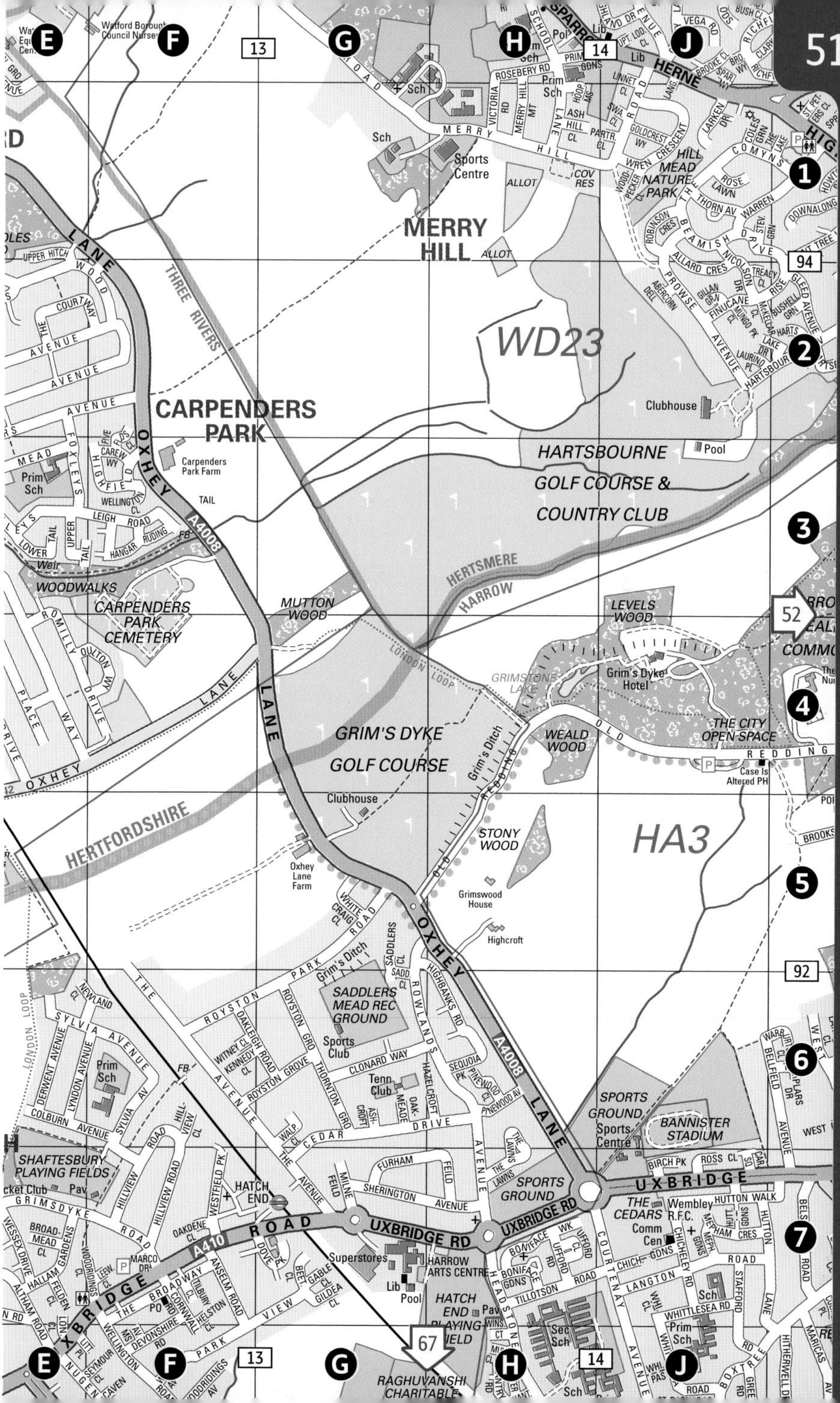
E
F
G
H
J
13
14
Watford Borough Council Nursery
MERRY HILL
Sch
Sports Centre
ALLOT
VICTORIA RD
MERRY HILL MT
ROSEBERY RD
Prim Sch
HOOP MS
ASH HILL CL
PARTR. CL
SWA. CL
LINNET CL
GOLDCREST WY
WREN CRESCENT
WOODPECKER CL
COV RES
HILL MEAD NATURE PARK
HERNE
Lib
VEGA RD
COMYNS
ROSE LAWN
THORN AV
WARREN
DOWNALONG
ROBINSON CRES
BEAMISH DRIVE
ALLARD CRES
NICOLSON DR
TREACY CL
RISE
GLEED AVENUE
PROWSE AVENUE
ABERCORN DELL
GILLAN GRN
FINUCANE
MUNGO PK CL
MCKELLAR CL
BUSHELL GRN
HARTS LAKE DR
LAURINO PL
HARTSBOURNE
94
1
2
3
4
5
6
7
WD23
Clubhouse
Pool
HARTSBOURNE GOLF COURSE & COUNTRY CLUB
THREE RIVERS
HERTSMERE
HARROW
HERTFORDSHIRE
CARPENDERS PARK
Carpenders Park Farm
TAIL
OXHEY LANE
A4008
UPPER HITCH
WOODWAY
COURT WAY
THE AVENUE
FOXLEYS
MEAD
Prim Sch
FIVE FLDS CL
CAREW WY
HIGHFIELD
WELLINGTON CL
LEIGH ROAD
RUDING
HANGAR
LOWER TAIL
UPPER TAIL
FB
Weir
WOODWALKS
CARPENDERS PARK CEMETERY
ROMILLY DRIVE
OULTON WAY
PLACE
WAY
OXHEY LANE
MUTTON WOOD
LONDON LOOP
LEVELS WOOD
52
COMMO
Grim's Dyke Hotel
GRIMSTONE LAKE
WEALD WOOD
OLD REDDING
THE CITY OPEN SPACE
Case Is Altered PH
GRIM'S DYKE GOLF COURSE
Clubhouse
Grim's Ditch
STONY WOOD
HA3
BROOKS
Oxhey Lane Farm
Grimswood House
Highcroft
WHITE CRAIG CL
92
ROYSTON PARK ROAD
Grim's Ditch
SADDLERS CL
SADDLERS MEAD REC GROUND
Sports Club
HIGHBANKS RD
ROWLANDS
ROYSTON GRO
OAKLEIGH ROAD
WITNEY CL
KENNEDY CL
ROYSTON GROVE
THORNTON GRO
CLONARD WAY
Tenn Club
HAZELCROFT
SEQUOIA PK
PINEWOOD CL
PINEWOOD AV
MEADE
OAK-CROFT
ASH-CROFT
DRIVE
CEDAR
NEWLAND
SYLVIA AVENUE
DERWENT AVENUE
LYNDON AVENUE
Prim Sch
SYLVIA AV
COLBURN AVENUE
FB
HILLVIEW CL
HILLVIEW ROAD
WALP. CL
THE AVENUE
SPORTS GROUND
Sports Centre
BANNISTER STADIUM
WARREN CL
BELLFIELD AVENUE
POPLARS DR
WEST
BIRCH PK
ROSS CL
UXBRIDGE
SHAFTESBURY PLAYING FIELDS
Cricket Club
Pav
GRIMSDYKE ROAD
WESTFIELD PK
HATCH END
FURHAM FEILD
MILNE FEILD
SHERINGTON AVENUE
THE LAWNS
SPORTS GROUND
UXBRIDGE RD
THE CEDARS
Wembley R.F.C.
Comm Cen
HUTTON WALK
MEPHAM CRES
HUTTON
BROADMEAD CL
WESSEX DRIVE
HALLAM GARDENS
FELDEN CL
ALTHAM ROAD
OAKDENE CL
A410
UXBRIDGE RD
MARCO DR
BROADWAY
ANSELM ROAD
DOVE PK
BEET
GABLE CL
GILDEA CL
Superstores
HARROW ARTS CENTRE
Lib
Pool
HATCH END PLAYING FIELD
Pav
BONIFACE WK
BONIFACE GDNS
UFFORD RD
UFFORD CL
TILLOTSON ROAD
HEADSTONE
COURTENAY AVENUE
CHICHELEY GDNS
CHICHELEY RD
LANGTON ROAD
STAFFORD ROAD
WHITTLESEA RD
Prim Sch
Sch
Sec Sch
LANE
HITHERWELL DR
BOXTREE RD
BELS ROAD
WELLINGTON
DEVONSHIRE RD
CORNWALL
HELSTON CL
TILBURY CL
PARK VIEW
SEYMOUR CL
NUGENT
CAVEN
WOODRIDINGS AV
PO
67
RAGHUVANSHI CHARITABLE

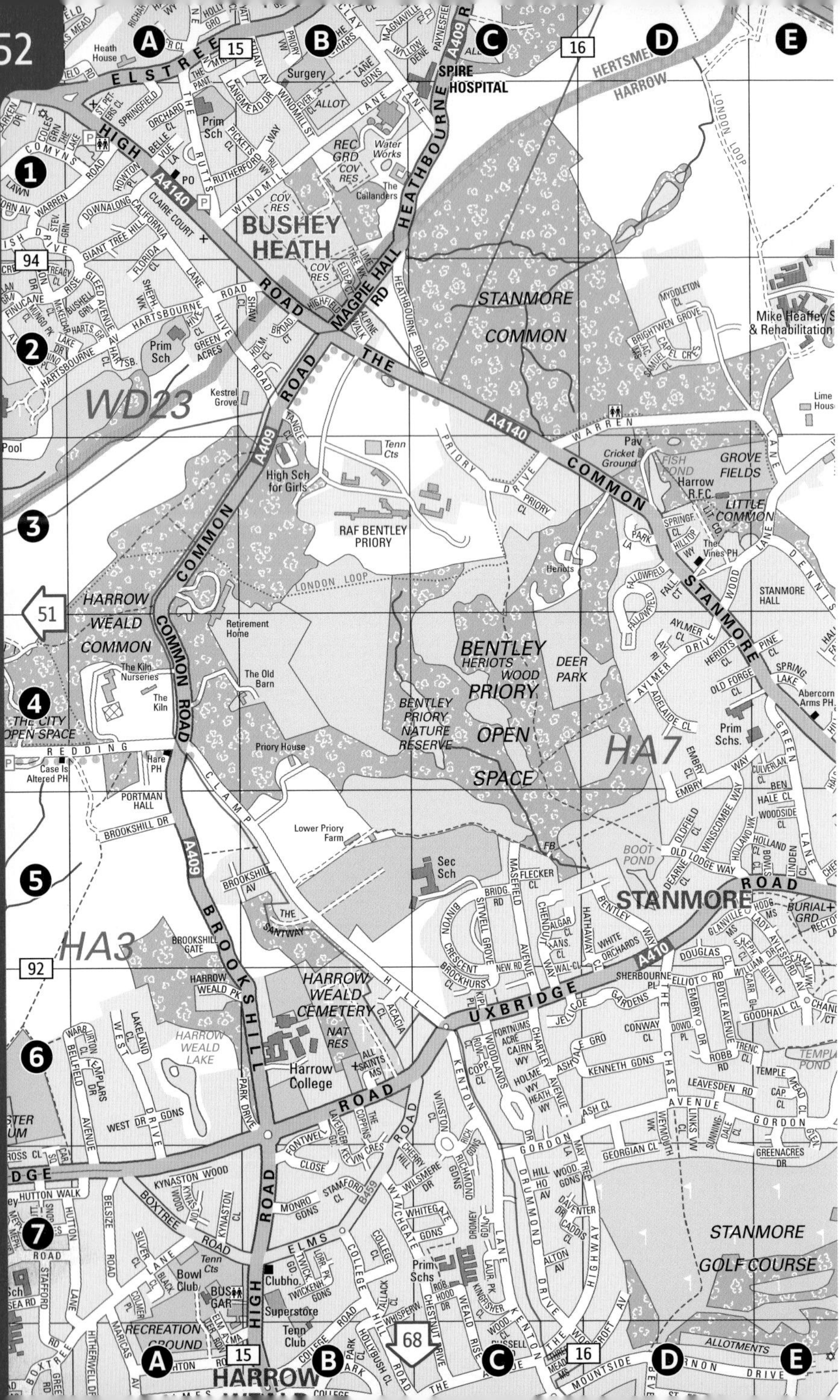
A
B
C
D
E
1
2
3
4
5
6
7
15
16
94
92
51
68
ELSTREE
HIGH ROAD
A4140
Heath House
Surgery
SPIRE HOSPITAL
A409
HEATHBOURNE
HERTSMERE
HARROW
LONDON LOOP
COMYNS ROAD
WARREN
CLAIRE COURT
CALIFORNIA
DOWNALONG
GIANT TREE HILL
FLORIDA
HARTSBOURNE AV
Prim Sch
WINDMILL
Water Works
The Callanders
REC GRD
COV RES
ALLOT
BUSHEY HEATH
MAGPIE HALL RD
HEATHBOURNE ROAD
THE COMMON
STANMORE COMMON
WD23
Kestrel Grove
Pool
GREEN ACRES
HIVE
BRIGHTWEN GROVE
CAPEL CRES
MYDDLETON CL
Mike Heaffey S & Rehabilitation
Lime House
Tenn Cts
High Sch for Girls
RAF BENTLEY PRIORY
PRIORY DRIVE
PRIORY CL
Pav
Cricket Ground
FISH POND
Harrow R.F.C.
GROVE FIELDS
LITTLE COMMON
The Vines PH
WOOD LANE
DENNIS
STANMORE HALL
HARROW WEALD COMMON
COMMON ROAD
Retirement Home
The Kiln Nurseries
The Kiln
The Old Barn
THE CITY OPEN SPACE
REDDING
Hare PH
Case Is Altered PH
PORTMAN HALL
BROOKSHILL DR
Priory House
CLAMP HILL
Lower Priory Farm
BENTLEY PRIORY OPEN SPACE
HERIOTS WOOD
DEER PARK
BENTLEY PRIORY NATURE RESERVE
Heriots
FALLOWFIELD
AYLMER DRIVE
ADELAIDE CL
HERIOTS CL
PINE CL
SPRING LAKE
OLD FORGE CL
Abercorn Arms PH
Prim Schs.
HA7
STANMORE
EMBRY WAY
WINSCOMBE WAY
BEN HALE CL
WOODSIDE CL
HOLLAND CL
OLD LODGE WAY
GREEN LANE
BOOT POND
Sec Sch
FLECKER CL
MASEFIELD AVENUE
SITWELL GROVE
BINYON CRESCENT
HATHAWAY CL
BENTLEY WAY
WHITE ORCHARDS
STANMORE ROAD
A410
BURIAL GRD
UXBRIDGE ROAD
BROOKSHILL
A409
BROOKSHILL AV
THE SANTWAY
BROOKSHILL GATE
HA3
HARROW WEALD PK
HARROW WEALD CEMETERY
NAT RES
ACACIA CL
HARROW WEALD LAKE
LAKELAND CL
BELLFIELD AVENUE
TEMPLARS DR
WEST DR GDNS
PARK DRIVE
Harrow College
ALL SAINTS MS
KENTON LANE
WOODLANDS
CHARTLEY AVENUE
ASHDALE GRO
KENNETH GDNS
CONWAY CL
JELLICOE GARDENS
SHERBOURNE PL
ELLIOT RD
BOYLE AVENUE
DOUGLAS
GOODHALL CL
ROBB RD
TEMPLE POND
TEMPLE MEAD CL
LEAVESDEN RD
AVENUE
GORDON AVENUE
GREENACRES DR
GEORGIAN CL
THE CHASE
WEYMOUTH WK
LINKS VW
STANMORE GOLF COURSE
DRUMMOND DRIVE
HIGHWAY
ALTON AV
DAVENTER DR
CADDIS CL
HILL HO AV
WINSTON CT
RICHMOND GDNS
WILSMERE DR
WHITEGATE GDNS
WYNCHGATE
CHERRY HILL
KEVIN CRES
FONTWELL CL
CLOSE
MONRO GDNS
STAMFORD CL
B459
ELMS ROAD
COLLEGE HILL ROAD
COLLEGE CL
Prim Schs
WEALD RISE
CHESTNUT DRIVE
KINGSHOTT
HIGH ROAD
Clubho.
Superstore
Tenn Club
BUS GAR
Bowl Club
Tenn Cts
RECREATION GROUND
KYNASTON WOOD
KYNASTON ROAD
BOXTREE ROAD
BELSIZE ROAD
SILVER CL
HUTTON WALK
HUTTON LANE
STAFFORD ROAD
HITHERWELL DR
MARICAS AV
HARROW
MOUNTSIDE
THE WOODCROFT AV
ALLOTMENTS
VERNON DRIVE
RUSSELL

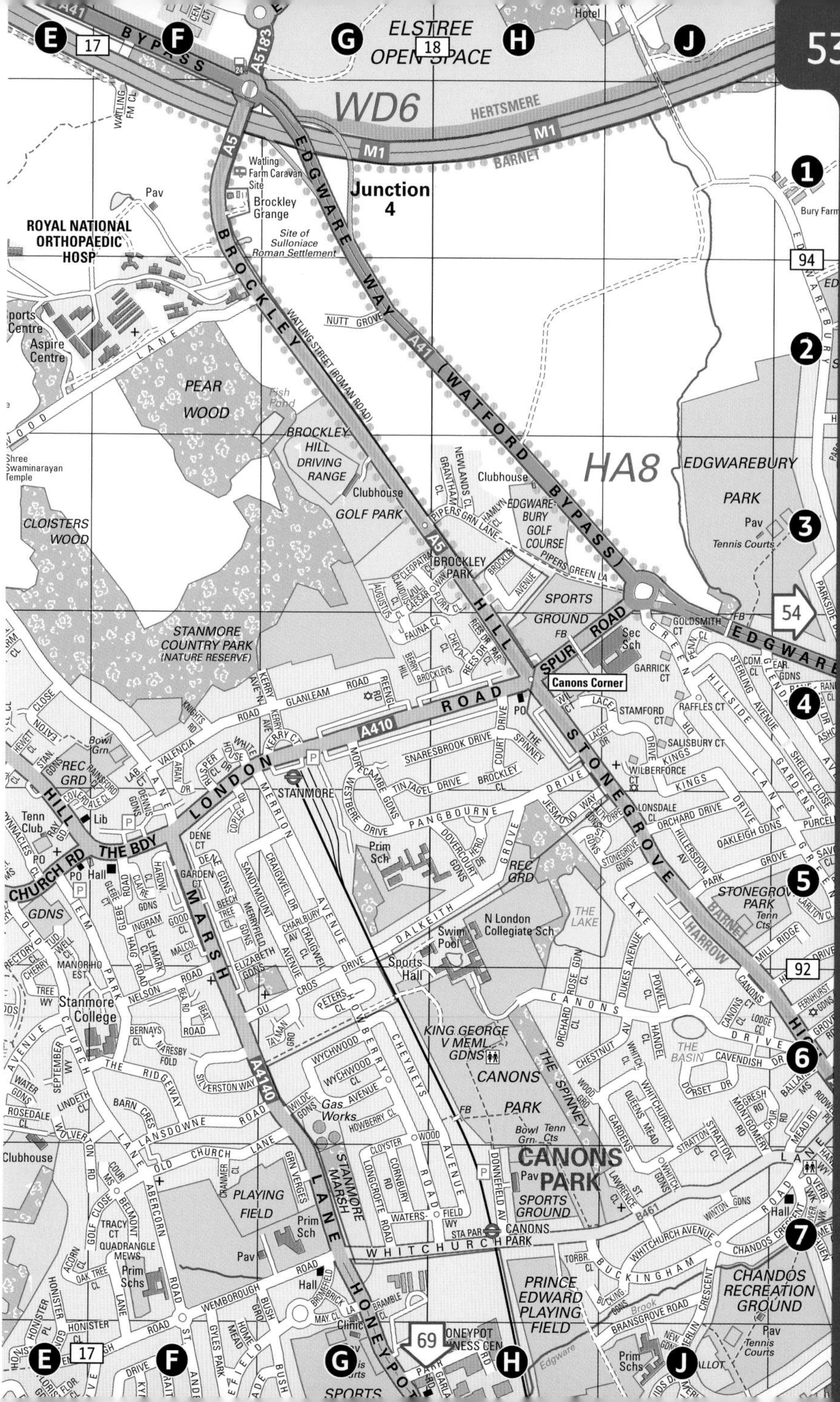
E
F
G
H
J
17
18
ELSTREE OPEN SPACE
Hotel
BYPASS
A41
A5183
WD6
HERTSMERE
M1
BARNET
A5
Watling Farm Caravan Site
Brockley Grange
Junction 4
Site of Sulloniace Roman Settlement
EDGWARE WAY
BROCKLEY
ROYAL NATIONAL ORTHOPAEDIC HOSP
Pav
Sports Centre
Aspire Centre
PEAR WOOD
Fish Pond
BROCKLEY HILL DRIVING RANGE
Clubhouse
GOLF PARK
WATLING STREET (ROMAN ROAD)
NUTT GROVE
A41 (WATFORD BYPASS)
Shree Swaminarayan Temple
CLOISTERS WOOD
HA8
EDGWAREBURY PARK
Bury Farm
Tennis Courts
EDGWAREBURY GOLF COURSE
BROCKLEY PARK
PIPERS GREEN LA
SPORTS GROUND
SPUR ROAD
Sec Sch
Canons Corner
STANMORE COUNTRY PARK (NATURE RESERVE)
GLANLEAM ROAD
A410
LONDON ROAD
STANMORE
SNARESBROOK DRIVE
TINTAGEL DRIVE
PANGBOURNE DRIVE
STONEGROVE
KINGS DRIVE
HILLSIDE AVENUE
GREEN LANE
EDGWARE
54
REC GRD
Tenn Club
Lib
HILL
CHURCH RD
THE BDY
MARSH
Prim Sch
REC GRD
N London Collegiate Sch
THE LAKE
STONEGROVE PARK
Tenn Cts
HARROW
BARNET
92
94
Stanmore College
DALKEITH
Swim Pool
Sports Hall
CANONS DRIVE
THE BASIN
KING GEORGE V MEML GDNS
CANONS PARK
THE SPINNEY
A4140
Gas Works
STANMORE MARSH
PLAYING FIELD
CANONS PARK SPORTS GROUND
Bowl Grn
Tenn Cts
WHITCHURCH LANE
B461
CANONS PARK
PRINCE EDWARD PLAYING FIELD
CHANDOS RECREATION GROUND
BUCKINGHAM
Brook
Edgware
Hall
Clinic
HONEYPOT LANE
69
Prim Schs
SPORTS
1
2
3
4
5
6
7

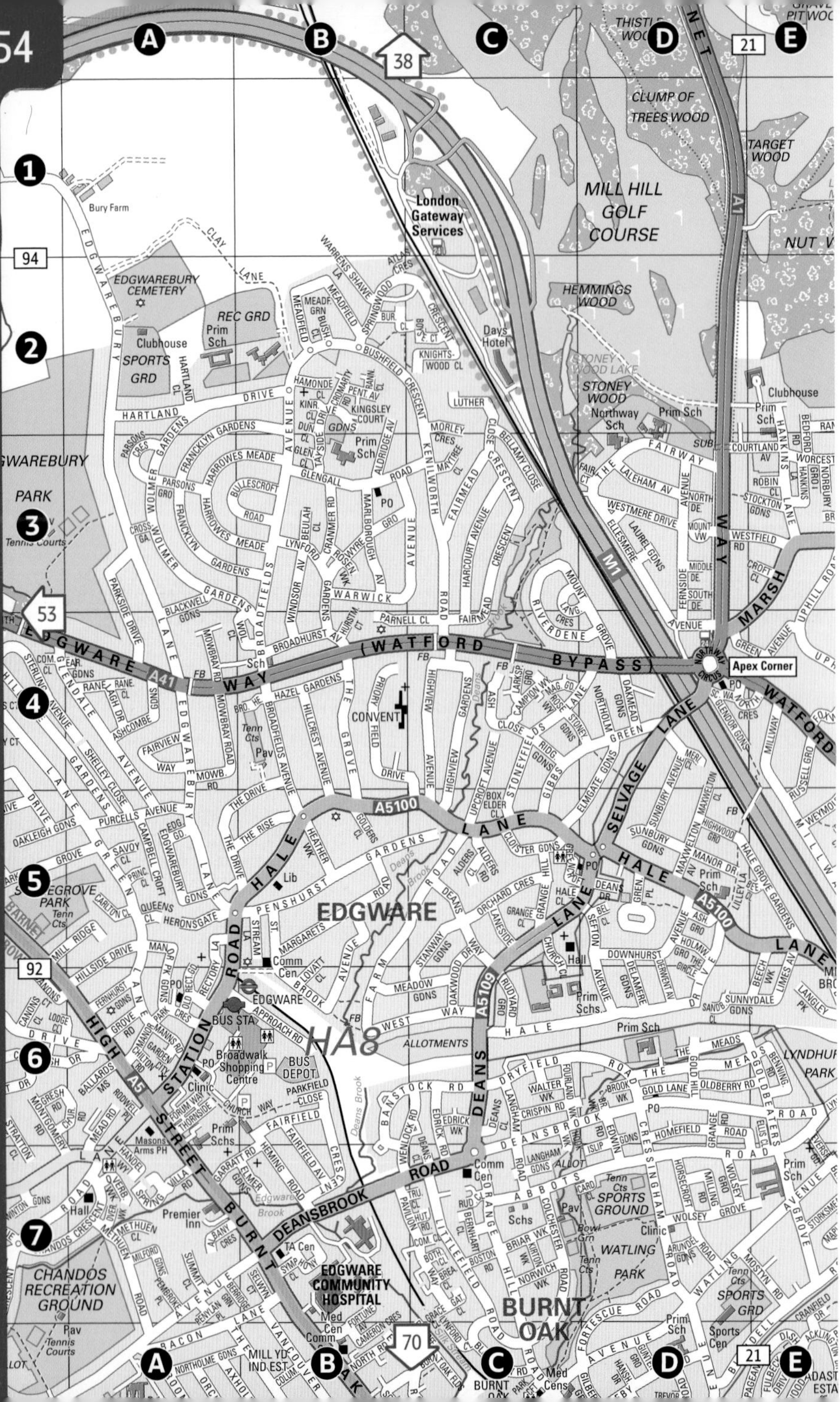
A
B
C
D
E
1
2
3
4
5
6
7
38
53
70
94
92
21
THISTLE WOOD
CLUMP OF TREES WOOD
TARGET WOOD
MILL HILL GOLF COURSE
NUT W
London Gateway Services
Bury Farm
EDGWAREBURY LANE
CLAY LANE
EDGWAREBURY CEMETERY
REC GRD
Prim Sch
Clubhouse
SPORTS GRD
HARTLAND CL
HARTLAND DRIVE
WARRENS SHAWE LA
MEADFIELD
SPRINGWOOD CRES
ATLAS CRES
BUSHFIELD CRESCENT
KNIGHTSWOOD CL
Days Hotel
HEMMINGS WOOD
STONEY WOOD LAKE
STONEY WOOD
Northway Sch
Prim Sch
Clubhouse
FAIRWAY
COURTLAND AV
ROBIN CL
STOCKTON GDNS
WESTFIELD RD
CROFT CL
MARSH
EDGWAREBURY PARK
Tennis Courts
FRANKLYN GARDENS
HARROWES MEADE
BULLESCROFT ROAD
PARSONS CRES
WOLMER GARDENS
GLENGALL ROAD
KINGSLEY COURT
Prim Sch
PO
KENILWORTH ROAD
MORLEY CRES
MAYTREE CL
FAIRMEAD
HARCOURT AVENUE
BELLAMY CLOSE
LUTHER CLOSE
LALEHAM AV
WESTMERE DRIVE
ELLESMERE
LAUREL GDNS
MOUNT GROVE
RIVERDENE
FERNSIDE AVENUE
M1
WARWICK AV
BLACKWELL GDNS
PARKSIDE DRIVE
BROADFIELDS AVENUE
BROADHURST AV
PARNELL CL
A41
EDGWARE WAY (WATFORD BYPASS)
Apex Corner
NORTHWAY CIRCUS
WATFORD WAY
SELVAGE LANE
HAZEL GARDENS
HILLCREST AVENUE
THE GROVE
PRIORY FIELD DRIVE
CONVENT
HIGHVIEW GARDENS
UPCROFT AVENUE
STONEYFIELDS LANE
NORTHOLM
OAKMEAD GDNS
SUNBURY AVENUE
MAXWELTON CL
MILLWAY
A5100
HALE LANE
THE DRIVE
THE RISE
HEATHER WK
GOLDERS CL
CLOISTER GDNS
SUNBURY GDNS
MANOR DR
HALE GROVE GARDENS
Lib
PENSHURST ROAD
EDGWARE
DEANS LANE
ORCHARD CRES
GRANGE CL
HALE DR
Hall
DOWNHURST
DELAMERE
DERWENT AV
SUNNYDALE GDNS
PURCELLS AVENUE
CAMPBELL CROFT
QUEENS CL
HERONSGATE
CANFORD ROAD
MILL RIDGE
HILLSIDE DRIVE
CANONS CL
FERNHURST GDNS
Comm Cen
EDGWARE
BUS STA
APPROACH RD
Broadwalk Shopping Centre
BUS DEPOT
HA8
ALLOTMENTS
WEST WAY
A5109
DEANS
Prim Schs
Prim Sch
THE MEADS
LYNDHURST PARK
OLDBERRY RD
GOLD LANE
STATION ROAD
Clinic
CHURCH WAY
PARKFIELD CLOSE
FAIRFIELD
HIGH STREET
A5
Prim Schs
Masons Arms PH
BANSTOCK RD
DRYFIELD ROAD
DEANSBROOK ROAD
HOMEFIELD ROAD
CRESSINGHAM
Comm Cen
Deans Brook
Edgware Brook
Premier Inn
METHUEN CL
CHANDOS CRESCENT
CHANDOS RECREATION GROUND
Pav
Tennis Courts
TA Cen
EDGWARE COMMUNITY HOSPITAL
Med Cen
Comm
BURNT OAK
SPORTS GROUND
WATLING PARK
Clinic
Schs
SPORTS GRD
Sports Cen
FORTESCUE ROAD
WATLING AVENUE
Med Cens
BURNT OAK BROADWAY
BACON LANE
MILL YD IND EST
VANCOUVER

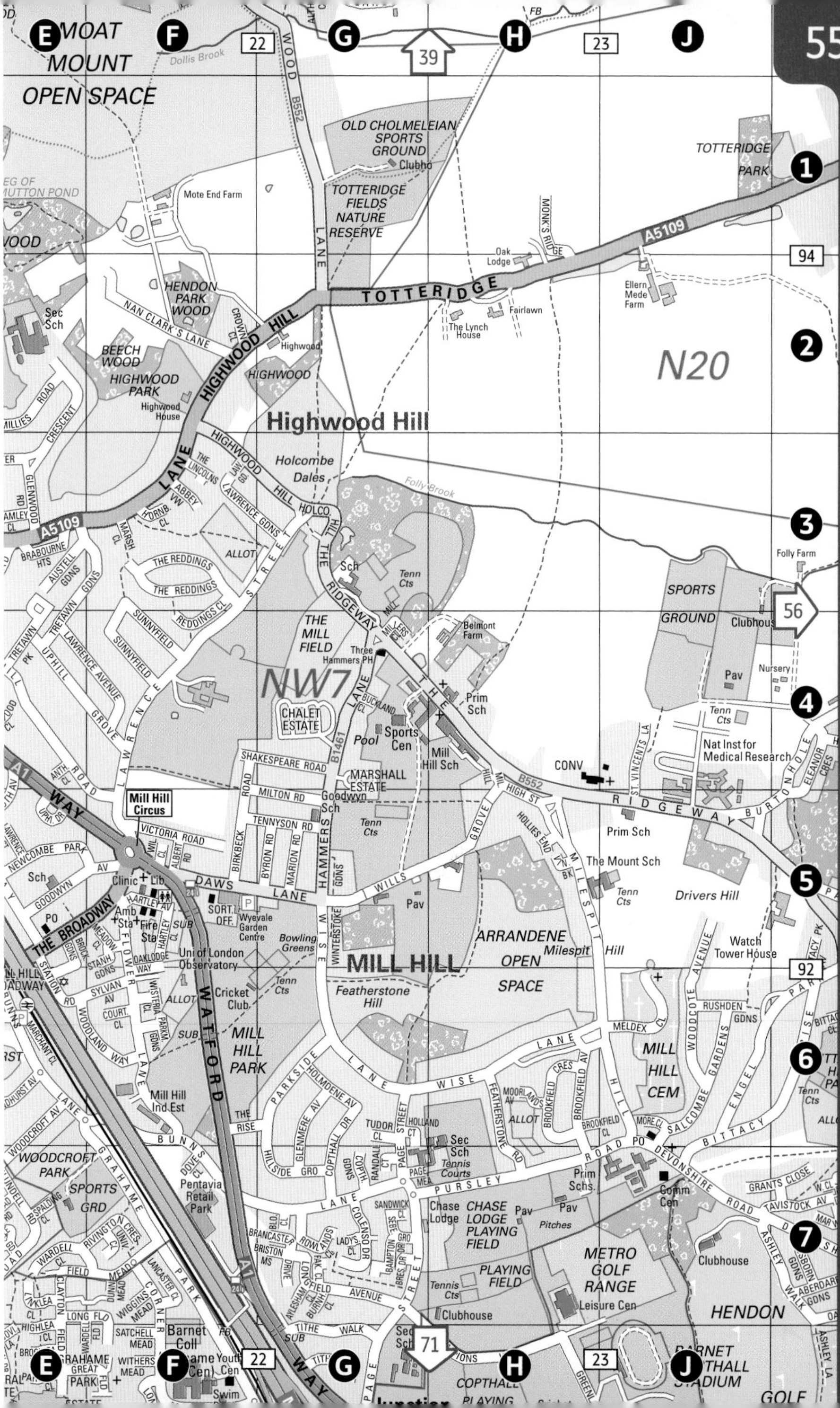
E
F
G
H
J
22
23
39
MOAT MOUNT OPEN SPACE
Dollis Brook
WOOD LANE
B552
OLD CHOLMELEIAN SPORTS GROUND
Clubho
TOTTERIDGE FIELDS NATURE RESERVE
TOTTERIDGE PARK
1
A5109
94
MONK'S RIDGE
Oak Lodge
Ellern Mede Farm
Mote End Farm
MUTTON POND
WOOD
HENDON PARK WOOD
TOTTERIDGE
Fairlawn
The Lynch House
Sec Sch
NAN CLARK'S LANE
CROWN CL
HIGHWOOD HILL
Highwood
BEECH WOOD
HIGHWOOD PARK
HIGHWOOD
Highwood House
2
N20
Highwood Hill
MILLIES ROAD
CRESCENT
GLENWOOD RD
THE LINCOLNS
LAWRENCE GDNS
ABBEY VW
HORNB. CL
Holcombe Dales
Folly Brook
HOLCO. HILL
LANE
A5109
BRABOURNE HTS
AUSTELL GDNS
MARSH CL
THE REDDINGS
ALLOT
STREET
Sch
Tenn Cts
3
Folly Farm
SPORTS GROUND
Clubhouse
56
TRETAWN PK
TRETAWN GDNS
UPHILL
LAWRENCE AVENUE
SUNNYFIELD
REDDINGS CL
THE RIDGEWAY
MILL FIELD
THE MILL FIELD
Three Hammers PH
MILLERS CL
Belmont Farm
NW7
BUCKLAND CL
Prim Sch
Pav
Nursery
4
Tenn Cts
Nat Inst for Medical Research
GROVE
LAWRENCE
CHALET ESTATE
Pool
Sports Cen
Mill Hill Sch
CONV
ST. VINCENTS LA
ANTH. CL
ROAD
A1 WAY
SHAKESPEARE ROAD
B1461
MARSHALL ESTATE
MILTON RD
Goodwyn Sch
HIGH ST
B552
RIDGEWAY
BURTON HOLE
ELEANOR CRES
Mill Hill Circus
UPHI. DR
VICTORIA ROAD
TENNYSON RD
Tenn Cts
HOLLIES END
Prim Sch
NEWCOMBE PARK
WIL CL
ALBERT RD
BIRKBECK
BYRON RD
MARION RD
HAMMERS
GDNS
GROVE
The Mount Sch
5
Sch
Clinic
Lib
DAWS LANE
WILLS
MILESPIT HILL
Tenn Cts
Drivers Hill
GOODWYN AV
PO
HARTLEY AV
Amb Sta
Fire Sta
SORT. OFF.
Wyevale Garden Centre
Pav
THE BROADWAY
MEADOW
Uni of London Observatory
Bowling Greens
WINTERSTOKE
ARRANDENE OPEN SPACE
Milespit Hill
Watch Tower House
AVENUE
STATION
SYLVAN AV
OAKLODGE WAY
Cricket Club
Tenn Cts
MILL HILL
Featherstone Hill
92
RUSHDEN GDNS
MILL HILL BROADWAY
ALLOT
COURT CL
WISTERIA
MELDEX CL
MILL HILL CEM
WOODLAND WAY
SUB
MILL HILL PARK
LANE
WOODCOTE
GARDENS
ENGEL
6
Mill Hill Ind Est
WATFORD
PARKSIDE
HOLMDENE AV
WISE LANE
FEATHERSTONE RD
MOORLANDS AV
BROOKFIELD CRES
BROOKFIELD AV
ALLOT
SALCOMBE
BITTACY
Tenn Cts
WOODCROFT AV
BUNNS
THE RISE
GLENMERE AV
COPTHALL DR
TUDOR CL
HOLLAND CT
Sec Sch
BROOKFIELD CL
MORE CL
PO
WOODCROFT PARK
GRAHAME PARK
SPORTS GRD
DOVE CL
Pentavia Retail Park
HILLSIDE GRO
RANDALL CT
PAGE MEA
Tennis Courts
Prim Schs
Comm Cen
DEVONSHIRE ROAD
GRANTS CLOSE
TAVISTOCK AV
PURSLEY
LANE
SANDWICK CL
Chase Lodge
CHASE LODGE PLAYING FIELD
Pav
Pav
Pitches
7
SPALDING CL
RIVINGTON CRES
COLENSO DR
ROWLANDS CL
BRANCASTER DR
BRISTON MS
LADYS CL
BAMPTON GRO
METRO GOLF RANGE
Clubhouse
ASHLEY WALK
ABERDARE GDNS
WARDELL CL
FIELD
DUNNMEAD
LANCASTER CL
PARK
A1
PLAYING FIELD
Tennis Cts
Leisure Cen
HENDON
CLAYTON FIELD
HIGHLEA CL
LONG FLD
WIGGINS MEAD
CORNER MEAD
LONGFIELD AVENUE
Clubhouse
SATCHELL MEAD
Barnet Coll
TITHE WALK
WAY
Sec Sch
71
BARNET COPTHALL STADIUM
WITHERS MEAD
Youth Cen
22
23
Swim
COPTHALL PLAYING
GOLF
ASHLEY LA

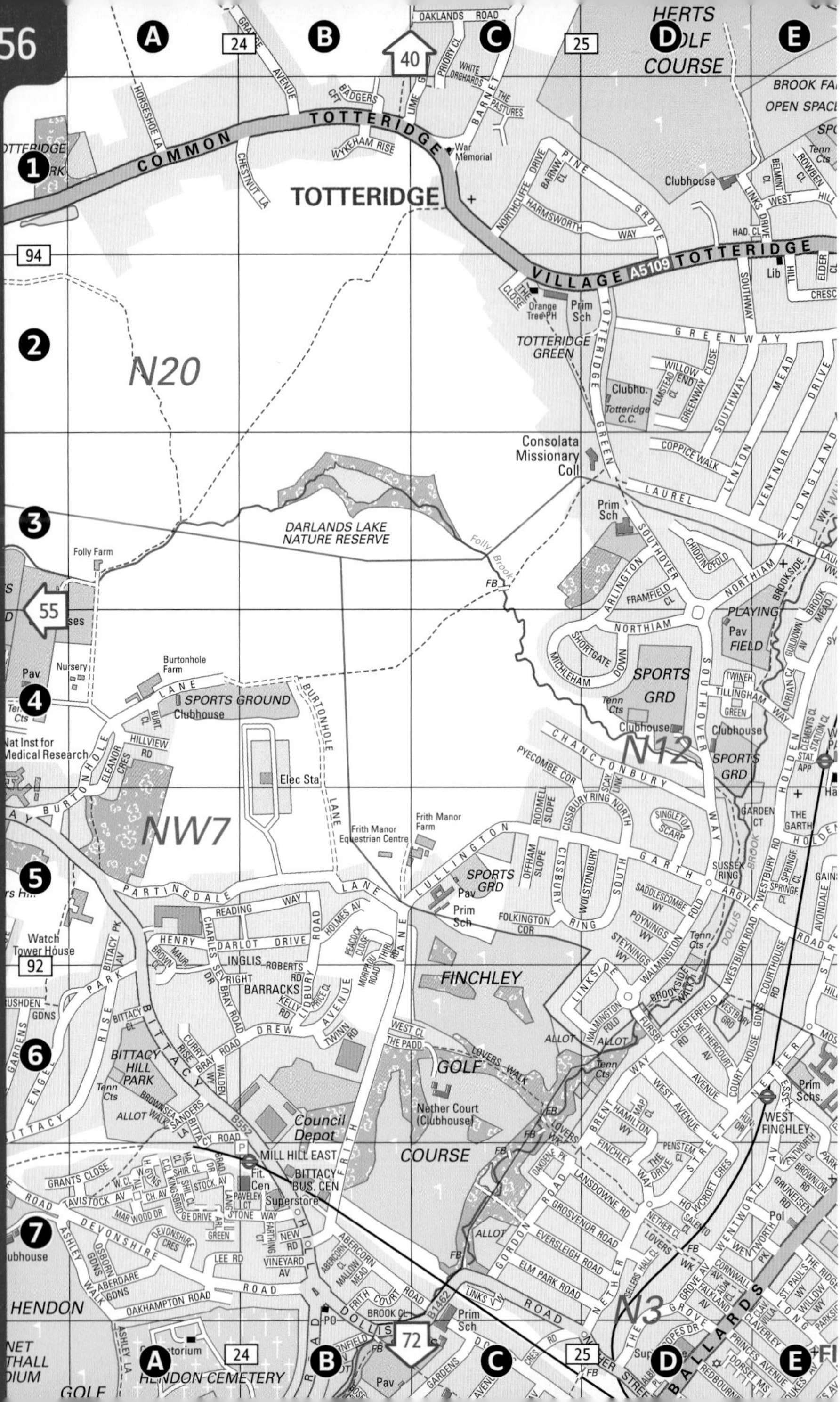
A
B
C
D
E
1
2
3
4
5
6
7
24
25
40
55
72
94
92
HERTS GOLF COURSE
BROOK FA
OPEN SPACE
OAKLANDS ROAD
GRANGE AVENUE
HORSESHOE LA
CHESTNUT LA
BADGERS CFT
LIME GR
PRIORY CL
WHITE ORCHARDS
BARNET LA
THE PASTURES
WYKEHAM RISE
War Memorial
COMMON
TOTTERIDGE
TOTTERIDGE PARK
NORTHCLIFFE DRIVE
BARNW CL
PINE GROVE
HARMSWORTH WAY
Clubhouse
LINKS DRIVE
BELMONT CL
ROWBEN CL
WEST HILL
HAD. CL
Tenn Cts
VILLAGE A5109 TOTTERIDGE
Lib
ELDER
CRESC
THE CLOSE
Orange Tree PH
Prim Sch
TOTTERIDGE GREEN
TOTTERIDGE GREEN
SOUTHWAY
GREENWAY
WILLOW END
ELMSTEAD CL
GREENWAY CLOSE
MEAD
DRIVE
Clubho.
Totteridge C.C.
COPPICE WALK
LYNTON
VENTNOR
LONGLAND
Consolata Missionary Coll
LAUREL WAY
N20
DARLANDS LAKE NATURE RESERVE
Folly Brook
FB
Folly Farm
SOUTHOVER
CHIDDINGFOLD
ARLINGTON
FRAMFIELD CL
NORTHIAM
BROOKSIDE
PLAYING FIELD
Pav
BROOK MEAD
GUILDOWN AV
SHORTGATE
MICHLEHAM DOWN
SPORTS GRD
Clubhouse
TWINEH.
TILLINGHAM WAY
GREEN
LORIAN CL
CLEMENTS CL
STATION APP
HOLDEN RD
Nursery
Burtonhole Farm
LANE
SPORTS GROUND
BURT. CL
BURTONHOLE LANE
Pav
Tenn Cts
Nat Inst for Medical Research
ELEANOR CRES
HILLVIEW RD
Elec Sta
CHANCTONBURY WAY
N12
PYECOMBE COR
SCAY LINK
CISSBURY RING NORTH
RODMELL SLOPE
SINGLETON SCARP
GARDEN CT
THE GARTH
NW7
Frith Manor Equestrian Centre
Frith Manor Farm
LULLINGTON GARTH
OFFHAM SLOPE
CISSBURY
WOLSTONBURY
SOUTH
SUSSEX RING
SADDLESCOMBE WY
ARGYLE ROAD
WESTBURY RD
SPRINGF. CL
AVONDALE
Watch Tower House
PARTINGDALE LANE
READING WAY
HOLMES AV
SPORTS GRD
Pav
Prim Sch
FOLKINGTON COR
RING
POYNINGS WY
STEYNINGS WY
WALMINGTON FOLD
Tenn Cts
DOLLIS
BITTACY PK AV
HENRY
CHARLES SEVRIGHT DR
DARLOT DRIVE
INGLIS
ROBERTS RD
BARRACKS
BRAY ROAD
PEACOCK CLOSE
MORPHOU ROAD
THIRL RD
LANE
FINCHLEY
LINKSIDE
BROOKSIDE WALK
CHESTERFIELD RD
NETHERCOURT AV
WESTBURY GRO
COURTHOUSE RD
RUSHDEN GDNS
BITTACY PARK
RISE
BITTACY CL
KELLY RD
LIDBURY
PRICE CL
AVENUE
DREW
TWINN RD
WEST CL
THE PADD.
LOVERS WALK
GOLF COURSE
ALLOT
FURSBY
WAY
WEST AVENUE
COURT HOUSE GDNS
NETHER ST
Prim Schs.
ENGEL
BITTACY HILL PARK
Tenn Cts
ALLOT
BROWNSEA WALK
SANDERS LA
CURRY RISE
WALDEN WY
B552
BITTACY ROAD
Nether Court (Clubhouse)
Council Depot
BRENT
HAMILTON WY
FINCHLEY WAY
THE DRIVE
PENSTEMON CL
HOWCROFT CRES
WEST FINCHLEY
WENTWORTH PARK
BROWNLOW RD
GRUNEISEN RD
MILL HILL EAST
BITTACY BUS. CEN
Fit. Cen
Superstore
GRANTS CLOSE
TAVISTOCK AV
MARWOOD DR
STOCK AV
PAVELEY CT
STONE WAY
FARTHING CT
NEW RD
VINEYARD AV
DEVONSHIRE
DEVONSHIRE CRES
GREEN
LEE RD
ROAD
ASHLEY
OSBORN GDNS
ABERDARE GDNS
WALK
OAKHAMPTON ROAD
HENDON
ABERCORN
MALLOW MEAD
FRITH COURT
ROAD
BROOK CL
PO
DOLLIS
B1462
LINKS VW
Prim Sch
OAKDENE PK
LANSDOWNE RD
GROSVENOR ROAD
EVERSLEIGH ROAD
ELM PARK ROAD
GORDON ROAD
ROAD
NETHER CL
LOVERS WK
SELLERS HALL CL
GROVE AV
FALKLAND AV
CORNWALL AV
WENTWORTH PK
Pol
BALLARDS LANE
N3
GROVE
CLAVERLEY GRO
PRINCES AVENUE
DORSET MS
ST. PAUL'S WY
WILLOW WY
LONG
THE RIDGE
ASHLEY LA
HENDON CEMETERY
GOLF
Pav
GARDENS
CRES
FB
REDBOURNE

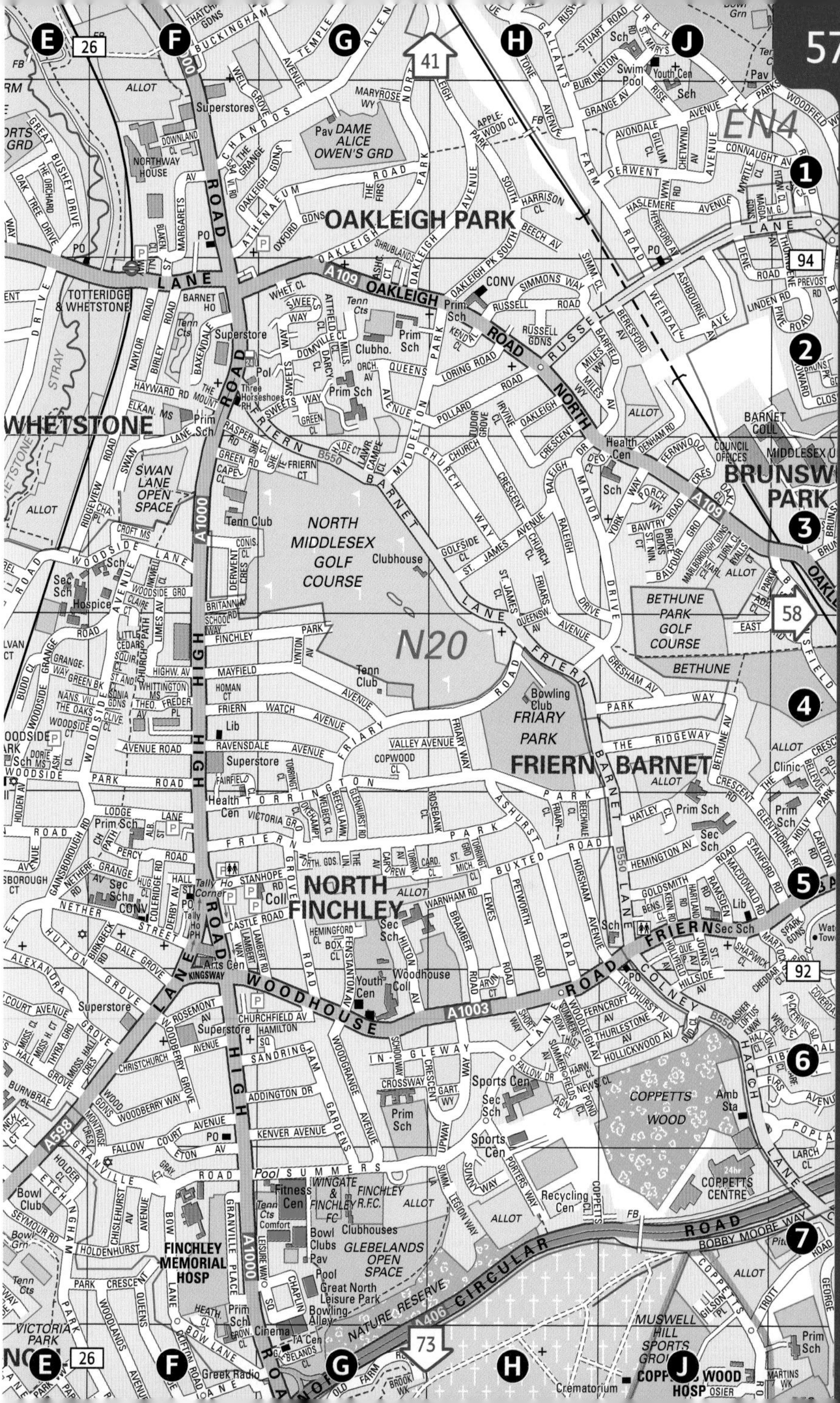
E
F
G
H
J
26
41
58
73
94
92
EN4
N20
OAKLEIGH PARK
WHETSTONE
TOTTERIDGE & WHETSTONE
BRUNSWICK PARK
FRIERN BARNET
NORTH FINCHLEY
DAME ALICE OWEN'S GRD
NORTH MIDDLESEX GOLF COURSE
FRIARY PARK
BETHUNE PARK GOLF COURSE
SWAN LANE OPEN SPACE
COPPETTS WOOD
GLEBELANDS OPEN SPACE
MUSWELL HILL SPORTS GROUND
COPPETTS CENTRE
FINCHLEY MEMORIAL HOSP
VICTORIA PARK
WINGATE & FINCHLEY FC
FINCHLEY R.F.C.
Great North Leisure Park
BARNET COLL
MIDDLESEX U
COUNCIL OFFICES
A109
A1000
A1003
A598
A406
B550
OAKLEIGH ROAD NORTH
FRIERN BARNET LANE
FRIERN BARNET ROAD
HIGH ROAD
WOODHOUSE ROAD
NORTH CIRCULAR ROAD
BOBBY MOORE WAY
COLNEY HATCH LANE
TOTTERIDGE LANE
OAKLEIGH PARK SOUTH
BETHUNE AVE
WOODSIDE PARK ROAD
FRIERN PARK
TORRINGTON PARK
BALLARDS LANE
NETHER STREET
Crematorium
COPPETTS WOOD HOSP
1
2
3
4
5
6
7

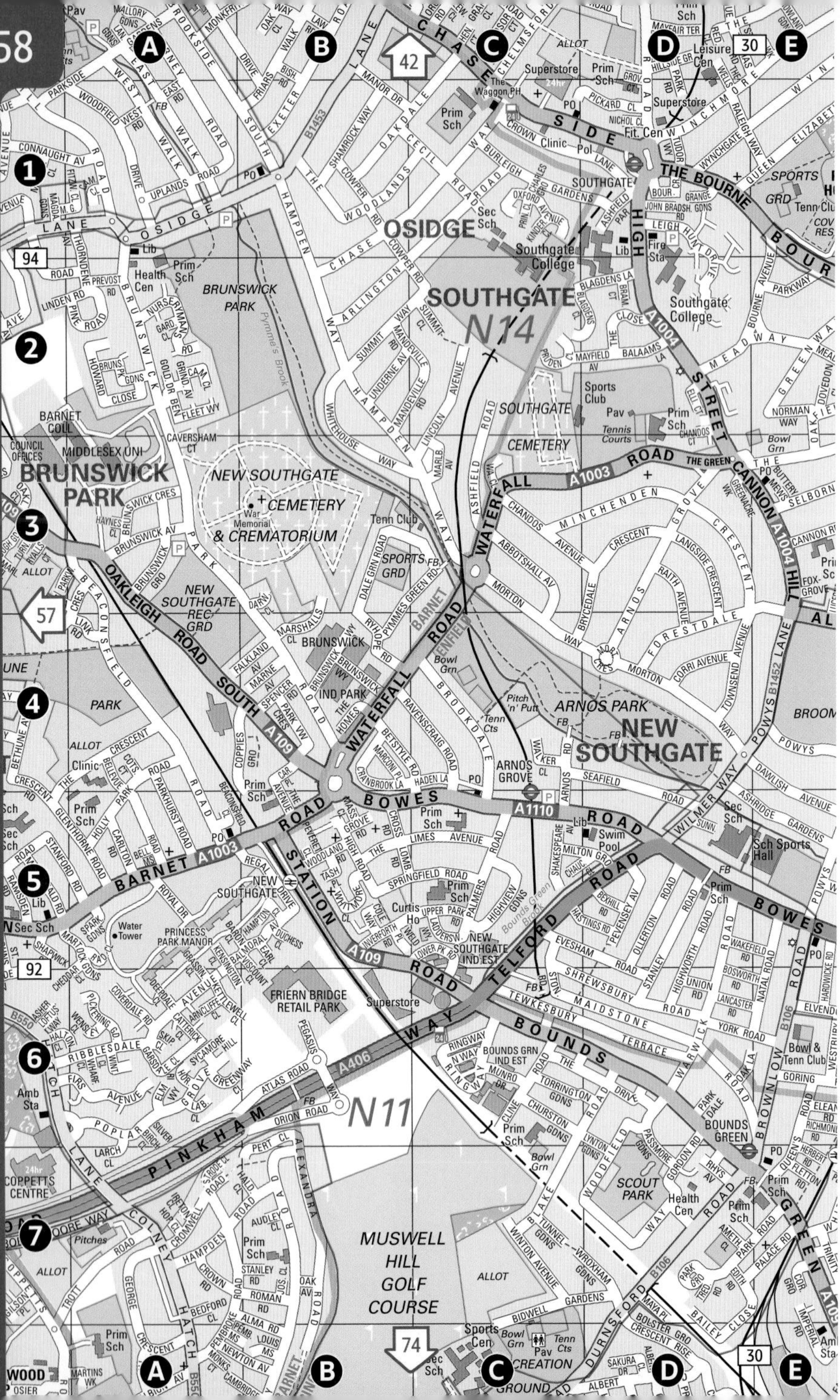
A
B
C
D
E
1
2
3
4
5
6
7
42
57
74
94
92
30
OSIDGE
SOUTHGATE
N14
BRUNSWICK PARK
NEW SOUTHGATE
N11
BRUNSWICK PARK
NEW SOUTHGATE CEMETERY & CREMATORIUM
SOUTHGATE CEMETERY
ARNOS PARK
NEW SOUTHGATE REC GRD
MUSWELL HILL GOLF COURSE
SCOUT PARK
FRIERN BRIDGE RETAIL PARK
COPPETTS CENTRE
PRINCESS PARK MANOR
BARNET COLL
MIDDLESEX UNI
COUNCIL OFFICES
Southgate College
SPORTS GRD
Sports Club
Superstore
Leisure Cen
Fit. Cen
Arnos Grove
Bounds Green
Waterfall Road
Chase Side
High Street
Cannon Hill
Bowes Road
Telford Road
Pinkham Way
Bounds Green Road
Station Road
Oakleigh Road South
Barnet Road
Osidge Lane
Colney Hatch Lane
Brunswick Park Road
Hampden Way
Powys Lane
Brownlow Road
Durnsford Road
Winchmore Hill Road
The Bourne
Green Lanes
Alexandra Road
Atlas Road
Orion Road
Pymme's Brook
Bounds Green Brook
A1003
A1004
A1110
A109
A406
B1453
B1452
B106
B550

GROVELANDS PARK
Boating Lake
Bandstand
PRIORY HOSPITAL
WINCHMORE HILL
N21
Bowl Club
Clubho.
Prim Sch
Cricket Club
THE PAULIN GROUND
FORDS GROVE
HIGHFIELD ROAD
Superstore
Sec Sch
Sports Hall
Recycling Cen
CLOWES SPORTS GROUND
FIRS FARM PLAYING FIELDS
Pumping Sta
The Woodman PH
SPORTS GRD
A111
A105
A1004
A406
A10
GREEN LANES
PALMERS GREEN
HEDGE LANE
BOWES PARK
N13
N22
ALLOTMENTS
Thea
The Fox PH
HAZELWOOD SPORTS GRD
TATEM PARK REC GRD
HOLLYWOOD GDNS
Great Cambridge Jnct
NORTH CIRCULAR ROAD
SPORTS GRD
TILE KILN LANE OPEN SPACE
Clockhouse Junction
TOTTENHALL SPORTS GROUND
BOUNDARY PLAYING FIELDS
ENFIELD
HARINGEY
NEW RIVER SPORTS CENTRE
ST. GEORGE'S IND EST
WOODSIDE PARK
Bowling Green
CEM
Glasshouse
PLAYING
HIGH ROAD
GREAT CAMBRIDGE ROAD
ROUNDWAY
43
60
75
31
32
92
94
E
F
G
H
J
1
2
3
4
5
6
7

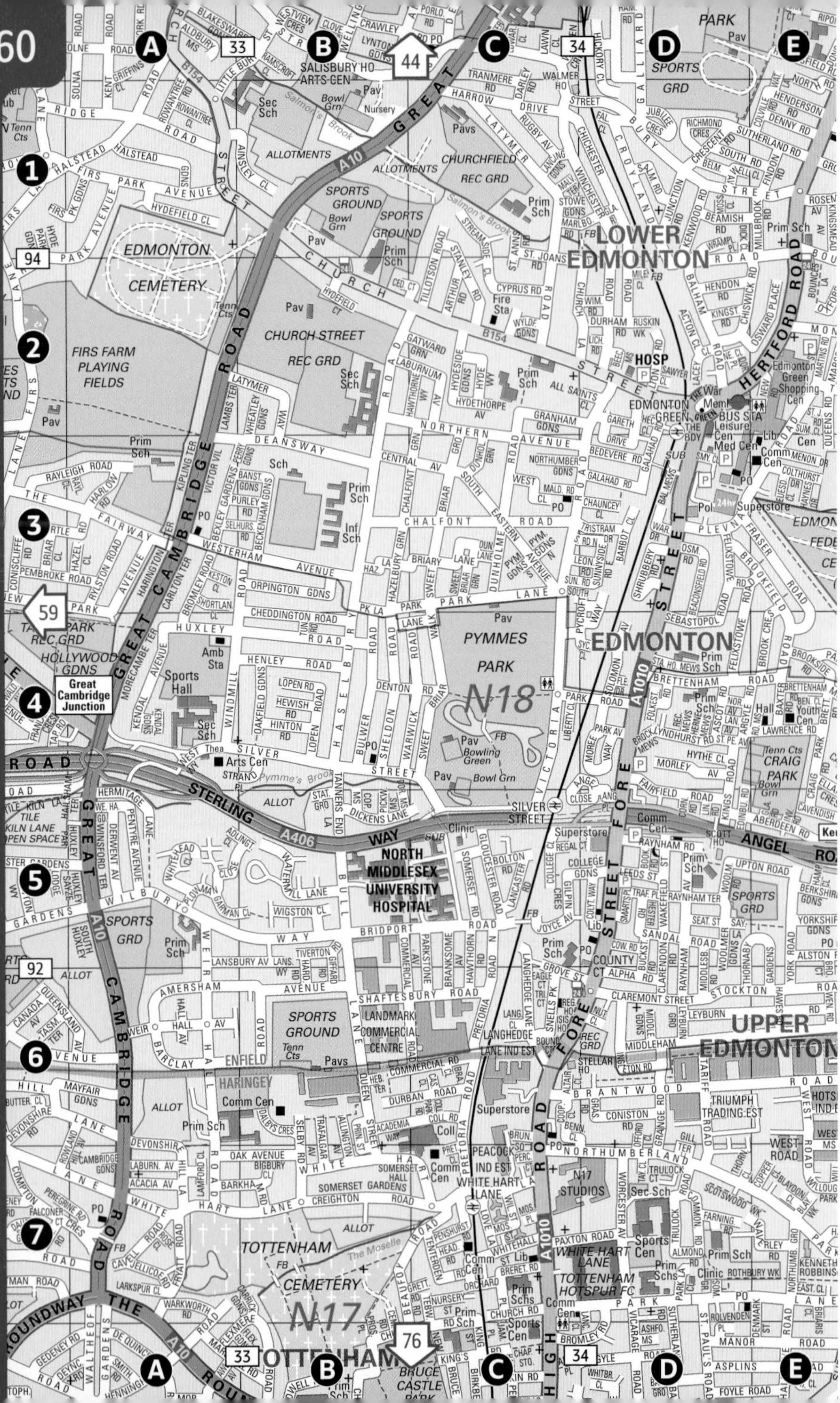
A
B
C
D
E
33
34
44
1
2
3
4
5
6
7
94
59
92
76
LOWER EDMONTON
EDMONTON
UPPER EDMONTON
TOTTENHAM
N18
N17
SPORTS GRD
SALISBURY HO ARTS CEN
ALLOTMENTS
CHURCHFIELD REC GRD
SPORTS GROUND
EDMONTON CEMETERY
FIRS FARM PLAYING FIELDS
CHURCH STREET REC GRD
HOSP
EDMONTON GREEN
BUS STA
Edmonton Green Shopping Cen
PYMMES PARK
Bowling Green
Great Cambridge Junction
HOLLYWOOD GDNS
Sports Hall
Amb Sta
Arts Cen
NORTH MIDDLESEX UNIVERSITY HOSPITAL
CRAIG PARK
TRIUMPH TRADING EST
LANDMARK COMMERCIAL CENTRE
LANGHEDGE LANE IND EST
PEACOCK IND EST
N17 STUDIOS
WHITE HART LANE
TOTTENHAM HOTSPUR FC
TOTTENHAM CEMETERY
HARINGEY
ENFIELD
GREAT CAMBRIDGE ROAD
A10
A406
STERLING WAY
A1010
FORE STREET
HIGH ROAD
HERTFORD ROAD
ANGEL ROAD
SILVER STREET
WHITE HART LANE
THE ROUNDWAY
CHURCH STREET
B154
BRUCE CASTLE PARK

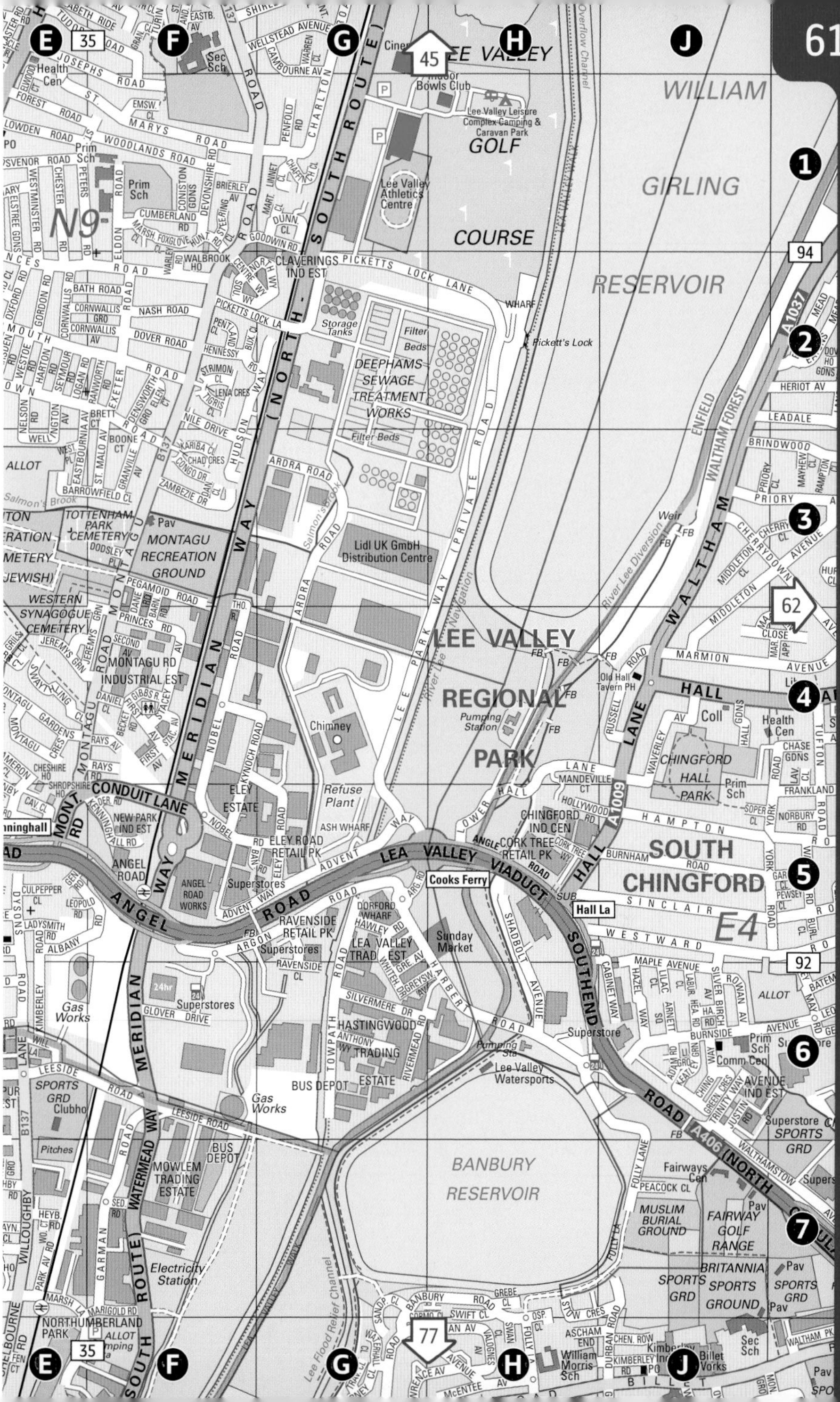
E
F
G
H
J
35
45
62
77
94
92
1
2
3
4
5
6
7
LEE VALLEY
Indoor Bowls Club
Lee Valley Leisure Complex Camping & Caravan Park
GOLF
COURSE
Lee Valley Athletics Centre
WILLIAM
GIRLING
RESERVOIR
N9
Health Cen
Sec Sch
Prim Sch
JOSEPHS ROAD
FOREST ROAD
ST. MARYS ROAD
WOODLANDS ROAD
WELLSTEAD AVENUE
CAMBOURNE AV
CHARLTON ROAD
SOUTH ROUTE
NORTH
MERIDIAN WAY
CUMBERLAND RD
WALBROOK HO
CLAVERINGS IND EST
PICKETTS LOCK LANE
PICKETTS LOCK LA
WHARF
Pickett's Lock
Storage Tanks
Filter Beds
DEEPHAMS SEWAGE TREATMENT WORKS
PRIVATE ROAD
BATH ROAD
CORNWALLIS RD
NASH ROAD
DOVER ROAD
NILE DRIVE
HUDSON WAY
ARDRA ROAD
Salmon's Brook
ALLOT
BARROWFIELD CL
TOTTENHAM PARK CEMETERY
MONTAGU RECREATION GROUND
Pav
Lidl UK GmbH Distribution Centre
WESTERN SYNAGOGUE CEMETERY
JEWISH
PEGAMOID ROAD
PRINCES RD
MONTAGU RD INDUSTRIAL EST
LEE PARK WAY
River Lee Navigation
LEE VALLEY
REGIONAL
PARK
Pumping Station
FB
River Lee Diversion
Weir
ENFIELD
WALTHAM FOREST
WALTHAM
A1037
A1009
HERIOT AV
LEADALE
BRINDWOOD
PRIORY
MIDDLETON
CHERRYDOWN AVENUE
MARMION AVENUE
Old Hall Tavern PH
HALL LANE
RUSSELL ROAD
Coll
CHINGFORD HALL PARK
Health Cen
Prim Sch
FRANKLAND
TUFTON
CHASE GDNS
NORBURY RD
YORK ROAD
HAMPTON
SOUTH
CHINGFORD
E4
SINCLAIR
WESTWARD
MAPLE AVENUE
CABINET WAY
ALLOT
Chimney
Refuse Plant
ASH WHARF
ELEY ESTATE
KYNOCH ROAD
NOBEL ROAD
CONDUIT LANE
MONT. RD
NEW PARK IND EST
ANGEL ROAD
ANGEL ROAD WORKS
ELEY ROAD RETAIL PK
Superstores
ADVENT WAY
LEA VALLEY VIADUCT
Cooks Ferry
Hall La
SOUTHEND ROAD
CHINGFORD IND CEN
CORK TREE RETAIL PK
MANDEVILLE CT
HOLLYWOOD
LOWER HALL LANE
BURNHAM ROAD
RAVENSIDE RETAIL PK
DORFORD WHARF
LEA VALLEY TRAD EST
Sunday Market
HARBET ROAD
SHADBOLT AVENUE
CULPEPPER CL
LEOPOLD RD
LADYSMITH RD
ALBANY
Gas Works
KIMBERLEY ROAD
GLOVER DRIVE
SILVERMERE DR
HASTINGWOOD TRADING ESTATE
TOWPATH ROAD
RIVERMEAD RD
BUS DEPOT
Pumping Sta
Lee Valley Watersports
Superstore
Prim Sch
Comm Cen
AVENUE IND EST
Superstore
SPORTS GRD
LEESIDE ROAD
SPORTS GRD
Clubho
Pitches
WATERMEAD WAY
MOWLEM TRADING ESTATE
BUS DEPOT
BANBURY RESERVOIR
FOLLY LANE
A406 (NORTH CIRCULAR)
WALTHAMSTOW
Fairways Cen
PEACOCK CL
MUSLIM BURIAL GROUND
FAIRWAY GOLF RANGE
BRITANNIA SPORTS GROUND
SPORTS GRD
Electricity Station
GARMAN ROAD
WILLOUGHBY LANE
NORTHUMBERLAND PARK
MARIGOLD RD
Lee Flood Relief Channel
BANBURY ROAD
GREBE CL
SWIFT CL
STOW CRES
ASCHAM END
CHEN. ROW
KIMBERLEY RD
William Morris Sch
Billet Works
BILLET
Sec Sch
McENTEE AV
WALTHAM PK
Overflow Channel

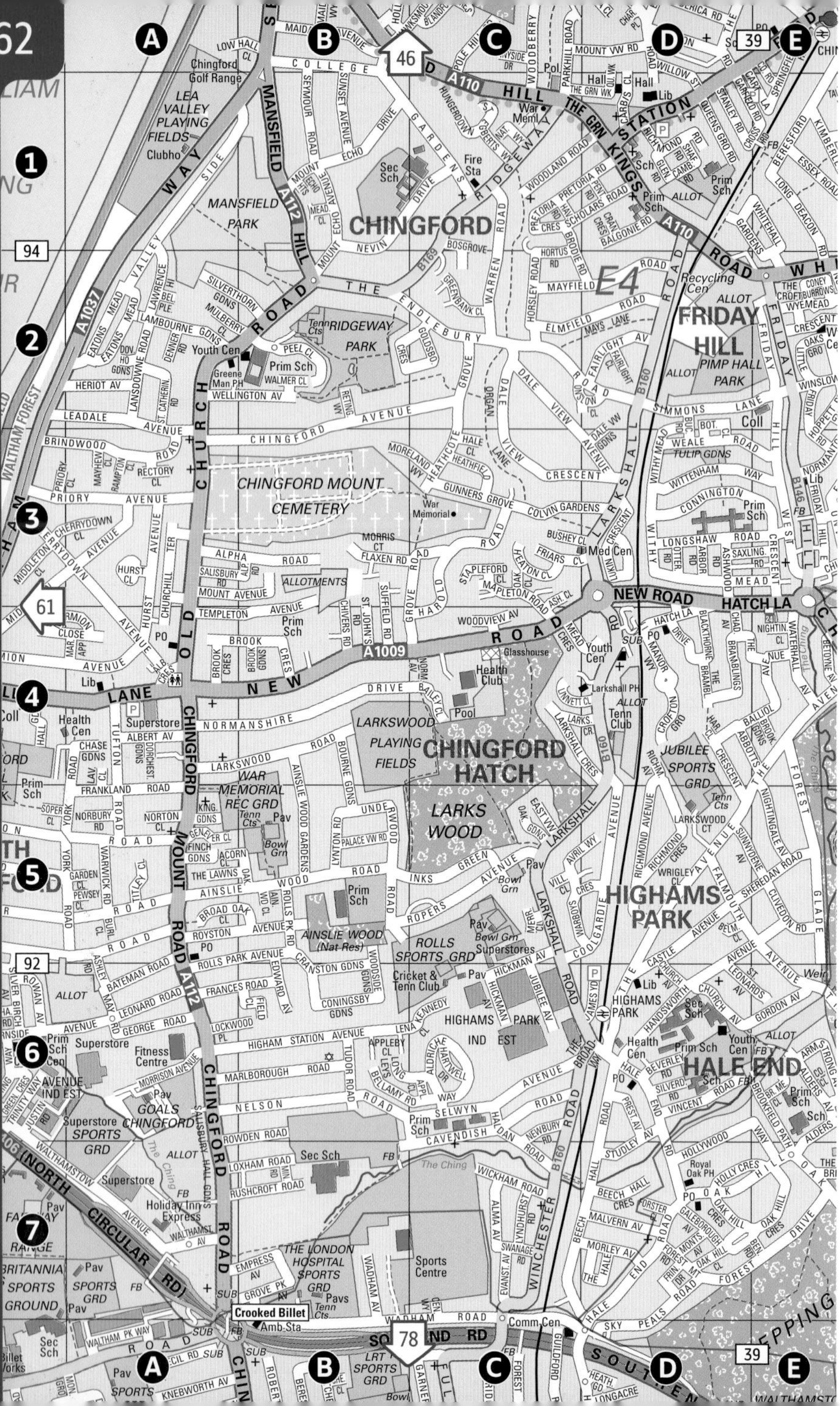
A
B
C
D
E
46
39
1
2
3
4
5
6
7
94
92
61
78
CHINGFORD
CHINGFORD HATCH
HIGHAMS PARK
HALE END
FRIDAY HILL
E4
LEA VALLEY PLAYING FIELDS
Chingford Golf Range
MANSFIELD PARK
RIDGEWAY PARK
CHINGFORD MOUNT CEMETERY
LARKSWOOD PLAYING FIELDS
LARKS WOOD
WAR MEMORIAL REC GRD
AINSLIE WOOD (Nat Res)
ROLLS SPORTS GRD
JUBILEE SPORTS GRD
PIMP HALL PARK
HIGHAMS PARK IND EST
GOALS CHINGFORD
SPORTS GRD
BRITANNIA SPORTS GROUND
THE LONDON HOSPITAL SPORTS GRD
LRT SPORTS GRD
Sports Centre
Holiday Inn Express
Crooked Billet
Amb Sta
Comm Cen
Recycling Cen
Glasshouse
Larkshall PH
Royal Oak PH
Greene Man PH
Fire Sta
War Meml
Youth Cen
Health Club
Cricket & Tenn Club
MANSFIELD HILL
A112
A110
A1037
A1009
A406 (NORTH CIRCULAR RD)
B160
B169
B146
OLD CHURCH ROAD
CHINGFORD MOUNT ROAD
CHINGFORD ROAD
NEW ROAD
HATCH LA
LARKSHALL ROAD
STATION ROAD
KINGS ROAD
THE GRN WK
THE RIDGEWAY
THE ENDLEBURY ROAD
WALTHAM FOREST
WALTHAM WAY
HALE END ROAD
FOREST ROAD
WINCHESTER ROAD
CHINGFORD AVENUE
PRIORY AVENUE
NORMANSHIRE DRIVE
LARKSWOOD ROAD
HIGHAM STATION AVENUE
MARLBOROUGH ROAD
NELSON ROAD
CAVENDISH ROAD
SELWYN AVENUE
WADHAM ROAD
SOUTHEND RD
ROLLS PARK AVENUE
AINSLIE WOOD ROAD
COOLGARDIE AVENUE
HICKMAN AV
DALE VIEW AVENUE
SIMMONS LANE
FRIDAY HILL
EPPING

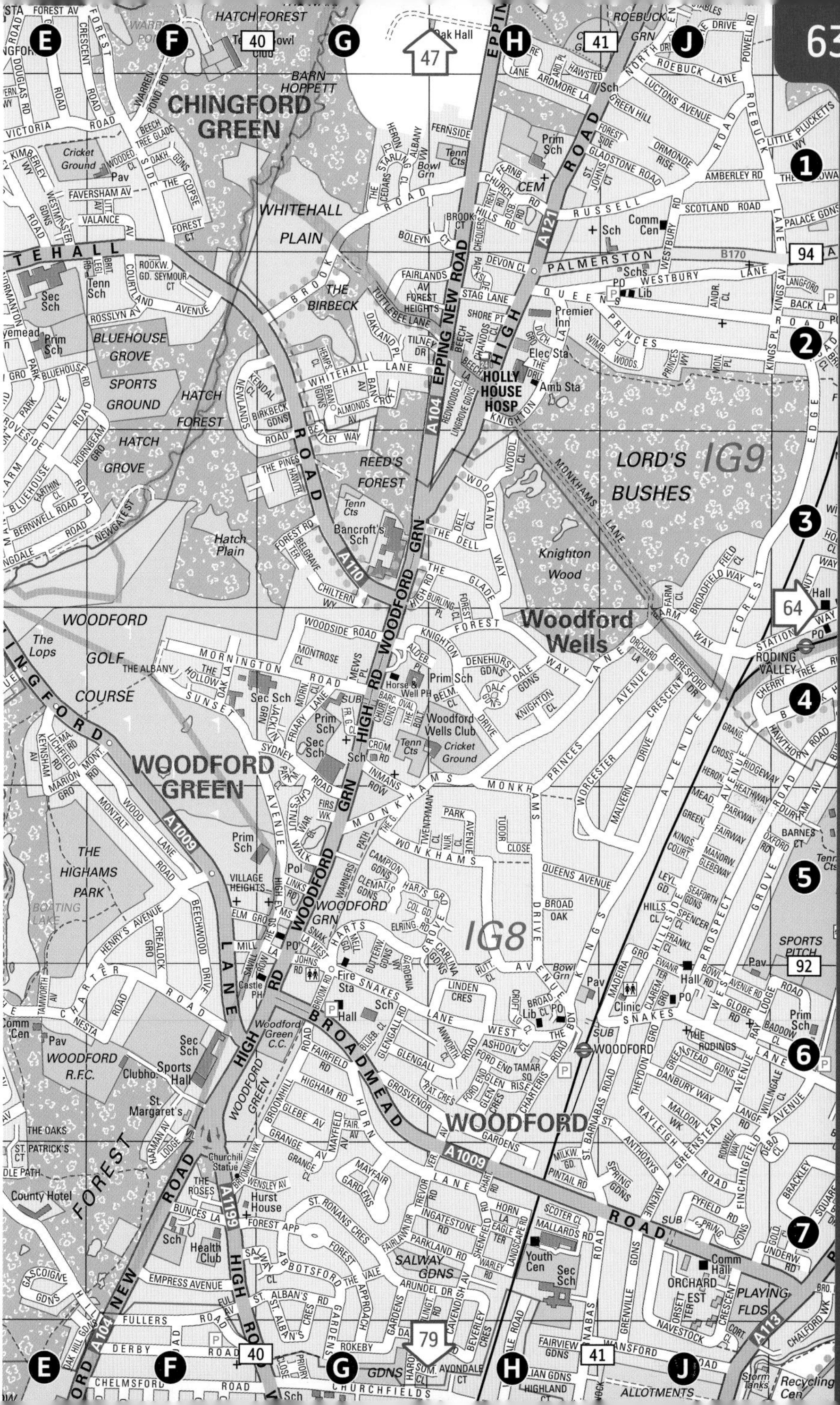
CHINGFORD GREEN
HATCH FOREST
BARN HOPPETT
WHITEHALL PLAIN
THE BIRBECK
BLUEHOUSE GROVE
SPORTS GROUND
HATCH FOREST
HATCH GROVE
REED'S FOREST
Hatch Plain
LORD'S BUSHES
IG9
Knighton Wood
Woodford Wells
WOODFORD GOLF COURSE
The Lops
WOODFORD GREEN
THE HIGHAMS PARK
BOATING LAKE
IG8
WOODFORD
WOODFORD GRN
WOODFORD R.F.C.
Woodford Green C.C.
HOLLY HOUSE HOSP
Bancroft's Sch
Woodford Wells Club
Cricket Ground
RODING VALLEY
SPORTS PITCH
ORCHARD EST
PLAYING FLDS
SALWAY GDNS
County Hotel
Hurst House
Churchill Statue
ALLOTMENTS
Recycling Cen
Storm Tanks
EPPING NEW ROAD
HIGH ROAD
WOODFORD GRN
HIGH RD
BROADMEAD ROAD
WOODFORD NEW ROAD
FOREST
A104
A121
A110
A1009
A1199
A113
B170
40
41
47
64
79
92
94
E
F
G
H
J
1
2
3
4
5
6
7

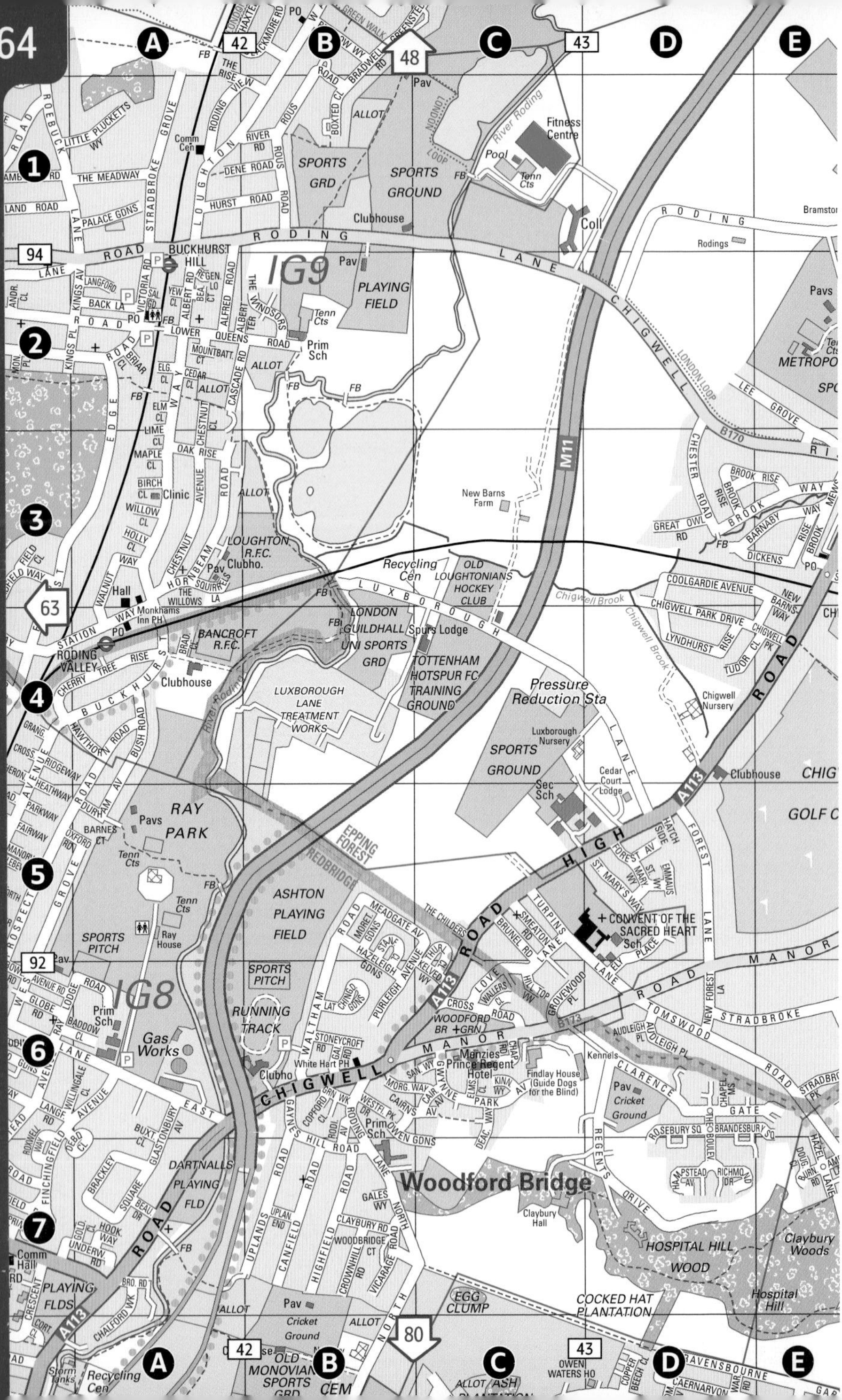
A
B
C
D
E
1
2
3
4
5
6
7
42
48
43
94
63
92
80
IG9
IG8
BUCKHURST HILL
RODING VALLEY
Woodford Bridge
M11
A113
B170
B173
RODING ROAD
RODING LANE
CHIGWELL LANE
RODING LANE
LONDON LOOP
River Roding
Fitness Centre
Pool
Tenn Cts
Coll
Rodings
Bramston
Pavs
METROPO
SPO
LEE GROVE
CHESTER ROAD
BROOK RISE
BROOK WAY
GREAT OWL RD
BARNABY WAY
DICKENS RISE
BROOK MEWS
COOLGARDIE AVENUE
NEW BARNS WAY
CHIGWELL PARK DRIVE
LYNDHURST RISE
TUDOR CL
CHIGWELL PK
Chigwell Brook
Chigwell Nursery
Clubhouse
CHIG
GOLF C
SPORTS GRD
SPORTS GROUND
ALLOT
Pav
Clubhouse
PLAYING FIELD
Tenn Cts
Prim Sch
New Barns Farm
Recycling Cen
OLD LOUGHTONIANS HOCKEY CLUB
LUXBOROUGH LANE
LONDON GUILDHALL UNI SPORTS GRD
Spurs Lodge
TOTTENHAM HOTSPUR FC TRAINING GROUND
LUXBOROUGH LANE TREATMENT WORKS
Pressure Reduction Sta
Luxborough Nursery
SPORTS GROUND
Cedar Court Lodge
Sec Sch
HIGH ROAD
HATCH SIDE
FOREST AV
FOREST LANE
ST. MARY'S WAY
EMMAUS WY
CONVENT OF THE SACRED HEART
Sch
ELY PLACE
TURPINS LANE
SMEATON RD
BRUNEL RD
HILL TOP VW
GROVEWOOD PL
MANOR ROAD
NEW FOREST LA
STRADBROKE
TOMSWOOD ROAD
AUDLEIGH PL
CLARENCE GATE
Kennels
Pav
Cricket Ground
ROSEBURY SQ
BRANDESBURY SQ
CHAPEL MS
HAMPSTEAD AV
RICHMOND DR
REGENTS DRIVE
Claybury Hall
HOSPITAL HILL WOOD
Claybury Woods
Hospital Hill
COCKED HAT PLANTATION
OWEN WATERS HO
COPPER BEECH CL
RAVENSBOURNE
CAERNARVON
EPPING FOREST
REDBRIDGE
THE CHILDERS
ASHTON PLAYING FIELD
SPORTS PITCH
RUNNING TRACK
MEADGATE AV
HAZELEIGH GDNS
PURLEIGH AVENUE
KELVEDON WY
LOVE LA
WALLERS CL
CROSS ROAD
WOODFORD BR
GRN
STONEYCROFT RD
WALTHAM ROAD
White Hart PH
CHIGWELL ROAD
Clubho
Menzies Prince Regent Hotel
Findlay House (Guide Dogs for the Blind)
PARK AV
CAIRNS AV
GWYNNE PARK
Prim Sch
OWEN GDNS
GAYNES HILL ROAD
RODING LANE NORTH
GALES WY
UPLANDS ROAD
CANFIELD ROAD
HIGHFIELD ROAD
CLAYBURY RD
WOODBRIDGE CT
CROWNHILL RD
VICARAGE ROAD
EGG CLUMP
Pav
Cricket Ground
ALLOT
OLD MONOVIAN SPORTS GRD
CEM
ALLOT / ASH PLANTATION
DARTNALLS PLAYING FLD
RAY PARK
Pavs
Tenn Cts
Ray House
SPORTS PITCH
Prim Sch
Gas Works
EAST
GLASTONBURY AV
BUXT. CL
BRACKLEY SQUARE
BEAU DR
HOOK WAY
UNDERW.
Comm Hall
PLAYING FLDS
CHALFORD WK
Storm Tanks
Recycling Cen
FB
THE RISE
RODING VIEW
LOUGHTON
RIVER RD
DENE ROAD
HURST ROAD
ROUS ROAD
BOXTED CL
BRADWELL RD
GREEN WALK
GREENSTED
THAXTED
BLACKMORE RD
ROEBUCK LANE
LITTLE PLUCKETTS WY
THE MEADWAY
PALACE GDNS
STRADBROKE GROVE
Comm Cen
KINGS AV
LANGFORD
BACK LA
VICTORIA RD
ALBERT RD
ALFRED ROAD
THE WINDSORS
QUEENS ROAD
LOWER
MOUNTBATT. CT
CASCADE RD
BRIAR CL
EDGE
ELM CL
LIME CL
MAPLE CL
BIRCH CL
Clinic
WILLOW CL
HOLLY CL
WALNUT WAY
CHESTNUT AVENUE
OAK RISE
CEDAR CL
HORNBEAM
SQUIRRELS
THE WILLOWS
Hall
Monkhams Inn PH
STATION WAY
LOUGHTON R.F.C.
Clubho.
BANCROFT R.F.C.
CHERRY TREE RISE
BUCKHURST WAY
Clubhouse
HAWTHORN ROAD
BUSH ROAD
RIDGEWAY
HEATHWAY
PARKWAY
FAIRWAY
DURHAM AV
OXFORD RD
BARNES CT
PROSPECT GROVE
AVENUE RD
GLOBE RD
RAY LODGE ROAD
BADDOW CL
LANE
WILLINGALE CL
AVENUE
LANGF. RD
FINCHINGFIELD
ROXWELL WAY
DEBD. CL
GOLD. WAY
BRO. RD
CRESCENT
CORT CL
Clubhouse

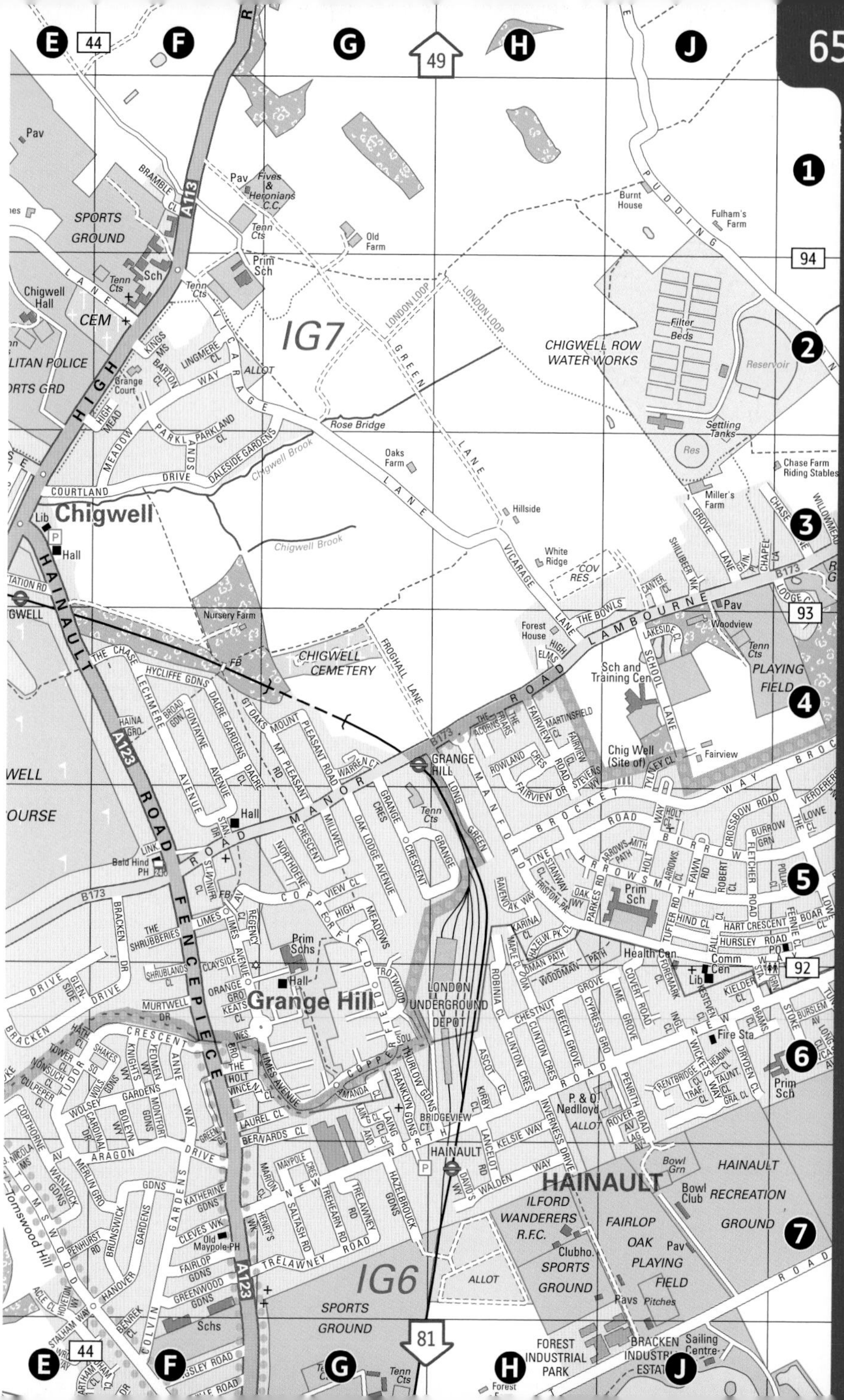
E
F
G
H
J
44
49
94
93
92
81
1
2
3
4
5
6
7
IG7
IG6
Chigwell
Grange Hill
HAINAULT
SPORTS GROUND
CEM
Chigwell Hall
Sch
Tenn Cts
Pav
Fives & Heronians C.C
Old Farm
Prim Sch
BRAMBLE CL
A113
HIGH ROAD
KINGS MS
LINGMERE CL
BARTON CL
WAY
ALLOT
VICARAGE LANE
Grange Court
HIGH MEAD
MEADOW
PARKLANDS
PARKLAND CL
DALESIDE GARDENS
DRIVE
COURTLAND
Chigwell Brook
Rose Bridge
LONDON LOOP
GREEN LANE
Oaks Farm
Hillside
White Ridge
COV RES
Burnt House
PUDDING LANE
Fulham's Farm
CHIGWELL ROW WATER WORKS
Filter Beds
Reservoir
Settling Tanks
Res
Chase Farm Riding Stables
Miller's Farm
GROVE LANE
SHILLIBEER WK
CANTER CL
CHAPEL LA
CHASE LANE
WILLOWMEAD
B173
LODGE CL
LAMBOURNE ROAD
THE BOWLS
Forest House
HIGH ELMS
Pav
Woodview
LAKESIDE CL
SCHOOL LANE
Sch and Training Cen
Tenn Cts
PLAYING FIELD
Chig Well (Site of)
Fairview
Lib
Hall
STATION RD
CHIGWELL
HAINAULT ROAD
A123
Nursery Farm
CHIGWELL CEMETERY
FROGHALL LANE
FB
THE CHASE
HYCLIFFE GDNS
LECHMERE AV
BROAD. GDN.
FONTAYNE AVENUE
DACRE GARDENS
DACRE CL
GT OAKS
MOUNT PLEASANT RD
MT PLEASANT
PLEASANT ROAD
WARREN CL
MANOR ROAD
GRANGE HILL
THE ACORNS
FRIARS
FAIRVIEW
MARTINSFIELD CL
ROWLAND CRES
FAIRVIEW DR
STEVENS WY
TYLNEY CL
BROCKET WAY
ROAD
LONG GREEN
MANFORD WAY
CROSSBOW ROAD
VERDERERS
LOWE
THE LOWE CL
BURROW GRN
BURROW RD
FLETCHER ROAD
POLLARD CL
ARROWSMITH PATH
ARROWSMITH RD
HOLT WAY
HOLT CL
ARROWS. CL
FAWN RD
ROBERT CL
TINE
STANWAY
FRISTON PATH
OAK WY
PARKES RD
Prim Sch
TUFTER RD
HIND CL
HART CRESCENT
BOAR CL
FERNIE CL
HURSLEY ROAD
PO
Health Cen
Comm Cen
Lib
KESTEVEN
KIELDER CL
BRAMS.
STOKE
BURSLEM AV
WELL
COURSE
HALL
STAN. DR
LINK.
Bald Hind PH
B173
ST WINIFR. CL
COPPERFIELD
VIEW CL
HIGH MEADOWS
OAK LODGE AVENUE
GRANGE CRES
GRANGE CRESCENT
MILLWELL CRESCENT
NORTHDENE
Tenn Cts
BRACKEN DR
THE SHRUBBERIES
SHRUBLANDS CL
LIMES AVENUE
REGENCY CL
CLAYSIDE
Prim Schs
ORANGE GRO
KEATS CL
MURTWELL DR
GLENSIDE
DRIVE
BRACKEN
TROTWOOD
LONDON UNDERGROUND DEPOT
RAVEN.
KARINA CL
MAPLE CL
HAZELW. PK CL
ROMAN PATH
WOODMAN PATH
ROBINIA CL
CHESTNUT
CLINTON CRES
BEECH GROVE
CYPRESS GRO
GROVE
LIME GROVE
COVERT ROAD
FOREMARK CL
INGL. CL
WICKETS WAY
Fire Sta
DRYDEN CL
Prim Sch
FENCEPIECE ROAD
CRESCENT
TUDOR
TOWER CL
NONSUCH CL
CULPEPER CL
SHAKES. SQ
KNIGHTS WY
YEOMEN WY
ANNE WAY
THE HOLT
VINCENT CL
AMANDA CL
THURLOW GDNS
FRANKLYN GDNS
LAING CL
ASCOT CL
KIRBY CL
LANCELOT RD
KELSIE WAY
INVERNESS DRIVE
P. & O. Nedlloyd
ALLOT
ROVER AV
PENRITH ROAD
TRENTBRIDGE CL
HEADIN. CL
TAUNT. CL
GRA. CL
LAUREL CL
BERNARDS CL
BRIDGEVIEW
NORTH
HAINAULT
WALDEN WAY
DAVID'S WY
Bowl Grn
Bowl Club
HAINAULT RECREATION GROUND
COPTHORNE AV
WOLSEY GDNS
CARDINAL DR
BOLEYN WY
MONTFORT GDNS
GARDENS
ARAGON DRIVE
WANNOCK GDNS
MERLIN GRO
MAYPOLE CRES
MARION CL
NEW NORTH ROAD
SALTASH RD
TREHEARN RD
TRELAWNEY RD
HAZELBROOK GDNS
TRELAWNEY ROAD
KATHERINE GDNS
CLEVES WK
Old Maypole PH
FAIRLOP GDNS
GREENWOOD GDNS
BRUNSWICK GARDENS
PENHURST RD
HANOVER
TOMSWOOD RD
Tomswood Hill
ST NICOLA MS
HOVETON WY
STALHAM WAY
BENREK CL
COLVIN
Schs
ILFORD WANDERERS R.F.C.
Clubho.
SPORTS GROUND
FAIRLOP OAK PLAYING FIELD
Pav
Pavs
Pitches
ALLOT
SPORTS GROUND
FOREST INDUSTRIAL PARK
BRACKEN INDUSTRIAL ESTATE
Sailing Centre
Tenn Cts
Forest

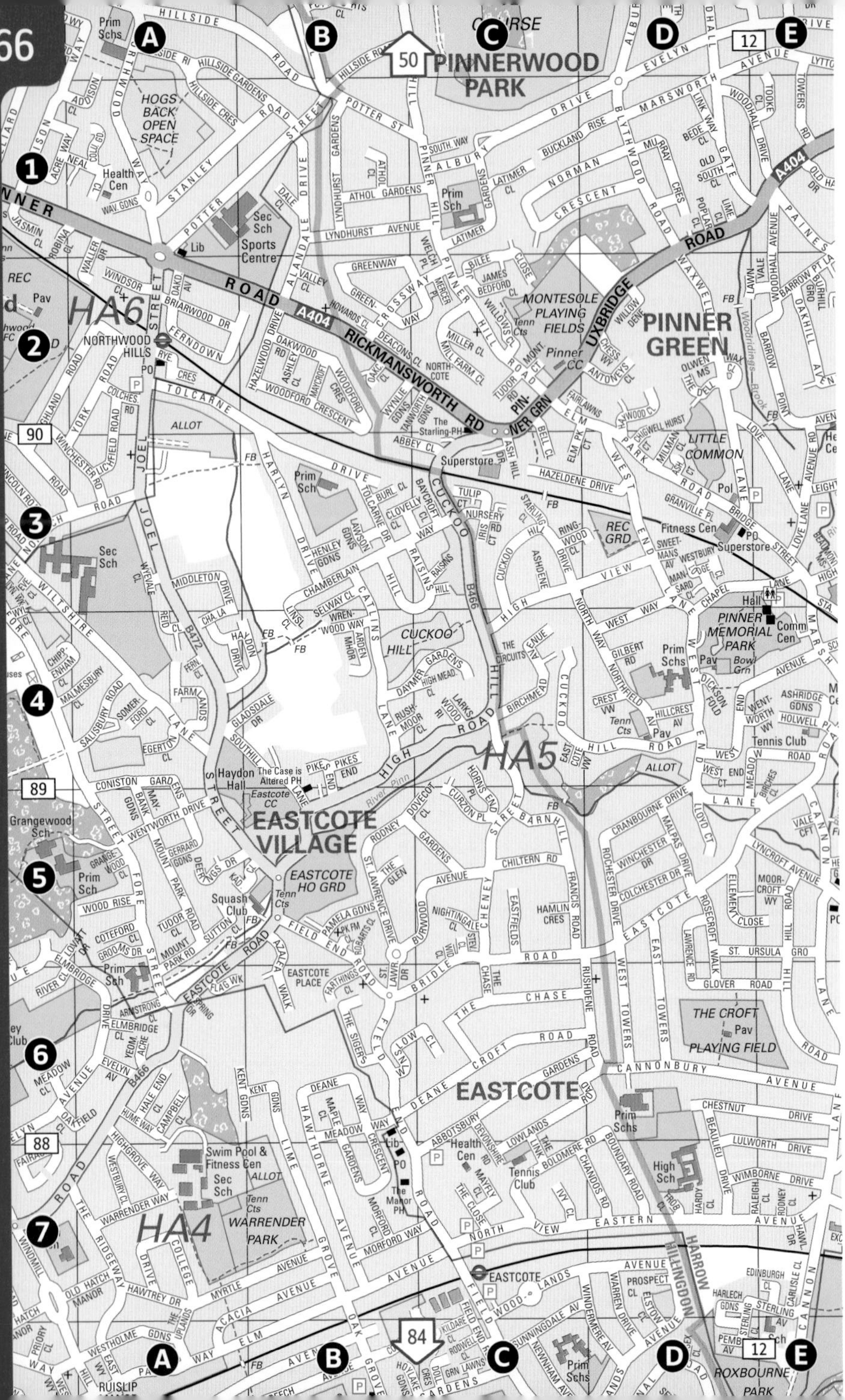
PINNERWOOD PARK
50
HOGS BACK OPEN SPACE
HILLSIDE ROAD
HILLSIDE GARDENS
HILLSIDE CRES
STANLEY ROAD
POTTER STREET
POTTER ST
EVELYN DRIVE
MARSWORTH AVENUE
BUCKLAND RISE
NORMAN CRESCENT
LATIMER GARDENS
ATHOL GARDENS
LYNDHURST AVENUE
LYNDHURST GARDENS
ALANDALE DRIVE
PINNER HILL
PINNER HILL ROAD
WOODHALL DRIVE
WOODHALL GATE
A404
UXBRIDGE ROAD
RICKMANSWORTH RD
Sec Sch
Sports Centre
Prim Sch
Prim Schs
Health Cen
Lib
HA6
NORTHWOOD HILLS
REC
Pav
MONTESOLE PLAYING FIELDS
Pinner CC
Tenn Cts
PINNER GREEN
TOLCARNE DRIVE
ALLOT
JOEL STREET
The Starling PH
Superstore
LITTLE COMMON
HAZELDENE DRIVE
REC GRD
Fitness Cen
PO
PINNER MEMORIAL PARK
Hall
Comm Cen
Bowl Grn
CUCKOO HILL
HIGH ROAD
HIGH VIEW
WEST END LANE
B466
B472
HA5
Tennis Club
EASTCOTE VILLAGE
EASTCOTE HO GRD
Haydon Hall
The Case is Altered PH
Eastcote CC
River Pinn
Squash Club
FIELD END ROAD
EASTCOTE ROAD
BRIDLE ROAD
THE CHASE
CANNONBURY AVENUE
THE CROFT PLAYING FIELD
EASTCOTE
High Sch
Swim Pool & Fitness Cen
WARRENDER PARK
HA4
Grangewood Sch
EASTERN AVENUE
EASTCOTE
HILLINGDON
HARROW
ROXBOURNE PARK
RUISLIP
90
89
88
84
12
The Manor PH

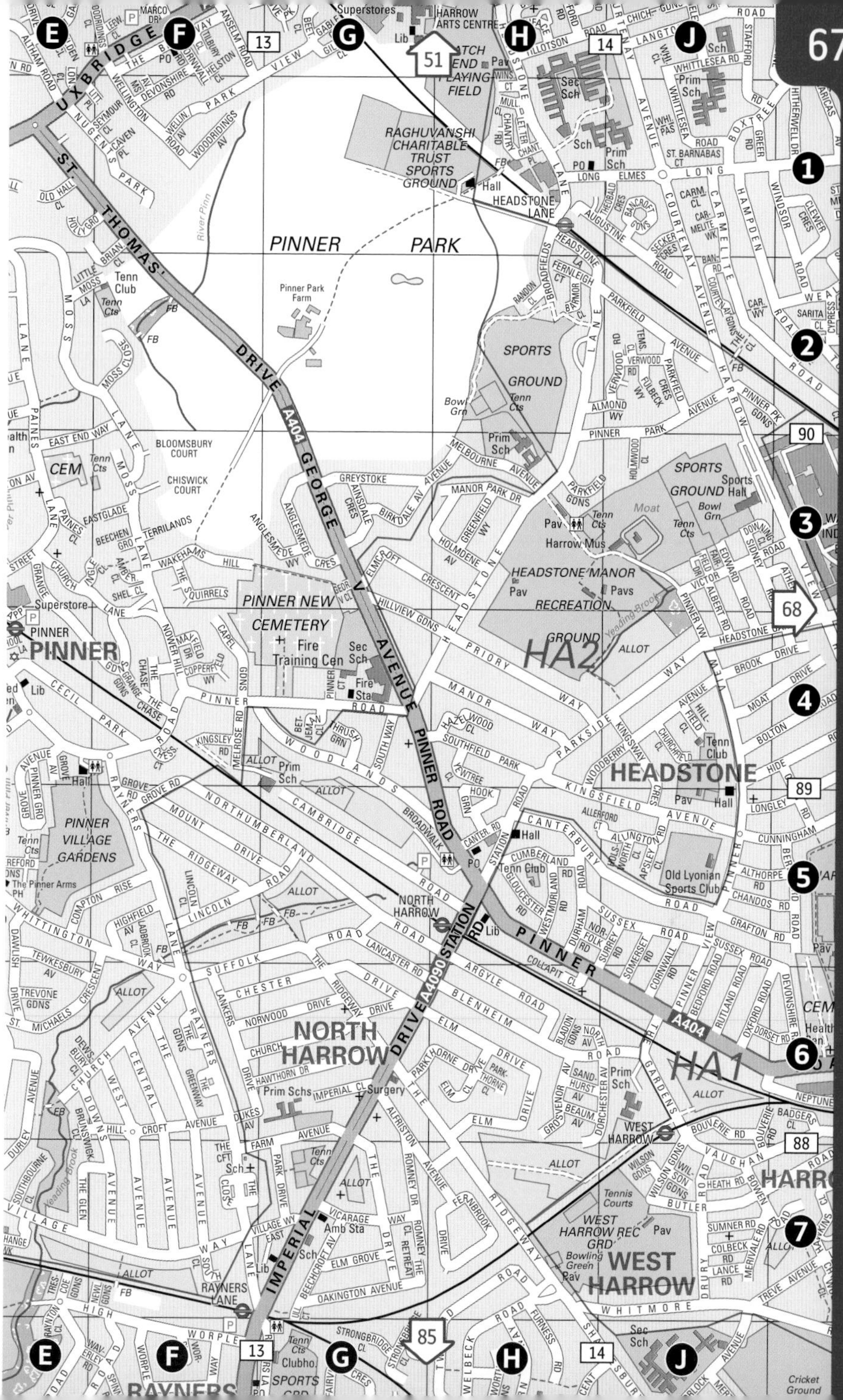
E
F
G
H
J
13
14
51
85
68
90
89
88
1
2
3
4
5
6
7
UXBRIDGE
Superstores
HARROW ARTS CENTRE
HATCH END PLAYING FIELD
RAGHUVANSHI CHARITABLE TRUST SPORTS GROUND
PINNER PARK
Pinner Park Farm
River Pinn
HEADSTONE LANE
ST. THOMAS' DRIVE
A404
GEORGE V AVENUE
PINNER ROAD
SPORTS GROUND
HEADSTONE MANOR RECREATION GROUND
Harrow Mus
Moat
Yeading Brook
HA2
HA1
PINNER NEW CEMETERY
Fire Training Cen
PINNER
Superstore
BLOOMSBURY COURT
CHISWICK COURT
CEM
PINNER VILLAGE GARDENS
The Pinner Arms PH
HEADSTONE
Old Lyonian Sports Club
NORTH HARROW
A4090
STATION RD
IMPERIAL DRIVE
WEST HARROW
WEST HARROW REC GRD
Bowling Green
Tennis Courts
RAYNERS LANE
Amb Sta
Surgery
Prim Schs
Cricket Ground
ALLOT
PARKFIELD AVENUE
CANTERBURY ROAD
KINGSFIELD AVENUE
PINNER VIEW
VAUGHAN ROAD
WHITMORE ROAD
ROAD
MAP

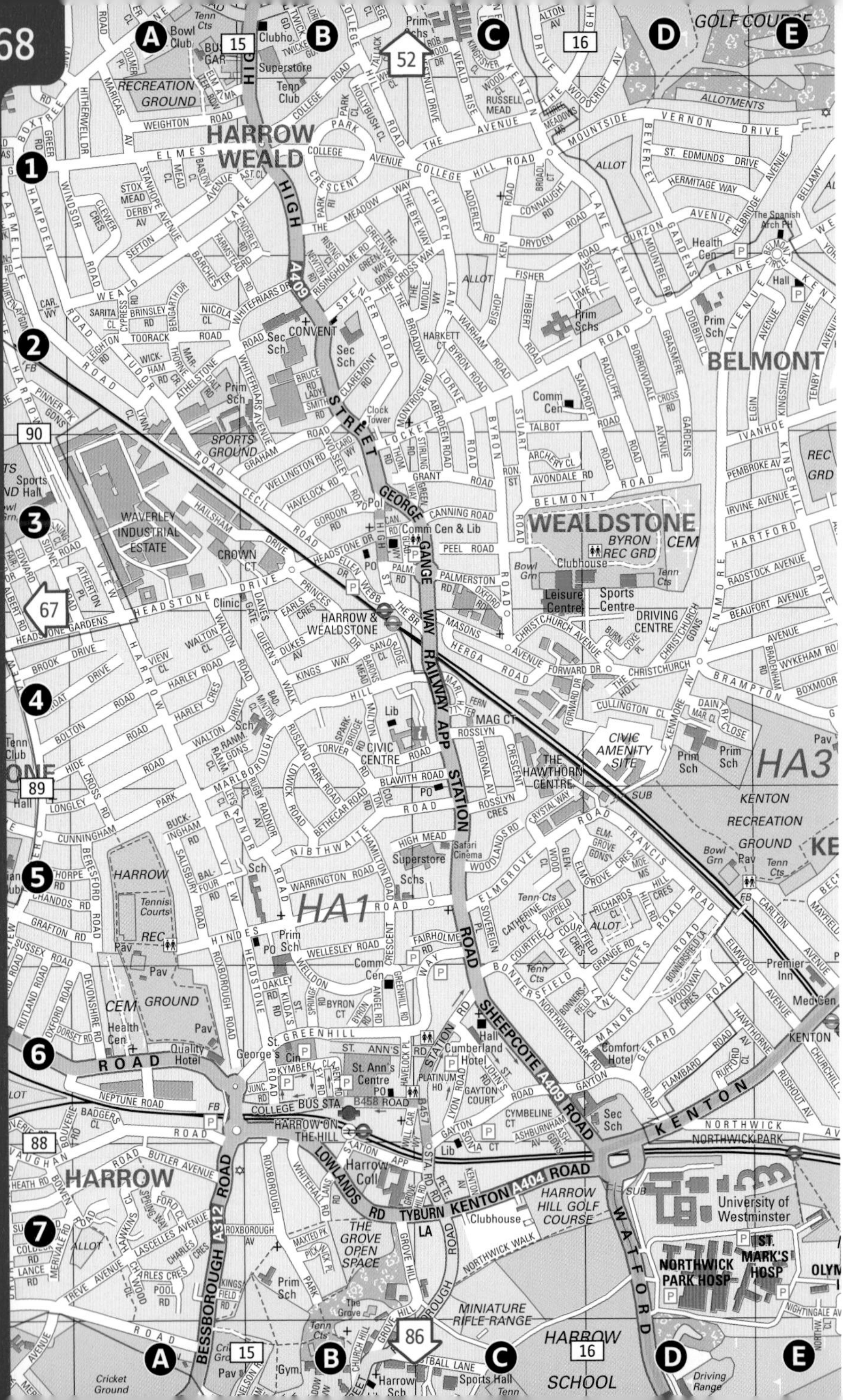
A
B
C
D
E
1
2
3
4
5
6
7
15
16
52
90
67
89
88
86
HARROW WEALD
BELMONT
WEALDSTONE
HARROW
HA1
HA3
GOLF COURSE
ALLOTMENTS
RECREATION GROUND
Bowl Club
Clubho.
Superstore
Tenn Club
Prim Schs
HIGH ROAD
COLLEGE ROAD
ELMES ROAD
WEIGHTON ROAD
MARICAS AV
HITHERWELL DR
BOXTREE RD
GREER RD
COLLEGE HILL ROAD
THE AVENUE
HOLLYBUSH CL
WEALD RISE
RUSSELL MEAD
KINGFISHER CL
KENTON LANE
WOODCROFT AV
MOUNTSIDE
VERNON DRIVE
ST. EDMUNDS DRIVE
HERMITAGE WAY
BEVERLEY
FELBRIDGE AVENUE
The Spanish Arch PH
BELMONT CIRCLE
Health Cen
CURZON AVENUE
MOUNTBEL RD
ALLOT
CONNAUGHT RD
ADDERLEY RD
DRYDEN ROAD
FISHER ROAD
HIBBERT ROAD
LIME CL
CHURCH LANE
THE MEADOW WAY
THE BYE WAY
THE CROSS WAY
THE GREENWAY
RISINGHOLME RD
WHITEFRIARS DR
WHITEFRIARS AVENUE
CONVENT
Sec Sch
Prim Sch
SPENCER ROAD
CLAREMONT RD
BRUCE RD
Clock Tower
HIGH STREET
A409
HARKETT CT
BYRON ROAD
WARHAM ROAD
BISHOP ROAD
THE BROADWAY
THE MIDDLE WY
LORNE RD
MONTROSE RD
ABERDEEN ROAD
STIRLING RD
GRANT ROAD
LOCKET ROAD
STUART ROAD
BYRON ROAD
Comm Cen
SANCROFT RD
RADCLIFFE RD
BORROWDALE AVENUE
GRASMERE AVENUE
CROSS RD
GARDENS
DOBBIN CL
TALBOT ROAD
ARCHERY CL
AVONDALE RD
BELMONT ROAD
IVANHOE
PEMBROKE AV
IRVINE AVENUE
HARTFORD
RADSTOCK AVENUE
BEAUFORT AVENUE
KENMORE AVENUE
KINGSHILL
ELGIN
TENBY
REC GRD
BYRON REC GRD
CEM
Clubhouse
Bowl Grn
Tenn Cts
Leisure Centre
Sports Centre
DRIVING CENTRE
CANNING ROAD
PEEL ROAD
PALMERSTON ROAD
OXFORD RD
MASONS AV
HERGA ROAD
CHRISTCHURCH AVENUE
FORWARD DR
CHRISTCHURCH GDNS
BRAMPTON
WYKEHAM RD
BOXMOOR
BRADENHAM
CULLINGTON CL
DAINTRY CLOSE
MAR CL
CIVIC AMENITY SITE
Prim Sch
KENTON RECREATION GROUND
Pav
Bowl Grn
SUB
GEORGE GANGE WAY
RAILWAY APP
STATION ROAD
Comm Cen & Lib
Pol
PO
HEADSTONE DR
ELLEN WEBB DR
PALM. RD
HARROW & WEALDSTONE
WEALD LANE
HAMPDEN ROAD
CARMELITE ROAD
WINDSOR ROAD
STANHOPE AVENUE
CLEWER CRES
STOX MEAD
DERBY AV
SEFTON AV
BARCHESTER CL
FARMSTEAD RD
ENDERLEY RD
SARITA CL
CYPRESS AV
BRINSLEY RD
BENGARTH DR
NICOLA CL
TOORACK ROAD
WICKHAM RD
ATHELSTONE ROAD
LEIGHTON RD
TUDOR ROAD
LYNN CL
PINNER PK GDNS
SPORTS GROUND
GRAHAM ROAD
WELLINGTON RD
HAVELOCK RD
GORDON RD
CECIL ROAD
HAILSHAM DRIVE
CROWN CT
WAVERLEY INDUSTRIAL ESTATE
HARROW VIEW
Sports Hall
SIDNEY ROAD
EDWARD RD
ALBERT RD
ATHERTON PL
HEADSTONE DRIVE
HEADSTONE GARDENS
Clinic
DANES GATE
PRINCES DRIVE
EARLS CRES
DUKES AV
QUEEN'S WALK
KINGS WAY
SANDRIDGE CL
BARONS MEAD
WALTON ROAD
WALTON CL
WALTON DRIVE
BROOK DRIVE
VIEW CL
HARLEY ROAD
HARLEY CRES
BOLTON ROAD
HIDE ROAD
CROSS RD
LONGLEY
Tenn Club
Hall
Lib
CIVIC CENTRE
MILTON ROAD
SPARKBRIDGE RD
TORVER RD
RUSLAND PARK ROAD
LOWICK ROAD
BLAWITH ROAD
BETHECAR ROAD
COLTON RD
PARK ROAD
MARLBOROUGH HILL
RUGBY RD
RADNOR AV
RANMOOR GDNS
MAG CT
ROSSLYN CRES
FROGNAL AV
CRESCENT
THE HAWTHORN CENTRE
CRYSTAL WAY
WOODLANDS RD
ELMGROVE
ELMGROVE CRES
ELMGROVE GDNS
FRANCIS ROAD
MOE MS
HILL CRES
RICHARDS CL
DUFFIELD
COURTFIELD CRES
CATHERINE PL
GRANGE RD
ALLOT
BONNERSFIELD LANE
CROFTS ROAD
WOODWAY CRES
MANOR ROAD
ELMWOOD AVENUE
CARLTON AVENUE
Premier Inn
Med Cen
KENTON
CHURCHILL
RUSHOUT AV
HAWTHORNE AV
RUFFORD CL
FLAMBARD ROAD
GERARD ROAD
Comfort Hotel
GAYTON ROAD
NORTHWICK PARK RD
SOVEREIGN PL
FAIRHOLME RD
HIGH MEAD
Safari Cinema
Superstore
Schs
NIBTHWAITE ROAD
HAMILTON ROAD
WARRINGTON ROAD
CUNNINGHAM PARK
BUCKINGHAM RD
SALISBURY ROAD
BALFOUR RD
HARROW REC
Tennis Courts
Pav
CEM GROUND
Health Cen
THORPE RD
CHANDOS RD
GRAFTON RD
SUSSEX ROAD
RUTLAND ROAD
OXFORD ROAD
DEVONSHIRE ROAD
DORSET RD
BERESFORD ROAD
HINDES ROAD
ROXBOROUGH ROAD
HEADSTONE ROAD
Prim Sch
WELLESLEY ROAD
WELLDON CRES
OAKLEY RD
KILDAS RD
ST. JOHN'S RD
SPRINGFIELD RD
BYRON CT
ANGEL RD
GREENHILL WAY
Comm Cen
St. GREENHILL
George's
Cin
ST. ANN'S RD
St. Ann's Centre
KYMBERLEY RD
CLARENDON RD
HAVELOCK PL
STATION RD
Cumberland Hotel
Hall
PLATINUM HO
GAYTON COURT
LYON ROAD
JOHN'S RD
SHEEPCOTE ROAD
CYMBELINE CT
ASHBURNHAM AV
Sec Sch
ROAD
Quality Hotel
NEPTUNE ROAD
COLLEGE BUS STA
B458 ROAD
HARROW ON THE HILL
BADGERS CL
BOUVERIE RD
VAUGHAN ROAD
BUTLER AVENUE
HEATH RD
BOWEN RD
FORD CL
SPRING WAY
HAWKINS CL
LASCELLES AVENUE
CHARLES CRES
MERIVALE RD
COLDEN RD
LANCE RD
ALLOT
TREVE AVENUE
POOL RD
CHARLWOOD CL
BESSBOROUGH ROAD
A312
ROXBOROUGH AV
KINGSFIELD RD
WHITEHALL RD
LOWLANDS RD
STATION APP
Harrow Coll
TYBURN LA
KENTON ROAD
A404
GROVE HILL RD
PETERBOROUGH ROAD
THE GROVE OPEN SPACE
MAXTED PK
PICKWICK PL
Prim Sch
The Grove
Tenn Cts
Gym
CHURCH HILL
FOOTBALL LANE
Harrow Sch
Sports Hall
MINIATURE RIFLE RANGE
HARROW SCHOOL
Clubhouse
HARROW HILL GOLF COURSE
NORTHWICK WALK
WATFORD ROAD
NORTHWICK PARK
NORTHWICK AV
University of Westminster
ST. MARK'S HOSP
NORTHWICK PARK HOSP
NIGHTINGALE AV
Driving Range
Cricket Ground
Pav
WELSON RD

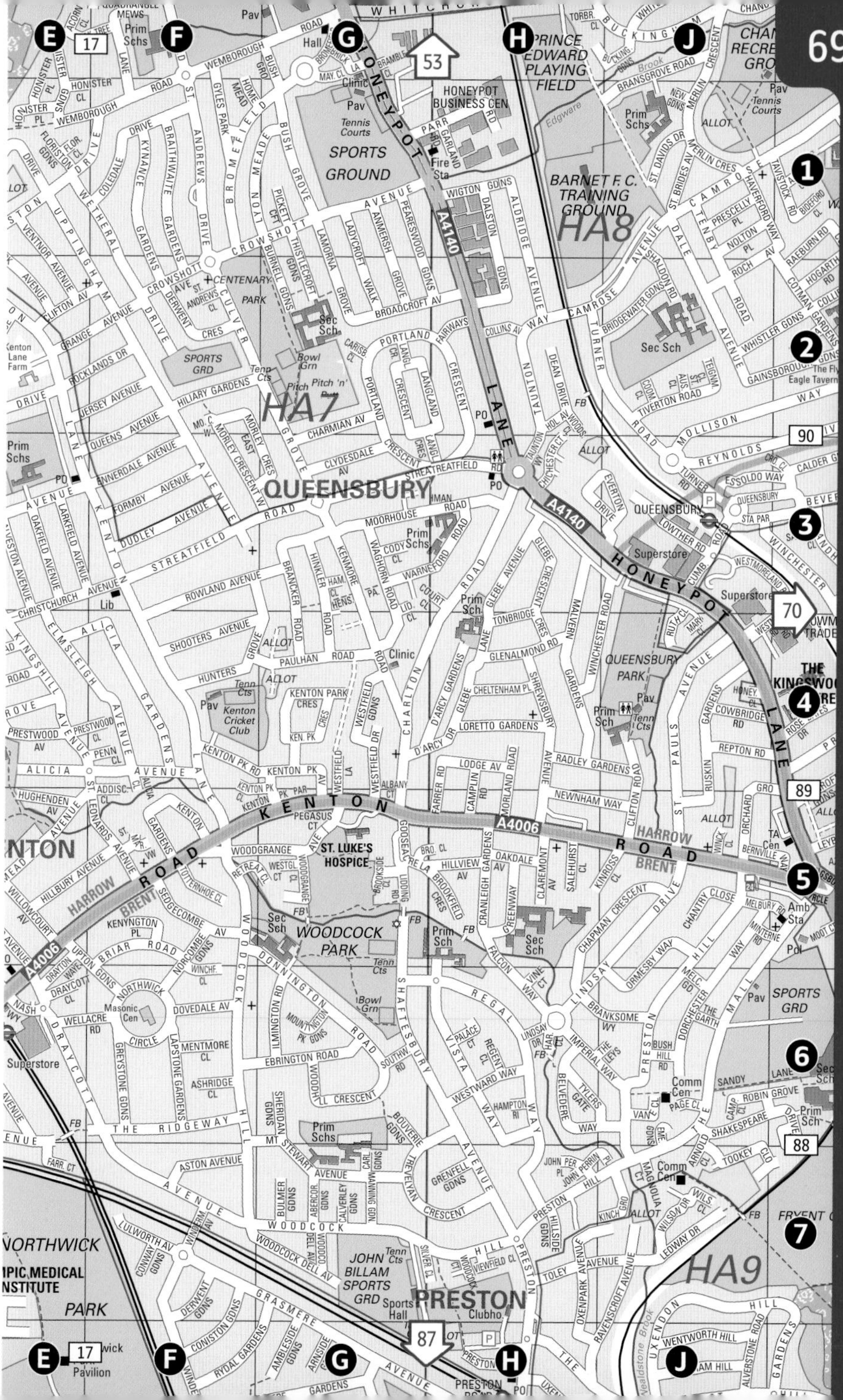
E
F
G
H
J
17
53
70
90
89
88
87
1
2
3
4
5
6
7
PRINCE EDWARD PLAYING FIELD
HONEYPOT BUSINESS CEN
SPORTS GROUND
BARNET F.C. TRAINING GROUND
HA8
HA7
HA9
CENTENARY PARK
SPORTS GRD
QUEENSBURY
QUEENSBURY PARK
KENTON
WOODCOCK PARK
ST. LUKE'S HOSPICE
JOHN BILLAM SPORTS GRD
PRESTON
NORTHWICK PARK
Kenton Cricket Club
Kenton Lane Farm
Masonic Cen
Superstore
Sec Sch
Prim Schs
Prim Sch
Eagle Tavern
HONEYPOT LANE
A4140
A4006
KENTON ROAD
HARROW ROAD
HARROW BRENT
WEMBOROUGH ROAD
WHITCHURCH
BUCKINGHAM
BRANSGROVE ROAD
CAMROSE AVENUE
CAMROSE WAY
MOLLISON WAY
REYNOLDS
CROWSHOTT AVENUE
CULVER GROVE
BROADCROFT AV
PORTLAND CRESCENT
CHARMIAN AV
CLYDESDALE
STREATFIELD ROAD
STREATFIELD AV
MOORHOUSE ROAD
ROWLAND AVENUE
CHRISTCHURCH AVENUE
SHOOTERS AVENUE
HUNTERS
PAULHAN ROAD
KENTON PARK CRES
KENTON PK RD
CHARLTON ROAD
GLEBE AVENUE
GLEBE CRESCENT
MALVERN
WINCHESTER ROAD
ST PAULS AVENUE
LORETTO GARDENS
RADLEY GARDENS
CLIFTON ROAD
WOODCOCK HILL
SHAFTESBURY AVENUE
REGAL WAY
LINDSAY DRIVE
PRESTON HILL
THE RIDGEWAY
WOODCOCK DELL AV
GRASMERE AVENUE
UXENDON HILL
WENTWORTH HILL
ALICIA AVENUE
ALICIA GARDENS
KENTON LANE
UPPINGHAM AVENUE
WETHERAL DRIVE
DRAYCOTT AVENUE
NORTHWICK CIRCLE
DONNINGTON ROAD
EBRINGTON ROAD
ASTON AVENUE
STEWART AVENUE
WESTWARD WAY
BELVEDERE WAY
FRYENT

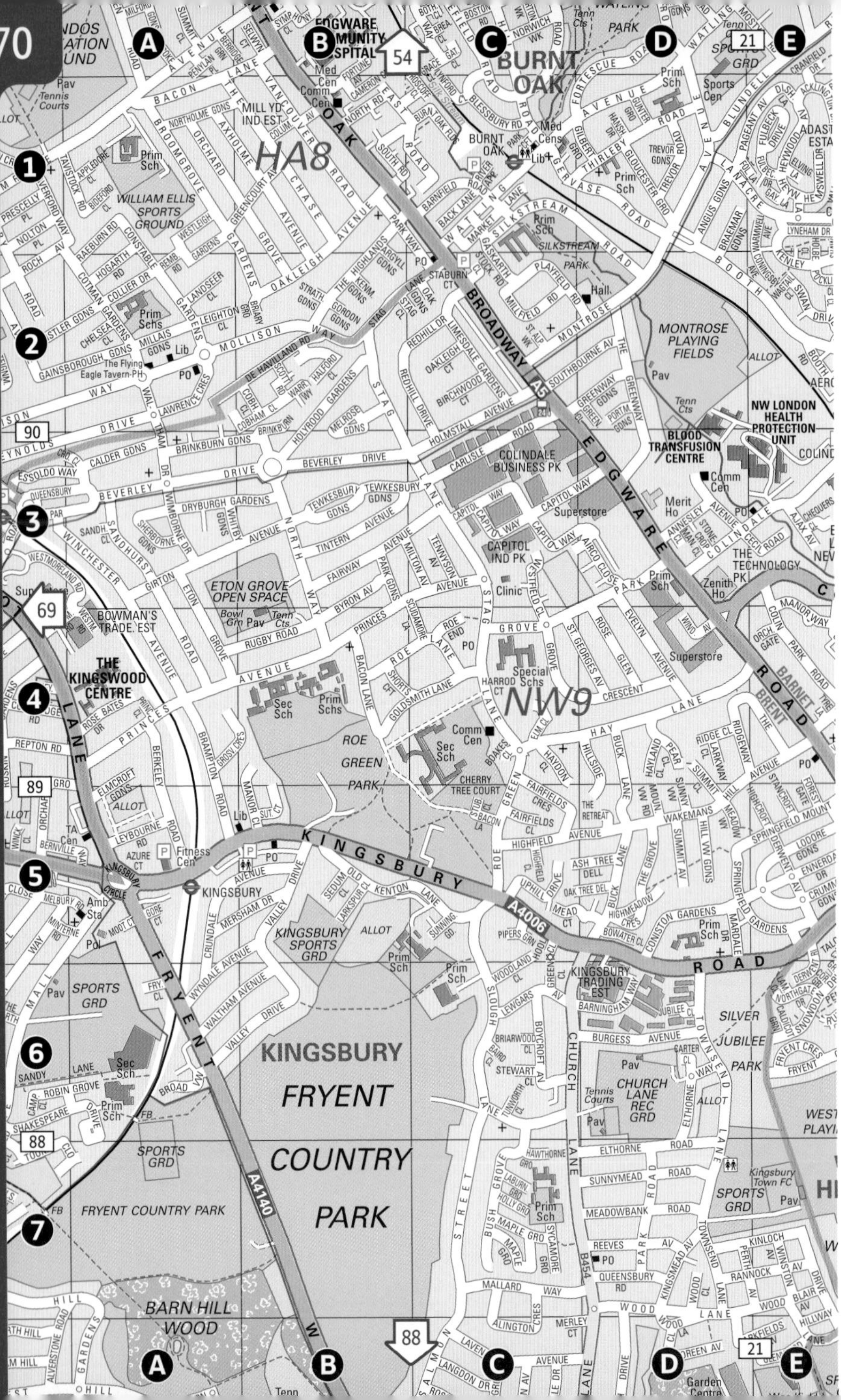
A
B
C
D
E
1
2
3
4
5
6
7
54
69
88
89
90
21
HA8
NW9
EDGWARE COMMUNITY HOSPITAL
BURNT OAK
WATLING PARK
WILLIAM ELLIS SPORTS GROUND
MILL YD IND EST
MONTROSE PLAYING FIELDS
NW LONDON HEALTH PROTECTION UNIT
BLOOD TRANSFUSION CENTRE
COLINDALE BUSINESS PK
CAPITOL IND PK
THE TECHNOLOGY PK
ETON GROVE OPEN SPACE
BOWMAN'S TRADE. EST
THE KINGSWOOD CENTRE
ROE GREEN PARK
SILKSTREAM PARK
KINGSBURY
KINGSBURY SPORTS GRD
KINGSBURY TRADING EST
SILVER JUBILEE PARK
CHURCH LANE REC GRD
KINGSBURY FRYENT COUNTRY PARK
FRYENT COUNTRY PARK
BARN HILL WOOD
SPORTS GRD
CHERRY TREE COURT
The Flying Eagle Tavern-PH
Kingsbury Town FC
BROADWAY
EDGWARE ROAD
KINGSBURY ROAD
FRYENT WAY
A5
A4006
A4140
B454
Prim Sch
Sec Sch
Special Schs
Comm Cen
Superstore
Clinic
Fitness Cen
Amb Sta
Lib
PO
Pav
ALLOT

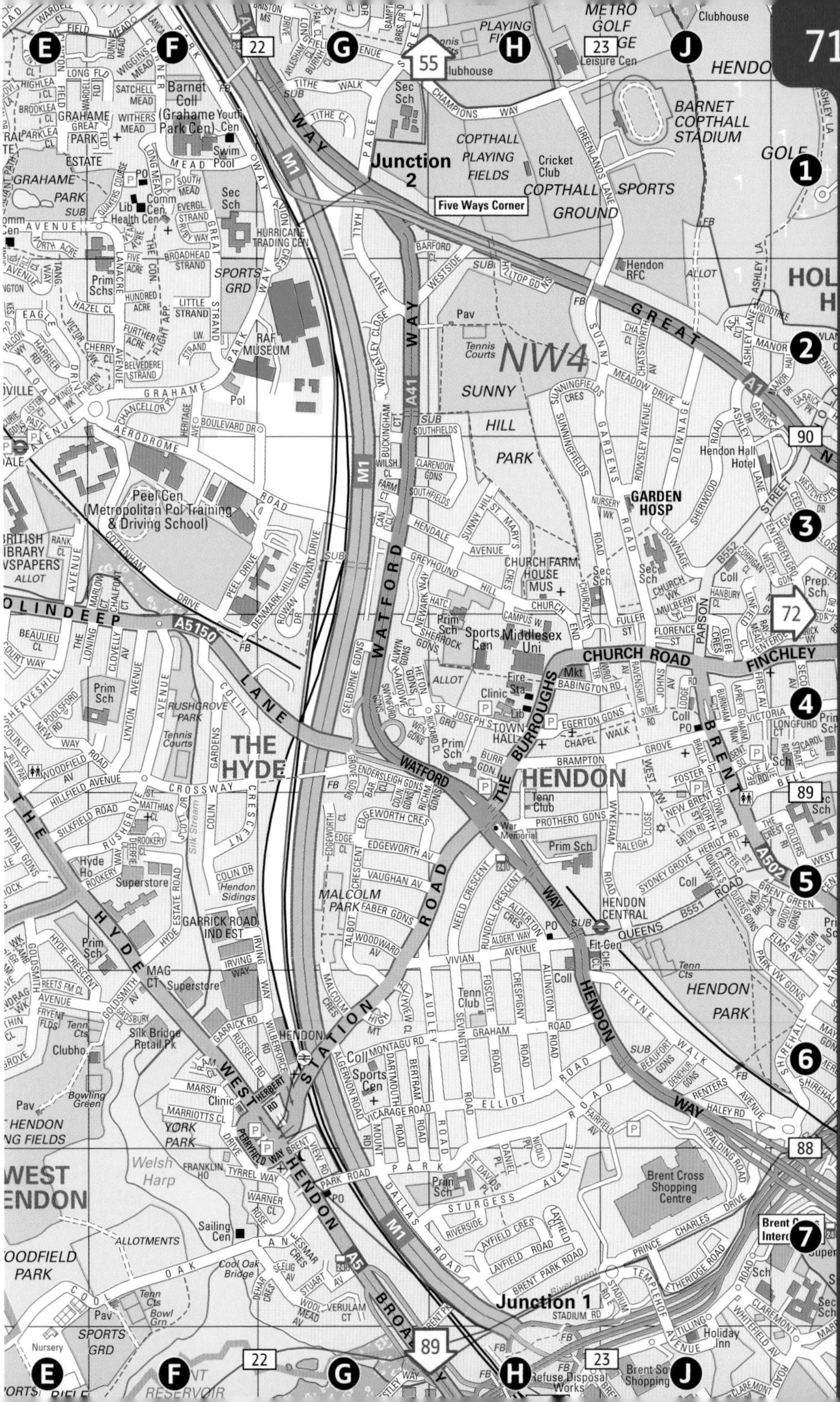
E
F
G
H
J
22
23
55
72
89
90
88
1
2
3
4
5
6
7
METRO GOLF
Clubhouse
Leisure Cen
HENDON
BARNET COPTHALL STADIUM
GOLF
Barnet Coll (Grahame Park Cen)
Youth Cen
Swim Pool
GRAHAME PARK ESTATE
GRAHAME PARK
Junction 2
Five Ways Corner
COPTHALL PLAYING FIELDS
Cricket Club
COPTHALL SPORTS GROUND
CHAMPIONS WAY
TITHE WALK
PAGE STREET
GREENLANDS LANE
HURRICANE TRADING CEN
Hendon RFC
ALLOT
GREAT NORTH WAY
A1
M1
A41
WATFORD WAY
SPORTS GRD
RAF MUSEUM
NW4
SUNNY HILL PARK
Tennis Courts
Pav
AERODROME ROAD
Peel Cen (Metropolitan Pol Training & Driving School)
GARDEN HOSP
Hendon Hall Hotel
BRITISH LIBRARY NEWSPAPERS
COLINDEEP LANE
A5150
CHURCH FARM HOUSE MUS
Middlesex Uni
Sports Cen
CHURCH ROAD
FINCHLEY
THE BURROUGHS
Fire Sta
Clinic
Lib
TOWN HALL
HENDON
THE HYDE
RUSHGROVE PARK
CROSSWAY
Tenn Club
War Memorial
Prim Sch
B552
B551
A502
HENDON CENTRAL
QUEENS ROAD
BRENT STREET
HENDON PARK
MALCOLM PARK
GARRICK ROAD IND EST
Superstore
Silk Bridge Retail Pk
Silk Stream
Hendon Sidings
STATION ROAD
HENDON WAY
VIVIAN AVENUE
WEST HENDON
Welsh Harp
YORK PARK
Bowling Green
ALLOTMENTS
Sailing Cen
COOL OAK LANE
Cool Oak Bridge
WOODFIELD PARK
SPORTS GRD
Nursery
BRENT RESERVOIR
A5
BROADWAY
Junction 1
STADIUM RD
River Brent
Brent Cross Shopping Centre
PRINCE CHARLES DRIVE
Holiday Inn
Brent Cross Interchange
Refuse Disposal Works
Brent South Shopping
CLAREMONT

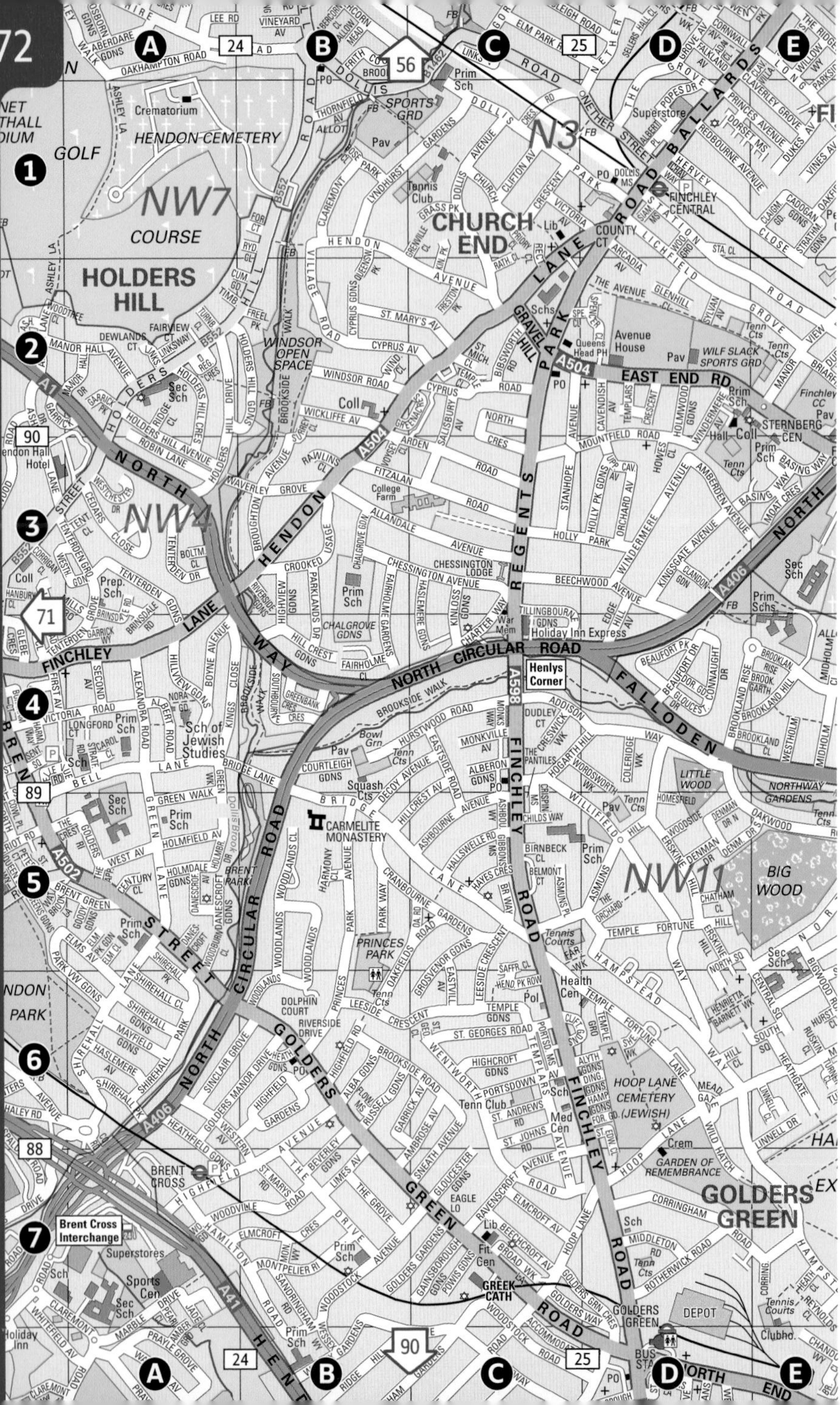
A
B
C
D
E
1
2
3
4
5
6
7
24
25
56
71
88
89
90
NW7
NW4
N3
NW11
HOLDERS HILL
CHURCH END
GOLDERS GREEN
GOLF
COURSE
Crematorium
HENDON CEMETERY
OAKHAMPTON ROAD
DOLLIS ROAD
SPORTS GRD
Prim Sch
Pav
Tennis Club
DOLLIS AVENUE
HENDON AVENUE
WINDSOR OPEN SPACE
CYPRUS AV
WINDSOR ROAD
WICKLIFFE AV
Coll
Superstore
FINCHLEY CENTRAL
BALLARDS LANE
REGENTS PARK ROAD
GRAVEL HILL
COUNTY CT
Lib
Avenue House
Queens Head PH
EAST END RD
WILF SLACK SPORTS GRD
STERNBERG CEN
Finchley CC
MOUNTFIELD ROAD
FITZALAN ROAD
College Farm
ALLANDALE AVENUE
HOLLY PARK
CHESSINGTON AVENUE
CHESSINGTON LODGE
BEECHWOOD AVENUE
Holiday Inn Express
War Mem
NORTH CIRCULAR ROAD
Henlys Corner
FALLODEN WAY
HENDON WAY
NORTH WAY
MANOR HALL AVENUE
HOLDERS HILL AVENUE
Hendon Hall Hotel
Sec Sch
Prep. Sch
TENTERDEN GDNS
FINCHLEY LANE
CHALGROVE GDNS
HILL CREST GDNS
BROOKSIDE WALK
VICTORIA ROAD
Sch of Jewish Studies
BELL LANE
BRIDGE LANE
COURTLEIGH GDNS
Squash Cts
CARMELITE MONASTERY
Bowl Grn
Tenn Cts
PRINCES PARK
FINCHLEY ROAD
LITTLE WOOD
NORTHWAY GARDENS
BIG WOOD
TEMPLE FORTUNE
HAMPSTEAD WAY
Health Cen
Pol
BRENT STREET
BRENT GREEN
A502
A406
A41
A504
A598
A1
B552
HOOP LANE CEMETERY (JEWISH)
Crem
GARDEN OF REMEMBRANCE
GOLDERS GREEN ROAD
BRENT CROSS
Brent Cross Interchange
Superstores
Sports Cen
Holiday Inn
Tenn Club
Med Cen
Lib
Fit. Cen
GREEK CATH
DEPOT
Tennis Courts
Clubho.
BUS STA
NORTH END
HENDON PARK
HOOP LANE
CORRINGHAM ROAD
ASHBOURNE AVENUE
HAMILTON ROAD
HIGHFIELD AVENUE
WOODVILLE ROAD
MIDDLETON RD

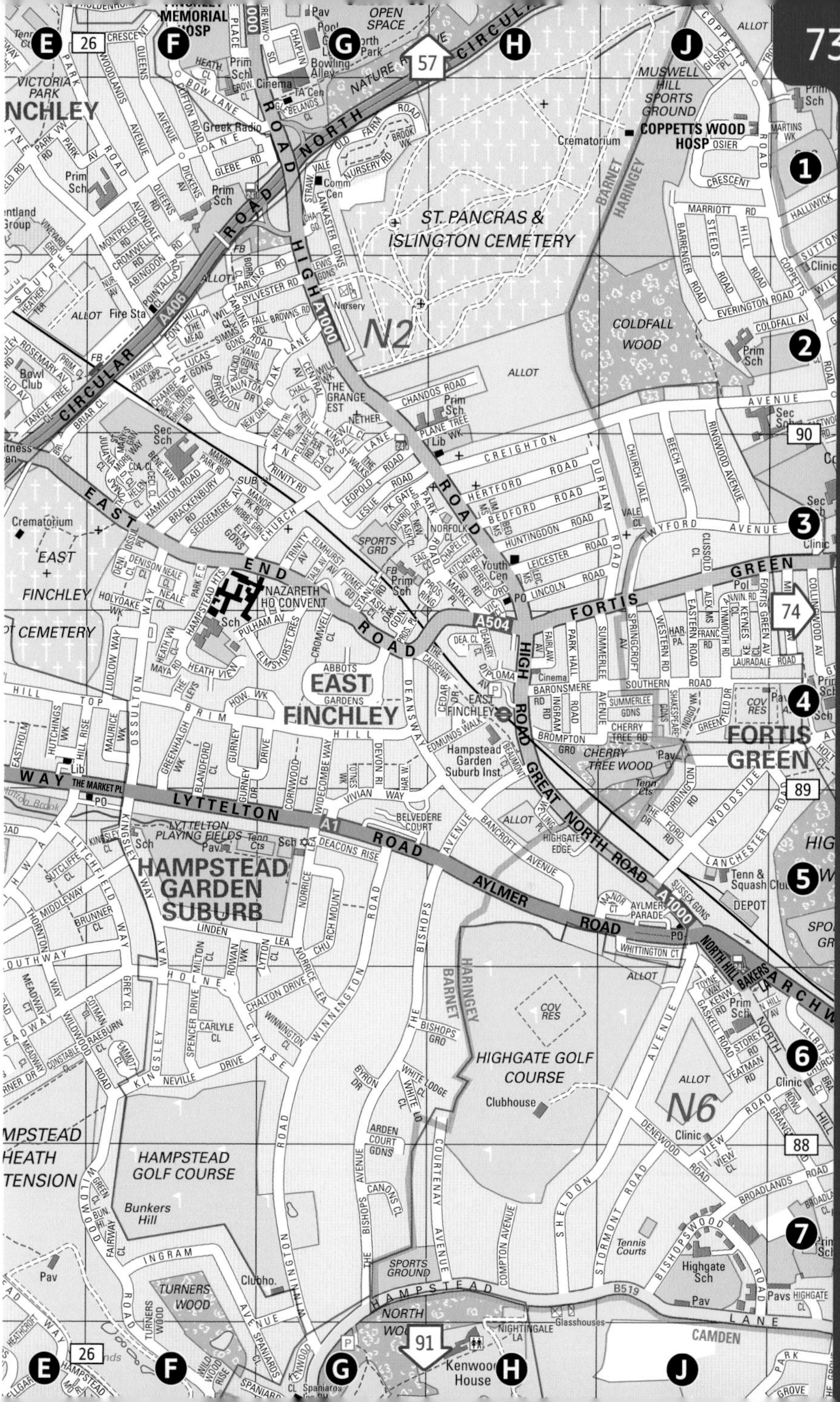
E
F
G
H
J
26
57
74
89
88
90
91
1
2
3
4
5
6
7
MEMORIAL HOSP
OPEN SPACE
VICTORIA PARK
NCHLEY
NATURE RESERVE
NORTH CIRCULAR ROAD
COPPETTS WOOD HOSP
MUSWELL HILL SPORTS GROUND
Crematorium
ST. PANCRAS & ISLINGTON CEMETERY
COLDFALL WOOD
ALLOT
N2
HIGH ROAD
A1000
A406
CIRCULAR
EAST END ROAD
CHURCH LANE
CREIGHTON AVENUE
TWYFORD AVENUE
FORTIS GREEN
A504
EAST FINCHLEY
CEMETERY
NAZARETH HO CONVENT
ABBOTS GARDENS
EAST FINCHLEY
Hampstead Garden Suburb Inst.
GREAT NORTH ROAD
CHERRY TREE WOOD
FORTIS GREEN
LYTTELTON ROAD
A1
LYTTELTON PLAYING FIELDS
HAMPSTEAD GARDEN SUBURB
AYLMER ROAD
HARINGEY
BARNET
HIGHGATE GOLF COURSE
Clubhouse
COV RES
N6
HAMPSTEAD HEATH EXTENSION
HAMPSTEAD GOLF COURSE
Bunkers Hill
TURNERS WOOD
SPORTS GROUND
HAMPSTEAD LANE
B519
Kenwood House
Highgate Sch
Tennis Courts
CAMDEN
Glasshouses
NIGHTINGALE LA

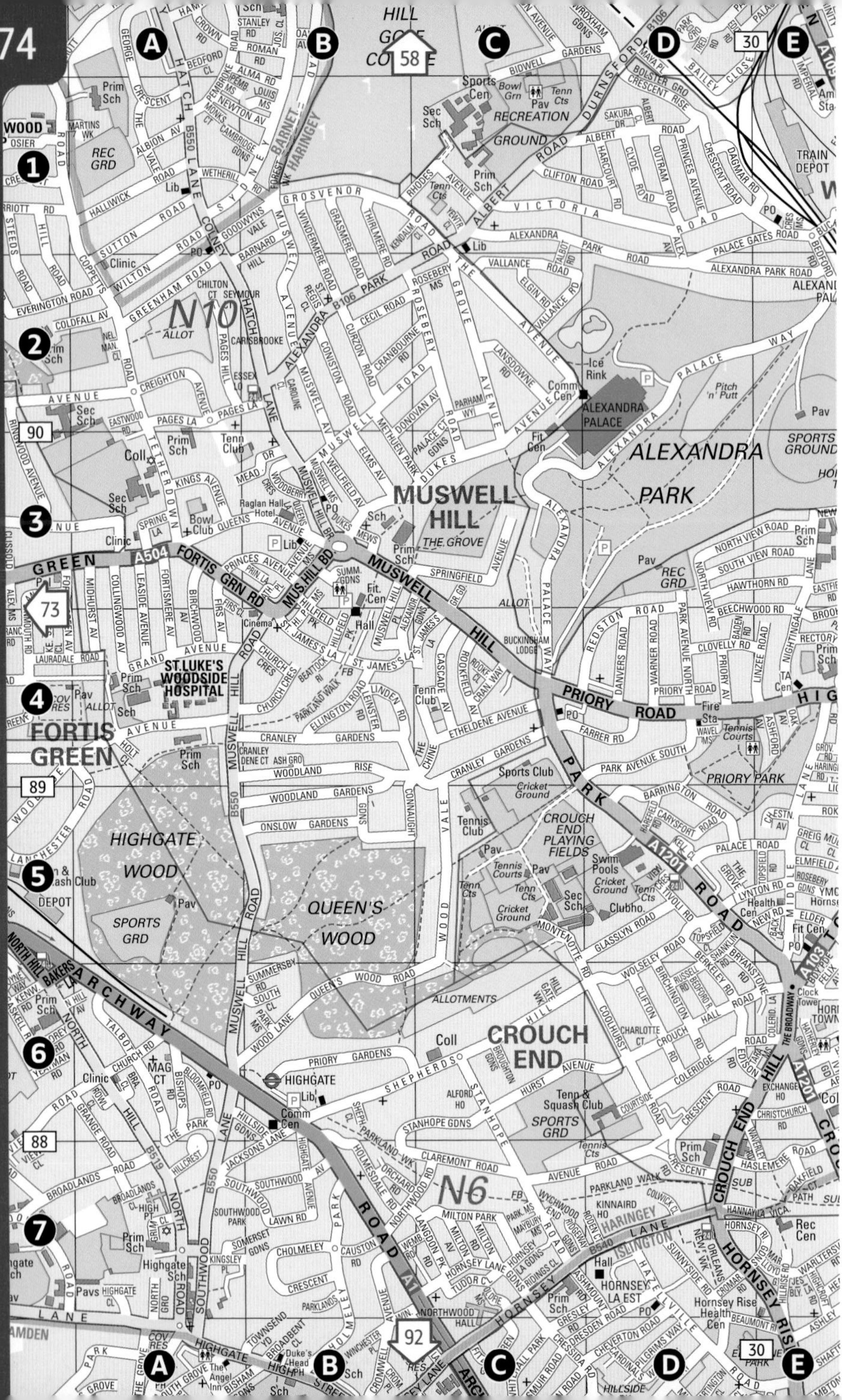
A
B
C
D
E
58
30
1
2
3
4
5
6
7
90
89
88
73
92
N10
N6
MUSWELL HILL
ALEXANDRA PALACE
ALEXANDRA PARK
FORTIS GREEN
HIGHGATE WOOD
QUEEN'S WOOD
CROUCH END
CROUCH END PLAYING FIELDS
PRIORY PARK
RECREATION GROUND
ST.LUKE'S WOODSIDE HOSPITAL
HIGHGATE
HARINGEY
ISLINGTON
CAMDEN
TRAIN DEPOT
MUSWELL HILL ROAD
MUSWELL HILL
FORTIS GRN RD
PRIORY ROAD
PARK ROAD
ARCHWAY ROAD
ALEXANDRA PARK ROAD
PALACE GATES ROAD
VICTORIA ROAD
DURNSFORD ROAD
COLNEY HATCH LANE
GROSVENOR ROAD
ALEXANDRA PALACE WAY
HORNSEY LANE
CROUCH END HILL
HORNSEY RISE
SHEPHERDS HILL
WOOD VALE
THE BROADWAY
A504
A1201
B550
B106
B540
B519
A1
A103

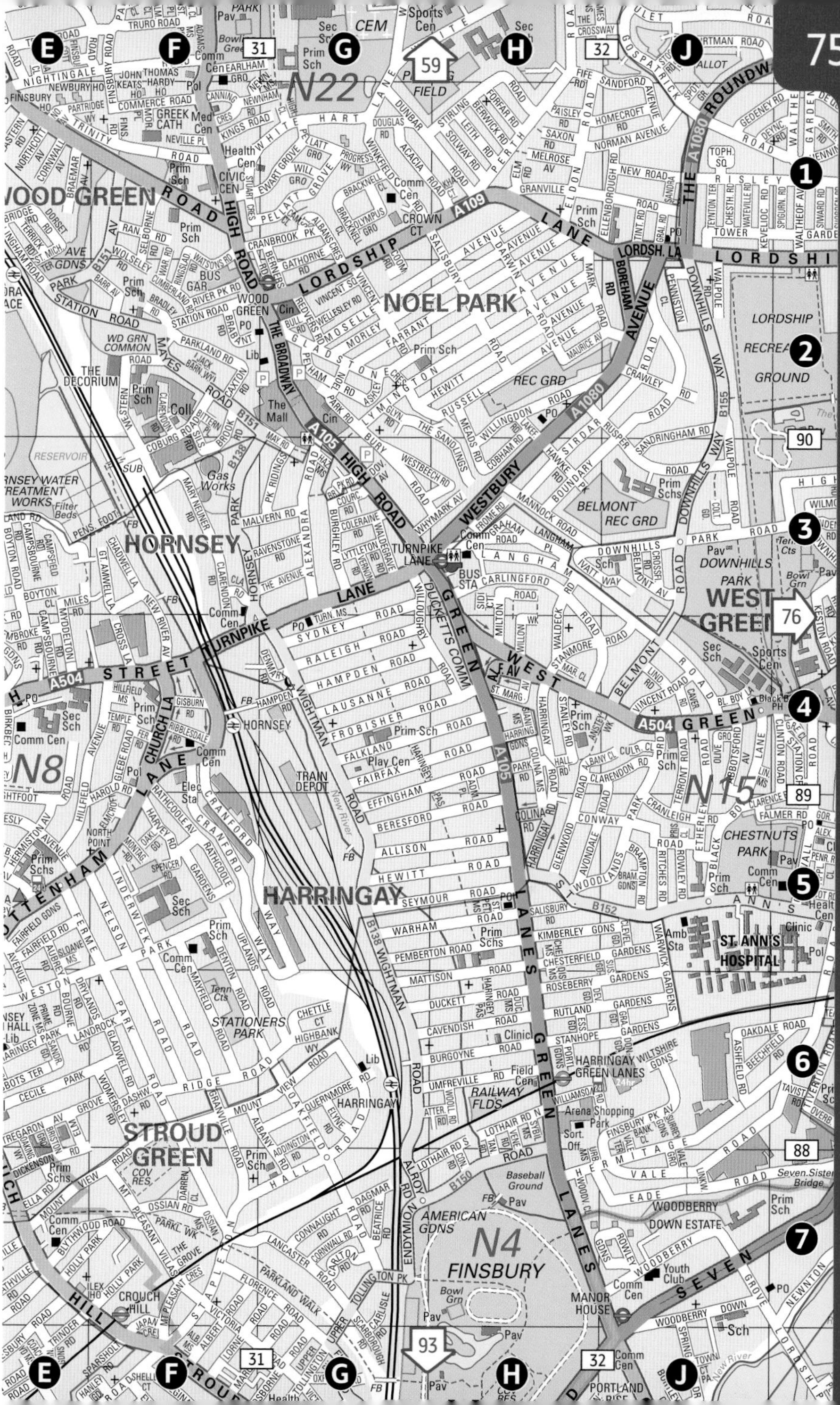
E
F
G
H
J
31
32
59
N22
WOOD GREEN
NOEL PARK
LORDSHIP RECREATION GROUND
HORNSEY
WEST GREEN
76
90
89
88
N8
N15
HARRINGAY
STROUD GREEN
N4
FINSBURY
93
CROUCH HILL
MANOR HOUSE
HARRINGAY GREEN LANES
TURNPIKE LANE
ST ANN'S HOSPITAL
CHESTNUTS PARK
DOWNHILLS PARK
BELMONT REC GRD
STATIONERS PARK
AMERICAN GDNS
RAILWAY FLDS
THE DECORIUM
The Mall
HORNSEY WATER TREATMENT WORKS
RESERVOIR
Gas Works
TRAIN DEPOT
WOODBERRY DOWN ESTATE
Seven Sisters Bridge
1
2
3
4
5
6
7

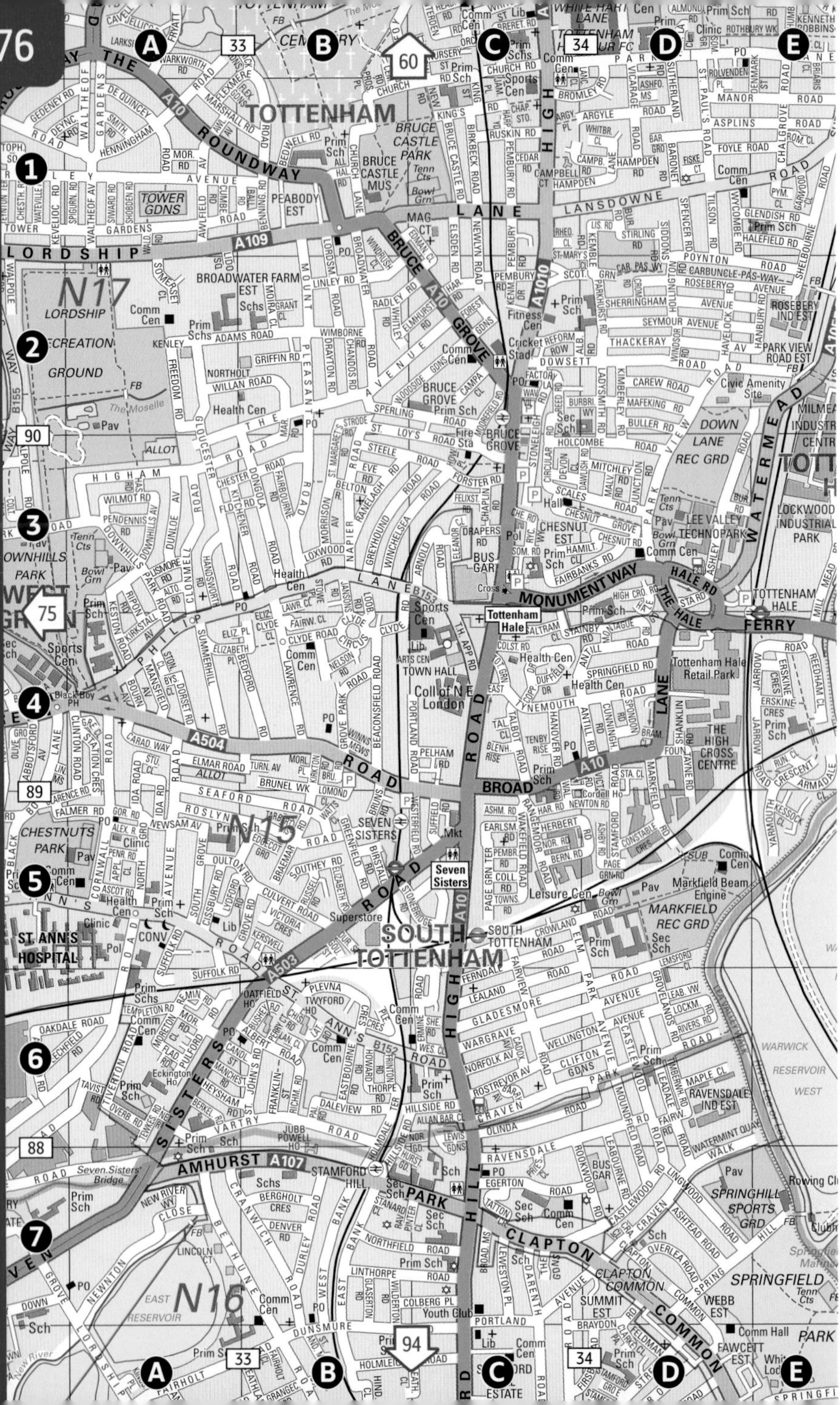
A
B
C
D
E
1
2
3
4
5
6
7
33
34
60
75
88
89
90
94
TOTTENHAM
BRUCE CASTLE PARK
BRUCE CASTLE MUS
TOWER GDNS
PEABODY EST
THE ROUNDWAY
A10
LORDSHIP LANE
A109
BROADWATER FARM EST
N17
LORDSHIP RECREATION GROUND
The Moselle
BRUCE GROVE
TOTTENHAM HOTSPUR FC
WHITE HART LANE
HIGH ROAD
A1010
LANSDOWNE ROAD
PARK VIEW ROAD EST
ROSEBERY IND EST
DOWN LANE REC GRD
LEE VALLEY TECHNOPARK
WATERMEAD WAY
LOCKWOOD INDUSTRIAL PARK
TOTTENHAM HALE
FERRY LANE
MONUMENT WAY
Tottenham Hale
Tottenham Hale Retail Park
THE HIGH CROSS CENTRE
CHESNUT EST
DOWNHILLS PARK
WEST GREEN
PHILIP LANE
TOWN HALL
Coll of N E London
BROAD LANE
A504
WEST GREEN ROAD
N15
SEVEN SISTERS
Seven Sisters
SEVEN SISTERS ROAD
A503
SOUTH TOTTENHAM
CHESTNUTS PARK
ST ANN'S HOSPITAL
ST ANN'S ROAD
B152
MARKFIELD REC GRD
Markfield Beam Engine
WARWICK RESERVOIR WEST
RAVENSDALE IND EST
SPRINGHILL SPORTS GRD
SPRINGFIELD PARK
AMHURST PARK
A107
STAMFORD HILL
CLAPTON COMMON
N16
EAST RESERVOIR
New River
SUMMIT EST
WEBB EST
FAWCETT EST
Seven Sisters' Bridge

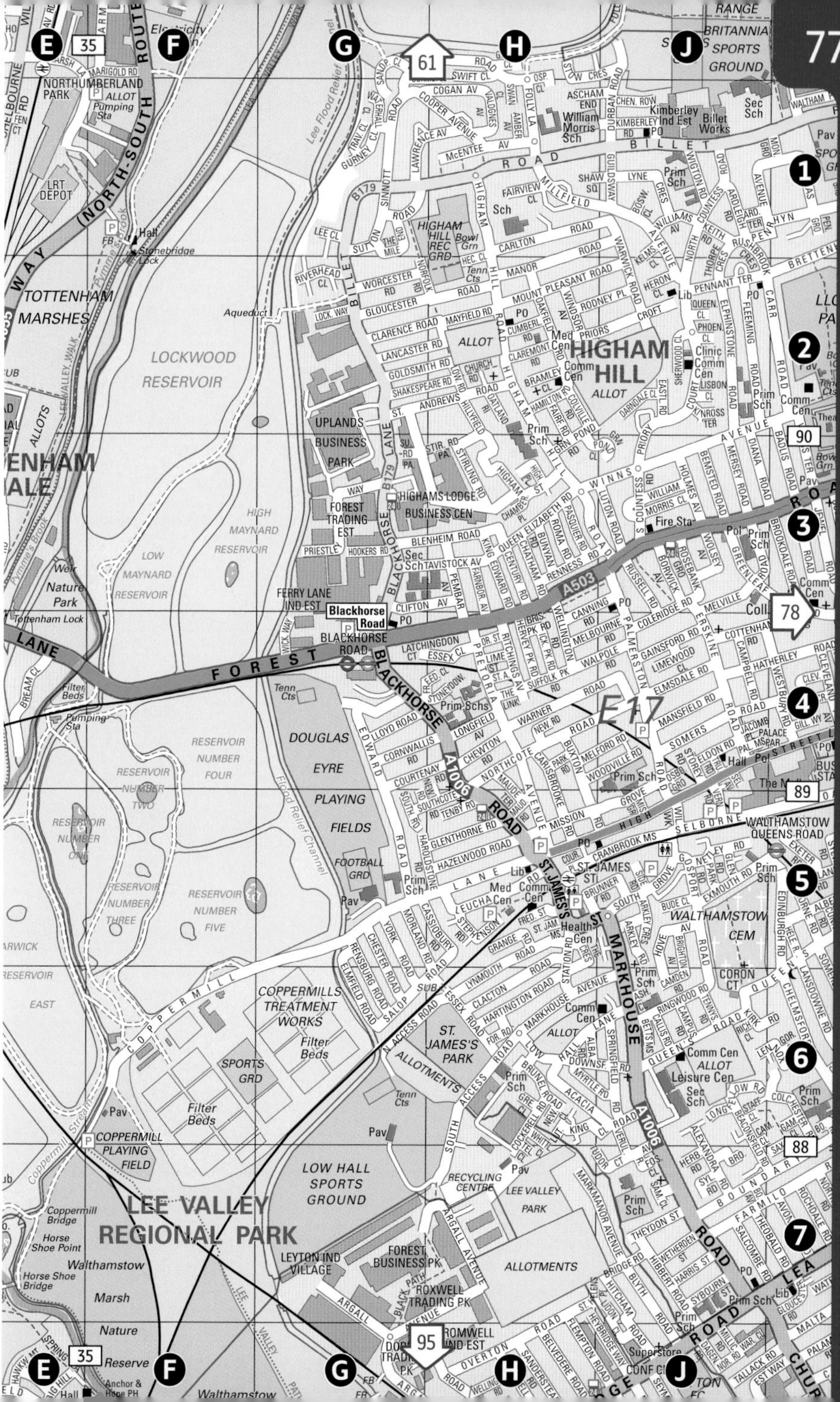
E
F
G
H
J
35
61
RANGE
BRITANNIA SPORTS GROUND
NORTHUMBERLAND PARK
ALLOT
Pumping Sta
LRT DEPOT
(NORTH-SOUTH ROUTE)
WAY
Stonebridge Lock
TOTTENHAM MARSHES
LOCKWOOD RESERVOIR
Aqueduct
Lee Flood Relief Channel
HIGH MAYNARD RESERVOIR
LOW MAYNARD RESERVOIR
Weir
Nature Park
Tottenham Lock
LANE
FOREST
Filter Beds
Pumping Sta
RESERVOIR NUMBER FOUR
RESERVOIR NUMBER TWO
RESERVOIR NUMBER ONE
RESERVOIR NUMBER THREE
RESERVOIR NUMBER FIVE
DOUGLAS EYRE PLAYING FIELDS
FOOTBALL GRD
COPPERMILLS TREATMENT WORKS
Filter Beds
SPORTS GRD
COPPERMILL PLAYING FIELD
LEE VALLEY REGIONAL PARK
Coppermill Bridge
Horse Shoe Point
Horse Shoe Bridge
Walthamstow Marsh Nature Reserve
Anchor & Hope PH
LOW HALL SPORTS GROUND
RECYCLING CENTRE
LEE VALLEY PARK
LEYTON IND VILLAGE
FOREST BUSINESS PK
ROXWELL TRADING PK
CROMWELL IND EST
95
ALLOTMENTS
ST. JAMES'S PARK
ALLOTMENTS
UPLANDS BUSINESS PARK
HIGHAMS LODGE BUSINESS CEN
FOREST TRADING EST
FERRY LANE IND EST
Blackhorse Road
BLACKHORSE ROAD
BLACKHORSE LANE
HIGHAM HILL REC GRD
HIGHAM HILL
ALLOT
Kimberley Ind Est
Billet Works
William Morris Sch
BILLET ROAD
A503
E17
A1006
BLACKHORSE ROAD
ST. JAMES'S ST
MARKHOUSE ROAD
HIGH ST
WALTHAMSTOW QUEENS ROAD
WALTHAMSTOW CEM
Leisure Cen
78
1
2
3
4
5
6
7
88
89
90
LEA BRIDGE ROAD
Superstore

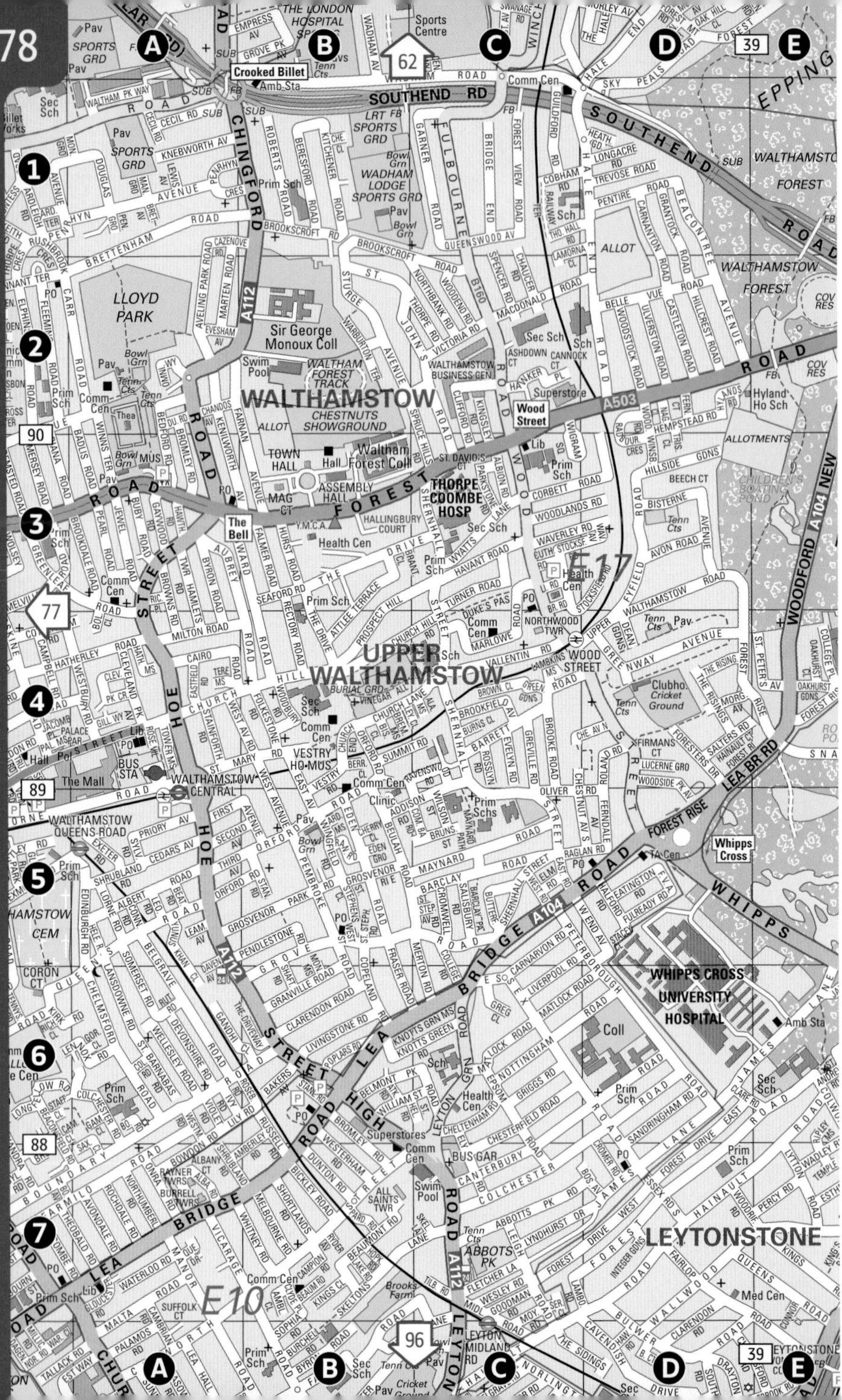
A
B
C
D
E
1
2
3
4
5
6
7
62
90
77
89
88
96
39
THE LONDON HOSPITAL SPORTS
Sports Centre
Crooked Billet
Amb Sta
SOUTHEND RD
SOUTHEND ROAD
EPPING
WALTHAMSTOW FOREST
CHINGFORD ROAD
A112
LLOYD PARK
Sir George Monoux Coll
WALTHAM FOREST TRACK
WALTHAMSTOW
CHESTNUTS SHOWGROUND
TOWN HALL
Waltham Forest Coll
ASSEMBLY HALL
FOREST ROAD
A503
Wood Street
THORPE COOMBE HOSP
The Bell
E17
UPPER WALTHAMSTOW
WADHAM LODGE SPORTS GRD
WALTHAMSTOW BUSINESS CEN
WOODFORD NEW ROAD
A104
The Mall
BUS STA
WALTHAMSTOW CENTRAL
WALTHAMSTOW QUEENS ROAD
HOE STREET
LEA BRIDGE ROAD
FOREST RISE
Whipps Cross
WHIPPS CROSS UNIVERSITY HOSPITAL
WHIPPS CROSS ROAD
HIGH ROAD
LEYTON
LEYTONSTONE
E10
LEYTON MIDLAND RD
ALL SAINTS TWR
Brooks Farm
ABBOTS PK
CHILDREN'S BOATING POND
ALLOTMENTS
Hyland Ho Sch
Clubho. Cricket Ground
BURIAL GRD
VESTRY HO MUS
Superstores
Swim Pool
BUS GAR
Coll

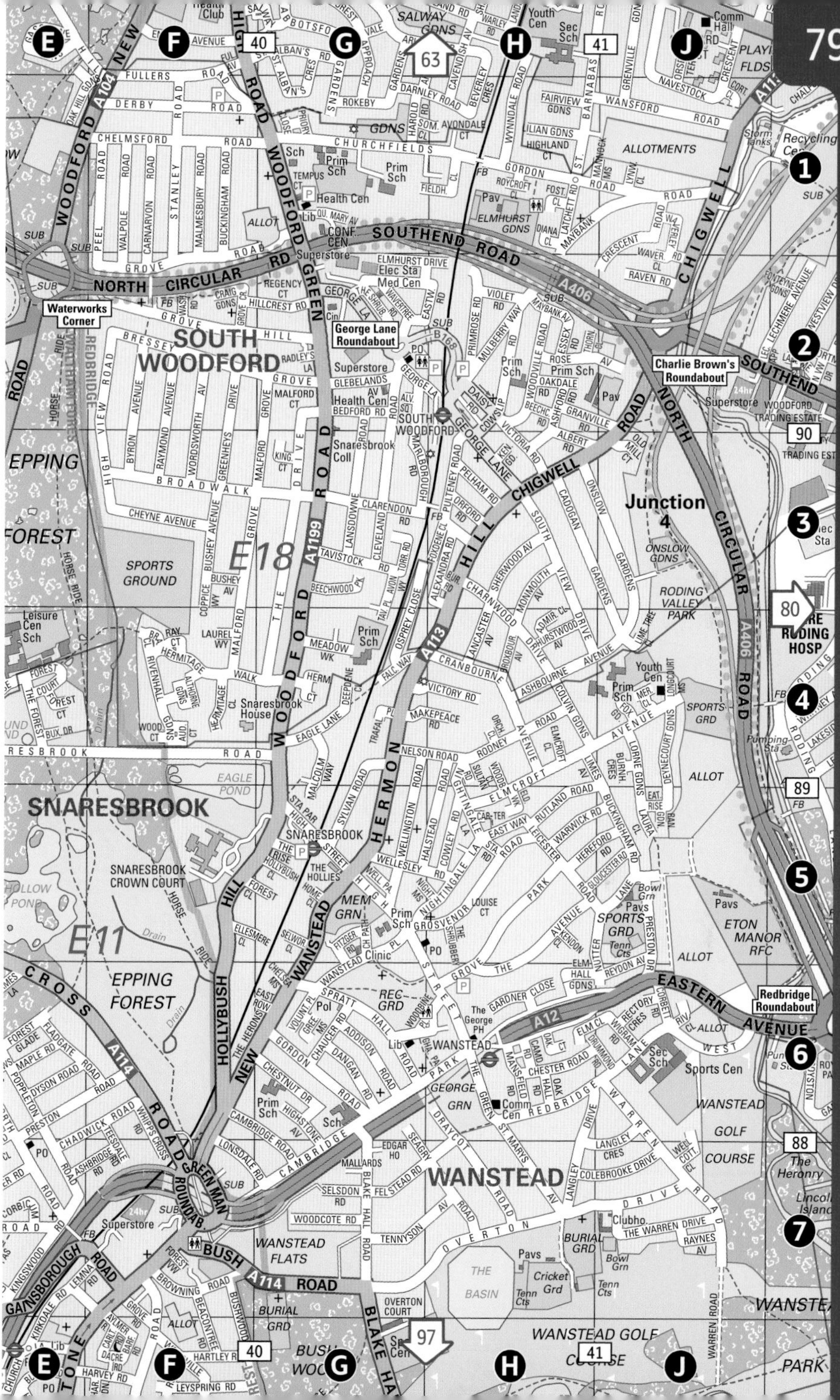
63
97
80
90
89
88
40
41
E
F
G
H
J
1
2
3
4
5
6
7
SOUTH WOODFORD
SNARESBROOK
WANSTEAD
E18
E11
EPPING FOREST
Junction 4
Waterworks Corner
George Lane Roundabout
Charlie Brown's Roundabout
Redbridge Roundabout
GREEN MAN ROUNDABOUT
NORTH CIRCULAR RD
SOUTHEND ROAD
A406
CHIGWELL ROAD
HIGH ROAD WOODFORD GREEN
WOODFORD NEW ROAD
A104
A1199
A113
A114
A12
EASTERN AVENUE
HERMON HILL
HOLLYBUSH HILL
NEW WANSTEAD
CROSS ROAD
BUSH ROAD
BLAKE HALL ROAD
SNARESBROOK ROAD
GEORGE LANE
CHIGWELL HILL
SNARESBROOK CROWN COURT
Snaresbrook House
EAGLE POND
HOLLOW POND
SPORTS GROUND
RODING VALLEY PARK
ONSLOW GDNS
ETON MANOR RFC
WANSTEAD GOLF COURSE
WANSTEAD FLATS
THE BASIN
RODING HOSP
Snaresbrook Coll
ALLOTMENTS
FULLERS ROAD
DERBY ROAD
CHELMSFORD ROAD
CHURCHFIELDS
GROVE ROAD
GROVE HILL
BROADWALK
CHEYNE AVENUE
EAGLE LANE
ELM CROFT
WANSTEAD PARK RD
REDBRIDGE LANE
WARREN ROAD
OVERTON DRIVE
CAMBRIDGE PARK
THE WARREN DRIVE
RAYNES AV
SALWAY GDNS
WANSFORD ROAD
GORDON ROAD
ELMHURST DRIVE
ELMHURST GDNS
SOUTH WOODFORD
SNARESBROOK
WANSTEAD
WOODFORD TRADING ESTATE
Superstore
Sports Cen
The Heronry
Lincoln Island
WANSTEAD PARK

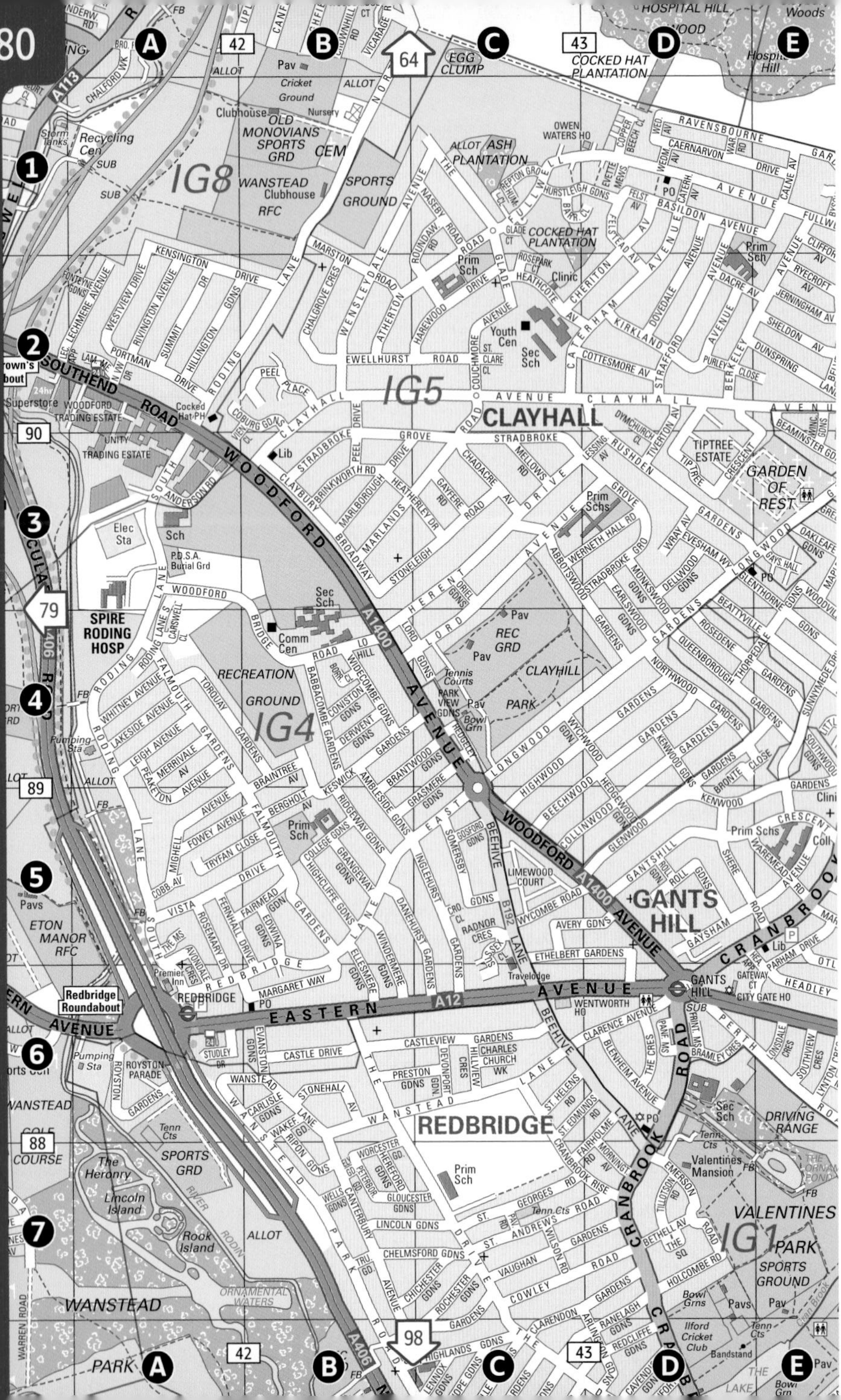
A
B
C
D
E
1
2
3
4
5
6
7
42
43
64
79
98
88
89
90
COCKED HAT PLANTATION
HOSPITAL HILL WOOD
Hospital Hill
Woods
EGG CLUMP
Cricket Ground
Clubhouse
OLD MONOVIANS SPORTS GRD
CEM
Nursery
Recycling Cen
Storm Tanks
IG8
WANSTEAD Clubhouse RFC
SPORTS GROUND
ALLOT
ASH PLANTATION
OWEN WATERS HO
RAVENSBOURNE AVENUE
CAERNARVON DRIVE
FULLWELL AVENUE
BASILDON AVENUE
KENSINGTON DRIVE
WESTVIEW DRIVE
RIVINGTON AVENUE
SUMMIT DR
HILLINGTON GDNS
PORTMAN DRIVE
RODING LANE
LECHMERE AVENUE
MARSTON ROAD
CHALGROVE CRES
WENSLEYDALE AVENUE
ATHERTON ROAD
HAREWOOD DRIVE
NASEBY ROAD
Prim Sch
Clinic
Youth Cen
Sec Sch
EWELLHURST ROAD
COUCHMORE AVENUE
CATERHAM AVENUE
KIRKLAND AV
DOVEDALE AVENUE
COTTESMORE AV
STRAFFORD AV
DACRE AV
RYECROFT AV
JERNINGHAM AV
SHELDON AV
DUNSPRING LANE
IG5
CLAYHALL AVENUE
CLAYHALL
STRADBROKE GROVE
PEEL DRIVE
Lib
Superstore
WOODFORD TRADING ESTATE
UNITY TRADING ESTATE
Cocked Hat PH
SOUTHEND ROAD
WOODFORD AVENUE
A1400
Elec Sta
Sch
P.D.S.A. Burial Grd
SPIRE RODING HOSP
WOODFORD BRIDGE ROAD
Sec Sch
Comm Cen
REC GRD
CLAYHILL PARK
Pav
Tennis Courts
Bowl Grn
TIPTREE ESTATE
GARDEN OF REST
RUSHDEN GARDENS
WERNETH HALL RD
LONGWOOD GARDENS
NORTHWOOD GARDENS
RECREATION GROUND
IG4
RODING LANE SOUTH
WHITNEY AVENUE
LAKESIDE AVENUE
LEIGH AVENUE
TORQUAY GARDENS
FALMOUTH GARDENS
BRAINTREE AV
BERGHOLT AV
FOWEY AVENUE
TRYFAN CLOSE
Pumping Sta
Pavs
ETON MANOR RFC
VISTA DRIVE
REDBRIDGE LANE
Premier Inn
REDBRIDGE
MARGARET WAY
Redbridge Roundabout
EASTERN AVENUE
A12
A406
WOODFORD AVENUE
BEEHIVE LANE
B192
LIMEWOOD COURT
WYCOMBE ROAD
GANTS HILL
GANTS HILL
CRANBROOK ROAD
WENTWORTH HO
Travelodge
ETHELBERT GARDENS
PERTH ROAD
CITY GATE HO
HEADLEY
Lib
Prim Schs
Coll
ROYSTON PARADE
CASTLE DRIVE
CASTLEVIEW GARDENS
CHARLES CHURCH WK
WANSTEAD PARK AVENUE
REDBRIDGE
Prim Sch
Sec Sch
DRIVING RANGE
Valentines Mansion
VALENTINES PARK
IG1
SPORTS GROUND
Ilford Cricket Club
Bandstand
THE LAKE
Bowl Grns
WANSTEAD GOLF COURSE
The Heronry
Lincoln Island
Rook Island
RIVER RODING
ORNAMENTAL WATERS
WANSTEAD PARK
SPORTS GRD
Tenn Cts
WARREN ROAD

E
44
F
G
H
J
65
SPORTS GROUND
Schs
ALLOT
Clubho.
SPORTS GROUND
PLAYING
Pavs
Pitches
FOREST INDUSTRIAL PARK
BRACKEN INDUSTRIAL ESTATE
Sailing Centre
Tenn Cts
Forest Farm
FOREST
Sports Cen
FAIRLOP
FAIRLOP WATER
Pav
1
OAKSIDE CT
Fullwell Cross
Health Cen
Lib
Sec Sch
IG6
DRIVING RANGE
2
Swim Pool
PO
FAIRLOP WATERS GOLF COURSE
90
Riding School
PAINTER
BARKINGSIDE CEM
Superstore
Prim Sch
BARKINGSIDE REC GRD
MAG CT
Barnardo's
3
BARKINGSIDE
BARNARDOS VILLAGE
ALDBOROUGH HATCH
Aldborough Hall Farm
82
SPORTS GRD
Pav
Clubho.
BARKINGSIDE
Redbridge FC & Barkingside FC
ALLOT
A123
4
Aldborough Hatch Farm
Cran Brook
Superstore
89
A12
Comm Cen
Prim Schs
Clubho.
High Sch
NEWBURY PARK
5
FORD'S SPORTS GROUND
Bowl Grn
Amb Sta
Sports Cen
TA Cen
Health Cen
Tennis Courts
Tenn Club
SPORTS GROUND
NEWBURY PARK
MEMORIAL HTS
War Mem
Holiday Inn Exp.
The Avenue PH
EASTERN AVENUE
Superstores
SEVEN KINGS PARK
Bandstand
6
IG2
IG3
Bowl Grn
Tenn Cts
PO
88
Tenn Cts
SPORTS GRD
Clubho.
Prim Sch
7
REC GRD
Sec Sch
Pav
SEVEN KINGS
Seven Kings Water
MELBOURNE FIELD
99
Schs
E
44
F
G
H
J

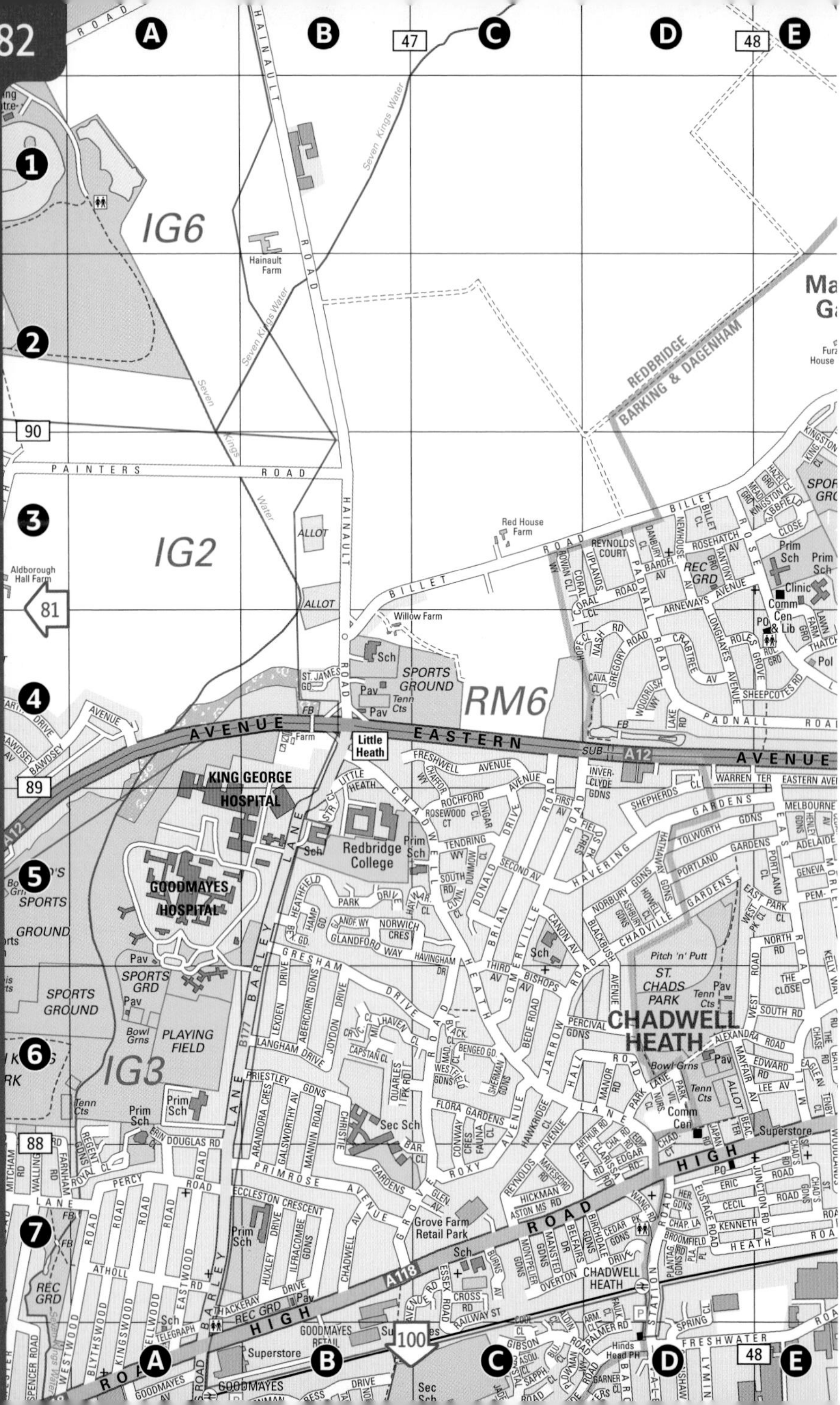
A
B
C
D
E
47
48
1
2
3
4
5
6
7
90
89
88
81
100
IG6
IG2
IG3
RM6
Hainault Farm
Seven Kings Water
HAINAULT ROAD
PAINTERS ROAD
ALLOT
Aldborough Hall Farm
Red House Farm
Willow Farm
BILLET ROAD
REDBRIDGE
BARKING & DAGENHAM
Furze House
SPORTS GROUND
Sch
Pav
Tenn Cts
ST. JAMES GD.
FB
Farm
Little Heath
EASTERN AVENUE
A12
KING GEORGE HOSPITAL
GOODMAYES HOSPITAL
Redbridge College
Prim Sch
SPORTS GRD
PLAYING FIELD
Bowl Grns
FRESHWELL AVENUE
ROCHFORD AV
ROSEWOOD CT
TENDRING WY
SECOND AV
THIRD AV
FIRST AV
HEATHFIELD
PARK DRIVE
NORWICH CRES
GLANDFORD WAY
HAVINGHAM DR
GRESHAM DRIVE
LEXDEN DRIVE
ABERCORN GDNS
JOYDON DRIVE
LANGHAM DRIVE
CAPSTAN CL
BENGEO GD.
WESTFIELD GDNS
FLORA GARDENS
CONWAY CRES
FAUNA CL
ROXY AVENUE
PRIESTLEY GDNS
ARANDORA CRES
GALSWORTHY AV
MANNIN ROAD
CHRISTIE GARDENS
Sec Sch
PRIMROSE AVENUE
ECCLESTON CRESCENT
HUXLEY DRIVE
ILFRACOMBE GDNS
CHADWELL AV
Grove Farm Retail Park
BARLEY LANE
B177
SOMERVILLE ROAD
BRIAN ROAD
DONALD DRIVE
BISHOPS ROAD
BEDE ROAD
JARROW ROAD
CANON AV
HAVERING GARDENS
TOLWORTH GDNS
PORTLAND GARDENS
CHADVILLE GARDENS
NORBURY GDNS
ASHBURY GDNS
HOWELL CL
HATHAWAY GDNS
BLACKBUSH AVENUE
SHEPHERDS CL
WARREN TER
EASTERN AVENUE
MELBOURNE
Pitch 'n' Putt
ST. CHADS PARK
CHADWELL HEATH
PERCIVAL GDNS
MANOR RD
HALL
PARK LANE
Comm Cen
Superstore
HIGH ROAD
ALEXANDRA ROAD
EDWARD RD
LEE AV
MAYFAIR AV
ALLOT
WEST ROAD
EAST ROAD
NORTH RD
SOUTH RD
THE CLOSE
REYNOLDS COURT
UPLANDS
CORAL CL
PADNALL ROAD
DANBURY CL
NEWHOUSE AV
BARDFIELD AV
REC GRD
ROSEHATCH AV
TANTONY GRO
ARNEWAYS AVENUE
CRABTREE AV
LONGHAYES AVENUE
ROLES GROVE
SHEEPCOTES RD
PADNALL ROAD
GREGORY ROAD
NASH RD
WOODRUSH WY
LAKE RD
KINGSTON CL
Prim Sch
Clinic
Comm Cen & Lib
PO
Pol
SPORTS GRD
HAWKRIDGE CL
REYNOLDS AVENUE
MAYESFORD RD
HICKMAN RD
ASTON MS RD
ARTHUR RD
CLARISSA RD
EDGAR RD
ERIC ROAD
CECIL ROAD
KENNETH RD
EUSTACE ROAD
JUNCTION RD W
BROOMFIELD
HEATH ROAD
MONTPELIER GDNS
MANSTED GDNS
BELFAIRS DR
BIRCHDALE GDNS
CEDAR PK GDNS
OVERTON DRIVE
CHADWELL HEATH
STATION ROAD
ESSEX ROAD
CROSS RD
RAILWAY ST
SPRING CL
FRESHWATER ROAD
GIBSON CL
PALMER RD
Hinds Head PH
A118
HIGH ROAD
GOODMAYES RETAIL PARK
Superstore
REC GRD
THACKERAY DRIVE
TELEGRAPH
PERCY ROAD
DOUGLAS RD
ROYAL CL
REGENT GDNS
FARNHAM RD
WALLINGTON RD
MITCHAM RD
ATHOLL RD
EASTWOOD RD
KINGSWOOD
BLYTHSWOOD
WESTWOOD
ELLWOOD
SPENCER ROAD
GOODMAYES AV
GOODMAYES
Sec Sch
SPORTS GROUND
SPORTS GRD
GROUND

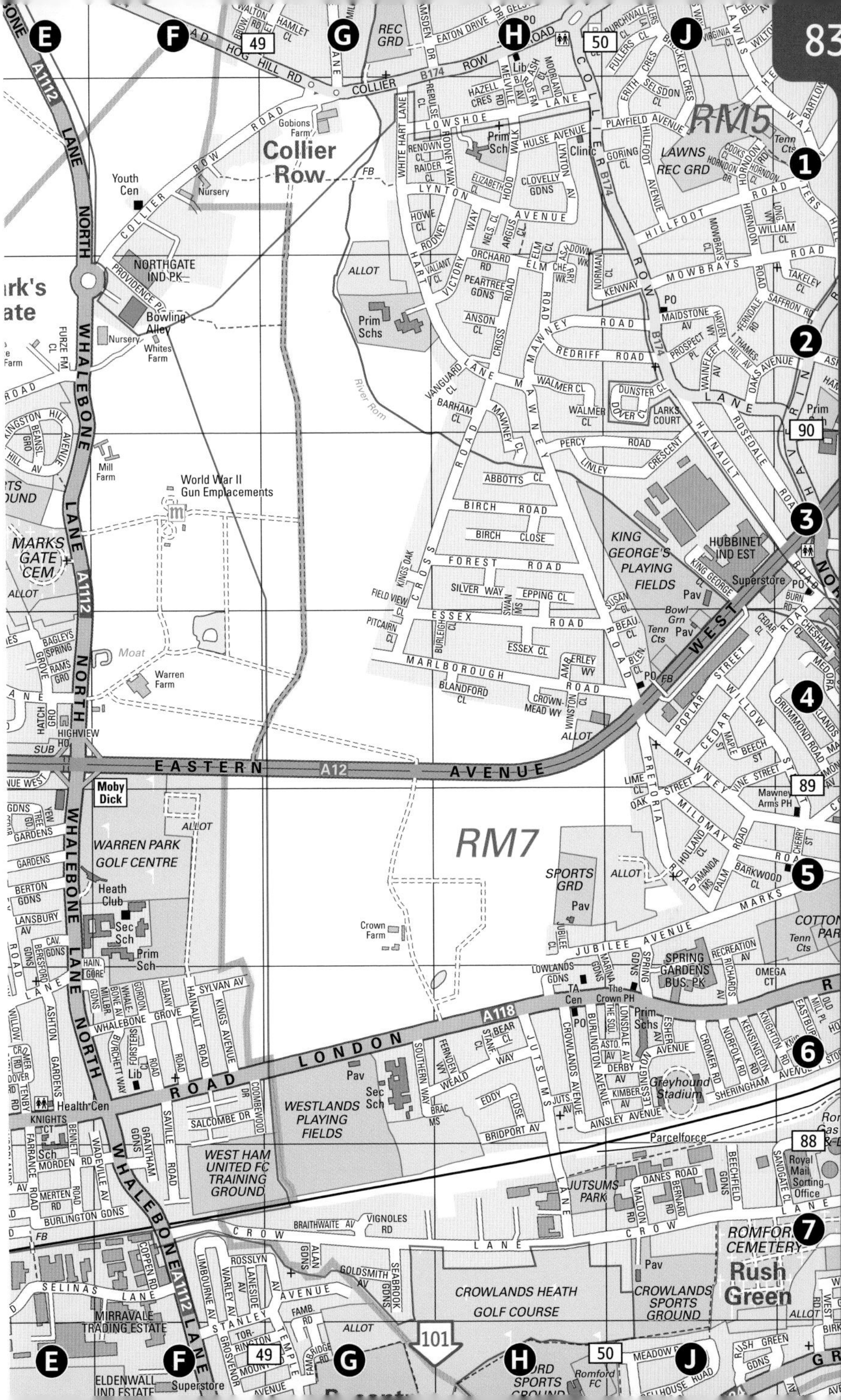

E
F
G
H
J
49
50
90
89
88
101
1
2
3
4
5
6
7
RM5
RM7
Collier Row
COLLIER ROW ROAD
HOG HILL RD
COLLIER ROW
B174
Gobions Farm
Youth Cen
Nursery
NORTHGATE IND PK
PROVIDENCE PL
Bowling Alley
Whites Farm
FURZE FM CL
KINGSTON HILL AVENUE
Mill Farm
World War II Gun Emplacements
MARKS GATE CEM
ALLOT
Moat
Warren Farm
BAGLEYS SPRING GROVE
RAMS GRO
HATCH GRO
HIGHVIEW HO
SUB
EASTERN AVENUE
A12
A1112
NORTH LANE
WHALEBONE LANE NORTH
Moby Dick
WARREN PARK GOLF CENTRE
Heath Club
Sec Sch
Prim Sch
REC GRD
EATON DRIVE
WALTON
HAMLET CL
LOWSHOE LANE
WHITE HART LANE
RENOWN CL
RAIDER CL
RODNEY WAY
HULSE AVENUE
Clinic
LYNTON AVENUE
ELIZABETH CL
HOOD WALK
CLOVELLY GDNS
HOWE CL
NELS. CL
ARGUS CL
ORCHARD RD
ELM CL
PEARTREE GDNS
VICTORY WAY
ANSON CL
CROSS ROAD
MAWNEY ROAD
REDRIFF ROAD
WALMER CL
DUNSTER CL
DOVER CL
LARKS COURT
VANGUARD CL
BARHAM CL
PERCY ROAD
LINLEY CRESCENT
ABBOTTS CL
BIRCH ROAD
BIRCH CLOSE
FOREST ROAD
SILVER WAY
EPPING CL
FIELD VIEW CL
ESSEX ROAD
PITCAIRN CL
BURLEIGH CL
ESSEX CL
MARLBOROUGH ROAD
ERLEY WY
BLANDFORD CL
CROWN-MEAD WY
WINSTON CL
Prim Schs
River Rom
KING GEORGE'S PLAYING FIELDS
Bowl Grn
Tenn Cts
Pav
HUBBINET IND EST
Superstore
KING GEORGE CL
NORTH STREET
WEST
NORMAN RD
KENWAY
MOWBRAYS ROAD
GORING CL
PLAYFIELD AVENUE
HILLFOOT AVENUE
HILLFOOT ROAD
LAWNS REC GRD
HORNDON RD
WILLIAM CL
TAKELEY CL
SAFFRON RD
MAIDSTONE AV
PROSPECT PL
HAYDEN WY
WAINFLEET AV
THAMES AV
OAKS AVENUE
HAINAULT ROAD
ROSEDALE ROAD
FERNDALE RD
ERITH CRES
SELSDON CL
BROCKLEY CRES
FULLERS CL
VIRGINIA CL
PO
Lib
POPLAR STREET
WILLOW ST
CEDAR ST
BEECH ST
MAPLE ST
PRETORIA ROAD
LIME CL
OAK STREET
MILDMAY ROAD
VINE STREET
Mawney Arms PH
HOLLAND CL
AMANDA MS
PALM
BARKWOOD CL
MARKS ROAD
SPORTS GRD
JUBILEE AVENUE
COTTONS PARK
RECREATION AV
SPRING GARDENS BUS. PK
OMEGA CT
LOWLANDS GDNS
TA Cen
The Crown PH
A118
LONDON ROAD
BEAR CL
STANLEY WAY
JUTSUMS LANE
CROWLANDS AVENUE
BURLINGTON AVENUE
LONSDALE AV
DERBY AV
KIMBER AV
AINSLEY AVENUE
Greyhound Stadium
SHERINGHAM AVENUE
CROMER RD
NORFOLK RD
KENSINGTON RD
KNIGHTON RD
EASTBURY RD
Parcelforce
Royal Mail Sorting Office
SANDGATE CL
DANES ROAD
BERNARD RD
MALDON RD
BEECHFIELD GDNS
JUTSUMS PARK
CROW LANE
ROMFORD CEMETERY
Rush Green
CROWLANDS HEATH GOLF COURSE
CROWLANDS SPORTS GROUND
WESTLANDS PLAYING FIELDS
SOUTHERN WAY
WEALD WAY
EDDY CLOSE
BRIDPORT AV
SALCOMBE DR
COOMBEWOOD DR
WEST HAM UNITED FC TRAINING GROUND
SAVILLE ROAD
GRANTHAM GDNS
WHALEBONE GROVE
SYLVAN AV
KINGS AVENUE
HAINAULT ROAD
ALBANY RD
GORDON RD
Crown Farm
Health Cen
KNIGHTS CT
MORDEN RD
MERTEN RD
WADEVILLE AV
BURLINGTON GDNS
BRAITHWAITE AV
VIGNOLES RD
SELINAS LANE
MIRRAVALE TRADING ESTATE
ELDENWALL IND ESTATE
ROSSLYN AV
LANESIDE AV
GOLDSMITH AVENUE
SEABROOK GDNS
STANLEY AV
TEMPLE AV
Romford FC
MEADOW RD
RUSH GREEN GDNS

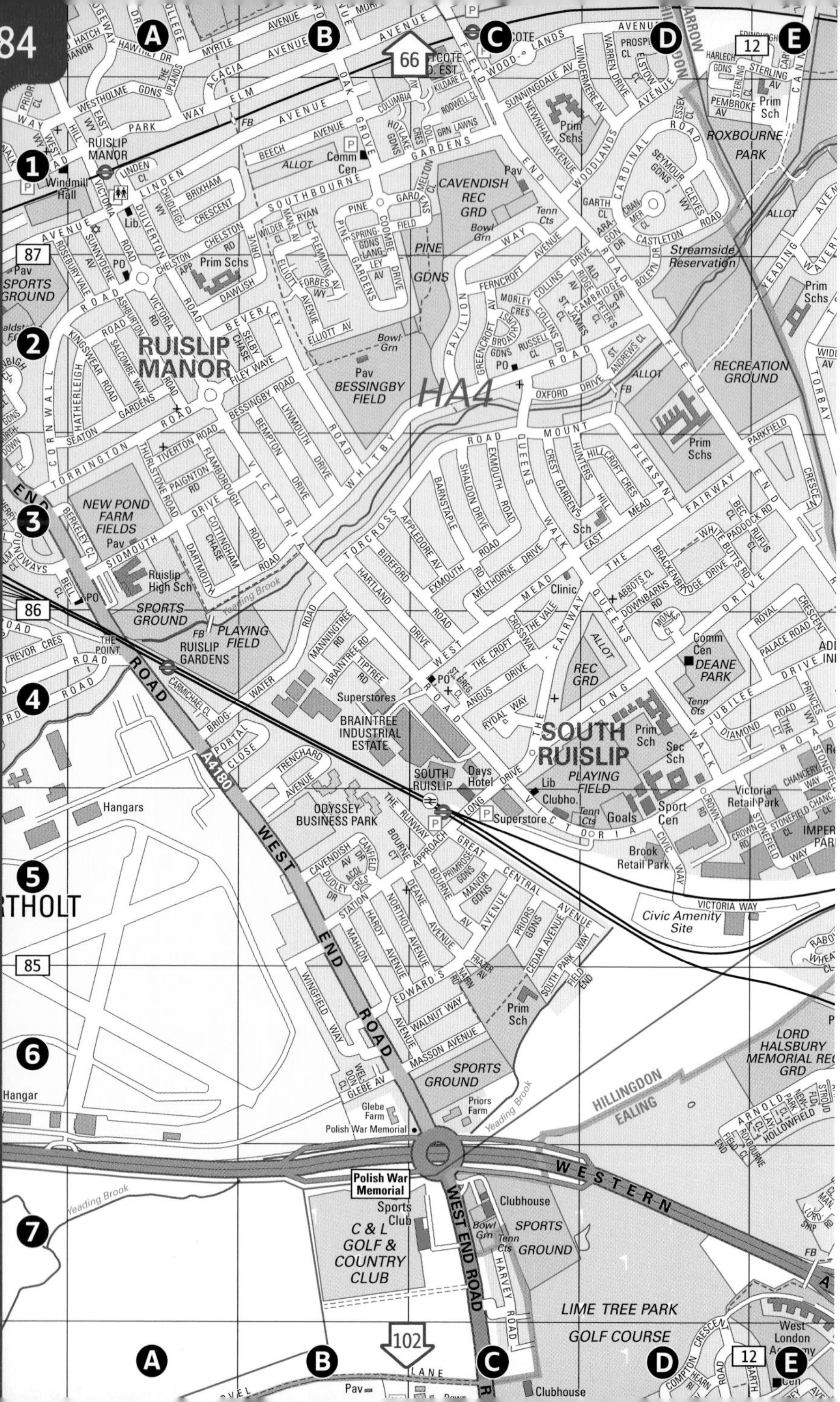

A
B
C
D
E
66
RUISLIP MANOR
RUISLIP
MANOR
Windmill Hall
Lib.
PO
Prim Schs
ALLOT
Comm Cen
CAVENDISH REC GRD
Pav
Tenn Cts
Bowl Grn
PINE GDNS
Streamside Reservation
ROXBOURNE PARK
Prim Sch
Prim Schs
RECREATION GROUND
87
SPORTS GROUND
BESSINGBY FIELD
HA4
NEW POND FARM FIELDS
Ruislip High Sch
86
SPORTS GROUND
PLAYING FIELD
RUISLIP GARDENS
Yeading Brook
Sch
Clinic
REC GRD
Superstores
BRAINTREE INDUSTRIAL ESTATE
SOUTH RUISLIP
Days Hotel
Lib
Clubho.
PLAYING FIELD
Goals
Sport Cen
Superstore
DEANE PARK
Victoria Retail Park
Brook Retail Park
Civic Amenity Site
ODYSSEY BUSINESS PARK
Hangars
A4180
WEST END ROAD
85
Hangar
SPORTS GROUND
Priors Farm
Glebe Farm
Polish War Memorial
LORD HALSBURY MEMORIAL REC GRD
HILLINGDON
EALING
WESTERN
Polish War Memorial
Sports Club
C & L GOLF & COUNTRY CLUB
Clubhouse
SPORTS GROUND
LIME TREE PARK
GOLF COURSE
West London Academy
102
12
Clubhouse
1
2
3
4
5
6
7

RAYNERS LANE
WEST HARROW
SOUTH HARROW
HA2
NORTHOLT
UB5
NORTHOLT PARK
ALEXANDRA PARK
NEWTON PARK WEST
NEWTON FM ECOLOGY PK
NORTHOLT RECREATION GRD
ISLIP MANOR PARK
ROXETH REC GRD
BELVUE PARK
BELVUE BUSINESS CENTRE
NORTHOLT TRADING ESTATE
KELVIN INDUSTRIAL ESTATE
GREENFORD PARK
EARLSMEAD STADIUM
Harrow Borough FC
Ruislip Retail Park
Target Roundabout
Air Traffic Radio Sta
ALEXANDRA AVENUE
A4090
NORTHOLT ROAD
A312
WHITTON AV W
MANDEVILLE ROAD
CHURCH ROAD
EASTCOTE LANE
SOMERVELL ROAD
ARUNDEL ROAD
RAYNERS LANE
VICTORIA ROAD
MALVERN AVENUE
ROXETH HILL
67
13
14
86
87
103
E
F
G
H
J
1
2
3
4
5
6
7

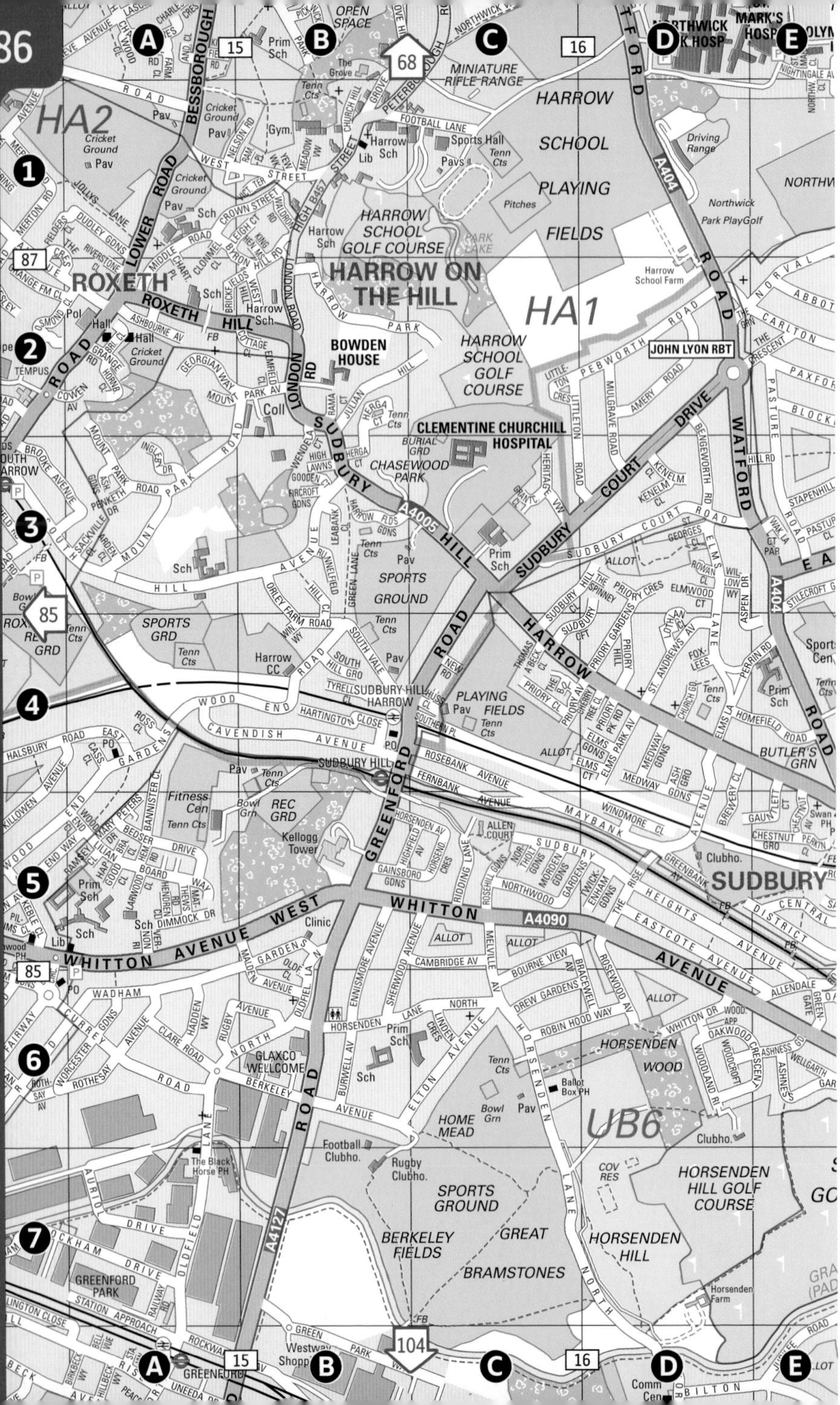
A
B
C
D
E
1
2
3
4
5
6
7
15
16
68
87
85
104
HA2
HA1
UB6
ROXETH
HARROW ON THE HILL
SUDBURY
BOWDEN HOUSE
CLEMENTINE CHURCHILL HOSPITAL
JOHN LYON RBT
HARROW SCHOOL PLAYING FIELDS
HARROW SCHOOL GOLF COURSE
MINIATURE RIFLE RANGE
OPEN SPACE
NORTHWICK PARK HOSP
ST MARK'S HOSP
Northwick Park PlayGolf
Driving Range
Harrow School Farm
PARK LAKE
CHASEWOOD PARK
BURIAL GRD
SPORTS GROUND
SPORTS GRD
PLAYING FIELDS
REC GRD
Kellogg Tower
Fitness Cen
Harrow CC
SUDBURY HILL HARROW
SUDBURY HILL
BUTLER'S GRN
HORSENDEN WOOD
HORSENDEN HILL GOLF COURSE
HORSENDEN HILL
Horsenden Farm
HOME MEAD
BERKELEY FIELDS
GREAT BRAMSTONES
GLAXCO WELLCOME
GREENFORD PARK
GREENFORD
Westway Shopp
The Black Horse PH
Ballot Box PH
Football Clubho.
Rugby Clubho.
COV RES
LOWER ROAD
BESSBOROUGH ROAD
WEST STREET
FOOTBALL LANE
CROWN STREET
HIGH STREET
LONDON ROAD
ROXETH HILL
SUDBURY HILL
MOUNT PARK ROAD
MOUNT PARK AV
HILL AVENUE
SOUTH HILL AVENUE
GREENFORD ROAD
HARROW ROAD
WATFORD ROAD
SUDBURY COURT DRIVE
SUDBURY COURT ROAD
PEBWORTH ROAD
WHITTON AVENUE WEST
WHITTON AVENUE EAST
EASTCOTE AVENUE
HORSENDEN LANE NORTH
HORSENDEN LANE
CAVENDISH AVENUE
WOOD END ROAD
WOOD END WAY
ROSEBANK AVENUE
FERNBANK AVENUE
MAYBANK AVENUE
STATION APPROACH
ROCKWARE AV
AURIOL DRIVE
ROCKHAM DRIVE
OLDFIELD LANE
BERKELEY AVENUE
ELTON AVENUE
NORTHWOOD GARDENS
RIDDING LANE
A404
A4005
A4090
A4127

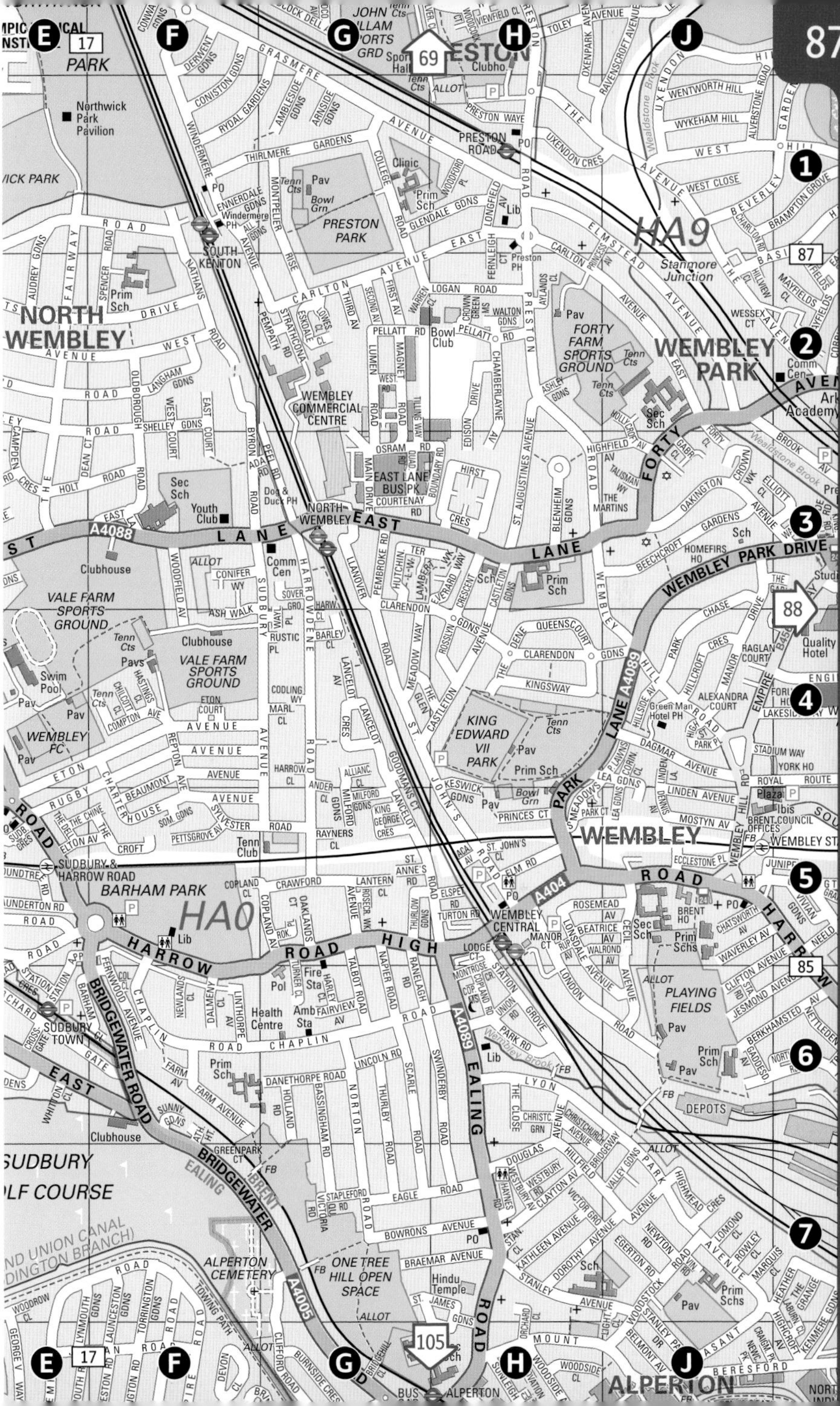
E
F
G
H
J
17
69
88
105
85
87
1
2
3
4
5
6
7
NORTH WEMBLEY
WEMBLEY PARK
WEMBLEY
ALPERTON
SUDBURY
HA9
HA0
PARK
Northwick Park Pavilion
PRESTON PARK
SOUTH KENTON
PRESTON ROAD
Stanmore Junction
WEMBLEY COMMERCIAL CENTRE
EAST LANE BUS PK
NORTH WEMBLEY
VALE FARM SPORTS GROUND
FORTY FARM SPORTS GROUND
KING EDWARD VII PARK
BARHAM PARK
WEMBLEY FC
WEMBLEY CENTRAL
SUDBURY & HARROW ROAD
SUDBURY TOWN
ALPERTON CEMETERY
ONE TREE HILL OPEN SPACE
PLAYING FIELDS
DEPOTS
Ark Academy
Quality Hotel
BRENT COUNCIL OFFICES
WEMBLEY STA
A4088
A4089
A404
A4005
EAST LANE
WEMBLEY PARK DRIVE
FORTY AVENUE
HARROW ROAD
HIGH ROAD
EALING ROAD
BRIDGEWATER ROAD
PRESTON ROAD
EAST AVENUE
CARLTON AVENUE
ELMSTEAD AVENUE
GRASMERE AVENUE
THIRLMERE GARDENS
WINDERMERE AVENUE
NATHANS ROAD
BYRON ROAD
SUDBURY AVENUE
HARROWDENE ROAD
LANCELOT ROAD
ST. JOHN'S ROAD
PARK LANE
CHAPLIN ROAD
EAGLE ROAD
STANLEY AVENUE
MOUNT PLEASANT
GRAND UNION CANAL (PADDINGTON BRANCH)
SUDBURY GOLF COURSE
Wealdstone Brook
Wembley Brook

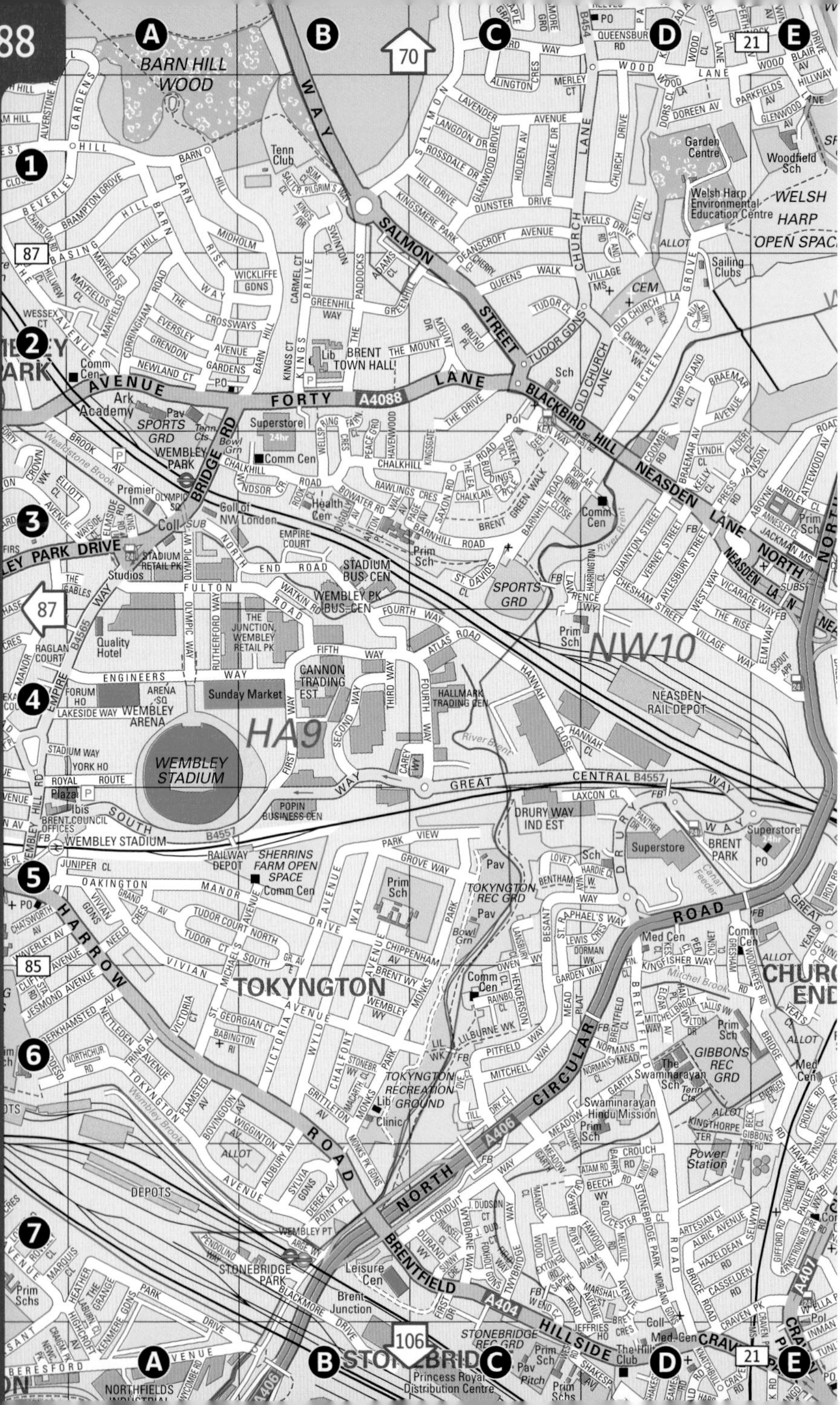
A
B
C
D
E
1
2
3
4
5
6
7
70
87
85
106
21
BARN HILL WOOD
Tenn Club
Garden Centre
Woodfield Sch
Welsh Harp Environmental Education Centre
WELSH HARP OPEN SPACE
Sailing Clubs
CEM
ALLOT
SALMON STREET
FORTY LANE
A4088
BLACKBIRD HILL
NEASDEN LANE
NEASDEN LANE NORTH
BRENT TOWN HALL
Lib
Superstore
Comm Cen
Ark Academy
SPORTS GRD
WEMBLEY PARK
BRIDGE RD
Premier Inn
Coll of NW London
WEMBLEY PARK DRIVE
STADIUM RETAIL PK
Studios
Quality Hotel
THE JUNCTION, WEMBLEY RETAIL PK
STADIUM BUS CEN
WEMBLEY PK BUS CEN
CANNON TRADING EST
HALLMARK TRADING CEN
Sunday Market
ENGINEERS WAY
WEMBLEY ARENA
WEMBLEY STADIUM
HA9
NW10
NEASDEN RAIL DEPOT
River Brent
GREAT CENTRAL WAY
B4557
DRURY WAY IND EST
BRENT PARK
POPIN BUSINESS CEN
Ibis
Plaza
BRENT COUNCIL OFFICES
SOUTH WAY
RAILWAY DEPOT
SHERRINS FARM OPEN SPACE
TOKYNGTON
TOKYNGTON REC GRD
TOKYNGTON RECREATION GROUND
HARROW ROAD
NORTH CIRCULAR ROAD
A406
GIBBONS REC GRD
Swaminarayan Hindu Mission
The Swaminarayan Sch
Power Station
CHURCH END
DEPOTS
STONEBRIDGE PARK
Brent Junction
Leisure Cen
BRENTFIELD
A404
HILLSIDE
STONEBRIDGE REC GRD
Princess Royal Distribution Centre
NORTHFIELDS INDUSTRIAL
A407
CRAVEN PARK

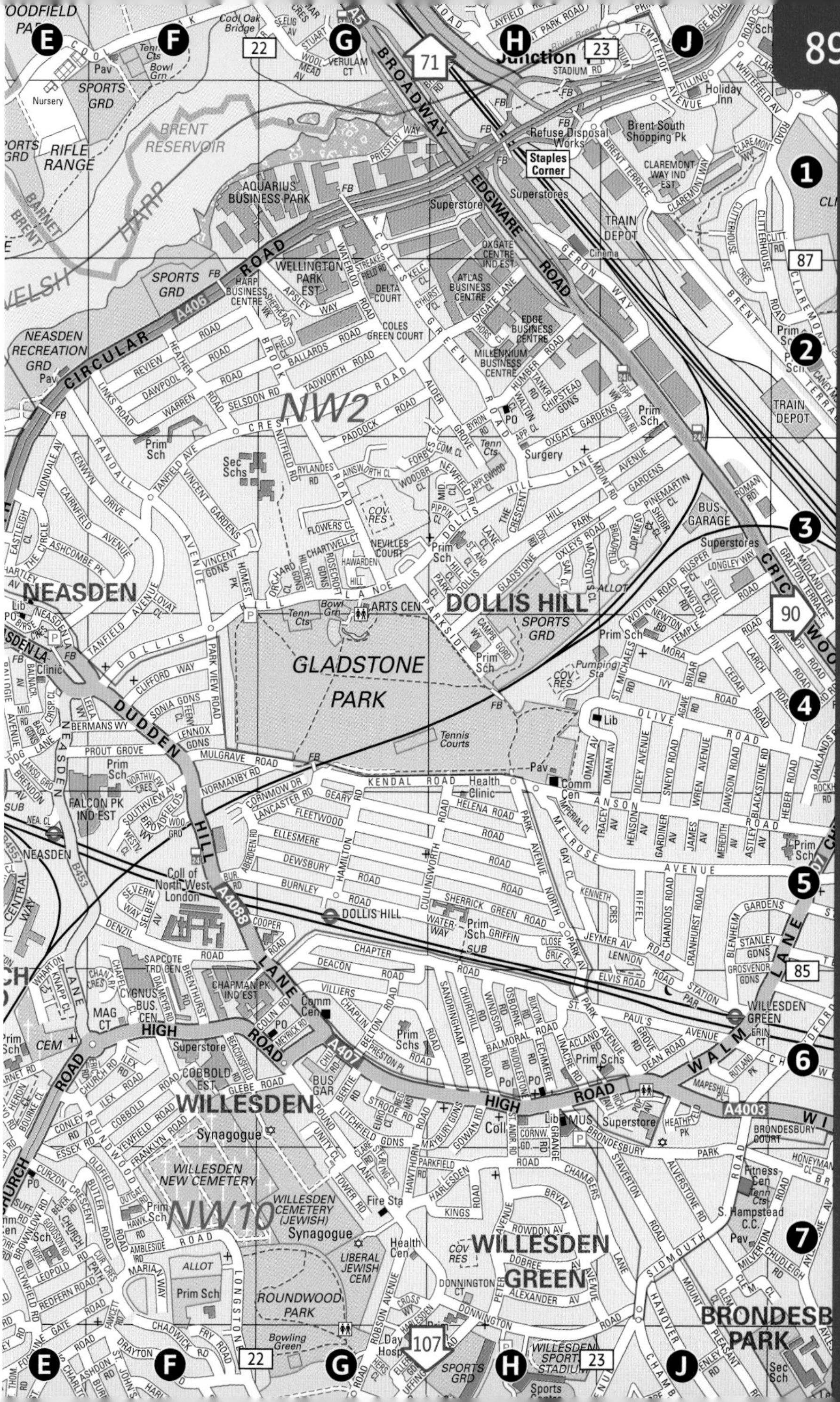

NW2
NW10
NEASDEN
DOLLIS HILL
WILLESDEN
WILLESDEN GREEN
BRONDESBURY PARK
GLADSTONE PARK
BRENT RESERVOIR
Staples Corner
Junction 1
BROADWAY
EDGWARE ROAD
CIRCULAR ROAD
A406
A5
A4088
A407
A4003
DUDDEN HILL LANE
HIGH ROAD
WALM LANE
DOLLIS HILL LANE
GERON WAY
NEASDEN RECREATION GRD
RIFLE RANGE
SPORTS GRD
AQUARIUS BUSINESS PARK
WELLINGTON PARK EST
HARP BUSINESS CENTRE
ATLAS BUSINESS CENTRE
OXGATE CENTRE IND EST
EDGE BUSINESS CENTRE
MILLENNIUM BUSINESS CENTRE
Brent South Shopping Pk
Refuse Disposal Works
CLAREMONT WAY IND EST
TRAIN DEPOT
BUS GARAGE
Holiday Inn
ARTS CEN
FALCON PK IND EST
Coll of North West London
DOLLIS HILL
NEASDEN
WILLESDEN GREEN
CHAPMAN PK IND EST
SAPCOTE TRD CEN
CYGNUS BUS. CEN
COBBOLD EST
WILLESDEN NEW CEMETERY
WILLESDEN CEMETERY (JEWISH)
LIBERAL JEWISH CEM
ROUNDWOOD PARK
WILLESDEN SPORTS STADIUM
S. Hampstead C.C.
E F G H J
1 2 3 4 5 6 7
22 23 71 87 85 90 107

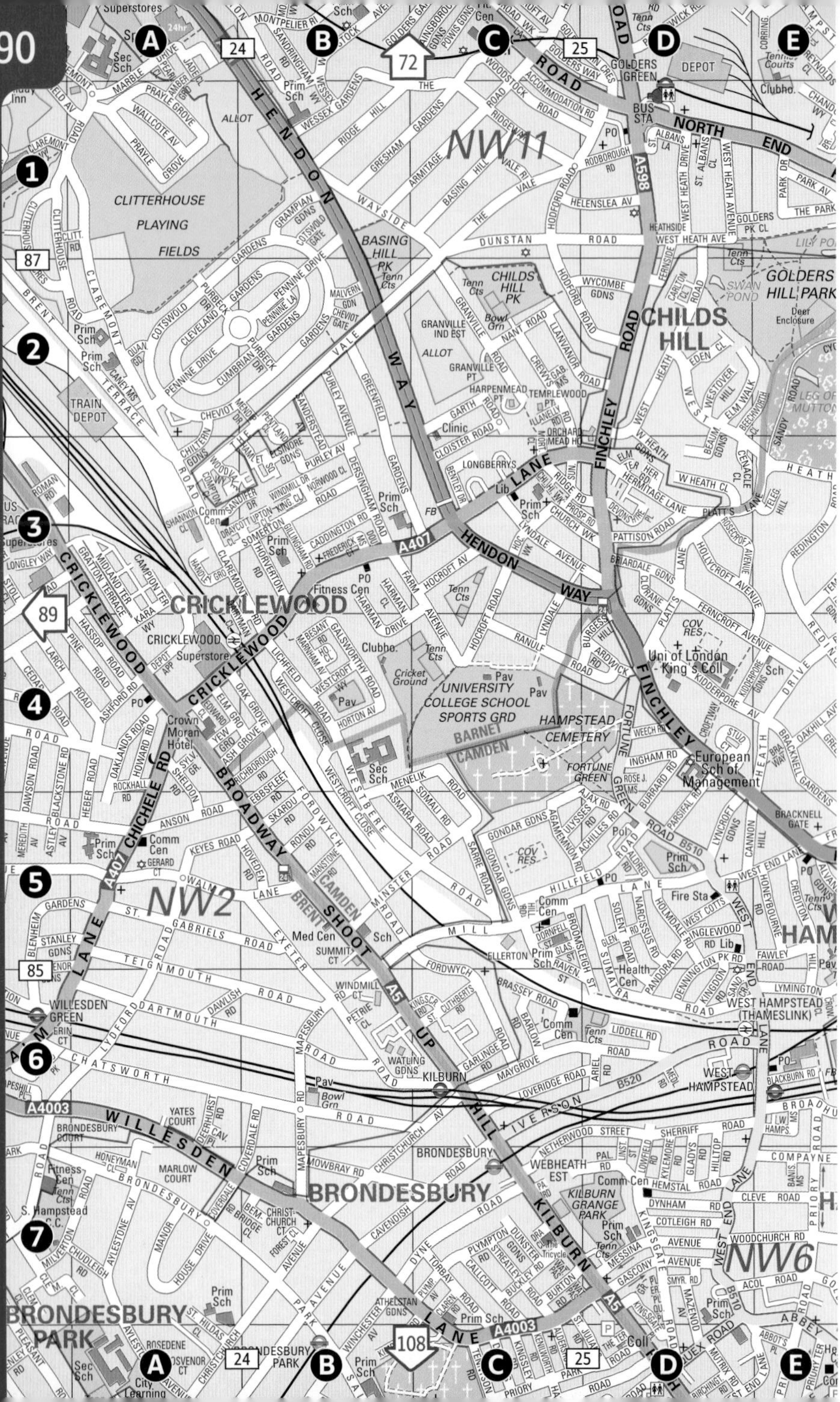
A
B
C
D
E
1
2
3
4
5
6
7
24
25
72
87
89
85
108
NW11
NW2
NW6
CRICKLEWOOD
CHILDS HILL
BRONDESBURY
BRONDESBURY PARK
CLITTERHOUSE PLAYING FIELDS
BASING HILL PK
CHILDS HILL PK
GOLDERS HILL PARK
UNIVERSITY COLLEGE SCHOOL SPORTS GRD
HAMPSTEAD CEMETERY
KILBURN GRANGE PARK
HENDON WAY
FINCHLEY ROAD
NORTH END ROAD
GOLDERS GREEN ROAD
CRICKLEWOOD LANE
CRICKLEWOOD BROADWAY
SHOOT UP HILL
KILBURN HIGH ROAD
WILLESDEN LANE
CHICHELE RD
WEST END LANE
MILL LANE
HILLFIELD LANE
FORTUNE GREEN ROAD
DUNSTAN ROAD
CLAREMONT ROAD
BRENT TERRACE
CRICKLEWOOD
WILLESDEN GREEN
KILBURN
WEST HAMPSTEAD
WEST HAMPSTEAD (THAMESLINK)
BRONDESBURY
BRONDESBURY PARK
GOLDERS GREEN
TRAIN DEPOT
DEPOT
Uni of London - King's Coll
European Sch of Management
A598
A407
A5
A4003
B510
B520
BARNET
CAMDEN
BRENT

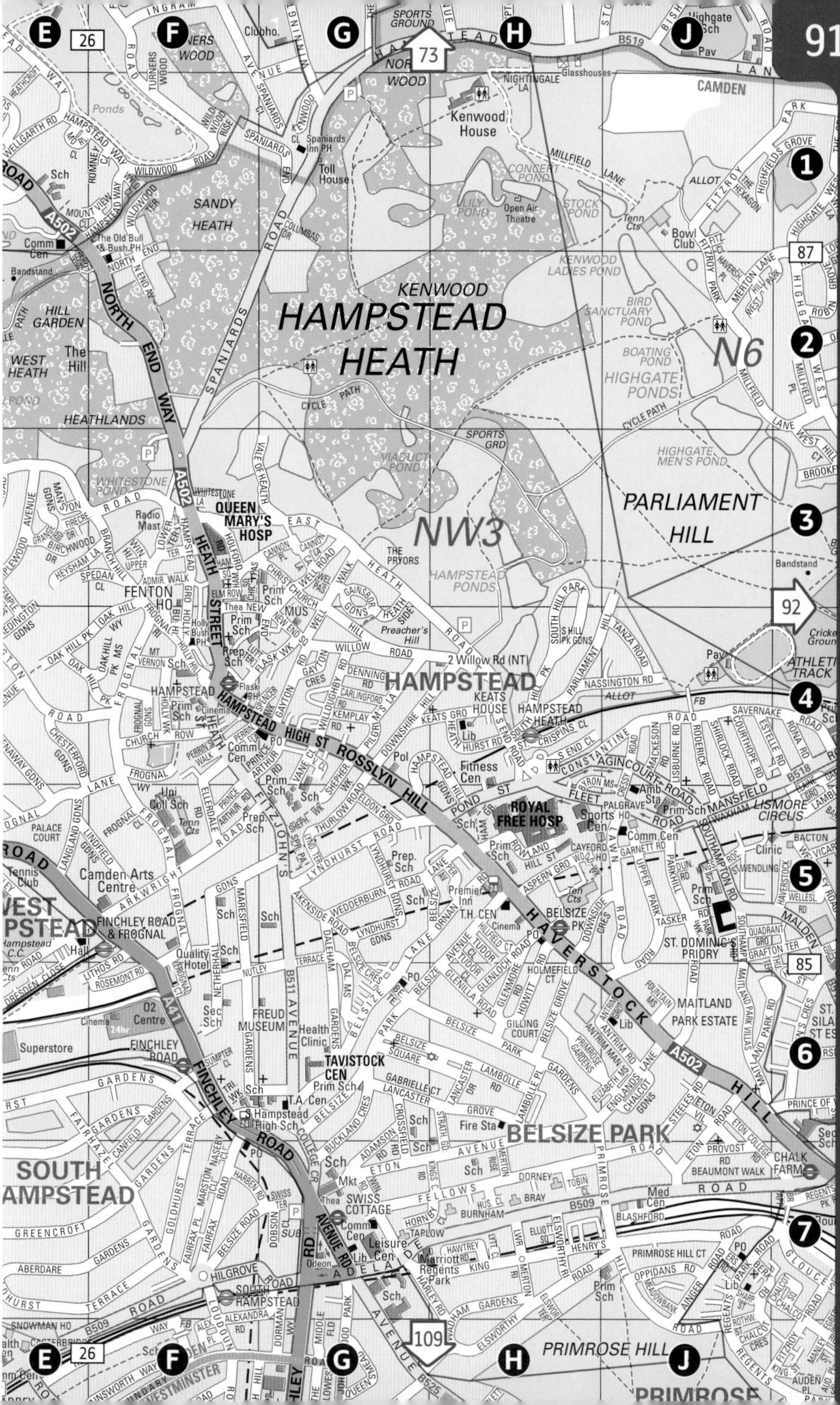
E
F
G
H
J
26
73
INGRAM
SPORTS GROUND
Clubho.
HAMPSTEAD LANE
B519
Highgate Sch
Pav
NORTH WOOD
Glasshouses
NIGHTINGALE LA
CAMDEN
TURNERS WOOD
Ponds
HEATHCROFT
WELLGARTH RD
HAMPSTEAD WAY
WILDWOOD ROAD
WILDWOOD RISE
SPANIARDS AVENUE
SPANIARDS END
KENWOOD
Spaniards Inn PH
Toll House
Kenwood House
MILLFIELD LANE
CONCERT POND
LILY POND
Open Air Theatre
STOCK POND
Tenn Cts
Bowl Club
ALLOT
FITZROY PARK
THE HEXAGON
HIGHFIELDS GROVE
1
87
Sch
ROMNEY CL
MOUNT VIEW
SANDY HEATH
A502
The Old Bull & Bush PH
Comm Cen
NORTH END
Bandstand
COLUMBAS DR
SPANIARDS ROAD
KENWOOD LADIES POND
MERTON LANE
HIGHGATE WEST HILL
KENWOOD
HAMPSTEAD HEATH
BIRD SANCTUARY POND
N6
2
HILL GARDEN
The Hill
WEST HEATH
NORTH END WAY
BOATING POND
HIGHGATE PONDS
MILLFIELD PL
CYCLE PATH
HEATHLANDS
SPORTS GRD
VIADUCT POND
HIGHGATE MEN'S POND
BROOKFIELD
WHITESTONE POND
WHITESTONE LA
QUEEN MARY'S HOSP
VALE OF HEALTH
EAST HEATH ROAD
PARLIAMENT HILL
3
Radio Mast
HEATH STREET
NW3
THE PRYORS
HAMPSTEAD PONDS
Bandstand
92
BIRCHWOOD DR
HEYSHAM LA
SPEDAN CL
FENTON HO
CHRISTCHURCH
Prim Sch
MUS
WELL WALK
GAINSBOROUGH GDNS
Preacher's Hill
SOUTH HILL PARK
S HILL PK GDNS
TANZA ROAD
Cricket Ground
OAK HILL PK
OAKHILL WY
Holly Bush PH
Prep. Sch
WILLOW ROAD
2 Willow Rd (NT)
PARLIAMENT HILL
Pav
ATHLETIC TRACK
HAMPSTEAD
FROGNAL
DENNING RD
CARLINGFORD RD
KEMPLAY RD
NASSINGTON RD
ALLOT
4
Cinema
HAMPSTEAD HIGH ST
ROSSLYN HILL
DOWNSHIRE HILL
KEATS GRO
KEATS HOUSE
HAMPSTEAD HEATH
ST CRISPINS CL
FB
SAVERNAKE ROAD
CHESTERFIELD GDNS
CHURCH ROW
Comm Cen
PO
Lib
HURST RD
Fitness Cen
CONSTANTINE ROAD
AGINCOURT ROAD
MACKESON ROAD
LISBURNE RD
RODERICK ROAD
SHIRLOCK ROAD
COURTHOPE RD
ESTELLE RD
RONA RD
FROGNAL LANE
Prim Sch
Sch
POND ST
FLEET RD
Amb Sta
Prim Sch
MANSFIELD
B518
LISMORE CIRCUS
PALACE COURT
Uni Coll Sch
Tenn Cts
ELLERDALE
PRINCE ARTHUR RD
THURLOW ROAD
ROYAL FREE HOSP
Sports Cen
PALGRAVE HO
Comm Cen
BACTON
Clinic
WENDLING
LANGLAND GDNS
LINDFIELD GDNS
ARKWRIGHT ROAD
FITZJOHN'S AVENUE
LYNDHURST ROAD
Prep. Sch
ROWLAND HILL ST
CAYFORD HO
GARNETT RD
UPPER PARK ROAD
PARKHILL
SOUTHAMPTON RD
5
Tennis Club
Camden Arts Centre
WEDDERBURN
LYNDHURST GDNS
Premier Inn
T.H. CEN
Ten Cts
Prim Sch
WEST HAMPSTEAD
FINCHLEY ROAD & FROGNAL
Hampstead C.C.
Hall
MARESFIELD
Sch
AKENSIDE ROAD
HAVERSTOCK
BELSIZE PK
Cinema
TASKER ROAD
ST. DOMINIC'S PRIORY
QUADRANT GRO
GRAFTON TER
MALDEN
LITHOS RD
ROSEMONT RD
Quality Hotel
NUTLEY TERRACE
BELSIZE LANE
HOLMEFIELD CT
85
DRESDEN CLOSE
NETHERHALL
B511 AVENUE
BELSIZE CRES
GLENLOCH ROAD
FOUNTAIN MS
MAITLAND PARK ESTATE
Cinema
24hr
O2 Centre
Sec Sch
FREUD MUSEUM
Health Clinic
BELSIZE PARK
GILLING COURT
BELSIZE GROVE
Lib
ANTRIM RD
ST. SILAS ST EST
A41
Superstore
FINCHLEY ROAD
TAVISTOCK CEN
BELSIZE SQUARE
LAMBOLLE RD
PRIMROSE GARDENS
6
GARDENS
Prim Sch
T.A. Cen
S Hampstead High Sch
GABRIELLE CT
LANCASTER
A502
HILL
PRINCE OF WALES
FAIRHAZEL GARDENS
CANFIELD GARDENS
Fire Sta
BELSIZE PARK
ETON VIL
PROVOST RD
BEAUMONT WALK
CHALK FARM
SOUTH HAMPSTEAD
GOLDHURST TERRACE
MARSTON CL
NASEBY CL
HARBEN RD
SWISS TER
COLLEGE CR
BUCKLAND CRES
ADAMSON RD
Sch
Mkt
Thea
SWISS COTTAGE
ETON AVENUE
FELLOWS ROAD
BURNHAM
DORNEY
TOBIN CL
BRAY
B509
Med Cen
BLASHFORD
REGENTS PK RD
GREENCROFT GARDENS
FAIRFAX PL
BELSIZE ROAD
DOBSON CL
SUB
AVENUE RD
Comm Cen
Leisure Cen
Lib
HORNBY CL
TAPLOW
HAWTREY RD
Marriott Regents Park
KING HENRY'S ROAD
ELLIOTT SQ
PRIMROSE HILL CT
OPPIDANS RD
7
ABERDARE GARDENS
HILGROVE ROAD
Odeon
ADELAIDE
MERTON RI
ELSWORTHY RD
Prim Sch
AINGER RD
PO
Lib
GLOUCESTER
SOUTH HAMPSTEAD
B509
ALEXANDRA
DORMAN WAY
Sch
HARLEY RD
WADHAM GARDENS
ELSWORTHY TER
CHALCOT CRES
SNOWMAN HO
CASTERBRIDGE
26
FB
109
PRIMROSE HILL
B525
WESTMINSTER
QUEEN'S
AUDEN PL
PRIMROSE

A
B
C
D
E
1
2
3
4
5
6
7
74
87
91
85
110
30
HIGHGATE
N6
HIGHGATE CEMETERY
WATERLOW PARK
WHITTINGTON HOSPITAL
ARCHWAY
ARCHWAY ROAD
HORNSEY LANE
HORNSEY RISE
HORNSEY LA EST
N19
ELTHORNE PARK
HILLSIDE PK
UPPER HOLLOWAY
HOLLOWAY
HOLLOWAY ROAD
ST. JOHNS GROVE
WHITTINGTON PARK
DARTMOUTH PARK
DARTMOUTH PARK HILL
HIGHGATE ROAD
HIGHGATE WEST HILL
SWAINS LANE
JUNCTION ROAD
TUFNELL PARK
TUFNELL PARK ROAD
BRECKNOCK ROAD
BRECKNOCK ROAD EST
London Met Uni
H.M. PRISON HOLLOWAY
HILLDROP ESTATE
GOSPEL OAK
LISMORE CIRCUS
ATHLETICS TRACK
Cricket Ground
Lido
Bandstand
NW5
KENTISH TOWN
KENTISH TOWN ROAD
KENTISH TOWN W
FORTESS ROAD
LEIGHTON ROAD
CAMDEN ROAD
CAMDEN SQUARE
CAMDEN PK RD
YORK WAY
ST. SILAS ST EST
PRINCE OF WALES RD
CHALK FARM
CHALK FARM RD
Roundhouse
Stables Mkt
Camden Lock Mkt
M.T.V. Studios
ROYAL COLLEGE ST
ST. PANCRAS WAY
AGAR GROVE EST
MARKET EST
SPORTS GRD
CLARENCE WAY EST
FORUM CLUB
Royal Mail Delivery Off
Recycle Cen
Holiday Inn
Superstore
Parcelforce
KING'S CROSS
A1
A400
A503
A5200
A5202
B518
B519

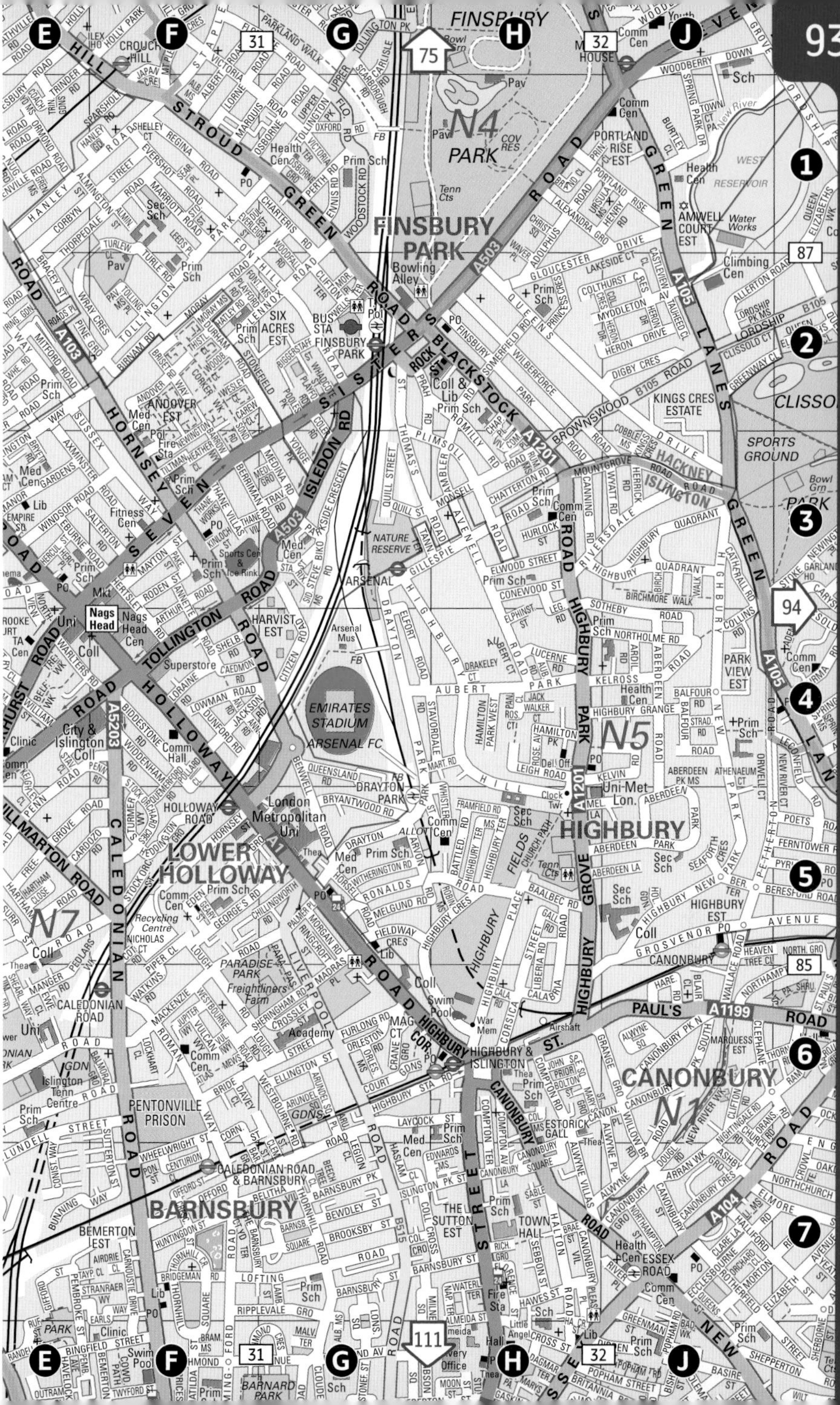
E
F
G
H
J
31
75
32
87
94
85
111
1
2
3
4
5
6
7
FINSBURY PARK
N4
FINSBURY
PARK
CROUCH HILL
STROUD GREEN ROAD
SEVEN SISTERS ROAD
BLACKSTOCK ROAD
ISLEDON RD
HORNSEY ROAD
HOLLOWAY ROAD
TOLLINGTON ROAD
GREEN LANES
BROWNSWOOD ROAD
HIGHBURY PARK
HIGHBURY GROVE
MOUNTGROVE ROAD
HACKNEY
ISLINGTON
CLISSOLD
SPORTS GROUND
WEST RESERVOIR
AMWELL COURT EST
Climbing Cen
KINGS CRES ESTATE
SIX ACRES EST
BUS STA
FINSBURY PARK
ANDOVER EST
NATURE RESERVE
ARSENAL
HARVIST EST
Arsenal Mus
EMIRATES STADIUM
ARSENAL FC
DRAYTON PARK
Nags Head
City & Islington Coll
HOLLOWAY ROAD
London Metropolitan Uni
LOWER HOLLOWAY
N5
HIGHBURY
N7
CALEDONIAN ROAD
CALEDONIAN ROAD
HILLMARTON ROAD
PARADISE PARK
Freightliners Farm
HIGHBURY FIELDS
HIGHBURY & ISLINGTON
HIGHBURY CORNER
PAUL'S ROAD
ST. PAUL'S ROAD
CANONBURY
N1
CANONBURY ROAD
UPPER STREET
ESTORICK GALL
PENTONVILLE PRISON
CALEDONIAN ROAD & BARNSBURY
BARNSBURY
BEMERTON EST
THE SUTTON EST
TOWN HALL
ESSEX ROAD
NEW NORTH ROAD
HIGHBURY EST
CANONBURY
A503
A1201
A103
A5203
A1
A105
B105
A1199
A104
B515

A
B
C
D
E
1
2
3
4
5
6
7
33
76
34
87
93
85
112
STAMFORD HILL
ABNEY PARK CEMETERY
STOKE NEWINGTON
N16
CLISSOLD
SPORTS GROUND
PARK
SHACKLEWELL
HACKNEY DOWNS
BUTTERFIELD GREEN
KINGSLAND
E8
N1
DALSTON
DE BEAUVOIR TOWN
LONDON FIELDS
HAGGERSTON
CLAPTON COMMON
SPRINGFIELD PARK
UPPER CLAPTON
RESERVOIR
Water Works
STAMFORD HILL ESTATE
HILLCOURT EST
GEORGE DOWNING EST
NORTHWOLD ESTATE
NIGHTINGALE EST
SHELLGROVE EST
Petchey Academy
Kingsland Shop Cen
DALSTON KINGSLAND
DALSTON JUNCTION
HACKNEY DOWNS
RECTORY ROAD
STOKE NEWINGTON HIGH ST
KINGSL. HIGH ST
BALLS POND ROAD
DALSTON LANE
GRAHAM ROAD
KINGSLAND ROAD
STAMFORD
UPPER CLAPTON
PEMBURY ROAD
A10
A104
A105
A107
A1199
A1207
B104
B105
B111
B102
B108

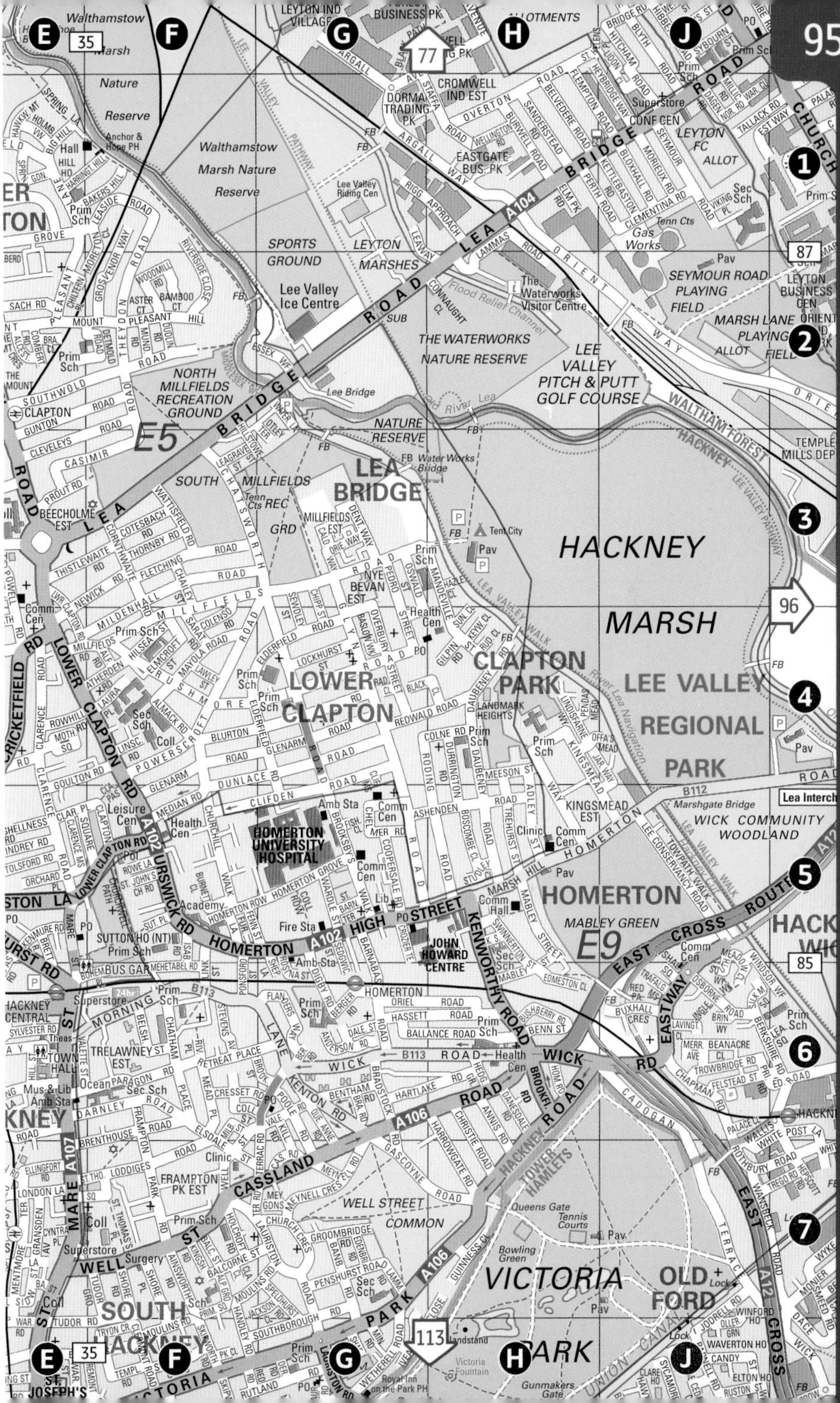
E
F
G
H
J
35
77
Walthamstow Marsh Nature Reserve
Walthamstow Marsh Nature Reserve
LEYTON IND VILLAGE
ALLOTMENTS
CROMWELL IND EST
DORMA TRADING PK
EASTGATE BUS. PK
Lee Valley Riding Cen
SPORTS GROUND
LEYTON MARSHES
Lee Valley Ice Centre
LEA BRIDGE ROAD
A104
Superstore
CONF CEN
LEYTON FC
ALLOT
Gas Works
Tenn Cts
SEYMOUR ROAD PLAYING FIELD
LEYTON BUSINESS CEN
MARSH LANE PLAYING FIELD
ALLOT
87
The Waterworks Visitor Centre
Flood Relief Channel
THE WATERWORKS NATURE RESERVE
LEE VALLEY PITCH & PUTT GOLF COURSE
ORIENT WAY
WALTHAM FOREST
HACKNEY
TEMPLE MILLS DEPOT
NORTH MILLFIELDS RECREATION GROUND
Lee Bridge
Old River Lea
NATURE RESERVE
CLAPTON
E5
SOUTH MILLFIELDS REC GRD
LEA BRIDGE
Water Works Bridge
Tent City
Pav
HACKNEY MARSH
96
BEECHOLME EST
MILLFIELDS EST
NYE BEVAN EST
Health Cen
CLAPTON PARK
LEE VALLEY REGIONAL PARK
River Lea Navigation
LOWER CLAPTON
LANDMARK HEIGHTS
KINGSMEAD EST
Marshgate Bridge
WICK COMMUNITY WOODLAND
Lea Interch
LOWER CLAPTON RD
A102
Leisure Cen
HOMERTON UNIVERSITY HOSPITAL
Amb Sta
Comm Cen
HOMERTON
MABLEY GREEN
E9
EAST CROSS ROUTE
A12
HACKNEY WICK
85
HOMERTON HIGH STREET
JOHN HOWARD CENTRE
Fire Sta
Academy
SUTTON HO (NT)
BUS GAR
HACKNEY CENTRAL
Superstore
TOWN HALL
TRELAWNEY EST
Mus & Lib
Ocean
HACKNEY
FRAMPTON PK EST
MARE ST
A107
CASSLAND ROAD
A106
WELL STREET COMMON
Queens Gate
Tennis Courts
Bowling Green
VICTORIA PARK
OLD FORD
Lock
UNION CANAL
SOUTH HACKNEY
113
Bandstand
Victoria Fountain
Royal Inn on the Park PH
Gunmakers Gate
ST JOSEPH'S
WAVERTON HO
TOWER HAMLETS
1
2
3
4
5
6
7

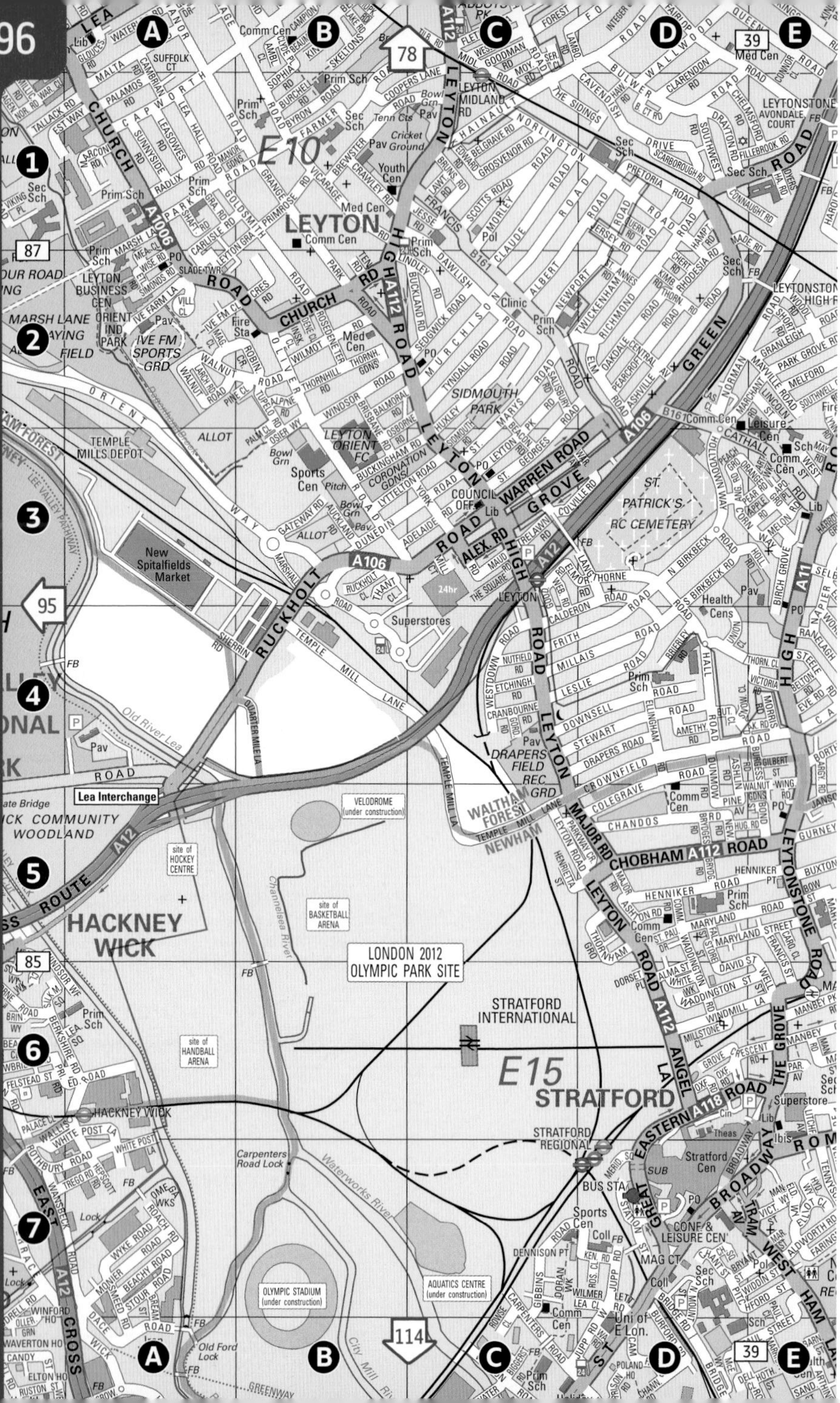
A
B
C
D
E
1
2
3
4
5
6
7
78
87
95
85
114
39
E10
LEYTON
E15
STRATFORD
HACKNEY WICK
LONDON 2012
OLYMPIC PARK SITE
STRATFORD INTERNATIONAL
STRATFORD REGIONAL
VELODROME (under construction)
site of HOCKEY CENTRE
site of BASKETBALL ARENA
site of HANDBALL ARENA
OLYMPIC STADIUM (under construction)
AQUATICS CENTRE (under construction)
New Spitalfields Market
Lea Interchange
TEMPLE MILLS DEPOT
LEYTON ORIENT FC
ST. PATRICK'S RC CEMETERY
SIDMOUTH PARK
DRAPERS FIELD REC GRD
IVE FM SPORTS GRD
MARSH LANE PLAYING FIELD
LEYTON BUSINESS CEN
ORIENT IND PARK
LEYTON MIDLAND RD
LEYTONSTONE
LEYTONSTONE HIGH RD
HACKNEY WICK
WALTHAM FOREST
NEWHAM
Stratford Cen
CONF & LEISURE CEN
Uni of E Lon.
Superstores
Superstore
Carpenters Road Lock
Old Ford Lock
Channelsea River
Waterworks River
City Mill River
Old River Lea
GREENWAY
CHURCH ROAD
HIGH ROAD
LEYTON HIGH ROAD
LEYTON ROAD
RUCKHOLT ROAD
TEMPLE MILL LANE
ORIENT WAY
GROVE GREEN ROAD
WARREN ROAD
CHOBHAM ROAD
LEYTONSTONE ROAD
ANGEL LA
GREAT EASTERN ROAD
BROADWAY
THE GROVE
WEST HAM LA
EAST CROSS ROUTE
A12
A106
A112
A118
A11
A1006
B161

E
F
G
H
J
1
2
3
4
5
6
7
40
41
79
87
98
85
115
BUSH WOOD
WANSTEAD GOLF COURSE
PARK
SHOULDER OF MUTTON POND
HERONRY POND
RESERVOIR WOOD
THE BASIN
Cricket Grd
BURIAL GRD
ALLOT
BLAKE HALL ROAD
WOODLANDS AVENUE
NORTHUMBERLAND AVENUE
ALDERSBROOK ROAD
A116
E11
E12
ALDERSBROOK
WANSTEAD FLATS
JUBILEE POND
CENTRE ROAD
A114
LEYTONSTONE ROAD
REDBRIDGE
NEWHAM
CAPEL ROAD
MANOR PARK CEMETERY
Crematorium
WEST HAM CEMETERY
JEWISH CEMETERY
WOODFORD ROAD
WOODGRANGE ROAD
WANSTEAD PARK
FOREST GATE
ROMFORD ROAD
A118
UPTON LANE
E7
WEST HAM PARK
SPORTS GRD
WEST HAM
UPTON
PORTWAY
Uni of East Lon
Newham Coll of F.E.
Clapton FC
Bandstand
Tennis Courts
HAMPTON ROAD
OSBORNE ROAD
CLAREMONT ROAD
WINDSOR ROAD
SEBERT ROAD
BALMORAL ROAD
GREEN STREET
B167
B165
B109
B161
B164

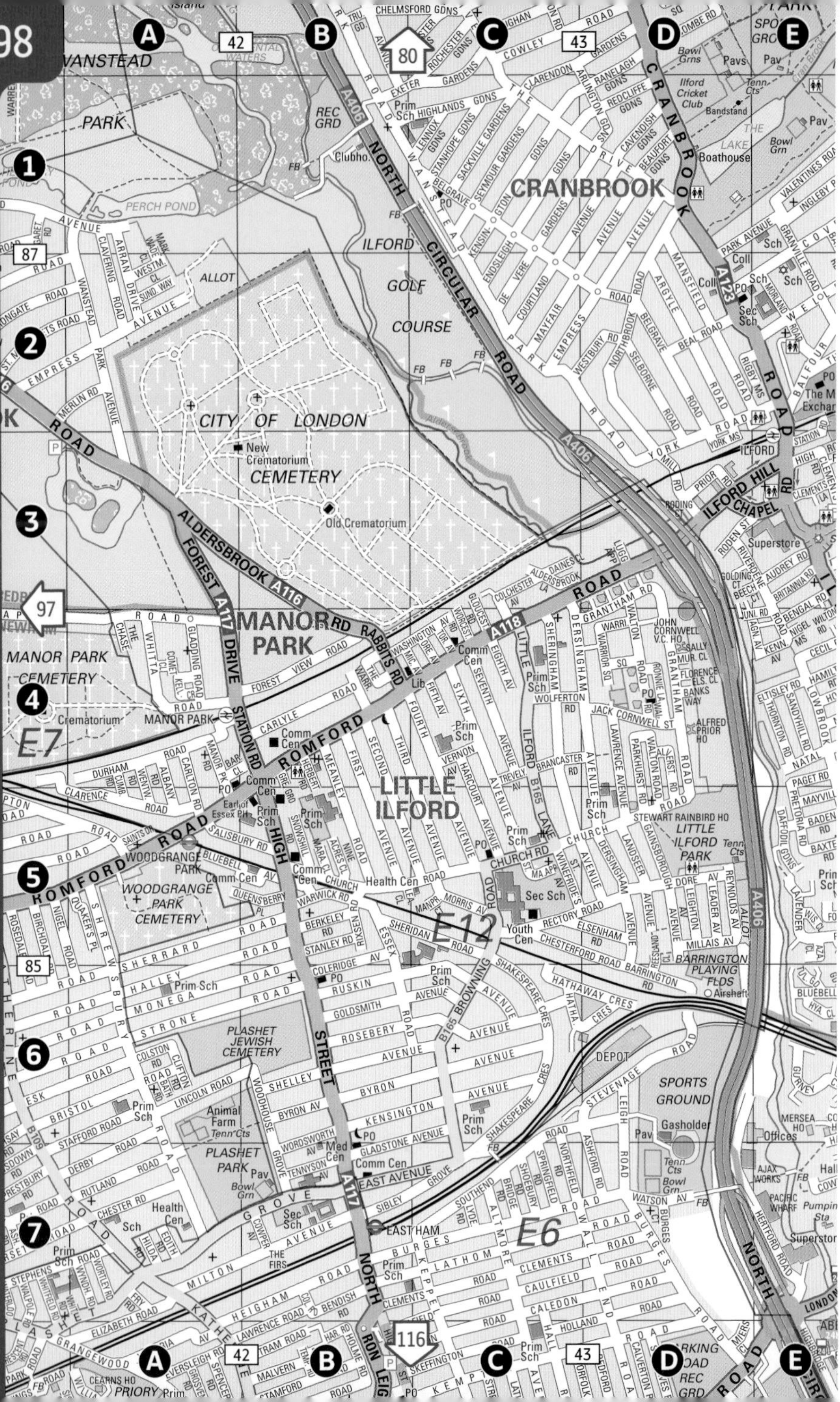
A
B
C
D
E
1
2
3
4
5
6
7
WANSTEAD
PARK
PERCH POND
42
43
80
87
97
85
116
REC GRD
Clubho.
NORTH CIRCULAR ROAD
A406
ILFORD GOLF COURSE
CRANBROOK
CRANBROOK ROAD
A123
Ilford Cricket Club
Bandstand
Boathouse
THE LAKE
Bowl Grns
Pavs
Pav
Tenn Cts
CHELMSFORD GDNS
ROCHESTER GDNS
EXETER GARDENS
COWLEY ROAD
CLARENDON GARDENS
HIGHLANDS GDNS
LENNOX GDNS
STANHOPE GDNS
SACKVILLE GARDENS
SEYMOUR GARDENS
RANELAGH GDNS
REDCLIFFE GDNS
ARLINGTON GD
CAVENDISH GDNS
BEAUFORT GDNS
THE DRIVE
WANSTEAD PARK ROAD
BELGRAVE
ENDSLEIGH GDNS
DE VERE GDNS
COURTLAND AVENUE
MAYFAIR AVENUE
EMPRESS AVENUE
WESTBURY RD
NORTHBROOK RD
BELGRAVE RD
SELBORNE RD
MANSFIELD ROAD
ARGYLE ROAD
BEAL ROAD
RIGBY MS
YORK ROAD
YORK MS
ILFORD
ILFORD HILL
CHAPEL RD
PRIOR RD
RODING
Superstore
PARK AVENUE
GRANVILLE ROAD
VALENTINES ROAD
INGLEBY RD
BALFOUR
The M Exchar
STATION RD
CLEMENTS
AVENUE
CLAVERING ROAD
ARRAN DRIVE
SUND. WAY
WESTM. CL
ALLOT
EMPRESS AVENUE
MERLIN RD
PARK AVENUE
CITY OF LONDON CEMETERY
New Crematorium
Old Crematorium
ALDERSBROOK ROAD
A116
FOREST DRIVE
A117
MANOR PARK
RABBITS RD
FOREST VIEW ROAD
MANOR PARK CEMETERY
Crematorium
E7
THE CHASE
WHITTA
GLADDING ROAD
STATION RD
CARLYLE ROAD
ROMFORD ROAD
A118
Comm Cen
Lib
WASHINGTON AV
GRANTHAM RD
SHERINGHAM AVENUE
DERSINGHAM AVENUE
WALTON ROAD
JOHN CORNWELL V.C. HO
SALLY MUR. CL
FLORENCE ELS. CL
BANKS WAY
WOLFERTON RD
JACK CORNWELL ST
ALFRED PRIOR HO
BRANCASTER RD
LAWRENCE AVENUE
PARKHURST RD
ILFORD LANE
B165
LITTLE ILFORD
STEWART RAINBIRD HO
LITTLE ILFORD PARK
CHURCH RD
Sec Sch
Youth Cen
RECTORY ROAD
ELSENHAM RD
CHESTERFORD ROAD
BARRINGTON ROAD
BARRINGTON PLAYING FLDS
Airshaft
HATHAWAY CRES
SHAKESPEARE CRES
BROWNING ROAD
E12
SHERIDAN ROAD
ESSEX
MANOR PK
DURHAM RD
ALBANY
CARLTON RD
CLARENCE ROAD
HIGH STREET NORTH
Earl of Essex PH
SALISBURY RD
BLUEBELL AV
WOODGRANGE PARK
WOODGRANGE PARK CEMETERY
QUEENSBERRY PL
WARWICK RD
BERKELEY RD
STANLEY RD
COLERIDGE AV
RUSKIN AVENUE
GOLDSMITH AVENUE
ROSEBERY AVENUE
SHERRARD ROAD
HALLEY ROAD
MONEGA ROAD
STRONE ROAD
SHREWSBURY ROAD
PLASHET JEWISH CEMETERY
COLSTON RD
CLIFTON RD
LINCOLN ROAD
SHELLEY AVENUE
BYRON AVENUE
KENSINGTON AVENUE
WOODHOUSE GROVE
Animal Farm
PLASHET PARK
BRISTOL ROAD
STAFFORD ROAD
DERBY ROAD
RUTLAND ROAD
CHESTER RD
WORDSWORTH AV
GLADSTONE AVENUE
EAST AVENUE
TENNYSON AV
PLASHET GROVE
Health Cen
Med Cen
Sec Sch
EAST HAM
THE FIRS
MILTON AVENUE
HEIGHAM ROAD
LAWRENCE ROAD
BENDISH RD
ELIZABETH ROAD
GRANGEWOOD
KATHERINE ROAD
PRIORY
SKEFFINGTON
KEPPEL ROAD
LATHOM ROAD
CLEMENTS ROAD
CAULFIELD ROAD
CALEDON ROAD
HOLLAND ROAD
WALL END ROAD
BURGES ROAD
ALTMORE AVENUE
SOUTHEND ROAD
SHOEBURY RD
SPRINGFIELD RD
NORTHFIELD RD
ASHFORD RD
LEIGH ROAD
STEVENAGE ROAD
DEPOT
SPORTS GROUND
Gasholder
WATSON AV
E6
BARKING ROAD REC GRD
HERTFORD ROAD
AJAX WORKS
PACIFIC WHARF
Pumping Sta
Superstore
Offices
MERSEA
LONDON
DAFFODIL GDNS
LAVENDER
PRETORIA RD
PAGET RD
NATAL
CECIL
BENGAL RD
BRITANNIA RD
AUDREY RD
RIVERDENE
GOLDING CT
ELTISLEY RD
HORNTON RD
SANDYHILL RD
LOWBROOK
BLUEBELL
REYNOLDS AV
LEADER AV
MILLAIS AV
DORE AV
GAINSBOROUGH
LANDSEER AVENUE

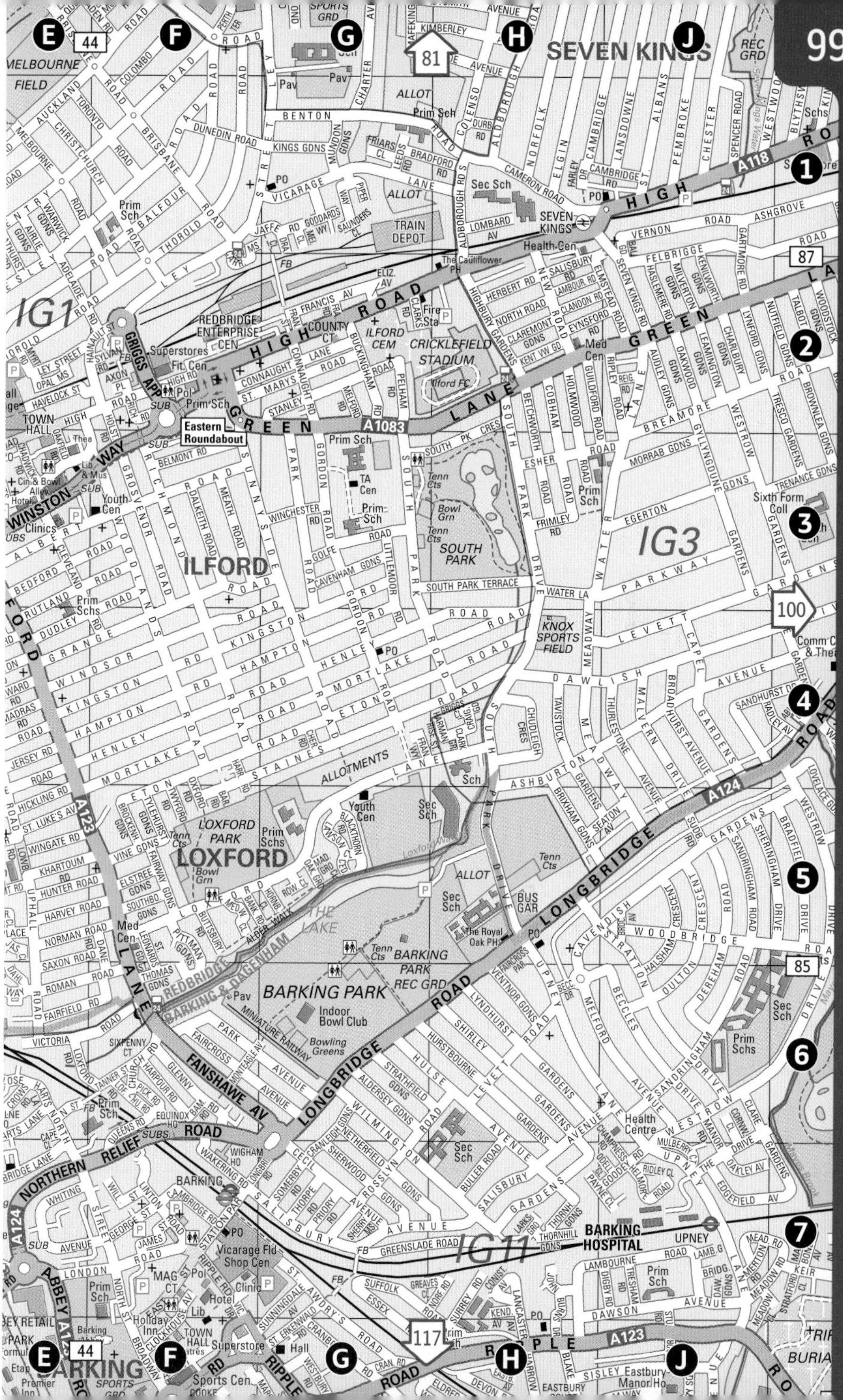
SEVEN KINGS
ILFORD
LOXFORD
BARKING
IG1
IG3
IG11
SOUTH PARK
BARKING PARK
CRICKLEFIELD STADIUM
KNOX SPORTS FIELD
LOXFORD PARK
Eastern Roundabout
HIGH ROAD
GREEN LANE
A1083
A118
A123
A124
LONGBRIDGE ROAD
NORTHERN RELIEF ROAD
WINSTON WAY
FANSHAWE AV
RIPPLE ROAD
UPNEY
BARKING HOSPITAL
Vicarage Fld Shop Cen
REDBRIDGE
BARKING & DAGENHAM
THE LAKE
TRAIN DEPOT
REDBRIDGE ENTERPRISE CEN
Sixth Form Coll
Indoor Bowl Club
81
87
100
85
117
44

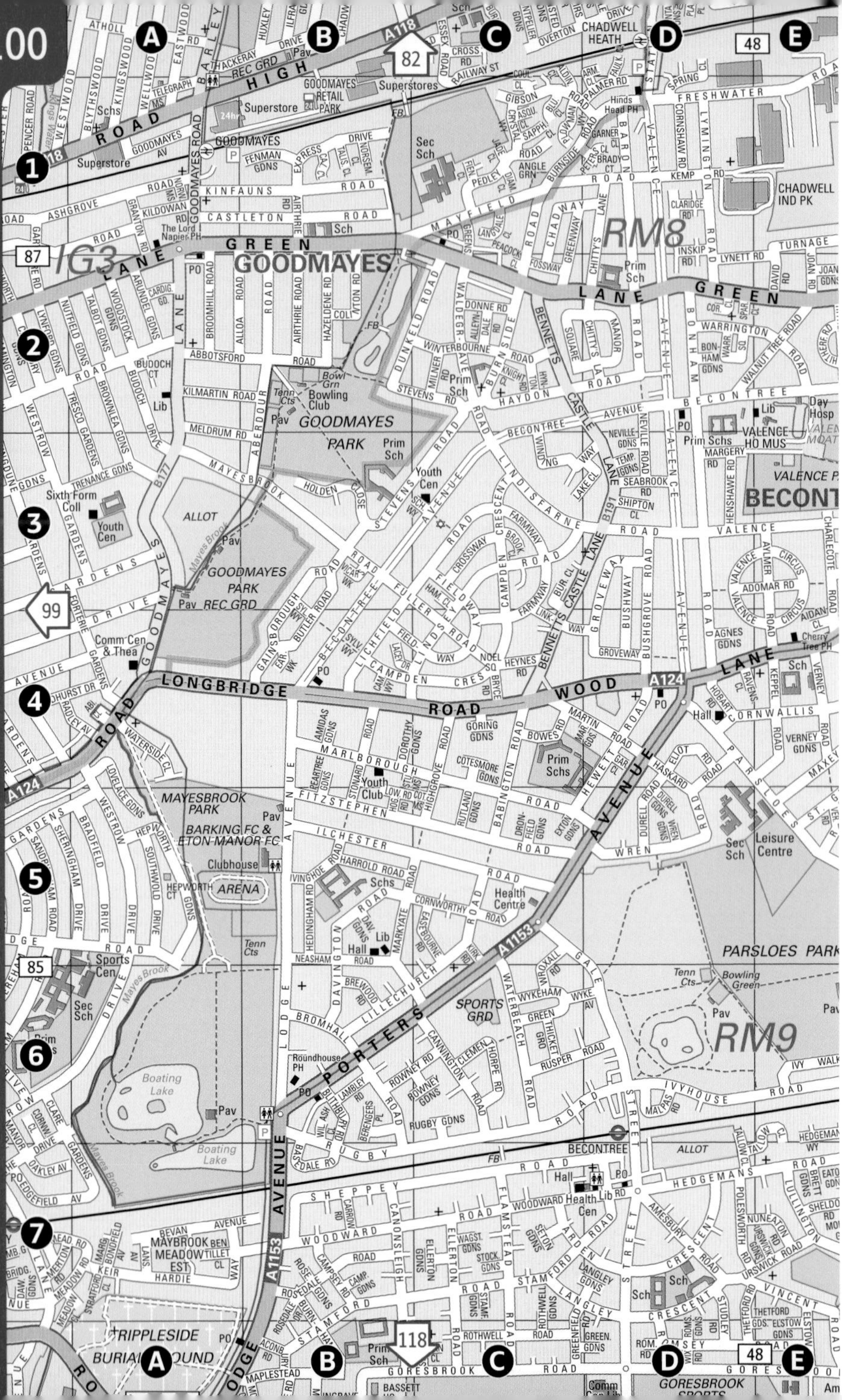
A
B
C
D
E
1
2
3
4
5
6
7
82
48
87
99
85
118
CHADWELL HEATH
GOODMAYES
RM8
IG3
RM9
BECONT
HIGH ROAD
A118
GREEN LANE
LONGBRIDGE ROAD
WOOD LANE
A124
A1153
PORTERS AVENUE
LODGE AVENUE
GOODMAYES LANE
GOODMAYES ROAD
BECONTREE AVENUE
STEVENS ROAD
BENNETTS CASTLE LANE
B177
B191
VALENCE AVENUE
VALENCE AVENUE
MAYESBROOK ROAD
MAYFIELD ROAD
KINFAUNS ROAD
CASTLETON ROAD
ASHGROVE ROAD
ABBOTSFORD ROAD
KILMARTIN ROAD
MELDRUM RD
ABERDOUR RD
DUNKELD ROAD
HAYDON ROAD
LINDISFARNE ROAD
FULLER ROAD
CAMPDEN CRES
MARLBOROUGH ROAD
FITZSTEPHEN ROAD
ILCHESTER ROAD
HARROLD ROAD
CORNWORTHY ROAD
LILLECHURCH ROAD
BROMHALL ROAD
RUGBY ROAD
SHEPPEY ROAD
WOODWARD ROAD
STAMFORD ROAD
GORESBROOK ROAD
IVYHOUSE ROAD
HEDGEMANS ROAD
VINCENT ROAD
RAMSEY RD
FRESHWATER ROAD
KEMP RD
TURNAGE ROAD
WARRINGTON ROAD
WALNUT TREE ROAD
CORNWALLIS ROAD
PARSLOES AVENUE
HASKARD RD
WREN ROAD
GALE ST
STREET
Superstore
Superstores
GOODMAYES RETAIL PARK
Sec Sch
Prim Sch
Prim Schs
Schs
Sixth Form Coll
Youth Cen
Youth Club
Lib
PO
Pav
Hall
Health Centre
Comm Cen & Thea
Clubhouse
ARENA
Tenn Cts
Bowling Club
Bowl Grn
GOODMAYES PARK
GOODMAYES PARK REC GRD
ALLOT
Mayes Brook
MAYESBROOK PARK
BARKING FC & ETON MANOR FC
Boating Lake
Sports Cen
SPORTS GRD
PARSLOES PARK
Bowling Green
Leisure Centre
VALENCE HO MUS
VALENCE PARK
Day Hosp
CHADWELL IND PK
Hinds Head PH
The Lord Napier PH
Cherry Tree PH
Roundhouse PH
BECONTREE
Health Cen
MAYBROOK MEADOW EST
TRIPPLESIDE BURIAL GROUND
GOODMAYES
FB

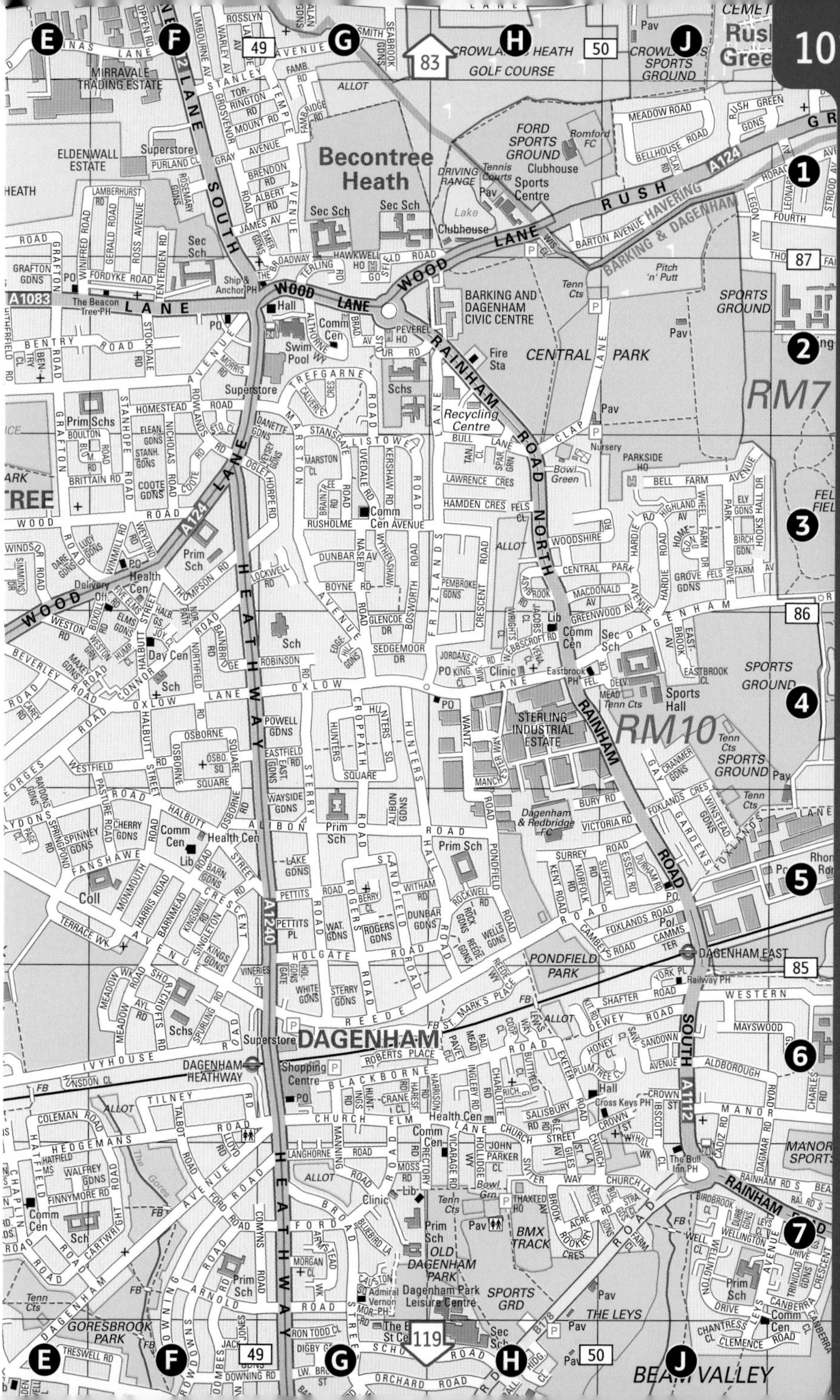
E
F
G
H
J
49
50
83
87
86
85
119
1
2
3
4
5
6
7
MIRRAVALE TRADING ESTATE
ELDENWALL ESTATE
Becontree Heath
CROWLANDS HEATH GOLF COURSE
CROWLANDS SPORTS GROUND
FORD SPORTS GROUND
Romford FC
RUSH GREEN ROAD
RUSH LANE
WOOD LANE
SOUTH LANE
BARKING AND DAGENHAM CIVIC CENTRE
CENTRAL PARK
RM7
RM10
RAINHAM ROAD NORTH
RAINHAM ROAD SOUTH
HEATHWAY
A1240
A124
A1083
A1112
STERLING INDUSTRIAL ESTATE
Dagenham & Redbridge FC
SPORTS GROUND
DAGENHAM EAST
PONDFIELD PARK
DAGENHAM
DAGENHAM HEATHWAY
OLD DAGENHAM PARK
Dagenham Park Leisure Centre
BMX TRACK
SPORTS GRD
THE LEYS
BEAM VALLEY
GORESBROOK PARK
OXLOW LANE
DAGENHAM ROAD
CHURCH ELM LANE
BLACKBORNE ROAD
HEDGEMANS ROAD
GOSFIELD ROAD
BALL FARM AVENUE
WESTERN AVENUE
MANOR ROAD

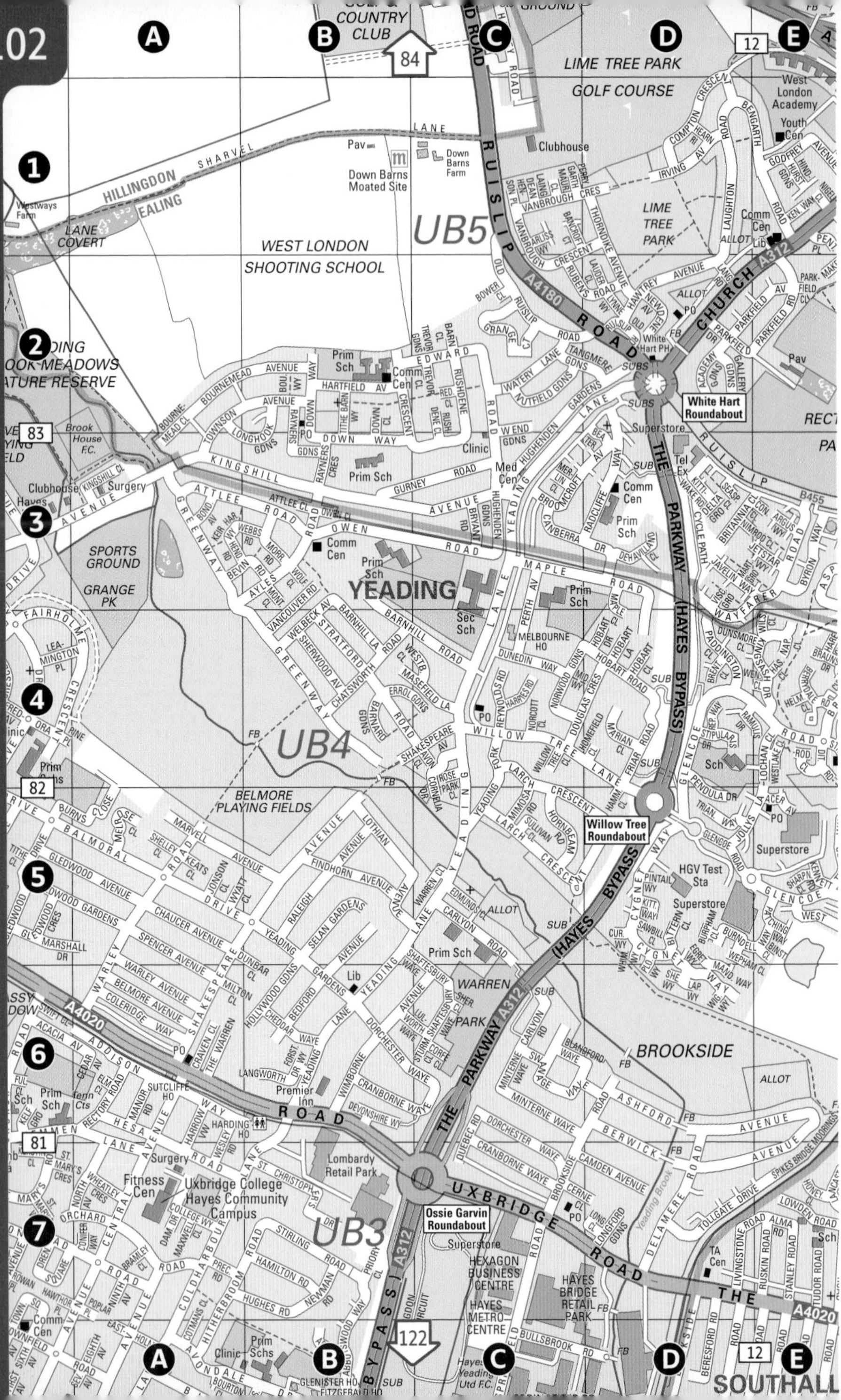
A
B
C
D
E
1
2
3
4
5
6
7
84
83
82
81
122
12
COUNTRY CLUB
LIME TREE PARK
GOLF COURSE
Clubhouse
SHARVEL LANE
HILLINGDON
EALING
Westways Farm
LANE COVERT
Pav
Down Barns Moated Site
Down Barns Farm
UB5
WEST LONDON
SHOOTING SCHOOL
RUISLIP ROAD
A4180
West London Academy
Youth Cen
LIME TREE PARK
Comm Cen
Lib
CHURCH
A312
ALLOT
PO
White Hart PH
White Hart Roundabout
SUBS
Superstore
Tel Ex
B455
PARKFIELD RD
Pav
Prim Sch
Comm Cen
BOURNEMEAD AVENUE
HARTFIELD AV
EDWARD
DOWN WAY
Clinic
Med Cen
Brook House F.C.
Clubhouse
Surgery
KINGSHILL AV
ATTLEE ROAD
OWEN ROAD
GURNEY ROAD
AVENUE
SPORTS GROUND
GRANGE PK
Comm Cen
Prim Sch
YEADING
Sec Sch
MAPLE ROAD
Prim Sch
MELBOURNE HO
BARNHILL ROAD
GREENWAY
DUNEDIN WAY
THE PARKWAY (HAYES BYPASS)
WILLOW TREE LANE
UB4
BELMORE PLAYING FIELDS
FB
Willow Tree Roundabout
GLENCOE RD
Sch
Superstore
HGV Test Sta
Superstore
PO
BALMORAL DRIVE
GLEDWOOD AVENUE
CHAUCER AVENUE
SPENCER AVENUE
WARLEY AVENUE
BELMORE AVENUE
COLERIDGE WAY
YEADING LANE
Lib
Prim Sch
WARREN PARK
ALLOT
BROOKSIDE
ALLOT
ASHFORD AVENUE
BERWICK AVENUE
A4020
ROAD
Premier Inn
Lombardy Retail Park
Ossie Garvin Roundabout
UXBRIDGE ROAD
Fitness Cen
Uxbridge College Hayes Community Campus
Surgery
UB3
Superstore
HEXAGON BUSINESS CENTRE
HAYES METRO CENTRE
HAYES BRIDGE RETAIL PARK
TA Cen
THE A4020
Comm Cen
Prim Schs
Clinic
Hayes Yeading Utd F.C.
SUB
SOUTHALL

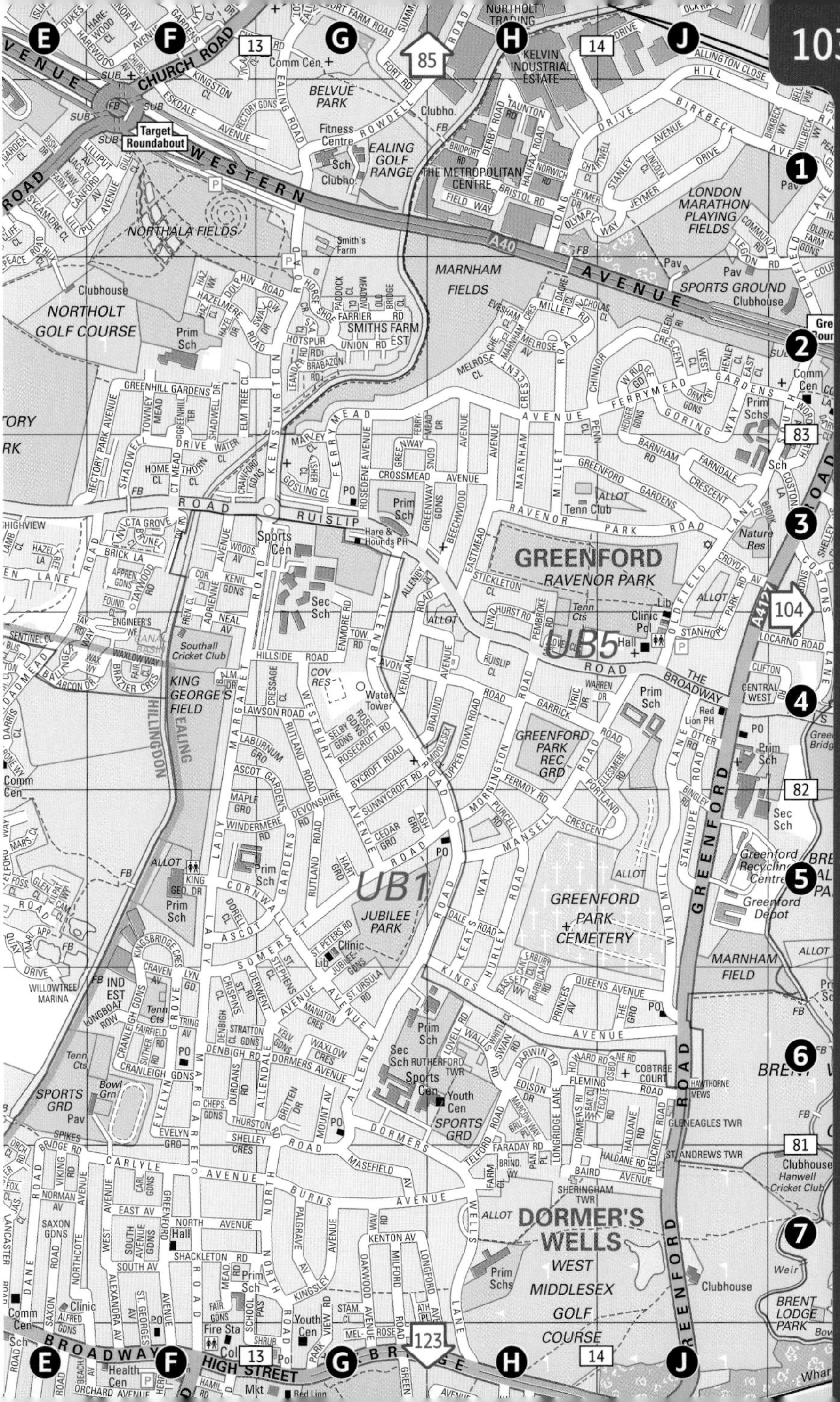
E
F
G
H
J
13
14
85
123
104
83
82
81
1
2
3
4
5
6
7
Target Roundabout
CHURCH ROAD
WESTERN AVENUE
A40
NORTHOLT TRADING
KELVIN INDUSTRIAL ESTATE
BELVUE PARK
Comm Cen
EALING ROAD
FORT RD
ROWDELL RD
Clubho.
Fitness Centre
EALING GOLF RANGE
THE METROPOLITAN CENTRE
BRISTOL RD
FIELD WAY
LONDON MARATHON PLAYING FIELDS
SPORTS GROUND
Clubhouse
NORTHALA FIELDS
MARNHAM FIELDS
NORTHOLT GOLF COURSE
SMITHS FARM EST
HOTSPUR RD
FERRYMEAD AVENUE
FERRYMEAD GARDENS
GREENHILL GARDENS
KENSINGTON ROAD
RUISLIP ROAD
Hare & Hounds PH
Sports Cen
Sec Sch
Prim Sch
RAVENOR PARK ROAD
GREENFORD
RAVENOR PARK
UB5
Clinic
Pol
Hall
Lib
OLDFIELD LANE
Nature Res
A4127
LOCARNO ROAD
Southall Cricket Club
KING GEORGE'S FIELD
HILLINGDON
EALING
ALLENBY ROAD
HILLSIDE ROAD
LAWSON ROAD
Water Tower
GREENFORD PARK REC GRD
THE BROADWAY
Red Lion PH
GREENFORD ROAD
UB1
JUBILEE PARK
GREENFORD PARK CEMETERY
Greenford Recycling Centre
Greenford Depot
MARNHAM FIELD
WINDMILL LANE
LADY MARGARET ROAD
CORNWALL ROAD
SOMERSET AVENUE
QUEENS AVENUE
IND EST
WILLOWTREE MARINA
SPORTS GRD
DORMERS AVENUE
DORMERS WELLS LANE
Youth Cen
COBTREE COURT
HAWTHORNE MEWS
GLENEAGLES TWR
ST. ANDREWS TWR
Clubhouse
Hanwell Cricket Club
CARLYLE AVENUE
BURNS AVENUE
DORMER'S WELLS
WEST MIDDLESEX GOLF COURSE
Weir
BRENT LODGE PARK
BROADWAY
HIGH STREET
Health Cen
Fire Sta
Mkt
Red Lion

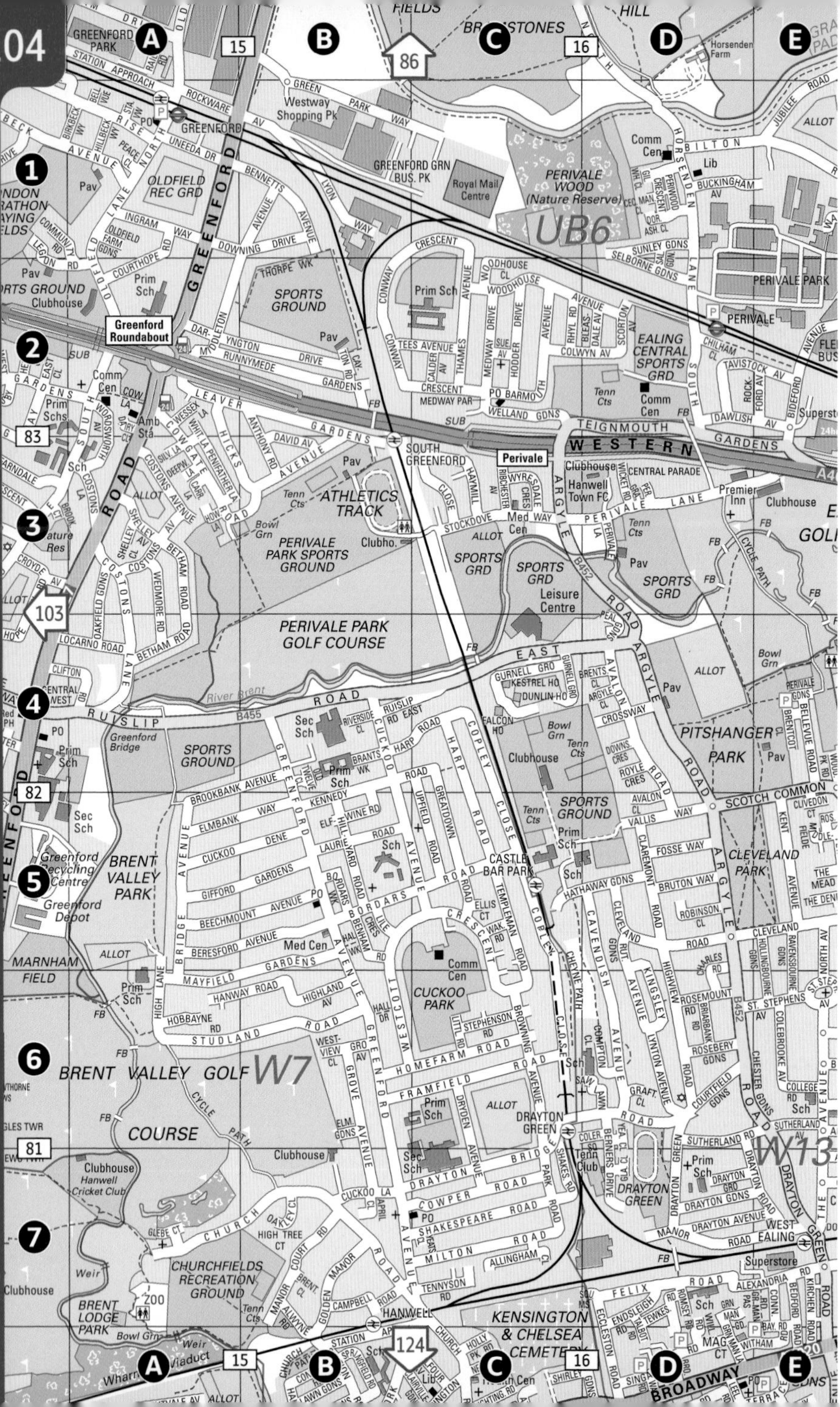
A
B
C
D
E
1
2
3
4
5
6
7
15
16
86
103
124
83
82
81
GREENFORD PARK
STATION APPROACH
FIELDS
BRABSTONES
HILL
Horsenden Farm
GREEN PARK WAY
Westway Shopping Pk
ROCKWARE AV
GREENFORD
UNEEDA DR
BIRKBECK AV
OLDFIELD REC GRD
OLDFIELD LANE NORTH
GREENFORD ROAD
BENNETTS AV
LYON WAY
GREENFORD GRN BUS. PK
Royal Mail Centre
PERIVALE WOOD (Nature Reserve)
UB6
Comm Cen
Lib
BILTON
BUCKINGHAM AV
HORSENDEN LANE
JUBILEE ROAD
ALLOT
INGRAM WAY
COMMUNITY RD
LEGION RD
COURTHOPE RD
DOWNING DRIVE
THORPE WK
SPORTS GROUND
CRESCENT
WOODHOUSE CL
WOODHOUSE AVENUE
SUNLEY GDNS
SELBORNE GDNS
PERIVALE PARK
PERIVALE
Prim Sch
Pav
SPORTS GROUND
Clubhouse
Greenford Roundabout
DARTYNGTON
MIDDLETON
RUNNYMEDE GARDENS
TEES AVENUE
CONWAY CRESCENT
MEDWAY DRIVE
HODDER DRIVE
COLWYN AV
EALING CENTRAL SPORTS GRD
CHILHAM CL
TAVISTOCK AV
BIDEFORD AV
Tenn Cts
Comm Cen
MEDWAY PAR
PO BARMOUTH
WELLAND GDNS
DAWLISH AV
Superstore
SUB
LEAVER GARDENS
WESSEX
COWGATE
HICKS AV
ANTHONY RD
DAVID AV
Amb Sta
SOUTH GREENFORD
Perivale
TEIGNMOUTH GARDENS
WESTERN
A40
WORDSWORTH
Prim Schs
Sch
ATHLETICS TRACK
Pav
Tenn Cts
HAYMILL CLOSE
RIBCHESTER AV
WYRESDALE CRES
Clubhouse
Hanwell Town FC
CENTRAL PARADE
PERIVALE LANE
Premier Inn
ARGYLE ROAD
Med Cen
STOCKDOVE WAY
ALLOT
COSTONS AVENUE
COSTONS LANE
BETHAM ROAD
WEDMORE RD
SHELLEY AV
Bowl Grn
PERIVALE PARK SPORTS GROUND
Clubho.
SPORTS GRD
SPORTS GRD
Leisure Centre
SPORTS GRD
GOLF
CYCLE PATH
FB
CROYDE AV
OAKFIELD GDNS
LOCARNO ROAD
PERIVALE PARK GOLF COURSE
EAST
B452
Bowl Grn
CLIFTON
CENTRAL WEST
River Brent
RUISLIP ROAD
B455
RUISLIP RD EAST
GURNELL GRO
KESTREL HO
DUNLIN HO
BRENTS CL
AVALON CL
CROSSWAY
ALLOT
Pav
PITSHANGER PARK
PERIVALE GDNS
BRENTCOT
BELLEVUE ROAD
Greenford Bridge
SPORTS GROUND
Sec Sch
RIVERSIDE CL
CUCKOO AV
HARP ROAD
COPLEY CLOSE
FALCON HO
Bowl Grn
Clubhouse
Tenn Cts
DOWNS CRES
ROYLE CRES
SCOTCH COMMON
CLIVEDON CT
PO
Prim Sch
Sec Sch
BROOKBANK AVENUE
ELMBANK WAY
GREENFORD AVENUE
KENNEDY RD
WINE RD
UPFIELD ROAD
GREATDOWN ROAD
HARP ROAD
SPORTS GROUND
AVALON CL
VALLIS WAY
Greenford Recycling Centre
Greenford Depot
BRENT VALLEY PARK
CUCKOO DENE
GIFFORD GARDENS
BEECHMOUNT AVENUE
BERESFORD AVENUE
LAURIE ROAD
HILL-YARD
BORDARS ROAD
CASTLE BAR PARK
TEMPLEMAN ROAD
ELLIS CT
CLAREMONT ROAD
FOSSE WAY
BRUTON WAY
HATHAWAY GDNS
CLEVELAND PARK
CLEVELAND ROAD
ROBINSON CL
KENT AVENUE
THE MEAD
THE DENE
NORTH AV
ALLOT
MARNHAM FIELD
Med Cen
MAYFIELD GARDENS
HANWAY ROAD
HIGHLAND AV
BRIDGE AVENUE
CUCKOO PARK
Comm Cen
COPLEY CLOSE
CHEYNE PATH
CAVENDISH AVENUE
KINGSLEY AVENUE
HIGHVIEW
CHARLES RD
ROSEMOUNT RD
BRIARBANK RD
ST. STEPHENS AV
COLEBROOKE AV
HIGH LANE
HOBBAYNE RD
STUDLAND ROAD
WESTVIEW CL
GROVE AVENUE
WESTCOTT
STEPHENSON RD
BROWNING AVENUE
HOMEFARM ROAD
COMPTON CL
LYNTON AVENUE
ROSEBERY GDNS
CHESTER GDNS
COLLEGE RD
BRENT VALLEY GOLF COURSE
W7
FRAMFIELD ROAD
DRYDEN AVENUE
ALLOT
DRAYTON GREEN
GRAFTON CL
COURTFIELD GDNS
SUTHERLAND
CYCLE PATH
ELM GDNS
Clubhouse
Prim Sch
Sec Sch
DRAYTON BRIDGE ROAD
PARK RD
SHAKESPEARE RD
BERNERS DRIVE
Tenn Club
DRAYTON GREEN
SUTHERLAND RD
DRAYTON GDNS
DRAYTON ROAD
W13
Clubhouse
Hanwell Cricket Club
CUCKOO LA
COWPER ROAD
SHAKESPEARE ROAD
MILTON ROAD
ALLINGHAM CL
TENNYSON RD
MANOR ROAD
DRAYTON AVENUE
WEST EALING
Superstore
GLEBE CT
CHURCH ROAD
OAKLEY CL
HIGH TREE CT
COURT RD
APRIL
PO
Weir
Clubhouse
CHURCHFIELDS RECREATION GROUND
MANOR CT
BRENT CL
GOLDEN MANOR
CAMPBELL ROAD
ALWYNE RD
HANWELL
KENSINGTON & CHELSEA CEMETERY
FELIX ROAD
ENDSLEIGH RD
TALBOT RD
TEWKESBURY RD
ECCLESTON ROAD
ALEXANDRIA RD
BEDFORD RD
KIRCHEN ROAD
Sch
MAG CT
WITHAM
ZOO
BRENT LODGE PARK
Bowl Grn
Weir
Wharncliffe Viaduct
STATION RD
CHURCH
Lib
Health Cen
BROADWAY
SHIRLEY GDNS

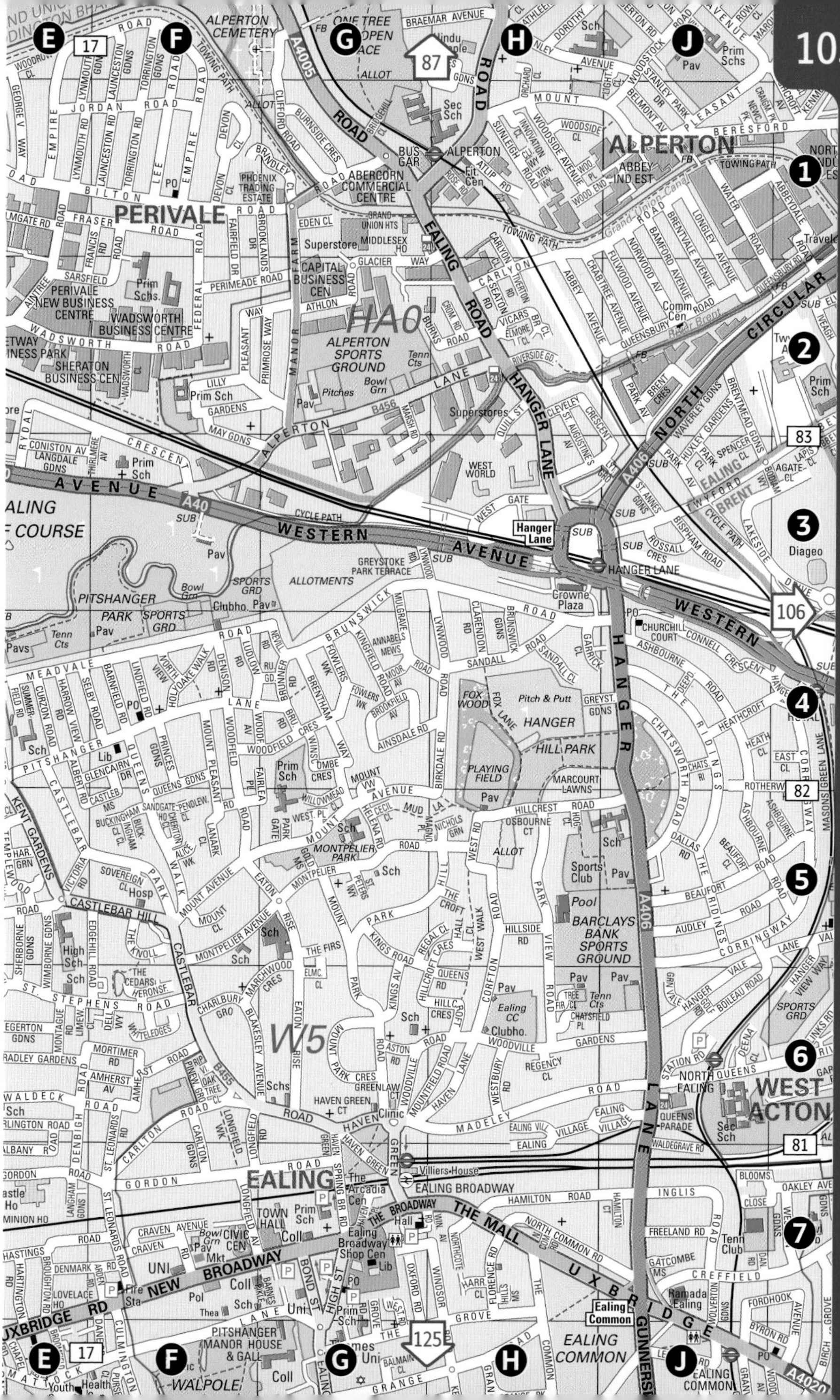
E
F
G
H
J
17
87
ALPERTON CEMETERY
ONE TREE OPEN SPACE
ALPERTON
PERIVALE
PERIVALE NEW BUSINESS CENTRE
WADSWORTH BUSINESS CENTRE
SHERATON BUSINESS CEN
ABERCORN COMMERCIAL CENTRE
PHOENIX TRADING ESTATE
CAPITAL BUSINESS CEN
ABBEY IND EST
HA0
ALPERTON SPORTS GROUND
EALING ROAD
HANGER LANE
NORTH CIRCULAR
WESTERN AVENUE
A40
A406
A4005
Grand Union Canal
River Brent
PITSHANGER PARK
HANGER HILL PARK
PLAYING FIELD
BARCLAYS BANK SPORTS GROUND
MONTPELIER PARK
W5
EALING
WEST ACTON
NORTH EALING
EALING COMMON
Ealing Broadway Shop Cen
TOWN HALL
THE BROADWAY
THE MALL
NEW BROADWAY
UXBRIDGE RD
UXBRIDGE ROAD
PITSHANGER MANOR HOUSE & GALL
WALPOLE
Hanger Lane
Ealing Common
Diageo
Crowne Plaza
1
2
3
4
5
6
7
83
82
81
106
125
A4020

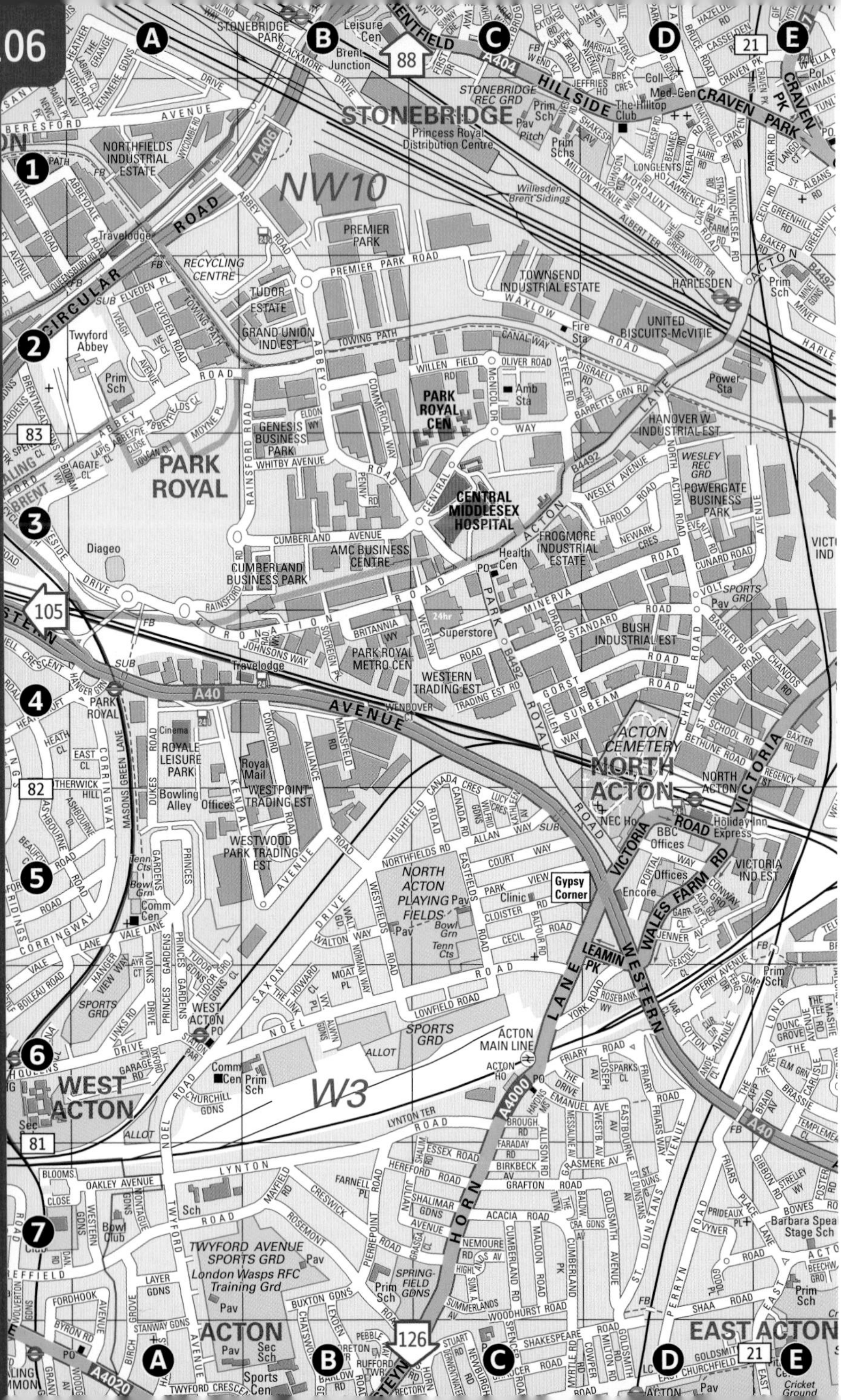
STONEBRIDGE
NW10
PARK ROYAL
NORTH ACTON
WEST ACTON
ACTON
EAST ACTON
W3
NORTHFIELDS INDUSTRIAL ESTATE
Princess Royal Distribution Centre
PREMIER PARK
RECYCLING CENTRE
TUDOR ESTATE
GRAND UNION IND EST
TOWNSEND INDUSTRIAL ESTATE
UNITED BISCUITS-McVITIE
HARLESDEN
PARK ROYAL CEN
GENESIS BUSINESS PARK
CENTRAL MIDDLESEX HOSPITAL
FROGMORE INDUSTRIAL ESTATE
HANOVER W INDUSTRIAL EST
POWERGATE BUSINESS PARK
AMC BUSINESS CENTRE
CUMBERLAND BUSINESS PARK
Diageo
Twyford Abbey
PARK ROYAL METRO CEN
WESTERN TRADING EST
BUSH INDUSTRIAL EST
ACTON CEMETERY
ROYALE LEISURE PARK
WESTPOINT TRADING EST
WESTWOOD PARK TRADING EST
NORTH ACTON PLAYING FIELDS
Gypsy Corner
BBC Offices
Holiday Inn Express
VICTORIA IND EST
ACTON MAIN LINE
TWYFORD AVENUE SPORTS GRD
London Wasps RFC Training Grd
Barbara Speake Stage Sch
A406
A404
A40
A4000
A4020
B4492
NORTH CIRCULAR ROAD
WESTERN AVENUE
HORN LANE
VICTORIA ROAD
WALES FARM RD
CORONATION ROAD
ACTON LANE
88
105
126
83
82
81
21

E
F
G
H
J
22
23
89
NW10
BRONDESBURY PARK
ROUNDWOOD PARK
WILLESDEN SPORTS STADIUM
Sports Centre
KING EDWARD VII SPORTS GRD
Capital City Academy
SPORTS GRD
CRAVEN PK RD
MANOR PK ROAD
HIGH STREET
HARLESDEN
STATION RD
TUBBS ROAD
A404
A4000
HARROW ROAD
KENSAL RISE
KENSAL GREEN
KENSAL GREEN CEMETERY
ST. MARY'S RC CEMETERY
Crematorium
W10
GRAND UNION CANAL (Paddington Branch)
Gas Holders
MAINTENANCE DEPOT
WILLESDEN JUNCTION
Willesden Freight Terminal
SCRUBS LANE
HYTHE RD IND EST
GATEWAY INDUSTRIAL ESTATE
Car Warehouses
OLD OAK LANE
A219
LITTLE WORMWOOD SCRUBS
NORTH POLE INTERNATIONAL DEPOT
OLD OAK COMMON
WORMWOOD SCRUBS
W12
LINFORD CHRISTIE STADIUM
QUEEN CHARLOTTE & CHELSEA HOSP
HAMMERSMITH HOSPITAL
H.M. PRISON WORMWOOD SCRUBS
EAST ACTON
DU CANE ROAD
WOOD LANE
NORTH KENSINGTON
B.B.C. Worldwide
Westway Sports Cen
WESTWAY
A40
Savoy Circus
WHITE CITY EST
B.B.C. Media Village
B.B.C. Offices
WHITE CITY
B.B.C. Television Centre
WORMHOLT PARK
HAMMERSMITH PARK
King Fahad Academy
SPORTS GROUND
LOFTUS ROAD STADIUM
SHEPHERD'S
A3220
82
83
81
108
127
1
2
3
4
5
6
7

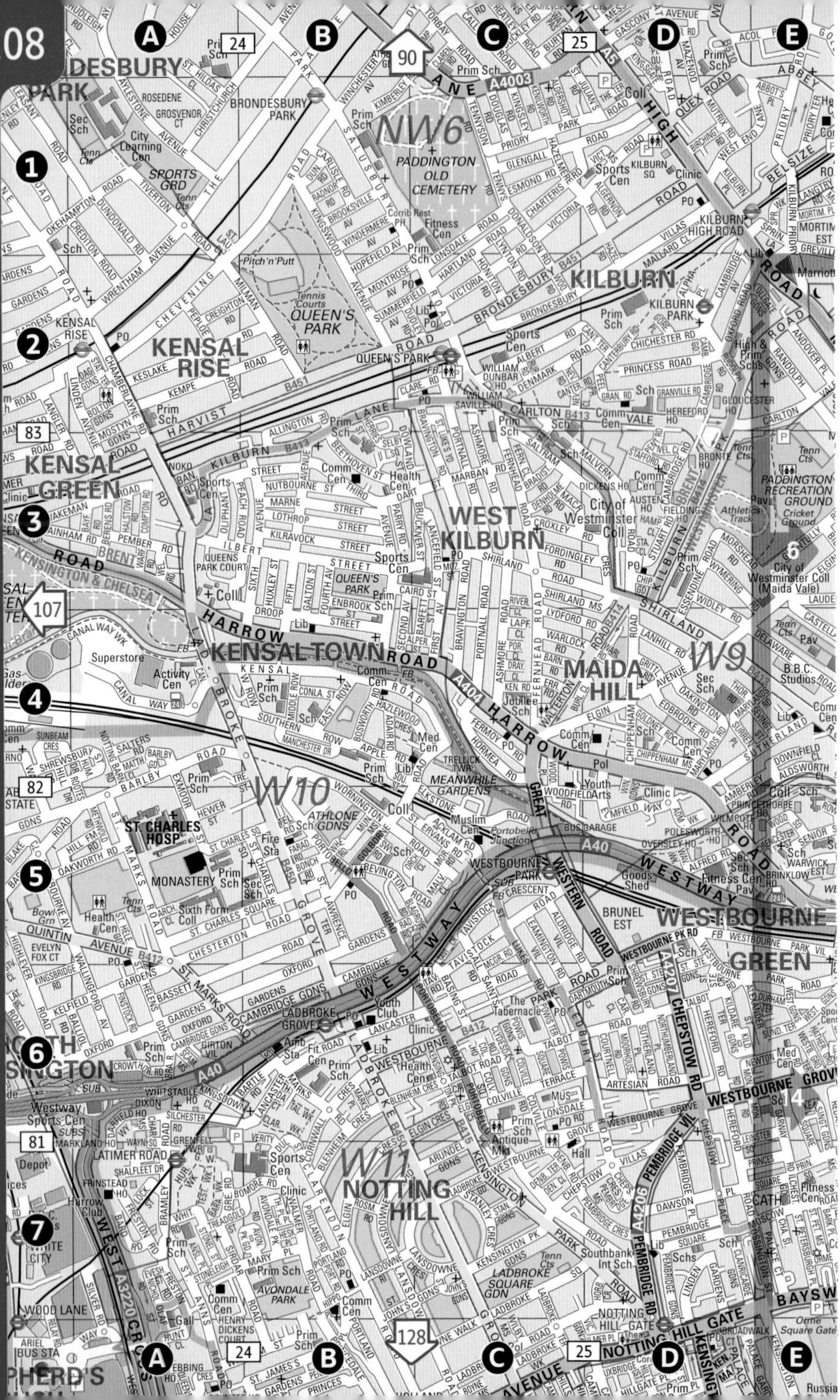

A
B
C
D
E
1
2
3
4
5
6
7
24
25
90
83
82
81
107
128
BRONDESBURY PARK
NW6
PADDINGTON OLD CEMETERY
QUEEN'S PARK
KILBURN
KILBURN HIGH ROAD
KILBURN PARK
KENSAL RISE
KENSAL GREEN
WEST KILBURN
MAIDA HILL
W9
KENSAL TOWN
HARROW ROAD
W10
ST. CHARLES HOSP
MONASTERY
WESTBOURNE PARK
WESTWAY
WESTBOURNE GREEN
A40
A404
A4003
A5
B451
B413
B412
B450
A4207
A4206
A3220
W11
NOTTING HILL
NOTTING HILL GATE
LADBROKE GROVE
LATIMER ROAD
WOOD LANE
WHITE CITY
LADBROKE SQUARE GDN
AVONDALE PARK
PADDINGTON RECREATION GROUND
City of Westminster Coll
B.B.C. Studios
KENSINGTON & CHELSEA
BRENT
BAYSWATER
Orme Square Gate

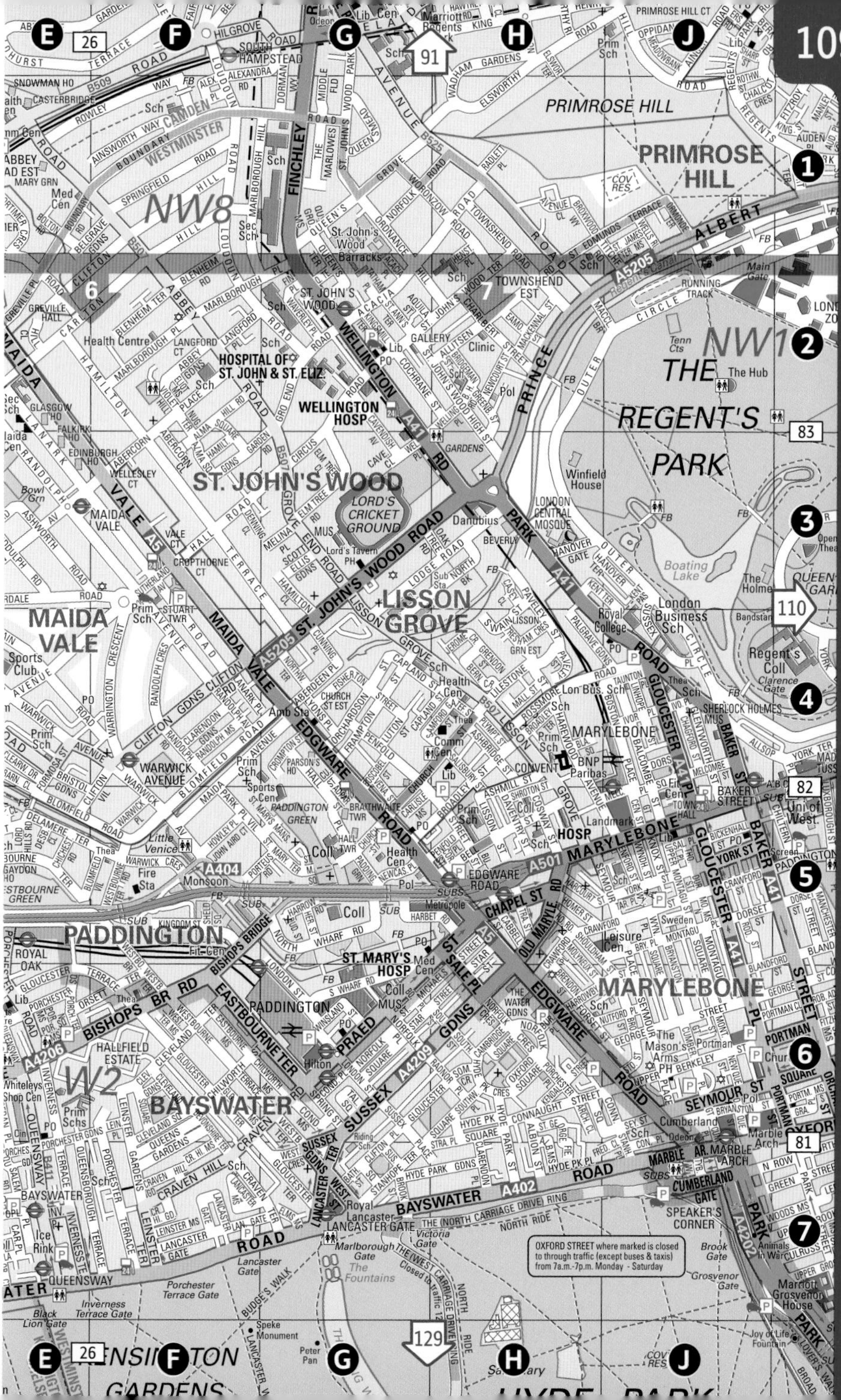
E
F
G
H
J
26
91
1
2
3
4
5
6
7
6
7
83
110
82
81
129
NW8
NW1
W2
PRIMROSE HILL
PRIMROSE HILL
THE REGENT'S PARK
ST. JOHN'S WOOD
LORD'S CRICKET GROUND
LISSON GROVE
MAIDA VALE
PADDINGTON
BAYSWATER
MARYLEBONE
MARYLEBONE
KENSINGTON GARDENS
HYDE PARK
SOUTH HAMPSTEAD
FINCHLEY ROAD
WELLINGTON ROAD
ST. JOHN'S WOOD ROAD
PRINCE ALBERT ROAD
OUTER CIRCLE
PARK ROAD
BAKER STREET
GLOUCESTER PL
MARYLEBONE ROAD
EDGWARE ROAD
MAIDA VALE
PRAED ST
SUSSEX GDNS
BAYSWATER ROAD
BISHOPS BR RD
EASTBOURNE TER
HOSPITAL OF ST. JOHN & ST. ELIZ.
WELLINGTON HOSP
ST. MARY'S HOSP
Winfield House
LONDON CENTRAL MOSQUE
Boating Lake
London Business Sch
Regent's Coll
SHERLOCK HOLMES MUS
WARWICK AVENUE
ROYAL OAK
QUEENSWAY
LANCASTER GATE
MARBLE ARCH
SPEAKER'S CORNER
The Fountains
Speke Monument
Peter Pan
OXFORD STREET where marked is closed to through traffic (except buses & taxis) from 7a.m.-7p.m. Monday - Saturday

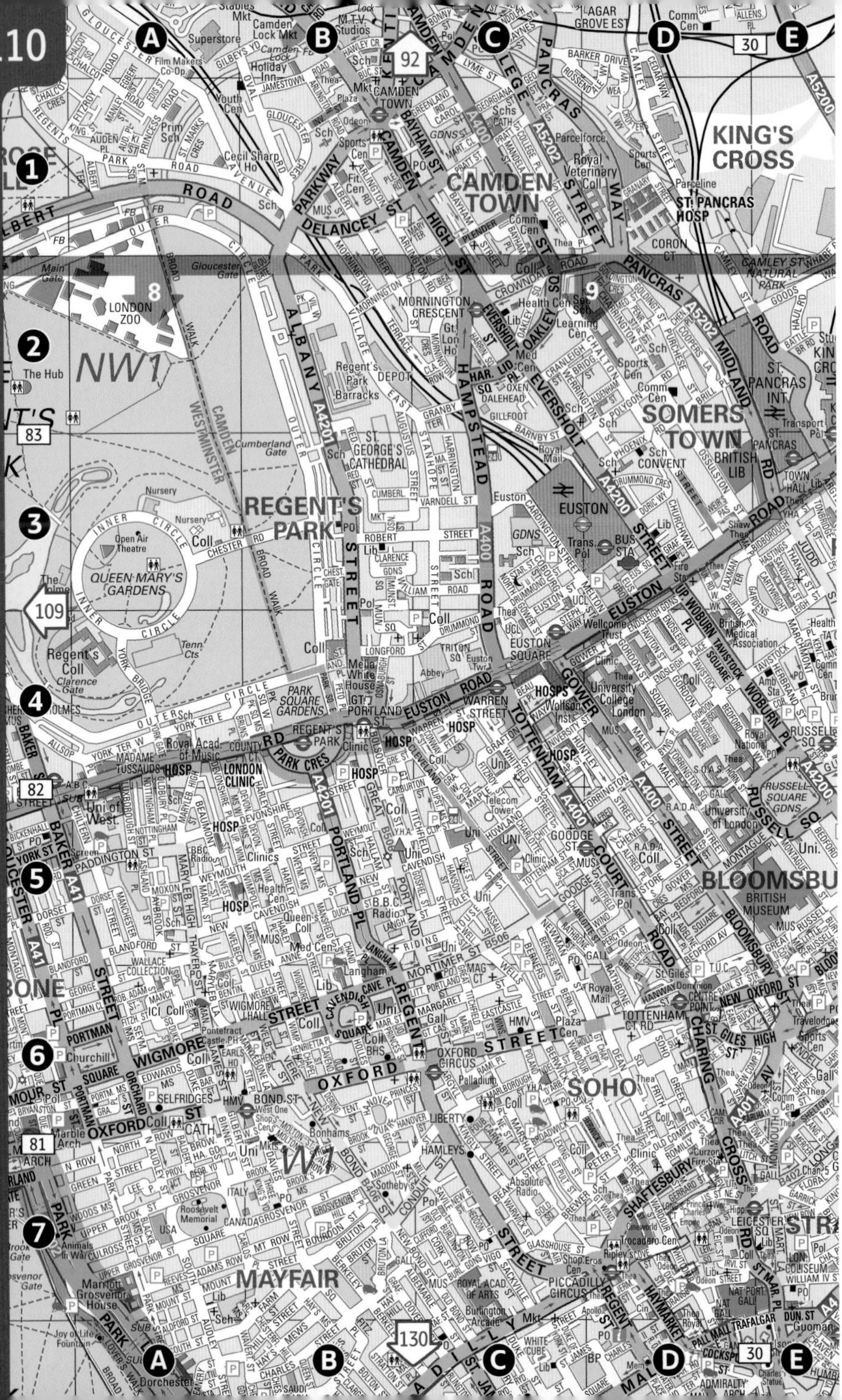
A
B
C
D
E
1
2
3
4
5
6
7
92
8
9
83
109
82
81
130
30
KING'S CROSS
CAMDEN TOWN
ST. PANCRAS HOSP
LONDON ZOO
NW1
SOMERS TOWN
BRITISH LIB
REGENT'S PARK
QUEEN MARY'S GARDENS
EUSTON
EUSTON ROAD
BLOOMSBU
BRITISH MUSEUM
University College London
SOHO
MAYFAIR
W1
OXFORD STREET
OXFORD CIRCUS
PICCADILLY CIRCUS
MARBLE ARCH
SELFRIDGES
TOTTENHAM COURT ROAD
HAMPSTEAD ROAD
REGENT STREET
PARK LANE
BAKER STREET
PORTLAND PL
CAVENDISH SQUARE
RUSSELL SQ
LEICESTER SQ
MADAME TUSSAUDS
LONDON CLINIC
CAMLEY ST NATURAL PARK
ST. PANCRAS INT
Telecom Tower
HAMLEYS
LIBERTY
Roosevelt Memorial
Royal Acad. of Music

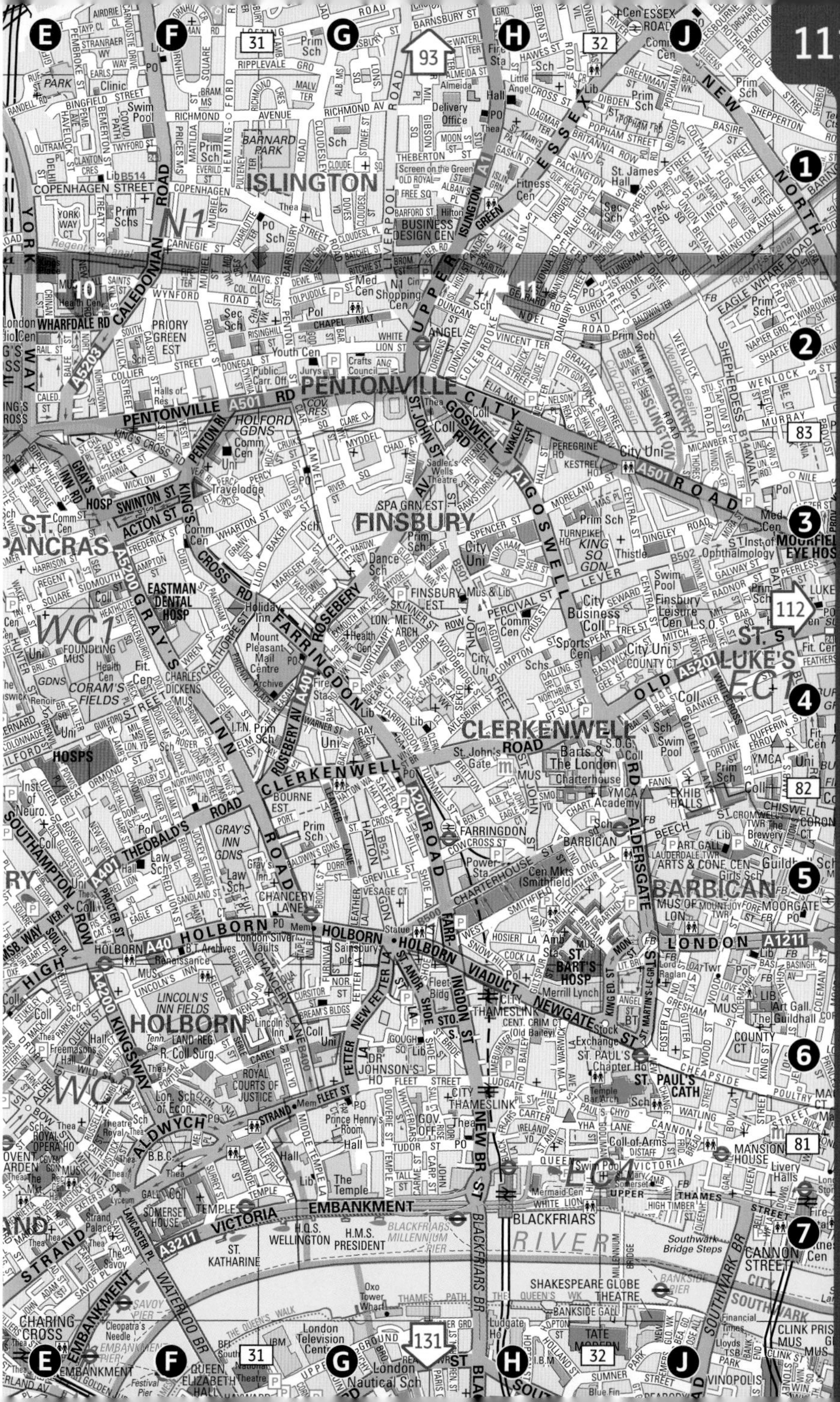
E
F
G
H
J
1
2
3
4
5
6
7
31
32
93
83
112
82
81
131
ISLINGTON
N1
PENTONVILLE
FINSBURY
ST. PANCRAS
WC1
CLERKENWELL
ST. LUKE'S
EC1
BARBICAN
HOLBORN
WC2
EC4
RIVER
CALEDONIAN ROAD
YORK WAY
PENTONVILLE RD
UPPER ST
CITY ROAD
GOSWELL RD
KING'S CROSS RD
GRAY'S INN ROAD
FARRINGDON RD
ROSEBERY AV
CLERKENWELL ROAD
THEOBALD'S ROAD
HOLBORN
HOLBORN VIADUCT
NEWGATE ST
ALDERSGATE ST
LONDON WALL
CHEAPSIDE
KINGSWAY
ALDWYCH
STRAND
FLEET ST
VICTORIA EMBANKMENT
UPPER THAMES STREET
BLACKFRIARS BR
WATERLOO BR
SOUTHWARK BR
NEW BR ST
ESSEX ROAD
NEW NORTH ROAD
OLD ST
ANGEL
FARRINGDON
BARBICAN
CHANCERY LANE
HOLBORN
TEMPLE
BLACKFRIARS
ST. PAUL'S
MANSION HOUSE
CANNON STREET
EMBANKMENT
CHARING CROSS
MOORGATE
Regent's Canal
City Rd Basin
Wenlock Basin
LINCOLN'S INN FIELDS
ROYAL COURTS OF JUSTICE
ST. PAUL'S CATH
TATE MODERN
SHAKESPEARE GLOBE THEATRE
SOMERSET HOUSE
H.Q.S. WELLINGTON
H.M.S. PRESIDENT
BLACKFRIARS MILLENNIUM PIER
SAVOY PIER
MOORFIELDS EYE HOSP
EASTMAN DENTAL HOSP
ST. BART'S HOSP
Mount Pleasant Mail Centre
CORAM'S FIELDS
GRAY'S INN GDNS
BUSINESS DESIGN CEN

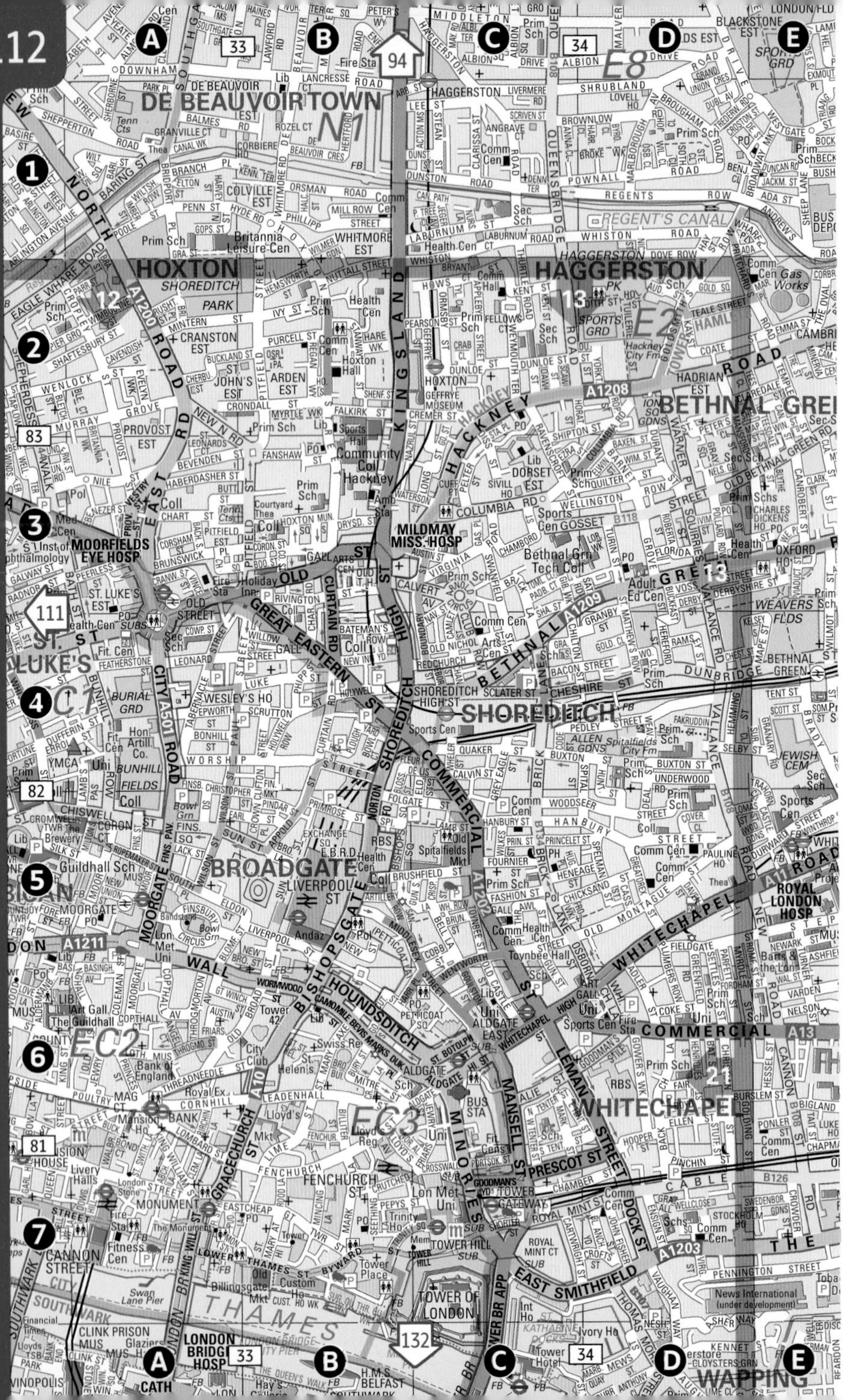
A
B
C
D
E
1
2
3
4
5
6
7
33
34
94
83
82
81
111
132
DE BEAUVOIR TOWN
N1
E8
HOXTON
SHOREDITCH PARK
HAGGERSTON
E2
BETHNAL GREEN
KINGSLAND
HACKNEY ROAD
REGENT'S CANAL
GREAT EASTERN ST
OLD STREET
CITY ROAD
SHOREDITCH
SHOREDITCH HIGH ST
COMMERCIAL ST
MOORFIELDS EYE HOSP
MILDMAY MISS. HOSP
ST. LUKE'S
EC1
BUNHILL FIELDS
BROADGATE
LIVERPOOL ST
BISHOPSGATE
HOUNDSDITCH
WHITECHAPEL
WHITECHAPEL ROAD
COMMERCIAL ROAD
ROYAL LONDON HOSP
EC2
EC3
MOORGATE
LONDON WALL
BANK
MONUMENT
FENCHURCH ST
ALDGATE
ALDGATE EAST
MINORIES
MANSELL ST
LEMAN STREET
PRESCOT ST
CABLE ST
EAST SMITHFIELD
TOWER HILL
TOWER OF LONDON
CANNON STREET
THAMES
LONDON BRIDGE HOSP
CLINK PRISON MUS
WAPPING
A1200
A1208
A1209
A501
A1211
A10
A1202
A11
A13
A1203
B108
B118
B126

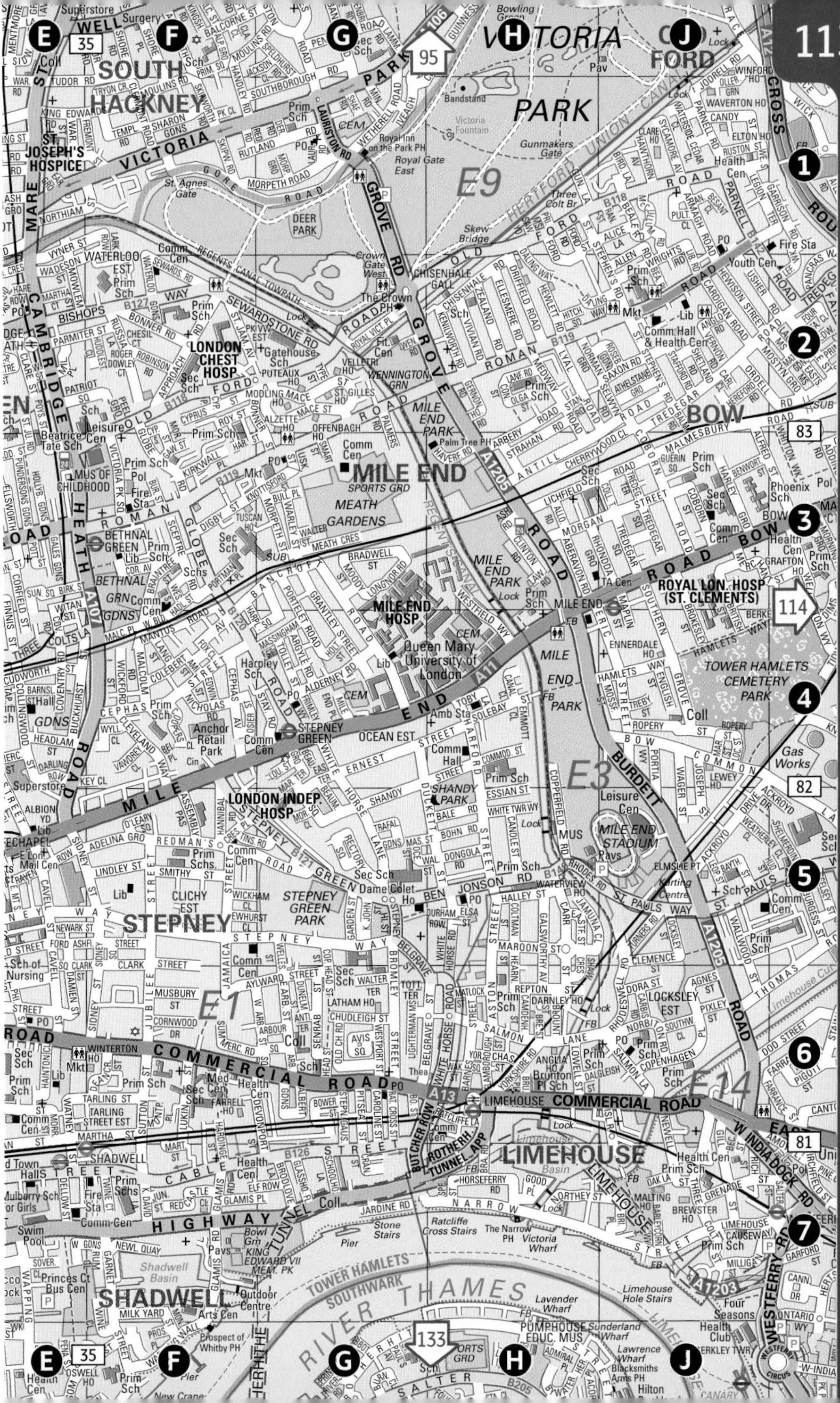
E
F
G
H
J
1
2
3
4
5
6
7
95
114
133
35
83
82
81
SOUTH HACKNEY
VICTORIA PARK
FORD
E9
E3
E1
E14
BOW
MILE END
STEPNEY
LIMEHOUSE
SHADWELL
VICTORIA PARK ROAD
GROVE ROAD
CAMBRIDGE HEATH ROAD
MARE ST
OLD FORD ROAD
ROMAN ROAD
MILE END ROAD
BOW ROAD
BURDETT ROAD
COMMERCIAL ROAD
CABLE STREET
HIGHWAY
WESTFERRY RD
W INDIA DOCK RD
RIVER THAMES
HERTFORD UNION CANAL
REGENT'S CANAL
ST. JOSEPH'S HOSPICE
LONDON CHEST HOSP
MILE END HOSP
LONDON INDEP. HOSP
ROYAL LON. HOSP (ST. CLEMENTS)
Queen Mary University of London
MILE END PARK
MILE END STADIUM
TOWER HAMLETS CEMETERY PARK
STEPNEY GREEN PARK
MEATH GARDENS
BETHNAL GRN GDNS
DEER PARK
Victoria Fountain
Bandstand
MUS OF CHILDHOOD
Shadwell Basin
Limehouse Basin
Gas Works
TOWER HAMLETS
SOUTHWARK

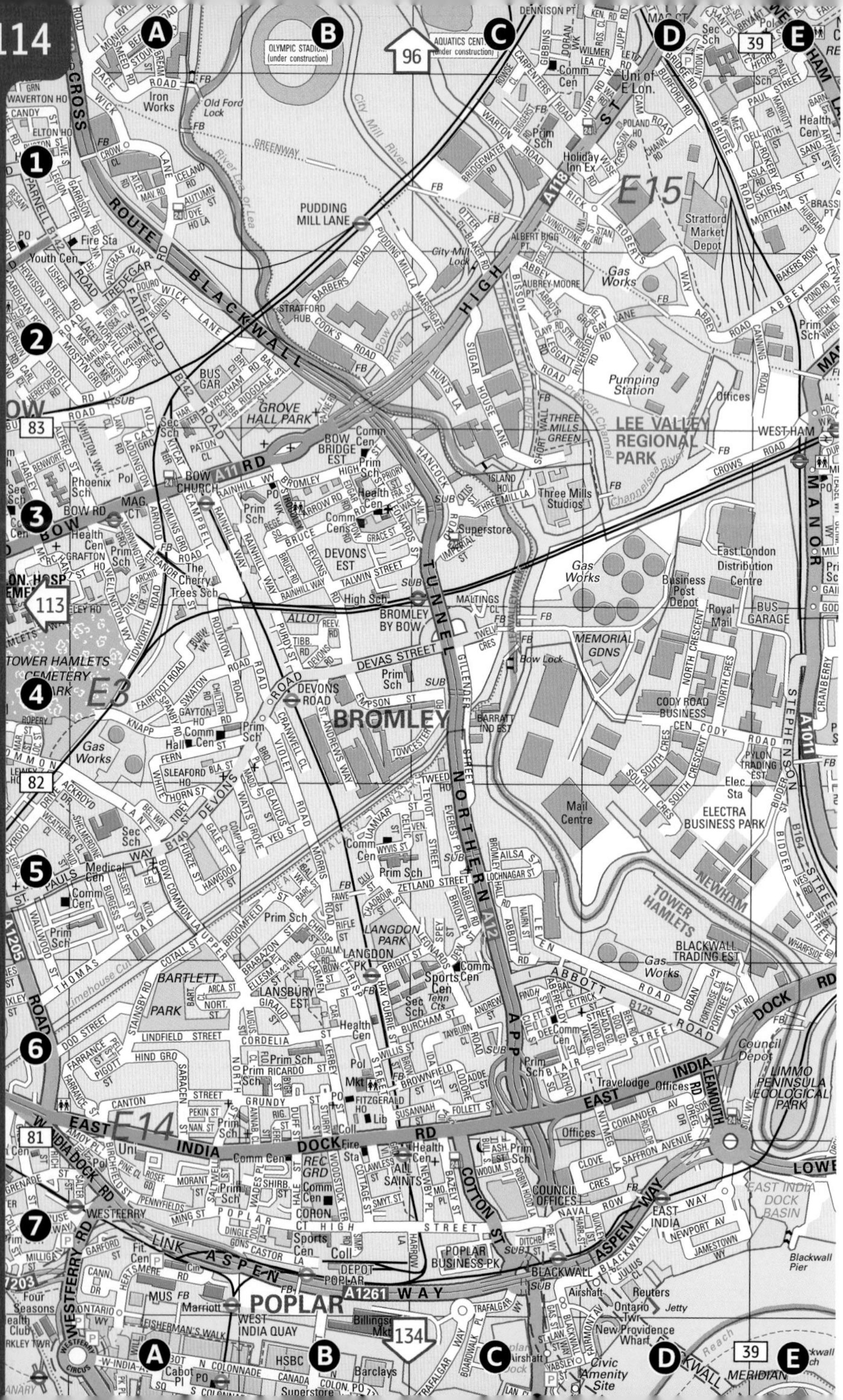
A
B
C
D
E
OLYMPIC STADIUM (under construction)
AQUATICS CENTRE (under construction)
96
39
1
2
3
4
5
6
7
83
113
82
81
134
E15
E3
E14
BROMLEY
POPLAR
BOW
BLACKWALL
ROUTE
TUNNEL
NORTHERN
APP
A12
A11
A118
A1011
A1205
A1261
B125
B140
B142
B164
HIGH ST
BOW RD
EAST INDIA DOCK RD
ASPEN WAY
LINK
COTTON ST
ABBOTT ROAD
DEVAS STREET
DEVONS ROAD
ST. PAULS WAY
BOW COMMON LA
UPPER NORTH STREET
CHRISP ST
WESTFERRY RD
WESTFERRY CIRCUS
MANOR
STEPHENSON
ABBEY ROAD
CARPENTERS ROAD
WARTON ROAD
PUDDING MILL LANE
SUGAR HOUSE LANE
THREE MILLS WALL RIVER
CROWS ROAD
LEAMOUTH RD
SAFFRON AVENUE
NEWPORT AV
JAMESTOWN WY
Iron Works
Old Ford Lock
GREENWAY
River Lea or Lea
City Mill River
City Mill Lock
Bow Back Rivers
Prescott Channel
Channelsea River
Limehouse Cut
Bow Lock
STRATFORD HUB
GROVE HALL PARK
BOW BRIDGE EST
DEVONS EST
BOW CHURCH
BROMLEY BY BOW
DEVONS ROAD
LANGDON PK
ALL SAINTS
WESTFERRY
WEST INDIA QUAY
BLACKWALL
EAST INDIA
WEST HAM
Three Mills Studios
THREE MILLS GREEN
LEE VALLEY REGIONAL PARK
Pumping Station
Gas Works
Holiday Inn Ex
Uni of E Lon.
Stratford Market Depot
East London Distribution Centre
Business Post Depot
Royal Mail
BUS GARAGE
MEMORIAL GDNS
Mail Centre
CODY ROAD BUSINESS CEN
PYLON TRADING EST
ELECTRA BUSINESS PARK
TOWER HAMLETS
NEWHAM
BLACKWALL TRADING EST
Council Depot
LIMMO PENINSULA ECOLOGICAL PARK
EAST INDIA DOCK BASIN
Blackwall Pier
TOWER HAMLETS CEMETERY PARK
LANGDON PARK
LANSBURY EST
BARTLETT PARK
REC GRD
POPLAR BUSINESS PK
COUNCIL OFFICES
Travelodge
Billingsgate Mkt
Marriott
HSBC
Barclays
Cabot Pl
Four Seasons
Health Club
Reuters
Airshaft
Ontario Twr
New Providence Wharf
Jetty
Civic Amenity Site
MERIDIAN
Superstore
Sports Cen
Prim Sch
Sec Sch
Health Cen
Comm Cen
Mkt
Lib
Fire Sta
Youth Cen

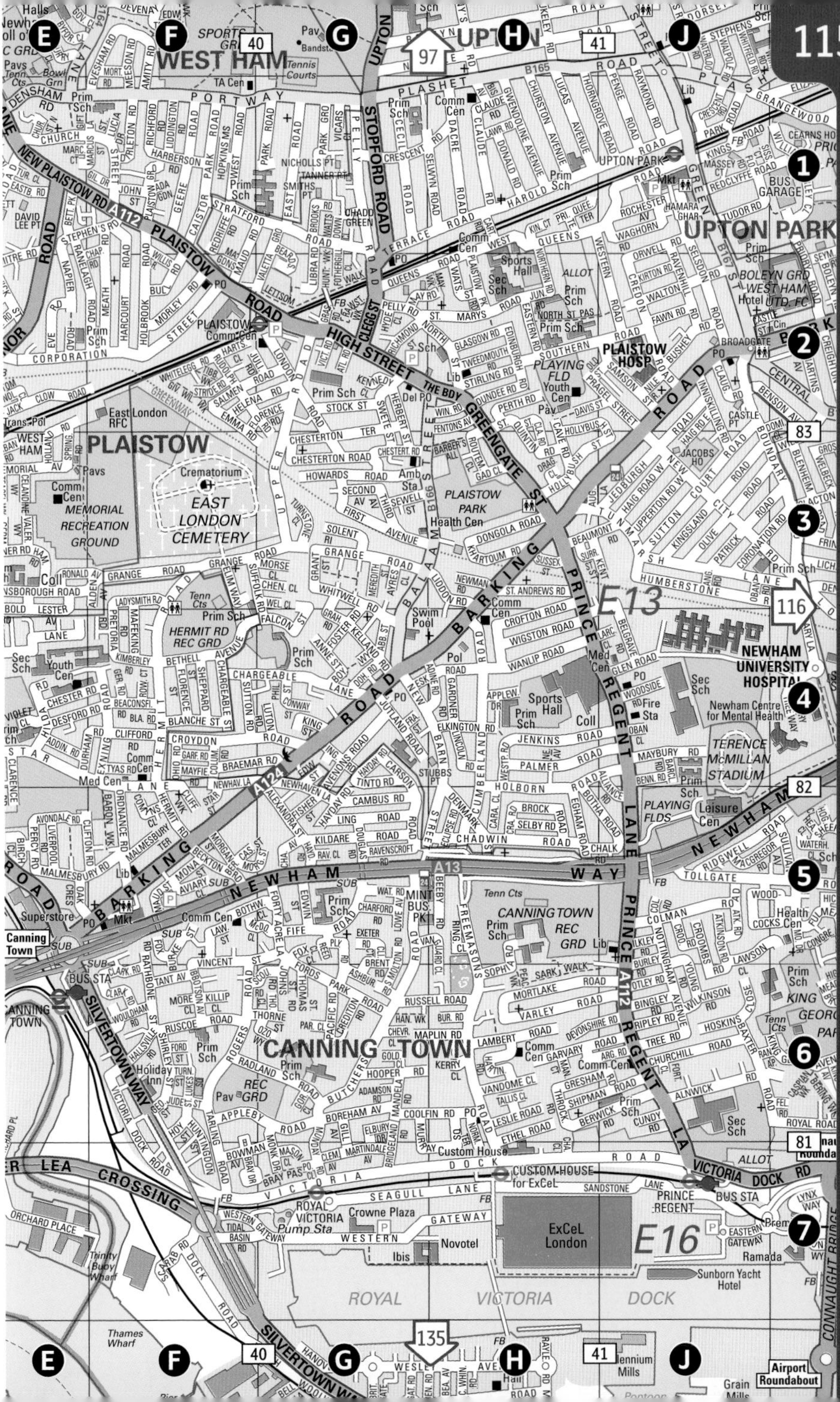
E
F
G
H
J
40
41
97
83
116
82
81
135
1
2
3
4
5
6
7
WEST HAM
UPTON
UPTON PARK
PLAISTOW
E13
CANNING TOWN
E16
NEWHAM UNIVERSITY HOSPITAL
Newham Centre for Mental Health
TERENCE McMILLAN STADIUM
PLAISTOW HOSP
BOLEYN GRD WEST HAM UTD. FC
EAST LONDON CEMETERY
Crematorium
MEMORIAL RECREATION GROUND
HERMIT RD REC GRD
CANNING TOWN REC GRD
PLAISTOW PARK
ExCeL London
ROYAL VICTORIA DOCK
Crowne Plaza
Novotel
Ibis
Ramada
Sunborn Yacht Hotel
Holiday Inn
East London RFC
Canning Town
CANNING TOWN
CUSTOM HOUSE for ExCeL
ROYAL VICTORIA
PRINCE REGENT
UPTON PARK
PLAISTOW
PLAISTOW ROAD
NEW PLAISTOW RD
A112
HIGH STREET
GREENGATE ST
BARKING ROAD
A124
PRINCE REGENT LANE
NEWHAM WAY
A13
VICTORIA DOCK ROAD
SILVERTOWN WAY
LEA CROSSING
STOPFORD ROAD
PORTWAY
PLASHET ROAD
GREEN STREET
BALAAM STREET
TUNMARSH LANE
HUMBERSTONE ROAD
Airport Roundabout
CONNAUGHT BRIDGE
Trinity Buoy Wharf
Thames Wharf
Pump Sta
Superstore
Millennium Mills
Grain Mills

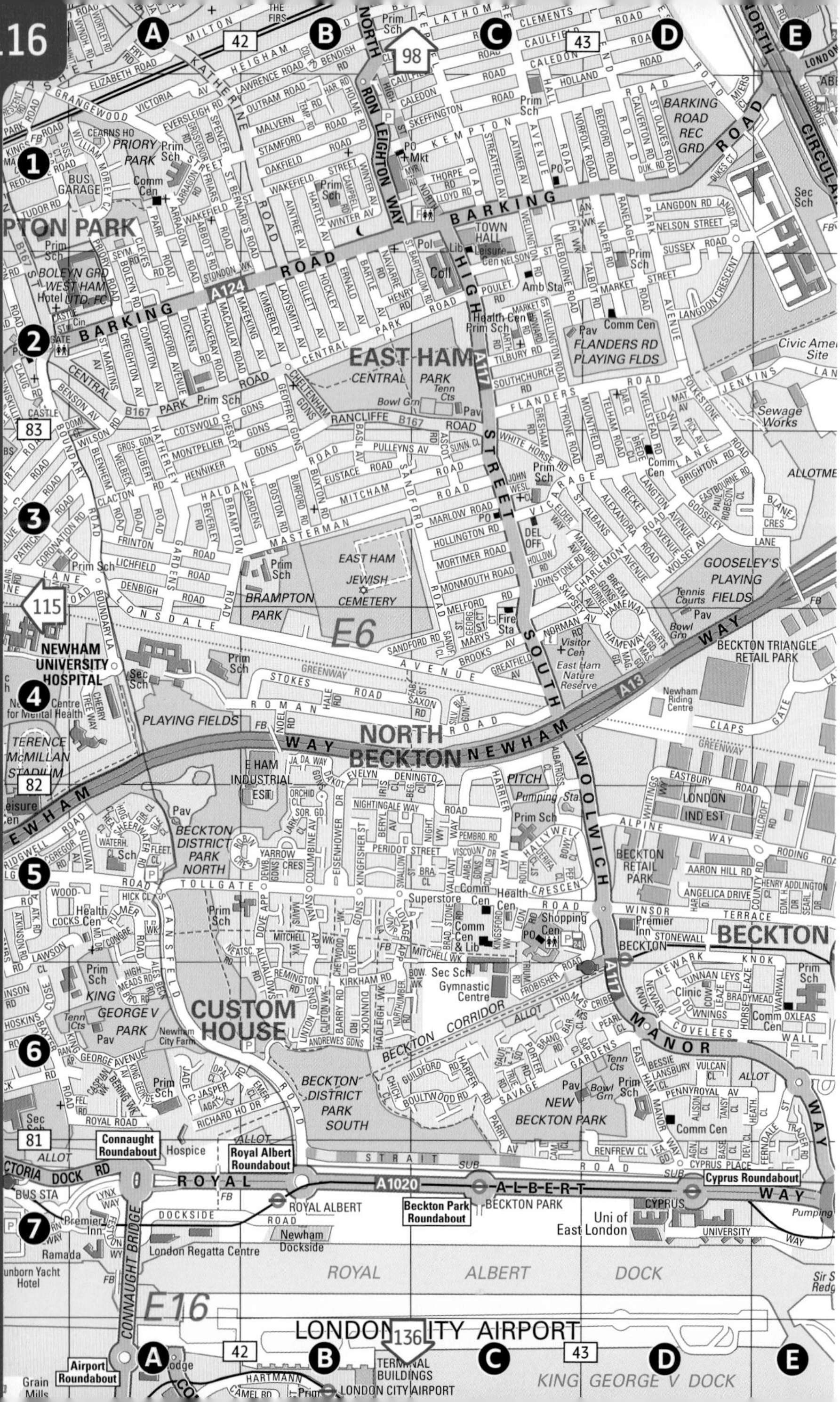
A
B
C
D
E
1
2
3
4
5
6
7
42
43
98
115
136
83
82
81
EAST HAM
NORTH BECKTON
BECKTON
CUSTOM HOUSE
E6
E16
PTON PARK
EAST HAM CENTRAL PARK
BRAMPTON PARK
EAST HAM JEWISH CEMETERY
PRIORY PARK
BUS GARAGE
BOLEYN GRD WEST HAM UTD. FC
BARKING ROAD REC GRD
FLANDERS RD PLAYING FLDS
GOOSELEY'S PLAYING FIELDS
PLAYING FIELDS
NEWHAM UNIVERSITY HOSPITAL
Newham Centre for Mental Health
TERENCE McMILLAN STADIUM
BECKTON DISTRICT PARK NORTH
BECKTON DISTRICT PARK SOUTH
KING GEORGE V PARK
NEW BECKTON PARK
E HAM INDUSTRIAL EST
LONDON IND EST
BECKTON RETAIL PARK
BECKTON TRIANGLE RETAIL PARK
Newham Riding Centre
East Ham Nature Reserve
Visitor Cen
Sewage Works
Civic Amen Site
ALLOTME
TOWN HALL
Leisure Cen
Health Cen
Comm Cen
Amb Sta
Fire Sta
Pumping Sta
Shopping Cen
Superstore
Gymnastic Centre
Newham City Farm
Hospice
Premier Inn
Ramada
Sunborn Yacht Hotel
London Regatta Centre
Newham Dockside
Uni of East London
ROYAL ALBERT DOCK
KING GEORGE V DOCK
LONDON CITY AIRPORT
TERMINAL BUILDINGS
Grain Mills
Connaught Roundabout
Royal Albert Roundabout
Beckton Park Roundabout
Cyprus Roundabout
Airport Roundabout
ROYAL ALBERT
BECKTON PARK
CYPRUS
BECKTON
BARKING ROAD
A124
HIGH STREET SOUTH
A117
NEWHAM WAY
A13
WOOLWICH MANOR WAY
ROYAL ALBERT WAY
A1020
RON LEIGHTON WAY
NORTH CIRCULAR
CONNAUGHT BRIDGE
VICTORIA DOCK RD
DOCKSIDE ROAD
UNIVERSITY WAY
STRAIT ROAD
BECKTON CORRIDOR
TOLLGATE ROAD
STANSFELD ROAD
ROMAN ROAD
STOKES ROAD
LONSDALE AVENUE
MASTERMAN ROAD
CENTRAL PARK ROAD
RANCLIFFE ROAD
B167
KATHERINE ROAD
HEIGHAM ROAD
MILTON AV
ST. BERNARD'S ROAD
WAKEFIELD STREET
GRANGEWOOD ST
CLEMENTS ROAD
CAULFIELD ROAD
CALEDON ROAD
HOLLAND ROAD
KEMPTON ROAD
LANGDON CRESCENT
FOLKESTONE ROAD
VICARAGE LANE
WHITE HORSE RD
SANDFORD ROAD
EASTBURY ROAD
ALPINE WAY
RODING ROAD
WINSOR TERRACE
NEWARK KNOK
COVELEES WALL
PENNYROYAL AV
SAVAGE GARDENS
ROYAL ROAD
HARTMANN
CAMEL RD

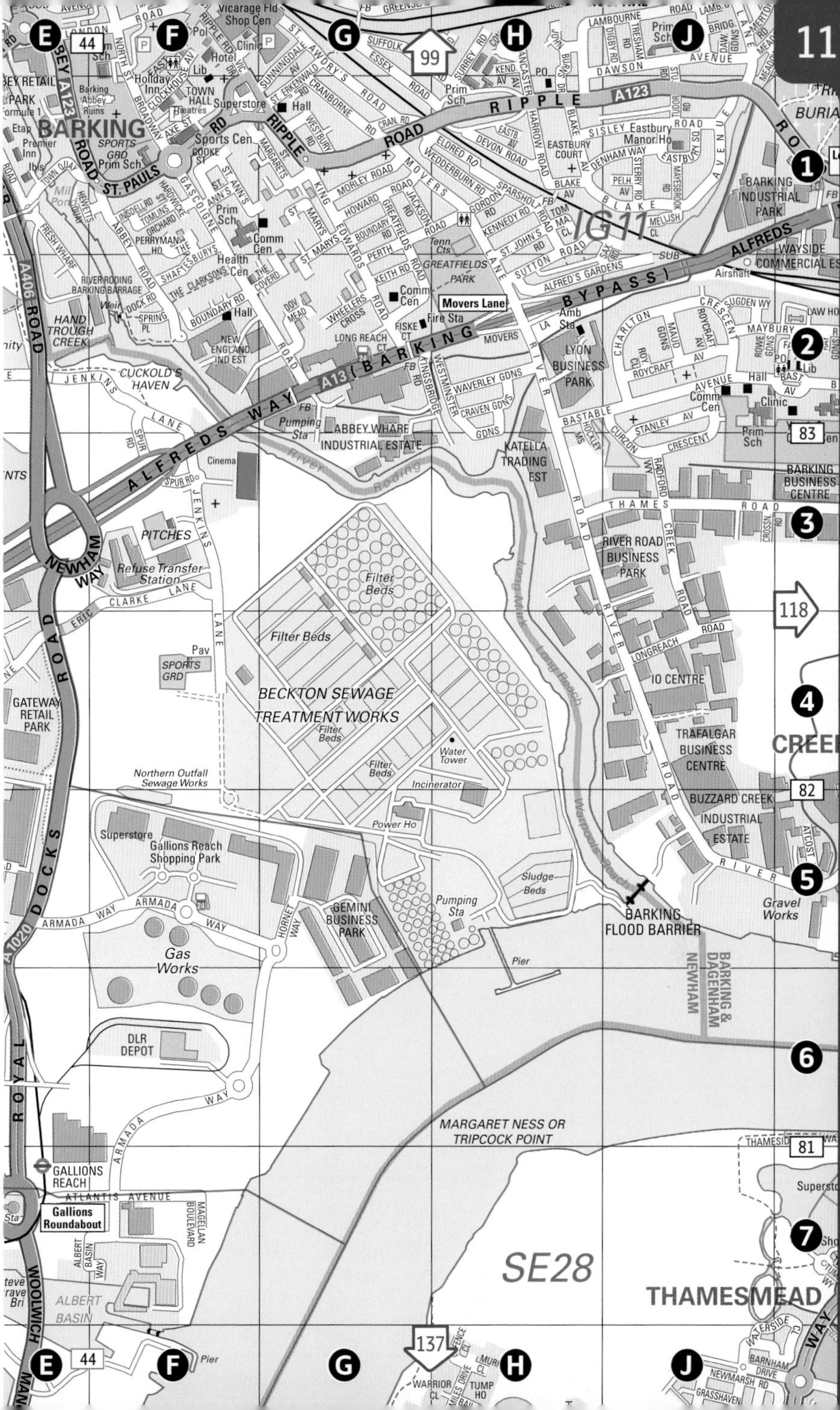
E
F
G
H
J
44
99
BARKING
IG11
SE28
THAMESMEAD
BARKING RETAIL PARK
Barking Abbey Ruins
Holiday Inn
TOWN HALL
Theatres
Vicarage Fld Shop Cen
Superstore
Sports Cen
Prim Sch
Premier Inn
Ibis
Formula 1
Etap
Mill Pond
RIPPLE ROAD
A123
ST. PAULS RD
ALFREDS WAY
A13 (BARKING BYPASS)
Movers Lane
Fire Sta
Comm Cen
Health Cen
Hall
GREATFIELDS PARK
Tenn Cts
Amb Sta
LYON BUSINESS PARK
KATELLA TRADING EST
ABBEY WHARF INDUSTRIAL ESTATE
NEW ENGLAND IND EST
Pumping Sta
RIVER RODING BARKING BARRAGE
Weir
HAND TROUGH CREEK
CUCKOLD'S HAVEN
River Roding
Cinema
PITCHES
Refuse Transfer Station
ERIC CLARKE LANE
JENKINS LANE
NEWHAM WAY
A406 ROAD
DOCKS ROAD
A1020
Pav
SPORTS GRD
GATEWAY RETAIL PARK
Filter Beds
BECKTON SEWAGE TREATMENT WORKS
Water Tower
Incinerator
Power Ho
Northern Outfall Sewage Works
Superstore
Gallions Reach Shopping Park
ARMADA WAY
HORNET WAY
GEMINI BUSINESS PARK
Gas Works
Sludge Beds
Pumping Sta
Pier
DLR DEPOT
Long Reach
Warpools Reach
BARKING FLOOD BARRIER
NEWHAM
BARKING & DAGENHAM
EASTBURY COURT
Eastbury Manor Ho
BARKING INDUSTRIAL PARK
WAYSIDE COMMERCIAL EST
Airshaft
RIVER ROAD
THAMES ROAD
RIVER ROAD BUSINESS PARK
IO CENTRE
TRAFALGAR BUSINESS CENTRE
BUZZARD CREEK INDUSTRIAL ESTATE
BARKING BUSINESS CENTRE
Gravel Works
CREEK
Clinic
Lib
Prim Sch
83
118
82
81
1
2
3
4
5
6
7
MARGARET NESS OR TRIPCOCK POINT
GALLIONS REACH
Gallions Roundabout
ATLANTIS AVENUE
MAGELLAN BOULEVARD
ALBERT BASIN WAY
ALBERT BASIN
ROYAL DOCKS ROAD
WOOLWICH MANOR WAY
137
Superstore
WATERSIDE CL
BARNHAM DRIVE
NEWMARSH RD
GRASSHAVEN
WARRIOR CL
TUMP HO

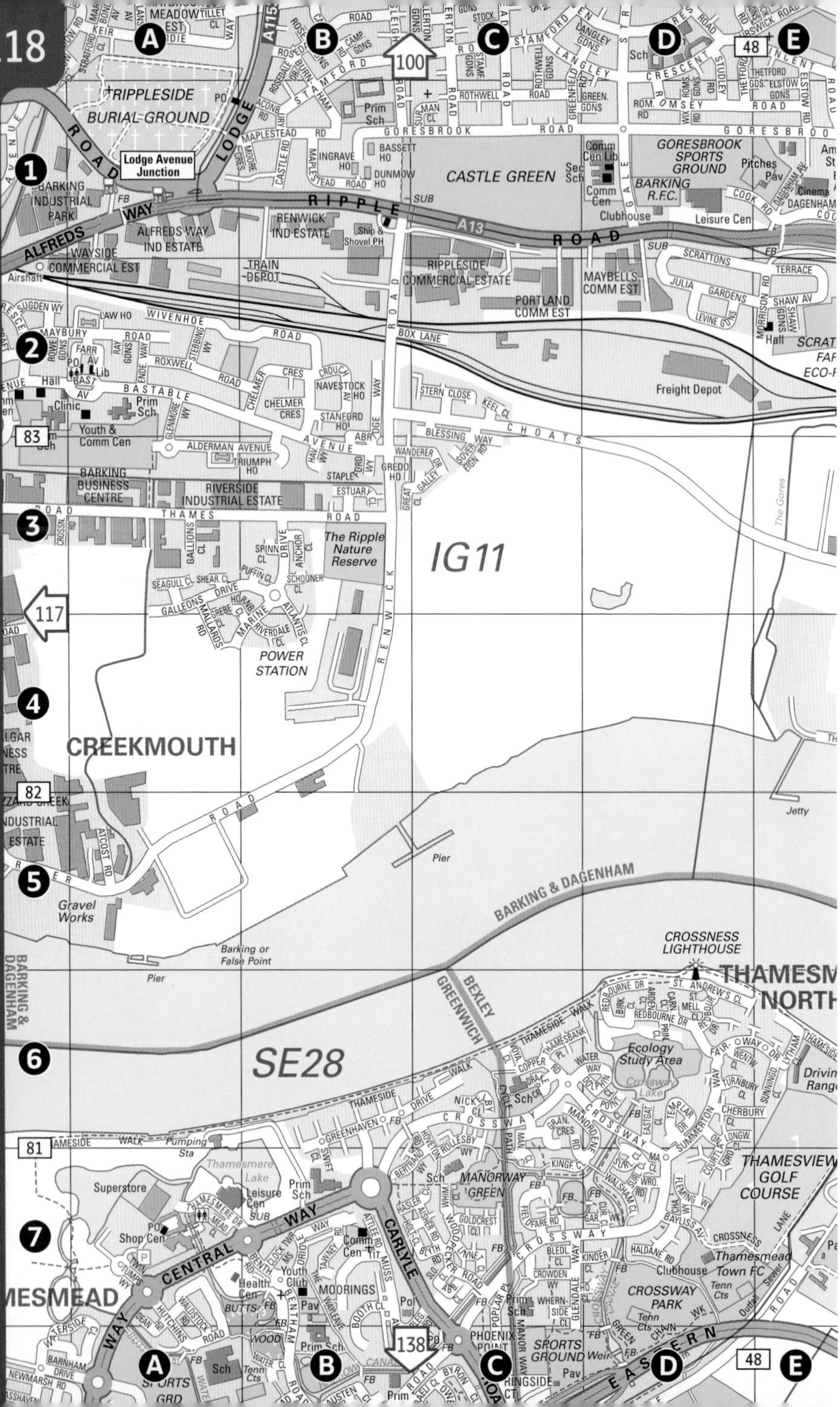
A
B
C
D
E
1
2
3
4
5
6
7
100
117
138
48
83
82
81
RIPPLESIDE
BURIAL GROUND
Lodge Avenue Junction
LODGE
ROAD
ALFREDS WAY
BARKING INDUSTRIAL PARK
ALFREDS WAY IND ESTATE
WAYSIDE COMMERCIAL EST
Airshaft
RENWICK IND ESTATE
Ship & Shovel PH
TRAIN DEPOT
RIPPLE ROAD
A13
CASTLE GREEN
GORESBROOK SPORTS GROUND
BARKING R.F.C.
Clubhouse
Leisure Cen
Pitches
Pav
Cinema
DAGENHAM
RIPPLESIDE COMMERCIAL ESTATE
MAYBELLS COMM EST
PORTLAND COMM EST
STAMFORD ROAD
GORESBROOK ROAD
MAPLESTEAD RD
BASSETT HO
DUNMOW HO
INGRAVE HO
CASTLE RD
ROTHWELL ROAD
LANGLEY CRESCENT
ROMSEY ROAD
STUDLEY
THETFORD GDS.
ELSTOW GDNS
COOK RD
SCRATTONS TERRACE
JULIA GARDENS
MORRISON RD
SHAW AV
LEVINE GDNS
Hall
Freight Depot
BOX LANE
MAYBURY ROAD
WIVENHOE ROAD
ROXWELL ROAD
BASTABLE AV
Clinic
Prim Sch
Youth & Comm Cen
CHELMER CRES
NAVESTOCK HO
STANFORD HO
CROUCH
AVENUE
ALDERMAN AVENUE
TRIUMPH HO
STERN CLOSE
KEEL CL
BLESSING WAY
CHOATS
WANDERER DR
SOVEREIGN RD
GREDO HO
GALLEY CL
STAPLE
ESTUARY CL
BARKING BUSINESS CENTRE
RIVERSIDE INDUSTRIAL ESTATE
THAMES ROAD
GALLIONS CL
SPINN CL
DRIVE
ANCHOR CL
SCHOONER CL
The Ripple Nature Reserve
IG11
The Gores
SEAGULL CL
SHEAR CL
PUFFIN CL
GALLEONS DRIVE
MALLARDS RD
GREBE CL
HORNBEAM
MARINE DR
RIVERDALE CL
ATLANTIS CL
POWER STATION
RENWICK ROAD
CREEKMOUTH
INDUSTRIAL ESTATE
ATCOST RD
Gravel Works
Pier
Barking or False Point
Jetty
BARKING & DAGENHAM
GREENWICH
BEXLEY
CROSSNESS LIGHTHOUSE
THAMESM
NORTH
SE28
THAMESIDE WALK
Ecology Study Area
Crossway Lake
Driving Range
THAMESVIEW GOLF COURSE
CROSSWAY
Sch
MANORWAY GREEN
FB
Pumping Sta
Thamesmere Lake
Superstore
Leisure Cen
SUB
Prim Sch
Shop Cen
PO
CENTRAL WAY
CARLYLE
Comm Cen
Youth Club
Health Cen
MOORINGS
Pav
BUTTS
WOOD
BENTHAM
Prim Sch
Tenn Cts
MESMEAD
SPORTS GRD
BARNHAM DRIVE
NEWMARSH RD
PHOENIX POINT
SPORTS GROUND
Weir
RINGSIDE CT
EASTERN
CROSSWAY PARK
Clubhouse
Thamesmead Town FC
Tenn Cts
CROSSNESS
BAYLISS AV
HALDANE RD
CHERBURY CL
TURNBURY CL
FAIRWAY DR
LYTHAM
Outfall Sewer

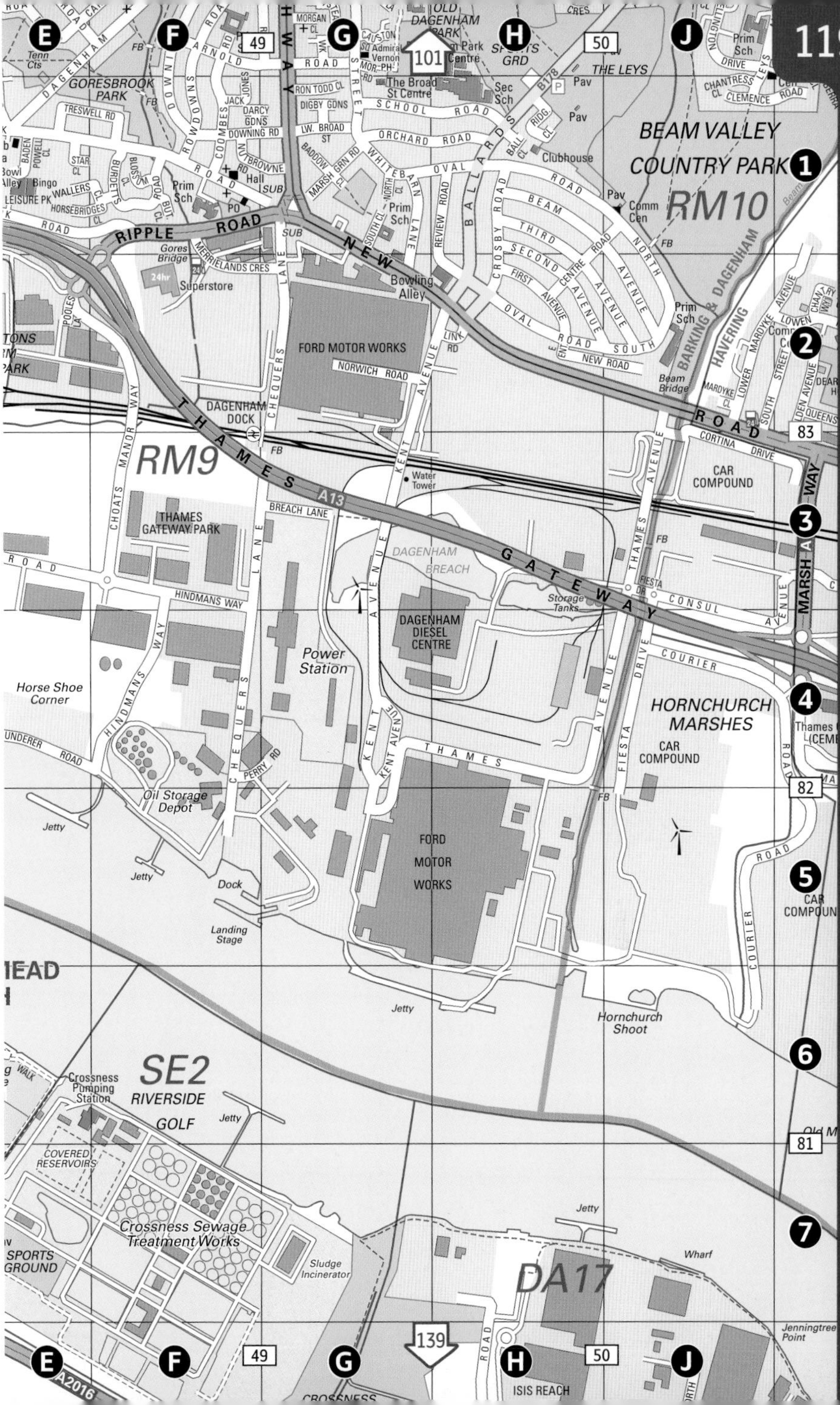
E
F
G
H
J
49
50
101
139
83
82
81
1
2
3
4
5
6
7
GORESBROOK PARK
DAGENHAM
ARNOLD ROAD
DOWNING RD
ROWDOWNS
COOMBES
JACK
JONES
DARCY GDNS
NUTBROWNE
TRESWELL RD
BADEN POWELL CL
STAR CL
BURDETTS
BLOSSOM
WALLERS CL
Bowl Alley
Bingo
LEISURE PK
HORSEBRIDGES CL
Prim Sch
Hall
PO
SUB
RIPPLE ROAD
Gores Bridge
24hr
Superstore
MERRIELANDS CRES
POOLES LA
MORGAN CL
RON TODD CL
DIGBY GDNS
LW. BROAD ST
BADDOW
MARSH GRN RD
WHITEBARN LANE
NORTH CL
SOUTH CL
SCHOOL ROAD
ORCHARD ROAD
The Broad St Centre
OLD DAGENHAM PARK
SPORTS GRD
Sec Sch
B178
THE LEYS
Pav
Clubhouse
RIDG. CL
BALL CL
BALLARDS
OVAL ROAD
REVIEW ROAD
CROSBY ROAD
BEAM
THIRD
SECOND
FIRST AVENUE
CENTRE ROAD
AVENUE
NORTH
OVAL ROAD SOUTH
NEW ROAD
Comm Cen
BEAM VALLEY COUNTRY PARK
RM10
FB
Prim Sch
BARKING & DAGENHAM
HAVERING
Beam Bridge
MARDYKE AVENUE
LOWER MARDYKE
SOUTH STREET
CHANTRESS CL
CLEMENCE ROAD
DRIVE
Prim Sch
Bowling Alley
LINK RD
NEW ROAD
FORD MOTOR WORKS
NORWICH ROAD
CHEQUERS LANE
KENT AVENUE
DAGENHAM DOCK
THAMES GATEWAY
A13
RM9
CHOATS MANOR WAY
BREACH LANE
Water Tower
THAMES GATEWAY PARK
DAGENHAM BREACH
DAGENHAM DIESEL CENTRE
Storage Tanks
HINDMANS WAY
Power Station
Horse Shoe Corner
UNDERER ROAD
PERRY RD
Oil Storage Depot
Jetty
Dock
Landing Stage
THAMES AVENUE
CORTINA DRIVE
CAR COMPOUND
FIESTA DR
CONSUL AVENUE
COURIER ROAD
FIESTA DRIVE
HORNCHURCH MARSHES
CAR COMPOUND
MARSH WAY
Thames
FORD MOTOR WORKS
Hornchurch Shoot
SE2
RIVERSIDE GOLF
Crossness Pumping Station
COVERED RESERVOIRS
Crossness Sewage Treatment Works
SPORTS GROUND
Sludge Incinerator
DA17
Wharf
Jenningtree Point
ISIS REACH
A2016
CROSSNESS

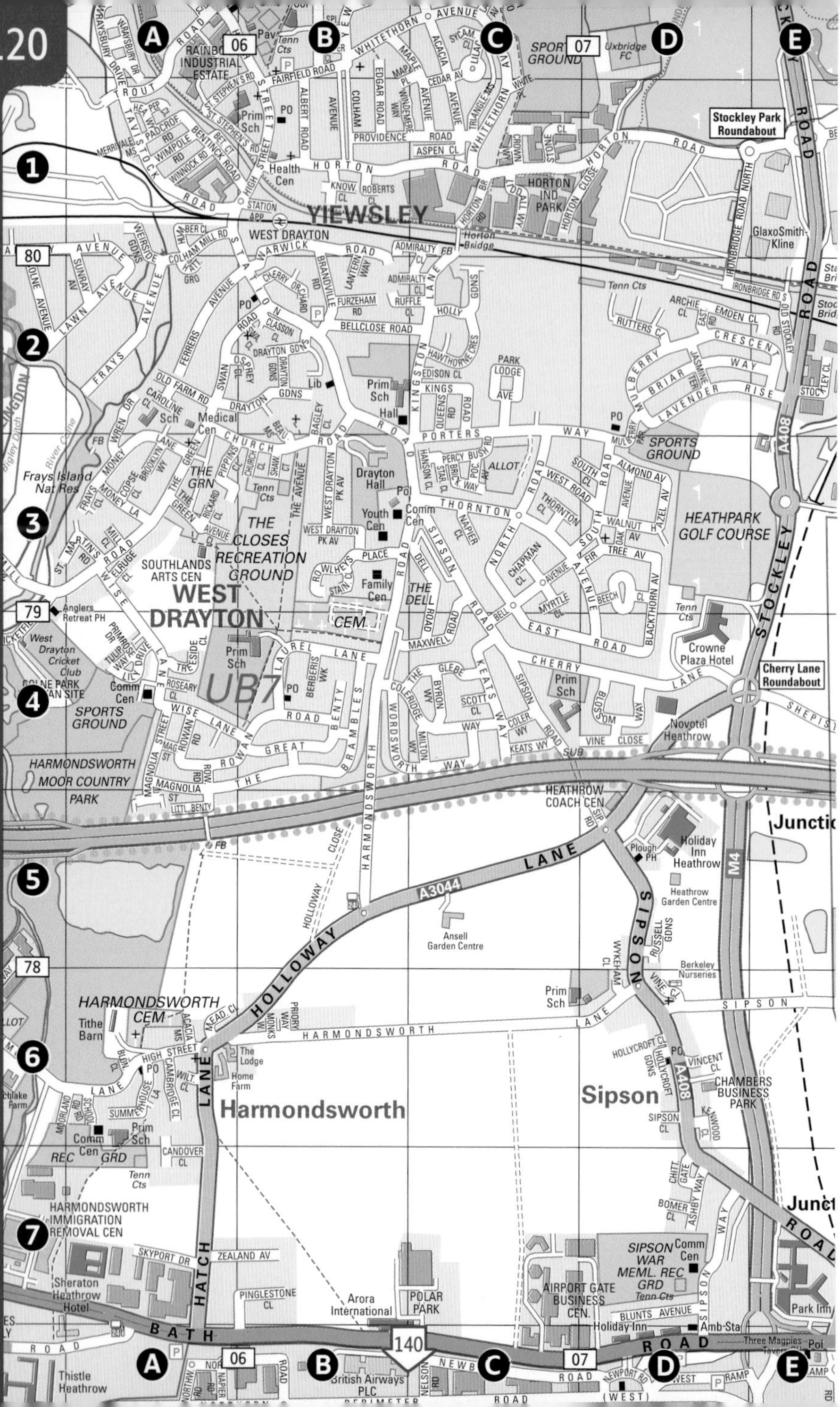
A
B
C
D
E
1
2
3
4
5
6
7
06
07
80
79
78
140
YIEWSLEY
WEST DRAYTON
West Drayton
Harmondsworth
Sipson
UB7
RAINBOW INDUSTRIAL ESTATE
SPORTS GROUND
Uxbridge FC
Stockley Park Roundabout
Cherry Lane Roundabout
GlaxoSmith-Kline
HORTON IND PARK
Horton Bridge
HEATHPARK GOLF COURSE
Crowne Plaza Hotel
Novotel Heathrow
HEATHROW COACH CEN
Holiday Inn Heathrow
Heathrow Garden Centre
Ansell Garden Centre
Berkeley Nurseries
CHAMBERS BUSINESS PARK
Junction
THE CLOSES RECREATION GROUND
SOUTHLANDS ARTS CEN
Anglers Retreat PH
West Drayton Cricket Club
COLNE PARK CARAVAN SITE
HARMONDSWORTH MOOR COUNTRY PARK
Frays Island Nat Res
River Colne
Bigley Ditch
Drayton Hall
Youth Cen
Family Cen
THE DELL
CEM
HARMONDSWORTH CEM
Tithe Barn
The Lodge
Home Farm
HARMONDSWORTH IMMIGRATION REMOVAL CEN
Sheraton Heathrow Hotel
Thistle Heathrow
Arora International
POLAR PARK
British Airways PLC
AIRPORT GATE BUSINESS CEN.
SIPSON WAR MEML. REC GRD
Holiday Inn
Amb Sta
Three Magpies Tavern PH
Park Inn
Plough PH
A408
A3044
M4
STOCKLEY ROAD
HORTON ROAD
PORTERS WAY
STATION ROAD
CHURCH ROAD
HOLLOWAY LANE
HARMONDSWORTH LANE
SIPSON ROAD
SIPSON LANE
HATCH LANE
BATH ROAD
CHERRY LANE
WISE LANE
FRAYS AVENUE
FERRERS AVENUE
THE GREEN
WEST DRAYTON PK AV
EAST ROAD
WEST ROAD
NORTH ROAD
SOUTH ROAD
THORNTON ROAD
LAUREL LANE
BRAMBLES
HARMONDSWORTH
GREAT BENTY
FAIRFIELD ROAD
WHITETHORN AVENUE
HIGH STREET
BENTINCK ROAD
TAVISTOCK ROAD
TROUT ROAD
IRONBRIDGE ROAD NORTH
CRESCENT WAY
LAVENDER RISE
BLUNTS AVENUE
ZEALAND AV
SKYPORT DR
PINGLESTONE CL
NEWPORT RD
PERIMETER ROAD

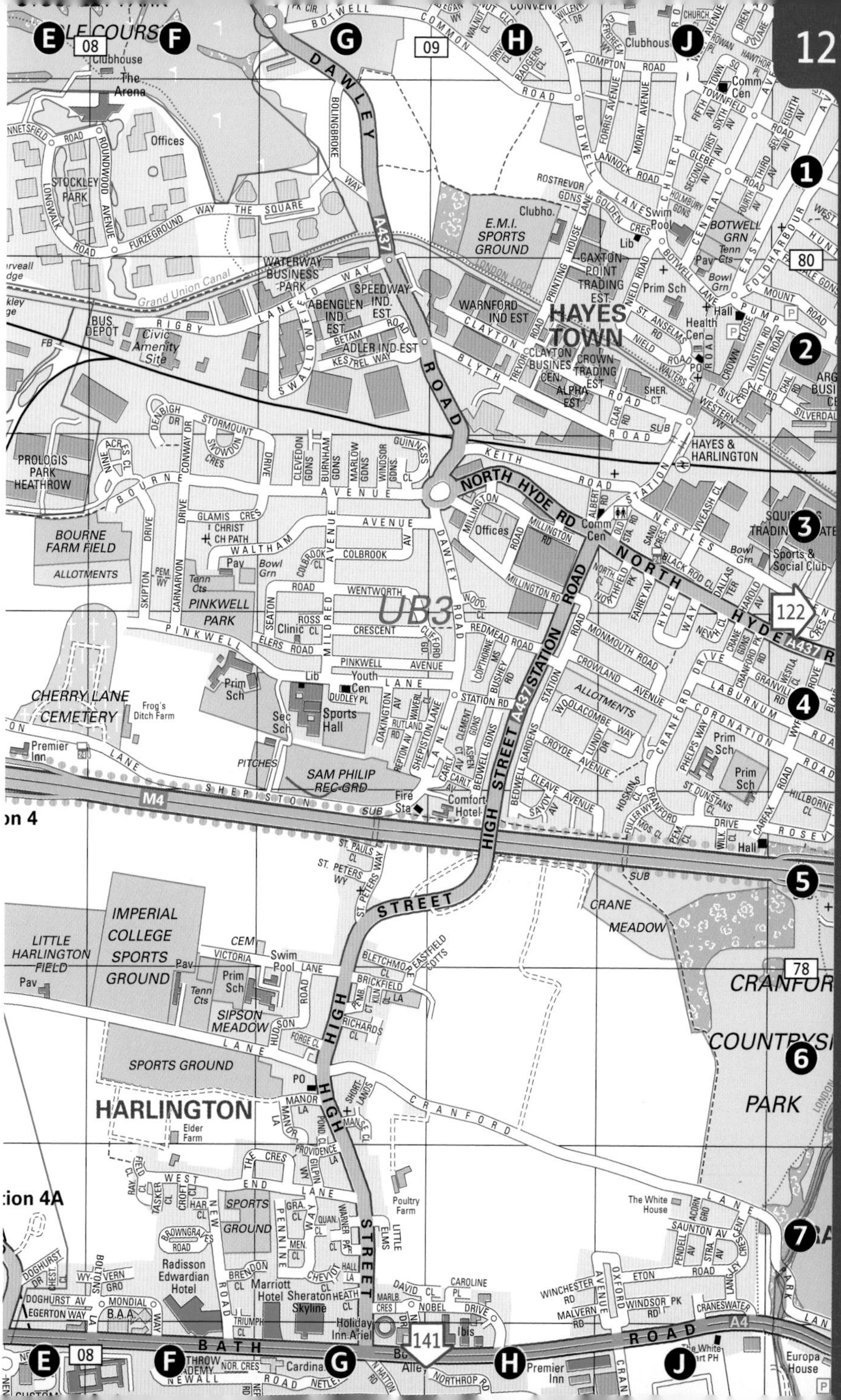
E
F
G
H
J
08
09
Clubhouse
The Arena
Offices
STOCKLEY PARK
ROUNDWOOD AVENUE
LONGWALK ROAD
FURZEGROUND WAY
THE SQUARE
DAWLEY ROAD
A437
BOLINGBROKE WAY
BOTWELL COMMON ROAD
COMPTON ROAD
FORRIS AVENUE
MORAY AVENUE
LANNOCK ROAD
CHURCH ROAD
CENTRAL AVENUE
Comm Cen
TOWNFIELD
1
2
3
4
5
6
7
E.M.I. SPORTS GROUND
Clubho.
LONDON LOOP
Grand Union Canal
WATERWAY BUSINESS PARK
SPEEDWAY IND. EST
ABENGLEN IND. EST
BETAM ROAD
ADLER IND EST
KESTREL WAY
SWALLOWFIELD WAY
LANEFIELD WAY
RIGBY LANE
BUS DEPOT
Civic Amenity Site
WARNFORD IND EST
CLAYTON ROAD
BLYTH ROAD
CAXTON POINT TRADING EST
HAYES TOWN
CLAYTON BUSINESS CEN.
CROWN TRADING EST
ALPHA EST
PRINTING HOUSE LANE
GOLDEN CRES
Swim Pool
Lib
Prim Sch
BOTWELL GRN
Tenn Cts
Pav
Bowl Grn
BOTWELL LANE
Hall
Health Cen
PUMP LANE
COLDHARBOUR LANE
MOUNT ROAD
80
WESTERN VW
SILVERDALE RD
HAYES & HARLINGTON
PROLOGIS PARK HEATHROW
BOURNE AVENUE
DENBIGH DR
STORMOUNT DR
SNOWDON CRES
CONWAY DR
KEITH ROAD
NORTH HYDE RD
Offices
MILLINGTON RD
Comm Cen
STATION ROAD
NESTLES AVENUE
SQUIRES TRADING ESTATE
Sports & Social Club
Bowl Grn
NORTH HYDE ROAD
122
BOURNE FARM FIELD
ALLOTMENTS
GLAMIS CRES
CHRIST CH PATH
WALTHAM AVENUE
Pav
Bowl Grn
Tenn Cts
PINKWELL PARK
COLBROOK AVENUE
WENTWORTH CRESCENT
UB3
MILDRED AVENUE
Clinic
ROSS
ELERS ROAD
PINKWELL LANE
PINKWELL AVENUE
REDMEAD ROAD
MONMOUTH ROAD
CROWLAND AVENUE
ALLOTMENTS
WOOLACOMBE WAY
LABURNUM
CORONATION ROAD
CRANFORD DRIVE
CHERRY LANE CEMETERY
Frog's Ditch Farm
Prim Sch
Lib
Youth Cen
Sec Sch
Sports Hall
Premier Inn
PITCHES
SAM PHILIP REC GRD
SHEPISTON LANE
STATION RD
HIGH STREET
Fire Sta
Comfort Hotel
CROYDE AVENUE
CLEAVE AVENUE
BEDWELL GARDENS
Prim Sch
Hall
M4
on 4
SUB
ST. PAULS CL
ST. PETERS WY
CRANE MEADOW
IMPERIAL COLLEGE SPORTS GROUND
LITTLE HARLINGTON FIELD
Pav
CEM
VICTORIA LANE
Swim Pool
Prim Sch
Tenn Cts
SIPSON MEADOW
BLETCHMORE CL
EASTFIELD COTTS
BRICKFIELD
RICHARDS CL
78
CRANFORD COUNTRYSIDE PARK
SPORTS GROUND
HARLINGTON
PO
Elder Farm
CRANFORD LANE
MANOR LA
SHORTLANDS
WEST END LANE
tion 4A
SPORTS GROUND
Poultry Farm
LITTLE ELMS
The White House
SAUNTON AV
Radisson Edwardian Hotel
Marriott Hotel
Sheraton Skyline
Holiday Inn Ariel
Ibis
B.A.A.
DOGHURST AV
EGERTON WAY
MONDIAL WAY
OXFORD AVENUE
ETON ROAD
WINCHESTER RD
MALVERN RD
WINDSOR PK
CRANESWATER
A4
BATH ROAD
141
Premier Inn
The White Hart PH
Europa House
Cardinal
NEWALL ROAD
NORTHROP RD

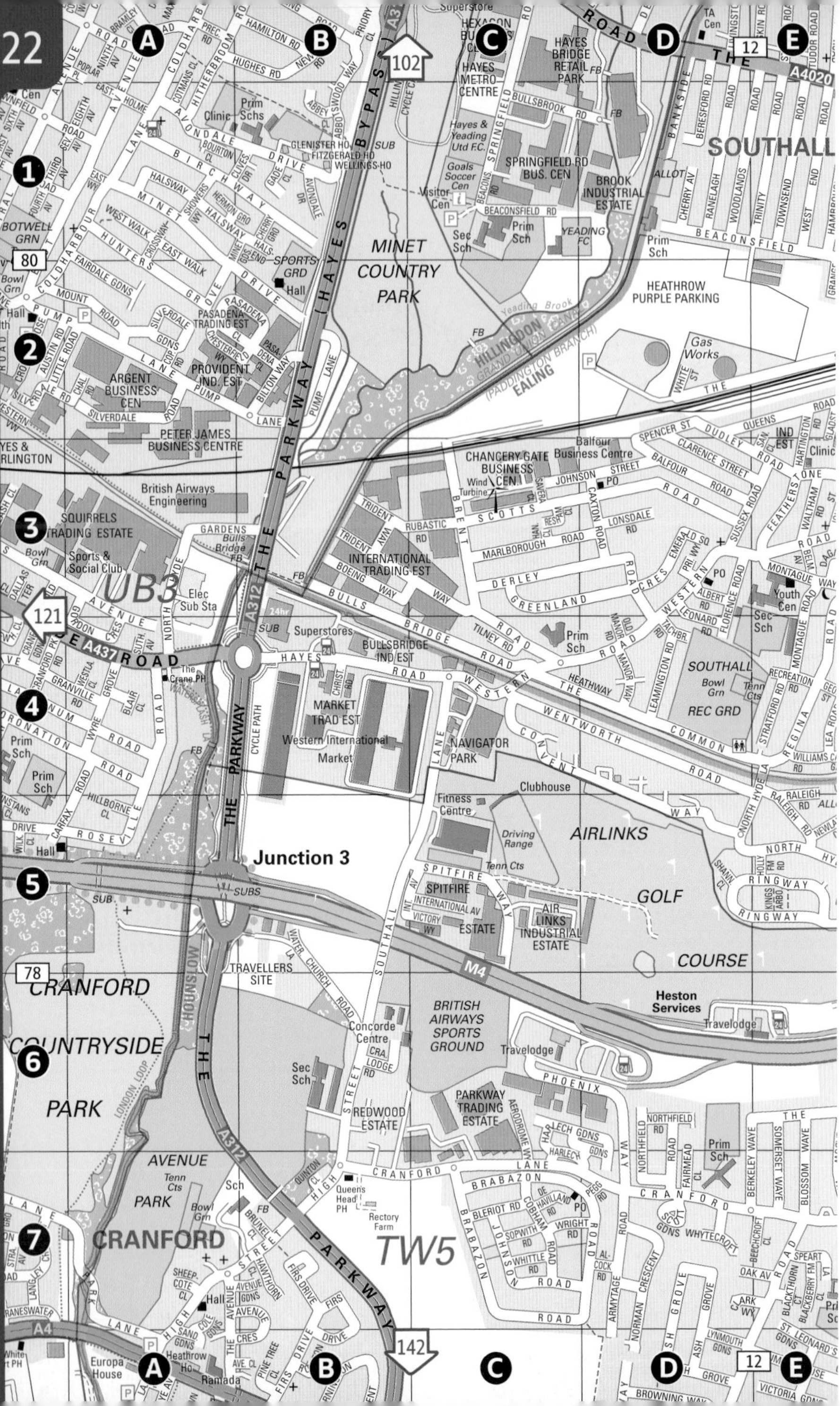
A
B
C
D
E
1
2
3
4
5
6
7
102
12
80
121
78
142
SOUTHALL
HAYES BRIDGE RETAIL PARK
HAYES METRO CENTRE
HEXAGON BUS. CEN
Superstore
TA Cen
A4020
BULLSBROOK RD
Hayes & Yeading Utd F.C.
Goals Soccer Cen
SPRINGFIELD RD BUS. CEN
BROOK INDUSTRIAL ESTATE
Visitor Cen
BEACONSFIELD RD
Sec Sch
Prim Sch
YEADING FC
MINET COUNTRY PARK
HEATHROW PURPLE PARKING
Gas Works
Yeading Brook
HILLINGDON
GRAND UNION CANAL
(PADDINGTON BRANCH)
EALING
THE PARKWAY (HAYES BYPASS)
A312
ARGENT BUSINESS CEN
PROVIDENT IND. EST
PASADENA TRADING EST
PETER JAMES BUSINESS CENTRE
SPORTS GRD
HAYES & HARLINGTON
British Airways Engineering
SQUIRRELS TRADING ESTATE
Sports & Social Club
UB3
Elec Sub Sta
A437
HAYES ROAD
Superstores
BULLSBRIDGE IND EST
MARKET TRAD EST
Western International Market
INTERNATIONAL TRADING EST
CHANCERY GATE BUSINESS CEN
Balfour Business Centre
Wind Turbine
BULLS BRIDGE ROAD
NAVIGATOR PARK
SOUTHALL REC GRD
AIRLINKS GOLF COURSE
Clubhouse
Driving Range
Fitness Centre
Junction 3
SPITFIRE ESTATE
AIR LINKS INDUSTRIAL ESTATE
M4
Heston Services
Travelodge
TRAVELLERS SITE
CRANFORD COUNTRYSIDE PARK
Concorde Centre
BRITISH AIRWAYS SPORTS GROUND
PARKWAY TRADING ESTATE
REDWOOD ESTATE
AVENUE PARK
CRANFORD
TW5
Queens Head PH
Rectory Farm
A4
Europa House
Heathrow Ho
Ramada
The Crane PH
HOUNSLOW
LONDON LOOP

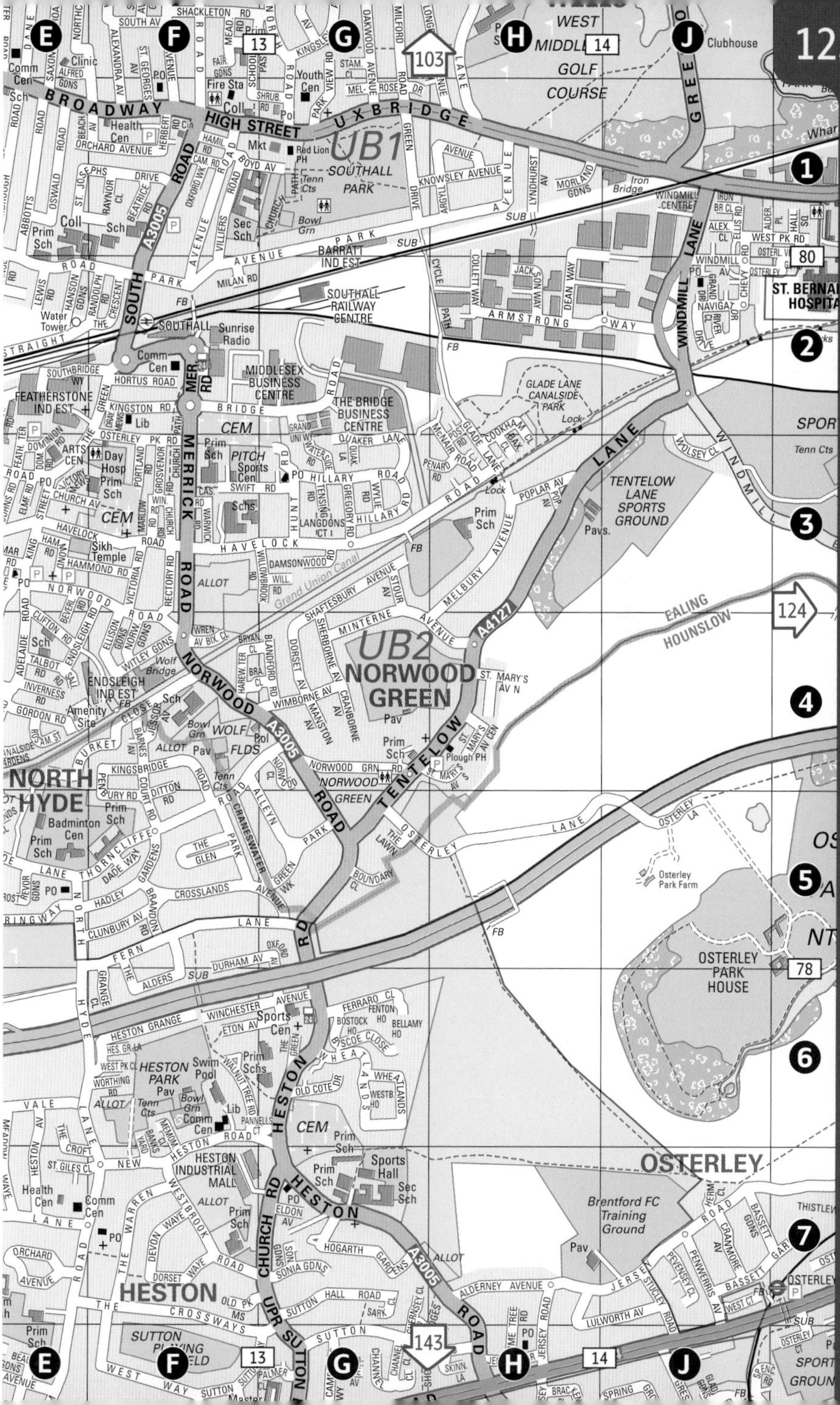
E
F
G
H
J
1
2
3
4
5
6
7
103
124
143
13
14
80
78
UB1
UB2
SOUTHALL
SOUTHALL PARK
NORWOOD GREEN
NORTH HYDE
HESTON
OSTERLEY
WEST MIDDLESEX GOLF COURSE
Clubhouse
BROADWAY
HIGH STREET
UXBRIDGE
SOUTH ROAD
A3005
MERRICK ROAD
NORWOOD ROAD
TENTELOW LANE
A4127
WINDMILL LANE
GREEN
SOUTH AV
SHACKLETON RD
ALEXANDRA AV
ST. GEORGES AV
ORCHARD AVENUE
KNOWSLEY AVENUE
MORLAND GDNS
LYNDHURST AV
Iron Bridge
WINDMILL CENTRE
WEST PK RD
ST. BERNARD'S HOSPITAL
PARK AVENUE
BARRATT IND EST
SOUTHALL RAILWAY CENTRE
ARMSTRONG WAY
COLLETT WAY
DEAN WAY
JACKSON WAY
MIDDLESEX BUSINESS CENTRE
THE BRIDGE BUSINESS CENTRE
BRIDGE ROAD
GLADE LANE CANALSIDE PARK
Lock
HILLARY ROAD
QUAKER LANE
HAVELOCK ROAD
Grand Union Canal
FEATHERSTONE IND EST
HORTUS ROAD
KINGSTON RD
OSTERLEY PK RD
Sikh Temple
NORWOOD ROAD
TENTELOW LANE SPORTS GROUND
Pavs.
EALING
HOUNSLOW
SHAFTESBURY AVENUE
MINTERNE AVENUE
MELBURY AVENUE
POPLAR AV
ST. MARY'S AV N
Plough PH
ENDSLEIGH IND EST
Amenity Site
Wolf Bridge
WOLF FLDS
Badminton Cen
OSTERLEY LANE
Osterley Park Farm
OSTERLEY PARK HOUSE
CROSSLANDS
RINGWAY
DURHAM AV
HESTON GRANGE
HESTON PARK
Swim Pool
HESTON INDUSTRIAL MALL
HESTON ROAD
CHURCH RD
UPR SUTTON
SUTTON HALL ROAD
SUTTON PLAYING FIELD
THE CROSSWAYS
WEST WAY
Brentford FC Training Ground
JERSEY ROAD
ALDERNEY AVENUE
LULWORTH AV
BASSETT GDNS
CRANMORE AV
OSTERLEY
SPORTS GROUND
HOGARTH GARDENS
DORSET WAYE
WESTBROOK
THE WARREN
VALE
ST. GILES CL
Health Cen
Comm Cen

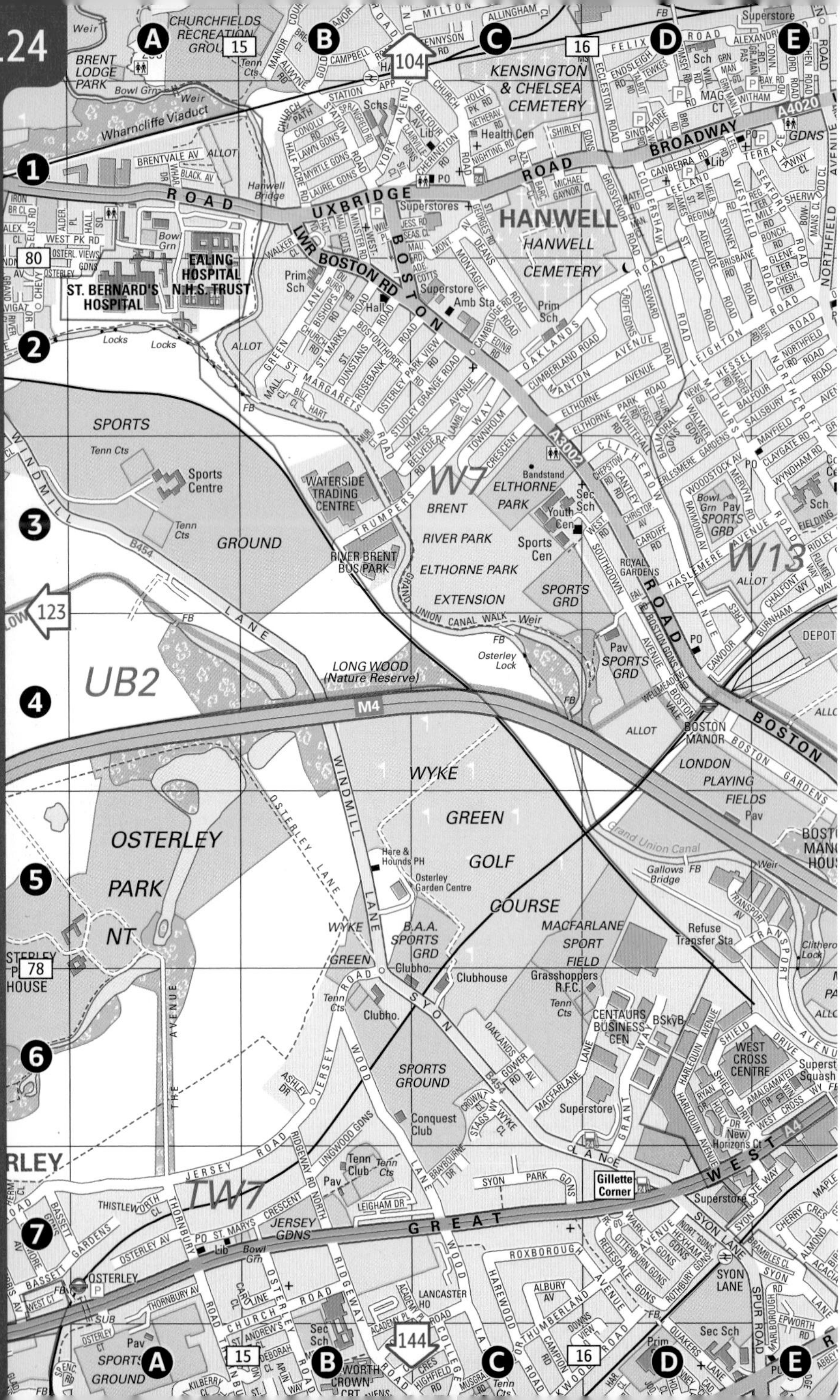
A
B
C
D
E
1
2
3
4
5
6
7
15
16
104
123
144
80
78
CHURCHFIELDS RECREATION GROUND
BRENT LODGE PARK
Weir
Bowl Grn
Wharncliffe Viaduct
MILTON
ALLINGHAM CL
TENNYSON RD
GOLD CAMPBELL
FELIX
ALEXANDRIA RD
Superstore
KENSINGTON & CHELSEA CEMETERY
ECCLESTON ROAD
ENDSLEIGH RD
Sch
MAG CT
WITHAM
A4020
BROADWAY
GDNS
Lib
Health Cen
SHIRLEY GDNS
STATION APP
CHURCH PATH
CONOLLY RD
LAWN GDNS
MYRTLE GDNS
LAUREL GDNS
HALF ACRE RD
Schs
YORK AVENUE
BALFOUR
CHERINGTON RD
NIGHTING RD
NETHERAV. RD
BRENTVALE AV
ALLOT
BLACK AV
ROAD
Hanwell Bridge
UXBRIDGE
ROAD
CANBERRA RD
LEELAND
Superstores
HANWELL
HANWELL CEMETERY
MICHAEL GAYNOR CL
GROSVENOR ROAD
WEST PK RD
OSTERLEY VIEWS
EALING HOSPITAL N.H.S. TRUST
ST. BERNARD'S HOSPITAL
LWR BOSTON RD
BOSTON
Prim Sch
Hall
Superstore
Amb Sta
Locks
ALLOT
ST. MARGARETS
BISHOPS RD
ST. MARKS
ST. DUNSTANS
BOSTONTHORPE
ROSEBANK
OSTERLEY PARK VIEW RD
OSTERLEY GRANGE ROAD
CAMBRIDGE ROAD
MONTAGUE ROAD
OAKLANDS
CUMBERLAND ROAD
MANTON AVENUE
ELTHORNE AVENUE
ELTHORNE PARK ROAD
LEIGHTON ROAD
NORTHFIELD AVENUE
SPORTS GROUND
Tenn Cts
Sports Centre
WINDMILL
B454
LANE
HUMES AVENUE
BELVEDERE RD
STUDLEY GRANGE ROAD
TOWNHOLM CRESCENT
A3002
WATERSIDE TRADING CENTRE
TRUMPERS
W7
BRENT
RIVER PARK
ELTHORNE PARK EXTENSION
ELTHORNE PARK
Bandstand
Sec Sch
Youth Cen
Sports Cen
SPORTS GRD
RIVER BRENT BUS PARK
GRAND UNION CANAL WALK
SOUTHDOWN
ROYAL GARDENS
BOSTON GDNS
CLITHEROW
CHEPSTOW RD
CANTLEY
CARDIFF RD
HASLEMERE AVENUE
WOODSTOCK AV
ERLESMERE GARDENS
MAYFIELD
CLAYGATE RD
WYNDHAM RD
W13
ALLOT
CHALFONT WAY
BURNHAM
DEPOT
PO
UB2
FB
LONG WOOD (Nature Reserve)
Osterley Lock
Pav
M4
ALLOT
BOSTON MANOR
LONDON PLAYING FIELDS
BOSTON GARDENS
WYKE
GREEN
GOLF
COURSE
OSTERLEY PARK NT
OSTERLEY LANE
Hare & Hounds PH
Osterley Garden Centre
Grand Union Canal
Gallows Bridge
Weir
TRANSPORT AV
Refuse Transfer Sta
Clitherow Lock
MACFARLANE SPORT FIELD
WYKE GREEN
B.A.A. SPORTS GRD
Clubho.
Clubhouse
Grasshoppers R.F.C.
SYON
OSTERLEY PARK HOUSE
THE AVENUE
CENTAURS BUSINESS CEN
BSkyB
HARLEQUIN AVENUE
WEST CROSS CENTRE
SHIELD DRIVE
WEST CROSS WY
SPORTS GROUND
JERSEY
WOOD
ASHLEY DR
OAKLANDS
GOWER RD
MACFARLANE LANE
Superstore
Conquest Club
STAGS WY
WYKE CL
GRANT WAY
New Horizons Ct
A4
WEST
OSTERLEY
JERSEY ROAD
RIDGEWAY RD NORTH
LINGWOOD GDNS
Tenn Club
BRAYBOURNE DR
SYON PARK GDNS
Gillette Corner
Superstore
SYON GATE WAY
TW7
THISTLEWORTH CL
THORNBURY
ST. MARYS CRESCENT
JERSEY GDNS
LEIGHAM DR
GREAT
ROXBOROUGH
OSTERLEY AV
BASSETT GARDENS
Lib
Bowl Grn
OSTERLEY
BASSETT
WEST CT
THORNBURY AV
CHURCH ROAD
ST ANDREW'S RD
Sec Sch
ACADEMY PL
LANCASTER HO
HAREWOOD ROAD
ALBURY AV
NORTHUMBERLAND AVENUE
REDESDALE GDNS
OTTERBURN GDNS
HEXHAM GDNS
ROTHBURY GDNS
SYON LANE
SPUR ROAD
Sec Sch
QUAKERS LANE
Prim
CHERRY CRES
BRAMBLES CL
EPWORTH RD
Pav
SPORTS GROUND
COLLEGE ROAD
WOOD LANE
DOWNS VIEW

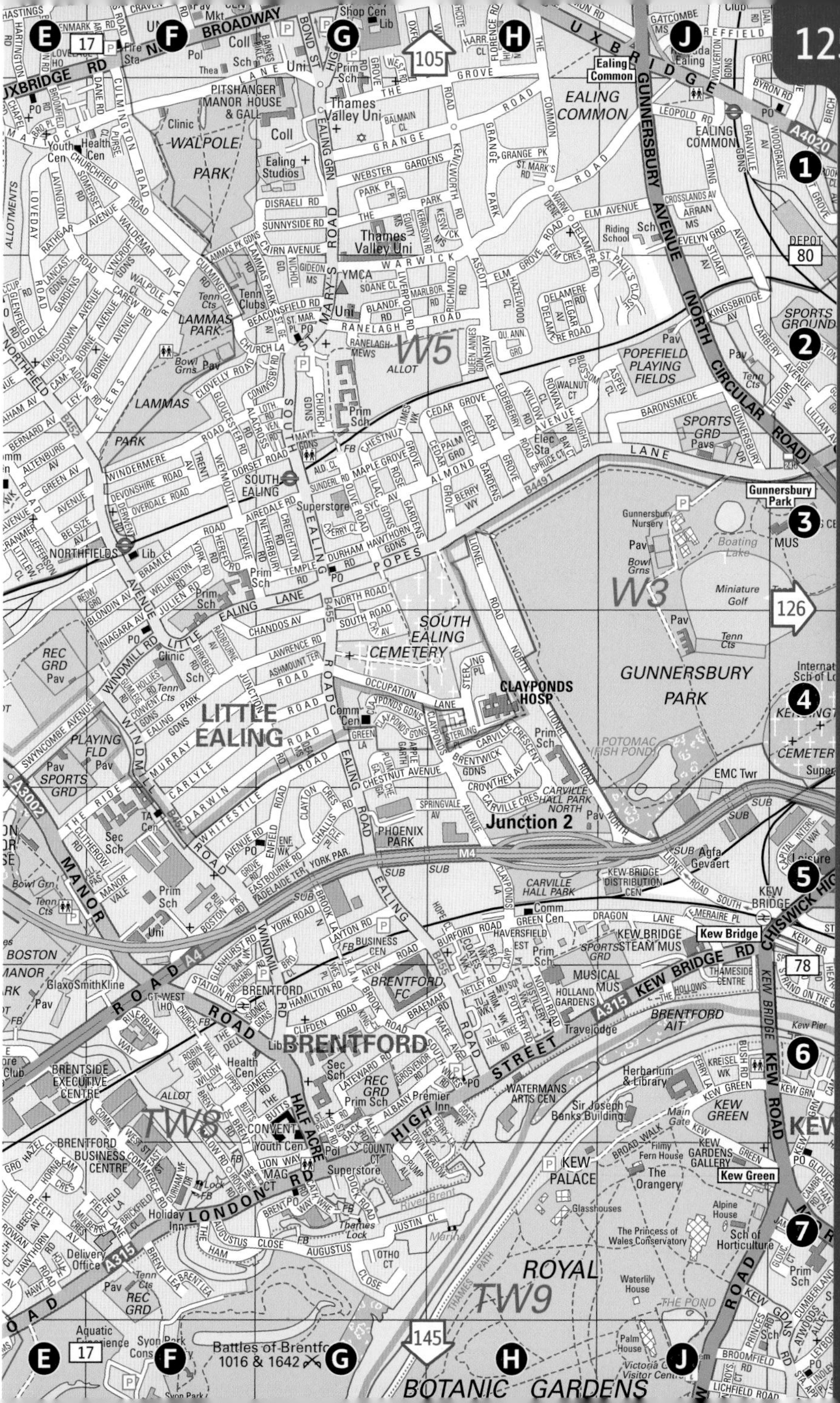
E
F
G
H
J
17
105
UXBRIDGE RD
BROADWAY
PITSHANGER MANOR HOUSE & GALL
Thames Valley Uni
Coll
WALPOLE PARK
Ealing Studios
Ealing Common
EALING COMMON
GUNNERSBURY AVENUE
A4020
1
80
DEPOT
SPORTS GROUNDS
2
POPEFIELD PLAYING FIELDS
NORTH CIRCULAR ROAD
LAMMAS PARK
W5
YMCA
SOUTH EALING
NORTHFIELDS
Superstore
Gunnersbury Park
3
Gunnersbury Nursery
Boating Lake
MUS
W3
Miniature Golf
126
SOUTH EALING CEMETERY
GUNNERSBURY PARK
CLAYPONDS HOSP
4
LITTLE EALING
POTOMAC (FISH POND)
EMC Twr
Junction 2
PHOENIX PARK
M4
A3002
SPORTS GRD
REC GRD
CARVILLE HALL PARK
KEW BRIDGE DISTRIBUTION CEN
Agfa Gevaert
5
KEW BRIDGE
Kew Bridge
KEW BRIDGE STEAM MUS
78
BOSTON MANOR
GlaxoSmithKline
BRENTFORD
BRENTFORD FC
MUSICAL MUS
KEW BRIDGE RD
A315
BRENTFORD AIT
Kew Pier
6
Travelodge
BRENTSIDE EXECUTIVE CENTRE
BRENTFORD
HIGH STREET
WATERMANS ARTS CEN
Herbarium & Library
KEW GREEN
TW8
Sir Joseph Banks Building
KEW
HALF ACRE
BRENTFORD BUSINESS CENTRE
Superstore
KEW PALACE
The Orangery
KEW GARDENS GALLERY
Kew Green
LONDON RD
River Brent
Holiday Inn
Thames Lock
Glasshouses
The Princess of Wales Conservatory
Alpine House
Sch of Horticulture
7
Delivery Office
ROYAL
TW9
Waterlily House
THE POND
Aquatic Experience
Syon Park
Battles of Brentford 1016 & 1642
145
Palm House
Victoria Gate Visitor Centre
BOTANIC GARDENS

A
B
C
D
E
1
2
3
4
5
6
7
106
125
146
80
78
21
ACTON
EAST ACTON
SOUTH ACTON
BEDFORD PARK
GUNNERSBURY
CHISWICK
KEW
GROVE PARK
W5
W3
W4
TW9
ACTON PARK
SOUTHFIELDS PLAYING FIELDS
ACTON PARK ESTATE
ACTON CENTRAL
ACTON TOWN
SOUTH ACTON
CHISWICK PARK
GUNNERSBURY
KEW BRIDGE
CHISWICK
Gunnersbury Park
Kew Bridge
Kew Green
Chiswick Rbt
Junction 1
KENSINGTON CEMETERY
International Sch of London
GUNNERSBURY TRIANGLE NATURE RESERVE
CHISWICK HOUSE GROUNDS
CHISWICK HOUSE
CHISWICK CEMETERY
THE NATIONAL ARCHIVES
OLIVER'S ISLAND
UNIVERSITY OF WESTMINSTER SPORTS GROUND
London Wasps RFC Training Grd
ACTON GRN COMMON
CHISWICK COMMON
ROWLEY IND PK
Kew Retail Park
Sewage Works
Chiswick & Latymer C.C.
A4020
A4000
A406
A315
A3000
A4
A316
B491
B490
B409
HIGH STREET
GUNNERSBURY AVENUE
NORTH CIRCULAR ROAD
CHISWICK HIGH ROAD
GREAT WEST RD
CEDARS RD
ELLESMERE ROAD
HOGARTH
KEW ROAD
MORTLAKE ROAD
BURLINGTON LANE
ALEXANDRA AV
HEATHFIELD TER
STEYNE RD
THE WARPLE
RIVER THAMES

E
F
G
H
J
22
23
107
80
128
78
147
1
2
3
4
5
6
7
SHEPHERD'S BUSH
Westfield
B.B.C. Television Centre
WOOD LANE
LOFTUS ROAD STADIUM QPR FC
W12
W6
SW13
UXBRIDGE ROAD
A4020
VALE
GOLDHAWK ROAD
A402
SHEPHERDS BUSH MARKET
SHEPHERDS BUSH COMMON
SHEPHERDS BUSH EMPIRE
Uni of the Arts
GREEK CATH
WENDELL PARK
STARCH GREEN
RAVENSCOURT PARK
STAMFORD BROOK
TURNHAM GREEN
RAVENSCOURT PARK
GLENTHORNE RD
BEADON RD
KING STREET
A315
HIGH ROAD
TOWN HALL
Kings Mall
LYRIC
Hammersmith Broadway
HAMMERSMITH FLYOVER
HAMMERSMITH
GREAT WEST ROAD
A4
CHISWICK LA
A316
Hogarth Rbt
Hogarth Club
HOMEFIELD REC. GRD
Wharves
UPPER MALL
THE DOVE PH
The Dove Pier
FURNIVAL GDNS
THE BLUE ANCHOR PH
QUEEN CAROLINE EST
APOLLO
FULHAM PALACE
FRANK BANFIELD PARK
RIVERSIDE STUDIOS
HAMMERSMITH BRIDGE
RICHMOND UPON THAMES
HAMMERSMITH & FULHAM
St. Paul's Sch
SPORTS GROUND
CASTELNAU
CHISWICK EYOT
Brewery
The Swedish Sch
LONSDALE ROAD
ST. MARY'S CONVENT
LEG OF MUTTON NATURE RESERVE
HARROD'S SPORTS GRD
The Harrodian
Chiswick Pier
THE WETLANDS CENTRE
Visitor Centre
A306
B350
RIVERSIDE RECREATION GROUND
Blakes Wharves
Harrods Wharf

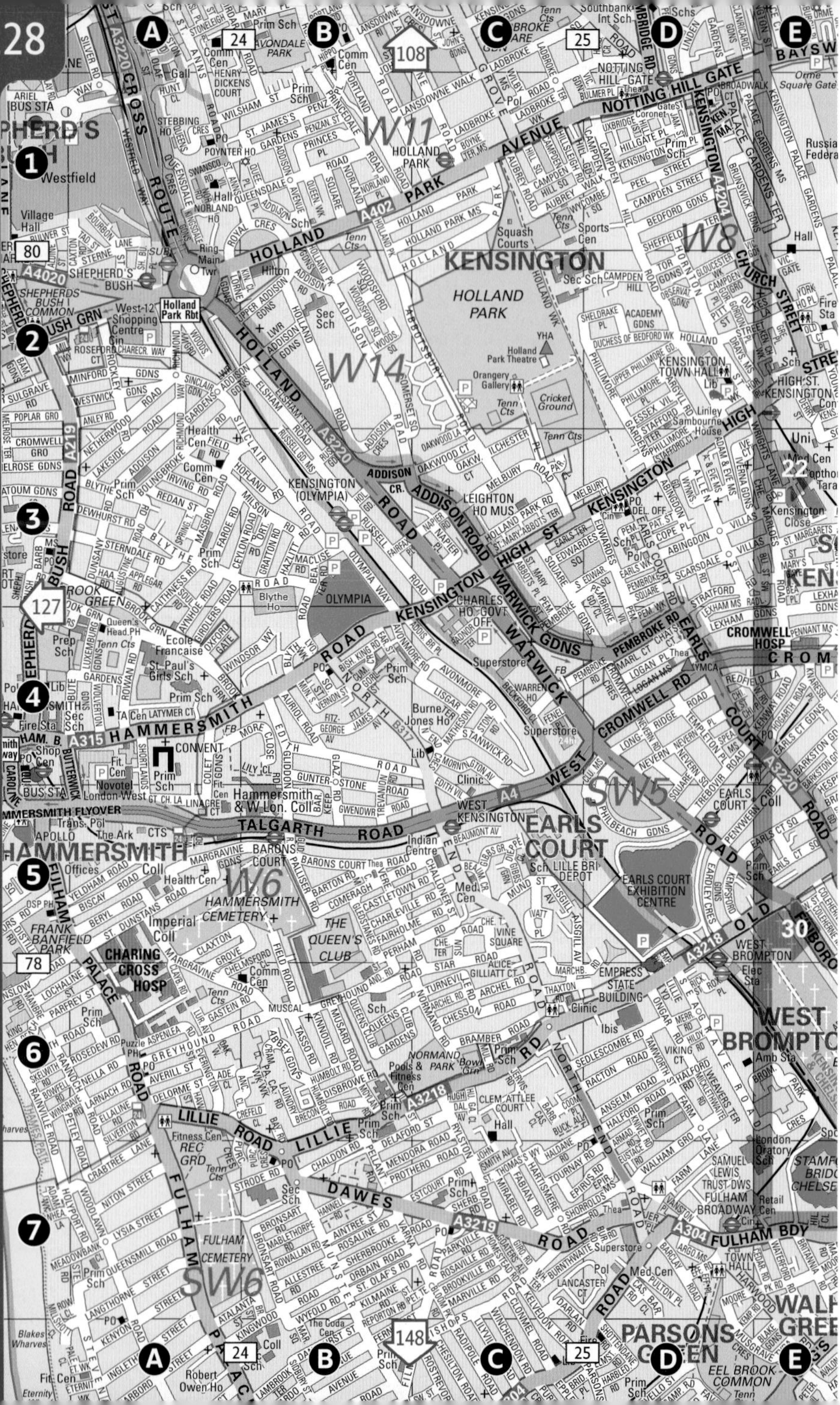
A
B
C
D
E
1
2
3
4
5
6
7
108
127
148
24
25
80
78
22
30
SHEPHERD'S BUSH
Westfield
W11
HOLLAND PARK
NOTTING HILL GATE
NOTTING HILL GATE
HOLLAND PARK AVENUE
W8
KENSINGTON
HOLLAND PARK
Holland Park Rbt
SHEPHERDS BUSH COMMON
W14
KENSINGTON (OLYMPIA)
OLYMPIA
KENSINGTON HIGH ST
WARWICK GDNS
WARWICK ROAD
HIGH ST. KENSINGTON
KENSINGTON TOWN HALL
CROMWELL RD
CROMWELL HOSP
BROOK GREEN
HAMMERSMITH ROAD
HAMMERSMITH FLYOVER
HAMMERSMITH
TALGARTH ROAD
WEST KENSINGTON
BARONS COURT
EARLS COURT
EARLS COURT EXHIBITION CENTRE
SW5
W6
HAMMERSMITH CEMETERY
THE QUEEN'S CLUB
CHARING CROSS HOSP
FULHAM PALACE ROAD
LILLIE ROAD
NORTH END ROAD
OLD BROMPTON ROAD
WEST BROMPTON
EMPRESS STATE BUILDING
DAWES ROAD
FULHAM CEMETERY
SW6
FULHAM BROADWAY
FULHAM BDY
PARSONS GREEN
EEL BROOK COMMON
WALHAM GREEN

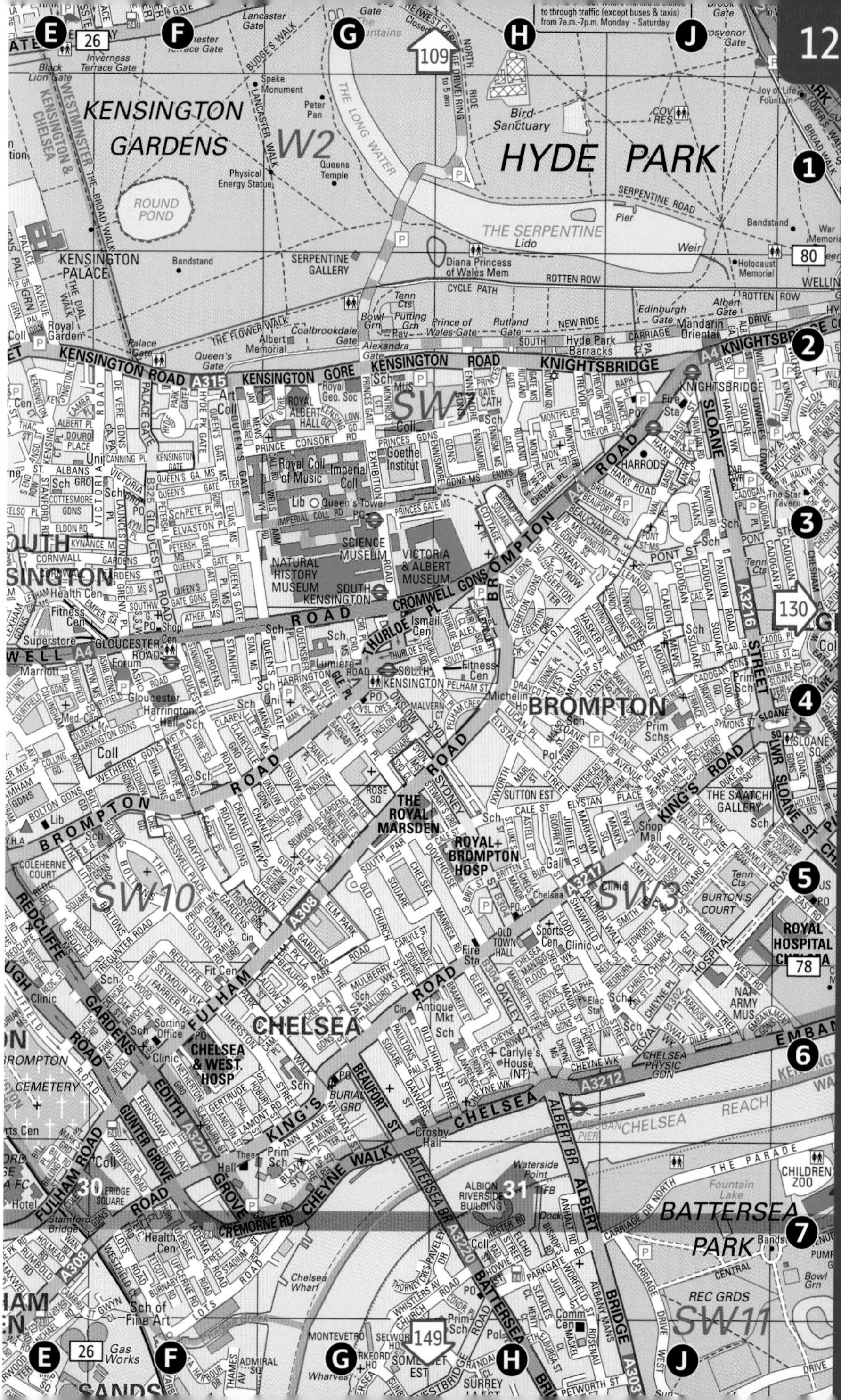

KENSINGTON GARDENS
W2
HYDE PARK
ROUND POND
THE LONG WATER
THE SERPENTINE
Lido
SERPENTINE ROAD
ROTTEN ROW
KENSINGTON PALACE
SERPENTINE GALLERY
Diana Princess of Wales Mem
Albert Memorial
Bird Sanctuary
Peter Pan
Speke Monument
Physical Energy Statue
Queens Temple
Holocaust Memorial
Hyde Park Barracks
KENSINGTON ROAD
KENSINGTON GORE
KNIGHTSBRIDGE
SW7
ROYAL ALBERT HALL
Royal Coll of Music
Imperial Coll
Queen's Tower
SCIENCE MUSEUM
NATURAL HISTORY MUSEUM
VICTORIA & ALBERT MUSEUM
SOUTH KENSINGTON
CROMWELL ROAD
BROMPTON ROAD
HARRODS
SLOANE STREET
BROMPTON
THE SAATCHI GALLERY
THE ROYAL MARSDEN
ROYAL BROMPTON HOSP
SW3
SW10
CHELSEA
CHELSEA & WEST. HOSP
KING'S ROAD
FULHAM ROAD
ROYAL HOSPITAL CHELSEA
NAT ARMY MUS
CHELSEA EMBANKMENT
CHELSEA PHYSIC GDN
CHEYNE WALK
Carlyle's House (NT)
CHELSEA REACH
ALBERT BR
BATTERSEA BR
BATTERSEA PARK
CHILDREN ZOO
SW11
BROMPTON CEMETERY
Chelsea Wharf
Gas Works
109
130
149
26
78
80

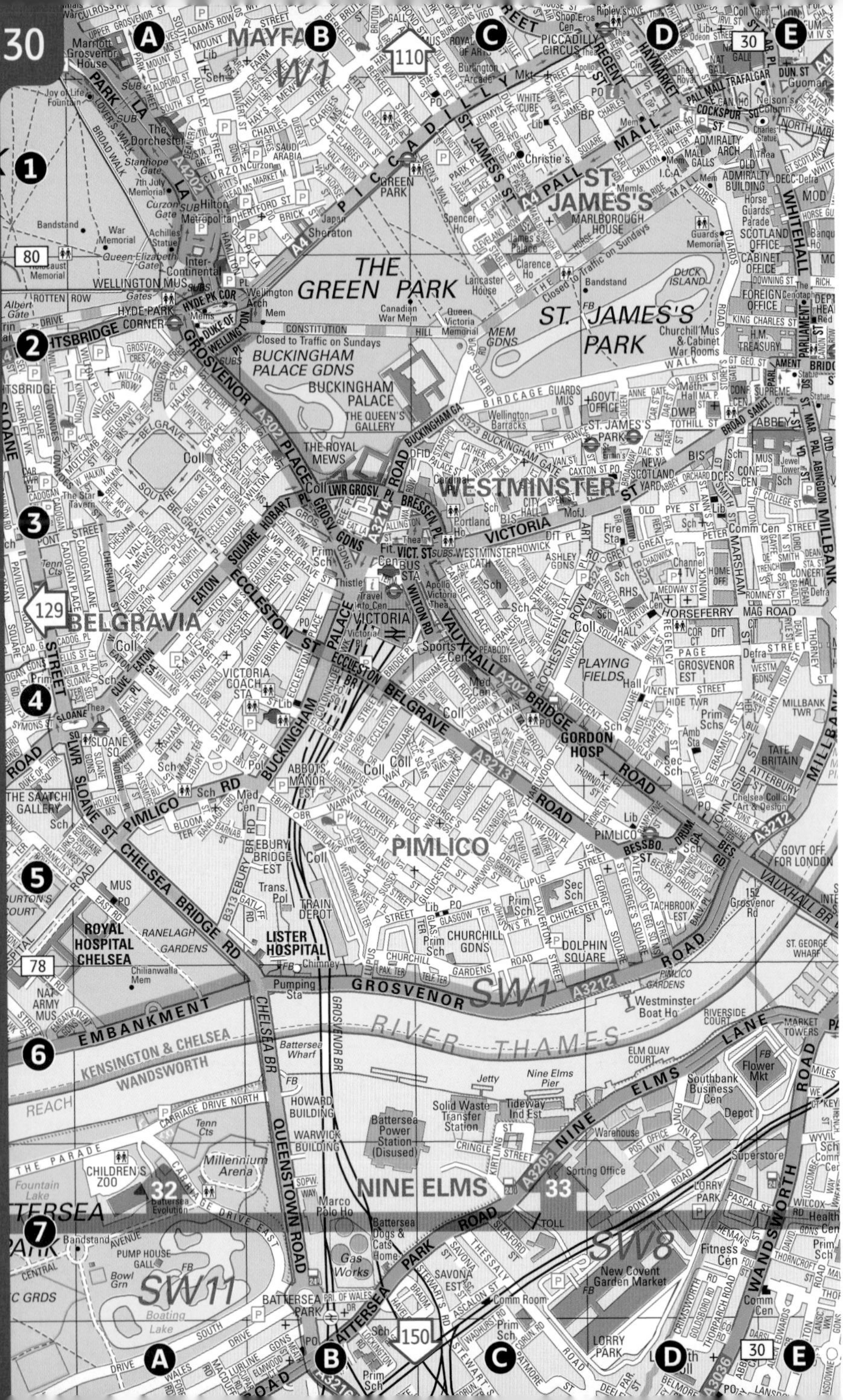
A
B
C
D
E
1
2
3
4
5
6
7
110
129
150
80
78
30
MAYFAIR
W1
PICCADILLY CIRCUS
PICCADILLY
HAYMARKET
REGENT ST
PALL MALL
TRAFALGAR
COCKSPUR
ADMIRALTY ARCH
Nelson's Column
WHITEHALL
ST JAMES'S
MARLBOROUGH HOUSE
Christie's
Burlington Arcade
ROYAL ACADEMY OF ARTS
GREEN PARK
THE GREEN PARK
Sheraton
The Dorchester
Hilton Metropolitan
PARK LA
Joy of Life Fountain
BROAD WALK
Stanhope Gate
7th July Memorial
Curzon Gate
Achilles Statue
Queen Elizabeth Gate
Bandstand
War Memorial
Holocaust Memorial
WELLINGTON MUS
ROTTEN ROW
Albert Gate
HYDE PARK CORNER
HYDE PARK
Wellington Arch
Inter-Continental
CONSTITUTION HILL
Closed to Traffic on Sundays
Canadian War Mem
Queen Victoria Memorial
Lancaster House
Clarence Ho
St. James's Palace
Spencer Ho
ST. JAMES'S PARK
DUCK ISLAND
Guards Memorial
HORSE GUARDS PARADE
SCOTLAND OFFICE
CABINET OFFICE
DOWNING ST
FOREIGN OFFICE
Cenotaph
KING CHARLES ST
H.M. TREASURY
Churchill Mus & Cabinet War Rooms
PARLIAMENT ST
BIRDCAGE WALK
BUCKINGHAM PALACE GDNS
BUCKINGHAM PALACE
THE QUEEN'S GALLERY
THE ROYAL MEWS
Wellington Barracks
GUARDS MUS
ST. JAMES'S PARK
NEW SCOTLAND YARD
BROADWAY
ABBEY
Jewel Tower
BROAD SANCT.
WESTMINSTER
VICTORIA ST
CITY HALL
WESTMINSTER CATH
VICTORIA
VICT. ST
BUS STA
Apollo Victoria Thea
Travel Info Cen
GROSVENOR PLACE
GROSVENOR CRES
BELGRAVE SQUARE
EATON SQUARE
BELGRAVIA
ECCLESTON ST
BUCKINGHAM PALACE RD
VICTORIA COACH STA
KNIGHTSBRIDGE
SLOANE ST
SLOANE SQ
LWR SLOANE ST
PIMLICO RD
THE SAATCHI GALLERY
DUKE OF YORK SQ
MILLBANK
HORSEFERRY ROAD
MARSHAM ST
PLAYING FIELDS
VAUXHALL BRIDGE ROAD
GORDON HOSP
TATE BRITAIN
Chelsea Coll of Art & Design
PIMLICO
BELGRAVE ROAD
WARWICK WAY
EBURY BRIDGE EST
ABBOTS MANOR EST
LISTER HOSPITAL
TRAIN DEPOT
CHURCHILL GDNS
DOLPHIN SQUARE
GOVT OFF FOR LONDON
152 Grosvenor Rd
GROSVENOR ROAD
SW1
A3212
PIMLICO GARDENS
Westminster Boat Ho
ROYAL HOSPITAL CHELSEA
RANELAGH GARDENS
Chilianwalla Mem
NAT ARMY MUS
CHELSEA BRIDGE RD
EMBANKMENT
KENSINGTON & CHELSEA
WANDSWORTH
RIVER THAMES
CHELSEA BR
GROSVENOR BR
Battersea Wharf
REACH
CARRIAGE DRIVE NORTH
HOWARD BUILDING
WARWICK BUILDING
Battersea Power Station (Disused)
Solid Waste Transfer Station
Nine Elms Pier
Tideway Ind Est
ELM QUAY COURT
RIVERSIDE COURT
MARKET TOWERS
Flower Mkt
Southbank Business Cen
Depot
NINE ELMS LANE
NINE ELMS
Sorting Office
Superstore
THE PARADE
CHILDREN'S ZOO
Millennium Arena
Fountain Lake
32
33
BATTERSEA PARK
Bandstand
PUMP HOUSE GALL
Bowl Grn
SW11
Boating Lake
QUEENSTOWN ROAD
Marco Polo Ho
Battersea Dogs & Cats Home
Gas Works
BATTERSEA PARK ROAD
PONTON ROAD
SW8
New Covent Garden Market
LORRY PARK
WANDSWORTH ROAD
Fitness Cen
Comm Room
Comm Cen
SAVONA EST
TOLL

E
F
G
H
J
31
111
32
CHARING CROSS
EMBANKMENT
London Television Centre
Nautical Sch
STAMFORD
SOUTHWARK
A3200
TATE MODERN
BLACKFRIARS
SE1
SOUTHWARK
QUEEN ELIZABETH HALL
ROYAL FESTIVAL HALL
HAYWARD GALLERY
London Eye
JUBILEE GARDENS
WATERLOO
WATERLOO EAST
VICTORIA
WESTMINSTER
WESTMINSTER BR
A302
HOUSES OF PARLIAMENT
ST. THOMAS' HOSP
THE BOROUGH
NEWINGTON
BOROUGH
LAMBETH NORTH
WESTMINSTER BRIDGE RD
ST. GEORGE'S CATHEDRAL
LAMBETH PALACE GDNS
GERALD. MARY HARMSWORTH PARK
IMPERIAL WAR MUSEUM
LAMBETH
A3203
A23
A201
132
ELEPHANT & CASTLE
SE17
SE11
80
78
WALWORTH
KENNINGTON
VAUXHALL
A3204
A3036
A203
THE OVAL (SURREY C.C.C.)
KENNINGTON OVAL
KENNINGTON PARK
OVAL
CAMBERWELL
34
35
A202
SOUTH LAMBETH
CAMBERWELL
SE5
151
1
2
3
4
5
6
7

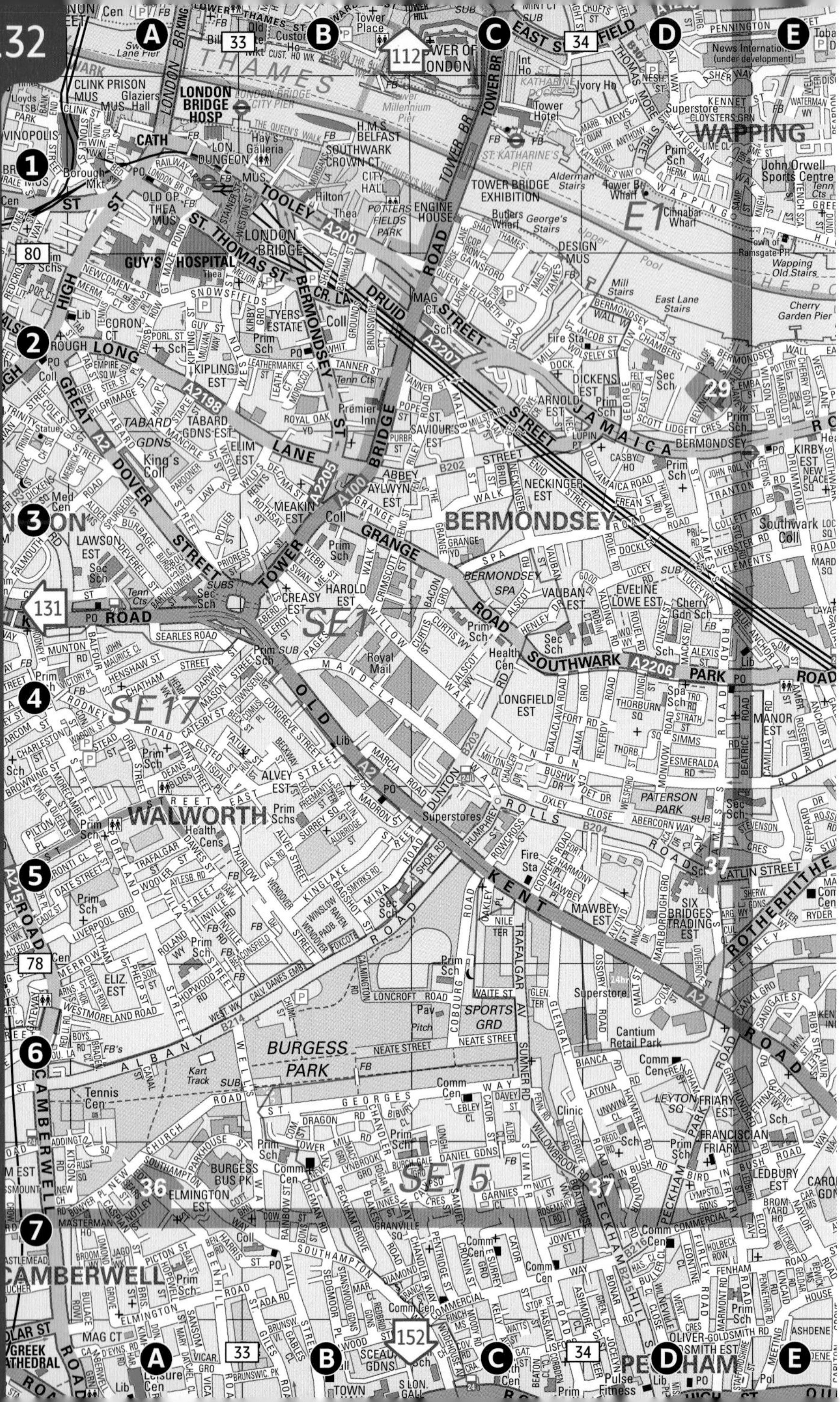
A
B
C
D
E
33
34
112
131
152
80
78
29
36
37
1
2
3
4
5
6
7
THAMES
CLINK PRISON MUS
Glaziers Hall
LONDON BRIDGE HOSP
CATH
Borough Mkt
OLD OP. THEA MUS
GUY'S HOSPITAL
TOOLEY ST
LON. DUNGEON
Hay's Galleria
H.M.S. BELFAST
SOUTHWARK CROWN CT
CITY HALL
POTTERS FIELDS PARK
ENGINE HOUSE
TOWER BRIDGE EXHIBITION
TOWER BR
TOWER BRIDGE ROAD
ST. THOMAS ST
LONDON BRIDGE
BERMONDSEY ST
Tower Millennium Pier
LONDON BRIDGE CITY PIER
THE QUEEN'S WALK
ST. KATHARINE'S PIER
ST KATHARINE DOCKS
Tower Hotel
Ivory Ho
WAPPING
E1
John Orwell Sports Centre
News International (under development)
PENNINGTON ST
Cinnabar Wharf
Alderman Stairs
Butlers Wharf
DESIGN MUS
Mill Stairs
East Lane Stairs
Cherry Garden Pier
Upper Pool
Town of Ramsgate PH
Wapping Old Stairs
DRUID STREET
A200
A2207
A2198
A2205
A100
A2206
A2
B202
B203
B204
B214
B216
B215
LONG LANE
HIGH ST
BOROUGH HIGH ST
GREAT DOVER STREET
TABARD GDNS EST
KIPLING EST
TYERS ESTATE
Premier Inn
ROYAL OAK YD
JAMAICA ROAD
BERMONDSEY
BERMONDSEY SPA
GRANGE ROAD
ABBEY STREET
NECKINGER EST
DICKENS EST
ARNOLD EST
SCOTT LIDGETT CRES
SOUTHWARK PARK ROAD
Southwark Coll
King's Coll
Med Cen
LAWSON EST
SE1
SE17
SE15
TOWER BRIDGE ROAD
HAROLD EST
CREASY EST
Royal Mail
MANDELA WAY
WILLOW WALK
OLD KENT ROAD
LONGFIELD EST
VAUBAN EST
EVELINE LOWE EST
MANOR EST
SEARLES ROAD
WALWORTH
ALVEY EST
EAST STREET
PATERSON PARK
ROLLS ROAD
Superstores
Fire Sta
MAWBEY EST
SIX BRIDGES TRADING EST
ROTHERHITHE NEW ROAD
CATLIN STREET
BURGESS PARK
SPORTS GRD
Kart Track
Tennis Cen
Cantium Retail Park
LEYTON SQ
FRIARY EST
FRANCISCAN FRIARY
LEDBURY EST
ALBANY ROAD
CAMBERWELL ROAD
CAMBERWELL
ELIZ. EST
BURGESS BUS PK
ELMINGTON EST
PECKHAM HILL ST
PECKHAM PARK ROAD
COMMERCIAL WAY
ST. GEORGES WAY
SOUTHAMPTON WAY
PECKHAM GROVE
PECKHAM
OLIVER GOLDSMITH EST
GREEK CATHEDRAL
Pulse Fitness
Leisure Cen

E
F
G
H
J
35
113
SHADWELL
MILK YARD
Outdoor Centre
Arts Cen
Prospect of Whitby PH
TOWER HAMLETS
SOUTHWARK
RIVER THAMES
Lavender Wharf
Limehouse Hole Stairs
Four Seasons
Health Club
BERKLEY TWR
WESTFERRY CIRCUS
T203
1
2
3
4
5
6
7
WAPPING WALL
New Crane Stairs
Pier
WAPPING
Wapping Dock Stairs
WATERSIDE GDNS
Wapping New Stairs
Health Cen
PUMPHOUSE EDUC. MUS
Sunderland Wharf
Lawrence Wharf
Blacksmiths Arms PH
Hilton Docklands
CANARY WHARF PIER
HILTON DOCKLANDS NELSON DOCK PIER
NELSON DOCK
MERMAID CT
CHRISTIAN CT
CASCADES TOWER
80
West India Dock Pier
MILLENNIUM HARBOUR
SEACON TOWER
OCEAN WHARF
SPORTS GRD
SALTER
ROTHERHITHE
Airshaft
YHA
Clubho.
MELLISH SPORTS GRD
SURREY WATER
Gas Holder
SE16
ECOLOGICAL PARK
STAVE HILL
RUSSIA DOCK WOODLAND
Health Cen
Surrey Docks Farm
Comm Cen
BRUNEL MUS
ROTHERHITHE
Princes Stairs
King's Stairs
KING'S STAIRS GDNS
AINSTY EST
ALBION ESTATE
Civic Cen
CANADA WATER
ROTHERHITHE
Associated Newspapers Print Works
CANADA WATER
Superstores
CANADA EST
HOWLAND EST
REDRIFF EST
CUSTOM HOUSE REACH
NEW CALEDONIAN WF
KING FREDERIK IX TWR
QUEEN OF DENMARK CT
PRINCES CT
NORWAY DOCK
TOWER HAMLETS
SOUTHWARK
LIMEHOUSE REACH
ARICA HOUSE
Seven Islands Leisure Cen
Bowling Alley
Cinema
MAST LEISURE PK
Surrey Quays Shopping Cen
GREENLAND DOCK
GREENLAND PIER
South Lock
St. George's Stairs
Surrey Docks Water Sports Cen
SOUTH DOCK
134
LOWER ROAD
A200
A2202 ROAD
REDRIFF
SURREY QUAYS
SOUTHWARK PARK EST
SOUTHWARK RUNNING TRACK
SOUTHWARK PARK
MAYDEW HOUSE
CAFE GALLERY
Lake
PLOUGH WAY
LEWISHAM
RAYMOUTH RD
ROTHERHITHE NEW RD
HAWKSTONE RD
Prim Sch
CANNON WHARF BUSINESS CEN
EVELYN
Med Cen
ARAGON TWR
THAMES PATH
RENNIE EST
Health Cen
HAWKSTONE EST
EDDYSTONE TWR
Youth Club
DAUBENEY TWR
SOUTH BERMONDSEY
PEPYS PARK
Landing Stage
DEPTFORD PARK
DEPTFORD
SE8
A2208
Lewisham Lions Cen
THE DEN MILLWALL FC
Power Station
Chimney
Recycling Cen
ORION BUSINESS CEN
SAYES COURT PARK
78
Fire Sta
DEPTFORD TRADING EST
SURREY CANAL ROAD
FOLKESTONE GDNS
Gas Works
SE14
BRIDGE HOUSE MEADOWS
SHARRATT Hall
PRINCE STREET
Med Cen
Comm Cen
Barnardo's Cen
Woodpecker Cen
Coll
Superstore
Tenn Cts
FORDHAM PARK
Comm Cen
Sec Sch
DEPTFORD
Health Cen
NEW CROSS
New Cross
A2
Superstore
SE15
HATCHAM GDNS
153
NEW CROSS GATE
NEW CROSS
BESSON ST
Health Cen

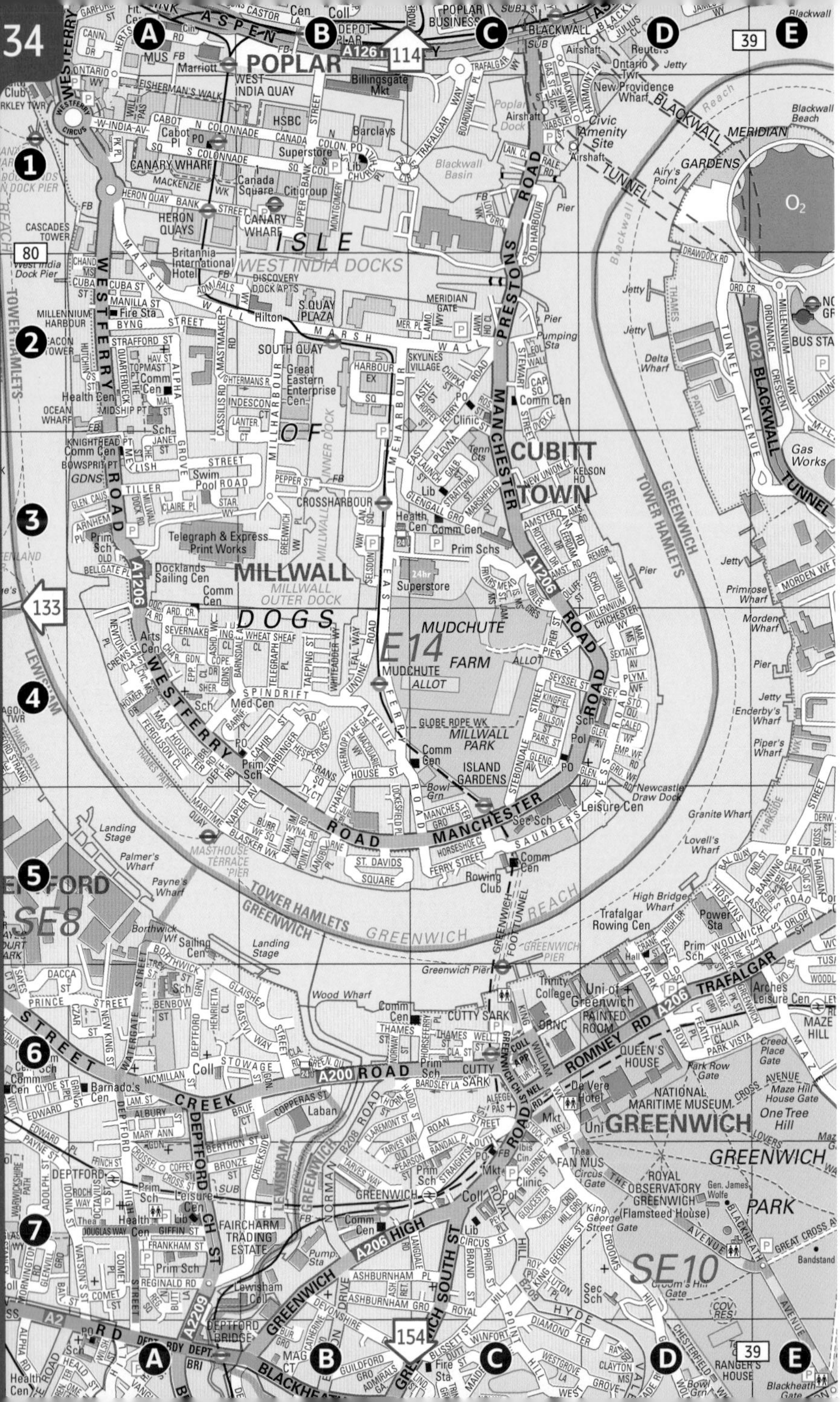
A
B
C
D
E
1
2
3
4
5
6
7
114
133
154
80
39
POPLAR
WEST INDIA QUAY
Billingsgate Mkt
POPLAR BUSINESS
BLACKWALL
ASPEN WAY
A1261
WESTFERRY CIRCUS
CANARY WHARF
Canada Square
HERON QUAYS
CANARY WHARF
Cabot Pl
N COLONNADE
S COLONNADE
HSBC
Barclays
Citigroup
Superstore
Blackwall Basin
Poplar Dock
Reuters
Ontario Twr
New Providence Wharf
Civic Amenity Site
BLACKWALL TUNNEL
MERIDIAN GARDENS
Blackwall Beach
Airy's Point
O₂
DRAWDOCK RD
CASCADES TOWER
West India Dock Pier
ISLE
WEST INDIA DOCKS
Britannia International Hotel
DISCOVERY DOCK APTS
S.QUAY PLAZA
MERIDIAN GATE
Hilton
MARSH WALL
SOUTH QUAY
MILLENNIUM HARBOUR
BEACON TOWER
PRESTONS ROAD
COLD HARBOUR
Pumping Sta
Great Eastern Enterprise Cen
HARBOUR EX SQ
SKYLINES VILLAGE
OF
INNER DOCK
MILLHARBOUR
LIMEHARBOUR
MANCHESTER ROAD
CUBITT TOWN
Comm Cen
Clinic
Tenn Cts
KELSON HO
NEW UNION CL
Health Cen
OCEAN WHARF
KNIGHTHEAD PT
Comm Cen
BOWSPRIT PT
GDNS
Swim Pool
CROSSHARBOUR
Telegraph & Express Print Works
Prim Schs
Superstore
MILLWALL
MILLWALL OUTER DOCK
Dockland Sailing Cen
DOGS
A1206
E14
MUDCHUTE
FARM
MUDCHUTE ALLOT
ALLOT
WESTFERRY ROAD
SPINDRIFT
Med Cen
GLOBE ROPE WK
MILLWALL PARK
ISLAND GARDENS
EAST FERRY ROAD
SAUNDERS NESS ROAD
Leisure Cen
Newcastle Draw Dock
Sec Sch
ST. DAVIDS SQUARE
FERRY STREET
Rowing Club
Landing Stage
Palmer's Wharf
Payne's Wharf
MASTHOUSE TERRACE PIER
TOWER HAMLETS
GREENWICH
REACH
GREENWICH FOOT TUNNEL
GREENWICH PIER
Greenwich Pier
DEPTFORD
SE8
Borthwick Wf
Sailing Cen
Landing Stage
Wood Wharf
CUTTY SARK
Trinity College
Uni of Greenwich
PAINTED ROOM
ORNC
ROMNEY RD
A206
TRAFALGAR
QUEEN'S HOUSE
NATIONAL MARITIME MUSEUM
GREENWICH
GREENWICH PARK
ROYAL OBSERVATORY GREENWICH (Flamsteed House)
Gen. James Wolfe
One Tree Hill
Maze Hill House Gate
Park Row Gate
Creed Place Gate
MAZE HILL
Arches Leisure Cen
Trafalgar Rowing Cen
Power Sta
High Bridge Wharf
Lovell's Wharf
Granite Wharf
Piper's Wharf
Enderby's Wharf
Primrose Wharf
Morden Wharf
Delta Wharf
Gas Works
BLACKWALL TUNNEL
A102
TUNNEL AVENUE
A200 ROAD
CREEK ROAD
DEPTFORD CH ST
Barnado's Cen
Laban
Coll
GREENWICH
Greenwich High Road
A206 HIGH
FAIRCHARM TRADING ESTATE
Lewisham Coll
DEPTFORD BRIDGE
A2209
A2
Prim Sch
Leisure Cen
Health Cen
King George Street Gate
Crooms Hill Gate
SE10
Sec Sch
HYDE
DIAMOND TER
RANGER'S HOUSE
Bandstand
GREAT CROSS AV
Blackheath Gate
BLACKHEATH

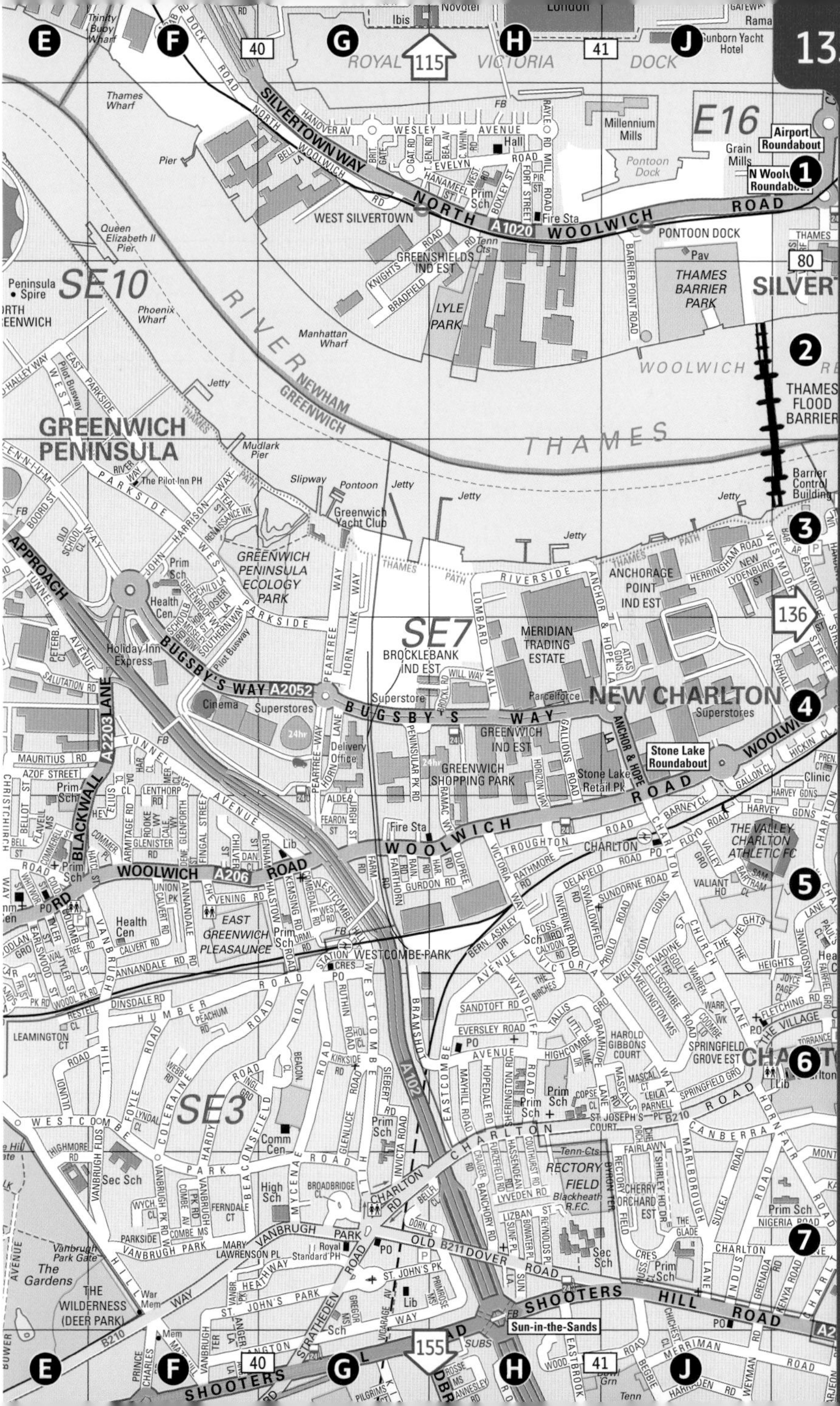
E
F
G
H
J
40
41
115
136
155
1
2
3
4
5
6
7
ROYAL VICTORIA DOCK
Ibis
Novotel
Sunborn Yacht Hotel
Trinity Buoy Wharf
Thames Wharf
Pier
Queen Elizabeth II Pier
E16
Millennium Mills
Grain Mills
Pontoon Dock
Airport Roundabout
SILVERTOWN WAY
NORTH WOOLWICH ROAD
A1020
WEST SILVERTOWN
PONTOON DOCK
WESLEY AVENUE
HANOVER AV
EVELYN ROAD
HANAMEEL ST
BOXLEY ST
FORT STREET
MILL ROAD
RAYLEIGH RD
Hall
Prim Sch
Fire Sta
GREENSHIELDS IND EST
KNIGHTS ROAD
BRADFIELD ROAD
LYLE PARK
BARRIER POINT ROAD
Pav
THAMES BARRIER PARK
80
SILVERT
Peninsula Spire
SE10
NORTH GREENWICH
Phoenix Wharf
RIVER THAMES
NEWHAM
GREENWICH
Manhattan Wharf
Jetty
WOOLWICH
THAMES FLOOD BARRIER
Barrier Control Building
GREENWICH PENINSULA
Mudlark Pier
Slipway
Pontoon
The Pilot Inn PH
PARKSIDE
JOHN HARRISON WAY
Greenwich Yacht Club
GREENWICH PENINSULA ECOLOGY PARK
THAMES PATH
RIVERSIDE
ANCHORAGE POINT IND EST
HERRINGHAM ROAD
WESTMOOR
EASTMOOR
APPROACH
BLACKWALL TUNNEL
Prim Sch
Health Cen.
Holiday Inn Express
BUGSBY'S WAY
A2052
SE7
BROCKLEBANK IND EST
MERIDIAN TRADING ESTATE
LOMBARD WALL
ANCHOR & HOPE LA
NEW CHARLTON
Parcelforce
Superstores
Superstore
Cinema
24hr
Delivery Office
GREENWICH IND EST
GALLIONS ROAD
GREENWICH SHOPPING PARK
Stone Lake Roundabout
Stone Lake Retail Pk
WOOLWICH ROAD
A2203
BLACKWALL LANE
MAURITIUS RD
AZOF STREET
CHRISTCHURCH
Lib
Fire Sta
A206
EAST GREENWICH PLEASAUNCE
Health Cen
VANBRUGH HILL
WESTCOMBE PARK
CHARLTON
THE VALLEY CHARLTON ATHLETIC FC
Clinic
HARVEY GDNS
FLOYD ROAD
VICTORIA WAY
DELAFIELD ROAD
SUNDORNE ROAD
WELLINGTON GDNS
CHURCH LANE
THE HEIGHTS
HUMBER ROAD
DINSDALE RD
LEAMINGTON CT
BRAMSHOT AV
A102
EVERSLEY ROAD
SANDTOFT RD
HAROLD GIBBONS COURT
SPRINGFIELD GROVE EST
THE VILLAGE
CHARLTON
SE3
WESTCOMBE PARK ROAD
Comm Cen
High Sch
Sec Sch
CHARLTON ROAD
RECTORY FIELD
Blackheath R.F.C.
Tenn Cts
CHERRY ORCHARD EST
Prim Sch
CANBERRA ROAD
HORNFAIR ROAD
NIGERIA ROAD
Vanbrugh Park Gate
The Gardens
THE WILDERNESS (DEER PARK)
VANBRUGH PARK
Royal Standard PH
OLD DOVER ROAD
B211
SHOOTERS HILL ROAD
Sun-in-the-Sands
ST. JOHN'S PARK
Lib
War Mem
B210
SHOOTERS

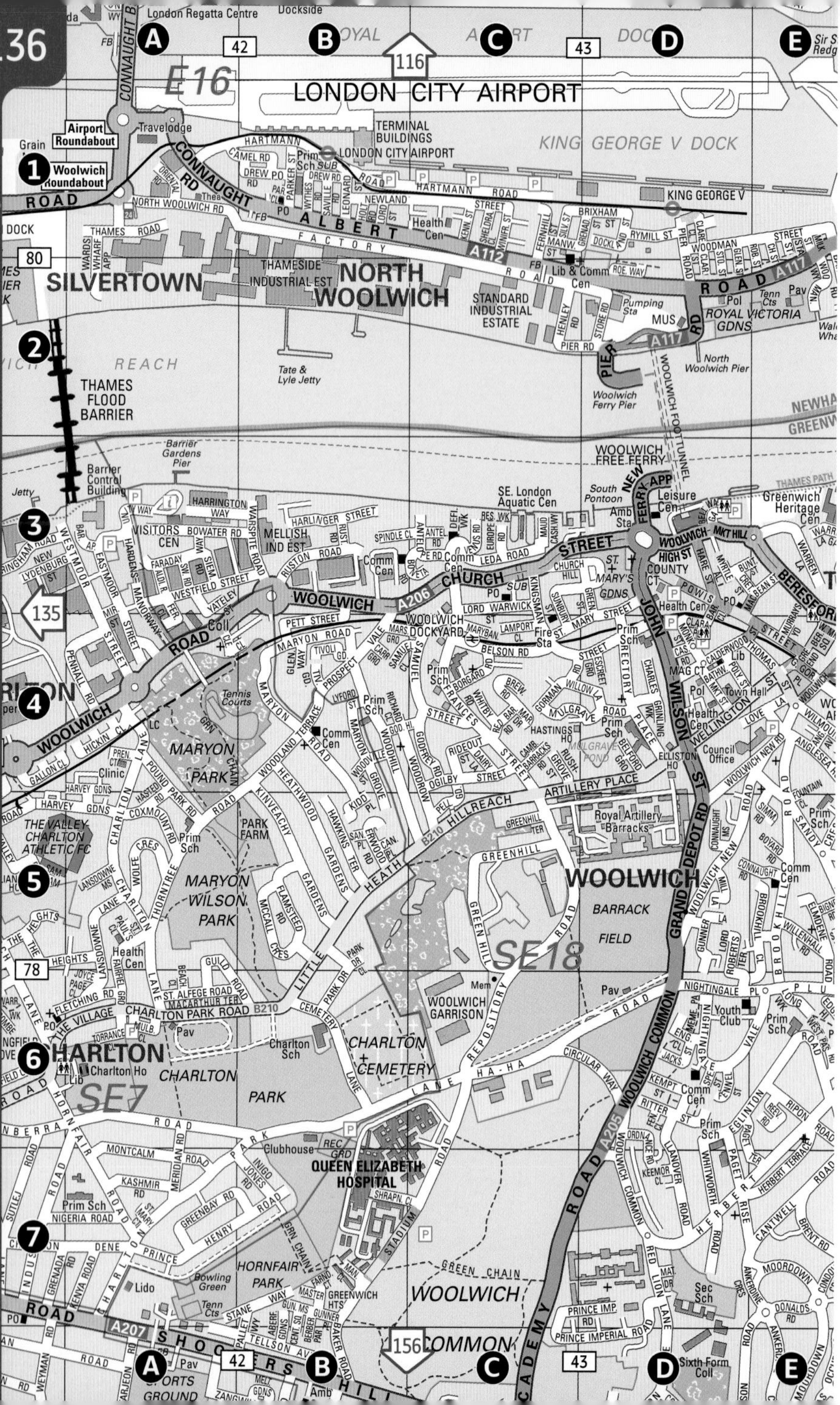
London Regatta Centre
Dockside
ROYAL ALBERT DOCK
116
42
43
E16
LONDON CITY AIRPORT
CONNAUGHT BRIDGE
Airport Roundabout
Travelodge
TERMINAL BUILDINGS
KING GEORGE V DOCK
Grain
Woolwich Roundabout
HARTMANN RD
LONDON CITY AIRPORT
CONNAUGHT RD
ALBERT ROAD
FACTORY ROAD
NORTH WOOLWICH RD
THAMES ROAD
KING GEORGE V
Health Cen
Lib & Comm Cen
A112
A117
80
SILVERTOWN
THAMESIDE INDUSTRIAL EST
NORTH WOOLWICH
STANDARD INDUSTRIAL ESTATE
ROYAL VICTORIA GDNS
Pumping Sta
MUS
PIER RD
North Woolwich Pier
REACH
THAMES FLOOD BARRIER
Tate & Lyle Jetty
Woolwich Ferry Pier
WOOLWICH FOOT TUNNEL
NEWHAM
GREENWICH
Barrier Gardens Pier
Barrier Control Building
WOOLWICH FREE FERRY
THAMES PATH
Jetty
HARRINGTON WAY
VISITORS CEN
BOWATER RD
MELLISH IND EST
SE. London Aquatic Cen
South Pontoon
NEW FERRY APP
Leisure Cen
Amb Sta
Greenwich Heritage Cen
WOOLWICH CHURCH STREET
A206
WOOLWICH HIGH ST
BERESFORD
135
WESTFIELD STREET
WOOLWICH DOCKYARD
JOHN WILSON ST
GRAND DEPOT RD
ST. MARY'S GDNS
ST. MARY STREET
Health Cen
WOOLWICH ROAD
MARYON PARK
Tennis Courts
Clinic
Comm Cen
Prim Sch
MULGRAVE POND
Town Hall
WELLINGTON
Council Office
HARVEY GDNS
THE VALLEY CHARLTON ATHLETIC FC
PARK FARM
HILLREACH
B210
ARTILLERY PLACE
Royal Artillery Barracks
MARYON WILSON PARK
WOOLWICH
BARRACK FIELD
SE18
78
Health Cen
CHARLTON PARK ROAD
WOOLWICH GARRISON
Mem
Pav
Youth Club
CHARLTON
Charlton Ho
Lib
SE7
CHARLTON PARK
Charlton Sch
CHARLTON CEMETERY
HA-HA LANE
CIRCULAR WAY
WOOLWICH COMMON
A205
Clubhouse
QUEEN ELIZABETH HOSPITAL
Prim Sch
HORNFAIR PARK
Bowling Green
Lido
Tenn Cts
GREEN CHAIN
WOOLWICH COMMON
156
A207
SHOOTERS HILL
SPORTS GROUND
Sec Sch
Sixth Form Coll
A B C D E
1 2 3 4 5 6 7

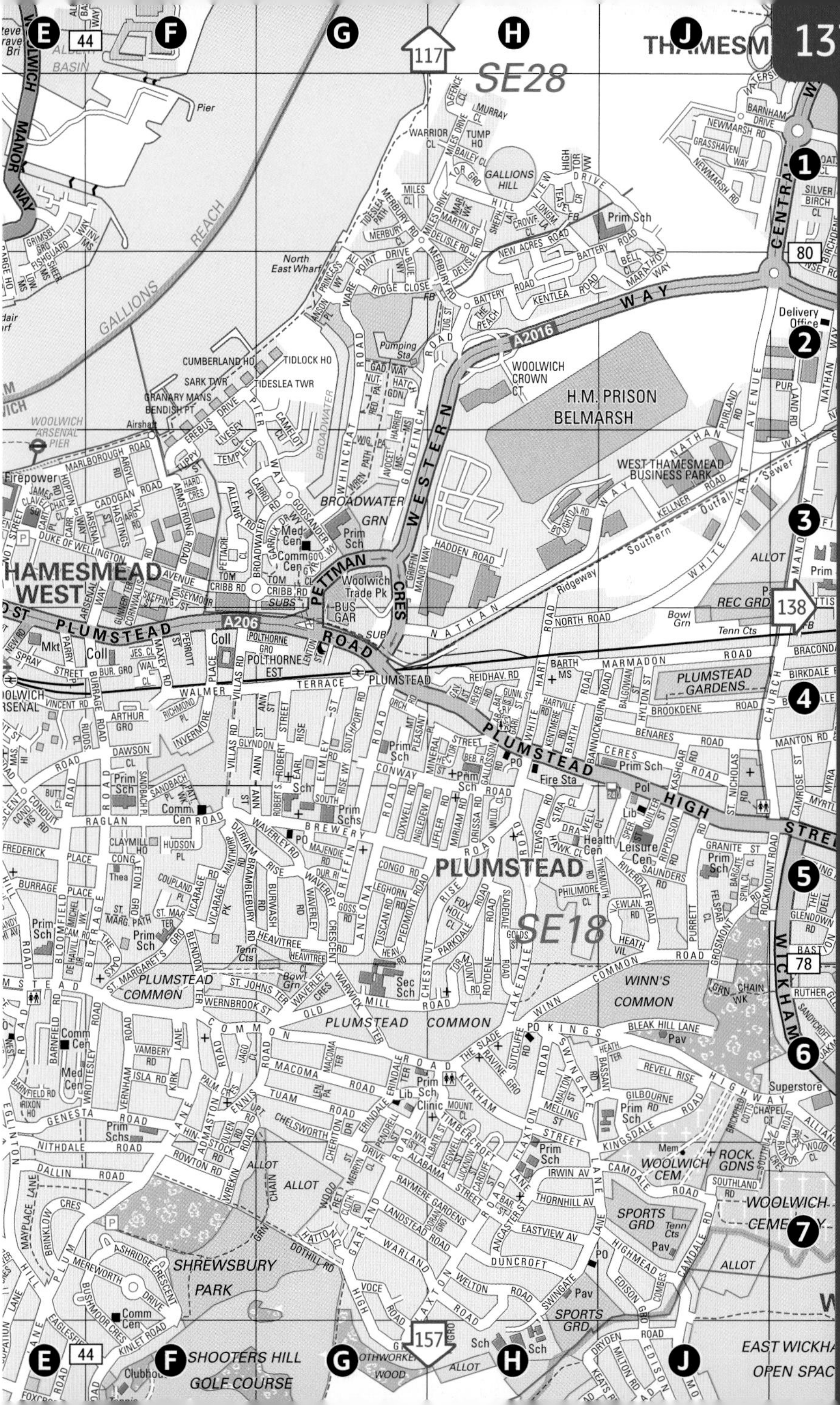

E
F
G
H
J
44
117
SE28
THAMESMEAD
ALBERT BASIN
Pier
GALLIONS REACH
MANOR WAY
WOOLWICH ARSENAL PIER
North East Wharf
GALLIONS HILL
MURRAY
TUMP HO
WARRIOR CL
MILES DRIVE
BAILEY CL
TOR GRO
MILES CL
HIGH VIEW DRIVE
Prim Sch
NEW ACRES ROAD
BATTERY ROAD
KENTLEA ROAD
MARATHON WAY
BELL CL
MERBURY RD
MARTIN ST
DELISLE RD
WARE POINT DRIVE
RIDGE CLOSE
BLUE WY
TIDESLEA PATH
PRINCESS WY
ANSON PL
FB
WAY
A2016
THE REACH
Pumping Sta
WOOLWICH CROWN CT
H.M. PRISON BELMARSH
CUMBERLAND HO
TIDLOCK HO
SARK TWR
TIDESLEA TWR
GRANARY MANS
BENDISH PT
Airshaft
EREBUS DRIVE
LIVESEY CL
TEMPLE CL
CAMELOT CL
PIER WAY
BROADWATER
WHINCHAT ROAD
GOLDFINCH ROAD
WESTERN
CRES
PETTMAN
BROADWATER GRN
Prim Sch
Med Cen
Comm Cen
Woolwich Trade Pk
BUS GAR
HADDEN ROAD
GRIFFIN MANOR WAY
WEST THAMESMEAD BUSINESS PARK
NATHAN WAY
KELLNER ROAD
BOUGHTON RD
Southern Outfall Sewer
WHITE HART AVENUE
PURLAND RD
Ridgeway
Delivery Office
NEWMARSH RD
GRASSHAVEN WAY
BARNHAM DRIVE
SILVER BIRCH CL
CENTRAL WAY
80
1
2
3
4
5
6
7
ALLOT
REC GRD
Bowl Grn
Tenn Cts
138
NORTH ROAD
MARLBOROUGH ROAD
Firepower
CADOGAN ROAD
ARMSTRONG ROAD
DUKE OF WELLINGTON AVENUE
THAMESMEAD WEST
TOM CRIBB RD
SUBS
PLUMSTEAD ROAD
A206
Mkt
Coll
POLTHORNE EST
PLUMSTEAD
WALMER TERRACE
WOOLWICH ARSENAL
VINCENT RD
ARTHUR GRO
INVERMORE
DAWSON CL
RAGLAN ROAD
FREDERICK PLACE
BURRAGE PLACE
BURRAGE ROAD
Prim Sch
Comm Cen
CLAYMILL HO
HUDSON PL
VICARAGE PK
MANTHORP RD
DURHAM RISE
WAVERLEY RD
BURWASH RD
CONWAY ROAD
PLUMSTEAD HIGH STREET
MARMADON ROAD
PLUMSTEAD GARDENS
BROOKDENE ROAD
BENARES ROAD
CERES ROAD
Prim Sch
Fire Sta
PO
Pol
Lib
Leisure Cen
Health Cen
MANTON RD
CAMROSE ST
GRANITE ST
SAUNDERS RD
ROCKMOUNT ROAD
PLUMSTEAD
SE18
HEATH VIL
WICKHAM LANE
WINN'S COMMON
WINN COMMON ROAD
PLUMSTEAD COMMON
PLUMSTEAD COMMON ROAD
HEAVITREE RD
Sec Sch
MILL ROAD
WERNBROOK ST
ST. JOHNS TER
BLEAK HILL LANE
KINGS HIGHWAY
Pav
REVELL RISE
GILBOURNE RD
Superstore
MACOMA ROAD
TUAM ROAD
CHELSWORTH DR
Lib
Clinic
KIRKHAM ST
TIMBERCROFT LANE
KINGSDALE ROAD
CAMDALE ROAD
WOOLWICH CEM
ROCK. GDNS
SOUTHLAND RD
WOOLWICH CEMETERY
VERNHAM RD
GENESTA ROAD
NITHDALE ROAD
DALLIN ROAD
ROWTON RD
HIN-STOCK RD
WREKIN RD
ALLOT
RAYMERE GARDENS
LANDSTEAD ROAD
WARLAND ROAD
WELTON ROAD
DUNCROFT
THORNHILL AV
EASTVIEW AV
IRWIN AV
SPORTS GRD
HIGHMEAD
EDISON GRO
SHREWSBURY PARK
MEREWORTH DRIVE
ASHRIDGE CRESCENT
BUSHMOOR CRES
KINLET ROAD
Comm Cen
SHOOTERS HILL GOLF COURSE
Clubhouse
157
ALLOT
Sch
78
EAST WICKHAM OPEN SPACE
DRYDEN ROAD
MILTON RD

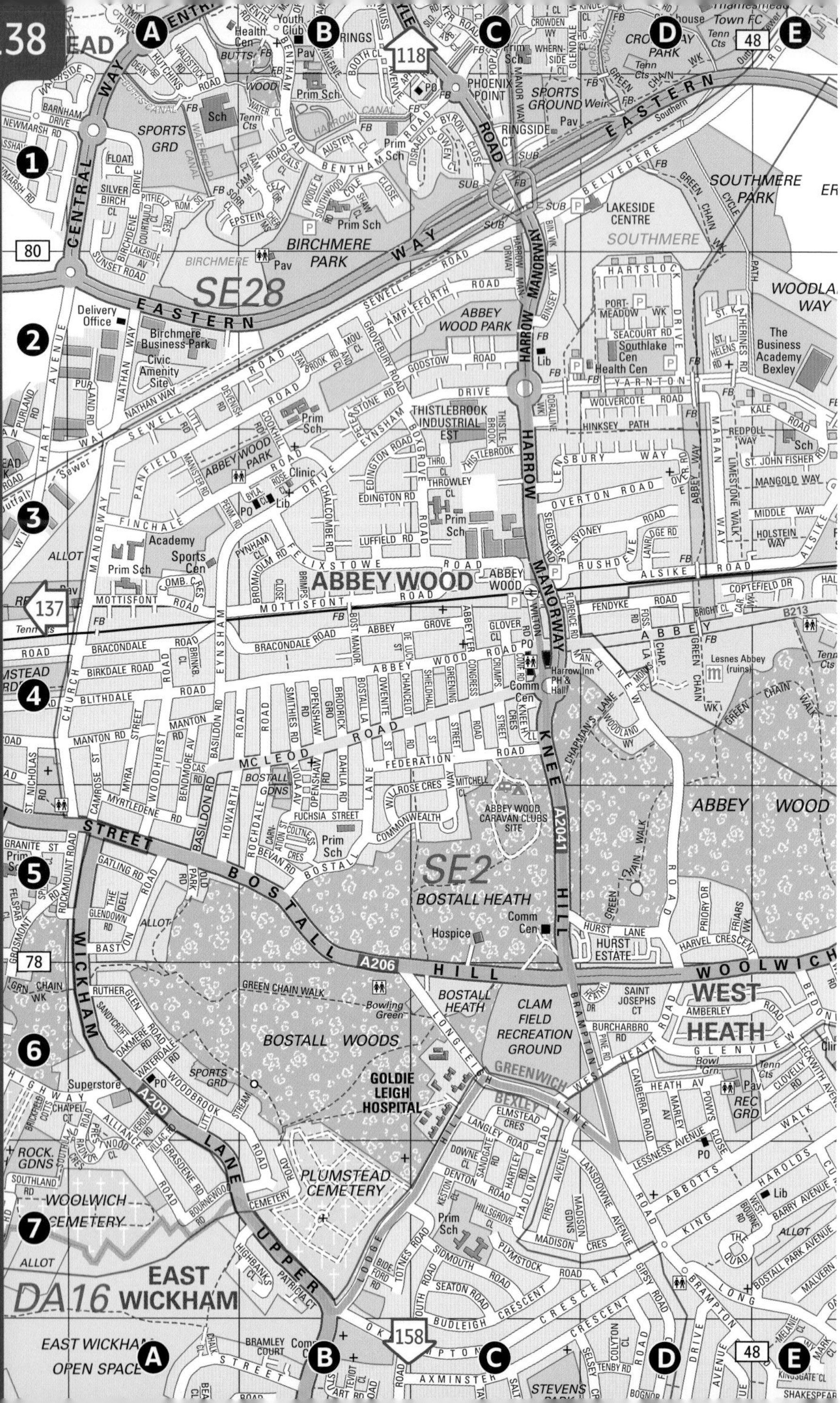

A
B
C
D
E
1
2
3
4
5
6
7
118
137
158
80
78
48
SE28
SE2
DA16
ABBEY WOOD
WEST HEATH
EAST WICKHAM
SPORTS GRD
BIRCHMERE PARK
BIRCHMERE
EASTERN WAY
CENTRAL WAY
HARROW MANORWAY
SOUTHMERE PARK
SOUTHMERE
LAKESIDE CENTRE
PHOENIX POINT
SPORTS GROUND
CROWN WAY PARK
Thamesmead Town FC
Youth Club
Health Cen
Prim Sch
Sch
Delivery Office
Birchmere Business Park
Civic Amenity Site
ABBEY WOOD PARK
THISTLEBROOK INDUSTRIAL EST
Southlake Cen
Health Cen
The Business Academy Bexley
Academy
Sports Cen
Clinic
Lib
PO
Harrow Inn PH & Hall
Comm Cen
Lesnes Abbey (ruins)
ABBEY WOOD CARAVAN CLUBS SITE
BOSTALL HEATH
Hospice
HURST ESTATE
BOSTALL WOODS
Bowling Green
GOLDIE LEIGH HOSPITAL
CLAM FIELD RECREATION GROUND
PLUMSTEAD CEMETERY
WOOLWICH CEMETERY
Superstore
EAST WICKHAM OPEN SPACE
REC GRD
BOSTALL HILL
WOOLWICH ROAD
WICKHAM LANE
UPPER WICKHAM LANE
KNEE HILL
A2041
A206
A209
B213
GREEN CHAIN WALK
FELIXSTOWE ROAD
MOTTISFONT ROAD
ABBEY GROVE
ABBEY WOOD ROAD
ABBEY ROAD
McLEOD ROAD
FEDERATION ROAD
BRAMPTON ROAD
LODGE LANE
LONG LANE
ABBOTTS WALK
KING HAROLDS WAY
BOSTALL PARK AVENUE
LESSNESS AVENUE
GIPSY ROAD
OKEHAMPTON CRESCENT
AXMINSTER CRESCENT
BUDLEIGH CRESCENT
SIDMOUTH ROAD
YARNTON WAY
ALSIKE ROAD
GODSTOW ROAD
SEWELL ROAD

E
F
49
G
117
H
50
J
Wharf
Sludge Inciner
SPORTS GROU
Jennings Point
A2016
CROSSNESS NATURE RESERVE
ITH MARSHES
Belvedere Sub Sta
NORMAN ROAD
ISIS REACH
NORTH FISHERS WAY
MANORWAY
BELVEDERE INDUSTRIAL ESTATE
80
1
DA18
WAY
EASTERN WY
ANDERSON WAY
JENNINGTREE WY
MULBERRY WAY
ST. THOMAS RD
CRABTREE
2
THAMESMEAD SPINE RD
KENCOT CL
BUS PARK
ALDER CL
WALDRIST WAY
VERID WAY
Prim Sch
HAILEY ROAD
EASTERN IND EST
HAILEY ROAD WAY
NORTH RD
POPPY CLOSE
MANORWAY
BELVEDERE BUS. PARK
FB
BRONZE
CHURCH MANORWAY INDUSTRIAL ESTATE
CHURCH
YARNTON WAY
PARKWAY
CENTURION WY
WATER CL
SUTHERLAND RD
CALDY ROAD
CRABTREE MANORWAY IND EST
GLIMPSING GRN
NORTHN PL
PO
LEATHERBOTTLE GRN
ASPEN GRN
Gas Works
MAIDA RD
STATION ROAD N
VIKING WAY
3
Prim Sch
BELVEDERE
KEATS ROAD
CRABTREE MANORWAY
ALLOT
DYLAN
RAIL PO
STATION RD
Comm Cen
SUB
Sch
MITCHELL CL
NORWAY
TUNSTOCK WAY
LAYMARSH CL
GILBERT RD
PICARDY ST
Superstore
Clinic
MON. RD
AMBROOKE
PAROMA
LOWER ROAD
B213
PO
79
ROAD
SHORT CL
HADLEY RD
ST AUGUSTINE'S RD
Prim Sch
ELSTREE GARDENS
KINGSWOOD AV
RIPLEY ROAD
COLEMAN RD
EDWARDS RD
SHERIDAN RD
GERTRUDE RD
LYNDON RD
LOWER PK RD
THORNTON RD
BRISTOW RD
GLADESWOOD RD
METHUEN RD
POPLAR MT
BELTWOOD RD
BULLBANKS RD
MAYFIELD RD
ASHBURNHAM RD
GORDON RD
STANMORE RD
GLENDALE
BATTLE ROAD
Sch
ALLOT
LEATHER BOTTLE LANE
Leather Bottle PH
UPPER ABBEY ROAD
ABBEY CRES
STICKLAND RD
ROBIN HALT ROAD
HALT ROBIN ROAD
PARKSIDE
DA17
BELVEDERE
4
GREEN CHAIN WALK
ALLOT
HATTER CL
MOR CL
HERON HILL
DRAPER CL
CLIVE RD
RUSKIN ROAD
KENTISH RD
B250
BUNKERS HILL
UPPER PARK ROAD
REGENCY SQUARE
FRANK'S PARK
VALLEY RD
Bexley Coll
BRAE CL
COW. CL
CLIVE RD
MILTON RD
ORCHARD RD
PRO. CL
Clinic
PICARDY
FREMANTLE RD
HEATHDENE DR
VALLEY
AVENUE
TOWER RD
BRAMBLE CROFT
HILLSIDE
RAGLAN RD
HAV RD
WELLBO RD
NAP HILL
LESSNESS PARK
BERKHAMSTEAD RD
MOSSDOWN CL
CALVERT CL
ELMBOURNE DR
FOX HO RD
Fire Sta
PLAYING FIELD
Trinity Sch
PEMBROKE
SANDCLIFF
NELSON RD
Eardley Arms PH
WALD CL
GLOU.
ESSENDEN RD
EARDLEY ROAD
ROAD
ERITH
ROAD
ROAD
UPPER HOLLY HILL RD
HOLMHURST RD
PO
ALFORD RD
CHURCH RD
CRUSOE RD
FRIDAY RD
THE VIEW
TREETOPS CL
COURT AV
A206
WOOLW. RD
ALBERT RD
REC GRD
Lib
Pol
Prim Sch
VANESSA CL
RUTLAND GATE
HOLLY HILL ROAD
ROBERTS RD
Bexley Coll
ATHOL RD
LUCAS RD
DE
FRASER ROAD
5
HAWTHORN PL
ALBERT ROAD ESTATE
HAROLD AVENUE
CROFT
BON. CL
TYESHURST CL
VICTORIA STREET
FLORA ST
ALFRED RD
BEDWELL ROAD
HODD. RD
CHESHUNT RD
STANDARD RD
SALMON RD
BROOK
LESSNESS HEATH
Atlas Trade Park
Clubhou
Tenn Cts
BELVEDERE SPORTS GRD
FAIRM.
ALBANY RD
LULLI CL
STAPLEY RD
CHAPMAN RD
RIVERDALE
WALK
MILFO RD CL
OSBORNE
BOEVEY PATH
BARNFIELD ROAD
Fox PH
WADE CL
LUMLEY CL
ALLOT
ERITH CEMETERY
78
DA8
GROSVENOR ROAD
WYN PL
STREET
SILVER SPRING CL
THORNE CL
BIRCH
UPPER GRO RD
GROVE RD
NUXLEY RD
CHAR CL
BROOK STREET CEMETERY
ORCHARD AV
DRYHILL RD
STREAMWAY
WALS. WK
BELLRING CL
THWAITE CL
KEMPTON CL
6
ELMHURST
MATFIELD RD
CRAY ROAD
SWANLANDS RD
CARLTON ROAD
HIGHFIELD AV
MEYER RD
WARD CL
LESNEY PARK
BEDONWELL ROAD
REDLEAF CL
ROSLEY RD
MANORWAY
LOCHMERE CL
COLLINDALE AV
CAMR. AV
CAVENDISH AV
OAKDENE AV
VICAR CL
MONASTERY
ERI & DIST HO
Prim Schs
EDWIN CL
IRIS CRESCENT
PARSONAGE
NORTHUMBERLAND HEATH
PARK
Prim Sch
LING RD
BEDONWELL ROAD
LENHAM ROAD
BRABOURNE CRES
STEELE WALK
REC GRD
THE DRIVE
BRANTWOOD AV
PEMBURY ROAD
KNOWLE AV
STAPLETON
CHIDD. AV
LYDD RD
SHINGLEWELL ROAD
LUDDESDON ROAD
EASTRY ROAD
PLAXTOL ROAD
SWANTON ROAD
Pav
PENDA RD
HENGIST RD
EMES ROAD
CRESCENT
BUXTON ELM RD
ASHBOURNE
WHITFIELD ROAD
AVENUE
DA7
CHESSINGTON
IGHTHAM ROAD
SUSSEX ROAD
SUSS PL
HORSA ROAD
AVENUE ROAD
Lib
LIMEWOOD RD
7
Sec Sch
RAMSDEN RD
HYTHE AVENUE
RAVIL GDNS
HURLINGHAM
NURSTEAD ROAD
LAWRENCE RD
COOKSON GRO
Prim Sch
NORTHUMBERLAND PK
ST PAUL'S RD
PO
BEXLEY
HURST RD
THE PANTILES
DRIVE
WINCHELSEA AV
PO
BELMONT
Prim Sch
LANGDALE CL
DICKENS CL
BYRON DR
WHEELOCK CL
TYLER CL
MILL ROAD
STONECROFT RD
NORTHUMBER HEATH
Earl Haig PH
AUSTEN RD
WILDE RD
BRONTE CL
ROAD
BROOK ST
OAKHURST
HEATH
ROMNEY GDNS
ROAD
CARTMEL
CRESCENT
159
BELMONT
The Pheasant PH
BECTON PL
YORK TER
NORTH
COLYERS
LITTLE
NORFOLK
HOLLINGBOURNE AVENUE
PENSHURST RD
CRAN
49
50
EAST HOLME
WEST HOLME
HEATH WAY
KIPLING
LONG
DUNWICH
DRIVE
BIRCHINGTON
ALBERT

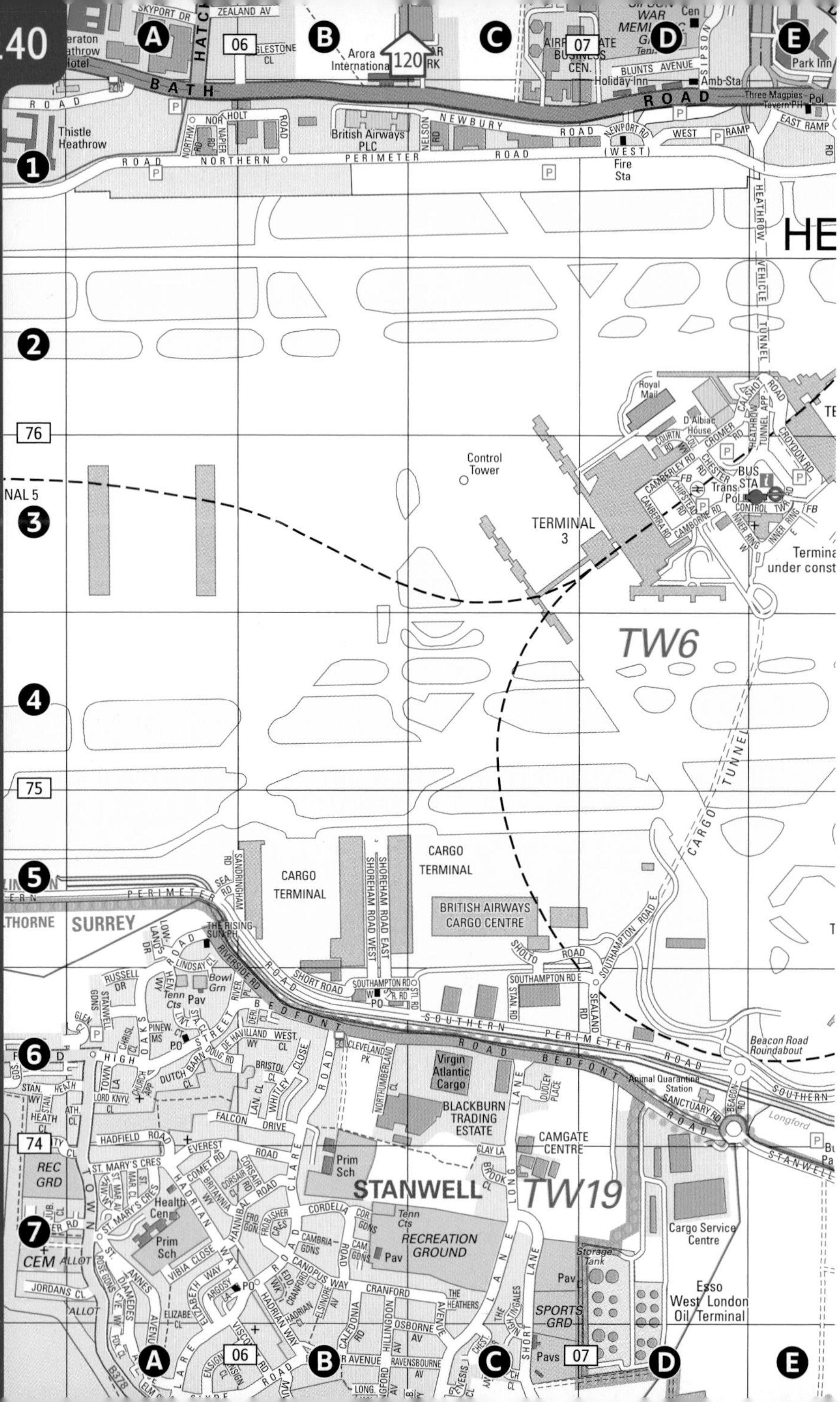
A
B
C
D
E
1
2
3
4
5
6
7
06
07
76
75
74
120
BATH ROAD
NORTHERN PERIMETER ROAD
ZEALAND AV
SKYPORT DR
Arora International
Thistle Heathrow
British Airways PLC
NEWBURY ROAD
WEST RAMP
EAST RAMP
Holiday Inn
Amb Sta
Three Magpies Tavern PH
Pol
Park Inn
BLUNTS AVENUE
Fire Sta
HEATHROW VEHICLE TUNNEL
HE
Royal Mail
D'Albiac House
Control Tower
TERMINAL 3
BUS STA
Trans. Pol
Terminal under const
TW6
CARGO TUNNEL
CARGO TERMINAL
CARGO TERMINAL
BRITISH AIRWAYS CARGO CENTRE
SHOREHAM ROAD EAST
SHOREHAM ROAD WEST
SANDRINGHAM RD
SOUTHAMPTON ROAD E
SOUTHERN PERIMETER ROAD
BEDFONT ROAD
SURREY
THE RISING SUN PH
Beacon Road Roundabout
Animal Quarantine Station
SANCTUARY RD
Longford
STANWELL
TW19
Virgin Atlantic Cargo
BLACKBURN TRADING ESTATE
CAMGATE CENTRE
FALCON DRIVE
HADFIELD ROAD
EVEREST ROAD
Health Cen
Prim Sch
REC GRD
CEM
RECREATION GROUND
Tenn Cts
Pav
SPORTS GRD
Storage Tank
Cargo Service Centre
Esso West London Oil Terminal
CRANFORD AVENUE
OSBORNE AV
HILLINGDON AV
CALEDONIA RD
RAVENSBOURNE AV
CANOPUS WAY
HADRIAN WAY
ELIZABETH WAY
VIBIA CLOSE
ST. MARY'S CRES
JORDANS CL
LONG LANE
SHORT LANE
THE HEATHERS
ALLOT
B378

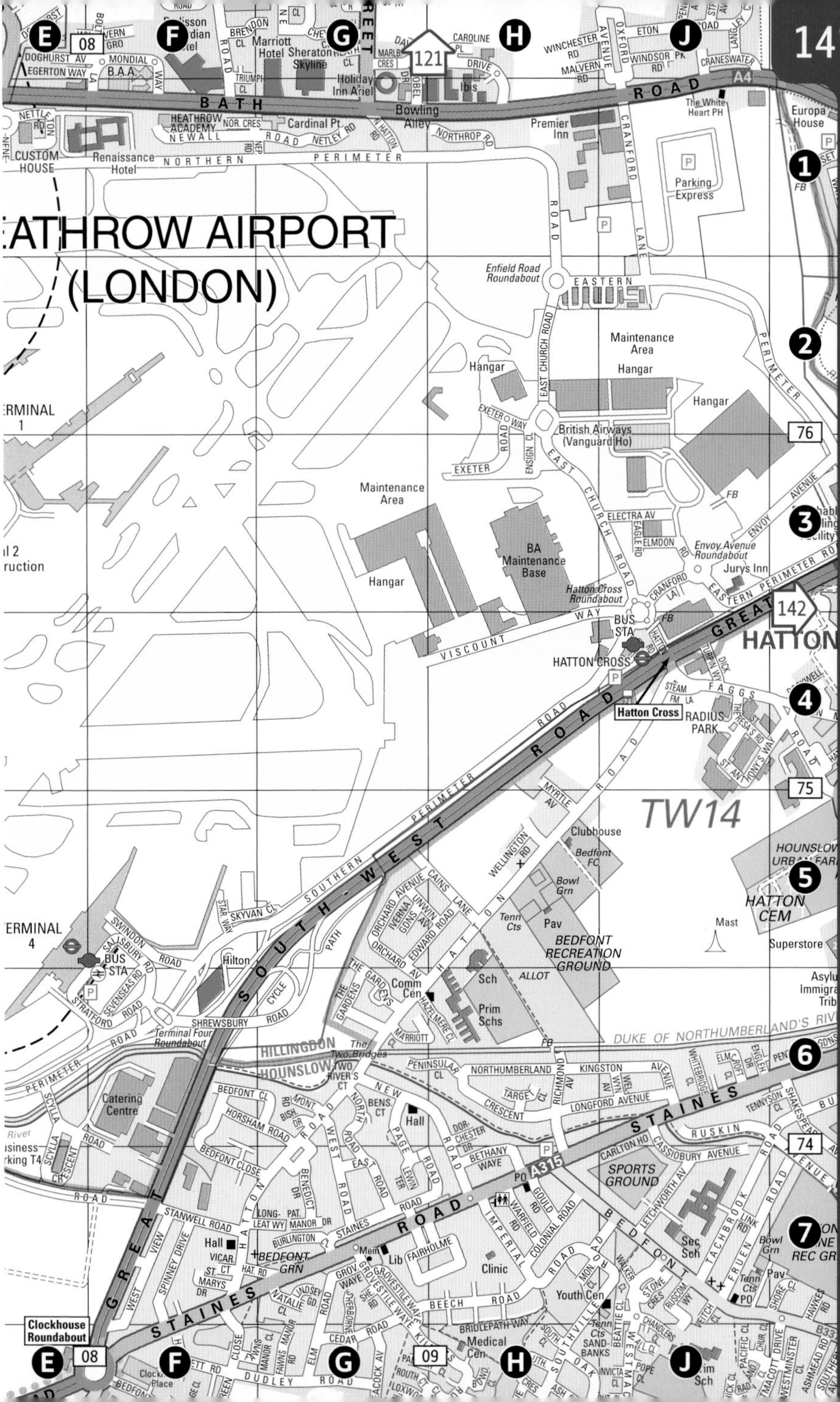
E
F
G
H
J
08
121
Marriott Hotel
Sheraton Skyline
Holiday Inn Ariel
Ibis
B.A.A.
DOGHURST AV
EGERTON WAY
MONDIAL WAY
BRENDON CL
TRIUMPH CL
CAROLINE PL
DRIVE
WINCHESTER RD
MALVERN RD
OXFORD AVENUE
ETON
WINDSOR PK
CRANESWATER
A4
BATH ROAD
Bowling Alley
The White Heart PH
Europa House
HEATHROW ACADEMY
NOR. CRES
Cardinal Pt.
NEWALL ROAD
NETLEY RD
NORTHROP RD
HATTON RD
NEP RD
Premier Inn
CUSTOM HOUSE
Renaissance Hotel
NORTHERN PERIMETER
CRANFORD LANE
ROAD
Parking Express
1
FB
HEATHROW AIRPORT (LONDON)
Enfield Road Roundabout
EASTERN
EAST CHURCH ROAD
Maintenance Area
Hangar
2
PERIMETER
TERMINAL 1
EXETER WAY
EXETER ROAD
ENSIGN CL
British Airways (Vanguard Ho)
76
Maintenance Area
ELECTRA AV
EAGLE RD
ELMDON
ENVOY AVENUE
3
Envoy Avenue Roundabout
Jurys Inn
Hangar
BA Maintenance Base
Hatton Cross Roundabout
CRANFORD LA
EASTERN PERIMETER ROAD
142
HATTON
VISCOUNT WAY
BUS STA
HATTON CROSS
Hatton Cross
GREAT SOUTH-WEST ROAD
DICK TURPIN WAY
STEAM FM LA
FAGGS ROAD
4
RADIUS PARK
ST. ANTONY'S WAY
75
MYRTLE AV
TW14
Clubhouse
Bedfont FC
HOUNSLOW URBAN FARM
5
WELLINGTON RD
Bowl Grn
Tenn Cts
Pav
BEDFONT RECREATION GROUND
HATTON CEM
Mast
Superstore
ALLOT
SOUTHERN PERIMETER
TERMINAL 4
SKYVAN CL
STAR WAY
SWINDON ROAD
SALISBURY RD
SEVENSEAS RD
STRATFORD ROAD
BUS STA
Hilton
CYCLE PATH
ORCHARD AVENUE
IVERNA GDNS
UNWIN AV
EDWARD ROAD
CAINS LANE
THE GARDENS
Comm Cen
HAZELMERE CL
Sch
Prim Schs
MARRIOTT
SHREWSBURY ROAD
Terminal Four Roundabout
PERIMETER ROAD
HILLINGDON
HOUNSLOW
The Two Bridges
TWO RIVER'S CT
PENINSULAR CL
DUKE OF NORTHUMBERLAND'S RIVER
FB
NORTHUMBERLAND AVENUE
KINGSTON AV
RICHMOND AV
TARGET CL
CRESCENT
LONGFORD AVENUE
WHITEBRIDGE CL
ELMCROFT CL
ENGLISH DR
6
SCYLLA ROAD
SCYLLA CRESCENT
Catering Centre
BEDFONT CL
MONT RD
BISH. RD
NEW ROAD
NORTH ROAD
BENS. CT
Hall
HORSHAM ROAD
BEDFONT CLOSE
WEST ROAD
EAST ROAD
PAGE ROAD
LENIN TER
DORCHESTER RD
BETHANY WAYE
A315
STAINES ROAD
TENNYSON
SHAKESPEARE
RUSKIN
CARLTON HO
CASSIOBURY AVENUE
SPORTS GROUND
74
LETCHWORTH AV
Sec Sch
TACHBROOK
LINK RD
FRUEN RD
7
Bowl Grn
Tenn Cts
Pav
PO
GOULD RD
WARFIELD RD
IMPERIAL
COLONIAL ROAD
HATTON ROAD
BENEDICT DR
LONG-LEAT WY
PAT. MANOR DR
BURLINGTON
FAIRHOLME
Lib
BEDFONT GRN
Hall
VICAR. CT
ST. MARYS DR
Clinic
Clockhouse Roundabout
GREAT
WEST
VIEW
SPINNEY DRIVE
STANWELL ROAD
NATALIE CL
LINDSEY GD.
GROVE WAYE
GROVESTILE WAYE
SHERBORNE
BEECH ROAD
BRIDLEPATH WAY
Medical Cen
Youth Cen
SOUTHVILLE CL
BEATTIE CL
WESTMACOTT
Tenn Cts
SAND-BANKS
MON. CL
WALKER CL
STONE CRES
RUSCOM. WY
CHANDLERS
VEITCH CL
PACIFIC CL
CHUR. CL
WESTMINSTER
MACOTT DRIVE
SHORE CL
HAWKES RD
ASHMEAD RD
B3
09
CEDAR ROAD
DUDLEY ROAD
ELM
FAWNS MANOR CL
CLOSE
Clockhouse Place
BEDFONT
INVICTA CL
POPE CL
Prim Sch
ROAD

A
B
C
D
E
1
2
3
4
5
6
7
122
141
160
12
76
75
74
TW5
TW4
TW14
HATTON
HOUNSLOW WEST
Waggoners Roundabout
Henlys Roundabout
BATH ROAD
GREAT SOUTH-WEST ROAD
A30
A4
A312
A315
A244
THE PARKWAY
THE CAUSEWAY
PERIMETER ROAD
STAINES ROAD
FAGGS ROAD
HARLINGTON ROAD WEST
HARLINGTON ROAD
HOUNSLOW ROAD
GREEN LANE
BEAVERS LANE
BEAVERS CRESCENT
BARRACK LANE
SALISBURY ROAD
CHINCHILLA DRIVE
ROSEMARY AVENUE
CLIFFORD ROAD
BASILDENE ROAD
BROWNING WAY
SHELLEY CRES
SPRINGWELL ROAD
BROAD WALK
ASH GROVE
NORMAN CRESCENT
SUMMERHOUSE
VICTORIA GDNS
CLAIRVALE ROAD
BERKELEY AVENUE
WAYE AVENUE
BYRON AVENUE
CHAUCER AVENUE
MORNINGTON CRESCENT
HIGH STREET
Europa House
Heathrow Ho
Ramada
Travelodge
Hall
Lib
Med Cen
PO
Comm Cen & Lib
Prim Schs
HASLEMERE HEATHROW ESTATE
British Airways PLC
HEATHROW CAUSEWAY CEN
HEATHROW INT TRADING ESTATE
REC GRD
RIFLE RANGE
GREEN LANE OPEN SPACE
Clubho
Perishable Handling Facility
Jurys Inn
ALLOT
ALLOTMENTS
BALANCING RESERVOIR
DONKEY WOOD
Civic Amenity Site
HOUNSLOW URBAN FARM
HATTON CEM
Amb Sta
Fire Sta
Superstore
24hr
Mast
MERCURY CENTRE
NORTH FELTHAM TRADING EST
FALCON EST
MARLIN PARK
GRIFFIN CENTRE
Asylum & Immigration Tribunal
Fagg's Bri
HOUNSLOW HEATH GOLF COURSE
Baber Bridge
BABER BRIDGE CARAVAN SITE
Clubhouse
Garden Centre
CENTRAL PARK EST
Cavalry Barracks
BEAVERSFORD PARK
Tenn Cts
Bowl Grn
VISTA OFF. CEN.
Prim Sch
SPORTS GRD
FELTHAM ARENAS
BEDFONT LANE REC GRD
GLEBELANDS PLAYING FIELDS
FELTHAM PARK
FRANK TOWELL COURT
STATION PARADE
St. Giles Hotel
Sorting Office
River Crane
RIVER CRANE
NORTHUMBERLAND'S RIVER
FB
Pav
Pavs.

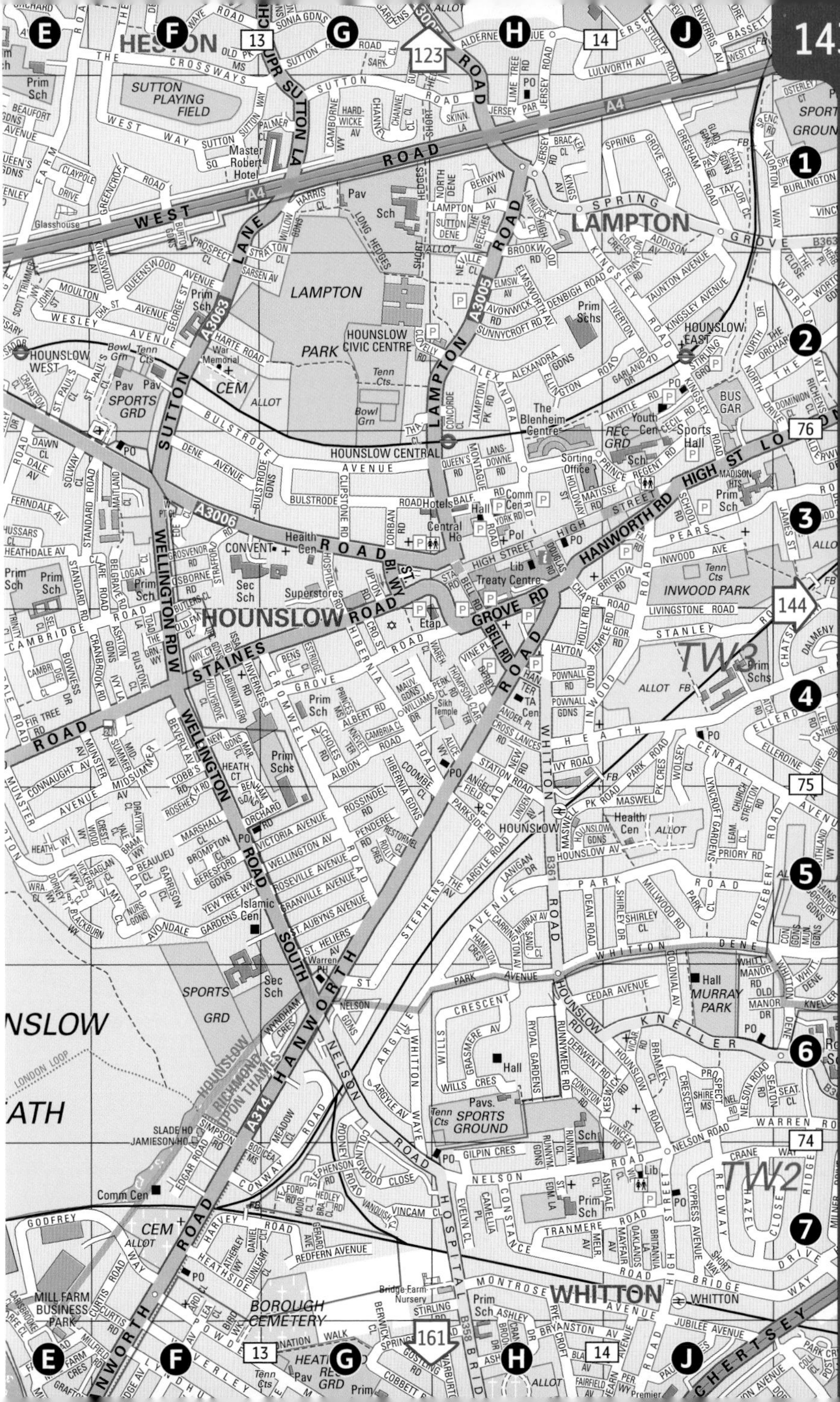

HESTON
LAMPTON
LAMPTON PARK
HOUNSLOW
HOUNSLOW ROAD
WHITTON
TW3
TW2
SUTTON PLAYING FIELD
WEST ROAD
A4
SUTTON LANE
UPR SUTTON LA
LAMPTON ROAD
A3005
A3063
A3006
HOUNSLOW WEST
HOUNSLOW EAST
HOUNSLOW CENTRAL
HOUNSLOW CIVIC CENTRE
The Blenheim Centre
Treaty Centre
HIGH STREET
HANWORTH RD
STAINES ROAD
WELLINGTON RD N
WELLINGTON ROAD SOUTH
GROVE RD
INWOOD PARK
MURRAY PARK
BOROUGH CEMETERY
MILL FARM BUSINESS PARK
SPORTS GROUND
WHITTON ROAD
HOUNSLOW RD
NELSON ROAD
HANWORTH ROAD
A314
CHERTSEY
SPRING GROVE
KNELLER RD
123
144
161
13
14
76
75
74
1
2
3
4
5
6
7
E
F
G
H
J

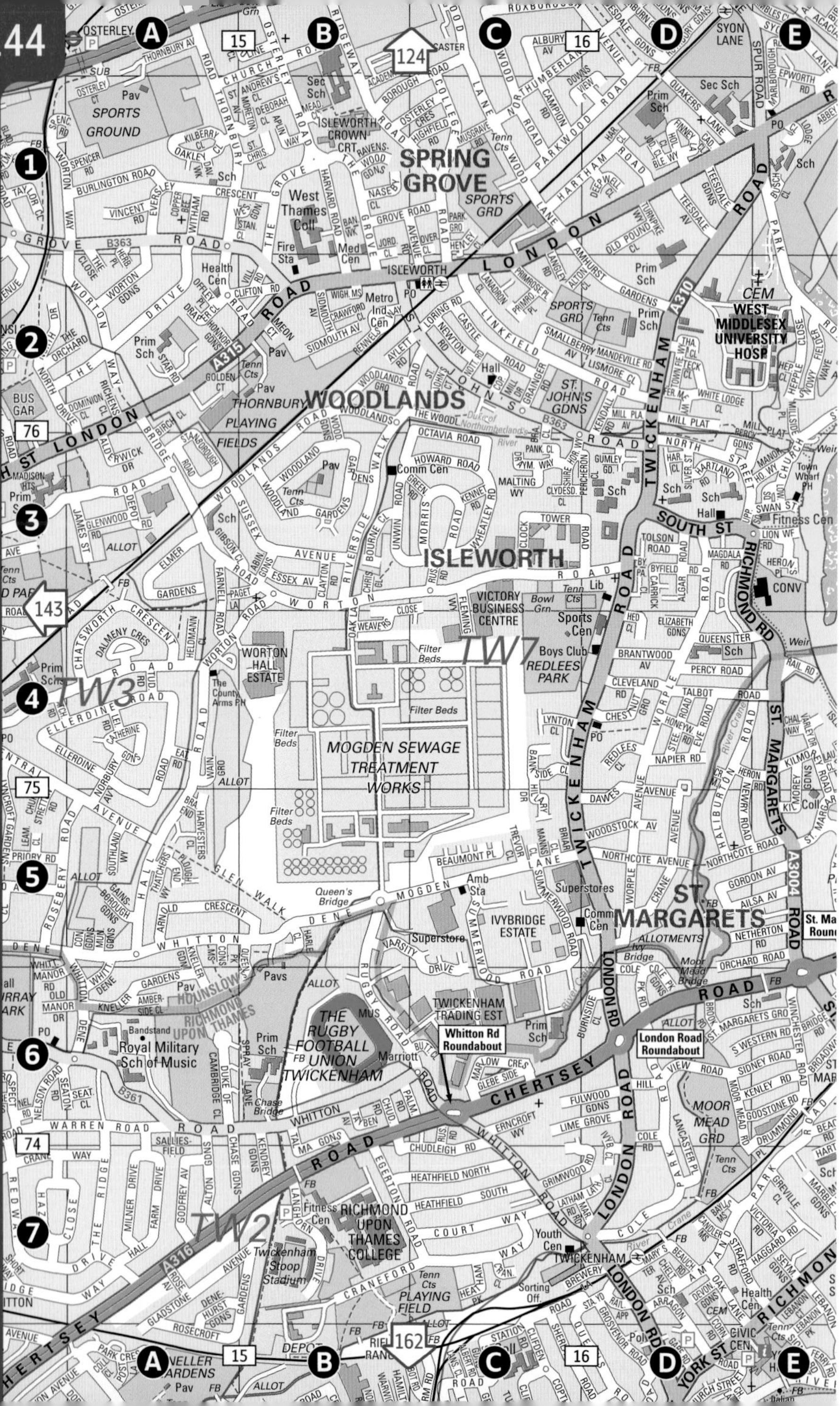
A
B
C
D
E
1
2
3
4
5
6
7
15
16
124
143
162
76
75
74
OSTERLEY
SYON LANE
SPORTS GROUND
Pav
Sec Sch
ISLEWORTH CROWN CRT
SPRING GROVE
SPORTS GRD
West Thames Coll
Fire Sta
Med Cen
Health Cen
Metro Ind Cen
ISLEWORTH
LONDON ROAD
GROVE ROAD
B363
A315
A310
Prim Sch
Sch
CEM
WEST MIDDLESEX UNIVERSITY HOSP
BUS GAR
THORNBURY PLAYING FIELDS
WOODLANDS
Duke of Northumberland's River
ST. JOHN'S GDNS
Comm Cen
Hall
Town Wharf PH
Fitness Cen
CONV
SOUTH ST
ISLEWORTH
VICTORY BUSINESS CENTRE
Bowl Grn
Lib
Sports Cen
Boys Club
REDLEES PARK
TW7
TW3
TW2
WORTON HALL ESTATE
The County Arms PH
Filter Beds
MOGDEN SEWAGE TREATMENT WORKS
ALLOT
Queen's Bridge
Amb Sta
Superstores
IVYBRIDGE ESTATE
ST. MARGARETS
ALLOTMENTS
St. Margarets Roundabout
A3004
RICHMOND RD
ST. MARGARETS ROAD
TWICKENHAM ROAD
LONDON ROAD
Superstore
TWICKENHAM TRADING EST
HOUNSLOW
RICHMOND UPON THAMES
Pavs
Bandstand
Royal Military Sch of Music
THE RUGBY FOOTBALL UNION TWICKENHAM
MUS
Marriott
Whitton Rd Roundabout
London Road Roundabout
CHERTSEY ROAD
A316
MOOR MEAD GRD
Tenn Cts
Fitness Cen
RICHMOND UPON THAMES COLLEGE
Twickenham Stoop Stadium
PLAYING FIELD
Youth Cen
TWICKENHAM
Sorting Off.
CIVIC CEN
Pol
DEPOT
KNELLER GARDENS
B361
WHITTON ROAD
WARREN ROAD
CRANEFORD WAY
HEATHFIELD NORTH
HEATHFIELD SOUTH
COURT WAY
YORK ST
RICHMOND

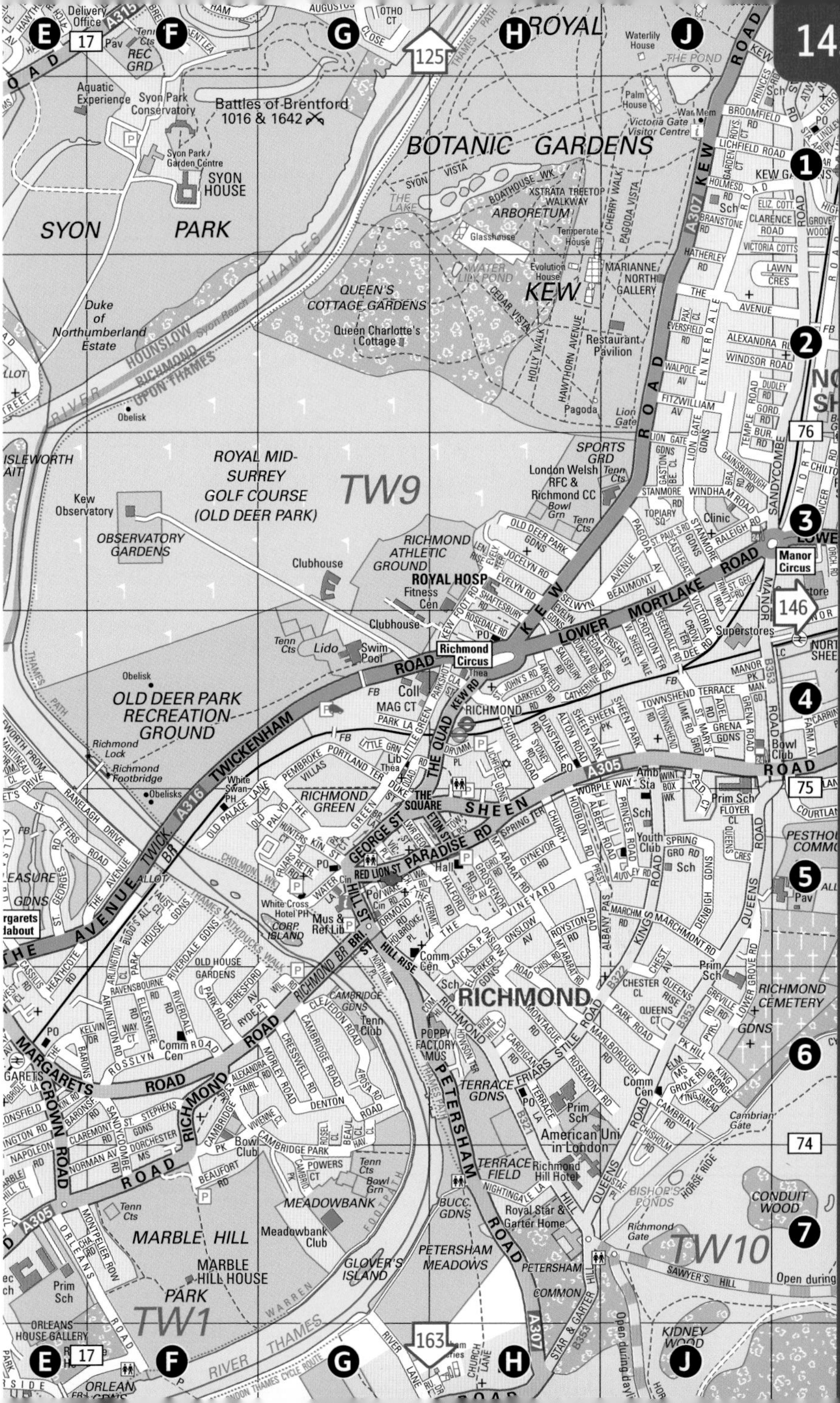
E
F
G
H
J
17
125
ROYAL
BOTANIC GARDENS
Waterlily House
THE POND
Palm House
Victoria Gate Visitor Centre
War Mem
Aquatic Experience
Syon Park Conservatory
Battles of Brentford 1016 & 1642
Syon Park Garden Centre
SYON HOUSE
SYON PARK
THE LAKE
SYON VISTA
BOATHOUSE WK
XSTRATA TREETOP WALKWAY
ARBORETUM
CHERRY WALK
PAGODA VISTA
Temperate House
Glasshouse
WATER LILY POND
Evolution House
MARIANNE NORTH GALLERY
KEW
QUEEN'S COTTAGE GARDENS
Queen Charlotte's Cottage
CEDAR VISTA
HOLLY WALK
HAWTHORN AVENUE
Restaurant Pavilion
Pagoda
Lion Gate
Duke of Northumberland Estate
RIVER THAMES
HOUNSLOW
RICHMOND UPON THAMES
Syon Reach
Obelisk
ISLEWORTH AIT
ROYAL MID-SURREY GOLF COURSE (OLD DEER PARK)
TW9
Kew Observatory
OBSERVATORY GARDENS
SPORTS GRD
London Welsh RFC & Richmond CC
RICHMOND ATHLETIC GROUND
Clubhouse
ROYAL HOSP
Fitness Cen
Lido
Swim Pool
Richmond Circus
OLD DEER PARK RECREATION GROUND
Richmond Lock
Richmond Footbridge
Obelisks
TWICKENHAM ROAD
A316
KEW ROAD
A307
LOWER MORTLAKE ROAD
Manor Circus
146
Superstores
KEW GARDENS
LICHFIELD ROAD
BROOMFIELD
NORTH SHEEN
76
3
1
2
4
5
6
7
75
74
RICHMOND
THE QUAD
PARADISE RD
SHEEN ROAD
A305
THE SQUARE
GEORGE ST
RED LION ST
HILL ST
RICHMOND GREEN
OLD PALACE LANE
White Swan PH
White Cross Hotel PH
Mus & Ref Lib
CORP. ISLAND
RICHMOND BR
HILL RISE
THE VINEYARD
ST. MARGARETS ROAD
CROWN ROAD
RICHMOND ROAD
THE AVENUE
PETERSHAM ROAD
POPPY FACTORY MUS
TERRACE GDNS
TERRACE FIELD
Richmond Hill Hotel
American Uni in London
Royal Star & Garter Home
PETERSHAM MEADOWS
PETERSHAM COMMON
GLOVER'S ISLAND
MEADOWBANK
Meadowbank Club
MARBLE HILL PARK
MARBLE HILL HOUSE
TW1
ORLEANS HOUSE GALLERY
163
RIVER LANE
CHURCH LANE
STAR & GARTER HILL
QUEENS ROAD
FRIARS STILE ROAD
BISHOP'S PONDS
Richmond Gate
TW10
SAWYER'S HILL
Open during
KIDNEY WOOD
CONDUIT WOOD
Cambrian Gate
HORSE RIDE
RICHMOND CEMETERY
PESTHOUSE COMMON
Manor Circus
Bowl Club
Prim Sch
Comm Cen

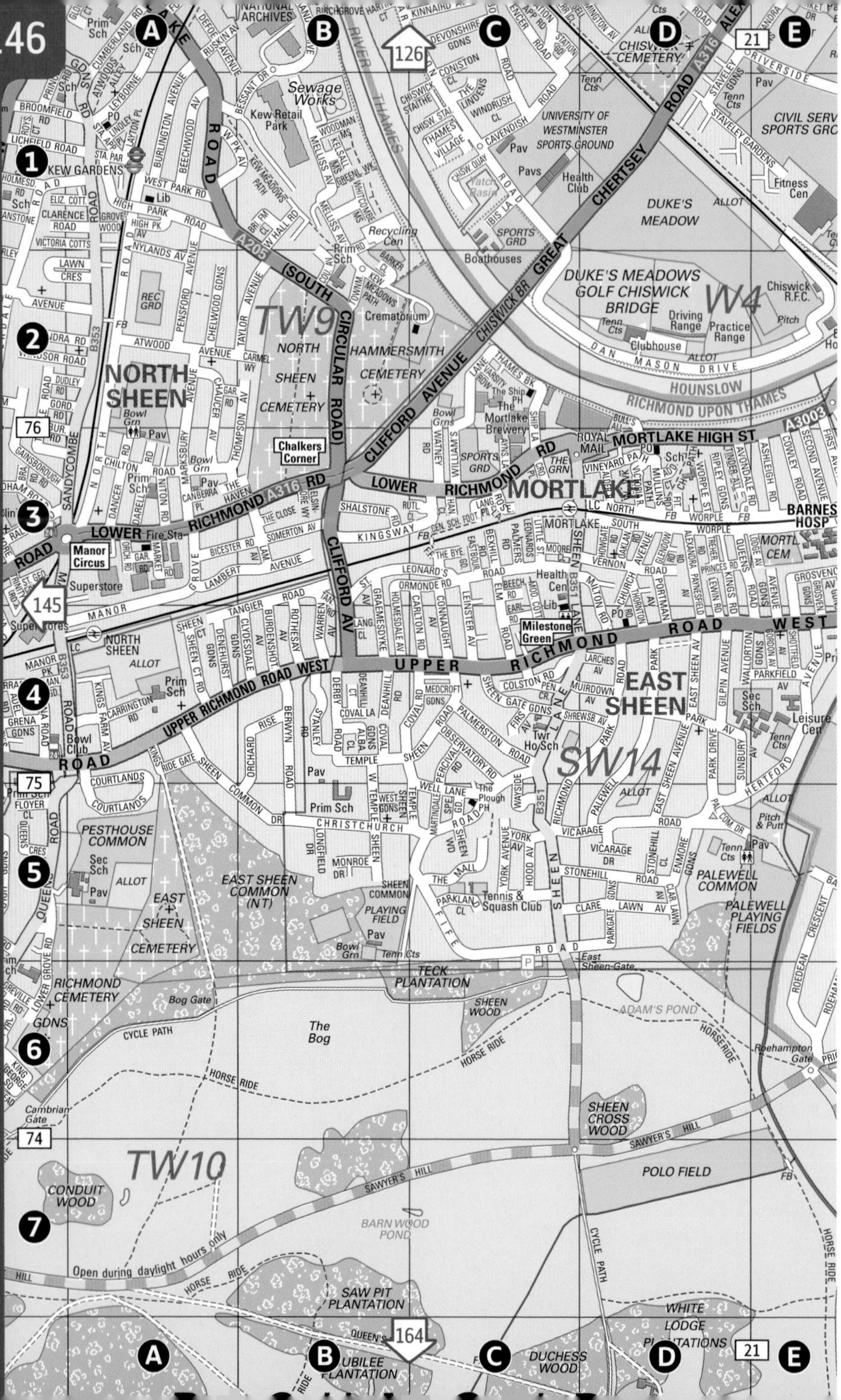
A
B
C
D
E
1
2
3
4
5
6
7
126
145
164
76
75
74
21
NATIONAL ARCHIVES
Sewage Works
Kew Retail Park
KEW GARDENS
NORTH SHEEN
TW9
NORTH SHEEN CEMETERY
HAMMERSMITH CEMETERY
Crematorium
Chalkers Corner
Manor Circus
Superstore
Superstores
RIVER THAMES
CHISWICK CEMETERY
UNIVERSITY OF WESTMINSTER SPORTS GROUND
DUKE'S MEADOW
DUKE'S MEADOWS GOLF CHISWICK BRIDGE
W4
Chiswick R.F.C.
CIVIL SERV SPORTS GRO
Driving Range
Practice Range
Clubhouse
DAN MASON DRIVE
HOUNSLOW
RICHMOND UPON THAMES
Boathouses
The Ship PH
The Mortlake Brewery
MORTLAKE
MORTLAKE HIGH ST
MORTLAKE
BARNES HOSP
MORTL CEM
SOUTH CIRCULAR ROAD
CLIFFORD AVENUE
CLIFFORD AV
GREAT CHERTSEY ROAD
CHISWICK BR
LOWER RICHMOND RD
LOWER RICHMOND ROAD
UPPER RICHMOND ROAD WEST
UPPER RICHMOND ROAD
UPPER RICHMOND ROAD WEST
KINGSWAY
SHEEN LANE
Milestone Green
Health Cen
EAST SHEEN
SW14
Leisure Cen
PESTHOUSE COMMON
EAST SHEEN COMMON (NT)
EAST SHEEN CEMETERY
RICHMOND CEMETERY
PALEWELL COMMON
PALEWELL PLAYING FIELDS
Tennis & Squash Club
The Plough PH
TECK PLANTATION
SHEEN WOOD
East Sheen Gate
ADAM'S POND
Bog Gate
The Bog
CYCLE PATH
HORSE RIDE
Roehampton Gate
SHEEN CROSS WOOD
SAWYER'S HILL
POLO FIELD
TW10
CONDUIT WOOD
Cambrian Gate
BARN WOOD POND
Open during daylight hours only
SAW PIT PLANTATION
JUBILEE PLANTATION
DUCHESS WOOD
WHITE LODGE PLANTATIONS
QUEEN'S

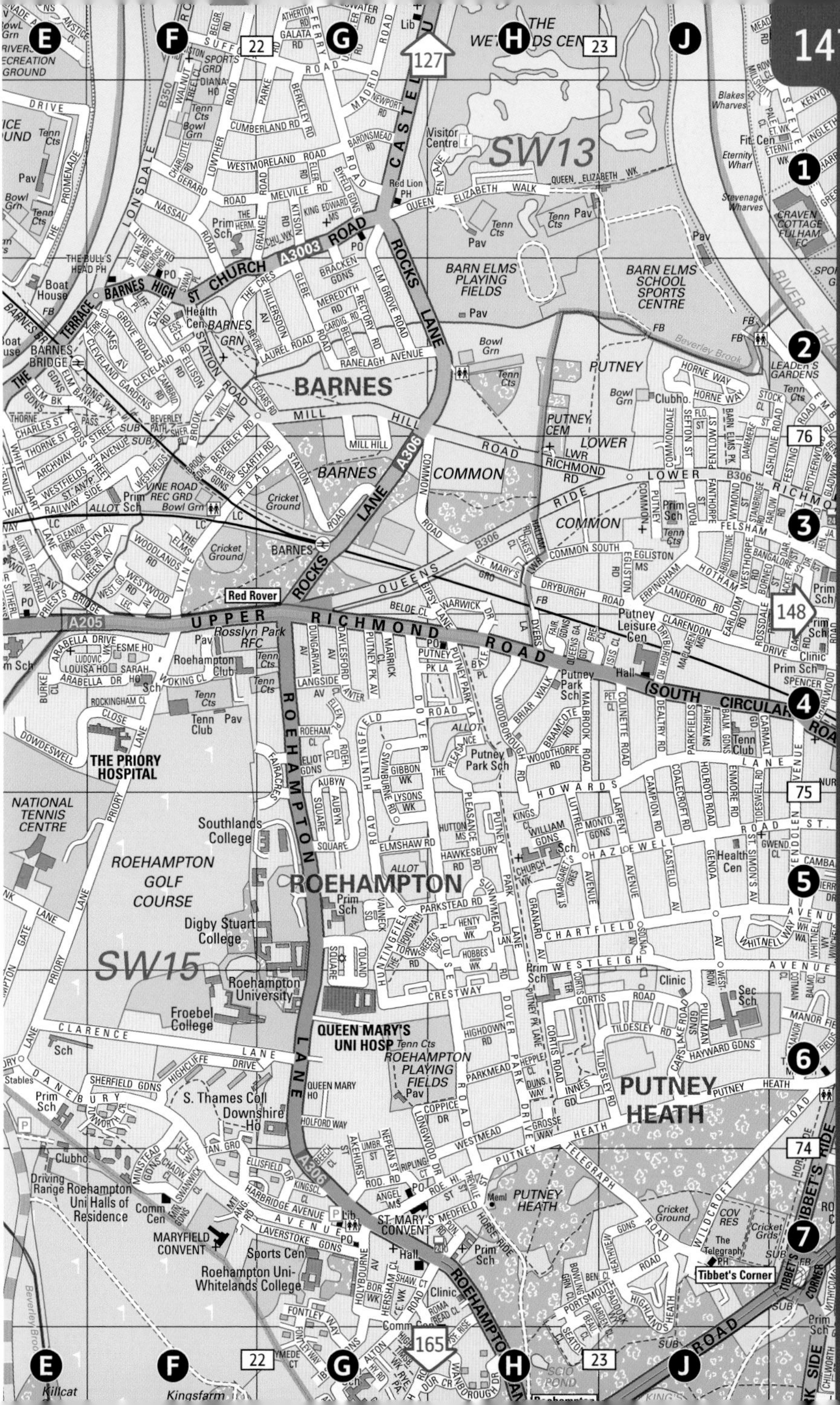
SW13
BARNES
BARNES COMMON
BARN ELMS PLAYING FIELDS
BARN ELMS SCHOOL SPORTS CENTRE
PUTNEY
LOWER RICHMOND RD
UPPER RICHMOND ROAD
(SOUTH CIRCULAR ROAD)
ROEHAMPTON
ROEHAMPTON LANE
ROEHAMPTON GOLF COURSE
NATIONAL TENNIS CENTRE
THE PRIORY HOSPITAL
SW15
QUEEN MARY'S UNI HOSP
ROEHAMPTON PLAYING FIELDS
PUTNEY HEATH
Tibbet's Corner
CRAVEN COTTAGE FULHAM FC
CASTELNAU
ROCKS LANE
CHURCH ROAD
BARNES HIGH ST
QUEEN ELIZABETH WALK
Red Rover
Southlands College
Digby Stuart College
Roehampton University
Froebel College
Roehampton Uni Halls of Residence
Roehampton Uni-Whitelands College
MARYFIELD CONVENT
ST MARY'S CONVENT
127
148
165
22
23
76
75
74
E
F
G
H
J
1
2
3
4
5
6
7

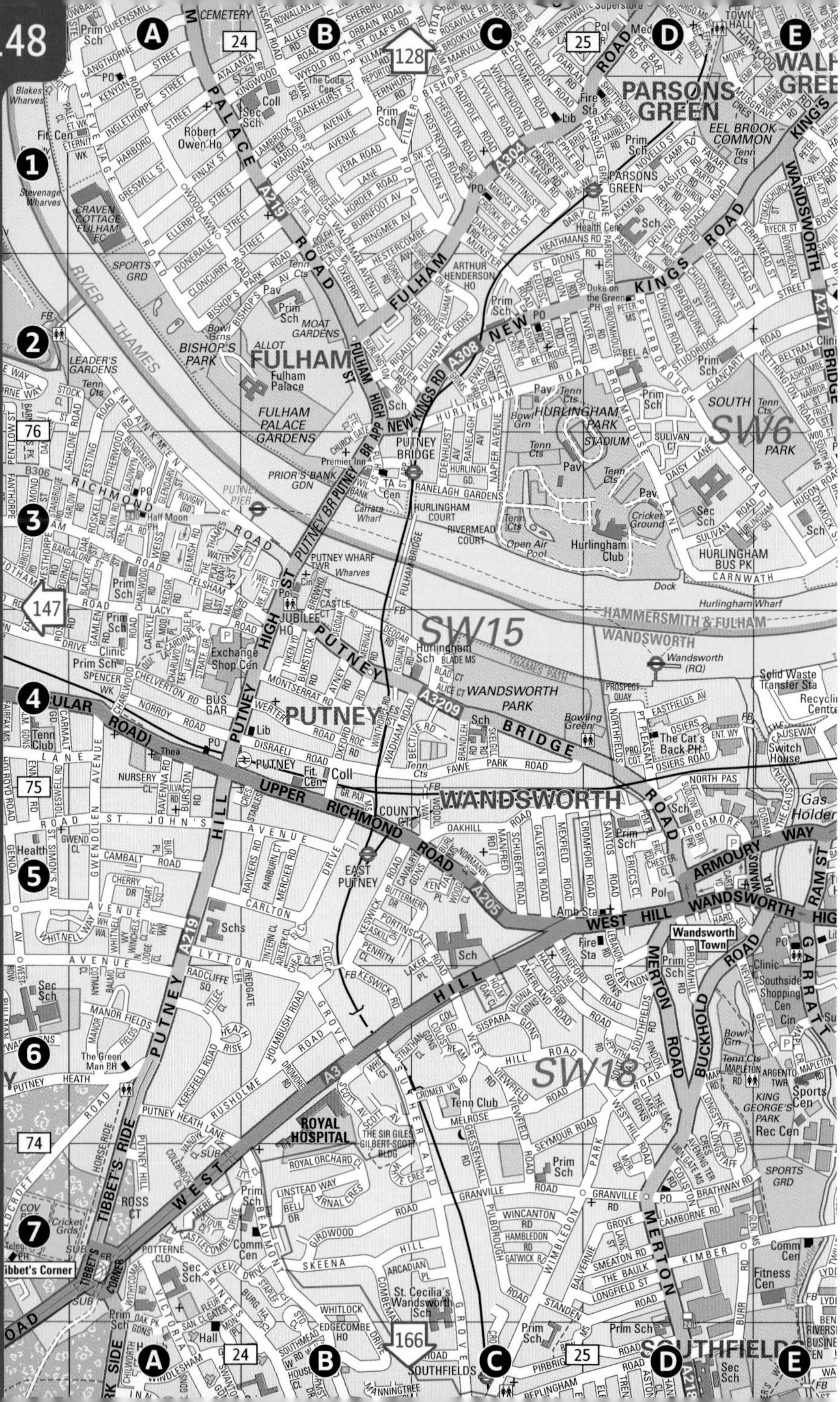

A
B
C
D
E
1
2
3
4
5
6
7
24
25
128
147
166
76
75
74
CEMETERY
PARSONS GREEN
EEL BROOK COMMON
WALHAM GREEN
PALACE ROAD
A219
FULHAM ROAD
A304
NEW KINGS ROAD
A308
KINGS ROAD
WANDSWORTH BRIDGE ROAD
A217
CRAVEN COTTAGE FULHAM FC
RIVER THAMES
BISHOP'S PARK
FULHAM
Fulham Palace
FULHAM PALACE GARDENS
MOAT GARDENS
LEADER'S GARDENS
Blakes Wharves
Stevenage Wharves
Robert Owen Ho
PUTNEY BRIDGE
HURLINGHAM PARK
STADIUM
Hurlingham Club
Open Air Pool
Cricket Ground
SOUTH PARK
SW6
HURLINGHAM BUS PK
CARNWATH
Hurlingham Wharf
HAMMERSMITH & FULHAM
WANDSWORTH
SW15
Wandsworth (RQ)
THAMES PATH
WANDSWORTH PARK
A3209
PUTNEY BRIDGE ROAD
PUTNEY HIGH ST
PUTNEY
PUTNEY WHARF TWR
Wharves
PRIOR'S BANK GDN
PUTNEY PIER
RICHMOND ROAD
LOWER RICHMOND ROAD
B306
Half Moon
Exchange Shop Cen
UPPER RICHMOND ROAD
A205
EAST PUTNEY
WANDSWORTH
WEST HILL
A3
SW18
ARMOURY WAY
Wandsworth Town
Southside Shopping Cen
KING GEORGE'S PARK
Rec Cen
SPORTS GRD
MERTON ROAD
BUCKHOLD ROAD
GARRATT LANE
ROYAL HOSPITAL
THE SIR GILES GILBERT SCOTT BLDG
PUTNEY HILL
PUTNEY HEATH
The Green Man PH
TIBBET'S RIDE
Tibbet's Corner
St. Cecilia's Wandsworth Sch
SOUTHFIELDS
Solid Waste Transfer Sta
Switch House
Gas Holder
The Cat's Back PH

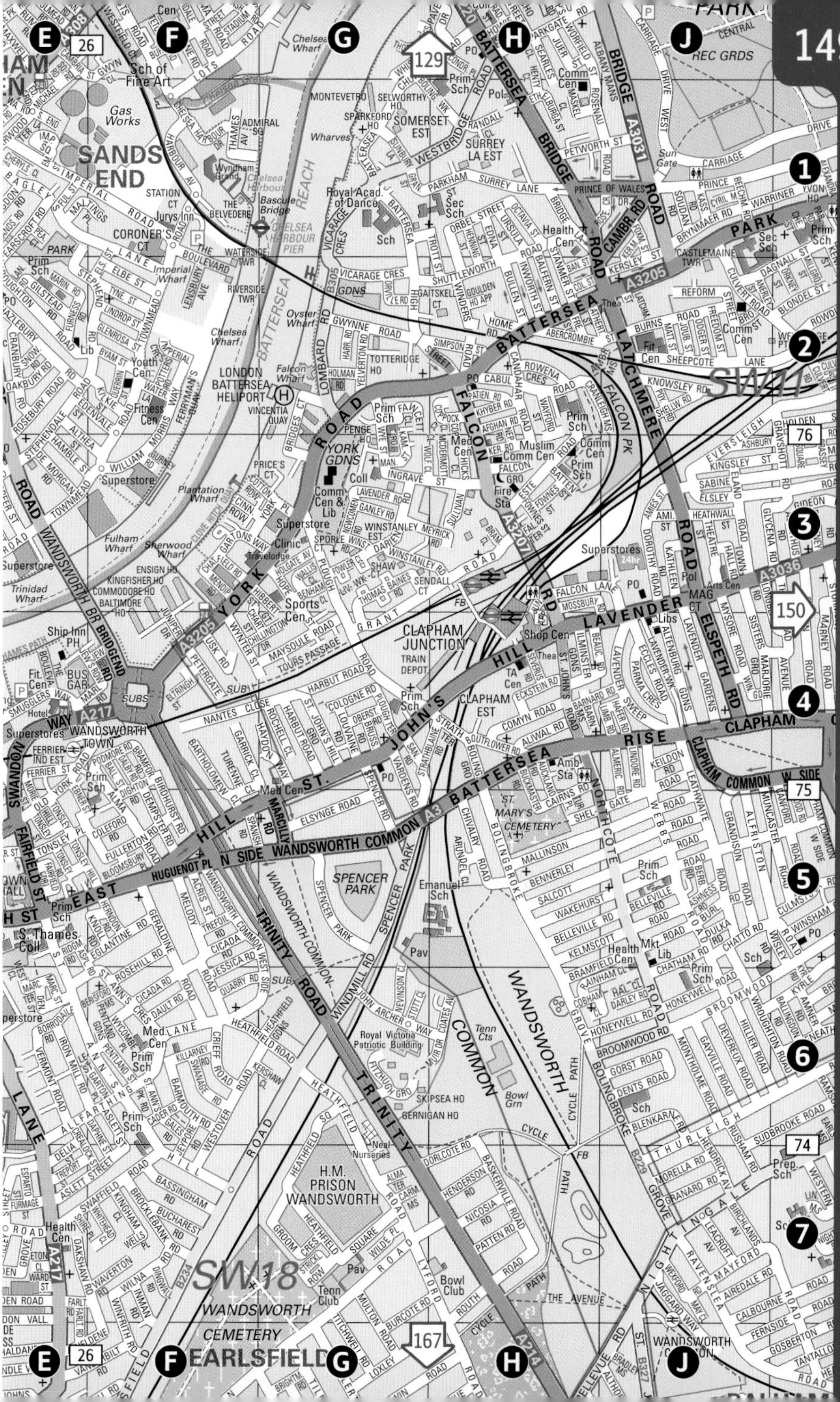

E
F
G
H
J
26
129
167
150
76
75
74
1
2
3
4
5
6
7
SANDS END
Gas Works
Sch of Fine Art
Chelsea Creek
Chelsea Wharf
MONTEVETRO
SELWORTHY HO
SOMERSET EST
SURREY LA EST
Wharves
Chelsea Harbour
Bascule Bridge
CHELSEA HARBOUR PIER
Royal Acad. of Dance
BATTERSEA REACH
BATTERSEA BRIDGE
BATTERSEA BRIDGE ROAD
BATTERSEA PARK ROAD
PRINCE OF WALES DRIVE
CARRIAGE DRIVE
REC GRDS
SW11
SW18
IMPERIAL ROAD
Imperial Wharf
CORONER'S CT
Jurys Inn
THE BELVEDERE
Chelsea Wharf
Oyster Wharf
Falcon Wharf
LONDON BATTERSEA HELIPORT
VINCENTIA QUAY
YORK GDNS
YORK ROAD
Plantation Wharf
Fulham Wharf
Sherwood Wharf
Trinidad Wharf
KINGFISHER HO
COMMODORE HO
BALTIMORE HO
ENSIGN HO
Superstore
Travelodge
Sports Cen
CLAPHAM JUNCTION
TRAIN DEPOT
LAVENDER HILL
FALCON ROAD
LATCHMERE ROAD
ELSPETH RD
ST. JOHN'S HILL
CLAPHAM EST
CLAPHAM COMMON W SIDE
CLAPHAM RISE
Superstores
Shop Cen
WANDSWORTH TOWN
WANDSWORTH BR RD
BRIDGEND RD
SWANDON WAY
FAIRFIELD ST
EAST HILL
HUGUENOT PL
WANDSWORTH COMMON N SIDE
WANDSWORTH COMMON WEST SIDE
SPENCER PARK
ST. MARY'S CEMETERY
Emanuel Sch
Royal Victoria Patriotic Building
WANDSWORTH COMMON
TRINITY ROAD
H.M. PRISON WANDSWORTH
WANDSWORTH CEMETERY
S. Thames Coll
BOLINGBROKE GROVE
NORTHCOTE ROAD
NIGHTINGALE LANE
WANDSWORTH COMMON
EARLSFIELD
THE AVENUE
CYCLE PATH
Bowl Club
Tenn Club

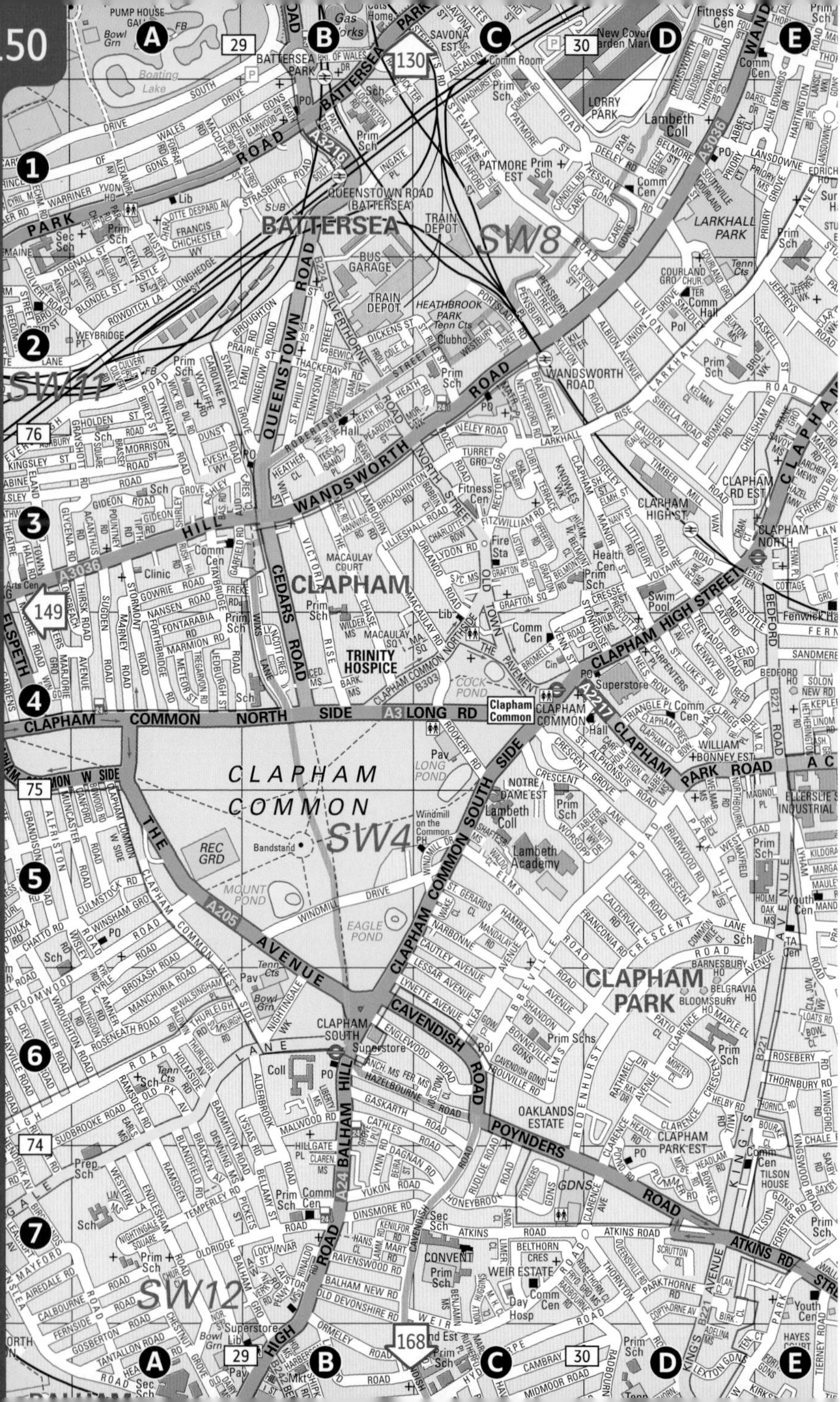
BATTERSEA
SW8
SW11
CLAPHAM
SW4
CLAPHAM COMMON
CLAPHAM PARK
SW12
QUEENSTOWN ROAD
WANDSWORTH ROAD
CEDARS ROAD
CLAPHAM COMMON NORTH SIDE
CLAPHAM HIGH STREET
CLAPHAM PARK ROAD
CLAPHAM COMMON SOUTH SIDE
THE AVENUE
CAVENDISH ROAD
POYNDERS ROAD
BALHAM HIGH ROAD
LARKHALL PARK
LAMBETH COLL
PATMORE EST
NEW COVENT GARDEN MARKET
LORRY PARK
TRINITY HOSPICE
LAMBETH ACADEMY
NOTRE DAME EST
OAKLANDS ESTATE
CLAPHAM PARK EST
WEIR ESTATE
ELLERSLIE INDUSTRIAL
QUEENSTOWN ROAD (BATTERSEA)
WANDSWORTH ROAD
CLAPHAM HIGH ST
CLAPHAM NORTH
CLAPHAM COMMON
CLAPHAM SOUTH
BATTERSEA PARK
Boating Lake
Bandstand
MOUNT POND
EAGLE POND
LONG POND
COCK POND
REC GRD
A3036
A3216
A3
A205
A24
A2217
B221
B224
B303
29
30
130
149
168
76
75
74
A
B
C
D
E
1
2
3
4
5
6
7

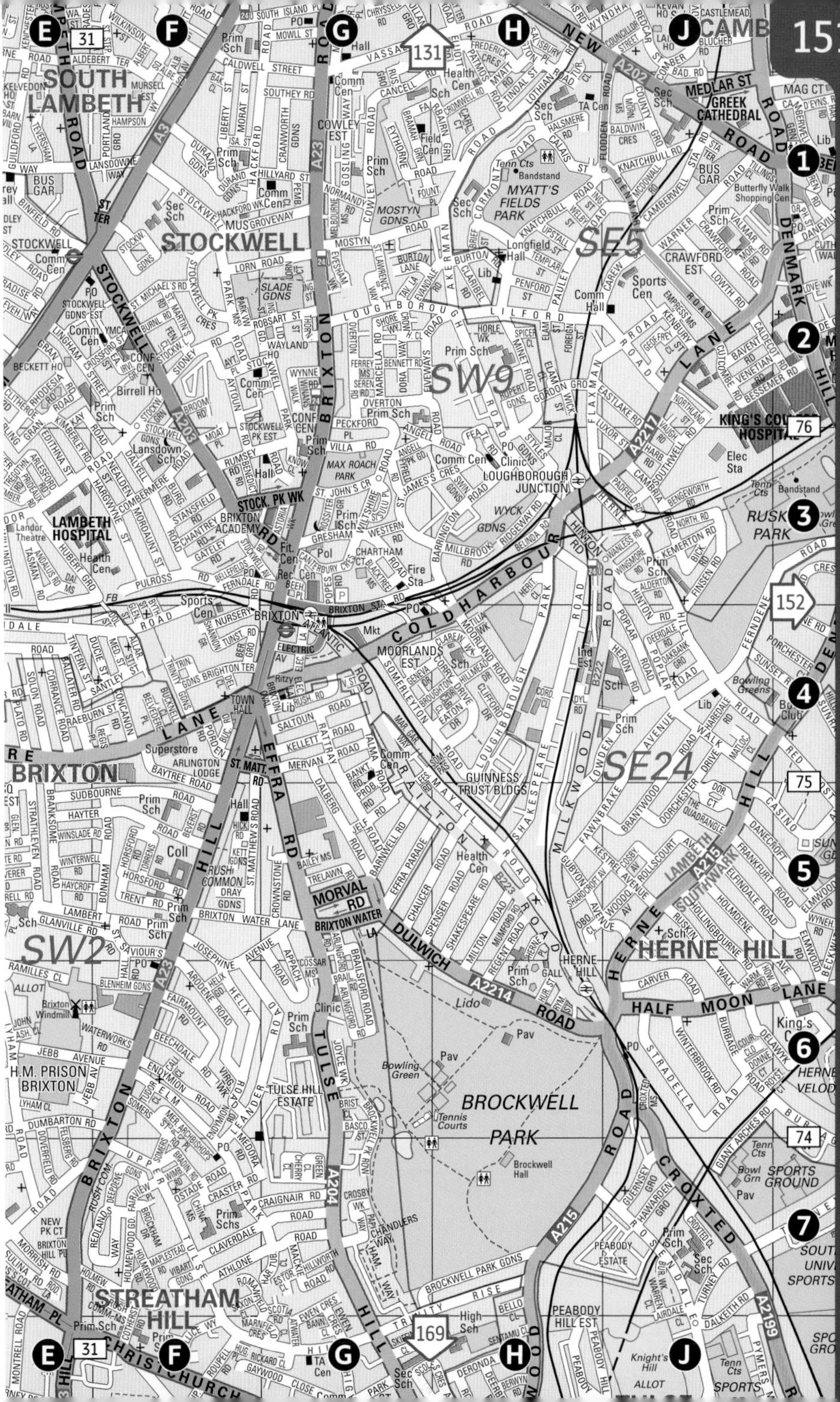
E
F
G
H
J
31
131
152
169
76
75
74
1
2
3
4
5
6
7
SOUTH LAMBETH
STOCKWELL
BRIXTON
SW9
SE5
SE24
SW2
HERNE HILL
STREATHAM HILL
MYATT'S FIELDS PARK
BROCKWELL PARK
RUSKIN PARK
LOUGHBOROUGH JUNCTION
KING'S COLLEGE HOSPITAL
LAMBETH HOSPITAL
H.M. PRISON BRIXTON
GREEK CATHEDRAL
TULSE HILL ESTATE
GUINNESS TRUST BLDGS
MOORLANDS EST
COWLEY EST
CRAWFORD EST
PEABODY ESTATE
PEABODY HILL EST
MAX ROACH PARK
SLADE GDNS
MOSTYN GDNS
WYCK GDNS
Brixton Windmill
Lido
Brockwell Hall
Butterfly Walk Shopping Cen
BRIXTON ROAD
STOCKWELL ROAD
COLDHARBOUR LANE
BRIXTON HILL
EFFRA RD
DULWICH ROAD
HERNE HILL
HALF MOON LANE
CROXTED ROAD
DENMARK HILL
CHAMPION HILL
TULSE HILL
NORWOOD ROAD
LOUGHBOROUGH RD
MILKWOOD ROAD
SHAKESPEARE ROAD
RAILTON ROAD
MAYALL ROAD
ATLANTIC RD
ACRE LANE
BRIXTON WATER LANE
MORVAL RD
CAMBERWELL NEW ROAD
A23
A3
A203
A202
A2217
A2214
A215
A204
A2199
B222
B223

A
B
C
D
E
1
2
3
4
5
6
7
33
34
132
151
170
76
75
74
PECKHAM
SE5
SE22
SE21
EAST DULWICH
DULWICH
MAUDSLEY HOSPITAL
KINGS COLLEGE HOSPITAL
RUSKIN PARK
William Booth College
DENMARK HILL
CAMBERWELL CH ST
PECKHAM ROAD
PECKHAM HIGH ST
LUCAS GDNS
WARWICK GDNS
CHAMPION PK
GROVE LANE
DOG KENNEL HILL
CHAMPION HILL EST
DENMARK HILL EST
GREENDALE PLAYING FIELDS
DULWICH COMMUNITY HOSP
ST. OLAVE'S REC GRD
SPORTS GROUND
SUNRAY GDNS
EAST DULWICH
GROVE VALE
EAST DULWICH ROAD
LORDSHIP LANE
PECKHAM RYE
PECKHAM RYE COMMON
HANOVER PK
COSSALL PARK
HERNE HILL VELODROME
King's Coll
VILLAGE WAY
HALF MOON LA
Alleyn's Sch
DULWICH PICTURE GALL
Dulwich Coll
DULWICH PARK
SOUTH BANK UNIVERSITY SPORTS GROUND
BELAIR PARK
COURT LANE
LORDSHIP LANE EST
DAWSON HEIGHTS ESTATE
CITYVIEW COURT
NORTH DULWICH
EAST DULWICH
DENMARK HILL
PECKHAM RYE
A215
A202
A2215
A2216
A2214
A2199
B219
HERNE HILL
LEWISHAM

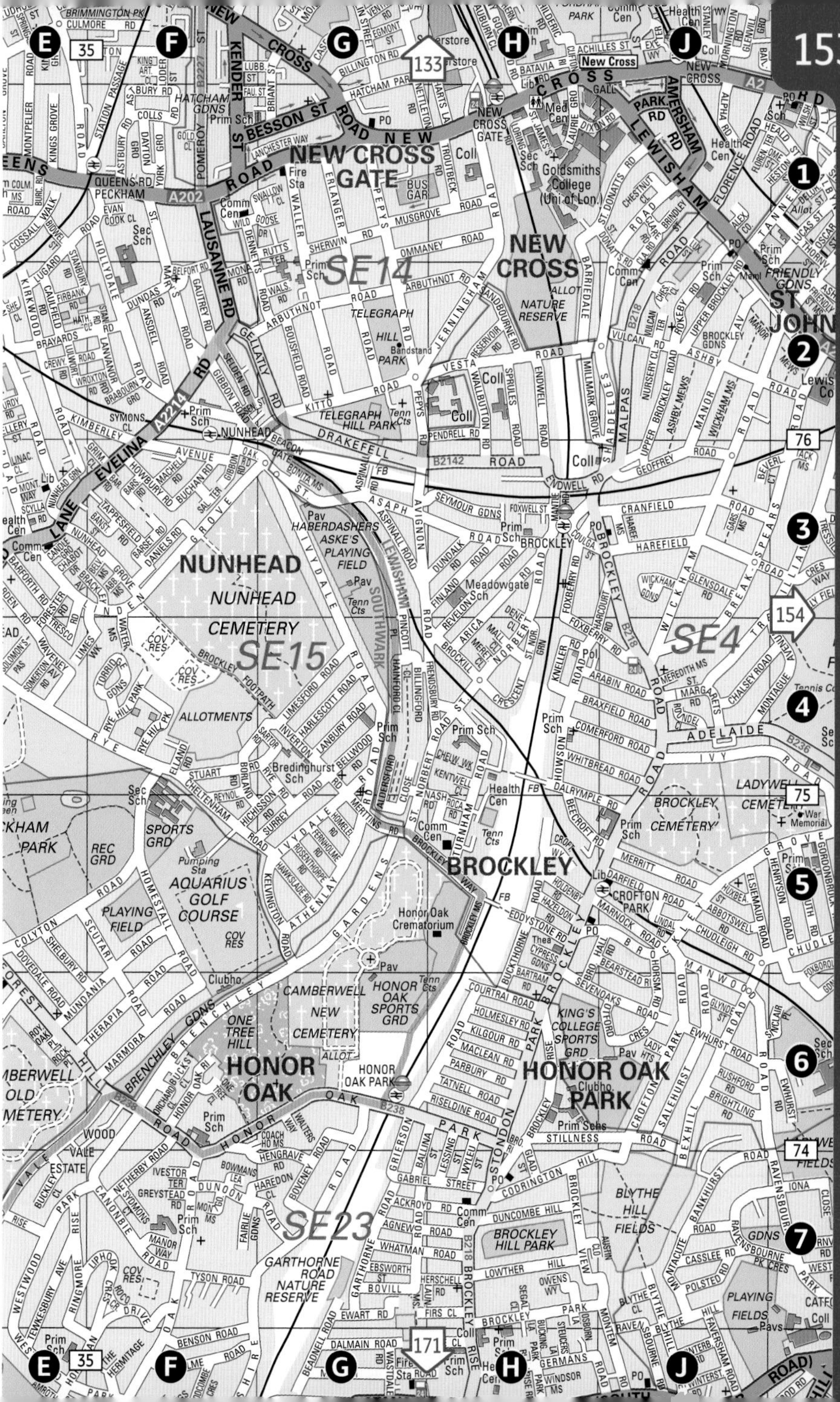
NEW CROSS GATE
NEW CROSS
SE14
NUNHEAD
NUNHEAD CEMETERY
SE15
BROCKLEY
BROCKLEY CEMETERY
LADYWELL CEMETERY
SE4
HONOR OAK
HONOR OAK PARK
SE23
CAMBERWELL NEW CEMETERY
CAMBERWELL OLD CEMETERY
ONE TREE HILL
AQUARIUS GOLF COURSE
TELEGRAPH HILL PARK
HABERDASHERS ASKE'S PLAYING FIELD
Goldsmiths College (Uni of Lon.)
NEW CROSS NATURE RESERVE
KING'S COLLEGE SPORTS GRD
HONOR OAK SPORTS GRD
Honor Oak Crematorium
BLYTHE HILL FIELDS
BROCKLEY HILL PARK
GARTHORNE ROAD NATURE RESERVE
PECKHAM PARK
QUEENS RD PECKHAM
NUNHEAD
BROCKLEY
CROFTON PARK
HONOR OAK PARK
NEW CROSS GATE
New Cross
133
154
171
35
74
75
76
E
F
G
H
J
1
2
3
4
5
6
7

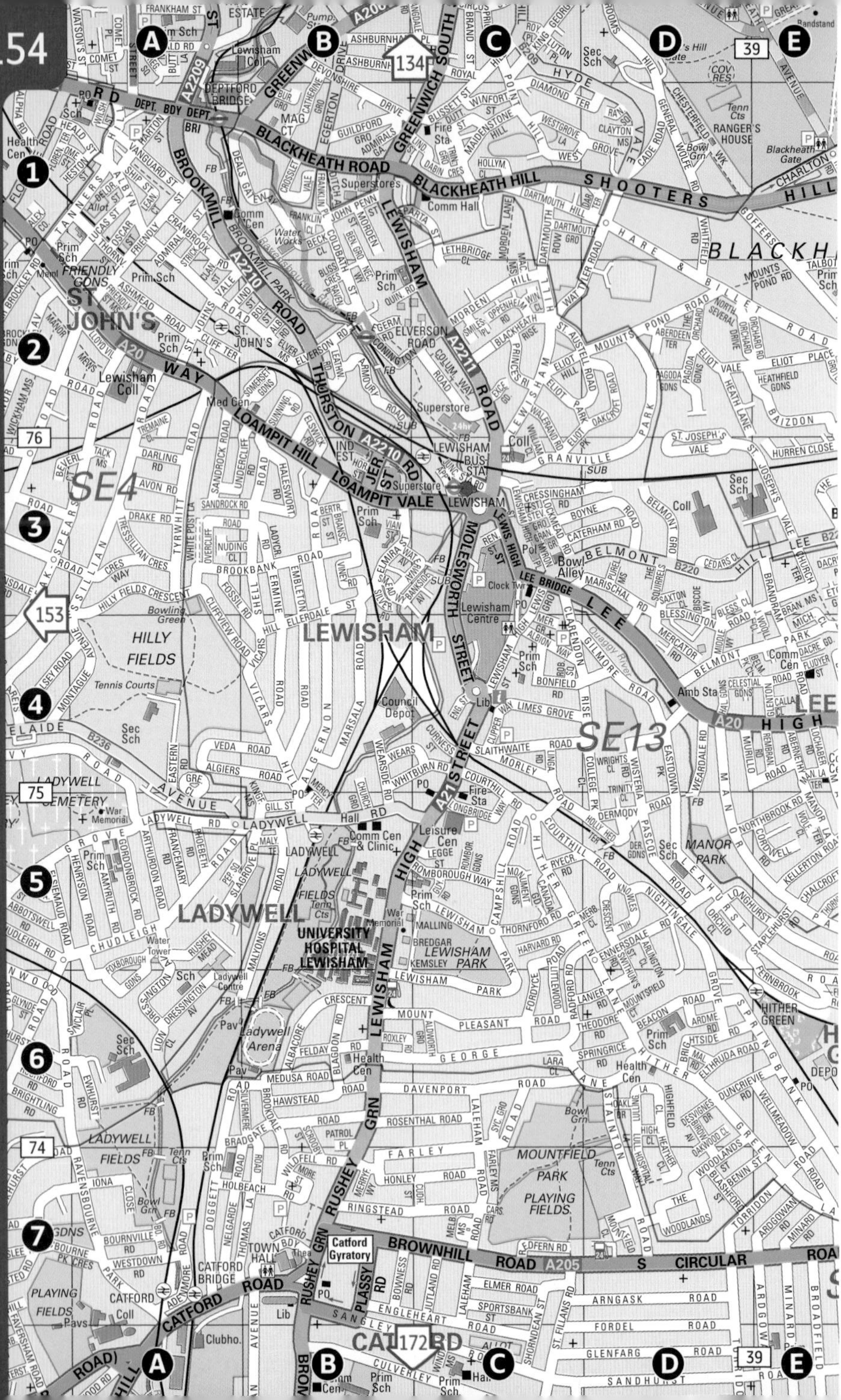
A
B
C
D
E
1
2
3
4
5
6
7
134
153
172
39
76
75
74
BLACKHEATH ROAD
BLACKHEATH HILL
SHOOTERS HILL
BLACKH
DEPTFORD BRIDGE
BROOKMILL ROAD
GREENWICH SOUTH ST
LEWISHAM ROAD
LEWISHAM HILL
HYDE VALE
RANGER'S HOUSE
Blackheath Gate
ST. JOHN'S
LEWISHAM WAY
Lewisham Coll
LOAMPIT HILL
LOAMPIT VALE
THURSTON ROAD
ELVERSON ROAD
LEWISHAM
SE4
SE13
HILLY FIELDS
Tennis Courts
MOLESWORTH STREET
Lewisham Centre
LEE BRIDGE
LEE HIGH ROAD
BELMONT HILL
LEWISHAM PARK
LADYWELL
LADYWELL CEMETERY
LADYWELL ROAD
UNIVERSITY HOSPITAL LEWISHAM
LEWISHAM HIGH STREET
MANOR PARK
HITHER GREEN
MOUNT PLEASANT ROAD
GEORGE LANE
LADYWELL FIELDS
Ladywell Arena
MOUNTFIELD PARK
PLAYING FIELDS
RUSHEY GRN
Catford Gyratory
BROWNHILL ROAD
S CIRCULAR ROAD
CATFORD ROAD
CATFORD BRIDGE
CATFORD
TOWN HALL
PLAYING FIELDS

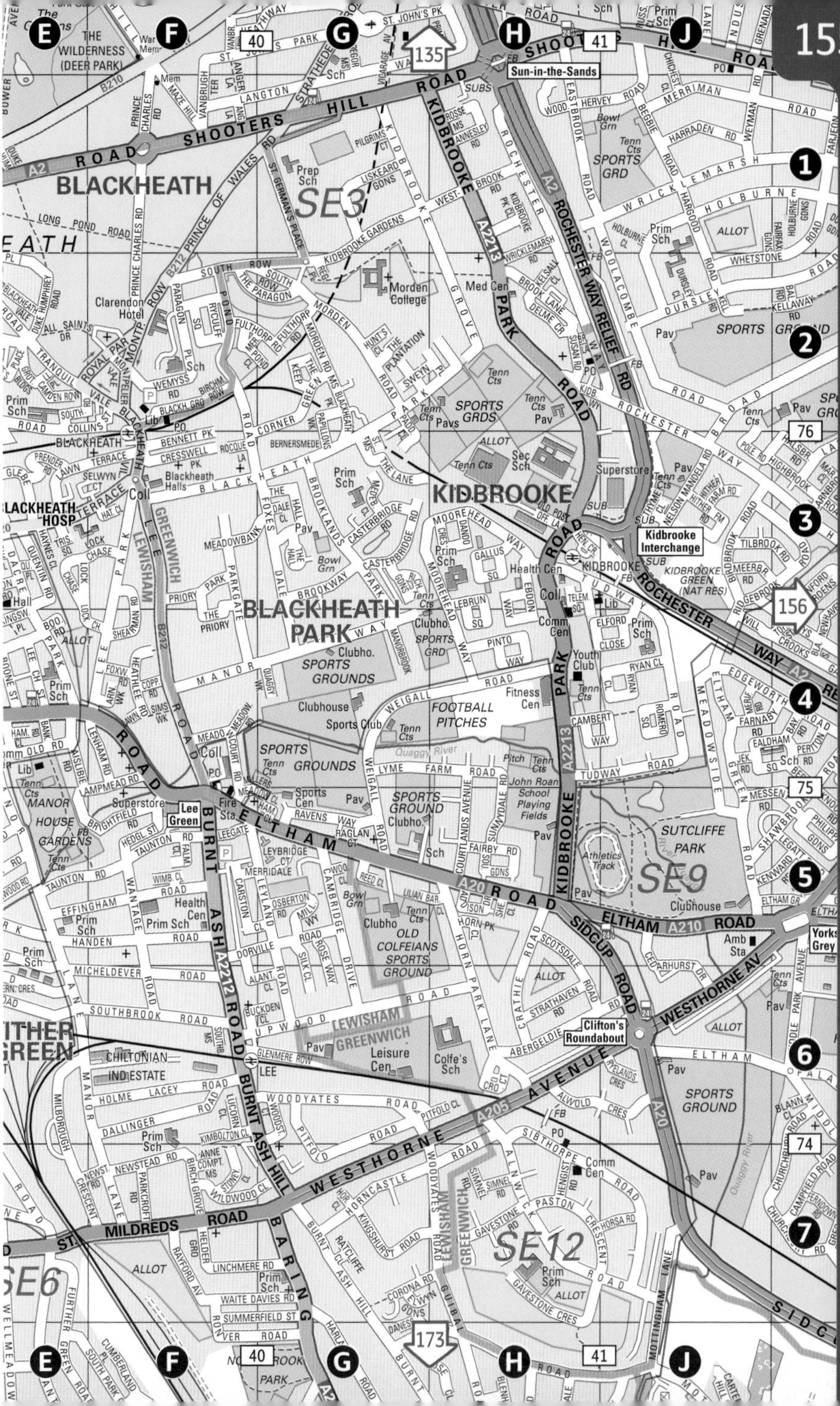
E
F
G
H
J
1
2
3
4
5
6
7
40
41
135
156
173
76
75
74
THE WILDERNESS (DEER PARK)
BLACKHEATH
SE3
KIDBROOKE
BLACKHEATH PARK
SE9
SE12
SE6
SHOOTERS HILL ROAD
Sun-in-the-Sands
ROCHESTER WAY RELIEF RD
KIDBROOKE PARK ROAD
PRINCE OF WALES RD
PRINCE CHARLES RD
LONG POND ROAD
KIDBROOKE GARDENS
KIDBROOKE GROVE
Morden College
Clarendon Hotel
SPORTS GRDS
Kidbrooke Interchange
KIDBROOKE GREEN (NAT RES)
ROCHESTER WAY
BLACKHEATH HOSP
Blackheath Halls
LEWISHAM
GREENWICH
MANOR WAY
SPORTS GROUNDS
FOOTBALL PITCHES
Quaggy River
John Roan School Playing Fields
SUTCLIFFE PARK
Athletics Track
ELTHAM ROAD
Lee Green
BURNT ASH ROAD
SIDCUP ROAD
WESTHORNE AV
Clifton's Roundabout
WESTHORNE AVENUE
OLD COLFEIANS SPORTS GROUND
Leisure Cen
Colfe's Sch
MANOR HOUSE GARDENS
HITHER GREEN
CHILTONIAN IND ESTATE
ST. MILDREDS ROAD
BURNT ASH HILL
BARING
SPORTS GROUND
Yorks Grey

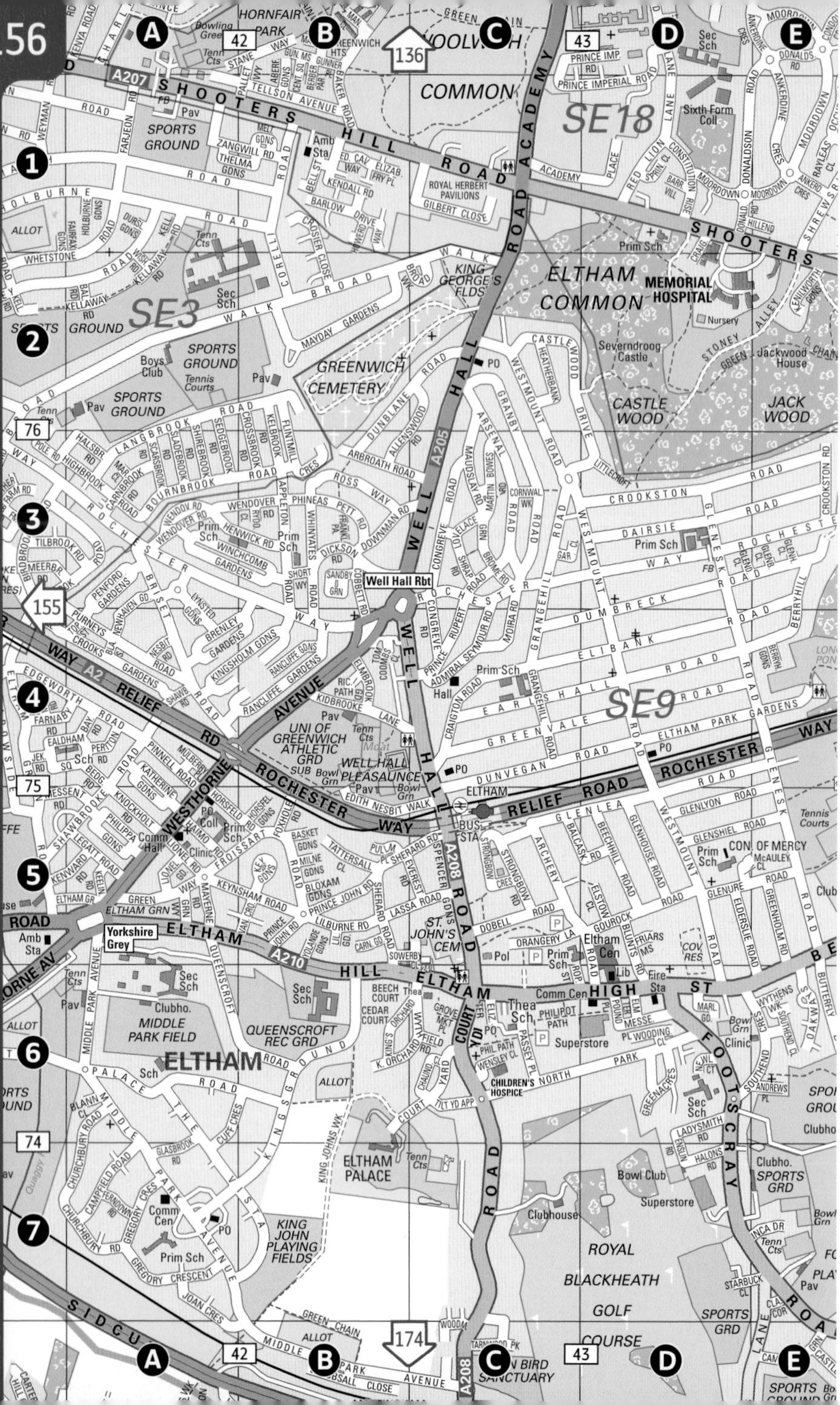
A
B
C
D
E
1
2
3
4
5
6
7
42
43
136
155
174
76
75
74
HORNFAIR PARK
Bowling Green
Tenn Cts
WOOLWICH COMMON
SE18
SE3
SE9
A207
SHOOTERS HILL ROAD
SHOOTERS
PRINCE IMP. RD
PRINCE IMPERIAL ROAD
Sec Sch
Sixth Form Coll
ACADEMY ROAD
ACADEMY PLACE
RED LION LANE
CONSTITUTION RISE
MOORDOWN
DONALDSON ROAD
ANKERDINE CRES
DONALDS RD
RAYLEAS CL
TELLSON AVENUE
STANE WAY
BAKER ROAD
SPORTS GROUND
ZANGWILL RD
THELMA GDNS
Amb Sta
ED. CAV WAY
ELIZAB. FRY PL
KENDALL RD
BARLOW DRIVE
ROYAL HERBERT PAVILIONS
GILBERT CLOSE
CROSIER CLOSE
WEYMAN ROAD
FARJEON RD
COLBURNE ROAD
ALLOT
WHETSTONE ROAD
KELLAWAY RD
CORELLI ROAD
BROAD WALK
KING GEORGE'S FLDS
ELTHAM COMMON
MEMORIAL HOSPITAL
Prim Sch
Nursery
Severndroog Castle
CASTLE WOOD
JACK WOOD
Jackwood House
STONEY ALLEY
GREEN CHAIN
KENILWORTH GDNS
MAYDAY GARDENS
GREENWICH CEMETERY
SPORTS GROUND
Boys Club
Tennis Courts
Pav
DUNBLANE ROAD
ALLENSWOOD RD
ARBROATH ROAD
A205
WELL HALL ROAD
PO
WESTMOUNT ROAD
HEATHERBANK
CASTLEWOOD DRIVE
GRANBY ROAD
ARSENAL ROAD
MAUDSLAY RD
BOWES RD
CORNWALLIS WK
LITTLECROFT
CROOKSTON ROAD
DAIRSIE ROAD
GLENESK ROAD
ROCHESTER WAY
LANGBROOK ROAD
HALSBROOK RD
HIGHBROOK RD
SCARSBROOK RD
SLADEBROOK RD
SHIREBROOK RD
SEDGEBROOK RD
CROSSBROOK RD
KELBROOK RD
FLINTMILL CRES
BOURNBROOK ROAD
CARNBROOK RD
ROSS WAY
WENDOVER RD
WENDOVER WAY
PHINEAS PETT RD
WHINYATES RD
APPLETON RD
DOWNMAN RD
HENWICK RD
WINCHCOMB GARDENS
DICKSON RD
SANDBY GRN
COBBETT RD
Well Hall Rbt
TILBROOK RD
MEERBROOK RD
PENFORD GARDENS
NEWHAVEN GD.
BRISET RD
LYNSTED GDNS
BRENLEY GARDENS
KINGSHOLM GDNS
RANCLIFFE GARDENS
PURNEYS RD
CROOKS RD
GARDENS
NESBIT RD
CONGREVE ROAD
RUPERT ROAD
ADMIRAL SEYMOUR RD
MOIRA RD
GRANGEHILL ROAD
DUMBRECK ROAD
ELIBANK ROAD
EARLSHALL ROAD
GREENVALE ROAD
ELTHAM PARK GARDENS
BERRYHILL
Hall
CRAIGTON ROAD
DUNVEGAN ROAD
A2
RELIEF RD
ROCHESTER WAY RELIEF ROAD
AVENUE
UNI OF GREENWICH ATHLETIC GRD
KIDBROOKE LANE
WELL HALL PLEASAUNCE
Moat
SUB
Bowl Grn
EDITH NESBIT WALK
ELTHAM
BUS STA
A208
GLENLEA ROAD
GLENLYON ROAD
GLENSHIEL ROAD
CON. OF MERCY
McAULEY CL
GLENURE ROAD
Tennis Courts
Club
EDGEWORTH RD
FARNABY RD
EALDHAM SQ
PERTON RD
PINNELL ROAD
KATHERINE GDNS
MULBERRY
KNOCKHOLT RD
PHILIPPA GDNS
WESTHORNE AVENUE
HORSFELD RD
PO Coll
Comm Hall
Clinic
FROISSART RD
FOXHOLE RD
BASKET GDNS
TATTERSALL CL
MILNE GDNS
BLOXAM GDNS
KEYNSHAM ROAD
PRINCE JOHN RD
LASSA ROAD
EVEREST RD
SPENCER GDNS
SHERARD RD
STRONGBOW RD
ARCHERY ROAD
BALCASKIE RD
BEECHHILL ROAD
GLENHOUSE ROAD
ELSTOW CL
ELDERSLIE ROAD
GREENHOLM RD
SHAWBROOKE RD
KENWARD RD
LEGATT ROAD
ELTHAM GR
ELTHAM GRN
LIONEL RD
ROAD
Amb Sta
Yorkshire Grey
ELTHAM HILL
A210
ST. JOHN'S CEM
DOBELL ROAD
ORANGERY LA
GOURCOCK RD
FRIARS MS
Eltham Cen
Lib
Fire Sta
COV. RES
Pol
Prim Sch
ELTHAM HIGH ST
Comm Cen
Thea Sch
PHILIPOT PATH
Superstore
MIDDLE PARK AVENUE
QUEENSCROFT ROAD
Sec Sch
Clubho.
MIDDLE PARK FIELD
QUEENSCROFT REC GRD
ELTHAM
BEECH COURT
CEDAR COURT
KING'S ORCHARD
WYTHFIELD RD
COURT YARD
CHILDREN'S HOSPICE
NORTH PARK
FOOTSCRAY ROAD
WYTHENS WK
OAKWAY
BUTTERFLY
SOUTHEND CRES
ANDREWS PL
PALACE ROAD
KINGSGROUND
CUFF CRES
ALLOT
KING JOHNS WK
ELTHAM PALACE
Tenn Cts
COURT ROAD
TILT YD APP
GREENACRES
LADYSMITH RD
ENSLIN RD
HALONS RD
Bowl Club
Superstore
Clubhouse
ROYAL BLACKHEATH GOLF COURSE
Clubho. SPORTS GRD
CHURCHBURY ROAD
CAMPFIELD ROAD
GLASBROOK RD
GREGORY CRES
PARK AVENUE
THE VISTA
Comm Cen
Prim Sch
GREGORY CRESCENT
JOAN CRES
KING JOHN PLAYING FIELDS
GREEN CHAIN WALK
MIDDLE PARK AVENUE
SIDCUP
ALLOT
WOODM
TARNWOOD PK
BIRD SANCTUARY
SPORTS GRD
STARBUCK CL
INCA DR
SPORTS GROUND

SHREWSBURY PARK
SHOOTERS HILL GOLF COURSE
SHOOTER'S HILL
Clubhouse
Tennis Courts
REC GRD
Bowl Grn
Comm Cen
KINLET ROAD
EAGLESFIELD RD
FOXCROFT RD
CLEANTHUS RD
Woodlands Farm Nature Reserve
CLOTHWORKERS WOOD
ALLOT
SPORTS GRD
Pav
Sch
EAST WICKHAM OPEN SPACE
Prim Schs
HILLVIEW CEMETERY
GREENWICH
BEXLEY
WICKHAM STREET
GLENMORE ROAD
EDISON ROAD
WORDSWORTH ROAD
CHAUCER ROAD
BLENHEIM DRIVE
EXETER RD
TIDFORD ROAD
MARINA DRIVE
SANDRINGHAM DRIVE
SHOULDER OF MUTTON GRN
LULWORTH ROAD
CLEVELAND ROAD
WELLING
A207
HILL
BELLEGROVE
Nursery
We Anchor in Hope PH
FALCONWOOD AVENUE
OXLEAS WOOD
OXLEAS MEADOW
ELTHAM COMMON
Prim Sch
ASHMORE GROVE
WELLING WAY
MONTROSE AVENUE
DA16
ROCHESTER WAY
FALCONWOOD FIELD
FALCONWOOD
Elec Sta
SHEPHERDLEAS WOOD
GREEN CHAIN
ELTHAM PARK NORTH
NORTHUMBERLAND AVENUE
WESTMORELAND AVENUE
CUMBERLAND AVENUE
CORNWALL AVENUE
YORKLAND AVENUE
WESTWOOD LANE
Sec Sch
Clinic
Comm Cen
PO
THE GREEN
SUTHERLAND AVENUE
HOOK LANE
A2 RELIEF ROAD
Falconwood
ELTHAM CEMETERY
Crematorium
EAST ROCHESTER WAY
ELTHAM PARK SOUTH
ELTHAM WARREN GOLF COURSE
COLEPITS WOOD ROAD
RIEFIELD ROAD
DA15
RIDGEWAY WEST
BOUNDARY ROAD
Greenwich Environment Curriculum Service
SPORTS GROUND
BEXLEY ROAD
A210
BLACKFEN ROAD
Jolly Fenman PH
REINICKENDORF AVENUE
ROAD
Uni
Winter Garden
AVERY HILL
AVERY HILL PARK
Pavs
University of Greenwich Avery Hill Campus
RESTONS CRESCENT
ALDERWOOD ROAD
RONALDSTONE ROAD
PARISH WOOD
Prim Sch
HOLBEACH GDNS
BERWICK CRESCENT
HARMAN DRIVE
HOLLY OAK WOOD PK
BLACKFEN
DAYS LANE
OAKLANDS AVENUE
ROSEBERY AV
CAMBRIDGE MISSION SPORTS GROUND
CHARLTON ATHLETIC FC TRAINING GRD
SPORTS GRDS
Sports Cen
MILLWALL FC
SPARROWS LANE
HALFWAY STREET
ANNANDALE ROAD
WILLERSLEY PK
A2
E
F
G
H
J
1
2
3
4
5
6
7
44
76
75
74
137
158
175

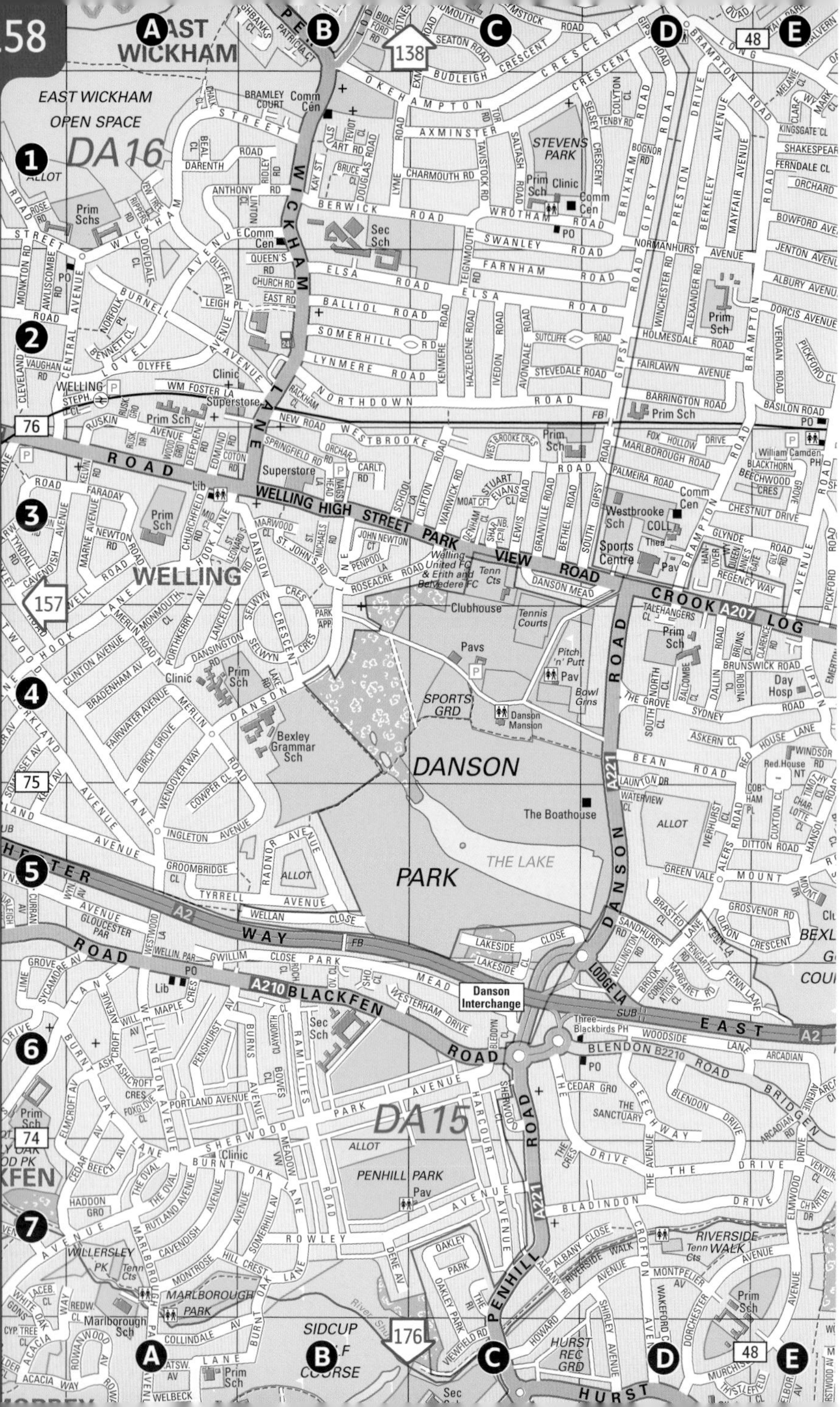
A
B
C
D
E
1
2
3
4
5
6
7
EAST WICKHAM
EAST WICKHAM OPEN SPACE
DA16
138
48
WELLING
157
76
75
74
DANSON
PARK
THE LAKE
The Boathouse
Danson Mansion
SPORTS GRD
Pitch 'n' Putt
Tennis Courts
Clubhouse
Welling United FC & Erith and Belvedere FC
Bexley Grammar Sch
Danson Interchange
DA15
PENHILL PARK
SIDCUP GOLF COURSE
176
HURST REC GRD
RIVERSIDE WALK
MARLBOROUGH PARK
Marlborough Sch
WILLERSLEY PK
Westbrooke Sch
Sports Centre
Red House NT
William Camden PH
Three Blackbirds PH
STEVENS PARK
WICKHAM LANE
WELLING HIGH STREET
PARK VIEW ROAD
CROOK LOG
BELLEGROVE ROAD
DANSON ROAD
BLACKFEN ROAD
ROCHESTER WAY
EAST ROCHESTER WAY
BLENDON ROAD
PENHILL ROAD
BRAMPTON ROAD
GIPSY ROAD
OKEHAMPTON CRESCENT
BUDLEIGH CRESCENT
BERWICK ROAD
SWANLEY ROAD
FARNHAM ROAD
ELSA ROAD
BALLIOL ROAD
SOMERHILL RD
LYNMERE ROAD
NORTHDOWN ROAD
WESTBROOKE ROAD
DANSON LANE
HOOK LANE
BURNT OAK LANE
SHERWOOD PARK AVENUE
ROWLEY AVENUE
BLADINDON DRIVE
A2
A207
A210
A221
B2210

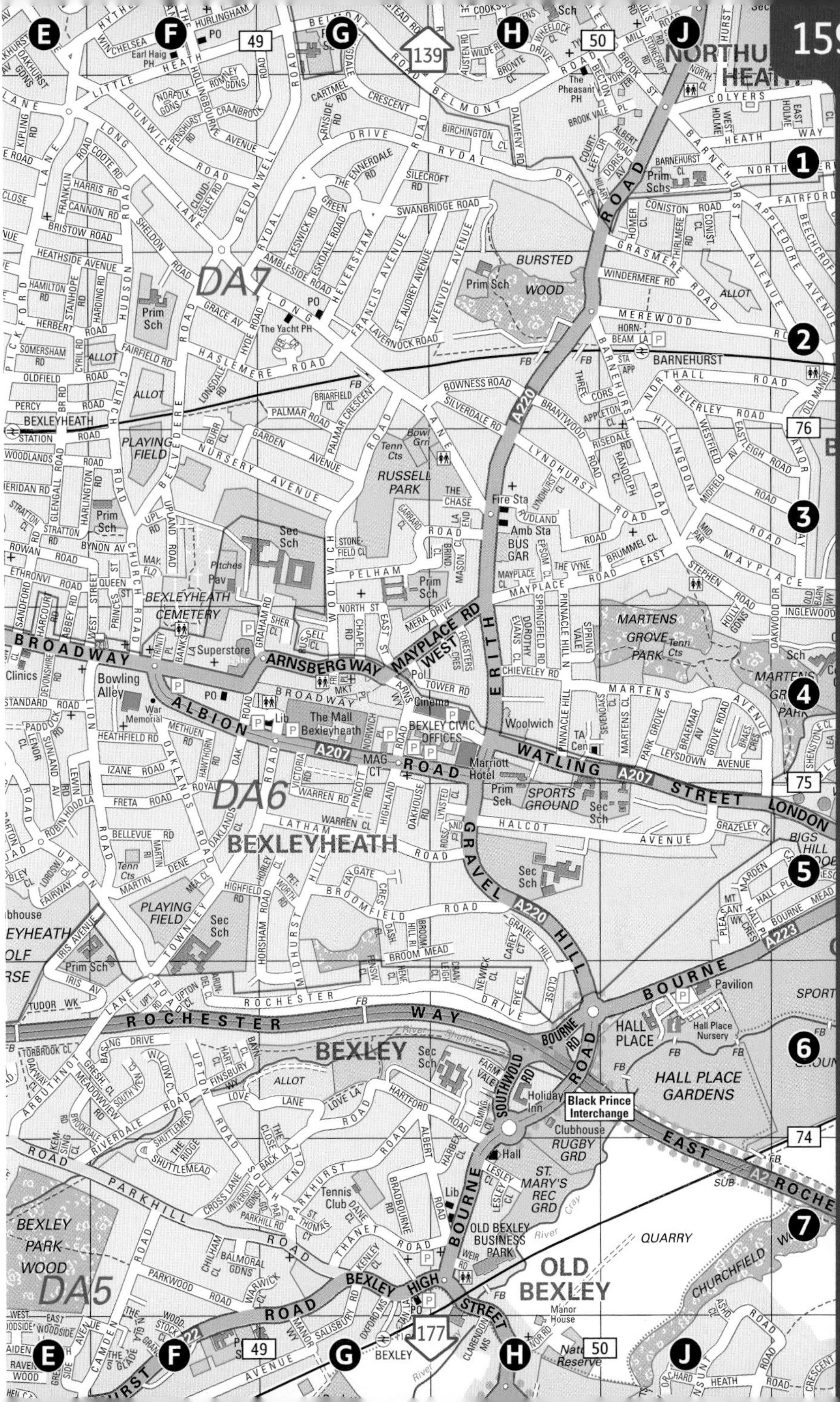

E
F
G
H
J
49
50
139
NORTHUMBERLAND HEATH
1
2
3
4
5
6
7
75
76
74
DA7
DA6
DA5
BEXLEYHEATH
BEXLEY
OLD BEXLEY
BURSTED WOOD
RUSSELL PARK
MARTENS GROVE PARK
HALL PLACE
HALL PLACE GARDENS
BEXLEY PARK WOOD
BEXLEYHEATH CEMETERY
PLAYING FIELD
ALLOT
SPORTS GROUND
RUGBY GRD
ST. MARY'S REC GRD
OLD BEXLEY BUSINESS PARK
QUARRY
Black Prince Interchange
Holiday Inn
Marriott Hotel
The Mall Bexleyheath
BEXLEY CIVIC OFFICES
Bowling Alley
War Memorial
Superstore
Cinema
Woolwich
Fire Sta
Amb Sta
BUS GAR
Prim Sch
Sec Sch
Lib
PO
The Yacht PH
The Pheasant PH
Earl Haig PH
Clinics
Tennis Club
Pavilion
Hall Place Nursery
Clubhouse
Manor House
Natr Reserve
BEXLEYHEATH STATION
BARNEHURST
BEXLEY
River Shuttle
River Cray
A220
A207
A223
A2
BROADWAY
ALBION ROAD
WATLING STREET
LONDON ROAD
ERITH ROAD
GRAVEL HILL
ROCHESTER WAY
BOURNE ROAD
BEXLEY HIGH STREET
ARNSBERG WAY
MAYPLACE RD WEST
MAYPLACE ROAD EAST
BARNEHURST ROAD
BELMONT ROAD
RYDAL DRIVE
LONG LANE
HASLEMERE ROAD
PALMAR ROAD
NURSERY AVENUE
UPTON ROAD
PARKHILL ROAD
HALCOT AVENUE
BROOMFIELD ROAD
MARTENS AVENUE
LOVE LANE
HURST ROAD
DANSON ROAD
ROCHESTER DRIVE
BRANTWOOD ROAD
LYNDHURST ROAD
NORTHALL ROAD
COLYERS LANE
FAIRFORD AVENUE
BOWNESS ROAD
SILVERDALE RD

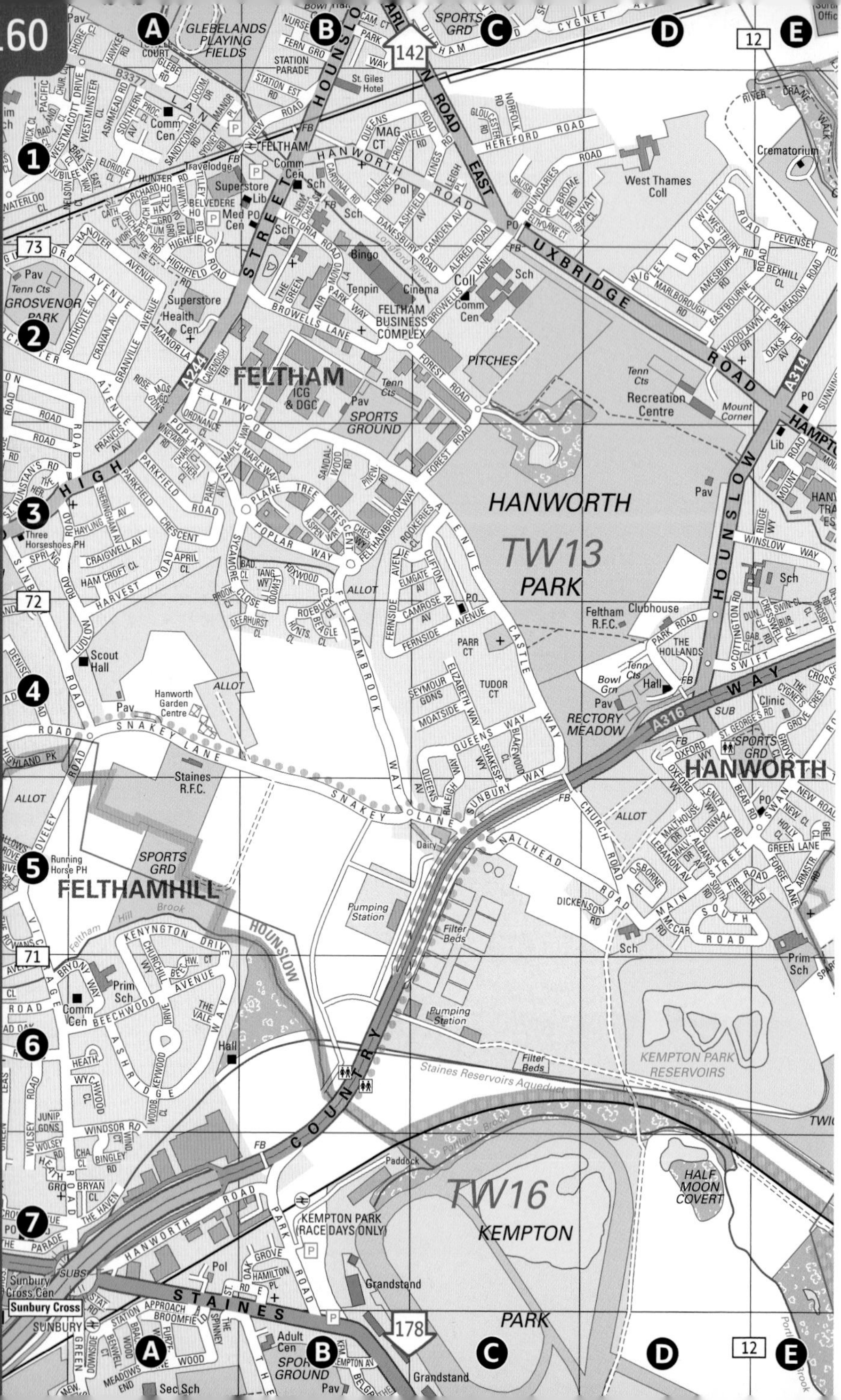
A
B
C
D
E
1
2
3
4
5
6
7
142
178
12
73
72
71
GLEBELANDS PLAYING FIELDS
SPORTS GRD
CYGNET
STATION PARADE
STATION EST
St. Giles Hotel
FERN GRO
NURSERY
HOUNSLOW ROAD
HOUNSLOW ROAD EAST
HAM
WAY
PARK
SHORE CL
HAWKES
COURT
GLEBE RD
B3377
LANE
LOCOM. DR
MANOR PL
PACIFIC
WESTMACOTT DRIVE
WESTMINSTER
ASHMEAD RD
SOUTHERN AV
Comm Cen
SANDYCOMBE RD
SYDNEY RD
NEW ROAD
FELTHAM
Travelodge
Comm Cen
HANWORTH ROAD
QUEENS ROAD
MAG CT
CROMWELL RD
NORFOLK RD
GLOUCESTER RD
HEREFORD ROAD
ROAD
West Thames Coll
RIVER CRANE WALK
Crematorium
JUBILEE WAY
ELDRIDGE CL
WATERLOO CL
NELSON CL
HUNTER RD
ORCHARD
TILLEY RD
Superstore
Lib
Sch
CARDINAL RD
FLORENCE RD
Pol
KINGS RD
LEIGH PL
SALISB RD
BOUNDARIES RD
BROME
WYATT CL
WIGLEY ROAD
WESTBURY RD
PEVENSEY ROAD
BELVEDERE
HIGHFIELD RD
Med Cen
PO
NEW CHAP. RD
VICTORIA ROAD
ASHFIELD AV
DANESBURY ROAD
CAMDEN AV
ALFRED ROAD
LANE
PO
UXBRIDGE ROAD
WIGLEY
MARLBOROUGH RD
AMESBURY RD
EASTBOURNE RD
BEXHILL CL
MEADOW ROAD
HANOVER AVENUE
Pav
Tenn Cts
GROSVENOR PARK
STREET
Bingo
Longford River
Tenpin
Cinema
Coll
Comm Cen
Sch
SOUTHCOTE AV
CRAVAN AV
GRANVILLE AVENUE
AVENUE
Superstore
Health Cen
MANOR LA
THE GREEN
BROWELLS LANE
FELTHAM BUSINESS COMPLEX
BROWELLS LA
WOODLAWN DR
LITTLE PARK DR
OAKS AV
A244
CAVENDISH TER
FELTHAM
ICG & DGC
FOREST ROAD
PITCHES
Tenn Cts
Recreation Centre
Mount Corner
A314
PO
HAMPTON
Lib
Pav
SPORTS GROUND
ELMWOOD
ORDNANCE CL
POPLAR WAY
VINEYARD
FRANCIS AV
ROAD
ROAD
HIGH
ST. DUNSTAN'S RD
PARKFIELD ROAD
PARK AV
MAPLE WAY
MAPLEWAY
SANDALWOOD RD
PINEW. RD
FELTHAMBROOK WAY
HANWORTH
TW13
PARK
HOUNSLOW ROAD
RIDGE WAY
WINSLOW WAY
Sch
SHERINGHAM AV
HAYLING AV
CRAIGWELL AV
HAM CROFT CL
HARVEST ROAD
APRIL CL
CRESCENT
Three Horseshoes PH
SPRING
PLANE TREE CRESCENT
ASPEN WAY
CHES. WY
POPLAR WAY
SYCAMORE CLOSE
ROOKERIES CL
AVENUE
CLIFTON AV
ELMGATE AV
CAMROSE AV
FERNSIDE AVENUE
PO
FOXWOOD
TANG. WY
LEWOOD
BROOK CL
DEERHURST CL
ROEBUCK CL
BEAGLE CL
HUNTS CL
ALLOT
Feltham R.F.C.
Clubhouse
PARK ROAD
THE HOLLANDS
COTTINGTON RD
SWIFT
CROSS
CRESSWELL
DUN. CL
GAB. CL
LUDLOW ROAD
Scout Hall
Hanworth Garden Centre
ALLOT
PARR CT
TUDOR CT
CASTLE WAY
SEYMOUR GDNS
ELIZABETH WAY
MOATSIDE
QUEENS WAY
BLAKEWOOD CL
Bowl Grn
Pav
Hall
RECTORY MEADOW
A316
WAY
SUB
Clinic
THE CYGNETS
ST. GEORGE'S RD
GROVE CRES
FB
OXFORD WY
SPORTS GRD
HANWORTH
ROAD
SNAKEY LANE
Pav
HIGHLAND PK
ALLOT
Staines R.F.C.
QUEENS AV
RALEIGH WAY
SHAKESP. WY
SUNBURY WAY
CHURCH ROAD
ALLOT
HENLEY WY
CONWAY RD
BEAR RD
SWAN
NEW ROAD
NEW CL
HOLLY CL
GREEN LANE
SNAKEY LANE
OVELEY
Running Horse PH
SPORTS GRD
FELTHAMHILL
Feltham Hill Brook
HOUNSLOW
Dairy
NALLHEAD ROAD
Pumping Station
Filter Beds
DICKENSON RD
OSBORNE CL
MALTHOUSE DR
LEBANON AV
ST. ALBANS AV
MAIN STREET
SOUTH RD
FIR RD
BIRCH RD
FORGE LANE
ARMSTR.
KENYNGTON DRIVE
CHURCHILL WY
BEC. CL
HW. CT
AVENUE
BRYONY WAY
Prim Sch
Comm Cen
BEECHWOOD AVENUE
THE VALE
WAY
ROAD
ASHRIDGE
KEYWOOD DRIVE
HEATH
WYCHWOOD CL
Pumping Station
McCAR. RD
SOUTH ROAD
Sch
Prim Sch
KEMPTON PARK RESERVOIRS
Hall
Filter Beds
Staines Reservoirs Aqueduct
COUNTRY
WOODB. CL
JUNIP. GDNS
WINDSOR RD
WOLSEY
CHA. CL
BINGLEY RD
BRYAN CL
THE HAVEN
Portland Brook
FB
Paddock
TW16
KEMPTON
HALF MOON COVERT
HANWORTH ROAD
KEMPTON PARK (RACE DAYS ONLY)
PARK ROAD
OAK GROVE
HAMILTON PL
Pol
PARADE
SUBS
Sunbury Cross Cen
Sunbury Cross
Grandstand
STAINES
STATION APPROACH
BROOMFIELD
THE SPINNEY
SUNBURY
Adult Cen
SPORTS GROUND
KEMPTON AV
PARK
FURZE
WOOD
MEADOWS END
DOWNSIDE
GREEN
Sec Sch
Pav
Grandstand

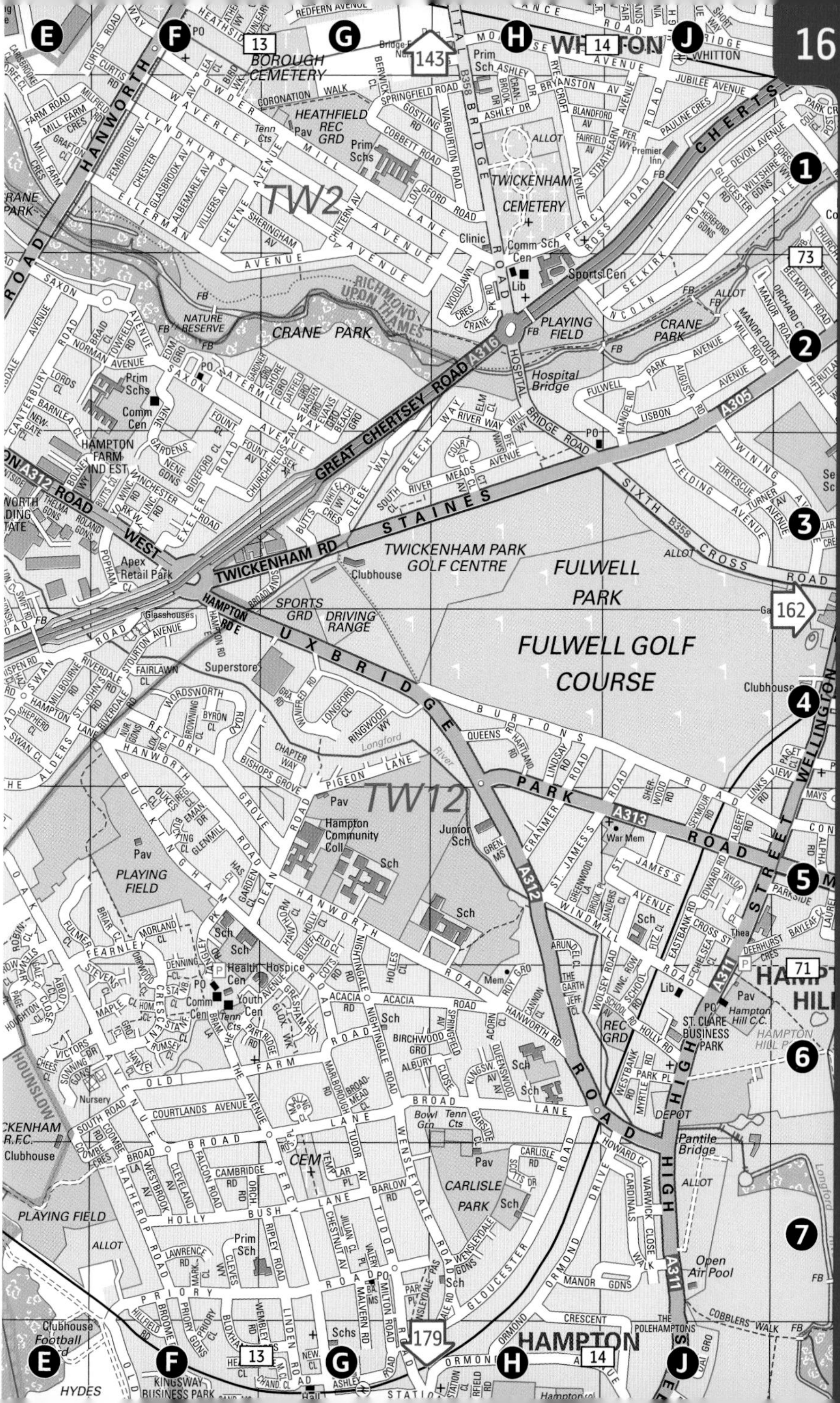
E
F
G
H
J
13
14
143
WHITTON
BOROUGH CEMETERY
HEATHFIELD REC GRD
TW2
TWICKENHAM CEMETERY
HANWORTH ROAD
GREAT CHERTSEY ROAD
A316
RICHMOND UPON THAMES
CRANE PARK
NATURE RESERVE
PLAYING FIELD
Sports Cen
Hospital Bridge
A305
STAINES
TWICKENHAM RD
TWICKENHAM PARK GOLF CENTRE
FULWELL PARK
FULWELL GOLF COURSE
SIXTH CROSS ROAD
B358
73
162
HAMPTON FARM IND EST
A312
Apex Retail Park
SPORTS GRD
DRIVING RANGE
UXBRIDGE
Superstore
Clubhouse
TW12
Hampton Community Coll
PARK ROAD
A313
WELLINGTON
STREET
HANWORTH ROAD
PLAYING FIELD
A311
HAMPTON HILL
71
ST. CLARE BUSINESS PARK
REC GRD
CARLISLE PARK
CEM
BROAD LANE
HIGH STREET
Pantile Bridge
Open Air Pool
COBBLERS WALK
TWICKENHAM R.F.C. Clubhouse
PLAYING FIELD
HOUNSLOW
Clubhouse Football
HAMPTON
179
KINGSWAY BUSINESS PARK
HYDES
1
2
3
4
5
6
7

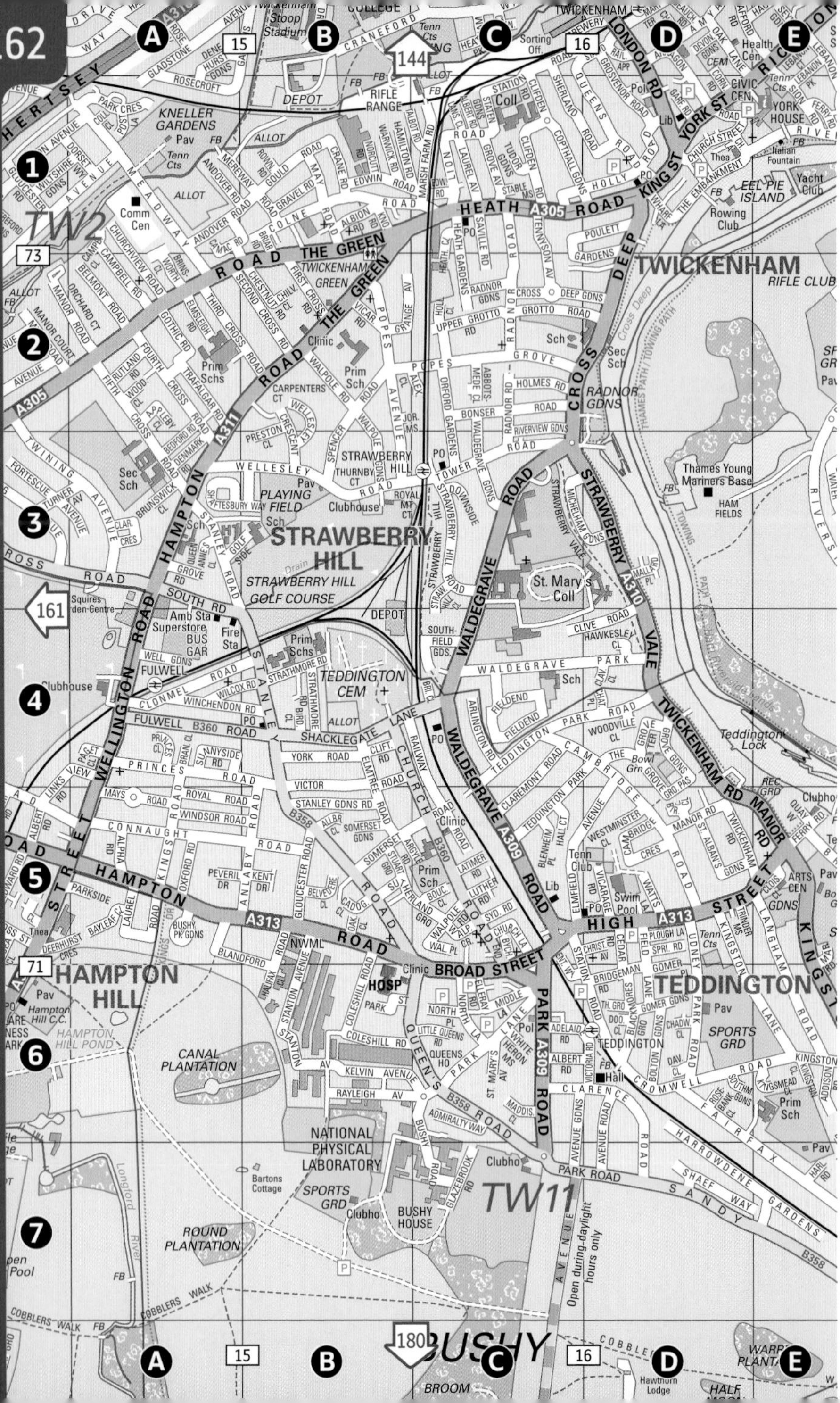
A
B
C
D
E
1
2
3
4
5
6
7
15
16
144
161
180
73
71
TW2
TW11
TWICKENHAM
RIFLE CLUB
STRAWBERRY HILL
STRAWBERRY HILL GOLF COURSE
TEDDINGTON
HAMPTON HILL
BUSHY
KNELLER GARDENS
TWICKENHAM GREEN
EEL PIE ISLAND
Yacht Club
Rowing Club
YORK HOUSE
CIVIC CEN
Italian Fountain
Thames Young Mariners Base
HAM FIELDS
Teddington Lock
TEDDINGTON CEM
St. Mary's Coll
NATIONAL PHYSICAL LABORATORY
BUSHY HOUSE
CANAL PLANTATION
ROUND PLANTATION
HAMPTON HILL POND
Hampton Hill C.C.
SPORTS GRD
Bartons Cottage
Squires Garden Centre
Superstore
BUS GAR
Fire Sta
Amb Sta
FULWELL
PLAYING FIELD
Clubhouse
HOSP
NWML
Swim Pool
Tenn Club
Lib
Hall
DEPOT
RIFLE RANGE
Sorting Off.
Comm Cen
Sec Sch
Prim Sch
Prim Schs
Sch
Clinic
Pav
ALLOT
Tenn Cts
HEATH A305 ROAD
THE GREEN
HAMPTON ROAD
HAMPTON A313 ROAD
WELLINGTON ROAD
HAMPTON A311 ROAD
STANLEY ROAD
WALDEGRAVE ROAD
WALDEGRAVE A309 ROAD
STRAWBERRY VALE
STRAWBERRY A310 VALE
CROSS DEEP
TWICKENHAM RD
MANOR RD
HIGH A313 STREET
BROAD STREET
PARK A309 ROAD
KINGS ST
YORK ST
LONDON RD
CHURCH STREET
THE EMBANKMENT
FULWELL B360 ROAD
SHACKLEGATE LANE
PRINCES ROAD
CONNAUGHT ROAD
TWINING AVENUE
SOUTH RD
WELLESLEY ROAD
TOWER ROAD
WALDEGRAVE PARK
TEDDINGTON PARK
CAMBRIDGE ROAD
CLARENCE ROAD
PARK ROAD
SANDY LANE
HARROWDENE GARDENS
FAIRFAX ROAD
CROMWELL ROAD
KINGSTON ROAD
QUEEN'S B358 ROAD
KELVIN AVENUE
COLESHILL RD
BUSHY ROAD
CHESTNUT AVENUE
COBBLERS WALK
Longford River
Open during daylight hours only
Open Pool
Hawthorn Lodge
BROOM

E
F
G
H
J
17
145
MARBLE HILL HOUSE
GLOVER'S ISLAND
PETERSHAM MEADOWS
PETERSHAM COMMON
TW1
RIVER THAMES
LONDON THAMES CYCLE ROUTE
ORLEANS HOUSE GALLERY
Riverside Ho
ORLEANS GDNS
Yacht Club
RIVER LANE
Petersham Nurseries
CHURCH LANE
Hall
Dysarts PH
STAR & GARTER HILL
A307
B353
Open during daylight hours only
KIDNEY WOOD
HORSE RIDE
ROAD
The German Sch
Stables
Ham Polo Club
Fox & Duck PH
CEDAR HTS
KING HENRY VIII MOUND
PETERSHAM
DRIFT WAY
1
73
HAM HOUSE (NT)
REC GRD
HAM HOUSE GARDENS
KING GEORGE'S FIELD
HAM STREET
Prim Sch
Sch
SANDPITS RD
SUDBROOK LA
BUTE AV
PETERSHAM
Pembroke Lodge
THE COPSE
MEADLANDS DRIVE
CLIFFORD RD
DICKENS CL
HAZEL LANE
PARK
2
ALLOT
RIVERSIDE DRIVE
BUCKINGHAM ROAD
SANDY LANE EST
TW10
SANDY LANE
Clubhouse
MURRAY RD
STRETTON RD
RUSSELL GDNS
NEVILLE RD
ASHBURNHAM RD
ARLINGTON RD
ASHLEY GDNS
LAUDERDALE DRIVE
SPORTS GRD
PETERSHAM
RICHMOND GOLF COURSE SUDBROOK PARK
The Wilderness
HORSE RIDE
Sec Sch
HAM
Clinic
Lib
Hall
WOODVILLE ROAD
MARTINGALES CL
BISHOPS CL
ST. MICHAEL'S CONVENT
3
MOWBRAY RD
SHERIDAN RD
LOVELL RD
CLEVES RD
MEAD RD
THE COMMON
PO
HAM COMMON
Ormeley Lodge
Ham Bottom
164
HAM
HORNBEAM WALK
BROUGHTON AVENUE
LOCK RD
NEW RD
CRAIG RD
MORNINGTON WK
UPPER HAM RD
HAM GATE AVENUE
B352
Ham Gate
4
THE CASSEL HOSPITAL
HAM FARM ROAD
CHURCH ROAD
COMMON
KINGFISHER DR
DUKES
MAGUIRE DRIVE
LAMMAS ROAD
BURNELL AVENUE
DYSART AVENUE
PARKLEYS
BARNFIELD
Parkgate House
CHURCH ROAD
TOWING PATH
Teddington Weir
RICHMOND
Fire Sta
ST. GEORGE'S IND EST
TUDOR DRIVE
HAM RIDINGS
ALLOT
Teddington Studios
SHELL SPORTS GRD
Pav
HORSLEY DR
Bowl Grn
Hawker Cen
ARAGON RD
LANCASTER GDNS
Remand Cen
Riding Sch
Comm Cen
5
SPORTS GRD
Clubho
BROOM WATER
TROWLOCK ISLAND
KINGSTON UPON THAMES
RICHMOND UPON THAMES
FERNHILL GDNS
CARDINAL
PO
Lib
WOODCOTE CL
71
ST. WINIFRED'S ROAD
BROOM ROAD
TROWLOCK AVE
Sec Sch
WOLSEY DRIVE
ALLOT
REC GRD
Coll
Prim Sch
Pav
ATBARA RD
KING EDWARDS GROVE
MELBOURNE RD
LOWER HAM ROAD
ALBANY PARK ROAD
DURLSTON RD
KT2
6
MUNSTER RD
Sec Sch
Clubho
Sailing Club
Sailing Cen
BROOM ROAD REC GRD
ST. ALBAN'S RD
LATCHMERE RD
STAUNTON RD
A310
HOLMESDALE ROAD
TROWLOCK WAY
Pav
FAIRWAYS
THAMESPOINT
Boathouse
BOCKHAMPTON RD
WYNDHAM ROAD
ST. MARK'S ROAD
THAMESIDE
STEVEN'S EYOT
BANK LANE
PARK FM RD
CHESFIELD RD
BURTON RD
KINGS ROAD
SHORTLANDS ROAD
7
LANGDON PK
Bowl Club
The Boater's Inn PH
WOODSIDE RD
CHESTNUT RD
EASTBURY RD
Clinic
YORK ROAD
CLIFTON ROAD
Family Cen
Prim Sch
BUSHY PARK ROAD
NORMANSFIELD AVENUE
Prim Sch
HAMBLE CT
Comm Cen
Pav
CANBURY GDNS
RICHMOND ROAD
KINGS RD
RICHMOND ROAD
DAGMAR RD
GLAMORGAN ROAD
Prim Sch
181
Fitness Cen
GIBBON
Superst
Coll
EAST ROAD
Prim Sch
Hall
BERESFORD RD
GLENVILLE RD
CEDARS ROAD
VICARAGE
UPPER TEDDINGTON RD

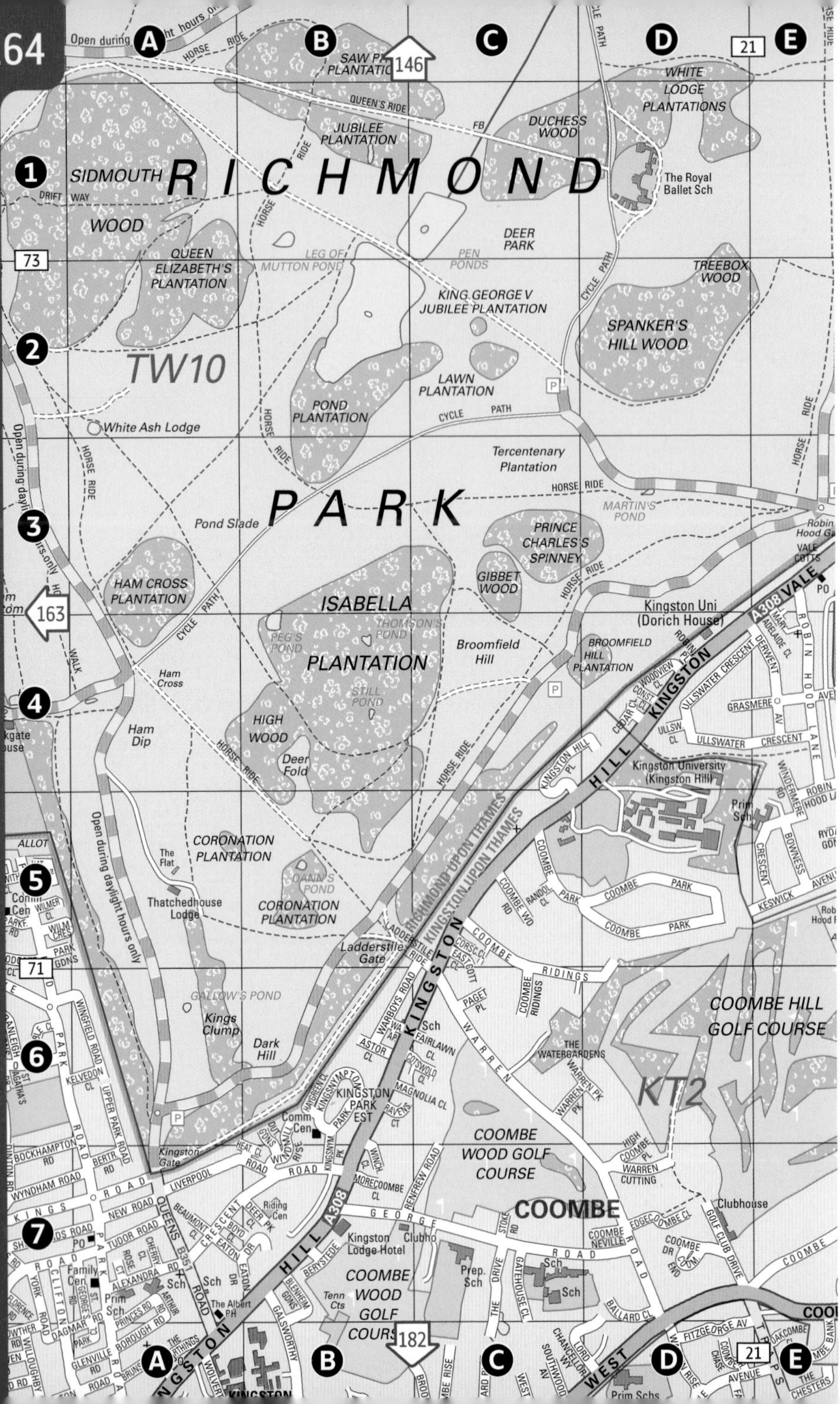
RICHMOND
PARK
TW10
KT2
SIDMOUTH
WOOD
DRIFT WAY
QUEEN ELIZABETH'S PLANTATION
SAW PIT PLANTATION
146
QUEEN'S RIDE
JUBILEE PLANTATION
HORSE RIDE
FB
DUCHESS WOOD
WHITE LODGE PLANTATIONS
The Royal Ballet Sch
21
73
DEER PARK
LEG OF MUTTON POND
PEN PONDS
KING GEORGE V JUBILEE PLANTATION
TREEBOX WOOD
SPANKER'S HILL WOOD
CYCLE PATH
LAWN PLANTATION
POND PLANTATION
White Ash Lodge
Open during daylight hours only
Tercentenary Plantation
MARTIN'S POND
Robin Hood Gate
VALE COTTS
Pond Slade
PRINCE CHARLES'S SPINNEY
GIBBET WOOD
HAM CROSS PLANTATION
163
ISABELLA PLANTATION
THOMSON'S POND
PEG'S POND
STILL POND
Broomfield Hill
BROOMFIELD HILL PLANTATION
Kingston Uni (Dorich House)
A308
KINGSTON VALE
Ham Cross
HIGH WOOD
Deer Fold
Ham Dip
WALK
CORONATION PLANTATION
DANN'S POND
The Flat
Thatchedhouse Lodge
Ladderstile Gate
GALLOW'S POND
Kings Clump
Dark Hill
Kingston Gate
KINGSTON HILL
RICHMOND UPON THAMES
KINGSTON UPON THAMES
Kingston University (Kingston Hill)
ULLSWATER CRESCENT
GRASMERE AV
ROBIN HOOD LANE
WINDERMERE RD
BOWNESS CRESCENT
KESWICK AVENUE
DERWENT RD
Prim Sch
COOMBE PARK
COOMBE RIDINGS
COOMBE WD RD
RANDOLPH CL
WARBOYS ROAD
FAIRLAWN CL
COTSWOLD CL
MAGNOLIA CL
PAGET PL
WARREN RISE
THE WATERGARDENS
WARREN PK
COOMBE HILL GOLF COURSE
COOMBE WOOD GOLF COURSE
HIGH COOMBE PL
WARREN CUTTING
COOMBE
Clubhouse
GOLF CLUB DRIVE
COOMBE LANE WEST
GEORGE ROAD
KINGSTON PARK EST
Comm Cen
Riding Cen
Kingston Lodge Hotel
Clubho
Prep. Sch
Sch
Tenn Cts
182
LIVERPOOL ROAD
QUEENS ROAD
PARK ROAD
KINGS ROAD
NEW ROAD
TUDOR ROAD
WYNDHAM ROAD
BOCKHAMPTON RD
UPPER PARK ROAD
WINGFIELD ROAD
KELVEDON CL
71
Family Cen
PO
Prim Sch
The Albert PH
ALLOT
A
B
C
D
E
1
2
3
4
5
6
7

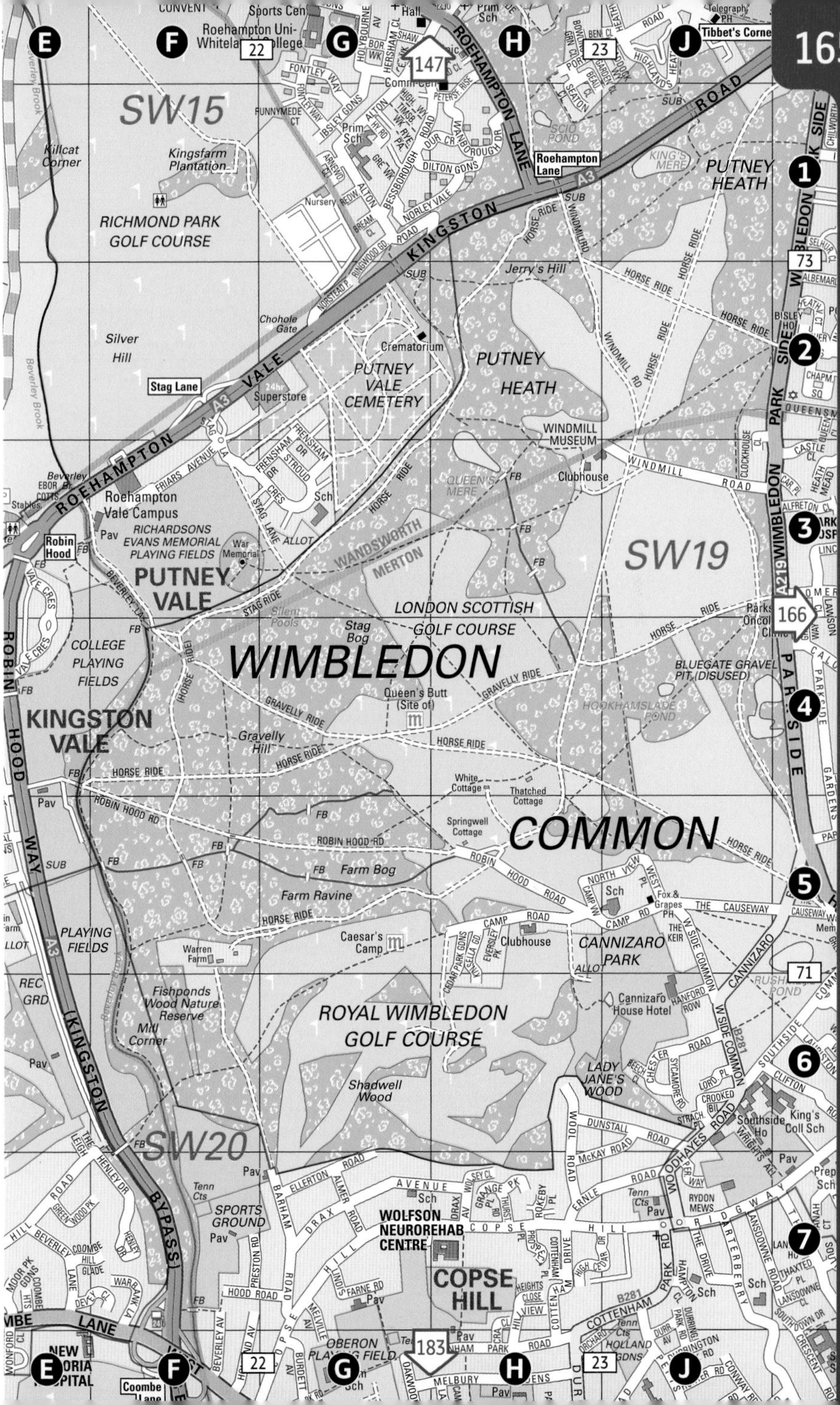
E
F
G
H
J
22
23
147
SW15
Killcat Corner
Kingsfarm Plantation
RICHMOND PARK GOLF COURSE
Roehampton Uni-Whitelands College
Sports Cen
CONVENT
Hall
Prim Sch
Tibbet's Corner
Telegraph PH
ROEHAMPTON LANE
Roehampton Lane
KINGSTON ROAD
A3
Comm Cen
FONTLEY WAY
IBSLEY GDNS
ALTON RD
DILTON GDNS
NORLEY VALE
BESSBOROUGH ROAD
DANEBURY AV
Nursery
SCIO POND
KING'S MERE
PUTNEY HEATH
1
73
Silver Hill
Chohole Gate
Crematorium
PUTNEY VALE CEMETERY
24hr Superstore
Stag Lane
A3 VALE
ROEHAMPTON
Jerry's Hill
HORSE RIDE
WINDMILL RD
PUTNEY HEATH
2
WINDMILL MUSEUM
Clubhouse
WINDMILL ROAD
QUEEN'S MERE
WIMBLEDON PARK SIDE
Beverley Brook
FRIARS AVENUE
Roehampton Vale Campus
RICHARDSONS EVANS MEMORIAL PLAYING FIELDS
War Memorial
PUTNEY VALE
Robin Hood
Stables
STAG LANE
FRENSHAM DR
Sch
WANDSWORTH
MERTON
SW19
3
A219
166
Parkside Oncology Clinic
LONDON SCOTTISH GOLF COURSE
Stag Bog
Silent Pools
STAG RIDE
COLLEGE PLAYING FIELDS
WIMBLEDON
GRAVELLY RIDE
Queen's Butt (Site of)
BLUEGATE GRAVEL PIT (DISUSED)
HOOKHAMSLADE POND
4
KINGSTON VALE
Gravelly Hill
ROBIN HOOD WAY
ROBIN HOOD RD
White Cottage
Thatched Cottage
Springwell Cottage
COMMON
5
Farm Bog
Farm Ravine
NORTH VIEW
Fox & Grapes PH
THE CAUSEWAY
CAMP ROAD
Caesar's Camp
Clubhouse
CANNIZARO PARK
PLAYING FIELDS
Warren Farm
REC GRD
71
RUSHMERE POND
Fishponds Wood Nature Reserve
Mill Corner
ROYAL WIMBLEDON GOLF COURSE
Cannizaro House Hotel
W SIDE COMMON
6
LADY JANE'S WOOD
Shadwell Wood
KINGSTON BYPASS
DUNSTALL ROAD
Southside Ho
King's Coll Sch
SW20
WOODHAYES ROAD
Tenn Cts
SPORTS GROUND
Pav
ELLERTON ROAD
DRAX AVENUE
RYDON MEWS
RIDGWAY
WOLFSON NEUROREHAB CENTRE
COPSE HILL
7
COPSE HILL
HOOD ROAD
COTTENHAM PARK RD
B281
COMBE LANE
NEW VICTORIA HOSPITAL
OBERON PLAYING FIELD
183
HOLLAND GDNS
MELBURY
Coombe Lane

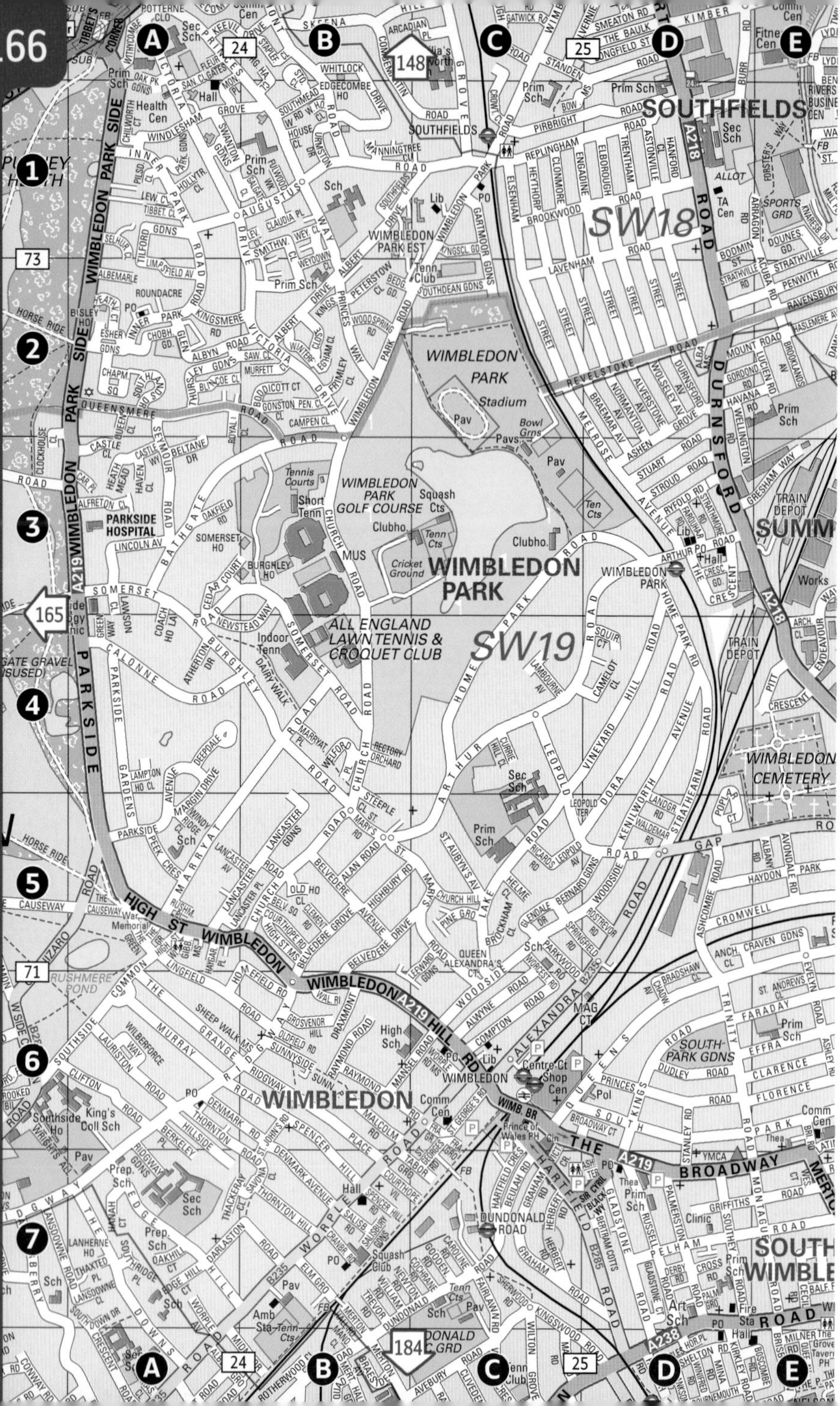
A
B
C
D
E
1
2
3
4
5
6
7
24
25
73
71
148
165
184
SOUTHFIELDS
SW18
SW19
WIMBLEDON PARK
WIMBLEDON
SOUTH WIMBLE
SUMM
PUTNEY HEATH
WIMBLEDON PARK SIDE
PARKSIDE
PARKSIDE HOSPITAL
QUEENSMERE ROAD
INNER PARK ROAD
AUGUSTUS ROAD
VICTORIA DRIVE
WIMBLEDON PARK ROAD
ARTHUR ROAD
HOME PARK ROAD
CHURCH ROAD
SOMERSET ROAD
BURGHLEY ROAD
CALONNE ROAD
MARRYAT ROAD
REVELSTOKE ROAD
DURNSFORD ROAD
MELROSE AVENUE
HIGH ST WIMBLEDON
WIMBLEDON HILL RD
THE BROADWAY
ALEXANDRA RD
QUEENS ROAD
WORPLE ROAD
RIDGWAY
SOUTHSIDE COMMON
CAUSEWAY
RUSHMERE POND
WIMBLEDON PARK GOLF COURSE
ALL ENGLAND LAWN TENNIS & CROQUET CLUB
WIMBLEDON CEMETERY
Stadium
Cricket Ground
Train Depot
Works
King's Coll Sch
Southside Ho
Centre Ct Shop Cen
DUNDONALD ROAD
DONALD REC GRD
A218
A219
A238
B235
B285

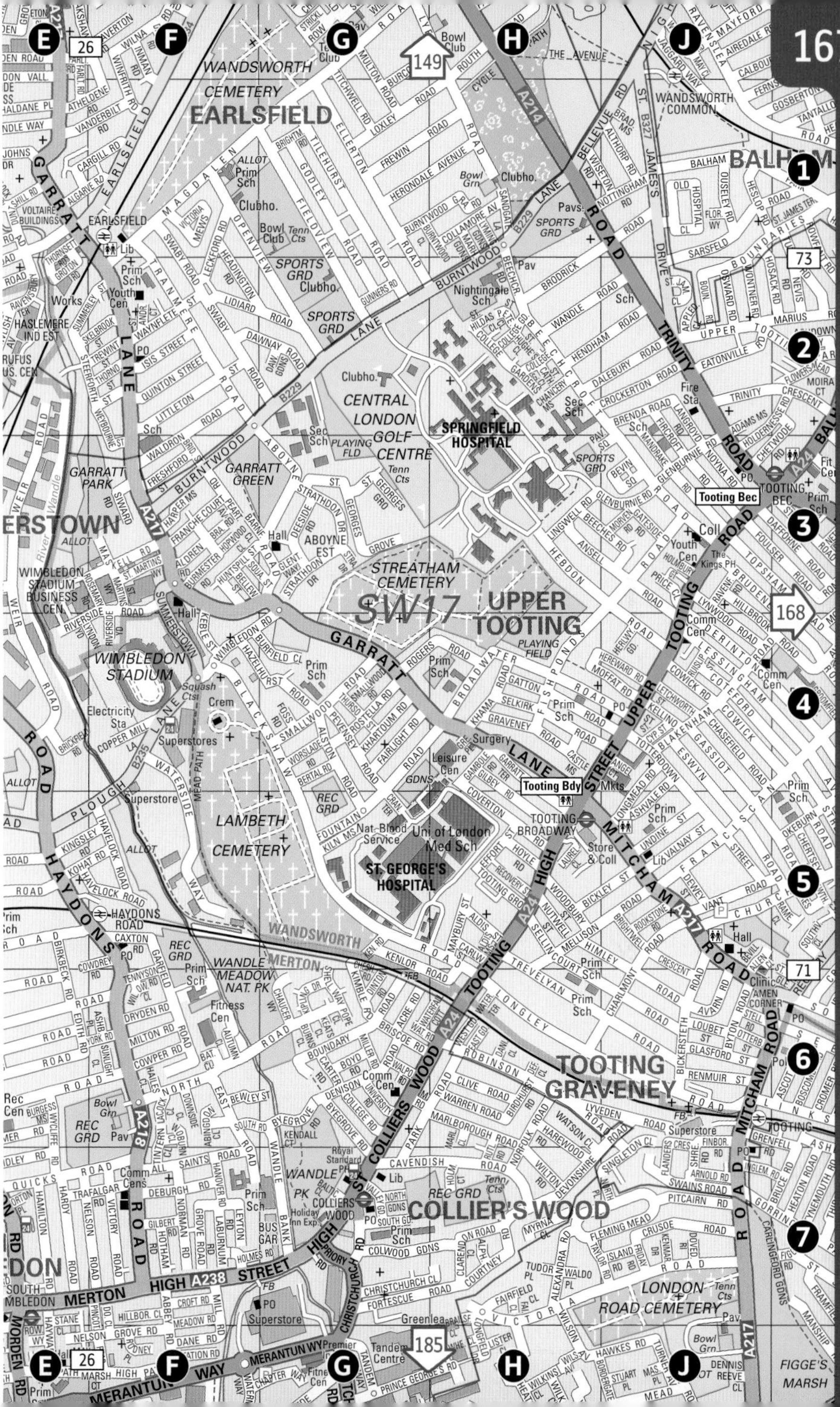
EARLSFIELD
WANDSWORTH CEMETERY
WANDSWORTH COMMON
BALHAM
CENTRAL LONDON GOLF CENTRE
SPRINGFIELD HOSPITAL
GARRATT GREEN
GARRATT PARK
STREATHAM CEMETERY
SW17
UPPER TOOTING
WIMBLEDON STADIUM
WIMBLEDON STADIUM BUSINESS CEN.
LAMBETH CEMETERY
ST. GEORGE'S HOSPITAL
Uni of London Med Sch
Tooting Bec
Tooting Bdy
TOOTING BROADWAY
TOOTING GRAVENEY
WANDLE MEADOW NAT. PK
WANDLE PK
COLLIER'S WOOD
LONDON ROAD CEMETERY
FIGGE'S MARSH
HAYDONS ROAD
HASLEMERE IND EST
GARRATT LANE
TRINITY ROAD
UPPER TOOTING ROAD
TOOTING HIGH STREET
MITCHAM ROAD
COLLIERS WOOD HIGH STREET
MERTON HIGH STREET
MERANTUN WAY
149
168
185
26
71
73
E
F
G
H
J
1
2
3
4
5
6
7

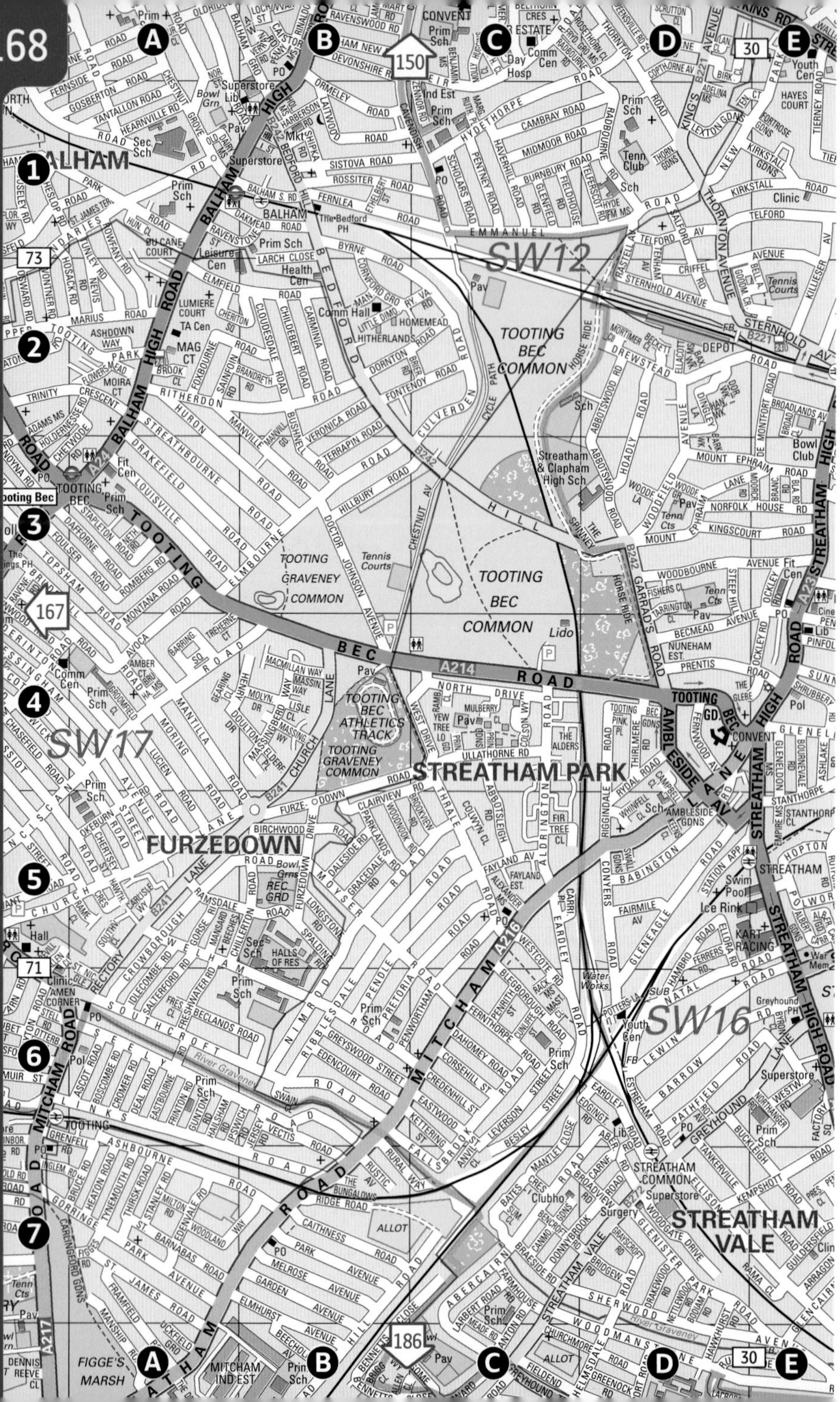

A
B
C
D
E
1
2
3
4
5
6
7
150
167
186
73
71
30
BALHAM
SW12
SW17
SW16
TOOTING BEC COMMON
TOOTING GRAVENEY COMMON
TOOTING BEC ATHLETICS TRACK
STREATHAM PARK
FURZEDOWN
STREATHAM VALE
STREATHAM COMMON
STREATHAM
TOOTING
TOOTING BEC
Tooting Bec
BALHAM HIGH ROAD
TOOTING BEC ROAD
BEC ROAD
A214
A24
A23
A216
A217
B242
B241
B221
B272
MITCHAM ROAD
MITCHAM LANE
STREATHAM HIGH ROAD
BEDFORD HILL
CULVERDEN ROAD
GARRAD'S ROAD
AMBLESIDE AV
CHURCH LANE
ELMBOURNE ROAD
DOCTOR JOHNSON AVENUE
CHESTNUT AV
CYCLE PATH
HORSE RIDE
THORNTON AVENUE
KING'S AVENUE
EMMANUEL ROAD
STERNHOLD AVENUE
TELFORD AV
DREWSTEAD ROAD
MOUNT EPHRAIM ROAD
KINGSCOURT ROAD
WOODBOURNE AVENUE
BECMEAD AVENUE
NUNEHAM EST.
PRENTIS ROAD
NORTH DRIVE
ULLATHORNE RD
HILLBURY ROAD
TERRAPIN ROAD
VERONICA ROAD
FONTENOY ROAD
DORNTON ROAD
HITHERLANDS
HOMEMEAD
RITHERDON ROAD
STREATHBOURNE ROAD
DRAKEFIELD ROAD
HURON ROAD
LOUISVILLE ROAD
MANVILLE ROAD
BUSHNELL ROAD
TOOTING BEC ROAD
MANTILLA ROAD
MORING ROAD
AVOCA ROAD
MONTANA ROAD
ROMBERG RD
TOPSHAM ROAD
FOULSER ROAD
DAFFORNE ROAD
CHASEFIELD ROAD
LUCIEN ROAD
FURZEDOWN ROAD
FURZEDOWN DRIVE
BIRCHWOOD ROAD
MOYSER ROAD
ROCHESTER WAY
LONGSTONE RD
SPALDING RD
ROCHESTER
RECTORY LANE
CROWBOROUGH ROAD
SOUTHCROFT ROAD
SEELY ROAD
LINKS ROAD
RIBBLESDALE ROAD
GREYSWOOD STREET
EDENCOURT ROAD
PENWORTHAM ROAD
PRETORIA ROAD
CORSEHILL ST
DAHOMEY ROAD
FERNTHORPE ROAD
BLEGBOROUGH ROAD
WESTCOTE RD
EARDLEY ROAD
FAYLAND AV
ABBOTSLEIGH RD
COLWYN CL
THRALE ROAD
CONVERS ROAD
GLENEAGLE ROAD
BABINGTON ROAD
FAIRMILE AV
NATAL ROAD
LEWIN ROAD
BARROW ROAD
PATHFIELD ROAD
GREYHOUND LANE
BUCKLEIGH
KEMPSHOTT ROAD
SHERWOOD AVENUE
WOODMANSTERNE
ESTREHAM ROAD
GLENISTER PARK ROAD
WOODGATE DRIVE
STREATHAM VALE
ASHBOURNE ROAD
FALLSBROOK ROAD
RURAL WAY
RIDGE ROAD
PARK AVENUE
CAITHNESS ROAD
MELROSE AVENUE
GARDEN AVENUE
ELMHURST AVENUE
ST. JAMES ROAD
ST. BARNABAS ROAD
GORRINGE PARK AVENUE
FIGGE'S MARSH
MITCHAM IND EST
River Graveney
Lido
Pav
Tennis Courts
REC GRD
ALLOT
Streatham & Clapham High Sch
CONVENT
Superstore
Swim Pool
Ice Rink
KART RACING
Water Works
Greyhound PH
The Bedford PH
Prim Sch
Sec Sch
HALLS OF RES
Health Cen
Comm Hall
Leisure Cen
Fit Cen
TA Cen
Bowl Club
Clinic
DEPOT
Day Hosp
Comm Cen
Youth Cen
HAYES COURT
Hall
AMEN CORNER
THE BUNGALOWS
Surgery
Clubho
Lib
PO
Pol
Mkt

E
F
G
H
J
31
32
151
STREATHAM HILL
SE21
TULSE HILL
Knight's Hill
ALLOT
SPORTS GRD
Tenn Cts
A199
1
2
3
4
5
6
7
73
170
71
187
CHRISTCHURCH ROAD
A205
A23
STREATHAM HILL
PULLMAN CT
COV RES
BUS GAR
PALACE ROAD ESTATE
ST. MARTINS EST
PALACE ROAD
Tulse Hill
TULSE HILL
THURLOW PARK ROAD
NORWOOD ROAD
A215
SW2
WYATT PARK ROAD
DOWNTON AVENUE
CRICKLADE AVENUE
BARCOMBE AVENUE
AMESBURY AVENUE
STREATHAM HILL
Bowl Grn
Coll
LEIGHAM VALE
HILLSIDE GDNS
Tenn Cts
KINGSMEAD ROAD
LANERCOST ROAD
CAMERON PL
LEIGHAM COURT ROAD
KNOLLYS ROAD
ROYAL CIRCUS
Superstore
YORK HILL EST
Fire Sta
LANCASTER AVENUE
IDMISTON ROAD
CHATSWORTH WAY
CHESTNUT ROAD
ROBSON ROAD
LANSDOWNE HILL
WEST NORWOOD CEMETERY
Crem
WEST NORWOOD
PARK HALL TRADING EST
AUCKLAND HILL
NORWOOD HIGH ST
KNIGHTS HILL
ERNEST AV
BUS GAR
THE WINDSOR CEN
ST. CLOUD ROAD
GIPSY ROAD
SACKVILLE ESTATE
Health Cen.
STREATHAM
WELLFIELD ROAD
Leigham Arms PH
SE27
CANTERBURY GROVE
CASEWICK ROAD
THORNLAW ROAD
ST. JULIAN'S FARM ROAD
CHAPEL ROAD
ROTHSCHILD ST
LINTON GROVE
Comm Cen
Prim Sch
WOODVALE EST
EYLEWOOD ROAD
NORWOOD PARK ROAD
SPORTS GRD
REC GRD
DASSETT ROAD
FURNEAUX AV
HOLDERNESS WY
VALLEYFIELD ROAD
OAKDALE ROAD
RUSSELL'S FOOTPATH
TRUSLOVE ROAD
LAKEVIEW ROAD
STREATHAM COMMON NORTH
A214
CROWN LANE
CROWN DALE
CENTRAL HILL
STREATHAM COMMON
THE ROOKERY
NORWOOD GROVE RECREATION GROUND
Social Cen
Bowling Green
Tennis Courts
NORWOOD NEW TOWN
CONVENT WOOD
BEULAH HILL
CROWN POND
SE19
PLAYING FIELD
BIGGIN WOOD
ALLOT
Pav
Tenn Cts
BIGGIN WAY
NORBURY HILL
UPPER NORWOOD
HERMITAGE
EVERSLEY
STREATHAM HIGH RD
GREEN LANE
B273
NORBURY PARK
NORBURY
ST. OSWALD'S ROAD
WADDINGTON WAY
DALE PARK
Sec Sch

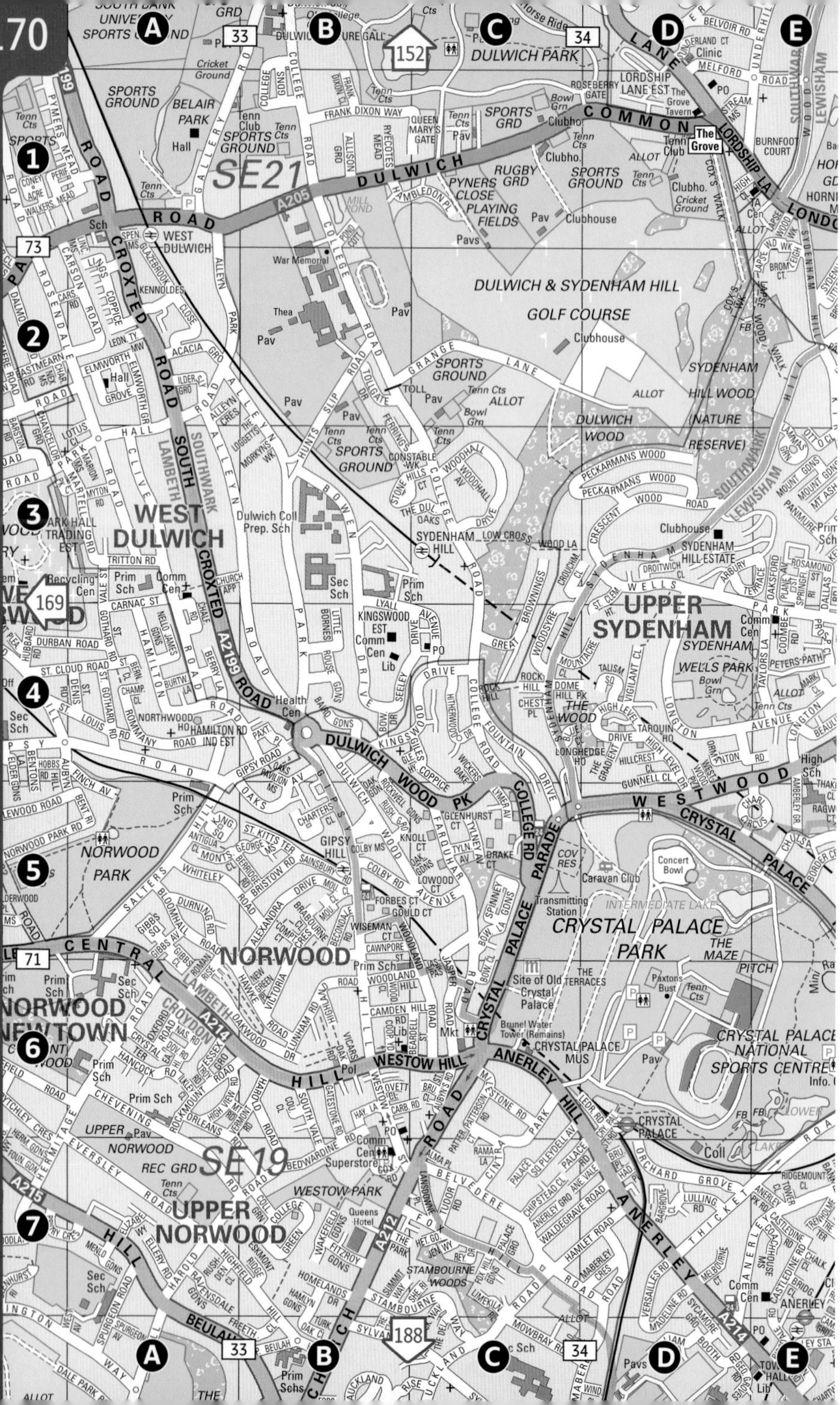
A
B
C
D
E
1
2
3
4
5
6
7
33
34
152
169
188
73
71
SE21
SE19
DULWICH PARK
DULWICH COMMON
DULWICH & SYDENHAM HILL
GOLF COURSE
BELAIR PARK
WEST DULWICH
DULWICH WOOD
SYDENHAM HILL WOOD (NATURE RESERVE)
UPPER SYDENHAM
SYDENHAM WELLS PARK
NORWOOD PARK
NORWOOD
NORWOOD NEW TOWN
UPPER NORWOOD
WESTOW PARK
CRYSTAL PALACE PARK
CRYSTAL PALACE NATIONAL SPORTS CENTRE
CRYSTAL PALACE
ANERLEY
GIPSY HILL
SYDENHAM HILL
LORDSHIP LANE EST
PYNERS CLOSE PLAYING FIELDS
SPORTS GROUND
SPORTS GRD
RUGBY GRD
Cricket Ground
War Memorial
Dulwich Coll Prep. Sch
KINGSWOOD EST
SYDENHAM HILL ESTATE
CROXTED ROAD
SOUTH CROXTED ROAD
DULWICH WOOD PK
COLLEGE RD
CRYSTAL PALACE PARADE
WESTWOOD
CRYSTAL PALACE PARADE
CENTRAL HILL
WESTOW HILL
ANERLEY HILL
ANERLEY ROAD
CHURCH ROAD
BEULAH HILL
GIPSY ROAD
NORWOOD ROAD
HALL ROAD
LORDSHIP LA
COX'S WALK
GRANGE LANE
SYDENHAM HILL
LONGTON AVENUE
Caravan Club
Transmitting Station
Concert Bowl
THE MAZE
INTERMEDIATE LAKE
Site of Old Crystal Palace
Brunel Water Tower (Remains)
CRYSTAL PALACE MUS
STAMBOURNE WOODS
REC GRD
Queens Hotel
Superstore
A205
A2199
A214
A212
A215

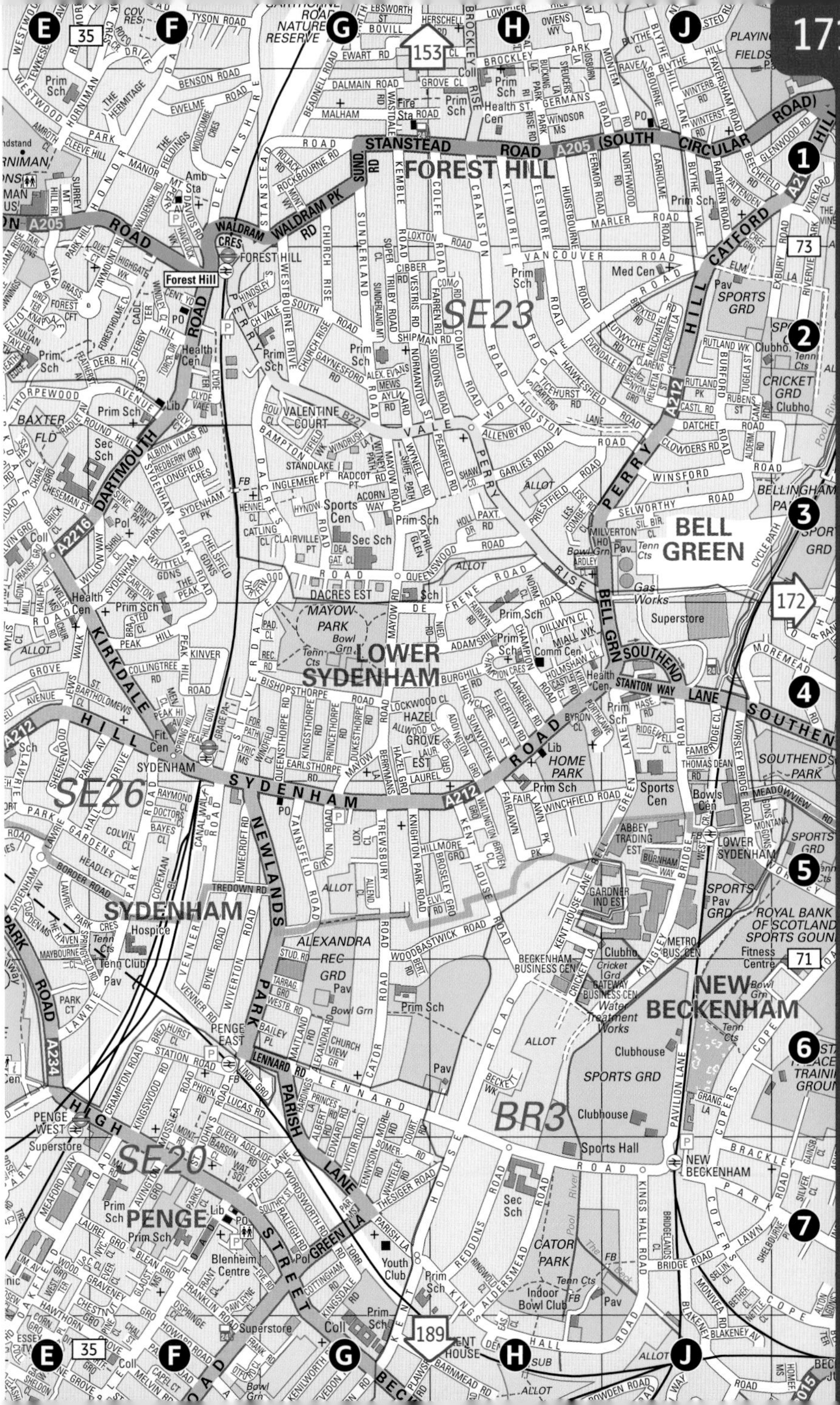
FOREST HILL
SE23
BELL GREEN
LOWER SYDENHAM
SYDENHAM
SE26
NEW BECKENHAM
BR3
PENGE
SE20
MAYOW PARK
ALEXANDRA REC GRD
CATOR PARK
HOME PARK
SOUTHEND PARK
STANSTEAD ROAD A205 (SOUTH CIRCULAR ROAD)
WALDRAM PK RD
DARTMOUTH ROAD
KIRKDALE
SYDENHAM ROAD A212
PERRY HILL A212
PERRY RISE
SOUTHEND LANE
NEWLANDS PARK
PARISH LANE
LENNARD ROAD
HIGH STREET
KENT HOUSE ROAD
BELL GRN
VALENTINE COURT
DACRES EST
HAZEL GROVE EST
BECKENHAM BUSINESS CEN
ABBEY TRADING EST
GARDNER IND EST
GATEWAY BUSINESS CEN
METRO BUS CEN
ROYAL BANK OF SCOTLAND SPORTS GOUND
Forest Hill
FOREST HILL
SYDENHAM
PENGE EAST
PENGE WEST
LOWER SYDENHAM
NEW BECKENHAM
Blenheim Centre
Superstore
Gas Works
153
172
189
73
71
35
E
F
G
H
J
1
2
3
4
5
6
7

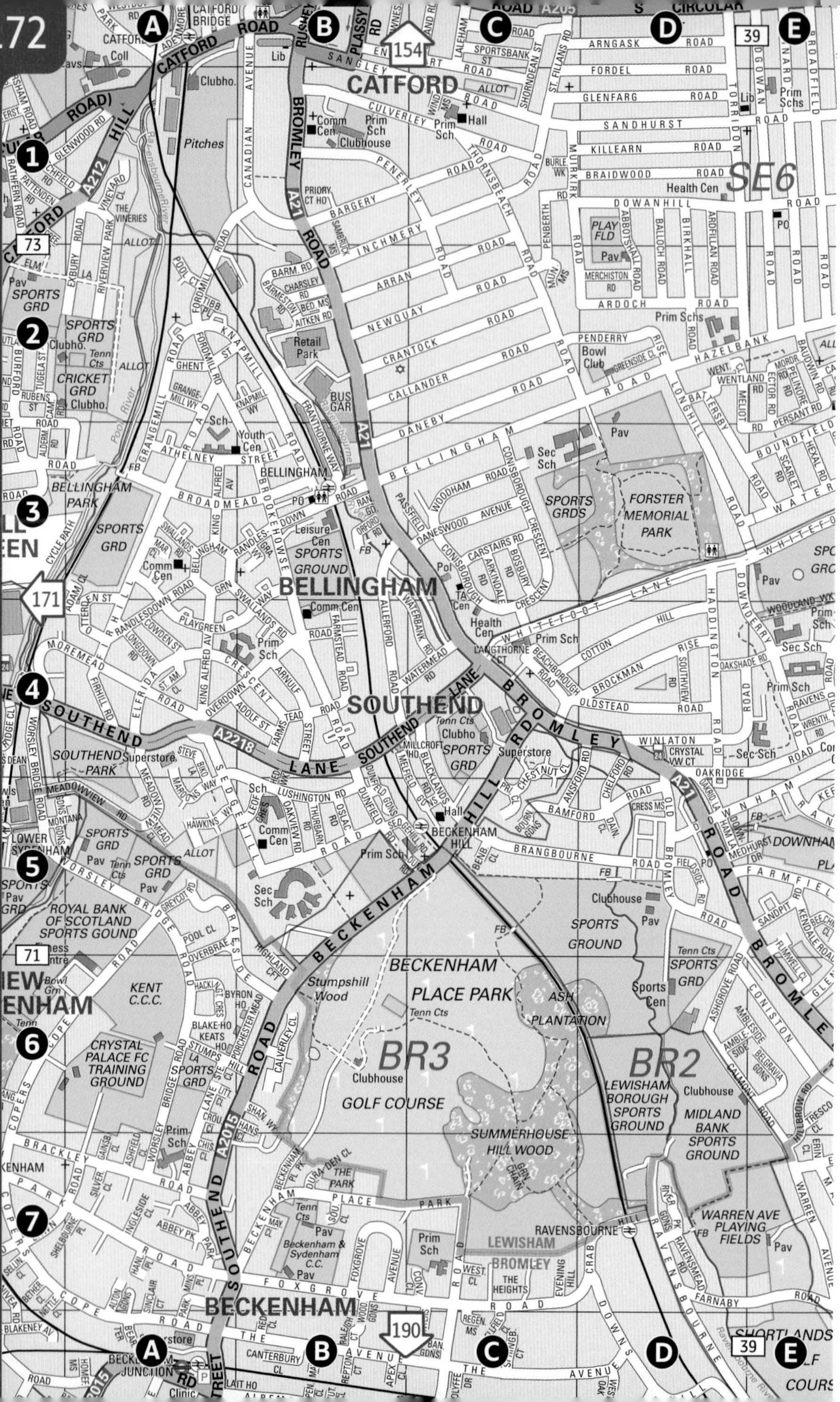
A
B
C
D
E
1
2
3
4
5
6
7
154
171
190
73
71
39
CATFORD
SE6
BELLINGHAM
SOUTHEND
BECKENHAM
BR3
BR2
CATFORD BRIDGE
CATFORD ROAD
CATFORD HILL
S CIRCULAR
ROAD A205
A212
A21
A2218
A2015
BROMLEY ROAD
SOUTHEND LANE
BECKENHAM HILL
SOUTHEND ROAD
ARNGASK ROAD
FORDEL ROAD
GLENFARG ROAD
SANDHURST ROAD
KILLEARN ROAD
BRAIDWOOD ROAD
DOWANHILL ROAD
ARDOCH ROAD
HAZELBANK ROAD
CULVERLEY ROAD
PENERLEY ROAD
BARGERY ROAD
INCHMERY ROAD
ARRAN ROAD
NEWQUAY ROAD
CRANTOCK ROAD
CALLANDER ROAD
DANEBY ROAD
BELLINGHAM ROAD
WHITEFOOT LANE
BROADMEAD
ATHELNEY STREET
RANDLESDOWN ROAD
MOREMEAD ROAD
BROMLEY HILL
FORSTER MEMORIAL PARK
SPORTS GRDS
BELLINGHAM PARK
SOUTHEND PARK
BECKENHAM PLACE PARK
GOLF COURSE
ASH PLANTATION
SUMMERHOUSE HILL WOOD
Stumpshill Wood
LEWISHAM BOROUGH SPORTS GROUND
MIDLAND BANK SPORTS GROUND
WARREN AVE PLAYING FIELDS
ROYAL BANK OF SCOTLAND SPORTS GOUND
KENT C.C.C.
CRYSTAL PALACE FC TRAINING GROUND
Beckenham & Sydenham C.C.
LOWER SYDENHAM
RAVENSBOURNE
BECKENHAM HILL
BELLINGHAM
LEWISHAM
BROMLEY
BECKENHAM PLACE
FOXGROVE ROAD
COPERS COPE ROAD
BRACKLEY ROAD
PARK ROAD
THE AVENUE
SHORTLANDS GOLF COURSE
FARNABY ROAD
RAVENSBOURNE AVENUE
WORSLEY BRIDGE ROAD
MEADOWVIEW ROAD
CONISTON ROAD
DOWNHAM WAY
Superstore
Sec Sch
Prim Sch
Comm Cen
Leisure Cen
Health Cen
Retail Park
BUS GAR
Clubhouse
Pav

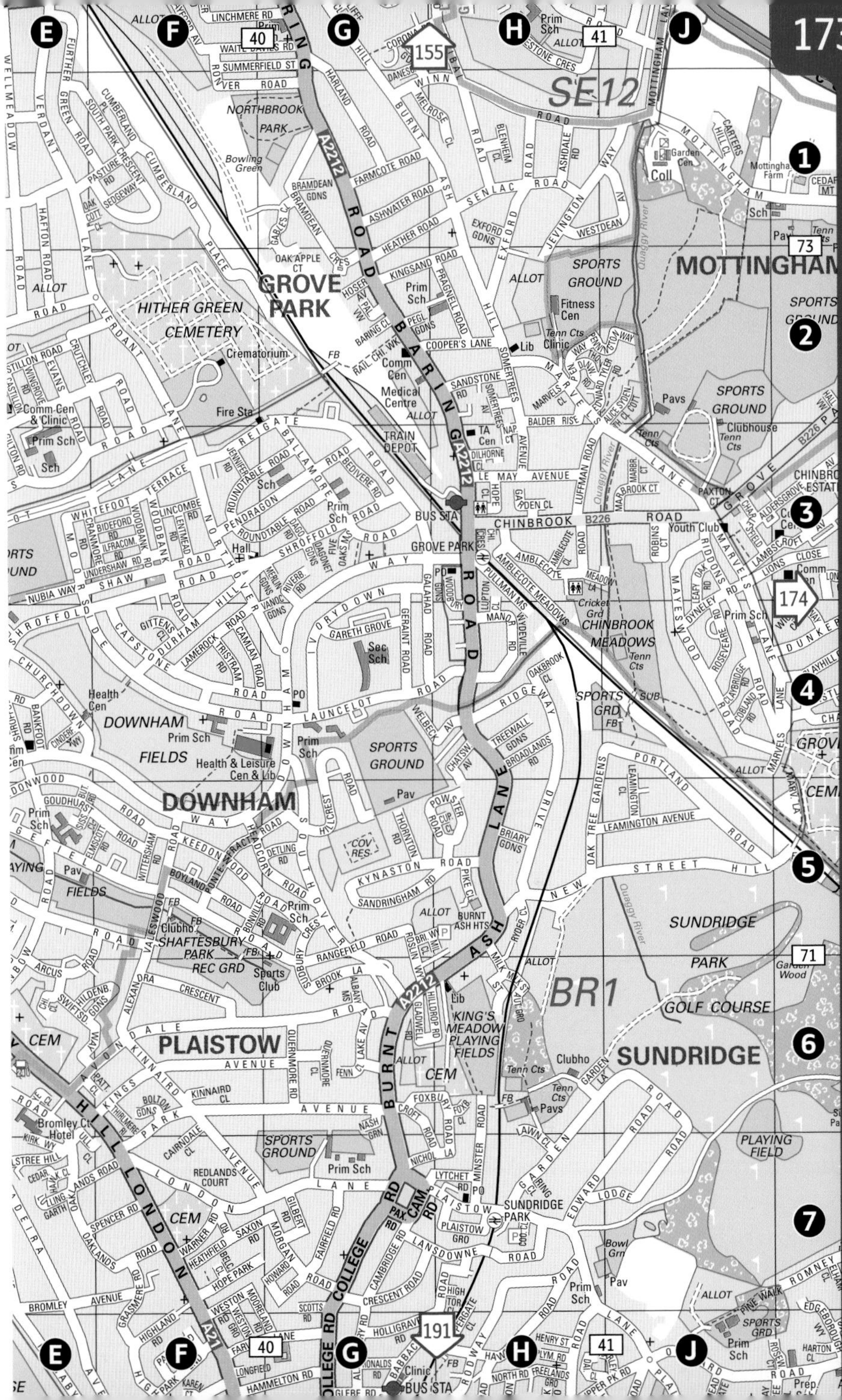
155
SE12
GROVE PARK
HITHER GREEN CEMETERY
Crematorium
NORTHBROOK PARK
Bowling Green
MOTTINGHAM
SPORTS GROUND
Fitness Cen
TRAIN DEPOT
BUS STA
GROVE PARK
CHINBROOK MEADOWS
174
DOWNHAM FIELDS
DOWNHAM
Health & Leisure Cen & Lib
SHAFTESBURY PARK REC GRD
BR1
SUNDRIDGE PARK GOLF COURSE
SUNDRIDGE
KING'S MEADOW PLAYING FIELDS
PLAISTOW
SUNDRIDGE PARK
Bromley Ct Hotel
CEM
PLAYING FIELD
191
40
41
73
71
A2212
A21
B226
E
F
G
H
J
1
2
3
4
5
6
7

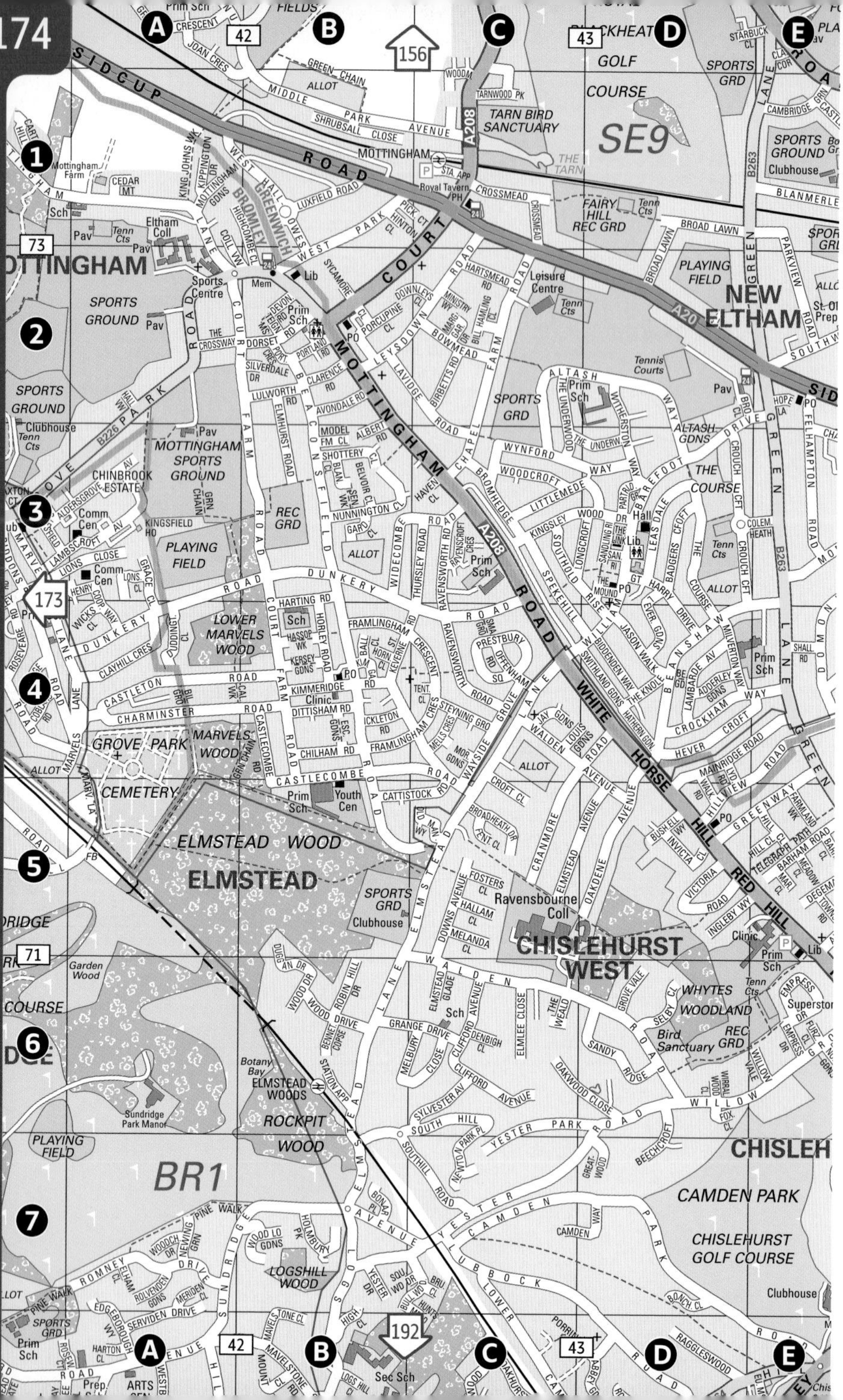

A
B
C
D
E
1
2
3
4
5
6
7
42
43
156
173
192
73
71
SIDCUP ROAD
MOTTINGHAM
NEW ELTHAM
SE9
BR1
BLACKHEATH GOLF COURSE
TARN BIRD SANCTUARY
THE TARN
FAIRY HILL REC GRD
PLAYING FIELD
SPORTS GROUND
SPORTS GRD
Clubhouse
Eltham Coll
Sports Centre
Leisure Centre
Mottingham Farm
MOTTINGHAM SPORTS GROUND
CHINBROOK ESTATE
LOWER MARVELS WOOD
MARVELS WOOD
GROVE PARK CEMETERY
ELMSTEAD WOOD
ELMSTEAD
ELMSTEAD WOODS
ROCKPIT WOOD
Botany Bay
Garden Wood
Sundridge Park Manor
LOGSHILL WOOD
Ravensbourne Coll
CHISLEHURST WEST
WHYTES WOODLAND
Bird Sanctuary
REC GRD
CAMDEN PARK
CHISLEHURST GOLF COURSE
COURT ROAD
MOTTINGHAM ROAD
WHITE HORSE HILL
RED HILL
DUNKERY ROAD
CASTLECOMBE ROAD
ELMSTEAD LANE
ELMSTEAD AVENUE
WALDEN ROAD
WILLOW GROVE
YESTER ROAD
YESTER PARK
SOUTHILL ROAD
LOWER CAMDEN
CAMDEN PARK ROAD
MIDDLE PARK AVENUE
WEST PARK
BEACONSFIELD ROAD
FARM ROAD
CHAPEL FARM ROAD
GREEN LANE
BEAUMONT
SUNDRIDGE AVENUE
A208
A20
B263
B226

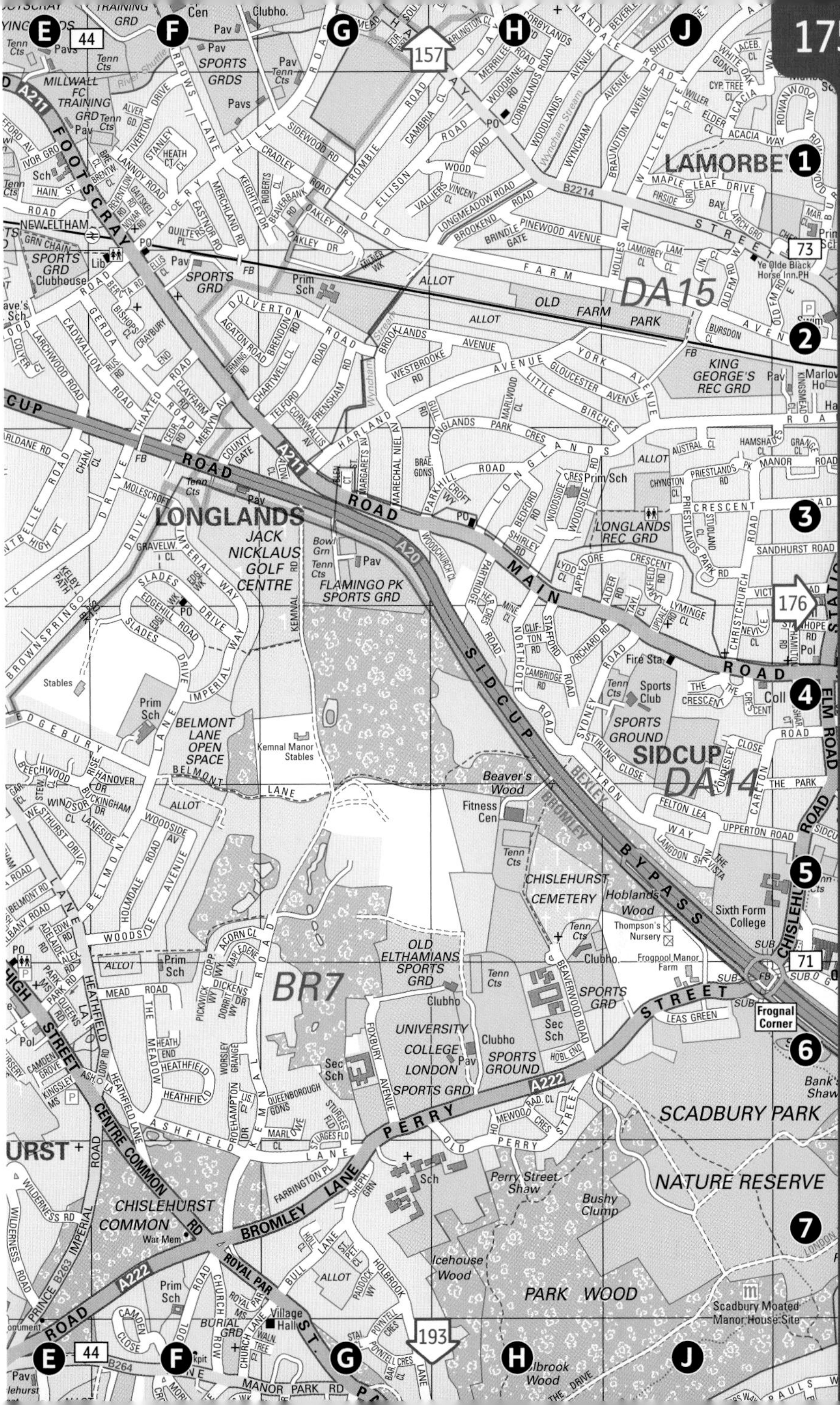
E
F
G
H
J
44
157
MILLWALL FC TRAINING GRD
SPORTS GRDS
FOOTSCRAY
A211
NEW ELTHAM
SPORTS GRD
Clubhouse
LAMORBEY
1
B2214
MAPLE LEAF DRIVE
PINEWOOD AVENUE
LONGMEADOW ROAD
73
Ye Olde Black Horse Inn.PH
DA15
OLD FARM PARK
ALLOT
2
KING GEORGE'S REC GRD
Marlow Ho
DULVERTON ROAD
WESTBROOKE RD
GLOUCESTER AVENUE
YORK AVENUE
LITTLE BIRCHES
HARLAND AV
LONGLANDS PARK CRES
LONGLANDS
LONGLANDS REC GRD
3
SIDCUP ROAD
A20
MAIN ROAD
JACK NICKLAUS GOLF CENTRE
FLAMINGO PK SPORTS GRD
176
4
SIDCUP
DA14
SPORTS GROUND
Sports Club
Fire Sta
ELM ROAD
BELMONT LANE OPEN SPACE
Kemnal Manor Stables
Stables
Prim Sch
Beaver's Wood
Fitness Cen
CHISLEHURST CEMETERY
Hoblands Wood
Thompson's Nursery
SIDCUP BYPASS
BEXLEY
BROMLEY
5
Sixth Form College
71
Frogpool Manor Farm
Frognal Corner
6
Bank's Shaw
OLD ELTHAMIANS SPORTS GRD
BR7
UNIVERSITY COLLEGE LONDON SPORTS GRD
SPORTS GROUND
SPORTS GRD
A222
PERRY STREET
SCADBURY PARK
NATURE RESERVE
Perry Street Shaw
Bushy Clump
7
Icehouse Wood
PARK WOOD
Scadbury Moated Manor House Site
URST
CHISLEHURST COMMON
War Mem
BROMLEY LANE
ROYAL PAR
Village Hall
BURIAL GRD
193
HIGH STREET
CENTRE COMMON RD
ROAD
MANOR PARK RD
Holbrook Wood

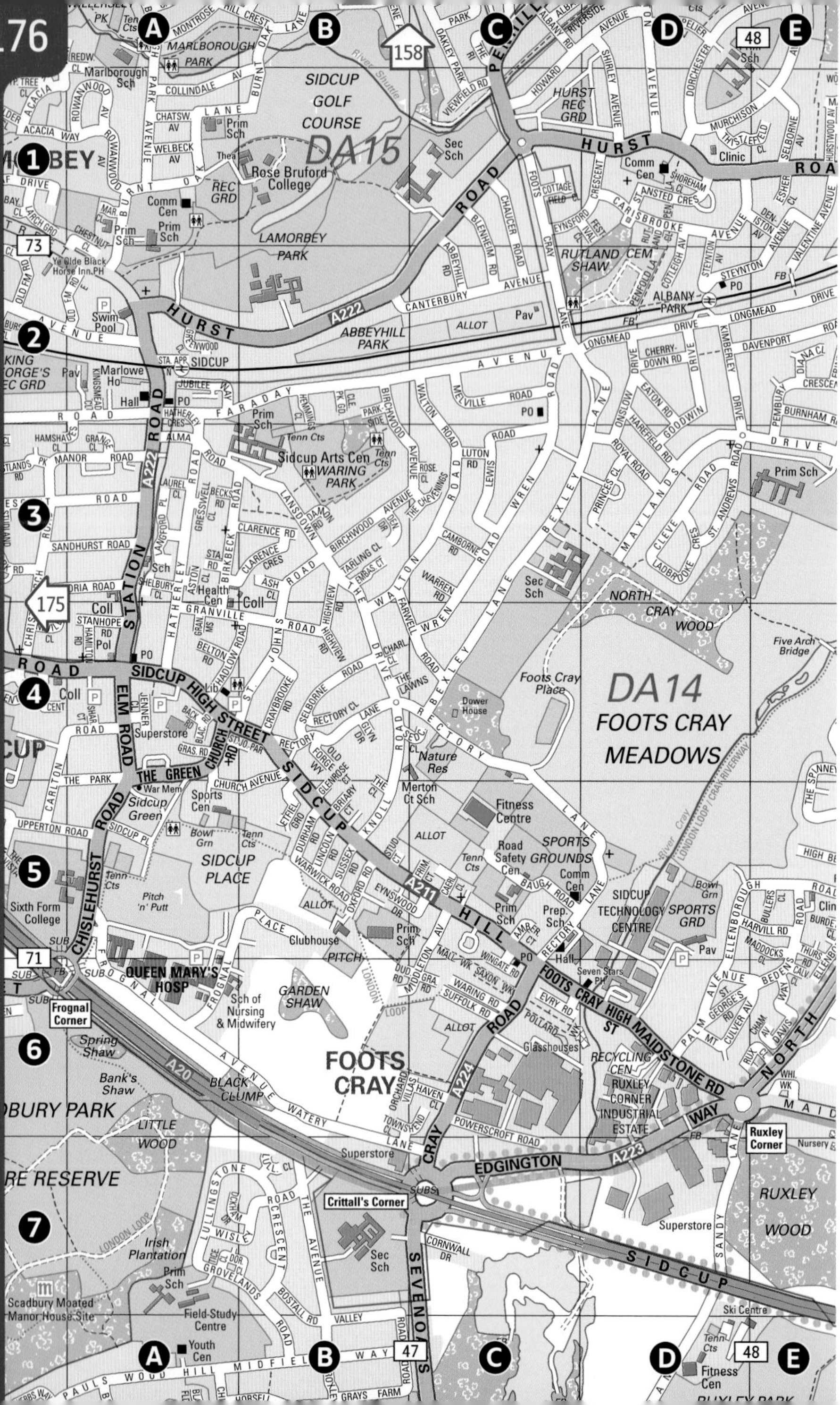
A
B
C
D
E
1
2
3
4
5
6
7
158
175
73
71
47
48
SIDCUP GOLF COURSE
DA15
DA14
FOOTS CRAY MEADOWS
FOOTS CRAY
LAMORBEY PARK
ABBEYHILL PARK
Rose Bruford College
Marlborough Sch
MARLBOROUGH PARK
REC GRD
HURST REC GRD
RUTLAND SHAW
CEM
ALBANY PARK
SIDCUP
Sidcup Arts Cen
WARING PARK
NORTH CRAY WOOD
Five Arch Bridge
Foots Cray Place
Dower House
Nature Res
Merton Ct Sch
Fitness Centre
SPORTS GROUNDS
Road Safety Cen
Comm Cen
SIDCUP TECHNOLOGY CENTRE
SPORTS GRD
Prep. Sch
Seven Stars PH
RECYCLING CEN
RUXLEY CORNER INDUSTRIAL ESTATE
Ruxley Corner
RUXLEY WOOD
Superstore
Ski Centre
Fitness Cen
Sidcup Green
SIDCUP PLACE
Pitch 'n' Putt
Sixth Form College
QUEEN MARY'S HOSP
Sch of Nursing & Midwifery
Frognal Corner
Spring Shaw
Bank's Shaw
LITTLE WOOD
GARDEN SHAW
BLACK CLUMP
Irish Plantation
Scadbury Moated Manor House Site
Field-Study Centre
Youth Cen
Crittall's Corner
Ye Olde Black Horse Inn PH
Swim Pool
Marlowe Ho
HURST ROAD
A222
STATION ROAD
SIDCUP HIGH STREET
ELM ROAD
THE GREEN
CHURCH AVENUE
CHISLEHURST ROAD
SIDCUP HILL
A211
FOOTS CRAY HIGH ST
MAIDSTONE RD
NORTH CRAY ROAD
EDGINGTON WAY
A223
A224
A20
SIDCUP BYPASS
SEVENOAKS ROAD
FROGNAL AVENUE
WATERY LANE
POWERSCROFT ROAD
CRAY ROAD
BEXLEY LANE
RECTORY LANE
FARADAY AVENUE
LONGMEAD DRIVE
KIMBERLEY DRIVE
MAYLANDS DRIVE
BURNT OAK LANE
ACACIA WAY
MIDFIELD WAY
SANDY LANE
LONDON LOOP
LONDON LOOP / CRAY RIVERWAY
River Cray
River Shuttle

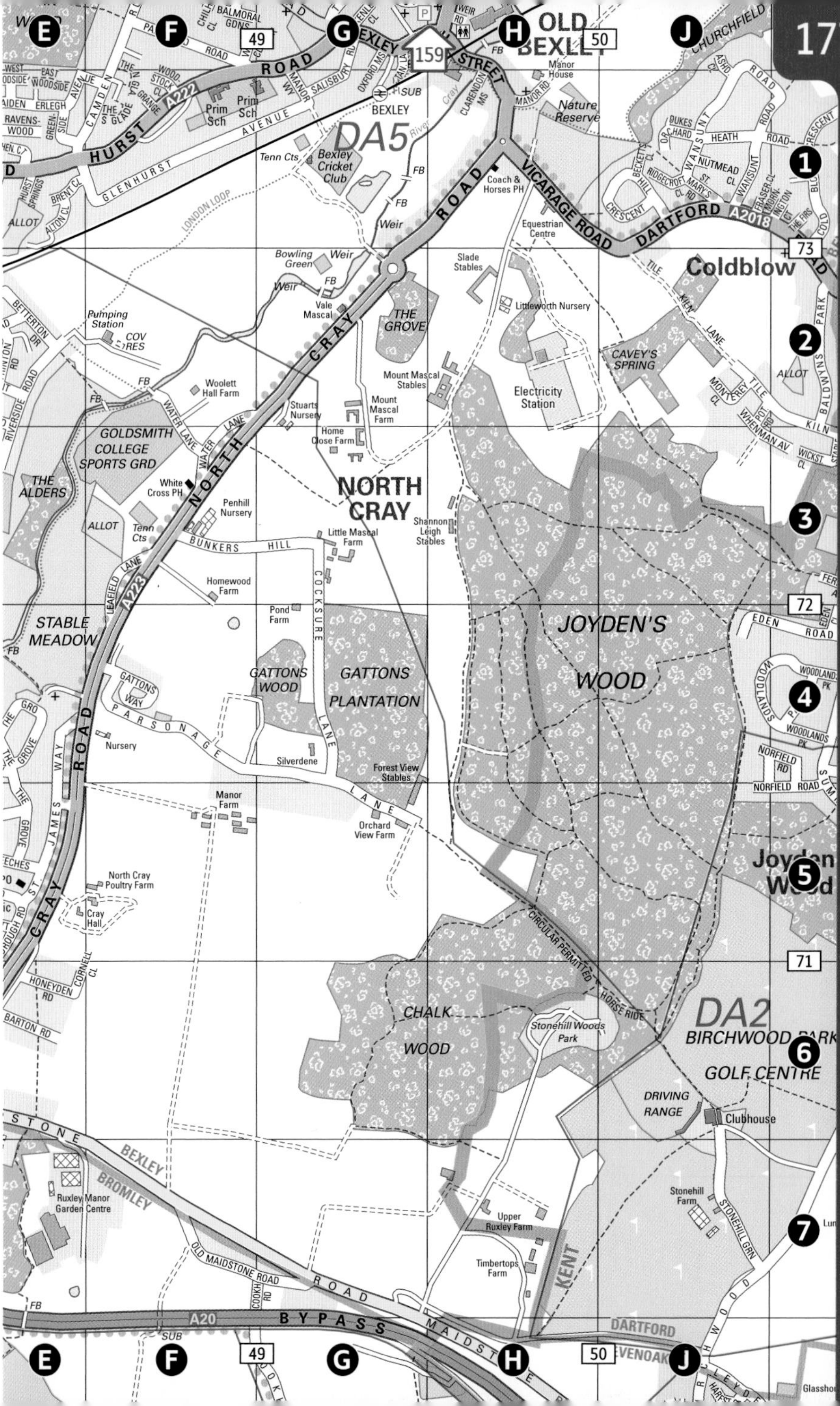
E
F
G
H
J
49
50
159
OLD BEXLEY
BEXLEY
DA5
HURST ROAD
A222
BEXLEY HIGH STREET
Prim Sch
Prim Sch
AVENUE
GLENHURST
BALMORAL GDNS
SALISBURY
MANOR WY
OXFORD MS
SUB
Tenn Cts
Bexley Cricket Club
River Cray
FB
Weir
LONDON LOOP
CLARENDON MS
MANOR RD
Manor House
Nature Reserve
CHURCHFIELD
HEATH ROAD
DUKES ORCHARD
WANSUNT
NUTMEAD CL
RIDGECROFT CL
MARY'S RD
BECKETTS CL
HILL CRESCENT
DARTFORD A2018
Coach & Horses PH
VICARAGE ROAD
Equestrian Centre
Coldblow
73
1
2
3
4
5
6
7
Bowling Green
Slade Stables
TILE KILN LANE
Littleworth Nursery
CAVEY'S SPRING
MONTREY CL
WHENMAN AV
WICKST
BALDWYNS PARK
ALLOT
Vale Mascal
THE GROVE
NORTH CRAY ROAD
Pumping Station
COV RES
BETTERTON DR
RIVERSIDE ROAD
Woolett Hall Farm
Mount Mascal Stables
Mount Mascal Farm
Electricity Station
Stuarts Nursery
WATER LANE
GOLDSMITH COLLEGE SPORTS GRD
Home Close Farm
THE ALDERS
White Cross PH
Penhill Nursery
NORTH CRAY
Shannon Leigh Stables
ALLOT
Tenn Cts
BUNKERS HILL
Little Mascal Farm
LEAFIELD LANE
A223
Homewood Farm
COCKSURE LANE
72
EDEN ROAD
JOYDEN'S WOOD
STABLE MEADOW
Pond Farm
GATTONS WOOD
GATTONS PLANTATION
WOODLANDS PK
WOODLANDS
GATTONS WAY
PARSONAGE LANE
Nursery
Silverdene
Forest View Stables
NORFIELD RD
NORFIELD ROAD
THE GROVE
JAMES WAY
Manor Farm
Orchard View Farm
Joyden's Wood
North Cray Poultry Farm
Cray Hall
CIRCULAR PERMITTED HORSE RIDE
71
CORNELL CL
HONEYDEN RD
BARTON RD
CHALK WOOD
Stonehill Woods Park
DA2
BIRCHWOOD PARK GOLF CENTRE
DRIVING RANGE
Clubhouse
BEXLEY
BROMLEY
Ruxley Manor Garden Centre
Stonehill Farm
STONEHILL GRN
Upper Ruxley Farm
KENT
Timbertops Farm
OLD MAIDSTONE ROAD
COOKHAM RD
MAIDSTONE ROAD
A20
BYPASS
DARTFORD
SEVENOAKS
BIRCHWOOD ROAD
SUB
Glasshouse

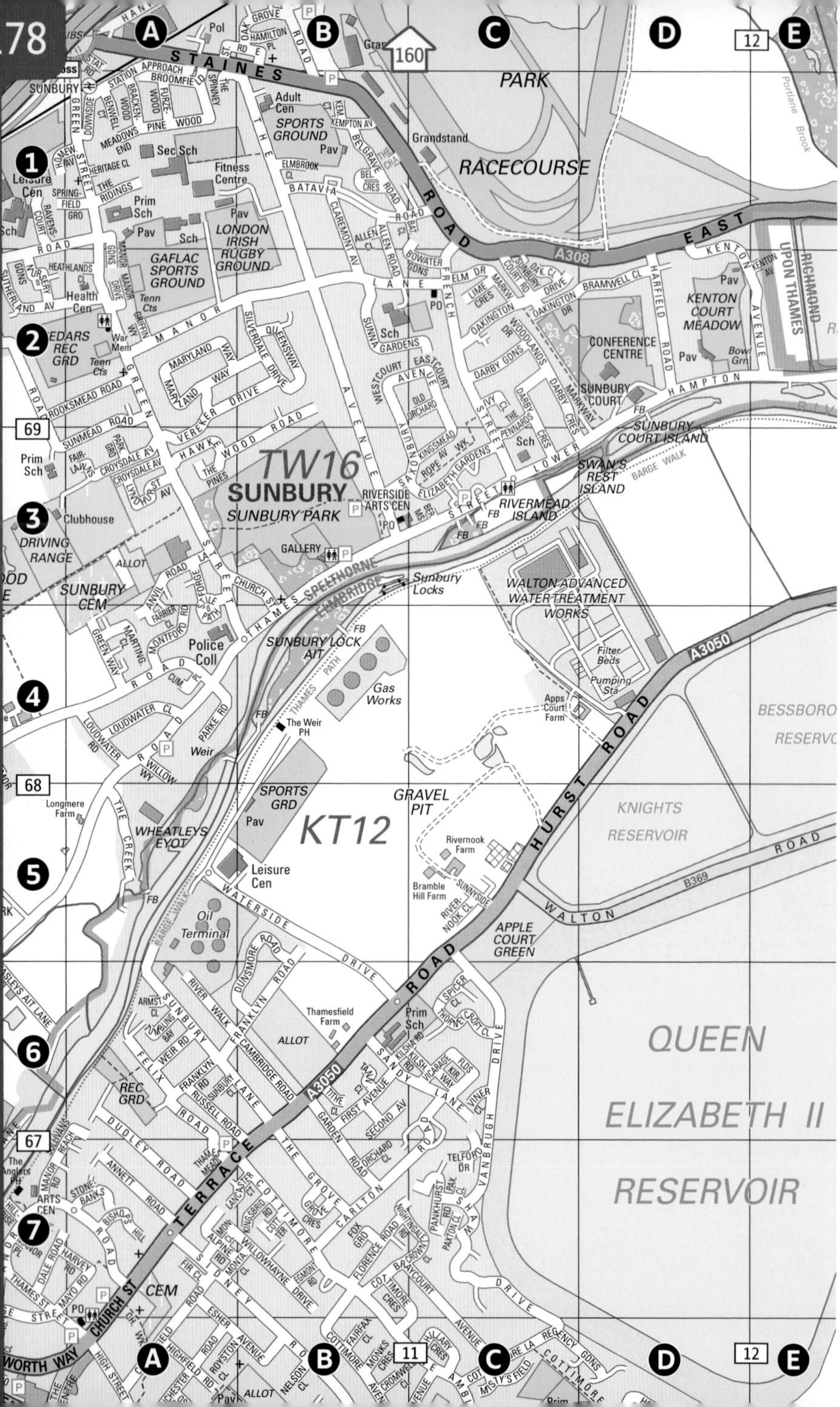
A
B
C
D
E
1
2
3
4
5
6
7
160
12
69
68
67
11
PARK
RACECOURSE
Grandstand
STAINES ROAD
EAST
A308
SUNBURY
Leisure Cen
Sec Sch
Adult Cen
SPORTS GROUND
Fitness Centre
Prim Sch
LONDON IRISH RUGBY GROUND
GAFLAC SPORTS GROUND
Health Cen
CEDARS REC GRD
War Mem
MANOR LANE
KENTON COURT MEADOW
CONFERENCE CENTRE
SUNBURY COURT
UPON THAMES
RICHMOND
Portlane Brook
HAMPTON
SUNBURY COURT ISLAND
SWAN'S REST ISLAND
RIVERMEAD ISLAND
BARGE WALK
TW16
SUNBURY
SUNBURY PARK
RIVERSIDE ARTS CEN
GALLERY
Clubhouse
DRIVING RANGE
SUNBURY CEM
ALLOT
SPELTHORNE
ELMBRIDGE
Sunbury Locks
WALTON ADVANCED WATER TREATMENT WORKS
Filter Beds
Pumping Sta
Apps Court Farm
SUNBURY LOCK AIT
Police Coll
THAMES PATH
Gas Works
The Weir PH
Weir
A3050
HURST ROAD
BESSBOROUGH RESERVOIR
KNIGHTS RESERVOIR
SPORTS GRD
Pav
GRAVEL PIT
KT12
Longmere Farm
WHEATLEYS EYOT
Leisure Cen
Rivernook Farm
Bramble Hill Farm
Oil Terminal
WATERSIDE DRIVE
WALTON ROAD
B369
APPLE COURT GREEN
Thamesfield Farm
ALLOT
Prim Sch
QUEEN ELIZABETH II RESERVOIR
REC GRD
TERRACE ROAD
The Anglers PH
ARTS CEN
CEM
CHURCH ST
PO
COTTIMORE LANE
HURSTFIELD ROAD
HIGH STREET

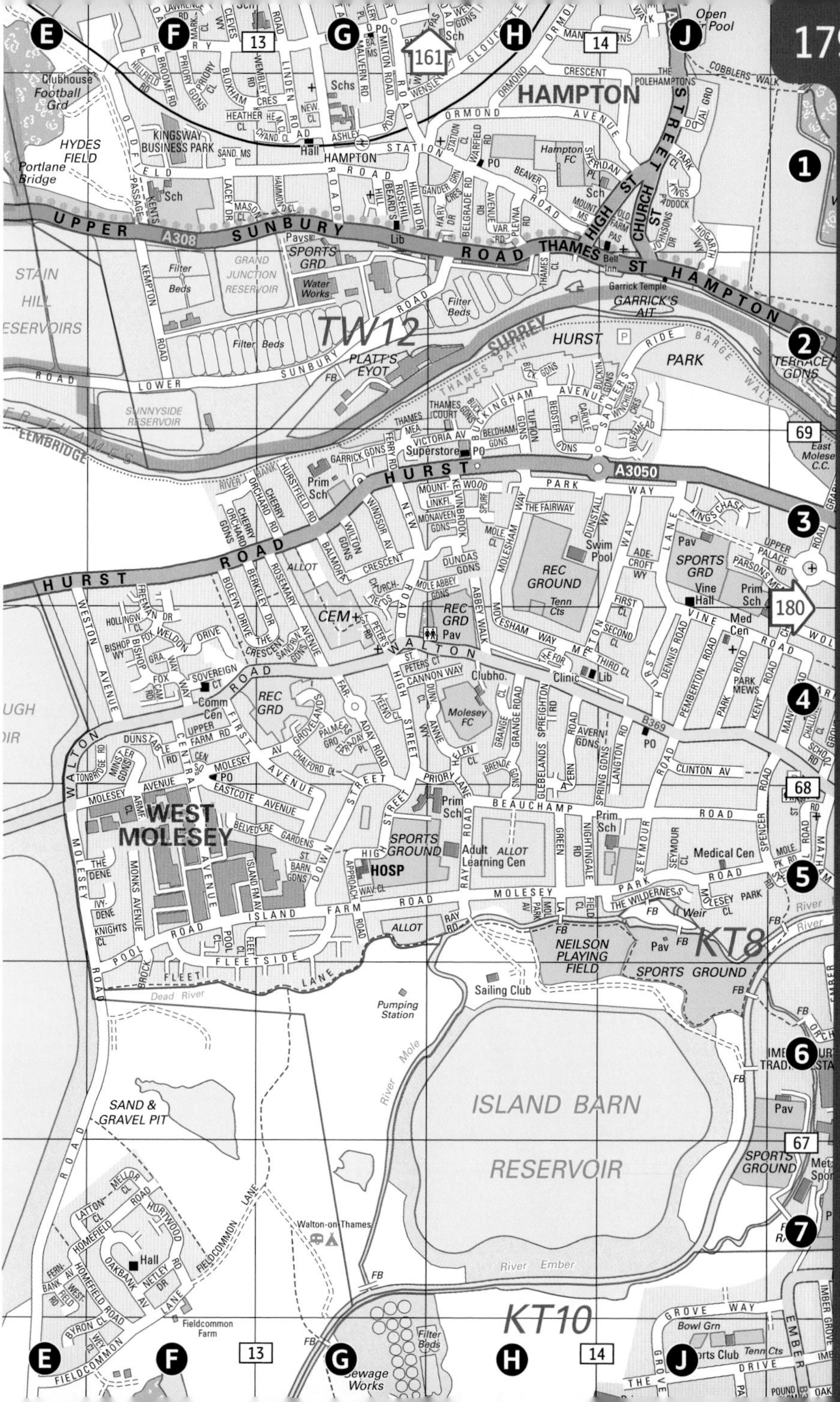
E
F
G
H
J
13
14
161
180
69
68
67
1
2
3
4
5
6
7
HAMPTON
WEST MOLESEY
TW12
KT8
KT10
UPPER SUNBURY ROAD
A308
THAMES ST
HAMPTON
A3050
HURST ROAD
WALTON ROAD
B369
HIGH ST
CHURCH ST
STATION ROAD
ORMOND AVENUE
OLDFIELD ROAD
LOWER SUNBURY ROAD
BUCKINGHAM AVENUE
PARK WAY
MOLESEY AVENUE
EASTCOTE AVENUE
BEAUCHAMP ROAD
MOLESEY ROAD
ISLAND FARM ROAD
FLEETSIDE
FLEET LANE
PARK ROAD
VINE ROAD
UPPER FARM RD
FIELDCOMMON LANE
HOMEFIELD ROAD
ISLAND BARN RESERVOIR
SAND & GRAVEL PIT
Clubhouse
Football Grd
HYDES FIELD
Portlane Bridge
KINGSWAY BUSINESS PARK
Hampton FC
STAIN HILL RESERVOIRS
GRAND JUNCTION RESERVOIR
Filter Beds
Water Works
SPORTS GRD
GARRICK'S AIT
Garrick Temple
HURST PARK
PLATT'S EYOT
SUNNYSIDE RESERVOIR
THAMES PATH
SURREY
East Molesey C.C.
REC GROUND
Swim Pool
Superstore
Prim Sch
CEM
REC GRD
Molesey FC
Clinic
Lib
Comm Cen
SPORTS GROUND
HOSP
Adult Learning Cen
Medical Cen
NEILSON PLAYING FIELD
Sailing Club
Pumping Station
River Mole
River Ember
Dead River
Walton-on-Thames
Fieldcommon Farm
Sewage Works
Bowl Grn
Sports Club
GROVE WAY
EMBER
Open Air Pool
Weir

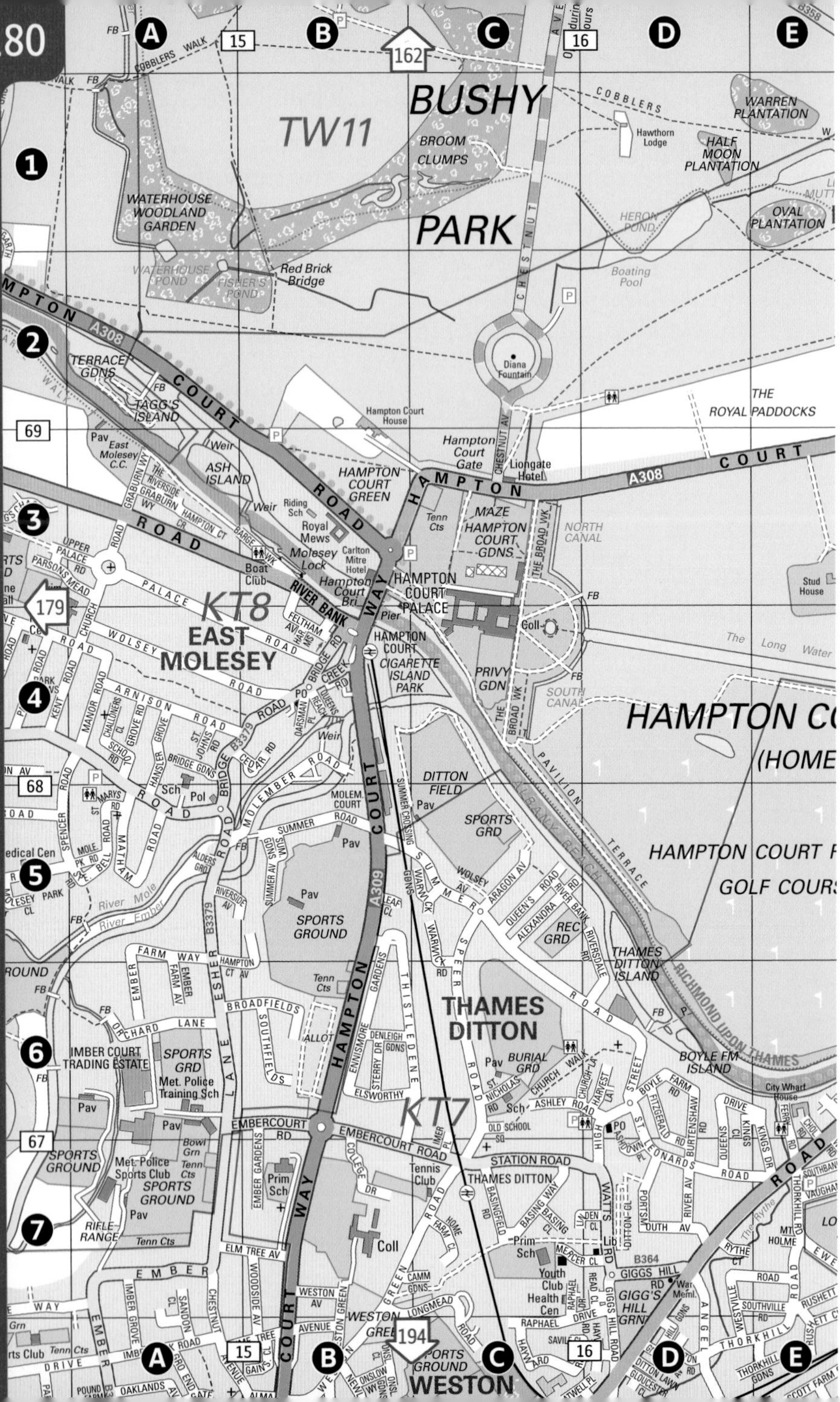

A
B
C
D
E
1
2
3
4
5
6
7
15
16
162
179
194
69
68
67
BUSHY
PARK
TW11
KT8
KT7
COBBLERS WALK
WATERHOUSE WOODLAND GARDEN
WATERHOUSE POND
FISHER'S POND
Red Brick Bridge
BROOM CLUMPS
Hawthorn Lodge
WARREN PLANTATION
HALF MOON PLANTATION
OVAL PLANTATION
HERON POND
Boating Pool
CHESTNUT AVE
Diana Fountain
THE ROYAL PADDOCKS
HAMPTON COURT ROAD
A308
TERRACE GDNS
TAGG'S ISLAND
ASH ISLAND
Weir
Hampton Court House
HAMPTON COURT GREEN
Hampton Court Gate
Liongate Hotel
Riding Sch
Royal Mews
Molesey Lock
Carlton Mitre Hotel
Boat Club
Hampton Court Bri
RIVER BANK
HAMPTON COURT PALACE
MAZE
HAMPTON COURT GDNS
NORTH CANAL
THE BROAD WK
Coll
Pier
Stud House
The Long Water
PRIVY GDN
SOUTH CANAL
HAMPTON COURT
CIGARETTE ISLAND PARK
HAMPTON CO
(HOME
HAMPTON COURT F
GOLF COURS
East Molesey C.C.
GRABURN WY
THE RIVERSIDE
HAMPTON CT
UPPER PALACE RD
PARSONS MEAD
PALACE ROAD
EAST MOLESEY
WOLSEY ROAD
CHURCH ROAD
FELTHAM AV
BRIDGE RD
CREEK RD
ARNISON ROAD
MANOR ROAD
KENT ROAD
PARK MEWS
CHALLONERS CL
GROVE RD
SCHOOL RD
HANSLER GROVE
ST. JOHNS RD
BRIDGE GDNS
B3379
CEDAR RD
QUEENS REACH
OARSMAN PL
MOLEMBER ROAD
MOLEM. COURT
Sch
Pol
SPENCER ROAD
ST MARYS RD
MATHAM ROAD
MOLE PK RD
BELL RD
MOLESEY PARK CL
Medical Cen
River Mole
River Ember
ALDERS GRO
RIVERSIDE AV
SUMMER ROAD
SUMMER AV
SUMMER GDNS
SUMMER CROSSING
Pav
SPORTS GROUND
DITTON FIELD
SPORTS GRD
ALBANY REACH
PAVILION TERRACE
WOLSEY AV
ARAGON AV
QUEEN'S ROAD
RIVER BANK
ALEXANDRA RD
REC GRD
RIVERSDALE RD
SPEER ROAD
WARWICK RD
WARWICK GDNS
THAMES DITTON ISLAND
RICHMOND UPON THAMES
LEAF CL
A309
HAMPTON COURT WAY
THISTLEDENE
GARDENS
ENNISMORE
STERRY DR
DENLEIGH GDNS
ELSWORTHY
THAMES DITTON
BURIAL GRD
CHURCH WALK
CHURCH LA
HARVEST LA
ST. NICHOLAS RD
ASHLEY ROAD
HIGH STREET
BOYLE FM ISLAND
BOYLE FARM RD
FITZGERALD RD
BURTENSHAW
DRIVE CL
KINGS DR
QUEENS
City Wharf House
FERRY RD
ST. LEONARDS ROAD
FARM WAY
EMBER FARM AV
EMBER FARM WAY
HAMPTON CT AV
BROADFIELDS
SOUTHFIELDS
ALLOT
ESHER LANE
ORCHARD LANE
IMBER COURT TRADING ESTATE
Met. Police Training Sch
FB
Tenn Cts
EMBERCOURT RD
EMBERCOURT ROAD
IMBER PL
OLD SCHOOL SQ
STATION ROAD
THAMES DITTON
Tennis Club
Bowl Grn
Met. Police Sports Club
RIFLE RANGE
EMBER GARDENS
Prim Sch
COLLEGE DR
HOME FARM CL
BASINGFIELD RD
BASING WAY
BASING CL
LINDEN CL
WATTS RD
DITTON CL
PORTSMOUTH AV
RIVER AV
Lib
Youth Club
Health Cen
MERCER CL
RAPHAEL DR
READ CL
GIGGS HILL
GIGGS HILL RD
B364
GIGG'S HILL GRN
War Meml.
ANGEL RD
HILL GDNS
RYTHE CT
The Rythe
WESTVILLE RD
SOUTHVILLE RD
THORKHILL RD
THORKHILL GDNS
RUSHETT CL
MT. HOLME
SOUTHBANK
VAUGHAN
ELM TREE AV
WOODSIDE AV
CHESTNUT AVENUE
EMBER LANE
IMBER GROVE
SANDON CL
WESTON AV
WESTON GREEN
CAMM GDNS
LONGMEAD ROAD
WESTON AVENUE
SPORTS GROUND
WESTON
IMBER PARK ROAD
DRIVE
OAKLANDS AV
POUND FARM
DITTON LAWN
GLOUCESTER
SAVILE CL
HAYWARD
SCOTT FARM
ALMA
Club

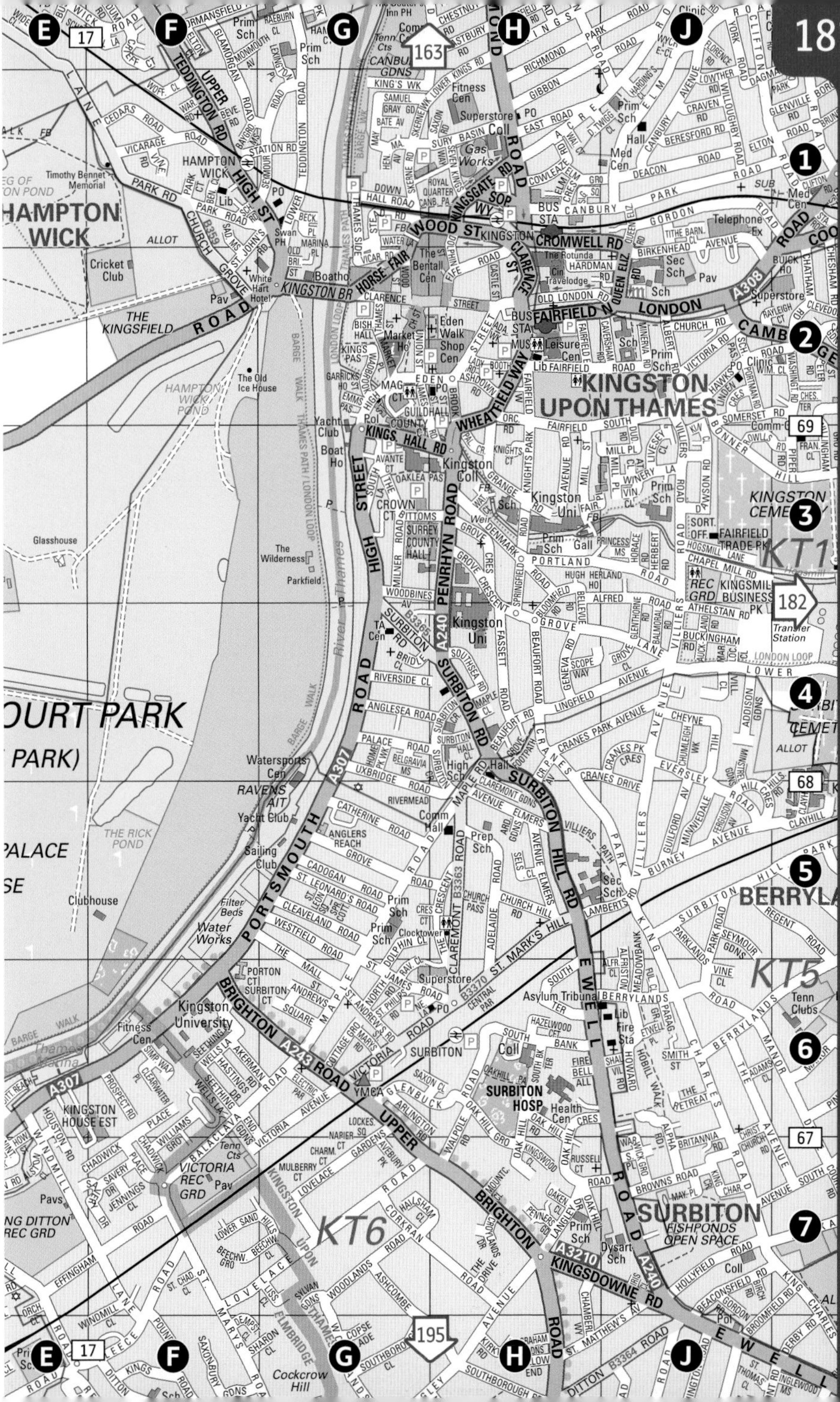
HAMPTON WICK
KINGSTON UPON THAMES
SURBITON
BERRYLANDS
KT1
KT5
KT6
River Thames
THE KINGSFIELD
HAMPTON WICK POND
THE RICK POND
Kingston Uni
Kingston Coll
Kingston University
KINGSTON CEMETERY
SURBITON HOSP
FISHPONDS OPEN SPACE
VICTORIA REC GRD
RAVENS AIT
Cockcrow Hill
Timothy Bennet Memorial
The Old Ice House
The Wilderness
Glasshouse
Clubhouse
Water Works
Filter Beds
The Bentall Cen
Eden Walk Shop Cen
GUILDHALL
COUNTY HALL
SURREY COUNTY HALL
The Rotunda
Telephone Ex
Gas Works
KINGSMILL BUSINESS PK
FAIRFIELD TRADE PK
Transfer Station
LONDON LOOP
THAMES PATH
KINGSTON BR
HIGH ST
PORTSMOUTH ROAD
PENRHYN ROAD
SURBITON HILL RD
EWELL ROAD
BRIGHTON ROAD
UPPER BRIGHTON ROAD
KINGSDOWNE RD
LONDON RD
CAMBRIDGE RD
RICHMOND RD
WOOD ST
CLARENCE ST
WHEATFIELD WAY
A307
A308
A240
A243
A3210
B3363
B3364
B3365
B3370
163
182
195
17
67
68
69
E
F
G
H
J
1
2
3
4
5
6
7

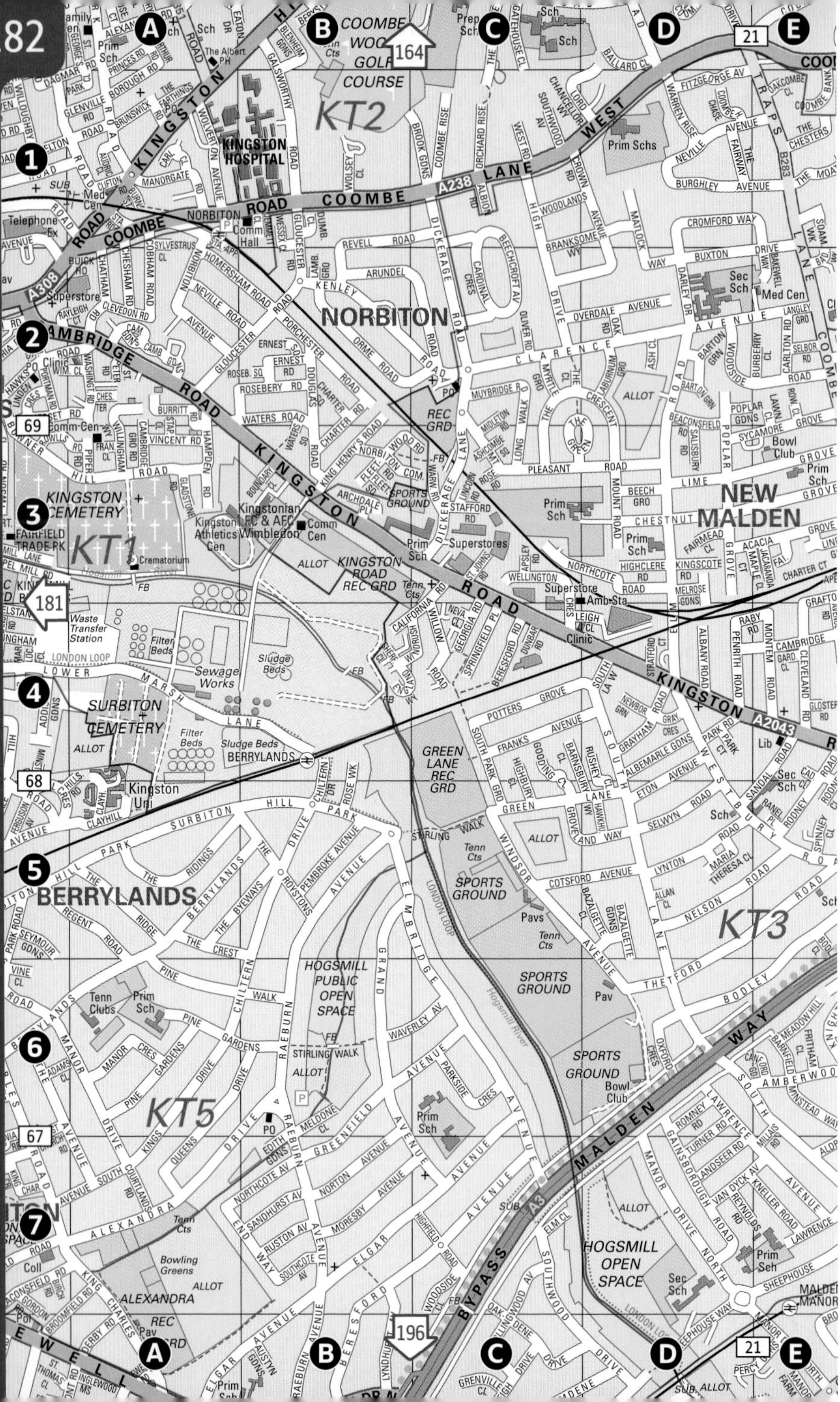
A
B
C
D
E
1
2
3
4
5
6
7
164
181
196
21
69
68
67
COOMBE WOOD GOLF COURSE
KT2
KINGSTON HOSPITAL
KINGSTON HILL
COOMBE LANE WEST
COOMBE ROAD
A238
A308
NORBITON
CAMBRIDGE ROAD
KINGSTON ROAD
KINGSTON CEMETERY
KT1
Crematorium
Kingstonian FC & AFC Wimbledon
Kingston Athletics Cen
KINGSTON ROAD REC GRD
Sewage Works
Sludge Beds
Filter Beds
Waste Transfer Station
LONDON LOOP
LOWER MARSH LANE
SURBITON CEMETERY
BERRYLANDS
Kingston Uni
GREEN LANE REC GRD
NEW MALDEN
KINGSTON ROAD A2043
KT3
SPORTS GROUND
HOGSMILL PUBLIC OPEN SPACE
Hogsmill River
KT5
MALDEN WAY
A3
BYPASS
HOGSMILL OPEN SPACE
ALEXANDRA REC GRD
Bowling Greens
EWELL
MALDEN MANOR

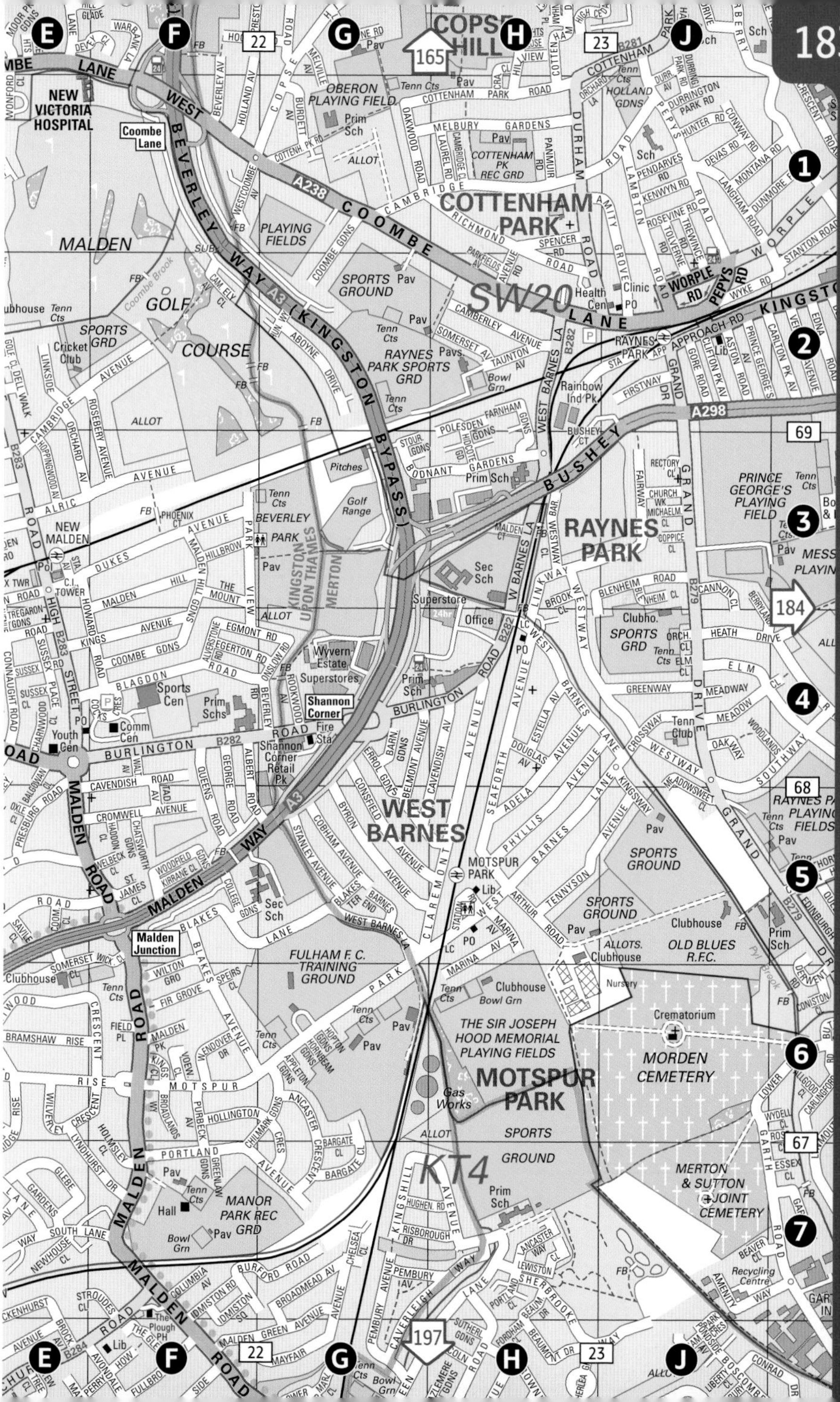
COPSE HILL
165
184
197
OBERON PLAYING FIELD
COTTENHAM PARK
COTTENHAM PK REC GRD
HOLLAND GDNS
NEW VICTORIA HOSPITAL
Coombe Lane
MALDEN
GOLF COURSE
SPORTS GRD
Cricket Club
PLAYING FIELDS
SPORTS GROUND
RAYNES PARK SPORTS GRD
SW20
COOMBE LANE
A238
WORPLE RD
RAYNES PARK
A298
BUSHEY RD
PRINCE GEORGE'S PLAYING FIELD
NEW MALDEN
BEVERLEY PARK
KINGSTON UPON THAMES
MERTON
Golf Range
Superstore
Wyvern Estate
Shannon Corner
Shannon Corner Retail Pk
KINGSTON BYPASS
A3
BEVERLEY WAY
WEST BARNES
MOTSPUR PARK
MALDEN WAY
Malden Junction
BURLINGTON ROAD
FULHAM F.C. TRAINING GROUND
THE SIR JOSEPH HOOD MEMORIAL PLAYING FIELDS
MOTSPUR PARK SPORTS GROUND
OLD BLUES R.F.C.
MORDEN CEMETERY
Crematorium
MERTON & SUTTON JOINT CEMETERY
Recycling Centre
MANOR PARK REC GRD
KT4
Gas Works
MALDEN ROAD
RAYNES PARK PLAYING FIELDS
The Plough PH
Lib
22
23
67
68
69
E
F
G
H
J
1
2
3
4
5
6
7

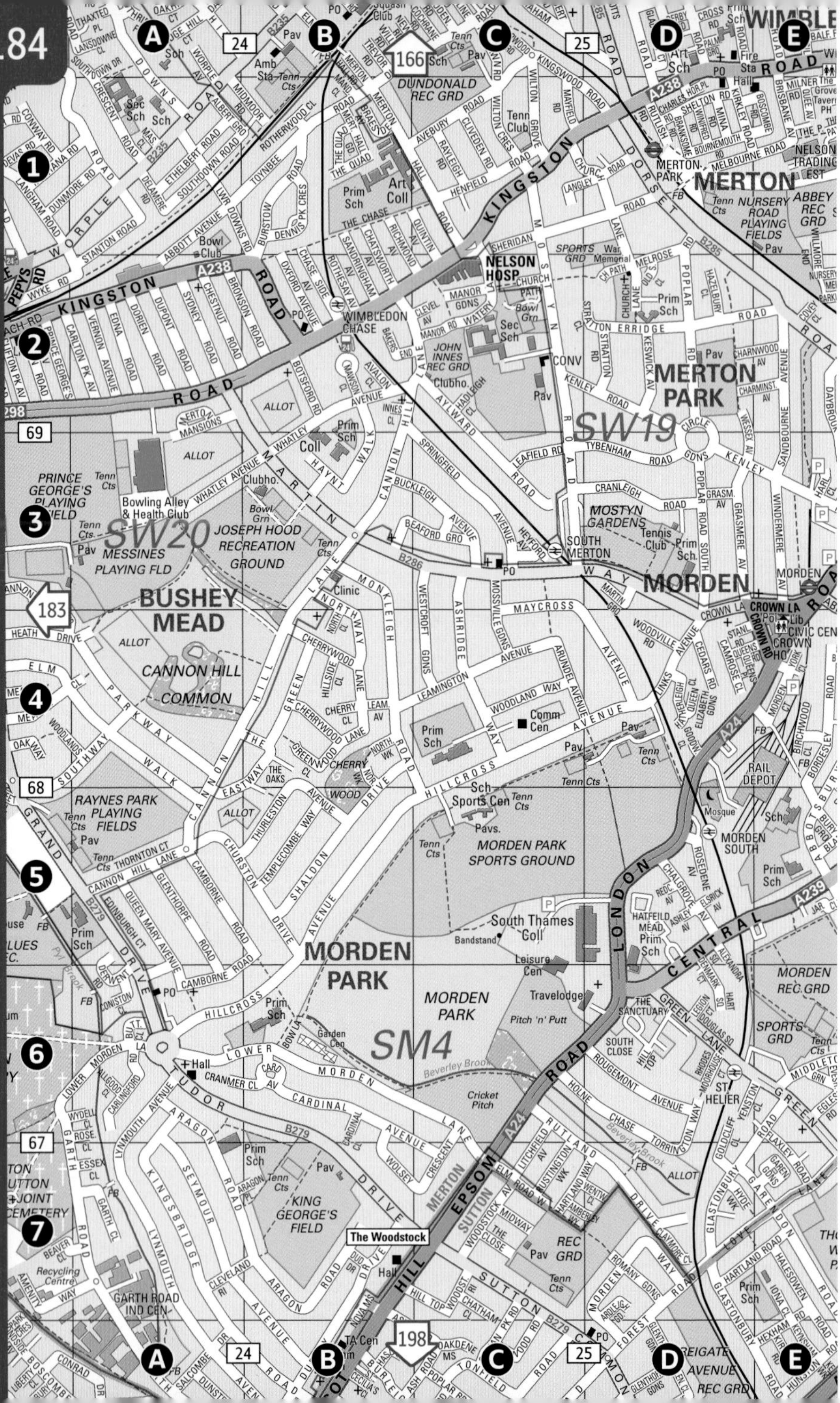

A
B
C
D
E
1
2
3
4
5
6
7
24
25
166
183
198
69
68
67
WIMBLEDON CHASE
DUNDONALD REC GRD
KINGSTON ROAD
A238
NELSON HOSP
MERTON PARK
MERTON
NURSERY ROAD PLAYING FIELDS
ABBEY REC GRD
NELSON TRADING EST
JOHN INNES REC GRD
SW19
SW20
PRINCE GEORGE'S PLAYING FIELD
MESSINES PLAYING FLD
JOSEPH HOOD RECREATION GROUND
BUSHEY MEAD
CANNON HILL COMMON
MARTIN WAY
B286
SOUTH MERTON
MORDEN
CROWN LA
CIVIC CEN
MOSTYN GARDENS
RAYNES PARK PLAYING FIELDS
MORDEN PARK SPORTS GROUND
South Thames Coll
MORDEN PARK
SM4
RAIL DEPOT
MORDEN SOUTH
MORDEN REC GRD
SPORTS GRD
ST HELIER
LONDON ROAD
A24
CENTRAL ROAD
A239
KING GEORGE'S FIELD
The Woodstock
EPSOM ROAD
REC GRD
GARTH ROAD IND CEN
Recycling Centre
Beverley Brook
Travelodge
Pitch 'n' Putt
REIGATE AVENUE REC GRD

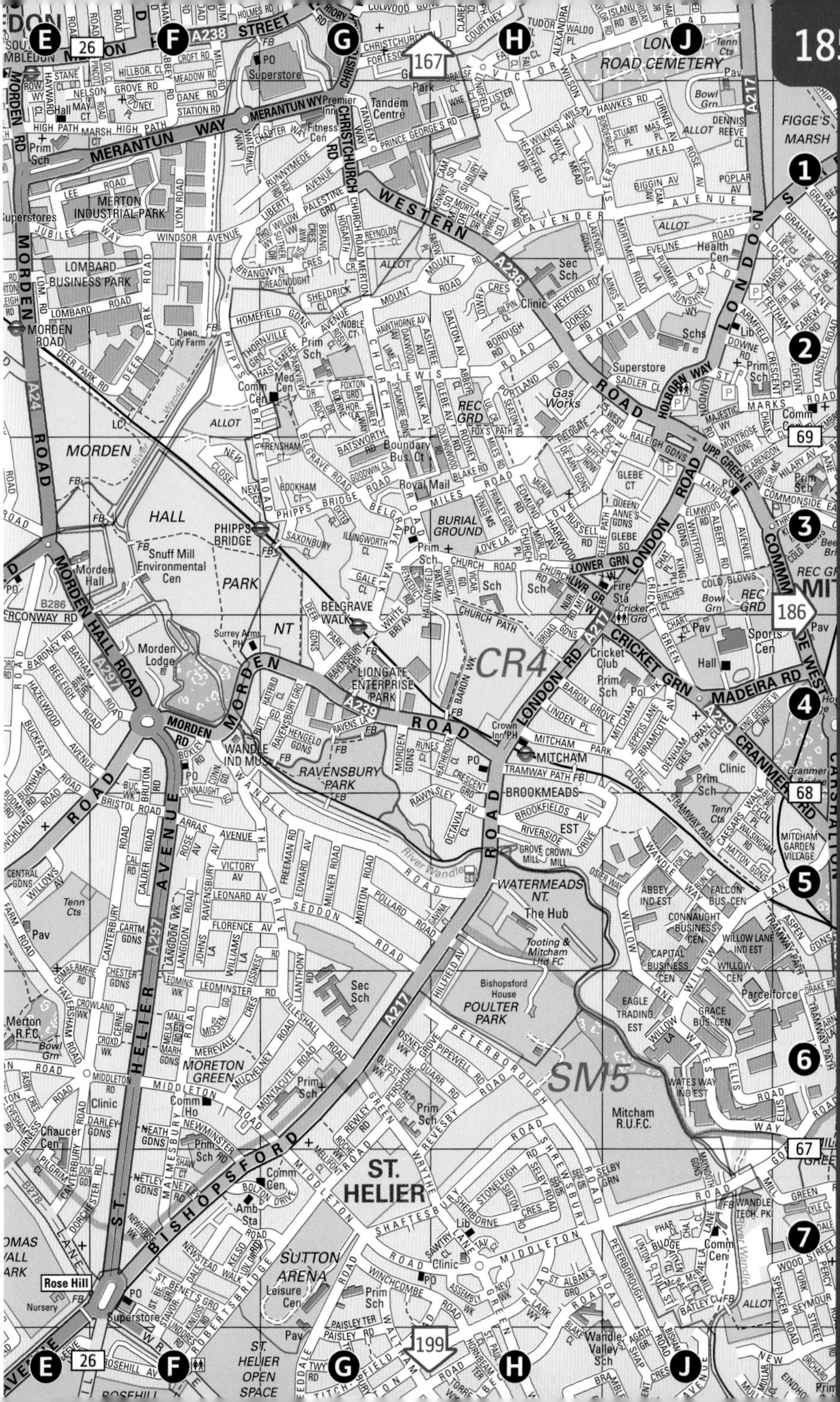
E
F
G
H
J
26
167
A238
STREET
CHRISTCHURCH
ROAD CEMETERY
Superstore
Tandem Centre
MERANTUN WAY
HIGH PATH
MERTON INDUSTRIAL PARK
Superstores
FIGGE'S MARSH
WESTERN
LAVENDER
AVENUE
LONDON
ROAD
JUBILEE WAY
WINDSOR AVENUE
LOMBARD BUSINESS PARK
MORDEN ROAD
MORDEN
A24
A236
MOUNT ROAD
CHURCH ROAD MERTON
Deen City Farm
ALLOT
Gas Works
Superstore
HOLBORN WAY
REC GRD
Boundary Bus. Ct
Royal Mail
BURIAL GROUND
HALL
PARK
PHIPPS BRIDGE
Snuff Mill Environmental Cen
Morden Hall
Morden Lodge
MORDEN HALL ROAD
A297
BELGRAVE WALK
NT
LIONGATE ENTERPRISE PARK
A239
CR4
MITCHAM
CRICKET GRN
MADEIRA RD
CRANMER RD
186
RAVENSBURY PARK
WANDLE IND MUS
BROOKMEADS
River Wandle
WATERMEADS NT.
The Hub
Tooting & Mitcham Utd FC
Bishopsford House
POULTER PARK
A217
ST. HELIER AVENUE
SM5
Mitcham R.U.F.C.
MORETON GREEN
BISHOPSFORD ROAD
ST. HELIER
SUTTON ARENA
Leisure Cen
ST. HELIER OPEN SPACE
Rose Hill
199
68
67
69
1
2
3
4
5
6
7
EAGLE TRADING EST
WILLOW LANE IND EST
CAPITAL BUSINESS CEN
Parcelforce
GRACE BUS. CEN
WATES WAY IND EST
ABBEY IND EST
FALCON BUS. CEN
CONNAUGHT BUSINESS CEN
MITCHAM GARDEN VILLAGE
WANDLE TECH. PK
Wandle Valley Sch
Merton R.F.C.
Chaucer Cen

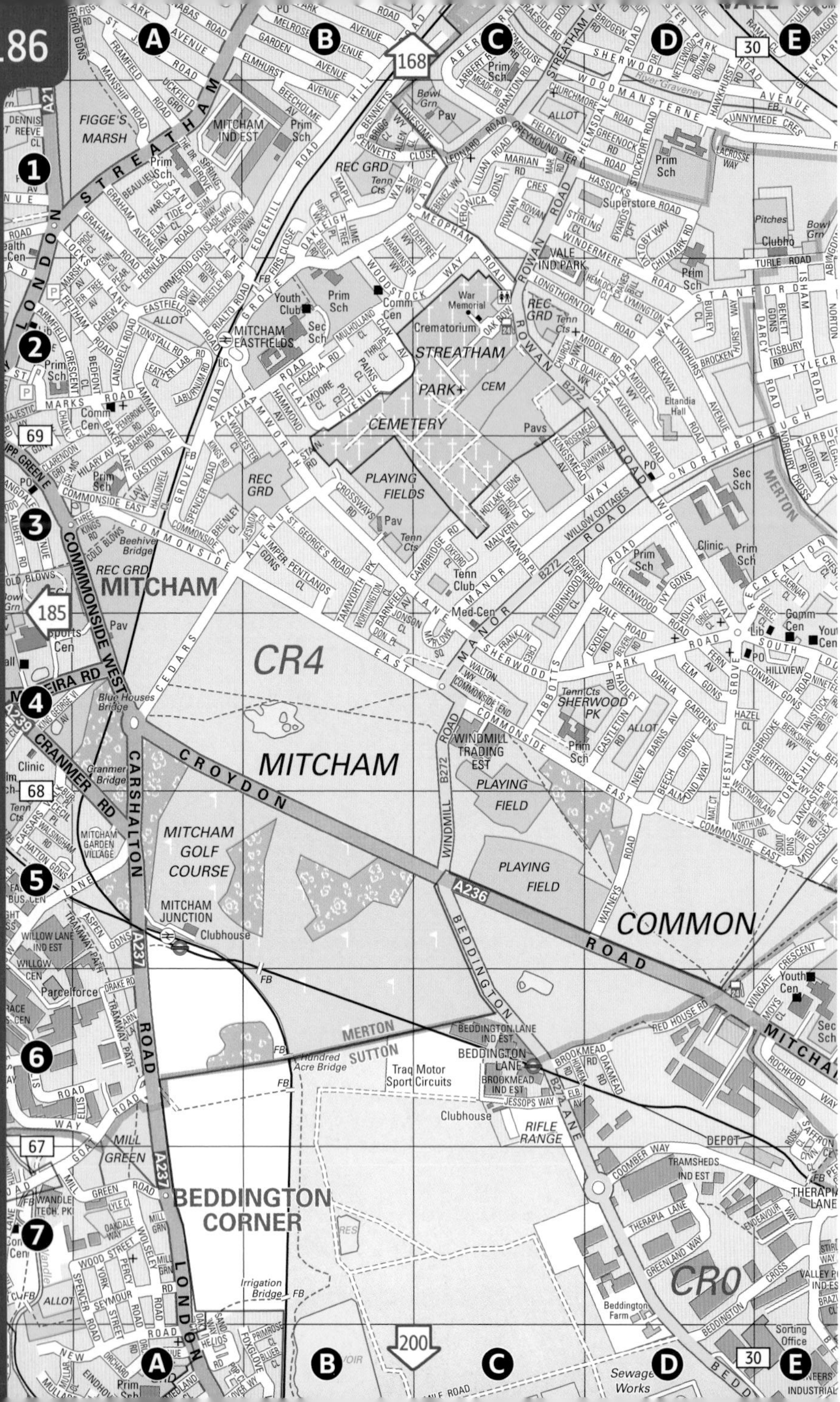
A
B
C
D
E
1
2
3
4
5
6
7
168
185
200
30
69
68
67
FIGGE'S MARSH
MITCHAM IND EST
STREATHAM ROAD
LONDON ROAD
MITCHAM EASTFIELDS
STREATHAM PARK CEMETERY
Crematorium
War Memorial
PLAYING FIELDS
REC GRD
MITCHAM
CR4
COMMONSIDE WEST
COMMONSIDE EAST
CROYDON ROAD
A236
MITCHAM GOLF COURSE
MITCHAM JUNCTION
Clubhouse
WINDMILL TRADING EST
PLAYING FIELD
COMMON
SHERWOOD PK
VALE IND PARK
ROWAN ROAD
NORTHBOROUGH ROAD
BEDDINGTON LANE
BEDDINGTON LANE IND EST
BROOKMEAD IND EST
Traq Motor Sport Circuits
RIFLE RANGE
TRAMSHEDS IND EST
THERAPIA LANE
CR0
Beddington Farm
Sewage Works
Sorting Office
CARSHALTON ROAD
A237
BEDDINGTON CORNER
MILL GREEN
WILLOW LANE IND EST
Parcelforce
CRANMER RD
Hundred Acre Bridge
Irrigation Bridge
MERTON
SUTTON
River Graveney
MITCHAM GARDEN VILLAGE
Blue Houses Bridge
Beehive Bridge
Cranmer Bridge

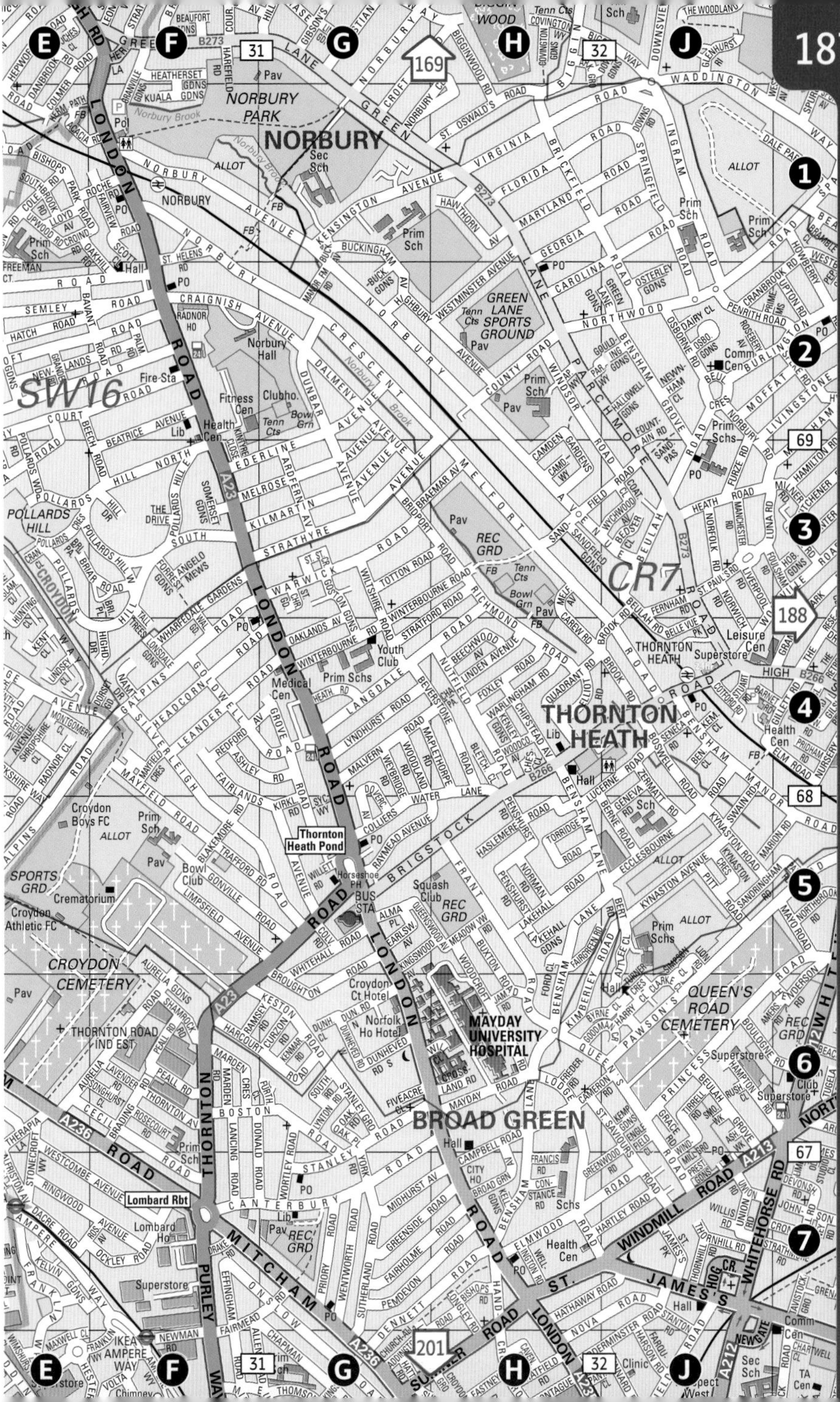
E
F
G
H
J
31
32
169
NORBURY PARK
NORBURY
NORBURY AVENUE
NORBURY CRESCENT
LONDON ROAD
A23
B273
B266
SW16
CR7
POLLARDS HILL
GREEN LANE SPORTS GROUND
Norbury Hall
REC GRD
THORNTON HEATH
Thornton Heath Pond
BRIGSTOCK ROAD
CROYDON CEMETERY
THORNTON ROAD IND EST
MAYDAY UNIVERSITY HOSPITAL
QUEEN'S ROAD CEMETERY
BROAD GREEN
A236 MITCHAM ROAD
Lombard Rbt
PURLEY WAY
WINDMILL ROAD
ST. JAMES'S ROAD
A213
A212
WHITEHORSE RD
188
201
1
2
3
4
5
6
7
69
68
67
Croydon Boys FC
Croydon Athletic FC
Crematorium
Croydon Ct Hotel
Norfolk Ho Hotel
IKEA
AMPERE WAY
Superstore
Leisure Cen

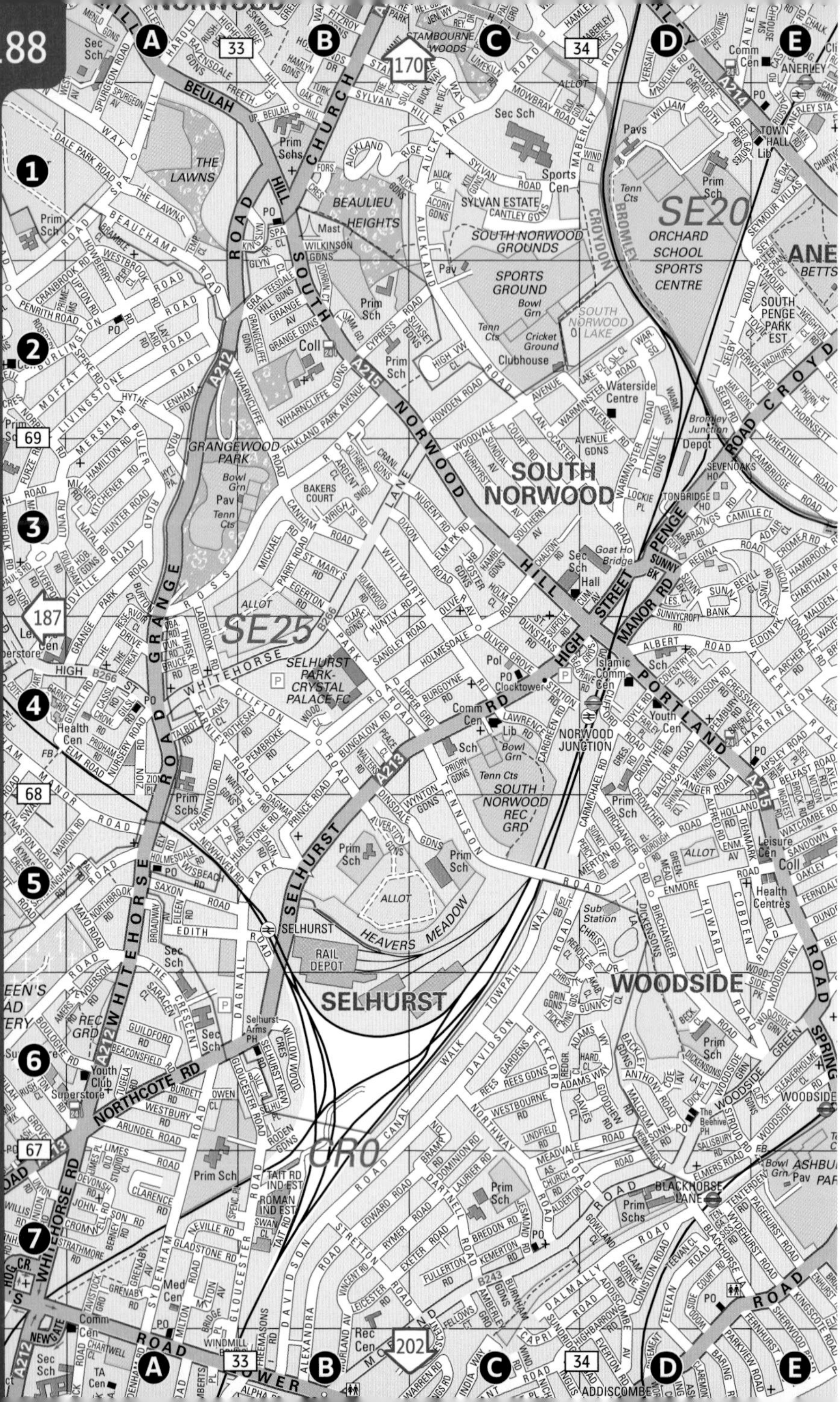
A
B
C
D
E
1
2
3
4
5
6
7
33
34
170
187
202
69
68
67
SOUTH NORWOOD
SE25
SE20
CR0
SELHURST
WOODSIDE
SOUTH NORWOOD GROUNDS
SPORTS GROUND
SOUTH NORWOOD LAKE
ORCHARD SCHOOL SPORTS CENTRE
BEAULIEU HEIGHTS
GRANGEWOOD PARK
THE LAWNS
SELHURST PARK-CRYSTAL PALACE FC
SOUTH NORWOOD REC GRD
RAIL DEPOT
HEAVERS MEADOW
NORWOOD JUNCTION
SELHURST
BLACKHORSE LANE
WOODSIDE
ANERLEY
STAMBOURNE WOODS
SYLVAN ESTATE
SOUTH PENGE PARK EST
BEULAH HILL
CHURCH ROAD
SOUTH NORWOOD HILL
GRANGE ROAD
WHITEHORSE ROAD
NORWOOD ROAD
SELHURST ROAD
HIGH STREET
PORTLAND ROAD
PENGE ROAD
CROYDON ROAD
NORTHCOTE RD
LOWER ADDISCOMBE ROAD
SPRING LANE
WOODSIDE GREEN
ADDISCOMBE
A212
A213
A214
A215
B266
B243
Selhurst Arms PH
The Beehive PH
Waterside Centre
Clocktower
Islamic Comm Cen
Leisure Cen
Health Centres
Bromley Junction Depot

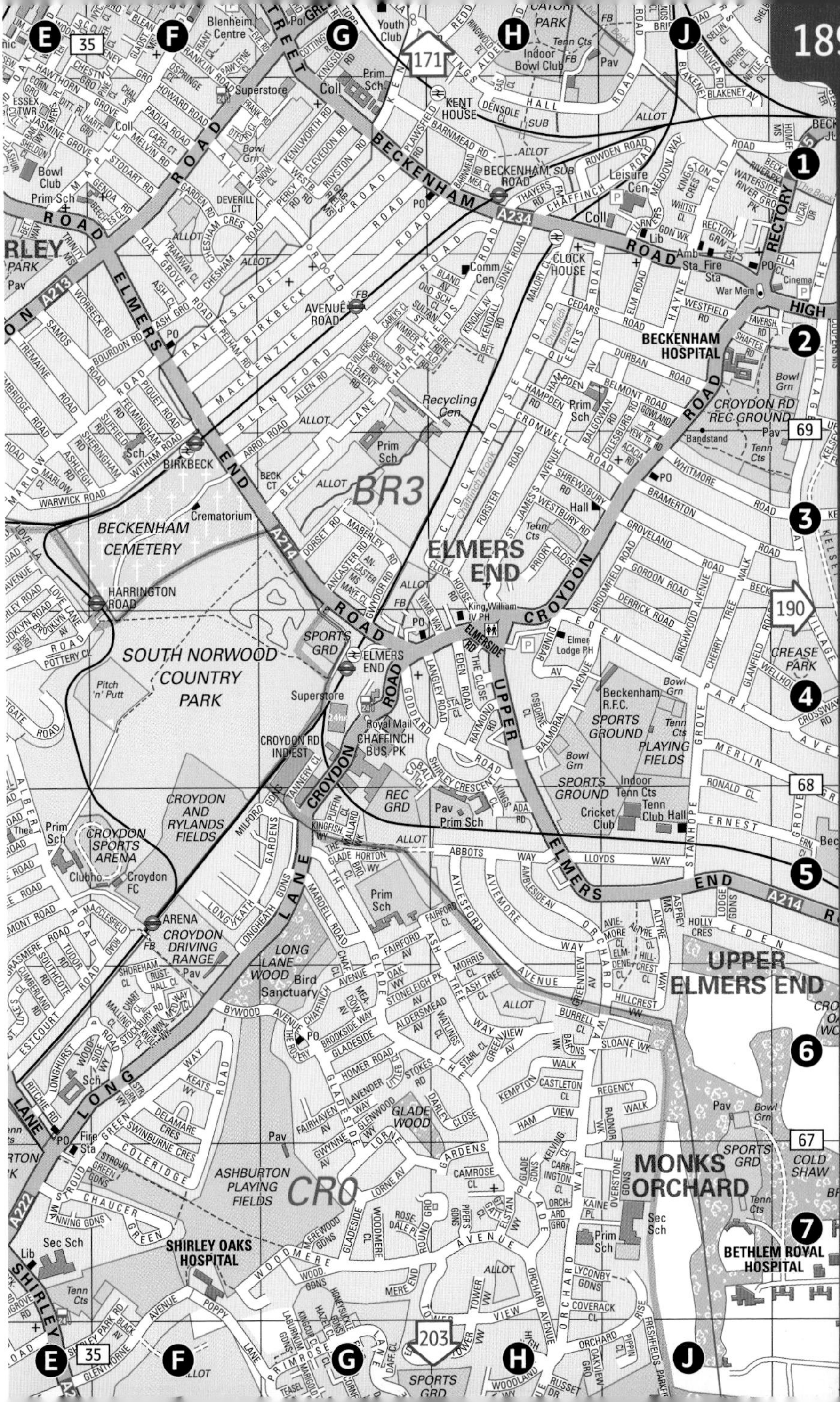
E
F
G
H
J
35
171
190
203
69
68
67
1
2
3
4
5
6
7
Blenheim Centre
Youth Club
Prim Sch
Coll
Superstore
KENT HOUSE
Indoor Bowl Club
Pav
ALLOT
BECKENHAM ROAD
A234
Leisure Cen
Coll
Lib
Amb Sta
Fire Sta
PO
Cinema
War Mem
HIGH
RECTORY
BECKENHAM HOSPITAL
CROYDON RD REC GROUND
Bandstand
Bowl Grn
Tenn Cts
Comm Cen
AVENUE ROAD
CLOCK HOUSE
Bowl Club
Prim Sch
ROAD
A213
ELMERS END
BIRKBECK
Crematorium
BECKENHAM CEMETERY
HARRINGTON ROAD
SOUTH NORWOOD COUNTRY PARK
Pitch 'n' Putt
Recycling Cen
BR3
ELMERS END
King William IV PH
CROYDON
A214
SPORTS GRD
ELMERS END
Superstore
Royal Mail
CROYDON RD IND EST
CHAFFINCH BUS PK
REC GRD
Pav
Prim Sch
Elmer Lodge PH
Beckenham R.F.C.
SPORTS GROUND
PLAYING FIELDS
Indoor Tenn Cts
Tenn Club Hall
Cricket Club
CREASE PARK
CROYDON AND RYLANDS FIELDS
CROYDON SPORTS ARENA
Clubho.
Croydon FC
ARENA
CROYDON DRIVING RANGE
LONG LANE WOOD
Bird Sanctuary
UPPER ELMERS END
MONKS ORCHARD
SPORTS GRD
COLD SHAW
BETHLEM ROYAL HOSPITAL
GLADE WOOD
ASHBURTON PLAYING FIELDS
CR0
SHIRLEY OAKS HOSPITAL
Sec Sch
Lib
Fire Sta
A222
SHIRLEY
LONG LANE
SPORTS GRD

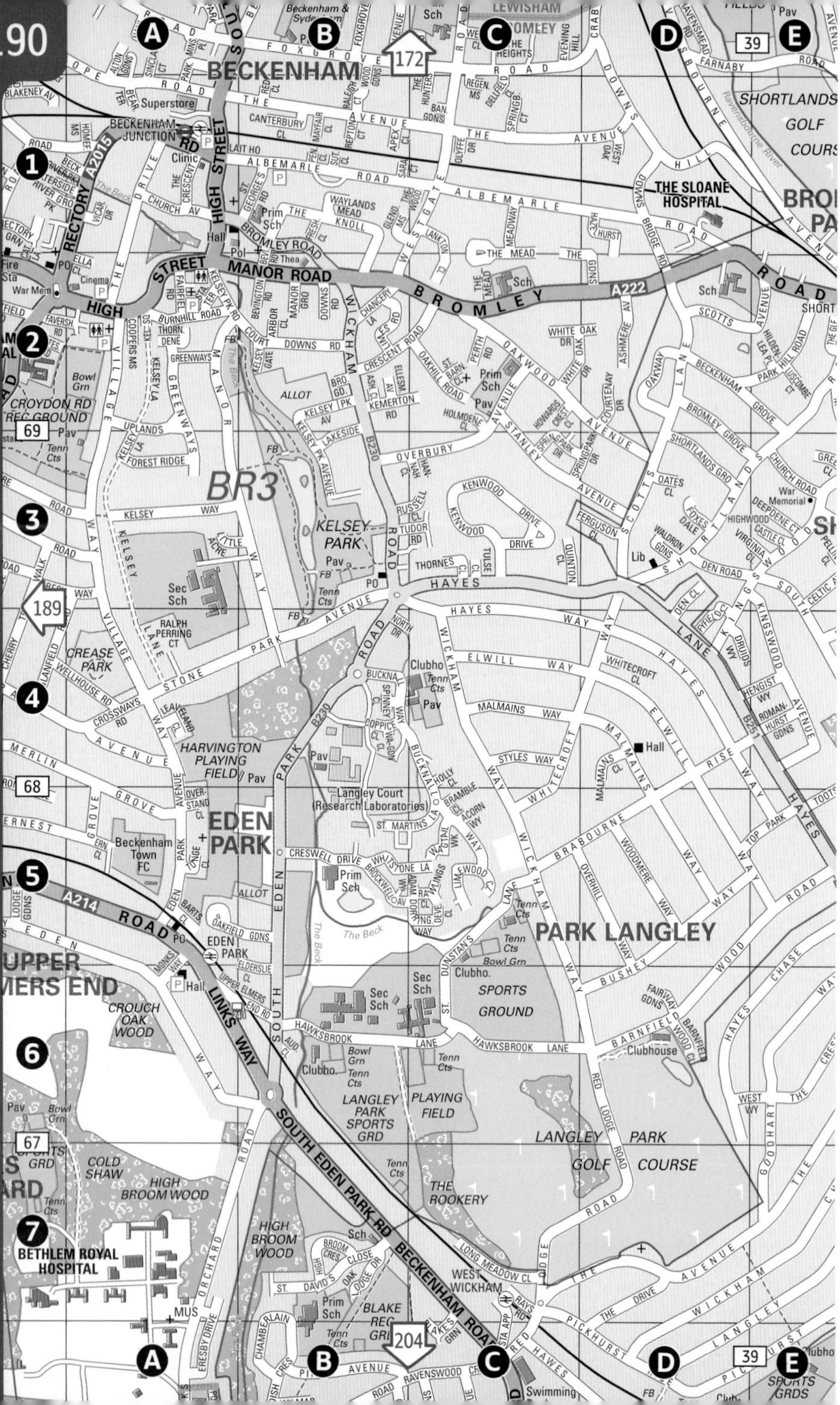
A
B
C
D
E
1
2
3
4
5
6
7
172
189
204
39
69
68
67
BECKENHAM
LEWISHAM
BROMLEY
SHORTLANDS GOLF COURSE
Ravensbourne River
THE SLOANE HOSPITAL
BECKENHAM JUNCTION
Superstore
Clinic
HIGH STREET
RECTORY RD
A2015
The Beck
MANOR ROAD
BROMLEY ROAD
BROMLEY RD
A222
ALBEMARLE ROAD
THE AVENUE
FOXGROVE ROAD
CANTERBURY CL
WESTGATE RD
THE MEAD
CROYDON RD REC GROUND
Bowl Grn
Tenn Cts
Pav
BR3
KELSEY PARK
KELSEY WAY
KELSEY LANE
ALLOT
CRESCENT ROAD
OAKWOOD AVENUE
STANLEY AVENUE
KENWOOD DRIVE
HAYES LANE
HAYES WAY
WICKHAM WAY
ELWILL WAY
MALMAINS WAY
STYLES WAY
WHITECROFT WAY
BRABOURNE RISE
B251
B230
KINGSWOOD ROAD
SOUTHEND ROAD
Sec Sch
Prim Sch
CREASE PARK
STONE PARK AVENUE
PARK ROAD
CROSSWAYS RD
HARVINGTON PLAYING FIELD
MERLIN GROVE
EDEN PARK
Beckenham Town FC
Langley Court (Research Laboratories)
CRESWELL DRIVE
SOUTH EDEN PARK RD
A214
UPPER ELMERS END
CROUCH OAK WOOD
HAWKSBROOK LANE
LANGLEY PARK SPORTS GRD
PLAYING FIELD
SPORTS GROUND
LANGLEY PARK GOLF COURSE
PARK LANGLEY
RED LODGE ROAD
BARNFIELD WOOD RD
Clubhouse
THE ROOKERY
HIGH BROOM WOOD
COLD SHAW
BETHLEM ROYAL HOSPITAL
LINKS WAY
BECKENHAM ROAD
WEST WICKHAM
LONG MEADOW CL
PICKHURST LANE
WICKHAM AVENUE
THE DRIVE
BLAKE REC GRD
ORCHARD
MUS
SPORTS GRDS
Swimming

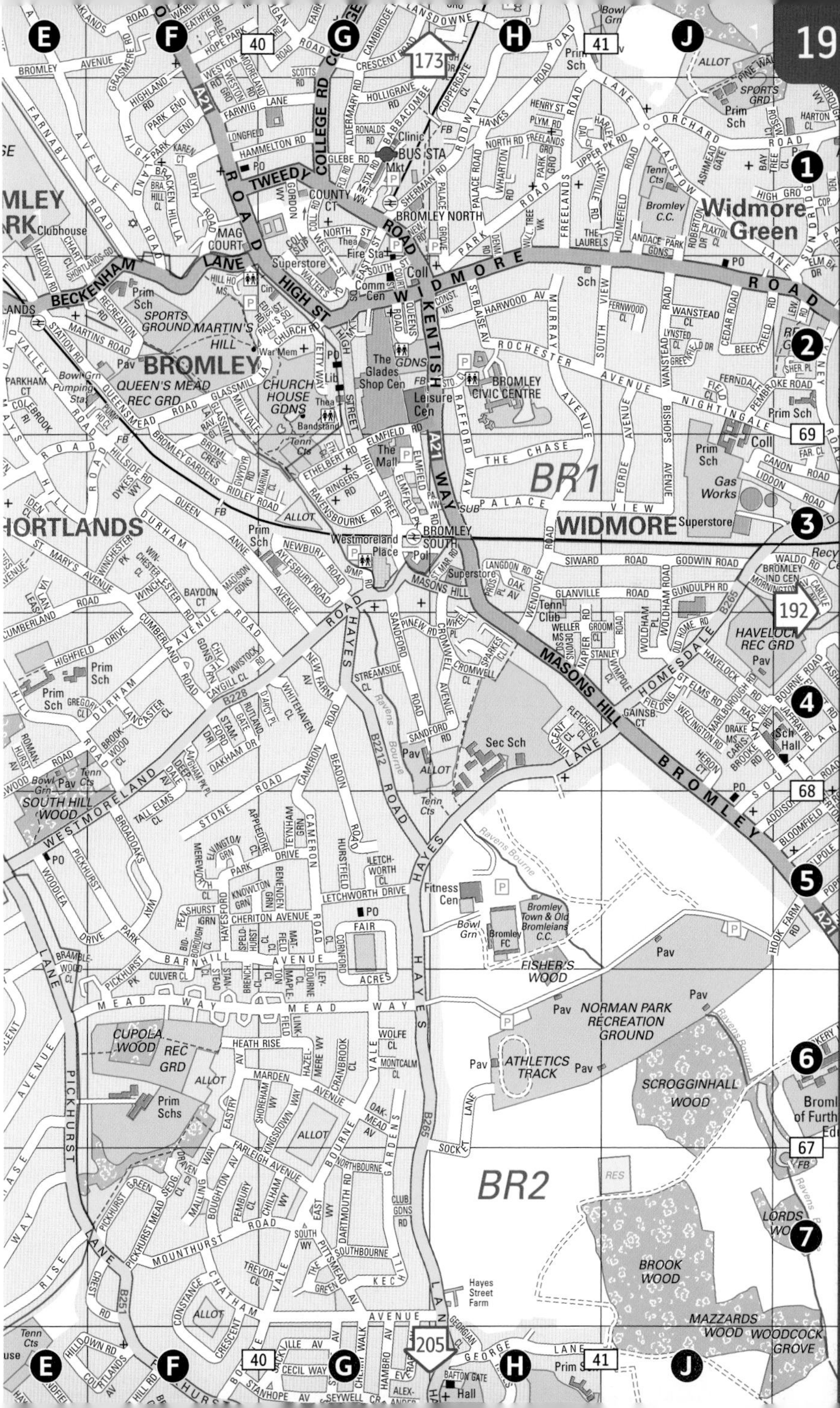

E
F
G
H
J
40
41
173
192
205
69
68
67
1
2
3
4
5
6
7
BROMLEY
BROMLEY NORTH
BROMLEY SOUTH
Widmore Green
WIDMORE
HORTLANDS
BR1
BR2
BECKENHAM LANE
HIGH ST
WIDMORE ROAD
TWEEDY ROAD
COLLEGE RD
KENTISH WAY
A21
MASONS HILL
BROMLEY COMMON
HAYES ROAD
HAYES LANE
WESTMORELAND ROAD
PICKHURST LANE
MEAD WAY
B228
B2212
B265
B251
SPORTS GROUND
MARTIN'S HILL
QUEEN'S MEAD REC GRD
CHURCH HOUSE GDNS
The Glades Shop Cen
Leisure Cen
BROMLEY CIVIC CENTRE
The Mall
Westmoreland Place
Bromley C.C.
HAVELOCK REC GRD
SOUTH HILL WOOD
CUPOLA WOOD
REC GRD
Prim Schs
Sec Sch
Fitness Cen
Bromley FC
Bromley Town & Old Bromleians C.C.
FISHER'S WOOD
NORMAN PARK RECREATION GROUND
ATHLETICS TRACK
SCROGGINHALL WOOD
BROOK WOOD
MAZZARDS WOOD
WOODCOCK GROVE
LORDS WOOD
Hayes Street Farm
Gas Works
Superstore
Ravens Bourne
FAIR ACRES

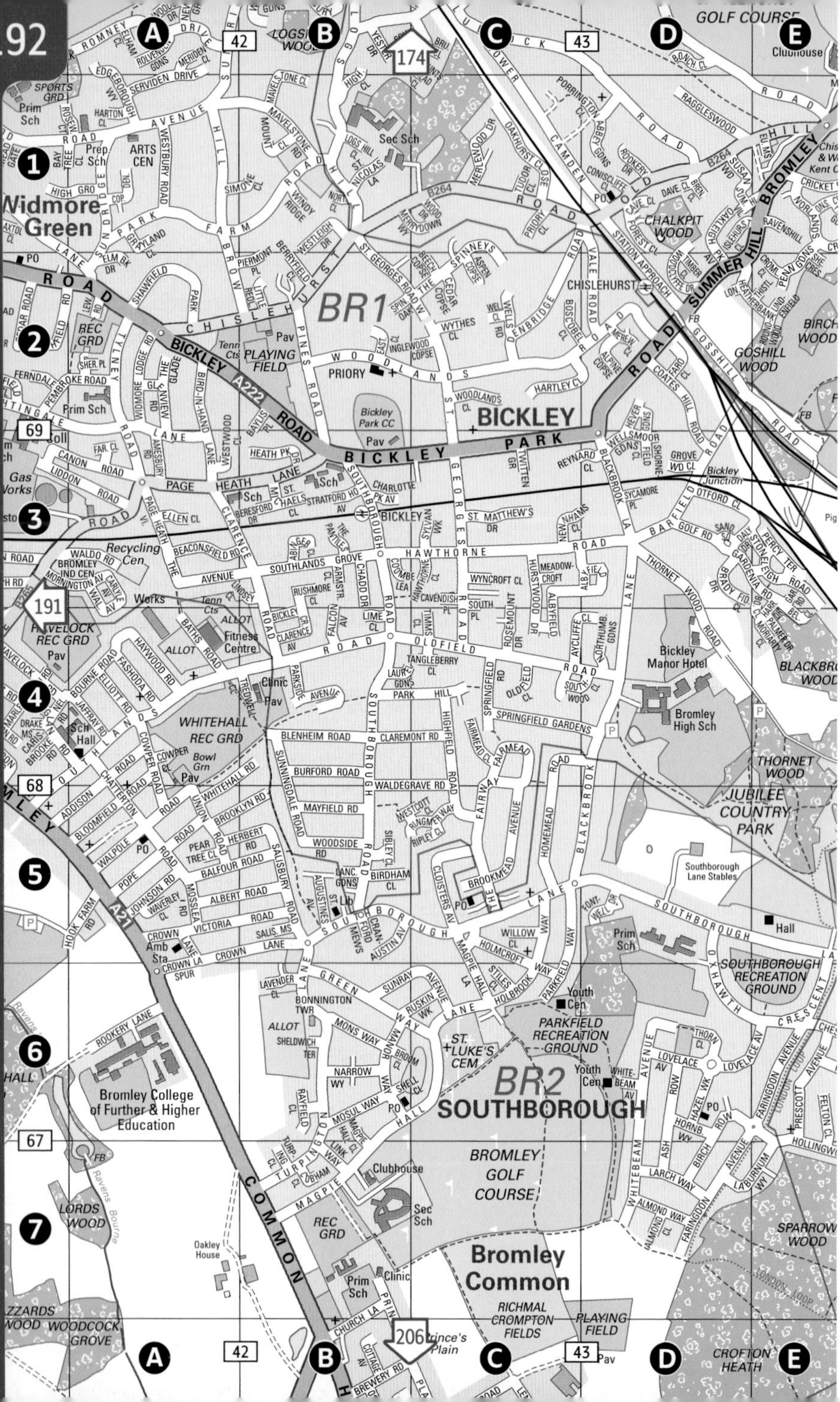
A
B
C
D
E
1
2
3
4
5
6
7
42
43
174
191
206
69
68
67
GOLF COURSE
Clubhouse
LOGSIDE WOOD
ROMNEY
ELHAM
ROLVENDEN GDNS
MERIDEN CL
DRIVE
SERVIDEN DRIVE
EDGEBOROUGH WY
SPORTS GRD
Prim Sch
HARTON CL
AVENUE
ROAD
Prep. Sch
ARTS CEN
BAY TREE CL
WESTBURY ROAD
HIGH GRO
Widmore Green
SUNDRIDGE
SUNDRIDGE PARK
TYLAND
ELM BK DR
LANE
PO
HILL
SIMONE CL
FARM
MAVELSTONE CL
MAVELSTONE RD
MOUNT
WINDY RIDGE
Sec Sch
LOGS HILL CL
ST. NICOLAS LA
NORTH CL
B264
WOOD DR
MERRYDOWN WY
WOOD RIDE
LUBBOCK
CAMDEN
PORRINGTON CL
ABBEY GDNS
CONISCLIFFE
ROOKERY
ROAD
RAGGLESWOOD
BONCH. CL
HILL
OAKHURST CLOSE
MERLEWOOD DR
TUDOR CL
CAMDEN ROAD
PRIORY CL
CHALKPIT WOOD
FOREST CL
CAVE CL
DAVE CL
STATION APPROACH
CHISLEHURST
BROMLEY
SUMMER HILL
ROAD
GOSSHILL
GOSHILL WOOD
BIRCH WOOD
Chislehurst & West Kent C
CRICKET
RAVENSHILL
PENN GDNS
FB
ROAD
BICKLEY
BR1
CHISLEHURST
PINES ROAD
WOODLANDS
PRIORY
Bickley Park CC
Pav
PLAYING FIELD
Tenn Cts
ST. GEORGES ROAD W
THE SPINNEYS
CEDAR COPSE
WYTHES CL
INGLEWOOD COPSE
DENBRIDGE
BOSCOBEL
HARTLEY CL
ALPINE COPSE
WOODLANDS CL
BICKLEY PARK
ROAD
BICKLEY ROAD
A222
PIERMONT PL
BERRYFIELD CL
WESTLEIGH DR
LITTLE REDLANDS
SHAWFIELD PARK
REC GRD
SHER. PL
FERNDALE
PEMBROKE ROAD
Prim Sch
NIGHTINGALE
LANE
TYLNEY ROAD
WIDMORE LODGE RD
THE GLADE
GLENVIEW
BIRD-IN-HAND LANE
WESTWOOD CL
AMESBURY RD
CANON ROAD
LIDDON ROAD
FAR. CL
Gas Works
PAGE HEATH LANE
HEATH PK DR
SOUTHBOROUGH
CHARLOTTE PK AV
Sch
ST. HAELS CL
STRATFORD HO AV
BICKLEY
SYLVAN WK
ST. MATTHEW'S DR
SYCAMORE PL
REYNARD CL
TWITTEN GR
WELLSMOOR GDNS
SHORNE FIELD
GROVE WD CL
OTFORD CL
Bickley Junction
BLACKBROOK LA
BARFIELD
GOLF RD
PERCY TER
ELLEN CL
BERESFORD DR
Recycling Cen
BEACONSFIELD RD
WALDO RD
BROMLEY IND CEN
MORNINGTON AV
CARLYLE AV
THE AVENUE
SOUTHLANDS GROVE
HAWTHORNE ROAD
CHADD DR
ARMSTR. CL
THE PANTILES
WYNCROFT CL
MEADOWCROFT
HURSTWOOD DR
ALBYFIELD
NEW NHAMS CL
THORNET WOOD ROAD
Works
Tenn Cts
ALLOT
RUSHMORE CL
BICKLEY CR
CLARENCE AV
FALCON AV
LIME CL
CAVENDISH PL
SOUTH PL
ROSEMOUNT DR
AYCLIFFE CL
NORTHUMB. GDNS
HAVELOCK REC GRD
Pav
BATHS ROAD
Fitness Centre
ALLOT
OLDFIELD ROAD
TANGLEBERRY CL
HAYWOOD RD
FASHODA RD
BOURNE ROAD
ELLIOTT RD
Clinic
Pav
PARKSIDE AVENUE
PARK HILL
SPRINGFIELD RD
OLDFIELD CL
SOUTH-WOOD CL
Bickley Manor Hotel
BLACKBROOK WOOD
Bromley High Sch
WHITEHALL REC GRD
TREDWELL
BLENHEIM ROAD
CLAREMONT RD
SPRINGFIELD GARDENS
FAIRMEAD CL
FAIRMEAD
THORNET WOOD
JUBILEE COUNTRY PARK
SOUTHLANDS RD
DRAKE MS
CARISBROOKE RD
Sch Hall
COWPER ROAD
Bowl Grn
Pav
WHITEHALL RD
BURFORD ROAD
WALDEGRAVE RD
MAYFIELD RD
FAIRWAY AVENUE
HOMEMEAD ROAD
BLACKBROOK
ADDISON
CHATTERTON ROAD
BLOOMFIELD ROAD
UNION ROAD
BROOKLYN RD
HERBERT RD
PEAR TREE CL
BALFOUR ROAD
SUNNINGDALE ROAD
SALISBURY ROAD
WOODSIDE RD
WESTCOTT CL
RINGMER WAY
RIPLEY CL
SIBLEY CL
Southborough Lane Stables
WALPOLE RD
PO
POPE ROAD
JOHNSON RD
WAVERLEY CL
MOSSLEA RD
ALBERT ROAD
VICTORIA ROAD
AUGUSTINES GDNS
LANC. GDNS
BIRDHAM CL
Lib
CLOISTERS AV
BROOKMEAD
PO
FONTWELL DR
SOUTHBOROUGH LANE
Hall
Prim Sch
HOOK FARM RD
CROWN LANE
Amb Sta
CROWN LA SPUR
SALIS. MS
CRANFORD MEWS
AUSTIN AV
WILLOW CL
HOLMCROFT WAY
MAGPIE HALL LA
PARKFIELD WAY
SOUTHBOROUGH RECREATION GROUND
OXHAWTH CRESCENT
A21
LAVENDER CL
GREEN LANE
SUNRAY AVENUE
RUSKIN WK
STILES CL
HOLBROOK WAY
Youth Cen
BONNINGTON TWR
ALLOT
SHELDWICH TER
MONS WAY
MANOR WAY
BROOM CL
ST. LUKE'S CEM
PARKFIELD RECREATION GROUND
BR2
SOUTHBOROUGH
Youth Cen
WHITEBEAM AV
THORN CL
LOVELACE AV
FARINGDON AVENUE
HOLLINGWORTH
PRESCOTT AVENUE
FELTON CL
ROOKERY LANE
Bromley College of Further & Higher Education
NARROW WY
SHELL CL
RAYFIELD CL
MOSUL WAY
PO
HALL
MAGPIE HALL CL
LINK WAY
TURPINGTON LANE
TURPING CL
BHAM WAY
ROW
HAZEL WK
PO
HORNB. WY
ASH ROW
BIRCH ROW
AVENUE
LABURNUM WY
LARCH WAY
ALMOND WAY
ALMOND CL
FARINGDON AV
WHITEBEAM AV
Clubhouse
BROMLEY GOLF COURSE
SPARROW WOOD
LONDON LOOP
MAGPIE
Sec Sch
REC GRD
COMMON
LORDS WOOD
Ravens Bourne
FB
Oakley House
Bromley Common
Clinic
Prim Sch
CHURCH LA
PRINCES PLAIN
COTTAGE AV
BREWERY RD
Prince's Plain
RICHMAL CROMPTON FIELDS
PLAYING FIELD
Pav
CROFTON HEATH
WOODCOCK GROVE
HALL

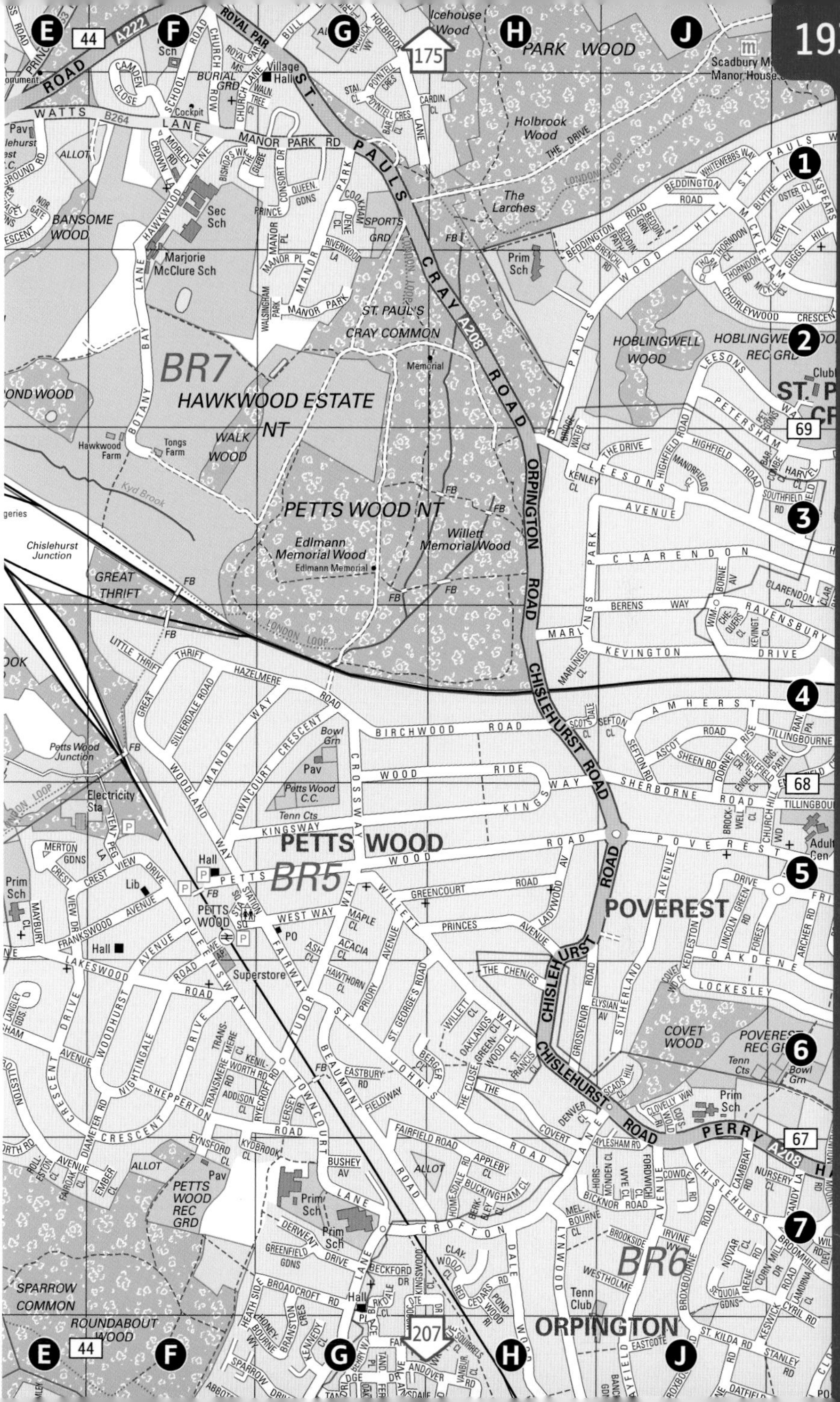
E
F
G
H
J
44
175
207
69
68
67
1
2
3
4
5
6
7
ROYAL PAR
A222
ROAD
Village Hall
Icehouse Wood
PARK WOOD
Scadbury Manor House
CAMDEN CLOSE
SCHOOL ROAD
CHURCH ROW
BURIAL GRD
Cockpit
WATTS LANE
B264
MANOR PARK RD
ST. PAULS CRAY ROAD
A208
Holbrook Wood
THE DRIVE
LONDON LOOP
The Larches
BEDDINGTON ROAD
WHITEWEBBS WAY
MICKLEHAM
CHORLEYWOOD CRESCENT
BANSOME WOOD
Sec Sch
Marjorie McClure Sch
HAWKWOOD LANE
BOTANY BAY LANE
Prim Sch
SPORTS GRD
MANOR PARK
ST. PAUL'S CRAY COMMON
Memorial
HOBLINGWELL WOOD
HOBLINGWELL REC GRD
BR7
HAWKWOOD ESTATE NT
WALK WOOD
Hawkwood Farm
Tongs Farm
Kyd Brook
PETTS WOOD NT
Edlmann Memorial Wood
Edlmann Memorial
Willett Memorial Wood
Chislehurst Junction
GREAT THRIFT
ORPINGTON ROAD
LEESONS HILL
HIGHFIELD ROAD
CLARENDON WAY
BERENS WAY
MARLINGS PARK
KEVINGTON DRIVE
RAVENSBURY
LITTLE THRIFT
HAZELMERE ROAD
SILVERDALE ROAD
CHISLEHURST ROAD
AMHERST
BIRCHWOOD ROAD
Petts Wood Junction
WOODLAND WAY
TOWNCOURT CRESCENT
Petts Wood C.C.
WOOD RIDE
KINGSWAY
SHERBORNE ROAD
Electricity Sta
PETTS WOOD
BR5
POVEREST ROAD
Hall
Lib
Superstore
QUEENSWAY
FAIRWAY
GREENCOURT ROAD
WEST WAY
PRINCES AVENUE
WILLETT WAY
POVEREST
THE CHENIES
LOCKESLEY
OAKDENE
COVET WOOD
POVEREST REC GRD
FRANKSWOOD AVENUE
LAKESWOOD ROAD
TUDOR WAY
ST. JOHN'S ROAD
ST. GEORGE'S ROAD
BEAUMONT ROAD
SHEPPERTON ROAD
CRESCENT DRIVE
TOWNCOURT LANE
FAIRFIELD ROAD
THE COVERT
PERRY HALL ROAD
ALLOT
PETTS WOOD REC GRD
SPARROW COMMON
ROUNDABOUT WOOD
CROFTON ROAD
BR6
ORPINGTON
Tenn Club
BROXBOURNE

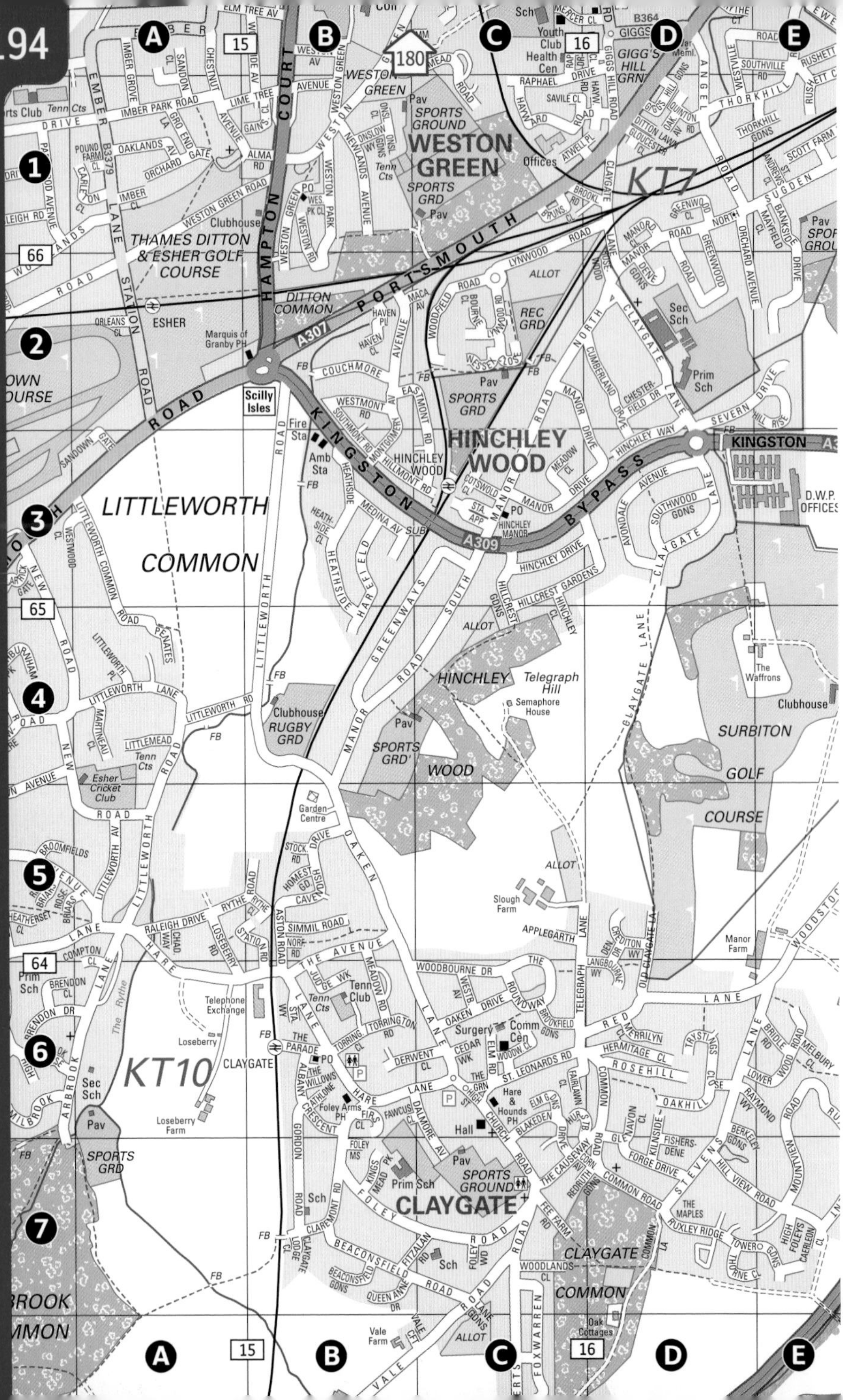
A
B
C
D
E
1
2
3
4
5
6
7
15
16
180
66
65
64
KT7
KT10
WESTON GREEN
HINCHLEY WOOD
CLAYGATE
LITTLEWORTH COMMON
THAMES DITTON & ESHER GOLF COURSE
SURBITON GOLF COURSE
CLAYGATE COMMON
DITTON COMMON
GIGG'S HILL GRN
ESHER
Scilly Isles
Marquis of Granby PH
HAMPTON COURT
PORTSMOUTH ROAD
A307
A309
KINGSTON BYPASS
KINGSTON ROAD
B3379
B364
EMBER LANE
STATION ROAD
WESTON GREEN ROAD
IMBER PARK ROAD
LITTLEWORTH ROAD
LITTLEWORTH COMMON ROAD
LITTLEWORTH LANE
NEW ROAD
MANOR ROAD SOUTH
GREENWAYS
CLAYGATE LANE
HARE LANE
OAKEN LANE
FOLEY ROAD
BEACONSFIELD ROAD
COMMON ROAD
RED LANE
TELEGRAPH LANE
HINCHLEY DRIVE
HILLCREST GARDENS
LINGFIELD
WESTON AVENUE
NEWLANDS AVENUE
COUCHMORE AV
WOODFIELD ROAD
Telegraph Hill
Semaphore House
The Waffrons
D.W.P. OFFICES
Clubhouse
RUGBY GRD
SPORTS GRD
SPORTS GROUND
Esher Cricket Club
Garden Centre
Slough Farm
Manor Farm
Loseberry Farm
Loseberry
Telephone Exchange
Foley Arms PH
Hare & Hounds PH
Prim Sch
Sec Sch
Fire Sta
Amb Sta
Youth Club
Health Cen
Vale Farm
Oak Cottages
ALLOT
REC GRD
FB
Pav
PO
Sch
Offices

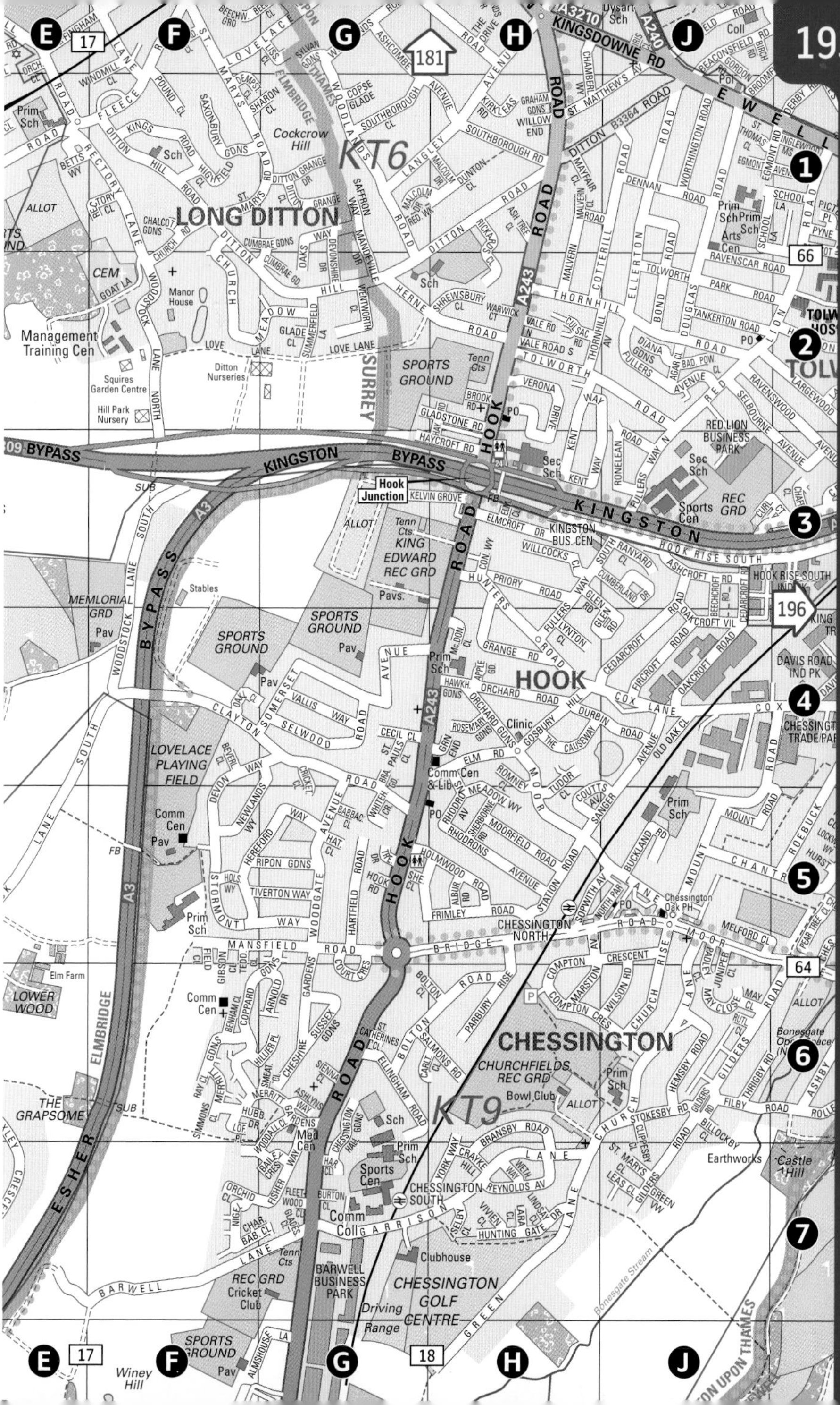
E
F
G
H
J
17
181
196
66
64
18
1
2
3
4
5
6
7
LONG DITTON
KT6
KT9
HOOK
CHESSINGTON
Cockcrow Hill
SURREY
ELMBRIDGE
THAMES
KINGSTON BYPASS
A3
A243
A3210
A240
B3364
KINGSDOWNE RD
EWELL
HOOK ROAD
DITTON ROAD
Hook Junction
Kelvin Grove
ALLOT
CEM
Manor House
Management Training Cen
Squires Garden Centre
Hill Park Nursery
Ditton Nurseries
SPORTS GROUND
MEMLORIAL GRD
Stables
KING EDWARD REC GRD
LOVELACE PLAYING FIELD
RED LION BUSINESS PARK
REC GRD
Sports Cen
KINGSTON BUS. CEN
HOOK RISE SOUTH
DAVIS ROAD IND PK
CHESSINGTON TRADE PARK
Chessington Oak PH
Chessington North
Chessington South
CHURCHFIELDS REC GRD
Bowl Club
Elm Farm
LOWER WOOD
THE GRAPSOME
Bonesgate Open Space
Castle Hill
Earthworks
Bonesgate Stream
BARWELL BUSINESS PARK
CHESSINGTON GOLF CENTRE
Driving Range
Clubhouse
Cricket Club
Winey Hill
KINGSTON UPON THAMES
ESHER BYPASS
BARWELL LANE
MANSFIELD ROAD
BRIDGE ROAD
NORTH PAR
CHURCH LANE
GARRISON LANE
CLAYTON ROAD
SOMERSET AVENUE
ORCHARD ROAD
COX LANE
GOSBURY HILL
MOOR LANE
HUNTERS ROAD
PRIORY ROAD
THORNHILL ROAD
TOLWORTH PARK ROAD
LOVE LANE
MEADOW HILL

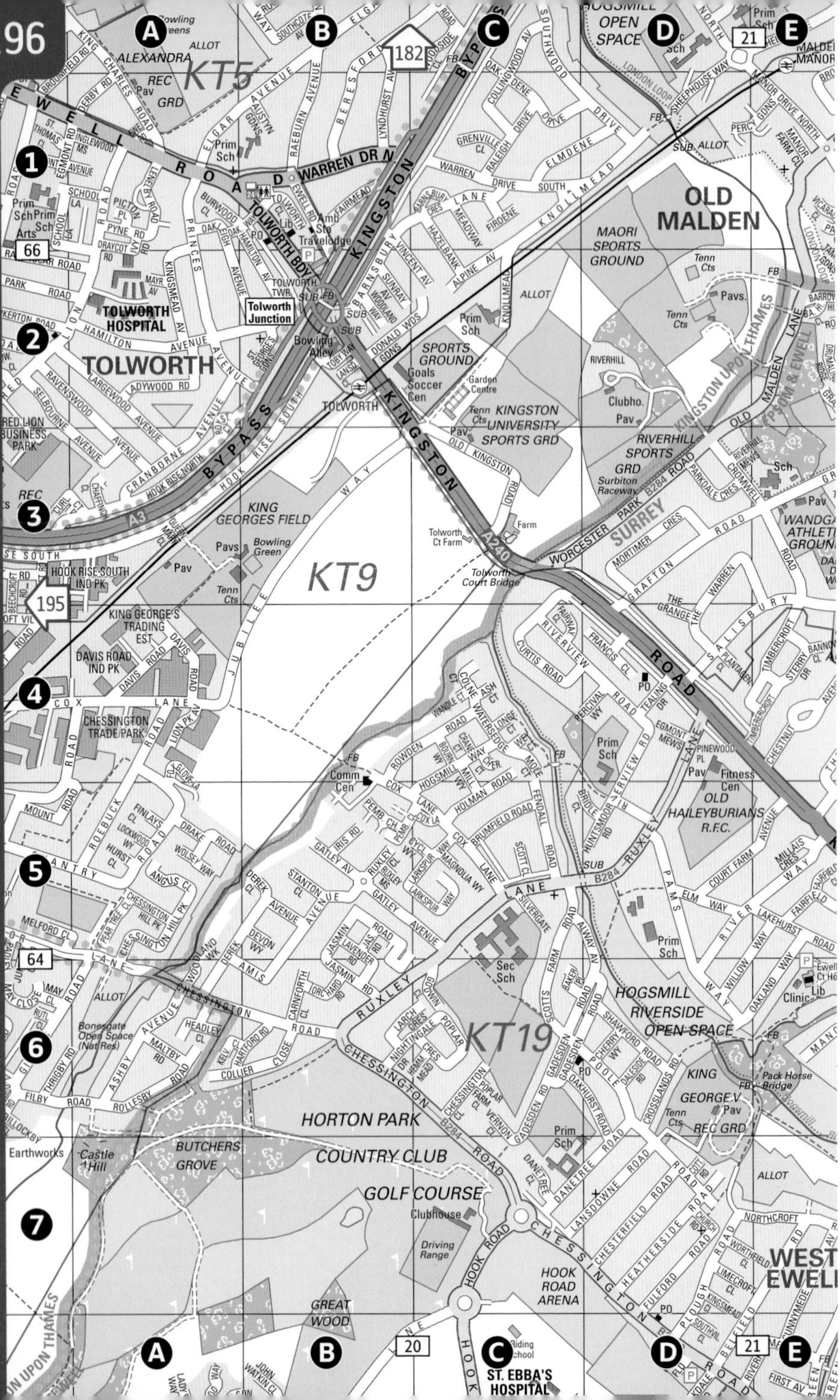
A
B
C
D
E
1
2
3
4
5
6
7
182
195
66
64
20
21
KT5
KT9
KT19
ALEXANDRA
REC
GRD
ALLOT
EWELL ROAD
WARREN DR N
KINGSTON BYPASS
TOLWORTH BDY
Tolworth Junction
TOLWORTH HOSPITAL
TOLWORTH
HOGSMILL OPEN SPACE
OLD MALDEN
MAORI SPORTS GROUND
SPORTS GROUND
Goals Soccer Cen
Garden Centre
KINGSTON UNIVERSITY SPORTS GRD
RIVERHILL SPORTS GRD
Surbiton Raceway
KING GEORGES FIELD
Bowling Green
SURREY
WORCESTER PARK ROAD
KINGSTON ROAD
A240
A3
B284
Tolworth Ct Farm
Tolworth Court Bridge
RED LION BUSINESS PARK
HOOK RISE SOUTH IND PK
KING GEORGE'S TRADING EST
DAVIS ROAD IND PK
CHESSINGTON TRADE PARK
COX LANE
JUBILEE WAY
OLD HAILEYBURIANS R.F.C.
WANDGAS ATHLETIC GROUND
Comm Cen
Sec Sch
HOGSMILL RIVERSIDE OPEN SPACE
KING GEORGE V REC GRD
Pack Horse Bridge
Bonesgate Open Space (Nat Res)
Earthworks
Castle Hill
BUTCHERS GROVE
HORTON PARK COUNTRY CLUB GOLF COURSE
Clubhouse
Driving Range
GREAT WOOD
HOOK ROAD ARENA
HOOK ROAD
CHESSINGTON ROAD
RUXLEY LANE
Riding School
ST. EBBA'S HOSPITAL
WEST EWELL
KINGSTON UPON THAMES
EPSOM & EWELL

E
F
G
H
J
22
23
183
198
66
64
1
2
3
4
5
6
7
MALDEN ROAD
CENTRAL ROAD
CHEAM COMMON ROAD
LONDON ROAD
KINGSTON ROAD
EWELL BYPASS
A2043
A24
A240
B284
B2200 ROAD
WORCESTER PARK
STONELEIGH
NORTH CHEAM
CUDDINGTON
NONSUCH PARK
KT4
KT17
SM3
SHADBOLT PK
KING GEORGE'S FIELD
AURIOL PARK
SPORTS GRD
REC GRD
ALLOT
Athletic Club
Superstore
Prim Sch
Prim Schs
Lib
PO
Pol
Clinic
Comm Cen
Tenn Cts
Bowl Grn
Pav
CEM
Beverley Brook
EPSOM & EWELL
SUTTON
Beggar's Hill
Organ Crossroads
Glasshouse
Cuddington Church (Site of)
Nonsuch Mansion
OAK PLANTATION
THE WOOD
Diana's Dyke
Chamber Mead
PLAYING FIELDS
Premier Inn
Stoneleigh Inn PH
The Plough PH
TA Cen
LONDON LOOP
MANOR DRIVE
LEYFIELD
HIGHDOWN
STONELEIGH PARK ROAD
SPARROW FARM ROAD
WICKHAM AVENUE
THE AVENUE

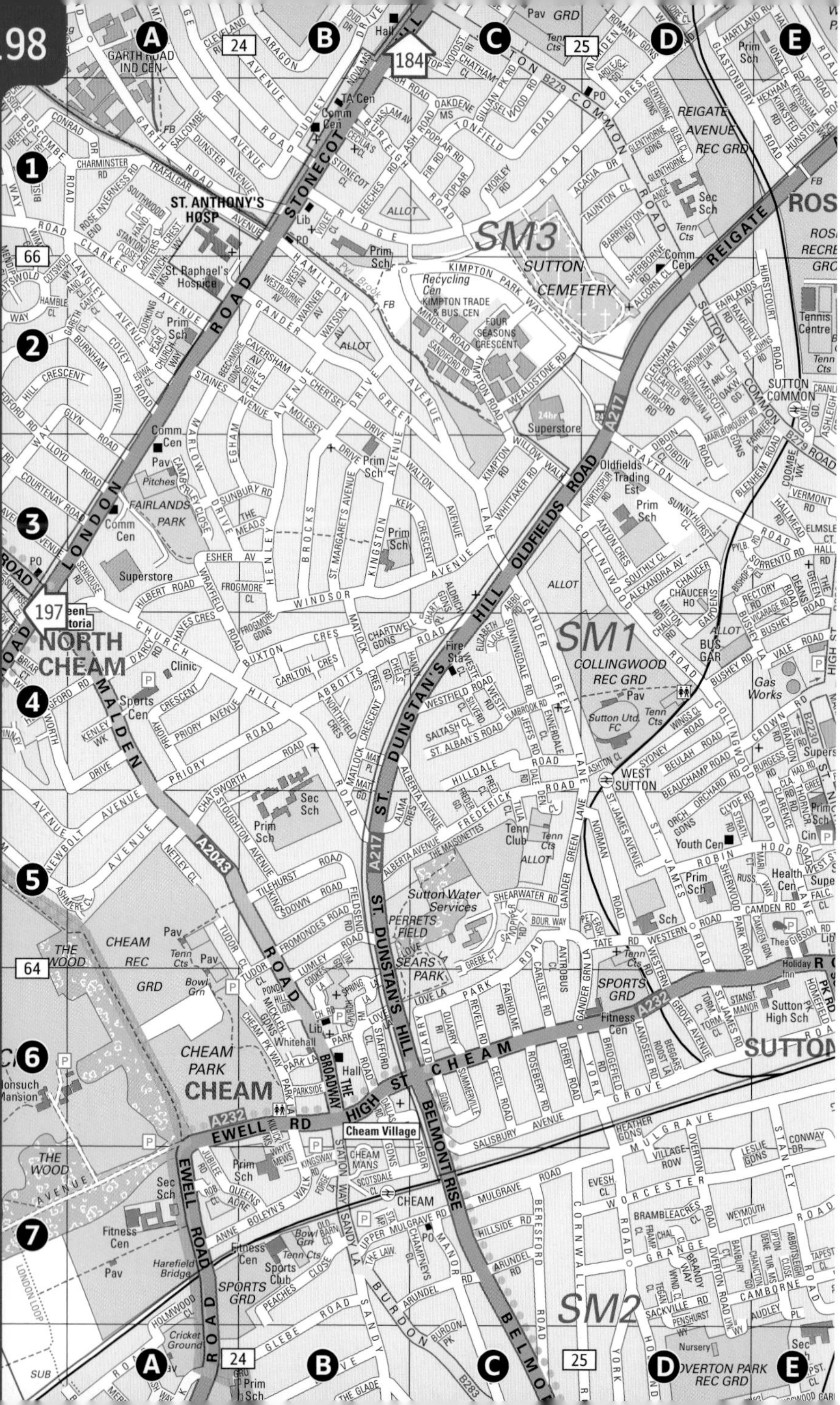
A
B
C
D
E
1
2
3
4
5
6
7
24
25
66
64
184
197
GARTH ROAD IND CEN
ST. ANTHONY'S HOSP
St. Raphael's Hospice
STONECOT HILL
LONDON ROAD
SM3
SUTTON CEMETERY
KIMPTON PARK WAY
Recycling Cen
KIMPTON TRADE & BUS. CEN
FOUR SEASONS CRESCENT
REIGATE AVENUE REC GRD
REIGATE AVENUE
ROSE
SUTTON COMMON ROAD
SUTTON COMMON
FAIRLANDS PARK
Superstore
NORTH CHEAM
MALDEN ROAD
A2043
A217
A232
B279
B2230
B283
OLDFIELDS ROAD
ST. DUNSTAN'S HILL
Oldfields Trading Est
SM1
COLLINGWOOD REC GRD
Sutton Utd. FC
WEST SUTTON
Gas Works
Sutton Water Services
PERRETS FIELD
SEARS PARK
SPORTS GRD
CHEAM REC GRD
THE WOOD
CHEAM PARK
CHEAM
Nonsuch Mansion
EWELL RD
EWELL ROAD
Cheam Village
HIGH ST
THE BROADWAY
BELMONT RISE
CHEAM ROAD
SUTTON
Sutton High Sch
MULGRAVE ROAD
WORCESTER ROAD
GRANGE ROAD
SM2
OVERTON PARK REC GRD
Harefield Bridge
Cricket Ground
LONDON LOOP

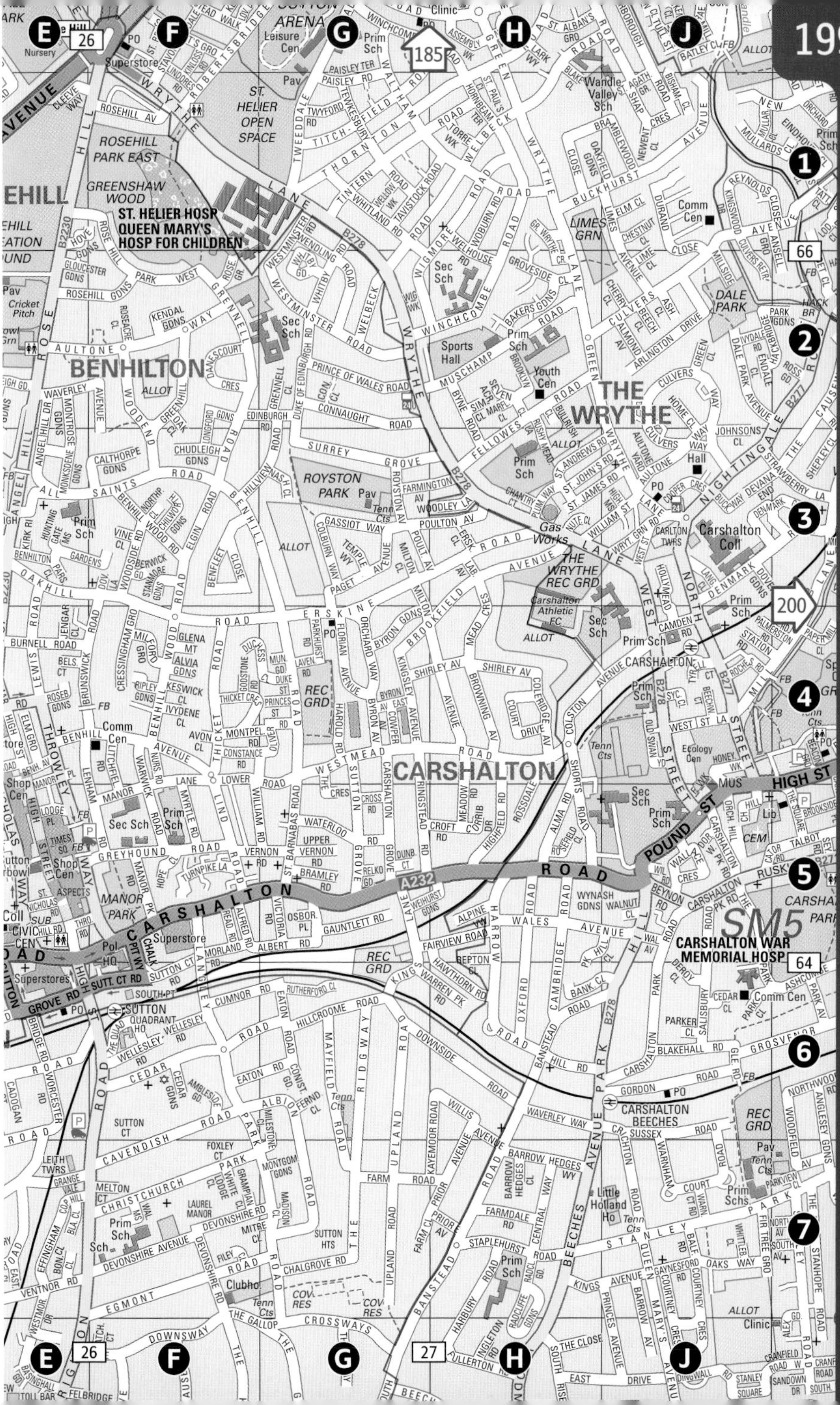
E
F
G
H
J
185
26
1
2
3
4
5
6
7
66
200
64
27
ST. HELIER OPEN SPACE
ROSEHILL PARK EAST
GREENSHAW WOOD
ST. HELIER HOSP
QUEEN MARY'S HOSP FOR CHILDREN
BENHILTON
THE WRYTHE
CARSHALTON
ROYSTON PARK
THE WRYTHE REC GRD
Carshalton Athletic FC
Carshalton Coll
LIMES GRN
DALE PARK
Wandle Valley Sch
Gas Works
MANOR PARK
SM5
CARSHALTON WAR MEMORIAL HOSP
CARSHALTON BEECHES
SUTTON
Superstore
Superstores
Shop Cen
Sports Hall
Youth Cen
Comm Cen
Little Holland Ho
Clubho
Sutton HTS
ROSEHILL AV
WRYTHE LANE
WRYTHE
GREEN WRYTHE LANE
BUCKHURST AVENUE
WESTMINSTER ROAD
WINCHCOMBE
MUSCHAMP ROAD
CULVERS AVENUE
ARLINGTON DRIVE
NIGHTINGALE ROAD
PRINCE OF WALES ROAD
CONNAUGHT ROAD
SURREY GROVE
ALL SAINTS ROAD
ERSKINE ROAD
OAKHILL ROAD
PAGET AVENUE
BENHILL AVENUE
WESTMEAD ROAD
LOWER ROAD
GREYHOUND ROAD
CARSHALTON ROAD
A232
HIGH ST
POUND ST
NORTH STREET
WEST STREET
BEECHES AVENUE
BANSTEAD ROAD
WAVERLEY WAY
STANLEY PARK ROAD
GROSVENOR AVENUE
DOWNSIDE ROAD
UPLAND ROAD
CAVENDISH ROAD
DEVONSHIRE AVENUE
EGMONT ROAD
DOWNSWAY
CROSSWAYS
THE GALLOP
STAPLEHURST ROAD
BARROW HEDGES WY
KINGS AVENUE
EAST DRIVE
FULLERTON RD
B278
B277
B2230

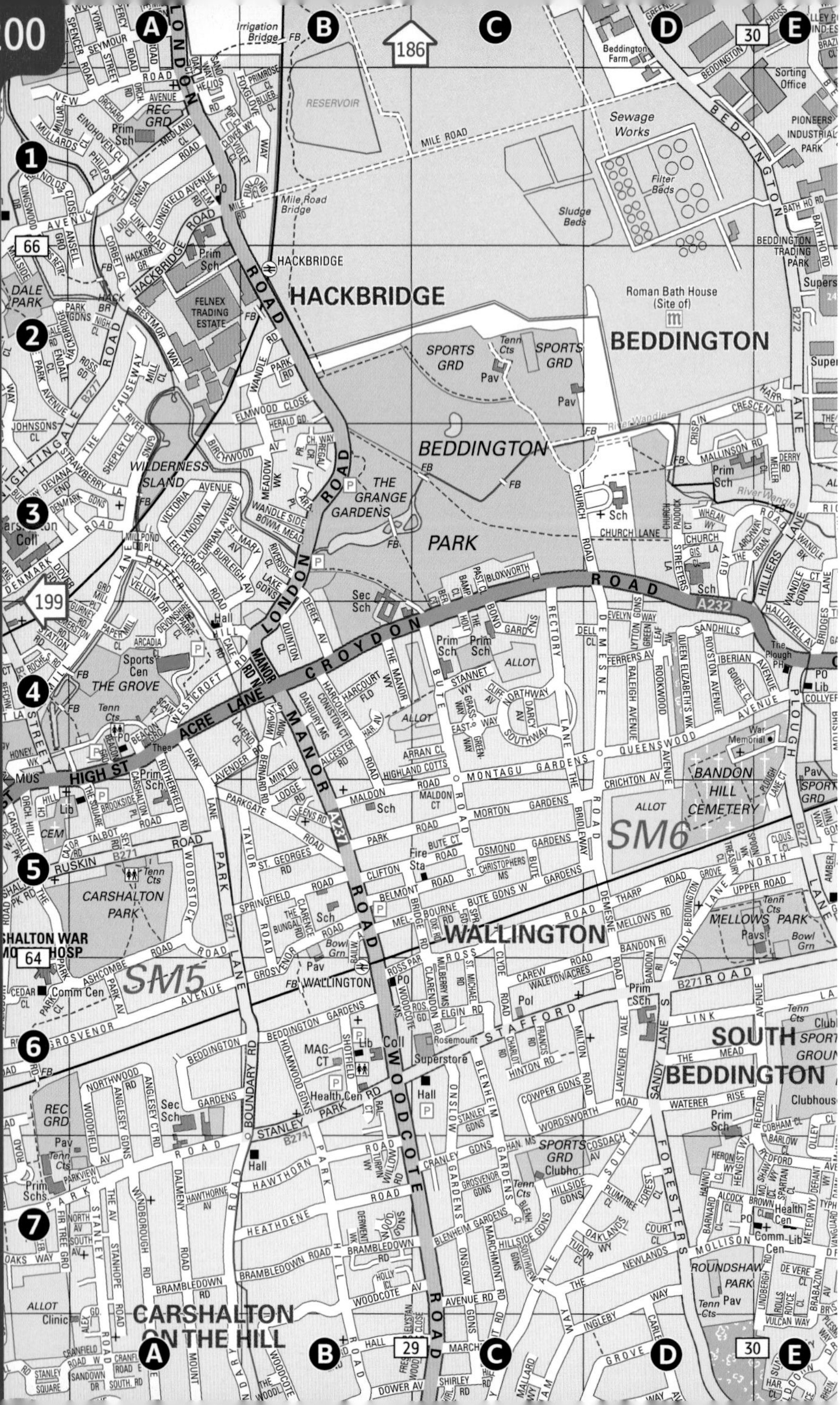
A
B
C
D
E
186
30
199
66
64
29
1
2
3
4
5
6
7
HACKBRIDGE
BEDDINGTON
BEDDINGTON PARK
THE GRANGE GARDENS
WALLINGTON
SOUTH BEDDINGTON
CARSHALTON ON THE HILL
CARSHALTON PARK
BANDON HILL CEMETERY
MELLOWS PARK
ROUNDSHAW PARK
SM5
SM6
RESERVOIR
Sewage Works
Filter Beds
Sludge Beds
Roman Bath House (Site of)
Irrigation Bridge
Mile Road Bridge
MILE ROAD
FELNEX TRADING ESTATE
PIONEERS INDUSTRIAL PARK
BEDDINGTON TRADING PARK
Sorting Office
Beddington Farm
THE GROVE
WILDERNESS ISLAND
DALE PARK
LONDON ROAD
CROYDON ROAD
A232
MANOR ROAD
A237
WOODCOTE ROAD
ACRE LANE
HIGH ST
PLOUGH LANE
B272
B271
B277
STAFFORD ROAD
QUEENSWOOD AVENUE
MONTAGU GARDENS
CHURCH LANE
River Wandle
HACKBRIDGE
WALLINGTON
Sports Cen
CARSHALTON WAR MEMORIAL HOSP
Superstore
Rosemount

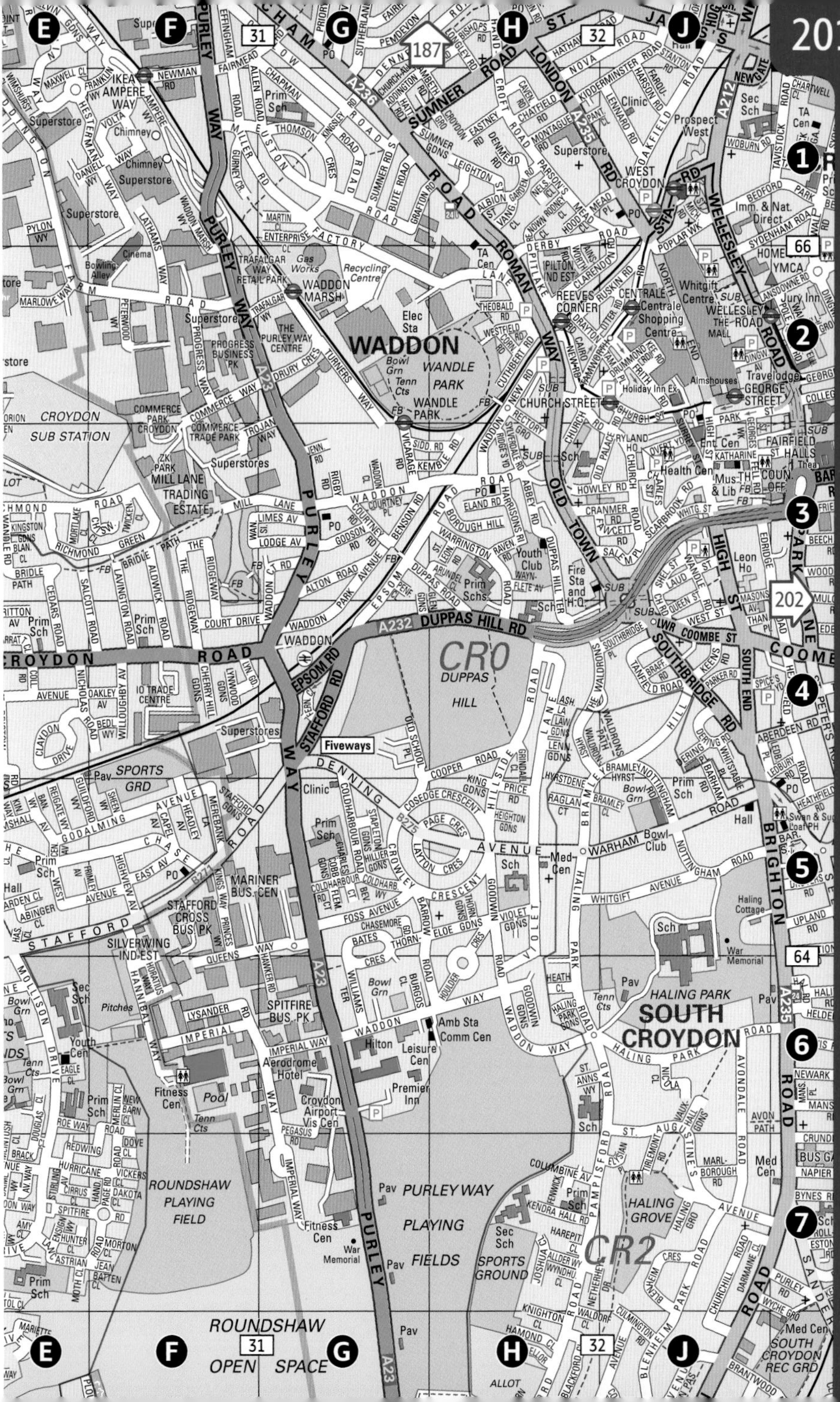
E
F
G
H
J
31
32
187
202
66
64
1
2
3
4
5
6
7
WADDON
CR0
CR2
SOUTH CROYDON
HALING PARK
DUPPAS HILL
WANDLE PARK
CROYDON SUB STATION
MILL LANE TRADING ESTATE
ROUNDSHAW PLAYING FIELD
PURLEY WAY PLAYING FIELDS
ROUNDSHAW OPEN SPACE
HALING GROVE
SPORTS GROUND
SPORTS GRD
SOUTH CROYDON REC GRD
PURLEY WAY
A23
A232
DUPPAS HILL RD
A236
A235
A212
B275
B271
ROMAN WAY
OLD TOWN
LONDON RD
SUMNER ROAD
WELLESLEY ROAD
SOUTHBRIDGE RD
HIGH ST
SOUTH END
BRIGHTON ROAD
CROYDON ROAD
STAFFORD ROAD
WADDON WAY
WADDON MARSH
WEST CROYDON
WEST CROYDON
REEVES CORNER
CENTRALE
CHURCH STREET
GEORGE STREET
WELLESLEY ROAD
AMPERE WAY
IKEA
Fiveways
Centrale Shopping Centre
Whitgift Centre
FAIRFIELD HALLS
Holiday Inn Ex.
Travelodge
Premier Inn
Hilton
Aerodrome Hotel
Croydon Airport Vis Cen
THE PURLEY WAY CENTRE
PROGRESS BUSINESS PK
COMMERCE PARK CROYDON
COMMERCE TRADE PARK
TRAFALGAR WAY RETAIL PARK
STAFFORD CROSS BUS PK
SILVERWING IND EST
SPITFIRE BUS PK
MARINER BUS CEN
PILTON IND EST
Superstore
Superstores
Gas Works
Recycling Centre
Elec Sta
Bowl Grn
Tenn Cts
Prim Sch
Sec Sch
Sch
Youth Club
Fire Sta and H.Q.
Health Cen
Mus TH & Lib
Almshouses
Imm. & Nat. Direct
YMCA
Jury Inn
Amb Sta Comm Cen
Leisure Cen
Fitness Cen
Swan & Sugar Loaf PH
Haling Cottage
War Memorial
Med Cen
Prospect West
CRANMER RD
WHITGIFT AVENUE
NOTTINGHAM ROAD
HALING PARK ROAD
WARHAM
PAMPISFORD ROAD
AVONDALE ROAD
CROWLEY CRESCENT
COSEDGE CRESCENT
PAGE CRES
LAYTON CRES
DENNING AVENUE
COOPER ROAD
VIOLET LANE
COLDHARBOUR ROAD
HARRISONS RI
FAIRMEAD RD
NEWMAN RD
FACTORY LANE
COMMERCE WAY
TROJAN WAY
MILL LANE
RICHMOND GREEN
DUPPAS AVENUE
IMPERIAL WAY
QUEENS WAY
LYSANDER RD
HANNIBAL WAY

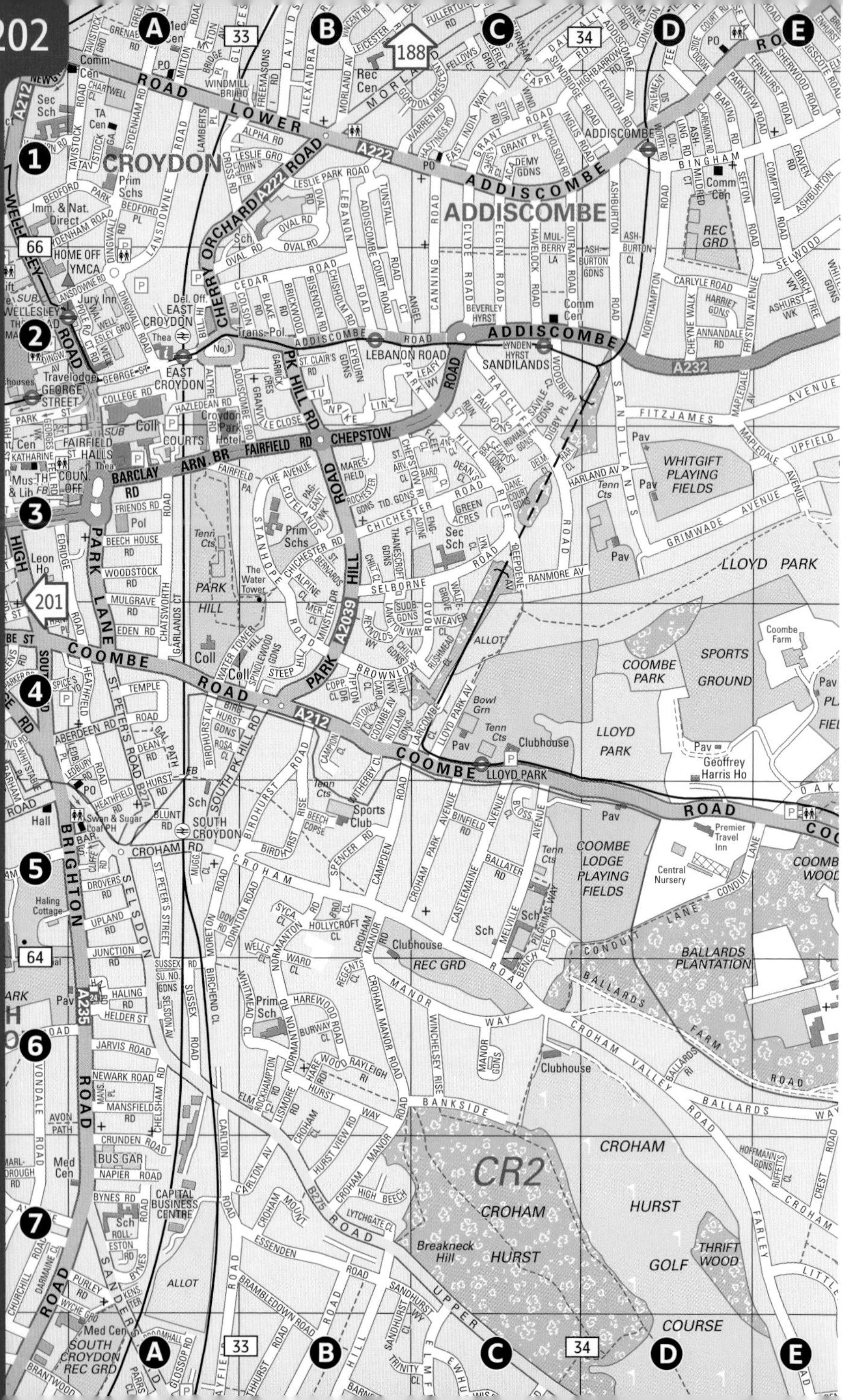
A
B
C
D
E
1
2
3
4
5
6
7
33
34
188
201
66
64
CROYDON
ADDISCOMBE
LOWER ADDISCOMBE ROAD
A222
A212
A232
A2039
A235
B275
B274
CHERRY ORCHARD ROAD
WELLESLEY ROAD
EAST CROYDON
GEORGE STREET
Travelodge
Jury Inn
YMCA
HOME OFF
FAIRFIELD HALLS
BARCLAY RD
PARK LANE
PK HILL RD
PARK HILL ROAD
CHEPSTOW ROAD
FAIRFIELD RD
ADDISCOMBE ROAD
LEBANON ROAD
SANDILANDS
LYNDEN HYRST
FITZJAMES AVENUE
WHITGIFT PLAYING FIELDS
LLOYD PARK
COOMBE PARK
SPORTS GROUND
Coombe Farm
COOMBE ROAD
LLOYD PARK AV
Bowl Grn
Clubhouse
Geoffrey Harris Ho
Premier Travel Inn
Central Nursery
COOMBE LODGE PLAYING FIELDS
COOMBE WOOD
BALLARDS PLANTATION
BALLARDS WAY
CONDUIT LANE
CROHAM VALLEY ROAD
CROHAM ROAD
CROHAM MANOR ROAD
MANOR WAY
REC GRD
BANKSIDE
CR2
CROHAM HURST
Breakneck Hill
CROHAM HURST GOLF COURSE
THRIFT WOOD
UPPER SELSDON ROAD
SOUTH CROYDON
BRIGHTON ROAD
SELSDON ROAD
ST. PETER'S STREET
SOUTH PK HILL RD
PARK HILL
The Water Tower
Sports Club
Haling Cottage
CAPITAL BUSINESS CENTRE
SOUTH CROYDON REC GRD
Swan & Sugar Loaf PH
ALLOT
Coll
Sch
Prim Schs
Sec Sch
Comm Cen
Med Cen
PO
Pav
Tenn Cts

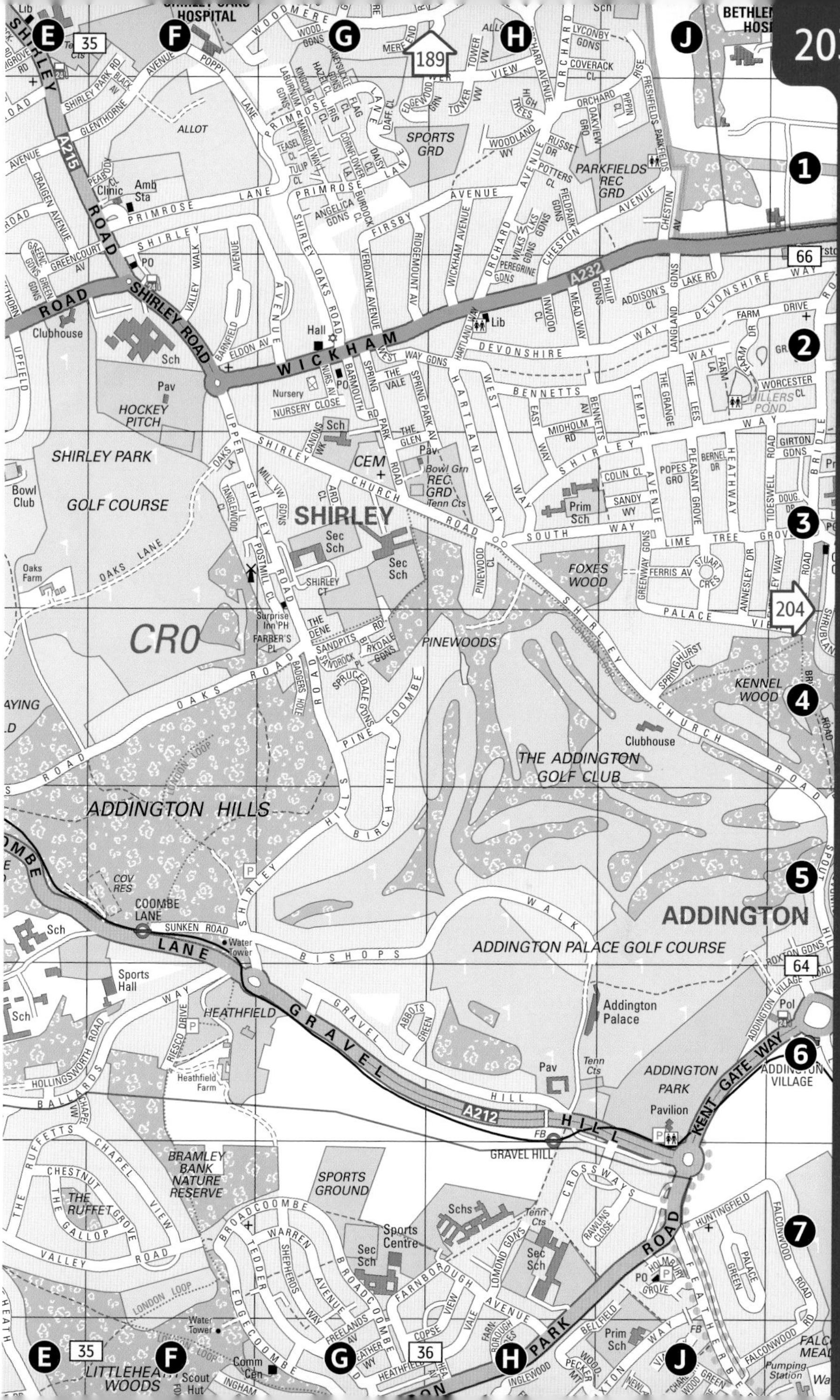
E
F
G
H
J
35
189
HOSPITAL
BETHLEM
1
2
3
4
5
6
7
66
64
204
36
A215
A232
A212
SHIRLEY ROAD
WICKHAM ROAD
SHIRLEY PARK RD
GLENTHORNE
POPPY LANE
ALLOT
PRIMROSE LANE
SPORTS GRD
Clinic
Amb Sta
PO
Clubhouse
Sch
Pav
HOCKEY PITCH
SHIRLEY PARK
GOLF COURSE
Bowl Club
OAKS LANE
Oaks Farm
CR0
OAKS ROAD
ADDINGTON HILLS
COV RES
COOMBE LANE
SUNKEN ROAD
Water Tower
Sports Hall
HEATHFIELD
Heathfield Farm
GRAVEL HILL
BISHOPS WALK
HOLLINGSWORTH ROAD
BALLARDS
THE RUFFETT
CHESTNUT GROVE
THE GALLOP
VALLEY ROAD
CHAPEL VIEW
BRAMLEY BANK NATURE RESERVE
LONDON LOOP
LITTLEHEATH WOODS
Scout Hut
Comm Cen
SPORTS GROUND
Sports Centre
Sec Sch
Schs
Tenn Cts
BROADCOOMBE
FARNBOROUGH AVENUE
PARK ROAD
KENT GATE WAY
ADDINGTON PARK
Pavilion
ADDINGTON VILLAGE
Addington Palace
ADDINGTON PALACE GOLF COURSE
ADDINGTON
ROXTON GDNS
Pol
HUNTINGFIELD
FALCONWOOD ROAD
Pumping Station
THE ADDINGTON GOLF CLUB
SHIRLEY CHURCH ROAD
KENNEL WOOD
SPRINGHURST CL
PINEWOODS
FOXES WOOD
SHIRLEY
CEM
Bowl Grn
REC GRD
Surprise Inn PH
FARRER'S PL
SANDPITS RD
UPPER SHIRLEY ROAD
SHIRLEY HILLS ROAD
PINE COOMBE
BIRCH HILL
HARTLAND WAY
DEVONSHIRE WAY
BENNETTS WAY
SHIRLEY WAY
SOUTH WAY
Prim Sch
LIME TREE GROVE
PALACE VIEW
FERRIS AV
STUART CRES
ANNESLEY DR
TIDESWELL ROAD
GIRTON GDNS
MILLERS POND
WORCESTER CL
FARM DRIVE
PARKFIELDS REC GRD
CHESTON AVENUE
FIRSBY AVENUE
ORCHARD AVENUE
WOODLAND WY
Lib
Hall
Nursery
NURSERY CLOSE

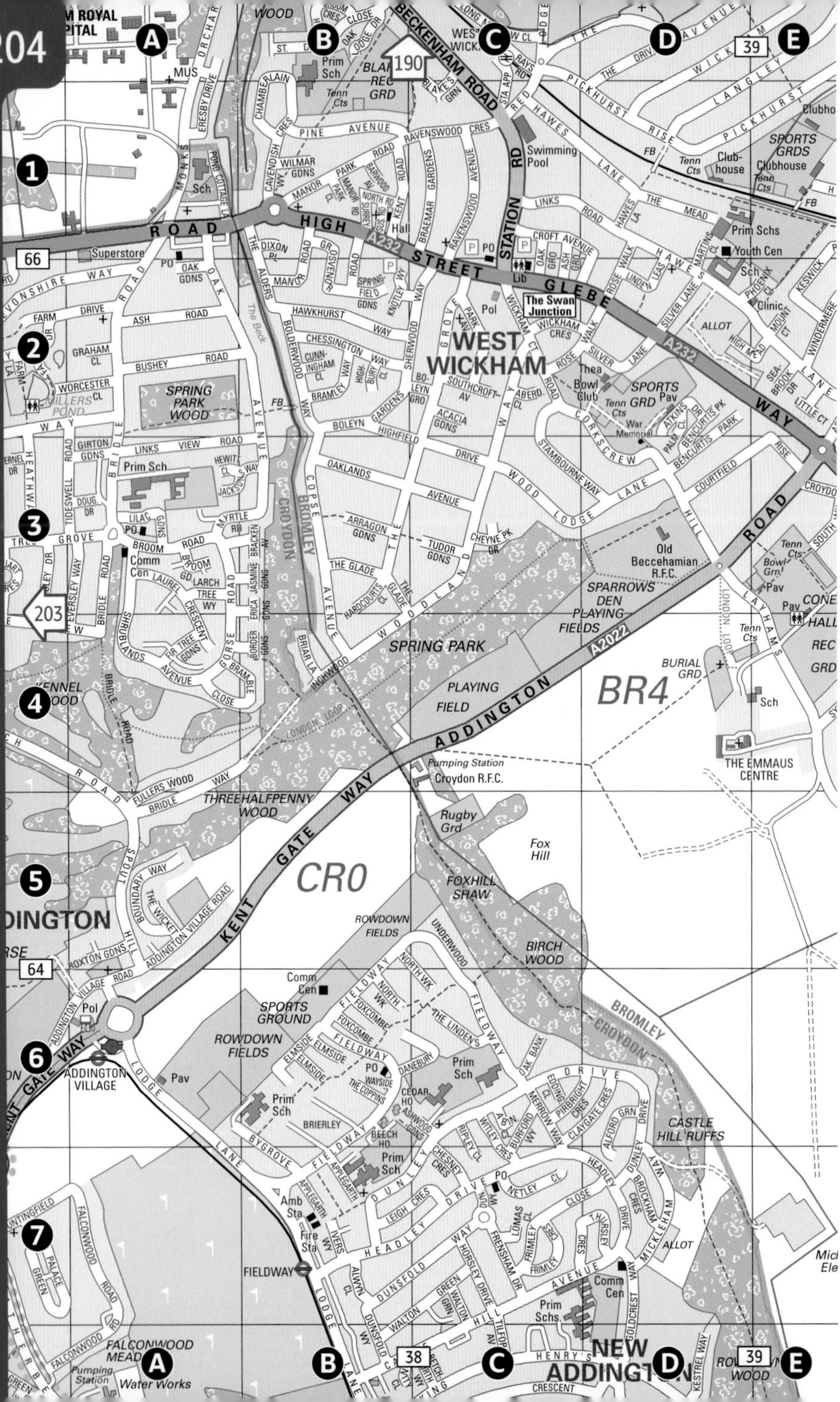
A
B
C
D
E
1
2
3
4
5
6
7
190
203
39
66
64
38
WOOD
Prim Sch
Tenn Cts
REC GRD
BECKENHAM ROAD
WEST WICKHAM
MUS
ERESBY DRIVE
ORCHARD
CHAMBERLAIN CRES
PINE AVENUE
RAVENSWOOD CRES
CAVENDISH WY
WILMAR GDNS
MANOR PARK ROAD
Sch
MONKS
POND COTTAGE LA
Swimming Pool
STATION RD
THE DRIVE
PICKHURST RISE
LANGLEY WAY
PICKHURST
HAWES LANE
FB
Tenn Cts
Club-house
Clubhouse
SPORTS GRDS
THE MEAD
Prim Schs
Youth Cen
LINKS ROAD
CROFT AVENUE
ROAD
HIGH STREET
A232
Superstore
PO
OAK GDNS
Hall
DIXON PL
MANOR ROAD
GROSVENOR ROAD
SPRINGFIELD GDNS
KNOTLEY WY
Lib
GLEBE WAY
The Swan Junction
Pol
WICKHAM CRES
ROSE WALK
SILVER LANE
HAYES
Sch
PHOENIX CL
Clinic
ALLOT
HIGH MEAD
MOUNT CT
SEABROOK DR
KESWICK
WINDERMERE
LITTLE CT
DEVONSHIRE WAY
FARM DRIVE
ASH ROAD
GRAHAM CL
BUSHEY ROAD
WORCESTER CL
MILLERS POND
SPRING PARK WOOD
HAWKHURST WAY
CHESSINGTON WAY
CUNNINGHAM CL
BRAMLEY WAY
HIGHBURY CL
SHERWOOD WAY
WEST WICKHAM
SOUTHCROFT AV
ABERD. CL
Thea
Bowl Club
Tenn Cts
SPORTS GRD
Pav
War Memorial
CORKSCREW
ATKINS DR
BENCURTIS PK
BENCURTIS PARK
STAMBOURNE WAY
ACACIA GDNS
BOLEYN GARDENS
BOLEYN GRO
HIGHFIELD DRIVE
OAKLANDS
AVENUE
WOOD LODGE LANE
COURTFIELD RISE
CROYDON ROAD
GIRTON GDNS
LINKS VIEW ROAD
Prim Sch
HEWITT CL
JACKSONS WAY
TIDESWELL ROAD
BRIDLE ROAD
AVENUE
DOUG. DR
LILAC GDNS
MYRTLE RD
BROOM ROAD
GROVE
Comm Cen
LARCH TREE WY
LAUREL CRESCENT
FIR TREE GDNS
SHRUBLANDS AVENUE
GORSE ROAD
BRAMBLE CLOSE
ERICA
JASMINE GDNS
BRACKEN AV
BORDER GDNS
CROYDON
BROMLEY
COPSE AVENUE
ARRAGON GDNS
THE GLADE
HARDCOURTS CL
TUDOR GDNS
CHEYNE PK DR
WOODLAND WAY
BRIAR LA
INCHWOOD
SPRING PARK
SPARROWS DEN PLAYING FIELDS
Old Beccehamian R.F.C.
A2022
LAYHAMS
LONDON LOOP
Pav
Bowl Grn
Tenn Cts
CONES
HALL REC GRD
BURIAL GRD
BR4
Sch
THE EMMAUS CENTRE
EVERSLEY WAY
KENNEL WOOD
PLAYING FIELD
ADDINGTON
Pumping Station
Croydon R.F.C.
Rugby Grd
FULLERS WOOD
BRIDLE WAY
THREEHALFPENNY WOOD
KENT GATE WAY
CR0
Fox Hill
FOXHILL SHAW
BOUNDARY WAY
THE WICKET
ADDINGTON VILLAGE ROAD
SPOUT HILL
ADDINGTON
ROXTON GDNS
ROWDOWN FIELDS
UNDERWOOD
BIRCH WOOD
NORTH WK
FIELDWAY
Comm Cen
SPORTS GROUND
FOXCOMBE
THE LINDENS
BROMLEY
CROYDON
ROWDOWN FIELDS
ELMSIDE
DANEBURY
Prim Sch
OAK BANK
Pol
ADDINGTON VILLAGE
Pav
LODGE LANE
WAYSIDE
THE COPPINS
CEDAR HO
ASHWOOD GDNS
Prim Sch
BRIERLEY
BYGROVE
BEECH HO
Prim Sch
CASTLE HILL RUFFS
DRIVE
EDDINGTON CL
PIRBRIGHT CRES
CLAYGATE CRES
ALFORD GRN
MERROW WAY
BURFORD WY
WITLEY CRES
RIPLEY CL
CHESNEY CRES
DUNLEY DRIVE
HEADLEY DRIVE
NETLEY CL
APPLEGARTH
Amb Sta
Fire Sta
IVERS WY
LEIGH CRES
CLOSE
LOMAS CL
FRIMLEY CRES
THURSLEY CRES
BROCKHAM CRES
MICKLEHAM WAY
ALLOT
FIELDWAY
ALWYN CL
DUNSFOLD WAY
HORSLEY DRIVE
FRENSHAM DR
AVENUE
Comm Cen
Prim Schs
WALTON GREEN
WALTON GRN
HILL
TILFORD AV
GOLDCREST WAY
KESTREL WAY
NEW ADDINGTON
HENRY'S
CRESCENT
ROWDOWN WOOD
HUNTINGFIELD
FALCONWOOD ROAD
PALACE GREEN
FALCONWOOD RD
FALCONWOOD MEAD
Pumping Station
Water Works
GATE WAY

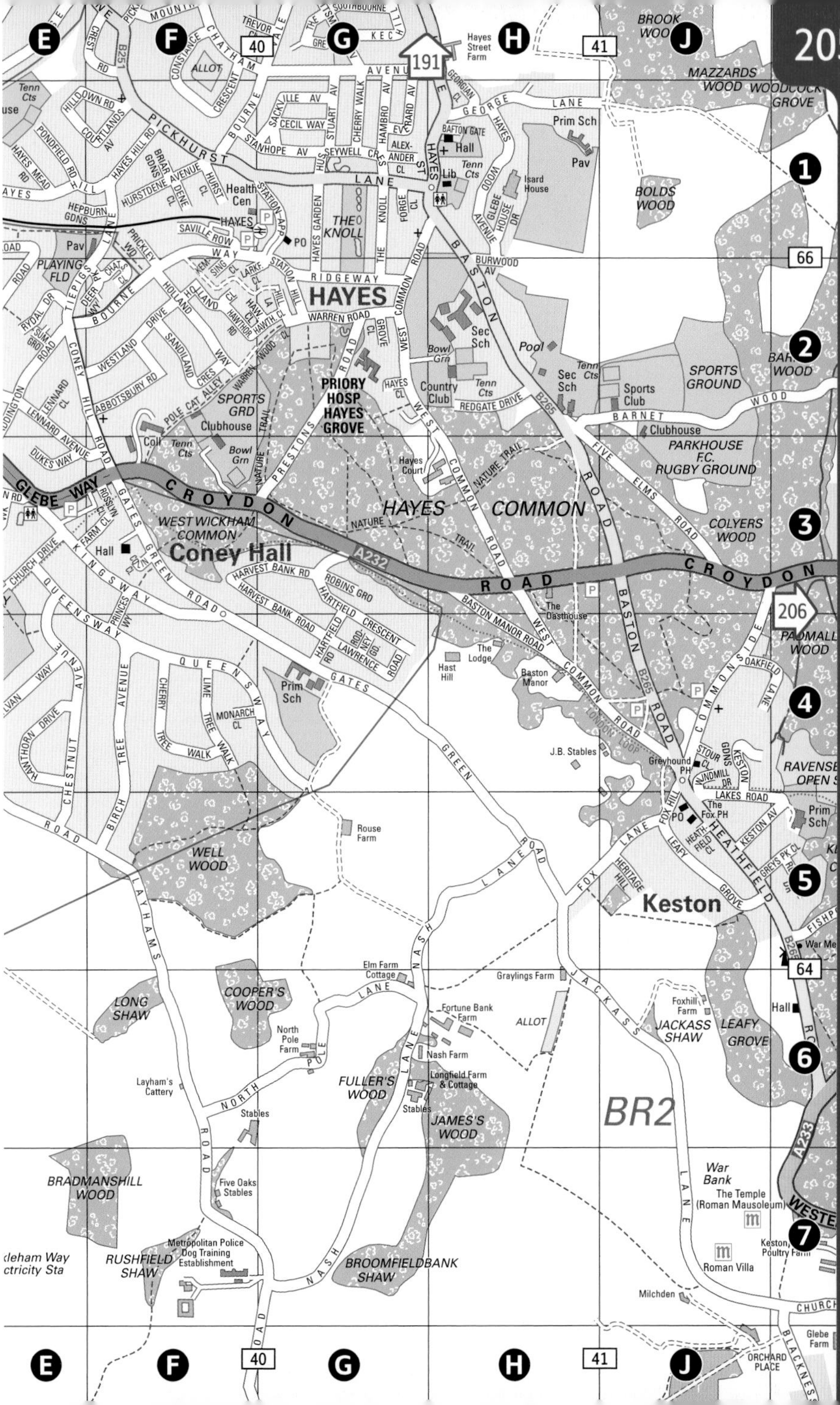
E
F
G
H
J
40
41
191
206
66
64
1
2
3
4
5
6
7
HAYES
Coney Hall
Keston
HAYES COMMON
WEST WICKHAM COMMON
BR2
CROYDON ROAD
A232
A233
B265
B251
GLEBE WAY
PICKHURST LANE
GEORGE LANE
BASTON ROAD
FIVE ELMS ROAD
BARNET WOOD
WEST COMMON ROAD
COMMONSIDE
HEATHFIELD
FOX LANE
JACKASS LANE
NASH LANE
NORTH POLE LANE
LAYHAMS ROAD
KINGSWAY
QUEENSWAY
GATES GREEN ROAD
CONEY HILL ROAD
BOURNE WAY
WARREN ROAD
RIDGEWAY
HAYES LANE
STATION APP
CHATHAM AVENUE
KECHILL GARDENS
CONSTANCE CRESCENT
HILLDOWN RD
COURTLANDS AV
PONDFIELD RD
HAYES HILL RD
HAYES MEAD RD
BRIAR GDNS
HURSTDENE AVENUE
DENE CL
HURST CL
HEPBURN GDNS
SAVILLE ROW
PRICKLEY WD
TIEPIGS LANE
HOLLAND WAY
HOLLAND DRIVE
WESTLAND DRIVE
SANDILAND CRES
ABBOTSBURY RD
LENNARD AVENUE
LENNARD CL
DUKES WAY
RYDAL DR
SUMMER GRD
POLE CAT ALLEY
WARREN WOOD CL
PRESTONS ROAD
NATURE TRAIL
HAYES CL
REDGATE DRIVE
BURWOOD AV
GLEBE HOUSE DR
HAYES WOOD AVENUE
GEORGIAN CL
BAFTON GATE
HAYES ST
ALEXANDER CL
FORGE CL
THE KNOLL
HAYES GARDEN
SEYWELL CL
STANHOPE AV
SACKVILLE AV
CECIL WAY
STUART AV
CHERRY WALK
HAMBRO AV
EVERARD AV
HARVEST BANK RD
HARVEST BANK ROAD
ROBINS GRO
HARTFIELD CRESCENT
HARTFIELD RD
LAWRENCE ROAD
BASTON MANOR ROAD
MONARCH CL
LIME TREE WALK
CHERRY TREE WALK
BIRCH TREE AVENUE
CHESTNUT AVENUE
HAWTHORN DRIVE
PRINCES WAY
CHURCH DRIVE
FARM CL
ROSSLYN CL
OAKFIELD LANE
LAKES ROAD
KESTON AV
STOUR CL
WINDMILL DR
KESTON GDNS
HEATHFIELD CL
LEAFY GROVE
HERITAGE HILL
GREYS PK CL
FISHPONDS
WESTERHAM
CHURCH
BLACKNESS
ORCHARD PLACE
THE KNOLL
PRIORY HOSP HAYES GROVE
Prim Sch
Pav
Health Cen
PO
Lib
Hall
Sec Sch
Pool
Tenn Cts
Bowl Grn
Country Club
Sports Club
SPORTS GROUND
Clubhouse
PARKHOUSE F.C. RUGBY GROUND
SPORTS GRD
PLAYING FLD
Coll
Hayes Court
The Oasthouse
The Lodge
Hast Hill
Baston Manor
LONDON LOOP
J.B. Stables
Greyhound PH
The Fox PH
Isard House
Hayes Street Farm
BROOK WOOD
MAZZARDS WOOD
WOODCOCK GROVE
BOLDS WOOD
COLYERS WOOD
PADMALL WOOD
RAVENSBOURNE OPEN SPACE
WELL WOOD
Rouse Farm
COOPER'S WOOD
LONG SHAW
Elm Farm Cottage
North Pole Farm
Fortune Bank Farm
Nash Farm
Longfield Farm & Cottage
Stables
FULLER'S WOOD
JAMES'S WOOD
Graylings Farm
ALLOT
Foxhill Farm
JACKASS SHAW
LEAFY GROVE
War Memorial
Layham's Cattery
Five Oaks Stables
BRADMANSHILL WOOD
RUSHFIELD SHAW
Metropolitan Police Dog Training Establishment
BROOMFIELDBANK SHAW
War Bank
The Temple (Roman Mausoleum)
Roman Villa
Keston Poultry Farm
Milchden
Glebe Farm
Addleham Way Electricity Sta

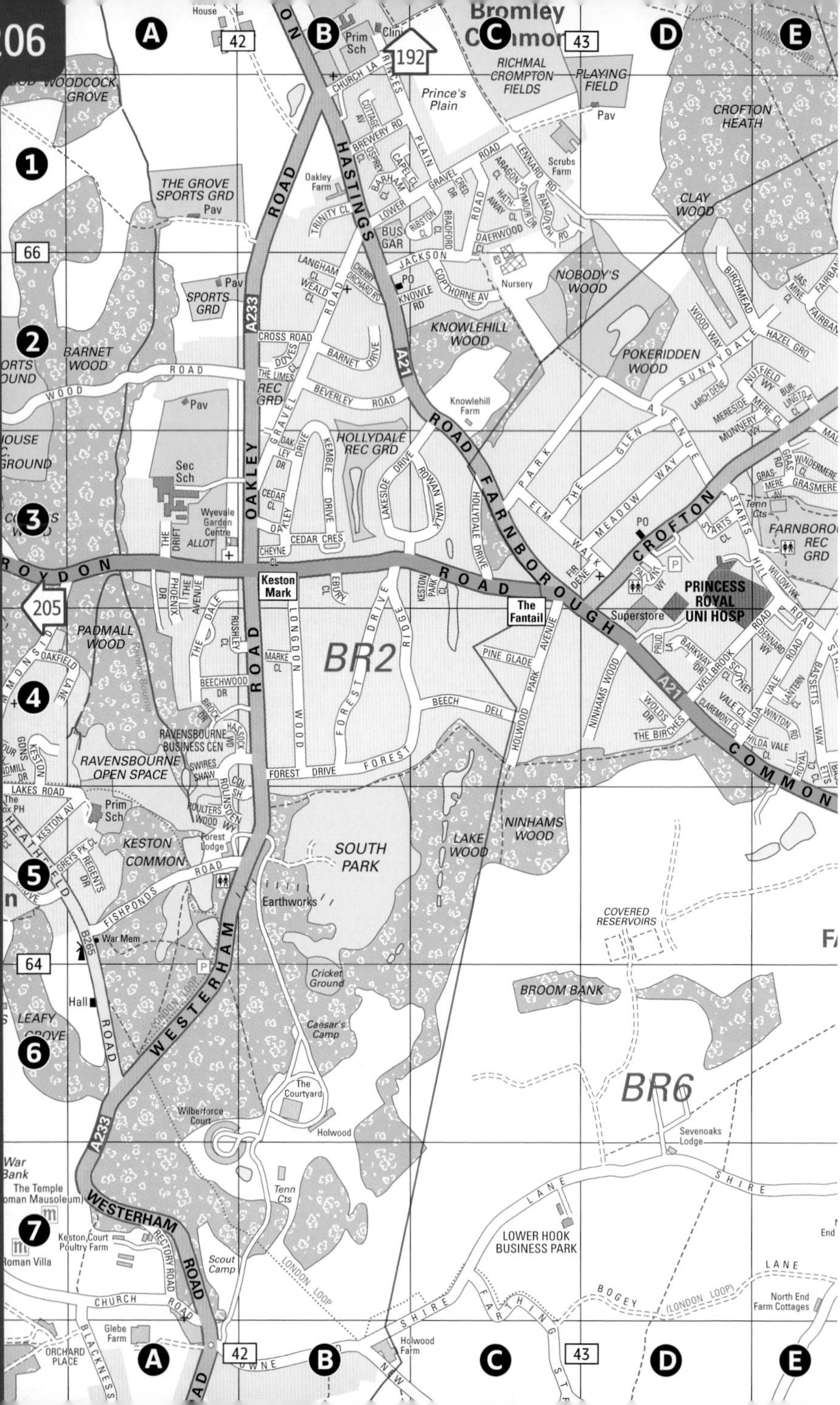
A
B
C
D
E
1
2
3
4
5
6
7
42
43
66
64
192
205
Bromley Common
House
Prim Sch
Clinic
WOODCOCK GROVE
CHURCH LA
PRINCES PLAIN
Prince's Plain
RICHMAL CROMPTON FIELDS
PLAYING FIELD
Pav
CROFTON HEATH
COTTAGE AV
BREWERY RD
OSPREY CL
CAPEL CL
BARHAM CL
GRAVEL ROAD
CRED. DR
ARAGON CL
SEYMOUR DR
LENNARD RD
RANDOLPH RD
Scrubs Farm
THE GROVE SPORTS GRD
Oakley Farm
TRINITY CL
LOWER
HASTINGS
ROAD
BUS GAR
RIBSTON CL
BRADFORD CL
HATH-AWAY
DAERWOOD CL
CLAY WOOD
LANGHAM CL
CHERRY ORCHARD RD
JACKSON
PO
KNOWLE RD
COPTHORNE AV
Nursery
NOBODY'S WOOD
BIRCHMEAD
JASMINE CL
FAIRBANK
SPORTS GRD
WEALD CL
A233
A21
CROSS ROAD
DOVES CL
BARNET DRIVE
KNOWLEHILL WOOD
WOOD WAY
SUNNYDALE
HAZEL GRO
BARNET WOOD
ROAD
WOOD
THE LIMES
REC GRD
BEVERLEY ROAD
POKERIDDEN WOOD
LARCH DENE
NUTFIELD WY
BURLINGTON CL
MERESIDE
MERE CL
MUNNERY WY
Knowlehill Farm
HOUSE REC. GROUND
Sec Sch
GRAVEL DAKLEY DR
DRIVE
KEMBLE DRIVE
HOLLYDALE REC GRD
LAKESIDE DRIVE
ROWAN WALK
HOLLYDALE DRIVE
FARNBOROUGH
PARK
THE GLEN
AVENUE
ELM WALK
MEADOW WAY
GRASMERE RD
GRAS-MERE AV
WINDERMERE CL
GRASMERE
Tenn Cts
CEDAR CL
OAKLEY
Wyevale Garden Centre
ALLOT
THE DRIFT
CEDAR CRES
CHEYNE CL
CROFTON
STARTS CL
STARTS HILL
FARNBOROUGH REC GRD
COOMBS WOOD
CROYDON
ROAD
Keston Mark
FIR DENE
PALLANT WY
P
PRINCESS ROYAL UNI HOSP
Superstore
WILLOW WK
PHOENIX DR
THE AVENUE
THE DALE
RUSHLEY CL
EBURY CL
KESTON PARK CL
The Fantail
PADMALL WOOD
OAKFIELD LANE
MARKE CL
LONGDON WOOD
BR2
FOREST DRIVE
RIDGE
PINE GLADE
AVENUE
PRUD LA
BARKWAY DR
DENNARD WY
ROAD
BEECHWOOD DR
BROCK WD
HASSOCK WD
Ravensbourne
NINHAMS WOOD
WELLBROOK
SCOTNEY CL
VALE CL
HILDA VALE
LANTERN CL
BASSETTS WAY
RAVENSBOURNE BUSINESS CEN
BEECH DELL
HOLWOOD PARK
WOLDS DR
CLAREMONT CL
WINTON RD
RAVENSBOURNE OPEN SPACE
SWIRES SHAW
COL-SH.
THE BIRCHES
HILDA VALE CL
ROYAL CL
ETTS
KESTON GDNS
WINDMILL DR
FOREST DRIVE
FOREST
COMMON
LAKES ROAD
The Fox PH
KESTON AV
Prim Sch
POULTERS WOOD
ROLINSDEN WY
NINHAMS WOOD
KESTON COMMON
Forest Lodge
SOUTH PARK
LAKE WOOD
HEATHFIELD
GREYS PK CL
REGENTS DR
FISHPONDS ROAD
Earthworks
COVERED RESERVOIRS
B265
War Mem
WESTERHAM
P
LONDON LOOP
Cricket Ground
BROOM BANK
Hall
LEAFY GROVE
ROAD
Caesar's Camp
BR6
The Courtyard
Wilberforce Court
Holwood
Sevenoaks Lodge
War Bank
The Temple (Roman Mausoleum)
Tenn Cts
SHIRE
LANE
Keston Court Poultry Farm
Roman Villa
RECTORY ROAD
WESTERHAM ROAD
LOWER HOOK BUSINESS PARK
Scout Camp
LANE
North End Farm Cottages
BOGEY (LONDON LOOP)
CHURCH ROAD
SHIRE
FARTHING ST
Glebe Farm
ORCHARD PLACE
BLACKNESS
Holwood Farm
DOWNE
NEW
FA

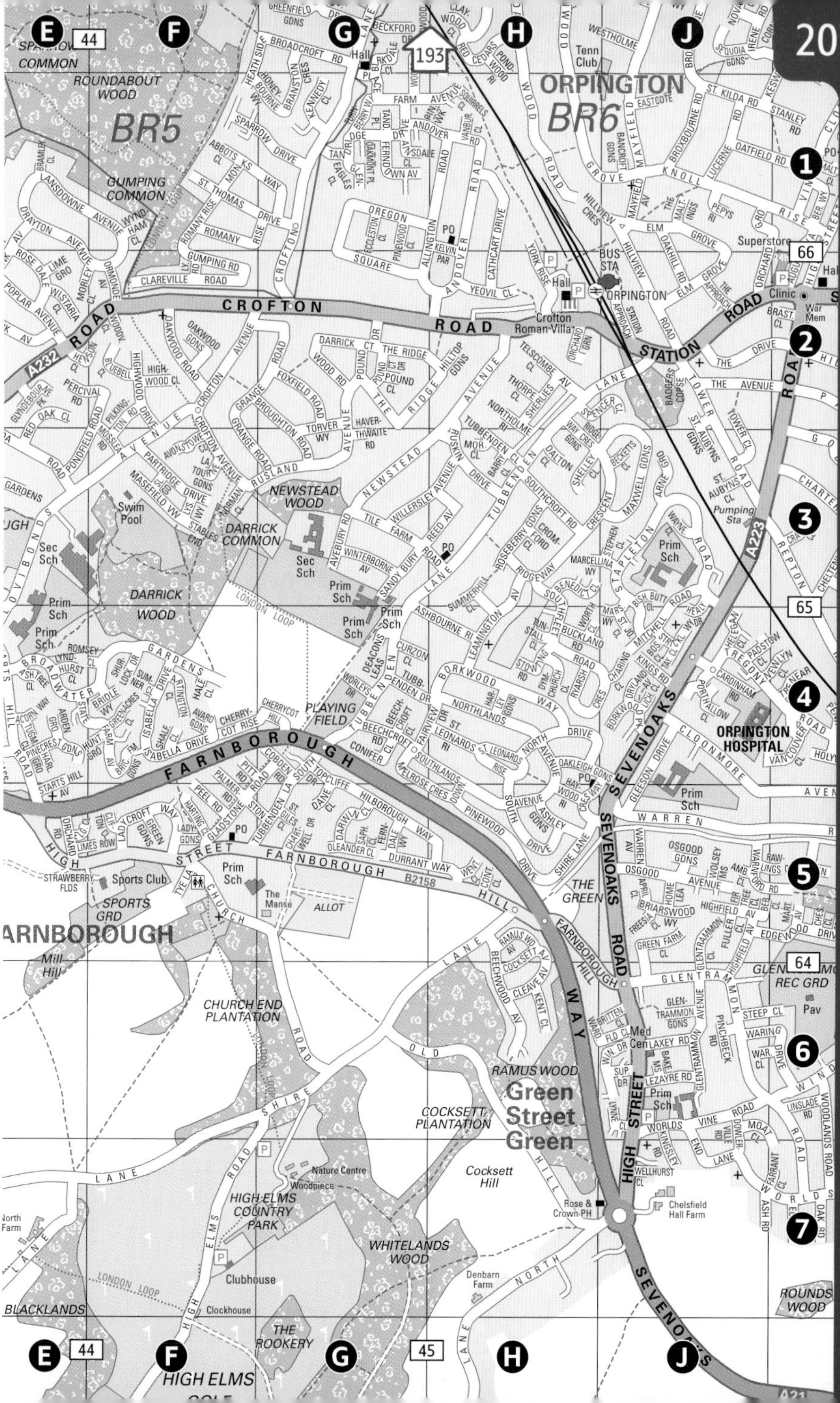
E
F
G
H
J
44
193
ORPINGTON
BR6
BR5
SPARROW COMMON
ROUNDABOUT WOOD
GUMPING COMMON
CROFTON ROAD
STATION ROAD
A232
A223
66
65
64
45
1
2
3
4
5
6
7
BUS STA
ORPINGTON
Crofton Roman Villa
Superstore
Clinic
War Mem
Tenn Club
NEWSTEAD WOOD
DARRICK COMMON
DARRICK WOOD
Swim Pool
Sec Sch
Prim Sch
PLAYING FIELD
FARNBOROUGH
FARNBOROUGH WAY
FARNBOROUGH HILL
HIGH STREET FARNBOROUGH
B2158
SEVENOAKS ROAD
SEVENOAKS WAY
ORPINGTON HOSPITAL
Pumping Sta
Sports Club
SPORTS GRD
Mill Hill
The Manse
ALLOT
THE GREEN
CHURCH END PLANTATION
RAMUS WOOD
Green Street Green
COCKSETT PLANTATION
Cocksett Hill
HIGH ELMS COUNTRY PARK
Nature Centre
Woodpiece
WHITELANDS WOOD
Clubhouse
Clockhouse
THE ROOKERY
BLACKLANDS
North Farm
Denbarn Farm
Rose & Crown PH
Chelsfield Hall Farm
Med Cen
GLENTRAMMON REC GRD
Pav
ROUNDS WOOD
HIGH ELMS
LONDON LOOP
A21

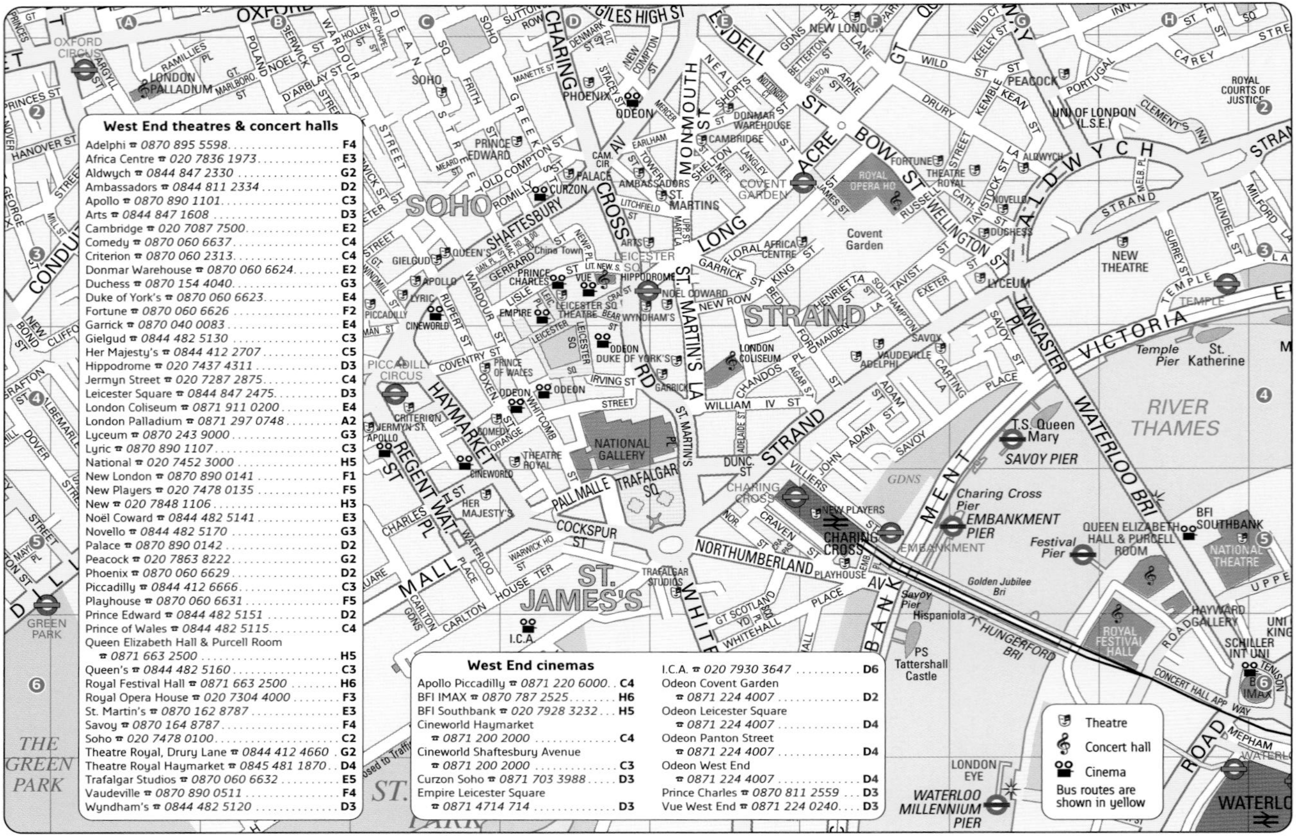

West End theatres & concert halls

Adelphi ☎ *0870 895 5598*		**F4**
Africa Centre ☎ *020 7836 1973*		**E3**
Aldwych ☎ *0844 847 2330*		**G2**
Ambassadors ☎ *0844 811 2334*		**D2**
Apollo ☎ *0870 890 1101*		**C3**
Arts ☎ *0844 847 1608*		**D3**
Cambridge ☎ *020 7087 7500*		**E2**
Comedy ☎ *0870 060 6637*		**C4**
Criterion ☎ *0870 060 2313*		**C4**
Donmar Warehouse ☎ *0870 060 6624*		**E2**
Duchess ☎ *0870 154 4040*		**G3**
Duke of York's ☎ *0870 060 6623*		**E4**
Fortune ☎ *0870 060 6626*		**F2**
Garrick ☎ *0870 040 0083*		**E4**
Gielgud ☎ *0844 482 5130*		**C3**
Her Majesty's ☎ *0844 412 2707*		**C5**
Hippodrome ☎ *020 7437 4311*		**D3**
Jermyn Street ☎ *020 7287 2875*		**C4**
Leicester Square ☎ *0844 847 2475*		**D3**
London Coliseum ☎ *0871 911 0200*		**E4**
London Palladium ☎ *0871 297 0748*		**A2**
Lyceum ☎ *0870 243 9000*		**G3**
Lyric ☎ *0870 890 1107*		**C3**
National ☎ *020 7452 3000*		**H5**
New London ☎ *0870 890 0141*		**F1**
New Players ☎ *020 7478 0135*		**F5**
New ☎ *020 7848 1106*		**H3**
Noël Coward ☎ *0844 482 5141*		**E3**
Novello ☎ *0844 482 5170*		**G3**
Palace ☎ *0870 890 0142*		**D2**
Peacock ☎ *020 7863 8222*		**G2**
Phoenix ☎ *0870 060 6629*		**D2**
Piccadilly ☎ *0844 412 6666*		**C3**
Playhouse ☎ *0870 060 6631*		**F5**
Prince Edward ☎ *0844 482 5151*		**D2**
Prince of Wales ☎ *0844 482 5115*		**C4**
Queen Elizabeth Hall & Purcell Room ☎ *0871 663 2500*		**H5**
Queen's ☎ *0844 482 5160*		**C3**
Royal Festival Hall ☎ *0871 663 2500*		**H6**
Royal Opera House ☎ *020 7304 4000*		**F3**
St. Martin's ☎ *0870 162 8787*		**E3**
Savoy ☎ *0870 164 8787*		**F4**
Soho ☎ *020 7478 0100*		**C2**
Theatre Royal, Drury Lane ☎ *0844 412 4660*		**G2**
Theatre Royal Haymarket ☎ *0845 481 1870*		**D4**
Trafalgar Studios ☎ *0870 060 6632*		**E5**
Vaudeville ☎ *0870 890 0511*		**F4**
Wyndham's ☎ *0844 482 5120*		**D3**

West End cinemas

Apollo Piccadilly ☎ *0871 220 6000*	**C4**
BFI IMAX ☎ *0870 787 2525*	**H6**
BFI Southbank ☎ *020 7928 3232*	**H5**
Cineworld Haymarket ☎ *0871 200 2000*	**C4**
Cineworld Shaftesbury Avenue ☎ *0871 200 2000*	**C3**
Curzon Soho ☎ *0871 703 3988*	**D3**
Empire Leicester Square ☎ *0871 4714 714*	**D3**
I.C.A. ☎ *020 7930 3647*	**D6**
Odeon Covent Garden ☎ *0871 224 4007*	**D2**
Odeon Leicester Square ☎ *0871 224 4007*	**D4**
Odeon Panton Street ☎ *0871 224 4007*	**D4**
Odeon West End ☎ *0871 224 4007*	**D4**
Prince Charles ☎ *0870 811 2559*	**D3**
Vue West End ☎ *0871 224 0240*	**D3**

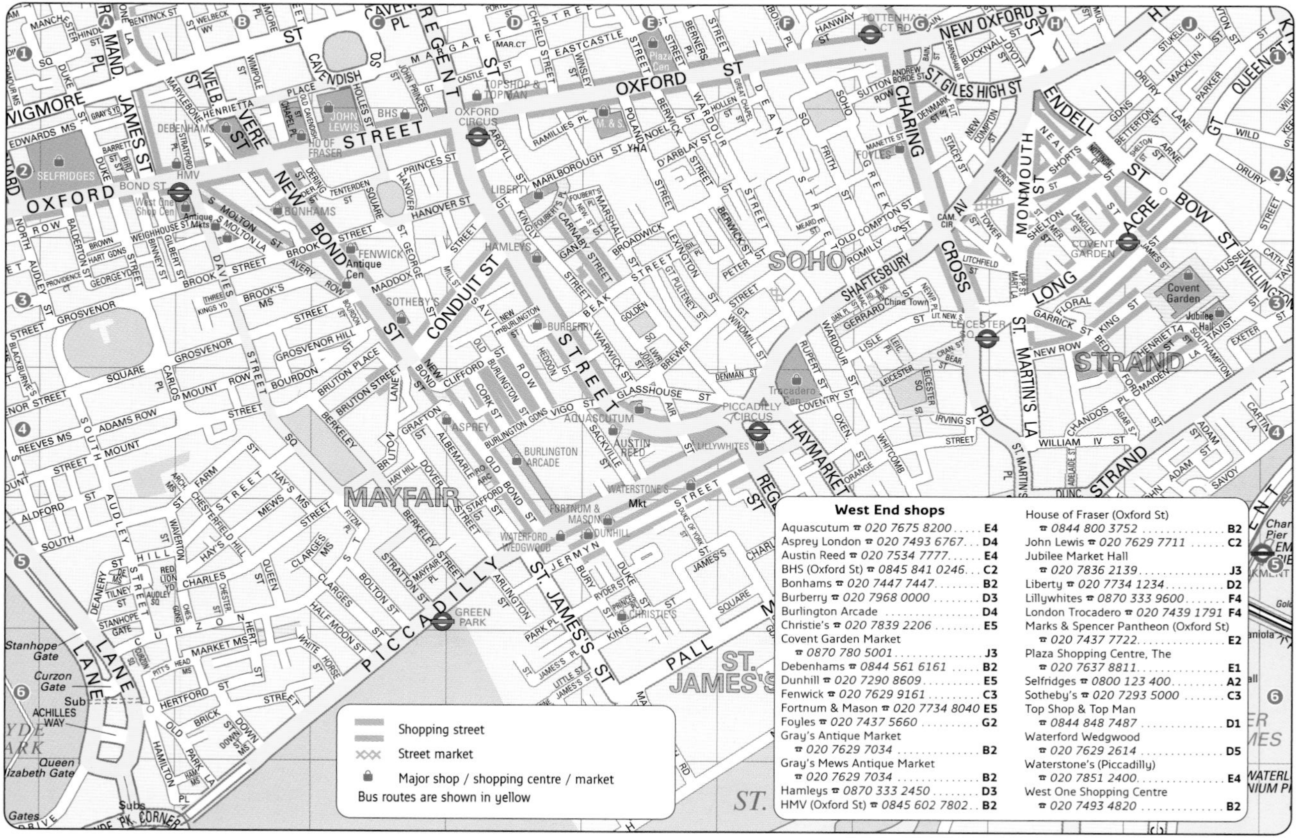
West End shops
Aquascutum ☎ 020 7675 8200 E4
Asprey London ☎ 020 7493 6767 D4
Austin Reed ☎ 020 7534 7777 E4
BHS (Oxford St) ☎ 0845 841 0246 C2
Bonhams ☎ 020 7447 7447 B2
Burberry ☎ 020 7968 0000 D3
Burlington Arcade D4
Christie's ☎ 020 7839 2206 E5
Covent Garden Market ☎ 0870 780 5001 J3
Debenhams ☎ 0844 561 6161 B2
Dunhill ☎ 020 7290 8609 E5
Fenwick ☎ 020 7629 9161 C3
Fortnum & Mason ☎ 020 7734 8040 E5
Foyles ☎ 020 7437 5660 G2
Gray's Antique Market ☎ 020 7629 7034 B2
Gray's Mews Antique Market ☎ 020 7629 7034 B2
Hamleys ☎ 0870 333 2450 D3
HMV (Oxford St) ☎ 0845 602 7802 B2
House of Fraser (Oxford St) ☎ 0844 800 3752 B2
John Lewis ☎ 020 7629 7711 C2
Jubilee Market Hall ☎ 020 7836 2139 J3
Liberty ☎ 020 7734 1234 D2
Lillywhites ☎ 0870 333 9600 F4
London Trocadero ☎ 020 7439 1791 F4
Marks & Spencer Pantheon (Oxford St) ☎ 020 7437 7722 E2
Plaza Shopping Centre, The ☎ 020 7637 8811 E1
Selfridges ☎ 0800 123 400 A2
Sotheby's ☎ 020 7293 5000 C3
Top Shop & Top Man ☎ 0844 848 7487 D1
Waterford Wedgwood ☎ 020 7629 2614 D5
Waterstone's (Piccadilly) ☎ 020 7851 2400 E4
West One Shopping Centre ☎ 020 7493 4820 B2
Shopping street
Street market
Major shop / shopping centre / market
Bus routes are shown in yellow

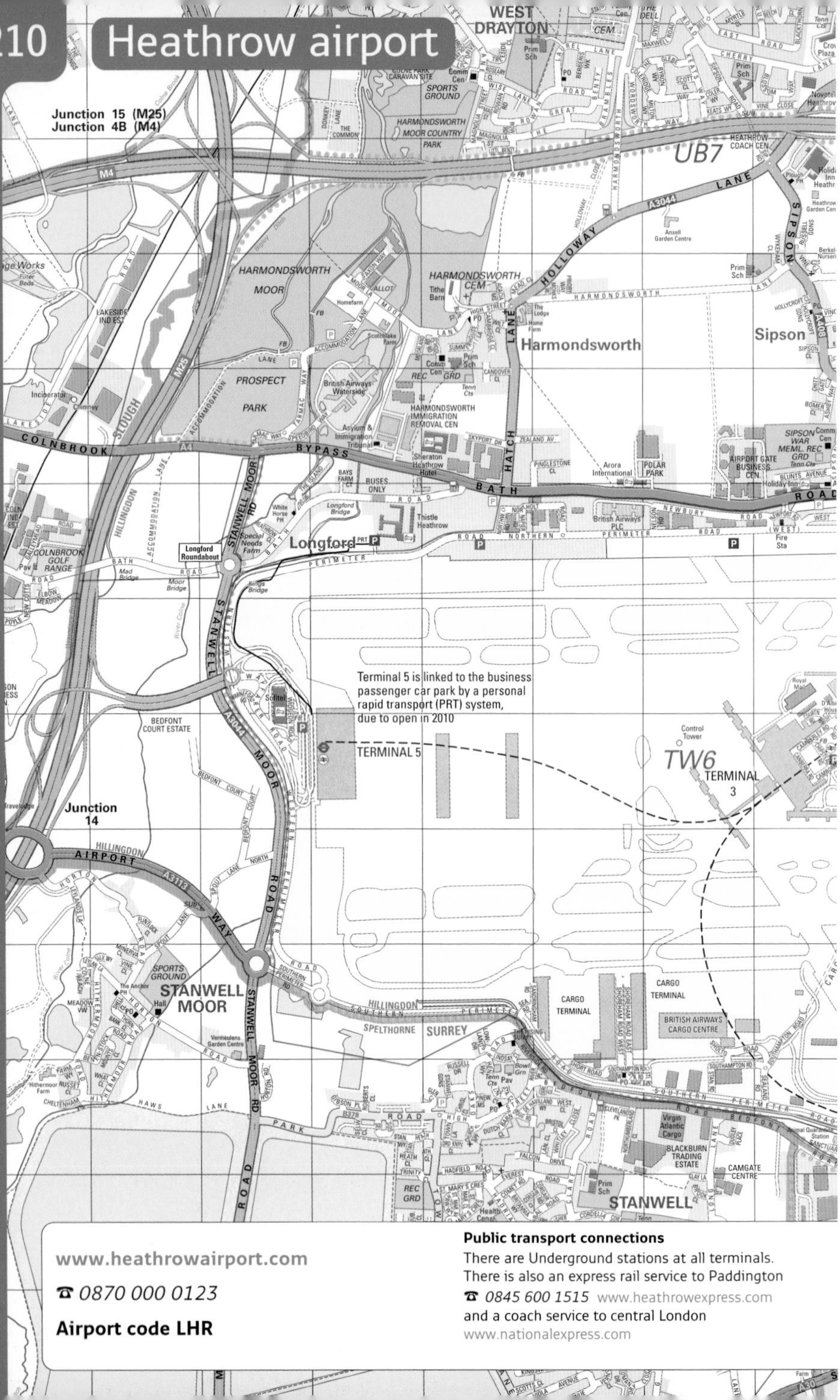

www.heathrowairport.com

☎ *0870 000 0123*

Airport code LHR

Public transport connections

There are Underground stations at all terminals. There is also an express rail service to Paddington

☎ *0845 600 1515* www.heathrowexpress.com

and a coach service to central London

www.nationalexpress.com

Parking

Short stay parking is available at all terminals and is recommended for stays of up to 5 hours. Long stay car parks operate courtesy coach services connecting them to the terminals. Parking Express Heathrow is the official long stay car park for Terminals 1, 3 and 4. Terminal 5 is served by a separate long stay car park.

Car parks

- P Short stay car park
- P Long stay car park
- P Business car park

Index

How to use this index

This index combines entries for street names, place names and places of interest.

Place names are shown in capital letters,

e.g. **ACTON**, W3 . . . .**126** A1

These include towns, villages and localities within the area covered by this atlas.

Places of interest are shown with a star symbol,

e.g. ★ **British Mus**, WC1 . . . . .**17** J2

These include parks, museums, galleries, and other important buildings or locations of tourist interest.

All other entries are for street names. When there is more than one street with exactly the same name then that name is shown only once in the index. It is then followed by a list of entries for each postal district that contains a street with that same name. For example, there are three streets called Appledore Close in this atlas and the index entry shows that one of these is in London postal district SW17, one is in Bromley, BR2 and one is in Edgware, HA8.

Appledore Cl, SW17 . . . . .**167** J2
Bromley BR2 . . . .**191** F5
Edgware HA8 . . . .**70** A1

All entries are followed by the page number and grid reference on which the name will be found. So, in the example above, **Appledore Close,** SW17 will be found on page **167** in square J2. All entries are indexed to the largest scale map on which they are shown.

The index also contains some street names which are not actually shown on the maps because there is not enough space to name them. In these cases the adjoining or nearest named thoroughfare to such streets is shown in the index in *italics,* and the reference indicates where the unnamed street is located *off* the named thoroughfare.

e.g. **Bacton St**, E2
off Roman Rd **113** F3

This means that Bacton Street is not named on the map, but it is located *off* Roman Road on page **113** in square F3.

A strict letter-by-letter alphabetical order is followed in this index. All non-alphabetic characters such as spaces, hyphens or apostrophes are not included in the index order. For example Belle Vue Road and Bellevue Road will be found listed together.

Standard terms such as Avenue, Close, Rise and Road are abbreviated in the index but are ordered alphabetically as if given in full. So, for example, **Alderton Ri** comes before **Alderton Rd**.

Names beginning with a definite article (i.e. The) are indexed from their second word onwards with the article being placed at the end of the name,

e.g. **Avenue, The**, E4 . . . .**62** D6

The alphabetical order extends to include postal information so that where two or more streets have exactly the same name, London postal district references are given first in alpha-numeric order and are followed by non-London post town references in alphabetical order, e.g. Appledore Close, SW17 is followed by Appledore Close, Bromley BR2 and then Appledore Close, Edgware HA8.

In cases where there are two or more streets of the same name in the same postal area, extra information is given in brackets to aid location. For example, High St, Orpington BR6 (Farnboro.), and High St, Orpington BR6 (Green St Grn), distinguishes between two streets called High Street which are both in the post town of Orpington, within the same postal district of BR6.

Extra locational information is also given for some localities within large post towns. This is also to aid location.

e.g. **Alford Grn**, Croy. (New Adgtn.) CR0

This street is within the locality of New Addington which is part of the post town of Croydon, and it is within postal district CR0.

A full list of locality and post town abbreviations used in this atlas is given below.

General abbreviations

Acad	Academy	BUPA	British United	Coll	College	Ctyd	Courtyard
All	Alley		Provident	Comb	Combined	Dep	Depot
Allot	Allotments		Association	Comm	Community	Dept	Department
Amb	Ambulance	C of E	Church of	Comp	Comprehensive	Dev	Development
Apts	Apartments		England	Conf	Conference	Dr	Drive
App	Approach	Cath	Cathedral	Cont	Continuing	Dws	Dwellings
Arc	Arcade	Cem	Cemetery	Conv	Convent	E	East
Assoc	Association	Cen	Central, Centre	Cor	Corner	Ed	Education,
Av	Avenue	Cft	Croft	Coron	Coroners		Educational
Bdy	Broadway	Cfts	Crofts	Cors	Corners	Elec	Electricity
Bk	Bank	Ch	Church	Cotts	Cottages	Embk	Embankment
Bldg	Building	Chyd	Churchyard	Cov	Covered	Est	Estate
Bldgs	Buildings	Cin	Cinema	Crem	Crematorium	Ex	Exchange
Boul	Boulevard	Circ	Circus	Cres	Crescent	Exhib	Exhibition
Bowl	Bowling	Cl	Close	Ct	Court	FB	Footbridge
Br	Bridge	Co	County	Cts	Courts	FC	Football Club

Fld	Field
Flds	Fields
Fm	Farm
GM	Grant Maintained
Gall	Gallery
Gar	Garage
Gdn	Garden
Gdns	Gardens
Gen	General
Govt	Government
Gra	Grange
Grad	Graduate
Gram	Grammar
Grd	Ground
Grds	Grounds
Grn	Green
Grns	Greens
Gro	Grove
Gros	Groves
Gt	Great
HQ	Headquarters
Ho	House
Hos	Houses
Hosp	Hospital
Hts	Heights
Ind	Industrial
Indep	Independent
Inf	Infant(s)
Inst	Institute
Int	International
JM	Junior Mixed
JMI	Junior Mixed & Infant(s)
Jun	Junior
Junct	Junction
La	Lane
Las	Lanes
Lib	Library
Lit	Literary
Lo	Lodge
Lwr	Lower
Mag	Magistrates
Mans	Mansions
Med	Medical, Medicine
Mem	Memorial
Met	Metropolitan
Mid	Middle
Mkt	Market
Mkts	Markets
Ms	Mews
Mt	Mount
Mus	Museum
N	North
NHS	National Health Service
NT	National Trust
Nat	National
Nurs	Nursery
PH	Public House
PO	Post Office
PRU	Pupil Referral Unit
Par	Parade
Pas	Passage
Pav	Pavilion
Pk	Park
Pl	Place
Pol	Police
Poly	Polytechnic
Prec	Precinct
Prep	Preparatory
Prim	Primary
Prom	Promenade
Pt	Point
Quad	Quadrant
Rbt	Roundabout
RC	Roman Catholic
Rd	Road
Rds	Roads
Rec	Recreation
Rehab	Rehabilitation
Res	Reservoir, Residence
Ri	Rise
S	South
SM	Secondary Mixed
Sch	School
Schs	Schools
Sec	Secondary
Sen	Senior
Shop	Shopping
Spec	Special
Sq	Square
St	Street
St.	Saint
Sta	Station
Sts	Streets
Sub	Subway
Swim	Swimming
TA	Territorial Army
TH	Town Hall
Tech	Technical, Technology
Tenn	Tennis
Ter	Terrace
Thea	Theatre
Trd	Trading
Twr	Tower
Twrs	Towers
Uni	University
Upr	Upper
VA	Voluntary Aided
VC	Voluntary Controlled
Vet	Veterinary
Vil	Villa
Vil	Villas
Vw	View
W	West
Wd	Wood
Wds	Woods
Wf	Wharf
Wk	Walk
Wks	Works
Yd	Yard

Locality and post town abbreviations

In the list of abbreviations shown below, post towns are in **bold** type

Bark.	**Barking**
Barn.	**Barnet**
Barne.	Barnehurst
Beck.	**Beckenham**
Bedd.	Beddington
Bedd.Cor.	Beddington Corner
Belv.	**Belvedere**
Bex.	**Bexley**
Bexh.	**Bexleyheath**
Borwd.	**Borehamwood**
Brent.	**Brentford**
Brom.	**Bromley**
Buck.H.	**Buckhurst Hill**
Bushey Hth	Bushey Heath
Carp.Pk	Carpenders Park
Cars.	**Carshalton**
Chad.Hth	Chadwell Heath
Chess.	**Chessington**
Chig.	**Chigwell**
Chis.	**Chislehurst**
Clay.	Claygate
Cockfos.	Cockfosters
Coll.Row	Collier Row
Cran.	Cranford
Croy.	**Croydon**
Dag.	**Dagenham**
Dart.	**Dartford**
E.Barn.	East Barnet
E.Bed.	East Bedfont
E.Mol.	**East Molesey**
Ealing Com.	Ealing Common
Eastcote Vill.	Eastcote Village
Edg.	**Edgware**
Elm.Wds	Elmstead Woods
Els.	Elstree
Enf.	**Enfield**
Epp.	**Epping**
Farnboro.	Farnborough
Felt.	**Feltham**
Grn St Grn	Green Street Green
Grnf.	**Greenford**
Hackbr.	Hackbridge
Han.	Hanworth
Har.	**Harrow**
Harling.	Harlington
Har.Hill	Harrow on the Hill
Har.Wld	Harrow Weald
Harm.	Harmondsworth
Hatt.Cr.	Hatton Cross
High Barn.	High Barnet
Highams Pk	Highams Park
Hinch.Wd	Hinchley Wood
Hmptn H.	Hampton Hill
Hmptn W.	Hampton Wick
Hmptn.	**Hampton**
Houns.	**Hounslow**
Houns.W.	Hounslow West
Ilf.	**Ilford**
Islw.	**Isleworth**
Kes.	**Keston**
Kings.T.	**Kingston upon Thames**
Lon.Hthrw Air.	London Heathrow Airport
Lon.Hthrw Air.N.	London Heathrow Airport North
Long Dit.	Long Ditton
Loug.	**Loughton**
Lt.Hth	Little Heath
Lwr Sydenham	Lower Sydenham
Mitch.	**Mitcham**
Mitch.Com.	Mitcham Common
Mord.	**Morden**
Mots.Pk	Motspur Park
N.Finchley	North Finchley
N.Har.	North Harrow
N.Mal.	**New Malden**
New Adgtn	New Addington
New Barn.	New Barnet
Northumb.Hth	Northumberland Heath
Norwood Junct.	Norwood Junction
Nthlt.	**Northolt**
Nthwd.	**Northwood**
Orp.	**Orpington**
Petts Wd	Petts Wood
Pnr.	**Pinner**
Pond.End	Ponders End
Pr.Bot.	Pratt's Bottom
Pur.	**Purley**
Rain.	**Rainham**
Rich.	**Richmond**
Rod.Val.	Roding Valley
Rom.	**Romford**
Ruis.	**Ruislip**
S.Croy.	**South Croydon**
S.Har.	South Harrow
S.Norwood	South Norwood
S.Oxhey	South Oxhey
S.Ruis.	South Ruislip
Scad.Pk	Scadbury Park
Short.	Shortlands
Sid.	**Sidcup**
St.P.Cray	St. Paul's Cray
Stai.	**Staines**
Stan.	**Stanmore**
Stanw.	Stanwell
Sthl Grn	Southall Green
Sthl.	**Southall**
Sun.	**Sunbury-on-Thames**
Surb.	**Surbiton**
Sutt.	**Sutton**
T.Ditt.	**Thames Ditton**
Tedd.	**Teddington**
Th.Hth.	**Thornton Heath**
They.B.	Theydon Bois
Tkgtn	Tokyngton
Twick.	**Twickenham**
Uxb.	**Uxbridge**
W.Ealing	West Ealing
W.Ewell	West Ewell
W.Mol.	**West Molesey**
W.Wick.	**West Wickham**
Wall.	**Wallington**
Walt.	**Walton-on-Thames**
Wat.	**Watford**
Wdf.Grn.	**Woodford Green**
Wealds.	Wealdstone
Well.	**Welling**
Wem.	**Wembley**
West Dr.	**West Drayton**
Woodside Pk	Woodside Park
Wor.Pk.	**Worcester Park**
Yiew.	Yiewsley

1 Canada Sq, E14 ... **134** B1
★ **2 Willow Rd (NT)**, NW3 . **91** H4
30 St. Mary Axe, EC3
off St. Mary Axe ... **20** E3
99 Bishopsgate, EC2
off Bishopsgate ... **20** D3

A

Aaron Hill Rd, E6 ... **116** D5
Abady Ho, SW1
off Page St ... **33** J1
Abberley Ms, SW4
off Cedars Rd ... **150** B3
Abbess Cl, E6
off Oliver Gdns ... **116** B5
SW2 ... **169** H1
Abbeville Ms, SW4 ... **150** D4
Abbeville Rd, N8
off Barrington Rd ... **74** D4
SW4 ... **150** C6
Abbey Av, Wem. HA0 ... **105** H2
Abbey Business Cen, SW8
off Ingate Pl ... **150** B1
Abbey Cl, E5 ... **94** D4
SW8 ... **150** D1
Hayes UB3 ... **122** B1
Northolt UB5
off Invicta Gro ... **103** F3
Pinner HA5 ... **66** B3
Abbey Cres, Belv. DA17 ... **139** G4
Abbeydale Rd, Wem. HA0 . **106** A1
Abbey Dr, SW17
off Church La ... **168** A5
Abbeyfield Cl, Mitch. CR4 . **185** H2
Abbeyfield Rd, SE16 ... **133** F4
Abbeyfields Cl, NW10 ... **106** A2
Abbey Gdns, NW8 ... **6** C2
SE16 ... **37** J1
SW1
off Great Coll St ... **26** A5
W6 ... **128** B6
Chislehurst BR7 ... **192** D1
Abbey Gro, SE2 ... **138** B4
Abbeyhill Rd, Sid. DA15 .. **176** C2
Abbey Ind Est, Mitch.
CR4 ... **185** J5
Wembley HA0 ... **105** J1
Abbey La, E15 ... **114** C2
Beckenham BR3 ... **172** A7
Abbey Ms, E17
off Leamington Av ... **78** A5
Isleworth TW7 ... **144** E1
Abbey Orchard St, SW1 ... **25** J5
Abbey Par, SW19
off Merton High St ... **167** F7
W5 *off Hanger La* ... **105** J3
Abbey Pk, Beck. BR3 ... **172** A7
Abbey Retail Pk, Bark.
IG11 ... **116** E1
Abbey Rd, E15 ... **114** E2
NW6 ... **90** E7
NW8 ... **109** F2
NW10 ... **106** B2
SE2 ... **138** D4
SW19 ... **167** F7
Barking IG11 ... **99** E7
Belvedere DA17 ... **138** D4
Bexleyheath DA7 ... **159** E4
Croydon CR0 ... **201** H3
Enfield EN1 ... **44** B5
Ilford IG2 ... **81** G5
Abbey Rd Est, NW8 ... **108** E1
Abbey St, E13 ... **115** G4
SE1 ... **28** E5
Abbey Ter, SE2 ... **138** C4
Abbey Trd Est, SE26 ... **171** J5
Abbey Vw, NW7 ... **55** F3
Abbey Wk, W.Mol. KT8 ... **179** H3
Abbey Way, SE2 ... **138** D3
Abbey Wf Ind Est, Bark.
IG11 ... **117** G2
ABBEY WOOD, SE2 ... **138** B3
Abbey Wd Caravan Club Site,
SE2 ... **138** C5
Abbey Wd Rd, SE2 ... **138** B4
Abbot Ct, SW8
off Hartington Rd ... **130** E7
Abbotsbury Cl, E15 ... **114** C2
W14
off Abbotsbury Rd ... **128** C2
Abbotsbury Gdns, Pnr.
HA5 ... **66** C6
Abbotsbury Ms, SE15 ... **153** F3
Abbotsbury Rd, W14 ... **128** B2
Bromley BR2 ... **205** F2
Morden SM4 ... **184** E5
Abbots Cl, Orp. BR5 ... **207** F1
Ruislip HA4 ... **84** D3
Abbots Dr, Har. HA2 ... **85** G2
Abbotsford Av, N15 ... **75** J4
Abbotsford Gdns, Wdf.Grn.
IG8 ... **63** G7
Abbotsford Rd, Ilf. IG3 ... **100** A2
Abbots Gdns, N2 ... **73** G4
W8 ... **22** A6
Abbots Grn, Croy. CR0 ... **203** G6
Abbotshade Rd, SE16 ... **133** G1
Abbotshall Av, N14 ... **58** C3
Abbotshall Rd, SE6 ... **172** D1
Abbots La, SE1 ... **28** E2
Abbotsleigh Cl, Sutt.
SM2 ... **198** E7
Abbotsleigh Rd, SW16 ... **168** C4
Abbots Manor Est, SW1 ... **32** D2
Abbotsmede Cl, Twick.
TW1 ... **162** C2
Abbots Pk, SW2 ... **169** G1
Abbot's Pl, NW6 ... **108** E1
Abbot's Rd, E6 ... **116** A1
Abbots Rd, Edg. HA8 ... **54** C7
Abbots Ter, N8 ... **74** E6
Abbotstone Rd, SW15 ... **147** J3
Abbot St, E8 ... **94** C6
Abbots Wk, W8 ... **22** A6
Abbots Way, Beck. BR3 ... **189** H5
Abbotswell Rd, SE4 ... **153** J5
Abbotswood Cl, Belv. DA17
off Coptefield Dr ... **138** E3
Abbotswood Gdns, Ilf.
IG5 ... **80** C3
Abbotswood Rd, SE22 ... **152** B4
SW16 ... **168** D3
Abbotswood Way, Hayes
UB3 ... **122** B1
Abbott Av, SW20 ... **184** A2
Abbott Cl, Hmptn. TW12 .. **161** E6
Northolt UB5 ... **85** F6
Abbott Rd, E14 ... **114** C5
Abbotts Cl, N1
off Alwyne Rd ... **93** J6
SE28 ... **118** C7
Romford RM7 ... **83** H3
Abbotts Cres, E4 ... **62** D4
Enfield EN2 ... **43** H2
Abbotts Dr, Wem. HA0 ... **86** E2
Abbotts Pk Rd, E10 ... **78** C7
Abbotts Rd, Barn. EN5 ... **40** E4
Mitcham CR4 ... **186** C4
Southall UB1 ... **123** E1
Sutton SM3 ... **198** C3
Abbotts Wk, Bexh. DA7 ... **138** D7
Abbotts Wf, E14
off Stainsby Rd ... **114** A6
Abchurch La, EC4 ... **20** C5
Abchurch Yd, EC4 ... **20** B5
Abdale Rd, W12 ... **127** H1
Aberavon Rd, E3 ... **113** H3
Abercairn Rd, SW16 ... **168** C7
Aberconway Rd, Mord.
SM4 ... **184** E3
Abercorn Cl, NW7 ... **56** B7
NW8 ... **6** C2
Abercorn Cres, Har. HA2 .. **85** H1
Abercorn Dell, Bushey
WD23 ... **51** J2
Abercorn Gdns, Har. HA3 .. **69** G7
Romford RM6 ... **82** B6
Abercorn Ms, Rich. TW10
off Kings Rd ... **145** J4
Abercorn Pl, NW8 ... **6** C3
Abercorn Rd, NW7 ... **56** B7
Stanmore HA7 ... **53** F7
Abercorn Wk, NW8 ... **6** C3
Abercorn Way, SE1 ... **37** H3
Abercrombie Dr, Enf. EN1
off Linwood Cres ... **44** D1
Abercrombie St, SW11 ... **149** H2
Aberdale Ct, SE16
off Poolmans St ... **133** G2
Aberdare Cl, W.Wick.
BR4 ... **204** C2
Aberdare Gdns, NW6 ... **91** E7
NW7 ... **56** A7
Aberdare Rd, Enf. EN3 ... **45** F4
Aberdeen La, N5 ... **93** H5
Aberdeen Par, N18
off Angel Rd ... **61** E5
Aberdeen Pk, N5 ... **93** H5
Aberdeen Pk Ms, N5 ... **93** J4
Aberdeen Pl, NW8 ... **6** E6
Aberdeen Rd, N5 ... **93** J4
N18 ... **60** E5
NW10 ... **89** F5
Croydon CR0 ... **201** J4
Harrow HA3 ... **68** C2
Aberdeen Sq, E14
off Westferry Circ ... **134** A1
Aberdeen Ter, SE3 ... **154** D2
Aberdour Rd, Ilf. IG3 ... **100** B3
Aberdour St, SE1 ... **36** D1
Aberfeldy St, E14 ... **114** C6
Aberford Gdns, SE18 ... **156** B1
Aberford Rd, Borwd.
WD6 ... **38** A2
Aberfoyle Rd, SW16 ... **168** D6
Abergeldie Rd, SE12 ... **155** H6
Aberglen Ind Est, Hayes
UB3 ... **121** G2
Abernethy Rd, SE13 ... **154** E4
Abersham Rd, E8 ... **94** C5
Abery St, SE18 ... **137** H4
Ability Twrs, EC1 ... **11** J3
Abingdon Cl, NW1
off Camden Ms ... **92** D6
SE1 ... **37** G3
SW19 ... **167** F6
Wor.Pk. KT4 ... **197** H3
Abingdon Rd, N3 ... **73** F2
SW16 ... **186** E2
W8 ... **128** D3
Abingdon St, SW1 ... **26** A5
Abingdon Vil, W8 ... **128** D3
Abinger Cl, Bark. IG11 ... **100** A4
Bromley BR1 ... **192** B3
Croydon (New Adgtn)
CR0 ... **204** C6
Wallington SM6 ... **201** E5
Abinger Gdns, Islw. TW7 .. **144** B3
Abinger Gro, SE8 ... **133** J6
Abinger Ms, W9
off Warlock Rd ... **108** D4
Abinger Rd, W4 ... **127** E3
Ablett St, SE16 ... **133** F5
Abney Gdns, N16
off Stoke Newington
High St ... **94** C2
Aboyne Dr, SW20 ... **183** G2
Aboyne Est, SW17 ... **167** G3
Aboyne Rd, NW10 ... **88** E3
SW17 ... **167** G3
Abraham Cl, Wat. WD19 ... **50** B4
Abridge Rd, Chig. IG7 ... **49** G6
Abridge Way, Bark. IG11 ... **118** B2
Abyssinia Cl, SW11
off Cairns Rd ... **149** H4
Abyssinia Rd, SW11
off Auckland Rd ... **149** H4
Acacia Av, N17 ... **60** A7
Brentford TW8 ... **124** E7
Mitcham CR4
off Acacia Rd ... **186** B2
Ruislip HA4 ... **84** A1
Wembley HA9 ... **87** H5
Acacia Cl, SE8 ... **133** H4
SE20 *off Selby Rd* ... **188** D2
Orpington BR5 ... **193** G5
Stanmore HA7 ... **52** B6
Acacia Dr, Sutt. SM3 ... **198** C1
Acacia Gdns, NW8 ... **7** F1
West Wickham BR4 ... **204** C2
Acacia Gro, SE21 ... **170** A2
New Malden KT3 ... **182** D3
Acacia Ms, West Dr. (Harm.)
UB7 ... **120** A6
Acacia Pl, NW8 ... **7** F1
Acacia Rd, E11 ... **97** E2
E17 ... **77** H6
N22 ... **75** G1
NW8 ... **7** F1
SW16 ... **187** E1
W3 ... **106** C7
Beckenham BR3 ... **189** J3
Enfield EN2 ... **44** A1
Hampton TW12 ... **161** G6
Mitcham CR4 ... **186** B2
Acacias, The, Barn. EN4 ... **41** G5
Acacia Way, Sid. DA15 ... **175** J1
Academia Way, N17 ... **60** B6
Academy Ct, Borwd. WD6 .. **38** A4
Academy Gdns, W8 ... **128** D2
Croydon CR0 ... **202** C1
Northolt UB5 ... **102** D2
Academy Pl, SE18 ... **156** C1
Academy Rd, SE18 ... **156** C1
Acanthus Dr, SE1 ... **37** H3
Acanthus Rd, SW11 ... **150** A3
Accommodation Rd,
NW11 ... **72** C7
A.C. Ct, T.Ditt. KT7
off Harvest La ... **180** D6
Ace Par, Chess. KT9
off Hook Rd ... **195** H3
Acer Av, Hayes UB4 ... **102** E5
Acer Ct, Enf. EN3 ... **45** H3
Acer Rd, E8 ... **94** C6
Acfold Rd, SW6 ... **148** E1
Achilles Cl, SE1 ... **37** J3
Achilles Rd, NW6 ... **90** D5
Achilles St, SE14 ... **133** H7
Achilles Way, W1 ... **24** B2
Acklam Rd, W10 ... **108** C5
Acklington Dr, NW9 ... **70** E1
Ackmar Rd, SW6 ... **148** D1
Ackroyd Dr, E3 ... **113** J5
Ackroyd Rd, SE23 ... **153** G7
Acland Cl, SE18
off Clothworkers Rd .. **137** G7
Acland Cres, SE5 ... **152** A4
Acland Rd, NW2 ... **89** H6
Acle Cl, Ilf. IG6 ... **65** E7
Acock Gro, Nthlt. UB5 ... **85** H4
Acol Cres, Ruis. HA4 ... **84** B5
Acol Rd, NW6 ... **90** D7
Aconbury Rd, Dag. RM9 .. **118** B1
Acorn Cl, E4 ... **62** A5
Chislehurst BR7 ... **175** F5
Enfield EN2 ... **43** H1
Hampton TW12 ... **161** H6
Stanmore HA7 ... **53** E7
Acorn Ct, Ilf. IG2 ... **81** H5
Acorn Gdns, SE19 ... **188** C1
W3 ... **106** D5
Acorn Gro, Hayes UB3 ... **121** J7
Acorn Par, SE15
off Carlton Gro ... **132** E7
Acorns, The, Chig. IG7 ... **65** H4
Acorn Wk, SE16 ... **133** H1
Acorn Way, SE23 ... **171** G3
Beckenham BR3 ... **190** C5
Orpington BR6 ... **207** E4
Acre Dr, SE22 ... **152** D4
Acre La, SW2 ... **150** E4
Carshalton SM5 ... **200** A4
Wallington SM6 ... **200** A4
Acre Path, Nthlt. UB5
off Arnold Rd ... **84** E6
Acre Rd, SW19 ... **167** G6
Dagenham RM10 ... **101** H7
Kingston upon Thames
KT2 ... **181** H1
Acris St, SW18 ... **149** F5
ACTON, W3 ... **126** A1
Acton Cl, N9 ... **60** D2
Acton Hill Ms, W3
off Uxbridge Rd ... **126** B1
Acton Ho, W3 ... **106** C6
Acton La, NW10 ... **106** E2
W3 ... **126** C2
W4 ... **126** D3
Acton Ms, E8 ... **112** C1
Acton Pk Est, W3 ... **126** D2
Acton St, WC1 ... **10** C4
Acuba Rd, SW18 ... **166** E2
Acworth Cl, N9 ... **45** F7
Ada Cl, N11 ... **57** J3
Ada Ct, W9 ... **6** D4
Ada Gdns, E14 ... **114** D6
E15 ... **115** F1
Adair Cl, SE25 ... **188** E3
Adair Rd, W10 ... **108** B4
Adair Twr, W10
off Appleford Rd ... **108** B4
Adam & Eve Ct, W1 ... **17** G3
Adam & Eve Ms, W8 ... **128** D3
Adam Cl, SE6 ... **171** J4
Adam Ct, SW7 ... **30** D1
Adam Meere Ho, E1
off Tarling St ... **113** F6
Adam Rd, E4 ... **61** J6
Adams Cl, N3 ... **56** D7
NW9 ... **88** B2
Surbiton KT5 ... **181** J6
Adams Ct, EC2 ... **20** C3
Adams Gdns Est, SE16
off St. Marychurch St . **133** F2
Adams Ms, N22 ... **59** F7
SW17 ... **167** J2
Adamson Rd, E16 ... **115** G6
NW3 ... **91** G7
Adamson Way, Beck.
BR3 ... **190** C5
Adams Pl, N7
off George's Rd ... **93** F5
Adams Quarter, Brent. TW8
off Tallow Rd ... **125** F6
Adamsrill Cl, Enf. EN1 ... **44** A6
Adamsrill Rd, SE26 ... **171** H4
Adams Rd, N17 ... **76** A2
Beckenham BR3 ... **189** H5
Adams Row, W1 ... **16** C6
Adams Sq, Bexh. DA6
off Regency Way ... **158** E3
Adam St, WC2 ... **18** B6
Adams Wk, Kings.T. KT1 .. **181** H2
Adams Way, Croy. CR0 ... **188** C6
Adam Wk, SW6 ... **127** J7
Ada Pl, E2 ... **112** D1
Adare Wk, SW16 ... **169** F3
Ada Rd, SE5 ... **132** B7
Wembley HA0 ... **87** F3
Adastral Est, NW9 ... **70** E1
Ada St, E8 ... **112** E1
Adcock Wk, Orp. BR6
off Borkwood Pk ... **207** J4
Adderley Gdns, SE9 ... **174** D4
Adderley Gro, SW11
off Culmstock Rd ... **150** A5
Adderley Rd, Har. HA3 ... **68** C1
Adderley St, E14 ... **114** C6
ADDINGTON, Croy. CR0 ... **203** J5
Addington Ct, SW14 ... **146** D3
Addington Dr, N12 ... **57** F6
Addington Gro, SE26 ... **171** H4
Addington Rd, E3 ... **114** A3
E16 ... **115** E4
N4 ... **75** G6
Croydon CR0 ... **201** G1
West Wickham BR4 ... **204** E2
Addington Sq, SE5 ... **36** A7
Addington St, SE1 ... **26** D4
Addington Village Rd, Croy.
CR0 ... **204** A5
Addis Cl, Enf. EN3 ... **45** G1
ADDISCOMBE, Croy. CR0 . **202** C1
Addiscombe Av, Croy.
CR0 ... **188** D7

Addiscombe Cl, Har. HA3 . .69 F5
Addiscombe Ct Rd, Croy.
CR0 . . . . .202 B1
Addiscombe Gro, Croy.
CR0 . . . . .202 A2
Addiscombe Rd, Croy.
CR0 . . . . .202 B2
Addison Av, N14 . . . . .42 B6
W11 . . . . .128 B1
Hounslow TW3 . . . . .143 J1
Addison Br Pl, W14 . . . . . .128 C4
Addison Cl, Nthwd. HA6 . . .66 A1
Orpington BR5 . . . . .193 F6
Addison Cres, W14 . . . . . . .128 B3
Addison Dr, SE12
off Eltham Rd 155 H5
Addison Gdns, W14 . . . . . .128 A3
Surbiton KT5 . . . . .181 J4
Addison Gro, W4 . . . . .127 E3
Addison Ind Est, Ruis. HA4
off Field End Rd 85 E4
Addison Pl, W11 . . . . .128 B1
Southall UB1
off Longford Av 103 G7
Addison Rd, E11 . . . . .79 G6
E17 . . . . .78 B5
SE25 . . . . .188 D4
W14 . . . . .128 C3
Bromley BR2 . . . . .191 J5
Enfield EN3 . . . . .45 F1
Ilford IG6 . . . . .81 F1
Teddington TW11 . . . . . .162 E6
Addison's Cl, Croy. CR0 . . .203 J2
Addison Way, NW11 . . . . . .72 C4
Hayes UB3 . . . . .102 A6
Addle Hill, EC4 . . . . .19 H5
Addle St, EC2 . . . . .20 A2
Addy Ho, SE16
off Rotherhithe New Rd 133 F4
Adecroft Way, W.Mol.
KT8 . . . . .179 J3
Adela Av, N.Mal. KT3 . . . . .183 H5
Adelaide Av, SE4 . . . . .153 J4
Adelaide Cl, SW9
off Broughton Dr 151 G4
Stanmore HA7 . . . . .52 D4
Adelaide Cotts, W7 . . . . . .124 C2
Adelaide Ct, E9
off Kenworthy Rd 95 H5
Adelaide Gdns, Rom. RM6 .82 E5
Adelaide Gro, W12 . . . . . . .127 G1
Adelaide Rd, E10 . . . . .96 B3
NW3 . . . . .91 G7
SW18
off Putney Br Rd 148 D5
W13 . . . . .124 D1
Chislehurst BR7 . . . . . . .175 E5
Hounslow TW5 . . . . .142 E1
Ilford IG1 . . . . .99 E2
Richmond TW9 . . . . .145 J4
Southall UB2 . . . . .123 E4
Surbiton KT6 . . . . .181 H5
Teddington TW11 . . . . . .162 C6
Adelaide St, WC2 . . . . .18 A6
Adelaide Ter, Brent. TW8 . .125 G5
Adela St, W10
off Kensal Rd 108 B4
Adelina Gro, E1 . . . . .113 F5
Adelina Ms, SW12 . . . . . . .168 D1
Adeline Pl, WC1 . . . . .17 J2
Adeliza Cl, Bark. IG11
off North St 99 F7
Adelphi Ct, SE16
off Poolmans St 133 G2
Adelphi Ter, WC2 . . . . .18 B6
Adeney Cl, W6 . . . . .128 A6
Aden Gro, N16 . . . . .94 A4
Adenmore Rd, SE6 . . . . . .154 A7
Aden Rd, Enf. EN3 . . . . .45 H4
Ilford IG1 . . . . .81 E7
Aden Ter, N16 . . . . .94 A4
Adie Rd, W6 . . . . .127 J3
Adine Rd, E13 . . . . .115 H4
Adisham Ho, E5
off Pembury Rd 94 E5
Adler Ind Est, Hayes UB3 .121 G2
Adler St, E1 . . . . .21 H3
Adley St, E5 . . . . .95 H5
Adlington Cl, N18 . . . . .60 A5
Admaston Rd, SE18 . . . . . .137 F7
Admiral Ct, NW4
off Barton Cl 71 G5
Admiral Ho, Tedd. TW11
off Twickenham Rd . . .162 D4
Admiral Hyson Trd Est, SE16
off Galleywall Rd 133 E5
Admiral Pl, N8 . . . . .75 H4
SE16 . . . . .133 H1
Admirals Cl, E18 . . . . .79 H4
Admiral Seymour Rd,
SE9 . . . . .156 C4
Admirals Gate, SE10 . . . . .154 B1
Admiral Sq, SW10 . . . . . . .149 F1
Admiral St, SE8 . . . . .154 A2
Admirals Wk, NW3 . . . . .91 F3
Admirals Way, E14 . . . . . . .134 A2
★ **Admiralty Arch**, SW1 . .25 J1
Admiralty Cl, SE8
off Reginald Sq 134 A7
West Drayton UB7
off Kingston La 120 C2
Admiralty Way, Tedd.
TW11 . . . . .162 C6
Admiral Wk, W9 . . . . .108 D5
Adolf St, SE6 . . . . .172 B4
Adolphus Rd, N4 . . . . .93 H2
Adolphus St, SE8 . . . . .133 J7
Adomar Rd, Dag. RM8 . . . .100 D3
Adpar St, W2 . . . . .7 E6
Adrian Av, NW2
off North Circular Rd . . .89 H1
Adrian Cl, Barn. EN5 . . . . . .40 A6
Adrian Ms, SW10 . . . . .30 B5
Adriatic Bldg, E14
off Narrow St 113 H7
Adrienne Av, Sthl. UB1 . . .103 F4
Advance Rd, SE27 . . . . . . .169 J4
Advent Ct, Wdf.Grn. IG8
off Wood La 63 F5
Adventurers Ct, E14
off Newport Av 114 D7
Advent Way, N18 . . . . .61 G5
Adys Rd, SE15 . . . . .152 C3
Aegean Apts, E16
off Western Gateway . .115 G7
Aerodrome Rd, NW4 . . . . . .71 F2
NW9 . . . . .71 F2
Aerodrome Way, Houns.
TW5 . . . . .122 C6
Aeroville, NW9 . . . . .70 E2
Affleck St, N1 . . . . .10 D2
Afghan Rd, SW11 . . . . .149 H2
★ **Africa Cen**, WC2 . . . . . . .18 A5
Agamemnon Rd, NW6 . . . .90 C5
Agar Cl, Surb. KT6 . . . . . . .195 J2
Agar Gro, NW1 . . . . .92 C7
Agar Gro Est, NW1 . . . . . . .92 D7
Agar Pl, NW1 . . . . .92 C7
Agar St, WC2 . . . . .18 A6
Agate Cl, E16 . . . . .116 A6
NW10 . . . . .106 A3
Agate Rd, W6 . . . . .127 J3
Agatha Cl, E1
off Prusom St 133 F1
Agaton Rd, SE9 . . . . .175 F2
Agave Rd, NW2 . . . . .89 J4
Agdon St, EC1 . . . . .11 G5
Agincourt Rd, NW3 . . . . . . .91 J4
Agnes Av, Ilf. IG1 . . . . .98 E4
Agnes Cl, E6 . . . . .116 D7
Agnesfield Cl, N12 . . . . .57 H6
Agnes Gdns, Dag. RM8 . . .100 D4
Agnes Rd, W3 . . . . .127 F1
Agnes St, E14 . . . . .113 J6
Agnew Rd, SE23 . . . . .153 G7
Agricola Ct, E3
off Parnell Rd 113 J1
Agricola Pl, Enf. EN1 . . . . . .44 C5
Aidan Cl, Dag. RM8 . . . . . .100 E4
Aileen Wk, E15 . . . . .97 F7
Ailsa Av, Twick. TW1 . . . . . .144 D5
Ailsa Rd, Twick. TW1 . . . . . .145 E5
Ailsa St, E14 . . . . .114 C5
Ainger Ms, NW3
off Ainger Rd 91 J7
Ainger Rd, NW3 . . . . .91 J7
Ainsdale Cl, Orp. BR6 . . . .207 G1
Ainsdale Cres, Pnr. HA5 . . .67 G3
Ainsdale Dr, SE1 . . . . .37 H4
Ainsdale Rd, W5 . . . . .105 G4
Watford WD19 . . . . .50 C3
Ainsley Av, Rom. RM7 . . . . .83 H6
Ainsley Cl, N9 . . . . .60 B1
Ainsley St, E2 . . . . .112 E3
Ainslie Wk, SW12 . . . . .150 B7
Ainslie Wd Cres, E4 . . . . . . .62 B5
Ainslie Wd Gdns, E4 . . . . . .62 B4
Ainslie Wd Rd, E4 . . . . .62 A5
Ainsty Est, SE16 . . . . .133 G2
Ainsworth Cl, NW2 . . . . .89 G3
SE15
off Lyndhurst Gro 152 B2
Ainsworth Rd, E9 . . . . .95 F7
Croydon CR0 . . . . .201 H2
Ainsworth Way, NW8 . . . .109 F1
Aintree Av, E6 . . . . .116 B1
Aintree Cres, Ilf. IG6 . . . . . .81 F2
Aintree Est, SW6
off Dawes Rd 128 B7
Aintree Rd, Grnf. (Perivale)
UB6 . . . . .105 E2
Aintree St, SW6 . . . . .128 B7
Airco Cl, NW9 . . . . .70 D3
Aird Ct, Hmptn. TW12
off Oldfield Rd 179 F1
Aird Ho, SE1
off Rockingham St 27 J6
Airdrie Cl, N1 . . . . .93 F7
Hayes UB4
off Glencoe Rd 103 E5
Airedale Av, W4 . . . . .127 F4
Airedale Av S, W4
off Netheravon Rd S . .127 F5
Airedale Rd, SW12 . . . . . . .149 J7
W5 . . . . .125 F3
Airlie Gdns, W8
off Campden Hill Rd . .128 D1
Ilford IG1 . . . . .99 E1
Air Links Ind Est, Houns.
TW5 . . . . .122 C5
Air Pk Way, Felt. TW13 . . . .160 B2
Airport Gate Business Cen,
West Dr. UB7 . . . . .120 C7
Airport Rbt, E16 . . . . .136 A1
Air St, W1 . . . . .17 G6
Airthrie Rd, Ilf. IG3 . . . . . . .100 B2
Aisgill Av, W14 . . . . .128 C5
Aisher Rd, SE28 . . . . .118 C7
Aislibie Rd, SE12 . . . . .155 E4
Aiten Pl, W6
off Standish Rd 127 G4
Aitken Cl, E8
off Pownall Rd 112 D1
Mitcham CR4 . . . . .185 J7
Aitken Rd, SE6 . . . . .172 B2
Barnet EN5 . . . . .39 J5
Aitman Dr, Brent. TW8
off Chiswick High Rd . .126 A5
Ait's Vw, W.Mol. KT8
off Victoria Av 179 H3
Ajax Av, NW9 . . . . .70 E3
Ajax Rd, NW6 . . . . .90 D5
Akabusi Cl, Croy. CR0 . . . .188 D6
Akehurst St, SW15 . . . . . .147 G6
Akenside Rd, NW3 . . . . .91 G5
Akerman Rd, SW9 . . . . . . .151 H2
Surbiton KT6 . . . . .181 F6
Alabama St, SE18 . . . . . . .137 G7
Alacross Rd, W5 . . . . .125 F2
Alamaro Lo, SE10
off Renaissance Wk . . .135 F3
Alandale Dr, Pnr. HA5 . . . . .66 B2
Aland Ct, SE16
off Finland St 133 H3
Alander Ms, E17 . . . . .78 C4
Alan Dr, Barn. EN5 . . . . .40 B6
Alan Gdns, Rom. RM7 . . . . .83 G7
Alan Hocken Way, E15 . . . .114 E2
Alan Rd, SW19 . . . . .166 B5
Alanthus Cl, SE12 . . . . . . .155 F6
Alaska Bldg, SE13
off Deals Gateway 154 B1
Alaska St, SE1 . . . . .27 E2
Alba Cl, Hayes UB4
off Ramulis Dr 102 D4
Albacore Cres, SE13 . . . . .154 B6
Alba Gdns, NW11 . . . . .72 B6
Alba Ms, SW18 . . . . .166 D2
Alban Cres, Borwd. WD6 . . .38 B1
Alban Highwalk, EC2
off London Wall 20 A2
Albany, W1 . . . . .17 F6
Albany, The, Wdf.Grn.
IG8 . . . . .63 F4
Albany Cl, N15 . . . . .75 H4
SW14 . . . . .146 B4
Bexley DA5 . . . . .158 C7
Albany Ct, E4
off Chelwood Cl 46 B6
Albany Ctyd, W1 . . . . .17 G6
Albany Cres, Edg. HA8 . . . . .54 A7
Esher (Clay.) KT10 . . . . .194 B6
Albany Mans, SW11 . . . . . .129 H7
Albany Ms, N1
off Barnsbury Pk 93 G7
SE5 . . . . .36 A6
Bromley BR1 . . . . .173 G6
Kingston upon Thames
KT2 . . . . .163 G6
Sutton SM1
off Camden Rd 198 E5
Albany Pk Av, Enf. EN3 . . . .45 F1
Albany Pk Rd, Kings.T.
KT2 . . . . .163 G6
Albany Pas, Rich. TW10 . . .145 J5
Albany Pl, Brent. TW8
off Albany Rd 125 H6
Albany Rd, E10 . . . . .78 A7
E12 . . . . .98 A4
E17 . . . . .77 H6
N4 . . . . .75 F6
N18 . . . . .61 E5
SE5 . . . . .36 B6
SE17 . . . . .36 B6
SW19 . . . . .166 E5
W13 . . . . .104 E7
Belvedere DA17 . . . . . . .139 F6
Bexley DA5 . . . . .158 C7
Brentford TW8 . . . . .125 G6
Chislehurst BR7 . . . . . . .174 E5
New Malden KT3 . . . . . .182 D4
Richmond TW10
off Albert Rd 145 J5
Romford RM6 . . . . .83 F6
Albany St, NW1 . . . . .8 D1
Albany Vw, Buck.H. IG9 . . . .63 G1
Alba Pl, W11
off Portobello Rd 108 C6
Albatross Cl, E6 . . . . .116 C4
Albatross St, SE18 . . . . . . .137 H7
Albatross Way, SE16 . . . . .133 G2
Albemarle, SW19 . . . . .166 A2
Albemarle App, Ilf. IG2 . . . .81 E6
Albemarle Av, Twick. TW2 .161 F1
Albemarle Gdns, Ilf. IG2 . . .81 E6
New Malden KT3 . . . . . .182 D4
Albemarle Pk, Stan. HA7
off Marsh La 53 F5
Albemarle Rd, Barn.
(E.Barn.) EN4 . . . . .41 H7
Beckenham BR3 . . . . . . .190 B1
Albemarle St, W1 . . . . .17 E6
Albemarle Way, EC1 . . . . . . .11 G6
Albermarle Pk, Beck. BR3
off Albemarle Rd 190 B1
Alberon Gdns, NW11 . . . . . .72 C4
Alberta Av, Sutt. SM1 . . . .198 B4
Alberta Est, SE17 . . . . .35 H3
Alberta Rd, Enf. EN1 . . . . . .44 C6
Erith DA8 . . . . .159 J1
Alberta St, SE17 . . . . .35 G3
Albert Av, E4 . . . . .62 A4
SW8 . . . . .131 F7
Albert Barnes Ho, SE1 . . . . .27 J6
Albert Basin, E16 . . . . .117 E7
Albert Basin Way, E16 . . . .117 E7
Albert Bigg Pt, E15 . . . . . . .114 C1
Albert Br, SW3 . . . . .31 H6
SW11 . . . . .31 H6
Albert Br Rd, SW11 . . . . . . .31 H7
Albert Carr Gdns, SW16 . . .168 E5
Albert Cl, E9
off Northiam St 113 E1
N22 . . . . .74 D1
Albert Ct, SW7 . . . . .23 E4
Albert Cres, E4 . . . . .62 A4
Albert Dr, SW19 . . . . .166 B2
Albert Embk, SE1 . . . . .34 B4
Albert Gdns, E1 . . . . .113 G6
Albert Gate, SW1 . . . . .24 A3
Albert Gro, SW20 . . . . .184 A1
Albert Hall Mans,
SW7 . . . . .23 E4
Albert Ho, SE28
off Erebus Dr 137 F3
Albert Mans, SW11
off Albert Br Rd 149 J1
★ **Albert Mem**, SW7 . . . . . .22 E3
Albert Ms, E14
off Narrow St 113 H7
N4 . . . . .93 F1
SE4 *off Arabin Rd* 153 H4
W8 . . . . .22 C5
Albert Pl, N3 . . . . .72 D1
N17 *off High Rd* 76 C3
W8 . . . . .22 B4
Albert Rd, E10 . . . . .96 C2
E16 . . . . .136 B1
E17 . . . . .78 A5
E18 . . . . .79 H3
N4 . . . . .93 F1
N15 . . . . .76 B6
N22 . . . . .74 C1
NW4 . . . . .72 A4
NW6 . . . . .108 C2
NW7 . . . . .55 F5
SE9 . . . . .174 B3
SE20 . . . . .171 G7
SE25 . . . . .188 D4
W5 . . . . .105 E4
Barnet EN4 . . . . .41 F4
Belvedere DA17 . . . . . . .139 F5
Bexley DA5 . . . . .159 G6
Bromley BR1 . . . . .173 G6
Bromley BR2 . . . . .192 A5
Buckhurst Hill IG9 . . . . . .64 A2
Dagenham RM8 . . . . . . .101 F1
Hampton (Hmptn H.)
TW12 . . . . .161 J5
Harrow HA2 . . . . .67 J3
Hayes UB3 . . . . .121 H3
Hounslow TW3 . . . . .143 G4
Ilford IG1 . . . . .99 E3
Kingston upon Thames
KT1 . . . . .181 J2
Mitcham CR4 . . . . .185 J3
New Malden KT3 . . . . . .183 F4
Richmond TW10 . . . . . . .145 H5
Southall UB2 . . . . .122 D3
Sutton SM1 . . . . .199 G5
Teddington TW11 . . . . . .162 C6
Twickenham TW1 . . . . . .162 C1
West Drayton UB7 . . . . .120 B1
Albert Rd Est, Belv.
DA17 . . . . .139 F5
Albert Sleet Ct, N9
off Colthurst Dr 60 E3
Albert Sq, E15 . . . . .97 E5
SW8 . . . . .131 F7
Albert St, N12 . . . . .57 F5
NW1 . . . . .110 B1
Albert Ter, NW1 . . . . .110 A1
NW10 . . . . .106 D1
W6 *off Beavor La* 127 G5
Buckhurst Hill IG9 . . . . . .64 A2
Albert Ter Ms, NW1
off Regents Pk Rd 110 A1
Albert Way, SE15 . . . . .132 E7

Albion Av, N10 74 A1
SW8 150 D2
Albion Cl, W2 15 H5
Albion Dr, E8 94 C7
Albion Est, SE16 133 F2
Albion Gro, N16 94 B4
Albion Hill, Loug. IG10 47 J5
Albion Ms, N1 111 G1
NW6
off Kilburn High Rd 90 C7
W2 15 H4
W6 off Galena Rd 127 H4
Albion Par, N16
off Albion Rd 94 A4
Albion Pk, Loug. IG10 48 A5
Albion Pl, EC1 19 G1
SE25 188 D3
W6 127 H4
Albion Riverside Bldg,
SW11 31 H7
Albion Rd, E17 78 C3
N16 94 A4
N17 76 C2
Bexleyheath DA6 159 F4
Hounslow TW3 143 G4
Kingston upon Thames
KT2 182 C1
Sutton SM2 199 G6
Twickenham TW2 162 B1
Albion Sq, E8 94 C7
Albion St, SE16 133 F2
W2 15 H4
Croydon CR0 201 H1
Albion Ter, E8 94 C7
Albion Vil Rd, SE26 171 F3
Albion Wk, N1 10 B2
Albion Way, EC1 19 J2
SE13 154 C4
Wembley HA9
off North End Rd 88 B3
Albion Yd, N1 10 B2
Albon Ho, SW18
off Neville Gill Cl 148 E6
Albrighton Rd, SE22 152 B3
Albuhera Cl, Enf. EN2 43 G1
Albury Av, Bexh. DA7 158 E2
Isleworth TW7 124 C7
Albury Cl, Hmptn. TW12 161 G6
Albury Ct, Sutt. SM1
off Ripley Gdns 199 F4
Albury Dr, Pnr. HA5 50 D7
Albury Ms, E12 97 J1
Albury Rd, Chess. KT9 195 H5
Albury St, SE8 134 A6
Albyfield, Brom. BR1 192 C3
Albyn Rd, SE8 154 A1
Alcester Cres, E5 95 E2
Alcester Rd, Wall. SM6 200 B4
Alcock Cl, Wall. SM6 200 D7
Alcock Rd, Houns. TW5 122 D7
Alconbury Rd, E5 94 D2
Alcorn Cl, Sutt. SM3 198 D2
Alcott Cl, W7
off Westcott Cres 104 C5
Alcuin Ct, Stan. HA7
off Old Ch La 53 F7
ALDBOROUGH HATCH, Ilf.
IG2 81 H3
Aldborough Rd, Dag.
RM10 101 J6
Aldborough Rd N, Ilf. IG2 81 J5
Aldborough Rd S, Ilf. IG3 99 H1
Aldbourne Rd, W12 127 F1
Aldbridge St, SE17 36 E3
Aldburgh Ms, W1 16 C3
Aldbury Av, Wem. HA9 88 B7
Aldbury Ms, N9 44 A7
Aldebert Ter, SW8 131 E7
Aldeburgh Cl, E5
off Southwold Rd 95 E2
Aldeburgh Pl, SE10
off Aldeburgh St 135 G4
Woodford Green IG8 63 G4
Aldeburgh St, SE10 135 G5
Alden Av, E15 115 F3
Aldenham St, NW1 9 G2
Aldensley Rd, W6 127 H3
Alderbrook Rd, SW12 150 B6
Alderbury Rd, SW13 127 G6
Alder Cl, SE15 37 G6
Erith DA18
off Waldrist Way 139 F2
Alder Ct, N11
off Cline Rd 58 C6
Alder Gro, NW2 89 H2
Aldergrove Gdns, Houns.
TW3 off Bath Rd 142 E2
Alder Ho, NW3
off Maitland Pk Vil 91 J6
Alderman Av, Bark. IG11 118 A3
Aldermanbury, EC2 20 A3
Aldermanbury Sq, EC2 20 A2
Alderman Judge Mall,
Kings.T. KT1
off Eden St 181 H2
Aldermans Hill, N13 58 E4
Alderman's Wk, EC2 20 D2
Aldermary Rd, Brom.
BR1 191 G1
Alder Ms, N19
off Bredgar Rd 92 C2
Aldermoor Rd, SE6 171 J3
Alderney Av, Houns. TW5 123 H7
Alderney Gdns, Nthlt.
UB5 85 F7
Alderney Ho, N1
off Arran Wk 93 J6
Alderney Ms, SE1 28 B5
Alderney Rd, E1 113 G4
Alderney St, SW1 32 E3
Alder Rd, SW14 146 D3
Sidcup DA14 175 J3
Alders, The, N21 43 G6
SW16 168 C4
Feltham TW13 160 E4
Hounslow TW5 123 F6
West Wickham BR4 204 B1
Alders Av, Wdf.Grn. IG8 62 E6
ALDERSBROOK, E12 97 H2
Aldersbrook Av, Enf. EN1 44 B2
Aldersbrook Dr, Kings.T.
KT2 163 J6
Aldersbrook La, E12 98 C3
Aldersbrook Rd, E11 97 H2
E12 98 A3
Alders Cl, E11 97 H2
W5 125 G3
Edgware HA8 54 C5
Aldersey Gdns, Bark.
IG11 99 G6
Aldersford Cl, SE4 153 G5
Aldersgate St, EC1 19 J3
Alders Gro, E.Mol. KT8
off Esher Rd 180 A5
Aldersgrove Av, SE9 173 J3
Aldershot Rd, NW6 108 C1
Aldersmead Av, Croy.
CR0 189 G6
Aldersmead Rd, Beck.
BR3 171 H7
Alderson Pl, Sthl. UB2 123 J1
Alderson St, W10
off Kensal Rd 108 B4
Alders Rd, Edg. HA8 54 C5
Alderton Cl, NW10 88 D3
Loughton IG10 48 D4
Alderton Cres, NW4 71 H5
Alderton Hall La, Loug.
IG10 48 D4
Alderton Hill, Loug. IG10 48 B5
Alderton Ms, Loug. IG10
off Alderton Hall La 48 D4
Alderton Ri, Loug. IG10 48 D4
Alderton Rd, SE24 151 J3
Croydon CR0 188 C7
Alderton Way, NW4 71 H5
Loughton IG10 48 C5
Alderville Rd, SW6 148 C2
Alder Wk, Ilf. IG1 99 F5
Alderwick Dr, Houns.
TW3 144 A3
Alderwood Rd, SE9 157 G6
Aldford St, W1 24 B1
Aldgate, EC3 21 F4
Aldgate Av, E1 21 F3
Aldgate Barrs Shop Cen,
E1 21 G3
Aldgate High St, EC3 21 F4
Aldine Ct, W12
off Aldine St 127 J1
Aldine Pl, W12
off Uxbridge Rd 127 J2
Aldine St, W12 127 J2
Aldington Cl, Dag. RM8 82 C7
Aldington Rd, SE18 136 A3
Aldis Ms, SW17 167 H5
Aldis St, SW17 167 H5
Aldred Rd, NW6 90 D5
Aldren Rd, SW17 167 F3
Aldriche Way, E4 62 C6
Aldrich Gdns, Sutt. SM3 198 C3
Aldrich Ter, SW18
off Lidiard Rd 167 F2
Aldridge Av, Edg. HA8 54 B3
Ruislip HA4 84 D2
Stanmore HA7 69 H1
Aldridge Ri, N.Mal. KT3 182 E7
Aldridge Rd Vil, W11 108 C5
Aldridge Wk, N14 42 E7
Aldrien Ct, N9
off Galahad Rd 60 D3
Aldrington Rd, SW16 168 C5
Aldsworth Cl, W9 6 A6
Aldwick Cl, SE9 175 G3
Aldwick Rd, Croy. CR0 201 F3
Aldworth Gro, SE13 154 C6
Aldworth Rd, E15 96 E7
Aldwych, WC2 18 C5
Aldwych Av, Ilf. IG6 81 F4
Aldwych Underpass, WC2
off Kingsway 18 C4
Alers Rd, Bexh. DA6 158 D5
Alesia Cl, N22 59 E7
Alestan Beck Rd, E16 116 A5
Alexa Ct, W8 30 A1
Sutton SM2
off Mulgrave Rd 198 D6
Alexander Av, NW10 89 H7
Alexander Cl,
Barn. EN4 41 G4
Bromley BR2 205 G1
Harrow HA2 85 J2
Sidcup DA15 157 H5
Southall UB2 123 J1
Twickenham TW2 162 C2
Alexander Evans Ms, SE23
off Sunderland Rd 171 G1
★ Alexander Fleming
Laboratory Mus, W2 15 F3
Alexander Ho, Kings.T. KT2
off Kingsgate Rd 181 H1
Alexander Ms, SW16 168 C5
W2 14 A3
Alexander Pl, SW7 31 G1
Alexander Rd, N19 92 E3
Bexleyheath DA7 158 D2
Chislehurst BR7 175 E5
Alexander Sq, SW3 31 G1
Alexander St, W2 108 D6
Alexandra Av, N22 74 D1
SW11 150 A1
W4 126 D7
Harrow HA2 85 F1
Southall UB1 103 F7
Sutton SM1 198 D3
Alexandra Cl, SE8 133 J6
Harrow HA2
off Alexandra Av 85 G3
Alexandra Cotts, SE14 153 J1
Alexandra Ct, N14 42 C5
N16 94 B4
W9 6 D5
Wembley HA9 87 J4
Alexandra Cres, Brom.
BR1 173 F6
Alexandra Dr, SE19 170 B5
Surbiton KT5 182 A7
Alexandra Gdns, N10 74 B4
W4 126 E7
Hounslow TW3 143 H2
Alexandra Gro, N4 93 H1
N12 57 E5
Alexandra Ms, N2 73 J3
SW19
off Alexandra Rd 166 C6
★ Alexandra Palace,
N22 74 D2
Alexandra Palace Way,
N22 74 C3
Alexandra Pk Rd, N10 74 B2
N22 74 D2
Alexandra Pl, NW8 109 F1
SE25 188 A5
Croydon CR0
off Alexandra Rd 202 B1
Alexandra Rd, E6 116 D3
E10 96 C3
E17 77 J6
E18 79 H3
N8 75 G3
N9 44 E7
N10 58 B6
N15 76 A5
NW4 72 A4
NW8 91 F7
SE26 171 G6
SW14 146 D3
SW19 166 C6
W4 126 D2
Brentford TW8 125 G6
Croydon CR0 202 B1
Enfield EN3 45 G4
Hounslow TW3 143 H2
Kingston upon Thames
KT2 164 A7
Mitcham CR4 167 H7
Richmond TW9 145 J2
Romford (Chad.Hth)
RM6 82 D6
Thames Ditton KT7 180 C5
Twickenham TW1 145 F6
Alexandra Sq, Mord.
SM4 184 D5
Alexandra St, E16 115 G5
SE14 133 H7
Alexandra Wk, SE19 170 B5
Alexandria Rd, W13 104 D7
Alexis St, SE16 37 H1
Alfearn Rd, E5 95 F4
Alford Grn, Croy.
(New Adgtn) CR0 204 D6
Alford Ho, N6 74 C6
Alford Pl, N1 12 A2
Alfoxton Av, N15 75 H4
Alfreda St, SW11 150 B1
Alfred Cl, W4
off Belmont Ter 126 D4
Alfred Gdns, Sthl. UB1 103 E7
Alfred Ms, W1 17 H1
Alfred Pl, WC1 17 H1
Alfred Prior Ho, E12 98 D4
Alfred Rd, E15 97 F5
SE25 188 D5
W2 108 D5
W3 126 C1
Belvedere DA17 139 F5
Buckhurst Hill IG9 64 A2
Feltham TW13 160 C2
Kingston upon Thames
KT1 181 H3
Sutton SM1 199 F5
Alfred's Gdns, Bark. IG11 117 H2
Alfred St, E3 113 J3
Alfreds Way, Bark. IG11 117 F3
Alfreds Way Ind Est, Bark.
IG11 118 A1
Alfreton Cl, SW19 166 A3
Alfriston, Surb. KT5 181 J5
Alfriston Av, Croy. CR0 186 E7
Harrow HA2 67 G6
Alfriston Cl, Surb. KT5 181 J6
Alfriston Rd, SW11 149 J5
Algar Cl, Islw. TW7
off Algar Rd 144 D3
Stanmore HA7 52 C5
Algar Rd, Islw. TW7 144 D3
Algarve Rd, SW18 167 E1
Algernon Rd, NW4 71 G6
NW6 108 D1
SE13 154 B4
Algers Cl, Loug. IG10 48 A5
Algers Mead, Loug. IG10 48 A5
Algers Rd, Loug. IG10 48 A5
Algiers Rd, SE13 154 A4
Alibon Gdns, Dag. RM10 101 G5
Alibon Rd, Dag. RM9,
RM10 101 F5
Alice Cl, Barn.
(New Barn.) EN5 41 F4
Alice Ct, SW15
off Deodar Rd 148 C4
Alice Gilliatt Ct, W14 128 C6
Alice La, E3 113 J1
Alice Ms, Tedd. TW11
off Luther Rd 162 C5
Alice St, SE1 28 D6
Alice Thompson Cl,
SE12 173 J2
Alice Wk, W5
off Queens Wk 105 F5
Alice Walker Cl, SE24
off Shakespeare Rd 151 H4
Alice Way, Houns. TW3 143 H4
Alicia Av, Har. HA3 69 E4
Alicia Cl, Har. HA3 69 F4
Alicia Gdns, Har. HA3 69 E4
Alie St, E1 21 G4
Alington Cres, NW9 88 C1
Alison Cl, E6 116 D6
Croydon CR0
off Shirley Oaks Rd 203 G1
Aliwal Rd, SW11 149 H4
Alkerden Rd, W4 127 E5
Alkham Rd, N16 94 C2
Allan Barclay Cl, N15
off High Rd 76 C6
Allan Cl, N.Mal. KT3 182 D5
Allandale Av, N3 72 B3
Allan Way, W3 106 C5
Allard Cres, Bushey
(Bushey Hth) WD23 51 J1
Allard Gdns, SW4 150 D5
Allardyce St, SW4 151 F4
Allbrook Cl, Tedd. TW11 162 B5
Allcroft Rd, NW5 92 A5
Allder Way, S.Croy. CR2 201 H7
Allenby Cl, Grnf. UB6 103 G3
Allenby Rd, SE23 171 H3
SE28 137 F3
Southall UB1 103 G6
Allen Cl, Mitch. CR4 186 B1
Sunbury-on-Thames
TW16 178 B1
Allen Ct, Grnf. UB6 86 C5
Allendale Av, Sthl. UB1 103 G6
Allendale Cl, SE5
off Daneville Rd 152 A1
SE26 171 G5
Allendale Rd, Grnf. UB6 86 E6
Allen Edwards Dr, SW8 150 E1
Allenford Ho, SW15
off Tunworth Cres 147 F6
Allen Pl, Twick. TW1
off Church St 162 D1
Allen Rd, E3 113 J2
N16 94 B4
Beckenham BR3 189 G2
Croydon CR0 187 F7
Sunbury-on-Thames
TW16 178 B1
Allensbury Pl, NW1 92 D7
Allens Rd, Enf. EN3 45 F5
Allen St, W8 128 D3
Allenswood, SW19
off Albert Dr 166 B1
Allenswood Rd, SE9 156 B3
Allerford Ct, Har. HA2 67 H5
Allerford Rd, SE6 172 B4

Allerton Ct, NW4
off Holders Hill Rd 72 A2
Allerton Rd, N16 93 J2
Allerton Wk, N7
off Durham Rd 93 F2
Allestree Rd, SW6 128 B7
Alleyn Cres, SE21 170 A2
Alleyndale Rd, Dag.
RM8 100 C2
Alleyn Pk, SE21 170 A2
Southall UB2 123 F4
Alleyn Rd, SE21 170 A3
Allfarthing La, SW18 149 E6
Allgood Cl, Mord. SM4 184 A6
Allgood St, E2 13 G2
Allhallows La, EC4 20 B6
★ **All Hallows-on-the-Wall C of E Ch**, EC2 20 C2
Allhallows Rd, E6 116 B5
All Hallows Rd, N17 76 B1
Alliance Cl, Houns. TW4
off Vickers Way 143 F5
Wembley HA0 87 G4
Alliance Ct, W3
off Alliance Rd 106 B5
Alliance Rd, E13 115 J4
SE18 138 A6
W3 106 B4
Allied Ct, N1
off Enfield Rd 94 B7
Allied Way, W3
off Larden Rd 127 E2
Allingham Cl, W7 104 C7
Allingham Ms, N1 11 J1
Allingham St, N1 11 J1
Allington Av, N17 60 B6
Allington Cl, SW19
off High St Wimbledon 166 A5
Greenford UB6 85 J7
Allington Ct, Enf. EN3 45 G5
Allington Rd, NW4 71 H5
W10 108 B2
Harrow HA2 67 J5
Orpington BR6 207 G2
Allington St, SW1 25 F6
Allison Cl, SE10
off Dartmouth Hill 154 C1
Allison Gro, SE21 170 B1
Allison Rd, N8 75 G5
W3 106 C6
Allitsen Rd, NW8 7 G2
Allnutt Way, SW4 150 D5
Alloa Rd, SE8 133 G5
Ilford IG3 100 A2
Allonby Gdns, Wem. HA9 87 F1
Allonby Ho, E14
off Aston St 113 H5
Allotment Way, NW2
off Midland Ter 90 A3
Alloway Rd, E3 113 H3
Allport Ms, E1
off Stepney Grn 113 F4
All Saints Cl, N9 60 C2
SW8
off Lansdowne Way 150 E1
All Saints Dr, SE3 155 E2
All Saints Ms, Har. HA3 52 B6
All Saints Pas, SW18
off Wandsworth High St 148 D5
All Saints Rd, SW19 167 F7
W3 126 C3
W11 108 C5
Sutton SM1 199 E3
All Saints St, N1 10 C1
All Saints Twr, E10 78 B7
Allsop Pl, NW1 8 A6
All Souls Av, NW10 107 H2
All Souls Pl, W1 17 E2
Allum Way, N20 57 F1
Allwood Cl, SE26 171 G4
Alma Av, E4 62 C7
Almack Rd, E5 95 F4
Alma Cres, Sutt. SM1 198 B5
Alma Gro, SE1 37 G2
Alma Pl, NW10
off Harrow Rd 107 H3
SE19 170 C7
Thornton Heath CR7 187 G5
Alma Rd, N10 58 A7
SW18 149 F5
Carshalton SM5 199 H5
Enfield EN3 45 H5
Esher KT10 194 B1
Sidcup DA14 176 A3
Southall UB1 102 E7
Alma Row, Har. HA3 68 A1
Alma Sq, NW8 6 D3
Alma St, E15 96 D6
NW5 92 B6
Alma Ter, SW18 149 G7
W8 *off Allen St* 128 D3
Almeida St, N1 93 H7
Almeric Rd, SW11 149 J4
Almer Rd, SW20 165 G7
Almington St, N4 93 F1
Almond Av, W5 125 H3
Carshalton SM5 199 J2
West Drayton UB7 120 D3
Almond Cl, SE15 152 D2
Bromley BR2 192 D7
Feltham TW13
off Highfield Rd 160 A1
Almond Gro, Brent. TW8 124 E7
Almond Rd, N17 60 D7
SE16 133 E4
Almonds Av, Buck.H. IG9 63 G2
Almond Way, Borwd. WD6 38 B4
Bromley BR2 192 D7
Harrow HA2 67 H2
Mitcham CR4 186 D5
Almorah Rd, N1 94 A7
Hounslow TW5 142 D1
Alnwick Gro, Mord. SM4
off Bordesley Rd 184 E4
Alnwick Rd, E16 115 J6
SE12 155 H7
ALPERTON, Wem. HA0 105 J1
Alperton La, Grnf. (Perivale) UB6 105 G3
Wembley HA0 105 G3
Alperton St, W10 108 B4
Alphabet Gdns, Cars.
SM5 185 G6
Alphabet Sq, E3
off Hawgood St 114 A5
Alpha Cl, NW1 7 H5
Alpha Gro, E14 134 A2
Alpha Pl, NW6 108 D2
SW3 31 H5
Alpha Rd, E4 62 B3
N18 60 D6
SE14 153 J1
Croydon CR0 202 B1
Enfield EN3 45 H4
Surbiton KT5 181 J6
Teddington TW11 162 A5
Alpha St, SE15 152 D2
Alphea Cl, SW19 167 H7
Alpine Av, Surb. KT5 196 C2
Alpine Cl, Croy. CR0 202 B3
Alpine Copse, Brom. BR1 192 D2
Alpine Gro, E9 95 F7
Alpine Rd, E10 96 B2
SE16 133 F4
Walton-on-Thames KT12 178 A7
Alpine Vw, Cars. SM5 199 H5
Alpine Wk, Stan. HA7 52 B2
Alpine Way, E6 116 D5
Alric Av, NW10 88 D7
New Malden KT3 183 E3
Alroy Rd, N4 75 G7
Alsace Rd, SE17 36 D3
Alscot Rd, SE1 37 G1
Alscot Way, SE1 37 F1
Alsike Rd, SE2 138 D3
Erith DA18 138 E3
Alsom Av, Wor.Pk. KT4 197 G4
Alston Cl, Surb. (Long Dit.) KT6 181 E7
Alston Rd, N18 60 E5
SW17 167 G4
Barnet EN5 40 B3
Alston Wks, Barn. EN5 40 B3
Altair Cl, N17 60 C6
Altash Way, SE9 174 C2
Altenburg Av, W13 125 E3
Altenburg Gdns, SW11 149 J4
Alt Gro, SW19
off St. George's Rd 166 C7
Altham Gdns, Wat.
WD19 50 D4
Altham Rd, Pnr. HA5 51 E7
Althea St, SW6 149 E2
Althorne Gdns, E18 79 F4
Althorne Way, Dag.
RM10 101 G2
Althorp Cl, Barn. EN5 39 G7
Althorpe Gro, SW11
off Westbridge Rd 149 G1
Althorpe Ms, SW11
off Battersea High St 149 G1
Althorpe Rd, Har. HA1 67 J5
Althorp Rd, SW17 167 J1
Altima Ct, SE22
off East Dulwich Rd 152 D4
Altmore Av, E6 98 C7
Alton Av, Stan. HA7 52 C7
Alton Cl, Bex. DA5 177 E1
Isleworth TW7 144 C2
Alton Gdns, Beck. BR3 172 A7
Twickenham TW2 144 A7
Alton Ho, E3
off Bromley High St 114 B3
Alton Rd, N17 76 A3
SW15 165 G1
Croydon CR0 201 G3
Richmond TW9 145 H4
Alton St, E14 114 B5
Altyre Cl, Beck. BR3 189 J5
Altyre Rd, Croy. CR0 202 A2
Altyre Way, Beck. BR3 189 J5
Alvanley Gdns, NW6 90 E5
Alva Way, Wat. WD19 50 D2
Alverstone Av, SW19 166 D2
Barnet (E.Barn.) EN4 41 H7
Alverstone Gdns, SE9 175 F1
Alverstone Rd, E12 98 D4
NW2 89 J7
New Malden KT3 183 F4
Wembley HA9 87 J1
Alverston Gdns, SE25 188 B5
Alverton St, SE8 133 J5
Alveston Av, Har. HA3 68 E3
Alveston Sq, E18
off Marlborough Rd 79 G2
Alvey Est, SE17 36 D2
Alvey St, SE17 36 D3
Alvia Gdns, Sutt. SM1 199 F4
Alvington Cres, E8 94 C5
Alway Av, Epsom KT19 196 C5
Alwold Cres, SE12 155 H6
Alwyn Av, W4 126 D5
Alwyn Cl, Croy. (New Adgtn) CR0 204 B7
Alwyne La, N1
off Alwyne Vil 93 H7
Alwyne Pl, N1 93 J6
Alwyne Rd, N1 93 J7
SW19 166 C6
W7 104 B7
Alwyne Sq, N1 93 J6
Alwyne Vil, N1 93 H7
Alwyn Gdns, NW4 71 G4
W3 106 B6
Alyth Gdns, NW11 72 D6
Alzette Ho, E2 113 G3
Amalgamated Dr, Brent.
TW8 124 D6
Amanda Cl, Chig. IG7 65 G6
Amanda Ms, Rom. RM7 83 J5
Amazon Apts, N8
off New River Av 75 F4
Amazon St, E1
off Hessel St 112 E6
Ambassador Cl, Houns.
TW3 142 E2
Ambassador Gdns, E6 116 C5
Ambassador's Ct, SW1 25 G2
Ambassador Sq, E14
off Cahir St 134 B4
Amber Av, E17 77 H1
Amber Cl, Barn. EN5 41 E6
Amber Ct, SW17 168 A4
Amberden Av, N3 72 D3
Ambergate St, SE17 35 H3
Amber Gro, NW2 90 A1
Amber La, Ilf. IG6 64 E7
Amberley Cl, Orp. BR6 207 J5
Pinner HA5 67 F3
Amberley Ct, Sid. DA14 176 C5
Amberley Gdns, Enf.
EN1 44 B7
Epsom KT19 197 F4
Amberley Gro, SE26 170 E4
Croydon CR0 188 C7
Amberley Rd, E10 78 A7
N13 59 F2
SE2 138 D6
W9 108 D5
Buckhurst Hill IG9 63 J1
Enfield EN1 44 C7
Amberley Way, Houns.
TW4 142 C5
Morden SM4 184 C7
Romford RM7 83 H4
Amber Ms, N22
off Brampton Pk Rd 75 G3
Amberside Cl, Islw. TW7 144 A6
Amber St, E15
off Great Eastern Rd 96 D6
Amber Wf, E2
off Nursery La 112 C1
Amberwood Cl, Wall.
SM6 200 E5
Amberwood Ri, N.Mal.
KT3 182 E6
Amblecote Cl, SE12 173 H3
Amblecote Meadows,
SE12 173 H3
Amblecote Rd, SE12 173 H3
Ambler Rd, N4 93 H3
Ambleside, SW19
off Albert Dr 166 B1
Bromley BR1 172 D6
Ambleside Av, SW16 168 D4
Beckenham BR3 189 H5
Ambleside Cl, E9
off Churchill Wk 95 F5
E10 78 B7
N17 *off Drapers Rd* 76 C3
Ambleside Cres,
Enfield EN3 45 G3
Ambleside Gdns, SW16 168 D5
Ilford IG4 80 B4
Sutton SM2 199 F6
Wembley HA9 87 G1
Ambleside Pt, SE15
off Ilderton Rd 133 F7
Ambleside Rd, NW10 89 F7
Bexleyheath DA7 159 G2
Ambrooke Rd, Belv.
DA17 139 G3
Ambrosden Av, SW1 25 G6
Ambrose Av, NW11 72 B7
Ambrose Cl, E6
off Lovage App 116 B5
Orpington BR6
off Stapleton Rd 207 J3
Ambrose Ms, SW11 149 H2
Ambrose St, SE16 132 E4
Ambrose Wk, E3
off Malmesbury Rd 114 A2
Amelia Cl, W3 126 B1
Amelia St, SE17 35 H3
Amen Cor, EC4 19 H4
SW17 167 J6
Amen Ct, EC4 19 H3
Amenity Way, Mord. SM4 183 J7
America Sq, EC3 21 F5
America St, SE1 27 J2
Amerland Rd, SW18 148 C6
Amersham Av, N18 60 A6
Amersham Gro, SE14 133 J7
Amersham Rd, SE14 133 J7
Croydon CR0 187 J6
Amersham Vale, SE14 133 J7
Amery Gdns, NW10 107 H1
Amery Rd, Har. HA1 86 D2
Amesbury Av, SW2 169 E2
Amesbury Cl, Wor.Pk.
KT4 197 J1
Amesbury Dr, E4 46 B6
Amesbury Rd, Brom.
BR1 192 A3
Dagenham RM9 100 D7
Feltham TW13 160 D2
Amesbury Twr, SW8
off Westbury St 150 C2
Amethyst Cl, N11 58 D7
Amethyst Ct, Enf. EN3
off Enstone Rd 45 H3
Amethyst Rd, E15 96 D4
Amherst Av, W13 105 F6
Amherst Dr, Orp. BR5 193 J4
Amherst Rd, W13 105 F6
Amhurst Gdns, Islw.
TW7 144 C1
Amhurst Par, N16
off Amhurst Pk 76 C7
Amhurst Pk, N16 76 A7
Amhurst Pas, E8 94 D4
Amhurst Rd, E8 94 E5
N16 94 C4
Amhurst Ter, E8 94 D4
Amhurst Wk, SE28
off Roman Sq 138 A1
Amidas Gdns, Dag.
RM8 100 B4
Amiel St, E1 113 F4
Amies St, SW11 149 J3
Amina Way, SE16 29 H6
Amis Av, Epsom KT19 196 B6
Amity Gro, SW20 183 J1
Amity Rd, E15 115 F1
Ammanford Grn, NW9
off Ruthin Cl 70 E6
Amner Rd, SW11 150 A6
Amor Rd, W6 127 J3
Amott Rd, SE15 152 D3
Amoy Pl, E14 114 A6
Ampere Way, Croy. CR0 187 E7
Ampleforth Rd, SE2 138 B2
Ampthill Sq Est, NW1 9 G2
Ampton Pl, WC1 10 C4
Ampton St, WC1 10 C4
Amroth Cl, SE23 171 E1
Amroth Grn, NW9
off Fryent Gro 71 E6
Amsterdam Rd, E14 134 C3
Amundsen Ct, E14
off Napier Av 134 A5
Amwell Cl, Enf. EN2 44 A5
Amwell Ct Est, N4 93 J1
Amwell St, EC1 11 E3
Amyand Cotts, Twick. TW1
off Amyand Pk Rd 144 E6
Amyand La, Twick. TW1
off Marble Hill Gdns 145 E7
Amyand Pk Gdns, Twick. TW1
off Amyand Pk Rd 144 E7
Amyand Pk Rd, Twick.
TW1 144 D7
Amy Cl, Wall. SM6 201 E7
Amyruth Rd, SE4 154 A5
Amy Warne Cl, E6
off Evelyn Denington Rd 116 B4
Anatola Rd, N19
off Dartmouth Pk Hill 92 B2
Ancaster Cres, N.Mal.
KT3 183 G6
Ancaster Ms, Beck. BR3 189 G3
Ancaster Rd, Beck. BR3 189 G3
Ancaster St, SE18 137 H7
Anchorage Cl, SW19 166 D5

Anchorage Pt, E14
off Cuba St **134** A2
Anchorage Pt Ind Est,
SE7 **135** J3
Anchor & Hope La, SE7 **135** H3
Anchor Cl, Bark. IG11 **118** B3
Anchor Ho, SW18
off Smugglers Way **149** E4
Anchor Ms, N1
off Balls Pond Rd **94** B6
SW11
off Westbridge Rd **149** G1
SW12 **150** B6
Anchor Retail Pk, E1 **113** F4
Anchor St, SE16 **132** E4
Anchor Ter, E1
off Cephas Av **113** F4
Anchor Wf, E3
off Watts Gro **114** B5
Anchor Yd, EC1 **12** A5
Ancill Cl, W6 **128** B6
Ancona Rd, NW10 **107** G2
SE18 **137** G5
Andace Pk Gdns, Brom.
BR1 **191** J1
Andalus Rd, SW9 **151** E3
Ander Cl, Wem. HA0 **87** G4
Anderson Cl, N21 **43** F5
W3 **106** D6
Sutton SM3 **198** D1
Anderson Ho, Bark. IG11
off The Coverdales **117** G2
Anderson Pl, Houns.
TW3 **143** H4
Anderson Rd, E9 **95** G6
Woodford Green IG8 **80** A3
Andersons Sq, N1
off Gaskin St **111** H1
Anderson St, SW3 **31** J3
Anderson Way, Belv.
DA17 **139** H2
Anderton Cl, SE5 **152** A3
Andmark Ct, Sthl. UB1
off Herbert Rd **123** F1
Andover Av, E16
off King George Av **116** A6
Andover Cl, Grnf. UB6
off Ruislip Rd **103** H4
Andover Pl, NW6 **6** A1
Andover Rd, N7 **93** F2
Orpington BR6 **207** G1
Twickenham TW2 **162** A1
Andre St, E8 **94** D5
Andrew Borde St, WC2 **17** J3
Andrew Cl, Ilf. IG6 **65** G6
Andrewes Gdns, E6 **116** B6
Andrewes Ho, EC2 **20** A2
Andrew Pl, SW8
off Cowthorpe Rd **150** D1
Andrew Reed Ho, SW18
off Linstead Way **148** B7
Andrews Cl, E6
off Linton Gdns **116** B6
Buckhurst Hill IG9 **63** J2
Harrow HA1
off Bessborough Rd **68** A7
Worcester Park KT4 **198** A2
Andrews Crosse, WC2 **18** E4
Andrews Pl, SE9 **156** E6
Andrew's Rd, E8 **112** E1
Andrew St, E14 **114** C6
Andrews Wk, SE17 **35** H6
Andwell Cl, SE2 **138** B2
Anemone Ct, Enf. EN3
off Enstone Rd **45** H3
ANERLEY, SE20 **188** E1
Anerley Gro, SE19 **170** C7
Anerley Hill, SE19 **170** C6
Anerley Pk, SE20 **170** D7
Anerley Pk Rd, SE20 **170** E7
Anerley Rd, SE19 **170** D7
SE20 **170** D7
Anerley Sta Rd, SE20 **188** E1
Anerley St, SW11 **149** J2
Anerley Vale, SE19 **170** C7
Anfield Cl, SW12
off Belthorn Cres **150** C7
Angel All, E1 **21** G3
Angel Cl, N18 **60** C4
Hampton TW12
off Windmill Rd **161** J6
Angel Cor Par, N18
off Fore St **60** D5
Angel Ct, EC2 **20** C3
SW1 **25** G2
SW17 **167** J4
Angel Edmonton, N18
off Angel Rd **60** D5
Angelfield, Houns. TW3 **143** H4
Angel Gate, EC1 **11** H3
Angel Hill, Sutt. SM1 **199** E3
Angel Hill Dr, Sutt. SM1 **199** E3
Angelica Dr, E6 **116** D5
Angelica Gdns, Croy.
CR0 **203** G1
Angelis Apts, N1
off Graham St **11** H2
Angel La, E15 **96** D6
Angell Pk Gdns, SW9 **151** G3
Angell Rd, SW9 **151** G3
Angell Town Est, SW9
off Overton Rd **151** G2
Angel Ms, E1
off Cable St **112** D7
N1 **11** F2
Angel Ms, SW15
off Roehampton
High St **147** G7
Angelo Ms, SW16 **187** F3
Angel Pas, EC4 **20** B6
Angel Pl, N18 **60** D5
SE1 **28** B3
Angel Rd, N18 **60** E5
Harrow HA1 **68** B6
Thames Ditton KT7 **180** D7
Angel Rd Wks, N18 **61** F5
Angel Southside, EC1 **11** F2
Angel Sq, EC1 **11** F2
Angel St, EC1 **19** J3
Angel Wf, N1 **12** A1
Angel Wk, W6 **127** J4
Angerstein La, SE3 **135** F7
Angle Grn, Dag. RM8 **100** C1
Anglers Cl, Rich. TW10
off Locksmeade Rd **163** F4
Angler's La, NW5 **92** B6
Anglers Reach, Surb.
KT6 **181** G5
Anglesea Av, SE18 **136** E4
Anglesea Ms, SE18
off Anglesea Av **136** E4
Anglesea Rd, SE18 **136** E4
Kingston upon Thames
KT1 **181** G4
Anglesea Ter, W6
off Wellesley Av **127** H3
Anglesey Ct Rd, Cars.
SM5 **200** A6
Anglesey Gdns, Cars.
SM5 **200** A6
Anglesey Rd, Enf. EN3 **45** E4
Watford WD19 **50** C5
Anglesmede Cres, Pnr.
HA5 **67** G3
Anglesmede Way, Pnr.
HA5 **67** F3
Angles Rd, SW16 **169** E4
Anglia Cl, N17
off Park La **60** E7
Anglia Ct, Dag. RM8
off Spring Cl **100** D1
Anglia Ho, E14 **113** H6
Anglian Rd, E11 **96** D3
Anglia Wk, E6 **116** C1
Anglo Rd, E3 **113** J2
Angrave Ct, E8 **112** C1
Angrave Pas, E8
off Haggerston Rd **112** C1
Angus Cl, Chess. KT9 **196** A5
Angus Dr, Ruis. HA4 **84** C4
Angus Gdns, NW9 **70** D1
Angus Rd, E13 **115** J3
Angus St, SE14 **133** H7
Anhalt Rd, SW11 **31** H7
Ankerdine Cres, SE18 **136** D7
Anlaby Rd, Tedd. TW11 **162** B5
Anley Rd, W14 **128** A2
Anmersh Gro, Stan. HA7 **69** G1
Annabel Cl, E14 **114** B6
Annabels Ms, W5 **105** G4
Anna Cl, E8 **112** C1
Annandale Rd, SE10 **135** F6
W4 **126** E4
Croydon CR0 **202** D2
Sidcup DA15 **157** H7
Anna Neagle Cl, E7
off Dames Rd **97** G4
Anne Boleyn Ct, SE9
off Avery Hill Rd **157** G6
Anne Boleyn's Wk,
Kings.T. KT2 **163** H5
Sutton SM3 **198** A7
Anne Case Ms, N.Mal. KT3
off Sycamore Gro **182** D3
Anne Compton Ms,
SE12 **155** F7
Anne Goodman Ho, E1
off Jubilee St **113** F6
Anne of Cleeves Ct, SE9
off Avery Hill Rd **157** G6
Annesley Av, NW9 **70** D3
Annesley Cl, NW10 **88** E3
Annesley Dr, Croy. CR0 **203** J3
Annesley Rd, SE3 **155** H1
Annesley Wk, N19 **92** C2
Annesmere Gdns, SE3
off Highbrook Rd **156** A3
Anne St, E13 **115** G4
Annette Cl, Har. HA3
off Spencer Rd **68** B2
Annette Cres, N1
off Essex Rd **93** J7
Annette Rd, N7 **93** F4
Annett Rd, Walt. KT12 **178** A7
Anne Way, Ilf. IG6 **65** F6
West Molesey KT8 **179** H4
Annie Besant Cl, E3 **113** J1
Annie Taylor Ho, E12
off Walton Rd **98** D4
Anning St, EC2 **13** E5
Annington Rd, N2 **73** J3
Annis Rd, E9 **95** H6
Ann La, SW10 **30** E7
Ann Moss Way, SE16 **133** F3
Ann's Cl, SW1 **24** A4
Ann's Pl, E1 **21** F2
Ann St, SE18 **137** G4
Annsworthy Av, Th.Hth. CR7
off Grange Pk Rd **188** A3
Annsworthy Cres, SE25
off Grange Rd **188** A2
Ansdell Rd, SE15 **153** F2
Ansdell St, W8 **22** B5
Ansdell Ter, W8 **22** B5
Ansell Gro, Cars. SM5 **200** A1
Ansell Rd, SW17 **167** H3
Anselm Cl, Croy. CR0 **202** C3
Anselm Rd, SW6 **128** D6
Pinner HA5 **51** F7
Ansford Rd, Brom. BR1 **172** C5
Ansleigh Pl, W11 **108** A7
Anson Cl, Rom. RM7 **83** H2
Anson Ho, E1
off Shandy St **113** H4
Anson Pl, SE28 **137** G2
Anson Rd, N7 **92** C4
NW2 **90** A5
Anson Ter, Nthlt. UB5 **85** H6
Anstey Rd, SE15 **152** D3
Anstey Wk, N15 **75** H4
Anstice Cl, W4 **127** E7
Anstridge Path, SE9 **157** G6
Anstridge Rd, SE9 **157** G6
Antelope Rd, SE18 **136** C3
Antelope Wk, Surb. KT6
off Maple Rd **181** G5
Anthony Cl, NW7 **55** E4
Watford WD19 **50** C1
Anthony Rd, SE25 **188** D6
Greenford UB6 **104** B2
Welling DA16 **158** A1
Anthony St, E1
off Commercial Rd **113** E6
Anthony Way, N18 **61** G6
Antigua Cl, SE19 **170** A5
Antigua Wk, SE19 **170** A5
Antill Rd, E3 **113** H3
N15 **76** C4
Antill Ter, E1 **113** G6
Antlers Hill, E4 **46** B5
Anton Cres, Sutt. SM1 **198** D3
Antoneys Cl, Pnr. HA5 **66** D2
Antonine Hts, SE1 **28** D4
Anton Pl, Wem. HA9 **88** B3
Anton St, E8 **94** D5
Antrim Gro, NW3 **91** J6
Antrim Mans, NW3 **91** H6
Antrim Rd, NW3 **91** J6
Antrobus Cl, Sutt. SM1 **198** C5
Antrobus Rd, W4 **126** C4
Anvil Cl, SW16 **168** C7
Anvil Rd, Sun. TW16 **178** A3
Anworth Cl, Wdf.Grn.
IG8 **63** H6
Apex Cl, Beck. BR3 **190** B1
Apex Cor, NW7 **54** D4
Apex Ind Est, NW10
off Hythe Rd **107** F4
Apex Retail Pk, Felt.
TW13 **161** F3
Apex Twr, N.Mal. KT3 **182** E3
Aplin Way, Islw. TW7 **144** B1
Apollo, E14
off Newton Pl **134** A4
Apollo Av, Brom. BR1
off Rodway Rd **191** H1
Northwood HA6 **50** A5
★ **Apollo Hammersmith**,
W6 **127** J5
Apollo Pl, E11 **96** E3
SW10 **31** E7
★ **Apollo Thea**, W1 **17** H5
★ **Apollo Victoria Thea**,
SW1 **25** F6
Apollo Way, SE28
off Broadwater Rd **137** G3
Apostle Way, Th.Hth. CR7 **187** H2
Apothecary St, EC4 **19** G4
Appach Rd, SW2 **151** G5
Apple Blossom Ct, SW8
off Pascal St **33** J7
Appleby Cl, E4 **62** C6
N15 **76** A5
Orpington (Petts Wd)
BR5 **193** H7
Twickenham TW2 **162** A2
Appleby Ct, W3
off Newport Rd **126** C2
Appleby Rd, E8 **94** D7
E16 **115** F6
Appleby St, E2 **13** F1
Appledore Av, Bexh.
DA7 **159** J1
Ruislip HA4 **84** B3
Appledore Cl, SW17 **167** J2
Bromley BR2 **191** F5
Edgware HA8 **70** A1
Appledore Cres, Sid.
DA14 **175** H3
Appledore Way, NW7
off Tavistock Av **56** A7
Appleford Rd, W10 **108** B4
Apple Garth, Brentford
TW8 **125** G4
Applegarth, Croy.
(New Adgtn) CR0 **204** B7
Esher (Clay.) KT10 **194** C5
Applegarth Dr, Ilf. IG2 **81** J4
Applegarth Rd, SE28 **138** B1
W14 **128** A3
Apple Gro, Chess. KT9 **195** H4
Enfield EN1 **44** B3
Apple Mkt, Kings.T. KT1
off Eden St **181** G2
Apple Rd, E11 **96** E3
Appleton Cl, Bexh. DA7 **159** H2
Appleton Gdns, N.Mal.
KT3 **183** G6
Appleton Rd, SE9 **156** B3
Loughton IG10 **49** E3
Appleton Sq, Mitch. CR4
off Silbury Av **185** H1
Appletree Cl, SE20
off Jasmine Gro **189** E1
Appletree Gdns, Barn.
EN4 **41** H4
Apple Tree Yd, SW1 **25** G1
Applewood Cl, N20 **57** H1
NW2 **89** H3
Applewood Dr, E13 **115** H4
Appold St, EC2 **20** D1
Apprentice Gdns, Nthlt.
UB5 *off Taywood Rd* **103** F3
Apprentice Way, E5
off Clarence Rd **95** E4
Approach, The, NW4 **72** A5
W3 **106** D6
Enfield EN1 **44** E2
Orpington BR6 **207** J2
Approach Cl, N16
off Cowper Rd **94** B4
Approach Rd, E2 **113** F2
SW20 **183** J2
Barnet EN4 **41** G4
Edgware HA8 **54** B6
West Molesey KT8 **179** G5
Aprey Gdns, NW4 **71** J4
April Cl, W7 **104** B7
Feltham TW13 **160** A3
Orpington BR6 **207** J5
April Glen, SE23 **171** G3
April St, E8 **94** C4
Apsley Cl, Har. HA2 **67** J5
★ **Apsley Ho**
(Wellington Mus), W1 **24** B3
Apsley Rd, SE25 **188** E4
New Malden KT3 **182** C3
Apsley Way, NW2 **89** G2
W1 **24** C3
Aquarius Business Pk,
NW2 **89** F1
Aquarius Way, Nthwd.
HA6 **50** A5
★ **Aquatic Experience**,
Brent. TW8 **145** E1
Aquila St, NW8 **7** F1
Aquinas St, SE1 **27** F1
Arabella Dr, SW15 **147** E4
Arabia Cl, E4 **46** D7
Arabin Rd, SE4 **153** H4
Aragon Av, T.Ditt. KT7 **180** C5
Aragon Cl, Brom. BR2 **206** C1
Loughton IG10 **48** B6
Aragon Dr, Ilf. IG6 **65** F7
Ruislip HA4 **84** D1
Aragon Pl, Mord. SM4 **184** A7
Aragon Rd, Kings.T. KT2 **163** H5
Morden SM4 **184** A6
Aragon Twr, SE8 **133** J4
Arandora Cres, Rom.
RM6 **82** B7
Aran Dr, Stan. HA7 **53** F4
Aran Ms, N7
off Barnsbury Gro **93** G7
Arbery Rd, E3 **113** H3
Arbor Cl, Beck. BR3 **190** B2
Arbor Ct, N16 **94** A2
Arborfield Cl, SW2 **169** F1
Arbor Rd, E4 **62** D3
Arbour Rd, Enf. EN3 **45** G4
Arbour Sq, E1 **113** G6
Arbroath Grn, Wat.
WD19 **50** A3
Arbroath Rd, SE9 **156** B3
Arbury Ter, SE26 **170** D3
Arbuthnot La, Bex. DA5 **159** E6
Arbuthnot Rd, SE14 **153** G2
Arbutus St, E8 **112** B1

Arcade, The, EC2 **20** D2
Croydon CR0
off High St **201** J3
Arcadia Av, N3 **72** D1
Arcadia Cen, The, W5 **105** G7
Arcadia Cl, Cars. SM5 **200** A4
Arcadian Av, Bex. DA5 **158** E6
Arcadian Cl, Bex. DA5 **158** E6
Arcadian Gdns, N22 **59** F7
Arcadian Pl, SW18 **148** B7
Arcadian Rd, Bex. DA5 **158** E6
Arcadia St, E14 **114** A6
Archangel St, SE16 **133** G2
Archbishops Pl, SW2 **151** F6
Archdale Pl, N.Mal. KT3 **182** B3
Archdale Rd, SE22 **152** C5
Archel Rd, W14 **128** C6
Archer Cl, Kings.T. KT2 **163** H7
Archer Ho, N1
off Phillipp St **112** B1
SW11
off Vicarage Cres **149** G2
Archer Ms, SW9 **150** E3
Hmptn. (Hmptn H.) TW12
off Windmill Rd **161** J6
Archer Rd, SE25 **188** E4
Archers Dr, Enf. EN3 **45** F2
Archer Sq, SE14
off Knoyle St **133** H6
Archer St, W1 **17** H5
Archery Cl, W2 **15** H4
Harrow HA3 **68** C3
Archery Rd, SE9 **156** C5
Archery Steps, W2
off St. Georges Flds **15** H5
Arches, SW9
off Ridgeway Rd **151** H3
Arches, The, SW6
off Munster Rd **148** C2
SW8
off New Covent Gdn Mkt **33** J7
WC2 **26** B1
Harrow HA2 **85** H2
Archgate Business Cen, N12
off High Rd **57** F5
Archibald Ms, W1 **16** C6
Archibald Rd, N7 **92** D4
Archibald St, E3 **114** A3
Archie Cl, West Dr. UB7 **120** D2
Archie St, SE1 **29** E4
Arch St, SE1 **27** J6
Archway Cl, N19
off Archway Rd **92** C2
SW19 **166** E4
W10 **108** A5
Wallington SM6 **200** D3
Archway Mall, N19
off Magdala Av **92** C2
Archway Ms, SW15
off Putney Br Rd **148** B4
Archway Rd, N6 **73** J6
N19 **92** C1
Archway St, SW13 **147** E3
Arcola St, E8 **94** C5
Arcon Dr, Nthlt. UB5 **103** E4
Arctic St, NW5
off Gillies St **92** B5
Arcus Rd, Brom. BR1 **173** E6
Ardbeg Rd, SE24 **152** A6
Arden Cl, SE28 **118** D6
Harrow HA1 **86** A3
Houns. TW4 **143** F7
Arden Ct Gdns, N2 **73** G6
Arden Cres, E14 **134** A4
Dagenham RM9 **100** C7
Arden Est, N1 **12** D2
Arden Gro, Orp. BR6 **207** E4
Arden Ho, SW9
off Grantham Rd **151** E2
Arden Ms, E17 **78** B5
Arden Mhor, Pnr. HA5 **66** B4
Arden Rd, N3 **72** B3
W13 **105** F7
Ardent Cl, SE25 **188** B3
Ardfern Av, SW16 **187** G3
Ardfillan Rd, SE6 **172** D1
Ardgowan Rd, SE6 **154** E7
Ardilaun Rd, N5 **93** J4
Ardingly Cl, Croy. CR0 **203** G3
Ardleigh Gdns, Sutt. SM3 **184** D7
Ardleigh Ms, Ilf. IG1
off Bengal Rd **98** E3
Ardleigh Rd, E17 **77** J1
N1 **94** A6
Ardleigh Ter, E17 **77** J1
Ardley Cl, NW10 **88** E3
SE6 **171** H3
Ardlui Rd, SE27 **169** J2
Ardmay Gdns, Surbiton KT6 **181** H5
Ardmere Rd, SE13 **154** D6
Ardmore La, Buck.H. IG9 **47** H7
Ardmore Pl, Buck.H. IG9 **47** H7
Ardoch Rd, SE6 **172** D2
Ardra Rd, N9 **61** G3
Ardrossan Gdns, Wor.Pk. KT4 **197** G3
Ardshiel Cl, SW15
off Bemish Rd **148** A3
Ardwell Av, Ilf. IG6 **81** F5
Ardwell Rd, SW2 **168** E2
Ardwick Rd, NW2 **90** D4
Arena Shop Pk, N4 **75** H6
Arena Sq, Wem. HA9 **88** A4
Arewater Grn, Loug. IG10 **48** C1
Argali Ho, Erith DA18
off Kale Rd **138** E3
Argall Av, E10 **77** G7
Argall Way, E10 **95** G1
Argenta Way, NW10 **88** B7
Argent Business Cen, Hayes UB3 **122** A2
Argent Ct, Barn. EN5 **41** F4
Argon Ms, SW6 **128** D7
Argon Rd, N18 **61** F5
Argosy La, Stai. (Stanw.) TW19 **140** A7
Argus Cl, Rom. RM7 **83** H1
Argus Way, Nthlt. UB5 **102** E3
Argyle Av, Houns. TW3 **143** G6
Argyle Cl, W13 **104** D4
Argyle Pas, N17 **76** C1
Argyle Pl, W6 **127** H4
Argyle Rd, E1 **113** G4
E15 **96** E4
E16 **115** J6
N12 **56** D5
N17 **76** D1
N18 **60** D4
W13 **104** D5
Barnet EN5 **39** J4
Greenford UB6 **104** C3
Harrow HA2 **67** H6
Hounslow TW3 **143** H5
Ilford IG1 **98** D2
Teddington TW11 **162** B5
Argyle Sq, WC1 **10** B3
Argyle St, WC1 **10** A3
Argyle Wk, WC1 **10** B4
Argyle Way, SE16 **37** J4
Argyll Av, Sthl. UB1 **123** H1
Argyll Cl, SW9
off Dalyell Rd **151** F3
Argyll Gdns, Edg. HA8 **70** B2
Argyll Rd, SE18 **137** F3
W8 **128** D2
Argyll St, W1 **17** F4
Aria Ho, WC2 **18** B3
Arica Ho, SE16 **133** E3
Arica Rd, SE4 **153** H4
Ariel Rd, NW6 **90** D6
Ariel Way, W12 **127** J1
Hounslow TW4 **142** B3
Aristotle Rd, SW4 **150** D3
Arizona Bldg, SE13
off Deals Gateway **154** B1
Arkell Gro, SE19 **169** H7
Arkindale Rd, SE6 **172** C3
ARKLEY, Barn. EN5 **39** G5
Arkley Cres, E17 **77** J5
Arkley Dr, Barn. EN5 **39** G4
Arkley La, Barn. EN5 **39** G3
Arkley Pk, Barn. EN5 **38** D6
Arkley Rd, E17 **77** J5
Arkley Vw, Barn. EN5 **39** H4
Arklow Ho, SE17 **36** B5
Arklow Ms, Surb. KT6
off Vale Rd S **195** H2
Arklow Rd, SE14 **133** J6
Arkwright Rd, NW3 **91** F5
Arlesey Cl, SW15 **148** B5
Arlesford Rd, SW9 **151** E3
Arlingford Rd, SW2 **151** G5
Arlington, N12 **56** D3
Arlington Av, N1 **111** J2
Arlington Bldg, E3
off Fairfield Rd **114** A2
Arlington Cl, SE13 **154** D5
Sidcup DA15 **157** H7
Sutton SM1 **198** D2
Twickenham TW1 **145** F6
Arlington Ct, W3
off Mill Hill Rd **126** B1
Hayes UB3
off Shepiston La **121** G5
Arlington Dr, Cars. SM5 **199** J2
Arlington Gdns, W4 **126** C5
Ilford IG1 **98** D1
Arlington Grn, NW7 **56** A7
Arlington Lo, SW2 **151** F4
Arlington Ms, Twick. TW1
off Arlington Rd **145** F6
Arlington Pl, SE10
off Greenwich S St **134** C7
Arlington Rd, N14 **58** B2
NW1 **110** B1
W13 **104** E6
Richmond TW10 **163** G2
Surbiton KT6 **181** G6
Teddington TW11 **162** C4
Twickenham TW1 **145** F6
Woodford Green IG8 **79** G1
Arlington Sq, N1 **111** J1
Arlington St, SW1 **25** F1
Arlington Way, EC1 **11** F3
Arliss Way, Nthlt. UB5 **102** C1
Arlow Rd, N21 **59** G1
Armada Ct, SE8
off Watergate St **134** A6
Armadale Cl, N17 **76** E4
Armadale Rd, SW6 **128** D7
Feltham TW14 **142** A5
Armada Way, E6 **117** F7
Armagh Rd, E3 **113** J1
Armfield Cl, W.Mol. KT8 **179** F5
Armfield Cres, Mitch. CR4 **185** J2
Armfield Rd, Enf. EN2 **44** A1
Arminger Rd, W12 **127** H1
Armistice Gdns, SE25 **188** D3
Armitage Rd, NW11 **90** C1
SE10 **135** F5
Armour Cl, N7
off Roman Way **93** F6
Armoury Rd, SE8 **154** B2
Armoury Way, SW18 **148** D5
Armstead Wk, Dag. RM10 **101** G7
Armstrong Av, Wdf.Grn. IG8 **62** E6
Armstrong Cl, E6
off Porter Rd **116** C6
Borehamwood WD6 **38** C3
Bromley BR1 **192** B3
Dagenham RM8 **82** D7
Pinner HA5 **66** A6
Walton-on-Thames KT12
off Sunbury La **178** A6
Armstrong Cres, Barn. (Cockfos.) EN4 **41** G3
Armstrong Rd, NW10 **88** E7
SE18 **137** F3
SW7 **22** E6
W3 **127** F1
Feltham TW13 **160** E5
Armstrong Way, Sthl. UB2 **123** H2
Armytage Rd, Houns. TW5 **122** D7
Arnal Cres, SW18 **148** B7
Arncliffe Cl, N11 **58** A6
Arncroft Ct, Bark. IG11
off Renwick Rd **118** B3
Arndale Wk, SW18
off Garratt La **148** E5
Arne Gro, Orp. BR6 **207** J3
Arne Ho, SE11 **34** C3
Arne St, WC2 **18** B4
Arnett Sq, E4 **61** J6
Arne Wk, SE3 **155** F4
Arneways Av, Rom. RM6 **82** D3
Arneway St, SW1 **25** J6
Arnewood Cl, SW15 **165** G1
Arney's La, Mitch. CR4 **186** A6
Arngask Rd, SE6 **154** D7
Arnhem Pl, E14 **134** A3
Arnhem Way, SE22
off East Dulwich Gro **152** B5
Arnhem Wf, E14
off Arnhem Pl **134** A3
Arnison Rd, E.Mol. KT8 **180** A4
Arnold Bennett Way, N8
off Burghley Rd **75** G3
Arnold Circ, E2 **13** F4
Arnold Cl, Har. HA3 **69** J7
Arnold Cres, Islw. TW7 **144** A5
Arnold Dr, Chess. KT9 **195** G6
Arnold Est, SE1 **29** G4
Arnold Gdns, N13 **59** H5
Arnold Rd, E3 **114** A3
N15 **76** C3
SW17 **167** J7
Dagenham RM9, RM10 **101** F7
Northolt UB5 **84** D6
Arnos Gro, N14 **58** D4
Arnos Rd, N11 **58** C5
Arnott Cl, SE28
off Applegarth Rd **118** C7
W4 **126** D4
Arnould Av, SE5 **152** A4
Arnsberg Way, Bexh. DA7 **159** G4
Arnside Gdns, Wem. HA9 **87** G1
Arnside Rd, Bexh. DA7 **159** G1
Arnside St, SE17 **36** A5
Arnulf St, SE6 **172** B4
Arnulls Rd, SW16 **169** G6
Arodene Rd, SW2 **151** F6
Arosa Rd, Twick. TW1 **145** G6
Arpley Sq, SE20
off High St **171** F7
Arragon Gdns, SW16 **168** E7
West Wickham BR4 **204** B3
Arragon Rd, E6 **116** A1
SW18 **166** E1
Twickenham TW1 **144** D7
Arran Cl, Wall. SM6 **200** B4
Arran Dr, E12 **98** A1
Arran Grn, Wat. WD19
off Prestwick Rd **50** D4
Arran Ms, W5 **125** J1
Arran Rd, SE6 **172** B2
Arran Wk, N1 **93** J7
Arras Av, Mord. SM4 **185** F5
Arrol Ho, SE1 **28** A6
Arrol Rd, Beck. BR3 **189** F3
Arrow Rd, E3 **114** B3
Arrowscout Wk, Nthlt. UB5
off Wayfarer Rd **102** E3
Arrowsmith Cl, Chig. IG7 **65** J5
Arrowsmith Ho, SE11 **34** C3
Arrowsmith Path, Chig. IG7 **65** J5
Arrowsmith Rd, Chig. IG7 **65** H5
Loughton IG10 **48** B3
★ **Arsenal FC**, N5 **93** G4
Arsenal Rd, SE9 **156** C2
Arsenal Way, SE18 **137** F3
Arta Ho, E1
off Devonport St **113** F6
Arterberry Rd, SW20 **165** J7
Artesian Cl, NW10 **88** D7
Artesian Gro, Barn. EN5 **41** F3
Artesian Rd, W2 **108** D6
Artesian Wk, E11 **96** E3
Arthingworth St, E15 **114** E1
Arthur Ct, SW11
off Charlotte Despard Av **150** A1
W2 **14** A3
Arthurdon Rd, SE4 **154** A5
Arthur Gro, SE18 **137** F4
Arthur Henderson Ho, SW6 **148** C2
Arthur Horsley Wk, E7
off Magpie Cl **97** F5
Arthur Newton Ho, SW11
off Lavender Rd **149** G3
Arthur Rd, E6 **116** C2
N7 **93** F4
N9 **60** C2
SW19 **166** D3
Kingston upon Thames KT2 **164** A7
New Malden KT3 **183** H5
Romford RM6 **82** C7
Arthur St, EC4 **20** C6
Arthur Walls Ho, E12
off Grantham Rd **98** D3
Artichoke Hill, E1
off Pennington St **112** E7
Artichoke Pl, SE5
off Camberwell Ch St **152** A1
Artillery Cl, Ilf. IG2
off Horns Rd **81** F6
Artillery La, E1 **20** E2
W12 **107** G6
Artillery Mans, SW1 **25** H5
Artillery Pas, E1 **21** E2
Artillery Pl, SE18 **136** C5
SW1 **25** H6
Harrow HA3
off Chicheley Rd **51** J7
Artillery Row, SW1 **25** H6
Artington Cl, Orp. BR6 **207** F4
Artisan Cl, E6
off Ferndale St **116** E7
Artizan St, E1 **21** E3
Arundel Av, Mord. SM4 **184** C4
Arundel Cl, E15 **97** E4
SW11 **149** H5
Bexley DA5 **159** F6
Croydon CR0 **201** H3
Hampton (Hmptn H.) TW12 **161** H5
Arundel Ct, N12 **57** H6
Harrow HA2 **85** G4
Arundel Dr, Borwd. WD6 **38** C5
Harrow HA2 **85** F4
Woodford Green IG8 **63** G7
Arundel Gdns, N21 **59** G1
W11 **108** C7
Edgware HA8 **54** D7
Ilford IG3 **100** A2
Arundel Gt Ct, WC2 **18** D5
Arundel Gro, N16 **94** B5
Arundel Pl, N1 **93** G6
Arundel Rd, Barn. (Cockfos.) EN4 **41** H3
Croydon CR0 **188** A6
Hounslow TW4 **142** C3
Kingston upon Thames KT1 **182** B2
Sutton SM2 **198** C7
Arundel Sq, N7 **93** G6
Arundel St, WC2 **18** D5
Arundel Ter, SW13 **127** H6
Arvon Rd, N5 **93** G5
Asbaston Ter, Ilf. IG1
off Buttsbury Rd **99** F5
Ascalon St, SW8 **130** C7
Ascham Dr, E4
off Rushcroft Rd **62** B7

Ascham End, E17 ... **77** H1
Ascham St, NW5 ... **92** C5
Aschurch Rd, Croy. CR0 .. **188** C7
Ascot Cl, Borwd. (Els.)
WD6 ... **38** A5
Ilford IG6 ... **65** H6
Northolt UB5 ... **85** G5
Ascot Gdns, Sthl. UB1 ... **103** F5
Ascot Rd, E6 ... **116** C3
N15 ... **76** A5
N18 ... **60** D4
SW17 ... **168** A6
Orpington BR5 ... **193** J4
Ascott Av, W5 ... **125** H2
Ashanti Ms, E8
off Lower Clapton Rd .. **95** E5
Ashbourne Av, E18 ... **79** H4
N20 ... **57** J2
NW11 ... **72** C5
Bexleyheath DA7 ... **139** E7
Harrow HA2 ... **86** A2
Ashbourne Cl, N12 ... **57** E4
W5 ... **106** A5
Ashbourne Ct, E5
off Daubeney Rd ... **95** H4
Ashbourne Gro, NW7 ... **54** D5
SE22 ... **152** C5
W4 ... **127** E5
Ashbourne Par, W5
off Ashbourne Rd ... **105** J4
Ashbourne Ri, Orp. BR6 .. **207** G4
Ashbourne Rd, W5 ... **105** J5
Mitcham CR4 ... **168** A6
Ashbourne Ter, SW19 ... **166** D7
Ashbourne Way, NW11
off Ashbourne Av ... **72** C5
Ashbridge Rd, E11 ... **79** E7
Ashbridge St, NW8 ... **7** G6
Ashbrook Rd, N19 ... **92** D1
Dagenham RM10 ... **101** H3
Ashburn Gdns, SW7 ... **30** C1
Ashburnham Av, Har. HA1 . **68** C6
Ashburnham Cl, N2 ... **73** G3
Watford WD19 ... **50** A3
Ashburnham Dr, Wat.
WD19 ... **50** A3
Ashburnham Gdns, Har.
HA1 ... **68** C6
Ashburnham Gro, SE10 ... **134** B7
Ashburnham Pl, SE10 ... **134** B7
Ashburnham Retreat,
SE10 ... **134** B7
Ashburnham Rd, NW10 ... **107** J3
SW10 ... **129** F7
Belvedere DA17 ... **139** J4
Richmond TW10 ... **163** E3
Ashburnham Twr, SW10
off Blantyre St ... **30** E7
Ashburn Pl, SW7 ... **30** C1
Ashburton Av, Croy. CR0 .. **202** E1
Ilford IG3 ... **99** H4
Ashburton Cl, Croy. CR0 .. **202** D1
Ashburton Ct, Pnr. HA5 ... **66** D3
Ashburton Gdns, Croy.
CR0 ... **202** D2
Ashburton Rd, E16 ... **115** G6
Croydon CR0 ... **202** D1
Ruislip HA4 ... **84** A2
Ashburton Ter, E13
off Grasmere Rd ... **115** G2
Ashburton Triangle, N5
off Drayton Pk ... **93** G4
Ashbury Gdns, Rom.
RM6 ... **82** D5
Ashbury Pl, SW19 ... **167** F6
Ashbury Rd, SW11 ... **149** J3
Ashby Av, Chess. KT9 ... **196** A6
Ashby Gro, N1 ... **93** J7
Ashby Ho, N1
off Essex Rd ... **93** J7
Ashby Ms, SE4 ... **153** J2
SW2 *off Prague Pl* ... **150** E5
Ashby Rd, N15 ... **76** D5
SE4 ... **153** J2
Ashby St, EC1 ... **11** H4
Ashby Wk, Croy. CR0 ... **187** J6
Ashby Way, West Dr.
(Sipson) UB7 ... **120** D7
Ashchurch Gro, W12 ... **127** G2
Ashchurch Pk Vil, W12 ... **127** G3
Ashchurch Ter, W12 ... **127** G3
Ash Cl, SE20 ... **189** F2
Carshalton SM5 ... **199** J2
Edgware HA8 ... **54** C4
New Malden KT3 ... **182** D2
Orpington BR5 ... **193** G5
Sidcup DA14 ... **176** B3
Stanmore HA7 ... **52** D6
Ashcombe Av, Surb. KT6 . **181** G7
Ashcombe Gdns, Edg.
HA8 ... **54** A4
Ashcombe Ho, Enf. EN3 ... **45** G3
Ashcombe Pk, NW2 ... **89** E3
Ashcombe Rd, SW19 ... **166** D5
Carshalton SM5 ... **200** A6
Ashcombe Sq, N.Mal.
KT3 ... **182** C3
Ashcombe St, SW6 ... **148** E2
Ash Ct, N11 *off Cline Rd* ... **58** C6
Epsom KT19 ... **196** C4
Ashcroft, Pnr. HA5 ... **51** G6
Ashcroft Av, Sid. DA15 ... **158** A6
Ashcroft Ct, N20 ... **57** G2
Ashcroft Cres, Sid. DA15 .. **158** A6
Ashcroft Rd, E3 ... **113** H3
Chessington KT9 ... **195** J3
Ashcroft Sq, W6
off King St ... **127** J4
Ashdale Cl, Twick. TW2 ... **143** J7
Ashdale Gro, Stan. HA7 ... **52** C6
Ashdale Rd, SE12 ... **173** H1
Ashdale Way, Twick. TW2
off Ashdale Cl ... **143** J7
Ashdene, SE15 ... **152** E1
Pinner HA5 ... **66** C3
Ashdon Cl, Wdf.Grn. IG8 ... **63** H6
Ashdon Rd, NW10 ... **107** E1
Ashdown Cl, Beck. BR3 ... **190** B2
Bexley DA5 ... **159** J7
Ashdown Ct, E17 ... **78** C2
Ashdown Cres, NW5
off Queen's Cres ... **92** A5
Ashdown Pl, T.Ditt. KT7 ... **180** D6
Ashdown Rd, Enf. EN3 ... **45** F3
Kingston upon Thames
KT1 ... **181** H2
Ashdown Wk, E14 ... **134** A4
Romford RM7 ... **83** H2
Ashdown Way, SW17 ... **168** A2
Ashen, E6
off Downings ... **116** D6
Ashenden, SE17 ... **35** J1
Ashenden Rd, E5 ... **95** G5
Ashen Gro, SW19 ... **166** D3
Ashentree Ct, EC4 ... **19** F4
Asher Loftus Way, N11 ... **57** J6
Asher Way, E1 ... **29** J1
Ashfield Av, Felt. TW13 ... **160** B1
Ashfield Cl, Beck. BR3 ... **172** A7
Richmond TW10 ... **163** H1
Ashfield La, Chis. BR7 ... **175** F6
Ashfield Par, N14 ... **58** D1
Ashfield Rd, N4 ... **75** J6
N14 ... **58** C3
W3 ... **127** F1
Ashfields, Loug. IG10 ... **48** C2
Ashfield St, E1 ... **112** E5
Ashfield Yd, E1
off Ashfield St ... **113** F5
Ashford Av, N8 ... **74** E4
Hayes UB4 ... **102** D6
Ashford Cl, E17 ... **77** J6
Ashford Cres, Enf. EN3 ... **45** F2
Ashford Grn, Wat. WD19 ... **50** D5
Ashford Ms, N17 ... **76** D1
Ashford Rd, E6 ... **98** D6
E18 ... **79** H2
NW2 ... **90** A4
Ashford St, N1 ... **12** D3
Ash Gro, E8 ... **113** E1
N13 ... **59** J3
NW2 ... **90** A4
SE20 ... **189** F2
W5 ... **125** H2
Enfield EN1 ... **44** B7
Hounslow TW5 ... **142** D1
Southall UB1 ... **103** G5
Wembley HA0 ... **86** D4
West Wickham BR4 ... **204** C2
Ashgrove Rd, Brom. BR1 . **172** D6
Ilford IG3 ... **99** J1
Ash Hill Cl, Bushey WD23 .. **51** H1
Ash Hill Dr, Pnr. HA5 ... **66** C3
Ash Ho, SE1
off Longfield Est ... **37** G2
Ashingdon Cl, E4 ... **62** C3
Ashington Ho, E1
off Barnsley St ... **113** E4
Ashington Rd, SW6 ... **148** C2
Ash Island, E.Mol. KT8 ... **180** A3
Ashlake Rd, SW16 ... **168** E4
Ashland Pl, W1 ... **16** B1
Ashlar Pl, SE18
off Masons Hill ... **137** E4
Ashleigh Gdns, Sutt.
SM1 ... **198** E2
Ashleigh Pt, SE23
off Dacres Rd ... **171** G3
Ashleigh Rd, SE20 ... **189** E3
SW14 ... **146** E3
Ashley Av, Ilf. IG6 ... **81** E2
Morden SM4 ... **184** D5
Ashley Cl, NW4 ... **71** J2
Pinner HA5 ... **66** B2
Ashley Cres, N22 ... **75** G2
SW11 ... **150** A3
Ashley Dr, Borwd. WD6 ... **38** C5
Isleworth TW7 ... **124** B6
Twickenham TW2 ... **143** H7
Ashley Gdns, N13 ... **59** J4
SW1 ... **25** G6
Orpington BR6 ... **207** H5
Richmond TW10 ... **163** G3
Wembley HA9 ... **87** H2
Ashley Gro, Loug. IG10
off Staples Rd ... **48** B3
Ashley La, NW4 ... **71** J2
NW7 ... **71** J2
Croydon CR0 ... **201** H4
Ashley Pl, SW1 ... **25** F6
Ashley Rd, E4 ... **62** A5
E7 ... **97** J7
N17 ... **76** D3
N19 ... **92** E1
SW19 ... **166** E6
Enfield EN3 ... **45** F2
Hampton TW12 ... **179** G1
Richmond TW9
off Jocelyn Rd ... **145** H3
Thames Ditton KT7 ... **180** C6
Thornton Heath CR7 ... **187** F4
Ashley Wk, NW7 ... **55** J7
Ashling Rd, Croy. CR0 ... **202** D1
Ashlin Rd, E15 ... **96** D4
Ashlone Rd, SW15 ... **147** J3
Ashlyns Way, Chess.
KT9 ... **195** G6
Ashmead, N14 ... **42** C5
Ashmead Gate, Brom.
BR1 ... **191** J1
Ashmead Ho, E9
off Kingsmead Way ... **95** H5
Ashmead Ms, SE4
off Ashmead Rd ... **154** A2
Ashmead Rd, SE8 ... **154** A2
Feltham TW14 ... **160** A1
Ashmere Av, Beck. BR3 ... **190** D2
Ashmere Cl, Sutt. SM3 ... **197** J5
Ashmere Gro, SW2 ... **150** E4
Ashmill St, NW1 ... **15** G1
Ashmole Pl, SW8 ... **34** D6
Ashmole St, SW8 ... **34** D6
Ashmore Cl, SE15 ... **132** C7
Ashmore Ct, Houns. TW5
off Wheatlands ... **123** G6
Ashmore Gro, Well. DA16 . **157** G3
Ashmore Rd, W9 ... **108** C4
Ashmount Rd, N15 ... **76** C5
N19 ... **74** C7
Ashmount Ter, W5 ... **125** G4
Ashneal Gdns, Har. HA1 ... **86** A3
Ashness Gdns, Grnf.
UB6 ... **86** E6
Ashness Rd, SW11 ... **149** J5
Ashridge Cl, Har. HA3 ... **69** F6
Ashridge Cres, SE18 ... **137** F7
Ashridge Dr, Wat. WD19 ... **50** C5
Ashridge Gdns, N13 ... **58** D5
Pinner HA5 ... **66** E4
Ashridge Way, Mord. SM4 . **184** C3
Sunbury-on-Thames
TW16 ... **160** A6
Ash Rd, E15 ... **97** E5
Croydon CR0 ... **204** A2
Orpington BR6 ... **207** J7
Sutton SM3 ... **184** B7
Ash Row, Brom. BR2 ... **192** D7
Ashtead Rd, E5 ... **76** D7
Ashton Cl, Sutt. SM1 ... **198** D4
Ashton Ct, E4
off Connington Cres ... **62** E3
Ashton Gdns, Houns.
TW4 ... **143** F4
Romford RM6 ... **83** E6
Ashton Rd, E15 ... **96** D5
Ashton St, E14 ... **114** C7
Ashtree Av, Mitch. CR4 ... **185** G2
Ash Tree Cl, Croy. CR0 ... **189** H6
Ashtree Cl, Orp. BR6 ... **207** E4
Ash Tree Cl, Surb. KT6 ... **195** H1
Ash Tree Dell, NW9 ... **70** C5
Ash Tree Way, Croy. CR0 .. **189** H5
Ashurst Cl, SE20 ... **189** E1
Ashurst Dr, Ilf. IG2, IG6 ... **81** E6
Ashurst Rd, N12 ... **57** H5
Barnet EN4 ... **41** J5
Ashurst Wk, Croy. CR0 ... **202** E2
Ashvale Rd, SW17 ... **167** J5
Ashville Rd, E11 ... **96** D2
Ash Wk, SW2 ... **169** F1
Wembley HA0 ... **87** F4
Ashwater Rd, SE12 ... **173** G1
Ashway Cen, The, Kings.T.
KT2 *off Elm Cres* ... **181** H1
Ashwell Cl, E6
*off Northumberland
Rd* ... **116** B6
Ashwin St, E8 ... **94** C6
Ashwood Gdns, Croy.
(New Adgtn) CR0 ... **204** B6
Hayes UB3
off Cranford Dr ... **121** J4
Ashwood Rd, E4 ... **62** D3
Ashworth Cl, SE5
off Love Wk ... **152** A2
Ashworth Rd, W9 ... **6** B3
Askern Cl, Bexh. DA6 ... **158** D4
Aske St, N1 ... **12** D3
Askew Cres, W12 ... **127** F2
Askew Rd, W12 ... **127** F1
Askham Ct, W12 ... **127** G1
Askham Rd, W12 ... **127** G1
Askill Dr, SW15 ... **148** B5
Asland Rd, E15 ... **114** E1
Aslett St, SW18 ... **149** E7
Asmara Rd, NW2 ... **90** B5
Asmuns Hill, NW11 ... **72** D5
Asmuns Pl, NW11 ... **72** C5
Asolando Dr, SE17 ... **36** A2
Aspect Ct, SW6
off Lensbury Av ... **149** F2
Aspects, Sutt. SM1 ... **199** E5
Aspen Cl, N19
off Hargrave Pk ... **92** C2
W5 ... **125** J2
West Drayton UB7 ... **120** C1
Aspen Copse, Brom.
BR1 ... **192** C2
Aspen Ct, Hayes UB3 ... **121** H4
Aspen Dr, Wem. HA0 ... **86** D4
Aspen Gdns, W6 ... **127** H5
Mitcham CR4 ... **186** A5
Aspen Grn, Erith DA18 ... **139** F3
Aspen Ho, NW3
off Maitland Pk Vil ... **91** J6
Aspen La, Nthlt. UB5 ... **102** E3
Aspenlea Rd, W6 ... **128** A6
Aspen Way, E14 ... **114** A7
Feltham TW13 ... **160** B3
Aspern Gro, NW3 ... **91** H5
Aspinall Rd, SE4 ... **153** G3
Aspinden Rd, SE16 ... **133** E4
Aspley Rd, SW18 ... **149** E5
Asplins Rd, N17 ... **76** D1
Asprey Ms, Beck. BR3 ... **189** J5
Asprey Pl, Brom. BR1
off Chislehurst Rd ... **192** B2
Asquith Cl, Dag. RM8 ... **100** C1
Assam St, E1 ... **21** H3
Assata Ms, N1
off St. Paul's Rd ... **93** H6
Assembly Pas, E1 ... **113** F5
Assembly Wk, Cars.
SM5 ... **185** H7
Assurance Cotts, Belv.
DA17 *off Heron Hill* ... **139** F5
Astall Cl, Har. HA3 ... **68** B1
Astbury Business Pk, SE15
off Station Pas ... **153** F1
Astbury Ho, SE11 ... **26** E6
Astbury Rd, SE15 ... **153** F1
Astell St, SW3 ... **31** H3
Aste St, E14 ... **134** C2
Asteys Row, N1
off River Pl ... **93** J7
Asthall Gdns, Ilf. IG6 ... **81** F4
Astle St, SW11 ... **150** A2
Astley Av, NW2 ... **89** J5
Astley Ho, SE1
off Rowcross St ... **37** G3
Aston Av, Har. HA3 ... **69** F7
Aston Cl, Sid. DA14 ... **176** A3
Aston Ct, N4
off Queens Dr ... **93** J2
Aston Grn, Houns. TW4 ... **142** C2
Aston Ho, SW8
off Wandsworth Rd ... **150** D1
Aston Ms, Rom. RM6 ... **82** C7
Aston Pl, SW16
off Averil Gro ... **169** H6
Aston Rd, SW20 ... **183** J2
W5 ... **105** G6
Esher (Clay.) KT10 ... **194** B5
Aston St, E14 ... **113** H6
Aston Ter, SW12
off Cathles Rd ... **150** B6
Astonville St, SW18 ... **166** D1
Astor Av, Rom. RM7 ... **83** J6
Astor Cl, Kings.T. KT2 ... **164** B6
Astoria Wk, SW9 ... **151** G3
Astrop Ms, W6 ... **127** J3
Astrop Ter, W6 ... **127** J3
Astwood Ms, SW7 ... **30** C1
Asylum Rd, SE15 ... **133** E7
Atalanta St, SW6 ... **148** A1
Atbara Ct, Tedd. TW11 ... **163** E6
Atbara Rd, Tedd. TW11 ... **163** E6
Atcham Rd, Houns. TW3 .. **143** J4
Atcost Rd, Bark. IG11 ... **118** A5
Atheldene Rd, SW18 ... **167** E1
Athelney St, SE6 ... **172** A3
Athelstane Gro, E3 ... **113** J2
Athelstane Ms, N4
off Stroud Grn Rd ... **93** G1
Athelstan Gdns, NW6 ... **90** B7
Athelstan Ho, E9
off Kingsmead Way ... **95** J5
Athelstan Rd, Kings.T.
KT1 ... **181** J4
Athelstone Rd, Harrow
HA3 ... **68** A2
Athena Cl, Har. HA2
off Byron Hill Rd ... **86** B2
Kingston upon Thames
KT1 ... **181** J3
Athena Ct, SE1
off Long La ... **28** D4
Athenaeum Ct, N5 ... **93** J4

Athenaeum Pl, N10
off Fortis Grn Rd 74 B3
Athenaeum Rd, N20 57 F1
Athenlay Rd, SE15 153 G5
Athens Gdns, W9
off Harrow Rd 108 D4
Atherden Rd, E5 95 F4
Atherfold Rd, SW9 150 E3
Atherley Way, Houns. TW4 143 F7
Atherstone Ct, W2 14 B1
Atherstone Ms, SW7 30 D1
Atherton Cl, Stai. (Stanw.) TW19 140 A6
Atherton Dr, SW19 166 A4
Atherton Hts, Wem. HA0 87 F6
Atherton Ms, E7 97 F6
Atherton Pl, Har. HA2 68 A3
Southall UB1 103 G7
Atherton Rd, E7 97 F5
SW13 127 G7
Ilford IG5 80 B2
Atherton St, SW11 149 H2
Athlone, Esher (Clay.) KT10 194 B6
Athlone Cl, E5
off Goulton Rd 95 E5
Athlone Rd, SW2 151 F7
Athlone St, NW5 92 A6
Athlon Rd, Wem. HA0 105 G2
Athol Cl, Pnr. HA5 66 B1
Athole Gdns, Enf. EN1 44 B5
Athol Gdns, Pnr. HA5 66 B1
Atholl Ho, W9 6 C4
Atholl Rd, Ilf. IG3 82 A7
Athol Rd, Erith DA8 139 J5
Athol Sq, E14 114 C6
Atkin Bldg, WC1
off Raymond Bldgs 18 D1
Atkins Dr, W.Wick. BR4 204 D2
Atkinson Ho, SW11
off Austin Rd 150 A1
Atkinson Rd, E16 115 J5
Atkins Rd, E10 78 B6
SW12 150 D7
Atlanta Bldg, SE13
off Deals Gateway 154 B1
Atlantic Rd, SW9 151 G4
Atlantis Cl, Bark. IG11 118 B3
Atlas Business Cen, NW2 89 H2
Atlas Cres, Edg. HA8 54 B2
Atlas Gdns, SE7 135 J4
Atlas Ms, E8
off Dalston La 94 C6
N7 93 F6
Atlas Rd, E13 115 G2
N11 58 B6
Atlas Rd, NW10 107 E3
Wembley HA9 88 C4
Atley Rd, E3 114 A1
Atlip Cen, Wem. HA0
off Atlip Rd 105 H1
Atlip Rd, Wem. HA0 105 H1
Atney Rd, SW15 148 B4
Atria Rd, Nthwd. HA6 50 A5
Attenborough Cl, Wat. WD19 50 E3
Atterbury Rd, N4 75 G6
Atterbury St, SW1 33 J2
Attewood Av, NW10 88 E3
Attewood Rd, Nthlt. UB5 85 E6
Attfield Cl, N20 57 G2
Attlee Cl, Hayes UB4 102 B3
Thornton Heath CR7 187 J6
Attlee Rd, SE28 118 B7
Hayes UB4 102 A3
Attlee Ter, E17 78 B4
Attneave St, WC1 10 E4
Atwater Cl, SW2 169 G1
Atwell Cl, E10
off Belmont Pk Rd 78 B6
Atwell Pl, T.Ditt. KT7 194 C1
Atwell Rd, SE15
off Rye La 152 D2
Atwood Av, Rich. TW9 146 A2
Atwood Rd, W6 127 H4
Atwoods Alley, Rich. TW9 146 A1
Aubert Ct, N5 93 H4
Aubert Pk, N5 93 H4
Aubert Rd, N5 93 H4
Aubrey Beardsley Ho, SW1
off Vauxhall Br Rd 33 G2
Aubrey Moore Pt, E15 114 C2
Aubrey Pl, NW8 6 C2
Aubrey Rd, E17 78 A3
N8 75 E5
W8 128 C1
Aubrey Wk, W8 128 C1
Auburn Cl, SE14 133 H7
Aubyn Hill, SE27 169 J4
Aubyn Sq, SW15 147 G4
Auckland Cl, SE19 188 C1
Auckland Gdns, SE19 188 B1
Auckland Hill, SE27 169 J4
Auckland Ri, SE19 188 B1
Auckland Rd, E10 96 B3
SE19 188 C1
SW11 149 H4
Ilford IG1 99 E1
Kingston upon Thames KT1 181 J4
Auckland St, SE11 34 C4
Auden Dr, Borwd. WD6 38 A5
Auden Pl, NW1 110 A1
Sutton SM3
off Wordsworth Dr 197 J4
Audleigh Pl, Chig. IG7 64 D6
Audley Cl, N10 58 B7
SW11 150 A3
Borehamwood WD6 38 A3
Audley Ct, E18 79 F4
Pinner HA5
off Rickmansworth Rd 66 C2
Audley Dr, E16
off Wesley Av 135 H1
Audley Gdns, Ilf. IG3 99 J2
Loughton IG10 49 F2
Audley Pl, Sutt. SM2 198 E7
Audley Rd, NW4 71 H6
W5 105 J5
Enfield EN2 43 H2
Richmond TW10 145 J5
Audley Sq, W1 24 C1
Audrey Cl, Beck. BR3 190 B6
Audrey Gdns, Wem. HA0 87 E2
Audrey Rd, Ilf. IG1 98 E3
Audrey St, E2 13 H1
Audric Cl, Kings.T. KT2 182 A1
Augurs La, E13 115 H3
Augusta Cl, W.Mol. KT8
off Freeman Dr 179 F3
Augusta Rd, Twick. TW2 161 J2
Augusta St, E14 114 B6
Augustine Rd, W14 128 A3
Harrow HA3 67 H1
Augustus Cl, W12
off Goldhawk Rd 127 H2
Brentford TW8 125 F7
Stanmore HA7 53 G3
Augustus Ct, SE1 36 D1
Augustus Ho, NW1
off Augustus St 9 F3
Augustus Rd, SW19 166 B1
Augustus St, NW1 9 E2
Aulay Lawrence Ct, N9
off Menon Dr 60 E3
Aultone Way, Cars. SM5 199 J3
Sutton SM1 199 E2
Aultone Yd, Cars. SM5 199 J3
Aulton Pl, SE11 35 F4
Aurelia Gdns, Croy. CR0 187 F5
Aurelia Rd, Croy. CR0 187 E6
Auriga Ms, N1 94 A5
Auriol Cl, Wor.Pk. KT4
off Auriol Pk Rd 197 E3
Auriol Dr, Grnf. UB6 86 A7
Auriol Pk Rd, Wor.Pk. KT4 197 E3
Auriol Rd, W14 128 B4
Austell Gdns, NW7 55 E3
Austen Apts, SE20
off Croydon Rd 188 E2
Austen Cl, SE28 138 B1
Loughton IG10 49 G3
Austen Ho, NW6 108 D3
Austen Rd, Erith DA8 139 H7
Harrow HA2 85 H2
Austin Av, Brom. BR2 192 B5
Austin Cl, SE23 153 J7
Twickenham TW1 145 F5
Austin Ct, E6
off Kings Rd 115 J1
Austin Friars, EC2 20 C3
Austin Friars Pas, EC2 20 C3
Austin Friars Sq, EC2 20 C3
Austin Rd, SW11 150 A1
Hayes UB3 121 J2
Austin St, E2 13 F4
Austral Cl, Sid. DA15 175 J3
Australia Rd, W12 107 H7
Austral St, SE11 35 G1
Austyn Gdns, Surb. KT5 196 B1
Autumn Cl, SW19 167 F6
Enfield EN1 44 D1
Autumn Gro, Bromley BR1 173 H6
Autumn St, E3 114 A1
Avalon Cl, SW20 184 B2
W13 104 D5
Enfield EN2 43 G2
Avalon Rd, SW6 148 E1
W13 104 D4
Avante Ct, Kings.T. KT1 181 G3
Avard Gdns, Orp. BR6 207 F4
Avarn Rd, SW17 167 J6
Avebury Ct, N1
off Poole St 112 A1
Avebury Pk, Surb. KT6 181 G7
Avebury Rd, E11
off Southwest Rd 96 D1
SW19 184 C1
Orpington BR6 207 G3
Avebury St, N1
off Poole St 112 A1
Aveline St, SE11 34 E3
Aveling Pk Rd, E17 78 A2
Ave Maria La, EC4 19 H4
Avenell Rd, N5 93 H3
Avening Rd, SW18
off Brathway Rd 148 D7
Avening Ter, SW18 148 D6
Avenons Rd, E13 115 G4
Avenue, The, E4 62 D6
E11 (Leytonstone) 97 F2
E11 (Wanstead) 79 H6
N3 72 D2
N8 75 G3
N10 74 C2
N11 58 B4
N17 76 B2
NW6 108 A1
SE10 134 D7
SW4 150 A5
SW11 149 H7
SW18 149 H7
W4 126 E3
W13 104 E7
Barnet EN5 40 B3
Beckenham BR3 190 B1
Bexley DA5 158 D7
Bromley BR1 192 A3
Carshalton SM5 200 A7
Croydon CR0 202 B3
Epsom KT17 197 H7
Esher (Clay.) KT10 194 B6
Hampton TW12 161 F6
Harrow HA3 68 C1
Hounslow TW3 143 H5
Hounslow (Cran.) TW5 142 A1
Isleworth TW7 124 A6
Keston BR2 206 A3
Loughton IG10 48 A6
Orpington BR6 207 J2
Orpington (St.P.Cray) BR5 176 B7
Pinner HA5 67 F6
Pinner (Hatch End) HA5 51 G7
Richmond TW9 145 J2
Sunbury-on-Thames TW16 178 B1
Surbiton KT5 181 J6
Sutton (Cheam) SM3 197 J7
Twickenham TW1 145 F5
Wembley HA9 87 J2
West Drayton UB7 120 B3
West Wickham BR4 190 C7
Worcester Park KT4 197 F2
Avenue Cl, N14 42 C6
NW8 109 H1
Hounslow TW5
off The Avenue 142 A1
West Drayton UB7 120 A3
Avenue Cres, W3 126 B2
Hounslow TW5 122 B7
Avenue Elmers, Surb. KT6 181 H5
Avenue Gdns, SE25 188 D3
SW14 146 E3
W3 126 B2
Hounslow TW5
off The Avenue 122 A7
Teddington TW11 162 C7
Avenue Gate, Loug. IG10 47 J6
Avenue Ind Est, E4 61 J6
Avenue Ms, N10 74 B3
Avenue Pk Rd, SE27 169 H2
Avenue Rd, E7 97 H5
N6 74 C7
N12 57 F4
N14 42 B7
N15 76 A5
NW3 91 G7
NW8 91 G7
NW10 107 F2
SE20 189 F1
SE25 188 D2
SW16 186 D2
SW20 183 H2
W3 126 B2
Beckenham BR3 189 F1
Belvedere DA17 139 J4
Bexleyheath DA7 158 E3
Brentford TW8 125 F5
Erith DA8 139 J7
Hampton TW12 179 H1
Isleworth TW7 144 C1
Kingston upon Thames KT1 181 H3
New Malden KT3 182 E4
Pinner HA5 66 E3
Romford (Chad.Hth) RM6 82 B7
Southall UB1 123 F2
Teddington TW11 162 D7
Wallington SM6 200 C7
Woodford Green IG8 63 J6
Avenue Rd Est, E11
off High Rd Leytonstone 96 D4
Avenue S, Surb. KT5 181 J7
Avenue Ter, N.Mal. KT3
off Kingston Rd 182 C3
Averil Gro, SW16 169 H6
Averill St, W6 128 A6
Avern Gdns, W.Mol. KT8 179 H4
Avern Rd, W.Mol. KT8 179 H5
Avery Fm Row, SW1 32 D2
Avery Gdns, Ilf. IG2 80 C5
AVERY HILL, SE9 157 F6
★ **Avery Hill Pk**, SE9 157 F6
Avery Hill Rd, SE9 157 G6
Avery Row, W1 16 D5
Avey La, Loug. (High Beach) IG10 47 H1
Aviary Cl, E16 115 F5
Aviemore Cl, Beck. BR3 189 J5
Aviemore Way, Beck. BR3 189 H5
Avignon Rd, SE4 153 G3
Avington Ct, SE1
off Old Kent Rd 36 E2
Avington Gro, SE20 171 F7
Avion Cres, NW9 71 G1
Avis Sq, E1 113 G6
Avoca Rd, SW17 168 A4
Avocet Cl, SE1 37 H3
Avocet Ms, SE28 137 G3
Avon Cl, Hayes UB4 102 C4
Sutton SM1 199 F4
Worcester Park KT4 197 G2
Avon Ct, Buck.H. IG9
off Chequers 63 H1
Greenford UB6
off Braund Av 103 H4
Avondale Av, N12 56 E5
NW2 89 E3
Barnet EN4 57 J1
Esher KT10 194 D3
Avondale Av, Worcester Park KT4 197 F1
Avondale Cl, Loug. IG10 48 C7
Avondale Ct, E11 96 E1
E16 *off Avondale Rd* 115 E5
E18 79 H1
Avondale Cres, Enf. EN3 45 H3
Ilford IG4 80 A5
Avondale Dr, Hayes UB3 122 A1
Loughton IG10 48 C7
Avondale Gdns, Houns. TW4 143 F5
Avondale Ho, SE1
off Avondale Sq 37 H4
Avondale Pk Gdns, W11 108 B7
Avondale Pk Rd, W11 108 B7
Avondale Ri, SE15 152 C3
Avondale Rd, E16 115 E5
E17 78 A7
N3 73 F1
N13 59 G2
N15 75 H5
SE9 174 B2
SW14 146 D3
SW19 166 E5
Bromley BR1 173 E6
Harrow HA3 68 C3
South Croydon CR2 201 J6
Welling DA16 158 C2
Avondale Sq, SE1 37 H4
Avonley Rd, SE14 133 F7
Avon Ms, Pnr. HA5 67 F1
Avonmore Gdns, W14
off Avonmore Rd 128 C4
Avonmore Pl, W14
off Avonmore Rd 128 B4
Avonmore Rd, W14 128 C4
Avonmouth St, SE1 27 J5
Avon Path, S.Croy. CR2 201 J6
Avon Pl, SE1 28 A4
Avon Rd, E17 78 D3
SE4 154 A3
Greenford UB6 103 G4
Avonstowe Cl, Orp. BR6 207 F3
Avon Way, E18 79 G3
Avonwick Rd, Houns. TW3 143 H2
Avril Way, E4 62 C5
Avro Way, Wall. SM6 201 E7
Awlfield Av, N17 76 A1
Awliscombe Rd, Well. DA16 157 J2
Axe St, Bark. IG11 117 F1
Axholme Av, Edg. HA8 70 A1
Axis Ct, SE10
off Woodland Cres 134 E6
SE16 *off East La* 29 J3
Axminster Cres, Well. DA16 158 C1
Axminster Rd, N7 93 E3
Axon Pl, Ilf. IG1 99 F2
Aybrook St, W1 16 B2
Aycliffe Cl, Brom. BR1 192 C4
Aycliffe Rd, W12 127 F1
Aylands Cl, Wem. HA9 87 H2
Aylesbury Cl, E7
off Atherton Rd 97 F6

Aylesbury Ct, Sutt. SM1
off Benhill Wd Rd **199** F3
Aylesbury Est, SE17 **36** C4
Aylesbury Rd, SE17 **36** C4
Bromley BR2 **191** G3
Aylesbury St, EC1 **11** G6
NW10 **88** D3
Aylesford Av, Beck. BR3 **189** H5
Aylesford St, SW1 **33** H3
Aylesham Cen, SE15 **152** D1
Aylesham Cl, NW7 **55** G7
Aylesham Rd, Orp. BR6 **193** J7
Ayles Rd, Hayes UB4 **102** B3
Aylestone Av, NW6 **108** A1
Aylett Rd, SE25 **188** E4
Isleworth TW7 **144** B2
Ayley Cft, Enf. EN1 **44** D5
Ayliffe Cl, Kings.T. KT1
off Cambridge Gdns **182** A2
Aylmer Cl, Stan. HA7 **52** D4
Aylmer Dr, Stan. HA7 **52** D4
Aylmer Par, N2 **73** J5
Aylmer Rd, E11 **97** F1
N2 **73** H5
W12 **127** E2
Dagenham RM8 **100** E3
Ayloffe Rd, Dag. RM9 **101** F6
Aylton Est, SE16
off Renforth St **133** F2
Aylward Rd, SE23 **171** G2
SW20 **184** C2
Aylwards Ri, Stan. HA7 **52** D4
Aylward St, E1 **113** F6
Aylwyn Est, SE1 **29** E5
Aynhoe Rd, W14 **128** A4
Aynscombe La, SW14 **146** C3
Aynscombe Path, SW14
off Thames Bk **146** C2
Ayr Ct, W3
off Monks Dr **106** A5
Ayres Cl, E13 **115** G3
Ayres St, SE1 **28** A3
Ayrsome Rd, N16 **94** B3
Ayrton Gould Ho, E2
off Smart St **113** G3
Ayrton Rd, SW7 **22** E5
Aysgarth Ct, Sutt. SM1
off Sutton Common Rd **198** E3
Aysgarth Rd, SE21 **152** B6
Aytoun Pl, SW9 **151** F2
Aytoun Rd, SW9 **151** F2
Azalea Cl, W7 **124** C1
Ilford IG1 **98** E5
Azalea Ct, Wdf.Grn. IG8
off The Bridle Path **63** E7
Azalea Ho, Felt. TW13
off Bedfont La **160** B1
Azalea Wk, Pnr. HA5 **66** B5
Southall UB2
off Navigator Dr **123** J2
Azania Ms, NW5 **92** B5
Azenby Rd, SE15 **152** C2
Azile Everitt Ho, SE18
off Blendon Ter **137** F5
Azof St, SE10 **135** E4

B

Baalbec Rd, N5 **93** H5
Babbacombe Cl, Chess. KT9 **195** G5
Babbacombe Gdns, Ilf. IG4 **80** B4
Babbacombe Rd, Brom. BR1 **191** G1
Baber Bridge Caravan Site, Felt. TW14 **142** C5
Baber Dr, Felt. TW14 **142** C6
Babington Ct, WC1
off Ormond Cl **18** B1
Babington Ri, Wem. HA9 **88** A6
Babington Rd, NW4 **71** H4
SW16 **168** D5
Dagenham RM8 **100** C5
Babmaes St, SW1 **17** H6
Bacchus Wk, N1 **12** D2
Baches St, N1 **12** C4
Back Ch La, E1 **21** H5
Back Hill, EC1 **11** E6
Backhouse Pl, SE17 **36** E2
Back La, N8 **74** E5
NW3 *off Heath St* **91** F4
Bexley DA5 **159** G7
Brentford TW8 **125** G6
Buckhurst Hill IG9 **64** A2
Edgware HA8 **70** C1
Richmond TW10 **163** F3
Romford RM6
off St. Chad's Rd **82** E7
Backley Gdns, SE25 **188** D6
Back Rd, Sid. DA14 **176** A4
Bacon Gro, SE1 **29** F6
Bacon La, NW9 **70** B4
Edgware HA8 **70** A1
Bacons La, N6 **92** A1
Bacon St, E1 **13** G5
E2 **13** G5
Bacon Ter, Dag. RM8
off Fitzstephen Rd **100** B5
Bacton, NW5 **92** A5
Bacton St, E2
off Roman Rd **113** F3
Baddow Cl, Dag. RM10 **119** G1
Woodford Green IG8 **64** A6
Baddow Wk, N1
off Popham Rd **111** J1
Baden Pl, SE1 **28** B3
Baden Powell Cl, Dag. RM9 **119** E1
Surbiton KT6 **195** J2
Baden Rd, N8 **74** D4
Ilford IG1 **98** E5
Badger Cl, Felt. TW13
off Sycamore Cl **160** A3
Hounslow TW4 **142** C3
Ilford IG2 **81** F7
Badgers Cl, Enf. EN2 **43** H3
Harrow HA1 **68** A6
Badgers Copse, Orp. BR6 **207** J2
Worcester Park KT4 **197** F2
Badgers Cft, N20 **56** B1
SE9 **174** D3
Badgers Hole, Croy. CR0 **203** G4
Badgers Wk, N.Mal. KT3 **182** E2
Badlis Rd, E17 **78** A2
Badma Cl, N9
off Hudson Way **61** F3
Badminton Cl, Borwd. WD6 **38** A2
Harrow HA1 **68** B4
Northolt UB5 **85** G6
Badminton Ms, E16
off Hanameel St **135** G1
Badminton Rd, SW12 **150** A6
Badric Ct, SW11
off Yelverton Rd **149** G2
Badsworth Rd, SE5 **131** J7
Baffin Way, E14
off Prestons Rd **114** C7
Bafton Gate, Brom. BR2 **205** H1
Bagley Cl, West Dr. UB7 **120** B2
Bagley's La, SW6 **149** E1
Bagleys Spring, Rom. RM6 **83** E4
Bagshot Ct, SE18
off Prince Imperial Rd **156** D1
Bagshot Rd, Enf. EN1 **44** C7
Bagshot St, SE17 **36** E4
Baildon St, SE8 **133** J7
Bailey Cl, E4 **62** C4
N11 **58** D7
SE28 **137** H1
Bailey Cres, Chess. KT9 **195** G7
Bailey Ms, SW2 **151** G5
W4 *off Herbert Gdns* **126** B6
Bailey Pl, SE26 **171** G6
Baillies Wk, W5
off Liverpool Rd **125** G2
Bainbridge Cl, Rich. (Ham) TW10
off Latchmere Cl **163** H5
Bainbridge Rd, Dag. RM9 **101** F4
Bainbridge St, WC1 **17** J3
Baines Cl, S.Croy. CR2
off Brighton Rd **202** A5
Baird Av, Sthl. UB1 **103** H7
Baird Cl, E10
off Marconi Rd **96** A1
NW9 **70** C6
Baird Gdns, SE19 **170** B4
Baird Rd, Enf. EN1 **44** E4
Baird St, EC1 **12** A5
Bairny Wd App, Wdf.Grn. IG8 *off Broadway Cl* **63** H6
Baizdon Rd, SE3 **154** E2
Bakehouse Ms, Hmptn. TW12 *off Malvern Rd* **161** G7
Baker La, Mitch. CR4 **186** A2
Baker Pas, NW10
off Baker Rd **106** E1
Baker Pl, Epsom KT19 **196** C6
Baker Rd, NW10 **106** E1
SE18 **136** B7
Bakers Av, E17 **78** B6
Bakers Ct, SE25 **188** B3
Bakers End, SW20 **184** B2
Bakers Fld, N7 **92** D4
Bakers Gdns, Cars. SM5 **199** H2
Bakers Hall Ct, EC3 **20** E6
Bakers Hill, E5 **95** F1
Barnet (New Barn.) EN5 **41** E2
Bakers La, N6 **73** J5
Baker's Ms, W1 **16** B3
Bakers Ms, Orp. BR6 **207** J6
Bakers Pas, NW3
off Heath St **91** F4
Baker's Rents, E2 **13** F4
Bakers Row, E15 **114** E2
Baker's Row, EC1 **11** E6
Baker St, NW1 **8** A6
W1 **16** A1
Enfield EN1 **44** A3
Baker's Yd, EC1 **11** E6
Bakery Cl, SW9 **151** F1
Bakery Path, Edg. HA8
off Station Rd **54** B6
Bakery Pl, SW11
off Altenburg Gdns **149** J4
Bakewell Way, N.Mal. KT3 **182** E2
Balaams La, N14 **58** D2
Balaam St, E13 **115** G3
Balaclava Rd, SE1 **37** G2
Surbiton KT6 **181** F7
Bala Grn, NW9
off Snowdon Dr **70** E6
Balcaskie Rd, SE9 **156** C5
Balchen Rd, SE3 **156** A2
Balchier Rd, SE22 **152** E6
Balcombe Cl, Bexh. DA6 **158** D4
Balcombe St, NW1 **7** J6
Balcon Ct, W5
off Boileau Rd **105** J6
Balcon Way, Borwd. WD6 **38** C1
Balcorne St, E9 **95** F7
Balder Ri, SE12 **173** H2
Balderton St, W1 **16** C4
Baldock St, E3 **114** B2
Baldry Gdns, SW16 **169** E6
Baldwin Cres, SE5 **151** J1
Baldwin Gdns, Houns. TW3 *off Chamberlain Gdns* **143** J1
Baldwin's Gdns, EC1 **18** E1
Baldwins Hill, Loug. IG10 **48** C2
Baldwin St, EC1 **12** B4
Baldwin Ter, N1 **11** J1
Baldwyn Gdns, W3 **106** C7
Balearic Apts, E16
off Western Gateway **115** G7
Bale Rd, E1 **113** H5
Balfern Gro, W4 **127** E5
Balfern St, SW11 **149** H1
Balfe St, N1 **10** B2
Balfour Av, W7 **124** C1
Balfour Business Cen, Sthl. UB2 **122** D3
Balfour Gro, N20 **57** J3
Balfour Ho, W10
off St. Charles Sq **108** A5
Balfour Ms, N9 **60** D3
W1 **24** C1
Balfour Pl, SW15 **147** H4
W1 **16** C6
Balfour Rd, N5 **93** J4
SE25 **188** D4
SW19 **166** E7
W3 **106** C5
W13 **124** D2
Bromley BR2 **192** A5
Carshalton SM5 **199** J7
Harrow HA1 **68** A5
Hounslow TW3 **143** H3
Ilford IG1 **98** E2
Southall UB2 **122** D3
Balfour St, SE17 **36** B1
Balfron Twr, E14
off St. Leonards Rd **114** C6
Balgonie Rd, E4 **62** D1
Balgowan Cl, N.Mal. KT3 **183** E5
Balgowan Rd, Beck. BR3 **189** H3
Balgowan St, SE18 **137** J4
BALHAM, SW12 **167** J1
Balham Continental Mkt, SW12 *off Shipka Rd* **168** B1
Balham Gro, SW12 **150** A7
Balham High Rd, SW12 **168** A1
SW17 **168** A2
Balham Hill, SW12 **150** B7
Balham New Rd, SW12 **150** B7
Balham Pk Rd, SW12 **167** J1
Balham Rd, N9 **60** D2
Balham Sta Rd, SW12 **168** B1
Balkan Wk, E1
off Tobacco Dock **112** E7
Balladier Wk, E14 **114** B5
Ballamore Rd, Brom. BR1 **173** G3
Ballance Rd, E9 **95** G6
Ballantine St, SW18 **149** F4
Ballantyne Cl, SE9 **174** B4
Ballard Cl, Kings.T. KT2 **164** D7
Ballards Cl, Dag. RM10 **119** H1
Ballards Fm Rd, Croy. CR0 **202** D6
South Croydon CR2 **202** D6
Ballards La, N3 **72** D1
N12 **72** D1
Ballards Ms, Edg. HA8 **54** A6
Ballards Ri, S.Croy. CR2 **202** D6
Ballards Rd, NW2 **89** G2
Dagenham RM10 **119** H1
Ballards Way, Croy. CR0 **203** E6
South Croydon CR2 **202** D6
Ballast Quay, SE10 **134** D5
Ballater Cl, Wat. WD19 **50** C4
Ballater Rd, SW2 **151** E4
South Croydon CR2 **202** C5
Ball Ct, EC3
off Castle Ct **20** C4
Ballina St, SE23 **153** G7
Ballingdon Rd, SW11 **150** A6
Ballinger Pt, E3
off Bromley High St **114** B3
Ballinger Way, Northolt UB5 **103** E4
Balliol Av, E4 **62** D4
Balliol Rd, N17 **76** B1
W10 **107** J6
Welling DA16 **158** B2
Balloch Rd, SE6 **172** D1
Ballogie Av, NW10 **89** E4
Ballow Cl, SE5
off Harris St **132** B7
Balls Pond Pl, N1
off Balls Pond Rd **94** A6
Balls Pond Rd, N1 **94** A6
Balmain Cl, W5 **125** G1
Balmer Rd, E3 **113** J2
Balmes Rd, N1 **112** A1
Balmoral Apts, W2
off Praed St **15** G2
Balmoral Av, N11 **58** A5
Beckenham BR3 **189** H4
Balmoral Cl, SW15 **148** A6
Balmoral Ct, Wor.Pk. KT4 **197** H2
Balmoral Cres, W.Mol. KT8 **179** G3
Balmoral Dr, Borwd. WD6 **38** D5
Southall UB1 **103** F4
Balmoral Gdns, W13 **124** D3
Bexley DA5 **159** F7
Ilford IG3 **99** J1
Balmoral Gro, N7 **93** F6
Balmoral Ms, W12 **127** F3
Balmoral Rd, E7 **97** J4
E10 **96** B2
NW2 **89** H6
Harrow HA2 **85** G4
Kingston upon Thames KT1 **181** J4
Worcester Park KT4 **197** H3
Balmore Cl, E14 **114** C6
Balmore Cres, Barn. EN4 **42** A5
Balmore St, N19 **92** B2
Balmuir Gdns, SW15 **147** J4
Balnacraig Av, NW10 **89** E4
Balniel Gate, SW1 **33** J3
Baltic Apts, E16
off Western Gateway **115** G7
Baltic Cl, SW19 **167** G7
Baltic Ct, SE16
off Timber Pond Rd **133** G2
Baltic Pl, N1
off Kingsland Rd **112** B1
Baltic Quay, SE16
off Sweden Gate **133** H4
Baltic St E, EC1 **11** J6
Baltic St W, EC1 **11** J6
Baltimore Ho, SW18
off Juniper Dr **149** F4
Baltimore Pl, Well. DA16 **157** J2
Balvaird Pl, SW1 **33** J4
Balvernie Gro, SW18 **148** C7
Bamber Ho, Bark. IG11
off St. Margarets **117** F1
Bamber Rd, SE15
off Moody Rd **152** C1
Bamborough Gdns, W12 **127** J2
Bamford Av, Wem. HA0 **105** J1
Bamford Rd, Bark. IG11 **99** F6
Bromley BR1 **172** C5
Bampfylde Cl, Wall. SM6 **200** C3
Bampton Dr, NW7 **55** G7
Bampton Rd, SE23 **171** G3
Banavie Gdns, Beck. BR3 **190** C1
Banbury Cl, Enf. EN2
off Holtwhites Hill **43** H1
Banbury Ct, WC2 **18** A5
Sutton SM2 **198** D7
Banbury Enterprise Cen, Croy. CR0
off Factory La **201** H2
Banbury Rd, E9 **95** G7
E17 **61** G7
Banbury St, SW11 **149** H2
Banbury Wk, Nthlt. UB5
off Brabazon Rd **103** G2
Banchory Rd, SE3 **135** H7
Bancroft Av, N2 **73** H5
Buckhurst Hill IG9 **63** G2
Bancroft Ct, SW8
off Allen Edwards Dr **150** E1
Northolt UB5 **102** C1

Bancroft Gdns, Har. HA3 **67** J1
Orpington BR6 **207** J1
Bancroft Rd, E1 **113** F3
Harrow HA3 **67** J2
Bandon Ri, Wall. SM6 **200** D5
Banfield Rd, SE15 **152** E3
Bangalore St, SW15 **147** J3
Bangor Cl, Nthlt. UB5 **85** H5
Banim St, W6 **127** H3
Banister Ms, NW6 **90** E7
Banister Rd, W10 **108** A3
Bank, The, N6
off Cholmeley Pk **92** B1
Bank Av, Mitch. CR4 **185** G2
Bank End, SE1 **28** A1
Bankfoot Rd, Brom. BR1 **173** E4
Bankhurst Rd, SE6 **153** J7
Bank La, SW15 **146** E5
Kingston upon Thames KT2 **163** H7
Bank Ms, Sutt. SM1
off Sutton Ct Rd **199** F6
★ **Bank of England**, EC2 **20** B4
★ **Bank of England Mus**, EC2 **20** C4
Banks Ho, SE1 **27** J6
Banksian Wk, Islw. TW7 **144** B1
Banksia Rd, N18 **61** F5
Bankside, SE1 **19** J6
Enfield EN2 **43** H1
South Croydon CR2 **202** C6
Southall UB1 **122** D1
Bankside Av, SE13 **154** B3
Northolt UB5
off Townson Av **102** A2
Bankside Cl, N4 **75** J6
Carshalton SM5 **199** H6
Isleworth TW7 **144** C4
Bankside Dr, T.Ditt. KT7 **194** E1
★ **Bankside Gall**, SE1 **19** H6
Bankside Lofts, SE1 **27** H1
Bankside Rd, Ilf. IG1 **99** F5
Bankside Way, SE19
off Lunham Rd **170** B6
Banks La, Bexh. DA6 **159** F4
Banks Rd, Borwd. WD6 **38** C2
Bank St, E14 **134** A1
Banks Way, E12 **98** D4
Banks Yard, Houns. TW5 **123** F6
Bankton Rd, SW2 **151** G4
Bankwell Rd, SE13 **155** E4
Bannerman Ho, SW8 **34** C6
Banner St, EC1 **12** A6
Banning St, SE10 **134** E5
Bannister Cl, SW2 **169** G1
Greenford UB6 **86** A5
Bannister Ho, E9
off Homerton High St **95** G5
Harrow HA3
off Headstone Dr **68** B3
Bannockburn Rd, SE18 **137** H4
Bannow Cl, Epsom KT19 **196** E4
★ **Banqueting Ho**, SW1 **26** A2
Banstead Ct, W12
off Hilary Rd **107** F7
Banstead Gdns, N9 **60** B3
Banstead Rd, Cars. SM5 **199** H6
Banstead St, SE15 **153** F3
Banstead Way, Wall. SM6 **201** E5
Banstock Rd, Edg. HA8 **54** B6
Banting Dr, N21 **43** F5
Banton Cl, Enf. EN1
off Central Av **44** E2
Bantry St, SE5 **132** A7
Banwell Rd, Bex. DA5
off Woodside La **158** D6
Banyard Rd, SE16
off Southwark Pk Rd **133** E3
Baptist Gdns, NW5
off Queen's Cres **92** A6
Barandon Wk, W11 **108** A7
Barbara Brosnan Ct, NW8 **6** E2
Barbara Castle Cl, SW6 **128** C6
Barbara Hucklesby Cl, N22
off The Sandlings **75** H2
Barbauld Rd, N16 **94** B3
Barber Cl, N21 **43** G7
Barber's All, E13 **115** H3
Barbers Rd, E15 **114** B2
BARBICAN, EC2 **19** J2
★ **Barbican Arts & Conf Cen**, EC2 **20** A1
Barbican Rd, Grnf. UB6 **103** H6
Barb Ms, W6 **127** J3
Barbon Cl, WC1 **18** B1
Barbot Cl, N9 **60** D3
Barchard St, SW18 **148** E5
Barchester Cl, W7 **124** C1
Barchester Rd, Har. HA3 **68** A2
Barchester St, E14 **114** B5
Barclay Cl, SW6 **128** D7
Barclay Oval, Wdf.Grn. IG8 **63** G4
Barclay Path, E17 **78** C5
Barclay Rd, E11 **97** E1
E13 **115** J4
E17 **78** C5
N18 **60** A6
SW6 **128** D7
Croydon CR0 **202** A3
Barcombe Av, SW2 **169** E2
Barcombe Cl, Orp. BR5 **193** J3
Barden St, SE18 **137** H7
Bardfield Av, Rom. RM6 **82** D3
Bardney Rd, Mord. SM4 **185** E4
Bardolph Rd, N7 **92** E4
Richmond TW9
off St. Georges Rd **145** J3
Bard Rd, W10 **108** A7
Bardsey Pl, E1
off Mile End Rd **113** F5
Bardsey Wk, N1
off Clephane Rd **93** J6
Bardsley Cl, Croy. CR0 **202** C3
Bardsley La, SE10 **134** C6
Barfett St, W10 **108** C4
Barfield Av, N20 **57** H2
Barfield Rd, E11 **97** F1
Bromley BR1 **192** D3
Barfields, Loug. IG10 **48** D4
Barfields Gdns, Loug. IG10
off Barfields **48** D4
Barfields Path, Loug. IG10 **48** D4
Barfleur La, SE8 **133** J4
Barford Cl, NW4 **71** G1
Barford St, N1 **111** G1
Barforth Rd, SE15 **153** E3
Barfreston Way, SE20 **189** E1
Bargate Cl, SE18 **137** J5
New Malden KT3 **183** G7
Barge Ho Rd, E16 **136** E1
Barge Ho St, SE1 **27** F1
Barge La, E3
off Birdsfield La **113** J1
Bargery Rd, SE6 **172** B1
Barge Wk, E.Mol. KT8 **180** A3
Kingston upon Thames KT1, KT2 **181** G1
Walton-on-Thames KT12 **178** D3
Bargrove Cl, SE20 **170** D7
Bargrove Cres, SE6
off Elm La **171** J2
Barham Cl, Brom. BR2 **206** B1
Chislehurst BR7 **174** E5
Romford RM7 **83** H2
Wembley HA0 **87** E6
Barham Rd, SW20 **165** G7
Chislehurst BR7 **174** E5
South Croydon CR2 **201** J4
Baring Cl, SE12 **173** G2
Baring Rd, SE12 **155** G7
Barnet (Cockfos.) EN4 **41** G3
Croydon CR0 **202** D1
Baring St, N1 **112** A1
Barkantine Shop Par, The, E14
off The Quarterdeck **134** A2
Barker Cl, N.Mal. KT3
off England Way **182** B4
Richmond TW9 **146** B2
Barker Dr, NW1 **92** C7
Barker Ms, SW4 **150** B4
Barker St, SW10 **30** C5
Barker Wk, SW16 **168** D3
Barkham Rd, N17 **60** A7
Barkham Ter, SE1 **27** F5
BARKING, IG11 **117** E1
Barking & Dagenham Civic Cen, Dag. RM10 **101** H2
Barking Ind Pk, Bark. IG11 **117** J1
Barking Rd, E6 **116** A2
E13 **115** H4
E16 **115** F5
BARKINGSIDE, Ilf. IG6 **81** E3
Bark Pl, W2 **14** A5
Barkston Gdns, SW5 **30** A3
Barkway Ct, N4
off Queens Dr **93** J2
Barkway Dr, Orp. BR6 **206** D4
Barkwood Cl, Rom. RM7 **83** J5
Barkworth Rd, SE16 **133** E5
Barlborough St, SE14 **133** F7
Barlby Gdns, W10 **108** A4
Barlby Rd, W10 **108** A5
Barley Cl, Wem. HA0 **87** G4
Barleycorn Way, E14 **113** J7
Barleyfields Cl, Rom. RM6 **82** B7
Barley La, Ilf. IG3 **100** A1
Romford RM6 **82** B6
Barley Mow Pas, EC1 **19** H2
W4 **126** D5
Barley Shotts Business Pk, W10 *off Acklam Rd* **108** C5
Barlow Cl, Wall. SM6 **200** E7
Barlow Dr, SE18 **156** B1
Barlow Ho, SE16
off Rennie Est **133** E4
Barlow Pl, W1 **17** E6
Barlow Rd, NW6 **90** C6
W3 **126** B1
Hampton TW12 **161** G7
Barlow St, SE17 **36** C1
Barmeston Rd, SE6 **172** B2
Barmor Cl, Har. HA2 **67** H2
Barmouth Av, Grnf. (Perivale) UB6 **104** C2
Barmouth Rd, SW18 **149** F6
Croydon CR0 **203** G2
Barnabas Ct, N21
off Cheyne Wk **43** G5
Barnabas Rd, E9 **95** G5
Barnaby Cl, Har. HA2 **85** J2
Barnaby Pl, SW7 **31** E2
Barnaby Way, Chig. IG7 **64** E3
Barnard Cl, SE18 **136** D4
Chislehurst BR7 **193** G1
Sunbury-on-Thames TW16 *off Oak Gro* **160** B7
Wallington SM6 **200** D7
Barnard Gdns, Hayes UB4 **102** B4
New Malden KT3 **183** G4
Barnard Gro, E15
off Vicarage La **97** F7
Barnard Hill, N10 **74** A2
Barnard Ms, SW11 **149** H4
Barnardo Dr, Ilf. IG6 **81** F4
Barnardo Gdns, E1
off Devonport St **113** G7
Barnardo St, E1
off Devonport St **113** G6
Barnardos Village, Ilford IG6 **81** F3
Barnard Rd, SW11 **149** H4
Enfield EN1 **45** E2
Mitcham CR4 **186** A3
Barnard's Inn, EC1 **19** F3
Barnby Sq, E15
off Barnby St **114** E1
Barnby St, E15 **114** E1
NW1 **9** G2
Barn Cl, Nthlt. UB5 **102** C2
Barn Cres, Stan. HA7 **53** F6
Barncroft Cl, Loug. IG10 **48** D5
Barncroft Grn, Loug. IG10 **48** D5
Barncroft Rd, Loug. IG10 **48** D5
Barneby Cl, Twick. TW2
off Rowntree Rd **162** B1
Barnehurst Av, Bexh. DA7 **159** J1
Erith DA8 **159** J1
Barnehurst Cl, Erith DA8 **159** J1
Barnehurst Rd, Bexh. DA7 **159** J2
Barn Elms Pk, SW15 **147** J2
BARNES, SW13 **147** G2
Barnes All, Hmptn. TW12
off Hampton Ct Rd **179** J2
Barnes Av, SW13 **127** G7
Southall UB2 **123** F4
Barnes Br, SW13 **147** E2
W4 **147** E2
Barnesbury Ho, SW4 **150** D5
Barnes Cl, E12 **98** A4
★ **Barnes Common**, SW13 **147** G3
Barnes Ct, E16
off Ridgwell Rd **115** J5
Barnet EN5 **41** E4
Woodford Green IG8 **64** A5
Barnes End, N.Mal. KT3 **183** G5
Barnes High St, SW13 **147** F2
Barnes Ho, Bark. IG11
off St. Marys **117** G1
Barnes Pikle, W5 **105** G7
Barnes Rd, N18 **61** F4
Ilford IG1 **99** F5
Barnes St, E14 **113** H6
Barnes Ter, SE8 **133** J5
BARNET, EN4 & EN5 **40** C3
Barnet Bypass, Barn. EN5 **38** E3
Borehamwood WD6 **38** E3
Barnet Dr, Brom. BR2 **206** B2
BARNET GATE, Barn. EN5 **39** F6
Barnet Gate La, Barn. EN5 **39** F6
Barnet Gro, E2 **13** H3
Barnet Hill, Barn. EN5 **40** D4
Barnet La, N20 **56** C1
Barnet EN5 **40** C6
★ **Barnet Mus**, Barn. EN5
off Wood St **40** B4
Barnet Rd, Barn. EN5 **39** H5
Barnet Trd Est, Barn. (High Barn.) EN5 **40** C3
Barnett St, E1
off Cannon St Rd **112** E6
Barnet Way, NW7 **38** D7
Barnet Wd Rd, Brom. BR2 **205** J2
Barney Cl, SE7 **135** J5
Barn Fld, NW3
off Upper Pk Rd **91** J5
Barnfield, N.Mal. KT3 **182** E6
Barnfield Av, Croy. CR0 **203** F2
Kingston upon Thames KT2 **163** H5
Mitcham CR4 **186** B4
Barnfield Cl, N4
off Crouch Hill **75** E7
SW17 **167** F3
Barnfield Gdns, SE18
off Barnfield Rd **137** E6
Kingston upon Thames KT2 **163** H4
Barnfield Pl, E14 **134** A4
Barnfield Rd, SE18 **137** E6
W5 **105** F4
Belvedere DA17 **139** F6
Edgware HA8 **70** C1
Barnfield Wd Cl, Beck. BR3 **190** D6
Barnfield Wd Rd, Beck. BR3 **190** D6
Barnham Dr, SE28 **137** J1
Barnham Rd, Grnf. UB6 **103** J3
Barnham St, SE1 **28** E3
Barnhill, Pnr. HA5 **66** C5
Barn Hill, Wem. HA9 **88** B2
Barnhill Av, Brom. BR2 **191** F5
Barnhill La, Hayes UB4 **102** B3
Barnhill Rd, Hayes UB4 **102** B4
Wembley HA9 **88** C3
Barnhurst Path, Wat. WD19 **50** C5
Barningham Way, NW9 **70** D6
Barnlea Cl, Felt. TW13 **161** E2
Barnmead Gdns, Dag. RM9 **101** F5
Barnmead Rd, Beck. BR3 **189** H1
Dagenham RM9 **101** F5
Barn Ri, Wem. HA9 **88** A1
BARNSBURY, N1 **93** F7
Barnsbury Cl, N.Mal. KT3 **182** C4
Barnsbury Cres, Surb. KT5 **196** C1
Barnsbury Est, N1
off Barnsbury Rd **111** F1
Barnsbury Gro, N7 **93** F7
Barnsbury La, Surbiton KT5 **196** B2
Barnsbury Pk, N1 **93** G7
Barnsbury Rd, N1 **10** E1
Barnsbury Sq, N1 **93** G7
Barnsbury St, N1 **93** G7
Barnsbury Ter, N1 **93** F7
Barnscroft, SW20 **183** H3
Barnsdale Av, E14 **134** A4
Barnsdale Rd, W9 **108** C4
Barnsley St, E1 **113** E4
Barnstaple La, SE13
off Lewisham High St **154** C4
Barnstaple Rd, Ruis. HA4 **84** C3
Barnston Wk, N1
off Popham St **111** J1
Barn St, N16
off Stoke Newington Ch St **94** B2
Barn Way, Wem. HA9 **88** A1
Barnwell Rd, SW2 **151** G5
Barnwood Cl, N20 **56** C1
W9 **6** A6
Baron Cl, N11 **58** A5
Baroness Rd, E2 **13** G3
Baronet Gro, N17 **76** D1
Baronet Rd, N17 **76** D1
Baron Gdns, Ilf. IG6 **81** F3
Baron Gro, Mitch. CR4 **185** H4
Baron Ho, SW19
off Chapter Way **185** G1
Baron Rd, Dag. RM8 **100** D1
Barons, The, Twick. TW1 **145** E6
Barons Ct, Wall. SM6
off Whelan Way **200** D3
Barons Ct Rd, W14 **128** B5
Baronsfield Rd, Twick. TW1 **145** E6
Barons Gate, Barn. EN4 **41** H6
Barons Keep, W14 **128** B5
Barons Mead, Har. HA1 **68** B4
Baronsmead Rd, SW13 **147** G1
Baronsmede, W5 **125** J2
Baronsmere Rd, N2 **73** H4
Barons Pl, SE1 **27** F4
Baron St, N1 **11** E1
Barons Wk, Croy. CR0 **189** H6
Baron Wk, E16 **115** F5
Mitcham CR4 **185** H4
Baroque Ct, Houns. TW3
off Prince Regent Rd **143** J3
Barque Ms, SE8
off Watergate St **134** A6
Barrack Rd, Houns. TW4 **142** D4
Barracks La, Barn. EN5
off High St **40** B3
Barratt Av, N22 **75** F2

Barratt Ind Pk, Sthl. UB1 .... **123** G2
Barratt Way, Har. HA3 *off Tudor Rd* **68** A3
Barrenger Rd, N10 .... **73** J1
Barrett Rd, E17 .... **78** C4
Barretts Grn Rd, NW10 .... **106** C2
Barretts Gro, N16 .... **94** B5
Barrett St, W1 .... **16** C4
Barrhill Rd, SW2 .... **169** E2
Barriedale, SE14 .... **153** H1
Barrie Est, W2 .... **14** E5
Barrier App, SE7 .... **136** A3
Barrier Pt Rd, E16 .... **135** J1
Barrier Pt Twr, E16 *off Barrier Pt Rd* **135** J2
Barringer Sq, SW17 .... **168** A4
Barrington Cl, NW5 .... **92** A5
Ilford IG5 .... **80** C1
Loughton IG10 .... **49** F4
Barrington Ct, W3 *off Cheltenham Pl* **126** B2
Barrington Grn, Loug. IG10 .... **49** F4
Barrington Rd, E12 .... **98** D6
N8 .... **74** D5
SW9 .... **151** H3
Bexleyheath DA7 .... **158** D2
Loughton IG10 .... **49** F3
Sutton SM3 .... **198** D1
Barrington Vil, SE18 .... **156** D1
Barrow Av, Cars. SM5 .... **199** J7
Barrow Cl, N21 .... **59** H3
Barrowdene Cl, Pnr. HA5 *off Paines La* **67** E2
Barrowell Grn, N21 .... **59** H2
Barrowfield Cl, N9 .... **61** E3
Barrowgate Rd, W4 .... **126** C5
Barrow Hedges Cl, Cars. SM5 .... **199** H7
Barrow Hedges Way, Cars. SM5 .... **199** H7
Barrow Hill, Wor.Pk. KT4 .... **196** E2
Barrow Hill Cl, Wor.Pk. KT4 .... **196** E2
Barrow Hill Est, NW8 .... **7** G2
Barrow Hill Rd, NW8 .... **7** G2
Barrow Pt Av, Pnr. HA5 .... **66** E2
Barrow Pt La, Pnr. HA5 .... **66** E2
Barrow Rd, SW16 .... **168** D6
Croydon CR0 .... **201** G5
Barrow Wk, Brent. TW8 .... **125** F5
Barrs Rd, NW10 .... **88** D7
Barry Av, N15 .... **76** C6
Bexleyheath DA7 .... **138** E7
Barry Cl, Orp. BR6 .... **207** H3
Barry Ho, SE16 *off Rennie Est* **133** E5
Barry Rd, E6 .... **116** B6
NW10 .... **88** C7
SE22 .... **152** D6
Barset Rd, SE15 .... **153** F3
Barson Cl, SE20 .... **171** F7
Barston Rd, SE27 .... **169** J2
Barstow Cres, SW2 .... **169** F1
Barter St, WC1 .... **18** B2
Barters Wk, Pnr. HA5 *off High St* **66** E3
Barth Ms, SE18 .... **137** H4
Bartholomew Cl, EC1 .... **19** J2
SW18 .... **149** F4
Bartholomew Ct, E14 *off Newport Av* **114** D7
Bartholomew La, EC2 .... **20** C4
Bartholomew Pl, EC1 .... **19** J2
Bartholomew Rd, NW5 .... **92** C6
Bartholomew Sq, E1 *off Coventry Rd* **113** E4
EC1 .... **12** A5
Bartholomew St, SE1 .... **28** B6
Bartholomew Vil, NW5 .... **92** C6
Barth Rd, SE18 .... **137** H4
Bartle Av, E6 .... **116** B2
Bartle Rd, W11 .... **108** B6
Bartlett Cl, E14 .... **114** A6
Bartlett Ct, EC4 .... **19** F3
Bartletts Pas, EC4 .... **19** F3
Bartlett St, S.Croy. CR2 .... **202** A5
Barton Av, Rom. RM7 .... **101** H1
Barton Cl, E6 .... **116** C6
E9 *off Churchill Wk* **95** F5
NW4 .... **71** G5
SE15 *off Kirkwood Rd* **153** E3
Bexleyheath DA6 .... **158** E5
Barton Cl, Chigwell IG7 .... **65** F2
Barton Grn, N.Mal. KT3 .... **182** D2
Barton Ho,
E3 *off Bow Rd* **114** B3
N1 *off Sable St* **93** H7
SW6 *off Wandsworth Br Rd* **149** E3
Barton Meadows, Ilf. IG6 .... **81** F4
Barton Rd, W14 .... **128** B5
Sidcup DA14 .... **177** E6
Barton St, SW1 .... **26** A5
Bartonway, NW8 *off Queen's Ter* **109** G1
Barton Way, Borwd. WD6 .... **38** A2
Bartram Rd, SE4 .... **153** H5
Barts Cl, Beck. BR3 .... **190** A5
Barville Cl, SE4 *off St. Norbert Rd* **153** H4
Barwell Business Pk, Chess. KT9 .... **195** G7
Barwell La, Chess. KT9 .... **195** F7
Barwick Ho, W3 .... **126** C2
Barwick Rd, E7 .... **97** H4
Barwood Av, W.Wick. BR4 .... **204** B1
Bascombe St, SW2 .... **151** G6
Basden Gro, Felt. TW13 .... **161** G2
Basedale Rd, Dag. RM9 .... **100** B7
Baseing Cl, E6 .... **116** D7
Basevi Way, SE8 .... **134** B6
Bashley Rd, NW10 .... **106** D4
Basil Av, E6 .... **116** B2
Basildene Rd, Houns. TW4 .... **142** D2
Basildon Av, Ilf. IG5 .... **80** D1
Basildon Rd, SE2 .... **138** A5
Basil Gdns, SE27 .... **169** J5
Croydon CR0 *off Primrose La* **203** G1
Basilon Rd, Bexh. DA7 .... **158** E2
Basil St, SW3 .... **23** J5
Basin App, E14 *off Commercial Rd* **113** H6
Basing Cl, T.Ditt. KT7 .... **180** C7
Basing Ct, SE15 .... **152** C1
Basingdon Way, SE5 .... **152** A4
Basing Dr, Bex. DA5 .... **159** F6
Basingfield Rd, T.Ditt. KT7 .... **180** C7
Basinghall Av, EC2 .... **20** B2
Basinghall St, EC2 .... **20** B3
Basing Hill, NW11 .... **90** C1
Wembley HA9 .... **87** J2
Basing Ho, Bark. IG11 *off St. Margarets* **117** G1
Basing Ho Yd, E2 .... **13** E3
Basing Pl, E2 .... **13** E3
Basing St, W11 .... **108** C6
Basing Way, N3 .... **72** D3
Thames Ditton KT7 .... **180** C7
Basire St, N1 .... **111** J1
Baskerville Gdns, NW10 *off Dog La* **89** E4
Baskerville Rd, SW18 .... **149** H7
Basket Gdns, SE9 .... **156** B5
Baslow Cl, Har. HA3 .... **68** A1
Baslow Wk, E5 *off Overbury St* **95** G4
Basnett Rd, SW11 .... **150** A3
Basque Ct, SE16 *off Poolmans St* **133** G2
Bassano St, SE22 .... **152** C5
Bassant Rd, SE18 .... **137** J6
Bassein Pk Rd, W12 .... **127** F2
Bassett Gdns, Islw. TW7 .... **123** J7
Bassett Ho, Dag. RM9 .... **118** B1
Bassett Rd, W10 .... **108** A6
Bassetts Cl, Orp. BR6 .... **206** E4
Bassett St, NW5 .... **92** A6
Bassetts Way, Orp. BR6 .... **206** E4
Bassett Way, Grnf. UB6 .... **103** H6
Bassingham Rd, SW18 .... **149** F7
Wembley HA0 .... **87** G6
Bassishaw Highwalk, EC2 *off Aldermanbury Sq* **20** A2
Bastable Av, Bark. IG11 .... **117** H2
Bastion Highwalk, EC2 .... **19** J2
Bastion Ho, EC2 *off London Wall* **19** J2
Bastion Rd, SE2 .... **138** A5
Baston Manor Rd, Brom. BR2 .... **205** H3
Baston Rd, Brom. BR2 .... **205** H1
Bastwick St, EC1 .... **11** J5
Basuto Rd, SW6 .... **148** D1
Batavia Cl, Sun. TW16 .... **178** C1
Batavia Ms, SE14 *off Goodwood Rd* **133** H7
Batavia Rd, SE14 .... **133** H7
Sunbury-on-Thames TW16 .... **178** B1
Batchelor St, N1 .... **11** E1
Bateman Cl, Bark. IG11 *off Glenny Rd* **99** F6
Bateman Ho, SE17 .... **35** G6
Bateman Rd, E4 .... **62** A6
Bateman's Bldgs, W1 .... **17** H4
Bateman's Row, EC2 .... **12** E5
Bateman St, W1 .... **17** H4
Bates Cres, SW16 .... **168** C7
Croydon CR0 .... **201** G5
Bateson St, SE18 .... **137** H4
Bate St, E14 *off Three Colt St* **113** J7
Bath Cl, SE15 *off Asylum Rd* **133** E7
Bath Ct, EC1 .... **11** E6
EC1 (St. Luke's Est) *off St. Luke's Est* **12** B4
Bathgate Rd, SW19 .... **166** A3
Bath Ho, SE1 *off Bath Ter* **28** A5
Bath Ho Rd, Croy. CR0 .... **200** E1
Bath Pas, Kings.T. KT1 *off St. James Rd* **181** G2
Bath Pl, EC2 .... **12** D4
Barnet EN5 .... **40** C3
Bath Rd, E7 .... **98** A6
N9 .... **61** E2
W4 .... **126** E4
Hayes (Harling.) UB3 .... **141** F1
Hounslow TW3, TW4, TW5, TW6 .... **142** D2
Romford RM6 .... **82** E6
West Drayton UB7 .... **140** A1
Baths Rd, Brom. BR2 .... **192** A4
Bath St, EC1 .... **12** A4
Bath Ter, SE1 .... **27** J6
Bathurst Av, SW19 *off Brisbane Av* **184** E1
Bathurst Gdns, NW10 .... **107** H2
Bathurst Ms, W2 .... **15** E5
Bathurst Rd, Ilf. IG1 .... **98** E1
Bathurst St, W2 .... **15** E5
Bathway, SE18 .... **136** D4
Batley Cl, Mitch. CR4 .... **185** J7
Batley Pl, N16 .... **94** C3
Batley Rd, N16 *off Stoke Newington High St* **94** C3
Enfield EN2 .... **43** J1
Batman Cl, W12 .... **127** H1
Batoum Gdns, W6 .... **127** J3
Batson Ho, E1 *off Fairclough St* **21** J4
Batson St, W12 .... **127** G2
Batsworth Rd, Mitch. CR4 .... **185** G3
Battenburg Wk, SE19 *off Brabourne Cl* **170** B5
Batten Cl, E6 *off Savage Gdns* **116** C6
Batten St, SW11 .... **149** H3
Battersby Rd, SE6 .... **172** D2
BATTERSEA, SW11 .... **150** B1
Battersea Br, SW3 .... **31** F7
SW11 .... **31** F7
Battersea Br Rd, SW11 .... **129** H7
Battersea Business Cen, SW11 *off Lavender Hill* **150** A3
Battersea Ch Rd, SW11 .... **149** G1
★ **Battersea Dogs Home**, SW8 .... **130** B7
Battersea High St, SW11 .... **149** G1
★ **Battersea Park**, SW11 .... **32** A7
Battersea Pk Rd, SW8 .... **150** B1
SW11 .... **149** H2
Battersea Ri, SW11 .... **149** H5
Battersea Sq, SW11 *off Battersea High St* **149** G1
Battery Rd, SE28 .... **137** H2
Battishill Gdns, N1 *off Waterloo Ter* **93** H7
Battishill St, N1 *off Waterloo Ter* **93** H7
Battlebridge Ct, N1 .... **10** B1
Battle Br La, SE1 .... **28** D2
Battle Br Rd, NW1 .... **10** A2
Battle Cl, SW19 .... **167** F6
Battledean Rd, N5 .... **93** H5
Battle Rd, Belv. DA17 .... **139** J4
Erith DA8 .... **139** J4
Batty St, E1 .... **21** J3
Batwa Ho, SE16 *off Verney Rd* **133** E5
Baudwin Rd, SE6 .... **172** E2
Baugh Rd, Sid. DA14 .... **176** C5
Baulk, The, SW18 .... **148** D7
Bavant Rd, SW16 .... **187** E2
Bavaria Rd, N19 .... **92** E2
Bavdene Ms, NW4 *off The Burroughs* **71** H4
Bavent Rd, SE5 .... **151** J2
Bawdale Rd, SE22 .... **152** C5
Bawdsey Av, Ilf. IG2 .... **81** J4
Bawtree Rd, SE14 .... **133** H7
Bawtry Rd, N20 .... **57** J3
Baxendale, N20 .... **57** F2
Baxendale St, E2 .... **13** H3
Baxter Cl, Brom. BR1 *off Stoneleigh Rd* **192** E3
Southall UB2 .... **123** H2
Baxter Ho, E3 *off Bromley High St* **114** B3
Baxter Rd, E16 .... **115** J6
N1 .... **94** A6
N18 .... **60** E4
NW10 .... **106** E4
Ilford IG1 .... **98** E5
Bay Ct, W5 *off Popes La* **125** H3
Baycroft Cl, Pnr. HA5 .... **66** C3
Baydon Ct, Brom. BR2 .... **191** F3
Bayes Cl, SE26 .... **171** F5
Bayeux Ho, SE7 *off Springfield Gro* **135** J6
Bayfield Rd, SE9 .... **156** A4
Bayford Ms, E8 *off Bayford St* **95** E7
Bayford Rd, NW10 .... **108** A3
Bayford St, E8 .... **95** E7
Baygrove Ms, Kings.T. (Hmptn W.) KT1 .... **181** F1
Bayham Pl, NW1 .... **9** F1
Bayham Rd, W4 .... **126** D3
W13 .... **104** E7
Morden SM4 .... **185** E4
Bayham St, NW1 .... **110** C1
Bayleaf Cl, Hmptn. TW12 *off Laurel Rd* **162** A5
Bayley St, WC1 .... **17** H2
Bayley Wk, SE2 *off Woolwich Rd* **139** E5
Baylis Ms, Twick. TW1 *off Amyand Pk Rd* **144** D7
Baylis Pl, Brom. BR1 .... **192** B2
Baylis Rd, SE1 .... **27** E4
Bayliss Av, SE28 .... **118** D7
Bayliss Cl, N21 .... **43** E5
Southall UB1 .... **103** H6
Bayne Cl, E6 *off Savage Gdns* **116** C6
Baynes Cl, Enf. EN1 .... **44** D2
Baynes Ms, NW3 *off Belsize La* **91** G6
Baynes St, NW1 .... **92** C7
Baynham Cl, Bex. DA5 .... **159** F6
Bayonne Rd, W6 .... **128** B6
Bayshill Ri, Nthlt. UB5 .... **85** H6
Bayston Rd, N16 .... **94** C3
BAYSWATER, W2 .... **14** B4
Bayswater Rd, W2 .... **15** F5
Baythorne St, E3 .... **113** J5
Bay Tree Cl, Brom. BR1 .... **191** J1
Ilford IG6 *off Hazel La* **64** E7
Baytree Cl, Sid. DA15 .... **175** J1
Baytree Ho, E4 *off Dells Cl* **46** B7
Baytree Ms, SE17 .... **36** B1
Baytree Rd, SW2 .... **151** F4
Bazalgette Cl, N.Mal. KT3 .... **182** D5
Bazalgette Gdns, N.Mal. KT3 .... **182** D5
Bazely St, E14 .... **114** C7
Bazile Rd, N21 .... **43** G6
Beacham Cl, SE7 .... **136** A5
Beachborough Rd, Brom. BR1 .... **172** C4
Beachcroft Rd, E11 .... **97** E3
Beachcroft Way, N19 .... **92** D1
Beach Gro, Felt. TW13 .... **161** G2
Beachy Rd, E3 .... **96** A7
Beacon Gate, SE14 .... **153** G3
Beacon Gro, Carshalton SM5 .... **200** A4
Beacon Hill, N7 .... **92** E5
Beacon Rd, SE13 .... **154** D6
Hounslow (Lon.Hthrw Air.) TW6 .... **140** D6
Beacon Rd Rbt, Houns. (Lon.Hthrw Air.) TW6 .... **140** E6
Beacons Cl, E6 *off Oliver Gdns* **116** B5
Beaconsfield Cl, N11 .... **58** A4
SE3 .... **135** G6
W4 .... **126** C5
Beaconsfield Gdns, Esher (Clay.) KT10 .... **194** B7
Beaconsfield Par, SE9 *off Beaconsfield Rd* **174** B4
Beaconsfield Rd, E10 .... **96** C2
E16 .... **115** F4
E17 .... **77** J6
N9 .... **60** D4
N11 .... **58** A3
N15 .... **76** B4
NW10 .... **89** F6
SE3 .... **135** F7
SE9 .... **174** B2
SE17 .... **36** C4
W4 .... **126** D3
W5 .... **125** F2
Bromley BR1 .... **192** A3
Croydon CR0 .... **188** A6
Esher (Clay.) KT10 .... **194** B7
Hayes UB4 .... **122** C1
New Malden KT3 .... **182** D2
Southall UB1 .... **122** D1
Surbiton KT5 .... **181** J7
Twickenham TW1 .... **144** E6
Beaconsfield Ter, Rom. RM6 .... **82** D6
Beaconsfield Ter Rd, W14 .... **128** B3
Beaconsfield Wk, E6 *off East Ham Manor Way* **116** D6
SW6 .... **148** C1
Beacontree Av, E17 .... **78** D1
Beacontree Rd, E11 .... **79** F7
Beadlow Cl, Cars. SM5 *off Olveston Wk* **185** G6

Beadman Pl, SE27
off Norwood High St **169** H4
Beadman St, SE27 **169** H4
Beadnell Rd, SE23 **171** G1
Beadon Rd, W6 **127** J4
Bromley BR2 **191** G4
Beaford Gro, SW20 **184** B3
Beagle Cl, Felt. TW13 **160** B4
Beak St, W1 **17** G5
Beal Cl, Well. DA16 **158** A1
Beale Cl, N13 **59** H5
Beale Pl, E3 **113** J2
Beale Rd, E3 **113** J1
Beal Rd, Ilf. IG1 **98** D2
Beam Av, Dag. RM10 **119** H1
Beames Rd, NW10 **106** D1
Beaminster Gdns, Ilf. IG6 **80** E2
Beaminster Ho, SW8
off Dorset Rd **34** C7
Beamish Dr, Bushey
(Bushey Hth) WD23 **51** J1
Beamish Ho, SE16
off Rennie Est **133** F4
Beamish Rd, N9 **60** D1
Beanacre Cl, E9 **95** J6
Bean Rd, Bexh. DA6 **158** D4
Beanshaw, SE9 **174** D4
Beansland Gro, Rom.
RM6 **83** E2
Bear All, EC4 **19** G3
Bear Cl, Rom. RM7 **83** H6
Beardell St, SE19 **170** C6
Beardow Gro, N14 **42** C6
Beard Rd, Kings.T. KT2 **163** J5
Beardsfield, E13
off Valetta Gro **115** G1
Beard's Hill, Hmptn.
TW12 **179** G1
Beard's Hill Cl, Hmptn.
TW12
off Beard's Hill **179** G1
Beardsley Ter, Dag. RM8
off Fitzstephen Rd **100** B5
Beardsley Way, W3 **126** D2
Bearfield Rd, Kings.T.
KT2 **163** H7
Bear Gdns, SE1 **27** J1
Bear La, SE1 **27** H1
Bear Rd, Felt. TW13 **160** D5
Bearstead Ri, SE4 **153** J5
Bearsted Ter, Beck. BR3 **190** A1
Bear St, WC2 **17** J5
Beaton Cl, SE15 **152** C1
Beatrice Av, SW16 **187** F3
Wembley HA9 **87** H5
Beatrice Cl, E13
off Chargeable La **115** G4
Pinner HA5 *off Reid Cl* **66** A4
Beatrice Ct, Buck.H. IG9 **64** A2
Beatrice Pl, W8 **22** A6
Beatrice Rd, E17 **78** A5
N4 **75** G7
N9 **45** F7
SE1 **37** J2
Richmond TW10
off Albert Rd **145** J5
Southall UB1 **123** F1
Beatson Wk, SE16 **133** G1
Beattock Ri, N10 **74** B4
Beatty Rd, N16 **94** B4
Stanmore HA7 **53** F6
Beatty St, NW1 **9** F1
Beattyville Gdns, Ilf.
IG6 **80** D3
Beauchamp Cl, W4
off Beaumont Rd **126** C3
Beauchamp Ct, Stan. HA7
off Hardwick Cl **53** F5
Beauchamp Pl, SW3 **23** H5
Beauchamp Rd, E7 **97** H7
SE19 **188** A1
SW11 **149** H4
East Molesey KT8 **179** H5
Sutton SM1 **198** D5
Twickenham TW1 **144** D7
West Molesey KT8 **179** H5
Beauchamp St, EC1 **19** E2
Beauchamp Ter, SW15
off Dryburgh Rd **147** H3
Beauclerc Rd, W6 **127** H3
Beauclerk Cl, Felt. TW13
off Florence Rd **160** B1
Beaudesert Ms, West Dr.
UB7 **120** B2
Beaufort, E6
off Newark Knok **116** D5
Beaufort Av, Har. HA3 **68** D4
Beaufort Cl, E4
off Higham Sta Av **62** B6
SW15 **147** H7
W5 **105** J5
Romford RM7 **83** J4
Beaufort Ct, SW6
off Lillie Rd **128** D6
Richmond TW10
off Beaufort Rd **163** F4
Beaufort Dr, NW11 **72** D4
Beaufort Gdns, NW4 **71** J6
SW3 **23** H5
SW16 **169** F7
Hounslow TW5 **143** E1
Ilford IG1 **98** D1
Beaufort Ms, SW6
off Lillie Rd **128** C6
Beaufort Pk, NW11 **72** D4
Beaufort Rd, W5 **105** J5
Kingston upon Thames
KT1 **181** H4
Richmond TW10 **163** F4
Twickenham TW1 **145** F7
Beaufort St, SW3 **31** F6
Beaufort Way, Epsom
KT17 **197** G7
Beaufoy Rd, N17 **60** B7
Beaufoy Wk, SE11 **34** D2
Beaulieu Av, E16 **135** H1
SE26 **170** E4
Beaulieu Cl, NW9 **71** E4
SE5 **152** A3
Hounslow TW4 **143** F5
Mitcham CR4 **186** A1
Twickenham TW1 **145** G7
Watford WD19 **50** C1
Beaulieu Dr, Pnr. HA5 **66** D6
Beaulieu Gdns, N21 **43** J7
Beaulieu Pl, W4 **126** C3
Beaumanor Gdns,
SE9 **174** D4
Beaumaris Dr, Wdf.Grn.
IG8 **64** A7
Beaumaris Gdns, SE19 **169** J7
Beaumaris Grn, NW9
off Goldsmith Av **71** E6
Beaumaris Twr, W3 **126** B2
Beaumont Av, W14 **128** C5
Harrow HA2 **67** H6
Richmond TW9 **145** J3
Wembley HA0 **87** F5
Beaumont Cl, N2 **73** H4
Kingston upon Thames
KT2 **164** A7
Beaumont Cres, W14 **128** C5
Beaumont Dr, Wor.Pk.
KT4 **197** H1
Beaumont Gdns, NW3 **90** D3
Beaumont Gro, E1 **113** G4
Beaumont Ms, W1 **16** C1
Pinner HA5 **66** E3
Beaumont Pl, W1 **9** G5
Barnet EN5 **40** C1
Isleworth TW7 **144** C5
Beaumont Ri, N19 **92** D1
Beaumont Rd, E10 **78** B7
E13 **115** H3
SE19 **169** J6
SW19 **148** B7
W4 **126** C3
Orpington BR5 **193** G6
Beaumont Sq, E1 **113** G4
Beaumont St, W1 **16** C1
Beaumont Wk, NW3 **91** J7
Beauvais Ter, Nthlt.
UB5 **102** D3
Beauval Rd, SE22 **152** C6
Beaverbank Rd, SE9 **175** G1
Beaver Cl, SE20
off Lullington Rd **170** D7
Hampton TW12 **179** H1
Morden SM4 **183** J7
Beaver Gro, Nthlt. UB5
off Jetstar Way **102** E3
Beavers Cres, Houns.
TW4 **142** C4
Beavers La, Houns. TW4 **142** C3
Beavers La Camp, Houns.
TW4 *off Beavers La* **142** C3
Beaverwood Rd, Chis.
BR7 **175** H6
Beavor Gro, W6
off Beavor La **127** G5
Beavor La, W6 **127** G4
Bebbington Rd, SE18 **137** H4
Beblets Cl, Orp. BR6 **207** J5
Beccles Dr, Bark. IG11 **99** H6
Beccles St, E14 **113** J7
Bec Cl, Ruis. HA4 **84** D3
Beck Cl, SE13 **154** B1
Beck Ct, Beck. BR3 **189** G3
BECKENHAM, BR3 **190** A1
Beckenham Business Cen,
Beck. BR3 **171** H6
Beckenham Gdns, N9 **60** B3
Beckenham Gro, Brom.
BR2 **190** D2
Beckenham Hill Rd,
SE6 **172** B5
Beckenham BR3 **172** B5
Beckenham La, Brom.
BR2 **191** E2
Beckenham Pl Pk, Beck.
BR3 **172** B7
Beckenham Rd, Beck.
BR3 **189** G1
West Wickham BR4 **190** B7
Beckers, The, N16 **94** D4
Becket Av, E6 **116** D3
Becket Cl, SE25 **188** D6
Becket Fold, Har. HA1
off Courtfield Cres **68** C5
Becket Rd, N18 **61** F4
Becket St, SE1 **28** B5
Beckett Cl, NW10 **88** D6
SW16 **168** D2
Belvedere DA17
off Tunstock Way **139** E3
Beckett Ho, SW9 **151** E2
Becketts Cl, Bex. DA5 **177** J1
Feltham TW14 **142** B6
Orpington BR6 **207** J3
Becketts Pl, Kings.T.
(Hmptn W.) KT1 **181** G1
Beckett Wk, Beck. BR3 **171** H6
Beckford Cl, W14 **128** C4
Beckford Dr, Orp. BR5 **193** G7
Beckford Pl, SE17 **36** A4
Beckford Rd, Croy. CR0 **188** C6
Beck La, Beck. BR3 **189** G3
Becklow Gdns, W12
off Becklow Rd **127** G2
Becklow Ms, W12
off Becklow Rd **127** F2
Becklow Rd, W12 **127** G2
Beck River Pk, Beck.
BR3 **189** J1
Beck Rd, E8 **112** E1
Becks Rd, Sid. DA14 **176** A3
BECKTON, E6 **116** D5
Beckton Pk Rbt, E16 **116** B7
Beckton Retail Pk, E6 **116** D5
Beckton Rd, E16 **115** F5
Beckton Triangle Retail Pk,
E6 **116** D4
Beck Way, Beck. BR3 **189** J3
Beckway Rd, SW16 **186** D2
Beckway St, SE17 **36** C2
Beckwith Rd, SE24 **152** A6
Beclands Rd, SW17 **168** A6
Becmead Av, SW16 **168** D4
Harrow HA3 **68** E5
Becondale Rd, SE19 **170** B5
BECONTREE, Dag. RM8 **100** E3
Becontree Av, Dag.
RM8 **100** B4
BECONTREE HEATH, Dag.
RM8 **101** G1
Becquerel Ct, SE10
off West Parkside **135** F3
Bective Pl, SW15
off Bective Rd **148** C4
Bective Rd, E7 **97** G4
SW15 **148** C4
Becton Pl, Erith DA8 **139** H7
Bedale St, SE1 **28** B2
BEDDINGTON, Croy.
CR0 **200** D2
BEDDINGTON CORNER,
Mitch. CR4 **186** A7
Beddington Cross, Croy.
CR0 **200** D1
Beddington Fm Rd, Croy.
CR0 **200** E1
Beddington Gdns, Cars.
SM5 **200** A6
Wallington SM6 **200** B6
Beddington Grn, Orp.
BR5 **193** J1
Beddington Gro, Wall.
SM6 **200** D5
Beddington La, Croy.
CR0 **186** C5
Beddington La Ind Est,
Croy. CR0 **186** C6
Beddington Path, Orp.
BR5 **193** J1
Beddington Rd, Ilf. IG3 **81** J7
Orpington BR5 **193** H2
Beddington Trd Pk, Croy.
CR0 **200** E1
Bede Cl, Pnr. HA5 **66** D1
Bedens Rd, Sid. DA14 **176** E6
Bede Rd, Rom. RM6 **82** C6
Bedevere Rd, N9 **60** D3
Bedfont Cl, Felt. TW14 **141** F6
Mitcham CR4 **186** A2
Bedfont La, Felt. TW13,
TW14 **141** J7
Bedfont Rd, Stai. (Stanw.)
TW19 **140** B6
Bedford Av, WC1 **17** J2
Barnet EN5 **40** C5
Hayes UB4 **102** B6
Bedfordbury, WC2 **18** A5
Bedford Cl, N10 **58** A7
W4 **127** E6
Bedford Cor, W4
off The Avenue **126** E4
Bedford Ct, WC2 **18** A6
Bedford Gdns, W8 **128** D1
Bedford Hill, SW12 **168** B1
SW16 **168** B1
Bedford Ho, SW4 **150** E4
Bedford Ms, N2 **73** H3
SE6 *off Aitken Rd* **172** B2
BEDFORD PARK, W4 **126** D3
Bedford Pk, Croy. CR0 **201** J1
Bedford Pk Cor, W4
off Bath Rd **126** E4
Bedford Pas, SW6
off Dawes Rd **128** B7
Bedford Pl, WC1 **18** A1
Croydon CR0 **202** A1
Bedford Rd, E6 **116** D1
E17 **78** A2
E18 **79** G2
N2 **73** H3
N8 **74** D6
N9 **44** E7
N15 **76** B4
N22 **74** E1
NW7 **54** E3
SW4 **150** E3
W4 **126** D3
W13 **104** E7
Harrow HA1 **67** J6
Ilford IG1 **99** E3
Sidcup DA15 **175** H3
Twickenham TW2 **162** A3
Worcester Park KT4 **197** J2
Bedford Row, WC1 **18** D1
Bedford Sq, WC1 **17** J2
Bedford St, WC2 **18** A5
Bedford Ter, SW2
off Lyham Rd **150** E5
Bedford Way, WC1 **9** J6
Bedgebury Gdns, SW19 **166** B2
Bedgebury Rd, SE9 **156** A4
Bedivere Rd, Brom. BR1 **173** G3
Bedlam Ms, SE11 **34** D1
Bedlow Way, Croy. CR0 **201** F4
Bedonwell Rd, SE2 **138** E6
Belvedere DA17 **139** G6
Bexleyheath DA7 **139** G6
Bedser Cl, SE11 **34** D5
Thornton Heath CR7 **187** J3
Bedser Dr, Grnf. UB6 **86** A5
Bedster Gdns, W.Mol.
KT8 **179** H2
Bedwardine Rd, SE19 **170** B7
Bedwell Gdns, Hayes
UB3 **121** H5
Bedwell Rd, N17 **76** B1
Belvedere DA17 **139** G5
Beeby Rd, E16 **115** H5
Beech Av, N20 **57** H1
W3 **126** E1
Brentford TW8 **125** E7
Buckhurst Hill IG9 **63** H2
Ruislip HA4 **84** B1
Beech Av, Sidcup
DA15 **158** A7
Beech Cl, N9 **44** D6
SE8 *off Clyde St* **133** J6
SW15 **147** G7
SW19 **165** J6
Carshalton SM5 **199** J2
Loughton IG10 **49** E3
Staines (Stanw.) TW19
off St. Mary's Cres **140** A7
Sunbury-on-Thames
TW16 *off Harfield Rd* **178** D2
West Drayton UB7 **120** D3
Beech Copse, Brom.
BR1 **192** C2
South Croydon CR2 **202** B5
Beech Ct, E17 **78** D3
SE9 **156** B6
Ilford IG1 **98** D3
Beechcroft, Chis. BR7 **174** D7
Beechcroft Av, NW11 **72** C7
Harrow HA2 **67** G7
New Malden KT3 **182** C1
Southall UB1 **123** F1
Beechcroft Cl, Houns.
TW5 **122** E7
Orpington BR6 **207** G4
Beechcroft Gdns, Wem.
HA9 **87** J3
Beechcroft Lo, Sutt. SM2
off Devonshire Rd **199** F7
Beechcroft Rd, E18 **79** H2
SW14 **146** C3
SW17 **167** H2
Chessington KT9 **195** J4
Orpington BR6 **207** G4
Beechdale, N21 **59** F2
Beechdale Rd, SW2 **151** F6
Beech Dell, Kes. BR2 **206** C4
Beech Dr, N2 **73** J3
Beechen Cliff Way, Islw.
TW7
off Henley Cl **144** C1
Beechen Gro, Pnr. HA5 **67** F3
Beeches, The, Houns.
TW3 **143** H1
Beeches Av, Cars. SM5 **199** H7
Beeches Cl, SE20 **189** F1
Beeches Rd, SW17 **167** H3
Sutton SM3 **198** B1

Beechfield Cotts, Brom. BR1 *off Widmore Rd* **191** J2
Beechfield Gdns, Rom. RM7 **83** J7
Beechfield Rd, N4 **75** J6
SE6 **171** J1
Bromley BR1 **191** J2
Beech Gdns, EC2 *off White Lyon Ct* **19** J1
W5 **125** H2
Dagenham RM10 **101** H7
Beech Gro, Ilf. IG6 **65** H6
Mitcham CR4 **186** D4
New Malden KT3 **182** D3
Beech Hall Cres, E4 **62** D7
Beech Hall Rd, E4 **62** C7
Beech Hill Av, Barn. EN4 **41** F1
Beechhill Rd, SE9 **156** D5
Beech Ho, NW3 *off Maitland Pk Vil* **91** J6
Croydon CR0 **204** B6
Beech Ho Rd, Croy. CR0 **202** A3
Beech La, Buck.H. IG9 **63** H2
Beech Lawns, N12 **57** G5
Beechmont Cl, Brom. BR1 **172** E5
Beechmore Gdns, Sutt. SM3 **198** A2
Beechmore Rd, SW11 **149** J1
Beechmount Av, W7 **104** A5
Beecholme Av, Mitch. CR4 **186** B1
Beecholme Est, E5 **95** E3
Beech Rd, N11 **59** E6
SW16 **187** E2
Feltham TW14 **141** H7
Beechrow, Rich. (Ham) TW10 **163** H4
Beech St, EC2 **19** J1
Romford RM7 **83** J4
Beech Tree Cl, N1 **93** G7
Stanmore HA7 **53** F5
Beech Tree Glade, E4 **63** F1
Beech Tree Pl, Sutt. SM1 *off St. Nicholas Way* **199** E5
Beechvale Cl, N12 **57** H5
Beech Wk, NW7 **54** E6
Beech Way, NW10 **88** D7
Beechway, Bex. DA5 **158** D6
Beech Way, Twick. TW2 **161** G3
Beechwood Av, N3 **72** C3
Greenford UB6 **103** H3
Beechwood Av, Harrow HA2 **85** H3
Orpington BR6 **207** H5
Richmond TW9 **146** A1
Sunbury-on-Thames TW16 **160** A6
Thornton Heath CR7 **187** H4
Beechwood Circle, Har. HA2 *off Beechwood Gdns* **85** H3
Beechwood Cl, NW7 **54** D5
Surbiton (Long Dit.) KT6 **181** F7
Beechwood Ct, Cars. SM5 **199** J4
Sunbury-on-Thames TW16 **160** A6
Beechwood Cres, Bexh. DA7 **158** D3
Beechwood Dr, Kes. BR2 **206** A4
Woodford Green IG8 **63** F5
Beechwood Gdns, NW10 *off St. Annes Gdns* **105** J3
Harrow HA2 **85** H3
Ilford IG5 **80** C5
Beechwood Gro, W3 **106** E7
Surbiton (Long Dit.) KT6 **181** F7
Beechwood Ms, N9 **60** D2
Beechwood Pk, E18 **79** G3
Beechwood Ri, Chis. BR7 **175** E4
Beechwood Rd, E8 **94** C6
N8 **74** D4
Beechwoods Ct, SE19 *off Crystal Palace Par* **170** C5
Beechworth Cl, NW3 **90** D2
Beecroft La, SE4 *off Beecroft Rd* **153** H5
Beecroft Ms, SE4 *off Beecroft Rd* **153** H5
Beecroft Rd, SE4 **153** H5
Beehive Cl, E8 **94** C7
Beehive La, Ilf. IG1, IG4 **80** C6
Beehive Pas, EC3 **20** D4
Beehive Pl, SW9 **151** G3
Beeken Dene, Orp. BR6 *off Isabella Dr* **207** F4
Beeleigh Rd, Mord. SM4 **185** E4
Beeston Cl, E8 *off Ferncliff Rd* **94** D5
Watford WD19 **50** D4
Beeston Pl, SW1 **24** E6
Beeston Rd, Barn. EN4 **41** G6
Beeston Way, Felt. TW14 **142** C6
Beethoven St, W10 **108** B3
Beeton Cl, Pnr. HA5 **51** G7
Begbie Rd, SE3 **155** J1
Beggars Hill, Epsom KT17 **197** F7
Beggar's Hill, Epsom (Junct) KT17 **197** F6
Beggars Roost La, Sutt. SM1 **198** D6
Begonia Cl, E6 **116** B5
Begonia Pl, Hmptn. TW12 *off Gresham Rd* **161** G6
Begonia Wk, W12 *off Du Cane Rd* **107** F6
Beira St, SW12 **150** B7
Bejun Ct, Barn. (New Barn.) EN5 *off Station App* **41** F4
Bekesbourne St, E14 *off Ratcliffe La* **113** H6
Belcroft Cl, Brom. BR1 **173** F7
Beldham Gdns, W.Mol. KT8 **179** H3
Belfairs Dr, Rom. RM6 **82** C7
Belfairs Grn, Wat. WD19 **50** D5
Belfast Rd, N16 **94** C2
SE25 **188** E4
Belfont Wk, N7 **93** E4
Belford Gro, SE18 **136** D4
Belfort Rd, SE15 **153** F2
Belfour Ter, N3 *off Squires La* **73** E2
Belfry Cl, SE16 *off Masters Dr* **133** E5
Bromley BR1 **192** E4
Belgrade Rd, N16 **94** B4
Hampton TW12 **179** H1
Belgrave Cl, N14 *off Prince George Av* **42** C5
NW7 **54** D5
W3 *off Avenue Rd* **126** B2
Belgrave Ct, E14 *off Westferry Circ* **113** J7
Belgrave Cres, Sun. TW16 **178** B1
Belgrave Gdns, N14 **42** D5
Belgrave Gdns, NW8 **109** E1
Stanmore HA7 *off Copley Rd* **53** F5
Belgrave Hts, E11 **97** G1
Belgrave Ms N, SW1 **24** B4
Belgrave Ms S, SW1 **24** C5
Belgrave Ms W, SW1 **24** B5
Belgrave Pl, SW1 **24** C5
Belgrave Rd, E10 **96** C1
E11 **97** G2
E13 **115** J4
E17 **78** A5
SE25 **188** C4
SW1 **33** F2
SW13 **127** F7
Hounslow TW4 **143** F3
Ilford IG1 **98** C1
Mitcham CR4 **185** G3
Sunbury-on-Thames TW16 **178** B1
Belgrave Sq, SW1 **24** B5
Belgrave St, E1 **113** G6
Belgrave Ter, Wdf.Grn. IG8 **63** G3
Belgrave Wk, Mitch. CR4 **185** G3
Belgrave Yd, SW1 **24** D6
BELGRAVIA, SW1 **24** B6
Belgravia Cl, Barn. EN5 **40** C3
Belgravia Gdns, Brom. BR1 **172** E6
Belgravia Ho, SW4 **150** D6
Belgravia Ms, Kings.T. KT1 **181** G4
Belgrove St, WC1 **10** A3
Belham Wk, SE5 *off Datchelor Pl* **152** A1
Belinda Rd, SW9 **151** H3
Belitha Vil, N1 **93** F7
Bell, The, E17 **78** A3
Bellamy Cl, E14 *off Manilla St* **134** A2
W14 *off Aisgill Av* **128** C5
Edgware HA8 **54** C3
Bellamy Dr, Stan. HA7 **68** E1
Bellamy Ho, SW17 *off Garratt La* **167** G4
Hounslow TW5 *off Biscoe Cl* **123** G6
Bellamy Rd, E4 **62** B6
Enfield EN2 **44** A2
Bellamy St, SW12 **150** B7
Bel La, Felt. TW13 *off Butts Cotts* **161** F3
Bellarmine Cl, SE28 **137** J2
Bellasis Av, SW2 **168** E2
Bell Av, West Dr. UB7 **120** C4
Bell Cl, Pnr. HA5 **66** C2
Bellclose Rd, West Dr. UB7 **120** B2
Bell Ct, Surb. KT5 *off Barnsbury La* **196** B2
Bell Dr, SW18 **148** B7
Bellefields Rd, SW9 **151** F3
Bellegrove Cl, Well. DA16 **157** J2
Bellegrove Par, Well. DA16 *off Bellegrove Rd* **157** J3
Bellegrove Rd, Well. DA16 **157** G2
Bellenden Rd, SE15 **152** C2
Bellestaines Pleasaunce, E4 **62** A2
Belleville Rd, SW11 **149** J5
Belle Vue, Grnf. UB6 **104** A1
Belle Vue Est, NW4 *off Bell La* **71** J4
Belle Vue La, Bushey (Bushey Hth) WD23 **52** A1
Bellevue Ms, N11 **58** A5
Bellevue Par, SW17 *off Bellevue Rd* **167** H1
Belle Vue Pk, Th.Hth. CR7 **187** J3
Bellevue Pl, E1 **113** F4
Belle Vue Rd, E17 **78** D2
Bellevue Rd, N11 **58** A4
Belle Vue Rd, NW4 **71** J4
Bellevue Rd, SW13 **147** G2
SW17 **167** H1
W13 **104** E4
Bexleyheath DA6 **159** F5
Kingston upon Thames KT1 **181** H3
Bellew St, SW17 **167** F3
Bell Fm Av, Dag. RM10 **101** J3
Bellfield Av, Har. HA3 **51** J6
Bellfield Cl, SE3 *off Charlton Rd* **135** H7
Bellflower Cl, E6 *off Sorrel Gdns* **116** B5
Bell Gdns, E17 *off Markhouse Rd* **77** J5
Bellgate Ms, NW5 *off York Ri* **92** B3
BELL GREEN, SE6 **171** J3
Bell Grn, SE26 **171** J3
Bell Grn La, SE26 **171** H5
Bell Hill, Croy. CR0 *off Surrey St* **201** J2
Bellhouse Rd, Rom. RM7 **101** J1
Bellina Ms, NW5 *off Fortess Rd* **92** C4
BELLINGHAM, SE6 **172** B3
Bellingham Ct, Bark. IG11 *off Renwick Rd* **118** B3
Bellingham Grn, SE6 **172** A3
Bellingham Rd, SE6 **172** B3
Bellingham Trd Est, SE6 *off Franthorne Way* **172** B3
Bell Inn Yd, EC3 **20** C4
Bell La, E1 **21** F2
E16 **135** G1
NW4 **72** A4
Twickenham TW1 *off The Embankment* **162** D1
Wembley HA9 *off Magnet Rd* **87** G2
Bellmaker Ct, E3 *off St. Pauls Way* **114** A5
Bell Meadow, SE19 *off Dulwich Wd Av* **170** B4
Bello Cl, SE24 **151** H7
Bellot Gdns, SE10 *off Bellot St* **135** E5
Bellot St, SE10 **135** E5
Bellring Cl, Belv. DA17 **139** G6
Bell Rd, E.Mol. KT8 **180** A5
Enfield EN1 **44** A1
Hounslow TW3 **143** H4
Bells All, SW6 **148** D2
Bells Gdn Est, SE15 *off Buller Cl* **132** D7
Bells Hill, Barn. EN5 **40** A5
Bell St, NW1 **15** G1
SE18 **156** B1
Belltrees Gro, SW16 **169** F5
Bell Water Gate, SE18 **136** D3
Bell Wf La, EC4 **20** A6
Bellwood Rd, SE15 **153** G4
Bell Yd, WC2 **18** E3
Bell Yd Ms, SE1 **28** E4
Belmarsh Rd, SE28 *off Western Way* **137** H2
BELMONT, Har. HA3 **68** D2
Belmont Av, N9 **60** D1
N13 **59** E5
N17 **75** J3
Barnet EN4 **41** J5
New Malden KT3 **183** G5
Southall UB2 **122** E3
Welling DA16 **157** H3
Wembley HA0 **105** J1
Belmont Circle, Har. HA3 **68** E1
Belmont Cl, E4 **62** D5
N20 **56** E1
Belmont Cl, SW4 **150** C3
Barnet (Cockfos.) EN4 **41** J4
Woodford Green IG8 **63** H4
Belmont Ct, NW11 **72** C5
Belmont Gro, SE13 **154** D3
W4 *off Belmont Ter* **126** D4
Belmont Hall Ct, SE13 *off Belmont Gro* **154** D3
Belmont Hill, SE13 **154** D3
Belmont La, Chis. BR7 **175** F5
Stanmore HA7 **53** F7
Belmont Ms, SW19 *off Chapman Sq* **166** A2
Belmont Pk, SE13 **154** D4
Belmont Pk Cl, SE13 **154** D4
Belmont Pk Rd, E10 **78** B6
Belmont Ri, Sutt. SM2 **198** C6
Belmont Rd, N15 **75** J4
N17 **75** J4
SE25 **188** E5
SW4 **150** C3
W4 *off Chiswick High Rd* **126** D4
Beckenham BR3 **189** J2
Chislehurst BR7 **175** E5
Erith DA8 **139** G7
Harrow HA3 **68** C3
Ilford IG1 **99** F3
Twickenham TW2 **162** A2
Wallington SM6 **200** B5
Belmont St, NW1 **92** A7
Belmont Ter, W4 **126** D4
Belmor, Borwd. (Els.) WD6 **38** A5
Belmore Av, Hayes UB4 **102** A6
Belmore La, N7 **92** D5
Belmore St, SW8 **150** D1
Beloe Cl, SW15 **147** G3
Belper Ct, E5 *off Pedro St* **95** G4
Belsham St, E9 **95** F6
Belsize Av, N13 **59** F6
NW3 **91** G6
W13 **125** E3
Belsize Ct, NW3 *off Belsize La* **91** H5
Sutt. SM1 **199** E4
Belsize Cres, NW3 **91** G5
Belsize Gro, NW3 **91** H6
Belsize La, NW3 **91** G6
Belsize Ms, NW3 *off Belsize La* **91** G6
BELSIZE PARK, NW3 **91** H6
Belsize Pk, NW3 **91** G6
Belsize Pk Gdns, NW3 **91** H6
Belsize Pk Ms, NW3 *off Belsize La* **91** G6
Belsize Pl, NW3 *off Belsize La* **91** G6
Belsize Rd, NW6 **108** E1
Harrow HA3 **52** A7
Belsize Sq, NW3 **91** G6
Belsize Ter, NW3 **91** G6
Belson Rd, SE18 **136** C4
Beltane Dr, SW19 **166** A3
Belthorn Cres, SW12 **150** C7
Belton Rd, E7 **97** H7
E11 **96** E4
N17 **76** B3
NW2 **89** G6
Sidcup DA14 **176** A4
Belton Way, E3 **114** A5
Beltran Rd, SW6 **148** E2
Beltwood Rd, Belv. DA17 **139** J4
BELVEDERE, DA17 **139** H4
Belvedere, The, SW10 **149** F1
Belvedere Av, SW19 **166** B5
Ilford IG5 **80** E2
Belvedere Bldgs, SE1 **27** H4
Belvedere Business Pk, Belv. DA17 *off Crabtree Manorway S* **139** H2
Belvedere Cl, Tedd. TW11 **162** B5
Belvedere Ct, N1 *off De Beauvoir Cres* **112** B1
N2 **73** G5
Belvedere Dr, SW19 **166** B5
Belvedere Gdns, W.Mol. KT8 **179** F5
Belvedere Gro, SW19 **166** B5
Belvedere Ho, Felt. TW13 **160** A1
Belvedere Ind Est, Belv. DA17 **139** J3
Belvedere Ms, SE3 *off Langton Way* **135** H7
SE15 **153** F3
Belvedere Pl, SE1 **27** H4
SW2 *off Acre La* **151** F4
Belvedere Rd, E10 **95** H1
SE1 **26** D3
SE2 **138** D1
SE19 **170** C7
W7 **124** C3

Belvedere Rd, Bexleyheath DA7 ... **159** F3
Belvedere Sq, SW19 ... **166** B5
Belvedere Strand, NW9 ... **71** F2
Belvedere Way, Har. HA3 ... **69** H6
Belvoir Cl, SE9 ... **174** B3
Belvoir Ho, SW1
off Vauxhall Br Rd ... **33** G1
Belvoir Rd, SE22 ... **152** D7
Belvue Business Cen, Nthlt. UB5 ... **85** H7
Belvue Cl, Nthlt. UB5 ... **85** G7
Belvue Rd, Nthlt. UB5 ... **85** G7
Bembridge Cl, NW6 ... **90** B7
Bemersyde Pt, E13
off Balaam St ... **115** H3
Bemerton Est, N1 ... **93** E7
Bemerton St, N1 ... **111** F1
Bemish Rd, SW15 ... **148** A3
Bempton Dr, Ruis. HA4 ... **84** B2
Bemsted Rd, E17 ... **77** J3
Benares Rd, SE18 ... **137** J4
Benbow Rd, W6 ... **127** H3
Benbow St, SE8 ... **134** A6
Benbury Cl, Brom. BR1 ... **172** C5
Bench Fld, S.Croy. CR2 ... **202** C6
Bencroft Rd, SW16 ... **168** C7
Bencurtis Pk, W.Wick. BR4 ... **204** D3
Bendall Ms, NW1 ... **15** H1
Bendemeer Rd, SW15 ... **148** A3
Bendish Pt, SE28 ... **137** F2
Bendish Rd, E6 ... **98** B7
Bendmore Av, SE2 ... **138** A5
Bendon Valley, SW18 ... **148** E7
Benedict Cl, Belv. DA17
off Tunstock Way ... **139** E3
Orpington BR6 ... **207** H3
Benedict Dr, Felt. TW14 ... **141** G7
Benedict Rd, SW9 ... **151** F3
Mitcham CR4 ... **185** G3
Benedict Way, N2 ... **73** F3
Benenden Grn, Brom. BR2 ... **191** G5
Benett Gdns, SW16 ... **186** E2
Benfleet Cl, Sutt. SM1 ... **199** F3
Benfleet Way, N11 ... **58** A2
Bengal Ct, EC3
off Birchin La ... **20** C4
Bengal Rd, Ilf. IG1 ... **98** E4
Bengarth Dr, Har. HA3 ... **68** A2
Bengarth Rd, Nthlt. UB5 ... **102** D1
Bengeo Gdns, Rom. RM6 ... **82** C6
Bengeworth Rd, SE5 ... **151** J3
Harrow HA1 ... **86** D2
Ben Hale Cl, Stan. HA7 ... **52** E4
Benham Cl, SW11 ... **149** G3
Chessington KT9
off Merritt Gdns ... **195** F6
Benham Gdns, Houns. TW4 ... **143** F5
Benham Rd, W7 ... **104** B5
Benhams Pl, NW3
off Holly Wk ... **91** F4
Benhill Av, Sutt. SM1 ... **199** E4
Benhill Rd, SE5 ... **132** A7
Sutton SM1 ... **199** F3
Benhill Wd Rd, Sutt. SM1 ... **199** F3
BENHILTON, Sutt. SM1 ... **199** E2
Benhilton Gdns, Sutt. SM1 ... **199** E3
Benhurst Ct, SW16 ... **169** G5
Benhurst La, SW16 ... **169** G5
Benington Ct, N4
off Brownswood Rd ... **93** J2
Benin St, SE13 ... **154** D7
Benjafield Cl, N18 ... **60** E4
Benjamin Cl, E8 ... **112** D1
Benjamin Ms, SW12 ... **150** C7
Benjamin St, EC1 ... **19** G1
Ben Jonson Ho, EC2
off The Barbican ... **20** A1
Ben Jonson Rd, E1 ... **113** H5
Benledi Rd, E14 ... **114** D6
Bennelong Cl, W12 ... **107** H7
Bennerley Rd, SW11 ... **149** H5
Bennet Ms, N19 ... **92** D3
Bennets Ctyd, SW19
off Watermill Way ... **185** F1
Bennetsfield Rd, Uxb. UB11 ... **120** E1
Bennet's Hill, EC4 ... **19** H5
Bennet St, SW1 ... **25** F1
Bennett Cl, Houns. TW4 ... **143** E5
Kingston upon Thames (Hmptn W.) KT1 ... **181** F1
Welling DA16 ... **158** A2
Bennett Gro, SE13 ... **154** B1
Bennett Ho, SW1
off Page St ... **33** J1
Bennett Pk, SE3 ... **155** F3
Bennett Rd, E13 ... **115** J4
N16 ... **94** B4
SW9 ... **151** G2
Romford RM6 ... **83** E6
Bennetts Av, Croy. CR0 ... **203** H2
Greenford UB6 ... **104** B1
Bennetts Castle La, Dag. RM8 ... **100** C4
Bennetts Cl, N17 ... **60** C6
Mitcham CR4 ... **186** B1
Bennetts Copse, Chis. BR7 ... **174** B6
Bennett St, W4 ... **126** E6
Bennetts Way, Croy. CR0 ... **203** H2
Bennetts Yd, SW1 ... **25** J6
Benningholme Rd, Edg. HA8 ... **54** E6
Bennington Rd, N17 ... **76** B1
Woodford Green IG8 ... **62** E7
Benn St, E9 ... **95** H6
Benn's Wk, Rich. TW9
off Rosedale Rd ... **145** H4
Benrek Cl, Ilf. IG6 ... **81** F1
Bensbury Cl, SW15 ... **147** H7
Bensham Cl, Th.Hth. CR7 ... **187** J4
Bensham Gro, Th.Hth. CR7 ... **187** J2
Bensham La, Croy. CR0 ... **187** H7
Thornton Heath CR7 ... **187** H4
Bensham Manor Rd, Th.Hth. CR7 ... **187** J4
Bensington Ct, Felt. TW14 ... **141** G6
Bensley Cl, N11 ... **57** J5
Ben Smith Way, SE16 ... **29** J5
Benson Av, E6 ... **115** J2
Benson Cl, Houns. TW3 ... **143** G4
Benson Ct, SW8
off Hartington Rd ... **150** E1
Benson Quay, E1
off Garnet St ... **113** F7
Benson Rd, SE23 ... **171** F1
Croydon CR0 ... **201** G3
Bentalls Cen, Kings.T. KT1 ... **181** G2
Bentfield Gdns, SE9
off Aldersgrove Av ... **173** J3
Benthal Rd, N16 ... **94** D2
Bentham Ct, N1
off Rotherfield St ... **93** J7
Bentham Ho, SE1
off Falmouth Rd ... **28** B5
Bentham Rd, E9 ... **95** G6
SE28 ... **118** B7
Bentham Wk, NW10 ... **88** C5
Ben Tillet Cl, Bark. IG11 ... **100** A7
Ben Tillett Cl, E16
off Newland St ... **136** C1
Bentinck Cl, NW8
off Prince Albert Rd ... **7** H2
Bentinck Ms, W1 ... **16** C3
Bentinck Rd, West Dr. UB7 ... **120** A1
Bentinck St, W1 ... **16** C3
Bentley Ct, SE13
off Whitburn Rd ... **154** C4
Bentley Dr, NW2 ... **90** C3
Ilford IG2 ... **81** F6
Bentley Ms, Enf. EN1 ... **44** A6
★ **Bentley Priory Open Space**, Stan. HA7 ... **52** C4
Bentley Rd, N1
off Tottenham Rd ... **94** B6
Bentley Way, Stan. HA7 ... **52** D5
Woodford Green IG8 ... **63** G3
Benton Rd, Ilf. IG1 ... **99** G1
Watford WD19 ... **50** D5
Bentons La, SE27 ... **169** J4
Bentons Ri, SE27 ... **170** A5
Bentry Cl, Dag. RM8 ... **101** E2
Bentry Rd, Dag. RM8 ... **101** E2
Bentworth Rd, W12 ... **107** H6
Benville Ho, SW8
off Oval Pl ... **131** F7
Benwell Ct, Sun. TW16 ... **178** A1
Benwell Rd, N7 ... **93** G4
Benwick Cl, SE16
off Aspinden Rd ... **133** E4
Benworth St, E3 ... **113** J3
Benyon Rd, N1
off Southgate Rd ... **112** A1
Benyon Wf, E8
off Kingsland Rd ... **112** B1
Berberis Ho, Felt. TW13
off Highfield Rd ... **160** A2
Berberis Wk, West Dr. UB7 ... **120** B4
Berber Pl, E14
off Birchfield St ... **114** A7
Berber Rd, SW11 ... **149** J5
Berberry Cl, Edg. HA8
off Larkspur Gro ... **54** C4
Bercta Rd, SE9 ... **175** F2
Berengers Pl, Dagenham RM9 ... **100** B6
Berenger Twr, SW10
off Blantyre St ... **31** E7
Berenger Wk, SW10
off Blantyre St ... **30** E7
Berens Rd, NW10 ... **108** A3
Berens Way, Chis. BR7 ... **193** J4
Beresford Av, N20 ... **57** J2
W7 ... **104** A5
Surbiton KT5 ... **196** B1
Twickenham TW1 ... **145** F6
Wembley HA0 ... **105** J1
Beresford Dr, Brom. BR1 ... **192** B3
Woodford Green IG8 ... **63** J4
Beresford Gdns, Enf. EN1 ... **44** B4
Hounslow TW4 ... **143** F5
Romford RM6 ... **83** E5
Beresford Rd, E4 ... **62** E1
E17 ... **78** B1
N2 ... **73** H3
N5 ... **93** J5
N8 ... **75** G5
Harrow HA1 ... **68** A5
Kingston upon Thames KT2 ... **181** J1
New Malden KT3 ... **182** C4
Southall UB1 ... **122** D1
Sutton SM2 ... **198** C7
Beresford Sq, SE18 ... **136** E4
Beresford St, SE18 ... **136** E3
Beresford Ter, N5 ... **93** J5
Berestede Rd, W6 ... **127** F5
Bere St, E1
off Cranford St ... **113** G7
Bergenia Ho, Felt. TW13
off Bedfont La ... **160** B1
Bergen Sq, SE16
off Norway Gate ... **133** H3
Berger Cl, Orp. BR5 ... **193** G6
Berger Rd, E9 ... **95** G6
Berghem Ms, W14
off Blythe Rd ... **128** A3
Bergholt Av, Ilf. IG4 ... **80** B5
Bergholt Cres, N16 ... **76** B7
Bergholt Ms, NW1
off Rossendale Way ... **92** C7
Berglen Ct, E14
off Branch Rd ... **113** H6
Bering Sq, E14
off Napier Av ... **134** A5
Bering Wk, E16 ... **116** A6
Berisford Ms, SW18 ... **149** E6
Berkeley Av, Bexh. DA7 ... **158** D1
Greenford UB6 ... **86** B6
Hounslow TW4 ... **142** A2
Ilford IG5 ... **80** D2
Berkeley Cl, Borwd. (Els.) WD6 ... **38** A5
Kingston upon Thames KT2 ... **163** H7
Orpington BR5 ... **193** H7
Ruislip HA4 ... **84** A3
Berkeley Ct, N14 ... **42** C6
Wallington SM6 ... **200** C3
Berkeley Cres, Barn. EN4 ... **41** G5
Berkeley Dr, W.Mol. KT8 ... **179** F3
Berkeley Gdns, N21 ... **44** A7
W8
off Brunswick Gdns ... **128** D1
Esher (Clay.) KT10 ... **194** D6
Berkeley Ho, E3 ... **113** J4
Berkeley Ms, W1 ... **16** A3
Berkeley Pl, SW19 ... **166** A6
Berkeley Rd, E12 ... **98** B5
N8 ... **74** D5
N15 ... **76** A6
NW9 ... **70** A4
SW13 ... **147** G1
Berkeley Sq, W1 ... **16** E6
Berkeley St, W1 ... **17** E6
Berkeley Twr, E14
off Westferry Circ ... **133** J1
Berkeley Wk, N7
off Durham Rd ... **93** F2
Berkeley Waye, Houns. TW5 ... **122** D7
Berkerley Ms, Sun. TW16
off Thames St ... **178** C3
Berkhampstead Rd, Belv. DA17 ... **139** G5
Berkhamsted Av, Wem. HA9 ... **87** J6
Berkley Gro, NW1
off Berkley Rd ... **92** A7
Berkley Rd, NW1 ... **91** J7
Berkshire Gdns, N13 ... **59** G6
N18 ... **60** E5
Berkshire Rd, E9 ... **95** J6
Berkshire Sq, Mitch. CR4
off Berkshire Way ... **187** E4
Berkshire Way, Mitch. CR4 ... **186** E4
Bermans Way, NW10 ... **89** E4
BERMONDSEY, SE1 ... **29** F6
Bermondsey Sq, SE1 ... **28** E5
Bermondsey St, SE1 ... **28** D2
Bermondsey Wall E, SE16 ... **29** J4
Bermondsey Wall W, SE16 ... **29** H3
Bernal Cl, SE28
off Haldane Rd ... **118** D7
Bernard Ashley Dr, SE7 ... **135** H5
Bernard Av, W13 ... **125** E3
Bernard Cassidy St, E16 ... **115** F5
Bernard Gdns, SW19 ... **166** C5
Bernard Rd, N15 ... **76** C5
Romford RM7 ... **83** J7
Wallington SM6 ... **200** B4
Bernards Cl, Ilf. IG6 ... **65** F6
Bernard Shaw Ho, NW10
off Knatchbull Rd ... **106** D1
Bernard St, WC1 ... **10** A6
Bernays Cl, Stan. HA7 ... **53** F6
Bernays Gro, SW9 ... **151** F4
Bernel Dr, Croy. CR0 ... **203** J3
Berne Rd, Th.Hth. CR7 ... **187** J5
Berners Dr, W13 ... **104** D6
Bernersmede, SE3 ... **155** G3
Berners Ms, W1 ... **17** G2
Berners Pl, W1 ... **17** G3
Berners Rd, N1 ... **11** F1
N22 ... **75** G1
Berners St, W1 ... **17** G2
Berney Rd, Croy. CR0 ... **188** A7
Bernhardt Cres, NW8 ... **7** G5
Bernhart Cl, Edg. HA8 ... **54** C7
Bernville Way, Har. HA3
off Orchard Gro ... **69** J5
Bernwell Rd, E4 ... **63** E3
Berridge Grn, Edg. HA8 ... **54** A7
Berridge Ms, NW6
off Hillfield Rd ... **90** D5
Berridge Rd, SE19 ... **170** B5
Berriman Rd, N7 ... **93** F3
Berriton Rd, Har. HA2 ... **85** F1
Berrybank Cl, E4
off Greenbank Cl ... **62** C2
Berry Cl, N21 ... **59** H1
Dagenham RM10 ... **101** G5
Berry Ct, Houns. TW4
off Raglan Cl ... **143** F5
Berrydale Rd, Hayes UB4 ... **102** E4
Berryfield Cl, E17 ... **78** B4
Bromley BR1 ... **192** B1
Berryfield Rd, SE17 ... **35** H3
Berryhill, SE9 ... **156** E4
Berry Hill, Stan. HA7 ... **53** G4
Berryhill Gdns, SE9 ... **156** E4
BERRYLANDS, Surb. KT5 ... **181** J5
Berrylands, SW20 ... **183** J3
Surbiton KT5 ... **182** A5
Berrylands Rd, Surb. KT5 ... **181** J6
Berry La, SE21 ... **170** A4
Berryman Cl, Dag. RM8
off Bennetts Castle La ... **100** C3
Berrymans La, SE26 ... **171** G4
Berrymead Gdns, W3 ... **126** C1
Berrymede Rd, W4 ... **126** D3
Berry Pl, EC1 ... **11** H4
Berry St, EC1 ... **11** H5
Berry Way, W5 ... **125** H3
Bertal Rd, SW17 ... **167** G4
Berthon St, SE8 ... **134** A7
Bertie Rd, NW10 ... **89** G6
SE26 ... **171** G6
Bertram Cotts, SW19 ... **166** D7
Bertram Rd, NW4 ... **71** G6
Enfield EN1 ... **44** D4
Kingston upon Thames KT2 ... **164** A7
Bertram St, N19 ... **92** B2
Bertram Way, Enf. EN1 ... **44** C4
Bertrand St, SE13 ... **154** B3
Bertrand Way, SE28 ... **118** B7
Bert Rd, Th.Hth. CR7 ... **187** J5
Berwick Av, Hayes UB4 ... **102** D6
Berwick Cl, Stan. HA7
off Gordon Av ... **52** C6
Twickenham TW2 ... **143** G7
Berwick Cres, Sid. DA15 ... **157** H6
Berwick Gdns, Sutt. SM1 ... **199** F3
Berwick Rd, E16 ... **115** H6
N22 ... **75** H1
Welling DA16 ... **158** B1
Berwick St, W1 ... **17** H4
Berwyn Av, Houns. TW3 ... **143** H1
Berwyn Rd, SE24 ... **169** H1
Richmond TW10 ... **146** B4
Beryl Av, E6 ... **116** B5
Beryl Ho, SE18
off Spinel Cl ... **137** J5
Beryl Rd, W6 ... **128** A5
Berystede, Kings.T. KT2 ... **164** B7
Besant Ct, N1
off Newington Grn Rd ... **94** A5
Besant Pl, SE22
off Hayes Gro ... **152** C4
Besant Rd, NW2 ... **90** B4
Besant Wk, N7
off Newington Barrow Way ... **93** F2
Besant Way, NW10 ... **88** C5
Besley St, SW16 ... **168** C6
Bessant Dr, Rich. TW9 ... **146** B1
Bessborough Gdns, SW1 ... **33** J3
Bessborough Pl, SW1 ... **33** H3
Bessborough Rd, SW15 ... **165** G1
Harrow HA1 ... **86** A1
Bessborough St, SW1 ... **33** H3
Bessemer Rd, SE5 ... **151** J2
Bessie Lansbury Cl, E6 ... **116** D6

Bessingby Rd, Ruis. HA4 ... **84** A2
Bessingham Wk, SE4
off Aldersford Cl ... **153** G5
Besson St, SE14 ... **153** F1
Bessy St, E2
off Roman Rd ... **113** F3
Bestwood St, SE8 ... **133** G4
Beswick Ms, NW6
off Dresden Cl ... **91** E6
Betam Rd, Hayes UB3 ... **121** G2
Beta Pl, SW4
off Santley St ... **151** F4
Betchworth Cl, Sutt. SM1
off St. Barnabas Rd ... **199** G5
Betchworth Rd, Ilf. IG3 ... **99** H2
Betham Rd, Grnf. UB6 ... **104** A3
Bethany Waye, Felt. TW14 ... **141** H7
Bethecar Rd, Har. HA1 ... **68** B5
Bethell Av, E16 ... **115** F4
Ilford IG1 ... **80** D7
Bethel Rd, Well. DA16 ... **158** C3
Bethersden Cl, Beck. BR3 ... **171** J7
BETHNAL GREEN, E2 ... **112** D2
Bethnal Grn Est, E2
off Roman Rd ... **113** F3
Bethnal Grn Rd, E1 ... **13** F5
E2 ... **13** F5
Bethune Av, N11 ... **57** J4
Bethune Rd, N16 ... **76** A7
NW10 ... **106** D4
Bethwin Rd, SE5 ... **35** H7
Betjeman Cl, Pnr. HA5 ... **67** G4
Betjeman Ct, West Dr. UB7 **120** A1
Betony Cl, Croy. CR0
off Primrose La ... **203** G1
Betoyne Av, E4 ... **62** E4
Betstyle Rd, N11 ... **58** B4
Betterton Dr, Sid. DA14 ... **177** E2
Betterton St, WC2 ... **18** A4
Bettons Pk, E15 ... **115** E1
Bettridge Rd, SW6 ... **148** C2
Betts Cl, Beck. BR3 ... **189** H2
Betts Ms, E17
off Ringwood Rd ... **77** J6
Betts St, E1
off The Highway ... **112** E7
Betts Way, SE20 ... **189** E1
Surbiton (Long Dit.) KT6 ... **195** E1
Beulah Av, Th.Hth. CR7
off Beulah Rd ... **187** J2
Beulah Cl, Edg. HA8 ... **54** B3
Beulah Cres, Th.Hth. CR7 ... **187** J2
Beulah Gro, Croy. CR0 ... **187** J6
Beulah Hill, SE19 ... **169** H6
Beulah Path, E17
off Addison Rd ... **78** B5
Beulah Rd, E17 ... **78** B5
SW19 ... **166** C7
Sutton SM1 ... **198** D4
Thornton Heath CR7 ... **187** J3
Bevan Av, Bark. IG11 ... **100** A7
Bevan Ct, Croy. CR0 ... **201** G5
Bevan Rd, SE2 ... **138** B5
Barnet EN4 ... **41** J4
Bevan St, N1 ... **111** J1
Bev Callender Cl, SW8
off Daley Thompson Way ... **150** B3
Bevenden St, N1 ... **12** C3
Bevercote Wk, Belv. DA17
off Osborne Rd ... **139** F6
Beveridge Rd, NW10 ... **89** E7
Beverley Av, SW20 ... **183** F1
Hounslow TW4 ... **143** F4
Sidcup DA15 ... **157** J7
Beverley Cl, N21 ... **59** J1
SW11
off Maysoule Rd ... **149** G4
SW13 ... **147** F2
Chessington KT9 ... **195** F4
Enfield EN1 ... **44** B4
Beverley Cotts, SW15
off Kingston Vale ... **165** E3
Beverley Ct, N14 ... **42** C7
N20 *off Farnham Cl* ... **41** F7
SE4 ... **153** J3
Beverley Cres, Wdf.Grn. IG8 ... **79** H1
Beverley Dr, Edg. HA8 ... **70** B3
Beverley Gdns, NW11 ... **72** B7
SW13 ... **147** F3
Stanmore HA7 ... **68** D1
Wembley HA9 ... **87** J1
Worcester Park KT4
off Green La ... **197** G1
Beverley La, SW15 ... **165** F3
Kingston upon Thames KT2 ... **165** E7
Beverley Ms, E4
off Beverley Rd ... **62** D6
Beverley Path, SW13 ... **147** F2
Beverley Rd, E4 ... **62** D6
E6 ... **116** A3
SE20 *off Wadhurst Cl* ... **188** E2
Beverley Rd, SW13 ... **147** F3
W4 ... **127** F5
Bexleyheath DA7 ... **159** J2
Bromley BR2 ... **206** B2
Dagenham RM9 ... **101** E4
Kingston upon Thames KT1 ... **181** F1
Beverley Rd, Mitcham CR4 ... **186** D4
New Malden KT3 ... **183** G4
Ruislip HA4 ... **84** A2
Southall UB2 ... **123** E3
Worcester Park KT4 ... **197** J2
Beverley Trd Est, Mord. SM4 *off Garth Rd* ... **184** A7
Beverley Way, SW20 ... **183** F1
New Malden KT3 ... **183** F1
Beverly, NW8 ... **7** G4
Beversbrook Rd, N19 ... **92** D3
Beverstone Rd, SW2 ... **151** F5
Thornton Heath CR7 ... **187** G4
Beverston Ms, W1 ... **15** J2
Bevill Allen Cl, SW17 ... **167** J5
Bevill Cl, SE25 ... **188** D3
Bevin Cl, SE16
off Stave Yd Rd ... **133** H1
Bevin Ct, WC1 ... **10** D3
Bevington Path, SE1
off Tanner St ... **29** F4
Bevington Rd, W10 ... **108** B5
Beckenham BR3 ... **190** B2
Bevington St, SE16 ... **29** J4
Bevin Rd, Hayes UB4 ... **102** A3
Bevin Sq, SW17 ... **167** J3
Bevin Way, WC1 ... **10** E3
Bevis Marks, EC3 ... **20** E3
Bewcastle Gdns, Enf. EN2 ... **43** E4
Bew Ct, SE22
off Lordship La ... **152** D7
Bewdley St, N1 ... **93** G7
Bewick Ms, SE15 ... **132** E7
Bewick St, SW8 ... **150** B2
Bewley St, E1
off Cable St ... **113** E7
SW19 ... **167** F6
Bewlys Rd, SE27 ... **169** H5
Bexhill Cl, Felt. TW13 ... **160** E2
Bexhill Rd, N11 ... **58** D5
SE4 ... **153** J7
SW14 ... **146** C3
Bexhill Wk, E15
off Mitre Rd ... **115** E1
BEXLEY, DA5 ... **159** G6
Bexley Gdns, N9 ... **60** A3
Romford (Chad.Hth) RM6 ... **82** B5
BEXLEYHEATH, DA6 & DA7 ... **159** F5
Bexley High St, Bex. DA5 ... **159** G7
Bexley La, Sid. DA14 ... **176** C3
Bexley Rd, SE9 ... **156** E5
Erith DA8 ... **139** J7
Beynon Rd, Cars. SM5 ... **199** J5
Bianca Rd, SE15 ... **37** H6
Bibsworth Rd, N3 ... **72** C2
Bibury Cl, SE15 ... **37** E6
Bicester Rd, Rich. TW9 ... **146** A3
Bickenhall St, W1 ... **16** A1
Bickersteth Rd, SW17 ... **167** J6
Bickerton Rd, N19 ... **92** C2
BICKLEY, Brom. BR1 ... **192** C3
Bickley Cres, Bromley BR1 ... **192** B4
Bickley Pk Rd, Brom. BR1 ... **192** B3
Bickley Rd, E10 ... **78** B7
Bromley BR1 ... **192** A2
Bickley St, SW17 ... **167** H5
Bicknell Rd, SE5 ... **151** J3
Bicknoller Rd, Enf. EN1 ... **44** C1
Bicknor Rd, Orp. BR6 ... **193** H7
Bidborough Cl, Brom. BR2 ... **191** F5
Bidborough St, WC1 ... **10** A4
Biddenden Way, SE9 ... **174** D4
Bidder St, E16 ... **114** E5
Biddestone Rd, N7 ... **93** F4
Biddulph Rd, W9 ... **6** A4
Bideford Av, Grnf. (Perivale) UB6 ... **104** E2
Bideford Cl, Edg. HA8 ... **70** A1
Feltham TW13 ... **161** F3
Bideford Gdns, Enf. EN1 ... **44** B7
Bideford Rd, Brom. BR1 ... **173** F3
Ruislip HA4 ... **84** B3
Welling DA16 ... **138** B7
Bidwell Gdns, N11 ... **58** C7
Bidwell St, SE15 ... **153** E1
★ **Big Ben** (St. Stephens Twr), SW1 ... **26** B4
Bigbury Cl, N17 ... **60** B7
Biggerstaff Rd, E15 ... **114** C1
Biggerstaff St, N4 ... **93** G2
Biggin Av, Mitch. CR4 ... **185** J1
Biggin Hill, SE19 ... **169** H7
Biggin Hill Cl, Kings.T. KT2 ... **163** F5
Biggin Way, SE19 ... **169** H7
Bigginwood Rd, SW16 ... **169** H7
Biggs Row, SW15
off Felsham Rd ... **148** A3
Big Hill, E5 ... **95** E1
Bigland St, E1 ... **112** E6
Bignell Rd, SE18 ... **136** E5
Bignold Rd, E7 ... **97** G4
Bigwood Rd, NW11 ... **72** E5
Billet Cl, Rom. RM6 ... **82** D3
Billet Rd, E17 ... **77** G2
Romford RM6 ... **82** B3
Billets Hart Cl, W7 ... **124** B2
Billet Wks, E17 ... **77** J1
Bill Faust Ho, E1
off Tarling St ... **113** F6
Bill Hamling Cl, SE9 ... **174** C2
Billingford Cl, SE4 ... **153** G4
Billing Pl, SW10 ... **30** B7
Billing Rd, SW10 ... **30** B7
Billings Cl, Dag. RM9
off Ellerton Rd ... **100** C7
★ **Billingsgate Mkt**, E14 ... **134** B1
Billing St, SW10 ... **30** B7
Billington Ms, W3
off High St ... **126** B1
Billington Rd, SE14 ... **133** G7
Billinton Hill, Croy. CR0 ... **202** A2
Billiter Sq, EC3 ... **20** E5
Billiter St, EC3 ... **20** E4
Bill Nicholson Way, N17
off High Rd ... **60** C7
Billockby Cl, Chess. KT9 ... **195** J6
Billson St, E14 ... **134** C4
Bilsby Gro, SE9 ... **174** A4
Bilton Rd, Grnf. UB6 ... **105** E1
Bilton Twrs, W1
off Great Cumberland Pl ... **16** A4
Bilton Way, Enf. EN3 ... **45** H1
Hayes UB3 ... **122** B2
Bina Gdns, SW5 ... **30** C2
Bincote Rd, Enf. EN2 ... **43** F3
Binden Rd, W12 ... **127** F3
Bindon Grn, Mord. SM4 ... **185** E4
Binfield Rd, SW4 ... **151** E1
South Croydon CR2 ... **202** C5
Bingfield St, N1 ... **111** E1
Bingham Ct, N1
off Halton Rd ... **93** H7
Bingham Pl, W1 ... **16** B1
Bingham Pt, SE18
off Wilmount St ... **137** E4
Bingham Rd, Croy. CR0 ... **202** D1
Bingham St, N1 ... **94** A6
Bingley Rd, E16 ... **115** J6
Greenford UB6 ... **103** J5
Sunbury-on-Thames TW16 ... **160** A7
Binley Ho, SW15
off Highcliffe Dr ... **147** G6
Binne Ho, SE1
off Bath Ter ... **27** J6
Binney St, W1 ... **16** C5
Binns Rd, W4 ... **126** E5
Binns Ter, W4
off Binns Rd ... **126** E5
Binsey Wk, SE2 ... **138** C1
Binstead Cl, Hayes UB4 ... **102** E5
Binyon Cres, Stan. HA7 ... **52** C5
Birbetts Rd, SE9 ... **174** C2
Bircham Path, SE4
off Aldersford Cl ... **153** G5
Birchanger Rd, SE25 ... **188** D5
Birch Av, N13 ... **59** J3
Birch Cl, E16 ... **115** E5
N19 *off Hargrave Pk* ... **92** C2
SE15
off Bournemouth Rd ... **152** D2
Brentford TW8 ... **124** E7
Buckhurst Hill IG9 ... **64** A3
Hounslow TW3 ... **144** A3
Romford RM7 ... **83** H3
Teddington TW11 ... **162** D5
Birchdale Gdns, Rom. RM6 ... **82** D7
Birchdale Rd, E7 ... **97** J5
Birchdene Dr, SE28 ... **138** A2
Birchdown Ho, E3
off Rainhill Way ... **114** B3
Birchen Cl, NW9 ... **88** D2
Birchend Cl, S.Croy. CR2 ... **202** A6
Birchen Gro, NW9 ... **88** D2
Birches, The, E12
off Station Rd ... **98** B4
N21 ... **43** F6
SE7 ... **135** H6
Orpington BR6 ... **206** D4
Birches Cl, Mitch. CR4 ... **185** J3
Pinner HA5 ... **66** E5
Birchfield St, E14 ... **114** A7
Birch Gdns, Dag. RM10 ... **101** J3
Birch Grn, NW9
off Clayton Fld ... **55** E7
Birch Gro, E11 ... **96** E3
SE12 ... **155** F7
W3 ... **126** A1
Welling DA16 ... **158** A4
Birchgrove Ho, Rich. TW9 ... **126** B7
Birch Hill, Croy. CR0 ... **203** G5
Birchington Cl, Bexh. DA7 ... **159** H1
Birchington Ho, E5
off Pembury Rd ... **94** E5
Birchington Rd, N8 ... **74** D6
NW6 ... **108** D1
Surbiton KT5 ... **181** J7
Birchin La, EC3 ... **20** C4
Birchlands Av, SW12 ... **149** J7
Birchmead, Orp. BR6 ... **206** D2
Birchmead Av, Pnr. HA5 ... **66** C4
Birchmere Business Pk, SE28 ... **138** A2
Birchmere Row, SE3 ... **155** F2
Birchmore Wk, N5 ... **93** J3
Birch Pk, Har. HA3 ... **51** J7
Birch Rd, Felt. TW13 ... **160** D5
Romford RM7 ... **83** H3
Birch Row, Brom. BR2 ... **192** D7
Birch Tree Av, W.Wick. BR4 ... **205** F5
Birch Tree Way, Croy. CR0 ... **202** E2
Birchville Ct, Bushey (Bushey Hth) WD23
off Heathbourne Rd ... **52** B1
Birch Wk, Borwd. WD6 ... **38** A1
Erith DA8 ... **139** J6
Mitcham CR4 ... **186** B1
Birchway, Hayes UB3 ... **122** A1
Birchwood Av, N10 ... **74** A3
Beckenham BR3 ... **189** J4
Sidcup DA14 ... **176** B2
Wallington SM6 ... **200** A3
Birchwood Cl, Mord. SM4 ... **184** E4
Birchwood Ct, N13 ... **59** H5
Edgware HA8 ... **70** C2
Birchwood Dr, NW3 ... **91** E3
Birchwood Gro, Hmptn. TW12 ... **161** G6
Birchwood Rd, SW17 ... **168** B5
Orpington BR5 ... **193** G4
Birdbrook Cl, Dag. RM10 ... **101** J7
Birdbrook Rd, SE3 ... **155** J3
Birdcage Wk, SW1 ... **25** G4
Birdham Cl, Brom. BR1 ... **192** B5
Birdhurst Av, S.Croy. CR2 ... **202** A4
Birdhurst Gdns, S.Croy. CR2 ... **202** A4
Birdhurst Ri, S.Croy. CR2 ... **202** B5
Birdhurst Rd, SW18 ... **149** F4
SW19 ... **167** H6
South Croydon CR2 ... **202** B5
Bird in Bush Rd, SE15 ... **37** J7
Bird-in-Hand La, Brom. BR1 ... **192** A2
Bird-in-Hand Ms, SE23
off Dartmouth Rd ... **171** F2
Bird-in-Hand Pas, SE23
off Dartmouth Rd ... **171** F2
Bird in Hand Yd, NW3
off Hampstead High St ... **91** F4
Birds Fm Av, Rom. RM5 ... **83** H1
Birdsfield La, E3 ... **113** J1
Bird St, W1 ... **16** C4
Bird Wk, Twick. TW2 ... **161** F1
Birdwood Av, SE13 ... **154** D6
Birdwood Cl, Tedd. TW11 ... **162** B4
Birkbeck Av, W3 ... **106** C7
Greenford UB6 ... **103** J1
Birkbeck Gdns, Wdf.Grn. IG8 ... **63** F2
Birkbeck Gro, W3 ... **126** D2
Birkbeck Hill, SE21 ... **169** H2
Birkbeck Ms, E8
off Sandringham Rd ... **94** C5
W3 *off Birkbeck Rd* ... **126** D1
Birkbeck Pl, SE21 ... **169** J1
Birkbeck Rd, E8 ... **94** C5
N8 ... **75** E4
N12 ... **57** F5
N17 ... **76** C1
NW7 ... **55** F5
Birkbeck Rd, SW19 ... **167** E5
W3 ... **126** D1
W5 ... **125** F4
Beckenham BR3 ... **189** F2
Enfield EN2 ... **44** A1
Ilford IG2 ... **81** G5
Sidcup DA14 ... **176** A3
Birkbeck St, E2 ... **113** E3
Birkbeck Way, Grnf. UB6 ... **103** J1

Birkdale Av, Pnr. HA5 67 G3
Birkdale Cl, SE16
off Masters Dr 132 E5
SE28 118 D6
Orpington BR6 193 G7
Birkdale Gdns, Croy. CR0 203 G4
Watford WD19 50 D3
Birkdale Rd, SE2 138 A4
W5 105 H4
Birkenhead Av, Kings.T. KT2 181 J2
Birkenhead St, WC1 10 B3
Birkhall Rd, SE6 172 D1
Birkwood Cl, SW12 150 D7
Birley Rd, N20 57 F2
Birley St, SW11 150 A2
Birnam Rd, N4 93 F2
Birnbeck Cl, NW11 72 C5
Birnbeck Ct, NW11
off Finchley Rd 72 C5
Birrell Ho, SW9 151 F2
Birse Cres, NW10 89 E4
Birstall Grn, Wat. WD19 50 D4
Birstall Rd, N15 76 B5
Biscayne Av, E14
off Fairmont Av 114 D7
Biscay Rd, W6 128 A5
Biscoe Cl, Houns. TW5 123 G6
Biscoe Way, SE13 154 D3
Bisenden Rd, Croy. CR0 202 B2
Bisham Cl, Cars. SM5 199 J1
Bisham Gdns, N6 92 A1
Bishop Butt Cl, Orp. BR6 207 J3
Bishop Fox Way, W.Mol. KT8 179 F4
Bishop Ken Rd, Har. HA3 68 C2
Bishop Kings Rd, W14 128 B4
Bishop Rd, N14 42 B7
Bishop's Av, E13 115 H1
SW6 148 A2
Bishops Av, Brom. BR1 191 J2
Romford RM6 82 C6
Bishops Av, The, N2 73 G7
Bishops Br, W2 14 D3
Bishops Br Rd, W2 14 B4
Bishops Cl, E17 78 B4
Bishop's Cl, N19 92 C3
Bishops Cl, SE9 175 F2
W4 126 C5
Barnet EN5 40 A6
Enfield EN1
off Central Av 44 E2
Richmond TW10 163 G3
Bishop's Cl, Sutt. SM1 198 D3
Bishop's Ct, EC4 19 G3
WC2 18 E3
Bishops Dr, Felt. TW14 141 G6
Northolt UB5 103 E1
Bishopsford Rd, Mord. SM4 185 F7
Bishopsgate, EC2 20 D4
Bishopsgate Arc, EC2 20 E2
Bishopsgate Chyd, EC2 20 D2
Bishops Gro, N2 73 G6
Hampton TW12 161 F4
Bishop's Hall, Kings.T. KT1 181 G2
Bishops Hill, Walt. KT12 178 A7
Bishops Ho, SW8
off South Lambeth Rd 131 E7
Bishopsmead, SE5
off Camberwell Rd 131 J7
Bishop's Pk, SW6 148 A2
Bishop's Pk Rd, SW6 148 A2
Bishops Pk Rd, SW16 187 E1
Bishops Pl, Sutt. SM1
off Lind Rd 199 F5
Bishops Rd, N6 74 A6
SW6 148 C1
Bishop's Rd, SW11 31 H7
Bishops Rd, W7 124 B2
Croydon CR0 187 H7
Bishops Sq, E1 21 E1
Bishops Ter, SE11 35 F1
Bishopsthorpe Rd, SE26 171 G4
Bishop St, N1 111 J1
Bishops Wk, Chis. BR7 193 F1
Croydon CR0 203 G5
Bishop's Wk, Pnr. HA5
off High St 66 E3
Bishops Way, E2 113 E2
Bishopswood Rd, N6 73 J7
Bishop Wilfred Wd Cl, SE15
off Moncrieff St 152 D2
Bisley Cl, Wor.Pk. KT4 197 J1
Bisley Ho, SW19 166 A2
Bispham Rd, NW10 105 J3
Bisson Rd, E15 114 C2
Bisterne Av, E17 78 D3
Bittacy Busines Cen, NW7 56 B7
Bittacy Cl, NW7 56 A6
Bittacy Ct, NW7
off Bittacy Hill 56 B7
Bittacy Hill, NW7 56 A6
Bittacy Pk Av, NW7 56 A6
Bittacy Ri, NW7 55 J6
Bittacy Rd, NW7 56 A6
Bittern Cl, Hayes UB4 102 D5
Bittern Pl, N22 75 F2
Bittern St, SE1 27 J4
Bittoms, The, Kings.T. KT1 181 G3
Bixley Cl, Sthl. UB2 123 F4
Blackall St, EC2 12 D5
Blackberry Fm Cl, Houns. TW5 122 E7
Blackbird Hill, NW9 88 C2
Blackbird Yd, E2 13 G3
Blackborne Rd, Dag. RM10 101 G6
Black Boy La, N15 75 J5
Blackbrook La, Brom. BR1, BR2 192 D3
Black Bull Yd, EC1
off Hatton Wall 19 E1
Blackburne's Ms, W1 16 B5
Blackburn Rd, NW6 90 E6
Blackburn Trd Est, Stai. (Stanw.) TW19 140 C6
Blackburn Way, Houns. TW4 off Vickers Way 143 E5
Blackbush Av, Rom. RM6 82 D5
Blackbush Cl, Sutt. SM2 199 E7
Blackdown Cl, N2 73 F2
Blackdown Ter, SE18
off Prince Imperial Rd 136 C7
Blackett St, SW15 148 A3
Black Fan Cl, Enf. EN2 43 J1
BLACKFEN, Sid. DA15 157 J7
Blackfen Par, Sid. DA15
off Blackfen Rd 158 A6
Blackfen Rd, Sid. DA15 157 H5
Blackford Rd, Wat. WD19 50 D5
Blackford's Path, SW15
off Roehampton High St 147 G7
Blackfriars Br, EC4 19 G5
SE1 19 G5
Blackfriars Ct, EC4 19 G5
Black Friars La, EC4 19 G5
Blackfriars Pas, EC4 19 G5
Blackfriars Rd, SE1 27 G4
Black Gates, Pnr. HA5
off Moss La 67 F3
BLACKHEATH, SE3 155 E1
★ Blackheath, SE3 154 D1
Blackheath Av, SE10 134 D7
Blackheath Gro, SE3 155 F2
Blackheath Hill, SE10 154 C1
BLACKHEATH PARK, SE3 155 F4
Blackheath Pk, SE3 155 F3
Blackheath Ri, SE13 154 C2
Blackheath Rd, SE10 154 B1
Blackheath Vale, SE3 155 E2
Blackheath Village, SE3 155 F2
Black Horse Ct, SE1 28 C5
Blackhorse La, E17 77 G3
Croydon CR0 188 D7
Blackhorse Ms, E17
off Blackhorse La 77 G3
Blackhorse Rd, E17 77 G4
SE8 133 H5
Sidcup DA14 176 A4
Blacklands Rd, SE6 172 C4
Blacklands Ter, SW3 31 J2
Black Lion La, W6 127 G4
Black Lion Ms, W6
off Black Lion La 127 G4
Blackmore Av, Sthl. UB1 124 A1
Blackmore Dr, NW10 88 B7
Blackmore Rd, Buck.H. IG9 48 B7
Blackmores Gro, Tedd. TW11 162 D6
Blackmore Twr, W3
off Stanley Rd 126 C3
Black Path, E10 77 G7
Blackpool Rd, SE15 152 E2
Black Prince Interchange, Bex. DA5 off East Rochester Way 159 H6
Black Prince Rd, SE1 34 C2
SE11 34 D2
Black Rod Cl, Hayes UB3 121 J3
Blackshaw Rd, SW17 167 F4
Blacksmiths Cl, Rom. RM6 82 C6
Blacks Rd, W6
off Queen Caroline St 127 J4
Blackstock Ms, N4
off Blackstock Rd 93 H2
Blackstock Rd, N4 93 H2
N5 93 H2
Blackstone Est, E8 94 D7
Blackstone Ho, SW1
off Churchill Gdns 33 F4
Blackstone Rd, NW2 89 J5
Black Swan Yd, SE1 28 D3
Blackthorn Av, West Dr. UB7 120 D4
Blackthorn Ct, Houns. TW5 122 E7
Blackthorne Av, Croy. CR0 189 F7
Blackthorne Dr, E4 62 D4
Blackthorn Gro, Bexh. DA7 158 D3
Blackthorn Rd, Ilf. IG1 99 G5
Blackthorn St, E3 114 A4
Blacktree Ms, SW9 151 G3
Blackwall La, SE10 135 E5
Blackwall Pier, E14 114 E7
Blackwall Trd Est, E14 114 D5
Blackwall Tunnel, E14 134 D1
Blackwall Tunnel App, SE10 134 E2
Blackwall Tunnel Northern App, E3 114 A2
E14 114 A2
Blackwall Way, E14 114 C7
Blackwater Cl, E7 97 F4
Blackwater Rd, Sutt. SM1
off High St 199 E4
Blackwater St, SE22 152 C5
Blackwell Cl, E5 95 G4
Harrow HA3 52 A7
Blackwell Gdns, Edg. HA8 54 A3
Blackwood Av, N18
off Harbet Rd 61 G5
Blackwood St, SE17 36 B3
Blade Ms, SW15
off Deodar Rd 148 C4
Blades Ct, SW15
off Deodar Rd 148 C4
Bladindon Dr, Bex. DA5 158 C7
Bladon Gdns, Har. HA2 67 H6
Blagdens Cl, N14 58 C2
Blagdens La, N14 58 D2
Blagdon Rd, SE13 154 B6
New Malden KT3 183 F4
Blagdon Wk, Tedd. TW11 163 F6
Blagrove Rd, W10 108 B5
Blair Av, NW9 70 E7
Blair Cl, N1 93 J6
Hayes UB3 122 A4
Sidcup DA15 157 H5
Blairderry Rd, SW2 169 E2
Blairhead Dr, Wat. WD19 50 B3
Blair Ho, SW9
off Stockwell Gdns 151 F2
Blair St, E14 114 C6
Blake Apts, N8
off New River Av 75 F3
Blake Av, Bark. IG11 117 H1
Blake Cl, W10 107 J5
Carshalton SM5 185 H7
Welling DA16 157 H1
Blakeden Dr, Esher (Clay.) KT10 194 C6
Blake Gdns, SW6 148 E1
Blake Hall Cres, E11 97 G1
Blake Hall Rd, E11 79 G7
Blakehall Rd, Cars. SM5 199 J6
Blake Ho, Beck. BR3 172 A6
Blake Ms, Rich. TW9
off High Pk Rd 146 A1
Blakemore Gdns, SW13
off Lonsdale Rd 127 H6
Blakemore Rd, SW16 168 E3
Thornton Heath CR7 187 F5
Blakemore Way, Belv. DA17 139 E3
Blakeney Av, Beck. BR3 189 J1
Blakeney Cl, E8
off Ferncliff Rd 94 D5
N20 57 F1
Blakeney Cl, NW1
off Rossendale Way 92 D7
Blakeney Rd, Beck. BR3 171 J7
Blakenham Rd, SW17 167 J4
Blaker Ct, SE7
off Fairlawn 135 J7
Blake Rd, E16 115 F4
N11 58 C7
Croydon CR0 202 B2
Mitcham CR4 185 H3
Blaker Rd, E15 114 C1
Blakes Av, N.Mal. KT3 183 F5
Blake's Grn, W.Wick. BR4 204 C1
Blakes La, N.Mal. KT3 183 F5
Blakesley Av, W5 105 F6
Blakesley Ho, E12
off Grantham Rd 98 D3
Blakesley Wk, SW20
off Kingston Rd 184 C2
Blakes Rd, SE15 36 E7
Blakes Ter, N.Mal. KT3 183 G5
Blake St, SE8
off Watergate St 134 A6
Blakesware Gdns, N9 44 A7
Blakewood Cl, Felt. TW13 160 C4
Blanchard Cl, SE9 174 B3
Blanchard Way, E8 94 D6
Blanch Cl, SE15
off Culmore Rd 133 F7
Blanchedowne, SE5 152 A4
Blanche St, E16 115 F4
Blanchland Rd, Mord. SM4 184 E5
Blandfield Rd, SW12 150 A6
Blandford Av, Beck. BR3 189 H2
Twickenham TW2 161 H1
Blandford Cl, N2 73 F4
Croydon CR0 201 E3
Romford RM7 83 H4
Blandford Cres, E4 46 C7
Blandford Rd, W4 126 E3
W5 125 G2
Beckenham BR3 189 F2
Southall UB2 123 G4
Teddington TW11 162 A5
Blandford Sq, NW1 7 H6
Blandford St, W1 16 A3
Blandford Waye, Hayes UB4 102 C6
Bland St, SE9 156 A4
Blaney Cres, E6 116 E3
Blanmerle Rd, SE9 174 E1
Blann Cl, SE9 156 A6
Blantyre St, SW10 30 E7
Blantyre Twr, SW10 30 E7
Blantyre Wk, SW10
off Blantyre St 30 E7
Blashford, NW3 91 J7
Blashford St, SE13 154 D7
Blasker Wk, E14 134 A5
Blawith Rd, Har. HA1 68 B4
Blaydon Cl, N17 60 E7
Blaydon Wk, N17 60 E7
Bleak Hill La, SE18 137 J6
Blean Gro, SE20 171 F7
Bleasdale Av, Grnf. (Perivale) UB6 104 D2
Blechynden St, W10
off Bramley Rd 108 A7
Bleddyn Cl, Sid. DA15 158 C6
Bledlow Cl, NW8 7 F6
SE28 118 C7
Bledlow Ri, Grnf. UB6 103 J2
Bleeding Heart Yd, EC1 19 F2
Blegborough Rd, SW16 168 C6
Blemundsbury, WC1
off Dombey St 18 C1
Blendon Dr, Bex. DA5 158 D6
Blendon Path, Brom. BR1
off Hope Pk 173 F7
Blendon Rd, Bex. DA5 158 D6
Blendon Ter, SE18 137 F5
Blendworth Pt, SW15
off Wanborough Dr 165 H1
Blenheim Av, Ilf. IG2 80 D6
Blenheim Cen, The, Houns. TW3
off Prince Regent Rd 143 H3
Blenheim Cl, N21
off Elm Pk Rd 59 J1
SE12 173 H1
SW20 183 J3
Enfield EN2 59 J1
Greenford UB6
off Leaver Gdns 104 A2
Romford RM7 83 J4
Wallington SM6 200 C7
Blenheim Ct, N19 92 E2
Bromley BR2
off Durham Av 191 F4
Sidcup DA14 175 G3
Blenheim Ct, Sutton SM2
off Wellesley Rd 199 F6
Woodford Green IG8
off Navestock Cres 63 J7
Blenheim Cres, W11 108 B6
South Croydon CR2 201 J7
Blenheim Dr, Welling DA16 157 J1
Blenheim Gdns, NW2 89 J5
SW2 151 F6
Kingston upon Thames KT2 164 B7
Wallington SM6 200 C6
Wembley HA9 87 H3
Blenheim Gro, SE15 152 D2
Blenheim Pas, NW8 6 C1
Blenheim Pl, Tedd. TW11 162 C5
Blenheim Ri, N15 76 C4
Blenheim Rd, E6 116 A3
E15 97 E4
E17 77 G3
NW8 6 C1
SE20 off Maple Rd 171 F7
SW20 183 J3
W4 126 E3
Barnet EN5 40 A3
Bromley BR1 192 B4
Harrow HA2 67 H6
Northolt UB5 85 H6
Sidcup DA15 176 C1
Sutton SM1 198 D3

Blenheim Shop Cen, SE20 **171** F7
Blenheim St, W1 **16** D4
Blenheim Ter, NW8 **6** C1
Blenheim Way, Islw. TW7 **144** D1
Blenkarne Rd, SW11 **149** J6
Bleriot Rd, Houns. TW5 **122** C7
Blessbury Rd, Edg. HA8 **70** C1
Blessington Cl, SE13 **154** D3
Blessington Rd, SE13 **154** D3
Blessing Way, Bark. IG11 **118** C3
Bletchingley Cl, Th.Hth. CR7 **187** H4
Bletchley Ct, N1 **12** B2
Bletchley St, N1 **12** A2
Bletchmore Cl, Hayes (Harling.) UB3 **121** G5
Bletsoe Wk, N1 **12** A1
Blewbury Ho, SE2 *off Yarnton Way* **138** D2
Blincoe Cl, SW19 **166** A2
Blind La, Loug. (High Beach) IG10 **46** E2
Bliss Cres, SE13 **154** B2
Blissett St, SE10 **154** C1
Bliss Ms, W10 *off Third Av* **108** B3
Blisworth Cl, Hayes UB4 *off Braunston Dr* **103** E4
Blithbury Rd, Dag. RM9 **100** B6
Blithdale Rd, SE2 **138** A4
Blithfield St, W8 **22** A6
Blockley Rd, Wem. HA0 **86** E2
Bloemfontein Av, W12 **127** H1
Bloemfontein Rd, W12 **107** H7
Bloemfontein Way, W12 *off Bloemfontein Rd* **127** H1
Blomfield Ct, SW11 *off Westbridge Rd* **149** H1
Blomfield Ms, W2 **14** C2
Blomfield Rd, W9 **14** C1
Blomfield St, EC2 **20** C2
Blomfield Vil, W2 **14** B2
Blomville Rd, Dag. RM8 **101** E3
Blondell Cl, West Dr. (Harm.) UB7 **120** A6
Blondel St, SW11 **150** A2
Blondin Av, W5 **125** F4
Blondin St, E3 **114** A2
Bloomburg St, SW1 **33** G2
Bloomfield Ct, E10 *off Brisbane Rd* **96** B3
Bloomfield Cres, Ilf. IG2 **81** E6
Bloomfield Pl, W1 **16** E5
Bloomfield Rd, N6 **74** A6
SE18 **137** E5
Bromley BR2 **192** A5
Kingston upon Thames KT1 **181** H4
Bloomfield Ter, SW1 **32** C3
Bloom Gro, SE27 **169** H3
Bloomhall Rd, SE19 **170** A5
Bloom Pk Rd, SW6 **128** C7
BLOOMSBURY, WC1 **17** J2
Bloomsbury Cl, NW7 **55** G7
W5 **105** J7
Bloomsbury Ct, WC1 **18** B2
Pinner HA5 **67** F3
Bloomsbury Ho, SW4 **150** D6
Bloomsbury Ms, Wdf.Grn. IG8 *off Waltham Rd* **64** B6
Bloomsbury Pl, SW18 *off Fullerton Rd* **149** F5
WC1 **18** B1
Bloomsbury Sq, WC1 **18** B2
Bloomsbury St, WC1 **17** J2
Bloomsbury Way, WC1 **18** A3
Blore Cl, SW8 *off Thessaly Rd* **150** D1
Blore Ct, W1 **17** H4
Blossom Cl, W5 **125** H2
Dagenham RM9 **119** F1
South Croydon CR2 **202** C5
Blossom La, Enf. EN2 **43** J1
Blossom St, E1 **21** E1
Blossom Way, West Dr. UB7 **120** D4
Blossom Waye, Houns. TW5 **122** E7
Blount St, E14 **113** H6
Bloxam Gdns, SE9 **156** B5
Bloxhall Rd, E10 **95** J1
Bloxham Cres, Hmptn. TW12 **161** F7
Bloxworth Cl, Wall. SM6 **200** C3
Blucher Rd, SE5 **131** J7
Blue Anchor All, Rich. TW9 *off Kew Rd* **145** H4
Blue Anchor La, SE16 **37** J1
Blue Anchor Yd, E1 **21** H5
Blue Ball Yd, SW1 **25** F2
Bluebell Av, E12 **98** A5
Bluebell Cl, E9 *off Moulins Rd* **113** F1
SE26 **170** C4
Northolt UB5 **85** F6
Bluebell Cl, Orp. BR6 **207** F2
Wallington SM6 **200** B1
Bluebell Way, Ilf. IG1 **98** E6
Blueberry Cl, Wdf.Grn. IG8 **63** G6
Bluebird La, Dag. RM10 **101** G7
Bluebird Way, SE28 **137** G2
Bluefield Cl, Hmptn. TW12 **161** G5
Bluegates, Epsom (Ewell) KT17 **197** G7
Bluehouse Rd, E4 **63** E3
Bluelion Pl, SE1 **28** D5
Blueprint Apts, SW12 *off Balham Gro* **150** B7
Bluewater Ho, SW18 *off Smugglers Way* **149** E4
Blundell Cl, E8 *off Amhurst Rd* **94** D4
Blundell Rd, Edg. HA8 **70** D1
Blundell St, N7 **92** E7
Blunden Cl, Dag. RM8 **100** C1
Blunt Rd, S.Croy. CR2 **202** A5
Blunts Av, West Dr. (Sipson) UB7 **120** D7
Blunts Rd, SE9 **156** D5
Blurton Rd, E5 **95** F4
Blyth Cl, E14 *off Manchester Rd* **134** D4
Twickenham TW1 *off Grimwood Rd* **144** C6
Blythe Cl, SE6 **153** J7
Blythe Hill, SE6 **153** J7
Orpington BR5 **193** J1
Blythe Hill La, SE6 **153** J7
Blythe Hill Pl, SE23 *off Brockley Pk* **153** H7
Blythe Ms, W14 *off Blythe Rd* **128** A3
Blythe Rd, W14 **128** A3
Blythe St, E2 **112** E3
Blytheswood Pl, SW16 *off Curtis Fld Rd* **169** F4
Blythe Vale, SE6 **171** J1
Blyth Rd, E17 **77** J7
SE28 **118** C7
Bromley BR1 **191** F1
Hayes UB3 **121** H2
Blyth's Wf, E14 *off Narrow St* **113** H7
Blythswood Rd, Ilford IG3 **100** A1
Blyth Wd Pk, Brom. BR1 *off Blyth Rd* **191** F1
Blythwood Rd, N4 **75** E7
Pinner HA5 **66** D1
Boades Ms, NW3 *off New End* **91** G4
Boadicea St, N1 *off Copenhagen St* **111** F1
Boakes Cl, NW9 **70** C4
Boardman Av, E4 **46** B5
Boardman Cl, Barn. EN5 **40** B5
Boardwalk Pl, E14 **134** C1
Boar's Head Yd, Brent. TW8 *off Brent Way* **125** G7
Boatemah Wk, SW9 *off Peckford Pl* **151** G2
Boathouse Wk, SE15 **37** G7
Richmond TW9 **145** H1
Boat Lifter Way, SE16 *off Sweden Gate* **133** H4
Bob Anker Cl, E13 *off Chesterton Rd* **115** G3
Bobbin Cl, SW4 **150** C3
Bobby Moore Way, N10 **57** J7
Bob Marley Way, SE24 *off Mayall Rd* **151** G4
Bockhampton Rd, Kings.T. KT2 **163** J7
Bocking St, E8 **112** E1
Boddicott Cl, SW19 **166** B2
Boddington Gdns, W3 **126** A2
Bodiam Cl, Enf. EN1 **44** A2
Bodiam Rd, SW16 **168** D7
Bodiam Way, NW10 **105** J3
Bodicea Ms, Houns. TW4 **143** F7
Bodley Cl, N.Mal. KT3 **182** E5
Bodley Manor Way, SW2 *off Hambridge Way* **151** G7
Bodley Rd, N.Mal. KT3 **182** D6
Bodmin Cl, Har. HA2 **85** F3
Bodmin Gro, Mord. SM4 **185** E5
Bodmin St, SW18 **166** D1
Bodnant Gdns, SW20 **183** G3
Bodney Rd, E8 **94** E5
Boeing Way, Sthl. UB2 **122** B3
Boevey Path, Belv. DA17 **139** F6
Bogey La, Orp. BR6 **206** D7
Bognor Gdns, Wat. WD19 **50** C5
Bognor Rd, Well. DA16 **158** D1
Bohemia Pl, E8 **95** E6
Bohn Rd, E1 **113** H5
Bohun Gro, Barn. EN4 **41** H6
Boileau Par, W5 *off Boileau Rd* **105** J6
Boileau Rd, SW13 **127** G7
W5 **105** J6
Bolden St, SE8 **154** B2
Bolderwood Way, W.Wick. BR4 **204** B2
Boldmere Rd, Pnr. HA5 **66** C7
Boleyn Av, Enf. EN1 **44** E1
Boleyn Cl, E17 **78** A4
Loughton IG10 *off Roding Gdns* **48** B6
Boleyn Ct, Buck.H. IG9 **63** G1
Boleyn Dr, Ruis. HA4 **84** D2
West Molesey KT8 **179** F3
Boleyn Gdns, Dag. RM10 **101** J7
West Wickham BR4 **204** B2
Boleyn Gro, W.Wick. BR4 **204** C2
Boleyn Rd, E6 **116** A2
E7 **97** G7
N16 **94** B5
Boleyn Way, Barn. EN5 **41** F3
Ilford IG6 **65** F6
Bolina Rd, SE16 **133** F5
Bolingbroke Gro, SW11 **149** H4
Bolingbroke Rd, W14 **128** A3
Bolingbroke Wk, SW11 **129** G7
Bolingbroke Way, Hayes UB3 **121** G1
Bolliger Ct, NW10 *off Park Royal Rd* **106** C4
Bollo Br Rd, W3 **126** B3
Bollo La, W3 **126** B2
W4 **126** C4
Bolney Gate, SW7 **23** G4
Bolney St, SW8 **131** F7
Bolney Way, Felt. TW13 **161** E3
Bolsover St, W1 **9** E6
Bolstead Rd, Mitch. CR4 **186** B1
Bolster Gro, N22 **58** D7
Bolt Ct, EC4 **19** F4
Boltmore Cl, NW4 **72** A3
Bolton Cl, SE20 *off Selby Rd* **188** D2
Chessington KT9 **195** G6
Bolton Cres, SE5 **35** F6
Bolton Dr, Mord. SM4 **185** F7
Bolton Gdns, NW10 **108** A2
SW5 **30** A3
Bromley BR1 **173** F6
Teddington TW11 **162** D6
Bolton Gdns Ms, SW10 **30** C3
Bolton Rd, E15 **97** F6
N18 **60** C5
NW8 **109** E1
NW10 **107** E1
W4 **126** C7
Chessington KT9 **195** G6
Harrow HA1 **67** J4
Boltons, The, SW10 **30** C3
Wembley HA0 **86** C4
Woodford Green IG8 **63** G4
Boltons La, Hayes (Harling.) UB3 **121** F7
Boltons Pl, SW5 **30** C3
Bolton St, W1 **24** E1
Bolton Wk, N7 *off Durham Rd* **93** F2
Bombay St, SE16 **132** E4
Bomer Cl, West Dr. (Sipson) UB7 **120** D7
Bomore Rd, W11 **108** A7
Bonar Pl, Chis. BR7 **174** B7
Bonar Rd, SE15 **132** D7
Bonchester Cl, Chis. BR7 **174** D7
Bonchurch Cl, Sutt. SM2 **199** E7
Bonchurch Rd, W10 **108** B5
W13 **124** E1
Bond Ct, EC4 **20** B4
Bondfield Av, Hayes UB4 **102** A3
Bondfield Rd, E6 *off Lovage App* **116** B5
Bond Gdns, Wall. SM6 **200** C4
Bonding Yd Wk, SE16 *off Finland St* **133** H3
Bond Rd, Mitch. CR4 **185** H2
Surbiton KT6 **195** J2
Bond St, E15 **96** E5
W4 **126** E4
W5 **105** G7
Bondway, SW8 **34** B6
Boneta Rd, SE18 **136** C3
Bonfield Rd, SE13 **154** C4
Bonham Cl, Belv. DA17 *off Croft Cl* **139** F5
Bonham Gdns, Dag. RM8 **100** D2
Bonham Rd, SW2 **151** F5
Dagenham RM8 **100** D2
Bonheur Rd, W4 **126** D2
Bonhill St, EC2 **12** C6
Boniface Gdns, Har. HA3 **51** H7
Boniface Wk, Har. HA3 **51** H7
Bonington Ho, Enf. EN1 *off Ayley Cft* **44** D5
Bonita Ms, SE4 **153** G3
Bon Marche Ter Ms, SE27 *off Gipsy Rd* **170** B4
Bonner Hill Rd, Kings.T. KT1 **181** J3
Bonner Rd, E2 **113** F2
Bonnersfield Cl, Har. HA1 **68** C6
Bonnersfield La, Har. HA1 **68** D6
Bonner St, E2 **113** F2
Bonneville Gdns, SW4 **150** C6
Bonnington Ho, N1 *off Killick St* **10** C2
Bonnington Sq, SW8 **34** C5
Bonnington Twr, Brom. BR2 **192** B6
Bonny St, NW1 **92** C7
Bonser Rd, Twick. TW1 **162** C2
Bonsor St, SE5 **132** B7
Bonville Gdns, NW4 *off Handowe Cl* **71** G4
Bonville Rd, Brom. BR1 **173** F5
Bookbinders' Cotts, N20 *off Manor Dr* **57** J3
Booker Cl, E14 *off Wallwood St* **113** J5
Booker Rd, N18 **60** D5
Bookham Ct, Mitch. CR4 **185** G3
Book Ms, WC2 **17** J4
Boone Ct, N9 **61** F3
Boones Rd, SE13 **155** E4
Boone St, SE13 **155** E4
Boord St, SE10 **135** E3
Boothby Rd, N19 **92** D2
Booth Cl, E9 *off Victoria Pk Rd* **113** E1
SE28 **118** B7
Booth Ho, Brent. TW8 *off High St* **125** F7
Booth La, EC4 **19** J5
Booth Rd, NW9 **70** E2
Croydon CR0 *off Waddon New Rd* **201** H2
Booth's Pl, W1 **17** G2
Boot St, N1 **12** D4
Bordars Rd, W7 **104** B5
Bordars Wk, W7 **104** B5
Borden Av, Enf. EN1 **44** A6
Border Cres, SE26 **170** E5
Border Gdns, Croy. CR0 **204** B4
Bordergate, Mitch. CR4 **185** H1
Border Rd, SE26 **171** E5
Borders La, Loug. IG10 **48** D4
Bordesley Rd, Mord. SM4 **184** E4
Bordon Wk, SW15 **147** G7
Boreas Wk, N1 **11** H2
Boreham Av, E16 **115** G6
Boreham Cl, E11 *off Hainault Rd* **96** C1
Boreham Rd, N22 **75** J2
BOREHAMWOOD, WD6 **38** B3
Borehamwood Ind Pk, Borwd. WD6 **38** D2
Borehamwood Shop Pk, Borwd. WD6 **38** A3
Borgard Rd, SE18 **136** C4
Borkwood Pk, Orp. BR6 **207** J4
Borkwood Way, Orp. BR6 **207** H4
Borland Rd, SE15 **153** F4
Teddington TW11 **162** E6
Borneo St, SW15 **147** J3
BOROUGH, THE, SE1 **27** J4
Borough High St, SE1 **27** J4
Borough Hill, Croy. CR0 **201** H3
★ **Borough Mkt**, SE1 **28** B2
Borough Rd, SE1 **27** G5
Isleworth TW7 **144** B1
Kingston upon Thames KT2 **182** A1
Mitcham CR4 **185** H2
Borough Sq, SE1 **27** J4
Borrett Cl, SE17 **35** J4
Borrodaile Rd, SW18 **149** E6
Borrowdale Av, Har. HA3 **68** D2
Borrowdale Cl, Ilf. IG4 **80** B4
Borrowdale Ct, Enf. EN2 **43** J1
Borthwick Ms, E15 *off Borthwick Rd* **96** E4
Borthwick Rd, E15 **96** E4
NW9 *off West Hendon Bdy* **71** F6
Borthwick St, SE8 **134** A5
Borwick Av, E17 **77** J3
Bosbury Rd, SE6 **172** C3
Boscastle Rd, NW5 **92** B3
Boscobel Cl, Brom. BR1 **192** C2
Boscobel Pl, SW1 **32** C1
Boscobel St, NW8 **7** F6
Bosco Cl, Orp. BR6 **207** J4
Boscombe Av, E10 **78** D7
Boscombe Circ, NW9 *off Warmwell Av* **70** D2
Boscombe Cl, E5 **95** H5

Boscombe Gdns, SW16 ... 169 E6
Boscombe Rd, SW17 ... 168 A6
SW19 ... 184 E1
W12 ... 127 G1
Worcester Park KT4 ... 197 J1
Bose Cl, N3 ... 72 B1
Bosgrove, E4 ... 62 C1
Boss Ho, SE1 ... 29 F3
Boss St, SE1 ... 29 F3
Bostall Heath, SE2 ... 138 C5
Bostall Hill, SE2 ... 138 B5
Bostall La, SE2 ... 138 B5
Bostall Manorway, SE2 ... 138 B4
Bostall Pk Av, Bexh. DA7 ... 138 E7
Bostall Rd, Orp. BR5 ... 176 B7
Bostal Row, Bexh. DA7
off Harlington Rd ... 159 F3
Bostock Ho, Houns. TW5
off Biscoe Cl ... 123 G6
Boston Gdns, W4 ... 127 E6
W7 ... 124 D4
Brentford TW8 ... 124 D4
★ **Boston Manor Ho**, Brent. TW8 ... 124 E5
Boston Manor Rd, Brent. TW8 ... 124 E4
Boston Pk Rd, Brent. TW8 ... 125 F5
Boston Pl, NW1 ... 7 J6
Boston Rd, E6 ... 116 B3
E17 ... 78 A6
W7 ... 124 B1
Croydon CR0 ... 187 F6
Edgware HA8 ... 54 C7
Bostonthorpe Rd, W7 ... 124 B2
Boston Vale, W7 ... 124 D4
Bosun Cl, E14
off Byng St ... 134 A2
Boswell Ct, WC1 ... 18 B1
Boswell Path, Hayes UB3
off Croyde Av ... 121 J4
Boswell Rd, Th.Hth. CR7 ... 187 J4
Boswell St, WC1 ... 18 B1
Bosworth Cl, E17 ... 77 J1
Bosworth Rd, N11 ... 58 D6
W10 ... 108 B4
Barnet EN5 ... 40 D3
Dagenham RM10 ... 101 G4
Botany Bay La, Chis. BR7 ... 193 F3
Botany Cl, Barn. EN4 ... 41 H4
Boteley Cl, E4 ... 62 D2
Botham Cl, Edg. HA8 ... 54 C7
Botha Rd, E13 ... 115 H5
Bothwell Cl, E16 ... 115 F5
Bothwell St, W6
off Delorme St ... 128 A6
Botolph All, EC3 ... 20 D5
Botolph La, EC3 ... 20 C6
Botsford Rd, SW20 ... 184 B2
Botts Ms, W2
off Chepstow Rd ... 108 D6
Botts Pas, W2
off Chepstow Rd ... 108 D6
Botwell La, Hayes UB3 ... 121 H1
Boucher Cl, Tedd. TW11 ... 162 C5
Boughton Av, Bromley BR2 ... 191 F7
Boughton Rd, SE28 ... 137 H3
Boulcott St, E1 ... 113 G6
Boulevard, The, SW6 ... 149 F1
SW17
off Balham High Rd ... 168 A2
SW18
off Smugglers Way ... 149 E4
Wembley HA9
off Engineers Way ... 88 A4
Woodford Green IG8 ... 64 D6
Boulogne Rd, Croy. CR0 ... 187 J6
Boulter Cl, Brom. BR1 ... 192 E3
Boulton Ho, Brent. TW8
off Green Dragon La ... 125 H5
Boulton Rd, Dag. RM8 ... 101 E3
Boultwood Rd, E6 ... 116 B6
Bounces La, N9 ... 60 E2
Bounces Rd, N9 ... 60 E1
Boundaries Rd, SW12 ... 167 J2
Feltham TW13 ... 160 C1
Boundary Av, E17 ... 77 J7
Boundary Business Ct, Mitch. CR4 185 G3
Boundary Cl, SE20
off Haysleigh Gdns ... 188 D2
Barnet EN5 ... 40 C1
Ilford IG3
off Loxford La ... 99 H4
Kingston upon Thames KT1 ... 182 B3
Southall UB2 ... 123 G5
Boundary Ct, N18 ... 60 C6
Boundary La, E13 ... 116 A3
SE17 ... 36 A6
Boundary Pas, E2 ... 13 F5
Boundary Rd, E13 ... 115 J2
E17 ... 77 J7
N9 ... 45 F6
N22 ... 75 H3
Boundary Rd, NW8 ... 109 E1
SW19 ... 167 G6
Barking IG11 ... 117 F2
Carshalton SM5 ... 200 B6
Pinner HA5 ... 66 D6
Sidcup DA15 ... 157 H5
Wallington SM6 ... 200 B6
Wembley HA9 ... 87 H3
Boundary Row, SE1 ... 27 G3
Boundary St, E2 ... 13 F4
Boundary Way, Croy. CR0 ... 204 A5
Boundfield Rd, SE6 ... 172 E3
Bounds Grn Ind Est, N11 ... 58 B6
Bounds Grn Rd, N11 ... 58 C6
N22 ... 58 C6
Bourchier St, W1 ... 17 H5
Bourdon Pl, W1 ... 16 E5
Bourdon Rd, SE20 ... 189 F2
Bourdon St, W1 ... 16 E5
Bourke Cl, NW10 ... 89 E6
SW4 ... 150 E6
Bourlet Cl, W1 ... 17 F2
Bourn Av, N15 ... 76 A4
Barnet EN4 ... 41 G5
Bournbrook Rd, SE3 ... 156 A3
Bourne, The, N14 ... 58 D1
Bourne Av, N14 ... 58 E2
Hayes UB3 ... 121 F3
Ruislip HA4 ... 84 C5
Bourne Cl, Islw. TW7 ... 144 B3
Thames Ditton KT7 ... 194 C2
Bourne Ct, Ruis. HA4 ... 84 B5
Bourne Dr, Mitch. CR4 ... 185 G2
Bourne Est, EC1 ... 18 E1
Bourne Gdns, E4 ... 62 B4
Bourne Hill, N13 ... 58 E1
Bourne Hill Cl, N13
off Bourne Hill ... 59 F2
Bournemead Av, Nthlt. UB5 102 A2
Bournemead Cl, Nthlt. UB5 102 A2
Bournemead Way, Nthlt. UB5 102 B2
Bournemouth Cl, SE15 ... 152 D2
Bournemouth Rd, SE15 ... 152 D2
SW19 ... 184 D1
Bourne Pl, W4
off Dukes Av ... 126 D5
Bourne Rd, E7 ... 97 F3
N8 ... 75 E6
Bexley DA5 ... 159 H6
Bromley BR2 ... 192 A4
Dartford DA1 ... 159 J6
Bourneside Cres, N14 ... 58 D1
Bourneside Gdns, SE6 ... 172 C5
Bourne St, SW1 ... 32 B2
Croydon CR0
off Waddon New Rd ... 201 H2
Bourne Ter, W2 ... 14 A1
Bourne Vale, Brom. BR2 ... 191 G7
Bournevale Rd, SW16 ... 168 E4
Bourne Vw, Grnf. UB6 ... 86 C6
Bourne Way, Brom. BR2 ... 205 F2
Epsom KT19 ... 196 C4
Sutton SM1 ... 198 C5
Bournewood Rd, SE18 ... 138 A7
Bournville Rd, SE6 ... 154 A7
Bournwell Cl, Barn. EN4 ... 41 J3
Bourton Cl, Hayes UB3 ... 122 A1
Bousfield Rd, SE14 ... 153 G2
Boutflower Rd, SW11 ... 149 H4
Boutique Hall, SE13
off Lewisham Cen ... 154 C4
Bouton Pl, N1
off Waterloo Ter ... 93 H7
Bouverie Gdns, Har. HA3 ... 69 G6
Bouverie Ms, N16 ... 94 B2
Bouverie Pl, W2 ... 15 F3
Bouverie Rd, N16 ... 94 B2
Harrow HA1 ... 67 J7
Bouverie St, EC4 ... 19 F4
Boveney Rd, SE23 ... 153 G7
Bovill Rd, SE23 ... 153 G7
Bovingdon Av, Wem. HA9 ... 88 A6
Bovingdon Cl, N19
off Brookside Rd ... 92 C2
Bovingdon La, NW9 ... 70 E1
Bovingdon Rd, SW6 ... 148 E1
Bovingdon Sq, Mitch. CR4
off Leicester Av ... 187 E4
BOW, E3 ... 113 J2
Bowater Cl, NW9 ... 70 D5
SW2 ... 150 E6
Bowater Gdns, Sun. TW16 ... 178 B2
Bowater Pl, SE3 ... 135 H7
Bowater Rd, SE18 ... 136 A3
Wembley HA9 ... 88 B3
Bow Back Rivers Wk, E15 ... 96 B7
Bow Br Est, E3 ... 114 B3
Bow Chyd, EC4 ... 20 A4
Bow Common La, E3 ... 113 J4
Bowden St, SE11 ... 35 F4
Bowditch, SE8 ... 133 J5
Bowdon Rd, E17 ... 78 A7
Bowen Dr, SE21 ... 170 B3
Bowen Rd, Har. HA1 ... 67 J7
Bowen St, E14 ... 114 B6
Bower Av, SE10 ... 154 E1
Bower Cl, Nthlt. UB5 ... 102 C2
Bowerdean St, SW6 ... 148 E1
Bowerman Av, SE14 ... 133 H6
Bower St, E1 ... 113 G6
Bowers Wk, E6 ... 116 B6
Bowery Ct, Dag. RM10
off Reede Way ... 101 H6
Bowes Cl, Sid. DA15 ... 158 B6
BOWES PARK, N22 ... 59 E6
Bowes Rd, N11 ... 58 B5
N13 ... 58 E5
W3 ... 106 E7
Dagenham RM8 ... 100 C4
Bowfell Rd, W6 ... 127 J6
Bowford Av, Bexh. DA7 ... 158 E1
Bowhill Cl, SW9 ... 35 F7
Bowie Cl, SW4 ... 150 D7
Bow Ind Est, E15 ... 96 A7
Bowland Rd, SW4 ... 150 D4
Woodford Green IG8 ... 63 J6
Bowland Yd, SW1 ... 24 A4
Bow La, EC4 ... 20 A4
N12 ... 73 F1
Morden SM4 ... 184 B6
Bowl Ct, EC2 ... 12 E6
Bowley Cl, SE19 ... 170 C6
Bowley La, SE19 ... 170 C5
Bowling Grn Cl, SW15 ... 147 H7
Bowling Grn La, EC1 ... 11 F5
Bowling Grn Pl, SE1 ... 28 B3
Bowling Grn Row, SE18
off Samuel St ... 136 C4
Bowling Grn St, SE11 ... 35 E5
Bowling Grn Wk, N1 ... 12 D3
Bowls, The, Chig. IG7 ... 65 H4
Bowls Cl, Stan. HA7 ... 52 E5
Bowman Av, E16 ... 115 F7
Bowman Ms, SW18 ... 166 C1
Bowmans Cl, W13 ... 124 E1
Bowmans Lea, SE23 ... 153 F7
Bowmans Meadow, Wall. SM6 ... 200 B3
Bowmans Ms, E1 ... 21 H5
Bowman's Ms, N7
off Seven Sisters Rd ... 93 E3
Bowmans Pl, N7
off Holloway Rd ... 93 E3
Bowman Trd Est, NW9 ... 70 A4
Bowmead, SE9 ... 174 C2
Bowmore Wk, NW1
off St. Paul's Cres ... 92 D7
Bowness Cl, E8
off Beechwood Rd ... 94 C6
Bowness Cres, SW15 ... 164 E5
Bowness Dr, Houns. TW4 ... 143 E4
Bowness Rd, SE6 ... 154 B7
Bexleyheath DA7 ... 159 H2
Bowood Rd, SW11 ... 150 A4
Enfield EN3 ... 45 G2
Bowring Grn, Wat. WD19 ... 50 C5
Bow Rd, E3 ... 113 J3
Bowrons Av, Wem. HA0 ... 87 G7
Bowsley Ct, Felt. TW13
off Highfield Rd ... 160 A2
Bowsprit Pt, E14 ... 134 A3
Bow St, E15 ... 96 E5
WC2 ... 18 B4
Bow Triangle Business Cen, E3
off Eleanor St ... 114 A4
Bowyer Cl, E6 ... 116 C5
Bowyer Ct, E4
off The Ridgeway ... 62 C1
Bowyer Pl, SE5 ... 36 A7
Bowyer St, SE5 ... 35 J7
Boxall Rd, SE21 ... 152 B6
Box Elder Cl, Edgware HA8 ... 54 C5
Boxgrove Rd, SE2 ... 138 C3
Box La, Bark. IG11 ... 118 B2
Boxley Rd, Mord. SM4 ... 185 F4
Boxley St, E16 ... 135 H1
Boxmoor Rd, Har. HA3 ... 68 E4
Boxoll Rd, Dag. RM9 ... 101 F4
Boxted Cl, Buck.H. IG9 ... 64 B1
Boxtree La, Har. HA3 ... 67 J1
Boxtree Rd, Har. HA3 ... 52 A7
Boxwood Cl, West Dr. UB7
off Hawthorne Cres ... 120 C2
Boxworth Cl, N12 ... 57 G5
Boxworth Gro, N1
off Richmond Av ... 111 F1
Boyard Rd, SE18 ... 136 E5
Boyce St, SE1 ... 26 D2
Boyce Way, E13 ... 115 G4
Boycroft Av, NW9 ... 70 C6
Boyd Av, Sthl. UB1 ... 123 F1
Boyd Cl, Kings.T. KT2 ... 164 A7
Boydell Ct, NW8
off St. John's Wd Pk ... 91 G7
Boyd Rd, SW19 ... 167 G6
Boyd St, E1 ... 21 H4
Boyfield St, SE1 ... 27 H4
Boyland Rd, Brom. BR1 ... 173 F5
Boyle Av, Stan. HA7 ... 52 D6
Boyle Fm Island, T.Ditt. KT7 ... 180 D6
Boyle Fm Rd, T.Ditt. KT7 ... 180 D6
Boyle St, W1 ... 17 F5
Boyne Av, NW4 ... 72 A4
Boyne Rd, SE13 ... 154 C3
Dagenham RM10 ... 101 G3
Boyne Ter Ms, W11 ... 128 C1
Boyseland Ct, Edg. HA8 ... 54 C2
Boyson Rd, SE17 ... 36 B5
Boyton Cl, E1
off Stayner's Rd ... 113 G4
N8 ... 75 E3
Boyton Rd, N8 ... 75 E3
Brabant Ct, EC3 ... 20 D5
Brabant Rd, N22 ... 75 F2
Brabazon Av, Wall. SM6 ... 200 E7
Brabazon Rd, Houns. TW5 ... 122 C7
Northolt UB5 ... 103 G2
Brabazon St, E14 ... 114 B6
Brabourne Cl, SE19 ... 170 B5
Brabourne Cres, Bexh. DA7 ... 139 F6
Brabourne Hts, NW7 ... 55 E3
Brabourne Ri, Beck. BR3 ... 190 C5
Brabourn Gro, SE15 ... 153 F2
Bracer Ho, N1
off Nuttall St ... 12 E1
Bracewell Av, Grnf. UB6 ... 86 C5
Bracewell Rd, W10 ... 107 J5
Bracewood Gdns, Croy. CR0 ... 202 C3
Bracey Ms, N4
off Bracey St ... 93 E2
Bracey St, N4 ... 93 E2
Bracken, The, E4
off Hortus Rd ... 62 C2
Bracken Av, SW12 ... 150 A6
Croydon CR0 ... 204 B3
Brackenbridge Dr, Ruis. HA4 ... 84 D3
Brackenbury Gdns, W6 ... 127 H3
Brackenbury Rd, N2 ... 73 F3
W6 ... 127 H3
Bracken Cl, E6 ... 116 C5
Borehamwood WD6 ... 38 B1
Twickenham TW2
off Hedley Rd ... 143 G7
Brackendale, N21 ... 59 F2
Brackendale Cl, Houns. TW3 ... 143 H1
Bracken Dr, Chig. IG7 ... 65 E6
Bracken End, Islw. TW7 ... 144 A5
Brackenfield Cl, E5 ... 94 E3
Bracken Gdns, SW13 ... 147 G2
Bracken Hill Cl, Brom. BR1 ... 191 F1
Bracken Hill La, Brom. BR1 ... 191 F1
Bracken Ind Est, Ilf. IG6 ... 65 J7
Bracken Ms, E4
off Hortus Rd ... 62 C2
Romford RM7 ... 83 G6
Brackens, The, Enf. EN1 ... 44 B7
Brackenwood, Sun. TW16 ... 178 A1
Brackley Av, SE15 ... 153 E3
Brackley Cl, Wall. SM6 ... 201 E7
Brackley Rd, W4 ... 127 E5
Beckenham BR3 ... 171 J7
Brackley Sq, Wdf.Grn. IG8 ... 64 A7
Brackley St, EC1 ... 19 J1
Brackley Ter, W4 ... 127 E5
Bracklyn Cl, N1 ... 12 B1
Bracklyn Ct, N1 ... 12 B1
Bracklyn St, N1 ... 12 B1
Bracknell Cl, N22 ... 75 G1
Bracknell Gdns, NW3 ... 90 E4
Bracknell Gate, NW3 ... 90 E5
Bracknell Way, NW3 ... 90 E4
Bracondale Rd, SE2 ... 138 A4
Bradbourne Rd, Bex. DA5 ... 159 G7
Bradbourne St, SW6 ... 148 D2
Bradbury Cl, Borwd. WD6 ... 38 B1
Southall UB2 ... 123 F4
Bradbury Ct, SW20
off Clifton Pk Av ... 183 J2
Bradbury Ms, N16
off Bradbury St ... 94 B5
Bradbury St, N16 ... 94 B5
Braddock Cl, Islw. TW7 ... 144 C3
Braddon Rd, Rich. TW9 ... 145 J3
Braddyll St, SE10 ... 134 E5
Bradenham Av, Well. DA16 ... 158 A4
Bradenham Cl, SE17 ... 36 B5
Bradenham Rd, Har. HA3 ... 68 E4
Braden St, W9 ... 6 A6
Bradfield Dr, Barking IG11 ... 100 A5
Bradfield Ho, SW8
off Wandsworth Rd ... 150 D2

Bradfield Rd, E16 .... **135** G2
Ruislip HA4 .... **85** E5
Bradford Cl, N17 .... **60** C6
SE26 *off Coombe Rd* **170** E4
Bromley BR2 .... **206** C1
Bradford Dr, Epsom
KT19 .... **197** F6
Bradford Rd, W3
off Warple Way **126** E2
Ilford IG1 .... **99** G1
Bradfords Cl, IG9 .... **64** A4
Bradgate Rd, SE6 .... **154** A6
Brading Cres, E11 .... **97** H2
Brading Rd, SW2 .... **151** F7
Croydon CR0 .... **187** F6
Brading Ter, W12 .... **127** H3
Bradiston Rd, W9 .... **108** C3
Bradley Cl, N1 .... **11** F1
N7 *off Sutterton St* **93** F6
Bradley Gdns, W13 .... **104** E6
Bradley Ho, E3
off Bromley High St **114** B2
Bradley Lynch Ct, E2
off Morpeth St **113** G3
Bradley Ms, SW17
off Bellevue Rd **167** J1
Bradley Rd, N22 .... **75** F2
SE19 .... **169** J6
Bradley Stone Rd, E6 .... **116** C5
Bradman Row, Edg. HA8
off Pavilion Way **54** C7
Bradmead, SW8 .... **130** B7
Bradmore Ct, Enf. EN3
off Enstone Rd **45** H3
Bradmore Pk Rd, W6 .... **127** H3
Bradshaw Cl, SW19 .... **166** D6
Bradshaw Dr, NW7 .... **56** A7
Bradshaws Cl, SE25 .... **188** D3
Bradstock Rd, E9 .... **95** G6
Epsom KT17 .... **197** G5
Brad St, SE1 .... **27** F2
Bradwell Av, Dag. RM10 .... **101** G2
Bradwell Cl, E18 .... **79** F4
Bradwell Ms, N18
off Lyndhurst Rd **60** D4
Bradwell Rd, Buck.H. IG9 .... **64** B1
Bradwell St, E1 .... **113** G3
Brady Av, Loug. IG10 .... **49** F2
Brady Ct, Dag. RM8 .... **100** D1
Brady Dr, Brom. BR1 .... **192** D3
Bradymead, E6 .... **116** D6
Brady St, E1 .... **112** E4
Braemar Av, N22 .... **75** E1
NW10 .... **88** D3
SW19 .... **166** D2
Bexleyheath DA7 .... **159** J4
Thornton Heath CR7 .... **187** G3
Wembley HA0 .... **87** G7
Braemar Cl, SE16
off Masters Dr **132** E5
Braemar Gdns, NW9 .... **70** D1
Sidcup DA15 .... **175** G3
West Wickham BR4 .... **204** C1
Braemar Rd, E13 .... **115** F4
N15 .... **76** B5
Brentford TW8 .... **125** G6
Worcester Park KT4 .... **197** H3
Braemer Ho, W9 .... **6** C4
Braeside, Beck. BR3 .... **172** A5
Braeside Av, SW19 .... **184** B1
Braeside Cl, Pnr. HA5
off The Avenue **51** G7
Braeside Cres, Bexh.
DA7 .... **159** J4
Braeside Rd, SW16 .... **168** C7
Braes St, N1 .... **93** H7
Braesyde Cl, Belv. DA17 .... **139** F4
Brafferton Rd, Croy. CR0 .... **201** J4
Braganza St, SE17 .... **35** G3
Bragg Cl, Dag. RM8
off Porters Av **100** B6
Braham St, E1 .... **21** G4
Braid Av, W3 .... **106** E6
Braid Cl, Felt. TW13 .... **161** F2
Braid Ct, W4
off Lawford Rd **126** C7
Braidwood Pas, EC1
off Cloth St **19** J1
Braidwood Rd, SE6 .... **172** D1
Braidwood St, SE1 .... **28** D2
Brailsford Cl, Mitch. CR4 .... **167** H7
Brailsford Rd, SW2 .... **151** G5
Brainton Av, Felt. TW14 .... **142** B7
Braintree Av, Ilf. IG4 .... **80** B4
Braintree Ind Est, Ruis.
HA4 .... **84** B4
Braintree Rd, Dag. RM10 .... **101** G3
Ruislip HA4 .... **84** B4
Braintree St, E2 .... **113** F3
Braithwaite Av, Rom. RM7 .... **83** G7
Braithwaite Gdns, Stan.
HA7 .... **69** F1
Braithwaite Ho, EC1 .... **12** A5
Braithwaite Rd, Enf. EN3 .... **45** J3
Braithwaite Twr, W2 .... **15** E1
Bramah Grn, SW9 .... **151** G1
★ **Bramah Mus**, SE1 .... **28** A2
Bramalea Cl, N6 .... **74** A6
Bramall Cl, E15
off Idmiston Rd **97** F5
Bramber Ct, Brent. TW8
off Sterling Pl **125** H4
Bramber Ho, Kings.T. KT2
off Kingsgate Rd **181** H1
Bramber Rd, N12 .... **57** H5
W14 .... **128** C6
Brambleacres Cl, Sutt.
SM2 .... **198** D7
Bramblebury Rd, SE18 .... **137** F5
Bramble Cl, N15
off Broad La **76** D4
SE19 .... **188** A1
Beckenham BR3 .... **190** C5
Chigwell IG7 .... **65** F1
Croydon CR0 .... **204** A4
Stanmore HA7 .... **53** G7
Bramble Cft, Erith DA8 .... **139** J4
Brambledown Cl, W.Wick.
BR4 .... **191** E5
Brambledown Rd, Cars.
SM5 .... **200** A7
South Croydon CR2 .... **202** B7
Wallington SM6 .... **200** B7
Bramble Gdns, W12 .... **107** F7
Bramble La, Hmptn.
TW12 .... **161** F6
Brambles, The, Chig. IG7
off Clayside **65** F6
West Drayton UB7 .... **120** B4
Brambles Cl, Islw. TW7 .... **124** E7
Bramblewood Cl, Cars.
SM5 .... **199** H1
Bramblings, The, E4 .... **62** D4
Bramcote Av, Mitch.
CR4 .... **185** J4
Bramcote Ct, Mitch. CR4
off Bramcote Av **185** J4
Bramcote Gro, SE16 .... **133** F5
Bramcote Rd, SW15 .... **147** H4
Bramdean Cres, SE12 .... **173** G1
Bramdean Gdns, SE12 .... **173** G1
Bramerton Rd, Beck.
BR3 .... **189** J3
Bramerton St, SW3 .... **31** G5
Bramfield Ct, N4
off Queens Dr **93** J2
Bramfield Rd, SW11 .... **149** H6
Bramford Ct, N14 .... **58** D2
Bramford Rd, SW18 .... **149** F4
Bramham Gdns, SW5 .... **30** A3
Chessington KT9 .... **195** G4
Bramhope La, SE7 .... **135** H6
Bramlands Cl, SW11 .... **149** H3
Bramley Cl, E17 .... **77** H2
N14 .... **42** B5
NW7 .... **55** E3
Hayes UB3 .... **102** A7
Orpington BR6 .... **207** E1
South Croydon CR2 .... **201** H5
Twickenham TW2 .... **143** J6
Woodford Green IG8
off Orsett Ter **63** J7
Bramley Ct, Well. DA16 .... **158** B1
Bramley Cres, SW8 .... **33** J7
Ilford IG2 .... **80** D6
Bramley Gdns, Wat.
WD19 .... **50** C5
Bramley Hill, S.Croy.
CR2 .... **201** H5
Bramley Ho, SW15
off Tunworth Cres **147** F6
W10 *off Bramley Rd* **108** A6
Bramley Hyrst, S.Croy.
CR2 .... **201** J4
Bramley Par, N14 .... **42** C4
Bramley Rd, N14 .... **42** B5
W5 .... **125** F3
W10 .... **108** A7
Sutton SM1 .... **199** G5
Bramley Way, Houns.
TW4 .... **143** F5
West Wickham BR4 .... **204** B2
Brampton Cl, E5 .... **95** E2
Brampton Gdns, N15
off Brampton Rd **75** J5
Brampton Gro, NW4 .... **71** H4
Harrow HA3 .... **68** D4
Wembley HA9 .... **88** A1
Brampton La, NW4 .... **71** J4
Brampton Pk Rd, N22 .... **75** G3
Brampton Rd, E6 .... **116** A3
N15 .... **75** J5
NW9 .... **70** A4
SE2 .... **138** C6
Bexleyheath DA7 .... **138** D7
Croydon CR0 .... **188** C7
Watford WD19 .... **50** A3
Bramshaw Gdns, Wat.
WD19 .... **50** D5
Bramshaw Ri, N.Mal.
KT3 .... **183** E6
Bramshaw Rd, E9 .... **95** G6
Bramshill Cl, Chig. IG7
off Tine Rd **65** H5
Bramshill Gdns, NW5 .... **92** B3
Bramshill Rd, NW10 .... **107** F2
Bramshot Av, SE7 .... **135** G6
Bramshot Way, Wat.
WD19 .... **50** A2
Bramston Cl, Ilf. IG6 .... **65** J6
Bramston Rd, NW10 .... **107** G2
SW17 .... **167** F3
Bramwell Cl, Sun. TW16 .... **178** D2
Bramwell Ho, SE1
off Harper Rd **28** A6
SW1 .... **33** F4
Bramwell Ms, N1 .... **111** F1
Brancaster Dr, NW7 .... **55** F7
Brancaster Pl, Loug.
IG10 .... **48** C3
Brancaster Rd, E12 .... **98** C4
SW16 .... **168** E3
Ilford IG2 .... **81** G6
Brancepeth Gdns, Buck.H.
IG9 .... **63** G2
Branch Hill, NW3 .... **91** F3
Branch Pl, N1 .... **112** A1
Branch Rd, E14 .... **113** H7
Branch St, SE15 .... **132** B7
Brancker Rd, Har. HA3 .... **69** G3
Brancroft Way, Enf. EN3 .... **45** H1
Brand Cl, N4 .... **93** H1
Brandesbury Sq, Wdf.Grn.
IG8 .... **64** D6
Brandlehow Rd, SW15 .... **148** C4
Brandon Est, SE17 .... **35** H6
Brandon Ms, EC2
off The Barbican **20** B2
Brandon Rd, E17 .... **78** C3
N7 .... **92** E7
Southall UB2 .... **123** F5
Sutton SM1 .... **198** E4
Brandon St, SE17 .... **35** J2
Brandram Ms, SE13 .... **154** E3
Brandram Rd, SE13 .... **154** E3
Brandreth Rd, E6 .... **116** C6
SW17 .... **168** B2
Brandries, The, Wall.
SM6 .... **200** D3
Brand St, SE10 .... **134** C7
Brandville Gdns, Ilf. IG6 .... **81** E4
Brandville Rd, West Dr.
UB7 .... **120** B2
Brandy Way, Sutt. SM2 .... **198** D7
Brangbourne Rd, Brom.
BR1 .... **172** C5
Brangton Rd, SE11 .... **34** D4
Brangwyn Cres, SW19 .... **185** G1
Branksea St, SW6 .... **128** B7
Branksome Av, N18 .... **60** C6
Branksome Cl, Tedd.
TW11 .... **162** A4
Branksome Rd, SW2 .... **151** E5
SW19 .... **184** D1
Branksome Way, Har.
HA3 .... **69** H6
New Malden KT3 .... **182** C1
Bransby Rd, Chess. KT9 .... **195** H6
Branscombe Gdns, N21 .... **43** G7
Branscombe St, SE13 .... **154** B3
Bransdale Cl, NW6
off West End La **108** E1
Bransgrove Rd, Edg. HA8 .... **69** J1
Branston Cres, Orp. BR5 .... **207** G1
Branstone Rd, Rich.
TW9 .... **145** J1
Brants Wk, W7 .... **104** B4
Brantwood Av, Erith
DA8 .... **139** J7
Isleworth TW7 .... **144** D4
Brantwood Cl, E17 .... **78** B3
Brantwood Gdns, Enf.
EN2 .... **42** E4
Ilford IG4 .... **80** B4
Brantwood Rd, N17 .... **60** C6
SE24 .... **151** J5
Bexleyheath DA7 .... **159** H2
Brasenose Dr, SW13 .... **127** J6
Brasher Cl, Grnf. UB6 .... **86** A5
Brassett Pt, E15 .... **114** E1
Brassey Cl, Felt. TW14 .... **160** A1
Brassey Rd, NW6 .... **90** C6
Brassey Sq, SW11 .... **150** A3
Brassie Av, W3 .... **106** E6
Brass Tally All, SE16
off Middleton Dr **133** G2
Brasted Cl, SE26 .... **171** F4
Bexleyheath DA6 .... **158** D5
Brathway Rd, SW18 .... **148** D7
Bratley St, E1 .... **13** H6
Braund Av, Grnf. UB6 .... **103** H4
Braundton Av, Sid.
DA15 .... **175** J1
Braunston Dr, Hayes
UB4 .... **102** E4
Bravington Pl, W9
off Bravington Rd **108** C4
Bravington Rd, W9 .... **108** C2
Bravingtons Wk, N1 .... **10** B2
Brawne Ho, SE17 .... **35** H6
Braxfield Rd, SE4 .... **153** H4
Braxted Pk, SW16 .... **169** F6
Bray, NW3 .... **91** H7
Brayards Rd, SE15 .... **152** E2
Braybourne Dr, Islw.
TW7 .... **124** C7
Braybrooke Gdns, SE19
off Fox Hill **170** B7
Braybrook St, W12 .... **107** F5
Brayburne Av, SW4 .... **150** C2
Bray Cl, Borwd. WD6 .... **38** C1
Braycourt Av, Walt.
KT12 .... **178** B7
Bray Cres, SE16
off Marlow Way **133** G2
Braydon Rd, N16 .... **94** C1
Bray Dr, E16 .... **115** F7
Brayfield Ter, N1
off Lofting Rd **93** G7
Brayford Sq, E1
off Summercourt Rd **113** F6
Bray Pas, E16 .... **115** G7
Bray Pl, SW3 .... **31** J2
Bray Rd, NW7 .... **56** A6
Brayton Gdns, Enf. EN2 .... **42** D4
Braywood Rd, SE9 .... **157** G4
Brazier Cres, Nthlt. UB5
off Waxlow Way **103** F4
Brazil Cl, Croy. (Bedd.)
CR0 .... **186** E7
Breach La, Dag. RM9 .... **119** G3
Bread St, EC4 .... **20** A4
Breakspears Ms, SE4
off Ashby Rd **154** A2
Breakspears Rd, SE4 .... **153** J3
Bream Cl, N17 .... **77** E4
Bream Gdns, E6 .... **116** D3
Breamore Cl, SW15 .... **165** G1
Breamore Rd, Ilf. IG3 .... **99** J2
Bream's Bldgs, EC4 .... **18** E3
Bream St, E3 .... **96** A7
Breamwater Gdns, Rich.
TW10 .... **163** E3
Brearley Cl, Edg. HA8 .... **54** C7
Breasley Cl, SW15 .... **147** H4
Brechin Pl, SW7 .... **30** D2
Brecknock Rd, N7 .... **92** C4
N19 .... **92** C4
Brecknock Rd Est, N19 .... **92** C4
Breckonmead, Brom. BR1
off Wanstead Rd **191** J2
Brecon Cl, Mitch. CR4 .... **186** E3
Worcester Park KT4 .... **197** J2
Brecon Grn, NW9
off Goldsmith Av **71** E6
Brecon Ms, N7
off Brecknock Rd **92** D5
Brecon Rd, W6 .... **128** B6
Enfield EN3 .... **45** F4
Brede Cl, E6 .... **116** D3
Bredgar, SE13 .... **154** C5
Bredgar Rd, N19 .... **92** C2
Bredhurst Cl, SE20 .... **171** F6
Bredinghurst, SE22 .... **152** D7
Bredon Rd, Croy. CR0 .... **188** C7
Breer St, SW6 .... **148** E3
Breezers Hill, E1 .... **21** J6
Brember Rd, Har. HA2 .... **85** J2
Bremer Ms, E17
off Church La **78** B4
Bremner Rd, SW7 .... **22** D4
Brenchley Cl, Brom. BR2 .... **191** F6
Chislehurst BR7 .... **192** D1
Brenchley Gdns, SE23 .... **153** F6
Brenchley Rd, Orp. BR5 .... **193** J1
Brenda Rd, SW17 .... **167** J2
Brende Gdns, W.Mol.
KT8 .... **179** H4
Brendon Av, NW10 .... **89** E4
Brendon Cl, Hayes
(Harling.) UB3 .... **121** F7
Brendon Gdns, Har.
HA2 .... **85** H4
Ilford IG2 .... **81** H5
Brendon Gro, N2 .... **73** F2
Brendon Rd, SE9 .... **175** G2
Dagenham RM8 .... **101** F1
Brendon St, W1 .... **15** H3
Brendon Way, Enf. EN1 .... **44** B7
Brenley Cl, Mitch. CR4 .... **186** A3
Brenley Gdns, SE9 .... **156** A4
Brent Cl, Bex. DA5 .... **177** E1
Brentcot Cl, W13 .... **104** E4
Brent Cres, NW10 .... **105** J2
Brent Cross Gdns, NW4
off Cooper Rd **72** A6
Brent Cross Interchange,
The, NW2 .... **72** A7
Brent Cross Shop Cen,
NW4 .... **71** J7
Brentfield, NW10 .... **88** B7
Brentfield Cl, NW10 .... **88** D6
Brentfield Gdns, NW2
off Hendon Way **72** A7
Brentfield Ho, NW10
off Stonebridge Pk **88** D7
Brentfield Rd, NW10 .... **88** D6
BRENTFORD, TW8 .... **125** G6

Brentford Business Cen, Brent.TW8 **125** E7
Brentford Cl, Hayes UB4 **102** D4
★ **Brentford FC**, Brent. TW8 **125** G6
Brent Grn, NW4 **71** J5
Brent Grn Wk, Wem. HA9 **88** C3
Brentham Way, W5 **105** G4
Brenthouse Rd, E9 **95** E7
Brenthurst Rd, NW10 **89** F5
Brent Lea, Brent. TW8 **125** F7
Brentmead Cl, W7 **104** B7
Brentmead Gdns, NW10 **105** J2
Brentmead Pl, NW11 *off North Circular Rd* **72** A6
Brenton St, E14 **113** H6
Brent Pk, NW10 **88** D5
Brent Pk Rd, NW4 **71** H7
NW9 **89** G1
Brent Pl, Barn. EN5 **40** D5
Brent Rd, E16 **115** G5
SE18 **136** E7
Brentford TW8 **125** F6
Southall UB2 **122** C3
Brent Side, Brent. TW8 **125** F6
Brentside Cl, W13 **104** D4
Brentside Executive Cen, Brent. TW8 **125** E6
Brent S Shop Pk, NW2 **89** J1
Brent St, NW4 **71** J4
Brent Ter, NW2 **89** J2
Brentvale Av, Sthl. UB1 **124** A1
Wembley HA0 **105** J1
Brent Vw Rd, NW9 **71** G7
Brent Way, N3 **56** D6
Brentford TW8 **125** G7
Wembley HA9 **88** B6
Brentwick Gdns, Brent. TW8 **125** H4
Brentwood Cl, SE9 **175** F1
Brentwood Ho, SE18 *off Shooters Hill Rd* **136** A7
Brereton Rd, N17 **60** C7
Bressay Dr, NW7 **55** G7
Bressenden Pl, SW1 **25** E5
Bressey Av, Enf. EN1 **44** D1
Bressey Gro, E18 **79** F2
Breton Ho, EC2 *off The Barbican* **20** A1
Brett Cl, N16 **94** B2
Northolt UB5 *off Broomcroft Av* **102** D3
Brett Ct, N9 **61** F2
Brett Cres, NW10 **88** D7
Brettell St, SE17 **36** C4
Brettenham Av, E17 **78** A1
Brettenham Rd, E17 **78** A2
N18 **60** E4
Brett Gdns, Dag. RM9 **100** E7
Brett Ho Cl, SW15 *off Putney Heath La* **148** A6
Brett Pas, E8 *off Kenmure Rd* **95** E5
Brett Rd, E8 **95** E5
Barnet EN5 **39** J5
Brewer's Grn, SW1 **25** H5
Brewers Hall Gdns, EC2 **20** A2
Brewers La, Rich. TW9 **145** G5
Brewer St, W1 **17** G5
★ **Brewery, The**, EC1 **20** A1
Brewery Cl, Wem. HA0 **86** D5
Brewery La, Twick. TW1 **144** C7
Brewery Rd, N7 **92** E7
SE18 **137** G5
Bromley BR2 **206** B1
Brewery Sq, EC1 **11** G5
SE1 **29** F2
Brewhouse La, E1 **133** E1
SW15 **148** B3
Brewhouse Rd, SE18 **136** C4
Brewhouse Wk, SE16 **133** H1
Brewhouse Yd, EC1 **11** H5
Brewood Rd, Dag. RM8 **100** B6
Brewster Gdns, W10 **107** J5
Brewster Ho, E14 **113** J7
Brewster Rd, E10 **96** B1
Brian Rd, Rom. RM6 **82** C5
Briant Est, SE1 **26** E6
Briant Ho, SE1 **26** D6
Briants Cl, Pnr. HA5 **67** F2
Briant St, SE14 **153** G1
Briar Av, SW16 **169** F7
Briarbank Rd, W13 **104** D6
Briar Cl, N2 **73** E3
N13 **59** J3
Buckhurst Hill IG9 **64** A2
Hampton TW12 **161** F5
Isleworth TW7 **144** C5
Briar Ct, Sutt. SM3 **197** J4
Briar Cres, Nthlt. UB5 **85** H6
Briardale Gdns, NW3 **90** D3
Briarfield Av, N3 **72** E2
Briarfield Cl, Bexh. DA7 **159** G2
Briar Gdns, Brom. BR2 **205** F1
Briaris Cl, N17 **60** E7
Briar La, Croy. CR0 **204** B4
Briar Pas, SW16 **187** E3
Briar Pl, SW16 **187** F3
Briar Rd, NW2 **89** J4
SW16 **187** E3
Harrow HA3 **69** F5
Twickenham TW2 **162** B1
Briarswood Way, Orp. BR6 **207** J5
Briar Wk, SW15 **147** H4
W10 *off Droop St* **108** B4
Edgware HA8 **54** C7
Briar Way, West Dr. UB7 **120** D2
Briarwood Cl, NW9 **70** C6
Briarwood Ct, Wor.Pk. KT4 *off The Avenue* **197** G1
Briarwood Dr, Nthwd. HA6 **66** A2
Briarwood Rd, SW4 **150** D5
Epsom KT17 **197** G6
Briary Cl, NW3 *off Fellows Rd* **91** H7
Briary Ct, E16 *off Turner St* **115** F6
Sidcup DA14 **176** B5
Briary Gdns, Bromley BR1 **173** H5
Briary Gro, Edg. HA8 **70** B2
Briary La, N9 **60** C3
Brick Ct, EC4 **18** E4
Brick Fm Cl, Rich. TW9 **146** B1
Brickfield Cl, Brent. TW8 **125** F7
Brickfield Cotts, SE18 **137** J6
Brickfield Fm Gdns, Orp. BR6 **207** F4
Brickfield La, Barn. EN5 **39** F6
Hayes (Harling.) UB3 **121** G6
Brickfield Rd, SW19 **167** E4
Thornton Heath CR7 **187** H1
Brickfields, Har. HA2 **86** A2
Brickfields Way, West Dr. UB7 **120** C3
Brickland Ct, N9 *off The Broadway* **60** D2
Brick La, E1 **13** G5
E2 **13** G4
Enfield EN1, EN3 **44** E2
Stanmore HA7 **53** G7
Bricklayer's Arms Distribution Cen, SE1 **36** E2
Bricklayer's Arms Rbt, SE1 **36** B1
Brick St, W1 **24** D2
Brickwood Cl, SE26 **171** E3
Brickwood Rd, Croy. CR0 **202** B2
Brideale Cl, SE15 **37** G6
Bride Ct, EC4 **19** G4
Bride La, EC4 **19** G4
Bridel Ms, N1 *off Colebrooke Row* **111** H1
Brides Pl, N1 *off De Beauvoir Rd* **94** B7
Bride St, N7 **93** F6
Bridewain St, SE1 **29** F5
Bridewell Pl, E1 *off Brewhouse La* **133** E1
EC4 **19** G4
Bridford Ms, W1 **16** E1
Bridge, The, SW8 *off Queenstown Rd* **130** B7
Harrow HA3 **68** B3
Bridge App, NW1 **92** A7
Bridge Av, W6 **127** J5
W7 **104** A5
Bridge Business Cen, The, Sthl. UB2 **123** G2
Bridge Cl, W10 *off Kingsdown Cl* **108** A6
Enfield EN1 **45** E2
Teddington TW11 *off Shacklegate La* **162** C4
Bridge Ct, E14 *off Newport Av* **114** D7
Harrow HA2 **85** J2
Bridge Dr, N13 **59** F4
Bridge End, E17 **78** C1
Bridge End Cl, Kings.T. KT2 *off Clifton Rd* **182** A1
Bridgefield Rd, Sutt. SM1 **198** D6
Bridgefoot, SE1 **34** A4
Bridge Gdns, N16 *off Green Las* **94** A4
East Molesey KT8 **180** A4
Bridge Gate, N21 *off Ridge Av* **43** J7
Bridgehill Cl, Wem. HA0 **105** G1
Bridge Ho, NW3 *off Adelaide Rd* **92** A7
SW8 *off St. George Wf* **34** A4
Bridge Ho Quay, E14 *off Prestons Rd* **134** C1
Bridgeland Rd, E16 **115** G7
Bridgelands Cl, Beck. BR3 **171** J7
Bridge La, NW11 **72** B5
SW11 **149** H1
Bridgeman Rd, N1 **93** F7
Teddington TW11 **162** D6
Bridgeman St, NW8 **7** G2
Bridge Meadows, SE14 **133** G6
Bridgend Rd, SW18 **149** F4
Bridgenhall Rd, Enf. EN1 **44** C1
Bridgen Rd, Bex. DA5 **158** E6
Bridge Pk, SW18 **148** D5
Bridge Pl, SW1 **33** E1
Croydon CR0 **188** A7
Bridgepoint Pl, N6 *off Hornsey La* **92** C1
Bridgeport Pl, E1 **29** J1
Bridge Rd, E6 **98** C7
E15 **96** D7
E17 **77** J7
N9 *off Fore St* **60** D3
N22 **74** E1
NW10 **88** E6
Beckenham BR3 **171** J7
Bexleyheath DA7 **159** E2
Chessington KT9 **195** H5
East Molesey KT8 **180** B4
Hounslow TW3 **144** A2
Isleworth TW7 **144** A3
Southall UB2 **123** F2
Sutton SM2 **199** E6
Twickenham TW1 **144** E6
Wallington SM6 **200** C5
Wembley HA9 **88** A3
Bridge Row, Croy. CR0 *off Cross Rd* **202** A1
Bridges Ct, SW11 **149** G3
Bridges La, Croy. CR0 **200** E4
Bridges Pl, SW6 **148** C1
Bridges Rd, SW19 **166** E6
Stanmore HA7 **52** C5
Bridges Rd Ms, SW19 *off Bridges Rd* **166** E6
Bridge St, SW1 **26** A4
W4 **126** D4
Pinner HA5 **66** D3
Richmond TW9 **145** G5
Bridge Ter, E15 *off Bridge Rd* **96** D7
SE13 *off Mercator Rd* **154** D4
Bridgetown Cl, SE19 *off St. Kitts Ter* **170** B5
Bridge Vw, W6 **127** J5
Bridgeview Ct, Ilf. IG6 **65** G6
Bridgewater Cl, Chis. BR7 **193** H3
Bridgewater Gdns, Edg. HA8 **69** J2
Bridgewater Rd, Ruis. HA4 **84** A4
Wembley HA0 **87** F7
Bridgewater Sq, EC2 **19** J1
Bridgewater St, EC2 **19** J1
Bridge Way, N11 *off Pymmes Grn Rd* **58** C3
NW11 **72** C5
Bridgeway, Bark. IG11 **99** J7
Bridge Way, Twick. TW2 **143** J7
Bridgeway, Wem. HA0 **87** H7
Bridgeway St, NW1 **9** G2
Bridge Wf Rd, Islw. TW7 *off Church St* **144** E3
Bridgewood Cl, SE20 **170** E7
Bridgewood Rd, SW16 **168** D7
Worcester Park KT4 **197** G4
Bridge Yd, SE1 **28** C1
Bridgford St, SW18 **167** F3
Bridgman Rd, W4 **126** C3
Bridgwater Rd, E15 **114** C1
Bridle Cl, Epsom KT19 **196** D5
Kingston upon Thames KT1 **181** G4
Sunbury-on-Thames TW16 *off Forge La* **178** A3
Bridle La, W1 **17** G5
Twickenham TW1 **145** E6
Bridle Ms, Barn. EN5 *off High St* **40** C4
Bridle Path, Croy. (Bedd.) CR0 **201** F3
Bridle Path, The, Wdf.Grn. IG8 **62** E7
Bridle Rd, Croy. CR0 **204** A3
Esher (Clay.) KT10 **194** E6
Pinner HA5 **66** C6
Bridle Way, Croy. CR0 **204** A5
Orpington BR6 **207** F4
Bridleway, The, Wall. SM6 **200** C4
Bridlington Rd, N9 **44** E7
Watford WD19 **50** D3
Bridport Av, Rom. RM7 **83** H6
Bridport Pl, N1 **12** C1
Bridport Rd, N18 **60** B5
Greenford UB6 **103** H1
Thornton Heath CR7 **187** G3
Bridport Ter, SW8 *off Wandsworth Rd* **150** D1
Bridstow Pl, W2 *off Talbot Rd* **108** D6
Brief St, SE5 **151** H1
Brierley, Croy. (New Adgtn) CR0 **204** B6
Brierley Av, N9 **61** F1
Brierley Cl, SE25 **188** D4
Brierley Rd, E11 **96** D4
SW12 **168** C2
Brierly Gdns, E2 *off Royston St* **113** F2
Brigade Cl, Har. HA2 **86** A2
Brigade St, SE3 *off Royal Par* **155** F2
Brigadier Av, Enf. EN2 **43** J1
Briggeford Cl, E5 *off Geldeston Rd* **94** D2
Briggs Cl, Mitch. CR4 **186** B1
Bright Cl, Belv. DA17 **138** D4
Brightfield Rd, SE12 **155** F5
Brightling Rd, SE4 **153** J6
Brightlingsea Pl, E14 **113** J7
Brightman Rd, SW18 **167** G1
Brighton Av, E17 **77** J5
Brighton Dr, Nthlt. UB5 **85** G6
Brighton Gro, SE14 *off Harts La* **153** H1
Brighton Rd, E6 **116** D3
N2 **73** F2
N16 **94** B4
South Croydon CR2 **201** J5
Surbiton KT6 **181** F6
Brighton Ter, SW9 **151** F4
Brightside, The, Enfield EN3 **45** G1
Brightside Rd, SE13 **154** D6
Bright St, E14 **114** B6
Brightwell Cl, Croy. CR0 *off Sumner Rd* **201** G1
Brightwell Cres, SW17 **167** J5
Brightwen Gro, Stan. HA7 **52** D2
Brig Ms, SE8 *off Watergate St* **134** A6
Brigstock Rd, Belv. DA17 **139** H4
Thornton Heath CR7 **187** G5
Brill Pl, NW1 **9** J2
Brim Hill, N2 **73** F4
Brimpsfield Cl, SE2 **138** B3
BRIMSDOWN, Enf. EN3 **45** H3
Brimsdown Av, Enf. EN3 **45** H2
Brimsdown Ind Est, Enf. EN3 **45** H1
Brimstone Ho, E15 *off Victoria St* **96** E7
Brindle Gate, Sidcup DA15 **175** H1
Brindley Cl, Bexh. DA7 **159** H3
Wembley HA0 **105** F1
Brindley Ho, SW2 *off New Pk Rd* **150** E7
Brindley St, SE14 **153** J1
Brindley Way, Brom. BR1 **173** G5
Southall UB1 **103** H7
Brindwood Rd, E4 **61** J3
Brinkburn Cl, SE2 **138** A4
Edgware HA8 **70** B2
Brinkburn Gdns, Edg. HA8 **70** A3
Brinkley, Kings.T. KT1 *off Burritt Rd* **182** A2
Brinkley Rd, Wor.Pk. KT4 **197** H2
Brinklow Cres, SE18 **137** E7
Brinklow Ho, W2 **108** E5
Brinkworth Rd, Ilf. IG5 **80** B3
Brinkworth Way, E9 **95** J6
Brinsdale Rd, NW4 **72** A4
Brinsley Ho, E1 *off Tarling St* **113** F6
Brinsley Rd, Har. HA3 **68** A2
Brinsworth Cl, Twick. TW2 **162** A2
Brinton Wk, SE1 **27** G2
Brion Pl, E14 **114** C5
Brisbane Av, SW19 **184** E1
Brisbane Rd, E10 **96** B2
W13 **124** D2
Ilford IG1 **81** E7
Brisbane St, SE5 **132** A7
Briscoe Cl, E11 **97** F2
Briscoe Rd, SW19 **167** G6
Briset Rd, SE9 **156** A3
Briset St, EC1 **19** G1
Briset Way, N7 **93** F2
Bristol Cl, Houns. TW4 *off Harvey Rd* **143** G7
Staines (Stanw.) TW19 **140** B6
Wallington SM6 **200** E7
Bristol Gdns, SW15 *off Portsmouth Rd* **147** J7
W9 **6** B6
Bristol Ho, SE11 *off Lambeth Wk* **26** E6
Bristol Ms, W9 **6** B6
Bristol Pk Rd, E17 **77** H4

Bristol Rd, E7 97 J6
Greenford UB6 103 H1
Morden SM4 185 F5
Briston Gro, N8 75 E6
Briston Ms, NW7 55 G7
Bristowe Cl, SW2
off Tulse Hill 151 G6
Bristow Rd, SE19 170 B5
Bexleyheath DA7 159 E1
Croydon CR0 200 E4
Hounslow TW3 143 J3
★ **Britain at War Experience**, SE1 28 D2
Britannia Bldg, N1
off Ebenezer St 12 B3
Britannia Cl, SW4
off Bowland Rd 150 D4
Northolt UB5 102 D3
Britannia Ct, Kings.T. KT2
off Skerne Wk 181 G1
Britannia Gate, E16 135 G1
Britannia La, Twick. TW2 143 J7
Britannia Rd, E14 134 A4
N12 57 F3
SW6 128 E7
Ilford IG1 98 E3
Surbiton KT5 181 J7
Britannia Row, N1 111 H1
Britannia St, WC1 10 C3
Britannia Wk, N1 12 B3
Britannia Way, NW10 106 B4
SW6 *off Britannia Rd* 129 E7
Staines (Stanw.) TW19 140 A7
★ **British Dental Assoc Mus**, W1 16 D2
British Gro, W4 127 F5
British Gro N, W4
off Middlesex Ct 127 F5
British Gro Pas, W4 127 F5
British Gro S, W4
off British Gro Pas 127 F5
British Legion Rd, E4 63 F2
★ **British Lib**, NW1 9 J3
★ **British Lib Newspapers**, NW9 70 E3
★ **British Med Assoc**, WC1 9 J5
★ **British Mus, The**, WC1 17 J2
★ **British Red Cross Mus & Archives**, SW1 20 B1
British St, E3 113 J3
Brittain Rd, Dag. RM8 101 E3
Brittany Pt, SE11 35 E2
Britten Cl, NW11 90 E1
Brittenden Cl, Orp. BR6 207 H6
Brittenden Par, Orp. (Grn St Grn) BR6
off Glentrammon Rd 207 J6
Britten Dr, Sthl. UB1 103 G6
Britten St, SW3 31 G4
Brittidge Rd, NW10
off Paulet Way 88 E7
Britton Cl, SE6
off Brownhill Rd 154 D7
Britton St, EC1 11 G6
Brixham Cres, Ruis. HA4 84 A1
Brixham Gdns, Ilf. IG3 99 H5
Brixham Rd, Well. DA16 158 D1
Brixham St, E16 136 C1
BRIXTON, SW2 151 E4
★ **Brixton Acad, The**, SW9 151 F3
Brixton Hill, SW2 151 E7
Brixton Hill Pl, SW2
off Brixton Hill 151 E7
Brixton Oval, SW2 151 G4
Brixton Rd, SW9 151 G2
Brixton Sta Rd, SW9 151 G4
Brixton Water La, SW2 151 F5
Broadbent Cl, N6 92 B1
Broadbent St, W1 16 D5
Broadberry Ct, N18 60 E5
Broadbridge Cl, SE3 135 G7
Broad Common Est, N16
off Osbaldeston Rd 94 D1
Broadcoombe, S.Croy. CR2 203 F7
Broad Ct, WC2 18 B4
Broadcroft Av, Stan. HA7 69 G2
Broadcroft Rd, Orp. BR5 193 G7
Broadeaves Cl, S.Croy. CR2 202 B5
Broadfield Cl, NW2 89 J3
Croydon CR0
off Progress Way 201 F2
Broadfield Ct, Bushey (Bushey Hth) WD23 52 B2
Broadfield La, NW1 92 E7
Broadfield Rd, SE6 154 E7
Broadfields, E.Mol. KT8 180 A6
Harrow HA2 67 H2
Broadfields Av, N21 43 G7
Edgware HA8 54 B4
Broadfields Hts, Edg. HA8 54 B4
Broadfields La, Wat. WD19 50 B1
Broadfield Sq, Enf. EN1 45 E2
Broadfields Way, NW10 89 F5
Broadfield Way, Buck.H. IG9 63 J3
BROADGATE, EC2 20 C1
Broadgate, E13 115 J2
Broadgate Circle, EC2 20 D1
Broadgate Rd, E16 116 A6
Broadgates Av, Barn. EN4 41 E1
Broadgates Rd, SW18
off Ellerton Rd 167 G1
BROAD GREEN, Croy. CR0 187 G6
Broad Grn Av, Croy. CR0 187 H7
Broadhead Strand, NW9 71 F1
Broadheath Dr, Chis. BR7 174 C5
Broadhinton Rd, SW4 150 B3
Broadhurst Av, Edg. HA8 54 B4
Ilford IG3 99 J4
Broadhurst Cl, NW6
off Broadhurst Gdns 91 F6
Richmond TW10
off Lower Gro Rd 145 J5
Broadhurst Gdns, NW6 90 E6
Chigwell IG7 65 F4
Ruislip HA4 84 C2
Broadlands, Felt. (Han.) TW13 161 F3
Broadlands Av, SW16 168 E2
Enfield EN3 45 E3
Broadlands Cl, N6 74 A7
SW16 168 E2
Enfield EN3 45 E3
Broadlands Rd, N6 73 J7
Bromley BR1 173 H4
Broadlands Way, N.Mal. KT3 183 F6
Broad La, EC2 20 D1
N8 *off Tottenham La* 75 F5
N15 76 C4
Hampton TW12 161 G6
Broad Lawn, SE9 174 D2
Broadlawns Ct, Har. HA3 68 C1
Broadley St, NW8 15 F1
Broadley Ter, NW1 7 H6
Broadmayne, SE17 36 A3
Broadmead, SE6 172 A3
Broadmead Av, Wor.Pk. KT4 183 G7
Broadmead Cl, Hmptn. TW12 161 G6
Pinner HA5 51 E7
Broadmead Rd, Hayes UB4 102 E4
Northolt UB5 102 E4
Woodford Green IG8 63 G6
Broad Oak, Wdf.Grn. IG8 63 H5
Broad Oak Cl, E4 62 A5
Broadoak Ct, SW9
off Gresham Rd 151 G3
Broadoaks Way, Brom. BR2 191 F5
Broad Sanctuary, SW1 25 J4
Broadstone Pl, W1 16 B2
Broad St, Dag. RM10 101 G7
Teddington TW11 162 C6
Broad St Av, EC2 20 D2
Broad St Pl, EC2 20 C2
Broad Vw, NW9 70 A6
Broadview Rd, SW16 168 C7
Broadwalk, E18 79 F3
Broad Wk, N21 59 F2
NW1 8 D4
SE3 155 J3
W1 24 B1
Broadwalk, Har. HA2 67 G5
Broad Wk, Houns. TW5 142 D1
Richmond TW9 125 J7
Broad Wk, The, W8 14 B6
East Molesey KT8 180 C3
Broadwalk Ct, W8 128 D1
Broad Wk La, NW11 72 C7
Broadwalk Shop Cen, Edg. HA8 54 B6
Broadwall, SE1 27 F1
Broadwater Fm Est, N17 76 A2
Broadwater Gdns, Orp. BR6 207 E4
Broadwater Rd, N17 76 B1
SE28 137 G3
SW17 167 H4
Broadway, E15 96 D7
SW1 25 H5
Barking IG11 117 F1
Bexleyheath DA6, DA7 159 E4
Broadway, The, E4 62 C6
E13 115 H2
N8 74 E6
N9 60 D2
N14
off Winchmore Hill Rd 58 D1
N22 75 G2
NW7 55 E5
SW13 *off The Terrace* 146 E2
SW19 166 C6
Broadway, The, W5 105 G7
W7 *off Cherington Rd* 124 B1
W7 (W.Ealing) 124 D1
W13 124 D1
Croydon CR0
off Croydon Rd 201 E4
Dagenham RM8 101 F2
Greenford UB6 103 J4
Harrow (Wealds.) HA3 68 B2
Loughton IG10 49 F4
Pinner HA5 51 F7
Southall UB1 102 D7
Stanmore HA7 53 F5
Sutton SM1
off Manor La 199 F5
Sutton (Cheam) SM3 198 B6
Thames Ditton KT7
off Hampton Ct Way 194 B1
Wembley HA9
off East La 87 H3
Woodford Green IG8 63 H6
Broadway Av, Croy. CR0 188 A5
Twickenham TW1 144 E6
Broadway Cl, Wdf.Grn. IG8 63 H6
Broadway Ct, SW19 166 C6
Broadway Gdns, Mitch. CR4 185 H4
Broadway Mkt, E8 112 E1
SW17 167 J4
Broadway Mkt Ms, E8
off Regents Row 112 D1
Broadway Ms, E5 76 C7
N13 *off Elmdale Rd* 59 F5
N21 59 H1
Broadway Par, N8 74 E6
Hayes UB3
off Coldharbour La 122 A1
Broadway Pl, SW19
off Hartfield Rd 166 C6
Broadway Shop Cen, W6
off Hammersmith Bdy 127 J4
Bexleyheath DA6 159 G4
Broadway Wk, E14
off Alpha Gro 134 A3
Broadwick St, W1 17 G5
Broadwood Ter, W8
off Pembroke Rd 128 C4
Broad Yd, EC1 11 G6
Brocas Cl, NW3
off Fellows Rd 91 H7
Brockbridge Ho, SW15
off Tangley Gro 147 F6
Brockdene Dr, Kes. BR2 206 A4
Brockdish Av, Bark. IG11 99 J5
Brockenhurst, W.Mol. KT8 179 F6
Brockenhurst Av, Wor.Pk. KT4 197 E1
Brockenhurst Gdns, NW7 55 E5
Ilford IG1 99 F5
Brockenhurst Ms, N18 60 D4
Brockenhurst Rd, Croy. CR0 188 E7
Brockenhurst Way, SW16 186 D2
Brocket Cl, Chig. IG7
off Brocket Way 65 J5
Brocket Way, Chig. IG7 65 H5
Brockham Cl, SW19 166 C5
Brockham Cres, Croy. (New Adgtn) CR0 204 D7
Brockham Dr, SW2
off Fairview Pl 151 F7
Ilford IG2 81 E6
Brockham St, SE1 28 A5
Brockhurst Cl, Stan. HA7 52 C6
Brockill Cres, SE4 153 H4
Brocklebank Rd, SE7 135 H4
SW18 149 F7
Brocklehurst St, SE14 133 G7
Brocklesby Rd, SE25 188 E4
BROCKLEY, SE4 153 H5
Brockley Av, Stan. HA7 53 H3
Brockley Cl, Stan. HA7 53 H4
Brockley Cross, SE4
off Endwell Rd 153 J3
Brockley Footpath, SE15 153 F4
Brockley Gdns, SE4 153 J2
Brockley Gro, SE4 153 J5
Brockley Hall Rd, SE4 153 H6
Brockley Hill, Stan. HA7 53 F1
Brockley Ms, SE4 153 H5
Brockley Pk, SE23 153 H7
Stanmore HA7 53 H3
Brockley Ri, SE23 153 H6
Brockley Rd, SE4 153 J3
Brockleyside, Stan. HA7 53 G4
Brockley Vw, SE23 153 H7
Brockley Way, SE4 153 G5
Brockman Ri, Brom. BR1 172 D4
Brock Pl, E3 114 B4
Brock Rd, E13 115 H5
Brocks Dr, Sutt. SM3 198 B3
Brockshot Cl, Brent. TW8 125 G6
Brock St, SE15
off Evelina Rd 153 F3
Brockway Cl, E11 97 E1
Brockweir, E2
off Cyprus St 113 F2
Brockwell Av, Beck. BR3 190 B5
Brockwell Cl, Orp. BR5 193 J5
★ **Brockwell Park**, SE24 151 H6
Brockwell Pk Gdns, SE24 151 G7
Brockwell Pk Row, SW2 151 G6
Brodewater Rd, Borwd. WD6 38 B2
Brodia Rd, N16 94 B3
Brodick Ho, E3
off Saxon Rd 113 J2
Brodie Ho, SE1
off Coopers Rd 37 G3
Brodie Rd, E4 62 C1
Brodie St, SE1 37 G3
Brodlove La, E1 113 G7
Brodrick Gro, SE2 138 B4
Brodrick Rd, SW17 167 H2
Brograve Gdns, Beck. BR3 190 B2
Broken Wf, EC4 19 J5
Brokesley St, E3 113 J4
Broke Wk, E8 112 D1
Bromar Rd, SE5 152 B3
Bromborough Grn, Wat. WD19 50 C5
Bromefield, Stan. HA7 69 F1
Bromehead Rd, E1
off Commercial Rd 113 F6
Bromehead St, E1
off Commercial Rd 113 F6
Bromell's Rd, SW4 150 C4
Brome Rd, SE9 156 C3
Bromfelde Rd, SW4 150 D3
Bromfelde Wk, SW4 150 D2
Bromfield St, N1 11 F1
Bromhall Rd, Dag. RM8, RM9 100 B6
Bromhedge, SE9 174 C3
Bromholm Rd, SE2 138 B3
Bromleigh Ct, SE23
off Lapse Wd Wk 170 E2
BROMLEY, E3 114 B4
BROMLEY, BR1 & BR2 191 F2
Bromley Av, Brom. BR1 173 E7
BROMLEY COMMON, Brom. BR2 192 C7
Bromley Common, Brom. BR2 191 J4
Bromley Cres, Brom. BR2 191 F3
Bromley Gdns, Brom. BR2 191 F3
Bromley Gro, Brom. BR2 190 D2
Bromley Hall Rd, E14 114 C5
Bromley High St, E3 114 B3
Bromley Hill, Brom. BR1 172 E5
Bromley Ind Cen, Brom. BR1 191 J3
Bromley La, Chis. BR7 175 F7
BROMLEY PARK, Brom. BR1 190 E1
Bromley Pk, Brom. BR1
off London Rd 191 F1
Bromley Pl, W1 17 F1
Bromley Rd, E10 78 B6
E17 78 A2
N17 76 C1
N18 60 A3
SE6 172 B1
Beckenham BR3 190 B1
Bromley (Downham) BR1 172 C4
Bromley (Short.) BR2 190 C2
Chislehurst BR7 192 E1
Bromley St, E1 113 G5
BROMPTON, SW3 23 G6
Brompton Arc, SW3 23 J4
Brompton Cl, SE20
off Selby Rd 188 D2
Hounslow TW4 143 F5
Brompton Gro, N2 73 H4
★ **Brompton Oratory**, SW7 23 G6
Brompton Pk Cres, SW6 30 A6
Brompton Pl, SW3 23 H5
Brompton Rd, SW1 23 H5
SW3 31 G1
SW7 23 H5
Brompton Sq, SW3 23 G5
Brompton Ter, SE18
off Prince Imperial Rd 156 D1
Bromwich Av, N6 92 A2
Bromyard Av, W3 127 E1
Bromyard Ho, SE15 132 E7
W3 127 E1
BRONDESBURY, NW2 90 B7
Brondesbury Ct, NW2 89 J6
Brondesbury Ms, NW6
off Willesden La 90 D7

BRONDESBURY PARK, NW6 89 J7
Brondesbury Pk, NW2 89 H6
NW6 90 A7
Brondesbury Rd, NW6 108 C2
Brondesbury Vil, NW6 108 C2
Bronsart Rd, SW6 128 B7
Bronson Rd, SW20 184 A2
Bronte Cl, E7
off Bective Rd 97 G4
Erith DA8 139 H7
Ilford IG2 80 D5
Bronte Ho, NW6 108 D3
Bronti Cl, SE17 36 A4
Bronze Age Way, Belv. DA17 139 J3
Erith DA8 139 J3
Bronze St, SE8 134 A7
Brook Av, Dag. RM10 101 H7
Edgware HA8 54 B6
Wembley HA9 88 A3
Brookbank Av, W7 104 A5
Brookbank Rd, SE13 154 A3
Brook Cl, NW7 56 B7
SW17 168 A2
SW20 183 H3
W3 *off West Lo Av* 126 A1
Borehamwood WD6 38 B3
Staines (Stanw.) TW19 140 C7
Brook Ct, Buck.H. IG9 63 H1
Brook Cres, E4 62 A4
N9 60 E4
Brookdale, N11 58 C4
Brookdale Rd, E17 78 A3
SE6 154 B6
Bexley DA5 159 E6
Brookdene Rd, SE18 137 J4
Brook Dr, SE11 27 F6
Harrow HA1 67 J4
Brooke Av, Har. HA2 85 J3
Brooke Ct, W10
off Kilburn La 108 B2
Brookehowse Rd, SE6 172 B3
Brookend Rd, Sid. DA15 175 H1
Brooke Rd, E5 94 D3
E17 78 C4
N16 94 C3
Brooke's Ct, EC1 19 E1
Brookes Mkt, EC1 19 F1
Brooke St, EC1 19 E2
Brookfield, N6 92 A3
Brookfield Av, E17 78 C4
NW7 55 H6
W5 105 G4
Sutton SM1 199 G4
Brookfield Cl, NW7 55 H6
Brookfield Ct, Grnf. UB6 103 J3
Harrow HA3 69 G5
Brookfield Cres, NW7 55 H6
Harrow HA3 69 H5
Brookfield Gdns, Esher (Clay.) KT10 194 C6
Brookfield Pk, NW5 92 B3
Brookfield Path, Wdf.Grn. IG8 62 E6
Brookfield Rd, E9 95 H6
N9 60 D3
W4 126 D2
Brookfields, Enf. EN3 45 G4
Brookfields Av, Mitch. CR4 185 H5
Brook Gdns, E4 62 B4
SW13 147 F3
Kingston upon Thames KT2 182 C1
Brook Gate, W1 16 A6
Brook Grn, W6 128 A4
Brookhill Cl, SE18 136 E5
Barnet (E.Barn.) EN4 41 H5
Brookhill Rd, SE18 136 E5
Barnet EN4 41 H5
Brookhouse Gdns, E4 62 E4
Brook Ind Est, Hayes UB4 122 D1
Brooking Cl, Dag. RM8 100 C3
Brooking Rd, E7 97 G5
Brookland Cl, NW11 72 D4
Brookland Garth, NW11 72 E4
Brookland Hill, NW11 72 D4
Brookland Ri, NW11 72 D4
Brooklands Av, SW19 166 E2
Sidcup DA15 175 G2
Brooklands Dr, Grnf. (Perivale) UB6 105 G1
Brooklands Pk, SE3 155 G3
Brooklands Pas, SW8
off Belmore St 150 D1
Brooklands Pl, Hmptn. TW12 161 H5
Brooklands Rd, T.Ditt. KT7 194 C1
Brook La, SE3 155 H2
Bexley DA5 158 D6
Bromley BR1 173 G6
Brook La N, Brentford TW8 125 G5
Brooklea Cl, NW9 71 E1
Brooklyn Av, SE25 189 E4
Loughton IG10 48 B4
Brooklyn Cl, Cars. SM5 199 H2
Brooklyn Gro, SE25 189 E4
Brooklyn Pas, W12
off Lime Gro 127 J2
Brooklyn Rd, SE25 188 E4
Bromley BR2 192 A5
Brooklyn Way, West Dr. UB7 120 A3
Brookmarsh Ind Est, SE10
off Norman Rd 134 B7
Brook Mead, Epsom KT19 197 E6
Brookmead Av, Brom. BR1 192 C5
Brookmead Ind Est, Croy. CR0 186 C6
Brook Meadow, N12 56 E4
Brook Meadow Cl, Wdf.Grn. IG8 62 E6
Brookmead Rd, Croy. CR0 186 C6
Brookmeads Est, Mitch. CR4 185 H5
Brook Ms, N13 59 G5
Chigwell IG7 64 E3
Brook Ms N, W2 14 D5
Brookmill Rd, SE8 154 A1
Brook Par, Chig. IG7
off High Rd 64 E3
Brook Pk Cl, N21 43 H6
Brook Path, Loug. IG10 48 B4
Brook Pl, Barn. EN5 40 D5
Brook Retail Pk, Ruis. HA4
off Victoria Rd 84 D5
Brook Ri, Chig. IG7 64 D3
Brook Rd, N8 74 E4
N22 75 F3
NW2 89 G2
Borehamwood WD6 38 A2
Buckhurst Hill IG9 63 G2
Ilford IG2 81 H6
Loughton IG10 48 B5
Surbiton KT6 195 H2
Thornton Heath CR7 187 J4
Twickenham TW1 144 D6
Brook Rd S, Brent. TW8 125 G6
Brooks Av, E6 116 C4
Brooksbank St, E9 95 F6
Brooksby Ms, N1
off Brooksby St 93 G7
Brooksby St, N1 93 G7
Brooksby's Wk, E9 95 G5
Brooks Cl, SE9 174 D2
Brookscroft Rd, E17 78 B1
Brookshill, Har. HA3 52 A5
Brookshill Av, Har. HA3 52 A5
Brookshill Dr, Har. HA3 52 A5
Brookshill Gate, Har. (Har.Wld) HA3 52 A5
Brookside, N21 43 F6
Barnet (E.Barn.) EN4 41 H6
Carshalton SM5 200 A5
Ilford IG6 65 F6
Orpington BR6 193 J7
Brookside Cl, Barn. EN5 40 B6
Feltham TW13
off Sycamore Cl 160 A3
Harrow (Kenton) HA3 69 G5
Harrow (S.Har.) HA2 85 E4
Brookside Cres, Wor.Pk. KT4 *off Green La* 197 G1
Brookside Rd, N9 60 E4
N19 92 C2
NW11 72 B6
Hayes UB4 102 C7
Brookside S, Barn. (E.Barn.) EN4 42 A7
Brookside Wk, N3 72 B2
N12 56 D6
NW4 72 B4
NW11 72 B4
Brookside Way, Croy. CR0 189 G6
Brooks La, W4 126 A6
Brook's Ms, W1 16 D5
Brook Sq, SE18
off Barlow Dr 156 B1
Brooks Rd, E13 115 G1
W4 126 A5
Brook St, N17
off High Rd 76 C2
W1 16 C5
W2 15 F5
Belvedere DA17 139 H5
Erith DA8 139 H6
Kingston upon Thames KT1 181 H2
Brooksville Av, NW6 108 B1
Brook Vale, Erith DA8 159 H1
Brookview Rd, SW16 168 C5
Brookville Rd, SW6 128 C7
Brook Wk, N2 73 G1
Edgware HA8 54 D6
Brookway, SE3 155 G3
Brook Way, Chig. IG7 64 D3
Brookwood Av, SW13 147 F3
Brookwood Cl, Brom. BR2 191 F4
Brookwood Rd, SW18 166 C1
Hounslow TW3 143 H1
Broom Cl, Brom. BR2 192 B6
Teddington TW11 163 G7
Broomcroft Av, Nthlt. UB5 102 C3
Broome Ho, E5
off Pembury Rd 94 E5
Broome Rd, Hmptn. TW12 161 F7
Broome Way, SE5 132 A7
Broomfield, E17 77 J7
Sunbury-on-Thames TW16 178 A1
Broomfield Av, N13 59 F5
Loughton IG10 48 C6
Broomfield La, N13 59 F4
Broomfield Pl, W13
off Broomfield Rd 125 E1
Broomfield Rd, N13 59 E5
W13 125 E1
Beckenham BR3 189 H3
Bexleyheath DA6 159 G5
Richmond TW9 145 J1
Romford RM6 82 D7
Surbiton KT5 195 J1
Teddington TW11
off Melbourne Rd 163 F6
Broomfield St, E14 114 A5
Broom Gdns, Croy. CR0 204 A3
Broomgrove Gdns, Edg. HA8 70 A1
Broomgrove Rd, SW9 151 F2
Broomhill Ct, Wdf.Grn. IG8
off Broomhill Rd 63 G6
Broomhill Ri, Bexh. DA6 159 G5
Broomhill Rd, SW18 148 D5
Ilford IG3 100 A2
Woodford Green IG8 63 G6
Broomhill Wk, Wdf.Grn. IG8 63 F7
Broomhouse La, SW6 148 D2
Broomhouse Rd, SW6 148 D2
Broomloan La, Sutt. SM1 198 D2
Broom Lock, Tedd. TW11 163 F6
Broom Mead, Bexh. DA6 159 G5
Broom Pk, Tedd. TW11 163 G7
Broom Rd, Croy. CR0 204 A3
Teddington TW11 163 F6
Broomsleigh Business Pk, SE26
off Worsley Br Rd 171 J5
Broomsleigh St, NW6 90 C5
Broom Water, Tedd. TW11 163 F6
Broom Water W, Tedd. TW11 163 F5
Broomwood Cl, Croy. CR0 189 G5
Broomwood Rd, SW11 149 J6
Broseley Gro, SE26 171 H5
Broster Gdns, SE25 188 C3
Brougham Rd, E8 112 D1
W3 106 C6
Brougham St, SW11 149 J2
Brough Cl, SW8
off Kenchester Cl 131 E7
Kingston upon Thames KT2 163 G5
Broughinge Rd, Borwd. WD6 38 B2
Broughton Av, N3 72 B3
Richmond TW10 163 E3
Broughton Dr, SW9 151 G4
Broughton Gdns, N6 74 C6
Broughton Rd, SW6 148 E2
W13 105 E7
Orpington BR6 207 G2
Thornton Heath CR7 187 G6
Broughton Rd App, SW6
off Wandsworth Br Rd 148 E2
Broughton St, SW8 150 A2
Brouncker Rd, W3 126 C2
Browells La, Felt. TW13 160 B2
Brown Cl, Wall. SM6 200 D7
Brownfield St, E14 114 B6
Browngraves Rd, Hayes (Harling.) UB3 121 F7
Brown Hart Gdns, W1 16 C5
Brownhill Rd, SE6 154 B7
Browning Av, W7 104 C6
Sutton SM1 199 H4
Worcester Park KT4 197 H1
Browning Cl, E17 78 C4
W9 6 D6
Hampton TW12 161 F4
Welling DA16 157 H1
Browning Ms, W1 16 D2
Browning Rd, E11 79 F7
E12 98 C6
Browning St, SE17 36 A3
Browning Way, Houns. TW5 142 D1
Brownlea Gdns, Ilf. IG3 100 A2
Brownlow Cl, Barn. EN4 41 G5
Brownlow Ms, WC1 10 D6
Brownlow Rd, E7
off Woodford Rd 97 G4
E8 112 C1
N3 56 E7
N11 58 E6
NW10 89 E7
W13 124 D1
Borehamwood WD6 38 A4
Croydon CR0 202 B4
Brownlow St, WC1 18 D2
Brown's Bldgs, EC3 20 E4
Brownsea Wk, NW7 56 A6
Browns La, NW5 92 B5
Brownspring Dr, SE9 175 E4
Browns Rd, E17 78 A3
Surbiton KT5 181 J7
Brown St, W1 15 J3
Brownswell Rd, N2 73 G2
Brownswood Rd, N4 93 H3
Broxash Rd, SW11 150 A6
Broxbourne Av, E18 79 H4
Broxbourne Rd, E7 97 G3
Orpington BR6 193 J7
Broxholme Cl, SE25
off Whitehorse La 188 A4
Broxholm Rd, SE27 169 G3
Broxted Rd, SE6 171 J2
Broxwood Way, NW8 109 H1
★ **Bruce Castle Mus**, N17 76 B1
Bruce Castle Rd, N17 76 C1
Bruce Cl, W10
off Ladbroke Gro 108 B5
Welling DA16 158 B1
Bruce Gdns, N20 57 J3
Bruce Gro, N17 76 B1
Bruce Hall Ms, SW17 168 A4
Bruce Rd, E3 114 B3
NW10 88 D7
SE25 188 A4
Barnet EN5
off St. Albans Rd 40 B3
Harrow HA3 68 B2
Mitcham CR4 168 A7
Bruckner St, W10 108 C3
Brudenell Rd, SW17 167 J3
Bruffs Meadow, Nthlt. UB5 85 E6
Bruford Ct, SE8 134 A6
Bruges Pl, NW1
off Randolph St 92 C7
Brumfield Rd, Epsom KT19 196 C5
Brummel Cl, Bexh. DA7 159 J3
★ **Brunei Gall**, WC1 17 J1
Brunel Cl, SE19 170 C6
Hounslow TW5 122 B7
Northolt UB5 103 F3
★ **Brunel Engine Ho**, SE16 133 F2
Brunel Est, W2 108 D5
Brunel Ms, W10
off Kilburn La 108 B3
Brunel Pl, Sthl. UB1 103 H6
Brunel Rd, E17 77 H6
SE16 133 F2
W3 106 E5
Woodford Green IG8 64 C5
Brunel St, E16
off Victoria Dock Rd 115 F6
Brunel Wk, N15 76 B4
Twickenham TW2
off Stephenson Rd 143 G7
Brune St, E1 21 F2
Brunlees Ho, SE1
off Bath Ter 27 J6
Brunner Cl, NW11 73 E5
Brunner Rd, E17 77 H5
W5 105 G4
Bruno Pl, NW9 88 C2
Brunswick Av, N11 58 A3
Brunswick Cl, Bexh. DA6 158 D4
Pinner HA5 67 E6
Thames Ditton KT7 194 C1
Twickenham TW2 162 A3
Brunswick Ct, EC1
off Tompion St 11 G4
SE1 29 E4
SW1 *off Regency St* 33 J2
Barnet EN4 41 G5
Brunswick Cres, N11 58 A3
Brunswick Gdns, W5 105 H3
W8 128 D1
Ilford IG6 65 F7
Brunswick Gro, N11 58 A3
Brunswick Ind Pk, N11 58 B4
Brunswick Ms, SW16
off Potters La 168 D6
W1 16 A3
BRUNSWICK PARK, N11 57 J3

Brunswick Pk, SE5 **152** A1
Brunswick Pk Gdns, N11 **58** A2
Brunswick Pk Rd, N11 **58** A2
Brunswick Pl, N1 **12** C4
NW1 **8** C5
SE19 **170** D7
Brunswick Quay, SE16 **133** G3
Brunswick Rd, E10 **96** C1
E14 *off Blackwall Tunnel Northern App* **114** C6
N15 **76** B5
W5 **105** G4
Bexleyheath DA6 **158** D4
Kingston upon Thames KT2 **182** A1
Sutton SM1 **199** E4
Brunswick Shop Cen, WC1 **10** A5
Brunswick Sq, N17 **60** C6
WC1 **10** B6
Brunswick St, E17 **78** C5
Brunswick Vil, SE5 **152** B1
Brunswick Way, N11 **58** B4
Brunton Pl, E14 **113** H6
Brushfield St, E1 **21** E1
Brushwood Cl, E14 *off Uamvar St* **114** B5
Brussels Rd, SW11 **149** G4
Bruton Cl, Chis. BR7 **174** C7
Bruton La, W1 **16** E6
Bruton Pl, W1 **16** E6
Bruton Rd, Mord. SM4 **185** F5
Bruton St, W1 **16** E6
Bruton Way, W13 **104** D5
Bryan Av, NW10 **89** H7
Bryan Cl, Sun. TW16 **160** A7
Bryan Rd, SE16 **133** J2
Bryan's All, SW6 *off Wandsworth Br Rd* **148** E2
Bryanston Av, Twick. TW2 **161** H1
Bryanston Cl, Sthl. UB2 **123** F4
Bryanstone Ct, Sutt. SM1 *off Oakhill Rd* **199** F4
Bryanstone Rd, N8 **74** D5
Bryanston Ms E, W1 **15** J2
Bryanston Ms W, W1 **15** J2
Bryanston Pl, W1 **15** J2
Bryanston Sq, W1 **15** J2
Bryanston St, W1 **15** J4
Bryant Cl, Barn. EN5 **40** C5
Bryant Ct, E2 **13** F1
Bryant Rd, Nthlt. UB5 **102** C3
Bryant St, E15 **96** D7
Bryantwood Rd, N7 **93** G5
Brycedale Cres, N14 **58** D4
Bryce Rd, Dag. RM8 **100** C4
Brydale Ho, SE16 *off Rotherhithe New Rd* **133** G4
Bryden Cl, SE26 **171** H5
Brydges Pl, WC2 **18** A6
Brydges Rd, E15 **96** D5
Brydon Wk, N1 *off Outram Pl* **111** E1
Bryer Ct, EC2 *off Bridgewater St* **19** J1
Bryett Rd, N7 **93** E3
Brymay Cl, E3 **114** A2
Brynmaer Rd, SW11 **149** J1
Bryn-y-Mawr Rd, Enf. EN1 **44** C4
Bryony Cl, Loug. IG10 **48** E4
Bryony Rd, W12 **107** G7
Buchanan Cl, N21 **43** F5
Buchanan Ct, Borwd. WD6 **38** C2
Buchanan Gdns, NW10 **107** H2
Buchan Rd, SE15 **153** F3
Bucharest Rd, SW18 **149** F7
Buckden Cl, N2 *off Southern Rd* **73** J4
SE12 *off Upwood Rd* **155** F6
Buckfast Ct, W13 *off Romsey Rd* **104** D7
Buckfast Rd, Mord. SM4 **185** E4
Buckfast St, E2 **13** J4
Buck Hill Wk, W2 **15** F6
Buckhold Rd, SW18 **148** D6
Buckhurst Av, Cars. SM5 **199** H1
BUCKHURST HILL, IG9 **47** H7
Buckhurst St, E1 **113** E4
Buckhurst Way, Buck.H. IG9 **64** A4
Buckingham Arc, WC2 **18** B6
Buckingham Av, N20 **41** F7
Feltham TW14 **142** B6
Greenford (Perivale) UB6 **104** D1
Thornton Heath CR7 **187** G1
Welling DA16 **157** H4
West Molesey KT8 **179** H3
Buckingham Chambers, SW1 *off Greencoat Pl* **33** G1
Buckingham Cl, W5 **105** F5
Enfield EN1 **44** B2
Hampton TW12 **161** F5
Orpington BR5 **193** H7
Buckingham Ct, NW4 **71** G3
Loughton IG10 *off Rectory La* **48** D2
Buckingham Dr, Chis. BR7 **175** E5
Buckingham Gdns, Edg. HA8 **53** J7
Thornton Heath CR7 **187** G2
West Molesey KT8 *off Buckingham Av* **179** H2
Buckingham Gate, SW1 **25** F4
Buckingham La, SE23 **153** H7
Buckingham Lo, N10 **74** C4
Buckingham Ms, N1 *off Buckingham Rd* **94** B6
NW10 *off Buckingham Rd* **107** F2
SW1 **25** F5
★ **Buckingham Palace**, SW1 **24** E4
Buckingham Palace Rd, SW1 **32** D2
Buckingham Pl, SW1 **25** F5
Buckingham Rd, E10 **96** B3
E11 **79** J5
E15 **97** F5
E18 **79** F1
N1 **94** B6
N22 **74** E1
NW10 **107** F2
Borehamwood WD6 **38** D4
Edgware HA8 **53** J7
Hampton TW12 **161** F4
Harrow HA1 **68** A5
Ilford IG1 **99** G2
Kingston upon Thames KT1 **181** J4
Mitcham CR4 **186** E5
Richmond TW10 **163** G2
Buckingham St, WC2 **18** B6
Buckland Cl, NW7 **55** G4
Buckland Cres, NW3 **91** G7
Buckland Ri, Pnr. HA5 **66** C1
Buckland Rd, E10 **96** C2
Chessington KT9 **195** J5
Orpington BR6 **207** H4
Bucklands Rd, Tedd. TW11 **163** F6
Buckland St, N1 **12** C2
Buckland Wk, W3 **126** C1
Morden SM4 **185** F4
Buckland Way, Wor.Pk. KT4 **197** J1
Buck La, NW9 **70** D5
Bucklebury, NW1 **9** F5
Buckleigh Av, SW20 **184** B3
Buckleigh Rd, SW16 **168** D6
Buckleigh Way, SE19 **188** C1
Buckler Ct, N7 *off Eden Gro* **93** F5
Buckler Gdns, SE9 *off Southold Ri* **174** C3
Bucklers All, SW6 **128** C6
Bucklersbury, EC4 **20** B4
Bucklersbury Pas, EC4 **20** B4
Bucklers Way, Cars. SM5 **199** J3
Buckles Ct, Belv. DA17 *off Fendyke Rd* **138** D3
Buckle St, E1 **21** G3
Buckley Cl, SE23 **153** E7
Buckley Rd, NW6 **90** C7
Buckley St, SE1 **26** E2
Buckmaster Cl, SW9 *off Stockwell Pk Rd* **151** F3
Buckmaster Rd, SW11 **149** H4
Bucknall St, WC2 **17** J3
Bucknall Way, Beck. BR3 **190** B4
Bucknell Cl, SW2 **151** F4
Buckner Rd, SW2 **151** F4
Buckrell Rd, E4 **62** D2
Buckstone Cl, SE23 **153** F6
Buckstone Rd, N18 **60** D6
Buck St, NW1 **92** B7
Buckters Rents, SE16 **133** H1
Buckthorne Rd, SE4 **153** H6
Buck Wk, E17 *off Wood St* **78** D4
Budd Cl, N12 **57** E4
Buddings Circle, Wem. HA9 **88** C3
Budd's All, Twick. TW1 *off Arlington Cl* **145** F5
Bude Cl, E17 **77** J5
Budge La, Mitch. CR4 **185** J7
Budge Row, EC4 **20** B5
Budge's Wk, W2 **22** C1
Budleigh Cres, Well. DA16 **158** C1
Budoch Ct, Ilf. IG3 **100** A2
Budoch Dr, Ilf. IG3 **100** A2
Buer Rd, SW6 **148** B2
Bugsby's Way, SE7 **135** G4
SE10 **135** F4
Buick Ho, Kings.T. KT2 **182** A2
Building 22, SE18 *off Carriage St* **137** E3
Building 36, SE18 *off Marlborough Rd* **137** F3
Building 45, SE18 *off Hopton Rd* **137** E3
Building 47, SE18 *off Marlborough Rd* **137** F3
Building 48, SE18 *off Marlborough Rd* **137** F3
Building 49, SE18 *off Argyll Rd* **137** F3
Building 50, SE18 *off Argyll Rd* **137** F3
Bulganak Rd, Th.Hth. CR7 **187** J4
Bulinga St, SW1 **33** J2
Bullace Row, SE5 **132** A7
Bull All, Well. DA16 *off Welling High St* **158** B3
Bullards Pl, E2 **113** G3
Bullbanks Rd, Belv. DA17 **139** J4
Bullen Ho, E1 *off Collingwood St* **113** E4
Bullen St, SW11 **149** H2
Buller Cl, SE15 **132** D7
Buller Rd, N17 **76** D2
N22 **75** G2
NW10 *off Chamberlayne Rd* **108** A3
Barking IG11 **99** H7
Thornton Heath CR7 **188** A2
Bullers Cl, Sid. DA14 **176** E5
Bullers Wd Dr, Chis. BR7 **174** B7
Bullescroft Rd, Edg. HA8 **54** A3
Bullhead Rd, Borwd. WD6 **38** C3
Bullied Way, SW1 **32** E2
Bull Inn Ct, WC2 **18** B6
Bullivant St, E14 **114** C7
Bull La, N18 **60** B5
Chislehurst BR7 **175** G7
Dagenham RM10 **101** H3
Bull Rd, E15 **115** F2
Bullrush Cl, Cars. SM5 **199** H2
Croydon CR0 **188** B6
Bull's All, SW14 **146** D2
Bulls Br Ind Est, Sthl. UB2 **122** B4
Bulls Br Rd, Sthl. UB2 **122** B3
Bullsbrook Rd, Hayes UB4 **122** C1
Bulls Gdns, SW3 **31** H1
Bull's Head Pas, EC3 **20** D4
Bull Yd, SE15 *off Peckham High St* **152** D1
Bulmer Gdns, Har. HA3 **69** G7
Bulmer Ms, W11 *off Ladbroke Rd* **108** D7
Bulmer Pl, W11 **128** D1
Bulow Est, SW6 *off Pearscroft Rd* **149** E1
Bulstrode Av, Houns. TW3 **143** F2
Bulstrode Gdns, Houns. TW3 **143** F3
Bulstrode Pl, W1 **16** C2
Bulstrode Rd, Houns. TW3 **143** G3
Bulstrode St, W1 **16** C3
Bulwer Ct Rd, E11 **96** D1
Bulwer Gdns, Barn. EN5 **41** F4
Bulwer Rd, E11 **78** D7
N18 **60** B4
Barnet EN5 **41** E4
Bulwer St, W12 **127** J1
Bunces La, Wdf.Grn. IG8 **63** F7
Bungalow Rd, SE25 **188** B4
Bungalows, The, SW16 **168** B7
Wallington SM6 **200** B5
Bunhill Row, EC1 **12** B5
Bunhouse Pl, SW1 **32** B3
Bunkers Hill, NW11 **73** F7
Belvedere DA17 **139** G4
Sidcup DA14 **177** F3
Bunning Way, N7 **93** E7
Bunns La, NW7 **55** F6
Bunsen St, E3 *off Kenilworth Rd* **113** H2
Buntingbridge Rd, Ilf. IG2 **81** G5
Bunting Cl, N9 *off Dunnock Cl* **61** G1
Mitcham CR4 **185** J5
Bunton St, SE18 **136** D3
Bunyan Ct, EC2 *off The Barbican* **19** J1
Bunyan Rd, E17 **77** H3
Buonaparte Ms, SW1 **33** H3
Burbage Cl, SE1 **28** B6
Burbage Rd, SE21 **152** A6
SE24 **151** J6
Burberry Cl, N.Mal. KT3 **182** E2
Burbridge Way, N17 **76** C2
Burcham St, E14 **114** B6
Burcharbro Rd, SE2 **138** D6
Burchell Rd, E10 **96** B1
SE15 **153** E1
Burcher Gale Gro, SE15 **37** E7
Burchett Way, Rom. RM6 **83** F6
Burcote Rd, SW18 **167** G1
Burden Cl, Brent. TW8 **125** F5
Burdenshott Av, Rich. TW10 **146** B4
Burden Way, E11 *off Brading Cres* **97** H2
Burder Cl, N1 **94** B6
Burder Rd, N1 *off Balls Pond Rd* **94** B6
Burdett Av, SW20 **183** G1
Burdett Cl, W7 *off Cherington Rd* **124** C2
Sidcup DA14 **176** E5
Burdett Ms, NW3 *off Belsize Cres* **91** G6
W2 **14** A3
Burdett Rd, E3 **113** J4
E14 **113** J4
Croydon CR0 **188** A6
Richmond TW9 **145** J2
Burdetts Rd, Dag. RM9 **119** F1
Burdett St, SE1 **27** E5
Burdock Cl, Croy. CR0 **203** G1
Burdock Rd, N17 **76** D3
Burdon La, Sutt. SM2 **198** B7
Burfield Cl, SW17 **167** G4
Burford Cl, Dag. RM8 **100** C3
Ilford IG6 **81** F4
Burford Gdns, N13 **59** F3
Burford Rd, E6 **116** B3
E15 **96** D7
SE6 **171** J2
Brentford TW8 **125** H5
Bromley BR1 **192** B4
Sutton SM1 **198** D2
Worcester Park KT4 **183** F7
Burford Wk, SW6 *off Cambria St* **129** E7
Burford Way, Croy. (New Adgtn) CR0 **204** C6
Burford Wf Apts, E15 *off Cam Rd* **114** D1
Burges Ct, E6 **98** D7
Burges Gro, SW13 **127** H7
Burges Rd, E6 **98** B7
Burgess Av, NW9 **70** D6
Burgess Business Pk, SE5 **36** C7
Burgess Cl, Felt. TW13 **160** E4
Burgess Hill, NW2 **90** D4
Burgess Ms, SW19 **167** E6
Burgess Rd, E15 **96** E4
Sutton SM1 **198** E4
Burgess St, E14 **114** A5
Burge St, SE1 **28** C6
★ **Burgh Ho** (Hampstead Mus), NW3 *off New End Sq* **91** G4
Burghill Rd, SE26 **171** H4
Burghley Av, Borwd. WD6 **38** C5
New Malden KT3 **182** D1
Burghley Hall Cl, SW19 **148** B7
Burghley Ho, SW19 **166** B3
Burghley Pl, Mitch. CR4 **185** J5
Burghley Rd, E11 **97** E1
N8 **75** G3
NW5 **92** B5
SW19 **166** A4
Burghley Twr, W3 **107** F7
Burgh St, N1 **11** H1
Burgon St, EC4 **19** H4
Burgos Cl, Croy. CR0 **201** G6
Burgos Gro, SE10 **154** B1
Burgoyne Rd, N4 **75** H6
SE25 **188** C4
SW9 **151** F3
Burgundy Pl, W12 *off Bourbon St* **128** A1
Burham Cl, SE20 *off Maple Rd* **171** F7
Burhill Gro, Pnr. HA5 **66** E2
Burke Cl, SW15 **147** E4
Burke Ho, SW11 *off Maysoule Rd* **149** G4
Burke St, E16 **115** F6
Burket Cl, Sthl. UB2 *off Kingsbridge Rd* **123** F4
Burland Rd, SW11 **149** J5
Burleigh Av, Sid. DA15 **157** J5
Wallington SM6 **200** A3
Burleigh Cl, Rom. RM7 **83** H4
Burleigh Gdns, N14 **58** C1
Burleigh Ho, W10 *off St. Charles Sq* **108** A5
Burleigh Pl, SW15 **148** A5
Burleigh Rd, Enfield EN1 **44** B4
Sutton SM3 **198** B1
Burleigh St, WC2 **18** C5

Burleigh Wk, SE6
off Muirkirk Rd **172** C1
Burleigh Way, Enfield EN2
off Church St **44** A3
Burley Cl, E4 **62** A5
SW16 **186** D2
Burley Rd, E16 **115** J6
Burlington Arc, W1 **17** F6
Burlington Av, Rich. TW9 **146** A1
Romford RM7 **83** H6
Burlington Cl, E6
off Northumberland Rd **116** B6
W9 **108** C4
Feltham TW14 **141** G7
Orpington BR6 **206** E2
Pinner HA5 **66** B3
Burlington Gdns, W1 **17** F6
W3 **126** C1
W4 **126** C5
Romford RM6 **83** E7
Burlington La, W4 **126** E7
Burlington Ms, SW15 **148** C5
W3 **126** C1
Burlington Pl, SW6
off Burlington Rd **148** B2
Woodford Green IG8 **63** G3
Burlington Ri, Barn. (E.Barn.) EN4 **57** H1
Burlington Rd, N10
off Tetherdown **74** A3
N17 **76** D1
SW6 **148** B2
W4 **126** C5
Enfield EN2 **44** A1
Isleworth TW7 **144** A1
New Malden KT3 **183** G4
Thornton Heath CR7 **187** J2
Burma Rd, N16 **94** A4
Burmester Rd, SW17 **167** F3
Burnaby Cres, W4 **126** B6
Burnaby Gdns, W4 **126** C6
Burnaby St, SW10 **129** F7
Burnbrae Cl, N12 **57** E6
Burnbury Rd, SW12 **168** C1
Burncroft Av, Enfield EN3 **45** F2
Burndell Way, Hayes UB4 **102** D5
Burne Jones Ho, W14 **128** C4
Burnell Av, Rich. TW10 **163** F5
Welling DA16 **158** A2
Burnell Gdns, Stan. HA7 **69** G1
Burnell Rd, Sutt. SM1 **199** E4
Burnell Wk, SE1 **37** G3
Burnels Av, E6 **116** D3
Burness Cl, N7
off Roman Way **93** F6
Burne St, NW1 **15** G1
Burnett Cl, E9 **95** F5
Burnett Rd, Ilf. IG6 **64** E7
Burney Av, Surb. KT5 **181** J5
Burney Dr, Loug. IG10 **49** E2
Burney St, SE10 **134** C7
Burnfoot Av, SW6 **148** B1
Burnfoot Ct, SE22 **170** E1
Burnham, NW3 **91** H7
Burnham Cl, NW7 **55** G7
SE1 **37** G2
Harrow (Wealds.) HA3 **68** D4
Burnham Ct, NW4 **71** J4
Burnham Cres, E11 **79** J4
Burnham Dr, Wor.Pk. KT4 **198** A2
Burnham Gdns, Croy. CR0 **188** C7
Hayes UB3 **121** G3
Hounslow TW4 **142** B1
Burnham Rd, E4 **61** J5
Dagenham RM9 **100** B7
Morden SM4 **185** E5
Sidcup DA14 **176** E2
Burnham St, E2 **113** F3
Kingston upon Thames KT2 **182** A1
Burnham Way, SE26 **171** J5
W13 **124** E4
Burnhill Cl, SE15
off Gervase St **133** E7
Burnhill Rd, Beckenham BR3 **190** A2
Burnley Cl, Wat. WD19 **50** C5
Burnley Rd, NW10 **89** G5
SW9 **151** F2
Burnsall St, SW3 **31** H3
Burns Av, Felt. TW14 **142** A6
Romford (Chad.Hth) RM6 **82** C7
Sidcup DA15 **158** B6
Southall UB1 **103** G7
Burns Cl, E17 **78** C4
SW19 **167** G6
Welling DA16 **157** J1
Burnside Av, E4 **61** J6
Burnside Cl, SE16 **133** G1
Barnet EN5 **40** D3
Twickenham TW1 **144** D6
Burnside Cres, Wem. HA0 **105** G1
Burnside Rd, Dag. RM8 **100** C2
Burns Rd, NW10 **107** F1
SW11 **149** J2
W13 **124** E2
Wembley HA0 **105** G2
Burns Way, Houns. TW5 **142** D2
Burnt Ash Hts, Brom. BR1 **173** H5
Burnt Ash Hill, SE12 **155** F6
Burnt Ash La, Brom. BR1 **173** G6
Burnt Ash Rd, SE12 **155** F5
Burnthwaite Rd, SW6 **128** D7
BURNT OAK, Edg. HA8 **54** C7
Burnt Oak Bdy, Edg. HA8 **54** A7
Burnt Oak Flds, Edg. HA8 **70** C1
Burnt Oak La, Sid. DA15 **158** A6
Burntwood Cl, SW18 **167** G1
Burntwood Gra Rd, SW18 **167** G1
Burntwood La, SW17 **167** H2
Burntwood Vw, SE19
off Bowley La **170** C5
Buross St, E1
off Commercial Rd **113** E6
Burpham Cl, Hayes UB4 **102** D5
Burrage Gro, SE18 **137** F4
Burrage Pl, SE18 **137** E5
Burrage Rd, SE18 **137** F6
Burrard Rd, E16 **115** H6
NW6 **90** D5
Burr Cl, E1 **29** H1
Bexleyheath DA7 **159** F3
Burrell Cl, Croy. CR0 **189** H6
Edgware HA8 **54** B2
Burrell Row, Beck. BR3
off High St **190** A2
Burrell St, SE1 **27** G1
Burrells Wf Sq, E14 **134** B5
Burrell Twr, E10 **78** A7
Burritt Rd, Kings.T. KT1 **182** A2
Burroughs, The, NW4 **71** H5
Burroughs Gdns, NW4 **71** H4
Burroughs Par, NW4
off The Burroughs **71** H4
Burrow Cl, Chig. IG7
off Burrow Rd **65** J5
Burrow Grn, Chig. IG7 **65** J5
Burrow Rd, SE22 **152** B4
Chigwell IG7 **65** J5
Burrows Ms, SE1 **27** G3
Burrows Rd, NW10 **107** J3
Burrow Wk, SE21 **151** J7
Burr Rd, SW18 **148** D7
Bursdon Cl, Sid. DA15 **175** J2
Bursland Rd, Enf. EN3 **45** G4
Burslem St, E1 **21** J4
Burstock Rd, SW15 **148** B4
Burston Rd, SW15 **148** A5
Burston Vil, SW15
off St. John's Av **148** A5
Burstow Rd, SW20 **184** B1
Burtenshaw Rd, T.Ditt. KT7 **180** D7
Burtley Cl, N4 **93** J1
Burton Cl, Chess. KT9 **195** G7
Thornton Heath CR7 **188** A3
Burton Ct, SW3
off Franklin's Row **32** A3
Burton Gdns, Houns. TW5 **143** F1
Burton Gro, SE17 **36** B4
Burtonhole Cl, NW7 **56** A4
Burtonhole La, NW7 **56** B4
Burton La, SW9 **151** G2
Burton Ms, SW1 **32** C2
Burton Pl, WC1 **9** J4
Burton Rd, E18 **79** H3
NW6 **90** C7
SW9 **151** H2
Kingston upon Thames KT2 **163** H7
Loughton IG10 **49** F4
Burtons Rd, Hmptn. (Hmptn H.) TW12 **161** H4
Burton St, WC1 **9** J4
Burtwell La, SE27 **170** A4
Burwash Ho, SE1 **28** C4
Burwash Rd, SE18 **137** G5
Burway Cl, S.Croy. CR2 **202** B6
Burwell Av, Grnf. UB6 **86** B6
Burwell Cl, E1
off Bigland St **113** E6
Burwell Rd, E10 **95** H1
Burwell Wk, E3 **114** A4
Burwood Av, Brom. BR2 **205** H2
Pinner HA5 **66** C5
Burwood Cl, Surb. KT6 **196** A1
Burwood Pl, W2 **15** H3
Barnet EN4 **41** F1
Bury Cl, SE16
off Rotherhithe St **133** G1
Bury Ct, EC3 **20** E3
Bury Gro, Mord. SM4 **184** E5
Bury Pl, WC1 **18** A2
Bury Rd, E4 **47** E5
N22 **75** G3
Dagenham RM10 **101** H5
Buryside Cl, Ilf. IG2 **81** J4
Bury St, EC3 **20** E4
N9 **60** D1
SW1 **25** G1
Bury St W, N9 **44** A7
Bury Wk, SW3 **31** G2
Busbridge Ho, E14
off Brabazon St **114** A5
Busby Ms, NW5
off Busby Pl **92** D6
Busby Pl, NW5 **92** D6
Busby St, E2 **13** G5
Busch Cl, Islw. TW7
off Park Rd **144** E1
Bushbaby Cl, SE1 **28** D6
Bushberry Rd, E9 **95** H6
Bush Cl, Ilf. IG2 **81** G5
Bush Cotts, SW18
off Putney Br Rd **148** D5
Bush Ct, W12
off Shepherds Bush Grn **128** A2
Bushell Cl, SW2 **169** F2
Bushell Grn, Bushey (Bushey Hth) WD23 **52** A2
Bushell St, E1 **29** J2
Bushell Way, Chis. BR7 **174** D5
Bushey Av, E18 **79** F3
Orpington BR5 **193** G7
Bushey Cl, E4 **62** C3
Bushey Ct, SW20 **183** H2
Bushey Down, SW12
off Bedford Hill **168** B2
BUSHEY HEATH, Bushey WD23 **52** B1
Bushey Hill Rd, SE5 **152** B1
Bushey La, Sutt. SM1 **198** D4
Bushey Lees, Sid. DA15
off Fen Gro **157** J6
BUSHEY MEAD, SW20 **184** A3
Bushey Rd, E13 **115** J2
N15 **76** B6
SW20 **183** H3
Croydon CR0 **204** A2
Hayes UB3 **121** H4
Sutton SM1 **198** E4
Bushey Way, Beck. BR3 **190** D6
Bushfield Cl, Edg. HA8 **54** B2
Bushfield Cres, Edg. HA8 **54** B2
Bushfields, Loug. IG10 **48** D5
Bush Gro, NW9 **70** C7
Stanmore HA7 **69** G1
Bushgrove Rd, Dag. RM8 **100** D4
Bush Hill, N21 **43** J7
BUSH HILL PARK, Enf. EN1 **44** B5
Bush Hill Rd, N21 **44** A6
Harrow HA3 **69** J6
Bush Ind Est, NW10 **106** D4
Bush La, EC4 **20** B5
Bushmead Cl, N15
off Copperfield Dr **76** C4
Bushmoor Cres, SE18 **137** F7
Bushnell Rd, SW17 **168** B2
Bush Rd, E8 **112** E1
E11 **79** F7
SE8 **133** G4
Buckhurst Hill IG9 **64** A4
Richmond TW9 **125** J6
Bushway, Dag. RM8 **100** D4
Bushwood, E11 **97** F1
Bushwood Dr, SE1 **37** G2
Bushwood Rd, Rich. TW9 **126** A6
★ **Bushy Park**, Tedd. TW11 **180** C1
Bushy Pk, Hmptn. (Hmptn H.) TW12 **180** C1
Teddington TW11 **180** C1
Bushy Pk Gdns, Tedd. TW11 **162** A5
Bushy Pk Rd, Tedd. TW11 **163** E7
Bushy Rd, Tedd. TW11 **162** C6
★ **Business Design Cen**, N1 **111** G1
Butcher Row, E1 **113** G7
E14 **113** G7
Butchers Rd, E16 **115** G6
Bute Av, Rich. TW10 **163** H2
Bute Ct, Wall. SM6 **200** C5
Bute Gdns, W6 **128** A4
Wallington SM6 **200** C5
Bute Gdns W, Wall. SM6 **200** C5
Bute Ms, NW11
off Northway **73** E5
Bute Rd, Croy. CR0 **201** G1
Ilford IG6 **81** E5
Wallington SM6 **200** C4
Bute St, SW7 **31** E1
Bute Wk, N1
off Marquess Rd **94** A6
Butler Av, Har. HA1 **68** A7
Butler Cl, Edg. HA8
off Scott Rd **70** B2
Butler Ct, Wem. HA0
off Harrow Rd **86** D4
Butler Pl, SW1 **25** H5
Butler Rd, NW10 **89** F7
Dagenham RM8 **100** B4
Harrow HA1 **67** J7
Butlers & Colonial Wf, SE1 **29** G3
Butlers Cl, Houns. TW4 **143** F3
Butler St, E2
off Knottisford St **113** F3
Butlers Wf, SE1 **29** F2
Buttercup Cl, Nthlt. UB5 **85** E6
Butterfield Cl, N17 **59** J6
SE16 *off Wilson Gro* **132** E2
Twickenham TW1
off Rugby Rd **144** C6
Butterfields, E17 **78** C5
Butterfield Sq, E6
off Harper Rd **116** C6
Butterfly La, SE9 **156** E6
Butterfly Wk, SE5
off Denmark Hill **152** A1
Butter Hill, Cars. SM5 **200** A3
Wallington SM6 **200** A3
Butteridges Cl, Dag. RM9 **119** F1
Buttermere Cl, E15 **96** D4
SE1 **37** F2
Morden SM4 **184** A6
Buttermere Dr, SW15 **148** B5
Buttermere Wk, E8 **94** C6
Butterwick, W6 **127** J4
Butterworth Gdns, Wdf.Grn. IG8 **63** G6
Buttery Ms, N14 **58** E3
Buttesland St, N1 **12** C3
Buttfield Cl, Dag. RM10 **101** H6
Buttmarsh Cl, SE18 **137** E5
Butts, The, Brent. TW8 **125** G6
Sunbury-on-Thames TW16
off Elizabeth Gdns **178** C3
Buttsbury Rd, Ilf. IG1 **99** F5
Butts Cotts, Felt. TW13 **161** F3
Butts Cres, Felt. (Han.) TW13 **161** G3
Butts Piece, Nthlt. UB5
off Longhook Gdns **102** B2
Butts Rd, Brom. BR1 **173** E5
Buxhall Cres, E9 **95** J6
Buxted Rd, E8 **94** C7
N12 **57** H5
SE22 **152** B4
Buxton Cl, N9 **61** F2
Woodford Green IG8 **64** A6
Buxton Ct, N1 **12** A3
Buxton Cres, Sutt. SM3 **198** B4
Buxton Dr, E11 **79** E4
New Malden KT3 **182** D2
Buxton Gdns, W3 **106** B7
Buxton Ho, SW11
off Maysoule Rd **149** G4
Buxton Ms, SW4 **150** D2
Buxton Path, Wat. WD19 **50** C3
Buxton Rd, E4 **46** D7
E6 **116** B3
E15 **96** E5
E17 **77** H4
N19 **92** D1
NW2 **89** H6
SW14 **147** E3
Ilford IG2 **81** H6
Thornton Heath CR7 **187** H5
Buxton St, E1 **13** G6
Buzzard Creek Ind Est, Bark. IG11 **117** J5
Byam St, SW6 **149** F2
Byards Cft, SW16 **186** D1
Byatt Wk, Hmptn. TW12
off Victors Dr **161** E6
Bychurch End, Tedd. TW11
off Church Rd **162** C5
Bycroft Rd, Sthl. UB1 **103** G4
Bycroft St, SE20
off Penge La **171** G7
Bycullah Av, Enf. EN2 **43** H3
Bycullah Rd, Enf. EN2 **43** H3
Bye, The, W3 **107** E6
Byegrove Ct, SW19
off Byegrove Rd **167** G7
Byegrove Rd, SW19 **167** G6
Byeway, The, SW14 **146** C3
Bye Way, The, Har. HA3 **68** B1
Byeways, Twick. TW2 **161** H3
Byeways, The, Surb. KT5 **182** A5
Byfeld Gdns, SW13 **147** G1
Byfield Cl, SE16 **133** H2

Byfield Pas, Islw. TW7 ... 144 D3
Byfield Rd, Islw. TW7 ... 144 D3
Byford Cl, E15 ... 97 E7
Bygrove, Croy. (New Adgtn) CR0 ... 204 B6
Bygrove St, E14 ... 114 B6
Byland Cl, N21 ... 43 F7
Morden SM4 *off Bolton Dr* ... 185 G7
Bylands Cl, SE2 *off Finchale Rd* ... 138 B3
SE16 *off Rotherhithe St* ... 133 G1
Byne Rd, SE26 ... 171 F6
Carshalton SM5 ... 199 H2
Bynes Rd, S.Croy. CR2 ... 202 A7
Byng Pl, WC1 ... 9 H6
Byng Rd, Barn. EN5 ... 40 A3
Byng St, E14 ... 134 A2
Bynon Av, Bexh. DA7 ... 159 E3
Byre, The, N14 ... 42 B6
Byre Rd, N14 ... 42 A6
Byrne Rd, SW12 ... 168 B1
Byron Av, E12 ... 98 B6
E18 ... 79 F3
NW9 ... 70 B4
Borehamwood WD6 ... 38 A5
Hounslow TW4 ... 142 A2
New Malden KT3 ... 183 G5
Sutton SM1 ... 199 G4
Byron Av E, Sutt. SM1 ... 199 G4
Byron Cl, E8 ... 112 D1
SE26 ... 171 H4
SE28 ... 138 C1
SW16 ... 168 E6
Hampton TW12 ... 161 F4
Byron Ct, W9 *off Lanhill Rd* ... 108 D4
Enfield EN2 ... 43 H2
Harrow HA1 ... 68 B6
Byron Dr, N2 ... 73 G6
Erith DA8 ... 139 H7
Byron Gdns, Sutt. SM1 ... 199 G4
Byron Hill Rd, Har. HA2 ... 86 A1
Byron Ho, Beck. BR3 ... 172 A6
Byron Ms, NW3 ... 91 H5
W9 *off Shirland Rd* ... 108 D4
Byron Rd, E10 ... 96 B1
E17 ... 78 A3
NW2 ... 89 H2
NW7 ... 55 G5
W5 ... 125 J1
Harrow HA1 ... 68 B6
Harrow (Wealds.) HA3 ... 68 C2
Wembley HA0 ... 87 F3
Byron St, E14 *off St. Leonards Rd* ... 114 C6
Byron Ter, N9 ... 45 F6
Byron Way, Nthlt. UB5 ... 102 E3
West Drayton UB7 ... 120 C4
Bysouth Cl, N15 ... 76 A4
Ilford IG5 ... 80 E1
By the Wd, Wat. WD19 ... 50 D2
Bythorn St, SW9 ... 151 F3
Byton Rd, SW17 ... 167 J6
Byward Av, Felt. TW14 ... 142 C6
Byward St, EC3 ... 20 E6
Bywater Pl, SE16 ... 133 H1
Bywater St, SW3 ... 31 J3
Byway, The, Epsom KT19 ... 197 F4
Bywell Pl, W1 ... 17 F2
Bywood Av, Croy. CR0 ... 189 F6
Byworth Wk, N19 *off Courtauld Rd* ... 92 E1

C

Cabbell St, NW1 ... 15 G2
Cabinet Way, E4 ... 61 J6
Cable Pl, SE10 *off Diamond Ter* ... 154 C1
Cable St, E1 ... 21 H5
Cable Trade Pk, SE7 ... 135 J4
Cabot Pl, E14 ... 134 A1
Cabot Sq, E14 ... 134 A1
Cabot Way, E6 *off Parr Rd* ... 116 A1
Cabul Rd, SW11 ... 149 H2
Cactus Cl, SE15 *off Lyndhurst Gro* ... 152 B2
Cactus Wk, W12 *off Du Cane Rd* ... 107 F6
Cadbury Cl, Islw. TW7 ... 144 D1
Cadbury Way, SE16 ... 29 G6
Caddington Cl, Barn. EN4 ... 41 H5
Caddington Rd, NW2 ... 90 B3
Caddis Cl, Stan. HA7 ... 52 C7
Cadell Cl, E2 ... 13 G2
Cade Rd, SE10 ... 154 D1
Cader Rd, SW18 ... 149 F6
Cadet Dr, SE1 ... 37 G3
Cadiz Rd, Dag. RM10 ... 101 J7
Cadiz St, SE17 ... 36 A4
Cadley Ter, SE23 ... 171 F2
Cadman Cl, SW9 *off Langton Rd* ... 131 H7
Cadmer Cl, N.Mal. KT3 ... 182 E4
Cadmus Cl, SW4 *off Aristotle Rd* ... 150 D3
Cadnam Pt, SW15 *off Dilton Gdns* ... 165 H1
Cadogan Cl, E9 *off Cadogan Ter* ... 95 J7
Beckenham BR3 *off Albemarle Rd* ... 190 D1
Harrow HA2 ... 85 H4
Teddington TW11 ... 162 B5
Cadogan Ct, Sutt. SM2 ... 199 E6
Cadogan Gdns, E18 ... 79 H3
N3 ... 72 E1
N21 ... 43 G5
SW3 ... 32 A1
Cadogan Gate, SW1 ... 32 A1
Cadogan La, SW1 ... 24 B6
Cadogan Pl, SW1 ... 24 A5
Cadogan Rd, SE18 ... 137 F3
Surbiton KT6 ... 181 G5
Cadogan Sq, SW1 ... 24 A6
Cadogan St, SW3 ... 31 J2
Cadogan Ter, E9 ... 95 J6
Cadoxton Av, N15 ... 76 C6
Cadwallon Rd, SE9 ... 175 E2
Caedmon Rd, N7 ... 93 F4
Caerleon Cl, Esher (Clay.) KT10 ... 194 E7
Sidcup DA14 ... 176 C5
Caerleon Ter, SE2 *off Blithdale Rd* ... 138 B4
Caernarvon Cl, Mitch. CR4 ... 186 E3
Caernarvon Dr, Ilf. IG5 ... 80 D1
Caesars Wk, Mitch. CR4 ... 185 J5
Cahill St, EC1 ... 12 A6
Cahir St, E14 ... 134 B4
Cains La, Felt. TW14 ... 141 H5
Caird St, W10 ... 108 B3
Cairn Av, W5 ... 125 G1
Cairncross Ms, N8 *off Felix Av* ... 75 E6
Cairndale Cl, Brom. BR1 ... 173 F7
Cairnfield Av, NW2 ... 89 E3
Cairngorm Cl, Tedd. TW11 *off Vicarage Rd* ... 162 D5
Cairns Av, Wdf.Grn. IG8 ... 64 B6
Cairns Ms, SE18 *off Bell St* ... 156 B1
Cairns Rd, SW11 ... 149 H5
Cairn Way, Stan. HA7 ... 52 C6
Cairo New Rd, Croy. CR0 ... 201 H2
Cairo Rd, E17 ... 78 A4
Caishowe Rd, Borwd. WD6 ... 38 B1
Caistor Ms, SW12 *off Caistor Rd* ... 150 B7
Caistor Pk Rd, E15 ... 115 F1
Caistor Rd, SW12 ... 150 B7
Caithness Gdns, Sid. DA15 ... 157 J6
Caithness Rd, W14 ... 128 A4
Mitcham CR4 ... 168 B7
Calabria Rd, N5 ... 93 H6
Calais Gate, SE5 *off Calais St* ... 151 H1
Calais St, SE5 ... 151 H1
Calbourne Rd, SW12 ... 149 J7
Calcott Wk, SE9 ... 174 A4
Caldbeck Av, Wor.Pk. KT4 ... 197 G2
Caldecot Rd, SE5 ... 151 J2
Caldecott Way, E5 ... 95 G3
Calder Av, Grnf. (Perivale) UB6 ... 104 C2
Calder Cl, Enf. EN1 ... 44 B3
Calder Gdns, Edg. HA8 ... 70 A3
Calderon Pl, W10 *off St. Quintin Gdns* ... 107 J5
Calderon Rd, E11 ... 96 C4
Calder Rd, Mord. SM4 ... 185 F5
Caldervale Rd, SW4 ... 150 D5
Calderwood Pl, Barn. EN4 ... 40 E1
Calderwood St, SE18 ... 136 D4
Caldicot Grn, NW9 ... 70 E6
Caldwell Gdns Est, SW9 *off Caldwell St* ... 151 G1
Caldwell Rd, Wat. WD19 ... 50 D4
Caldwell St, SW9 ... 131 F7
Caldy Rd, Belv. DA17 ... 139 H3
Caldy Wk, N1 *off Clifton Rd* ... 93 J6
Caleb St, SE1 ... 27 J3
Caledonian Cl, Ilf. IG3 ... 100 B1
Caledonian Rd, N1 ... 10 B2
N7 ... 93 F5
Caledonian Sq, NW1 *off Canal Boul* ... 92 D6
Caledonian Wf, E14 ... 134 D4
Caledonia St, N1 ... 10 B2
Caledon Rd, E6 ... 116 B1
Wallington SM6 ... 200 A4
Cale St, SW3 ... 31 G3
Caletock Way, SE10 ... 135 F5
Calico Row, SW11 *off York Pl* ... 149 F3
Calidore Cl, SW2 ... 151 F6
California Bldg, SE13 *off Deals Gateway* ... 154 B1
California La, Bushey (Bushey Hth) WD23 ... 52 A1
California Rd, N.Mal. KT3 ... 182 B4
Callaby Ter, N1 *off Wakeham St* ... 94 A6
Callaghan Cl, SE13 ... 154 E4
Callander Rd, SE6 ... 172 B2
Callard Av, N13 ... 59 H5
Callcott Rd, NW6 ... 90 C7
Callcott St, W8 *off Hillgate Pl* ... 128 D1
Callendar Rd, SW7 ... 22 E5
Callingham Cl, E14 *off Wallwood St* ... 113 J5
Callis Fm Cl, Stai. (Stanw.) TW19 *off Bedfont Rd* ... 140 B6
Callisons Pl, SE10 *off Bellot St* ... 135 E5
Callis Rd, E17 ... 77 J6
Callow St, SW3 ... 30 D5
Calmington Rd, SE5 ... 36 E4
Calmont Rd, Brom. BR1 ... 172 D6
Calne Av, Ilf. IG5 ... 80 E1
Calonne Rd, SW19 ... 166 A4
Calshot Rd, Houns. (Lon.Hthrw Air.) TW6 ... 140 D2
Calshot St, N1 ... 10 C1
Calshot Way, Enf. EN2 ... 43 H3
Hounslow (Lon.Hthrw Air.) TW6 *off Calshot Rd* ... 140 E2
Calthorpe Gdns, Edg. HA8 *off Jesmond Way* ... 53 H5
Sutton SM1 ... 199 F3
Calthorpe St, WC1 ... 10 D5
Calton Av, SE21 ... 152 B5
Calton Rd, Barn. (New Barn.) EN5 ... 41 F6
Calverley Cl, Beck. BR3 ... 172 B6
Calverley Ct, Epsom KT19 *off Kingston Rd* ... 196 D4
Calverley Cres, Dag. RM10 ... 101 G2
Calverley Gdns, Har. HA3 ... 69 G7
Calverley Gro, N19 ... 92 D1
Calverley Rd, Epsom KT17 ... 197 G6
Calvert Av, E2 ... 13 E4
Calvert Cl, Belv. DA17 ... 139 G4
Sidcup DA14 ... 176 E6
Calverton, SE5 ... 36 C5
Calverton Rd, E6 ... 116 D1
Calvert Rd, SE10 ... 135 F5
Barnet EN5 ... 40 A2
Calvert's Bldgs, SE1 ... 28 B2
Calvert St, NW1 *off Chalcot Rd* ... 110 A1
Calvin St, E1 ... 13 F6
Calydon Rd, SE7 ... 135 H5
Calypso Cres, SE15 ... 37 F7
Calypso Way, SE16 ... 133 J3
Camac Rd, Twick. TW2 ... 162 A1
Camarthen Grn, NW9 *off Snowdon Dr* ... 70 E6
Cambalt Rd, SW15 ... 148 A5
Camberley Av, SW20 ... 183 H2
Enfield EN1 ... 44 B4
Camberley Cl, Sutt. SM3 ... 198 A3
Camberley Rd, Houns. (Lon.Hthrw Air.) TW6 ... 140 D3
Cambert Way, SE3 ... 155 H4
CAMBERWELL, SE5 ... 131 J7
Camberwell Business Cen, SE5 *off Lomond Gro* ... 132 A7
Camberwell Ch St, SE5 ... 152 A1
Camberwell Glebe, SE5 ... 152 A1
Camberwell Grn, SE5 ... 152 A1
Camberwell Gro, SE5 ... 152 A1
Camberwell New Rd, SE5 ... 35 E6
Camberwell Pas, SE5 *off Camberwell New Rd* ... 151 J1
Camberwell Rd, SE5 ... 36 A6
Camberwell Sta Rd, SE5 ... 151 J1
Cambeys Rd, Dag. RM10 ... 101 H5
Camborne Av, W13 ... 125 E2
Camborne Cl, Houns. (Lon.Hthrw Air.) TW6 *off Camborne Rd* ... 140 D3
Camborne Ms, SW18 *off Camborne Rd* ... 148 D7
W11 *off St. Marks Rd* ... 108 B6
Camborne Rd, SW18 ... 148 D7
Croydon CR0 ... 188 D7
Hounslow (Lon.Hthrw Air.) TW6 ... 140 D3
Camborne Rd, Morden SM4 ... 184 A5
Sidcup DA14 ... 176 C3
Sutton SM2 ... 198 D7
Welling DA16 ... 157 J2
Camborne Way, Houns. TW5 ... 143 G1
Hounslow (Lon.Hthrw Air.) TW6 *off Camborne Rd* ... 140 D3
Cambourne Av, N9 ... 45 G7
Cambray Rd, SW12 ... 168 C1
Orpington BR6 ... 193 J7
Cambria Cl, Houns. TW3 ... 143 G4
Sidcup DA15 ... 175 G1
Cambria Ct, Felt. TW14 ... 142 B7
Cambria Gdns, Stai. TW19 ... 140 B7
Cambria Ho, SE26 *off High Level Dr* ... 170 D4
Cambrian Av, Ilf. IG2 ... 81 H5
Cambrian Cl, SE27 ... 169 H3
Cambrian Grn, NW9 *off Snowdon Dr* ... 71 E5
Cambrian Rd, E10 ... 78 A7
Richmond TW10 ... 145 J6
Cambria Rd, SE5 ... 151 J3
Cambria St, SW6 ... 129 E7
Cambridge Av, NW6 ... 108 D2
Greenford UB6 ... 86 C5
New Malden KT3 ... 183 F2
Welling DA16 ... 157 J4
Cambridge Barracks Rd, SE18 ... 136 C4
Cambridge Circ, WC2 ... 17 J4
Cambridge Cl, E17 ... 77 J6
N22 ... 75 G1
NW10 *off Lawrence Way* ... 88 C3
SW20 ... 183 H1
Barnet (E.Barn.) EN4 ... 58 A1
Hounslow TW4 ... 143 E4
West Drayton (Harm.) UB7 ... 120 A6
Cambridge Cotts, Rich. TW9 ... 126 A6
Cambridge Cres, E2 ... 112 E2
Teddington TW11 ... 162 D5
Cambridge Dr, SE12 ... 155 G5
Ruislip HA4 ... 84 C2
Cambridge Gdns, N10 ... 74 A1
N13 ... 59 G5
N17 ... 60 A7
N21 ... 44 A7
NW6 ... 108 D2
W10 ... 108 B6
Enfield EN1 ... 44 D2
Kingston upon Thames KT1 ... 182 A2
Cambridge Gate, NW1 ... 8 E4
Cambridge Gate Ms, NW1 ... 8 E4
Cambridge Grn, SE9 ... 174 E1
Cambridge Gro, SE20 ... 188 E1
W6 ... 127 H4
Cambridge Gro Rd, Kings.T. KT1 ... 182 A2
Cambridge Heath Rd, E1 ... 113 E2
E2 ... 113 E2
Cambridge Mans, SW11 *off Cambridge Rd* ... 149 J1
Cambridge Par, Enf. EN1 *off Great Cambridge Rd* ... 44 D1
Cambridge Pk, E11 ... 79 G7
Twickenham TW1 ... 145 G7
Cambridge Pk Rd, E11 *off Cambridge Pk* ... 79 G7
Cambridge Pl, W8 ... 22 B4
Cambridge Rd, E4 ... 62 D1
E11 ... 79 F6
NW6 ... 108 D3
SE20 ... 188 E3
SW11 ... 149 J1
SW13 ... 147 F2
SW20 ... 183 G1
W7 ... 124 C2
Barking IG11 ... 99 F7
Bromley BR1 ... 173 G7
Carshalton SM5 ... 199 H6
Hampton TW12 ... 161 F7
Harrow HA2 ... 67 G5
Hounslow TW4 ... 143 E4
Ilford IG3 ... 99 H1
Kingston upon Thames KT1, KT2 ... 181 J2
Mitcham CR4 ... 186 C3
New Malden KT3 ... 182 E4
Richmond TW9 ... 126 A7
Sidcup DA14 ... 175 H4
Southall UB1 ... 123 F1
Teddington TW11 ... 162 C4
Twickenham TW1 ... 145 G6
Walton-on-Thames KT12 ... 178 B6
West Molesey KT8 ... 179 F4
Cambridge Rd N, W4 ... 126 B5
Cambridge Rd S, W4 ... 126 B5
Cambridge Row, SE18 ... 137 E5

Cambridge Sq, W2 ....15 G3
Cambridge St, SW1 ....32 E2
Cambridge Ter, N13 ....59 G5
NW1 ....8 E4
Cambridge Ter Ms, NW1 ....8 E4
Cambstone Cl, N11 ....58 A2
Cambus Cl, Hayes UB4 ...103 E5
Cambus Rd, E16 ....115 G5
Camdale Rd, SE18 ....137 J7
★ Camden Arts Cen,
NW3 ....91 E5
Camden Av, Felt. TW13 ...160 C2
Hayes UB4 ....102 C7
Camden Cl, Chis. BR7 ....175 F7
Camden Gdns, NW1
off Kentish Town Rd ...92 B7
Sutton SM1 ....198 E5
Thornton Heath CR7 ...187 H3
Camden Gro, Chiswick
BR7 ....175 E6
Camden High St, NW1 ...110 B1
Camden Hill Rd, SE19 ....170 B6
Camdenhurst St, E14 ....113 H6
Camden La, N7
off Rowstock Gdns 92 D6
★ Camden Lock Mkt &
Waterbuses, NW1 ....92 B7
Camden Lock Pl, NW1
off Chalk Fm Rd 92 B7
Camden Ms, NW1 ....92 D6
Camden Pk Rd, NW1 ....92 D6
Chislehurst BR7 ....174 C7
Camden Pas, N1 ....11 G1
Camden Rd, E11 ....79 H6
E17 ....77 J6
N7 ....92 D5
NW1 ....110 C1
Bexley DA5 ....177 F1
Carshalton SM5 ....199 J4
Sutton SM1 ....198 D5
Camden Row, SE3 ....155 E2
Camden Sq, NW1 ....92 D6
SE15
off Watts St 152 C1
Camden St, NW1 ....92 B7
Camden Ter, NW1
off North Vil 92 D6
CAMDEN TOWN, NW1 ....110 C1
Camden Wk, N1 ....111 H1
Camden Way, Chis. BR7 ..174 C7
Thornton Heath CR7 ...187 H3
Camelford Wk, W11
off St. Marks Rd 108 B6
Camel Gro, Kings.T.
KT2 ....163 G5
Camellia Ct, Wdf.Grn. IG8
off The Bridle Path 63 E7
Camellia Ho, Felt. TW13
off Tilley Rd 160 B1
Camellia Pl, Twick.
TW2 ....143 H7
Camellia St, SW8
off Hartington Rd 130 E7
Camelot Cl, SE28 ....137 G2
SW19 ....166 D4
Camelot Ho, NW1
off Camden Pk Rd 92 D6
Camelot St, SE15
off Bird in Bush Rd ...132 E7
Camel Rd, E16 ....136 A1
Camera Pl, SW10 ....30 E6
Cameron Cl, N18 ....60 E4
N20 off Myddelton Pk ...57 H2
N22 ....59 F7
Cameron Cres, Edg. HA8 ...70 B1
Cameron Ho, SE5
off Comber Gro 131 J7
Cameron Pl, E1
off Varden St 113 E6
SW16 ....169 G2
Cameron Rd, SE6 ....171 J2
Bromley BR2 ....191 G4
Croydon CR0 ....187 H6
Ilford IG3 ....99 H1
Cameron Sq, Mitch.
CR4 ....185 H1
Camerton Cl, E8
off Buttermere Wk 94 C6
Camgate Cen, Stai.
(Stanw.) TW19 ....140 C6
Camilla Rd, SE16 ....132 E4
Camille Cl, SE25 ....188 D3
Camlan Rd, Brom. BR1 ...173 F4
Camlet St, E2 ....13 F5
Camlet Way, Barn. EN4 ....40 D2
Camley St, NW1 ....9 J1
★ Camley St Natural Pk,
NW1 ....9 J1
Camm Gdns, Kings.T. KT1
off Church Rd 181 J2
Thames Ditton KT7 ....180 B7
Camms Ter, Dag. RM10 ...101 J5
Camomile Av, Mitch.
CR4 ....185 J1
Camomile St, EC3 ....20 D3
Campana Rd, SW6 ....148 D1
Campbell Av, Ilf. IG6 ....81 F4
Campbell Cl, SE18
off Moordown 156 D1
SW16 ....168 D4
Ruislip HA4 ....66 A6
Twickenham TW2 ....162 A2
Campbell Ct, N17 ....76 C1
SE22 off Lordship La ...152 D7
Campbell Cft, Edg. HA8 ...54 A5
Campbell Gordon Way,
NW2 ....89 H4
Campbell Rd, E3 ....114 A3
E6 ....116 B1
E15 off Trevelyan Rd 97 F4
E17 ....77 J4
N17 ....76 D1
W7 ....104 B7
Croydon CR0 ....187 H7
East Molesey KT8
off Hampton Ct Rd ...180 C3
Twickenham TW2 ....162 A2
Campbell Wk, N1
off Outram Pl 111 E1
Campdale Rd, N7 ....92 D3
Campden Cres, Dag.
RM8 ....100 B4
Wembley HA0 ....87 E2
Campden Gro, W8 ....128 D2
Campden Hill, W8 ....128 D2
Campden Hill Ct, W8
off Campden Hill Rd ..128 D2
Campden Hill Gdns, W8 ..128 D1
Campden Hill Gate, W8
off Duchess of
Bedford's Wk 128 D2
Campden Hill Pl, W11
off Holland Pk Av 128 C1
Campden Hill Rd, W8 ....128 D1
Campden Hill Sq, W8 ....128 C1
Campden Hill Twrs, W11
off Notting Hill Gate ..128 D1
Campden Ho Cl, W8
off Hornton St 128 D2
Campden Rd, S.Croy.
CR2 ....202 B5
Campden St, W8 ....128 D1
Campden Way, Dag. RM8
off Campden Cres 100 B4
Campen Cl, SW19 ....166 B2
Camperdown St, E1 ....21 G4
Campfield Rd, SE9 ....156 A7
Campion Cl, E6 ....116 C7
Croydon CR0 ....202 B4
Harrow HA3 ....69 J6
Campion Ct, Wem. HA0
off Elmore Cl 105 H2
Campion Gdns, Wdf.Grn.
IG8 ....63 G5
Campion Pl, SE28 ....138 B1
Campion Rd, E10 ....78 B7
SW15 ....147 J4
Isleworth TW7 ....144 C1
Campion Ter, NW2 ....90 A3
Campion Way, Edg. HA8 ...54 C4
Camplin Rd, Har. HA3 ....69 H5
Camplin St, SE14 ....133 G7
Camp Rd, SW19 ....165 H5
Campsbourne, The, N8
off High St 75 E4
Campsbourne Rd, N8 ....75 E3
Campsey Gdns, Dag.
RM9 ....100 B7
Campsey Rd, Dag. RM9 ...100 B7
Campsfield Rd, N8 ....75 E3
Campshill Pl, SE13
off Campshill Rd 154 C5
Campshill Rd, SE13 ....154 C5
Campus Rd, E17 ....77 J6
Campus Way, NW4
off Greyhound Hill 71 H3
Camp Vw, SW19 ....165 H5
Cam Rd, E15 ....114 D1
Camrose Av, Edg. HA8 ....69 J1
Erith DA8 ....139 H6
Feltham TW13 ....160 B4
Camrose Cl, Croy. CR0 ...189 H7
Morden SM4 ....184 D4
Camrose St, SE2 ....138 A5
Canada Av, N18 ....59 J6
Canada Cres, W3 ....106 C5
Canada Est, SE16 ....133 F3
Canada Gdns, SE13 ....154 C5
Canada Rd, W3 ....106 C4
Canada Sq, E14 ....134 B1
Canada St, SE16 ....133 G2
Canada Way, W12 ....107 H7
Canadian Av, SE6 ....172 B1
Canal App, SE8 ....133 H6
Canal Boul, NW1 ....92 D6
Canal Cl, E1 ....113 H4
W10 ....108 A4
Canal Gro, SE15 ....37 J5
Canal Path, E2 ....112 C1
Canalside Gdns, Sthl. UB2 123 E4
Canal St, SE5 ....36 B6
Canal Wk, N1 ....112 A1
NW10
off West End Cl 88 C7
Canal Wk, SE26 ....171 F5
Croydon CR0 ....188 B6
Canal Way, N1 ....12 A1
NW1 ....7 H3
NW8 ....7 G4
NW10 ....107 F4
W2 ....14 B1
W9
off Great Western Rd ..108 C5
W10 ....108 A4
Canal Way Wk, W10 ....108 A4
Canberra Cl, NW4 ....71 G3
Canberra Dr, Hayes UB4 ..102 C3
Northolt UB5 ....102 C3
Canberra Pl, Rich. TW9 ...146 A3
Canberra Rd, E6
off Barking Rd 116 C1
SE7 ....135 J6
W13 ....124 D1
Bexleyheath DA7 ....138 D6
Hounslow
(Lon.Hthrw Air.) TW6 ..140 D3
Canbury Av, Kings.T.
KT2 ....181 J1
Canbury Business Pk,
Kings.T. KT2
off Elm Cres 181 H1
Canbury Ms, SE26
off Wells Pk Rd 170 D3
Canbury Pk Rd, Kings.T.
KT2 ....181 H1
Canbury Pas, Kings.T.
KT2 ....181 G1
Cancell Rd, SW9 ....151 G1
Candahar Rd, SW11 ....149 H2
Candle Gro, SE15 ....153 E3
Candlemakers Apts,
SW11 off York Rd 149 G3
Candler St, N15 ....76 A6
Candover Cl, West Dr.
(Harm.) UB7 ....120 A7
Candover St, W1 ....17 F2
Candy St, E3 ....113 J1
Caney Ms, NW2
off Claremont Rd 90 A2
Canfield Dr, Ruis. HA4 ....84 B5
Canfield Gdns, NW6 ....91 F7
Canfield Pl, NW6
off Canfield Gdns 91 F6
Canfield Rd, Wdf.Grn.
IG8 ....64 B7
Canford Av, Nthlt. UB5 ...103 E1
Canford Cl, Enf. EN2 ....43 G2
Canford Gdns, N.Mal.
KT3 ....182 D6
Canford Pl, Tedd. TW11 ...163 E6
Canford Rd, SW11 ....150 A5
Canham Rd, SE25 ....188 B3
W3 ....126 E2
Canmore Gdns, SW16 ....168 C7
Cann Hall Rd, E11 ....96 E4
Canning Cres, N22 ....75 F1
Canning Cross, SE5 ....152 B2
Canning Pas, W8 ....22 C5
Canning Pl, W8 ....22 C5
Canning Pl Ms, W8 ....22 C4
Canning Rd, E15 ....114 E2
E17 ....77 H4
N5 ....93 H3
Croydon CR0 ....202 C2
Harrow HA3 ....68 C3
Cannington Rd, Dag.
RM9 ....100 C6
CANNING TOWN, E16 ....115 G6
Canning Town, E16 ....115 E5
Cannizaro Rd, SW19 ....165 J6
Cannonbury Av, Pnr.
HA5 ....66 D6
Cannon Cl, SW20 ....183 J3
Hampton TW12
off Hanworth Rd 161 H6
Cannon Ct, EC1
off Brewhouse Yd 11 H5
Cannon Dr, E14 ....114 A7
Cannon Hill, N14 ....58 D3
NW6 ....90 D5
Cannon Hill La, SW20 ....184 B3
Cannon La, NW3 ....91 G3
Pinner HA5 ....84 E1
Cannon Pl, NW3 ....91 G3
SE7 ....136 B5
Cannon Rd, N14 ....58 E3
Bexleyheath DA7 ....159 E1
Cannon St, EC4 ....19 J4
Cannon St Rd, E1 ....112 E6
Cannon Trd Est, Wem.
HA9 ....88 B4
Cannon Way, W.Mol.
KT8 ....179 G4
Cannon Wf Business Cen,
SE8 ....133 H4
Cannon Workshops, E14
off Cannon Dr 114 A7
Canon All, EC4
off St. Paul's Chyd 19 H4
Canon Av, Rom. RM6 ....82 C5
Canon Beck Rd, SE16 ....133 F2
Canonbie Rd, SE23 ....153 F7
CANONBURY, N1 ....93 J6
Canonbury Cres, N1 ....93 J7
Canonbury Gro, N1 ....93 J7
Canonbury La, N1 ....93 H7
Canonbury Pk N, N1 ....93 J6
Canonbury Pk S, N1 ....93 J6
Canonbury Pl, N1 ....93 H6
Canonbury Rd, N1 ....93 H6
Enfield EN1 ....44 B1
Canonbury Sq, N1 ....93 H7
Canonbury St, N1 ....93 J7
Canonbury Vil, N1 ....93 H7
Canonbury Yd, N1
off New N Rd 111 J1
Canonbury Yd W, N1
off Compton Rd 93 H6
Canon Mohan Cl, N14
off Farm La 42 B6
Canon Rd, Brom. BR1 ....191 J3
Canon Row, SW1 ....26 A4
Canons Cl, N2 ....73 G7
Edgware HA8 ....53 J6
Canons Cor, Edg. HA8 ....53 H4
Canons Ct, Edg. HA8 ....53 J6
Canons Dr, Edg. HA8 ....53 H6
Canonsleigh Rd, Dag.
RM9 ....100 B7
CANONS PARK, Edg.
HA8 ....53 H7
Canons Pk Cl, Edg. HA8
off Donnefield Av 53 H7
Canon St, N1 ....111 J1
Canons Wk, Croy. CR0 ....203 G3
Canopus Way, Nthwd.
HA6 ....50 A4
Staines TW19 ....140 B7
Canrobert St, E2 ....112 E3
Cantelowes Rd, NW1 ....92 D6
Canterbury Av, Ilf. IG1 ....80 B7
Sidcup DA15 ....176 C2
Canterbury Cl, E6
off Harper Rd 116 C6
Beckenham BR3 ....190 B1
Chigwell IG7 ....65 J3
Greenford UB6 ....103 H6
Worcester Park KT4 ....198 A2
Canterbury Cres, SW9 ....151 G3
Canterbury Gro, SE27 ....169 H3
Canterbury Ho, E3
off Bow Rd 114 B3
SE1 ....26 D5
Borehamwood WD6 ....38 A2
Canterbury Pl, SE17 ....35 H2
Canterbury Rd, E10 ....78 C7
NW6 ....108 D2
Borehamwood WD6 ....38 A2
Croydon CR0 ....187 F7
Feltham TW13 ....161 E3
Harrow HA1, HA2 ....67 H5
Morden SM4 ....185 F5
Canterbury Ter, NW6 ....108 D2
Cantium Retail Pk, SE1 ....37 H5
Cantley Gdns, SE19 ....188 C1
Ilford IG2 ....81 F6
Cantley Rd, W7 ....124 D3
Canton St, E14 ....114 A6
Cantrell Rd, E3 ....113 J4
Cantwell Rd, SE18 ....136 E7
Canute Gdns, SE16 ....133 G4
Canvey St, SE1 ....27 H1
Cape Cl, Bark. IG11
off North St 99 E6
Capel Av, Wall. SM6 ....201 F5
Capel Cl, N20 ....57 F3
Bromley BR2 ....206 B1
Capel Ct, EC2 ....20 C4
SE20 ....189 F1
Capel Cres, Stan. HA7 ....52 D2
Capel Gdns, Ilf. IG3 ....99 J4
Pinner HA5 ....67 F4
Capel Pt, E7 ....97 H4
Capel Rd, E7 ....97 H4
E12 ....97 J4
Barnet EN4 ....41 H6
Capener's Cl, SW1 ....24 B4
Capern Rd, SW18
off Cargill Rd 167 F1
Cape Rd, N17
off High Cross Rd 76 D3
Cape Yd, E1 ....29 J1
Capital Business Cen,
Mitch. CR4 ....185 J5
S.Croy. CR2 ....202 A7
Wembley HA0 ....105 G2
Capital Business Pk,
Borwd. WD6 ....38 C3
Capital E Apts, E16
off Western Gateway ..115 G7
Capital Interchange Way,
Brent. TW8 ....126 A5
Capitol Ind Pk, NW9 ....70 C3
Capitol Way, NW9 ....70 C3
Capland St, NW8 ....7 F5
Caple Par, NW10
off Harley Rd 106 E2
Caple Rd, NW10 ....107 F2

Capper St, WC1 .... 9 G6
Caprea Cl, Hayes UB4 *off Triandra Way* 102 D5
Capri Rd, Croy. CR0 ...... 202 C1
Capstan Cl, Rom. RM6 .... 82 B6
Capstan Ride, Enf. EN2 .... 43 G2
Capstan Rd, SE8 .... 133 J4
Capstan Sq, E14 .... 134 C2
Capstan Way, SE16 ...... 133 H1
Capstone Rd, Brom. BR1 .173 F4
Capthorne Av, Har. HA2 ... 85 E1
Capuchin Cl, Stan. HA7 .... 52 E6
Capulet Ms, E16 *off Hanover Av* 135 G1
Capulet Sq, E3 *off Talwin St* 114 B3
Capworth St, E10 .... 96 A1
Caradoc Cl, W2 .... 108 D6
Caradoc St, SE10 .... 134 E5
Caradon Cl, E11 .... 97 E1
Caradon Way, N15 .... 76 A4
Caravel Cl, E14 *off Tiller Rd* 134 A3
Caravelle Gdns, Nthlt. UB5 *off Javelin Way* 102 D3
Caravel Ms, SE8 *off Watergate St* 134 A6
Caraway Cl, E13 .... 115 H5
Caraway Pl, Wall. SM6 ... 200 B3
Carberry Rd, SE19 .... 170 B6
Carbery Av, W3 .... 125 J2
Carbis Cl, E4 .... 62 D1
Carbis Rd, E14 .... 113 J6
Carbuncle Pas Way, N17 ... 76 D2
Carburton St, W1 .... 17 E1
Cardale St, E14 *off Plevna St* 134 C3
Carden Rd, SE15 .... 152 E3
Cardiff Rd, W7 .... 124 D3
Enfield EN3 .... 45 E4
Cardiff St, SE18 .... 137 H7
Cardigan Gdns, Ilf. IG3 ... 100 A2
Cardigan Rd, E3 .... 113 J2
SW13 .... 147 G2
SW19 *off Haydons Rd* .. 167 F6
Richmond TW10 .... 145 H6
Cardigan St, SE11 .... 34 E3
Cardigan Wk, N1 *off Ashby Gro* 93 J7
Cardinal Av, Borwd. WD6 .... 38 B3
Kingston upon Thames KT2 .... 163 H5
Morden SM4 .... 184 B6
Cardinal Bourne St, SE1 .... 28 C6
Cardinal Cap All, SE1 *off New Globe Wk* 19 J6
Cardinal Cl, Chis. BR7 .... 193 G1
Edgware HA8 .... 54 D7
Morden SM4 .... 184 B7
Worcester Park KT4 ...... 197 G4
Cardinal Ct, Borwd. WD6 .. 38 B3
Cardinal Cres, N.Mal. KT3 .... 182 C2
Cardinal Dr, Ilf. IG6 .... 65 F6
Cardinal Hinsley Cl, NW10 .... 107 G2
Cardinal Pl, SW15 .... 148 A4
Cardinal Rd, Felt. TW13 ... 160 B1
Ruislip HA4 .... 84 D1
Cardinals Wk, Hmptn. TW12 .... 161 J7
Cardinals Way, N19 .... 92 D1
Cardinal Wk, SW1 *off Palace St* 25 F5
Cardinal Way, Har. HA3 .... 68 B3
Cardine Ms, SE15 .... 132 E7
Cardington Sq, Houns. TW4 .... 142 D4
Cardington St, NW1 .... 9 F3
Cardinham Rd, Orp. BR6 .... 207 J4
Cardozo Rd, N7 .... 93 E5
Cardrew Av, N12 .... 57 G5
Cardrew Cl, N12 .... 57 G5
Cardross St, W6 .... 127 H3
Cardwell Rd, N7 .... 92 E4
Carew Cl, N7 .... 93 F2
Carew Rd, N17 .... 76 D2
W13 .... 125 F2
Mitcham CR4 .... 186 A2
Thornton Heath CR7 ... 187 H3
Wallington SM6 .... 200 C6
Carew St, SE5 .... 151 J2
Carew Way, Wat. WD19 .... 51 F3
Carey Ct, Bexh. DA6 ...... 159 H5
Carey Gdns, SW8 .... 150 C1
Carey La, EC2 .... 19 J3
Carey Pl, SW1 .... 33 H2
Carey Rd, Dag. RM9 .... 101 E4
Carey St, WC2 .... 18 D4
Carey Way, Wem. HA9 ..... 88 B4
Carfax Pl, SW4 .... 150 D4
Carfax Rd, Hayes UB3 .... 121 J5
Carfree Cl, N1 *off Bewdley St* 93 G7
Cargill Rd, SW18 .... 167 E1
Cargreen Pl, SE25 *off Cargreen Rd* 188 C4
Cargreen Rd, SE25 .... 188 C4
Carholme Rd, SE23 .... 171 J1
Carisbrook Cl, Enf. EN1 .... 44 C1
Carisbrooke, N10 .... 74 A2
Carisbrooke Av, Bex. DA5 .... 176 D1
Carisbrooke Cl, Houns. TW4 *off Farm Rd* 161 E1
Stanmore HA7 .... 69 G2
Carisbrooke Gdns, SE15 ... 37 G7
Carisbrooke Ho, Kings.T. KT2 *off Kingsgate Rd* ... 181 H1
Carisbrooke Rd, E17 ...... 77 H4
Bromley BR2 .... 191 J4
Mitcham CR4 .... 186 D4
Carker's La, NW5 .... 92 B5
Carleton Cl, Esher KT10 ... 194 A1
Carleton Rd, N7 .... 92 D5
Carlile Cl, E3 .... 113 J2
Carlina Gdns, Wdf.Grn. IG8 .... 63 H5
Carlingford Gdns, Mitch. CR4 .... 167 J7
Carlingford Rd, N15 .... 75 H3
NW3 .... 91 G4
Morden SM4 .... 184 A6
Carlisle Av, EC3 .... 21 E4
W3 .... 106 E6
Carlisle Cl, Kings.T. KT2 .... 182 A1
Pinner HA5 .... 66 E7
Carlisle Gdns, Har. HA3 .... 69 G7
Ilford IG1 .... 80 B6
Carlisle La, SE1 .... 26 D6
Carlisle Ms, NW8 .... 15 F1
Carlisle Pl, N11 .... 58 B4
SW1 .... 25 F6
Carlisle Rd, E10 .... 96 A2
N4 .... 75 G7
NW6 .... 108 B1
NW9 .... 70 C3
Hampton TW12 .... 161 H7
Sutton SM1 .... 198 C5
Carlisle St, W1 .... 17 H4
Carlisle Wk, E8 *off Cumberland Cl* 94 C6
Carlisle Way, SW17 ...... 168 A5
Carlos Pl, W1 .... 16 C6
Carlow St, NW1 .... 9 F1
Carlton Av, N14 .... 42 D5
Feltham TW14 .... 142 C6
Harrow HA3 .... 68 E5
Hayes UB3 .... 121 H4
South Croydon CR2 ... 202 B7
Carlton Av E, Wem. HA9 ... 87 H1
Carlton Av W, Wem. HA0 ... 86 E2
Carlton Cl, NW3 .... 90 D2
Borehamwood WD6 ... 38 D4
Chessington KT9 .... 195 G6
Edgware HA8 .... 54 A5
Northolt UB5 *off Whitton Av W* 85 J5
Carlton Ct, SW9 .... 151 H1
Ilford IG6 .... 81 G3
Carlton Cres, Sutt. SM3 ... 198 B4
Carlton Dr, SW15 .... 148 B5
Ilford IG6 .... 81 G3
Carlton Gdns, SW1 .... 25 H2
W5 .... 105 F6
Carlton Gro, SE15 .... 152 E1
Carlton Hill, NW8 .... 109 E2
Carlton Ho, Felt. TW14 .... 141 J7
Carlton Ho Ter, SW1 .... 25 H2
Carlton Pk Av, SW20 ...... 183 J2
Carlton Rd, E11 .... 97 F1
E12 .... 98 A4
E17 .... 77 H1
N4 .... 75 G7
N11 .... 58 A5
SW14 .... 146 C3
W4 .... 126 D2
W5 .... 105 F7
Erith DA8 .... 139 H6
New Malden KT3 ...... 182 E2
Sidcup DA14 .... 175 J5
South Croydon CR2 ... 202 A6
Walton-on-Thames KT12 .... 178 B7
Welling DA16 .... 158 B3
Carlton Sq, E1 *off Argyle Rd* 113 G4
Carlton St, SW1 .... 17 H6
Carlton Ter, E11 .... 79 H5
N18 .... 60 A3
SE26 .... 171 F3
Carlton Twr Pl, SW1 .... 24 A5
Carlton Twrs, Carshalton SM5 .... 199 J5
Carlton Vale, NW6 .... 108 E2
Carlton Vil, SW15 *off St. John's Av* 148 A5
Carlwell St, SW17 .... 167 H5
Carlyle Av, Brom. BR1 .... 192 A3
Southall UB1 .... 103 F7
Carlyle Cl, N2 .... 73 F6
West Molesey KT8 ..... 179 H2
Carlyle Ct, SW10 *off Chelsea Harbour* .. 149 F1
Carlyle Gdns, Sthl. UB1 ... 103 F7
Carlyle Lo, Barn. (New Barn.) EN5 *off Richmond Rd* 41 F5
Carlyle Ms, E1 *off Alderney Rd* 113 G4
Carlyle Pl, SW15 .... 148 A4
Carlyle Rd, E12 .... 98 B4
NW10 .... 106 D1
SE28 .... 118 B7
W5 .... 125 F5
Croydon CR0 .... 202 D2
★ **Carlyle's Ho**, SW3 ..... 31 G6
Carlyle Sq, SW3 .... 31 F4
Carly Ms, E2 .... 13 H4
Carlyon Av, Har. HA2 ...... 85 F4
Carlyon Cl, Wem. HA0 .... 105 H1
Carlyon Rd, Hayes UB4 ... 102 C6
Wembley HA0 .... 105 H2
Carlys Cl, Beck. BR3 ...... 189 G2
Carmalt Gdns, SW15 ..... 147 J4
Carmarthen Pl, SE1 .... 28 D3
Carmel Ct, W8 .... 22 A3
Wembley HA9 .... 88 B2
Carmelite Cl, Har. HA3 ..... 67 J1
Carmelite Rd, Har. HA3 .... 67 J1
Carmelite St, EC4 .... 19 F5
Carmelite Wk, Har. HA3 .... 67 J1
Carmelite Way, Har. HA3 ... 67 J2
Carmel Way, Rich. TW9 ... 146 B2
Carmen St, E14 .... 114 B6
Carmichael Cl, SW11 *off Darien Rd* 149 G3
Ruislip HA4 .... 84 A4
Carmichael Ms, SW18 ... 149 G7
Carmichael Rd, SE25 ..... 188 D5
Carminia Rd, SW17 .... 168 B2
Carnaby St, W1 .... 17 F4
Carnac St, SE27 .... 170 A4
Carnanton Rd, E17 .... 78 D1
Carnarvon Av, Enf. EN1 .... 44 C3
Carnarvon Dr, Hayes UB3 .121 F3
Carnarvon Rd, E10 .... 78 C6
E15 .... 97 F6
E18 .... 79 F1
Barnet EN5 .... 40 B3
Carnation St, SE2 .... 138 B5
Carnbrook Ms, SE3 *off Carnbrook Rd* 156 A3
Carnbrook Rd, SE3 .... 156 A3
Carnecke Gdns, SE9 ..... 156 B5
Carnegie Cl, Surb. KT6 *off Fullers Av* 195 J2
Carnegie Pl, SW19 .... 166 A3
Carnegie St, N1 .... 111 F1
Carnforth Cl, Epsom KT19 .... 196 B6
Carnforth Rd, SW16 ...... 168 D7
Carnie Lo, SW17 *off Manville Rd* 168 B3
Carnoustie Cl, SE28 ...... 118 D6
Carnoustie Dr, N1 .... 93 F7
Carnwath Rd, SW6 .... 148 D3
Carol Cl, NW4 .... 72 A4
Carolina Cl, E15 .... 96 E5
Carolina Rd, Th.Hth. CR7 .... 187 H2
Caroline Cl, N10 *off Alexandra Pk Rd* 74 B2
SW16 .... 169 F3
W2 .... 14 B6
Croydon CR0 .... 202 B4
Isleworth TW7 .... 124 A7
West Drayton UB7 ..... 120 A2
Caroline Ct, Stan. HA7 *off The Chase* 52 D6
Caroline Gdns, E2 .... 13 E3
SE15 .... 132 E7
Caroline Pl, SW11 .... 150 A2
W2 .... 14 B5
Hayes (Harling.) UB3 ... 121 H7
Caroline Pl Ms, W2 .... 14 B6
Caroline Rd, SW19 .... 166 C7
Caroline St, E1 .... 113 G6
Caroline Ter, SW1 .... 32 B2
Caroline Wk, W6 .... 128 B6
Carol St, NW1 .... 110 C1
Carolyn Ho, Croy. CR0 *off Dingwall Rd* 202 A2
Carpenders Av, Wat. WD19 .... 50 E3
CARPENDERS PARK, Wat. WD19 .... 51 F2
Carpenter Gdns, N21 ...... 59 H2
Carpenters Arms Path, SE9 *off Eltham High St* 156 C6
Carpenters Business Pk, E15 .... 96 A7
Carpenters Cl, Barn. EN5 .. 41 E6
Carpenters Ct, Twick. TW2 .... 162 B2
Carpenters Ms, N7 *off North Rd* 93 E5
Carpenters Pl, SW4 ...... 150 D4
Carpenters Rd, E15 .... 96 A6
Carpenter St, W1 .... 16 D6
Carrara Cl, SW9 *off Eaton Dr* 151 H4
Carrara Ms, E8 .... 94 D6
Carrara Wf, SW6 .... 148 B3
Carr Cl, Stan. HA7 .... 52 D6
Carre Ms, SE5 *off Calais St* 151 H1
Carr Gro, SE18 .... 136 B4
Carriage Dr E, SW11 .... 32 B7
Carriage Dr N, SW11 ...... 32 C6
Carriage Dr S, SW11 ..... 149 J1
Carriage Dr W, SW11 ..... 129 J7
Carriage Ms, Ilf. IG1 .... 99 F2
Carriage Pl, N16 .... 94 A3
SW16 .... 168 C5
Carriage St, SE18 .... 137 E3
Carrick Cl, Islw. TW7 ..... 144 D3
Carrick Dr, Ilf. IG6 .... 81 F1
Carrick Gdns, N17 .... 60 B7
Carrick Ms, SE8 *off Watergate St* 134 A6
Carrill Way, Belv. DA17 ... 138 D4
Carrington Av, Borwd. WD6 .... 38 B5
Hounslow TW3 .... 143 H5
Carrington Cl, Barn. (Arkley) EN5 .... 39 G5
Borehamwood WD6 .... 38 C5
Croydon CR0 .... 189 H7
Carrington Gdns, E7 *off Woodford Rd* 97 G4
Carrington Rd, Rich. TW10 .... 146 A4
Carrington Sq, Har. HA3 ... 51 J7
Carrington St, W1 .... 24 D2
Carrol Cl, NW5 .... 92 B4
Carroll Cl, E15 .... 97 F5
Carroll Hill, Loug. IG10 .... 48 C3
Carronade Ct, N7 *off Eden Gro* 93 F5
Carronade Pl, SE28 ...... 137 F3
Carron Cl, E14 .... 114 B6
Carroun Rd, SW8 .... 34 C7
Carroway La, Grnf. UB6 *off Cowgate Rd* 104 A3
Carrow Rd, Dag. RM9 .... 100 B7
Carr Rd, E17 .... 77 J2
Northolt UB5 .... 85 G6
Carrs La, N21 .... 43 J5
Carr St, E14 .... 113 H5
CARSHALTON, SM5 ...... 199 G4
Carshalton Gro, Sutt. SM1 .... 199 G4
Carshalton Pk Rd, Cars. SM5 .... 199 J5
Carshalton Pl, Cars. SM5 .... 200 A4
Carshalton Rd, Cars. SM5 .... 199 F5
Mitcham CR4 .... 186 A4
Sutton SM1 .... 199 F5
Carslake Rd, SW15 ...... 147 J6
Carson Rd, E16 .... 115 G4
SE21 .... 169 J2
Barnet (Cockfos.) EN4 ... 41 J4
Carstairs Rd, SE6 .... 172 C3
Carston Cl, SE12 .... 155 F5
Carswell Cl, Ilf. IG4 *off Roding La S* 80 A4
Carswell Rd, SE6 .... 154 C7
Carter Cl, NW9 .... 70 D6
Carteret St, SW1 .... 25 H4
Carteret Way, SE8 .... 133 H4
Carterhatch La, Enf. EN1 ... 44 D2
Carterhatch Rd, Enf. EN3 .. 45 F2
Carter La, EC4 .... 19 H4
Carter Pl, SE17 .... 36 A4
Carter Rd, E13 .... 115 H1
SW19 .... 167 G6
Carters Cl, Wor.Pk. KT4 ... 198 A2
Carters Hill Cl, SE9 .... 173 J1
Carters La, SE23 .... 171 H2
Carter St, SE17 .... 35 J5
Carters Yd, SW18 *off Wandsworth High St* 148 D5
Carthew Rd, W6 .... 127 H3
Carthew Vil, W6 .... 127 H3
Carthusian St, EC1 .... 19 J1
Cartier Circle, E14 .... 134 B1
Carting La, WC2 .... 18 B6
Cart La, E4 .... 46 D7
Cartmel, NW1 .... 9 F3
Cartmel Cl, N17 *off Heybourne Rd* 61 E7
Cartmel Gdns, Mord. SM4 .... 185 F5
Cartmel Rd, Bexh. DA7 ... 159 G1
Carton St, W1 .... 16 A3
Cartridge Pl, SE18 .... 137 E3
Cartwright Gdns, WC1 ..... 10 A4
Cartwright Rd, Dag. RM9 .... 101 F7
Cartwright St, E1 .... 21 G5

Cartwright Way, SW13 127 H7
Carver Cl, W4 126 C3
Carver Rd, SE24 151 J6
Carville Cres, Brent. TW8 125 H4
Cary Rd, E11 97 E4
Carysfort Rd, N8 74 D5
N16 94 A3
Casby Ho, SE16 29 H5
Cascade Av, N10 74 C4
Cascade Cl, Buck.H. IG9
off Cascade Rd 64 A2
Cascade Rd, Buck.H. IG9 64 A2
Cascades Twr, E14 133 J1
Casella Rd, SE14 133 G7
Casewick Rd, SE27 169 H4
Casey Cl, NW8 7 G4
Casimir Rd, E5 95 E3
Casino Av, SE24 151 J5
Caspian St, SE5 36 B7
Caspian Wk, E16 116 A6
Caspian Wf, E3
off Violet Rd 114 B5
Cassandra Cl, Nthlt.
UB5 86 A4
Casselden Rd, NW10 88 D7
Cassidy Rd, SW6 128 D7
Cassilda Rd, SE2 138 A4
Cassilis Rd, E14 134 A2
Twickenham TW1 145 E5
Cassiobury Av, Felt.
TW14 141 J6
Cassiobury Rd, E17 77 G5
Cassis Ct, Loug. IG10 49 F4
Cassland Rd, E9 95 F7
Thornton Heath CR7 188 A4
Casslee Rd, SE6 153 J7
Casson St, E1 21 H2
Castalia Sq, E14
off Roserton St 134 C2
Castalia St, E14
off Plevna St 134 C2
Castellain Rd, W9 6 C6
Castellane Cl, Stan. HA7
off Daventer Dr 52 C7
Castello Av, SW15 147 J5
Castell Rd, Loug. IG10 49 F1
CASTELNAU, SW13 127 G6
Castelnau, SW13 127 H6
Castelnau Gdns, SW13
off Arundel Ter 127 H6
Castelnau Pl, SW13
off Castelnau 127 H6
Castelnau Row, SW13
off Lonsdale Rd 127 H6
Casterbridge, NW6 109 E1
Casterbridge Rd, SE3 155 G3
Casterton St, E8
off Wilton Way 95 E6
Castile Rd, SE18 136 D4
Castillon Rd, SE6 172 E2
Castlands Rd, SE6 171 J2
Castle Av, E4 62 D5
Castlebar Hill, W5 105 E5
Castlebar Ms, W5 105 F5
Castlebar Pk, W5 105 E4
Castlebar Rd, W5 105 F5
Castle Baynard St, EC4 19 H5
Castlebrook Cl, SE11 35 G1
Castle Cl, E9
off Swinnerton St 95 H5
SW19 166 A3
W3 126 B2
Bromley BR2 190 E3
Castlecombe Dr, SW19 148 A7
Castlecombe Rd, SE9 174 B4
Castle Ct, EC3 20 C4
SE26 171 H4
SW15 148 B3
Castledine Rd, SE20 170 E7
Castle Dr, Ilf. IG4 80 B6
Castleford Av, SE9 174 E1
Castleford Cl, N17 60 C6
Castlegate, Rich. TW9 145 J3
Castlehaven Rd, NW1 92 B7
Castle La, SW1 25 G5
Castleleigh Ct, Enf. EN2 44 A5
Castlemaine Av, S.Croy.
CR2 202 C5
Castlemaine Twr, SW11 149 J1
Castlemain St, E1 112 E5
Castlemead, SE5 131 J7
Castle Ms, N12
off Castle Rd 57 F5
NW1 *off Castle Rd* 92 B6
SW17 167 H4
Hampton TW12
off Station Rd 179 H1
Castle Par, Epsom KT17
off Ewell Bypass 197 G7
Castle Pl, NW1 92 B6
W4 *off Windmill Rd* 126 E4
Castle Pt, E13 115 J2
Castlereagh St, W1 15 H3
Castle Rd, N12 57 F5
NW1 92 B6
Dagenham RM9 118 B1
Enfield EN3 45 H1
Castle Rd, Isleworth TW7 144 C2
Northolt UB5 85 H6
Southall UB2 123 F3
Castle St, E6 115 J2
Kingston upon Thames
KT1 181 H2
Castleton Av, Wem. HA9 87 H4
Castleton Cl, Croy. CR0 189 H6
Castleton Gdns, Wem.
HA9 87 H3
Castleton Rd, E17 78 D2
SE9 174 A4
Ilford IG3 100 A1
Mitcham CR4 186 D4
Ruislip HA4 84 D1
Castletown Rd, W14 128 B5
Castleview Cl, N4 93 J1
Castleview Gdns, Ilf. IG1 80 B6
Castle Wk, Sun. TW16
off Elizabeth Gdns 178 C3
Castle Way, SW19 166 A3
Feltham TW13 160 C4
Castlewood Dr, SE9 156 C2
Castlewood Rd, N15 76 D6
N16 76 D7
Barnet (Cockfos.) EN4 41 G3
Castle Yd, N6
off North Rd 74 A7
SE1 27 H1
Richmond TW10
off Hill St 145 G5
Caston Pt Trd Est, Hayes
UB3 121 H2
Castor La, E14 114 B7
Catalina Rd, Houns.
(Lon.Hthrw Air.) TW6
off Cromer Rd 140 D2
Catalpa Ct, SE13
off Hither Grn La 154 D6
Caterham Av, Ilf. IG5 80 C2
Caterham Rd, SE13 154 C3
Catesby St, SE17 36 C2
CATFORD, SE6 172 B1
Catford Br, SE6 154 A7
Catford Bdy, SE6 154 B7
Catford Gyratory, SE6 154 B7
Catford Hill, SE6 171 J2
Catford Ms, SE6
off Holbeach Rd 154 B7
Catford Rd, SE6 172 A1
Cathall Rd, E11 96 D3
Cathay St, SE16 133 E2
Cathay Wk, Nthlt. UB5
off Brabazon Rd 103 G2
Cathcart Dr, Orp. BR6 207 H2
Cathcart Hill, N19 92 C3
Cathcart Rd, SW10 30 B5
Cathcart St, NW5 92 B6
Cathedral Piazza, SW1 25 F6
Cathedral St, SE1 28 B1
Cathedral Wk, SW1 25 F5
Catherall Rd, N5 93 J3
Catherine Cl, Loug. IG10
off Roding Gdns 48 C6
Catherine Ct, N14
off Conisbee Ct 42 C5
Catherine Dr, Rich. TW9 145 H4
Catherine Gdns, Houns.
TW3 144 A4
Catherine Griffiths Ct,
EC1 11 F5
Catherine Gro, SE10 154 B1
Catherine Ho, N1
off Phillipp St 112 B1
Catherine Howard Ct, SE9
off Avery Hill Rd 157 G6
Catherine of Aragon Ct,
SE9 *off Avery Hill Rd* 157 F6
Catherine Parr Ct, SE9
off Avery Hill Rd 157 G6
Catherine Pl, SW1 25 F5
Harrow HA1 68 C5
Catherine Rd, Surb.
KT6 181 G5
Catherine's Cl, West Dr. UB7
off Money La 120 A3
Catherine St, WC2 18 C5
Catherine Wheel All, E1 20 E2
Catherine Wheel Rd, Brent.
TW8 125 G7
Catherine Wheel Yd,
SW1 25 F2
Catherwood Ct, N1
off Murray Gro 12 B2
Cat Hill, Barn. EN4 41 H6
Cathles Rd, SW12 150 B6
Cathnor Rd, W12 127 H2
Catling Cl, SE23 171 F3
Catlins La, Pnr. HA5 66 B3
Catlin St, SE16 37 J4
Cator La, Beck. BR3 189 J2
Cato Rd, SW4 150 D3
Cator Rd, SE26 171 G6
Carshalton SM5 199 J5
Cator St, SE15 37 F6
Cato St, W1 15 H2
Catterick Cl, N11 58 A6
Cattistock Rd, SE9 174 B5
Cattley Cl, Barn. EN5 40 B4
Catton St, WC1 18 C2
Caughley Ho, SE11
off Lambeth Wk 26 E6
Caulfield Rd, E6 98 C7
SE15 153 E2
Causeway, The, N2 73 H4
SW18 148 E4
SW19 166 A5
Carshalton SM5 200 A3
Chessington KT9 195 H4
Esher (Clay.) KT10 194 C7
Feltham TW14 142 A4
Hounslow TW4 142 A4
Teddington TW11
off Broad St 162 C6
Causeyware Rd, N9 45 E7
Causton Rd, N6 74 B7
Causton Sq, Dag. RM10 101 G7
Causton St, SW1 33 J2
Cautley Av, SW4 150 C5
Cavalier Cl, Rom. RM6 82 D4
Cavalier Ho, W5
off Uxbridge Rd 105 F7
Cavalry Barracks, Houns.
TW4 142 D3
Cavalry Cres, Houns.
TW4 142 D4
Cavalry Gdns, SW15 148 B5
Cavan Pl, Pnr. HA5 67 F1
Cavaye Pl, SW10 30 D4
Cavell Dr, Enf. EN2 43 G2
Cavell Rd, N17 60 A7
Cavell St, E1 113 E5
Cavendish Av, N3 72 D2
NW8 7 F2
W13 104 D5
Erith DA8 139 J6
Harrow HA1 86 A4
New Malden KT3 183 H5
Ruislip HA4 84 B5
Sidcup DA15 158 A7
Welling DA16 157 J3
Woodford Green IG8 79 H1
Cavendish Cl, N18 61 E5
NW6
off Cavendish Rd 90 C7
NW8 7 F3
Cavendish Ct, EC3 20 E3
Cavendish Cres, Borwd.
(Els.) WD6 38 A4
Cavendish Dr, E11 96 D1
Edgware HA8 53 J6
Esher (Clay.) KT10 194 B5
Cavendish Gdns, SW4 150 C6
Barking IG11 99 H5
Ilford IG1 98 D1
Romford RM6 83 E5
Cavendish Ms N, W1 16 E1
Cavendish Ms S, W1 16 E2
Cavendish Par, SW4
off Clapham Common
S Side 150 B6
Hounslow TW4
off Bath Rd 142 E2
Cavendish Pl, NW2 90 A6
W1 16 E3
Bromley BR1 192 C3
Cavendish Rd, E4 62 C6
N4 75 G6
N18 60 E5
NW6 90 B7
SW12 150 B6
SW19 167 G7
W4 146 C1
Barnet EN5 39 J3
Croydon CR0 201 H1
New Malden KT3 183 F5
Sutton SM2 199 F7
Cavendish Sq, W1 16 E3
Cavendish St, N1 12 B2
Cavendish Ter, Felt. TW13
off High St 160 A2
Cavendish Way, W.Wick.
BR4 204 B1
Cavenham Gdns, Ilf. IG1 99 G3
Caverleigh Way, Wor.Pk.
KT4 197 G1
Cave Rd, E13 115 H2
Richmond TW10 163 F4
Caversham Av, N13 59 G3
Sutton SM3 198 B2
Caversham Ct, N11 58 A3
Caversham Flats, SW3 31 J5
Caversham Rd, N15 75 J4
NW5 92 C6
Kingston upon Thames
KT1 181 J2
Caversham St, SW3 31 J5
Caverswall St, W12 107 J6
Caveside Cl, Chis. BR7 192 D1
Cawdor Cres, W7 124 D4
Cawnpore St, SE19 170 B5
Caxton Gro, E3 114 A3
Caxton Ms, Brent. TW8
off The Butts 125 G6
Caxton Rd, N22 75 F2
SW19 167 F5
W12 128 A2
Southall UB2 122 D3
Caxton St, SW1 25 G5
Caxton St N, E16
off Victoria Dock Rd 115 F7
Cayenne Ct, SE1 29 G2
Cayford Ho, NW3 91 H5
Caygill Cl, Brom. BR2 191 F4
Cayley Rd, Sthl. UB2
off McNair Rd 123 H3
Cayton Pl, EC1 12 B4
Cayton Rd, Grnf. UB6 104 B2
Cayton St, EC1 12 B4
Cazenove Rd, E17 78 A1
N16 94 C2
Cearns Ho, E6 116 A1
Cecil Av, Bark. IG11 99 G7
Enfield EN1 44 C4
Wembley HA9 87 J5
Cecil Cl, W5 105 G5
Chessington KT9 195 G4
Cecil Ct, WC2 17 J6
Barnet EN5 40 A3
Cecile Pk, N8 75 E6
Cecilia Cl, N2 73 F3
★ **Cecilia Coleman Gall**,
NW8 7 F1
Cecilia Rd, E8 94 D5
Cecil Manning Cl,
Grnf. UB6
off Horsenden La S 104 D1
Cecil Pk, Pnr. HA5 67 E4
Cecil Pl, Mitch. CR4 185 J5
Cecil Rd, E11 97 E3
E13 115 G1
E17 78 A1
N10 74 B2
N14 58 C1
NW9 70 E3
NW10 106 E1
SW19 166 E7
W3 106 C5
Croydon CR0 187 F6
Enfield EN2 44 A4
Harrow HA3 68 B3
Hounslow TW3 143 J2
Ilford IG1 98 E4
Romford RM6 82 D7
Sutton SM1 198 C6
★ **Cecil Sharp Ho**,
NW1 110 A1
Cecil Way, Brom. BR2 205 G1
Cedar Av, Barn. EN4 41 H7
Enfield EN3 45 F2
Hayes UB3 102 A6
Romford RM6 82 E5
Ruislip HA4 84 C6
Sidcup DA15 158 A7
Twickenham TW2 143 H6
West Drayton UB7 120 C1
Cedar Cl, E3 113 J1
SE21 169 J1
SW15 164 D4
Borehamwood WD6 38 B4
Bromley BR2 206 B3
Buckhurst Hill IG9 64 A2
Carshalton SM5 199 J6
East Molesey KT8
off Cedar Rd 180 B4
Ilford IG1 99 G5
Romford RM7 83 J4
Cedar Copse, Brom. BR1 192 C2
Cedar Ct, E11
off Grosvenor Rd 79 H5
N1 *off Essex Rd* 93 J7
SE7 *off Fairlawn* 135 J6
SE9 156 B6
SW19 166 A3
Cedar Cres, Brom. BR2 206 B3
Cedarcroft Rd, Chess.
KT9 195 J4
Cedar Dr, N2 73 H4
Loughton IG10 49 E2
Pinner HA5 51 G6
Cedar Gdns, Sutt. SM2 199 F6
Cedar Gro, W5 125 H3
Bexley DA5 158 C6
Southall UB1 103 G5
Cedar Hts, Rich. TW10 163 H1
Cedar Ho, Croy. CR0 204 B6
Cedarhurst, Brom. BR1 173 E7
Cedarhurst Dr, SE9 155 J5
Cedar Lawn Av, Barn.
EN5 40 B5
Cedar Ms, SW15
off Cambalt Rd 148 A5
Cedar Mt, SE9 174 A1
Cedarne Rd, SW6 128 E7
Cedar Pk, Chig. IG7
off High Rd 65 E4
Cedar Pk Gdns, SW19 165 H5
Romford RM6 82 D7
Cedar Pl, SE7
off Floyd Rd 135 J5
Cedar Ri, N14 42 A7

Cedar Rd, N17 76 C1
NW2 89 J4
Bromley BR1 191 J2
Croydon CR0 202 B2
East Molesey KT8 180 B4
Hounslow TW4 142 C2
Romford RM7 83 J4
Sutton SM2 199 F6
Teddington TW11 162 D5
Cedars, The, E15
off Portway 115 F1
W13
off Heronsforde 105 F6
Buckhurst Hill IG9 63 G1
Teddington TW11
off Adelaide Rd 162 C6
Cedars Av, E17 78 A5
Mitcham CR4 186 A4
Cedars Cl, NW4 72 A3
SE13 154 D3
Cedars Ct, N9 60 B2
Cedars Ms, SW4
off Cedars Rd 150 B4
Cedars Rd, E15 97 E6
N21 59 H2
SW4 150 B3
SW13 147 F2
W4 126 C5
Beckenham BR3 189 H2
Croydon CR0 201 E3
Kingston upon Thames (Hmptn W.) KT1 181 F1
Morden SM4 184 D4
Cedar Ter, Rich. TW9 145 H4
Cedar Tree Gro, SE27 169 H5
Cedarville Gdns, SW16 169 F6
Cedar Vista, Rich. (Kew) TW9 145 H2
Cedar Wk, Esher (Clay.) KT10 194 C6
Cedar Way, NW1 92 D7
Cedra Ct, N16 94 D1
Cedric Rd, SE9 175 F3
Celadon Cl, Enf. EN3 45 H3
Celandine Cl, E14 114 A5
Celandine Dr, E8 94 C7
SE28 138 B1
Celandine Gro, N14 42 C5
Celandine Way, E15 115 E3
Celbridge Ms, W2 14 B3
Celestial Gdns, SE13 154 D4
Celia Rd, N19 92 C4
Celtic Av, Brom. BR2 190 E3
Celtic St, E14 114 B5
Cemetery La, SE7 136 B6
Cemetery Rd, E7 97 F4
N17 60 B7
SE2 138 B7
Cenacle Cl, NW3 90 D3
★ **Cenotaph, The**, SW1 26 A3
Centaurs Business Cen, Islw. TW7 124 D6
Centaur St, SE1 26 D5
Centenary Ind Est, Enf. EN3 45 J4
Centenary Rd, Enf. EN3 45 J4
Centenary Wk, Loug. IG10 47 H3
Central Av, E11 96 D2
N2 73 G2
N9 60 B3
SW11 129 J7
Enfield EN1 44 E2
Hayes UB3 102 A7
Hounslow TW3 143 J4
Pinner HA5 67 F6
Wallington SM6 201 E5
Welling DA16 157 J2
West Molesey KT8 179 F4
Central Circ, NW4
off Hendon Way 71 H5
★ **Central Criminal Ct** (Old Bailey), EC4 19 H3
Centrale Shop Cen, Croy. CR0 201 J2
Central Gdns, Mord. SM4 185 E5
Central Hill, SE19 170 A5
Central Ho, E15
off High St 114 C2
Barking IG11
off Cambridge Rd 99 F7
Central Par, E17
off Hoe St 78 A4
Feltham TW14 142 C7
Greenford (Perivale) UB6 104 D3
Hounslow TW5
off Heston Rd 123 G7
Surbiton KT6 181 H6
Central Pk Av, Dag. RM10 101 H3
Central Pk Est, Houns. TW4 142 D5
Central Pk Rd, E6 116 A2
Central Pl, SE25
off Portland Rd 188 E4
Central Rd, Mord. SM4 184 D6
Wembley HA0 86 E5
Worcester Park KT4 197 G2
Central Sch Footpath, SW14 146 C3
Central Sq, NW11 72 E6
Wembley HA9
off Station Gro 87 H5
West Molesey KT8 179 F4
Central St, EC1 11 J4
Central Way, NW10 106 C3
SE28 138 A1
Carshalton SM5 199 H7
Feltham TW14 142 B5
Central West, Grnf. UB6 103 J4
Centre, The, Felt. TW13 160 A2
Centre Av, W3 126 D1
W10 *off Harrow Rd* 107 J3
Centre Common Rd, Chis. BR7 175 F6
Centre Ct Shop Cen, SW19 166 C6
Centre Pt, SE1 37 H3
Centrepoint, WC1 17 J3
Centre Rd, E7 97 G2
E11 97 G2
Dagenham RM10 119 H2
Centre St, E2 112 E2
Centre Way, E17 62 C7
N9 61 F2
Centreway Apts, Ilf. IG1
off High Rd 99 F2
Centric Cl, NW1
off Oval Rd 110 B1
Centrillion Pt, Croy. CR0
off Masons Av 201 J4
Centurion Bldg, SW8 32 D6
Centurion Cl, N7 93 F7
Centurion Ct, SE18
off Rushgrove St 136 D4
Wallington (Hackbr.) SM6 *off Wandle Rd* 200 B3
Centurion La, E3
off Libra Rd 113 J2
Centurion Sq, SE18 156 B1
Centurion Way, Erith DA18 139 G3
Century Cl, NW4 72 A5
Century Ms, E5
off Lower Clapton Rd 95 F4
Century Rd, E17 77 H3
Century Yd, SE23 171 F2
Cephas Av, E1 113 F4
Cephas St, E1 113 F4
Ceres Rd, SE18 137 J4
Cerise Rd, SE15 152 D1
Cerne Cl, Hayes UB4 102 D7
Cerne Rd, Mord. SM4 185 F6
Cerney Ms, W2 14 E5
Cervantes Ct, W2 14 B4
Cester St, E2
off Whiston Rd 112 D1
Ceylon Rd, W14 128 A3
Chabot Dr, SE15 153 E3
Chadacre Av, Ilf. IG5 80 C3
Chadacre Rd, Epsom KT17 197 H6
Chadbourn St, E14 114 B5
Chad Cres, N9 61 F3
Chadd Dr, Brom. BR1 192 B3
Chadd Grn, E13 115 G1
Chadview Ct, Rom. (Chad.Hth) RM6 82 D7
Chadville Gdns, Rom. RM6 82 D5
Chadway, Dag. RM8 100 C1
Chadwell Av, Rom. RM6 82 B7
CHADWELL HEATH, Rom. RM6 82 D6
Chadwell Heath La, Rom. RM6 82 B5
Chadwell La, N8 75 F3
Chadwell St, EC1 11 F3
Chadwick Av, E4 62 D4
N21 43 F4
SW19 166 D6
Chadwick Cl, SW15 147 F7
W7 *off Westcott Cres* 104 C5
Teddington TW11 162 D6
Chadwick Ms, W4
off Thames Rd 126 B6
Chadwick Pl, Surb. (Long Dit.) KT6 181 F7
Chadwick Rd, E11 79 E7
NW10 107 F1
SE15 152 C2
Ilford IG1 99 E3
Chadwick St, SW1 25 J6
Chadwick Way, SE28 118 D7
Chadwin Rd, E13 115 H5
Chadworth Way, Esher (Clay.) KT10 194 A5
Chaffinch Av, Croy. CR0 189 G6
Chaffinch Business Pk, Beck. BR3 189 G4
Chaffinch Cl, N9 61 G1
Croydon CR0 189 G5
Chaffinch Cl, Surbiton KT6 196 A3
Chaffinch Rd, Beck. BR3 189 H1
Chafford Way, Rom. RM6 82 C4
Chagford St, NW1 7 J6
Chailey Av, Enf. EN1 44 C2
Chailey Cl, Houns. TW5 142 D1
Chailey St, E5 95 F3
Chalbury Wk, N1 10 D1
Chalcombe Rd, SE2 138 B3
Chalcot Cl, Sutt. SM2 198 D7
Chalcot Cres, NW1 109 J1
Chalcot Gdns, NW3 91 J6
Chalcot Ms, SW16 168 E3
Chalcot Rd, NW1 92 A7
Chalcot Sq, NW1 92 A7
Chalcott Gdns, Surb. (Long Dit.) KT6 195 F1
Chalcroft Rd, SE13 154 E5
Chaldon Path, Th.Hth. CR7 187 H4
Chaldon Rd, SW6 128 B7
Chale Rd, SW2 150 E6
Chalet Est, NW7 55 G4
Chalfont Av, Wem. HA9 88 B6
Chalfont Ct, NW9 71 F3
Chalfont Grn, N9 60 B3
Chalfont Ms, SW19
off Augustus Rd 166 C1
Chalfont Rd, N9 60 B3
SE25 188 C3
Hayes UB3 122 A2
Chalfont Wk, Pnr. HA5
off Willows Cl 66 C2
Chalfont Way, W13 124 E3
Chalford Cl, W.Mol. KT8 179 G4
Chalford Rd, SE21 170 A4
Chalford Wk, Wdf.Grn. IG8 80 A1
Chalgrove Av, Mord. SM4 184 D5
Chalgrove Cres, Ilf. IG5 80 B2
Chalgrove Gdns, N3 72 B3
Chalgrove Rd, N17 76 E1
Sutton SM2 199 G7
Chalice Cl, Wall. SM6
off Lavender Vale 200 D6
Chalkenden Cl, SE20 170 E7
Chalkers Cor, SW14 146 B3
Chalk Fm Rd, NW1 92 A7
Chalk Hill Rd, W6
off Shortlands 128 A4
Chalkhill Rd, Wem. HA9 88 B3
Chalklands, Wem. HA9 88 C3
Chalk La, Barn. EN4 41 J4
Chalkley Cl, Mitch. CR4 185 J2
Chalkmill Dr, Enf. EN1 44 E3
Chalk Pit Way, Sutt. SM1 199 F5
Chalk Rd, E13 115 H5
Chalkstone Cl, Well. DA16 158 A1
Chalkwell Pk Av, Enf. EN1 44 B4
Challenge Ct, Twick. TW2
off Langhorn Dr 144 B7
Challice Way, SW2 169 F1
Challin St, SE20 189 F1
Challis Rd, Brent. TW8 125 G5
Challoner Cl, N2 73 G2
Challoner Cres, W14
off Challoner St 128 C5
Challoners Cl, E.Mol. KT8 180 A4
Challoner St, W14 128 C5
Chalmers Ho, SW11
off York Rd 149 F3
Chalmers Wk, SE17 35 H6
Chalmers Way, Felt. TW14 142 A5
Chaloner Ct, SE1 28 B3
Chalsey Rd, SE4 153 J4
Chalton Dr, N2 73 F6
Chalton St, NW1 9 J3
Chamberlain Cl, SE28
off Broadwater Rd 137 G3
Ilford IG1
off Richmond Rd 99 F3
Chamberlain Cotts, SE5
off Camberwell Gro 152 A1
Chamberlain Cres, W.Wick. BR4 204 B1
Chamberlain Gdns, Houns. TW3 143 J1
Chamberlain La, Pnr. HA5 66 A4
Chamberlain Pl, E17 77 H3
Chamberlain Rd, N2 73 F2
W13 *off Midhurst Rd* 124 D2
Chamberlain St, NW1
off Regents Pk Rd 91 J7
Chamberlain Wk, Felt. TW13 *off Burgess Cl* 160 E4
Chamberlain Way, Pnr. HA5 66 B3
Surbiton KT6 181 H7
Chamberlayne Av, Wem. HA9 87 H2
Chamberlayne Rd, NW10 108 A3
Chambers Av, Sid. DA14
off Bedens Rd 176 E6
Chambers Business Pk, West Dr. UB7 120 D6
Chambers Gdns, N2 73 G1
Chambers Ho, SW16
off Pringle Gdns 168 C4
Chambers La, NW10 89 H7
Chambers Pl, S.Croy. CR2
off Rolleston Rd 202 A7
Chambers Rd, N7 92 E4
Chambers St, SE16 29 H3
Chamber St, E1 21 G5
Chambers Wk, Stan. HA7 52 E5
Chambon Pl, W6
off Beavor La 127 G4
Chambord St, E2 13 G4
Chamers Ct, W12
off Heathstan Rd 107 G6
Champa Cl, N17 76 C2
Champion Cres, SE26 171 H4
Champion Gro, SE5 152 A3
Champion Hill, SE5 152 A3
Champion Hill Est, SE5 152 B3
Champion Pk, SE5 152 A2
Champion Pk Est, SE5
off Denmark Hill 152 A3
Champion Rd, SE26 171 H4
Champions Way, NW4 71 H1
NW7 71 H1
Champness Cl, SE27 170 A4
Champness Rd, Bark. IG11 99 J6
Champneys Cl, Sutt. SM2 198 C7
Chancellor Gro, SE21 169 J2
Chancellor Pas, E14
off The South Colonnade 134 A1
Chancellor Pl, NW9 71 F2
Chancellors Ct, WC1
off Orde Hall St 18 C1
Chancellors Rd, W6 127 J5
Chancellors St, W6 127 J5
Chancellors Wf, W6
off Crisp Rd 127 J5
Chancelot Rd, SE2 138 B4
Chancel St, SE1 27 G1
Chancery Gate Bus Cen, Sthl. UB2 122 C3
Chancerygate Cl, Ruis. HA4 84 E5
Chancerygate Way, Ruis. HA4 84 E4
Chancery La, WC2 18 E3
Beckenham BR3 190 B2
Chancery Ms, SW17 167 H2
Chance St, E1 13 F5
E2 13 F5
Chanctonbury Cl, SE9 175 E3
Chanctonbury Gdns, Sutt. SM2 198 E7
Chanctonbury Way, N12 56 C4
Chandler Av, E16 115 G5
Chandler Cl, Hmptn. TW12 179 G1
Chandler Ct, Th.Hth. CR7
off Bensham La 187 H5
Chandler Ms, Twick. TW1 144 D7
Chandler Rd, Loug. IG10 49 E1
Chandlers Cl, Felt. TW14 141 J7
Chandlers Ms, E14 134 A2
Chandler St, E1
off Wapping La 133 E1
Chandlers Way, SW2 151 G7
Chandler Way, SE15 37 E6
Chandon Lo, Sutt. SM2
off Devonshire Rd 199 F7
Chandos Av, E17 78 A2
N14 58 C3
N20 57 F1
W5 125 F4
Chandos Cl, Buck.H. IG9 63 H2
Chandos Ct, Stan. HA7 52 E6
Chandos Cres, Edg. HA8 53 J7
Chandos Par, Edg. HA8
off Chandos Cres 53 J7
Chandos Pl, WC2 18 A6
Chandos Rd, E15 96 D5
N2 73 G2
N17 76 B2
NW2 89 J5
NW10 106 E4
Harrow HA1 67 J5
Pinner HA5 66 C7
Chandos St, W1 16 E2
Chandos Way, NW11 90 E1
Change All, EC3 20 C4
Channel Cl, Houns. TW5 143 G1
Channel Gate Rd, NW10
off Old Oak La 107 F3
Channel Ho, E14
off Aston St 113 H5
Channel Islands Est, N1
off Clifton Rd 93 J6

Channelsea Ho
Business Cen, E15
off Canning Rd 114 D2
Channelsea Rd, E15 114 D1
Chantress Cl, Dag.
RM10 119 J1
Chantrey Rd, SW9 151 F3
Chantry, The, E4
off The Ridgeway 62 C1
Chantry Cl, NW7 39 F7
SE2 *off Felixstowe Rd* 138 C3
W9 *off Elgin Av* 108 C4
Harrow HA3 69 J5
Sidcup DA14
off Ellenborough Rd 176 E5
Sunbury-on-Thames
TW16 160 A7
Chantry Ct, Cars. SM5 199 H3
Chantry Cres, NW10 89 F6
Chantry La, Brom. BR2
off Bromley
Common 192 A5
Chantry Pl, Har. HA3 67 H1
Chantry Rd, Chess. KT9 195 J5
Harrow HA3 67 H1
Chantry Sq, W8
off St. Mary's Pl 22 A6
Chantry St, N1 111 H1
Chantry Way, Mitch. CR4
off Church Rd 185 G3
Chant Sq, E15 96 D7
Chant St, E15 96 D7
Chapel Cl, NW10 89 F5
Chapel Ct, N2 73 H3
SE1 28 B3
SE18 137 J6
Chapel Fm Rd, SE9 174 C3
Chapel Gate Ms, SW4
off Bedford Rd 150 E3
Chapel Ho St, E14 134 B5
Chapelier Ho, SW18
off Eastfields Av 148 D4
Chapel La, Chig. IG7 65 J3
Pinner HA5 66 D3
Romford RM6 82 D7
Chapel Mkt, N1 10 E1
Chapel Ms, Wdf.Grn. IG8 64 D6
Chapel Mill Rd, Kings.T.
KT1 181 J3
Chapelmount Rd, Wdf.Grn.
IG8 64 C6
Chapel Path, E11 79 G6
Chapel Pl, EC2 12 D4
N1 11 F1
N17
off White Hart La 60 C7
W1 16 D4
Chapel Rd, SE27 169 H4
W13 125 E1
Bexleyheath DA7 159 G4
Hounslow TW3 143 H3
Ilford IG1 98 D3
Twickenham TW1 145 E7
Chapel Side, W2 14 A5
Chapel Stones, N17 76 C1
Chapel St, NW1 15 G2
SW1 24 C5
Enfield EN2 43 J3
Chapel Ter, Loug. IG10
off Forest Rd 48 B4
Chapel Vw, S.Croy. CR2 203 E6
Chapel Wk, NW4 71 H4
Croydon CR0
off Whitgift Cen 201 J2
Chapel Way, N7
off Sussex Way 93 F3
Chapel Yd, SW18
off Wandsworth
High St 148 D5
Chaplin Cl, SE1 27 F3
Chaplin Rd, E15 115 E2
N17 76 C3
NW2 89 G6
Dagenham RM9 101 E7
Wembley HA0 87 F6
Chaplin Sq, N12 57 G7
Chapman Cl, West Dr.
UB7 120 C3
Chapman Cres, Har. HA3 69 H5
Chapman Pk Ind Est,
NW10 89 F6
Chapman Pl, N4 93 H2
Chapman Rd, E9 95 J6
Belvedere DA17 139 G5
Croydon CR0 201 G1
Chapman's La, SE2 138 C4
Belvedere DA17 138 D4
Chapman Sq, SW19 166 A2
Chapman St, E1 112 E7
Chapone Pl, W1 17 H4
Chapter Chambers, SW1
off Chapter St 33 H2
Chapter Cl, W4
off Church Path 126 C3
Chapter Ho Ct, EC4 19 J4
Chapter Rd, NW2 89 G5
SE17 35 H4
Chapter St, SW1 33 H2
Chapter Way, SW19 185 F1
Hampton TW12 161 G4
Chara Pl, W4 126 D6
Charcot Ho, SW15
off Highcliffe Dr 147 F6
Charcroft Gdns, Enf.
EN3 45 G4
Chardin Rd, W4
off Elliott Rd 126 E4
Chardmore Rd, N16 94 D1
Chard Rd, Houns.
(Lon.Hthrw Air.) TW6
off Heathrow
Tunnel App 140 E2
Chardwell Cl, E6
off Northumberland
Rd 116 B6
Charecroft Way, W12 128 A2
W14 128 A2
Charfield Ct, W9 6 A6
Charford Rd, E16 115 G5
Chargeable La, E13 115 F4
Chargeable St, E16 115 F4
Chargrove Cl, SE16
off Marlow Way 133 G2
Charing Cl, Orp. BR6 207 J4
Charing Cross, SW1 25 J1
Charing Cross Rd, WC2 17 J3
Chariot Cl, E3
off Garrison Rd 114 A1
Charlbert St, NW8 7 G1
Charlbury Av, Stan. HA7 53 G5
Charlbury Gdns, Ilf. IG3 99 J2
Charlbury Gro, W5 105 F6
Charlbury Ho, E12
off Grantham Rd 98 D3
Charldane Rd, SE9 174 E3
Charlecote Gro, SE26 171 E3
Charlecote Rd, Dag. RM8 100 E3
Charlemont Rd, E6 116 C3
Charles Babbage Cl,
Chess. KT9 195 F7
Charles Barry Cl, SW4 150 C3
Charles Burton Ct, E5
off Ashenden Rd 95 H5
Charles Ch Wk, Ilf. IG1 80 C6
Charles Cl, Sid. DA14 176 B4
Charles Cobb Gdns, Croy.
CR0 201 G5
Charles Coveney Rd,
SE15 152 C1
Charles Cres, Har. HA1 68 A7
Charles Dickens Ho, E2 112 E3
★ **Charles Dickens Mus**,
WC1 10 D5
Charles Dickens Ter, SE20
off Maple Rd 171 F7
Charlesfield, SE9 173 J3
Charles Flemwell Ms, E16
off Hanameel St 135 G1
Charles Gardner Ct, N1 12 C3
Charles Grinling Wk,
SE18 136 D4
Charles Gro, N14 58 C1
Charles Haller St, SW2
off Tulse Hill 151 G7
Charles Hocking Ho, W3
off Bollo Br Rd 126 C2
Charles Ho, N17
off Love La 60 C7
Charles La, NW8 7 F2
Charles Mackenzie Ho, SE16
off Linsey St 37 H1
Charlesmere Gdns, SE28
off Battery Rd 137 H2
Charles Nex Ms, SE21 169 J2
Charles Pl, E4 46 D7
NW1 9 G4
Charles Rd, E7
off Lens Rd 97 J7
SW19 184 D1
W13 104 D6
Romford RM6 82 D7
Charles Rowan Ho, WC1 11 E4
Charles II Pl, SW3
off King's Rd 31 J4
Charles II St, SW1 25 H1
Charles Sevright Dr,
NW7 56 A5
Charles Sq, N1 12 C4
Charles Sq Est, N1 12 C4
Charles St, SW13 147 E2
W1 24 D1
Croydon CR0 201 J3
Enfield EN1 44 C5
Hounslow TW3 143 F2
Charleston Cl, Felt. TW13
off Poplar Way 160 A3
Charleston St, SE17 36 A2
Charles Townsend Ho,
EC1 11 F5
Charles Whincup Rd,
E16 135 H1
Charlesworth Pl, SW13
off Eleanor Gro 147 F3
Charleville Circ, SE26 170 D5
Charleville Ms, Islw. TW7
off Railshead Rd 144 E4
Charleville Rd, W14 128 B5
Charlie Brown's Rbt, E18 79 J2
Charlie Chaplin Wk, SE1
off Waterloo Br 26 D2
Charlieville Rd, Erith DA8
off Northumberland
Pk 139 J7
Charlmont Rd, SW17 167 J6
Charlotte Cl, Bexh. DA6 158 E5
Ilford IG6
off Connor Cl 81 F1
Charlotte Ct, N8 74 D6
W6 *off Invermead Cl* 127 G4
Charlotte Despard Av,
SW11 150 A1
Charlotte Ms, W1 17 G1
W10 108 A6
W14 *off Munden St* 128 B4
Charlotte Pk Av, Brom.
BR1 192 B3
Charlotte Pl, NW9
off Uphill Dr 70 C5
SW1 33 F2
W1 17 G2
Charlotte Rd, EC2 12 D5
SW13 147 F1
Dagenham RM10 101 H6
Wallington SM6 200 C6
Charlotte Row, SW4 150 C3
Charlotte Sq, Rich. TW10
off Greville Rd 145 J6
Charlotte St, W1 17 G1
Charlotte Ter, N1 111 F1
Charlow Cl, SW6
off Townmead Rd 149 F2
CHARLTON, SE7 135 J6
★ **Charlton Athletic FC**,
SE7 135 J5
Charlton Ch La, SE7 135 J5
Charlton Cres, Bark. IG11 117 J2
Charlton Dene, SE7 135 J7
Charlton Kings Rd, NW5 92 D5
Charlton La, SE7 136 A5
Charlton Pk La, SE7 136 A7
Charlton Pk Rd, SE7 136 A6
Charlton Pl, N1 11 G1
Charlton Rd, N9 61 G1
NW10 107 E1
SE3 135 G7
SE7 135 H7
Harrow HA3 69 G4
Wembley HA9 87 J1
Charlton Way, SE3 154 E1
Charlwood Cl, Har. HA3
off Kelvin Cres 52 B6
Charlwood Ho, SW1
off Vauxhall Br Rd 33 H2
Richmond TW9 126 B7
Charlwood Pl, SW1 33 G2
Charlwood Rd, SW15 148 A3
Charlwood St, SW1 33 G2
Charlwood Ter, SW15
off Cardinal Pl 148 A4
Charmian Av, Stan. HA7 69 G3
Charminster Av, SW19 184 D2
Charminster Ct, Surb. KT6
off Lovelace Gdns 181 G7
Charminster Rd, SE9 174 A4
Worcester Park KT4 198 A1
Charmouth Ho, SW8
off Dorset Rd 34 C7
Charmouth Rd, Well.
DA16 158 C1
Charnock Rd, E5 94 E3
Charnwood Av, SW19 184 D2
Charnwood Cl, N.Mal.
KT3 183 E4
Charnwood Dr, E18 79 H3
Charnwood Gdns, E14 134 A4
Charnwood Pl, N20 57 F3
Charnwood Rd, SE25 188 A5
Charnwood St, E5 94 D2
Charrington Rd, Croy. CR0
off Drayton Rd 201 H2
Charrington St, NW1 9 H1
Charsley Rd, SE6 172 B2
Chart Cl, Brom. BR2 191 E1
Croydon CR0 189 F6
Mitcham CR4 185 J4
Charter Av, Ilf. IG2 99 G1
Charter Ct, N.Mal. KT3 182 E3
Charter Cres, Houns.
TW4 142 E4
Charter Dr, Bex. DA5 158 E7
★ **Charterhouse**, EC1 19 H1
Charterhouse Av, Wem.
HA0 87 F4
Charterhouse Bldgs, EC1 11 H6
Charterhouse Ms, EC1 19 H1
Charterhouse Rd, E8 94 D4
Charterhouse Sq, EC1 19 H1
Charterhouse St, EC1 19 F2
Charteris Rd, N4 93 G1
NW6 108 C1
Woodford Green IG8 63 H7
Charter Rd, Kings.T. KT1 182 B3
Charter Rd, The, Wdf.Grn.
IG8 62 E6
Charters Cl, SE19 170 B5
Charter Sq, Kings.T.
KT1 182 B2
Charter Way, N3 72 C4
N14 42 C6
Chartfield Av, SW15 147 H5
Chartfield Sq, SW15 148 A5
Chartham Ct, SW9 151 G3
Chartham Gro, SE27
off Royal Circ 169 G3
Chartham Rd, SE25 188 E3
Chart Hills Cl, SE28
off Fairway Dr 118 E6
Chartley Av, NW2 88 E3
Stanmore HA7 52 C6
Charton Cl, Belv. DA17
off Nuxley Rd 139 F6
Chartridge Cl, Barn. EN5 39 G5
Chart St, N1 12 C3
Chartwell Cl, SE9 175 F2
Croydon CR0 202 A1
Greenford UB6 103 H1
Chartwell Ct, NW2 89 G3
Chartwell Dr, Orp. BR6 207 G5
Chartwell Gdns, Sutt.
SM3 198 B4
Chartwell Pl, Har. HA2 86 A2
Sutton SM3 198 C4
Chartwell Way, SE20 188 E1
Charwood, SW16 169 G4
Chase, The, E12 98 A4
SW4 150 B3
SW16 169 F7
SW20 184 B1
Bexleyheath DA7 159 H3
Bromley BR1 191 H3
Chigwell IG7 65 F4
Edgware HA8 70 B1
Loughton IG10 47 J7
Pinner HA5 67 F4
Pinner (Eastcote) HA5 66 C6
Romford (Chad.Hth)
RM6 82 E6
Stanmore HA7 52 D5
Sunbury-on-Thames
TW16 178 B1
Wallington SM6 200 E5
Chase Ct Gdns, Enf. EN2 43 J3
Chasefield Rd, SW17 167 J4
Chase Gdns, E4 62 A4
Twickenham TW2 144 A6
Chase Grn, Enf. EN2 43 J3
Chase Grn Av, Enf. EN2 43 H2
Chase Hill, Enf. EN2 43 J3
Chase La, Ilf. IG6 81 G5
Chaseley Dr, W4 126 B5
Chaseley St, E14 113 H6
Chasemore Cl, Mitch.
CR4 185 J7
Chasemore Gdns, Croy.
CR0 201 G5
Chase Ridings, Enf. EN2 43 G2
Chase Rd, N14 42 C6
NW10 106 D4
W3 106 D4
Chase Side, N14 42 A6
Enfield EN2 43 J3
Chase Side Av, SW20 184 B1
Enfield EN2 43 J2
Chase Side Cres, Enf.
EN2 43 J1
Chase Side Pl, Enf. EN2
off Chase Side 43 J2
Chaseville Par, N21 43 F5
Chaseville Pk Rd, N21 43 E5
Chase Way, N14 58 B2
Chasewood Av, Enf. EN2 43 H2
Chasewood Pk, Har. HA1 86 C3
Chaston Pl, NW5
off Grafton Ter 92 A5
Chater Ho, E2
off Roman Rd 113 G3
Chatfield Rd, SW11 149 F3
Croydon CR0 201 H1
Chatham Av, Brom. BR2 191 F7
Chatham Cl, NW11 72 D5
SE18 137 E3
Sutton SM3 184 C7
Chatham Pl, E9 95 F6
Chatham Rd, E17 77 H3
E18 *off Grove Hill* 79 F2
SW11 149 J6
Kingston upon Thames
KT1 182 A2
Orpington BR6
off Gladstone Rd 207 F5
Chatham St, SE17 36 B1
Chatsfield Pl, W5 105 H6
Chatsworth Av,
NW4 71 J2
SW20 184 B1
Bromley BR1 173 H4
Sidcup DA15 176 A1
Wembley HA9 87 J5

Chatsworth Cl, NW4 71 J2
Borehamwood WD6 38 A3
West Wickham BR4 205 F2
Chatsworth Ct, W8 128 D4
Stanmore HA7
off Marsh La 53 F5
Chatsworth Cres, Houns.
TW3 144 A4
Chatsworth Dr, Enf. EN1 44 D7
Chatsworth Est, E5
off Elderfield Rd 95 G4
Chatsworth Gdns, W3 106 B7
Harrow HA2 85 H1
New Malden KT3 183 F5
Chatsworth Par, Orp. BR5
off Queensway 193 F5
Chatsworth Pl, Mitch.
CR4 185 J3
Teddington TW11 162 D4
Chatsworth Ri, W5 105 J4
Chatsworth Rd, E5 95 F3
E15 97 F5
NW2 90 A6
W4 126 C6
W5 105 J4
Croydon CR0 202 A4
Hayes UB4 102 B4
Sutton SM3 198 A5
Chatsworth Way, SE27 169 H3
Chatterton Ms, N4
off Chatterton Rd 93 H3
Chatterton Rd, N4 93 H3
Bromley BR2 192 A4
Chatto Rd, SW11 149 J5
Chaucer Av, Hayes UB4 102 A5
Hounslow TW4 142 B2
Richmond TW9 146 A2
Chaucer Cl, N11 58 C5
Chaucer Ct, N16 94 B4
Chaucer Dr, SE1 37 G2
Chaucer Gdns, Sutt.
SM1 198 D3
Chaucer Grn, Croydon
CR0 189 E7
Chaucer Ho, SW1 33 F4
Sutton SM1 198 D3
Chaucer Rd, E7 97 G6
E11 79 G6
E17 78 C2
SE24 151 G5
W3 126 C1
Sidcup DA15 176 C1
Sutton SM1 198 D4
Welling DA16 157 H1
Chaucer Way, SW19 167 G6
Chauncey Cl, N9 60 D3
Chaundrye Cl, SE9 156 C6
Chauntler Cl, E16 115 H6
Chaville Way, N3 72 D1
CHEAM, Sutt. SM3 198 A6
Cheam Common Rd,
Wor.Pk. KT4 197 H2
Cheam Mans, Sutt. SM3 198 B7
Cheam Pk Way, Sutt.
SM3 198 B6
Cheam Rd, Sutt. SM1 198 C6
Cheam St, SE15
off Nunhead La 153 E3
Cheam Village, Sutt.
SM3 198 B6
Cheapside, EC2 20 A4
N13 *off Taplow Rd* 59 J4
Chearsley, SE17
off Deacon Way 36 A1
Cheddar Cl, N11 57 J6
Cheddar Rd, Houns.
(Lon.Hthrw Air.) TW6
off Cromer Rd 140 D2
Cheddar Waye, Hayes
UB4 102 B6
Cheddington Rd, N18 60 B3
Chedworth Cl, E16
off Hallsville Rd 115 F6
Cheeseman Cl, Hmptn.
TW12 161 E6
Cheesemans Ter, W14 128 C5
Cheldon Av, NW7 56 A7
Chelford Rd, Brom. BR1 172 D5
Chelmer Cres, Bark.
IG11 118 B2
Chelmer Rd, E9 95 G5
Chelmsford Cl, E6
off Guildford Rd 116 C6
W6 128 A6
Chelmsford Gdns, Ilf. IG1 80 B7
Chelmsford Rd, E11 96 D1
E17 78 A6
E18 79 F1
N14 42 C7
Chelmsford Sq, NW10 107 J1
CHELSEA, SW3 31 E5
★ **Chelsea Antique Mkt**,
SW3 31 F5
Chelsea Br, SW1 32 D5
SW8 32 D5
Chelsea Br Rd, SW1 32 B3
Chelsea Cloisters, SW3 31 H2
Chelsea Cl, NW10
off Winchelsea Rd 106 D1
Edgware HA8 70 A2
Hampton (Hmptn H.)
TW12 161 J6
Worcester Park KT4 183 G7
Chelsea Cres, SW10
off Harbour Av 149 F1
Chelsea Embk, SW3 31 H6
★ **Chelsea FC**, SW6 30 A7
Chelsea Gdns, SW1
off Chelsea Br Rd 32 C4
W13
off Hathaway Gdns 104 C5
Sutton SM3 198 B4
Chelsea Harbour,
SW10 149 F1
Chelsea Harbour Dr,
SW10 149 F1
Chelsea Manor Ct, SW3 31 H5
Chelsea Manor Gdns,
SW3 31 G5
Chelsea Manor St, SW3 31 G4
Chelsea Ms, E11 79 G6
Chelsea Pk Gdns, SW3 30 E5
★ **Chelsea Physic Gdn**,
SW3 31 J5
Chelsea Reach Twr,
SW10 30 E7
Chelsea Sq, SW3 31 F3
Chelsea Twrs, SW3
off Chelsea
Manor Gdns 31 H4
Chelsea Village, SW6
off Fulham Rd 129 E7
Chelsea Vista, SW6
off The Boulevard 149 F1
Chelsea Wf, SW10 129 G7
Chelsfield Av, N9 45 G7
Chelsfield Gdns, SE26 171 F3
Chelsfield Grn, N9
off Chelsfield Av 45 G7
Chelsham Rd, SW4 150 D3
South Croydon CR2 202 A6
Chelston App, Ruis. HA4 84 A2
Chelston Rd, Ruis. HA4 84 A1
Chelsworth Dr, SE18 137 G6
Cheltenham Av, Twick.
TW1 144 D7
Cheltenham Cl, N.Mal. KT3
off Northcote Rd 182 C3
Northolt UB5 85 H6
Cheltenham Gdns, E6 116 B2
Loughton IG10 48 B6
Cheltenham Pl, W3 126 B1
Harrow HA3 69 H4
Cheltenham Rd, E10 78 C6
SE15 153 F4
Cheltenham Ter, SW3 32 A3
Chelverton Rd, SW15 148 A4
Chelwood, N20
off Oakleigh Rd N 57 G2
Chelwood Cl, E4 46 B6
Chelwood Gdns, Rich.
TW9 146 A2
Chelwood Gdns Pas,
Rich. TW9
off Chelwood Gdns 146 A2
Chelwood Wk, SE4 153 H4
Chenappa Cl, E13 115 G3
Chenduit Way, Stan. HA7 52 C5
Cheney Row, E17 77 J1
Cheneys Rd, E11 97 E3
Cheney St, Pnr. HA5 66 C5
Chenies, The, Orp. BR6 193 H6
Chenies Ms, WC1 9 H6
Chenies Pl, NW1 9 H1
Barn. EN5 39 G5
Chenies St, WC1 17 H1
Cheniston Gdns, W8 22 A5
Chepstow Cl, SW15 148 B6
Chepstow Cres, W11 108 D7
Ilford IG3 81 H6
Chepstow Gdns, Sthl.
UB1 103 F6
Chepstow Pl, W2 108 D6
Chepstow Ri, Croy. CR0 202 B3
Chepstow Rd, W2 108 D6
W7 124 D3
Croydon CR0 202 B3
Chepstow Vil, W11 108 C7
Chequers, Buck.H. IG9 63 H1
Chequers Cl, NW9 70 E3
Orpington BR5 193 J4
Chequers Gdns, N13 59 H5
Chequers La, Dag. RM9 119 F4
Chequers Par, SE9
off Eltham High St 156 C6
Chequers Rd, Loughton
IG10 48 D5
Chequer St, EC1 12 A6
Chequers Way, N13 59 J5
Cherbury Cl, SE28 118 D6
Cherbury Ct, N1 12 C2
Cherbury St, N1 12 C2
Cherchefelle Ms, Stan.
HA7 52 E5
Cherimoya Gdns,
W.Mol. KT8
off Kelvinbrook 179 H3
Cherington Rd, W7 124 C1
Cheriton Av, Brom. BR2 191 F5
Ilford IG5 80 C2
Cheriton Cl, W5 105 F5
Barnet EN4 41 J3
Cheriton Dr, SE18 137 G7
Cheriton Ho, E5
off Pembury Rd 94 E5
Cheriton Sq, SW17 168 A2
Cherry Av, Sthl. UB1 122 D1
Cherry Blossom Cl, N13 59 H5
Cherry Cl, E17
off Eden Rd 78 B5
NW9 71 F2
SW2 *off Tulse Hill* 151 G7
W5 125 G3
Carshalton SM5 199 J2
Morden SM4 184 B4
Cherrycot Hill, Orp. BR6 207 G4
Cherrycot Ri, Orp. BR6 207 F4
Cherry Cres, Brent. TW8 124 E7
Cherrycroft Gdns, Pnr. HA5
off Westfield Pk 51 F7
Cherrydown Av, E4 61 J3
Cherrydown Cl, E4 61 J3
Cherrydown Rd, Sid.
DA14 176 D2
Cherrydown Wk, Rom.
RM7 83 H2
Cherry Gdns, Dag. RM9 101 F5
Northolt UB5 85 H7
Cherry Gdn St, SE16 132 E2
Cherry Garth, Brent. TW8 125 G4
Cherry Gro, Hayes UB3 122 B1
Cherry Hill, Barn.
(New Barn.) EN5 41 E6
Harrow HA3 52 B6
Cherry Hill Gdns, Croy.
CR0 201 F4
Cherry Hills, Wat. WD19 50 E5
Cherrylands Cl, NW9 88 C2
Cherry La, West Dr. UB7 120 C4
Cherry La Rbt, West Dr.
UB7 120 E4
Cherry Laurel Wk, SW2
off Beechdale Rd 151 F6
Cherry Orchard, West Dr.
UB7 120 B2
Cherry Orchard Est, SE7 135 J7
Cherry Orchard Gdns,
Croy. CR0
off Oval Rd 202 A2
West Molesey KT8 179 F3
Cherry Orchard Rd, Brom.
BR2 206 B2
Croydon CR0 202 A2
West Molesey KT8 179 G3
Cherry Tree Cl, E9
off Moulins Rd 113 F1
Wembley HA0 86 C4
Cherry Tree Ct, NW9
off Boakes Cl 70 C4
SE7 *off Fairlawn* 135 J6
Cherry Tree Dr, SW16 169 E3
Cherry Tree Ri, Buck.H.
IG9 63 J4
Cherry Tree Rd, E15
off Wingfield Rd 96 E5
N2 73 J4
Cherry Tree Wk, EC1 12 A6
Beckenham BR3 189 J4
West Wickham BR4 205 F4
Cherry Tree Way, E13 116 A4
Stanmore HA7 53 E6
Cherry Wk, Brom. BR2 205 G1
Richmond TW9 145 H2
Cherry Way, Epsom
KT19 196 D6
Cherrywood Cl, E3 113 H3
Kingston upon Thames KT2 164
A7
Cherrywood Dr, SW15 148 A5
Cherrywood La, Mord.
SM4 184 B4
Cherrywood Lo, SE13
off Oakwood Cl 154 D6
Cherry Wd Way, W5
off Hanger Vale La 106 A5
Cherston Gdns, Loug.
IG10 48 D4
Cherston Rd, Loug. IG10 48 D4
Chertsey Dr, Sutt. SM3 198 B2
Chertsey Rd, E11 96 D2
Ilford IG1 99 G4
Twickenham TW1, TW2 144 C6
Chertsey St, SW17 168 A5
Chervil Cl, Felt. TW13 160 A3
Chervil Ms, SE28 138 B1
Cherwell Ct, Epsom
KT19 196 C4
Cherwell Ho, NW8
off Church St Est 7 F6
Cheryls Cl, SW6 149 E1
Cheseman St, SE26 171 E3
Chesfield Rd, Kings.T.
KT2 163 H7
Chesham Av, Orp. BR5 192 E6
Chesham Cl, SW1 24 B6
Chesham Cres, SE20 189 F2
Chesham Ms, SW1 24 B5
Chesham Pl, SW1 24 B6
Chesham Rd, SE20 189 F2
SW19 167 G5
Kingston upon Thames
KT1 182 A1
Chesham St, NW10 88 D3
SW1 24 B6
Chesham Ter, W13 124 E2
Cheshire Cl, E17 78 B1
SE4 153 J2
Mitcham CR4 186 E3
Cheshire Ct, EC4 19 F4
Cheshire Gdns, Chess.
KT9 195 G6
Cheshire Ho, N18 61 E4
Cheshire Rd, N22 59 F7
Cheshire St, E2 13 G5
Chesholm Rd, N16 94 B3
Cheshunt Rd, E7 97 H6
Belvedere DA17 139 G5
Chesil Ct, E2 113 F2
Chesilton Rd, SW6 148 C1
Chesley Gdns, E6 116 A2
Chesney Cres, Croy.
(New Adgtn) CR0 204 C7
Chesney St, SW11 150 A1
Chesnut Est, N17 76 C3
Chesnut Gro, N17
off Chesnut Rd 76 D3
Chesnut Rd, N17 76 C3
Chessell Cl, Th.Hth. CR7 187 H4
CHESSINGTON, KT9 195 H6
Chessington Av, N3 72 B3
Bexleyheath DA7 139 E7
Chessington Cl, Epsom
KT19 196 C6
Chessington Ct, Pnr.
HA5 67 F4
Chessington Hall Gdns,
Chess. KT9 195 G7
Chessington Hill Pk,
Chess. KT9 196 A5
Chessington Lo, N3 72 C3
Chessington Mans, E10
off Albany Rd 78 A7
Chessington Trade Pk,
Chess. KT9 196 A4
Chessington Way, W.Wick.
BR4 204 B2
Chesson Rd, W14 128 C6
Chesswood Way, Pnr.
HA5 66 D2
Chester Av, Rich. TW10 145 J6
Twickenham TW2 161 F1
Chester Cl, SW1 24 C4
SW13 147 H3
Loughton IG10 49 F1
Richmond TW10 145 J6
Sutton SM1 198 D2
Chester Cl N, NW1 8 E3
Chester Cl S, NW1 8 E4
Chester Cotts, SW1 32 B2
Chester Ct, NW1
off Albany St 8 E4
SE5 *off Lomond Gro* 132 A7
Chester Cres, E8
off Ridley Rd 94 C5
Chester Dr, Har. HA2 67 F6
Chesterfield Dr, Esher
KT10 194 D2
Chesterfield Gdns, N4 75 H5
SE10 *off Crooms Hill* 134 D7
W1 24 D1
Chesterfield Gro, SE22 152 C5
Chesterfield Hill, W1 16 D6
Chesterfield Ms, N4
off Chesterfield Gdns 75 H5
Chesterfield Rd, E10 78 C6
N3 56 D6
W4 126 C6
Barnet EN5 40 A5
Epsom KT19 196 D7
Chesterfield St, W1 24 D1
Chesterfield Wk, SE10 154 D1
Chesterfield Way, SE15 133 F7
Hayes UB3 122 A2
Chesterford Gdns, NW3 91 E4
Chesterford Ho, SE18
off Shooters Hill Rd 156 A1
Chesterford Rd, E12 98 C5
Chester Gdns, W13 104 D6
Enfield EN3 45 E6
Morden SM4 185 F6
Chester Gate, NW1 8 D4
Chester Grn, Loug.
IG10 49 F1
Chester Ms, E17
off Chingford Rd 78 A2
SW1 24 D5
Chester Path, Loug.
IG10 49 F1

Chester Pl, NW1 ....**8** D3
Chester Rd, E7 ....**98** A7
E11 ....**79** H6
E16 ....**115** E4
E17 ....**77** G5
N9 ....**61** E1
N17 ....**76** A3
N19 ....**92** B2
NW1 ....**8** C4
SW19 ....**165** J6
Borehamwood WD6 ....**38** C3
Chigwell IG7 ....**64** D3
Hounslow TW4 ....**142** B3
Hounslow (Lon.Hthrw Air.) TW6 ..**140** D3
Ilford IG3 ....**99** J1
Loughton IG10 ....**48** E2
Sidcup DA15 ....**157** H5
Chester Row, SW1 ....**32** B2
Chesters, The, N.Mal. KT3 ....**182** E1
Chester Sq, SW1 ....**32** D1
Chester Sq Ms, SW1 ......**24** D6
Chester St, E2 ....**13** J5
SW1 ....**24** C5
Chester Ter, NW1 ....**8** D3
Chesterton Cl, SW18 .....**148** D5
Greenford UB6 ....**103** H2
Chesterton Ho, SW11
off Ingrave St **149** G3
Chesterton Rd, E13 ......**115** G3
W10 ....**108** A5
Chesterton Sq, W8
off Pembroke Rd **128** C4
Chesterton Ter, E13 ......**115** G3
Kingston upon Thames KT1 ....**182** A2
Chester Way, SE11 ....**35** F2
Chesthunte Rd, N17 ......**75** J1
Chestnut All, SW6
off Lillie Rd **128** C6
Chestnut Av, E7 ....**97** H4
N8 ....**74** E5
SW14
off Thornton Rd **146** D3
SW17 ....**168** C3
Brentford TW8 ....**125** G4
Buckhurst Hill IG9 ......**64** A3
East Molesey KT8 .....**180** C3
Edgware HA8 ....**53** H6
Epsom KT19 ....**196** E4
Esher KT10 ....**180** A7
Hampton TW12 ....**161** G7
Teddington TW11 ......**180** C2
Wembley HA0 ....**86** E5
West Wickham BR4 ....**205** E5
Chestnut Av N, E17 ....**78** C4
Chestnut Av S, E17 ....**78** C4
Chestnut Cl, N14 ....**42** C5
N16
off Grazebrook Rd **94** A2
SE6 ....**172** C5
SE14 ....**153** J1
SW16 ....**169** G4
Buckhurst Hill IG9 ......**64** A3
Carshalton SM5 ....**199** J1
Sidcup DA15 ....**176** A1
West Drayton UB7 .....**121** E7
Chestnut Ct, SW6
off North End Rd **128** C6
Surbiton KT6
off Penners Gdns **181** H7
Chestnut Dr, E11 ....**79** G6
Bexleyheath DA7 ......**158** D3
Harrow HA3 ....**52** C7
Pinner HA5 ....**66** D6
Chestnut Gro, SE20 ......**171** E7
SW12 ....**150** A7
W5 ....**125** G3
Barnet EN4 ....**41** J5
Ilford IG6 ....**65** H6
Isleworth TW7 ....**144** D4
Mitcham CR4 ....**186** D4
New Malden KT3 ......**182** D3
South Croydon CR2 ....**203** E7
Wembley HA0 ....**86** E5
Chestnut Ho, NW3
off Maitland Pk Vil **91** J6
Chestnut La, N20 ....**56** B1
Chestnut Pl, SE26 ....**170** C4
Chestnut Ri, SE18 ....**137** G6
Chestnut Rd, SE27 ....**169** H3
SW20 ....**184** A2
Kingston upon Thames KT2 ....**163** H7
Twickenham TW2 ......**162** B2
Chestnut Row, N3
off Nether St **56** D7
Chestnut Wk, Wdf.Grn. IG8 ....**63** G5
Chestnut Way, Felt. TW13 ....**160** B3
Cheston Av, Croy. CR0 ...**203** H2
Chettle Cl, SE1 ....**28** B5
Chettle Ct, N8 ....**75** G6
Chetwode Rd, SW17 .....**167** J3
Chetwood Wk, E6 ....**116** B6
Chetwynd Av, Barn. (E.Barn.) EN4 ....**57** J1
Chetwynd Rd, NW5 ....**92** B4
Chevalier Cl, Stan. HA7 ....**53** H4
Cheval Pl, SW7 ....**23** H5
Cheval St, E14 ....**134** A3
Cheveney Wk, Brom. BR2
off Marina Cl **191** G3
Chevening Rd, NW6 ......**108** A2
SE10 ....**135** F5
SE19 ....**170** A6
Chevenings, The, Sid. DA14 ....**176** C3
Cheverton Rd, N19 ....**92** D1
Chevet St, E9
off Kenworthy Rd **95** H5
Cheviot Cl, Enf. EN1 ......**44** A2
Hayes (Harling.) UB3 ...**121** G7
Cheviot Gdns, NW2 ....**90** A2
SE27 ....**169** H4
Cheviot Gate, NW2 ....**90** B2
Cheviot Rd, SE27 ....**169** G5
Cheviot Way, Ilf. IG2 ......**81** H4
Chevron Cl, E16 ....**115** G6
Chevy Rd, Sthl. UB2 ......**123** J2
Chewton Rd, E17 ....**77** H4
Cheyne Av, E18 ....**79** F3
Twickenham TW2 ......**161** F1
Cheyne Cl, NW4 ....**71** J5
Bromley BR2 ....**206** B3
Cheyne Ct, SW3 ....**31** J5
Cheyne Gdns, SW3 ....**31** H5
Cheyne Hill, Surb. KT5 ...**181** J4
Cheyne Ms, SW3 ....**31** H5
Cheyne Pk Dr, W.Wick. BR4 ....**204** C3
Cheyne Path, W7 ....**104** C5
W13 ....**104** C6
Cheyne Pl, SW3 ....**31** J5
Cheyne Row, SW3 ....**31** G6
Cheyne Wk, N21 ....**43** H5
NW4 ....**71** J6
SW3 ....**31** H6
SW10 ....**30** E7
Croydon CR0 ....**202** D2
Cheyneys Av, Edg. HA8 ....**53** G6
Chichele Gdns, Croy. CR0 ....**202** B4
Chichele Rd, NW2 ....**90** A5
Chicheley Gdns, Har. HA3 ....**51** J7
Chicheley Rd, Har. HA3 ....**51** J7
Chicheley St, SE1 ....**26** D3
Chichester Cl, E6 ....**116** B6
SE3 ....**135** J7
Hampton TW12
off Maple Cl **161** F6
Chichester Ct, NW1
off Royal Coll St **92** C7
Stanmore HA7 ....**69** H3
Chichester Gdns, Ilf. IG1 ...**80** B7
Chichester Ms, SE27 .....**169** G4
Chichester Rents, WC2 ....**18** E3
Chichester Rd, E11 ....**97** E3
N9 ....**60** D1
NW6 ....**108** D2
W2 ....**14** B1
Croydon CR0 ....**202** B3
Chichester St, SW1 ....**33** G4
Chichester Way, E14 .....**134** D4
Feltham TW14 ....**142** B7
Chicksand St, E1 ....**21** G2
Chiddingfold, N12 ....**56** D3
Chiddingstone Av, Bexh. DA7 ....**139** F7
Chiddingstone St, SW6 ....**148** D2
Chieveley Rd, Bexh. DA7 ....**159** H4
Chignell Pl, W13
off The Broadway **124** D1
CHIGWELL, IG7 ....**65** E3
Chigwell Hill, E1
off Pennington St **112** E7
Chigwell Hurst Ct, Pnr. HA5 ....**66** D3
Chigwell La, Loug. IG10 ...**49** F5
Chigwell Pk, Chig. IG7 .....**64** E4
Chigwell Pk Dr, Chig. IG7 ..**64** D3
Chigwell Ri, Chig. IG7 .....**64** D2
Chigwell Rd, E18 ....**79** H3
Woodford Green IG8 ....**79** J2
Chilcombe Ho, SW15
off Fontley Way **147** G7
Chilcot Cl, E14
off Grundy St **114** B6
Chilcott Cl, Wem. HA0 .....**87** F4
Childebert Rd, SW17 ......**168** B2
Childeric Rd, SE14 ....**133** H7
Childerley, Kings.T. KT1
off Burritt Rd **182** A3
Childerley St, SW6
off Fulham Palace Rd **148** B1
Childers, The, Wdf.Grn. IG8 ....**64** C5
Childers St, SE8 ....**133** H6
Child La, SE10 ....**135** F3
CHILDS HILL, NW2 ....**90** D2
Childs Hill Wk, NW2 ....**90** C3
Childs La, SE19
off Westow St **170** B6
Child's Ms, SW5
off Child's Pl **30** A2
Child's Pl, SW5 ....**128** D4
Child's St, SW5 ....**128** D4
Child's Wk, SW5
off Child's St **128** D4
Childs Way, NW11 ....**72** C5
Chilham Cl, Bex. DA5 ....**159** F7
Greenford (Perivale) UB6 ....**104** D2
Chilham Rd, SE9 ....**174** B4
Chilham Way, Brom. BR2 .**191** G7
Chillerton Rd, SW17 .....**168** A5
Chillingford Ho, SW17
off Blackshaw Rd **167** F4
Chillington Dr, SW11 .....**149** F4
Chillingworth Gdns, Twick. TW1
off Tower Rd **162** C3
Chillingworth Rd, N7 ......**93** F5
Chilmark Gdns, N.Mal. KT3 ....**183** F7
Chilmark Rd, SW16 ......**186** D2
Chiltern Av, Twick. TW2 ...**161** G1
Chiltern Cl, Croy. CR0 ....**202** B3
Worcester Park KT4
off Cotswold Way **197** J2
Chiltern Ct, N10 ....**74** A2
Chiltern Dene, Enf. EN2 ....**43** F4
Chiltern Dr, Surb. KT5 ....**182** B5
Chiltern Gdns, NW2 ....**90** A3
Bromley BR2 ....**191** F4
Chiltern Rd, E3 ....**114** A4
Ilford IG2 ....**81** H4
Pinner HA5 ....**66** C5
Chiltern St, W1 ....**16** B1
Chiltern Way, Wdf.Grn. IG8 ....**63** G3
Chilthorne Cl, SE6
off Ravensbourne Pk Cres **153** J7
Chilton Av, W5 ....**125** G4
Chilton Gro, SE8 ....**133** G4
Chiltonian Ind Est, SE12 ....**155** F6
Chilton Rd, Edg. HA8 ......**54** A6
Richmond TW9 ....**146** A3
Chiltons, The, E18
off Grove Hill **79** G2
Chilton St, E2 ....**13** G5
Chilvers Cl, Twick. TW2
off Chestnut Rd **162** B2
Chilver St, SE10 ....**135** F5
Chilwell Gdns, Wat. WD19 ....**50** C4
Chilworth Ct, SW19 ......**166** A1
Chilworth Gdns, Sutt. SM1 ....**199** F3
Chilworth Ms, W2 ....**14** D4
Chilworth St, W2 ....**14** D4
Chimes Av, N13 ....**59** G5
China Hall Ms, SE16
off Lower Rd **133** F3
China Ms, SW2 ....**151** F7
★ **Chinatown**, W1
off Gerrard St **17** H5
Chinbrook Cres, SE12 .....**173** H3
Chinbrook Est, SE9 ......**174** A3
Chinbrook Rd, SE12 ......**173** H3
Chinchilla Dr, Houns. TW4 ....**142** C2
Chine, The, N10 ....**74** C4
N21 ....**43** H6
Wembley HA0 ....**87** E5
Ching Ct, WC2 ....**18** A4
Chingdale Rd, E4 ....**62** E3
CHINGFORD, E4 ....**62** B1
Chingford Av, E4 ....**62** B3
CHINGFORD GREEN, E4 ...**63** F1
CHINGFORD HATCH, E4 ...**62** C4
Chingford Ind Cen, E4 .....**61** H5
Chingford La, Wdf.Grn. IG8 ....**62** E4
Chingford Mt Rd, E4 ......**62** A4
Chingford Rd, E4 ....**62** A6
E17 ....**78** B1
Chingley Cl, Brom. BR1 ...**173** E6
Ching Way, E4 ....**61** J6
Chinnery Cl, Enf. EN1 .....**44** C1
Chinnor Cres, Grnf. UB6 ..**103** H2
Chipka St, E14 ....**134** C2
Chipley St, SE14 ....**133** H6
Chipmunk Gro, Nthlt. UB5
off Argus Way **102** E3
Chippendale Ho, SW1 .....**33** E4
Chippendale St, E5 ....**95** G3
Chippenham Av, Wem. HA9 ....**88** B5
Chippenham Gdns, NW6 ....**108** D3
Chippenham Ms, W9 .....**108** D4
Chippenham Rd, W9 .....**108** D4
CHIPPING BARNET, Barn. EN5 ....**40** B4
Chipping Cl, Barn. EN5
off St. Albans Rd **40** B3
Chipstead Av, Th.Hth. CR7 ....**187** H4
Chipstead Cl, SE19 ....**170** C7
Chipstead Gdns, NW2 .....**89** H2
Chipstead Rd, Houns. TW6 **140** D3
Chipstead St, SW6 ....**148** D1
Chip St, SW4 ....**150** D3
Chirk Cl, Hayes UB4
off Braunston Dr **103** E4
Chisenhale Rd, E3 ....**113** H2
Chisholm Rd, Croy. CR0 ..**202** B2
Richmond TW10 ....**145** J6
Chisledon Wk, E9
off Southmoor Way **95** J6
CHISLEHURST, BR7 ......**174** D7
Chislehurst Av, N12 ....**57** F7
★ **Chislehurst Caves**, Chis. BR7
off Caveside Cl **192** D1
Chislehurst Rd, Brom. BR1 ....**192** A2
Chislehurst BR7 ....**192** A2
Orpington BR5, BR6 ...**193** H4
Richmond TW10 ....**145** H6
Sidcup DA14 ....**176** A5
CHISLEHURST WEST, Chis. BR7 ....**174** C5
Chislet Cl, Beck. BR3 .....**172** A7
Chisley Rd, N15 ....**76** B6
Chiswell Sq, SE3
off Brook La **155** H2
Chiswell St, EC1 ....**20** A1
SE5 ....**36** C7
CHISWICK, W4 ....**126** D6
Chiswick Br, SW14 ......**146** C2
W4 ....**146** C2
Chiswick Cl, Croy. CR0 ...**201** F3
Chiswick Common Rd, W4 ....**126** D4
Chiswick Ct, Pnr. HA5 .....**67** F3
Chiswick Grn Studios, W4
off Evershed Wk **126** C4
Chiswick High Rd, W4 ....**126** D4
Brentford TW8 ....**125** J5
★ **Chiswick Ho**, W4 .....**126** E6
Chiswick Ho Grds, W4 ....**126** D6
Chiswick La, W4 ....**127** E5
Chiswick La S, W4 ....**127** F5
Chiswick Mall, W4 ....**127** F6
W6 ....**127** F6
Chiswick Pk, W4 ....**126** B4
Chiswick Pier, W4 ....**127** F7
Chiswick Quay, W4 ......**146** C1
Chiswick Rd, N9 ....**60** D2
W4 ....**126** C4
Chiswick Rbt, W4 ....**126** A5
Chiswick Sq, W4
off Hogarth Rbt **127** E6
Chiswick Staithe, W4 ....**146** C1
Chiswick Ter, W4
off Acton La **126** C4
Chiswick Village, W4 .....**126** B5
Chiswick Wf, W4 ....**127** F6
Chitterfield Gate, West Dr. (Sipson) UB7 ....**120** D7
Chitty's La, Dag. RM8 ....**100** D2
Chitty St, W1 ....**17** G1
Chivalry Rd, SW11 ....**149** H5
Chivenor Gro, Kings.T. KT2 ....**163** G5
Chivers Rd, E4 ....**62** B3
Choats Manor Way, Dag. RM9 ....**119** F3
Choats Rd, Bark. IG11 ....**118** C2
Dagenham RM9 ....**118** C2
Chobham Gdns, SW19 ....**166** A2
Chobham Rd, E15 ....**96** D5
Choice Vw, Ilf. IG1
off Axon Pl **99** F2
Cholmeley Cres, N6 ....**74** B7
Cholmeley Pk, N6 ....**92** B1
Cholmley Gdns, NW6
off Fortune Grn Rd **90** D5
Cholmley Rd, T.Ditt. KT7 ..**180** E6
Cholmondeley Av, NW10 ....**107** G2
Cholmondeley Wk, Rich. TW9 ....**145** F5
Choppins Ct, E1
off Wapping La **133** E1
Chopwell Cl, E15
off Bryant St **96** E7
Chorleywood Cres, Orp. BR5 ....**193** J2
Choumert Gro, SE15 ......**152** D2
Choumert Ms, SE15 ......**152** D2
Choumert Rd, SE15 ......**152** C3
Choumert Sq, SE15 ......**152** D2
Chow Sq, E8
off Arcola St **94** C5
Chrislaine Cl, Stai. (Stanw.) TW19 ....**140** A6
Chrisp St, E14 ....**114** B5

Christabel Cl, Islw. TW7 . . . **144** B3
Christchurch Av, N12 . . . . . . **57** F6
NW6 . . . . **90** B7
Harrow HA3 . . . . **69** E4
Teddington TW11 . . . . . . **162** D5
Wembley HA0 . . . . **87** H6
Christchurch Cl, N12
off Summers La **57** G7
SW19 . . . . **167** G7
Enfield EN2 . . . . **43** J2
Christchurch Ct, NW6 . . . . . **90** B7
Christchurch Gdns, Har.
HA3 . . . . **68** D4
Christchurch Grn, Wem.
HA0 . . . . **87** H6
Christchurch Hill, NW3 . . . . **91** G3
Christchurch La, Barn.
EN5 . . . . **40** B2
Christchurch Pk, Sutt.
SM2 . . . . **199** F7
Christ Ch Pas, EC1 . . . . **19** H3
Christchurch Pas, NW3 . . . . **91** F3
Barnet EN5 . . . . **40** B3
Christ Ch Path, Hayes
UB3 . . . . **121** F3
Christchurch Rd, N8 . . . . **74** E6
SW2 . . . . **169** F1
SW14 . . . . **146** B5
SW19 . . . . **185** G1
Christ Ch Rd, Beck. BR3
off Fairfield Rd **190** A2
Christchurch Rd, Ilf. IG1 . . . **99** E1
Sidcup DA15 . . . . **175** J4
Christ Ch Rd, Surb. KT5 . . **181** J6
Christchurch Sq, E9
off Victoria Pk Rd **113** F1
Christchurch St, SW3 . . . . . **31** J5
Christchurch Ter, SW3 . . . . . **31** J5
Christchurch Way, SE10 . . **135** E4
Christian Ct, SE16 . . . . **133** J1
Christian Flds, SW16 . . . . . **169** G7
Christian St, E1 . . . . **21** J3
Christie Ct, N19
off Hornsey Rd **93** E2
Christie Dr, Croy. CR0 . . . . **188** D5
Christie Gdns, Rom.
RM6 . . . . **82** B6
Christie Rd, E9 . . . . **95** H6
Christina Sq, N4 . . . . **93** H1
Christina St, EC2 . . . . **12** D5
Christine Worsley Cl, N21
off Highfield Rd **59** H2
Christopher Av, W7 . . . . . . **124** D3
Christopher Cl, SE16 . . . . . **133** G2
Sidcup DA15 . . . . **157** J5
Christopher Gdns, Dag.
RM9 *off Wren Rd* **100** D5
Christopher Pl, NW1 . . . . **9** J4
Christopher Rd, Sthl.
UB2 . . . . **122** B4
Christopher's Ms, W11
off Penzance St **128** B1
Christopher St, EC2 . . . . **12** C6
Chryssell Rd, SW9 . . . . **131** G7
Chubworthy St, SE14 . . . . **133** H6
Chudleigh Cres, Ilf. IG3 . . . . **99** H4
Chudleigh Gdns, Sutt.
SM1 . . . . **199** F3
Chudleigh Rd, NW6 . . . . **90** A7
SE4 . . . . **153** J5
Twickenham TW2 . . . . . . **144** C7
Chudleigh St, E1 . . . . **113** G6
Chudleigh Way, Ruis.
HA4 . . . . **84** A1
Chulsa Rd, SE26 . . . . **170** E5
Chumleigh St, SE5 . . . . **36** D5
Chumleigh Wk, Surb.
KT5 . . . . **181** J4
Church All, Croy. CR0 . . . . . **201** G1
Church App, SE21 . . . . **170** A3
Staines (Stanw.) TW19 . **140** A6
Church Av, E4 . . . . **62** D6
NW1
off Kentish Town Rd . . . **92** B6
SW14 . . . . **146** D3
Beckenham BR3 . . . . **190** A1
Northolt UB5 . . . . **85** F7
Pinner HA5 . . . . **67** E6
Sidcup DA14 . . . . **176** A5
Southall UB2 . . . . **123** E3
Churchbury Cl, Enf. EN1 . . . **44** B2
Churchbury La, Enf. EN1 . . . **44** A3
Churchbury Rd, SE9 . . . . . **156** A7
Enfield EN1 . . . . **44** A2
Church Cl, N20 . . . . **57** H3
W8 . . . . **22** A3
Edgware HA8 . . . . **54** C5
Hounslow TW3
off Bath Rd **143** F3
Loughton IG10 . . . . **48** C2
West Drayton UB7 . . . . . **120** B3
Church Cor, SW17
off Mitcham Rd **167** J5
Church Ct, Rich. TW9
off George St **145** G5
Church Cres, E9 . . . . **95** G7
N3 . . . . **72** C1
Church Cres, N10 . . . . **74** B4
N20 . . . . **57** H3
Churchcroft Cl, SW12 . . . . **150** A7
Churchdown, Brom. BR1 . . **173** E4
Church Dr, NW9 . . . . **88** D1
Harrow HA2 . . . . **67** F6
West Wickham BR4 . . . . **205** E3
Church Elm La, Dag. RM10 . **101** G6
CHURCH END, N3 . . . . **72** C1
CHURCH END, NW10 . . . . . **88** E6
Church End, E17 . . . . **78** B4
NW4 . . . . **71** H3
Church Entry, EC4 . . . . **19** H4
Church Est Almshouses,
Rich. TW9
off St. Mary's Gro **145** J4
★ **Church Farm Ho Mus**,
NW4 . . . . **71** H3
Church Fm La, Sutt. SM3 . **198** B6
Churchfield Av, N12 . . . . **57** F6
Churchfield Cl, Har. HA2 . . **67** J4
Churchfield Rd, W3 . . . . . . **126** C1
W7 . . . . **124** B2
W13 . . . . **125** E1
Welling DA16 . . . . **158** A3
Churchfields, E18 . . . . **79** G1
SE10 *off Roan St* **134** C6
Loughton IG10 . . . . **48** B4
West Molesey KT8 . . . . . **179** G3
Churchfields Av, Felt.
TW13 . . . . **161** F3
Churchfields Rd, Beck.
BR3 . . . . **189** G2
Church Gdns, W5 . . . . **125** G2
Wembley HA0 . . . . **86** D4
Church Garth, N19
off Pemberton Gdns . . . **92** D2
Church Gate, SW6 . . . . **148** B3
Church Gro, SE13 . . . . **154** B4
Kingston upon Thames
KT1 . . . . **181** F1
Church Hill, E17 . . . . **78** A4
N21 . . . . **43** F7
SE18 . . . . **136** C3
SW19 . . . . **166** C5
Carshalton SM5 . . . . **199** J5
Harrow HA1 . . . . **86** B1
Loughton IG10 . . . . **48** B3
Church Hill Rd, E17 . . . . **78** B4
Barnet EN4 . . . . **41** J7
Surbiton KT6 . . . . **181** H5
Sutton SM3 . . . . **198** A4
Church Hill Wd, Orp.
BR5 . . . . **193** J5
Church Hyde, SE18
off Old Mill Rd **137** H6
Churchill Av, Har. HA3 . . . . . **68** E6
Churchill Ct, SE18
off Rushgrove St **136** C4
W5 . . . . **105** J4
Northolt UB5 . . . . **85** G5
Churchill Gdns, SW1 . . . . . . **33** F4
W3 . . . . **106** A6
Churchill Gdns Rd, SW1 . . . **33** E4
Churchill Ms, Wdf.Grn. IG8
off High Rd
Woodford Grn **63** F6
★ **Churchill Mus & Cabinet**
War Rooms, SW1 . . . . . **25** J3
Churchill Pl, E14 . . . . **134** B1
Harrow HA1
off Sandridge Cl **68** B4
Churchill Rd, E16 . . . . **115** J6
NW2 . . . . **89** H6
NW5 . . . . **92** B4
Edgware HA8 . . . . **53** J6
Churchill Ter, E4 . . . . **62** A4
Churchill Wk, E9 . . . . **95** F5
Churchill Way, Brom. BR1
off Ethelbert Rd **191** G3
Sunbury-on-Thames
TW16 . . . . **160** A5
Churchlands Way, Sutton
SM3 . . . . **198** A2
Church La, E11 . . . . **97** E1
E17 . . . . **78** B4
N2 . . . . **73** G3
N8 . . . . **75** F4
N9 . . . . **60** D2
N17 . . . . **76** B1
NW9 . . . . **88** C2
SW17 . . . . **168** B4
SW19 . . . . **184** C1
W5 . . . . **125** F2
Bromley BR2 . . . . **206** B1
Chessington KT9 . . . . . . **195** J6
Chislehurst BR7 . . . . **193** F1
Dagenham RM10 . . . . . . **101** H6
Enfield EN1 . . . . **44** A3
Harrow HA3 . . . . **68** C1
Loughton IG10 . . . . **48** C3
Pinner HA5 . . . . **67** E3
Richmond TW10 . . . . **163** H1
Teddington TW11 . . . . . . **162** C5
Thames Ditton KT7 . . . . **180** C6
Twickenham TW1 . . . . . . **162** D1
Wallington SM6 . . . . **200** D3
Churchley Rd, SE26 . . . . . . **171** E4
Church Manor Est, SW9
off Vassall Rd **131** G7
Church Manorway,
SE2 . . . . **137** J4
Church Manorway Ind Est,
Erith DA8 . . . . **139** J3
Churchmead, SE5
off Camberwell Rd . . . **131** J7
Churchmead Cl, Barn.
(E.Barn.) EN4 . . . . **41** H6
Church Meadow, Surb.
(Long Dit.) KT6 . . . . **195** F2
Churchmead Rd,
NW10 . . . . **89** G6
Churchmore Rd, SW16 . . . **186** C1
Church Mt, N2 . . . . **73** G5
Church Paddock Ct, Wall.
SM6 . . . . **200** D3
Church Pas, EC2
off Gresham St **20** A3
Barnet EN5
off Wood St **40** C4
Surbiton KT6 . . . . **181** H5
Church Path, E11 . . . . **79** G5
E17
off St. Mary Rd **78** B4
N5 . . . . **93** H5
N12 . . . . **57** F5
N17
off White Hart La **60** B7
N20 . . . . **57** F4
NW10 . . . . **89** E7
SW14 . . . . **146** D3
SW19 . . . . **184** D2
W4 . . . . **126** C3
W7 . . . . **124** B1
Mitcham CR4 . . . . **185** H3
Southall UB1 . . . . **123** G1
Southall (Sthl Grn)
UB2 . . . . **123** F3
Church Pl, SW1 . . . . **17** G6
W5
off Church Gdns **125** G2
Mitcham CR4 . . . . **185** H3
Twickenham TW1
off Church St **162** D1
Church Ri, SE23 . . . . **171** G1
Chessington KT9 . . . . . . **195** J6
Church Rd, E10 . . . . **96** B2
E12 . . . . **98** B5
E17 . . . . **77** H2
N1 . . . . **93** J6
N6 . . . . **74** A6
N17 . . . . **76** B1
NW4 . . . . **71** H4
NW10 . . . . **89** E6
SE19 . . . . **188** B1
SW13 . . . . **147** F2
SW19 (Wimbledon) **166** B3
W3 . . . . **126** C2
W7 . . . . **124** C1
Barking IG11 . . . . **99** F6
Bexleyheath DA7 . . . . . . **159** F2
Bromley BR2 . . . . **191** G2
Bromley (Short.)
BR2 . . . . **190** E3
Buckhurst Hill IG9 . . . . . . **63** H1
Croydon CR0 . . . . **201** H3
East Molesey KT8 . . . . . **180** A4
Enfield EN3 . . . . **45** F6
Epsom (W.Ewell)
KT19 . . . . **196** D7
Esher (Clay.) KT10 . . . . . **194** C6
Feltham TW13 . . . . **160** D5
Hayes UB3 . . . . **121** J1
Hounslow (Cran.)
TW5 . . . . **122** B5
Hounslow (Heston)
TW5 . . . . **123** G7
Ilford IG2 . . . . **81** G6
Isleworth TW7 . . . . **144** A1
Keston BR2 . . . . **206** A7
Kingston upon Thames
KT1 . . . . **181** J2
Loughton (High Beach)
IG10 . . . . **47** H2
Mitcham CR4 . . . . **185** G2
Northolt UB5 . . . . **85** F7
Orpington (Farnboro.)
BR6 . . . . **207** F5
Richmond TW9, TW10 . . **145** H5
Richmond (Ham)
TW10 . . . . **163** J5
Sidcup DA14 . . . . **176** A4
Southall UB2 . . . . **123** F3
Stanmore HA7 . . . . **53** E5
Surbiton (Long Dit.)
KT6 . . . . **195** F2
Sutton SM3 . . . . **198** B6
Teddington TW11 . . . . . . **162** B4
Wallington SM6 . . . . **200** C3
Welling DA16 . . . . **158** B2
West Drayton UB7 . . . . . **120** A3
Worcester Park KT4 . . . . **196** E1
Church Rd Merton,
SW19 . . . . **185** G1
Church Rd Twr Block, Stan. HA7
off Church Rd **53** F5
Church Row, NW3 . . . . **91** F4
Chislehurst BR7 . . . . **175** F7
Church St, E15 . . . . **115** E1
E16 . . . . **136** E1
N9 . . . . **60** B2
NW8 . . . . **15** F1
W2 . . . . **15** F1
W4 . . . . **127** E6
Croydon CR0 . . . . **201** J2
Dagenham RM10 . . . . . . **101** H6
Enfield EN2 . . . . **44** A3
Hampton TW12 . . . . **179** J1
Isleworth TW7 . . . . **144** E3
Kingston upon Thames
KT1 . . . . **181** G2
Sunbury-on-Thames
TW16 . . . . **178** B3
Sutton SM1
off High St **199** E5
Twickenham TW1 . . . . . . **162** D1
Church St Est, NW8 . . . . **7** F6
Church St N, E15 . . . . **115** E1
Church St Pas, E15
off Church St **115** E1
Church Stretton Rd, Houns.
TW3 . . . . **143** J5
Church Ter, NW4 . . . . **71** H3
SE13 . . . . **154** E3
SW8 . . . . **150** D2
Richmond TW10 . . . . **145** G5
Church Vale, N2 . . . . **73** J3
SE23 . . . . **171** F2
Church View Gro, SE26 . . . **171** G6
Churchview Rd, Twick. TW2 **162** A1
Church Wk, N6
off Swains La **92** A3
N16 . . . . **94** A4
NW2 . . . . **90** C3
NW4 . . . . **71** J3
NW9 . . . . **88** D2
SW13 . . . . **147** G1
SW15 . . . . **147** H5
SW16 . . . . **186** C2
SW20 . . . . **183** J3
Brentford TW8 . . . . **125** F6
Enfield EN2 . . . . **44** A3
Richmond TW9
off Red Lion St **145** G5
Thames Ditton KT7 . . . . **180** C6
Churchward Ho, W14
off Ivatt Pl **128** C5
Church Way, N20 . . . . **57** G3
Churchway, NW1 . . . . **9** J3
Church Way, Barn. EN4 . . . . **41** J4
Edgware HA8 . . . . **54** A6
Churchwell Path, E9 . . . . . . **95** F5
Churchwood Gdns,
Wdf.Grn. IG8 . . . . **63** G4
Churchyard Row, SE11 . . . . **35** H1
Church Yd Wk, W2 . . . . **15** E1
Churston Av, E13 . . . . **115** H1
Churston Cl, SW2
off Tulse Hill **169** H1
Churston Dr, Mord. SM4 . . **184** A5
Churston Gdns, N11 . . . . . . **58** C6
Churton Pl, SW1 . . . . **33** G2
Churton St, SW1 . . . . **33** G2
Chusan Pl, E14
off Commercial Rd . . . **113** J6
Chyngton Cl, Sid. DA15 . . **175** J3
Cibber Rd, SE23 . . . . **171** G2
Cicada Rd, SW18 . . . . **149** F5
Cicely Rd, SE15 . . . . **152** D1
Cinderella Path, NW11
off North End Rd **91** E1
Cinderford Way, Brom.
BR1 . . . . **173** E4
Cinnabar Wf, E1 . . . . **29** J2
Cinnamon Cl, SE15 . . . . **37** F7
Croydon CR0 . . . . **186** E7
Cinnamon Row, SW11 . . . . **149** F3
Cinnamon St, E1 . . . . **133** E1
Cintra Pk, SE19 . . . . **170** C7
Circle, The, NW2 . . . . **89** E3
NW7 . . . . **54** D5
SE1 . . . . **29** F3
Circle Gdns, SW19 . . . . **184** D2
Circuits, The, Pnr. HA5 . . . . . **66** C4
Circular Rd, N17 . . . . **76** C3
Circular Way, SE18 . . . . . . **136** C6
Circus Lo, NW8 . . . . **6** E3
Circus Ms, W1 . . . . **15** J1
Circus Pl, EC2 . . . . **20** C2
Circus Rd, NW8 . . . . **6** E3
Circus St, SE10 . . . . **134** C7
Cirencester St, W2 . . . . **14** A1
Cirrus Cl, Wall. SM6 . . . . . . **201** E7
Cissbury Ring N, N12 . . . . . . **56** C5
Cissbury Ring S, N12 . . . . . . **56** C5
Cissbury Rd, N15 . . . . **76** A5
Citadel Pl, SE11 . . . . **34** C3
Citizen Ho, N7
off Harvist Est **93** G4
Citizen Rd, N7 . . . . **93** G4
C.I. Twr, N.Mal. KT3 . . . . . . **183** E3

Citron Ter, SE15
 off Nunhead La **153** E3
City Business Cen, SE16
 off Lower Rd **133** F2
City Cross Business Pk,
 SE10 *off Salutation Rd* **135** E4
City Forum, EC1 **11** J3
City Gdn Row, N1 **11** H2
City Gate Ho, Ilf. IG2 **80** E6
City Ho, Croy. CR0 **187** H7
City Mill River Towpath,
 E15 **96** B7
★ **City of Westminster**
 Archives Cen, SW1 **25** J5
City Pt, EC2 **20** B1
City Rd, EC1 **11** G2
City Twr, E14
 off Limeharbour **134** B2
★ **City Uni**, EC1 **11** G4
City Vw, Ilf. IG1
 off Axon Pl **99** F2
City Vw Apts, N1
 off Essex Rd **93** J7
Cityview Ct, SE22 **152** D7
City Wk, SE1 **28** D4
Civic Way, Ilf. IG6 **81** F4
 Ruislip HA4 **84** D5
Clabon Ms, SW1 **23** J6
Clack St, SE16 **133** F2
Clacton Rd, E6 **116** A3
 E17 **77** H6
 N17 *off Sperling Rd* **76** C2
Claigmar Gdns, N3 **72** E1
Claire Ct, N12 **57** F3
 Bushey (Bushey Hth)
 WD23 **52** A1
 Pinner HA5
 off Westfield Pk **51** F7
Claire Gdns, Stan. HA7 **53** F5
Claire Pl, E14 **134** A3
Clairvale Rd, Houns. TW5 **142** D1
Clairview Rd, SW16 **168** B5
Clairville Gdns, W7 **124** B1
Clairville Pt, SE23 **171** G3
Clamp Hill, Stan. HA7 **52** A4
Clancarty Rd, SW6 **148** D2
Clandon Cl, W3 **126** B2
 Epsom KT17 **197** F6
Clandon Gdns, N3 **72** D3
Clandon Rd, Ilf. IG3 **99** H2
Clandon St, SE8 **154** A2
Clanricarde Gdns, W2 **108** D7
CLAPHAM, SW4 **150** B3
★ **Clapham Common**,
 SW4 **150** A4
Clapham Common, SW4 **150** C4
Clapham Common N Side,
 SW4 **150** B4
Clapham Common S Side,
 SW4 **150** B6
Clapham Common W Side,
 SW4 **150** A4
Clapham Cres, SW4 **150** D4
Clapham Est, SW11 **149** H4
Clapham High St, SW4 **150** D4
Clapham Junct Sta,
 SW11 **149** G4
Clapham Manor St, SW4 **150** C3
CLAPHAM PARK, SW4 **150** D6
Clapham Pk Est, SW4 **150** D6
Clapham Pk Rd, SW4 **150** D4
Clapham Rd, SW9 **150** E3
Clapham Rd Est, SW4 **150** D3
Clap La, Dag. RM10 **101** H3
Claps Gate La, E6 **116** D4
Clapton Common, E5 **76** C7
CLAPTON PARK, E5 **95** H4
Clapton Pk Est, E5
 off Blackwell Cl **95** G4
Clapton Pas, E5 **95** F5
Clapton Sq, E5 **95** F5
Clapton Ter, N16
 off Oldhill St **94** D1
Clapton Way, E5 **94** D4
Clara Pl, SE18 **136** D4
Clare Cl, N2 **73** F3
Clare Cor, SE9 **156** E7
Claredale St, E2 **13** J2
Clare Gdns, E7 **97** G4
 W11
 off Westbourne Pk Rd **108** B6
 Barking IG11 **99** J6
Clare Ho, E3 **113** J1
Clare La, N1 **93** J7
Clare Lawn Av, SW14 **146** D5
Clare Mkt, WC2 **18** C4
Clare Ms, SW6
 off Waterford Rd **128** E7
Claremont Av, Har. HA3 **69** H5
 New Malden KT3 **183** G5
 Sunbury-on-Thames
 TW16 **178** B1
Claremont Cl, E16 **136** D1
 N1 **11** F2
 SW2
 off Christchurch Rd **169** F1
 Orpington BR6 **206** D4
Claremont Ct, Surb. KT6
 off St. James Rd **181** G6
Claremont Gdns, Ilf. IG3 **99** H2
 Surbiton KT6 **181** H5
Claremont Gro, W4
 off Edensor Gdns **127** E7
 Woodford Green IG8 **63** J6
Claremont Pk, N3 **72** B1
Claremont Rd, E7 **97** H5
 E11 *off Grove Grn Rd* **96** D3
 E17 **77** H2
 N6 **74** C7
 NW2 **90** A3
 W9 **108** B2
 W13 **104** D5
 Bromley BR1 **192** B4
 Croydon CR0 **202** D1
 Esher (Clay.) KT10 **194** B7
 Harrow HA3 **68** B2
 Surbiton KT6 **181** H6
 Teddington TW11 **162** C5
 Twickenham TW1 **145** E6
Claremont Sq, N1 **10** E2
Claremont St, E16 **136** D1
 N18 **60** D6
 SE10 **134** B7
Claremont Way, NW2 **89** J1
Clarence Av, SW4 **150** D6
 Bromley BR1 **192** B4
 Ilford IG2 **80** D6
 New Malden KT3 **182** C2
Clarence Cl, Barn.
 EN4 **41** G5
Clarence Cres, SW4 **150** D6
 Sidcup DA14 **176** B3
Clarence Gdns, NW1 **9** E4
Clarence Gate, Wdf.Grn.
 IG8 **64** D6
Clarence Gate Gdns, NW1
 off Glentworth St **8** A6
★ **Clarence Ho**, SW1 **25** G3
Clarence La, SW15 **147** E6
Clarence Ms, E5 **95** E5
 SE16 **133** G1
 SW12 **150** B7
Clarence Pl, E5 **95** E5
Clarence Rd, E5 **95** E4
 E12 **98** A5
 E16 **115** E4
 E17 **77** G2
 N15 **75** J5
 N22 **59** E7
 NW6 **90** C7
 SE8 **134** B6
 SE9 **174** B2
 SW19 **166** E6
 W4 **126** A5
 Bexleyheath DA6 **158** E4
 Bromley BR1 **192** A3
 Croydon CR0 **188** A7
 Enfield EN3 **45** E5
 Richmond TW9 **145** J1
 Sidcup DA14 **176** B3
 Sutton SM1 **198** E4
 Teddington TW11 **162** C6
 Wallington SM6 **200** B5
Clarence St, Kings.T.
 KT1 **181** H2
 Richmond TW9 **145** H4
 Southall UB2 **122** D3
Clarence Ter, NW1 **8** A5
 Hounslow TW3 **143** H4
Clarence Wk, SW4 **150** E2
Clarence Way, NW1 **92** B7
Clarence Way Est, NW1 **92** B7
Clarendon Cl, E9 **95** F7
 W2 **15** G5
Clarendon Cres, Twick.
 TW2 **162** A3
Clarendon Cross, W11
 off Portland Rd **108** B7
Clarendon Dr, SW15 **147** J4
Clarendon Gdns, NW4 **71** G3
 W9 **6** D6
 Ilford IG1 **98** C1
 Wembley HA9 **87** H4
Clarendon Gro, NW1 **9** H3
 Mitcham CR4 **185** J3
Clarendon Ms, W2 **15** G4
 Bexley DA5 **177** H1
 Borehamwood WD6
 off Clarendon Rd **38** A3
Clarendon Pl, W2 **15** G5
Clarendon Ri, SE13 **154** C3
Clarendon Rd, E11 **96** D1
 E17 **78** B6
 E18 **79** G3
 N8 **75** F3
 N15 **75** H4
 N18 **60** D6
 N22 **75** F2
 SW19 **167** H7
 W5 **105** H3
 W11 **108** B7
 Borehamwood WD6 **38** A3
 Croydon CR0 **201** H2
 Harrow HA1 **68** B6
Clarendon Rd, Hayes UB3 **121** J2
 Wallington SM6 **200** C6
Clarendon St, SW1 **32** E4
Clarendon Ter, W9 **6** D5
Clarendon Wk, W11 **108** B6
Clarendon Way, N21 **43** J6
 Chislehurst BR7 **193** J3
 Orpington BR5 **193** J3
Clarens St, SE6 **171** J2
Clare Pl, SW15
 off Minstead Gdns **147** F7
Clare Pt, NW2
 off Claremont Rd **90** A1
Clare Rd, E11 **78** D6
 NW10 **89** G7
 SE14 **153** J1
 Greenford UB6 **86** A6
 Hounslow TW4 **143** F3
 Staines (Stanw.)
 TW19 **140** B7
Clare St, E2 **113** E2
Claret Gdns, SE25 **188** B4
Clareville Gro, SW7 **30** D2
Clareville Gro Ms, SW7 **30** D2
Clareville Rd, Orp. BR5 **207** F2
Clareville St, SW7 **30** D2
Clare Way, Bexh. DA7 **158** E1
Clarewood Wk, SW9 **151** H4
Clarges Ms, W1 **24** D1
Clarges St, W1 **24** E1
Claribel Rd, SW9 **151** H2
Claridge Rd, Dag. RM8 **100** D1
Clarissa Rd, Rom. RM6 **82** D7
Clarissa St, E8 **112** C1
Clarke Ms, N9
 off Plevna Rd **60** E3
Clarke Path, N16 **94** D1
Clarkes Av, Wor.Pk. KT4 **198** A1
Clarke's Ms, W1 **16** C1
Clark Gro, Ilf. IG3 **99** H4
Clark Lawrence Ct, SW11
 off Winstanley Rd **149** G3
Clarkson Rd, E16 **115** F6
Clarkson Row, NW1 **9** F2
Clarksons, The, Bark.
 IG11 **117** F2
Clarkson St, E2 **112** E3
Clarks Pl, EC2 **20** D3
Clarks Rd, Ilf. IG1 **99** G2
Clark St, E1 **113** E5
Clark Way, Houns. TW5 **122** D7
Classon Cl, West Dr.
 UB7 **120** B2
Claude Rd, E10 **96** C2
 E13 **115** H1
 SE15 **152** E2
Claude St, E14 **134** A4
Claudia Jones Way, SW2 **150** E6
Claudia Pl, SW19 **166** B1
Claudius Cl, Stan. HA7 **53** G3
Claughton Rd, E13 **115** J2
Clauson Av, Nthlt. UB5 **85** H5
Clavell St, SE10 **134** C6
Claverdale Rd, SW2 **151** F7
Clavering Av, SW13 **127** H6
Clavering Cl, Twick. TW1 **162** D4
Clavering Rd, E12 **98** A1
Claverings Ind Est, N9 **61** G2
Claverley Gro, N3 **56** D7
Claverley Vil, N3 **56** E7
Claverton St, SW1 **33** G4
Clave St, E1
 off Cinnamon St **133** F1
Claxton Gro, W6 **128** A5
Claxton Path, SE4
 off Hainford Cl **153** G4
Clay Av, Mitch. CR4 **186** B2
Claybank Gro, SE13
 off Algernon Rd **154** B3
Claybourne Ms, SE19
 off Church Rd **170** B7
Claybridge Rd, SE12 **173** J4
Claybrook Cl, N2 **73** G3
Claybrook Rd, W6 **128** A6
Claybury Bdy, Ilf. IG5 **80** B3
Claybury Hall, Wdf.Grn.
 IG8 **64** C7
Claybury Rd, Wdf.Grn.
 IG8 **64** B7
Claydon, SE17
 off Deacon Way **35** J1
Claydon Dr, Croy. CR0 **201** E4
Claydown Ms, SE18
 off Woolwich
 New Rd **136** D5
Clayfarm Rd, SE9 **175** F2
CLAYGATE, Esher KT10 **194** B7
Claygate Cres, Croy.
 (New Adgtn) CR0 **204** C6
Claygate La, Esher KT10 **194** D2
 Thames Ditton KT7 **194** D1
Claygate Lo Cl, Esher
 (Clay.) KT10 **194** B7
Claygate Rd, W13 **124** E3
CLAYHALL, Ilf. IG5 **80** C2
Clayhall Av, Ilf. IG5 **80** B3
Clayhill, Surb. KT5 **182** A5
Clayhill Cres, SE9 **174** A4
Claylands Pl, SW8 **34** E7
Claylands Rd, SW8 **34** D6
Clay La, Edg. HA8 **54** A1
 Staines (Stanw.) TW19 **140** C7
Claymill Ho, SE18 **137** F5
Claymore Cl, Mord.
 SM4 **184** D7
Claymore Ct, E17
 off Billet Rd **77** H1
Claypole Dr, Houns. TW5 **143** E1
Claypole Rd, E15 **114** C2
Clayponds Av, Brent. TW8 **125** H4
Clayponds Gdns, W5 **125** G4
Clayponds La, Brent.
 TW8 **125** H5
Clay Rd, The, Loug. IG10 **48** B1
Clayside, Chig. IG7 **65** F6
Clay's La, Loug. IG10 **48** D1
Clay St, W1 **16** A2
Clayton Av, Wem. HA0 **87** H7
Clayton Business Pk,
 Hayes UB3 **121** H2
Clayton Cl, E6
 off Brandreth Rd **116** C6
Clayton Cres, N1 **111** E1
 Brentford TW8 **125** G5
Clayton Dr, SE8
 off Sapphire Rd **133** H5
Clayton Fld, NW9 **55** E7
Clayton Ms, SE10 **154** D1
Clayton Rd, SE15 **152** D1
 Chessington KT9 **195** F4
 Hayes UB3 **121** H2
 Isleworth TW7 **144** B3
 Romford RM7 **101** J1
Clayton St, SE11 **34** E5
Clayton Ter, Hayes UB4
 off Jollys La **102** D5
Claywood Cl, Orp. BR6 **193** H7
Clayworth Cl, Sid. DA15 **158** B6
Cleanthus Cl, SE18 **157** E1
Cleanthus Rd, SE18 **157** E1
Clearbrook Way, E1
 off West Arbour St **113** F6
Clearwater Pl, Surb. KT6
 off Portsmouth Rd **181** F6
Clearwater Ter, W11
 off Lorne Gdns **128** A2
Clearwell Dr, W9 **6** A6
Cleave Av, Hayes UB3 **121** H4
 Orpington BR6 **207** H6
Cleaveland Rd, Surb.
 KT6 **181** G5
Cleaverholme Cl, SE25 **188** E6
Cleaver Sq, SE11 **35** F3
Cleaver St, SE11 **35** F3
Cleeve Hill, SE23 **171** E1
Cleeve Pk Gdns, Sid.
 DA14 **176** B2
Cleeve Way, SW15 **147** F7
 Sutton SM1 **199** E1
Clegg Ho, SE3
 off Pinto Way **155** H4
Clegg St, E1
 off Prusom St **133** E1
 E13 **115** G2
Cleland Path, Loug. IG10 **49** E1
Clematis Gdns, Wdf.Grn.
 IG8 **63** G5
Clematis St, W12 **107** F7
Clem Attlee Ct, SW6 **128** C6
Clem Attlee Par, SW6
 off North End Rd **128** C6
Clemence Rd, Dag.
 RM10 **119** J1
Clemence St, E14 **113** J5
Clement Av, SW4 **150** D4
Clement Cl, NW6 **89** J7
 W4 *off Acton La* **126** D4
Clement Gdns, Hayes
 UB3 **121** H4
Clementhorpe Rd, Dag.
 RM9 **100** C6
Clementina Rd, E10 **95** J1
Clementine Cl, W13
 off Balfour Rd **124** E2
Clementine Wk, Wdf.Grn.
 IG8 *off Salway Cl* **63** G7
Clement Rd, SW19 **166** B5
 Beckenham BR3 **189** G2
Clements Av, E16 **115** G7
Clements Cl, N12 **56** E4
Clements Ct, Houns.
 TW4 **142** D4
 Ilford IG1
 off Clements La **98** E3
Clement's Inn, WC2 **18** D4
Clement's Inn Pas, WC2 **18** D4
Clements La, EC4 **20** C5
 Ilford IG1 **98** E3
Clements Pl, Brent. TW8 **125** G5
Clements Rd, E6 **98** C7
 SE16 **29** J6
 Ilford IG1 **98** E3
Clendon Way, SE18
 off Polthorne Gro **137** G4

Clennam St, SE1 **28** A3
Clensham Ct, Sutt. SM1 *off Sutton Common Rd* **198** D2
Clensham La, Sutt. SM1 **198** D2
Clenston Ms, W1 **15** J3
Cleopatra's Cl, Stan. HA7 **53** G3
★ **Cleopatra's Needle**, WC2 **26** C1
Clephane Rd, N1 **93** J6
Clere St, EC2 **12** C5
CLERKENWELL, EC1 **11** G6
Clerkenwell Cl, EC1 **11** F5
Clerkenwell Grn, EC1 **11** F6
Clerkenwell Rd, EC1 **10** E6
Clerks Piece, Loug. IG10 **48** C3
Clermont Rd, E9 **113** F1
Clevedon Cl, N16 *off Smalley Cl* **94** C3
Clevedon Gdns, Hayes UB3 **121** G3
Hounslow TW5 **142** B1
Clevedon Rd, SE20 **189** G1
Kingston upon Thames KT1 **182** A2
Twickenham TW1 **145** G6
Cleveland Av, SW20 **184** C2
W4 **127** F4
Hampton TW12 **161** F7
Cleveland Cres, Borwd. WD6 **38** C5
Cleveland Gdns, N4 **75** J5
NW2 **90** A2
SW13 **147** F2
W2 **14** C4
Worcester Park KT4 **197** E2
Cleveland Gro, E1 *off Cleveland Way* **113** F4
Cleveland Ms, W1 **17** F1
Cleveland Pk, Stai. TW19 **140** B6
Cleveland Pk Av, E17 **78** A4
Cleveland Pk Cres, E17 **78** A4
Cleveland Pl, SW1 **25** G1
Cleveland Ri, Mord. SM4 **184** A7
Cleveland Rd, E18 **79** G3
N1 **94** A7
N9 **45** E7
SW13 **147** F2
W4 *off Antrobus Rd* **126** C3
W13 **104** E5
Ilford IG1 **99** E3
Isleworth TW7 **144** D4
New Malden KT3 **182** E4
Welling DA16 **157** J2
Worcester Park KT4 **197** E2
Cleveland Row, SW1 **25** F2
Cleveland Sq, W2 **14** C4
Cleveland St, W1 **9** F6
Cleveland Ter, W2 **14** D3
Cleveland Way, E1 **113** F4
Cleveley Cl, SE7 **136** A4
Cleveley Cres, W5 **105** H2
Cleveleys Rd, E5 **95** E3
Cleverly Est, W12 **127** G1
Cleve Rd, NW6 **90** D7
Sidcup DA14 **176** D3
Cleves Cl, Loug. IG10 **48** B6
Cleves Rd, E6 **116** A1
Richmond TW10 **163** F3
Cleves Wk, Ilf. IG6 **65** F7
Cleves Way, Hmptn. TW12 **161** F7
Ruislip HA4 **84** D1
Clewer Cres, Har. HA3 **68** A1
Clewer Ho, SE2 *off Wolvercote Rd* **138** D2
Clichy Est, E1 **113** F5
Clifden Ms, E5 *off Clifden Rd* **95** G4
Clifden Rd, E5 **95** F5
Brentford TW8 **125** G6
Twickenham TW1 **162** C1
Cliffe Rd, S.Croy. CR2 **202** A5
Cliffe Wk, Sutt. SM1 *off Turnpike La* **199** F5
Clifford Av, SW14 **146** B3
Chislehurst BR7 **174** C6
Ilford IG5 **80** E1
Wallington SM6 **200** C4
Clifford Cl, Nthlt. UB5 **103** E1
Clifford Dr, SW9 **151** H4
Clifford Gdns, NW10 **107** J2
Hayes UB3 **121** G4
Clifford Haigh Ho, SW6 *off Fulham Palace Rd* **128** A7
Clifford Rd, E16 **115** F4
E17 **78** C2
N9 **45** F6
SE25 **188** D4
Barnet EN5 **41** E3
Hounslow TW4 **142** D3
Richmond TW10 **163** G2
Wembley HA0 **105** G1
Clifford's Inn Pas, EC4 **19** E4
Clifford St, W1 **17** F6
Clifford Way, NW10 **89** F4
Cliff Rd, NW1 **92** D6
Cliff Ter, SE8 **154** A2
Cliffview Rd, SE13 **154** A3
Cliff Vil, NW1 **92** D6
Cliff Wk, E16 **115** F5
Clifton Av, E17 **77** G3
N3 **72** C1
W12 **127** F1
Feltham TW13 **160** C3
Stanmore HA7 **69** E2
Wembley HA9 **87** J6
Clifton Cl, Orp. BR6 **207** F5
Clifton Ct, N4 *off Biggerstaff St* **93** G2
NW8 **6** E5
Woodford Green IG8 *off Snakes La W* **63** G6
Clifton Cres, SE15 **133** E7
Clifton Est, SE15 *off Consort Rd* **152** E1
Clifton Gdns, N15 **76** C6
NW11 **72** C6
W4 *off Dolman Rd* **126** D4
W9 **6** C6
Enfield EN2 **42** E4
Clifton Gro, E8 **94** D6
Clifton Hill, NW8 **109** E2
Clifton Pk Av, SW20 **183** J2
Clifton Pl, SE16 *off Canon Beck Rd* **133** F2
W2 **15** F5
Clifton Ri, SE14 **133** H7
Clifton Rd, E7 **98** A6
E16 **115** E5
N1 **93** J6
N3 **73** F1
N8 **74** D6
N22 **74** C1
NW10 **107** G2
SE25 **188** B4
SW19 **166** A6
W9 **6** D5
Greenford UB6 **103** J4
Harrow HA3 **69** J5
Hounslow (Lon.Hthrw Air.) TW6 *off Inner Ring E* **140** E3
Ilford IG2 **81** G6
Isleworth TW7 **144** A2
Kingston upon Thames KT2 **163** J7
Loughton IG10 **48** B4
Sidcup DA14 **175** H4
Southall UB2 **123** E4
Teddington TW11 **162** B4
Wallington SM6 **200** B5
Welling DA16 **158** C3
Clifton's Rbt, SE12 **155** H6
Clifton St, EC2 **20** D1
Clifton Ter, N4 **93** G2
Clifton Vil, W9 **14** B1
Clifton Wk, E6 **116** B6
W6 *off Galena Rd* **127** H4
Clifton Way, SE15 **133** E7
Borehamwood WD6 **38** A1
Wembley HA0 **105** H1
Clinch Ct, E16 **115** G5
Cline Rd, N11 **58** C6
Clinger Ct, N1 *off Pitfield St* **112** B1
★ **Clink Prison Mus**, SE1 **28** B1
Clink St, SE1 **28** A1
Clinton Av, E.Mol. KT8 **179** J4
Welling DA16 **157** J4
Clinton Cres, Ilf. IG6 **65** H6
Clinton Rd, E3 **113** H3
E7 **97** G4
N15 **76** A4
Clinton Ter, Sutt. SM1 *off Manor La* **199** F4
Clipper Cl, SE16 *off Kinburn St* **133** G2
Clipper Way, SE13 **154** C4
Clippesby Cl, Chess. KT9 **195** J7
Clipstone Ms, W1 **9** F6
Clipstone Rd, Houns. TW3 **143** G3
Clipstone St, W1 **17** E1
Clissold Cl, N2 **73** J3
Clissold Ct, N4 **93** J2
Clissold Cres, N16 **94** A3
Clissold Rd, N16 **94** A3
Clitheroe Av, Har. HA2 **85** G1
Clitheroe Gdns, Wat. WD19 **50** D3
Clitheroe Rd, SW9 **151** E2
Clitherow Av, W7 **124** D3
Clitherow Pas, Brent. TW8 **125** F5
Clitherow Rd, Brent. TW8 **125** E5
Clitterhouse Cres, NW2 **89** J1
Clitterhouse Rd, NW2 **89** J1
Clive Av, N18 *off Claremont St* **60** D6
Clive Ct, W9 **6** D5
Cliveden Cl, N12 **57** F4
Cliveden Pl, SW1 **32** B1
Cliveden Rd, SW19 **184** C1
Clivedon Ct, W13 **104** E5
Clivedon Rd, E4 **62** E5
Clive Pas, SE21 *off Clive Rd* **170** A3
Clive Rd, SE21 **170** A3
SW19 **167** H6
Belvedere DA17 **139** G4
Enfield EN1 **44** D4
Feltham TW14 **142** A6
Twickenham TW1 **162** C4
Clivesdale Dr, Hayes UB3 **122** B1
Clive Way, Enf. EN1 **44** D4
Cloak La, EC4 **20** A5
Clockhouse Av, Bark. IG11 **117** F1
Clockhouse Cl, SW19 **165** J3
Clockhouse Junct, N13 **59** F5
Clockhouse Pl, SW15 **148** B5
Clock Ho Rd, Beck. BR3 **189** H3
★ **Clockmakers Company Collection, The** (Guildhall Lib), EC2 **20** A3
Clock Twr Ms, N1 *off Arlington Av* **111** J1
SE28 **118** B7
W7 *off Uxbridge Rd* **124** B1
Clock Twr Pl, N7 **92** E6
Clock Twr Rd, Islw. TW7 **144** C3
Cloister Cl, Tedd. TW11 **162** E5
Cloister Gdns, SE25 **188** E6
Edgware HA8 **54** C5
Cloister Rd, NW2 **90** C3
W3 **106** C5
Cloisters Av, Brom. BR2 **192** C5
Cloisters Business Cen, SW8 *off Battersea Pk Rd* **130** B7
Cloisters Mall, Kings.T. KT1 *off Union St* **181** G2
Clonard Way, Pnr. HA5 **51** G6
Clonbrock Rd, N16 **94** B4
Cloncurry St, SW6 **148** A2
Clonmel Cl, Har. HA2 **86** A2
Clonmell Rd, N17 **76** A3
Clonmel Rd, SW6 **128** C7
Teddington TW11 **162** A4
Clonmore St, SW18 **166** C1
Cloonmore Av, Orp. BR6 **207** J4
Clorane Gdns, NW3 **90** D3
Close, The, E4 *off Beech Hall Rd* **62** C7
N14 **58** D2
N20 **56** C2
SE3 *off Heath La* **154** D2
Barnet (E.Barn.) EN4 **41** J6
Beckenham BR3 **189** H4
Bexley DA5 **159** G6
Harrow HA2 **67** J2
Isleworth TW7 **144** A2
Mitcham CR4 **185** J4
New Malden KT3 **182** C2
Orpington BR5 **193** H6
Pinner (Eastcote) HA5 **66** C7
Pinner (Rayners La) HA5 **67** F7
Richmond TW9 **146** B3
Romford RM6 **82** E6
Sidcup DA14 **176** B4
Sutton SM3 **184** C7
Wembley (Barnhill Rd) HA9 **88** C3
Wembley (Lyon Pk Av) HA0 **87** H6
Cloth Ct, EC1 **19** H2
Cloth Fair, EC1 **19** H2
Clothier St, E1 **21** E3
Cloth St, EC1 **19** J1
Clothworkers Rd, SE18 **137** G7
Cloudesdale Rd, SW17 **168** B2
Cloudesley Cl, Sid. DA14 **175** J4
Cloudesley Pl, N1 **111** G1
Cloudesley Rd, N1 **111** G1
Bexleyheath DA7 **159** F1
Cloudesley Sq, N1 **111** G1
Cloudesley St, N1 **111** G1
Clouston Cl, Wall. SM6 **200** E5
Clova Rd, E7 **97** F6
Clove Cres, E14 **114** D7
Clove Hitch Quay, SW11 **149** F3
Clovelly Av, NW9 **71** F4
Clovelly Cl, Pnr. HA5 **66** B3
Clovelly Gdns, SE19 **188** C1
Enfield EN1 **44** B7
Romford RM7 **83** H1
Clovelly Rd, N8 **74** D4
W4 **126** C2
W5 **125** F2
Bexleyheath DA7 **138** E6
Hounslow TW3 **143** G2
Clovelly Way, E1 *off Jamaica St* **113** F6
Harrow HA2 **85** F2
Orpington BR6 **193** J6
Clover Cl, E11 *off Norman Rd* **96** D2
Cloverdale Gdns, Sid. DA15 **157** J6
Cloverleys, Loug. IG10 **48** A5
Clover Ms, SW3 **31** J5
Clover Way, Wall. SM6 **200** A1
Clove St, E13 *off Barking Rd* **115** G4
Clowders Rd, SE6 **171** J3
Clowser Cl, Sutt. SM1 *off Turnpike La* **199** F5
Cloysters Grn, E1 **29** H1
Cloyster Wd, Edg. HA8 **53** G7
Club Gdns Rd, Brom. BR2 **191** G7
Club Row, E1 **13** F5
E2 **13** F5
Clunbury Av, Sthl. UB2 **123** F5
Clunbury St, N1 **12** C2
Cluny Est, SE1 **28** D5
Cluny Ms, SW5 **128** D4
Cluny Pl, SE1 **28** D5
Cluse Ct, N1 **11** J1
Clutton St, E14 **114** B5
Clydach Rd, Enf. EN1 **44** C4
Clyde Circ, N15 **76** B4
Clyde Pl, E10 **78** B7
Clyde Rd, N15 **76** B4
N22 **74** D1
Croydon CR0 **202** C1
Sutton SM1 **198** D5
Wallington SM6 **200** C5
Clydesdale, Enf. EN3 **45** G4
Clydesdale Av, Stan. HA7 **69** G3
Clydesdale Cl, Borwd. WD6 **38** D5
Isleworth TW7 **144** C3
Clydesdale Gdns, Rich. TW10 **146** B4
Clydesdale Ho, Erith DA18 *off Kale Rd* **138** E2
Clydesdale Rd, W11 **108** C6
Clyde St, SE8 **133** J6
Clyde Ter, SE23 **171** F2
Clyde Vale, SE23 **171** F2
Clymping Dene, Felt. TW14 **142** B7
Clyston St, SW8 **150** C2
Coach & Horses Yd, W1 **17** E5
Coach Ho La, N5 *off Highbury Hill* **93** H4
SW19 **166** A4
Coach Ho Ms, SE14 *off Waller Rd* **153** G2
Coachhouse Ms, SE20 **170** E7
Coach Ho Ms, SE23 **153** G6
Coach Ho Yd, SW18 *off Ebner St* **149** E4
Coachmaker Ms, SW4 *off Fenwick Pl* **150** E3
W4 *off Berrymede Rd* **126** D3
Coach Yd Ms, N19 *off Trinder Gdns* **93** E1
Coaldale Wk, SE21 *off Lairdale Cl* **151** J7
Coalecroft Rd, SW15 **147** J4
Coalport Ho, SE11 *off Walnut Tree Wk* **34** E1
Coal Post Cl, Orp. (Grn St Grn) BR6 *off Lynne Cl* **207** J6
Coates Av, SW18 **149** H6
Coates Cl, Th.Hth. CR7 **187** J3
Coates Hill Rd, Brom. BR1 **192** D2
Coate St, E2 **13** J2
Coates Wk, Brent. TW8 **125** H5
Cobalt Cl, Beck. BR3 **189** G4
Cobb Cl, Borwd. WD6 **38** C5
Cobbett Rd, SE9 **156** B3
Twickenham TW2 **161** G1
Cobbetts Av, Ilf. IG4 **80** A5
Cobbett St, SW8 **131** F7
Cobble La, N1 *off Edwards Ms* **93** H7
Cobble Ms, N5 **93** J3
N6 *off Highgate W Hill* **92** A1
Cobblers Wk, E.Mol. KT8 **180** D1
Hampton TW12 **161** J7
Kingston upon Thames KT2 **180** D1
Teddington TW11 **180** D1
Cobblestone Pl, Croy. CR0 *off Oakfield Rd* **201** J1
Cobbold Est, NW10 **89** F6
Cobbold Ms, W12 *off Cobbold Rd* **127** F2
Cobbold Rd, E11 **97** F3
NW10 **89** F6
W12 **127** E2
Cobb's Ct, EC4 *off Pilgrim St* **19** H4
Cobb's Rd, Houns. TW4 **143** F4
Cobb St, E1 **21** F2
Cobden Ms, SE26 **171** E5

Cobden Rd, E11 **97** E3
SE25 **188** D5
Orpington BR6 **207** G4
Cobham Av, N.Mal.
KT3 **183** G5
Cobham Cl, SW11 **149** H6
Bromley BR2 **192** B7
Edgware HA8 **70** B2
Enfield EN1 **44** D3
Sidcup DA15
off Park Mead **158** B6
Wallington SM6 **200** E6
Cobham Ho, Bark. IG11
off St. Margarets **117** F1
Cobham Ms, NW1
off Agar Gro **92** D7
Cobham Pl, Bexh. DA6 **158** D5
Cobham Rd, E17 **78** C1
N22 **75** H3
Hounslow TW5 **122** C7
Ilford IG3 **99** H2
Kingston upon Thames
KT1 **182** A1
Cobland Rd, SE12 **173** J4
Coborn Rd, E3 **113** J3
Coborn St, E3 **113** J3
Cobourg Rd, SE5 **37** F5
Cobourg St, NW1 **9** G4
Cobtree Ct, Sthl. UB1 **103** J6
Coburg Cl, SW1 **33** G1
Coburg Cres, SW2 **169** F1
Coburg Gdns, Ilf. IG5 **80** A2
Coburg Rd, N22 **75** F3
Cochrane Ms, NW8 **7** F2
Cochrane Rd, SW19 **166** C7
Cochrane St, NW8 **7** F2
Cockayne Way, SE8 **133** H5
Cockerell Rd, E17 **77** H7
COCKFOSTERS, Barn.
EN4 **41** H4
Cockfosters Par, Barn. EN4
off Cockfosters Rd **42** A4
Cockfosters Rd, Barn.
EN4 **41** J2
Cock Hill, E1 **21** E2
Cock La, EC1 **19** G2
Cockpit Steps, SW1 **25** J4
Cockpit Yd, WC1 **18** D1
Cocks Cres, N.Mal. KT3 **183** F4
Cocksett Av, Orp. BR6 **207** H6
Cockspur Ct, SW1 **25** J1
Cockspur St, SW1 **25** J1
Cocksure La, Sid. DA14 **177** G3
Coda Cen, The, SW6 **148** B1
Code St, E1 **13** G6
Codling Cl, E1 **29** J1
Codling Way, Wem. HA0 **87** G4
Codrington Hill, SE23 **153** H7
Codrington Ms, W11
off Blenheim Cres **108** B6
Cody Cl, Har. HA3 **69** G3
Wallington SM6
off Alcock Cl **200** D7
Cody Rd, E16 **114** D4
Cody Rd Business Cen,
E16 **114** D4
Coe Av, SE25 **188** D6
Coe's All, Barn. EN5
off Wood St **40** B4
Coffey St, SE8 **134** A7
Cogan Av, E17 **77** H1
Coin St, SE1 **27** E1
Coity Rd, NW5 **92** A6
Cokers La, SE21
off Perifield **169** J1
Coke St, E1 **21** H3
Colas Ms, NW6
off Birchington Rd **108** D1
Colbeck Ms, SW7 **30** B2
Colbeck Rd, Har. HA1 **67** J7
Colberg Pl, N16 **76** B7
Colborne Way, Wor.Pk.
KT4 **197** J3
Colbrook Av, Hayes
UB3 **121** G3
Colbrook Cl, Hayes UB3 **121** G3
Colburn Av, Pnr. HA5 **51** E6
Colburn Way, Sutton
SM1 **199** G3
Colby Ms, SE19 **170** B5
Colby Rd, SE19 **170** B5
Colchester Av, E12 **98** C3
Colchester Dr, Pnr. HA5 **66** D5
Colchester Rd, E10 **78** C7
E17 **78** A6
Edgware HA8 **54** C7
Northwood HA6 **66** A2
Coldbath Sq, EC1 **11** E5
Coldbath St, SE13 **154** B1
COLDBLOW, Bex. DA5 **177** J2
Cold Blow La, SE14 **133** G7
Cold Blows, Mitch. CR4 **185** J3
Coldershaw Rd, W13 **124** D1
Coldfall Av, N10 **73** J2
Cold Harbour, E14 **134** C2
Coldharbour Crest, SE9
off Great Harry Dr **174** D3
Coldharbour La, SE5 **151** G4
SW9 **151** G4
Hayes UB3 **102** A7
Coldharbour La
Ind Est, SE5
off Coldharbour La **151** J2
Coldharbour Pl, SE5
off Denmark Hill **152** A2
Coldharbour Rd, Croy.
CR0 **201** G5
Coldharbour Way, Croy.
CR0 **201** G5
Coldstream Gdns, SW18 **148** C6
Colebeck Ms, N1 **93** H6
Colebert Av, E1 **113** F4
Colebrook Cl, NW7 **56** A7
SW15
off West Hill **148** A7
Colebrooke Av, W13 **104** E6
Colebrooke Dr, E11 **79** H7
Colebrooke Pl, N1
off St. Peters St **111** H1
Colebrooke Ri, Brom.
BR2 **191** E2
Colebrooke Row, N1 **11** G2
Colebrook Gdns, Loug.
IG10 **49** E2
Colebrook Ho, E14
off Brabazon St **114** B6
Colebrook La, Loug. IG10 **49** E2
Colebrook Path, Loug.
IG10 **49** E2
Colebrook Rd, SW16 **187** E1
Colebrook Way, N11 **58** B5
Coleby Path, SE5
off Harris St **132** A7
Colechurch Ho, SE1
off Avondale Sq **37** H4
Cole Cl, SE28 **138** B1
Coledale Dr, Stan. HA7 **69** F1
Coleford Rd, SW18 **149** F5
Cole Gdns, Houns. TW5 **122** A7
Colegrave Rd, E15 **96** D5
Colegrove Rd, SE15 **37** G6
Coleherne Ct, SW5 **30** B4
Coleherne Ms, SW10 **30** A4
Coleherne Rd, SW10 **30** A4
Colehill Gdns, SW6
off Fulham Palace Rd **148** B1
Colehill La, SW6 **148** B1
Coleman Cl, SE25 **188** D2
Coleman Flds, N1 **111** J1
Coleman Rd, SE5 **36** D7
Belvedere DA17 **139** G4
Dagenham RM9 **101** E6
Colemans Heath, SE9 **174** E3
Coleman St, EC2 **20** B3
Colenso Dr, NW7 **55** G7
Colenso Rd, E5 **95** F4
Ilford IG2 **99** H1
Cole Pk Gdns, Twick. TW1 **144** D6
Cole Pk Rd, Twick. TW1 **144** D6
Cole Pk Vw, Twick. TW1
off Hill Vw Rd **144** D6
Colepits Wd Rd, SE9 **157** F5
Coleraine Rd, N8 **75** G3
SE3 **135** F6
Coleridge Av, E12 **98** B6
Sutton SM1 **199** H4
Coleridge Cl, SW8 **150** B2
Coleridge Gdns, NW6
off Fairhazel Gdns **91** F7
SW10 **30** B7
Coleridge Ho, SW1 **33** F4
Coleridge La, N8
off Coleridge Rd **74** E6
Coleridge Rd, E17 **77** J4
N4 **93** G2
N8 **74** D6
N12 **57** F5
Croydon CR0 **189** F7
Coleridge Sq, SW10 **30** C7
W13 *off Berners Dr* **104** D6
Coleridge Wk, NW11 **72** D4
Coleridge Way, Borwd.
WD6 **38** A4
Hayes UB4 **102** A6
West Drayton UB7 **120** C4
Cole Rd, Twick. TW1 **144** D6
Colesburg Rd, Beck. BR3 **189** J3
Coles Cres, Har. HA2 **85** H2
Coles Grn, Bushey
(Bushey Hth) WD23 **51** J1
Loughton IG10 **48** D1
Coles Grn Ct, NW2 **89** G2
Coles Grn Rd, NW2 **89** G1
Coleshill Flats, SW1
off Pimlico Rd **32** C2
Coleshill Rd, Tedd. TW11 **162** B6
Colestown St, SW11 **149** H2
Cole St, SE1 **28** A4
Colet Cl, N13 **59** H6
Colet Gdns, W14 **128** A4
Coley St, WC1 **10** D6
Colfe Rd, SE23 **171** H1
Colham Av, West Dr.
UB7 **120** B1
Colham Mill Rd, West Dr.
UB7 **120** A2
Colina Ms, N15
off Harringay Rd **75** H5
Colina Rd, N15 **75** H5
Colin Cl, NW9 **71** E4
Croydon CR0 **203** J3
West Wickham BR4 **205** F3
Colin Cres, NW9 **71** F4
Colindale Av, NW9 **70** D3
Colindale Business Pk,
NW9 **70** C3
Colindeep Gdns, NW4 **71** G5
Colindeep La, NW4 **70** E3
NW9 **70** E3
Colin Dr, NW9 **71** F5
Colinette Rd, SW15 **147** J4
Colin Gdns, NW9 **71** F5
Colin Par, NW9
off Edgware Rd **70** E4
Colin Pk Rd, NW9 **70** E4
Colin Rd, NW10 **89** G6
Colinsdale, N1
off Camden Wk **111** H1
Colinton Rd, Ilf. IG3 **100** B2
Coliston Pas, SW18
off Coliston Rd **148** D7
Coliston Rd, SW18 **148** D7
Collamore Av, SW18 **167** H1
Collapit Cl, Har. HA1 **67** H5
Collard Av, Loug. IG10 **49** F2
Collard Grn, Loug. IG10 **49** F2
Collard Pl, NW1
off Harmood St **92** B7
College App, SE10 **134** C6
College Av, Har. HA3 **68** B1
College Cl, E9
off Median Rd **95** F5
N18 **60** C5
Harrow HA3 **52** B7
Twickenham TW2
off Meadway **162** A1
College Cres, NW3 **91** G6
College Cross, N1 **93** G7
College Dr, Ruis. HA4 **66** A7
Thames Ditton KT7 **180** B7
College Gdns, E4 **46** B7
N18 **60** C5
SE21 **170** B1
SW17 **167** H2
Enfield EN2 **44** A1
Ilford IG4 **80** B5
New Malden KT3 **183** F5
College Grn, SE19 **170** B7
College Gro, NW1
off St. Pancras Way **110** D1
College Hill, EC4 **20** A5
College Hill Rd, Har. HA3 **68** C1
College La, NW5 **92** B4
College Ms, SW1 **26** A5
SW18
off St. Ann's Hill **149** E5
★ **College of Arms**, EC4 **19** H5
College Pk Cl, SE13 **154** D4
College Pk Rd, N17 **60** C6
College Pl, E17 **78** E4
NW1 **110** C1
SW10 **30** C7
College Pt, E15 **97** F6
College Rd, E17 **78** C5
N17 **60** C6
N21 **59** G2
NW10 **107** J2
SE19 **170** C5
SE21 **152** B7
SW19 **167** G6
W13 **104** E6
Bromley BR1 **173** G7
Croydon CR0 **202** A2
Enfield EN2 **44** A2
Harrow (Har.Hill) HA1 **68** B6
Harrow (Har.Wld) HA3 **68** B1
Isleworth TW7 **144** C1
Wembley HA9 **87** G1
College Row, E9 **95** G5
College Slip, Bromley
BR1 **191** G1
College St, EC4 **20** A5
College Ter, E3 **113** J3
N3 *off Hendon La* **72** C2
College Vw, SE9 **174** A1
College Wk, Kings.T. KT1
off Grange Rd **181** H3
College Way, Hayes
UB3 **102** A7
College Yd, NW5
off College La **92** B4
Collent St, E9 **95** F6
Colless Rd, N15 **76** C5
Collett Rd, SE16 **29** J6
Collett Way, Sthl. UB2 **123** H1
Collier Cl, E6
off Trader Rd **116** E7
Epsom KT19 **196** A6
Collier Dr, Edg. HA8 **70** A2
COLLIER ROW, Rom.
RM5 **83** G1
Collier Row Rd, Rom.
RM5 **83** F1
Colliers Shaw, Kes. BR2 **206** A4
Collier St, N1 **10** C2
Colliers Water La, Th.Hth.
CR7 **187** G5
COLLIER'S WOOD, SW19 **167** G7
Collindale Av, Erith DA8 **139** H6
Sidcup DA15 **176** A1
Collingbourne Rd, W12 **127** H1
Collingham Gdns, SW5 **30** B2
Collingham Pl, SW5 **30** A2
Collingham Rd, SW5 **30** B1
Collings Cl, N13 **59** F6
N22
off Whittington Rd **59** F6
Collington St, SE10
off Hoskins St **134** D5
Collingtree Rd, SE26 **171** F4
Collingwood Av, N10 **74** A3
Surbiton KT5 **196** C1
Collingwood Cl, SE20 **189** E1
Twickenham TW2 **143** G6
Collingwood Rd, E17 **78** A6
N15 **76** B4
Mitcham CR4 **185** H2
Sutton SM1 **198** D3
Collingwood St, E1 **113** E4
Collins Av, Stan. HA7 **69** H2
Collins Dr, Ruis. HA4 **84** C2
Collinson St, SE1 **27** J4
Collinson Wk, SE1 **27** J4
Collins Rd, N5 **93** J4
Collins Sq, SE3
off Tranquil Vale **155** F2
Collins St, SE3 **155** E2
Collin's Yd, N1
off Islington Grn **111** H1
Collinwood Av, Enf. EN3 **45** F3
Collinwood Gdns, Ilf. IG5 **80** C5
Collis All, Twick. TW2
off The Green **162** B1
Collison Pl, N16 **94** B2
Colls Rd, SE15 **153** F1
Collyer Av, Croy. CR0 **200** E4
Collyer Pl, SE15
off Peckham High St **152** D1
Collyer Rd, Croy. CR0 **201** E4
Colman Rd, E16 **115** J5
Colmar Cl, E1
off Alderney Rd **113** G4
Colmer Pl, Har. HA3 **52** A7
Colmer Rd, SW16 **187** E1
Colmore Ms, SE15 **153** E1
Colmore Rd, Enf. EN3 **45** F4
Colnbrook St, SE1 **27** G6
Colne Ct, Epsom KT19 **196** C4
Colne Ho, Bark. IG11 **99** E6
Colne Rd, E5 **95** H4
N21 **44** A7
Twickenham TW1, TW2 **162** B1
Colne St, E13
off Grange Rd **115** G3
Colney Hatch La, N10 **58** A7
N11 **57** J6
Cologne Rd, SW11 **149** G4
Colombo Rd, Ilf. IG1 **99** F1
Colombo St, SE1 **27** G2
Colomb St, SE10 **135** E5
Colonels Wk, Enf. EN2 **43** H2
Colonial Av, Twick. TW2 **143** J5
Colonial Dr, W4 **126** C4
Colonial Rd, Felt. TW14 **141** H7
Colonnade, WC1 **10** A6
Colonnade Wk, SW1 **32** D2
Colony Ms, N1
off Mildmay Gro N **94** A5
Colorado Apts, N8
off Great Amwell La **75** F3
Colorado Bldg, SE13
off Deals Gateway **154** B1
Colosseum Ter, NW1
off Albany St **8** E5
Colson Gdns, Loug. IG10 **48** D4
Colson Grn, Loug. IG10
off Colson Rd **48** E4
Colson Path, Loug. IG10 **48** D4
Colson Rd, Croy. CR0 **202** B2
Loughton IG10 **48** E4
Colson Way, SW16 **168** C4
Colsterworth Rd, N15 **76** C4
Colston Av, Cars. SM5 **199** H4
Colston Cl, Cars. SM5
off West St **199** J4
Colston Rd, E7 **98** A6
SW14 **146** C4
Colthurst Cres, N4 **93** J2
Colthurst Dr, N9 **60** E3
Coltman St, E14 **113** H5
Coltness Cres, SE2 **138** B5
Colton Gdns, N17 **75** J3
Colton Rd, Har. HA1 **68** B5
Columbia Av, Edg. HA8 **70** B1
Ruislip HA4 **84** B1
Worcester Park KT4 **183** F7
Columbia Pt, SE16
off Moodkee St **133** F3

Columbia Rd, E2 .... **13** F3
E13 .... **115** F4
Columbia Sq, SW14
off Upper Richmond Rd W **146** C4
Columbine Av, E6 .... **116** B5
South Croydon CR2 .... **201** H7
Columbine Way, SE13 .... **154** C2
Columbus Ct, SE16
off Rotherhithe St **133** F1
Columbus Ctyd, E14
off West India Av **134** A1
Columbus Gdns, Nthwd. HA6 .... **66** A1
Colva Wk, N19
off Chester Rd **92** B2
Colvestone Cres, E8 .... **94** C5
Colview Ct, SE9
off Mottingham La **174** A1
Colville Est, N1 .... **112** A1
Colville Gdns, W11 .... **108** C6
Colville Hos, W11 .... **108** C6
Colville Ms, W11
off Lonsdale Rd **108** C6
Colville Pl, W1 .... **17** G2
Colville Rd, E11 .... **96** C3
E17 .... **77** H2
N9 .... **60** E1
W3 .... **126** B3
W11 .... **108** C6
Colville Sq, W11 .... **108** C6
Colville Ter, W11 .... **108** C6
Colvin Cl, SE26 .... **171** F5
Colvin Gdns, E4 .... **62** C3
E11 .... **79** H4
Ilford IG6 .... **81** F1
Colvin Rd, E6 .... **98** B7
Thornton Heath CR7 ... **187** G5
Colwall Gdns, Wdf.Grn. IG8 .... **63** G5
Colwell Rd, SE22 .... **152** C5
Colwick Cl, N6 .... **74** D7
Colwith Rd, W6 .... **127** J6
Colwood Gdns, SW19 .... **167** G7
Colworth Gro, SE17 .... **36** A2
Colworth Rd, E11 .... **78** E6
Croydon CR0 .... **202** D1
Colwyn Av, Grnf. (Perivale) UB6 .... **104** C2
Colwyn Cl, SW16 .... **168** C5
Colwyn Cres, Houns. TW3 .... **143** J1
Colwyn Grn, NW9
off Snowdon Dr **70** E6
Colwyn Ho, SE1
off Briant Est **26** E6
Colwyn Rd, NW2 .... **89** H3
Colyer Cl, N1 .... **10** D1
SE9 .... **175** E2
Colyers La, Erith DA8 .... **159** J1
Colyton Cl, Well. DA16 ... **158** D1
Wembley HA0 .... **87** F6
Colyton La, SW16 .... **169** G5
Colyton Rd, SE22 .... **153** E5
Colyton Way, N18 .... **60** D5
Combe, The, NW1 .... **9** E4
Combe Av, SE3 .... **135** F7
Combedale Rd, SE10 ..... **135** G5
Combemartin Rd, SW18 .... **148** B7
Combe Ms, SE3 .... **135** F7
Comber Cl, NW2 .... **89** H3
Comber Gro, SE5 .... **151** J1
Comber Ho, SE5
off Comber Gro **131** J7
Combermere Rd, SW9 .... **151** F3
Morden SM4 .... **185** E6
Comberton Rd, E5 .... **95** E2
Combeside, SE18 .... **137** J7
Combwell Cres, SE2 ..... **138** A3
Comely Bk Rd, E17 .... **78** C5
Comeragh Ms, W14 ...... **128** B5
Comeragh Rd, W14 ...... **128** B5
Comer Cres, Sthl. UB2
off Windmill Av **123** J2
Comerford Rd, SE4 ...... **153** H4
Comer Ho, Barn. EN5
off Station Rd **41** F4
Comet Cl, E12 .... **98** A4
Comet Pl, SE8 .... **134** A7
Comet Rd, Stai. (Stanw.) TW19 .... **140** A7
Comet St, SE8 .... **134** A7
Comfort St, SE15 .... **36** D6
Commerce Park Croydon, CRO **201** F2
Commerce Rd, N22 .... **75** F1
Brentford TW8 .... **125** F7
Commerce Trade Park, Croy. CRO **201** F3
Commerce Way, Croy. CR0 .... **201** F2
Commercial Rd, E1 .... **21** H3
E14 .... **113** F6
N17 .... **60** B6
N18 .... **60** B5
Commercial St, E1 .... **13** F6
Commercial Way, NW10 .. **106** B2
SE15 .... **132** C7
Commerell Pl, SE10 ...... **135** F5
Commerell St, SE10 ...... **135** E5
Commodity Quay, E1 ..... **21** G6
Commodore Ho, SW18
off Juniper Dr **149** F4
Commodore St, E1 ...... **113** H4
Common, The, E15 .... **97** E6
W5 .... **105** H7
Richmond TW10 .... **163** G3
Southall UB2 .... **122** C4
Stanmore HA7 .... **52** B2
Commondale, SW15 ..... **147** J3
Common La, Esher (Clay.) KT10 .... **194** D7
Common Mile Cl, SW4 ... **150** D5
Common Rd, SW13 ...... **147** G3
Esher (Clay.) KT10 ..... **194** D6
Stanmore HA7 .... **52** A4
Commonside, Kes. BR2 .. **205** J4
Commonside E, Mitch. CR4 .... **185** J3
Commonside W, Mitch. CR4 .... **185** J3
Commonwealth Av, W12 .... **107** H7
Commonwealth Rd, N17 ... **60** D7
Commonwealth Way, SE2 .... **138** B5
Community Cl, Houns. TW5 .... **142** B1
Community La, N7 .... **92** D5
Community Rd, E15 ...... **96** D5
Greenford UB6 .... **103** J1
Como Rd, SE23 .... **171** H2
Compass Cl, Edg. HA8 .... **53** J4
Compass Hill, Rich. TW10 . **145** G6
Compass Ho, SW18
off Smugglers Way ... **149** E4
Compass La, Brom. BR1
off North St **191** G1
Compayne Gdns, NW6 .... **90** E7
Compter Pass, EC2 .... **20** A3
Compton Av, E6 .... **116** A2
N1 .... **93** H6
N6 .... **73** H7
Wembley HA0 .... **87** F4
Compton Cl, E3 .... **114** A5
NW1 .... **9** E4
NW11 *off The Vale* **90** A3
SE15
off Commercial Way .. **132** D7
W13 .... **104** D6
Edgware HA8 .... **54** C7
Compton Ct, SE19 .... **170** B5
Compton Cres, N17 .... **59** J7
W4 .... **126** C6
Chessington KT9 ...... **195** H6
Northolt UB5 .... **102** D1
Compton Ho, SW11
off Parkham St **149** H1
Compton Pas, EC1 .... **11** H5
Compton Pl, WC1 .... **10** A5
Watford WD19 .... **50** E3
Compton Ri, Pnr. HA5 ..... **67** E5
Compton Rd, N1 .... **93** H6
N21 .... **59** G1
NW10 .... **108** A3
SW19 .... **166** C6
Croydon CR0 .... **202** E1
Compton St, EC1 .... **11** G5
Compton Ter, N1 .... **93** H6
Computer Ho, Brent. TW8 .... **125** F6
Comreddy Cl, Enf. EN2 .... **43** H1
Comus Pl, SE17 .... **36** D2
Comyn Rd, SW11 .... **149** H4
Comyns, The, Bushey (Bushey Hth) WD23 ..... **51** J1
Comyns Cl, E16 .... **115** F5
Comyns Rd, Dag. RM9 .... **101** G7
Conant Ms, E1 .... **21** H5
Concanon Rd, SW2 ...... **151** F4
Concert Hall App, SE1 ..... **26** D2
Concord Cl, Nthlt. UB5 ... **102** E3
Concorde Cl, Houns. TW3 .... **143** H2
Concorde Dr, E6 .... **116** C5
Concorde Way, SE16 ..... **133** G4
Concord Rd, W3 .... **106** B4
Enfield EN3 .... **45** F5
Concord Ter, Har. HA2
off Coles Cres **85** H2
Concourse, The, N9
off Edmonton Grn Shop Cen **60** D2
NW9 .... **71** F1
Condell Rd, SW8 .... **150** C1
Conder St, E14
off Salmon La **113** H6
Condor Path, Nthlt. UB5
off Brabazon Rd **103** G2
Condover Cres, SE18 ..... **136** E7
Condray Pl, SW11 .... **129** H7
Conduit Av, SE10
off Crooms Hill **134** D7
Conduit Ct, WC2 .... **18** A5
Conduit La, N18 .... **61** F5
Croydon CR0 .... **202** D5
Enfield EN3
off Morson Rd **45** H6
South Croydon CR2 ... **202** D5
Conduit Ms, SE18 .... **137** E5
W2 .... **14** E4
Conduit Pas, W2 .... **15** E4
Conduit Pl, W2 .... **15** E4
Conduit Rd, SE18 .... **137** E5
Conduit St, W1 .... **17** E5
Conduit Way, NW10 .... **88** C7
Conewood St, N5 .... **93** H3
Coney Acre, SE21 .... **169** J1
Coney Burrows, E4 .... **62** E2
Coneygrove Path, Nthlt. UB5 *off Arnold Rd* **84** E6
CONEY HALL, W.Wick. BR4 .... **205** F3
Coney Hill Rd, W.Wick. BR4 .... **205** E2
Coney Way, SW8 .... **34** D6
Conference Cl, E4
off Greenbank Cl **62** C2
Conference Rd, SE2 ...... **138** C4
Congleton Gro, SE18 ..... **137** F5
Congo Dr, N9 .... **61** F3
Congo Rd, SE18 .... **137** G5
Congress Rd, SE2 .... **138** C4
Congreve Rd, SE9 .... **156** C3
Congreve St, SE17 .... **36** D1
Congreve Wk, E16 .... **116** A5
Conical Cor, Enf. EN2 ..... **43** J2
Conifer Cl, Orp. BR6 ..... **207** G4
Conifer Gdns, SW16 ..... **169** E3
Enfield EN1 .... **44** B6
Sutton SM1 .... **198** E2
Conifers Cl, Teddington TW11 .... **163** E7
Conifer Way, Wem. HA0 .... **87** F3
Coniger Rd, SW6 .... **148** D2
Coningham Ms, W12
off Percy Rd **127** G1
Coningham Rd, W12 ..... **127** H2
Coningsby Av, NW9 .... **70** E2
Coningsby Cotts, W5
off Coningsby Rd **125** G2
Coningsby Gdns, E4 ...... **62** B6
Coningsby Rd, N4 .... **75** H7
W5 .... **125** F2
Conington Rd, SE13 ..... **154** B2
Conisbee Ct, N14 .... **42** C5
Conisborough Cres, SE6 .... **172** C3
Coniscliffe Cl, Chislehurst BR7 .... **192** D1
Coniscliffe Rd, N13 .... **59** J3
Coniston Av, Bark. IG11 .... **99** H7
Greenford (Perivale) UB6 .... **105** E3
Welling DA16 .... **157** H3
Coniston Cl, N20 .... **57** F3
SW13 *off Lonsdale Rd* . **127** F7
SW20 .... **184** A6
W4 .... **146** C1
Barking IG11
off Coniston Av **99** H7
Bexleyheath DA7 ...... **159** J1
Coniston Ct, NW7
off Langstone Way **56** B7
Wallington SM6 .... **200** B4
Conistone Way, N7 .... **93** E7
Coniston Gdns, N9 .... **61** F1
NW9 .... **70** D5
Ilford IG4 .... **80** B4
Pinner HA5 .... **66** A4
Sutton SM2 .... **199** G6
Wembley HA9 .... **87** F1
Coniston Ho, SE5 .... **35** J7
Coniston Rd, N10 .... **74** B2
N17 .... **60** D6
Bexleyheath DA7 ...... **159** J1
Bromley BR1 .... **172** E6
Croydon CR0 .... **188** D7
Twickenham TW2 ...... **143** H6
Coniston Wk, E9
off Clifden Rd **95** F5
Coniston Way, Chess. KT9 .... **195** H3
Conlan St, W10 .... **108** B4
Conley Rd, NW10 .... **89** E6
Conley St, SE10
off Pelton Rd **135** E5
Connaught Av, E4 .... **46** D7
SW14 .... **146** C3
Barnet EN4 .... **57** J1
Enfield EN1 .... **44** B2
Hounslow TW4 .... **143** E5
Loughton IG10 .... **48** A4
Connaught Br, E16 ...... **136** A1
Connaught Business Cen, Mitch. CR4 .... **185** J5
Connaught Cl, E10 .... **95** H2
W2 .... **15** G4
Enfield EN1 .... **44** B2
Sutton SM1 .... **199** G2
Connaught Ct, E17
off Orford Rd **78** B4
Buckhurst Hill IG9
off Chequers **63** H1
Connaught Dr, NW11 ...... **72** D4
Connaught Gdns, N10 ..... **74** B5
N13 .... **59** H4
Morden SM4 .... **185** F4
Connaught Hill, Loug. IG10 .... **48** A4
Connaught La, Ilf. IG1 ..... **99** F2
Connaught Ms, NW3
off Pond St **91** H5
SE18 .... **136** D5
Ilford IG1
off Connaught Rd **99** G2
Connaught Pl, W2 .... **15** J5
Connaught Rd, E4 .... **46** E7
E11 .... **96** D1
E16 .... **136** A1
E17 .... **78** A5
N4 .... **75** G7
NW10 .... **107** E1
SE18 .... **136** D5
W13 .... **104** E7
Barnet EN5 .... **40** A6
Harrow HA3 .... **68** C1
Ilford IG1 .... **99** G2
New Malden KT3 ...... **183** E4
Richmond TW10
off Albert Rd **145** J5
Sutton SM1 .... **199** G2
Teddington TW11 ...... **162** A5
Connaught Rbt, E16 ...... **116** A7
Connaught Sq, W2 .... **15** J4
Connaught St, W2 .... **15** G4
Connaught Way, N13 ...... **59** H4
Connect La, Ilf. (Barkingside) IG6 .... **81** F2
Connell Cres, W5 .... **105** J4
Connemara Cl, Borwd. WD6 .... **38** C6
Connington Cres, E4 ...... **62** D3
Connor Cl, E11 .... **96** E1
Ilford IG6 .... **81** E1
Connor Ct, SW11
off Alfreda St **150** B1
Connor Rd, Dag. RM9 .... **101** F4
Connor St, E9
off Lauriston Rd **113** G1
Conolly Rd, W7 .... **124** B1
Conrad Dr, Wor.Pk. KT4 ... **197** J1
Conrad Ho, N16 .... **94** B5
Consfield Av, N.Mal. KT3 .... **183** G4
Consort Ms, Islw. TW7 .... **144** A5
Consort Rd, SE15 .... **152** E1
Cons St, SE1 .... **27** F3
Constable Av, E16
off Wesley Av **135** H1
Constable Cl, N11
off Friern Barnet La **57** J5
NW11 .... **73** E6
Constable Cres, N15 ...... **76** D5
Constable Gdns, Edg. HA8 .... **70** A1
Isleworth TW7 .... **144** A5
Constable Ho, E14
off Cassilis Rd **134** A2
NW3 *off Adelaide Rd* **91** J7
Constable Ms, Brom. BR1 . **191** H2
Dagenham RM8
off Stonard Rd **100** B4
Constable Wk, SE21 ...... **170** B3
Constance Cl, SW15 ..... **164** D4
Constance Cres, Brom. BR2 .... **191** F7
Constance Rd, Croy. CR0 .... **187** H7
Enfield EN1 .... **44** B6
Sutton SM1 .... **199** F4
Twickenham TW2 ...... **143** H7
Constance St, E16
off Albert Rd **136** B1
Constantine Rd, NW3 ..... **91** H4
Constitution Hill, SW1 .... **24** D3
Constitution Ri, SE18 .... **156** D1
Consul Av, Dag. RM9 ..... **119** J3
Content St, SE17 .... **36** A2
Contessa Cl, Orp. BR6 .... **207** H5
Control Twr Rd, Houns. (Lon.Hthrw Air.) TW6 ... **140** D3
Convair Wk, Nthlt. UB5
off Kittiwake Rd **102** D3
Convent Cl, Barn. EN5 ..... **40** C2
Beckenham BR3 .... **172** C7
Convent Gdns, W5 .... **125** F4
W11
off Kensington Pk Rd . **108** C6
Convent Hill, SE19 .... **169** J6
Convent Way, Sthl. UB2 .. **122** C4
Conway Cl, Stan. HA7 ..... **52** D6
Conway Cres, Grnf. (Perivale) UB6 .... **104** B2
Romford RM6 .... **82** C7
Conway Dr, Hayes UB3 ... **121** F3
Sutton SM2 .... **198** E6

Conway Gdns, Mitch.
CR4 . . . . **186** D4
Wembley HA9 . . . . **69** F7
Conway Gro, W3 . . . . **106** D5
Conway Ms, W1 . . . . **17** F1
Conway Rd, N14 . . . . **59** E3
N15 . . . . **75** H5
NW2 . . . . **89** J2
SE18 . . . . **137** G4
SW20 . . . . **183** J1
Feltham TW13 . . . . **160** D5
Hounslow TW4 . . . . **143** F7
Hounslow
(Lon.Hthrw Air.) TW6
off Inner Ring E **140** E3
Conway St, E13 . . . . **115** G4
W1 . . . . **9** F6
Conway Wk, Hmptn. TW12
off Fearnley Cres **161** F6
Conybeare, NW3
off King Henry's Rd **91** H7
Conyers Cl, Wdf.Grn. IG8 . . **62** E6
Conyers Rd, SW16 . . . . **168** D5
Conyer St, E3 . . . . **113** H2
Conyers Way, Loug. IG10 . . **49** E3
Cooden Cl, Brom. BR1 . . . . **173** H7
Cook Ct, SE16
off Rotherhithe St **133** F1
Cookes Cl, E11 . . . . **97** F2
Cookes La, Sutt. SM3 . . . . **198** B6
Cooke St, Bark. IG11 . . . . . **117** F1
Cookham Cl, Sthl. UB2 . . . **123** H2
Cookham Cres, SE16
off Marlow Way **133** G2
Cookham Dene Cl, Chis.
BR7 . . . . **193** G1
Cookham Rd, Sid. DA14 . . **177** G7
Cookhill Rd, SE2 . . . . **138** B2
Cook Rd, Dag. RM9 . . . . . . **118** E1
Cooks Cl, E14
off Cabot Sq **134** A1
Romford RM5 . . . . **83** J1
Cooks Ferry, N18 . . . . **61** H5
Cooks Ferry Rbt, N18
off Advent Way **61** G5
Cookson Gro, Erith DA8 . . **139** H7
Cook's Rd, E15 . . . . **114** B2
Cooks Rd, SE17 . . . . **35** G5
Coolfin Rd, E16 . . . . **115** G6
Coolgardie Av, E4 . . . . **62** C5
Chigwell IG7 . . . . **64** D3
Coolhurst Rd, N8 . . . . **74** D6
Cool Oak La, NW9 . . . . **71** E7
Coomassie Rd, W9
off Bravington Rd **108** C4
COOMBE, Kings.T. KT2 . . . **164** C7
Coombe Av, Croy. CR0 . . . **202** B4
Coombe Bk, Kings.T.
KT2 . . . . **182** E1
Coombe Cl, Edg. HA8 . . . . . **69** J2
Hounslow TW3 . . . . **143** G4
Coombe Cor, N21 . . . . **59** H1
Coombe Cres, Hmptn.
TW12 . . . . **161** E7
Coombe Dr, Kings.T. KT2 . **164** D7
Ruislip HA4 . . . . **84** B1
Coombe End, Kings.T.
KT2 . . . . **164** D7
Coombefield Cl, N.Mal.
KT3 . . . . **183** E5
Coombe Gdns, SW20 . . . . **183** G2
New Malden KT3 . . . . . . **183** F4
Coombe Hts, Kings.T.
KT2 . . . . **165** E7
Coombe Hill Glade,
Kings.T. KT2 . . . . **165** E7
Coombe Hill Rd, Kings.T.
KT2 . . . . **164** E7
Coombe Ho Chase, N.Mal.
KT3 . . . . **182** D1
Coombehurst Cl, Barn.
EN4 . . . . **41** J2
Coombe La, SW20 . . . . **183** G1
Croydon CR0 . . . . **202** E5
Coombe La W, Kings.T.
KT2 . . . . **164** E7
Coombe Lea, Brom. BR1 . . **192** B3
Coombe Lo, SE7 . . . . **135** J6
Coombe Neville, Kings.T. KT2**164**
D7
Coombe Pk, Kings.T. KT2 . **164** D5
Coombe Ridings, Kings.T. KT2**164**
C5
Coombe Ri, Kings.T. KT2 . . **182** C1
Coombe Rd, N22 . . . . **75** G1
NW10 . . . . **88** D3
SE26 . . . . **170** E4
W4 . . . . **127** E5
W13
off Northcroft Rd **124** E3
Croydon CR0 . . . . **202** A4
Hampton TW12 . . . . **161** F6
Kingston upon Thames
KT2 . . . . **182** A1
New Malden KT3 . . . . . . **182** E2
Coomber Way, Croy. CR0 . **186** D7
Coombes Rd, Dag. RM9 . . **119** F1
Coombe Wk, Sutt. SM1 . . . **198** E3
Coombewood Dr, Rom.
RM6 . . . . **83** F6
Coombe Wd Rd, Kings.T.
KT2 . . . . **164** C5
Coombs St, N1 . . . . **11** H2
Coomer Ms, SW6
off Coomer Pl **128** C6
Coomer Pl, SW6 . . . . **128** C6
Coomer Rd, SW6
off Coomer Pl **128** C6
Cooms Wk, Edg. HA8
off East Rd **70** C1
Cooperage Cl, N17
off Brantwood Rd **60** C6
Cooper Av, E17 . . . . **77** G1
Cooper Cl, SE1 . . . . **27** F4
Cooper Cres, Cars. SM5 . . **199** J3
Cooper Rd, NW4 . . . . **72** A6
NW10 . . . . **89** F5
Croydon CR0 . . . . **201** G4
Coopersale Cl, Wdf.Grn. IG8
off Navestock Cres **63** J7
Coopersale Rd, E9 . . . . **95** G5
Coopers Cl, E1 . . . . **113** F4
Dagenham RM10 . . . . . . **101** H6
Coopers Cres, Borwd.
WD6 . . . . **38** C1
Coopers La, E10 . . . . **96** B1
NW1 . . . . **9** J1
Cooper's La, SE12 . . . . **173** H2
Coopers Ms, Beck. BR3 . . . **190** A2
Coopers Rd, SE1 . . . . **37** G4
Cooper's Row, EC3 . . . . **21** F5
Cooper St, E16
off Lawrence St **115** F5
Coopers Wk, E15
off Maryland St **96** E5
Coopers Yd, N1
off Upper St **93** H7
Cooper's Yd, SE19 . . . . **170** B6
Coote Gdns, Dag. RM8 . . . **101** F3
Coote Rd, Bexh. DA7 . . . . . **159** F1
Dagenham RM8 . . . . **101** F3
Copeland Dr, E14 . . . . **134** A4
Copeland Ho, SE11 . . . . **26** D6
Copeland Rd, E17 . . . . **78** B5
SE15 . . . . **152** D2
Copeman Cl, SE26 . . . . **171** F5
Copenhagen Gdns, W4 . . . **126** C2
Copenhagen Pl, E14 . . . . . . **113** J6
Copenhagen St, N1 . . . . . . **111** E1
Cope Pl, W8 . . . . **128** D3
Copers Cope Rd, Beck.
BR3 . . . . **171** J6
Cope St, SE16 . . . . **133** G4
Copford Cl, Wdf.Grn. IG8 . . . **64** B6
Copford Wk, N1
off Popham St **111** J1
Copgate Path, SW16 . . . . . **169** F6
Copinger Wk, Edg. HA8
off North Rd **70** B1
Copland Av, Wem. HA0 . . . . **87** G5
Copland Cl, Wem. HA0 . . . . **87** F5
Copland Ms, Wem. HA0
off Copland Rd **87** H6
Copland Rd, Wem. HA0 . . . . **87** H6
Copleston Ms, SE15
off Copleston Rd **152** C3
Copleston Pas, SE15 . . . . . **152** C3
Copleston Rd, SE15 . . . . . . **152** C3
Copley Cl, SE17 . . . . **35** H6
W7 . . . . **104** C5
Copley Dene, Brom.
BR1 . . . . **192** A1
Copley Pk, SW16 . . . . **169** F6
Copley Rd, Stan. HA7 . . . . . **53** F5
Copley St, E1 . . . . **113** G5
Coppard Gdns, Chess.
KT9 . . . . **195** F6
Copped Hall, SE21
off Glazebrook Cl **170** A2
Coppelia Rd, SE3 . . . . **155** F4
Coppen Rd, Dag. RM8 . . . . . **83** F7
Copperas St, SE8 . . . . **134** B6
Copper Beech Cl, Ilf. IG5 . . . **80** D1
Copper Beech Ct, Loug.
IG10 . . . . **48** D1
Copper Beeches, Islw. TW7
off Eversley Cres **144** A1
Copper Cl, N17 . . . . **60** E7
SE19 *off Auckland Rd* . . **170** C7
Copperdale Rd, Hayes
UB3 . . . . **122** A2
Copperfield, Chig. IG7 . . . . . **65** G6
Copperfield Ct, Pnr. HA5
off Copperfield Way . . . **67** F4
Copperfield Dr, N15 . . . . **76** C4
Copperfield Ms, N18 . . . . . . **60** B5
Copperfield Rd, E3 . . . . **113** H4
SE28 . . . . **118** C6
Copperfield St, SE1 . . . . **27** H3
Copperfield Way, Chis.
BR7 . . . . **175** F6
Pinner HA5 . . . . **67** F4
Coppergate Cl, Brom.
BR1 . . . . **191** H1
Copper Mead Cl, NW2 . . . . . **89** J3
Copper Ms, W4
off Reynolds Rd **126** C3
Copper Mill Dr, Islw.
TW7 . . . . **144** C2
Coppermill La, E17 . . . . **77** F6
Copper Mill La, SW17 . . . . **167** F4
Copper Row, SE1 . . . . **29** F2
Coppetts Centre, N12 . . . . . **57** J7
Coppetts Cl, N12 . . . . **57** H7
Coppetts Rd, N10 . . . . **74** A2
Coppice, The, Enf. EN2 . . . . **43** H4
Coppice Cl, SW20 . . . . **183** J3
Beckenham BR3 . . . . **190** B4
Stanmore HA7 . . . . **52** C6
Coppice Dr, SW15 . . . . **147** H6
Coppice Wk, N20 . . . . **56** D3
Coppice Way, E18 . . . . **79** F4
Coppies Gro, N11 . . . . **58** A4
Copping Cl, Croy. CR0 . . . . **202** B4
Coppins, The, Croy.
(New Adgtn) CR0 . . . . . . **204** B6
Harrow HA3 . . . . **52** B6
Coppock Cl, SW11 . . . . **149** H2
Coppsfield, W.Mol. KT8
off Hurst Rd **179** G3
Copse, The, E4 . . . . **63** F1
Copse Av, W.Wick. BR4 . . . **204** B3
Copse Cl, SE7 . . . . **135** H6
West Drayton UB7 . . . . . **120** A3
Copse Glade, Surb. KT6 . . . **195** G1
COPSE HILL, SW20 . . . . . . **165** H7
Copse Hill, SW20 . . . . **165** H7
Sutton SM2 . . . . **199** E7
Copsewood Cl, Sid.
DA15 . . . . **157** H6
Coptain Ho, SW18
off Eastfields Av **148** D4
Coptefield Dr, Belv.
DA17 . . . . **138** D3
Copthall Av, EC2 . . . . **20** C3
Copthall Bldgs, EC2 . . . . **20** B3
Copthall Cl, EC2 . . . . **20** B3
Copthall Ct, EC2 . . . . **20** B3
Copthall Dr, NW7 . . . . **55** G7
Copthall Gdns, NW7 . . . . . . **55** G7
Twickenham TW1 . . . . . . **162** C1
Copthorne Av, SW12 . . . . . **150** D7
Bromley BR2 . . . . **206** C2
Ilford IG6 . . . . **65** E6
Copthorne Ms, Hayes
UB3 . . . . **121** H4
Coptic St, WC1 . . . . **18** A2
Copwood Cl, N12 . . . . **57** G4
Coral Apts, E16
off Western Gateway . . **115** G7
Coral Cl, Rom. RM6 . . . . **82** C4
Coraline Cl, Sthl. UB1 . . . . **103** F3
Coralline Wk, SE2 . . . . **138** C2
Coral Row, SW11
off Gartons Way **149** F3
Coral St, SE1 . . . . **27** F4
★ **Coram's Flds**, WC1 . . . . **10** C5
Coram St, WC1 . . . . **10** A6
Coran Cl, N9 . . . . **45** G7
Corban Rd, Houns. TW3 . . **143** G3
Corbden Cl, SE15 . . . . **152** C1
Corbet Cl, Wall. SM6 . . . . . **200** A1
Corbet Ct, EC3 . . . . **20** C4
Corbet Pl, E1 . . . . **21** F1
Corbett Gro, N22 . . . . **58** E7
Corbett Rd, E11 . . . . **79** J6
E17 . . . . **78** C3
Corbetts La, SE16
off Rotherhithe New Rd **133** F4
Corbetts Pas, SE16
off Silwood St **133** F4
Corbicum, E11 . . . . **79** E7
Corbidge Ct, SE8
off Glaisher St **134** B6
Corbiere Ct, SW19
off Thornton Rd **166** A6
Corbiere Ho, N1 . . . . **112** B1
Corbin Ho, E3
off Bromley High St . . **114** B3
Corbins La, Har. HA2 . . . . . . **85** H3
Corbridge Cres, E2 . . . . **112** E2
Corby Cres, Enf. EN2 . . . . . . **43** E4
Corbylands Rd, Sid.
DA15 . . . . **157** H7
Corbyn St, N4 . . . . **93** E1
Corby Rd, NW10 . . . . **106** D2
Corby Way, E3
off Knapp Rd **114** A4
Cordelia Cl, SE24 . . . . **151** H4
Cordelia Gdns, Stai.
TW19 . . . . **140** B7
Cordelia Rd, Stai.
TW19 . . . . **140** B7
Cordelia St, E14 . . . . **114** B6
Cordell Ho, N15 . . . . **76** D5
Cording St, E14
off Chrisp St **114** B5
Cordwainers Wk, E13
off Richmond St **115** G2
Cord Way, E14
off Mellish St **134** A3
Cordwell Rd, SE13 . . . . **154** E5
Corefield Cl, N11
off Benfleet Way **58** A2
Corelli Rd, SE3 . . . . **156** B2
Corfe Av, Har. HA2 . . . . **85** G4
Corfe Cl, Borwd. WD6 . . . . . **38** D3
Hayes UB4 . . . . **102** C6
Hounslow TW4
off Farm Rd **161** E1
Corfe Ho, SW8
off Dorset Rd **34** C7
Corfe Twr, W3 . . . . **126** B2
Corfield Rd, N21 . . . . **43** F5
Corfield St, E2 . . . . **113** E3
Corfton Rd, W5 . . . . **105** H6
Coriander Av, E14 . . . . **114** D6
Cories Cl, Dag. RM8 . . . . . . **100** D2
Corinium Cl, Wem. HA9 . . . . **87** J4
Corinne Rd, N19 . . . . **92** C4
Corinthian Way, Stai.
(Stanw.) TW19
off Clare Rd **140** A7
Corker Wk, N7 . . . . **93** F2
Corkran Rd, Surb. KT6 . . . . **181** G7
Corkscrew Hill, W.Wick.
BR4 . . . . **204** D2
Cork Sq, E1
off Smeaton St **132** E1
Cork St, W1 . . . . **17** F6
Cork St Ms, W1 . . . . **17** F6
Cork Tree Retail Pk, E4 . . . . . **61** H5
Cork Tree Way, E4 . . . . **61** H5
Corlett St, NW1 . . . . **15** G1
Cormont Rd, SE5 . . . . **151** H1
Cormorant Cl, E17 . . . . **77** G1
Cormorant Ho, Enf. EN3
off Alma Rd **45** G5
Cormorant Pl, Sutt. SM1
off Sandpiper Rd **198** C5
Cormorant Rd, E7 . . . . **97** F4
Cornbury Rd, Edg. HA8 . . . . **53** G7
Cornelia Dr, Hayes UB4 . . . **102** C4
Cornelia St, N7 . . . . **93** F6
Cornell Cl, Sid. DA14 . . . . . **177** E6
Cornell Ct, Enf. EN3 . . . . **45** H3
Corner Fielde, SW2
off Streatham Hill **169** E1
Corner Grn, SE3 . . . . **155** G3
Corner Ho St, WC2 . . . . **26** A1
Corner Mead, NW9 . . . . **55** F7
Corney Reach Way, W4 . . . **127** E7
Corney Rd, W4 . . . . **127** E6
Cornflower La, Croy.
CR0 . . . . **203** G1
Cornflower Ter, SE22 . . . . . **152** E6
Cornford Cl, Brom. BR2 . . . **191** G5
Cornford Gro, SW12 . . . . . **168** B2
Cornhill, EC3 . . . . **20** C4
Cornish Ct, N9 . . . . **44** E7
Cornish Gro, SE20 . . . . **171** E7
Cornish Ho, SE17 . . . . **35** G6
Brentford TW8
off Green Dragon La . . **125** J5
Corn Mill Dr, Orp. BR6 . . . . **193** J7
Cornmill La, SE13 . . . . **154** B3
Cornmow Dr, NW10 . . . . **89** F5
Cornshaw Rd, Dag. RM8 . . **100** D1
Cornthwaite Rd, E5 . . . . **95** F3
Cornwall Av, E2 . . . . **113** F3
N3 . . . . **56** D7
N22 . . . . **75** E1
Esher (Clay.) KT10
off The Causeway **194** C7
Southall UB1 . . . . **103** F5
Welling DA16 . . . . **157** H3
Cornwall Cl, Bark. IG11 . . . . **99** J6
Cornwall Cres, W11 . . . . . . **108** B7
Cornwall Dr, Orp. BR5 . . . . **176** C7
Cornwall Gdns, NW10 . . . . . **89** H6
SW7 . . . . **22** B6
Cornwall Gdns Wk, SW7 . . . **22** B6
Cornwall Gro, W4 . . . . **127** E5
Cornwallis Av, N9 . . . . **61** E2
SE9 . . . . **175** G2
Cornwallis Ct, SW8
off Allen Edwards Dr . . **150** E1
Cornwallis Gro, N9 . . . . **61** E2
Cornwallis Rd, E17 . . . . **77** G4
N9 . . . . **61** E2
N19 . . . . **92** E2
SE18 . . . . **137** F4
Dagenham RM9 . . . . **100** D4
Cornwallis Sq, N19 . . . . **92** E2
Cornwallis Wk, SE9 . . . . . . **156** C3
Cornwall Ms S, SW7 . . . . . . **22** C6
Cornwall Ms W, SW7 . . . . . . **22** B6
Cornwall Rd, N4 . . . . **75** G7
N15 . . . . **76** A5
N18 . . . . **60** D5
SE1 . . . . **26** E1
Croydon CR0 . . . . **201** H2
Esher (Clay.) KT10 . . . . . **194** D7
Harrow HA1 . . . . **67** J6
Pinner HA5 . . . . **51** F7
Sutton SM2 . . . . **198** C7
Twickenham TW1 . . . . . . **162** D1
Cornwall Sq, SE11 . . . . **35** F3

Cornwall St, E1
off Watney St **113** E7
Cornwall Ter, NW1 . . . . **8** A6
Cornwall Ter Ms, NW1 . . . . . . **8** A6
Corn Way, E11 . . . . **96** D3
Cornwood Cl, N2 . . . . **73** G5
Cornwood Dr, E1 . . . . **113** F6
Cornworthy Rd, Dag. RM8 . . . . **100** C5
Corona Rd, SE12 . . . . **155** G7
Coronation Av, N16
off Victorian Rd **94** C3
Coronation Cl, Bex. DA5 . . **158** D6
Ilford IG6 . . . . **81** F4
Coronation Rd, E13 . . . . . . **115** J3
NW10 . . . . **106** A4
Hayes UB3 . . . . **121** J4
Coronation Wk, Twick. TW2 . . . . **161** F1
Coronet St, N1 . . . . **12** D4
Corporation Av, Houns. TW4 . . . . **142** E4
Corporation Row, EC1 . . . . . **11** F5
Corporation St, E15 . . . . . . **115** E2
N7 . . . . **92** E5
Corrance Rd, SW2 . . . . **151** E4
Corri Av, N14 . . . . **58** D4
Corrib Dr, Sutt. SM1 . . . . . **199** H5
Corrigan Cl, NW4 . . . . **71** J3
Corringham Ct, NW11
off Corringham Rd **72** D7
Corringham Rd, NW11 . . . . . **72** D7
Wembley HA9 . . . . **88** A2
Corringway, NW11 . . . . **72** E7
W5 . . . . **106** A4
Corris Grn, NW9
off Snowdon Dr **70** E6
Corry Dr, SW9 . . . . **151** H4
Corsair Cl, Stai. TW19 . . . . **140** A7
Corsair Rd, Stai. TW19 . . . . **140** B7
Corscombe Cl, Kings.T. KT2 . . . . **164** C5
Corsehill St, SW16 . . . . **168** C6
Corsham St, N1 . . . . **12** C4
Corsica St, N5 . . . . **93** H6
Cortayne Rd, SW6 . . . . **148** C2
Cortina Dr, Dag. RM9 . . . . . **119** J3
Cortis Rd, SW15 . . . . **147** H6
Cortis Ter, SW15 . . . . **147** H6
Cortland Cl, Wdf.Grn. IG8 . . **79** J1
Corunna Rd, SW8 . . . . **150** C1
Corunna Ter, SW8 . . . . **150** C1
Corvette Sq, SE10
off Feathers Pl **134** D6
Coryton Path, W9
off Fernhead Rd **108** C4
Cosbycote Av, SE24 . . . . . . **151** J5
Cosdach Av, Wall. SM6 . . . **200** D7
Cosedge Cres, Croy. CR0 . . . . **201** G5
Cosgrove Cl, N21 . . . . **59** J2
Hayes UB4
off Kingsash Dr **102** E4
Cosmo Pl, WC1 . . . . **18** B1
Cosmur Cl, W12 . . . . **127** F3
Cossall Wk, SE15 . . . . **153** E1
Cossar Ms, SW2 . . . . **151** G6
Cosser St, SE1 . . . . **26** E5
Costa St, SE15 . . . . **152** D2
Costons Av, Grnf. UB6 . . . . **104** A3
Costons La, Grnf. UB6 . . . . **104** A3
Coston Wk, SE4
off Hainford Cl **153** G4
Cosway St, NW1 . . . . **15** H1
Cotall St, E14 . . . . **114** A6
Coteford Cl, Loug. IG10 . . . . **48** E2
Pinner HA5 . . . . **66** A5
Coteford St, SW17 . . . . **167** J4
Cotelands, Croy. CR0 . . . . . **202** B3
Cotesbach Rd, E5 . . . . **95** F3
Cotesmore Gdns, Dag. RM8 . . . . **100** C4
Cotford Rd, Th.Hth. CR7 . . **187** J4
Cotham St, SE17 . . . . **36** A2
Cotherstone Rd, SW2 . . . . **169** F1
Cotleigh Av, Bex. DA5 . . . . **176** D2
Cotleigh Rd, NW6 . . . . **90** D7
Cotman Cl, NW11 . . . . **73** F6
SW15 . . . . **148** A6
Cotman Gdns, Edgware HA8 . . . . **70** A2
Cotman Ms, Dag. RM8
off Highgrove Rd **100** C5
Cotmans Cl, Hayes UB3 . . **122** A1
Coton Rd, Well. DA16 . . . . . **158** A3
Cotsford Av, N.Mal. KT3 . . **182** C5
Cotswold Cl, Esher (Hinch.Wd) KT10 . . . . . . **194** C3
Kingston upon Thames KT2 . . . . **164** B6
Cotswold Ct, EC1 . . . . **11** J5
N11 . . . . **58** A4
Cotswold Gdns, E6 . . . . . . **116** A3
NW2 . . . . **90** A2
Ilford IG2 . . . . **81** G7
Cotswold Gate, NW2
off Cotswold Gdns **90** B1
Cotswold Grn, Enf. EN2
off Cotswold Way **43** F4
Cotswold Ms, SW11
off Battersea High St . . **149** G1
Cotswold Ri, Orp. BR6 . . . **193** J6
Cotswold Rd, Hmptn. TW12 . . . . **161** G6
Cotswold St, SE27
off Norwood High St . . **169** H4
Cotswold Way, Enf. EN2 . . . **43** F4
Worcester Park KT4 . . . . **197** J2
Cottage Av, Brom. BR2 . . . **206** B1
Cottage Cl, Har. HA2 . . . . . . **86** B2
Cottage Fld Cl, Sid. DA14 . . . . **176** C1
Cottage Grn, SE5 . . . . **36** C7
Cottage Gro, SW9 . . . . **150** E3
Surbiton KT6 . . . . **181** G6
Cottage Pl, SW3 . . . . **23** G5
Cottage Rd, N7 . . . . **93** F5
Epsom KT19 . . . . **196** D7
Cottage St, E14 . . . . **114** B7
Cottage Wk, N16
off Brooke Rd **94** C3
Cottenham Dr, NW9 . . . . . . **71** F3
SW20 . . . . **165** H7
Cottenham Par, SW20
off Durham Rd **183** H2
COTTENHAM PARK, SW20 . . . . **183** H1
Cottenham Pk Rd, SW20 . . . . **165** H7
Cottenham Pl, SW20 . . . . . **165** H7
Cottenham Rd, E17 . . . . **77** J4
Cotterill Rd, Surb. KT6 . . . **195** H2
Cottesbrook St, SE14
off Nynehead St **133** H7
Cottesloe Ms, SE1 . . . . **27** F5
Cottesmore Av, Ilf. IG5 . . . . **80** D2
Cottesmore Gdns, W8 . . . . . **22** B5
Cottimore Cres, Walt. KT12 . . . . **178** B7
Cottimore La, Walt. KT12 . . . . **178** B7
Cottimore Ter, Walt. KT12 . . . . **178** B7
Cottingham Chase, Ruis. HA4 . . . . **84** A3
Cottingham Rd, SE20 . . . . **171** G7
SW8 . . . . **34** D6
Cottington Rd, Felt. TW13 . . . . **160** D4
Cottington St, SE11 . . . . **35** F3
Cottle Way, SE16
off St. Marychurch St . **133** F2
Cotton Av, W3 . . . . **106** D6
Cotton Cl, E11 . . . . **97** E2
Dagenham RM9
off Flamstead Rd **100** C7
Cottongrass Cl, Croy. CR0
off Cornflower La **203** G1
Cotton Hill, Brom. BR1 . . . **172** D4
Cotton Row, SW11 . . . . **149** F3
Cottons Gdns, E2 . . . . **13** E3
Cottons La, SE1 . . . . **28** C1
Cotton St, E14 . . . . **114** C7
Cottrell Ct, SE10
off Greenroof Way **135** F4
Cottrill Gdns, E8
off Marcon Pl **94** E6
Cotts Cl, W7
off Westcott Cres **104** C6
Couchmore Av, Esher KT10 . . . . **194** B2
Ilford IG5 . . . . **80** C2
Coulgate St, SE4 . . . . **153** H3
Coulson Cl, Dag. RM8 . . . . . **82** C7
Coulson St, SW3 . . . . **31** J3
Coulter Cl, Hayes UB4
off Berrydale Rd **102** E4
Coulter Rd, W6 . . . . **127** H3
Councillor St, SE5 . . . . **131** J7
Counter Ct, SE1
off Borough High St . . . **28** B2
Counter St, SE1 . . . . **28** D1
Countess Rd, NW5 . . . . **92** C5
Countisbury Av, Enf. EN1 . . **44** C7
Country Way, Felt. (Han.) TW13 . . . . **160** B7
Sunbury-on-Thames TW16 . . . . **160** B7
County Gate, SE9 . . . . **175** F3
Barnet (New Barn.) EN5 . . . . **41** E6
County Gro, SE5 . . . . **151** J1
★ **County Hall**, SE1 . . . . . . **26** C3
County Rd, E6 . . . . **116** E5
Thornton Heath CR7 . . . **187** H2
County St, SE1 . . . . **28** A6
Coupland Pl, SE18 . . . . **137** F5
Courcy Rd, N8 . . . . **75** G3
Courier Rd, Dag. RM9 . . . . **119** J4
Courland Gro, SW8 . . . . . . **150** D1
Courland Gro Hall, SW8 . . **150** D2
Courland St, SW8 . . . . **150** D1
Course, The, SE9 . . . . **174** D3
Court, The, Ruis. HA4 . . . . . **84** E4
Courtauld Cl, SE28 . . . . . . **138** A1
★ **Courtauld Inst of Art**, WC2 . . . . **18** C5
Courtauld Rd, N19 . . . . **92** D1
Court Av, Belv. DA17 . . . . . **139** F5
Court Cl, Har. HA3 . . . . **69** H3
Twickenham TW2 . . . . . . **161** H3
Wallington SM6 . . . . **200** D7
Court Cl Av, Twick. TW2 . . . **161** H3
Court Cres, Chess. KT9 . . . **195** G5
Court Downs Rd, Beck. BR3 . . . . **190** B2
Court Dr, Croy. CR0 . . . . . . **201** F4
Stanmore HA7 . . . . **53** H4
Sutton SM1 . . . . **199** H4
Courtenay Av, N6 . . . . **73** H6
Harrow HA3 . . . . **67** J1
Courtenay Dr, Beck. BR3 . . **190** D2
Courtenay Gdns, Har. HA3 . . . . **67** J2
Courtenay Ms, E17
off Cranbrook Ms **77** H5
Courtenay Pl, E17 . . . . **77** H5
Courtenay Rd, E11 . . . . **97** F3
E17 . . . . **77** G4
SE20 . . . . **171** G7
Wembley HA9 . . . . **87** G3
Worcester Park KT4 . . . . **197** J3
Courtenay Sq, SE11 . . . . **34** E4
Courtenay St, SE11 . . . . **34** E3
Courtens Ms, Stan. HA7 . . . **53** F7
Court Fm Av, Epsom KT19 . . . . **196** D5
Court Fm Rd, SE9 . . . . **174** A2
Northolt UB5 . . . . **85** G7
Courtfield, W5
off Castlebar Hill **105** F5
Courtfield Av, Har. HA1 . . . . **68** C5
Courtfield Cres, Har. HA1 . . **68** C5
Courtfield Gdns, SW5 . . . . . **30** B1
W13 . . . . **104** D6
Courtfield Ms, SW5 . . . . **30** C2
Courtfield Ri, W.Wick. BR4 . . . . **204** D3
Courtfield Rd, SW7 . . . . **30** B2
Court Gdns, N7 . . . . **93** G6
Courtgate Cl, NW7 . . . . **55** F6
Courthill Rd, SE13 . . . . **154** C4
Courthope Rd, NW3 . . . . **91** J4
SW19 . . . . **166** B5
Greenford UB6 . . . . **104** A2
Courthope Vil, SW19 . . . . . **166** B7
Court Ho Gdns, N3 . . . . **56** D6
Courthouse Rd, N12 . . . . . . **56** E6
Courtland Av, E4 . . . . **63** F2
NW7 . . . . **54** D3
SW16 . . . . **169** F7
Ilford IG1 . . . . **98** C2
Courtland Dr, Chig. IG7 . . . . **65** E3
Courtland Gro, SE28 . . . . . **118** D7
Courtland Rd, E6
off Harrow Rd **116** B1
Courtlands, Rich. TW10 . . . **146** A4
Courtlands Av, SE12 . . . . . **155** H5
Bromley BR2 . . . . **205** F1
Hampton TW12 . . . . **161** F6
Richmond TW9 . . . . **146** B2
Courtlands Dr, Epsom KT19 . . . . **197** E6
Courtlands Rd, Surb. KT5 . . . . **182** A7
Court La, SE21 . . . . **152** B6
Court La Gdns, SE21 . . . . . **152** B7
Courtleet Dr, Erith DA8 . . . . **159** H1
Courtleigh Gdns, NW11 . . . . **72** B4
Courtman Rd, N17 . . . . **59** J7
Court Mead, Nthlt. UB5 . . . **103** F3
Courtmead Cl, SE24 . . . . . **151** J6
Courtnell St, W2 . . . . **108** D6
Courtney Cl, SE19 . . . . **170** B6
Courtney Cres, Cars. SM5 . . . . **199** J7
Courtney Pl, Croy. CR0 . . . **201** G3
Courtney Rd, N7
off Bryantwood Rd **93** G5
SW19 . . . . **167** H7
Croydon CR0 . . . . **201** G3
Hounslow (Lon.Hthrw Air.) TW6 . . **140** D3
Courtney Way, Houns. (Lon.Hthrw Air.) TW6 . . . **140** D3
Court Par, Wem. HA0 . . . . . . **86** E3
Courtrai Rd, SE23 . . . . **153** H6
Court Rd, SE9 . . . . **174** B2
SE25 . . . . **188** C2
Southall UB2 . . . . **123** F4
Courtside, N8 . . . . **74** D6
Court St, E1
off Whitechapel Rd . . . **112** E5
Bromley BR1 . . . . **191** G2
Court Way, NW9 . . . . **71** E4
W3 . . . . **106** C5
Ilford IG6 . . . . **81** F3
Twickenham TW2 . . . . . . **144** C7
Courtway, Wdf.Grn. IG8 . . . **63** J5
Courtway, The, Wat. WD19 . . . . **51** E2
Court Yd, SE9 . . . . **156** B6
Courtyard, The, N1 . . . . **93** F7
Keston BR2 . . . . **206** B6
Courtyard Ho, SW6
off Lensbury Av **149** F2
Courtyard Ms, Orp. BR5
off Dorchester Cl **176** A7
Cousin La, EC4 . . . . **20** B6
Couthurst Rd, SE3 . . . . **135** H6
Coutts Av, Chess. KT9 . . . . **195** H5
Coutts Cres, NW5 . . . . **92** A3
Coval Gdns, SW14 . . . . **146** B4
Coval La, SW14 . . . . **146** B4
Coval Pas, SW14
off Coval Rd **146** C4
Coval Rd, SW14 . . . . **146** B4
Covelees Wall, E6 . . . . **116** D6
Covell Ct, SE8
off Reginald Sq **134** A7
★ **Covent Garden**, WC2 . . . **18** B5
Covent Gdn Mkt, WC2 . . . . . **18** B5
Coventry Cl, E6
off Harper Rd **116** C6
NW6
off Kilburn High Rd . . . **108** D1
Coventry Rd, E1 . . . . **113** E4
E2 . . . . **113** E4
SE25 . . . . **188** D4
Ilford IG1 . . . . **98** E1
Coventry St, W1 . . . . **17** H6
Coverack Cl, N14 . . . . **42** C6
Croydon CR0 . . . . **189** H7
Coverdale Cl, Stan. HA7 . . . **53** E5
Coverdale Gdns, Croy. CR0
off Park Hill Ri **202** C3
Coverdale Rd, N11 . . . . **58** A6
NW2 . . . . **90** A7
W12 . . . . **127** H1
Coverdales, The, Bark. IG11 . . . . **117** F2
Coverley Cl, E1 . . . . **21** J1
Covert, The, Orp. BR6 . . . . **193** H6
Coverton Rd, SW17 . . . . . . **167** H5
Covert Rd, Ilf. IG6 . . . . **65** J6
Covert Way, Barn. EN4 . . . . **41** F2
Covet Wd Cl, Orp. BR5 . . . **193** J6
Covey Cl, SW19 . . . . **184** E2
Covington Gdns, SW16 . . . **169** H7
Covington Way, SW16 . . . . **169** F6
Cowan Cl, E6
off Oliver Gdns **116** B5
Cowbridge La, Bark. IG11 . . **98** E7
Cowbridge Rd, Har. HA3 . . . **69** J4
Cowcross St, EC1 . . . . **19** G1
Cowdenbeath Path, N1 . . . **111** F1
Cowden Rd, Orp. BR6 . . . . **193** J7
Cowden St, SE6 . . . . **172** A4
Cowdrey Cl, Enf. EN1 . . . . . **44** B2
Cowdrey Rd, SW19 . . . . . . **167** E5
Cowdry Rd, E9
off East Cross Route . . . **95** J6
Cowen Av, Har. HA2 . . . . **85** J2
Cowgate Rd, Grnf. UB6 . . . **104** A2
Cowick Rd, SW17 . . . . **167** J4
Cowings Mead, Nthlt. UB5 . . . . **85** E7
Cowland Av, Enf. EN3 . . . . . **45** F4
Cow La, Grnf. UB6 . . . . **104** A2
Cow Leaze, E6 . . . . **116** D6
Cowleaze Rd, Kings.T. KT2 . . . . **181** H1
Cowley Est, SW9 . . . . **151** G1
Cowley Pl, NW4 . . . . **71** J5
Cowley Rd, E11 . . . . **79** H5
SW9 . . . . **151** G1
SW14 . . . . **146** E3
W3 . . . . **127** F1
Ilford IG1 . . . . **80** C7
Cowley St, SW1 . . . . **26** A5
Cowling Cl, W11
off Wilsham St **128** B1
Cowper Av, E6 . . . . **98** B7
Sutton SM1 . . . . **199** G4
Cowper Cl, Brom. BR2 . . . . **192** A4
Welling DA16 . . . . **158** A5
Cowper Gdns, N14 . . . . **42** C6
Wallington SM6 . . . . **200** C6
Cowper Rd, N14 . . . . **58** B1
N16 . . . . **94** B5
N18 . . . . **60** D5
SW19 . . . . **167** F6
W3 . . . . **126** D1
W7 . . . . **104** C7
Belvedere DA17 . . . . **139** G4
Bromley BR2 . . . . **192** A4
Kingston upon Thames KT2 . . . . **163** J5
Cowpers Ct, EC3
off Birchin La **20** C4
Cowper St, EC2 . . . . **12** C5
Cowper Ter, W10
off St. Quintin Av **108** A5
Cowslip Rd, E18 . . . . **79** H2
Cowthorpe Rd, SW8 . . . . . **150** D1

Coxe Pl, Har. (Wealds.) HA3 **68** D4
Cox La, Chess. KT9 **195** J4
Epsom KT19 **196** B5
Coxmount Rd, SE7 **136** A5
Coxson Way, SE1 **29** F4
Cox's Wk, SE21 **170** D1
Coxwell Rd, SE18 **137** G5
SE19 **170** B7
Coxwold Path, Chess. KT9
off Garrison La **195** H7
Crabbs Cft Cl, Orp. BR6
off Ladycroft Way **207** F5
Crab Hill, Beck. BR3 **172** D7
Crabtree Av, Rom. RM6 **82** D4
Wembley HA0 **105** H2
Crabtree Cl, E2 **13** F1
Crabtree La, SW6 **128** A7
Crabtree Manorway Ind Est, Belv. DA17 **139** H3
Crabtree Manorway N, Belv. DA17 **139** J2
Crabtree Manorway S, Belv. DA17 **139** J3
Crace St, NW1 **9** H3
Craddock Rd, Enf. EN1 **44** C3
Craddock St, NW5
off Prince of Wales Rd **92** A6
Cradley Rd, SE9 **175** G1
Craigen Av, Croy. CR0 **203** E1
Craigen Gdns, Ilf. IG3 **99** H4
Craigerne Rd, SE3 **135** H7
Craig Gdns, E18 **79** F2
Craigholm, SE18 **156** D2
Craigmuir Pk, Wem. HA0 **105** J1
Craignair Rd, SW2 **151** G7
Craignish Av, SW16 **187** F2
Craig Pk Rd, N18 **60** E5
Craig Rd, Rich. TW10 **163** F4
Craigs Ct, SW1 **26** A1
Craigton Rd, SE9 **156** C4
Craigweil Cl, Stan. HA7 **53** G5
Craigweil Dr, Stan. HA7 **53** G5
Craigwell Av, Felt. TW13 **160** A3
Craik Ct, NW6
off Carlton Vale **108** C2
Crail Row, SE17 **36** C2
Cramer Ct, N.Mal. KT3
off Warwick Rd **182** C3
Cramer St, W1 **16** C2
Crammond Cl, W6 **128** B6
Crampton Rd, SE20 **171** F6
Crampton St, SE17 **35** J2
Cranberry Cl, Nthlt. UB5
off Parkfield Av **102** D2
Cranberry La, E16 **114** E4
Cranborne Av, Sthl. UB2 **123** G4
Surbiton KT6 **196** A3
Cranborne Rd, Bark. IG11 **117** G1
Cranborne Waye, Hayes UB4 **102** C7
Cranbourn All, WC2
off Cranbourn St **17** J5
Cranbourne Av, E11 **79** H4
Cranbourne Cl, SW16 **187** E3
Cranbourne Dr, Pnr. HA5 **66** D5
Cranbourne Gdns, NW11 **72** B5
Ilford IG6 **81** F3
Cranbourne Pas, SE16
off Marigold St **132** E2
Cranbourne Rd, E12
off High St N **98** B5
E15 **96** C4
N10 **74** B2
Cranbourn St, WC2 **17** J5
CRANBROOK, Ilf. IG1 **98** C1
Cranbrook Cl, Bromley BR2 **191** G6
Cranbrook Dr, Twick. TW2 **161** H1
Cranbrook Ho, E5
off Pembury Rd **94** E5
Cranbrook La, N11 **58** B4
Cranbrook Ms, E17 **77** H5
Cranbrook Pk, N22 **75** F1
Cranbrook Ri, Ilf. IG1 **80** C7
Cranbrook Rd, SE8 **154** A1
SW19 **166** B7
W4 **127** E5
Barnet EN4 **41** G6
Bexleyheath DA7 **159** F1
Hounslow TW4 **143** F4
Ilford IG1, IG2, IG6 **80** D7
Thornton Heath CR7 **187** J2
Cranbrook St, E2
off Mace St **113** G2
Cranbury Rd, SW6 **149** E2
Crandale Ho, E5
off Pembury Rd **94** E5
Crane Av, W3 **106** C7
Isleworth TW7 **144** D5
Cranebank Ms, Twick. TW1 **144** D4
Cranebrook, Twick. TW2
off Manor Rd **161** J2
Crane Cl, Dag. RM10 **101** G6
Harrow HA2 **85** J3
Crane Ct, EC4 **19** F4
Epsom KT19 **196** C4
Craneford Cl, Twick. TW2 **144** C7
Craneford Way, Twick. TW2 **144** B7
Crane Gdns, Hayes UB3 **121** J4
Crane Gro, N7 **93** G6
Crane Ho, SE15
off Talfourd Pl **152** C1
Crane Lo Rd, Houns. TW5 **122** B6
Crane Pk Rd, Twick. TW2 **161** H2
Crane Rd, Twick. TW2 **162** B1
Cranesbill Cl, NW9
off Annesley Av **70** D3
Cranes Dr, Surb. KT5 **181** H4
Cranes Pk, Surb. KT5 **181** H4
Cranes Pk Av, Surb. KT5 **181** H4
Cranes Pk Cres, Surb. KT5 **181** J4
Crane St, SE10 **134** D5
SE15 **152** C1
Craneswater, Hayes UB3 **121** J7
Craneswater Pk, Sthl. UB2 **123** F5
Cranes Way, Borwd. WD6 **38** C5
Crane Way, Twick. TW2 **143** J7
Cranfield Cl, SE27
off Norwood High St **169** J3
Cranfield Dr, NW9 **54** E7
Cranfield Rd, SE4 **153** J3
Cranfield Row, SE1 **27** F5
CRANFORD, Houns. TW5 **122** A7
Cranford Av, N13 **59** E5
Staines TW19 **140** B7
Cranford Cl, SW20 **183** H1
Staines TW19 **140** B7
Cranford Cotts, E1
off Cranford St **113** G7
Cranford Dr, Hayes UB3 **121** J4
Cranford La, Hayes UB3 **121** G6
Hounslow (Heston) TW5 **122** D7
Hounslow (Lon.Hthrw Air.) TW6 **141** J3
Hounslow (Lon.Hthrw Air.N) TW6 **141** J1
Cranford Ms, Kes. BR2 **192** B5
Cranford Pk Rd, Hayes UB3 **121** J4
Cranford St, E1 **113** G7
Cranford Way, N8 **75** F5
Cranhurst Rd, NW2 **89** J5
Cranleigh Cl, SE20 **188** E2
Bexley DA5 **159** H6
Cranleigh Ct, Mitch. CR4
off Phipps Br Rd **185** G3
Cranleigh Gdns, N21 **43** G5
SE25 **188** B3
Barking IG11 **99** G7
Harrow HA3 **69** H5
Kingston upon Thames KT2 **163** J6
Loughton IG10 **48** C6
Southall UB1 **103** F6
Sutton SM1 **198** E2
Cranleigh Gdns Ind Est, Sthl. UB1
off Cranleigh Gdns **103** F5
Cranleigh Ms, SW11 **149** H2
Cranleigh Rd, N15 **75** J5
SW19 **184** D3
Cranleigh St, NW1 **9** G2
Cranley Dene Ct, N10 **74** B4
Cranley Dr, Ilf. IG2 **81** F7
Cranley Gdns, N10 **74** C4
N13 **59** F3
SW7 **30** D3
Wallington SM6 **200** C7
Cranley Ms, SW7 **30** D3
Cranley Par, SE9
off Beaconsfield Rd **174** B4
Cranley Pl, SW7 **31** E2
Cranley Rd, E13 **115** H5
Ilford IG2 **81** F6
Cranmer Av, W13 **124** E3
Cranmer Cl, Mord. SM4 **184** A6
Ruislip HA4 **84** D1
Stanmore HA7 **53** F7
Cranmer Ct, SW3 **31** H2
SW4 **150** D3
Hampton (Hmptn H.) TW12
off Cranmer Rd **161** H5
Cranmer Fm Cl, Mitch. CR4 **185** J4
Cranmer Gdns, Dag. RM10 **101** J4
Cranmer Ho, SW11
off Surrey La **149** H1
Cranmer Rd, E7 **97** H4
SW9 **35** F7
Cranmer Rd,
Croydon CR0 **201** H3
Edgware HA8 **54** B3
Hampton (Hmptn H.) TW12 **161** H5
Kingston upon Thames KT2 **163** H5
Mitcham CR4 **185** J4
Cranmer Ter, SW17 **167** G5
Cranmore Av, Islw. TW7 **123** J7
Cranmore Rd, Brom. BR1 **173** E3
Chislehurst BR7 **174** C5
Cranmore Way, N10 **74** C4
Cranston Cl, Houns. TW3 **143** E2
Cranston Est, N1 **12** C2
Cranston Gdns, E4 **62** B5
Cranston Rd, SE23 **171** H1
Cranswick Rd, SE16 **133** E5
Crantock Rd, SE6 **172** B2
Cranwell Cl, E3 **114** B4
Cranwich Av, N21 **44** A7
Cranwich Rd, N16 **76** A7
Cranwood St, EC1 **12** B4
Cranworth Cres, E4 **62** D1
Cranworth Gdns, SW9 **151** G1
Craster Rd, SW2 **151** F7
Crathie Rd, SE12 **155** H6
Cravan Av, Felt. TW13 **160** A2
Craven Av, W5 **105** F7
Southall UB1 **103** F5
Craven Cl, N16
off Craven Wk **76** D7
Hayes UB4 **102** A6
Craven Gdns, SW19 **166** D5
Barking IG11 **117** H2
Ilford IG6 **81** G2
Craven Hill, W2 **14** D5
Craven Hill Gdns, W2 **14** C5
Craven Hill Ms, W2 **14** D5
Craven Ms, SW11
off Taybridge Rd **150** A3
Craven Pk, NW10 **106** E1
Craven Pk Ms, NW10 **88** E7
Craven Pk Rd, N15 **76** C6
NW10 **106** E1
Craven Pas, WC2 **26** A1
Craven Rd, NW10 **106** D1
W2 **14** D5
W5 **105** F7
Croydon CR0 **202** E1
Kingston upon Thames KT2 **181** J1
Craven St, WC2 **26** A1
Craven Ter, W2 **14** D5
Craven Wk, N16 **76** D7
Crawford Av, Wem. HA0 **87** G5
Crawford Cl, Islw. TW7 **144** B2
Crawford Est, SE5 **151** J2
Crawford Gdns, N13 **59** H3
Northolt UB5 **103** F3
Crawford Ms, W1 **15** J2
Crawford Pas, EC1 **11** E6
Crawford Pl, W1 **15** H3
Crawford Rd, SE5 **151** J1
Crawford St, NW10
off Fawood Av **88** D7
W1 **15** J2
Crawley Rd, E10 **96** B1
N22 **75** J2
Enfield EN1 **44** B7
Crawshay Ct, SW9
off Eythorne Rd **151** G1
Crawthew Gro, SE22 **152** C4
Craybrooke Rd, Sid. DA14 **176** B4
Craybury End, SE9 **175** F2
Crayford Cl, E6
off Neatscourt Rd **116** B5
Crayford Rd, N7 **92** D4
Crayke Hill, Chess. KT9 **195** H7
Cray Rd, Belv. DA17 **139** G6
Sidcup DA14 **176** C7
Crealock Gro, Wdf.Grn. IG8 **63** F5
Crealock St, SW18 **149** E6
Creasy Est, SE1 **28** D6
Crebor St, SE22 **152** D6
Credenhall Dr, Brom. BR2 **206** C1
Credenhill St, SW16 **168** C6
Crediton Hill, NW6 **90** E5
Crediton Rd, E16
off Pacific Rd **115** G6
NW10 **108** A1
Crediton Way, Esher (Clay.) KT10 **194** D5
Credon Rd, E13 **115** J2
SE16 **133** E5
Creechurch La, EC3 **20** E4
Creechurch Pl, EC3 **21** E4
Creed Ct, EC4
off Ludgate Sq **19** H4
Creed La, EC4 **19** H4
Creek, The, Sun. TW16 **178** A5
CREEKMOUTH, Bark. IG11 **118** A4
Creek Rd, SE8 **134** A6
SE10 **134** A6
Barking IG11 **117** J3
East Molesey KT8 **180** B4
Creekside, SE8 **134** B7
Creeland Gro, SE6
off Catford Hill **171** J1
Crefeld Cl, W6 **128** A6
Creffield Rd, W3 **105** J7
W5 **105** J7
Creighton Av, E6 **116** A2
N2 **73** H3
N10 **74** A2
Creighton Cl, W12 **107** G7
Creighton Rd, N17 **60** B7
NW6 **108** A2
W5 **125** G3
Cremer St, E2 **13** F2
Cremorne Est, SW10 **31** E7
Cremorne Rd, SW10 **129** F7
Crescent, EC3 **21** F5
Crescent, The, E17 **77** H5
N11 **57** J4
NW2 **89** H3
SW13 **147** F2
SW19 **166** D3
W3 **106** E6
Barnet EN5 **40** E3
Beckenham BR3 **190** A1
Bexley DA5 **158** C7
Croydon CR0 **188** A5
Harrow HA2 **86** A1
Hayes (Harling.) UB3 **121** F7
Ilford IG2 **80** D6
Loughton IG10 **48** A5
New Malden KT3 **182** C2
Sidcup DA14 **175** J4
Southall UB1 **123** F2
Surbiton KT6 **181** H5
Sutton SM1 **199** G4
Wembley HA0 **86** E2
West Molesey KT8 **179** G4
West Wickham BR4 **190** E6
Crescent Arc, SE10
off Creek Rd **134** C6
Crescent Ct, Surb. KT6 **181** G5
Crescent Dr, Orp. BR5 **193** E6
Crescent Gdns, SW19 **166** D3
Ruislip HA4 **66** B6
Crescent Gro, SW4 **150** C4
Mitcham CR4 **185** H4
Crescent Ho, SE13
off Ravensbourne Pl **154** B2
Crescent La, SW4 **150** D5
Crescent Ms, N22 **74** E1
Crescent Pl, SW3 **31** G1
Crescent Ri, N22 **74** D1
Barnet EN4 **41** H5
Crescent Rd, E4 **47** E7
E6 **115** J1
E10 **96** B2
E13 **115** G1
E18 **79** J2
N3 **72** C1
N8 **74** D7
N9 **60** D1
N11 **57** J4
N15
off Carlingford Rd **75** H3
N22 **74** D1
SE18 **136** E5
SW20 **184** A1
Barnet EN4 **41** H5
Beckenham BR3 **190** B2
Bromley BR1 **173** G7
Dagenham RM10 **101** H4
Enfield EN2 **43** H3
Kingston upon Thames KT2 **164** A7
Sidcup DA15 **175** J3
Crescent Row, EC1 **11** J6
Crescent Stables, SW15 **148** B5
Crescent St, N1 **93** F7
Crescent Vw, Loug. IG10 **48** A6
Crescent Way, N12 **57** H6
SE4 **154** A3
SW16 **169** F7
Orpington BR6 **207** H5
Crescent Wd Rd, SE26 **170** D3
Cresford Rd, SW6 **148** E1
Crespigny Rd, NW4 **71** H6
Cressage Cl, Sthl. UB1 **103** G4
Cresset Rd, E9 **95** F6
Cresset St, SW4 **150** D3
Cressfield Cl, NW5 **92** A5
Cressida Rd, N19 **92** C1
Cressingham Gro, Sutt. SM1 **199** F4
Cressingham Rd, SE13 **154** C3
Edgware HA8 **54** D6
Cressington Cl, N16
off Wordsworth Rd **94** B5
Cress Ms, Brom. BR1 **172** D5
Cresswell Gdns, SW5 **30** C3
Cresswell Pk, SE3 **155** F3
Cresswell Pl, SW10 **30** C3
Cresswell Rd, SE25 **188** D4

Cresswell Rd, Felt. TW13 **160** E4
Twickenham TW1 **145** G6
Cresswell Way, N21 **43** G7
Cressy Ct, E1
off Cressy Pl **113** F5
W6 **127** H3
Cressy Ho, E1
off Hannibal Rd **113** F5
Cressy Pl, E1 **113** F5
Cressy Rd, NW3 **91** J5
Crest, The, N13 **59** G4
NW4 **71** J5
Surbiton KT5 **182** A5
Crestbrook Av, N13 **59** H3
Crestbrook Pl, N13 **59** H3
Crestfield St, WC1 **10** B3
Crest Gdns, Ruis. HA4 **84** C3
Creston Way, Wor.Pk. KT4 **198** A1
Crest Rd, NW2 **89** F2
Bromley BR2 **191** F7
South Croydon CR2 **202** E7
Crest Vw, Pnr. HA5 **66** D4
Crest Vw Dr, Orp. BR5 **193** E5
Crestway, SW15 **147** H6
Crestwood Way, Houns. TW4 **143** F5
Creswell Dr, Beck. BR3 **190** B5
Creswick Rd, W3 **106** B7
Creswick Wk, E3
off Addington Rd **114** A3
NW11 **72** C4
Creton St, SE18 **136** D3
Creukhorne Rd, NW10 **88** E7
Crewdson Rd, SW9 **131** G7
Crewe Pl, NW10 **107** F3
Crews St, E14 **134** A4
Crewys Rd, NW2 **90** C2
SE15 **153** E2
Crichton Av, Wall. SM6 **200** D5
Crichton Rd, Cars. SM5 **199** J6
Crichton St, SW8
off Westbury St **150** C2
Cricketers Arms Rd, Enf. EN2 **43** J2
Cricketers Cl, N14 **42** C7
Chessington KT9 **195** G4
Cricketers Ct, SE11 **35** G2
Cricketers Ms, SW18
off East Hill **149** E5
Cricketers Ter, Cars. SM5
off Wrythe La **199** H3
Cricketers Wk, SE26
off Doctors Cl **171** F5
Cricketfield Rd, E5 **94** E4
Cricket Grn, Mitch. CR4 **185** J3
Cricket Grd Rd, Chis. BR7 **192** E1
Cricket La, Beck. BR3 **171** H6
Cricklade Av, SW2 **169** E2
CRICKLEWOOD, NW2 **90** A3
Cricklewood Bdy, NW2 **89** J3
Cricklewood La, NW2 **90** A4
Cridland St, E15
off Church St **115** F1
Crieff Ct, Tedd. TW11 **163** F7
Crieff Rd, SW18 **149** F6
Criffel Av, SW2 **168** D2
Crimscott St, SE1 **29** E6
Crimsworth Rd, SW8 **150** D1
Crinan St, N1 **10** B1
Cringle St, SW8 **33** F7
Cripplegate St, EC2 **19** J1
Cripps Grn, Hayes UB4
off Stratford Rd **102** B4
Crispe Ho, Bark. IG11
off Dovehouse Mead **117** G2
Crispen Rd, Felt. TW13 **160** E4
Crispian Cl, NW10 **89** E4
Crispin Cl, Croy. CR0
off Harrington Cl **200** E2
Crispin Cres, Croy. CR0 **200** D3
Crispin Ms, NW11 **72** C5
Crispin Pl, E1 **21** F1
Crispin Rd, Edg. HA8 **54** C6
Crispin St, E1 **21** F2
Crisp Rd, W6 **127** J5
Cristowe Rd, SW6 **148** C2
Criterion Ms, N19 **92** D2
Crittall's Cor, Sid. DA14 **176** B7
Crockerton Rd, SW17 **167** J2
Crockham Way, SE9 **174** D4
Crocus Cl, Croy. CR0
off Cornflower La **203** G1
Crocus Fld, Barn. EN5 **40** C6
Croft, The, E4 **62** E2
NW10 **107** F2
W5 **105** H5
Barnet EN5 **40** A4
Hounslow TW5 **123** E6
Loughton IG10 **48** D2
Pinner HA5 **67** F7
Ruislip HA4 **84** C4
Wembley HA0 **87** F5
Croft Av, W.Wick. BR4 **204** C1
Croft Cl, NW7 **54** E3
Croft Cl, Belv. DA17 **139** F5
Chislehurst BR7 **174** C4
Hayes (Harling.) UB3 **121** F7
Croft Ct, Borhamwood WD6 **38** D3
Croftdown Rd, NW5 **92** A3
Croft End Cl, Chess. KT9
off Ashcroft Rd **195** J3
Crofters Cl, Islw. TW7
off Ploughmans End **144** A5
Crofters Ct, SE8
off Croft St **133** H4
Crofters Way, NW1 **110** D1
Croft Gdns, W7 **124** D2
Croft Lo Cl, Wdf.Grn. IG8 **63** H6
Croft Ms, N12 **57** F3
Crofton Av, W4 **126** D7
Bexley DA5 **158** D7
Orpington BR6 **207** F2
Croftongate Way, SE4 **153** H5
Crofton Gro, E4 **62** D4
Crofton La, Orp. BR5, BR6 **193** G7
Crofton Pk Rd, SE4 **153** J6
Crofton Rd, E13 **115** H4
SE5 **152** B1
Orpington BR6 **206** D3
Crofton Ter, E5
off Studley Cl **95** H5
Richmond TW9 **145** J4
Crofton Way, Barn. EN5
off Wycherley Cres **40** E6
Enfield EN2 **43** G2
Croft Rd, SW16 **187** G1
SW19 **167** F7
Bromley BR1 **173** G6
Enfield EN3 **45** H1
Sutton SM1 **199** H5
Croftside, SE25
off Sunny Bk **188** D3
Crofts La, N22 **59** G7
Crofts Rd, Har. HA1 **68** D6
Crofts St, E1 **21** H6
Croft St, SE8 **133** H4
Croftway, NW3 **90** D4
Richmond TW10 **163** E3
Croft Way, Sid. DA15 **175** H3
Crogsland Rd, NW1 **92** A7
Croham Cl, S.Croy. CR2 **202** B7
Croham Manor Rd, S.Croy. CR2 **202** B5
Croham Mt, S.Croy. CR2 **202** B7
Croham Pk Av, S.Croy. CR2 **202** C5
Croham Rd, S.Croy. CR2 **202** A5
Croham Valley Rd, S.Croy. CR2 **202** C6
Croindene Rd, SW16 **187** E1
Cromartie Rd, N19 **74** D7
Cromarty Rd, Edg. HA8 **54** B2
Crombie Cl, Ilf. IG4 **80** C5
Crombie Rd, Sid. DA15 **175** G1
Crome Rd, NW10 **88** E6
Cromer Pl, Orp. BR6
off Andover Rd **207** G1
Cromer Rd, E10
off James La **78** D6
N17 **76** D2
SE25 **188** E3
SW17 **168** A6
Barnet (New Barn.) EN5 **41** F4
Hounslow (Lon.Hthrw Air.) TW6 **140** D3
Romford RM7 **83** J6
Romford (Chad.Hth) RM6 **83** E6
Woodford Green IG8 **63** G4
Cromer St, WC1 **10** B4
Cromer Ter, E8
off Ferncliff Rd **94** D5
Cromer Vil Rd, SW18 **148** C6
Cromford Cl, Orp. BR6 **207** H3
Cromford Path, E5
off Overbury St **95** G4
Cromford Rd, SW18 **148** D5
Cromford Way, N.Mal. KT3 **182** D1
Cromlix Cl, Chis. BR7 **192** E2
Crompton St, W2 **6** E6
Cromwell Av, N6 **92** B1
W6 **127** H5
Bromley BR2 **191** H4
New Malden KT3 **183** F5
Cromwell Cl, N2 **73** G4
W3 *off High St* **126** C1
Bromley BR2 **191** H4
Cromwell Cres, SW5 **128** D4
Cromwell Gdns, SW7 **23** F6
Cromwell Gro, W6 **127** J3
Cromwell Highwalk, EC2
off Silk St **20** A1
Cromwell Ind Est, E10 **95** H1
Cromwell Ms, SW7 **31** F1
Cromwell Pl, N6 **92** B1
SW7 **31** F1
SW14 **146** C3
W3 *off Grove Pl* **126** C1
Cromwell Rd, E7 **97** J7
E17 **78** C5
N3 **73** F2
N10 **58** A7
SW5 **128** E4
SW7 **30** E1
SW9 **151** H1
SW19 **166** D5
Beckenham BR3 **189** H2
Croydon CR0 **188** A7
Feltham TW13 **160** B1
Hounslow TW3 **143** G4
Kingston upon Thames KT2 **181** H1
Teddington TW11 **162** D6
Wembley HA0 **105** H2
Worcester Park KT4 **196** D3
Cromwell St, Houns. TW3 **143** G4
Cromwell Twr, EC2 **20** A1
Crondace Rd, SW6 **148** D1
Crondall Ct, N1 **12** D2
Crondall Ho, SW15
off Fontley Way **165** G1
Crondall St, N1 **12** C2
Cronin St, SE15 **132** C7
Crooked Billet, E17 **62** B7
SW19 **165** J6
Crooked Billet Yd, E2 **12** E3
Crooked Usage, N3 **72** B3
Crooke Rd, SE8 **133** H5
Crookham Rd, SW6 **148** C1
Crook Log, Bexh. DA6 **158** D3
Crookston Rd, SE9 **156** D3
Croombs Rd, E16 **115** J5
Crooms Hill, SE10 **134** D7
Crooms Hill Gro, SE10 **134** C7
Cropley Ct, N1 **12** B1
Cropley St, N1 **12** B1
Croppath Rd, Dag. RM10 **101** G4
Cropthorne Ct, W9 **6** D4
Crosby Cl, Felt. TW13 **160** E4
Crosby Ct, SE1 **28** B3
Crosby Rd, E7 **97** G6
Dagenham RM10 **119** H2
Crosby Row, SE1 **28** B4
Crosby Sq, EC3 **20** D4
Crosby Wk, E8
off Beechwood Rd **94** C6
SW2 **151** G7
Crosier Cl, SE3 **156** B1
Crosland Pl, SW11
off Taybridge Rd **150** A3
Cross Av, SE10 **134** D6
Crossbow Rd, Chig. IG7 **65** J5
Crossbrook Rd, SE3 **156** B2
Cross Cl, SE15
off Gordon Rd **152** E2
Cross Deep, Twick. TW1 **162** C2
Cross Deep Gdns, Twick. TW1 **162** C2
Crossfield Rd, N17 **75** J3
NW3 **91** G7
Crossfields, Loug. IG10 **48** E5
Crossfield St, SE8 **134** A7
Crossford St, SW9 **151** F2
Crossgate, Edg. HA8 **54** A3
Greenford UB6 **87** E6
Cross Keys Cl, N9
off Balham Rd **60** D2
W1 **16** C2
Cross Keys Sq, EC1 **19** J2
Cross Lances Rd, Houns. TW3 **143** H4
Crossland Rd, Th.Hth. CR7 **187** H6
Crosslands Av, W5 **125** J1
Southall UB2 **123** F5
Crosslands Rd, Epsom KT19 **196** D6
Cross La, EC3 **20** D6
N8 **75** F4
Bexley DA5 **159** F7
Crosslet St, SE17 **36** C1
Crosslet Vale, SE10 **154** B1
Crossley St, N7 **93** G6
Crossmead, SE9 **174** C1
Crossmead Av, Grnf. UB6 **103** G3
Crossmount Ho, SE5 **35** J7
Crossness La, SE28 **118** D7
★ **Crossness Pumping Sta**, SE2 **119** E6
Crossness Rd, Bark. IG11 **117** J3
Cross Rd, E4 **62** D1
N11 **58** B5
N22 **59** G7
SE5 **152** B2
SW19 **166** D7
Bromley BR2 **206** B2
Cross Rd, Croydon CR0 **202** A1
Enfield EN1 **44** B4
Feltham TW13 **160** E4
Harrow HA1 **68** A4
Harrow (S.Har.) HA2 **85** H3
Harrow (Wealds.) HA3 **68** D2
Kingston upon Thames KT2 **163** J7
Romford RM7 **83** G3
Romford (Chad.Hth) RM6 **82** C7
Sidcup DA14
off Sidcup Hill **176** B4
Sutton SM2 **199** G5
Woodford Green IG8 **64** C6
Cross Rds, Loug. (High Beach) IG10 **47** H2
Cross St, N1 **111** H1
SW13 **147** E2
Hampton (Hmptn H.) TW12 **161** J5
Crossthwaite Av, SE5 **152** A4
Crosstrees Ho, E14
off Cassilis Rd **134** A3
Crosswall, EC3 **21** F5
Crossway, N12 **57** G6
N16 **94** B5
NW9 **71** F4
SE28 **118** C6
SW20 **183** J4
W13 **104** D4
Dagenham RM8 **100** C3
Enfield EN1 **44** B7
Hayes UB3 **122** A1
Orpington BR5 **193** G4
Pinner HA5 **66** B2
Ruislip HA4 **84** C4
Woodford Green IG8 **63** J4
Crossway, The, N22 **59** H7
SE9 **174** A2
Cross Way, The, Har. HA3 **68** B2
Crossways, N21 **43** J6
South Croydon CR2 **203** H7
Crossways, The, Houns. TW5 **123** F7
Wembley HA9 **88** A2
Crossways Rd, Beckenham BR3 **190** A4
Mitcham CR4 **186** B3
Croston St, E8 **112** D1
Crothall Cl, N13 **59** F3
Crouch Av, Bark. IG11 **118** B2
Crouch Cl, Beck. BR3 **172** A6
Crouch Cft, SE9 **174** D3
CROUCH END, N8 **74** C6
Crouch End Hill, N8 **74** D7
Crouch Hall Rd, N8 **74** D6
Crouch Hill, N4 **74** E6
N8 **74** E6
Crouchman's Cl, SE26 **170** C3
Crouch Rd, NW10 **88** D7
Crowborough Path, Wat. WD19 **50** D4
Crowborough Rd, SW17 **168** A6
Crowden Way, SE28 **118** C7
Crowder Cl, N12 **73** F1
Crowder St, E1 **112** E7
Crowfoot Cl, E9
off Lee Conservancy Rd **95** J5
SE28 **137** H1
Crowhurst Cl, SW9 **151** G2
Crowland Av, Hayes UB3 **121** H4
Crowland Gdns, N14 **42** E7
Crowland Rd, N15 **76** C5
Thornton Heath CR7 **188** A4
Crowlands Av, Rom. RM7 **83** H6
Crowland Ter, N1 **94** A7
Crowland Wk, Mord. SM4 **185** E6
Crow La, Rom. RM7 **83** F7
Crowley Cres, Croy. CR0 **201** G5
Crowline Wk, N1
off Clephane Rd **93** J6
Crowmarsh Gdns, SE23
off Tyson Rd **153** F7
Crown Arc, Kings.T. KT1
off Union St **181** G2
Crownbourne Ct, Sutt. SM1
off St. Nicholas Way **198** E4
Crown Cl, E3 **114** A1
N22 *off Winkfield Rd* **75** G1
NW6 **90** E6
NW7 **55** F2
Hayes UB3 **121** J2
Walton-on-Thames KT12 **178** C7
Crown Ct, EC2 **20** A4
SE12 **155** H6
WC2 **18** B4
Crown Dale, SE19 **169** H6
Crowndale Rd, NW1 **9** F1
Crownfield Av, Ilf. IG2 **81** H5
Crownfield Rd, E15 **96** D5
Crowngate Ho, E3
off Hereford Rd **113** J2

Crown Green Ms, Wembley HA9 .... **87** H2
Crown Hill, Croy. CR0 *off Church St* **201** J2
Crownhill Rd, NW10 .... **107** F1
Woodford Green IG8 .... **64** B7
Crown Ho, Bark. IG11 *off Linton Rd* **99** F7
Crown La, N14 .... **58** C1
SW16 .... **169** G5
Bromley BR2 .... **192** A5
Chislehurst BR7 .... **193** F1
Morden SM4 .... **184** E3
Crown La Gdns, SW16 .... **169** G5
Crown La Spur, Brom. BR2 .... **192** A6
Crownmead Way, Rom. RM7 .... **83** H4
Crown Ms, E13 *off Waghorn Rd* **115** J1
W6 .... **127** G4
Crown Mill, Mitch. CR4 .... **185** H5
Crown Office Row, EC4 .... **19** E5
Crown Pas, SW1 .... **25** G2
Kingston upon Thames KT1 *off Church St* **181** G2
Crown Pl, EC2 .... **20** D1
NW5 *off Kentish Town Rd* **92** B6
SE16 *off Varcoe Rd* **133** E5
Crown Pt Par, SE19 *off Beulah Hill* **169** H6
Crown Reach, SW1 .... **33** J4
Crown Rd, N10 .... **58** A7
Borehamwood WD6 .... **38** A1
Enfield EN1 .... **44** E4
Ilford IG6 .... **81** G4
Morden SM4 .... **184** E4
New Malden KT3 .... **182** C1
Ruislip HA4 .... **84** D5
Sutton SM1 .... **198** E4
Twickenham TW1 .... **145** E6
Crownstone Rd, SW2 .... **151** G5
Crown St, SE5 .... **36** A7
W3 .... **126** B1
Dagenham RM10 .... **101** J6
Harrow HA2 .... **86** A1
Crown Ter, Rich. TW9 .... **145** J4
Crown Trd Est, Hayes UB3 **121** H2
Crowntree Cl, Islw. TW7 .... **124** C6
Crown Wk, Wem. HA9 .... **87** J3
Crown Way, West Dr. UB7 .... **120** C1
Crown Wds La, SE9 .... **157** E2
SE18 .... **157** E2
Crown Wds Way, SE9 .... **157** G5
Crown Wks, E2 *off Temple St* **112** E2
Crown Yd, Houns. TW3 *off High St* **143** J3
Crowshott Av, Stan. HA7 .... **69** F1
Crows Rd, E15 .... **114** D3
Barking IG11 .... **99** E6
Crowther Av, Brent. TW8 .... **125** H4
Crowther Cl, SW6 *off Coomer Pl* **128** C6
Crowther Rd, SE25 .... **188** D4
Crowthorne Cl, SW18 .... **166** C1
Crowthorne Rd, W10 .... **108** A6
Croxden Cl, Edg. HA8 .... **69** J3
Croxden Wk, Mord. SM4 .... **185** F6
Croxford Gdns, N22 .... **59** H7
Croxley Rd, W9 .... **108** C3
Croxted Cl, SE21 .... **151** J7
Croxted Ms, SE24 *off Croxted Rd* **151** J6
Croxted Rd, SE21 .... **151** J7
SE24 .... **151** J7
Croxteth Ho, SW8 *off Wandsworth Rd* **150** D2
Croyde Av, Grnf. UB6 .... **103** J3
Hayes UB3 .... **121** H4
Croyde Cl, Sid. DA15 .... **157** G7
CROYDON, CR0 .... **202** A1
Croydon Flyover, Croy. CR0 .... **201** H4
Croydon Gro, Croy. CR0 .... **201** H1
Croydon Rd, E13 .... **115** F4
SE20 .... **188** E2
Beckenham BR3 .... **189** H4
Bromley BR2 .... **205** F3
Croydon (Bedd.) CR0 .... **201** E4
Croydon (Mitch.Com.) CR0 .... **186** A4
Hounslow (Lon.Hthrw Air.) TW6 .... **140** E2
Keston BR2 .... **205** J3
Mitcham CR4 .... **186** A4
Wallington SM6 .... **200** B4
West Wickham BR4 .... **204** E3
Croydon Rd Ind Est, Beck. BR3 .... **189** G4
Croydon Valley Trade Pk, Croy. CR0 *off Beddington Fm Rd* **186** E7
Croyland Rd, N9 .... **60** D1
Croylands Dr, Surb. KT6 .... **181** H7
Croysdale Av, Sun. TW16 .... **178** A3
Crozier Ho, SE3 *off Ebdon Way* **155** H3
Crozier Ter, E9 .... **95** G5
Crucible Cl, Rom. RM6 .... **82** B6
Crucifix La, SE1 .... **28** D3
Cruden Ho, SE17 .... **35** G6
Cruden St, N1 .... **111** H1
Cruikshank Rd, E15 .... **97** E4
Cruikshank St, WC1 .... **10** E3
Crummock Gdns, NW9 .... **70** E5
Crumpsall St, SE2 .... **138** C4
Crundale Av, NW9 .... **70** A5
Crunden Rd, S.Croy. CR2 .... **202** A7
Crusader Gdns, Croy. CR0 *off Cotelands* **202** B3
Crusader Industral Est, N4 *off Hermitage Rd* **75** J6
Crusoe Ms, N16 .... **94** A2
Crusoe Rd, Mitch. CR4 .... **167** J7
Crutched Friars, EC3 .... **21** E5
Crutchley Rd, SE6 .... **173** E2
Crystal Ct, SE19 *off College Rd* **170** C5
Crystal Ho, SE18 *off Spinel Cl* **137** J5
★ **Crystal Palace FC**, SE25 .... **188** B4
★ **Crystal Palace Nat Sports Cen**, SE19 .... **170** D6
Crystal Palace Par, SE19 .... **170** C6
★ **Crystal Palace Pk**, SE19 .... **170** C5
Crystal Palace Pk Rd, SE26 .... **170** D5
Crystal Palace Rd, SE22 .... **152** D4
Crystal Palace Sta Rd, SE19 .... **170** D6
Crystal Ter, SE19 .... **170** A6
Crystal Vw Ct, Brom. BR1 .... **172** D4
Crystal Way, Dag. RM8 .... **100** C1
Harrow HA1 .... **68** C5
Crystal Wf, N1 .... **11** H2
Cuba Dr, Enf. EN3 .... **45** F2
Cuba St, E14 .... **134** A2
Cubitt Bldg, SW1 .... **32** D4
Cubitt Sq, Sthl. UB2 *off Windmill Av* **123** J1
Cubitt Steps, E14 *off Cabot Sq* **134** A1
Cubitt St, WC1 .... **10** D4
Cubitts Yd, WC2 .... **18** B5
Cubitt Ter, SW4 .... **150** C3
CUBITT TOWN, E14 .... **134** C3
Cuckoo Av, W7 .... **104** B4
Cuckoo Dene, W7 .... **104** A5
Cuckoo Hall La, N9 .... **45** F7
Cuckoo Hill, Pnr. HA5 .... **66** C3
Cuckoo Hill Dr, Pnr. HA5 .... **66** C3
Cuckoo Hill Rd, Pnr. HA5 .... **66** C4
Cuckoo La, W7 .... **104** B7
Cudas Cl, Epsom KT19 .... **197** F4
Cuddington, SE17 .... **35** J1
Cuddington Av, Wor.Pk. KT4 .... **197** F3
Cudham St, SE6 .... **154** C7
Cudworth St, E1 .... **113** E4
Cuff Cres, SE9 .... **156** A6
Cuff Pt, E2 .... **13** F3
Culford Gdns, SW3 .... **32** A2
Culford Gro, N1 .... **94** B6
Culford Ms, N1 *off Culford Rd* **94** B6
Culford Rd, N1 .... **94** B7
Culgaith Gdns, Enf. EN2 .... **42** E4
Cullen Way, NW10 .... **106** C4
Culling Rd, SE16 *off Lower Rd* **133** F3
Cullington Cl, Har. HA3 .... **68** D4
Cullingworth Rd, NW10 .... **89** G5
Culloden Cl, SE16 .... **37** J4
Culloden Rd, Enf. EN2 .... **43** H2
Culloden St, E14 .... **114** C6
Cullum St, EC3 .... **20** D5
Culmington Rd, W13 .... **125** F2
Culmore Rd, SE15 .... **133** E7
Culmstock Rd, SW11 .... **150** A5
Culpeper Cl, Ilf. IG6 .... **65** E6
Culpepper Cl, N18 .... **61** E5
Culross Cl, N15 .... **75** J4
Culross St, W1 .... **16** B6
Culsac Rd, Surb. KT6 .... **195** H2
Culverden Rd, SW12 .... **168** C2
Watford WD19 .... **50** B3
Culver Gro, Stan. HA7 .... **69** F2
Culverhouse Gdns, SW16 .... **169** F3
Culverlands Cl, Stan. HA7 .... **52** E4
Culverley Rd, SE6 .... **172** B1
Culvers Av, Carshalton SM5 .... **199** J2
Culvers Retreat, Cars. SM5 .... **199** J1
Culverstone Cl, Brom. BR2 .... **191** F6
Culvers Way, Carshalton SM5 .... **199** J2
Culvert Pl, SW11 .... **150** A2
Culvert Rd, N15 .... **76** B5
SW11 .... **149** J2
Culworth St, NW8 .... **7** G2
Culzean Cl, SE27 *off Chatsworth Way* **169** H3
Cumberland Av, NW10 .... **106** B3
Welling DA16 .... **157** H3
Cumberland Business Pk, NW10 .... **106** A3
Cumberland Cl, E8 .... **94** C6
SW20 *off Lansdowne Rd* **166** A7
Ilford IG6 .... **81** F1
Twickenham TW1 *off Westmorland Cl* **145** E6
Cumberland Ct, Welling DA16 *off Bellegrove Rd* **157** H2
Cumberland Cres, W14 .... **128** B4
Cumberland Dr, Bexh. DA7 .... **138** E7
Chessington KT9 .... **195** J3
Esher KT10 .... **194** D2
Cumberland Gdns, NW4 .... **72** A2
WC1 .... **10** D3
Cumberland Gate, W1 .... **15** J5
Cumberland Ho, SE28 .... **137** F2
Cumberland Mkt, NW1 .... **9** E3
Cumberland Mkt Est, NW1 .... **8** E3
Cumberland Ms, SE11 .... **35** F4
Cumberland Mills Sq, E14 *off Saunders Ness Rd* **134** D5
Cumberland Pk, NW10 .... **107** G3
W3 .... **106** C7
Cumberland Pl, NW1 .... **8** D3
SE6 .... **173** F1
Sunbury-on-Thames TW16 .... **178** A4
Cumberland Rd, E12 .... **98** A4
E13 .... **115** H5
E17 .... **77** H2
N9 .... **61** F1
N22 .... **75** F2
SE25 .... **189** E6
SW13 .... **147** F1
W3 .... **106** C7
W7 .... **124** C2
Bromley BR2 .... **190** E4
Harrow HA1 .... **67** H5
Richmond TW9 .... **126** A7
Stanmore HA7 .... **69** J3
Cumberland St, SW1 .... **32** E3
Cumberland Ter, NW1 .... **8** D2
Cumberland Ter Ms, NW1 .... **8** D2
Cumberland Vil, W3 *off Cumberland Rd* **106** C7
Cumberlow Av, SE25 .... **188** D3
Cumberton Rd, N17 .... **76** A1
Cumbrae Gdns, Surb. (Long Dit.) KT6 .... **195** G2
Cumbrian Gdns, NW2 .... **90** A2
★ **Cuming Mus**, SE17 .... **35** J2
Cumming St, N1 .... **10** C2
Cumnor Gdns, Epsom KT17 .... **197** G6
Cumnor Rd, Sutt. SM2 .... **199** F6
Cunard Cres, N21 .... **44** A6
Cunard Pl, EC3 .... **20** E4
Cunard Rd, NW10 .... **106** D3
Cunard Wk, SE16 .... **133** H4
Cundy Rd, E16 .... **115** J6
Cundy St, SW1 .... **32** C2
Cundy St Est, SW1 .... **32** C2
Cunliffe Rd, Epsom KT19 .... **197** F4
Cunliffe St, SW16 .... **168** C6
Cunningham Cl, Rom. RM6 .... **82** C5
West Wickham BR4 .... **204** B2
Cunningham Ct, E10 *off Oliver Rd* **96** B3
Cunningham Pk, Har. HA1 .... **67** J5
Cunningham Pl, NW8 .... **7** E5
Cunningham Rd, N15 .... **76** D4
Cunnington St, W4 .... **126** C3
Cupar Rd, SW11 .... **150** A1
Cupola Cl, Brom. BR1 .... **173** H5
Cureton St, SW1 .... **33** J2
Curie Gdns, NW9 .... **71** E2
Curlew Cl, SE28 .... **118** D7
Curlew Ct, Surb. KT6 .... **195** J3
Curlew Ho, Enf. EN3 *off Allington Ct* **45** G5
Curlew St, SE1 .... **29** F3
Curlew Ter, Ilf. IG5 *off Tiptree Cres* **80** D3
Curlew Way, Hayes UB4 .... **102** D5
Curness St, SE13 .... **154** C4
Curnick's La, SE27 *off Chapel Rd* **169** J4
Curnock Est, NW1 *off Plender St* **110** C1
Curran Av, Sidcup DA15 .... **157** J5
Wallington SM6 .... **200** A3
Currey Rd, Grnf. UB6 .... **86** A6
Curricle St, W3 .... **126** E1
Currie Hill Cl, SW19 .... **166** C4
Curry Ri, NW7 .... **56** A6
Cursitor St, EC4 .... **18** E3
Curtain Pl, EC2 .... **12** E5
Curtain Rd, EC2 .... **12** D6
Curthwaite Gdns, Enf. EN2 .... **42** D4
Curtis Dr, W3 .... **106** D6
Curtis Fld Rd, SW16 .... **169** F4
Curtis Ho, N11 .... **58** B5
Curtis La, Wem. HA0 *off Montrose Cres* **87** H6
Curtis Rd, Epsom KT19 .... **196** C4
Hounslow TW4 .... **143** F7
Curtis St, SE1 .... **37** F1
Curtis Way, SE1 .... **37** F1
SE28 *off Tawney Rd* **118** B7
Curve, The, W12 .... **107** G7
Curwen Av, E7 *off Woodford Rd* **97** H4
Curwen Rd, W12 .... **127** G2
Curzon Av, Enf. EN3 .... **45** G5
Stanmore HA7 .... **68** D1
Curzon Cl, Orp. BR6 .... **207** G4
Curzon Cres, NW10 .... **89** F7
Barking IG11 .... **117** J2
Curzon Gate, W1 .... **24** B2
Curzon Pl, Pnr. HA5 .... **66** C5
Curzon Rd, N10 .... **74** B2
W5 .... **105** E4
Thornton Heath CR7 .... **187** G6
Curzon Sq, W1 .... **24** C2
Curzon St, W1 .... **24** C2
Cusack Cl, Twick. TW1 *off Waldegrave Rd* **162** C4
CUSTOM HOUSE, E16 .... **116** A6
Custom Ho Reach, SE16 .... **133** J2
Custom Ho Wk, EC3 .... **20** D6
Cut, The, SE1 .... **27** F3
Cutcombe Rd, SE5 .... **151** J2
Cuthberga Cl, Bark. IG11 *off George St* **99** F7
Cuthbert Gdns, SE25 .... **188** B3
Cuthbert Rd, E17 .... **78** C3
N18 *off Fairfield Rd* **60** D5
Croydon CR0 .... **201** H2
Cuthbert St, W2 .... **15** E1
Cuthill Wk, SE5 .... **152** A1
Cutlers Gdns, E1 .... **21** E3
Cutlers Gdns Arc, EC2 *off Devonshire Sq* **21** E3
Cutlers Sq, E14 *off Britannia Rd* **134** A4
Cutlers Ter, N1 *off Balls Pond Rd* **94** B6
Cutler St, E1 .... **21** E3
Cutthroat All, Rich. TW10 *off Ham St* **163** F2
★ **Cutty Sark**, SE10 .... **134** C6
Cutty Sark Gdns, SE10 *off King William Wk* **134** C6
Cuxton Cl, Bexh. DA6 .... **158** E5
Cyclamen Cl, Hmptn. TW12 *off Gresham Rd* **161** G6
Cyclamen Way, Epsom KT19 .... **196** B5
Cyclops Ms, E14 .... **134** A4
Cygnet Av, Felt. TW14 .... **142** C7
Cygnet Cl, NW10 .... **88** D5
Borehamwood WD6 .... **38** C1
Cygnets, The, Felt. TW13 .... **160** E4
Cygnet St, E1 .... **13** G5
Cygnet Way, Hayes UB4 .... **102** D5
Cygnus Business Cen, NW10 .... **89** F6
Cymbeline Ct, Har. HA1 .... **68** C6
Cynthia St, N1 .... **10** D2
Cyntra Pl, E8 .... **95** E7
Cypress Av, Twickenham TW2 .... **143** J7
Cypress Cl, E5 .... **94** D2
Cypress Gdns, SE4 .... **153** H5
Cypress Gro, Ilf. IG6 .... **65** H6
Cypress Pl, W1 .... **9** G6
Cypress Rd, SE25 .... **188** B2
Harrow HA3 .... **68** A2
Cypress Tree Cl, Sid. DA15 .... **175** J1
Cyprus Av, N3 .... **72** B2
Cyprus Cl, N4 *off Atterbury Rd* **75** H6
Cyprus Gdns, N3 .... **72** B2
Cyprus Pl, E2 .... **113** F2
E6 .... **116** D7
Cyprus Rd, N3 .... **72** C2
N9 .... **60** C2
Cyprus Rbt, E16 .... **116** D7
Cyprus St, E2 .... **113** F2
Cyrena Rd, SE22 .... **152** C6
Cyril Mans, SW11 .... **149** J1

Cyril Rd, Bexh. DA7 **159** E2
Cyrus St, EC1 **11** H5
Czar St, SE8 **134** A6

D

Dabbs Hill La, Northolt
UB5 **85** H5
Dabin Cres, SE10 **154** C1
Dacca St, SE8 **133** J6
Dace Rd, E3 **96** A7
Dacre Av, Ilf. IG5 **80** D2
Dacre Cl, Chig. IG7 **65** F4
Greenford UB6 **103** H2
Dacre Gdns, SE13 **154** E4
Borehamwood WD6 **38** D5
Chigwell IG7 **65** F4
Dacre Pk, SE13 **155** E3
Dacre Pl, SE13 **154** E3
Dacre Rd, E11 **97** F1
E13 **115** H1
Croydon CR0 **187** E7
Dacres Est, SE23 **171** G3
Dacres Rd, SE23 **171** G3
Dacre St, SW1 **25** H5
Dade Way, Sthl. UB2 **123** F5
Daerwood Cl, Brom. BR2 **206** C1
Daffodil Cl, Croy. CR0 **203** G1
Daffodil Gdns, Ilf. IG1 **98** E5
Daffodil Pl, Hmptn. TW12
off Gresham Rd **161** G6
Daffodil St, W12 **107** F7
Dafforne Rd, SW17 **168** A3
DAGENHAM,
RM8-RM10 **101** G6
Dagenham Av, Dag.
RM9 **118** E1
Dagenham Leisure Pk, Dag.
RM9 *off Cook Rd* **118** E1
Dagenham Rd, E10 **95** J1
Dagenham RM10 **101** J4
Dagmar Av, Wem. HA9 **87** J4
Dagmar Gdns, NW10 **108** A2
Dagmar Ms, Sthl. UB2
off Dagmar Rd **123** E3
Dagmar Pas, N1
off Cross St **111** H1
Dagmar Rd, N4 **75** G7
N15 *off Cornwall Rd* **76** A4
N22 **74** D1
SE5 **152** B1
SE25 **188** B5
Dagenham RM10 **101** J7
Kingston upon Thames
KT2 **181** J1
Southall UB2 **122** E3
Dagmar Ter, N1 **111** H1
Dagnall Pk, SE25 **188** B6
Dagnall Rd, SE25 **188** B5
Dagnall St, SW11 **149** J2
Dagnan Rd, SW12 **150** B7
Dagonet Gdns, Brom.
BR1 **173** G3
Dagonet Rd, Brom. BR1 **173** G3
Dahlia Gdns, Ilf. IG1 **99** E6
Mitcham CR4 **186** D4
Dahlia Rd, SE2 **138** B4
Dahomey Rd, SW16 **168** C6
Daimler Way, Wall. SM6 **200** E7
Daines Cl, E12 **98** C3
Dainford Cl, Brom. BR1 **172** D5
Dainton Cl, Brom. BR1 **191** H1
Daintry Cl, Har. HA3 **68** D4
Daintry Way, E9
off Osborne Rd **95** J6
Dairsie Rd, SE9 **156** D3
Dairy Cl, NW10 **107** G1
SW6 **148** C1
Bromley BR1
off Plaistow La **173** H7
Grnf. UB6 **104** A2
Thornton Heath CR7 **187** J2
Dairy Fm Pl, SE15
off Queens Rd **153** F1
Dairy La, SE18 **136** C4
Dairyman Cl, NW2 **90** A4
Dairy Ms, N2
off East End Rd **73** H4
SW9 **151** E3
Dairy Wk, SW19 **166** B4
Daisy Cl, Croy. CR0 **203** G1
Daisy Dobbins Wk, N19
off Hillrise Rd **74** E7
Daisy La, SW6 **148** D3
Daisy Rd, E16
off Cranberry La **114** E4
E18 **79** H2
Dakin Pl, E1
off White Horse Rd **113** H5
Dakota Bldg, SE13
off Deals Gateway **154** A1
Dakota Cl, Wall. SM6 **201** F7
Dakota Gdns, E6 **116** B4
Northolt UB5
off Argus Way **102** E3
Dalberg Rd, SW2 **151** G4
Dalberg Way, SE2
off Lanridge Rd **138** D3
Dalby Rd, SW18 **149** F4
Dalbys Cres, N17 **60** B6
Dalby St, NW5 **92** B6
Dalcross Rd, Houns.
TW4 **142** E2
Dale, The, Kes. BR2 **206** A4
Dale Av, Edg. HA8 **69** J1
Hounslow TW4 **143** E3
Dalebury Rd, SW17 **167** H2
Dale Cl, SE3 **155** G3
Barnet (New Barn.)
EN5 **41** E6
Pinner HA5 **66** B1
Dale Gdns, Wdf.Grn. IG8 **63** H4
Dale Grn Rd, N11 **58** B3
Dale Gro, N12 **57** F5
Daleham Gdns, NW3 **91** G5
Daleham Ms, NW3 **91** G6
Dalehead, NW1 **9** F2
Dalemain Ms, E16
off Hanover Av **135** G1
Dale Pk Av, Cars. SM5 **199** J2
Dale Pk Rd, SE19 **187** J1
Dale Rd, NW5
off Grafton Rd **92** A5
SE17 **35** H6
Greenford UB6 **103** H5
Sutton SM1 **198** C4
Dale Row, W11
off St. Marks Rd **108** B6
Daleside Gdns, Chig. IG7 **65** F3
Daleside Rd, SW16 **168** B5
Epsom KT19 **196** D6
Dales Path, Borwd. WD6
off Farriers Way **38** D5
Dales Rd, Borwd. WD6 **38** D5
Dale St, W4 **126** E5
Dale Vw Av, E4 **62** C2
Dale Vw Cres, E4 **62** C2
Dale Vw Gdns, E4 **62** D3
Daleview Rd, N15 **76** B6
Dalewood Gdns, Wor.Pk.
KT4 **197** H2
Dale Wd Rd, Orp. BR6 **193** H7
Daley St, E9 **95** G6
Daley Thompson Way,
SW8 **150** B2
Dalgarno Gdns, W10 **107** J5
Dalgarno Way, W10 **107** J4
Dalgleish St, E14 **113** H6
Daling Way, E3 **113** H1
Dalkeith Gro, Stan. HA7 **53** G5
Dalkeith Rd, SE21 **169** J1
Ilford IG1 **99** F3
Dallas Rd, NW4 **71** G7
SE26 **170** E3
W5 **105** J5
Sutton SM3 **198** B6
Dallas Ter, Hayes UB3 **121** J3
Dallinger Rd, SE12 **155** F6
Dalling Rd, W6 **127** H3
Dallington Sq, EC1
off Dallington St **11** H5
Dallington St, EC1 **11** H5
Dallin Rd, SE18 **137** E7
Bexleyheath DA6 **158** D4
Dalmain Rd, SE23 **171** G1
Dalmally Rd, Croy. CR0 **188** C7
Dalmeny Av, N7 **92** D4
SW16 **187** G2
Dalmeny Cl, Wem. HA0 **87** F6
Dalmeny Cres, Houns.
TW3 **144** A4
Dalmeny Rd, N7 **92** D3
Barnet (New Barn.)
EN5 **41** F6
Carshalton SM5 **200** A7
Erith DA8 **159** H1
Worcester Park KT4 **197** H3
Dalmeyer Rd, NW10 **89** F6
Dalmore Av, Esher (Clay.)
KT10 **194** C6
Dalmore Rd, SE21 **169** J2
Dalrymple Cl, N14 **42** D7
Dalrymple Rd, SE4 **153** H4
DALSTON, E8 **94** D7
Dalston Gdns, Stan. HA7 **69** H1
Dalston La, E8 **94** C6
Dalton Av, Mitch. CR4 **185** H2
Dalton Cl, Orp. BR6 **207** H3
Dalton Rd, Har. (Har.Wld)
HA3 **68** A2
Dalton St, SE27 **169** H2
Dalwood St, SE5 **152** B1
Daly Dr, Brom. BR1 **192** D3
Dalyell Rd, SW9 **151** F3
Damascene Wk, SE21
off Lovelace Rd **169** J1
Damask Ct, Sutt. SM1
off Cleeve Way **199** E1
Damask Cres, E16
off Cranberry La **115** E4
Damer Ter, SW10
off Tadema Rd **129** F7
Dames Rd, E7 **97** G3
Dame St, N1 **11** J1
Damien St, E1 **113** E6
Damon Cl, Sid. DA14 **176** B3
Damson Dr, Hayes UB3 **102** A7
Damsonwood Rd, Sthl.
UB2 **123** G3
Danbrook Rd, SW16 **187** E1
Danbury Cl, Rom. RM6 **82** D3
Danbury Ms, Wall. SM6 **200** B4
Danbury Rd, Loug. IG10 **48** B7
Danbury St, N1 **11** H1
Danbury Way, Wdf.Grn.
IG8 **63** J6
Danby St, SE15 **152** C3
Dancer Rd, SW6 **148** C1
Richmond TW9 **146** A3
Dando Cres, SE3 **155** H3
Dandridge Cl, SE10 **135** F5
Danebury, Croy.
(New Adgtn) CR0 **204** B6
Danebury Av, SW15 **147** E6
Daneby Rd, SE6 **172** B3
Dane Cl, Bex. DA5 **159** G7
Orpington BR6 **207** G5
Danecourt Gdns, Croy.
CR0 **202** C3
Danecroft Rd, SE24 **151** J5
Danehill Wk, Sid. DA14
off Hatherley Rd **176** A3
Danehurst Gdns, Ilf. IG4 **80** B5
Danehurst St, SW6 **148** B1
Daneland, Barn. EN4 **41** J6
Danemead Gro, Nthlt.
UB5 **85** H5
Danemere St, SW15 **147** J3
Dane Pl, E3
off Roman Rd **113** J2
Dane Rd, N18 **61** F4
SW19 **185** F1
W13 **125** F1
Ilford IG1 **99** F5
Southall UB1 **103** E7
Danesbury Rd, Felt.
TW13 **160** B1
Danescombe, SE12
off Winn Rd **173** G1
Danes Ct, Wem. HA9
off North End Rd **88** B3
Danescourt Cres, Sutt.
SM1 **199** F2
Danescroft, NW4 **72** A5
Danescroft Av, NW4 **72** A5
Danescroft Gdns, NW4 **72** A5
Danesdale Rd, E9 **95** H6
Danesfield, SE5 **36** D5
Danes Gate, Har. HA1 **68** B3
Danes Rd, Rom. RM7 **83** J7
Dane St, WC1 **18** C2
Daneswood Av, SE6 **172** C3
Danethorpe Rd, Wem.
HA0 **87** G6
Danetree Cl, Epsom
KT19 **196** C7
Danetree Rd, Epsom
KT19 **196** C7
Danette Gdns, Dag.
RM10 **101** F2
Daneville Rd, SE5 **152** A1
Dangan Rd, E11 **79** G6
Daniel Bolt Cl, E14
off Uamvar St **114** B5
Daniel Cl, N18 **61** F4
SW17 **167** H6
Hounslow TW4
off Harvey Rd **143** F7
Daniel Gdns, SE15 **37** F7
Daniell Way, Croy. CR0 **201** E1
Daniel Pl, NW4 **71** H6
Daniel Rd, W5 **105** J7
Daniels Rd, SE15 **153** F3
Dan Leno Wk, SW6
off Britannia Rd **128** E7
Dan Mason Dr, W4 **146** D2
Dansey Pl, W1 **17** H5
Dansington Rd, Well.
DA16 **158** A4
Danson Cres, Well.
DA16 **158** B3
Danson Interchange,
Sid. DA15
off East Rochester
Way **158** C6
Danson La, Well. DA16 **158** A4
Danson Mead, Well.
DA16 **158** C3
★ **Danson Park**, Well.
DA16 **158** C4
Danson Pk, Bexh. DA6 **158** C4
Danson Rd, Bex. DA5 **158** D5
Bexleyheath DA6 **158** D5
Danson Underpass, Sid.
DA15 *off Danson Rd* **158** C5
Dante Pl, SE11 **35** H1
Dante Rd, SE11 **35** G1
Danube Apts, N8
off Great Amwell La **75** F3
Danube Cl, N9 **61** F3
Danube St, SW3 **31** H3
Danvers Rd, N8 **74** D4
Danvers St, SW3 **31** F6
Danziger Way, Borwd.
WD6 **38** C1
Daphne Gdns, E4
off Gunners Gro **62** C3
Daphne St, SW18 **149** F6
Daplyn St, E1 **21** H1
D'Arblay St, W1 **17** G4
Darby Cres, Sun. TW16 **178** C2
Darby Gdns, Sun. TW16 **178** C2
Darcy Av, Wall. SM6 **200** C4
Darcy Cl, N20 **57** G2
D'Arcy Dr, Har. HA3 **69** G4
Darcy Gdns, Dag. RM9 **119** F1
D'Arcy Gdns, Har. HA3 **69** H4
Darcy Ho, E8
off Warburton Rd **112** E1
D'Arcy Pl, Brom. BR2 **191** G4
Darcy Rd, SW16 **186** E2
Isleworth TW7
off London Rd **144** D1
D'Arcy Rd, Sutt. SM3 **198** A4
Dare Gdns, Dag. RM8 **101** E3
Darell Rd, Rich. TW9 **146** A3
Darenth Rd, N16 **76** C7
Welling DA16 **158** A1
Darfield Rd, SE4 **153** J5
Darfield Way, W10 **108** A6
Darfur St, SW15 **148** A3
Dargate Cl, SE19
off Chipstead Cl **170** C7
Darien Rd, SW11 **149** G3
Dark Ho Wk, EC3
off Grant's Quay Wf **20** C6
Darlands Dr, Barn. EN5 **40** A5
Darlan Rd, SW6 **128** C7
Darlaston Rd, SW19 **166** A7
Darley Cl, Croy. CR0 **189** H6
Darley Dr, N.Mal. KT3 **182** D2
Darley Gdns, Mord. SM4 **185** E6
Darley Rd, N9 **60** C1
SW11 **149** J6
Darling Rd, SE4 **154** A3
Darling Row, E1 **113** E4
Darlington Rd, SE27 **169** H5
Darmaine Cl, S.Croy. CR2 **201** J7
Darnaway Pl, E14
off Abbott Rd **114** C6
Darndale Cl, E17 **77** J2
Darnley Ho, E14 **113** H6
Darnley Rd, E9 **95** E6
Woodford Green IG8 **79** G1
Darnley Ter, W11
off St. James's Gdns **128** A1
Darrell Rd, SE22 **152** D5
Darren Cl, N4 **75** F7
Darrick Wd Rd, Orp.
BR6 **207** G2
Darris Cl, Hayes UB4 **103** E4
Darsley Dr, SW8 **150** D1
Dartford Av, N9 **45** F6
Dartford Gdns, Rom.
(Chad.Hth) RM6
off Heathfield Pk Dr **82** B5
Dartford Ho, SE1
off Longfield Est **37** G2
Dartford Rd, Bex. DA5 **177** J1
Dartford St, SE17 **36** A5
Dartmoor Wk, E14
off Charnwood Gdns **134** A4
Dartmouth Cl, W11 **108** C6
Dartmouth Gro, SE10 **154** C1
Dartmouth Hill, SE10 **154** C1
Dartmouth Ho, Kings.T.
KT2 *off Kingsgate Rd* **181** H1
DARTMOUTH PARK, NW5 **92** B3
Dartmouth Pk Av, NW5 **92** B3
Dartmouth Pk Hill, N19 **92** B1
NW5 **92** B1
Dartmouth Pk Rd, NW5 **92** B4
Dartmouth Pl, SE23
off Dartmouth Rd **171** F2
W4 **127** E6
Dartmouth Rd, NW2 **90** A6
NW4 **71** G6
SE23 **171** F3
SE26 **171** F3
Bromley BR2 **191** G7
Ruislip HA4 **84** A3
Dartmouth Row, SE10 **154** C2
Dartmouth St, SW1 **25** H4
Dartmouth Ter, SE10 **154** D1
Dartnell Rd, Croy. CR0 **188** C7
Dartrey Twr, SW10
off Blantyre St **30** E7
Dartrey Wk, SW10
off Blantyre St **30** E7
Dart St, W10 **108** B3
Darville Rd, N16 **94** C3
Darwell Cl, E6 **116** D2
Darwen Pl, E2
off Wharf Pl **112** E1
Darwin Cl, N11 **58** B3
Orpington BR6 **207** G5
Darwin Ct, SE17 **36** C2

Darwin Dr, Sthl. UB1 **103** H6
Darwin Gdns, Wat. WD19 **50** C5
Darwin Rd, N22 **75** H1
W5 **125** F5
Welling DA16 **157** J3
Darwin St, SE17 **36** C1
Daryngton Dr, Grnf. UB6 **104** A2
Dashwood Cl, Bexh. DA6 **159** G5
Dashwood Rd, N8 **75** F6
Dassett Rd, SE27 **169** H5
Datchelor Pl, SE5 **152** A1
Datchet Rd, SE6 **171** J3
Datchworth Ct, N4
off Queens Dr **93** J3
Date St, SE17 **36** B4
Daubeney Gdns, N17 **59** J7
Daubeney Pl, Hmptn. TW12
off High St **179** J1
Daubeney Rd, E5 **95** H4
N17 **59** J7
Daubeney Twr, SE8 **133** J5
Dault Rd, SW18 **149** F6
Davema Cl, Chis. BR7 **192** D1
Davenant Rd, N19 **92** D2
Croydon CR0
off Duppas Hill Rd **201** H4
Davenant St, E1 **21** J2
Davenport Cl, Tedd. TW11 **162** D6
Davenport Ho, SE11
off Walnut Tree Wk **34** E1
Davenport Rd, SE6 **154** B6
Sidcup DA14 **176** D2
Daventer Dr, Stan. HA7 **52** C7
Daventry Av, E17 **78** A6
Daventry St, NW1 **15** G1
Davern Cl, SE10 **135** F4
Davey Cl, N7 **93** F6
N13 **59** F5
Davey Rd, E9 **96** A7
Davey St, SE15 **37** G6
David Av, Grnf. UB6 **104** B3
David Cl, Hayes (Harling.) UB3 **121** G7
Davidge St, SE1 **27** G4
David Lee Pt, E15 **115** E1
David Ms, W1 **16** A1
David Rd, Dag. RM8 **100** E2
Davidson Gdns, SW8 **130** E7
Davidson La, Har. HA1
off Grove Hill **68** C7
Davidson Rd, Croy. CR0 **188** C6
Davidson Terraces, E7
off Windsor Rd **97** H5
Davids Rd, SE23 **171** F1
David St, E15 **96** D6
David's Way, Ilf. IG6 **65** H7
David Twigg Cl, Kings.T. KT2 **181** H1
Davies Cl, Croy. CR0 **188** D6
Davies La, E11 **97** E2
Davies Ms, W1 **16** D5
Davies St, W1 **16** D5
Davies Wk, Islw. TW7
off Oakley Cl **144** A1
Davington Gdns, Dag. RM8 **100** B5
Davington Rd, Dag. RM8 **100** B6
Davinia Cl, Wdf.Grn. IG8
off Deacon Way **64** C6
Davis Rd, W3 **127** F1
Chessington KT9 **196** A4
Davis Rd Ind Pk, Chess. KT9 **196** A4
Davis St, E13 **115** H2
Davisville Rd, W12 **127** G2
Davis Way, Sid. DA14
off Bedens Rd **176** E6
Dawes Av, Islw. TW7 **144** D5
Dawes Ho, SE17 **36** B2
Dawes Rd, SW6 **128** B7
Dawes St, SE17 **36** C3
Dawlish Av, N13 **58** E4
SW18 **166** E2
Greenford (Perivale) UB6 **104** D2
Dawlish Dr, Ilf. IG3 **99** H4
Pinner HA5 **67** E5
Ruislip HA4 **84** A2
Dawlish Rd, E10 **96** C2
N17 **76** D3
NW2 **90** A6
Dawnay Gdns, SW18 **167** G2
Dawnay Rd, SW18 **167** F2
Dawn Cl, Houns. TW4 **143** E3
Dawn Cres, E15
off Bridge Rd **114** D1
Dawpool Rd, NW2 **89** F2
Daws Hill, E4 **46** C3
Daws La, NW7 **55** F5
Dawson Av, Bark. IG11 **99** H7
Dawson Cl, SE18 **137** F4
Dawson Gdns, Barking IG11 **99** J7
Dawson Hts Est, SE22 **152** D7
Dawson Pl, W2 **108** D7
Dawson Rd, NW2 **89** J5
Kingston upon Thames KT1 **181** J3
Dawson St, E2 **13** G2
Dawson Ter, N9 **45** F7
Dax Ct, Sun. TW16
off Thames St **178** C3
Daybrook Rd, SW19 **184** E2
Daylesford Av, SW15 **147** G4
Daymer Gdns, Pinner HA5 **66** B4
Daysbrook Rd, SW2 **169** F2
Days La, Sid. DA15 **157** H7
Dayton Gro, SE15 **153** F1
Deacon Ms, N1 **94** A7
Deacon Rd, NW2 **89** G5
Kingston upon Thames KT2 **181** J1
Deacons Cl, Borwd. (Els.) WD6 **38** A4
Pinner HA5 **66** B2
Deacons Hts, WD6 **38** A6
Deacons Leas, Orp. BR6 **207** G4
Deacons Ri, N2 **73** G5
Deacons Wk, Hmptn. TW12
off Bishops Gro **161** F4
Deacon Trd Est, E4
off Cabinet Way **61** J6
Deacon Way, SE17 **35** J1
Woodford Green IG8 **64** C7
Deal Ms, W5
off Darwin Rd **125** G4
Deal Porters Way, SE16 **133** F3
Deal Rd, SW17 **168** A6
Deals Gateway, SE13 **154** A1
Deal St, E1 **21** H1
Dealtry Rd, SW15 **147** J4
Deal Wk, SW9
off Mandela St **131** G7
Dean Bradley St, SW1 **26** A6
Dean Cl, E9
off Churchill Wk **95** F5
SE16
off Surrey Water Rd **133** G1
Dean Ct, SW8
off Thorncroft St **130** E7
Wembley HA0 **87** E3
Deancross St, E1 **113** F6
Dean Dr, Stan. HA7 **69** H2
Deane Av, Ruis. HA4 **84** C5
Deane Cft Rd, Pnr. HA5 **66** B6
Deanery Cl, N2 **73** H4
Deanery Ms, W1 **24** C1
Deanery Rd, E15 **97** E6
Deanery St, W1 **24** C1
Deane Way, Ruis. HA4 **66** B6
Dean Farrar St, SW1 **25** H5
Dean Gdns, E17 **78** D4
W13
off Northfield Av **124** E1
Deanhill Ct, SW14
off Coval La **146** B4
Deanhill Rd, SW14 **146** B4
Dean Ho, E1
off Tarling St **113** F6
Dean Rd, NW2 **89** J6
SE28 **118** A7
Croydon CR0 **202** A4
Hampton TW12 **161** G5
Hounslow TW3 **143** H5
Dean Ryle St, SW1 **34** A1
Deansbrook Cl, Edg. HA8 **54** C6
Deansbrook Rd, Edg. HA8 **54** C7
Deans Bldgs, SE17 **36** B2
Deans Cl, W4 **126** B6
Dean's Cl, Croy. CR0 **202** C3
Deans Cl, Edg. HA8 **54** C6
Deans Ct, EC4 **19** H4
Deanscroft Av, NW9 **88** C2
Deans Dr, N13 **59** H6
Edgware HA8 **54** D5
Dean's Gate Cl, SE23 **171** G3
Deans La, W4
off Deans Cl **126** B6
Edgware HA8 **54** C6
Deans Ms, W1 **16** E3
Deans Rd, W7 **124** C1
Sutton SM1 **198** E3
Dean Stanley St, SW1 **26** A6
Dean St, E7 **97** G5
W1 **17** H3
Deansway, N2 **73** G4
N9 **60** B3
Deans Way, Edg. HA8 **54** C5
Dean's Yd, SW1 **25** J5
Dean Trench St, SW1 **26** A6
Dean Wk, Edg. HA8
off Deansbrook Rd **54** C6
Dean Way, Sthl. UB2 **123** H2
Dearne Cl, Stan. HA7 **52** D5
De'Arn Gdns, Mitch. CR4 **185** H3
Dearsley Rd, Enf. EN1 **44** D3
Deason St, E15
off High St **114** C1
De Barowe Ms, N5
off Leigh Rd **93** H4
DEBDEN, Loug. IG10 **49** G3
Debden Cl, NW9
off Kenley Av **70** E2
Kingston upon Thames KT2 **163** G5
Woodford Green IG8 **63** J7
De Beauvoir Cres, N1 **112** B1
De Beauvoir Est, N1 **112** A1
De Beauvoir Rd, N1 **112** B1
De Beauvoir Sq, N1 **94** B7
DE BEAUVOIR TOWN, N1 **112** A1
Debnams Rd, SE16
off Rotherhithe New Rd **133** F4
De Bohun Av, N14 **42** B6
Deborah Cl, Islw. TW7 **144** B1
De Brome Rd, Felt. TW13 **160** C1
Deburgh Rd, SW19 **167** F7
Decima St, SE1 **28** D5
Deck Cl, SE16
off Thame Rd **133** G2
Decoy Av, NW11 **72** B5
De Crespigny Pk, SE5 **152** A2
Deeley Rd, SW8 **150** D1
Deena Cl, W3 **105** J6
Deepdale, SW19 **166** A4
Deepdale Av, Brom. BR2 **191** F4
Deepdale Cl, N11 **58** A6
Deepdene, W5 **105** J4
Deepdene Av, Croy. CR0 **202** C3
Deepdene Cl, E11 **79** G4
Deepdene Ct, N21 **43** H6
Bromley BR2 **190** E3
Deepdene Gdns, SW2 **151** F7
Deepdene Path, Loug. IG10 **48** D4
Deepdene Pt, SE23
off Dacres Rd **171** G3
Deepdene Rd, SE5 **152** A4
Loughton IG10 **48** D4
Welling DA16 **158** A3
Deepwell Cl, Islw. TW7 **144** D1
Deepwood La, Grnf. UB6
off Cowgate Rd **104** A3
Deerbrook Rd, SE24 **169** H1
Deerdale Rd, SE24 **151** J4
Deerfield Cl, NW9 **71** F5
Deerhurst Cl, Felt. TW13 **160** A4
Deerhurst Cres, Hmptn. (Hmptn H.) TW12 **161** J5
Deerhurst Rd, NW2 **90** A6
SW16 **169** F5
Deerings Dr, Pnr. HA5 **66** A5
Deerleap Gro, E4 **46** B5
Dee Rd, Rich. TW9 **145** J4
Deer Pk Cl, Kings.T. KT2 **164** B7
Deer Pk Gdns, Mitch. CR4 **185** G3
Deer Pk Rd, SW19 **185** E2
Deer Pk Way, W.Wick. BR4 **205** F2
Deeside Rd, SW17 **167** G3
Dee St, E14 **114** C6
Defence Cl, SE28 **137** H1
Defiance Wk, SE18 **136** C3
Defiant Way, Wall. SM6 **200** E7
Defoe Av, Rich. TW9 **126** A7
Defoe Cl, SE16
off Vaughan St **133** J2
SW17 **167** H6
Defoe Ho, EC2
off The Barbican **19** J1
Defoe Pl, EC2
off The Barbican **20** A1
SW17
off Lessingham Av **167** J4
Defoe Rd, N16 **94** B2
De Frene Rd, SE26 **171** G4
De Gama Pl, E14
off Maritime Quay **134** A5
Degema Rd, Chis. BR7 **174** E5
Dehar Cres, NW9 **71** G7
Dehavilland Cl, Nthlt. UB5 **102** D3
De Havilland Ct, Ilf. IG1
off Piper Way **99** G1
De Havilland Dr, SE18 **137** E6
De Havilland Rd, Edg. HA8 **70** B2
Hounslow TW5 **122** C7
De Havilland Way, Stai. (Stanw.) TW19 **140** A6
Dekker Rd, SE21 **152** B6
Delacourt Rd, SE3
off Old Dover Rd **135** H7
Delafield Ho, E1 **21** J4
Delafield Rd, SE7 **135** H5
Delaford Rd, SE16 **133** E5
Delaford St, SW6 **128** B7
Delamare Cres, Croy. CR0 **189** F6
Delamere Ct, E17
off Hawker Pl **78** C2
Delamere Gdns, NW7 **54** D6
Delamere Rd, SW20 **184** A1
W5 **125** H1
Delamere Rd, Borehamwood WD6 **38** B1
Hayes UB4 **102** D7
Delamere St, W2 **14** C1
Delamere Ter, W2 **14** B1
Delancey Pas, NW1
off Delancey St **110** B1
Delancey St, NW1 **110** B1
De Laune St, SE17 **35** G4
Delaware Rd, W9 **6** A5
Delawyk Cres, SE24 **151** J6
Delcombe Av, Wor.Pk. KT4 **197** J1
Delft Way, SE22
off East Dulwich Gro **152** B5
Delhi Rd, Enf. EN1 **44** C7
Delhi St, N1 **111** E1
Delia St, SW18 **149** E7
Delisle Rd, SE28 **137** H1
Delius Gro, E15 **114** D2
Dell, The, SE2 **138** A5
SE19 **188** C1
Brentford TW8 **125** F6
Feltham TW14 **142** B7
Pinner HA5 **66** D2
Wembley HA0 **87** E5
Woodford Green IG8 **63** H3
Della Path, E5 **94** E3
Dellbow Rd, Felt. TW14
off Central Way **142** B5
Dell Cl, E15 **114** D1
Wallington SM6 **200** C4
Woodford Green IG8 **63** H3
Dellfield Cl, Beck. BR3 **190** C1
Dell La, Epsom KT17 **197** G5
Dellors Cl, Barn. EN5 **40** A5
Dellow Cl, Ilf. IG2 **81** G7
Dellow St, E1 **113** E7
Dell Rd, Epsom KT17 **197** G6
West Drayton UB7 **120** C3
Dells Cl, E4 **46** B7
Teddington TW11
off Middle La **162** C6
Dell's Ms, SW1 **33** G2
Dell Wk, N.Mal. KT3 **183** E2
Dell Way, W13 **105** F6
Dellwood Gdns, Ilf. IG5 **80** D3
Delmare Cl, SW9
off Brighton Ter **151** F4
Delme Cres, SE3 **155** H2
Delmey Cl, Croy. CR0 **202** C3
Deloraine St, SE8 **154** A1
Delorme St, W6 **128** A6
Delta Cl, Wor.Pk. KT4 **197** E3
Delta Ct, NW2 **89** G2
Delta Gain, Wat. WD19 **50** D2
Delta Gro, Nthlt. UB5 **102** D3
Delta Pk Ind Est, Enf. EN3 **45** J2
Delta Rd, Wor.Pk. KT4 **197** E3
Delta St, E2 **13** H3
De Luci Rd, Erith DA8 **139** J5
De Lucy St, SE2 **138** B4
Delvan Cl, SE18
off Ordnance Rd **136** D7
Delvers Mead, Dag. RM10 **101** J4
Delverton Rd, SE17 **35** H4
Delvino Rd, SW6 **148** D1
De Mandeville Gate, Enf. EN1 *off Southbury Rd* **44** D4
Demesne Rd, Wall. SM6 **200** D5
Demeta Cl, Wem. HA9 **88** C3
De Montfort Par, SW16
off Streatham High Rd **168** E3
De Montfort Rd, SW16 **168** E3
De Morgan Rd, SW6 **149** E3
Dempster Cl, Surb. (Long Dit.) KT6 **195** F1
Dempster Rd, SW18 **149** F5
Denbar Par, Rom. RM7
off Mawney Rd **83** J4
Denberry Dr, Sid. DA14 **176** B3
Denbigh Cl, W11 **108** C7
Chislehurst BR7 **174** C6
Southall UB1 **103** F6
Sutton SM1 **198** C5
Denbigh Dr, Hayes UB3 **121** F2
Denbigh Gdns, Rich. TW10 **145** J5
Denbigh Ms, SW1 **33** F2
Denbigh Pl, SW1 **33** F3
Denbigh Rd, E6 **116** A3
W11 **108** C7
W13 **105** E7
Hounslow TW3 **143** H2
Southall UB1 **103** F6
Denbigh St, SW1 **33** F2
Denbigh Ter, W11 **108** C7
Denbridge Rd, Brom. BR1 **192** C2
Den Cl, Beck. BR3 **190** D3
Dene, The, W13 **104** E5
Croydon CR0 **203** G4
Wembley HA9 **87** H4
West Molesey KT8 **179** F5

Dene Av, Houns. TW3 **143** F3
Sidcup DA15 **158** B7
Dene Cl, E10 **96** B2
SE4 **153** H3
Bromley BR2 **205** F1
Worcester Park KT4 **197** F2
Dene Ct, Stan. HA7 **53** F5
Dene Gdns, Stan. HA7 **53** F5
Thames Ditton KT7 **194** D2
Denehurst Gdns, NW4 **71** J6
W3 **126** B1
Richmond TW10 **146** A4
Twickenham TW2 **144** A7
Woodford Green IG8 **63** H4
Dene Rd, N11 **57** J1
Buckhurst Hill IG9 **64** A1
Denewood, Barn. (New Barn.) EN5 **41** F5
Denewood Rd, N6 **73** J6
Denford St, SE10
off Woolwich Rd **135** F5
Dengie Wk, N1
off Basire St **111** J1
Denham Cl, Well. DA16 **158** C3
Denham Cres, Mitch. CR4 **185** J4
Denham Dr, Ilf. IG2 **81** F6
Denham Rd, N20 **57** J3
Feltham TW14 **142** C6
Denham St, SE10 **135** G5
Denham Way, Bark. IG11 **117** H1
Borehamwood WD6 **38** D1
Denholme Rd, W9 **108** C3
Denis Bland Nature Reserve, Barnet EN5 **40** A3
Denison Cl, N2 **73** F3
Denison Rd, SW19 **167** G6
W5 **105** F4
Deniston Av, Bex. DA5 **176** E1
Denis Way, SW4
off Gauden Rd **150** D3
Denleigh Gdns, N21 **59** G1
Thames Ditton KT7 **180** B6
Denman Dr, NW11 **72** D5
Esher (Clay.) KT10 **194** D5
Denman Dr N, NW11 **72** D5
Denman Dr S, NW11 **72** D5
Denman Pl, W1
off Great Windmill St **17** H6
Denman Rd, SE15 **152** C1
Denman St, W1 **17** H6
Denmark Av, SW19 **166** B7
Denmark Ct, Mord. SM4 **184** D5
Denmark Gdns, Cars. SM5 **199** J3
Denmark Gro, N1 **11** E1
Denmark Hill, SE5 **152** A1
Denmark Hill Dr, NW9 **71** F4
Denmark Hill Est, SE5 **152** A4
Denmark Pl, E3
off Kitcat Ter **114** A3
WC2 **17** J3
Denmark Rd, N8 **75** G4
NW6 **108** C2
SE5 **151** J1
SE25 **188** D5
SW19 **166** A6
W13 **105** E7
Bromley BR1 **191** H1
Carshalton SM5 **199** J3
Kingston upon Thames KT1 **181** H3
Twickenham TW2 **162** A3
Denmark St, E11
off High Rd Leytonstone **96** E3
E13 **115** H5
N17 **76** E1
WC2 **17** J4
Denmark Ter, N2
off Fortis Grn **73** J3
Denmark Wk, SE27 **169** J4
Denmead Ho, SW15
off Highcliffe Dr **147** F6
Denmead Rd, Croy. CR0 **201** H1
Dennan Rd, Surb. KT6 **195** J1
Dennard Way, Orp. (Farnboro.) BR6 **206** E4
Denner Rd, E4 **62** A2
Denne Ter, E8 **112** C1
Dennett Rd, Croy. CR0 **201** G1
Dennetts Gro, SE14
off Dennetts Rd **153** G2
Dennetts Rd, SE14 **153** F1
Denning Av, Croy. CR0 **201** G4
Denning Cl, NW8 **6** D3
Hampton TW12 **161** F6
Denning Pt, E1 **21** F3
Denning Rd, NW3 **91** G4
Dennington Cl, E5
off Detmold Rd **95** E2
Dennington Pk Rd, NW6 **90** D6
Denningtons, The, Wor.Pk. KT4 **197** E2
Dennis Av, Wem. HA9 **87** J5
Dennis Gdns, Stan. HA7 **53** F5
Dennis La, Stan. HA7 **52** E3
Dennison Pt, E15 **96** C7
Dennis Pk Cres, SW20 **184** B1
Dennis Reeve Cl, Mitch. CR4 **185** J1
Dennis Rd, E.Mol. KT8 **179** J4
Denny Cl, E6
off Linton Gdns **116** B5
Denny Cres, SE11 **35** F2
Denny Gdns, Dag. RM9
off Canonsleigh Rd **100** B7
Denny Rd, N9 **60** E1
Denny St, SE11 **35** F3
Den Rd, Brom. BR2 **190** D3
Densham Rd, E15 **115** E1
Densole Cl, Beck. BR3 **189** H1
Densworth Gro, N9 **61** F2
Denton, NW1
off Malden Cres **92** A6
Denton Cl, Barn. EN5 **39** J5
Denton Rd, N8 **75** F5
N18 **60** B4
Twickenham TW1 **145** G6
Welling DA16 **138** C7
Denton St, SW18 **149** E6
Denton Way, E5 **95** G3
Dents Rd, SW11 **149** J6
Denver Cl, Orp. BR6 **193** H6
Denver Rd, N16 **76** B7
Denyer St, SW3 **31** H2
Denzil Rd, NW10 **89** F5
Deodar Rd, SW15 **148** B4
Deodora Cl, N20 **57** H3
★ **Department for Constitutional Affairs (DCA)**, SW1 **25** G5
★ **Department for Environment, Food & Rural Affairs (D.E.F.R.A.)**, SW1 **26** A1
★ **Department for Transport (DfT)**, SW1 **33** J1
★ **Department of Health & Dept for Work & Pensions (D.W.P.)**, SW1 **26** A3
Depot App, NW2 **90** A4
Depot Rd, W12 **107** J7
Hounslow TW3 **144** A3
DEPTFORD, SE8 **133** J5
Deptford Br, SE8 **154** A1
Deptford Bdy, SE8 **154** A1
Deptford Ch St, SE8 **134** A6
Deptford Ferry Rd, E14 **134** A4
Deptford Grn, SE8 **134** A6
Deptford High St, SE8 **134** A6
Deptford Strand, SE8 **133** J4
Deptford Wf, SE8 **133** J4
De Quincey Ho, SW1
off Lupus St **33** F4
De Quincey Ms, E16
off Wesley Av **135** G1
De Quincey Rd, N17 **76** A1
Derby Av, N12 **57** F5
Harrow HA3 **68** A1
Romford RM7 **83** J6
Derby Ct, E5
off Overbury St **95** G4
Derby Gate, SW1 **26** A3
Derby Hill, SE23 **171** F2
Derby Hill Cres, SE23 **171** F2
Derby Ho, SE11
off Walnut Tree Wk **34** E1
Derby Rd, E7 **97** J7
E9 **113** G1
E18 **79** F1
N18 **61** F5
SW14 **146** B4
SW19 **166** D7
Croydon CR0 **201** H2
Enfield EN3 **45** E5
Greenford UB6 **103** H1
Hounslow TW3 **143** H4
Surbiton KT5 **196** A1
Sutton SM1 **198** C6
Derby Rd Ind Est, Houns. TW3 *off Derby Rd* **143** H4
Derbyshire St, E2 **13** J4
Derby St, W1 **24** C2
Dereham Pl, EC2 **12** E4
Dereham Rd, Bark. IG11 **99** J6
Derek Av, Epsom KT19 **196** A5
Wallington SM6 **200** B4
Wembley HA9 **88** B7
Derek Cl, Epsom (Ewell) KT19 **196** B5
Derek Walcott Cl, SE24
off Shakespeare Rd **151** H5
Dericote St, E8 **112** D1
Deridene Cl, Stai. (Stanw.) TW19 *off Bedfont Rd* **140** B6
Derifall Cl, E6 **116** C5
Dering Pl, Croy. CR0 **201** J4
Dering Rd, Croy. CR0 **201** J4
Dering St, W1 **16** D4
Derinton Rd, SW17 **167** J4
Derley Rd, Sthl. UB2 **122** C3
Dermody Gdns, SE13 **154** D5
Dermody Rd, SE13 **154** D5
Deronda Rd, SE24 **169** H1
Deroy Cl, Cars. SM5 **199** J6
Derrick Gdns, SE7
off Anchor & Hope La **135** J4
Derrick Rd, Beck. BR3 **189** J3
Derry Rd, Croy. CR0 **200** E3
Derry St, W8 **22** A4
Dersingham Av, E12 **98** D5
Dersingham Rd, NW2 **90** B3
Derwent Av, N18 **60** A5
NW7 **54** D5
NW9 **70** E5
SW15 **164** E4
Barnet EN4 **57** J1
Pinner HA5 **51** E6
Derwent Cl, Esher (Clay.) KT10 **194** B6
Derwent Cres, N20 **57** F3
Bexleyheath DA7 **159** G2
Stanmore HA7 **69** F2
Derwent Dr, Orp. BR5 **193** G7
Derwent Gdns, Ilf. IG4 **80** B4
Wembley HA9 **69** F7
Derwent Gro, SE22 **152** C4
Derwent Ri, NW9 **70** E6
Derwent Rd, N13 **59** F4
SE20 **188** D2
SW20 **184** A6
W5 **125** F3
Southall UB1 **103** G6
Twickenham TW2 **143** H6
Derwent St, SE10 **134** E5
Derwent Wk, Wall. SM6 **200** B7
Derwentwater Rd, W3 **126** C1
Derwent Yd, W5
off Northfield Av **125** F3
Desborough Cl, W2 **14** B1
Desborough Ho, W14
off North End Rd **128** C6
Desborough St, W2 **14** A1
Desenfans Rd, SE21 **152** B6
Desford Ms, E16
off Desford Rd **115** E4
Desford Rd, E16 **115** E4
★ **Design Mus**, SE1 **29** G2
Desmond St, SE14 **133** H6
Desmond Tutu Dr, SE23
off St. Germans Rd **171** H1
Despard Rd, N19 **92** C1
Desvignes Dr, SE13 **154** D6
Detling Rd, Brom. BR1 **173** G5
Detmold Rd, E5 **95** F2
Devalls Cl, E6 **116** D7
Devana End, Cars. SM5 **199** J3
Devas Rd, SW20 **183** J1
Devas St, E3 **114** B4
Devenay Rd, E15 **97** F7
Devenish Rd, SE2 **138** A2
Deventer Cres, SE22 **152** B5
Deveraux Cl, Beck. BR3 **190** C5
De Vere Cl, Wall. SM6 **200** E7
De Vere Gdns, W8 **22** C4
Ilford IG1 **98** C2
Deverell St, SE1 **28** B6
De Vere Ms, W8 **22** C5
Devereux Ct, WC2 **18** E4
Devereux La, SW13 **127** H7
Devereux Rd, SW11 **149** J6
Deverill Ct, SE20 **189** F1
Devey Cl, Kings.T. KT2 **165** E7
Devizes St, N1
off Poole St **112** A1
Devon Av, Twickenham TW2 **161** J1
Devon Cl, N17 **76** C3
Buckhurst Hill IG9 **63** H2
Greenford (Perivale) UB6 **105** F1
Devon Ct, Buck.H. IG9
off Chequers **63** H1
Devoncroft Gdns, Twick. TW1 **144** D7
Devon Gdns, N4 **75** H6
Devonhurst Pl, W4
off Heathfield Ter **126** D5
Devonia Gdns, N18 **59** J6
Devonia Rd, N1 **11** H1
Devon Mans, SE1
off Tooley St **29** F3
Devonport Gdns, Ilf. IG1 **80** C6
Devonport Ms, W12
off Devonport Rd **127** H1
Devonport Rd, W12 **127** H2
Devonport St, E1 **113** F6
Devon Ri, N2 **73** G4
Devon Rd, Bark. IG11 **117** H1
Devons Est, E3 **114** B3
Devonshire Av, Sutt. SM2 **199** F7
Devonshire Business Pk, Borwd. WD6 **38** D3
Devonshire Cl, E15 **97** E4
N13 **59** G4
W1 **16** D1
Devonshire Cres, NW7 **56** A7
Devonshire Dr, SE10 **134** B7
Surbiton (Long Dit.) KT6 **195** G1
Devonshire Gdns, N17 **59** J6
N21 **43** J7
W4 **126** C7
Devonshire Gro, SE15 **133** E6
Devonshire Hill La, N17 **59** J6
Devonshire Ho, SE1
off Bath Ter **27** J5
Sutton SM2
off Devonshire Av **199** F7
Devonshire Ms, SW10
off Park Wk **30** E5
W4 *off Glebe St* **126** E5
Devonshire Ms N, W1 **16** D1
Devonshire Ms S, W1 **16** D1
Devonshire Ms W, W1 **8** D6
Devonshire Pas, W4 **126** E5
Devonshire Pl, NW2 **90** D3
W1 **8** C6
W8 **22** A6
Devonshire Pl Ms, W1 **8** C6
Devonshire Rd, E16 **115** H6
E17 **78** A6
N9 **61** F1
N13 **59** F4
N17 **59** J6
NW7 **56** A7
SE9 **174** B2
SE23 **171** F1
SW19 **167** H7
W4 **126** E5
W5 **125** F3
Bexleyheath DA6 **159** E4
Carshalton SM5 **200** A4
Croydon CR0 **188** A7
Feltham TW13 **160** E3
Harrow HA1 **68** A6
Ilford IG2 **81** G7
Pinner (Eastcote) HA5 **66** C6
Pinner (Hatch End) HA5 **67** F1
Southall UB1 **103** G5
Sutton SM2 **199** F7
Devonshire Row, EC2 **20** E2
Devonshire Row Ms, W1 **8** E6
Devonshire Sq, EC2 **20** E3
Bromley BR2 **191** H4
Devonshire St, W1 **16** C1
W4 **126** E5
Devonshire Ter, W2 **14** D4
Devonshire Way, Croy. CR0 **203** H2
Hayes UB4 **102** B6
Devons Rd, E3 **114** A5
Devon St, SE15 **132** E6
Devon Way, Chess. KT9 **195** F5
Epsom KT19 **196** B5
Devon Waye, Houns. TW5 **123** F7
De Walden St, W1 **16** C2
Dewar St, SE15 **152** D3
Dewberry Gdns, E6 **116** B5
Dewberry St, E14 **114** C5
Dewey Rd, N1 **10** E1
Dagenham RM10 **101** H6
Dewey St, SW17 **167** J5
Dewhurst Rd, W14 **128** A3
Dewlands Ct, NW4
off Holders Hill Rd **72** A2
Dewsbury Cl, Pnr. HA5 **67** E6
Dewsbury Ct, W4
off Chiswick Rd **126** C4
Dewsbury Gdns, Wor.Pk. KT4 **197** G3
Dewsbury Rd, NW10 **89** G5
Dewsbury Ter, NW1
off Camden High St **110** B1
Dexter Ho, Erith DA18
off Kale Rd **139** E3
Dexter Rd, Barn. EN5 **40** A6
Deyncourt Rd, N17 **75** J1
Deynecourt Gdns, E11 **79** J4
D'Eynsford Rd, SE5 **152** A1
Dhonan Ho, SE1
off Longfield Est **37** G1
Diadem Ct, W1 **17** H4
Dial Wk, The, W8 **22** B3
Diamedes Av, Stai. (Stanw.) TW19 **140** A7
Diameter Rd, Orp. BR5 **193** E7
Diamond Cl, Dag. RM8 **100** C1
Diamond Rd, Ruis. HA4 **84** D4
Diamond St, NW10 **88** D7
SE15 **132** B7
Diamond Ter, SE10 **154** C1
Diamond Way, SE8
off Crossfield St **134** A7
Diana Cl, E18 **79** H1
SE8 *off Staunton St* **133** J6
Sidcup DA14 **176** E2
Diana Gdns, Surb. KT6 **195** J2
Diana Ho, SW13 **147** F1
★ **Diana Princess of Wales Mem**, W2 **23** F2

Diana Rd, E17 **77** J3
Dianne Way, Barn. EN4 **41** H5
Dianthus Cl, SE2
off Carnation St **138** B5
Dibden St, N1 **111** H1
Dibdin Cl, Sutt. SM1 **198** D3
Dibdin Ho, W9 **6** A1
Dibdin Rd, Sutt. SM1 **198** D3
Dicey Av, NW2 **89** J5
Dickens Av, N3 **73** F1
Dickens Cl, Erith DA8 **139** H7
Hayes UB3
off Croyde Av **121** H4
Richmond TW10 **163** H2
Dickens Dr, Chis. BR7 **175** F6
Dickens Est, SE1 **29** H4
SE16 **29** H4
Dickens Ho, NW6 **108** D3
Dickens La, N18 **60** B5
Dickens Ms, EC1 **19** G1
Dickenson Cl, N9 **60** D1
Dickenson Rd, N8 **75** E7
Feltham TW13 **160** C5
Dickensons La, SE25 **188** D5
Dickensons Pl, SE25 **188** D6
Dickens Ri, Chig. IG7 **64** D3
Dickens Rd, E6 **116** A2
Dickens Sq, SE1 **28** A5
Dickens St, SW8 **150** B2
Dickenswood Cl, SE19 **169** H7
Dickerage La, N.Mal. KT3 **182** C3
Dickerage Rd, Kings.T. KT1 **182** C1
New Malden KT3 **182** C1
Dickinson Ct, EC1
off Brewhouse Yd **11** H6
Dickson Fold, Pnr. HA5 **66** D4
Dickson Rd, SE9 **156** B3
Dick Turpin Way, Felt. TW14 **141** J4
Didsbury Cl, E6
off Barking Rd **116** C1
Dieppe Cl, W14 **128** C5
Digby Cres, N4 **93** J2
Digby Gdns, Dag. RM10 **119** G1
Digby Pl, Croy. CR0 **202** C3
Digby Rd, E9 **95** G6
Barking IG11 **99** J7
Digby St, E2 **113** F3
Diggon St, E1
off Stepney Way **113** G5
Dighton Ct, SE5 **35** J6
Dighton Rd, SW18 **149** F5
Dignum St, N1 **11** E1
Digswell St, N7
off Holloway Rd **93** G6
Dilhorne Cl, SE12 **173** H3
Dilke St, SW3 **32** A5
Dilloway Yd, Sthl. UB2
off The Green **123** E2
Dillwyn Cl, SE26 **171** H4
Dilston Cl, Nthlt. UB5
off Yeading La **102** C3
Dilston Gro, SE16
off Abbeyfield Rd **133** F4
Dilton Gdns, SW15 **165** G1
Dilwyn Ct, E17
off Hillyfield **77** H2
Dimes Pl, W6 *off King St* **127** H4
Dimmock Dr, Grnf. UB6 **86** A5
Dimond Cl, E7 **97** G4
Dimsdale Dr, NW9 **88** C1
Enfield EN1 **44** D6
Dimsdale Wk, E13
off Stratford Rd **115** G1
Dimson Cres, E3 **114** A4
Dingle Cl, Barn. EN5 **39** F6
Dingle Gdns, E14 **114** A7
Dingley La, SW16 **168** D2
Dingley Pl, EC1 **12** A4
Dingley Rd, EC1 **11** J4
Dingwall Av, Croy. CR0 **201** J2
Dingwall Gdns, NW11 **72** D6
Dingwall Rd, SW18 **149** F7
Croydon CR0 **202** A2
Dinmont St, E2
off Coate St **112** E2
Dinsdale Gdns, SE25 **188** B4
Barnet (New Barn.) EN5 **41** E5
Dinsdale Rd, SE3 **135** F6
Dinsmore Rd, SW12 **150** B7
Dinton Rd, SW19 **167** G6
Kingston upon Thames KT2 **163** J7
Diploma Av, N2 **73** H4
Diploma Ct, N2
off Diploma Av **73** H4
Dirleton Rd, E15 **115** F1
Disbrowe Rd, W6 **128** B6
Discovery Business Pk, SE16
off St. James's Rd **29** J6
Discovery Wk, E1 **132** E1
Dishforth La, NW9 **70** E1
Disney Ms, N4
off Chesterfield Gdns **75** H5
Disney Pl, SE1 **28** A3
Disney St, SE1 **28** A3
Dison Cl, Enf. EN3 **45** G1
Disraeli Cl, SE28 **138** C1
W4 *off Acton La* **126** D3
Disraeli Gdns, SW15
off Fawe Pk Rd **148** C4
Disraeli Rd, E7 **97** G6
NW10 **106** C2
SW15 **148** B4
W5 **125** G1
Diss St, E2 **13** F3
Distaff La, EC4 **19** J5
Distillery La, W6
off Fulham Palace Rd **127** J5
Distillery Rd, W6 **127** J5
Distillery Wk, Brent. TW8 **125** H6
Distin St, SE11 **34** E2
District Rd, Wem. HA0 **86** E5
Ditch All, SE10 **154** B1
Ditchburn St, E14 **114** C7
Ditchfield Rd, Hayes UB4 **102** E4
Dittisham Rd, SE9 **174** B4
Ditton Cl, T.Ditt. KT7 **180** D7
Dittoncroft Cl, Croy. CR0 **202** B4
Ditton Gra Cl, Surb. (Long Dit.) KT6 **195** G1
Ditton Gra Dr, Surb. (Long Dit.) KT6 **195** G1
Ditton Hill, Surb. (Long Dit.) KT6 **195** F1
Ditton Hill Rd, Surb. (Long Dit.) KT6 **195** F1
Ditton Lawn, T.Ditt. KT7 **194** D1
Ditton Pl, SE20 **189** E1
Ditton Reach, T.Ditt. KT7 **180** E6
Ditton Rd, Bexh. DA6 **158** D5
Southall UB2 **123** F4
Surbiton KT6 **195** H1
Divis Way, SW15 **147** H6
Dixon Clark Ct, N1
off Canonbury Rd **93** H6
Dixon Cl, E6
off Brandreth Rd **116** C6
Dixon Ho, W10 **108** A6
Dixon Pl, W.Wick. BR4 **204** B1
Dixon Rd, SE14 **153** H1
SE25 **188** B3
Dixon's All, SE16 **132** E2
Dobbin Cl, Har. HA3 **68** D2
Dobell Path, SE9
off Dobell Rd **156** C5
Dobell Rd, SE9 **156** C5
Dobree Av, NW10 **89** H7
Dobson Cl, NW6 **91** G7
Doby Ct, EC4 **20** A5
Dockers Tanner Rd, E14 **134** A3
Dockhead, SE1 **29** G4
Dock Hill Av, SE16 **133** G2
Dockland St, E16 **136** D1
Dockley Rd, SE16 **29** H6
Dock Rd, E16 **115** F7
Brentford TW8 **125** G7
Dockside Rd, E16 **116** A7
Dock St, E1 **21** H5
Dockwell Cl, Felt. TW14 **142** A4
Doctor Johnson Av, SW17 **168** B3
★ **Doctor Johnson's Ho**, EC4 **19** F4
Doctors Cl, SE26 **171** F5
Docwra's Bldgs, N1 **94** B6
Dodbrooke Rd, SE27 **169** G3
Dodd Ho, SE16
off Rennie Est **133** E4
Doddington Gro, SE17 **35** G5
Doddington Pl, SE17 **35** G5
Dodsley Pl, N9 **61** F3
Dodson St, SE1 **27** F4
Dod St, E14 **113** J6
Doebury Wk, SE18
off Prestwood Cl **138** A6
Doel Cl, SW19 **167** F7
Doggett Rd, SE6 **154** A7
Doggetts Cl, Barn. (E.Barn.) EN4 **41** H5
Doghurst Av, Hayes (Harling.) UB3 **121** E7
Doghurst Dr, West Dr. UB7 **121** E7
Dog Kennel Hill, SE22 **152** B3
Dog Kennel Hill Est, SE22 **152** B3
Dog La, NW10 **89** E4
Doherty Rd, E13 **115** G4
Dokal Ind Est, Sthl. UB2
off Hartington Rd **122** E3
Dolben St, SE1 **27** G2
Dolby Rd, SW6 **148** C2
Dolland St, SE11 **34** D4
Dollis Av, N3 **72** C1
Dollis Brook Wk, Barn. EN5 **40** B6
Dollis Cres, Ruis. HA4 **84** C1
DOLLIS HILL, NW2 **89** H3
Dollis Hill Av, NW2 **89** H3
Dollis Hill La, NW2 **89** H3
Dollis Ms, N3 **72** D1
Dollis Pk, N3 **72** C1
Dollis Rd, N3 **56** B7
NW7 **56** B7
Dollis Valley Dr, Barn. EN5 **40** C6
Dollis Valley Grn Wk, N20
off Totteridge La **57** F2
Barnet EN5 **40** B6
Dollis Valley Way, Barn. EN5 **40** C6
Dolman Cl, N3
off Avondale Rd **73** F2
Dolman Rd, W4 **126** D4
Dolman St, SW4 **151** F4
Dolphin Cl, SE16
off Kinburn St **133** G2
SE28 **118** D6
Surbiton KT6 **181** G6
Dolphin Ct, NW11 **72** B6
Dolphin Ho, SW18
off Smugglers Way **149** E4
Dolphin La, E14 **114** B7
Dolphin Rd, Nthlt. UB5 **103** F2
Dolphin Sq, SW1 **33** G4
W4 **126** E7
Dolphin St, Kings.T. KT1 **181** H1
Dolphin Twr, SE8
off Abinger Gro **133** J6
Dombey St, WC1 **18** C1
Dome Hill Pk, SE26 **170** C4
Domett Cl, SE5 **152** A4
Domfe Pl, E5
off Rushmore Rd **95** F4
Domingo St, EC1 **11** J5
Dominica Cl, E13 **115** J2
Dominion Business Pk, N9 *off Goodwin Rd* **61** G2
Dominion Cl, Houns. TW3 **144** A2
Dominion Ho, W13 **104** E7
Dominion Rd, Croy. CR0 **188** C7
Southall UB2 **123** E3
Dominion St, EC2 **20** C1
★ **Dominion Thea**, W1 **17** J3
Domonic Dr, SE9 **174** E4
Domville Cl, N20 **57** G2
Donald Dr, Rom. RM6 **82** C5
Donald Rd, E13 **115** H1
Croydon CR0 **187** F6
Donaldson Rd, NW6 **108** C1
SE18 **156** D1
Donald Wds Gdns, Surb. KT5 **196** B2
Donato Dr, SE15 **36** D6
Doncaster Dr, Nthlt. UB5 **85** F5
Doncaster Gdns, N4
off Stanhope Gdns **75** J6
Northolt UB5 **85** F5
Doncaster Grn, Wat. WD19 **50** C5
Doncaster Rd, N9 **44** E7
Doncel Ct, E4 **46** D7
Donegal St, N1 **10** D2
Doneraile St, SW6 **148** A2
Dongola Rd, E1 **113** H5
E13 **115** H3
N17 **76** B3
Dongola Rd W, E13
off Balaam St **115** H3
Donington Av, Ilf. IG6 **81** F5
Donkey All, SE22 **152** D7
Donkey La, Enf. EN1 **44** D2
Donkin Ho, SE16
off Rennie Est **133** E4
Donne Ct, SE24 **151** J6
Donnefield Av, Edg. HA8 **53** H7
Donne Pl, SW3 **31** H1
Mitcham CR4 **186** B4
Donne Rd, Dag. RM8 **100** C2
Donnington Ct, NW10 **89** H7
Donnington Rd, NW10 **89** H7
Harrow HA3 **69** G5
Worcester Park KT4 **197** G2
Donnybrook Rd, SW16 **168** C7
Donovan Av, N10 **74** B2
Donovan Ct, SW10
off Drayton Gdns **30** E4
Donovan Pl, N21 **43** F5
Don Phelan Cl, SE5 **152** A1
Doone Cl, Tedd. TW11 **162** D6
Doon St, SE1 **26** E2
Doral Way, Cars. SM5 **199** J5
Dorando Cl, W12 **107** H7
Doran Gro, SE18 **137** H7
Doran Wk, E15 **96** C7
Dora Rd, SW19 **166** D5
Dora St, E14 **113** J6
Dora Way, SW9 **151** G2
Dorchester Av, N13 **59** J4
Bexley DA5 **176** D1
Harrow HA2 **67** J6
Dorchester Cl, Northolt UB5 **85** H5
Orpington BR5 **176** A7
Dorchester Ct, N14 **42** B7
SE24 **151** J5
Dorchester Dr, SE24 **151** J5
Feltham TW14 **141** H6
Dorchester Gdns, E4 **62** A4
NW11 **72** D4
Dorchester Gro, W4 **127** E5
Dorchester Ho, Richmond TW9 **126** B7
Dorchester Ms, N.Mal. KT3
off Elm Rd **182** D4
Twickenham TW1 **145** F7
Dorchester Rd, Mord. SM4 **185** E7
Northolt UB5 **85** H5
Worcester Park KT4 **197** J1
Dorchester Way, Har. HA3 **69** J6
Dorchester Waye, Hayes UB4 **102** C6
Dorcis Av, Bexh. DA7 **158** E2
Dordrecht Rd, W3 **127** E1
Dore Av, E12 **98** D5
Doreen Av, NW9 **88** D1
Dore Gdns, Mord. SM4 **185** E7
Dorell Cl, Sthl. UB1 **103** F5
Dorey Ho, Brent. TW8
off High St **125** F7
Doria Rd, SW6 **148** C2
Doric Way, NW1 **9** H3
Dorie Ms, N12 **57** E4
Dorien Rd, SW20 **184** A2
Doris Ashby Cl, Grnf. UB6
off Horsenden La S **104** D1
Doris Av, Erith DA8 **159** J1
Doris Rd, E7 **97** G7
Dorking Cl, SE8 **133** J6
Worcester Park KT4 **198** A2
Dorlcote Rd, SW18 **149** G7
Dorman Pl, N9 **60** D2
Dorman Wk, NW10
off Garden Way **88** D5
Dorman Way, NW8 **109** G1
Dorma Trd Pk, E10 **95** G1
Dormay St, SW18 **148** E5
Dormer Cl, E15 **97** F6
Barnet EN5 **40** A5
Dormers Av, Sthl. UB1 **103** G6
Dormers Ri, Sthl. UB1 **103** H6
DORMER'S WELLS, Sthl. UB1 **103** H7
Dormers Wells La, Sthl. UB1 **103** G6
Dornberg Cl, SE3 **135** G7
Dornberg Rd, SE3
off Banchory Rd **135** H7
Dorncliffe Rd, SW6 **148** B2
Dorney, NW3 **91** H7
Dorney Ri, Orp. BR5 **193** J4
Dorney Way, Houns. TW4 **143** E5
Dornfell St, NW6 **90** C5
Dornton Rd, SW12 **168** B2
South Croydon CR2 **202** A5
Dorothy Av, Wem. HA0 **87** H7
Dorothy Evans Cl, Bexh. DA7 **159** H4
Dorothy Gdns, Dag. RM8 **100** B4
Dorothy Rd, SW11 **149** J3
Dorrell Pl, SW9
off Brixton Rd **151** G4
Dorrien Wk, SW16 **168** D2
Dorrington Ct, SE25 **188** B2
Dorrington Pt, E3
off Bromley High St **114** B3
Dorrington St, EC1 **19** E1
Dorrington Way, Beck. BR3 **190** C5
Dorrit Ms, N18 **60** B4
Dorrit St, SE1 **28** A3
Dorrit Way, Chis. BR7 **175** F6
Dors Cl, NW9 **88** D1
Dorset Av, Sthl. UB2 **123** G4
Welling DA16 **157** J4
Dorset Bldgs, EC4 **19** G4
Dorset Cl, NW1 **15** J1
Dorset Dr, Edg. HA8 **53** J6
Dorset Est, E2 **13** G3
Dorset Gdns, Mitch. CR4 **187** F4
Dorset Ms, N3 **72** D1
SW1 **24** D5
Dorset Pl, E15 **96** D6
Dorset Ri, EC4 **19** G4
Dorset Rd, E7 **97** J7
N15 **76** A4
N22 **75** E1
SE9 **174** B2
SW8 **34** B7
SW19 **184** D1
W5 **125** F3
Beckenham BR3 **189** G3
Harrow HA1 **67** J6
Mitcham CR4 **185** H2
Dorset Sq, NW1 **7** J6
Dorset St, W1 **16** A2
Dorset Way, Twick. TW2 **162** A1

Dorset Waye, Houns. TW5 123 F7
Dorton Cl, SE15 off Chandler Way 132 B7
Dorville Cres, W6 127 H3
Dorville Rd, SE12 155 F5
Dothill Rd, SE18 137 G7
Douai Gro, Hmptn. TW12 179 J1
Doubleday Rd, Loug. IG10 49 F3
Doughty Ms, WC1 10 C6
Doughty St, WC1 10 C5
Douglas Av, E17 78 A1
New Malden KT3 183 H4
Wembley HA0 87 H7
Douglas Cl, Ilf. IG6 64 E7
Stanmore HA7 52 D5
Wallington SM6 201 E7
Douglas Cres, Hayes UB4 102 C4
Douglas Dr, Croy. CR0 204 A3
Douglas Ms, NW2 90 B3
Douglas Path, E14 off Manchester Rd 134 C5
Douglas Rd, E4 47 E7
E16 115 G5
N1 93 J7
N22 75 G1
NW6 108 C1
Hounslow TW3 143 H3
Ilford IG3 82 A6
Kingston upon Thames KT1 182 B2
Staines (Stanw.) TW19 140 A6
Surbiton KT6 195 J2
Welling DA16 158 B1
Douglas Sq, Mord. SM4 184 D6
Douglas St, SW1 33 H2
Douglas Ter, E17 off Penrhyn Av 77 J1
Douglas Way, SE8 133 J7
Doulton Ho, SE11 off Lambeth Wk 26 D6
Doulton Ms, NW6 off Dresden Cl 91 E6
Dounesforth Gdns, SW18 166 E1
Douro Pl, W8 22 B5
Douro St, E3 114 A2
Douthwaite Sq, E1 29 J1
Dove App, E6 116 B5
Dove Cl, NW7 55 F7
Northolt UB5 off Wayfarer Rd 102 D4
Wallington SM6 201 F7
Dovecot Cl, Pnr. HA5 66 B5
Dovecote Av, N22 75 G3
Dovecote Gdns, SW14 off Avondale Rd 146 D3
Dove Ct, EC2 20 B4
Dovedale Av, Har. HA3 69 F6
Ilford IG5 80 D2
Dovedale Cl, Well. DA16 158 A1
Dovedale Ri, Mitch. CR4 167 J7
Dovedale Rd, SE22 153 E5
Dovedon Cl, N14 58 E2
Dove Ho Gdns, E4 62 A2
Dovehouse Mead, Bark. IG11 117 G2
Dovehouse St, SW3 31 G3
Dove Ms, SW5 30 C2
Dove Pk, Pnr. HA5 51 G7
Dover Cl, NW2 off Brent Ter 90 A2
Romford RM5 83 J2
Dovercourt Av, Th.Hth. CR7 187 G4
Dovercourt Est, N1 94 A6
Dovercourt Gdns, Stan. HA7 53 H5
Dovercourt La, Sutt. SM1 199 F3
Dovercourt Rd, SE22 152 B6
Doverfield Rd, SW2 151 E6
Dover Flats, SE1 36 E2
Dover Gdns, Cars. SM5 199 J3
Dover Ho Rd, SW15 147 G4
Doveridge Gdns, N13 59 H4
Dove Rd, N1 94 A6
Dove Row, E2 112 D1
Dover Pk Dr, SW15 147 H6
Dover Patrol, SE3 off Kidbrooke Way 155 H2
Dover Rd, E12 97 J2
N9 61 F2
SE19 170 A6
Romford RM6 82 E6
Dover St, W1 17 E6
Dover Yd, W1 25 F1
Doves Cl, Brom. BR2 206 B2
Doves Yd, N1 111 G1
Dovet Ct, SW8 off Mursell Est 151 F1
Doveton Rd, South Croydon CR2 202 A5
Doveton St, E1 off Malcolm Rd 113 F4
Dove Wk, SW1 32 B3
Dowanhill Rd, SE6 172 D1
Dowd Cl, N11 off Nurserymans Rd 58 A2
Dowdeswell Cl, SW15 147 E4
Dowding Pl, Stan. HA7 52 D6
Dowdney Cl, NW5 92 C5
Dowgate Hill, EC4 20 B5
Dowland St, W10 108 B2
Dowlas Est, SE5 36 D7
Dowlas St, SE5 36 D7
Dowlerville Rd, Orp. BR6 207 J6
Dowman Cl, SW19 off Nelson Gro Rd 185 E1
Downage, NW4 71 J3
Downalong, Bushey (Bushey Hth) WD23 52 A1
Downbarns Rd, Ruis. HA4 84 D3
Downbury Ms, SW18 off Merton Rd 148 D6
Down Cl, Nthlt. UB5 102 B2
Downderry Rd, Brom. BR1 172 D3
Downe Cl, Well. DA16 138 C7
Downe Ho, SE7 off Springfield Gro 135 J6
Downend, SE18 off Moordown 136 E7
Downe Rd, Mitch. CR4 185 J2
Downers Cotts, SW4 off Old Town 150 C4
Downes Cl, Twick. TW1 off St. Margarets Rd 145 E6
Downes Ct, N21 59 G1
Downfield, Wor.Pk. KT4 197 F1
Downfield Cl, W9 6 A6
Down Hall Rd, Kings.T. KT2 181 G1
DOWNHAM, Brom. BR1 173 F5
Downham La, Brom. BR1 172 D5
Downham Rd, N1 94 A7
Downham Way, Brom. BR1 172 D5
Downhills Av, N17 76 A3
Downhills Pk Rd, N17 75 J3
Downhills Way, N17 75 J3
Downhurst Av, NW7 54 D5
Downing Cl, Har. HA2 67 J3
Downing Dr, Grnf. UB6 104 A1
Downing Rd, Dag. RM9 119 F1
Downings, E6 116 D6
Downing St, SW1 26 A3
Downland Cl, N20 57 F1
Downleys Cl, SE9 174 B2
Downman Rd, SE9 156 B3
Down Pl, W6 127 H4
Down Rd, Tedd. TW11 163 E6
Downs, The, SW20 166 A7
Downs Av, Chis. BR7 174 C5
Pinner HA5 67 F6
Downs Br Rd, Beck. BR3 190 D1
Downsbury Ms, SW18 off Merton Rd 148 D5
Downsell Rd, E15 96 C4
Downsfield Rd, E17 77 H6
Downshall Av, Ilf. IG3 81 H6
Downs Hill, Beck. BR3 172 D7
Downshire Hill, NW3 91 G4
Downside, Sun. TW16 178 A1
Twickenham TW1 162 C3
Downside Cl, SW19 167 F6
Downside Cres, NW3 91 H5
W13 104 D4
Downside Rd, Sutt. SM2 199 G6
Downside Wk, Brent. TW8 off Sidney Gdns 125 F6
Northolt UB5 103 F3
Downs La, E5 off Downs Rd 94 E4
Downs Pk Rd, E5 94 D5
E8 94 C5
Downs Rd, E5 94 D4
Beckenham BR3 190 B2
Enfield EN1 44 B4
Thornton Heath CR7 187 J1
Down St, W1 24 D2
West Molesey KT8 179 G5
Down St Ms, W1 24 D2
Downs Vw, Islw. TW7 144 C1
Downsview Gdns, SE19 169 H7
Downsview Rd, SE19 169 J7
Downsway, Orp. BR6 207 H5
Downton Av, SW2 169 E2
Downtown Rd, SE16 133 H2
Down Way, Nthlt. UB5 102 B3
Dowrey St, N1 off Richmond Av 111 G1
Dowsett Rd, N17 76 C2
Dowson Cl, SE5 152 A4
Doyce St, SE1 27 J3
Doyle Gdns, NW10 107 G1
Doyle Rd, SE25 188 D4
D'Oyley St, SW1 32 B1
Doynton St, N19 92 B2
Draco Gate, SW15 off Erpingham Rd 147 J3
Draco St, SE17 35 J5
Dragonfly Cl, E13 115 H3
Dragon Rd, SE15 36 D6
Dragoon Rd, SE8 133 J5
Dragor Rd, NW10 106 C4
Drake Cl, SE16 off Middleton Dr 133 G2
Drake Ct, SE19 170 C5
W12 127 J2
Harrow HA2 85 F1
Drake Cres, SE28 118 C6
Drakefell Rd, SE4 153 G2
SE14 153 G2
Drakefield Rd, SW17 168 A3
Drake Ho, SW8 off St. George Wf 34 A4
Drakeley Ct, N5 93 H4
Drake Ms, Brom. BR2 191 J4
Drake Rd, SE4 154 A3
Chessington KT9 196 A5
Croydon CR0 187 F7
Harrow HA2 85 F2
Mitcham CR4 186 A6
Drakes Ctyd, NW6 90 C7
Drake St, WC1 18 C2
Enfield EN2 44 A1
Drakes Wk, E6 116 C1
Drakewood Rd, SW16 168 D7
Draper Cl, Belv. DA17 139 F4
Isleworth TW7 144 A2
Draper Ho, SE1 35 H1
Draper Pl, N1 off Dagmar Ter 111 H1
Drapers' Ct, SW11 off Lurline Gdns 150 A1
Drapers Rd, E15 96 D4
N17 76 C3
Enfield EN2 43 H2
Drappers Way, SE16 37 J1
Draven Cl, Brom. BR2 191 F7
Drawdock Rd, SE10 134 D1
Drawell Cl, SE18 137 H5
Drax Av, SW20 165 H7
Draxmont, SW19 166 B6
Draycot Rd, E11 79 H6
Surbiton KT6 196 A1
Draycott Av, SW3 31 H1
Harrow HA3 69 E6
Draycott Cl, NW2 90 A3
SE5 off Caspian St 132 A7
Harrow HA3 69 E6
Draycott Ms, SW6 off New Kings Rd 148 C2
Draycott Pl, SW3 31 J2
Draycott Ter, SW3 32 A1
Drayford Cl, W9 108 C4
Dray Gdns, SW2 151 F5
Draymans Ms, SE15 off Chadwick Rd 152 C2
Draymans Way, Islw. TW7 144 C3
Drayside Ms, Sthl. UB2 123 F2
Drayson Ms, W8 128 D2
Drayton Av, W13 104 D7
Loughton IG10 48 C6
Orpington BR6 207 E1
Drayton Br Rd, W7 104 C7
W13 104 C7
Drayton Cl, Houns. TW4 143 F5
Ilford IG1 99 G1
Drayton Gdns, N21 43 H7
SW10 30 D3
W13 104 D7
West Drayton UB7 120 B2
Drayton Grn, W13 104 D7
Drayton Grn Rd, W13 104 E7
Drayton Gro, W13 104 D7
Drayton Pk, N5 93 G5
Drayton Pk Ms, N5 off Drayton Pk 93 G5
Drayton Rd, E11 96 D1
N17 76 B2
NW10 107 F1
W13 104 D7
Borehamwood WD6 38 A4
Croydon CR0 201 H2
Drayton Waye, Har. HA3 69 E6
Dreadnought Cl, SW19 185 G2
Dreadnought St, SE10 off Blackwall Tun App 135 E3
Dresden Cl, NW6 91 E6
Dresden Ho, SE11 off Lambeth Wk 34 D1
Dresden Rd, N19 92 C1
Dressington Av, SE4 154 A6
Drew Av, NW7 56 B6
Drew Gdns, Grnf. UB6 86 C6
Drew Rd, E16 136 B1
Drewstead Rd, SW16 168 D2
Driffield Rd, E3 113 H2
Drift, The, Brom. BR2 206 A3
Drift Way, Rich. TW10 163 J1
Driftway, The, Mitch. CR4 186 A1
Drinkwater Rd, Har. HA2 85 H2
Drive, The, E4 46 D7
E17 78 B4
Drive, The, E18 79 G4
N3 56 D7
N6 73 J5
N11 58 C6
NW10 off Longstone Av 107 F1
NW11 72 B7
SW6 off Fulham Rd 148 B2
SW16 187 F3
SW20 165 J7
W3 106 C6
Barking IG11 99 J7
Barnet (High Barn.) EN5 40 B3
Barnet (New Barn.) EN5 41 F6
Beckenham BR3 190 A2
Bexley DA5 158 C6
Buckhurst Hill IG9 47 J7
Chislehurst BR7 193 J3
Chislehurst (Scad.Pk) BR7 193 H1
Edgware HA8 54 A5
Enfield EN2 44 A1
Epsom KT19 197 F6
Erith DA8 139 H7
Feltham TW14 142 C7
Harrow HA2 67 G7
Hounslow TW3 144 A2
Ilford IG1 98 C1
Isleworth TW7 144 A2
Kingston upon Thames KT2 164 C7
Loughton IG10 48 B3
Morden SM4 185 G5
Orpington BR6 207 J2
Romford (Coll.Row) RM5 83 J1
Sidcup DA14 176 B3
Surbiton KT6 181 H7
Thornton Heath CR7 188 A4
Wembley HA9 88 C2
West Wickham BR4 190 D7
Driveway, The, E17 off Hoe St 78 B6
Droitwich Cl, SE26 170 D3
Dromey Gdns, Har. HA3 52 C7
Dromore Rd, SW15 148 B6
Dronfield Gdns, Dag. RM8 100 C5
Droop St, W10 108 B4
Drovers Pl, SE15 133 E7
Drovers Rd, S.Croy. CR2 202 A5
Droveway, Loug. IG10 49 E2
Druce Rd, SE21 152 B6
Druid St, SE1 29 E3
Druids Way, Brom. BR2 190 D4
Drumaline Ridge, Wor.Pk. KT4 197 E2
Drummond Cres, NW1 9 H3
Drummond Dr, Stan. HA7 52 C7
Drummond Gate, SW1 33 J3
Drummond Pl, Twick. TW1 144 E6
Drummond Rd, E11 79 H6
SE16 132 E3
Croydon CR0 201 J2
Drummonds, The, Buck.H. IG9 63 H2
Drummonds Pl, Rich. TW9 145 H4
Drummond St, NW1 9 F5
Drum St, E1 21 G3
Drury Cres, Croy. CR0 201 G2
Drury La, WC2 18 B4
Drury Rd, Har. HA1 67 J7
Drury Way, NW10 88 D5
Drury Way Ind Est, NW10 88 C5
Dryad St, SW15 148 A3
Dryburgh Gdns, NW9 70 A3
Dryburgh Rd, SW15 147 H3
Dryden Av, W7 104 C6
Dryden Cl, SW4 150 D5
Ilford IG6 65 J6
Dryden Ct, SE11 35 F2
Dryden Rd, SW19 167 F6
Enfield EN1 44 B6
Harrow HA3 68 C1
Welling DA16 157 H1
Dryden St, WC2 18 B4
Dryfield Cl, NW10 88 C6
Dryfield Rd, Edg. HA8 54 C6
Dryfield Wk, SE8 off New King St 134 A6
Dryhill Rd, Belv. DA17 139 F6
Dryland Av, Orp. BR6 207 J4
Drylands Rd, N8 75 E6
Drysdale Av, E4 46 B7
Drysdale Pl, N1 12 E3
Drysdale St, N1 12 E4
Dublin Av, E8 112 D1
Du Burstow Ter, W7 124 B2
Ducal St, E2 13 G4
Du Cane Cl, W12 107 J6
Du Cane Ct, SW17 168 A1

Du Cane Rd, W12 ...107 F6
Duchess Cl, N11 ...58 B5
Sutton SM1 ...199 F4
Duchess Gro, Buck.H. IG9 ...63 H2
Duchess Ms, W1 ...16 E2
Duchess of Bedford's Wk, W8 ...128 D2
Duchess St, W1 ...16 E2
Duchy St, SE1 ...27 F1
Ducie Ho, SE7
off Springfield Gro ...135 J6
Ducie St, SW4 ...151 F4
Duckett Ms, N4
off Duckett Rd ...75 H6
Duckett Rd, N4 ...75 H6
Duckett St, E1 ...113 G4
Duck La, W1 ...17 H4
Duck Lees La, Enf. EN3 ...45 H4
DUCKS ISLAND, Barn. EN5 ...40 A6
Ducks Wk, Twick. TW1 ...145 F5
Du Cros Dr, Stan. HA7 ...53 G6
Du Cros Rd, W3
off The Vale ...126 E1
Dudden Hill La, NW10 ...89 F4
Duddington Cl, SE9 ...174 A4
Dudley Av, Har. HA3 ...69 F3
Dudley Ct, NW11 ...72 C4
Dudley Dr, Mord. SM4 ...184 B7
Ruislip HA4 ...84 B5
Dudley Gdns, W13 ...125 E2
Harrow HA2 ...86 A1
Dudley Ho, W2
off North Wf Rd ...14 E2
Dudley Ms, SW2
off Bascombe St ...151 G6
Dudley Pl, Hayes UB3 ...121 G4
TW19 ...140 C6
Dudley Rd, E17 ...78 A2
N3 ...72 E2
NW6 ...108 B2
SW19 ...166 D6
Harrow HA2 ...85 J2
Ilford IG1 ...99 E4
Kingston upon Thames KT1 ...181 J3
Richmond TW9 ...145 J2
Southall UB2 ...122 D2
Walton-on-Thames KT12 ...178 A6
Dudley St, W2 ...14 E2
Dudlington Rd, E5 ...95 F2
Dudmaston Ms, SW3 ...31 F3
Dudrich Cl, N11 ...57 J6
Dudrich Ms, SE22
off Melbourne Gro ...152 C5
Dudsbury Rd, Sid. DA14 ...176 B6
Dudset La, Houns. TW5 ...142 A1
Duffell Ho, SE11 ...34 D3
Dufferin Av, EC1 ...12 B6
Dufferin St, EC1 ...12 A6
Duffield Cl, Har. HA1 ...68 C5
Duffield Dr, N15
off Copperfield Dr ...76 C4
Duff St, E14 ...114 B6
Dufour's Pl, W1 ...17 G4
Dugard Way, SE11 ...35 G1
Duggan Dr, Chis. BR7 ...174 B5
Dugolly Av, Wem. HA9 ...88 B3
Duke Gdns, Ilf. IG6
off Duke Rd ...81 G4
Duke Humphrey Rd, SE3 ...155 E1
Duke of Cambridge Cl, Twick. TW2 ...144 A6
Duke of Edinburgh Rd, Sutt. SM1 ...199 G2
Duke of Wellington Av, SE18 ...137 E3
Duke of Wellington Pl, SW1 ...24 C3
Duke of York Sq, SW3 ...32 A2
Duke of York St, SW1 ...25 G1
Duke Rd, W4 ...126 D5
Ilford IG6 ...81 G4
Dukes Av, N3 ...72 E1
N10 ...74 C3
W4 ...126 D5
Edgware HA8 ...53 J6
Harrow HA1 ...68 B4
Harrow (N.Har.) HA2 ...67 F6
Hounslow TW4 ...142 E4
Kingston upon Thames KT2 ...163 F4
New Malden KT3 ...183 F3
Northolt UB5 ...85 E7
Richmond TW10 ...163 F4
Dukes Cl, Hmptn. TW12 ...161 F5
Dukes Ct, E6 ...116 D1
Dukes Gate, W4 ...126 C4
Dukes Grn Av, Felt. TW14 ...142 A5
Dukes Head Yd, N6
off Highgate High St ...92 B1
Duke Shore Pl, E14
off Narrow St ...113 J7
Duke Shore Wf, E14
off Narrow St ...113 J7
Dukes La, W8 ...128 D2
Duke's Meadows, W4 ...146 D1
Dukes Ms, N10 ...74 B3
Duke's Ms, W1 ...16 C3
Dukes Orchard, Bex. DA5 ...177 J1
Duke's Pas, E17 ...78 C4
Dukes Pl, EC3 ...21 E4
Dukes Rd, E6 ...116 D1
W3 ...106 A5
Duke's Rd, WC1 ...9 J4
Dukesthorpe Rd, SE26 ...171 G4
Duke St, SW1 ...25 G1
W1 ...16 C3
Richmond TW9 ...145 G4
Sutton SM1 ...199 G4
Duke St Hill, SE1 ...28 C1
Dukes Way, W.Wick. BR4 ...205 E3
Duke's Yd, W1 ...16 C5
Dulas St, N4 ...93 F1
Dulford St, W11 ...108 B7
Dulka Rd, SW11 ...149 J5
Dulverton Rd, SE9 ...175 F2
Ruislip HA4 ...84 A1
DULWICH, SE21 ...152 B7
★ **Dulwich Coll Picture Gall**, SE21 ...152 B7
Dulwich Common, SE21 ...170 B1
SE22 ...170 B1
Dulwich Lawn Cl, SE22
off Colwell Rd ...152 C5
Dulwich Oaks, The, SE21 ...170 B3
Dulwich Ri Gdns, SE22
off Lordship La ...152 C5
Dulwich Rd, SE24 ...151 G5
Dulwich Village, SE21 ...152 B6
Dulwich Wd Av, SE19 ...170 B4
Dulwich Wd Pk, SE19 ...170 B4
Dumbarton Rd, SW2 ...151 E6
Dumbleton Cl, Kings.T. KT1 ...182 B1
Dumbreck Rd, SE9 ...156 C4
Dumont Rd, N16 ...94 B3
Dumpton Pl, NW1
off Gloucester Av ...92 A7
Dunbar Av, SW16 ...187 G2
Beckenham BR3 ...189 H4
Dagenham RM10 ...101 G3
Dunbar Cl, Hayes UB4 ...102 A5
Dunbar Ct, Sutt. SM1 ...199 G5
Dunbar Gdns, Dag. RM10 ...101 G5
Dunbar Rd, E7 ...97 G6
N22 ...75 G1
New Malden KT3 ...182 C4
Dunbar St, SE27 ...169 J3
Dunblane Cl, Edg. HA8 ...54 B2
Dunblane Rd, SE9 ...156 B3
Dunboyne Rd, NW3 ...91 J5
Dunbridge Ho, SW15
off Highcliffe Dr ...147 F6
Dunbridge St, E2 ...13 J5
Duncan Cl, Barn. EN5 ...41 F4
Duncan Gro, W3 ...106 E6
Duncannon St, WC2 ...18 A6
Duncan Rd, E8 ...112 E1
Richmond TW9 ...145 H4
Duncan St, N1 ...11 G1
Duncan Ter, N1 ...11 G2
Dunch St, E1
off Watney St ...113 E6
Duncombe Hill, SE23 ...153 H7
Duncombe Rd, N19 ...92 D1
Duncrievie Rd, SE13 ...154 D6
Duncroft, SE18 ...137 H7
Dundalk Rd, SE4 ...153 H3
Dundas Gdns, W.Mol. KT8 ...179 H3
Dundas Rd, SE15 ...153 F2
Dundee Ho, W9 ...6 C3
Dundee Rd, E13 ...115 H2
SE25 ...188 E5
Dundee St, E1 ...132 E1
Dundee Way, Enf. EN3 ...45 H3
Dundela Gdns, Wor.Pk. KT4 ...197 H4
Dundonald Cl, E6
off Northumberland Rd ...116 B6
Dundonald Rd, NW10 ...108 A1
SW19 ...166 B7
Dunedin Ho, E16
off Manwood St ...136 C1
Dunedin Rd, E10 ...96 B3
Ilford IG1 ...99 F1
Dunedin Way, Hayes UB4 ...102 C4
Dunelm Gro, SE27 ...169 J4
Dunelm St, E1 ...113 G6
Dunfield Gdns, SE6 ...172 B4
Dunfield Rd, SE6 ...172 B5
Dunford Rd, N7 ...93 F4
Dungarvan Av, SW15 ...147 G4
Dunheved Cl, Th.Hth. CR7 ...187 G6
Dunheved Rd N, Th.Hth. CR7 ...187 G6
Dunheved Rd S, Th.Hth. CR7 ...187 G6
Dunheved Rd W, Th.Hth. CR7 ...187 G6
Dunhill Pt, SW15
off Dilton Gdns ...165 H1
Dunholme Grn, N9 ...60 C3
Dunholme La, N9 ...60 D3
Dunholme Rd, N9 ...60 C3
Dunkeld Rd, SE25 ...188 A4
Dagenham RM8 ...100 B2
Dunkery Rd, SE9 ...174 A4
Dunkirk St, SE27 ...169 J4
Dunlace Rd, E5 ...95 F4
Dunleary Cl, Houns. TW4 ...143 F7
Dunley Dr, Croy. (New Adgtn) CR0 ...204 B7
Dunlin Ho, W13 ...104 C4
Dunloe Av, N17 ...76 A3
Dunloe St, E2 ...13 F2
Dunlop Pl, SE16 ...29 G6
Dunmore Pt, E2 ...13 F4
Dunmore Rd, NW6 ...108 B1
SW20 ...183 J1
Dunmow Cl, Felt. TW13 ...160 D4
Loughton IG10 ...48 B6
Romford RM6 ...82 C5
Dunmow Ho, Dag. RM9 ...118 B1
Dunmow Rd, E15 ...96 D4
Dunmow Wk, N1
off Popham St ...111 J1
Dunnage Cres, SE16
off Plough Way ...133 H4
Dunn Mead, NW9 ...55 F7
Dunnock Cl, N9 ...61 G1
Borehamwood WD6 ...38 A4
Dunnock Rd, E6 ...116 B6
Dunns Pas, WC1 ...18 B3
Dunn St, E8 ...94 C5
Dunollie Pl, NW5
off Dunollie Rd ...92 C5
Dunollie Rd, NW5 ...92 C5
Dunoon Rd, SE23 ...153 F7
Dunraven Dr, Enf. EN2 ...43 G2
Dunraven Rd, W12 ...127 G1
Dunraven St, W1 ...16 A5
Dunsany Rd, W14 ...128 A3
Dunsfold Way, Croy. (New Adgtn) CR0 ...204 B7
Dunsford Way, SW15
off Dover Pk Dr ...147 H6
Dunsmore Cl, Hayes UB4 ...102 D4
Dunsmore Rd, Walt. KT12 ...178 B6
Dunsmure Rd, N16 ...94 B1
Dunspring La, Ilf. IG5 ...80 E2
Dunstable Ms, W1 ...16 C1
Dunstable Rd, Rich. TW9 ...145 H4
West Molesey KT8 ...179 F4
Dunstall Rd, SW20 ...165 H6
Dunstall Way, W.Mol. KT8 ...179 H3
Dunstall Welling Est, Well. DA16 *off Leigh Pl* ...158 B2
Dunstan Cl, N2 ...73 F3
Dunstan Ho, E1
off Stepney Grn ...113 F5
Dunstan Rd, NW11 ...90 C1
Dunstans Gro, SE22 ...152 E6
Dunstans Rd, SE22 ...152 D7
Dunster Av, Mord. SM4 ...198 A1
Dunster Cl, Barn. EN5 ...40 A4
Romford RM5 ...83 J2
Dunster Ct, EC3 ...20 D5
Borehamwood WD6
off Kensington Way ...38 D3
Dunster Dr, NW9 ...88 C1
Dunster Gdns, NW6 ...90 C7
Dunsterville Way, SE1 ...28 C4
Dunster Way, Har. HA2 ...85 E3
Wallington SM6
off Helios Rd ...200 A1
Dunston Rd, E8 ...112 C1
SW11 ...150 A2
Dunston St, E8 ...112 C1
Dunton Cl, Surb. KT6 ...195 H1
Dunton Rd, E10 ...78 B7
SE1 ...37 F3
Duntshill Rd, SW18 ...167 E1
Dunvegan Cl, W.Mol. KT8 ...179 H4
Dunvegan Rd, SE9 ...156 C4
Dunwich Rd, Bexh. DA7 ...159 F1
Dunworth Ms, W11
off Portobello Rd ...108 C6
Duplex Ride, SW1 ...24 A4
Dupont Rd, SW20 ...184 A2
Duppas Av, Croy. CR0
off Violet La ...201 H4
Duppas Hill La, Croy. CR0
off Duppas Hill Rd ...201 H4
Duppas Hill Rd, Croy. CR0 ...201 H4
Duppas Hill Ter, Croy. CR0 ...201 H3
Duppas Rd, Croy. CR0 ...201 G3
Dupree Rd, SE7 ...135 H5
Dura Den Cl, Beck. BR3 ...172 B7
Durand Cl, Cars. SM5 ...199 J1
Durand Gdns, SW9 ...151 F1
Durands Wk, SE16 ...133 J2
Durand Way, NW10 ...88 C7
Durants Pk Av, Enf. EN3 ...45 G4
Durants Rd, Enf. EN3 ...45 F4
Durant St, E2 ...13 H3
Durban Gdns, Dag. RM10 ...101 J7
Durban Rd, E15 ...114 E3
E17 ...77 J1
N17 ...60 B6
SE27 ...169 J4
Beckenham BR3 ...189 J2
Ilford IG2 ...99 H1
Durbin Rd, Chess. KT9 ...195 H4
Durdans Rd, Sthl. UB1 ...103 F6
Durell Gdns, Dag. RM9 ...100 D5
Durell Rd, Dag. RM9 ...100 D5
Durfey Pl, SE5 ...36 C7
Durford Cres, SW15 ...165 G1
Durham Av, Brom. BR2 ...191 F4
Hounslow TW5 ...123 F5
Woodford Green IG8 ...64 A5
Durham Cl, SW20
off Durham Rd ...183 H2
Durham Hill, Brom. BR1 ...173 F4
Durham Ho St, WC2 ...18 B6
Durham Pl, SW3 ...31 J4
Ilford IG1
off Eton Rd ...99 F4
Durham Ri, SE18 ...137 F5
Durham Rd, E12 ...98 A4
E16 ...115 E4
N2 ...73 H3
N7 ...93 F2
N9 ...60 D2
SW20 ...183 H1
W5 ...125 G3
Borehamwood WD6 ...38 C3
Bromley BR2 ...191 F3
Dagenham RM10 ...101 J5
Feltham TW14 ...142 C7
Harrow HA1 ...67 H5
Sidcup DA14 ...176 B5
Durham Row, E1 ...113 H5
Durham St, SE11 ...34 C4
Durham Ter, W2 ...14 A3
Durham Wf Dr, Brent. TW8
off Commerce Rd ...125 F7
Durham Yd, E2
off Teesdale St ...112 E3
Durley Av, Pnr. HA5 ...67 E7
Durley Rd, N16 ...76 B7
Durlston Rd, E5 ...94 D2
Kingston upon Thames KT2 ...163 H6
Durnell Way, Loug. IG10 ...48 D3
Durnford St, N15 ...76 B5
SE10
off Greenwich Ch St ...134 C6
Durning Rd, SE19 ...170 A5
Durnsford Av, SW19 ...166 D2
Durnsford Ct, Enf. EN3
off Enstone Rd ...45 H3
Durnsford Rd, N11 ...74 D1
SW19 ...166 D2
Durrant Way, Orp. BR6 ...207 G5
Durrell Rd, SW6 ...148 C1
Durrington Av, SW20 ...183 J1
Durrington Pk Rd, SW20 ...165 J7
Durrington Rd, E5 ...95 H4
Durrington Twr, SW8
off Westbury St ...150 C2
Dursley Cl, SE3 ...155 J2
Dursley Gdns, SE3 ...156 A1
Dursley Rd, SE3 ...155 J2
Durward St, E1 ...112 E5
Durweston Ms, W1 ...16 A1
Durweston St, W1 ...16 A1
Dury Rd, Barn. EN5 ...40 C1
Dutch Barn Cl, Stai. (Stanw.) TW19 ...140 A6
Dutch Gdns, Kings.T. KT2 ...164 B6
Dutch Yd, SW18
off Wandsworth High St ...148 D5
Dutton St, SE10 ...154 C1
Duxberry Cl, Brom. BR2
off Southborough La ...192 B5
Duxford Ho, SE2
off Wolvercote Rd ...138 D2
Dwight Ct, SW6
off Burlington Rd ...148 B2
Dye Ho La, E3 ...114 A1
Dyer's Bldgs, EC1 ...19 E2
Dyers Hall Rd, E11 ...96 E1
Dyers La, SW15 ...147 H4
Dykes Way, Brom. BR2 ...191 F3
Dylan Rd, SE24 ...151 H4
Belvedere DA17 ...139 G3
Dylways, SE5 ...152 A4
Dymchurch Cl, Ilf. IG5 ...80 D2
Orpington BR6 ...207 H4

Dymes Path, SW19
off Queensmere Rd **166** A2
Dymock St, SW6 **148** E3
Dymond Est, SW17
off Glenburnie Rd **167** H3
Dyneley Rd, SE12 **173** J4
Dyne Rd, NW6 **90** C7
Dynevor Rd, N16 **94** B3
Richmond TW10 **145** H5
Dynham Rd, NW6 **90** D7
Dyott St, WC1 **18** A3
Dysart Av, Kings.T. KT2 **163** F5
Dysart St, EC2 **12** C6
Dyson Rd, E11 **79** E6
E15 **97** F6
Dysons Rd, N18 **61** E5

E

Eade Rd, N4 **75** J7
Eagans Cl, N2 **73** G3
Eagle Av, Rom. RM6 **82** E6
Eagle Cl, SE16
off Varcoe Rd **133** F5
Enfield EN3 **45** F4
Wallington SM6 **201** E6
Eagle Ct, EC1 **19** G1
N18 **60** C6
Eagle Dr, NW9 **71** E2
Eagle Hts, SW11
off Bramlands Cl **149** H3
Eagle Hill, SE19 **170** A6
Eagle Ho Ms, SW4
off Narbonne Av **150** C5
Eagle La, E11 **79** G4
Eagle Lo, NW11 **72** C7
Eagle Ms, N1
off Tottenham Rd **94** B6
Eagle Pl, SW1 **17** G6
SW7 **30** D3
Eagle Rd, Houns. TW6
off Elmdon Rd **141** J3
Wembley HA0 **87** G7
Eaglesfield Rd, SE18 **137** E7
Eagle St, WC1 **18** C2
Eagle Ter, Wdf.Grn. IG8 **63** H7
Eagle Trd Est, Mitch.
CR4 **185** J6
Eagle Wf Rd, N1 **12** A1
Eagling Cl, E3
off Rounton Rd **114** A3
Ealdham Sq, SE9 **155** J4
EALING, W5 **105** F7
Ealing Bdy Shop Cen,
W5 **105** G7
Ealing Cl, Borwd. WD6 **38** D1
★ **Ealing Common**, W5 **125** H1
Ealing Common, W5 **105** J7
Ealing Downs Ct, Grnf.
UB6 *off Perivale La* **104** D3
Ealing Grn, W5 **125** G1
Ealing Pk Gdns, W5 **125** F4
Ealing Rd, Brent. TW8 **125** G5
Northolt UB5 **85** G7
Wembley HA0 **105** G1
Ealing Village, W5 **105** H6
Eamont St, NW8 **7** G1
Eardley Cres, SW5 **128** D5
Eardley Pt, SE18
off Wilmount St **137** E4
Eardley Rd, SW16 **168** C5
Belvedere DA17 **139** G5
Earhart Way, Houns. TW4 **142** A3
Earl Cl, N11 **58** B5
Earldom Rd, SW15 **147** J4
Earle Gdns, Kings.T. KT2 **163** H6
Earlham Gro, E7 **97** F5
N22 **59** F7
Earlham St, WC2 **17** J4
Earl Ri, SE18 **137** G4
Earl Rd, SW14 **146** C4
Earlsbury Gdns, Edg. HA8 **54** A4
EARLS COURT, SW5 **128** C5
★ **Earls Court Exhib Cen**,
SW5 **128** D5
Earls Ct Gdns, SW5 **30** A2
Earls Ct Rd, SW5 **128** D4
W8 **128** D4
Earls Ct Sq, SW5 **30** A3
Earls Cres, Har. HA1 **68** B4
Earlsdown Ho, Bark. IG11
off Wheelers Cross **117** G2
Earlsferry Way, N1 **93** F7
EARLSFIELD, SW18 **167** F1
Earlsfield Ho, Kings.T. KT2
off Kingsgate Rd **181** G1
Earlsfield Rd, SW18 **167** F1
Earlshall Rd, SE9 **156** C4
Earls Ho, Rich. TW9 **126** B7
Earlsmead, Har. HA2 **85** F4
Earlsmead Rd, N15 **76** C5
NW10 **107** J2
Earl's Path, Loug. IG10 **47** J2
Earls Ter, W8 **128** C3
Earlsthorpe Ms, SW12 **150** A6
Earlsthorpe Rd, SE26 **171** G4
Earlstoke St, EC1 **11** G3
Earlston Gro, E9 **113** E1
Earl St, EC2 **20** D1
Earls Wk, W8 **128** D3
Dagenham RM8 **100** B4
Earls Way, Orp. BR6
off Station Rd **207** J2
Earlswood Av, Th.Hth.
CR7 **187** G5
Earlswood Gdns, Ilf. IG5 **80** D3
Earlswood St, SE10 **135** E5
Early Ms, NW1
off Arlington Rd **110** B1
Earnshaw St, WC2 **17** J3
Earsby St, W14 **128** B4
Easby Cres, Mord. SM4 **185** E6
Easebourne Rd, Dag.
RM8 **100** C5
Easedale Ho, Islw. TW7
off Summerwood Rd **144** C5
Eashing Pt, SW15
off Wanborough Dr **165** H1
Easley's Ms, W1 **16** C3
East 10 Enterprise Pk, E10
off Argall Way **95** H1
EAST ACTON, W3 **126** D1
East Acton La, W3 **106** E7
East Arbour St, E1 **113** G6
East Av, E12 **98** B7
E17 **78** B4
Hayes UB3 **121** J2
Southall UB1 **103** F7
Wallington SM6 **201** F5
East Bk, N16 **76** B7
Eastbank Rd, Hmptn.
(Hmptn H.) TW12 **161** J5
EAST BARNET, Barn.
EN4 **41** H6
East Barnet Rd, Barn.
EN4 **41** H6
Eastbourne Av, W3 **106** D6
Eastbourne Gdns, SW14 **146** C3
Eastbourne Ms, W2 **14** D3
Eastbourne Rd, E6 **116** D3
E15 **115** E1
N15 **76** B6
SW17 **168** A6
W4 **126** C6
Brentford TW8 **125** F5
Feltham TW13 **160** D2
Eastbourne Ter, W2 **14** D3
Eastbournia Av, N9 **61** E3
Eastbrook Av, N9 **45** F7
Dagenham RM10 **101** J4
Eastbrook Cl, Dag. RM10 **101** J4
Eastbrook Rd, SE3 **135** H7
Eastbury Av, Bark. IG11 **117** H1
Enfield EN1 **44** B1
Eastbury Ct, Bark. IG11 **117** H1
Eastbury Gro, W4 **127** E5
★ **Eastbury Manor Ho**,
Bark. IG11 **117** J1
Eastbury Rd, E6 **116** D4
Kingston upon Thames
KT2 **163** H7
Orpington BR5 **193** G6
Eastbury Sq, Bark. IG11 **117** J1
Eastbury Ter, E1 **113** G4
Eastcastle St, W1 **17** F3
Eastcheap, EC3 **20** C5
East Churchfield Rd, W3 **126** D1
Eastchurch Rd, Houns.
(Lon.Hthrw Air.) TW6 **141** H2
East Cl, W5 **106** A4
Barnet EN4 **42** A4
Greenford UB6 **103** J2
Eastcombe Av, SE7 **135** H6
EASTCOTE, Pnr. HA5 **66** C6
Eastcote, Orp. BR6 **207** J1
Eastcote Av, Grnf. UB6 **86** D5
Harrow HA2 **85** H2
West Molesey KT8 **179** F5
Eastcote La, Har. HA2 **85** G3
Northolt UB5 **85** G7
Eastcote La N, Nthlt. UB5 **85** F6
Eastcote Pl, Pnr. HA5 **66** B6
Eastcote Rd, Har. HA2 **85** J3
Pinner HA5 **66** D5
Pinner (Eastcote Vill.)
HA5 **66** A6
Welling DA16 **157** G2
Eastcote St, SW9 **151** F2
Eastcote Vw, Pnr. HA5 **66** C4
EASTCOTE VILLAGE, Pnr.
HA5 **66** B5
Eastcott Cl, Kings.T.
KT2 **164** C5
Eastcourt, Sun. TW16 **178** C2
East Ct, Wem. HA0 **87** F2
East Cres, N11 **57** J4
Enfield EN1 **44** C5
Eastcroft Rd, Epsom
KT19 **197** E7
East Cross Cen, E15 **96** A6
East Cross Route, E3 **95** J7
E9 **95** J7
Eastdown Pk, SE13 **154** D4
East Duck Lees La, Enf.
EN3 **45** H4
EAST DULWICH, SE22 **152** D6
East Dulwich Gro, SE22 **152** B6
East Dulwich Rd, SE15 **152** C4
SE22 **152** C4
East End Rd, N2 **73** F3
N3 **72** D2
East End Way, Pnr. HA5 **67** E3
East Entrance, Dag.
RM10 **119** H2
Eastern Av, E11 **79** J6
Ilford IG2, IG4 **80** B6
Pinner HA5 **66** D7
Romford RM6 **82** C4
Eastern Av W, Rom. RM1,
RM5, RM6, RM7 **82** E4
Eastern Gateway, E16 **115** J7
Eastern Ind Est, Erith
DA18 **139** G2
Eastern Perimeter Rd,
Houns. (Lon.Hthrw Air.)
TW6 **141** J3
Eastern Quay Apts, E16
off Rayleigh Rd **135** H1
Eastern Rd, E13 **115** H2
E17 **78** C5
N2 **73** J3
N22 **74** E1
SE4 **154** A4
Eastern Rbt, Ilf. IG1 **99** F2
Easternville Gdns, Ilf.
IG2 **81** F6
Eastern Way, SE2 **138** D1
SE28 **138** A2
Belvedere DA17 **139** H2
Erith DA18 **138** D1
East Ferry Rd, E14 **134** B3
Eastfield Cotts, Hayes
UB3 **121** H5
Eastfield Gdns, Dag.
RM10 **101** G4
Eastfield Rd, E17 **78** A4
N8 **74** E3
Dagenham
RM9, RM10 **101** G4
Eastfields, Pnr. HA5 **66** C5
Eastfields Av, SW18 **148** D4
Eastfields Rd, W3 **106** C5
Mitcham CR4 **186** A2
Eastfield St, E14 **113** H5
EAST FINCHLEY, N2 **73** G4
East Gdns, SW17 **167** H6
Eastgate Business Pk,
E10 **95** H1
Eastgate Cl, SE28 **118** D6
Eastglade, Pnr. HA5 **67** E3
EAST HAM, E6 **116** B2
Eastham Cl, Barn. EN5 **40** B5
East Ham Ind Est, E6 **116** B4
East Ham Manor Way,
E6 **116** D6
East Ham Mkt Hall, E6
off Myrtle Rd **116** B1
★ **East Ham Nature
Reserve & Visitor Cen**,
E6 *off Norman Rd* **116** C4
East Harding St, EC4 **19** F3
East Heath Rd, NW3 **91** G3
East Hill, SW18 **149** E5
Wembley HA9 **88** A2
Eastholm, NW11 **73** E4
Eastholme, Hayes UB3 **122** A1
East India Dock Rd, E14 **114** A6
East India Way, Croy.
CR0 **202** C1
Eastlake Ho, NW8
off Frampton St **7** F6
Eastlake Rd, SE5 **151** H2
Eastlands Cres, SE21 **152** C6
East La, SE16 **29** H4
Kingston upon Thames
KT1 *off High St* **181** G3
Wembley HA0, HA9 **87** G3
East La Business Pk, Wem.
HA9 **87** G3
Eastlea Ms, E16
off Desford Rd **115** E4
Eastleigh Av, Har. HA2 **85** H2
Eastleigh Cl, NW2 **89** E3
Sutton SM2 **199** E7
Eastleigh Rd, E17 **77** J2
Bexleyheath DA7 **159** J2
Hounslow
(Lon.Hthrw Air.) TW6
off Cranford La **141** J3
Eastleigh Wk, SW15 **147** G7
Eastleigh Way, Felt.
TW14 **160** A1
Eastman Rd, W3 **126** D1
East Mascalls, SE7
off Mascalls Rd **135** J6
East Mead, Ruis. HA4 **84** D3
Eastmead Av, Grnf. UB6 **103** H3
Eastmead Cl, Brom. BR1 **192** B2
Eastmearn Rd, SE21 **169** J2
EAST MOLESEY, KT8 **180** A4
Eastmont Rd, Esher
KT10 **194** B2
Eastmoor Pl, SE7
off Eastmoor St **136** A3
Eastmoor St, SE7 **136** A3
East Mt St, E1 **113** E5
Eastney Rd, Croy. CR0 **201** H1
Eastney St, SE10 **134** D5
Eastnor Rd, SE9 **175** F1
Easton Gdns, Borwd.
WD6 **38** D4
Easton St, WC1 **10** E4
East Pk Cl, Rom. RM6 **82** D5
East Parkside, SE10 **135** E2
East Pas, EC1 **19** H1
East Pier, E1
off Wapping High St **132** E1
East Pl, SE27
off Pilgrim Hill **169** J4
East Pt, SE1 **37** H3
East Poultry Av, EC1 **19** G2
East Ramp, Houns.
(Lon.Hthrw Air.) TW6 **140** E1
East Rd, E15 **115** G1
N1 **12** B4
SW3 **32** B4
SW19 **167** F6
Barnet EN4 **58** A1
Edgware HA8 **70** B1
Feltham TW14 **141** G7
Kingston upon Thames
KT2 **181** H1
Romford (Chad.Hth)
RM6 **82** E5
Welling DA16 **158** B2
West Drayton UB7 **120** C4
East Rochester Way, SE9 **157** H4
Bexley DA5 **158** D6
Sidcup DA15 **157** H4
East Row, E11 **79** G6
W10 **108** B4
Eastry Av, Brom. BR2 **191** F6
Eastry Rd, Erith DA8 **139** G7
EAST SHEEN, SW14 **146** D4
East Sheen Av, SW14 **146** D4
Eastside Rd, NW11 **72** C4
East Smithfield, E1 **21** G6
East St, SE17 **36** A3
Barking IG11 **99** F7
Bexleyheath DA7 **159** G4
Brentford TW8 **125** F7
Bromley BR1 **191** G2
East Surrey Gro, SE15 **132** C7
East Tenter St, E1 **21** G4
East Twrs, Pnr. HA5 **66** D5
East Vale, W3
off The Vale **127** F1
East Vw, E4 **62** C5
Barnet EN5 **40** C3
Eastview Av, SE18 **137** H7
Eastville Av, NW11 **72** C6
East Wk, Barn. (E.Barn.)
EN4 **42** A7
Hayes UB3 **122** A1
Eastway, E9 **95** J6
East Way, E11 **79** H5
Bromley BR2 **191** G7
Croydon CR0 **203** H2
Hayes UB3 **122** A1
Eastway, Mord. SM4 **184** A5
East Way, Ruis. HA4 **84** A1
Eastway, Wall. SM6 **200** C4
Eastway Commercial Cen,
E9 **96** A5
Eastway Cres, Har. HA2
off Eliot Dr **85** H2
Eastwell Cl, Beck. BR3 **189** H1
Eastwick Ct, SW19
off Victoria Dr **166** A1
EAST WICKHAM, Well.
DA16 **138** A7
Eastwood Cl, E18
off George La **79** G2
N7 *off Eden Gro* **93** G5
N17 **60** E7
Eastwood Rd, E18 **79** G2
N10 **74** A2
Ilford IG3 **82** A7
West Drayton UB7 **120** D2
East Woodside, Bex. DA5 **177** E1
Eastwood St, SW16 **168** C6
Eatington Rd, E10 **78** D5
Eaton Cl, SW1 **32** B2
Stanmore HA7 **53** E4
Eaton Dr, SW9 **151** H4
Kingston upon Thames
KT2 **164** A7
Eaton Gdns, Dag. RM9 **100** E7
Eaton Gate, SW1 **32** B1
Eaton Ho, E14
off Westferry Circ **113** J7
Eaton La, SW1 **24** E6
Eaton Ms N, SW1 **32** B1
Eaton Ms S, SW1 **32** C1
Eaton Ms W, SW1 **32** C1
Eaton Pk Rd, N13 **59** G2
Eaton Pl, SW1 **24** B6

Eaton Ri, E11 ...79 J5
W5 ...105 G6
Eaton Rd, NW4 ...71 J5
Enfield EN1 ...44 B3
Hounslow TW3 ...144 A4
Sidcup DA14 ...176 D2
Sutton SM2 ...199 G6
Eaton Row, SW1 ...24 D5
Eatons Mead, E4 ...62 A2
Eaton Sq, SW1 ...24 D5
Eaton Ter, SW1 ...32 B1
Eaton Ter Ms, SW1 ...32 B1
Eatonville Rd, SW17 ...167 J2
Eatonville Vil, SW17
off Eatonville Rd ...167 J2
Ebb Ct, E16
off Albert Basin Way ..117 F7
Ebbisham Dr, SW8 ...34 C5
Ebbisham Rd, Wor.Pk.
KT4 ...197 J2
Ebbsfleet Rd, NW2 ...90 B5
Ebdon Way, SE3 ...155 H3
Ebenezer Ho, SE11 ...35 F2
Ebenezer St, N1 ...12 B3
Ebenezer Wk, SW16 ...186 C1
Ebley Cl, SE15 ...37 F6
Ebner St, SW18 ...149 E5
Ebor Cotts, SW15 ...165 E3
Ebor St, E1 ...13 F5
Ebrington Rd, Har. HA3 ...69 G6
Ebsworth St, SE23 ...153 G7
Eburne Rd, N7 ...93 E3
Ebury Br, SW1 ...32 D3
Ebury Br Est, SW1 ...32 D3
Ebury Br Rd, SW1 ...32 C4
Ebury Cl, Kes. BR2 ...206 B3
Ebury Ms, SE27 ...169 H3
SW1 ...32 C1
Ebury Ms E, SW1 ...32 D1
Ebury Sq, SW1 ...32 C2
Ebury St, SW1 ...32 D1
Ecclesbourne Cl, N13 ...59 G5
Ecclesbourne Gdns, N13 ...59 G5
Ecclesbourne Rd, N1 ...93 J7
Thornton Heath CR7 ...187 J5
Eccles Rd, SW11 ...149 J4
Eccleston Br, SW1 ...32 E1
Eccleston Cl, Barn.
(Cockfos.) EN4 ...41 J4
Orpington BR6 ...207 G1
Eccleston Cres, Rom.
RM6 ...82 A7
Ecclestone Ct, Wem. HA9
off St. John's Rd ...87 H5
Ecclestone Pl, Wem. HA9 ..87 J5
Eccleston Ms, SW1 ...24 C6
Eccleston Pl, SW1 ...32 D1
Eccleston Rd, W13 ...104 D7
Eccleston Sq, SW1 ...32 E2
Eccleston Sq Ms, SW1 ...33 F2
Eccleston St, SW1 ...24 D6
Echo Hts, E4 ...62 B1
Eckford St, N1 ...10 E1
Eckington Ho, N15
off Fladbury Rd ...76 A6
Eckstein Rd, SW11 ...149 H4
Eclipse Ho, N22
off Station Rd ...75 F2
Eclipse Rd, E13 ...115 H5
Ector Rd, SE6 ...172 E2
Edbrooke Rd, W9 ...108 D4
Eddinton Cl, Croy. CR0 ...204 C6
Eddiscombe Rd, SW6 ...148 C2
Eddy Cl, Rom. RM7 ...83 H6
Eddystone Rd, SE4 ...153 H5
Eddystone Twr, SE8 ...133 H4
Eddystone Wk, Stai.
TW19 ...140 B7
Ede Cl, Houns. TW3 ...143 F3
Edenbridge Cl, SE16
off Masters Dr ...133 E5
Edenbridge Rd, E9 ...95 G7
Enfield EN1 ...44 B6
Eden Cl, NW3 ...90 D2
W8 off Adam &
Eve Ms ...128 D3
Wembley HA0 ...105 G1
Edencourt Rd, SW16 ...168 B6
Edenfield Gdns, Wor.Pk.
KT4 ...197 F3
Eden Gro, E17 ...78 B5
N7 ...93 F5
NW10
off St. Andrews Rd ...89 H6
Edenham Way, W10
off Elkstone Rd ...108 C5
Edenhurst Av, SW6 ...148 C3
Eden Ms, SW17
off Huntspill St ...167 F3
EDEN PARK, Beck. BR3 ...190 A5
Eden Pk Av, Beck. BR3 ...189 H4
Eden Rd, E17 ...78 B5
SE27 ...169 H5
Beckenham BR3 ...189 H4
Bexley DA5 ...177 J4
Croydon CR0 ...202 A4
Edensor Gdns, W4 ...127 E7
Edensor Rd, W4 ...126 E7
Eden St, Kings.T. KT1 ...181 G2
Edenvale Cl, Mitch. CR4
off Edenvale Rd ...168 A7
Edenvale Rd, Mitch. CR4 ..168 A7
Edenvale St, SW6 ...149 E2
Eden Wk, Kings.T. KT1
off Eden St ...181 H2
Eden Wk Shop Cen, Kings.
T. KT1 ...181 H2
Eden Way, E3
off Old Ford Rd ...113 J1
Beckenham BR3 ...189 J5
Ederline Av, SW16 ...187 F3
Edgar Kail Way, SE22 ...152 B4
Edgarley Ter, SW6 ...148 B1
Edgar Rd, E3 ...114 B3
Hounslow TW4 ...143 F7
Romford RM6 ...82 D7
Edgar Wallace Cl, SE15 ...37 E7
Edgbaston Rd, Wat. WD19 ..50 B3
Edgeborough Way, Brom.
BR1 ...174 A7
Edgebury, Chis. BR7 ...175 E4
Edgebury Wk, Chis.
BR7 ...175 F4
Edgecombe Ho, SW19 ...166 B1
Edgecoombe, S.Croy.
CR2 ...203 F7
Edgecoombe Cl, Kings.T.
KT2 ...164 D7
Edgecote Cl, W3
off Cheltenham Pl ...126 C1
Edgecot Gro, N15
off Oulton Rd ...76 B5
Edgefield Av, Bark. IG11 ...99 J7
Edge Hill, SE18 ...136 E6
SW19 ...166 A7
Edge Hill Av, N3 ...72 D4
Edge Hill Ct, SW19 ...166 A7
Edgehill Gdns, Dag.
RM10 ...101 G4
Edgehill Rd, W13 ...105 F5
Chislehurst BR7 ...175 F3
Mitcham CR4 ...186 B1
Edgeley La, SW4
off Edgeley Rd ...150 D3
Edgeley Rd, SW4 ...150 D3
Edgel St, SW18
off Ferrier St ...149 E4
Edge Pt Cl, SE27 ...169 H5
Edge St, W8
off Kensington Ch St ..128 D1
Edgewood Dr, Orp. BR6 ..207 J5
Edgewood Grn, Croy.
CR0 ...203 G1
Edgeworth Av, NW4 ...71 G5
Edgeworth Cl, NW4 ...71 G5
Edgeworth Cres, NW4 ...71 G5
Edgeworth Rd, SE9 ...155 J4
Barnet (Cockfos.) EN4 ...41 H4
Edgington Rd, SW16 ...168 D6
Edgington Way, Sid.
DA14 ...176 C7
Edgson Ho, SW1
off Ebury Br Rd ...32 D3
EDGWARE, HA8 ...54 B5
Edgwarebury Gdns, Edg.
HA8 ...54 A5
Edgwarebury La, Edg.
HA8 ...54 A4
Edgware Ct, Edg. HA8
off High St ...54 A6
Edgware Rd, NW2 ...89 H1
NW9 ...70 D3
W2 ...15 H3
Edgware Rd Sub, W2
off Edgware Rd ...15 G2
Edgware Way, Edg. HA8 ...53 J4
Edinburgh Cl, E2
off Russia La ...113 F2
Pinner HA5 ...66 D7
Edinburgh Ct, SW20 ...184 A5
Kingston upon Thames
KT1 off Watersplash Cl .181 H3
Edinburgh Dr, Rom. RM7
off Eastern Av W ...83 J4
Edinburgh Gate, SW1 ...23 J3
Edinburgh Ho, W9 ...6 B3
Edinburgh Rd, E13 ...115 H2
E17 ...78 A5
N18 ...60 D5
W7 ...124 C2
Sutton SM1 ...199 F2
Edington Rd, SE2 ...138 B3
Enfield EN3 ...45 F2
Edison Cl, E17
off Exeter Rd ...78 A5
West Drayton UB7 ...120 C2
Edison Ct, SE10
off Greenroof Way ...135 F3
Edison Dr, Sthl. UB1 ...103 H6
Wembley HA9 ...87 H3
Edison Gro, SE18 ...137 J7
Edison Rd, N8 ...74 D6
Bromley BR2 ...191 G2
Enfield EN3 ...45 J2
Edison Rd, Welling DA16 ..157 J1
Edis St, NW1 ...110 A1
Edith Cavell Cl, N19
off Hillrise Rd ...74 E7
Edith Cavell Way, SE18 ...156 B1
Edith Gdns, Surb. KT5 ...182 B7
Edith Gro, SW10 ...30 C6
Edithna St, SW9 ...151 E3
Edith Nesbit Wk, SE9 ...156 B5
Edith Rd, E6 ...98 A7
E15 off Chandos Rd ...96 D5
N11 ...58 D7
SE25 ...188 A5
SW19 ...167 E6
W14 ...128 B4
Romford RM6 ...82 D6
Edith Row, SW6 ...149 E1
Edith St, E2 ...13 H1
Edith Summerskill Ho, SW6
off Clem Attlee Ct ...128 C7
Edith Ter, SW10 ...30 C7
Edith Vil, SW15
off Bective Rd ...148 B4
W14 ...128 C4
Edith Yd, SW10 ...30 D7
Edmansons Cl, N17 ...76 C1
Edmeston Cl, E9 ...95 H6
Edmonds Ct, W.Mol. KT8
off Avern Rd ...179 H4
EDMONTON, N9 ...60 D4
Edmonton Grn, N9
off The Green ...60 D2
Edmonton Grn Mkt, N9
off Edmonton Grn
Shop Cen ...60 E2
Edmonton Grn Shop Cen,
N9 ...60 E2
Edmonton Trade Pk, N18
off Eley Rd ...61 F5
Edmund Gro, Felt. TW13 ..161 F2
Edmund Halley Way,
SE10 ...134 E2
Edmund Hurst Dr, E6 ...116 E5
Edmund Rd, Mitch. CR4 ..185 H3
Welling DA16 ...158 A3
Edmunds Cl, Hayes UB4 ..102 C5
Edmund St, SE5 ...36 B7
Edmunds Wk, N2 ...73 H4
Edna Rd, SW20 ...184 A2
Edna St, SW11 ...149 H1
Edrich Ho, SW4 ...150 E1
Edric Ho, SW1
off Page St ...33 J1
Edrick Rd, Edg. HA8 ...54 C6
Edrick Wk, Edg. HA8 ...54 C6
Edric Rd, SE14 ...133 G7
Edridge Rd, Croy. CR0 ...201 J3
Edulf Rd, Borwd. WD6 ...38 B1
Edward Av, E4 ...62 B6
Morden SM4 ...185 G5
Edward Cl, N9 ...44 C7
NW2 ...90 A4
Hampton (Hmptn H.)
TW12 off Edward Rd ...161 J5
Northolt UB5 ...102 C2
Edward Ct, E16
off Alexandra St ...115 G5
Edwardes Pl, W8
off Edwardes Sq ...128 C3
Edwardes Sq, W8 ...128 D3
Edward Gro, Barn. EN4 ...41 G5
Edward Ms, NW1 ...8 E2
Edward Pl, SE8 ...133 J6
Edward Rd, E17 ...77 G4
SE20 ...171 G7
Barnet EN4 ...41 G5
Bromley BR1 ...173 H7
Chislehurst BR7 ...175 E5
Croydon CR0 ...188 B7
Feltham TW14 ...141 G5
Hampton (Hmptn H.)
TW12 ...161 J5
Harrow HA2 ...67 J3
Northolt UB5 ...102 C2
Romford RM6 ...82 E6
Edward's Av, Ruis. HA4 ...84 B6
Edwards Cl, Wor.Pk. KT4 ..198 A2
Edwards Cotts, N1
off Compton Av ...93 H6
Edwards Dr, N11
off Gordon Rd ...58 D7
Edwards La, N16 ...94 A2
Edwards Ms, N1 ...93 G7
W1 ...16 B4
Edward Sq, N1
off Copenhagen St ...111 F1
SE16
off Rotherhithe St ...133 H1
Edwards Rd, Belv. DA17 ..139 G4
Edward St, E16 ...115 G4
SE8 ...133 J6
SE14 ...133 H7
Edward's Way, SE4
off Adelaide Av ...154 A5
Edwards Yd, Wem. HA0
off Mount Pleasant ...105 H1
Edward Temme Av, E15 ...97 F7
Edward Tyler Rd, SE12 ...173 H2
Edwina Gdns, Ilf. IG4 ...80 B5
Edwin Av, E6 ...116 D2
Edwin Cl, Bexh. DA7 ...139 F6
Edwin Hall Pl, SE13
off Hither Grn La ...154 D6
Edwin Pl, Croy. CR0
off Cross Rd ...202 A1
Edwin Rd, Edg. HA8 ...54 D6
Twickenham TW1,
TW2 ...162 C1
Edwin's Mead, E9
off Lindisfarne Way ...95 H4
Edwin St, E1 ...113 F4
E16 ...115 G5
Edwyn Cl, Barn. EN5 ...39 J6
Edwyn Ho, SW18
off Neville Gill Cl ...148 E6
Eel Brook Cl, SW6
off King's Rd ...148 E1
Eel Brook Studios, SW6
off Moore Pk Rd ...128 D7
Eel Pie Island, Twick.
TW1 ...162 D1
Effie Pl, SW6 ...128 D7
Effie Rd, SW6 ...128 D7
Effingham Cl, Sutt. SM2 ..199 E7
Effingham Rd, N8 ...75 G5
SE12 ...155 E5
Croydon CR0 ...187 F7
Surbiton (Long Dit.)
KT6 ...181 E7
Effort St, SW17 ...167 H5
Effra Par, SW2 ...151 G5
Effra Rd, SW2 ...151 G4
SW19 ...166 E6
Egbert St, NW1 ...110 A1
Egbury Ho, SW15
off Tangley Gro ...147 F6
Egeremont Rd, SE13 ...154 B2
Egerton Cl, Pnr.
HA5 ...66 A4
Egerton Cres, SW3 ...31 H1
Egerton Dr, SE10 ...154 B1
Egerton Gdns, NW4 ...71 H4
NW10 ...107 J1
SW3 ...23 G6
W13 ...105 E6
Ilford IG3 ...99 J3
Egerton Gdns Ms, SW3 ...23 H6
Egerton Pl, SW3 ...23 H6
Egerton Rd, N16 ...76 C7
SE25 ...188 B3
New Malden KT3 ...183 F4
Twickenham TW2 ...144 B7
Wembley HA0 ...87 J7
Egerton Ter, SW3 ...23 H6
Egerton Way, Hayes UB3 .121 E7
Eggardon Ct, Nthlt. UB5
off Lancaster Rd ...85 J6
Egham Cl, SW19 ...166 B2
Sutton SM3 ...198 B2
Egham Cres, Sutt. SM3 ...198 A3
Egham Rd, E13 ...115 H5
Eglantine Rd, SW18 ...149 F5
Egleston Rd, Mord. SM4 ..184 E6
Eglington Ct, SE17 ...35 J5
Eglington Rd, E4 ...46 D7
Eglinton Hill, SE18 ...137 E6
Eglinton Rd, SE18 ...136 D6
Egliston Ms, SW15 ...147 J3
Egliston Rd, SW15 ...147 J3
Eglon Ms, NW1
off Berkley Rd ...91 J7
Egmont Av, Surb. KT6 ...195 J1
Egmont Ms, KT19 ...196 D4
Egmont Rd, N.Mal. KT3 ..183 F4
Surbiton KT6 ...195 J1
Sutton SM2 ...199 F7
Walton-on-Thames
KT12 ...178 B7
Egmont St, SE14 ...133 G7
Egremont Ho, SE13
off Conington Rd ...154 B2
Egremont Rd, SE27 ...169 G3
Egret Way, Hayes UB4 ...102 D5
Eider Cl, E7 ...97 F5
Hayes UB4
off Cygnet Way ...102 D5
Eighteenth Rd, Mitch.
CR4 ...186 E4
Eighth Av, E12 ...98 C4
Hayes UB3 ...122 A1
Eileen Rd, SE25 ...188 A5
Eindhoven Cl, Cars. SM5 .200 A1
Eisenhower Dr, E6 ...116 B5
Elaine Gro, NW5 ...92 A5
Elam Cl, SE5 ...151 H2
Elam St, SE5 ...151 H2
Eland Pl, Croy. CR0
off Eland Rd ...201 H3
Eland Rd, SW11 ...149 J3
Croydon CR0 ...201 H3
Elba Pl, SE17 ...36 A1
Elberon Av, Croy. CR0 ...186 C6
Elbe St, SW6 ...149 F2
Elborough Rd, SE25 ...188 D5

Elborough St, SW18 . . . . .166 D1
Elbury Dr, E16 . . . . .115 G6
Elcho St, SW11 . . . . .129 H7
Elcot Av, SE15 . . . . .132 E7
Eldenwall Ind Est,
Dag. RM8
off Whalebone La S . . .101 F1
Elder Av, N8 . . . . .74 E5
Elderberry Cl, Ilf. IG6
off Hazel La 65 E7
Elderberry Gro, SE27
off Linton Gro 169 J4
Elderberry Rd, W5 . . . . . . .125 H2
Elderberry Way, E6 . . . . . . .116 C3
Elder Cl, N20 . . . . .56 E2
Sidcup DA15 . . . . .175 J1
Elder Ct, Bushey
(Bushey Hth) WD23 . . . . .52 B2
Elderfield Pl, SW17 . . . . . .168 B4
Elderfield Rd, E5 . . . . .95 F4
Elderfield Wk, E11 . . . . .79 H5
Elderflower Way, E15 . . . . . .96 E7
Elder Gdns, SE27 . . . . .169 J4
Elder Oak Cl, SE20 . . . . . . .188 E1
Elder Rd, SE27 . . . . .169 J5
Elderslie Cl, Beck. BR3 . . . .190 B5
Elderslie Rd, SE9 . . . . .156 D5
Elder St, E1 . . . . .21 F1
Elderton Rd, SE26 . . . . . . .171 H4
Eldertree Pl, Mitch. CR4
off Eldertree Way 186 C1
Eldertree Way, Mitch.
CR4 . . . . .186 B1
Elder Wk, N1
off Essex Rd 111 H1
SE13 *off Bankside Av* . .154 C3
Elderwood Pl, SE27 . . . . . .169 J5
Eldon Av, Borwd. WD6 . . . .38 A2
Croydon CR0 . . . . .203 F2
Hounslow TW5 . . . . .123 G7
Eldon Gro, NW3 . . . . .91 G5
Eldon Pk, SE25 . . . . .188 E4
Eldon Rd, E17 . . . . .77 J4
N9 . . . . .61 F2
N22 . . . . .75 H1
W8 . . . . .22 B6
Eldon St, EC2 . . . . .20 C2
Eldon Way, NW10 . . . . .106 B2
Eldred Rd, Bark. IG11 . . . . .117 H1
Eldridge Cl, Felt. TW14 . . . .160 A1
Eldridge Ct, Dag. RM10
off Reede Way 101 H6
Eleanor Cl, N15
off Arnold Rd 76 C3
SE16 . . . . .133 G2
Eleanor Cres, NW7 . . . . .56 A4
Eleanor Gdns, Barn. EN5 . .40 A5
Dagenham RM8 . . . . . . .101 F3
Eleanor Gro, SW13 . . . . . .147 E3
Eleanor Rd, E8 . . . . .94 E6
E15 . . . . .97 F6
N11 . . . . .58 E6
Eleanor St, E3 . . . . .114 A3
Eleanor Wk, SE18
off Samuel St 136 C4
Electra Av, Houns. TW6
off Eastchurch Rd 141 J3
Electra Business Pk,
E16 . . . . .114 D5
Electric Av, SW9 . . . . .151 G4
Electric La, SW9 . . . . .151 G4
Electric Par, E18
off George La 79 G2
Surbiton KT6 . . . . .181 G6
Elektron Ho, E14
off Blackwall Way 114 D7
Elephant & Castle, SE1 . . . .27 H6
Elephant & Castle
Shop Cen, SE1
off Elephant & Castle . .35 J1
Elephant La, SE16 . . . . . . .133 F2
Elephant Rd, SE17 . . . . .35 J1
Elers Rd, W13 . . . . .125 F2
Hayes UB3 . . . . .121 G4
Eleven Acre Ri, Loug.
IG10 . . . . .48 C3
Eley Est, N18 . . . . .61 F5
Eley Rd, N18 . . . . .61 G5
Eley Rd Retail Pk, N18 . . . . .61 G5
Elfindale Rd, SE24 . . . . . . .151 J5
Elfin Gro, Tedd. TW11
off Broad St 162 C5
Elford Cl, SE3 . . . . .155 H4
Elfort Rd, N5 . . . . .93 G4
Elfrida Cres, SE6 . . . . .172 A4
Elf Row, E1 . . . . .113 F7
Elfwine Rd, W7 . . . . .104 B5
Elgal Cl, Orp. BR6 . . . . .207 E5
Elgar Av, NW10 . . . . .88 D6
SW16 . . . . .186 E3
W5 . . . . .125 H2
Surbiton KT5 . . . . .182 B7
Elgar Cl, E13
off Bushey Rd 115 J2
SE8 *off Comet St* 134 A7
Buckhurst Hill IG9 . . . . . .64 A2
Elgar St, SE16 . . . . .133 H3
Elgin Av, W9 . . . . .6 A4
W12 . . . . .127 G2
Harrow HA3 . . . . .68 E2
Elgin Cl, W12 . . . . .127 H2
Elgin Cres, W11 . . . . .108 C6
Hounslow (Lon.Hthrw Air.)
TW6 *off Eastern*
Perimeter Rd 141 H2
Elgin Ms, W11
off Ladbroke Gro 108 B6
Elgin Ms N, W9 . . . . .6 B3
Elgin Ms S, W9 . . . . .6 B3
Elgin Rd, N22 . . . . .74 C2
Croydon CR0 . . . . .202 C1
Ilford IG3 . . . . .99 H1
Sutton SM1 . . . . .199 F3
Wallington SM6 . . . . . . .200 C6
Elgood Av, Nthwd. HA6 . . . .50 A6
Elgood Cl, W11
off Avondale Pk Rd . . .108 B7
Elham Cl, Brom. BR1 . . . . .174 A7
Elham Ho, E5
off Pembury Rd 94 E5
Elia Ms, N1 . . . . .11 G2
Elias Pl, SW8 . . . . .34 E6
Elia St, N1 . . . . .11 G2
Elibank Rd, SE9 . . . . .156 D4
Elim Est, SE1 . . . . .28 D5
Elim St, SE1 . . . . .28 C5
Elim Way, E13 . . . . .115 F3
Eliot Bk, SE23 . . . . .170 E2
Eliot Cotts, SE3
off Eliot Pl 155 E2
Eliot Ct, N15
off Tynemouth Rd 76 C4
Eliot Dr, Har. HA2 . . . . .85 H2
Eliot Gdns, SW15 . . . . .147 G4
Eliot Hill, SE13 . . . . .154 C2
Eliot Ms, NW8 . . . . .6 D2
Eliot Pk, SE13 . . . . .154 C3
Eliot Pl, SE3 . . . . .154 E2
Eliot Rd, Dag. RM9 . . . . . .100 D4
Eliot Vale, SE3 . . . . .154 D2
Elizabethan Cl, Stai.
(Stanw.) TW19
off Elizabethan Way . . .140 A7
Elizabethan Way, Stai.
(Stanw.) TW19 . . . . .140 A7
Elizabeth Av, N1 . . . . .93 J7
Enfield EN2 . . . . .43 H3
Ilford IG1 . . . . .99 G2
Elizabeth Blackwell Ho, N22
off Progress Way 75 G1
Elizabeth Br, SW1 . . . . .32 D2
Elizabeth Cl, E14
off Grundy St 114 B6
W9 .6 D5
Barnet EN5 . . . . .40 A3
Romford RM7 . . . . .83 H1
Sutton SM1 . . . . .198 C4
Elizabeth Clyde Cl, N15 . . . .76 B4
Elizabeth Cotts, Rich.
(Kew) TW9 . . . . .145 J1
Elizabeth Ct, SW1 . . . . .25 J6
Kingston upon Thames
KT2 *off Lower*
Kings Rd 181 H1
Woodford Green IG8
off Navestock Cres 63 J7
Elizabeth Est, SE17 . . . . . . .36 B5
Elizabeth Fry Pl, SE18 . . . .156 B1
Elizabeth Fry Rd, E8
off Lamb La 95 E7
Elizabeth Gdns, W3 . . . . . .127 F1
Isleworth TW7 . . . . .144 D4
Stanmore HA7 . . . . .53 F6
Sunbury-on-Thames
TW16 . . . . .178 C3
Elizabeth Ms, NW3 . . . . . . .91 H6
Elizabeth Pl, N15 . . . . .76 A4
Elizabeth Ride, N9 . . . . .45 E7
Elizabeth Rd, E6 . . . . .116 A1
N15 . . . . .76 B5
Elizabeth Sq, SE16
off Rotherhithe St 113 H7
Elizabeth St, SW1 . . . . .32 C1
Elizabeth Ter, SE9 . . . . . . .156 C6
Elizabeth Way, SE19 . . . . . .170 A7
Feltham TW13 . . . . .160 C4
Elizabeth Wheeler Ho,
Brom. BR1
off The Mall 191 G3
Elkanette Ms, N20 . . . . .57 F2
Elkington Pt, SE11 . . . . .34 E2
Elkington Rd, E13 . . . . .115 H4
Elkstone Rd, W10 . . . . .108 C5
Ella Cl, Beck. BR3 . . . . .190 A2
Ellacott Ms, SW16 . . . . .168 D2
Ellaline Rd, W6 . . . . .128 A6
Ella Ms, NW3
off Cressy Rd 91 J5
Ellanby Cres, N18 . . . . .60 E4
Elland Cl, Barn. EN5 . . . . . . .41 G5
Elland Rd, SE15 . . . . .153 F4
Ella Rd, N8 . . . . .75 E7
Ellement Cl, Pnr. HA5 . . . . .66 D5
Ellenborough Pl, SW15 . . .147 G4
Ellenborough Rd, N22 . . . . .75 J1
Sidcup DA14 . . . . .176 D5
Ellen Cl, Brom. BR1 . . . . . .192 A3
Ellen Ct, N9 . . . . .61 F2
Ellen St, E1 . . . . .21 J4
Ellen Webb Dr, Har.
(Wealds.) HA3 . . . . .68 B3
Ellen Wilkinson Ho, E2
off Usk St 113 G3
Elleray Rd, Tedd. TW11 . . . .162 C6
Ellerby St, SW6 . . . . .148 A1
Ellerdale Cl, NW3
off Ellerdale Rd 91 F4
Ellerdale Rd, NW3 . . . . .91 F5
Ellerdale St, SE13 . . . . . . .154 B4
Ellerdine Rd, Houns.
TW3 . . . . .143 J4
Ellerker Gdns, Rich.
TW10 . . . . .145 H6
Ellerman Av, Twick. TW2 . .161 F1
Ellerslie Gdns, NW10 . . . . .107 G1
Ellerslie Rd, W12 . . . . .127 H1
Ellerslie Sq Ind Est, SW2 .150 E5
Ellerton, NW6
off Mill La 90 C5
Ellerton Gdns, Dag.
RM9 . . . . .100 C7
Ellerton Rd, SW13 . . . . . . .147 G1
SW18 . . . . .167 G1
SW20 . . . . .165 G7
Dagenham RM9 . . . . . . .100 C7
Surbiton KT6 . . . . .195 J2
Ellery Rd, SE19 . . . . .170 A7
Ellery St, SE15 . . . . .152 E2
Ellesborough Cl, Wat.
WD19 . . . . .50 C5
Ellesmere Av, NW7 . . . . .54 D3
Beckenham BR3 . . . . . . .190 B2
Ellesmere Cl, E11 . . . . .79 F5
Ellesmere Gdns, Ilf. IG4 . . . .80 B5
Ellesmere Gro, Barn.
EN5 . . . . .40 C5
Ellesmere Rd, E3 . . . . .113 H2
NW10 . . . . .89 G5
W4 . . . . .126 D6
Greenford UB6 . . . . .103 J4
Twickenham TW1 . . . . . .145 F6
Ellesmere St, E14 . . . . .114 B6
Ellingfort Rd, E8 . . . . .95 E7
Ellingham Rd, E15 . . . . .96 D4
W12 . . . . .127 G2
Chessington KT9 . . . . . .195 G6
Ellington Ct, N14 . . . . .58 D2
Ellington Ho, SE1 . . . . .28 A5
Ellington Rd, N10 . . . . .74 B4
Hounslow TW3 . . . . .143 H2
Ellington St, N7 . . . . .93 G6
Elliot Cl, E15 . . . . .96 E7
Elliot Rd, NW4 . . . . .71 H6
Stanmore HA7 . . . . .52 D6
Elliott Av, Ruis. HA4 . . . . . . .84 B2
Elliott Cl, Wem. HA9 . . . . . . .87 J3
Elliott Rd, SW9 . . . . .131 H7
W4 . . . . .126 E4
Bromley BR2 . . . . .192 A4
Thornton Heath CR7 . . .187 H4
Elliott's Pl, N1
off St. Peters St 111 H1
Elliott Sq, NW3 . . . . .91 H7
Elliotts Row, SE11 . . . . .35 G1
Ellis Cl, NW10
off High Rd 89 H6
SE9 . . . . .175 F2
Edgware HA8 . . . . .54 E6
Elliscombe Rd, SE7 . . . . . .135 J5
Ellis Ct, W7 . . . . .104 C5
Ellisfield Dr, SW15 . . . . . . .147 F7
Ellison Gdns, Sthl. UB2 . . .123 F4
Ellison Ho, SE13
off Lewisham Rd 154 C2
Ellison Rd, SW13 . . . . .147 F2
SW16 . . . . .168 D7
Sidcup DA15 . . . . .175 G1
Ellis Rd, Mitch. CR4 . . . . . .185 J6
Southall UB2 . . . . .123 J1
Ellis St, SW1 . . . . .32 A1
Elliston Ho, SE18 . . . . .136 D4
Ellora Rd, SW16 . . . . .168 D5
Ellsworth St, E2 . . . . .113 E3
Ellwood Ct, W9 . . . . .6 A6
Elmar Rd, N15 . . . . .76 A4
Elm Av, W5 . . . . .125 H1
Ruislip HA4 . . . . .84 A1
Elmbank, N14 . . . . .43 E7
Elmbank Av, Barn. EN5 . . . .39 J4
Elm Bk Dr, Brom. BR1 . . . .192 A2
Elm Bk Gdns, SW13 . . . . . .147 E2
Elmbank Way, W7 . . . . .104 A5
Elmbourne Dr, Belv.
DA17 . . . . .139 H4
Elmbourne Rd, SW17 . . . .168 A3
Elmbridge Av, Surb. KT5 . .182 B5
Elmbridge Cl, Ruis. HA4 . . .66 A6
Elmbridge Wk, E8
off Wilman Gro 94 D7
Elmbrook Cl, Sun. TW16 . .178 B1
Elmbrook Gdns, SE9 . . . . .156 B4
Elmbrook Rd, Sutt. SM1 . .198 C4
Elm Cl, E11 . . . . .79 H6
N19 *off Hargrave Pk* 92 C2
NW4 . . . . .72 A5
SW20 . . . . .183 J4
Buckhurst Hill IG9 . . . . . .64 A2
Carshalton SM5 . . . . . . .199 J1
Harrow HA2 . . . . .67 H6
Hayes UB3 . . . . .102 A6
Romford RM7 . . . . .83 H2
South Croydon CR2 . . .202 B6
Surbiton KT5 . . . . .182 C7
Twickenham TW2 . . . . . .161 H2
Elm Ct, EC4 . . . . .19 E5
Mitcham CR4
off Armfield Cres 185 J2
Elmcourt Rd, SE27 . . . . . . .169 H2
Elm Cres, W5 . . . . .125 H1
Kingston upon Thames
KT2 . . . . .181 H1
Elmcroft, N8 . . . . .75 F5
Elmcroft Av, E11 . . . . .79 H5
N9 . . . . .44 E6
NW11 . . . . .72 C7
Sidcup DA15 . . . . .157 J6
Elmcroft Cl, E11 . . . . .79 H4
W5 . . . . .105 G6
Chessington KT9 . . . . . .195 H3
Feltham TW14 . . . . .141 J6
Elmcroft Cres, NW11 . . . . . .72 B7
Harrow HA2 . . . . .67 G3
Elmcroft Dr, Chess. KT9 . .195 H3
Elmcroft Gdns, NW9 . . . . . .70 A5
Elmcroft St, E5 . . . . .95 F4
Elmdale Rd, N13 . . . . .59 F5
Elmdene, Surb. KT5 . . . . . .196 C1
Elmdene Cl, Beck. BR3 . . .189 J5
Elmdene Rd, SE18 . . . . . . .136 E5
Elmdon Rd, Houns. TW4 . .142 D2
Hounslow (Hatt.Cr.)
TW6 . . . . .141 J3
Elm Dr, Har. HA2 . . . . .67 H6
Sunbury-on-Thames
TW16 . . . . .178 C2
Elmer Cl, Enf. EN2 . . . . .43 F3
Elmer Gdns, Edg. HA8 . . . . .54 B7
Isleworth TW7 . . . . .144 A3
Elmer Rd, SE6 . . . . .154 C7
Elmers Dr, Tedd. TW11
off Kingston Rd 163 E6
ELMERS END, Beck. BR3 . .189 H3
Elmers End Rd, SE20 . . . . .189 F2
Beckenham BR3 . . . . . . .189 F2
Elmerside Rd, Beck. BR3 . .189 H4
Elmers Rd, SE25 . . . . .188 D7
Elmfield Av, N8 . . . . .74 E5
Mitcham CR4 . . . . .186 A1
Teddington TW11 . . . . . .162 C5
Elmfield Cl, Har. HA1 . . . . . .86 B2
Elmfield Pk, Brom. BR1 . . .191 G3
Elmfield Rd, E4 . . . . .62 C2
E17 . . . . .77 G6
N2 . . . . .73 G3
SW17 . . . . .168 A2
Bromley BR1 . . . . .191 G3
Southall UB2 . . . . .123 E3
Elmfield Way, W9 . . . . .108 D5
Elm Friars Wk, NW1 . . . . . . .92 D7
Elm Gdns, N2 . . . . .73 F3
Esher (Clay.) KT10 . . . . .194 C6
Mitcham CR4 . . . . .186 D4
Elmgate Av, Felt. TW13 . . .160 B3
Elmgate Gdns, Edg. HA8 . .54 D5
Elm Grn, W3 . . . . .106 E6
Elmgreen Cl, E15
off Church St N 115 E1
Elm Gro, N8 . . . . .75 E6
NW2 . . . . .90 A4
SE15 . . . . .152 C2
SW19 . . . . .166 B7
Harrow HA2 . . . . .67 G7
Kingston upon Thames
KT2 . . . . .181 H1
Orpington BR6 . . . . .207 J1
Sutton SM1 . . . . .199 E4
Woodford Green IG8 . . . .63 F5
Elmgrove Cres, Har. HA1 . . .68 C5
Elmgrove Gdns, Har. HA1 . .68 D5
Elm Gro Par, Wall. SM6
off Butter Hill 200 A3
Elm Gro Rd, SW13 . . . . . . .147 G2
W5 . . . . .125 H2
Elmgrove Rd, Croy. CR0 . .188 E7
Harrow HA1 . . . . .68 C5
Elm Hall Gdns, E11 . . . . . . .79 H6
Elmhurst, Belv. DA17 . . . . .139 E6
Elmhurst Av, N2 . . . . .73 G3
Mitcham CR4 . . . . .168 B7
Elmhurst Dr, E18 . . . . .79 G2
Elmhurst Mans, SW4
off Edgeley Rd 150 D3
Elmhurst Rd, E7 . . . . .97 H7
N17 . . . . .76 B2
SE9 . . . . .174 B2
Elmhurst St, SW4 . . . . . . .150 D3
Elmhurst Vil, SE15
off Cheltenham Rd . . .153 F4

Elmhurst Way, Loug. IG10 48 C7
Elmington Cl, Bex. DA5 159 H6
Elmington Est, SE5 36 C7
Elmington Rd, SE5 152 A1
Elmira St, SE13 154 B3
Elm La, SE6 171 J2
Elmlee Cl, Chis. BR7 174 C6
Elmley Cl, E6
off Lovage App 116 B5
Elmley St, SE18 137 G4
Elm Ms, Rich. TW10 145 J6
Elmore Cl, Wem. HA0 105 H2
Elmore Rd, E11 96 C3
Enfield EN3 45 G1
Elmores, Loug. IG10 48 D3
Elmore St, N1 93 J7
Elm Par, Sid. DA14
off Main Rd 176 A4
Elm Pk, SW2 151 F6
Stanmore HA7 53 E5
Elm Pk Av, N15 76 C5
Elm Pk Ct, Pnr. HA5 66 C3
Elm Pk Gdns, NW4 72 A5
SW10 31 E4
Elm Pk La, SW3 30 E4
Elm Pk Mans, SW10 30 D5
Elm Pk Rd, E10 95 H1
N3 56 C7
N21 43 J7
SE25 188 C3
SW3 30 E5
Pinner HA5 66 C2
Elm Pl, SW7 31 E3
Elm Quay Ct, SW8 33 H5
Elm Rd, E7 97 F6
E11 96 D2
E17 78 C5
N22 75 H1
SW14 146 C3
Barnet EN5 40 C4
Beckenham BR3 189 J2
Chessington KT9 195 H4
Epsom KT17 197 F6
Esher (Clay.) KT10 194 C6
Kingston upon Thames KT2 181 J1
New Malden KT3 182 D4
Romford RM7 83 H2
Sidcup DA14 176 A4
Thornton Heath CR7 188 A4
Wallington SM6 200 A1
Wembley HA9 87 H5
Elm Rd W, Sutt. SM3 184 C7
Elm Row, NW3 91 F3
Elms, The, SW13 147 F3
Loughton IG10 47 F2
Elms Av, N10 74 B3
NW4 72 A5
Elmscott Gdns, N21 43 J6
Elmscott Rd, Brom. BR1 173 E5
Elms Ct, Wem. HA0 86 C4
Elms Cres, SW4 150 C6
Elmsdale Rd, E17 77 J4
Elms Gdns, Dag. RM9 101 F4
Wembley HA0 86 D4
Elmshaw Rd, SW15 147 G5
Elmshurst Cres, N2 73 G4
Elmside, Croy. (New Adgtn) CR0 204 B6
Elmside Rd, Wem. HA9 88 A3
Elms La, Wem. HA0 86 D4
Elmsleigh Av, Har. HA3 69 E4
Elmsleigh Ct, Sutt. SM1 198 E3
Elmsleigh Rd, Twick. TW2 162 A2
Elmslie Cl, Wdf.Grn. IG8 64 C6
Elmslie Pt, E3 113 J5
Elms Ms, W2 14 E5
Elms Pk Av, Wem. HA0 86 D4
Elms Rd, SW4 150 C5
Harrow HA3 52 B7
ELMSTEAD, Chis. BR7 174 A5
Elmstead Av, Chis. BR7 174 C5
Wembley HA9 87 H1
Elmstead Cl, N20 56 D2
Epsom KT19 197 E5
Elmstead Cres, Well. DA16 138 C6
Elmstead Gdns, Wor.Pk. KT4 197 G3
Elmstead Glade, Chis. BR7 174 C6
Elmstead La, Chis. BR7 174 C5
Elmstead Rd, Ilf. IG3 99 H2
Elmstone Rd, SW6 148 D1
Elm St, WC1 10 D6
Elmswood, Chig. IG7
off Copperfield 65 G6
Elmsworth Av, Houns. TW3 143 H2
Elm Ter, NW2 90 D3
SE9 156 D6
Harrow HA3 52 A7
Elm Tree Av, Esher KT10 180 A7
Elm Tree Cl, NW8 7 E3
Northolt UB5 103 F2
Elm Tree Ct, SE7
off Fairlawn 135 J6
Elm Tree Rd, NW8 7 E3
Elmtree Rd, Tedd. TW11 162 B4
Elm Wk, NW3 90 D2
SW20 183 J4
Orpington BR6 206 C3
Elm Way, N11 58 A6
NW10 88 E4
Epsom KT19 196 D5
Worcester Park KT4 197 J3
Elmwood Av, N13 59 E5
Borehamwood WD6 38 B4
Feltham TW13 160 A2
Harrow HA3 68 D5
Elmwood Cl, Epsom KT17 197 G7
Wallington SM6 200 A2
Elmwood Ct, SW11 150 B1
Wembley HA0 86 D3
Elmwood Cres, NW9 70 C4
Elmwood Dr, Bex. DA5 158 E7
Epsom KT17 197 G6
Elmwood Gdns, W7 104 B6
Elmwood Rd, SE24 152 A5
W4 126 C6
Croydon CR0 187 H7
Mitcham CR4 185 J3
Elmworth Gro, SE21 170 A2
Elnathan Ms, W9 6 B6
Elphinstone Rd, E17 77 J2
Elphinstone St, N5 93 H4
Elrington Rd, E8 94 D6
Woodford Green IG8 63 G5
Elruge Cl, West Dr. UB7 120 A3
Elsa Rd, Well. DA16 158 B2
Elsa St, E1 113 H5
Elsdale St, E9 95 F6
Elsden Ms, E2
off Old Ford Rd 113 F2
Elsden Rd, N17 76 C1
Elsenham Rd, E12 98 C5
Elsenham St, SW18 166 C1
Elsham Rd, E11 96 E3
W14 128 B2
Elsham Ter, W14 128 B2
Elsiedene Rd, N21 43 J7
Elsiemaud Rd, SE4 153 J5
Elsie Rd, SE22 152 C4
Elsinore Av, Stai. TW19 140 B7
Elsinore Gdns, NW2 90 B3
Elsinore Rd, SE23 171 H1
Elsinore Way, Rich. TW9 146 B3
Elsley Rd, SW11 149 J3
Elspeth Rd, SW11 149 J4
Wembley HA0 87 H5
Elsrick Av, Mord. SM4 184 D5
Elstan Way, Croy. CR0 189 H7
Elstead Ct, Sutt. SM3
off Stonecot Hill 198 B1
Elsted St, SE17 36 C2
Elstow Cl, SE9 156 D5
Ruislip HA4 66 D7
Elstow Gdns, Dag. RM9 118 E1
Elstow Rd, Dag. RM9 100 E7
Elstree Business Centre, WD6 38 D3
Elstree Gdns, N9 61 E1
Belvedere DA17 139 E4
Ilford IG1 99 F5
Elstree Hill, Brom. BR1 172 E7
Elstree Pk, Borwd. WD6 38 D6
Elstree Way, Borwd. WD6 38 B3
Elswick Rd, SE13 154 B2
Elswick St, SW6 149 F2
Elsworthy, T.Ditt. KT7 180 B6
Elsworthy Ri, NW3 91 H7
Elsworthy Rd, NW3 109 H1
Elsworthy Ter, NW3 91 H7
Elsynge Rd, SW18 149 G5
ELTHAM, SE9 156 A6
Eltham Grn, SE9 155 J5
Eltham Grn Rd, SE9 155 J4
Eltham High St, SE9 156 C6
Eltham Hill, SE9 156 A5
★ **Eltham Palace**, SE9 156 B7
Eltham Palace Rd, SE9 155 J6
Eltham Pk Gdns, SE9 156 D4
Eltham Rd, SE9 155 J5
SE12 155 F5
Elthiron Rd, SW6 148 D1
Elthorne Av, W7 124 C2
Elthorne Ct, Felt. TW13 160 C1
Elthorne Pk Rd, W7 124 C2
Elthorne Rd, N19 92 D2
NW9 70 D7
Elthorne Way, NW9 70 D6
Elthruda Rd, SE13 154 D6
Eltisley Rd, Ilf. IG1 98 E4
Elton Av, Barn. EN5 40 C5
Greenford UB6 86 C6
Wembley HA0 87 E5
Elton Cl, Kings.T. KT1 163 F7
Elton Ho, E3 113 J1
Elton Pl, N16 94 B5
Elton Rd, Kings.T. KT2 181 J1
Eltringham St, SW18 149 F4
Elvaston Ms, SW7 22 D5
Elvaston Pl, SW7 22 C6
Elveden Pl, NW10 106 A2
Elveden Rd, NW10 106 A2
Elvendon Rd, N13 58 E6
Elver Gdns, E2 13 J3
Elverson Ms, SE8 154 B2
Elverson Rd, SE8 154 B2
Elverton St, SW1 33 H1
Elvington Grn, Brom. BR2 191 F5
Elvington La, NW9 70 E1
Elvino Rd, SE26 171 H5
Elvis Rd, NW2 89 J6
Elwill Way, Beck. BR3 190 C4
Elwin St, E2 13 H3
Elwood Cl, Barn. EN5 41 F4
Elwood Ct, N9 60 E1
Elwood St, N5 93 H3
Elwyn Gdns, SE12 155 G7
Ely Cl, N.Mal. KT3 183 F2
Ely Ct, EC1 19 F2
Ely Gdns, Borwd. WD6 38 D5
Dagenham RM10 101 J3
Ilford IG1 80 B7
Elyne Rd, N4 75 G6
Ely Pl, EC1 19 F2
Woodford Green IG8 64 D6
Ely Rd, E10 78 C6
Croydon CR0 188 A5
Hounslow (Houns.W.) TW4 142 C3
Hounslow (Lon.Hthrw Air.) TW6 *off Eastern Perimeter Rd* 141 J2
Elysian Av, Orp. BR5 193 H6
Elysian Pl, S.Croy. CR2 201 J7
Elysium Bldg, The, SE8
off Trundleys Rd 133 G5
Elysium Pl, SW6
off Fulham Pk Gdns 148 C2
Elysium St, SW6
off Fulham Pk Gdns 148 C2
Elystan Business Cen, Hayes UB4 102 C7
Elystan Pl, SW3 31 H3
Elystan St, SW3 31 G2
Elystan Wk, N1
off Cloudesley Rd 111 G1
Emanuel Av, W3 106 C6
Emanuel Dr, Hmptn. TW12 161 F5
Embankment, SW15 148 A2
Embankment, The, Twick. TW1 162 D1
Embankment Gdns, SW3 32 A5
Embankment Pier, WC2 26 C1
Embankment Pl, WC2 26 B1
Embassy Ct, Sid. DA14 176 B3
Welling DA16
off Welling High St 158 B3
Embassy Gdns, Beck. BR3
off Blakeney Rd 189 J1
Emba St, SE16 29 J4
Ember Cl, Orp. BR5 193 F7
Embercourt Rd, T.Ditt. KT7 180 B6
Ember Fm Av, E.Mol. KT8 180 A6
Ember Fm Way, E.Mol. KT8 180 A6
Ember Gdns, T.Ditt. KT7 180 B7
Ember La, E.Mol. KT8 180 A7
Esher KT10 180 A7
Emberton, SE5 36 D5
Emberton Ct, EC1
off Tompion St 11 G4
Embleton Rd, SE13 154 B3
Watford WD19 50 A3
Embleton Wk, Hmptn. TW12
off Fearnley Cres 161 F6
Embry Cl, Stan. HA7 52 D4
Embry Dr, Stan. HA7 52 D6
Embry Way, Stan. HA7 52 D5
Emden Cl, West Dr. UB7 120 D2
Emden St, SW6 149 E1
Emerald Cl, E16 116 B6
Emerald Gdns, Dag. RM8 101 G1
Emerald Rd, NW10 106 D1
Emerald Sq, Sthl. UB2 122 D3
Emerald St, WC1 18 C1
Emerson Apts, N8
off Chadwell La 75 F3
Emerson Gdns, Har. HA3 69 J6
Emerson Rd, Ilf. IG1 80 D7
Emerson St, SE1 27 J1
Emerton Cl, Bexh. DA6 158 E4
Emery Hill St, SW1 25 G6
Emery St, SE1 27 F5
Emes Rd, Erith DA8 139 J7
Emilia Cl, Enf. EN3 45 E5
Emily Duncan Pl, E7 97 H4
Emlyn Gdns, W12 127 E2
Emlyn Rd, W12 127 E2
Emmanuel Rd, SW12 168 C1
Emma Rd, E13 115 F2
Emma St, E2 112 E2
Emmaus Way, Chig. IG7 64 D5
Emmott Av, Ilf. IG6 81 F5
Emmott Cl, E1 113 H4
NW11 73 F6
Emms Pas, Kings.T. KT1 181 G2
Emperor's Gate, SW7 22 B6
Empire Av, N18 59 J5
Empire Ct, Wem. HA9 88 B3
Empire Ms, SW16 168 E5
Empire Par, N18
off Empire Av 60 A6
Empire Rd, Grnf. (Perivale) UB6 105 F1
Empire Sq, N7 93 E3
SE1 28 B4
SE20 *off High St* 171 G7
Empire Sq E, SE1
off Empire Sq 28 B4
Empire Sq S, SE1
off Empire Sq 28 B4
Empire Sq W, SE1
off Empire Sq 28 B4
Empire Way, Wem. HA9 87 J4
Empire Wf Rd, E14 134 D4
Empress App, SW6
off Lillie Rd 128 D6
Empress Av, E4 62 B7
E12 97 J2
Ilford IG1 98 C2
Woodford Green IG8 63 F7
Empress Dr, Chis. BR7 174 E6
Empress Ms, SE5 151 J2
Empress Pl, SW6 128 D5
Empress St, SE17 36 A5
Empson St, E3 114 B4
Emsworth Cl, N9 61 F1
Emsworth Rd, Ilf. IG6 81 E2
Emsworth St, SW2 169 F2
Emu Rd, SW8 150 B2
Ena Rd, SW16 186 E3
Enbrook St, W10 108 B3
Endale Cl, Cars. SM5 199 J2
Endeavour Way, SW19 166 E4
Barking IG11 118 A2
Croydon CR0 186 D7
Endell St, WC2 18 A3
Enderby St, SE10 134 E5
Enderley Cl, Har. HA3
off Enderley Rd 68 B1
Enderley Rd, Har. HA3 68 B1
Endersby Rd, Barn. EN5 39 J5
Endersleigh Gdns, NW4 71 G4
Endlebury Rd, E4 62 B2
Endlesham Rd, SW12 150 A7
Endsleigh Gdns, WC1 9 H5
Ilford IG1 98 C2
Surbiton KT6 181 F6
Endsleigh Ind Est, Sthl. UB2 123 F4
Endsleigh Pl, WC1 9 J5
Endsleigh Rd, W13 104 D7
Southall UB2 123 E4
Endsleigh St, WC1 9 H5
Endway, Surb. KT5 182 A7
Endwell Rd, SE4 153 H2
Endymion Rd, N4 75 G7
SW2 151 F6
Energen Cl, NW10 88 E6
ENFIELD, EN1 - EN3 44 C3
Enfield Enterprise Cen, Enf. EN3 *off Queensway* 45 F5
ENFIELD HIGHWAY, Enf. EN3 45 F3
Enfield Retail Pk, Enf. EN1 44 E3
Enfield Rd, N1 94 B7
W3 126 B2
Brentford TW8 125 G5
Enfield EN2 42 D4
Hounslow (Lon.Hthrw Air.) TW6 *off Eastern Perimeter Rd* 141 H2
Enfield Rd Rbt, Houns. TW6 *off Northern Perimeter Rd* 141 H2
ENFIELD TOWN, Enf. EN2 44 A2
Enfield Wk, Brent. TW8 125 G5
Enford St, W1 15 J1
Engadine Cl, Croy. CR0 202 C3
Engadine St, SW18 166 C1
Engate St, SE13 154 C4
Engel Pk, NW7 55 J6
Engineer Cl, SE18 136 D6
Engineers Way, Wem. HA9 88 A4
Engineer's Wf, Nthlt. UB5
off Taywood Rd 103 F4
Englands La, NW3 91 J6
Loughton IG10 48 D2
England Way, N.Mal. KT3 182 B4
Englefield Cl, Croy. CR0 187 J6
Enfield EN2 43 G2
Orpington BR5 193 J5
Englefield Cres, Orp. BR5 193 J4

Englefield Path, Orp. BR5 **193** J4
Englefield Rd, N1 **94** A6
Engleheart Dr, Felt. TW14 **141** J6
Engleheart Rd, SE6 **154** B7
Englewood Rd, SW12 **150** B6
English Grds, SE1 **28** D2
English St, E3 **113** J4
Enid St, SE16 **29** G5
Enmore Av, SE25 **188** D5
Enmore Gdns, SW14 **146** D5
Enmore Rd, SE25 **188** D5
SW15 **147** J4
Southall UB1 **103** G4
Ennerdale Av, Stan. HA7 **69** F3
Ennerdale Cl, Sutt. SM1 **198** C4
Ennerdale Dr, NW9 **70** E5
Ennerdale Gdns, Wem. HA9 **87** F1
Ennerdale Ho, E3 **113** J4
Ennerdale Rd, Bexh. DA7 **159** G1
Richmond TW9 **145** J2
Ennersdale Rd, SE13 **154** D5
Ennismore Av, W4 **127** F4
Greenford UB6 **86** B6
Ennismore Gdns, SW7 **23** G4
Thames Ditton KT7 **180** B6
Ennismore Gdns Ms, SW7 **23** G5
Ennismore Ms, SW7 **23** G5
Ennismore St, SW7 **23** G5
Ennis Rd, N4 **93** G1
SE18 **137** F6
Ensign Cl, Houns. TW6 *off Exeter Way* **141** H2
Ensign Dr, N13 **59** J3
Ensign Ho, SW8 *off St. George Wf* **34** A5
Ensign St, E1 **21** H5
Ensign Way, Wall. SM6 **201** E7
Enslin Rd, SE9 **156** D6
Ensor Ms, SW7 **30** E3
Enstone Rd, Enf. EN3 **45** H3
Enterprise Cl, Croy. CR0 **201** G1
Enterprise Ind Est, SE16 *off Bolina Rd* **133** F5
Enterprise Way, NW10 **107** G3
SW18 **148** D4
Teddington TW11 **162** C5
Enterprize Way, SE8 **133** J4
Envoy Av, Houns. TW6 *off Eastern Perimeter Rd* **142** A3
Envoy Av Rbt, Houns. TW6 *off Cranford La* **141** J3
Epirus Ms, SW6 **128** D7
Epirus Rd, SW6 **128** C7
Epping Cl, E14 **134** A4
Romford RM7 **83** H3
★ **Epping Forest**, Epp. & Loug. **47** J1
Epping Glade, E4 **46** C6
Epping New Rd, Buck.H. IG9 **63** H2
Loughton IG10 **47** H5
Epping Pl, N1 *off Liverpool Rd* **93** G6
Epping Way, E4 **46** B6
Epple Rd, SW6 **148** C1
Epsom Cl, Bexh. DA7 **159** H3
Northolt UB5 **85** F5
Epsom Rd, E10 **78** C6
Croydon CR0 **201** G4
Ilford IG3 **81** J6
Morden SM4 **184** C7
Sutton SM3 **184** C7
Epsom Sq, Houns. (Lon.Hthrw Air.) TW6 *off Eastern Perimeter Rd* **141** J2
Epstein Rd, SE28 **138** A1
Epworth Rd, Islw. TW7 **124** E7
Epworth St, EC2 **12** C6
Equana Apts, SE8 *off Evelyn St* **133** H5
Equinox Ho, Bark. IG11 **99** F6
Equity Sq, E2 **13** G4
Erasmus St, SW1 **33** J2
Erbin Ct, N9 *off Galahad Rd* **60** D2
Erconwald St, W12 **107** F6
Erebus Dr, SE28 **137** F3
Eresby Dr, Beck. BR3 **204** A1
Eresby Pl, NW6 **90** D7
Erica Gdns, Croy. CR0 **204** B4
Erica St, W12 **107** G7
Eric Clarke La, Bark. IG11 **117** E4
Eric Cl, E7 **97** G4
Ericcson Cl, SW18 **148** D5
Eric Fletches Ct, N1 *off Essex Rd* **93** J7
Eric Rd, E7 **97** G4
NW10 *off Church Rd* **89** F6
Romford RM6 **82** D7
Eric St, E3 **113** J4
Eridge Rd, W4 **126** D3
Erin Cl, Brom. BR1 **172** E7
Ilford IG3 **82** A6
Erin Ct, NW2 **89** J6
Erindale, SE18 **137** G6
Erindale Ter, SE18 **137** G6
Erith Cres, Rom. RM5 **83** J1
Erith Rd, Belv. DA17 **139** G5
Bexleyheath DA7 **159** H4
Erith DA8 **159** H4
Erlanger Rd, SE14 **153** G1
Erlesmere Gdns, W13 **124** D3
Ermine Cl, Houns. TW4 **142** C2
Ermine Ho, N17 *off Moselle St* **60** C7
Ermine Ms, E2 *off Laburnum St* **112** C1
Ermine Rd, N15 **76** C6
SE13 **154** B3
Ermine Side, Enf. EN1 **44** D5
Ermington Rd, SE9 **175** F2
Ernald Av, E6 **116** B2
Erncroft Way, Twick. TW1 **144** C6
Ernest Av, SE27 **169** H4
Ernest Cl, Beck. BR3 **190** A5
Ernest Gdns, W4 **126** B6
Ernest Gro, Beck. BR3 **189** J5
Ernest Rd, Kings.T. KT1 **182** B2
Ernest Sq, Kings.T. KT1 **182** B2
Ernest St, E1 **113** G4
Ernle Rd, SW20 **165** H7
Ernshaw Pl, SW15 *off Carlton Dr* **148** B5
★ **Eros**, W1 **17** H6
Erpingham Rd, SW15 **147** J3
Erridge Rd, SW19 **184** D2
Errington Rd, W9 **108** C4
Errol Gdns, Hayes UB4 **102** B4
New Malden KT3 **183** G4
Errol St, EC1 **12** A6
Erskine Cl, Sutt. SM1 **199** H3
Erskine Cres, N17 **76** E4
Erskine Hill, NW11 **72** D5
Erskine Ho, SE7 *off Springfield Gro* **135** J6
Erskine Ms, NW3 *off Erskine Rd* **91** J7
Erskine Rd, E17 **77** J4
NW3 **91** J7
Sutton SM1 **199** G4
Watford WD19 **50** C3
Erwood Rd, SE7 **136** B5
Esam Way, SW16 **169** G5
Escott Gdns, SE9 **174** B4
Escot Way, Barn. EN5 **39** J5
Escreet Gro, SE18 **136** D4
Esher Av, Rom. RM7 **83** J6
Sutton SM3 **198** A3
Walton-on-Thames KT12 **178** A7
Esher Bypass, Chess. KT9 **195** E7
Esher KT10 **195** E7
Esher Cl, Bex. DA5 **176** E1
Esher Cres, Houns. (Lon.Hthrw Air.) TW6 *off Eastern Perimeter Rd* **141** H2
Esher Gdns, SW19 **166** A2
Esher Ms, Mitch. CR4 **185** J3
Esher Rd, E.Mol. KT8 **180** A6
Ilford IG3 **99** H3
Eskdale, NW1 **9** F2
Eskdale Av, Nthlt. UB5 **103** F1
Eskdale Cl, Wem. HA9 **87** G2
Eskdale Rd, Bexh. DA7 **159** G2
Eskmont Ridge, SE19 **170** B7
Esk Rd, E13 **115** G4
Esmar Cres, NW9 **71** G7
Esme Ho, SW15 **147** F4
Esmeralda Rd, SE1 **37** J2
Esmond Gdns, W4 *off South Par* **126** D4
Esmond Rd, NW6 **108** C1
W4 **126** D4
Esmond St, SW15 **148** B4
Esparto St, SW18 **149** E7
Essenden Rd, Belv. DA17 **139** G5
South Croydon CR2 **202** B7
Essendine Rd, W9 **108** D4
Essex Av, Islw. TW7 **144** B3
Essex Cl, E17 **77** H4
Morden SM4 **184** A7
Romford RM7 **83** H4
Ruislip HA4 **84** D1
Essex Ct, EC4 **18** E4
SW13 **147** F2
Essex Gdns, N4 **75** H6
Essex Gro, SE19 **170** A6
Essex Ho, E14 *off Giraud St* **114** B6
Essex Lo, N10 **74** A2
Essex Pk, N3 **56** E6
Essex Pk Ms, W3 **126** E1
Essex Pl, W4 **126** C4
Essex Pl Sq, W4 *off Chiswick High Rd* **126** D4
Essex Rd, E4 **62** E1
E10 **78** C6
E12 **98** B5
Essex Rd, E17 **77** H6
E18 **79** H2
N1 **111** H1
NW10 **89** E7
W3 **106** C7
W4 *off Belmont Ter* **126** D4
Barking IG11 **99** G7
Borehamwood WD6 **38** A3
Dagenham RM10 **101** J5
Enfield EN2 **44** A4
Romford RM7 **83** H4
Romford (Chad.Hth) RM6 **82** C7
Essex Rd S, E11 **78** D7
Essex St, E7 **97** G5
WC2 **18** E5
Essex Twr, SE20 **189** E1
Essex Vil, W8 **128** D2
Essex Wf, E5 **95** F2
Essian St, E1 **113** H5
Essoldo Way, Edg. HA8 **69** J3
Estate Way, E10 **95** J1
Estcourt Rd, SE25 **189** E6
SW6 **128** C7
Estella Av, N.Mal. KT3 **183** H4
Estelle Rd, NW3 **91** J4
Esterbrooke St, SW1 **33** H2
Este Rd, SW11 **149** H3
Esther Cl, N21 **43** G7
Esther Rd, E11 **78** E7
Estoria Cl, SW2 **151** G7
★ **Estorick Collection of Modern Italian Art**, N1 **93** H6
Estreham Rd, SW16 **168** D6
Estridge Cl, Houns. TW3 **143** G4
Estuary Cl, Bark. IG11 **118** B3
Eswyn Rd, SW17 **167** J4
Etchingham Pk Rd, N3 **57** E7
Etchingham Rd, E15 **96** C4
Eternit Wk, SW6 **147** J1
Etfield Gro, Sid. DA14 **176** B5
Ethelbert Cl, Brom. BR1 **191** G3
Ethelbert Gdns, Ilf. IG2 **80** C5
Ethelbert Rd, SW20 **184** A1
Bromley BR1 **191** G3
Erith DA8 **139** J7
Ethelbert St, SW12 **168** B1
Ethelburga St, SW11 **149** H1
Ethelburga Twr, SW11 *off Rosenau Rd* **149** H1
Etheldene Av, N10 **74** C4
Ethelden Rd, W12 **127** H1
Ethelred Est, SE11 *off Hotspur St* **131** G4
Ethel Rd, E16 **115** H6
Ethel St, SE17 **35** J2
Etheridge Grn, Loug. IG10 **49** F3
Etheridge Rd, NW2 **71** J7
Loughton IG10 **49** E2
Etherley Rd, N15 **75** J5
Etherow St, SE22 **152** D6
Etherstone Grn, SW16 **169** G4
Etherstone Rd, SW16 **169** G4
Ethnard Rd, SE15 **132** E6
Ethronvi Rd, Bexh. DA7 **159** E3
Etloe Rd, E10 **96** A2
Eton Av, N12 **57** F7
NW3 **91** G7
Barnet EN4 **41** H6
Hounslow TW5 **123** F6
New Malden KT3 **182** D5
Wembley HA0 **87** E4
Eton Cl, SW18 **149** E7
Eton Coll Rd, NW3 **91** J6
Eton Ct, NW3 *off Eton Av* **91** G7
Wembley HA0 **87** F4
Eton Garages, NW3 *off Lambolle Pl* **91** H6
Eton Gro, NW9 **70** A3
SE13 **154** E3
Eton Hall, NW3 *off Eton Coll Rd* **91** J6
Eton Pl, NW3 *off Haverstock Hill* **92** A7
Eton Ri, NW3 *off Eton Coll Rd* **91** J6
Eton Rd, NW3 **91** J7
Hayes UB3 **121** J7
Ilford IG1 **99** F5
Eton St, Rich. TW9 **145** H5
Eton Vil, NW3 **91** J6
Etta St, SE8 **133** H6
Ettrick St, E14 **114** C6
Etwell Pl, Surb. KT5 **181** J6
Euesden Cl, N9 **60** E3
Eugenia Rd, SE16 **133** F4
Eugenie Ms, Chiswick BR7 **192** E1
Eureka Rd, Kings.T. KT1 *off Washington Rd* **182** A2
Euro Cl, NW10 **89** G6
Europa Pl, EC1 **11** J4
Europe Rd, SE18 **136** C3
Eustace Bldg, SW8 **32** D6
Eustace Pl, SE18 *off Borgard Rd* **136** C4
Eustace Rd, E6 **116** B3
SW6 **128** D7
Romford RM6 **82** D7
Euston Cen, NW1 *off Triton Sq* **9** F5
Euston Gro, NW1 **9** H4
Euston Rd, N1 **10** A3
NW1 **9** E6
Croydon CR0 **201** G1
Euston Sq, NW1 **9** H4
Euston Sta, NW1 **9** G3
Euston Sta Colonnade, NW1 **9** H4
Euston St, NW1 **9** G5
Euston Twr, NW1 **9** F5
Evan Cook Cl, SE15 **153** F1
Evandale Rd, SW9 **151** G2
Evangelist Rd, NW5 **92** B4
Evans Cl, E8 *off Buttermere Wk* **94** C6
Evans Gro, Felt. TW13 **161** G2
Evans Rd, SE6 **173** E2
Evanston Av, E4 **62** C7
Evanston Gdns, Ilf. IG4 **80** B6
Eva Rd, Rom. RM6 **82** C7
Evelina Rd, SE15 **153** F3
SE20 **171** G7
Eveline Lowe Est, SE16 **29** H6
Eveline Rd, Mitch. CR4 **185** J1
Evelyn Av, NW9 **70** D4
Evelyn Cl, Twick. TW2 **143** H7
Evelyn Ct, N1 **12** B2
Evelyn Denington Rd, E6 **116** B4
Evelyn Dr, Pnr. HA5 **50** D7
Evelyn Fox Ct, W10 **107** J5
Evelyn Gdns, SW7 **30** E4
Richmond TW9 *off Kew Rd* **145** H4
Evelyn Gro, W5 **125** J1
Southall UB1 **103** F6
Evelyn Rd, E16 **135** H1
E17 **78** C4
SW19 **166** E5
W4 **126** D3
Barnet (Cockfos.) EN4 **41** J4
Richmond TW9 **145** H3
Richmond (Ham) TW10 **163** F3
Evelyn St, SE8 **133** H5
Evelyn Ter, Rich. TW9 **145** H3
Evelyn Wk, N1 **12** B2
Evelyn Way, Wall. SM6 **200** D4
Evelyn Yd, W1 **17** H3
Evening Hill, Beck. BR3 **172** C7
Evenwood Cl, SW15 **148** B5
Everard Av, Brom. BR2 **205** G1
Everard Way, Wem. HA9 **87** H3
Everatt Cl, SW18 *off Amerland Rd* **148** C6
Everdon Rd, SW13 **127** G6
Everest Pl, E14 **114** C5
Everest Rd, SE9 **156** C5
Staines (Stanw.) TW19 **140** A7
Everett Cl, Bushey (Bushey Hth) WD23 **52** B1
Everett Wk, Belv. DA17 *off Osborne Rd* **139** F5
Everglade Strand, NW9 **71** F1
Evergreen Cl, SE20 **171** F7
Evergreen Ct, Stai. (Stanw.) TW19 *off Evergreen Way* **140** A7
Evergreen Sq, E8 **94** C7
Evergreen Way, Stai. (Stanw.) TW19 **140** A7
Everilda St, N1 **111** F1
Evering Rd, E5 **94** C3
N16 **94** C3
Everington Rd, N10 **73** J2
Everington St, W6 **128** A6
Everitt Rd, NW10 **106** D3
Everleigh St, N4 **93** F1
Eve Rd, E11 **96** E4
E15 **115** E2
N17 **76** B3
Isleworth TW7 **144** D4
Eversfield Gdns, NW7 **54** E6
Eversfield Rd, Richmond TW9 **145** J2
Evershed Wk, W4 **126** C3
Eversholt Ct, Barn. EN5 *off Lyonsdown Rd* **41** F5
Eversholt St, NW1 **9** G1
Evershot Rd, N4 **93** F1
Eversleigh Rd, E6 **116** A1
N3 **56** C7
SW11 **149** J3
Barnet EN5 **41** F5
Eversley Av, Wembley HA9 **88** A2
Eversley Cl, N21 **43** F6
Loughton IG10 **49** F3
Eversley Cres, N21 **43** F6
Isleworth TW7 **144** A1
Eversley Mt, N21 **43** F6
Eversley Pk, SW19 **165** H5
Eversley Pk Rd, N21 **43** F6

Eversley Rd, SE7 **135** H6
SE19 **170** A7
Surbiton KT5 **181** J4
Eversley Way, Croy. CR0 **204** A4
Everthorpe Rd, SE15 **152** C3
Everton Bldgs, NW1 **9** F4
Everton Dr, Stan. HA7 **69** J3
Everton Rd, Croy. CR0 **202** D1
Evesham Av, E17 **78** A2
Evesham Cl, Grnf. UB6 **103** H2
Sutton SM2 **198** D7
Evesham Ct, W13 *off Tewkesbury Rd* **124** D1
Evesham Grn, Mord. SM4 **184** E6
Evesham Rd, E15 **115** F1
N11 **58** C5
Morden SM4 **185** E6
Evesham St, W11 **108** A7
Evesham Wk, SE5 *off Love Wk* **152** A2
SW9 **151** G2
Evesham Way, SW11 **150** A3
Ilford IG5 **80** D3
Evette Ms, Ilf. IG5 **80** D1
Evry Rd, Sid. DA14 **176** C6
Ewald Rd, SW6 **148** C2
Ewanrigg Ter, Wdf.Grn. IG8 **63** J5
Ewart Gro, N22 **75** G1
Ewart Pl, E3 *off Roman Rd* **113** J2
Ewart Rd, SE23 **153** G7
Ewe Cl, N7 **93** E6
Ewell Bypass, Epsom KT17 **197** G7
Ewell Ct Av, Epsom KT19 **197** E5
Ewellhurst Rd, Ilf. IG5 **80** B2
Ewell Pk Gdns, Epsom KT17 **197** G7
Ewell Pk Way, Epsom (Ewell) KT17 **197** G6
Ewell Rd, Surb. KT6 **181** H6
Surbiton (Long Dit.) KT6 **180** E7
Sutton SM3 **198** B6
Ewelme Rd, SE23 **171** F1
Ewen Cres, SW2 **151** G7
Ewer St, SE1 **27** J2
Ewhurst Cl, E1 **113** F5
Ewhurst Ct, Mitch. CR4 *off Phipps Br Rd* **185** G3
Ewhurst Rd, SE4 **153** J6
Exbury Rd, SE6 **172** A2
Excalibur Ct, N9 *off Galahad Rd* **60** D3
Excel Ct, WC2 **17** J6
★ **ExCeL London**, E16 **115** H7
ExCeL Marina, E16 *off Western Gateway* **115** G7
Excelsior Cl, Kings.T. KT1 *off Washington Rd* **182** A2
Excelsior Gdns, SE13 **154** C2
ExCeL Waterfront, E16 *off Western Gateway* **115** H7
Exchange, The, E1 *off Commercial St* **13** F6
Exchange Arc, EC2 **20** E1
Exchange Cl, N11 *off Benfleet Way* **58** A2
Exchange Ct, WC2 **18** B6
Exchange Ho, N8 **74** E6
Exchange Pl, EC2 **20** D1
Exchange Sq, EC2 **20** D1
Exchange Wk, Pnr. HA5 **66** E7
Exeter Cl, E6 *off Harper Rd* **116** C6
Exeter Ct, Surb. KT6 *off Maple Rd* **181** H5
Exeter Gdns, Ilf. IG1 **98** B1
Exeter Ho, SW15 *off Putney Heath* **147** J6
Exeter Ms, NW6 *off West Hampstead Ms* **90** E6
SW6 *off Farm La* **128** D7
Exeter Rd, E16 **115** G5
E17 **78** A5
N9 **61** F2
N14 **58** B1
NW2 **90** B5
Croydon CR0 **188** B7
Dagenham RM10 **101** H6
Enfield EN3 **45** G3
Feltham TW13 **161** F3
Harrow HA2 **85** E2
Hounslow (Lon.Hthrw Air.) TW6 **141** H2
Welling DA16 **157** J2
Exeter St, WC2 **18** B5
Exeter Way, SE14 **133** J7
Hounslow (Lon.Hthrw Air.) TW6 **141** H3
Exford Gdns, SE12 **173** H1
Exford Rd, SE12 **173** H2
Exhibition Cl, W12 **107** J7
Exhibition Rd, SW7 **23** F4
Exmoor Cl, Ilf. IG6 **81** F1
Exmoor St, W10 **108** A4
Exmouth Mkt, EC1 **11** E5
Exmouth Ms, NW1 **9** G4
Exmouth Pl, E8 **94** E7
Exmouth Rd, E17 **77** J5
Ruislip HA4 **84** C3
Welling DA16 **158** C1
Exmouth St, E1 *off Commercial Rd* **113** F6
Exning Rd, E16 **115** F4
Exon St, SE17 **36** D2
Express Dr, Ilf. IG3 **100** B1
Exton Gdns, Dag. RM8 **100** C5
Exton Rd, NW10 **88** C7
Exton St, SE1 **27** E2
Eyebright Cl, Croy. CR0 *off Primrose La* **203** G1
Eyhurst Cl, NW2 **89** G2
Eylewood Rd, SE27 **169** J5
Eynella Rd, SE22 **152** C7
Eynham Rd, W12 **107** J6
Eynsford Cl, Orp. BR5 **193** F7
Eynsford Cres, Bex. DA5 **176** C1
Eynsford Rd, Ilf. IG3 **99** H2
Eynsham Dr, SE2 **138** A4
Eynswood Dr, Sid. DA14 **176** B5
Eyot Gdns, W6 **127** F5
Eyot Grn, W4 *off Chiswick Mall* **127** F5
Eyre Ct, NW8 **6** E1
Eyre St Hill, EC1 **11** E6
Eythorne Rd, SW9 **151** G1
Ezra St, E2 **13** G3

F

Faber Gdns, NW4 **71** G5
Fabian Rd, SW6 **128** C7
Fabian St, E6 **116** C4
Factory La, N17 **76** C2
Croydon CR0 **201** G1
Factory Rd, E16 **136** B1
Factory Sq, SW16 **168** E6
Factory Yd, W7 *off Uxbridge Rd* **124** B1
Faggs Rd, Felt. TW14 **142** A5
Fairacre, N.Mal. KT3 **182** E3
Fairacres, SW15 **147** G4
Fair Acres, Brom. BR2 **191** G5
Fairbairn Grn, SW9 **151** G1
Fairbank Av, Orp. BR6 **206** E2
Fairbank Est, N1 **12** C2
Fairbanks Rd, N17 **76** C3
Fairbourne Rd, N17 **76** B3
Fairbridge Rd, N19 **92** D2
Fairbrook Cl, N13 **59** G5
Fairbrook Rd, N13 **59** G6
Fairburn Cl, Borwd. WD6 **38** A1
Fairburn Ct, SW15 **148** B5
Fairburn Ho, W14 *off Ivatt Pl* **128** C5
Fairby Ho, SE1 **37** G1
Fairby Rd, SE12 **155** H5
Faircharm Trd Est, SE8 **134** A7
Fairchild Cl, SW11 *off Wye St* **149** G2
Fairchild Pl, EC2 **13** E6
Fairchild St, EC2 **13** E6
Fairclough Cl, Nthlt. UB5 *off Waxlow Way* **103** F4
Fairclough St, E1 **21** J4
Faircross Av, Bark. IG11 **99** F6
Faircross Par, Bark. IG11 **99** H6
Fairdale Gdns, SW15 **147** H4
Hayes UB3 **122** A1
Fairey Av, Hayes UB3 **121** J4
Fairfax Gdns, SE3 **156** A1
Fairfax Ms, E16 *off Wesley Av* **135** H1
SW15 **147** J4
Fairfax Pl, NW6 **91** F7
W14 **128** B3
Fairfax Rd, N8 **75** G4
NW6 **91** F7
W4 **127** E3
Teddington TW11 **162** D6
Fairfield Av, NW4 **71** H6
Edgware HA8 **54** B6
Twickenham TW2 **161** H1
Watford WD19 **50** C3
Fairfield Cl, N12 **57** F4
Enfield EN3 *off Scotland Grn Rd N* **45** H4
Epsom (Ewell) KT19 **196** E5
Mitcham CR4 **167** H7
Sidcup DA15 **157** J6
Fairfield Ct, NW10 **107** G1
Northwood HA6 *off Windsor Cl* **66** A2
Fairfield Cres, Edg. HA8 **54** B6
Fairfield Dr, SW18 **149** E5
Greenford (Perivale) UB6 **105** F1
Harrow HA2 **67** J3
Fairfield E, Kings.T. KT1 **181** H2
Fairfield Gdns, N8 **75** E5
Fairfield Gro, SE7 **136** A5
★ **Fairfield Halls**, Croy. CR0 **202** A3
Fairfield N, Kings.T. KT1 **181** H2
Fairfield Path, Croy. CR0 **202** A3
Fairfield Pl, Kings.T. KT1 **181** H3
Fairfield Rd, E3 **114** A2
E17 **77** H2
N8 **75** E5
N18 **60** D4
W7 **124** D3
Beckenham BR3 **190** A2
Bexleyheath DA7 **159** F2
Bromley BR1 **173** G7
Croydon CR0 **202** B3
Ilford IG1 **99** E6
Kingston upon Thames KT1 **181** H2
Orpington BR5 **193** G6
Southall UB1 **103** F6
West Drayton UB7 **120** B1
Woodford Green IG8 **63** G6
Fairfields Cl, NW9 **70** C5
Fairfields Cres, NW9 **70** C4
Fairfield S, Kings.T. KT1 **181** H3
Fairfields Rd, Houns. TW3 **143** J3
Fairfield St, SW18 **149** E5
Fairfield Trade Pk, Kings.T. KT1 **181** J3
Fairfield Way, Barn. EN5 **40** D5
Epsom KT19 **196** E5
Fairfield W, Kings.T. KT1 **181** H2
Fairfoot Rd, E3 **114** A4
Fairford Av, Croy. CR0 **189** G5
Fairford Cl, Croy. CR0 **189** H5
Fairford Ct, Sutt. SM2 *off Grange Rd* **198** E7
Fairford Gdns, Wor.Pk. KT4 **197** F3
Fairford Ho, SE11 **35** F2
Fairgreen, Barn. EN4 **41** J3
Fairgreen E, Barn. EN4 **41** J3
Fairgreen Par, Mitch. CR4 *off London Rd* **185** J3
Fairgreen Rd, Th.Hth. CR7 **187** H5
Fairhaven Av, Croy. CR0 **189** G6
Fairhaven Cres, Wat. WD19 **50** A3
Fairhazel Gdns, NW6 **91** E6
Fairholme, Felt. TW14 **141** G7
Fairholme Cl, N3 **72** B4
Fairholme Gdns, N3 **72** B3
Fairholme Rd, W14 **128** B5
Croydon CR0 **187** G7
Harrow HA1 **68** C5
Ilford IG1 **80** C7
Sutton SM1 **198** C6
Fairholt Cl, N16 **94** B1
Fairholt Rd, N16 **94** A1
Fairholt St, SW7 **23** H5
Fairland Rd, E15 **97** F6
Fairlands Av, Buck.H. IG9 **63** G2
Sutton SM1 **198** D2
Thornton Heath CR7 **187** F4
Fairlands Ct, SE9 *off North Pk* **156** D6
Fairlawn, SE7 **135** J6
Fairlawn Av, N2 **73** H4
W4 **126** C4
Bexleyheath DA7 **158** D2
Fairlawn Cl, N14 **42** C6
Esher (Clay.) KT10 **194** C6
Feltham TW13 **161** F4
Kingston upon Thames KT2 **164** C6
Fairlawn Ct, SE7 *off Fairlawn* **135** J7
Fairlawn Dr, Wdf.Grn. IG8 **63** G7
Fairlawnes, Wall. SM6 *off Maldon Rd* **200** B5
Fairlawn Gdns, Sthl. UB1 **103** F7
Fairlawn Gro, W4 **126** C4
Fairlawn Pk, SE26 **171** H5
Fairlawn Rd, SW19 **166** C7
Fairlawns, Pnr. HA5 **66** C2
Sunbury-on-Thames TW16 **178** A3
Twickenham TW1 **145** F6
Fairlead Ho, E14 *off Cassilis Rd* **134** A3
Fairlea Pl, W5 **105** G4
Fairlie Ct, E3 *off Stroudley Wk* **114** B3
Fairlie Gdns, SE23 **153** F7
Fairlight Av, E4 **62** D2
NW10 **107** E2
Woodford Green IG8 **63** G6
Fairlight Cl, E4 **62** D2
Worcester Park KT4 **197** J4
Fairlight Rd, SW17 **167** G4
Fairlop Gdns, Ilford IG6 **65** F7
Fairlop Rd, E11 **78** D7
Ilford IG6 **81** F2
Fairmead, Brom. BR1 **192** C4
Surbiton KT5 **196** B1
Fairmead Cl, Brom. BR1 **192** C4
Hounslow TW5 **122** D7
New Malden KT3 **182** D3
Fairmead Cres, Edg. HA8 **54** C3
Fairmead Gdns, Ilf. IG4 **80** B5
Fairmead Ho, E9 *off Kingsmead Way* **95** H4
Fairmead Rd, N19 **92** D3
Croydon CR0 **201** F1
Loughton IG10 **47** H4
Fairmeads, Loug. IG10 **48** E2
Fairmeadside, Loug. IG10 **47** J5
Fairmile Av, SW16 **168** D5
Fairmile Ho, Tedd. TW11 *off Twickenham Rd* **162** D4
Fairmont Av, E14 **134** D1
Fairmont Cl, Belv. DA17 **139** F5
Fairmount Rd, SW2 **151** F6
Fairoak Cl, Orp. BR5 **193** E7
Fairoak Dr, SE9 **157** G5
Fair Oak Pl, Ilf. IG6 **81** F2
Fairseat Cl, Bushey (Bushey Hth) WD23 *off Hive Rd* **52** B2
Fairstead Wk, N1 *off Popham Rd* **111** J1
Fair St, SE1 **29** E3
Hounslow TW3 *off High St* **143** J3
Fairthorn Rd, SE7 **135** G5
Fairview, Ruis. HA4 *off The Fairway* **84** C4
Fairview Av, Wem. HA0 **87** G6
Fairview Cl, E17 **77** H1
Chigwell IG7 **65** H4
Fairview Ct, NW4 **72** A2
Fairview Cres, Har. HA2 **85** G1
Fairview Dr, Chig. IG7 **65** H4
Orpington BR6 **207** G4
Fairview Gdns, Wdf.Grn. IG8 **79** H1
Fairview Pl, SW2 **151** F7
Fairview Rd, N15 **76** C5
SW16 **187** F1
Chigwell IG7 **65** H4
Enfield EN2 **43** G1
Sutton SM1 **199** G5
Fairview Way, Edg. HA8 **54** A4
Fairwater Av, Well. DA16 **158** A4
Fairway, SW20 **183** J3
Bexleyheath DA6 **159** E5
Orpington BR5 **193** G5
Woodford Green IG8 **63** J5
Fairway, The, N13 **59** J3
N14 **42** B6
NW7 **54** D3
W3 **106** E6
Barnet (New Barn.) EN5 **41** E6
Bromley BR1 **192** C5
New Malden KT3 **182** D1
Northolt UB5 **85** J6
Ruislip HA4 **84** D3
Wembley HA0 **87** E3
West Molesey KT8 **179** H3
Fairway Av, NW9 **70** B3
Borehamwood WD6 **38** B2
Fairway Cl, NW11 **73** F7
Croydon CR0 **189** H5
Epsom KT19 **196** C4
Hounslow TW4 **142** C5
Fairway Ct, NW7 **54** D3
Fairway Dr, SE28 **118** D6
Greenford UB6 **85** H7
Fairway Gdns, Beck. BR3 **190** D6
Ilford IG1 **99** F5
Fairways, Stan. HA7 **69** H2
Teddington TW11 **163** G7
Fairweather Cl, N15 **76** B4
Fairweather Rd, N16 **76** D6
Fairwyn Rd, SE26 **171** H4
Fakenham Cl, NW7 **55** G7
Northolt UB5 *off Goodwood Dr* **85** G6
Fakruddin St, E1 **13** J6
Falcon Av, Bromley BR1 **192** B4
Falconberg Ct, W1 **17** J3
Falconberg Ms, W1 **17** H3
Falcon Business Cen, Mitch. CR4 **185** J5
Falcon Cl, W4 *off Sutton La S* **126** C6
Falcon Ct, EC4 **19** E4
Falcon Cres, Enf. EN3 **45** G5
Falcon Dr, Stai. (Stanw.) TW19 **140** A6
Falconer Ct, N17 *off Compton Cres* **59** J7
Falconer Wk, N7 *off Newington Barrow Way* **93** F2

Falcon Est, Felt. TW14 *off Central Way* 142 B5
Falcon Gro, SW11 149 H3
Falcon Ho, W13 104 C4
Falcon La, SW11 149 H3
Falcon Pk Ind Est, NW10 89 F5
Falcon Rd, SW11 149 H2
Enfield EN3 45 G5
Hampton TW12 161 F7
Falcon St, E13 115 G4
Falcon Ter, SW11 149 H3
Falcon Way, E11 79 G4
E14 134 B4
NW9 71 E2
Feltham TW14 142 B5
Harrow HA3 69 H5
FALCONWOOD, Well. DA16 157 G3
Falconwood, SE9 157 F4
Falconwood Av, Well. DA16 157 G2
Falconwood Par, Well. DA16 157 H4
Falconwood Rd, Croy. CR0 204 A7
Falcourt Cl, Sutt. SM1 198 E5
Falkirk Gdns, Wat. WD19 50 D5
Falkirk Ho, W9 6 B3
Falkirk St, N1 12 E2
Falkland Av, N3 56 D7
N11 58 A4
Falkland Pk Av, SE25 188 B3
Falkland Pl, NW5 *off Falkland Rd* 92 C5
Falkland Rd, N8 75 G4
NW5 92 C5
Barnet EN5 40 B2
Fallaize Av, Ilf. IG1 *off Riverdene Rd* 98 E4
Falloden Way, NW11 72 D4
Fallow Cl, Chig. IG7 65 J5
Fallow Ct, SE16 37 J4
Fallow Ct Av, N12 57 F7
Fallowfield, N4 *off Six Acres Est* 93 F2
Stanmore HA7 52 D3
Fallowfield Ct, Stan. HA7 52 D3
Fallow Flds, Loug. IG10 47 J7
Fallowfields Dr, N12 57 H6
Fallows Cl, N2 73 F2
Fallsbrook Rd, SW16 168 C7
Falman Cl, N9 60 D1
Falmer Rd, E17 78 B3
N15 75 J5
Enfield EN1 44 B4
Falmouth Av, E4 62 D5
Falmouth Cl, N22 59 F7
SE12 155 F5
Falmouth Gdns, Ilf. IG4 80 B5
Falmouth Ho, Kings.T. KT2 *off Kingsgate Rd* 181 G1
Falmouth Rd, SE1 28 A5
Falmouth St, E15 96 D5
Falmouth Way, E17 *off Gosport Rd* 77 J5
Falstaff Ms, Hmptn. (Hmptn H.) TW12 *off Hampton Rd* 162 A5
Fambridge Cl, SE26 171 J4
Fambridge Rd, Dag. RM8 101 G1
Fane St, W14 *off North End Rd* 128 C6
★ **Fan Mus**, SE10 134 C7
Fann St, EC1 11 J6
EC2 11 J6
Fanshawe, The, Dag. RM9 *off Gale St* 100 D7
Fanshawe Av, Bark. IG11 99 F6
Fanshawe Cres, Dag. RM9 101 E5
Fanshawe Rd, Rich. TW10 163 F4
Fanshaw St, N1 12 D3
Fantail, The, Orp. BR6 206 C4
Fantail Cl, SE28 *off Greenhaven Dr* 118 C6
Fanthorpe St, SW15 147 J3
Faraday Av, Sid. DA14 176 A2
Faraday Cl, N7 *off Bride St* 93 F6
Faraday Lo, SE10 *off Renaissance Wk* 135 F3
★ **Faraday Mus**, W1 17 F6
Faraday Pl, W.Mol. KT8 179 G4
Faraday Rd, E15 97 F6
SW19 166 D6
W3 106 C7
W10 108 B5
Southall UB1 103 H7
Welling DA16 158 A3
West Molesey KT8 179 G4
Faraday Way, SE18 136 A3
Croydon CR0 *off Ampere Way* 201 F1
Fareham Rd, Felt. TW14 142 C7
Fareham St, W1 17 H3
Farewell Pl, Mitch. CR4 185 H1
Faringdon Av, Brom. BR2 192 E6
Faringford Rd, E15 96 E7
Farjeon Rd, SE3 156 A1
Farleigh Av, Brom. BR2 191 F6
Farleigh Pl, N16 94 C4
Farleigh Rd, N16 94 C4
Farley Dr, Ilf. IG3 99 H1
Farley Ms, SE6 154 C7
Farley Pl, SE25 188 D4
Farley Rd, SE6 154 B7
South Croydon CR2 202 E7
Farlington Pl, SW15 *off Roehampton La* 147 H7
Farlow Rd, SW15 148 A3
Farlton Rd, SW18 149 E7
Farman Gro, Nthlt. UB5 *off Wayfarer Rd* 102 D3
Farm Av, NW2 90 B3
SW16 169 E4
Harrow HA2 67 F7
Wembley HA0 87 F6
Farmborough Cl, Har. HA1 *off Pool Rd* 68 A7
Farm Cl, SW6 *off Farm La* 128 D7
Barnet EN5 39 J5
Buckhurst Hill IG9 63 J3
Dagenham RM10 101 J7
Southall UB1 103 H7
Sutton SM2 199 G7
West Wickham BR4 205 E3
Farmcote Rd, SE12 173 G1
Farm Ct, NW4 71 G3
Farmdale Rd, SE10 135 G5
Carshalton SM5 199 H7
Farm Dr, Croy. CR0 203 J2
Farm End, E4 46 E5
Farmer Rd, E10 96 B1
Farmers Rd, SE5 35 H7
Farmer St, W8 *off Uxbridge St* 128 D1
Farmfield Rd, Brom. BR1 172 E5
Farmhouse Rd, SW16 168 C7
Farmilo Rd, E17 77 J7
Farmington Av, Sutt. SM1 199 G3
Farmlands, Enf. EN2 43 G1
Pinner HA5 66 A4
Farmlands, The, Nthlt. UB5 85 F6
Farmland Wk, Chis. BR7 174 E5
Farm La, N14 42 A6
SW6 128 D6
Croydon CR0 203 J2
Farm La Trd Cen, SW6 *off Farm La* 128 D6
Farmleigh, N14 42 C7
Farm Pl, W8 *off Uxbridge St* 128 D1
Farm Rd, N21 59 H1
NW10 106 D1
Edgware HA8 54 B6
Hounslow TW4 161 E1
Morden SM4 185 E5
Sutton SM2 199 G7
Farmstead Rd, SE6 172 B4
Harrow HA3 68 A1
Farm St, W1 16 D6
Farm Vale, Bex. DA5 159 H6
Farm Wk, NW11 72 C5
Farm Way, Buck.H. IG9 63 J4
Farmway, Dag. RM8 100 C4
Farm Way, Wor.Pk. KT4 197 J3
Farnaby Rd, SE9 155 J4
Bromley BR1, BR2 172 D7
Farnan Av, E17 78 A2
Farnan Rd, SW16 169 E5
FARNBOROUGH, Orp. BR6 206 E5
Farnborough Av, E17 77 H3
South Croydon CR2 203 G7
Farnborough Cl, Wem. HA9 88 B2
Farnborough Common, Orp. BR6 206 C3
Farnborough Cres, Brom. BR2 *off Saville Row* 205 F1
Farnborough Hill, Orp. BR6 207 G5
Farnborough Ho, SW15 *off Fontley Way* 165 G1
Farnborough Way, Orp. BR6 207 F4
Farncombe St, SE16 29 J4
Farndale Av, N13 59 H3
Farndale Cres, Grnf. UB6 103 J3
Farnell Ms, SW5 30 A3
Farnell Pl, W3 106 B7
Farnell Rd, Islw. TW7 144 A3
Farnham Cl, N20 41 F7
Farnham Gdns, SW20 183 H2
Farnham Pl, SE1 27 H2
Farnham Rd, Ilf. IG3 81 J7
Welling DA16 158 C2
Farnham Royal, SE11 34 D4
Farningham Rd, N17 60 D7
Farnley Rd, E4 46 E7
SE25 188 A4
Farnsworth Ct, SE10 *off West Parkside* 135 F3
Faro Cl, Brom. BR1 192 D2
Faroe Rd, W14 128 A3
Farorna Wk, Enf. EN2 43 G1
Farquhar Rd, SE19 170 C5
SW19 166 D3
Farquharson Rd, Croy. CR0 201 J1
Farrance Rd, Rom. RM6 83 E6
Farrance St, E14 113 J6
Farrans Ct, Har. HA3 69 E7
Farrant Av, N22 75 G2
Farr Av, Bark. IG11 118 A2
Farrell Ho, E1 113 F6
Farren Rd, SE23 171 H2
Farrer Ms, N8 *off Farrer Rd* 74 C4
Farrer Rd, N8 74 C4
Harrow HA3 69 H5
Farrer's Pl, Croy. CR0 203 G4
Farrier Cl, Brom. BR1 192 A3
Sunbury-on-Thames TW16 178 A4
Farrier Pl, Sutt. SM1 198 D3
Farrier Rd, Nthlt. UB5 103 G2
Farriers Ct, Sutt. SM3 *off Forge La* 198 B7
Farriers Ms, SE15 *off Machell Rd* 153 F3
Farrier St, NW1 92 B7
Farriers Way, Borwd. WD6 38 C6
Farrier Wk, SW10 30 C5
Farringdon Ho, Rich. TW9 126 B7
Farringdon La, EC1 11 F6
Farringdon Rd, EC1 10 E5
Farringdon St, EC4 19 G3
Farrington Pl, Chis. BR7 175 G7
Farrins Rents, SE16 133 H1
Farrow La, SE14 133 F7
Farrow Pl, SE16 *off Ropemaker Rd* 133 H3
Farr Rd, Enf. EN2 44 A1
Farthingale Wk, E15 96 D7
Farthing All, SE1 29 H4
Farthing Ct, NW7 56 B7
Farthing Flds, E1 *off Raine St* 133 E1
Farthings, The, Kings.T. KT2 182 A1
Farthings Cl, E4 63 E3
Pinner HA5 66 B6
Farthing St, Orp. BR6 206 C7
Farwell Rd, Sid. DA14 176 B3
Farwig La, Brom. BR1 191 F1
Fashion St, E1 21 F2
Fashoda Rd, Brom. BR2 192 A4
Fassett Rd, E8 94 D6
Kingston upon Thames KT1 181 H4
Fassett Sq, E8 94 D6
Fauconberg Rd, W4 126 C6
Faulkner Cl, Dag. RM8 82 D7
Faulkner's All, EC1 19 G1
Faulkner St, SE14 153 F1
Fauna Cl, Rom. RM6 82 C7
Stanmore HA7 53 G4
Faunce St, SE17 35 G5
Favart Rd, SW6 148 D1
Faversham Av, E4 63 E1
Enfield EN1 44 A6
Faversham Rd, SE6 153 J7
Beckenham BR3 189 J2
Morden SM4 185 E6
Fawcett Cl, SW11 149 G2
SW16 169 G4
Fawcett Est, E5 94 D1
Fawcett Rd, NW10 107 F1
Croydon CR0 201 J3
Fawcett St, SW10 30 C5
Fawcus Cl, Esher (Clay.) KT10 *off Dalmore Av* 194 C6
Fawe Pk Rd, SW15 148 C4
Fawe St, E14 114 B5
Fawkham Ho, SE1 *off Longfield Est* 37 G2
Fawley Rd, NW6 90 E5
Fawnbrake Av, SE24 151 H5
Fawn Rd, E13 115 J2
Chigwell IG7 65 J5
Fawood Av, NW10 88 D7
Faygate Cres, Bexh. DA6 159 G5
Faygate Rd, SW2 169 F2
Fayland Av, SW16 168 C5
Fayland Estate, SW16 168 C5
Fearnley Cres, Hmptn. TW12 161 E5
Fearon St, SE10 135 G5
Featherbed La, Croy. CR0 203 J7
Feathers Pl, SE10 134 D6
Featherstone Av, SE23 171 E2
Featherstone Gdns, Borwd. WD6 38 C4
Featherstone Ind Est, Sthl. UB2 123 E2
Featherstone Rd, NW7 55 H6
Southall UB2 122 E3
Featherstone St, EC1 12 B5
Featherstone Ter, Sthl. UB2 123 E3
Featley Rd, SW9 151 H3
Federal Rd, Grnf. (Perivale) UB6 105 F2
Federation Rd, SE2 138 B4
Fee Fm Rd, Esher (Clay.) KT10 194 C7
Feeny Cl, NW10 89 F4
Felbridge Av, Stan. HA7 68 D1
Felbridge Cl, SW16 169 G4
Felbridge Ho, SE22 *off Pytchley Rd* 152 B3
Felbrigge Rd, Ilf. IG3 99 J2
Felday Rd, SE13 154 B6
Felden Cl, Pnr. HA5 51 E7
Felden St, SW6 148 C1
Feldman Cl, N16 94 D1
Feldspar Ct, Enf. EN3 *off Enstone Rd* 45 H3
Felgate Ms, W6 127 H4
Felhampton Rd, SE9 174 E2
Felhurst Cres, Dag. RM10 101 H4
Felix Av, N8 74 E6
Felix Pl, SW2 *off Talma Rd* 151 G5
Felix Rd, W13 104 D7
Walton-on-Thames KT12 178 A6
Felixstowe Ct, E16 *off Fishguard Way* 137 E1
Felixstowe Rd, N9 60 D4
N17 76 C3
NW10 107 H3
SE2 138 B3
Fellbrigg Rd, SE22 152 C5
Fellbrigg St, E1 *off Headlam St* 113 E4
Fellbrook, Rich. TW10 163 E3
Fellmongers Path, SE1 29 E4
Fellmongers Yd, Croy. CR0 *off Surrey St* 201 J3
Fellowes Cl, Hayes UB4 *off Paddington Cl* 102 D4
Fellowes Rd, Cars. SM5 199 H3
Fellows Ct, E2 13 F2
Croy. CRO 188 C7
Fellows Rd, NW3 91 G7
Fell Rd, Croy. CR0 201 J3
Felltram Ms, SE7 *off Woolwich Rd* 135 G5
Felltram Way, SE7 *off Woolwich Rd* 135 G5
Fell Wk, Edg. HA8 *off East Rd* 70 C1
Felmersham Cl, SW4 *off Haselrigge Rd* 150 D4
Felmingham Rd, SE20 189 F2
Felnex Trd Est, Wall. SM6 200 A2
Felsberg Rd, SW2 151 E6
Fels Cl, Dag. RM10 101 H3
Fels Fm Av, Dag. RM10 101 J3
Felsham Rd, SW15 148 A3
Felspar Cl, SE18 137 J5
Felstead Av, Ilf. IG5 80 D1
Felstead Cl, N13 59 G5
Felstead Gdns, E14 *off Ferry St* 134 C5
Felstead Rd, E11 79 G7
Loughton IG10 48 B7
Felstead St, E9 95 J6
Felsted Rd, E16 116 A6
FELTHAM, TW13 & TW14 160 A2
Feltham Av, E.Mol. KT8 180 B4
Felthambrook Way, Felt. TW13 160 B3
Feltham Business Complex, Felt. TW13 160 B2
Feltham Rd, Mitch. CR4 185 J2
Felton Cl, Orp. BR5 192 E6
Felton Gdns, Bark. IG11 *off Sutton Rd* 117 H1
Felton Ho, SE3 *off Ryan Cl* 155 H4
Felton Lea, Sid. DA14 175 J5
Felton Rd, W13 *off Camborne Av* 125 F2
Barking IG11 *off Sutton Rd* 117 H2
Felton St, N1 112 A1
Fencepiece Rd, Chig. IG7 65 F5
Ilford IG6 65 F5
Fenchurch Av, EC3 20 D4
Fenchurch Bldgs, EC3 20 E4
Fenchurch Pl, EC3 20 E5
Fenchurch St, EC3 20 D5
Fen Ct, EC3 20 D4
Fendall Rd, Epsom KT19 196 C5
Fendall St, SE1 29 E6
Fendt Cl, E16 *off Bowman Av* 115 F7

Fendyke Rd, Belv. DA17 **138** D3
Fenelon Pl, W14 **128** C4
Fen Gro, Sid. DA15 **157** J6
Fenham Rd, SE15 **132** D7
Fen La, SW13 **147** H1
Fenman Ct, N17 **76** E1
Fenman Gdns, Ilf. IG3 **100** B1
Fenn Cl, Brom. BR1 **173** G6
Fennel Cl, E16
off Cranberry La **115** E4
Croydon CR0
off Primrose La **203** G1
Fennel St, SE18 **136** D6
Fenner Cl, SE16
off Layard Rd **133** E4
Fenner Sq, SW11
off Thomas Baines Rd **149** G3
Fenning St, SE1 **28** D3
Fenn St, E9 **95** F5
Fenstanton Av, N12 **57** G5
Fen St, E16
off Huntingdon St **115** F7
Fenswood Cl, Bex. DA5 **159** G5
Fentiman Rd, SW8 **34** B6
Fentiman Way, Har. HA2 **85** H2
Fenton Cl, E8
off Laurel St **94** C6
SW9 **151** F2
Chislehurst BR7 **174** C5
★ **Fenton Ho**, NW3 **91** F3
Fenton Ho, Houns. TW5
off Biscoe Cl **123** G6
Fenton Rd, N17 **59** J7
Fentons Av, E13 **115** H2
Fenton St, E1
off Commercial Rd **113** E6
Fenwick Cl, SE18 **136** D6
Fenwick Gro, SE15 **152** D3
Fenwick Pl, SW9 **150** E3
South Croydon CR2 **201** H7
Fenwick Rd, SE15 **152** D3
Ferdinand Pl, NW1
off Ferdinand St **92** A7
Ferdinand St, NW1 **92** A6
Ferguson Av, Surb. KT5 **181** J5
Ferguson Cl, E14 **134** A4
Bromley BR2 **190** D3
Ferguson Dr, W3 **106** D6
Fergus Rd, N5
off Calabria Rd **93** H5
Ferme Pk Rd, N4 **75** E5
N8 **75** E5
Fermor Rd, SE23 **171** H1
Fermoy Rd, W9 **108** C4
Greenford UB6 **103** H4
Fern Av, Mitch. CR4 **186** D4
Fernbank, Buck.H. IG9 **63** H1
Fernbank Av, Walt. KT12 **179** E7
Wembley HA0 **86** C4
Fernbank Ms, SW12 **150** B6
Fernbrook Av, Sid. DA15
off Blackfen Rd **157** H5
Fernbrook Cres, SE13 **154** E6
Fernbrook Dr, Har. HA2 **67** H7
Fernbrook Rd, SE13 **154** E6
Ferncliff Rd, E8 **94** D5
Fern Cl, N1 **12** D1
Ferncroft Av, N12 **57** H6
NW3 **90** D3
Ruislip HA4 **84** C2
Ferndale, Brom. BR1 **191** J2
Ferndale Av, E17 **78** D5
Hounslow TW4 **143** E3
Ferndale Cl, Bexh. DA7 **158** E1
Ferndale Ct, SE3 **135** F7
Ferndale Rd, E7 **97** H7
E11 **97** E2
N15 **76** C6
SE25 **188** E5
SW4 **150** E4
SW9 **151** F3
Romford RM5 **83** J2
Ferndale St, E6 **116** E7
Ferndale Ter, Har. HA1 **68** C4
Ferndale Way, Orp. BR6 **207** G5
Fern Dene, W13
off Templewood **105** E5
Ferndene Rd, SE24 **151** J4
Fernden Way, Rom. RM7 **83** H6
Ferndown, Nthwd. HA6 **66** A2
Ferndown Av, Orp. BR6 **207** G1
Ferndown Cl, Pnr. HA5 **50** E7
Sutton SM2 **199** G6
Ferndown Rd, SE9 **156** A7
Watford WD19 **50** C3
Ferney Meade Way, Islw. TW7 **144** D2
Ferney Rd, Barn. (E.Barn.) EN4 **42** A7
Fern Gro, Felt. TW14 **142** B7
Fernhall Dr, Ilf. IG4 **80** A5
Fernham Rd, Th.Hth. CR7 **187** J3
Fernhead Rd, W9 **108** C4
Fernhill Ct, E17 **78** D2
Fernhill Gdns, Kings.T. KT2 **163** G5
Fernhill St, E16 **136** C1
Fernholme Rd, SE15 **153** G5
Fernhurst Gdns, Edg. HA8 **54** A6
Fernhurst Rd, SW6 **148** B1
Croydon CR0 **188** D7
Fern La, Houns. TW5 **123** F5
Fernlea Rd, SW12 **168** B1
Mitcham CR4 **186** A2
Fernleigh Cl, W9 **108** C3
Croydon CR0 **201** G4
Fernleigh Ct, Har. HA2 **67** H2
Wembley HA9 **87** H2
Fernleigh Rd, N21 **59** G2
Fernley Cl, Pnr. (Eastcote) HA5 **66** A4
Fernsbury St, WC1 **10** E4
Fernshaw Rd, SW10 **30** C6
Fernside, NW11 **90** D2
Buckhurst Hill IG9 **63** H1
Fernside Av, NW7 **54** D3
Feltham TW13 **160** B4
Fernside Rd, SW12 **167** J1
Ferns Rd, E15 **97** F6
Fern St, E3 **114** A4
Fernthorpe Rd, SW16 **168** C6
Ferntower Rd, N5 **94** A5
Fern Wk, SE16 **37** J4
Fernways, Ilf. IG1
off Cecil Rd **98** E4
Fernwood, SW19
off Albert Dr **166** C1
Fernwood Av, SW16 **168** D4
Wembley HA0
off Bridgewater Rd **87** F5
Fernwood Cl, Brom. BR1 **191** J2
Fernwood Cres, N20 **57** J3
Ferranti Cl, SE18 **136** A3
Ferraro Cl, Houns. TW5 **123** G6
Ferrers Av, Wall. SM6 **200** D4
West Drayton UB7 **120** A2
Ferrers Rd, SW16 **168** D5
Ferrestone Rd, N8 **75** F4
Ferrey Ms, SW9 **151** G2
Ferriby Cl, N1
off Bewdley St **93** G7
Ferrier Pt, E16
off Forty Acre La **115** G5
Ferrier St, SW18 **149** E4
Ferring Cl, Har. HA2 **85** J1
Ferrings, SE21 **170** B2
Ferris Av, Croy. CR0 **203** J3
Ferris Rd, SE22 **152** D4
Ferron Rd, E5 **94** E3
Ferrour Ct, N2 **73** G3
Ferrybridge Ho, SE11 **26** D6
Ferryhills Cl, Wat. WD19 **50** C3
Ferry Ho, E5
off Harrington Hill **95** F1
Ferry La, N17 **76** D4
SW13 **127** F6
Brentford TW8 **125** H6
Richmond TW9 **125** J6
Ferryman's Quay, SW6 **149** F2
Ferrymead Av, Grnf. UB6 **103** G3
Ferrymead Dr, Grnf. UB6 **103** G2
Ferrymead Gdns, Grnf. UB6 **103** J2
Ferrymoor, Rich. TW10 **163** E3
Ferry Pl, SE18
off Woolwich High St **136** D3
Ferry Rd, SW13 **127** G7
Teddington TW11 **162** E5
Thames Ditton KT7 **180** E6
Twickenham TW1 **162** E1
West Molesey KT8 **179** G3
Ferry Sq, Brent. TW8 **125** G6
Ferry St, E14 **134** C5
Festing Rd, SW15 **148** A3
Festival Cl, Bex. DA5 **176** D1
Festival Ct, Sutt. SM1
off Cleeve Way **185** E7
Festival Wk, Cars. SM5 **199** J5
Festoon Way, E16 **116** A7
Fetter La, EC4 **19** F4
Ffinch St, SE8 **134** A7
Fidgeon Cl, Brom. BR1 **192** D3
Field Cl, E4 **62** B6
NW2 **89** G2
Bromley BR1 **191** J2
Buckhurst Hill IG9 **63** J3
Chessington KT9 **195** F5
Hayes (Harling.) UB3 **121** F7
Hounslow TW4 **142** B1
West Molesey KT8 **179** H5
Fieldcommon La, Walt. KT12 **179** F7
Field Ct, WC1 **18** D2
Field End, Barn. EN5 **39** H4
Northolt UB5 **84** D6
Ruislip HA4 **84** C6
Fieldend, Twick. TW1 **162** C4
Fieldend Rd, SW16 **186** C1
Field End Rd, Pnr. HA5 **66** B6
Ruislip HA4 **85** E4
Fielders Cl, Enf. EN1
off Woodfield Cl **44** B4
Harrow HA2 **85** J1
Fieldfare Rd, SE28 **118** C7
Fieldgate La, Mitch. CR4 **185** H3
Fieldgate St, E1 **21** J2
Fieldhouse Cl, E18 **79** G1
Fieldhouse Rd, SW12 **168** C1
Fielding Av, Twick. TW2 **161** J3
Fielding Ho, NW6 **108** D3
Fielding La, Brom. BR2 **191** J4
Fielding Ms, SW13
off Castelnau **127** H6
Fielding Rd, W4 **126** D3
W14 **128** A3
Fieldings, The, SE23 **171** F1
Fielding St, SE17 **35** J5
Fielding Wk, W13 **124** E3
Field La, Brent. TW8 **125** F7
Teddington TW11 **162** D5
Field Mead, NW7 **55** E7
NW9 **55** E7
Fieldpark Gdns, Croy. CR0 **203** H1
Field Pl, N.Mal. KT3 **183** F6
Field Pt, E7
off Station Rd **97** G4
Field Rd, E7 **97** F4
N17 **76** A3
W6 **128** B5
Feltham TW14 **142** B6
Fieldsend Rd, Sutt. SM3 **198** B5
Fields Est, E8 **94** D7
Fieldside Cl, Orp. BR6
off State Fm Av **207** F4
Fieldside Rd, Brom. BR1 **172** D5
Fields Pk Cres, Rom. RM6 **82** D5
Field St, WC1 **10** C3
Fieldview, SW18 **167** G1
Field Vw Cl, Rom. RM7 **83** G3
Field Way, NW10
off Twybridge Way **88** C7
Fieldway, Croy. (New Adgtn) CR0 **204** B6
Dagenham RM8 **100** B4
Field Way, Grnf. UB6 **103** H1
Fieldway, Orp. BR5 **193** G6
Fieldway Cres, N5 **93** G5
Fiennes Cl, Dag. RM8 **100** C1
Fiesta Dr, Dag. RM9 **119** J4
Fife Rd, E16 **115** G5
N22 **59** H7
SW14 **146** C5
Kingston upon Thames KT1 **181** H2
Fife Ter, N1 **10** D1
Fifield Path, SE23
off Bampton Rd **171** G3
Fifield Wk, SE23 **171** G3
Fifth Av, E12 **98** C4
W10 **108** B3
Hayes UB3 **121** J1
Fifth Cross Rd, Twick. TW2 **162** A2
Fifth Way, Wem. HA9 **88** B4
Figges Rd, Mitch. CR4 **168** A7
Fig Tree Cl, NW10
off Craven Pk **106** E1
Filby Rd, Chess. KT9 **195** J6
Filey Av, N16 **94** D1
Filey Cl, Sutt. SM2 **199** F7
Filey Waye, Ruis. HA4 **84** A2
Filigree Ct, SE16
off Silver Wk **133** J1
Fillebrook Av, Enf. EN1 **44** B2
Fillebrook Rd, E11 **96** D1
Filmer Rd, SW6 **148** B1
Filston Rd, Erith DA8
off Riverdale Rd **139** J5
Filton Cl, NW9 **71** E2
Finborough Rd, SW10 **30** A5
SW17 **167** J6
Finchale Rd, SE2 **138** A3
Finch Av, SE27 **170** A4
Finch Cl, NW10 **88** D5
Barnet EN5 **40** D5
Finchdean Ho, SW15
off Tangley Gro **147** F7
Finch Dr, Felt. TW14 **142** D7
Finch Gdns, E4 **62** A5
Finchingfield Av, Wdf.Grn. IG8 **63** J7
Finch La, EC3 **20** C4
FINCHLEY, N3 **72** E1
Finchley Ct, N3 **57** E6
Finchley La, NW4 **71** J4
Finchley Pk, N12 **57** F4
Finchley Pl, NW8 **6** E1
Finchley Rd, NW2 **90** D3
NW3 **91** F6
NW8 **109** G1
NW11 **72** C6
Finchley Way, N3 **56** D7
Finch Ms, SE15 **132** C7
Finden Rd, E7 **97** H5
Findhorn Av, Hayes UB4 **102** B5
Findhorn St, E14 **114** C6
Findon Cl, SW18 **148** D6
Harrow HA2 **85** H3
Findon Rd, N9 **60** E1
W12 **127** G2
Fingal St, SE10 **135** F5
Finland Quay, SE16
off Finland St **133** H3
Finland Rd, SE4 **153** H3
Finland St, SE16 **133** H3
Finlays Cl, Chess. KT9 **196** A5
Finlay St, SW6 **148** A1
Finney La, Islw. TW7 **144** D1
Finnis St, E2 **113** E3
Finnymore Rd, Dag. RM9 **101** E7
FINSBURY, EC1 **11** F3
Finsbury Av, EC2 **20** C2
Finsbury Av Sq, EC2 **20** C2
Finsbury Circ, EC2 **20** C2
Finsbury Cotts, N22 **59** E7
Finsbury Est, EC1 **11** F4
Finsbury Ho, N22 **75** E1
Finsbury Mkt, EC2 **12** D6
FINSBURY PARK, N4 **93** G1
★ **Finsbury Park**, N4 **75** H7
Finsbury Pk Av, N4 **75** J6
Finsbury Pk Rd, N4 **93** H2
Finsbury Pavement, EC2 **20** C1
Finsbury Rd, N22 **75** F1
Finsbury Sq, EC2 **20** C1
Finsbury St, EC2 **20** B1
Finsbury Twr, EC1 **12** B6
Finsbury Way, Bex. DA5 **159** F6
Finsen Rd, SE5 **151** J3
Finstock Rd, W10 **108** A6
Finucane Ri, Bushey (Bushey Hth) WD23 **51** J2
Firbank Cl, E16 **116** A5
Enfield EN2
off Gladbeck Way **43** J4
Firbank Rd, SE15 **153** E2
Fir Cl, Walt. KT12 **178** A7
Fircroft Gdns, Har. HA1 **86** B3
Fircroft Rd, SW17 **167** J2
Chessington KT9 **195** J4
Fir Dene, Orp. BR6 **206** C3
Firdene, Surb. KT5 **196** C1
Fire Bell All, Surb. KT6 **181** H6
Firecrest Dr, NW3 **91** E3
Firefly Gdns, E6
off Jack Dash Way **116** B4
★ **Firepower**, SE18 **137** E3
Fire Sta All, Barn. EN5
off Christchurch La **40** B2
Firethorn Cl, Edg. HA8
off Larkspur Gro **54** C4
Fir Gro, N.Mal. KT3 **183** F6
Fir Gro Rd, SW9
off Marcella Rd **151** G2
Firhill Rd, SE6 **172** A4
Firmans Ct, E17 **78** D4
Fir Rd, Felt. TW13 **160** D5
Sutton SM3 **198** C1
Firs, The, E6 **98** B7
E17 *off Leucha Rd* **77** H5
N20 **57** G1
W5 **105** G5
Firs Av, N10 **74** A3
N11 **58** A6
SW14 **146** C4
Firsby Av, Croy. CR0 **203** G1
Firsby Rd, N16 **94** C1
Firs Cl, N10 *off Firs Av* **74** A3
SE23 **153** G7
Esher (Clay.) KT10 **194** B6
Mitcham CR4 **186** B2
Firscroft, N13 **59** J3
Firs Dr, Houns. TW5 **122** B7
Loughton IG10 **48** D1
Firside Gro, Sid. DA15 **175** J1
Firs La, N13 **59** J3
N21 **59** J2
Firs Pk Av, N21 **60** A1
Firs Pk Gdns, N21 **59** J1
First Av, E12 **98** B4
E13 **115** G3
E17 **78** A5
N18 **61** F4
NW4 **71** J4
SW14 **146** E3
W3 **127** F1
W10 **108** C4
Bexleyheath DA7 **138** C7
Dagenham RM10 **119** H2
Enfield EN1 **44** C6
Greenford UB6 **86** A7
Hayes UB3 **121** J1
Romford RM6 **82** C5
Walton-on-Thames KT12 **178** B6
Wembley HA9 **87** G2
West Molesey KT8 **179** F4
First Cl, W.Mol. KT8 **179** J3
First Cross Rd, Twick. TW2 **162** B2
First Dr, NW10 **88** C7
First St, SW3 **31** H1
Firstway, SW20 **183** J2
First Way, Wem. HA9 **88** B4
Firs Wk, Wdf.Grn. IG8 **63** G5

Firswood Av, Epsom KT19 **197** F5
Firth Gdns, SW6 **148** B1
Fir Tree Av, Mitch. CR4 **186** A2
West Drayton UB7 **120** D3
Fir Tree Cl, SW16 **168** C5
W5 **105** H6
Epsom (Ewell) KT19 **197** F4
Orpington BR6 **207** J5
Fir Tree Gdns, Croy. CR0 **204** A4
Fir Tree Gro, Cars. SM5 **199** J7
Fir Tree Rd, Houns. TW4 **143** E4
Fir Trees Cl, SE16 **133** H1
Fir Tree Wk, Dag. RM10 *off Wheel Fm Dr* **101** J3
Enfield EN1 **44** A3
Fisher Cl, E9 *off Brooksby's Wk* **95** G5
Croydon CR0 **202** C1
Greenford UB6 **103** G3
Fisherman Cl, Rich. TW10 *off Locksmeade Rd* **163** F4
Fishermans Dr, SE16 **133** G2
Fisherman's Wk, E14 **134** A1
Fishermans Wk, SE28 *off Tugboat St* **137** H2
Fisher Rd, Har. HA3 **68** C2
Fishers Cl, SW16 **168** D3
Fishers Ct, SE14 *off Besson St* **153** G1
Fishersdene, Esher (Clay.) KT10 **194** D7
Fishers La, W4 **126** D4
Fisher St, E16 **115** G5
WC1 **18** B2
Fishers Way, Belv. DA17 **139** J1
Fisherton St, NW8 **7** E6
Fishguard Way, E16 **137** E2
Fishponds Rd, SW17 **167** H4
Keston BR2 **206** A5
Fish St Hill, EC3 **20** C5
Fiske Ct, N17 **76** D1
Fitzalan Rd, N3 **72** B3
Esher (Clay.) KT10 **194** B7
Fitzalan St, SE11 **34** E1
Fitzgeorge Av, W14 **128** B4
New Malden KT3 **182** D1
Fitzgerald Av, SW14 **147** E3
Fitzgerald Cl, E11 *off Fitzgerald Rd* **79** G5
Fitzgerald Ho, E14 **114** B6
SW9 *off Stockwell Pk Rd* **151** G2
Hayes UB3 **122** B1
Fitzgerald Rd, E11 **79** G5
SW14 **146** D3
Thames Ditton KT7 **180** D6
Fitzhardinge St, W1 **16** B3
Fitzherbert Ho, Rich. TW10 *off Kingsmead* **145** J6
Fitzhugh Gro, SW18 **149** G6
Fitzjames Av, W14 **128** B4
Croydon CR0 **202** D2
Fitzjohn Av, Barn. EN5 **40** B5
Fitzjohn's Av, NW3 **91** G5
Fitzmaurice Ho, SE16 *off Rennie Est* **133** E4
Fitzmaurice Pl, W1 **24** E1
Fitzneal St, W12 **107** F6
Fitzroy Cl, N6 **91** J1
Fitzroy Ct, W1 **9** G6
Fitzroy Cres, W4 **126** D7
Fitzroy Gdns, SE19 **170** B7
Fitzroy Ms, W1 **9** F6
Fitzroy Pk, N6 **91** J1
Fitzroy Rd, NW1 **110** A1
Fitzroy Sq, W1 **9** F6
Fitzroy St, W1 **9** F6
Fitzroy Yd, NW1 *off Fitzroy Rd* **110** A1
Fitzsimmons Ct, NW10 *off Knatchbull Rd* **106** D1
Fitzstephen Rd, Dag. RM8 **100** B5
Fitzwarren Gdns, N19 **92** C1
Fitzwilliam Av, Rich. TW9 **145** J2
Fitzwilliam Cl, N20 **58** A1
Fitzwilliam Ms, E16 *off Hanover Av* **135** G1
Fitzwilliam Rd, SW4 **150** C3
Fitzwygram Cl, Hmptn. (Hmptn H.) TW12 **161** J5
Five Acre, NW9 **71** F1
Fiveacre Cl, Th.Hth. CR7 **187** G6
Five Bell All, E14 *off Three Colt St* **113** J7
Five Elms Rd, Brom. BR2 **205** H3
Dagenham RM9 **101** F3
Five Flds Cl, Wat. WD19 **51** F3
Five Oaks Ms, Brom. BR1 **173** G3
Fives Ct, SE11 **35** G1
Fiveways, Croy. CR0 **201** G4
Five Ways Cor, NW4 **71** H1
Fiveways Rd, SW9 **151** G2
Fladbury Rd, N15 **76** A6
Fladgate Rd, E11 **79** E6
Flag Cl, Croy. CR0 **203** G1
Flagon Ct, Croy. CR0 *off Lower Coombe St* **201** J4
Flagstaff Ho, SW8 *off St. George Wf* **34** A5
Flag Wk, Pnr. HA5 **66** A6
Flambard Rd, Har. HA1 **68** D6
Flamborough Rd, Ruis. HA4 **84** A3
Flamborough St, E14 **113** H6
Flamborough Wk, E14 *off Flamborough St* **113** H6
Flamingo Gdns, Nthlt. UB5 *off Jetstar Way* **102** E3
Flamstead Gdns, Dag. RM9 *off Flamstead Rd* **100** C7
Flamstead Rd, Dag. RM9 **100** C7
Flamsted Av, Wem. HA9 **88** A6
Flamsteed Rd, SE7 **136** B5
Flanchford Rd, W12 **127** F3
Flanders Cres, SW17 **167** J7
Flanders Rd, E6 **116** C2
W4 **127** E4
Flanders Way, E9 **95** G6
Flank St, E1 **21** H5
Flask Cotts, NW3 *off New End Sq* **91** G4
Flask Wk, NW3 **91** G4
Flather Cl, SW16 *off Blegborough Rd* **168** C5
Flat Iron Sq, SE1 *off Union St* **28** A2
Flavell Ms, SE10 **135** E5
Flaxen Cl, E4 *off Flaxen Rd* **62** B3
Flaxen Rd, E4 **62** B3
Flaxley Rd, Mord. SM4 **184** E6
Flaxman Ct, W1 **17** H4
Flaxman Rd, SE5 **151** H2
Flaxman Ter, WC1 **9** J4
Flaxmere Gdns, N17 **76** B1
Flaxton Rd, SE18 **157** G1
Flecker Cl, Stan. HA7 **52** C5
Fleece Dr, N9 **60** D4
Fleece Rd, Surb. (Long Dit.) KT6 **195** F1
Fleece Wk, N7 *off Manger Rd* **93** E6
Fleeming Cl, E17 *off Pennant Ter* **77** J2
Fleeming Rd, E17 **77** J2
Fleet Cl, W.Mol. KT8 **179** F5
Fleet La, W.Mol. KT8 **179** F6
Fleet Pl, EC4 *off Limeburner La* **19** G3
Fleet Rd, NW3 **91** H5
Fleetside, W.Mol. KT8 **179** F6
Fleet Sq, WC1 **10** D4
Fleet St, EC4 **19** E4
Fleet St Hill, E1 **13** H6
Fleetway Business Pk, Grnf. (Perivale) UB6 **105** E2
Fleetwood Cl, E16 **116** A5
Chessington KT9 **195** G7
Croydon CR0 **202** C3
Fleetwood Ct, E6 *off Evelyn Denington Rd* **116** C5
Fleetwood Gro, W3 *off East Acton La* **106** E7
Fleetwood Rd, NW10 **89** G5
Kingston upon Thames KT1 **182** B3
Fleetwood Sq, Kings.T. KT1 **182** B3
Fleetwood St, N16 *off Stoke Newington Ch St* **94** B2
Fleetwood Way, Wat. WD19 **50** C4
Fleming Cl, W9 *off Chippenham Rd* **108** D4
Fleming Ct, W2 **14** E1
Croydon CR0 **201** G5
Fleming Dr, N21 **43** F5
Fleming Mead, Mitch. CR4 **167** H7
Fleming Rd, SE17 **35** H5
Southall UB1 **103** H6
Fleming Wk, NW9 *off Pasteur Cl* **71** E2
Fleming Way, SE28 **118** D7
Isleworth TW7 **144** C3
Flemming Av, Ruis. HA4 **84** B1
Flempton Rd, E10 **77** H7
Fletcher Cl, E6 *off Trader Rd* **116** E6
Fletcher La, E10 **78** C7
Fletcher Path, SE8 *off New Butt La* **134** A7
Fletcher Rd, W4 **126** C3
Chigwell IG7 **65** J5
Fletchers Cl, Bromley BR2 **191** H4
Fletcher St, E1 **21** J5
Fletching Rd, E5 **95** F3
SE7 **135** J6
Fletton Rd, N11 **58** E7
Fleur de Lis St, E1 **13** E6
Fleur Gates, SW19 *off Princes Way* **148** A7
Flexmere Gdns, N17 *off Flexmere Rd* **76** A1
Flexmere Rd, N17 **76** A1
Flight App, NW9 **71** F2
Flimwell Cl, Brom. BR1 **172** E5
Flint Cl, E15 **97** F7
Orpington (Grn St Grn) BR6 *off Lynne Cl* **207** J6
Flintmill Cres, SE3 **156** B2
Flinton St, SE17 **36** E3
Flint St, SE17 **36** C2
Flitcroft St, WC2 **17** J3
Floathaven Cl, SE28 **138** A1
Flock Mill Pl, SW18 **166** E1
Flockton St, SE16 **29** H4
Flodden Rd, SE5 **151** J1
Flood La, Twick. TW1 *off Church La* **162** D1
Flood Pas, SE18 *off Samuel St* **136** C4
Flood St, SW3 **31** H4
Flood Wk, SW3 **31** H5
Flora Cl, E14 **114** B6
Stanmore HA7 **53** H3
Flora Gdns, W6 **127** H4
Romford RM6 **82** C6
Flora Ho, E3 *off Garrison Rd* **114** A1
Floral Pl, N1 *off Northampton Gro* **94** A5
Floral St, WC2 **18** A5
Flora St, Belv. DA17 *off Victoria St* **139** F5
Florence Av, Enf. EN2 **43** J3
Morden SM4 **185** F5
Florence Cantwell Wk, N19 *off Hillrise Rd* **74** E7
Florence Cl, Walt. KT12 *off Florence Rd* **178** B7
Florence Ct, W9 *off Maida Vale* **6** D4
Florence Dr, Enf. EN2 **43** J3
Florence Elson Cl, E12 **98** D4
Florence Gdns, W4 **126** C6
Romford RM6 *off Roxy Av* **82** C7
Florence Nightingale Ho, N1 *off Nightingale Rd* **93** J6
★ **Florence Nightingale Mus**, SE1 **26** C4
Florence Rd, E6 **115** J1
E13 **115** F2
N4 **93** G1
SE2 **138** C3
SE14 **153** J1
SW19 **166** E6
W4 **126** D3
W5 **105** H7
Beckenham BR3 **189** G2
Bromley BR1 **191** G1
Feltham TW13 **160** B1
Kingston upon Thames KT2 **163** J7
Southall UB2 **122** D4
Walton-on-Thames KT12 **178** B7
Florence St, E16 **115** F4
N1 **93** H7
NW4 **71** J4
Florence Ter, SE14 **153** J1
SW15 *off Roehampton Vale* **165** E3
Florence Way, SW12 **167** J1
Florence White Ct, N9 *off Colthurst Dr* **60** E3
Florey Sq, N21 *off Highlands Av* **43** F5
Florfield Pas, E8 *off Reading La* **95** E6
Florfield Rd, E8 *off Reading La* **95** E6
Florian Av, Sutt. SM1 **199** G4
Florian Rd, SW15 **148** B4
Florida Cl, Bushey (Bushey Hth) WD23 **52** A2
Florida Ct, Brom. BR2 *off Westmoreland Rd* **191** F4
Florida Rd, Th.Hth. CR7 **187** H1
Florida St, E2 **13** H4
Florin Ct, SE1 *off Tanner St* **29** F4
Floris Pl, SW4 *off Fitzwilliam Rd* **150** C3
Floriston Cl, Stan. HA7 **69** E1
Floriston Ct, Nthlt. UB5 **85** H5
Floriston Gdns, Stan. HA7 **69** E1
Floss St, SW15 **147** J2
Flower & Dean Wk, E1 **21** G2
Flower La, NW7 **55** F5
Flower Ms, NW11 **72** B6
Flower Pot Cl, N15 *off St. Ann's Rd* **76** C6
Flowers Cl, NW2 **89** G3
Flowersmead, SW17 **168** A2
Flowers Ms, N19 *off Archway Rd* **92** C2
Flower Wk, The, SW7 **22** C4
Floyd Rd, SE7 **135** J5
Floyer Cl, Rich. TW10 **145** J5
Fludyer St, SE13 **154** E4
Foley Ho, E1 *off Tarling St* **113** F6
Foley Ms, Esher (Clay.) KT10 **194** B7
Foley Rd, Esher (Clay.) KT10 **194** B7
Foley St, W1 **17** F2
Foley Wood., Esher KT10 *off Foley Rd* **194** C7
Folgate St, E1 **21** E1
Foliot Ho, N1 *off Priory Grn Est* **10** C1
Foliot St, W12 **107** F6
Folkestone Rd, E6 **116** D2
E17 **78** B4
N18 **60** D4
Folkingham La, NW9 **70** D1
Folkington Cor, N12 **56** C5
Follett St, E14 **114** C6
Folly La, E4 **61** J7
E17 **77** H1
Folly Ms, W11 *off Portobello Rd* **108** C6
Folly Wall, E14 **134** C2
Fontaine Rd, SW16 **169** F7
Fontarabia Rd, SW11 **150** A4
Fontayne Av, Chig. IG7 **65** F4
Fontenelle, SE5 *off Sceaux Gdns* **152** B1
Fontenoy Rd, SW12 **168** B2
Fonteyne Gdns, Wdf.Grn. IG8 **79** J2
Fonthill Cl, SE20 *off Selby Rd* **188** D2
Fonthill Ms, N4 **93** F2
Fonthill Rd, N4 **93** F1
Font Hills, N2 **73** F2
Fontley Way, SW15 **147** G7
Fontwell Cl, Har. HA3 **52** B7
Northolt UB5 **85** G6
Fontwell Dr, Brom. BR2 **192** D5
Football La, Har. HA1 **86** B1
Footpath, The, SW15 **147** G5
FOOTS CRAY, Sid. DA14 **176** B6
Foots Cray High St, Sid. DA14 **176** C6
Foots Cray La, Sid. DA14 **176** C1
Footscray Rd, SE9 **156** D6
Forbes Cl, NW2 **89** G3
Forbes Ct, SE19 **170** B5
Forbes St, E1 **21** J4
Forbes Way, Ruis. HA4 **84** B2
Forburg Rd, N16 **94** D1
Ford Cl, E3 *off Roman Rd* **113** H2
Harrow HA1 **68** A7
Thornton Heath CR7 **187** H6
Forde Av, Brom. BR1 **191** J3
Fordel Rd, SE6 **172** D1
Ford End, Wdf.Grn. IG8 **63** H6
Fordham Cl, Barn. EN4 **41** H3
Worcester Park KT4 **197** H1
Fordham Rd, Barn. EN4 **41** G3
Fordham St, E1 **21** J3
Fordhook Av, W5 **105** J7
Fordingley Rd, W9 **108** C3
Fordington Ho, SE26 *off Sydenham Hill Est* **170** E3
Fordington Rd, N6 **73** J5
Fordmill Rd, SE6 **172** A2
Ford Rd, E3 **113** H1
Dagenham RM9, RM10 **101** F7
Fords Gro, N21 **59** J1
Fords Pk Rd, E16 **115** G6
Ford Sq, E1 **113** E5
Ford St, E3 **113** H1
E16 **115** F6
Fordwich Cl, Orp. BR6 **193** J7
Fordwych Rd, NW2 **90** B4
Fordyce Ho, SW16 *off Colson Way* **168** C4
Fordyce Rd, SE13 **154** C6
Fordyke Rd, Dag. RM8 **101** F2
★ **Foreign & Commonwealth Office**, SW1 **25** J3
Foreign St, SE5 **151** H2
Foreland Ct, NW4 **72** B1
Foreland St, SE18 *off Plumstead Rd* **137** G4
Foremark Cl, Ilford IG6 **65** J5
Foreshore, SE8 **133** J4
Forest, The, E11 **79** E4
Forest App, E4 **47** E7
Woodford Green IG8 **63** F7

Forest Av, E4 47 E7
Chigwell IG7 64 D5
Forest Business Pk, E10 77 G7
Forest Cl, E11 79 F5
NW6 90 B7
Chislehurst BR7 192 D1
Woodford Green IG8 63 H3
Forest Ct, E4 63 F1
E11 79 E4
Forest Cft, SE23 171 E2
Forestdale, N14 58 D4
Forestdale Cen, The, Croy. CR0
off Holmbury Gro 203 J7
Forest Dr, E12 98 A3
Keston BR2 206 B4
Woodford Green IG8 62 D7
Forest Dr E, E11 78 D7
Forest Dr W, E11 78 C7
Forest Edge, Buck.H. IG9 63 J4
Forester Rd, SE15 153 E4
Foresters Cl, Wall. SM6 200 D7
Foresters Cres, Bexh. DA7 159 H4
Foresters Dr, E17 78 D4
Wallington SM6 200 D7
Forest Gdns, N17 76 C2
FOREST GATE, E7 97 G5
Forest Gate, NW9 70 E4
Forest Glade, E4 62 E4
E11 79 E6
Forest Gro, E8 94 C6
Forest Hts, Buck.H. IG9 63 G2
FOREST HILL, SE23 171 G1
Forest Hill, SE23 171 F2
Forest Hill Business Cen, SE23 *off Clyde Vale* 171 F2
Forest Hill Ind Est, SE23
off Perry Vale 171 F2
Forest Hill Rd, SE22 152 E5
SE23 152 E5
Forestholme Cl, SE23 171 F2
Forest Ind Pk, Ilf. IG6 81 H1
Forest La, E7 97 E5
E15 97 E5
Chigwell IG7 64 D5
Forest Mt Rd, Wdf.Grn. IG8 62 D7
Forest Pt, E7
off Windsor Rd 97 H5
Fore St, EC2 20 A2
N9 60 D5
N18 60 C6
Pinner HA5 66 A5
Fore St Av, EC2 20 B2
Forest Ridge, Beck. BR3 190 A3
Keston BR2 206 B4
Forest Ri, E17 78 D5
Forest Rd, E7 97 G4
E8 94 C6
E11 78 D7
E17 77 F4
N9 61 E1
N17 77 F4
Feltham TW13 160 C2
Ilford IG6 81 H1
Loughton IG10 48 A3
Richmond TW9 126 A7
Romford RM7 83 H3
Sutton SM3 198 D1
Woodford Green IG8 63 G3
Forest Side, E4 47 F7
E7 *off Capel Rd* 97 H4
Buckhurst Hill IG9 63 J1
Worcester Park KT4 197 F1
Forest St, E7 97 G5
Forest Vw, E4 46 D7
E11 *off High Rd Leytonstone* 79 F7
Forest Vw Av, E10 78 D5
Forest Vw Rd, E12 98 B4
E17 78 C1
Loughton IG10 48 A4
Forest Wk, N10 74 B1
Forest Way, N19
off Hargrave Pk 92 C2
Loughton IG10 48 B3
Orpington BR5 193 J5
Sidcup DA15 157 G7
Woodford Green IG8 63 H4
Forfar Rd, N22 75 H1
SW11 150 A1
Forge Cl, Brom. BR2 205 G1
Hayes (Harling.) UB3 121 G6
Forge Dr, Esher (Clay.) KT10 194 D7
Forge La, Felt. TW13 160 E5
Richmond TW10
off Petersham Rd 163 H1
Sunbury-on-Thames TW16 178 A3
Sutton SM3 198 B7
Forge Ms, Croy. CR0
off Addington Village Rd 204 A5
Forge Pl, NW1
off Malden Cres 92 A6
Forlong Path, Nthlt. UB5
off Cowings Mead 85 E6
Forman Pl, N16
off Farleigh Rd 94 C4
Formation, The, E16
off Woolwich Manor Way 136 E2
Formby Av, Stan. HA7 69 F3
Formosa St, W9 6 C6
Formunt Cl, E16
off Vincent St 115 F5
Forres Gdns, NW11 72 D6
Forrester Path, SE26 171 F4
Forrest Gdns, SW16 187 F3
Forris Av, Hayes UB3 121 J1
Forset St, W1 15 H3
Forstal Cl, Brom. BR2
off Ridley Rd 191 G3
Forster Cl, Wdf.Grn. IG8 62 D7
Forster Rd, E17 77 H6
N17 76 C3
SW2 150 E7
Beckenham BR3 189 H3
Croydon CR0
off Windmill Rd 187 J7
Forsters Cl, Rom. RM6 83 F6
Forster's Way, SW18 166 E1
Forsters Way, Hayes UB4 102 B6
Forston St, N1 12 B1
Forsyte Cres, SE19 188 B1
Forsyth Gdns, SE17 35 H5
Forsyth Ho, SW1
off Tachbrook St 33 G3
Forsythia Cl, Ilf. IG1 98 E5
Forsyth Pl, Enf. EN1 44 B5
Forterie Gdns, Ilf. IG3 100 A3
Fortescue Av, E8
off Mentmore Ter 95 E7
Twickenham TW2 161 J3
Fortescue Rd, SW19 167 G7
Edgware HA8 70 D1
Fortess Gro, NW5
off Fortess Rd 92 C5
Fortess Rd, NW5 92 B5
Fortess Wk, NW5
off Fortess Rd 92 B5
Fortess Yd, NW5
off Fortess Rd 92 B4
Forthbridge Rd, SW11 150 A4
Fortis Cl, E16 115 J6
FORTIS GREEN, N2 73 J4
Fortis Grn, N2 73 H4
N10 73 H4
Fortis Grn Av, N2 73 J3
Fortis Grn Rd, N10 74 A3
Fortismere Av, N10 74 A3
Fortnam Rd, N19 92 D2
★ **Fortnum & Mason**, W1 25 F1
Fortnums Acre, Stan. HA7 52 C6
Fort Rd, SE1 37 G2
Northolt UB5 85 G7
Fortrose Cl, E14 114 D6
Fortrose Gdns, SW2 168 E1
Fort St, E1 21 E2
E16 135 H1
Fortuna Cl, N7
off Jupiter Way 93 F6
Fortune Gate Rd, NW10 107 E1
Fortune Grn Rd, NW6 90 D4
Fortune Pl, SE1 37 G4
Fortunes Mead, Nthlt. UB5 85 E6
Fortune St, EC1 12 A6
Fortune Wk, SE28
off Broadwater Rd 137 G3
Fortune Way, NW10 107 G3
Forty Acre La, E16 115 G5
Forty Av, Wem. HA9 87 J3
Forty Cl, Wem. HA9 87 J2
Forty Footpath, SW14 146 C3
Forty La, Wem. HA9 88 B2
Forum, The, W.Mol. KT8 179 H4
Forum Cl, E3
off Garrison Rd 114 A1
★ **Forum Club**, NW5 92 B5
Forum Magnum Sq, SE1 26 C3
Forumside, Edg. HA8
off Station Rd 54 A6
Forum Way, Edg. HA8 54 A6
Forval Cl, Mitch. CR4 185 J5
Forward Dr, Har. HA3 68 C4
Fosbury Ms, W2 14 B6
Foscote Ms, W9
off Amberley Rd 108 D5
Foscote Rd, NW4 71 H6
Foskett Ms, E8 94 C5
Foskett Rd, SW6 148 C2
Foss Av, Croy. CR0 201 G5
Fossdene Rd, SE7 135 H5
Fossdyke Cl, Hayes UB4 103 E5
Fosse Way, W13 104 D5
Fossil Rd, SE13 154 A3
Fossington Rd, Belv. DA17 138 D4
Foss Rd, SW17 167 G4
Fossway, Dag. RM8 100 C2
Foster La, EC2 19 J3
Foster Rd, E13 115 G4
W3 106 E7
W4 126 D5
Fosters Cl, E18 79 H1
Chislehurst BR7 174 C5
Foster St, NW4 71 J4
Foster Wk, NW4
off Foster St 71 J4
Fothergill Cl, E13 115 G2
Fothergill Dr, N21 43 E5
Fotheringham Rd, Enf. EN1 44 C4
Foubert's Pl, W1 17 F4
Foulden Rd, N16 94 C4
Foulden Ter, N16
off Foulden Rd 94 C4
Foulis Ter, SW7 31 F3
Foulser Rd, SW17 167 J3
Foulsham Rd, Th.Hth. CR7 187 J3
Founder Cl, E6
off Trader Rd 116 E6
Founders Cl, Nthlt. UB5
off Taywood Rd 103 F3
Founders Ct, EC2 20 B3
Founders Gdns, SE19 169 J7
★ **Foundling Mus**, WC1 10 B5
Foundry Cl, SE16 133 H1
Foundry Ms, NW1 9 G5
Hounslow TW3
off New Rd 143 H4
Foundry Pl, E1
off Redman's Rd 113 F5
Fountain Cl, E5
off Lower Clapton Rd 95 E3
SE18 136 E5
Fountain Ct, EC4 18 E5
WD6 38 A2
Fountain Dr, SE19 170 C4
Fountain Grn Sq, SE16 29 J4
Fountain Ho, SW6
off The Boulevard 149 F2
SW8
off St. George Wf 34 B4
Fountain Ms, N5
off Highbury Gra 93 J4
NW3 91 J6
Fountain Pl, SW9 151 G1
Fountain Rd, SW17 167 G5
Thornton Heath CR7 187 J2
Fountains, The, Loug. IG10
off Fallow Flds 48 A7
Fountains Av, Felt. TW13 161 F3
Fountains Cl, Felt. TW13 161 F2
Fountains Cres, N14 42 E7
Fountain Sq, SW1 32 D1
Fountayne Rd, N15 76 D4
N16 94 D2
Fount St, SW8 130 D7
Fouracres, SW12
off Little Dimocks 168 B2
Enfield EN3 45 H1
Fourland Wk, Edg. HA8 54 C6
Fournier St, E1 21 F1
Four Seasons Cl, E3 114 A2
Four Seasons Cres, Sutt. SM3 198 C2
Fourth Av, E12 98 C4
W10 108 B4
Hayes UB3 121 J1
Fourth Cross Rd, Twick. TW2 162 A2
Fourth Way, Wem. HA9 88 C4
Four Wents, The, E4
off Kings Rd 62 D2
Fowey Av, Ilf. IG4 80 A5
Fowey Cl, E1
off Kennet St 132 E1
Fowler Cl, SW11 149 G3
Fowler Rd, E7 97 G4
N1 *off Halton Rd* 93 H7
Mitcham CR4 186 A2
Fowlers Cl, Sid. DA14
off Thursland Rd 176 E5
Fowlers Wk, W5 105 G4
Fownes St, SW11 149 H3
Fox & Knot St, EC1 19 H1
Foxberry Rd, SE4 153 H3
Foxborough Gdns, SE4 154 A6
Foxbourne Rd, SW17 168 A2
Foxbury Av, Chis. BR7 175 G6
Foxbury Cl, Brom. BR1 173 H6
Foxbury Rd, Bromley BR1 173 G6
Fox Cl, E1 113 F4
E16 115 G5
Foxcombe, Croy. (New Adgtn) CR0 204 B6
Foxcombe Cl, E6
off Boleyn Rd 116 A2
Foxcombe Rd, SW15
off Alton Rd 165 G1
Foxcote, SE5 36 E4
Foxcroft Rd, SE18 157 E1
Foxes Dale, SE3 155 G3
Bromley BR2 190 D3
Foxfield Rd, Orp. BR6 207 G2
Foxglove Cl, N9 61 F1
Sidcup DA15 158 A6
Southall UB1 103 E7
Foxglove Gdns, E11 79 J4
Foxglove La, Chess. KT9 196 A4
Foxglove Path, SE28
off Crowfoot Cl 137 H1
Foxglove St, W12 107 F7
Foxglove Way, Wall. SM6 200 B1
Foxgrove, N14 58 E3
Fox Gro, Walt. KT12 178 B7
Foxgrove Av, Beck. BR3 172 B7
Foxgrove Path, Wat. WD19 50 D5
Foxgrove Rd, Beck. BR3 172 B7
Foxham Rd, N19 92 D3
Fox Hill, SE19 170 C7
Keston BR2 205 J5
Fox Hill Gdns, SE19 170 C7
Foxhole Rd, SE9 156 B5
Fox Hollow Cl, SE18 137 H5
Fox Hollow Dr, Bexh. DA7 158 D3
Foxholt Gdns, NW10 88 C7
Foxhome Cl, Chis. BR7 174 D6
Fox Ho, SW11
off Maysoule Rd 149 G4
Fox Ho Rd, Belv. DA17 139 H4
Foxlands Cres, Dag. RM10 101 J5
Foxlands La, Dag. RM10 101 J5
Foxlands Rd, Dag. RM10 101 J5
Fox La, N13 59 F3
W5 105 H4
Keston BR2 205 H5
Foxlees, Wem. HA0 86 D4
Foxley Cl, E8
off Ferncliff Rd 94 D5
Loughton IG10 49 E2
Foxley Ct, Sutt. SM2 199 F7
Foxley Ho, E3
off Bromley High St 114 B3
Foxley Rd, SW9 35 F7
Thornton Heath CR7 187 H4
Foxleys, Wat. WD19 51 E3
Foxley Sq, SW9
off Cancell Rd 131 H7
Foxmead Cl, Enf. EN2 43 F3
Foxmore St, SW11 149 J1
Fox Rd, E16 115 F5
Fox's Path, Mitch. CR4 185 H2
Foxton Gro, Mitch. CR4 185 G2
Foxwell Ms, SE4
off Foxwell St 153 H3
Foxwell St, SE4 153 H3
Foxwood Cl, NW7 54 E4
Feltham TW13 160 B3
Foxwood Grn Cl, Enf. EN1 44 B6
Foxwood Rd, SE3 155 F4
Foyle Rd, N17 76 D1
SE3 135 F6
Framfield Cl, N12 56 D3
Framfield Ct, Enf. EN1 44 B6
Framfield Rd, N5 93 H5
W7 104 B6
Mitcham CR4 168 A7
Framlingham Cl, E5
off Detmold Rd 95 F2
Framlingham Cres, SE9 174 B4
Frampton Cl, Sutt. SM2 198 D7
Frampton Pk Est, E9 95 F7
Frampton Pk Rd, E9 95 F6
Frampton Rd, Houns. TW4 142 E5
Frampton St, NW8 7 E6
Francemary Rd, SE4 154 A5
Frances & Dick James Ct, NW7 *off Langstone Way* 56 B7
Frances Rd, E4 62 A6
Frances St, SE18 136 C4
Franche Ct Rd, SW17 167 F3
Francis Av, Bexh. DA7 159 G2
Feltham TW13 160 A3
Ilford IG1 99 G2
Francis Barber Cl, SW16
off Well Cl 169 F4
Franciscan Rd, SW17 167 J5
Francis Chichester Way, SW11 150 A1
Francis Cl, E14
off Saunders Ness Rd 134 D4
Epsom KT19 196 D4
Francis Gro, SW19 166 C6
Francis Pl, N6
off Holmesdale Rd 74 B7
Francis Rd, E10 96 C1
N2 73 J4
Croydon CR0 187 H7
Greenford (Perivale) UB6 105 E2

Francis Rd, Harrow HA1 ...68 D5
Hounslow TW4 ...142 D2
Ilford IG1 ...99 G2
Pinner HA5 ...66 C5
Wallington SM6 ...200 C6
Francis St, E15 ...96 E5
SW1 ...33 F1
Ilford IG1 ...99 G2
Francis Ter, N19 ...92 C3
Francis Ter Ms, N19
off Francis Ter ...92 C3
Francis Wk, N1
off Bingfield St ...111 F1
Francklyn Gdns, Edg. HA8 .54 A3
Franconia Rd, SW4 ...150 C5
Frank Bailey Wk, E12
off Gainsborough Av ...98 D5
Frank Burton Cl, SE7
off Victoria Way ...135 H5
Frank Dixon Cl, SE21 ...170 B1
Frank Dixon Way, SE21 ...170 B1
Frankfurt Rd, SE24 ...151 J5
Frankham St, SE8 ...134 A7
Frankland Cl, SE16 ...133 E3
Woodford Green IG8 ...63 J5
Frankland Rd, E4 ...62 A5
SW7 ...23 E6
Franklin Cl, N20 ...41 F7
SE13 ...154 B1
SE27 ...169 H3
Kingston upon Thames KT1 ...182 A3
Franklin Cres, Mitch. CR4 ...186 C4
Franklin Ho, NW9 ...71 F7
Franklin Pas, SE9 ...156 B3
Franklin Pl, SE13 ...154 B1
Franklin Rd, SE20 ...171 F7
Bexleyheath DA7 ...159 E1
Franklins Ms, Har. HA2 ...85 J2
Franklin Sq, W14
off Marchbank Rd ...128 C5
Franklin's Row, SW3 ...32 A3
Franklin St, E3 ...114 B3
N15 ...76 B6
Franklin Way, Croy. CR0 ...187 E7
Franklyn Gdns, Ilford IG6 ...65 G6
Franklyn Rd, NW10 ...89 F7
Walton-on-Thames KT12 ...178 A6
Franks Av, N.Mal. KT3 ...182 C4
Frank St, E13 ...115 G4
Frankswood Av, Orp. BR5 ...193 E5
Frank Towell Ct, Felt. TW14 ...142 A7
Franlaw Cres, N13 ...59 J4
Fransfield Gro, SE26 ...171 E3
Frant Cl, SE20 ...171 F7
Franthorne Way, SE6 ...172 B2
Frant Rd, Th.Hth. CR7 ...187 H5
Fraser Cl, E6
off Linton Gdns ...116 B6
Bexley DA5
off Dartford Rd ...177 J1
Fraser Ct, W12
off Heathstan Rd ...107 G6
Fraser Ho, Brent. TW8
off Green Dragon La ...125 J5
Fraser Rd, E17 ...78 B5
N9 ...60 E3
Erith DA8 ...139 J5
Greenford (Perivale) UB6 ...105 E1
Fraser St, W4 ...126 E5
Frating Cres, Wdf.Grn. IG8 ...63 G6
Frays Av, West Dr. UB7 ...120 A2
Frays Cl, West Dr. UB7 ...120 A3
Frazer Av, Ruis. HA4 ...84 C5
Frazier St, SE1 ...26 E4
Frean St, SE16 ...29 H5
Freda Corbett Cl, SE15 ...37 H7
Frederica Rd, E4 ...46 D7
Frederica St, N7
off Caledonian Rd ...93 F7
Frederick Cl, W2 ...15 H5
Sutton SM1 ...198 C4
Frederick Ct, NW2
off Douglas Ms ...90 B3
Frederick Cres, SW9 ...131 H7
Enfield EN3 ...45 F2
Frederick Gdns, Croy. CR0 ...187 H6
Sutton SM1 ...198 C5
Frederick Pl, SE18 ...137 E5
Frederick Rd, SE17 ...35 H5
Sutton SM1 ...198 C5
Frederick's Pl, EC2 ...20 B4
Fredericks Pl, N12 ...57 F4
Frederick Sq, SE16
off Rotherhithe St ...113 H7
Frederick's Row, EC1 ...11 G3
Frederick St, WC1 ...10 C4
Frederick Ter, E8
off Arbutus St ...112 C1
Frederick Vil, W7
off Lower Boston Rd ...124 B1
Frederic Ms, SW1 ...24 A4
Frederic St, E17 ...77 H5
Fred White Wk, N7
off Market Rd ...93 E6
Fred Wigg Twr, E11 ...97 F2
Freedom Cl, E17 ...77 H4
Freedom Rd, N17 ...76 A2
Freedom St, SW11 ...149 J2
Freegrove Rd, N7 ...93 E5
Freeland Pk, NW4 ...72 B2
Freeland Rd, W5 ...105 J7
Freelands Gro, Brom. BR1 ...191 H1
Freelands Rd, Brom. BR1 ...191 H1
Freeling St, N1
off Caledonian Rd ...93 F7
Freeman Cl, Nthlt. UB5 ...85 E7
Freeman Ct, N7
off Tollington Way ...93 E3
SW16 ...187 E2
Freeman Dr, W.Mol. KT8 ...179 F3
Freeman Rd, Mord. SM4 ...185 G5
Freemantle Av, Enf. EN3 ...45 G5
Freemantle St, SE17 ...36 D3
★ **Freemason's Hall** (United Grand Lodge of England), WC2 ...18 B3
Freemasons Pl, Croy. CR0
off Freemasons Rd ...202 B1
Freemasons Rd, E16 ...115 H5
Croydon CR0 ...202 B1
Freesia Cl, Orp. BR6 ...207 J5
Freethorpe Cl, SE19 ...188 A1
Free Trade Wf, E1
off The Highway ...113 G7
★ **Freightliners Fm**, N7 ...93 F6
Freke Rd, SW11 ...150 A3
Fremantle Rd, Belv. DA17 ...139 G4
Ilford IG6 ...81 F2
Fremont St, E9 ...113 F1
French Ordinary Ct, EC3 ...21 E5
French Pl, E1 ...13 E5
French St, Sun. TW16 ...178 C2
Frendsbury Rd, SE4 ...153 H4
Frensham Cl, Sthl. UB1 ...103 F4
Frensham Ct, Mitch. CR4 ...185 G3
Frensham Dr, SW15 ...165 G2
Croydon (New Adgtn) CR0 ...204 C7
Frensham Rd, SE9 ...175 G2
Frensham St, SE15 ...37 J6
Frere St, SW11 ...149 H2
Freshfield Av, E8 ...94 C7
Freshfield Cl, SE13
off Mercator Rd ...154 D4
Freshfield Dr, N14 ...42 B7
Freshfields, Croy. CR0 ...189 J7
Freshford St, SW18 ...167 F3
Freshwater Cl, SW17 ...168 A6
Freshwater Rd, SW17 ...168 A6
Dagenham RM8 ...100 D1
Freshwell Av, Rom. RM6 ...82 C4
Fresh Wf Est, Bark. IG11
off Fresh Wf Rd ...117 E1
Fresh Wf Rd, Bark. IG11 ...117 E1
Freshwood Cl, Beck. BR3 ...190 B1
Freston Gdns, Barn. EN4 ...42 A5
Freston Pk, N3 ...72 C2
Freston Rd, W10 ...108 A7
W11 ...108 A7
Freta Rd, Bexh. DA6 ...159 F5
★ **Freud Mus**, NW3 ...91 F6
Frewin Rd, SW18 ...167 G1
Friar Ms, SE27 ...169 H3
Friar Rd, Hayes UB4 ...102 D4
Friars, The, Chig. IG7 ...65 H4
Friars Av, N20 ...57 H3
SW15 ...165 F3
Friars Cl, E4 ...62 C3
SE1 ...27 G2
Ilford IG1 ...99 G1
Northolt UB5
off Broomcroft Av ...102 D3
Friars Gdns, W3
off St. Dunstans Av ...106 D6
Friars Gate Cl, Wdf.Grn. IG8 ...63 G4
Friars La, Rich. TW9 ...145 G5
Friars Mead, E14 ...134 C3
Friars Ms, SE9 ...156 D5
Friars Pl La, W3 ...106 D7
Friars Rd, E6 ...116 A1
Friars Stile Pl, Rich. TW10
off Friars Stile Rd ...145 H6
Friars Stile Rd, Rich. TW10 ...145 H6
Friar St, EC4 ...19 H4
Friars Wk, N14 ...58 B1
SE2 ...138 D5
Friars Way, W3 ...106 D6
Friary Cl, N12 ...57 H5
Friary Ct, SW1 ...25 G2
Friary Est, SE15 ...37 J6
Friary La, Wdf.Grn. IG8 ...63 G4
Friary Pk Est, W3
off Friary Rd ...106 D6
Friary Rd, N12 ...57 G4
SE15 ...37 J6
W3 ...106 D6
Friary Way, N12 ...57 H4
FRIDAY HILL, E4 ...62 D2
Friday Hill, E4 ...62 E2
Friday Hill E, E4 ...62 E3
Friday Hill W, E4 ...62 E2
Friday Rd, Mitch. CR4 ...167 J7
Friday St, EC4 ...19 J4
Frideswide Pl, NW5
off Islip St ...92 C5
Friendly Pl, SE13
off Lewisham Rd ...154 B1
Friendly St, SE8 ...154 A1
Friendly St Ms, SE4 ...154 A2
Friendship Wk, Nthlt. UB5
off Wayfarer Rd ...102 D3
Friendship Way, E15
off Carpenters Rd ...114 C1
Friends Rd, Croy. CR0 ...202 A3
Friend St, EC1 ...11 G3
FRIERN BARNET, N11 ...57 H4
Friern Barnet La, N11 ...57 H4
N20 ...57 H4
Friern Barnet Rd, N11 ...57 J5
Friern Br Retail Pk, N11 ...58 B6
Friern Ct, N20 ...57 G3
Friern Mt Dr, N20 ...41 F7
Friern Pk, N12 ...57 F5
Friern Rd, SE22 ...152 D6
Friern Watch Av, N12 ...57 F4
Frigate Ms, SE8
off Watergate St ...134 A6
Frimley Av, Wall. SM6 ...201 E5
Frimley Cl, SW19 ...166 B2
Croydon (New Adgtn) CR0 ...204 C7
Frimley Ct, Sid. DA14 ...176 B5
Frimley Cres, Croy. (New Adgtn) CR0 ...204 C7
Frimley Gdns, Mitch. CR4 .185 H3
Frimley Rd, Chess. KT9 ...195 H5
Ilford IG3 ...99 H3
Frimley Way, E1 ...113 G4
Frinstead Ho, W10 ...108 A7
Frinton Cl, Wat. WD19 ...50 B2
Frinton Dr, Wdf.Grn. IG8 ...62 D7
Frinton Ms, Ilf. IG2
off Bramley Cres ...80 D6
Frinton Rd, E6 ...116 A3
N15 ...76 B6
SW17 ...168 A6
Sidcup DA14 ...176 E2
Friston Path, Chig. IG7 ...65 H5
Friston St, SW6 ...148 E2
Friswell Pl, Bexh. DA6 ...159 G4
Fritham Cl, N.Mal. KT3 ...182 E6
Frith Ct, NW7 ...56 B7
Frith La, NW7 ...56 B7
Frith Rd, E11 ...96 C4
Croydon CR0 ...201 J2
Frith St, W1 ...17 H4
Frithville Gdns, W12 ...127 J1
Frizlands La, Dag. RM10 ...101 H4
Frobisher Cl, Pnr. HA5 ...66 D7
Frobisher Cres, EC2
off The Barbican ...20 A1
Staines TW19 ...140 B7
Frobisher Gdns, Stai. TW19 ...140 B7
Frobisher Ms, Enf. EN2 ...44 A4
Frobisher Pas, E14
off The North Colonnade ...134 A1
Frobisher Pl, SE15
off St. Mary's Rd ...153 F1
Frobisher Rd, E6 ...116 C6
N8 ...75 G4
Frobisher St, SE10 ...135 E6
Froghall La, Chig. IG7 ...65 G4
Frogley Rd, SE22 ...152 C4
Frogmore, SW18 ...148 D5
Frogmore Cl, Sutt. SM3 ...198 A3
Frogmore Est, Ruis. HA4 ...84 D5
Frogmore Gdns, Sutt. SM3 ...198 B4
Frogmore Ind Est, NW10 ...106 C3
Frognal, NW3 ...91 F5
Frognal Av, Har. HA1 ...68 C4
Sidcup DA14 ...176 A5
Frognal Cl, NW3 ...91 F5
Frognal Cor, Sid. DA14 ...175 J6
Frognal Ct, NW3 ...91 F6
Frognal Gdns, NW3 ...91 F4
Frognal La, NW3 ...90 E5
Frognal Par, NW3
off Frognal Ct ...91 F6
Frognal Pl, Sid. DA14 ...176 A6
Frognal Ri, NW3 ...91 F4
Frognal Way, NW3 ...91 F4
Froissart Rd, SE9 ...156 A5
Frome Rd, N22
off Westbury Av ...75 H3
Frome St, N1 ...11 J1
Fromondes Rd, Sutt. SM3 ...198 B5
Frostic Wk, E1 ...21 G2
Froude St, SW8 ...150 B2
Fruen Rd, Felt. TW14 ...141 J7
Fruiterers Pas, EC4
off Southwark Br ...20 A6
Fryatt Rd, N17 ...60 A7
Fryday Gro Ms, SW12
off Weir Rd ...150 C7
Fryent Cl, NW9 ...70 A6
Fryent Cres, NW9 ...70 E6
Fryent Flds, NW9 ...71 E6
Fryent Gro, NW9 ...70 E6
Fryent Way, NW9 ...70 A5
Frying Pan All, E1 ...21 F2
Fry Rd, E6 ...98 A7
NW10 ...107 F1
Fryston Av, Croy. CR0 ...202 D2
Fuchsia St, SE2 ...138 B5
Fulbeck Dr, NW9 ...70 E1
Fulbeck Wk, Edg. HA8
off Burrell Cl ...54 B2
Fulbeck Way, Har. HA2 ...67 J2
Fulbourne Rd, E17 ...78 C1
Fulbourne St, E1
off Durward St ...112 E5
Fulbrook Ms, N19
off Junction Rd ...92 C4
Fulbrook Rd, N19
off Junction Rd ...92 C4
Fulford Gro, Wat. WD19 ...50 B2
Fulford Rd, Epsom KT19 ...196 D7
Fulford St, SE16 ...133 E2
FULHAM, SW6 ...148 B2
Fulham Bdy, SW6 ...128 D7
Fulham Bdy Retail Cen, SW6 *off Fulham Bdy* ...128 D7
Fulham Br, SW6 ...148 B3
Fulham Ct, SW6
off Shottendane Rd ...148 D1
★ **Fulham FC**, SW6 ...148 A1
Fulham High St, SW6 ...148 B2
★ **Fulham Palace**, SW6 ...148 B2
Fulham Palace Rd, SW6 ...128 A7
W6 ...127 J5
Fulham Pk Gdns, SW6 ...148 C2
Fulham Pk Rd, SW6 ...148 C2
Fulham Rd, SW3 ...30 E4
SW6 ...30 B7
SW10 ...30 E4
Fullbrooks Av, Wor.Pk. KT4 ...197 F1
Fuller Cl, E2 ...13 H5
Orpington BR6 ...207 J5
Fuller Rd, Dag. RM8 ...100 B3
Fullers Av, Surb. KT6 ...195 J2
Woodford Green IG8 ...63 F7
★ **Fuller's Griffin Brewery**, W4 ...127 F6
Fullers Rd, E18 ...79 F1
Fuller St, NW4 ...71 J4
Fullers Way N, Surb. KT6 ...195 J3
Fullers Way S, Chess. KT9 ...195 H4
Fullers Wd, Croy. CR0 ...204 A5
Fuller Ter, Ilf. IG1
off Oaktree Gro ...99 G5
Fullerton Rd, SW18 ...149 F5
Croydon CR0 ...188 C7
Fuller Way, Hayes UB3 ...121 J5
Fullwell Av, Ilf. IG5, IG6 ...80 C1
FULLWELL CROSS, Ilf. IG6 ...81 G1
Fullwell Cross Rbt, Ilf. IG6
off High St ...81 G2
Fullwoods Ms, N1 ...12 C3
Fulmar Cl, Surb. KT5 ...181 J6
Fulmead St, SW6 ...149 E1
Fulmer Cl, Hmptn. TW12 ...161 E5
Fulmer Rd, E16 ...116 A5
Fulmer Way, W13 ...124 E3
Fulready Rd, E10 ...78 D5
Fulstone Cl, Houns. TW4 ...143 F4
Fulthorp Rd, SE3 ...155 F2
Fulton Ms, W2 ...14 C5
Fulton Rd, Wem. HA9 ...88 A3
Fulwell Pk Av, Twick. TW2 .161 H2
Fulwell Rd, Tedd. TW11 ...162 A4
Fulwood Av, Wem. HA0 ...105 J1
Fulwood Gdns, Twick. TW1 ...144 C6
Fulwood Pl, WC1 ...18 D2
Fulwood Wk, SW19 ...166 B1
Furber St, W6 ...127 H3
Furham Feild, Pnr. HA5 ...51 G7
Furley Rd, SE15 ...132 D7
Furlong Cl, Wall. SM6 ...200 B1
Furlong Rd, N7 ...93 G6
Furmage St, SW18 ...149 E7
Furneaux Av, SE27 ...169 H5
Furness Rd, NW10 ...107 G2
SW6 ...149 E2
Harrow HA2 ...67 H7
Morden SM4 ...185 E7

Furnival St, EC4 19 E3
Furrow La, E9 95 F5
Fursby Av, N3 56 D6
Further Acre, NW9 71 F2
Furtherfield Cl, Croy. CR0 187 G6
Further Grn Rd, SE6 155 E7
Furze Cl, Wat. WD19 50 C5
FURZEDOWN, SW17 168 A5
Furzedown Dr, SW17 168 B5
Furzedown Hall, SW17
off Spalding Rd 168 B5
Furzedown Rd, SW17 168 B5
Furze Fm Cl, Rom. RM6 83 E2
Furzefield Cl, Chis. BR7 174 E6
Furzefield Rd, SE3 135 H6
Furzeground Way, Uxb. UB11 121 F1
Furzeham Rd, West Dr. UB7 120 B2
Furzehill Par, Borwd. WD6
off Shenley Rd 38 A3
Furzehill Rd, Borwd. WD6 38 A4
Furze Rd, Th.Hth. CR7 187 J3
Furze St, E3 114 A5
Furzewood, Sun. TW16 178 A1
Fuschia Ct, Wdf.Grn. IG8
off The Bridle Path 63 E7
Fyfe Way, Brom. BR1
off Widmore Rd 191 G2
Fyfield, N4
off Six Acres Est 93 G2
Fyfield Cl, Brom. BR2 190 D4
Fyfield Ct, E7 97 G6
Fyfield Rd, E17 78 D3
SW9 151 G3
Enfield EN1 44 B3
Woodford Green IG8 63 J7
Fynes St, SW1 33 H1

G

Gable Cl, Pnr. HA5 51 G7
Gable Ct, SE26
off Lawrie Pk Av 171 E4
Gables, The, Wem. HA9 88 A3
Gables Cl, SE5 152 B1
SE12 173 G1
Gabriel Cl, Felt. TW13 160 D4
Gabrielle Cl, Wem. HA9 87 J3
Gabrielle Ct, NW3 91 G6
Gabriel Ms, NW2 90 C2
Gabriel's Ms, Beck. BR3 189 G1
Gabriel St, SE23 153 G7
Gabriel's Wf, SE1 27 E1
Gad Cl, E13 115 H3
Gaddesden Av, Wem. HA9 87 J6
Gade Cl, Hayes UB3 122 B1
Gadesden Rd, Epsom KT19 196 C6
Gadsbury Cl, NW9 71 F6
Gadwall Cl, E16
off Freemasons Rd 115 H6
Gadwall Way, SE28 137 G2
Gage Rd, E16
off Malmesbury Rd 115 E5
Gage St, WC1 18 B1
Gainford St, N1
off Richmond Av 111 G1
Gainsboro Gdns, Grnf. UB6 86 B5
Gainsborough Av, E12 98 D5
Gainsborough Cl, Beck. BR3 172 A7
Esher KT10
off Lime Tree Av 194 B1
Gainsborough Ct, N12 56 E5
W12 *off Lime Gro* 127 J2
Bromley BR2 191 J4
Gainsborough Gdns,
NW3 91 G3
NW11 72 C7
Edgware HA8 69 J2
Isleworth TW7 144 A5
Gainsborough Ho, E14
off Cassilis Rd 134 A2
Enfield EN1
off Ayley Cft 44 D5
Gainsborough Ms, SE26
off Panmure Rd 170 E3
Gainsborough Pl, Chig. IG7 65 J3
Gainsborough Rd, E11 79 E7
E15 114 E3
N12 57 E5
W4 127 F4
Dagenham RM8 100 B4
New Malden KT3 182 D7
Richmond TW9 145 J3
Woodford Green IG8 64 B6
Gainsborough Sq, Bexh. DA6
off Regency Way 158 D3
Gainsborough St, E9
off Trowbridge Rd 95 J6
Gainsborough Studios, N1
off Poole St 112 A1
Gainsford Rd, E17 77 J4
Gainsford St, SE1 29 F3
Gairloch Rd, SE5 152 B2
Gaisford St, NW5 92 C6
Gaitskell Ct, SW11 149 G2
Gaitskell Ho, WD4 38 D4
Gaitskell Rd, SE9 175 F1
Gaitskell Way, SE1
off Weller St 27 J3
Galahad Rd, N9 60 D3
Bromley BR1 173 G3
Galata Rd, SW13 127 G7
Galatea Sq, SE15
off Scylla Rd 152 E3
Galaxy, E14
off Crews St 134 A4
Galba Ct, Brent. TW8
off Augustus Cl 125 G7
Galbraith St, E14 134 C3
Galdana Av, Barn. EN5 41 F3
Galeborough Av, Wdf.Grn. IG8 62 D7
Gale Cl, Hmptn. TW12
off Stewart Cl 161 E6
Mitcham CR4 185 G3
Galena Ho, SE18
off Grosmont Rd 137 J5
Galena Rd, W6 127 H4
Galen Pl, WC1 18 B2
Galesbury Rd, SW18 149 F6
Gales Gdns, E2 113 E3
Gale St, E3 114 A5
Dagenham RM9 118 D1
Gales Way, Wdf.Grn. IG8 64 B7
Galgate Cl, SW19 166 B1
Gallants Fm Rd, Barn. (E.Barn.) EN4 41 H7
Galleon Cl, SE16
off Kinburn St 133 G2
Galleon Ho, SW8
off St. George Wf 34 A5
Galleons Dr, Bark. IG11 118 A3
Gallery Gdns, Nthlt. UB5 102 D2
Gallery Rd, SE21 170 A1
Galley La, Barn. EN5 39 H3
Galleywall Rd, SE16 132 E4
Galliard Cl, N9 45 F6
Galliard Rd, N9 60 D1
Gallia Rd, N5 93 H5
Gallica Ct, Sutt. SM1
off Cleeve Way 199 E1
Gallions Cl, Bark. IG11 118 A3
Gallions Reach Shop Pk, E6 117 F5
Gallions Rd, E16 117 F7
SE7 135 H4
Gallions Rbt, E16 116 E7
Gallions Vw Rd, SE28
off Goldfinch Rd 137 H2
Gallon Cl, SE7 135 J4
Gallop, The, S.Croy. CR2 203 E7
Sutton SM2 199 F7
Gallosson Rd, SE18 137 H4
Galloway Path, Croy. CR0 202 A4
Galloway Rd, W12 127 G1
Gallus Cl, N21 43 F6
Gallus Sq, SE3 155 H3
Galpins Rd, Th.Hth. CR7 187 F4
Galsworthy Av, E14 113 H5
Romford RM6 82 B7
Galsworthy Cl, SE28 138 B1
Galsworthy Cres, SE3
off Merriman Rd 155 J1
Galsworthy Rd, NW2 90 B4
Kingston upon Thames KT2 164 B7
Galsworthy Ter, N16
off Hawksley Rd 94 B3
Galton St, W10 108 B4
Galva Cl, Barn. EN4 42 A4
Galvani Way, Croy. CR0
off Ampere Way 201 F1
Galveston Rd, SW15 148 C5
Galway Cl, SE16
off Masters Dr 133 E5
Galway Ho, EC1 12 A4
Galway St, EC1 12 A4
Gambetta St, SW8 150 B2
Gambia St, SE1 27 H2
Gambier Ho, EC1 12 A3
Gambole Rd, SW17 167 H4
Games Ho, SE7
off Springfield Gro 135 J6
Games Rd, Barn. EN4 41 J3
Gamlen Rd, SW15 148 A4
Gamuel Cl, E17 78 A6
Gander Grn Cres, Hmptn. TW12 179 G1
Gander Grn La, Sutt. SM1, SM3 198 B2
Gandhi Cl, E17 78 A6
Gandolfi St, SE15 36 D6
Ganton St, W1 17 F5
Ganton Wk, Wat. WD19 50 D4
GANTS HILL, Ilf. IG2 80 D5
Gants Hill, Ilf. IG2
off Eastern Av 80 D6
Gantshill Cres, Ilf. IG2 80 D5
Gap Rd, SW19 166 D5
Garage Rd, W3 106 A6
Garand Ct, N7
off Eden Gro 93 F5
Garbutt Pl, W1 16 C1
Garden Av, Bexh. DA7 159 G3
Mitcham CR4 168 B7
Garden City, Edg. HA8 54 A6
Garden Cl, E4 62 A5
SE12 173 H3
SW15 147 H7
Barnet (Arkley) EN5 39 J4
Hampton TW12 161 F5
New Malden KT3 182 E4
Northolt UB5 103 E1
Wallington SM6 200 E5
Garden Ct, N12 56 E5
Richmond TW9 145 J1
Stanmore HA7 53 F5
West Molesey KT8
off Avern Rd 179 H4
Gardeners Cl, N11 58 A2
SE9 174 B3
Gardeners Rd, Croy. CR0 201 H1
Gardenia Rd, Brom. BR1 192 D3
Enfield EN1 44 B6
Gardenia Way, Wdf.Grn. IG8 63 G5
Garden La, SW2
off Christchurch Rd 169 F1
Bromley BR1 173 H6
Garden Ms, W2
off Linden Gdns 108 D7
Garden Pl, E8
off Haggerston Rd 112 C1
Garden Rd, NW8 6 D3
SE20 189 F1
Bromley BR1 173 H7
Richmond TW9 146 A3
Walton-on-Thames KT12 178 B6
Garden Row, SE1 27 G6
Gardens, The, E5 76 C7
SE22 152 D4
Beckenham BR3 190 C2
Feltham TW14 141 G5
Harrow HA1 67 J6
Pinner HA5 67 F6
Garden St, E1 113 G5
Garden Ter, SW1 33 H3
Garden Wk, EC2 12 D4
Beckenham BR3 189 J1
Garden Way, NW10 88 C6
Gardiner Av, NW2 89 J5
Gardiner Cl, Dag. RM8 100 D4
Enfield EN3 45 G6
Gardner Cl, E11 79 H6
Gardner Ct, EC1
off Brewery Sq 11 G5
N5 *off Kelvin Rd* 93 J4
Gardner Gro, Felt. TW13 161 F2
Gardner Ind Est, Beck. BR3 171 H5
Gardner Pl, Felt. TW14 142 B6
Gardner Rd, E13 115 H4
Gardners La, EC4 19 J5
Gardnor Rd, NW3
off Flask Wk 91 G4
Gard St, EC1 11 H3
Garendon Gdns, Mord. SM4 184 E7
Garendon Rd, Mord. SM4 184 E7
Gareth Cl, Wor.Pk. KT4
off Burnham Dr 198 A2
Gareth Dr, N9 60 D2
Gareth Gro, Brom. BR1 173 G4
Garfield Ms, SW11
off Garfield Rd 150 B3
Garfield Rd, E4 62 D1
E13 115 F4
SW11 150 A3
SW19 167 F5
Enfield EN3 45 F4
Twickenham TW1 162 D1
Garford St, E14 114 A7
Garganey Wk, SE28 118 D7
Garibaldi St, SE18 137 H4
Garland Ct, SE17
off Wansey St 36 A2
Croy. CRO 202 A4
Garland Dr, Houns. TW3 143 J2
Garland Ho, Kings.T. KT2
off Kingsgate Rd 181 H1
Garland Rd, SE18 137 G7
Bromley BR1 192 E3
Stanmore HA7 69 H1
Garlands Ct, Croy. CR0
off Chatsworth Rd 202 A4
Garlick Hill, EC4 20 A5
Garlies Rd, SE23 171 H3
Garlinge Rd, NW2 90 C6
Garman Cl, N18 60 A5
Garman Rd, N17 61 F7
Garnault Ms, EC1 11 F4
Garnault Pl, EC1 11 F4
Garner Cl, Dag. RM8 100 D1
Garner Rd, E17 78 C1
Garner St, E2 13 J2
Garnet Rd, NW10 89 E6
Thornton Heath CR7 188 A4
Garnet St, E1 113 F7
Garnett Cl, SE9 156 C3
Garnett Rd, NW3 91 J5
Garnett Way, E17
off McEntee Av 77 H1
Garnet Wk, E6
off Kingfisher St 116 B5
Garnham Cl, N16
off Garnham St 94 C2
Garnham St, N16 94 C2
Garnies Cl, SE15 37 F7
Garrad's Rd, SW16 168 D3
Garrard Cl, Bexh. DA7 159 G3
Chislehurst BR7 175 E5
Garrard Wk, NW10
off Garnet Rd 89 E6
Garratt Cl, Croy. CR0 200 E4
Garratt La, SW17 167 G4
SW18 148 E5
Garratt Rd, Edg. HA8 54 A7
Garratt Ter, SW17 167 H4
Garrett Cl, W3 106 D5
Garrett St, EC1 12 A5
Garrick Av, NW11 72 B6
Garrick Cl, SW18 149 F4
W5 105 H4
Richmond TW9
off Old Palace La 145 G5
Garrick Ct, Edg. HA8 53 J4
Garrick Cres, Croy. CR0 202 B2
Garrick Dr, NW4 71 J2
SE28 137 G3
Garrick Gdns, W.Mol. KT8 179 G3
Garrick Pk, NW4 72 A2
Garrick Rd, NW9 71 F6
Greenford UB6 103 H4
Richmond TW9 146 A2
Garricks Ho, Kings.T. KT1 181 G2
Garrick St, WC2 18 A5
Garrick Way, NW4 72 A4
Garrick Yd, WC2 18 A5
Garrison Cl, SE18
off Red Lion La 136 D7
Hounslow TW4 143 F5
Garrison La, Chess. KT9 195 G7
Garrison Rd, E3 114 A1
Garrowsfield, Barn. EN5 40 C5
Garsdale Cl, N11 58 A6
Garside Cl, SE28 137 G3
Hampton TW12 161 H6
Garsington Ms, SE4 153 J3
Garter Way, SE16
off Poolmans St 133 G2
Garth, The, N12 56 E5
Hampton (Hmptn H.) TW12 *off Uxbridge Rd* 161 H6
Harrow HA3 69 J6
Garth Cl, W4 126 D5
Kingston upon Thames KT2 163 J5
Morden SM4 184 A7
Ruislip HA4 84 D1
Garth Ct, W4
off Garth Rd 126 D5
Garth Ho, NW2
off Granville Rd 90 C2
Garthland Dr, Barn. EN5 39 H5
Garth Ms, W5
off Greystoke Gdns 105 H4
Garthorne Rd, SE23 153 G7
Garth Rd, NW2 90 C2
W4 126 D6
Kingston upon Thames KT2 163 J5
Morden SM4 183 J6
Garth Rd Ind Cen, Mord. SM4 184 A7
Garthside, Rich. (Ham) TW10 163 H5
Garthway, N12 57 H6
Gartmoor Gdns, SW19 166 C1
Gartmore Rd, Ilf. IG3 99 J1
Garton Pl, SW18 149 F6
Gartons Cl, Enf. EN3 45 F5
Gartons Way, SW11 149 F3
Garvary Rd, E16 115 H6
Garway Rd, W2 14 A4
Garwood Cl, N17 76 E1
Gascoigne Gdns, Wdf.Grn. IG8 63 E7
Gascoigne Pl, E2 13 F4
Gascoigne Rd, Bark. IG11 117 F1
Gascony Av, NW6 90 D7
Gascony Pl, W12
off Bourbon St 128 A1
Gascoyne Rd, E9 95 G7

Gaselee St, E14 .....114 C7
Gaskarth Rd, SW12 .....150 B6
Edgware HA8 .....70 C1
Gaskell Rd, N6 .....73 J6
Gaskell St, SW4 .....150 E2
Gaskin St, N1 .....111 H1
Gaspar Cl, SW5 .....30 B1
Gaspar Ms, SW5 .....30 B1
Gassiot Rd, SW17 .....167 J4
Gassiot Way, Sutt. SM1 ...199 G3
Gastein Rd, W6 .....128 A6
Gaston Bell Cl, Rich. TW9 .145 J3
Gaston Rd, Mitch. CR4 ...186 A3
★ **Gasworks Gall**, SE11 ...34 D5
Gataker St, SE16 .....133 E3
Gatcombe Ho, SE22
off Pytchley Rd 152 B3
Gatcombe Ms, W5 .....105 J7
Gatcombe Rd, E16 .....135 G1
N19 .....92 D3
Gatcombe Way, Barn. EN4 .41 J3
Gate Cl, Borwd. WD6 .....38 C1
Gate End, Nthwd. HA6 ....50 A7
Gateforth St, NW8 .....7 G6
Gatehouse Cl, Kings.T.
KT2 .....164 C7
Gate Ho Sq, SE1 .....28 A1
Gateley Rd, SW9 .....151 F3
Gate Ms, SW7 .....23 H4
Gater Dr, Enf. EN2 .....44 A1
Gatesborough St, EC2 .....12 D5
Gates Grn Rd, Kes. BR2 ...205 G4
West Wickham BR4 ....205 F3
Gateside Rd, SW17 .....167 J3
Gatestone Rd, SE19 .....170 B6
Gate St, WC2 .....18 C3
Gate Studios, Borwd.
WD6 .....38 A4
Gateway, SE17 .....36 A5
Gateway Business Cen,
SE26 .....171 H6
Gateway Ind Est, NW10 ..107 F3
Gateway Ms, E8
off Shacklewell La 94 C5
Gateway Retail Pk, E6 ....117 E4
Gateway Rd, E10 .....96 B3
Gateways, The, SW3 .....31 H2
Gatfield Gro, Felt. TW13 ..161 G2
Gathorne Rd, N22 .....75 G2
Gathorne St, E2
off Mace St 113 G2
Gatley Av, Epsom KT19 ...196 B5
Gatliff Cl, SW1
off Ebury Br Rd 32 D4
Gatliff Rd, SW1 .....32 C4
Gatling Rd, SE2 .....138 A5
Gatonby St, SE15 .....152 C1
Gatting Cl, Edg. HA8 .....54 C7
Gatton Rd, SW17 .....167 H4
Gattons Way, Sid. DA14 ..177 F4
Gatward Cl, N21 .....43 H6
Gatward Grn, N9 .....60 B2
Gatwick Rd, SW18 .....148 C7
Gauden Cl, SW4 .....150 D3
Gauden Rd, SW4 .....150 D2
Gaumont Ter, W12
off Lime Gro 127 J2
Gauntlet Cl, Nthlt. UB5 ....84 E7
Gauntlett Ct, Wem. HA0 ...86 E5
Gauntlett Rd, Sutt. SM1 ..199 G5
Gaunt St, SE1 .....27 H5
Gautrey Rd, SE15 .....153 F2
Gautrey Sq, E6 .....116 C6
Gavel St, SE17 .....36 C1
Gaverick Ms, E14
off Westferry Rd 134 A4
Gavestone Cres, SE12 ....155 H7
Gavestone Rd, SE12 .....155 H7
Gaviller Pl, E5
off Clarence Rd 95 E4
Gavina Cl, Mord. SM4 ....185 H5
Gavin St, SE18 .....137 H4
Gawain Wk, N9
off Galahad Rd 60 D3
Gawber St, E2 .....113 F3
Gawsworth Cl, E15
off Ash Rd 97 E5
Gawthorne Ct, E3
off Mostyn Gro 114 A2
Gay Cl, NW2 .....89 H5
Gaydon Ho, W2 .....14 B1
Gaydon La, NW9 .....70 E1
Gayfere Rd, Epsom KT17 .197 G5
Ilford IG5 .....80 C3
Gayfere St, SW1 .....26 A6
Gayford Rd, W12 .....127 F2
Gay Gdns, Dag. RM10 ....101 J4
Gayhurst, SE17 .....36 C5
Gayhurst Rd, E8 .....94 D7
Gaylor Rd, Nthlt. UB5 .....85 F5
Gaynesford Rd, SE23 .....171 G2
Carshalton SM5 .....199 J7
Gaynes Hill Rd, Wdf.Grn.
IG8 .....64 B6
Gay Rd, E15 .....114 D2
Gaysham Av, Ilf. IG2 .....80 D5
Gaysham Hall, Ilf. IG5 .....80 E3
Gay St, SW15 .....148 A3
Gayton Ct, Har. HA1 .....68 C6
Gayton Cres, NW3 .....91 G4
Gayton Ho, E3 .....114 A4
Gayton Rd, NW3 .....91 G4
SE2 off Florence Rd 138 C3
Harrow HA1 .....68 C6
Gayville Rd, SW11 .....149 J6
Gaywood Cl, SW2 .....169 F1
Gaywood Est, SE1 .....27 G6
Gaywood Rd, E17 .....78 A3
Gaywood St, SE1 .....27 H6
Gaza St, SE17 .....35 G4
Gazelle Ho, E15
off Manbey Pk Rd 96 E6
Gean Ct, N11
off Cline Rd 58 C6
Gearies ville Gdns, Ilf. IG6 ..81 E4
Gearing Cl, SW17 .....168 A4
Geary Ct, N9
off The Broadway 60 D2
Geary Rd, NW10 .....89 G5
Geary St, N7 .....93 F5
Geddes Pl, Bexh. DA6
off Market Pl 159 G4
Gedeney Rd, N17 .....75 J1
Gedling Ho, SE22
off Quorn Rd 152 C3
Gedling Pl, SE1 .....29 G5
Geere Rd, E15 .....115 F1
Gees Ct, W1 .....16 C4
Gee St, EC1 .....11 J5
Geffrye Ct, N1 .....12 E2
Geffrye Est, N1 .....13 E2
★ **Geffrye Mus**, E2 .....13 E2
Geffrye St, E2 .....13 F1
Geldart Rd, SE15 .....132 E7
Geldeston Rd, E5 .....94 D2
Gellatly Rd, SE14 .....153 F2
Gemini Business Pk, E6 ...117 G5
Gemini Gro, Nthlt. UB5
off Javelin Way 102 E3
Gemini Ho, E3
off Garrison Rd 114 A1
Gemini Project, SE14
off Landmann Way ...133 G5
Genas Cl, Ilf. IG6 .....81 E1
General Gordon Pl, SE18 .136 E4
General Wolfe Rd, SE10 ...154 D1
Genesis Business Pk,
NW10 .....106 B2
Genesta Rd, SE18 .....137 E6
Geneva Dr, SW9 .....151 G4
Geneva Gdns, Rom. RM6 ..82 E5
Geneva Rd, Kings.T. KT1 ..181 H4
Thornton Heath CR7 ...187 J5
Genever Cl, E4 .....62 A5
Genista Rd, N18 .....61 E5
Genoa Av, SW15 .....147 J5
Genoa Rd, SE20 .....189 F1
Genotin Rd, Enf. EN1 .....44 A3
Genotin Ter, Enf. EN1
off Genotin Rd 44 A3
Gentian Row, SE13
off Sparta St 154 C1
Gentlemans Row, Enf.
EN2 .....43 J3
Gentry Gdns, E13
off Whitwell Rd 115 G4
Geoffrey Cl, SE5 .....151 J2
Geoffrey Gdns, E6 .....116 B2
Geoffrey Rd, SE4 .....153 J3
George Beard Rd, SE8 ....133 J4
George Belt Ho, E2
off Smart St 113 G3
George Comberton Wk, E12
off Gainsborough Av ...98 D5
George Ct, WC2 .....18 B6
George Cres, N10 .....58 A7
George Downing Est, N16 .94 C2
George Eliot Ho, SW1
off Vauxhall Br Rd 33 G2
George Elliston Ho, SE1
off Old Kent Rd 37 H4
George V Av, Pnr. HA5 .....67 G3
George V Cl, Pnr. HA5 .....67 G3
George V Way, Grnf.
(Perivale) UB6 .....105 E1
George Gange Way, Har. (Wealds.)
HA3 .....68 B3
George Gros Rd, SE20 ....188 D1
★ **George Inn**, SE1 .....28 B2
George Inn Yd, SE1 .....28 B2
George La, E18 .....79 G2
SE13 .....154 C6
Bromley BR2 .....205 H1
George La Rbt, E18 .....79 G2
George Lansbury Ho, N22
off Progress Way 75 G1
George Loveless Ho, E2 ...13 G3
George Lowe Ct, W2 .....14 A1
George Mathers Rd,
SE11 .....35 G1
George Ms, NW1 .....9 F4
SW9 off Brixton Rd 151 G2
Enfield EN2
off Church St 44 A3
George Rd, E4 .....62 A6
Kingston upon Thames
KT2 .....164 B7
New Malden KT3 .....183 F4
George Row, SE16 .....29 H4
George Sq, SW19
off Mostyn Rd 184 C3
George's Rd, N7 .....93 F5
Georges Sq, SW6
off North End Rd 128 C6
George St, E16 .....115 F6
W1 .....16 A3
W7 off The Broadway ..124 B1
Barking IG11 .....99 F7
Croydon CR0 .....202 A2
Hounslow TW3 .....143 F2
Richmond TW9 .....145 G5
Southall UB2 .....122 E4
George Taylor Ct, N9
off Colthurst Dr 60 E3
Georgetown Cl, SE19 ....170 B5
Georgette Pl, SE10
off King George St ...134 C7
Georgeville Gdns, Ilf. IG6 ..81 E4
George Wyver Cl, SW19
off Beaumont Rd 148 B7
George Yd, EC3 .....20 C4
W1 .....16 C5
Georgiana St, NW1 .....110 C1
Georgian Cl, Brom. BR2 ..191 H7
Stanmore HA7 .....52 D7
Georgian Ct, SW16
off Gleneldon Rd 169 E4
Wembley HA9 .....88 A6
Georgian Way, Har. HA1 ...86 A2
Georgia Rd, N.Mal. KT3 ..182 C4
Thornton Heath CR7 ...187 H1
Georgina Gdns, E2 .....13 G3
Geraint Rd, Brom. BR1 ...173 G4
Geraldine Rd, SW18 .....149 F5
W4 .....126 A6
Geraldine St, SE11 .....27 G6
Gerald Ms, SW1 .....32 C1
Gerald Rd, E16 .....115 F4
SW1 .....32 C1
Dagenham RM8 .....101 F2
Gerard Av, Houns. TW4 ...143 G7
Gerard Pl, E9
off Groombridge Rd ...95 G7
Gerard Rd, SW13 .....147 F1
Harrow HA1 .....68 D6
Gerards Cl, SE16 .....133 F5
Gerards Pl, SW4
off Magnolia Pl 150 D5
Gerda Rd, SE9 .....175 F2
Germander Way, E15 .....115 E3
Gernigan Ho, SW18
off Fitzhugh Gro 149 G6
Gernon Rd, E3 .....113 H2
Geron Way, NW2 .....89 H1
Gerrard Gdns, Pnr. HA5 ....66 A5
Gerrard Ho, SE14
off Briant St 133 G7
Gerrard Pl, W1 .....17 J5
Gerrard Rd, N1 .....11 H1
Gerrards Cl, N14 .....42 C5
Gerrard St, W1 .....17 H5
Gerridge St, SE1 .....27 F4
Gerry Raffles Sq, E15
off Great Eastern Rd ...96 D6
Gertrude Rd, Belv. DA17 ..139 G4
Gertrude St, SW10 .....30 D6
Gervase Cl, Wem. HA9 ....88 C3
Gervase Rd, Edg. HA8 .....70 C1
Gervase St, SE15 .....133 E7
Ghent St, SE6 .....172 A2
Ghent Way, E8
off Tyssen St 94 C6
Giant Arches Rd, SE24 ...151 J7
Giant Tree Hill, Bushey
(Bushey Hth) WD23 .....52 A1
Gibbard Ms, SW19 .....166 A5
Gibbfield Cl, Rom. RM6 ....82 E3
Gibbins Rd, E15 .....96 C7
Gibbon Rd, SE15 .....153 F2
W3 .....106 E7
Kingston upon Thames
KT2 .....181 H1
Gibbons Ms, NW11
off Hayes Cres 72 C5
Gibbons Rents, SE1
off Magdalen St 28 D2
Gibbons Rd, NW10 .....88 D6
Gibbon Wk, SW15 .....147 G4
Gibbs Av, SE19 .....170 A5
Gibbs Cl, SE19 .....170 A5
Gibbs Couch, Wat.
WD19 .....50 D3
Gibbs Grn, W14 .....128 C5
Edgware HA8 .....54 C5
Gibbs Rd, N18 .....61 F4
Gibbs Sq, SE19 .....170 A5
Gibney Ter, Brom. BR1
off Durham Hill 173 F4
Gibraltar Wk, E2 .....13 G4
Gibson Business Cen, N17
off High Rd 60 C7
Gibson Cl, E1
off Colebert Av 113 F4
N21 .....43 G6
Chessington KT9 .....195 F6
Isleworth TW7 .....144 A3
Gibson Gdns, N16
off Northwold Rd 94 C2
Gibson Ms, Twick. TW1
off Richmond Rd 145 F7
Gibson Rd, SE11 .....34 D2
Dagenham RM8 .....100 C1
Sutton SM1 .....198 E5
Gibson's Hill, SW16 .....169 G6
Gibson Sq, N1 .....111 G1
Gibson St, SE10 .....134 E5
Gideon Cl, Belv. DA17 ....139 H4
Gideon Ms, W5 .....125 G2
Gideon Rd, SW11 .....150 A3
Giesbach Rd, N19 .....92 C2
Giffard Rd, N18 .....60 B5
Giffin St, SE8 .....134 A7
Gifford Gdns, W7 .....104 A5
Gifford St, N1 .....93 E7
Gift La, E15 .....115 E1
Giggs Hill Gdns, T.Ditt.
KT7 .....194 D1
Giggs Hill Rd, T.Ditt. KT7 ..180 D7
Gilbert Cl, SE18 .....156 C1
Gilbert Gro, Edg. HA8 .....70 D1
Gilbert Ho, EC2
off The Barbican 20 A1
SE8 off McMillan St ...134 A6
SW1 .....33 E4
Gilbert Pl, WC1 .....18 A2
Gilbert Rd, SE11 .....35 F2
SW19 .....167 F7
Belvedere DA17 .....139 G3
Bromley BR1 .....173 G7
Pinner HA5 .....66 D4
Gilbert St, E15 .....96 E4
W1 .....16 C4
Hounslow TW3
off High St 143 J3
Gilbert Way, Croy. CR0
off Beddington
Fm Rd 201 E1
Gilbert White Cl, Grnf. UB6
off Horsenden La S ...104 D1
Gilbey Rd, SW17 .....167 H4
Gilbeys Yd, NW1 .....92 A7
Gilbourne Rd, SE18 .....137 J6
Gilda Av, Enf. EN3 .....45 H5
Gilda Cres, N16 .....94 D1
Gildea Cl, Pnr. HA5 .....51 G7
Gildea St, W1 .....17 E2
Gilden Cres, NW5 .....92 A5
Gildersome St, SE18
off Nightingale Vale ...136 D6
Gilders Rd, Chess. KT9 ...195 J6
Giles Coppice, SE19 .....170 C4
Gilkes Cres, SE21 .....152 B6
Gilkes Pl, SE21 .....152 B6
Gillan Grn, Bushey
(Bushey Hth) WD23 .....51 J2
Gillards Ms, E17
off Gillards Way 78 A4
Gillards Way, E17 .....78 A4
Gill Av, E16 .....115 G6
Gillender St, E3 .....114 C4
E14 .....114 C4
Gillespie Rd, N5 .....93 G3
Gillett Av, E6 .....116 B2
Gillette Cor, Islw. TW7 ....124 D7
Gillett Pl, N16
off Gillett St 94 B5
Gillett Rd, Th.Hth. CR7 ....188 A4
Gillett St, N16 .....94 B5
Gillfoot, NW1 .....9 F2
Gillham Ter, N17 .....60 D6
Gillian Pk Rd, Sutt. SM3 ..198 C1
Gillian St, SE13 .....154 B5
Gillies St, NW5 .....92 A5
Gilling Ct, NW3 .....91 H6
Gillingham Rd, NW2 .....90 B3
Gillingham Row, SW1 .....33 F1
Gillingham St, SW1 .....33 E1
Gillison Wk, SE16
off Tranton Rd 29 J5
Gillman Dr, E15 .....115 F1
Gill St, E14 .....113 J6
Gillum Cl, Barn. (E.Barn.)
EN4 .....57 J1
Gilmore Rd, SE13 .....154 D4
Gilpin Av, SW14 .....146 D4
Gilpin Cl, W2 .....14 E1
Mitcham CR4 .....185 H2
Gilpin Cres, N18 .....60 C5
Twickenham TW2 .....143 H7
Gilpin Rd, E5 .....95 H4
Gilpin Way, Hayes
(Harling.) UB3 .....121 G7
Gilsland Pl, Th.Hth. CR7
off Gilsland Rd 188 A4
Gilsland Rd, Th.Hth. CR7 ..188 A4
Gilstead Ho, Bark. IG11 ...118 B2
Gilstead Rd, SW6 .....149 E2
Gilston Rd, SW10 .....30 D4

Gilton Rd, SE6 173 E3
Giltspur St, EC1 19 H3
Gilwell Cl, E4 off Antlers Hill 46 B4
Gilwell La, E4 46 C4
Gilwell Pk, E4 46 C3
Ginsburg Yd, NW3 off Heath St 91 F4
Gippeswyck Cl, Pnr. HA5 off Uxbridge Rd 66 D1
Gipsy Hill, SE19 170 B4
Gipsy La, SW15 147 G3
Gipsy Rd, SE27 169 J4
Welling DA16 158 D1
Gipsy Rd Gdns, SE27 169 J4
Giralda Cl, E16 off Fulmer Rd 116 A5
Giraud St, E14 114 B6
Girdlers Rd, W14 128 A4
Girdlestone Wk, N19 92 C2
Girdwood Rd, SW18 148 B7
Girling Way, Felt. TW14 142 A3
Gironde Rd, SW6 128 C7
Girton Av, NW9 70 A3
Girton Cl, Nthlt. UB5 85 J6
Girton Gdns, Croy. CR0 204 A3
Girton Rd, SE26 171 G5
Northolt UB5 85 J6
Girton Vil, W10 108 A6
Gisbourne Cl, Wall. SM6 200 D3
Gisburn Rd, N8 75 F4
Gissing Wk, N1 off Lofting Rd 93 G7
Gittens Cl, Brom. BR1 173 F4
Given Wilson Wk, E13 115 F2
Glacier Way, Wem. HA0 105 G2
Gladbeck Way, Enf. EN2 43 H4
Gladding Rd, E12 98 A4
Glade, The, N21 43 F6
SE7 135 J7
Bromley BR1 192 A2
Croydon CR0 189 G5
Enfield EN2 43 G3
Epsom KT17 197 G5
Ilford IG5 80 C1
West Wickham BR4 204 B3
Woodford Green IG8 63 H3
Glade Cl, Surb. (Long Dit.) KT6 195 G2
Glade Ct, Ilf. IG5 80 C1
Glade Gdns, Croy. CR0 189 H7
Glade La, Sthl. UB2 123 H2
Gladeside, N21 43 F6
Croydon CR0 189 G6
Gladeside Cl, Chess. KT9 195 G7
Gladesmore Rd, N15 76 C6
Glades Shop Cen, The, Brom. BR1 191 G2
Gladeswood Rd, Belv. DA17 139 H4
Gladiator St, SE23 153 H6
Glading Ter, N16 94 C3
Gladioli Cl, Hmptn. TW12 off Gresham Rd 161 G6
Gladsdale Dr, Pnr. HA5 66 A4
Gladsmuir Rd, N19 92 C1
Barnet EN5 40 B2
Gladstone Av, E12 98 B7
N22 75 G2
Feltham TW14 142 A6
Twickenham TW2 144 A7
Gladstone Ct, SW1 off Regency St 33 J2
SW8 off Havelock Ter 150 B1
SW19 166 D7
Gladstone Gdns, Houns. TW3 143 J1
Gladstone Ms, N22 off Pelham Rd 75 G2
NW6 off Cavendish Rd 90 C7
SE20 171 F7
Gladstone Par, NW2 off Edgware Rd 89 H1
Gladstone Pk Gdns, NW2 89 H3
Gladstone Pl, E3 off Roman Rd 113 J2
Barnet EN5 40 A4
Gladstone Rd, SW19 166 D7
W4 off Acton La 126 D3
Buckhurst Hill IG9 63 H1
Croydon CR0 188 A7
Kingston upon Thames KT1 182 A3
Orpington BR6 207 F5
Southall UB2 122 E3
Surbiton KT6 195 G2
Gladstone St, SE1 27 G5
Gladstone Ter, SE27 off Bentons La 169 J4
Gladstone Way, Har. (Wealds.) HA3 68 B3
Gladwell Rd, N8 75 F6
Bromley BR1 173 G6
Gladwyn Rd, SW15 148 A3
Gladys Rd, NW6 90 D7
Glaisher St, SE8 134 A6
Glamis Cres, Hayes UB3 121 F3
Glamis Pl, E1 113 F7
Glamis Rd, E1 113 F7
Glamis Way, Nthlt. UB5 85 J6
Glamorgan Cl, Mitch. CR4 186 E3
Glamorgan Rd, Kings.T. KT1 163 F7
Glandford Way, Rom. (Chad.Hth) RM6 82 B5
Glanfield Rd, Beck. BR3 189 J4
Glanleam Rd, Stan. HA7 53 G4
Glanville Ms, Stan. HA7 52 D5
Glanville Rd, SW2 151 E5
Bromley BR2 191 H3
Glasbrook Av, Twick. TW2 161 F1
Glasbrook Rd, SE9 156 A7
Glaserton Rd, N16 76 B7
Glasford St, SW17 167 J6
Glasgow Ho, W9 6 B2
Glasgow Rd, E13 115 H2
N18 60 D4
Glasgow Ter, SW1 33 F4
Glasier Ct, E15 off Glenavon Rd 97 E7
Glaskin Ms, E9 off Danesdale Rd 95 H6
Glasse Cl, W13 104 D7
Glasshill St, SE1 27 H3
Glasshouse Flds, E1 113 G7
Glasshouse St, W1 17 G6
Glasshouse Wk, SE11 34 B3
Glasshouse Yd, EC1 11 J6
Glasslyn Rd, N8 74 D5
Glassmill La, Brom. BR2 191 F2
Glass St, E2 off Coventry Rd 113 E4
Glass Yd, SE18 off Woolwich High St 136 D3
Glastonbury Av, Wdf.Grn. IG8 64 A7
Glastonbury Ho, SW1 32 D3
Glastonbury Pl, E1 off Sutton St 113 F6
Glastonbury Rd, N9 60 D1
Morden SM4 184 D7
Glastonbury St, NW6 90 C5
Glaucus St, E3 114 B5
Glazbury Rd, W14 128 B4
Glazebrook Cl, SE21 170 A2
Glazebrook Rd, Tedd. TW11 162 C7
Glebe, The, SE3 154 E3
SW16 168 D4
Chislehurst BR7 193 F1
West Drayton UB7 120 C4
Worcester Park KT4 197 F1
Glebe Av, Enf. EN2 43 H3
Harrow HA3 69 H3
Mitcham CR4 185 H2
Ruislip HA4 84 B6
Woodford Green IG8 63 G6
Glebe Cl, W4 off Prince of Wales Ter 126 E5
Glebe Cotts, Sutt. SM1 off Vale Rd 198 E4
Glebe Ct, W7 104 A7
Mitcham CR4 185 J3
Stanmore HA7 53 F5
Glebe Cres, NW4 71 J4
Harrow HA3 69 H3
Glebe Gdns, N.Mal. KT3 183 E7
Glebe Ho Dr, Brom. BR2 205 H1
Glebe Hyrst, SE19 170 B4
Glebelands, W.Mol. KT8 179 H5
Glebelands Av, E18 79 G2
Ilford IG2 81 G7
Glebelands Cl, N12 73 G1
Glebelands Rd, Felt. TW14 142 A7
Glebe La, Barn. EN5 39 G5
Harrow HA3 69 H4
Glebe Ms, Sid. DA15 157 J5
Glebe Path, Mitch. CR4 185 H3
Glebe Pl, SW3 31 G5
Glebe Rd, E8 off Middleton Rd 94 C7
N3 73 F1
N8 75 F4
NW10 89 F6
SW13 147 G2
Bromley BR1 191 G1
Carshalton SM5 199 J6
Dagenham RM10 101 H6
Hayes UB3 121 J1
Stanmore HA7 53 F5
Glebe Side, Twick. TW1 144 C6
Glebe Sq, Mitch. CR4 185 J3
Glebe St, W4 126 E5
Glebe Ter, W4 off Glebe St 126 E5
Glebe Way, Felt. (Han.) TW13 161 G3
West Wickham BR4 204 C2
Glebeway, Wdf.Grn. IG8 63 J5
Gledhow Gdns, SW5 30 C2
Gledstanes Rd, W14 128 B5
Gleed Av, Bushey (Bushey Hth) WD23 52 A2
Gleeson Dr, Orp. BR6 207 J5
Glegg Pl, SW15 148 A4
Glen, The, Brom. BR2 190 E2
Croydon CR0 203 G3
Enfield EN2 43 H4
Orpington BR6 206 C3
Pinner HA5 67 E7
Pinner (Eastcote) HA5 66 B5
Southall UB2 123 F5
Wembley HA9 87 G4
Glenaffric Av, E14 134 D4
Glen Albyn Rd, SW19 166 A2
Glenalmond Rd, Har. HA3 69 H4
Glenalvon Way, SE18 136 B4
Glena Mt, Sutt. SM1 199 F4
Glenarm Rd, E5 95 F5
Glenavon Cl, Esher (Clay.) KT10 194 D7
Glenavon Rd, E15 97 E7
Glenbarr Cl, SE9 off Dumbreck Rd 156 E3
Glenbow Rd, Brom. BR1 172 E6
Glenbrook N, Enf. EN2 43 F4
Glenbrook Rd, NW6 90 D5
Glenbrook S, Enf. EN2 43 F4
Glenbuck Ct, Surb. KT6 off Glenbuck Rd 181 H6
Glenbuck Rd, Surb. KT6 181 G6
Glenburnie Rd, SW17 167 J3
Glencairn Dr, W5 105 E4
Glencairne Cl, E16 116 A5
Glencairn Rd, SW16 186 E1
Glencoe Av, Ilf. IG2 81 G7
Glencoe Dr, Dag. RM10 101 G4
Glencoe Rd, Hayes UB4 102 E5
Glencorse Grn, Wat. WD19 50 D4
Glen Cres, Wdf.Grn. IG8 63 H6
Glendale Av, N22 59 G7
Edgware HA8 53 J4
Romford RM6 82 C7
Glendale Cl, SE9 off Dumbreck Rd 156 D3
Glendale Dr, SW19 166 C5
Glendale Gdns, Wem. HA9 87 G1
Glendale Ms, Beck. BR3 190 B1
Glendale Rd, Erith DA8 139 J4
Glendale Way, SE28 118 C7
Glendall St, SW9 151 F4
Glendarvon St, SW15 148 A3
Glendevon Cl, Edg. HA8 54 B3
Glendish Rd, N17 76 D1
Glendor Gdns, NW7 54 D4
Glendower Gdns, SW14 off Glendower Rd 146 D3
Glendower Pl, SW7 31 E1
Glendower Rd, E4 62 D1
SW14 146 D3
Glendown Rd, SE2 138 A5
Glendun Rd, W3 107 E7
Gleneagle Ms, SW16 off Ambleside Av 168 D5
Gleneagle Rd, SW16 168 D5
Gleneagles, Stan. HA7 52 E6
Gleneagles Cl, SE16 off Ryder Dr 132 E5
Orpington BR6 207 G1
Staines (Stanw.) TW19 140 A6
Watford WD19 50 D4
Gleneagles Grn, Orp. BR6 off Tandridge Dr 207 G1
Gleneagles Twr, Sthl. UB1 103 J6
Gleneldon Ms, SW16 168 E4
Gleneldon Rd, SW16 168 E4
Glenelg Rd, SW2 151 E5
Glenesk Rd, SE9 156 D3
Glenfarg Rd, SE6 172 D1
Glenfield Rd, SW12 168 C1
W13 125 E2
Glenfield Ter, W13 124 E2
Glenfinlas Way, SE5 35 H7
Glenforth St, SE10 135 F5
Glengall Causeway, E14 134 A3
Glengall Gro, E14 134 B3
Glengall Rd, NW6 108 C1
SE15 37 G5
Bexleyheath DA7 159 E3
Edgware HA8 54 B3
Woodford Green IG8 63 G6
Glengall Ter, SE15 37 G5
Glen Gdns, Croy. CR0 201 H3
Glengarnock Av, E14 134 C4
Glengarry Rd, SE22 152 B5
Glenham Dr, Ilf. IG2 80 E5
Glenhaven Av, Borwd. WD6 38 A3
Glenhead Cl, SE9 off Dumbreck Rd 156 E3
Glenhill Cl, N3 72 D2
Glenhouse Rd, SE9 156 D5
Glenhurst Av, NW5 92 A4
Bexley DA5 177 F1
Glenhurst Ct, SE19 170 C5
Glenhurst Ri, SE19 169 J7
Glenhurst Rd, N12 57 G5
Brentford TW8 125 F6
Glenilla Rd, NW3 91 H6
Glenister Ho, Hayes UB3 122 B1
Glenister Pk Rd, SW16 168 D7
Glenister Rd, SE10 135 F5
Glenister St, E16 136 D1
Glenkerry Ho, E14 off Burcham St 114 C6
Glenlea Path, SE9 off Well Hall Rd 156 C5
Glenlea Rd, SE9 156 C5
Glenloch Rd, NW3 91 H6
Enfield EN3 45 F2
Glenluce Rd, SE3 135 G7
Glenlyon Rd, SE9 156 D5
Glenmere Av, NW7 55 G7
Glenmere Row, SE12 155 G6
Glen Ms, E17 off Glen Rd 77 J5
Glenmill, Hmptn. TW12 161 F5
Glenmore Rd, NW3 91 H6
Welling DA16 157 J1
Glenmore Way, Bark. IG11 118 A3
Glenmount Path, SE18 off Raglan Rd 137 F5
Glennie Rd, SE27 169 G3
Glenny Rd, Bark. IG11 99 F6
Glenorchy Cl, Hayes UB4 103 E5
Glenparke Rd, E7 97 H6
Glen Ri, Wdf.Grn. IG8 63 H6
Glen Rd, E13 115 J4
E17 77 J5
Chessington KT9 195 H3
Glenrosa St, SW6 149 F2
Glenrose Ct, Sid. DA14 176 B5
Glenroy St, W12 107 J6
Glensdale Rd, SE4 153 J3
Glenshiel Rd, SE9 156 D5
Glenside, Chig. IG7 65 E6
Glentanner Way, SW17 167 G3
Glen Ter, E14 off Manchester Rd 134 C2
Glentham Gdns, SW13 off Glentham Rd 127 H6
Glentham Rd, SW13 127 G6
Glenthorne Av, Croy. CR0 203 E1
Glenthorne Cl, Sutt. SM3 198 D1
Glenthorne Gdns, Ilf. IG6 80 D3
Sutton SM3 198 D1
Glenthorne Ms, W6 off Glenthorne Rd 127 H4
Glenthorne Rd, E17 77 H5
N11 57 J5
W6 127 J4
Kingston upon Thames KT1 181 J4
Glenthorpe Rd, Mord. SM4 184 A5
Glenton Rd, SE13 154 E4
Glentrammon Av, Orp. BR6 207 J6
Glentrammon Cl, Orp. BR6 207 J6
Glentrammon Gdns, Orp. BR6 207 J6
Glentrammon Rd, Orp. BR6 207 J6
Glentworth St, NW1 8 A6
Glenure Rd, SE9 156 D5
Glenview, SE2 138 D6
Glenview Rd, Brom. BR1 192 A2
Glenville Gro, SE8 133 J7
Glenville Ms, SW18 148 E7
Glenville Rd, Kings.T. KT2 182 A1
Glen Wk, Islw. TW7 144 A5
Glenwood Av, NW9 88 E1
Glenwood Cl, Harrow HA1 68 C5
Glenwood Ct, E18 off Clarendon Rd 79 G3
Glenwood Gdns, Ilford IG2 80 D5
Glenwood Gro, NW9 88 C1
Glenwood Rd, N15 75 H5
NW7 55 E3
SE6 171 J1
Epsom KT17 197 G6
Hounslow TW3 144 A3
Glenwood Way, Croy. CR0 189 G6
Glenworth Av, E14 134 D4
Gliddon Dr, E5 94 D4
Gliddon Rd, W14 128 B4
Glimpsing Grn, Erith DA18 139 E3
Global App, E3 off Hancock Rd 114 B2
Globe Pond Rd, SE16 133 H1

Globe Rd, E1 113 F3
E2 113 F3
E15 97 F5
Woodford Green IG8 63 J6
Globe Rope Wk, E14 134 C4
Globe St, SE1 28 A5
Globe Ter, E2
off Globe Rd 113 F3
Globe Town, E2
off Mace St 113 G2
Globe Wf, SE16
off Rotherhithe St 113 G7
Globe Yd, W1 16 D4
Gloster Rd, N.Mal. KT3 182 E4
Gloucester Arc, SW7 30 C1
Gloucester Av, NW1 92 A7
Sidcup DA15 175 H2
Welling DA16 157 J4
Gloucester Circ, SE10 134 C7
Gloucester Cl, NW10 88 D7
Thames Ditton KT7 194 D1
Gloucester Ct, Rich. TW9 126 A7
Gloucester Cres, NW1 110 B1
Gloucester Dr, N4 93 H2
NW11 72 D4
Gloucester Gdns, NW11 72 C7
W2 14 B3
Barnet (Cockfos.) EN4 42 A4
Ilford IG1 80 B7
Sutton SM1 199 E2
Gloucester Gate, NW1 8 D1
Gloucester Gate Ms, NW1 8 D1
Gloucester Gro, Edg. HA8 70 D1
Gloucester Ho, NW6 108 D2
Gloucester Ms, E10
off Gloucester Rd 78 A7
W2 14 D4
Gloucester Ms W, W2 14 C4
Gloucester Par, Sid. DA15 158 A5
Gloucester Pk, SW7 30 C1
Gloucester Pl, NW1 7 J5
W1 16 A1
Gloucester Pl Ms, W1 16 A2
Gloucester Rd, E10 78 A7
E11 79 H5
E12 98 C3
E17 77 G2
N17 76 A2
N18 60 C5
SW7 22 C5
W3 126 C2
W5 125 F2
Barnet EN5 41 F5
Belvedere DA17 139 F5
Croydon CR0 188 A6
Feltham TW13 160 C1
Hampton TW12 161 H7
Harrow HA1 67 H5
Hounslow TW4 142 E4
Kingston upon Thames KT1 182 B2
Richmond TW9 126 A7
Teddington TW11 162 B5
Twickenham TW2 161 J1
Gloucester Sq, E2
off Whiston Rd 112 D1
W2 15 F4
Gloucester St, SW1 33 F4
Gloucester Ter, W2 14 C3
Gloucester Wk, W8 128 D2
Gloucester Way, EC1 11 F4
Glover Cl, SE2 138 C4
Glover Dr, N18 61 F6
Glover Rd, Pnr. HA5 66 D6
Gloxinia Wk, Hmptn. TW12 161 G6
Glycena Rd, SW11 149 J3
Glyn Av, Barn. EN4 41 G4
Glyn Cl, SE25 188 B2
Glyn Ct, SW16 169 G3
Stanmore HA7 52 E6
Glyndebourne Pk, Orp. BR6 207 E2
Glynde Ms, SW3 23 H6
Glynde Rd, Bexh. DA7 158 D3
Glynde St, SE4 153 J6
Glyndon Rd, SE18 137 F4
Glyn Dr, Sid. DA14 176 B4
Glynfield Rd, NW10 89 E7
Glynne Rd, N22 75 G2
Glyn Rd, E5 95 G3
Enfield EN3 45 F4
Worcester Park KT4 198 A2
Glyn St, SE11 34 C4
Glynwood Ct, SE23 171 F2
Goaters All, SW6 128 C7
Goat La, Surb. KT6 195 F2
Goat Rd, Mitch. CR4 186 A7
Goat Wf, Brent. TW8 125 H6
Godalming Av, Wall. SM6 201 E5
Godalming Rd, E14 114 B5
Godbold Rd, E15 114 E3
Goddard Pl, N19 92 C3
Goddard Rd, Beck. BR3 189 G4
Goddards Way, Ilf. IG1 99 G1
Godfrey Av, Nthlt. UB5 102 E1
Twickenham TW2 144 A7
Godfrey Hill, SE18 136 B4
Godfrey Ho, EC1 12 B4
Godfrey Pl, E2 13 F4
Godfrey Rd, SE18 136 C4
Godfrey St, E15 114 C2
SW3 31 H3
Godfrey Way, Houns. TW4 143 E7
Goding St, SE11 34 B4
Godley Cl, SE14
off Kender St 153 F1
Godley Rd, SW18 167 G1
Godliman St, EC4 19 J4
Godman Rd, SE15 152 E2
Godolphin Cl, N13 59 H6
Godolphin Pl, W3 106 D7
Godolphin Rd, W12 127 H2
Godson Rd, Croy. CR0 201 G3
Godson St, N1 11 E1
Godstone Rd, Sutt. SM1 199 F4
Twickenham TW1 144 D6
Godstow Rd, SE2 138 C2
Godwin Cl, N1 12 A1
Epsom KT19 196 C6
Godwin Ct, NW1 9 G1
Godwin Ho, NW6
off Tollgate Gdns 6 A1
Godwin Rd, E7 97 H4
Bromley BR2 191 J3
Goffers Rd, SE3 154 D1
Goidel Cl, Wall. SM6 200 D4
Golborne Gdns, W10
off Golborne Rd 108 C4
Golborne Ms, W10
off Portobello Rd 108 B5
Golborne Rd, W10 108 B5
Golda Cl, Barn. EN5 40 A6
Goldbeaters Gro, Edg. HA8 54 E6
Goldcliff Cl, Mord. SM4 184 D7
Goldcrest Cl, E16
off Sheerwater Rd 116 A5
SE28 118 C7
Goldcrest Ms, W5 105 G5
Goldcrest Way, Bushey WD23 51 J1
Golden Ct, Islw. TW7
off London Rd 144 A2
Richmond TW9
off George St 145 G5
Golden Cres, Hayes UB3 121 J1
Golden Cross Ms, W11
off Basing St 108 C6
★ **Golden Hinde**, SE1 28 B1
Golden Jubilee Br, SE1 26 C2
WC2 26 B1
Golden La, EC1 11 J6
Golden La Est, EC1 11 J6
Golden Manor, W7 104 B7
Golden Plover Cl, E16
off Maplin Rd 115 H6
Golden Sq, W1 17 G5
Golden Yd, NW3
off Heath St 91 F4
Golders Cl, Edg. HA8 54 B5
Golders Gdns, NW11 72 B7
GOLDERS GREEN, NW11 72 D7
Golders Grn Cres, NW11 72 C7
Golders Grn Rd, NW11 72 B6
Golders Manor Dr, NW11 72 A6
Golders Pk Cl, NW11 90 D1
Golders Ri, NW4 72 A5
Golders Way, NW11 72 C7
Goldfinch Rd, SE28 137 G3
Goldfinch Way, Borwd. WD6 38 A4
Goldhawk Ms, W12
off Devonport Rd 127 H2
Goldhawk Rd, W6 127 F4
W12 127 G3
Goldhaze Cl, Wdf.Grn. IG8 64 A7
Gold Hill, Edg. HA8 54 D6
Goldhurst Ter, NW6 90 E7
Golding Cl, Chess. KT9
off Coppard Gdns 195 F6
Golding Ct, Ilf. IG1 98 D3
Goldingham Av, Loug. IG10 49 F2
Goldings Hill, Loug. IG10 48 D1
Goldings Ri, Loug. IG10 48 D1
Goldings Rd, Loug. IG10 48 D1
Golding St, E1 21 J4
Golding Ter, SW11
off Longhedge St 150 A2
Goldington Cres, NW1 9 H1
Goldington St, NW1 9 H1
Gold La, Edg. HA8 54 D6
Goldman Cl, E2 13 H5
Goldmark Ho, SE3
off Lebrun Sq 155 H3
Goldney Rd, W9 108 D4
Goldrill Dr, N11 58 A2
Goldsboro Rd, SW8 150 D1
Goldsborough Cres, E4 62 C2
Goldsdown Cl, Enf. EN3 45 H2
Goldsdown Rd, Enf. EN3 45 G2
Goldsmid St, SE18
off Sladedale Rd 137 H5
Goldsmith Av, E12 98 B6
NW9 71 F6
W3 106 D7
Romford RM7 83 G7
Goldsmith Cl, W3 126 D1
Harrow HA2 85 H1
Goldsmith Ct, Edg. HA8 53 J4
Goldsmith La, NW9 70 B4
Goldsmith Rd, E10 96 A1
E17 77 G2
N11 57 J5
SE15 152 D1
W3 126 D1
★ **Goldsmiths' Hall**, EC2 19 J3
Goldsmith's Pl, NW6
off Springfield La 108 E1
Goldsmith's Row, E2 13 H2
Goldsmith's Sq, E2 13 J1
Goldsmith St, EC2 20 A3
Goldsworthy Gdns, SE16 133 F4
Goldwell Ho, SE22
off Quorn Rd 152 B3
Goldwell Rd, Th.Hth. CR7 187 F4
Goldwin Cl, SE14 153 F1
Goldwing Cl, E16 115 G6
Golf Cl, Stan. HA7 53 F7
Thornton Heath CR7
off Kensington Av 187 G1
Golf Club Dr, Kings.T. KT2 164 D7
Golfe Rd, Ilf. IG1 99 G3
Golf Rd, W5
off Boileau Rd 105 J6
Bromley BR1 192 D3
Golf Side, Twick. TW2 162 A3
Golfside Cl, N20 57 H3
New Malden KT3 183 E2
Gollogly Ter, SE7 135 J5
Gomer Gdns, Tedd. TW11 162 D6
Gomer Pl, Tedd. TW11 162 D6
Gomm Rd, SE16 133 F3
Gomshall Av, Wall. SM6 200 E5
Gondar Gdns, NW6 90 C5
Gonson St, SE8 134 B6
Gonston Cl, SW19 166 B2
Gonville Cres, Nthlt. UB5 85 H6
Gonville Rd, Th.Hth. CR7 187 F5
Gonville St, SW6
off Putney Br App 148 B3
Gooch Ho, E5 94 E3
Goodall Rd, E11 96 C3
Gooden Ct, Har. HA1 86 B3
Goodenough Rd, SW19 166 C7
Goodey Rd, Bark. IG11 99 J7
Goodge Pl, W1 17 G2
Goodge St, W1 17 G2
Goodhall Cl, Stan. HA7 52 D6
Goodhall St, NW10 107 E3
Goodhart Pl, E14 113 H7
Goodhart Way, W.Wick. BR4 190 E7
Goodhew Rd, Croy. CR0 188 D6
Gooding Cl, N.Mal. KT3 182 C4
Goodinge Cl, N7 92 E6
Goodman Cres, SW2 168 D2
Goodman Rd, E10 78 C7
Goodmans Ct, E1 21 F5
Wembley HA0 87 G4
Goodman's Stile, E1 21 H3
Goodmans Yd, E1 21 F5
GOODMAYES, Ilf. IG3 100 B2
Goodmayes Av, Ilf. IG3 100 A1
Goodmayes La, Ilf. IG3 100 A4
Goodmayes Retail Pk, Rom. RM6 *off High Rd* 100 B1
Goodmayes Rd, Ilf. IG3 100 A1
Goodrich Rd, SE22 152 C6
Goodson Rd, NW10 89 E7
Goods Way, NW1 10 A1
Goodway Gdns, E14 114 D6
Goodwill Dr, Har. HA2 85 G1
Goodwin Cl, SE16 29 G6
Mitcham CR4 185 G3
Goodwin Ct, Barn. EN4 41 H6
Goodwin Dr, Sid. DA14 176 D3
Goodwin Gdns, Croy. CR0 201 H6
Goodwin Rd, N9 61 F1
W12 127 G2
Croydon CR0 201 H5
Goodwins Ct, WC2 18 A5
Goodwin St, N4
off Fonthill Rd 93 G2
Goodwood Cl, Mord. SM4 184 D4
Stanmore HA7 53 F5
Goodwood Dr, Nthlt. UB5 85 G6
Goodwood Path, Borwd. WD6 38 A2
Goodwood Rd, SE14 133 H7
Goodwyn Av, NW7 55 E5
Goodwyns Vale, N10 74 A1
Goodyers Gdns, NW4 72 A5
Goosander Way, SE28 137 G3
Gooseacre La, Har. HA3 69 G5
Gooseley La, E6 116 D3
Goosens Cl, Sutt. SM1
off Turnpike La 199 F5
Goose Sq, E6
off Harper Rd 116 C6
Gophir La, EC4 20 B5
Gopsall St, N1 112 A1
Goran Ct, N9
off Bedevere Rd 60 D3
Gordon Av, E4 62 E6
SW14 146 E4
Stanmore HA7 52 E6
Twickenham TW1 144 D5
Gordonbrock Rd, SE4 154 A5
Gordon Cl, E17 78 A6
N19
off Highgate Hill 92 C1
Gordon Cres, Croy. CR0 202 B1
Hayes UB3 122 A3
Gordondale Rd, SW19 166 D2
Gordon Gdns, Edg. HA8 70 B2
Gordon Gro, SE5 151 H2
Gordon Hill, Enf. EN2 43 J1
Gordon Ho, E1
off Glamis Rd 113 F7
Gordon Ho Rd, NW5 92 A4
Gordon Pl, W8 128 D2
Gordon Rd, E4 47 E7
E11 79 G6
E15 96 C4
E18 79 H1
N3 56 C7
N9 61 E2
N11 58 D7
SE15 152 E2
W4 126 B6
W5 105 F7
W13 104 E7
Barking IG11 117 H1
Beckenham BR3 189 J3
Belvedere DA17 139 J4
Carshalton SM5 199 J6
Enfield EN2 43 J1
Esher (Clay.) KT10 194 B6
Harrow HA3 68 B3
Hounslow TW3 143 J4
Ilford IG1 99 G3
Kingston upon Thames KT2 181 J1
Richmond TW9 145 J2
Romford RM6 83 F6
Sidcup DA15 157 H5
Southall UB2 123 E4
Surbiton KT5 181 J7
Gordon Sq, WC1 9 J6
Gordon St, E13
off Grange Rd 115 G3
WC1 9 H5
Gordon Way, Barn. EN5 40 C4
Bromley BR1 191 G1
Gore Ct, NW9 70 A5
Gorefield Pl, NW6 108 D2
Gore Rd, E9 113 F1
SW20 183 J2
Goresbrook Rd, Dag. RM9 118 B1
Goresbrook Village, Dag. RM9
off Goresbrook Rd 118 B1
Gore St, SW7 22 D5
Gorham Pl, W11
off Mary Pl 108 B7
Goring Cl, Rom. RM5 83 J1
Goring Gdns, Dag. RM8 100 C4
Goring Rd, N11 58 E6
Goring St, EC3 21 E3
Goring Way, Grnf. UB6 103 J2
Gorleston Rd, N15 76 A5
Gorleston St, W14 128 B4
Gorman Rd, SE18 136 C4
Gorringe Pk Av, Mitch. CR4 167 J7
Gorse Cl, E16 115 G6
Gorse Ri, SW17 168 A5
Gorse Rd, Croy. CR0 204 A4
Gorst Rd, NW10 106 C4
SW11 149 J6
Gorsuch Pl, E2 13 F3
Gorsuch St, E2 13 F3
Gosberton Rd, SW12 168 A1
Gosbury Hill, Chess. KT9 195 H4
Gosfield Rd, Dag. RM8 101 G2
Gosfield St, W1 17 F1
Gosford Gdns, Ilf. IG4 80 C5
Gosforth La, Wat. WD19 50 C3
Gosforth Path, Wat. WD19 50 A3
Goshawk Way, Felt. TW14
off Falcon Way 142 B5
Goslett Yd, WC2 17 J4
Gosling Cl, Grnf. UB6 103 G3
Gosling Way, SW9 151 G1
Gospatrick Rd, N17 59 J7
GOSPEL OAK, NW5 92 A4
Gosport Rd, E17 77 J5
Gosport Wk, N17
off Yarmouth Cres 76 E5

Gossage Rd, SE18 .... **137** G5
Gosset St, E2 .... **13** G3
Gosshill Rd, Chis. BR7 .... **192** D2
Gossington Cl, Chis. BR7 *off Beechwood Ri* **175** E4
Gosterwood St, SE8 .... **133** H6
Gostling Rd, Twick. TW2 .... **161** G1
Goston Gdns, Th.Hth. CR7 .... **187** G3
Goswell Rd, EC1 .... **11** J6
Gothic Ct, Hayes UB3 *off Sipson La* **121** G6
Gothic Rd, Twick. TW2 .... **162** A2
Gottfried Ms, NW5 *off Fortess Rd* **92** C4
Goudhurst Rd, Brom. BR1 .... **173** E5
Gough Rd, E15 .... **97** F4
Enfield EN1 .... **44** E2
Gough Sq, EC4 .... **19** F3
Gough St, WC1 .... **10** D5
Gough Wk, E14 *off Saracen St* **114** A6
Gould Ct, SE19 .... **170** B5
Goulden Ho App, SW11 .... **149** H2
Goulding Gdns, Th.Hth. CR7 .... **187** H2
Gould Rd, Felt. TW14 .... **141** H7
Twickenham TW2 .... **162** B1
Gould Ter, E8 *off Kenmure Rd* **95** E5
Goulston St, E1 .... **21** F3
Goulton Rd, E5 .... **95** E4
Gourley Pl, N15 *off Gourley St* **76** B5
Gourley St, N15 .... **76** B5
Gourock Rd, SE9 .... **156** D5
Govan St, E2 *off Whiston Rd* **112** D1
Govier Cl, E15 .... **97** E7
Gowan Av, SW6 .... **148** B1
Gowan Rd, NW10 .... **89** H6
Gower Cl, SW4 .... **150** C6
Gower Ct, WC1 .... **9** H5
Gower Ms, WC1 .... **17** H2
Gower Pl, WC1 .... **9** G5
Gower Rd, E7 .... **97** G6
Isleworth TW7 .... **124** C6
Gower St, WC1 .... **9** G5
Gower's Wk, E1 .... **21** H3
Gowland Pl, Beck. BR3 .... **189** J2
Gowlett Rd, SE15 .... **152** D3
Gowlland Cl, Croy. CR0 .... **188** D7
Gowrie Rd, SW11 .... **150** A3
Graburn Way, E.Mol. KT8 .... **180** A3
Grace Av, Bexh. DA7 .... **159** F2
Grace Business Cen, Mitch. CR4 .... **185** J6
Gracechurch St, EC3 .... **20** C5
Grace Cl, SE9 .... **174** A3
Borehamwood WD6 .... **38** D1
Edgware HA8 .... **54** C7
Ilford IG6 .... **65** J6
Gracedale Rd, SW16 .... **168** B5
Gracefield Gdns, SW16 .... **169** E3
Grace Jones Cl, E8 *off Parkholme Rd* **94** D6
Grace Path, SE26 .... **171** F4
Grace Pl, E3 *off St. Leonards St* **114** B3
Grace Rd, Croy. CR0 .... **187** J6
Grace's All, E1 .... **21** H5
Graces Ms, SE5 .... **152** B2
Graces Rd, SE5 .... **152** B2
Grace St, E3 .... **114** B3
Gradient, The, SE26 .... **170** D4
Graduate Pl, SE1 *off Long La* **28** D5
Graeme Rd, Enf. EN1 .... **44** A2
Graemesdyke Av, SW14 .... **146** B3
Grafton Cl, W13 .... **104** D6
Hounslow TW4 .... **161** E1
Worcester Park KT4 .... **197** E3
Grafton Cres, NW1 .... **92** B6
Grafton Gdns, N4 .... **75** J6
Dagenham RM8 .... **101** E2
Grafton Ho, E3 .... **114** A3
Grafton Ms, W1 .... **9** F6
Grafton Pk Rd, Wor.Pk. KT4 .... **196** E2
Grafton Pl, NW1 .... **9** H4
Grafton Rd, NW5 .... **92** A5
W3 .... **106** C7
Croydon CR0 .... **201** G1
Dagenham RM8 .... **101** E2
Enfield EN2 .... **43** F3
Harrow HA1 .... **67** J5
New Malden KT3 .... **182** E3
Worcester Park KT4 .... **196** D3
Graftons, The, NW2 *off Hermitage La* **90** D3
Grafton Sq, SW4 .... **150** C3
Grafton St, W1 .... **17** E6
Grafton Ter, NW5 .... **91** J5
Grafton Way, W1 .... **9** F6
WC1 .... **9** F6
West Molesey KT8 .... **179** F4
Grafton Yd, NW5 *off Prince of Wales Rd* **92** B6
Graham Av, W13 .... **124** E2
Mitcham CR4 .... **186** A1
Graham Cl, Croy. CR0 .... **204** A2
Grahame Pk Est, NW9 .... **71** E1
Grahame Pk Way, NW7 .... **55** F7
NW9 .... **71** F2
Graham Gdns, Surb. KT6 .... **195** H1
Graham Rd, E8 .... **94** C6
E13 .... **115** G4
N15 .... **75** H3
NW4 .... **71** H6
SW19 .... **166** C7
W4 .... **126** D3
Bexleyheath DA6 .... **159** G4
Hampton TW12 .... **161** G4
Harrow HA3 .... **68** B3
Mitcham CR4 .... **186** A1
Graham St, N1 .... **11** H2
Graham Ter, SW1 .... **32** B2
Grainger Cl, Nthlt. UB5 *off Lancaster Rd* **85** J5
Grainger Rd, N22 .... **75** J1
Isleworth TW7 .... **144** C2
Gramer Cl, E11 *off Norman Rd* **96** D2
Grampian Cl, Hayes (Harling.) UB3 .... **121** G7
Orpington BR6 *off Clovelly Way* **193** J6
Sutton SM2 .... **199** F7
Grampian Gdns, NW2 .... **90** B1
Grampian Ho, N9 *off Edmonton Grn Shop Cen* **60** E2
Gramsci Way, SE6 .... **172** B3
Granard Av, SW15 .... **147** H5
Granard Business Cen, NW7 *off Bunns La* **55** E6
Granard Rd, SW12 .... **149** J7
Granary Cl, N9 .... **45** F7
Granary Mans, SE28 .... **137** F2
Granary Rd, E1 .... **112** E4
Granary Sq, N1 *off Liverpool Rd* **93** G6
Granary St, NW1 .... **110** D1
Granby Pl, SE1 .... **26** E4
Granby Rd, SE9 .... **156** C2
Granby St, E2 .... **13** G5
Granby Ter, NW1 .... **9** F2
Grand Arc, N12 *off Ballards La* **57** F5
Grand Av, EC1 .... **19** H1
N10 .... **74** A4
Surbiton KT5 .... **182** B5
Wembley HA9 .... **88** A5
Grand Av E, Wem. HA9 .... **88** B5
Grand Dep Rd, SE18 .... **136** D5
Grand Dr, SW20 .... **183** J2
Southall UB2 .... **123** J2
Granden Rd, SW16 .... **187** E2
Grandison Rd, SW11 .... **149** J5
Worcester Park KT4 .... **197** J2
Grand Junct Wf, N1 .... **11** J2
Grand Par, N4 *off Green Las* **75** H6
Wembley HA9 *off Forty Av* **88** A2
Grand Par Ms, SW15 .... **148** B5
Grand Union Canal Wk, W7 .... **124** B3
Grand Union Cl, W9 *off Woodfield Rd* **108** C5
Grand Union Cres, E8 .... **94** D7
Grand Union Hts, Wem. HA0 .... **105** G1
Grand Union Ind Est, NW10 .... **106** B2
Grand Union Wk, NW1 .... **92** B7
Grand Union Way, Sthl. UB2 *off Bridge Rd* **123** G2
Grand Wk, E1 *off Solebay St* **113** H4
Granfield St, SW11 .... **149** G1
Grange, The, N20 .... **57** F1
SE1 .... **29** F5
SW19 .... **166** A6
W14 *off Lisgar Ter* **128** C4
Croydon CR0 .... **203** J2
Wembley HA0 .... **88** A7
Worcester Park KT4 .... **196** D3
Grange Av, N12 .... **57** F5
N20 .... **40** B7
SE25 .... **188** B2
Barnet (E.Barn.) EN4 .... **57** H1
Stanmore HA7 .... **69** E2
Twickenham TW2 .... **162** B2
Woodford Green IG8 .... **63** G6
Grangecliffe Gdns, SE25 .... **188** B2
Grange Cl, Edg. HA8 .... **54** C5
Hounslow TW5 .... **123** F6
Sidcup DA15 .... **176** A3
West Molesey KT8 .... **179** H4
Woodford Green IG8 .... **63** G7
Grange Ct, WC2 .... **18** D4
Chigwell IG7 .... **65** F2
Grange Ct, Loughton IG10 .... **48** A5
Northolt UB5 .... **102** C2
Grangecourt Rd, N16 .... **94** B1
Grange Cres, SE28 .... **118** C6
Chigwell IG7 .... **65** G5
Grange Dr, Chis. BR7 .... **174** B6
Grange Est, The, N2 .... **73** G2
Grange Fm Cl, Har. HA2 .... **85** J2
Grange Gdns, N14 .... **58** D1
NW3 .... **91** E3
SE25 .... **188** B2
Pinner HA5 .... **67** F4
Grange Gro, N1 .... **93** H6
GRANGE HILL, Chig. IG7 .... **65** G6
Grange Hill, SE25 .... **188** B2
Edgware HA8 .... **54** C5
Grangehill Pl, SE9 *off Westmount Rd* **156** C3
Grangehill Rd, SE9 .... **156** C4
Grange Ho, Bark. IG11 *off St. Margarets* **117** G1
Grange La, SE21 .... **170** C2
Grange Mans, Epsom KT17 .... **197** F7
Grangemill Rd, SE6 .... **172** A3
Grangemill Way, SE6 .... **172** A2
GRANGE PARK, N21 .... **43** H5
Grange Pk, W5 .... **125** H1
Grange Pk Av, N21 .... **43** H6
Grange Pk Pl, SW20 .... **165** H7
Grange Pk Rd, E10 .... **96** B1
Thornton Heath CR7 .... **188** A4
Grange Pl, NW6 .... **90** D7
Grange Rd, E10 .... **96** A1
E13 .... **115** F3
E17 .... **77** H5
N6 .... **74** A6
N17 .... **60** D6
N18 .... **60** D6
NW10 .... **89** H6
SE1 .... **28** E5
SE19 .... **188** A4
SE25 .... **188** A4
SW13 .... **147** G1
W4 .... **126** B5
W5 .... **125** G1
Chessington KT9 .... **195** H4
Edgware HA8 .... **54** D6
Harrow HA1 .... **68** D6
Harrow (S.Har.) HA2 .... **86** A2
Ilford IG1 .... **99** E4
Kingston upon Thames KT1 .... **181** H3
Orpington BR6 .... **207** F2
Southall UB1 .... **122** E2
Sutton SM2 .... **198** D7
Thornton Heath CR7 .... **188** A4
West Molesey KT8 .... **179** H4
Grange St, N1 .... **112** A1
Grange Vale, Sutt. SM2 .... **199** E7
Grange Vw Rd, N20 .... **57** F1
Grange Wk, SE1 .... **28** E5
Grange Wk Ms, SE1 .... **29** E6
Grangeway, N12 .... **57** E4
NW6 *off Messina Av* **90** D7
Woodford Green IG8 .... **63** J4
Grangeway, The, N21 .... **43** H6
Grangeway Gdns, Ilf. IG4 .... **80** B5
Grangewood, Bex. DA5 *off Hurst Rd* **177** F1
Grangewood Cl, Pnr. HA5 .... **66** A5
Grangewood La, Beck. BR3 .... **171** J6
Grangewood St, E6 .... **115** J1
Grangewood Ter, SE25 *off Grange Rd* **188** A2
Grange Yd, SE1 .... **29** F6
Granham Gdns, N9 .... **60** C2
Granite Apts, E15 *off Windmill La* **96** D6
Granite St, SE18 .... **137** J5
Granleigh Rd, E11 .... **96** E2
Gransden Av, E8 .... **95** E7
Gransden Rd, W12 *off Wendell Rd* **127** F2
Grantbridge St, N1 .... **11** H1
Grantchester Cl, Har. HA1 .... **86** C3
Grant Cl, N14 .... **42** C7
N17 .... **76** B2
Grant Ct, E4 *off The Ridgeway* **62** C1
Grantham Cl, Edg. HA8 .... **53** H3
Grantham Gdns, Rom. RM6 .... **83** F6
Grantham Grn, Borwd. WD6 .... **38** C5
Grantham Pl, W1 .... **24** D2
Grantham Rd, E12 .... **98** D4
SW9 .... **151** E2
W4 .... **126** E7
Grantley Rd, Houns. TW4 .... **142** C2
Grantley St, E1 .... **113** G3
Grantock Rd, E17 .... **78** D1
Granton Rd, SW16 .... **186** C1
Ilford IG3 .... **100** A1
Sidcup DA14 .... **176** C6
Grant Pl, Croy. CR0 .... **202** C1
Grant Rd, SW11 .... **149** G4
Croydon CR0 .... **202** C1
Harrow HA3 .... **68** B3
Grants Cl, NW7 .... **55** J7
Grant's Quay Wf, EC3 .... **20** C6
Grant St, E13 .... **115** G3
N1 .... **11** E1
Grantully Rd, W9 .... **6** A4
Grant Way, Islw. TW7 .... **124** D6
Granville Av, N9 .... **61** F3
Feltham TW13 .... **160** A2
Hounslow TW3 .... **143** G5
Granville Cl, Croy. CR0 .... **202** B2
Granville Ct, N1 .... **112** A1
Granville Gdns, SW16 .... **187** F1
W5 .... **125** J1
Granville Gro, SE13 .... **154** C3
Granville Ind Est, NW2 .... **90** C2
Granville Ms, Sid. DA14 .... **176** A4
Granville Pk, SE13 .... **154** C3
Granville Pl,
N12 (N.Finchley) **57** F7
SW6 *off Maxwell Rd* **129** E7
W1 .... **16** B4
Pinner HA5 .... **66** D3
Granville Pt, NW2 .... **90** C2
Granville Rd, E17 .... **78** B6
E18 .... **79** H2
N4 .... **75** F6
N12 .... **57** E7
N13 .... **59** F6
N22 .... **75** H1
NW2 .... **90** C2
NW6 .... **108** D2
SW18 .... **148** D7
SW19 *off Russell Rd* **166** D7
Barnet EN5 .... **39** J4
Hayes UB3 .... **121** J4
Ilford IG1 .... **98** E1
Sidcup DA14 .... **176** A4
Welling DA16 .... **158** C3
Granville Sq, SE15 .... **36** E7
WC1 .... **10** D4
Granville St, WC1 .... **10** D4
Grape St, WC2 .... **18** A3
Graphite Sq, SE11 .... **34** C3
Grapsome Cl, Chess. KT9 *off Nigel Fisher Way* **195** F7
Grasdene Rd, SE18 .... **138** A7
Grasgarth Cl, W3 .... **106** C7
Grasmere Av, SW15 .... **164** D4
SW19 .... **184** D3
W3 .... **106** C7
Hounslow TW3 .... **143** H6
Orpington BR6 .... **206** E3
Wembley HA9 .... **69** G7
Grasmere Cl, Loug. IG10 .... **48** C2
Grasmere Ct, N22 .... **59** F6
Grasmere Gdns, Har. HA3 .... **68** D2
Ilford IG4 .... **80** C5
Orpington BR6 .... **206** E3
Grasmere Pt, SE15 *off Ilderton Rd* **133** F7
Grasmere Rd, E13 .... **115** G2
N10 .... **74** B1
N17 .... **60** D6
SE25 .... **189** E6
SW16 .... **169** F5
Bexleyheath DA7 .... **159** J1
Bromley BR1 .... **191** F1
Orpington BR6 .... **206** E3
Grasshaven Way, SE28 .... **137** J1
Grassington Cl, N11 .... **58** A5
Grassington Rd, Sid. DA14 .... **176** A4
Grassmount, SE23 .... **171** E2
Grass Pk, N3 .... **72** C1
Grassway, Wall. SM6 .... **200** C4
Grasvenor Av, Barn. EN5 .... **40** D6
Gratton Rd, W14 .... **128** B3
Gratton Ter, NW2 .... **90** A3
Graveley, Kings.T. KT1 *off Willingham Way* **182** A2
Graveley Av, Borwd. WD6 .... **38** C4
Gravel Hill, N3 .... **72** C2
Bexleyheath DA6 .... **159** H5
Croydon CR0 .... **203** G6
Gravel Hill Cl, Bexh. DA6 .... **159** H5
Gravel La, E1 .... **21** F3
Gravelly Ride, SW19 .... **165** H4
Gravel Pit La, SE9 .... **157** F5
Gravel Rd, Brom. BR2 .... **206** B2
Twickenham TW2 .... **162** B1
Gravelwood Cl, Chis. BR7 .... **175** F3
Gravenel Gdns, SW17 *off Nutwell St* **167** H5
Graveney Gro, SE20 .... **171** F7
Graveney Rd, SW17 .... **167** H4
Gravesend Rd, W12 .... **107** G7
Graves Yd Ind Est, Well. DA16 *off Upper Wickham La* **158** B2
Gray Av, Dag. RM8 .... **101** F1
Grayham Cres, N.Mal. KT3 .... **182** D4

Grayham Rd, N.Mal. KT3 .182 D4
Grayland Cl, Brom. BR1 . .192 A1
Grayling Cl, E16
off Cranberry La 115 E4
Grayling Rd, N16 . . . . .94 A2
Grayling Sq, E2 . . . . .13 J3
Grayscroft Rd, SW16 . . . . .168 D7
Grayshott Rd, SW11 . . . . .150 A2
★ **Gray's Inn**, WC1 . . . . . . .18 D1
Gray's Inn Pl, WC1 . . . . .18 D2
Gray's Inn Rd, WC1 . . . . . . .10 C4
Gray's Inn Sq, WC1 . . . . . . .18 E1
Grayson Ho, EC1 . . . . .12 A4
Gray St, SE1 . . . . .27 F4
Grayswood Gdns, SW20
off Farnham Gdns 183 H2
Grayswood Pt, SW15
off Norley Vale 165 G1
Gray's Yd, W1 . . . . .16 C4
Graywood Ct, N12 . . . . .57 F7
Grazebrook Rd, N16 . . . . . .94 A2
Grazeley Cl, Bexh. DA6 . . .159 J5
Grazeley Ct, SE19
off Gipsy Hill 170 B5
Great Acre Ct, SW4
off Clapham Pk Rd . . .150 D4
Great Amwell La, N8 . . . . . .75 F3
Great Arthur Ho, EC1 . . . . . .11 J6
Great Bell All, EC2 . . . . . . .20 B3
Great Benty, West Dr.
UB7 . . . . .120 B4
Great Brownings, SE21 . . .170 C4
Great Bushey Dr, N20 . . . . .57 E1
Great Cambridge Ind Est,
Enf. EN1 . . . . .44 D5
Great Cambridge Junct,
N18 . . . . .60 A4
Great Cambridge Rd, N9 . . .60 B1
N17 . . . . .60 A5
N18 . . . . .60 A5
Enfield EN1 . . . . .44 D4
Great Castle St, W1 . . . . . . .17 E3
Great Cen Av, Ruis. HA4 . . .84 C5
Great Cen St, NW1 . . . . . . .15 J1
Great Cen Way, NW10 . . . . .88 E5
Wembley HA9 . . . . .88 C4
Great Chapel St, W1 . . . . . .17 H3
Great Chart St, SW11 . . . . .149 G4
Great Chertsey Rd, W4 . . .146 C2
Feltham TW13 . . . . .161 G3
Great Ch La, W6 . . . . .128 A5
Great Coll St, SW1 . . . . . . .26 A5
Great Cross Av, SE10 . . . . .134 E7
Great Cumberland Ms,
W1 . . . . .15 J4
Great Cumberland Pl, W1 . .15 J3
Great Dover St, SE1 . . . . . .28 A4
Greatdown Rd, W7 . . . . . . .104 C4
**Great Eastern Enterprise
Cen**, E14 . . . . .134 B2
Great Eastern Rd, E15 . . . . .96 D7
Great Eastern St, EC2 . . . . .12 D4
Great Eastern Wk, EC2 . . . .20 E2
Great Elms Rd, Brom.
BR2 . . . . .191 J4
Great Fld, NW9 . . . . .71 E1
Greatfield Av, E6 . . . . .116 C4
Greatfield Cl, N19
off Warrender Rd 92 C4
SE4 . . . . .154 A4
Greatfields Rd, Bark.
IG11 . . . . .117 G1
Great Fleete Way, Bark. IG11
off Choats Rd 118 C2
Great Galley Cl, Bark.
IG11 . . . . .118 B3
Great Gatton Cl, Croy.
CR0 . . . . .189 H7
Great George St, SW1 . . . . .25 J4
Great Guildford St, SE1 . . .27 J1
Great Hall, SW11
off Battersea Pk Rd . . .150 A1
Greatham Wk, SW15 . . . . . .165 G1
Great Harry Dr, SE9 . . . . . .174 D3
Great James St, WC1 . . . . .10 C6
Great Marlborough St,
W1 . . . . .17 F4
Great Maze Pond, SE1 . . . .28 C3
Great Newport St, WC2
off Charing Cross Rd . . .17 J5
Great New St, EC4 . . . . . . .19 F3
Great N Leisure Pk, N12 . . .57 G7
Great N Rd, N2 . . . . .73 H4
N6 . . . . .73 H4
Barnet (New Barn.)
EN5 . . . . .40 D5
Great N Way, NW4 . . . . . . .71 J2
Great Oaks, Chig. IG7 . . . . .65 F4
Greatorex St, E1 . . . . .21 H1
Great Ormond St, WC1 . . . .18 B1
Great Owl Rd, Chig. IG7 . . . .64 D3
Great Percy St, WC1 . . . . . .10 D3
Great Peter St, SW1 . . . . . .25 H6
Great Portland St, W1 . . . . .17 E1
Great Pulteney St, W1 . . . . .17 G5
Great Queen St, WC2 . . . . .18 B4
Great Russell St, WC1 . . . . .17 J3
Great St. Helens, EC3 . . . . .20 D3
Great St. Thomas Apostle,
EC4 . . . . .20 A5
Great Scotland Yd, SW1 . . .26 A2
Great Smith St, SW1 . . . . . .25 J5
Great South-West Rd, Felt.
TW14 . . . . .141 F7
Hounslow TW4 . . . . .141 J4
Great Spilmans, SE22 . . . .152 B5
Great Strand, NW9 . . . . . . .71 F1
Great Suffolk St, SE1 . . . . .27 H2
Great Sutton St, EC1 . . . . . .11 H6
Great Swan All, EC2 . . . . . .20 B3
Great Thrift, Orp. BR5 . . . .193 F4
Great Titchfield St, W1 . . . . .17 F3
Great Twr St, EC3 . . . . .20 D5
Great Trade Cen, NW10
off Hythe Rd 107 G4
Great Trinity La, EC4 . . . . . .20 A5
Great Turnstile, WC1 . . . . . .18 D2
Great Western Rd, W2 . . . .108 C5
W9 . . . . .108 C5
W11 . . . . .108 C5
Great W Rd, W4 . . . . .126 B5
W6 . . . . .127 F5
Brentford TW8 . . . . .126 B5
Hounslow TW5 . . . . .142 D2
Isleworth TW7 . . . . .124 B7
Great Winchester St,
EC2 . . . . .20 C3
Great Windmill St, W1 . . . . .17 H5
Greatwood, Chis. BR7 . . . .174 D7
Great Yd, SE1 . . . . .28 E3
Greaves Cl, Bark. IG11 . . . . .99 G7
Greaves Pl, SW17 . . . . .167 H4
Greaves Twr, SW10 . . . . . . .30 D7
Grebe Av, Hayes UB4
off Cygnet Way 102 D6
Grebe Cl, E7
off Cormorant Rd 97 F5
E17 . . . . .61 H7
Barking IG11 . . . . .118 A4
Grebe Ct, Sutt. SM1 . . . . . .198 C5
Grecian Cres, SE19 . . . . . .169 H6
Gredo Ho, Bark. IG11 . . . . .118 B3
Greek Ct, W1 . . . . .17 J4
★ **Greek Orthodox Cath
of the Divine Wisdom
(St. Sophia)**, W2 . . . . . .14 A5
Greek St, W1 . . . . .17 J4
Green, The, E4 . . . . .62 C1
E11 . . . . .79 H6
E15 . . . . .97 E6
N9 . . . . .60 D2
N14 . . . . .58 D3
N17 . . . . .59 J6
N21 . . . . .43 G7
SW14 . . . . .146 C3
SW19 . . . . .166 A5
W3 . . . . .107 E6
W5 *off High St* 105 G7
Bexleyheath DA7 . . . . . .159 G1
Bromley BR1
off Downham Way 173 G3
Bromley (Hayes) BR2 . . .191 G7
Carshalton SM5
off High St 200 A4
Esher (Clay.) KT10 . . . . .194 C6
Feltham TW13 . . . . .160 B2
Hounslow TW5
off Heston Rd 123 G6
Morden SM4 . . . . .184 B4
New Malden KT3 . . . . . .182 C3
Orpington (St.P.Cray)
BR5 *off The Avenue* . . .176 B7
Richmond TW9 . . . . .145 G5
Sidcup DA14 . . . . .176 A4
Southall UB2 . . . . .123 G6
Sutton SM1 . . . . .198 E3
Twickenham TW2 . . . . . .162 B1
Welling DA16 . . . . .157 H4
Wembley HA0 . . . . .86 D2
West Drayton UB7 . . . . .120 A3
Woodford Green IG8 . . . .63 G5
Greenacre Cl, Nthlt. UB5 . . .85 F5
Greenacre Gdns, E17 . . . . . .78 C4
Greenacre Pl, Wall. (Hackbr.)
SM6 *off Park Rd* 200 B2
Greenacres, N3 . . . . .72 B2
SE9 . . . . .156 D6
Barnet EN4 . . . . .41 G4
Bushey (Bushey Hth)
WD23 . . . . .52 A2
Green Acres, Croy. CR0 . . .202 C3
Greenacres Cl, Orp. BR6 . . .207 F4
Greenacres Dr, Stan. HA7 . .52 E7
Greenacre Sq, SE16
off Fishermans Dr 133 G2
Greenacre Wk, N14 . . . . . . .58 D3
Green Arbour Ct, EC1 . . . . .19 G3
Green Av, NW7 . . . . .54 D4
W13 . . . . .125 E3
Greenaway Av, N18 . . . . . . .61 G6
Greenaway Gdns, NW3 . . . .90 E4
Green Bk, E1 . . . . .132 E1
N12 . . . . .57 E4
Greenbank Av, Wem. HA0 . .86 D5
Greenbank Cl, E4 . . . . .62 C2
Greenbank Cres, NW4 . . . . .72 B4
Greenbay Rd, SE7 . . . . . . .136 A7
Greenberry St, NW8 . . . . . . .7 G2
Greenbrook Av, Barn. EN4 .41 F1
Green Cl, NW9 . . . . .70 C6
NW11 . . . . .73 F7
Bromley BR2 . . . . .190 E3
Carshalton SM5 . . . . . . .199 J2
Feltham TW13 . . . . .160 E5
Greencoat Pl, SW1 . . . . .33 G1
Greencoat Row, SW1 . . . . .25 G6
Greencourt Av, Croy.
CR0 . . . . .203 E2
Edgware HA8 . . . . .70 B1
Greencourt Gdns, Croy.
CR0 . . . . .203 E1
Greencourt Rd, Orp. BR5 .193 G5
Greencrest Pl, NW2
off Dollis Hill La 89 G3
Greencroft, Edg. HA8 . . . . .54 C5
Greencroft Av, Ruis. HA4 . . .84 C2
Greencroft Cl, E6
off Neatscourt Rd 116 B5
Greencroft Gdns, NW6 . . . .91 E7
Enfield EN1 . . . . .44 B3
Greencroft Rd, Houns.
TW5 . . . . .143 F1
Green Dale, SE5 . . . . .152 A4
SE22 . . . . .152 B5
Green Dale Cl, SE22
off Green Dale 152 B5
Green Dragon Ct, SE1 . . . . .28 B1
Green Dragon La, N21 . . . . .43 H6
Brentford TW8 . . . . .125 H5
Green Dragon Yd, E1 . . . . . .21 H2
Green Dr, Sthl. UB1 . . . . . .123 G1
Green End, N21 . . . . .59 H2
Chessington KT9 . . . . . .195 H4
Greenend Rd, W4 . . . . . . .126 E2
Green Fm Cl, Orp. BR6 . . .207 J5
Greenfell Mans, SE8
off Glaisher St 134 B6
Greenfield Av, Surb. KT5 . .182 B7
Watford WD19 . . . . .50 D2
Greenfield Dr, N2 . . . . .73 J4
Bromley BR1 . . . . .191 J2
Greenfield Gdns, NW2 . . . . .90 B2
Dagenham RM9 . . . . . . .118 D1
Orpington BR5 . . . . .193 G7
Greenfield Rd, E1 . . . . .21 J2
N15 . . . . .76 B5
Dagenham RM9 . . . . . . .118 C1
Greenfields, Loug. IG10 . . . .48 D4
Greenfields Cl, Loug. IG10 .48 D4
Greenfield Way, Har. HA2 . .67 H3
GREENFORD, UB6 . . . . . . .103 H3
Greenford Av, W7 . . . . . . .104 B4
Southall UB1 . . . . .103 F7
Greenford Gdns, Grnf.
UB6 . . . . .103 H3
Greenford Grn Business Pk,
Grnf. UB6
off Green Pk Way 104 C1
Greenford Rd, Grnf. UB6 . .103 J5
Harrow HA1 . . . . .86 B5
Southall UB1 . . . . .123 J1
Sutton SM1 . . . . .198 E4
Greenford Rbt, Grnf. UB6 .104 A2
Green Gdns, Orp. BR6 . . . .207 F5
Greengate, Grnf. UB6 . . . . .86 E6
Greengate St, E13 . . . . . . .115 H2
Greenhalgh Wk, N2 . . . . . . .73 F4
Greenham Cl, SE1 . . . . .27 E4
Greenham Cres, E4 . . . . . . .61 J6
Greenham Rd, N10 . . . . . . .74 A2
Greenhaven Dr, SE28 . . . . .118 B6
Greenheath Business Cen,
E2 *off Three Colts La* . . .113 E4
Greenheys Dr, E18 . . . . .79 F3
Greenhill, NW3
off Prince Arthur Rd . . .91 G4
Green Hill, SE18 . . . . .136 C5
Buckhurst Hill IG9 . . . . . .63 J1
Greenhill, Sutt. SM1 . . . . .199 F2
Wembley HA9 . . . . .88 B2
Greenhill Gdns, Nthlt.
UB5 . . . . .103 F2
Greenhill Gro, E12 . . . . .98 B4
Greenhill Par, Barn.
(New Barn.) EN5
off Great N Rd 40 E5
Greenhill Pk, NW10 . . . . . .106 E1
Barnet (New Barn.)
EN5 . . . . .40 E5
Greenhill Rd, NW10 . . . . . .106 E1
Harrow HA1 . . . . .68 B6
Greenhill's Rents, EC1 . . . . .19 G1
Greenhills Ter, N1
off Baxter Rd 94 A6
Greenhill Ter, SE18 . . . . . .136 C5
Northolt UB5 . . . . .103 F2
Greenhill Way, Har. HA1 . . .68 B6
Wembley HA9 . . . . .88 B2
Greenhithe Cl, Sid. DA15 .157 H7
Greenholm Rd, SE9 . . . . . .156 E5
Green Hundred Rd, SE15 . .37 J6
Greenhurst Rd, SE27 . . . . .169 G5
Greening St, SE2 . . . . .138 C4
Green Knight Ct, N9
off Galahad Rd 60 D3
Greenland Cres, Sthl.
UB2 . . . . .122 C3
Greenland Ms, SE8
off Trundleys Rd 133 G5
Greenland Pl, NW1
off Greenland Rd 110 B1
Greenland Quay, SE16 . . .133 G4
Greenland Rd, NW1 . . . . . .110 C1
Barnet EN5 . . . . .39 J6
Greenlands La, NW4 . . . . . .71 H1
Greenland St, NW1
off Camden High St . . .110 B1
Greenland Way, Croy.
CR0 . . . . .186 D7
Green La, E4 . . . . .46 E3
NW4 . . . . .72 A5
SE9 . . . . .174 D2
SE20 . . . . .171 G7
SW16 . . . . .169 F7
W7 . . . . .124 B2
Chigwell IG7 . . . . .65 G2
Chislehurst BR7 . . . . . . .174 E4
Dagenham RM8 . . . . . . .100 A1
Edgware HA8 . . . . .54 A5
Feltham TW13 . . . . .160 E5
Harrow HA1 . . . . .86 B3
Hounslow TW4 . . . . .142 B3
Ilford IG1, IG3 . . . . .99 F2
Morden SM4 . . . . .184 E6
New Malden KT3 . . . . . .182 C5
Stanmore HA7 . . . . .52 E4
Thornton Heath CR7 . . . .187 G1
Watford WD19 . . . . .50 C1
West Molesey KT8 . . . . .179 H5
Worcester Park KT4 . . . .197 G1
Green La Gdns, Th.Hth.
CR7 . . . . .187 J2
Green Las, N4 . . . . .93 J1
N8 . . . . .75 H3
N13 . . . . .59 F6
N15 . . . . .75 H3
N16 . . . . .93 J3
N21 . . . . .59 H1
Greenlaw Ct, W5 . . . . .105 G6
Greenlaw Gdns, N.Mal.
KT3 . . . . .183 F7
Greenlawn La, Brent.
TW8 . . . . .125 G4
Green Lawns, Ruis. HA4 . . .84 C1
Greenlaw St, SE18 . . . . . . .136 D3
Green Leaf Av, Wall. SM6 .200 D4
Greenleaf Cl, SW2
off Tulse Hill 151 G7
Greenleafe Dr, Ilf. IG6 . . . . .81 E4
Greenleaf Rd, E6
off Redclyffe Rd 115 J1
E17 . . . . .77 J3
Greenleaf Way, Har. HA3 . . .68 C3
Greenlea Pk, SW19 . . . . . .167 G7
Greenlink Wk, Rich. TW9 . .146 B1
Green Man Gdns, W13 . . . .104 D7
Green Man La, W13 . . . . . .124 D1
Feltham TW14 . . . . .142 A4
Green Man Pas, W13 . . . . .104 D7
Green Man Rbt, E11 . . . . . . .79 F7
Greenman St, N1 . . . . .93 J7
Greenmead Cl, SE25 . . . . .188 D5
Green Moor Link, N21 . . . . .43 H7
Greenmoor Rd, Enf. EN3 . . .45 F2
Greenoak Pl, Barn.
(Cockfos.) EN4 . . . . .41 J2
Greenoak Way, SW19 . . . .166 A4
Greenock Rd, SW16 . . . . . .186 D1
W3 . . . . .126 B3
★ **Green Park, The**, SW1 . .24 E2
Greenpark Ct, Wem. HA0 . .87 F7
Green Pk Way, Grnf. UB6 .104 B1
Green Pl, SE10
off Millennium Way . . .134 E2
Green Pt, E15 . . . . .97 E6
Green Pond Cl, E17 . . . . . . .77 J3
Green Pond Rd, E17 . . . . . . .77 H3
Green Ride, Loug. IG10 . . . .47 G5
Green Rd, N14 . . . . .42 B6
N20 . . . . .57 F3
Greenroof Way, SE10 . . . . .135 F3
Greens Cl, The, Loug. IG10 .48 D2
Green's Ct, W1 . . . . .17 H5
Green's End, SE18 . . . . . . .136 E4
Greenshank Cl, E17
off Banbury Rd 61 H7
Greenshields Ind Est,
E16 . . . . .135 H1
Greenside, Bex. DA5 . . . . .177 E1
Dagenham RM8 . . . . . . .100 C1
Greenside Cl, N20 . . . . .57 G2
SE6 . . . . .172 D2
Ilford IG6 . . . . .65 F6
Greenside Rd, W12 . . . . . .127 G3
Croydon CR0 . . . . .187 G7
Greenslade Rd, Bark. IG11 . .99 G7
Greenstead Av, Wdf.Grn.
IG8 . . . . .63 J7

Greenstead Cl, Wdf.Grn. IG8 *off Greenstead Gdns* **63** J6
Greenstead Gdns, SW15 **147** G5
Woodford Green IG8 **63** J6
Greensted Rd, Loug. IG10 **48** B7
Greenstone Ms, E11 **79** G6
Green St, E7 **97** H6
E13 **115** J1
W1 **16** A5
Enfield EN3 **45** F2
Sunbury-on-Thames TW16 **178** A1
GREEN STREET GREEN, Orp. BR6 **207** H6
Green Ter, EC1 **11** F4
Green Vale, W5 **105** J6
Bexleyheath DA6 **158** D5
Greenvale Rd, SE9 **156** C4
Green Verges, Stan. HA7 **53** G7
Green Vw, Chess. KT9 **195** J7
Greenview Av, Beck. BR3 **189** H6
Croydon CR0 **189** H6
Greenview Cl, W3 **126** E1
Green Wk, NW4 **72** A5
SE1 **28** D6
Buckhurst Hill IG9 **48** B7
Hampton TW12 *off Orpwood Cl* **161** F6
Southall UB2 **123** G5
Woodford Green IG8 **64** B6
Green Wk, The, E4 **62** C1
Greenway, N14 **58** E2
N20 **56** D2
Green Way, SE9 **156** A5
Greenway, SW20 **183** J4
Green Way, Brom. BR2 **192** B6
Greenway, Chis. BR7 **174** D5
Dagenham RM8 **100** C2
Harrow HA3 **69** H5
Hayes UB4 **102** B4
Pinner HA5 **66** B2
Green Way, Sun. TW16 **178** A4
Greenway, Wall. SM6 **200** C4
Woodford Green IG8 **63** J5
Greenway, The, NW9 **70** D2
Harrow (Har.Wld) HA3 **68** B1
Hounslow TW4 **143** F4
Pinner HA5 **67** F6
Greenway Av, E17 **78** D4
Greenway Cl, N4 **93** J2
N11 **58** A6
N15 *off Copperfield Dr* **76** C4
N20 **56** D2
NW9 **70** D2
Greenway Gdns, NW9 **70** D2
Croydon CR0 **203** J3
Greenford UB6 **103** G3
Harrow HA3 **68** B2
Greenways, Beck. BR3 **190** A2
Esher KT10 **194** B4
Greenways, The, Twick. TW1 *off South Western Rd* **144** D6
Greenwell St, W1 **9** E6
GREENWICH, SE10 **134** D6
Greenwich Cen Business Pk, SE10 *off Norman Rd* **134** B7
Greenwich Ch St, SE10 **134** C6
Greenwich Cres, E6 *off Swan App* **116** B5
Greenwich Foot Tunnel, E14 **134** C5
SE10 **134** C5
Greenwich Hts, SE18 **136** B7
Greenwich High Rd, SE10 **154** B1
Greenwich Ho, SE13 *off Hither Grn La* **154** D6
Greenwich Ind Est, SE7 **135** H4
Greenwich Mkt, SE10 *off King William Wk* **134** C6
★ **Greenwich Park**, SE10 **134** D7
Greenwich Pk St, SE10 **134** D5
Greenwich Quay, SE8 **134** B6
Greenwich Shop Pk, SE7 **135** H4
Greenwich S St, SE10 **154** B1
Greenwich Vw Pl, E14 **134** B3
Greenwood Av, Dag. RM10 **101** H4
Enfield EN3 **45** H2
Greenwood Cl, Mord. SM4 **184** B4
Orpington BR5 **193** H6
Sidcup DA15 **176** A2
Thames Ditton KT7 **194** D1
Greenwood Ct, SW1 **33** F3
Greenwood Dr, E4 *off Avril Way* **62** C5
Greenwood Gdns, N13 **59** H3
Ilford IG6 **65** F7
Greenwood La, Hmptn. (Hmptn H.) TW12 **161** H5
Greenwood Pk, Kings.T. KT2 **165** E7
Greenwood Pl, NW5 *off Highgate Rd* **92** B5
Greenwood Rd, E8 **94** D6
E13 *off Valetta Gro* **115** F2
Croydon CR0 **187** H7
Isleworth TW7 **144** B3
Mitcham CR4 **186** D3
Thames Ditton KT7 **194** D1
Greenwoods, The, Har. (S.Har.) HA2 **85** J3
Greenwood Ter, NW10 **106** D1
Green Wrythe Cres, Cars. SM5 **199** H1
Green Wrythe La, Cars. SM5 **185** G6
Greer Rd, Har. HA3 **67** J1
Greet St, SE1 **27** F2
Greg Cl, E10 **78** C6
Gregor Ms, SE3 **135** G7
Gregory Cl, Brom. BR2 **191** E4
Gregory Cres, SE9 **156** A7
Gregory Pl, W8 **22** A3
Gregory Rd, Rom. RM6 **82** D4
Southall UB2 **123** G3
Gregson Cl, Borwd. WD6 **38** C1
Greig Cl, N8 **74** E5
Greig Ter, SE17 **35** H5
Grenaby Av, Croy. CR0 **188** A7
Grenaby Rd, Croy. CR0 **188** A7
Grenada Rd, SE7 **135** J7
Grenade St, E14 **113** J7
Grenadier St, E16 **136** D1
Grena Gdns, Rich. TW9 **145** J4
Grenard Cl, SE15 **132** D7
Grena Rd, Rich. TW9 **145** J4
Grendon Gdns, Wem. HA9 **88** A2
Grendon Ho, N1 *off Priory Grn Est* **10** C2
Grendon St, NW8 **7** G5
Grenfell Cl, Borwd. WD6 **38** C1
Grenfell Gdns, Har. HA3 **69** H7
Grenfell Ho, SE5 *off Comber Gro* **131** J7
Grenfell Rd, W11 **108** A7
Mitcham CR4 **167** J6
Grenfell Twr, W11 **108** A7
Grenfell Wk, W11 **108** A7
Grennell Cl, Sutt. SM1 **199** G2
Grennell Rd, Sutt. SM1 **199** F2
Grenoble Gdns, N13 **59** G6
Grenville Cl, N3 **72** C1
Surbiton KT5 **196** C1
Grenville Ct, SE19 *off Lymer Av* **170** C5
Grenville Gdns, Wdf.Grn. IG8 **79** J1
Grenville Ms, N19 **93** E1
Hampton TW12 **161** H5
Grenville Pl, NW7 **54** D5
SW7 **22** C6
Grenville Rd, N19 **92** E1
Grenville St, WC1 **10** B6
Gresham Av, N20 **57** J4
Gresham Cl, Bex. DA5 **159** E6
Enfield EN2 **43** J3
Gresham Dr, Rom. RM6 **82** B5
Gresham Gdns, NW11 **90** B1
Gresham Pl, N19 **92** D2
Gresham Rd, E6 **116** C2
E16 **115** H6
NW10 **88** D5
SE25 **188** D4
SW9 **151** G3
Beckenham BR3 **189** H2
Edgware HA8 **53** J6
Hampton TW12 **161** G6
Hounslow TW3 **143** J1
Gresham St, EC2 **19** J3
Gresham Way, SW19 **166** D3
Gresley Cl, E17 **77** H6
N15 *off Clinton Rd* **76** A4
Gresley Rd, N19 **92** C1
Gressenhall Rd, SW18 **148** C6
Gresse St, W1 **17** H2
Gresswell Cl, Sid. DA14 **176** A3
Greswell St, SW6 **148** A1
Gretton Rd, N17 **60** B7
Greville Cl, Twick. TW1 **144** E7
Greville Ct, E5 *off Napoleon Rd* **94** E3
Greville Hall, NW6 **6** A1
Greville Ms, NW6 *off Greville Rd* **108** E2
Greville Pl, NW6 **6** B1
Greville Rd, E17 **78** C4
NW6 **6** A1
Richmond TW10 **145** J6
Greville St, EC1 **19** F2
Grey Cl, NW11 **73** F6
Greycoat Gdns, SW1 *off Greycoat St* **25** H6
Greycoat Pl, SW1 **25** H6
Greycoat St, SW1 **25** H6
Greycot Rd, Beck. BR3 **172** A5
Grey Eagle St, E1 **21** F1
Greyfell Cl, Stan. HA7 *off Coverdale Cl* **53** E5
Greyfriars Pas, EC1 **19** H3
Greyhound Hill, NW4 **71** G3
Greyhound La, SW16 **168** D6
Greyhound Rd, N17 **76** B3
NW10 **107** H3
W6 **128** A6
W14 **128** B6
Sutton SM1 **199** F5
Greyhound Ter, SW16 **186** C1
Greyladies Gdns, SE10 *off Wat Tyler Rd* **154** C1
Greys Pk Cl, Kes. BR2 **205** J5
Greystead Rd, SE23 **153** F7
Greystoke Av, Pnr. HA5 **67** G3
Greystoke Gdns, W5 **105** H4
Enfield EN2 **42** D4
Greystoke Pk Ter, W5 **105** G3
Greystoke Pl, EC4 **19** E3
Greystone Gdns, Har. HA3 **69** F6
Ilford IG6 **81** F2
Greystone Path, E11 *off Grove Rd* **79** F7
Greyswood Av, N18 **61** G6
Greyswood St, SW16 **168** B6
Grierson Rd, SE23 **153** G7
Griffin Cen, The, Felt. TW14 **142** B5
Griffin Cl, NW10 **89** H5
Griffin Manor Way, SE28 **137** G3
Griffin Rd, N17 **76** B2
SE18 **137** G5
Griffins Cl, N21 **44** A7
Griffin Way, Sun. TW16 **178** A2
Griffith Cl, Dag. RM8 *off Gibson Rd* **100** C1
Griffiths Cl, Wor.Pk. KT4 **197** H2
Griffiths Rd, SW19 **166** D7
Griggs App, Ilf. IG1 **99** F2
Griggs Cl, Ilf. IG3 **99** H4
Griggs Pl, SE1 **28** E6
Griggs Rd, E10 **78** C6
Grilse Cl, N9 **61** E4
Grimsby Gro, E16 **137** E1
Grimsby St, E2 **13** G6
Grimsdyke Cres, Barn. EN5 **39** J3
Grimsdyke Rd, Pnr. HA5 **51** E7
Grimsel Path, SE5 **35** H7
Grimshaw Cl, N6 **74** A7
Grimston Rd, SW6 **148** C2
Grimthorpe Ho, EC1 **11** G5
Grimwade Av, Croy. CR0 **202** D3
Grimwade Cl, SE15 **153** F3
Grimwood Rd, Twick. TW1 **144** C7
Grindall Cl, Croy. CR0 **201** H4
Grindal St, SE1 **26** E4
Grindleford Av, N11 **58** A2
Grindley Gdns, Croy. CR0 **188** C6
Grinling Pl, SE8 **134** A6
Grinstead Rd, SE8 **133** H5
Grittleton Av, Wem. HA9 **88** B6
Grittleton Rd, W9 **108** D4
Grizedale Ter, SE23 **171** E2
Grocer's Hall Ct, EC2 **20** B4
Grogan Cl, Hmptn. TW12 **161** F6
Groombridge Cl, Well. DA16 **158** A5
Groombridge Rd, E9 **95** G7
Groom Cl, Brom. BR2 **191** H4
Groom Cres, SW18 **149** G7
Groomfield Cl, SW17 **168** A4
Groom Pl, SW1 **24** C5
Grooms Dr, Pnr. HA5 **66** A5
Grosmont Rd, SE18 **137** J5
Grosse Way, SW15 **147** H6
Grosvenor Av, N5 **93** J5
SW14 **146** E3
Carshalton SM5 **199** J6
Harrow HA2 **67** H6
Richmond TW10 **145** H5
Grosvenor Cl, Loug. IG10 **48** E1
Grosvenor Cotts, SW1 **32** B1
Grosvenor Ct, N14 **42** C7
NW6 **108** A1
Grosvenor Cres, NW9 **70** A4
SW1 **24** C4
Grosvenor Cres Ms, SW1 **24** B4
Grosvenor Dr, Loug. IG10 **49** E1
Grosvenor Est, SW1 **33** J1
Grosvenor Gdns, E6 **116** A3
N10 **74** C3
N14 **42** D5
NW2 **89** J5
NW11 **72** C6
SW1 **24** D5
SW14 **146** E3
Kingston upon Thames KT2 **163** G6
Wallington SM6 **200** C7
Woodford Green IG8 **63** G6
Grosvenor Gdns Ms E, SW1 **24** E5
Grosvenor Gdns Ms N, SW1 **24** D6
Grosvenor Gdns Ms S, SW1 **24** E6
Grosvenor Gate, W1 **16** A6
Grosvenor Hill, SW19 **166** B6
W1 **16** D5
Grosvenor Pk, SE5 **35** J6
Grosvenor Pk Rd, E17 **78** A5
Grosvenor Path, Loug. IG10 **49** E1
Grosvenor Pl, SW1 **24** C4
Grosvenor Ri E, E17 **78** B5
Grosvenor Rd, E6 **116** A1
E7 **97** H6
E10 **96** C1
E11 **79** G5
N3 **56** C7
N9 **60** E1
N10 **74** B1
SE25 **188** D4
SW1 **32** D5
W4 **126** B5
W7 **124** D1
Belvedere DA17 **139** G6
Bexleyheath DA6 **158** D5
Borehamwood WD6 **38** A3
Brentford TW8 **125** G6
Dagenham RM8 **101** F1
Hounslow TW3 **143** F3
Ilford IG1 **99** F3
Orpington BR5 **193** H6
Richmond TW10 **145** H5
Southall UB2 **123** F3
Twickenham TW1 **144** D7
Wallington SM6 **200** B6
West Wickham BR4 **204** B1
Grosvenor Sq, W1 **16** C5
Grosvenor St, W1 **16** D5
Grosvenor Ter, SE5 **35** H7
Grosvenor Way, E5 **95** F2
Grosvenor Wf Rd, E14 **134** D4
Grote's Bldgs, SE3 **155** E2
Grote's Pl, SE3 **154** E2
Groton Rd, SW18 **167** E2
Grotto Pas, W1 **16** C1
Grotto Rd, Twick. TW1 **162** C2
Grove, The, E15 **96** E6
N3 **72** D1
N4 **75** F7
N6 **92** A1
N8 **74** D5
N13 **59** G5
N14 **42** C5
NW9 **70** D5
NW11 **72** B7
SE22 **170** D1
W5 **125** G1
Bexleyheath DA6 **158** D4
Edgware HA8 **54** B4
Enfield EN2 **43** G2
Greenford UB6 **103** J6
Isleworth TW7 **144** B1
Sidcup DA14 **177** E4
Teddington TW11 **162** D4
Twickenham TW1 *off Bridge Rd* **144** E6
Walton-on-Thames KT12 **178** B7
West Wickham BR4 **204** B3
Grove Av, N3 **56** D7
N10 **74** C2
W7 **104** B6
Pinner HA5 **67** E4
Sutton SM1 **198** D6
Twickenham TW1 **162** C1
Grove Bk, Wat. WD19 **50** D1
Grovebury Rd, SE2 **138** B2
Grove Cl, N14 **42** C7
SE23 **171** G1
Bromley BR2 **205** G2
Feltham TW13 **160** E4
Kingston upon Thames KT1 **181** J4
Grove Cotts, SW3 **31** H5
Grove Ct, Barn. EN5 *off High St* **40** C3
East Molesey KT8 *off Walton Rd* **180** A5
Grove Cres, E18 **79** F2
NW9 **70** C4
Feltham TW13 **160** E4
Kingston upon Thames KT1 **181** H3
Walton-on-Thames KT12 **178** B7
Grove Cres Rd, E15 **96** D6
Grovedale Rd, N19 **92** D2
Grove Dws, E1 *off Adelina Gro* **113** F5
Grove End, E18 *off Grove Hill* **79** F2
NW5 *off Chetwynd Rd* **92** B4
Grove End Gdns, NW8 *off Grove End Rd* **6** E2
Grove End La, Esher KT10 **194** A1
Grove End Rd, NW8 **6** E2
Grove Fm Ct, Mitch. CR4 *off Brookfields Av* **185** J4

Grove Fm Retail Pk, Rom. (Chad.Hth) RM6 ....82 C7
Grove Footpath, Surb. KT5 ....181 H4
Grove Gdns, NW4 ....71 G4
NW8 ....7 H4
Dagenham RM10 ....101 J3
Enfield EN3 ....45 G1
Teddington TW11 ....162 D4
Grove Grn Rd, E11 ....96 C3
Grove Hall Ct, NW8 ....6 D3
Grove Hill, E18 ....79 F2
Harrow HA1 ....68 B7
Grove Hill Rd, SE5 ....152 B3
Harrow HA1 ....68 B7
Grove Ho Rd, N8 ....74 E4
Groveland Av, SW16 ....169 F7
Groveland Ct, EC4 ....20 A4
Groveland Rd, Beck. BR3 ....189 J3
Grovelands, W.Mol. KT8 ....179 G4
Grovelands Cl, SE5 ....152 B2
Harrow HA2 ....85 H3
Grovelands Ct, N14 ....42 D7
Grovelands Rd, N13 ....59 F4
N15 ....76 D6
Orpington BR5 ....176 A7
Groveland Way, N.Mal. KT3 ....182 C5
Grove La, SE5 ....152 A1
Chigwell IG7 ....65 J3
Kingston upon Thames KT1 ....181 H4
Grove La Ter, SE5 off Grove La 152 B3
Grove Mkt Pl, SE9 ....156 C6
Grove Ms, W6 ....127 J3
W11 off Portobello Rd 108 C6
Grove Mill, Mitch. CR4 ....185 H5
Grove Mill Pl, Cars. SM5 ....200 A3
GROVE PARK, SE12 ....173 G2
GROVE PARK, W4 ....126 B7
Grove Pk, E11 ....79 H6
NW9 ....70 C4
SE5 ....152 B2
Grove Pk Av, E4 ....62 B7
Grove Pk Br, W4 ....126 C7
Grove Pk Gdns, W4 ....126 B6
Grove Pk Ms, W4 ....126 C7
Grove Pk Rd, N15 ....76 B4
SE9 ....173 J3
W4 ....126 B7
Grove Pk Ter, W4 ....126 B6
Grove Pas, E2 ....113 E2
Teddington TW11 ....162 D5
Grove Pl, NW3 off Christchurch Hill 91 G3
SW12 ....150 B6
W3 ....126 C1
Barking IG11 off Clockhouse Av 117 F1
Grove Rd, E3 ....113 G1
E4 ....62 B4
E11 ....79 F7
E17 ....78 B6
E18 ....79 F2
N11 ....58 B5
N12 ....57 G5
N15 ....76 B5
NW2 ....89 J6
SW13 ....147 F2
SW19 ....167 F7
W3 ....126 C1
W5 ....105 G7
Barnet (Cockfos.) EN4 ....41 H3
Belvedere DA17 ....139 F6
Bexleyheath DA7 ....159 J4
Borehamwood WD6 ....38 A1
Brentford TW8 ....125 F5
East Molesey KT8 ....180 A4
Edgware HA8 ....54 A6
Hounslow TW3 ....143 H4
Isleworth TW7 ....144 B1
Mitcham CR4 ....186 B2
Pinner HA5 ....67 F5
Richmond TW10 ....145 J6
Romford RM6 ....82 B7
Surbiton KT6 ....181 G5
Sutton SM1 ....199 E6
Thornton Heath CR7 ....187 G4
Twickenham TW2 ....162 A3
Groveside Cl, W3 ....106 A6
Carshalton SM5 ....199 H2
Groveside Rd, E4 ....62 E2
Grovestile Waye, Felt. TW14 ....141 G7
Grove St, N18 ....60 C6
SE8 ....133 J4
Grove Ter, NW5 ....92 B3
Teddington TW11 ....162 D4
Grove Ter Ms, NW5 off Grove Ter 92 B3
Grove Vale, SE22 ....152 B4
Chislehurst BR7 ....174 D6
Grove Vil, E14 ....114 B7
Groveway, SW9 ....151 F1
Dagenham RM8 ....100 D4
Grove Way, Esher KT10 ....179 J7
Wembley HA9 ....88 B5
Grovewood, Rich. TW9 ....146 A1
Grove Wd Cl, Brom. BR1 ....192 D3
Grovewood Pl, Wdf.Grn. IG8 ....64 C6
Grummant Rd, SE15 ....152 C1
Grundy St, E14 ....114 B6
Gruneisen Rd, N3 ....56 E7
★ Guards Mus, SW1 ....25 G4
Gubyon Av, SE24 ....151 H5
Guerin Sq, E3 ....113 J3
Guernsey Cl, Houns. TW5 ....143 G1
Guernsey Gro, SE24 ....151 J7
Guernsey Ho, N1 off Clifton Rd 93 J6
Guernsey Rd, E11 ....96 D1
Guibal Rd, SE12 ....155 H7
Guildersfield Rd, SW16 ....168 E7
Guildford Gro, SE10 ....154 B1
Guildford Rd, E6 ....116 B6
E17 ....78 C1
SW8 ....151 E1
Croydon CR0 ....188 A6
Ilford IG3 ....99 H2
Guildford Way, Wall. SM6 ....201 E5
★ Guildhall, The, EC2 ....20 B3
★ Guildhall Art Gall (Guildhall Lib), EC2 ....20 A3
Guildhall Bldgs, EC2 ....20 B3
Guildhall Yd, EC2 ....20 A3
Guildhouse St, SW1 ....33 F1
Guildown Av, N12 ....56 E4
Guild Rd, SE7 ....136 A5
Guildsway, E17 ....77 J1
Guilford Av, Surb. KT5 ....181 J5
Guilford Pl, WC1 ....10 C6
Guilford St, WC1 ....10 B6
Guinness Cl, E9 ....95 H7
Hayes UB3 ....121 G3
Guinness Ct, E1 ....21 G4
Guinness Sq, SE1 ....36 D1
Guinness Trust Bldgs, SE1 off Snowsfields 28 D3
SE11 ....35 G3
SW3 ....31 J2
SW9 ....151 H4
W6 off Fulham Palace Rd 127 J5
Guinness Trust Est, N16 off Holmleigh Rd 94 B1
Guion Rd, SW6 ....148 C2
Gulland Wk, N1 off Nightingale Rd 93 J6
Gulliver Cl, Nthlt. UB5 ....103 F1
Gulliver Rd, Sid. DA15 ....175 H2
Gulliver St, SE16 ....133 J3
Gulston Wk, SW3 ....32 A2
Gumleigh Rd, W5 ....125 F4
Gumley Gdns, Islw. TW7 ....144 D3
Gumping Rd, Orp. BR5 ....207 F2
Gundulph Rd, Brom. BR2 ....191 J3
Gunmakers La, E3 ....113 H1
Gunnell Cl, SE26 ....170 D5
Croydon CR0 ....188 D6
Gunner La, SE18 ....136 D5
GUNNERSBURY, W4 ....126 B4
Gunnersbury Av, W3 ....126 A3
W4 ....126 A3
W5 ....125 J1
Gunnersbury Cl, W4 off Grange Rd 126 B5
Gunnersbury Ct, W3 ....126 B2
Gunnersbury Cres, W3 ....126 A2
Gunnersbury Dr, W5 ....125 J2
Gunnersbury Gdns, W3 ....126 A2
Gunnersbury La, W3 ....126 A3
Gunnersbury Ms, W4 off Chiswick High Rd 126 B5
★ Gunnersbury Park, W3 ....125 J4
Gunnersbury Pk, W3 ....125 J4
W5 ....125 J4
★ Gunnersbury Park Mus & Art Cen, W3 ....126 A3
Gunners Gro, E4 ....62 C3
Gunners Rd, SW18 ....167 G2
Gunnery Ter, SE18 ....137 F4
Gunning St, SE18 ....137 H4
Gunpowder Sq, EC4 ....19 F3
Gunstor Rd, N16 ....94 B4
Gun St, E1 ....21 F2
Gunter Gro, SW10 ....30 C6
Edgware HA8 ....70 D1
Gunterstone Rd, W14 ....128 B4
Gunthorpe St, E1 ....21 G2
Gunton Rd, E5 ....95 E3
SW17 ....168 A6
Gunwhale Cl, SE16 ....133 G1
Gurdon Rd, SE7 ....135 G5
Gurnell Gro, W13 ....104 C4
Gurney Cl, E15 off Gurney Rd 97 E5
Gurney Cl, E17 ....77 G1
Barking IG11 ....98 E6
Gurney Cres, Croydon CR0 ....201 F1
Gurney Dr, N2 ....73 F5
Gurney Rd, E15 ....96 E5
SW6 ....149 F3
Carshalton SM5 ....200 A4
Northolt UB5 ....102 B3
Guthrie St, SW3 ....31 G3
Gutter La, EC2 ....20 A3
Guyatt Gdns, Mitch. CR4 off Ormerod Gdns 186 A2
Guy Barnett Gro, SE3 off Casterbridge Rd 155 G3
Guy Rd, Wall. SM6 ....200 D3
Guyscliff Rd, SE13 ....154 C5
Guy St, SE1 ....28 C3
Gwalior Rd, SW15 off Felsham Rd 148 A3
Gwendolen Av, SW15 ....148 A5
Gwendolen Cl, SW15 ....147 J5
Gwendoline Av, E13 ....115 H1
Gwendwr Rd, W14 ....128 B5
Gwillim Cl, Sid. DA15 ....158 A5
Gwydor Rd, Beck. BR3 ....189 G4
Gwydyr Rd, Brom. BR2 ....191 F3
Gwyn Cl, SW6 ....129 F7
Gwynne Av, Croy. CR0 ....189 G7
Gwynne Cl, W4 off Pumping Sta Rd 127 F6
Gwynne Pk Av, Wdf.Grn. IG8 ....64 C6
Gwynne Pl, WC1 ....10 D4
Gwynne Rd, SW11 ....149 G2
Gylcote Cl, SE5 ....152 A4
Gyles Pk, Stan. HA7 ....69 F1
Gyllyngdune Gdns, Ilf. IG3 ....99 J2
Gypsy Cor, W3 ....106 C5

H

Haarlem Rd, W14 ....128 A3
Haberdasher Est, N1 off Haberdasher St 12 C3
Haberdasher Pl, N1 ....12 C3
Haberdasher St, N1 ....12 C3
Habgood Rd, Loug. IG10 ....48 B3
Habitat Cl, SE15 off Gordon Rd 153 E2
Haccombe Rd, SW19 off Haydons Rd 167 F6
HACKBRIDGE, Wall. SM6 ....200 B2
Hackbridge Grn, Wall. SM6 ....200 A2
Hackbridge Pk Gdns, Cars. SM5 ....200 A2
Hackbridge Rd, Wall. SM6 ....200 A2
Hackford Rd, SW9 ....151 F1
Hackford Wk, SW9 ....151 F1
Hackforth Cl, Barn. EN5 ....39 H5
Hackington Cres, Beck. BR3 ....172 A6
HACKNEY, E8 ....94 E6
★ Hackney City Fm, E2 ....13 H2
Hackney Cl, Borwd. WD6 ....38 D5
Hackney Gro, E8 off Reading La 95 E6
★ Hackney Marsh, E9 ....95 H3
★ Hackney Mus, E8 ....95 E6
Hackney Rd, E2 ....13 F4
HACKNEY WICK, E9 ....96 A5
Hackworth Pt, E3 off Rainhill Way 114 B3
Hacon Sq, E8 off Richmond Rd 95 E7
Hadar Cl, N20 ....56 D1
Hadden Rd, SE28 ....137 H3
Hadden Way, Grnf. UB6 ....86 A6
Haddington Rd, Brom. BR1 ....172 D3
Haddo Ho, SE10 off Haddo St 134 B6
Haddon Cl, Borwd. WD6 ....38 A2
Enfield EN1 ....44 D6
New Malden KT3 ....183 F5
Haddonfield, SE8 ....133 G4
Haddon Gro, Sid. DA15 ....158 A7
Haddon Rd, Sutt. SM1 ....198 E4
Haddo St, SE10 ....134 B6
Haden Ct, N4 off Lennox Rd 93 G2
Haden La, N11 ....58 C4
Hadfield Cl, Sthl. UB1 off Adrienne Av 103 F3
Hadfield Rd, Stai. (Stanw.) TW19 ....140 A6
Hadleigh Cl, E1 off Mantus Rd 113 F4
SW20 ....184 C2
Hadleigh Rd, N9 ....44 E7
Hadleigh St, E2 ....113 F4
Hadleigh Wk, E6 ....116 B6
HADLEY, Barn. EN5 ....40 C2
Hadley Cl, N21 ....43 G6
Hadley Common, Barn. EN5 ....40 D2
Hadley Gdns, W4 ....126 D5
Southall UB2 ....123 F5
Hadley Grn, Barn. EN5 ....40 C2
Hadley Grn Rd, Barn. EN5 ....40 C2
Hadley Grn W, Barn. EN5 ....40 C2
Hadley Gro, Barn. EN5 ....40 B2
Hadley Hts, Barn. EN5 off Hadley Rd 41 E2
Hadley Highstone, Barn. EN5 ....40 C1
Hadley Ridge, Barn. EN5 ....40 C3
Hadley Rd, Barn. (New Barn.) EN5 ....41 E4
Belvedere DA17 ....139 F4
Mitcham CR4 ....186 D4
Hadley St, NW1 ....92 B6
Hadley Way, N21 ....43 G6
Hadlow Pl, SE19 ....170 D7
Hadlow Rd, Sid. DA14 ....176 A4
Welling DA16 ....138 C7
Hadrian Cl, E3 off Garrison Rd 114 A1
Staines TW19 ....140 B7
Hadrian Ct, Sutt. SM2 off Stanley Rd 198 E7
Hadrian Est, E2 ....13 J2
Hadrian Ms, N7 off Roman Way 93 F7
Hadrians Ride, Enf. EN1 ....44 C5
Hadrian St, SE10 ....134 E5
Hadrian Way, Stai. (Stanw.) TW19 ....140 B7
Hadyn Pk Rd, W12 ....127 G2
Hafer Rd, SW11 ....149 J4
Hafton Rd, SE6 ....173 E1
Haggard Rd, Twick. TW1 ....144 E7
HAGGERSTON, E2 ....13 G1
Haggerston Rd, E8 ....94 C7
Haggerston Studios, E8 off Kingsland Rd 112 C1
Hague St, E2 ....13 J4
Ha-Ha Rd, SE18 ....136 C6
Haig Pl, Mord. SM4 off Green La 184 D6
Haig Rd, Stan. HA7 ....53 F5
Haig Rd E, E13 ....115 J3
Haig Rd W, E13 ....115 J3
Haigville Gdns, Ilf. IG6 ....81 E4
Hailes Cl, SW19 ....167 F6
Haileybury Av, Enf. EN1 ....44 C6
Hailey Rd, Erith DA18 ....139 G2
Hailsham Av, SW2 ....169 F2
Hailsham Cl, Surb. KT6 ....181 G7
Hailsham Dr, Har. HA1 ....68 A3
Hailsham Rd, SW17 ....168 A6
Hailsham Ter, N18 ....59 J5
Haimo Rd, SE9 ....156 A5
HAINAULT, Ilf. IG6 ....65 H7
Hainault Ct, E17 ....78 D4
Hainault Gore, Rom. RM6 ....83 E5
Hainault Gro, Chig. IG7 ....65 F4
Hainault Rd, E11 ....96 C1
Chigwell IG7 ....65 E3
Romford RM5 ....83 J2
Romford (Chad.Hth) RM6 ....83 F6
Romford (Lt.Hth) RM6 ....82 B3
Hainault St, SE9 ....175 E1
Ilford IG1 ....99 E2
Haines Cl, N1 ....94 B7
Haines Wk, Mord. SM4 off Dorchester Rd 185 E7
Hainford Cl, SE4 ....153 G4
Haining Cl, W4 off Wellesley Rd 126 A5
Hainthorpe Rd, SE27 ....169 H3
Hainton Cl, E1 ....113 E6
Halberd Ms, E5 off Knightland Rd 94 E2
Halbutt Gdns, Dag. RM9 ....101 F3
Halbutt St, Dag. RM9 ....101 F4
Halcomb St, N1 ....112 B1
Halcot Av, Bexh. DA6 ....159 H5
Halcrow St, E1 off Newark St 113 E5
Haldane Cl, N10 ....58 B7
Haldane Pl, SW18 ....166 E1
Haldane Rd, E6 ....116 A3
SE28 ....118 D7
SW6 ....128 C7
Southall UB1 ....103 J6
Haldan Rd, E4 ....62 C6
Haldon Cl, Chig. IG7 off Arrowsmith Rd 65 H5
Haldon Rd, SW18 ....148 C5
Hale, The, E4 ....62 D7
N17 ....76 D3
Hale Cl, E4 ....62 C3
Edgware HA8 ....54 C5
Orpington BR6 ....207 F4
Hale Dr, NW7 ....54 C6
HALE END, E4 ....62 D6
Hale End Cl, Ruis. HA4 ....66 A6

Hale End Rd, E4 62 D6
E17 78 D1
Woodford Green IG8 62 D7
Halefield Rd, N17 76 D1
Hale Gdns, N17 76 D3
W3 126 A1
Hale Gro Gdns, NW7 54 D5
Hale La, NW7 54 D5
Edgware HA8 54 B5
Hale Path, SE27 169 H4
Hale Rd, E6 116 B4
N17 76 D3
Halesowen Rd, Mord. SM4 184 E7
Hales Prior, N1 *off Calshot St* 10 C2
Hales St, SE8 *off Deptford High St* 134 A7
Hale St, E14 114 B7
Halesworth Cl, E5 *off Theydon Rd* 95 F2
Halesworth Rd, SE13 154 B3
Hale Wk, W7 104 B5
Haley Rd, NW4 71 J6
Half Acre, Brent. TW8 125 G6
Half Acre Rd, W7 124 B1
Half Moon Ct, EC1 19 J2
Half Moon Cres, N1 10 D1
Half Moon La, SE24 151 J6
Half Moon Pas, E1 21 G4
Half Moon St, W1 24 E1
Halford Cl, Edg. HA8 70 B2
Halford Rd, E10 78 D5
SW6 128 D6
Richmond TW10 145 H5
Halfway St, Sid. DA15 157 G7
Haliburton Rd, Twick. TW1 144 D5
Haliday Wk, N1 *off Balls Pond Rd* 94 A6
Halidon Cl, E9 *off Urswick Rd* 95 F5
Halifax Cl, Tedd. TW11 162 A6
Halifax Rd, Enf. EN2 43 J2
Greenford UB6 103 H1
Halifax St, SE26 171 E4
Halifield Dr, Belv. DA17 138 E3
Haling Gro, S.Croy. CR2 201 J7
Haling Pk, S.Croy. CR2 201 J6
Haling Pk Gdns, S.Croy. CR2 201 H6
Haling Pk Rd, S.Croy. CR2 201 H5
Haling Rd, S.Croy. CR2 202 A6
Halkin Arc, SW1 24 B5
Halkin Ms, SW1 24 B5
Halkin Pl, SW1 24 B5
Halkin St, SW1 24 C4
Hall, The, SE3 155 G3
Hallam Cl, Chis. BR7 174 C5
Hallam Gdns, Pnr. HA5 51 E7
Hallam Ms, W1 16 E1
Hallam Rd, N15 75 H4
SW13 147 H3
Hallam St, W1 8 E6
Hallane Ho, SE27 *off Elder Rd* 169 J5
Hall Av, N18 60 A6
Hall Cl, W5 105 H5
Hall Ct, Tedd. TW11 162 C5
Hall Dr, SE26 171 F5
W7 104 B6
Halley Gdns, SE13 154 D4
Halley Rd, E7 97 J6
E12 98 A6
Halley St, E14 113 H5
Hall Fm Cl, Stan. HA7 52 E4
Hall Fm Dr, Twick. TW2 144 A7
Hallfield Est, W2 14 C3
Hall Gdns, E4 61 J4
Hall Gate, NW8 6 D3
Halliards, The, Walt. KT12 *off Felix Rd* 178 A6
Halliday Ho, E1 *off Christian St* 21 J4
Halliday Sq, Sthl. UB2 124 A1
Halliford St, N1 93 J7
Hallingbury Ct, E17 78 B3
Hallings Wf Studios, E15 *off Channelsea Rd* 114 D1
Halliwell Rd, SW2 151 F6
Halliwick Rd, N10 74 A1
Hall La, E4 61 H5
NW4 71 G1
Hayes (Harling.) UB3 121 G7
Hallmark Trd Cen, Wem. HA9 88 C4
Hallmead Rd, Sutt. SM1 198 E3
Hall Oak Wk, NW6 *off Barlow Rd* 90 C6
Hallowell Av, Croy. CR0 200 E4
Hallowell Cl, Mitch. CR4 186 A3
Hallowell Gdns, Th.Hth. CR7 187 J2
Hallowes Cres, Wat. WD19 50 A3
Hallowfield Way, Mitch. CR4 185 G3
★ **Hall Pl**, Bex. DA5 159 J6
Hall Pl, W2 6 E6
Hall Pl Cres, Bex. DA5 159 J5
Hall Rd, E6 116 C1
E15 96 D4
NW8 6 D4
Isleworth TW7 144 A5
Romford (Chad.Hth) RM6 82 C6
Hall St, EC1 11 H3
N12 57 F5
Hallsville Rd, E16 115 F6
Hallswelle Rd, NW11 72 C5
Hall Twr, W2 15 F1
Hall Vw, SE9 174 A2
Hallywell Cres, E6 116 C5
Halons Rd, SE9 156 D7
Halpin Pl, SE17 36 C2
Halsbrook Rd, SE3 156 A3
Halsbury Cl, Stan. HA7 52 E4
Halsbury Rd, W12 127 H1
Halsbury Rd E, Nthlt. UB5 85 J4
Halsbury Rd W, Nthlt. UB5 85 H5
Halsend, Hayes UB3 122 B1
Halsey Ms, SW3 31 J1
Halsey St, SW3 31 J1
Halsham Cres, Bark. IG11 99 J6
Halsmere Rd, SE5 151 H1
Halstead Cl, Croy. CR0 *off Charles St* 201 J3
Halstead Ct, N1 12 B2
Halstead Gdns, N21 60 A1
Halstead Rd, E11 79 G5
N21 59 J1
Enfield EN1 44 B4
Halston Cl, SW11 149 J6
Halstow Rd, NW10 108 A3
SE10 135 G5
Halsway, Hayes UB3 122 A1
Halter Cl, Borwd. WD6 38 D5
Halton Cl, N11 57 J6
Halton Cross St, N1 111 H1
Halton Pl, N1 *off Dibden St* 111 J1
Halton Rd, N1 93 H7
Halt Robin La, Belv. DA17 *off Halt Robin Rd* 139 H4
Halt Robin Rd, Belv. DA17 139 G4
HAM, Rich. TW10 163 G3
Ham, The, Brent. TW8 125 F7
Hambalt Rd, SW4 150 C5
Hamble Ct, Tedd. TW11 163 G7
Hambledon Gdns, SE25 188 C3
Hambledon Pl, SE21 170 B1
Hambledon Rd, SW18 148 C7
Hambledown Rd, Sid. DA15 157 G7
Hamble St, SW6 149 E3
Hambleton Cl, Wor.Pk. KT4 197 J2
Hamble Wk, Nthlt. UB5 *off Brabazon Rd* 103 G2
Hambley Ho, SE16 *off Manor Est* 132 E4
Hambridge Way, SW2 151 G7
Hambro Av, Brom. BR2 205 G1
Hambrook Rd, SE25 188 E3
Hambro Rd, SW16 168 D6
Hambrough Rd, Sthl. UB1 122 E1
Ham Cl, Rich. TW10 163 F3
Ham Common, Rich. TW10 163 J4
Ham Cft Cl, Felt. TW13 160 A3
Hamden Cres, Dag. RM10 101 H3
Hamel Cl, Har. HA3 69 G3
Hamelin St, E14 *off St. Leonards Rd* 114 C6
Hameway, E6 116 D4
Ham Fm Rd, Rich. TW10 163 G4
Ham Flds, Rich. TW10 *off Riverside Dr* 162 E3
Hamfrith Rd, E15 97 F6
Ham Gate Av, Rich. TW10 163 G3
★ **Ham Ho**, Rich. TW10 163 F1
Hamilton Av, N9 44 D7
Ilford IG6 81 E4
Surbiton KT6 196 B1
Sutton SM3 198 B2
Hamilton Cl, N17 76 C3
NW8 6 E4
SE16 *off Somerford Way* 133 H2
Barnet (Cockfos.) EN4 41 H4
Teddington TW11 *off Munster Rd* 163 F6
Hamilton Ct, W5 105 J7
W9 6 C3
Hamilton Cres, N13 59 G4
Harrow HA2 85 F3
Hounslow TW3 143 H5
Hamilton Gdns, NW8 6 D3
Hamilton Ho, SW8 *off St. George Wf* 34 A5
Hamilton La, N5 *off Hamilton Pk* 93 H4
Hamilton Ms, SW18 *off Merton Rd* 166 D1
W1 24 D3
Hamilton Pk, N5 93 H4
Hamilton Pk W, N5 93 H4
Hamilton Pl, N19 92 D3
W1 24 C2
Sunbury-on-Thames TW16 160 B7
Hamilton Rd, E15 115 E3
E17 77 H2
N2 73 F3
N9 44 D7
NW10 89 G5
NW11 72 A7
SE27 170 A4
SW19 167 E7
W4 126 E2
W5 105 H7
Barnet (Cockfos.) EN4 41 H4
Bexleyheath DA7 159 E2
Brentford TW8 125 G6
Harrow HA1 68 B5
Hayes UB3 102 B7
Ilford IG1 98 E4
Sidcup DA15 176 A4
Southall UB1 123 F1
Thornton Heath CR7 188 A3
Twickenham TW2 162 B1
Watford WD19 50 B3
Hamilton Rd Ind Est, SE27 170 A4
Hamilton Rd Ms, SW19 *off Hamilton Rd* 167 E7
Hamilton Sq, N12 57 G6
SE1 28 C3
Hamilton St, SE8 *off Deptford High St* 134 A6
Hamilton Ter, NW8 6 D3
Hamilton Way, N3 56 D6
N13 59 H4
Hamlea Cl, SE12 155 F5
Hamlet, The, SE5 152 A3
Hamlet Cl, SE13 155 E4
Hamlet Gdns, W6 127 G4
Hamlet Ms, SE21 *off Thurlow Pk Rd* 170 A1
Hamleton Ter, Dag. RM9 *off Flamstead Rd* 100 C7
Hamlet Rd, SE19 170 C7
Hamlet Sq, NW2 90 B3
Hamlets Way, E3 113 J4
Hamlet Way, SE1 28 C3
★ **Hamleys**, W1 17 F5
Hamlin Cres, Pnr. HA5 66 C5
Hamlyn Cl, Edg. HA8 53 H3
Hamlyn Gdns, SE19 170 B7
Hamlyn Ho, Felt. TW13 *off High St* 160 B1
Hammelton Grn, SW9 *off Cromwell Rd* 151 H1
Hammelton Rd, Brom. BR1 191 F1
Hammers La, NW7 55 G5
HAMMERSMITH, W6 127 J5
Hammersmith Br, SW13 127 H6
W6 127 H6
Hammersmith Br Rd, W6 127 J5
Hammersmith Bdy, W6 127 J4
Hammersmith Flyover, W6 127 J5
Hammersmith Gro, W6 127 J3
Hammersmith Rd, W6 128 A4
W14 128 A4
Hammersmith Ter, W6 127 G5
Hammet Cl, Hayes UB4 102 D5
Hammett St, EC3 21 F5
Hammond Av, Mitch. CR4 186 B2
Hammond Cl, Barn. EN5 40 B5
Greenford UB6 *off Lilian Board Way* 86 A5
Hampton TW12 179 G1
Hammond Ho, SE14 *off Lubbock St* 133 F7
Hammond Rd, Enf. EN1 45 E2
Southall UB2 123 E3
Hammonds Cl, Dag. RM8 100 C3
Hammond St, NW5 92 C6
Hammond Way, SE28 *off Oriole Way* 118 B7
Hamonde Cl, Edg. HA8 54 B2
Hamond Sq, N1 12 D1
Ham Pk Rd, E7 97 F7
E15 97 F7
Hampden Av, Beck. BR3 189 H2
Hampden Cl, NW1 9 J2
Hampden Gurney St, W1 15 J4
Hampden La, N17 76 C1
Hampden Rd, N8 75 G4
N10 58 A7
N17 76 D1
N19 *off Holloway Rd* 92 D2
Beckenham BR3 189 H2
Hampden Rd, Harrow HA3 67 J1
Kingston upon Thames KT1 182 A3
Hampden Sq, N14 *off Osidge La* 58 B1
Hampden Way, N14 58 B2
Hampshire Cl, N18 60 E5
Hampshire Hog La, W6 *off King St* 127 H4
Hampshire Rd, N22 59 F7
Hampshire St, NW5 *off Torriano Av* 92 D6
Hampson Way, SW8 151 F1
HAMPSTEAD, NW3 91 G4
Hampstead Av, Wdf.Grn. IG8 64 D7
Hampstead Cl, SE28 138 B1
Hampstead Gdns, NW11 72 D6
Romford (Chad.Hth) RM6 82 B5
HAMPSTEAD GARDEN SUBURB, N2 73 F5
Hampstead Grn, NW3 91 H5
Hampstead Gro, NW3 91 F3
★ **Hampstead Heath**, NW3 91 G2
Hampstead Hts, N2 73 F4
Hampstead High St, NW3 91 F4
Hampstead Hill Gdns, NW3 91 G4
Hampstead La, N6 73 G7
NW3 73 G7
Hampstead Rd, NW1 9 F1
Hampstead Sq, NW3 91 F3
Hampstead Wk, E3 *off Waterside Cl* 113 J1
Hampstead Way, NW11 91 F1
HAMPTON, TW12 179 H1
Hampton Cl, N11 58 B5
NW6 108 D3
SW20 165 J7
Borehamwood WD6 38 C5
Hampton Ct, N1 *off Upper St* 93 H6
Hampton Ct Av, E.Mol. KT8 180 A5
Hampton Ct Cres, E.Mol. KT8 180 A3
★ **Hampton Court Palace & Pk**, E.Mol. KT8 180 B3
Hampton Ct Par, E.Mol. KT8 *off Creek Rd* 180 B4
Hampton Ct Pk, E.Mol. (Home Pk) KT8 180 D4
Kingston upon Thames (Home Pk) KT1 180 D4
Hampton Ct Rd, E.Mol. KT8 180 C3
Hampton TW12 179 J2
Kingston upon Thames KT1 180 C3
Hampton Ct Way, E.Mol. KT8 180 B6
Esher KT10 194 B2
Thames Ditton KT7 194 B2
Hampton Fm Ind Est, Felt. TW13 161 F3
HAMPTON HILL, Hmptn. TW12 161 J6
Hampton Hill Business Pk, Hmptn. TW12 *off Wellington Rd* 161 J5
Hampton La, Felt. TW13 161 E4
Hampton Mead, Loug. IG10 48 E3
Hampton Ms, NW10 *off Minerva Rd* 106 D3
Hampton Ri, Har. HA3 69 H6
Hampton Rd, E4 61 J5
E7 97 H5
E11 96 D1
Croydon CR0 187 J6
Hampton (Hmptn H.) TW12 162 A5
Ilford IG1 99 E4
Teddington TW11 162 A5
Twickenham TW2 162 A3
Worcester Park KT4 197 G2
Hampton Rd E, Felt. (Han.) TW13 161 F3
Hampton Rd W, Felt. TW13 160 E2
Hampton St, SE1 35 H2
SE17 35 H2
HAMPTON WICK, Kings.T. KT1 181 E1
Ham Ridings, Rich. TW10 163 J5
Hamshades Cl, Sid. DA15 175 J3
Ham St, Rich. TW10 163 F2
Ham Vw, Croy. CR0 189 H6
Ham Yd, W1 17 H5
Hanah Ct, SW19 166 A7
Hanameel St, E16 135 G1
Hana Ms, E5 *off Goulton Rd* 95 F4

Hanbury Cl, NW4 ... **71** J3
Hanbury Dr, E11 *off High Rd Leytonstone* ... **79** F7
N21 ... **43** F5
Hanbury Ms, N1 *off Mary St* ... **111** J1
Hanbury Rd, N17 ... **76** E2
W3 ... **126** B2
Hanbury St, E1 ... **21** F1
Hancock Ct, Borwd. WD6 ... **38** C1
Hancock Rd, E3 ... **114** C3
SE19 ... **170** A6
Handa Wk, N1 *off Clephane Rd* ... **93** J6
Hand Ct, WC1 ... **18** D2
Handcroft Rd, Croy. CR0 ... **187** H7
Handel Cl, Edg. HA8 ... **53** J6
Handel Pl, NW10 ... **88** D6
Handel St, WC1 ... **10** A5
Handel Way, Edg. HA8 ... **54** A7
Handen Rd, SE12 ... **155** E5
Handforth Rd, SW9 ... **34** E7
Ilford IG1 *off Winston Way* ... **99** E3
Handley Gro, NW2 ... **90** A3
Handley Page Rd, Wall. SM6 ... **201** F7
Handley Rd, E9 ... **95** F7
Handowe Cl, NW4 ... **71** G4
Handside Cl, Wor.Pk. KT4 ... **198** A1
Hands Wk, E16 ... **115** G6
Handsworth Av, E4 ... **62** D6
Handsworth Rd, N17 ... **76** A3
Handsworth Way, Wat. WD19 ... **50** A3
Handtrough Way, Bark. IG11 *off Fresh Wf Rd* ... **117** E2
Hanford Cl, SW18 ... **166** D1
Hanford Row, SW19 ... **165** J6
Hangar Ruding, Wat. WD19 ... **51** F3
Hanger Grn, W5 ... **106** A4
Hanger La, W5 ... **105** J4
Hanger Vale La, W5 ... **105** J6
Hanger Vw Way, W3 ... **106** A6
Hanging Sword All, EC4 ... **19** F4
Hankey Pl, SE1 ... **28** C4
Hankins La, NW7 ... **54** E3
Hanley Gdns, N4 ... **93** E1
Hanley Pl, Beck. BR3 ... **172** A7
Hanley Rd, N4 ... **93** E1
Hanmer Wk, N7 *off Newington Barrow Way* ... **93** F3
Hannah Cl, NW10 ... **88** C4
Beckenham BR3 ... **190** C3
Hannah Ct, N13 ... **59** F2
Hannah Mary Way, SE1 ... **37** J2
Hannah Ms, Wall. SM6 ... **200** C7
Hannay La, N8 ... **74** D7
Hannay Wk, SW16 ... **168** D2
Hannell Rd, SW6 ... **128** B7
Hannen Rd, SE27 *off Norwood High St* ... **169** H3
Hannibal Rd, E1 ... **113** F5
Staines (Stanw.) TW19 ... **140** A7
Hannibal Way, Croy. CR0 ... **201** F6
Hannington Rd, SW4 ... **150** B3
Hanover Av, E16 ... **135** G1
Feltham TW13 ... **160** A1
Hanover Cl, Rich. TW9 ... **126** A7
Sutton SM3 ... **198** C4
Hanover Ct, SE19 *off Anerley Rd* ... **170** C7
W12 *off Uxbridge Rd* ... **127** G1
Hanover Dr, Chis. BR7 ... **175** F4
Hanover Gdns, SE11 ... **34** E6
Ilford IG6 ... **65** F7
Hanover Gate, NW1 ... **7** H4
Hanover Gate Mans, NW1 ... **7** H5
Hanover Ho, Surb. KT6 *off Lenelby Rd* ... **196** A1
Hanover Pk, SE15 ... **152** D1
Hanover Pl, E3 *off Brokesley St* ... **113** J3
WC2 ... **18** B4
Hanover Rd, N15 ... **76** C4
NW10 ... **89** J7
SW19 ... **167** F7
Hanover Sq, W1 ... **17** E4
Hanover Steps, W2 *off St. Georges Flds* ... **15** H4
Hanover St, W1 ... **17** E4
Croydon CR0 *off Abbey Rd* ... **201** H3
Hanover Ter, NW1 ... **7** H4
Hanover Ter Ms, NW1 ... **7** H4
Hanover Way, Bexh. DA6 ... **158** D3
Hanover W Ind Est, NW10 ... **106** D2
Hanover Yd, N1 ... **11** H1
Hansa Cl, Sthl. UB2 ... **122** C3
Hansard Ms, W14 *off Holland Rd* ... **128** A2
Hansart Way, Enf. EN2 *off The Ridgeway* ... **43** G1
Hanscomb Ms, SW4 *off Bromell's Rd* ... **150** C4
Hans Cres, SW1 ... **23** J5
Hanselin Cl, Stan. HA7 ... **52** C5
Hansen Dr, N21 ... **43** F5
Hanshaw Dr, Edg. HA8 ... **70** D1
Hansler Gro, E.Mol. KT8 ... **180** A4
Hansler Rd, SE22 ... **152** C5
Hansol Rd, Bexh. DA6 ... **158** E5
Hanson Cl, SW12 ... **150** B7
SW14 ... **146** C3
Beckenham BR3 ... **172** B6
Loughton IG10 ... **49** F2
West Drayton UB7 ... **120** C3
Hanson Dr, Loug. IG10 ... **49** F2
Hanson Gdns, Sthl. UB1 ... **123** E2
Hanson Grn, Loug. IG10 ... **49** F2
Hanson St, W1 ... **17** F1
Hans Pl, SW1 ... **24** A5
Hans Rd, SW3 ... **23** J5
Hans St, SW1 ... **24** A6
Hanway Pl, W1 ... **17** H3
Hanway Rd, W7 ... **104** A6
Hanway St, W1 ... **17** H3
HANWELL, W7 ... **124** C1
HANWORTH, Felt. TW13 ... **160** D4
Hanworth Rd, Felt. TW13 ... **160** B1
Hampton TW12 ... **161** H6
Hounslow TW3, TW4 ... **143** H3
Sunbury-on-Thames TW16 ... **160** A7
Hanworth Ter, Houns. TW3 ... **143** H4
Hanworth Trd Est, Felt. TW13 ... **161** E3
Hapgood Cl, Grnf. UB6 ... **86** A5
Harads Pl, E1 ... **21** J6
Harben Rd, NW6 ... **91** F7
Harberson Rd, E15 ... **115** F1
SW12 ... **168** B1
Harberton Rd, N19 ... **92** C1
Harbet Rd, E4 ... **61** G5
N18 ... **61** G5
W2 ... **15** F2
Harbex Cl, Bex. DA5 ... **159** H7
Harbinger Rd, E14 ... **134** B4
Harbledown Rd, SW6 ... **148** D1
Harbord Cl, SE5 *off De Crespigny Pk* ... **152** A2
Harbord St, SW6 ... **148** A1
Harborne Cl, Wat. WD19 ... **50** C5
Harborough Av, Sid. DA15 ... **157** H7
Harborough Rd, SW16 ... **169** F4
Harbour Av, SW10 ... **149** F1
Harbour Cl, Mitch. CR4 ... **186** A1
Harbour Ex Sq, E14 ... **134** B2
Harbour Reach, SW6 *off The Boulevard* ... **149** F1
Harbour Rd, SE5 ... **151** J3
Harbour Yd, SW10 *off Harbour Av* ... **149** F1
Harbridge Av, SW15 ... **147** F7
Harbut Rd, SW11 ... **149** G4
Harcombe Rd, N16 ... **94** B3
Harcourt Av, E12 ... **98** C4
Edgware HA8 ... **54** C3
Sidcup DA15 ... **158** C6
Wallington SM6 ... **200** B4
Harcourt Cl, Islw. TW7 ... **144** D3
Harcourt Fld, Wall. SM6 ... **200** B4
Harcourt Lo, Wall. SM6 *off Croydon Rd* ... **200** B4
Harcourt Rd, E15 ... **115** F2
N22 ... **74** D1
SE4 ... **153** H4
SW19 *off Russell Rd* ... **166** D7
Bexleyheath DA6 ... **159** E4
Thornton Heath CR7 ... **187** F6
Wallington SM6 ... **200** B4
Harcourt St, W1 ... **15** H2
Harcourt Ter, SW10 ... **30** B4
Hardcastle Cl, Croy. CR0 ... **188** D6
Hardcourts Cl, W.Wick. BR4 ... **204** B3
Hardel Ri, SW2 ... **169** H2
Hardel Wk, SW2 *off Papworth Way* ... **151** G7
Hardens Manorway, SE7 ... **136** A3
Harders Rd, SE15 ... **152** E2
Hardess St, SE24 *off Herne Hill Rd* ... **151** J3
Hardie Cl, NW10 ... **88** D5
Hardie Rd, Dag. RM10 ... **101** J3
Harding Cl, SE17 ... **35** J5
Croydon CR0 ... **202** C3
Hardinge Cres, SE18 ... **137** F3
Hardinge Rd, N18 ... **60** B5
NW10 ... **107** H1
Hardinge St, E1 ... **113** F6
Harding Ho, Hayes UB3 ... **102** B6
Harding Rd, Bexh. DA7 ... **159** F2
Harding's Cl, Kings.T. KT2 ... **181** J1
Hardings La, SE20 ... **171** G6
Hardman Rd, SE7 ... **135** H5
Kingston upon Thames KT2 ... **181** H2
Hardwick Cl, Stan. HA7 ... **53** F5
Hardwicke Av, Houns. TW5 ... **143** G1
Hardwicke Ho, E3 *off Bromley High St* ... **114** B3
Hardwicke Ms, WC1 ... **10** D4
Hardwicke Rd, N13 ... **58** E6
W4 ... **126** C4
Richmond TW10 ... **163** F4
Hardwicke St, Bark. IG11 ... **117** F1
Hardwick Grn, W13 ... **105** E5
Hardwick's Sq, SW18 ... **148** D5
Hardwick St, EC1 ... **11** F4
Hardwidge St, SE1 ... **28** D3
Hardy Av, E16 *off Wesley Av* ... **135** G1
Ruislip HA4 ... **84** B5
Hardy Cl, SE16 *off Middleton Dr* ... **133** G2
Barnet EN5 ... **40** B6
Pinner HA5 ... **66** D7
Hardy Pas, N22 *off Berners Rd* ... **75** G2
Hardy Rd, E4 ... **61** J6
SE3 ... **135** F7
SW19 ... **167** E7
Hardy's Ms, E.Mol. KT8 ... **180** B4
Hardy Way, Enf. EN2 ... **43** G1
Hare & Billet Rd, SE3 ... **154** D1
Harebell Dr, E6 ... **116** D5
Harecastle Cl, Hayes UB4 ... **102** E4
Hare Ct, EC4 ... **19** E4
Harecourt Rd, N1 ... **93** J6
Haredale Rd, SE24 ... **151** J4
Haredon Cl, SE23 ... **153** F7
Harefield, Esher KT10 ... **194** B4
Harefield Cl, Enf. EN2 ... **43** G1
Harefield Ms, SE4 ... **153** J3
Harefield Rd, N8 ... **74** D5
SE4 ... **153** J3
SW16 ... **169** F7
Sidcup DA14 ... **176** D2
Hare La, Esher (Clay.) KT10 ... **194** B6
Hare Marsh, E2 ... **13** H5
Harepit Cl, S.Croy. CR2 ... **201** H7
Hare Pl, EC4 ... **19** F4
Hare Row, E2 ... **113** E2
Haresfield Rd, Dag. RM10 ... **101** G6
Hare St, SE18 ... **136** D3
Hare Wk, N1 ... **12** E2
Harewood Av, NW1 ... **7** H6
Northolt UB5 ... **85** E7
Harewood Cl, Nthlt. UB5 ... **85** F7
Harewood Dr, Ilf. IG5 ... **80** C2
Harewood Pl, W1 ... **16** E4
Harewood Rd, SW19 ... **167** H6
Isleworth TW7 ... **124** C7
South Croydon CR2 ... **202** B6
Watford WD19 ... **50** B3
Harewood Row, NW1 ... **15** H1
Harewood Ter, Sthl. UB2 ... **123** F4
Harfield Gdns, SE5 ... **152** B3
Harfield Rd, Sun. TW16 ... **178** D2
Harford Cl, E4 ... **46** B7
Harford Ms, N19 ... **92** D3
Harford Rd, E4 ... **46** B7
Harford St, E1 ... **113** H4
Harford Wk, N2 ... **73** G5
Hargood Cl, Har. HA3 ... **69** H6
Hargood Rd, SE3 ... **155** J1
Hargrave Pk, N19 ... **92** C2
Hargrave Pl, N7 *off Brecknock Rd* ... **92** D5
Hargrave Rd, N19 ... **92** C2
Hargwyne St, SW9 ... **151** F3
Hari Cl, Nthlt. UB5 ... **85** H5
Haringey Pk, N8 ... **74** E6
Haringey Pas, N4 ... **75** H6
N8 ... **75** G4
Haringey Rd, N8 ... **74** E4
Harington Ter, N9 ... **60** A3
N18 ... **60** A3
Harkett Cl, Har. HA3 *off Byron Rd* ... **68** C2
Harkett Ct, Har. HA3 ... **68** C2
Harkness Ct, Sutt. SM1 *off Cleeve Way* ... **199** F1
Harkness Ho, E1 *off Christian St* ... **21** J4
Harland Av, Croy. CR0 ... **202** C3
Sidcup DA15 ... **175** G3
Harland Cl, SW19 ... **184** E3
Harland Rd, SE12 ... **173** G1
Harlands Gro, Orp. BR6 ... **207** E4
Harlech Gdns, Houns. TW5 ... **122** C6
Pinner HA5 ... **66** D7
Harlech Rd, N14 ... **59** E3
Harlech Twr, W3 ... **126** B2
Harlequin Av, Brent. TW8 ... **124** D6
Harlequin Cl, Hayes UB4 *off Cygnet Way* ... **102** D5
Isleworth TW7 ... **144** B5
Harlequin Ho, Erith DA18 *off Kale Rd* ... **138** E3
Harlequin Rd, Tedd. TW11 ... **162** E7
★ **Harlequins RL**, Twick. TW2 ... **144** B7
Harlescott Rd, SE15 ... **153** G4
HARLESDEN, NW10 ... **106** E2
Harlesden Gdns, NW10 ... **107** F1
Harlesden La, NW10 ... **107** G1
Harlesden Rd, NW10 ... **107** G1
Harleston Cl, E5 *off Theydon Rd* ... **95** F2
Harley Cl, Wem. HA0 ... **87** G6
Harley Ct, E11 *off Blake Hall Rd* ... **79** G7
Harley Cres, Har. HA1 ... **68** A4
Harleyford, Brom. BR1 ... **191** H1
Harleyford Rd, SE11 ... **34** C5
Harleyford St, SE11 ... **34** E6
Harley Gdns, SW10 ... **30** D4
Orpington BR6 ... **207** H4
Harley Gro, E3 ... **113** J3
Harley Pl, W1 ... **16** D2
Harley Rd, NW3 ... **91** G7
NW10 ... **106** E2
Harrow HA1 ... **68** A4
Harley St, W1 ... **16** D2
Harling Ct, SW11 *off Latchmere Rd* ... **149** J2
Harlinger St, SE18 ... **136** B3
HARLINGTON, Hayes UB3 ... **121** F6
Harlington Cl, Hayes (Harling.) UB3 ... **121** F7
Harlington Cor, Hayes UB3 *off Bath Rd* ... **141** G1
Harlington Rd, Bexh. DA7 ... **159** E3
Hounslow (Lon.Hthrw Air.) TW6 ... **141** J4
Harlington Rd E, Felt. TW13, TW14 ... **142** B7
Harlington Rd W, Felt. TW14 ... **142** B6
Harlow Rd, N13 ... **60** A3
Harlyn Dr, Pnr. HA5 ... **66** B3
Harman Av, Wdf.Grn. IG8 ... **63** F7
Harman Cl, E4 ... **62** D4
NW2 ... **90** B3
SE1 *off Avondale Sq* ... **37** H4
Harman Dr, NW2 ... **90** B3
Sidcup DA15 ... **157** J6
Harman Rise, Ilf. IG3 ... **99** H4
Harman Rd, Enf. EN1 ... **44** C5
HARMONDSWORTH, West Dr. UB7 ... **120** A6
Harmondsworth La, West Dr. UB7 ... **120** B6
Harmondsworth Rd, West Dr. UB7 ... **120** B5
Harmony Cl, NW11 ... **72** B5
Harmony Pl, SE1 ... **37** G3
Harmony Ter, Har. HA2 *off Goldsmith Cl* ... **85** H1
Harmony Way, NW4 *off Victoria Rd* ... **71** J4
Harmood Gro, NW1 *off Clarence Way* ... **92** B7
Harmood Pl, NW1 *off Harmood St* ... **92** B7
Harmood St, NW1 ... **92** B7
Harmsworth Ms, SE11 ... **27** G6
Harmsworth St, SE17 ... **35** G4
Harmsworth Way, N20 ... **56** C1
Harold Av, Belv. DA17 ... **139** F5
Hayes UB3 ... **121** J3
Harold Est, SE1 ... **28** E6
Harold Gibbons Ct, SE7 ... **135** J6
Harold Laski Ho, EC1 ... **11** G4
Harold Pl, SE11 *off Kennington La* ... **34** E4
Harold Rd, E4 ... **62** C4
E11 ... **96** E1
E13 ... **115** H1
N8 ... **75** F5
N15 ... **76** C5
NW10 ... **106** D3
SE19 ... **170** B6
Sutton SM1 ... **199** G4
Woodford Green IG8 ... **79** G1
Haroldstone Rd, E17 ... **77** G5
Harp All, EC4 ... **19** G3
Harpenden Rd, E12 ... **97** J2
SE27 ... **169** H3
Harpenmead Pt, NW2 ... **90** C2
Harper Cl, N14 *off Alexandra Ct* ... **42** C5
Harper Ms, SW17 ... **167** F3
Harper Rd, E6 ... **116** C6
SE1 ... **27** J5
Harpers Yd, N17 ... **76** C1
Harp Island Cl, NW10 ... **88** D2
Harp La, EC3 ... **20** D6
Harpley Sq, E1 ... **113** F3
Harpour Rd, Barking IG11 ... **99** F6
Harp Rd, W7 ... **104** C4

Harpsden St, SW11
off Battersea Pk Rd . . . **150** A1
Harpur Ms, WC1 . . . . **18** C1
Harpur St, WC1 . . . . **18** C1
Harraden Rd, SE3 . . . . **155** J1
Harrap St, E14 . . . . **114** C7
Harrier Av, E11
off Eastern Av **79** H6
Harrier Ms, SE28 . . . . **137** G3
Harrier Rd, NW9 . . . . **71** E2
Harriers Cl, W5 . . . . **105** H7
Harrier Way, E6 . . . . **116** C4
Harries Rd, Hayes UB4 . . . **102** C4
Harriet Cl, E8 . . . . **112** D1
Harriet Gdns, Croy. CR0 . . **202** D2
Harriet St, SW1 . . . . **24** A4
Harriet Tubman Cl, SW2 . . **151** G7
Harriet Wk, SW1 . . . . **24** A4
HARRINGAY, N8 . . . . **75** G5
Harringay Gdns, N8 . . . . **75** H4
Harringay Rd, N15 . . . . **75** H5
Harrington Cl, NW10 . . . . . . **88** D3
Croydon CR0 . . . . **200** E2
Harrington Ct, W10
off Dart St **108** C3
Croydon CR0
off Altyre Rd **202** A2
Harrington Gdns, SW7 . . . . **30** B2
Harrington Hill, E5 . . . . **95** E1
Harrington Ho, NW1 . . . . **9** F3
Harrington Rd, E11 . . . . **97** E1
SE25 . . . . **188** D4
SW7 . . . . **30** E1
Harrington Sq, NW1 . . . . **9** F2
Harrington St, NW1 . . . . **9** F3
Harrington Way, SE18 . . . . **136** A3
Harriott Cl, SE10 . . . . **135** F4
Harris Cl, Enf. EN2 . . . . **43** H1
Hounslow TW3 . . . . **143** G1
Harrison Cl, N20 . . . . **57** H1
Harrison Dr, Brom. BR1 . . . **192** E4
Harrison Rd, NW10 . . . . **106** D1
Dagenham RM10 . . . . . . **101** H6
Harrisons Ri, Croy. CR0 . . . **201** H3
Harrison St, WC1 . . . . **10** B4
Harris Rd, Bexh. DA7 . . . . . **159** E1
Dagenham RM9 . . . . **101** F5
Harris St, E17 . . . . **77** J7
SE5 . . . . **132** A7
★ **Harrods**, SW1 . . . . **23** J5
Harrogate Rd, Wat. WD19 . . **50** C3
Harrold Rd, Dag. RM8 . . . . **100** B5
HARROW, HA1 - HA3 . . . . . **68** A7
★ **Harrow Arts Cen**, Pnr. HA5 . . . . **51** H7
Harrow Av, Enf. EN1 . . . . . . **44** C6
Harroway Rd, SW11 . . . . . . **149** G2
Harrowby St, W1 . . . . **15** H3
Harrow Cl, Chess. KT9 . . . . **195** G7
Harrowdene Cl, Wem. HA0 . . . . **87** G4
Harrowdene Gdns, Tedd. TW11 . . . . **162** D6
Harrowdene Rd, Wem. HA0 . . . . **87** G3
Harrow Dr, N9 . . . . **60** C1
Harrowes Meade, Edg. HA8 . . . . **54** A3
Harrow Flds Gdns, Har. HA1 . . . . **86** B3
Harrowgate Rd, E9 . . . . **95** H6
Harrow Grn, E11 . . . . **96** E3
Harrow La, E14 . . . . **114** C7
Harrow Manorway, SE2 . . . . **138** C1
★ **Harrow Mus**, Har. HA2 . . . . **67** J3
HARROW ON THE HILL, Har. HA1 . . . . **86** B2
Harrow Pk, Har. HA1 . . . . . . **86** B2
Harrow Pas, Kings.T. KT1
off Market Pl **181** G2
Harrow Pl, E1 . . . . **21** E3
Harrow Rd, E6 . . . . **116** B1
E11 . . . . **97** E3
NW10 . . . . **107** H3
W2 . . . . **14** A2
W9 . . . . **108** C4
W10 . . . . **108** A4
Barking IG11 . . . . **117** H1
Carshalton SM5 . . . . . . **199** H5
Ilford IG1 . . . . **99** F4
Wembley HA0 . . . . **87** F5
Wembley (Tkgtn) HA9 . . . **87** J5
★ **Harrow Sch**, Har. HA1 . . **86** B1
Harrow Vw, Har. HA1, HA2 . . . . **68** A4
Hayes UB3 . . . . **102** A6
Harrow Vw Rd, W5 . . . . **105** E4
Harrow Way, Wat. WD19 . . . **50** E3
HARROW WEALD, Har. HA3 . . . . **68** A1
Harrow Weald Pk, Har. HA3 . . . . **52** A6
Hart Cres, Chig. IG7 . . . . **65** J5
Harte Rd, Hounslow TW3 . . . . **143** F2
Hartfield Av, Borwd. (Els.) WD6 . . . . **38** A5
Northolt UB5 . . . . **102** B2
Hartfield Cl, Borwd. (Els.) WD6 . . . . **38** A5
Hartfield Cres, SW19 . . . . . **166** C7
West Wickham BR4 . . . . **205** G3
Hartfield Gro, SE20 . . . . . . **189** E1
Hartfield Rd, SW19 . . . . . . **166** C7
Chessington KT9 . . . . . . **195** G5
West Wickham BR4 . . . . **205** G4
Hartfield Ter, E3 . . . . **114** A2
Hartford Av, Har. HA3 . . . . . **68** D3
Hartforde Rd, Borwd. WD6 . . . . **38** A2
Hartford Rd, Bex. DA5 . . . . **159** G6
Epsom KT19 . . . . **196** A6
Hart Gro, W5 . . . . **126** A1
Southall UB1 . . . . **103** G5
Hartham Cl, N7 . . . . **93** E5
Isleworth TW7 . . . . **144** D1
Hartham Rd, N7 . . . . **92** E5
N17 . . . . **76** C2
Isleworth TW7 . . . . **144** C1
Harting Rd, SE9 . . . . **174** B4
Hartington Cl, Har. HA1 . . . . **86** B4
Orpington (Farnboro.) BR6 . . . . **207** F5
Hartington Ct, W4 . . . . **126** B7
Hartington Rd, E16 . . . . . . **115** H6
E17 . . . . **77** H6
SW8 . . . . **150** E1
W4 . . . . **126** B7
W13 . . . . **105** E7
Southall UB2 . . . . **122** E3
Twickenham TW1 . . . . . . **144** E7
Hartismere Rd, SW6 . . . . . **128** C7
Hartlake Rd, E9 . . . . **95** G6
Hartland Cl, N21
off Elmscott Gdns **43** J6
Edgware HA8 . . . . **54** A2
Hartland Dr, Edg. HA8 . . . . . **54** A2
Ruislip HA4 . . . . **84** B3
Hartland Rd, E15 . . . . **97** F7
N11 . . . . **57** J5
NW1 . . . . **92** B7
NW6 . . . . **108** C2
Hampton (Hmptn H.) TW12 . . . . **161** H4
Isleworth TW7 . . . . **144** D3
Morden SM4 . . . . **184** D7
Hartlands Cl, Bex. DA5 . . . **159** F6
Hartland Way, Croy. CR0 . . **203** H2
Morden SM4 . . . . **184** C7
Hartlepool Ct, E16
off Fishguard Way **137** E1
Hartley Av, E6 . . . . **116** B1
NW7 . . . . **55** F5
Hartley Cl, NW7 . . . . **55** F5
Bromley BR1 . . . . **192** C2
Hartley Ho, SE1
off Longfield Est **37** G1
Hartley Rd, E11 . . . . **97** F1
Croydon CR0 . . . . **187** H7
Welling DA16 . . . . **138** C7
Hartley St, E2 . . . . **113** F3
Hartmann Rd, E16 . . . . **136** B1
Hartnoll St, N7
off Eden Gro **93** F5
Harton Cl, Brom. BR1 . . . . **192** A1
Harton Rd, N9 . . . . **61** E2
Harton St, SE8 . . . . **154** A1
Hartopp Pt, SW6
off Pellant Rd **128** B7
Hartsbourne Av, Bushey (Bushey Hth) WD23 . . . . . **51** J2
Hartsbourne Cl, Bushey (Bushey Hth) WD23 . . . . . **52** A2
Hartsbourne Rd, Bushey (Bushey Hth) WD23 . . . . . **52** A2
Harts Gro, Wdf.Grn. IG8 . . . **63** G5
Hartshorn All, EC3 . . . . **21** E4
Hartshorn Gdns, E6 . . . . . . **116** D4
Harts La, SE14 . . . . **133** H7
Barking IG11 . . . . **98** E6
Hartslock Dr, SE2 . . . . **138** D2
Hartsmead Rd, SE9 . . . . . . **174** C2
Hart Sq, Mord. SM4 . . . . . **184** D6
Hart St, EC3 . . . . **20** E5
Hartsway, Enf. EN3 . . . . **45** F4
Hartswood Gdns, W12 . . . **127** F3
Hartswood Grn, Bushey (Bushey Hth) WD23 . . . . . **52** A2
Hartswood Rd, W12 . . . . . . **127** F2
Hartsworth Cl, E13 . . . . . . **115** F2
Hartville Rd, SE18 . . . . **137** H4
Hartwell Cl, SW2
off Challice Way **169** F1
Hartwell Dr, E4 . . . . **62** C6
Hartwell St, E8
off Dalston La **94** C6
Harvard Hill, W4 . . . . **126** B6
Harvard La, W4 . . . . **126** B5
Harvard Rd, SE13 . . . . **154** C5
W4 . . . . **126** B5
Isleworth TW7 . . . . **144** B1
Harvel Cres, SE2 . . . . **138** D5
Harvest Bk Rd, W.Wick. BR4 . . . . **205** F3
Harvesters Cl, Islw. TW7 . . **144** A5
Harvest La, Loug. IG10 . . . . **48** A7
Thames Ditton KT7 . . . . **180** D6
Harvest Rd, Felt. TW13 . . . **160** A4
Harvey Dr, Hmptn. TW12 . . **179** H1
Harvey Gdns, E11
off Harvey Rd **97** F1
SE7 . . . . **135** J5
Loughton IG10 . . . . **49** E3
Harvey Ho, Brent. TW8
off Green Dragon La . . **125** H5
Harvey Rd, E11 . . . . **97** E1
N8 . . . . **75** F5
SE5 . . . . **152** A1
Hounslow TW4 . . . . **143** F7
Ilford IG1 . . . . **99** E5
Northolt UB5 . . . . **84** C7
Walton-on-Thames KT12 . . . . **178** A7
Harvey St, N1 . . . . **112** A1
Harvill Rd, Sid. DA14 . . . . . **176** D5
Harvington Wk, E8
off Wilman Gro **94** D7
Harvist Est, N7 . . . . **93** F4
Harvist Rd, NW6 . . . . **108** A3
Harwater Dr, Loug. IG10 . . . **48** C2
Harwell Pas, N2 . . . . **73** J4
Harwood Av, Brom. BR1 . . **191** H2
Mitcham CR4 . . . . **185** H3
Harwood Cl, N12 . . . . **57** H6
Wembley HA0 . . . . **87** G3
Harwood Rd, SW6 . . . . **128** D7
Harwoods Yd, N21
off Wades Hill **43** G7
Harwood Ter, SW6 . . . . **148** E1
Hascombe Ter, SE5
off Love Wk **152** A2
Haselbury Rd, N9 . . . . **60** B4
N18 . . . . **60** B4
Haseley End, SE23
off Tyson Rd **153** F7
Haselrigge Rd, SW4 . . . . . . **150** D4
Haseltine Rd, SE26 . . . . . . **171** J4
Haselwood Dr, Enf. EN2 . . . **43** H4
Haskard Rd, Dag. RM9 . . . **100** D4
Hasker St, SW3 . . . . **31** H1
Haslam Av, Sutt. SM3 . . . . **198** B1
Haslam Cl, N1 . . . . **93** G7
Haslam Ct, N11
off Waterfall Rd **58** B4
Haslam St, SE15 . . . . **132** C7
Haslemere Av, NW4 . . . . **72** A6
SW18 . . . . **166** E2
W7 . . . . **124** D3
W13 . . . . **124** D3
Barnet EN4 . . . . **57** J1
Hounslow TW5 . . . . **142** C2
Mitcham CR4 . . . . **185** G2
Haslemere Business Cen, Enf. EN1 . . . . **44** E5
Haslemere Cl, Hmptn. TW12 . . . . **161** F5
Wallington SM6 . . . . **201** E5
Haslemere Gdns, N3 . . . . . . **72** C3
Haslemere Heathrow Est, Houns. TW4 . . . . **142** B2
Haslemere Ind Est, SW18 . . . . **167** E2
Haslemere Rd, N8 . . . . **74** D7
N21 . . . . **59** H2
Bexleyheath DA7 . . . . . . **159** F2
Ilford IG3 . . . . **99** J2
Thornton Heath CR7 . . . **187** H5
Hasler Cl, SE28 . . . . **118** B7
Hasluck Gdns, Barn. (New Barn.) EN5 . . . . **41** F6
Hassard St, E2 . . . . **13** G2
Hassendean Rd, SE3 . . . . . **135** H6
Hassett Rd, E9 . . . . **95** G6
Hassocks Cl, SE26 . . . . **171** E3
Hassocks Rd, SW16 . . . . . . **186** D1
Hassock Wd, Kes. BR2 . . . . **206** A4
Hassop Rd, NW2 . . . . **90** A4
Hassop Wk, SE9 . . . . **174** B4
Hasted Rd, SE7 . . . . **136** A5
Hastings Av, Ilf. IG6 . . . . **81** F4
Hastings Cl, SE15 . . . . **132** D7
Barnet EN5 . . . . **41** F4
Wembley HA0 . . . . **87** F4
Hastings Dr, Surb. KT6 . . . **181** F6
Hastings Ho, SE18 . . . . **136** C4
Hastings Pl, Croy. CR0
off Hastings Rd **202** C1
Hastings Rd, N11 . . . . **58** C5
N17 . . . . **76** A3
W13 . . . . **104** E7
Bromley BR2 . . . . **206** B1
Croydon CR0 . . . . **202** C1
Hastings St, SE18 . . . . **137** F3
WC1 . . . . **10** A4
Hastingwood Trd Est, N18 . . **61** G6
Hastoe Cl, Hayes UB4 . . . . **102** E4
Hasty Cl, Mitch. CR4
off Slade Way **186** A1
Hat & Mitre Ct, EC1 . . . . **11** H6
Hatch, The, Enf. EN3 . . . . . . **45** G1
Hatcham Ms Business Cen, SE14
off Hatcham Pk Rd **153** G1
Hatcham Pk Ms, SE14
off Hatcham Pk Rd **153** G1
Hatcham Pk Rd, SE14 . . . . **153** G1
Hatcham Rd, SE15 . . . . **133** F6
Hatchard Rd, N19 . . . . **92** D2
Hatchcroft, NW4 . . . . **71** H3
HATCH END, Pnr. HA5 . . . . . **50** E7
Hatchers Ms, SE1 . . . . **28** E4
Hatch Gro, Rom. RM6 . . . . . **83** E4
Hatch La, E4 . . . . **62** D4
West Drayton (Harm.) UB7 . . . . **120** A7
Hatch Pl, Kings.T. KT2 . . . . **163** J5
Hatch Rd, SW16 . . . . **187** E2
Hatch Side, Chig. IG7 . . . . . **64** D5
Hatchwood Cl, Wdf.Grn. IG8 *off Sunset Av* **63** F4
Hatcliffe Cl, SE3 . . . . **155** F3
Hatcliffe St, SE10 . . . . **135** F5
Hatfeild Cl, Mitch. CR4 . . . . **185** G4
Hatfeild Mead, Mord. SM4 . . . . **184** D5
Hatfield Cl, SE14
off Reaston St **133** G7
Ilford IG6 . . . . **81** E3
Hatfield Ms, Dag. RM9 . . . . **101** E7
Hatfield Rd, E15 . . . . **97** E5
W4 . . . . **126** D2
W13 . . . . **124** D1
Dagenham RM9 . . . . **101** E6
Hatfields, SE1 . . . . **27** F1
Loughton IG10 . . . . **48** E3
Hathaway Cl, Brom. BR2 . . **206** C1
Ilford IG6 . . . . **65** E6
Stanmore HA7 . . . . **52** D5
Hathaway Cres, E12 . . . . **98** C6
Hathaway Gdns, W13 . . . . **104** C5
Romford RM6 . . . . **82** D5
Hathaway Rd, Croy. CR0 . . **187** H7
Hatherleigh Cl, NW7 . . . . . . **56** A7
Chessington KT9 . . . . . . **195** G5
Morden SM4 . . . . **184** D4
Hatherleigh Rd, Ruis. HA4 . **84** A2
Hatherley Cres, Sid. DA14 . **176** A2
Hatherley Gdns, E6 . . . . . . **116** A2
N8 . . . . **74** E6
Hatherley Gro, W2 . . . . **14** A3
Hatherley Ms, E17 . . . . **78** A4
Hatherley Rd, E17 . . . . **77** J4
Richmond TW9 . . . . **145** J1
Sidcup DA14 . . . . **176** A4
Hatherley St, SW1 . . . . **33** G2
Hathern Gdns, SE9 . . . . . . **174** D4
Hatherop Rd, Hmptn. TW12 . . . . **161** F7
Hathersage Ct, N1
off Newington Grn **94** A5
Hathorne Cl, SE15 . . . . **153** E2
Hathway St, SE15
off Gibbon Rd **153** F2
Hathway Ter, SE14
off Gibbon Rd **153** G2
Hatley Av, Ilf. IG6 . . . . **81** F4
Hatley Cl, N11 . . . . **57** J5
Hatley Rd, N4 . . . . **93** F2
Hatteraick St, SE16
off Brunel Rd **133** F2
Hattersfield Cl, Belv. DA17 . . . . **139** F4
HATTON, Felt. TW14 . . . . . . **141** J4
Hatton Cl, SE18 . . . . **137** G7
Hatton Cross, Felt. TW14
off Great South-West Rd **141** J4
Hatton Cross Rbt, Houns. TW6 *off Southern Perimeter Rd* **141** J3
Hatton Gdn, EC1 . . . . **19** F1
Hatton Gdns, Mitch. CR4 . . **185** J5
Hatton Grn, Felt. TW14 . . . **142** A4
Hatton Gro, West Dr. UB7 . . . . **120** A2
Hatton Ho, E1 . . . . **21** J5
Hatton Pl, EC1 . . . . **11** F6
Hatton Rd, Croy. CR0 . . . . . **201** G1
Feltham TW14 . . . . **141** H5
Hatton Row, NW8 . . . . **7** F6
Hatton St, NW8 . . . . **7** F6
Hatton Wk, Enf. EN2
off London Rd **44** A4
Hatton Wall, EC1 . . . . **19** E1
Haul Rd, NW1 . . . . **10** A1
Haunch of Venison Yd, W1 . **16** D4
Hauteville Ct Gdns, W6
off Stamford Brook Av **127** F3
Havana Rd, SW19 . . . . **166** D2
Havannah St, E14 . . . . **134** A2
Havant Rd, E17 . . . . **78** C3
Havelock Cl, W12
off India Way **107** H7
Havelock Pl, Harrow HA1 . . . . **68** B6

Havelock Rd, N17 .76 D2
SW19 .167 F5
Belvedere DA17 .139 F4
Bromley BR2 .191 J4
Croydon CR0 .202 C1
Harrow HA3 .68 B3
Southall UB2 .123 F3
Havelock St, N1 .111 E1
Ilford IG1 .99 E2
Havelock Ter, SW8 .130 B7
Havelock Wk, SE23 .171 F1
Haven, The, SE26 .171 E5
Richmond TW9 .146 A3
Sunbury-on-Thames TW16 .160 A7
Haven Cl, SE9 .174 C3
SW19 .166 A3
Esher KT10 .194 B2
Sidcup DA14 .176 C6
Haven Ct, Esher KT10
off Portsmouth Rd .194 B2
Haven Grn, W5 .105 G6
Haven Grn Ct, W5 .105 G6
Havenhurst Ri, Enf. EN2 .43 G2
Haven La, W5 .105 H6
Haven Ms, N1
off Liverpool Rd .93 G7
Haven Pl, W5 .105 G7
Esher KT10 .194 B2
Haven St, NW1
off Castlehaven Rd .92 B7
Havenwood, Wem. HA9 .88 B3
Haverfield Gdns, Rich. TW9 .126 A7
Haverfield Rd, E3 .113 H3
Haverford Way, Edg. HA8 .69 J1
Haverhill Rd, E4 .62 C1
SW12 .168 C1
Havering Gdns, Rom. RM6 .82 C5
Havering St, E1
off Devonport St .113 G6
Havering Way, Bark. IG11 .118 B3
Haversfield Est, Brent. TW8 .125 H5
Haversham Cl, Twick. TW1 .145 G6
Haversham Pl, N6 .91 J2
Haverstock Hill, NW3 .91 H5
Haverstock Pl, N1
off Haverstock St .11 H3
Haverstock Rd, NW5 .92 A5
Haverstock St, N1 .11 H2
Haverthwaite Rd, Orp. BR6 .207 G2
Havil St, SE5 .132 B7
Havisham Pl, SE19 .169 H6
Hawarden Gro, SE24 .151 J7
Hawarden Hill, NW2 .89 G3
Hawarden Rd, E17 .77 G4
Hawbridge Rd, E11 .96 D1
Hawes La, W.Wick. BR4 .204 C1
Hawes Rd, N18 .60 E6
Bromley BR1 .191 H1
Hawes St, N1 .93 H7
Haweswater Ho, Islw. TW7
off Summerwood Rd .144 C5
Hawgood St, E3 .114 A5
Hawkdene, E4 .46 B6
Hawke Pk Rd, N22 .75 H3
Hawke Pl, SE16
off Middleton Dr .133 G2
Hawke Rd, SE19 .170 B6
Hawker Pl, E17 .78 C2
Hawker Rd, Croy. CRO .201 G6
Hawkesbury Rd, SW15 .147 H5
Hawkesfield Rd, SE23 .171 H2
Hawkesley Cl, Twick. TW1 .162 D4
Hawkes Rd, Felt. TW14 .142 A7
Mitcham CR4 .185 H1
Hawke Twr, SE14
off Nynehead St .133 H6
Hawkewood Rd, Sun. TW16 .178 A3
Hawkhurst Gdns, Chess. KT9 .195 H4
Hawkhurst Rd, SW16 .186 D1
Hawkhurst Way, N.Mal. KT3 .182 D5
West Wickham BR4 .204 B2
Hawkins Cl, NW7
off Hale La .54 D5
Borehamwood WD6
off Banks Rd .38 C2
Harrow HA1 .68 A7
Hawkins Rd, NW10 .88 E7
Teddington TW11 .163 E6
Hawkins Ter, SE7 .136 B5
Hawkins Way, SE6 .172 A5
Hawkley Gdns, SE27 .169 H2
Hawkridge, NW5
off Warden Rd .92 A6
Hawkridge Cl, Rom. RM6 .82 C7
Hawksbrook La, Beck. BR3 .190 B6
Hawkshaw Cl, SW2
off Tierney Rd .150 E7
Hawkshead, NW1 .9 F3
Hawkshead Cl, Brom. BR1 .173 E7
Hawkshead Rd, NW10 .89 F7
W4 .126 E2
Hawkslade Rd, SE15 .153 G5
Hawksley Rd, N16 .94 B3
Hawks Ms, SE10
off Luton Pl .134 C7
Hawksmoor Cl, E6
off Allhallows Rd .116 B6
SE18 .137 H5
Hawksmoor Ms, E1
off Cable St .112 E7
Hawksmoor St, W6 .128 A6
Hawksmouth, E4 .46 B7
Hawks Rd, Kings.T. KT1 .181 J2
Hawkstone Est, SE16 .133 F4
Hawkstone Rd, SE16 .133 F4
Hawk Ter, Ilf. IG5
off Tiptree Cres .80 D3
Hawkwell Ct, E4
off Colvin Gdns .62 C3
Hawkwell Ho, Dag. RM8 .101 G1
Hawkwell Wk, N1
off Basire St .111 J1
Hawkwood Cres, E4 .46 B6
Hawkwood La, Chis. BR7 .193 F1
Hawkwood Mt, E5 .95 E1
Hawlands Dr, Pnr. HA5 .66 E7
Hawley Cl, Hmptn. TW12 .161 F6
Hawley Cres, NW1 .92 B7
Hawley Ms, NW1
off Hawley St .92 B7
Hawley Rd, N18 .61 G5
NW1 .92 B7
Hawley St, NW1 .92 B7
Hawstead Rd, SE6 .154 B6
Hawsted, Buck.H. IG9 .47 H7
Hawthorn Av, E3 .113 J1
N13 .59 E5
Richmond (Kew) TW9 .145 H2
Thornton Heath CR7 .187 H1
Hawthorn Cen, The, Har. HA1 .68 C4
Hawthorn Cl, Hmptn. TW12 .161 G5
Hounslow TW5 .122 B7
Orpington BR5 .193 G6
Hawthorn Cres, SW17 .168 A5
Hawthornden Cl, N12
off Fallowfields Dr .57 H6
Hawthorndene Cl, Brom. BR2 .205 F2
Hawthorndene Rd, Brom. BR2 .205 F2
Hawthorn Dr, Har. HA2 .67 F6
West Wickham BR4 .205 E4
Hawthorne Av, Cars. SM5 .200 A7
Harrow HA3 .68 D6
Mitcham CR4 .185 G2
Ruislip HA4 .66 B6
Hawthorne Cl, N1 .94 B6
Bromley BR1 .192 C3
Sutton SM1
off Aultone Way .199 F2
Hawthorne Ct, Nthwd. HA6
off Ryefield Cres .66 A2
Hawthorne Cres, West Dr. UB7 .120 C2
Hawthorne Fm Av, Nthlt. UB5 .103 E1
Hawthorne Gro, NW9 .70 C7
Hawthorne Ms, W7 .103 J6
Grnf. UB6
off Greenford Rd .103 J6
Hawthorne Rd, E17 .78 A3
Bromley BR1 .192 B3
Hawthorne Way, N9 .60 B2
Staines (Stanw.) TW19 .140 A7
Hawthorn Gdns, W5 .125 G3
Hawthorn Gro, SE20 .171 E7
Barnet EN5 .39 F6
Hawthorn Hatch, Brent. TW8 .125 E7
Hawthorn Ms, NW7
off Holders Hill Rd .72 B1
Hawthorn Pl, Erith DA8 .139 J5
Hawthorn Rd, N8 .74 D3
N18 .60 C6
NW10 .89 G7
Bexleyheath DA6 .159 F4
Brentford TW8 .125 E7
Buckhurst Hill IG9 .64 A4
Feltham TW13 .160 A1
Sutton SM1 .199 H6
Wallington SM6 .200 B7
Hawthorns, Wdf.Grn. IG8 .63 G3
Hawthorns, The, Epsom KT17 *off Kingston Rd* .197 F6
Loughton IG10 .48 D4
Hawthorn Wk, W10
off Fifth Av .108 B4
Hawtrey Av, Nthlt. UB5 .102 D2
Hawtrey Dr, Ruis. HA4 .66 A7
Hawtrey Rd, NW3 .91 H7
Haxted Rd, Brom. BR1
off North Rd .191 H1
Hay Cl, E15 .97 E7
Borehamwood WD6 .38 C2
Haycroft Gdns, NW10 .107 G1
Haycroft Rd, SW2 .151 E5
Surbiton KT6 .195 H3
Hay Currie St, E14 .114 B6
Hayday Rd, E16 .115 G5
Haydens Pl, W11
off Portobello Rd .108 C6
Hayden Way, Rom. RM5 .83 J2
Haydns Ms, W3 .106 C6
Haydock Av, Nthlt. UB5 .85 G6
Haydock Grn, Nthlt. UB5
off Haydock Av .85 G6
Haydon Cl, NW9 .70 C4
Enfield EN1
off Mortimer Dr .44 B6
Haydon Dr, Pnr. HA5 .66 A4
Haydon Pk Rd, SW19 .166 E5
Haydon Rd, Dag. RM8 .100 C2
Haydons Rd, SW19 .167 E5
Haydon St, EC3 .21 F5
Haydon Wk, E1 .21 G4
Haydon Way, SW11 .149 G4
HAYES, Brom. BR2 .205 G2
Hayes Br Retail Pk, Hayes UB4 .102 D7
Hayes Bypass, Hayes UB3, UB4 .102 D4
Hayes Chase, W.Wick. BR4 .190 E5
Hayes Cl, Brom. BR2 .205 G2
Hayes Ct, SW2 .168 E1
Hayes Cres, NW11 .72 C5
Sutton SM3 .198 A4
Hayesend Ho, SW17
off Blackshaw Rd .167 F4
Hayesford Pk Dr, Brom. BR2 .191 F5
Hayes Gdn, Brom. BR2 .205 G2
Hayes Gro, SE22 .152 C4
Hayes Hill, Brom. BR2 .204 E1
Hayes Hill Rd, Brom. BR2 .205 F1
Hayes La, Beck. BR3 .190 C3
Bromley BR2 .191 G5
Hayes Mead Rd, Brom. BR2 .205 E1
Hayes Metro Cen, Hayes UB4 .102 C7
Hayes Pl, NW1 .7 H6
Hayes Rd, Brom. BR2 .191 G4
Southall UB2 .122 B4
Hayes St, Brom. BR2 .205 H1
HAYES TOWN, Hayes UB3 .121 H2
Hayes Way, Beck. BR3 .190 C4
Hayes Wd Av, Brom. BR2 .205 H1
Hayfield Pas, E1
off Stepney Grn .113 F4
Hayfield Yd, E1
off Mile End Rd .113 F4
Haygarth Pl, SW19 .166 A5
Haygreen Cl, Kings.T. KT2 .164 B6
Hay Hill, W1 .17 E6
Hayland Cl, NW9 .70 D4
Hay La, NW9 .70 D4
Hayles St, SE11 .35 G1
Haylett Gdns, Kings.T. KT1
off Anglesea Rd .181 G4
Hayling Av, Felt. TW13 .160 A3
Hayling Cl, N16
off Boleyn Rd .94 B5
Hayling Rd, Wat. WD19 .50 B2
Hayman St, N1
off Hawes St .93 H7
Haymarket, SW1 .17 H6
Haymarket Arc, SW1 .17 H6
Haymer Gdns, Wor.Pk. KT4 .197 G3
Haymerle Rd, SE15 .37 H6
Haymill Cl, Grnf. (Perivale) UB6 .104 C3
Hayne Rd, Beck. BR3 .189 J2
Haynes Cl, N11 .58 A3
N17 .60 E7
SE3 .155 E3
Haynes Dr, N9 .60 E3
Haynes La, SE19 .170 B6
Haynes Rd, Wem. HA0 .87 H7
Hayne St, EC1 .19 H1
Haynt Wk, SW20 .184 B3
★ **Hay's Galleria**, SE1 .28 D1
Hay's La, SE1 .28 D2
Haysleigh Gdns, SE20 .188 D2
Hay's Ms, W1 .16 D6
Hay St, E2 .112 D1
Hayter Ct, E11 .97 H2
Hayter Rd, SW2 .151 E5
Hayton Cl, E8
off Buttermere Wk .94 C6
Hayward Cl, SW19 .185 E1
★ **Hayward Gall**, SE1 .26 D1
Hayward Gdns, SW15 .147 J6
Hayward Rd, N20 .57 F2
Thames Ditton KT7 .194 D1
Haywards Cl, Rom. (Chad.Hth) RM6 .82 B5
Hayward's Pl, EC1 .11 G6
Haywood Cl, Pnr. HA5 .66 D2
Haywood Ri, Orp. BR6 .207 H4
Haywood Rd, Brom. BR2 .192 A4
Hazel Av, West Dr. UB7 .120 D3
Hazelbank, Surb. KT5 .196 C1
Hazelbank Rd, SE6 .172 D2
Hazelbourne Rd, SW12 .150 B6
Hazelbrouck Gdns, Ilf. IG6 .65 G7
Hazelbury Cl, SW19 .184 D2
Hazelbury Grn, N9 .60 B3
Hazelbury La, N9 .60 B3
Hazel Cl, N13 .60 A3
N19 *off Hargrave Pk* .92 C2
NW9 .71 E2
SE15 .152 D2
Brentford TW8 .125 E7
Croydon CR0 .189 G7
Mitcham CR4 .186 D4
Twickenham TW2 .143 J7
Hazelcroft, Pnr. HA5 .51 G6
Hazeldean Rd, NW10 .88 D7
Hazeldene Dr, Pnr. HA5 .66 C3
Hazeldene Rd, Ilf. IG3 .100 B2
Welling DA16 .158 C2
Hazeldon Rd, SE4 .153 H5
Hazeleigh Gdns, Wdf.Grn. IG8 .64 B5
Hazel Gdns, Edg. HA8 .54 B4
Hazelgreen Cl, N21 .59 H1
Hazel Gro, SE26 .171 G4
Enfield EN1
off Dimsdale Dr .44 D6
Feltham TW13 .160 A1
Orpington BR6 .206 E2
Romford RM6 .82 E3
Wembley HA0
off Carlyon Rd .105 H1
Hazel Gro Est, SE26 .171 G4
Hazel Ho, NW3
off Maitland Pk Rd .91 J6
Hazelhurst, Beck. BR3 .190 D1
Hazelhurst Rd, SW17 .167 F4
Hazel La, Ilf. IG6 .64 E7
Richmond TW10 .163 H2
Hazell Cres, Rom. RM5 .83 H1
Hazellville Rd, N19 .74 D7
Hazel Mead, Barn. EN5 .39 H5
Hazelmere Cl, Felt. TW14 .141 G6
Northolt UB5 .103 F2
Hazelmere Dr, Nthlt. UB5 .103 F2
Hazelmere Rd, NW6 .108 D1
Northolt UB5 .103 F2
Orpington BR5 .193 F4
Hazelmere Wk, Nthlt. UB5 .103 F2
Hazelmere Way, Brom. BR2 .191 G6
Hazel Ms, N8
off Alexandra Rd .75 G3
Hazel Rd, E15
off Burgess Rd .96 E5
NW10 .107 J3
Hazeltree La, Nthlt. UB5 .103 E3
Hazel Wk, Brom. BR2 .192 D6
Hazel Way, E4 .61 J6
SE1 .37 F1
Hazelwood, Loug. IG10 .48 A5
Hazelwood Av, Mord. SM4 .185 E4
Hazelwood Cl, W5 .125 H2
Harrow HA2 .67 H4
Hazelwood Ct, NW10
off Neasden La N .88 E3
Hazelwood Cres, N13 .59 G4
Hazelwood Cft, Surb. KT6 .181 H6
Hazelwood Dr, Pnr. HA5 .66 B2
Hazelwood La, N13 .59 G4
Hazelwood Ms, SW9 .150 E3
Hazelwood Pk Cl, Chigwell IG7 .65 H5
Hazelwood Rd, E17 .77 H5
Enfield EN1 .44 C6
Hazlebury Rd, SW6 .148 E2
Hazledean Rd, Croy. CR0 .202 A2
Hazledene Rd, W4 .126 C6
Hazlemere Gdns, Wor.Pk. KT4 .197 H1
Hazlewell Rd, SW15 .147 H5
Hazlewood Cl, E5 .95 H3
Hazlewood Cres, W10 .108 B4
Hazlewood Twr, W10
off Golborne Rd .108 C4
Hazlitt Cl, Felt. TW13 .161 E4
Hazlitt Ms, W14
off Hazlitt Rd .128 B3
Hazlitt Rd, W14 .128 B3
Headcorn Pl, Th.Hth. CR7
off Headcorn Rd .187 F4
Headcorn Rd, N17 .60 C7
Bromley BR1 .173 F5
Thornton Heath CR7 .187 F4

Headfort Pl, SW1 24 C4
Headingley Cl, Ilf. IG6 65 J6
Headington Rd, SW18 167 F1
Headlam Rd, SW4 150 D6
Headlam St, E1 113 E4
Headley App, Ilf. IG2 80 D5
Headley Av, Wall. SM6 201 F5
Headley Cl, Epsom KT19 196 A6
Headley Ct, SE26 171 E5
Headley Dr, Croy. (New Adgtn) CR0 204 B7
Ilford IG2 80 E6
Head's Ms, W11 *off Westbourne Gro* 108 D6
HEADSTONE, Har. HA2 67 J4
Headstone Dr, Har. HA1, HA3 68 B3
Headstone Gdns, Har. HA2 67 J4
Headstone La, Har. HA2, HA3 67 H4
Headstone Rd, Har. HA1 68 B5
Head St, E1 113 G6
Headway Cl, Rich. TW10 *off Locksmeade Rd* 163 F4
Heald St, SE14 153 J1
Healey St, NW1 92 B6
Healy Dr, Orp. BR6 207 J4
Heanor Ct, E5 *off Pedro St* 95 G4
Hearne Rd, W4 126 A6
Hearn Ri, Nthlt. UB5 102 D1
Hearn's Bldgs, SE17 36 C2
Hearnshaw St, E14 113 H5
Hearn St, EC2 12 E6
Hearnville Rd, SW12 168 A1
Heath, The, W7 *off Lower Boston Rd* 124 B1
Heatham Pk, Twick. TW2 144 C7
Heath Av, Bexh. DA7 138 D6
Heathbourne Rd, Bushey (Bushey Hth) WD23 52 B2
Stanmore HA7 52 B2
Heath Brow, NW3 *off North End Way* 91 F3
Heath Cl, NW11 72 E7
W5 105 J4
Hayes (Harling.) UB3 121 G7
South Croydon CR2 201 H6
Heathcock Ct, WC2 *off Exchange Ct* 18 B6
Heathcote Av, Ilf. IG5 80 C2
Heathcote Ct, Ilf. IG5 *off Heathcote Av* 80 C2
Heathcote Gro, E4 62 C3
Heathcote Pt, E9 *off Wick Rd* 95 G6
Heathcote Rd, Twick. TW1 145 E6
Heathcote St, WC1 10 C5
Heathcote Way, West Dr. UB7 *off Tavistock Rd* 120 A1
Heath Ct, SE9 175 F1
Hounslow TW4 143 F4
Heathcroft, NW11 91 E1
W5 105 J4
Heathcroft Gdns, E17 78 D1
Heathdale Av, Houns. TW4 143 E3
Heathdene Dr, Belv. DA17 139 H4
Heathdene Rd, SW16 169 F7
Wallington SM6 200 B7
Heath Dr, NW3 90 E4
SW20 183 J4
Heathedge, SE26 170 E2
Heatherbank, SE9 156 C2
Chislehurst BR7 192 D2
Heather Cl, E6 116 E6
N7 *off Newington Barrow Way* 93 F3
SE13 154 D6
SW8 150 B3
Hampton TW12 179 F1
Isleworth TW7 *off Harvesters Cl* 144 A5
Heatherdale Cl, Kings.T. KT2 164 A6
Heatherdene Cl, N12 57 F7
Mitcham CR4 185 H4
Heather Dr, Enf. EN2 43 H2
Heather Gdns, NW11 72 B6
Sutton SM2 198 D6
Heatherlands, Sun. TW16 160 A6
Heatherley Dr, Ilf. IG5 80 B3
Heather Pk Dr, Wem. HA0 88 A7
Heather Rd, E4 61 J6
NW2 89 F2
SE12 173 G2
Heathers, The, Stai. TW19 140 C7
Heatherset Gdns, SW16 169 F7
Heatherside Rd, Epsom KT19 196 D7
Sidcup DA14 *off Wren Rd* 176 C3
Heatherton Ter, N3 73 E2
Heather Wk, W10 *off Droop St* 108 B4
Edgware HA8 54 B5
Twickenham TW2 *off Stephenson Rd* 143 G7
Heather Way, Stan. HA7 52 C6
Heatherwood Cl, E12 97 J2
Heathfield, E4 62 C3
Chislehurst BR7 175 F6
Heathfield Av, SW18 *off Heathfield Rd* 149 G7
Heathfield Cl, E16 116 A5
Keston BR2 205 J5
Heathfield Dr, Mitch. CR4 185 H1
Heathfield Gdns, NW11 72 A6
SE3 154 E2
SW18 149 G6
W4 126 C5
Croydon CR0 *off Coombe Rd* 201 J4
Heathfield La, Chis. BR7 175 E6
Heathfield N, Twick. TW2 144 C7
Heathfield Pk, NW2 89 J6
Heathfield Pk Dr, Rom. (Chad.Hth) RM6 82 B5
Heathfield Rd, SW18 149 F6
W3 126 B2
Bexleyheath DA6 159 F4
Bromley BR1 173 F7
Croydon CR0 202 A4
Keston BR2 205 J5
Heathfields Ct, Houns. TW4 *off Heathlands Way* 143 E5
Heathfield S, Twick. TW2 144 C7
Heathfield Sq, SW18 149 G7
Heathfield St, W11 *off Portland Rd* 108 B7
Heathfield Ter, SE18 137 J6
W4 126 C5
Heath Gdns, Twick. TW1 162 C1
Heathgate, NW11 72 E6
Heathgate Pl, NW3 *off Agincourt Rd* 91 J5
Heath Gro, SE20 *off Maple Rd* 171 F7
Heath Hurst Rd, NW3 91 H4
Heathland Rd, N16 94 B1
Heathlands Cl, Sun. TW16 178 A2
Twickenham TW1 162 C2
Heathlands Way, Houns. TW4 143 E5
Heath La, SE3 154 D2
Heathlee Rd, SE3 155 F4
Heathley End, Chis. BR7 175 F6
Heathmans Rd, SW6 148 C1
Heath Mead, SW19 166 A3
Heath Pk Dr, Brom. BR1 192 B3
Heath Pas, NW3 91 E2
Heath Ri, SW15 148 A6
Bromley BR2 191 F6
Heath Rd, SW8 150 B2
Bexley DA5 177 J1
Harrow HA1 67 J7
Hounslow TW3 143 H4
Romford RM6 82 D7
Thornton Heath CR7 187 J3
Twickenham TW1, TW2 162 C1
★ **Heathrow Airport (London)**, Houns. TW6 140 E1
Heathrow Causeway Cen, Houns. TW4 142 B3
Heathrow Ho, Houns. TW5 *off Bath Rd* 142 A1
Heathrow Interchange, Hayes UB4 122 C1
Heathrow Int Trd Est, Houns. TW4 142 B3
Heathrow Tunnel App, Houns. (Lon.Hthrw Air.) TW6 140 E3
Heathrow Vehicle Tunnel, Houns. (Lon.Hthrw Air.) TW6 140 E1
Heaths Cl, Enf. EN1 44 B2
Heath Side, NW3 91 G4
Heathside, Esher KT10 194 B3
Hounslow TW4 143 F7
Heath Side, Orp. BR5 207 F1
Heathside Av, Bexh. DA7 159 E1
Heathside Cl, Esher KT10 194 B3
Ilford IG2 81 G5
Heathstan Rd, W12 107 G6
Heath St, NW3 91 F3
Heath Vw, N2 73 F4
Heath Vw Cl, N2 73 F4
Heathview Ct, SW19 166 A2
Heathview Dr, SE2 138 D6
Heathview Gdns, SW15 147 J7
Heathview Rd, Th.Hth. CR7 187 G4
Heath Vil, SE18 137 J5
SW18 *off Cargill Rd* 167 F1
Heathville Rd, N19 74 E7
Heathwall St, SW11 149 J3
Heathway, SE3 135 F7
Croydon CR0 203 J3
Dagenham RM9, RM10 101 G7
Heath Way, Erith DA8 159 J1
Heathway, Sthl. UB2 122 C4
Wdf.Grn. IG8 63 J4
Heathway Ind Est, Dag. RM10 *off Manchester Way* 101 H4
Heathwood Gdns, SE7 136 B4
Heathwood Pt, SE23 *off Dacres Rd* 171 G3
Heaton Cl, E4 62 C3
Heaton Rd, SE15 152 D3
Mitcham CR4 168 A7
Heaven Tree Cl, N1 93 J5
Heaver Rd, SW11 *off Wye St* 149 G3
Heavitree Cl, SE18 137 G5
Heavitree Rd, SE18 137 G5
Hebden Ct, E2 *off Laburnum St* 112 C1
Hebden Ter, N17 60 B6
Hebdon Rd, SW17 167 H3
Heber Rd, NW2 90 A5
SE22 152 C6
Hebron Rd, W6 127 H3
Hecham Cl, E17 77 H2
Heckfield Pl, SW6 *off Fulham Rd* 128 D7
Heckford St, E1 *off The Highway* 113 G7
Hector Cl, N9 60 D2
Hector St, SE18 137 H4
Heddington Gro, N7 93 F5
Heddon Cl, Islw. TW7 144 D4
Heddon Ct Av, Barn. EN4 41 J5
Heddon Ct Par, Barn. EN4 *off Cockfosters Rd* 42 A5
Heddon Rd, Barn. (Cockfos.) EN4 41 J5
Heddon St, W1 17 F5
Hedge Hill, Enf. EN2 43 H1
Hedge La, N13 59 H3
Hedgeley, Ilf. IG4 80 C4
Hedgemans Rd, Dag. RM9 100 D7
Hedgemans Way, Dag. RM9 100 E6
Hedgerley Gdns, Grnf. UB6 103 J2
Hedgerow La, Barn. (Arkley) EN5 39 H5
Hedgers Cl, Loug. IG10 *off Newmans La* 48 D4
Hedgers Gro, E9 95 H6
Hedger St, SE11 35 G1
Hedge Wk, SE6 172 B5
Hedgewood Gdns, Ilf. IG5 80 D4
Hedgley St, SE12 155 F5
Hedingham Cl, N1 *off Popham Rd* 93 J7
Hedingham Ho, Kings.T. KT2 *off Kingsgate Rd* 181 H1
Hedingham Rd, Dag. RM8 100 B5
Hedley Rd, Twick. TW2 143 G7
Hedley Row, N5 *off Poets Rd* 94 A5
Heenan Cl, Bark. IG11 *off Glenny Rd* 99 F6
Heene Rd, Enf. EN2 44 A1
Heidegger Cres, SW13 *off Wyatt Dr* 127 H7
Heigham Rd, E6 98 A7
Heighton Gdns, Croy. CR0 201 H5
Heights, The, SE7 135 J5
Beckenham BR3 172 C7
Loughton IG10 48 C2
Northolt UB5 85 F5
Heights Cl, SW20 165 H7
Heiron St, SE17 35 H6
Helby Rd, SW4 150 D6
Helder Gro, SE12 155 F7
Helder St, S.Croy. CR2 202 A6
Heldmann Cl, Houns. TW3 144 A4
Helegan Cl, Orp. BR6 207 J4
Helena Pl, E9 *off Fremont St* 113 F1
Helena Rd, E13 115 F2
E17 78 A5
NW10 89 H5
W5 105 G5
Helena Sq, SE16 *off Rotherhithe St* 113 H7
Helen Av, Felt. TW14 142 B7
Helen Cl, N2 73 F3
West Molesey KT8 179 H4
Helenslea Av, NW11 90 C1
Helen's Pl, E2 *off Roman Rd* 113 F3
Helen St, SE18 *off Wilmount St* 137 E4
Helios Rd, Wall. SM6 200 A1
Helix Gdns, SW2 *off Helix Rd* 151 F6
Helix Rd, SW2 151 F6
Hellen Way, Wat. WD19 50 C4
Hellings St, E1 29 J2
Helme Cl, SW19 166 C5
Helmet Row, EC1 12 A5
Helmore Rd, Bark. IG11 99 J7
Helmsdale Cl, Hayes UB4 102 E4
Helmsdale Rd, SW16 186 C1
Helmsley Pl, E8 94 E7
Helperby Rd, NW10 88 E7
Helsinki Sq, SE16 133 H3
Helston Cl, Pnr. HA5 51 F7
Helvetia St, SE6 171 J2
Hemans St, SW8 33 J7
Hemberton Rd, SW9 150 E3
Hemery Rd, Grnf. UB6 86 A5
Hemingford Cl, N12 57 G5
Hemingford Rd, N1 111 F1
Sutton SM3 197 J4
Heming Rd, Edg. HA8 54 B7
Hemington Av, N11 57 J5
Hemingway Cl, NW5 92 A4
Hemlock Rd, W12 107 F7
Hemming Cl, Hmptn. TW12 *off Chandler Cl* 179 G1
Hemmings Cl, Sid. DA14 176 B2
Hemmings Mead, Epsom KT19 196 B6
Hemming St, E1 13 J6
Hempstead Cl, Buck.H. IG9 63 G2
Hempstead Rd, E17 78 D2
Hemp Wk, SE17 36 C1
Hemsby Rd, Chess. KT9 195 J6
Hemstal Rd, NW6 90 D7
Hemswell Dr, NW9 70 E1
Hemsworth Ct, N1 *off Hemsworth St* 112 B2
Hemsworth St, N1 12 D1
Hemus Pl, SW3 31 H4
Hen & Chicken Ct, EC4 19 E4
Henbury Way, Wat. WD19 50 D3
Henchman St, W12 107 F6
Hendale Av, NW4 71 G3
Henderson Cl, NW10 88 C6
Henderson Dr, NW8 7 E5
Henderson Rd, E7 97 J6
N9 60 E1
SW18 149 H7
Croydon CR0 188 A6
Hayes UB4 102 A3
Hendham Rd, SW17 167 H2
HENDON, NW4 71 H4
Hendon Av, N3 72 B1
Hendon Hall Ct, NW4 *off Parson St* 72 A3
Hendon La, N3 72 B3
Hendon Pk Row, NW11 72 C6
Hendon Rd, N9 60 D2
Hendon Way, NW2 90 C3
NW4 71 H6
Staines (Stanw.) TW19 140 A6
Hendon Wd La, NW7 39 F6
Hendren Cl, Grnf. UB6 86 A5
Hendre Rd, SE1 36 E2
Hendrick Av, SW12 149 J6
Heneage La, EC3 21 E4
Heneage St, E1 21 G1
Henfield Cl, N19 92 C1
Bexley DA5 159 G6
Henfield Rd, SW19 184 C1
Hengelo Gdns, Mitch. CR4 185 G4
Hengist Rd, SE12 155 H7
Erith DA8 139 H7
Hengist Way, Brom. BR2 190 E4
Hengrave Rd, SE23 153 G7
Hengrove Ct, Bex. DA5 *off Hurst Rd* 177 E1
Henley Av, Sutt. SM3 198 B3
Henley Cl, SE16 *off St. Marychurch St* 133 F2
Greenford UB6 103 J2
Isleworth TW7 144 C1
Henley Ct, N14 42 C7
Henley Cross, SE3 155 H3
Henley Dr, SE1 37 G1
Kingston upon Thames KT2 165 F7
Henley Gdns, Pnr. HA5 66 B3
Romford RM6 82 E5
Henley Prior, N1 *off Collier St* 10 C2
Henley Rd, E16 136 C2
N18 60 B4
NW10 107 J1
Ilford IG1 99 F4
Henley St, SW11 150 A2
Henley Way, Felt. TW13 160 D5
Henlow Pl, Rich. TW10 163 G2
Henlys Cor, N3 72 C4
Henlys Rbt, Houns. TW5 *off Bath Rd* 142 D2

Hennel Cl, SE23 ... **171** F3
Hennessy Rd, N9 ... **61** F2
Henniker Gdns, E6 ... **116** A3
Henniker Ms, SW3 ... **30** E5
Henniker Pt, E15 ... **96** D5
Henniker Rd, E15 ... **96** D5
Henningham Rd, N17 ... **76** A1
Henning St, SW11 ... **149** H1
Henrietta Cl, SE8 ... **134** A6
Henrietta Ms, WC1 ... **10** B5
Henrietta Pl, W1 ... **16** D4
Henrietta St, E15 ... **96** C5
WC2 ... **18** B5
Henriques St, E1 ... **21** J3
Henry Addlington Cl, E6 ... **116** E5
Henry Cooper Way, SE9 ... **174** A3
Henry Darlot Dr, NW7 ... **56** A5
Henry Dent Cl, SE5 ... **152** A3
Henry Dickens Ct, W11 ... **128** A1
Henry Doulton Dr, SW17 ... **168** B4
Henry Jackson Rd, SW15 ... **148** A3
Henry Macaulay Av,
Kings.T. KT2 ... **181** G1
Henry Peters Dr, Tedd. TW11
off Somerset Gdns ... **162** B5
Henry Rd, E6 ... **116** B2
N4 ... **93** J1
Barnet EN4 ... **41** G5
Henry's Av, Wdf.Grn. IG8 ... **63** F5
Henryson Rd, SE4 ... **154** A5
Henry St, Brom. BR1 ... **191** H1
Henry's Wk, Ilf. IG6 ... **65** G7
Henry Tate Ms, SW16 ... **169** G5
Henry Wise Ho, SW1
off Vauxhall Br Rd ... **33** G2
Hensford Gdns, SE26
off Wells Pk Rd ... **171** E4
Henshall Pt, E3
off Bromley High St ... **114** B3
Henshall St, N1 ... **94** A6
Henshawe Rd, Dag. RM8 ... **100** D3
Henshaw St, SE17 ... **36** B1
Hensley Pt, E9
off Wick Rd ... **95** G6
Henslowe Rd, SE22 ... **152** D5
Henson Av, NW2 ... **89** J5
Henson Cl, Orp. BR6 ... **207** E2
Henson Path, Har. HA3 ... **69** G3
Henson Pl, Nthlt. UB5 ... **102** C1
Henstridge Pl, NW8 ... **7** G1
Henty Cl, SW11 ... **129** H7
Henty Wk, SW15 ... **147** H5
Henville Rd, Brom. BR1 ... **191** H1
Henwick Rd, SE9 ... **156** A3
Henwood Side, Wdf.Grn.
IG8 *off Love La* ... **64** C6
Hepburn Gdns, Brom.
BR2 ... **205** E1
Hepburn Ms, SW11
off Webbs Rd ... **149** J5
Hepple Cl, Islw. TW7 ... **144** E2
Hepplestone Cl, SW15 ... **147** H6
Hepscott Rd, E9 ... **96** A7
Hepworth Ct, SW1 ... **32** C4
Barking IG11 ... **100** A5
Hepworth Gdns, Bark.
IG11 ... **100** A5
Hepworth Rd, SW16 ... **169** E7
Hepworth Wk, NW3
off Haverstock Hill ... **91** H5
Herald Gdns, Wall. SM6 ... **200** B3
Herald's Pl, SE11 ... **35** G1
Herald St, E2
off Three Colts La ... **113** E4
Herbal Hill, EC1 ... **11** F6
Herbert Cres, SW1 ... **24** A5
Herbert Gdns, NW10 ... **107** H2
W4 ... **126** B6
Romford RM6 ... **82** D7
Herbert Ms, SW2
off Bascombe St ... **151** G6
Herbert Morrison Ho, SW6
off Clem Attlee Ct ... **128** C6
Herbert Pl, SE18
off Plumstead
Common Rd ... **137** E6
Isleworth TW7
off Spring Gro Rd ... **144** A1
Herbert Rd, E12 ... **98** B4
E17 ... **77** J7
N11 ... **58** E7
N15 ... **76** C5
NW9 ... **71** G6
SE18 ... **136** D7
SW19 ... **166** C7
Bexleyheath DA7 ... **159** E2
Bromley BR2 ... **192** A5
Ilford IG3 ... **99** H2
Kingston upon Thames
KT1 ... **181** J3
Southall UB1 ... **123** F1
Herbert St, E13 ... **115** G2
NW5 ... **92** A6
Herbert Ter, SE18 ... **136** E7
Herbrand St, WC1 ... **10** A5
Hercules Pl, N7
off Hercules St ... **93** E3
Hercules Rd, SE1 ... **26** D6
Hercules St, N7 ... **93** E3
Hereford Av, Barn. EN4 ... **57** J1
Hereford Ct, Sutt. SM2
off Worcester Rd ... **198** D7
Hereford Gdns, SE13
off Longhurst Rd ... **155** E5
Ilford IG1 ... **80** B7
Pinner HA5 ... **66** E5
Twickenham TW2 ... **161** J1
Hereford Ho, NW6 ... **108** D2
Hereford Ms, W2
off Hereford Rd ... **108** D6
Hereford Pl, SE14
off Royal Naval Pl ... **133** J7
Hereford Retreat, SE15 ... **37** H6
Hereford Rd, E3 ... **113** J2
E11 ... **79** H5
W2 ... **108** D6
W3 ... **106** B7
W5 ... **125** F3
Feltham TW13 ... **160** C1
Hereford Sq, SW7 ... **30** D2
Hereford St, E2 ... **13** H5
Hereford Way, Chess.
KT9 ... **195** F5
Herent Dr, Ilf. IG5 ... **80** B4
Hereward Gdns, N13 ... **59** G5
Hereward Grn, Loug. IG10 ... **49** F1
Hereward Rd, SW17 ... **167** J4
Herga Ct, Har. HA1 ... **86** B3
Herga Rd, Har. HA3 ... **68** C4
Heriot Av, E4 ... **62** A2
Heriot Rd, NW4 ... **71** J5
Heriots Cl, Stan. HA7 ... **52** D4
Heritage Cl, SW9 ... **151** H3
Sunbury-on-Thames
TW16 *off Green St* ... **178** A1
Heritage Hill, Kes. BR2 ... **205** J5
Heritage Pl, SW18
off Earlsfield Rd ... **167** F1
Heritage Vw, Har. HA1 ... **86** C3
Herlwyn Gdns, SW17 ... **167** J4
Herm Cl, Islw. TW7
off Jersey Rd ... **123** J7
Herme Ms, N18 ... **60** D4
Hermes Cl, W9
off Chippenham Rd ... **108** D4
Hermes St, N1 ... **10** E2
Hermes Wk, Nthlt. UB5
off Hotspur Rd ... **103** G2
Hermiston Av, N8 ... **75** E5
Hermitage, The, SE23 ... **171** F1
SW13 ... **147** F1
Richmond TW10 ... **145** G5
Hermitage Cl, E18 ... **79** F4
SE2
off Felixstowe Rd ... **138** C3
Enfield EN2 ... **43** H2
Esher (Clay.) KT10 ... **194** D6
Hermitage Ct, E18 ... **79** G4
NW2 *off Hermitage La* ... **90** D3
Hermitage Gdns, NW2 ... **90** D3
SE19 ... **169** J6
Hermitage La, N18 ... **60** A5
NW2 ... **90** D3
SE25 ... **188** D6
SW16 ... **169** F7
Croydon CR0 ... **188** D6
Hermitage Path, SW16 ... **187** E1
Hermitage Rd, N4 ... **75** H7
N15 ... **75** H7
SE19 ... **169** J7
Hermitage Row, E8 ... **94** D5
Hermitage St, W2 ... **15** E2
Hermitage Wk, E18 ... **79** F4
Hermitage Wall, E1 ... **29** J2
Hermitage Waterside, E1 ... **29** H1
Hermitage Way, Stan. HA7 ... **68** D1
Hermit Pl, NW6
off Belsize Rd ... **108** E1
Hermit Rd, E16 ... **115** F5
Hermit St, EC1 ... **11** G3
Hermon Gro, Hayes UB3 ... **122** A1
Hermon Hill, E11 ... **79** G5
E18 ... **79** G5
Herndon Rd, SW18 ... **149** F5
Herne Cl, NW10
off North Circular Rd ... **88** D5
HERNE HILL, SE24 ... **151** J5
Herne Hill, SE24 ... **151** J6
Herne Hill Ho, SE24
off Railton Rd ... **151** H6
Herne Hill Rd, SE24 ... **151** J3
Herne Ms, N18
off Lyndhurst Rd ... **60** D4
Herne Pl, SE24 ... **151** H5
Herne Rd, Surb. KT6 ... **195** G2
Heron Cl, E17 ... **77** J2
NW10 ... **89** E6
Buckhurst Hill IG9 ... **63** G1
Sutton SM1
off Sandpiper Rd ... **198** C5
Heron Ct, E5
off Big Hill ... **95** E1
Bromley BR2 ... **191** J4
Heron Cres, Sid. DA14 ... **175** H3
Herondale Av, SW18 ... **167** G1
Heron Dr, N4 ... **93** J2
Herongate Rd, E12 ... **97** J2
Heron Hill, Belv. DA17 ... **139** F4
Heron Ms, Ilf. IG1
off Balfour Rd ... **98** E2
Heron Pl, SE16 ... **133** H1
Heron Quay, E14 ... **134** A1
Heron Rd, SE24 ... **151** J4
Croydon CR0
off Tunstall Rd ... **202** B2
Twickenham TW1 ... **144** D4
Herons, The, E11 ... **79** F6
Heronsforde, W13 ... **105** F6
Heronsgate, Edg. HA8 ... **54** A5
Heronslea Dr, Stan. HA7 ... **53** H5
Heron's Pl, Islw. TW7 ... **144** E3
Heron Sq, Rich. TW9
off Bridge St ... **145** G5
Herons Ri, Barn.
(New Barn.) EN4 ... **41** H4
Heron Trd Est, W3
off Alliance Rd ... **106** B4
Heron Way, Felt. TW14 ... **142** A4
Wall. SM6 ... **200** D7
Heronway, Wdf.Grn. IG8 ... **63** J4
Herrick Rd, N5 ... **93** J3
Herrick St, SW1 ... **33** J1
Herries St, W10 ... **108** B2
Herringham Rd, SE7 ... **135** J3
Herrongate Cl, Enf. EN1 ... **44** C2
Hersant Cl, NW10 ... **107** G1
Herschell Ms, SE5
off Bicknell Rd ... **151** J3
Herschell Rd, SE23 ... **153** G7
Hersham Cl, SW15 ... **147** G7
Hertford Av, SW14 ... **146** D5
Hertford Cl, Barn. EN4 ... **41** G3
Hertford Ct, N13
off Green Las ... **59** G3
Hertford Pl, W1 ... **9** F6
Hertford Rd, N1 ... **112** B1
N2 ... **73** H3
N9 ... **60** E2
Barking IG11 ... **98** E7
Barnet EN4 ... **41** F3
Enfield EN3 ... **45** F3
Ilford IG2 ... **81** H6
Hertford Sq, Mitch. CR4
off Hertford Way ... **186** E4
Hertford St, W1 ... **24** D1
Hertford Wk, Belv. DA17
off Hoddesdon Rd ... **139** G5
Hertford Way, Mitch. CR4 ... **186** E4
Hertslet Rd, N7 ... **93** F3
Hertsmere Ind Pk, Borwd.
WD6 ... **38** D3
Hertsmere Rd, E14 ... **114** A7
Hertswood Ct, Barn. EN5
off Hillside Gdns ... **40** B4
Hervey Cl, N3 ... **72** D1
Hervey Pk Rd, E17 ... **77** H4
Hervey Rd, SE3 ... **155** H1
Hesa Rd, Hayes UB3 ... **102** A6
Hesewall Cl, SW4
off Brayburne Av ... **150** C2
Hesketh Pl, W11 ... **108** B7
Hesketh Rd, E7 ... **97** G3
Heslop Rd, SW12 ... **167** J1
Hesper Ms, SW5 ... **30** A3
Hesperus Cres, E14 ... **134** B4
Hessel Rd, W13 ... **124** D2
Hessel St, E1 ... **112** E6
Hestercombe Av, SW6 ... **148** B2
Hesterman Way, Croy.
CR0 ... **201** E1
Hester Rd, N18 ... **60** D5
SW11 ... **129** H7
Hester Ter, Rich. TW9
off Chilton Rd ... **146** A3
Hestia Ho, SE1
off Royal Oak Yd ... **28** D4
HESTON, Houns. TW5 ... **123** F7
Heston Av, Houns. TW5 ... **123** E7
Heston Gra, Houns. TW5
off North Hyde La ... **123** F6
Heston Gra La, Houns.
TW5 ... **123** F6
Heston Ind Mall, Houns.
TW5 ... **123** F7
Heston Rd, Houns. TW5 ... **123** G7
Heston St, SE14 ... **153** J1
Heswell Grn, Wat. WD19
off Fairhaven Cres ... **50** A3
Hetherington Rd, SW4 ... **150** E4
Hetley Gdns, SE19 ... **170** C7
Hetley Rd, W12 ... **127** H1
Heton Gdns, NW4 ... **71** G4
Hevelius Cl, SE10 ... **135** F5
Hever Cft, SE9 ... **174** D4
Hever Gdns, Brom. BR1 ... **192** D2
Heverham Rd, SE18 ... **137** H4
Heversham Rd, Bexh.
DA7 ... **159** G2
Hevingham Dr, Rom.
(Chad.Hth) RM6 ... **82** C5
Hewer St, W10 ... **108** A5
Hewett Cl, Stan. HA7 ... **53** E4
Hewett Rd, Dag. RM8 ... **100** D5
Hewetts Quay, Bark. IG11 ... **117** E1
Hewett St, EC2 ... **12** E6
Hewish Rd, N18 ... **60** B4
Hewison St, E3 ... **113** J2
Hewitt Av, N22 ... **75** H2
Hewitt Cl, Croy. CR0 ... **204** A3
Hewitt Rd, N8 ... **75** G5
Hewlett Rd, E3 ... **113** H2
Hexagon, The, N6 ... **91** J1
Hexal Rd, SE6 ... **172** E3
Hexham Gdns, Islw. TW7 ... **124** D7
Hexham Rd, SE27 ... **169** J2
Barnet EN5 ... **41** E4
Morden SM4 ... **198** E1
Hexton Ct, N4
off Brownswood Rd ... **93** J2
Heybourne Rd, N17 ... **61** E7
Heybridge Av, SW16 ... **169** E7
Heybridge Dr, Ilf. IG6 ... **81** G2
Heybridge Way, E10 ... **77** H7
Heyford Av, SW8 ... **34** B7
SW20 ... **184** C3
Heyford Rd, Mitch. CR4 ... **185** H2
Heyford Ter, SW8
off Heyford Av ... **34** B7
Heygate St, SE17 ... **35** J2
Heylyn Sq, E3
off Malmesbury Rd ... **113** J3
Heynes Rd, Dag. RM8 ... **100** C4
Heysham Dr, Wat. WD19 ... **50** C5
Heysham La, NW3 ... **91** E3
Heysham Rd, N15 ... **76** A6
Heythorp St, SW18 ... **166** C1
Heywood Av, NW9 ... **70** E1
Heyworth Rd, E5 ... **94** E4
E15 ... **97** F5
Hibbert Rd, E17 ... **77** J7
Harrow HA3 ... **68** C2
Hibbert St, SW11 ... **149** F3
Hibernia Gdns, Houns.
TW3 ... **143** G4
Hibernia Pt, SE2
off Wolvercote Rd ... **138** D2
Hibernia Rd, Houns. TW3 ... **143** G4
Hibiscus Cl, Edg. HA8
off Campion Way ... **54** C4
Hibiscus Ho, Felt. TW13
off High St ... **160** B1
Hichisson Rd, SE15 ... **153** F5
Hickeys Almshouses, Rich. TW9
off St. Mary's Gro ... **145** J4
Hickin Cl, SE7 ... **136** A4
Hickin St, E14
off Plevna St ... **134** C3
Hickling Rd, Ilf. IG1 ... **99** E5
Hickman Av, E4 ... **62** C6
Hickman Cl, E16 ... **116** A5
Hickman Rd, Rom. RM6 ... **82** C7
Hickmore Wk, SW4 ... **150** C3
Hickory Cl, N9 ... **44** D7
Hicks Av, Grnf. UB6 ... **104** A2
Hicks Cl, SW11 ... **149** H3
Hicks St, SE8 ... **133** H5
Hidcote Gdns, SW20 ... **183** H3
Hide, E6 *off Downings* ... **116** D6
Hide Pl, SW1 ... **33** H2
Hide Rd, Har. HA1 ... **68** A4
Hides St, N7
off Sheringham Rd ... **93** F6
Hide Twr, SW1 ... **33** H2
Higgins Wk, Hmptn. TW12
off Abbott Cl ... **161** E6
High Acres, Enf. EN2
off Old Pk Vw ... **43** G3
HIGHAM HILL, E17 ... **77** H2
Higham Hill Rd, E17 ... **77** H2
Higham Ms, Nthlt. UB5
off Taywood Rd ... **103** F4
Higham Pl, E17 ... **77** H3
Higham Rd, N17 ... **76** A3
Woodford Green IG8 ... **63** G6
Highams Ct, E4
off Friars Cl ... **62** D3
Highams Lo Business Cen,
E17 ... **77** H3
HIGHAMS PARK, E4 ... **62** D5
Highams Pk Ind Est, E4 ... **62** C6
Higham Sta Av, E4 ... **62** B6
Higham St, E17 ... **77** H3
Highbanks Cl, Well. DA16 ... **138** B7
Highbanks Rd, Pnr. HA5 ... **51** H5
Highbank Way, N8 ... **75** G6
HIGH BARNET, Barn. EN5 ... **40** A2
Highbarrow Rd, Croy.
CR0 ... **188** D7
HIGH BEACH, Loug. IG10 ... **47** G1
High Beech, S.Croy. CR2 ... **202** B7
High Beeches, Sid. DA14 ... **176** E5
High Beech Rd, Loug.
IG10 ... **48** A4
High Br, SE10 ... **134** D5
Highbridge Rd, Barking
IG11 ... **116** E1
High Br Wf, SE10 ... **134** D5
Highbrook Rd, SE3 ... **156** A3

High Broom Cres, W.Wick. BR4 **190** B7
HIGHBURY, N5 **93** H5
Highbury Av, Th.Hth. CR7 **187** G2
Highbury Cl, N.Mal. KT3 **182** C4
West Wickham BR4 **204** B2
Highbury Cor, N5 **93** G6
Highbury Cres, N5 **93** G5
Highbury Est, N5 **93** J5
Highbury Gdns, Ilf. IG3 **99** H2
Highbury Gra, N5 **93** H4
Highbury Gro, N5 **93** H6
Highbury Hill, N5 **93** G3
Highbury New Pk, N5 **93** J5
Highbury Pk, N5 **93** H3
Highbury Pl, N5 **93** H6
Highbury Quad, N5 **93** H3
Highbury Rd, SW19 **166** B5
Highbury Sq, N14 *off Burleigh Gdns* **58** C1
Highbury Sta Rd, N1 **93** G6
Highbury Ter, N5 **93** H5
Highbury Ter Ms, N5 **93** H5
High Cedar Dr, SW20 **165** H7
Highclere Rd, N.Mal. KT3 **182** D3
Highclere St, SE26 **171** H4
Highcliffe Dr, SW15 **147** F6
Highcliffe Gdns, Ilf. IG4 **80** B5
Highcombe, SE7 **135** H6
Highcombe Cl, SE9 **174** A1
High Coombe Pl, Kings.T. KT2 **164** D7
Highcroft, NW9 **70** E5
Highcroft Av, Wem. HA0 **106** A1
Highcroft Gdns, NW11 **72** C6
Highcroft Rd, N19 **74** E7
High Cross Cen, The, N15 **76** D4
High Cross Rd, N17 **76** D3
Highcross Way, SW15 **165** G1
Highdaun Dr, SW16 **187** F4
Highdown, Wor.Pk. KT4 **197** E2
Highdown Rd, SW15 **147** H6
High Dr, N.Mal. KT3 **182** C1
High Elms, Chig. IG7 **65** H4
Woodford Green IG8 **63** G5
Highfield, Bushey (Bushey Hth) WD23 **52** B2
Watford WD19 **51** F3
Highfield Av, NW9 **70** C5
NW11 **72** A7
Erith DA8 **139** H6
Greenford UB6 **86** B5
Orpington BR6 **207** J5
Pinner HA5 **67** F5
Wembley HA9 **87** H3
Highfield Cl, N22 **75** G1
NW9 **70** C5
SE13 **154** D6
Surbiton (Long Dit.) KT6 **195** F1
Highfield Ct, N14 **42** C6
Highfield Dr, Brom. BR2 **191** E4
Epsom KT19 **197** F7
West Wickham BR4 **204** B2
Highfield Gdns, NW11 **72** B6
Highfield Hill, SE19 **170** A7
Highfield Ms, NW6 *off Compayne Gdns* **90** E7
Highfield Rd, N21 **59** H2
NW11 **72** B6
W3 **106** B5
Bexleyheath DA6 **159** F5
Bromley BR1 **192** C4
Chislehurst BR7 **193** J3
Feltham TW13 **160** A2
Isleworth TW7 **144** C1
Surbiton KT5 **182** C7
Sutton SM1 **199** H5
Woodford Green IG8 **64** B7
Highfields Gro, N6 **91** J1
High Foleys, Esher (Clay.) KT10 **194** E7
High Gables, Loug. IG10 **48** A5
HIGHGATE, N6 **92** A2
Highgate Av, N6 **74** B6
★ **Highgate Cem**, N6 **92** A1
Highgate Cl, N6 **74** A7
Highgate Edge, N2 **73** H5
Highgate High St, N6 **92** A1
Highgate Hill, N6 **92** B1
N19 **92** B1
Highgate Ho, SE26 *off Sydenham Hill Est* **170** D3
Highgate Rd, NW5 **92** B4
Highgate Spinney, N8 *off Crescent Rd* **74** D6
Highgate Wk, SE23 **171** F2
Highgate W Hill, N6 **92** A2
High Gro, SE18 **137** G7
Bromley BR1 **191** J1
Highgrove Cl, N11 *off Balmoral Av* **58** A5
Chislehurst BR7 **192** B1
Highgrove Ms, Cars. SM5 **199** J3
Highgrove Rd, Dag. RM8 **100** C5
Highgrove Way, Ruis. HA4 **66** A6
High Hill, E5 *off Mount Pleasant La* **95** E1
High Hill Ferry, E5 *off Big Hill* **95** E1
High Holborn, WC1 **18** B3
Highland Av, W7 **104** B6
Dagenham RM10 **101** J3
Loughton IG10 **48** B6
Highland Cotts, Wall. SM6 **200** B4
Highland Ct, E18 **79** H1
Highland Cft, Beck. BR3 **172** B5
Highland Rd, SE19 **170** B6
Bexleyheath DA6 **159** G5
Bromley BR1, BR2 **191** F1
Highlands, Wat. WD19 **50** C1
Highlands, The, Barn. EN5 **40** E5
Edgware HA8 **70** B2
Highlands Av, N21 **43** F5
W3 **106** C7
Highlands Cl, N4 *off Mount Vw Rd* **75** E7
Hounslow TW3 **143** H1
Highlands Gdns, Ilf. IG1 **98** C1
Highlands Heath, SW15 **147** J7
Highlands Rd, Barn. EN5 **40** D5
High La, W7 **104** A6
High Lawns, Har. HA1 **86** B3
Highlea Cl, NW9 **71** E1
High Level Dr, SE26 **170** D4
Highlever Rd, W10 **107** J5
Highmead, SE18 **137** J7
High Mead, Chig. IG7 **65** F2
Harrow HA1 **68** B5
West Wickham BR4 **204** D2
Highmead Cres, Wem. HA0 **87** J7
High Meadow Cl, Pnr. HA5 **66** C4
Highmeadow Cres, NW9 **70** D5
High Meadows, Chig. IG7 **65** G5
High Meads Rd, E16 **116** A6
Highmore Rd, SE3 **135** E7
High Mt, NW4 **71** G6
High Pk Av, Rich. TW9 **146** A1
High Pk Rd, Rich. TW9 **146** A1
High Path, SW19 **185** E1
High Pt, N6 **74** A7
SE9 **175** E3
High Rd, N2 **73** H4
N11 **58** B5
N12 **57** F6
N15 **76** C6
N17 **76** C1
N20 **41** F7
N22 **75** G3
NW10 (Willesden) **89** H6
Buckhurst Hill IG9 **63** H2
Bushey (Bushey Hth) WD23 **52** A1
Chigwell IG7 **64** C5
Harrow (Har.Wld) HA3 **52** B7
Ilford IG1 **98** E3
Ilford (Seven Kings) IG3 **99** J1
Loughton IG10 **47** J7
Pinner (Eastcote) HA5 **66** B4
Romford (Chad.Hth) RM6 **100** B1
Wembley HA0, HA9 **87** G5
High Rd Leyton, E10 **96** B1
E15 **96** C3
High Rd Leytonstone, E11 **96** E4
E15 **96** E4
High Rd Woodford Grn, E18 **63** F7
Woodford Green IG8 **63** F7
Highshore Rd, SE15 **152** C2
High Silver, Loug. IG10 **48** A4
Highstone Av, E11 **79** G6
High St, E11 **79** G5
E13 **115** G2
E15 **114** C2
E17 **77** J5
N8 **74** E4
N14 **58** D1
NW7 **55** H4
NW10 (Harlesden) **107** F2
SE20 **171** E6
SE25 (S.Norwood) **188** C4
W3 **126** B1
W5 **105** G7
Barnet EN5 **40** B3
Beckenham BR3 **190** A2
Brentford TW8 **125** G6
Bromley BR1 **191** G2
Carshalton SM5 **200** A4
Chislehurst BR7 **174** E6
Croydon CR0 **201** J2
Edgware HA8 **54** A6
Enfield (Pond.End) EN3 **45** F5
Esher (Clay.) KT10 **194** C6
Feltham TW13 **160** A3
Hampton TW12 **161** J6
Harrow HA1, HA2 **86** B1
Harrow (Wealds.) HA3 **68** B3
Hayes (Harling.) UB3 **121** H5
High St, Hounslow TW3 **143** J3
Hounslow (Cran.) TW5 **122** B7
Ilford (Barkingside) IG6 **81** F2
Kingston upon Thames KT1 **181** G2
Kingston upon Thames (Hmptn W.) KT1 **181** F1
New Malden KT3 **183** E3
Orpington (Farnboro.) BR6 **207** E5
Orpington (Grn St Grn) BR6 **207** J7
Pinner HA5 **66** E3
Southall UB1 **123** F1
Staines (Stanw.) TW19 **140** A6
Sutton SM1 **198** E4
Sutton (Cheam) SM3 **198** B6
Teddington TW11 **162** D5
Thames Ditton KT7 **180** D7
Thornton Heath CR7 **187** J4
Twickenham (Whitton) TW2 **143** J7
Wembley HA9 **87** J4
West Drayton (Harm.) UB7 **120** A6
West Drayton (Yiew.) UB7 **120** A1
West Molesey KT8 **179** G4
West Wickham BR4 **204** B1
High St Colliers Wd, SW19 **167** G7
High St Ms, SW19 **166** B5
High St N, E6 **116** B1
E12 **98** B5
High St S, E6 **116** C2
High St Wimbledon, SW19 **166** A5
High Timber St, EC4 **19** J5
High Tor Cl, Brom. BR1 **173** H7
High Tor Vw, SE28 **137** H1
High Tree Ct, W7 **104** B7
High Trees, SW2 **169** G1
Barnet EN4 **41** H5
Croydon CR0 **203** H1
Highview, Nthlt. UB5 **103** E3
High Vw, Pnr. HA5 **66** C4
Highview Av, Edg. HA8 **54** C4
Wallington SM6 **201** F5
High Vw Cl, SE19 **188** C2
Loughton IG10 **47** J5
Highview Gdns, N3 **72** B4
N11 **58** C5
Edgware HA8 **54** C4
Highview Ho, Rom. RM6 **83** E4
High Vw Rd, E18 **79** F3
SE19 **170** A6
Highview Rd, W13 **104** D5
Sidcup DA14 **176** B4
Highway, The, E1 **21** J6
E14 **21** J6
Stanmore HA7 **68** C1
Highwood, Brom. BR2 **190** D3
Highwood Av, N12 **57** F4
Highwood Cl, SE22 **170** D1
Orpington BR6 **207** F2
Highwood Dr, Orp. BR6 **207** F2
Highwood Gdns, Ilf. IG5 **80** C5
Highwood Gro, NW7 **54** D5
HIGHWOOD HILL, NW7 **55** G2
Highwood Hill, NW7 **55** F2
Highwood La, Loug. IG10 **48** D5
Highwood Rd, N19 **92** E3
High Worple, Har. HA2 **67** F7
Highworth Rd, N11 **58** D6
Hilary Av, Mitch. CR4 **186** A3
Hilary Cl, SW6 **30** A7
Erith DA8 **159** J1
Hilary Rd, W12 **107** F6
Hilbert Rd, Sutt. SM3 **198** A3
Hilborough Way, Orp. BR6 **207** G5
Hilda Lockert Wk, SW9 *off Fiveways Rd* **151** H2
Hilda Rd, E6 **98** A7
E16 **115** E4
Hilda Ter, SW9 **151** G2
Hilda Vale Cl, Orp. BR6 **206** D4
Hilda Vale Rd, Orp. BR6 **206** D4
Hildenborough Gdns, Brom. BR1 **173** E6
Hildenlea Pl, Brom. BR2 **190** E2
Hildreth St, SW12 **168** B1
Hildreth St Ms, SW12 *off Hildreth St* **168** B1
Hildyard Rd, SW6 **128** D6
Hiley Rd, NW10 **107** J3
Hilgrove Rd, NW6 **91** F7
Hiliary Gdns, Stan. HA7 **69** F2
Hillary Dr, Islw. TW7 **144** C4
Hillary Ri, Barn. EN5 **40** D4
Hillary Rd, Sthl. UB2 **123** G3
Hillbeck Cl, SE15 **133** F7
Hillbeck Way, Grnf. UB6 **104** A1
Hillborne Cl, Hayes UB3 **122** A5
Hillborough Cl, SW19 **167** F7
Hillbrook Rd, SW17 **167** J3
Hill Brow, Brom. BR1 **192** A1
Hillbrow, N.Mal. KT3 **183** F3
Hillbrow Rd, Brom. BR1 **172** E7
Hillbury Av, Har. HA3 **69** E5
Hillbury Rd, SW17 **168** B3
Hill Cl, NW2 **89** H3
NW11 **72** D6
Barnet EN5 **39** J5
Chislehurst BR7 **174** E5
Harrow HA1 **86** B3
Stanmore HA7 **52** E4
Hillcote Av, SW16 **169** G7
Hill Ct, Nthlt. UB5 **85** G5
Hillcourt Av, N12 **56** E6
Hillcourt Est, N16 **94** A1
Hillcourt Rd, SE22 **152** E6
Hill Cres, N20 **56** E2
Bexley DA5 **177** J1
Harrow HA1 **68** D5
Surbiton KT5 **181** J5
Worcester Park KT4 **197** J2
Hillcrest, N6 **74** A7
N21 **43** H7
SE24 **152** A4
Hill Crest, Sid. DA15 **158** A7
Hillcrest Av, NW11 **72** B5
Edgware HA8 **54** B4
Pinner HA5 **66** D4
Hillcrest Cl, SE26 **170** D4
Beckenham BR3 **189** J5
Hillcrest Ct, Sutt. SM2 *off Eaton Rd* **199** G6
Hillcrest Gdns, N3 **72** B4
NW2 **89** G3
Esher KT10 **194** C3
Hillcrest Rd, E17 **78** D2
E18 **79** F2
W3 **126** A1
W5 **105** H5
Bromley BR1 **173** G5
Loughton IG10 **48** A6
Hillcrest Vw, Beck. BR3 **189** J6
Hillcroft, Loug. IG10 **48** D2
Hillcroft Av, Pnr. HA5 **67** F6
Hillcroft Cres, W5 **105** H6
Ruislip HA4 **84** D3
Watford WD19 **50** B1
Wembley HA9 **87** J4
Hillcroft Rd, E6 **116** E5
Hillcroome Rd, Sutt. SM2 **199** G6
Hillcross Av, Mord. SM4 **184** C5
Hilldale Rd, Sutt. SM1 **198** C4
Hilldown Rd, SW16 **169** E7
Bromley BR2 **205** E1
Hill Dr, NW9 **88** C1
SW16 **187** F3
Hilldrop Cres, N7 **92** D5
Hilldrop Est, N7 **92** D5
Hilldrop La, N7 **92** D5
Hilldrop Rd, N7 **92** D5
Bromley BR1 **173** G6
Hillend, SE18 **156** D1
Hill End, Orp. BR6 *off The Approach* **207** J2
Hillersdon Av, SW13 **147** G2
Edgware HA8 **53** J5
Hillery Cl, SE17 **36** C2
Hill Fm Rd, W10 **107** J5
Hillfield Av, N8 **75** E5
NW9 **71** E5
Morden SM4 **185** H6
Wembley HA0 **87** H7
Hillfield Cl, Har. HA2 **67** J4
Hillfield Ct, NW3 **91** H5
Hillfield Ms, N8 **75** F4
Hillfield Pk, N10 **74** B4
N21 **59** G2
Hillfield Pk Ms, N10 **74** B4
Hillfield Rd, NW6 **90** C5
Hampton TW12 **161** F7
Hillfoot Av, Rom. RM5 **83** J1
Hillfoot Rd, Rom. RM5 **83** J1
Hillgate Pl, SW12 **150** B7
W8 **128** D1
Hillgate St, W8 **128** D1
Hill Gate Wk, N6 **74** C6
Hill Gro, Felt. TW13 *off Watermill Way* **161** F2
Hill Ho, E5 **95** E1
Hill Ho Av, Stan. HA7 **52** C7
Hill Ho Cl, N21 **43** G7
Hill Ho Dr, Hmptn. TW12 **179** G1
Hill Ho Ms, Brom. BR2 **191** F2
Hill Ho Rd, SW16 **169** F5
Hilliards Ct, E1 *off Wapping High St* **133** F1
Hillier Cl, Barn. (New Barn.) EN5 **40** E6
Hillier Gdns, Croy. CR0 **201** G5
Hillier Pl, Chess. KT9 **195** G6
Hillier Rd, SW11 **149** J6
Hilliers La, Croy. CR0 **200** E3
Hillingdon Rd, Bexh. DA7 **159** J2
Hillingdon St, SE17 **35** H6
Hillington Gdns, Wdf.Grn. IG8 **80** A2
Hillman Dr, W10 **107** J4

Hillman St, E8 ..... 95 E6
Hillmarton Rd, N7 ..... 93 E5
Hillmead Dr, SW9 ..... 151 H4
Hillmont Rd, Esher KT10 .. 194 B3
Hillmore Gro, SE26 ..... 171 G5
Hill Path, SW16
off Valley Rd 169 F5
Hillreach, SE18 ..... 136 C5
Hill Ri, N9 ..... 45 E6
NW11 ..... 73 E4
SE23 *off London Rd* ... 171 E1
Esher KT10 ..... 194 E2
Greenford UB6 ..... 85 J7
Richmond TW10 ..... 145 G5
Hillrise Rd, N19 ..... 74 E7
Hill Rd, N10 ..... 73 J1
NW8 ..... 6 D2
Carshalton SM5 ..... 199 H6
Harrow HA1 ..... 68 D5
Mitcham CR4 ..... 186 B1
Pinner HA5 ..... 66 E5
Sutton SM1 ..... 199 E5
Wembley HA0 ..... 86 E3
Hillsboro Rd, SE22 ..... 152 B5
Hillsborough Grn, Wat.
WD19 ..... 50 A3
Hillsgrove, Well. DA16 .... 138 C7
Hillside, NW9 ..... 70 D4
NW10 ..... 106 C1
SW19 ..... 166 A6
Barnet (New Barn.)
EN5 ..... 41 F5
Hillside Av, N11 ..... 57 J6
Borehamwood WD6 .... 38 B4
Wembley HA9 ..... 87 J4
Woodford Green IG8 .... 63 J5
Hillside Cl, NW8 ..... 6 B1
Morden SM4 ..... 184 B4
Woodford Green IG8 .... 63 J5
Hillside Cres, Har. HA2 .... 85 J1
Northwood HA6 ..... 66 A1
Hillside Dr, Edg. HA8 ..... 54 A6
Hillside Gdns, E17 ..... 78 D3
N6 ..... 74 A6
SW2 ..... 169 G2
Barnet EN5 ..... 40 B4
Edgware HA8 ..... 53 J4
Harrow HA3 ..... 69 H7
Northwood HA6 ..... 50 A7
Wallington SM6 ..... 200 C7
Hillside Gro, N14 ..... 42 D7
NW7 ..... 55 G7
Hillside La, Brom. BR2 ..... 205 G2
Hillside Pas, SW2 ..... 169 F2
Hillside Ri, Nthwd. HA6 .... 50 A7
Hillside Rd, N15 ..... 76 B7
SW2 ..... 169 G2
W5 ..... 105 H5
Bromley BR2 ..... 191 F3
Croydon CR0 ..... 201 H5
Northwood HA6 ..... 50 A7
Pinner HA5 ..... 50 B7
Southall UB1 ..... 103 G4
Surbiton KT5 ..... 181 J5
Sutton SM2 ..... 198 C7
Hillsleigh Rd, W8 ..... 128 C1
Hills Ms, W5 ..... 105 H7
Hills Pl, W1 ..... 17 F4
Hills Rd, Buck.H. IG9 ..... 63 H1
Hillstowe St, E5 ..... 95 F2
Hill St, W1 ..... 24 C1
Richmond TW9 ..... 145 G5
Hill Top, NW11 ..... 73 E4
Hilltop, Loug. IG10 ..... 48 D2
Hill Top, Mord. SM4 ..... 184 D6
Sutton SM3 ..... 184 C7
Hilltop Av, NW10 ..... 88 C7
Hill Top Cl, Loug. IG10 ..... 48 D3
Hilltop Gdns, NW4 ..... 71 H2
Orpington BR6 ..... 207 H2
Hill Top Pl, Loug. IG10 ..... 48 D3
Hilltop Rd, NW6 ..... 90 D7
Hill Top Vw, Wdf.Grn. IG8 .. 64 C6
Hilltop Way, Stan. HA7 ..... 52 D3
Hillview, SW20 ..... 165 H7
Mitcham CR4 ..... 186 E4
Hillview Av, Har. HA3 ..... 69 H5
Hillview Cl, Pnr. HA5 ..... 51 F6
Wembley HA9 ..... 87 J2
Hillview Cres, Ilf. IG1 ..... 80 C6
Orpington BR6 ..... 207 H1
Hill Vw Dr, SE28 ..... 137 H1
Welling DA16 ..... 157 H2
Hillview Gdns, NW4 ..... 72 A4
Hill Vw Gdns, NW9 ..... 70 D5
Hillview Gdns, Har. HA2 ... 67 G3
Hillview Rd, NW7 ..... 56 A4
Chislehurst BR7 ..... 174 D5
Hill Vw Rd, Esher (Clay.)
KT10 ..... 194 D7
Hillview Rd, Orp. BR6 .... 207 J1
Pinner HA5 ..... 51 F7
Sutton SM1 ..... 199 F3
Hill Vw Rd, Twick. TW1 .... 144 D6
Hillway, N6 ..... 92 A2
NW9 ..... 88 E1
Hillworth Rd, SW2 ..... 151 G7
Hillyard Rd, W7 ..... 104 B5
Hillyard St, SW9 ..... 151 G1
Hillyfield, E17 ..... 77 H2
Hillyfield Cl, E9
off Mabley St 95 H5
Hillyfields, Loug. IG10 ..... 48 D2
Hilly Flds Cres, SE4 ..... 154 A3
Hilsea Pt, SW15
off Wanborough Dr ... 165 H1
Hilsea St, E5 ..... 95 F4
Hilton Av, N12 ..... 57 G5
Hilversum Cres, SE22
off East Dulwich Gro .. 152 B5
Himley Rd, SW17 ..... 167 H5
Hinchley Cl, Esher KT10 .. 194 C3
Hinchley Dr, Esher KT10 .. 194 C3
Hinchley Manor, Esher
KT10 ..... 194 C3
Hinchley Way, Esher
KT10 ..... 194 D3
HINCHLEY WOOD, Esher
KT10 ..... 194 C3
Hinckley Rd, SE15 ..... 152 D4
Hind Cl, Chig. IG7 ..... 65 J5
Hind Ct, EC4 ..... 19 F4
Hinde Ms, W1
off Marylebone La 16 C3
Hindes Rd, Har. HA1 ..... 68 A5
Hinde St, W1 ..... 16 C3
Hind Gro, E14 ..... 114 A6
Hindhead Cl, N16 ..... 94 B1
Hindhead Gdns, Nthlt.
UB5 ..... 102 E1
Hindhead Grn, Wat. WD19 .. 50 C5
Hindhead Pt, SW15
off Wanborough Dr ... 165 H1
Hindhead Way, Wall.
SM6 ..... 200 E5
Hind Ho, N7
off Harvist Est 93 G4
Hindle Ho, E8
off Arcola St 94 C5
Hindmans Rd, SE22 ..... 152 D5
Hindmans Way, Dag.
RM9 ..... 119 F4
Hindmarsh Cl, E1 ..... 21 J5
Hindon Ct, SW1 ..... 33 F1
Hindrey Rd, E5 ..... 94 E5
Hindsley's Pl, SE23 ..... 171 F2
Hinkler Rd, Har. HA3 ..... 69 G3
Hinksey Path, SE2 ..... 138 D3
Hinstock Rd, SE18 ..... 137 F6
Hinton Av, Houns. TW4 ... 142 D4
Hinton Cl, SE9 ..... 174 B1
Hinton Rd, N18 ..... 60 B4
SE24 ..... 151 H3
Wallington SM6 ..... 200 C6
Hippodrome Ms, W11
off Portland Rd 108 B7
Hippodrome Pl, W11 ..... 108 B7
Hirst Ct, SW1 ..... 32 D4
Hirst Cres, Wem. HA9 ..... 87 H3
Hitcham Rd, E17 ..... 77 J7
Hitchin Sq, E3 ..... 113 H2
Hithe Gro, SE16
off Lower Rd 133 F3
Hitherbroom Rd, Hayes
UB3 ..... 122 A1
Hither Fm Rd, SE3 ..... 155 J3
Hitherfield Rd, SW16 ..... 169 F2
Dagenham RM8 ..... 100 E2
HITHER GREEN, SE13 ..... 154 E6
Hither Grn La, SE13 ..... 154 C5
Hitherlands, SW12 ..... 168 B2
Hitherwell Dr, Har. HA3 .... 68 A1
Hitherwood Dr, SE19 ..... 170 C4
Hive Cl, Bushey
(Bushey Hth) WD23 ..... 52 A2
Hive Rd, Bushey
(Bushey Hth) WD23 ..... 52 A2
★ **H.M.S. Belfast**, SE1 .... 28 E1
★ **H.M.S. President**, EC4 .. 19 F6
★ **H.M. Treasury**, SW1 .... 26 A3
Hoadly Rd, SW16 ..... 168 D3
Hobart Cl, N20
off Oakleigh Rd N 57 H2
Hayes UB4 ..... 102 D4
Hobart Dr, Hayes UB4 .... 102 D4
Hobart Gdns, Th.Hth.
CR7 ..... 188 A3
Hobart La, Hayes UB4 .... 102 D4
Hobart Pl, SW1 ..... 24 D5
Richmond TW10
off Chisholm Rd 145 J6
Hobart Rd, Dag. RM9 ..... 100 D4
Hayes UB4 ..... 102 D4
Ilford IG6 ..... 81 F2
Worcester Park KT4 .... 197 H3
Hobbayne Rd, W7 ..... 104 A6
Hobbes Wk, SW15 ..... 147 H5
Hobbs Grn, N2 ..... 73 F3
Hobbs Ms, Ilf. IG3
off Ripley Rd 99 J2
Hobbs Pl Est, N1
off Pitfield St 112 B1
Hobbs Rd, SE27 ..... 169 J4
Hobby St, Enf. EN3 ..... 45 G5
Hobday St, E14 ..... 114 B5
Hobill Wk, Surb. KT5 ..... 181 J6
Hoblands End, Chis.
BR7 ..... 175 H6
Hobsons Pl, E1 ..... 21 H1
Hobury St, SW10 ..... 30 D6
Hocker St, E2 ..... 13 F4
Hockett Cl, SE8
off Grove St 133 J4
Hockley Av, E6 ..... 116 B2
Hockley Ct, E18
off Churchfields 79 G1
Hockley Ms, Bark. IG11 ... 117 H2
Hocroft Av, NW2 ..... 90 C3
Hocroft Rd, NW2 ..... 90 C4
Hocroft Wk, NW2 ..... 90 C3
Hodder Dr, Grnf. (Perivale)
UB6 ..... 104 C2
Hoddesdon Rd, Belv.
DA17 ..... 139 G5
Hodes Row, NW3
off Estelle Rd 92 A4
Hodford Rd, NW11 ..... 90 C2
Hodgkin Cl, SE28
off Fleming Way 118 D7
Hodgkins Ms, Stan. HA7 ... 52 E5
Hodister Cl, SE5
off Badsworth Rd 131 J7
Hodnet Gro, SE16 ..... 133 G4
Hodson Cl, Har. HA2 ..... 85 F3
Hoe, The, Wat. WD19 ..... 50 D2
Hoechst, Houns. TW4 .... 142 C3
Hoe St, E17 ..... 78 A4
Hoffmann Gdns, S.Croy.
CR2 ..... 202 D7
Hoffman Sq, N1
off Chart St 12 C3
Hofland Rd, W14 ..... 128 A3
Hogan Ms, W2 ..... 14 E1
Hogan Way, E5
off Geldeston Rd 94 D2
Hogarth Business Pk, W4 . 126 E6
Hogarth Cl, E16 ..... 116 A5
W5 ..... 105 H5
Hogarth Ct, EC3 ..... 20 E5
SE19 *off Fountain Dr* .. 170 C4
Hogarth Cres, SW19 ..... 185 G1
Croydon CR0 ..... 187 J7
Hogarth Gdns, Houns.
TW5 ..... 123 G7
Hogarth Hill, NW11 ..... 72 C4
Hogarth La, W4 ..... 126 E6
Hogarth Pl, SW5 ..... 30 A2
Hogarth Reach, Loug.
IG10 ..... 48 C5
Hogarth Rd, SW5 ..... 30 A2
Dagenham RM8 ..... 100 B5
Edgware HA8 ..... 70 A2
Hogarth Rbt, W4 ..... 127 F6
Hogarth Rbt Flyover, W4
off Burlington La 127 E6
★ **Hogarth's Ho**, W4
off Hogarth La 126 E6
Hogarth Way, Hmptn.
TW12 ..... 179 J1
Hogshead Pas, E1
off Tobacco Dock 113 E7
Hogsmill La, Kings.T. KT1 . 181 J3
Hogsmill Way, Epsom
KT19 ..... 196 C5
Holbeach Cl, NW9 ..... 70 E1
Holbeach Gdns, Sid.
DA15 ..... 157 H6
Holbeach Ms, SW12
off Harberson Rd 168 B1
Holbeach Rd, SE6 ..... 154 A7
Holbeck Row, SE15 ..... 132 D7
Holbein Ms, SW1 ..... 32 B3
Holbein Pl, SW1 ..... 32 B2
Holbein Ter, Dag. RM8
off Marlborough Rd .. 100 B4
Holberton Gdns, NW10 ... 107 H3
HOLBORN, WC2 ..... 18 C3
Holborn, EC1 ..... 18 E2
Holborn Circ, EC1 ..... 19 F2
Holborn Pl, WC1 ..... 18 C2
Holborn Rd, E13 ..... 115 H4
Holborn Viaduct, EC1 ..... 19 F2
Holborn Way, Mitch. CR4 .. 185 J2
Holbrook Cl, N19
off Dartmouth Pk Hill .. 92 B1
Enfield EN1 ..... 44 C1
Holbrooke Ct, N7 ..... 92 E4
Holbrooke Pl, Rich. TW10 . 145 G5
Holbrook La, Chis. BR7 ... 175 G7
Holbrook Rd, E15 ..... 115 F2
Holbrook Way, Brom.
BR2 ..... 192 C6
Holburne Cl, SE3 ..... 155 J1
Holburne Gdns, SE3 ..... 156 A1
Holburne Rd, SE3 ..... 155 J1
Holcombe Hill, NW7 ..... 55 G3
Holcombe Rd, N17 ..... 76 C3
Ilford IG1 ..... 80 D7
Holcombe St, W6 ..... 127 H5
Holcote Cl, Belv. DA17
off Blakemore Way ... 139 E3
Holcroft Rd, E9 ..... 95 F7
Holden Av, N12 ..... 57 E5
NW9 ..... 88 C1
Holdenby Rd, SE4 ..... 153 H5
Holden Cl, Dag. RM8 ..... 100 B3
Holdenhurst Av, N12 ..... 57 E7
Holden Pt, E15
off Waddington Rd 96 D6
Holden Rd, N12 ..... 56 E5
Holden St, SW11 ..... 150 A2
Holder Cl, N3 ..... 57 E7
Holdernesse Cl, Islw.
TW7 ..... 144 D1
Holdernesse Rd, SW17 ... 167 J3
Holderness Way, SE27 .... 169 H5
HOLDERS HILL, NW4 ..... 72 A2
Holders Hill Av, NW4 ..... 72 A2
Holders Hill Circ, NW7
off Dollis Rd 56 B7
Holders Hill Cres, NW4 .... 72 A2
Holders Hill Dr, NW4 ..... 72 A3
Holders Hill Gdns, NW4 ... 72 B2
Holders Hill Rd, NW4 ..... 72 A2
NW7 ..... 72 A2
Holegate St, SE7
off Westmoor St 136 A3
Holford Ho, SE16
off Manor Est 132 E4
Holford Ms, WC1 ..... 10 E2
Holford Pl, WC1 ..... 10 D3
Holford Rd, NW3 ..... 91 F3
Holford St, WC1 ..... 10 E3
Holford Yd, WC1 ..... 10 D2
Holgate Av, SW11 ..... 149 G3
Holgate Gdns, Dag.
RM10 ..... 101 G5
Holgate Rd, Dag. RM10 ... 101 G5
Holland Av, SW20 ..... 183 F1
Holland Cl, Barn.
(New Barn.) EN5 ..... 41 G7
Bromley BR2 ..... 205 F2
Romford RM7 ..... 83 J5
Stanmore HA7 ..... 52 E5
Holland Ct, E17
off Evelyn Rd 78 C4
NW7 ..... 55 G6
Holland Dr, SE23 ..... 171 H3
Holland Gdns, W14 ..... 128 B3
Brentford TW8 ..... 125 H6
Holland Gro, SW9 ..... 131 G7
★ **Holland Pk**, W8 ..... 128 C2
Holland Pk, W11 ..... 128 B2
Holland Pk Av, W11 ..... 128 B2
Ilford IG3 ..... 81 H6
Holland Pk Gdns, W14 .... 128 B1
Holland Pk Ms, W11 ..... 128 B1
Holland Pk Rd, W14 ..... 128 C3
Holland Pk Rbt, W11 ..... 128 A2
Holland Pas, N1
off Basire St 111 J1
Holland Pl, W8 ..... 22 A3
Holland Ri Ho, SW9
off Clapham Rd 131 F7
Holland Rd, E6 ..... 116 C1
E15 ..... 115 E3
NW10 ..... 107 G1
SE25 ..... 188 D5
W14 ..... 128 A2
Wembley HA0 ..... 87 G6
Hollands, The, Felt. TW13 . 160 D4
Worcester Park KT4 .... 197 F1
Holland St, SE1 ..... 27 H1
W8 ..... 128 D2
Holland Town Est, SW9
off Brixton Rd 131 G7
Holland Vil Rd, W14 ..... 128 B2
Holland Wk, N19
off Duncombe Rd 92 D1
W8 ..... 128 C2
Stanmore HA7 ..... 52 D5
Holland Way, Brom. BR2 .. 205 F2
Hollar Rd, N16
*off Stoke Newington
High St* 94 C3
Hollen St, W1 ..... 17 H3
Holles Cl, Hmptn. TW12 ... 161 G6
Holles St, W1 ..... 16 E3
Holley Rd, W3 ..... 127 E2
Hollickwood Av, N12 ..... 57 J6
Holliday Sq, SW11
off Fowler Cl 149 G3
Hollidge Way, Dag.
RM10 ..... 101 H6
Hollies, The, E11 ..... 79 G5
N20
off Oakleigh Pk N 57 G1
Harrow HA3 ..... 68 D4
Hollies Av, Sidcup
DA15 ..... 175 J2
Hollies Cl, SW16 ..... 169 G6
Twickenham TW1 ..... 162 C2
Hollies End, NW7 ..... 55 H5
Hollies Rd, W5 ..... 125 F4
Hollies Way, SW12
off Bracken Av 150 A7
Holligrave Rd, Brom.
BR1 ..... 191 G1

Hollingbourne Av, Bexh. DA7 .139 F7
Hollingbourne Gdns, W13 .104 E5
Hollingbourne Rd, SE24 .151 J5
Hollingsworth Rd, Croy. CR0 .203 E6
Hollington Cres, N.Mal. KT3 .183 F6
Hollington Rd, E6 .116 C3
N17 .76 D2
Hollingworth Cl, W.Mol. KT8 .179 F4
Hollingworth Rd, Orp. BR5 .192 E6
Hollman Gdns, SW16 .169 H6
Hollow, The, Wdf.Grn. IG8 .63 F4
HOLLOWAY, N7 .92 D5
Holloway Cl, West Dr. UB7 .120 B5
Holloway La, West Dr. UB7 .120 B6
Holloway Rd, E6 .116 C3
E11 .96 E3
N7 .93 F4
N19 .92 D2
Holloway St, Houns. TW3 .143 H3
Hollowfield Wk, Nthlt. UB5 .84 E6
Hollows, The, Brent. TW8 .125 J6
Hollow Wk, Rich. (Kew) TW9 off Royal Botanic Gdns .125 H7
Holly Av, Stan. HA7 .69 H2
Hollybank Cl, Hmptn. TW12 .161 G5
Hollyberry La, NW3 off Holly Wk .91 F4
Hollybrake Cl, Chis. BR7 .175 G7
Hollybush Cl, E11 .79 G5
Harrow HA3 .68 B1
Hollybush Gdns, E2 .113 E3
Hollybush Hill, E11 .79 F6
Holly Bush Hill, NW3 .91 F4
Holly Bush La, Hmptn. TW12 .161 F7
Hollybush Pl, E2 off Bethnal Grn Rd .113 E3
Hollybush Rd, Kings.T. KT2 .163 H5
Holly Bush Steps, NW3 off Heath St .91 F4
Hollybush St, E13 .115 H3
Holly Bush Vale, NW3 off Heath St .91 F4
Holly Cl, Beck. BR3 .190 C4
Buckhurst Hill IG9 .64 A3
Feltham TW13 .160 E5
Wallington SM6 .200 B7
Holly Ct, SE10 off West Parkside .135 F3
Sutton SM2 off Worcester Rd .198 D7
Holly Cres, Beck. BR3 .189 J5
Woodford Green IG8 .62 D7
Hollycroft Av, NW3 .90 D3
Wembley HA9 .87 J2
Hollycroft Cl, S.Croy. CR2 .202 B5
West Drayton (Sipson) UB7 .120 D6
Hollycroft Gdns, West Dr. (Sipson) UB7 .120 D6
Hollydale Cl, Nthlt. UB5 off Dorchester Rd .85 H4
Hollydale Dr, Brom. BR2 .206 C3
Hollydale Rd, SE15 .153 F1
Hollydene, SE15 .152 E1
Hollydown Way, E11 .96 D3
Holly Dr, E4 .46 B7
Brentford TW8 .124 D6
Holly Fm Rd, Sthl. UB2 .122 E5
Hollyfield Av, N11 .57 J5
Hollyfield Rd, Surb. KT5 .181 J7
Holly Gdns, Bexh. DA7 .159 J4
West Drayton UB7 .120 C2
Holly Gro, NW9 .70 C7
SE15 .152 C2
Pinner HA5 .67 E1
Hollygrove Cl, Houns. TW3 off Staines Rd .143 F4
Holly Hedge Ter, SE13 .154 D5
Holly Hill, N21 .43 F6
NW3 .91 F4
Holly Hill Rd, Belv. DA17 .139 H5
Erith DA8 .139 H5
Holly Lo Gdns, N6 .92 A2
Hollymead, Cars. SM5 .199 J3
Holly Ms, SW10 .30 D4
Holly Mt, NW3 off Holly Bush Hill .91 F4
Hollymount Cl, SE10 .154 C1
Holly Pk, N3 .72 C3
N4 .75 F7
Holly Pk Est, N4 off Blythwood Rd .75 E7
Holly Pk Gdns, N3 .72 D3
Holly Pk Rd, N11 .58 A5
W7 .124 C1
Holly Pl, NW3 off Holly Wk .91 F4
Holly Rd, E11 .79 F7
W4 off Dolman Rd .126 D4
Hampton (Hmptn H.) TW12 .161 J6
Hounslow TW3 .143 H4
Twickenham TW1 .162 D1
Holly St, E8 .94 C6
Holly Ter, N6 off Highgate W Hill .92 A1
N20 off Swan La .57 F2
Hollytree Cl, SW19 .166 A1
Hollyview Cl, NW4 .71 G6
Holly Village, N6 off Swains La .92 B2
Holly Wk, NW3 .91 F4
Enfield EN2 .43 J3
Richmond TW9 .145 H2
Holly Way, Mitch. CR4 .186 D4
Hollywood Gdns, Hayes UB4 .102 B6
Hollywood Ms, SW10 .30 C5
Hollywood Rd, E4 .61 H5
SW10 .30 C4
Hollywood Way, Wdf.Grn. IG8 .62 D7
Holman Ho, E2 off Roman Rd .113 G3
Holman Rd, SW11 .149 G2
Epsom KT19 .196 C5
Holmbridge Gdns, Enf. EN3 .45 G4
Holmbrook Dr, NW4 .72 A5
Holmbury Ct, SW17 .167 J3
SW19 .167 H7
Holmbury Gdns, Hayes UB3 off Church Rd .121 J1
Holmbury Gro, Croy. CR0 .203 J7
Holmbury Pk, Brom. BR1 .174 B7
Holmbury Vw, E5 .95 E1
Holmbush Rd, SW15 .148 B6
Holmcote Gdns, N5 .93 J5
Holmcroft Way, Brom. BR2 .192 C5
Holmdale Gdns, NW4 .72 A5
Holmdale Rd, NW6 .90 D5
Chislehurst BR7 .175 F5
Holmdale Ter, N15 .76 B7
Holmdene Av, NW7 .55 G6
SE24 .151 J5
Harrow HA2 .67 H3
Holmdene Cl, Beck. BR3 .190 C2
Holmead Rd, SW6 .129 E7
Holmebury Cl, Bushey (Bushey Hth) WD23 .52 B2
Holme Ct, Islw. TW7 off Twickenham Rd .144 D3
Holmefield Ct, NW3 .91 H6
Holme Lacey Rd, SE12 .155 F6
Holme Rd, E6 .116 B1
Holmes Av, E17 .77 J3
NW7 .56 B5
Holmes Cl, SE22 .152 D4
Holmesdale Av, SW14 .146 B3
Holmesdale Cl, SE25 .188 C3
Holmesdale Rd, N6 .74 B7
SE25 .188 A5
Bexleyheath DA7 .158 D2
Croydon CR0 .188 A5
Richmond TW9 .145 J1
Teddington TW11 .163 F6
Holmesley Rd, SE23 .153 H6
Holmes Pl, SW10 .30 D5
Holmes Rd, NW5 .92 B5
SW19 .167 F7
Twickenham TW1 .162 C2
Holmes Ter, SE1 .27 E3
Holme Way, Stan. HA7 .52 C6
Holmewood Gdns, SW2 .151 F7
Holmewood Rd, SE25 .188 B3
SW2 .151 E7
Holmfield Av, NW4 .72 A5
Holmhurst Rd, Belv. DA17 .139 H5
Holmleigh Rd, N16 .94 B1
Holmleigh Rd Est, N16 off Holmleigh Rd .94 B1
Holm Oak Cl, SW15 .148 C6
Holm Oak Ms, SW4 .150 D5
Holmshaw Cl, SE26 .171 H4
Holmside Ri, Wat. WD19 .50 B3
Holmside Rd, SW12 .150 A6
Holmsley Cl, N.Mal. KT3 .183 F6
Holmsley Ho, SW15 off Tangley Gro .147 F7
Holms St, E2 .13 H1
Holmstall Av, Edg. HA8 .70 C3
Holm Wk, SE3 off Blackheath Pk .155 G2
Holmwood Cl, Har. HA2 .67 J3
Northolt UB5 .85 H6
Holmwood Gdns, N3 .72 D2
Wallington SM6 .200 B6
Holmwood Gro, NW7 .54 D5
Holmwood Rd, Chess. KT9 .195 G5
Ilford IG3 .99 H2
Holmwood Vil, SE7 off Woolwich Rd .135 G5
Holne Chase, N2 .73 F6
Morden SM4 .184 C6
Holness Rd, E15 .97 F6
Holroyd Rd, SW15 .147 J4
Holstein Way, Erith DA18 .138 E3
Holstock Rd, Ilf. IG1 .99 F2
Holsworth Cl, Har. HA2 .67 J5
Holsworthy Sq, WC1 .10 D6
Holsworthy Way, Chess. KT9 .195 F5
Holt, The, Ilf. IG6 .65 F6
Morden SM4 off London Rd .184 D4
Wallington SM6 .200 C4
Holt Cl, N10 .74 A4
SE28 .118 B7
Chigwell IG7 .65 J5
Holton St, E1 .113 G4
Holt Rd, E16 .136 B1
Wembley HA0 .87 E3
Holt Way, Chig. IG7 .65 J5
Holtwhite Av, Enf. EN2 .43 J2
Holtwhites Hill, Enf. EN2 .43 H1
Holwell Pl, Pnr. HA5 .66 E4
Holwood Pk Av, Orp. BR6 .206 C4
Holwood Pl, SW4 .150 D4
Holybourne Av, SW15 .147 G7
Holyhead Cl, E3 off Campbell Rd .114 A3
E6 off Valiant Way .116 C5
Holyoake Ct, SE16 off Bryan Rd .133 J2
Holyoake Wk, N2 .73 F3
W5 .105 F4
Holyoak Rd, SE11 .35 G1
Holyport Rd, SW6 .127 J7
Holyrood Av, Har. HA2 .85 E4
Holyrood Gdns, Edg. HA8 .70 B3
Holyrood Ms, E16 off Wesley Av .135 G1
Holyrood Rd, Barn. (New Barn.) EN5 .41 F6
Holyrood St, SE1 .28 D2
Holywell Cl, SE3 .135 G6
SE16 off Masters Dr .133 E5
Holywell La, EC2 .12 E5
Holywell Row, EC2 .12 D6
Homan Ct, N12 .57 F4
Home Cl, Cars. SM5 .199 J2
Northolt UB5 .103 F3
Homecroft Gdns, Loug. IG10 .48 E4
Homecroft Rd, N22 .75 H1
SE26 .171 F5
Home Fm Cl, T.Ditt. KT7 .180 C7
Homefarm Rd, W7 .104 B6
Homefield Av, Ilf. IG2 .81 H5
Homefield Cl, NW10 .88 C6
Hayes UB4 .102 C4
Homefield Gdns, N2 .73 G3
Mitcham CR4 .185 F2
Homefield Ms, Beck. BR3 .190 A1
Homefield Pk, Sutt. SM1 .198 E6
Homefield Rd, SW19 .166 A6
W4 .127 F4
Bromley BR1 .191 J1
Edgware HA8 .54 D6
Walton-on-Thames KT12 .179 E7
Wembley HA0 .86 D4
Homefield St, N1 .12 D2
Homefirs Ho, Wembley HA9 .87 J3
Home Gdns, Dag. RM10 .101 J3
Homelands Dr, SE19 .170 B7
Home Lea, Orp. BR6 .207 J5
Homeleigh Rd, SE15 .153 G5
Homemead, SW12 .168 B2
Home Mead, Stan. HA7 .69 F1
Homemead Rd, Brom. BR2 .192 C5
Croydon CR0 .186 C6
★ Home Office, SW1 .25 J6
Home Pk, E.Mol. (Hampton Ct Pk) KT8 .180 E4
Kingston upon Thames (Hampton Ct Pk) KT1 .180 E4
Home Pk Par, Kings.T. KT1 off High St .181 G2
Home Pk Rd, SW19 .166 D3
Home Pk Wk, Kings.T. KT1 .181 G4
Homer Cl, Bexh. DA7 .159 J1
Homer Dr, E14 .134 A4
Home Rd, SW11 .149 H2
Homer Rd, E9 .95 H6
Croydon CR0 .189 G6
Homer Row, W1 .15 H2
Homersham Rd, Kings.T. KT1 .182 A2
Homer St, W1 .15 H2
HOMERTON, E9 .95 H5
Homerton Gro, E9 .95 G5
Homerton High St, E9 .95 F5
Homerton Rd, E9 .95 H5
Homerton Row, E9 .95 F5
Homerton Ter, E9 off Morning La .95 F6
Homesdale Cl, E11 .79 G5
Homesdale Rd, Brom. BR1, BR2 .191 J4
Orpington BR5 .193 H7
Homesfield, NW11 .72 D5
Homestall Rd, SE22 .153 F5
Homestead, The, N11 .58 B4
Homestead Gdns, Esher (Clay.) KT10 .194 B5
Homestead Paddock, N14 .42 B5
Homestead Pk, NW2 .89 F3
Homestead Rd, SW6 .128 C7
Dagenham RM8 .101 F2
Homewillow Cl, N21 .43 H6
Homewood Cl, Hmptn. TW12 off Fearnley Cres .161 F6
Homewood Cres, Chis. BR7 .175 H6
Homildon Ho, SE26 off Sydenham Hill Est .170 D3
Honduras St, EC1 .11 J5
Honeybourne Rd, NW6 .90 E5
Honeybourne Way, Orp. BR5 .207 G1
Honeybrook Rd, SW12 .150 C7
Honey Cl, Dag. RM10 .101 H6
Honeycroft, Loug. IG10 .48 D4
Honeyden Rd, Sid. DA14 .177 E6
Honey La, EC2 .20 A4
Honeyman Cl, NW6 .90 A7
Honeypot Business Cen, Stan. HA7 .69 H1
Honeypot Cl, NW9 .69 J4
Honeypot La, NW9 .69 J3
Stanmore HA7 .69 J3
Honeysett Rd, N17 off Reform Row .76 C2
Honeysuckle Cl, Sthl. UB1 .102 E7
Honeysuckle Gdns, Croy. CR0 .189 G7
Honeywell Rd, SW11 .149 J6
★ Honeywood Heritage Cen, Cars. SM5 .199 J4
Honeywood Rd, NW10 .107 F2
Isleworth TW7 .144 D4
Honeywood Wk, Cars. SM5 .199 J4
Honister Cl, Stan. HA7 .69 E1
Honister Gdns, Stan. HA7 .53 E7
Honister Pl, Stan. HA7 .69 E1
Honiton Gdns, NW7 .56 A7
SE15 off Gibbon Rd .153 F2
Honiton Ho, Enf. EN3 off Exeter Rd .45 G3
Honiton Rd, NW6 .108 C2
Welling DA16 .157 J2
Honley Rd, SE6 .154 B7
Honnor Gdns, Islw. TW7 .144 A2
HONOR OAK, SE23 .153 F6
HONOR OAK PARK, SE4 .153 H6
Honor Oak Pk, SE23 .153 F6
Honor Oak Ri, SE23 .153 F6
Honor Oak Rd, SE23 .171 F1
Hood Av, N14 .42 B6
SW14 .146 C5
Hood Cl, Croy. CR0 .201 H1
Hoodcote Gdns, N21 .43 H7
Hood Ct, EC4 .19 F4
Hood Rd, SW20 .165 F7
Hood Wk, Rom. RM7 .83 H1
HOOK, Chess. KT9 .195 H4
Hook, The, Barn. (New Barn.) EN5 .41 G6
Hookers Rd, E17 .77 G3
Hook Fm Rd, Brom. BR2 .192 A5
Hooking Grn, Har. HA2 .67 H5
Hook Junct, Surb. KT6 .195 G3
Hook La, Well. DA16 .157 J5
Hook Ri N, Surb. KT6 .196 A3
Hook Ri S, Surb. KT6 .196 B3
Hook Ri S Business Cen, Surb. KT6 .196 A3
Hook Ri S Ind Pk, Surb. KT6 .195 J3
Hook Rd, Chess. KT9 .195 G5
Surbiton KT6 .195 H3
Hooks Cl, SE15 off Woods Rd .152 E1
Hooks Hall Dr, Dag. RM10 .101 J3
Hookstone Way, Wdf.Grn. IG8 .64 A7
Hook Wk, Edg. HA8 .54 C6
Hool Cl, NW9 off Kingsbury Rd .70 C5

Hooper Rd, E16 115 G6
Hooper's Ct, SW3 23 J4
Hoopers Ms, W3 126 C1
Hooper's Ms, Bushey WD23 51 H1
Hooper St, E1 21 H5
Hoop La, NW11 72 C7
Hope Cl, N1 *off Wallace Rd* 93 J6
SE12 173 H3
Brentford TW8 *off Burford Rd* 125 H5
Romford (Chad.Hth) RM6 82 C4
Sutton SM1 199 F5
Woodford Green IG8 *off West Gro* 63 J6
Hopedale Rd, SE7 135 H6
Hopefield Av, NW6 108 B2
Hope Gdns, W3 *off Park Rd N* 126 B2
Hope La, SE9 174 E2
Hope Pk, Brom. BR1 173 F7
Hopes Cl, Houns. TW5 *off Old Cote Dr* 123 G6
Hope St, SW11 149 G3
Hopetown St, E1 21 G2
Hopewell St, SE5 132 A7
Hopewell Yd, SE5 *off Hopewell St* 132 A7
Hope Wf, SE16 *off St. Marychurch St* 133 F2
Hop Gdns, WC2 18 A6
Hopgood St, W12 *off Macfarlane Rd* 127 J1
Hopkins Cl, N10 58 A7
Hopkins Ms, E15 *off West Rd* 115 F1
Hopkinsons Pl, NW1 *off Fitzroy Rd* 110 A1
Hopkins Rd, E10 78 B7
Hopkins St, W1 17 G4
Hoppers Rd, N13 59 G2
N21 59 G2
Hoppett Rd, E4 62 E3
Hopping La, N1 *off St. Mary's Gro* 93 H6
Hoppingwood Av, N.Mal. KT3 183 E3
Hop St, SE10 135 F4
Hopton Gdns, N.Mal. KT3 183 G6
Hopton Rd, SE18 137 E3
SW16 168 E5
Hopton's Gdns, SE1 27 H1
Hopton St, SE1 27 H1
Hoptree Cl, N12 *off Woodside Pk Rd* 56 E4
Hopwood Cl, SW17 167 F3
Hopwood Rd, SE17 36 C5
Hopwood Wk, E8 *off Wilman Gro* 94 D7
Horace Av, Rom. RM7 101 J1
Horace Bldg, SW8 *off Queenstown Rd* 32 D7
Horace Rd, E7 97 H4
Ilford IG6 81 F3
Kingston upon Thames KT1 181 J3
Horatio Ct, SE16 *off Rotherhithe St* 133 F1
Horatio Pl, E14 *off Cold Harbour* 134 C2
SW19 184 D1
Horatio St, E2 13 H2
Horatius Way, Croydon CR0 201 F6
Horbury Cres, W11 108 D7
Horbury Ms, W11 *off Ladbroke Rd* 108 C7
Horder Rd, SW6 148 B1
Horizon Business Cen, N9 *off Goodwin Rd* 61 G1
Horizon Way, SE7 135 H4
Horle Wk, SE5 151 H2
Horley Cl, Bexleyheath DA6 159 G5
Horley Rd, SE9 174 B4
Hormead Rd, W9 108 C4
Hornbeam Cl, NW7 55 F3
SE11 34 E1
Barking IG11 118 A3
Borehamwood WD6 38 A1
Buckhurst Hill IG9 *off Hornbeam Rd* 64 A3
Ilford IG1 99 G5
Northolt UB5 85 F5
Hornbeam Cres, Brent. TW8 125 E7
Hornbeam Gdns, N.Mal. KT3 183 G6
Hornbeam Gro, E4 63 E3
Hornbeam Ho, NW3 *off Maitland Pk Vil* 91 J6
Hornbeam La, E4 47 E5
Bexleyheath DA7 159 J2
Hornbeam Rd, Buck.H. IG9 64 A3
Hayes UB4 102 C5
Hornbeam Sq, E3 *off Hawthorn Av* 113 J1
Hornbeams Ri, N11 58 A6
Hornbeam Ter, Cars. SM5 199 H1
Hornbeam Wk, Rich. TW10 163 J3
Hornbeam Way, Brom. BR2 192 D6
Hornblower Cl, SE16 *off Greenland Quay* 133 H4
Hornbuckle Cl, Har. HA2 86 A2
Hornby Cl, NW3 91 G7
Horncastle Cl, SE12 155 G7
Horncastle Rd, SE12 155 G7
Hornchurch Cl, Kings.T. KT2 163 G4
Horndean Cl, SW15 *off Bessborough Rd* 165 G1
Horndon Cl, Rom. RM5 83 J1
Horndon Grn, Rom. RM5 83 J1
Horndon Rd, Rom. RM5 83 J1
Horner La, Mitch. CR4 185 G2
Hornet Way, E6 *off Armada Way* 117 G5
Horne Way, SW15 147 J2
Hornfair Rd, SE7 135 J6
Horniman Dr, SE23 171 E1
★ **Horniman Mus**, SE23 170 E1
Horning Cl, SE9 174 B4
Horn La, SE10 135 G4
W3 106 C7
Woodford Green IG8 63 G6
Horn Link Way, SE10 135 G4
Horn Pk Cl, SE12 155 H5
Horn Pk La, SE12 155 H5
Horns Cft Cl, Bark. IG11 *off Thornhill Gdns* 99 H7
Horns End Pl, Pnr. HA5 66 C4
HORNSEY, N8 75 F3
Hornsey La, N6 92 B1
Hornsey La Est, N19 74 D7
Hornsey La Gdns, N6 74 C7
Hornsey Pk Rd, N8 75 F3
Hornsey Ri, N19 74 D7
Hornsey Ri Gdns, N19 74 D7
Hornsey Rd, N7 93 F2
N19 92 E1
Hornsey St, N7 93 F5
Hornshay St, SE15 133 F6
Horns Rd, Ilf. IG2, IG6 81 F5
Hornton Pl, W8 128 D2
Hornton St, W8 128 D1
Horsa Rd, SE12 155 J7
Erith DA8 139 J7
Horse & Dolphin Yd, W1 17 J5
Horsebridge Cl, Dag. RM9 119 E1
Horsecroft Rd, Edg. HA8 54 D7
Horse Fair, Kings.T. KT1 181 G2
Horseferry Pl, SE10 134 C6
Horseferry Rd, E14 113 H7
SW1 25 H6
Horse Guards Av, SW1 26 A2
★ **Horse Guards Par**, SW1 25 J2
Horse Guards Rd, SW1 25 J2
Horse Leaze, E6 116 D6
Horsell Rd, N5 93 G5
Horselydown La, SE1 29 F3
Horsemongers Ms, SE1 28 A4
Horsenden Av, Grnf. UB6 86 B5
Horsenden Cres, Grnf. UB6 86 C5
Horsenden La N, Grnf. UB6 86 C6
Horsenden La S, Grnf. (Perivale) UB6 104 D1
Horse Ride, SW1 25 G2
Horse Rd, E7 *off Centre Rd* 97 H3
Horseshoe Cl, E14 134 C5
NW2 89 H2
Horse Shoe Ct, EC1 *off Brewhouse Yd* 11 H5
Horse Shoe Cres, Nthlt. UB5 103 G2
Horse Shoe Grn, Sutt. SM1 *off Aultone Way* 199 E2
Horseshoe La, N20 56 A1
Enfield EN2 *off Chase Side* 43 J3
Horseshoe Ms, SW2 *off Acre La* 151 E4
Horse Yd, N1 *off Essex Rd* 111 H1
Horsfeld Gdns, SE9 156 B5
Horsfeld Rd, SE9 156 A5
Horsford Rd, SW2 151 F5
Horsham Av, N12 57 H5
Horsham Rd, Bexh. DA6 159 G5
Feltham TW14 141 F6
Horsleydown Old Stairs, SE1 29 F2
Horsley Dr, Croy. (New Adgtn) CR0 204 C7
Kingston upon Thames KT2 163 G5
Horsley Rd, E4 62 C2
Bromley BR1 *off Palace Rd* 191 H1
Horsley St, SE17 36 B5
Horsmonden Cl, Orp. BR6 193 H7
Horsmonden Rd, SE4 153 J5
Hortensia Rd, SW10 30 C6
Horticultural Pl, W4 *off Heathfield Ter* 126 D5
Horton Av, NW2 90 B4
Horton Br Rd, West Dr. UB7 120 C1
Horton Cl, West Dr. UB7 120 C1
Horton Ho, SW8 34 C7
Horton Ind Pk, West Dr. UB7 120 C1
Horton Rd, E8 94 E6
West Drayton UB7 120 D1
Horton St, SE13 154 B3
Horton Way, Croydon CR0 189 G5
Hortus Rd, E4 62 C2
Southall UB2 123 F2
Hosack Rd, SW17 167 J2
Hoser Av, SE12 173 G2
Hosier La, EC1 19 G2
Hoskins Cl, E16 115 J6
Hayes UB3 121 J5
Hoskins St, SE10 134 D5
Hospital Br Rd, Twick. TW2 143 H7
Hospital Rd, E9 *off Homerton Row* 95 G5
Hounslow TW3 143 G3
Hospital Way, SE13 154 D7
Hotham Cl, W.Mol. KT8 *off Garrick Gdns* 179 G3
Hotham Rd, SW15 147 J3
SW19 167 F7
Hotham Rd Ms, SW19 *off Haydons Rd* 167 F7
Hotham St, E15 114 E1
Hothfield Pl, SE16 *off Lower Rd* 133 F3
Hotspur Ind Est, N17 60 E6
Hotspur Rd, Nthlt. UB5 103 G2
Hotspur St, SE11 34 E3
Houblon Rd, Rich. TW10 145 H5
Houghton Cl, E8 *off Buttermere Wk* 94 C6
Hampton TW12 161 E6
Houghton Rd, N15 *off West Grn Rd* 76 C4
Houghton Sq, SW9 *off Clapham Rd* 150 E2
Houghton St, WC2 18 D4
Houlder Cres, Croy. CR0 201 H6
Houndsden Rd, N21 43 F6
Houndsditch, EC3 20 E3
Houndsfield Rd, N9 44 E7
HOUNSLOW, TW3 - TW6 143 F4
Hounslow Av, Houns. TW3 143 H5
Hounslow Business Pk, Houns. TW3 *off Alice Way* 143 H4
Hounslow Gdns, Houns. TW3 143 H5
★ **Hounslow Heath**, Houns. TW4 142 E6
Hounslow Rd, Felt. TW14 160 B1
Feltham (Han.) TW13 160 D4
Twickenham TW2 143 J6
HOUNSLOW WEST, Houns. TW4 142 D3
Houseman Way, SE5 *off Hopewell St* 132 A7
★ **Houses of Parliament**, SW1 26 B4
Houston Pl, Esher KT10 *off Lime Tree Av* 194 B1
Houston Rd, SE23 171 H2
Surbiton (Long Dit.) KT6 181 E6
Hove Av, E17 77 J5
Hoveden Rd, NW2 90 B5
Hove Gdns, Sutt. SM1 199 E1
Hoveton Rd, SE28 118 C6
Hoveton Way, Ilf. IG6 65 E7
Howard Av, Bex. DA5 176 C1
Howard Bldg, SW8 32 D6
Howard Cl, N11 58 A2
NW2 90 B4
W3 106 B6
Hampton TW12 161 J6
Loughton IG10 48 B6
Howard Dr, Borwd. WD6 38 D4
Howard Ms, N5 *off Hamilton Pk* 93 H4
Howard Rd, E6 116 C2
E11 97 E3
E17 78 A3
N15 76 B6
N16 94 A4
NW2 90 A4
SE20 189 F1
SE25 188 D5
Barking IG11 117 G1
Bromley BR1 173 G7
Ilford IG1 98 E4
Isleworth TW7 144 C3
New Malden KT3 183 E3
Southall UB1 103 H6
Surbiton KT5 181 J6
Howards Cl, Pnr. HA5 66 B2
Howards Crest Cl, Beck. BR3 190 C2
Howards La, SW15 147 H5
Howards Rd, E13 115 G3
Howard St, T.Ditt. KT7 181 E7
Howard Wk, N2 73 F4
Howard Way, Barn. EN5 40 A5
Howarth Rd, SE2 138 A5
Howberry Cl, Edg. HA8 53 G6
Howberry Rd, Edg. HA8 53 G6
Stanmore HA7 53 G6
Thornton Heath CR7 188 A1
Howbury Rd, SE15 153 F3
Howcroft Cres, N3 56 D7
Howcroft La, Grnf. UB6 *off Cowgate Rd* 104 A3
Howden Cl, SE28 118 D7
Howden Rd, SE25 188 C2
Howden St, SE15 152 D3
Howe Cl, Rom. RM7 83 G1
Howell Cl, Rom. RM6 82 D5
Howell Wk, SE1 35 H2
Howerd Way, SE18 156 B1
Howes Cl, N3 72 D3
Howfield Pl, N17 76 C3
Howgate Rd, SW14 146 D3
Howick Pl, SW1 25 G6
Howie St, SW11 129 H7
Howitt Cl, N16 *off Allen Rd* 94 B4
NW3 *off Howitt Rd* 91 H6
Howitt Rd, NW3 91 H6
Howland Est, SE16 133 F3
Howland Ms E, W1 17 G1
Howland St, W1 17 F1
Howland Way, SE16 133 H2
Howletts Rd, SE24 151 J6
Howley Pl, W2 14 D1
Howley Rd, Croy. CR0 201 H3
Howsman Rd, SW13 127 G6
Howson Rd, SE4 153 H4
Howson Ter, Rich. TW10 145 H6
Hows St, E2 13 F1
Howton Pl, Bushey (Bushey Hth) WD23 52 A1
HOXTON, N1 12 D2
Hoxton Mkt, N1 12 D4
Hoxton Sq, N1 12 D4
Hoxton St, N1 12 E4
Hoylake Gdns, Mitch. CR4 186 C3
Ruislip HA4 84 B1
Watford WD19 50 D4
Hoylake Rd, W3 107 E6
Hoyland Cl, SE15 *off Commercial Way* 132 E7
Hoyle Rd, SW17 167 H5
Hoy St, E16 115 F6
★ **H.Q.S. Wellington, Master Mariners' Hall**, WC2 18 E5
Hubbard Dr, Chess. KT9 195 F6
Hubbard Rd, SE27 169 J4
Hubbard St, E15 114 E1
Hubbinet Ind Est, Rom. RM7 83 J3
Hubert Gro, SW9 151 E3
Hubert Rd, E6 116 A3
Huddart St, E3 113 J5
Huddleston Cl, E2 113 F2
Huddlestone Rd, E7 97 F4
NW2 89 H6
Huddleston Rd, N7 92 D4
Hudson Apts, N8 *off Chadwell La* 75 F3
Hudson Cl, E15 *off Park Gro* 115 G1
W12 *off Canada Way* 107 H7
Hudson Ct, E14 *off Maritime Quay* 134 A5
SW19 167 E7
Hudson Gdns, Orp. (Grn St Grn) BR6 *off Superior Dr* 207 J6
Hudson Pl, SE18 137 F5
Hudson Rd, Bexh. DA7 159 F2
Hayes (Harling.) UB3 121 G6
Hudson's Pl, SW1 33 E1
Hudson Way, N9 61 F3
NW2 *off Gratton Ter* 90 A3
Huggin Ct, EC4 20 A5
Huggin Hill, EC4 20 A5

Huggins Pl, SW2
off Roupell Rd ... **169** F1
Hughan Rd, E15 ... **96** D5
Hugh Dalton Av, SW6 ... **128** C6
Hughenden Av, Har. HA3 ... **69** E5
Hughenden Gdns, Nthlt.
UB5 ... **102** C3
Hughenden Rd, Wor.Pk.
KT4 ... **183** G7
Hughendon Ter, E15
off Westdown Rd ... **96** C4
Hughes Cl, N12 ... **57** F5
Hughes Rd, Hayes UB3 ... **102** B7
Hughes Ter, SW9
off Styles Gdns ... **151** H3
Hughes Wk, Croy. CR0
off St. Saviours Rd ... **187** J7
Hugh Gaitskell Cl, SW6 ... **128** C6
Hugh Herland Ho, Kings.T.
KT1 ... **181** H3
Hugh Ms, SW1 ... **32** E2
Hugh St, SW1 ... **32** E2
Hugon Rd, SW6 ... **148** E3
Hugo Rd, N19 ... **92** C4
Huguenot Pl, E1 ... **21** G1
SW18 ... **149** F5
Huguenot Sq, SE15
off Scylla Rd ... **152** E3
Hullbridge Ms, N1
off Sherborne St ... **112** A1
Hull Cl, SE16 ... **133** G2
Hull Pl, E16
off Fishguard Way ... **137** F1
Hull St, EC1 ... **11** J4
Hulme Pl, SE1 ... **28** A4
Hulse Av, Bark. IG11 ... **99** G6
Romford RM7 ... **83** H1
Hulse Ter, Ilf. IG1
off Buttsbury Rd ... **99** F5
Humber Cl, West Dr. UB7 ... **120** A1
Humber Dr, W10 ... **108** A4
Humber Rd, NW2 ... **89** H2
SE3 ... **135** F6
Humberstone Rd, E13 ... **115** J3
Humberton Cl, E9
off Marsh Hill ... **95** H5
Humbolt Rd, W6 ... **128** B6
Humes Av, W7 ... **124** B3
Hume Ter, E16
off Prince Regent La ... **115** J6
Hume Way, Ruis. HA4 ... **66** A6
Humphrey Cl, Ilf. IG5 ... **80** C1
Humphrey St, SE1 ... **37** F3
Humphries Cl, Dag. RM9 ... **101** F4
Hundred Acre, NW9 ... **71** F2
Hungerdown, E4 ... **62** C1
Hungerford Br, SE1 ... **26** B1
WC2 ... **26** B1
Hungerford La, WC2 ... **26** A1
Hungerford Rd, N7 ... **92** D5
Hungerford St, E1
off Commercial Rd ... **113** E6
Hunsdon Cl, Dag. RM9 ... **101** E6
Hunsdon Rd, SE14 ... **133** G6
Hunslett St, E2
off Royston St ... **113** F2
Hunston Rd, Mord. SM4 ... **198** E1
Hunt Cl, W11 ... **128** A1
Hunter Cl, SE1 ... **28** C6
SW12
off Balham Pk Rd ... **168** A1
Borehamwood WD6 ... **38** C5
Wallington SM6 ... **201** E7
Huntercrombe Gdns, Wat.
WD19 ... **50** C5
Hunter Ho, Felt. TW13 ... **160** A1
Hunter Rd, SW20 ... **183** J1
Ilford IG1 ... **99** E5
Thornton Heath CR7 ... **188** A3
Hunters, The, Beckenham
BR3 ... **190** C1
Hunters Ct, Rich. TW9
off Friars La ... **145** G5
Hunters Gro, Har. HA3 ... **69** F4
Hayes UB3 ... **122** A1
Orpington BR6 ... **207** E4
Hunters Hall Rd, Dag.
RM10 ... **101** G4
Hunters Hill, Ruis. HA4 ... **84** C3
Hunters Meadow, SE19
off Dulwich Wd Av ... **170** B4
Hunters Rd, Chess. KT9 ... **195** H3
Hunters Sq, Dag. RM10 ... **101** G4
Hunter St, WC1 ... **10** B5
Hunters Way, Croy. CR0 ... **202** B4
Enfield EN2 ... **43** G1
Hunter Wk, E13 ... **115** G2
Borehamwood WD6
off Hunter Cl ... **38** C5
Huntingdon Cl, Mitch.
CR4 ... **187** E3
Northolt UB5
off Plumpton Cl ... **85** G6
Huntingdon Gdns, W4 ... **126** C7
Worcester Park KT4 ... **197** J3
Huntingdon Rd, N2 ... **73** H3
N9 ... **61** F1
Huntingdon St, E16 ... **115** F6
N1 ... **93** F7
Huntingfield, Croy. CR0 ... **203** J7
Huntingfield Rd, SW15 ... **147** G4
Hunting Gate Cl, Enf. EN2 ... **43** G3
Hunting Gate Dr, Chess.
KT9 ... **195** H7
Hunting Gate Ms, Sutt.
SM1 ... **199** E3
Twickenham TW2
off Colne Rd ... **162** B1
Huntings Rd, Dag. RM10 ... **101** G6
Huntley Cl, Stai.
(Stanw.) TW19
off Cambria Gdns ... **140** B7
Huntley St, WC1 ... **9** G6
Huntley Way, SW20 ... **183** G2
Huntly Dr, N3 ... **56** D6
Huntly Rd, SE25 ... **188** B4
Hunton St, E1 ... **13** H6
Hunt Rd, Sthl. UB2 ... **123** G3
Hunt's Cl, SE3 ... **155** G2
Hunt's Ct, WC2 ... **17** J6
Hunts La, E15 ... **114** C2
Huntsmans Cl, Felt.
TW13 ... **160** B4
Huntsman St, SE17 ... **36** C2
Hunts Mead, Enf. EN3 ... **45** G3
Hunts Mead Cl, Chis.
BR7 ... **174** C7
Huntsmoor Rd, Epsom
KT19 ... **196** D5
Huntspill St, SW17 ... **167** F3
Hunts Slip Rd, SE21 ... **170** B3
Huntsworth Ms, NW1 ... **7** J6
Hurdwick Pl, NW1
off Harrington Sq ... **9** F1
Hurley Cres, SE16
off Marlow Way ... **133** G2
Hurley Ho, SE11 ... **35** F2
Hurley Rd, Grnf. UB6 ... **103** H6
Hurlingham Business Pk,
SW6 ... **148** D3
★ **Hurlingham Club**,
SW6 ... **148** C3
Hurlingham Ct, SW6 ... **148** C3
Hurlingham Gdns, SW6 ... **148** C3
★ **Hurlingham Park**,
SW6 ... **148** C2
Hurlingham Retail Pk, SW6
off Carnwath Rd ... **149** E3
Hurlingham Rd, SW6 ... **148** C2
Bexleyheath DA7 ... **139** F7
Hurlingham Sq, SW6 ... **148** D3
Hurlock St, N5 ... **93** H3
Hurlstone Rd, SE25 ... **188** A5
Hurn Ct Rd, Houns. TW4 ... **142** D2
Huron Cl, Orp.
(Grn St Grn) BR6
off Winnipeg Dr ... **207** J6
Huron Rd, SW17 ... **168** A2
Hurren Cl, SE3 ... **154** E3
Hurricane Rd, Wall. SM6 ... **201** E7
Hurricane Trd Cen, NW9 ... **71** G1
Hurry Cl, E15 ... **97** E7
Hursley Rd, Chig. IG7 ... **65** J5
Hurst Av, E4 ... **62** A4
N6 ... **74** C6
Hurstbourne, Esher (Clay.)
KT10 ... **194** C6
Hurstbourne Gdns, Bark.
IG11 ... **99** H6
Hurstbourne Ho, SW15
off Tangley Gro ... **147** F6
Hurstbourne Rd, SE23 ... **171** H1
Hurst Cl, E4 ... **62** A3
NW11 ... **72** E6
Bromley BR2 ... **205** F1
Chessington KT9 ... **196** A5
Northolt UB5 ... **85** F6
Hurstcourt Rd, Sutt. SM1 ... **198** E2
Hurstdene Av, Brom.
BR2 ... **205** F1
Hurstdene Gdns, N15 ... **76** B7
Hurst Est, SE2 ... **138** D5
Hurstfield, Brom. BR2 ... **191** G5
Hurstfield Rd, W.Mol.
KT8 ... **179** G3
Hurst La, SE2 ... **138** D5
East Molesey KT8 ... **179** J4
Hurstleigh Gdns, Ilf. IG5 ... **80** C1
Hurstmead Ct, Edg. HA8 ... **54** B4
Hurst Ri, Barn. EN5 ... **40** D3
Hurst Rd, E17 ... **78** B3
N21 ... **59** G1
Bexley DA5 ... **176** D1
Buckhurst Hill IG9 ... **64** A1
Croydon CR0 ... **202** A5
East Molesey KT8 ... **179** G3
Erith DA8 ... **139** J7
Sidcup DA15 ... **176** A2
Walton-on-Thames
KT12 ... **178** C5
West Molesey KT8 ... **179** E3
Hurst Springs, Bexley
DA5 ... **177** E1
Hurst St, SE24 ... **151** H6
Hurst Vw Rd, S.Croy.
CR2 ... **202** B7
Hurst Way, S.Croy. CR2 ... **202** B6
Hurstway Wk, W11 ... **108** A7
Hurstwood Av, E18 ... **79** H4
Bexley DA5 ... **176** E1
Hurstwood Dr, Brom.
BR1 ... **192** C3
Hurstwood Rd, NW11 ... **72** B4
Hurtwood Rd, Walt. KT12 ... **179** F7
Huson Cl, NW3 ... **91** H7
Hussain Cl, Har. HA1 ... **86** C4
Hussars Cl, Houns. TW4 ... **142** E3
Husseywell Cres, Brom.
BR2 ... **205** G1
Hutchings St, E14 ... **134** A2
Hutchings Wk, NW11 ... **73** E4
Hutchins Cl, E15
off Gibbins Rd ... **96** C7
Hutchinson Ter, Wem.
HA9 ... **87** G3
Hutchins Rd, SE28 ... **118** A7
Hutton Cl, Grnf. UB6
off Mary Peters Dr ... **86** A5
Woodford Green IG8 ... **63** H6
Hutton Gdns, Har. HA3 ... **51** J7
Hutton Gro, N12 ... **57** E5
Hutton La, Har. HA3 ... **51** J7
Hutton Row, Edg. HA8 ... **54** C7
Hutton St, EC4 ... **19** F4
Hutton Wk, Har. HA3 ... **51** J7
Huxbear St, SE4 ... **153** J5
Huxley Cl, Nthlt. UB5 ... **103** E1
Huxley Dr, Rom. RM6 ... **82** B7
Huxley Gdns, NW10 ... **105** J3
Huxley Par, N18 ... **60** A5
Huxley Pl, N13 ... **59** H4
Huxley Rd, E10 ... **96** C2
N18 ... **60** A4
Welling DA16 ... **157** J3
Huxley Sayze, N18 ... **60** A5
Huxley St, W10 ... **108** B3
Hyacinth Cl, Hmptn. TW12
off Gresham Rd ... **161** G6
Ilford IG1 ... **98** E6
Hyacinth Ct, Pnr. HA5
off Tulip Ct ... **66** C3
Hyacinth Rd, SW15 ... **165** G1
Hycliffe Gdns, Chig. IG7 ... **65** F4
HYDE, THE, NW9 ... **71** F4
Hyde, The, NW9 ... **71** E5
Hyde Cl, E13 ... **115** G2
Barnet EN5 ... **40** C3
Hyde Ct, N20 ... **57** G3
Hyde Cres, NW9 ... **71** E5
Hyde Est Rd, NW9 ... **71** F5
Hyde Fm Ms, SW12
off Telferscot Rd ... **168** D1
Hydefield Cl, N21 ... **60** A1
Hydefield Ct, N9 ... **60** B2
Hyde Ho, NW9 ... **71** E5
Hyde La, SW11
off Battersea Br Rd ... **149** H1
★ **Hyde Park**, W2 ... **23** G1
Hyde Pk, SW7 ... **23** G1
W1 ... **23** G1
Hyde Pk Av, N21 ... **59** J2
Hyde Pk Cor, W1 ... **24** C3
Hyde Pk Cres, W2 ... **15** G4
Hyde Pk Gdns, N21 ... **59** J1
W2 ... **15** F5
Hyde Pk Gdns Ms, W2 ... **15** F5
Hyde Pk Gate, SW7 ... **22** D4
Hyde Pk Gate Ms, SW7 ... **22** D4
Hyde Pk Pl, W2 ... **15** H5
Hyde Pk Sq, W2 ... **15** G4
Hyde Pk Sq Ms, W2 ... **15** G4
Hyde Pk St, W2 ... **15** G4
Hyderabad Way, E15 ... **96** E7
Hyde Rd, N1 ... **112** A1
Bexleyheath DA7 ... **159** F2
Richmond TW10
off Albert Rd ... **145** J5
Hydeside Gdns, N9 ... **60** C2
Hydes Pl, N1
off Compton Av ... **93** H7
Hyde St, SE8
off Deptford High St ... **134** A6
Hydethorpe Av, N9 ... **60** C2
Hydethorpe Rd, SW12 ... **168** C1
Hyde Vale, SE10 ... **134** C7
Hyde Wk, Mord. SM4 ... **184** D7
Hyde Way, N9 ... **60** C2
Hayes UB3 ... **121** J4
Hylands Rd, E17 ... **78** D2
Hylton St, SE18 ... **137** J4
Hyndewood, SE23 ... **171** G3
Hyndman St, SE15 ... **132** E6
Hynton Rd, Dag. RM8 ... **100** C2
Hyperion Ho, E3
off Arbery Rd ... **113** H2
Hyrstdene, S.Croy. CR2 ... **201** H4
Hyson Rd, SE16
off Galleywall Rd ... **133** E4
Hythe Av, Bexh. DA7 ... **139** F7
Hythe Cl, N18 ... **60** D4
Hythe Path, Th.Hth. CR7 ... **188** A3
Hythe Rd, NW10 ... **107** G4
Thornton Heath CR7 ... **188** A2
Hythe Rd Ind Est, NW10 ... **107** G3
Hyver Hill, NW7 ... **38** D6

I

Ian Sq, Enf. EN3
off Lansbury Rd ... **45** G1
Ibbetson Path, Loug. IG10 ... **49** E3
Ibbotson Av, E16 ... **115** F6
Ibbott St, E1
off Mantus Rd ... **113** F4
Iberian Av, Wall. SM6 ... **200** D4
Ibex Ho, E15
off Forest La ... **97** E6
Ibis La, W4 ... **146** C1
Ibis Way, Hayes UB4
off Cygnet Way ... **102** D6
Ibscott Cl, Dag. RM10 ... **101** J6
Ibsley Gdns, SW15 ... **165** G1
Ibsley Way, Barn.
(Cockfos.) EN4 ... **41** H5
Iceland Rd, E3 ... **114** A1
Iceland Wf, SE16
off Plough Way ... **133** H4
Iceni Ct, E3
off Roman Rd ... **113** J1
Ice Wf, N1 ... **10** B1
Ice Wf Marina, N1
off New Wf Rd ... **10** B1
Ickburgh Est, E5
off Ickburgh Rd ... **94** E2
Ickburgh Rd, E5 ... **94** E3
Ickleton Rd, SE9 ... **174** B4
Icknield Dr, Ilf. IG2 ... **81** E5
Ickworth Pk Rd, E17 ... **77** H4
Idaho Bldg, SE13
off Deals Gateway ... **154** B1
Ida Rd, N15 ... **76** A5
Ida St, E14 ... **114** C6
Iden Cl, Brom. BR2 ... **191** E3
Idlecombe Rd, SW17 ... **168** A6
Idmiston Rd, E15 ... **97** F5
SE27 ... **169** J3
Worcester Park KT4 ... **183** F7
Idmiston Sq, Wor.Pk. KT4 ... **183** F7
Idol La, EC3 ... **20** D6
Idonia St, SE8 ... **133** J7
Idris Ct, N9
off Galahad Rd ... **60** D3
Iffley Rd, W6 ... **127** H3
Ifield Rd, SW10 ... **30** B5
Ifor Evans Pl, E1
off Mile End Rd ... **113** G4
Ightham Rd, Erith DA8 ... **139** G7
Igraine Ct, N9
off Galahad Rd ... **60** D3
Ikea Twr, NW10 ... **88** D5
Ilbert St, W10 ... **108** A3
Ilchester Gdns, W2 ... **14** A5
Ilchester Pl, W14 ... **128** C3
Ilchester Rd, Dag. RM8 ... **100** B5
Ildersly Gro, SE21 ... **170** A2
Ilderton Rd, SE15 ... **133** F7
SE16 ... **133** E5
Ilex Cl, Sun. TW16
off Oakington Dr ... **178** C2
Ilex Ho, N4 ... **75** F7
Ilex Rd, NW10 ... **89** F6
Ilex Way, SW16 ... **169** G5
ILFORD, IG1 - IG6 ... **99** F3
Ilford Hill, Ilf. IG1 ... **98** D3
Ilford La, Ilf. IG1 ... **98** E3
Ilfracombe Gdns, Rom.
RM6 ... **82** B7
Ilfracombe Rd, Brom.
BR1 ... **173** F3
Iliffe St, SE17 ... **35** H3
Iliffe Yd, SE17 ... **35** H3
Ilkeston Ct, E5
off Overbury St ... **95** G4
Ilkley Cl, SE19 ... **170** A6
Ilkley Rd, E16 ... **115** J5
Watford WD19 ... **50** D5
Illingworth Cl, Mitch.
CR4 ... **185** G3
Illingworth Way, Enf.
EN1 ... **44** B4
Ilmington Rd, Har. HA3 ... **69** G6
Ilminster Gdns, SW11 ... **149** H4
Imber Cl, N14 ... **42** C7
Esher KT10
off Ember La ... **194** A1
Imber Ct Trd Est, E.Mol.
KT8 ... **180** A6
Imber Gro, Esher KT10 ... **180** A7
Imber Pk Rd, Esher KT10 ... **194** A1
Imber St, N1 ... **112** A1
Imer Pl, T.Ditt. KT7 ... **180** C7
Imperial Av, N16
off Victorian Rd ... **94** C3
Imperial Cl, Har. HA2 ... **67** G6
★ **Imperial Coll London**,
SW7 ... **23** E5
Imperial Coll Rd, SW7 ... **22** E6

Imperial Ct, NW8 .... 7 H1
Imperial Cres, SW6 ...... 149 F2
Imperial Dr, Har. HA2 ..... 67 G7
Imperial Gdns, Mitch.
CR4 .... 186 B3
Imperial Ms, E6
off Central Pk Rd 115 J2
Imperial Pk, Ruis. HA4 ..... 84 E5
Imperial Pl, Chis. BR7
off Forest Cl 192 D1
Imperial Rd, N22 .... 74 E1
SW6 .... 149 E1
Feltham TW14 .... 141 H7
Imperial Sq, SW6 .... 149 E1
Imperial St, E3 .... 114 C3
★ **Imperial War Mus**,
SE1 .... 27 F6
Imperial Way, Chis. BR7 .. 175 F3
Croydon CR0 .... 201 F6
Harrow HA3 .... 69 H6
Imperial Wf, SW6 .... 149 F2
Imprimo Pk, Loug. IG10 .... 49 F4
Imre Cl, W12 .... 127 H1
Inca Dr, SE9 .... 156 E7
Inca Ter, N15
off Milton Rd 75 H3
Inchmery Rd, SE6 .... 172 B2
Inchwood, Croy. CR0 ..... 204 B4
Independence Ho, SW19
off Chapter Way 185 G1
Independent Pl, E8
off Downs Pk Rd 94 C5
Independents Rd, SE3
off Blackheath Village . 155 F3
Inderwick Rd, N8 .... 75 F5
Indescon Ct, E14 .... 134 A2
Indiana Bldg, SE13
off Deals Gateway 154 A1
India Pl, WC2 .... 18 C5
India St, EC3 .... 21 F4
India Way, W12 .... 107 H7
Indigo Ms, E14
off Ashton St 114 C7
N16 .... 94 A3
Indigo Wk, N2 .... 73 J4
N6 .... 73 J4
Indus Rd, SE7 .... 135 J7
Industry Ter, SW9
off Canterbury Cres .. 151 G3
Ingal Rd, E13 .... 115 G4
Ingate Pl, SW8 .... 150 B1
Ingatestone Rd, E12 ...... 97 J1
SE25 .... 188 E4
Woodford Green IG8 .... 63 G7
Ingelow Rd, SW8 .... 150 B2
Ingersoll Rd, W12 .... 127 H1
Ingestre Ct, W1
off Ingestre Pl 17 G5
Ingestre Pl, W1 .... 17 G4
Ingestre Rd, E7 .... 97 G4
NW5 .... 92 B4
Ingham Rd, NW6 .... 90 D4
Inglebert St, EC1 .... 11 E3
Ingleborough St, SW9 .... 151 G2
Ingleby Dr, Har. HA1 ...... 86 A3
Ingleby Rd, N7
off Bryett Rd 93 E3
Dagenham RM10 ...... 101 H6
Ilford IG1 .... 98 E1
Ingleby Way, Chis. BR7 ... 174 D5
Ingle Cl, Pnr. HA5 .... 67 E3
Ingledew Rd, SE18 .... 137 G5
Inglehurst Gdns, Ilf. IG4 ... 80 C5
Inglemere Rd, SE23 ...... 171 G3
Mitcham CR4 .... 167 J7
Ingle Ms, EC1 .... 11 E3
Inglesham Wk, E9 .... 95 J6
Ingleside Cl, Beck. BR3 ... 172 A7
Ingleside Gro, SE3 .... 135 F6
Inglethorpe St, SW6 ..... 148 A1
Ingleton Av, Well. DA16 ... 158 A5
Ingleton Rd, N18 .... 60 D6
Ingleton St, SW9 .... 151 G2
Ingleway, N12 .... 57 G6
Inglewood Cl, E14 .... 134 A4
Ilford IG6 .... 65 J6
Inglewood Copse, Brom.
BR1 .... 192 B2
Inglewood Ms, Surb.
KT6 .... 196 A1
Inglewood Rd, NW6 ...... 90 D5
Inglis Barracks, NW7 ..... 56 A5
Inglis Rd, W5 .... 105 J7
Croydon CR0 .... 202 C1
Inglis St, SE5 .... 151 H1
Ingram Av, NW11 .... 73 F7
Ingram Cl, SE11 .... 34 D1
Stanmore HA7 .... 53 F5
Ingram Ho, E3
off Daling Way 113 H2
Ingram Rd, N2 .... 73 H4
Thornton Heath CR7 ... 187 J1
Ingram Way, Grnf. UB6 ... 104 A1
Ingrave Ho, Dag. RM9 .... 118 B1
Ingrave St, SW11 .... 149 G3
Ingress St, W4
off Devonshire Rd 126 E5
Inigo Jones Rd, SE7 ..... 136 B7
Inigo Pl, WC2 .... 18 A5
Inkerman Rd, NW5 .... 92 B6
Inkerman Ter, W8
off Allen St 128 D3
Inks Grn, E4 .... 62 C5
Inkster Ho, SW11
off Ingrave St 149 H3
Inkwell Cl, N12 .... 57 F3
Inman Rd, NW10 .... 106 E1
SW18 .... 149 F7
Inmans Row, Wdf.Grn.
IG8 .... 63 G4
Inner Circle, NW1 .... 8 B4
Inner Pk Rd, SW19 .... 166 A1
Inner Ring E, Houns.
(Lon.Hthrw Air.) TW6 ... 140 E3
Inner Ring W, Houns.
(Lon.Hthrw Air.) TW6 ... 140 D3
Inner Temple La, EC4 ...... 19 E4
Innes Cl, SW20 .... 184 B2
Innes Gdns, SW15 .... 147 H6
Innes St, SE15 .... 37 E7
Innes Yd, Croy. CR0
off Whitgift St 201 J3
Inniskilling Rd, E13 ...... 115 J2
Innovation Cl, Wem. HA0 . 105 H1
Inskip Cl, E10 .... 96 B2
Inskip Rd, Dag. RM8 ..... 100 D1
Insley Ho, E3 *off Bow Rd* . 114 B3
★ **Institute of Contemporary
Arts (I.C.A.)**, SW1 ..... 25 J1
Institute Pl, E8 .... 94 E5
Integer Gdns, E11 .... 78 D7
Interchange E Ind Est, E5
off Grosvenor Way 95 F2
International Av, Houns.
TW5 .... 122 C5
International Trd Est, Sthl.
UB2 .... 122 B3
Inveraray Pl, SE18
off Old Mill Rd 137 G6
Inver Cl, E5
off Theydon Rd 95 F2
Inverclyde Gdns, Rom.
RM6 .... 82 D4
Inver Ct, W2 .... 14 B4
W6 *off Invermead Cl* ... 127 G3
Inveresk Gdns, Wor.Pk.
KT4 .... 197 F3
Inverforth Cl, NW3
off North End Way 91 F2
Inverforth Rd, N11 .... 58 B5
Inverine Rd, SE7 .... 135 H5
Invermead Cl, W6 .... 127 G4
Invermore Pl, SE18 .... 137 F4
Inverness Av, Enf. EN1 ..... 44 B1
Inverness Dr, Ilf. IG6 ...... 65 H6
Inverness Gdns, W8 .... 22 A2
Inverness Ms, E16 .... 137 F1
W2 .... 14 B5
Inverness Pl, W2 .... 14 B5
Inverness Rd, N18 .... 60 E5
Hounslow TW3 .... 143 F4
Southall UB2 .... 123 E4
Worcester Park KT4 .... 198 A1
Inverness St, NW1 .... 110 B1
Inverness Ter, W2 .... 14 B5
Inverton Rd, SE15 .... 153 G4
Invicta Cl, E3
off Hawgood St 114 A5
Chislehurst BR7 ...... 174 D5
Invicta Gro, Nthlt. UB5 ... 103 F3
Invicta Plaza, SE1 .... 27 G1
Invicta Rd, SE3 .... 135 G7
Inville Rd, SE17 .... 36 C4
Inwen Ct, SE8 .... 133 H5
Inwood Av, Houns. TW3 .. 143 J3
Inwood Cl, Croy. CR0 .... 203 H2
Inwood Ho, SE22
off Pytchley Rd 152 B3
Inwood Rd, Hounslow
TW3 .... 143 H4
Inworth St, SW11 .... 149 H2
Inworth Wk, N1
off Popham St 111 J1
IO Cen, SE18
off Armstrong Rd 137 F3
Iona Cl, SE6 .... 154 A7
Morden SM4 .... 184 E7
Ionian Bldg, E14
off Narrow St 113 H7
Ion Sq, E2 .... 13 H2
IO Trade Centre, Croydon
CR0 .... 201 F4
Ipswich Rd, SW17 .... 168 A6
Ireland Cl, E6
off Bradley Stone Rd . . 116 C5
Ireland Pl, N22 .... 59 E7
Ireland Yd, EC4 .... 19 H4
Irene Rd, SW6 .... 148 D1
Orpington BR6 .... 193 J7
Ireton Cl, N10 .... 58 A7
Ireton St, E3
off Tidworth Rd 114 A4
Iris Av, Bex. DA5 .... 159 E5
Iris Cl, E6 .... 116 B5
Iris Cl, Croydon CR0 ..... 203 G1
Surbiton KT6 .... 181 J7
Iris Ct, Pnr. HA5 .... 66 C3
Iris Cres, Bexh. DA7 ...... 139 F6
Iris Rd, Epsom (W.Ewell)
KT19 .... 196 B5
Iris Wk, Edg. HA8
off Ash Cl 54 C4
Irkdale Av, Enf. EN1 .... 44 C1
Iron Br Cl, NW10 .... 88 E5
Southall UB2 .... 123 J1
Iron Br Rd, Uxb. UB11 .... 120 D2
West Drayton UB7 ..... 120 D2
Iron Mill Pl, SW18
off Garratt La 149 E6
Iron Mill Rd, SW18 .... 149 E6
Ironmonger La, EC2 .... 20 B4
Ironmonger Pas, EC1 ...... 12 A5
Ironmonger Row, EC1 ..... 12 A4
Ironmongers Pl, E14
off Spindrift Av 134 A4
Ironside Cl, SE16
off Kinburn St 133 G2
Ironside Rd, Brent. TW8 ... 125 F7
Iron Wks, E3 .... 114 A1
Irvine Av, Har. HA3 .... 68 D3
Irvine Cl, E14
off Uamvar St 114 C5
N20 .... 57 H2
Irvine Way, Orp. BR6 ..... 193 J7
Irving Av, Nthlt. UB5 ..... 102 D1
Irving Gro, SW9 .... 151 F2
Irving Ms, N1
off Alwyne Rd 93 J6
Irving Rd, W14 .... 128 A3
Irving St, WC2 .... 17 J6
Irving Way, NW9 .... 71 F5
Irwell Est, SE16
off Neptune St 133 F2
Irwin Av, SE18 .... 137 H7
Irwin Gdns, NW10 .... 107 H1
Isaac Way, SE1 .... 28 A3
Isabel Hill Cl, Hmptn.
TW12 *off Upper
Sunbury Rd* 179 H1
Isabella Cl, N14 .... 42 C7
Isabella Ct, Rich. TW10
off Grove Rd 145 J6
Isabella Dr, Orp. BR6 ..... 207 F4
Isabella Ms, N1
off Balls Pond Rd 94 B6
Isabella Pl, Kings.T. KT2 .. 163 J5
Isabella Rd, E9 .... 95 F5
Isabella St, SE1 .... 27 G2
Isabel St, SW9 .... 151 F1
Isambard Ms, E14 .... 134 C3
Isambard Pl, SE16
off Rotherhithe St 133 F1
Isel Way, SE22
off East Dulwich Gro . . 152 B5
Isham Rd, SW16 .... 186 E2
Isis Cl, SW15 .... 147 J4
Isis Ho, N18 .... 60 C6
Isis Reach, Belv. DA17
off Norman Rd 139 H1
Isis St, SW18 .... 167 F2
Island Fm Av, W.Mol.
KT8 .... 179 F5
Island Fm Rd, W.Mol.
KT8 .... 179 F5
Island Rd, SE16 .... 133 G4
Mitcham CR4 .... 167 J7
Island Row, E14 .... 113 J6
Isla Rd, SE18 .... 137 F6
Islay Gdns, Houns. TW4 .. 142 D5
Islay Wk, N1
off Douglas Rd 93 J6
Isledon Rd, N7 .... 93 G3
Islehurst Cl, Chis. BR7 .... 192 D1
ISLEWORTH, TW7 .... 144 C3
Isleworth Business Complex,
Islw. TW7
off St. John's Rd 144 C2
Isleworth Prom, Twick.
TW1 .... 144 E4
ISLINGTON, N1 .... 111 F1
Islington Grn, N1 .... 111 H1
Islington High St, N1 ...... 11 F2
Islington Pk Ms, N1
off Islington Pk St 93 H7
Islington Pk St, N1 .... 93 G7
Islip Gdns, Edg. HA8 ...... 54 D7
Northolt UB5 .... 85 E7
Islip Manor Rd, Nthlt. UB5 . 85 E7
Islip St, NW5 .... 92 C5
Ismailia Rd, E7 .... 97 H7
★ **Ismaili Cen**, SW7 .... 31 F1
Isom Cl, E13
off Belgrave Rd 115 H3
Issa Rd, Houns. TW3
off Staines Rd 143 F4
Ivanhoe Dr, Har. HA3 ...... 68 D3
Ivanhoe Rd, SE5 .... 152 C3
Hounslow TW4 .... 142 D3
Ivatt Pl, W14 .... 128 C5
Ivatt Way, N17 .... 75 H3
Iveagh Av, NW10 .... 106 A2
Iveagh Cl, E9 .... 113 G1
NW10 .... 106 A2
Iveagh Ter, NW10
off Iveagh Av 106 A2
Ivedon Rd, Well. DA16 .... 158 C2
Ive Fm Cl, E10 .... 96 A2
Ive Fm La, E10 .... 96 A2
Iveley Rd, SW4 .... 150 C2
Ivere Dr, Barn. (New Barn.)
EN5 .... 40 E6
Iverhurst Cl, Bexh. DA6 ... 158 D5
Iverna Ct, W8 .... 128 D3
Iverna Gdns, W8 .... 128 D3
Feltham TW14 .... 141 G5
Iverson Rd, NW6 .... 90 C6
Ivers Way, Croy.
(New Adgtn) CR0 ...... 204 B7
Ives Rd, E16 .... 114 E5
Ives St, SW3 .... 31 H1
Ivestor Ter, SE23 .... 153 F7
Ivimey St, E2 .... 13 J3
Ivinghoe Cl, Enf. EN1 ...... 44 B2
Ivinghoe Rd, Dag. RM8 .... 100 B5
Ivor Gro, SE9 .... 175 E1
Ivor Pl, NW1 .... 7 J6
Ivor St, NW1 .... 92 C7
Ivory Ct, Felt. TW13 ...... 160 A1
Ivorydown, Brom. BR1 ... 173 G4
Ivory Sq, SW11
off Gartons Way 149 F3
Ivybridge Cl, Twick. TW1 .. 144 D6
Ivybridge Est, Islw. TW7 .. 144 C5
Ivybridge Ho, SE22
off Pytchley Rd 152 B3
Ivybridge La, WC2 .... 18 B6
Ivychurch Cl, SE20 .... 171 F7
Ivychurch La, SE17 .... 37 F3
Ivy Cl, Har. HA2 .... 85 F4
Pinner HA5 .... 66 C7
Sunbury-on-Thames
TW16 .... 178 C2
Ivy Cotts, E14
off Grove Vil 114 B7
Ivy Ct, SE16 .... 37 J4
Ivy Cres, W4 .... 126 C4
Ivydale Rd, SE15 .... 153 G3
Carshalton SM5 .... 199 J2
Ivyday Gro, SW16 .... 169 F3
Ivydene, W.Mol. KT8 ..... 179 F5
Ivydene Cl, Sutt. SM1 .... 199 F4
Ivy Gdns, N8 .... 74 E6
Mitcham CR4 .... 186 D3
Ivyhouse Rd, Dag. RM9 ... 100 D6
Ivy La, Houns. TW4 .... 143 F4
Ivymount Rd, SE27 ...... 169 G3
Ivy Rd, E16
off Pacific Rd 115 G6
E17 .... 78 A6
N14 .... 42 C7
NW2 .... 89 J4
SE4 .... 153 J4
SW17
off Tooting High St ... 167 H5
Hounslow TW3 .... 143 H4
Surbiton KT6 .... 196 A1
Ivy St, N1 .... 12 D1
Ivy Wk, Dag. RM9 .... 100 E6
Ixworth Pl, SW3 .... 31 G3
Izane Rd, Bexh. DA6 ..... 159 F4

J

Jacaranda Cl, N.Mal. KT3 . 182 E3
Jacaranda Gro, E8 .... 94 C7
Jackass La, Kes. BR2 ..... 205 H6
Jack Barnett Way, N22 .... 75 F2
Jack Clow Rd, E15 .... 115 E2
Jack Cornwell St, E12 ..... 98 D4
Jack Dash Way, E6 .... 116 B4
Jack Goodchild Way,
Kings.T. KT1
off Kingston Rd 182 B3
Jack Jones, Dag. RM9 .... 119 F1
Jacklin Grn, Wdf.Grn. IG8 .. 63 G4
Jackman Ms, NW2 .... 88 E3
Jackman St, E8 .... 112 E1
Jackson Cl, E9 .... 95 F7
Jackson Ct, E11
off Brading Cres 97 H1
Jackson Rd, N7 .... 93 F4
Barking IG11 .... 117 G1
Barnet EN4 .... 41 H6
Bromley BR2 .... 206 B2
Jacksons La, N6 .... 74 A7
Jacksons Pl, Croy. CR0
off Cross Rd 202 A1
Jackson St, SE18 .... 136 D6
Jacksons Way, Croy. CR0 . 204 A3
Jackson Way, Sthl. UB2 ... 123 H2
Jack Walker Ct, N5 .... 93 H4
Jacob Ho, Erith DA18
off Kale Rd 138 D2
Jacob Ms, Stan. HA7 ...... 52 D2
Jacobs Cl, Dag. RM10 .... 101 H4
Jacobs Ho, E13 .... 115 J3
Jacob St, SE1 .... 29 G3

Jacob's Well Ms, W1 **16** C3
Jacqueline Cl, Nthlt. UB5 *off Canford Av* **103** F1
Jade Cl, E16 **116** A6
NW2 **72** A7
Dagenham RM8 **100** C1
Jaffe Rd, Ilf. IG1 **99** F1
Jaffray Pl, SE27 **169** H4
Jaffray Rd, Brom. BR2 **192** A4
Jaggard Way, SW12 **149** J7
Jago Cl, SE18 **137** F6
Jago Wk, SE5 **132** A7
Jamaica Rd, SE1 **29** G4
SE16 **132** C2
Thornton Heath CR7 **187** H6
Jamaica St, E1 **113** F6
James Av, NW2 **89** J5
Dagenham RM8 **101** F1
James Bedford Cl, Pnr. HA5 **66** C2
James Boswell Cl, SW16 *off Samuel Johnson Cl* **169** G4
James Clavell Sq, SE18 **137** E3
James Cl, E13 *off Richmond St* **115** G2
NW11 *off Woodlands* **72** B6
James Collins Cl, W9 *off Fermoy Rd* **108** C4
James Ct, N1 *off Morton Rd* **93** J7
James Dudson Ct, NW10 **88** C7
James Gdns, N22 **59** H7
James Hammett Ho, E2 **13** G2
James Joyce Wk, SE24 *off Shakespeare Rd* **151** H4
James La, E10 **78** D7
E11 **78** D6
James Newman Ct, SE9 *off Great Harry Dr* **174** D3
Jameson Cl, W3 *off Acton La* **126** C2
Jameson Ct, E2 **113** F2
Jameson Ho, SE11 *off Glasshouse Wk* **34** C3
Jameson St, W8 **128** D1
James Pl, N17 **76** C1
James Riley Pt, E15 *off Carpenters Rd* **114** C1
James's Cotts, Rich. TW9 *off Kew Rd* **126** A7
James Sinclair Pt, E13 **115** J1
James St, W1 **16** C3
WC2 **18** B5
Barking IG11 **99** F7
Enfield EN1 **44** C5
Hounslow TW3 **144** A3
James Ter, SW14 *off Mullins Path* **146** D3
Jamestown Rd, NW1 **110** B1
Jamestown Way, E14 **114** D7
James Way, Wat. WD19 **50** D4
James Yd, E4 **62** D6
Jamieson Ho, Houns. TW4 **143** F7
Jamuna Cl, E14 **113** H5
Jane Seymour Ct, SE9 *off Avery Hill Rd* **157** G7
Jane St, E1 *off Commercial Rd* **112** E6
Janet St, E14 **134** A3
Janeway Pl, SE16 *off Janeway St* **132** E2
Janeway St, SE16 **29** J4
Janice Ms, Ilf. IG1 *off Oakfield Rd* **99** E3
Jansen Wk, SW11 *off Hope St* **149** G4
Janson Cl, E15 *off Janson Rd* **96** E5
NW10 **88** D3
Janson Rd, E15 **96** E5
Jansons Rd, N15 **76** B3
Japan Cres, N4 **93** F1
Japan Rd, Rom. RM6 **82** D6
Jardine Rd, E1 **113** G7
Jarman Ho, E1 *off Jubilee St* **113** F5
Jarrett Cl, SW2 **169** H1
Jarrow Cl, Mord. SM4 **184** E5
Jarrow Rd, N17 **76** E4
SE16 **133** F4
Romford RM6 **82** C6
Jarrow Way, E9 **95** H4
Jarvis Cl, Bark. IG11 *off Westbury Rd* **117** G1
Barnet EN5 **40** A5
Jarvis Rd, SE22 *off Melbourne Gro* **152** B4
South Croydon CR2 **202** A6
Jasmine Cl, Ilf. IG1 **99** E5
Orpington BR6 **206** E2
Southall UB1 **103** E7
Jasmine Gdns, Croy. CR0 **204** B3
Harrow HA2 **85** G2
Jasmine Gro, SE20 **189** E1
Jasmine Sq, E3 *off Birdsfield La* **113** J1
Jasmine Ter, West Dr. UB7 **120** D2
Jasmine Way, E.Mol. KT8 *off Hampton Ct Way* **180** B4
Jasmin Rd, Epsom KT19 **196** B5
Jason Ct, W1 *off Marylebone La* **16** C3
Jason Wk, SE9 **174** D4
Jasper Pas, SE19 **170** C6
Jasper Rd, E16 **116** A6
SE19 **170** C5
Jasper Wk, N1 **12** B3
Javelin Way, Nthlt. UB5 **102** D3
Jaycroft, Enf. EN2 *off The Ridgeway* **43** G1
Jay Gdns, Chis. BR7 **174** C4
Jay Ms, SW7 **22** D4
Jazzfern Ter, Wem. HA0 *off Maybank Av* **86** D5
Jean Batten Cl, Wall. SM6 **201** F7
Jebb Av, SW2 **151** E6
Jebb St, E3 **114** A2
Jedburgh Rd, E13 **115** J3
Jedburgh St, SW11 **150** A4
Jeddo Rd, W12 **127** F2
Jefferson Cl, W13 **125** E3
Ilford IG2 **81** E5
Jefferson Wk, SE18 *off Kempt St* **136** D6
Jeffreys Pl, NW1 *off Jeffreys St* **92** C7
Jeffreys Rd, SW4 **150** E2
Enfield EN3 **45** J3
Jeffreys St, NW1 **92** B7
Jeffreys Wk, SW4 **150** E2
Jeffries Ho, NW10 **106** C1
Jeffs Cl, Hmptn. TW12 *off Uxbridge Rd* **161** H6
Jeffs Rd, Sutt. SM1 **198** C4
Jeger Av, E2 **112** C1
Jeken Rd, SE9 **155** J4
Jelf Rd, SW2 **151** G5
Jellicoe Gdns, Stan. HA7 **52** C6
Jellicoe Ho, SW8 *off St. George Wf* **34** A5
Jellicoe Rd, E13 *off Jutland Rd* **115** G4
N17 **60** A7
Jemma Knowles Cl, SW2 *off Neil Wates Cres* **169** G1
Jemmett Cl, Kings.T. KT2 **182** B1
Jengar Cl, Sutt. SM1 **199** E4
Jenkins La, E6 **116** D2
Barking IG11 **117** E2
Jenkinson Ho, E2 *off Usk St* **113** G3
Jenkins Rd, E13 **115** H4
Jenner Av, W3 **106** D5
Jenner Cl, Sid. DA14 **176** A4
Jenner Pl, SW13 **127** H6
Jenner Rd, N16 **94** C2
Jennett Rd, Croy. CR0 **201** G3
Jennifer Rd, Brom. BR1 **173** F3
Jennings Cl, Surb. (Long Dit.) KT6 **181** F7
Jennings Rd, SE22 **152** C6
Jennings Way, Barn. EN5 **39** J3
Jenningtree Way, Belv. DA17 **139** J2
Jenny Hammond Cl, E11 *off Newcomen Rd* **97** F3
Jenson Way, SE19 **170** C7
Jenton Av, Bexh. DA7 **158** E1
Jephson Rd, E7 **97** J7
Jephson St, SE5 *off Grove La* **152** A1
Jephtha Rd, SW18 **148** D6
Jeppos La, Mitch. CR4 **185** J4
Jepson Ho, SW6 *off Pearscroft Rd* **149** E1
Jerdan Pl, SW6 **128** D7
Jeremiah St, E14 **114** B6
Jeremys Grn, N18 **61** E4
Jermyn St, SW1 **25** F1
Jerningham Av, Ilf. IG5 **80** E2
Jerningham Rd, SE14 **153** H2
Jerome Cres, NW8 **7** G5
Jerome Pl, Kings.T. KT1 *off Wadbrook St* **181** G2
Jerome St, E1 **21** F1
Jerome Twr, W3 **126** B2
Jerrard St, N1 **12** E2
SE13 **154** B3
Jersey Av, Stan. HA7 **69** E2
Jersey Dr, Orp. BR5 **193** G6
Jersey Ho, N1 *off Clifton Rd* **93** J6
Jersey Par, Hounslow TW5 **143** H1
Jersey Rd, E11 **96** D1
E16 *off Prince Regent La* **115** J6
SW17 **168** B6
Jersey Rd, W7 **124** D2
Hounslow TW3, TW5 **143** H1
Ilford IG1 **99** E4
Isleworth TW7 **124** B6
Jersey St, E2 *off Bethnal Grn Rd* **113** E3
Jerusalem Pas, EC1 **11** G6
Jervis Ct, W1 **17** E4
Jervis Rd, SW6 *off Lillie Rd* **128** C6
Jerviston Gdns, SW16 **169** G6
Jesmond Av, Wem. HA9 **87** J6
Jesmond Cl, Mitch. CR4 **186** B3
Jesmond Rd, Croy. CR0 **188** C7
Jesmond Way, Stan. HA7 **53** H5
Jessam Av, E5 **94** E1
Jessamine Rd, W7 **124** B1
Jessel Dr, Loug. IG10 **49** F1
Jessel Ho, SW1 *off Page St* **33** J1
Jesse Rd, E10 **96** C1
Jessica Rd, SW18 **149** F6
Jessie Blythe La, N19 **74** E7
Jessop Av, Sthl. UB2 **123** F4
Jessop Rd, SE24 *off Milkwood Rd* **151** H4
Jessop Sq, E14 *off Heron Quay* **134** A1
Jessops Way, Croy. CR0 **186** C6
Jessup Cl, SE18 **137** F4
Jethou Ho, N1 *off Nightingale Rd* **93** J6
Jetstar Way, Northolt UB5 **102** E3
Jevington Way, SE12 **173** H2
Jewel Rd, E17 **78** A3
★ **Jewel Twr** (Houses of Parliament), SW1 **26** A5
★ **Jewish Mus**, NW1 *off Albert St* **110** B1
Jewry St, EC3 **21** F4
Jew's Row, SW18 **149** E4
Jews Wk, SE26 **171** E4
Jeymer Av, NW2 **89** H5
Jeymer Dr, Grnf. UB6 **103** J1
Jeypore Pas, SW18 *off Jeypore Rd* **149** F6
Jeypore Rd, SW18 **149** F7
Jigger Mast Ho, SE18 *off Woolwich Ch St* **136** C3
Jillian Cl, Hmptn. TW12 **161** G7
Jim Bradley Cl, SE18 *off John Wilson St* **136** D4
Jim Griffiths Ho, SW6 *off Clem Attlee Ct* **128** C6
Jim O'Neill Wk, Ruis. HA4 *off Sidmouth Dr* **84** A3
Joan Cres, SE9 **156** A7
Joan Gdns, Dag. RM8 **100** E2
Joan Rd, Dag. RM8 **100** E2
Joan St, SE1 **27** G2
Jocelyn Rd, Rich. TW9 **145** H3
Jocelyn St, SE15 **152** D1
Jockey's Flds, WC1 **18** D1
Jodane St, SE8 **133** J4
Jodrell Cl, Islw. TW7 **144** D1
Jodrell Rd, E3 **113** J1
Joel St, Nthwd. HA6 **66** A3
Pinner HA5 **66** A3
Johanna St, SE1 **27** E4
John Adam St, WC2 **26** B1
John Aird Ct, W2 **14** D1
John Archer Way, SW18 **149** G6
John Ashby Cl, SW2 **151** E6
John Austin Cl, Kings.T. KT2 *off Queen Elizabeth Rd* **181** J1
John Barnes Wk, E15 **97** F6
John Bradshaw Rd, N14 **58** D1
John Burns Dr, Bark. IG11 **99** H7
John Campbell Rd, N16 **94** B5
John Carpenter St, EC4 **19** G5
John Cornwell VC Ho, E12 **98** D4
John Drinkwater Cl, E11 *off Browning Rd* **79** F7
John Fearon Wk, W10 *off Dart St* **108** B3
John Felton Rd, SE16 **29** H4
John Fisher St, E1 **21** H5
John Gooch Dr, Enf. EN2 **43** H1
John Harrison Ho, E1 *off Philpot St* **113** E6
John Harrison Way, SE10 **135** F3
John Horner Ms, N1 **11** J1
John Islip St, SW1 **34** A2
John Keats Ho, N22 **59** F7
John Kennedy Ho, SE16 *off Rotherhithe Old Rd* **133** G4
John Maurice Cl, SE17 **36** B1
John McKenna Wk, SE16 **29** J5
John Milton Pass, EC2 **20** A4
John Newton Ct, Well. DA16 **158** B3
John Parker Cl, Dag. RM10 **101** H7
John Parker Sq, SW11 *off Thomas Baines Rd* **149** G3
John Penn St, SE13 **154** B1
John Perrin Pl, Har. HA3 **69** H7
John Princes St, W1 **17** E3
John Rennie Wk, E1 *off Wine Cl* **133** F1
John Roll Way, SE16 **29** J5
John Ruskin St, SE5 **35** G7
Johns Av, NW4 **71** J4
John Silkin La, SE8 **133** G5
Johns La, Mord. SM4 **185** F5
John's Ms, WC1 **10** D6
John Smith Av, SW6 **128** C7
John Smith Ms, E14 *off Newport Av* **114** D7
Johnson Cl, E8 **112** D1
Johnson Ho, E2 **13** J3
Johnson Rd, NW10 **106** D1
Bromley BR2 **192** A5
Croydon CR0 **188** A7
Hounslow TW5 **122** C7
Johnsons Cl, Cars. SM5 **199** J3
Johnson's Ct, EC4 *off Fleet St* **19** F4
Johnsons Dr, Hmptn. TW12 **179** J1
Johnson's Pl, SW1 **33** F4
Johnson St, E1 *off Cable St* **113** F7
Southall UB2 **122** C3
Johnsons Way, NW10 **106** B4
John Spencer Sq, N1 **93** H6
John's Pl, E1 *off Damien St* **113** E6
John's Ter, Croy. CR0 **202** A1
Johnston Cl, SW9 *off Hackford Rd* **151** F1
Johnston Ct, E10 *off Oliver Rd* **96** B3
Johnstone Rd, E6 **116** C3
Johnston Rd, Wdf.Grn. IG8 **63** G5
Johnston Ter, NW2 *off Kara Way* **90** A3
John St, E15 **115** F1
SE25 **188** D4
WC1 **10** D6
Enfield EN1 **44** C5
Hounslow TW3 **143** E2
John Trundle Ct, EC2 *off The Barbican* **19** J1
John Walsh Twr, E11 **97** F2
John Wesley Cl, E6 **116** C3
John Williams Cl, SE14 **133** G6
Kingston upon Thames KT2 *off Henry Macaulay Av* **181** G1
John Wilson St, SE18 **136** D3
John Woolley Cl, SE13 **154** E4
Joiner's Arms Yd, SE5 *off Denmark Hill* **152** A1
Joiners Pl, N5 *off Leconfield Rd* **94** A4
Joiner St, SE1 **28** C2
Joiners Yd, N1 *off Caledonia St* **10** B2
Jolles Ho, E3 *off Bromley High St* **114** B3
Jollys La, Har. HA2 **86** A1
Hayes UB4 **102** D5
Jonathan Ct, W4 *off Windmill Rd* **127** E4
Jonathan St, SE11 **34** C3
Jones Rd, E13 *off Holborn Rd* **115** H4
Jones St, W1 **16** D6
Jones Wk, Rich. TW10 *off Lower Gro Rd* **145** J6
Jonquil Gdns, Hmptn. TW12 *off Partridge Rd* **161** F6
Jonson Cl, Hayes UB4 **102** A5
Mitcham CR4 **186** B4
Jordan Cl, Dag. RM10 *off Muggeridge Rd* **101** H4
Harrow HA2 **85** F3
Jordan Ct, SW15 *off Charlwood Rd* **148** A4
Jordan Rd, Grnf. (Perivale) UB6 **105** E1
Jordans Cl, Islw. TW7 **144** B1
Jordans Ms, Twick. TW2 *off Popes Av* **162** B2
Joseph Av, W3 **106** D6
Joseph Conrad Ho, SW1 *off Tachbrook St* **33** G2
Joseph Hardcastle Cl, SE14 **133** G7
Josephine Av, SW2 **151** F5
Joseph Powell Cl, SW12 **150** C6
Joseph Ray Rd, E11 **97** E2
Joseph St, E3 **113** J4
Joseph Trotter Cl, EC1 *off Myddelton St* **11** F4
Joshua Cl, N10 **58** B7
South Croydon CR2 **201** H7

Joshua St, E14
off St. Leonards Rd 114 C6
Joslings Cl, W12 107 H7
Joubert St, SW11 149 J2
Jowett St, SE15 132 C7
Joyce Av, N18 60 C5
Joyce Dawson Way, SE28
off Thamesmere Dr 118 A7
Joyce Dawson Way Shop Arc, SE28
off Thamesmere Dr 118 A7
Joyce Lattimore Ct, N9
off Colthurst Dr 60 E3
Joyce Page Cl, SE7 136 A6
Joyce Wk, SW2 151 G6
JOYDENS WOOD, Bex. DA5 177 J5
Joydon Dr, Rom. RM6 82 B6
Joyners Cl, Dag. RM9 101 F4
Jubb Powell Ho, N15 76 B6
Jubilee Av, E4 62 C6
Romford RM7 83 H5
Twickenham TW2 161 J1
Jubilee Cl, NW9 70 D6
NW10 107 E2
Kingston upon Thames KT1 *off High St* 181 F1
Pinner HA5 66 C2
Romford RM7 83 H5
Jubilee Cres, E14 134 C3
N9 60 D1
Jubilee Dr, Ruis. HA4 84 D4
★ **Jubilee Gdns**, SE1 26 C2
Jubilee Gdns, Sthl. UB1 103 G6
Jubilee La, W5
off Haven La 105 H6
Jubilee Mkt Hall, WC2 18 B5
Jubilee Par, Wdf.Grn. IG8
off Snakes La E 63 J6
Jubilee Pl, SW3 31 H3
Jubilee Rd, Grnf. (Perivale) UB6 104 E1
Sutton SM3 198 A7
Jubilee St, E1 113 F6
Jubilee Trust, SE10
off Egerton Dr 134 B7
Jubilee Wk, Wat. WD19 50 B4
Jubilee Way, SW19 185 E1
Chessington KT9 196 A4
Sidcup DA14 176 A2
Judd St, WC1 10 A4
Jude St, E16 115 F6
Judge Wk, Esher (Clay.) KT10 194 B6
Juer St, SW11 129 H7
Jules Thorn Av, Enf. EN1 44 C3
Julia Gdns, Bark. IG11 118 D2
Julia Garfield Ms, E16
off Evelyn Rd 135 H1
Juliana Cl, N2 73 F3
Julian Av, W3 106 B7
Julian Cl, Barn. (New Barn.) EN5 40 E3
Julian Hill, Har. HA1 86 B2
Julian Ho, SE21
off Kingswood Est 170 B4
Julian Pl, E14 134 B5
Julian Tayler Path, SE23 170 E2
Julia St, NW5
off Oak Village 92 A4
Julien Rd, W5 125 F3
Juliette Rd, E13 115 F2
Julius Caesar Way, Stan. HA7 53 G4
Julius Nyerere Cl, N1
off Copenhagen St 111 F1
Junction, The, Wem. HA9 88 B4
Junction App, SE13 154 C3
SW11 149 H3
Junction Av, W10
off Harrow Rd 107 J3
Junction Ms, W2 15 G3
Junction Pl, W2 15 F3
Junction Rd, E13 115 H2
N9 60 D1
N17 76 D3
N19 92 C4
W5 125 G4
Brentford TW8 125 G4
Harrow HA1 68 B6
South Croydon CR2 202 A5
Junction Rd E, Rom. RM6
off Kenneth Rd 82 E7
Junction Rd W, Rom. RM6 82 E7
Junction Shop Cen, The, SW11 *off St. John's Hill* 149 H4
Juniper Cl, Barn. EN5 40 A5
Chessington KT9 195 J6
Wembley HA9 87 J5
Juniper Cres, NW1 92 A7
Juniper Dr, SW18 149 F4
Juniper Gdns, SW16
off Leonard Rd 186 C1
Juniper La, E6 116 B5
Juniper Rd, Ilf. IG1 98 D4
Juniper St, E1 113 F7
Juno Ho, E3
off Garrison Rd 114 A1
Juno Way, SE14 133 G6
Jupiter Way, N7 93 F6
Jupp Rd, E15 96 D7
Jupp Rd W, E15 114 C1
Justice Wk, SW3 31 G6
Justin Cl, Brent. TW8 125 G7
Justines Pl, E2
off Palmers Rd 113 G3
Justin Pl, N22 59 F7
Justin Rd, E4 61 J6
Jute La, Enf. EN3 45 H2
Jutland Cl, N19
off Sussex Way 92 E1
Jutland Rd, E13 115 G4
SE6 154 C7
Jutsums Av, Rom. RM7 83 H6
Jutsums La, Rom. RM7 83 H6
Juxon Cl, Har. HA3
off Augustine Rd 67 H1
Juxon St, SE11 34 D1

K

Kaduna Cl, Pnr. HA5 66 A5
Kaine Pl, Croy. CRO 189 H7
Kale Rd, Erith DA18 138 E2
Kambala Rd, SW11 149 G2
Kangley Br Rd, SE26 171 J6
Kara Way, NW2 90 A4
Karen Ct, SE4
off Wickham Rd 153 J3
Bromley BR1 191 F1
Karen Ter, E11
off Montague Rd 97 F2
Karenza Ct, Wem. HA9
off Lulworth Av 69 F7
Kariba Cl, N9 61 F3
Karina Cl, Chig. IG7 65 H5
Karma Way, Har. HA2 85 G1
Karoline Gdns, Grnf. UB6
off Oldfield La N 104 A2
Kashgar Rd, SE18 137 J5
Kashmir Rd, SE7 136 A7
Kassala Rd, SW11 149 J1
Katella Trd Est, Bark. IG11 117 H3
Kates Cl, Barn. EN5 39 G5
Katharine St, Croy. CR0 201 J3
Katherine Cl, SE16
off Rotherhithe St 133 G1
Katherine Gdns, SE9 156 A4
Ilford IG6 65 F7
Katherine Rd, E6 98 A7
E7 97 J5
Twickenham TW1
off London Rd 162 D1
Katherine Sq, W11
off Wilsham St 128 B1
Kathleen Av, W3 106 C5
Wembley HA0 87 H7
Kathleen Rd, SW11 149 J3
Kayemoor Rd, Sutt. SM2 199 H7
Kay Rd, SW9 151 E2
Kays Ter, E18
off Walpole Rd 79 F1
Kay St, E2 13 J1
Welling DA16 158 B1
Kay Way, SE10
off Greenwich High Rd 134 B7
Kean St, WC2 18 C4
Keatley Grn, E4 61 J6
Keats Av, E16
off Wesley Av 135 H1
Keats Cl, E11
off Nightingale La 79 H5
NW3 *off Keats Gro* 91 H4
SE1 37 F2
SW19 167 G6
Chigwell IG7 65 F6
Enfield EN3 45 G5
Hayes UB4 102 A5
Keats Gro, NW3 91 G4
★ **Keats Ho**, NW3 91 H4
Keats Ho, SW1 33 G5
Beckenham BR3 172 A6
Keats Pl, EC2 20 B2
Keats Rd, Belv. DA17 139 J3
Welling DA16 157 H1
Keats Way, Croy. CR0 189 F6
Greenford UB6 103 H5
West Drayton UB7 120 C4
Kebbell Ter, E7 97 H5
Keble Cl, Nthlt. UB5 85 J5
Worcester Park KT4 197 F1
Keble Pl, SW13
off Somerville Av 127 H6
Keble St, SW17 167 F4
Kechill Gdns, Brom. BR2 191 G7
Kedelston Ct, E5
off Redwald Rd 95 H4
Kedeston Ct, Sutt. SM1
off Hurstcourt Rd 198 E1
Kedleston Dr, Orp. BR5 193 J6
Kedleston Wk, E2
off Middleton St 113 E3
Keedonwood Rd, Brom. BR1 172 E5
Keel Cl, SE16 133 G1
Barking IG11 118 C2
Keel Ct, E14
off Newport Av 114 D7
Keeley Rd, Croy. CR0 201 J2
Keeley St, WC2 18 C4
Keeling Ho, E2
off Claredale St 112 E2
Keeling Rd, SE9 156 A5
Keely Cl, Barn. EN4 41 H5
Keemor Cl, SE18 136 D7
Keens Cl, SW16 168 D5
Keens Rd, Croy. CR0 201 J4
Keens Yd, N1
off St. Paul's Rd 93 H6
Keep, The, SE3 155 G2
Kingston upon Thames KT2 163 J6
Keepers Ms, Tedd. TW11 163 F6
Keep La, N11
off Gardeners Cl 58 A2
Keetons Rd, SE16 132 E3
Keevil Dr, SW19 148 A7
Keighley Cl, N7 93 E4
Keightley Dr, SE9 175 F1
Keildon Rd, SW11 149 J4
Keir, The, SW19 165 J5
Keir Hardie Est, E5
off Springfield 94 E1
Keir Hardie Ho, W6
off Lochaline St 127 J6
Keir Hardie Way, Bark. IG11 100 A7
Hayes UB4 102 A3
Keith Connor Cl, SW8
off Daley Thompson Way 150 B3
Keith Gro, W12 127 G2
Keith Rd, E17 77 J1
Barking IG11 117 G2
Hayes UB3 121 H3
Kelbrook Rd, SE3 156 B3
Kelby Path, SE9 175 E3
Kelceda Cl, NW2 89 G2
Kelfield Gdns, W10 107 J6
Kelfield Ms, W10
off Kelfield Gdns 108 A6
Kelland Cl, N8
off Palace Rd 74 D5
Kelland Rd, E13 115 G4
Kellaway Rd, SE3 155 J2
Keller Cres, E12 98 A4
Kellerton Rd, SE13 154 E5
Kellett Rd, SW2 151 G4
Kelling Gdns, Croy. CR0 187 H7
Kellino St, SW17 167 J4
Kellner Rd, SE28 137 J3
Kell St, SE1 27 H5
Kelly Av, SE15 132 C7
Kelly Cl, NW10 88 D3
Kelly Ct, Borwd. WD6 38 C2
Kelly Ms, W9
off Woodfield Rd 108 C5
Kelly Rd, NW7 56 B6
Kelly St, NW1 92 B6
Kelly Way, Rom. RM6 82 E5
Kelman Cl, SW4 150 D2
Kelmore Gro, SE22 152 D4
Kelmscott Cl, E17 77 J2
Kelmscott Gdns, W12 127 G3
Kelmscott Rd, SW11 149 H5
Kelross Pas, N5
off Kelross Rd 93 J4
Kelross Rd, N5 93 H4
Kelsall Cl, SE3 155 H2
Kelsall Ms, Rich. TW9 146 B1
Kelsey Gate, Beck. BR3 190 B2
Kelsey La, Beck. BR3 190 A3
Kelsey Pk Av, Beck. BR3 190 B2
Kelsey Pk Rd, Beck. BR3 190 A2
Kelsey Sq, Beck. BR3 190 A2
Kelsey St, E2 13 J5
Kelsey Way, Beck. BR3 190 A3
Kelshall Ct, N4
off Brownswood Rd 93 J2
Kelsie Way, Ilf. IG6 65 H7
Kelson Ho, E14 134 C3
Kelso Pl, W8 22 B5
Kelso Rd, Cars. SM5 185 F7
Kelston Rd, Ilf. IG6 81 E2
Kelvedon Cl, Kings.T. KT2 163 J6
Kelvedon Ho, SW8 150 E1
Kelvedon Rd, SW6 128 C7
Kelvedon Way, Wdf.Grn. IG8 64 C6
Kelvin Av, N13 59 F6
Teddington TW11 162 B6
Kelvinbrook, W.Mol. KT8 179 H3
Kelvin Cl, Epsom KT19 196 A6
Kelvin Cres, Har. HA3 52 B7
Kelvin Dr, Twick. TW1 145 E6
Kelvin Gdns, Croy. CR0 187 E7
Southall UB1 103 G6
Kelvin Gro, SE26 170 E3
Chessington KT9 195 G3
Kelvington Cl, Croy. CR0 189 H7
Kelvington Rd, SE15 153 G5
Kelvin Ind Est, Grnf. UB6 85 H7
Kelvin Par, Orp. BR6 207 H1
Kelvin Rd, N5 93 H4
Welling DA16 158 A3
Kember St, N1
off Carnoustie Dr 93 F7
Kemble Dr, Brom. BR2 206 B3
Kemble Rd, N17 76 D1
SE23 171 G1
Croydon CR0 201 G3
Kemble St, WC2 18 C4
Kemerton Rd, SE5 151 J3
Beckenham BR3 190 B2
Croydon CR0 188 C7
Kemeys St, E9 95 H5
Kemnal Rd, Chis. BR7 175 G4
Kemp Ct, SW8
off Allen Edwards Dr 130 E7
Kempe Rd, NW6 108 A2
Kemp Gdns, Croy. CR0 187 J6
Kemp Ho, W1
off Berwick St 17 H5
Kempis Way, SE22
off East Dulwich Gro 152 B5
Kemplay Rd, NW3 91 G4
Kemp Rd, Dag. RM8 100 D1
Kemp's Ct, W1 17 G4
Kemps Dr, E14
off Morant St 114 A7
Kempsford Gdns, SW5 128 D5
Kempsford Rd, SE11 35 F2
Kemps Gdns, SE13
off Thornford Rd 154 C5
Kempshott Rd, SW16 168 D7
Kempson Rd, SW6 148 D1
Kempthorne Rd, SE8 133 H4
Kempton Av, Nthlt. UB5 85 G6
Sunbury-on-Thames TW16 178 B1
Kempton Cl, Erith DA8 139 J6
Kempton Ct, E1
off Durward St 112 E5
Sunbury-on-Thames TW16 178 B1
★ **Kempton Park Racecourse**, Sun. TW16 160 C7
Kempton Rd, E6 116 C1
Hampton TW12 179 F2
Kempton Wk, Croy. CR0 189 H6
Kempt St, SE18 136 D6
Kemsing Cl, Bex. DA5 159 E7
Bromley BR2 205 F2
Thornton Heath CR7 187 J4
Kemsing Rd, SE10 135 G5
Kemsley, SE13 154 C5
Kenbury Gdns, SE5
off Kenbury St 151 J2
Kenbury St, SE5 151 J2
Kenchester Cl, SW8 131 E7
Kencot Cl, Erith DA18 139 F2
Kencot Cl Business Pk, Erith DA18 139 F2
Kendal Av, N18 60 A4
W3 106 A4
Barking IG11 99 H7
Kendal Cl, N20 57 H2
SW9 35 G7
Woodford Green IG8 63 F2
Kendale Rd, Brom. BR1 172 E5
Kendal Gdns, N18 60 A4
Sutton SM1 199 F2
Kendal Ho, N1 10 D1
Kendall Av, Beck. BR3 189 H2
Kendall Ct, SW19 167 G6
Borehamwood WD6
off Gregson Cl 38 C1
Kendall Pl, W1 16 B2
Kendall Rd, SE18 156 B1
Beckenham BR3 189 H2
Isleworth TW7 144 D2
Kendalmere Cl, N10 74 B1
Kendal Par, N18
off Great Cambridge Rd 60 A4
Kendal Pl, SW15 148 C5
Kendal Rd, NW10 89 G4
Kendal Steps, W2
off St. Georges Flds 15 H4
Kendal St, W2 15 H4
Kender St, SE14 133 F7
Kendoa Rd, SW4 150 D4
Kendon Cl, E11 79 H5
Kendra Hall Rd, S.Croy. CR2 201 H7
Kendrey Gdns, Twick. TW2 144 B6
Kendrick Ms, SW7 31 E1
Kendrick Pl, SW7 31 E2
Kenelm Cl, Har. HA1 86 D3
Kenerne Dr, Barn. EN5 40 B5
Kenilford Rd, SW12 150 B7

Kenilworth Av, E17 .78 A2
SW19 .166 D5
Harrow HA2 .85 F4
Kenilworth Cl, Borwd. WD6 .38 C3
Kenilworth Ct, SW15 *off Lower Richmond Rd* .148 A3
Kenilworth Cres, Enf. EN1 .44 B1
Kenilworth Dr, Borwd. WD6 .38 C3
Kenilworth Gdns, SE18 .156 E2
Ilford IG3 .99 J2
Loughton IG10 .48 C6
Southall UB1 .103 F3
Watford WD19 .50 C5
Kenilworth Rd, E3 .113 H2
NW6 .108 C1
SE20 .189 G1
W5 .125 H1
Edgware HA8 .54 C3
Epsom KT17 .197 G6
Orpington BR5 .193 F6
Kenley, N17 .76 A2
Kenley Av, NW9 .70 E2
Kenley Cl, Barn. EN4 .41 H4
Bexley DA5 .159 G7
Chislehurst BR7 .193 H3
Kenley Gdns, Th.Hth. CR7 .187 H4
Kenley Rd, SW19 .184 C2
Kingston upon Thames KT1 .182 B2
Twickenham TW1 .144 D6
Kenley Wk, W11 .108 B7
Sutton SM3 .198 A4
Kenlor Rd, SW17 .167 G5
Kenmare Dr, N17 .76 C2
Mitcham CR4 .167 J7
Kenmare Gdns, N13 .59 H4
Kenmare Rd, Th.Hth. CR7 .187 G6
Kenmere Gdns, Wem. HA0 .106 A1
Kenmere Rd, Well. DA16 .158 C2
Kenmont Gdns, NW10 .107 H3
Kenmore Av, Har. HA3 .68 D4
Kenmore Cl, Rich. TW9 *off Kent Rd* .126 A7
Kenmore Gdns, Edg. HA8 .70 B2
Kenmore Rd, Har. HA3 .69 G3
Kenmure Rd, E8 .95 E5
Kenmure Yd, E8 *off Kenmure Rd* .95 E5
Kennacraig Cl, E16 *off Hanameel St* .135 G1
Kennard Rd, E15 .96 D7
N11 .57 J5
Kennard St, E16 .136 C1
SW11 .150 A1
Kennedy Av, Enf. EN3 .45 F6
Kennedy Cl, E13 .115 G2
Mitcham CR4 .186 A2
Orpington BR5 .207 G1
Pinner HA5 .51 F6
Kennedy Ho, SE11 *off Vauxhall Wk* .34 C3
Kennedy Path, W7 *off Harp Rd* .104 C4
Kennedy Rd, W7 .104 B5
Barking IG11 .117 H1
Kennedy Wk, SE17 *off Flint St* .36 C2
Kennet Cl, SW11 *off Maysoule Rd* .149 G4
Kenneth Av, Ilf. IG1 .98 E4
Kenneth Cres, NW2 .89 H5
Kenneth Gdns, Stan. HA7 .52 D6
Kenneth More Rd, Ilf. IG1 *off Oakfield Rd* .99 E3
Kennet Ho, NW8 .15 F1
Kenneth Rd, Rom. RM6 .82 D7
Kenneth Robbins Ho, N17 .60 E7
Kennet Rd, W9 .108 C4
Isleworth TW7 .144 C3
Kennet Sq, Mitch. CR4 .185 H1
Kennet St, E1 .29 J1
Kennett Dr, Hayes UB4 .102 E5
Kennet Wf La, EC4 .20 A5
Kenninghall, N18 .60 E5
Kenninghall Rd, E5 .94 D3
N18 .61 F5
Kenning St, SE16 *off Railway Av* .133 F2
Kennings Way, SE11 .35 G3
Kenning Ter, N1 .112 B1
KENNINGTON, SE11 .35 E6
Kennington Grn, SE11 .35 E4
Kennington La, SE11 .35 F3
Kennington Oval, SE11 .34 D5
Kennington Pk, SW9 .35 F7
Kennington Pk Est, SE11 .35 E6
Kennington Pk Gdns, SE11 .35 G5
Kennington Pk Pl, SE11 .35 F4
Kennington Pk Rd, SE11 .35 F5
Kennington Rd, SE1 .27 E5
SE11 .27 E6
Kennoldes, SE21 .170 A2
Kenrick Pl, W1 .16 B1
KENSAL GREEN, NW10 .107 J3
★ **Kensal Green Cem**, W10 .107 J3
KENSAL RISE, NW6 .108 A2
Kensal Rd, W10 .108 B4
KENSAL TOWN, W10 .108 A4
Kensal Wf, W10 *off Ladbroke Gro* .108 A4
KENSINGTON, W8 .128 C2
Kensington Av, E12 .98 B6
Thornton Heath CR7 .187 G1
Kensington Ch Ct, W8 .22 A4
Kensington Ch St, W8 .128 D1
Kensington Ch Wk, W8 .22 A3
Kensington Cl, N11 .58 A5
Kensington Ct, NW7 *off Grenville Pl* .54 D5
W8 .22 B4
Kensington Ct Gdns, W8 *off Kensington Ct Pl* .22 B5
Kensington Ct Ms, W8 .22 B4
Kensington Ct Pl, W8 .22 B5
Kensington Dr, Wdf.Grn. IG8 .80 A1
★ **Kensington Gdns**, W2 .22 D2
Kensington Gdns, Ilf. IG1 .98 C2
Kingston upon Thames KT1 *off Portsmouth Rd* .181 G3
Kensington Gdns Sq, W2 .14 A4
Kensington Gate, W8 .22 C5
Kensington Gore, SW7 .23 E4
Kensington Grn, W8 .22 A6
Kensington Hall Gdns, W14 *off Beaumont Av* .128 C5
Kensington High St, W8 .128 D3
W14 .128 B4
Kensington Mall, W8 .128 D1
★ **Kensington Palace**, W8 .22 B2
Kensington Palace Gdns, W8 .22 A1
Kensington Pk Gdns, W11 .108 C7
Kensington Pk Ms, W11 *off Kensington Pk Rd* .108 C6
Kensington Pk Rd, W11 .108 C7
Kensington Path, E10 *off Balmoral Rd* .96 B2
Kensington Pl, W8 .128 D1
Kensington Rd, SW7 .23 F4
W8 .22 B4
Northolt UB5 .103 G3
Romford RM7 .83 J6
Kensington Sq, W8 .22 A4
Kensington Ter, S.Croy. CR2 .202 A7
Kensington Village, W14 *off Avonmore Rd* .128 C4
Kensington Way, Borwd. WD6 .38 D3
Kent Av, W13 .104 E5
Dagenham RM9 .119 G4
Welling DA16 .157 J5
Kent Cl, Mitch. CR4 .187 E4
Orpington BR6 .207 H6
Kent Dr, Barn. (Cockfos.) EN4 .42 A4
Teddington TW11 .162 B5
Kentford Way, Nthlt. UB5 .102 E1
Kent Gdns, W13 .105 E5
Ruislip HA4 .66 B6
Kent Gate Way, Croy. CR0 .204 A5
Kent Ho La, Beck. BR3 .171 H5
Kent Ho Rd, SE26 .189 G1
Beckenham BR3 .171 H5
Kentish Bldgs, SE1 .28 B2
Kentish Rd, Belv. DA17 .139 G4
KENTISH TOWN, NW5 .92 C6
Kentish Town Rd, NW1 .92 B7
NW5 .92 B7
Kentish Way, Brom. BR1 .191 G2
Kentlea Rd, SE28 .137 H2
Kentmere Rd, SE18 .137 H4
KENTON, Har. HA3 .68 E5
Kenton Av, Har. HA1 .68 C7
Southall UB1 .103 G7
Sunbury-on-Thames TW16 .178 E2
Kenton Ct, W14 *off Kensington High St* .128 C3
Kenton Gdns, Har. HA3 .69 F5
Kenton La, Har. HA3 .69 F3
Kenton Pk Av, Har. HA3 .69 G4
Kenton Pk Cl, Har. HA3 .69 F4
Kenton Pk Cres, Har. HA3 .69 G4
Kenton Pk Rd, Har. HA3 .69 F4
Kenton Rd, E9 .95 G6
Harrow HA1, HA3 .69 G5
Kenton St, WC1 .10 A5
Kent Pas, NW1 .7 J5
Kent Rd, N21 .60 A1
W4 .126 C3
Dagenham RM10 .101 H5
East Molesey KT8 .179 J4
Kingston upon Thames KT1 *off The Bittoms* .181 G3
Richmond TW9 .126 A7
West Wickham BR4 .204 B1
Kents Pas, Hmptn. TW12 .179 F1
Kent St, E2 .13 G1
E13 .115 J3
Kent Ter, NW1 .7 H4
Kent Vw Gdns, Ilf. IG3 .99 H2
Kent Way, Surb. KT6 .195 H3
Kentwell Cl, SE4 .153 H4
Kentwode Grn, SW13 .127 G7
Kent Yd, SW7 .23 H4
Kenver Av, N12 .57 G6
Kenward Rd, SE9 .155 J5
Kenway, Rom. RM5 .83 J2
Ken Way, Wem. HA9 .88 C2
Kenway Rd, SW5 .30 A2
Kenwood Av, N14 .42 D5
SE14 *off Briant St* .153 G1
Kenwood Cl, NW3 .91 G1
West Drayton (Sipson) UB7 .120 D6
Kenwood Dr, Beckenham BR3 .190 C3
Kenwood Gdns, E18 .79 H3
Ilford IG2 .80 D4
★ **Kenwood Ho**, NW3 .91 H1
Kenwood Rd, N6 .73 J6
N9 .60 D1
Kenworthy Rd, E9 .95 H5
Kenwyn Dr, NW2 .89 E3
Kenwyn Rd, SW4 .150 D4
SW20 .183 J1
Kenya Rd, SE7 .136 A7
Kenyngton Dr, Sun. TW16 .160 A5
Kenyngton Pl, Har. HA3 .69 F5
Kenyon St, SW6 .148 A1
Keogh Rd, E15 .97 E6
Kepler Rd, SW4 .150 E4
Keppel Rd, E6 .98 C7
Dagenham RM9 .100 E4
Keppel Row, SE1 .27 J2
Keppel St, WC1 .17 J1
Kerbela St, E2 .13 H5
Kerbey St, E14 .114 B6
Kerfield Cres, SE5 .152 A1
Kerfield Pl, SE5 .152 A1
Kerri Cl, Barn. EN5 .39 J4
Kerridge Ct, N1 .94 B6
Kerrison Pl, W5 .125 G1
Kerrison Rd, E15 .114 D1
SW11 .149 H3
W5 .125 G1
Kerrison Vil, W5 *off Kerrison Pl* .125 G1
Kerry Av, Stan. HA7 .53 G4
Kerry Av N, Stan. HA7 .53 G4
Kerry Cl, E16 .115 H6
N13 .59 F2
Kerry Ct, Stan. HA7 .53 G4
Kerry Ho, E1 *off Sidney St* .113 F6
Kerry Path, SE14 .133 J6
Kerry Rd, SE14 .133 J6
Kersey Gdns, SE9 .174 B4
Kersfield Rd, SW15 .148 A6
Kershaw Cl, SW18 .149 F6
Kershaw Rd, Dag. RM10 .101 G3
Kersley Ms, SW11 .149 J2
Kersley Rd, N16 .94 B3
Kersley St, SW11 .149 J2
Kerswell Cl, N15 .76 B5
Kerwick Cl, N7 *off Sutterton St* .93 F7
Keslake Rd, NW6 .108 A2
Kessock Cl, N17 .76 E5
Kesteven Cl, Ilf. IG6 .65 J6
Kestlake Rd, Bex. DA5 *off East Rochester Way* .158 C6
KESTON, BR2 .205 J5
Keston Av, Kes. BR2 .205 J5
Keston Cl, N18 .60 A3
Welling DA16 .138 C7
Keston Gdns, Kes. BR2 .205 J4
Keston Mark, Kes. BR2 .206 B3
Keston Pk Cl, Kes. BR2 .206 C3
Keston Rd, N17 .76 A3
SE15 .152 D3
Thornton Heath CR7 .187 G6
Kestral Ct, Wall. SM6 *off Carew Rd* .200 C5
Kestrel Av, E6 *off Swan App* .116 B5
SE24 .151 H5
Kestrel Cl, NW9 .70 E2
NW10 .88 D5
Kingston upon Thames KT2 .163 G4
Kestrel Ho, EC1 .11 J3
SW8 *off St. George Wf* .34 A5
W13 .104 C4
Enfield EN3 *off Alma Rd* .45 H5
Kestrel Pl, SE14 *off Milton Ct Rd* .133 H6
Kestrel Way, Felt. TW14 *off Falcon Way* .142 B5
Hayes UB3 .121 G2
Keswick Av, SW15 .164 E5
SW19 .184 D2
Keswick Bdy, SW15 *off Upper Richmond Rd* .148 C5
Keswick Cl, Sutt. SM1 .199 F4
Keswick Gdns, Ilf. IG4 .80 B5
Wembley HA9 .87 H4
Keswick Ms, W5 .125 H1
Keswick Rd, SW15 .148 B5
Bexleyheath DA7 .159 G2
Orpington BR6 .207 J1
Twickenham TW2 .143 J6
West Wickham BR4 .204 E2
Kettering St, SW16 .168 C6
Kett Gdns, SW2 .151 F5
Kettlebaston Rd, E10 .95 J1
Kettlewell Cl, N11 .58 A6
Kevan Ho, SE5 .131 J7
Kevelioc Rd, N17 .75 J1
Kevin Cl, Houns. TW4 .142 D2
Kevington Cl, Orp. BR5 .193 J4
Kevington Dr, Chis. BR7 .193 J4
Orpington BR5 .193 J4
KEW, Rich. TW9 .126 A6
Kew Br, Brent. TW8 .125 J6
Richmond TW9 .125 J6
Kew Br Arches, Rich. TW9 *off Kew Br* .125 J6
Kew Br Ct, W4 .126 A5
Kew Br Rd, Brent. TW8 .125 J6
★ **Kew Bridge Steam Mus**, Brent. TW8 .125 J5
Kew Cres, Sutt. SM3 .198 B3
Kew Foot Rd, Rich. TW9 .145 H4
Kew Gdns Rd, Rich. TW9 .125 J7
Kew Grn, Rich. TW9 .126 A7
Kew Meadows Path, Rich. TW9 .146 B2
★ **Kew Observatory**, Rich. TW9 .145 E3
★ **Kew Palace** (Royal Botanic Gdns), Rich. TW9 .125 H7
Kew Retail Pk, Rich. TW9 .146 B1
Kew Rd, Rich. TW9 .126 A6
Key Cl, E1 .113 E4
Keyes Rd, NW2 .90 A5
Keyham Ho, W2 *off Westbourne Pk Rd* .108 D5
Keymer Rd, SW2 .169 F2
Keynes Cl, N2 .73 J3
Keynsham Av, Wdf.Grn. IG8 .63 E4
Keynsham Gdns, SE9 .156 B5
Keynsham Rd, SE9 .156 A5
Morden SM4 .198 E1
Keynsham Wk, Mord. SM4 .198 E1
Keyse Rd, SE1 .29 F6
Keysham Av, Houns. TW5 *off The Avenue* .142 A1
Keystone Cres, N1 .10 B2
Keywood Dr, Sun. TW16 .160 A6
Keyworth Cl, E5 .95 H4
Keyworth Pl, SE1 .27 H5
Keyworth St, SE1 .27 H5
Kezia Ms, SE8 *off Trundleys Rd* .133 H5
Kezia St, SE8 *off Trundleys Rd* .133 H5
Khalsa Ct, N22 .75 H1
Khama Rd, SW17 .167 H4
Khartoum Rd, E13 .115 H3
SW17 .167 G4
Ilford IG1 .99 E5
Khyber Rd, SW11 .149 H2
Kibworth St, SW8 .131 F7
KIDBROOKE, SE3 .155 H3
Kidbrooke Gdns, SE3 .155 G2
Kidbrooke Gro, SE3 .155 G1
Kidbrooke Interchange, SE3 .155 J3
Kidbrooke La, SE9 .156 B4
Kidbrooke Pk Cl, SE3 .155 H1
Kidbrooke Pk Rd, SE3 .155 H1
Kidbrooke Way, SE3 .155 H2
Kidderminster Pl, Croy. CR0 *off Kidderminster Rd* .201 H1
Kidderminster Rd, Croy. CR0 .201 H1
Kidderpore Av, NW3 .90 D4
Kidderpore Gdns, NW3 .90 D4
Kidd Pl, SE7 .136 B5
Kielder Cl, Ilf. IG6 .65 J6
Kiffen St, EC2 .12 C5

Kilberry Cl, Islw. TW7 .....144 A1
KILBURN, NW6 ....108 C2
Kilburn Br, NW6 *off Kilburn High Rd* ...108 D1
Kilburn Gate, NW6 ....6 A1
Kilburn High Rd, NW6 .....90 C7
Kilburn La, W9 ....108 A3
W10 ....108 A3
Kilburn Pk Rd, NW6 ......108 D3
Kilburn Pl, NW6 ....108 D1
Kilburn Priory, NW6 ......108 E1
Kilburn Sq, NW6 ....108 D1
Kilburn Vale, NW6 *off Belsize Rd* 108 E1
Kilby Ct, SE10 *off Child La* 135 F3
Kildare Cl, Ruis. HA4 ......84 C1
Kildare Gdns, W2 ....108 D6
Kildare Rd, E16 ....115 G5
Kildare Ter, W2 ....108 D6
Kildare Wk, E14 *off Farrance St* 114 A6
Kildoran Rd, SW2 ....150 E5
Kildowan Rd, Ilf. IG3 .....100 A1
Kilgour Rd, SE23 ....153 H6
Kilkie St, SW6 ....149 F2
Killarney Rd, SW18 ......149 F6
Killburns Mill Cl, Wall. SM6 *off London Rd* 200 B2
Killearn Rd, SE6 ....172 D1
Killester Gdns, Wor.Pk. KT4 ....197 H4
Killick Ms, Sutt. SM3 .....198 B6
Killick St, N1 ....10 C1
Killieser Av, SW2 ....168 E2
Killip Cl, E16 ....115 F6
Killowen Av, Nthlt. UB5 ....85 J5
Killowen Rd, E9 ....95 G6
Killyon Rd, SW8 ....150 C2
Killyon Ter, SW8 ....150 C2
Kilmaine Rd, SW6 ....128 B7
Kilmarnock Gdns, Dag. RM8 *off Lindsey Rd* 100 C3
Kilmarnock Rd, Wat. WD19 .50 D4
Kilmarsh Rd, W6 ....127 J4
Kilmartin Av, SW16 ......187 F3
Kilmartin Rd, Ilf. IG3 .....100 A2
Kilmington Rd, SW13 ....127 G6
Kilmorey Gdns, Twick. TW1 ....144 E5
Kilmorey Rd, Twick. TW1 ..144 E4
Kilmorie Rd, SE23 ....171 H1
Kiln Cl, Hayes (Harling.) UB3 ....121 G6
Kilner St, E14 ....114 A5
Kiln Ms, SW17 ....167 G5
Kiln Pl, NW5 ....92 A5
Kilnside, Esher (Clay.) KT10 ....194 D7
Kilpatrick Way, Hayes UB4 ....103 E5
Kilravock St, W10 ....108 B3
Kilsby Wk, Dag. RM9 *off Rugby Rd* 100 B6
Kilsha Rd, Walt. KT12 .....178 B6
Kimbell Gdns, SW6 ......148 B1
Kimbell Pl, SE3 *off Tudway Rd* 155 J4
Kimberley Av, E6 ....116 B2
SE15 ....153 E2
Ilford IG2 ....81 G7
Romford RM7 ....83 J6
Kimberley Dr, Sid. DA14 ..176 D2
Kimberley Gdns, N4 ......75 H5
Enfield EN1 ....44 C3
Kimberley Ind Est, E17 ....77 J1
Kimberley Rd, E4 ....62 E1
E11 ....96 D2
E16 ....115 F4
E17 ....77 J1
N17 ....76 D2
N18 ....61 E6
NW6 ....108 B1
SW9 ....151 E2
Beckenham BR3 ....189 G2
Croydon CR0 ....187 H6
Kimberley Wk, Walt. KT12 *off Cottimore La* 178 B7
Kimberley Way, E4 ....63 E1
Kimber Rd, SW18 ....148 D7
Kimble Rd, SW19 ....167 G6
Kimbolton Cl, SE12 ......155 F6
Kimbolton Grn, Borwd. WD6 ....38 C4
Kimbolton Row, SW3 .....31 G2
Kimmeridge Gdns, SE9 ....174 B4
Kimmeridge Rd, SE9 .....174 B4
Kimpton Ho, SW15 *off Fontley Way* 147 G7
Kimpton Link Business Cen, Sutt. SM3 *off Kimpton Rd* 198 C2
Kimpton Pk Way, Sutt. SM3 ....198 C2
Kimpton Rd, SE5 ....152 A1
Sutton SM3 ....198 C2
Kimpton Trade & Business Cen, Sutt. SM3 ....198 C2
Kinburn St, SE16 ....133 G2
Kincaid Rd, SE15 ....132 E7
Kincardine Gdns, W9 *off Harrow Rd* 108 D4
Kinch Gro, Wem. HA9 .....69 J7
Kinder Cl, SE28 ....118 D7
Kinder St, E1 *off Cannon St Rd* 112 E6
Kinderton Cl, N14 ....58 C1
Kinefold Ho, N7 *off York Way* 92 E6
Kinetic Business Centre, WD6 ....38 A3
Kinfauns Rd, SW2 ....169 G2
Ilford IG3 ....100 A1
King Alfred Av, SE6 ......172 A3
King & Queen Cl, SE9 *off St. Keverne Rd* 174 B4
King & Queen St, SE17 ....36 A2
King & Queen Wf, SE16 *off Rotherhithe St* 133 G1
King Arthur Cl, SE15 .....133 F7
King Charles Cres, Surb. KT5 ....181 J7
King Charles Rd, Surb. KT5 ....181 J5
King Charles St, SW1 .....25 J3
King Charles Ter, E1 *off Sovereign Cl* 113 E7
King Charles Wk, SW19 *off Princes Way* 166 B1
Kingcup Cl, Croy. CR0 ....189 G7
King David La, E1 ....113 F7
Kingdon Rd, NW6 ....90 D6
King Edward Dr, Chess. KT9 *off Kelvin Gro* 195 H3
King Edward Ms, SW13 ..147 G1
King Edward Rd, E10 ......96 C1
E17 ....77 H3
Barnet EN5 ....40 D4
King Edward's Gdns, W3 ....126 A1
King Edwards Gro, Tedd. TW11 ....163 E6
King Edward's Pl, W3 *off King Edward's Gdns* 126 A1
King Edwards Rd, E9 .....113 E1
N9 ....44 E7
Barking IG11 ....117 G1
King Edward's Rd, Enf. EN3 ....45 G4
King Edward St, EC1 ......19 J3
King Edward III Ms, SE16 *off Paradise St* 133 E2
King Edward Wk, SE1 .....27 F5
Kingfield Rd, W5 ....105 G4
Kingfield St, E14 ....134 C4
Kingfisher Av, E11 *off Eastern Av* 79 H6
Kingfisher Cl, SE28 ......118 C7
Harrow (Har.Wld) HA3 ..52 C7
Kingfisher Ct, SW19 *off Queensmere Rd* ...166 B2
Surbiton KT6 *off Ewell Rd* 181 J7
Sutton SM1 *off Sandpiper Rd* 198 C5
Kingfisher Dr, Rich. TW10 .163 E4
Kingfisher Ho, SW18 *off Juniper Dr* 149 F3
Kingfisher Ms, SE13 .....154 B4
Kingfisher Pl, N22 *off Clarendon Rd* 75 F2
Kingfisher Sq, SE8 ....133 J6
Kingfisher St, E6 ....116 B5
Kingfisher Wk, NW9 ......71 E2
Kingfisher Way, NW10 .....88 D5
Beckenham BR3 ....189 G5
King Frederik IX Twr, SE16 ....133 J3
King Gdns, Croy. CR0 ....201 H5
King George Av, E16 .....116 A6
Ilford IG2 ....81 G5
King George Cl, Rom. RM7 ....83 J3
King George V Dock, E16 .136 C1
King Georges Dr, Sthl. UB1 ....103 F5
King George VI Av, Mitch. CR4 ....185 J4
King George Sq, Rich. TW10 ....145 J6
King George's Trd Est, Chess. KT9 ....196 A4
King George St, SE10 ....134 C7
Kingham Cl, SW18 ....149 F7
W11 ....128 B2
King Harolds Way, Bexh. DA7 ....138 D7
King Henry Ms, Har. HA2 ..86 B1
Orpington BR6 *off Osgood Av* 207 J5
King Henry's Reach, W6 ....127 J6
King Henry's Rd, NW3 .....91 H7
Kingston upon Thames KT1 ....182 B3
King Henry St, N16 ....94 B5
King Henry's Wk, N1 ......94 B6
King Henry Ter, E1 *off Sovereign Cl* 113 E7
Kinghorn St, EC1 ....19 J2
King James Ct, SE1 ....27 H4
King James St, SE1 ....27 H4
King John Ct, EC2 ....12 E5
King John St, E1 ....113 G5
King Johns Wk, SE9 ......174 A1
Kinglake Est, SE17 ....36 E3
Kinglake St, SE17 ....36 D4
Kinglet Cl, E7 *off Romford Rd* 97 G6
Kingly Ct, W1 ....17 F5
Kingly St, W1 ....17 F4
Kingsand Rd, SE12 ......173 G2
Kings Arbour, Sthl. UB2 ..122 E5
Kings Arms Ct, E1 ....21 H2
Kings Arms Yd, EC2 ....20 B3
Kingsash Dr, Hayes UB4 ....102 E4
Kings Av, N10 ....74 A3
N21 ....59 H1
King's Av, SW4 ....150 D7
SW12 ....168 D1
Kings Av, W5 ....105 G6
Bromley BR1 ....173 F6
Buckhurst Hill IG9 ......64 A2
Carshalton SM5 ....199 H7
Greenford UB6 ....103 H6
Hounslow TW3 ....143 H1
New Malden KT3 ......183 E4
Romford RM6 ....83 F6
Woodford Green IG8 ....63 H6
Kings Bench St, SE1 ......27 H3
Kings Bench Wk, EC4 ......19 F4
Kingsbridge Av, W3 ......125 J2
Kingsbridge Ct, E14 *off Dockers Tanner Rd* 134 A3
Kingsbridge Cres, Sthl. UB1 ....103 F5
Kingsbridge Dr, NW7 ......56 A7
Kingsbridge Rd, W10 .....107 J6
Barking IG11 ....117 G2
Morden SM4 ....184 A7
Southall UB2 ....123 F4
Walton-on-Thames KT12 ....178 B7
KINGSBURY, NW9 ....70 B6
Kingsbury Circle, NW9 ....70 A5
Kingsbury Rd, N1 ....94 B6
NW9 ....70 B5
Kingsbury Ter, N1 ....94 B6
Kingsbury Trd Est, NW9 ...70 C6
Kings Butts, SE9 *off Strongbow Cres* ...156 C5
Kings Chace Vw, Enf. EN2 *off Crofton Way* 43 G2
Kings Chase, E.Mol. KT8 ....179 J3
Kingsclere Cl, SW15 .....147 G7
Kingsclere Ct, Barn. EN5 *off Gloucester Rd* 41 F5
Kingsclere Pl, Enf. EN2 ...43 J2
Kingscliffe Gdns, SW19 ...166 C1
Kings Cl, E10 ....78 B7
NW4 ....72 A4
Thames Ditton KT7 .....180 D6
Kings Coll Rd, NW3 ....91 H7
Kingscote Rd, W4 ....126 D3
Croydon CR0 ....188 E7
New Malden KT3 ......182 D3
Kingscote St, EC4 ....19 G5
Kings Ct, E13 ....115 H1
W6 *off Hamlet Gdns* ...127 G4
Wembley HA9 ....88 B2
Kingscourt Rd, SW16 ....168 D3
Kings Ct S, SW3 *off Chelsea Manor Gdns* 31 H4
Kings Cres, N4 ....93 J3
Kings Cres Est, N4 ....93 J2
Kingscroft Rd, NW2 ....90 C6
KING'S CROSS, N1 ....110 D1
King's Cross Br, N1 ....10 B3
King's Cross Rd, WC1 .....10 D3
King's Cross Sta, N1 ......10 A2
Kingsdale Gdns, W11 ....128 A1
Kingsdale Rd, SE18 ......137 J7
SE20 ....171 G7
Kingsdown Av, W3 ....107 E7
W13 ....125 E2
Kingsdown Cl, SE16 *off Masters Dr* 133 E5
W10 ....108 A6
Kingsdowne Rd, Surb. KT6 ....181 H7
Kingsdown Rd, E11 ....97 E3
N19 ....92 E2
Sutton SM3 ....198 B5
Kingsdown Way, Brom. BR2 ....191 G7
Kings Dr, Edg. HA8 ....53 J4
Surbiton KT5 ....182 A7
Teddington TW11 ......162 A5
Thames Ditton KT7 ....180 E6
Wembley HA9 ....88 B2
Kings Fm Av, Rich. TW10 ..146 A4
Kingsfield Av, Har. HA2 ....67 H4
Kingsfield Ho, SE9 ....174 A3
Kingsfield Rd, Har. HA1 ....68 A7
Kingsford St, NW5 ....91 J5
Kingsford Way, E6 ....116 C5
Kings Gdns, NW6 *off West End La* 90 D7
Ilford IG1 ....99 G1
King's Garth Ms, SE23 *off London Rd* 171 F2
Kingsgate, Wem. HA9 .....88 C3
Kingsgate Av, N3 ....72 D3
Kingsgate Cl, Bexh. DA7 ..158 E1
Kingsgate Est, N1 *off Tottenham Rd* 94 B6
Kingsgate Pl, NW6 ....90 D7
Kingsgate Rd, NW6 ....90 D7
Kingston upon Thames KT2 ....181 H1
Kings Grn, Loug. IG10 .....48 B3
Kingsground, SE9 ....156 B7
Kings Gro, SE15 ....133 E7
Kings Hall Ms, SE13 *off Lewisham Rd* 154 C3
Kings Hall Rd, Beck. BR3 ....171 H7
Kings Head Hill, E4 ....46 B7
Kings Head Yd, SE1 ....28 B2
Kings Highway, SE18 ....137 H6
Kingshill, SE17 ....36 A2
Kings Hill, Loug. IG10 .....48 B2
Kingshill Av, Har. HA3 .....69 E4
Northolt UB5 ....102 A3
Worcester Park KT4 ....183 G7
Kingshill Cl, Hayes UB4 ....102 A3
Kingshill Dr, Har. HA3 .....68 E3
Kingshold Est, E9 *off Victoria Pk Rd* 113 F1
Kingshold Rd, E9 ....95 F7
Kingsholm Gdns, SE9 ....156 A4
King's Ho, SW8 ....34 B7
Kingshurst Rd, SE12 .....155 G7
Kingside, SE18 *off Woolwich Ch St* ...136 B3
King's Keep, SW15 *off Westleigh Av* 148 A5
Kings Keep, Kings.T. KT1 *off Beaufort Rd* 181 H4
KINGSLAND, N1 ....94 B6
Kingsland, NW8 *off Broxwood Way* 109 H1
Kingsland Basin, N1 *off Kingsland Rd* 112 B1
Kingsland Grn, E8 ....94 B6
Kingsland High St, E8 .....94 C5
Kingsland Pas, E8 *off Kingsland Grn* 94 B6
Kingsland Rd, E2 ....13 E3
E8 ....112 B2
E13 ....115 J3
Kingsland Shop Cen, E8 ..94 C6
Kings La, Sutt. SM1 ......199 G6
Kingslawn Cl, SW15 .....147 H5
Kingsleigh Cl, Brent. TW8 ....125 G6
Kingsleigh Pl, Mitch. CR4 .185 J3
Kingsleigh Wk, Brom. BR2 *off Stamford Dr* 191 F4
Kingsley Av, W13 ....104 D6
Hounslow TW3 ....143 J2
Southall UB1 ....103 G7
Sutton SM1 ....199 G4
Kingsley Cl, N2 ....73 F5
Dagenham RM10 ....101 H4
Kingsley Ct, Edg. HA8 .....54 B2
Kingsley Dr, Wor.Pk. KT4 *off Badgers Copse* 197 F2
Kingsley Flats, SE1 ....36 D1
Kingsley Gdns, E4 ....62 A5
Kingsley Ms, E1 *off Wapping La* 113 E7
W8 ....22 B6
Chislehurst BR7 ....175 E6
Kingsley Pl, N6 ....74 A7
Kingsley Rd, E7 ....97 G7
E17 ....78 C2
N13 ....59 G4
NW6 ....108 C1
SW19 ....167 E5
Croydon CR0 ....201 G1
Harrow HA2 ....85 J4
Hounslow TW3 ....143 J2
Ilford IG6 ....81 F1
Loughton IG10 ....49 G3
Orpington BR6 ....207 J6
Pinner HA5 ....67 F4
Kingsley St, SW11 ....149 J3
Kingsley Way, N2 ....73 F6
Kingsley Wd Dr, SE9 .....174 C3
Kingslyn Cres, SE19 ......188 B1

Kings Mall, W6 . . . . .127 J4
Kingsman Par, SE18
off Woolwich Ch St . . .136 C3
Kingsman St, SE18 . . . . . .136 C3
Kingsmead, Barn. EN5 . . . .40 D4
Richmond TW10 . . . . . . .145 J6
Kingsmead Av, N9 . . . . . . .60 E1
NW9 . . . . .70 D7
Mitcham CR4 . . . . .186 C3
Sunbury-on-Thames
TW16 . . . . .178 C3
Surbiton KT6 . . . . .196 A2
Worcester Park KT4 . . . .197 H3
Kingsmead Cl, Epsom
KT19 . . . . .196 D7
Sidcup DA15 . . . . .176 A2
Teddington TW11 . . . . . .162 E6
Kingsmead Dr, Nthlt. UB5 . .85 F7
Kingsmead Est, E9 . . . . .95 H5
Kingsmead Ho, E9
off Kingsmead Way 95 H4
Kings Mead Pk, Esher
(Clay.) KT10 . . . . .194 B7
Kingsmead Rd, SW2 . . . . .169 G2
Kingsmead Way, E9 . . . . . . .95 H4
Kingsmere Cl, SW15
off Felsham Rd 148 A3
Kingsmere Pk, NW9 . . . . . . .88 B1
Kingsmere Pl, N16 . . . . .94 A1
Kingsmere Rd, SW19 . . . . .166 A2
Kings Ms, SW4
off King's Av 150 E5
King's Ms, WC1 . . . . .10 D6
Kings Ms, Chig. IG7 . . . . . . .65 F2
Kingsmill Business Pk,
Kings.T. KT1 . . . . .181 J3
Kingsmill Gdns, Dag.
RM9 . . . . .101 F5
Kingsmill Rd, Dag. RM9 . . .101 F5
Kingsmill Ter, NW8 . . . . .7 F1
Kingsnympton Pk, Kings.T.
KT2 . . . . .164 B6
Kings Oak, Rom. RM7 . . . . .83 G3
King's Orchard, SE9 . . . . . .156 B6
Kings Paddock, Hmptn.
TW12 . . . . .179 J1
Kings Par, Cars. SM5
off Wrythe La 199 H3
Kingspark Ct, E18 . . . . .79 G3
King's Pas, E11 . . . . .78 E7
Kings Pas, Kings.T. KT1 . . .181 G2
Kings Pl, SE1 . . . . .27 J4
W4 . . . . .126 C5
Buckhurst Hill IG9 . . . . . .63 J2
Loughton IG10 . . . . .48 A7
King Sq, EC1 . . . . .11 J4
King's Quay, SW10
off Chelsea Harbour . .149 F1
King's Reach Twr, SE1 . . . . .27 F1
Kings Ride Gate, Rich.
TW10 . . . . .146 A4
Kingsridge, SW19 . . . . .166 B2
Kings Rd, E4 . . . . .62 D1
E6 . . . . .115 J1
E11 . . . . .78 E7
King's Rd, N17 . . . . .76 C1
Kings Rd, N18 . . . . .60 D5
N22 . . . . .75 F1
NW10 . . . . .89 H7
SE25 . . . . .188 D3
King's Rd, SW1 . . . . .31 H3
SW3 . . . . .31 H3
SW6 . . . . .148 E1
SW10 . . . . .148 E1
Kings Rd, SW14 . . . . .146 D3
SW19 . . . . .166 D6
W5 . . . . .105 G5
Barking IG11
off North St 99 F7
Barnet EN5 . . . . .39 J3
Feltham TW13 . . . . .160 C1
Harrow HA2 . . . . .85 F2
Kingston upon Thames
KT2 . . . . .163 H7
Mitcham CR4 . . . . .186 A3
Orpington BR6 . . . . .207 J4
Richmond TW10 . . . . . . .145 J5
Surbiton (Long Dit.)
KT6 . . . . .195 F1
Teddington TW11 . . . . . .162 A5
Twickenham TW1 . . . . . .145 E6
West Drayton UB7 . . . . .120 C2
Kings Rd Bungalows, Har.
HA2 *off Kings Rd* 85 F3
King's Scholars' Pas, SW1 .25 F6
King Stairs Cl, SE16
off Elephant La 133 F2
King's Ter, NW1
off Plender St 110 C1
Kings Ter, Islw. TW7
off Worple Rd 144 D3
Kingsthorpe Rd, SE26 . . . .171 G4
Kingston Av, Feltham
TW14 . . . . .141 H6
Sutton SM3 . . . . .198 B3
Kingston Br, Kings.T.
KT1 . . . . .181 G2
Kingston Business Cen,
Chess. KT9 . . . . .195 H3
Kingston Bypass, SW15 . .165 E6
SW20 . . . . .165 E6
Esher KT10 . . . . .194 D3
New Malden KT3 . . . . . .183 G2
Surbiton KT5, KT6 . . . . .195 H3
Kingston Cl, Nthlt. UB5 . . . .85 F7
Romford RM6 . . . . .82 E3
Teddington TW11 . . . . . .162 E6
Kingston Cres, Beck. BR3 .189 J1
Kingston Gdns, Croy.
CR0 . . . . .201 E3
Kingston Hall Rd, Kings.T.
KT1 . . . . .181 G3
Kingston Hill, Kings.T.
KT2 . . . . .164 C6
Kingston Hill Av, Rom.
RM6 . . . . .82 E2
Kingston Hill Pl, Kings.T.
KT2 . . . . .164 C4
Kingston Ho Est, Surb. KT6
off Portsmouth Rd 181 E6
Kingston La, Tedd. TW11 . .162 D5
West Drayton UB7 . . . . .120 C2
Kingston Lo, N.Mal. KT3
off Kingston Rd 182 E4
★ **Kingston Mus & Heritage Cen**, Kings.T. KT1 . . . .181 H2
Kingston Pk Est, Kings.T.
KT2 . . . . .164 B6
Kingston Pl, Har. HA3
off Richmond Gdns 52 C7
Kingston Rd, N9 . . . . .60 D2
SW15 . . . . .165 G1
SW19 . . . . .184 C1
SW20 . . . . .183 J2
Barnet EN4 . . . . .41 G5
Epsom KT17, KT19 . . . . .196 E5
Ilford IG1 . . . . .99 E4
Kingston upon Thames
KT1 . . . . .182 B3
New Malden KT3 . . . . . .182 D4
Southall UB2 . . . . .123 F2
Surbiton KT5 . . . . .196 B2
Teddington TW11 . . . . . .162 E5
Worcester Park KT4 . . . .196 B2
Kingston Sq, SE19 . . . . . . .170 A5
KINGSTON UPON THAMES,
KT1 & KT2 . . . . .181 H2
KINGSTON VALE, SW15 . .165 E4
Kingston Vale, SW15 . . . . .164 D4
Kingstown St, NW1 . . . . . .110 A1
King St, E13 . . . . .115 G4
EC2 . . . . .20 A4
N2 . . . . .73 G3
N17 . . . . .76 C1
SW1 . . . . .25 G2
W3 . . . . .126 B1
W6 . . . . .127 G4
WC2 . . . . .18 A5
Richmond TW9 . . . . .145 G5
Southall UB2 . . . . .123 E3
Twickenham TW1 . . . . . .162 D1
King St Ms, N2
off King St 73 G3
King's Wk, Kings.T. KT2 . . .181 G1
Kings Wk Shop Mall, SW3
off King's Rd 31 J3
Kingswater Pl, SW11
off Battersea Ch Rd . . .129 H7
Kingsway, N12 . . . . .57 F6
SW14 . . . . .146 B3
WC2 . . . . .18 C3
Kings Way, Croy. CR0 . . . .201 F5
Kingsway, Enf. EN3 . . . . . . .45 E5
Kings Way, Har. HA1 . . . . . .68 B4
Kingsway, N.Mal. KT3 . . . .183 J4
Orpington BR5 . . . . .193 H5
Wembley HA9 . . . . .87 H4
West Wickham BR4 . . . .205 E3
Woodford Green IG8 . . . .63 J5
Kingsway Business Pk,
Hmptn. TW12 . . . . .179 F1
Kingsway Cres, Har. HA2 . .67 J4
Kingsway Pl, EC1 . . . . .11 F5
Kingsway Rd, Sutt. SM3 . .198 B7
Kingsway Shop Cen, NW3
off Hampstead High St . .91 F4
Kingswear Rd, NW5 . . . . . .92 B3
Ruislip HA4 . . . . .84 A2
Kings Wf, E8
off Kingsland Rd 112 B1
Kingswood Av, NW6 . . . . .108 B1
Belvedere DA17 . . . . . . .139 F4
Bromley BR2 . . . . .190 E3
Hampton TW12 . . . . . . .161 H6
Hounslow TW3 . . . . .143 F1
Thornton Heath CR7 . . .187 G5
Kingswood Cl, N20 . . . . . . .41 F6
SW8 . . . . .131 E7
Enfield EN1 . . . . .44 B5
New Malden KT3 . . . . . .183 F6
Orpington BR6 . . . . .193 G7
Surbiton KT6 . . . . .181 H7
Kingswood Ct, SE13
off Hither Grn La 154 D6
Kingswood Dr, SE19 . . . . .170 B4
Carshalton SM5 . . . . . . .199 J1
Kingswood Est, SE21 . . . .170 B4
Kingswood Ms, N15
off Harringay Rd 75 H5
Kingswood Pk, N3 . . . . .72 C2
Kingswood Pl, SE13 . . . . . .155 E4
Kingswood Rd, E11 . . . . . . .79 E7
SE20 . . . . .171 F6
SW2 . . . . .150 E6
SW19 . . . . .166 C7
W4 . . . . .126 C3
Bromley BR2 . . . . .190 D4
Ilford IG3 . . . . .100 A1
Wembley HA9 . . . . .88 A3
Kingswood Ter, W4
off Kingswood Rd 126 C3
Kingswood Way, Wall.
SM6 . . . . .201 E5
Kingsworth Cl, Beck.
BR3 . . . . .189 H5
Kingsworthy Cl, Kings.T.
KT1 . . . . .181 J3
King's Yd, SW15
off Stanbridge Rd 147 J3
Kingthorpe Rd, NW10 . . . . .88 D7
Kingthorpe Ter, NW10 . . . . .88 D6
Kingweston Cl, NW2
off Windmill Dr 90 B3
King William IV Gdns, SE20
off St. John's Rd 171 F6
King William La, SE10
off Trafalgar Rd 134 E5
King William St, EC4 . . . . . .20 C6
King William Wk, SE10 . . .134 C6
Kingwood Rd, SW6 . . . . . .148 A1
Kinlet Rd, SE18 . . . . .157 F1
Kinloch Dr, NW9 . . . . .70 E7
Kinloch St, N7
off Hornsey Rd 93 F3
Kinloss Ct, N3
off Kinloss Gdns 72 C4
Kinloss Gdns, N3 . . . . .72 C4
Kinloss Rd, Cars. SM5 . . . .185 F7
Kinnaird Av, W4 . . . . .126 C7
Bromley BR1 . . . . .173 F6
Kinnaird Cl, Brom.
BR1 . . . . .173 F6
Kinnaird Ho, N6 . . . . .74 D7
Kinnaird Way, Wdf.Grn.
IG8 . . . . .64 C6
Kinnear Rd, W12 . . . . .127 F2
Kinnerton Pl N, SW1 . . . . . .24 A4
Kinnerton Pl S, SW1 . . . . . .24 A4
Kinnerton St, SW1 . . . . .24 B4
Kinnerton Yd, SW1 . . . . .24 A4
Kinnoul Rd, W6 . . . . .128 B6
Kinross Av, Wor.Pk.
KT4 . . . . .197 G2
Kinross Cl, Edg. HA8 . . . . . .54 B2
Harrow HA3 . . . . .69 J5
Kinross Ter, E17 . . . . .77 J2
Kinsale Rd, SE15 . . . . .152 D3
Kinsella Gdns, SW19 . . . . .165 H5
Kinsey Ho, SE21
off Kingswood Est 170 B4
Kintore Way, SE1 . . . . .37 F1
Kintyre Cl, SW16 . . . . .187 F2
Kinveachy Gdns, SE7 . . . . .136 B5
Kinver Rd, SE26 . . . . .171 F4
Kipling Dr, SW19 . . . . .167 G6
Kipling Est, SE1 . . . . .28 C4
Kipling Pl, Stan. HA7 . . . . . .52 C6
Kipling Rd, Bexh. DA7 . . . .159 E1
Kipling St, SE1 . . . . .28 C4
Kipling Ter, N9 . . . . .60 A3
Kipling Twr, W3 . . . . .126 C3
Kippington Dr, SE9 . . . . . .174 A1
Kirby Cl, Epsom KT19 . . . .197 F5
Ilford IG6 . . . . .65 H6
Loughton IG10 . . . . .48 B7
Kirby Est, SE16 . . . . .132 E3
Kirby Gro, SE1 . . . . .28 D3
Kirby St, EC1 . . . . .19 F1
Kirby Way, Walt. KT12 . . . .178 C6
Kirchen Rd, W13 . . . . .104 E7
Kirkby Cl, N11
off Coverdale Rd 58 A6
Kirkcaldy Grn, Wat. WD19
off Trevose Way 50 C3
Kirkdale, SE26 . . . . .170 E2
Kirkdale Rd, E11 . . . . .97 E1
Kirkfield Cl, W13
off Broomfield Rd 125 E1
Kirkham Rd, E6 . . . . .116 B6
Kirkham St, SE18 . . . . .137 H6
Kirkland Av, Ilf. IG5 . . . . . . .80 D2
Kirkland Cl, Sid. DA15 . . . .157 H6
Kirkland Dr, Enf. EN2 . . . . . .43 H1
Kirkland Wk, E8 . . . . .94 C6
Kirk La, SE18 . . . . .137 F6
Kirkleas Rd, Surb. KT6 . . . .195 H1
Kirklees Rd, Dagenham
RM8 . . . . .100 C5
Thornton Heath CR7 . . .187 G5
Kirkley Rd, SW19 . . . . .184 D1
Kirkman Pl, W1 . . . . .17 H2
Kirkmichael Rd, E14
off Dee St 114 C6
Kirk Ri, Sutt. SM1 . . . . .199 E3
Kirk Rd, E17 . . . . .77 J6
Kirkside Rd, SE3 . . . . .135 G6
Kirkstall Av, N17 . . . . .76 A4
Kirkstall Gdns, SW2 . . . . . .168 D1
Kirkstall Rd, SW2 . . . . .168 D1
Kirkstead Ct, E5
off Mandeville St 95 H4
Kirksted Rd, Mord. SM4 . .198 E1
Kirkstone Lo, Islw. TW7
off Summerwood Rd .144 C5
Kirkstone Way, Brom.
BR1 . . . . .173 E7
Kirk St, WC1 . . . . .10 C6
Kirkton Rd, N15 . . . . .76 B4
Kirkwall Pl, E2 . . . . .113 F3
Kirkwood Rd, SE15 . . . . . .153 E2
Kirn Rd, W13
off Kirchen Rd 104 E7
Kirrane Cl, N.Mal. KT3 . . . .183 F5
Kirtley Rd, SE26 . . . . .171 H4
Kirtling St, SW8 . . . . .33 F7
Kirton Cl, W4 . . . . .126 D4
Kirton Gdns, E2 . . . . .13 G4
Kirton Rd, E13 . . . . .115 J2
Kirton Wk, Edg. HA8 . . . . . .54 C7
Kirwyn Way, SE5 . . . . .35 H7
Kitcat Ter, E3 . . . . .114 A3
Kitchen Ct, E10
off Brisbane Rd 96 B2
Kitchener Rd, E7 . . . . .97 H6
E17 . . . . .78 B1
N2 . . . . .73 H3
N17 . . . . .76 A3
Dagenham RM10 . . . . . .101 H6
Thornton Heath CR7 . . .188 A3
Kite Pl, E2 . . . . .13 J3
Kite Yd, SW11
off Cambridge Rd 149 J1
Kitley Gdns, SE19 . . . . . . .188 C1
Kitson Rd, SE5 . . . . .36 A7
SW13 . . . . .147 G1
Kittiwake Pl, Sutt. SM1
off Sandpiper Rd 198 C5
Kittiwake Rd, Nthlt. UB5 . .102 D3
Kittiwake Way, Hayes
UB4 . . . . .102 D5
Kitto Rd, SE14 . . . . .153 G2
Kiver Rd, N19 . . . . .92 D2
Klea Av, SW4 . . . . .150 C6
Kleine Wf, N1
off Orsman Rd 112 B1
Knapdale Cl, SE23 . . . . . . .171 E2
Knapmill Rd, SE6 . . . . .172 A2
Knapmill Way, SE6 . . . . . . .172 B2
Knapp Cl, NW10 . . . . .89 E6
Knapp Rd, E3 . . . . .114 A4
Knapton Ms, SW17
off Seely Rd 168 A6
Knaresborough Dr,
SW18 . . . . .166 E1
Knaresborough Pl, SW5 . . .30 A1
Knatchbull Rd, NW10 . . . . .106 D1
SE5 . . . . .151 J1
Knebworth Av, E17 . . . . . . .78 A1
Knebworth Cl, Barn. EN5 . .41 E4
Knebworth Path, Borwd.
WD6 . . . . .38 D4
Knebworth Rd, N16
off Nevill Rd 94 B4
Knee Hill, SE2 . . . . .138 C4
Knee Hill Cres, SE2 . . . . . .138 C4
Kneller Gdns, Islw. TW7 . . .144 A5
Kneller Rd, SE4 . . . . .153 H4
New Malden KT3 . . . . . .182 E7
Twickenham TW2 . . . . . .143 J6
Knevett Ter, Hounslow
TW3 . . . . .143 G4
Knight Cl, Dagenham
RM8 . . . . .100 C2
Knight Ct, E4
off The Ridgeway 62 C1
Knighten St, E1 . . . . .132 E1
Knighthead Pt, E14 . . . . . .134 A3
Knightland Rd, E5 . . . . .94 E2
Knighton Cl, S.Croy. CR2 .201 H7
Woodford Green IG8 . . . .63 H4
Knighton Dr, Wdf.Grn. IG8 .63 G4
Knighton Grn, Buck.H. IG9
off High Rd 63 H2
Knighton La, Buck.H. IG9 . .63 H2
Knighton Pk Rd, SE26 . . . .171 G5
Knighton Rd, E7 . . . . .97 G3
Romford RM7 . . . . .83 J6
Knightrider Ct, EC4
off Knightrider St 19 J5
Knightrider St, EC4 . . . . . . .19 J5
Knights Arc, SW1 . . . . .23 J4
Knights Av, W5 . . . . .125 H2
Knightsbridge, SW1 . . . . . . .24 A4
SW7 . . . . .23 H4
**Knightsbridge Apts,
The**, SW7
off Knightsbridge 23 J4
Knightsbridge Grn, SW1 . . .23 J4

Knights Cl, E9
off *Churchill Wk* 95 F5
West Molesey KT8 179 F5
Knights Ct, Kings.T. KT1 181 H3
Romford RM6 83 E6
Knights Hill, SE27 169 H5
Knights Hill Sq, SE27 169 H4
Knights Ms, Sutt. SM2
off *York Rd* 198 D7
Knights Pk, Kings.T. KT1 181 H3
Knight's Pl, Twick. TW2
off *May Rd* 162 B1
Knights Rd, E16 135 G2
Stanmore HA7 53 F4
Knights Wk, SE11 35 G2
Knights Way, Ilf. IG6 65 F6
Knightswood Cl, Edg. HA8 54 C2
Knightwood Cres, N.Mal. KT3 182 E6
Knivet Rd, SW6 128 D6
Knobs Hill Rd, E15 114 B1
Knockholt Rd, SE9 156 A5
Knole, The, SE9 174 D4
Knole Cl, Croy. CR0 189 F6
Knole Gate, Sid. DA15
off *Woodside Cres* 175 H3
Knoll, The, W13 105 F5
Beckenham BR3 190 B1
Bromley BR2 205 G2
Knoll Ct, SE19 170 B5
Knoll Dr, N14 42 A7
Knollmead, Surb. KT5 196 C1
Knoll Ri, Orp. BR6 207 J1
Knoll Rd, SW18 149 F5
Bexley DA5 159 G7
Sidcup DA14 176 B5
Knolls Cl, Wor.Pk. KT4 197 H3
Knollys Cl, SW16 169 G3
Knollys Rd, SW16 169 G3
Knottisford St, E2 113 F3
Knotts Grn Ms, E10 78 B6
Knotts Grn Rd, E10 78 B6
Knowle Av, Bexh. DA7 139 E7
Knowle Cl, SW9 151 G3
Knowle Rd, Brom. BR2 206 B2
Twickenham TW2 162 B1
Knowles Cl, West Dr. UB7 120 B1
Knowles Hill Cres, SE13 154 D5
Knowles Ho, SW18
off *Neville Gill Cl* 148 E6
Knowles Wk, SW4 150 C3
Knowlton Grn, Brom. BR2 191 F5
Knowsley Av, Sthl. UB1 123 G1
Knowsley Rd, SW11 149 J2
Knox Rd, E7 97 F6
Knox St, W1 15 J1
Knoyle St, SE14 133 H6
Kohat Rd, SW19 167 E5
Kossuth St, SE10 134 E5
Kotree Way, SE1 37 J2
Kramer Ms, SW5
off *Kempsford Gdns* 128 D5
Kreedman Wk, E8 94 D5
Kreisel Wk, Rich. TW9 125 J6
Kuala Gdns, SW16 187 F1
Kuhn Way, E7
off *Forest La* 97 G5
Kwesi Ms, SE27 169 G5
Kydbrook Cl, Orp. BR5 193 F7
Kylemore Cl, E6
off *Parr Rd* 116 A2
Kylemore Rd, NW6 90 D7
Kymberley Rd, Harrow HA1 68 B6
Kynance Gdns, Stan. HA7 69 F1
Kynance Ms, SW7 22 C6
Kynance Pl, SW7 22 C6
Kynaston Av, N16
off *Dynevor Rd* 94 C3
Thornton Heath CR7 187 J5
Kynaston Cl, Har. HA3 52 A7
Kynaston Cres, Th.Hth. CR7 187 J5
Kynaston Rd, N16 94 B3
Bromley BR1 173 G5
Enfield EN2 44 A1
Thornton Heath CR7 187 J5
Kynaston Wd, Har. HA3 52 A7
Kynersley Cl, Cars. SM5
off *William St* 199 J3
Kynoch Rd, N18 61 F4
Kyrle Rd, SW11 150 A5
Kyverdale Rd, N16 94 C2

L

Laburnum Av, N9 60 B2
N17 60 A7
Sutton SM1 199 H3
Laburnum Cl, E4 61 J6
N11 58 A6
SE15 off *Clifton Way* 133 F7
Wembley HA0 88 A7
Laburnum Ct, E2 112 C1
Stanmore HA7 53 F4
Laburnum Cres, Sun. TW16
off *Batavia Rd* 178 B1
Laburnum Gdns, N21 59 J2
Croydon CR0 189 G7
Laburnum Gro, N21 59 J2
NW9 70 C7
Hounslow TW3 143 F4
New Malden KT3 182 D2
Southall UB1 103 F4
Laburnum Ho, Dag. RM10
off *Bradwell Av* 101 G2
Laburnum Rd, SW19 167 F7
Hayes UB3 121 J4
Mitcham CR4 186 A2
Laburnum St, E2 112 C1
Laburnum Way, Brom. BR2 192 D7
Lacebark Cl, Sid. DA15 157 J7
Lacewing Cl, E13
off *Sewell St* 115 G3
Lacey Cl, N9 60 D2
Lacey Dr, Dag. RM8 100 B4
Edgware HA8 53 H4
Hampton TW12 179 F1
Lacey Ms, E3 114 A2
Lackington St, EC2 20 C1
Lacock Cl, SW19 167 F6
Lacock Ct, W13
off *Singapore Rd* 124 D1
Lacon Rd, SE22 152 D4
Lacrosse Way, SW16 186 D1
Lacy Rd, SW15 148 A4
Ladas Rd, SE27 169 J4
Ladbroke Cres, W11
off *Ladbroke Gro* 108 B6
Ladbroke Gdns, W11 108 C7
Ladbroke Gro, W10 108 A4
W11 108 B6
Ladbroke Ms, W11
off *Ladbroke Rd* 128 B1
Ladbroke Rd, W11 128 C1
Enfield EN1 44 C6
Ladbroke Sq, W11 108 C7
Ladbroke Ter, W11 108 C7
Ladbroke Wk, W11 128 C1
Ladbrook Cl, Pnr. HA5 67 F5
Ladbrooke Cres, Sid. DA14 176 D3
Ladbrook Rd, SE25 188 A3
Ladderstile Ride, Kings.T. KT2 164 B5
Ladderswood Way, N11 58 C5
Ladlands, SE22 152 D7
Lady Aylesford Av, Stan. HA7 52 E5
Lady Booth Rd, Kings.T. KT1 181 H2
Ladycroft Gdns, Orp. BR6 207 F5
Ladycroft Rd, SE13 154 B3
Ladycroft Wk, Stan. HA7 69 G1
Ladycroft Way, Orp. BR6 207 F5
Lady Dock Path, SE16
off *Salter Rd* 133 H2
Ladyfield Cl, Loug. IG10 49 E4
Ladyfields, Loug. IG10 49 E4
Lady Hay, Wor.Pk. KT4 197 F2
Lady Margaret Rd, N19 92 C4
NW5 92 C5
Southall UB1 103 F5
Ladysmith Av, E6 116 B2
Ilford IG2 81 G7
Ladysmith Cl, NW7 55 G7
Ladysmith Rd, E16 115 F3
N17 76 D2
N18 61 E5
SE9 156 D6
Enfield EN1 44 B3
Harrow HA3 68 B2
Lady Somerset Rd, NW5 92 B4
LADYWELL, SE13 154 A5
Ladywell Cl, SE4
off *Adelaide Av* 154 A4
Ladywell Hts, SE4 153 J6
Ladywell Rd, SE13 154 A5
Ladywell St, E15
off *Plaistow Gro* 115 F1
Ladywood Av, Orp. BR5 193 H5
Ladywood Rd, Surb. KT6 196 A2
Lafone Av, Felt. TW13
off *Alfred Rd* 160 C1
Lafone St, SE1 29 F3
Lagado Ms, SE16 133 G1
Lagonda Av, Ilf. IG6 65 J6
Laidlaw Dr, N21 43 F4
Laing Cl, Ilf. IG6 65 G6
Laing Dean, Nthlt. UB5 102 C1
Laing Ho, SE5
off *Comber Gro* 131 J7
Laings Av, Mitch. CR4 185 J2
Lainlock Pl, Hounslow TW3 143 H1
Lainson St, SW18 148 D7
Lairdale Cl, SE21 169 J1
Laird Ho, SE5 131 J7
Lairs Cl, N7
off *Manger Rd* 93 E6
Lait Ho, Beck. BR3 190 A1
Laitwood Rd, SW12 168 B1
Lakanal, SE5
off *Sceaux Gdns* 152 B1
Lake, The, Bushey (Bushey Hth) WD23 51 J1
Lake Av, Brom. BR1 173 G6
Lake Business Cen, N17
off *Tariff Rd* 60 D7
Lake Cl, SW19
off *Lake Rd* 166 C5
Dagenham RM8 100 C3
Lakedale Rd, SE18 137 H6
Lake Dr, Bushey (Bushey Hth) WD23 51 J2
Lakefield Cl, SE20
off *Limes Av* 171 E7
Lakefield Rd, N22 75 H2
Lake Gdns, Dag. RM10 101 G5
Richmond TW10 163 E2
Wallington SM6 200 B3
Lakehall Gdns, Th.Hth. CR7 187 H5
Lakehall Rd, Th.Hth. CR7 187 H5
Lake Ho Rd, E11 97 G3
Lakehurst Rd, Epsom KT19 196 E5
Lakeland Cl, Har. HA3 52 A6
Lakenheath, N14 42 D6
Lake Rd, E10 78 B7
SW19 166 C5
Croydon CR0 203 J2
Romford RM6 82 D4
Laker Pl, SW15 148 B6
Lakeside, W13
off *Edgehill Rd* 105 F6
Beckenham BR3 190 B3
Enfield EN2 42 D4
Wallington SM6
off *Derek Av* 200 B3
Lakeside Av, SE28 138 A1
Ilford IG4 80 A4
Lakeside Cl, SE25 188 D2
Chigwell IG7 65 J4
Sidcup DA15 158 C5
Lakeside Ct, N4 93 H2
Borehamwood (Els.) WD6 38 A5
Lakeside Cres, Barn. EN4 41 J5
Lakeside Dr, NW10 105 J3
Bromley BR2 206 B3
Lakeside Rd, N13 59 F4
W14 128 A3
Lakeside Way, Wem. HA9 87 J4
Lakes Rd, Kes. BR2 205 J5
Lakeswood Rd, Orp. BR5 193 E6
Lake Vw, Edg. HA8 53 J5
Lakeview Ct, SW19
off *Victoria Dr* 166 B2
Lakeview Est, E3
off *Old Ford Rd* 113 G2
Lakeview Rd, SE27 169 G5
Welling DA16 158 B4
Lakis Cl, NW3
off *Flask Wk* 91 F4
Laleham Av, NW7 54 D3
Laleham Rd, SE6 154 C6
Lalor St, SW6 148 B2
Lambarde Av, SE9 174 D4
Lamb Cl, Nthlt. UB5 103 E3
Lamberhurst Rd, SE27 169 G4
Dagenham RM8 101 F1
Lambert Av, Rich. TW9 146 B3
Lambert Jones Ms, EC2
off *The Barbican* 19 J1
Lambert Rd, E16 115 H6
N12 57 F5
SW2 151 E5
Lamberts Pl, Croy. CR0 202 A1
Lamberts Rd, Surb. KT5 181 H5
Lambert St, N1 93 G7
Lambert Wk, Wem. HA9 87 G3
Lambert Way, N12 57 F5
LAMBETH, SE1 26 C5
Lambeth Br, SE1 34 B1
SW1 34 B1
Lambeth High St, SE1 34 C2
Lambeth Hill, EC4 19 J5
★ **Lambeth Palace**, SE1 26 C6
Lambeth Palace Rd, SE1 26 C6
Lambeth Pier, SE1 26 B6
Lambeth Rd, SE1 26 D6
SE11 26 D6
Croydon CR0 187 G7
Lambeth Twrs, SE11 27 E6
Lambeth Wk, SE1 34 D1
SE11 34 D1
Lambfold Ho, N7
off *York Way* 92 E6
Lambkins Ms, E17 78 C4
Lamb La, E8 94 E7
Lamble St, NW5 92 A5
Lambley Rd, Dagenham RM9 100 B6
Lambolle Pl, NW3 91 H6
Lambolle Rd, NW3 91 H6
Lambourn Cl, W7 124 C2
Lambourne Av, SW19 166 C4
Lambourne Ct, Wdf.Grn. IG8
off *Navestock Cres* 63 J7
Lambourne Gdns, E4 62 A2
Barking IG11 99 J7
Enfield EN1 44 C2
Lambourne Gro, SE16 133 G4
Lambourne Pl, SE3
off *Shooters Hill Rd* 155 H1
Lambourne Rd, E11 78 C7
Barking IG11 99 H7
Chigwell IG7 65 H4
Ilford IG3 99 H2
Lambourn Gro, Kings.T. KT1 182 B2
Lambourn Rd, SW4 150 B3
Lambrook Ter, SW6 148 B1
Lamb's Bldgs, EC1 12 B6
Lambs Cl, N9
off *Winchester Rd* 60 D2
Lambs Conduit Pas, WC1 18 C1
Lamb's Conduit St, WC1 10 C6
Lambscroft Av, SE9 173 J3
Lambs Meadow, Wdf.Grn. IG8 80 A2
Lambs Ms, N1
off *Colebrooke Row* 111 H1
Lamb's Pas, EC1 20 B1
Lambs Ter, N9 60 A2
Lamb St, E1 21 F1
Lambs Wk, Enf. EN2 43 J2
Lambton Ms, N19
off *Lambton Rd* 92 E1
Lambton Pl, W11
off *Westbourne Gro* 108 C6
Lambton Rd, N19 92 E1
SW20 183 J1
Lamb Wk, SE1 28 D4
Lamerock Rd, Brom. BR1 173 F4
Lamerton Rd, Ilf. IG6 81 E2
Lamerton St, SE8 134 A6
Lamford Cl, N17 60 A7
Lamington St, W6 127 H4
Lamlash St, SE11 35 G1
Lammas Av, Mitch. CR4 186 A2
Lammas Grn, SE26 170 E3
Lammas Pk, W5 125 F2
Lammas Pk Gdns, W5 125 F2
Lammas Pk Rd, W5 125 F1
Lammas Rd, E9 95 G7
E10 95 H2
Richmond TW10 163 F4
Lammermoor Rd, SW12 150 B7
Lamont Rd, SW10 30 D6
Lamont Rd Pas, SW10
off *Lamont Rd* 30 E6
LAMORBEY, Sid. DA15 175 J1
Lamorbey Cl, Sid. DA15 175 J1
Lamorna Cl, E17 78 C2
Lamorna Gro, Stan. HA7 69 G1
Lampard Gro, N16 94 C1
Lampern Sq, E2 13 J3
Lampeter Cl, NW9 70 E6
Lampeter Sq, W6
off *Humbolt Rd* 128 B6
Lamplighter Cl, E1
off *Cleveland Way* 113 F4
Lampmead Rd, SE12 155 E5
Lamp Office Ct, WC1 10 C6
Lamport Cl, SE18 136 C4
LAMPTON, Houns. TW3 143 H1
Lampton Av, Houns. TW3 143 H1
Lampton Ho Cl, SW19 166 A4
Lampton Pk Rd, Houns. TW3 143 H2
Lampton Rd, Houns. TW3 143 H2
Lanacre Av, NW9 71 F1
Lanadron Cl, Islw. TW7
off *London Rd* 144 C2
Lanark Cl, W5 105 F5
Lanark Ms, W9 6 C4
Lanark Pl, W9 6 D5
Lanark Rd, W9 6 C4
Lanark Sq, E14 134 B3
Lanata Wk, Hayes UB4
off *Ramulis Dr* 102 D4
Lanbury Rd, SE15 153 G4
Lancashire Ct, W1 16 E5
Lancaster Av, E18 79 H4
SE27 169 H2
SW19 166 A5
Barking IG11 99 H7
Mitcham CR4 186 E5
Lancaster Cl, N1
off *Hertford Rd* 94 B7
N17 60 D7
NW9 55 F7
Bromley BR2 191 F4
Kingston upon Thames KT2 163 G5
Staines (Stanw.) TW19 140 B6
Lancaster Cotts, Rich. TW10 off *Lancaster Pk* 145 H6

Lancaster Ct, SE27 169 H2
SW6 128 C7
W2 14 D6
Walton-on-Thames KT12 178 A7
Lancaster Dr, E14
off Prestons Rd 134 C1
NW3 91 H6
Loughton IG10 48 B6
Lancaster Gdns, SW19 166 B5
W13 125 E2
Bromley BR1 192 B5
Kingston upon Thames KT2 163 G5
Lancaster Gate, W2 14 D6
Lancaster Gro, NW3 91 G6
★ **Lancaster Ho**, SW1 25 F3
Lancaster Ho, Islw. TW7 124 C7
Lancaster Ms, SW18
off East Hill 149 E5
W2 14 D5
Richmond TW10
off Richmond Hill 145 H6
Lancaster Pk, Rich. TW10 145 H5
Lancaster Pl, SW19 166 A5
WC2 18 C5
Hounslow TW4 142 C2
Ilford IG1
off Staines Rd 99 F4
Twickenham TW1 144 D6
Lancaster Rd, E7 97 G7
E11 97 E2
E17 77 G2
N4 75 G7
N11 58 D6
N18 60 C5
NW10 89 F5
SE25 188 C2
SW19 166 A5
W11 108 B6
Barnet EN4 41 G5
Enfield EN2 44 A1
Harrow HA2 67 G5
Northolt UB5 85 J6
Southall UB1 103 E7
Lancaster St, SE1 27 H4
Lancaster Ter, W2 15 E5
Lancaster Wk, W2 22 E3
Lancaster Way, Wor.Pk. KT4 183 H7
Lancaster W, W11
off Grenfell Rd 108 A7
Lancastrian Rd, Wall. SM6 201 E7
Lancefield St, W10 108 C3
Lancell St, N16
off Stoke Newington Ch St 94 B2
Lancelot Av, Wem. HA0 87 G4
Lancelot Cres, Wembley HA0 87 G4
Lancelot Gdns, Barn. (E.Barn.) EN4 42 A7
Lancelot Pl, SW7 23 J4
Lancelot Rd, Ilf. IG6 65 H6
Welling DA16 158 A4
Wembley HA0 87 G5
Lance Rd, Har. HA1 67 J7
Lancer Sq, W8 22 A3
Lancey Cl, SE7
off Cleveley Cl 136 A4
Lanchester Rd, N6 73 J5
Lanchester Way, SE14 153 F1
Lancing Gdns, N9 60 C1
Lancing Rd, W13
off Drayton Grn Rd 104 E7
Croydon CR0 187 F6
Ilford IG2 81 G6
Lancing St, NW1 9 H4
Lancresse Ct, N1 112 B1
Landcroft Rd, SE22 152 C6
Landells Rd, SE22 152 C6
Landford Rd, SW15 147 J3
Landgrove Rd, SW19 166 D5
Landmann Ho, SE16 133 E4
Landmann Way, SE14 133 G6
Landmark Commercial Cen, N18 60 B6
Landmark Hts, E5 95 H4
Landon Pl, SW1 23 J5
Landons Cl, E14 134 C1
Landon Wk, E14
off Cottage St 114 B7
Landor Rd, SW9 150 E3
Landor Wk, W12 127 G2
Landra Gdns, N21 43 H6
Landridge Rd, SW6 148 C2
Landrock Rd, N8 75 E6
Landscape Rd, Wdf.Grn. IG8 63 H7
Landsdown Cl, Barn. (New Barn.) EN5 41 F4
Landseer Av, E12 98 D5
Landseer Cl, SW19
off Thorburn Way 185 G1
Edgware HA8 70 A2
Landseer Rd, N19 92 E3
Enfield EN1 44 D5
New Malden KT3 182 D7
Sutton SM1 198 D6
Landstead Rd, SE18 137 G7
Lane, The, NW8 6 C1
SE3 155 G3
Lane Cl, NW2 89 H3
Lane End, Bexh. DA7 159 H3
Lane Gdns, Esher (Clay.) KT10 194 C7
Lane Ms, E12
off Colchester Av 98 C3
Lanercost Cl, SW2 169 G2
Lanercost Gdns, N14 42 E7
Lanercost Rd, SW2 169 G2
Lanesborough Pl, SW1 24 C3
Laneside, Chis. BR7 175 E5
Edgware HA8 54 C5
Laneside Av, Dag. RM8 83 F7
Laneway, SW15 147 H5
Lanfranc Rd, E3 113 H2
Lanfrey Pl, W14
off North End Rd 128 C5
Langbourne Av, N6 92 A2
Langbourne Pl, E14 134 B5
Langbourne Way, Esher (Clay.) KT10 194 D6
Langbrook Rd, SE3 156 A3
Langcroft Cl, Cars. SM5 199 J3
Langdale, NW1 9 F3
Langdale Av, Mitch. CR4 185 J3
Langdale Cl, SE17 35 J5
SW14 146 B4
Dagenham RM8 100 C1
Orpington BR6
off Grasmere Rd 206 E3
Langdale Cres, Bexh. DA7 139 G7
Langdale Gdns, Grnf. (Perivale) UB6 105 E3
Langdale Rd, SE10 134 C7
Thornton Heath CR7 187 G4
Langdale St, E1
off Burslem St 112 E6
Langdon Ct, NW10 106 E1
Langdon Cres, E6 116 D2
Langdon Dr, NW9 88 C1
Langdon Pk, Tedd. TW11 163 F7
Langdon Pk Rd, N6 74 C7
Langdon Pl, SW14 146 C3
Langdon Rd, E6 116 D1
Bromley BR2 191 H3
Morden SM4 185 F5
Langdons Ct, Sthl. UB2 123 G3
Langdon Shaw, Sid. DA14 175 J5
Langdon Wk, Mord. SM4 185 F5
Langdon Way, SE1 37 J2
Langford Cl, E8 94 D5
N15 76 B6
NW8 6 D1
W3 126 B2
Langford Ct, NW8 6 C2
Langford Cres, Barn. (Cockfos.) EN4 41 J4
Langford Grn, SE5 152 B3
Langford Ms, N1
off Liverpool Rd 93 G7
SW11
off Plough Rd 149 G4
Langford Pl, NW8 6 D2
Sidcup DA14 176 A3
Langford Rd, SW6 149 E2
Barnet (Cockfos.) EN4 41 H4
Woodford Green IG8 63 J6
Langfords, Buck.H. IG9 64 A2
Langham Cl, N15
off Langham Rd 75 H3
Kes. BR2 206 B2
Langham Dr, Rom. RM6 82 B6
Langham Gdns, N21 43 G5
W13 105 E7
Edgware HA8 54 C7
Richmond TW10 163 F4
Wembley HA0 87 F2
Langham Ho Cl, Rich. TW10 163 G4
Langham Pk Pl, Brom. BR2 191 F4
Langham Pl, N15 75 H3
W1 16 E2
W4 *off Hogarth Rbt* 127 E6
Langham Rd, N15 75 H3
SW20 183 J1
Edgware HA8 54 C6
Teddington TW11 162 E5
Langham St, W1 17 E2
Langhedge Cl, N18 60 C6
Langhedge La, N18 60 C5
Langhedge La Ind Est, N18 60 C6
Langholm Cl, SW12
off King's Av 150 D7
Langholme, Bushey WD23 51 J1
Langhorn Dr, Twick. TW2 144 B7
Langhorne Ho, SE7
off Springfield Gro 135 J6
Langhorne Rd, Dag. RM10 101 G7
Langland Cres, Stan. HA7 69 H3
Langland Dr, Pnr. HA5 50 E7
Langland Gdns, NW3 91 E5
Croydon CR0 203 J2
Langler Rd, NW10 107 J2
Langley Av, Ruis. HA4 84 B1
Surbiton KT6 195 G1
Worcester Park KT4 198 A2
Langley Ct, WC2 18 A5
Beckenham BR3 190 B5
Langley Cres, E11 79 J7
Dagenham RM9 100 C7
Edgware HA8 54 C3
Hayes UB3 121 J7
Langley Dr, E11 79 H7
W3 126 B1
Langley Gdns, Brom. BR2
off Great Elms Rd 191 J4
Dagenham RM9 100 C7
Orpington BR5 193 E6
Langley Gro, N.Mal. KT3 182 E2
Langley La, SW8 34 B5
Langley Meadow, Loug. IG10 49 G2
Langley Pk, NW7 54 E6
Langley Pk Rd, Sutt. SM1, SM2 199 F5
Langley Rd, SW19 184 C1
Beckenham BR3 189 H4
Isleworth TW7 144 C2
Surbiton KT6 181 H7
Welling DA16 138 C6
Langley Row, Barn. EN5 40 C1
Langley St, WC2 18 A4
Langley Way, W.Wick. BR4 204 D1
Langmead Dr, Bushey (Bushey Hth) WD23 52 A1
Langmead St, SE27
off Beadman St 169 H4
Langmore Ct, Bexh. DA6
off Regency Way 158 D3
Langridge Ms, Hmptn. TW12 *off Oak Av* 161 F6
Langroyd Rd, SW17 167 J2
Langside Av, SW15 147 G4
Langside Cres, N14 58 D3
Langstone Way, NW7 56 A7
Langston Hughes Cl, SE24
off Shakespeare Rd 151 H4
Langston Rd, Loug. IG10 49 F5
Lang St, E1 113 F4
Langthorn Ct, EC2 20 B3
Langthorne Ct, Brom. BR1 172 C4
Langthorne Rd, E11 96 D3
Langthorne St, SW6 128 A7
Langton Av, E6 116 D3
N20 41 F7
Langton Cl, WC1 10 D4
Langton Ho, SW16
off Colson Way 168 C4
Langton Pl, SW18
off Merton Rd 166 D1
Langton Ri, SE23 152 E7
Langton Rd, NW2 89 J3
SW9 131 H7
Harrow HA3 51 J7
West Molesey KT8 179 J4
Langton St, SW10 30 D6
Langton Way, SE3 155 F1
Croydon CR0 202 B4
Langtry Pl, SW6
off Seagrave Rd 128 D6
Langtry Rd, NW8 108 E1
Northolt UB5 102 D2
Langtry Wk, NW8
off Alexandra Pl 109 F1
Langwood Chase, Tedd. TW11 163 F6
Langworth Dr, Hayes UB4 102 A6
Lanherne Ho, SW20 166 A7
Lanhill Rd, W9 108 D4
Lanier Rd, SE13 154 C6
Lanigan Dr, Houns. TW3 143 H5
Lankaster Gdns, N2 73 G1
Lankers Dr, Har. HA2 67 F6
Lankton Cl, Beck. BR3 190 C1
Lannock Rd, Hayes UB3 121 H1
Lannoy Pt, SW6
off Pellant Rd 128 B7
Lannoy Rd, SE9 175 F1
Lanrick Rd, E14 114 D6
Lanridge Rd, SE2 138 D3
Lansbury Av, N18 60 A5
Barking IG11 100 A7
Feltham TW14 142 B6
Romford RM6 83 E5
Lansbury Cl, NW10 88 C5
Lansbury Est, E14 114 B6
Lansbury Gdns, E14 114 D6
Lansbury Rd, Enf. EN3 45 G1
Lansbury Way, N18 60 B5
Lanscombe Wk, SW8 150 E1
Lansdell Rd, Mitch. CR4 186 A2
Lansdowne Av, Bexh. DA7 138 D7
Orpington BR6 207 E1
Lansdowne Cl, SW20 166 A7
Surbiton KT5 196 B2
Twickenham TW1
off Lion Rd 162 C1
Lansdowne Copse, Wor.Pk. KT4 197 G2
Lansdowne Ct, Wor.Pk. KT4 197 G2
Lansdowne Cres, W11 108 B7
Lansdowne Dr, E8 94 D6
Lansdowne Gdns, SW8 150 E1
Lansdowne Grn, SW8
off Hartington Rd 150 E1
Lansdowne Gro, NW10 89 E4
Lansdowne Hill, SE27 169 H3
Lansdowne La, SE7 136 A6
Lansdowne Ms, SE7 136 A5
W11 *off Lansdowne Rd* 128 C1
Lansdowne Pl, SE1 28 C5
SE19 170 C7
Lansdowne Ri, W11 108 B7
Lansdowne Rd, E4 62 A2
E11 97 F2
E17 78 A5
E18 79 G3
N3 56 C7
N10 74 C2
N17 76 C1
SW20 165 J7
W11 108 B7
Bromley BR1 173 G7
Croydon CR0 202 A2
Epsom KT19 196 C7
Harrow HA1 68 B7
Hounslow TW3 143 H3
Ilford IG3 99 J1
Stanmore HA7 53 F6
Lansdowne Row, W1 24 E1
Lansdowne Ter, WC1 10 B6
Lansdowne Wk, W11 128 B1
Lansdowne Way, SW8 150 D1
Lansdowne Wd Cl, SE27 169 H3
Lansdown Rd, E7 97 J7
Sidcup DA14 176 B3
Lansfield Av, N18 60 D4
Lantern Cl, SW15 147 G4
Orpington BR6 206 E4
Wembley HA0 87 G5
Lanterns Ct, E14 134 A2
Lantern Way, West Dr. UB7 120 B2
Lant St, SE1 27 J3
Lanvanor Rd, SE15 153 F2
Lapford Cl, W9 108 C4
Lapponum Wk, Hayes UB4
off Lochan Cl 102 D5
Lapse Wd Wk, SE23 170 E2
Lapstone Gdns, Har. HA3 69 F6
Lapwing Ct, Surb. KT6
off Chaffinch Cl 196 A3
Lapwing Ter, E7
off Hampton Rd 98 A5
Lapwing Twr, SE8
off Abinger Gro 133 J6
Lapwing Way, Hayes UB4 102 D6
Lara Cl, SE13 154 C6
Chessington KT9 195 H7
Larbert Rd, SW16 186 C1
Larch Av, W3 126 E1
Larch Cl, E13 115 H4
N11 58 A7
N19 *off Bredgar Rd* 92 C2
SE8 *off Clyde St* 133 J6
SW12 168 B2
Larch Cres, Epsom KT19 196 B6
Hayes UB4 102 C4
Larch Dene, Orp. BR6 206 D2
Larch Dr, W4
off Gunnersbury Av 126 A5
Larches, The, N13 59 J3
Larches Av, SW14 146 D4
Larch Grn, NW9
off Clayton Fld 71 E1
Larch Gro, Sid. DA15 175 J1
Larch Rd, E10
off Walnut Rd 96 A2
NW2 89 J4
Larch Tree Way, Croy. CR0 204 A3
Larch Way, Brom. BR2 192 D7
Larchwood Rd, SE9 175 E2
Larcombe Cl, Croy. CR0 202 C4
Larcom St, SE17 36 A2
Larden Rd, W3 127 E1
Largewood Av, Surb. KT6 196 A2
Larissa St, SE17 36 C3
Larkbere Rd, SE26 171 H4
Larken Cl, Bushey WD23
off Larken Dr 51 J1

Larken Dr, Bushey WD23 **51** J1
Larkfield Av, Har. HA3 **69** E3
Larkfield Cl, Brom. BR2 **205** F2
Larkfield Rd, Rich. TW9 **145** H4
Sidcup DA14 **175** J3
Larkhall La, SW4 **150** D2
Larkhall Ri, SW4 **150** C3
Larkhill Ter, SE18
off Prince Imperial Rd **136** D7
Lark Row, E2 **113** F1
Larksfield Gro, Enf. EN1 **45** E1
Larks Gro, Bark. IG11 **99** H7
Larkshall Ct, Rom. RM7 **83** J2
Larkshall Cres, E4 **62** C4
Larkshall Rd, E4 **62** C5
Larkspur Cl, E6 **116** B5
N17 **60** A7
NW9 **70** B5
Larkspur Gro, Edg. HA8 **54** C4
Larkspur Way, Epsom KT19 **196** C5
Larkswood Ct, E4 **62** D5
Larkswood Leisure Pk, E4
off New Rd **62** C4
Larkswood Ri, Pnr. HA5 **66** C4
Larkswood Rd, E4 **62** A4
Lark Way, Cars. SM5 **185** H7
Larkway Cl, NW9 **70** D4
Larnach Rd, W6 **128** A6
Larner Ct, W12
off Heathstan Rd **107** G6
Larpent Av, SW15 **147** J5
Larwood Cl, Grnf. UB6 **86** A5
Lascelles Av, Har. HA1 **68** A7
Lascelles Cl, E11 **96** D2
Lascotts Rd, N22 **59** F6
Lassa Rd, SE9 **156** B5
Lassell St, SE10 **134** D5
Lasseter Pl, SE3
off Vanbrugh Hill **135** F6
Latchett Rd, E18 **79** H1
Latchingdon Ct, E17 **77** G4
Latchingdon Gdns, Wdf.Grn. IG8 **64** B6
Latchmere Cl, Rich. TW10 **163** H5
Latchmere La, Kings.T. KT2 **163** J6
Latchmere Pas, SW11
off Cabul Rd **149** H2
Latchmere Rd, SW11 **149** J2
Kingston upon Thames KT2 **163** H7
Latchmere St, SW11 **149** J2
Lateward Rd, Brent. TW8 **125** G6
Latham Cl, E6
off Oliver Gdns **116** B6
Twickenham TW1 **144** D7
Latham Ho, E1 **113** G6
Latham Rd, Bexh. DA6 **159** G5
Twickenham TW1 **144** C7
Lathams Way, Croy. CR0 **201** F1
Lathkill Cl, Enf. EN1 **44** D7
Lathom Rd, E6 **98** C7
Latimer, SE17 **36** D4
Latimer Av, E6 **116** C1
Latimer Cl, Pnr. HA5 **66** C1
Worcester Park KT4 **197** H4
Latimer Gdns, Pnr. HA5 **66** C1
Latimer Pl, W10 **107** J6
Latimer Rd, E7 **97** H4
N15 **76** B6
SW19 **166** E6
W10 **107** J6
Barnet EN5 **40** E3
Croydon CR0
off Abbey Rd **201** H3
Teddington TW11 **162** C5
Latitude Ct, E16
off Albert Basin Way **117** F7
Latona Rd, SE15 **37** H6
La Tourne Gdns, Orp. BR6 **207** F3
Lattimer Pl, W4 **127** E6
Latton Cl, Walt. KT12 **179** E7
Latymer Ct, W6 **128** A4
Latymer Rd, N9 **60** C1
Latymer Way, N9 **60** A2
Laubin Cl, Twick. TW1
off St. Margaret's Dr **144** E4
Lauder Cl, Nthlt. UB5 **102** D2
Lauderdale Dr, Rich. TW10 **163** G3
Lauderdale Pl, EC2
off The Barbican **19** J1
Lauderdale Rd, W9 **6** A4
Lauderdale Twr, EC2 **19** J1
Laud St, SE11 **34** C3
Croydon CR0 **201** J3
Laugan Wk, SE17
off East St **36** A3
Laughton Ct, Borwd. WD6
off Banks Rd **38** D2
Laughton Rd, Northolt UB5 **102** D1
Launcelot Rd, Brom. BR1 **173** G4
Launcelot St, SE1 **26** E4
Launceston Gdns, Grnf. (Perivale) UB6 **105** F1
Launceston Pl, W8 **22** C5
Launceston Rd, Grnf. (Perivale) UB6 **105** F1
Launch St, E14 **134** C3
Launders Gate, W3 **126** B2
Laundress La, N16 **94** D3
Laundry La, N1
off Greenman St **111** J1
Laundry Ms, SE23 **153** H7
Laundry Rd, W6 **128** B6
Launton Dr, Bexh. DA6 **158** D4
Laura Cl, E11 **79** J5
Enfield EN1 **44** B5
Lauradale Rd, N2 **73** J4
Laura Pl, E5 **95** F4
Laurel Apts, SE17
off Townsend St **36** D1
Laurel Av, Twick. TW1 **162** C1
Laurel Bk Gdns, SW6
off New Kings Rd **148** C2
Laurel Bk Rd, Enf. EN2 **43** J1
Laurel Bk Vil, W7
off Lower Boston Rd **124** B1
Laurel Cl, N19
off Hargrave Pk **92** C2
SW17 **167** H5
Ilford IG6 **65** F6
Sidcup DA14 **176** A3
Laurel Cres, Croy. CR0 **204** A3
Laurel Dr, N21 **43** G7
Laurel Gdns, E4 **46** B7
NW7 **54** D3
W7 **124** B1
Bromley BR1 **192** B4
Hounslow TW4 **142** E4
Laurel Gro, SE20 **171** E7
SE26 **171** G4
Laurel La, West Dr. UB7 **120** B4
Laurel Manor, Sutt. SM2 **199** F7
Laurel Pk, Har. HA3 **52** C7
Laurel Rd, SW13 **147** G2
SW20 **183** H1
Hampton (Hmptn H.) TW12 **162** A5
Laurels, The, Brom. BR1 **191** H1
Laurel St, E8 **94** C6
Laurel Vw, N12 **56** E3
Laurel Way, E18 **79** F4
N20 **56** D3
Laurence Ms, W12
off Askew Rd **127** G2
Laurence Pountney Hill, EC4 **20** B5
Laurence Pountney La, EC4 **20** B5
Laurie Gro, SE14 **153** H1
Laurie Rd, W7 **104** B5
Laurier Rd, NW5 **92** B3
Croydon CR0 **188** C7
Laurimel Cl, Stan. HA7
off September Way **53** E6
Laurino Pl, Bushey (Bushey Hth) WD23 **51** J2
Lauriston Rd, E9 **113** G1
SW19 **166** A6
Lausanne Rd, N8 **75** G4
SE15 **153** F1
Lavell St, N16 **94** A4
Lavender Av, NW9 **88** C1
Mitcham CR4 **185** H1
Worcester Park KT4 **197** J3
Lavender Cl, E4 **62** A4
SW3 **31** F6
Bromley BR2 **192** B6
Carshalton SM5 **200** A4
Lavender Ct, W.Mol. KT8
off Molesham Way **179** H3
Lavender Gdns, SW11 **149** J4
Enfield EN2 **43** H1
Harrow (Har.Wld) HA3 **52** B6
Lavender Gro, E8 **94** C7
Mitcham CR4 **185** H1
Lavender Hill, SW11 **149** H4
Enfield EN2 **43** G1
Lavender Pl, Ilf. IG1 **98** E5
Lavender Ri, West Dr. UB7 **120** D2
Lavender Rd, SE16 **133** H1
SW11 **149** G3
Carshalton SM5 **200** A4
Croydon CR0 **187** F6
Enfield EN2 **44** A1
Epsom KT19 **196** B5
Sutton SM1 **199** G4
Lavender St, E15
off Manbey Gro **96** E6
Lavender Sweep, SW11 **149** J4
Lavender Ter, SW11
off Falcon Rd **149** H3
Lavender Vale, Wall. SM6 **200** D6
Lavender Wk, SW11 **149** J4
Mitcham CR4 **186** A3
Lavender Way, Croy. CR0 **189** G6
Lavengro Rd, SE27 **169** J2
Lavenham Rd, SW18 **166** C2
Lavernock Rd, Bexh. DA7 **159** G2
Lavers Rd, N16 **94** B3
Laverstoke Gdns, SW15 **147** G7
Laverton Ms, SW5 **30** B2
Laverton Pl, SW5 **30** B2
Lavidge Rd, SE9 **174** B2
Lavina Gro, N1 **10** C1
Lavington Cl, E9 **95** J6
Lavington Rd, W13 **125** E1
Croydon CR0 **201** F3
Lavington St, SE1 **27** H2
Lawdons Gdns, Croy. CR0 **201** H4
Lawford Rd, N1 **94** B7
NW5 **92** C6
W4 **126** C7
Law Ho, Bark. IG11 **118** A2
Lawless St, E14 **114** B7
Lawley Rd, N14 **42** B7
Lawley St, E5 **95** F4
Lawn, The, Sthl. UB2 **123** G5
Lawn Cl, N9 **44** C7
Bromley BR1 **173** H6
New Malden KT3 **182** E2
Lawn Cres, Rich. TW9 **145** J2
Lawn Fm Gro, Rom. RM6 **82** E4
Lawn Gdns, W7 **124** B1
Lawn Ho Cl, E14 **134** C2
Lawn La, SW8 **34** B5
Lawn Rd, NW3 **91** J5
Beckenham BR3 **171** J7
Lawns, The, E4 **62** A5
SE3 *off Lee Ter* **155** F3
SE19 **188** A1
Pinner HA5 **51** H7
Sidcup DA14 **176** B4
Sutton SM2 **198** B7
Lawns Ct, Wem. HA9
off The Avenue **87** J2
Lawnside, SE3 **155** F4
Lawn Ter, SE3 **155** E3
Lawn Vale, Pnr. HA5 **66** D2
Lawrence Av, E12 **98** D4
E17 **77** G1
N13 **59** H4
NW7 **55** E4
NW10 **106** D1
New Malden KT3 **182** D6
Lawrence Bldgs, N16 **94** C3
Lawrence Campe Cl, N20 **57** G3
Lawrence Cl, E3 **114** A2
N15 *off Lawrence Rd* **76** B3
W12 *off Australia Rd* **107** H7
Lawrence Ct, NW7 **55** E5
Lawrence Cres, Dag. RM10 **101** H3
Edgware HA8 **70** A2
Lawrence Gdns, NW7 **55** F3
Lawrence Hall, E13
off Cumberland Rd **115** H4
Lawrence Hill, E4 **62** A2
Lawrence La, EC2 **20** A4
Lawrence Pl, N1
off Outram Pl **111** E1
Lawrence Rd, E6 **116** A1
E13 **115** H1
N15 **76** B4
N18 **60** E4
SE25 **188** C4
W5 **125** G4
Erith DA8 **139** H7
Hampton TW12 **161** F7
Hounslow TW4 **142** C4
Pinner HA5 **66** D5
Richmond TW10 **163** F4
West Wickham BR4 **205** G4
Lawrence St, E16 **115** F5
NW7 **55** F4
SW3 **31** G6
Lawrence Way, NW10 **88** C3
Lawrence Weaver Cl, Mord. SM4
off Green La **184** D6
Lawrie Pk Av, SE26 **171** E5
Lawrie Pk Cres, SE26 **171** E5
Lawrie Pk Gdns, SE26 **171** E4
Lawrie Pk Rd, SE26 **171** E6
Laws Cl, SE25 **188** A4
Lawson Cl, E16 **115** J5
SW19 **166** A3
Ilford IG1 **99** G5
Lawson Ct, N11
off Ringway **58** C6
Lawson Est, SE1 **28** B6
Lawson Gdns, Pinner HA5 **66** B3
Lawson Rd, Enf. EN3 **45** F1
Southall UB1 **103** F4
Law St, SE1 **28** C5
Lawton Rd, E3 **113** H3
E10 **96** C1
Barnet (Cockfos.) EN4 **41** G3
Loughton IG10 **48** E3
Laxcon Cl, NW10 **88** C5
Laxey Rd, Orp. BR6 **207** J6
Laxley Cl, SE5 **35** H7
Laxton Pl, NW1 **9** E5
Layard Rd, SE16 **133** E4
Enfield EN1 **44** C1
Thornton Heath CR7 **188** A2
Layard Sq, SE16 **132** E4
Laycock St, N1 **93** G6
Layer Gdns, W3 **106** A7
Layfield Cl, NW4 **71** H7
Layfield Cres, NW4 **71** H7
Layfield Rd, NW4 **71** H7
Layhams Rd, Kes. BR2 **205** F5
West Wickham BR4 **204** D3
Laymarsh Cl, Belv. DA17 **139** F3
Laymead Cl, Nthlt. UB5 **84** E6
Laystall St, EC1 **10** E6
Layton Cres, Croy. CR0 **201** G5
Layton Pl, Richmond (Kew) TW9 **146** A1
Layton Rd, Brent. TW8 **125** G5
Hounslow TW3 **143** H4
Laytons Bldgs, SE1 **28** A3
Layzell Wk, SE9
off Mottingham La **174** A1
Lazar Wk, N7
off Briset Way **93** F2
Lazenby Ct, WC2 **18** A5
Leabank Cl, Har. HA1 **86** B3
Leabank Sq, E9 **96** A6
Leabank Vw, N15 **76** D6
Leabourne Rd, N16 **76** D6
LEA BRIDGE, E5 **95** G3
Lea Br Rd, E5 **95** F3
E10 **95** H1
E17 **78** D4
Lea Cl, Twick. TW2 **143** F7
Leacroft Av, SW12 **149** J7
Leacroft Cl, N21 **59** H2
Leadale Av, E4 **62** A2
Leadale Rd, N15 **76** D6
N16 **76** D6
Leadbeaters Cl, N11
off Goldsmith Rd **57** J5
★ **Leadenhall Mkt**, EC3 **20** D4
Leadenhall Pl, EC3 **20** D4
Leadenhall St, EC3 **20** D4
Leadenham Ct, E3
off Spanby Rd **114** A4
Leader Av, E12 **98** D5
Leadings, The, Wem. HA9 **88** C3
Leaf Cl, T.Ditt. KT7 **180** B5
Leaf Gro, SE27 **169** G5
Leafield Cl, SW16 **169** H6
Leafield La, Sid. DA14 **177** F4
Leafield Rd, SW20 **184** C3
Sutton SM1 **198** D2
Leafy Gro, Kes. BR2 **205** J5
Leafy Oak Rd, SE12 **173** J3
Leafy Way, Croy. CR0 **202** C2
Lea Gdns, Wem. HA9 **87** H4
Leagrave St, E5 **95** F3
Lea Hall Gdns, E10
off Lea Hall Rd **96** A1
Lea Hall Rd, E10 **96** A1
Leahurst Rd, SE13 **154** D5
Lea Interchange, E9 **96** A5
Leake St, SE1 **26** D3
Lealand Rd, N15 **76** C6
Leamington Av, E17 **78** A5
Bromley BR1 **173** J5
Morden SM4 **184** C4
Orpington BR6 **207** H4
Leamington Cl, E12 **98** B5
Bromley BR1 **173** J4
Hounslow TW3 **143** J5
Leamington Cres, Har. HA2 **85** E3
Leamington Gdns, Ilf. IG3 **99** J2
Leamington Pk, W3 **106** D5
Leamington Rd, Sthl. UB2 **122** D4
Leamington Rd Vil, W11 **108** C5
Leamore St, W6 **127** H4
Leamouth Rd, E6
off Remington Rd **116** B6
E14 **114** D6
Leander Ct, SE8 **154** A1
Leander Rd, SW2 **151** F6
Northolt UB5 **103** G2
Thornton Heath CR7 **187** F4
Learner Dr, Har. HA2 **85** G2
Lea Rd, Beck. BR3
off Fairfield Rd **190** A2
Enfield EN2 **44** A1
Southall UB2 **122** E4
Learoyd Gdns, E6 **116** D7
Leas Cl, Chess. KT9 **195** J7
Leas Dale, SE9 **174** D3
Leas Grn, Chis. BR7 **175** J6
Leaside Av, N10 **74** A3
Leaside Rd, E5 **95** F1
Leasowes Rd, E10 **96** A1
Lea Sq, E3
off Legion Ter **113** J1
Leatherbottle Grn, Erith DA18 **139** F3
Leather Bottle La, Belv. DA17 **139** E4
Leather Cl, Mitch. CR4 **186** A2

Leatherdale St, E1 *off Portelet Rd* 113 G3
Leather Gdns, E15 *off Abbey Rd* 115 E1
Leatherhead Cl, N16 94 C1
Leather La, EC1 19 F2
Leather Mkt, The, SE1 28 D4
Leathermarket Ct, SE1 28 D4
Leathermarket St, SE1 28 D4
Leather Rd, SE16 133 G4
Leathersellers Cl, Barn. EN5 *off The Avenue* 40 B4
Leathsail Rd, Har. HA2 85 H3
Leathwaite Rd, SW11 149 J4
Leathwell Rd, SE8 154 B2
Lea Valley Rd, E4 45 H5
Enfield EN3 45 H5
Lea Valley Trd Est, N18 61 G5
Lea Valley Viaduct, E4 61 G5
N18 61 G5
Lea Valley Wk, E3 114 C4
E5 95 H3
E9 95 H3
E10 95 H3
E14 114 B5
E15 114 C3
E17 77 F1
N9 61 H1
N15 76 D6
N16 76 D6
N17 77 F1
N18 77 F1
Enfield EN3 45 J3
Leaveland Cl, Beck. BR3 190 A4
Leaver Gdns, Grnf. UB6 104 A2
Leavesden Rd, Stan. HA7 52 D6
Lea Vw Ho, E5 *off Springfield* 94 E1
Leaway, E10 95 G1
Lebanon Av, Felt. TW13 160 D5
Lebanon Ct, Twick. TW1 144 E7
Lebanon Gdns, SW18 148 D6
Lebanon Pk, Twick. TW1 144 E7
Lebanon Rd, SW18 148 D5
Croydon CR0 202 B1
Lebrun Sq, SE3 155 H3
Lechmere App, Wdf.Grn. IG8 79 J2
Lechmere Av, Chig. IG7 65 F4
Woodford Green IG8 80 A2
Lechmere Rd, NW2 89 H6
Leckford Rd, SW18 167 F2
Leckhampton Pl, SW2 *off Scotia Rd* 151 G7
Leckwith Av, Bexh. DA7 138 E6
Lecky St, SW7 31 E3
Leclair Ho, SE3 *off Gallus Sq* 155 H3
Leconfield Av, SW13 147 F3
Leconfield Rd, N5 94 A4
Leda Av, Enf. EN3 45 G1
Leda Rd, SE18 136 C3
Ledbury Est, SE15 132 E7
Ledbury Ho, SE22 *off Pytchley Rd* 152 B3
Ledbury Ms N, W11 *off Ledbury Rd* 108 D7
Ledbury Ms W, W11 *off Ledbury Rd* 108 D7
Ledbury Pl, Croy. CR0 202 A4
Ledbury Rd, W11 108 C6
Croydon CR0 201 J4
Ledbury St, SE15 37 J7
Ledrington Rd, SE19 170 D6
Ledway Dr, Wem. HA9 69 J7
LEE, SE12 154 E4
Lee Av, Rom. RM6 82 E6
Lee Br, SE13 154 C3
Leechcroft Av, Sid. DA15 157 J5
Leechcroft Rd, Wall. SM6 200 A3
Lee Ch St, SE13 155 E4
Lee Cl, E17 77 G1
Barnet EN5 41 F4
Lee Conservancy Rd, E9 95 J5
Leecroft Rd, Barn. EN5 40 B5
Leeds Pl, N4 93 F1
Leeds Rd, Ilf. IG1 99 G1
Leeds St, N18 60 D5
Leefern Rd, W12 127 G2
Leegate, SE12 155 F5
Lee Grn, SE12 *off Lee High Rd* 155 F5
Lee Gro, Chig. IG7 64 D2
Lee High Rd, SE12 154 D3
SE13 154 D3
Leeke St, WC1 10 C3
Leeland Rd, W13 124 D1
Leeland Ter, W13 124 D1
Leeland Way, NW10 89 E4
Lee Pk, SE3 155 F4
Lee Pk Way, N9 61 G4
N18 61 G4
Leerdam Dr, E14 134 C3
Lee Rd, NW7 56 A7
SE3 155 F3
SW19 185 E1
Enfield EN1 44 D6
Lee Rd, Greenford (Perivale) UB6 105 F1
Lees, The, Croy. CR0 203 J2
Leeside, Barn. EN5 40 B5
Leeside Business Cen, Enf. EN3 45 J2
Leeside Ct, SE16 *off Rotherhithe St* 133 G1
Leeside Cres, NW11 72 C6
Leeside Ind Est, N17 *off Garman Rd* 61 F7
Leeside Rd, N17 61 E6
Leeson Rd, SE24 151 G4
Leesons Hill, Chis. BR7 193 H3
Leesons Way, Orp. BR5 193 J2
Lees Pl, W1 16 B5
Lee St, E8 112 C1
Lee Ter, SE3 154 E3
SE13 154 E3
Lee Valley Pathway, E9 95 J3
E10 77 F7
E17 77 F7
Lee Valley Technopark, N17 76 D3
Lee Vw, Enf. EN2 43 H1
Leeward Gdns, SW19 166 C6
Leeway, SE8 133 J5
Leeway Cl, Pnr. (Hatch End) HA5 51 F7
Leewood Cl, SE12 *off Upwood Rd* 155 F6
Le Fay Ct, N9 *off Galahad Rd* 60 D3
Lefevre Wk, E3 *off Parnell Rd* 114 A2
Lefroy Rd, W12 127 F2
Legard Rd, N5 93 H4
Legatt Rd, SE9 156 A5
Leggatt Rd, E15 114 C2
Legge St, SE13 154 C5
Leghorn Rd, NW10 107 F2
SE18 137 G5
Legion Cl, N1 93 G6
Legion Ct, Mord. SM4 184 D6
Legion Rd, Grnf. UB6 103 J1
Legion Ter, E3 113 J1
Legion Way, N12 57 H7
Legon Av, Rom. RM7 101 J1
Legrace Av, Houns. TW4 142 D2
Leicester Av, Mitch. CR4 187 E4
Leicester Cl, Wor.Pk. KT4 197 J4
Leicester Ct, WC2 17 J5
Leicester Gdns, Ilf. IG3 81 H7
Leicester Ms, N2 *off Leicester Rd* 73 H3
Leicester Pl, WC2 17 J5
Leicester Rd, E11 79 H5
N2 73 H3
Barnet EN5 40 E5
Croydon CR0 188 B7
Leicester Sq, WC2 17 J6
Leicester St, WC2 17 J5
Leigh, The, Kings.T. KT2 165 E6
Leigham Av, SW16 169 E3
Leigham Cl, SW16 169 F3
Leigham Ct, Wall. SM6 *off Clyde Rd* 200 C6
Leigham Ct Rd, SW16 169 E2
Leigham Dr, Islw. TW7 124 B7
Leigham Vale, SW2 169 F3
SW16 169 F3
Leigh Av, Ilf. IG4 80 A4
Leigh Cl, N.Mal. KT3 182 C4
Leigh Cl Ind Est, N.Mal. KT3 *off Leigh Cl* 182 D4
Leigh Ct, SE4 *off Lewisham Way* 154 A2
Borehamwood WD6 *off Banks Rd* 38 D2
Harrow HA2 86 B1
Leigh Cres, Croy. (New Adgtn) CR0 204 B7
Leigh Gdns, NW10 107 J2
Leigh Hunt Dr, N14 58 D1
Leigh Hunt St, SE1 27 J3
Leigh Orchard Cl, SW16 169 F3
Leigh Pl, EC1 19 E1
Feltham TW13 160 C1
Welling DA16 158 A2
Leigh Rd, E6 98 D6
E10 78 C7
N5 93 H4
Hounslow TW3 144 A4
Leigh Rodd, Watford WD19 51 F3
Leigh St, WC1 10 A5
Leighton Av, E12 98 D5
Pinner HA5 66 E3
Leighton Cl, Edgware HA8 70 A2
Leighton Cres, NW5 92 C5
Leighton Gdns, NW10 107 H2
Leighton Gro, NW5 92 C5
★ **Leighton Ho Mus**, W14 128 C3
Leighton Pl, NW5 92 C5
Leighton Rd, NW5 92 D5
W13 124 D2
Enfield EN1 44 C5
Harrow (Har.Wld) HA3 68 A2
Leighton St, Croy. CR0 201 H1
Leila Parnell Pl, SE7 135 J6
Leinster Av, SW14 146 C3
Leinster Gdns, W2 14 C4
Leinster Ms, W2 14 C5
Barnet EN5 40 B3
Leinster Pl, W2 14 C4
Leinster Rd, N10 74 B4
Leinster Sq, W2 108 D6
Leinster Ter, W2 14 C5
Leisure Way, N12 57 G7
Leith Cl, NW9 88 D1
Leithcote Gdns, SW16 169 F4
Leithcote Path, SW16 169 F3
Leith Rd, N22 75 H1
Leith Twrs, Sutt. SM2 199 E7
Leith Yd, NW6 *off Quex Rd* 108 D1
Lela Av, Houns. TW4 142 C2
Lelitia Cl, E8 *off Pownall Rd* 112 D1
Leman St, E1 21 G4
Lemark Cl, Stan. HA7 53 F5
Le May Av, SE12 173 H3
Lemmon Rd, SE10 134 E6
Lemna Rd, E11 79 E7
Lemon Gro, Felt. TW13 160 A1
Lemonwell Ct, SE9 *off Lemonwell Dr* 157 F5
Lemonwell Dr, SE9 157 F5
Lemsford Cl, N15 76 D5
Lemsford Ct, N4 *off Brownswood Rd* 93 J2
Borehamwood WD6 38 C4
Lemuel St, SW18 149 E6
Lena Cres, N9 61 F2
Lena Gdns, W6 127 J3
Lena Kennedy Cl, E4 62 B6
Lenanton Steps, E14 *off Manilla St* 134 A2
Lendal Ter, SW4 150 D3
Lenelby Rd, Surb. KT6 196 A1
Len Freeman Pl, SW6 *off John Smith Av* 128 C7
Lenham Rd, SE12 155 F4
Bexleyheath DA7 139 F6
Sutton SM1 199 E4
Thornton Heath CR7 188 A2
Lennard Av, W.Wick. BR4 205 E2
Lennard Cl, W.Wick. BR4 205 E2
Lennard Rd, SE20 171 F6
Beckenham BR3 171 G6
Bromley BR2 206 C1
Croydon CR0 201 J1
Lennon Rd, NW2 89 J5
Lennox Gdns, NW10 89 F4
SW1 23 J6
Croydon CR0 201 H4
Ilford IG1 98 C1
Lennox Gdns Ms, SW1 23 J6
Lennox Rd, E17 77 J6
N4 93 F2
Lenor Cl, Bexh. DA6 159 E4
Lensbury Av, SW6 149 F2
Lensbury Way, SE2 138 C3
Lens Rd, E7 97 J7
Lenthall Ho, SW1 33 G4
Lenthall Rd, E8 94 C7
Loughton IG10 49 G4
Lenthorp Rd, SE10 135 F4
Lentmead Rd, Brom. BR1 173 F3
Lenton Path, SE18 137 G6
Lenton Ri, Rich. TW9 145 H3
Lenton St, SE18 137 G4
Lenton Ter, N4 *off Fonthill Rd* 93 G2
Leof Cres, SE6 172 B5
Leominster Rd, Mord. SM4 185 F6
Leominster Wk, Mord. SM4 185 F6
Leonard Av, Mord. SM4 185 F5
Leonard Pl, N16 *off Allen Rd* 94 B4
Leonard Rd, E4 62 A6
E7 97 G4
N9 60 C3
SW16 186 C1
Southall UB2 122 D3
Leonard Robbins Path, SE28 *off Tawney Rd* 118 B7
Leonard St, E16 136 B1
EC2 12 C5
Leonora Tyson Ms, SE21 170 A2
Leontine Cl, SE15 132 D7
Leopards Ct, EC1 19 E1
Leopold Av, SW19 166 C5
Leopold Ms, E9 *off Fremont St* 113 F1
Leopold Rd, E17 78 A5
N2 73 G3
N18 61 E5
NW10 89 E7
SW19 166 C4
W5 125 J1
Leopold St, E3 113 J5
Leopold Ter, SW19 166 C5
Leo St, SE15 133 E7
Leo Yd, EC1 11 H6
Leppoc Rd, SW4 150 D5
Leroy St, SE1 36 D1
Lerry Cl, W14 *off Thaxton Rd* 128 C6
Lescombe Cl, SE23 171 H3
Lescombe Rd, SE23 171 H3
Lesley Cl, Bex. DA5 159 H7
Leslie Gdns, Sutt. SM2 198 D7
Leslie Gro, Croy. CR0 202 B1
Leslie Gro Pl, Croy. CR0 *off Leslie Gro* 202 B1
Leslie Pk Rd, Croy. CR0 202 B1
Leslie Rd, E11 96 C4
E16 115 H6
N2 73 G3
Leslie Smith Sq, SE18 *off Nightingale Vale* 136 D6
★ **Lesnes Abbey (ruins)**, Erith DA18 138 D4
Lessar Av, SW4 150 C5
Lessingham Av, SW17 167 J4
Ilford IG5 80 D3
Lessing St, SE23 153 H7
Lessington Av, Rom. RM7 83 J6
Lessness Av, Bexh. DA7 138 D7
LESSNESS HEATH, Belv. DA17 139 H5
Lessness Pk, Belv. DA17 139 F5
Lessness Rd, Belv. DA17 *off Stapley Rd* 139 G5
Morden SM4 185 F6
Lester Av, E15 115 E3
Lestock Cl, SE25 188 D3
Leswin Pl, N16 *off Leswin Rd* 94 C3
Leswin Rd, N16 94 C3
Letchford Gdns, NW10 107 G3
Letchford Ms, NW10 *off Letchford Gdns* 107 G3
Letchford Ter, Har. HA3 67 H1
Letchworth Av, Felt. TW14 141 J7
Letchworth Cl, Brom. BR2 191 G5
Watford WD19 50 D5
Letchworth Dr, Brom. BR2 191 G5
Letchworth St, SW17 167 J4
Lethbridge Cl, SE13 154 C1
Letterstone Rd, SW6 *off Varna Rd* 128 C7
Lettice St, SW6 148 C1
Lett Rd, E15 96 D7
Lettsom St, SE5 152 B2
Lettsom Wk, E13 115 G2
Leucha Rd, E17 77 H5
Levana Cl, SW19 166 B1
Levehurst Ho, SE27 *off Elder Rd* 169 J5
Levehurst Way, SW4 150 E2
Leven Cl, Wat. WD19 50 D5
Levendale Rd, SE23 171 H2
Leven Rd, E14 114 C5
Leverett St, SW3 31 H1
Leverholme Gdns, SE9 174 D3
Leverson St, SW16 168 C6
Lever St, EC1 11 H4
Leverton Pl, NW5 *off Leverton St* 92 C5
Leverton St, NW5 92 C5
Levett Gdns, Ilf. IG3 99 J4
Levett Rd, Bark. IG11 99 H6
Levine Gdns, Bark. IG11 118 D2
Levison Way, N19 *off Grovedale Rd* 92 D2
Lewes Cl, Nthlt. UB5 85 G6
Lewesdon Cl, SW19 166 A1
Lewes Rd, N12 57 H5
Bromley BR1 192 A2
Leweston Pl, N16 76 C7
Lewey Ho, E3 113 J4
Lewgars Av, NW9 70 C6
Lewing Cl, Orp. BR6 *off Place Fm Av* 207 H1
Lewin Rd, SW14 146 D3
SW16 168 D6
Bexleyheath DA6 159 E4
Lewin Ter, Felt. TW14 *off Page Rd* 141 G7
Lewis Av, E17 78 A1
Lewis Cl, N14 42 C7
Lewis Cres, NW10 88 C5
Lewis Gdns, N2 73 G2
N16 76 C6
Lewis Gro, SE13 154 C3
LEWISHAM, SE13 154 B4

Lewisham Cen, SE13 154 C3
Lewisham High St, SE13 154 C3
Lewisham Hill, SE13 154 C2
Lewisham Pk, SE13 154 B6
Lewisham Rd, SE13 154 B1
Lewisham St, SW1 25 J4
Lewisham Way, SE4 153 J1
SE14 153 J1
Lewis Pl, E8 94 D5
Lewis Rd, Mitch. CR4 185 G2
Richmond TW10
off Red Lion St 145 G5
Sidcup DA14 176 C3
Southall UB1 123 E2
Sutton SM1 199 E4
Welling DA16 158 C3
Lewis St, NW1 92 B6
Lewiston Cl, Wor.Pk. KT4 183 H7
Lewis Way, Dag. RM10 101 H6
Lexden Dr, Rom. RM6 82 B6
Lexden Rd, W3 106 B7
Mitcham CR4 186 D4
Lexham Ct, Grnf. UB6 104 A1
Lexham Gdns, W8 30 A1
Lexham Gdns Ms, W8 22 B6
Lexham Ho, Bark. IG11
off St. Margarets 117 G1
Lexham Ms, W8 128 D4
Lexham Wk, W8 22 B6
Lexington Apts, EC1 12 B5
Lexington Bldg, E3
off Fairfield Rd 114 A2
Lexington Pl, Kings.T.
KT1 163 G7
Lexington St, W1 17 G4
Lexington Way, Barn.
EN5 40 A4
Lexton Gdns, SW12 168 D1
Leyborne Av, W13 125 E2
Leyborne Pk, Rich. TW9 146 A1
Leybourne Cl, Brom. BR2 191 G6
Leybourne Rd, E11 97 F1
NW1 92 B7
NW9 70 A5
Leybourne St, NW1
off Hawley St 92 B7
Leybridge Ct, SE12 155 G5
Leyburn Cl, E17
off Church La 78 B4
Leyburn Gdns, Croy.
CR0 202 B2
Leyburn Gro, N18 60 D6
Leyburn Rd, N18 60 D6
Leycroft Cl, Loug. IG10 48 D5
Leyden St, E1 21 F2
Leydon Cl, SE16
off Lagado Ms 133 G1
Leyfield, Wor.Pk. KT4 197 E1
Leyland Av, Enf. EN3 45 H2
Leyland Gdns, Wdf.Grn.
IG8 63 J5
Leyland Rd, SE12 155 G5
Leylang Rd, SE14 133 G7
Leys, The, N2 73 F4
Harrow HA3 69 J6
Leys Av, Dag. RM10 101 J7
Leys Cl, Dag. RM10 101 J7
Harrow HA1 68 A5
Leysdown Av, Bexh.
DA7 159 J4
Leysdown Rd, SE9 174 B2
Leysfield Rd, W12 127 G2
Leys Gdns, Barn. EN4 42 A5
Leyspring Rd, E11 97 F1
Leys Rd E, Enf. EN3 45 H1
Leys Rd W, Enf. EN3 45 H1
Ley St, Ilf. IG1, IG2 99 E2
Leyswood Dr, Ilf. IG2 81 H5
Leythe Rd, W3 126 C2
LEYTON, E11 96 B1
Leyton Business Cen, E10 96 A2
Leyton Gra, E10 96 A2
Leyton Gra Est, E10
off Leyton Gra 96 A2
Leyton Grn Rd, E10 78 C6
Leyton Ind Village, E10 77 G7
★ Leyton Orient FC, E10 96 B3
Leyton Pk Rd, E10 96 C3
Leyton Rd, E15 96 D5
SW19 167 F7
LEYTONSTONE, E11 78 D7
Leytonstone Rd, E15 96 E5
Leywick St, E15 114 E2
Lezayre Rd, Orp. BR6 207 J6
Liardet St, SE14 133 H6
Liberia Rd, N5 93 H6
★ Liberty, W1 17 F4
Liberty Av, SW19 185 G1
Liberty Cl, N18 60 C4
Wor.Pk. KT4 197 J1
Liberty Ms, SW12 150 B6
Liberty St, SW9 151 F1
Libra Rd, E3 113 J1
E13 115 G2
Library Pl, E1
off Cable St 113 E7
Library St, SE1 27 G4
Library Way, Twick. TW2
off Nelson Rd 143 J7
Lichfield Cl, Barn. EN4 41 J3
Lichfield Ct, Rich. TW9
off Sheen Rd 145 H5
Lichfield Gdns, Rich. TW9 145 H4
Lichfield Gro, N3 72 D1
Lichfield Rd, E3 113 H3
E6 116 A3
N9 60 D2
NW2 90 B4
Dagenham RM8 100 B4
Hounslow TW4 142 C3
Northwood HA6 66 A3
Richmond TW9 145 J1
Woodford Green IG8 63 E4
Lichlade Cl, Orp. BR6 207 J4
Lickey Ho, W14
off North End Rd 128 C6
Lidbury Rd, NW7 56 B6
Lidcote Gdns, SW9 151 G2
Liddall Way, West Dr.
UB7 120 C1
Liddell Cl, Har. HA3 69 G3
Liddell Gdns, NW10 107 J2
Liddell Rd, NW6 90 D6
Lidding Rd, Har. HA3 69 G5
Liddington Rd, E15 115 F1
Liddon Rd, E13 115 H3
Bromley BR1 191 J3
Liden Cl, E17
off Hitcham Rd 95 J1
Lidfield Rd, N16 94 A4
Lidgate Rd, SE15
off Chandler Way 132 C7
Lidiard Rd, SW18 167 F2
Lidlington Pl, NW1 9 F2
Lido Ho, W13
off Northfield Av 125 E1
Lido Sq, N17 76 A1
Lidyard Rd, N19 92 C1
★ Lifetimes Mus
(Croydon Central Lib),
Croy. CR0 201 J3
Liffler Rd, SE18 137 H5
Liffords Pl, SW13 147 F2
Lifford St, SW15 148 A4
Lightcliffe Rd, N13 59 G4
Lighter Cl, SE16 133 H4
Lighterman Ms, E1 113 G6
Lightermans Rd, E14 134 A2
Lightfoot Rd, N8 74 E5
Lightley Cl, Wem. HA0
off Stanley Av 87 J7
Ligonier St, E2 13 F5
Lilac Cl, E4 61 J6
Lilac Gdns, W5 125 G3
Croydon CR0 204 A3
Lilac Ms, N8
off Courcy Rd 75 G3
Lilac Pl, SE11 34 C2
Lilac St, W12 107 G7
Lilah Ms, Brom. BR2
off Beckenham La 191 E2
Lilburne Gdns, SE9 156 B5
Lilburne Rd, SE9 156 B5
Lilburne Wk, NW10 88 C6
Lile Cres, W7 104 B5
Lilestone St, NW8 7 G5
Lilford Rd, SE5 151 H2
Lilian Barker Cl, SE12 155 G5
Lilian Board Way, Grnf.
UB6 86 A5
Lilian Cl, N16
off Barbauld Rd 94 B3
Lilian Gdns, Wdf.Grn. IG8 79 H1
Lilian Rd, SW16 186 C1
Lillechurch Rd, Dag. RM8 100 B6
Lilleshall Rd, Mord. SM4 185 G6
Lilley Cl, E1 29 J2
Lilley La, NW7 54 D5
Lillian Av, W3 126 A2
Lillian Rd, SW13 127 G6
Lillie Rd, SW6 128 B7
Lillieshall Rd, SW4 150 B3
Lillie Yd, SW6 128 D6
Lillingston Ho, N7
off Harvist Est 93 G4
Lillington Gdns Est, SW1 33 G2
Lilliput Av, Nthlt. UB5 103 F1
Lily Cl, W14 128 B4
Lily Dr, West Dr. UB7 120 A4
Lily Gdns, Wem. HA0 105 F2
Lily Pl, EC1 19 F1
Lily Rd, E17 78 A6
Lilyville Rd, SW6 148 C1
Limbourne Av, Dag. RM8 83 F7
Limburg Rd, SW11 149 J4
Limeburner La, EC4 19 G4
Lime Cl, E1 29 J1
Bromley BR1 192 B4
Buckhurst Hill IG9 64 A3
Carshalton SM5 199 J2
Harrow HA3 68 C2
Romford RM7 83 J4
Lime Ct, Mitch. CR4 185 G2
Lime Cres, Sun. TW16 178 C2
Limecroft Cl, Epsom
KT19 196 D7
Limedene Cl, Pnr. HA5 66 D1
Lime Gro, E4 61 J6
N20 56 C1
W12 127 J2
Ilford IG6 65 J6
New Malden KT3 182 D3
Orpington BR6 207 E2
Ruislip HA4 66 B7
Sidcup DA15 157 J6
Twickenham TW1 144 C6
Limeharbour, E14 134 B3
LIMEHOUSE, E14 113 H7
Limehouse Causeway,
E14 113 J7
Limehouse Link, E14 113 H7
Limekiln Dr, SE7 135 H6
Limekiln Pl, SE19 170 C7
Limerick Cl, SW12 150 C7
Limerick Ms, N2
off Bedford Rd 73 H3
Lime Rd, Rich. TW9
off St. Mary's Gro 145 J4
Lime Row, Erith DA18
off Northwood Pl 139 F3
Limerston St, SW10 30 D5
Limes, The, SW18 148 D6
W2 off Linden Gdns 108 D7
Bromley BR2 206 B2
Limes Av, E11 79 H4
N12 57 F4
NW7 54 E6
NW11 72 B7
SE20 171 E7
SW13 147 F2
Carshalton SM5 199 J1
Chigwell IG7 65 F5
Croydon CR0 201 G3
Limes Av, The, N11 58 B5
Limesdale Gdns, Edg.
HA8 70 C2
Limes Fld Rd, SW14
off White Hart La 147 E3
Limesford Rd, SE15 153 G4
Limes Gdns, SW18 148 D6
Limes Gro, SE13 154 C4
Limes Pl, Croy. CR0 188 A7
Limes Rd, Beck. BR3 190 B2
Croydon CR0 188 A6
Limes Row, Orp.
(Farnboro.) BR6 207 E5
Limestone Wk, Erith
DA18 138 D3
Lime St, E17 77 H4
EC3 20 D5
Lime St Pas, EC3 20 D4
Limes Wk, SE15 153 E4
W5 125 G2
Lime Ter, W7
off Manor Ct Rd 104 B7
Lime Tree Av, Esher KT10 194 A1
Thames Ditton KT7 194 A1
Lime Tree Cl, E18 79 J4
Limetree Cl, SW2 169 F1
Lime Tree Gro, Croy. CR0 203 J3
Lime Tree Pl, Mitch. CR4 186 B1
Lime Tree Rd, Houns.
TW5 143 H1
Limetree Wk, SW17
off Hawthorn Cres 168 A5
Lime Tree Wk, Bushey
(Bushey Hth) WD23 52 B1
West Wickham BR4 205 F4
Lime Wk, E15
off Church St N 115 E1
Limewood Cl, E17 77 J4
W13
off St. Stephens Rd 105 E6
Beckenham BR3 190 C5
Limewood Ct, Ilf. IG4 80 C5
Limewood Rd, Erith DA8 139 J7
Limpsfield Av, SW19 166 A2
Thornton Heath CR7 187 F5
Linacre Cl, SE15 153 E3
Linacre Ct, W6 128 A5
Linacre Rd, NW2 89 H6
Linale Ho, N1
off Murray Gro 12 B2
Linberry Wk, SE8 133 J4
Linchmere Rd, SE12 155 F7
Lincoln Av, N14 58 C3
SW19 166 A3
Twickenham TW2 161 H2
Lincoln Cl, SE25
off Woodside Grn 188 E6
Greenford UB6 103 J1
Harrow HA2 67 F5
Lincoln Ct, N16 76 A7
Borehamwood WD6 38 D5
Lincoln Cres, Enf. EN1 44 B5
Lincoln Dr, Wat. WD19 50 C3
Lincoln Gdns, Ilf. IG1 80 B7
Lincoln Grn Rd, Orp. BR5 193 J5
Lincoln Ms, NW6
off Willesden La 108 C1
SE21 170 A1
Lincoln Rd, E7 98 A6
E13 115 H4
E18 off Grove Rd 79 G1
N2 73 H3
SE25 188 E3
Enfield EN1, EN3 44 D5
Feltham TW13 161 F3
Harrow HA2 67 F5
Mitcham CR4 186 E5
New Malden KT3 182 C3
Sidcup DA14 176 B5
Wembley HA0 87 G6
Worcester Park KT4 197 H1
Lincolns, The, NW7 55 F3
★ Lincoln's Inn, WC2 18 D3
Lincoln's Inn Flds, WC2 18 C3
Lincoln St, E11 96 E2
SW3 31 J2
Lincoln Way, Enf. EN1 44 E5
Lincombe Rd, Brom. BR1 173 F3
Lindal Cres, Enf. EN2 43 E4
Lindales, The, N17
off Brantwood Rd 60 C6
Lindal Rd, SE4 153 J5
Lindbergh Rd, Wall. SM6 200 E7
Linden Av, NW10 108 A2
Enfield EN1 44 D1
Hounslow TW3 143 H5
Ruislip HA4 84 A1
Thornton Heath CR7 187 H4
Wembley HA9 87 J5
Linden Cl, N14 42 C6
Ruislip HA4 84 A1
Stanmore HA7 52 E5
Thames Ditton KT7 180 C7
Linden Ct, W12 127 J1
Linden Cres, Grnf. UB6 86 C6
Kingston upon Thames
KT1 181 J2
Woodford Green IG8 63 H6
Lindenfield, Chis. BR7 192 E2
Linden Gdns, W2 108 D7
W4 126 D5
Enfield EN1 44 D1
Linden Gro, SE15 153 E3
SE26 171 F6
New Malden KT3 182 E3
Teddington TW11
off Waldegrave Rd 162 C5
Linden Lawns, Wem. HA9 87 J4
Linden Lea, N2 73 F5
Linden Leas, W.Wick.
BR4 204 D2
Linden Ms, N1 94 A5
W2 off Linden Gdns 108 D7
Linden Pas, W4
off Linden Gdns 126 D5
Linden Pl, Mitch. CR4 185 H4
Linden Rd, E17
off High St 77 J5
N10 74 B4
N11 57 J2
N15 75 J4
Hampton TW12 161 G7
Lindens, The, N12 57 G5
W4 146 C1
Croydon (New Adgtn)
CR0 204 C6
Loughton IG10 48 C5
Linden Wk, N19
off Hargrave Pk 92 C2
Linden Way, N14 42 C6
Lindeth Cl, Stan. HA7 53 E6
Lindfield Gdns, NW3 91 E5
Lindfield Rd, W5 105 F4
Croydon CR0 188 C6
Lindfield St, E14 114 A6
Lindhill Cl, Enf. EN3 45 G1
Lindisfarne Rd, SW20 165 G7
Dagenham RM8 100 C3
Lindisfarne Way, E9 95 H4
Lindley Est, SE15 37 H7
Lindley Pl, Rich. (Kew)
TW9 146 A1
Lindley Rd, E10 96 B2
Lindley St, E1 113 F5
Lindore Rd, SW11 149 J4
Lindores Rd, Cars. SM5 185 F7
Lindo St, SE15
off Selden Rd 153 F2
Lind Rd, Sutt. SM1 199 F5
Lindrop St, SW6 149 F2
Lindsay Cl, Chess. KT9 195 H7
Staines (Stanw.) TW19 140 A5
Lindsay Ct, SW11
off Battersea High St 149 G1
Lindsay Dr, Har. HA3 69 H6
Lindsay Rd, Hmptn.
(Hmptn H.) TW12 161 H4
Worcester Park KT4 197 H2
Lindsay Sq, SW1 33 J3
Lindsell St, SE10 154 C1
Lindsey Cl, Brom. BR1 192 A3
Mitcham CR4 187 E4
Lindsey Gdns, Felt. TW14 141 G7
Lindsey Ms, N1 93 J7
Lindsey Rd, Dag. RM8 100 C4

Lindsey St, EC1 **19** H1
Lind St, SE8 **154** B2
Lindum Rd, Tedd. TW11 **163** F7
Lindway, SE27 **169** H5
Lindwood Cl, E6
off Northumberland Rd **116** B5
Linfield Cl, NW4 **71** J3
Linford Rd, E17 **78** C3
Linford St, SW8 **150** C1
Lingards Rd, SE13 **154** C4
Lingey Cl, Sid. DA15 **175** J2
Lingfield Av, Kings.T. KT1 **181** H4
Lingfield Cl, Enf. EN1 **44** B6
Lingfield Cres, SE9 **157** G4
Lingfield Gdns, N9 **45** E7
Lingfield Rd, SW19 **166** A5
Worcester Park KT4 **197** J3
Lingham St, SW9 **151** E2
Lingholm Way, Barn. EN5 **40** A5
Lingmere Cl, Chig. IG7 **65** F2
Ling Rd, E16 **115** G5
Erith DA8 **139** J6
Lingrove Gdns, Buck.H. IG9 **63** H3
Lings Coppice, SE21 **170** A2
Lingwell Rd, SW17 **167** H3
Lingwood Gdns, Islw. TW7 **124** B7
Lingwood Rd, E5 **76** D7
Linhope St, NW1 **7** J5
Link, The, SE9 **174** D3
W3 **106** B6
Enfield EN3 **45** H1
Northolt UB5
off Eastcote La **85** F5
Pinner (Eastcote) HA5 **66** C7
Wembley HA0
off Nathans Rd **87** F1
Link Cen, The, Dag. RM10
off Heathway **101** G6
Linkfield, Brom. BR2 **191** G6
West Molesey KT8 **179** G3
Linkfield Rd, Islw. TW7 **144** C2
Link La, Wall. SM6 **200** D6
Linklea Cl, NW9 **55** E7
Link Rd, N11 **58** A4
Dagenham RM9 **119** H2
Feltham TW14 **141** J7
Wallington SM6 **200** A1
Links, The, E17 **77** H4
Links Av, Mord. SM4 **184** D4
Links Dr, N20 **56** D1
Links Gdns, SW16 **169** G7
Linkside, N12 **56** C6
Chigwell IG7 **65** F5
New Malden KT3 **183** E2
Linkside Cl, Enf. EN2 **43** F3
Linkside Gdns, Enf. EN2 **43** F3
Links Rd, NW2 **89** F2
SW17 **167** J6
W3 **106** A6
West Wickham BR4 **204** C1
Woodford Green IG8 **63** G5
Links Side, Enf. EN2 **43** G3
Link St, E9 **95** F6
Links Vw, N3 **56** C7
Links Vw Cl, Stan. HA7 **52** D6
Links Vw Rd, Croy. CR0 **204** A3
Hampton (Hmptn H.) TW12 **161** J5
Linksway, NW4 **72** A2
Links Way, Beck. BR3 **190** A6
Links Yd, E1 **21** H1
Linkway, N4 **75** J7
SW20 **183** H3
Link Way, Brom. BR2 **192** B7
Linkway, Dag. RM8 **100** C4
Link Way, Pnr. HA5 **66** D1
Linkway, Rich. TW10 **163** E2
Linkway, The, Barn. EN5 **40** E6
Linkwood Wk, NW1
off Maiden La **92** D7
Linley Cres, Rom. RM7 **83** H3
Linley Rd, N17 **76** B2
★ **Linley Sambourne Ho**, W8 **128** D2
Linnell Cl, NW11 **72** E6
Linnell Dr, NW11 **72** E6
Linnell Rd, N18 **60** D5
SE5 **152** B2
Linnet Cl, N9 **61** G1
SE28 **118** C7
Linnet Ms, SW12 **150** A7
Linnett Cl, E4 **62** C4
Linnet Ter, Ilf. IG5
off Tiptree Cres **80** D3
Linom Rd, SW4 **150** E4
Linscott Rd, E5 **95** F4
Linsdell Rd, Bark. IG11 **117** F1
Linsey St, SE16 **37** H1
Linslade Cl, Houns. TW4
off Heathlands Way **143** E5
Pinner HA5 **66** B3
Linstead St, NW6 **90** D7
Linstead Way, SW18 **148** B7
Linsted Ct, SE9 **157** H6
Linster Gro, Borwd. WD6 **38** C5
Lintaine Cl, W6
off Moylan Rd **128** B6
Linthorpe Av, Wem. HA0 **87** F6
Linthorpe Rd, N16 **76** B7
Barnet (Cockfos.) EN4 **41** H3
Linton Cl, Mitch. CR4 **185** J7
Welling DA16 **158** B1
Linton Gdns, E6 **116** B6
Linton Gro, SE27 **169** H5
Linton Rd, Bark. IG11 **99** F7
Lintons, The, Bark. IG11 **99** F7
Linton St, N1 **111** J1
Lintott Ct, Stai. (Stanw.) TW19 **140** A6
Linver Rd, SW6 **148** D2
Linwood Cl, SE5 **152** C2
Linwood Cres, Enf. EN1 **44** D1
Linzee Rd, N8 **74** E4
Lion Av, Twick. TW1
off Lion Rd **162** C1
Lion Cl, SE4 **154** A6
Lion Ct, Borwd. WD6 **38** C1
Lionel Gdns, SE9 **156** A5
Lionel Ms, W10
off Telford Rd **108** B5
Lionel Rd, SE9 **156** A5
Lionel Rd N, Brent. TW8 **125** H4
Lionel Rd S, Brent. TW8 **125** J5
Liongate Enterprise Pk, Mitch. CR4 **185** G4
Lion Gate Gdns, Rich. TW9 **145** J3
Lion Gate Ms, SW18
off Merton Rd **148** D7
Lion Mills, E2 **13** J2
Lion Pk Av, Chess. KT9 **196** A4
Lion Plaza, EC2
off Lothbury **20** B3
Lion Rd, E6 **116** C5
N9 **60** D2
Bexleyheath DA6 **159** F4
Croydon CR0 **187** J5
Twickenham TW1 **162** C1
Lions Cl, SE9 **173** J3
Lion Way, Brent. TW8 **125** G7
Lion Wf Rd, Islw. TW7 **144** E3
Lion Yd, SW4
off Tremadoc Rd **150** D4
Liphook Cres, SE23 **153** F7
Liphook Rd, Wat. WD19 **50** D4
Lippitts Hill, Loug. (High Beach) IG10 **47** E1
Lipton Cl, SE28
off Aisher Rd **118** C7
Lipton Rd, E1
off Bower St **113** G6
Lisbon Av, Twick. TW2 **161** J2
Lisbon Cl, E17 **77** J2
Lisburne Rd, NW3 **91** J4
Lisford St, SE15 **152** C1
Lisgar Ter, W14 **128** C4
Liskeard Cl, Chis. BR7 **175** F6
Liskeard Gdns, SE3 **155** G1
Lisle Cl, SW17 **168** B4
Lisle St, WC2 **17** J5
Lismore Circ, NW5 **91** J5
Lismore Cl, Islw. TW7 **144** D2
Lismore Rd, N17 **76** A3
South Croydon CR2 **202** B6
Lismore Wk, N1
off Clephane Rd **93** J6
Lissant Cl, Surb. (Long Dit.) KT6 **181** G7
Lissenden Gdns, NW5 **92** A4
Lisson Grn Est, NW8 **7** G4
LISSON GROVE, NW8 **7** F5
Lisson Gro, NW1 **7** G5
NW8 **7** F4
Lisson St, NW1 **15** G1
Lister Cl, W3 **106** D5
Mitcham CR4 **185** H1
Lister Ct, NW9 **71** E2
Lister Gdns, N18 **59** J5
Lister Rd, E11 **97** E1
Lister Wk, SE28
off Haldane Rd **118** D7
Liston Rd, N17 **76** D1
SW4 **150** C3
Liston Way, Wdf.Grn. IG8
off Navestock Cres **63** J7
Listowel Cl, SW9 **35** F7
Listowel Rd, Dag. RM10 **101** G3
Listria Pk, N16 **94** B2
Litchfield Av, E15 **96** E6
Morden SM4 **184** C7
Litchfield Gdns, NW10 **89** G6
Litchfield Rd, Sutt. SM1 **199** F4
Litchfield St, WC2 **17** J5
Litchfield Way, NW11 **73** E5
Lithos Rd, NW3 **91** E6
Little Acre, Beck. BR3 **190** A3
Little Albany St, NW1 **8** E5
Little Argyll St, W1 **17** F4
Little Benty, West Dr. UB7 **120** A5
Little Birches, Sid. DA15 **175** H2
Little Boltons, The, SW5 **30** B3
SW10 **30** B3
Little Bornes, SE21 **170** B4
Little Britain, EC1 **19** J3
Littlebrook Cl, Croy. CR0 **189** G6
Little Brownings, SE23 **170** E2
Littlebury Rd, SW4 **150** D3
Little Bury St, N9 **60** A1
Little Cedars, N12 **57** F4
Little Chester St, SW1 **24** C5
Little Cloisters, SW1
off College Ms **26** A5
Little Coll La, EC4
off College St **20** B5
Little Coll St, SW1 **26** A5
Littlecombe, SE7 **135** H6
Littlecombe Cl, SW15 **148** A6
Little Common, Stan. HA7 **52** D3
Littlecote Cl, SW19 **148** A7
Littlecote Pl, Pnr. HA5 **67** E1
Little Cottage Pl, SE10
off Tarves Way **134** B7
Little Ct, W.Wick. BR4 **204** E2
Littlecroft, SE9 **156** D3
Littledale, SE2 **138** A6
Little Dean's Yd, SW1 **26** A5
Little Dimocks, SW12 **168** B2
Little Dorrit Ct, SE1 **28** A3
Little Dragons, Loug. IG10 **48** A4
LITTLE EALING, W5 **125** F4
Little Ealing La, W5 **125** F4
Little Edward St, NW1 **8** E3
Little Elms, Hayes (Harling.) UB3 **121** G7
Little Essex St, WC2 **18** E5
Little Ferry Rd, Twick. TW1
off Ferry Rd **162** E1
Littlefield Cl, N19
off Tufnell Pk Rd **92** C4
Kingston upon Thames KT1 *off Fairfield W* **181** H2
Littlefield Rd, Edg. HA8 **54** C7
Little Friday Rd, E4 **62** E2
Little Gearies, Ilf. IG6 **80** E4
Little George St, SW1 **26** A4
Little Gra, Grnf. UB6
off Perivale La **104** D3
Little Grn, Rich. TW9 **145** G4
Little Grn St, NW5
off College La **92** B4
Littlegrove, Barn. (E.Barn.) EN4 **41** H6
Little Halliards, Walt. KT12
off Felix Rd **178** A6
Little Heath, SE7 **136** B6
Romford (Chad.Hth) RM6 **82** B4
Romford (Junct) RM6 **82** B4
Little Heath Rd, Bexh. DA7 **159** F1
Littleheath Rd, S.Croy. CR2 **202** E7
★ **Little Holland Ho**, Cars. SM5 **199** H7
LITTLE ILFORD, E12 **98** B5
Little Ilford La, E12 **98** C4
Littlejohn Rd, W7 **104** C6
Little London, Chig. IG7 **49** J4
Little London Ct, SE1
off Mill St **29** G4
Little Marlborough St, W1
off Foubert's Pl **17** F4
Littlemead, Esher KT10 **194** A4
Littlemede, SE9 **174** C3
Littlemoor Rd, Ilf. IG1 **99** G3
Littlemore Rd, SE2 **138** A2
Little Moss La, Pnr. HA5 **67** E2
Little Newport St, WC2 **17** J5
Little New St, EC4 **19** F3
Little Orchard Cl, Pnr. HA5
off Barrow Pt La **66** E2
Little Oxhey La, Wat. WD19 **50** D5
Little Pk Dr, Felt. TW13 **160** D2
Little Pk Gdns, Enf. EN2 **43** J3
Little Pluckets Way, Buck.H. IG9 **63** J1
Little Portland St, W1 **17** F3
Little Queens Rd, Tedd. TW11 **162** C6
Little Redlands, Brom. BR1 **192** B2
Little Rd, Croy. CR0
off Lower Addiscombe Rd **202** B1
Hayes UB3 **121** J2
Littlers Cl, SW19
off Runnymede **185** G1
Little Russell St, WC1 **18** A2
Little St. James's St, SW1 **25** F2
Little St. Leonards, SW14 **146** C3
Little Sanctuary, SW1 **25** J4
Little Smith St, SW1 **25** J5
Little Somerset St, E1 **21** F4
Littlestone Cl, Beck. BR3 **172** A6
Little Strand, NW9 **71** F2
Little Thrift, Orp. BR5 **193** F4
Little Titchfield St, W1 **17** F2
Littleton Av, E4 **63** F1
Littleton Cres, Har. HA1 **86** C2
Littleton Ho, SW1
off Lupus St **33** F4
Littleton Rd, Har. HA1 **86** C2
Littleton St, SW18 **167** F2
Little Trinity La, EC4 **20** A5
Little Turnstile, WC1 **18** C3
★ **Little Venice (Waterbuses)**, W2 **14** C1
Littlewood, SE13 **154** C5
Littlewood Cl, W13 **125** E3
Littleworth Av, Esher KT10 **194** A5
Littleworth Common Rd, Esher KT10 **194** A3
Littleworth La, Esher KT10 **194** A4
Littleworth Pl, Esher KT10 **194** A4
Littleworth Rd, Esher KT10 **194** B4
Livermere Rd, E8 **112** C1
Liverpool Gro, SE17 **36** A4
Liverpool Rd, E10 **78** C6
E16 **115** E5
N1 **111** G2
N7 **93** G5
W5 **125** G2
Kingston upon Thames KT2 **164** A7
Thornton Heath CR7 **187** J3
Liverpool St, EC2 **20** D2
Livesey Cl, SE28 **137** F3
Kingston upon Thames KT1 **181** J3
★ **Livesey Mus for Children**, SE15 **132** E6
Livesey Pl, SE15 **37** J5
Livingstone Ct, E10
off Matlock Rd **78** C6
Barnet EN5
off Christchurch La **40** B2
Livingstone Pl, E14
off Ferry St **134** C5
Livingstone Rd, E15 **114** C1
E17 **78** B6
N13 **59** E6
SW11
off Winstanley Rd **149** G3
Hounslow TW3 **143** J4
Southall UB1 **102** D7
Thornton Heath CR7 **187** J2
Livingstone Wk, SW11 **149** G3
Livonia St, W1 **17** G4
Lizard St, EC1 **12** A4
Lizban St, SE3 **135** H7
Llanelly Rd, NW2 **90** C2
Llanover Rd, SE18 **136** D6
Wembley HA9 **87** G3
Llanthony Rd, Mord. SM4 **185** G6
Llanvanor Rd, NW2 **90** C2
Llewellyn St, SE16 **29** J4
Lloyd Av, SW16 **187** E1
Lloyd Baker St, WC1 **10** D4
Lloyd Ct, Pnr. HA5 **66** D5
Lloyd Pk, E17 **78** A2
Lloyd Pk Av, Croy. CR0 **202** C4
Lloyd Rd, E6 **116** C1
E17 **77** G4
Dagenham RM9 **101** F6
Worcester Park KT4 **197** J3
Lloyd's Av, EC3 **21** E4
★ **Lloyd's of London**, EC3 **20** D4
Lloyds Pl, SE3 **155** E2
Lloyd Sq, WC1 **10** E3
Lloyd's Row, EC1 **11** F4
Lloyd St, WC1 **10** E3
Lloyds Way, Beck. BR3 **189** H5
Lloyd Vil, SE4 **154** A2
Loampit Hill, SE13 **154** A2
Loampit Vale, SE13 **154** B3
Loanda Cl, E8
off Clarissa St **112** C1
Loats Rd, SW2 **150** E6
Lobelia Cl, E6
off Sorrel Gdns **116** B5
Locarno Rd, W3 **126** C1
Greenford UB6 **103** J4
Lochaber Rd, SE13 **154** E4
Lochaline St, W6 **127** J6
Lochan Cl, Hayes UB4 **102** E4
Lochinvar St, SW12 **150** B7
Lochmere Cl, Erith DA8 **139** H6
Lochnagar St, E14 **114** C5
Lock Bldg, The, E15
off High St **114** C2
Lock Chase, SE3 **155** E3
Lock Cl, Sthl. UB2
off Navigator Dr **123** J2
Lockesfield Pl, E14 **134** B5
Lockesley Dr, Orp. BR5 **193** J6

Lockesley Sq, Surb. KT6
off Lovelace Gdns 181 G6
Locket Rd, Har. HA3 68 B3
Locket Rd Ms, Har. HA3
off Locket Rd 68 B3
Lockfield Av, Enf. EN3 45 H2
Lockgate Cl, E9
off Lee Conservancy Rd 95 J5
Lockhart Cl, N7 93 F6
Enfield EN3 45 E5
Lockhart St, E3 113 J4
Lockhurst St, E5 95 G4
Lockie Pl, SE25 188 D3
Lockier Wk, Wem. HA9 87 G3
Lockington Rd, SW8 150 B1
Lockmead Rd, N15 76 D6
SE13 154 C3
Lock Ms, NW1
off Northpoint Sq 92 D6
Lock Rd, Rich. TW10 163 F4
Locks La, Mitch. CR4 185 J1
Locksley Est, E14 113 J6
Locksley St, E14 113 J5
Locksmeade Rd, Rich.
TW10 163 F4
Locksons Cl, E14
off Broomfield St 114 B5
Lockswood Cl, Barn. EN4 41 J4
Lockton St, W10 108 A7
Lockwell Rd, Dag. RM10
off Heathway 101 F3
Lockwood Cl, SE26 171 G4
Lockwood Ind Pk, N17 76 E3
Lockwood Pl, E4 62 A6
Lockwood Sq, SE16 132 E3
Lockwood Way, E17 77 G2
Chessington KT9 196 A5
Lockyer Est, SE1 28 C3
Lockyer St, SE1 28 C4
Locomotive Dr, Felt.
TW14 160 A1
Locton Grn, E3
off Ruston St 113 J1
Loddiges Rd, E9 95 F7
Loder St, SE15 153 F1
Lodge Av, SW14 146 E3
Croydon CR0 201 G3
Dagenham RM8, RM9 118 A1
Harrow HA3 69 H4
Lodge Av Junct, Bark.
IG11 118 A1
Lodge Cl, N18 59 J5
Edgware HA8 53 J6
Isleworth TW7 144 E1
Wallington SM6 200 A1
Lodge Ct, Wem. HA0 87 H5
Lodge Dr, N13 59 G4
Lodge Gdns, Beck. BR3 189 J5
Lodge Hill, SE2 138 B7
Ilford IG4 80 B4
Welling DA16 138 B7
Lodgehill Pk Cl, Har. HA2 85 H2
Lodge La, N12 57 F5
Bexley DA5 158 D6
Croydon (New Adgtn)
CR0 204 A6
Lodge Pl, Sutt. SM1 199 E5
Lodge Rd, NW4 71 J4
NW8 7 F4
Bromley BR1 173 H7
Croydon CR0 187 H6
Wallington SM6 200 B5
Lodge Vil, Wdf.Grn. IG8 63 F7
Lodore Gdns, NW9 70 E5
Lodore St, E14 114 C6
Lofthouse Pl, Chess. KT9 195 F6
Loftie St, SE16 29 J4
Lofting Rd, N1 93 F7
Loftus Rd, W12 127 H1
Barking IG11 99 F6
Logan Cl, Enf. EN3 45 G1
Hounslow TW4 143 F3
Logan Ms, W8 128 D4
Logan Pl, W8 128 D4
Logan Rd, N9 61 E2
Wembley HA9 87 H2
Loggetts, The, SE21 170 B3
Logs Hill, Brom. BR1 174 B7
Chislehurst BR7 174 B7
Logs Hill Cl, Chis. BR7 192 B1
Lolesworth Cl, E1 21 F2
Lollard St, SE11 34 D1
Loman St, SE1 27 H3
Lomas Cl, Croy. CR0 204 C7
Lomas Dr, E8 94 C7
Lomas St, E1 21 J1
Lombard Av,
Enfield EN3 45 F1
Ilford IG3 99 H1
Lombard Business Pk,
SW19 185 E2
Lombard Ct, EC3 20 C5
W3 *off Crown St* 126 B1
Lombard La, EC4 19 F4
Lombard Rd, N11 58 B5
SW11 149 G2
Lombard Rd, SW19 185 E2
Lombard Rbt, Croy.
CR0 187 F7
Lombard St, EC3 20 C4
Lombard Wall, SE7 135 H3
Lombardy Cl, Ilf. IG6
off Hazel La 64 E7
Lombardy Pl, W2 14 A6
Lombardy Retail Pk, Hayes
UB3 102 B7
Lomond Cl, N15 76 B4
Wembley HA0 87 J7
Lomond Gdns, S.Croy.
CR2 203 H7
Lomond Gro, SE5 36 B7
Loncroft Rd, SE5 37 E5
Londesborough Rd,
N16 94 B4
Londinium Twr, E1
off Mansell St 21 G5
★ **London Aquarium**,
SE1 26 C3
★ **London Brass Rubbing Cen**
(St. Martin-in-the-Fields Ch),
WC2 18 A6
London Br, EC4 28 C1
SE1 28 C1
London Br St, SE1 28 B2
★ **London Butterfly Ho**,
Brent. TW8 145 E1
★ **London Canal Mus, The**,
N1 *off New Wf Rd* 10 B1
★ **London Cen Mkts**
(Smithfield Mkt), EC1 19 G1
★ **London Cen Mosque**,
NW8 7 H3
★ **London City Airport**,
E16 136 B1
★ **London Coliseum**,
WC2 18 A6
★ **London Dungeon**, SE1 28 C2
★ **London Eye**, SE1 26 C3
London Flds, E8 94 E7
London Flds E Side, E8 94 E7
London Flds W Side, E8 94 D7
★ **London Fire Brigade**
Mus, SE1 27 J3
London Fruit Ex, E1
off Brushfield St 21 F2
★ **London Heathrow**
Airport, Houns. TW6 140 E1
London Ind Est, E6 116 D5
London La, E8 95 E7
Bromley BR1 173 F7
London Master Bakers
Almshouses, E10
off Lea Br Rd 78 B6
★ **London Met Archives**,
EC1 11 F5
London Ms, W2 15 F4
★ **London Palladium**, W1 17 F4
London Pav, The, W1 17 H6
★ **London Peace Pagoda**,
SW11 32 A7
★ **London Regatta Cen**,
E16 116 A7
London Rd, E13 115 G2
SE1 27 G5
SE23 170 E1
SW16 187 F1
SW17 185 J2
Barking IG11 98 E7
Brentford TW8 125 F7
Bromley BR1 173 F7
Croydon CR0 187 H7
Enfield EN2 44 A3
Harrow HA1 86 B2
Hounslow TW3 143 J3
Isleworth TW7 144 C2
Kingston upon Thames
KT2 181 J2
Mitcham CR4 185 J2
Mitcham (Bedd.Cor.)
CR4 186 A7
Morden SM4 184 D5
Romford (Abridge)
RM4 49 J4
Romford (Chad.Hth)
RM6, RM7 83 G6
Stanmore HA7 53 F5
Sutton SM3 198 A3
Thornton Heath CR7 187 G5
Twickenham TW1 144 D5
Wallington SM6 200 B4
Wembley HA9 87 H6
London Rd Rbt, Twick.
TW1 *off Chertsey Rd* 144 D6
★ **London Silver Vaults**,
WC2 18 E2
London Stile, W4
off Wellesley Rd 126 A5
★ **London Stone**, EC4 20 B5
London St, EC3 20 E5
W2 15 E4
★ **London Television Cen**,
SE1 27 E1
London Ter, E2 13 H2
★ **London Transport Mus**,
WC2 18 B5
★ **London Trocadero, The**,
W1 17 H6
London Wall, EC2 20 A2
London Wall Bldgs, EC2 20 C2
★ **London Zoo**, NW1 8 B1
Lonesome Way, SW16 186 B1
Long Acre, WC2 18 A5
Longacre Pl, Cars. SM5
off Beddington Gdns 200 A6
Longacre Rd, E17 78 D1
Longbeach Rd, SW11 149 J3
Longberrys, NW2 90 C3
Longboat Row, Sthl.
UB1 103 F6
Longbridge Rd, Bark.
IG11 99 F7
Dagenham RM8 100 A4
Longbridge Way, SE13 154 C5
Longcliffe Path, Wat.
WD19 50 A3
Longcourt Ms, E11 79 J4
Longcroft, SE9 174 C3
Longcrofte Rd, Edg. HA8 53 G7
Longcroft Ri, Loug. IG10 48 D5
Long Deacon Rd, E4 62 E1
LONG DITTON, Surb.
KT6 195 F1
Longdon Wd, Kes. BR2 206 B4
Longdown Rd, SE6 172 A4
Long Dr, W3 106 E6
Greenford UB6 103 H1
Ruislip HA4 84 D4
Long Elmes, Har. HA3 67 H1
Longfellow Rd, E17 77 J6
Worcester Park KT4 197 G2
Longfellow Way, SE1 37 G2
Long Fld, NW9 55 E7
Longfield, Brom. BR1 191 F1
Loughton IG10 47 J5
Longfield Av, E17 77 H4
NW7 55 G7
W5 105 F7
Wallington SM6 200 A1
Wembley HA9 87 H1
Longfield Cres, SE26 171 F3
Longfield Dr, SW14 146 B5
Mitcham CR4 167 H7
Longfield Est, SE1 37 G2
Longfield Rd, W5 105 F7
Longfield St, SW18 148 D7
Longfield Wk, W5 105 F6
Longford Av, Felt. TW14 141 H6
Southall UB1 103 G7
Longford Cl, Felt. TW13
off Swift Rd 161 E3
Hampton (Hmptn H.)
TW12 161 G4
Hayes UB4
off Longford Gdns 102 D7
Longford Ct, E5
off Pedro St 95 G4
NW4 72 A4
Epsom KT19 196 C4
Longford Gdns, Hayes
UB4 102 D7
Sutton SM1 199 F3
Longford Ho, E1
off Jubilee St 113 F6
Longford Rd, Twick. TW2 161 G1
Longford St, NW1 8 E5
Longford Wk, SW2
off Papworth Way 151 G7
Long Grn, Chig. IG7 65 H4
Longhayes Av, Rom. RM6 82 D4
Longhayes Ct, Rom. RM6
off Longhayes Av 82 D4
Longheath Gdns, Croy.
CR0 189 F5
Longhedge Ho, SE26 170 C4
Long Hedges, Houns.
TW3 143 G1
Longhedge St, SW11 150 A2
Longhill Rd, SE6 172 D2
Longhook Gdns, Nthlt.
UB5 102 A2
Longhope Cl, SE15 37 F6
Longhurst Rd, SE13 154 D5
Croydon CR0 189 E6
Longland Ct, SE1 37 H3
Longland Dr, N20 56 E3
LONGLANDS, Chis. BR7 175 F3
Longlands Ct, W11
off Portobello Rd 108 C7
Mitcham CR4
off Summerhill Way 186 A1
Longlands Pk Cres, Sid.
DA15 175 H3
Longlands Rd, Sid. DA15 175 H3
Long La, EC1 19 H1
N2 73 F2
N3 56 E7
SE1 28 B4
Bexleyheath DA7 138 D7
Croydon CR0 189 F5
Staines (Stanw.) TW19 140 C7
Longleat Ho, SW1
off Rampayne St 33 H3
Longleat Rd, Enf. EN1 44 B5
Longleat Way, Felt. TW14 141 G7
Longleigh La, SE2 138 C6
Bexleyheath DA7 138 C6
Longlents Ho, NW10 106 D1
Longley Av, Wem. HA0 105 J1
Longley Ct, SW8
off Lansdowne Way 150 E1
Longley Rd, SW17 167 H6
Croydon CR0 187 H7
Harrow HA1 67 J5
Long Leys, E4 62 B6
Longley St, SE1 37 H2
Longley Way, NW2 89 J3
Long Mark Rd, E16
off Fulmer Rd 116 A5
Longmarsh La, SE28 137 H1
Long Mead, NW9 71 F1
Longmead, Chis. BR7 192 D2
Longmead Dr, Sid.
DA14 176 D2
Longmead Ho, SE27
off Elder Rd 169 J5
Long Meadow, NW5
off Torriano Av 92 D5
Long Meadow Cl, W.Wick.
BR4 190 C7
Longmeadow Rd, Sid.
DA15 175 H1
Longmead Rd, SW17 167 J5
Thames Ditton KT7 180 B7
Longmoore St, SW1 33 F2
Longmoor Pt, SW15
off Norley Vale 165 G1
Longmore Av, Barn. EN4,
EN5 41 F6
Longnor Rd, E1 113 G3
Long Pond Rd, SE3 155 E1
Long Reach Ct, Bark.
IG11 117 G2
Longreach Rd, Bark. IG11 117 J4
Longridge Ho, SE1 28 A6
Longridge La, Sthl. UB1 103 H7
Longridge Rd, SW5 128 D4
Long Rd, SW4 150 B4
Long's Ct, WC2 17 H5
Longs Ct, Rich. TW9
off Crown Ter 145 J4
Longshaw Rd, E4 62 D3
Longshore, SE8 133 J4
Longstaff Cres, SW18 148 D6
Longstaff Rd, SW18 148 D6
Longstone Av, NW10 89 F7
Longstone Ct, SE1 28 A4
Longstone Rd, SW17 168 B5
Long St, E2 13 F3
Longthornton Rd, SW16 186 C2
Longthorpe Ct, W6
off Invermead Cl 127 G3
Longton Av, SE26 170 D4
Longton Gro, SE26 170 E4
Longton Ho, SE11
off Lambeth Wk 34 D1
Longville Rd, SE11 35 G1
Long Wk, SE1 28 E5
SE18 136 E6
SW13 147 E2
New Malden KT3 182 C3
Longwalk Rd, Uxb.
UB11 121 E1
Longwood Dr, SW15 147 G6
Longwood Gdns, Ilf.
IG5, IG6 80 C4
Longworth Cl, SE28 118 D6
Long Yd, WC1 10 C6
Loning, The, NW9 71 E4
Lonsdale Av, E6 116 A3
Romford RM7 83 J6
Wembley HA9 87 H5
Lonsdale Cl, E6
off Lonsdale Av 116 B4
SE9 174 A3
Edgware HA8 53 J5
Pinner HA5 51 E7
Lonsdale Cres, Ilf. IG2 80 E6
Lonsdale Dr, Enf. EN2 43 E5
Lonsdale Gdns, Th.Hth.
CR7 187 F4
Lonsdale Ms, W11
off Lonsdale Rd 108 C6
Richmond TW9
off Elizabeth Cotts 146 A1
Lonsdale Pl, N1
off Barnsbury St 93 G7
Lonsdale Rd, E11 79 F7
NW6 108 C2
SE25 188 E4
SW13 127 G6
W4 127 F4
W11 108 C6
Bexleyheath DA7 159 F2
Southall UB2 122 D3
Lonsdale Sq, N1 93 G7
Loobert Rd, N15 76 B3
Looe Gdns, Ilf. IG6 81 E3

Loop Rd, Chis. BR7 . . . . . . 175 F6
Lopen Rd, N18 . . . . 60 B4
Loraine Cl, Enf. EN3 . . . . 45 F5
Loraine Rd, N7 . . . . 93 F4
W4 . . . . 126 B6
Lord Amory Way, E14 . . . . 134 C2
Lord Av, Ilf. IG5 . . . . 80 C4
Lord Chancellor Wk, Kings.T. KT2 . . . . 182 C1
Lordell Pl, SW19 . . . . 165 J6
Lorden Wk, E2 . . . . 13 H4
Lord Gdns, Ilf. IG5 . . . . 80 B4
Lord Hills Br, W2 . . . . 14 B2
Lord Hills Rd, W2 . . . . 14 B1
Lord Holland La, SW9 *off Urlwin Wk* 151 G2
Lord Knyvett Cl, Stai. (Stanw.) TW19 . . . . 140 A6
Lord Knyvetts Ct, Stai. (Stanw.) TW19 *off De Havilland Way* . . 140 B6
Lord Napier Pl, W6 *off Oil Mill La* 127 G5
Lord N St, SW1 . . . . 26 A6
Lord Roberts Ms, SW6 *off Waterford Rd* 128 E7
Lord Roberts Ter, SE18 . . . 136 D5
★ **Lord's** (Marylebone CC & Mus, Middlesex CCC), NW8 . . . . 7 F3
Lord's Cl, SE21 . . . . 169 J2
Lords Cl, Felt. TW13 . . . . . . 161 E2
Lordship Gro, N16 . . . . 94 A2
Lordship La, N17 . . . . 75 J1
N22 . . . . 75 G2
SE22 . . . . 152 C6
Lordship La Est, SE22 . . . . 170 D1
Lordship Pk, N16 . . . . 93 J2
Lordship Pk Ms, N16 . . . . . . 93 J2
Lordship Pl, SW3 . . . . 31 G6
Lordship Rd, N16 . . . . 94 A2
Northolt UB5 . . . . 84 E7
Lordship Ter, N16 . . . . 94 A2
Lordsmead Rd, N17 . . . . 76 B1
Lord St, E16 . . . . 136 B1
Lord's Vw, NW8 . . . . 7 F4
Lordswood Cl, Bexh. DA6 . . . . 159 E5
Lord Warwick St, SE18 . . . 136 C3
Lorenzo St, WC1 . . . . 10 C3
Loretto Gdns, Har. HA3 . . . . 69 H4
Lorian Cl, N12 . . . . 56 E4
Loring Rd, N20 . . . . 57 H2
SE14 . . . . 153 H1
Isleworth TW7 . . . . 144 C2
Loris Rd, W6 . . . . 127 J3
Lorn Ct, SW9 . . . . 151 G2
Lorne Av, Croy. CR0 . . . . . . 189 G7
Lorne Cl, NW8 . . . . 7 H4
Lorne Gdns, E11 . . . . 79 J4
W11 . . . . 128 A2
Croydon CR0 . . . . 189 G7
Lorne Rd, E7 . . . . 97 H4
E17 . . . . 78 A5
N4 . . . . 93 F1
Harrow HA3 . . . . 68 C2
Richmond TW10 *off Albert Rd* 145 J5
Lorn Rd, SW9 . . . . 151 F2
Lorraine Pk, Har. HA3 . . . . . 52 B7
Lorrimore Rd, SE17 . . . . 35 H5
Lorrimore Sq, SE17 . . . . 35 H5
Loseberry Rd, Esher (Clay.) KT10 . . . . 194 A5
Lothair Rd, W5 . . . . 125 G2
Lothair Rd N, N4 . . . . 75 H6
Lothair Rd S, N4 . . . . 75 G7
Lothair St, SW11 *off Grant Rd* 149 H3
Lothbury, EC2 . . . . 20 B3
Lothian Av, Hayes UB4 . . . 102 B5
Lothian Cl, Wem. HA0 . . . . . 86 D4
Lothian Rd, SW9 . . . . 151 H1
Lothrop St, W10 . . . . 108 B3
Lots Rd, SW10 . . . . 129 F7
Lotus Cl, SE21 . . . . 169 J3
Loubet St, SW17 . . . . 167 J6
Loudoun Av, Ilf. IG6 . . . . 81 E5
Loudoun Rd, NW8 . . . . 6 D1
Loudwater Cl, Sun. TW16 . 178 A4
Loudwater Rd, Sun. TW16 . . . . 178 A4
Loughborough Est, SW9 *off Loughborough Rd* . . 151 H2
Loughborough Pk, SW9 . . 151 H4
Loughborough Rd, SW9 . . . . 151 G2
Loughborough St, SE11 . . . 34 D3
Lough Rd, N7 . . . . 93 F6
LOUGHTON, IG10 . . . . 48 C5
Loughton Business Cen, Loughton IG10 . . . . 49 F4
Loughton Seedbed Cen, Loughton IG10 *off Langston Rd* 49 G4
Loughton Way, Buck.H. IG9 . . . . 64 A1
Louisa Cl, E9 *off Wetherell Rd* 113 G1
Louisa Gdns, E1 *off Louisa St* 113 G4
Louisa Ho, SW15 . . . . 147 E4
Louisa St, E1 . . . . 113 G4
Louise Aumonier Wk, N19 *off Hillrise Rd* 74 E7
Louise Bennett Cl, SE24 *off Shakespeare Rd* . . . 151 H4
Louise Ct, E11 *off Grosvenor Rd* 79 H5
Louise Rd, E15 . . . . 97 E6
Louis Gdns, Chis. BR7 . . . . 174 C4
Louis Ms, N10 . . . . 74 B1
Louisville Rd, SW17 . . . . . . 168 A3
Louvaine Rd, SW11 . . . . . . 149 G4
Lovage App, E6 . . . . 116 B5
Lovat Cl, NW2 . . . . 89 F3
Lovat La, EC3 . . . . 20 D6
Lovatt Cl, Edg. HA8 . . . . 54 B6
Lovat Wk, Houns. TW5 *off Cranford La* 122 E7
Loveday Rd, W13 . . . . 125 E1
Lovegrove St, SE1 . . . . 37 J4
Lovegrove Wk, E14 . . . . . . 134 C1
Lovekyn Cl, Kings.T. KT2 *off Queen Elizabeth Rd* . 181 J2
Lovelace Av, Brom. BR2 . . 192 D6
Lovelace Gdns, Bark. IG11 . . . . 100 A4
Surbiton KT6 . . . . 181 G7
Lovelace Grn, SE9 . . . . 156 C3
Lovelace Ho, W13 *off Uxbridge Rd* 105 E7
Lovelace Rd, SE21 . . . . 169 J2
Barnet EN4 . . . . 41 H7
Surbiton KT6 . . . . 181 F7
Love La, EC2 . . . . 20 A3
N17 . . . . 60 C7
SE18 . . . . 136 E4
SE25 . . . . 189 E3
Bexley DA5 . . . . 159 F6
Mitcham CR4 . . . . 185 H3
Morden SM4 . . . . 184 D7
Pinner HA5 . . . . 66 E3
Surbiton KT6 . . . . 195 G2
Sutton SM3 . . . . 198 B6
Woodford Green IG8 . . . . 64 C6
Lovel Av, Well. DA16 . . . . . 158 A2
Lovelinch Cl, SE15 . . . . 133 F6
Lovell Ho, E8 . . . . 112 D1
Lovell Pl, SE16 *off Ropemaker Rd* 133 H3
Lovell Rd, Rich. TW10 . . . . 163 F3
Southall UB1 . . . . 103 H6
Loveridge Ms, NW6 *off Loveridge Rd* 90 C6
Loveridge Rd, NW6 . . . . 90 C6
Lovers Wk, N3 . . . . 56 D7
NW7 . . . . 56 C6
SE10 . . . . 134 E6
Lover's Wk, W1 . . . . 24 B1
Lovett Dr, Cars. SM5 . . . . . 185 F7
Lovett's Pl, SW18 *off Old York Rd* 149 E4
Lovett Way, NW10 . . . . 88 C5
Love Wk, SE5 . . . . 152 A2
Lovibonds Av, Orpington BR6 . . . . 207 E4
Lowbrook Rd, Ilf. IG1 . . . . . . 99 E5
Low Cross Wd La, SE21 . . . 170 C3
Lowden Rd, N9 . . . . 61 E1
SE24 . . . . 151 H4
Southall UB1 . . . . 102 E7
Lowe Av, E16 . . . . 115 G5
Lowell St, E14 . . . . 113 H6
Lower Addiscombe Rd, Croy. CR0 . . . . 202 B1
Lower Addison Gdns, W14 . . . . 128 B2
Lower Alderton Hall La, Loug. IG10 . . . . 48 D5
Lower Belgrave St, SW1 . . . 24 D6
Lower Boston Rd, W7 . . . . 124 B1
Lower Broad St, Dag. RM10 . . . . 119 G1
Lower Camden, Chis. BR7 . . . . 174 C7
Lower Ch St, Croy. CR0 *off Waddon New Rd* . . 201 H2
LOWER CLAPTON, E5 . . . . . 95 G4
Lower Clapton Rd, E5 . . . . . 95 E5
Lower Clarendon Wk, W11 *off Lancaster Rd* 108 B6
Lower Common S, SW15 . . . . 147 H3
Lower Coombe St, Croy. CR0 . . . . 201 J4
Lower Downs Rd, SW20 . . 184 A1
Lower Drayton Pl, Croy. CR0 *off Drayton Rd* 201 H2
LOWER EDMONTON, N9 . . 60 D1
Lower George St, Rich. TW9 . . . . 145 G5
Lower Gravel Rd, Brom. BR2 . . . . 206 B1
Lower Grn Gdns, Wor.Pk. KT4 . . . . 197 G1
Lower Grn W, Mitch. CR4 . 185 H3
Lower Grosvenor Pl, SW1 . . 24 D5
Lower Gro Rd, Rich. TW10 . . . . 145 J6
Lower Hall La, E4 . . . . 61 H5
Lower Hampton Rd, Sun. TW16 . . . . 178 C3
Lower Ham Rd, Kings.T. KT2 . . . . 163 G6
LOWER HOLLOWAY, N7 . . . 93 F5
Lower James St, W1 . . . . . . 17 G5
Lower John St, W1 . . . . 17 G5
Lower Kenwood Av, Enf. EN2 . . . . 42 D5
Lower Kings Rd, Kings.T. KT2 . . . . 181 H1
Lower Lea Crossing, E14 . . . . 114 E7
E16 . . . . 114 E7
Lower Maidstone Rd, N11 *off Telford Rd* 58 C6
Lower Mall, W6 . . . . 127 H5
Lower Mardyke Av, Rain. RM13 . . . . 119 J2
Lower Marsh, SE1 . . . . 26 E4
Lower Marsh La, Kings.T. KT1 . . . . 181 J4
Lower Mast Ho, SE18 *off Woolwich Ch St* . . . 136 C3
Lower Merton Ri, NW3 . . . . 91 H7
Lower Morden La, Mord. SM4 . . . . 183 J6
Lower Mortlake Rd, Rich. TW9 . . . . 145 H4
Lower Pk Rd, N11 . . . . 58 C5
Belvedere DA17 . . . . 139 G3
Loughton IG10 . . . . 48 A5
Lower Queens Rd, Buck.H. IG9 . . . . 64 A2
Lower Richmond Rd, SW14 . . . . 146 B3
SW15 . . . . 147 J3
Richmond TW9 . . . . 146 A3
Lower Rd, SE1 . . . . 26 E3
SE8 . . . . 133 F3
SE16 . . . . 133 F3
Belvedere DA17 . . . . 139 G3
Harrow HA2 . . . . 86 A2
Loughton IG10 . . . . 48 D2
Sutton SM1 . . . . 199 F4
Lower Robert St, WC2 *off John Adam St* 18 B6
Lower Sand Hills, T.Ditt. (Long Dit.) KT7 . . . . 181 F7
Lower Sloane St, SW1 . . . . 32 B2
Lower Sq, Islw. TW7 . . . . . 144 E3
Lower Strand, NW9 . . . . 71 F2
Lower Sunbury Rd, Hmptn. TW12 . . . . 179 F2
LOWER SYDENHAM, SE26 . . . . 171 G4
Lower Sydenham Ind Est, SE26 *off Kangley Br Rd* 171 J5
Lower Tail, Wat. WD19 . . . . . 51 E3
Lower Talbot Wk, W11 *off Talbot Wk* 108 B6
Lower Teddington Rd, Kings.T. KT1 . . . . 181 G1
Lower Ter, NW3 . . . . 91 F3
Lower Thames St, EC3 . . . . 20 C6
Lower Wd Rd, Esher (Clay.) KT10 . . . . 194 D6
Lowestoft Cl, E5 *off Theydon Rd* 95 F2
Lowestoft Ms, E16 . . . . 137 E2
Loweswater Cl, Wem. HA9 . . . . 87 G2
Lowfield Rd, NW6 . . . . 90 D7
W3 . . . . 106 C6
Low Hall Cl, E4 . . . . 46 A7
Low Hall La, E17 . . . . 77 H6
Lowick Rd, Har. HA1 . . . . . . 68 B4
Lowlands Dr, Stai. (Stanw.) TW19 . . . . 140 A5
Lowlands Gdns, Rom. RM7 . . . . 83 H6
Lowlands Rd, Har. HA1 . . . . 68 B7
Pinner HA5 . . . . 66 C7
Lowman Rd, N7 . . . . 93 F4
Lowndes Cl, SW1 . . . . 24 C6
Lowndes Ct, W1 . . . . 17 F4
Bromley BR1 *off Queens Rd* 191 G2
Lowndes Pl, SW1 . . . . 24 B6
Lowndes Sq, SW1 . . . . 24 A4
Lowndes St, SW1 . . . . 24 A5
Lowood Ct, SE19 . . . . 170 C5
Lowood St, E1 *off Dellow St* 113 E7
Lowry Cres, Mitch. CR4 . . . 185 H2
Lowry Ho, E14 *off Cassilis Rd* 134 A2
Lowry Rd, Dag. RM8 . . . . . 100 B4
Lowshoe La, Rom. RM5 . . . 83 H1
Lowther Dr, Enf. EN2 . . . . . 42 E4
Lowther Gdns, SW7 . . . . . . 23 E5
Lowther Hill, SE23 . . . . 153 H7
Lowther Rd, E17 . . . . 77 H2
N7 *off Liverpool Rd* 93 G5
SW13 . . . . 147 F1
Kingston upon Thames KT2 . . . . 181 J1
Stanmore HA7 . . . . 69 J3
Lowth Rd, SE5 . . . . 151 J2
LOXFORD, Ilf. IG1 . . . . 99 F5
Loxford Av, E6 . . . . 116 A2
Loxford La, Ilf. IG1, IG3 . . . . 99 F5
Loxford Rd, Bark. IG11 . . . . 99 E6
Loxford Ter, Bark. IG11 *off Fanshawe Av* 99 F6
Loxham Rd, E4 . . . . 62 A7
Loxham St, WC1 . . . . 10 B4
Loxley Cl, SE26 . . . . 171 G5
Loxley Rd, SW18 . . . . 167 G1
Hampton TW12 . . . . 161 F4
Loxton Rd, SE23 . . . . 171 G1
Loxwood Rd, N17 . . . . 76 B3
Lubbock Rd, Chis. BR7 . . . 174 C7
Lubbock St, SE14 . . . . 133 F7
Lucan Pl, SW3 . . . . 31 G2
Lucan Rd, Barn. EN5 . . . . . . 40 B3
Lucas Av, E13 . . . . 115 H1
Harrow HA2 . . . . 85 G2
Lucas Cl, NW10 *off Pound La* 89 G7
Lucas Ct, SW11 *off Strasburg Rd* 150 A1
Harrow HA2 . . . . 85 G1
Lucas Gdns, N2 . . . . 73 F2
Lucas Rd, SE20 . . . . 171 F6
Lucas Sq, NW11 *off Hampstead Way* 72 D6
Lucas St, SE8 . . . . 154 A1
Lucerne Cl, N13 . . . . 58 E4
Lucerne Ct, Erith DA18 *off Middle Way* 138 E3
Lucerne Gro, E17 . . . . 78 D4
Lucerne Ms, W8 *off Kensington Mall* . . . 128 D1
Lucerne Rd, N5 . . . . 93 H4
Orpington BR6 . . . . 207 J1
Thornton Heath CR7 . . . 187 H5
Lucey Rd, SE16 . . . . 29 H6
Lucey Way, SE16 . . . . 29 J6
Lucien Rd, SW17 . . . . 168 A4
SW19 . . . . 166 E2
Lucknow St, SE18 . . . . 137 H7
Lucorn Cl, SE12 . . . . 155 F6
Lucton Ms, Loug. IG10 . . . . 48 E4
Luctons Av, Buck.H. IG9 . . . 63 J1
Lucy Cres, W3 . . . . 106 C5
Lucy Gdns, Dag. RM8 . . . . 101 E3
Luddesdon Rd, Erith DA8 . . . . 139 G7
Ludford Cl, Croy. CR0 *off Warrington Rd* 201 H4
Ludgate Bdy, EC4 . . . . 19 G4
Ludgate Circ, EC4 . . . . 19 G4
Ludgate Hill, EC4 . . . . 19 G4
Ludgate Sq, EC4 . . . . 19 H4
Ludham Cl, SE28 *off Rollesby Way* 118 C6
Ilford IG6 . . . . 81 F1
Ludlow Cl, Brom. BR2 *off Aylesbury Rd* 191 G3
Harrow HA2 . . . . 85 F4
Ludlow Mead, Wat. WD19 . . 50 B3
Ludlow Rd, W5 . . . . 105 F4
Feltham TW13 . . . . 160 A4
Ludlow St, EC1 . . . . 11 J5
Ludlow Way, N2 . . . . 73 F4
Ludovick Wk, SW15 . . . . . . 147 E4
Ludwick Ms, SE14 . . . . 133 H7
Luffield Rd, SE2 . . . . 138 B3
Luffman Rd, SE12 . . . . 173 H3
Lugard Rd, SE15 . . . . 153 E2
Lugg App, E12 . . . . 98 D3
Luke Ho, E1 . . . . 112 E6
Luke St, EC2 . . . . 12 D5
Lukin Cres, E4 . . . . 62 D3
Lukin St, E1 . . . . 113 F6
Lukintone Cl, Loug. IG10 . . . 48 B6
Lullingstone Cl, Orp. BR5 *off Lullingstone Cres* . . 176 B7
Lullingstone Cres, Orp. BR5 . . . . 176 A7
Lullingstone La, SE13 . . . . 154 D6
Lullingstone Rd, Belv. DA17 . . . . 139 F6
Lullington Garth, N12 . . . . . 56 C5
Borehamwood WD6 . . . . 38 B5
Bromley BR1 . . . . 173 E7
Lullington Rd, SE20 . . . . . . 170 D7
Dagenham RM9 . . . . 100 E7
Lulot Gdns, N19 . . . . 92 B2
Lulworth, NW1 *off Agar Pl* 92 D7
SE17 . . . . 36 B3
Lulworth Av, Houns. TW5 . . . . 123 H7
Wembley HA9 . . . . 69 F7

Lulworth Cl, Har. HA2 .....85 F3
Lulworth Cres, Mitch.
CR4 ....185 H2
Lulworth Dr, Pnr. HA5 .....66 D7
Lulworth Gdns, Har. HA2 ..85 E2
Lulworth Ho, SW8 ....34 C7
Lulworth Rd, SE9 ....174 B2
SE15 ....153 E2
Welling DA16 ....157 J2
Lulworth Waye, Hayes
UB4 ....102 C6
Lumen Rd, Wem. HA9 .....87 G2
Lumiere Ct, SW17 ....168 A2
Lumley Cl, Belv. DA17 ....139 G6
Lumley Ct, WC2 ....18 B6
Lumley Flats, SW1
off Holbein Pl 32 B3
Lumley Gdns, Sutt. SM3 ..198 B5
Lumley Rd, Sutt. SM3 ....198 B6
Lumley St, W1 ....16 C4
Luna Ho, SE16 ....29 J3
Luna Rd, Th.Hth. CR7 .....187 J3
Lundin Wk, Wat. WD19 .....50 D4
Lund Pt, E15
off Carpenters Rd 114 C1
Lundy Dr, Hayes UB3 ....121 H4
Lundy Wk, N1
off Clifton Rd 93 J6
Lunham Rd, SE19 ....170 B6
Lupin Cl, SW2
off Palace Rd 169 H2
Croydon CR0
off Primrose La 203 G1
West Drayton UB7
off Magnolia St 120 A5
Lupin Cres, Ilf. IG1
off Bluebell Way 99 E6
Lupino Ct, SE11 ....34 D2
Lupin Pt, SE1 ....29 G4
Lupton Cl, SE12 ....173 H4
Lupton St, NW5 ....92 C4
Lupus St, SW1 ....33 G4
Luralda Gdns, E14
off Saunders Ness Rd ..134 C5
Lurgan Av, W6 ....128 A6
Lurline Gdns, SW11 ......150 A1
Luscombe Ct, Brom. BR2 .190 E2
Luscombe Way, SW8 ......34 A7
Lushes Ct, Loug. IG10
off Lushes Rd 49 E5
Lushes Rd, Loug. IG10 .....49 E5
Lushington Rd, NW10 ....107 H2
SE6 ....172 B5
Lushington Ter, E8
off Wayland Av 94 D5
Luther Cl, Edg. HA8 ......54 C2
Luther King Cl, E17 ....77 H6
Luther Ms, Tedd. TW11
off Luther Rd 162 C5
Luther Rd, Tedd. TW11 ....162 C5
Luton Pl, SE10 ....134 C7
Luton Rd, E13 ....115 G4
E17 ....77 J3
Sidcup DA14 ....176 C3
Luton St, NW8 ....7 F6
Lutton Ter, NW3 ....91 F4
Luttrell Av, SW15 ....147 H5
Lutwyche Rd, SE6 ....171 J2
Lutyens Ho, SW1
off Churchill Gdns 33 F4
Luxborough La, Chig. IG7 ..64 B3
Luxborough St, W1 ....16 B1
Luxborough Twr, W1
off Luxborough St 16 B1
Luxembourg Ms, E15
off Leytonstone Rd 96 E5
Luxemburg Gdns, W6 ....128 A4
Luxfield Rd, SE9 ....174 B1
Luxford St, SE16 ....133 G4
Luxmore St, SE4 ....153 J1
Luxor St, SE5 ....151 H2
Lyall Av, SE21 ....170 B3
Lyall Ms, SW1 ....24 B6
Lyall Ms W, SW1 ....24 B6
Lyall St, SW1 ....24 B6
Lyal Rd, E3 ....113 H2
Lycée, The, SE11 ....35 F4
Lycett Pl, W12
off Becklow Rd 127 G2
Lyconby Gdns, Croy. CR0 .189 H7
Lydd Cl, Sid. DA14 ....175 H3
Lydden Ct, SE9 ....157 H6
Lydden Gro, SW18 ....148 E7
Lydden Rd, SW18 ....148 E7
Lydd Rd, Bexh. DA7 ......139 F7
Lydeard Rd, E6 ....98 C7
Lydford Cl, N16
off Pellerin Rd 94 B5
Lydford Rd, N15 ....76 A5
NW2 ....90 A6
W9 ....108 C4
Lydhurst Av, SW2 ....169 F2
Lydney Cl, SW19
off Princes Way 166 B2
Lydon Rd, SW4 ....150 C3
Lydstep Rd, Chis. BR7 ....174 D4
Lyford Rd, SW18 ....149 G7
Lyford St, SE18 ....136 B4
Lygon Ho, SW6
off Fulham Palace Rd .148 B1
Lygon Pl, SW1 ....24 D6
Lyham Cl, SW2 ....151 E6
Lyham Rd, SW2 ....150 E5
Lyle Cl, Mitch. CR4 ....186 A7
Lyme Fm Rd, SE12 ....155 G4
Lyme Gro, E9
off St. Thomas's Sq 95 F7
Lymer Av, SE19 ....170 C5
Lyme Rd, Well. DA16 .....158 B1
Lymescote Gdns, Sutt.
SM1 ....198 D2
Lyme St, NW1 ....92 C7
Lyme Ter, NW1
off Royal Coll St 92 C7
Lyminge Cl, Sid. DA14 ....175 J4
Lyminge Gdns, SW18 ....167 H1
Lymington Av, N22 ....75 G2
Lymington Cl, E6
off Valiant Way 116 C5
SW16 ....186 D2
Lymington Ct, Sutt. SM1
off All Saints Rd 199 F3
Lymington Gdns, Epsom
KT19 ....197 F5
Lymington Rd, NW6 ......90 E6
Dagenham RM8 ....100 D1
Lyminster Cl, Hayes UB4
off West Quay Dr 102 E5
Lympstone Gdns, SE15 ....37 J7
Lynbridge Gdns, N13 ......59 H4
Lynbrook Gro, SE15 ....36 E7
Lynch Cl, SE3
off Paragon Pl 155 F2
Lynchen Cl, Houns. TW5
off The Avenue 142 A1
Lynch Wk, SE8
off Prince St 133 J6
Lyncott Cres, SW4 ....150 B4
Lyncroft Av, Pnr. HA5 .....66 E5
Lyncroft Gdns, NW6 ......90 D5
W13 ....125 F2
Hounslow TW3 ....143 J4
Lyndale, NW2 ....90 C4
Lyndale Av, NW2 ....90 C3
Lyndale Cl, SE3 ....135 F6
Lynden Hyrst, Croy. CRO .202 C2
Lyndhurst Av, N12 ....57 J6
NW7 ....54 E6
SW16 ....186 D2
Pinner HA5 ....66 B1
Southall UB1 ....123 H1
Sunbury-on-Thames
TW16 ....178 A3
Surbiton KT5 ....196 B1
Twickenham TW2 ......161 F1
Lyndhurst Cl, NW10 ....88 D3
Bexleyheath DA7 ......159 H3
Croydon CR0 ....202 C3
Orpington BR6 ....207 E4
Lyndhurst Ct, E18
off Churchfields 79 G1
Sutton SM2
off Overton Rd 198 D7
Lyndhurst Dr, E10 ....78 C7
New Malden KT3 ......183 E6
Lyndhurst Gdns, N3 ......72 B1
NW3 ....91 G5
Barking IG11 ....99 H6
Enfield EN1 ....44 B4
Ilford IG2 ....81 G6
Pinner HA5 ....66 B1
Lyndhurst Gro, SE15 .....152 B2
Lyndhurst Ho, SW15
off Ellisfield Dr 147 G7
Lyndhurst Ri, Chig. IG7 ....64 D4
Lyndhurst Rd, E4 ....62 C7
N18 ....60 D4
N22 ....59 F6
NW3 ....91 G5
Bexleyheath DA7 ......159 H3
Greenford UB6 ....103 H4
Thornton Heath CR7 ...187 G4
Lyndhurst Sq, SE15 .....152 C1
Lyndhurst Ter, NW3 ....91 G5
Lyndhurst Way, SE15 .....152 C1
Sutton SM2 ....198 D7
Lyndon Av, Pnr. HA5 ......51 E6
Sidcup DA15 ....157 J5
Wallington SM6 ....200 A3
Lyndon Rd, Belv. DA17 ...139 G4
Lyndon Yd, SW17 ....167 E4
Lyne Cres, E17 ....77 J1
Lyneham Dr, NW9 ....70 E1
Lyneham Wk, E5
off Boscombe Cl 95 H5
Lynette Av, SW4 ....150 B6
Lynett Rd, Dagenham
RM8 ....100 D2
Lynford Cl, Barn. EN5 .....39 F5
Edgware HA8 ....54 C7
Lynford Gdns, Edg. HA8 ...54 B3
Ilford IG3 ....99 J2
Lynmere Rd, Well.
DA16 ....158 B2
Lyn Ms, E3
off Tredegar Sq 113 J3
N16 ....94 B4
Lynmouth Av, Enf. EN1 ....44 C6
Morden SM4 ....184 A7
Lynmouth Dr, Ruis. HA4 ...84 B2
Lynmouth Gdns, Grnf.
(Perivale) UB6 ....105 E1
Hounslow TW5 ....142 D1
Lynmouth Rd, E17 ....77 H6
N2 ....73 J3
N16 ....94 C1
Greenford (Perivale)
UB6 ....105 E1
Lynn Cl, Har. HA3 ....68 A2
Lynne Cl, Orp.
(Grn St Grn) BR6 ......207 J6
Lynne Way, Nthlt. UB5 ....102 D2
Lynn Ms, E11 off Lynn Rd ..97 E2
Lynn Rd, E11 ....96 E2
SW12 ....150 B7
Ilford IG2 ....81 G7
Lynn St, Enf. EN2 ....44 A1
Lynsted Cl, Bexh. DA6 ....159 H5
Bromley BR1 ....191 J2
Lynsted Ct, Beck. BR3
off Churchfields Rd ...189 H2
Lynsted Gdns, SE9 ......156 A3
Lynton Av, N12 ....57 G4
NW9 ....71 F4
W13 ....104 D6
Romford RM7 ....83 G1
Lynton Cl, NW10 ....88 E5
Chessington KT9 ......195 H4
Isleworth TW7 ....144 C4
Lynton Cres, Ilf. IG2 ....80 E6
Lynton Est, SE1 ....37 H2
Lynton Gdns, N11 ....58 D6
Enfield EN1 ....44 B7
Lynton Mead, N20 ....56 D3
Lynton Rd, E4 ....62 B5
N8 ....74 D5
NW6 ....108 C1
SE1 ....37 G2
W3 ....106 A7
Croydon CR0 ....187 G6
Harrow HA2 ....85 E2
New Malden KT3 ......182 D5
Lynton Ter, W3 ....106 B6
Lynwood Cl, E18 ....79 J1
Harrow HA2 ....85 E3
Lynwood Dr, Wor.Pk. KT4 .197 G2
Lynwood Gdns, Croy.
CR0 ....201 F4
Southall UB1 ....103 F6
Lynwood Gro, N21 ....59 G1
Orpington BR6 ....193 H7
Lynwood Rd, SW17 ......167 J3
W5 ....105 H4
Thames Ditton KT7 ....194 C2
Lynx Way, E16 ....116 A7
Lyon Business Pk, Bark.
IG11 ....117 H2
Lyon Meade, Stan. HA7 ....69 F1
Lyon Pk Av, Wem. HA0 ....87 H6
Lyon Rd, SW19 ....185 F1
Harrow HA1 ....68 C6
Lyonsdown Av, Barn.
(New Barn.) EN5 ....41 F6
Lyonsdown Rd, Barn.
(New Barn.) EN5 ....41 F6
Lyons Pl, NW8 ....7 E5
Lyon St, N1
off Caledonian Rd 93 F7
Lyons Wk, W14 ....128 B4
Lyon Way, Grnf. UB6 .....104 B1
Lyoth Rd, Orp. BR5 ......207 F2
Lyric Dr, Grnf. UB6 ....103 H4
★ Lyric Hammersmith,
W6 ....127 J4
Lyric Ms, SE26 ....171 F4
Lyric Rd, SW13 ....147 F1
Lyric Sq, W6 off King St ..127 J4
Lysander Gdns, Surb. KT6
off Ewell Rd 181 J6
Lysander Gro, N19 ....92 D1
Lysander Ho, E2
off Temple St 112 E2
Lysander Ms, N19
off Lysander Gro 92 D1
Lysander Rd, Croy. CR0 ...201 F6
Lysander Way, Orp.
BR6 ....207 F3
Lysias Rd, SW12 ....150 A6
Lysia St, SW6 ....128 A7
Lysons Wk, SW15 ....147 G5
Lytchet Rd, Brom. BR1 ....173 H7
Lytchet Way, Enf. EN3 .....45 F1
Lytchgate Cl, S.Croy.
CR2 ....202 B7
Lytcott Dr, W.Mol. KT8
off Freeman Dr 179 F4
Lytcott Gro, SE22 ....152 C5
Lyte St, E2
off Bishops Way 113 F2
Lytham Av, Wat. WD19 ....50 D5
Lytham Cl, SE28 ....118 E6
Lytham Gro, W5 ....105 J3
Lytham St, SE17 ....36 B4
Lyttelton Cl, NW3 ....91 H7
Lyttelton Rd, E10 ....96 B3
N2 ....73 F5
Lyttleton Rd, N8 ....75 G3
Lytton Av, N13 ....59 G2
Lytton Cl, N2 ....73 G5
Loughton IG10 ....49 G3
Northolt UB5 ....85 F7
Lytton Gdns, Wall. SM6 ...200 D4
Lytton Gro, SW15 ....148 A5
Lytton Rd, E11 ....78 E7
Barnet EN5 ....41 F4
Pinner HA5 ....50 E7
Lytton Strachey Path, SE28
off Titmuss Av 118 B7
Lyveden Rd, SE3 ....135 H7
SW17 ....167 H6

M

Maberley Cres, SE19 .....170 D7
Maberley Rd, SE19 ....188 C1
Beckenham BR3 ....189 G3
Mabledon Pl, WC1 ....9 J4
Mablethorpe Rd, SW6 ....128 B7
Mabley St, E9 ....95 H6
McAdam Dr, Enf. EN2 .....43 H2
Macaret Cl, N20 ....41 E7
MacArthur Cl, E7 ....97 G6
Wembley HA9 ....88 B6
MacArthur Ter, SE7 ....136 A6
Macaulay Av, Esher KT10 .194 B2
Macaulay Ct, SW4 ....150 B3
Macaulay Rd, E6 ....116 A2
SW4 ....150 B3
Macaulay Sq, SW4 ......150 B4
Macaulay Way, SE28
off Booth Cl 118 B7
McAuley Cl, SE1 ....26 E5
SE9 ....156 E5
Macauley Ms, SE13 ......154 C2
Macbean St, SE18 ....136 D3
Macbeth St, W6 ....127 H5
McCall Cl, SW4
off Jeffreys Rd 150 E2
McCall Cres, SE7 ....136 B5
McCarthy Rd, Felt. TW13 ..160 D5
Macclesfield Br, NW1 ......7 H1
Macclesfield Rd, EC1 ......11 J3
SE25 ....189 E5
Macclesfield St, W1 ....17 J5
McCoid Way, SE1 ....27 J4
McCrone Ms, NW3
off Belsize La 91 G6
McCullum Rd, E3 ....113 J1
McDermott Cl, SW11 .....149 H3
McDermott Rd, SE15 .....152 D3
Macdonald Av, Dag.
RM10 ....101 H3
Macdonald Rd, E7 ....97 G4
E17 ....78 C2
N11 ....57 J5
N19 ....92 C2
McDonough Cl, Chess.
KT9 ....195 H4
McDowall Cl, E16 ....115 F5
McDowall Rd, SE5 ....151 J1
Macduff Rd, SW11 ....150 A1
Mace Cl, E1
off Kennet St 132 E1
McEntee Av, E17 ....77 H1
Mace St, E2 ....113 G2
McEwen Way, E15 ....114 D1
Macey Ho, SW11
off Surrey La 149 H1
Macfarland Gro, SE15 .....36 E7
MacFarlane La, Islw. TW7 .124 C6
Macfarlane Rd, W12 .....127 J1
Macfarren Pl, NW1 ....8 C6
McGrath Rd, E15 ....97 F5
Macgregor Rd, E16 ....115 J5
McGregor Rd, W11 ....108 C6
Machell Rd, SE15 ....153 F3
McIntosh Cl, Wall. SM6 ...200 E7
Mackay Rd, SW4 ....150 B3
McKay Rd, SW20 ....165 H7
McKellar Cl, Bushey
(Bushey Hth) WD23 .....51 J2
Mackennal St, NW8 ....7 H2
Mackenzie Cl, W12
off Australia Rd 107 H7
Mackenzie Rd, N7 ....93 F6
Beckenham BR3 ....189 F2
Mackenzie Wk, E14 ......134 A1
McKerrell Rd, SE15 ......152 D1
Mackeson Rd, NW3 ....91 J4
Mackie Rd, SW2 ....151 G7
Mackintosh La, E9
off Homerton High St ..95 G5
Macklin St, WC2 ....18 B3
Mackrow Wk, E14
off Robin Hood La 114 C7
Macks Rd, SE16 ....37 J1
Mackworth St, NW1 ....9 F3

Maclaren Ms, SW15
off Clarendon Dr 147 J4
Maclean Rd, SE23 153 H6
Macleod Rd, N21 43 E5
McLeod Rd, SE2 138 B4
McLeod's Ms, SW7 22 B6
Macleod St, SE17 36 A4
Maclise Rd, W14 128 B3
McMillan St, SE8 134 A6
McMillan Student Village, SE8 *off Creek Rd* 134 A6
Macmillan Way, SW17 168 B4
McNair Rd, Sthl. UB2 123 H2
McNeil Rd, SE5 152 B2
McNicol Dr, NW10 106 C2
Macoma Rd, SE18 137 G6
Macoma Ter, SE18 137 G6
Maconochies Rd, E14 134 B5
Macquarie Way, E14 134 B4
McRae La, Mitch. CR4 185 J7
Macroom Rd, W9 108 C3
Mac's Pl, EC4 19 F3
★ **Madame Tussauds**, NW1 8 B6
Mada Rd, Orp. BR6 206 E3
Maddams St, E3 114 B4
Maddison Cl, N2
off Long La 73 F2
Teddington TW11 162 C6
Maddocks Cl, Sid. DA14 176 E5
Maddock Way, SE17 35 H6
Maddox St, W1 16 E5
Madeira Av, Brom. BR1 172 E7
Madeira Gro, Wdf.Grn. IG8 63 J6
Madeira Rd, E11 96 D1
N13 59 H4
SW16 169 E5
Mitcham CR4 185 J4
Madeleine Cl, Rom. RM6 82 C6
Madeleine Terr, SE5 152 C1
Madeley Rd, W5 105 H6
Madeline Gro, Ilf. IG1 99 G5
Madeline Rd, SE20 188 D1
Madge Gill Way, E6
off Ron Leighton Way 116 B1
Madinah Rd, E8 94 D6
Madingley, Kings.T. KT1
off St. Peters Rd 182 A2
Madison Bldg, SE10
off Blackheath Rd 154 B1
Madison Ct, Dag. RM10
off Reede Way 101 H6
Madison Cres, Bexh. DA7 138 C7
Madison Gdns, Bexh. DA7 138 C7
Bromley BR2 191 F3
Madison Hts, Houns. TW3
off High St 143 J3
Madras Pl, N7 93 G6
Madras Rd, Ilf. IG1 98 E4
Madrid Rd, SW13 147 G1
Madrigal La, SE5 131 H7
Madron St, SE17 36 E3
Mafeking Av, E6 116 A2
Brentford TW8 125 H6
Ilford IG2 81 G7
Mafeking Rd, E16 115 F4
N17 76 D2
Enfield EN1 44 C3
Magdala Av, N19 92 B2
Magdala Rd, Islw. TW7 144 D3
South Croydon CR2
off Napier Rd 202 A7
Magdalene Cl, SE15
off Pilkington Rd 152 E2
Magdalene Gdns, E6 116 D4
N20 57 J1
Magdalen Ms, NW3
off Frognal 91 F6
Magdalen Pas, E1 21 G5
Magdalen Rd, SW18 167 F1
Magdalen St, SE1 28 D2
Magee St, SE11 35 E5
Magellan Boul, E16 117 F7
Magellan Pl, E14
off Maritime Quay 134 A4
Maggie Blakes Causeway, SE1 *off Shad Thames* 29 F2
Magnet Rd, Wem. HA9 87 G2
Magnin Cl, E8
off Wilde Cl 112 D1
Magnolia Cl, E10 96 A2
Kingston upon Thames KT2 164 B6
Magnolia Ct, Felt. TW13
off Highfield Rd 160 A1
Harrow HA3 69 J7
Wallington SM6
off Parkgate Rd 200 B5
Magnolia Gdns, Edg. HA8 54 C4
Magnolia Pl, SW4 150 D5
W5 105 G5
Magnolia Rd, W4 126 B6
Magnolia St, West Dr. UB7 120 A4
Magnolia Way, Epsom KT19 196 C5
Magnum Ho, Kings.T. KT2
off London Rd 182 A1
Magnus Ct, N9
off Bedevere Rd 60 D3
Magpie All, EC4 19 F4
Magpie Cl, E7 97 F5
NW9 *off Eagle Dr* 71 E2
Enfield EN1 44 D1
Magpie Hall Cl, Brom. BR2 192 B6
Magpie Hall La, Brom. BR2 192 C5
Magpie Hall Rd, Bushey (Bushey Hth) WD23 52 B2
Magpie Pl, SE14
off Milton Ct Rd 133 H6
Magri Wk, E1
off Ashfield St 113 F5
Maguire Dr, Rich. TW10 163 F4
Maguire St, SE1 29 G3
Mahatma Gandhi Ind Est, SE24 *off Milkwood Rd* 151 H4
Mahlon Av, Ruis. HA4 84 B5
Mahogany Cl, SE16 133 H1
Mahon Cl, Enf. EN1 44 C1
Maida Av, E4 46 B7
W2 14 D1
MAIDA HILL, W9 108 C4
Maida Rd, Belv. DA17 139 G3
MAIDA VALE, W9 6 B5
Maida Vale, W9 6 C4
Maida Way, E4 46 B7
Maiden Erlegh Av, Bex. DA5 176 E1
Maiden La, NW1 92 D7
SE1 28 A1
WC2 18 B6
Maiden Pl, NW5 92 C3
Maiden Rd, E15 97 E7
Maidenstone Hill, SE10 154 C1
Maids of Honour Row, Rich. TW9
off The Green 145 G5
Maidstone Av, Rom. RM5 83 J2
Maidstone Bldgs Ms, SE1 28 A2
Maidstone Ho, E14
off Carmen St 114 B6
Maidstone Rd, N11 58 C6
Sidcup DA14 176 D6
Main Av, Enf. EN1 44 C5
Main Dr, Wem. HA9 87 G3
Mainridge Rd, Chis. BR7 174 D4
Main Rd, Sid. DA14 175 H3
Main St, Felt. TW13 160 D5
Maismore St, SE15 37 J6
Maisonettes, The, Sutt. SM1 198 C5
Maitland Cl, Houns. TW4 143 F3
Maitland Cl Est, SE10
off Greenwich High Rd 134 B7
Maitland Pk Est, NW3 91 J6
Maitland Pk Rd, NW3 91 J6
Maitland Pk Vil, NW3 91 J6
Maitland Pl, E5
off Lower Clapton Rd 95 F4
Maitland Rd, E15 97 F6
SE26 171 G6
Majendie Rd, SE18 137 G5
Majestic Way, Mitch. CR4 185 J2
Major Cl, SW9 151 H3
Major Rd, E15 96 C5
SE16 29 J5
Makepeace Av, N6 92 A2
Makepeace Rd, E11 79 G4
Northolt UB5 102 E2
Makins St, SW3 31 H2
Malabar St, E14 134 A2
Malam Gdns, E14
off Wades Pl 114 B7
Malbrook Rd, SW15 147 H4
Malcolm Ct, Stan. HA7 53 F5
Malcolm Cres, NW4 71 G6
Malcolm Dr, Surb. KT6 195 H1
Malcolm Pl, E2 113 F4
Malcolm Rd, E1 113 F4
SE20 171 F7
SE25 188 D6
SW19 166 B6
Malcolms Way, N14 42 C5
Malcolm Way, E11 79 G5
Malden Av, SE25 188 E4
Greenford UB6 86 B5
Malden Ct, N.Mal. KT3 183 H3
Malden Cres, NW1 92 A6
Malden Grn Av, Wor.Pk. KT4 197 F1
Malden Grn Ms, Wor.Pk. KT4 *off Malden Rd* 197 G1
Malden Hill, N.Mal. KT3 183 F3
Malden Hill Gdns, N.Mal. KT3 183 F3
Malden Junct, N.Mal. KT3 183 F5
Malden Pk, N.Mal. KT3 183 F6
Malden Pl, NW5
off Grafton Ter 92 A5
Malden Rd, NW5 92 A5
Borehamwood WD6 38 A3
New Malden KT3 183 E5
Sutton SM3 198 A4
Worcester Park KT4 183 F7
Malden Way, N.Mal. KT3 183 F5
Maldon Cl, E15
off Maryland St 96 D5
N1 111 J1
SE5 152 B3
Maldon Ct, Wall. SM6 200 C5
Maldon Rd, N9 60 C3
W3 106 C7
Romford RM7 83 J7
Wallington SM6 200 B5
Maldon Wk, Wdf.Grn. IG8 63 J6
Malet Pl, WC1 9 H6
Malet St, WC1 9 H6
Maley Av, SE27 169 H2
Malford Ct, E18 79 G2
Malford Gro, E18 79 F4
Malfort Rd, SE5 152 B3
Malham Cl, N11
off Catterick Cl 58 A6
Malham Rd, SE23 171 G1
Malham Ter, N18
off Dysons Rd 61 E6
Malins Cl, Barn. EN5 39 H5
Mall, The, N14 58 E3
SW1 25 G3
SW14 146 C5
W5 105 H7
Bromley BR1 191 G3
Croydon CR0 201 J2
Harrow HA3 69 J6
Surbiton KT6 181 G5
Mallams Ms, SW9
off St. James's Cres 151 H3
Mallard Cl, E9
off Berkshire Rd 95 J6
NW6 108 D2
W7 124 B2
Barnet (New Barn.) EN5
off The Hook 41 G6
Twickenham TW2
off Stephenson Rd 143 G7
Mallard Path, SE28
off Goosander Way 137 G3
Mallard Pl, Twick. TW1 162 D3
Mallard Pt, E3
off Rainhill Way 114 B3
Mallards, E11 79 G7
Mallards Rd, Bark. IG11 118 A3
Woodford Green IG8 63 H7
Mallard Wk, Beck. BR3 189 G5
Sidcup DA14 176 C5
Mallard Way, NW9 70 C7
Mall Chambers, W8
off Kensington Mall 128 D1
Mallet Dr, Nthlt. UB5 85 F5
Mallet Rd, SE13 154 D6
Mall Ex, The, Ilf. IG1 98 E2
★ **Mall Galleries**, SW1 25 J1
Malling, SE13 154 C5
Malling Cl, Croy. CR0 189 F6
Malling Gdns, Mord. SM4 185 F6
Malling Way, Brom. BR2 191 F7
Mallinson Rd, SW11 149 H5
Croydon CR0 200 D3
Mallord St, SW3 31 F5
Mallory Cl, E14
off Uamvar St 114 B5
SE4 153 H4
Mallory Gdns, Barn. (E.Barn.) EN4 42 A7
Mallory St, NW8 7 H5
Mallow Cl, Croy. CR0
off Marigold Way 203 G1
Mallow Mead, NW7 56 B7
Mallow St, EC1 12 B5
Mall Rd, W6 127 H5
Mall Shop Cen, The, Dag. RM10 *off Heathway* 101 G6
Mall Walthamstow, The, E17 77 J4
Malmains Cl, Beck. BR3 190 D5
Malmains Way, Beck. BR3 190 C4
Malmesbury, E2
off Cyprus St 113 F2
Malmesbury Rd, E3 113 J3
E16 115 E5
E18 79 F1
Morden SM4 185 F7
Malmesbury Ter, E16 115 F5
Malmsmead Ho, E9
off Kingsmead Way 95 H5
Malory Cl, Beck. BR3 189 H2
Malory Ct, N9
off Galahad Rd 60 D3
Malpas Dr, Pnr. HA5 66 D5
Malpas Rd, E8 94 E6
SE4 153 J2
Dagenham RM9 100 D6
Malta Rd, E10 96 A1
Malta St, EC1 11 H5
Maltby Rd, Chess. KT9 196 A6
Maltby St, SE1 29 F4
Malthouse Dr, W4 127 E6
Feltham TW13 160 D5
Malthouse Pas, SW13
off The Terrace 147 E2
Malthus Path, SE28
off Owen Cl 138 C1
Malting Ho, E14 113 J7
Maltings, The, Orp. BR6 207 J1
Worcester Park KT4
off Sherbrooke Way 183 H7
Maltings Cl, E3 114 C3
SW13
off Cleveland Gdns 147 E2
Maltings Ms, Sid. DA15
off Station Rd 176 A3
Maltings Pl, SE1 29 E4
SW6 149 E1
Malting Way, Islw. TW7 144 C3
Malton Ms, SE18
off Malton St 137 H6
W10
off Cambridge Gdns 108 B6
Malton Rd, W10
off St. Marks Rd 108 B6
Malton St, SE18 137 H6
Maltravers St, WC2 18 D5
Malt St, SE1 37 H5
Malva Cl, SW18
off St. Ann's Hill 149 E5
Malvern Av, E4 62 D7
Bexleyheath DA7 138 E7
Harrow HA2 85 E3
Malvern Cl, SE20
off Derwent Rd 188 D2
W10 108 C5
Mitcham CR4 186 C3
Surbiton KT6 195 H1
Malvern Ct, SE14
off Avonley Rd 133 F7
SW7 31 F2
Sutton SM2
off Overton Rd 198 D7
Malvern Dr,
Feltham TW13 160 D5
Ilford IG3 99 J4
Woodford Green IG8 63 J5
Malvern Gdns, NW2 90 B2
NW6 *off Carlton Vale* 108 C2
Harrow HA3 69 H3
Loughton IG10 48 C6
Malvern Ms, NW6
off Malvern Rd 108 D3
Malvern Pl, NW6 108 C3
Malvern Rd, E6 116 B1
E8 94 D7
E11 97 E2
N8 75 F3
N17 76 D3
NW6 108 D3
Hampton TW12 161 G7
Hayes UB3 121 H7
Surbiton KT6 195 H2
Thornton Heath CR7 187 G4
Malvern Ter, N1 111 G1
N9 60 C1
Malvern Way, W13
off Templewood 105 E5
Malwood Rd, SW12 150 B6
Malyons Rd, SE13 154 B5
Malyons Ter, SE13 154 B5
Managers St, E14
off Prestons Rd 134 C1
Manatee Pl, Wall. SM6
off Croydon Rd 200 D3
Manaton Cl, SE15 152 E3
Manaton Cres, Sthl. UB1 103 G6
Manbey Gro, E15 96 E6
Manbey Pk Rd, E15 96 E6
Manbey Rd, E15 96 E6
Manbey St, E15 96 E6
Manbre Rd, W6 127 J6
Manbrough Av, E6 116 C3
Manchester Ct, E16 115 H6
Manchester Dr, W10 108 B4
Manchester Gro, E14 134 C5
Manchester Ms, W1 16 B2
Manchester Rd, E14 134 C5
N15 76 A6
Thornton Heath CR7 187 J3
Manchester Sq, W1 16 B3
Manchester St, W1 16 B2
Manchester Way, Dag. RM10 101 H4
Manchuria Rd, SW11 150 A6
Manciple St, SE1 28 B4
Mandalay Rd, SW4 150 C5
Mandarin Way, Hayes UB4 102 D6
Mandela Cl, NW10 88 C7
Mandela Rd, E16 115 G6

Mandela St, NW1 ....110 C1
SW9 ....131 G7
Mandela Way, SE1 ....36 E1
Mandel Ho, SW18
off Eastfields Av 148 D4
Mandeville Cl, SE3
off Vanbrugh Pk 135 F7
SW20 ....184 B1
Mandeville Ct, E4 ....61 H4
Mandeville Dr, Surb. KT6 .195 G1
Mandeville Ho, SE1 ....37 G3
Mandeville Ms, SW4
off Clapham Pk Rd ...150 E4
Mandeville Pl, W1 ....16 C3
Mandeville Rd, N14 ....58 B2
Isleworth TW7 ....144 D2
Northolt UB5 ....85 G7
Mandeville St, E5 ....95 H3
Mandrake Rd, SW17 ....167 J3
Mandrake Way, E15 ....96 E7
Mandrell Rd, SW2 ....150 E5
Manette St, W1 ....17 J4
Manford Way, Chig. IG7 ...65 H4
Manfred Rd, SW15 ....148 C5
Manger Rd, N7 ....93 E6
Mangold Way, Erith
DA18 ....138 E3
Manhattan Bldg, E3
off Fairfield Rd 114 A2
Manhattan Wf, E16 ....135 G2
Manilla St, E14 ....134 A2
Manister Rd, SE2 ....138 A3
Manitoba Ct, SE16
off Renforth St 133 F2
Manitoba Gdns, Orp.
(Grn St Grn) BR6
off Superior Dr 207 J6
Manley Ct, N16
off Stoke Newington
High St 94 C3
Manley St, NW1 ....110 A1
Mann Cl, Croy. CR0
off Scarbrook Rd 201 J3
Manneby Prior, N1
off Cumming St 10 D2
Manningford Cl, EC1 ....11 G3
Manning Gdns, Har. HA3 ..69 G7
Manning Pl, Rich. TW10
off Grove Rd 145 J6
Manning Rd, E17
off Southcote Rd 77 H5
Dagenham RM10 ....101 G6
Manningtree Cl, SW19 ...166 B1
Manningtree Rd, Ruis.
HA4 ....84 B4
Manningtree St, E1 ....21 H3
Mannin Rd, Rom. RM6 ...82 B7
Mannock Cl, NW9 ....70 D3
Mannock Dr, Loug. IG10 ...49 F2
Mannock Ms, E18 ....79 H1
Mannock Rd, N22 ....75 H3
Manns Cl, Islw. TW7 ....144 C5
Manns Rd, Edg. HA8 ....54 A6
Manoel Rd, Twickenham
TW2 ....161 J2
Manor Av, SE4 ....153 J2
Hounslow TW4 ....142 D3
Northolt UB5 ....85 F7
Manorbrook, SE3 ....155 G4
Manor Circ, Rich. TW9 ....146 A3
Manor Cl, E17
off Manor Rd 77 H2
NW7 off Manor Dr 54 D5
NW9 ....70 B5
SE28 ....118 C6
Barnet EN5 ....40 B4
Worcester Park KT4 ....197 E1
Manor Cotts App, N2 ....73 F2
Manor Ct, E10
off Grange Pk Rd 96 B1
N2 ....73 H5
SW6 off Bagley's La ...149 E1
Twickenham TW2 ....161 J2
Wembley HA9 ....87 H5
Manor Ct Rd, W7 ....104 B7
Manor Cres, Surb. KT5 ...182 A6
Manordene Cl, T.Ditt. KT7 .194 D1
Manordene Rd, SE28 ....118 C6
Manor Dr, N14 ....42 B7
N20 ....57 H3
NW7 ....54 D5
Epsom KT19 ....196 E6
Esher KT10 ....194 C2
Feltham TW13
off Lebanon Av 160 D5
Sunbury-on-Thames
TW16 ....178 A2
Surbiton KT5 ....181 J6
Wembley HA9 ....87 J4
Manor Dr, The, Wor.Pk.
KT4 ....197 E1
Manor Dr N, N.Mal. KT3 ..182 D7
Worcester Park KT4 ....196 E1
Manor Est, SE16 ....132 E4
Manor Fm Cl, Wor.Pk.
KT4 ....196 E1
Manor Fm Dr, E4 ....63 E3
Manor Fm Rd, Th.Hth.
CR7 ....187 G2
Wembley HA0 ....105 G2
Manorfield Cl, N19
off Junction Rd 92 C4
Manor Flds, SW15 ....148 A6
Manorfields Cl, Chis.
BR7 ....193 J3
Manor Gdns, N7 ....92 E3
SW20 ....184 C2
W3 ....126 A4
W4 off Devonshire Rd ..127 E5
Hampton TW12 ....161 H7
Richmond TW9 ....145 J4
Ruislip HA4 ....84 C5
South Croydon CR2 ...202 C6
Sunbury-on-Thames
TW16 ....178 A2
Manor Gate, Nthlt. UB5 ...84 E7
Manorgate Rd, Kings.T.
KT2 ....182 A1
Manor Gro, SE15 ....133 F6
Beckenham BR3 ....190 B2
Richmond TW9 ....146 A4
Manor Hall Av, NW4 ....71 J2
Manor Hall Dr, NW4 ....72 A2
Manorhall Gdns, E10 ....96 A1
Manor Ho Dr, NW6 ....90 A7
Manor Ho Est, Stan. HA7 ..53 E6
Manor Ho Way, Islw.
TW7 ....144 E3
Manor La, SE12 ....155 E6
SE13 ....154 E4
Feltham TW13 ....160 A2
Hayes (Harling.) UB3 ...121 G6
Sunbury-on-Thames
TW16 ....178 A2
Sutton SM1 ....199 F5
Manor La Ter, SE13 ....154 E4
Manor Ms, NW6
off Cambridge Av 108 D2
SE4 ....153 J2
Manor Mt, SE23 ....171 F1
Manor Par, NW10
off Station Rd 107 F2
MANOR PARK, E12 ....98 B4
Manor Pk, SE13 ....154 D4
Chislehurst BR7 ....193 G2
Richmond TW9 ....145 J4
Manor Pk Cl, W.Wick.
BR4 ....204 B1
Manor Pk Cres, Edg. HA8 ..54 A6
Manor Pk Dr, Har. HA2 ....67 H3
Manor Pk Gdns, Edg. HA8 .54 A5
Manor Pk Par, SE13
off Lee High Rd 154 D4
Manor Pk Rd, E12 ....98 A4
N2 ....73 F3
NW10 ....107 F1
Chislehurst BR7 ....193 F1
Sutton SM1 ....199 F5
West Wickham BR4 ....204 B1
Manor Pl, SE17 ....35 H4
Chislehurst BR7 ....193 G1
Feltham TW14 ....160 A1
Mitcham CR4 ....186 C3
Sutton SM1 ....199 E4
Manor Rd, E10 ....78 A7
E15 ....114 E3
E16 ....114 E3
E17 ....77 H2
N16 ....94 A2
N17 ....76 D1
N22 ....59 E6
SE25 ....188 D4
SW20 ....184 C2
W13 ....104 D7
Barking IG11 ....99 J6
Barnet EN5 ....40 B5
Beckenham BR3 ....190 B2
Bexley DA5 ....177 H1
Chigwell IG7 ....64 E5
Dagenham RM10 ....101 J6
East Molesey KT8 ....180 A4
Enfield EN2 ....44 A2
Harrow HA1 ....68 D6
Hayes UB3 ....102 A6
Loughton IG10 ....47 H6
Mitcham CR4 ....186 C4
Richmond TW9 ....145 J3
Romford (Chad.Hth)
RM6 ....82 D6
Sidcup DA15 ....175 J3
Sutton SM2 ....198 C7
Teddington TW11 ....162 E5
Twickenham TW2 ....161 J2
Wallington SM6 ....200 B4
West Wickham BR4 ....204 B2
Woodford Green IG8 ....64 C6
Manor Rd N, Esher KT10 ..194 C3
Thames Ditton KT7 ....194 D2
Wallington SM6 ....200 B4
Manor Rd S, Esher KT10 ..194 B4
Manorside, Barn. EN5 ....40 B4
Manorside Cl, SE2 ....138 C4
Manor Sq, Dag. RM8 ....100 D2
Manor Vale, Brent. TW8 ...125 F5
Manor Vw, N3 ....72 E2
Manor Way, E4 ....62 D4
NW9 ....70 E3
SE3 ....155 F4
SE23 ....153 F7
SE28 ....138 C1
Beckenham BR3 ....190 A2
Bexley DA5 ....177 G1
Borehamwood WD6 ....38 C4
Bromley BR2 ....192 B6
Manorway, Enf. EN1 ....44 B7
Manor Way, Har. HA2 ....67 H4
Mitcham CR4 ....186 C3
Orpington BR5 ....193 F4
South Croydon CR2 ...202 B6
Southall UB2 ....122 D4
Manorway, Wdf.Grn. IG8 ..63 J5
Manor Way, Wor.Pk. KT4 .197 E1
Manor Way, The, Wall.
SM6 ....200 B4
Manpreet Ct, E12
off Morris Av 98 C5
Manresa Rd, SW3 ....31 G4
Mansard Beeches, SW17 .168 A5
Mansard Cl, Pnr. HA5 ....66 D3
Manse Cl, Hayes
(Harling.) UB3 ....121 G6
Mansel Gro, E17 ....78 A1
Mansell Rd, W3 ....126 D2
Greenford UB6 ....103 H5
Mansell St, E1 ....21 G6
Mansel Rd, SW19 ....166 B6
Mansergh Cl, SE18 ....136 B7
Manse Rd, N16 ....94 C3
Mansfield Av, N15 ....76 A4
Barnet EN4 ....41 J6
Ruislip HA4 ....84 B1
Mansfield Cl, N9 ....44 D6
Mansfield Hill, E4 ....62 B1
Mansfield Ms, W1 ....16 D2
Mansfield Pl, NW3
off New End 91 F4
South Croydon CR2 ...202 A6
Mansfield Rd, E11 ....79 H6
E17 ....77 J4
NW3 ....91 J5
W3 ....106 B4
Chessington KT9 ....195 F5
Ilford IG1 ....98 D2
South Croydon CR2 ...202 A6
Mansfield St, W1 ....16 D2
Mansford St, E2 ....13 J2
Manship Rd, Mitch. CR4 ..168 A7
Mansion Cl, SW9
off Cowley Rd 151 G1
Mansion Gdns, NW3 ....91 E3
★ Mansion Ho, EC4 ....20 B4
Mansion Ho Pl, EC4 ....20 B4
Mansion Ho St, EC4 ....20 B4
Mansions, The, SW5
off Earls Ct Rd 30 A3
Manson Ms, SW7 ....30 D2
Manson Pl, SW7 ....30 E2
Mansted Gdns, Rom.
RM6 ....82 C7
Manston Av, Sthl. UB2 ...123 G4
Manston Cl, SE20
off Garden Rd 189 F1
Manstone Rd, NW2 ....90 B5
Manston Gro, Kings.T.
KT2 ....163 G5
Manthorp Rd, SE18 ....137 F5
Mantilla Rd, SW17 ....168 A4
Mantle Rd, SE4 ....153 H3
Mantlet Cl, SW16 ....168 C7
Mantle Way, E15
off Romford Rd 96 E7
Manton Av, W7 ....124 C2
Manton Rd, SE2 ....138 A4
Mantua St, SW11 ....149 G3
Mantus Cl, E1
off Mantus Rd 113 F4
Mantus Rd, E1 ....113 F4
Manuka Cl, W7
off Grosvenor Rd 124 D1
Manus Way, N20
off Blakeney Cl 57 F1
Manville Gdns, SW17 ....168 B3
Manville Rd, SW17 ....168 A2
Manwood Rd, SE4 ....153 J5
Manwood St, E16 ....136 C1
Manygates, SW12 ....168 B2
Mapesbury Ms, NW4
off Station Rd 71 G6
Mapesbury Rd,
NW2 ....90 B7
Mapeshill Pl, NW2 ....89 J6
Mape St, E2 ....112 E4
Maple Av, E4 ....61 J5
W3 ....127 E1
Harrow HA2 ....85 H2
Maple Cl, N3 ....56 D6
N16 ....76 D6
SW4 ....150 D6
Buckhurst Hill IG9 ....64 A3
Hampton TW12 ....161 F6
Hayes UB4 ....102 D3
Maple Cl, Ilford IG6 ....65 H5
Mitcham CR4 ....186 B1
Orpington BR5 ....193 G5
Ruislip HA4 ....66 B6
Maple Ct, N.Mal. KT3 ....182 D3
Maple Cres, Sid. DA15 ....158 A6
Maplecroft Cl, E6
off Allhallows Rd 116 B6
Mapledale Av, Croy. CR0 ..202 D2
Mapledene, Chis. BR7 ....175 F5
Mapledene Est, E8
off Mapledene Rd 94 D7
Mapledene Rd, E8 ....94 C7
Maple Gdns, Edg. HA8 ....54 E7
Maple Gate, Loug. IG10 ...48 D2
Maple Gro, NW9 ....70 C7
W5 ....125 G3
Brentford TW8 ....124 E7
Southall UB1 ....103 F5
Maple Ho, NW3
off Maitland Pk Vil 91 J6
Maplehurst Cl, Kings.T.
KT1 ....181 H4
Maple Ind Est, Felt. TW13
off Maple Way 160 B3
Maple Leaf Dr, Sid. DA15 .175 J1
Mapleleafe Gdns, Ilf. IG6 ...80 E3
Maple Leaf Sq, SE16
off Fishermans Dr 133 G2
Maple Ms, NW6 ....6 A1
SW16 ....169 F5
Maple Pl, N17
off Park La 60 D7
W1 ....9 G6
Maple Rd, E11 ....79 E6
SE20 ....189 E1
Hayes UB4 ....102 C3
Surbiton KT6 ....181 H5
Maples, The, Esher (Clay.)
KT10 ....194 D7
Maples Pl, E1
off Raven Row 113 E5
Maplestead Rd, SW2 ....151 F7
Dagenham RM9 ....118 B1
Maple St, E2 ....13 J2
W1 ....17 F1
Romford RM7 ....83 J4
Maplethorpe Rd, Th.Hth.
CR7 ....187 G4
Mapleton Cl, Brom. BR2 ..191 G6
Mapleton Cres, SW18 ....148 E6
Mapleton Rd, E4 ....62 C3
SW18 ....148 E6
Enfield EN1 ....45 E2
Maple Wk, W10
off Sixth Av 108 B4
Maple Way, Felt. TW13 ....160 A3
Maplin Cl, N21 ....43 F6
Maplin Ho, SE2
off Wolvercote Rd 138 D2
Maplin Rd, E16 ....115 G6
Maplin St, E3 ....113 J3
Mapperley Dr, Wdf.Grn.
IG8 off Forest Dr 62 E7
Marabou Cl, E12 ....98 B5
Maran Way, Erith DA18 ...138 D2
Marathon Ho, NW1 ....15 J1
Marathon Way, SE28 ....137 J2
Marban Rd, W9 ....108 C3
★ Marble Arch, W1 ....16 A5
Marble Arch Apts, W1
off Harrowby St 15 H3
Marble Cl, W3 ....126 B1
Marble Dr, NW2 ....90 A1
Marble Hill Cl, Twick.
TW1 ....144 E7
Marble Hill Gdns, Twick.
TW1 ....144 E7
★ Marble Hill Ho, Twick.
TW1 ....145 F7
Marble Ho, SE18
off Felspar Cl 137 J5
Marble Quay, E1 ....29 H1
Marbrook Ct, SE12 ....173 J3
Marcella Rd, SW9 ....151 G2
Marcellina Way, Orp.
BR6 ....207 H3
Marchant Cl, NW7 ....55 E6
Marchant Rd, E11 ....96 D2
Marchant St, SE14 ....133 H6
Marchbank Rd, W14 ....128 C6
Marchmont Gdns, Rich.
TW10
off Marchmont Rd 145 J5
Marchmont Rd, Rich.
TW10 ....145 J5
Wallington SM6 ....200 C7
Marchmont St, WC1 ....10 A5
March Rd, Twick. TW1 ....144 D7
Marchside Cl, Houns.
TW5 ....142 D1
Marchwood Cl, SE5 ....132 B7
Marchwood Cres, W5 ....105 F6
Marcia Rd, SE1 ....37 E2
Marcilly Rd, SW18 ....149 G5
Marco Dr, Pnr. HA5 ....51 F7
Marconi Pl, N11 ....58 B4

Marconi Rd, E10 ...96 A1
Marconi Way, Sthl. UB1 ...103 H6
Marcon Pl, E8 ...94 E6
Marco Rd, W6 ...127 J3
Marcourt Lawns, W5 ...105 H4
Marcus Ct, E15 ...115 E1
Marcus Garvey Ms, SE22 off St. Aidan's Rd ...152 E5
Marcus Garvey Way, SE24 ...151 G4
Marcus St, E15 ...115 F1
SW18 ...149 E6
Marcus Ter, SW18 ...149 E6
Mardale Dr, NW9 ...70 D5
Mardell Rd, Croy. CR0 ...189 G5
Marden Av, Brom. BR2 ...191 G6
Marden Cres, Bex. DA5 ...159 J5
Croydon CR0 ...187 F6
Marden Ho, E8 off Bodney Rd ...94 E5
Marden Rd, N17 ...76 B3
Croydon CR0 ...187 F6
Marden Sq, SE16 ...132 E3
Marder Rd, W13 ...124 D2
Mardyke Cl, Rain. RM13 ...119 J2
Mardyke Ho, SE17 off Crosslet St ...36 C1
Marechal Niel Av, Sid. DA15 ...175 G3
Maresfield, Croy. CR0 ...202 B3
Maresfield Gdns, NW3 ...91 F5
Mare St, E8 ...113 E1
Marfleet Cl, Cars. SM5 ...199 H2
Margaret Av, E4 ...46 B6
Margaret Bondfield Av, Bark. IG11 ...100 A7
Margaret Bldgs, N16 off Margaret Rd ...94 C1
Margaret Ct, W1 ...17 F3
Margaret Gardner Dr, SE9 ...174 C2
Margaret Ingram Cl, SW6 off John Smith Av ...128 C7
Margaret Lockwood Cl, Kings.T. KT1 ...181 J4
Margaret Rd, N16 ...94 C1
Barnet EN4 ...41 G5
Bexley DA5 ...158 D6
Margaret Rutherford Pl, SW12 ...168 C1
Margaret St, W1 ...17 E3
Margaretta Ter, SW3 ...31 G5
Margaretting Rd, E12 ...97 J2
Margaret Way, Ilf. IG4 ...80 B6
Margate Rd, SW2 ...150 E5
Margeholes, Wat. WD19 ...50 E2
Margery Pk Rd, E7 ...97 G6
Margery Rd, Dag. RM8 ...100 D3
Margery St, WC1 ...10 E4
Margin Dr, SW19 ...166 A5
Margravine Gdns, W6 ...128 A5
Margravine Rd, W6 ...128 A5
Marham Dr, NW9 off Kenley Av ...70 E1
Marham Gdns, SW18 ...167 H1
Morden SM4 ...185 F6
Mar Ho, SE7 off Springfield Gro ...135 J6
Maria Cl, SE1 ...37 J1
Marian Cl, Hayes UB4 ...102 D4
Marian Ct, Sutt. SM1 ...198 E5
Marian Pl, E2 ...112 E2
Marian Rd, SW16 ...186 C1
Marian Sq, E2 ...13 J1
Marian St, E2 off Hackney Rd ...112 E2
Marian Way, NW10 ...89 F7
Maria Ter, E1 ...113 G5
Maria Theresa Cl, N.Mal. KT3 ...182 D5
Maricas Av, Har. HA3 ...68 A1
Marie Curie, SE5 off Sceaux Gdns ...152 B1
Marie Lloyd Gdns, N19 ...74 E7
Marie Lloyd Ho, N1 ...12 B2
Marie Lloyd Wk, E8 off Forest Rd ...94 D6
Marigold All, SE1 ...19 G6
Marigold Cl, Sthl. UB1 off Lancaster Rd ...103 E7
Marigold Rd, N17 ...61 F7
Marigold St, SE16 ...132 E2
Marigold Way, E4 off Silver Birch Av ...61 J6
Croydon CR0 ...203 G1
Marina App, Hayes UB4 ...103 E5
Marina Av, N.Mal. KT3 ...183 H5
Marina Cl, Brom. BR2 ...191 G3
Marina Dr, Well. DA16 ...157 H2
Marina Gdns, Rom. RM7 ...83 J6
Marina Pl, Kings.T. (Hmptn W.) KT1 ...181 G1
Marina Way, Tedd. TW11 off Fairways ...163 G7
Marine Dr, SE18 ...136 C4
Barking IG11 ...118 B4
Marinefield Rd, SW6 ...149 E2
Mariner Business Cen, Croy. CR0 ...201 F5
Mariner Gdns, Rich. TW10 ...163 F3
Mariner Rd, E12 off Dersingham Av ...98 D4
Mariners Cl, Barn. EN4 ...41 G5
Mariners Ms, E14 ...134 D4
Marine St, SE16 ...29 H5
Marine Twr, SE8 off Abinger Gro ...133 J6
Marion Cl, Ilf. IG6 ...65 G7
Marion Gro, Wdf.Grn. IG8 ...63 E5
Marion Ms, SE21 ...170 A3
Marion Rd, NW7 ...55 G5
Thornton Heath CR7 ...187 J5
Marischal Rd, SE13 ...154 D3
Maritime Ho, SE18 off Green's End ...136 E4
Barking IG11 off Linton Rd ...99 F7
Maritime Quay, E14 ...134 A5
Maritime St, E3 ...113 J4
Marius Pas, SW17 off Marius Rd ...168 A2
Marius Rd, SW17 ...168 A2
Marjorams Av, Loug. IG10 ...48 C2
Marjorie Gro, SW11 ...149 J4
Marjorie Ms, E1 off Arbour Sq ...113 G6
Mark Av, E4 ...46 B6
Mark Cl, Bexh. DA7 ...158 E1
Southall UB1 off Longford Av ...123 H1
Marke Cl, Kes. BR2 ...206 B4
Markeston Grn, Wat. WD19 ...50 D4
Market, The, Cars. SM5 off Wrythe La ...199 F1
Sutton SM1 off Rose Hill ...199 F1
Market App, W12 off Lime Gro ...127 J2
Market Ct, W1 ...17 F3
Market Dr, W4 ...126 E7
Market Est, N7 ...92 E6
Market Hill, SE18 ...136 D3
Market La, W12 off Goldhawk Rd ...127 J2
Edgware HA8 ...70 C1
Market Ms, W1 ...24 D2
Market Pl, N2 ...73 H3
NW11 ...73 F4
SE16 ...37 J1
W1 ...17 F3
W3 ...126 C1
Bexleyheath DA6 ...159 G4
Brentford TW8 ...125 F7
Enfield EN2 off The Town ...44 A3
Kingston upon Thames KT1 ...181 G2
Market Rd, N7 ...92 E6
Richmond TW9 ...146 A3
Market Row, SW9 off Atlantic Rd ...151 G4
Market Service Rd, The, Sutt. SM1 off Rosehill Av ...199 F1
Market Sq, E14 off Chrisp St ...114 B6
N9 off Edmonton Grn Shop Cen ...60 E2
Bromley BR1 ...191 G2
Market St, E1 ...21 F1
E6 ...116 C2
SE18 ...136 D4
Market Trd Est, Sthl. UB2 ...122 B4
Market Way, E14 off Kerbey St ...114 B6
Wembley HA0 off Turton Rd ...87 H5
Market Yd Ms, SE1 ...28 D5
Markfield Gdns, E4 ...46 B7
Markfield Rd, N15 ...76 D4
Markham Pl, SW3 ...31 J3
Markham Sq, SW3 ...31 J3
Markham St, SW3 ...31 H3
Markhole Cl, Hmptn. TW12 off Priory Rd ...161 F7
Markhouse Av, E17 ...77 H6
Markhouse Rd, E17 ...77 J5
Markland Ho, W10 ...108 A7
Mark La, EC3 ...20 E6
Markmanor Av, E17 ...77 H7
Mark Rd, N22 ...75 H2
Marksbury Av, Rich. TW9 ...146 A3
MARK'S GATE, Rom. RM6 ...82 E2
Mark Sq, EC2 ...12 D5
Marks Rd, Rom. RM7 ...83 J5
Mark St, E15 ...96 E7
EC2 ...12 D5
Mark Wade Cl, E12 ...98 A1
Markway, Sun. TW16 ...178 C2
Markwell Cl, SE26 ...170 E4
Markyate Rd, Dag. RM8 ...100 B5
Marlands Rd, Ilf. IG5 ...80 B3
Marlborough, SW3 ...31 H1
Marlborough Av, E8 ...112 D1
N14 ...58 C3
Edgware HA8 ...54 B3
Marlborough Cl, N20 ...57 J3
SE17 ...35 H2
SW19 ...167 H6
Orpington BR6 off Aylesham Rd ...193 J7
Marlborough Ct, W1 ...17 F4
W8 ...128 D4
Wallington SM6 off Cranley Gdns ...200 C7
Marlborough Cres, W4 ...126 D3
Hayes (Harling.) UB3 ...121 G7
Marlborough Dr, Ilf. IG5 ...80 B3
Marlborough Gdns, N20 ...57 J3
Marlborough Gate Ho, W2 ...14 E5
Marlborough Gro, SE1 ...37 H4
Marlborough Hill, NW8 ...109 F1
Harrow HA1 ...68 C4
★ Marlborough Ho, SW1 ...25 G2
Marlborough La, SE7 ...135 J6
Marlborough Ms, SW2 off Acre La ...151 F4
Marlborough Pk Av, Sid. DA15 ...158 A7
Marlborough Pl, NW8 ...6 C2
Marlborough Rd, E4 ...62 A6
E7 ...97 J7
E15 off Borthwick Rd ...97 E4
E18 ...79 G3
N9 ...60 C1
N19 ...92 D2
N22 ...59 E7
SE18 ...137 E3
SW1 ...25 G2
SW19 ...167 H6
W4 ...126 C5
W5 ...125 G2
Bexleyheath DA7 ...158 D3
Bromley BR2 ...191 J4
Dagenham RM8 ...100 B4
Feltham TW13 ...160 D2
Hampton TW12 ...161 G6
Isleworth TW7 ...144 E1
Richmond TW10 ...145 H6
Romford RM7 ...83 G4
South Croydon CR2 ...201 J7
Southall UB2 ...122 C3
Sutton SM1 ...198 D3
Marlborough St, SW3 ...31 G2
Marlborough Yd, N19 ...92 D2
Marler Rd, SE23 ...171 H1
Marlescroft Way, Loug. IG10 ...48 E5
Marley Av, Bexh. DA7 ...138 D6
Marley Cl, N15 off Stanmore Rd ...75 H4
Greenford UB6 ...103 G3
Marley St, SE16 ...133 G4
Marley Wk, NW2 off Lennon Rd ...89 J5
Marl Fld Cl, Wor.Pk. KT4 ...197 G1
Marlingdene Cl, Hmptn. TW12 ...161 G6
Marlings Cl, Chis. BR7 ...193 H4
Marlings Pk Av, Chis. BR7 ...193 H4
Marlin Pk, Houns. TW4 ...142 B5
Marlins Cl, Sutt. SM1 off Turnpike La ...199 F5
Marloes Cl, Wem. HA0 ...87 G4
Marloes Rd, W8 ...22 A6
Marlow Cl, SE20 ...189 E3
Marlow Ct, NW6 ...90 A7
NW9 ...71 F3
Marlow Cres, Twick. TW1 ...144 C6
Marlow Dr, Sutt. SM3 ...198 A2
Marlowe Cl, Chis. BR7 ...175 G6
Ilford IG6 ...81 F1
Marlowe Ct, SE19 off Lymer Av ...170 C5
Marlowe Gdns, SE9 ...156 D6
Marlowe Path, SE8 off Glaisher St ...134 B6
Marlowe Rd, E17 ...78 C4
Marlowes, The, NW8 ...109 G1
Marlowe Sq, Mitch. CR4 ...186 C4
Marlowe Way, Croy. CR0 ...201 E2
Marlow Gdns, Hayes UB3 ...121 G3
Marlow Rd, E6 ...116 C3
SE20 ...189 E3
Southall UB2 ...123 F3
Marlow Way, SE16 ...133 G2
Marl Rd, SW18 ...149 E4
Marlton St, SE10 off Woolwich Rd ...135 F5
Marlwood Cl, Sid. DA15 ...175 H2
Marmadon Rd, SE18 ...137 J4
Marmara Apts, E16 off Western Gateway ...115 G7
Marmion App, E4 ...62 A4
Marmion Av, E4 ...61 J4
Marmion Cl, E4 ...61 J4
Marmion Ms, SW11 off Taybridge Rd ...150 A3
Marmion Rd, SW11 ...150 A4
Marmont Rd, SE15 ...152 D1
Marmora Rd, SE22 ...153 F6
Marmot Rd, Houns. TW4 ...142 D3
Marne Av, N11 ...58 B4
Welling DA16 ...158 A3
Marnell Way, Houns. TW4 ...142 D3
Marne St, W10 ...108 B3
Marney Rd, SW11 ...150 A4
Marnfield Cres, SW2 ...169 F1
Marnham Av, NW2 ...90 B4
Marnham Cres, Grnf. UB6 ...103 H3
Marnock Rd, SE4 ...153 H5
Maroon St, E14 ...113 H5
Maroons Way, SE6 ...172 A5
Marquess Est, N1 ...93 J6
Marquess Rd, N1 ...94 A6
Marquis Cl, Wem. HA0 ...87 J7
Marquis Rd, N4 ...93 F1
N22 ...59 F6
NW1 ...92 D6
Marrabon Cl, Sid. DA15 ...176 A1
Marrick Cl, SW15 ...147 G4
Marriott Cl, Felt. TW14 ...141 G6
Marriott Rd, E15 ...114 E1
N4 ...93 F1
N10 ...73 J1
Barnet EN5 ...40 A3
Marriotts Cl, NW9 ...71 F6
Marryat Cl, Houns. TW4 ...143 F4
Marryat Pl, SW19 ...166 B4
Marryat Rd, SW19 ...166 A5
Marryat Sq, SW6 ...148 B1
Marsala Rd, SE13 ...154 B4
Marsden Rd, N9 ...60 E2
SE15 ...152 C3
Marsden St, NW5 ...92 A6
Marsden Way, Orp. BR6 ...207 J4
Marshall, W2 off Hermitage St ...14 E2
Marshall Cl, SW18 off Allfarthing La ...149 F6
Harrow HA1 off Bowen Rd ...68 A7
Hounslow TW4 ...143 F5
Marshall Est, NW7 ...55 G4
Marshall Path, SE28 off Attlee Rd ...118 B7
Marshall Rd, E10 ...96 B3
N17 ...76 A1
Marshalls Cl, N11 ...58 B4
Marshall's Gro, SE18 ...136 B4
Marshalls Pl, SE16 ...29 G6
Marshall's Rd, Sutt. SM1 ...198 E4
Marshall St, NW10 ...88 D7
W1 ...17 G4
Marshalsea Rd, SE1 ...28 A3
Marsham Cl, Chis. BR7 ...174 E5
Marsham St, SW1 ...25 J6
Marsh Av, Mitch. CR4 ...185 J2
Marshbrook Cl, SE3 ...156 A3
Marsh Cl, NW7 ...55 F3
Marsh Ct, SW19 ...185 F1
Marsh Dr, NW9 ...71 F6
Marsh Fm Rd, Twick. TW2 ...162 C1
Marshfield St, E14 ...134 C3
Marshgate La, E15 ...114 B1
Marshgate Path, SE28 off Tom Cribb Rd ...137 F3
Marshgate Sidings, E15 ...114 B1
Marsh Grn Rd, Dag. RM10 ...119 G1
Marsh Hill, E9 ...95 H5
Marsh La, E10 ...96 A2
N17 ...61 E7
NW7 ...54 E4
Stanmore HA7 ...53 F5
Marsh Rd, Pnr. HA5 ...66 E4
Wembley HA0 ...105 G2
Marshside Cl, N9 ...61 F1
Marsh St, E14 off Harbinger Rd ...134 B4
Marsh Wall, E14 ...134 A1
Marsland Cl, SE17 ...35 H4
Marston, SE17 off Deacon Way ...36 A1
Marston Av, Chess. KT9 ...195 H6
Dagenham RM10 ...101 G2
Marston Cl, NW6 ...91 F7
Dagenham RM10 ...101 G3
Marston Rd, Ilf. IG5 ...80 B1
Teddington TW11 ...162 E5
Marston Way, SE19 ...169 H7
Marsworth Av, Pnr. HA5 ...66 D1
Marsworth Cl, Hayes UB4 ...103 E5
Marsworth Ho, E2 off Whiston Rd ...112 D1
Martaban Rd, N16 ...94 B2
Martara Ms, SE17 ...35 J4
Martello St, E8 ...94 E7
Martello Ter, E8 ...94 E7

Martell Rd, SE21 . . . .**170** A3
Martel Pl, E8
off Dalston La **94** C6
Marten Rd, E17 . . . .**78** A2
Martens Av, Bexh. DA7 . . .**159** J4
Martens Cl, Bexh. DA7 . . .**159** J4
Martha Ct, E2 . . . .**113** E2
Martham Cl, SE28 . . . .**118** D7
Ilford IG6 . . . .**81** E1
Martha Rd, E15 . . . .**97** E6
Martha's Bldgs, EC1 . . . . . .**12** B5
Martha St, E1 . . . .**113** E6
Marthorne Cres, Har.
HA3 . . . .**68** A2
Martina Ter, Chig. IG7
off Manford Way **65** H5
Martin Bowes Rd, SE9 . . .**156** C3
Martinbridge Trd Est, Enf.
EN1 . . . .**44** D5
Martin Cl, N9 . . . .**61** G1
Martin Cres, Croy. CR0 . . .**201** G1
Martindale, SW14 . . . .**146** C5
Martindale Av, E16 . . . .**115** G7
Martindale Rd, SW12 . . . .**150** B7
Hounslow TW4 . . . .**142** E3
Martin Dene, Bexh. DA6 . . .**159** F5
Martin Dr, Nthlt. UB5 . . . . .**85** F5
Martineau Cl, Esher
KT10 . . . .**194** A4
Martineau Dr, Twick. TW1
off St. Margaret's Dr . .**145** E4
Martineau Ms, N5
off Martineau Rd **93** H4
Martineau Rd, N5 . . . .**93** H4
Martineau St, E1 . . . .**113** F7
Martingale Cl, Sun. TW16 . **178** A4
Martingales Cl, Rich.
TW10 . . . .**163** G3
Martin Gdns, Dag. RM8 . . .**100** C4
Martin Gro, Mord. SM4 . . .**184** D3
Martin Ho, SE1 . . . .**28** A6
Martin La, EC4 . . . .**20** C5
Martin Ri, Bexh. DA6 . . . . .**159** F5
Martin Rd, Dag. RM8 . . . . .**100** C4
Martins, The, Wem. HA9 . . .**87** J3
Martins Cl, W.Wick. BR4 . .**204** D1
Martinsfield Cl, Chig. IG7 . .**65** H4
Martins Mt, Barn.
(New Barn.) EN5 . . . .**40** D4
Martins Pl, SE28
off Martin St **137** H1
Martins Rd, Brom. BR2 . . .**191** E2
Martin St, SE28 . . . .**137** H1
Martins Wk, N8
off Alexandra Rd **75** G3
N10 . . . .**74** A1
SE28 . . . .**137** H1
Borehamwood WD6
off Siskin Cl **38** A4
Martin Way, SW20 . . . .**184** B3
Morden SM4 . . . .**184** B3
Martlesham Wk, NW9
off Kenley Av **70** E2
Martlet Gro, Nthlt. UB5 . . .**102** D3
Martlett Ct, WC2 . . . .**18** B4
Martley Dr, Ilf. IG2 . . . .**80** E5
Martock Cl, Har. HA3 . . . . . .**68** D4
Martock Gdns, N11 . . . .**57** J5
Marton Cl, SE6 . . . .**172** A3
Marton Rd, N16 . . . .**94** B2
Martys Yd, NW3
off Hampstead High St . .**91** G4
Marvell Av, Hayes UB4 . . .**102** A5
Marvels Cl, SE12 . . . .**173** H2
Marvels La, SE12 . . . .**173** H2
Marville Rd, SW6 . . . .**128** C7
Marvin St, E8
off Sylvester Rd **95** E6
Marwell Cl, W.Wick. BR4
off Deer Pk Way **205** F2
Marwood Cl, Well.
DA16 . . . .**158** B3
Marwood Dr, NW7 . . . .**56** A7
Mary Adelaide Cl, SW15 . .**164** E4
Mary Ann Gdns, SE8 . . . . .**134** A6
Maryatt Av, Har. HA2 . . . . . .**85** H2
Marybank, SE18 . . . .**136** C4
Mary Cl, Stan. HA7 . . . .**69** J4
Mary Datchelor Cl, SE5 . . .**152** A1
Mary Grn, NW8 . . . .**109** E1
Maryland Ind Est, E15
off Maryland Rd **96** D5
Maryland Pk, E15 . . . .**96** E5
Maryland Pt, E15
off The Grove **96** E6
Maryland Rd, E15 . . . .**96** D5
N22 . . . .**59** F6
Thornton Heath CR7 . . .**187** H1
Maryland Sq, E15 . . . .**97** E5
Marylands Rd, W9 . . . .**108** D4
Maryland St, E15 . . . .**96** D5
Maryland Wk, N1
off Popham St **111** J1
Maryland Way, Sun.
TW16 . . . .**178** A2
Mary Lawrenson Pl, SE3 . .**135** F7
MARYLEBONE, NW1 . . . . . .**15** J3
Marylebone Flyover, NW1 .**15** F2
W2 . . . .**15** F2
Marylebone Gdns, Rich.
TW9 *off Manor Rd* **145** J4
Marylebone High St, W1 . . .**16** C1
Marylebone La, W1 . . . .**16** D4
Marylebone Ms, W1 . . . .**16** D2
Marylebone Pas, W1 . . . . . .**17** G3
Marylebone Rd, NW1 . . . . .**15** H1
Marylebone St, W1 . . . .**16** C2
Marylee Way, SE11 . . . .**34** D3
Mary Macarthur Ho, E2
off Warley St **113** G3
W6 *off Field Rd* **128** B6
Mary Neuner Rd, N8 . . . . . .**75** F3
Maryon Gro, SE7 . . . .**136** B4
Maryon Ms, NW3
off South End Rd **91** H4
Maryon Rd, SE7 . . . .**136** B4
SE18 . . . .**136** B4
Mary Peters Dr, Grnf. UB6 .**86** A5
Mary Pl, W11 . . . .**108** B7
Mary Rose Cl, Hmptn.
TW12 *off Ashley Rd* **179** G1
Mary Rose Mall, E6
off Frobisher Rd **116** D5
Maryrose Way, N20 . . . .**57** G1
Mary Seacole Cl, E8
off Clarissa St **112** C1
Mary's Ter, Twick. TW1 . . . .**144** D7
Mary St, E16
off Barking Rd **115** F5
N1 . . . .**111** J1
Mary Ter, NW1 . . . .**110** B1
Mary Way, Wat. WD19 . . . . .**50** C4
Masbro Rd, W14 . . . .**128** A3
Mascalls Ct, SE7 . . . .**135** J6
Mascalls Rd, SE7 . . . .**135** J6
Mascotte Rd, SW15 . . . . . .**148** A4
Mascotts Cl, NW2 . . . .**89** H3
Masefield Av, Borwd.
WD6 . . . .**38** B5
Southall UB1 . . . .**103** G7
Stanmore HA7 . . . .**52** C5
Masefield Cres, N14 . . . . . .**42** C6
Masefield Gdns, E6 . . . . . .**116** D4
Masefield La, Hayes UB4 .**102** B4
Masefield Rd, Hmptn. TW12
off Wordsworth Rd . . .**161** F4
Masefield Vw, Orp. BR6 . .**207** F3
Masham Ho, Erith DA18
off Kale Rd **138** D2
Mashie Rd, W3 . . . .**106** E6
Maskall Cl, SW2 . . . .**169** G1
Maskani Wk, SW16
off Bates Cres **168** C7
Maskell Rd, SW17 . . . .**167** F3
Maskelyne Cl, SW11 . . . . .**149** H1
Mason Cl, E16 . . . .**115** G7
SE16 . . . .**37** J3
SW20 . . . .**184** A1
Bexleyheath DA7 . . . . . .**159** H3
Borehamwood WD6 . . . .**38** C2
Hampton TW12 . . . .**179** F1
Mason Ct, Wem. HA9
off The Avenue **88** A2
Mason Rd, Sutt. SM1
off Manor Pl **199** E5
Woodford Green IG8 . . . .**63** E4
Masons Arms Ms, W1 . . . . .**17** E4
Masons Av, EC2 . . . .**20** B3
Croydon CR0 . . . .**201** J3
Harrow HA3 . . . .**68** C4
Masons Grn La, W3 . . . . . .**106** A5
Masons Hill, SE18 . . . .**137** E4
Bromley BR1, BR2 . . . . .**191** G3
Masons Pl, EC1 . . . .**11** H3
Mitcham CR4 . . . .**185** J1
Mason St, SE17 . . . .**36** C2
Masons Yd, EC1 . . . .**11** H3
Mason's Yd, SW1 . . . .**25** G1
SW19 *off High St*
Wimbledon **166** A5
Massey Cl, N11 . . . .**58** B5
Massey Ct, E6 . . . .**115** J1
Massie Rd, E8
off Graham Rd **94** D6
Massingberd Way, SW17 . .**168** B4
Massinger St, SE17 . . . .**36** D2
Massingham St, E1 . . . . . .**113** G4
Masson Av, Ruis. HA4 . . . . .**84** C6
Master Gunner Pl, SE18 . . **136** B7
Masterman Ho, SE5 . . . .**36** A7
Masterman Rd, E6 . . . .**116** B3
Masters Cl, SW16 . . . .**168** C6
Masters Dr, SE16 . . . .**132** E5
Masters St, E1 . . . .**113** G5
Mast Ho Ter, E14 . . . .**134** A4
Mast Leisure Pk, SE16 . . . .**133** G3
Mastmaker Rd, E14 . . . .**134** A2
Mast Quay, SE18
off Woolwich Ch St . . .**136** C3
Maswell Pk Cres, Houns.
TW3 . . . .**143** J5
Maswell Pk Rd, Houns.
TW3 . . . .**143** H5
Matcham Rd, E11 . . . .**97** E3
Matchless Dr, SE18 . . . . . .**136** D7
Matfield Cl, Brom. BR2 . . . .**191** G5
Matfield Rd, Belv. DA17 . .**139** G6
Matham Gro, SE22 . . . . . .**152** C4
Matham Rd, E.Mol. KT8 . .**180** A5
Matheson Rd, W14 . . . .**128** C4
Mathews Av, E6 . . . .**116** D2
Mathews Pk Av, E15 . . . . . .**97** F6
Matilda Cl, SE19
off Elizabeth Way **170** A7
Matilda Gdns, E3 . . . .**114** A2
Matilda St, N1 . . . .**111** F1
Matisse Rd, Houns. TW3
off Prince Regent Rd . .**143** H3
Matlock Cl, SE24 . . . .**151** J4
Barnet EN5 . . . .**40** A5
Matlock Ct, SE5
off Denmark Hill Est . .**152** A4
Matlock Cres, Sutt. SM3 . .**198** B4
Watford WD19 . . . .**50** C3
Matlock Gdns, Sutt. SM3 .**198** B4
Matlock Pl, Sutt. SM3 . . . .**198** B4
Matlock Rd, E10 . . . .**78** C6
Matlock St, E14 . . . .**113** H6
Matlock Way, N.Mal. KT3 .**182** D1
Matrimony Pl, SW8 . . . . . .**150** C2
Matson Ct, Wdf.Grn. IG8
off The Bridle Path **62** E7
Matson Ho, SE16
off Slippers Pl **133** E3
Matthew Cl, W10 . . . .**108** A4
Matthew Ct, Mitch. CR4 . . .**186** D5
Matthew Parker St, SW1 . .**25** J4
Matthews Rd, Grnf. UB6 . . .**86** A5
Matthews St, SW11 . . . . . .**149** J2
Matthews Yd, WC2 . . . .**18** A4
Matthias Rd, N16 . . . .**94** A5
Mattingley Way, SE15 . . . . .**37** F7
Mattison Rd, N4 . . . .**75** G6
Mattock La, W5 . . . .**125** E1
W13 . . . .**125** E1
Maud Cashmore Way,
SE18 . . . .**136** C3
Maud Chadburn Pl, SW4
off Balham Hill **150** B6
Maude Rd, E17 . . . .**77** H5
SE5 . . . .**152** B1
Maudesville Cotts, W7
off The Broadway **124** B1
Maude Ter, E17 . . . .**77** H4
Maud Gdns, E13 . . . .**115** F1
Barking IG11 . . . .**117** J2
Maudlin's Grn, E1 . . . .**29** H1
Maud Rd, E10 . . . .**96** C3
E13 . . . .**115** F2
Maudslay Rd, SE9 . . . .**156** C3
Maudsley Ho, Brent. TW8
off Green Dragon La . .**125** H5
Maud St, E16 . . . .**115** F5
Maud Wilkes Cl, NW5 . . . . . .**92** C5
Mauleverer Rd, SW2 . . . . .**150** E5
Maundeby Wk, NW10
off Neasden La **89** E6
Maunder Rd, W7 . . . .**124** C1
Maunsel St, SW1 . . . .**33** H1
Maurer Ct, SE10
off John Harrison Way .**135** F3
Maurice Av, N22 . . . .**75** H2
Maurice Brown Cl, NW7 . . .**56** A5
Maurice St, W12 . . . .**107** H6
Maurice Wk, NW11 . . . .**73** F4
Maurier Cl, Nthlt. UB5 . . . .**102** C1
Mauritius Rd, SE10 . . . . . .**135** E4
Maury Rd, N16 . . . .**94** D2
Mauveine Gdns, Houns.
TW3 . . . .**143** G4
Mavelstone Cl, Brom.
BR1 . . . .**192** B1
Mavelstone Rd, Brom.
BR1 . . . .**192** B1
Maverton Rd, E3 . . . .**114** A1
Mavis Av, Epsom KT19 . . .**197** E5
Mavis Cl, Epsom KT19 . . . .**197** E5
Mavis Wk, E6 . . . .**116** B5
Mawbey Est, SE1 . . . .**37** H4
Mawbey Ho, SE1
off Old Kent Rd **37** G4
Mawbey Pl, SE1 . . . .**37** G4
Mawbey Rd, SE1 . . . .**37** G4
Mawbey St, SW8 . . . .**130** E7
Mawney Cl, Rom. RM7 . . . .**83** H2
Mawney Rd, Rom. RM7 . . .**83** J4
Mawson Cl, SW20 . . . .**184** B2
Mawson La, W4
off Great W Rd **127** F6
Maxey Gdns, Dag. RM9 . . .**101** E4
Maxey Rd, SE18 . . . .**137** F4
Dagenham RM9 . . . .**100** E4
Maxfield Cl, N20 . . . .**41** F7
Maxilla Gdns, W10
off Cambridge Gdns . .**108** A6
Maxilla Wk, W10
off Kingsdown Cl **108** A6
Maxim Rd, N21 . . . .**43** G6
Maxted Pk, Harrow
HA1 . . . .**68** B7
Maxted Rd, SE15 . . . .**152** C3
Maxwell Cl, Croy. CR0 . . . .**201** E1
Hayes UB3 . . . .**102** A7
Maxwell Gdns, Orp. BR6 . .**207** J3
Maxwell Rd, SW6 . . . .**128** E7
Borehamwood WD6 . . . .**38** B3
Welling DA16 . . . .**158** A4
West Drayton UB7 . . . . .**120** C4
Maxwelton Av, NW7 . . . . . .**54** D5
Maxwelton Cl, NW7 . . . . . .**54** D5
Maya Angelou Ct, E4
off Bailey Cl **62** C4
Maya Cl, SE15 . . . .**152** E2
Mayall Rd, SE24 . . . .**151** H5
Maya Pl, N11 . . . .**58** D7
Maya Rd, N2 . . . .**73** F4
Maybank Av, E18 . . . .**79** H2
Wembley HA0 . . . .**86** C5
Maybank Gdns, Pnr. HA5 . .**66** A5
Maybank Rd, E18 . . . .**79** H1
May Bate Av, Kings.T.
KT2 . . . .**181** G1
Maybells Commercial Est,
Bark. IG11 . . . .**118** D2
Mayberry Pl, Surb. KT5 . . .**181** J7
Maybourne Cl, SE26 . . . . .**171** E5
Maybrook Meadow Est,
Bark. IG11 . . . .**100** A7
Maybury Cl, Loug. IG10 . . . .**48** E4
Orpington BR5 . . . .**193** E5
Maybury Gdns, NW10 . . . . .**89** H6
Maybury Ms, N6 . . . .**74** C7
Maybury Rd, E13 . . . .**115** J4
Barking IG11 . . . .**117** J2
Maybury St, SW17 . . . .**167** H5
Maychurch Cl, Stan. HA7 . . .**53** G7
May Cl, Chess. KT9 . . . . . .**195** J6
May Ct, SW19 . . . .**185** E1
Maycroft, Pnr. HA5 . . . .**66** B2
Maycross Av, Mord. SM4 . .**184** C3
Mayday Gdns, SE3 . . . . . .**156** B2
Mayday Rd, Th.Hth. CR7 . .**187** H6
Maydew Ho, SE16 . . . .**133** F4
Mayerne Rd, SE9 . . . .**156** A5
Mayesbrook Rd, Bark.
IG11 . . . .**117** J1
Dagenham RM8 . . . .**100** A3
Ilford IG3 . . . .**100** A3
Mayesford Rd, Rom. RM6 . .**82** C7
Mayes Rd, N22 . . . .**75** G2
Mayeswood Rd, SE12 . . . .**173** J3
MAYFAIR, W1 . . . .**16** D6
Mayfair Av, Bexh. DA7 . . . .**158** D1
Ilford IG1 . . . .**98** C2
Romford RM6 . . . .**82** D6
Twickenham TW2 . . . . . .**143** J7
Worcester Park KT4 . . . .**197** G1
Mayfair Cl, Beck. BR3 . . . . .**190** B1
Surbiton KT6 . . . .**195** H1
Mayfair Gdns, N17 . . . .**60** A6
Woodford Green IG8 . . . .**63** G7
Mayfair Ms, NW1
off Regents Pk Rd **91** J7
Mayfair Pl, W1 . . . .**25** E1
Mayfair Ter, N14 . . . .**42** D7
Mayfield, Bexh. DA7 . . . . .**159** F3
Mayfield Av, N12 . . . .**57** F4
N14 . . . .**58** C2
W4 . . . .**127** E4
W13 . . . .**124** E3
Harrow HA3 . . . .**68** E5
Orpington BR6 . . . .**207** J1
Woodford Green IG8 . . . .**63** G7
Mayfield Cl, E8
off Forest Rd **94** C6
SW4 . . . .**150** D5
Thames Ditton KT7 . . . .**194** E1
Mayfield Cres, N9 . . . .**44** E6
Thornton Heath CR7 . . .**187** F4
Mayfield Dr, Pnr. HA5 . . . . .**67** F4
Mayfield Gdns, NW4 . . . . . .**72** A6
W7 . . . .**104** A6
Mayfield Mans, SW15
off West Hill **148** A7
Mayfield Rd, E4 . . . .**62** C2
E8 . . . .**94** C7
E13 . . . .**115** F4
E17 . . . .**77** H2
N8 . . . .**75** F6
SW19 . . . .**184** C1
W3 . . . .**106** B7
W12 . . . .**127** E2
Belvedere DA17 . . . .**139** J4
Bromley BR1 . . . .**192** B5
Dagenham RM8 . . . .**100** C1
Enfield EN3 . . . .**45** G2
Sutton SM2 . . . .**199** G6
Thornton Heath CR7 . . .**187** F4
Mayfields, Wem. HA9 . . . . .**88** A2
Mayfields Cl, Wem. HA9 . . .**88** A2
Mayflower Cl, SE16
off Greenland Quay . .**133** G4
Mayflower Ct, SE16
off St. Marychurch St .**133** F2
Mayflower Rd, SW9 . . . . . .**150** E3
Mayflower St, SE16 . . . . . .**133** F2
Mayfly Cl, Pnr. (Eastcote)
HA5 . . . .**66** C7

Mayfly Gdns, Nthlt. UB5
off Ruislip Rd ... **102** D3
Mayford Cl, SW12 ... **149** J7
Beckenham BR3 ... **189** G3
Mayford Rd, SW12 ... **149** J7
May Gdns, Wem. HA0 ... **105** F2
Maygood St, N1 ... **10** D1
Maygrove Rd, NW6 ... **90** C6
Mayhew Cl, E4 ... **62** A3
Mayhill Rd, SE7 ... **135** H6
Barnet EN5 ... **40** B6
Maylands Dr, Sid. DA14 ... **176** D3
Maylands Rd, Wat. WD19 ... **50** C4
Maynard Cl, N15
off Brunswick Rd ... **76** B5
SW6 *off Cambria St* ... **129** E7
Maynard Path, E17 ... **78** C5
Maynard Rd, E17 ... **78** C5
Maynards Quay, E1
off Garnet St ... **113** F7
Maynooth Gdns, Cars.
SM5 ... **185** J7
Mayola Rd, E5 ... **95** F4
Mayo Rd, NW10 ... **88** E6
Croydon CR0 ... **188** A5
Mayow Rd, SE23 ... **171** G3
SE26 ... **171** G4
Mayplace Cl, Bexh. DA7 ... **159** H3
Mayplace La, SE18 ... **137** E7
Mayplace Rd E, Bexh.
DA7 ... **159** H3
Dartford DA1 ... **159** J3
Mayplace Rd W, Bexh.
DA7 ... **159** G4
Maypole Cres, Ilf. IG6 ... **65** G7
May Rd, E4 ... **62** A6
E13 ... **115** G2
Twickenham TW2 ... **162** B1
Mayroyd Av, Surb. KT6 ... **196** A2
May's Bldgs Ms, SE10
off Crooms Hill ... **134** C7
Mays Ct, WC2 ... **18** A6
Mays Hill Rd, Brom. BR2 ... **191** E2
Mays La, E4 ... **62** D2
Barnet EN5 ... **40** B5
Maysoule Rd, SW11 ... **149** G4
Mays Rd, Tedd. TW11 ... **162** A5
Mayston Ms, SE10
off Westcombe Hill ... **135** G5
May St, W14
off North End Rd ... **128** C5
Mayswood Gdns, Dag.
RM10 ... **101** J6
Mayton St, N7 ... **93** F3
Maytree Cl, Edg. HA8 ... **54** C3
Maytree Gdns, W5
off South Ealing Rd ... **125** G3
May Tree La, Stan. HA7 ... **52** C7
Maytree Wk, SW2 ... **169** G2
Mayville Est, N16
off King Henry St ... **94** B5
Mayville Rd, E11 ... **96** E2
Ilford IG1 ... **98** E5
May Wk, E13 ... **115** H2
Maywood Cl, Beck. BR3 ... **172** B7
Maze Hill, SE3 ... **134** E6
SE10 ... **134** E6
Mazenod Av, NW6 ... **90** D7
Maze Rd, Rich. TW9 ... **126** A7
Mead, The, N2 ... **73** F2
W13 ... **104** E5
Beckenham BR3 ... **190** C1
Wallington SM6 ... **200** D6
Watford WD19 ... **50** E3
West Wickham BR4 ... **204** D1
Mead Cl, NW1
off Belmont St ... **92** A7
Harrow HA3 ... **68** A1
Loughton IG10 ... **48** E2
Mead Ct, NW9 ... **70** C5
Mead Cres, E4 ... **62** C4
Sutton SM1 ... **199** H4
Meadcroft Rd, SE11 ... **35** G6
Meade Cl, W4 ... **126** A6
Meadfield, Edg. HA8 ... **54** B2
Mead Fld, Har. HA2
off Kings Rd ... **85** F3
Meadfield Grn, Edg. HA8 ... **54** B2
Meadfoot Rd, SW16 ... **168** C7
Meadgate Av, Wdf.Grn.
IG8 ... **64** B5
Mead Gro, Rom. RM6 ... **82** D3
Meadlands Dr, Rich.
TW10 ... **163** G2
Meadow, The, Chis. BR7 ... **175** F6
Meadow Av, Croy. CR0 ... **189** G6
Meadow Bk, N21 ... **43** F6
Meadowbank, NW3 ... **91** J7
SE3 ... **155** F3
Surbiton KT5 ... **181** J6
Meadowbank Cl, SW6 ... **127** J7
Islw. TW7 ... **144** B1
Meadowbank Gdns,
Houns. TW5 ... **142** A2
Meadowbank Rd, NW9 ... **70** D7
Meadowbanks, Barn.
EN5 ... **39** F5
Meadow Cl, E4 ... **62** B1
E9 ... **95** J5
SE6 ... **172** A5
SW20 ... **183** J4
Barking IG11 ... **117** J1
Barnet EN5 ... **40** C6
Bexleyheath DA6 ... **159** F5
Chislehurst BR7 ... **174** E5
Esher KT10 ... **194** C3
Hounslow TW4 ... **143** G6
Northolt UB5 ... **103** G2
Richmond TW10 ... **163** H1
Sutton SM1
off Aultone Way ... **199** F2
Meadowcourt Rd, SE3 ... **155** F4
Meadowcroft, Brom. BR1 ... **192** C3
Meadowcroft Rd, N13 ... **59** G2
Meadow Dr, N10 ... **74** B3
NW4 ... **71** J2
Meadowford Cl, SE28 ... **118** A7
Meadow Gdns, Edg. HA8 ... **54** B6
Meadow Garth, NW10 ... **88** C6
Meadowgate Cl, NW7 ... **55** F5
Meadow Hill, N.Mal. KT3 ... **182** E6
Meadow La, SE12 ... **173** H3
Meadowlea Cl, West Dr.
(Harm.) UB7 ... **120** A6
Meadow Ms, SW8 ... **34** C6
Meadow Pl, SW8 ... **34** B7
W4 *off Edensor Rd* ... **126** E7
Meadow Rd, SW8 ... **34** C7
SW19 ... **167** F7
Barking IG11 ... **99** J7
Borehamwood WD6 ... **38** B2
Bromley BR2 ... **191** E1
Dagenham RM9 ... **101** F6
Esher (Clay.) KT10 ... **194** B6
Feltham TW13 ... **160** E2
Loughton IG10 ... **48** B5
Pinner HA5 ... **66** D5
Romford RM7 ... **101** J1
Southall UB1 ... **103** F7
Sutton SM1 ... **199** H5
Meadow Row, SE1 ... **27** J6
Meadows Cl, E10 ... **96** A2
Meadows End, Sun.
TW16 ... **178** A1
Meadowside, SE9 ... **155** J4
Meadow Stile, Croy. CR0
off High St ... **201** J3
Meadowsweet Cl, E16
off Monarch Dr ... **116** A5
SW20 ... **183** J4
Meadow Vw, Har. HA1 ... **86** B1
Sidcup DA15 ... **158** B7
Meadowview Rd, SE6 ... **171** J5
Bexley DA5 ... **159** E6
Meadow Vw Rd, Th.Hth.
CR7 ... **187** H5
Meadow Wk, E18 ... **79** G4
Dagenham RM9 ... **101** F6
Epsom KT17, KT19 ... **197** E6
Wallington SM6 ... **200** B3
Meadow Way, NW9 ... **70** D5
Chessington KT9 ... **195** H5
Chigwell IG7 ... **65** F3
Orpington BR6 ... **206** D3
Ruislip HA4 ... **66** B6
Wembley HA9 ... **87** G4
Meadow Way, The, Har.
HA3 ... **68** B1
Meadow Waye, Houns.
TW5 ... **123** E6
Mead Path, SW17 ... **167** F5
Mead Pl, E9 ... **95** F6
Croydon CR0 ... **201** H1
Mead Plat, NW10 ... **88** C6
Mead Rd, Chis. BR7 ... **175** F6
Edgware HA8 ... **54** A6
Richmond TW10 ... **163** F3
Mead Row, SE1 ... **27** E5
Meads, The, Edg. HA8 ... **54** D6
Sutton SM3 ... **198** B3
Meadside Cl, Beck. BR3 ... **189** H1
Meads La, Ilf. IG3 ... **81** H7
Meads Rd, N22 ... **75** H2
Enfield EN3 ... **45** H1
Mead Ter, Wem. HA9
off Meadow Way ... **87** G4
Meadvale Rd, W5 ... **105** E4
Croydon CR0 ... **188** C7
Meadway, N14 ... **58** D2
NW11 ... **72** E6
SW20 ... **183** J4
Barnet EN5 ... **40** D4
Beckenham BR3 ... **190** C1
Mead Way, Brom. BR2 ... **191** F6
Croydon CR0 ... **203** H2
Meadway, Ilf. IG3 ... **99** H4
Surbiton KT5 ... **196** C1
Twickenham TW2 ... **162** A1
Woodford Green
IG8 ... **63** J5
Meadway, The, SE3
off Heath La ... **154** D2
Buckhurst Hill IG9 ... **64** A1
Loughton IG10 ... **48** C6
Meadway Cl, NW11 ... **73** E6
Barnet EN5 ... **40** D4
Pinner HA5
off Highbanks Rd ... **51** H6
Meadway Ct, NW11 ... **73** E6
Meadway Gate, NW11 ... **72** D6
Meaford Way, SE20 ... **171** E7
Meakin Est, SE1 ... **28** D5
Meanley Rd, E12 ... **98** B4
Meard St, W1 ... **17** H4
Meath Cres, E2 ... **113** G3
Meath Rd, E15 ... **115** F2
Ilford IG1 ... **99** F3
Meath St, SW11 ... **150** B1
Mecklenburgh Pl, WC1 ... **10** C5
Mecklenburgh Sq, WC1 ... **10** C5
Mecklenburgh St, WC1 ... **10** C5
Medburn St, NW1 ... **9** H1
Medcroft Gdns, SW14 ... **146** C4
Medebourne Cl, SE3 ... **155** G3
Medesenge Way, N13 ... **59** H6
Medfield St, SW15 ... **147** H7
Medhurst Cl, E3
off Arbery Rd ... **113** H2
Medhurst Dr, Brom. BR1 ... **172** E5
Median Rd, E5 ... **95** F5
★ **Medici Galleries**, W1 ... **16** E6
Medina Av, Esher KT10 ... **194** B3
Medina Gro, N7
off Medina Rd ... **93** G3
Medina Rd, N7 ... **93** G3
Medland Cl, Wall. SM6 ... **200** A1
Medland Ho, E14
off Branch Rd ... **113** H7
Medlar Cl, Nthlt. UB5
off Parkfield Av ... **102** E2
Medlar St, SE5 ... **151** J1
Medley Rd, NW6 ... **90** D6
Medora Rd, SW2 ... **151** F7
Medusa Rd, SE6 ... **154** B6
Medway Bldgs, E3
off Medway Rd ... **113** H2
Medway Cl, Croy. CR0 ... **189** F6
Ilford IG1 ... **99** F5
Medway Dr, Grnf.
(Perivale) UB6 ... **104** C2
Medway Gdns, Wem.
HA0 ... **86** D4
Medway Ms, E3
off Medway Rd ... **113** H2
Medway Par, Grnf.
(Perivale) UB6 ... **104** C2
Medway Rd, E3 ... **113** H2
Medway St, SW1 ... **25** J6
Medwin St, SW4 ... **151** F4
Meecham Ct, SW11
off Shuttleworth Rd ... **149** G2
Meerbrook Rd, SE3 ... **155** J3
Meeson Rd, E15 ... **115** F1
Meeson St, E5 ... **95** H4
Meeting Fld Path, E9
off Chatham Pl ... **95** F6
Meeting Ho All, E1
off Watts St ... **133** E1
Meeting Ho La, SE15 ... **152** E1
Mehetabel Rd, E9 ... **95** F6
Meister Cl, Ilf. IG1 ... **99** G1
Melancholy Wk, Rich.
TW10 ... **163** F2
Melanda Cl, Chis. BR7 ... **174** C5
Melanie Cl, Bexh. DA7 ... **158** E1
Melba Way, SE13 ... **154** B1
Melbourne Av, N13 ... **59** F6
W13 ... **124** D1
Pinner HA5 ... **67** H3
Melbourne Cl, Orp. BR6 ... **193** H7
Wallington SM6
off Melbourne Rd ... **200** C5
Melbourne Ct, E5
off Daubeney Rd ... **95** H4
SE20 ... **170** D7
Melbourne Gdns, Rom.
RM6 ... **82** E5
Melbourne Gro, SE22 ... **152** B4
Melbourne Ho, Hayes
UB4 ... **102** C4
Melbourne Ms, SE6 ... **154** C7
SW9 ... **151** G1
Melbourne Pl, WC2 ... **18** D5
Melbourne Rd, E6 ... **116** C1
E10 ... **78** B7
E17 ... **77** H4
SW19 ... **184** D1
Ilford IG1 ... **99** E1
Teddington TW11 ... **163** F6
Wallington SM6 ... **200** B5
Melbourne Sq, SW9
off Melbourne Ms ... **151** G1
Melbourne Ter, SW6
off Moore Pk Rd ... **128** E7
Melbourne Way, Enfield
EN1 ... **44** C6
Melbray Ms, SW6
off Hurlingham Rd ... **148** C2
Melbreak Ho, SE22
off Pytchley Rd ... **152** B3
Melbury Av, Sthl. UB2 ... **123** H3
Melbury Cl, Chis. BR7 ... **174** B6
Esher (Clay.) KT10 ... **194** E6
Melbury Ct, W8 ... **128** C3
Melbury Dr, SE5
off Sedgmoor Pl ... **132** B7
Melbury Gdns, SW20 ... **183** H1
Melbury Rd, W14 ... **128** C3
Harrow HA3 ... **69** J5
Melcombe Gdns, Har.
HA3 ... **69** J6
Melcombe Ho, SW8
off Dorset Rd ... **131** F7
Melcombe Pl, NW1 ... **15** J1
Melcombe St, NW1 ... **8** A6
Meldex Cl, NW7 ... **55** J6
Meldon Cl, SW6
off Bagley's La ... **149** E1
Meldone Cl, Surb. KT5 ... **182** B6
Meldrum Rd, Ilf. IG3 ... **100** A2
Melfield Gdns, SE6 ... **172** B4
Melford Av, Bark. IG11 ... **99** H6
Melford Cl, Chess. KT9 ... **195** J5
Melford Rd, E6 ... **116** C4
E11 ... **96** E2
E17 ... **77** H4
SE22 ... **152** D7
Ilford IG1 ... **99** G2
Melfort Av, Th.Hth. CR7 ... **187** H3
Melfort Rd, Th.Hth. CR7 ... **187** H3
Melgund Rd, N5 ... **93** G5
Melina Pl, NW8 ... **6** E4
Melina Rd, W12 ... **127** H2
Melior Pl, SE1 ... **28** D3
Melior St, SE1 ... **28** C3
Meliot Rd, SE6 ... **172** D2
Meller Cl, Croy. CR0 ... **200** E3
Mellifont Cl, Cars. SM5 ... **185** G7
Melling Dr, Enf. EN1 ... **44** D1
Melling St, SE18 ... **137** H6
Mellish Cl, Bark. IG11 ... **117** J1
Mellish Gdns, Wdf.Grn.
IG8 ... **63** G5
Mellish Ind Est, SE18 ... **136** B3
Mellish St, E14 ... **134** A3
Mellison Rd, SW17 ... **167** H5
Melliss Av, Rich. TW9 ... **146** B1
Mellitus St, W12 ... **107** F6
Mellor Cl, Walt. KT12 ... **179** F7
Mellows Rd, Ilf. IG5 ... **80** C3
Wallington SM6 ... **200** D5
Mells Cres, SE9 ... **174** C4
Mell St, SE10
off Trafalgar Rd ... **134** E5
Melody La, N5 ... **93** H5
Melody Rd, SW18 ... **149** F5
Melon Pl, W8 ... **22** A3
Melon Rd, E11 ... **96** E3
SE15 ... **152** D1
Melrose Av, N22 ... **75** H1
NW2 ... **89** H5
SW16 ... **187** F3
SW19 ... **166** D2
Borehamwood WD6 ... **38** B5
Greenford UB6 ... **103** H2
Mitcham CR4 ... **168** B7
Twickenham TW2 ... **143** H7
Melrose Cl, SE12 ... **173** G1
Greenford UB6 ... **103** H2
Hayes UB4 ... **102** A5
Melrose Ct, W13
off Williams Rd ... **124** D1
Melrose Cres, Orp. BR6 ... **207** G4
Melrose Dr, Sthl. UB1 ... **123** G1
Melrose Gdns, W6 ... **127** J3
Edgware HA8 ... **70** B2
New Malden KT3 ... **182** D3
Melrose Rd, SW13 ... **147** F2
SW18 ... **148** C6
SW19 ... **184** D2
W3 *off Stanley Rd* ... **126** C3
Pinner HA5 ... **67** F4
Melrose Ter, W6 ... **127** J2
Melsa Rd, Mord. SM4 ... **185** F6
Melthorne Dr, Ruis. HA4 ... **84** C3
Melthorpe Gdns, SE3 ... **156** B1
Melton Cl, Ruis. HA4 ... **84** C1
Melton Ct, SW7 ... **31** F2
Sutton SM2 ... **199** F7
Melton St, NW1 ... **9** G4
Melville Av, SW20 ... **165** G7
Greenford UB6 ... **86** C5
South Croydon CR2 ... **202** C5
Melville Gdns, N13 ... **59** H5
Melville Pl, N1
off Essex Rd ... **93** J7
Melville Rd, E17 ... **77** J3
NW10 ... **88** D7
SW13 ... **147** G1
Sidcup DA14 ... **176** C2
Melville Vil Rd, W3
off High St ... **126** D1
Melvin Rd, SE20 ... **189** F1
Melwas Ct, N9
off Galahad Rd ... **60** D3
Melyn Cl, N7
off Anson Rd ... **92** C4
Memel Ct, EC1 ... **11** J6

Memel St, EC1 11 J6
Memess Path, SE18 136 D6
Memorial Av, E15 114 E3
Memorial Cl, Houns. TW5 123 F6
Memorial Hts, Ilf. IG2 81 G6
Menai Pl, E3
off Blondin St 114 A2
Mendip Cl, SE26 171 F4
Hayes (Harling.) UB3 121 G7
Worcester Park KT4 197 J1
Mendip Dr, NW2 90 A2
Mendip Ho, N9
off Edmonton Grn Shop Cen 60 D2
Mendip Hos, E2
off Globe Rd 113 F3
Mendip Rd, SW11 149 F3
Ilford IG2 81 H5
Mendora Rd, SW6 128 B7
Menelik Rd, NW2 90 B4
Menlo Gdns, SE19 170 A7
Menon Dr, N9 60 E3
Menotti St, E2 13 J5
Mentmore Cl, Har. HA3 69 F6
Mentmore Ter, E8 95 E7
Meon Ct, Islw. TW7 144 B2
Meon Rd, W3 126 C2
Meopham Rd, Mitch. CR4 186 C1
Mepham Cres, Har. HA3 51 J7
Mepham Gdns, Har. HA3 51 J7
Mepham St, SE1 26 D2
Mera Dr, Bexh. DA7 159 G4
Merantun Way, SW19 185 F1
Merbury Cl, SE13 154 C5
SE28 137 G1
Merbury Rd, SE28 137 H2
Mercator Pl, E14
off Napier Av 134 B5
Mercator Rd, SE13 154 D4
Mercer Cl, T.Ditt. KT7 180 C7
Merceron Hos, E2
off Globe Rd 113 F3
Merceron St, E1 112 E4
Mercer Pl, Pnr. HA5 66 C2
Mercers Cl, SE10 135 F4
Mercers Ms, N19
off Mercers Rd 92 D3
Mercers Pl, W6 127 J4
Mercers Rd, N19 92 D3
Mercer St, WC2 18 A4
Merchants Cl, SE25
off Clifford Rd 188 D4
Merchants Ho, SE10
off Hoskins St 134 D5
Merchants Row, SE10
off Hoskins St 134 D5
Merchant St, E3 113 J3
Merchiston Rd, SE6 172 D2
Merchland Rd, SE9 175 F1
Mercia Gro, SE13 154 C4
Mercier Rd, SW15 148 B5
Mercury Cen, Felt. TW14 142 B5
Mercury Ho, E3
off Garrison Rd 114 A1
Mercury Way, SE14 133 G6
Mercy Ter, SE13 154 B4
Merebank La, Croy. CR0 201 F5
Mere Cl, SW15 148 A7
Orpington BR6 206 E2
Meredith Av, NW2 89 J5
Meredith Cl, Pnr. HA5 50 D7
Meredith Ms, SE4 153 J4
Meredith St, E13 115 G3
EC1 11 G4
Meredyth Rd, SW13 147 G2
Mere End, Croy. CR0 189 G7
Mereside, Orp. BR6 206 D2
Meretone Cl, SE4 153 H4
Mereton Mans, SE8
off Brookmill Rd 154 A1
Merevale Cres, Mord. SM4 185 F6
Mereway Rd, Twick. TW2 162 A1
Merewood Cl, Brom. BR1 192 D2
Merewood Gdns, Croy. CR0 189 G7
Merewood Rd, Bexh. DA7 159 J2
Mereworth Cl, Brom. BR2 191 F5
Mereworth Dr, SE18 137 E7
Merganser Gdns, SE28
off Avocet Ms 137 G3
Meriden Cl, Brom. BR1 174 A7
Ilford IG6 81 F1
Meridian Business Pk, Enf. EN3 45 H6
Meridian Cl, NW7 54 D4
Meridian Ct, SE16
off East La 29 H3
Meridian Gate, E14 134 C2
Meridian Pl, E14 134 B2
Meridian Rd, SE7 136 A7
Meridian Sq, E15 96 D7
Meridian Trd Est, SE7 135 H4
Meridian Wk, N17
off Commercial Rd 60 B6
Meridian Way, N9 61 F5
N18 61 F6
Enfield EN3 45 G6
Merifield Rd, SE9 155 J4
Merino Cl, E11 79 J4
Merino Pl, Sid. DA15
off Blackfen Rd 158 A6
Merivale Rd, SW15 148 B4
Harrow HA1 67 J7
Merlewood Dr, Chis. BR7 192 C1
Merley Ct, NW9 88 C1
Merlin Cl, Croy. CR0 202 B4
Mitcham CR4 185 H3
Northolt UB5 102 C3
Wallington SM6 201 F6
Merlin Ct, Brom. BR2
off Durham Av 191 F4
Merlin Cres, Edg. HA8 69 J1
Merlin Gdns, Brom. BR1 173 G3
Merling Cl, Chess. KT9
off Coppard Gdns 195 G5
Merlin Gro, Beck. BR3 189 J4
Ilford IG6 65 E7
Merlin Ho, Enf. EN3
off Allington Ct 45 G5
Merlin Rd, E12 97 J2
Welling DA16 158 A4
Merlin Rd N, Well. DA16 158 A4
Merlins Av, Har. HA2 85 F3
Merlin St, WC1 11 E4
Mermaid Ct, SE1 28 B3
SE16 133 J1
Mermaid Twr, SE8
off Abinger Gro 133 J6
Merredene St, SW2 151 F6
Merriam Av, E9 95 J6
Merriam Cl, E4 62 C5
Merrick Rd, Sthl. UB2 123 F2
Merrick Sq, SE1 28 A5
Merridale, SE12 155 G5
Merridene, N21 43 H6
Merrielands Cres, Dag. RM9 119 F1
Merrilands Rd, Wor.Pk. KT4 197 J1
Merrilees Rd, Sid. DA15 175 H1
Merrilyn Cl, Esher (Clay.) KT10 194 D6
Merriman Rd, SE3 155 J1
Merrington Rd, SW6 128 D6
Merrion Av, Stan. HA7 53 G5
Merritt Gdns, Chess. KT9 195 F6
Merritt Rd, SE4 153 J5
Merrivale, N14 42 D6
Merrivale Av, Ilf. IG4 80 A4
Merrivale Ms, West Dr. UB7 120 A1
Merrow St, SE17 36 B5
Merrow Wk, SE17 36 C3
Merrow Way, Croy. (New Adgtn) CR0 204 C6
Merrydown Way, Chis. BR7 192 B1
Merryfield, SE3 155 F2
Merryfield Gdns, Stan. HA7 53 F5
Merryfield Ho, SE9
off Grove Pk Rd 173 J3
Merryfields Way, SE6 154 B7
MERRY HILL, Bushey WD23 51 G1
Merryhill Cl, E4 46 B7
Merry Hill Mt, Bushey WD23 51 H1
Merry Hill Rd, Bushey WD23 51 H1
Merryhills Ct, N14 42 C5
Merryhills Dr, Enf. EN2 42 D4
Merryweather Ct, N.Mal. KT3 *off Rodney Cl* 182 E5
Mersea Ho, Bark. IG11 98 E6
Mersey Rd, E17 77 J3
Mersey Wk, Nthlt. UB5
off Brabazon Rd 103 G2
Mersham Dr, NW9 70 A5
Mersham Pl, SE20 189 E1
Mersham Rd, Th.Hth. CR7 188 A3
Merten Rd, Rom. RM6 83 E7
Merthyr Ter, SW13 127 H6
MERTON, SW19 184 D1
Merton Abbey Mills, SW19
off Watermill Way 185 F1
Merton Av, W4 127 F4
Northolt UB5 85 J5
Merton Ct, Ilf. IG1
off Castleview Gdns 80 B6
Merton Gdns, Orp. BR5 193 E5
Merton Hall Gdns, SW20 184 B1
Merton Hall Rd, SW19 184 B1
Merton High St, SW19 167 E7
Merton Ind Pk, SW19 185 F1
Merton La, N6 91 J2
Merton Mans, SW20 184 A2
MERTON PARK, SW19 184 D2
Merton Pk Par, SW19
off Kingston Rd 184 C1
Merton Ri, NW3 91 H7
Merton Rd, E17 78 C5
SE25 188 D5
SW18 148 D5
SW19 166 E7
Barking IG11 99 J7
Harrow HA2 85 J1
Ilford IG3 81 J7
Merton Way, W.Mol. KT8 179 H4
Merttins Rd, SE15 153 G5
Meru Cl, NW5 92 A5
Mervan Rd, SW2 151 G4
Mervyn Av, SE9 175 F3
Mervyn Rd, W13 124 D3
Messaline Av, W3 106 C6
Messent Rd, SE9 155 J5
Messeter Pl, SE9 156 D6
Messina Av, NW6 90 D7
Metcalf Wk, Felt. TW13
off Cresswell Rd 160 E4
Meteor St, SW11 150 A4
Meteor Way, Wall. SM6 200 E7
Methley St, SE11 35 F4
★ **Methodist Cen Hall**, SW1 25 J4
Methuen Cl, Edg. HA8 54 A7
Methuen Pk, N10 74 B2
Methuen Rd, Belv. DA17 139 H4
Bexleyheath DA6 159 F4
Edgware HA8 54 A7
Methven Ct, N9
off The Broadway 60 D3
Methwold Rd, W10 108 A5
Metro Business Cen, SE26 171 J5
Metro Cen Hts, SE1 27 J6
Metro Ind Cen, Islw. TW7 144 B2
Metropolitan Cen, The, Grnf. UB6 103 H1
Metropolitan Cl, E14
off Broomfield St 114 A5
Mews, The, N1
off St. Paul St 111 J1
N8 *off Turnpike La* 75 G3
Ilford IG4 80 A5
Twickenham TW1
off Bridge Rd 144 E6
Mews Deck, E1
off Sovereign Cl 113 E7
Mews Pl, Wdf.Grn. IG8 63 G4
Mews St, E1 29 H1
Mexfield Rd, SW15 148 C5
Meyer Rd, Erith DA8 139 J6
Meymott St, SE1 27 G2
Meynell Cres, E9 95 G7
Meynell Gdns, E9 95 G7
Meynell Rd, E9 95 G7
Meyrick Rd, NW10 89 G6
SW11 149 G3
★ **MI5 (Security Service) Thames Ho**, SW1 34 A1
Miah Ter, E1 29 J2
Miall Wk, SE26 171 H4
Micawber St, N1 12 A3
Michael Cliffe Ho, EC1 11 F4
Michael Faraday Ho, SE17 36 C4
Michael Gaynor Cl, W7 124 C1
Michaelmas Cl, SW20 183 J3
Michael Rd, E11 97 E1
SE25 188 B3
SW6 149 E1
Michaels Cl, SE13 154 E4
Michael Stewart Ho, SW6
off Clem Attlee Ct 128 C6
Micheldever Rd, SE12 155 E6
Michelham Gdns, Twick. TW1 162 C3
Michels Row, Rich. TW9
off Kew Foot Rd 145 H4
Michel Wk, SE18 137 E5
Michigan Av, E12 98 B4
Michigan Bldg, E14
off Blackwall Way 114 C7
Michleham Down, N12 56 C4
Mickleham Cl, Orp. BR5 193 J2
Mickleham Gdns, Sutt. SM3 198 B6
Mickleham Rd, Orp. BR5 193 J1
Mickleham Way, Croy. (New Adgtn) CR0 204 D7
Micklethwaite Rd, SW6 128 D6
Middle Dartrey Wk, SW10
off Blantyre St 30 E7
Middle Dene, NW7 54 D3
Middle Fld, NW8 109 G1
Middlefielde, W13 104 E5
Middlefield Gdns, Ilf. IG2 81 E6
Middle Grn Cl, Surb. KT5
off Alpha Rd 181 J6
Middleham Gdns, N18 60 D6
Middleham Rd, N18 60 D6
Middle La, N8 74 E5
Teddington TW11 162 C6
Middle La Ms, N8
off Middle La 74 E5
Middle Pk Av, SE9 156 A6
Middle Path, Har. HA2
off Middle Rd 86 A1
Middle Rd, E13
off London Rd 115 G2
SW16 186 D2
Barnet (E.Barn.) EN4 41 H6
Harrow HA2 86 A2
Middle Row, W10 108 B4
Middlesborough Rd, N18 60 D6
Middlesex Business Cen, Sthl. UB2 123 G2
Middlesex Cl, Sthl. UB1 103 H4
Middlesex Ct, W4 127 F5
Middlesex Ho, Wem. HA0 105 G1
Middlesex Pas, EC1 19 H2
Middlesex Rd, Mitch. CR4 186 E5
Middlesex St, E1 20 E2
Middlesex Wf, E5 95 F2
Middle St, EC1 19 J1
Croydon CR0
off Surrey St 201 J2
Middle Temple, EC4 19 E5
Middle Temple La, EC4 18 E4
Middleton Av, E4 61 J4
Greenford UB6 104 A2
Sidcup DA14 176 C6
Middleton Cl, E4 61 J3
Middleton Dr, SE16 133 G2
Pinner HA5 66 A3
Middleton Gdns, Ilf. IG2 80 E6
Middleton Gro, N7 92 E5
Middleton Ms, N7
off Middleton Gro 92 E5
Middleton Pl, W1 17 F2
Middleton Rd, E8 94 C7
NW11 72 D7
Carshalton SM5 185 H7
Morden SM4 185 F6
Middleton St, E2 112 E3
Middleton Way, SE13 154 D4
Middleway, NW11 73 E5
Middle Way, SW16 186 D2
Erith DA18 138 E3
Hayes UB4 102 C4
Middle Way, The, Har. HA3 68 C2
Middle Yd, SE1 28 D1
Midfield Av, Bexh. DA7 159 J3
Midfield Par, Bexh. DA7 159 J3
Midford Pl, W1 9 G6
Midholm, NW11 72 E4
Wembley HA9 88 A1
Midholm Cl, NW11 72 E4
Midholm Rd, Croy. CR0 203 H2
Midhope St, WC1 10 B4
Midhurst Av, N10 74 A3
Croydon CR0 187 G7
Midhurst Hill, Bexh. DA6 159 G6
Midhurst Rd, W13 124 D2
Midhurst Way, E5 94 D4
Midland Cres, NW3
off Finchley Rd 91 F6
Midland Pl, E14
off Ferry St 134 C5
Midland Rd, E10 78 C7
NW1 9 J2
Midland Ter, NW2 90 A3
NW10 107 E4
Midleton Rd, N.Mal. KT3 182 C3
Midlothian Rd, E3
off Burdett Rd 113 J4
Midmoor Rd, SW12 168 C1
SW19 184 A1
Midship Cl, SE16
off Surrey Water Rd 133 G1
Midship Pt, E14 134 A2
Midstrath Rd, NW10 89 E4
Midsummer Av, Houns. TW4 143 F4
Midway, Sutt. SM3 184 C7
Midwinter Cl, Well. DA16
off Hook La 158 A3
Midwood Cl, NW2 89 H3
Miers Cl, E6 116 D1
Mighell Av, Ilf. IG4 80 A5
Milan Rd, Sthl. UB1 123 F2
Milborne Gro, SW10 30 D4
Milborne St, E9 95 F6
Milborough Cres, SE12 155 E6
Milcote St, SE1 27 G4
Mildenhall Rd, E5 95 F4
Mildmay Av, N1 94 A6
Mildmay Gro N, N1 94 A5
Mildmay Gro S, N1 94 A5
Mildmay Pk, N1 94 A5
Mildmay Pl, N16
off Boleyn Rd 94 B5

Mildmay Rd, N1 .... 94 B5
Ilford IG1
off Albert Rd 99 E3
Romford RM7 .... 83 J5
Mildmay St, N1 .... 94 A6
Mildred Av, Borwd. WD6 .... 38 A4
Hayes UB3 .... 121 G4
Northolt UB5 .... 85 H5
Mildred Ct, Croy. CRO 202 D1
MILE END, E1 .... 113 G3
Mile End, The, E17 .... 77 G1
Mile End Pl, E1 .... 113 G4
Mile End Rd, E1 .... 113 F5
E3 .... 113 F5
Mile Rd, Wall. SM6 .... 200 A1
Miles Cl, SE28 .... 137 G1
Miles Dr, SE28 .... 137 G1
Milespit Hill, NW7 .... 55 H5
Miles Pl, NW1 .... 15 F1
Surbiton KT5
off Villiers Av 181 J4
Miles Rd, N8 .... 75 E3
Mitcham CR4 .... 185 H3
Miles St, SW8 .... 34 A6
Milestone Cl, N9 .... 60 D2
Sutton SM2 .... 199 G6
Milestone Grn, SW14 .... 146 C4
Milestone Rd, SE19 .... 170 C6
Miles Way, N20 .... 57 H2
Milfoil St, W12 .... 107 G7
Milford Cl, SE2 .... 139 E6
Milford Gdns, Croy. CR0 .... 189 F5
Edgware HA8 .... 54 A7
Wembley HA0 .... 87 G5
Milford Gro, Sutt. SM1 .... 199 F4
Milford La, WC2 .... 18 D5
Milford Ms, SW16 .... 169 F3
Milford Rd, W13 .... 124 E1
Southall UB1 .... 103 G7
Milford Twrs, SE6
off Thomas La 154 B7
Milk St, E16 .... 136 E1
EC2 .... 20 A4
Bromley BR1 .... 173 H6
Milkwell Gdns, Wdf.Grn.
IG8 .... 63 H7
Milkwell Yd, SE5 .... 151 J1
Milkwood Rd, SE24 .... 151 H5
Milk Yd, E1 .... 113 F7
Millais Av, E12 .... 98 D5
Millais Cres, Epsom
KT19 .... 196 E5
Millais Gdns, Edg. HA8 .... 70 A2
Millais Rd, E11 .... 96 C4
Enfield EN1 .... 44 C5
New Malden KT3 .... 182 E7
Millais Way, Epsom
KT19 .... 196 C4
Milland Ct, Borwd. WD6 .... 38 D1
Millard Cl, N16
off Boleyn Rd 94 B5
Millard Ter, Dag. RM10
off Church Elm La 101 G6
Millbank, SW1 .... 26 A6
Millbank Ct, SW1 .... 34 A1
Millbank Twr, SW1 .... 34 A2
Millbank Way, SE12 .... 155 G5
Millbourne Rd, Felt.
TW13 .... 161 E4
Mill Br, Barn. EN5 .... 40 C6
Millbrook Av, Well.
DA16 .... 157 G4
Millbrook Gdns, Rom.
(Chad.Hth) RM6 .... 83 F6
Millbrook Pl, NW1
off Hampstead Rd 9 F1
Millbrook Rd, N9 .... 60 E1
SW9 .... 151 H3
Mill Cl, Cars. SM5 .... 200 A2
West Drayton UB7 .... 120 A3
Mill Cor, Barn. EN5 .... 40 C1
Mill Ct, E10 .... 96 C3
Millcroft Ho, SE6 .... 172 C4
Millender Wk, SE16 .... 133 F4
Millennium Br, EC4 .... 19 J5
SE1 .... 19 J5
Millennium Cl, E16
off Russell Rd 115 H6
Millennium Dr, E14 .... 134 D4
Millennium Harbour, E14 .... 133 J2
Millennium Pl, E2 .... 113 E2
Millennium Sq, SE1 .... 29 F3
Millennium Way, SE10 .... 134 E2
Miller Cl, Brom. BR1 .... 173 G5
Mitcham CR4 .... 185 J7
Pinner HA5 .... 66 C2
Miller Rd, SW19 .... 167 G6
Croydon CR0 .... 201 F1
Miller's Av, E8 .... 94 C5
Millers Cl, NW7 .... 55 G4
Millers Ct, W4
off Chiswick Mall 127 F5
Millers Grn Cl, Enf. EN2 .... 43 H3
Millers Meadow Cl, SE3 .... 155 F5
Miller's Ter, E8 .... 94 C5
Miller St, NW1 .... 9 F1
Millers Way, W6 .... 127 J2
Miller Wk, SE1 .... 27 F2
Millet Rd, Grnf. UB6 .... 103 H3
Mill Fm Business Pk,
Houns. TW4 .... 143 E7
Mill Fm Cl, Pnr. HA5 .... 66 C2
Mill Fm Cres, Houns.
TW4 .... 161 E1
Millfield, N4
off Six Acres Est 93 G2
Millfield Av, E17 .... 77 H1
Millfield La, N6 .... 91 J2
Millfield Pl, N6 .... 92 A2
Millfield Rd, Edg. HA8 .... 70 C2
Hounslow TW4 .... 161 E1
Millfields Est, E5 .... 95 G3
Millfields Rd, E5 .... 95 F4
Mill Gdns, SE26 .... 171 E4
Mill Grn, Mitch. CR4 .... 186 A7
Mill Grn Business Pk,
Mitch. CR4
off Mill Grn Rd 186 A7
Mill Grn Rd, Mitch. CR4 .... 185 J7
Millgrove St, SW11 .... 150 A2
Millharbour, E14 .... 134 B3
Millhaven Cl, Rom. RM6 .... 82 B6
MILL HILL, NW7 .... 55 G5
Mill Hill, SW13
off Mill Hill Rd 147 G2
Mill Hill Circ, NW7 .... 55 F5
Mill Hill Gro, W3 .... 126 B1
Mill Hill Ind Est, NW7 .... 55 F6
Mill Hill Rd, SW13 .... 147 G2
W3 .... 126 B2
Mill Hill Ter, W3
off Mill Hill Rd 126 C1
Millhouse Pl, SE27 .... 169 H4
Millicent Rd, E10 .... 95 J1
Milligan St, E14 .... 113 J7
Milliners Ct, Loug. IG10
off The Croft 48 D2
Milliners Ho, SW18
off Eastfields Av 148 D4
Milling Rd, Edg. HA8 .... 54 D7
Millington Rd, Hayes
UB3 .... 121 H3
Mill La, E4 .... 46 B3
NW6 .... 90 C5
SE18 .... 136 D5
Carshalton SM5 .... 199 J4
Croydon CR0 .... 201 F3
Romford (Chad.Hth)
RM6 .... 82 E6
Woodford Green IG8 .... 63 F5
Mill La Trd Est, Croy. CR0 .... 201 F3
Millman Ms, WC1 .... 10 C6
Millman Pl, WC1
off Millman St 10 C6
Millman St, WC1 .... 10 C6
Millmark Gro, SE14 .... 153 H2
Millmarsh La, Enf. EN3 .... 45 H2
Mill Mead Rd, N17 .... 76 E4
Mill Pl, E14
off Commercial Rd 113 H6
Chislehurst BR7
off Old Hill 192 E1
Kingston upon Thames
KT1 .... 181 J3
Mill Plat, Islw. TW7 .... 144 D2
Mill Plat Av, Islw. TW7 .... 144 D2
Mill Pond Cl, SW8
off Thorparch Rd 130 D7
Millpond Est, SE16
off West La 132 E2
Millpond Pl, Cars. SM5 .... 200 A3
Mill Ridge, Edg. HA8 .... 53 J5
Mill Rd, E16 .... 135 H1
SW19 .... 167 F7
Erith DA8 .... 139 J7
Ilford IG1 .... 98 D3
Twickenham TW2 .... 161 J2
Mill Row, N1 .... 112 B1
Mills Ct, EC2 .... 12 E4
Mills Gro, E14
off Dewberry St 114 C5
NW4 .... 72 A3
Millshott Cl, SW6 .... 127 J7
Millside, Cars. SM5 .... 199 J2
Millside Pl, Islw. TW7 .... 144 E2
Millsmead Way, Loug.
IG10 .... 48 C2
Millson Cl, N20 .... 57 G2
Mills Row, W4 .... 126 D4
Millstream Cl, N13 .... 59 G5
Millstream Rd, SE1 .... 29 F4
Mill St, SE1 .... 29 G4
W1 .... 17 E5
Kingston upon Thames
KT1 .... 181 H3
Mill Vale, Brom. BR2 .... 191 F2
Mill Vw Cl, Epsom (Ewell)
KT17 .... 197 F7
Mill Vw Gdns, Croy. CR0 .... 203 G3
MILLWALL, E14 .... 134 B3
Millwall Dock Rd, E14 .... 134 A3
★ **Millwall FC**, SE16 .... 133 F5
Millway, NW7 .... 54 E5
Mill Way, Felt. TW14 .... 142 B5
Millway Gdns, Nthlt. UB5 .... 85 F6
Millwell Cres, Chig. IG7 .... 65 G5
Millwood Rd, Houns.
TW3 .... 143 J5
Millwood St, W10
off St. Charles Sq 108 B5
Mill Yd, E1 .... 21 H5
Mill Yd Indusrial Est, Edg.
HA8 .... 70 B1
Milman Cl, Pnr. HA5 .... 66 D3
Milman Rd, NW6 .... 108 B2
Milman's St, SW10 .... 31 E6
Milmead Ind Cen, N17 .... 76 E2
Milne Ct, E18
off Churchfields 79 G1
Milne Feild, Pnr. HA5 .... 51 G7
Milne Gdns, SE9 .... 156 B5
Milner Dr, Twick. TW2 .... 144 A7
Milner Pl, N1 .... 111 G1
Carshalton SM5
off High St 200 A4
Milner Rd, E15 .... 114 E3
SW19 .... 184 E1
Dagenham RM8 .... 100 C2
Kingston upon Thames
KT1 .... 181 G3
Morden SM4 .... 185 G5
Thornton Heath CR7 .... 188 A3
Milner Sq, N1 .... 93 H7
Milner St, SW3 .... 31 J1
Milner Wk, SE9 .... 175 G2
Milnthorpe Rd, W4 .... 126 D6
Milo Gdns, SE22
off Milo Rd 152 C6
Milo Rd, SE22 .... 152 C6
Milroy Wk, SE1 .... 27 G1
Milson Rd, W14 .... 128 B3
Milstead Ho, E5
off Pembury Rd 94 E5
Milton Av, E6 .... 98 A7
N6 .... 74 C7
NW9 .... 70 C3
NW10 .... 106 C1
Barnet EN5 .... 40 C5
Croydon CR0 .... 188 A7
Sutton SM1 .... 199 G3
Milton Cl, N2 .... 73 F5
SE1 .... 37 F2
Hayes UB4 .... 102 A6
Sutton SM1 .... 199 G3
Milton Ct, EC2 .... 20 B1
Romford (Chad.Hth)
RM6 *off Cross Rd* 82 C7
Milton Ct Rd, SE14 .... 133 H6
Milton Cres, Ilf. IG2 .... 81 F7
Milton Dr, Borwd. WD6 .... 38 B5
Milton Gdn Est, N16
off Milton Gro 94 B4
Milton Gro, N11 .... 58 C5
N16 .... 94 A4
Milton Pk, N6 .... 74 C7
Milton Pl, N7
off George's Rd 93 G5
Milton Rd, E17 .... 78 A4
N6 .... 74 C7
N15 .... 75 H4
NW7 .... 55 G5
NW9
off West Hendon Bdy 71 G7
SE24 .... 151 H6
SW14 .... 146 D3
SW19 .... 167 F6
W3 .... 126 D1
W7 .... 104 C7
Belvedere DA17 .... 139 G4
Croydon CR0 .... 202 A1
Hampton TW12 .... 161 G7
Harrow HA1 .... 68 B4
Mitcham CR4 .... 168 A7
Sutton SM1 .... 198 D3
Wallington SM6 .... 200 C6
Welling DA16 .... 157 J1
Milton St, EC2 .... 20 B1
Milton Way, West Dr.
UB7 .... 120 C4
Milverton Gdns, Ilf. IG3 .... 99 J2
Milverton Ho, SE23 .... 171 H3
Milverton Rd, NW6 .... 89 J7
Milverton St, SE11 .... 35 F4
Milverton Way, SE9 .... 174 D4
Milward St, E1
off Stepney Way 113 E5
Milward Wk, SE18
off Spearman St 136 D6
Mimosa Rd, Hayes UB4 .... 102 C5
Mimosa St, SW6 .... 148 C1
Minard Rd, SE6 .... 154 E7
Mina Rd, SE17 .... 36 E4
SW19 .... 184 D1
Minchenden Cres, N14 .... 58 C3
Mincing La, EC3 .... 20 D5
Minden Rd, SE20 .... 188 E1
Sutton SM3 .... 198 C2
Minehead Rd, SW16 .... 169 F5
Harrow HA2 .... 85 G3
Mineral Cl, Barn. EN5 .... 39 J6
Mineral St, SE18 .... 137 H4
Minera Ms, SW1 .... 32 C1
Minerva Cl, SW9 .... 131 G7
Sidcup DA14 .... 175 H3
Minerva Rd, E4 .... 62 B7
NW10 .... 106 C4
Kingston upon Thames
KT1 .... 181 J2
Minerva St, E2 .... 112 E2
Minet Av, NW10 .... 106 E2
Minet Dr, Hayes UB3 .... 122 A1
Minet Gdns, NW10 .... 106 E2
Hayes UB3 .... 122 A1
Minet Rd, SW9 .... 151 H2
Minford Gdns, W14 .... 128 A2
Mingard Wk, N7
off Hornsey Rd 93 F3
Ming St, E14 .... 114 A7
★ **Ministry of Defence**,
SW1 .... 26 A2
Ministry Way, SE9 .... 174 C2
Miniver Pl, EC4
off Garlick Hill 20 A5
Mink Ct, Houns. TW4 .... 142 C3
Minniedale, Surb. KT5 .... 181 J5
Minnow St, SE17 .... 36 E2
Minnow Wk, SE17
off Minnow St 36 E2
Minories, EC3 .... 21 F5
Minshull Pl, Beck. BR3 .... 172 A7
Minshull St, SW8
off Wandsworth Rd 150 D1
Minson Rd, E9 .... 113 G1
Minstead Gdns, SW15 .... 147 F7
Minstead Way, N.Mal.
KT3 .... 182 E6
Minster Av, Sutt. SM1
off Leafield Rd 198 D2
Minster Ct, EC3 .... 20 D5
Minster Dr, Croy. CR0 .... 202 B4
Minster Gdns, W.Mol.
KT8 .... 179 F4
Minster Pavement, EC3
off Mincing La 20 D5
Minster Rd, NW2 .... 90 B5
Bromley BR1 .... 173 H7
Minster Wk, N8
off Lightfoot Rd 74 E4
Minstrel Gdns, Surb.
KT5 .... 181 J4
Mint Business Pk, E16 .... 115 G5
Mintern Cl, N13 .... 59 H3
Minterne Av, Sthl. UB2 .... 123 G4
Minterne Rd, Har. HA3 .... 69 J5
Minterne Waye, Hayes
UB4 .... 102 C6
Mintern St, N1 .... 12 C1
Minton Ho, SE11
off Walnut Tree Wk 34 E1
Minton Ms, NW6
off Dresden Cl 91 E6
Mint Rd, Wall. SM6 .... 200 B4
Mint St, SE1 .... 27 J3
Mint Wk, Croy. CR0
off High St 201 J3
Mirabel Rd, SW6 .... 128 C7
Miranda Cl, E1
off Sidney St 113 F5
Miranda Ct, W3
off Queens Dr 105 J6
Miranda Rd, N19 .... 92 C1
Mirfield St, SE7 .... 136 A4
Miriam Rd, SE18 .... 137 H5
Mirravale Trd Est, Dag.
RM8 .... 83 F7
Mirren Cl, Har. HA2 .... 85 F4
Mirror Path, SE9
off Lambscroft Av 173 J3
Missenden Gdns, Mord.
SM4 .... 185 F6
Mission Gro, E17 .... 77 H5
Mission Pl, SE15 .... 152 D1
Mission Sq, Brent. TW8 .... 125 H6
Mistletoe Cl, Croy. CR0
off Marigold Way 203 G1
Mistral, SE5
off Sceaux Gdns 152 B1
Mitali Pas, E1 .... 21 H4
MITCHAM, CR4 .... 186 A3
Mitcham Gdn Village,
Mitch. CR4 .... 186 A5
Mitcham Ind Est, Mitch.
CR4 .... 186 A1
Mitcham La, SW16 .... 168 C6
Mitcham Pk, Mitch. CR4 .... 185 J4
Mitcham Rd, E6 .... 116 B3
SW17 .... 167 J5
Croydon CR0 .... 186 E6
Ilford IG3 .... 81 J7
Mitchellbrook Way, NW10 .... 88 D6
Mitchell Cl, SE2 .... 138 C4
Belvedere DA17 .... 139 J3
Mitchell Rd, N13 .... 59 H5
Orpington BR6 .... 207 J4
Mitchell's Pl, SE21
off Dulwich Village 152 B7
Mitchell St, EC1 .... 11 J5
Mitchell Wk, E6 .... 116 B5

Mitchell Way, NW10 88 C6
Bromley BR1 191 G1
Mitchison Rd, N1 94 A6
Mitchley Rd, N17 76 D3
Mitford Cl, Chess. KT9
off Merritt Gdns 195 F6
Mitford Rd, N19 93 E2
Mitre, The, E14
off Three Colt St 113 J7
Mitre Av, E17
off Greenleaf Rd 77 J3
Mitre Cl, Brom. BR2
off Beckenham La 191 F2
Sutton SM2 199 F7
Mitre Ct, EC2 20 A3
Mitre Rd, E15 114 E2
SE1 27 F3
Mitre Sq, EC3 21 E4
Mitre St, EC3 21 E4
Mitre Way, W10 107 H4
Mizzen Mast Ho, SE18
off Woolwich Ch St 136 D3
Moat, The, N.Mal. KT3 182 E1
Moat Cl, Orp. BR6 207 J6
Moat Cres, N3 72 E3
Moat Cft, Well. DA16 158 C3
Moat Dr, E13
off Boundary Rd 115 J2
Harrow HA1 67 J4
Moat Fm Rd, Nthlt. UB5 85 F6
Moat Pl, SW9 151 F3
W3 106 B6
Moatside, Enf. EN3 45 G4
Feltham TW13 160 C4
Moberly Rd, SW4 150 D7
Moby Dick, Rom. RM6 83 F4
Modbury Gdns, NW5
off Queen's Cres 92 A6
Modder Pl, SW15 148 A4
Model Cotts, SW14 146 C3
Model Fm Cl, SE9 174 B3
Modling Ho, E2 113 F2
Moelwyn Hughes Ct, N7
off Hilldrop Cres 92 D5
Moelyn Ms, Har. HA1 68 D5
Moffat Ho, SE5
off Comber Gro 131 J7
Moffat Rd, N13 59 E6
SW17 167 H4
Thornton Heath CR7 187 J2
Mogden La, Islw. TW7 144 B5
Mohmmad Khan Rd, E11
off Harvey Rd 97 F1
Moira Cl, N17 76 B2
Moira Ct, SW17 168 A2
Moira Rd, SE9 156 C4
Molasses Row, SW11
off Cinnamon Row 149 F3
Mole Abbey Gdns, W.Mol. KT8 *off New Rd* 179 G3
Mole Ct, Epsom KT19 196 C4
Molember Ct, E.Mol. KT8 180 B5
Molember Rd, E.Mol. KT8 180 B5
Molescroft, SE9 175 F3
Molesey Av, W.Mol. KT8 179 F4
Molesey Dr, Sutt. SM3 198 B2
Molesey Pk Av, W.Mol. KT8 179 H5
Molesey Pk Cl, E.Mol. KT8 179 J5
Molesey Pk Rd, E.Mol. KT8 180 A5
West Molesey KT8 179 H5
Molesey Rd, W.Mol. KT8 179 E5
Molesford Rd, SW6 148 D1
Molesham Cl, W.Mol. KT8 179 H3
Molesham Way, W.Mol. KT8 179 H3
Molesworth St, SE13 154 C3
Mollison Av, Enf. EN3 45 H5
Mollison Dr, Wall. SM6 201 E6
Mollison Sq, Wall. SM6
off Mollison Dr 200 E7
Mollison Way, Edg. HA8 70 A2
Molly Huggins Cl, SW12 150 C7
Molyneux Dr, SW17 168 B4
Molyneux St, W1 15 H2
Monarch Cl, Felt. TW14 141 H7
West Wickham BR4 205 F4
Monarch Dr, E16 116 A5
Monarch Ms, E17 78 B5
SW16 169 G5
Monarch Par, Mitch. CR4
off London Rd 185 J2
Monarch Pl, Buck.H. IG9 63 J2
Monarch Rd, Belv. DA17 139 G3
Monarchs Ct, NW7
off Grenville Pl 54 D5
Monarch Way, Ilf. IG2 81 G6
Mona Rd, SE15 153 F2
Monastery Gdns, Enf. EN2 44 A2
Mona St, E16 115 F5
Monaveen Gdns, W.Mol. KT8 179 G3
Monck St, SW1 25 J6
Monclar Rd, SE5 152 A4
Moncorvo Cl, SW7 23 G4
Moncrieff Cl, E6
off Linton Gdns 116 B6
Moncrieff Pl, SE15
off Rye La 152 D2
Moncrieff St, SE15 152 D2
Mondial Way, Hayes (Harling.) UB3 121 F7
Monega Rd, E7 97 J6
E12 98 A6
Money La, West Dr. UB7 120 A3
Monier Rd, E3 96 A7
Monivea Rd, Beck. BR3 171 J7
Monkchester Cl, Loug. IG10 48 D1
Monk Dr, E16 115 G6
MONKEN HADLEY, Barn. EN5 40 C1
Monkfrith Av, N14 42 B6
Monkfrith Cl, N14 42 B7
Monkfrith Way, N14 42 B7
Monkhams Av, Wdf.Grn. IG8 63 G5
Monkhams Dr, Wdf.Grn. IG8 63 H4
Monkhams La, Buck.H. IG9 63 H3
Woodford Green IG8 63 G5
Monkleigh Rd, Mord. SM4 184 B3
Monk Pas, E16
off Monk Dr 115 G7
Monks Av, Barn. EN5 41 F6
West Molesey KT8 179 F5
Monks Cl, SE2 138 D4
Enfield EN2 43 J2
Harrow HA2 85 H2
Ruislip HA4 84 D4
Monksdene Gdns, Sutt. SM1 199 E3
Monks Dr, W3 106 A5
Monksgrove, Loug. IG10 48 D5
Monksmead, Borwd. WD6 38 C4
MONKS ORCHARD, Croy. CR0 189 J7
Monks Orchard Rd, Beck. BR3 204 A1
Monks Pk, Wem. HA9 88 C6
Monks Pk Gdns, Wem. HA9 88 B6
Monk's Ridge, N20 55 H1
Monks Rd, Enf. EN2 43 J2
Monk St, SE18 136 D4
Monks Way, NW11 72 C4
Beckenham BR3 190 A6
Orpington BR5 207 F1
West Drayton (Harm.) UB7 120 B6
Monkswell Ct, N10 74 A1
Monkswood Gdns, Borwd. WD6 38 D5
Ilford IG5 80 D3
Monkton Ho, E5
off Pembury Rd 94 E5
Monkton Rd, Well. DA16 157 J2
Monkton St, SE11 35 F1
Monkville Av, NW11 72 C4
Monkwell Sq, EC2 20 A2
Monmouth Av, E18 79 H4
Kingston upon Thames KT1 163 F7
Monmouth Cl, W4
off Beaumont Rd 126 D3
Mitcham CR4
off Recreation Way 187 E4
Welling DA16 158 A4
Monmouth Gro, Brent. TW8 *off Sterling Pl* 125 H4
Monmouth Ho, NW5
off Raglan St 92 B6
Monmouth Pl, W2
off Monmouth Rd 108 D6
Monmouth Rd, E6 116 C3
N9 60 E2
W2 108 D6
Dagenham RM9 101 F5
Hayes UB3 121 H4
Monmouth St, WC2 18 A4
Monnery Rd, N19 92 C3
Monnow Rd, SE1 37 H3
Mono La, Felt. TW13 160 B2
Monoux Gro, E17 78 A1
Monroe Cres, Enf. EN1 44 E1
Monroe Dr, SW14 146 B5
Monro Gdns, Har. HA3 52 B7
Monro Way, E5 94 D4
Monsal Ct, E5
off Redwald Rd 95 H4
Monsell Ct, N4
off Monsell Rd 93 H3
Monsell Rd, N4 93 H3
Monson Rd, NW10 107 G2
SE14 133 G7
Mons Way, Brom. BR2 192 B6
Montacute Rd, SE6 153 J7
Morden SM4 185 G6
Montagu Cres, N18 61 E4
Montague Av, SE4 153 J4
W7 124 C1
Montague Cl, SE1 28 B1
Barnet EN5 40 C4
Walton-on-Thames KT12 178 A7
Montague Gdns, W3 106 A7
Montague Pl, WC1 17 J1
Montague Rd, E8 94 D5
E11 97 F2
N8 75 F5
N15 76 D4
SW19 166 E7
W7 124 C1
W13 105 E6
Croydon CR0 201 H1
Hounslow TW3 143 H3
Richmond TW10 145 H6
Southall UB2 122 E4
Montague Sq, SE15
off Clifton Way 133 F7
Montague St, EC1 19 J2
WC1 18 A1
Montague Waye, Sthl. UB2 122 E3
Montagu Gdns, N18 60 E4
Wallington SM6 200 C4
Montagu Mans, W1 16 A1
Montagu Ms N, W1 16 A2
Montagu Ms S, W1 16 A3
Montagu Ms W, W1 16 A3
Montagu Pl, W1 15 J2
Montagu Rd, N9 61 F4
N18 61 E5
NW4 71 G6
Montagu Rd Ind Est, N18 61 F4
Montagu Row, W1 16 A2
Montagu Sq, W1 16 A2
Montagu St, W1 16 A3
Montaigne Cl, SW1 33 J2
Montalt Rd, Wdf.Grn. IG8 63 F5
Montana Bldg, SE13
off Deals Gateway 154 B1
Montana Gdns, SE26 171 J5
Sutton SM1
off Lind Rd 199 F5
Montana Rd, SW17 168 A4
SW20 183 J1
Montbelle Rd, SE9 174 E3
Montcalm Cl, Brom. BR2 191 G6
Hayes UB4
off Ayles Rd 102 B3
Montcalm Rd, SE7 136 A7
Montclare St, E2 13 F4
Monteagle Av, Bark. IG11 99 F6
Monteagle Way, E5 94 D3
SE15 153 E3
Montefiore St, SW8 150 B2
Montego Cl, SE24
off Railton Rd 151 G4
Montem Rd, SE23 153 J7
New Malden KT3 182 E4
Montem St, N4
off Thorpedale Rd 93 F1
Montenotte Rd, N8 74 C5
Monterey Cl, NW7
off The Broadway 55 E5
Bexley DA5 177 J2
Montesole Ct, Pnr. HA5 66 C2
Montevetro, SW11 149 G1
Montford Pl, SE11 34 E4
Montford Rd, Sun. TW16 178 A4
Montfort Gdns, Ilf. IG6 65 F6
Montfort Pl, SW19 166 A1
Montgolfier Wk, Nthlt. UB5
off Wayfarer Rd 102 E3
Montgomerie Ms, SE23 153 F7
Montgomery Av, Esher KT10 194 B3
Montgomery Cl, Mitch. CR4 187 E4
Sidcup DA15 157 J6
Montgomery Ct, W2
off Harrow Rd 14 E2
W4
off St. Thomas' Rd 126 C6
Montgomery Gdns, Sutt. SM2 199 G7
Montgomery Rd, W4 126 C4
Edgware HA8 53 J6
Montgomery St, E14 134 B1
Montholme Rd, SW11 149 J6
Monthope Rd, E1 21 H2
Montolieu Gdns, SW15 147 H5
Montpelier Av, W5 105 F5
Bexley DA5 158 D7
Montpelier Gdns, E6 116 A3
Romford RM6 82 C7
Montpelier Gro, NW5 92 C5
Montpelier Ms, SW7 23 H5
Montpelier Pl, E1 113 F6
SW7 23 H5
Montpelier Ri, NW11 72 B7
Wembley HA9 87 G1
Montpelier Rd, N3 73 F1
SE15 153 E1
W5 105 G5
Sutton SM1 199 F4
Montpelier Row, SE3 155 F2
Twickenham TW1 145 E7
Montpelier Sq, SW7 23 H4
Montpelier St, SW7 23 H4
Montpelier Ter, SW7 23 H4
Montpelier Vale, SE3 155 F2
Montpelier Wk, SW7 23 H5
Montpelier Way, NW11 72 B7
Montrave Rd, SE20 171 F6
Montreal Pl, WC2 18 C5
Montreal Rd, Ilf. IG1 81 F7
Montrell Rd, SW2 169 E1
Montrose Av, NW6 108 B2
Edgware HA8 70 C2
Sidcup DA15 158 A7
Twickenham TW2 143 H7
Welling DA16 157 G3
Montrose Cl, Well. DA16 157 J3
Woodford Green IG8 63 G4
Montrose Ct, SW7 23 F4
Montrose Cres, N12 57 F6
Wembley HA0 87 H6
Montrose Gdns, Mitch. CR4 185 J3
Sutton SM1 199 E2
Montrose Pl, SW1 24 C4
Montrose Rd, Felt. TW14 141 G6
Harrow HA3 68 B2
Montrose Way, SE23 171 G1
Montserrat Av, Wdf.Grn. IG8 62 D7
Montserrat Cl, SE19 170 A5
Montserrat Rd, SW15 148 B4
★ **Monument, The**, EC3 20 C6
Monument Gdns, SE13 154 C5
Monument St, EC3 20 C6
Monument Way, N17 76 C3
Monza St, E1 113 F7
Moodkee St, SE16 133 F3
Moody Rd, SE15 132 C7
Moody St, E1 113 G3
Moon La, Barn. EN5 40 C3
Moon St, N1 111 H1
Moorcroft Gdns, Brom. BR2
off Southborough Rd 192 B5
Moorcroft Rd, SW16 168 E3
Moorcroft Way, Pnr. HA5 66 E5
Moordown, SE18 156 D1
Moore Cl, SW14 146 C3
Mitcham CR4 186 B2
Moore Cres, Dag. RM9 118 B1
Moorefield Rd, N17 76 C2
Moorehead Way, SE3 155 H3
Moore Ho, E14
off Cassilis Rd 134 A2
Mooreland Rd, Brom. BR1 173 F7
Moore Pk Rd, SW6 128 E7
Moore Rd, SE19 169 J6
Moore St, SW3 31 J1
Moore Wk, E7
off Stracey Rd 97 G4
Moorey Cl, E15
off Stephen's Rd 115 F1
Moorfield Av, W5 105 G4
Moorfield Rd, Chess. KT9 195 H5
Enfield EN3 45 F1
Moorfields, EC2 20 B2
Moorfields Highwalk, EC2 20 B2
Moorgate, EC2 20 B3
Moorgate Pl, EC2 20 B3
Moorhouse Rd, W2 108 D6
Harrow HA3 69 G3
Moorings, SE28 118 B7
Moorings, The, E16
off Prince Regent La 115 J5
Moorings Ho, Brent. TW8
off Tallow Rd 125 F7
Moorland Cl, Twick. TW2
off Telford Rd 143 G7
Moorland Rd, SW9 151 H4
Moorlands Av, NW7 55 H6
Moorlands Est, SW9 151 G4
Moor La, EC2 20 B2
Chessington KT9 195 H4
Moormead Dr, Epsom KT19 197 E5
Moor Mead Rd, Twick. TW1 144 D6
Moor Pk Gdns, Kings.T. KT2 165 E7
Moor Pl, EC2 20 B2
Moorside Rd, Brom. BR1 173 E3
Moor St, W1 17 J4
Moortown Rd, Wat. WD19 50 C4
Moot Ct, NW9 70 A5
Morant Pl, N22 75 F1
Morant St, E14 114 A7
Mora Rd, NW2 89 J4

Mora St, EC1 . . . . **12** A4
Morat St, SW9 . . . . **151** F1
Moravian Pl, SW10 . . . . **31** F6
Moravian St, E2 . . . . **113** F2
Moray Av, Hayes UB3 . . . . **121** J1
Moray Cl, Edg. HA8 *off Pentland Av* **54** B2
Moray Ms, N7 *off Durham Rd* **93** F2
Moray Rd, N4 . . . . **93** F2
Mordaunt Gdns, Dag. RM9 . . . . **100** E7
Mordaunt Ho, NW10 . . . . . **106** D1
Mordaunt Rd, NW10 . . . . . **106** D1
Mordaunt St, SW9 . . . . **151** F3
MORDEN, SM4 . . . . **184** D3
Morden Ct, Mord. SM4 . . . **184** E4
Morden Gdns, Grnf. UB6 . . **86** C5
Mitcham CR4 . . . . **185** G4
★ **Morden Hall Pk N.T.**, Mord. SM4 . . . . **185** E3
Morden Hall Rd, Mord. SM4 . . . . **185** E3
Morden Hill, SE13 . . . . **154** C2
Morden La, SE13 . . . . **154** C1
MORDEN PARK, Mord. SM4 . . . . **184** B5
Morden Rd, SE3 . . . . **155** G2
SW19 . . . . **167** E7
Mitcham CR4 . . . . **185** F4
Romford RM6 . . . . **83** E7
Morden Rd Ms, SE3 . . . . . . **155** G2
Morden St, SE13 . . . . **154** B1
Morden Way, Sutt. SM3 . . **184** D7
Morden Wf Rd, SE10 . . . . . **134** E3
Mordon Rd, Ilf. IG3 . . . . **81** J7
Mordred Ct, N9 *off Galahad Rd* **60** D2
Mordred Rd, SE6 . . . . **172** E2
Morecambe Cl, E1 . . . . **113** G5
Morecambe Gdns, Stan. HA7 . . . . **53** G4
Morecambe St, SE17 . . . . . . **36** A2
Morecambe Ter, N18 . . . . . . **60** A4
More Cl, E16 . . . . **115** F6
W14 . . . . **128** B4
Morecoombe Cl, Kings.T. KT2 . . . . **164** B7
Moree Way, N18 . . . . **60** D4
Moreland St, EC1 . . . . **11** H3
Moreland Way, E4 . . . . **62** B3
Morella Rd, SW12 . . . . **149** J7
Morell Cl, Barn. EN5 . . . . . . **41** F3
More London Pl, SE1 . . . . . . **28** D2
More London Riverside, SE1 . . . . **28** E2
Moremead Rd, SE6 . . . . . . **171** J4
Morena St, SE6 . . . . **154** B7
Moresby Av, Surb. KT5 . . . **182** B7
Moresby Rd, E5 . . . . **94** E1
Moresby Wk, SW8 . . . . **150** B2
Moreton Av, Islw. TW7 . . . . **144** B1
Moreton Cl, E5 . . . . **95** F2
N15 . . . . **76** A6
NW7 . . . . **55** J6
SW1 . . . . **33** G3
Moreton Gdns, Wdf.Grn. IG8 . . . . **64** B5
Moreton Ho, SE16 *off Slippers Pl* **133** E3
Moreton Pl, SW1 . . . . **33** G3
Moreton Rd, N15 . . . . **76** A6
South Croydon CR2 . . . **202** A5
Worcester Park KT4 . . . . **197** G2
Moreton St, SW1 . . . . **33** G3
Moreton Ter, SW1 . . . . **33** G3
Moreton Ter Ms N, SW1 . . . **33** G3
Moreton Ter Ms S, SW1 . . . **33** G3
Moreton Twr, W3 . . . . **126** B1
Morford Cl, Ruis. HA4 . . . . . **66** B7
Morford Way, Ruis. HA4 . . . **66** B7
Morgan Av, E17 . . . . **78** D4
Morgan Cl, Dag. RM10 . . . . **101** G7
Morgan Ct, N9 *off Galahad Rd* **60** D3
SW11 *off Battersea High St* . . **149** G1
Morgan Ho, SW1 *off Vauxhall Br Rd* **33** G2
Morgan Rd, N7 . . . . **93** G5
W10 . . . . **108** C5
Bromley BR1 . . . . **173** G7
Morgans La, SE1 . . . . **28** D2
Morgan St, E3 . . . . **113** H3
E16 . . . . **115** F5
Morgan Way, Wdf.Grn. IG8 . . . . **64** B6
Moriarty Cl, Brom. BR1 . . . **192** E4
Moriatry Cl, N7 . . . . **92** E4
Morie St, SW18 . . . . **149** E4
Morieux Rd, E10 . . . . **95** J1
Moring Rd, SW17 . . . . **168** A4
Morkyns Wk, SE21 . . . . **170** B3
Morland Av, Croy. CR0 . . . **202** B1
Morland Cl, NW11 . . . . **91** E1
Hampton TW12 . . . . **161** F5
Mitcham CR4 . . . . **185** H3
Morland Est, E8 *off Richmond Rd* **94** D7
Morland Gdns, NW10 . . . . . **88** D7
Southall UB1 . . . . **123** H1
Morland Ms, N1 *off Lofting Rd* **93** G7
Morland Rd, E17 . . . . **77** G5
SE20 . . . . **171** G6
Croydon CR0 . . . . **202** B1
Dagenham RM10 . . . . . . **101** G7
Harrow HA3 . . . . **69** H5
Ilford IG1 . . . . **98** E2
Sutton SM1 . . . . **199** F5
Morley Av, E4 . . . . **62** D7
N18 . . . . **60** D4
N22 . . . . **75** G2
Morley Cl, Orp. BR6 . . . . . . **207** E2
Morley Cres, Edg. HA8 . . . . **54** C2
Ruislip HA4 . . . . **84** C2
Morley Cres E, Stan. HA7 . . **69** F2
Morley Cres W, Stan. HA7 . . **69** F2
Morley Rd, E10 . . . . **96** C1
E15 . . . . **115** F2
SE13 . . . . **154** C4
Barking IG11 . . . . **117** G1
Chislehurst BR7 . . . . **193** F1
Romford RM6 . . . . **82** E5
Sutton SM3 . . . . **198** C1
Twickenham TW1 . . . . . . **145** G6
Morley St, SE1 . . . . **27** F5
Morna Rd, SE5 . . . . **151** J2
Morning La, E9 . . . . **95** F6
Morningside Rd, Wor.Pk. KT4 . . . . **197** H2
Mornington Av, W14 . . . . . **128** C4
Bromley BR1 . . . . **191** J3
Ilford IG1 . . . . **80** D7
Mornington Cl, Wdf.Grn. IG8 . . . . **63** G4
Mornington Ct, Bex. DA5 . **177** J1
Mornington Cres, NW1 . . . . . **9** F1
Hounslow TW5 . . . . **142** B1
Mornington Gro, E3 . . . . . . **114** A3
Mornington Ms, SE5 . . . . . **151** J1
Mornington Pl, NW1 . . . . **9** E1
Mornington Rd, E4 . . . . **46** D7
E11 . . . . **97** F1
SE8 . . . . **133** J7
Greenford UB6 . . . . **103** H5
Loughton IG10 . . . . **49** F3
Woodford Green IG8 . . . . **63** F4
Mornington St, NW1 . . . . **8** E1
Mornington Ter, NW1 . . . . . **110** B1
Mornington Wk, Rich. TW10 . . . . **163** F4
Morocco St, SE1 . . . . **28** D4
Morpeth Gro, E9 . . . . **113** G1
Morpeth Rd, E9 . . . . **113** F1
Morpeth St, E2 . . . . **113** G3
Morpeth Ter, SW1 . . . . **25** F6
Morpeth Wk, N17 *off West Rd* **60** E7
Morrab Gdns, Ilf. IG3 . . . . . . **99** J3
Morrells Yd, SE11 . . . . **35** F3
Morris Av, E12 . . . . **98** C5
Morris Cl, Croy. CR0 . . . . . **189** H6
Orpington BR6 . . . . **207** H3
Morris Ct, E4 . . . . **62** B3
Morris Gdns, SW18 . . . . . . **148** D7
Morrish Rd, SW2 . . . . **151** E7
Morrison Av, E4 . . . . **62** A6
N17 . . . . **76** B3
Morrison Rd, SW9 *off Marcella Rd* **151** G2
Barking IG11 . . . . **118** E2
Hayes UB4 . . . . **102** B3
Morrison St, SW11 . . . . **150** A3
Morris Pl, N4 . . . . **93** G2
Morris Rd, E14 . . . . **114** B5
E15 . . . . **96** E4
Dagenham RM8 . . . . **101** F2
Isleworth TW7 . . . . **144** C3
Morris St, E1 . . . . **113** E6
Morriston Cl, Wat. WD19 . . . **50** C5
Morse Cl, E13 . . . . **115** G3
Morshead Rd, W9 . . . . **108** D3
Morson Rd, Enf. EN3 . . . . . . **45** H6
Morston Gdns, SE9 . . . . . . **174** C4
Morten Cl, SW4 . . . . **150** D6
Morteyne Rd, N17 . . . . **76** A1
Mortham St, E15 . . . . **114** D1
Mortimer Cl, NW2 . . . . **90** C3
SW16 . . . . **168** D2
Mortimer Cres, NW6 . . . . . **108** E1
Worcester Park KT4 . . . . **196** D3
Mortimer Dr, Enfield EN1 . . . . **44** A5
Mortimer Est, NW6 . . . . . . **108** E1
Mortimer Ho, W11 *off St. Anns Rd* **128** A1
Mortimer Mkt, WC1 . . . . **9** G6
Mortimer Pl, NW6 . . . . **108** E1
Mortimer Rd, E6 . . . . **116** C3
N1 . . . . **94** B7
NW10 . . . . **107** J3
W13 . . . . **105** F6
Mitcham CR4 . . . . **185** J1
Mortimer Sq, W11 *off St. Anns Rd* **108** A7
Mortimer St, W1 . . . . **17** F3
Mortimer Ter, NW5 *off Gordon Ho Rd* **92** B4
MORTLAKE, SW14 . . . . **146** C3
Mortlake Cl, Croy. CR0 . . . **201** E3
Mortlake Dr, Mitch. CR4 . . **185** H1
Mortlake High St, SW14 . . **146** D3
Mortlake Rd, E16 . . . . **115** H6
Ilford IG1 . . . . **99** F4
Richmond TW9 . . . . **126** A7
Mortlake Sta Pas, SW14 *off Sheen La* **146** C3
Mortlake Ter, Rich. TW9 *off Kew Rd* **126** A7
Mortlock Cl, SE15 *off Cossall Wk* **152** E2
Morton Cl, E1 *off Deancross St* **113** F6
Wallington SM6 . . . . **201** F7
Morton Ct, Nthlt. UB5 . . . . . **85** J5
Morton Cres, N14 . . . . **58** D4
Morton Gdns, Wall. SM6 . . . . **200** C5
Morton Ms, SW5 . . . . **30** A2
Morton Pl, SE1 . . . . **26** E6
Morton Rd, E15 . . . . **97** F7
N1 . . . . **93** J7
Morden SM4 . . . . **185** G5
Morton Way, N14 . . . . **58** C3
Morvale Cl, Belv. DA17 . . . **139** F4
Morval Rd, SW2 . . . . **151** G5
Morven Rd, SW17 . . . . **167** J3
Morville Ho, SW18 *off Fitzhugh Gro* **149** G6
Morville St, E3 . . . . **114** A2
Morwell St, WC1 . . . . **17** J2
Moscow Pl, W2 . . . . **14** A5
Moscow Rd, W2 . . . . **14** A5
Moseley Row, SE10 . . . . . . **135** F4
Moselle Av, N22 . . . . **75** G2
Moselle Cl, N8 *off Miles Rd* **75** E3
Moselle Ho, N17 *off William St* **60** C7
Moselle Pl, N17 . . . . **60** C7
Moselle St, N17 . . . . **60** C7
Mosquito Cl, Wall. SM6 . . . **200** E7
Mossborough Cl, N12 . . . . . **57** E6
Mossbury Rd, SW11 . . . . . **149** H3
Moss Cl, E1 . . . . **21** J1
N9 . . . . **60** D1
Pinner HA5 . . . . **67** F2
Mossdown Cl, Belv. DA17 . . . . **139** G4
Mossford Ct, Ilf. IG6 . . . . **81** E3
Mossford Grn, Ilf. IG6 . . . . . **81** E3
Mossford La, Ilf. IG6 . . . . . . **81** E2
Mossford St, E3 . . . . **113** J4
Moss Gdns, Felt. TW13 . . . **160** A2
South Croydon CR2 *off Warren Av* **203** G7
Moss Hall Ct, N12 . . . . **57** E6
Moss Hall Cres, N12 . . . . . . **57** E6
Moss Hall Gro, N12 . . . . **56** E6
Mossington Gdns, SE16 *off Abbeyfield Rd* **133** F4
Moss La, Pnr. HA5 . . . . **67** F3
Mosslea Rd, SE20 . . . . **171** F7
Bromley BR2 . . . . **192** A5
Orpington BR6 . . . . **207** F3
Mossop St, SW3 . . . . **31** H1
Moss Rd, Dag. RM10 . . . . . **101** G7
Mossville Gdns, Mord. SM4 . . . . **184** C3
Moston Cl, Hayes UB3 . . . . **121** J5
Mostyn Av, Wem. HA9 . . . . . **87** J5
Mostyn Gdns, NW10 . . . . . **108** A3
Mostyn Gro, E3 . . . . **113** J2
Mostyn Rd, SW9 . . . . **151** G1
SW19 . . . . **184** C1
Edgware HA8 . . . . **54** D7
Mosul Way, Brom. BR2 . . . **192** B6
Motcomb St, SW1 . . . . **24** A5
Moth Cl, Wall. SM6 . . . . . . **201** E7
Mothers' Sq, E5 . . . . **95** E4
Motley Av, EC2 . . . . **12** D5
Motley St, SW8 *off St. Rule St* **150** C2
MOTSPUR PARK, N.Mal. KT3 . . . . **183** H6
Motspur Pk, N.Mal. KT3 . . **183** F6
MOTTINGHAM, SE9 . . . . . **173** J2
Mottingham Gdns, SE9 . . . . **174** A1
Mottingham La, SE9 . . . . . **173** J1
SE12 . . . . **173** J1
Mottingham Rd, N9 . . . . **45** G6
SE9 . . . . **174** B2
Mottisfont Rd, SE2 . . . . . . **138** A3
Motts La, Dag. RM8 *off Green La* **101** F2
Mott St, Loug. (High Beach) IG10 . . . . . . **47** F1
Moulins Rd, E9 . . . . **113** F1
Moulsford Ho, N7 . . . . **92** D5
Moulton Av, Houns. TW3 . . . . **143** E2
Mound, The, SE9 . . . . **174** D3
Moundfield Rd, N16 . . . . **76** D6
Mount, The, E5 . . . . **94** E2
N20 . . . . **57** F2
NW3 *off Heath St* **91** F4
W3 . . . . **126** B1
New Malden KT3 . . . . . . **183** F3
Wembley HA9 . . . . **88** B2
Worcester Park KT4 . . . . **197** H4
Mountacre Cl, SE26 . . . . . . **170** C4
Mount Adon Pk, SE22 . . . . **152** D7
Mountague Pl, E14 . . . . **114** C7
Mountain Ho, SE11 . . . . **34** C3
Mount Angelus Rd, SW15 . . . . **147** F7
Mount Ararat Rd, Rich. TW10 . . . . **145** H5
Mount Ash Rd, SE26 . . . . . **170** E3
Mount Av, E4 . . . . **62** A3
W5 . . . . **105** G5
Southall UB1 . . . . **103** G6
Mountbatten Cl, SE18 . . . . **137** H6
SE19 . . . . **170** B5
Mountbatten Ct, SE16 *off Rotherhithe St* **133** F1
Buckhurst Hill IG9 . . . . . . **64** A2
Mountbatten Gdns, Beck. BR3 *off Balmoral Av* **189** H4
Mountbatten Ms, SW18 *off Inman Rd* **167** F1
Mountbel Rd, Stan. HA7 . . . **68** D1
Mount Cl, W5 . . . . **105** F5
Barnet (Cockfos.) EN4 . . . **42** A4
Bromley BR1 . . . . **192** B1
Mountcombe Cl, Surb. KT6 . . . . **181** H7
Mount Cor, Felt. TW13 . . . . **160** D2
Mount Ct, SW15 *off Weimar St* **148** B3
West Wickham BR4 . . . . **204** E2
Mount Culver Av, Sid. DA14 . . . . **176** D6
Mount Dr, Bexh. DA6 . . . . **158** E5
Harrow HA2 . . . . **67** F5
Wembley HA9 . . . . **88** C2
Mountearl Gdns, SW16 . . . **169** F3
Mount Echo Av, E4 . . . . **62** B2
Mount Echo Dr, E4 . . . . **62** B1
Mount Ephraim La, SW16 . . . . **168** D3
Mount Ephraim Rd, SW16 . . . . **168** D3
Mountfield Cl, SE6 . . . . **154** D7
Mountfield Rd, E6 . . . . **116** D2
N3 . . . . **72** D3
W5 . . . . **105** G6
Mountfield Ter, SE6 *off Mountfield Cl* **154** D7
Mountford Mans, SW11 *off Battersea Pk Rd* . . . **150** A1
Mountfort Cres, N1 *off Barnsbury Sq* **93** G7
Mountfort Ter, N1 *off Barnsbury Sq* **93** G7
Mount Gdns, SE26 . . . . **170** E3
Mount Gro, Edg. HA8 . . . . . **54** C3
Mountgrove Rd, N5 . . . . **93** H3
Mount Holme, T.Ditt. KT7 *off Thorkhill Rd* **180** E7
Mounthurst Rd, Brom. BR2 . . . . **191** F7
Mountington Pk Cl, Har. HA3 . . . . **69** G6
Mountjoy Cl, SE2 . . . . **138** B2
Mountjoy Ho, EC2 *off The Barbican* **20** A2
Mount Ms, Hmptn. TW12 . **179** H1
Mount Mills, EC1 . . . . **11** H4
Mount Nod Rd, SW16 . . . . **169** F3
Mount Pk Av, Har. HA1 . . . . **86** A2
Mount Pk Cres, W5 . . . . . . **105** G6
Mount Pk Rd, W5 . . . . **105** G5
Harrow HA1 . . . . **86** A3
Pinner HA5 . . . . **66** A5
Mount Pl, W3 *off High St* . **126** B1
Mount Pleasant, SE27 . . . . **169** J4
WC1 . . . . **10** D6
Barnet EN4 . . . . **41** H4
Ruislip HA4 . . . . **84** C2
Wembley HA0 . . . . **105** H1
Mount Pleasant Cres, N4 . . **75** F7
Mount Pleasant Est, Ilf. IG1 *off Ilford La* **99** F5
Mount Pleasant Hill, E5 . . . . **95** E2
Mount Pleasant La, E5 . . . . **94** E2
Mount Pleasant Pl, SE18 . . . . **137** G4
Mount Pleasant Rd, E17 . . . **77** H2
N17 . . . . **76** B2
NW10 . . . . **89** J7
SE13 . . . . **154** B6
W5 . . . . **105** F4
Chigwell IG7 . . . . **65** G4
New Malden KT3 . . . . . . **182** C3
Mount Pleasant Vil, N4 . . . **75** F7

Mount Pleasant Wk, Bex. DA5 **159** J5
Mount Rd, NW2 **89** H3
NW4 **71** G6
SE19 **170** A6
SW19 **166** D2
Barnet EN4 **41** H5
Bexleyheath DA6 **158** D5
Chessington KT9 **195** J5
Dagenham RM8 **101** F1
Feltham TW13 **160** E3
Hayes UB3 **121** J2
Ilford IG1 **98** E5
Mitcham CR4 **185** H2
New Malden KT3 **182** D3
Mount Row, W1 **16** D6
Mountsfield Ct, SE13 **154** D6
Mountside, Felt. TW13 **161** E3
Stanmore HA7 **68** C1
Mounts Pond Rd, SE3 **154** D2
Mount Sq, The, NW3
off Heath St **91** F3
Mount Stewart Av, Har. HA3 **69** G6
Mount St, W1 **16** C6
Mount St Ms, W1 **16** D6
Mount Ter, E1
off New Rd **112** E5
Mount Vernon, NW3 **91** F4
Mount Vw, NW7 **54** D3
W5 **105** G4
Mountview Cl, NW11 **91** E1
Mountview Ct, N8
off Green Las **75** H4
Mount Vw Rd, E4 **46** C7
N4 **75** E7
NW9 **70** D4
Mountview Rd, Esher (Clay.) KT10 **194** E7
Mount Vil, SE27 **169** H3
Mountwood, W.Mol. KT8 **179** G3
Movers La, Bark. IG11 **117** G1
Mowatt Cl, N19 **92** D1
Mowbray Rd, NW6 **90** B7
SE19 **188** C1
Barnet (New Barn.) EN5 **41** F4
Edgware HA8 **54** A4
Richmond TW10 **163** F3
Mowbrays Cl, Rom. RM5 **83** J1
Mowbrays Rd, Rom. RM5 **83** J2
Mowbrey Gdns, Loug. IG10 **49** F2
Mowlem St, E2 **113** E2
Mowlem Trd Est, N17 **61** F7
Mowll St, SW9 **131** G7
Moxon Cl, E13
off Whitelegg Rd **115** F2
Moxon St, W1 **16** B2
Barnet EN5 **40** C3
Moye Cl, E2 **13** J1
Moyers Rd, E10 **78** C7
Moylan Rd, W6 **128** B6
Moyne Pl, NW10 **106** A2
Moynihan Dr, N21 **43** E5
Moys Cl, Croy. CR0 **186** E6
Moyser Rd, SW16 **168** B5
Mozart St, W10 **108** C3
Mozart Ter, SW1 **32** C2
Muchelney Rd, Mord. SM4 **185** F6
Mud La, W5 **105** G5
Mudlarks Boul, SE10
off John Harrison Way **135** F3
Muggeridge Cl, S.Croy. CR2 **202** A5
Muggeridge Rd, Dag. RM10 **101** H4
Muirdown Av, SW14 **146** C4
Muir Dr, SW18 **149** H6
Muirfield, W3 **107** E6
Muirfield Cl, SE16
off Ryder Dr **133** E5
Watford WD19 **50** C4
Muirfield Cres, E14
off Millharbour **134** B3
Muirfield Grn, Wat. WD19 **50** C4
Muirfield Rd, Wat. WD19 **50** D4
Muirkirk Rd, SE6 **172** C1
Muir Rd, E5 **94** D3
Muir St, E16
off Newland St **136** C1
Mulberry Business Cen, SE16 *off Quebec Way* **133** G2
Mulberry Cl, E4 **62** A2
N8 **74** E5
NW3
off Hampstead High St **91** G4
NW4 **71** J3
SE7 **136** A6
SE22 **152** D5
SW3 *off Beaufort St* **31** F6
SW16 **168** C4
Barnet EN4 **41** G4
Northolt UB5
off Parkfield Av **102** E2
Mulberry Ct, EC1
off Tompion St **11** H4
N2 *off Great N Rd* **73** H3
Barking IG11 **99** J7
Surbiton KT6 **181** G7
Mulberry Cres, Brent. TW8 **125** E7
West Drayton UB7 **120** D2
Mulberry La, Croy. CR0 **202** C1
Mulberry Ms, SE14
off Lewisham Way **153** J1
Wallington SM6 **200** C6
Mulberry Par, West Dr. UB7 **120** D3
Mulberry Pl, SE9 **156** A4
W6 *off Chiswick Mall* **127** G5
Mulberry Rd, E8 **94** C7
Mulberry St, E1 **21** H3
Mulberry Tree Ms, W4
off Clovelly Rd **126** C2
Mulberry Wk, SW3 **31** F5
Mulberry Way, E18 **79** H2
Belvedere DA17 **139** J2
Ilford IG6 **81** F4
Mulgrave Rd, NW10 **89** F4
SE18 **136** C4
SW6 **128** C6
W5 **105** G3
Croydon CR0 **202** A3
Harrow HA1 **86** D2
Sutton SM2 **198** D6
Mulholland Cl, Mitch. CR4 **186** B2
Mulkern Rd, N19 **92** D1
Mullards Cl, Mitch. CR4 **199** J1
Muller Ho, SE18
off Connaught Rd **136** D5
Muller Rd, SW4 **150** D6
Mullet Gdns, E2 **13** J3
Mullins Path, SW14 **146** D3
Mullion Cl, Har. HA3 **67** H1
Mullion Wk, Wat. WD19
off Ormskirk Rd **50** D4
Mull Wk, N1
off Clephane Rd **93** J6
Mulready St, NW8 **7** G6
Multi-way, W3
off Valetta Rd **127** E2
Multon Rd, SW18 **149** G7
Mulvaney Way, SE1 **28** C4
Mumford Mills, SE10
off Greenwich High Rd **154** B1
Mumford Rd, SE24
off Railton Rd **151** H5
Muncaster Rd, SW11 **149** J5
Muncies Ms, SE6 **172** C2
Mundania Rd, SE22 **153** E6
Munday Rd, E16 **115** G6
Munden Ho, E3
off Bromley High St **114** B3
Munden St, W14 **128** B4
Mundesley Cl, Wat. WD19 **50** C4
Mundford Rd, E5 **95** F2
Mundon Gdns, Ilf. IG1 **99** G1
Mund St, W14 **128** C5
Mundy St, N1 **12** D3
Mungo Pk Cl, Bushey (Bushey Hth) WD23 **51** J2
Munkenbeck, W2
off Hermitage St **15** E2
Munnery Way, Orp. BR6 **206** D3
Munnings Gdns, Islw. TW7 **144** A5
Munro Dr, N11 **58** C6
Munro Ms, W10 **108** B5
Munro Ter, SW10 **31** E6
Munslow Gdns, Sutt. SM1 **199** G4
Munster Av, Houns. TW4 **143** F4
Munster Ct, Tedd. TW11 **163** F6
Munster Gdns, N13 **59** H4
Munster Ms, SW6
off Lillie Rd **128** B7
Munster Rd, SW6 **148** C1
Teddington TW11 **163** E6
Munster Sq, NW1 **9** E4
Munton Rd, SE17 **36** A1
Murchison Av, Bex. DA5 **176** D1
Murchison Rd, E10 **96** C2
Murdock Cl, E16
off Rogers Rd **115** F6
Murdock St, SE15 **132** E6
Murfett Cl, SW19 **166** B2
Muriel St, N1 **10** D1
Murillo Rd, SE13 **154** D4
Murphy St, SE1 **26** E4
Murray Av, Brom. BR1 **191** H2
Hounslow TW3 **143** H5
Murray Cl, SE28 **137** H1
Murray Ct, W7
off St. Margarets Rd **124** B2
Murray Cres, Pnr. HA5 **66** D1
Murray Gro, N1 **12** A2
Murray Ms, NW1 **92** D7
Murray Rd, SW19 **166** A6
W5 **125** F4
Richmond TW10 **163** E2
Murray Sq, E16 **115** G6
Murray St, NW1 **92** D7
Murrays Yd, SE18 **136** E4
Murray Ter, NW3
off Flask Wk **91** G4
W5 *off Murray Rd* **125** G4
Mursell Est, SW8 **151** F1
Murtwell Dr, Chig. IG7 **65** F6
Musard Rd, W6 **128** B6
W14 **128** B6
Musbury St, E1 **113** F6
Muscal, W6 **128** B6
Muscatel Pl, SE5
off Dalwood St **152** B1
Muschamp Rd, SE15 **152** C3
Carshalton SM5 **199** H2
Muscovy Ho, Erith DA18
off Kale Rd **138** E2
Muscovy St, EC3 **21** E6
★ **Museum in Docklands**, E14 *off Hertsmere Rd* **114** A7
Museum La, SW7 **23** F6
★ **Museum of Childhood at Bethnal Green**, E2 **113** E3
★ **Museum of Croydon**, Croy. CR0 **201** J3
★ **Museum of Gdn History**, SE1 **26** C6
★ **Museum of Instruments** (Royal College of Music), SW7 **22** E5
★ **Museum of London**, EC2 **19** J2
★ **Museum of Richmond**, Rich. TW9 **145** G5
Museum Pas, E2
off Victoria Pk Sq **113** F3
Museum St, WC1 **18** A2
Museum Way, W3 **126** A2
Musgrave Cl, Barnet EN4 **41** F1
Musgrave Cres, SW6 **148** D1
Musgrave Rd, Islw. TW7 **144** C1
Musgrove Rd, SE14 **153** G1
Musjid Rd, SW11
off Kambala Rd **149** G2
Musket Cl, Barn. (E.Barn.) EN4
off East Barnet Rd **41** G5
Musquash Way, Houns. TW4 **142** C2
Muston Rd, E5 **94** E2
Mustow Pl, SW6
off Munster Rd **148** C2
Muswell Av, N10 **74** B2
MUSWELL HILL, N10 **74** B3
Muswell Hill, N10 **74** B3
Muswell Hill Bdy, N10 **74** B3
Muswell Hill Pl, N10 **74** B4
Muswell Hill Rd, N6 **74** A6
N10 **74** A4
Muswell Ms, N10
off Muswell Rd **74** B3
Muswell Rd, N10 **74** B3
Mutrix Rd, NW6 **108** D1
Mutton Pl, NW1
off Harmood St **92** B6
Muybridge Rd, N.Mal. KT3 **182** C2
Myatt Rd, SW9 **151** H1
Myatts Flds S, SW9
off St. Lawrence Way **151** G2
Myatts N, SW9
off Fairbairn Grn **151** G1
Mycenae Rd, SE3 **135** G7
Myddelton Cl, Enf. EN1 **44** C1
Myddelton Gdns, N21 **43** H7
Myddelton Pk, N20 **57** G3
Myddelton Pas, EC1 **11** F3
Myddelton Rd, N8 **75** E4
Myddelton Sq, EC1 **11** F3
Myddelton St, EC1 **11** F4
Myddleton Av, N4 **93** J2
Myddleton Cl, Stan. HA7 **52** D2
Myddleton Ms, N22 **59** E7
Myddleton Rd, N22 **59** E7
Myers La, SE14 **133** G6
Mylis Cl, SE26 **171** E4
Mylius Cl, SE14
off Kender St **153** F1
Mylne St, EC1 **11** E2
Mynterne Ct, SW19
off Swanton Gdns **166** A1
Myra St, SE2 **138** A5
Myrdle St, E1 **21** J2
Myrna Cl, SW19 **167** H7
Myron Pl, SE13 **154** C3
Myrtle Av, Felt. TW14 **141** H4
Ruislip HA4 **66** A7
Myrtleberry Cl, E8
off Beechwood Rd **94** C6
Myrtle Cl, Barn. (E.Barn.) EN4 **57** J1
West Drayton UB7 **120** C3
Myrtledene Rd, SE2 **138** A5
Myrtle Gdns, W7 **124** B1
Myrtle Gro, N.Mal. KT3 **182** C2
Myrtle Rd, E6 **116** B1
E17 **77** H6
N13 **59** J3
W3 **126** C1
Croydon CR0 **204** A3
Hampton (Hmptn H.) TW12 **161** J6
Hounslow TW3 **143** J2
Ilford IG1 **99** E2
Sutton SM1 **199** F5
Myrtle Wk, N1 **12** D2
Mysore Rd, SW11 **149** J3
Myton Rd, SE21 **170** A3

N

N17 Studios, N17 **60** C7
N1 Shop Cen, N1 **11** F1
Nadine St, SE7 **135** J5
Nafferton Ri, Loug. IG10 **48** A5
Nagle Cl, E17 **78** D2
Nags Head, N7 **93** F4
Nags Head Cen, N7 **93** F4
Nag's Head Ct, EC1 **11** J6
Nags Head La, Well. DA16 **158** B3
Nags Head Rd, Enf. EN3 **45** F4
Nairne Gro, SE24 **152** A5
Nairn Grn, Wat. WD19 **50** A3
Nairn Rd, Ruis. HA4 **84** C6
Nairn St, E14 **114** C5
Nallhead Rd, Felt. TW13 **160** C5
Namba Roy Cl, SW16 **169** F4
Namton Dr, Th.Hth. CR7 **187** F4
Nan Clark's La, NW7 **55** F2
Nankin St, E14 **114** A6
Nansen Rd, SW11 **150** A4
Nansen Village, N12 **57** E4
Nant Ct, NW2
off Granville Rd **90** C2
Nantes Cl, SW18 **149** F4
Nantes Pas, E1 **21** F1
Nant Rd, NW2 **90** C2
Nant St, E2
off Cambridge Heath Rd **113** E3
Naoroji St, WC1 **11** E4
Napier Av, E14 **134** A5
SW6 **148** C3
Napier Cl, SE8
off Amersham Vale **133** J7
W14 *off Napier Rd* **128** C3
West Drayton UB7 **120** C3
Napier Ct, SE12 **173** H3
SW6
off Ranelagh Gdns **148** C3
Surbiton KT6 **181** G6
Napier Gro, N1 **12** A2
Napier Pl, W14 **128** C3
Napier Rd, E6 **116** D1
E11 **96** E4
E15 **115** E2
N17 **76** B3
NW10 **107** H3
SE25 **188** E4
W14 **128** C3
Belvedere DA17 **139** F4
Bromley BR2 **191** H4
Enfield EN3 **45** G5
Hounslow (Lon.Hthrw Air.) TW6 **140** A1
Isleworth TW7 **144** D4
South Croydon CR2 **202** A7
Wembley HA0 **87** G5
Napier Ter, N1 **93** H7
Napoleon Rd, E5 **94** E3
Twickenham TW1 **145** E7
Napton Cl, Hayes UB4 **102** E4
Narbonne Av, SW4 **150** C5
Narborough St, SW6 **148** E2
Narcissus Rd, NW6 **90** D5
Naresby Fold, Stan. HA7 **53** F6
Narford Rd, E5 **94** D3
Narrow Boat Cl, SE28
off Ridge Cl **137** G2
Narrow St, E14 **113** H7
Narrow Way, Brom. BR2 **192** B6
Nascot St, W12 **107** J6
Naseberry Ct, E4
off Merriam Cl **62** C5
Naseby Cl, NW6 **91** F7
Isleworth TW7 **144** B1
Naseby Rd, SE19 **170** A6
Dagenham RM10 **101** G3
Ilford IG5 **80** C1
Nash Cl, Sutt. SM1 **199** G3
Nash Grn, Brom. BR1 **173** G6
Nash Ho, SW1 **33** E4
Nash La, Kes. BR2 **205** G5
Nash Rd, N9 **61** F2
SE4 **153** G4
Romford RM6 **82** D4
Nash St, NW1 **8** E4
Nash Way, Har. (Kenton) HA3 **69** E6
Nasmyth St, W6 **127** H3

Nassau Path, SE28
off Disraeli Cl 138 C1
Nassau Rd, SW13 . . . . . . .147 F1
Nassau St, W1 . . . . .17 F2
Nassington Rd, NW3 . . . . . .91 H4
Natalie Cl, Felt. TW14 . . . . .141 G7
Natalie Ms, Twick. TW2
off Sixth Cross Rd 162 A3
Natal Rd, N11 . . . . .58 E6
SW16 . . . . .168 D6
Ilford IG1 . . . . .98 E4
Thornton Heath CR7 . . .188 A3
Nathaniel Cl, E1 . . . . .21 G2
Nathans Rd, Wem. HA0 . . . .87 F2
Nathan Way, SE28 . . . . . . .137 H4
★ **National Archives, The**,
Rich. TW9 . . . . .126 B7
★ **National Army Mus**,
SW3 . . . . .32 A5
★ **National Gall**, WC2 . . . .17 J6
★ **National Maritime Mus**,
SE10 . . . . .134 D6
★ **National Portrait Gall**,
WC2 . . . . .17 J6
National Ter, SE16
off Bermondsey Wall E 132 E2
★ **National Thea**, SE1 . . . .26 D1
Nation Way, E4 . . . . .62 C1
★ **Natural History Mus**,
SW7 . . . . .23 E6
Naval Row, E14 . . . . .114 C7
Naval Wk, Brom. BR1
off High St 191 G2
Navarino Gro, E8 . . . . .94 D6
Navarino Rd, E8 . . . . .94 D6
Navarre Rd, E6 . . . . .116 B2
Navarre St, E2 . . . . .13 F5
Navenby Wk, E3
off Burwell Wk 114 A4
Navestock Cl, E4
off Mapleton Rd 62 C3
Navestock Cres, Wdf.Grn.
IG8 . . . . .79 J1
Navestock Ho, Bark. IG11 .118 B2
Navigation Ct, E16
off Gallions Rd 117 F7
Navigator Dr, Sthl. UB2 . . .123 J2
Navigator Pk, Sthl. UB2 . .122 C4
Navy St, SW4 . . . . .150 D3
Naxos Bldg, E14
off Hutchings St 134 A2
Nayim Pl, E8
off Amhurst Rd 94 E5
Naylor Gro, Enf. EN3
off South St 45 G5
Naylor Rd, N20 . . . . .57 F2
SE15 . . . . .132 E7
Nazareth Gdns, SE15 . . . .152 E2
Nazrul St, E2 . . . . .13 F3
Neagle Cl, Borwd. WD6
off Balcon Way 38 C1
Neal Av, Sthl. UB1 . . . . . . .103 F4
Neal Cl, Nthwd. HA6 . . . . . .66 A1
Nealden St, SW9 . . . . .151 F3
Neale Cl, N2 . . . . .73 F3
Neal St, WC2 . . . . .18 A4
Neal's Yd, WC2 . . . . .18 A4
Near Acre, NW9 . . . . .71 F1
NEASDEN, NW2 . . . . .89 E3
Neasden Cl, NW10 . . . . .89 E5
Neasden Junct, NW10
off North Circular Rd . . .88 E4
Neasden La, NW10 . . . . . . .89 E4
Neasden La N, NW10 . . . . .88 D3
Neasham Rd, Dag. RM8 . .100 B5
Neate St, SE5 . . . . .37 F5
Neath Gdns, Mord. SM4 . .185 F6
Neathouse Pl, SW1 . . . . . . .33 F1
Neatscourt Rd, E6 . . . . . . .116 A5
Nebraska Bldg, SE13
off Deals Gateway 154 B1
Nebraska St, SE1 . . . . .28 B4
★ **NEC Harlequins RFC**,
Twick. TW2 . . . . .144 B7
Neckinger, SE16 . . . . .29 G5
Neckinger Est, SE16 . . . . . .29 G5
Neckinger St, SE1 . . . . .29 G4
Nectarine Way, SE13 . . . . .154 B2
Needham Rd, W11
off Westbourne Gro . . .108 D6
Needham Ter, NW2
off Kara Way 90 A3
Needleman St, SE16 . . . . .133 G2
Neeld Cres, NW4 . . . . .71 H5
Wembley HA9 . . . . .88 A5
Neeld Par, Wem. HA9
off Harrow Rd 88 A5
Neil Wates Cres, SW2 . . . .169 G1
Nelgarde Rd, SE6 . . . . .154 A7
Nella Rd, W6 . . . . .128 A6
Nelldale Rd, SE16 . . . . . . .133 F4
Nello James Gdns,
SE27 . . . . .170 A4
Nelson Cl, NW6 . . . . .108 D3
Croydon CR0 . . . . .201 H1
Romford RM7 . . . . .83 H1
Nelson Ct, SE16
off Brunel Rd 133 F1
Nelson Gdns, E2 . . . . .13 J3
Hounslow TW3 . . . . .143 G6
Nelson Gro Rd, SW19 . . . .185 E1
Nelson Mandela Cl, N10 . . .74 A2
Nelson Mandela Rd, SE3 .155 J3
Nelson Pas, EC1 . . . . .12 A4
Nelson Pl, N1 . . . . .11 H2
Sidcup DA14
off Sidcup High St 176 A4
Nelson Rd, E4 . . . . .62 B6
E11 . . . . .79 G4
N8 . . . . .75 F5
N9 . . . . .61 E2
N15 . . . . .76 B4
SE10 . . . . .134 C6
SW19 . . . . .167 E7
Belvedere DA17 . . . . . . .139 F5
Bromley BR2 . . . . .191 J4
Enfield EN3 . . . . .45 G6
Harrow HA1 . . . . .86 A1
Hounslow TW3, TW4 . . .143 G6
Hounslow
(Lon.Hthrw Air.) TW6 . .140 C1
New Malden KT3 . . . . . .182 D5
Sidcup DA14
off Sidcup High St 176 A4
Stanmore HA7 . . . . .53 F6
Twickenham TW2 . . . . . .143 J6
★ **Nelson's Column**,
WC2 . . . . .26 A1
Nelson Sq, SE1 . . . . .27 G3
Nelson's Row, SW4 . . . . . .150 D4
Nelson St, E1 . . . . .112 E6
E6 . . . . .116 C2
E16
off Huntingdon St 115 F6
Nelsons Yd, NW1 . . . . .9 F1
Nelson Ter, N1 . . . . .11 H2
Nelson Trd Est, SW19 . . . . .184 E1
Nelson Wk, SE16
off Salter Rd 133 H1
Nemoure Rd, W3 . . . . .106 C7
Nene Gdns, Felt. TW13 . . .161 F2
Nene Rd, Houns.
(Lon.Hthrw Air.) TW6 . . .141 E1
Nepaul Rd, SW11 . . . . .149 H2
Nepean St, SW15 . . . . . . .147 G6
Neptune Ct, Borwd. WD6
off Clarendon Rd 38 A3
Neptune Ho, E3
off Garrison Rd 114 A1
Neptune Rd, Har. HA1 . . . . .68 A6
Hounslow
(Lon.Hthrw Air.) TW6 . .141 G1
Neptune St, SE16 . . . . . . .133 F3
Nero Ct, Brent. TW8
off Justin Cl 125 G7
Nesbit Rd, SE9 . . . . .156 A4
Nesbitt Cl, SE3
off Hurren Cl 154 E3
Nesbitts All, Barn. EN5
off Bath Pl 40 C3
Nesbitt Sq, SE19
off Coxwell Rd 170 B7
Nesham St, E1 . . . . .29 H1
Ness St, SE16 . . . . .29 H5
Nesta Rd, Wdf.Grn. IG8 . . .63 E6
Nestles Av, Hayes UB3 . . .121 J3
Nestor Av, N21 . . . . .43 H6
Netheravon Rd, W4 . . . . . .127 F4
W7 . . . . .124 C1
Netheravon Rd S, W4 . . . .127 F5
Netherbury Rd, W5 . . . . . .125 G3
Netherby Gdns, Enf. EN2 . . .42 E4
Netherby Rd, SE23 . . . . . .153 F7
Nether Cl, N3 . . . . .56 D7
Nethercourt Av, N3 . . . . . . .56 D6
Netherfield Gdns, Bark.
IG11 . . . . .99 G6
Netherfield Rd, N12 . . . . . . .57 E5
SW17 . . . . .168 A3
Netherford Rd, SW4 . . . . .150 C2
Netherhall Gdns, NW3 . . . .91 F6
Netherhall Way, NW3
off Netherhall Gdns . . .91 F5
Netherheys Dr, S.Croy.
CR2 . . . . .201 H7
Netherlands Rd, Barn.
(New Barn.) EN5 . . . . . . .41 G6
Netherleigh Cl, N6 . . . . .92 B1
Nether St, N3 . . . . .72 D1
N12 . . . . .56 D7
Netherton Gro, SW10 . . . . .30 D6
Netherton Rd, N15 . . . . . . .76 A6
Twickenham TW1 . . . . . .144 D5
Netherwood, N2 . . . . .73 G2
Netherwood Pl, W14
off Netherwood Rd . . .128 A3
Netherwood Rd, W14 . . . .128 A3
Netherwood St, NW6 . . . . .90 C7
Netley Cl, Croy.
(New Adgtn) CR0 . . . . . .204 C7
Sutton SM3 . . . . .198 A5
Netley Dr, Walt. KT12 . . . . .179 F7
Netley Gdns, Mord. SM4 .185 F7
Netley Rd, E17 . . . . .77 J5
Brentford TW8 . . . . .125 H6
Hounslow
(Lon.Hthrw Air.) TW6 . .141 G1
Ilford IG2 . . . . .81 G5
Morden SM4 . . . . .185 F7
Netley St, NW1 . . . . .9 F4
Nettleden Av, Wem. HA9 . . .88 A6
Nettlefold Pl, SE27 . . . . . . .169 H3
Nettlestead Cl, Beck.
BR3 . . . . .189 J1
Nettleton Rd, SE14 . . . . . .153 G1
Hounslow
(Lon.Hthrw Air.) TW6 . .141 E1
Nettlewood Rd, SW16 . . . .168 D7
Neuchatel Rd, SE6 . . . . . . .171 J2
Nevada Bldg, SE10
off Blackheath Rd 154 B1
Nevada Cl, N.Mal. KT3 . . .182 C4
Nevada St, SE10 . . . . .134 C6
Nevern Pl, SW5 . . . . .128 D4
Nevern Rd, SW5 . . . . .128 D4
Nevern Sq, SW5 . . . . .128 D4
Neville Av, N.Mal. KT3 . . .182 D1
Neville Cl, E11 . . . . .97 F3
NW1 . . . . .9 J2
NW6 . . . . .108 C2
SE15 . . . . .132 D7
W3 *off Acton La* 126 C2
Hounslow TW3 . . . . .143 H2
Sidcup DA15 . . . . .175 J4
Neville Dr, N2 . . . . .73 F6
Neville Gdns, Dag. RM8 . .100 D3
Neville Gill Cl, SW18 . . . . .148 D6
Neville Pl, N22 . . . . .75 F1
Neville Rd, E7 . . . . .97 G7
NW6 . . . . .108 C2
W5 . . . . .105 G4
Croydon CR0 . . . . .188 A7
Dagenham RM8 . . . . . . .100 D2
Ilford IG6 . . . . .81 F1
Kingston upon Thames
KT1 . . . . .182 A2
Richmond TW10 . . . . . . .163 F3
Nevilles Ct, NW2 . . . . .89 G3
Neville St, SW7 . . . . .31 E3
Neville Ter, SW7 . . . . .31 E3
Neville Wk, Cars. SM5 . . . .185 H7
Nevill Rd, N16 . . . . .94 B4
Nevill Way, Loug. IG10
off Valley Hill 48 B7
Nevin Dr, E4 . . . . .62 B1
Nevinson Cl, SW18 . . . . . .149 G6
Nevis Rd, SW17 . . . . .168 A2
New Acres Rd, SE28 . . . . .137 H2
Newall Ct, W12
off Heathstan Rd 107 G6
Newall Ho, SE1 . . . . .28 A5
Newall Rd, Houns.
(Lon.Hthrw Air.) TW6 . . .141 F1
Newark Cres, NW10 . . . . . .106 D3
Newark Grn, Borwd. WD6 . .38 D3
Newark Knok, E6 . . . . .116 D6
Newark Rd, S.Croy. CR2 . .202 A6
Newark St, E1 . . . . .112 E5
Newark Way, NW4 . . . . .71 G4
New Ash Cl, N2 . . . . .73 G3
New Atlas Wf, E14
off Arnhem Pl 134 A3
New Barn Cl, Wall. SM6 . .201 F6
NEW BARNET, Barn. EN5 . .41 E4
New Barns Av, Mitch.
CR4 . . . . .186 D4
New Barn St, E13 . . . . .115 G4
New Barns Way, Chig. IG7 .64 E3
NEW BECKENHAM, Beck.
BR3 . . . . .171 J6
New Bell Yd, EC4 . . . . .19 H5
Newbiggin Path, Wat.
WD19 . . . . .50 C4
Newbolt Av, Sutt. SM3 . . .197 J5
Newbolt Rd, Stan. HA7 . . . .52 C6
New Bond St, W1 . . . . .16 D4
Newborough Grn, N.Mal.
KT3 . . . . .182 D4
New Brent St, NW4 . . . . . . .71 J5
Newbridge Pt, SE23
off Windrush La 171 G3
New Br St, EC4 . . . . .19 G4
New Broad St, EC2 . . . . . . .20 D2
New Bdy, W5 . . . . .105 F7
Hampton (Hmptn H.)
TW12
off Hampton Rd 162 A5
New Bdy Bldgs, W5
off New Bdy 105 G7
Newburgh Rd, W3 . . . . . . .126 C1
Newburgh St, W1 . . . . .17 F4
New Burlington Ms, W1 . . .17 F5
New Burlington Pl, W1 . . . .17 F5
New Burlington St, W1 . . . .17 F5
Newburn St, SE11 . . . . .34 D4
Newbury Cl, Northolt
UB5 . . . . .85 F6
Newbury Gdns, Epsom
KT19 . . . . .197 F4
Newbury Ho, N22 . . . . .75 E1
Newbury Ms, NW5
off Malden Rd 92 A6
NEWBURY PARK, Ilf. IG2 . . .81 G5
Newbury Rd, E4 . . . . .62 C6
Bromley BR2 . . . . .191 G3
Hounslow
(Lon.Hthrw Air.) TW6 . .140 C1
Ilford IG2 . . . . .81 G6
Newbury St, EC1 . . . . .19 J2
Newbury Way, Nthlt. UB5 . .85 E6
New Butt La, SE8 . . . . . . .134 A7
New Butt La N, SE8
off Reginald Rd 134 A7
Newby Cl, Enf. EN1 . . . . . . .44 B2
Newby Pl, E14 . . . . .114 C7
Newby St, SW8 . . . . .150 B3
New Caledonian Wf,
SE16 . . . . .133 J3
Newcastle Cl, EC4 . . . . .19 G3
Newcastle Pl, W2 . . . . .15 F2
Newcastle Row, EC1 . . . . . .11 F5
New Cavendish St, W1 . . . .17 E1
New Change, EC4 . . . . .19 J4
New Chapel Rd, Felt. TW13
off High St 160 B1
New Chapel Sq, Felt.
TW13 . . . . .160 B1
New Charles St, EC1 . . . . . .11 H3
NEW CHARLTON, SE7 . . . .135 J4
New Ch Ct, SE19
off Waldegrave Rd 170 D7
New Ch Rd, SE5 . . . . .36 A7
New City Rd, E13 . . . . .115 J3
New Cl, SW19 . . . . .185 F3
Feltham TW13 . . . . .160 E5
New Coll Ct, NW3
off Finchley Rd 91 F6
New Coll Ms, N1
off Islington Pk St 93 G7
New Coll Par, NW3
off Finchley Rd 91 G6
Newcombe Gdns, SW16 . . .169 E4
Hounslow TW4 . . . . .143 F4
Newcombe Pk, NW7 . . . . . .55 E5
Wembley HA0 . . . . .105 J1
Newcombe St, W8
off Kensington Pl 128 D1
Newcomen Rd, E11 . . . . . . .97 F3
SW11 . . . . .149 G3
Newcomen St, SE1 . . . . . . .28 B3
New Compton St, WC2 . . . .17 J4
New Concordia Wf, SE1 . . .29 G3
Newcourt St, NW8 . . . . .7 G2
★ **New Covent Garden Flower Mkt**, SW8 . . . . .33 J6
★ **New Covent Garden Mkt**, SW8 . . . . .130 D7
New Crane Pl, E1
off Garnet St 133 F1
NEW CROSS, SE14 . . . . . .153 H1
New Cross, SE14 . . . . .133 J7
NEW CROSS GATE,
SE14 . . . . .153 G1
New Cross Rd, SE14 . . . . .133 F7
Newdales Cl, N9 . . . . .60 D2
Newdene Av, Nthlt. UB5 . .102 D2
New Ealing Bdy, W5
off Haven Grn 105 G7
Newell St, E14 . . . . .113 J6
NEW ELTHAM, SE9 . . . . . .174 D2
New End, NW3 . . . . .91 F4
New End Sq, NW3 . . . . .91 G4
Newent Cl, SE15 . . . . .36 D7
Carshalton SM5 . . . . . . .199 J1
New Fm Av, Brom. BR2 . . .191 G4
New Ferry App, SE18 . . . .136 D3
New Fetter La, EC4 . . . . . . .19 F3
Newfield Cl, Hmptn.
TW12 *off Percy Rd* 179 G1
Newfield Ri, NW2 . . . . .89 H3
New Forest La, Chig. IG7 . .64 D6
Newgale Gdns, Edg. HA8 . .69 J1
New Gdn Dr, West Dr.
UB7 *off Drayton Gdns* . .120 B2
Newgate, Croy. CR0 . . . . . .201 J1
Newgate Cl, Felt. TW13 . . .161 E2
Newgate St, E4 . . . . .63 F3
EC1 . . . . .19 H3
New Globe Wk, SE1 . . . . . .27 J1
New Goulston St, E1 . . . . . .21 F3
New Grn Pl, SE19 . . . . .170 B6
Newhams Row, SE1 . . . . . .28 E4
Newham Way, E6 . . . . .115 J5
E16 . . . . .115 F5
Newhaven Cl, Hayes
UB3 . . . . .121 J4
Newhaven Gdns, SE9 . . . .156 A4
Newhaven La, E16 . . . . . . .115 F4
Newhaven Rd, SE25 . . . . .188 A5
New Heston Rd, Houns.
TW5 . . . . .123 F7
New Horizons, WD6 . . . . . . .38 C2
New Horizons Ct, Brent.
TW8
off Shield Dr 124 D6
Newhouse Av, Rom.
RM6 . . . . .82 D3

Newhouse Cl, N.Mal. KT3 . . . 183 E7
Newhouse Wk, Mord. SM4 . . . 185 F7
Newick Cl, Bex. DA5 . . . 159 H6
Newick Rd, E5 . . . 95 E3
Newing Grn, Brom. BR1 . . 174 A7
NEWINGTON, SE1 . . . 35 J1
Newington Barrow Way, N7 . . . 93 F3
Newington Butts, SE1 . . . 35 H2
SE11 . . . 35 H2
Newington Causeway, SE1 . . . 27 H6
Newington Grn, N1 . . . 94 A5
N16 . . . 94 A5
Newington Grn Rd, N1 . . . 94 A6
New Inn Bdy, EC2 . . . 12 E5
New Inn Pas, WC2 . . . 18 D4
New Inn Sq, EC2 . . . 12 E5
New Inn St, EC2 . . . 12 E5
New Inn Yd, EC2 . . . 12 E5
New James Ct, SE15 *off Nunhead La* . . . 153 E3
New Jersey Ter, SE15 *off Nunhead La* . . . 152 E3
New Jubilee Ct, Wdf.Grn. IG8 *off Grange Av* . . . 63 G7
New Kent Rd, SE1 . . . 27 J6
New Kings Rd, SW6 . . . 148 C2
New King St, SE8 . . . 134 A6
Newland Cl, Pnr. HA5 . . . 51 E6
Newland Ct, EC1 *off St. Luke's Est* . . . 12 B5
Wembley HA9 *off Barn Ri* . . . 88 A2
Newland Dr, Enf. EN1 . . . 44 E1
Newland Gdns, W13 . . . 124 D2
Newland Rd, N8 . . . 74 E3
Newlands, The, Wall. SM6 . . . 200 C7
Newlands Av, T.Ditt. KT7 . . 194 B1
Newlands Cl, Edg. HA8 . . . 53 H3
Southall UB2 . . . 122 E5
Wembley HA0 . . . 87 F6
Newlands Ct, SE9 . . . 156 D6
Newlands Pk, SE26 . . . 171 G5
Newlands Pl, Barn. EN5 . . . 40 A5
Newlands Quay, E1 . . . 113 F7
Newlands Rd, SW16 . . . 187 E2
Woodford Green IG8 . . . 63 F2
Newlands Ter, SW8 *off Queenstown Rd* . . . 150 B2
Newland St, E16 . . . 136 B1
Newlands Way, Chess. KT9 . . . 195 F5
Newling Cl, E6 *off Porter Rd* . . . 116 C6
New London St, EC3 . . . 21 E5
New Lydenburg Commercial Est, SE7 *off New Lydenburg St* . . 135 J3
New Lydenburg St, SE7 . . 135 J3
Newlyn Cl, Orp. BR6 . . . 207 J4
Newlyn Gdns, Har. HA2 . . . 67 F7
Newlyn Rd, N17 . . . 76 C1
Barnet EN5 . . . 40 C4
Welling DA16 . . . 157 J2
NEW MALDEN, KT3 . . . 182 D3
Newman Pas, W1 . . . 17 G2
Newman Rd, E13 . . . 115 H3
E17 *off Southcote Rd* . . . 77 G5
Bromley BR1 . . . 191 G1
Croydon CR0 . . . 201 F1
Hayes UB3 . . . 102 B7
Newmans Cl, Loug. IG10 . . 48 E3
Newman's Ct, EC3 . . . 20 C4
Newmans La, Loug. IG10 . . 48 D3
Surbiton KT6 . . . 181 G6
Newman's Row, WC2 . . . 18 D2
Newman St, W1 . . . 17 G2
Newmans Way, Barn. EN4 . 41 F1
Newman Yd, W1 . . . 17 G3
Newmarket Av, Nthlt. UB5 . 85 G5
Newmarket Grn, SE9 *off Middle Pk Av* . . . 156 A7
Newmarsh Rd, SE28 . . . 137 J1
Newminster Rd, Mord. SM4 . . . 185 F6
New Mt St, E15 . . . 96 D7
Newnes Path, SW15 *off Putney Pk La* . . . 147 H4
Newnham Av, Ruis. HA4 . . 84 C1
Newnham Cl, Loug. IG10 . . 48 A6
Northolt UB5 . . . 85 J5
Thornton Heath CR7 . . . 187 J2
Newnham Gdns, Nthlt. UB5 . . . 85 J5
Newnham Ms, N22 . . . 75 F1
Newnham Rd, N22 . . . 75 F1
Newnhams Cl, Brom. BR1 . . . 192 C3
Newnham Ter, SE1 . . . 26 E5
Newnham Way, Har. HA3 . . 69 H5
New N Pl, EC2 . . . 12 D6
New N Rd, N1 . . . 12 C2
Ilford IG6 . . . 65 G7
New N St, WC1 . . . 18 C1
Newnton Cl, N4 . . . 76 A7
New Oak Rd, N2 . . . 73 F2
New Orleans Wk, N19 . . . 74 D7
New Oxford St, WC1 . . . 17 J3
New Pk Av, N13 . . . 59 J3
New Pk Cl, Nthlt. UB5 . . . 84 E6
New Pk Ct, SW2 . . . 151 E7
New Pk Ind Est, N18 . . . 61 F5
New Pk Par, SW2 *off New Pk Rd* . . . 151 E7
New Pk Rd, SW2 . . . 168 D1
Newpiece, Loug. IG10 . . . 48 E3
New Pl Sq, SE16 . . . 132 E3
New Plaistow Rd, E15 . . . 115 E1
Newport Av, E13 . . . 115 H4
E14 . . . 114 D7
Newport Ct, WC2 . . . 17 J5
Newport Mead, Wat. WD19 *off Kilmarnock Rd* . . . 50 D4
Newport Pl, WC2 . . . 17 J5
Newport Rd, E10 . . . 96 C2
E17 . . . 77 H4
SW13 . . . 147 G1
W3 . . . 126 C2
Hounslow (Lon.Hthrw Air.) TW6 . . 140 D1
Newport St, SE11 . . . 34 C2
New Priory Ct, NW6 *off Mazenod Av* . . . 90 D7
New Providence Wf, E14 . . 134 D1
Newquay Cres, Har. HA2 . . 85 E2
Newquay Gdns, Wat. WD19 *off Fulford Gro* . . . 50 B2
Newquay Rd, SE6 . . . 172 B2
New Quebec St, W1 . . . 16 A4
New Ride, SW7 . . . 23 J3
New River Av, N8 . . . 75 F3
New River Ct, N5 . . . 94 A4
New River Cres, N13 . . . 59 H4
New River Head, EC1 . . . 11 F3
New River Wk, N1 . . . 93 J6
New River Way, N4 . . . 76 A7
New Rd, E1 . . . 112 E5
E4 . . . 62 B4
N8 . . . 74 E5
N9 . . . 60 E2
N17 . . . 76 C1
N22 . . . 75 J1
NW7 . . . 56 B7
NW7 (Barnet Gate) . . . 39 F7
SE2 . . . 138 D4
Brentford TW8 . . . 125 G6
Dagenham RM9, RM10 . . . 119 G1
Feltham TW14 . . . 160 B1
Feltham (E.Bed.) TW14 . 141 G6
Feltham (Han.) TW13 . . . 160 E5
Harrow HA1 . . . 86 C4
Hayes (Harling.) UB3 . . . 121 F7
Hounslow TW3 . . . 143 H4
Ilford IG3 . . . 99 H2
Kingston upon Thames KT2 . . . 164 A7
Mitcham CR4 . . . 199 J1
Richmond TW10 . . . 163 F4
Welling DA16 . . . 158 B2
West Molesey KT8 . . . 179 G3
New Row, WC2 . . . 18 A5
Newry Rd, Twick. TW1 . . . 144 D4
Newsam Av, N15 . . . 76 A5
★ **New Scotland Yd**, SW1 . . . 25 H5
Newsholme Dr, N21 . . . 43 F5
NEW SOUTHGATE, N11 . . . 58 D4
New Southgate Ind Est, N11 . . . 58 C5
New Spitalfields Mkt, E10 . . . 96 A3
New Spring Gdns Wk, SE11 . . . 34 B4
New Sq, WC2 . . . 18 D3
Newstead Av, Orp. BR6 . . . 207 G3
Newstead Cl, N12 . . . 57 H6
Newstead Rd, SE12 . . . 155 E7
Newstead Wk, Cars. SM5 . . . 185 F7
Newstead Way, SW19 . . . 166 A4
New St, EC2 . . . 20 E2
New St Hill, Brom. BR1 . . . 173 H5
New St Sq, EC4 . . . 19 F3
Newton Av, N10 . . . 74 A1
W3 . . . 126 C2
Newton Cl, E17 . . . 77 H6
Harrow HA2 . . . 85 G2
Newton Cres, Borwd. WD6 . . . 38 C4
Newton Gro, W4 . . . 126 E4
Newton Ho, Enf. EN3 *off Exeter Rd* . . . 45 G3
Newton Pl, E14 . . . 134 A4
Newton Rd, E15 . . . 96 D5
N15 . . . 76 C5
NW2 . . . 89 J3
SW19 . . . 166 B7
W2 . . . 108 D6
Harrow HA3 . . . 68 B2
Newton Rd, Isleworth TW7 144 C2
Welling DA16 . . . 158 A3
Wembley HA0 . . . 87 J7
Newton St, WC2 . . . 18 B3
Newtons Yd, SW18 *off Wandsworth High St* 148 D5
Newton Wk, Edg. HA8 *off Roscoff Cl* . . . 70 C1
Newton Way, N18 . . . 59 J5
Newtown St, SW11 *off Strasburg Rd* . . . 150 B1
New Trinity Rd, N2 . . . 73 G3
New Turnstile, WC1 . . . 18 C2
New Union Cl, E14 . . . 134 C3
New Union St, EC2 . . . 20 B2
New Wanstead, E11 . . . 79 F6
New Way Rd, NW9 . . . 71 E4
New Wf Rd, N1 . . . 10 B1
New Zealand Way, W12 . . . 107 H7
Niagara Av, W5 . . . 125 F4
Niagara Cl, N1 *off Cropley St* . . . 12 A1
Nibthwaite Rd, Har. HA1 . . . 68 B5
Nicholas Cl, Grnf. UB6 . . . 103 H2
Nicholas Ct, E13 *off Tunmarsh La* . . . 115 H3
Nicholas Gdns, W5 . . . 125 G2
Nicholas La, EC4 . . . 20 C5
Nicholas Ms, W4 *off Short Rd* . . . 126 E6
Nicholas Pas, EC4 . . . 20 C5
Nicholas Rd, E1 . . . 113 F4
Croydon CR0 . . . 201 E4
Dagenham RM8 . . . 101 F2
Nicholay Rd, N19 . . . 92 D2
Nichol Cl, N14 . . . 58 D1
Nicholes Rd, Houns. TW3 . 143 G4
Nichol La, Brom. BR1 . . . 173 G7
Nichollsfield Wk, N7 *off Hillmarton Rd* . . . 93 F5
Nicholls Pt, E15 . . . 115 G1
Nicholl St, E2 . . . 112 D1
Nichols Cl, N4 *off Osborne Rd* . . . 93 G1
Chessington KT9 *off Merritt Gdns* . . . 195 F6
Nichols Ct, E2 . . . 13 F2
Nichols Grn, W5 . . . 105 H5
Nicholson Rd, Croy. CR0 . . . 202 C1
Nicholson St, SE1 . . . 27 G2
Nickelby Cl, SE28 . . . 118 C6
Nickols Wk, SW18 *off Jew's Row* . . . 149 E4
Nicola Cl, Har. HA3 . . . 68 A2
South Croydon CR2 . . . 201 J6
Nicola Ms, Ilf. IG6 . . . 65 E7
Nicol Cl, Twick. TW1 *off Cassilis Rd* . . . 145 E6
Nicoll Pl, NW4 . . . 71 H6
Nicoll Rd, NW10 . . . 107 E1
Nicoll Way, Borwd. WD6 . . 38 D5
Nicolson Dr, Bushey (Bushey Hth) WD23 . . . 51 J1
Nicosia Rd, SW18 . . . 149 H7
Niederwald Rd, SE26 . . . 171 H4
Nield Rd, Hayes UB3 . . . 121 J2
Nigel Cl, Nthlt. UB5 . . . 102 E1
Nigel Fisher Way, Chess. KT9 . . . 195 F7
Nigel Ms, Ilf. IG1 . . . 98 E4
Nigel Playfair Av, W6 *off King St* . . . 127 H4
Nigel Rd, E7 . . . 97 J5
SE15 . . . 152 D3
Nigeria Rd, SE7 . . . 135 J7
Nightingale Av, E4 . . . 62 E5
Harrow HA1 . . . 68 E7
Nightingale Cl, E4 . . . 62 E4
W4 *off Grove Pk Ter* . . . 126 C6
Carshalton SM5 . . . 200 A2
Pinner HA5 . . . 66 C5
Nightingale Ct, E11 *off Nightingale La* . . . 79 H5
Sutton SM1 *off Lind Rd* . . . 199 F5
Nightingale Dr, Epsom KT19 . . . 196 B6
Nightingale Est, E5 . . . 94 D3
Nightingale Gro, SE13 . . . 154 D5
Nightingale Hts, SE18 *off Nightingale Vale* . . . 136 E6
Nightingale Ho, E1 *off Thomas More St* . . . 29 H1
Nightingale La, E11 . . . 79 G5
N6 . . . 91 H1
N8 . . . 74 E4
SW4 . . . 149 J7
SW12 . . . 149 J7
Bromley BR1 . . . 191 J2
Richmond TW10 . . . 145 H7
Nightingale Ms, E3 *off Chisenhale Rd* . . . 113 H2
E11 . . . 79 G5
SE11 . . . 35 F1
Kingston upon Thames KT1 *off South La* . . . 181 G3
Nightingale Pl, SE18 . . . 136 D6
SW10 . . . 30 D5
Nightingale Rd, E5 . . . 94 E3
N1 . . . 93 J6
N9 . . . 45 F6
N22 . . . 75 E1
NW10 . . . 107 F2
W7 . . . 124 C1
Carshalton SM5 . . . 199 J3
Hampton TW12 . . . 161 G5
Orpington BR5 . . . 193 F6
Walton-on-Thames KT12 . . . 178 B7
West Molesey KT8 . . . 179 H5
Nightingales, The, Stai. TW19 . . . 140 C7
Nightingale Sq, SW12 . . . 150 A7
Nightingale Vale, SE18 . . . 136 D6
Nightingale Wk, SW4 . . . 150 B6
Nightingale Way, E6 . . . 116 B5
Nile Cl, N16 *off Evering Rd* . . . 94 C3
Nile Dr, N9 . . . 61 F2
Nile Path, SE18 *off Jackson St* . . . 136 D6
Nile Rd, E13 . . . 115 J2
Nile St, N1 . . . 12 A3
Nile Ter, SE15 . . . 37 F4
Nimegen Way, SE22 . . . 152 B5
Nimrod Cl, Nthlt. UB5 . . . 102 D3
Nimrod Pas, N1 *off Tottenham Rd* . . . 94 B6
Nimrod Rd, SW16 . . . 168 B6
Nina Mackay Cl, E15 *off Arthingworth St* . . . 114 E1
Nine Acres Cl, E12 . . . 98 B5
Hayes UB3 *off Bourne Av* . . . 121 F3
NINE ELMS, SW8 . . . 33 G7
Nine Elms La, SW8 . . . 33 G6
Nineteenth Rd, Mitch. CR4 . . . 186 E4
Ninhams Wd, Orp. BR6 . . 206 D4
Ninth Av, Hayes UB3 . . . 102 A7
Nisbet Ho, E9 *off Homerton High St* . . 95 G5
Nisbett Wk, Sid. DA14 *off Sidcup High St* . . . 176 A4
Nithdale Rd, SE18 . . . 137 E7
Niton Cl, Barn. EN5 . . . 40 A6
Niton Rd, Rich. TW9 . . . 146 A3
Niton St, SW6 . . . 128 A7
Niven Cl, Borwd. WD6 . . . 38 C1
N.L.A. Twr, Croy. CR0 . . . 202 A2
No. 1 St, SE18 . . . 137 E3
Nobel Dr, Hayes (Harling.) UB3 . . . 121 G7
Nobel Rd, N18 . . . 61 F5
Noble Ct, Mitch. CR4 . . . 185 G2
Noble St, EC2 . . . 19 J3
Noel Coward Ho, SW1 *off Vauxhall Br Rd* . . . 33 G2
NOEL PARK, N22 . . . 75 G2
Noel Pk Rd, N22 . . . 75 G2
Noel Rd, E6 . . . 116 B4
N1 . . . 11 G1
W3 . . . 106 B6
Noel Sq, Dag. RM8 . . . 100 C4
Noel St, W1 . . . 17 G4
Noel Ter, SE23 *off Dartmouth Rd* . . . 171 F2
Noko, W10 . . . 108 A3
Nolan Way, E5 . . . 94 D4
Nolton Pl, Edg. HA8 . . . 69 J1
Nonsuch Cl, Ilf. IG6 . . . 65 E6
Nonsuch Ho, SW19 *off Chapter Way* . . . 185 G1
★ **Nonsuch Mansion**, Sutt. SM3 . . . 197 J6
Nora Gdns, NW4 . . . 72 A4
NORBITON, Kings.T. KT2 . 182 B2
Norbiton Av, Kings.T. KT1 . . . 182 A2
Norbiton Common Rd, Kings.T. KT1 . . . 182 B3
Norbiton Rd, E14 . . . 113 J6
Norbreck Gdns, NW10 *off Lytham Gro* . . . 105 J3
Norbreck Par, NW10 *off Lytham Gro* . . . 105 J3
Norbroke St, W12 . . . 107 F7
Norburn St, W10 *off Chesterton Rd* . . . 108 B5
NORBURY, SW16 . . . 187 G1
Norbury Av, SW16 . . . 187 F1
Hounslow TW3 . . . 144 A5
Thornton Heath CR7 . . . 187 G2
Norbury Cl, SW16 . . . 187 G1
Norbury Ct Rd, SW16 . . . 186 E3
Norbury Cres, SW16 . . . 187 F1
Norbury Cross, SW16 . . . 186 E3
Norbury Gdns, Rom. RM6 . 82 D5
Norbury Gro, NW7 . . . 54 E3
Norbury Hill, SW16 . . . 169 G7
Norbury Ri, SW16 . . . 186 E3
Norbury Rd, E4 . . . 62 A5
Thornton Heath CR7 . . . 187 J2

Norcombe Gdns, Har. HA3 69 F6
Norcott Cl, Hayes UB4 102 C4
Norcott Rd, N16 94 D2
Norcroft Gdns, SE22 152 D7
Norcutt Rd, Twick. TW2 162 B1
Norfield Rd, Dart. DA2 177 J4
Norfolk Av, N13 59 H6
N15 76 C6
Norfolk Cl, N2 73 H3
N13 59 H6
Barnet EN4 42 A4
Twickenham TW1 *off Cassilis Rd* 145 E6
Norfolk Cres, W2 15 H3
Sidcup DA15 157 H7
Norfolk Gdns, Bexh. DA7 159 F1
Borehamwood WD6 38 D4
Norfolk Ho, SE3 135 E6
SW1 *off Regency St* 33 J1
Norfolk Ho Rd, SW16 168 D3
Norfolk Ms, W10 *off Blagrove Rd* 108 C5
Norfolk Pl, W2 15 F3
Welling DA16 158 A2
Norfolk Rd, E6 116 C1
E17 77 G2
NW8 109 G1
NW10 88 E7
SW19 167 H7
Barking IG11 99 H7
Barnet EN5 40 D3
Dagenham RM10 101 H5
Enfield EN3 45 E6
Esher (Clay.) KT10 194 B5
Feltham TW13 160 C1
Harrow HA1 67 H5
Ilford IG3 99 H1
Romford RM7 83 J6
Thornton Heath CR7 187 J3
Norfolk Row, SE1 34 C1
Norfolk Sq, W2 15 F4
Norfolk Sq Ms, W2 15 F4
Norfolk St, E7 97 G4
Norfolk Ter, W6 *off Field Rd* 128 B5
Norgrove St, SW12 150 A7
Norhyrst Av, SE25 188 C3
Norland Ho, W11 128 A1
Norland Pl, W11 128 B1
Norland Rd, W11 128 A1
Norlands Cres, Chis. BR7 192 E1
Norlands Gate, Chis. BR7 193 E1
Norland Sq, W11 128 B1
Norley Vale, SW15 165 G1
Norlington Rd, E10 96 C1
E11 96 C1
Norman Av, N22 75 H1
Feltham TW13 161 E2
Southall UB1 103 E7
Twickenham TW1 145 E7
Normanby Cl, SW15 148 C5
Normanby Rd, NW10 89 F4
Norman Cl, Orp. BR6 207 F3
Romford RM5 83 H2
Norman Ct, Ilf. IG2 81 G7
Woodford Green IG8 *off Monkhams Av* 63 H5
Norman Cres, Houns. TW5 142 D1
Pinner HA5 66 C1
Normand Gdns, W14 *off Greyhound Rd* 128 B6
Normand Ms, W14 *off Normand Rd* 128 C6
Normand Rd, W14 128 C6
Normandy Av, Barn. EN5 40 C5
Normandy Cl, SE26 171 H3
Normandy Rd, SW9 151 G1
Normandy Ter, E16 115 H6
Norman Gro, E3 113 H2
Normanhurst Av, Bexh. DA7 158 D1
Normanhurst Dr, Twick. TW1 *off St. Margarets Rd* 144 E5
Normanhurst Rd, SW2 169 F2
Norman Rd, E6 116 C4
E11 96 D2
N15 76 C5
SE10 134 B7
SW19 167 F7
Belvedere DA17 139 H3
Ilford IG1 99 E5
Sutton SM1 198 D5
Thornton Heath CR7 187 H5
Normans Cl, NW10 88 D6
Normansfield Av, Tedd. TW11 163 F7
Normanshire Av, E4 62 C4
Normanshire Dr, E4 62 A4
Normans Mead, NW10 88 D6
Norman St, EC1 11 J4
Normanton Av, SW19 166 D2
Normanton Pk, E4 62 E3
Normanton Rd, S.Croy. CR2 202 B6
Normanton St, SE23 171 G2
Norman Way, N14 58 E2
W3 106 B5
Normington Cl, SW16 169 G5
Norrice Lea, N2 73 G5
Norris St, SW1 17 H6
Norroy Rd, SW15 148 A4
Norrys Cl, Barn. (Cockfos.) EN4 41 J5
Norrys Rd, Barn. (Cockfos.) EN4 41 J4
Norseman Cl, Ilf. IG3 100 B1
Norseman Way, Grnf. UB6 *off Olympic Way* 103 H1
Norstead Pl, SW15 165 G2
North Access Rd, E17 77 G6
North Acre, NW9 71 E1
NORTH ACTON, W3 106 D4
North Acton Rd, NW10 106 D3
Northall Rd, Bexh. DA7 159 J2
Northampton Gro, N1 94 A5
Northampton Pk, N1 93 J6
Northampton Rd, EC1 11 F5
Croydon CR0 202 D2
Enfield EN3 45 H4
Northampton Row, EC1 11 F4
Northampton Sq, EC1 11 G4
Northampton St, N1 93 J7
Northanger Rd, SW16 168 E6
North Arc, Croy. CR0 *off North End* 201 J2
North Audley St, W1 16 B4
North Av, N18 60 D4
W13 104 E6
Carshalton SM5 200 A7
Harrow HA2 67 H6
Hayes UB3 102 A7
Richmond TW9 *off Sandycombe Rd* 146 A1
Southall UB1 103 F7
North Bk, NW8 7 F4
Northbank Rd, E17 78 C2
NORTH BECKTON, E6 116 B4
North Birkbeck Rd, E11 96 D3
Northborough Rd, SW16 186 D3
Northbourne, Brom. BR2 191 G7
Northbourne Ho, E5 *off Pembury Rd* 94 E5
Northbourne Rd, SW4 150 D4
North Branch Av, W10 *off Harrow Rd* 107 J3
Northbrook Rd, N22 59 E7
SE13 154 D5
Barnet EN5 40 B6
Croydon CR0 188 A5
Ilford IG1 98 D2
Northburgh St, EC1 11 H5
North Carriage Dr, W2 15 G5
NORTH CHEAM, Sutt. SM3 197 J4
Northchurch, SE17 36 C3
Northchurch Rd, N1 94 A7
Wembley HA9 87 J6
Northchurch Ter, N1 94 B7
North Circular Rd,
E4 (A406) 61 J7
E6 (A406) 117 E2
E11 (A406) 79 J2
E12 (A406) 98 E5
E17 (A406) 61 J7
E18 (A406) 79 J2
N3 (A406) 72 E3
N11 (A406) 73 G1
N12 (A406) 73 G1
N13 (A406) 59 G5
N18 (A406) 60 B5
NW2 (A406) 88 E3
NW10 (A406) 88 B7
NW11 (A406) 72 B4
W3 (A406) 125 J2
W4 (A406) 125 J2
W5 (A406) 125 J2
Barking (A406) IG11 117 E2
Ilford (A406) IG1, IG4 98 B1
Northcliffe Cl, Wor.Pk. KT4 197 E3
Northcliffe Dr, N20 56 C1
North Cl, Barn. EN5 39 J5
Bexleyheath DA6 158 D4
Dagenham RM10 119 G1
Feltham TW14 *off North Rd* 141 G6
Morden SM4 184 B4
North Colonnade, The, E14 134 A1
North Common Rd, W5 105 H7
Northcote, Pnr. HA5 66 C2
Northcote Av, W5 105 H7
Isleworth TW7 144 D5
Southall UB1 103 E7
Surbiton KT5 182 A7
Northcote Ms, SW11 *off Northcote Rd* 149 H4
Northcote Rd, E17 77 H4
NW10 89 E7
Northcote Rd, SW11 149 H4
Croydon CR0 188 A6
New Malden KT3 182 C3
Sidcup DA14 175 H4
Twickenham TW1 144 D5
Northcott Av, N22 75 E1
North Countess Rd, E17 77 J2
NORTH CRAY, Sid. DA14 177 G3
North Cray Rd, Bex. DA5 177 F3
Sidcup DA14 176 E6
North Cres, E16 114 D4
N3 72 C2
WC1 17 H1
Northcroft Rd, W13 124 E2
Epsom KT19 196 D7
Northcroft Ter, W13 *off Northcroft Rd* 125 E2
North Cross Rd, SE22 152 C5
Ilford IG6 81 F4
North Dene, NW7 54 D3
Northdene, Chig. IG7 65 G5
North Dene, Houns. TW3 143 H1
Northdene Gdns, N15 76 C6
Northdown Gdns, Ilf. IG2 81 H5
Northdown Rd, Well. DA16 158 B2
Northdown St, N1 10 B1
North Dr, SW16 168 C4
Beckenham BR3 190 B4
Hounslow TW3 143 J2
Orpington BR6 207 H4
North End, NW3 91 F2
North End, Buckhurst Hill IG9 47 J7
Croydon CR0 201 J2
North End Av, NW3 91 F2
North End Cres, W14 128 C4
North End Ho, W14 128 B4
North End Par, W14 *off North End Rd* 128 B4
North End Rd, NW11 90 D1
SW6 128 C6
W14 128 B4
Wembley HA9 88 A3
North End Way, NW3 91 F2
Northern Av, N9 60 C2
Northernhay Wk, Mord. SM4 184 B4
Northern Perimeter Rd, Houns. (Lon.Hthrw Air.) TW6 141 F1
Northern Perimeter Rd W, Houns. (Lon.Hthrw Air.) TW6 140 A1
Northern Relief Rd, Bark. IG11 99 E7
Northern Rd, E13 115 H1
Northern Service Rd, Barn. EN5 40 B3
North Eyot Gdns, W6 127 G5
Northey St, E14 113 H7
North Feltham Trd Est, Houns. TW4 142 B5
Northfield, Loug. IG10 48 A4
Northfield Av, W5 125 E2
W13 125 E2
Pinner HA5 66 D4
Northfield Cl, Brom. BR1 192 B1
Hayes UB3 121 H3
Northfield Cres, Sutt. SM3 198 B4
Northfield Gdns, Dag. RM9 *off Northfield Rd* 101 F4
Northfield Pk, Hayes UB3 121 J3
Northfield Path, Dag. RM9 101 F3
Northfield Rd, E6 98 C7
N16 76 B7
W13 124 E2
Barnet EN4 41 H3
Borehamwood WD6 38 B1
Dagenham RM9 101 F4
Enfield EN3 44 E5
Hounslow TW5 122 D6
Northfields, SW18 148 D4
Northfields Ind Est, Wem. HA0 106 A1
Northfields Rd, W3 106 B5
NORTH FINCHLEY, N12 57 G5
North Flockton St, SE16 29 H3
North Gdn, E14 *off Westferry Circ* 133 J1
North Gdns, SW19 167 G7
North Gate, NW8 7 G2
Northgate Ct, SW9 *off Canterbury Cres* 151 G3
Northgate Dr, NW9 70 E6
Northgate Ind Pk, Rom. RM5 83 F2
North Glade, The, Bex. DA5 159 F7
North Gower St, NW1 9 G4
North Grn, NW9 *off Clayton Fld* 55 E7
North Gro, N6 74 A7
N15 76 A5
NORTH HARROW, Har. HA2 67 G6
North Hatton Rd, Houns. (Lon.Hthrw Air.) TW6 141 G1
North Hill, N6 73 J6
North Hill Av, N6 74 A6
NORTH HYDE, Sthl. UB2 123 E4
North Hyde Gdns, Hayes UB3 122 A4
North Hyde La, Houns. TW5 123 E5
Southall UB2 123 E5
North Hyde Rd, Hayes UB3 121 J3
Northiam, N12 56 D3
Northiam St, E9 113 E1
Northington St, WC1 10 C6
NORTH KENSINGTON, W10 107 J6
Northlands Av, Orp. BR6 207 H4
Northlands St, SE5 151 J2
North La, Tedd. TW11 162 C6
North Lo Cl, SW15 148 A5
North London Business Pk, N11 57 J2
North Mall, N9 *off Edmonton Grn Shop Cen* 60 E2
North Ms, WC1 10 D6
Northolm, Edg. HA8 54 D4
Northolme Gdns, Edg. HA8 70 A1
Northolme Ri, Orp. BR6 207 H2
Northolme Rd, N5 93 J4
NORTHOLT, UB5 85 F7
Northolt, N17 76 A2
Northolt Av, Ruis. HA4 84 B5
Northolt Gdns, Grnf. UB6 86 C5
Northolt Rd, Har. HA2 85 H4
Hounslow (Lon.Hthrw Air.) TW6 140 A1
Northolt Trd Est, Nthlt. UB5 85 H7
Northover, Brom. BR1 173 F3
North Par, Chess. KT9 195 H5
Edgware HA8 *off Mollison Way* 70 A2
North Pk, SE9 156 C6
North Pas, SW18 148 D4
North Pl, Mitch. CR4 167 J7
Teddington TW11 162 C6
Northpoint, Brom. BR1 *off Sherman Rd* 191 G1
Northpoint Cl, Sutt. SM1 199 F3
Northpoint Sq, NW1 92 D6
North Pole La, Kes. BR2 205 F6
North Pole Rd, W10 107 J5
Northport St, N1 112 A1
North Ride, W2 15 G6
North Ri, W2 *off St. Georges Flds* 15 H4
North Rd, N6 74 A7
N7 92 E6
N9 60 E1
SE18 137 H4
SW19 167 F6
W5 125 G3
Belvedere DA17 139 H3
Brentford TW8 125 H6
Bromley BR1 191 H1
Edgware HA8 70 B1
Feltham TW14 141 G6
Ilford IG3 99 H2
Richmond TW9 146 A3
Romford (Chad.Hth) RM6 82 E5
Southall UB1 103 G7
Surbiton KT6 181 G6
West Drayton UB7 120 C3
West Wickham BR4 204 B1
Northrop Rd, Houns. (Lon.Hthrw Air.) TW6 141 H1
North Row, W1 16 A5
North Several, SE3 *off Orchard Rd* 154 D2
NORTH SHEEN, Rich. TW9 146 A2
Northside Rd, Brom. BR1 *off Mitchell Way* 191 G1
North Side Wandsworth Common, SW18 149 F5
Northspur Rd, Sutt. SM1 198 D3
North Sq, N9 *off Edmonton Grn Shop Cen* 60 E2
NW11 72 D5
Northstead Rd, SW2 169 G2
North St, E13 115 G2
NW4 71 J5
SW4 150 C3
Barking IG11 99 E6
Bexleyheath DA7 159 G4
Bromley BR1 191 G1
Carshalton SM5 199 J3
Isleworth TW7 144 D3
North St Pas, E13 115 H2
North Tenter St, E1 21 G4

North Ter, SW3 . . . . .23 G6
Northumberland All, EC3 . .21 E4
Northumberland Av, E12 . . .97 J1
WC2 . . . . .26 A1
Enfield EN1 . . . . .45 E1
Isleworth TW7 . . . . .144 C1
Welling DA16 . . . . .157 G4
Northumberland Cl,
Erith DA8 . . . . .139 J7
Staines (Stanw.) TW19 .140 B6
Northumberland Cres,
Felt. TW14 . . . . .141 H6
Northumberland Gdns,
N9 . . . . .60 C3
Bromley BR1 . . . . .192 D4
Isleworth TW7 . . . . .124 D7
Mitcham CR4 . . . . .186 D5
Northumberland Gro, N17 .60 E7
NORTHUMBERLAND HEATH, Erith DA8 . . . . .139 J7
Northumberland Pk, N17 . .60 C7
Erith DA8 . . . . .139 J7
Northumberland Pk Ind Est, N17
off Willoughby La 61 E7
Northumberland Pl, W2 . . .108 D6
Richmond TW10 . . . . . . .145 G5
Northumberland Rd, E6 . . .116 B6
E17 . . . . .78 A7
Barnet (New Barn.)
EN5 . . . . .41 F6
Harrow HA2 . . . . .67 F5
Northumberland Row,
Twick. TW2
off Colne Rd 162 B1
Northumberland St, WC2 . .26 A1
Northumberland Way,
Erith DA8 . . . . .159 J1
Northumbria St, E14 . . . . .114 A6
North Verbena Gdns, W6
off St. Peter's Sq 127 G5
Northview, N7 . . . . .93 E3
North Vw, SW19 . . . . .165 H5
W5 . . . . .105 F4
Pinner HA5 . . . . .66 C7
Northview Cres, NW10 . . . .89 F4
North Vw Dr, Wdf.Grn.
IG8 . . . . .80 A2
North Vw Rd, N8 . . . . .74 D3
North Vil, NW1 . . . . .92 D6
North Wk, W2 . . . . .14 C6
Croydon (New Adgtn)
CR0 . . . . .204 B5
North Way, N9 . . . . .61 F2
N11 . . . . .58 C6
NW9 . . . . .70 B3
Northway, NW11 . . . . .72 E5
Morden SM4 . . . . .184 B3
North Way, Pnr. HA5 . . . . . .66 C3
Northway, Wall. SM6 . . . . .200 C4
Northway Circ, NW7 . . . . . .54 D4
Northway Cres, NW7 . . . . . .54 D4
Northway Ho, N20 . . . . .57 F1
Northway Rd, SE5 . . . . . . .151 J3
Croydon CR0 . . . . .188 C6
Northways Par, NW3
off Finchley Rd 91 G7
Northweald La, Kings.T.
KT2 . . . . .163 G5
NORTH WEMBLEY, Wem.
HA0 . . . . .87 E2
Northwest Pl, N1 . . . . .11 F1
North Wf Rd, W2 . . . . .14 E2
Northwick Av, Harrow
HA3 . . . . .68 D6
Northwick Circle, Har.
HA3 . . . . .69 F6
Northwick Cl, NW8 . . . . .6 E5
Harrow HA1 . . . . .86 E1
Northwick Pk Rd, Har.
HA1 . . . . .68 C6
Northwick Rd,
Watford WD19 . . . . .50 C4
Wembley HA0 . . . . .105 G1
Northwick Ter, NW8 . . . . .6 E5
Northwick Wk, Har. HA1 . . .68 C7
Northwold Dr, Pnr. HA5
off Cuckoo Hill 66 C3
Northwold Est, E5 . . . . .94 D2
Northwold Rd, E5 . . . . .94 C2
N16 . . . . .94 C2
North Wd Ct, SE25
off Regina Rd 188 D3
Northwood Gdns, N12 . . . .57 G5
Greenford UB6 . . . . .86 C5
Ilford IG5 . . . . .80 D4
Northwood Hall, N6 . . . . . . .74 C7
Northwood Ho, SE27 . . . .170 A4
Northwood Pl, Erith
DA18 . . . . .139 F3
Northwood Rd, N6 . . . . .74 B7
SE23 . . . . .171 J1
Carshalton SM5 . . . . . . .200 A6
Hounslow
(Lon.Hthrw Air.) TW6 . .140 A1
Thornton Heath CR7 . . .187 H2
Northwood Twr, E17 . . . . . .78 C4
Northwood Way, SE19
off Roman Ri 170 A6
Northwood HA6 . . . . .50 A7
NORTH WOOLWICH, E16 . .136 B2
★ **North Woolwich Old Sta Mus**, E16 . . . . . . .136 D2
North Woolwich Rd, E16 . .135 G1
North Woolwich Rbt, E16 .135 J1
North Worple Way, SW14 .146 D3
Norton Av, Surb. KT5 . . . .182 B7
Norton Cl, E4 . . . . .62 A5
Borehamwood WD6 . . . .38 A1
Enfield EN1
off Brick La 44 E2
Norton Folgate, E1 . . . . .21 E1
Norton Gdns, SW16 . . . . .186 E2
Norton Rd, E10 . . . . .95 J1
Wembley HA0 . . . . .87 G6
Norval Rd, Wem. HA0 . . . . .86 E2
Norway Gate, SE16 . . . . . .133 H3
Norway Pl, E14
off Commercial Rd . . .113 J6
Norway St, SE10 . . . . .134 B6
Norwich Cres, Rom.
(Chad.Hth) RM6 . . . . .82 B5
Norwich Ho, E14
off Cordelia St 114 B6
Norwich Ms, Ilf. IG3
off Ashgrove Rd 100 A1
Norwich Pl, Bexh.
DA6 . . . . .159 G4
Norwich Rd, E7 . . . . .97 G5
Dagenham RM9 . . . . . . .119 G2
Greenford UB6 . . . . .103 H1
Thornton Heath CR7 . . .187 J3
Norwich St, EC4 . . . . .19 E3
Norwich Wk, Edg. HA8 . . . .54 C7
NORWOOD, SE19 . . . . .170 A6
Norwood Av, Wem. HA0 . .105 J1
Norwood Cl, NW2 . . . . .90 B3
Southall UB2 . . . . .123 G4
Twickenham TW2
off Fourth Cross Rd . . .162 A2
Norwood Cres, Houns. (Lon.Hthrw Air.) TW6 . . . . .141 F1
Norwood Dr, Har. HA2 . . . .67 F6
Norwood Gdns, Hayes
UB4 . . . . .102 C4
Southall UB2 . . . . .123 F4
NORWOOD GREEN, Sthl.
UB2 . . . . .123 G4
Norwood Grn Rd, Sthl.
UB2 . . . . .123 G4
Norwood High St, SE27 . .169 H3
NORWOOD NEW TOWN,
SE19 . . . . .169 J6
Norwood Pk Rd, SE27 . . . .169 J5
Norwood Rd, SE24 . . . . . .169 H1
SE27 . . . . .169 H2
Southall UB2 . . . . .123 F4
Norwood Ter, Sthl. UB2
off Tentelow La 123 H4
Notley St, SE5 . . . . .36 B7
Notre Dame Est, SW4 . . . .150 C4
Notson Rd, SE25 . . . . .188 E4
Notting Barn Rd, W10 . . . .108 A4
Nottingdale Sq, W11
off Wilsham St 128 B1
Nottingham Av, E16 . . . . . .115 J5
Nottingham Ct, WC2 . . . . . .18 A4
Nottingham Pl, W1 . . . . .8 B6
Nottingham Rd, E10 . . . . . .78 C6
SW17 . . . . .167 J1
Isleworth TW7 . . . . .144 C2
South Croydon CR2 . . . .201 J4
Nottingham St, W1 . . . . . . .16 B1
Nottingham Ter, NW1 . . . . . .8 B6
NOTTING HILL, W11 . . . . . .108 B7
Notting Hill Gate, W11 . . . .128 D1
Nova, E14 *off Newton Pl* . .134 A4
Nova Ms, Sutt. SM3 . . . . . .198 B1
Novar Cl, Orp. BR6 . . . . . . .193 J7
Nova Rd, Croy. CR0 . . . . . .201 H1
Novar Rd, SE9 . . . . .175 F1
Novello St, SW6 . . . . .148 D1
Novello Way, Borwd. WD6 .38 D1
Nowell Rd, SW13 . . . . .127 G6
Nower Hill, Pnr. HA5 . . . . . .67 F4
Noyna Rd, SW17 . . . . .167 J3
Nubia Way, Brom. BR1 . . . .173 E3
Nuding Cl, SE13 . . . . .154 A3
Nugent Rd, N19 . . . . .93 E1
SE25 . . . . .188 C3
Nugents Ct, Pnr. HA5
off St. Thomas' Dr 67 E1
Nugents Pk, Pnr. HA5 . . . . .67 E1
Nugent Ter, NW8 . . . . .6 D2
Numa Ct, Brent. TW8
off Justin Cl 125 G7
Nun Ct, EC2 . . . . .20 B3
Nuneaton Rd, Dag.
RM9 . . . . .100 D7
Nuneham Est, SW16
off Prentis Rd 168 D4
NUNHEAD, SE15 . . . . .153 F3
Nunhead Cres, SE15 . . . . .152 E3
Nunhead Est, SE15 . . . . . .152 E4
Nunhead Grn, SE15 . . . . . .153 E3
Nunhead Gro, SE15 . . . . . .153 E3
Nunhead La, SE15 . . . . . . .152 E3
Nunhead Pas, SE15
off Peckham Rye 152 D3
Nunnington Cl, SE9 . . . . . .174 B3
Nunns Rd, Enf. EN2 . . . . . . .43 J2
Nupton Dr, Barn. EN5 . . . . .39 J6
Nurse Cl, Edg. HA8
off Gervase Rd 70 C1
Nursery Av, N3 . . . . .73 F2
Bexleyheath DA7 . . . . . .159 F3
Croydon CR0 . . . . .203 G2
Nursery Cl, SE4 . . . . .153 J2
SW15 . . . . .148 A4
Croydon CR0 . . . . .203 G2
Enfield EN3 . . . . .45 G1
Feltham TW14 . . . . .142 B7
Orpington BR6 . . . . .193 J7
Romford RM6 . . . . .82 D6
Watford WD19 . . . . .50 B1
Woodford Green IG8 . . . .63 H5
Nursery Ct, N17
off Nursery St 60 C7
Nursery Gdns, Chis.
BR7 . . . . .174 E6
Enfield EN3 . . . . .45 G1
Hampton TW12
off Hanworth Rd 161 F4
Hounslow TW4 . . . . .143 F5
Nursery La, E2 . . . . .112 C1
E7 . . . . .97 G6
W10 . . . . .107 J5
Nurserymans Rd, N11 . . . . .58 A2
Nursery Rd, E9
off Morning La 95 F6
N2 . . . . .73 G1
N14 . . . . .42 C7
SW9 . . . . .151 F4
Loughton IG10 . . . . .47 J5
Pinner HA5 . . . . .66 C3
Sutton SM1 . . . . .199 F4
Thornton Heath CR7 . . .188 A4
Nursery Rd Merton,
SW19 . . . . .184 E2
Nursery Rd Mitcham,
Mitch. CR4 . . . . .185 H3
Nursery Rd Wimbledon,
SW19 *off Worple Rd* . . .166 B7
Nursery Row, SE17 . . . . . . .36 B2
Barnet EN5
off St. Albans Rd 40 B3
Nursery St, N17 . . . . .60 C7
Nursery Wk, NW4 . . . . .71 H3
Nurstead Rd, Erith DA8 . . .139 G7
Nutbourne St, W10 . . . . . .108 B3
Nutbrook St, SE15 . . . . . . .152 D3
Nutbrowne Rd, Dag.
RM9 . . . . .119 F1
Nutcroft Rd, SE15 . . . . . . .132 E7
Nutfield Cl, N18 . . . . .60 D6
Carshalton SM5 . . . . . . .199 H3
Nutfield Gdns, Ilf. IG3 . . . . .99 J2
Northolt UB5 . . . . .102 C2
Nutfield Rd, E15 . . . . .96 C4
NW2 . . . . .89 G2
SE22 . . . . .152 C5
Thornton Heath CR7 . . .187 H4
Nutfield Way, Orp. BR6 . . .206 D2
Nutford Pl, W1 . . . . .15 H3
Nuthatch Gdns, SE28 . . . .137 G2
Nuthurst Av, SW2 . . . . . . .169 F2
Nutley Ter, NW3 . . . . .91 F6
Nutmead Cl, Bex. DA5 . . .177 J1
Nutmeg Cl, E16
off Cranberry La 115 E4
Nutmeg La, E14 . . . . .114 D6
Nuttall St, N1 . . . . .12 E1
Nutter La, E11 . . . . .79 J6
Nutt Gro, Edg. HA8 . . . . . . .53 G2
Nutt St, SE15 . . . . .37 G7
Nutwell St, SW17 . . . . . . .167 H5
Nuxley Rd, Belv. DA17 . . . .139 F6
Nyanza St, SE18 . . . . .137 G6
Nye Bevan Est, E5 . . . . .95 G3
Nylands Av, Rich. TW9 . . . .146 A1
Nymans Gdns, SW20
off Hidcote Gdns 183 H3
Nynehead St, SE14 . . . . . .133 H7
Nyon Gro, SE6 . . . . .171 J2
Nyssa Cl, Wdf.Grn. IG8
off Gwynne Pk Av 64 C6
Nyton Cl, N19
off Courtauld Rd 92 E1

O

★ **O2, The**, SE10 . . . . .134 E1
O2 Shop Cen, NW3
off Finchley Rd 91 F6
Oak Apple Ct, SE12 . . . . . .173 G2
Oak Av, N8 . . . . .74 E4
N10 . . . . .58 B7
N17 . . . . .60 A7
Croydon CR0 . . . . .204 A2
Hampton TW12 . . . . .161 E5
Oak Av, Hounslow TW5 . . .122 D7
West Drayton UB7 . . . . .120 D3
Oak Bk, Croy.
(New Adgtn) CR0 . . . . . .204 C6
Oakbank Av, Walt. KT12 . . .179 F7
Oakbank Gro, SE24 . . . . . .151 J4
Oakbark Ho, Brent. TW8
off High St 125 F7
Oakbrook Cl, Brom. BR1 . .173 H4
Oakbury Rd, SW6 . . . . . . .149 E2
Oak Cl, N14 . . . . .42 B7
Sutton SM1 . . . . .199 F2
Oakcombe Cl, N.Mal.
KT3 . . . . .182 E1
Oak Cottage Cl, SE6 . . . . .173 F1
Oak Cres, E16 . . . . .115 E5
Oakcroft Cl, Pnr. HA5 . . . . . .66 B2
Oakcroft Rd, SE13 . . . . . . .154 D2
Chessington KT9 . . . . . .195 J4
Oakcroft Vil, Chess. KT9 . .195 J4
Oakdale, N14 . . . . .58 B1
Oakdale Av, Har. HA3 . . . . .69 H5
Northwood HA6 . . . . .66 A2
Oakdale Cl, Wat. WD19 . . . .50 C4
Oakdale Gdns, E4 . . . . .62 C5
Oakdale Rd, E7 . . . . .97 H7
E11 . . . . .96 D2
E18 . . . . .79 H2
N4 . . . . .75 J6
SE15 . . . . .153 F3
SW16 . . . . .169 E5
Watford WD19 . . . . .50 C3
Oakdale Way, Mitch.
CR4 . . . . .186 A7
Oakdene, SE15
off Carlton Gro 152 E1
Oak Dene, W13
off The Dene 104 E5
Oakdene Av, Chis. BR7 . . .174 D5
Erith DA8 . . . . .139 J6
Thames Ditton KT7 . . . .194 D1
Oakdene Cl, Pnr. HA5 . . . . .51 F7
Oakdene Dr, Surb. KT5 . . .182 C7
Oakdene Ms, Sutt. SM3 . . .198 C1
Oakdene Pk, N3 . . . . .56 C7
Oakdene Rd, Orp. BR5 . . .193 J5
Oakden St, SE11 . . . . .35 F1
Oake Ct, SW15
off Portinscale Rd 148 B5
Oaken Dr, Esher (Clay.)
KT10 . . . . .194 C6
Oakenholt Ho, SE2
off Hartslock Dr 138 D2
Oaken La, Esher (Clay.)
KT10 . . . . .194 B5
Oakenshaw Cl, Surb.
KT6 . . . . .181 H7
Oakes Cl, E6
off Savage Gdns 116 C6
Oakeshott Av, N6 . . . . .92 A2
Oakey La, SE1 . . . . .27 E5
Oak Fm, Borwd. WD6 . . . . .38 C5
Oakfield, E4 . . . . .62 B5
Oakfield Av, Har. HA3 . . . . .69 E3
Oakfield Cl, N.Mal. KT3
off Blakes La 183 F5
Oakfield Ct, N8 . . . . .74 E7
NW2 *off Hendon Way* . . .72 A7
Borehamwood WD6 . . . .38 B3
Oakfield Gdns, N18 . . . . . . .60 B4
SE19 . . . . .170 B5
Beckenham BR3 . . . . . . .190 A5
Carshalton SM5 . . . . . . .199 H1
Greenford UB6 . . . . .104 A4
Oakfield La, Kes. BR2 . . . .205 J4
Oakfield Lo, Ilf. IG1
off Albert Rd 99 E3
Oakfield Rd, E6 . . . . .116 B1
E17 . . . . .77 H2
N3 . . . . .72 E1
N4 . . . . .75 G6
N14 . . . . .58 E3
SE20 . . . . .171 E7
SW19 . . . . .166 A3
Croydon CR0 . . . . .201 J1
Ilford IG1 . . . . .99 E2
Oakfield Rd Ind Est, SE20
off Oakfield Rd 171 E7
Oakfields Rd, NW11 . . . . . . .72 B6
Oakfield St, SW10 . . . . .30 C5
Oakford Rd, NW5 . . . . .92 C4
Oak Gdns, Croy. CR0 . . . . .204 A2
Edgware HA8 . . . . .70 C2
Oak Gro, NW2 . . . . .90 B4
Ruislip HA4 . . . . .66 B7
Sunbury-on-Thames
TW16 . . . . .160 B7
West Wickham BR4 . . . .204 C2
Oak Gro Rd, SE20 . . . . . . .189 F1
Oakhall Ct, E11 . . . . .79 H6
Oak Hall Rd, E11 . . . . .79 H6
Oakham Cl, SE6
off Rutland Wk 171 J2
Barnet EN4 . . . . .41 J3
Oakham Dr, Bromley
BR2 . . . . .191 F4
Oakhampton Rd, NW7 . . . .56 A7

Oakhill, Esher (Clay.) KT10 194 D6
Oak Hill, Surb. KT6 181 H7
Woodford Green IG8 62 D7
Oakhill Av, NW3 90 E4
Pinner HA5 66 E2
Oak Hill Cl, Wdf.Grn. IG8 62 D7
Oakhill Ct, SW19 166 A7
Oak Hill Cres, Surb. KT6 181 H7
Woodford Green IG8 62 D7
Oakhill Dr, Surb. KT6 181 H7
Oak Hill Gdns, Wdf.Grn. IG8 79 E1
Oak Hill Gro, Surb. KT6 181 H6
Oak Hill Pk, NW3 91 E4
Oak Hill Pk Ms, NW3 91 F4
Oakhill Path, Surb. KT6 181 H6
Oakhill Pl, SW15 *off Oakhill Rd* 148 D5
Oakhill Rd, SW15 148 C5
SW16 187 E1
Beckenham BR3 190 C2
Orpington BR6 207 J1
Oak Hill Rd, Surb. KT6 181 H6
Oakhill Rd, Sutt. SM1 199 E3
Oak Hill Way, NW3 91 F4
Oak Ho, NW3 *off Maitland Pk Vil* 91 J6
Oakhouse Rd, Bexh. DA6 159 G5
Oakhurst Av, Barn. (E.Barn.) EN4 41 H7
Bexleyheath DA7 138 E7
Oakhurst Cl, E17 78 E4
Chislehurst BR7 192 C1
Ilford IG6 81 F1
Teddington TW11 162 B5
Oakhurst Gdns, E4 63 F1
E17 78 E4
Bexleyheath DA7 139 E7
Oakhurst Gro, SE22 152 D4
Oakhurst Rd, Epsom KT19 196 C6
Oakington Av, Har. HA2 67 G7
Hayes UB3 121 G4
Wembley HA9 87 J3
Oakington Cl, Sun. TW16 178 C2
Oakington Dr, Sun. TW16 178 C2
Oakington Manor Dr, Wem. HA9 88 A5
Oakington Rd, W9 108 D4
Oakington Way, N8 75 E6
Oakland Pl, Buck.H. IG9 63 G2
Oakland Rd, E15 96 D4
Oaklands, N21 59 F2
Twickenham TW2 143 J7
Oaklands Av, N9 44 E6
Esher KT10 194 A1
Isleworth TW7 124 C6
Sidcup DA15 157 J7
Thornton Heath CR7 187 G4
Watford WD19 50 B1
West Wickham BR4 204 B3
Oaklands Cl, Bexh. DA6 159 F5
Chessington KT9 195 F4
Orpington BR5 193 H6
Oaklands Ct, W12 *off Uxbridge Rd* 127 H1
Wembley HA0 87 G5
Oaklands Est, SW4 150 C6
Oaklands Gro, W12 127 G1
Oaklands La, Barn. EN5 39 H4
Oaklands Ms, NW2 *off Oaklands Rd* 90 A4
Oaklands Pk Av, Ilf. IG1 *off High Rd* 99 G2
Oaklands Pl, SW4 *off St. Alphonsus Rd* 150 C4
Oaklands Rd, N20 40 C7
NW2 90 A4
SW14 146 D3
W7 124 C2
Bexleyheath DA6 159 F4
Bromley BR1 173 E7
Oaklands Way, Wall. SM6 200 D7
Oakland Way, Epsom KT19 196 D6
Oak La, E14 113 J7
N2 73 G2
N11 58 D6
Isleworth TW7 144 B4
Twickenham TW1 144 D7
Woodford Green IG8 63 F4
Oakleafe Gdns, Ilford IG6 80 E3
Oaklea Pas, Kings.T. KT1 181 G3
Oakleigh Av, N20 57 G2
Edgware HA8 70 B2
Surbiton KT6 196 A1
Oakleigh Cl, N20 57 J3
Oakleigh Ct, Barnet EN4 41 H6
Edgware HA8 70 C2
Oakleigh Cres, N20 57 H2
Oakleigh Gdns, N20 57 F1
Edgware HA8 53 J5
Orpington BR6 207 H4
Oakleigh Ms, N20 *off Oakleigh Rd N* 57 F2
OAKLEIGH PARK, N20 57 G1
Oakleigh Pk Av, Chis. BR7 192 D1
Oakleigh Pk N, N20 57 G1
Oakleigh Pk S, N20 57 H2
Oakleigh Rd, Pnr. HA5 51 F6
Oakleigh Rd N, N20 57 G2
Oakleigh Rd S, N11 58 A3
Oakleigh Way, Mitch. CR4 186 B1
Surbiton KT6 196 A1
Oakley Av, W5 106 A7
Barking IG11 99 J7
Croydon CR0 201 E4
Oakley Cl, E4 62 C3
E6 *off Northumberland Rd* 116 B6
W7 104 B7
Isleworth TW7 144 A1
Oakley Ct, Loug. IG10 *off Hillyfields* 48 D2
Mitcham CR4 186 A7
Oakley Cres, EC1 11 H2
Oakley Dr, SE9 175 G1
SE13 154 D6
Bromley BR2 206 B3
Oakley Gdns, N8 75 F5
SW3 31 H5
Oakley Pk, Bex. DA5 158 C7
Oakley Pl, SE1 37 F4
Oakley Rd, N1 94 A7
SE25 188 E5
Bromley BR2 206 B3
Harrow HA1 68 B6
Oakley Sq, NW1 9 G2
Oakley St, SW3 31 G5
Oakley Wk, W6 128 A6
Oakley Yd, E2 13 G5
Oak Lo Av, Chig. IG7 65 G5
Oak Lo Cl, Stan. HA7 *off Dennis La* 53 F5
Oak Lo Dr, W.Wick. BR4 190 B7
Oak Lo Ms, W4 126 E5
Oaklodge Way, NW7 55 F5
Oak Manor Dr, Wem. HA9 *off Oakington Manor Dr* 87 J5
Oakmead Av, Brom. BR2 191 G6
Oakmeade, Pnr. HA5 51 G6
Oakmead Gdns, Edg. HA8 54 D4
Oakmead Pl, Mitch. CR4 185 H1
Oakmead Rd, SW12 168 A1
Croydon CR0 186 D6
Oakmere Rd, SE2 138 A6
Oakmont Pl, Orp. BR6 207 G1
Oakmoor Way, Chig. IG7 65 H5
Oak Pk Gdns, SW19 148 A7
Oak Pk Ms, N16 *off Brooke Rd* 94 C3
Oak Pl, SW18 *off East Hill* 149 E5
Oakridge Dr, N2 73 G3
Oakridge La, Brom. BR1 172 D5
Oakridge Rd, Brom. BR1 172 D4
Oak Ri, Buck.H. IG9 64 A3
Oak Rd, W5 *off The Broadway* 105 G7
Erith (Northumb.Hth) DA8 139 J7
New Malden KT3 182 D2
Oak Row, SW16 186 C2
Oaks, The, N12 57 E4
SE18 137 F5
Morden SM4 184 B4
Watford WD19 50 C1
Woodford Green IG8 63 E6
Oaks Av, SE19 170 B5
Feltham TW13 160 E2
Romford RM5 83 J2
Worcester Park KT4 197 H3
Oaksford Av, SE26 170 E3
Oaks Gro, E4 62 E2
Oakshade Rd, Brom. BR1 172 D4
Oakshaw Rd, SW18 149 E7
Oakside Ct, Ilf. IG6 81 G1
Oaks La, Croy. CR0 203 F3
Ilford IG2 81 H5
Oaks Pavilion Ms, SE19 170 B4
Oaks Rd, Croy. CR0 202 E5
Staines (Stanw.) TW19 140 A6
Oaks Shop Cen, W3 *off High St* 126 C1
Oak St, Rom. RM7 83 J5
Oaks Way, Cars. SM5 199 J7
Surbiton (Long Dit.) KT6 195 G2
Oakthorpe Rd, N13 59 G5
Oaktree Av, N13 59 H3
Oak Tree Cl, W5 *off Pinewood Gro* 105 F6
Loughton IG10 49 F1
Stanmore HA7 53 F7
Oak Tree Dell, NW9 70 C5
Oak Tree Dr, N20 57 E1
Oak Tree Gdns, Brom. BR1 173 H5
Oaktree Gro, Ilf. IG1 99 G5
Oak Tree Rd, NW8 7 F4
Oakview Gdns, N2 73 G4
Oakview Gro, Croy. CR0 203 H1
Oakview Rd, SE6 172 B5
Oak Village, NW5 92 A4
Oak Wk, Wall. SM6 *off Helios Rd* 200 A1
Oak Way, N14 42 B7
Oakway, SW20 183 J4
Oak Way, W3 126 E1
Oakway, Brom. BR2 190 D2
Oak Way, Croy. CR0 189 G6
Oakway Cl, Bex. DA5 159 E6
Oakways, SE9 156 E6
OAKWOOD, N14 42 D6
Oakwood Av, N14 42 D7
Beckenham BR3 190 C2
Borehamwood WD6 38 B4
Bromley BR2 191 H3
Mitcham CR4 185 G2
Southall UB1 103 G7
Oakwood Cl, N14 42 C6
SE13 154 D7
Chislehurst BR7 174 C6
Woodford Green IG8 *off Green Wk* 64 B6
Oakwood Ct, W14 128 C3
Oakwood Cres, N21 43 E6
Greenford UB6 86 D6
Oakwood Dr, SE19 170 A6
Edgware HA8 54 C6
Oakwood Gdns, Ilford IG3 99 J2
Orpington BR6 207 F2
Sutton SM1 198 D2
Oakwood Hill, Loug. IG10 48 C6
Oakwood Hill Ind Est, Loug. IG10 49 E5
Oakwood La, W14 128 C3
Oakwood Pk Rd, N14 42 D7
Oakwood Pl, Croy. CR0 187 G6
Oakwood Rd, NW11 72 E5
SW20 183 G1
Croydon CR0 187 G6
Orpington BR6 207 F2
Pinner HA5 66 B2
Oakwood Vw, N14 42 D6
Oakworth Rd, W10 107 J5
Oarsman Pl, E.Mol. KT8 180 B4
Oates Cl, Brom. BR2 190 D3
Oatfield Ho, N15 76 B6
Oatfield Rd, Orp. BR6 207 J1
Oatland Ri, E17 77 H2
Oatlands Rd, Enf. EN3 45 F1
Oat La, EC2 19 J3
Oban Cl, E13 115 J4
Oban Ho, E14 *off Oban St* 114 D6
Barking IG11 *off Wheelers Cross* 117 G2
Oban Rd, E13 115 J3
SE25 188 A4
Oban St, E14 114 D6
Oberon Cl, Borwd. WD6 38 C1
Oberstein Rd, SW11 149 G4
Oborne Cl, SE24 151 H5
O'Brien Ho, E2 *off Smart St* 113 G3
Observatory Gdns, W8 128 D2
Observatory Ms, E14 *off Storers Quay* 134 D4
Observatory Rd, SW14 146 C4
Occupation La, SE18 156 E1
W5 125 G4
Occupation Rd, SE17 35 J3
W13 124 E2
Ocean Est, E1 113 G4
Ocean St, E1 113 G5
Ocean Wf, E14 133 J2
Ockendon Ms, N1 *off Ockendon Rd* 94 A6
Ockendon Rd, N1 94 A6
Ockham Dr, Orp. BR5 176 A7
Ockley Ct, Sutt. SM1 *off Oakhill Rd* 199 F4
Ockley Rd, SW16 168 E3
Croydon CR0 187 F7
Octagon Arc, EC2 20 D2
Octavia Cl, Mitch. CR4 185 H5
Octavia Ms, W9 *off Bravington Rd* 108 C4
Octavia Rd, Islw. TW7 144 C2
Octavia St, SW11 149 H1
Octavia Way, SE28 *off Booth Cl* 118 B7
Octavius St, SE8 134 A7
Odard Rd, W.Mol. KT8 *off Down St* 179 G4
Oddesey Rd, Borwd. WD6 38 B1
Odell Cl, Bark. IG11 99 J7
Odell Wk, SE13 *off Bankside Av* 154 B3
Odeon, The, Bark. IG11 *off Longbridge Rd* 99 G7
Odessa Rd, E7 97 F3
NW10 107 G2
Odessa St, SE16 133 J2
Odger St, SW11 149 J2
Odhams Wk, WC2 18 B4
Odyssey Business Pk, Ruis. HA4 84 B5
Offa's Mead, E9 *off Lindisfarne Way* 95 H4
Offenbach Ho, E2 113 G2
Offenham Rd, SE9 174 C4
Offers Ct, Kings.T. KT1 *off Winery La* 181 J3
Offerton Rd, SW4 150 C3
Offham Slope, N12 56 C5
Offley Pl, Islw. TW7 144 A2
Offley Rd, SW9 35 E7
Offord Cl, N17 60 D6
Offord Rd, N1 93 F7
Offord St, N1 93 F7
Ogilby St, SE18 136 C4
Oglander Rd, SE15 152 C4
Ogle St, W1 17 F1
Oglethorpe Rd, Dag. RM10 101 F3
Ohio Bldg, SE13 *off Deals Gateway* 154 B1
Ohio Rd, E13 115 F4
Oil Mill La, W6 127 G5
Okeburn Rd, SW17 168 A5
Okehampton Cl, N12 57 G5
Okehampton Cres, Well. DA16 158 B1
Okehampton Rd, NW10 107 J1
Olaf St, W11 108 A7
Oldacre Ms, SW12 *off Balham Gro* 150 B7
★ **Old Admiralty Bldg** (M.o.D.), SW1 25 J2
Old Bailey, EC4 19 H4
Old Barge Ho All, SE1 *off Upper Grd* 27 F1
Old Barn Cl, Sutt. SM2 198 B7
Old Barrack Yd, SW1 24 B3
Old Barrowfield, E15 *off Stephen's Rd* 115 F1
Old Bellgate Pl, E14 134 A3
Oldberry Rd, Edg. HA8 54 D6
Old Bethnal Grn Rd, E2 13 H3
OLD BEXLEY, Bex. DA5 159 H7
Old Bexley Business Pk, Bex. DA5 159 H7
Old Billingsgate Wk, EC3 *off Lower Thames St* 20 D6
Old Bond St, W1 17 F6
Oldborough Rd, Wem. HA0 87 F2
Old Brewers Yd, WC2 18 A4
Old Brewery Ms, NW3 *off Hampstead High St* 91 G4
Old Br Cl, Nthlt. UB5 103 G2
Old Br St, Kings.T. (Hmptn W.) KT1 181 G2
Old Broad St, EC2 20 C4
Old Bromley Rd, Brom. BR1 172 D5
Old Brompton Rd, SW5 128 D5
SW7 128 D5
Old Bldgs, WC2 18 E3
Old Burlington St, W1 17 F5
Oldbury Pl, W1 16 C1
Oldbury Rd, Enf. EN1 44 D2
Old Canal Ms, SE15 37 G4
Old Castle St, E1 21 F2
Old Cavendish St, W1 16 D3
Old Change Ct, EC4 *off Carter La* 19 J4
Old Chelsea Ms, SW3 31 F6
Old Ch La, NW9 88 C2
Greenford (Perivale) UB6 *off Perivale La* 104 D3
Stanmore HA7 53 F7
Old Ch Rd, E1 113 G6
E4 62 A4
Old Ch St, SW3 31 F4
Old Claygate La, Esher (Clay.) KT10 194 D6
Old Clem Sq, SE18 *off Kempt St* 136 D6
Old Coal Yd, SE28 *off Pettman Cres* 137 G4
Old Compton St, W1 17 H5
Old Cote Dr, Houns. TW5 123 G6
Old Ct Pl, W8 22 A3
★ **Old Curiosity Shop**, WC2 18 C3
Old Dairy Ms, SW12 168 A1
Old Dairy Sq, N21 *off Wades Hill* 43 G7
Old Deer Pk Gdns, Rich. TW9 145 H3
Old Devonshire Rd, SW12 150 B7

Old Dock Cl, Rich. TW9
off Watcombe Cotts . . .126 A6
Old Dover Rd, SE3 . . . . .135 G7
Old Fm Av, N14 . . . . .42 C7
Sidcup DA15 . . . . .175 G1
Old Fm Cl, Houns. TW4 . . .143 F4
Old Fm Pas, Hmptn.
TW12 . . . . .179 J1
Old Fm Rd, N2 . . . . .73 G1
Hampton TW12 . . . . .161 F6
West Drayton UB7 . . . . .120 A2
Old Fm Rd E, Sid. DA15 . .176 A2
Old Fm Rd W, Sid. DA15 . .175 J2
Oldfield Cl, Brom. BR1 . . . .192 C4
Greenford UB6 . . . . .86 B5
Stanmore HA7 . . . . .52 D5
Oldfield Fm Gdns, Grnf.
UB6 . . . . .104 A1
Oldfield Gro, SE16 . . . . . . .133 G4
Oldfield La N, Grnf.
UB6 . . . . .86 B6
Oldfield La S, Grnf. UB6 . .103 J4
Oldfield Ms, N6 . . . . .74 C7
Oldfield Rd, N16 . . . . .94 B3
NW10 . . . . .89 F7
SW19 . . . . .166 B6
W3 *off Valetta Rd* 127 F2
Bexleyheath DA7 . . . . . .159 E2
Bromley BR1 . . . . .192 C4
Hampton TW12 . . . . .179 F1
Oldfields Circ, Nthlt. UB5 . .85 J6
Oldfields Rd, Sutt. SM1 . . .198 C3
Oldfields Trd Est, Sutt.
SM1 . . . . .198 D3
Old Fish St Hill, EC4 . . . . . .19 J5
Old Fleet La, EC4 . . . . .19 G3
Old Fold Cl, Barn. EN5
off Old Fold La 40 C1
Old Fold La, Barn. EN5 . . . .40 C1
Old Fold Vw, Barn. EN5 . . . .39 J3
OLD FORD, E3 . . . . .95 J7
Old Ford Rd, E2 . . . . .113 F2
E3 . . . . .113 H2
Old Forge Cl, Stan. HA7 . . .52 D4
Old Forge Ms, W12
off Goodwin Rd 127 H2
Old Forge Rd, N19
off Elthorne Rd 92 D2
Old Forge Way, Sid.
DA14 . . . . .176 B4
Old Fox Footpath, S.Croy.
CR2 *off Essenden Rd* . . .202 B7
Old Gloucester St, WC1 . . .18 B1
Old Hall Cl, Pnr. HA5 . . . . . .67 E1
Old Hall Dr, Pnr. HA5 . . . . . .66 E1
Oldham Ter, W3 . . . . .126 C1
Old Hill, Chis. BR7 . . . . . . .192 D1
Orpington BR6 . . . . .207 G6
Oldhill St, N16 . . . . .94 D1
Old Homesdale Rd, Brom.
BR2 . . . . .191 J4
Old Hosp Cl, SW12 . . . . . .167 J1
Old Ho Cl, SW19 . . . . .166 B5
Old Ho Gdns, Twick. TW1 . .145 F5
Old Jamaica Rd, SE16 . . . . .29 H5
Old James St, SE15 . . . . . .152 E3
Old Jewry, EC2 . . . . .20 B4
Old Kenton La, NW9 . . . . . .70 B5
Old Kent Rd, SE1 . . . . .28 C6
SE15 . . . . .37 J5
Old Kingston Rd, Wor.Pk.
KT4 . . . . .196 C3
Old Lo Pl, Twick. TW1
off St. Margarets Rd . .145 E6
Old Lo Way, Stan. HA7 . . . .52 D5
Old London Rd, Kings.T.
KT2 . . . . .181 H2
Old Maidstone Rd, Sid.
DA14 . . . . .177 F7
OLD MALDEN, Wor.Pk.
KT4 . . . . .196 D1
Old Malden La, Wor.Pk.
KT4 . . . . .196 D2
Old Manor Dr, Islw. TW7 . .143 J6
Old Manor Rd, Sthl. UB2 .122 D4
Old Manor Way, Chis.
BR7 . . . . .174 C5
Old Manor Yd, SW5
off Earls Ct Rd 128 E4
Old Mkt Sq, E2 . . . . .13 F3
Old Marylebone Rd, NW1 . .15 H2
Old Ms, Har. HA1
off Hindes Rd 68 B5
Old Mill Ct, E18 . . . . .79 J3
Old Mill Rd, SE18 . . . . .137 G6
Old Mitre Ct, EC4 . . . . .19 F4
Old Montague St, E1 . . . . . .21 H2
Old Nichol St, E2 . . . . .13 F5
Old N St, WC1 . . . . .18 C1
Old Oak Cl, Chess. KT9 . . .195 J4
OLD OAK COMMON,
NW10 . . . . .107 F5
Old Oak Common La,
NW10 . . . . .107 E5
W3 . . . . .107 E5
Old Oak La, NW10 . . . . . . .107 E3
Old Oak Rd, W3 . . . . .107 F7
★ **Old Operating Thea Mus & Herb Garret**,
SE1 . . . . .28 C2
Old Orchard, Sun. TW16 . .178 C2
Old Orchard, The, NW3
off Nassington Rd 91 J4
Old Palace La, Rich. TW9 . .145 F5
Old Palace Rd, Croy. CR0 .201 H3
Old Palace Ter, Rich. TW9
off King St 145 G5
Old Palace Yd, SW1 . . . . . . .26 A5
Richmond TW9 . . . . .145 F5
Old Paradise St, SE11 . . . . .34 C1
Old Pk Av, SW12 . . . . .150 A6
Enfield EN2 . . . . .43 J4
Old Pk Gro, Enf. EN2 . . . . . .43 J4
Old Pk La, W1 . . . . .24 C2
Old Pk Ms, Houns. TW5 . . .123 F7
Old Pk Ridings, N21 . . . . . .43 H6
Old Pk Rd, N13 . . . . .59 F4
SE2 . . . . .138 A5
Enfield EN2 . . . . .43 H3
Old Pk Rd S, Enf. EN2 . . . .43 H4
Old Pk Vw, Enf. EN2 . . . . . .43 G3
Old Pearson St, SE10 . . . .134 B7
Old Perry St, Chis. BR7 . . .175 H7
Old PO La, SE3 . . . . .155 H3
Old Pound Cl, Islw. TW7 . .144 D1
Old Pye St, SW1 . . . . .25 H5
Old Quebec St, W1 . . . . . . .16 A4
Old Queen St, SW1 . . . . . . .25 J4
Old Rectory Gdns, Edg.
HA8 . . . . .54 A6
Old Redding, Har. HA3 . . . .51 J4
Oldridge Rd, SW12 . . . . . .150 A7
Old River Lea Towpath,
E15 *off City Mill River Towpath* 96 B7
Old Rd, SE13 . . . . .155 E4
Enfield EN3 . . . . .45 F1
Old Rope Wk, Sun. TW16
off The Avenue 178 B3
Old Royal Free Pl, N1
off Liverpool Rd 111 G1
Old Royal Free Sq, N1 . . . .111 G1
Old Ruislip Rd, Nthlt.
UB5 . . . . .102 D2
Old Savill's Cotts, Chig.
IG7 . . . . .65 F4
Old Sch Cl, SE10 . . . . .135 E3
SW19 . . . . .184 D2
Beckenham BR3 . . . . . . .189 G2
Old Sch Cres, E7 . . . . .97 G6
Old Sch Pl, Croy. CR0 . . . .201 G4
Old Sch Sq, E14
off Pelling St 114 A6
Thames Ditton KT7 . . . .180 C6
Old Seacoal La, EC4 . . . . . .19 G3
Old S Cl, Pnr. (Hatch End)
HA5 . . . . .66 D1
Old S Lambeth Rd, SW8 . . .34 B7
★ **Old Spitalfields Mkt**,
E1 . . . . .21 F1
Old Sq, WC2 . . . . .18 D3
Old Sta Rd, Hayes UB3 . . .121 J3
Loughton IG10 . . . . .48 B5
Old Sta Way, SW4
off Voltaire Rd 150 D3
Old Sta Yd, Brom. BR2
off Bourne Way 205 F1
Oldstead Rd, Brom. BR1 . .172 D4
Old Stockley Rd, West Dr.
UB7 . . . . .120 E2
Old St, E13 . . . . .115 H2
EC1 . . . . .11 J5
Old Studio Cl, Croy. CR0 . . .188 A7
Old Swan Yd, Cars. SM5 . .199 J4
Old Thea Ct, SE1
off Porter St 28 A1
Old Town, SW4 . . . . .150 C3
Croydon CR0 . . . . .201 H3
Old Tram Yd, SE18
off Lakedale Rd 137 H4
Old Twelve Cl, W7
off Greenford Av 104 B4
Old Woolwich Rd, SE10 . . .134 D6
Old York Rd, SW18 . . . . . . .149 E5
Oleander Cl, Orp. BR6 . . . .207 G5
O'Leary Sq, E1 . . . . .113 F5
Olga St, E3 . . . . .113 H2
Olinda Rd, N16 . . . . .76 C6
Oliphant St, W10 . . . . .108 A3
Olive Gro, N15 . . . . .75 J4
Oliver Av, SE25 . . . . .188 C3
Oliver Cl, W4 . . . . .126 B6
Oliver Gdns, E6 . . . . .116 B6
Oliver-Goldsmith Est,
SE15 . . . . .152 D1
Oliver Gro, SE25 . . . . .188 C4
Oliver Ms, SE15 . . . . .152 D2
Olive Rd, E13 . . . . .115 J3
NW2 . . . . .89 J4
SW19 *off Norman Rd* . . .167 F7
W5 . . . . .125 G3
Oliver Rd, E10 . . . . .96 B2
E17 . . . . .78 C5
NW10 . . . . .106 C2
Oliver Rd,
New Malden KT3 . . . . . .182 C2
Sutton SM1 . . . . .199 G4
Olivers Yd, EC1 . . . . .12 C5
Olivette St, SW15 . . . . . . .148 A3
Ollards Gro, Loughton
IG10 . . . . .48 A4
Ollerton Grn, E3 . . . . .113 J1
Ollerton Rd, N11 . . . . .58 D5
Olley Cl, Wall. SM6 . . . . . .200 E7
Ollgar Cl, W12 . . . . .127 F1
Olliffe St, E14 . . . . .134 C3
Olmar St, SE1 . . . . .37 H5
Olney Rd, SE17 . . . . .35 J5
Olron Cres, Bexh. DA6 . . . .158 D5
Olven Rd, SE18 . . . . .137 F7
Olveston Wk, Cars. SM5 . .185 G6
Olwen Ms, Pnr. HA5 . . . . . .66 D2
Olyffe Av, Well. DA16 . . . . .158 A2
Olyffe Dr, Beck. BR3 . . . . .190 C1
★ **Olympia**, W14 . . . . . . .128 B3
Olympia Ms, W2 . . . . .14 B6
Olympia Way, W14 . . . . . . .128 B3
Olympic Way, Grnf. UB6 . .103 H1
Wembley HA9 . . . . .88 A4
Olympus Gro, N22 . . . . .75 G1
Olympus Sq, E5
off Nolan Way 94 D3
Oman Av, NW2 . . . . .89 J4
O'Meara St, SE1 . . . . .28 A2
Omega Bldg, SW18
off Smugglers Way . . .149 E4
Omega Cl, E14
off Tiller Rd 134 B3
Omega Ct, Rom. RM7 . . . . .83 J6
Omega Pl, N1 . . . . .10 B2
Omega St, SE14 . . . . .154 A1
Omega Wks, E3 . . . . .96 A7
Ommaney Rd, SE14 . . . . . .153 G1
Omnibus Way, E17 . . . . .78 A2
Ondine Rd, SE15 . . . . .152 C4
Onega Gate, SE16 . . . . . . .133 H3
O'Neill Path, SE18
off Kempt St 136 D6
One Tree Cl, SE23 . . . . . . .153 F6
Ongar Cl, Rom. RM6 . . . . . .82 C5
Ongar Rd, SW6 . . . . .128 D6
Onra Rd, E17 . . . . .78 A7
Onslow Av, Rich. TW10 . . .145 H5
Onslow Cl, E4 . . . . .62 C2
W10 *off Dowland St* . . .108 C3
Thames Ditton KT7 . . . .194 B1
Onslow Cres, SW7 . . . . .31 F2
Chislehurst BR7 . . . . . . .192 E1
Onslow Dr, Sid. DA14 . . . .176 D2
Onslow Gdns, E18 . . . . .79 H3
N10 . . . . .74 B5
N21 . . . . .43 G5
SW7 . . . . .30 E2
Thames Ditton KT7 . . . .194 B1
Wallington SM6 . . . . . . .200 C6
Onslow Ms E, SW7 . . . . . . .31 E2
Onslow Ms W, SW7 . . . . . . .30 E2
Onslow Par, N14
off Osidge La 58 B1
Onslow Rd, Croy. CR0 . . . .187 F7
New Malden KT3 . . . . . .183 G4
Richmond TW10 . . . . . . .145 H5
Onslow Sq, SW7 . . . . .31 F1
Onslow St, EC1 . . . . .11 F6
Onslow Way, T.Ditt. KT7 . . .194 B1
Ontario St, SE1 . . . . .27 H6
Ontario Twr, E14 . . . . .114 D7
Ontario Way, E14 . . . . .114 A7
On The Hill, Wat. WD19 . . . .50 E2
Onyx Ms, E15
off Vicarage La 97 E6
Opal Cl, E16 . . . . .116 A6
Opal Ms, NW6
off Priory Pk Rd 108 D1
Ilford IG1 . . . . .99 E2
Opal St, SE11 . . . . .35 G2
Openshaw Rd, SE2 . . . . . .138 B4
Openview, SW18 . . . . .167 F1
Ophelia Gdns, NW2
off Hamlet Sq 90 B3
Ophir Ter, SE15 . . . . .152 D1
Opossum Way, Houns.
TW4 . . . . .142 C2
Oppenheim Rd, SE13 . . . .154 C2
Oppidans Ms, NW3
off Meadowbank 91 J7
Oppidans Rd, NW3 . . . . . . .91 J7
Orange Ct, E1
off Hermitage Wall 29 J2
Orange Gro, E11 . . . . .96 D3
Chigwell IG7 . . . . .65 F6
Orange Hill Rd, Edg. HA8 . .54 C7
Orange Pl, SE16
off Lower Rd 133 F3
Orangery, The, Rich.
TW10 . . . . .163 F2
Orangery La, SE9 . . . . . . .156 C5
Orange Sq, SW1 . . . . .32 C2
Orange St, WC2 . . . . .17 H6
Orange Yd, W1 . . . . .17 J4
Oransay Rd, N1 . . . . .93 J6
Oransay Wk, N1
off Oransay Rd 93 J6
Oratory La, SW3 . . . . .31 F3
Orbain Rd, SW6 . . . . .128 B7
Orbel St, SW11 . . . . .149 H1
Orb St, SE17 . . . . .36 B2
Orchard, The, N14 . . . . .42 B5
N20 . . . . .57 E1
N21 . . . . .44 A6
NW11 . . . . .72 D5
SE3 . . . . .154 D2
W4 . . . . .126 D4
W5 *off Montpelier Rd* . .105 G5
Epsom KT17 . . . . .197 F7
Hounslow TW3 . . . . .143 J2
Orchard Av, N3 . . . . .72 D3
N14 . . . . .42 C6
N20 . . . . .57 G2
Belvedere DA17 . . . . . . .139 E6
Croydon CR0 . . . . .189 H7
Feltham TW14 . . . . .141 G5
Hounslow TW5 . . . . .123 E7
Mitcham CR4 . . . . .200 A1
New Malden KT3 . . . . . .183 E2
Southall UB1 . . . . .123 E1
Thames Ditton KT7 . . . .194 D1
Orchard Cl, E4
off Chingford Mt Rd . . .62 A4
E11 . . . . .79 H4
N1 . . . . .93 J7
NW2 . . . . .89 G3
SE23
off Brenchley Gdns . . .153 F6
SW20 . . . . .183 J4
W10 . . . . .108 B5
Bexleyheath DA7 . . . . . .158 E1
Bushey (Bushey Hth)
WD23 . . . . .52 A1
Edgware HA8 . . . . .53 H6
Epsom (W.Ewell)
KT19 . . . . .196 B6
Northolt UB5 . . . . .85 J5
Surbiton (Long Dit.)
KT6 . . . . .181 E7
Walton-on-Thames
KT12 . . . . .178 B7
Wembley HA0 . . . . .105 H1
Orchard Ct, Islw. TW7
off Thornbury Av 124 A7
Twickenham TW2 . . . . . .162 A2
Wallington SM6
off Parkgate Rd 200 B5
Worcester Park KT4 . . . .197 G1
Orchard Cres, Edg. HA8 . . .54 C5
Enfield EN1 . . . . .44 C1
Orchard Dr, SE3
off Orchard Rd 154 E2
Edgware HA8 . . . . .53 J5
Orchard Est, Wdf.Grn. IG8 . .63 J7
Orchard Gdns, Chess.
KT9 . . . . .195 H4
Sutton SM1 . . . . .198 D5
Orchard Gate, NW9 . . . . . . .70 E4
Esher KT10 . . . . .194 A1
Greenford UB6 . . . . .86 E6
Orchard Grn, Orp. BR6 . . .207 H2
Orchard Gro, SE20 . . . . . . .170 D7
Croydon CR0 . . . . .189 H7
Edgware HA8 . . . . .70 A1
Harrow HA3 . . . . .69 J5
Orpington BR6 . . . . .207 J2
Orchard Hill, SE13
off Coldbath St 154 B2
Carshalton SM5 . . . . . . .199 J5
Orchard La, SW20 . . . . . . .183 H1
East Molesey KT8 . . . . .180 A6
Woodford Green IG8 . . . .63 J4
Orchardleigh Av, Enf.
EN3 . . . . .45 F2
Orchardmede, N21 . . . . .44 A6
Orchard Ms, N1
off Southgate Gro 94 A7
N6 *off Orchard Rd* 74 B7
SW17
off Franche Ct Rd 167 F3
Orchard Pl, E5 . . . . .95 E5
E14 . . . . .114 E7
N17 . . . . .60 C7
Orchard Ri, Croy. CR0 . . . .203 H1
Kingston upon Thames
KT2 . . . . .182 C1
Richmond TW10 . . . . . . .146 B4
Orchard Ri E, Sid. DA15 . . .157 J5
Orchard Ri W, Sid. DA15 . .157 H5
Orchard Rd, N6 . . . . .74 B7
SE3 . . . . .154 E2
SE18 . . . . .137 G4
Barnet EN5 . . . . .40 C4
Belvedere DA17 . . . . . . .139 G4
Brentford TW8 . . . . .125 F6
Bromley BR1 . . . . .191 J1
Chessington KT9 . . . . . .195 H4
Dagenham RM10 . . . . . .119 G1
Enfield EN3 . . . . .45 F5
Feltham TW13 . . . . .160 A1
Hampton TW12 . . . . .161 F7
Hounslow TW4 . . . . .143 F5

Orchard Rd, Kings.T. KT1 181 H2
Mitcham CR4 200 A1
Orpington (Farnboro.) BR6 207 E5
Richmond TW9 146 A3
Romford RM7 83 H1
Sidcup DA14 175 H4
Sunbury-on-Thames TW16 *off Hanworth Rd* 160 B7
Sutton SM1 198 D5
Twickenham TW1 144 D5
Welling DA16 158 B3
Orchardson Ho, NW8 *off Orchardson St* 7 F5
Orchardson St, NW8 7 E6
Orchard Sq, W14 *off Sun Rd* 128 C5
Orchard St, E17 77 H4
W1 16 B4
Orchard Ter, Enf. EN1 44 D6
Orchard Vil, Sid. DA14 176 B6
Orchard Wk, Kings.T. KT2 *off Clifton Rd* 182 A1
Orchard Way, Beck. BR3 189 H5
Croydon CR0 203 H1
Enfield EN1 44 B3
Sutton SM1 199 G4
Orchestra Cl, Edg. HA8 *off Symphony Cl* 54 B7
Orchid Cl, E6 116 B5
SE13 154 D5
Chessington KT9 195 F7
Southall UB1 103 E6
Orchid Gdns, Houns. TW3 *off Staines Rd* 143 F4
Orchid Rd, N14 42 C7
Orchid St, W12 107 G7
Orde Hall St, WC1 10 C6
Ordell Rd, E3 113 J2
Ordnance Cl, Felt. TW13 160 A3
Ordnance Cres, SE10 134 D2
Ordnance Hill, NW8 109 G1
Ordnance Ms, NW8 7 F1
Ordnance Rd, E16 115 F5
SE18 136 D6
Oregano Dr, E14 114 D6
Oregon Av, E12 98 C4
Oregon Bldg, SE13 *off Deals Gateway* 154 B1
Oregon Cl, N.Mal. KT3 *off Georgia Rd* 182 C4
Oregon Sq, Orp. BR6 207 G1
Orestes Ms, NW6 *off Aldred Rd* 90 D5
Orford Ct, SE27 169 H2
Orford Gdns, Twick. TW1 162 C2
Orford Rd, E17 78 A5
E18 79 H3
SE6 172 B3
Organ Crossroads, Epsom KT17 197 G7
Organ La, E4 62 C2
Oriel Cl, Mitch. CR4 186 D4
Oriel Ct, NW3 *off Heath St* 91 F4
Oriel Dr, SW13 127 H6
Oriel Gdns, Ilf. IG5 80 C3
Oriel Pl, NW3 *off Heath St* 91 F4
Oriel Rd, E9 95 G6
Oriel Way, Nthlt. UB5 85 H7
Oriental Rd, E16 136 A1
Oriental St, E14 *off Morant St* 114 A7
Orient Ind Pk, E10 96 A2
Orient St, SE11 35 G1
Orient Way, E5 95 G3
E10 95 H2
Oriole Way, SE28 118 B7
Orion Cen, The, Croy. CR0 200 E2
Orion Ho, E1 *off Coventry Rd* 113 E4
Orion Pt, E14 *off Crews St* 134 A4
Orion Rd, N11 58 B6
Orissa Rd, SE18 137 H5
Orkney St, SW11 150 A2
Orlando Rd, SW4 150 C3
Orleans Cl, Esher KT10 194 A2
★ **Orleans Ho Gall**, Twick. TW1 163 E1
Orleans Rd, SE19 170 A6
Twickenham TW1 145 E7
Orleston Ms, N7 93 G6
Orleston Rd, N7 93 G6
Orley Fm Rd, Har. HA1 86 B3
Orlop St, SE10 134 E5
Ormanton Rd, SE26 170 D4
Orme Ct, W2 14 A6
Orme Ct Ms, W2 14 B6
Orme La, W2 14 A6
Ormeley Rd, SW12 168 B1
Orme Rd, Kings.T. KT1 182 B2
Sutton SM1 *off Grove Rd* 199 E6
Ormerod Gdns, Mitch. CR4 186 A2
Ormesby Cl, SE28 *off Wroxham Rd* 118 D7
Ormesby Way, Har. HA3 69 J6
Orme Sq, W2 14 A6
Ormiston Gro, W12 127 H1
Ormiston Rd, SE10 135 G5
Ormond Av, Hmptn. TW12 179 H1
Richmond TW10 *off Ormond Rd* 145 G5
Ormond Cl, WC1 18 B1
Ormond Cres, Hmptn. TW12 179 H1
Ormond Dr, Hmptn. TW12 161 H7
Ormonde Av, Orp. BR6 207 F2
Ormonde Gate, SW3 32 A4
Ormonde Pl, SW1 32 B2
Ormonde Ri, Buck.H. IG9 63 J1
Ormonde Rd, SW14 146 B3
Ormonde Ter, NW8 109 J1
Ormond Ms, WC1 10 B6
Ormond Rd, N19 93 E1
Richmond TW10 145 G5
Ormond Yd, SW1 25 G1
Ormsby, Sutt. SM2 *off Grange Rd* 198 E7
Ormsby Gdns, Grnf. UB6 103 J2
Ormsby Pl, N16 *off Victorian Gro* 94 C3
Ormsby Pt, SE18 *off Vincent Rd* 137 E4
Ormsby St, E2 13 F1
Ormside St, SE15 133 F6
Ormskirk Rd, Wat. WD19 50 D4
Ornan Rd, NW3 91 H5
Orpen Wk, N16 94 B3
Orpheus St, SE5 152 A1
ORPINGTON, BR5 & BR6 207 H1
Orpington Gdns, N18 60 B3
Orpington Rd, N21 59 H1
Chislehurst BR7 193 H3
Orpwood Cl, Hmptn. TW12 161 F5
Orsett St, SE11 34 D3
Orsett Ter, W2 14 B3
Woodford Green IG8 79 J1
Orsman Rd, N1 112 B1
Orton Gro, Enf. EN1 44 D1
Orton Pl, SW19 167 E7
Orton St, E1 29 H2
Orville Rd, SW11 149 G2
Orwell Ct, N5 93 J4
Orwell Rd, E13 115 J2
Osbaldeston Rd, N16 94 D2
Osberton Rd, SE12 155 G5
Osbert St, SW1 33 H2
Osborn Cl, E8 112 D1
Osborne Cl, Barn. EN4 41 J3
Beckenham BR3 189 H4
Feltham TW13 160 D5
Osborne Gdns, Th.Hth. CR7 187 J2
Osborne Gro, E17 77 J4
N4 93 G1
Osborne Ms, E17 *off Osborne Gro* 77 J4
Osborne Pl, Sutt. SM1 199 G5
Osborne Rd, E7 97 H5
E9 95 J6
E10 96 B3
N4 93 F1
N13 59 G3
NW2 89 H6
W3 126 B3
Belvedere DA17 139 F5
Buckhurst Hill IG9 63 H1
Dagenham RM9 101 F5
Enfield EN3 45 H2
Hounslow TW3 143 F3
Kingston upon Thames KT2 163 H7
Southall UB1 103 J6
Thornton Heath CR7 187 J2
Osborne Sq, Dag. RM9 101 F4
Osborne Ter, SW17 *off Church La* 168 A5
Osborne Way, Chess. KT9 *off Bridge Rd* 195 J5
Osborn Gdns, NW7 56 A7
Osborn La, SE23 153 H7
Osborn St, E1 21 G2
Osborn Ter, SE3 *off Lee Rd* 155 F4
Osbourne Ct, W5 105 H5
Oscar Faber Pl, N1 *off St. Peter's Way* 94 B7
Oscar St, SE8 154 A1
Oseney Cres, NW5 92 C6
Osgood Av, Orp. BR6 207 J5
Osgood Gdns, Orp. BR6 207 J5
OSIDGE, N14 58 B1
Osidge La, N14 58 A1
Osier Cres, N10 73 J1
Osier La, SE10 135 F3
Osier Ms, W4 127 F6
Osiers Rd, SW18 148 D4
Osier St, E1 113 F4
Osier Way, E10 96 B3
Mitcham CR4 185 H5
Oslac Rd, SE6 172 B5
Oslo Ct, NW8 7 G2
Oslo Sq, SE16 133 H3
Osman Cl, N15 *off Tewkesbury Rd* 76 A6
Osman Rd, N9 60 D3
W6 *off Batoum Gdns* 127 J3
Osmington Ho, SW8 *off Dorset Rd* 131 F7
Osmond Cl, Har. HA2 85 J2
Osmond Gdns, Wall. SM6 200 C5
Osmund St, W12 *off Braybrook St* 107 F5
Osnaburgh St, NW1 9 E6
NW1 (north section) 9 E4
Osnaburgh Ter, NW1 8 E5
Osney Ho, SE2 *off Hartslock Dr* 138 D2
Osney Wk, Cars. SM5 185 G6
Osprey Cl, E6 *off Dove App* 116 B5
E11 79 G4
E17 61 H7
Bromley BR2 206 B1
Sutton SM1 *off Sandpiper Rd* 198 C5
West Drayton UB7 120 A2
Osprey Hts, SW11 *off Bramlands Cl* 149 H3
Osprey Ms, Enf. EN3 45 E5
Ospringe Cl, SE20 171 F7
Ospringe Ct, SE9 157 G6
Ospringe Rd, NW5 92 C4
Osram Ct, W6 *off Lena Gdns* 127 J3
Osram Rd, Wem. HA9 87 G3
Osric Path, N1 12 D2
Ossian Ms, N4 75 F7
Ossian Rd, N4 75 F7
Ossie Garvin Rbt, Hayes UB4 *off The Parkway* 102 C7
Ossington Bldgs, W1 16 B1
Ossington Cl, W2 *off Ossington St* 108 D7
Ossington St, W2 108 D7
Ossory Rd, SE1 37 H4
Ossulston St, NW1 9 H2
Ossulton Pl, N2 *off East End Rd* 73 F3
Ossulton Way, N2 73 F4
Ostade Rd, SW2 151 F7
Osten Ms, SW7 22 B6
OSTERLEY, Islw. TW7 123 J7
Osterley Av, Islw. TW7 124 A7
Osterley Ct, Islw. TW7 144 A1
Osterley Cres, Islw. TW7 144 B1
Osterley Gdns, Sthl. UB2 *off Chevy Rd* 124 A2
Thornton Heath CR7 187 J2
Osterley Ho, E14 *off Giraud St* 114 B6
Osterley La, Islw. TW7 124 B5
Southall UB2 123 G5
Osterley Pk, Islw. TW7 124 A5
★ **Osterley Park Ho**, Islw. TW7 123 J5
Osterley Pk Rd, Sthl. UB2 123 F3
Osterley Pk Vw Rd, W7 124 B2
Osterley Rd, N16 94 B4
Isleworth TW7 124 B7
Osterley Views, Sthl. UB2 *off West Pk Rd* 124 A1
Oster Ter, E17 *off Southcote Rd* 77 G5
Ostliffe Rd, N13 59 J5
Oswald Bldg, SW8 32 D6
Oswald Rd, Sthl. UB1 123 E1
Oswald's Mead, E9 *off Lindisfarne Way* 95 H4
Oswald St, E5 95 G3
Oswald Ter, NW2 *off Temple Rd* 89 J3
Osward Pl, N9 60 E2
Osward Rd, SW17 167 J2
Oswell Ho, E1 133 E1
Oswin St, SE11 35 H1
Oswyth Rd, SE5 152 B2
Otford Cl, SE20 189 F1
Bexley DA5 *off Southwold Rd* 159 H6
Bromley BR1 192 D3
Otford Cres, SE4 153 J6
Othello Cl, SE11 35 G3
Otho Ct, Brent. TW8 125 G7
Otis St, E3 114 C3
Otley App, Ilf. IG2 81 E6
Otley Dr, Ilf. IG2 80 E5
Otley Rd, E16 115 J6
Otley Ter, E5 95 G2
Otley Way, Wat. WD19 50 C3
Ottaway St, E5 94 D3
Ottenden Cl, Orp. BR6 *off Southfleet Rd* 207 H4
Otterbourne Rd, E4 62 D3
Croydon CR0 201 J2
Otterburn Gdns, Islw. TW7 124 D7
Otterburn Ho, SE5 35 J7
Otterburn St, SW17 167 J6
Otter Cl, E15 114 C1
Otterden St, SE6 172 A4
Otter Rd, Grnf. UB6 103 J4
Otto Cl, SE26 170 E3
Otto St, SE17 35 G6
Oulton Cl, E5 *off Mundford Rd* 95 F2
SE28 *off Rollesby Way* 118 C6
Oulton Cres, Bark. IG11 99 J6
Oulton Rd, N15 76 A5
Oulton Way, Wat. WD19 51 E4
Ouseley Rd, SW12 167 J1
Outer Circle, NW1 8 B6
Outgate Rd, NW10 89 F7
Outram Pl, N1 111 E1
Outram Rd, E6 116 B1
N22 74 D1
Croydon CR0 202 C1
Outwich St, EC3 20 E3
★ **Oval, The** (Surrey CCC), SE11 34 D5
Oval, The, E2 112 E2
Sidcup DA15 158 A7
Oval Pl, SW8 34 C7
Oval Rd, NW1 110 B1
Croydon CR0 202 B1
Oval Rd N, Dag. RM10 119 H1
Oval Rd S, Dag. RM10 119 H2
Oval Way, SE11 34 D4
Overbrae, Beck. BR3 172 A6
Overbrook Wk, Edg. HA8 54 A7
Overbury Av, Beck. BR3 190 B3
Overbury Rd, N15 76 A6
Overbury St, E5 95 G4
Overcliff Rd, SE13 154 A3
Overcourt Cl, Sid. DA15 158 B6
Overdale Av, N.Mal. KT3 182 C2
Overdale Rd, W5 125 F3
Overdown Rd, SE6 172 A4
Overhill Rd, SE22 152 D7
Overhill Way, Beck. BR3 190 D5
Overlea Rd, E5 76 D7
Overmead, Sid. DA15 157 G7
Oversley Ho, W2 108 D5
Overstand Cl, Beck. BR3 190 A5
Overstone Gdns, Croy. CR0 189 J7
Overstone Rd, W6 127 J3
Overton Cl, NW10 88 C6
Isleworth TW7 *off Avenue Rd* 144 C1
Overton Ct, E11 79 G7
Overton Dr, E11 79 H7
Romford RM6 82 C7
Overton Ho, SW15 *off Tangley Gro* 147 F7
Overton Rd, E10 95 H1
N14 42 E5
SE2 138 C3
SW9 151 G2
Sutton SM2 198 D6
Overton Rd E, SE2 138 D3
Overtons Yd, Croy. CR0 201 J3
Ovesdon Av, Har. HA2 85 F1
Ovett Cl, SE19 170 B6
Ovex Cl, E14 134 C2
Ovington Gdns, SW3 23 H6
Ovington Ms, SW3 23 H6
Ovington Sq, SW3 23 H6
Ovington St, SW3 23 H6
Owen Cl, SE28 138 C1
Croydon CR0 188 A6
Hayes UB4 102 B3
Northolt UB5 85 E6
Owen Gdns, Wdf.Grn. IG8 64 B6
Owenite St, SE2 138 B4
Owen Rd, N13 59 J5
Hayes UB4 102 B3
Owens Ms, E11 *off Short Rd* 96 E2
Owen's Row, EC1 11 G3
Owen St, EC1 11 G2
Owens Way, SE23 153 H7
Owen Wk, SE20 *off Sycamore Gro* 188 D1
Owen Waters Ho, Ilf. IG5 80 C1
Owen Way, NW10 88 C6
Owgan Cl, SE5 *off Benhill Rd* 132 A7
Owl, The, Loug. (High Beach) IG10 47 F2
Oxberry Av, SW6 148 B2
Oxendon St, SW1 17 H6
Oxenford St, SE15 152 C3
Oxenholme, NW1 9 G2
Oxenpark Av, Wem. HA9 69 H7

Oxestalls Rd, SE8 133 H5
Oxford Av, N14 58 C1
SW20 184 B2
Hayes UB3 121 J7
Hounslow TW5 123 G5
★ **Oxford Circ**, W1 17 F3
Oxford Circ Av, W1 17 F4
Oxford Cl, N9 60 E2
Mitcham CR4 186 C3
Oxford Ct, EC4 20 B5
W3 106 A6
Feltham TW13 *off Oxford Way* 160 D4
Oxford Cres, N.Mal. KT3 182 D6
Oxford Dr, SE1 28 D2
Ruislip HA4 84 C2
Oxford Gdns, N20 57 G1
N21 43 J7
W4 126 A5
W10 108 B6
Oxford Gate, W6 128 A4
Oxford Ms, Bex. DA5 177 G1
Oxford Pl, NW10 *off Press Rd* 88 D3
Oxford Rd, E15 96 D6
N4 93 G1
N9 61 E2
NW6 108 D2
SE19 170 A6
SW15 148 B4
W5 105 G7
Carshalton SM5 199 H6
Enfield EN3 45 E5
Harrow HA1 67 J6
Harrow (Wealds.) HA3 68 C3
Ilford IG1 99 F4
Sidcup DA14 176 B5
Teddington TW11 162 A5
Wallington SM6 200 C5
Woodford Green IG8 63 J5
Oxford Rd N, W4 126 B5
Oxford Rd S, W4 126 A5
Oxford Sq, W2 15 H4
Oxford St, W1 17 G3
Oxford Wk, Sthl. UB1 123 F1
Oxford Way, Felt. TW13 160 D4
Oxgate Cen Ind Est, The, NW2 89 H1
Oxgate Gdns, NW2 89 H3
Oxgate La, NW2 89 H2
Oxhawth Cres, Brom. BR2 192 D5
Oxhey Dr, Nthwd. HA6 50 B5
Watford WD19 50 C3
Oxhey Dr S, Nthwd. HA6 50 B5
Oxhey La, Har. HA3 51 G5
Pinner HA5 51 G5
Watford WD19 51 F2
Oxhey Ridge Cl, Nthwd. HA6 50 A5
Oxleas, E6 116 E6
Oxleas Cl, Well. DA16 157 G2
Oxleay Ct, Har. HA2 85 G1
Oxleay Rd, Har. HA2 85 G1
Oxleigh Cl, N.Mal. KT3 183 E5
Oxley Cl, SE1 37 G3
Oxleys Rd, NW2 89 H3
Oxlip Cl, Croy. CR0 *off Marigold Way* 203 G1
Oxlow La, Dag. RM9, RM10 101 G4
Oxonian St, SE22 152 C4
Oxo Twr Wf, SE1 19 F6
Oxted Cl, Mitch. CR4 185 G3
Oxtoby Way, SW16 186 D2
Oyster Catchers Cl, E16 *off Freemasons Rd* 115 H6
Oyster Catcher Ter, Ilf. IG5 *off Tiptree Cres* 80 D3
Oystergate Wk, EC4 *off Swan La* 20 B6
Oyster Row, E1 *off Lukin St* 113 F6
Oyster Wf, SW11 149 G2
Ozolins Way, E16 115 G6

P

Pablo Neruda Cl, SE24 *off Shakespeare Rd* 151 H4
Pace Pl, E1 *off Bigland St* 113 E6
Pacific Ms, SW9 *off Saltoun Rd* 151 G4
Pacific Rd, E16 115 G6
Pacific Wf, SE16 *off Rotherhithe St* 133 G1
Packham Ct, Wor.Pk. KT4 *off Lavender Av* 197 J3
Packington Rd, W3 126 C3
Packington Sq, N1 111 J1
Packington St, N1 111 H1
Packmores Rd, SE9 157 G5
Padbury, SE17 36 D4
Padbury Ct, E2 13 G4
Padcroft Rd, West Dr. UB7 120 A1
Paddenswick Rd, W6 127 G3
PADDINGTON, W2 14 C2
Paddington Cl, Hayes UB4 102 D4
Paddington Grn, W2 15 F1
Paddington Sta, W2 14 E3
Paddington St, W1 16 B1
Paddington Underground Sta, W2 14 E3
Paddock Cl, SE3 155 G2
SE26 171 G4
Northolt UB5 103 G2
Orpington (Farnboro.) BR6 *off State Fm Av* 207 E4
Worcester Park KT4 196 E1
Paddock Gdns, SE19 *off Westow St* 170 B6
Paddock Rd, NW2 89 G3
Bexleyheath DA6 159 E4
Ruislip HA4 84 D3
Paddocks, The, NW7 56 B6
Barnet (Cockfos.) EN4 41 J3
Wembley HA9 88 B2
Paddocks Cl, Har. HA2 85 H4
Paddock Way, SW15 147 J7
Chislehurst BR7 175 G7
Padfield Ct, Wem. HA9 *off Forty Av* 87 J3
Padfield Rd, SE5 151 J3
SW9 151 J3
Padley Cl, Chess. KT9 195 J5
Padnall Ct, Rom. RM6 *off Padnall Rd* 82 D3
Padnall Rd, Rom. RM6 82 D4
Padstow Cl, Orp. BR6 207 J4
Padstow Rd, Enf. EN2 43 H2
Padua Rd, SE20 189 F1
Pagden St, SW8 150 B1
Pageant Av, NW9 70 D1
Pageant Cres, SE16 *off Rotherhithe St* 133 H1
Pageantmaster Ct, EC4 19 G4
Pageant Wk, Croy. CR0 202 B3
Page Av, Wem. HA9 88 C3
Page Cl, Dag. RM9 101 E5
Hampton TW12 161 E6
Harrow HA3 69 J6
Page Cres, Croy. CR0 201 G5
Page Grn Rd, N15 76 D5
Page Grn Ter, N15 76 C5
Page Heath La, Brom. BR1 192 A3
Page Heath Vil, Brom. BR1 192 A3
Pagehurst Rd, Croy. CR0 188 E7
Page Meadow, NW7 55 G7
Page Rd, Felt. TW14 141 G6
Pages Hill, N10 74 A2
Pages La, N10 74 A2
Page St, NW7 71 G1
SW1 33 J1
Pages Wk, SE1 36 D1
Pages Yd, W4 *off Church St* 127 E6
Paget Av, Sutt. SM1 199 G3
Paget Cl, Hmptn. TW12 162 A4
Paget Gdns, Chis. BR7 192 E1
Paget La, Islw. TW7 144 A3
Paget Pl, Kings.T. KT2 164 C6
Thames Ditton KT7 *off Brooklands Rd* 194 D1
Paget Ri, SE18 136 D7
Paget Rd, N16 94 A1
Ilford IG1 98 E4
Paget St, EC1 11 G3
Paget Ter, SE18 136 D6
Pagitts Gro, Barn. EN4 40 E1
Pagnell St, SE14 133 J7
Pagoda Av, Rich. TW9 145 J3
Pagoda Gdns, SE3 154 D2
Pagoda Gro, SE27 169 J2
Pagoda Vista, Rich. TW9 145 J2
Paignton Rd, N15 76 B6
Ruislip HA4 84 A3
Paines Cl, Pnr. HA5 67 E3
Paines La, Pnr. HA5 66 E1
Pains Cl, Mitch. CR4 186 B2
Painsthorpe Rd, N16 *off Oldfield Rd* 94 B3
Painters Ms, SE16 *off Macks Rd* 37 J1
Painters Rd, Ilf. IG2 81 J3
Paisley Rd, N22 75 H1
Carshalton SM5 199 G1
Paisley Ter, Cars. SM5 185 G7
Pakeman St, N7 93 F3
Pakenham Cl, SW12 *off Balham Pk Rd* 168 A1
Pakenham St, WC1 10 D4
Palace Av, W8 22 B2
Palace Ct, NW3 91 E5
W2 14 A5
Harrow HA3 69 H6
Palace Ct Gdns, N10 74 C3
Palace Ex, Enf. EN2 44 A4
Palace Gdns, Buck.H. IG9 64 A1
Enfield EN2 44 A4
Palace Gdns Ms, W8 128 D1
Palace Gdns Ter, W8 128 D1
Palace Gate, W8 22 C4
Palace Gates Rd, N22 74 D1
Palace Grn, W8 22 B3
Croydon CR0 203 J7
Palace Gro, SE19 170 C7
Bromley BR1 191 H1
Palace Ms, E17 77 J4
SW1 32 C2
SW6 *off Hartismere Rd* 128 C7
Palace of Industry, Wem. HA9 *off Fulton Rd* 88 A4
Palace Par, E17 78 A4
Palace Pl, SW1 25 F5
Palace Rd, N8 74 D5
N11 58 E7
SE19 170 C7
SW2 169 F1
Bromley BR1 191 H1
East Molesey KT8 180 A3
Kingston upon Thames KT1 181 G4
Ruislip HA4 84 E4
Palace Rd Est, SW2 169 F1
Palace Sq, SE19 170 C7
Palace St, SW1 25 F5
Palace Vw, SE12 173 G2
Bromley BR1 191 G3
Croydon CR0 203 J4
Palace Vw Rd, E4 62 B5
Palamos Rd, E10 96 A1
Palatine Av, N16 *off Stoke Newington Rd* 94 C4
Palatine Rd, N16 94 B4
Palemead Cl, SW6 147 J1
Palermo Rd, NW10 107 G2
Palestine Gro, SW19 185 G1
Palewell Common Dr, SW14 146 D5
Palewell Pk, SW14 146 D5
Paley Gdns, Loug. IG10 49 E3
Palfrey Pl, SW8 34 D7
Palgrave Av, Sthl. UB1 103 G7
Palgrave Gdns, NW1 7 H5
Palgrave Ho, NW3 91 J5
Palgrave Rd, W12 127 F3
Palissy St, E2 13 F4
Palladino Ho, SW17 *off Laurel Cl* 167 H5
Pallant Way, Orp. BR6 206 D3
Pallet Way, SE18 156 B1
Palliser Rd, W14 128 B5
Pallister Ter, SW15 *off Roehampton Vale* 165 F3
Pall Mall, SW1 25 G2
Pall Mall E, SW1 25 J1
Palmar Cres, Bexh. DA7 159 G3
Palmar Rd, Bexh. DA7 159 G2
Palm Av, Sid. DA14 176 D6
Palm Cl, E10 96 B3
Palmeira Rd, Bexh. DA7 158 D3
Palmer Av, Sutt. SM3 197 J4
Palmer Cl, Houns. TW5 143 G1
Northolt UB5 85 E6
West Wickham BR4 204 D3
Palmer Cres, Kings.T. KT1 181 H3
Palmer Dr, Brom. BR1 192 E4
Palmer Gdns, Barn. EN5 40 A5
Palmer Ho, SE14 *off Lubbock St* 133 G7
Palmer Pl, N7 93 G5
Palmer Rd, E13 115 H4
Dagenham RM8 100 D1
PALMERS GREEN, N13 59 G3
Palmers Gro, W.Mol. KT8 179 G4
Palmers La, Enf. EN1, EN3 45 E1
Palmers Pas, SW14 *off Palmers Rd* 146 C3
Palmers Rd, E2 113 G2
N11 58 C5
SW14 146 C3
SW16 187 F2
Borehamwood WD6 38 B1
Palmerston Cres, N13 59 F5
SE18 137 F6
Palmerston Gro, SW19 166 D7
Palmerston Ho, SW11 *off Strasburg Rd* 150 A1
W8 *off Kensington Pl* 128 D1
Palmerston Rd, E7 97 H5
E17 77 J4
N22 59 F7
NW6 90 D7
SW14 146 C4
SW19 166 D7
W3 126 C3
Buckhurst Hill IG9 63 H2
Carshalton SM5 199 J4
Croydon CR0 188 A5
Palmerston Rd, Har. HA3 68 C3
Hounslow TW3 143 J1
Orpington BR6 207 F4
Sutton SM1 *off Vernon Rd* 199 F5
Twickenham TW2 144 C6
Palmerston Way, SW8 *off Bradmead* 130 B7
Palmer St, SW1 25 H4
Palm Gro, W5 125 H3
Palm Rd, Rom. RM7 83 J5
Pamela Gdns, Pnr. HA5 66 B5
Pamela Wk, E8 *off Marlborough Av* 112 D1
Pampisford Rd, S.Croy. CR2 201 H7
Pams Way, Epsom KT19 196 D5
Pancras La, EC4 20 A4
Pancras Rd, NW1 9 H1
Pancras Way, E3 114 A2
Pandian Way, NW1 *off Busby Pl* 92 D6
Pandora Rd, NW6 90 D6
Panfield Ms, Ilf. IG2 *off Cranbrook Rd* 80 D6
Panfield Rd, SE2 138 A3
Pangbourne Av, W10 107 J5
Pangbourne Dr, Stan. HA7 53 G5
Pangbourne Ho, N7 92 E5
Panhard Pl, Sthl. UB1 103 H7
Pank Av, Barn. EN5 41 F5
Pankhurst Av, E16 *off Wesley Av* 135 H1
Pankhurst Cl, SE14 *off Briant St* 133 G7
Isleworth TW7 144 C3
Pankhurst Rd, Walt. KT12 178 C7
Panmuir Rd, SW20 183 H1
Panmure Cl, N5 93 H4
Panmure Rd, SE26 170 E3
Pannells Ct, Houns. TW5 *off Heston Rd* 123 G6
Panoramic, The, NW3 *off Pond St* 91 H5
Pansy Gdns, W12 107 G7
Panther Dr, NW10 88 D5
Pantiles, The, NW11 *off Willifield Way* 72 C4
Bexleyheath DA7 139 F7
Bromley BR1 192 B3
Pantiles Cl, N13 59 H5
Panton Cl, Croy. CR0 201 H1
Panton St, SW1 17 H6
Panyer All, EC4 19 J4
Papermill Cl, Cars. SM5 200 A4
Papillons Wk, SE3 155 G2
Papworth Gdns, N7 *off Chillingworth Rd* 93 F5
Papworth Way, SW2 151 G7
Parade, The, SW11 32 A7
Carshalton SM5 *off Beynon Rd* 199 J5
Esher (Clay.) KT10 194 B6
Hampton TW12 *off Hampton Rd* 162 A5
Watford (Carp.Pk) WD19 50 E3
Watford (S.Oxhey) WD19 *off Prestwick Rd* 50 D3
Parade Ms, SE27 169 H2
Paradise Pas, N7 93 G5
Paradise Path, SE28 *off Birchdene Dr* 138 A1
Paradise Pl, SE18 *off Godfrey Hill* 136 B4
Paradise Rd, SW4 150 E2
Richmond TW9 145 G5
Paradise Row, E2 *off Bethnal Grn Rd* 113 E3
Paradise St, SE16 132 E2
Paradise Wk, SW3 31 J5
Paragon, The, SE3 155 F2
Paragon Cl, E16 115 G6
Paragon Gro, Surb. KT5 181 J6
Paragon Ms, SE1 36 C1
Paragon Pl, SE3 155 F2
Surbiton KT5 *off Berrylands Rd* 181 J6
Paragon Rd, E9 95 F6
Parbury Ri, Chess. KT9 195 H6
Parbury Rd, SE23 153 H6
Parchmore Rd, Th.Hth. CR7 187 H2
Parchmore Way, Th.Hth. CR7 187 H2
Pardoe Rd, E10 78 B7
Pardoner St, SE1 28 C5
Pardon St, EC1 11 H5
Parfett St, E1 21 J2
Parfitt Cl, NW3 *off North End* 91 F2
Parfrey St, W6 127 J6
Parham Dr, Ilf. IG2 80 E6
Parham Way, N10 74 C2
Paris Gdn, SE1 27 G1

Parish Gate Dr, Sid. DA15 157 H6
Parish La, SE20 171 G6
Parish Ms, SE20 171 G7
Parish Wf, SE18 *off Woodhill* 136 B4
Park, The, N6 74 A6
NW11 90 E1
SE19 170 B7
SE23 *off Park Hill* 171 F1
W5 125 G1
Carshalton SM5 199 J5
Sidcup DA14 176 A5
Park App, Well. DA16 158 B4
Park Av, E6 116 D1
E15 96 E6
N3 73 E1
N13 59 G3
N18 60 D4
N22 75 E2
NW2 89 H6
NW10 105 J3
NW11 90 E1
SW14 146 D4
Barking IG11 99 F6
Bromley BR1 173 F6
Carshalton SM5 200 A6
Enfield EN1 44 B6
Hounslow TW3 143 H6
Ilford IG1 98 D2
Mitcham CR4 168 B7
Orpington (Farnboro.) BR6 206 C3
Southall UB1 123 G1
West Wickham BR4 204 C2
Woodford Green IG8 63 H5
Park Av E, Epsom KT17 197 G6
Park Av Ms, Mitch. CR4 *off Park Av* 168 B7
Park Av N, N8 74 D3
NW10 89 H5
Park Av Rd, N17 61 E7
Park Av S, N8 74 D4
Park Av W, Epsom KT17 197 G6
Park Cen Bldg, E3 *off Fairfield Rd* 114 A2
Park Chase, Wem. HA9 87 J4
Park Cl, E9 113 F1
NW2 89 H3
NW10 105 J3
SW1 23 J4
W4 126 D5
W14 128 C3
Carshalton SM5 199 J6
Hampton TW12 179 J1
Harrow HA3 68 B1
Hounslow TW3 143 J5
Kingston upon Thames KT2 182 A1
Park Ct, SE21 169 J3
SE26 171 E6
SW11 *off Battersea Pk Rd* 150 B1
Kingston upon Thames (Hmptn W.) KT1 181 F1
New Malden KT3 182 D4
Wembley HA9 87 H5
Park Cres, N3 57 E7
W1 8 D6
Enfield EN2 44 A4
Erith DA8 139 J6
Harrow HA3 68 B1
Twickenham TW2 162 A1
Park Cres Ms E, W1 8 E6
Park Cres Ms W, W1 16 D1
Park Cft, Edg. HA8 70 C1
Parkcroft Rd, SE12 155 F7
Park Dale, N11 58 D6
Parkdale Cres, Wor.Pk. KT4 196 D3
Parkdale Rd, SE18 137 H5
Park Dr, N21 43 J6
NW11 90 E1
SE7 136 B6
SW14 146 D4
W3 126 A3
Dagenham RM10 101 J3
Harrow (Har.Wld) HA3 52 B6
Harrow (N.Har.) HA2 67 G7
Park Dr Cl, SE7 136 B5
Park E Bldg, E3 *off Fairfield Rd* 114 A2
Park End, NW3 *off South Hill Pk* 91 H4
Bromley BR1 191 F1
Parker Cl, E16 136 B1
Carshalton SM5 199 J6
Parker Ms, WC2 18 B3
Parke Rd, SW13 147 G1
Sunbury-on-Thames TW16 178 A4
Parker Rd, Croy. CR0 201 J4
Parkers Row, SE1 29 G4
Parker St, E16 136 B1
WC2 18 B3
Parkes Rd, Chigwell IG7 65 H5
Park Fm Cl, N2 73 F3
Pinner HA5 66 B5
Park Fm Rd, Brom. BR1 192 A1
Kingston upon Thames KT2 163 H7
Parkfield Av, SW14 146 E4
Feltham TW13 160 A3
Harrow HA2 67 J2
Northolt UB5 102 D2
Parkfield Cl, Edg. HA8 54 B6
Northolt UB5 102 E2
Parkfield Cres, Felt. TW13 160 A3
Harrow HA2 67 J2
Ruislip HA4 84 E3
Parkfield Dr, Nthlt. UB5 102 D2
Parkfield Gdns, Har. HA2 67 H3
Parkfield Rd, NW10 89 G7
SE14 153 J1
Feltham TW13 160 A3
Harrow HA2 85 J3
Northolt UB5 102 E2
Parkfields, SW15 147 J4
Croydon CR0 203 J1
Parkfields Av, NW9 88 D1
SW20 183 H1
Parkfields Cl, Cars. SM5 200 A4
Parkfields Rd, Kings.T. KT2 163 J5
Parkfield St, N1 11 F1
Parkfield Way, Brom. BR2 192 C6
Park Gdns, NW9 70 B3
Kingston upon Thames KT2 163 J5
Park Gate, N2 73 G3
N21 43 F7
Parkgate, SE3 155 F3
Park Gate, W5 105 G5
Parkgate Av, Barn. EN4 41 F1
Parkgate Cl, Kings.T. KT2 *off Warboys App* 164 B6
Parkgate Cres, Barn. EN4 41 F2
Parkgate Gdns, SW14 146 D5
Parkgate Ms, N6 74 C7
Parkgate Rd, SW11 129 H7
Wallington SM6 200 A5
Park Gates, Har. HA2 85 G4
Park Gro, E15 115 G1
N11 58 D7
Bexleyheath DA7 159 J4
Bromley BR1 191 H1
Edgware HA8 53 J5
Park Gro Rd, E11 96 E2
Park Hall Rd, N2 73 H4
SE21 169 J3
Park Hall Trd Est, SE21 169 J3
Parkham Ct, Brom. BR2 191 E2
Parkham St, SW11 149 H1
Park Hill, SE23 171 E2
SW4 150 D5
W5 105 G5
Bromley BR1 192 B4
Carshalton SM5 199 H6
Loughton IG10 48 A5
Richmond TW10 145 J6
Park Hill Cl, Cars. SM5 199 H5
Park Hill Ct, SW17 *off Beeches Rd* 167 J3
Park Hill Ri, Croy. CR0 202 B2
Parkhill Rd, E4 62 C1
NW3 91 J5
Bexley DA5 159 F7
Park Hill Rd, Brom. BR2 190 E2
Croydon CR0 202 B2
Parkhill Rd, Sid. DA15 175 G3
Park Hill Rd, Wall. SM6 200 B7
Parkhill Wk, NW3 91 J5
Parkholme Rd, E8 94 C6
Park Ho, N21 43 F7
Park Ho Gdns, Twick. TW1 145 F6
Parkhouse St, SE5 36 C7
Parkhurst Gdns, Bex. DA5 159 G7
Parkhurst Rd, E12 98 D4
E17 77 H4
N7 92 E4
N11 58 A4
N17 76 D2
N22 59 F7
Bexley DA5 159 G7
Sutton SM1 199 G4
Parkinson Ho, SW1 *off Tachbrook St* 33 H3
Parkland Cl, Chig. IG7 65 F3
Parkland Gdns, SW19 166 A1
Parkland Mead, Brom. BR1 *off Gardenia Rd* 192 E3
Parkland Rd, N22 75 F2
Woodford Green IG8 63 G7
Parklands, N6 74 B7
Chigwell IG7 65 F3
Surbiton KT5 181 J5
Parklands Cl, SW14 146 C5
Ilford IG2 81 F7
Parklands Ct, Houns. TW5 142 D2
Parklands Dr, N3 72 B3
Parklands Gro, Islw. TW7 *off College Rd* 144 C1
Parklands Rd, SW16 168 B5
Parklands Way, Wor.Pk. KT4 197 E3
Parkland Wk, N4 75 F7
N6 74 D7
N10 74 B4
Park La, E15 *off High St* 114 D1
N9 60 C3
N17 60 D7
W1 24 C2
Carshalton SM5 200 A4
Croydon CR0 202 A3
Harrow HA2 85 H3
Hounslow (Cran.) TW5 122 A7
Richmond TW9 145 G4
Romford (Chad.Hth) RM6 82 D6
Stanmore HA7 52 D3
Sutton SM3 198 B6
Teddington TW11 162 C6
Wallington SM6 200 A4
Wembley HA9 87 H5
Park La Cl, N17 60 D7
PARK LANGLEY, Beck. BR3 190 C5
Park Lawns, Wem. HA9 87 J4
Parklea Cl, NW9 71 E1
Parkleigh Rd, SW19 184 E2
Parkleys, Rich. TW10 163 G4
Park Lo Av, West Dr. UB7 120 C2
Park Mans, SW1 *off Knightsbridge* 23 J4
SW8 34 B5
Parkmead, SW15 147 H6
Park Mead, Har. HA2 85 H3
Parkmead, Loug. IG10 48 D5
Park Mead, Sid. DA15 158 B5
Parkmead Gdns, NW7 55 F6
Park Ms, SE10 *off Calvert Rd* 135 F5
SE24 *off Croxted Rd* 151 J6
Chislehurst BR7 175 E6
East Molesey KT8 179 J4
Hampton (Hmptn H.) TW12 *off Park Rd* 161 J5
Parkmore Cl, Wdf.Grn. IG8 63 G4
Park Par, NW10 107 F2
Park Pl, E14 134 A1
N1 112 A1
SW1 25 F2
W3 126 A4
W5 125 G1
Hampton (Hmptn H.) TW12 161 J6
Wembley HA9 87 J4
Park Pl Vil, W2 14 D1
Park Ridings, N8 75 G3
Park Ri, SE23 171 H1
Harrow HA3 68 B1
Park Ri Rd, SE23 171 H1
Park Rd, E6 115 J1
E10 96 A1
E12 97 H1
E15 115 G1
E17 77 J5
N2 73 G3
N8 74 C4
N11 58 D7
N14 42 D7
N15 75 H4
N18 60 C4
NW1 7 G3
NW4 71 G7
NW8 7 G3
NW9 70 D7
NW10 106 E1
SE25 188 B4
SW19 167 G6
W4 126 C7
W7 104 C7
Barnet (High Barn.) EN5 40 C4
Barnet (New Barn.) EN4 41 H4
Beckenham BR3 171 J7
Bromley BR1 191 H1
Chislehurst BR7 175 E6
East Molesey KT8 179 J4
Feltham TW13 160 D4
Hampton (Hmptn H.) TW12 161 H4
Hounslow TW3 143 J4
Ilford IG1 99 G3
Isleworth TW7 144 E1
Kingston upon Thames KT2 163 J5
Kingston upon Thames (Hmptn W.) KT1 181 F1
New Malden KT3 182 D4
Richmond TW10 145 J6
Park Rd, Sunbury-on-Thames TW16 160 B7
Surbiton KT5 181 J5
Sutton SM3 198 B6
Teddington TW11 162 C6
Twickenham TW1 145 F6
Wallington SM6 200 B5
Wallington (Hackbr.) SM6 200 B2
Wembley HA0 87 H6
Park Rd E, W3 126 B2
Park Rd N, W3 126 B2
W4 126 D5
Park Row, SE10 134 D6
PARK ROYAL, NW10 106 A3
Park Royal Metro Cen, NW10 106 B4
Park Royal Rd, NW10 106 C3
W3 106 C3
Parkshot, Rich. TW9 145 H4
Parkside, N3 72 E1
NW2 89 G3
NW7 55 G6
SE3 135 F7
SW19 166 A4
Buckhurst Hill IG9 63 H2
Hampton (Hmptn H.) TW12 162 A5
Sidcup DA14 176 B2
Sutton SM3 198 B6
Parkside Av, SW19 166 A5
Bromley BR1 192 B4
Parkside Business Est, SE8 *off Rolt St* 133 H6
Parkside Cl, SE20 171 F7
Parkside Cres, N7 93 G3
Surbiton KT5 182 C6
Parkside Dr, Edg. HA8 54 A3
Parkside Est, E9 *off Rutland Rd* 113 G1
Parkside Gdns, SW19 166 A4
Barnet (E.Barn.) EN4 57 J1
Parkside Ho, Dag. RM10 101 J3
Parkside Rd, SW11 150 A1
Belvedere DA17 139 J4
Hounslow TW3 143 H5
Parkside Ter, N18 *off Great Cambridge Rd* 60 A4
Orpington BR6 *off Willow Wk* 206 E3
Parkside Wk, SE10 134 E5
Parkside Way, Har. HA2 67 H4
Park S, SW11 *off Austin Rd* 150 A1
Park Sq E, NW1 8 D5
Park Sq Ms, NW1 8 D6
Park Sq W, NW1 8 D5
Parkstead Rd, SW15 147 G5
Park Steps, W2 *off St. Georges Flds* 15 H5
Parkstone Av, N18 60 C5
Parkstone Rd, E17 78 C3
SE15 *off Rye La* 152 D2
Park St, SE1 27 J1
W1 16 B5
Croydon CR0 201 J2
Teddington TW11 162 B6
Park Ter, Wor.Pk. KT4 197 G1
Parkthorne Cl, Har. HA2 67 H6
Parkthorne Dr, Har. HA2 67 G6
Parkthorne Rd, SW12 150 D7
Park Twrs, W1 *off Brick St* 24 D2
Park Vw, N21 43 F7
W3 106 C5
New Malden KT3 183 F3
Pinner HA5 67 F1
Wembley HA9 88 B5
Parkview Cl, Cars. SM5 199 J7
Parkview Ct, SW18 *off Broomhill Rd* 148 D6
Park Vw Ct, Ilf. IG2 *off Brancaster Rd* 81 H6
Parkview Cres, Wor.Pk. KT4 197 J1
Park Vw Cres, N11 58 B4
Parkview Dr, Mitch. CR4 185 G2
Park Vw Est, E2 113 F2
N5 93 J4
Park Vw Gdns, NW4 71 J5
Ilford IG4 80 C4
Park Vw Ho, SE24 *off Hurst St* 151 H6
Park Vw Ms, SW9 151 F2
Park Vw Rd, N3 73 E1
N17 76 D3
NW10 89 F4
Parkview Rd, SE9 174 E1
Park Vw Rd, W5 105 H5
Parkview Rd, Croy. CR0 202 D1
Park Vw Rd, Pnr. HA5 50 B7
Southall UB1 123 G1
Welling DA16 158 C3
Park Vw Rd Est, N17 76 E2
Park Village E, NW1 110 B2
Park Village W, NW1 8 D1

Park Vil, Rom. RM6 ....**82** D6
Parkville Rd, SW6 ....**128** C7
Park Vista, SE10 ....**134** D6
Park Wk, N6
off North Rd **74** A7
SE10
off Crooms Hill **134** D7
SW10 ....**30** D5
Parkway, N14 ....**58** E2
Park Way, N20 ....**57** J4
Parkway, NW1 ....**110** B1
Park Way, NW11 ....**72** B5
Parkway, SW20 ....**184** A4
Park Way, Edg. HA8 ....**70** B1
Enfield EN2 ....**43** G2
Parkway, Erith DA18 .....**139** E3
Park Way, Felt. TW14 .....**142** B7
Parkway, Ilf. IG3 ....**99** J3
Park Way, Ruis. HA4 ....**84** A1
West Molesey KT8 .....**179** H3
Parkway, Wdf.Grn. IG8 ....**63** J5
Parkway, The, Hayes UB3,
UB4 ....**102** C6
Hounslow (Cran.) TW4,
TW5 ....**142** B2
Northolt UB5 ....**102** D3
Southall UB2 ....**122** A5
Parkway Trd Est, Houns.
TW5 ....**122** C6
Park W, W2 ....**15** H4
Park W Bldg, E3
off Fairfield Rd **114** A2
Park W Pl, W2 ....**15** H3
Parkwood, N20 ....**57** J3
Beckenham BR3 ....**190** A1
Parkwood Gro, Sun.
TW16 ....**178** A3
Parkwood Ms, N6 ....**74** B6
Parkwood Rd, SW19 .....**166** C5
Bexley DA5 ....**159** F7
Isleworth TW7 ....**144** C1
Parliament Ct, E1 ....**21** E2
Parliament Hill, NW3 ......**91** H4
Parliament Ms, SW14
off Thames Bk **146** C2
Parliament Sq, SW1 ....**26** A4
Parliament St, SW1 ....**26** A4
Parliament Vw Apts, SE1 ..**34** C1
Parma Cres, SW11 ....**149** J4
Parmiter St, E2 ....**113** E2
Parmoor Ct, EC1 ....**11** J5
Parnell Cl, W12 ....**127** H3
Edgware HA8 ....**54** B4
Parnell Rd, E3 ....**113** J1
Parnham Cl, Brom. BR1
off Stoneleigh Rd **192** E3
Parnham St, E14
off Blount St **113** H6
Parolles Rd, N19 ....**92** C1
Paroma Rd, Belv. DA17 ...**139** G3
Parr Cl, N9 ....**60** E4
N18 ....**60** E4
Parr Ct, N1 ....**12** B1
Feltham TW13 ....**160** C4
Parr Pl, W4
off Chiswick High Rd ..**127** F4
Parr Rd, E6 ....**116** A1
Stanmore HA7 ....**69** G1
Parrs Pl, Hmptn. TW12 ....**161** G7
Parr St, N1 ....**12** B1
Parry Av, E6 ....**116** C6
Parry Cl, Epsom KT17 ....**197** G7
Parry Pl, SE18 ....**137** E4
Parry Rd, SE25 ....**188** B3
W10 ....**108** B3
Parry St, SW8 ....**34** A5
Parsifal Rd, NW6 ....**90** D5
Parsley Gdns, Croy. CR0
off Primrose La **203** G1
Parsloes Av, Dag. RM9 ...**100** D4
Parsonage Ct, Loug. IG10 ..**49** E3
Parsonage Gdns, Enf. EN2 .**43** J2
Parsonage La, Enf. EN1,
EN2 ....**44** A2
Sidcup DA14 ....**177** F4
Parsonage Manorway,
Belv. DA17 ....**139** G6
Parsonage St, E14 ....**134** C4
Parsons Cl, Sutt. SM1 ....**199** E3
Parsons Cres, Edg. HA8 ...**54** A3
PARSONS GREEN, SW6 ..**148** D1
Parsons Grn, SW6 ....**148** D1
Parsons Grn La, SW6 .....**148** D1
Parsons Gro, Edg. HA8 ....**54** A3
Parsons Ho, SW2
off New Pk Rd **150** E7
Parson's Ho, W2 ....**7** E6
Parson's Mead, Croy.
CR0 ....**201** H1
Parsons Mead, E.Mol.
KT8 ....**179** J3
Parsons Rd, E13
off Old St **115** J2
Parson St, NW4 ....**71** J4
Parthenia Rd, SW6 ....**148** D1
Partingdale La, NW7 ......**56** A5
Partington Cl, N19 ....**92** D1
Partridge Cl, E16
off Fulmer Rd **116** A5
Barnet EN5 ....**39** J6
Bushey WD23 ....**51** H1
Stanmore HA7 ....**53** H4
Partridge Dr, Orp. BR6 ....**207** F3
Partridge Grn, SE9 ....**174** D3
Partridge Rd, Hmptn.
TW12 ....**161** F6
Sidcup DA14 ....**175** H3
Partridge Sq, E6
off Nightingale Way ...**116** B5
Partridge Way, N22 ....**75** E1
Parvin St, SW8 ....**150** D1
Pasadena Cl, Hayes UB3 ..**122** B2
Pasadena Cl Trd Est, Hayes
UB3 *off Pasadena Cl* ...**122** B2
Pasadena Trd Est, Hayes
UB3 *off Pasadena Cl* ...**122** B2
Pascal Ms, SE19
off Anerley Hill **170** D7
Pascal St, SW8 ....**33** J7
Pascoe Rd, SE13 ....**154** D5
Pasgen Ct, N9
off Galahad Rd **60** D2
Pasley Cl, SE17 ....**35** J4
Pasquier Rd, E17 ....**77** H3
Passey Pl, SE9 ....**156** C6
Passfield Dr, E14
off Uamvar St **114** B5
Passfield Path, SE28
off Booth Cl **118** B7
Passfields, SE6 ....**172** C3
Passing All, EC1 ....**11** H6
Passmore Gdns, N11 ....**58** D6
Passmore St, SW1 ....**32** B2
★ **Passport Office**, SW1 ..**33** E1
Pasteur Cl, NW9 ....**71** E2
Pasteur Gdns, N18 ....**59** H5
Paston Cl, E5
off Caldecott Way **95** G3
Wallington SM6 ....**200** C3
Paston Cres, SE12 ....**155** H7
Pastor St, SE11 ....**35** H1
Pasture Cl, Wem. HA0 .....**86** E3
Pasture Rd, SE6 ....**173** F1
Dagenham RM9 ....**101** F4
Wembley HA0 ....**86** E2
Pastures, The, N20 ....**56** C1
Pastures Path, E11 ....**97** E1
Patcham Ter, SW8 ....**150** B1
Patching Way, Hayes
UB4 ....**102** E5
Paternoster La, EC4
off Warwick La **19** H4
Paternoster Row, EC4 .....**19** J4
Paternoster Sq, EC4 ....**19** H4
Paterson Ct, EC1
off St. Luke's Est **12** B4
Pater St, W8 ....**128** D3
Pates Manor Dr, Felt.
TW14 ....**141** G7
Path, The, SW19 ....**184** E1
Pathfield Rd, SW16 ......**168** D6
Pathway, The, Wat. WD19
off Anthony Cl **50** D1
Patience Rd, SW11 ....**149** H2
Patio Cl, SW4 ....**150** D6
Patmore Est, SW8 ....**150** C1
Patmore St, SW8 ....**150** C1
Patmos Rd, SW9 ....**131** H7
Paton Cl, E3 ....**114** A3
Paton St, EC1 ....**11** J4
Patricia Ct, Chis. BR7
off Manor Pk Rd **193** G1
Welling DA16 ....**138** B7
Patrick Connolly Gdns, E3
off Talwin St **114** B3
Patrick Rd, E13 ....**115** J3
Patriot Sq, E2 ....**113** E2
Patrol Pl, SE6 ....**154** B6
Patshull Pl, NW5
off Patshull Rd **92** C6
Patshull Rd, NW5 ....**92** C6
Patten All, Rich. TW10
off The Hermitage **145** G5
Pattenden Rd, SE6 ....**171** J1
Patten Rd, SW18 ....**149** H7
Patterdale Cl, Brom. BR1 ..**173** F6
Patterdale Rd, SE15 ......**133** F7
Patterson Ct, SE19 ....**170** C7
Patterson Rd, SE19 ......**170** C6
Pattina Wk, SE16 ....**133** J1
Pattison Rd, NW2 ....**90** D3
Pattison Wk, SE18 ....**137** F5
Paul Cl, E15 ....**96** E7
Paulet Rd, SE5 ....**151** H2
Paulet Way, NW10 ....**88** E7
Paul Gdns, Croy. CR0 ....**202** C2
Paulhan Rd, Har. HA3 .....**69** G4
Paulin Dr, N21 ....**43** G7
Pauline Cres, Twick. TW2 ..**161** J1
Pauline Ho, E1 ....**21** J1
Paul Julius Cl, E14 ....**114** D7
Paul Robeson Cl, E6 ......**116** D3
Paul's Nurs Rd, Loug. (High
Beach) IG10 ....**47** H1
Paul St, E15 ....**114** D1
EC2 ....**12** C6
Paul's Wk, EC4 ....**19** H5
Paultons Sq, SW3 ....**31** F5
Paultons St, SW3 ....**31** F6
Pauntley St, N19 ....**92** C1
Paved Ct, Rich. TW9 ......**145** G5
Paveley Ct, NW7 ....**56** A7
Paveley Dr, SW11 ....**129** H7
Paveley Ho, N1
off Priory Grn Est **10** C2
Paveley St, NW8 ....**7** H5
Pavement, The, SW4 ......**150** C4
W5 *off Popes La* **125** H3
Isleworth TW7
off South St **144** D3
Pavement Ms, Rom. RM6
off Clarissa Rd **82** D7
Pavement Sq, Croy. CR0 ..**202** D1
Pavet Cl, Dag. RM10 ......**101** H6
Pavilion La, Beck. BR3 ....**171** J6
Pavilion Ms, N3
off Windermere Av **72** D2
Pavilion Par, W12
off Wood La **107** J6
Pavilion Rd, SW1 ....**24** A6
Ilford IG1 ....**80** C7
Pavilion Sq, SW17 ....**167** H3
Pavilion St, SW1 ....**24** A6
Pavilion Ter, W12
off Wood La **107** J6
East Molesey KT8 .....**180** C4
Ilford IG2
off Southdown Cres ...**81** H5
Pavilion Way, Edg. HA8 ....**54** B7
Ruislip HA4 ....**84** C2
Pavillion Ms, N4 ....**93** F2
Pawleyne Cl, SE20 ....**171** F7
Pawsey Cl, E13
off Plashet Rd **115** G1
Pawson's Rd, Croy. CR0 ..**187** J6
Paxford Rd, Wem. HA0 ....**86** E2
Paxton Cl, Rich. TW9 .....**145** J2
Walton-on-Thames
KT12 ....**178** C7
Paxton Ct, SE12 ....**173** J3
Borwd. WD6
off Manor Way **38** C4
Paxton Pl, SE27 ....**170** B4
Paxton Rd, N17 ....**60** C7
SE23 ....**171** H3
W4 ....**126** E6
Bromley BR1 ....**173** G7
Paxton Ter, SW1 ....**33** E5
Payne Cl, Bark. IG11 ....**99** H7
Paynell Ct, SE3
off Lawn Ter **155** E3
Payne Rd, E3 ....**114** B2
Paynesfield Av, SW14 ....**146** D3
Payne St, SE8 ....**133** J6
Paynes Wk, W6 ....**128** B6
Payzes Gdns, Wdf.Grn.
IG8 *off Chingford La* **63** F5
Peabody Av, SW1 ....**32** D3
Peabody Cl, SE10
off Devonshire Dr **154** B1
SW1 ....**32** E5
Croydon CR0 ....**203** F1
Peabody Cotts, SE24
off Rosendale Rd **151** J7
Peabody Dws, WC1 ....**10** A5
Peabody Est, EC1
(Clerkenwell)
off Farringdon La **11** F6
EC1 (St. Luke's) **12** A6
N1 (Islington)
off Greenman St **111** J1
N17 ....**76** B1
SE1 ....**27** F2
SE17 ....**36** B2
SE24 ....**151** H7
SW1 ....**33** F1
SW3 ....**31** H5
SW6 *off Lillie Rd* **128** D6
W6 *off The Square* **127** J5
W10 ....**107** J5
Peabody Hill, SE21 ....**169** H1
Peabody Hill Est, SE21 ...**151** H7
Peabody Sq, SE1 ....**27** G4
Peabody Twr, EC1
off Golden La **12** A6
Peabody Trust, SE1 ....**27** J2
**Peabody Trust Camberwell
Grn Est**, SE5
off Camberwell Grn ..**152** A1
**Peabody Trust Old Pye St
Est**, SW1
off Old Pye St **25** H6
Peabody Yd, N1
off Greenman St **111** J1
Peace Cl, N14 ....**42** B5
SE25 ....**188** B4
Greenford UB6
off Oldfield La N **104** A1
Peace Gro, Wem. HA9 .....**88** B3
Peace St, SE18
off Nightingale Vale ...**136** E6
Peaches Cl, Sutt. SM2 ....**198** B7
Peach Gro, E11 ....**96** D3
Peach Rd, W10 ....**108** A3
Feltham TW13 ....**160** A1
Peachum Rd, SE3 ....**135** F6
Peachwalk Ms, E3
off Grove Rd **113** G2
Peachy Cl, Edg. HA8
off Manor Pk Cres **54** A6
Peacock Cl, E4 ....**61** J7
Dagenham RM8 ....**100** C1
Peacock Ind Est, N17 ......**60** C7
Peacock St, SE17 ....**35** H2
Peacock Wk, E16 ....**115** H6
Peacock Yd, SE17 ....**35** H2
Peak, The, SE26 ....**171** F3
Peaketon Av, Ilf. IG4 ....**80** A4
Peak Hill, SE26 ....**171** F4
Peak Hill Av, SE26 ....**171** F4
Peak Hill Gdns, SE26 .....**171** F4
Peal Gdns, W13 ....**104** D4
Peall Rd, Croy. CR0 ......**187** F6
Pearce Cl, Mitch. CR4 .....**186** A2
Pearcefield Av, SE23 .....**171** F1
Pear Cl, NW9 ....**70** D4
SE14
off Southerngate Way ..**133** H7
Pearcroft Rd, E11 ....**96** D2
Peardon St, SW8 ....**150** B3
Peareswood Gdns, Stan.
HA7 ....**69** G1
Pearfield Rd, SE23 ....**171** H3
Pearing Cl, Sutt. SM3 .....**198** A2
Pearl Cl, E6 ....**116** D6
NW2 ....**72** A7
Pearl Rd, E17 ....**78** A3
Pearl St, E1
off Penang St **133** E1
Pearman St, SE1 ....**27** F5
Pear Pl, SE1 ....**27** E3
Pear Rd, E11 ....**96** D3
Pearscroft Ct, SW6 ....**149** E1
Pearscroft Rd, SW6 ....**148** E1
Pearse St, SE15 ....**36** E6
Pearson Cl, SE5
off Medlar St **151** J1
Barnet EN5 ....**40** E4
Pearson Ms, SW4 ....**150** D3
Pearsons Av, SE14
off Tanners Hill **154** A1
Pearson St, E2 ....**13** E1
Pearson Way, Mitch. CR4 ..**186** A1
Pears Rd, Houns. TW3 ....**143** J3
Peartree Av, SW17 ....**167** F3
Pear Tree Cl, E2 ....**112** C1
Bromley BR2 ....**192** A5
Chessington KT9 ......**196** A5
Mitcham CR4 ....**185** H2
Peartree Ct, E18
off Churchfields **79** H1
Pear Tree Ct, EC1 ....**11** F6
Peartree Gdns, Dag. RM8 .**100** B4
Romford RM7 ....**83** H2
Peartree La, E1
off Glamis Rd **113** F7
Peartree Rd, Enf. EN1 .....**44** B3
Pear Tree St, EC1 ....**11** H5
Peartree Way, SE10 ......**135** G4
Peary Pl, E2
off Kirkwall Pl **113** F3
Peatfield Cl, Sid. DA15
off Woodside Rd **175** H3
Pebble Way, W3 ....**126** B1
Pebworth Rd, Har. HA1 ....**86** D2
Peckarmans Wd, SE26 ....**170** D3
Peckett Sq, N5
off Highbury Gra **93** H4
Peckford Pl, SW9 ....**151** G2
PECKHAM, SE15 ....**152** D1
Peckham Gro, SE15 ....**36** E7
Peckham High St, SE15 ...**152** D1
Peckham Hill St, SE15 .....**37** H7
Peckham Pk Rd, SE15 .....**37** H7
Peckham Rd, SE5 ....**152** B1
SE15 ....**152** B1
Peckham Rye, SE15 ......**152** D3
SE22 ....**152** D4
Pecks Yd, E1 ....**21** F1
Peckwater St, NW5 ....**92** C5
Pedlars Wk, N7 ....**93** E6
Pedley Rd, Dag. RM8 .....**100** C1
Pedley St, E1 ....**13** G6
Pedro St, E5 ....**95** G3
Pedworth Gdns, SE16
*off Rotherhithe
New Rd* **133** F4
Peek Cres, SW19 ....**166** A5
Peel Cl, E4 ....**62** B2
N9
off Plevna Rd **60** D3
Peel Dr, NW9 ....**71** F3
Ilford IG5 ....**80** B3
Peel Gro, E2 ....**113** F2
Peel Pas, W8
off Peel St **128** D1
Peel Pl, Ilf. IG5 ....**80** B2
Peel Prec, NW6 ....**108** D2

Peel Rd, E18 79 F1
NW6 108 C3
Harrow (Wealds.) HA3 68 C3
Orpington BR6 207 F5
Wembley HA9 87 G3
Peel St, W8 128 D1
Peerglow Est, Enf. EN3 45 F4
Peerless St, EC1 12 B4
Pegamoid Rd, N18 61 F3
Pegasus Cl, N16
off Green Las 94 A4
Pegasus Ct, W3
off Horn La 106 C6
Harrow HA3 69 G5
Pegasus Pl, SE11 35 E5
SW6 *off Ackmar Rd* 148 D1
Pegasus Rd, Croy. CR0 201 G6
Pegasus Way, N11 58 B6
Pegg Rd, Houns. TW5 122 D7
Pegley Gdns, SE12 173 G2
Pegwell St, SE18 137 H7
Pekin Cl, E14
off Pekin St 114 A6
Pekin St, E14 114 A6
Peldon Ct, Rich. TW9 145 J4
Peldon Pas, Rich. TW10
off Worple Way 145 J4
Peldon Wk, N1
off Britannia Row 111 H1
Pelham Av, Bark. IG11 117 J1
Pelham Cl, SE5 152 B2
Pelham Cres, SW7 31 G2
Pelham Ho, W14
off Mornington Av 128 C4
Pelham Pl, SW7 31 G2
W13 *off Ruislip Rd E* 104 C4
Pelham Rd, E18 79 H3
N15 76 C4
N22 75 G2
SW19 166 D7
Beckenham BR3 189 F2
Bexleyheath DA7 159 G3
Ilford IG1 99 G2
Pelham St, SW7 31 F1
Pelican Est, SE15 152 C1
Pelican Ho, SE5
off Peckham Rd 152 C1
Pelican Pas, E1
off Cambridge Heath Rd 113 F4
Pelier St, SE17 36 A5
Pelinore Rd, SE6 172 E2
Pellant Rd, SW6 128 B7
Pellatt Gro, N22 75 G1
Pellatt Rd, SE22 152 C5
Wembley HA9 87 H2
Pellerin Rd, N16 94 B5
Pellings Cl, Bromley BR2 190 E3
Pelling St, E14 114 A6
Pellipar Cl, N13 59 G3
Pellipar Gdns, SE18 136 C5
Pellow Cl, Barn. EN5 40 C6
Pelly Rd, E13 115 G2
Pelter St, E2 13 F3
Pelton Rd, SE10 134 E5
Pembar Av, E17 77 H3
Pemberley Chase, Epsom (W.Ewell) KT19 196 B5
Pemberley Cl, Epsom (W.Ewell) KT19 196 B5
Pember Rd, NW10 108 A3
Pemberton Gdns, N19 92 C3
Romford RM6 82 E5
Pemberton Ho, SE26
off High Level Dr 170 D4
Pemberton Pl, E8
off Mare St 95 E7
Pemberton Rd, N4 75 G5
East Molesey KT8 179 J4
Pemberton Row, EC4 19 F3
Pemberton Ter, N19 92 C3
Pembridge Av, Twick. TW2 161 F1
Pembridge Cres, W11 108 D7
Pembridge Gdns, W2 108 D7
Pembridge Ms, W11 108 D7
Pembridge Pl, SW15 148 D5
W2 108 D7
Pembridge Rd, W11 108 D7
Pembridge Sq, W2 108 D7
Pembridge Vil, W2 108 D7
W11 108 D7
Pembroke Av, N1 111 E1
Harrow HA3 68 D3
Pinner HA5 84 D1
Surbiton KT5 182 B5
Pembroke Cl, SW1 24 C4
Pembroke Cotts, W8
off Pembroke Sq 128 D3
Pembroke Gdns, W8 128 C4
Dagenham RM10 101 H3
Pembroke Gdns Cl, W8 128 D3
Pembroke Ms, E3
off Morgan St 113 H3
N10 74 A1
Pembroke Ms, W8
off Earls Wk 128 D3
Pembroke Pl, W8 128 D3
Edgware HA8 54 A7
Isleworth TW7
off Thornbury Rd 144 B2
Pembroke Rd, E6 116 C5
E17 78 B5
N8 74 E4
N10 74 A1
N13 59 J3
N15 76 C5
SE25 188 B4
W8 128 D4
Bromley BR1 191 J2
Erith DA8 139 J5
Greenford UB6 103 H4
Ilford IG3 99 J1
Mitcham CR4 186 A2
Wembley HA9 87 G3
Pembroke Sq, W8 128 D3
Pembroke St, N1 93 E7
Pembroke Studios, W8 128 C3
Pembroke Vil, W8 128 D4
Richmond TW9 145 G4
Pembroke Wk, W8 128 D4
Pembroke Way, Hayes UB3 121 F3
Pembry Cl, SW9 151 G1
Pembury Av, Wor.Pk. KT4 183 G7
Pembury Cl, E5
off Shellness Rd 95 E5
Bromley BR2 191 F7
Pembury Ct, Hayes (Harling.) UB3 121 G6
Pembury Cres, Sid. DA14 176 E2
Pembury Pl, E5 94 E5
Pembury Rd, E5 94 E5
N17 76 C2
SE25 188 D4
Bexleyheath DA7 139 E7
Pemdevon Rd, Croy. CR0 187 G7
Pemell Cl, E1
off Colebert Av 113 F4
Pemerich Cl, Hayes UB3 121 J5
Pempath Pl, Wem. HA9 87 G2
Penally Pl, N1
off Shepperton Rd 112 A1
Penang St, E1 133 E1
Penard Rd, Sthl. UB2 123 G3
Penarth St, SE15 133 F6
Penates, Esher KT10 194 A4
Penberth Rd, SE6 172 C2
Penbury Rd, Sthl. UB2 123 F4
Pencombe Ms, W11
off Denbigh Rd 108 C7
Pencraig Way, SE15 132 E6
Pendall Cl, Barn. EN4 41 H4
Penda Rd, Erith DA8 139 H7
Pendarves Rd, SW20 183 J1
Penda's Mead, E9
off Lindisfarne Way 95 H4
Pendell Av, Hayes UB3 121 J7
Pendennis Rd, N17 76 A3
SW16 168 E4
Penderel Rd, Houns. TW3 143 G5
Penderry Ri, SE6 172 D2
Penderyn Way, N7 92 D4
Pendle Rd, SW16 168 B6
Pendlestone Rd, E17 78 A5
Pendlewood Cl, W5
off Queens Wk 105 F5
Pendolino Way, NW10 88 A7
Pendragon Rd, Brom. BR1 173 F3
Pendragon Wk, NW9 70 E6
Pendrell Rd, SE4 153 H2
Pendrell St, SE18 137 G7
Pendula Dr, Hayes UB4 102 D4
Pendulum Ms, E8
off Birkbeck Rd 94 C5
Penerley Rd, SE6 172 B1
Penfields Ho, N7
off York Way 92 E6
Penfold Cl, Croy. CR0 201 G3
Penfold La, Bex. DA5 176 D2
Penfold Pl, NW1 15 F1
Penfold Rd, N9 61 G1
Penfold St, NW1 7 F6
NW8 7 F6
Penford Gdns, SE9 156 A3
Penford St, SE5 151 H2
Pengarth Rd, Bex. DA5 158 D5
PENGE, SE20 171 F7
Penge Ho, SW11
off Wye St 149 G3
Penge La, SE20 171 F7
Penge Rd, E13 97 J7
SE20 188 D3
SE25 188 D3
Penhall Rd, SE7 136 A4
Penhill Rd, Bex. DA5 158 C7
Penhurst Pl, SE1 26 D6
Penhurst Rd, Ilf. IG6 65 E7
Penifather La, Grnf. UB6 104 A3
Peninsula Apts, W2
off Praed St 15 G2
Peninsula Hts, SE1 34 B3
Peninsular Cl, Felt. TW14 141 G6
Peninsular Pk Rd, SE7 135 G4
Penistone Rd, SW16 168 E7
Penketh Dr, Har. HA1 86 A3
Penmon Rd, SE2 138 A3
Pennack Rd, SE15 37 G6
Pennant Ms, W8 30 A1
Pennant Ter, E17 77 J2
Pennard Rd, W12 127 J2
Pennards, The, Sun. TW16 178 C2
Penn Cl, Grnf. UB6 103 H2
Harrow HA3 69 F4
Penner Cl, SW19 166 B2
Penners Gdns, Surb. KT6 181 H7
Pennethorne Cl, E9
off Victoria Pk Rd 113 F1
Pennethorne Ho, SW11
off Wye St 149 G3
Pennethorne Rd, SE15 132 E7
Penn Gdns, Chis. BR7 192 E2
Pennine Dr, NW2 90 B2
Pennine Ho, N9
off Edmonton Grn Shop Cen 60 D3
Pennine La, NW2
off Pennine Dr 90 B2
Pennine Way, Hayes (Harling.) UB3 121 G7
Pennington Cl, SE27
off Hamilton Rd 170 A4
Pennington Dr, N21 43 E5
Pennington St, E1 21 J6
Pennington Way, SE12 173 H2
Penniston Cl, N17 75 J2
Penniwell Cl, Edg. HA8 53 J4
Penn La, Bex. DA5 158 D5
Penn Rd, N7 93 E5
Penn St, N1 112 A1
Pennyfather La, Enf. EN2 43 J2
Pennyfields, E14 114 A7
Penny Ms, SW12 150 B7
Pennymoor Wk, W9
off Riverton Cl 108 C3
Penny Rd, NW10 106 B3
Pennyroyal Av, E6 116 D6
Penpoll Rd, E8 94 E6
Penpool La, Well. DA16 158 B3
Penrhyn Av, E17 77 J1
Penrhyn Cres, E17 78 A1
SW14 146 C4
Penrhyn Gdns, Kings.T. KT1 *off Surbiton Rd* 181 G4
Penrhyn Gro, E17 78 A1
Penrhyn Rd, Kings.T. KT1 181 H3
Penrith Cl, SW15 148 B5
Beckenham BR3 190 B1
Penrith Pl, SE27 169 H2
Penrith Rd, N15 76 A5
Ilford IG6 65 J6
New Malden KT3 182 D4
Thornton Heath CR7 187 J2
Penrith St, SW16 168 C6
Penrose Av, Wat. WD19 50 D2
Penrose Gro, SE17 35 J4
Penrose Ho, SE17 35 J4
Penrose St, SE17 35 J4
Penryn St, NW1 9 H1
Penry St, SE1 37 E2
Pensbury Pl, SW8 150 C2
Pensbury St, SW8 150 C2
Penscroft Gdns, Borwd. WD6 38 D4
Pensford Av, Rich. TW9 146 A2
Penshurst Av, Sid. DA15 158 A6
Penshurst Gdns, Edg. HA8 54 B5
Penshurst Grn, Brom. BR2 191 F5
Penshurst Rd, E9 95 G7
N17 60 C7
Bexleyheath DA7 159 F1
Thornton Heath CR7 187 H5
Penshurst Wk, Brom. BR2
off Penshurst Grn 191 F5
Penshurst Way, Sutt. SM2 198 D7
Pensilver Cl, Barn. EN4 41 H4
Penstemon Cl, N3 56 D7
Penstock Footpath, N22 75 E3
Pentavia Retail Pk, NW7 55 F7
Pentelow Gdns, Felt. TW14 142 A6
Pentire Rd, E17 78 D1
Pentland Av, Edg. HA8 54 B2
Pentland Cl, N9 61 F2
NW11 90 B2
Pentland Gdns, SW18
off St. Ann's Hill 149 F6
Pentland Pl, Nthlt. UB5 102 E1
Pentland Rd, NW6 108 D3
Pentlands Cl, Mitch. CR4 186 B3
Pentland St, SW18 149 F6
Pentlow St, SW15 147 J3
Pentlow Way, Buck.H. IG9 48 B7
Pentney Rd, E4 62 D1
SW12 168 C1
SW19
off Midmoor Rd 184 B1
Penton Gro, N1 11 E2
Penton Ho, SE2
off Hartslock Dr 138 D2
Penton Pl, SE17 35 H3
Penton Ri, WC1 10 D3
Penton St, N1 10 E1
PENTONVILLE, N1 10 E2
Pentonville Rd, N1 10 C2
Pentridge St, SE15 37 F7
Pentyre Av, N18 60 A5
Penwerris Av, Islw. TW7 123 J7
Penwith Rd, SW18 166 E2
Penwood Ho, SW15
off Tunworth Cres 147 F6
Penwortham Rd, SW16 168 B6
Penylan Pl, Edg. HA8 54 A7
Penywern Rd, SW5 128 D5
Penzance Pl, W11 128 B1
Penzance St, W11 128 B1
Peony Ct, Wdf.Grn. IG8
off The Bridle Path 63 E7
Peony Gdns, W12 107 G7
Pepler Ms, SE5 37 F5
Peploe Rd, NW6 108 A2
Peplow Cl, West Dr. UB7 120 A1
Pepper All, Loug. (High Beach) IG10 47 G1
Pepper Cl, E6 116 C5
Peppercorn Cl, Th.Hth. CR7 188 A2
Peppermead Sq, SE13 154 A5
Peppermint Cl, Croy. CR0 186 E7
Peppermint Pl, E11
off Birch Gro 96 E3
Pepper St, E14 134 B3
SE1 27 J3
Peppie Cl, N16 94 B2
Pepys Cres, E16
off Britannia Gate 135 G1
Barnet EN5 39 J5
Pepys Ri, Orp. BR6 207 J1
Pepys Rd, SE14 153 G1
SW20 183 J1
Pepys St, EC3 21 E5
Perceval Av, NW3 91 H5
Percheron Cl, Islw. TW7 144 D3
Percheron Rd, Borwd. WD6 38 D6
Perch St, E8 94 C4
Percival Ct, N17 60 C7
Northolt UB5 85 G5
★ **Percival David Foundation of Chinese Art**, WC1 9 J5
Percival Gdns, Rom. RM6 82 C6
Percival Rd, SW14 146 C4
Enfield EN1 44 C4
Orpington BR6 207 E2
Percival St, EC1 11 G5
Percival Way, Epsom KT19 196 C4
Percy Bush Rd, West Dr. UB7 120 C3
Percy Circ, WC1 10 D3
Percy Gdns, Enf. EN3 45 G5
Isleworth TW7 144 D2
Worcester Park KT4 196 D1
Percy Ho, SW16
off Pringle Gdns 168 C4
Percy Ms, W1 17 H2
Percy Pas, W1 17 G2
Percy Rd, E11 78 E7
E16 115 E5
N12 57 F5
N21 43 J7
SE20 189 G1
SE25 188 D5
W12 127 G2
Bexleyheath DA7 159 E2
Hampton TW12 161 G7
Ilford IG3 82 A7
Isleworth TW7 144 D4
Mitcham CR4 186 A7
Romford RM7 83 H3
Twickenham TW2 161 H1
Percy St, W1 17 H2
Percy Ter, Brom. BR1 192 E3
Percy Way, Twick. TW2 161 J1
Percy Yd, WC1 10 D3
Peregrine Cl, NW10 88 D5
Peregrine Ct, SW16 169 F4
Welling DA16 157 J1
Peregrine Gdns, Croy. CR0 203 H2
Peregrine Ho, EC1 11 H3
Peregrine Rd, N17 59 J7
Peregrine Way, SW19 165 J7
Perham Rd, W14 128 B5
Peridot St, E6 116 B5
Perifield, SE21 169 J1
Perimeade Rd, Grnf. UB6 105 F2
Periton Rd, SE9 156 A4
PERIVALE, Grnf. UB6 105 F1

Perivale, Grnf. UB6 **104** C3
Perivale Gdns, W13
off Bellevue Rd **104** E4
Perivale Gra, Grnf. (Perivale) UB6 **104** D3
Perivale Ind Pk, Grnf. (Perivale) UB6 **104** D2
Perivale La, Grnf. (Perivale) UB6 **104** D3
Perivale New Business Cen, Grnf. (Perivale) UB6 **105** E2
Periwood Cres, Grnf. UB6
off Horsenden La S **104** D1
Perkin Cl, Houns. TW3 **143** H4
Wembley HA0 **86** E5
Perkin's Rents, SW1 **25** H5
Perkins Rd, Ilf. IG2 **81** G5
Perkins Sq, SE1 **28** A1
Perks Cl, SE3
off Hurren Cl **154** E3
Perpins Rd, SE9 **157** H6
Perran Rd, SW2
off Christchurch Rd **169** H2
Perran Wk, Brent. TW8 **125** H5
Perren St, NW5
off Ryland Rd **92** B6
Perrers Rd, W6 **127** H4
Perrin Rd, Wem. HA0 **86** D4
Perrins Ct, NW3
off Hampstead High St **91** F4
Perrins La, NW3 **91** F4
Perrin's Wk, NW3 **91** F4
Perrott St, SE18 **137** F4
Perry Av, W3 **106** D6
Perry Ct, E14
off Maritime Quay **134** A5
N15 **76** B6
Perryfield Way, NW9 **71** F6
Richmond TW10 **163** E2
Perry Gdns, N13 **60** A3
Perry Garth, Nthlt. UB5 **102** C1
Perry Hall Rd, Orp. BR6 **193** J6
Perry Hill, SE6 **171** J3
Perry Ho, SW2
off Tierney Rd **150** E7
Perry How, Wor.Pk. KT4 **197** F1
Perryman Ho, Bark. IG11 **117** F1
Perrymans Fm Rd, Ilford IG2 **81** G6
Perry Mead, Enf. EN2 **43** H2
Perrymead St, SW6 **148** D1
Perryn Rd, SE16
off Drummond Rd **132** E3
W3 **106** D7
Perry Ri, SE23 **171** H3
Perry Rd, Dag. RM9 **119** F4
Perrys Pl, W1 **17** H3
Perry St, Chis. BR7 **175** G6
Perry St Gdns, Chis. BR7
off Old Perry St **175** H6
Perry Vale, SE23 **171** F2
Perrywood Ho, E5
off Pembury Rd **94** E5
Persant Rd, SE6 **172** E2
Perseverance Pl, SW9 **131** G7
Richmond TW9
off Shaftesbury Rd **145** H3
Pershore Cl, Ilf. IG2 **81** E5
Pershore Gro, Cars. SM5 **185** G6
Pert Cl, N10 **58** B7
Perth Av, NW9 **70** D7
Hayes UB4 **102** C4
Perth Cl, SW20
off Huntley Way **183** G2
Northolt UB5
off Ascot Cl **85** G5
Perth Rd, E10 **95** H1
E13 **115** H2
N4 **93** G1
N22 **75** H1
Barking IG11 **117** G2
Beckenham BR3 **190** C2
Ilford IG2 **80** D6
Perth Ter, Ilf. IG2 **81** F7
Perwell Av, Har. HA2 **85** F1
Perwell Ct, Har. HA2 **85** F1
Peter Av, NW10 **89** H7
Peterboat Cl, SE10
off Tunnel Av **135** E4
Peterborough Gdns, Ilf. IG1 **80** B7
Peterborough Ms, SW6 **148** D2
Peterborough Rd, E10 **78** C5
SW6 **148** D2
Carshalton SM5 **185** H6
Harrow HA1 **86** B1
Peterborough Vil, SW6 **148** E1
Peterchurch Ho, SE15
off Commercial Way **132** E6
Petergate, SW11 **149** F4
Peter Heathfield Ho, E15
off High St **114** D1
Peterhouse Gdns, SW6
off Bagley's La **149** E1
Peter James Business Cen, Hayes UB3 **122** A2
Peterley Business Cen, E2
off Hackney Rd **113** E2
Peter Moore Ct, N9
off Menon Dr **60** E3
★ **Peter Pan Statue**, W2 **23** E1
Peters Cl, Dag. RM8 **100** D1
Stanmore HA7 **53** G6
Welling DA16 **157** H2
Petersfield Cl, N18 **59** J5
Petersfield Ri, SW15 **165** H1
Petersfield Rd, W3 **126** C2
PETERSHAM, Rich. TW10 **163** H1
Petersham Cl, Rich. TW10 **163** G2
Sutton SM1 **198** D5
Petersham Dr, Orp. BR5 **193** J2
Petersham Gdns, Orp. BR5 **193** J2
Petersham La, SW7 **22** C5
Petersham Ms, SW7 **22** C6
Petersham Pl, SW7 **22** C5
Petersham Rd, Rich. TW10 **145** H6
Peters Hill, EC4 **19** J5
Peter's La, EC1 **19** H1
Peters Path, SE26 **170** E4
Peterstone Rd, SE2 **138** B3
Peterstow Cl, SW19 **166** B2
Peter St, W1 **17** G5
Peterwood Way, Croy. CR0 **201** F2
Petherton Rd, N5 **93** J5
Petiver Cl, E9
off Frampton Pk Rd **95** F7
Petley Rd, W6 **127** J6
Peto Pl, NW1 **8** E5
Peto St N, E16
off Victoria Dock Rd **115** F7
Petrie Cl, NW2 **90** B6
★ **Petrie Mus of Egyptian Archaeology**, WC1
off Malet Pl **9** H6
Petros Gdns, NW3
off Lithos Rd **91** F5
Pettacre Cl, SE28 **137** F3
★ **Petticoat Lane Mkt**, E1 **21** E2
Petticoat Sq, E1 **21** F3
Petticoat Twr, E1 **21** F3
Pettits Pl, Dag. RM10 **101** G5
Pettits Rd, Dag. RM10 **101** G5
Pettiward Cl, SW15 **147** J4
Pettman Cres, SE28 **137** G3
Pettsgrove Av, Wem. HA0 **87** F5
Petts Hill, Nthlt. UB5 **85** H5
Pett St, SE18 **136** B4
PETTS WOOD, Orp. BR5 **193** G5
Petts Wd Rd, Orp. BR5 **193** F5
Petty France, SW1 **25** G5
Petty Wales, EC3 **21** E6
Petworth Cl, Nthlt. UB5 **85** F7
Petworth Gdns, SW20
off Hidcote Gdns **183** H3
Petworth Ho, SE22
off Pytchley Rd **152** B3
Petworth Rd, N12 **57** H5
Bexleyheath DA6 **159** G5
Petworth St, SW11 **149** H1
Petyt Pl, SW3 **31** G6
Petyward, SW3 **31** H2
Pevensey Av, N11 **58** D5
Enfield EN1 **44** A2
Pevensey Cl, Islw. TW7 **123** J7
Pevensey Rd, E7 **97** F4
SW17 **167** G4
Feltham TW13 **160** E1
Peverel, E6 *off Downings* **116** D6
Peverel Ho, Dag. RM10 **101** G2
Peveret Cl, N11 **58** B5
Peveril Dr, Tedd. TW11 **162** A5
Pewsey Cl, E4 **62** A5
Peyton Pl, SE10 **134** C7
Pharaoh Cl, Mitch. CR4 **185** J7
Pheasant Cl, E16
off Maplin Rd **115** G6
Phelp St, SE17 **36** B5
Phelps Way, Hayes UB3 **121** J4
Phene St, SW3 **31** H5
Pheonix Cl, W12 **107** H7
Philbeach Gdns, SW5 **128** D5
Phil Brown Pl, SW8
off Daley Thompson Way **150** B3
Philchurch Pl, E1 **21** J4
Philimore Cl, SE18 **137** H5
Philip Gdns, Croy. CR0 **203** J2
Philip La, N15 **76** A4
Philipot Path, SE9 **156** C6
Philippa Gdns, SE9 **156** A5
Philips Cl, Cars. SM5 **200** A1
Philip St, E13 **115** G4
Philip Wk, SE15 **152** D3
Phillimore Gdns, NW10 **107** J1
W8 **128** D2
Phillimore Gdns Cl, W8
off Phillimore Gdns **128** D3
Phillimore Pl, W8 **128** D2
Phillimore Wk, W8 **128** D3
Phillipp St, N1 **112** B1
Philpot La, EC3 **20** D5
Philpot Path, Ilf. IG1
off Richmond Rd **99** F3
Philpot Sq, SW6
off Peterborough Rd **148** E3
Philpot St, E1 **113** E6
Phineas Pett Rd, SE9 **156** B3
Phipps Br Rd, SW19 **185** F2
Mitcham CR4 **185** F2
Phipp's Ms, SW1 **24** E6
Phipp St, EC2 **12** D5
Phoebeth Rd, SE4 **154** A5
Phoenix Cl, E8
off Stean St **112** C1
E17 **77** J2
West Wickham BR4 **204** E2
Phoenix Ct, N.Mal. KT3 **183** F3
Phoenix Dr, Kes. BR2 **206** A3
Phoenix Pk, Brent. TW8 **125** G5
Phoenix Pl, WC1 **10** D5
Phoenix Pt, SE28 **138** C1
Phoenix Rd, NW1 **9** H3
SE20 **171** F6
Phoenix St, WC2 **17** J4
Phoenix Way, SW18
off North Side Wandsworth Common **149** F5
Hounslow TW5 **122** C6
Phoenix Wf, SE10 **135** F2
Phoenix Wf Rd, SE1 **29** G4
Phoenix Yd, WC1 **10** D4
★ **Photographers' Gall**, WC2 **17** J5
Phyllis Av, N.Mal. KT3 **183** H5
★ **Physical Energy Statue**, W2 **22** D2
Physic Pl, SW3 **31** J5
Picardy Manorway, Belv. DA17 **139** H3
Picardy Rd, Belv. DA17 **139** G4
Picardy St, Belv. DA17 **139** G3
Piccadilly, W1 **24** E2
Piccadilly Arc, SW1 **25** F1
Piccadilly Circ, W1 **17** H6
Piccadilly Ct, N7
off Caledonian Rd **93** F6
Piccadilly Pl, W1 **17** G6
Pickard Cl, N14 **58** D1
Pickard St, EC1 **11** H3
Pickering Av, E6 **116** D2
Pickering Cl, E9
off Cassland Rd **95** G7
Pickering Gdns, N11 **58** A6
Croydon CR0 **188** C6
Pickering Ms, W2 **14** B3
Pickering Pl, SW1 **25** G2
Pickering Rd, Bark. IG11 **99** F6
Pickering St, N1
off Essex Rd **111** H1
Pickets Cl, Bushey (Bushey Hth) WD23 **52** A1
Pickets St, SW12 **150** B7
Pickett Cft, Stan. HA7 **69** G1
Picketts Lock La, N9 **61** F2
Pickford Cl, Bexh. DA7 **158** E2
Pickford La, Bexh. DA7 **159** E2
Pickford Rd, Bexh. DA7 **158** E3
Pickfords Wf, N1 **11** J2
Pickhurst Grn, Brom. BR2 **191** F7
Pickhurst La, Brom. BR2 **205** F1
West Wickham BR4 **191** E6
Pickhurst Mead, Brom. BR2 **191** F7
Pickhurst Pk, Brom. BR2 **191** E5
Pickhurst Ri, W.Wick. BR4 **190** C7
Pickwick Cl, Houns. TW4
off Dorney Way **143** E5
Pickwick Ct, SE9 **174** B1
Pickwick Ms, N18 **60** B5
Pickwick Pl, Har. HA1 **68** B7
Pickwick Rd, SE21 **152** A7
Pickwick St, SE1 **27** J4
Pickwick Way, Chis. BR7 **175** F6
Pickworth Cl, SW8
off Kenchester Cl **131** E7
Picton Pl, W1 **16** C4
Surbiton KT6 **196** A1
Picton St, SE5 **132** A7
Picture Ho, SW16
off Streatham High Rd **168** E2
Pied Bull Yd, N1
off Theberton St **111** H1
Piedmont Rd, SE18 **137** G5
Pier Head, E1
off Wapping High St **132** E1
Pieris Ho, Felt. TW13
off High St **160** A2
Piermont Grn, SE22 **152** E5
Piermont Pl, Brom. BR1 **192** B2
Piermont Rd, SE22 **152** E5
Pier Par, E16
off Pier Rd **136** D1
Pierrepoint Arc, N1 **11** G1
Pierrepoint Rd, W3 **106** B7
Pierrepoint Row, N1 **11** G1
Pier Rd, E16 **136** D2
Feltham TW14 **142** B5
Pier St, E14 **134** C4
Pier Ter, SW18
off Jew's Row **149** E4
Pier Way, SE28 **137** G3
Pigeon La, Hmptn. TW12 **161** G4
Pigott St, E14 **114** A6
Pike Cl, Brom. BR1 **173** H5
Pike Rd, NW7
off Ellesmere Av **54** D4
Pikes End, Pnr. HA5 **66** B4
Pikestone Cl, Hayes UB4
off Berrydale Rd **102** E4
Pilgrimage St, SE1 **28** B4
Pilgrim Cl, Mord. SM4 **185** E7
Pilgrim Hill, SE27 **169** J4
Pilgrims Cl, N13 **59** F4
Northolt UB5 **85** J5
Pilgrims Ct, SE3 **155** G1
Pilgrim's La, NW3 **91** G4
Pilgrims Ms, E14
off Newport Av **114** D7
Pilgrims Pl, NW3
off Hampstead High St **91** G4
Pilgrims Ri, Barn. EN4 **41** H5
Pilgrim St, EC4 **19** G4
Pilgrims Way, E6
off High St N **116** B1
N19 **92** D1
South Croydon CR2 **202** C5
Pilgrim's Way, Wem. HA9 **88** B1
Pilkington Rd, SE15 **152** E2
Orpington BR6 **207** F2
Pilot Busway, SE10 **135** E2
Pilot Cl, SE8 **133** J6
Pilsdon Cl, SW19
off Inner Pk Rd **166** A1
Piltdown Rd, Wat. WD19 **50** D4
Pilton Ind Est, Croy. CR0 **201** H2
Pilton Pl, SE17 **36** A3
Pimento Ct, W5
off Olive Rd **125** G3
PIMLICO, SW1 **33** F3
Pimlico Rd, SW1 **32** B3
Pimlico Wk, N1 **12** D3
Pinchbeck Rd, Orp. BR6 **207** J6
Pinchin St, E1 **21** J5
Pincott Pl, SE4 **153** G4
Pincott Rd, SW19 **167** F7
Bexleyheath DA6 **159** G5
Pindar St, EC2 **20** D1
Pindock Ms, W9 **6** B6
Pineapple Ct, SW1 **25** F5
Pine Av, E15 **96** D5
West Wickham BR4 **204** B1
Pine Cl, E10
off Walnut Rd **96** B2
N14 **42** C7
N19 *off Hargrave Pk* **92** C2
SE20 **189** F1
Stanmore HA7 **52** E4
Pine Coombe, Croy. CR0 **203** G4
Pinecrest Gdns, Orp. BR6 **207** E4
Pinecroft Cres, Barn. EN5 **40** B4
Pinedene, SE15
off Meeting Ho La **152** E1
Pinefield Cl, E14 **114** A7
Pine Gdns, Ruis. HA4 **84** B1
Surbiton KT5 **182** A6
Pine Glade, Orp. BR6 **206** C4
Pine Gro, N4 **93** E2
N20 **56** C1
SW19 **166** C5
Pinehurst Wk, Orp. BR6 **207** H1
Pinelands Cl, SE3
off St. John's Pk **135** F7
Pinemartin Cl, NW2 **89** J3
Pine Ms, NW10
off Clifford Gdns **108** A2
Pine Rd, N11 **58** A2
NW2 **89** J4
Pines, The, N14 **42** C5
Sunbury-on-Thames TW16 **178** A3
Woodford Green IG8 **63** G3
Pines Rd, Brom. BR1 **192** B2
Pine St, EC1 **11** E5
Pine Tree Cl, Houns. TW5 **142** B1
Pine Tree Way, SE13
off Elmira St **154** B3
Pine Wk, Brom. BR1 **191** J1
Surbiton KT5 **182** A6
Pine Wd, Sun. TW16 **178** A1
Pinewood Av, Pnr. HA5 **51** H6
Sidcup DA15 **175** H1
Pinewood Cl, Borwd. WD6 **38** D1
Croydon CR0 **203** H3
Northwood HA6 **50** B5
Orpington BR6 **207** G2
Pinner HA5 **51** H6
Pinewood Dr, Orp. BR6 **207** H5

Pinewood Gro, W5 105 F6
Pinewood Ms, Stai. (Stanw.) TW19 140 A6
Pinewood Pl, Epsom KT19 196 D4
Pinewood Rd, SE2 138 D6
Bromley BR2 191 G4
Feltham TW13 160 B3
Pinfold Rd, SW16 168 E4
Pinglestone Cl, West Dr. (Harm.) UB7 120 B7
Pinkcoat Cl, Felt. TW13
off Tanglewood Way 160 B3
Pinkerton Pl, SW16 168 D4
Pinkham Way, N11 58 A7
Pinkwell Av, Hayes UB3 121 G4
Pinkwell La, Hayes UB3 121 F4
Pinley Gdns, Dag. RM9
off Stamford Rd 118 B1
Pinnacle Hill, Bexh. DA7 159 H4
Pinnacle Hill N, Bexh. DA7 159 H3
Pinnata Cl, Enf. EN2 43 J1
Pinnell Rd, SE9 156 A4
PINNER, HA5 67 E4
Pinner Ct, Pnr. HA5 67 G4
PINNER GREEN, Pnr. HA5 66 D2
Pinner Grn, Pnr. HA5 66 C2
Pinner Gro, Pnr. HA5 67 E4
Pinner Hill, Pnr. HA5 66 C1
Pinner Hill Rd, Pnr. HA5 66 C2
Pinner Pk, Pnr. HA5 67 G1
Pinner Pk Av, Har. HA2 67 H3
Pinner Pk Gdns, Har. HA2 67 J2
Pinner Rd, Har. HA1, HA2 67 H5
Pinner HA5 67 F4
Pinner Vw, Har. HA1, HA2 67 J6
PINNERWOOD PARK, Pnr. HA5 50 C7
Pintail Cl, E6
off Swan App 116 B5
Pintail Rd, Wdf.Grn. IG8 63 H7
Pintail Way, Hayes UB4 102 D5
Pinter Ho, SW9
off Grantham Rd 151 E2
Pinto Cl, Borwd. WD6 38 D6
Pinto Way, SE3 155 H4
Pioneer Cl, E14
off Broomfield St 114 B5
Pioneers Ind Pk, Croy. CR0 200 E1
Pioneer St, SE15 152 D1
Pioneer Way, W12
off Du Cane Rd 107 H6
Piper Cl, N7 93 F6
Piper Rd, Kings.T. KT1 182 A3
Piper's Gdns, Croy. CR0 189 H7
Pipers Grn, NW9 70 C5
Pipers Grn La, Edg. HA8 53 H3
Piper Way, Ilf. IG1 99 G1
Pipewell Rd, Cars. SM5 185 H6
Pippin Cl, NW2 89 H3
Croydon CR0 203 J1
Pippins Cl, West Dr. UB7 120 A3
Piquet Rd, SE20 189 F2
Pirbright Cres, Croy. (New Adgtn) CR0 204 C6
Pirbright Rd, SW18 166 C1
Pirie Cl, SE5
off Denmark Hill 152 A3
Pirie St, E16 135 H1
Pitcairn Cl, Rom. RM7 83 G4
Pitcairn Rd, Mitch. CR4 167 J7
Pitcairn's Path, Har. HA2
off Eastcote Rd 85 J3
Pitchford St, E15 96 D7
Pitfield Cres, SE28 138 A1
Pitfield Est, N1 12 C3
Pitfield St, N1 12 D4
Pitfield Way, NW10 88 C6
Enfield EN3 45 F1
Pitfold Cl, SE12 155 G6
Pitfold Rd, SE12 155 G6
Pitlake, Croy. CR0 201 H2
Pitman Ho, SE8
off Tanners Hill 154 A1
Pitman St, SE5 35 J7
Pitmaston Ho, SE13
off Lewisham Rd 154 C2
Pitmaston Rd, SE13
off Morden Hill 154 C2
Pitsea Pl, E1
off Pitsea St 113 G6
Pitsea St, E1 113 G6
Pitshanger La, W5 105 E4
★ **Pitshanger Manor Ho & Gall**, W5 125 F1
Pitshanger Pk, W13 105 F3
Pitt Cres, SW19 166 E4
Pitt Ho, SW11
off Maysoule Rd 149 G4
Pittman Gdns, Ilf. IG1 99 F5
Pitt Rd, Croy. CR0 187 J5
Orpington BR6 207 F4
Thornton Heath CR7 187 J5
Pitt's Head Ms, W1 24 C2
Pittsmead Av, Brom. BR2 191 G7
Pitt St, W8 128 D2
Pittville Gdns, SE25 188 D3
Pixfield Ct, Brom. BR2
off Beckenham La 191 F2
Pixley St, E14 113 J6
Place Fm Av, Orp. BR6 207 G1
PLAISTOW, E13 115 F3
PLAISTOW, Brom. BR1 173 F6
Plaistow Gro, E15 115 F1
Bromley BR1 173 H7
Plaistow La, Brom. BR1 173 G7
Plaistow Pk Rd, E13 115 H2
Plaistow Rd, E13 115 F1
E15 115 F1
Plane St, SE26 170 E3
Plane Tree Cres, Felt. TW13 160 B3
Plane Tree Wk, N2 73 G3
SE19 *off Lunham Rd* 170 B6
Plantagenet Cl, Wor.Pk. KT4 196 D4
Plantagenet Gdns, Rom. RM6 82 D7
Plantagenet Pl, Rom. RM6 82 D7
Plantagenet Rd, Barn. EN5 41 F4
Plantain Gdns, E11
off Hollydown Way 96 D3
Plantain Pl, SE1 28 B3
Plantation, The, SE3 155 G2
Plantation Cl, SW4
off King's Av 150 E5
Plantation La, EC3
off Rood La 20 D5
Plantation Wf, SW11 149 F3
Plashet Gro, E6 115 J1
Plashet Rd, E13 115 G1
Plassy Rd, SE6 154 B7
Platina St, EC2 12 C5
Platinum Ho, Har. HA1 68 C6
Plato Rd, SW2 151 E4
Platt, The, SW15 148 A3
Platt's Eyot, Hmptn. TW12 179 G2
Platt's La, NW3 90 D4
Platts Rd, Enf. EN3 45 F1
Platt St, NW1 9 H1
Plawsfield Rd, Beck. BR3 189 G1
Plaxtol Cl, Brom. BR1 191 J1
Plaxtol Rd, Erith DA8 139 G7
Plaxton Ct, E11
off Woodhouse Rd 97 F3
Playfair St, W6
off Winslow Rd 127 J5
Playfield Av, Rom. RM5 83 J1
Playfield Cres, SE22 152 C5
Playfield Rd, Edg. HA8 70 C2
Playford Rd, N4 93 F2
Playgreen Way, SE6 172 A4
Playground Cl, Beck. BR3
off Churchfields Rd 189 G2
Playhouse Ct, SE1
off Southwark Br Rd 27 J3
Playhouse Yd, EC4 19 G4
Plaza Business Cen, Enf. EN3
off Stockingswater La 45 J2
Plaza Par, NW6
off Kilburn High Rd 6 A1
Plaza Shop Cen, The, W1 17 G3
Plaza W, Houns. TW3 143 H1
Pleasance, The, SW15 147 H4
Pleasance Rd, SW15 147 H5
Pleasant Gro, Croy. CR0 203 J3
Pleasant Pl, N1 93 H7
Pleasant Row, NW1 110 B1
Pleasant Vw Pl, Orp. BR6
off High St 207 E5
Pleasant Way, Wem. HA0 105 F2
Plender St, NW1 110 C1
Pleshey Rd, N7 92 D4
Plevna Cres, N15 76 B6
Plevna Rd, N9 60 D3
Hampton TW12 179 H1
Plevna St, E14 134 C3
Pleydell Av, SE19 170 C7
W6 127 F4
Pleydell Ct, EC4 19 F4
Pleydell Est, EC1
off Radnor St 12 A4
Pleydell St, EC4 19 F4
Plimley Pl, W12
off Sterne St 128 A2
Plimsoll Cl, E14
off Grundy St 114 B6
Plimsoll Rd, N4 93 G3
Plough Ct, EC3 20 C5
Plough La, SE22 152 C6
SW17 167 E5
SW19 167 E5
Teddington TW11 162 D5
Wallington SM6 200 E4
Plough La Cl, Wall. SM6 200 E5
Ploughmans Cl, NW1
off Crofters Way 110 D1
Ploughmans End, Islw. TW7 144 A5
Ploughmans Wk, N2
off Long La 73 F2
Plough Ms, SW11
off Plough Ter 149 G4
Plough Pl, EC4 19 F3
Plough Rd, SW11 149 G3
Plough St, E1 21 H3
Plough Ter, SW11 149 G4
Plough Way, SE16 133 G4
Plough Yd, EC2 12 E6
Plover Way, SE16 133 H3
Hayes UB4 102 D6
Plowden Bldgs, EC4
off Middle Temple La 19 E5
Plowman Cl, N18 60 A5
Plowman Way, Dag. RM8 100 C1
Plumbers Row, E1 21 H2
Plumbridge St, SE10
off Blackheath Hill 154 C1
Plum Cl, Felt. TW13 160 A1
Plum Garth, Brent. TW8 125 G4
Plum La, SE18 137 E7
Plummer La, Mitch. CR4 185 J2
Plummer Rd, SW4 150 D7
Plumpton Cl, Nthlt. UB5 85 G6
Plumpton Way, Cars. SM5 199 H3
PLUMSTEAD, SE18 137 H5
Plumstead Common Rd, SE18 136 E6
Plumstead High St, SE18 137 H4
Plumstead Rd, SE18 137 E4
Plumtree Cl, Dag. RM10 101 H6
Wallington SM6 200 D7
Plumtree Ct, EC4 19 F3
Plumtree Mead, Loug. IG10 48 D3
Plymouth Rd, E16 115 G5
Bromley BR1 191 H1
Plymouth Wf, E14 134 D4
Plympton Av, NW6 90 C7
Plympton Cl, Belv. DA17
off Halifield Dr 139 E3
Plympton Pl, NW8 7 G6
Plympton Rd, NW6 90 C7
Plympton St, NW8 7 G6
Plymstock Rd, Well. DA16 138 C7
Pocklington Cl, NW9 70 E2
Pocock Av, West Dr. UB7 120 C3
Pocock St, SE1 27 G3
Podium, The, E2
off Roman Rd 113 F3
Podmore Rd, SW18 149 F4
Poets Rd, N5 94 A5
Poets Way, Har. HA1
off Blawith Rd 68 B4
Point, The, E17
off Tower Ms 78 A4
Pointalls Cl, N3 73 F2
Point Cl, SE10
off Point Hill 154 C1
Pointer Cl, SE28 118 D6
Pointers Cl, E14 134 B5
Point Hill, SE10 134 C7
Point of Thomas Path, E1
off Glamis Rd 113 F7
Point Pl, Wem. HA9 88 B7
Point Pleasant, SW18 148 D4
Point W, SW7 30 B1
Point Wf La, Brent. TW8
off Town Meadow 125 H7
Poland Ho, E15 114 D1
Poland St, W1 17 G4
Polar Pk, West Dr. UB7 120 C7
Polebrook Rd, SE3 155 J3
Pole Cat All, Brom. BR2 205 F2
Polecroft La, SE6 171 J2
Polehamptons, The, Hmptn. TW12
off High St 161 J7
Pole Hill Rd, E4 46 C7
Polesden Gdns, SW20 183 H2
Polesworth Ho, W2 108 D5
Polesworth Rd, Dag. RM9 100 D7
★ **Polish Inst & Sikorski Mus**, SW7
off Princes Gate 23 F4
Polish War Mem, Ruis. HA4 84 B7
Pollard Cl, E16 115 G7
N7 93 F5
Pollard Rd, N20 57 H2
Morden SM4 185 G5
Pollard Row, E2 13 J3
Pollards Cl, Loug. IG10 47 J5
Pollards Cres, SW16 187 E3
Pollards Hill E, SW16 187 F3
Pollards Hill N, SW16 187 E3
Pollards Hill S, SW16 187 E3
Pollards Hill W, SW16 187 E3
Pollard St, E2 13 J3
Pollards Wd Rd, SW16 187 E2
Pollard Wk, Sid. DA14 176 C6
Pollen St, W1 17 E4
Pollitt Dr, NW8 7 E5
★ **Pollock's Toy Mus**, W1 17 G1
Polperro Cl, Orp. BR6
off Cotswold Ri 193 J6
Polperro Ms, SE11 35 F1
Polsted Rd, SE6 153 J7
Polthorne Est, SE18 137 F4
Polthorne Gro, SE18 137 F4
Polworth Rd, SW16 168 E5
Polygon, The, SW4
off Old Town 150 C4
Polygon Rd, NW1 9 H2
Polytechnic St, SE18 136 D4
Pomell Way, E1 21 G3
Pomeroy Cl, Twick. TW1
off St. Margaret's Dr 145 E4
Pomeroy St, SE14 153 F1
Pomfret Rd, SE5
off Flaxman Rd 151 H3
Pomoja La, N19 92 D2
Pond Cl, N12 57 H6
SE3 155 F2
Pond Cottage La, W.Wick. BR4 204 A1
Pond Cotts, SE21 170 B1
PONDERS END, Enf. EN3 45 F5
Ponders End Ind Est, Enf. EN3 45 J4
Ponder St, N7 93 F7
Pond Fm Est, E5
off Millfields Rd 95 F3
Pond Fld End, Loug. IG10 47 J7
Pondfield Ho, SE27
off Elder Rd 169 J5
Pondfield Rd, Brom. BR2 205 E1
Dagenham RM10 101 H5
Orpington BR6 207 E3
Pond Hill Gdns, Sutt. SM3 198 B6
Pond Mead, SE21 152 A6
Pond Path, Chis. BR7
off Heathfield La 175 F6
Pond Pl, SW3 31 G2
Pond Rd, E15 114 E2
SE3 155 F2
Pondside Cl, Hayes (Harling.) UB3 121 G7
Pond Sq, N6
off South Gro 92 A1
Pond St, NW3 91 H5
Pond Way, Tedd. TW11
off Holmesdale Rd 163 F6
Pondwood Ri, Orp. BR6 193 H7
Ponler St, E1 112 E6
Ponsard Rd, NW10 107 H3
Ponsford St, E9 95 F6
Ponsonby Pl, SW1 33 J3
Ponsonby Rd, SW15 147 H7
Ponsonby Ter, SW1 33 J3
Pontefract Rd, Brom. BR1 173 F5
Ponton Rd, SW8 33 J6
Pont St, SW1 23 J6
Pont St Ms, SW1 23 J6
Pontypool Pl, SE1 27 G3
Pool Cl, Beck. BR3 172 A5
West Molesey KT8 179 F5
Pool Ct, SE6 172 A2
Poole Ct Rd, Houns. TW4
off Vicarage Fm Rd 142 E2
Poole Ho, SE11
off Lambeth Wk 26 D6
Poole Rd, E9 95 G6
Epsom KT19 196 D6
Pooles Bldgs, EC1 10 E6
Pooles La, SW10
off Lots Rd 129 F7
Dagenham RM9 119 E2
Pooles Pk, N4 93 G2
Poole St, N1 112 A1
Pooley Dr, SW14
off Moore Cl 146 C3
Poolmans St, SE16 133 G2
Pool Rd, Har. HA1 68 A7
West Molesey KT8 179 F6
Poolsford Rd, NW9 71 E4
Poonah St, E1
off Hardinge St 113 F6
Pope Cl, SW19 167 G6
Pope Ho, SE16
off Manor Est 132 E4
Pope Rd, Brom. BR2 192 A5
Popes Av, Twick. TW2 162 B2
Popes Dr, N3 72 D1
Popes Gro, Croy. CR0 203 J3
Twickenham TW1, TW2 162 C2
Pope's Head All, EC3
off Cornhill 20 C4
Popes La, W5 125 G3
Popes Rd, SW9 151 G3
Pope St, SE1 29 E4
Popham Cl, Felt. (Han.) TW13 161 F3
Popham Gdns, Rich. TW9 *off Lower Richmond Rd* 146 A3

Popham Rd, N1 111 J1
Popham St, N1 111 H1
Popin Business Cen, Wem. HA9 88 B5
POPLAR, E14 114 B7
Poplar Av, Mitch. CR4 185 J1
Orpington BR6 207 E2
Southall UB2 123 H3
Poplar Bath St, E14 *off Lawless St* 114 B7
Poplar Business Pk, E14 114 C7
Poplar Cl, E9 *off Lee Conservancy Rd* 95 J5
Pinner HA5 66 D1
Poplar Ct, SW19 166 D5
Poplar Cres, Epsom KT19 196 C6
Poplar Fm Cl, Epsom KT19 196 C6
Poplar Gdns, N.Mal. KT3 182 D2
Poplar Gro, N11 58 A6
W6 127 J2
New Malden KT3 182 D3
Wembley HA9 88 C3
Poplar High St, E14 114 A7
Poplar Mt, Belv. DA17 139 H4
Poplar Pl, SE28 118 C7
W2 14 A5
Hayes UB3 *off Central Av* 102 A7
Poplar Rd, SE24 151 J4
SW19 184 D2
Sutton SM3 198 C1
Poplar Rd S, SW19 184 D3
Poplars, The, N14 42 B5
Borehamwood WD6 *off Grove Rd* 38 A1
Poplars Av, NW10 89 J6
Poplars Rd, E17 78 B6
Poplar St, Rom. RM7 83 J4
Poplar Vw, Wem. HA9 *off Magnet Rd* 87 G2
Poplar Wk, SE24 151 J4
Croydon CR0 201 J2
Poplar Way, Felt. TW13 160 A3
Ilford IG6 81 F4
Poppins Ct, EC4 19 G4
Poppleton Rd, E11 79 E6
Poppy Cl, Barn. EN5 41 F6
Belvedere DA17 139 H3
Northolt UB5 85 F6
Wallington SM6 200 A1
★ **Poppy Factory Mus, The**, Rich. TW10 145 G6
Poppy La, Croy. CR0 189 F7
Porchester Cl, SE5 151 J4
Porchester Gdns, W2 14 A5
Porchester Gdns Ms, W2 14 B4
Porchester Gate, W2 *off Bayswater Rd* 14 C6
Porchester Mead, Beck. BR3 172 A6
Porchester Ms, W2 14 B3
Porchester Pl, W2 15 H4
Porchester Rd, W2 14 A3
Kingston upon Thames KT1 182 B2
Porchester Sq, W2 14 B3
Porchester Sq Ms, W2 14 B3
Porchester Ter, W2 14 C4
Porchester Ter N, W2 14 B3
Porch Way, N20 57 J3
Porcupine Cl, SE9 174 B2
Porden Rd, SW2 151 F4
Porlock Av, Har. HA2 85 J1
Porlock Rd, Enf. EN1 44 C7
Porlock St, SE1 28 B3
Porrington Cl, Chis. BR7 192 C1
Portal Cl, SE27 169 G3
Ruislip HA4 84 A4
Portal Way, W3 106 D5
Portbury Cl, SE15 *off Clayton Rd* 152 D1
Port Cres, E13 *off Jenkins Rd* 115 H4
★ **Portcullis Ho**, SW1 *off Bridge St* 26 A4
Portcullis Lo Rd, Enf. EN2 44 A3
Portelet Ct, N1 *off De Beauvoir Est* 112 B1
Portelet Rd, E1 113 G3
Porten Rd, W14 128 B3
Porter Rd, E6 116 C6
Porters Av, Dag. RM8, RM9 100 B6
Portersfield Rd, Enf. EN1 44 B4
Porter Sq, N19 92 E1
Porter St, SE1 28 A1
W1 16 A1
Porters Wk, E1 *off Tobacco Dock* 113 E7
Porters Way, N12 57 H7
West Drayton UB7 120 C3
Porteus Rd, W2 14 D2
Portgate Cl, W9 108 C4
Porthallow Cl, Orpington BR6 207 J4
Porthcawe Rd, SE26 171 H4
Porthkerry Av, Well. DA16 158 A4
Portia Way, E3 113 J4
Portinscale Rd, SW15 148 B5
Portland Av, N16 76 C7
New Malden KT3 183 F7
Sidcup DA15 158 A6
Portland Cl, Rom. RM6 82 E5
Worcester Park KT4 183 H7
Portland Commercial Est, Bark. IG11 118 C2
Portland Ct, SE1 *off Falmouth Rd* 28 B5
Portland Cres, SE9 174 B2
Greenford UB6 103 H4
Stanmore HA7 69 G2
Portland Gdns, N4 75 H6
Romford RM6 82 D5
Portland Gro, SW8 151 F1
Portland Ms, W1 17 G4
Portland Pl, W1 16 E2
Portland Ri, N4 93 H1
Portland Ri Est, N4 93 H1
Portland Rd, N15 76 C4
SE9 174 B2
SE25 188 D4
W11 108 B7
Bromley BR1 173 J4
Kingston upon Thames KT1 181 H3
Mitcham CR4 185 H2
Southall UB2 123 F3
Portland Sq, E1 *off Reardon St* 132 E1
Portland St, SE17 36 B3
Portland Ter, Richmond TW9 145 G4
Portland Wk, SE17 36 C5
Portman Av, SW14 146 D3
Portman Cl, W1 16 A3
Bexleyheath DA7 *off Queen Anne's Gate* 158 D3
Portman Dr, Wdf.Grn. IG8 80 A2
Portman Gdns, NW9 70 D2
Portman Gate, NW1 7 H6
Portman Hall, Har. HA3 52 A5
Portman Ms S, W1 16 B4
Portman Pl, E2 113 F3
Portman Rd, Kings.T. KT1 181 J2
Portman Sq, W1 16 A3
Portman St, W1 16 B4
Portmeadow Wk, SE2 138 D2
Portmeers Cl, E17 *off Lennox Rd* 78 A6
Portnall Rd, W9 108 C2
Portobello Ct, W11 *off Westbourne Gro* 108 C6
Portobello Ms, W11 *off Portobello Rd* 108 D7
Portobello Rd, W10 108 C6
W11 108 C6
Porton Ct, Surb. KT6 181 F6
Portpool La, EC1 18 E1
Portree Cl, N22 59 F7
Portree St, E14 114 D6
Portsdown, Edg. HA8 *off Rectory La* 54 A5
Portsdown Av, NW11 72 C6
Portsdown Ms, NW11 72 C6
Portsea Ms, W2 15 H4
Portsea Pl, W2 15 H4
Portslade Rd, SW8 150 C2
Portsmouth Av, T.Ditt. KT7 180 D7
Portsmouth Ms, E16 *off Wesley Av* 135 H1
Portsmouth Rd, SW15 147 H7
Esher KT10 194 B2
Kingston upon Thames KT1 181 F5
Surbiton KT6 181 F5
Thames Ditton KT7 194 B2
Portsmouth St, WC2 18 C4
Portsoken St, E1 21 F5
Portugal Gdns, Twick. TW2 *off Fulwell Pk Av* 161 J2
Portugal St, WC2 18 C4
Portway, E15 115 F1
Portway Gdns, SE18 *off Shooters Hill Rd* 156 A1
Postern Grn, Enf. EN2 43 G2
Post La, Twick. TW2 162 A1
Postmill Cl, Croy. CR0 203 G3
Post Office App, E7 97 H5
Post Office Ct, EC3 20 C4
Post Office Way, SW8 33 H7
Post Rd, Sthl. UB2 123 H3
Postway Ms, Ilf. IG1 *off Clements Rd* 98 E3
Potier St, SE1 28 C6
Potter Cl, Mitch. CR4 186 B2
Potteries, The, Barnet EN5 40 D5
Potterne Cl, SW19 148 A7
Potters Cl, SE15 37 E7
Croydon CR0 203 H1
Loughton IG10 48 B2
Potters Flds, SE1 29 E2
Potters Gro, N.Mal. KT3 182 C4
Potters Hts Cl, Pnr. HA5 50 B7
Potters La, SW16 168 D6
Barnet EN5 40 D4
Borehamwood WD6 38 C1
Potters Rd, SW6 149 F2
Barnet EN5 40 E4
Potter St, Nthwd. HA6 66 A1
Pinner HA5 66 B1
Potter St Hill, Pnr. HA5 50 B6
Pottery Cl, SE25 189 E4
Pottery La, W11 *off Penzance Pl* 128 B1
Pottery Rd, Bex. DA5 177 J2
Brentford TW8 125 H6
Pottery St, SE16 132 E2
Pott St, E2 113 E3
Poulett Gdns, Twick. TW1 162 D1
Poulett Rd, E6 116 C2
Poulters Wd, Kes. BR2 206 A5
Poulton Av, Sutt. SM1 199 G3
Poulton Cl, E8 *off Marcon Pl* 94 E5
Poultry, EC2 20 B4
Pound Cl, Orp. BR6 207 G2
Surbiton (Long Dit.) KT6 195 F1
Pound Ct Dr, Orp. BR6 207 G2
Pound Fm Cl, Esher KT10 194 A1
Poundfield Rd, Loug. IG10 48 D5
Pound La, NW10 89 G6
Pound Pk Rd, SE7 136 A4
Pound Pl, SE9 156 D6
Pound St, Cars. SM5 199 J5
Pountney Rd, SW11 150 A3
POVEREST, Orp. BR5 193 J5
Poverest Rd, Orp. BR5 193 J5
Powder Mill La, Twick. TW2 161 F1
Powell Cl, Chess. KT9 *off Coppard Gdns* 195 G5
Edgware HA8 53 J6
Wallington SM6 200 D7
Powell Gdns, Dag. RM10 101 G4
Powell Rd, E5 95 E3
Buckhurst Hill IG9 47 J7
Powell's Wk, W4 127 E6
Powergate Business Pk, NW10 106 D3
Power Rd, W4 126 A4
Powers Ct, Twick. TW1 145 G7
Powerscroft Rd, E5 95 F4
Sidcup DA14 176 C6
Powis Gdns, NW11 72 C7
W11 108 C6
Powis Ms, W11 *off Westbourne Pk Rd* 108 C6
Powis Pl, WC1 10 B6
Powis Rd, E3 114 B3
Powis Sq, W11 108 C6
Powis St, SE18 136 D3
Powis Ter, W11 108 C6
Powle Ter, Ilf. IG1 *off Oaktree Gro* 99 G5
Powlett Pl, NW1 *off Harmood St* 92 B6
Pownall Gdns, Houns. TW3 143 H4
Pownall Rd, E8 112 C1
Hounslow TW3 143 H4
Pownsett Ter, Ilf. IG1 *off Buttsbury Rd* 99 F5
Powster Rd, Brom. BR1 173 H5
Powys Cl, Bexh. DA7 138 D6
Powys Ct, Borwd. WD6 38 D3
Powys La, N13 58 E5
N14 58 E4
Poynders Ct, SW4 *off Poynders Rd* 150 C6
Poynders Gdns, SW4 150 C7
Poynders Rd, SW4 150 C6
Poynings Rd, N19 92 C3
Poynings Way, N12 56 D5
Poyntell Cres, Chis. BR7 193 G1
Poynter Ho, W11 128 A1
Poynter Rd, Enf. EN1 44 D5
Poynton Rd, N17 76 D2
Poyntz Rd, SW11 149 J2
Poyser St, E2 113 E2
Praed Ms, W2 15 F3
Praed St, W2 15 G2
Pragel St, E13 115 H2
Pragnell Rd, SE12 173 H2
Prague Pl, SW2 150 E5
Prah Rd, N4 93 G2
Prairie St, SW8 150 A2
Pratt Ms, NW1 *off Pratt St* 110 C1
Pratts Pas, Kings.T. KT1 *off Clarence St* 181 H2
Pratt St, NW1 110 C1
Pratt Wk, SE11 34 D1
Prayle Gro, NW2 90 A1
Prebend Gdns, W4 127 F3
W6 127 F3
Prebend St, N1 111 J1
Precinct, The, W.Mol. KT8 *off Victoria Av* 179 H3
Precinct Rd, Hayes UB3 102 A7
Precincts, The, Mord. SM4 *off Green La* 184 D6
Premier Cor, W9 *off Kilburn La* 108 C2
Premiere Pl, E14 *off Garford St* 114 A7
Premier Pk, NW10 106 B1
Premier Pk Rd, NW10 106 B2
Prendergast Rd, SE3 155 E3
Prentis Rd, SW16 168 D4
Prentiss Ct, SE7 136 A4
Presburg Rd, N.Mal. KT3 183 E5
Prescelly Pl, Edg. HA8 69 J1
Prescot St, E1 21 G5
Prescott Av, Orp. BR5 192 E6
Prescott Cl, SW16 168 E7
Prescott Grn, Loug. IG10 49 F3
Prescott Ho, SE17 35 H6
Prescott Pl, SW4 150 D3
Presentation Ms, SW2 *off Palace Rd* 169 F1
Preshaw Cres, Mitch. CR4 *off Lower Grn W* 185 H3
President Dr, E1 *off Waterman Way* 132 E1
President St, EC1 11 J3
Prespa Cl, N9 *off Hudson Way* 61 F2
Press Ct, SE1 37 H3
Press Rd, NW10 88 D3
Prestage Way, E14 114 C7
Prestbury Rd, E7 97 J7
Prestbury Sq, SE9 174 C4
Prested Rd, SW11 *off St. John's Hill* 149 H4
Prestige Way, NW4 *off Heriot Rd* 71 J5
PRESTON, Wem. HA9 69 G7
Preston Av, E4 62 D6
Preston Cl, SE1 36 D1
Twickenham TW2 162 B3
Preston Dr, E11 79 J5
Bexleyheath DA7 158 D1
Epsom KT19 197 E6
Preston Gdns, NW10 *off Church Rd* 89 E6
Ilford IG1 80 B6
Preston Hill, Har. HA3 69 J6
Preston Pl, NW2 89 G6
Richmond TW10 145 H5
Preston Rd, E11 79 E6
SE19 169 H6
SW20 165 F7
Harrow HA3 69 H7
Wembley HA9 87 H2
Prestons Rd, E14 134 C2
Bromley BR2 205 G3
Preston Waye, Har. HA3 87 H1
Prestwick Cl, Sthl. UB2 *off Ringway* 122 E5
Prestwick Rd, Wat. WD19 50 D5
Prestwood Av, Har. HA3 69 E4
Prestwood Cl, SE18 138 A7
Harrow HA3 69 E4
Prestwood Gdns, Croy. CR0 187 J7
Prestwood St, N1 12 A2
Pretoria Av, E17 77 H4
Pretoria Cl, N17 60 C7
Pretoria Cres, E4 62 C1
Pretoria Rd, E4 62 C1
E11 96 D1
E16 115 F3
N17 60 C7
SW16 168 B6
Ilford IG1 98 E5
Romford RM7 83 J4
Pretoria Rd N, N18 60 C6
Prevost Rd, N11 58 A2
Price Cl, NW7 56 B6
SW17 167 J3
Price Rd, Croy. CR0 201 H5
Price's Ct, SW11 149 G3
Prices Ms, N1 111 F1
Price's St, SE1 27 H2
Price Way, Hmptn. TW12 *off Victors Dr* 161 E6
Pricklers Hill, Barn. EN5 41 E6
Prickley Wd, Brom. BR2 205 F1
Priddy's Yd, Croy. CR0 *off Church St* 201 J2
Prideaux Pl, W3 106 D7
WC1 10 D3
Prideaux Rd, SW9 151 E3
Pridham Rd, Th.Hth. CR7 188 A4
Priest Ct, EC2 19 J3
Priestfield Rd, SE23 171 H3

Priestlands Pk Rd, Sid. DA15 **175** J3
Priestley Cl, N16 *off Ravensdale Rd* **76** C7
Priestley Gdns, Rom. RM6 **82** B6
Priestley Rd, Mitch. CR4 **186** A2
Priestley Way, E17 **77** G3
NW2 **89** G1
Priestman Pt, E3 *off Rainhill Way* **114** B3
Priest Pk Av, Har. HA2 **85** G2
Priests Br, SW14 **147** E4
SW15 **147** E4
Prima Rd, SW9 **35** E7
Primeplace Ms, Th.Hth. CR7 **187** J2
Primrose Av, Enf. EN2 **44** A1
Romford RM6 **82** B7
Primrose Cl, E3 **114** A2
N3 **73** E2
SE6 **172** C5
Harrow HA2 **85** F4
Wallington SM6 **200** B1
Primrose Dr, West Dr. UB7 **120** A4
Primrose Gdns, NW3 **91** H6
Ruislip HA4 **84** C5
PRIMROSE HILL, NW8 **109** J1
Primrose Hill, EC4 **19** F4
Primrose Hill Ct, NW3 **91** J7
Primrose Hill Rd, NW3 **91** H7
Primrose Hill Studios, NW1 *off Fitzroy Rd* **110** A1
Primrose La, Croy. CR0 **203** G1
Primrose Ms, NW1 *off Sharpleshall St* **91** J7
SE3 **135** H7
W5 *off St. Mary's Rd* **125** G2
Primrose Pl, Islw. TW7 **144** C2
Primrose Rd, E10 **96** B1
E18 **79** H2
Primrose Sq, E9 **95** F7
Primrose St, EC2 **20** D1
Primrose Wk, SE14 *off Alexandra St* **133** H7
Epsom (Ewell) KT17 **197** F7
Primrose Way, Wem. HA0 **105** G2
Primula St, W12 **107** G6
Prince Albert Rd, NW1 **7** H2
NW8 **7** H2
Prince Arthur Ms, NW3 *off Perrins La* **91** F4
Prince Arthur Rd, NW3 **91** F5
Prince Charles Dr, NW4 **71** J7
Prince Charles Rd, SE3 **155** F1
Prince Charles Way, Wall. SM6 **200** B3
Prince Consort Dr, Chis. BR7 **193** G1
Prince Consort Rd, SW7 **22** D5
Princedale Rd, W11 **128** B1
Prince Edward Rd, E9 **95** J6
Prince George Av, N14 **42** C4
Prince George Duke of Kent Ct, Chis. BR7 *off Holbrook La* **175** G7
Prince George Rd, N16 **94** B4
Prince George's Av, SW20 **183** J2
Prince George's Rd, SW19 **185** G1
Prince Henry Rd, SE7 **136** A7
★ **Prince Henry's Room**, EC4 **19** E4
Prince Imperial Rd, SE18 **156** C1
Chislehurst BR7 **175** E7
Prince John Rd, SE9 **156** B5
Princelet St, E1 **21** G1
Prince of Orange La, SE10 *off Greenwich High Rd* **134** C7
Prince of Wales Cl, NW4 *off Church Ter* **71** H4
Prince of Wales Dr, SW8 **130** B7
SW11 **149** J1
Prince of Wales Gate, SW7 **23** G3
Prince of Wales Pas, NW1 **9** F4
Prince of Wales Rd, NW5 **92** A6
SE3 **155** F1
Sutton SM1 **199** G2
Prince of Wales Ter, W4 **126** E5
W8 **22** B4
Prince Regent La, E13 **115** H3
E16 **115** J5
Prince Regent Ms, NW1 **9** F4
Prince Regent Rd, Houns. TW3 **143** J3
Prince Rd, SE25 **188** B5
Prince Rupert Rd, SE9 **156** C4
Prince's Arc, SW1 **25** G1
Princes Av, N3 **72** D1
N10 **74** A3
N13 **59** G5
N22 **74** D1
NW9 **70** B4
W3 **126** A3
Carshalton SM5 **199** J7
Princes Av, Greenford UB6 **103** H6
Orpington BR5 **193** H5
Surbiton KT6 **196** A1
Woodford Green IG8 **63** H4
Princes Cl, N4 **93** H1
NW9 **70** A4
SW4 *off Old Town* **150** C3
Edgware HA8 **54** A5
Sidcup DA14 **176** D3
Teddington TW11 **162** A4
Princes Ct, SE16 **133** J3
SW3 *off Brompton Rd* **23** J5
Wembley HA9 **87** H5
Princes Ct Business Cen, E1 **113** E7
Princes Dr, Har. HA1 **68** B3
Princes Gdns, SW7 **23** F5
W3 **106** A5
W5 **105** F4
Princes Gate, SW7 **23** G4
Princes Gate Ct, SW7 **23** F4
Princes Gate Ms, SW7 **23** F5
Princes La, N10 **74** B3
Princes Ms, W2 **14** A5
Hounslow TW3 *off Albert Rd* **143** G4
Princes Pk Av, NW11 **72** B6
Princes Pl, SW1 **25** G1
W11 **128** B1
Princes Plain, Brom. BR2 **192** B7
Princes Ri, SE13 **154** C2
Princes Riverside Rd, SE16 **133** G1
Princes Rd, N18 **61** F4
SE20 **171** G6
SW14 **146** D3
SW19 **166** D6
W13 *off Broomfield Rd* **125** E1
Buckhurst Hill IG9 **63** J2
Ilford IG6 **81** G4
Kingston upon Thames KT2 **164** A7
Richmond TW10 **145** J5
Richmond (Kew) TW9 **145** J1
Teddington TW11 **162** A4
Princess Alice Way, SE28 **137** G2
Princess Av, Wem. HA9 **87** H2
Princess Cl, SE28 **118** D6
Princess Cres, N4 **93** H2
Princesses Wk, Rich. (Kew) TW9 *off Royal Botanic Gdns* **125** H7
Princess Louise Cl, W2 **15** F1
Princess May Rd, N16 **94** B4
Princess Ms, NW3 *off Belsize Cres* **91** G6
Kingston upon Thames KT1 **181** J3
Princess Par, Orp. BR6 *off Crofton Rd* **206** D3
Princess Pk Manor, N11 **58** A5
Princes Sq, W2 **14** A5
Princess Rd, NW1 **110** A1
NW6 **108** D2
Croydon CR0 **187** J6
Princess St, SE1 **27** H6
Princes St, EC2 **20** B3
N17 **60** B6
W1 **17** E4
Bexleyheath DA7 **159** F4
Richmond TW9 *off Sheen Rd* **145** H5
Sutton SM1 **199** G4
Princes Ter, E13 **115** H1
Prince St, SE8 **133** J6
Princes Way, SW19 **148** A7
Buckhurst Hill IG9 **63** J2
Croydon CR0 **201** F5
Ruislip HA4 **84** E4
West Wickham BR4 **205** F4
Princes Yd, W11 *off Princedale Rd* **128** B1
Princethorpe Ho, W2 **108** D5
Princethorpe Rd, SE26 **171** G4
Princeton Ct, SW15 *off Felsham Rd* **148** A3
Princeton St, WC1 **18** C1
Principal Cl, N14 **58** C1
Principal Sq, E9 *off Chelmer Rd* **95** G5
Pringle Gdns, SW16 **168** C4
Printers Inn Ct, EC4 **19** E3
Printers Ms, E3 **113** H1
Printer St, EC4 **19** F3
Printing Ho La, Hayes UB3 **121** H2
Printing Ho Yd, E2 **13** E3
Print Village, SE15 *off Chadwick Rd* **152** C2
Priolo Rd, SE7 **135** J5
Prior Av, Sutt. SM2 **199** H7
Prior Bolton St, N1 **93** H6
Prioress Ho, E3 *off Bromley High St* **114** B3
Prioress Rd, SE27 **169** H3
Prioress St, SE1 **28** C6
Prior Rd, Ilf. IG1 **98** D3
Priors Cft, E17 **77** H2
Priors Fm La, Nthlt. UB5 **85** F6
Priors Fld, Nthlt. UB5 *off Arnold Rd* **85** E6
Priors Gdns, Ruis. HA4 **84** C5
Priors Mead, Enf. EN1 **44** B1
Prior St, SE10 **134** C7
Priory, The, SE3 **155** F4
Croydon CR0 *off Epsom Rd* **201** G4
Priory Av, E4 **61** J3
E17 **78** A5
N8 **74** D4
W4 **127** E4
Orpington BR5 **193** G6
Sutton SM3 **198** A4
Wembley HA0 **86** C4
Priory Cl, E4 **61** J3
E18 **79** G1
N3 **72** C1
N14 **42** B5
N20 **40** C7
SW19 *off High Path* **185** E1
Beckenham BR3 **189** H3
Chislehurst BR7 **192** C1
Hampton TW12 *off Priory Gdns* **179** F1
Hayes UB3 **102** B7
Stanmore HA7 **52** C3
Sunbury-on-Thames TW16 *off Staines Rd E* **160** A7
Wembley (Sudbury) HA0 **86** C4
Priory Ct, E17 **77** J3
EC4 *off Carter La* **19** H4
SW8 **150** D1
Priory Ct Est, E17 *off Priory Ct* **77** J2
Priory Ct Ho, SE6 **172** B1
Priory Cres, SE19 **169** J7
Sutton SM3 **198** A4
Wembley HA0 **86** D3
Priory Dr, SE2 **138** D5
Stanmore HA7 **52** C3
Priory Fld Dr, Edg. HA8 **54** B4
Priory Gdns, N6 **74** B6
SE25 **188** C4
SW13 **147** F3
W4 **127** E4
W5 *off Hanger La* **105** J3
Hampton TW12 **161** F7
Wembley HA0 **86** D4
Priory Grn Est, N1 **10** C1
Priory Gro, SW8 **150** E1
Barnet EN5 **40** D5
Priory Hts, N1 **10** C1
Priory Hill, Wem. HA0 **86** D4
Priory Ho, SE7 *off Springfield Gro* **135** J6
Priory La, SW15 **147** E6
Richmond TW9 *off Forest Rd* **126** A7
West Molesey KT8 **179** G4
Priory Ms, SW8 **150** D1
Priory Pk, SE3 **155** F3
Priory Pk Rd, NW6 **108** C1
Wembley HA0 **86** D4
Priory Rd, E6 **116** A1
N8 **74** D4
NW6 **108** E1
SW19 **167** G7
W4 **126** D3
Barking IG11 **99** G7
Chessington KT9 **195** H3
Croydon CR0 **187** G7
Hampton TW12 **161** F7
Hounslow TW3 **143** J5
Loughton IG10 **48** B4
Richmond TW9 **126** A6
Sutton SM3 **198** A4
Priory St, E3 **114** B3
Priory Ter, NW6 **108** E1
Sunbury-on-Thames TW16 *off Staines Rd E* **160** A7
Priory Wk, SW10 **30** D4
Priory Way, Har. HA2 **67** H4
Southall UB2 **122** D3
West Drayton (Harm.) UB7 **120** B6
Priscilla Cl, N15 *off Conway Rd* **75** J5
Pritchard's Rd, E2 **112** D1
Priter Rd, SE16 **29** J6
Private Rd, Enf. EN1 **44** B5
Probert Rd, SW2 **151** G5
Probyn Ho, SW1 *off Page St* **33** J1
Probyn Rd, SW2 **169** H2
Procter Ho, SE1 **37** H3
Procter St, WC1 **18** C2
Proctor Cl, Mitch. CR4 **186** A1
Proctors Cl, Felt. TW14 **160** A1
Progress Business Pk, Croy. CR0 **201** F2
Progress Way, N22 **75** G1
Croydon CR0 **201** F2
Enfield EN1 **44** D5
Prologis Pk Heathrow, West Dr. UB7 **121** E3
Promenade, Edg. HA8 **54** A5
Promenade, The, W4 **147** E1
Promenade App Rd, W4 **126** E7
Promenade Mans, Edg. HA8 *off Hale La* **54** A5
Prospect Business Pk, Loug. IG10 **49** G4
Prospect Cl, SE26 **170** E4
Belvedere DA17 **139** G4
Hounslow TW3 **143** F1
Ruislip HA4 **66** D7
Prospect Cotts, SW18 *off Point Pleasant* **148** D4
Prospect Cres, Twick. TW2 **143** J6
Prospect Hill, E17 **78** B4
Prospect Ho, SW19 *off Chapter Way* **185** G1
Prospect Pl, E1 **133** F1
N2 **73** G4
N7 *off Parkhurst Rd* **93** E4
N17 **60** B7
NW2 *off Ridge Rd* **90** C3
NW3 *off Holly Wk* **91** F4
SW20 **165** H7
W4 *off Chiswick High Rd* **126** D5
Bromley BR2 **191** H3
Romford RM5 **83** J2
Prospect Quay, SW18 **148** D4
Prospect Ring, N2 **73** G3
Prospect Rd, NW2 **90** C3
Barnet EN5 **40** D5
Surbiton (Long Dit.) KT6 **181** F6
Woodford Green IG8 **63** J5
Prospect St, SE16 *off Jamaica Rd* **133** E2
Prospect Vale, SE18 **136** B4
Prospero Rd, N19 **92** C1
Protea Cl, E16 *off Hermit Rd* **115** F4
Prothero Gdns, NW4 **71** H5
Prothero Ho, NW10 **88** D7
Prothero Rd, SW6 **128** B7
Prout Gro, NW10 **89** E4
Prout Rd, E5 **95** E3
Provence St, N1 **11** J1
Providence Av, Har. HA2 *off Goodwill Dr* **85** G1
Providence Cl, E9 *off Wetherell Rd* **113** G1
Providence Ct, W1 **16** C5
Providence La, Hayes (Harling.) UB3 **121** G7
Providence Pl, N1 *off Upper St* **111** H1
Romford RM5 **83** F2
Providence Rd, West Dr. UB7 **120** B1
Providence Row, N1 *off Pentonville Rd* **10** C2
Providence Row Cl, E2 *off Ainsley St* **113** E3
Providence Sq, SE1 *off Jacob St* **29** H3
Providence Yd, E2 **13** H3
Provident Ind Est, Hayes UB3 **122** A2
Provost Est, N1 **12** B3
Provost Rd, NW3 **91** J7
Provost St, N1 **12** B4
Prowse Av, Bushey (Bushey Hth) WD23 **51** J2
Prowse Pl, NW1 *off Bonny St* **92** B7
Prudence La, Orp. BR6 **206** D4
Pruden Cl, N14 **58** C2
Prudent Pas, EC2 **20** A3
Prusom St, E1 **133** E1
Pryors, The, NW3 **91** G3
★ **P.S. Tattershall Castle**, SW1 **26** B2
Pudding La, EC3 **20** C6
Chigwell IG7 **65** J1
Pudding Mill La, E15 **114** B1
Puddle Dock, EC4 **19** H5
Puffin Cl, Bark. IG11 **118** B3
Beckenham BR3 **189** G5
Puffin Ter, Ilf. IG5 *off Tiptree Cres* **80** D3
Pulborough Rd, SW18 **148** C7
Pulborough Way, Houns. TW4 **142** C4
Pulford Rd, N15 **76** A6
Pulham Av, N2 **73** F4
Pulham Ho, SW8 *off Dorset Rd* **131** F7
Puller Rd, Barn. EN5 **40** B2
Pulleyns Av, E6 **116** B3
Pullman Ct, SW2 **169** E1
Pullman Gdns, SW15 **147** J6

Pullman Ms, SE12 . . . . . . .173 H3
Pullman Pl, SE9 . . . . .156 B5
Pulross Rd, SW9 . . . . .151 F3
Pulse Apts, NW6
off Lymington Rd 91 E5
Pulteney Cl, E3 . . . . .113 J1
Isleworth TW7
off Gumley Gdns 144 D3
Pulteney Gdns, E18
off Pulteney Rd 79 H3
Pulteney Rd, E18 . . . . .79 H3
Pulteney Ter, N1 . . . . .111 F1
Pulton Pl, SW6 . . . . .128 D7
Puma Ct, E1 . . . . .21 F1
Pump All, Brent. TW8 . . . . .125 G7
Pump Cl, Nthlt. UB5
off Union Rd 103 G2
Pumphandle Path, N2
off Tarling Rd 73 F2
Pump Hill, Loug. IG10 . . . . .48 C2
Pump Ho Cl, SE16
off Renforth St 133 F2
Bromley BR2 . . . . .191 F2
★ **Pumphouse Ed Mus, Rotherhithe**, SE16 . . . .133 H1
Pump Ho Ms, E1 . . . . .21 H5
Pumping Sta Rd, W4 . . . . .127 E7
Pump La, SE14 . . . . .133 F7
Hayes UB3 . . . . .122 B2
Pump Pail N, Croy. CR0
off Old Town 201 J3
Pump Pail S, Croy. CR0
off Southbridge Rd . . .201 J3
Pundersons Gdns, E2 . . . .113 E3
Punjab La, Sthl. UB1
off Herbert Rd 123 F1
Purbeck Av, N.Mal. KT3 . . .183 F6
Purbeck Dr, NW2 . . . . .90 B2
Purbeck Ho, SW8
off Bolney St 131 F7
Purbrook Est, SE1 . . . . .29 E4
Purbrook St, SE1 . . . . .29 E5
Purcell Cres, SW6 . . . . . . .128 B7
Purcell Rd, Grnf. UB6 . . . . .103 H5
Purcells Av, Edg. HA8 . . . . .54 A5
Purcell St, N1 . . . . .12 D1
Purchese St, NW1 . . . . .9 J1
Purdy St, E3 . . . . .114 B4
Purelake Ms, SE13 . . . . . . .154 D3
Purland Cl, Dag. RM8 . . . . .101 F1
Purland Rd, SE28 . . . . .137 J2
Purleigh Av, Wdf.Grn. IG8 . . . . .64 B6
Purley Av, NW2 . . . . .90 B3
Purley Cl, Ilf. IG5 . . . . .80 D2
Purley Pl, N1
off Islington Pk St 93 H7
Purley Rd, N9 . . . . .60 A3
South Croydon CR2 . . .202 A7
Purley Way, Croy. CR0 . . . .187 F7
Purley CR8 . . . . .201 G7
Purley Way Centre, The, Croy. CRO 201 G2
Purley Way Cres, Croy. CR0 *off Purley Way* 187 F7
Purneys Rd, SE9 . . . . .156 A4
Purrett Rd, SE18 . . . . .137 J5
Purser's Cross Rd, SW6 . . .148 C1
Pursewardens Cl, W13 . . . .125 F1
Pursley Rd, NW7 . . . . .55 H7
Purves Rd, NW10 . . . . .107 J2
Puteaux Ho, E2 . . . . .113 G2
PUTNEY, SW15 . . . . .148 B4
Putney Br, SW6 . . . . .148 B3
SW15 . . . . .148 B3
Putney Br App, SW6 . . . . .148 B3
Putney Br Rd, SW15 . . . . .148 B4
SW18 . . . . .148 B4
Putney Common, SW15 . .147 J3
Putney Ex Shop Cen, SW15 . . . . .148 A4
Putney Gdns, Rom. (Chad.Hth) RM6
off Heathfield Pk Dr 82 B5
PUTNEY HEATH, SW15 . . .147 J6
Putney Heath, SW15 . . . . .147 J6
Putney Heath La, SW15 . .148 A6
Putney High St, SW15 . . . .148 A4
Putney Hill, SW15 . . . . . . .148 A6
Putney Pk Av, SW15 . . . . .147 G4
Putney Pk La, SW15 . . . . .147 H4
PUTNEY VALE, SW15 . . . .165 F3
Putney Wf Twr, SW15 . . . .148 B3
Puttenham Cl, Wat. WD19 . .50 C3
Pycroft Way, N9 . . . . .60 D4
Pyecombe Cor, N12 . . . . . . .56 C4
Pylbrook Rd, Sutt. SM1 . . .198 D3
Pylon Way, Croy. CR0 . . . .201 E1
Pym Cl, Barn. (E.Barn.) EN4 . . . . .41 G5
Pymers Mead, SE21 . . . . .169 J1
Pymmes Brook Dr, Barn. EN4 . . . . .41 H4
Pymmes Cl, N13 . . . . .59 F5
N17 . . . . .76 E1
Pymmes Gdns N, N9 . . . . . .60 C3
Pymmes Gdns S, N9 . . . . . .60 C3
Pymmes Grn Rd, N11 . . . . .58 B4
Pymmes Rd, N13 . . . . .59 E6
Pyne Rd, Surb. KT6 . . . . . .196 A1
Pynfolds, SE16
off Paradise St 133 E2
Pynham Cl, SE2 . . . . .138 A3
Pynnacles Cl, Stan. HA7 . . .52 E5
Pyrland Rd, N5 . . . . .94 A5
Richmond TW10 . . . . . . .145 J6
Pyrles Grn, Loug. IG10 . . . . .48 E1
Pyrles La, Loug. IG10 . . . . . .48 E2
Pyrmont Gro, SE27 . . . . . .169 H3
Pyrmont Rd, W4 . . . . .126 A6
Pytchley Cres, SE19 . . . . . .169 J6
Pytchley Rd, SE22 . . . . . . .152 B3

Q

Quadrangle, The, SE24 . . .151 J5
SW10
off Chelsea Harbour . .149 F1
W2 . . . . .15 G3
Quadrangle Cl, SE1 . . . . . . .36 D1
Quadrangle Ho, E15
off Romford Rd 97 E6
Quadrangle Ms, Stan. HA7 . . . . .53 F7
Quadrant, The, SW20 . . . . .184 B1
Bexleyheath DA7 . . . . . .138 D7
Richmond TW9 . . . . .145 H4
Sutton SM2 . . . . .199 F6
Quadrant Arc, W1 . . . . .17 G6
Quadrant Cl, NW4
off The Burroughs 71 H5
Quadrant Gro, NW5 . . . . . . .91 J5
Quadrant Ho, Sutt. SM2 . .199 F6
Quadrant Rd, Rich. TW9 . .145 G4
Thornton Heath CR7 . . .187 H4
Quad Rd, Wem. HA9 . . . . . .87 G3
Quaggy Wk, SE3 . . . . .155 G4
Quainton St, NW10 . . . . . . .88 D3
Quaker Ct, E1 . . . . .13 F6
EC1 . . . . .12 B5
Quaker La, Sthl. UB2 . . . . .123 G3
Quakers Course, NW9 . . . . .71 F1
Quakers La, Islw. TW7 . . . .144 D1
Quaker's Pl, E7 . . . . .98 A5
Quaker St, E1 . . . . .13 F6
Quakers Wk, N21 . . . . .44 A6
Quality Ct, WC2 . . . . .18 E3
Quantock Cl, Hayes (Harling.) UB3 . . . . .121 G7
Quantock Dr, Wor.Pk. KT4 . . . . .197 J2
Quantock Gdns, NW2 . . . . .90 A2
Quantock Ms, SE15
off Choumert Gro 152 D2
Quarles Pk Rd, Rom. RM6 . . . . .82 B6
Quarrendon St, SW6 . . . . .148 D2
Quarr Rd, Cars. SM5 . . . . .185 G6
Quarry Pk Rd, Sutt. SM1 . . . . .198 C6
Quarry Ri, Sutt. SM1 . . . . .198 C6
Quarry Rd, SW18 . . . . .149 F6
Quarterdeck, The, E14 . . . .134 A2
Quarter Mile La, E10 . . . . . .96 B4
Quayside Wk, Kings.T. KT1 *off Bishop's Hall* . . .181 G2
Quay W, Tedd. TW11 . . . . . .162 E5
Quebec Ms, W1 . . . . .16 A4
Quebec Rd, Hayes UB4 . . .102 C7
Ilford IG1, IG2 . . . . .81 E7
Quebec Way, SE16 . . . . . . .133 G2
Queen Adelaide Rd, SE20 . . . . .171 F6
Queen Alexandra's Ct, SW19 . . . . .166 C5
Queen Anne Av, N15
off Suffield Rd 76 C5
Bromley BR2 . . . . .191 F3
Queen Anne Dr, Esher (Clay.) KT10 . . . . .194 B7
Queen Anne Ms, W1 . . . . . .16 E2
Queen Anne Rd, E9 . . . . . . .95 G6
Queen Anne's Cl, Twick. TW2 . . . . .162 A3
Queen Anne's Gdns, W4 . .127 E3
Queen Annes Gdns, W5 . .125 H2
Enfield EN1 . . . . .44 B6
Queen Anne's Gdns, Mitch. CR4 . . . . .185 J3
Queen Anne's Gate, SW1 . .25 H4
Bexleyheath DA7 . . . . . .158 D3
Queen Anne's Gro, W4 . . .126 E3
Queen Annes Gro, W5 . . . .125 H2
Enfield EN1 . . . . .44 A7
Queen Annes Pl, Enf. EN1 . .44 B6
Queen Anne St, W1 . . . . . . .16 D3
Queen Anne's Wk, WC1
off Queen Sq 10 B6
Queen Anne Ter, E1
off Sovereign Cl 113 E7
Queenborough Gdns, Chis. BR7 . . . . .175 G6
Ilford IG2 . . . . .80 D4
Queen Caroline Est, W6 . .127 J5
Queen Caroline St, W6 . . .127 J4
Queen Elizabeth Gdns, Mord. SM4 . . . . .184 D4
★ **Queen Elizabeth Hall & Purcell Room**, SE1 . . . .26 C1
Queen Elizabeth Rd, E17 . . .77 H3
Kingston upon Thames KT2 . . . . .181 J1
Queen Elizabeths Cl, N16 . .94 A2
Queen Elizabeth's Coll, SE10 *off Greenwich High Rd* 134 C7
Queen Elizabeths Dr, N14 . .58 E1
★ **Queen Elizabeth II Conf Cen**, SW1 . . . . . . .25 J4
★ **Queen Elizabeth's Hunting Lo**, E4 . . . . .47 F7
Queen Elizabeth St, SE1 . . .29 E3
Queen Elizabeths Wk, N16 .94 A2
Queen Elizabeth's Wk, Wall. SM6 . . . . .200 D4
Queen Elizabeth Wk, SW13 . . . . .147 H1
Queenhithe, EC4 . . . . .20 A5
Queen Margaret's Gro, N1 .94 B5
Queen Mary Av, E18 . . . . . .79 G1
Mord. SM4 . . . . .184 A5
Queen Mary Cl, Surb. KT6 . . . . .196 A3
Queen Mary Ho, SW15 . . . .147 G6
Queen Mary Rd, SE19 . . . .169 H6
Queen Mary's Av, Cars. SM5 . . . . .199 J7
Queen Marys Bldgs, SW1
off Stillington St 33 G1
★ **Queen Mary's Gdns**, NW1 . . . . .8 B4
Queen of Denmark Ct, SE16 . . . . .133 J3
Queens Acre, Sutt. SM3 . . .198 A7
Queens Av, N3 . . . . .57 F7
N10 . . . . .74 A3
N20 . . . . .57 G2
Queen's Av, N21 . . . . .59 H1
Queens Av, Felt. TW13 . . . .160 C4
Greenford UB6 . . . . .103 H6
Stanmore HA7 . . . . .69 F3
Woodford Green IG8 . . . .63 H5
Queensberry Ms W, SW7 . .30 E1
Queensberry Pl, E12 . . . . . .98 A5
SW7 . . . . .30 E1
Richmond TW9
off Friars La 145 G5
Queensberry Way, SW7 . . . .31 E1
Queensborough Ms, W2 . . .14 C5
Queensborough Pas, W2 . . .14 C5
Queensborough Studios, W2 . . . . .14 C5
Queensborough Ter, W2 . . .14 B5
Queensbridge Pk, Islw. TW7 . . . . .144 B5
Queensbridge Rd, E2 . . . . .112 C1
E8 . . . . .94 C7
QUEENSBURY, Har. HA3 . .69 G3
Queensbury Circle Par, Har. HA3
off Streatfield Rd 69 H3
Stanmore HA7
off Streatfield Rd 69 H3
Queensbury Rd, NW9 . . . . .70 D7
Wembley HA0 . . . . .105 J2
Queensbury Sta Par, Edg. HA8 . . . . .69 J3
Queensbury St, N1 . . . . . . .93 J7
Queen's Circ, SW8
off Queenstown Rd . . .130 B7
SW11
off Queenstown Rd . . .130 B7
Queens Cl, Edg. HA8 . . . . . .54 A5
Wallington SM6
off Queens Rd 200 B5
★ **Queens Club (Tennis Cen)**, W14 . . . .128 B5
Queens Club Gdns, W14 . .128 B6
Queens Ct, SE23 . . . . .171 F1
Richmond TW10 . . . . . . .145 J6
Queenscourt, Wem. HA9 . . .87 H4
Queen's Cres, NW5 . . . . . . .92 A6
Queens Cres, Rich. TW10 . .145 J5
Queenscroft Rd, SE9 . . . . .156 A5
Queensdale Cres, W11 . . . .128 A1
Queensdale Pl, W11 . . . . . .128 B1
Queensdale Rd, W11 . . . . .128 A1
Queensdale Wk, W11 . . . . .128 B1
Queensdown Rd, E5 . . . . . .94 E4
Queens Dr, E10 . . . . .78 A7
N4 . . . . .93 H2
W3 . . . . .105 J6
W5 . . . . .105 J6
Surbiton KT5 . . . . .182 A7
Thames Ditton KT7 . . . .180 D7
Queens Elm Par, SW3
off Old Ch St 31 F3
Queen's Elm Sq, SW3 . . . . .31 F4
Queensferry Wk, N17
off Jarrow Rd 76 E4
★ **Queen's Gall, The**, SW1 . . . . .24 E4
Queens Gdns, NW4 . . . . . . .71 J5
W2 . . . . .14 C5
W5 . . . . .105 F4
Queen's Gdns, Houns. TW5 . . . . .142 E1
Queens Gate, SW7 . . . . . . .22 D4
Queen's Gate Gdns, SW7 . . . . .22 D6
Queens Gate Gdns, SW15 *off Upper Richmond Rd* 147 H4
Queensgate Gdns, Chis. BR7 . . . . .193 G1
Queensgate Ho, E3
off Hereford Rd 113 J2
Queen's Gate Ms, SW7 . . . .22 D4
Queensgate Ms, Beck. BR3 *off Queens Rd* 189 H1
Queensgate Pl, NW6 . . . . . .90 D7
Queen's Gate Pl, SW7 . . . . .22 D6
Queen's Gate Pl Ms, SW7 . . . . .22 D6
Queen's Gate Ter, SW7 . . . .22 C5
Queen's Gro, NW8 . . . . . . .109 G1
Queen's Gro Ms, NW8 . . . .109 G1
Queens Gro Rd, E4 . . . . . . .62 D1
Queen's Head Pas, EC4 . . . .19 J3
Queen's Head St, N1 . . . . .111 H1
Queens Head Yd, SE1 . . . . .28 B2
Queens Ho, Tedd. TW11 . . .162 C6
★ **Queen's Ice & Bowl**, W2 . . . . .14 B6
Queensland Av, N18 . . . . . .59 J6
SW19 . . . . .184 E1
Queensland Cl, E17 . . . . . . .77 J2
Queensland Ho, E16
off Rymill St 136 D1
Queensland Rd, N7 . . . . . . .93 G4
Queens La, N10 . . . . .74 B3
Queens Mkt, E13
off Green St 115 J1
Queensmead, NW8 . . . . . .109 G1
Queens Mead, Edg. HA8 . . .53 J6
Queensmead Rd, Brom. BR2 . . . . .191 F2
Queensmere Cl, SW19 . . . .166 A2
Queensmere Rd, SW19 . . .166 A2
Queens Ms, W2 . . . . .14 B5
Queensmill Rd, SW6 . . . . .128 A7
Queens Par, N11 . . . . .57 J5
W5 . . . . .105 J6
Queens Par Cl, N11
off Colney Hatch La 57 J5
Queens Pk Ct, W10 . . . . . .108 A3
★ **Queens Park Rangers FC**, W12 . . . . .127 H1
Queens Pas, Chis. BR7
off High St 175 E6
Queens Pl, Mord. SM4 . . .184 D4
Queen's Prom, Kings.T. KT1
off Portsmouth Rd 181 G3
Queen Sq, WC1 . . . . .10 B6
Queen Sq Pl, WC1 . . . . .10 B6
Queens Reach, E.Mol. KT8 . . . . .180 B4
Queens Ride, SW13 . . . . . .147 G3
SW15 . . . . .147 G3
Queen's Ride, Rich. TW10 . . . . .164 B1
Queens Ri, Rich. TW10 . . . .145 J6
Queens Rd, E11 . . . . .78 D7
E13 . . . . .115 H1
Queen's Rd, E17 . . . . .77 J6
Queens Rd, N3 . . . . .73 F1
N9 . . . . .60 E3
Queen's Rd, N11 . . . . .58 E7
Queens Rd, NW4 . . . . .71 J5
SE14 . . . . .152 E1
SE15 . . . . .152 E1
SW14 . . . . .146 D3
SW19 . . . . .166 C6
W5 . . . . .105 H6
Barking IG11 . . . . .99 F7
Barnet EN5 . . . . .40 A3
Beckenham BR3 . . . . . . .189 H2
Bromley BR1 . . . . .191 G2
Buckhurst Hill IG9 . . . . . .63 H2
Chislehurst BR7 . . . . . . .175 E6
Queen's Rd, Croy. CR0 . . .187 H6
Queens Rd, Enf. EN1 . . . . . .44 B4
Feltham TW13 . . . . .160 B1
Hampton (Hmptn H.) TW12 . . . . .161 H4
Queen's Rd, Houns. TW3 . .143 H3
Queens Rd, Kings.T. KT2 . . . . .164 A7
Loughton IG10 . . . . .48 B3
Morden SM4 . . . . .184 D4
New Malden KT3 . . . . . .183 F4
Richmond TW10 . . . . . . .145 J5
Southall UB2 . . . . .122 D2
Queen's Rd, Teddington TW11 . . . . .162 B6
Thames Ditton KT7 . . . .180 C5

Queens Rd, Twick. TW1 . . . 162 C1
Wallington SM6 . . . . 200 B5
Queen's Rd, Well. DA16 . . . . 158 B2
Queens Rd, West Dr. UB7 . . . . 120 C2
Queens Rd W, E13 . . . . 115 G2
Queen's Row, SE17 . . . . 36 B5
Queens Ter, E13 . . . . 115 H1
Queen's Ter, NW8 . . . . 7 E1
Queens Ter, Islw. TW7 . . . . 144 D4
Queens Ter Cotts, W7 *off Boston Rd* 124 B2
Queensthorpe Rd, SE26 . . 171 G4
★ **Queen's Twr**, SW7 . . . . . 23 E5
Queenstown Ms, SW8 *off Queenstown Rd* . . . 150 B1
Queenstown Rd, SW8 . . . . . 32 D6
Queen St, EC4 . . . . 20 A5
N17 . . . . 60 B6
W1 . . . . 24 D1
Bexleyheath DA7 . . . . . . 159 F3
Croydon CR0 . . . . 201 J4
Queen St Pl, EC4 . . . . 20 A6
Queensville Rd, SW12 . . . . 150 D7
Queens Wk, E4 . . . . 62 D1
NW9 . . . . 88 C2
Queen's Wk, SW1 . . . . 25 F2
Queens Wk, W5 . . . . 105 F4
Queen's Wk, Har. HA1 . . . . . 68 B4
Queens Wk, Ruis. HA4 . . . . . 84 D3
Queen's Wk, The, SE1 . . . . . . 26 C2
Queens Way, NW4 . . . . 71 J5
Queensway, W2 . . . . 14 B4
Queens Way, Croy. CR0 . . . 201 F6
Queensway, Enf. EN3 . . . . . . 45 E4
Queens Way, Felt. TW13 . . 160 C4
Queensway, Orp. BR5 . . . . 193 F5
Sunbury-on-Thames TW16 . . . . 178 B2
West Wickham BR4 . . . . 205 E3
Queensway Business Cen, Enf. EN3 *off Queensway* 45 F4
Queenswell Av, N20 . . . . . . 57 H4
Queenswood Av, E17 . . . . . 78 C1
Hampton TW12 . . . . 161 H6
Hounslow TW3 . . . . 143 F2
Thornton Heath CR7 . . . 187 G5
Wallington SM6 . . . . 200 D4
Queenswood Gdns, E11 . . . 97 G1
Queenswood Pk, N3 . . . . . . 72 B2
Queen's Wd Rd, N10 . . . . . . 74 B6
Queenswood Rd, SE23 . . . 171 G3
Sidcup DA15 . . . . 157 J5
Queens Yd, WC1 . . . . 9 G6
Queen Victoria, Sutt. SM3 . . . . 197 J4
Queen Victoria Av, Wem. HA0 . . . . 87 G7
★ **Queen Victoria Mem**, SW1 . . . . 25 F3
Queen Victoria St, EC4 . . . . 19 H5
Queen Victoria Ter, E1 *off Sovereign Cl* 113 E7
Quemerford Rd, N7 . . . . 93 F5
Quentin Pl, SE13 . . . . 155 E3
Quentin Rd, SE13 . . . . 155 E3
Quernmore Cl, Brom. BR1 . . . . 173 G6
Quernmore Rd, N4 . . . . 75 G6
Bromley BR1 . . . . 173 G6
Querrin St, SW6 . . . . 149 F2
Quex Ms, NW6 *off Quex Rd* 108 D1
Quex Rd, NW6 . . . . 108 D1
Quick Rd, W4 . . . . 126 E5
Quicks Rd, SW19 . . . . 167 E7
Quick St, N1 . . . . 11 H2
Quick St Ms, N1 . . . . 11 G2
Quickswood, NW3 *off King Henry's Rd* 91 H7
Quiet Nook, Brom. BR2 *off Croydon Rd* 206 A3
Quill La, SW15 . . . . 148 A4
Quill St, N4 . . . . 93 G3
W5 . . . . 105 H3
Quilp St, SE1 . . . . 27 J3
Quilters Pl, SE9 . . . . 175 F1
Quilter St, E2 . . . . 13 H3
SE18 . . . . 137 J5
Quilting Ct, SE16 *off Poolmans St* 133 G2
Quince Ho, Felt. TW13 *off High St* 160 B1
Quince Rd, SE13 . . . . 154 B2
Quinnell Cl, SE18 *off Rippolson Rd* 137 J5
Quinta Dr, Barn. EN5 . . . . . . 39 H5
Quintin Av, SW20 . . . . 184 C1
Quintin Cl, Pnr. HA5 *off High Rd* 66 B5
Quinton Cl, Beck. BR3 . . . . 190 C3
Hounslow TW5 . . . . 122 B7
Wallington SM6 . . . . 200 B4
Quinton Rd, T.Ditt. KT7 . . . 194 D1
Quinton St, SW18 . . . . 167 F2
Quixley St, E14 . . . . 114 D7
Quorn Rd, SE22 . . . . 152 B4

R

Rabbit Row, W8 *off Kensington Mall* . . . 128 D1
Rabbits Rd, E12 . . . . 98 B4
Rabournmead Dr, Nthlt. UB5 . . . . 84 E5
Raby Rd, N.Mal. KT3 . . . . . 182 D4
Raby St, E14 *off Salmon La* 113 H6
Raccoon Way, Houns. TW4 . . . . 142 C2
Rachel Cl, Ilf. IG6 . . . . 81 G3
Rackham Cl, Well. DA16 . . 158 B2
Rackham Ms, SW16 . . . . . . 168 C6
Racton Rd, SW6 . . . . 128 D6
Radbourne Av, W5 . . . . 125 F4
Radbourne Cl, E5 *off Overbury St* 95 G4
Radbourne Cres, E17 . . . . . . 78 D2
Radbourne Rd, SW12 . . . . 168 D1
Radcliffe Av, NW10 . . . . 107 G2
Enfield EN2 . . . . 43 J1
Radcliffe Gdns, Cars. SM5 . . . . 199 H7
Radcliffe Ms, Hmptn. (Hmptn H.) TW12 *off Taylor Cl* 161 J5
Radcliffe Path, SW8 *off Robertson St* 150 B2
Radcliffe Rd, N21 . . . . 59 H1
SE1 . . . . 29 E5
Croydon CR0 . . . . 202 C2
Harrow HA3 . . . . 68 D2
Radcliffe Sq, SW15 . . . . . . 148 A6
Radcliffe Way, Nthlt. UB5 . 102 D3
Radcot Pt, SE23 . . . . 171 G3
Radcot St, SE11 . . . . 35 F4
Raddington Rd, W10 . . . . . 108 B5
Radfield Way, Sid. DA15 . . 157 G7
Radford Rd, SE13 . . . . 154 C6
Radford Way, Bark. IG11 . . . 117 J3
Radipole Rd, SW6 . . . . 148 C1
Radius Pk, Felt. TW14 . . . . 141 J4
Radland Rd, E16 . . . . 115 F6
Radlet Av, SE26 . . . . 171 E3
Radlett Cl, E7 . . . . 97 F6
Radlett Pl, NW8 . . . . 109 H1
Radley Av, Ilf. IG3 . . . . 99 J4
Radley Ct, SE16 *off Marlow Way* 133 G2
Radley Gdns, Har. HA3 . . . . 69 H4
Radley Ho, SE2 *off Wolvercote Rd* 138 D2
Radley Ms, W8 . . . . 128 D3
Radley Rd, N17 . . . . 76 B2
Radley's La, E18 . . . . 79 G2
Radleys Mead, Dag. RM10 . . . . 101 H6
Radley Sq, E5 *off Dudlington Rd* 95 F2
Radlix Rd, E10 . . . . 96 A1
Radnor Av, Har. HA1 . . . . . . 68 B5
Welling DA16 . . . . 158 B5
Radnor Cl, Chis. BR7 . . . . . 175 H6
Mitcham CR4 . . . . 187 E4
Radnor Cres, SE18 . . . . 138 A6
Ilford IG4 . . . . 80 C5
Radnor Gdns, Enf. EN1 . . . . 44 B1
Twickenham TW1 . . . . . . 162 C2
Radnor Ho, SW16 . . . . 187 F2
Radnor Ms, W2 . . . . 15 F4
Radnor Pl, W2 . . . . 15 G4
Radnor Rd, NW6 . . . . 108 B1
SE15 . . . . 37 H7
Harrow HA1 . . . . 68 A5
Twickenham TW1 . . . . . . 162 C2
Radnor St, EC1 . . . . 12 A4
Radnor Ter, W14 . . . . 128 C4
Radnor Wk, E14 *off Copeland Dr* 134 A4
SW3 . . . . 31 H4
Croydon CR0 . . . . 189 J6
Radnor Way, NW10 . . . . . . 106 B4
Radstock Av, Har. HA3 . . . . . 68 D3
Radstock Cl, N11 . . . . 58 A5
Radstock St, SW11 . . . . 129 H7
Raebarn Gdns, Barn. EN5 . . . 39 H5
Raeburn Av, Surb. KT5 . . . 182 B6
Raeburn Cl, NW11 . . . . 73 F6
Kingston upon Thames KT1 . . . . 163 G7
Raeburn Rd, Edg. HA8 . . . . . 70 A2
Sidcup DA15 . . . . 157 H6
Raeburn St, SW2 . . . . 151 E4
Raffles Ct, Edg. HA8 . . . . . . 53 J4
Rafford Way, Brom. BR1 . . 191 H2
Raft Rd, SW18 *off North Pas* 148 D4
★ **Ragged Sch Mus**, E3 *off Copperfield Rd* 113 H5
Raggleswood, Chis. BR7 . . 192 D1
Raglan Cl, Houns. TW4 . . . 143 F5
Raglan Ct, SE12 . . . . 155 G5
South Croydon CR2 . . . . 201 H5
Wembley HA9 . . . . 87 J4
Raglan Gdns, Wat. WD19 . . . 50 B1
Raglan Rd, E17 . . . . 78 C5
SE18 . . . . 137 F5
Belvedere DA17 . . . . 139 F4
Bromley BR2 . . . . 191 J4
Enfield EN1 . . . . 44 B7
Raglan St, NW5 . . . . 92 B6
Raglan Ter, Har. HA2 . . . . . . 85 H4
Raglan Way, Nthlt. UB5 . . . . 85 J6
Ragley Cl, W3 *off Church Rd* 126 C2
Ragwort Ct, SE26 . . . . 170 E5
Rahere Ho, EC1 . . . . 11 J3
Raider Cl, Rom. RM7 . . . . . . 83 G1
Railey Ms, NW5 . . . . 92 C5
Railshead Rd, Islw. TW7 . . 144 E4
Railton Rd, SE24 . . . . 151 G4
Railway App, N4 *off Wightman Rd* 75 G6
SE1 . . . . 28 C1
Harrow HA1, HA3 . . . . . . 68 C4
Twickenham TW1 . . . . . . 144 D7
Wallington SM6 . . . . 200 B6
Railway Arches, W12 *off Shepherds Bush Mkt* 127 J2
Railway Av, SE16 . . . . 133 F2
Railway Children Wk, SE12 . . . . 173 G2
Bromley BR1 . . . . 173 G2
Railway Ms, E3 *off Wellington Way* 114 A3
W10 *off Ladbroke Gro* . . . 108 B6
Railway Pas, Tedd. TW11 *off Victoria Rd* 162 D6
Railway Pl, SW19 *off Hartfield Rd* 166 C6
Belvedere DA17 . . . . 139 G3
Railway Ri, SE22 *off Grove Vale* 152 B4
Railway Rd, Tedd. TW11 . . . 162 C4
Railway Side, SW13 . . . . . 147 E3
Railway St, N1 . . . . 10 B2
Romford RM6 . . . . 100 C1
Railway Ter, E17 . . . . 78 C1
SE13 *off Ladywell Rd* . . . 154 B5
Rainborough Cl, NW10 . . . . 88 C6
Rainbow Av, E14 . . . . 134 B5
Rainbow Ind Pk, SW20 . . . 183 H2
Rainbow Quay, SE16 . . . . . 133 H3
Rainbow St, SE5 . . . . 132 B7
Raines Ct, N16 *off Northwold Rd* 94 C2
Raine St, E1 . . . . 133 E1
Rainham Cl, SE9 . . . . 157 G6
SW11 . . . . 149 H6
Rainham Rd, NW10 . . . . . . 107 J3
Rainham Rd N, Dag. RM10 . . . . 101 H2
Rainham Rd S, Dag. RM10 . . . . 101 H4
Rainhill Way, E3 . . . . 114 A3
Rainsborough Av, SE8 . . . . 133 H4
Rainsford Cl, Stan. HA7 . . . . 53 F4
Rainsford Rd, NW10 . . . . . . 106 B3
Rainsford St, W2 . . . . 15 G3
Rainton Rd, SE7 . . . . 135 G5
Rainville Rd, W6 . . . . 127 J6
Raisins Hill, Pnr. HA5 . . . . . 66 C3
Raith Av, N14 . . . . 58 D3
Raleana Rd, E14 . . . . 134 C1
Raleigh Av, Hayes UB4 . . . . 102 B5
Wallington SM6 . . . . 200 D4
Raleigh Cl, NW4 . . . . 71 J5
Pinner HA5 . . . . 66 D7
Raleigh Ct, SE19 *off Lymer Av* 170 C5
Beckenham BR3 . . . . 190 B1
Wallington SM6 . . . . 200 B6
Raleigh Dr, N20 . . . . 57 H3
Esher (Clay.) KT10 . . . . . 194 A5
Surbiton KT5 . . . . 196 C1
Raleigh Gdns, SW2 *off Brixton Hill* 151 F6
Mitcham CR4 . . . . 185 J2
Raleigh Ms, N1 *off Queen's Head St* . . . 111 H1
Orpington BR6 *off Osgood Av* 207 J5
Raleigh Rd, N8 . . . . 75 G4
SE20 . . . . 171 G7
Enfield EN2 . . . . 44 A4
Richmond TW9 . . . . 145 J3
Southall UB2 . . . . 122 E5
Raleigh St, N1 . . . . 111 H1
Raleigh Way, N14 . . . . 58 D1
Feltham TW13 . . . . 160 C5
Rale La, E4 . . . . 46 D7
Ralph Ct, W2 . . . . 14 B3
Ralph Perring Ct, Beck. BR3 . . . . 190 A4
Ralston St, SW3 . . . . 31 J4
Ralston Way, Wat. WD19 . . . 50 D2
Rama Cl, SW16 . . . . 168 D7
Rama Ct, Har. HA1 . . . . 86 B2
Ramac Way, SE7 . . . . 135 H4
Rama La, SE19 . . . . 170 C7
Rambler Cl, SW16 . . . . 168 C4
Rame Cl, SW17 . . . . 168 A5
Ramilles Cl, SW2 . . . . 151 E6
Ramillies Pl, W1 . . . . 17 F4
Ramillies Rd, NW7 . . . . 54 E2
W4 . . . . 126 D4
Sidcup DA15 . . . . 158 B6
Ramillies St, W1 . . . . 17 F4
Rampart St, E1 *off Commercial Rd* . . . 112 E6
Ram Pas, Kings.T. KT1 *off High St* 181 G2
Rampayne St, SW1 . . . . 33 H3
Ram Pl, E9 *off Chatham Pl* 95 F6
Rampton Cl, E4 . . . . 62 A3
Ramsay Ms, SW3 . . . . 31 G5
Ramsay Pl, Har. HA1 . . . . . . 86 B1
Ramsay Rd, E7 . . . . 97 E4
W3 . . . . 126 C3
Ramscroft Cl, N9 . . . . 44 B7
Ramsdale Rd, SW17 . . . . . . 168 A5
Ramsden Rd, N11 . . . . 57 J5
SW12 . . . . 150 A6
Ramsey Cl, NW9 . . . . 71 F6
Greenford UB6 . . . . 85 J5
Ramsey Ho, SW11 *off Maysoule Rd* 149 G4
Wembley HA9 . . . . 87 H6
Ramsey Rd, Th.Hth. CR7 . . 187 F6
Ramsey St, E2 . . . . 13 J5
Ramsey Wk, N1 . . . . 94 A6
Ramsey Way, N14 . . . . 42 C7
Ramsfort Ho, SE16 *off Manor Est* 132 E4
Ramsgate Cl, E16 *off Hanameel St* 135 H1
Ramsgate St, E8 *off Dalston La* 94 C6
Ramsgill App, Ilf. IG2 . . . . . . 81 J4
Ramsgill Dr, Ilf. IG2 . . . . 81 J5
Rams Gro, Rom. RM6 . . . . . 83 E4
Ram St, SW18 . . . . 148 E5
Ramulis Dr, Hayes UB4 . . . 102 D4
Ramus Wd Av, Orp. BR6 . . 207 H5
Rancliffe Gdns, SE9 . . . . . . 156 B4
Rancliffe Rd, E6 . . . . 116 B2
Randall Av, NW2 . . . . 89 F3
Randall Cl, SW11 . . . . 149 H1
Erith DA8 . . . . 139 J6
Randall Ct, NW7 . . . . 55 G7
Randall Pl, SE10 . . . . 134 C7
Randall Rd, SE11 . . . . 34 C3
Randall Row, SE11 . . . . 34 C2
Randell's Rd, N1 . . . . 111 E1
Randisbourne Gdns, SE6 . . . . 172 B3
Randle Rd, Rich. TW10 . . . . 163 F4
Randlesdown Rd, SE6 . . . . 172 A4
Randolph App, E16 . . . . . . 116 A6
Randolph Av, W9 . . . . 6 D5
Randolph Cl, Bexh. DA7 . . 159 J3
Kingston upon Thames KT2 . . . . 164 C5
Randolph Cres, W9 . . . . 6 C6
Randolph Gdns, NW6 . . . . . . 6 A2
Randolph Gro, Rom. RM6 *off Donald Dr* 82 C5
Randolph Ho, Croy. CR0 . . 201 J1
Randolph Ms, W9 . . . . 6 D6
Randolph Rd, E17 . . . . 78 B5
W9 . . . . 6 C6
Bromley BR2 . . . . 206 C1
Southall UB1 . . . . 123 F2
Randolph St, NW1 . . . . 92 C7
Randon Cl, Har. HA2 . . . . . . 67 H2
Ranelagh Av, SW6 . . . . 148 C3
SW13 . . . . 147 G2
Ranelagh Br, W2 *off Gloucester Ter* 14 B2
Ranelagh Cl, Edg. HA8 . . . . 54 A4
Ranelagh Dr, Edg. HA8 . . . . 54 A4
Twickenham TW1 . . . . . . 145 E5
★ **Ranelagh Gdns**, SW3 . . 32 B4
Ranelagh Gdns, E11 . . . . 79 J5
SW6 . . . . 148 C3
W4 . . . . 126 C7
W6 . . . . 127 F3
Ilford IG1 . . . . 98 D1
Ranelagh Gdns Mans, SW6 *off Ranelagh Gdns* 148 B3
Ranelagh Gro, SW1 . . . . 32 C3
Ranelagh Ms, W5 . . . . 125 G2
Ranelagh Pl, N.Mal. KT3 . . 182 E5
Ranelagh Rd, E6 . . . . 116 D1
E11 . . . . 96 E4
E15 . . . . 115 E1
N17 . . . . 76 B3
N22 . . . . 75 F1
NW10 . . . . 107 F2
SW1 . . . . 33 G4
W5 . . . . 125 G2
Southall UB1 . . . . 122 D1

Ranelagh Rd, Wem. HA0 . . . **87** G5
Ranfurly Rd, Sutt. SM1 . . . **198** D2
Rangefield Rd, Brom. BR1 . . . **172** E5
Rangemoor Rd, N15 . . . **76** C5
Rangers Rd, E4 . . . **47** E7
Loughton IG10 . . . **47** E7
Rangers Sq, SE10 . . . **154** D1
Rangeworth Pl, Sid. DA15 *off Priestlands Pk Rd* . . **175** J3
Rangoon St, EC3 . . . **21** F4
Rankin Cl, NW9 . . . **71** E3
Rankine Ho, SE1 *off Bath Ter* . . . **27** J6
Ranleigh Gdns, Bexh. DA7 . . . **139** F7
Ranmere St, SW12 *off Ormeley Rd* . . . **168** B1
Ranmoor Cl, Har. HA1 . . . **68** A4
Ranmoor Gdns, Har. HA1 . . **68** A4
Ranmore Av, Croy. CR0 . . . **202** C3
Rannoch Cl, Edg. HA8 . . . **54** B2
Rannoch Rd, W6 . . . **127** J6
Rannock Av, NW9 . . . **70** E7
Ranskill Rd, Borwd. WD6 . . **38** A1
Ransome's Dock Business Cen, SW11 *off Parkgate Rd* . . . **129** H7
Ransom Rd, SE7 *off Floyd Rd* . . . **135** J5
Ransom Wk, SE7 *off Woolwich Rd* . . . **135** J4
Ranston St, NW1 . . . **15** G1
Ranulf Rd, NW2 . . . **90** C4
Ranwell Cl, E3 *off Beale Rd* . . . **113** J1
Ranwell St, E3 . . . **113** J1
Ranworth Rd, N9 . . . **61** F2
Ranyard Cl, Chess. KT9 . . . **195** J3
Raphael Dr, Loug. IG10 . . . **48** E2
T.Ditt. KT7 . . . **180** C7
Raphael St, SW7 . . . **23** J4
Rashleigh St, SW8 *off Peardon St* . . . **150** B2
Rasper Rd, N20 . . . **57** F2
Rastell Av, SW2 . . . **168** D2
Ratcliffe Cl, SE12 . . . **155** G7
Ratcliffe Cross St, E1 . . . **113** G6
Ratcliffe La, E14 . . . **113** H6
Ratcliffe Orchard, E1 *off Cranford St* . . . **113** G7
Ratcliff Rd, E7 . . . **97** J5
Rathbone Mkt, E16 *off Barking Rd* . . . **115** F5
Rathbone Pl, W1 . . . **17** H3
Rathbone St, E16 . . . **115** F5
W1 . . . **17** G2
Rathcoole Av, N8 . . . **75** F4
Rathcoole Gdns, N8 . . . **75** F5
Rathfern Rd, SE6 . . . **171** J1
Rathgar Av, W13 . . . **125** E1
Rathgar Cl, N3 . . . **72** C2
Rathgar Rd, SW9 *off Coldharbour La* . . . **151** H3
Rathmell Dr, SW4 . . . **150** D6
Rathmore Rd, SE7 . . . **135** H5
Rattray Rd, SW2 . . . **151** G4
Raul Rd, SE15 . . . **152** D2
Raveley St, NW5 . . . **92** C4
Raven Cl, NW9 . . . **71** E2
Raven Ct, E5 *off Stellman Cl* . . . **94** D3
Ravenet St, SW11 *off Strasburg Rd* . . . **150** B1
Ravenfield Rd, SW17 . . . **167** J3
Ravenhill Rd, E13 . . . **115** J2
Ravenna Rd, SW15 . . . **148** A5
Ravenoak Way, Chig. IG7 . . **65** H5
Ravenor Pk Rd, Grnf. UB6 . . . **103** H3
Raven Rd, E18 . . . **79** J2
Raven Row, E1 . . . **113** E5
Ravensbourne Av, Beck. BR3 . . . **172** D7
Bromley BR2 . . . **172** D7
Ravensbourne Business Cen, Kes. BR2 . . . **206** A4
Ravensbourne Gdns, W13 . . . **104** E5
Ilford IG5 . . . **80** D1
Ravensbourne Pk, SE6 . . . **154** A7
Ravensbourne Pk Cres, SE6 . . . **153** J7
Ravensbourne Pl, SE13 . . . **154** B2
Ravensbourne Rd, SE6 . . . **153** J7
Bromley BR1 . . . **191** G3
Twickenham TW1 . . . **145** F6
Ravensbury Av, Mord. SM4 . . . **185** F5
Ravensbury Ct, Mitch. CR4 *off Ravensbury Gro* . . . **185** G4
Ravensbury Gro, Mitch. CR4 . . . **185** G4
Ravensbury La, Mitch. CR4 . . . **185** G4
Ravensbury Path, Mitch. CR4 . . . **185** G4
Ravensbury Rd, SW18 . . . **166** D2
Orpington BR5 . . . **193** J4
Ravensbury Ter, SW18 . . . **166** E2
Ravenscar Rd, Brom. BR1 . . . **172** E4
Surbiton KT6 . . . **195** J2
Ravens Cl, Brom. BR2 . . . **191** F2
Enfield EN1 . . . **44** B2
Surbiton KT6 . . . **181** G6
Ravenscourt Av, W6 . . . **127** G4
Ravenscourt Gdns, W6 . . . **127** G4
Ravenscourt Pk, W6 . . . **127** G3
Ravenscourt Pl, W6 . . . **127** H4
Ravenscourt Rd, W6 . . . **127** H4
Ravenscourt Sq, W6 . . . **127** G3
Ravenscraig Rd, N11 . . . **58** B4
Ravenscroft Av, NW11 . . . **72** C7
Wembley HA9 . . . **87** J1
Ravenscroft Cl, E16 . . . **115** G5
Ravenscroft Cres, SE9 . . . **174** C3
Ravenscroft Pk, Barn. EN5 . . . **40** A4
Ravenscroft Pt, E9 *off Kenton Rd* . . . **95** G6
Ravenscroft Rd, E16 . . . **115** G5
W4 . . . **126** C4
Beckenham BR3 . . . **189** F2
Ravenscroft St, E2 . . . **13** G2
Ravensdale Av, N12 . . . **57** F4
Ravensdale Gdns, SE19 . . . **170** A7
Hounslow TW4 . . . **142** E3
Ravensdale Ind Est, N16 . . . **76** D6
Ravensdale Rd, N16 . . . **76** C7
Hounslow TW4 . . . **142** E3
Ravensdon St, SE11 . . . **35** F4
Ravensfield Cl, Dag. RM9 . **100** D4
Ravensfield Gdns, Epsom KT19 . . . **197** E5
Ravens Gate Ms, Brom. BR2 *off Meadow Rd* . . . **191** E2
Ravenshaw St, NW6 . . . **90** C5
Ravenshill, Chis. BR7 . . . **192** E1
Ravenshurst Av, NW4 . . . **71** J4
Ravenside Cl, N18 . . . **61** G6
Ravenside Retail Pk, N18 . . **61** G5
Ravenslea Rd, SW12 . . . **149** J7
Ravensleigh Gdns, Brom. BR1 *off Pike Cl* . . . **173** H5
Ravensmead Rd, Brom. BR2 . . . **172** D7
Ravensmede Way, W4 . . . **127** F4
Ravens Ms, SE12 *off Ravens Way* . . . **155** G5
Ravenstone, SE17 . . . **36** E4
Ravenstone Rd, N8 . . . **75** F3
NW9 *off West Hendon Bdy* . . **71** F6
Ravenstone St, SW12 . . . **168** A1
Ravens Way, SE12 . . . **155** G5
Ravenswood, Bex. DA5 . . . **177** E1
Ravenswood Av, Surb. KT6 . . . **195** J2
West Wickham BR4 . . . **204** C1
Ravenswood Ct, Kings.T. KT2 . . . **164** B6
Ravenswood Cres, Har. HA2 . . . **85** F2
West Wickham BR4 . . . **204** C1
Ravenswood Gdns, Islw. TW7 . . . **144** B1
Ravenswood Pk, Nthwd. HA6 . . . **50** A6
Ravenswood Rd, E17 . . . **78** B4
SW12 . . . **150** B7
Croydon CR0 . . . **201** H3
Ravensworth Rd, NW10 . . **107** H3
SE9 . . . **174** C4
Ravey St, EC2 . . . **12** D5
Ravine Gro, SE18 . . . **137** H6
Rav Pinter Cl, N16 . . . **76** B7
Rawlings Cl, Beck. BR3 . . . **190** C5
Orpington BR6 . . . **207** J5
Rawlings Cres, Wem. HA9 . **88** B3
Rawlings St, SW3 . . . **31** J1
Rawlins Cl, N3 . . . **72** B3
South Croydon CR2 . . . **203** H7
Rawlinson Ho, SE13 *off Mercator Rd* . . . **154** D4
Rawnsley Av, Mitch. CR4 . . **185** G5
Rawreth Wk, N1 *off Basire St* . . . **111** J1
Rawson Ct, SW11 *off Strasburg Rd* . . . **150** B1
Rawson St, SW11 *off Alfreda St* . . . **150** B1
Rawsthorne Cl, E16 *off Kennard St* . . . **136** C1
Rawstone Wk, E13 . . . **115** G2
Rawstorne Pl, EC1 . . . **11** G3
Rawstorne St, EC1 . . . **11** G3
Ray Cl, Chess. KT9 *off Merritt Gdns* . . . **195** F6
Raydean Rd, Barn. (New Barn.) EN5 . . . **40** E5
Raydons Gdns, Dag. RM9 . . . **101** E5
Raydons Rd, Dag. RM9 . . . **100** E5
Raydon St, N19 . . . **92** B2
Rayfield Cl, Brom. BR2 . . . **192** B6
Rayford Av, SE12 . . . **155** F7
Ray Gdns, Bark. IG11 . . . **118** A2
Stanmore HA7 . . . **53** E5
Rayleas Cl, SE18 . . . **156** E1
Rayleigh Av, Tedd. TW11 . . . **162** B6
Rayleigh Cl, N13 . . . **60** A3
Rayleigh Ct, Kings.T. KT1 . **181** J2
Rayleigh Ri, S.Croy. CR2 . . **202** B6
Rayleigh Rd, E16 . . . **135** H1
N13 . . . **59** J3
SW19 . . . **184** C1
Woodford Green IG8 . . . **63** J6
Ray Lo Rd, Wdf.Grn. IG8 . . . **63** J6
Ray Massey Way, E6 *off Ron Leighton Way* . **116** B1
Raymead, NW4 *off Tenterden Gro* . . . **71** J4
Raymead Av, Th.Hth. CR7 . **187** G5
Raymead Pas, Th.Hth. CR7 *off Raymead Av* . . . **187** G5
Raymere Gdns, SE18 . . . **137** G7
Raymond Av, E18 . . . **79** F3
W13 . . . **124** D3
Raymond Bldgs, WC1 . . . **18** D1
Raymond Cl, SE26 . . . **171** F5
Raymond Ct, N10 *off Pembroke Rd* . . . **58** A7
Raymond Rd, E13 . . . **97** J7
SW19 . . . **166** B6
Beckenham BR3 . . . **189** H4
Ilford IG2 . . . **81** G7
Raymond Way, Esher (Clay.) KT10 . . . **194** D6
Raymouth Rd, SE16 . . . **133** E4
Rayne Ct, E18 . . . **79** F4
Rayners Cl, Wem. HA0 . . . **87** G5
Rayners Ct, Har. HA2 . . . **85** G1
Rayners Cres, Nthlt. UB5 . **102** B3
Rayners Gdns, Nthlt. UB5 . . . **102** B2
RAYNERS LANE, Har. HA2 . **85** F1
Rayners La, Har. HA2 . . . **85** H2
Pinner HA5 . . . **67** F6
Rayners Rd, SW15 . . . **148** B5
Rayner Twr, E10 . . . **78** A7
Raynes Av, E11 . . . **79** J7
RAYNES PARK, SW20 . . . **183** H3
Raynham, W2 . . . **15** G4
Raynham Av, N18 . . . **60** D6
Raynham Rd, N18 . . . **60** D5
W6 . . . **127** H4
Raynham Ter, N18 . . . **60** D5
Raynor Cl, Sthl. UB1 . . . **123** F1
Raynor Pl, N1 *off Elizabeth Av* . . . **111** J1
Raynton Cl, Har. HA2 . . . **85** E1
Ray Rd, W.Mol. KT8 . . . **179** H5
Rays Av, N18 . . . **61** F4
Rays Rd, N18 . . . **61** F4
West Wickham BR4 . . . **190** C7
Ray St, EC1 . . . **11** F6
Ray St Br, EC1 . . . **11** F6
Ray Wk, N7 *off Andover Rd* . . . **93** F2
Raywood Cl, Hayes (Harling.) UB3 . . . **121** F7
Reach, The, SE28 . . . **137** H2
Reachview Cl, NW1 *off Baynes St* . . . **92** C7
Read Cl, T.Ditt. KT7 . . . **180** D7
Reading Cl, SE22 . . . **152** D6
Reading La, E8 . . . **94** E6
Reading Rd, Nthlt. UB5 . . . **85** H5
Sutton SM1 . . . **199** F5
Reading Way, NW7 . . . **56** A5
Reads Cl, Ilf. IG1 *off Chapel Rd* . . . **98** E3
Reapers Cl, NW1 *off Crofters Way* . . . **110** D1
Reapers Way, Islw. TW7 *off Hall Rd* . . . **144** A5
Reardon Ct, N21 . . . **59** J2
Reardon Path, E1 . . . **133** E1
Reardon St, E1 . . . **132** E1
Reaston St, SE14 . . . **133** F7
Reckitt Rd, W4 . . . **126** E5
Record St, SE15 . . . **133** F6
Recovery St, SW17 . . . **167** H5
Recreation Av, Rom. RM7 . . **83** J5
Recreation Rd, SE26 . . . **171** G4
Bromley BR2 . . . **191** F2
Sidcup DA15 *off Woodside Rd* . . . **175** H3
Southall UB2 . . . **122** E4
Recreation Way, Mitch. CR4 . . . **186** D3
Rector St, N1 . . . **111** J1
Rectory Cl, E4 . . . **62** A3
N3 . . . **72** C1
SW20 . . . **183** J3
Sidcup DA14 . . . **176** B4
Stanmore HA7 . . . **53** E6
Rectory Cl, Surb. (Long Dit.) KT6 . . . **195** F1
Rectory Cres, E11 . . . **79** J6
Rectory Fld Cres, SE7 . . . **135** J7
Rectory Gdns, N8 . . . **74** E4
SW4 *off Fitzwilliam Rd* . . . **150** C3
Northolt UB5 . . . **103** F1
Rectory Grn, Beck. BR3 . . . **189** J1
Rectory Gro, SW4 . . . **150** C3
Croydon CR0 . . . **201** H2
Hampton TW12 . . . **161** F4
Rectory La, SW17 . . . **168** A6
Edgware HA8 . . . **54** A6
Loughton IG10 . . . **48** D2
Sidcup DA14 . . . **176** B4
Stanmore HA7 . . . **52** E5
Surbiton (Long Dit.) KT6 . . . **195** E1
Wallington SM6 . . . **200** C4
Rectory Orchard, SW19 . . . **166** B4
Rectory Pk Av, Nthlt. UB5 . . . **103** F3
Rectory Pl, SE18 . . . **136** D4
Rectory Rd, E12 . . . **98** C5
E17 . . . **78** B3
N16 . . . **94** C3
SW13 . . . **147** G2
W3 . . . **126** B1
Beckenham BR3 . . . **190** A1
Dagenham RM10 . . . **101** G7
Hayes UB3 . . . **102** A6
Hounslow TW4 . . . **142** B1
Keston BR2 . . . **206** A7
Southall UB2 . . . **123** F3
Sutton SM1 . . . **198** D3
Rectory Sq, E1 . . . **113** G5
Reculver Ms, N18 . . . **60** D4
Reculver Rd, SE16 . . . **133** G5
Red Anchor Cl, SW3 . . . **31** G6
Redan Pl, W2 . . . **14** A4
Redan St, W14 . . . **128** A3
Redan Ter, SE5 *off Flaxman Rd* . . . **151** J2
Red Barracks Rd, SE18 . . . **136** C4
Redberry Gro, SE26 . . . **171** F3
Redbourne Av, N3 . . . **72** D1
Redbourne Dr, SE28 . . . **118** D6
REDBRIDGE, Ilf. IG1 . . . **80** C6
Redbridge Enterprise Cen, Ilf. IG1 . . . **99** F2
Redbridge Gdns, SE5 . . . **132** B7
Redbridge La E, Ilf. IG4 . . . **80** A6
Redbridge La W, E11 . . . **79** H6
Redbridge Rbt, Ilf. IG4 . . . **79** J6
Redburn St, SW3 . . . **31** J5
Redcar Cl, Nthlt. UB5 . . . **85** H5
Redcar St, SE5 . . . **131** J7
Redcastle Cl, E1 . . . **113** F7
Red Cedars Rd, Orp. BR6 . . . **193** H7
Redchurch St, E2 . . . **13** F5
Redcliffe Cl, SW5 *off Old Brompton Rd* . . **30** A4
Redcliffe Ct, E5 *off Napoleon Rd* . . . **94** E3
Redcliffe Gdns, SW5 . . . **30** B4
SW10 . . . **30** B4
W4 . . . **126** B7
Ilford IG1 . . . **98** D1
Redcliffe Ms, SW10 . . . **30** B4
Redcliffe Pl, SW10 . . . **30** C6
Redcliffe Rd, SW10 . . . **30** C4
Redcliffe Sq, SW10 . . . **30** B4
Redcliffe St, SW10 . . . **30** B5
Redclose Av, Mord. SM4 . . **184** D5
Redclyffe Rd, E6 . . . **115** J1
Redcroft Rd, Sthl. UB1 . . . **103** J7
Redcross Way, SE1 . . . **28** A3
Reddings, The, NW7 . . . **55** F3
Reddings Cl, NW7 . . . **55** F4
Reddington Ho, N1 . . . **10** D1
Reddins Rd, SE15 . . . **37** H6
Reddons Rd, Beck. BR3 . . . **171** H7
Redenham Ho, SW15 *off Tangley Gro* . . . **147** F7
Rede Pl, W2 *off Chepstow Pl* . . . **108** D6
Redesdale Gdns, Islw. TW7 . . . **124** D7
Redesdale St, SW3 . . . **31** H5
Redfern Av, Houns. TW4 . . **143** G7
Redfern Rd, NW10 . . . **89** E7
SE6 . . . **154** C7
Redfield La, SW5 . . . **128** D4
Redfield Ms, SW5 *off Redfield La* . . . **128** D4
Redford Av, Th.Hth. CR7 . . **187** F4
Wallington SM6 . . . **200** E6
Redford Wk, N1 *off Britannia Row* . . . **111** H1
Redgate Dr, Brom. BR2 . . . **205** H2
Redgate Ter, SW15 . . . **148** B6
Redgrave Cl, Croy. CR0 . . . **188** C6
Redgrave Rd, SW15 . . . **148** A3
Red Hill, Chis. BR7 . . . **174** D5
Redhill Dr, Edg. HA8 . . . **70** C2

Redhill St, NW1 8 E3
★ **Red Ho, The** (William Morris Ho), Bexh. DA6 158 E4
Red Ho La, Bexh. DA6 158 D4
Red Ho Rd, Croy. CR0 186 D6
Red Ho Sq, N1 *off Ashby Gro* 93 J7
Redington Gdns, NW3 90 E4
Redington Rd, NW3 90 E4
Redland Gdns, W.Mol. KT8 *off Dunstable Rd* 179 F4
Redlands Ct, Brom. BR1 173 F7
Redlands Rd, Enf. EN3 45 H1
Redlands Way, SW2 151 F7
Red La, Esher (Clay.) KT10 194 D6
Redleaf Cl, Belv. DA17 139 G6
Redlees Cl, Islw. TW7 144 D4
Red Lion Business Pk, Surb. KT6 195 J2
Red Lion Cl, SE17 36 A5
Red Lion Ct, EC4 19 F3
Red Lion Hill, N2 73 G2
Red Lion La, SE18 136 D7
Red Lion Pl, SE18 *off Shooters Hill Rd* 156 D1
Red Lion Rd, Surb. KT6 195 J2
Red Lion Row, SE17 36 A5
Red Lion Sq, SW18 *off Wandsworth High St* 148 D5
WC1 18 C2
Red Lion St, WC1 18 C1
Richmond TW9 145 G5
Red Lion Yd, W1 24 C1
Red Lo Rd, Beck. BR3 190 D6
West Wickham BR4 204 C1
Redman Cl, Nthlt. UB5 102 C2
Redman's Rd, E1 113 F5
Redmead La, E1 29 H2
Redmead Rd, Hayes UB3 121 H4
Redmore Rd, W6 127 H4
Red Oak Cl, Orp. BR6 207 E3
Red Path, E9 95 J6
Red Pl, W1 16 B5
Redpoll Way, Erith DA18 138 D3
Red Post Hill, SE21 152 A5
SE24 152 A4
Redriffe Rd, E13 115 F1
Redriff Est, SE16 133 J3
Redriff Rd, SE16 133 G4
Romford RM7 83 H2
Redroofs Cl, Beck. BR3 190 B1
Red Rover, SW15 147 F3
Redruth Cl, N22 59 F7
Redruth Gdns, Esher KT10 *off Common Rd* 194 D7
Redruth Rd, E9 113 G1
Red Sq, N16 94 A3
Redstart Cl, E6 *off Columbine Av* 116 B5
SE14 *off Southerngate Way* 133 H7
Redstart Mans, Ilf. IG1 *off Mill Rd* 98 D3
Redston Rd, N8 74 D4
Redvers Rd, N22 75 G2
Redvers St, N1 13 E3
Redwald Rd, E5 95 G4
Redway Dr, Twick. TW2 143 J7
Redwing Ms, SE5 *off Vaughan Rd* 151 J2
Redwing Path, SE28 137 G2
Redwing Rd, Wall. SM6 201 E7
Redwood Cl, E3 114 A2
N14 42 D7
SE16 133 H1
Sidcup DA15 158 A7
Watford WD19 50 C4
Redwood Ct, NW6 *off The Avenue* 90 B7
Redwood Est, Houns. TW5 122 B6
Redwood Gdns, E4 46 B6
Redwood Gro, W5 *off Northfield Av* 125 F3
Redwood Ms, SW4 *off Hannington Rd* 150 B3
Redwoods, SW15 165 G1
Redwoods Cl, Buck.H. IG9 63 H2
Redwood Wk, Surb. KT6 195 G1
Redwood Way, Barn. EN5 40 A5
Reece Ms, SW7 30 E1
Reed Av, Orp. BR6 207 H3
Reed Cl, E16 115 G5
SE12 155 G5
Reede Gdns, Dag. RM10 101 H5
Reede Rd, Dag. RM10 101 G6
Reede Way, Dag. RM10 101 H6
Reedham Cl, N17 76 E4
Reedham St, SE15 152 D2
Reedholm Vil, N16 *off Winston Rd* 94 A4
Reed Pl, SW4 150 D4
Reed Rd, N17 76 C2
Reeds Pl, NW1 *off Royal Coll St* 92 C7
Reedworth St, SE11 35 F2
Ree La Cotts, Loug. IG10 *off Englands La* 48 D1
Reenglass Rd, Stan. HA7 53 G4
Rees Dr, Stan. HA7 53 H4
Rees Gdns, Croy. CR0 188 C6
Reesland Cl, E12 98 D6
Rees St, N1 111 J1
Reets Fm Cl, NW9 71 E6
Reeves Av, NW9 70 D7
Reeves Cor, Croy. CR0 *off Roman Way* 201 H2
Reeves Ms, W1 16 B6
Reeves Rd, E3 114 B4
SE18 136 E6
Reflection, The, E16 *off Woolwich Manor Way* 136 E2
Reform Row, N17 76 C2
Reform St, SW11 149 J2
Regal Cl, E1 21 J1
W5 105 G5
Regal Ct, N18 60 C5
Regal Cres, Wall. SM6 200 B3
Regal Dr, N11 58 B5
Regal Ho, SW6 *off Lensbury Av* 149 F2
Ilford IG2 *off Royal Cres* 81 G6
Regal La, NW1 *off Regents Pk Rd* 110 A1
Regal Pl, E3 *off Coborn St* 113 J3
SW6 *off Maxwell Rd* 129 E7
Regal Row, SE15 *off Astbury Rd* 153 F1
Regal Way, Har. HA3 69 H6
Regan Ho, N18 60 C6
Regan Way, N1 12 D2
Regatta Ho, Tedd. TW11 *off Twickenham Rd* 162 D4
Regency Cl, W5 105 H6
Chigwell IG7 65 F5
Hampton TW12 161 F5
Regency Ct, E18 79 G2
Sutton SM1 *off Brunswick Rd* 199 E4
Regency Cres, NW4 72 A2
Regency Ho, SW6 *off The Boulevard* 149 F1
Regency Lo, Buck.H. IG9 64 A2
Regency Ms, NW10 *off High Rd* 89 G6
SW9 *off Lothian Rd* 131 H7
Beckenham BR3 190 C1
Isleworth TW7 *off Queensbridge Pk* 144 B5
Regency Pl, SW1 33 J1
Regency St, NW10 106 E4
SW1 33 H1
Regency Ter, SW7 *off Fulham Rd* 31 E3
Regency Wk, Croy. CR0 189 H6
Richmond TW10 *off Grosvenor Rd* 145 H5
Regency Way, Bexh. DA6 158 D3
Regeneration Rd, SE16 133 G4
Regent Cl, N12 *off Nether St* 57 F5
Harrow HA3 69 H6
Hounslow TW4 142 B1
Regent Gdns, Ilf. IG3 82 A6
Regent Pk, Barn. EN4 40 E1
Regent Pl, SW19 *off Haydons Rd* 167 E5
W1 17 G5
Croydon CR0 *off Grant Rd* 202 C1
Regent Rd, SE24 151 H6
Surbiton KT5 181 J5
Regents Av, N13 59 F5
Regents Br Gdns, SW8 34 B7
Regents Cl, S.Croy. CR2 202 B6
Regents Dr, Kes. BR2 206 A5
Woodford Green IG8 64 D6
Regents Ms, NW8 6 D1
REGENT'S PARK, NW1 8 C2
★ **Regent's Park, The**, NW1 8 A2
Regent's Pk Est, NW1 9 E4
Regents Pk Rd, N3 72 C3
NW1 109 J1
Regents Pk Ter, NW1 *off Oval Rd* 110 B1
Regent's Pl, SE3 155 G2
Regents Pl, Loug. IG10 48 A7
Regent Sq, E3 114 B3
WC1 10 B4
Belvedere DA17 139 H4
Regents Row, E8 112 D1
Regent St, NW10 *off Wellington Rd* 108 A3
SW1 17 H6
W1 17 E3
W4 126 A5
Regents Wf, N1 10 C1
Regina Cl, Barn. EN5 40 A3
Reginald Rd, E7 97 G7
SE8 134 A7
Reginald Sq, SE8 134 A7
Regina Pt, SE16 *off Renforth St* 133 F3
Regina Rd, N4 93 F1
SE25 188 D3
W13 124 D1
Southall UB2 122 E4
Regina Ter, W13 124 D1
Regis Pl, SW2 151 F4
Regis Rd, NW5 92 B5
Regnart Bldgs, NW1 9 G5
Reid Cl, Pnr. HA5 66 A4
Reidhaven Rd, SE18 137 H4
Reigate Av, Sutt. SM1 198 D1
Reigate Rd, Brom. BR1 173 F3
Ilford IG3 99 J2
Reigate Way, Wall. SM6 201 E5
Reighton Rd, E5 94 D3
Reindeer Cl, E13 *off Stratford Rd* 115 G1
Reinickendorf Av, SE9 157 F5
Reizel Cl, N16 94 C1
Relay Rd, W12 107 J7
Relf Rd, SE15 152 D3
Reliance Sq, EC2 13 E5
Relko Gdns, Sutt. SM1 199 G5
Relton Ms, SW7 23 H5
Rembrandt Cl, E14 134 D3
SW1 32 B2
Rembrandt Ct, Epsom KT19 197 F6
Rembrandt Rd, SE13 154 E4
Edgware HA8 70 A2
Remington Rd, E6 116 B6
N15 76 A6
Remington St, N1 11 H2
Remnant St, WC2 18 C3
Remus Rd, E3 *off Monier Rd* 96 A7
Renaissance Ct, Houns. TW3 *off Prince Regent Rd* 143 J3
Renaissance Wk, SE10 135 F3
Rendle Cl, Croy. CR0 188 C5
Rendlesham Rd, E5 94 D4
Enfield EN2 43 H1
Renforth St, SE16 133 F2
Renfrew Cl, E6 116 D7
Renfrew Ho, E17 *off Sherwood Cl* 77 J2
Renfrew Rd, SE11 35 G1
Hounslow TW4 142 D2
Kingston upon Thames KT2 164 B7
Renmuir St, SW17 167 J6
Rennell St, SE13 154 C3
Rennels Way, Islw. TW7 144 B2
Renness Rd, E17 77 H3
Rennets Cl, SE9 157 H5
Rennets Wd Rd, SE9 157 G5
Rennie Ct, SE1 *off Upper Grd* 27 G1
Rennie Est, SE16 133 E4
Rennie Ho, SE1 *off Bath Ter* 27 J6
Rennie St, SE1 27 G1
Renovation, The, E16 *off Woolwich Manor Way* 136 E2
Renown Cl, Croy. CR0 201 H1
Romford RM7 83 G1
Rensburg Rd, E17 77 G5
Renshaw Cl, Belv. DA17 *off Grove Rd* 139 F6
Renters Av, NW4 71 J6
Renwick Ind Est, Bark. IG11 118 B1
Renwick Rd, Bark. IG11 118 B4
Repens Way, Hayes UB4 *off Stipularis Dr* 102 D4
Rephidim St, SE1 28 D6
Replingham Rd, SW18 166 C1
Reporton Rd, SW6 148 B1
Repository Rd, SE18 136 C6
Repton Av, Hayes UB3 121 G4
Wembley HA0 87 F4
Repton Cl, Cars. SM5 199 H5
Repton Ct, Beck. BR3 190 B1
Ilford IG5 *off Repton Gro* 80 C1
Repton Gro, Ilf. IG5 80 C1
Repton Rd, Har. HA3 69 J4
Repton St, E14 113 H6
Repulse Cl, Rom. RM5 83 G1
Reservoir Cl, Th.Hth. CR7 188 A4
Reservoir Rd, N14 42 C5
SE4 153 H2
Resham Cl, Sthl. UB2 122 C3
Resolution Wk, SE18 136 C3
Resolution Way, SE8 *off Deptford High St* 134 A7
Restell Cl, SE3 135 E6
Restmor Way, Wall. SM6 200 A2
Reston Pl, SW7 22 C4
Restons Cres, SE9 157 G6
Restoration Sq, SW11 *off Battersea High St* 149 G1
Restormel Cl, Houns. TW3 143 G5
Retcar Cl, N19 *off Dartmouth Pk Hill* 92 B2
Retcar Pl, N19 92 B2
Retford St, N1 13 E2
Retingham Way, E4 62 B2
Retreat, The, NW9 70 D5
SW14 *off South Worple Way* 147 E3
Harrow HA2 67 G7
Surbiton KT5 181 J6
Thornton Heath CR7 188 A4
Worcester Park KT4 197 H3
Retreat Cl, Har. HA3 69 F5
Retreat Pl, E9 95 F6
Retreat Rd, Rich. TW9 145 G5
Reunion Row, E1 *off Tobacco Dock* 113 E7
Reuters Plaza, E14 *off The South Colonnade* 134 B1
Reveley Sq, SE16 *off Howland Way* 133 H2
Revell Ri, SE18 137 J6
Revell Rd, Kings.T. KT1 182 B1
Sutton SM1 198 C6
Revelon Rd, SE4 153 H4
Revelstoke Rd, SW18 166 C2
Reventlow Rd, SE9 175 F1
Reverdy Rd, SE1 37 H2
Reverend Cl, Har. HA2 85 H3
Revesby Rd, Cars. SM5 185 G6
Review Rd, NW2 89 F2
Dagenham RM10 119 H1
Rewell St, SW6 *off King's Rd* 129 F7
Rewley Rd, Cars. SM5 185 G6
Rex Pl, W1 16 C6
Reydon Av, E11 79 J6
Reynard Cl, SE4 *off Foxwell St* 153 H3
Bromley BR1 192 C3
Reynard Dr, SE19 170 C7
Reynard Pl, SE14 *off Milton Ct Rd* 133 H6
Reynardson Rd, N17 59 J7
Reynolah Gdns, SE7 *off Rathmore Rd* 135 H5
Reynolds Av, E12 98 D5
Chessington KT9 195 H7
Romford RM6 82 C7
Reynolds Cl, NW11 72 E7
SW19 185 G1
Carshalton SM5 199 J1
Reynolds Ct, E11 *off Cobbold Rd* 97 F3
Romford RM6 82 D3
Reynolds Dr, Edg. HA8 69 J3
Reynolds Pl, SE3 135 H7
Richmond TW10 *off Cambrian Rd* 145 J6
Reynolds Rd, SE15 153 F5
W4 126 C3
Hayes UB4 102 C4
New Malden KT3 182 D7
Reynolds Way, Croy. CR0 202 B4
Rheidol Ms, N1 11 J1
Rheidol Ter, N1 11 H1
Rheola Cl, N17 76 C1
Rhoda St, E2 13 G5
Rhodes Av, N22 74 C1
Rhodesia Rd, E11 96 D2
SW9 151 E2
Rhodes Moorhouse Ct, Mord. SM4 184 D6
Rhodes St, N7 *off Mackenzie Rd* 93 F5
Rhodeswell Rd, E14 113 H5
Rhodrons Av, Chess. KT9 195 H5
Rhondda Gro, E3 113 H3
Rhyl Rd, Grnf. (Perivale) UB6 104 C2
Rhyl St, NW5 92 A6
Rhys Av, N11 58 D7
Rialto Rd, Mitch. CR4 186 A2
Ribble Cl, Wdf.Grn. IG8 *off Prospect Rd* 63 J6
Ribblesdale Av, N11 58 A6
Northolt UB5 85 H6
Ribblesdale Rd, N8 75 F4
SW16 168 B6
Ribbon Dance Ms, SE5 *off Camberwell Gro* 152 A1
Ribchester Av, Grnf. (Perivale) UB6 104 C3
Ribston Cl, Bromley BR2 206 C1
Ricardo Path, SE28 *off Byron Cl* 138 C1
Ricardo St, E14 114 B6
Ricards Rd, SW19 166 C5
Richard Cl, SE18 136 B4

Richard Fell Ho, E12
off Walton Rd 98 D4
Richard Foster Cl, E17 77 J7
Richard Ho Dr, E16 116 A6
Richard Robert Res, The,
E15 *off Broadway* 96 D6
Richards Av, Rom. RM7 83 J5
Richards Cl, Har. HA1 68 D5
Hayes (Harling.) UB3 121 G6
Richardson Cl, E8
off Clarissa St 112 C1
Richardson Gdns, Dag.
RM10 101 H6
Richardson Rd, E15 114 E2
Richardson's Ms, W1 9 F6
Richards Pl, E17 78 A3
SW3 31 H1
Richard St, E1
off Commercial Rd 112 E6
Richbell Pl, WC1 18 C1
Richborne Ter, SW8 34 D7
Richborough Ho, E5
off Pembury Rd 94 E5
Richborough Rd, NW2 90 A4
Richbourne Ct, W1
off Harrowby St 15 H3
Richens Cl, Houns. TW3 144 A2
Riches Rd, Ilf. IG1 99 F2
Richford Gate, W6
off Richford St 127 J3
Richford Rd, E15 115 F1
Richford St, W6 127 J2
Rich Ind Est, SE1 29 E6
Richlands Av, Epsom
KT17 197 G4
Rich La, SW5 30 A4
RICHMOND,
TW9 & TW10 145 H6
Richmond Av, E4 62 D5
N1 111 F1
NW10 89 J6
SW20 184 B1
Feltham TW14 141 H6
Richmond Br, Rich. TW9 145 G6
Twickenham TW1 145 G6
Richmond Bldgs, W1 17 H4
Richmond Circ, Rich.
TW9 145 H4
Richmond Cl, E17 77 J6
Borehamwood WD6 38 D5
Richmond Ct, Mitch. CR4
off Phipps Br Rd 185 G3
Richmond Cres, E4 62 D5
N1 111 F1
N9 60 D1
Richmond Dr, Wdf.Grn.
IG8 64 D7
Richmond Gdns, NW4 71 G5
Harrow HA3 52 C6
Richmond Grn, Croy.
CR0 201 E3
Richmond Gro, N1 93 H7
Surbiton KT5
off Ewell Rd 181 J6
Richmond Hill, Rich.
TW10 145 H6
Richmond Hill Ct, Rich.
TW10 145 H6
Richmond Ho, NW1
off Park Village E 9 E2
Richmond Ms, W1 17 H4
Teddington TW11
off Broad St 162 C6
★ **Richmond Park**, Rich.
TW10 164 A1
Richmond Pk, Kings.T.
KT2 164 A1
Loughton IG10
off Fallow Flds 48 A7
Richmond TW10 164 A1
Richmond Pk Rd, SW14 146 C5
Kingston upon Thames
KT2 163 H7
Richmond Pl, SE18 137 F4
Richmond Rd, E4 62 D1
E7 97 H5
E8 94 C7
E11 96 D2
N2 73 F2
N11 58 E6
N15 76 B6
SW20 183 H1
W5 125 H2
Barnet (New Barn.)
EN5 41 E5
Croydon CR0 200 E3
Ilford IG1 99 F3
Isleworth TW7 144 D3
Kingston upon Thames
KT2 163 G5
Thornton Heath CR7 187 H3
Twickenham TW1 145 F6
Richmond St, E13 115 G2
Richmond Ter, SW1 26 A3
Richmond Way, E11 97 G2
W12 128 A2
W14 128 A3
Richmount Gdns, SE3 155 G3
Rich St, E14 113 J7
Rickard Cl, NW4 71 H4
SW2 169 F1
West Drayton UB7 120 A3
Rickards Cl, Surb. KT6 195 H1
Rickett St, SW6 128 D6
Rickman St, E1
off Mantus Rd 113 F3
Rickmansworth Rd, Pnr.
HA5 66 B2
Rick Roberts Way, E15 114 C1
Rickthorne Rd, N19 92 E2
Rickyard Path, SE9 156 B4
Ridding La, Grnf. UB6 86 C5
Riddons Rd, SE12 173 J3
Ride, The, Brent. TW8 125 E5
Enfield EN3 45 F3
Rideout St, SE18 136 C4
Rider Cl, Sid. DA15 157 H6
Ridgdale St, E3 114 B2
Ridge, The, Barn. EN5 40 C5
Bexley DA5 159 F7
Orpington BR6 207 G2
Surbiton KT5 182 A5
Twickenham TW2 144 A7
Ridge Av, N21 43 J7
Ridgebrook Rd, SE3 155 J4
Ridge Cl, NW4 72 A2
NW9 70 D4
SE28 137 G2
Ridge Crest, Enf. EN2 43 F1
Ridgecroft Cl, Bexley
DA5 177 J1
Ridge Hill, NW11 90 B1
Ridgemead Cl, N14 59 E2
Ridgemont Gdns, Edg.
HA8 54 C4
Ridgemount Av, Croy.
CR0 203 G1
Ridgemount Cl, SE20 170 E7
Ridgemount Gdns, Enf.
EN2 43 H2
Ridge Rd, N8 75 F6
N21 59 J1
NW2 90 C3
Mitcham CR4 168 B7
Sutton SM3 198 B1
Ridge's Yd, Croy. CR0 201 H3
Ridgeview Cl, Barn. EN5 40 A6
Ridgeview Rd, N20 57 E3
Ridge Way, SE19
off Vicars Oak Rd 170 B6
Ridgeway, SE28
off Pettman Cres 137 G4
Bromley BR2 205 G2
Ridge Way, Felt.
TW13 160 E3
Ridgeway, Wdf.Grn.
IG8 63 J4
Ridgeway, The, E4 62 B2
N3 56 E7
N11 57 J4
N14 59 E2
NW7 55 G4
NW9 70 E4
NW11 90 C1
W3 126 A2
Croydon CR0 201 F3
Enfield EN2 43 G1
Harrow (Kenton) HA3 69 F6
Harrow (N.Har.) HA2 67 G6
Ruislip HA4 66 A7
Stanmore HA7 53 F6
Ridgeway Av, Barn. EN4 41 J6
Ridgeway Cres, Orp. BR6 207 H3
Ridgeway Cres Gdns, Orp.
BR6 207 H2
Ridgeway Dr, Bromley
BR1 173 H4
Ridgeway E, Sid. DA15 157 J5
Ridgeway Gdns, N6 74 C7
Ilford IG4 80 B5
Ridgeway Rd, SW9 151 H3
Isleworth TW7 124 B7
Ridgeway Rd N, Islw.
TW7 124 B6
Ridgeway Wk, Nthlt. UB5
off Arnold Rd 85 E6
Ridgeway W, Sid. DA15 157 H5
Ridgewell Cl, N1
off Basire St 111 J1
SE26 171 J4
Dagenham RM10 119 H1
Ridgmount Gdns, WC1 9 H6
Ridgmount Pl, WC1 17 H1
Ridgmount Rd, SW18 149 E5
Ridgmount St, WC1 17 H1
Ridgway, SW19 166 A6
Ridgway, The, Sutton
SM2 199 G7
Ridgway Gdns, SW19 166 A6
Ridgway Pl, SW19 166 B6
Ridgwell Rd, E16 115 J5
Riding, The, NW11
off Golders Grn Rd 72 C7
Riding Ho St, W1 17 F2
Ridings, The, E11
off Malcolm Way 79 G5
W5 105 J4
Sunbury-on-Thames
TW16 178 A1
Surbiton KT5 182 A5
Ridings Av, N21 43 H4
Ridings Cl, N6
off Hornsey La Gdns 74 C7
Ridley Av, W13 124 E3
Ridley Cl, Bark. IG11 99 J7
Ridley Rd, E7 97 J4
E8 94 C5
NW10 107 G2
SW19 166 E7
Bromley BR2 191 F3
Welling DA16 158 B1
Ridsdale Rd, SE20 188 E1
Riefield Rd, SE9 157 F4
Riesco Dr, Croy. CR0 203 F6
Riffel Rd, NW2 89 J5
Rifle Ct, SE11 35 F5
Rifle St, E14 114 B5
Riga Ms, E1
off Commercial Rd 21 H3
Rigault Rd, SW6 148 B2
Rigby Cl, Croy. CR0 201 G3
Rigby La, Hayes UB3 121 G2
Rigby Ms, Ilf. IG1 98 D2
Rigden St, E14 114 B6
Rigeley Rd, NW10 107 G3
Rigg App, E10 95 G1
Rigge Pl, SW4 150 D4
Riggindale Rd, SW16 168 D5
Riley Rd, SE1 29 E5
Riley St, SW10 31 E7
Rinaldo Rd, SW12 150 B7
Ring, The, W2 15 G5
Ring Cl, Brom. BR1 173 H7
Ringcroft St, N7 93 G5
Ringers Rd, Brom. BR1 191 G3
Ringford Rd, SW18 148 C5
Ringlet Cl, E16 115 H5
Ringlewell Cl, Enf. EN1
off Central Av 44 E2
Ringmer Av, SW6 148 B1
Ringmer Gdns, N19 93 E2
Ringmer Ho, SE22
off Pytchley Rd 152 B3
Ringmer Pl, N21 44 A5
Ringmer Way, Brom. BR1 192 C5
Ringmore Ri, SE23 153 E7
Ringmore Vw, SE23
off Ringmore Ri 153 E7
Ring Rd, W12 107 J7
Ringside Ct, SE28 138 C1
Ringslade Rd, N22 75 F2
Ringstead Rd, SE6 154 B7
Sutton SM1 199 G4
Ringway, N11 58 C6
Southall UB2 123 E5
Ringwold Cl, Beck. BR3 171 H7
Ringwood Av, N2 73 J2
Croydon CR0 187 E7
Ringwood Cl, Pnr. HA5 66 C3
Ringwood Gdns, E14
off Inglewood Cl 134 A4
SW15 165 G2
Ringwood Rd, E17 77 J6
Ringwood Way, N21 59 H1
Hampton (Hmptn H.)
TW12 161 G4
Ripley Cl, Brom. BR1 192 C5
Croydon (New Adgtn)
CR0 204 C6
Ripley Gdns, SW14 146 D3
Sutton SM1 199 F4
Ripley Ms, E11 78 E6
Ripley Rd, E16 115 J6
Belvedere DA17 139 G4
Enfield EN2 43 J1
Hampton TW12 161 G7
Ilford IG3 99 J2
Ripley Vil, W5
off Castlebar Rd 105 F6
Riplington Ct, SW15 147 G7
Ripon Cl, Nthlt. UB5 85 G5
Ripon Gdns, Chess. KT9 195 G5
Ilford IG1 80 B6
Ripon Rd, N9 44 E7
N17 76 A3
SE18 136 E6
Ripon Way, Borwd. WD6 38 C5
Rippersley Rd, Well.
DA16 158 A1
Ripple Rd, Bark. IG11 99 F7
Dagenham RM9 118 B1
Rippleside Commercial Est,
Bark. IG11 118 C2
Ripplevale Gro, N1 93 F7
Rippolson Rd, SE18 137 J5
Risborough, SE17
off Deacon Way 35 J1
Risborough Dr, Wor.Pk.
KT4 183 G7
Risborough St, SE1 27 H3
Risdon St, SE16 133 F2
Rise, The, E11 79 G5
N13 59 G4
NW7 55 F6
NW10 88 D4
Bexley DA5 158 C7
Buckhurst Hill IG9 48 A7
Edgware HA8 54 B5
Greenford UB6 86 D5
Risedale Rd, Bexleyheath
DA7 159 H3
Riseholme Ho, SE22
off Albrighton Rd 152 B3
Riseldine Rd, SE23 153 H6
Risinghill St, N1 10 D1
Risingholme Cl, Har. HA3 68 B1
Risingholme Rd, Har. HA3 68 B2
Risings, The, E17 78 D4
Rising Sun Ct, EC1 19 H2
Risley Av, N17 75 J1
Rita Rd, SW8 34 B6
Ritches Rd, N15 75 J5
Ritchie Rd, Croy. CR0 189 E6
Ritchie St, N1 11 F1
Ritchings Av, E17 77 H4
Ritherdon Rd, SW17 168 A2
Ritson Rd, E8 94 D6
Ritter St, SE18 136 D6
Ritz Par, W5
off Connell Cres 105 J4
Rivaz Pl, E9 95 F6
Rivenhall Gdns, E18 79 F4
River App, Edg. HA8 70 C1
River Av, N13 59 H3
Thames Ditton KT7 180 D7
River Bk, N21 43 J7
East Molesey KT8 180 B3
Thames Ditton KT7 180 C5
West Molesey KT8 179 F3
Riverbank Rd, Brom.
BR1 173 G3
Riverbank Way, Brent.
TW8 125 F6
River Barge Cl, E14
off Stewart St 134 C2
River Brent Business Pk,
W7 124 B3
River Cl, E11 79 J6
Southall UB2 123 J2
Surbiton KT6
off Catherine Rd 181 G5
River Ct, SE1 19 G6
Rivercourt Rd, W6 127 H4
River Crane Wk, Felt.
TW13 160 D1
Hounslow TW4 160 D1
River Crane Way, Felt.
TW13
off Watermill Way 161 F2
Riverdale, SE13
off Lewisham High St 154 C3
Riverdale Cl, Bark. IG11 118 B4
Riverdale Dr, SW18
off Knaresborough Dr 166 E1
Riverdale Gdns, Twick.
TW1 145 F6
Riverdale Rd, SE18 137 J5
Bexley DA5 159 F7
Erith DA8 139 H5
Feltham TW13 161 E4
Twickenham TW1 145 F6
Riverdene, Edg. HA8 54 C3
Riverdene Rd, Ilf. IG1 98 D3
River Front, Enf. EN1 44 A3
River Gdns, Cars. SM5 200 A2
Feltham TW14 142 B5
River Gro Pk, Beck. BR3 189 J1
Riverhead Cl, E17 77 G2
Riverhill, Wor.Pk. KT4 196 D2
Riverhill Ms, Wor.Pk. KT4 196 D3
River La, Rich. TW10 163 G1
Rivermead, E.Mol. KT8 179 J3
Kingston upon Thames
KT1 181 G5
Rivermead Cl, Tedd.
TW11 163 E5
Rivermead Ct, SW6 148 C3
Rivermead Ho, E9
off Kingsmead Way 95 H5
Rivermead Rd, N18 61 G6
Rivermeads Av, Twick.
TW2 161 G3
Rivermill, SW1 33 J4
Rivernook Cl, Walt. KT12 178 C5
River Pk Gdns, Brom.
BR2 172 D7
River Pk Rd, N22 75 F2
River Pl, N1 93 J7
River Reach, Tedd. TW11 163 F5
River Rd, Bark. IG11 117 H2
Buckhurst Hill IG9 64 B1
River Rd Business Pk, Bark.
IG11 117 J3
Riversdale Rd, N5 93 H3
Thames Ditton KT7 180 D5
Riversfield Rd, Enf. EN1 44 B3
Rivers Ho, Brent. TW8
off Chiswick High Rd 126 A5

Riverside, NW4 ... 71 H7
SE7 ... 135 H3
Richmond TW9, TW10
off Water La ... 145 G5
Twickenham TW1 ... 162 E1
Riverside, The, E.Mol.
KT8 ... 180 A3
Riverside Av, E.Mol. KT8 ... 180 A5
Riverside Business Cen,
SW18 ... 166 E1
Riverside Cl, E5 ... 95 F1
W7 ... 104 B4
Kingston upon Thames
KT1 ... 181 G4
Wallington SM6 ... 200 B3
Riverside Ct, E4
off Chelwood Cl ... 46 B6
SW8 ... 33 J5
Riverside Dr, NW11 ... 72 B6
W4 ... 126 E7
Mitcham CR4 ... 185 H5
Richmond TW10 ... 162 E2
Riverside Gdns, N3 ... 72 B3
W6 ... 127 H5
Enfield EN2 ... 43 J2
Wembley HA0 ... 105 H2
Riverside Ind Est, Bark.
IG11 ... 118 A3
Riverside Mans, E1
off Milk Yd ... 113 F7
Riverside Pl, Stai.
(Stanw.) TW19 ... 140 A6
Riverside Rd, E15 ... 114 C2
N15 ... 76 D6
SW17 ... 167 E4
Sidcup DA14 ... 177 E3
Staines (Stanw.) TW19 ... 140 A5
Riverside Twr, SW6 ... 149 F2
Riverside Wk, E14
off Ferry St ... 134 C5
Bexley DA5 ... 158 C7
Isleworth TW7 ... 144 B3
Kingston upon Thames
KT1 off High St ... 181 G3
Loughton IG10 ... 48 E6
West Wickham BR4
off The Alders ... 204 B1
Riverside Yd, SW17 ... 167 F4
Riverstone Cl, Har. HA2 ... 86 A1
Riverstone Ct, Kings.T.
KT2 off Queen
Elizabeth Rd ... 181 J1
River St, EC1 ... 11 E3
River Ter, W6
off Crisp Rd ... 127 J5
Riverton Cl, W9 ... 108 C3
River Vw, Enf. EN2
off Chase Side ... 43 J3
Riverview Gdns,
SW13 ... 127 H6
Twickenham TW1 ... 162 C2
Riverview Gro, W4 ... 126 B6
River Vw Hts, SE16 ... 29 H3
Riverview Pk, SE6 ... 172 A2
Riverview Rd, W4 ... 126 B7
Epsom KT19 ... 196 C4
River Wk, E4
off Winchester Rd ... 62 C7
Walton-on-Thames
KT12 ... 178 A6
Riverwalk Business Pk,
Enf. EN3 ... 45 J3
Riverwalk Rd, Enf. EN3 ... 45 J4
Riverway, N13 ... 59 G5
River Way, SE10 ... 135 F3
Epsom KT19 ... 196 D5
Loughton IG10 ... 48 D6
Twickenham TW2 ... 161 H2
Riverwood La, Chis. BR7 ... 193 G1
Rivet Ho, SE1 ... 37 G3
Rivington Av, Wdf.Grn.
IG8 ... 80 A2
Rivington Ct, NW10 ... 107 G1
Dagenham RM10
off Reede Way ... 101 H6
Rivington Cres, NW7 ... 55 F7
Rivington Pl, EC2 ... 12 E4
Rivington St, EC2 ... 12 D4
Rivington Wk, E8
off Wilde Cl ... 112 D1
Rivulet Rd, N17 ... 59 J7
Rixon Ho, SE18 ... 137 E6
Rixon St, N7 ... 93 G3
Rixsen Rd, E12 ... 98 B5
Roach Rd, E3 ... 96 A7
Roads Pl, N19 ... 93 E2
Roan St, SE10 ... 134 C6
Robarts Cl, Pnr. HA5 ... 66 B5
Robb Rd, Stan. HA7 ... 52 D6
Robert Adam St, W1 ... 16 B3
Roberta St, E2 ... 13 H3
Robert Burns Ms, SE24
off Mayall Rd ... 151 H5
Robert Cl, W9 ... 6 D6
Chigwell IG7 ... 65 J5
Robert Dashwood Way,
SE17 ... 35 J2
Robert Keen Cl, SE15
off Cicely Rd ... 152 D1
Robert Lowe Cl, SE14 ... 133 G7
Roberton Dr, Bromley
BR1 ... 191 J1
Robert Owen Ho, SW6 ... 148 A1
Robertsbridge Rd, Cars.
SM5 ... 199 F1
Roberts Cl, SE9 ... 175 G1
SE16 ... 133 G2
Barking IG11
off Tanner St ... 99 F6
Sutton SM3 ... 198 A7
Thornton Heath CR7
off Kitchener Rd ... 188 A3
West Drayton UB7 ... 120 B1
Roberts Ms, SW1 ... 24 B6
Robertson St, SW8 ... 150 B3
Robert's Pl, EC1 ... 11 F5
Roberts Pl, Dag. RM10 ... 101 G6
Robert Sq, SE13 ... 154 C4
Roberts Rd, E17 ... 78 B1
NW7 ... 56 B6
Belvedere DA17 ... 139 G5
Robert St, E16 ... 136 E1
NW1 ... 8 E4
SE18 ... 137 G4
WC2 ... 18 B6
Croydon CR0
off High St ... 201 J3
Robert Sutton Ho, E1
off Tarling St ... 113 F6
Robeson St, E3
off Ackroyd Dr ... 113 J5
Robeson Way, Borwd.
WD6 ... 38 C1
Robina Cl, Bexh. DA6 ... 158 D4
Robin Cl, NW7 ... 54 E3
Hampton TW12 ... 161 E5
Robin Ct, SE16 ... 37 H1
Wallington SM6
off Carew Rd ... 200 C6
Robin Cres, E6 ... 116 A5
Robin Gro, N6 ... 92 A2
Brentford TW8 ... 125 F6
Harrow HA3 ... 69 J6
Robin Hill Dr, Chis. BR7 ... 174 B6
Robin Hood, SW15 ... 165 E3
Robinhood Cl, Mitch.
CR4 ... 186 C3
Robin Hood Dr, Har. HA3 ... 52 C7
Robin Hood Gdns, E14
off Woolmore St ... 114 C7
Robin Hood La, E14 ... 114 C7
SW15 ... 164 E4
Bexleyheath DA6 ... 159 E5
Robinhood La, Mitch.
CR4 ... 186 C3
Robin Hood La, Sutt.
SM1 ... 198 D5
Robin Hood Rd, SW19 ... 165 H5
Robin Hood Way,
SW15 ... 165 E4
SW20 ... 165 E4
Greenford UB6 ... 86 C6
Robin Ho, NW8
off Newcourt St ... 7 G2
Robinia Cl, SE20
off Sycamore Gro ... 188 D1
Ilford IG6 ... 65 H6
Robinia Cres, E10 ... 96 B2
Robin La, NW4 ... 72 A3
Robins Ct, SE12 ... 173 J3
Robinscroft Ms, SE10
off Sparta St ... 154 B1
Robins Gro, W.Wick. BR4 ... 205 G3
Robinson Cl, E11 ... 97 E3
Enfield EN2 ... 43 J3
Robinson Cres, Bushey
(Bushey Hth) WD23 ... 51 J1
Robinson Ho, W10
off Bramley Rd ... 108 A6
Robinson Rd, E2 ... 113 F2
SW17 ... 167 H6
Dagenham RM10 ... 101 G4
Robinsons Cl, W13 ... 104 D5
Robinson St, SW3 ... 31 J5
Robinwood Pl, SW15 ... 164 D4
Robsart St, SW9 ... 151 F2
Robson Av, NW10 ... 107 G1
Robson Cl, E6
off Linton Gdns ... 116 B6
Enfield EN2 ... 43 H2
Robson Rd, SE27 ... 169 H3
Rocastle Rd, SE4 ... 153 H5
Roch Av, Edg. HA8 ... 69 J2
Rochdale Rd, E17 ... 78 A7
SE2 ... 138 B5
Rochdale Way, SE8
off Octavius St ... 134 A7
Rochelle Cl, SW11 ... 149 G4
Rochelle St, E2 ... 13 F4
Rochemont Wk, E8
off Pownall Rd ... 112 C1
Roche Rd, SW16 ... 187 F1
Rochester Av, E13 ... 115 J1
Bromley BR1 ... 191 H2
Rochester Cl, SW16 ... 169 E7
Enfield EN1 ... 44 B1
Sidcup DA15 ... 158 B6
Rochester Dr, Bex. DA5 ... 159 F6
Pinner HA5 ... 66 D5
Rochester Gdns, Croy.
CR0 ... 202 B3
Ilford IG1 ... 80 C7
Rochester Ms, NW1 ... 92 C7
Rochester Pl, NW1 ... 92 C6
Rochester Rd, NW1 ... 92 C6
Carshalton SM5 ... 199 J4
Rochester Row, SW1 ... 33 G1
Rochester Sq, NW1 ... 92 C7
Rochester St, SW1 ... 25 H6
Rochester Ter, NW1 ... 92 C6
Rochester Wk, SE1 ... 28 B1
Rochester Way, SE3 ... 155 H1
SE9 ... 156 C3
Rochester Way Relief Rd,
SE3 ... 155 H1
SE9 ... 156 B4
Roche Wk, Cars. SM5 ... 185 G6
Rochford Av, Loug. IG10 ... 49 F3
Romford RM6 ... 82 C5
Rochford Cl, E6
off Boleyn Rd ... 116 A2
Rochford Grn, Loug. IG10 ... 49 F3
Rochford St, NW5 ... 91 J5
Rochford Wk, E8
off Wilman Gro ... 94 D7
Rochford Way, Croy. CR0 ... 186 E6
Rock Av, SW14
off South Worple Way ... 146 D3
Rockbourne Rd, SE23 ... 171 G1
Rock Cl, Mitch. CR4 ... 185 G2
Rockells Pl, SE22 ... 153 E6
Rockford Av, Grnf.
(Perivale) UB6 ... 104 D2
Rock Gdns, Dag. RM10 ... 101 H5
Rock Gro Way, SE16 ... 37 J1
Rockhall Rd, NW2 ... 90 A4
Rockhall Way, NW2
off Midland Ter ... 90 A3
Rockhampton Cl, SE27 ... 169 G4
Rockhampton Rd, SE27 ... 169 G4
South Croydon CR2 ... 202 B6
Rock Hill, SE26 ... 170 C4
Rockingham Cl, SW15 ... 147 F4
Rockingham Est, SE1 ... 27 J6
Rockingham St, SE1 ... 27 J6
Rockland Rd, SW15 ... 148 B4
Rocklands Dr, Stan. HA7 ... 69 E2
Rockley Rd, W14 ... 128 A2
Rockmount Rd, SE18 ... 137 J5
SE19 ... 170 A6
Rocks La, SW13 ... 147 G1
Rock St, N4 ... 93 G2
Rockware Av, Grnf. UB6 ... 104 A1
Rockways, Barn. EN5 ... 39 F6
Rockwell Gdns, SE19 ... 170 B5
Rockwell Rd, Dag. RM10 ... 101 H5
Rockwood Pl, W12 ... 127 J2
Rocliffe St, N1 ... 11 H2
Rocombe Cres, SE23 ... 153 F7
Rocque La, SE3 ... 155 F3
Rodborough Rd, NW11 ... 90 D1
Roden Ct, N6 ... 74 D7
Roden Gdns, Croy. CR0 ... 188 B6
Rodenhurst Rd, SW4 ... 150 C6
Roden St, N7 ... 93 F3
Ilford IG1 ... 98 D3
Roderick Rd, NW3 ... 91 J4
Roding Av, Wdf.Grn. IG8 ... 64 B6
Roding Gdns, Loug. IG10 ... 48 B6
Roding La, Buck.H. IG9 ... 64 B1
Chigwell IG7 ... 64 D1
Roding La N, Wdf.Grn.
IG8 ... 80 A2
Roding La S, Ilf. IG4 ... 80 A4
Woodford Green IG8 ... 80 A4
Roding Ms, E1 ... 29 J1
Roding Rd, E5 ... 95 G4
E6 ... 116 E5
Loughton IG10 ... 48 B5
Rodings, The, Wdf.Grn.
IG8 ... 63 J6
Rodings Row, Barn. EN5
off Leecroft Rd ... 40 B5
Roding Trd Est, Bark. IG11 ... 98 E7
Roding Vw, Buck.H. IG9 ... 64 A1
Rodmarton St, W1 ... 16 A2
Rodmell Cl, Hayes UB4 ... 102 E4
Rodmell Slope, N12 ... 56 C5
Rodmere St, SE10
off Trafalgar Rd ... 135 E5
Rodmill La, SW2 ... 151 E7
Rodney Cl, Croy. CR0 ... 201 H1
New Malden KT3 ... 182 E5
Pinner HA5 ... 66 E7
Rodney Ct, W9 ... 6 D5
Rodney Gdns, Pinner
HA5 ... 66 B5
West Wickham BR4 ... 205 G4
Rodney Pl, E17 ... 77 H2
SE17 ... 36 A1
SW19 ... 185 F1
Rodney Rd, E11 ... 79 H4
SE17 ... 36 A1
Mitcham CR4 ... 185 H2
New Malden KT3 ... 182 E5
Twickenham TW2 ... 143 G6
Rodney St, N1 ... 10 D1
Rodney Way, Rom. RM7 ... 83 G1
Rodway Rd, SW15 ... 147 G7
Bromley BR1 ... 191 H1
Rodwell Cl, Ruis. HA4 ... 84 C1
Rodwell Pl, Edg. HA8 ... 54 A6
Rodwell Rd, SE22 ... 152 C6
Roebourne Way, E16 ... 136 D2
Roebuck Cl, Felt. TW13 ... 160 B4
Roebuck La, N17
off High Rd ... 60 C6
Buckhurst Hill IG9 ... 47 J7
Roebuck Rd, Chess. KT9 ... 196 A5
Roedean Av, Enf. EN3 ... 45 F1
Roedean Cl, Enf. EN3 ... 45 F1
Roedean Cres, SW15 ... 146 E6
Roe End, NW9 ... 70 C4
Roe Grn, NW9 ... 70 C5
ROEHAMPTON, SW15 ... 147 G5
Roehampton Cl, SW15 ... 147 G4
Roehampton Dr, Chis.
BR7 ... 175 F6
Roehampton Gate,
SW15 ... 146 E6
Roehampton High St,
SW15 ... 147 H7
Roehampton La, SW15 ... 147 G4
Roehampton Vale, SW15 ... 165 E3
Roe La, NW9 ... 70 B4
Roe Way, Wall. SM6 ... 201 E6
Roffey St, E14 ... 134 C2
Rogate Ho, E5
off Muir Rd ... 94 E3
Roger Dowley Ct, E2 ... 113 F2
Rogers Est, E2
off Globe Rd ... 113 F3
Rogers Gdns, Dag. RM10 ... 101 G5
Rogers Ho, SW1
off Page St ... 33 J1
Rogers Rd, E16 ... 115 F6
SW17 ... 167 G4
Dagenham RM10 ... 101 G5
Roger St, WC1 ... 10 D6
Rogers Wk, N12
off Holden Rd ... 57 E3
Rojack Rd, SE23 ... 171 G1
Rokeby Gdns, Wdf.Grn.
IG8 ... 79 G1
Rokeby Pl, SW20 ... 165 H7
Rokeby Rd, SE4 ... 153 J2
Rokeby St, E15 ... 114 E1
Rokesby Cl, Well. DA16 ... 157 G2
Rokesby Pl, Wem. HA0 ... 87 G5
Rokesly Av, N8 ... 74 E5
Roland Gdns, SW7 ... 30 D3
Feltham TW13 ... 161 E3
Roland Ms, E1
off Stepney Grn ... 113 G5
Roland Rd, E17 ... 78 D4
Roland Way, SE17 ... 36 C4
SW7 ... 30 D3
Worcester Park KT4 ... 197 F2
Roles Gro, Rom. RM6 ... 82 D4
Rolfe Cl, Barn. EN4 ... 41 H4
Rolinsden Way, Kes. BR2 ... 206 A4
Rollesby Rd, Chess. KT9 ... 196 A6
Rollesby Way, SE28 ... 118 C7
Rolleston Av, Orp. BR5 ... 192 E6
Rolleston Cl, Orp. BR5 ... 193 E7
Rolleston Rd, S.Croy.
CR2 ... 202 A7
Roll Gdns, Ilf. IG2 ... 80 D5
Rollins St, SE15 ... 133 F6
Rollit Cres, Houns. TW3 ... 143 G5
Rollit St, N7
off Hornsey Rd ... 93 G5
Rolls Bldgs, EC4 ... 19 E3
Rollscourt Av, SE24 ... 151 J5
Rolls Pk Av, E4 ... 62 A6
Rolls Pk Rd, E4 ... 62 B5
Rolls Pk Rbt, Chig. IG7 ... 49 G7
Rolls Pas, EC4 ... 18 E3
Rolls Rd, SE1 ... 37 G3
Rolls Royce Cl, Wall.
SM6 ... 200 E7
Rolt St, SE8 ... 133 H6
Rolvenden Gdns, Brom.
BR1 ... 174 A7
Rolvenden Pl, N17 ... 60 D7
Roman Cl, W3
off Avenue Gdns ... 126 B2
Feltham TW14 ... 142 C5
Romanfield Rd, SW2 ... 151 F7
Romanhurst Av, Brom.
BR2 ... 191 E4
Romanhurst Gdns, Brom.
BR2 ... 190 E4
Roman Ind Est, Croy.
CR0 ... 188 B7
Roman Ri, SE19 ... 170 A6
Roman Rd, E2 ... 113 F3
E3 ... 113 H2

Roman Rd, E6 **116** B4
N10 **58** B7
NW2 **89** J3
W4 **127** E4
Ilford IG1 **99** E6
Roman Sq, SE28 **138** A1
Roman Way, N7 **93** F6
SE15 *off Clifton Way* **133** F7
Croydon CR0 **201** H2
Enfield EN1 **44** C5
Roman Way Ind Est, N1
off Offord St **93** F7
Romany Gdns, E17
off McEntee Av **77** H1
Sutton SM3 **184** D7
Romany Ri, Orp. BR5 **207** F1
Roma Read Cl, SW15 **147** H7
Roma Rd, E17 **77** H3
Romberg Rd, SW17 **168** A3
Romborough Gdns,
SE13 **154** C5
Romborough Way, SE13 **154** C5
Romero Cl, SW9
off Stockwell Rd **151** F3
Romero Sq, SE3 **155** J4
Romeyn Rd, SW16 **169** F3
Romford Rd, E7 **97** H5
E12 **98** B4
E15 **96** E7
Romford St, E1 **21** J2
Romilly Dr, Wat. WD19 **51** E4
Romilly Rd, N4 **93** H2
Romilly St, W1 **17** H5
Rommany Rd, SE27 **170** A4
Romney Cl, N17 **76** E1
NW11 **91** F1
SE14 *off Kender St* **133** F7
Chessington KT9 **195** H4
Harrow HA2 **67** G7
Romney Dr, Brom. BR1 **174** A7
Harrow HA2 **67** G7
Romney Gdns, Bexh.
DA7 **159** F1
Romney Ms, W1 **16** B1
Romney Rd, SE10 **134** C6
New Malden KT3 **182** D6
Romney Row, NW2
off Brent Ter **90** A2
Romney St, SW1 **25** J6
Romola Rd, SE24 **169** H1
Romsey Cl, Orp. BR6 **207** E4
Romsey Gdns, Dag. RM9 **118** D1
Romsey Rd, W13 **104** D7
Dagenham RM9 **118** D1
Romulus Ct, Brent. TW8
off Justin Cl **125** G7
Ronald Av, E15 **115** E3
Ronald Cl, Beck. BR3 **189** J4
Ronald Ho, SE3
off Cambert Way **155** J4
Ronalds Rd, N5 **93** G5
Bromley BR1 **191** G1
Ronaldstone Rd, Sid.
DA15 **157** H6
Ronald St, E1
off Devonport St **113** F6
Rona Rd, NW3 **92** A4
Ronart St, Har. (Wealds.)
HA3 **68** C3
Rona Wk, N1
off Ramsey Wk **94** A6
Rondu Rd, NW2 **90** B5
Ronelean Rd, Surb. KT6 **195** J3
Ron Leighton Way, E6 **116** B1
Ronnie La, E12 **98** D4
Ron Todd Cl, Dag. RM10
off Heathway **119** G1
Ronver Rd, SE12 **155** F7
Rood La, EC3 **20** D5
Rookby Ct, N21 **59** H2
Rook Cl, Wem. HA9 **88** B3
Rookeries Cl, Felt. TW13 **160** B3
Rookery Cl, NW9 **71** F5
Rookery Cres, Dag. RM10 **101** H7
Rookery Dr, Chis. BR7 **192** D1
Rookery La, Brom. BR2 **192** A6
Rookery Rd, SW4 **150** C4
Rookery Way, NW9 **71** F5
Rooke Way, SE10 **135** F5
Rookfield Av, N10 **74** C4
Rookfield Cl, N10 **74** C4
Rookstone Rd, SW17 **167** J5
Rook Wk, E6
off Allhallows Rd **116** B6
Rookwood Av, Loug. IG10 **49** F3
New Malden KT3 **183** G4
Wallington SM6 **200** D4
Rookwood Gdns, E4 **63** F2
Loughton IG10 **49** F3
Rookwood Ho, Bark. IG11
off St. Marys **117** G2
Rookwood Rd, N16 **76** C7
★ **Roosevelt Mem**, W1 **16** C5
Rootes Dr, W10 **108** A4
Ropemaker Rd, SE16 **133** H3
Ropemakers Flds, E14
off Narrow St **113** J7
Ropemaker St, EC2 **20** B1
Roper La, SE1 **29** E3
Ropers Av, E4 **62** C5
Ropers Orchard, SW3 **31** F6
Roper St, SE9 **156** C6
Ropers Wk, SW2
off Brockwell Pk Gdns **151** G7
Roper Way, Mitch. CR4 **186** A2
Ropery St, E3 **113** J4
Rope St, SE16 **133** H4
Rope Wk, Sun. TW16 **178** C3
Ropewalk Gdns, E1 **21** J4
Ropewalk Ms, E8
off Middleton Rd **94** D7
Ropley St, E2 **13** H2
Rosa Alba Ms, N5
off Kelross Rd **93** J4
Rosaline Rd, SW6 **128** B7
Rosamond St, SE26 **170** E3
Rosamund Cl, S.Croy.
CR2 **202** A4
Rosamun St, Sthl. UB2 **123** E4
Rosary Cl, Houns. TW3 **142** E2
Rosary Gdns, SW7 **30** C2
Rosaville Rd, SW6 **128** C7
Roscoe St, EC1 **12** A6
Roscoff Cl, Edg. HA8 **70** C1
Roseacre Cl, W13
off Middlefielde **104** E5
Sutton SM1 **199** F2
Roseacre Rd, Well. DA16 **158** B3
Rose All, EC2 *off New St* **20** E2
SE1 **28** A1
Rose & Crown Ct, EC2 **19** J3
Rose & Crown Yd, SW1 **25** G1
Roseary Cl, West Dr. UB7 **120** A4
Rose Av, E18 **79** H2
Mitcham CR4 **185** J1
Morden SM4 **185** F5
Rosebank, SE20 **170** E7
Rosebank Av, Wem. HA0 **86** C4
Rosebank Cl, N12 **57** H5
Teddington TW11 **162** D6
Rosebank Gdns, E3 **113** J2
Rosebank Gro, E17 **77** J3
Rosebank Rd, E17 **78** B6
W7 **124** B2
Rosebank Vil, E17 **78** A4
Rosebank Wk, NW1
off Maiden La **92** D7
SE18 *off Woodhill* **136** B4
Rosebank Way, W3 **106** D6
Rose Bates Dr, NW9 **70** A4
Roseberry Gdns, N4 **75** H6
Orpington BR6 **207** H3
Roseberry Pl, E8 **94** C6
Roseberry St, SE16 **132** E4
Rosebery Av, E12 **98** B6
EC1 **10** E6
N17 **76** D2
Harrow HA2 **85** F4
New Malden KT3 **183** F2
Sidcup DA15 **157** H7
Thornton Heath CR7 **187** J2
Rosebery Cl, Mord. SM4 **184** A6
Rosebery Ct, EC1
off Rosebery Av **11** E5
Rosebery Gdns, N8 **74** E5
W13 **104** D6
Sutton SM1 **199** E4
Rosebery Ind Pk, N17 **76** E2
Rosebery Ms, N10 **74** C2
SW2 *off Rosebery Rd* **150** E6
Rosebery Rd, N10 **74** C2
SW2 **150** E6
Hounslow TW3 **143** J5
Kingston upon Thames
KT1 **182** B2
Sutton SM1 **198** C6
Rosebery Sq, EC1 **10** E6
Kingston upon Thames
KT1 **182** A2
Rosebine Av, Twick. TW2 **144** A7
Rosebury Rd, SW6 **149** E2
Rosebury Sq, Wdf.Grn.
IG8 **64** D7
Rose Ct, E1 **21** F2
Pinner HA5
off Nursery Rd **66** C3
Rosecourt Rd, Croy. CR0 **187** F6
Rosecroft Av, NW3 **90** D3
Rosecroft Gdns, NW2 **89** G3
Twickenham TW2 **162** A1
Rosecroft Rd, Sthl. UB1 **103** G4
Rosecroft Wk, Pnr. HA5 **66** D5
Wembley HA0 **87** G5
Rose Dale, Orp. BR6 **207** E2
Rosedale Cl, SE2
off Finchale Rd **138** B3
W7 *off Boston Rd* **124** C2
Stanmore HA7 **53** E6
Rosedale Ct, N5 **93** H4
Rosedale Dr, Dag. RM9 **118** B1
Rosedale Gdns, Dag.
RM9 **100** B7
Rosedale Pl, Croydon
CR0 **189** G7
Rosedale Rd, E7 **97** J5
Dagenham RM9 **100** B7
Epsom KT17 **197** G5
Richmond TW9 **145** H4
Romford RM1 **83** J2
Rosedale Ter, W6
off Dalling Rd **127** H3
Rosedene, NW6 **108** A1
Rosedene Av, SW16 **169** F3
Croydon CR0 **187** F7
Greenford UB6 **103** G3
Morden SM4 **184** D5
Rosedene Gdns, Ilf. IG2 **80** D4
Rosedene Ter, E10 **96** B2
Rosedew Rd, W6 **128** A6
Rose End, Wor.Pk. KT4 **198** A1
Rosefield Cl, Cars. SM5 **199** H5
Rosefield Gdns, E14 **114** A7
Roseford Ct, W12 **128** A2
Rose Gdn Cl, Edg. HA8 **53** H6
Rose Gdns, W5 **125** G3
Feltham TW13 **160** A2
Southall UB1 **103** G4
Staines (Stanw.) TW19
off Diamedes Av **140** A7
Rosegate Ho, E3
off Hereford Rd **113** J2
Rose Glen, NW9 **70** D4
Rosehart Ms, W11
off Westbourne Gro **108** D6
Rose Hatch Av, Rom. RM6 **82** D3
Roseheath Rd, Houns.
TW4 **143** F5
ROSEHILL, Sutt. SM1 **198** E1
Rosehill, Esher (Clay.)
KT10 **194** D6
Hampton TW12 **179** G1
Rose Hill, Sutt. SM1 **199** E2
Rosehill Av, Sutt. SM1 **199** F1
Rosehill Gdns, Grnf. UB6 **86** C5
Sutton SM1 **199** E2
Rose Hill Pk W, Sutt. SM1 **199** F1
Rosehill Rd, SW18 **149** F6
Rose Joan Ms, NW6 **90** D4
Roseland Cl, N17 **60** A7
Rose La, Rom. RM6 **82** D3
Rose Lawn, Bushey
(Bushey Hth) WD23 **51** J1
Roseleigh Av, N5 **93** H4
Roseleigh Cl, Twick. TW1 **145** G6
Rosemary Av, N3 **73** E2
N9 **60** E1
Enfield EN2 **44** A1
Hounslow TW4 **142** D2
West Molesey KT8 **179** G3
Rosemary Cl, Croy.
CR0 **186** E6
Rosemary Dr, E14 **114** D6
Ilford IG4 **80** A5
Rosemary Gdns, SW14
off Rosemary La **146** C3
Chessington KT9 **195** H4
Dagenham RM8 **101** F1
Rosemary La, SW14 **146** C3
Rosemary Rd, SE15 **37** G7
SW17 **167** F3
Welling DA16 **157** J1
Rosemary St, N1
off Shepperton Rd **112** A1
Rosemead, NW9 **71** F7
Rosemead Av, Mitch.
CR4 **186** C2
Wembley HA9 **87** H5
Rose Ms, N18 **60** E4
Rosemont Av, N12 **57** F6
Rosemont Rd, NW3 **91** F6
W3 **106** B7
New Malden KT3 **182** C3
Richmond TW10 **145** H6
Wembley HA0 **105** H1
Rosemoor St, SW3 **31** J2
Rosemount, Wall. SM6 **200** C6
Rosemount Cl,
Wdf.Grn. IG8
off Chapelmount Rd **64** C6
Rosemount Dr, Brom.
BR1 **192** C4
Rosemount Pt, SE23
off Dacres Rd **171** G3
Rosemount Rd, W13 **104** D6
Rosenau Cres, SW11 **149** H1
Rosenau Rd, SW11 **149** H1
Rosendale Rd, SE21 **151** J7
SE24 **151** J7
Roseneath Av, N21 **59** H1
Roseneath Pl, SW16
off Curtis Fld Rd **169** F4
Roseneath Rd, SW11 **150** A6
Roseneath Wk, Enf. EN1 **44** A4
Rosens Wk, Edg. HA8 **54** B3
Rosenthal Rd, SE6 **154** B6
Rosenthorpe Rd, SE15 **153** G5
Rose Pk Cl, Hayes UB4 **102** C4
Rosepark Ct, Ilf. IG5 **80** C2
Roserton St, E14 **134** C2
Rosery, The, Croy. CR0 **189** G6
Roses, The, Wdf.Grn. IG8 **63** F7
Rose Sq, SW3 **31** F3
Rose St, EC4 **19** H3
WC2 **18** A5
Rosethorn Cl, SW12 **150** C7
Rose Tree Ms, Wdf.Grn.
IG8 *off Chigwell Rd* **64** B6
Rosetree Pl, Hmptn.
TW12 *off Broad La* **161** G6
Rosetta Cl, SW8 **131** E7
Rosetti Ter, Dag. RM8
off Marlborough Rd **100** B4
Roseveare Rd, SE12 **173** J4
Roseville Av, Houns. TW3 **143** G5
Roseville Rd, Hayes UB3 **122** A5
Rosevine Rd, SW20 **183** J1
Rose Wk, Surb. KT5 **182** B5
West Wickham BR4 **204** D2
Rose Way, SE12 **155** G5
Roseway, SE21 **152** A6
Rose Way, Edg. HA8 **54** C4
Rosewell Cl, SE20 **170** E7
Rosewood, Esher KT10 **194** D2
Rosewood Av, Grnf. UB6 **86** D5
Rosewood Cl, Sid. DA14 **176** C3
Rosewood Ct, Brom.
BR1 **191** J1
Kings.T. KT2 **164** A7
Romford RM6 **82** C5
Rosewood Gdns, SE13
off Morden Hill **154** C2
Rosewood Gro, Sutt.
SM1 **199** F2
Rosewood Sq, W12
off Primula St **107** G6
Rosewood Ter, SE20
off Laurel Gro **171** F7
Rosher Cl, E15 **96** D7
Rosina St, E9 **95** G5
Roskell Rd, SW15 **148** A3
Roslin Rd, W3 **126** B3
Roslin Sq, W3 **126** B3
Roslin Way, Brom. BR1 **173** G5
Roslyn Cl, Mitch. CR4 **185** G2
Roslyn Rd, N15 **76** A5
Rosmead Rd, W11 **108** B7
Rosoman Pl, EC1 **11** F5
Rosoman St, EC1 **11** F4
Rossall Cres, NW10 **105** J3
Ross Av, Dag. RM8 **101** F2
Ross Cl, Har. HA3 **51** J7
Hayes UB3 **121** G4
Northolt UB5 **86** A4
Ross Ct, E5
off Napoleon Rd **94** E4
SW15 **148** A7
Rossdale, Sutt. SM1 **199** H5
Rossdale Dr, N9 **45** F6
NW9 **88** C1
Rossdale Rd, SW15 **147** J4
Rosse Gdns, SE13
off Desvignes Dr **154** D6
Rosse Ms, SE3 **155** H1
Rossendale St, E5 **94** E2
Rossendale Way, NW1 **92** C7
Rossetti Ms, NW8
off Ordnance Hill **109** G1
Rossetti Rd, SE16 **132** E5
Rossignol Gdns, Cars.
SM5 **200** A2
Rossindel Rd, Houns.
TW3 **143** G5
Rossington St, E5 **94** D2
Rossiter Cl, SE19 **169** J7
Rossiter Flds, Barn. EN5 **40** B6
Rossiter Gro, SW9 **151** G3
Rossiter Rd, SW12 **168** B1
Rossland Cl, Bexh. DA6 **159** H5
Rosslyn Av, E4 **63** F2
SW13 **147** E3
Barnet (E.Barn.) EN4 **41** H6
Dagenham RM8 **83** F7
Feltham TW14 **142** A6
Rosslyn Cl, W.Wick. BR4 **205** F3
Rosslyn Cres, Har. HA1 **68** C5
Wembley HA9 **87** H4
Rosslyn Gdns, Wem. HA9
off Rosslyn Cres **87** H3
Rosslyn Hill, NW3 **91** G4
Rosslyn Ms, NW3
off Rosslyn Hill **91** G4
Rosslyn Pk Ms, NW3
off Lyndhurst Rd **91** G5
Rosslyn Rd, E17 **78** C4
Barking IG11 **99** G7
Twickenham TW1 **145** F6
Rossmore Cl, Enf. EN3 **45** G4
Rossmore Ct, NW1 **7** J5
Rossmore Rd, NW1 **7** H6
Ross Par, Wall. SM6 **200** B6
Ross Rd, SE25 **188** A3
Twickenham TW2 **161** H1
Wallington SM6 **200** C5
Ross Way, SE9 **156** B3
Rosswood Gdns, Wall.
SM6 **200** C6
Rostella Rd, SW17 **167** G4
Rostrevor Av, N15 **76** C6

Rostrevor Gdns, Hayes UB3 121 H1
Southall UB2 122 E5
Rostrevor Ms, SW6 148 C1
Rostrevor Rd, SW6 148 C1
SW19 166 D5
Rotary St, SE1 27 G5
Rothbury Gdns, Islw. TW7 124 D7
Rothbury Rd, E9 95 J7
Rothbury Wk, N17 60 D7
Rotherfield Rd, Cars. SM5 200 A4
Rotherfield St, N1 93 J7
Rotherham Wk, SE1 27 G2
Rotherhill Av, SW16 168 D6
ROTHERHITHE, SE16 133 G3
Rotherhithe New Rd, SE16 37 J4
Rotherhithe Old Rd, SE16 133 G4
Rotherhithe St, SE16 133 F2
Rotherhithe Tunnel, E1 133 F1
Rotherhithe Tunnel App, E14 113 H7
SE16 133 F2
Rotherwick Hill, W5 105 J4
Rotherwick Rd, NW11 72 D7
Rotherwood Cl, SW20 184 B1
Rotherwood Rd, SW15 148 A3
Rothery St, N1 *off Gaskin St* 111 H1
Rothery Ter, SW9 131 H7
Rothesay Av, SW20 184 B2
Greenford UB6 86 A6
Richmond TW10 146 B4
Rothesay Rd, SE25 188 A4
Rothsay Rd, E7 97 J7
Rothsay St, SE1 28 D5
Rothsay Wk, E14 *off Charnwood Gdns* 134 A4
Rothschild Rd, W4 126 C4
Rothschild St, SE27 169 H4
Roth Wk, N7 *off Durham Rd* 93 G2
Rothwell Gdns, Dag. RM9 118 C1
Rothwell Ho, Houns. TW5 *off Biscoe Cl* 123 G6
Rothwell Rd, Dag. RM9 118 C1
Rothwell St, NW1 109 J1
Rotten Row, SW1 24 B3
SW7 23 G3
Rotterdam Dr, E14 134 C3
Rouel Rd, SE16 29 H6
Rougemont Av, Mord. SM4 184 D6
Roundacre, SW19 166 A2
Roundaway Rd, Ilf. IG5 80 C2
Roundel Cl, SE4 *off Adelaide Av* 153 J4
Round Gro, Croy. CR0 189 G7
Roundhay Cl, SE23 171 G2
Round Hill, SE26 171 F2
Roundhill Dr, Enf. EN2 43 F4
Roundmead Av, Loug. IG10 48 D3
Roundmead Cl, Loug. IG10 48 D3
Roundtable Rd, Brom. BR1 173 F3
Roundtree Rd, Wem. HA0 86 E5
Roundway, The, N17 75 J1
Esher (Clay.) KT10 194 C5
Roundwood, Chiswick BR7 192 E2
Roundwood Av, Uxb. UB11 121 F1
Roundwood Pk, NW10 89 G7
Roundwood Rd, NW10 89 F6
Rounton Rd, E3 114 A4
Roupell Rd, SW2 169 F1
Roupell St, SE1 27 F2
Rousden St, NW1 92 C7
Rouse Gdns, SE21 170 B4
Rous Rd, Buck.H. IG9 64 B1
Routemaster Cl, E13 115 H3
Routh Rd, SW18 149 H7
Routh St, E6 116 C5
Rover Av, Ilf. IG6 65 J6
Rover Ho, N1 *off Phillipp St* 112 B1
Rowallan Rd, SW6 128 B7
Rowan Av, E4 61 J6
Rowan Cl, SW16 186 C1
W5 125 H2
Ilford IG1 99 G5
New Malden KT3 182 E2
Stanmore HA7 52 C6
Wembley HA0 86 D3
Rowan Cres, SW16 186 C1
Rowan Dr, NW9 71 G4
Rowan Gdns, Croydon CR0 202 C3
Rowan Ho, NW3 *off Maitland Pk Rd* 91 J6
Rowan Rd, SW16 186 C2
W6 128 A4
Bexleyheath DA7 159 E3
Brentford TW8 125 E7
West Drayton UB7 120 A4
Rowans, The, N13 59 H3
Rowans Way, Loug. IG10 48 C4
Rowan Ter, SE20 *off Sycamore Gro* 188 D1
W6 *off Bute Gdns* 128 A4
Rowantree Cl, N21 60 A1
Rowantree Rd, N21 60 A1
Enfield EN2 43 H2
Rowan Wk, N2 73 F6
N19 *off Bredgar Rd* 92 C2
W10 *off Sixth Av* 108 B4
Barnet EN5 40 E5
Bromley BR2 206 C3
Rowan Way, Rom. RM6 82 C3
Rowanwood Av, Sid. DA15 176 A1
Rowanwood Ms, Enf. EN2 43 H2
Rowben Cl, N20 56 E1
Rowberry Cl, SW6 127 J7
Rowcross St, SE1 37 F3
Rowdell Rd, Nthlt. UB5 103 G1
Rowden Pk Gdns, E4 *off Rowden Rd* 62 A6
Rowden Rd, E4 62 A6
Beckenham BR3 189 H1
Epsom KT19 196 B4
Rowditch La, SW11 150 A2
Rowdon Av, NW10 89 H7
Rowdowns Rd, Dag. RM9 119 F1
Rowe Gdns, Bark. IG11 117 J2
Rowe La, E9 95 F5
Rowena Cres, SW11 149 H2
Rowe Wk, Har. HA2 85 G3
Rowfant Rd, SW17 168 A1
Rowhill Rd, E5 95 E4
Rowington Cl, W2 14 A1
Rowland Av, Har. HA3 69 F3
Rowland Ct, E16 115 F4
Rowland Cres, Chig. IG7 65 H4
Rowland Gro, SE26 *off Dallas Rd* 171 E3
Rowland Hill Av, N17 59 J7
Rowland Hill St, NW3 91 H5
Rowlands Av, Pnr. HA5 51 G6
Rowlands Cl, N6 *off North Hill* 74 A6
NW7 55 G7
Rowlands Rd, Dag. RM8 101 F2
Rowland Way, SW19 185 E1
Rowley Av, Sid. DA15 158 B7
Rowley Cl, Wem. HA0 87 J7
Rowley Gdns, N4 75 J7
ROWLEY GREEN, Barn. EN5 39 F4
Rowley Grn Rd, Barn. EN5 39 F5
Rowley Ind Pk, W3 126 B3
Rowley La, Barn. EN5 39 F5
Borehamwood WD6 38 D1
Rowley Rd, N15 75 J5
Rowley Way, NW8 109 E1
Rowlheys Pl, West Dr. UB7 120 B3
Rowlls Rd, Kings.T. KT1 181 J3
Rowney Gdns, Dag. RM9 100 C6
Rowney Rd, Dag. RM9 100 B6
Rowntree Clifford Cl, E13 *off Liddon Rd* 115 H3
Rowntree Cl, NW6 *off Iverson Rd* 90 D6
Rowntree Path, SE28 *off Booth Cl* 118 B7
Rowntree Rd, Twick. TW2 162 B1
Rowse Cl, E15 114 C1
Rowsley Av, NW4 71 J3
Rowstock Gdns, N7 92 D5
Rowton Rd, SE18 137 F7
Roxborough Av, Har. HA1 68 A7
Isleworth TW7 124 C7
Roxborough Pk, Har. HA1 68 B7
Roxborough Rd, Har. HA1 68 A5
Roxbourne Cl, Nthlt. UB5 84 D6
Roxburgh Rd, SE27 169 H5
Roxby Pl, SW6 128 D6
ROXETH, Har. HA2 86 A2
Roxeth Grn Av, Har. HA2 85 H3
Roxeth Gro, Har. HA2 85 H4
Roxeth Hill, Har. HA2 86 A2
Roxley Rd, SE13 154 B6
Roxton Gdns, Croydon CR0 204 A5
Roxwell Rd, W12 127 G2
Barking IG11 118 A2
Roxwell Trd Pk, E10 77 G7
Roxwell Way, Wdf.Grn. IG8 63 J7
Roxy Av, Rom. RM6 82 C7
★ **Royal Acad of Arts**, W1 17 F6
★ **Royal Acad of Dramatic Art (R.A.D.A.)**, WC1 17 J1
★ **Royal Acad of Music**, NW1 8 C6
★ **Royal Air Force Mus**, NW9 71 G2
Royal Albert Dock, E16 116 B7
★ **Royal Albert Hall**, SW7 22 E4
Royal Albert Rbt, E16 116 A7
Royal Albert Way, E16 116 A7
Royal Arc, W1 17 F6
Royal Artillery Barracks, SE18 *off Repository Rd* 136 D5
Royal Av, SW3 31 J3
Worcester Park KT4 197 E2
★ **Royal Botanic Gdns, Kew**, Rich. TW9 125 H7
Royal Carriage Ms, SE18 137 E3
Royal Circ, SE27 169 G3
Royal Cl, N16 *off Manor Rd* 94 B1
SE8 133 J6
SW19 166 A3
Ilford IG3 82 A7
Orpington BR6 206 E4
Worcester Park KT4 196 E2
★ **Royal Coll of Art**, SW7 22 D4
★ **Royal Coll of Music**, SW7 22 E5
★ **Royal College of Surgeons of England**, WC2 18 D3
Royal Coll St, NW1 92 C7
Royal Ct, EC3 *off Royal Ex Bldgs* 20 C4
SE16 133 J3
★ **Royal Courts of Justice**, WC2 18 D4
Royal Cres, W11 128 A1
Ilford IG2 81 G6
Ruislip HA4 84 E4
Royal Cres Ms, W11 *off Queensdale Rd* 128 A1
Royal Docks Rd, E6 117 E6
★ **Royal Dress Collection** (Kensington Palace), W8 22 B2
Royal Dr, N11 58 A5
Royal Duchess Ms, SW12 *off Dinsmore Rd* 150 B7
Royale Leisure Pk, W3 106 A4
★ **Royal Exchange**, EC3 20 C4
Royal Ex Av, EC3 20 C4
Royal Ex Bldgs, EC3 20 C4
★ **Royal Festival Hall**, SE1 26 D2
Royal Gdns, W7 124 D3
★ **Royal Geographical Society**, SW7 23 E4
Royal Herbert Pavilions, SE18 156 C1
Royal Hill, SE10 134 C7
★ **Royal Horticultural Society (Lawrence Hall)**, SW1 25 H6
★ **Royal Horticultural Society (Lindley Hall)**, SW1 33 H1
★ **Royal Hosp Chelsea & Mus**, SW3 32 B4
Royal Hosp Rd, SW3 31 J5
★ **Royal Mews, The**, SW1 24 E5
Royal Mint Ct, EC3 21 G6
Royal Mint Pl, E1 21 G5
Royal Mint St, E1 21 G5
Royal Mt Ct, Twick. TW2 162 B3
Royal Naval Pl, SE14 133 J7
Royal Oak Ct, N1 12 D3
Royal Oak Ms, Tedd. TW11 *off High St* 162 D5
Royal Oak Pl, SE22 153 E6
Royal Oak Rd, E8 94 E6
Bexleyheath DA6 159 F5
Royal Oak Yd, SE1 28 D4
★ **Royal Observatory Greenwich** (Flamsteed Ho), SE10 134 D7
Royal Opera Arc, SW1 25 H1
★ **Royal Opera Ho**, WC2 18 B4
Royal Orchard Cl, SW18 148 B7
Royal Par, SE3 155 E2
SW6 *off Dawes Rd* 128 B7
W5 *off Western Av* 105 H3
Chislehurst BR7 175 F7
Richmond TW9 *off Station App* 146 A1
Royal Par Ms, SE3 *off Royal Par* 155 F2
Chislehurst BR7 175 F7
Royal Pl, SE10 134 C7
Royal Quarter, Kings.T. KT2 181 H1
Royal Rd, E16 116 A6
SE17 35 G5
Sidcup DA14 176 D3
Teddington TW11 162 A5
Royal Route, Wem. HA9 87 J4
Royals Business Pk, The, E16 116 B7
Royal St, SE1 26 D5
Royalty Ms, W1 17 H4
Royal Victoria Dock, E16 115 G7
Royal Victoria Patriotic Bldg, SW18 149 G6
Royal Victoria Pl, E16 *off Wesley Av* 135 H1
Royal Victoria Sq, E16 *off Western Gateway* 115 H7
Royal Victor Pl, E3 113 G2
Royal Wk, Wall. SM6 *off Prince Charles Way* 200 B3
Roycraft Av, Bark. IG11 117 J2
Roycraft Cl, Bark. IG11 117 J2
Roycroft Cl, E18 79 H1
SW2 169 G1
Roydene Rd, SE18 137 H6
Roydon Cl, SW11 *off Reform St* 149 J2
Loughton IG10 48 B7
Roydon St, SW11 *off Southolm St* 150 B1
Roy Gdns, Ilf. IG2 81 H4
Roy Gro, Hmptn. TW12 161 H6
Royle Bldg, N1 11 J1
Royle Cres, W13 104 D4
Roy Sq, E14 *off Narrow St* 113 H7
Royston Av, E4 62 A5
Sutton SM1 199 G3
Wallington SM6 200 D4
Royston Cl, Houns. TW5 142 B1
Royston Ct, SE24 *off Burbage Rd* 151 J6
Richmond TW9 145 J1
Surbiton KT6 196 A3
Royston Gdns, Ilf. IG1 80 A6
Royston Gro, Pnr. HA5 51 F6
Royston Par, Ilf. IG1 80 A6
Royston Pk Rd, Pnr. HA5 51 F6
Royston Rd, SE20 189 G1
Richmond TW10 145 H5
Roystons, The, Surb. KT5 182 B5
Royston St, E2 113 F2
Rozel Ct, N1 112 B1
Rozel Rd, SW4 150 C2
Rubastic Rd, Sthl. UB2 122 C3
Rubens Pl, SW4 *off Dolman St* 151 F4
Rubens Rd, Nthlt. UB5 102 C2
Rubens St, SE6 171 J2
Ruby Ms, E17 *off Ruby Rd* 78 A3
Ruby Rd, E17 78 A3
Ruby St, NW10 88 C7
SE15 132 E6
Ruby Triangle, SE15 *off Sandgate St* 132 E6
Ruby Way, NW9 71 F1
Ruckholt Cl, E10 96 B3
Ruckholt Rd, E10 96 A4
Rucklidge Av, NW10 107 F2
Rudall Cres, NW3 *off Willoughby Rd* 91 G4
Ruddington Cl, E5 95 H4
Ruddock Cl, Edg. HA8 54 C7
Ruddstreet Cl, SE18 137 E4
Rudgwick Ter, NW8 *off Avenue Rd* 109 H1
Rudland Rd, Bexh. DA7 159 H3
Rudloe Rd, SW12 150 C7
Rudolf Pl, SW8 34 B6
Rudolph Rd, E13 115 F2
NW6 108 D2
Rudstone Ho, E3 *off Bromley High St* 114 B3
Rudyard Gro, NW7 54 C6
Ruffetts, The, S.Croy. CR2 203 E7
Ruffetts Cl, S.Croy. CR2 202 E7
Ruffle Cl, West Dr. UB7 120 B2
Rufford Cl, Har. HA3 68 D6
Rufford St, N1 111 E1
Rufford Twr, W3 126 B1
Rufus Business Cen, SW18 167 E2
Rufus Cl, Ruis. HA4 84 E3
Rufus St, N1 12 D4
Rugby Av, N9 60 C1
Greenford UB6 86 A6
Wembley HA0 87 E5
Rugby Cl, Har. HA1 68 B5
★ **Rugby Football Union Twickenham**, Twick. TW1 144 B6
Rugby Gdns, Dag. RM9 100 C6
Rugby Rd, NW9 70 B4
W4 126 E2

Rugby Rd, Dagenham RM9 **100** B7
Twickenham TW1 **144** B6
Rugby St, WC1 **10** C6
Rugg St, E14 **114** A7
Ruislip Cl, Grnf. UB6 **103** H4
RUISLIP MANOR, Ruis. HA4 **84** A2
Ruislip Retail Pk, Ruis. HA4 *off Victoria Rd* **85** E4
Ruislip Rd, Grnf. UB6 **103** G3
Northolt UB5 **102** D2
Southall UB1 **103** G3
Ruislip Rd E, W7 **104** A4
W13 **104** A4
Greenford UB6 **104** A4
Ruislip St, SW17 **167** J4
Rumbold Rd, SW6 **129** E7
Rum Cl, E1 **113** F7
Rumford Ho, SE1 *off Bath Ter* **27** J5
Rumsey Cl, Hmptn. TW12 **161** F6
Rumsey Ms, N4 *off Monsell Rd* **93** H3
Rumsey Rd, SW9 **151** F3
Runbury Circle, NW9 **88** D2
Runcorn Cl, N17 **76** E4
Runcorn Pl, W11 **108** B7
Rundell Cres, NW4 **71** H5
Rundell Twr, SW8 *off Portland Gro* **151** F1
Runes Cl, Mitch. CR4 **185** G4
Runnel Fld, Har. HA1 **86** B3
Running Horse Yd, Brent. TW8 *off Pottery Rd* **125** H6
Runnymede, SW19 **185** G1
Runnymede Cl, Twick. TW2 **143** H6
Runnymede Ct, Croy. CR0 **202** C2
Runnymede Cres, SW16 **186** D1
Runnymede Gdns, Grnf. UB6 **104** A2
Twickenham TW2 **143** H6
Runnymede Ho, E9 *off Kingsmead Way* **95** H4
Runnymede Rd, Twick. TW2 **143** H6
Runway, The, Ruis. HA4 **84** B5
Runway Cl, NW9 *off Great Strand* **71** F2
Rupack St, SE16 *off St. Marychurch St* **133** F2
Rupert Av, Wem. HA9 **87** H5
Rupert Ct, W1 **17** H5
West Molesey KT8 *off St. Peter's Rd* **179** G4
Rupert Gdns, SW9 **151** H2
Rupert Rd, N19 *off Holloway Rd* **92** D2
NW6 **108** C2
W4 **127** E3
Rupert St, W1 **17** H5
Rural Way, SW16 **168** B7
Rusbridge Cl, E8 *off Amhurst Rd* **94** D5
Ruscoe Rd, E16 **115** F6
Ruscombe Way, Felt. TW14 **141** J7
Rush, The, SW19 *off Kingston Rd* **184** C1
Rusham Rd, SW12 **149** J6
Rushbridge Cl, Croy. CRO **187** J6
Rushbrook Cres, E17 **77** J1
Rushbrook Rd, SE9 **175** F2
Rush Common Ms, SW2 **151** F7
Rushcroft Rd, E4 **62** A7
SW2 **151** G4
Rushden Cl, SE19 **170** A7
Rushdene, SE2 **138** D3
Rushdene Av, Barn. EN4 **41** H7
Rushdene Cl, Nthlt. UB5 **102** C3
Rushdene Cres, Nthlt. UB5 **102** C2
Rushdene Rd, Pnr. HA5 **66** D6
Rushden Gdns, NW7 **55** J6
Ilford IG5 **80** D3
Rushen Wk, Cars. SM5 *off Paisley Rd* **199** G1
Rushett Cl, T.Ditt. KT7 **194** E1
Rushett Rd, T.Ditt. KT7 **180** E7
Rushey Cl, N.Mal. KT3 **182** D4
Rushey Grn, SE6 **154** B7
Rushey Hill, Enf. EN2 **43** F4
Rushey Mead, SE4 **154** A5
Rushford Rd, SE4 **153** J6
RUSH GREEN, Rom. RM7 **83** J7
Rush Grn Gdns, Rom. RM7 **101** J1
Rush Grn Rd, Rom. RM7 **101** J1
Rushgrove Av, NW9 **71** F5
Rushgrove St, SE18 **136** C4
Rush Hill Ms, SW11 *off Rush Hill Rd* **150** A3
Rush Hill Rd, SW11 **150** A3
Rushley Cl, Kes. BR2 **206** A4
Rushmead, E2 *off Florida St* **112** E3
Richmond TW10 **163** E3
Rushmead Cl, Croy. CR0 **202** C4
Rushmere Ct, Wor.Pk. KT4 *off The Avenue* **197** G2
Rushmere Ho, SW15 *off Fontley Way* **165** G1
Rushmere Pl, SW19 **166** A5
Rushmoor Cl, Pnr. HA5 **66** B4
Rushmore Cl, Brom. BR1 **192** B3
Rushmore Cres, E5 *off Rushmore Rd* **95** G4
Rushmore Rd, E5 **95** F4
Rusholme Av, Dag. RM10 **101** G3
Rusholme Gro, SE19 **170** B5
Rusholme Rd, SW15 **148** A6
Rushout Av, Har. HA3 **68** E6
Rushton St, N1 **12** C1
Rushworth St, SE1 **27** H3
Rushy Meadow La, Cars. SM5 **199** H2
Ruskin Av, E12 **98** B6
Feltham TW14 **141** J6
Richmond TW9 **126** A7
Welling DA16 **158** A3
Ruskin Cl, NW11 **72** E6
Ruskin Dr, Orp. BR6 **207** H3
Welling DA16 **158** A3
Worcester Park KT4 **197** H2
Ruskin Gdns, W5 **105** G4
Harrow HA3 **69** J4
Ruskin Gro, Welling DA16 **158** A2
Ruskin Pk Ho, SE5 **152** A3
Ruskin Rd, N17 **76** C1
Belvedere DA17 **139** G4
Carshalton SM5 **199** J5
Croydon CR0 **201** H2
Isleworth TW7 **144** C3
Southall UB1 **102** E7
Ruskin Wk, N9 **60** D2
SE24 **151** J5
Bromley BR2 **192** C6
Ruskin Way, SW19 **185** G1
Rusland Av, Orp. BR6 **207** G3
Rusland Hts, Har. HA1 *off Rusland Pk Rd* **68** B4
Rusland Pk Rd, Har. HA1 **68** B4
Rusper Cl, NW2 **89** J3
Stanmore HA7 **53** F4
Rusper Rd, N22 **75** J2
Dagenham RM9 **100** C6
Russell Av, N22 **75** H2
Russell Cl, NW10 **88** C7
SE7 **135** J7
W4 **127** F6
Beckenham BR3 **190** B3
Bexleyheath DA7 **159** G4
Ruislip HA4 **84** C2
Russell Ct, SW1 **25** G2
Surbiton KT6 **181** H7
Russell Dr, Stai. (Stanw.) TW19 **140** A6
Russell Gdns, N20 **57** H2
NW11 **72** B6
W14 **128** B3
Richmond TW10 **163** F2
West Drayton (Sipson) UB7 **120** D5
Russell Gdns Ms, W14 **128** B3
Russell Gro, NW7 **54** E5
SW9 **131** G7
Russell Kerr Cl, W4 *off Burlington La* **126** C7
Russell La, N20 **57** H2
Russell Lo, SE1 *off Spurgeon St* **28** B5
Russell Mead, Har. (Har.Wld) HA3 **68** C1
Russell Par, NW11 *off Golders Grn Rd* **72** B6
Russell Pl, NW3 *off Aspern Gro* **91** H5
SE16 *off Onega Gate* **133** H3
Russell Rd, E4 **61** J4
E10 **78** B6
E16 **115** G6
E17 **77** J3
N8 **74** D6
N13 **59** F6
N15 **76** B5
N20 **57** H2
NW9 **71** F6
SW19 **166** D7
W14 **128** B3
Buckhurst Hill IG9 **63** H1
Mitcham CR4 **185** H3
Northolt UB5 **85** J5
Twickenham TW2 **144** C6
Walton-on-Thames KT12 **178** A6
Russell's Footpath, SW16 **169** E5
Russell Sq, WC1 **10** A6
Russell St, WC2 **18** B5
Russell's Wf Flats, W10 *off Harrow Rd* **108** C4
Russell Wk, Rich. TW10 *off Park Hill* **145** J6
Russell Way, Sutt. SM1 **198** D5
Russet Cres, N7 *off Stock Orchard Cres* **93** F5
Russet Dr, Croy. CR0 **203** H1
Russets Cl, E4 *off Larkshall Rd* **62** D4
Russia Dock Rd, SE16 **133** H1
Russia La, E2 **113** F2
Russia Row, EC2 **20** A4
Russia Wk, SE16 **133** H2
Rusthall Av, W4 **126** D4
Rusthall Cl, Croy. CR0 **189** F6
Rustic Av, SW16 **168** B7
Rustic Pl, Wem. HA0 **87** G4
Rustic Wk, E16 *off Lambert Rd* **115** H6
Rustington Wk, Mord. SM4 **184** C7
Ruston Av, Surb. KT5 **182** B7
Ruston Gdns, N14 *off Byre Rd* **42** A6
Ruston Ms, W11 *off St. Marks Rd* **108** B6
Ruston Rd, SE18 **136** B3
Ruston St, E3 **113** J1
Rust Sq, SE5 **36** B7
Rutford Rd, SW16 **168** E5
Ruth Cl, Stan. HA7 **69** J4
Rutherford Cl, Borwd. WD6 **38** C2
Sutton SM2 **199** G6
Rutherford St, SW1 **33** H1
Rutherford Twr, Sthl. UB1 **103** H6
Rutherford Way, Bushey (Bushey Hth) WD23 **52** A1
Wembley HA9 **88** A4
Rutherglen Rd, SE2 **138** A6
Rutherwyke Cl, Epsom KT17 **197** G6
Ruthin Cl, NW9 **70** E6
Ruthin Rd, SE3 **135** G6
Ruthven St, E9 *off Lauriston Rd* **113** G1
Rutland Av, Sid. DA15 **158** A7
Rutland Cl, SW14 **146** B3
SW19 *off Rutland Rd* **167** H7
Bexley DA5 **176** D1
Chessington KT9 **195** J6
Rutland Ct, SW7 *off Rutland Gdns* **23** H4
Enfield EN3 **45** F5
Rutland Dr, Mord. SM4 **184** C6
Richmond TW10 **163** G1
Rutland Gdns, N4 **75** H6
SW7 **23** H4
W13 **104** D5
Croydon CR0 **202** B4
Dagenham RM8 **100** C5
Rutland Gdns Ms, SW7 **23** H4
Rutland Gate, SW7 **23** H4
Belvedere DA17 **139** H5
Bromley BR2 **191** F4
Rutland Gate Ms, SW7 **23** G4
Rutland Gro, W6 **127** H5
Rutland Ms, NW8 *off Boundary Rd* **109** E1
Rutland Ms E, SW7 **23** G5
Rutland Ms S, SW7 **23** G5
Rutland Ms W, SW7 *off Ennismore St* **23** G5
Rutland Pk, NW2 **89** J6
SE6 **171** J2
Rutland Pk Gdns, NW2 *off Rutland Pk* **89** J6
Rutland Pk Mans, NW2 *off Rutland Pk* **89** J6
Rutland Pl, EC1 **11** J6
Bushey (Bushey Hth) WD23 *off The Rutts* **52** A1
Rutland Rd, E7 **98** A7
E9 **113** F1
E11 **79** H5
E17 **78** A6
SW19 **167** H7
Harrow HA1 **67** J6
Hayes UB3 **121** G4
Ilford IG1 **99** E4
Southall UB1 **103** G5
Twickenham TW2 **162** A2
Rutland St, SW7 **23** H5
Rutland Wk, SE6 **171** J2
Rutley Cl, SE17 **35** G5
Rutlish Rd, SW19 **184** D1
Rutter Gdns, Mitch. CR4 **185** F4
Rutters Cl, West Dr. UB7 **120** D2
Rutts, The, Bushey (Bushey Hth) WD23 **52** A1
Rutts Ter, SE14 **153** G1
Ruvigny Gdns, SW15 **148** A3
Ruxley Cl, Epsom KT19 **196** B5
Sidcup DA14 **176** D6
Ruxley Cor, Sid. DA14 **176** E6
Ruxley Cor Ind Est, Sid. DA14 **176** D6
Ruxley Cres, Esher (Clay.) KT10 **194** E6
Ruxley La, Epsom KT19 **196** D5
Ruxley Ms, Epsom KT19 **196** B5
Ruxley Ridge, Esher (Clay.) KT10 **194** D7
Ryalls Ct, N20 **57** J3
Ryan Cl, SE3 **155** J4
Ruislip HA4 **84** B1
Ryan Dr, Brent. TW8 **124** D6
Ryarsh Cres, Orp. BR6 **207** H4
Rycott Path, SE22 *off Lordship La* **152** D7
Rycroft Way, N17 **76** C3
Ryculff Sq, SE3 **155** F2
Rydal Cl, NW4 **72** B1
Rydal Cres, Grnf. (Perivale) UB6 **105** E3
Rydal Dr, Bexh. DA7 **159** G1
West Wickham BR4 **205** E2
Rydal Gdns, NW9 **71** E5
SW15 **164** E5
Hounslow TW3 **143** H6
Wembley HA9 **87** F1
Rydal Rd, SW16 **168** D4
Rydal Way, Enf. EN3 **45** F6
Ruislip HA4 **84** C4
Ryde Pl, Twick. TW1 **145** F6
Ryder Av, E10 **78** B7
Ryder Cl, Brom. BR1 **173** H5
Ryder Ct, SW1 **25** G1
Ryder Dr, SE16 **132** E5
Ryder Ms, E9 *off Homerton High St* **95** F5
Ryders Ter, NW8 **6** C1
Ryder St, SW1 **25** G1
Ryder Yd, SW1 **25** G1
Ryde Vale Rd, SW12 **168** B2
Rydon Ms, SW19 **165** J7
Rydons Cl, SE9 **156** B3
Rydon St, N1 *off St. Paul St* **111** J1
Rydston Cl, N7 *off Sutterton St* **93** F7
Rye, The, N14 **42** C7
Rye Cl, Bex. DA5 **159** H6
Borehamwood WD6 **38** D4
Ryecotes Mead, SE21 **170** B1
Ryecroft Av, Ilf. IG5 **80** E2
Twickenham TW2 **143** H7
Ryecroft Cres, Barn. EN5 **39** H5
Ryecroft Rd, SE13 **154** C5
SW16 **169** G6
Orpington BR5 **193** G6
Ryecroft St, SW6 **148** E1
Ryedale, SE22 **152** E6
Ryefield Ct, Nthwd. HA6 *off Ryefield Cres* **66** A2
Ryefield Cres, Nthwd. HA6 **66** A2
Ryefield Par, Nthwd. HA6 *off Ryefield Cres* **66** A2
Ryefield Path, SW15 **165** G1
Ryefield Rd, SE19 **169** J6
Ryegates, SE15 *off Caulfield Rd* **153** E2
Rye Hill Pk, SE15 **153** F4
Ryelands Cres, SE12 **155** J6
Rye La, SE15 **152** D1
Rye Pas, SE15 **152** D3
Rye Rd, SE15 **153** G4
Rye Wk, SW15 **148** A5
Rye Way, Edg. HA8 *off Canons Dr* **53** J6
Ryfold Rd, SW19 **166** D3
Ryhope Rd, N11 **58** B4
Rylandes Rd, NW2 **89** G3
Ryland Ho, Croy. CR0 **201** J3
Ryland Rd, NW5 **92** B6
Rylett Cres, W12 **127** F3
Rylett Rd, W12 **127** F2
Rylston Rd, N13 **60** A3
SW6 **128** C6
Rymer Rd, Croy. CR0 **188** B7
Rymer St, SE24 **151** H6
Rymill St, E16 **136** D1
Rysbrack St, SW3 **23** J5
Rythe Cl, Chess. KT9 *off Nigel Fisher Way* **195** F7
Esher KT10 *off Rythe Rd* **194** B5
Rythe Ct, T.Ditt. KT7 **180** D7
Rythe Rd, Esher (Clay.) KT10 **194** A5

S

★ **Saatchi Gall, The**, SW3 **32** A3
Sabbarton St, E16 *off Silvertown Way* **115** F6
Sabella Ct, E3 *off Mostyn Gro* **113** J2
Sabine Rd, SW11 **149** J3

Sable Cl, Houns. TW4 .... 142 C3
Sable St, N1 .... 93 H7
Sach Rd, E5 .... 95 E2
Sackville Av, Brom. BR2 .. 205 G1
Sackville Cl, Har. HA2 .... 86 A3
Sackville Est, SW16 .... 169 E3
Sackville Gdns, Ilf. IG1 .... 98 C1
Sackville Rd, Sutt. SM2 ... 198 D7
Sackville St, W1 .... 17 G6
Saddlers Cl, Barn. (Arkley) EN5 .... 39 H5
Borehamwood WD6 *off Farriers Way* 38 D6
Pinner HA5 .... 51 G6
Saddlers Ms, SW8 *off Portland Gro* 151 E1
Kingston upon Thames (Hmptn W.) KT1 .... 181 F1
Wembley HA0 *off The Boltons* 86 C4
Saddlers Path, Borwd. WD6 .... 38 D5
Saddlescombe Way, N12 ... 56 D5
Saddle Yd, W1 .... 24 D1
Sadler Cl, Mitch. CR4 .... 185 J2
Sadler Ho, E3 *off Bromley High St* .. 114 B3
Sadlers Gate Ms, SW15 *off Commondale* 147 J3
Sadlers Ride, W.Mol. KT8 .... 179 J2
★ **Sadler's Wells Thea**, EC1 .... 11 G3
Saffron Av, E14 .... 114 D7
Saffron Cl, NW11 .... 72 C5
Croydon CR0 .... 186 E6
Saffron Ct, Felt. TW14 *off Staines Rd* 141 F7
Saffron Hill, EC1 .... 11 F6
Saffron Rd, Rom. RM5 .... 83 J2
Saffron St, EC1 .... 19 F1
Saffron Way, Surb. KT6 ... 195 G1
Sage Cl, E6 *off Bradley Stone Rd* .. 116 C5
Sage Ms, SE22 *off Lordship La* 152 C5
Sage St, E1 *off Cable St* .. 113 F7
Sage Way, WC1 .... 10 C4
Saigasso Cl, E16 *off Royal Rd* 116 A6
Sailacre Ho, SE10 *off Calvert Rd* 135 F5
Sail Ct, E14 *off Newport Av* 114 D7
Sailmakers Ct, SW6 *off William Morris Way* 149 F3
Sail St, SE11 .... 34 D1
Saimese Ms, N3 .... 72 D1
Sainfoin Rd, SW17 .... 168 A2
Sainsbury Rd, SE19 .... 170 B5
St. Agatha's Dr, Kings.T. KT2 .... 163 J6
St. Agathas Gro, Cars. SM5 .... 199 J1
St. Agnes Cl, E9 *off Gore Rd* 113 F1
St. Agnes Pl, SE11 .... 35 G6
St. Agnes Well, EC1 *off Old St* 12 C5
St. Aidans Ct, W13 *off St. Aidans Rd* 125 F2
Barking IG11 *off Choats Rd* 118 B3
St. Aidan's Rd, SE22 .... 152 E6
St. Aidans Rd, W13 .... 125 E2
St. Albans Av, E6 .... 116 C3
St. Alban's Av, W4 .... 126 D4
St. Albans Av, Felt. TW13 .. 160 D5
St. Albans Cl, NW11 .... 90 D1
St. Albans Ct, EC2 .... 20 A3
St. Albans Cres, N22 .... 75 G1
St. Alban's Cres, Wdf.Grn. IG8 .... 63 G7
St. Alban's Gdns, Tedd. TW11 .... 162 D5
St. Albans Gro, W8 .... 22 B5
St. Alban's Gro, Cars. SM5 .... 185 H7
St. Albans La, NW11 .... 90 D1
St. Alban's Pl, N1 .... 111 H1
St. Albans Rd, NW5 .... 92 A3
NW10 .... 106 E1
Barnet EN5 .... 40 A1
Ilford IG3 .... 99 J1
St. Alban's Rd, Kings.T. KT2 .... 163 H6
Sutton SM1 .... 198 C4
Woodford Green IG8 .... 63 G7
St. Albans St, SW1 .... 17 H6
St. Albans Ter, W6 *off Margravine Rd* 128 B6
St. Alban's Vil, NW5 *off Highgate Rd* 92 A3
St. Alfege Pas, SE10 .... 134 C6
St. Alfege Rd, SE7 .... 136 A6
St. Alphage Gdns, EC2 .... 20 A2
St. Alphage Highwalk, EC2 .... 20 B2
St. Alphage Wk, Edg. HA8 .... 70 C2
St. Alphege Rd, N9 .... 45 F7
St. Alphonsus Rd, SW4 ... 150 C4
St. Amunds Cl, SE6 .... 172 A4
St. Andrews Av, Wem. HA0 .... 86 D4
St. Andrew's Cl, N12 .... 57 F4
St. Andrews Cl, NW2 .... 89 H3
SE16 *off Ryder Dr* 133 E5
SE28 .... 118 D6
SW19 .... 166 E6
St. Andrew's Cl, Islw. TW7 144 A1
St. Andrews Cl, Ruis. HA4 .. 84 D2
Stanmore HA7 .... 69 F2
Thames Ditton KT7 .... 194 E1
St. Andrew's Ct, SW18 ... 167 F2
St. Andrews Dr, Stan. HA7 .... 69 F1
St. Andrew's Gro, N16 .... 94 A1
St. Andrew's Hill, EC4 .... 19 H5
St. Andrew's Ms, N16 .... 94 B1
St. Andrews Ms, SE3 *off Mycenae Rd* 135 G7
SW12 *off Emmanuel Rd* 168 D1
St. Andrews Pl, NW1 .... 8 E5
St. Andrews Rd, E11 .... 78 E6
E13 .... 115 H3
E17 .... 77 G2
N9 .... 45 F7
NW9 .... 88 D1
NW10 .... 89 H6
NW11 .... 72 C6
W3 .... 107 E7
W7 *off Churchfield Rd* 124 B2
W14 .... 128 B6
Carshalton SM5 .... 199 H3
Croydon CR0 *off Lower Coombe St* . 201 J4
Enfield EN1 .... 44 A3
Ilford IG1 .... 80 C7
Sidcup DA14 .... 176 D3
St. Andrew's Rd, Surb. KT6 .... 181 G6
St. Andrews Rd, Wat. WD19 .... 50 D3
St. Andrews Sq, W11 *off Bartle Rd* 108 B6
St. Andrew's Sq, Surb. KT6 .... 181 G6
St. Andrews Twr, Sthl. UB1 .... 103 J7
St. Andrew St, EC4 .... 19 F2
St. Andrews Way, E3 .... 114 B4
St. Anna Rd, Barn. EN5 *off Sampson Av* 40 A5
St. Annes Av, Stai. (Stanw.) TW19 .... 140 A7
St. Anne's Cl, N6 .... 92 A3
Watford WD19 .... 50 C4
St. Anne's Ct, W1 .... 17 H4
St. Annes Gdns, NW10 ... 105 J3
St. Annes Pas, E14 *off Newell St* 113 J6
St. Annes Rd, E11 .... 96 D2
St. Anne's Rd, Wem. HA0 .. 87 G5
St. Anne's Row, E14 *off Commercial Rd* ... 113 J6
St. Anne St, E14 *off Commercial Rd* ... 113 J6
St. Ann's, Bark. IG11 .... 117 F1
St. Ann's Cres, SW18 .... 149 F6
St. Ann's Gdns, NW5 *off Queen's Cres* 92 A6
St. Ann's Hill, SW18 .... 149 E5
St. Ann's La, SW1 .... 25 J5
St. Ann's Pk Rd, SW18 .... 149 F6
St. Ann's Pas, SW13 .... 147 E3
St. Anns Rd, N9 .... 60 C2
St. Ann's Rd, N15 .... 75 H5
SW13 .... 147 F2
St. Anns Rd, W11 .... 108 A7
St. Ann's Rd, Bark. IG11 *off Axe St* 117 F1
Harrow HA1 .... 68 B6
St. Ann's Shop Cen, Har. HA1 .... 68 B6
St. Ann's St, SW1 .... 25 J5
St. Ann's Ter, NW8 .... 7 F1
St. Anns Vil, W11 .... 128 A1
St. Anns Way, S.Croy. CR2 .... 201 H6
St. Anselm's Pl, W1 .... 16 D4
St. Anselms Rd, Hayes UB3 .... 121 J2
St. Anthonys Av, Wdf.Grn. IG8 .... 63 J6
St. Anthonys Cl, E1 .... 29 H1
SW17 *off College Gdns* 167 H2
St. Anthony's Way, Felt. TW14 .... 141 J4
St. Antony's Rd, E7 .... 97 H7
St. Arvans Cl, Croy. CR0 .. 202 B3
St. Asaph Rd, SE4 .... 153 G3
St. Aubins Ct, N1 *off De Beauvoir Est* ... 112 A1
St. Aubyn's Av, SW19 .... 166 C5
St. Aubyns Av, Houns. TW3 .... 143 G5
St. Aubyns Cl, Orp. BR6 .. 207 J3
St. Aubyns Gdns, Orp. BR6 .... 207 J2
St. Aubyn's Rd, SE19 .... 170 C6
St. Audrey Av, Bexh. DA7 . 159 G2
St. Augustine's Av, W5 .... 105 H2
St. Augustines Av, Brom. BR2 .... 192 B5
St. Augustine's Av, S.Croy. CR2 .... 201 J6
St. Augustines Av, Wem. HA9 .... 87 H3
St. Augustines Ct, SE1 *off Lynton Rd* 132 E5
St. Augustine's Path, N5 *off Highbury New Pk* .. 93 J4
St. Augustines Rd, NW1 ... 92 D7
St. Augustine's Rd, Belv. DA17 .... 139 F4
St. Austell Cl, Edg. HA8 .... 69 J2
St. Austell Rd, SE13 .... 154 C2
St. Awdry's Rd, Bark. IG11 . 99 G7
St. Awdry's Wk, Bark. IG11 *off Station Par* 99 F7
St. Barnabas Cl, SE22 *off East Dulwich Gro* .. 152 B5
Beckenham BR3 .... 190 C2
St. Barnabas Ct, Har. HA3 .. 67 J1
St. Barnabas Gdns, W.Mol. KT8 .... 179 G5
St. Barnabas Ms, SW1 .... 32 C3
St. Barnabas Rd, E17 .... 78 A6
Mitcham CR4 .... 168 A7
Sutton SM1 .... 199 G5
Woodford Green IG8 .... 79 H1
St. Barnabas St, SW1 .... 32 C3
St. Barnabas Ter, E9 .... 95 G5
St. Barnabas Vil, SW8 .... 151 E1
St. Bartholomews Cl, SE26 .... 171 F4
St. Bartholomew's Rd, E6 .... 116 B1
★ **St. Bartholomew-the-Great Ch**, EC1 .... 19 H2
St. Benedict's Cl, SW17 *off Church La* 168 A5
St. Benet's Cl, SW17 *off College Gdns* 167 H2
St. Benet's Gro, Cars. SM5 .... 185 F7
St. Benet's Pl, EC3 .... 20 C5
St. Bernards, Croy. CR0 ... 202 B3
St. Bernard's Cl, SE27 .... 170 A4
St. Bernard's Rd, E6 .... 116 A1
St. Blaise Av, Brom. BR1 .. 191 H2
St. Botolph Row, EC3 .... 21 F4
St. Botolph St, EC3 .... 21 F4
St. Brelades Ct, N1 *off Balmes Rd* 112 A1
St. Brides Av, EC4 .... 19 G4
Edgware HA8 .... 69 J1
★ **St. Bride's Ch**, EC4 .... 19 G4
St. Brides Cl, Erith DA18 *off St. Katherines Rd* .. 138 D2
St. Bride's Pas, EC4 *off Salisbury Ct* 19 G4
St. Bride St, EC4 .... 19 G3
St. Catherines Cl, SW17 .. 167 H2
Chessington KT9 .... 195 G6
St. Catherines Ct, Felt. TW13 .... 160 A1
St. Catherines Dr, SE14 *off Kitto Rd* 153 G2
St. Catherine's Ms, SW3 ... 31 J1
St. Catherines Rd, E4 .... 62 A2
St. Cecelia's Pl, SE3 *off Humber Rd* 135 G5
St. Cecilia's Cl, Sutt. SM3 . 198 B1
St. Chads Cl, Surb. (Long Dit.) KT6 .... 181 F7
St. Chad's Gdns, Rom. RM6 .... 82 E7
St. Chad's Pl, WC1 .... 10 B3
St. Chad's Rd, Rom. RM6 .... 82 E6
St. Chad's St, WC1 .... 10 B3
St. Charles Pl, W10 *off Chesterton Rd* 108 B5
St. Charles Sq, W10 .... 108 B5
St. Christopher's Cl, Islw. TW7 .... 144 B1
St. Christopher's Dr, Hayes UB3 .... 102 B7
St. Christophers Gdns, Th.Hth. CR7 .... 187 G3
St. Christophers Ms, Wall. SM6 .... 200 C5
St. Christopher's Pl, W1 .... 16 C3
St. Clair Cl, Ilf. IG5 .... 80 C2
St. Clair Dr, Wor.Pk. KT4 .. 197 H3
St. Clair Rd, E13 .... 115 H2
St. Clair's Rd, Croydon CR0 .... 202 B2
St. Clare Business Pk, Hmptn. TW12 .... 161 J6
St. Clare St, EC3 .... 21 F4
★ **St. Clement Danes Ch**, WC2 .... 18 D4
St. Clements Ct, EC4 *off Clements La* 20 C5
N7 *off Arundel Sq* 93 F6
St. Clements Hts, SE26 ... 170 D3
St. Clement's La, WC2 .... 18 D4
St. Clements St, N7 .... 93 G6
St. Clements Yd, SE22 *off Archdale Rd* 152 C5
St. Cloud Rd, SE27 .... 169 J4
St. Crispins Cl, NW3 .... 91 H4
Southall UB1 .... 103 F6
St. Cross St, EC1 .... 19 F1
St. Cuthberts Gdns, Pnr. HA5 *off Westfield Pk* 51 F7
St. Cuthberts Rd, N13 .... 59 G6
NW2 .... 90 C6
St. Cyprian's St, SW17 ... 167 J4
St. Davids Cl, SE16 *off Masters Dr* 133 E5
Wembley HA9 .... 88 C3
St. David's Cl, W.Wick. BR4 .... 190 B7
St. David's Ct, E17 .... 78 C3
St. Davids Dr, Edg. HA8 ... 69 J1
St. Davids Ms, E3 *off Morgan St* 113 H3
St. Davids Pl, NW4 .... 71 H7
St. Davids Sq, E14 .... 134 B5
St. Denis Rd, SE27 .... 170 A4
St. Dionis Rd, SW6 .... 148 C2
St. Donatts Rd, SE14 .... 153 J1
St. Dunstans, Sutt. SM1 *off Cheam Rd* 198 C6
St. Dunstan's All, EC3 .... 20 D5
St. Dunstans Av, W3 .... 106 D7
St. Dunstans Cl, Hayes UB3 .... 121 J4
St. Dunstan's Ct, EC4 *off Fleet St* 19 F4
St. Dunstans Gdns, W3 *off St. Dunstans Av* ... 106 D7
St. Dunstan's Hill, EC3 .... 20 D6
Sutton SM1 .... 198 B5
St. Dunstan's La, EC3 .... 20 D6
Beckenham BR3 .... 190 C6
St. Dunstan's Rd, E7 .... 97 J6
St. Dunstans Rd, SE25 ... 188 C4
W6 .... 128 A5
W7 .... 124 B2
Hounslow TW4 .... 142 C2
St. Edmunds Cl, NW8 *off St. Edmunds Ter* ... 109 J1
SW17 *off College Gdns* 167 H2
Erith DA18 *off St. Katherines Rd* . 138 D2
St. Edmunds Dr, Stan. HA7 .... 68 D1
St. Edmund's La, Twick. TW2 .... 143 H7
St. Edmunds Rd, N9 .... 44 D7
Ilford IG1 .... 80 C6
St. Edmunds Sq, SW13 ... 127 J6
St. Edmunds Ter, NW8 .... 7 H1
St. Edwards Cl, NW11 .... 72 D6
St. Egberts Way, E4 .... 62 C1
St. Elmo Rd, W12 .... 127 F1
St. Elmos Rd, SE16 .... 133 G2
St. Erkenwald Ms, Bark. IG11 *off St. Erkenwald Rd* .. 117 G1
St. Erkenwald Rd, Bark. IG11 .... 117 G1
St. Ermin's Hill, SW1 .... 25 H5
St. Ervans Rd, W10 .... 108 B5
St. Faiths Cl, Enf. EN2 .... 43 J1
St. Faith's Rd, SE21 .... 169 H1
St. Fillans Rd, SE6 .... 172 C1
St. Francis Cl, Orp. BR5 .. 193 H6
Watford WD19 .... 50 B1
St. Francis Pl, SW12 *off Malwood Rd* 150 B6
St. Francis Rd, SE22 .... 152 B4
St. Francis Way, Ilf. IG1 .... 99 H4
St. Frideswides Ms, E14 *off Lodore St* 114 C6
St. Gabriel's Cl, E11 .... 97 H2
E14 *off Morris Rd* 114 B5
St. Gabriels Rd, NW2 .... 90 A5
St. George's, Harrow HA1 .... 68 B6
St. Georges Av, E7 .... 97 H7
N7 .... 92 D4
NW9 .... 70 C4
St. George's Av, W5 .... 125 G2
St. Georges Av, Sthl. UB1 .... 103 F7
St. Georges Circ, SE1 .... 27 G5

St. Georges Cl, NW11 .....72 C6
SE28
off Redbourne Dr 118 D6
St. George's Cl, SW8
off Patmore St 150 C1
St. Georges Cl, Wem. HA0 .86 D3
St. Georges Ct, E6 ....116 C4
EC4 ....19 G3
SW7 ....22 C5
St. George's Dr, SW1 ......32 E2
St. Georges Dr, Wat.
WD19 ....50 E3
St. Georges Flds, W2 ......15 H4
St. George's Gdns, Surb.
KT6 ....196 B2
St. Georges Gro, SW17 ...167 G3
St. George's Ind Est, N22 ..59 H7
St. Georges Ind Est,
Kings.T. KT2 ....163 G5
St. Georges La, EC3
off Pudding La 20 C5
St. Georges Ms, NW1
off Regents Pk Rd 91 J7
SE1 ....27 F5
SE8 *off Grove St* 133 J4
St. Georges Pl, Twick.
TW1 *off Church St* 162 D1
St. Georges Rd, E7 ....97 H6
E10 ....96 C3
N13 ....59 F3
NW11 ....72 C6
SE1 ....27 F5
St. George's Rd, SW19 ...166 C6
St. Georges Rd, W4 ......126 E2
W7 ....124 C1
St. George's Rd, Beck.
BR3 ....190 B1
St. Georges Rd, Brom.
BR1 ....192 C2
Dagenham RM9 ....100 E5
St. George's Rd, Felt.
TW13 ....160 D4
St. Georges Rd, Ilf. IG1 ....80 C7
St. George's Rd, Kings.T.
KT2 ....164 A7
Mitcham CR4 ....186 B3
Orpington BR5 ....193 G6
St. Georges Rd, Rich.
TW9 ....145 J3
St. George's Rd, Sid.
DA14 ....176 D6
St. Georges Rd, Twick.
TW1 ....145 E5
Wallington SM6 ....200 B5
St. Georges Rd W, Brom.
BR1 ....192 B1
St. Georges Sq, E7 ....97 H7
E14 *off Narrow St* 113 H7
SE8 ....133 J4
St. George's Sq, SW1 .....33 H3
New Malden KT3
off High St 183 E3
St. George's Sq Ms, SW1 ..33 H4
St. Georges Ter, NW1
off Regents Pk Rd 91 J7
St. George St, W1 ....17 E4
St. Georges Wk, Croy.
CR0 ....201 J3
St. Georges Way, SE15 ....36 D6
St. George Wf, SW8 ....34 A4
St. Gerards Cl, SW4 ......150 C5
St. German's Pl, SE3 .....155 G1
St. Germans Rd, SE23 ....171 H1
St. Giles Av, Dag. RM10 ...101 H7
St. Giles Cl, Dag. RM10
off St. Giles Av 101 H7
Hounslow TW5 ....123 E7
Orpington BR6 ....207 G5
St. Giles Ct, WC2
off St. Giles High St ...18 A3
St. Giles High St, WC2 .....17 J3
St. Giles Pas, WC2 ....17 J4
St. Giles Rd, SE5 ....132 B7
St. Gilles Ho, E2 ....113 G2
St. Gothard Rd, SE27 ....170 A4
St. Gregory Cl, Ruis. HA4 ..84 C4
St. Helena Rd, SE16 ......133 G4
St. Helena St, WC1 ....10 E4
St. Helens Cres, SW16
off St. Helens Rd 187 F1
St. Helens Gdns, W10 ....108 A6
St. Helens Pl, EC3 ....20 D3
St. Helens Rd, SW16 .....187 F1
St. Helen's Rd, W13
off Dane Rd 125 F1
St. Helens Rd, Erith
DA18 ....138 D2
Ilford IG1 ....80 C6
ST. HELIER, Cars. SM5 ....185 G7
St. Helier Av, Mord. SM4 .185 F7
St. Heliers Av, Houns.
TW3 ....143 G5
St. Heliers Rd, E10 ....78 C6
St. Hildas Cl, NW6 ....90 A7
SW17 ....167 H2
St. Hilda's Rd, SW13 .....127 H6
St. Hughe's Cl, SW17 .....167 H2
St. Hughs Rd, SE20
off Ridsdale Rd 188 E1
St. James Av, N20 ....57 H3
W13 ....124 D1
Sutton SM1 ....198 D5
St. James Cl, N20 ....57 H3
NW8
off Prince Albert Rd ...109 J1
SE18
off Congleton Gro 137 F5
Barnet EN4 ....41 G4
New Malden KT3 ......183 F5
Ruislip HA4 ....84 C2
St. James Gdns, Rom.
(Lt.Hth) RM6 ....82 B4
Wembley HA0 ....87 G7
St. James Gate, NW1
off St. Paul's Cres 92 D7
St. James Gro, SW11
off Reform St 149 J2
St. James Ms, E14 ....134 C3
E17
off St. James's St 77 H5
St. James Rd, E15 ....97 F5
N9 ....60 E2
Carshalton SM5 ....199 H3
Kingston upon Thames
KT1 ....181 H2
Mitcham CR4 ....168 A7
Surbiton KT6 ....181 G6
Sutton SM1 ....198 D5
ST. JAMES'S, SW1 ....25 G2
St. James's, SE14 ....153 H1
St. James's Av, E2 ....113 F2
Beckenham BR3 ....189 H3
Hampton (Hmptn H.)
TW12 ....161 J5
St. James's Cl, SW17 .....167 J2
St. James's Cotts, Rich.
TW9 *off Paradise Rd* ...145 H5
St. James's Ct, SW1 ......25 G5
St. James's Cres, SW9 ....151 G3
St. James's Dr, SW12 ....167 J1
SW17 ....167 J1
St. James's Gdns, W11 ...128 B1
St. James's La, N10 ....74 B4
St. James's Mkt, SW1 .....17 H6
★ **St. James's Palace**,
SW1 ....25 G3
★ **St. James's Park**,
SW1 ....25 H3
St. James's Pk, Croy.
CR0 ....187 J7
St. James's Pas, EC3 ......21 E4
St. James's Pl, SW1 ....25 F2
St. James's Rd, SE1 ....37 J3
SE16 ....29 J5
Croydon CR0 ....187 H7
Hampton (Hmptn H.)
TW12 ....161 H5
St. James's Sq, SW1 ......25 G1
St. James's St, E17 ....77 H5
SW1 ....25 F1
St. James's Ter, NW8 ....7 J1
St. James's Ter Ms, NW8 ..109 J1
St. James St, W6 ....127 J5
St. James's Wk, EC1 ....11 G5
St. James Ter, SW12 .....168 A1
St. James Way, Sid.
DA14 ....177 E5
St. Joans Rd, N9 ....60 C1
St. John Fisher Rd, Erith
DA18 ....138 D3
ST. JOHN'S, SE8 ....154 A2
St. Johns Av, N11 ....57 J5
St. John's Av, NW10 .....107 F1
SW15 ....148 A5
St. John's Ch Rd, E9 ....95 F5
St. Johns Cl, N14 ....42 C6
St. John's Cl, SW6
off Dawes Rd 128 D7
Wembley HA9 ....87 H5
St. John's Cotts, SE20
off Maple Rd 171 F7
St. Johns Cotts, Rich. TW9
off Kew Foot Rd 145 H3
St. Johns Ct, Buck.H. IG9 ..63 H1
St. John's Ct, Islw. TW7 ...144 C2
St. John's Cres, SW9 .....151 G3
St. Johns Dr, SW18 ......166 E1
St. John's Est, N1 ....12 C2
SE1 ....29 F4
St. John's Gdns, W11 .....108 C7
★ **St. John's Gate & Mus**
of the Order of St. John,
EC1 ....11 G6
St. Johns Gro, N19 ....92 C2
SW13
off Terrace Gdns 147 F2
Richmond TW9
off Kew Foot Rd 145 H4
St. John's Hill, SW11 .....149 G4
St. John's Hill Gro, SW11 .149 G4
St. John's La, EC1 ....11 G6
St. John's Ms, W11
off Ledbury Rd 108 D6
St. Johns Par, Sid. DA14 ..176 A4
St. John's Pk, SE3 ....135 F7
St. John's Pas, SW19
off Ridgway Pl 166 B6
St. John's Path, EC1 ....11 G6
St. Johns Pathway, SE23
off Devonshire Rd 171 F1
St. John's Pl, EC1 ....11 G6
St. John's Rd, E4 ....62 B3
E6
off Ron Leighton Way .116 B1
St. Johns Rd, E16 ....115 G6
St. John's Rd, E17 ....78 B2
N15 ....76 B6
St. Johns Rd, NW11 ....72 C6
St. John's Rd, SE20 ......171 F7
SW11 ....149 H4
SW19 ....166 B7
Barking IG11 ....117 H1
Carshalton SM5 ....199 H3
St. Johns Rd, Croy. CR0
off Waddon Rd 201 H3
East Molesey KT8 .....180 A4
St. John's Rd, Felt. TW13 ..161 E4
Harrow HA1 ....68 C6
St. Johns Rd, Ilf. IG2 ......81 G7
St. John's Rd, Islw. TW7 ..144 B2
Kingston upon Thames
(Hmptn W.) KT1 ......181 F2
St. Johns Rd, Loug. IG10 ..48 C2
New Malden KT3 ......182 C3
St. John's Rd, Orp. BR5 ...193 G6
Richmond TW9 ....145 H4
St. Johns Rd, Sid. DA14 ..176 B4
Southall UB2 ....122 E3
Sutton SM1 ....198 D2
St. John's Rd, Well. DA16 .158 B3
Wembley HA9 ....87 G4
St. John's Sq, EC1 ....11 G6
St. Johns Ter, E7 ....97 H6
SE18 ....137 F6
SW15
off Kingston Vale 164 E3
W10 *off Harrow Rd* 108 A4
St. John St, EC1 ....11 H6
St. Johns Vale, SE8 ......154 A2
St. Johns Vil, N19 ....92 D2
St. John's Vil, W8 ....22 B6
St. Johns Way, N19 ....92 D1
ST. JOHN'S WOOD, NW8 ...6 E3
St. John's Wd Ct, NW8 .....7 F4
St. John's Wd High St,
NW8 ....7 F2
St. John's Wd Pk, NW8 ...109 G1
St. John's Wd Rd, NW8 .....6 E5
St. John's Wd Ter, NW8 .....7 G1
St. Josephs Cl, W10
off Bevington Rd 108 B5
St. Joseph's Cl, Orp. BR6 .207 J4
St. Josephs Ct, SE2 ......138 D6
St. Joseph's Ct, SE7 ......135 H6
St. Josephs Dr, Sthl. UB1 .123 E1
St. Joseph's Gro, NW4 ....71 H4
St. Josephs Rd, N9 ....45 E7
St. Josephs St, SW8
off Battersea Pk Rd ...150 B1
St. Joseph's Vale, SE3 ...154 D2
St. Jude's Rd, E2 ....113 E2
St. Jude St, N16 ....94 B5
St. Julian's Cl, SW16 .....169 G4
St. Julian's Fm Rd, SE27 ..169 G4
St. Julian's Rd, NW6 ......90 C7
★ **St. Katharine Docks**,
E1 ....21 G6
St. Katharines Prec, NW1 ...8 D1
St. Katharine's Way, E1 ....29 G1
St. Katherines Rd, Erith
DA18 ....138 D2
St. Katherine's Row, EC3
off Fenchurch St 21 E4
St. Katherine's Wk, W11
off Freston Rd 108 A7
St. Keverne Rd, SE9 ......174 B4
St. Kilda Rd, W13 ....124 D1
Orpington BR6 ....207 J1
St. Kilda's Rd, N16 ....94 A1
Harrow HA1 ....68 B6
St. Kitts Ter, SE19 ....170 B5
St. Laurence Cl, NW6 .....108 A1
St. Lawrence Cl, Edg. HA8 .53 J7
St. Lawrence Dr, Pnr. HA5 .66 B6
★ **St. Lawrence Jewry Ch**,
EC2 ....20 A3
St. Lawrence St, E14 .....134 C1
St. Lawrence Ter, W10 ....108 B5
St. Lawrence Way,
SW9 ....151 G1
St. Leonards Av, E4 ....62 D6
Harrow HA3 ....69 F4
St. Leonard's Cl, Well.
DA16 *off Hook La* 158 A3
St. Leonards Ct, N1 ....12 C3
St. Leonard's Gdns,
Houns. TW5 ....122 E7
St. Leonards Gdns, Ilford
IG1 ....99 F5
St. Leonards Ri, Orp.
BR6 ....207 H4
St. Leonards Rd, E14 .....114 B5
NW10 ....106 D4
St. Leonard's Rd,
SW14 ....146 B3
St. Leonards Rd, W13 ....105 F7
Croydon CR0 ....201 H3
Esher (Clay.) KT10 .....194 C6
St. Leonard's Rd, Surb.
KT6 ....181 G5
St. Leonards Rd, T.Ditt.
KT7 ....180 D6
St. Leonards Sq, NW5 .....92 A6
St. Leonard's Sq, Surb.
KT6 ....181 G5
St. Leonards St, E3 ....114 B3
St. Leonard's Ter, SW3 .....31 J4
St. Leonards Wk, SW16 ...169 F7
St. Loo Av, SW3 ....31 H5
St. Louis Rd, SE27 ....169 J4
St. Loy's Rd, N17 ....76 B2
St. Lucia Dr, E15 ....115 F1
ST. LUKE'S, EC1 ....12 A5
St. Luke's Av, SW4 ....150 D4
Ilford IG1 ....99 E5
St. Luke's Cl, EC1 ....12 A5
SE25 ....189 E6
St. Luke's Est, EC1 ....12 B4
St. Lukes Ms, W11
off Basing St 108 C6
St. Lukes Rd, W11 ....108 C5
St. Lukes Sq, E16 ....115 F6
St. Luke's St, SW3 ....31 G3
St. Luke's Yd, W9 ....108 C2
St. Malo Av, N9 ....61 F3
ST. MARGARETS, Twick.
TW1 ....144 D5
St. Margarets, Bark. IG11 ..117 G1
St. Margarets Av, N15 .....75 H4
N20 ....57 F2
Harrow HA2 ....85 J3
Sidcup DA15 ....175 G3
St. Margaret's Av, Sutt.
SM3 ....198 B3
St. Margarets Cl, EC2
off Lothbury 20 B3
St. Margaret's Ct, SE1 .....28 A2
St. Margaret's Cres,
SW15 ....147 H5
St. Margaret's Dr, Twick.
TW1 ....144 E5
St. Margaret's Gro, E11 ....97 F3
SE18 ....137 F6
St. Margarets Gro, Twick.
TW1 ....144 D6
St. Margarets La, W8 ......22 A6
St. Margarets Pas, SE13
off Church Ter 154 E3
St. Margarets Path,
SE18 ....137 F5
St. Margarets Rd, E12 .....97 J2
St. Margaret's Rd, N17 .....76 B3
NW10 ....107 J3
St. Margarets Rd, SE4 ....153 J4
W7 ....124 B2
Edgware HA8 ....54 B5
Isleworth TW7 ....144 E4
Twickenham TW1 ......144 E4
St. Margarets Rbt, Twick.
TW1 *off Chertsey Rd* ...144 E6
St. Margarets Sq, SE4
off Adelaide Av 153 J4
St. Margaret's St, SW1 ....26 A4
St. Margaret's Ter, SE18 ..137 F5
St. Marks Cl, SE10
off Ashburnham Gro ..134 C7
SW6 *off Ackmar Rd* 148 D1
W11 *off St. Marks Rd* ...108 B6
St. Mark's Cl, Barn. EN5 ...40 E3
St. Marks Cl, Har. HA1
off Nightingale Av 68 E7
St. Marks Cres, NW1 .....110 A1
St. Mark's Gate, E9
off Cadogan Ter 95 J7
St. Mark's Gro, SW10 .....30 B6
St. Mark's Hill, Surb. KT6 .181 H6
St. Mark's Pl, SW19
off Wimbledon Hill Rd ..166 C6
St. Marks Pl, W11 ....108 B6
St. Mark's Pl, Dag. RM10
off Reede Way 101 H6
St. Marks Ri, E8 ....94 C5
St. Marks Rd, SE25
off Coventry Rd 188 D4
St. Mark's Rd, W5 ....125 H1
St. Marks Rd, W7 ....124 B2
W10 ....108 A6
W11 ....108 B6
Bromley BR2 ....191 H3
Enfield EN1 ....44 C6
Mitcham CR4 ....185 J2
St. Mark's Rd, Tedd.
TW11 ....163 E7
St. Marks Sq, NW1 ....110 A1
St. Mark St, E1 ....21 G4
★ **St. Martin-in-the-Fields**
Ch, WC2 ....18 A6
St. Martins Av, E6 ....116 A2

St. Martins Cl, NW1 ... **110** C1
Enfield EN1 ... **44** E1
Erith DA18 *off St. Helens Rd* ... **138** D2
St. Martin's Cl, Wat. WD19 ... **50** C4
West Drayton UB7 *off St. Martin's Rd* ... **120** A3
St. Martin's Ct, WC2 *off St. Martin's La* ... **18** A5
St. Martins Est, SW2 ... **169** G1
St. Martin's La, WC2 ... **18** A5
St. Martins La, Beck. BR3 ... **190** B5
St. Martin's-le-Grand, EC1 ... **19** J3
St. Martin's Ms, WC2 ... **18** A6
St. Martin's Pl, WC2 ... **18** A6
St. Martins Rd, N9 ... **60** E2
St. Martin's Rd, SW9 ... **151** F2
West Drayton UB7 ... **120** A3
St. Martin's St, WC2 ... **17** J6
St. Martins Ter, N10 *off Pages La* ... **74** A2
St. Martins Way, SW17 ... **167** F3
St. Mary Abbots Pl, W8 ... **128** C3
St. Mary Abbots Ter, W14 ... **128** C3
St. Mary at Hill, EC3 ... **20** D6
★ **St. Mary at Hill Ch**, EC3 ... **20** D6
St. Mary Av, Wall. SM6 ... **200** A3
St. Mary Axe, EC3 ... **20** D4
St. Marychurch St, SE16 ... **133** F2
St. Mary Graces Ct, E1 ... **21** G5
St. Marylebone Cl, NW10 *off Craven Pk* ... **106** E1
★ **St. Mary-le-Bow Ch**, EC2 ... **20** A4
St. Mary Newington Cl, SE17 *off Surrey Sq* ... **36** E3
St. Mary Rd, E17 ... **78** A4
St. Marys, Bark. IG11 ... **117** G1
St. Marys App, E12 ... **98** C5
St. Marys Av, E11 ... **79** H6
St. Mary's Av, N3 ... **72** B2
Bromley BR2 ... **191** E3
Staines (Stanw.) TW19 ... **140** A7
Teddington TW11 ... **162** C6
St. Mary's Av Cen, Sthl. UB2 ... **123** H4
St. Mary's Av N, Sthl. UB2 ... **123** H4
St. Mary's Av S, Sthl. UB2 ... **123** H4
St. Mary's Cl, N17 *off Kemble Rd* ... **76** C1
St. Marys Cl, Chess. KT9 ... **195** J7
Epsom KT17 ... **197** G7
St. Mary's Cl, Stai. (Stanw.) TW19 ... **140** A7
Sunbury-on-Thames TW16 *off Green Way* ... **178** A4
St. Mary's Copse, Wor.Pk. KT4 ... **197** E2
St. Marys Ct, E6 ... **116** C4
St. Mary's Ct, SE7 ... **136** A7
W5 *off St. Mary's Rd* ... **125** G2
St. Mary's Cres, NW4 ... **71** H3
St. Marys Cres, Islw. TW7 ... **124** A7
St. Mary's Cres, Stai. (Stanw.) TW19 ... **140** A7
St. Marys Dr, Felt. TW14 ... **141** F7
St. Marys Est, SE16 *off St. Marychurch St* ... **133** F2
St. Mary's Gdns, SE11 ... **35** F1
St. Mary's Gate, W8 ... **22** A6
St. Marys Grn, N2 ... **73** F3
St. Mary's Gro, N1 ... **93** H6
SW13 ... **147** H3
W4 ... **126** B6
Richmond TW9 ... **145** J4
St. Marys Mans, W2 ... **14** E1
St. Mary's Ms, NW6 *off Priory Rd* ... **90** E7
Richmond TW10 ... **163** F2
St. Marys Path, N1 ... **111** H1
St. Mary's Pl, SE9 *off Eltham High St* ... **156** D6
W5 *off St. Mary's Rd* ... **125** G2
W8 ... **22** A6
St. Marys Rd, E10 ... **96** C3
E13 ... **115** H2
N8 *off High St* ... **75** E4
N9 ... **61** F1
St. Mary's Rd, NW10 ... **107** E1
St. Marys Rd, NW11 ... **72** B7
St. Mary's Rd, SE15 ... **153** F1
SE25 ... **188** B3
SW19 (Wimbledon) ... **166** B5
W5 ... **125** G2
Barnet EN4 ... **41** J7
Bexley DA5 ... **177** J1
St. Marys Rd, E.Mol. KT8 ... **180** A5
Ilford IG1 ... **99** F2
Surbiton KT6 ... **181** G6
Surbiton (Long Dit.) KT6 ... **181** F7
St. Mary's Rd, Wor.Pk. KT4 ... **197** E2
St. Marys Sq, W2 ... **14** E1
St. Mary's Sq, W5 *off St. Mary's Rd* ... **125** G2
St. Marys Ter, W2 ... **14** E1
St. Mary's Twr, EC1 *off Fortune St* ... **12** A6
St. Mary St, SE18 ... **136** C4
St. Marys Vw, Har. HA3 ... **69** F5
St. Mary's Wk, SE11 ... **35** F1
St. Mary's Way, Chig. IG7 ... **64** D5
St. Matthew's Av, Surb. KT6 ... **195** H1
St. Matthew's Dr, Brom. BR1 ... **192** C3
St. Matthew's Rd, SW2 ... **151** F4
St. Matthews Rd, W5 *off The Common* ... **125** H1
St. Matthew's Row, E2 ... **13** H4
St. Matthew St, SW1 ... **25** H6
St. Matthias Cl, NW9 ... **71** F5
St. Maur Rd, SW6 ... **148** C1
St. Mellion Cl, SE28 ... **118** D6
St. Merryn Cl, SE18 ... **137** G7
St. Michael's All, EC3 ... **20** C4
St. Michaels Av, N9 ... **45** F7
St. Michael's Av, Wem. HA9 ... **88** A6
St. Michaels Cl, E16 *off Fulmer Rd* ... **116** A5
St. Michael's Cl, N3 ... **72** C2
St. Michaels Cl, N12 ... **57** H5
Bromley BR1 ... **192** B3
Erith DA18 *off St. Helens Rd* ... **138** D2
Worcester Park KT4 ... **197** F2
St. Michaels Cres, Pnr. HA5 ... **67** E6
St. Michaels Gdns, W10 *off St. Lawrence Ter* ... **108** B5
St. Michael's Ms, SW1 ... **32** B2
St. Michaels Rd, NW2 ... **89** J4
St. Michael's Rd, SW9 ... **151** F2
St. Michaels Rd, Croy. CR0 ... **201** J1
Wallington SM6 ... **200** C6
Welling DA16 ... **158** B3
St. Michaels St, W2 ... **15** F3
St. Michaels Ter, N22 ... **75** E2
St. Mildred's Ct, EC2 *off Poultry* ... **20** B4
St. Mildreds Rd, SE12 ... **155** E7
St. Nicholas Cen, Sutt. SM1 *off St. Nicholas Way* ... **199** E5
St. Nicholas Glebe, SW17 ... **168** A6
St. Nicholas Pl, Loug. IG10 ... **48** D4
St. Nicholas Rd, SE18 ... **137** J5
Sutton SM1 ... **199** E5
Thames Ditton KT7 ... **180** C6
St. Nicholas St, SE8 *off Lucas St* ... **154** A1
St. Nicholas Way, Sutt. SM1 ... **198** E4
St. Nicolas La, Chis. BR7 ... **192** B1
St. Ninian's Ct, N20 ... **57** J3
St. Norbert Grn, SE4 ... **153** H4
St. Norbert Rd, SE4 ... **153** H4
St. Olaf's Rd, SW6 ... **128** B7
St. Olaves Ct, EC2 ... **20** B4
St. Olave's Est, SE1 ... **29** E3
St. Olaves Gdns, SE11 ... **34** E1
St. Olaves Rd, E6 ... **116** D1
St. Olave's Wk, SW16 ... **186** C2
St. Olav's Sq, SE16 ... **133** F2
St. Oswald's Pl, SE11 ... **34** C4
St. Oswald's Rd, SW16 ... **187** H1
St. Oswulf St, SW1 ... **33** J2
ST. PANCRAS, WC1 ... **10** A4
St. Pancras Way, NW1 ... **92** C7
St. Patrick's Ct, Wdf.Grn. IG8 ... **63** E7
St. Paul's All, EC4 *off St. Paul's Chyd* ... **19** H4
St. Paul's Av, NW2 ... **89** H6
SE16 ... **133** G1
St. Pauls Av, Har. HA3 ... **69** J5
★ **St. Paul's Cath**, EC4 ... **19** J4
St. Paul's Chyd, EC4 ... **19** H4
St. Paul's Cl, SE7 ... **136** A5
W5 ... **125** J2
St. Pauls Cl, Borwd. WD6 ... **38** C5
St. Paul's Cl, Cars. SM5 ... **199** H1
St. Pauls Cl, Chess. KT9 ... **195** G4
Hayes (Harling.) UB3 ... **121** G5
St. Paul's Cl, Houns. TW3 ... **143** E2
St. Paul's Ct, W14 *off Colet Gdns* ... **128** A4
St. Pauls Ctyd, SE8 *off Deptford High St* ... **134** A6
St. Pauls Cray Rd, Chis. BR7 ... **193** G1
St. Paul's Cres, NW1 ... **92** D7
St. Pauls Dr, E15 ... **96** D5
St. Paul's Ms, NW1 ... **92** D7
St. Paul's Pl, N1 ... **94** A6
St. Pauls Ri, N13 ... **59** H6
St. Paul's Rd, N1 ... **93** H6
N17 ... **60** D7
Barking IG11 ... **117** F1
Brentford TW8 ... **125** G6
Erith DA8 ... **139** J7
Richmond TW9 ... **145** J3
Thornton Heath CR7 ... **187** J3
St. Paul's Shrubbery, N1 ... **94** A6
St. Pauls Sq, Brom. BR2 ... **191** G2
St. Paul's Ter, SE17 ... **35** H5
St. Paul St, N1 ... **111** J1
St. Pauls Wk, Kings.T. KT2 *off Alexandra Rd* ... **164** A7
St. Pauls Way, E3 ... **113** J5
E14 ... **113** J5
St. Paul's Way, N3 ... **56** E7
St. Pauls Wd Hill, Orp. BR5 ... **193** H2
St. Peter's All, EC3 ... **20** C4
St. Peter's Av, E2 ... **13** J2
E17 ... **78** E4
St. Peters Av, N18 ... **60** D4
St. Petersburgh Ms, W2 ... **14** A5
St. Petersburgh Pl, W2 ... **14** A5
St. Peter's Cl, E2 ... **13** J2
St. Peters Cl, SW17 ... **167** H2
St. Peter's Cl, Barn. EN5 ... **39** H5
St. Peters Cl, Bushey (Bushey Hth) WD23 ... **52** A1
Chislehurst BR7 ... **175** G7
Ilford IG2 ... **81** H4
St. Peter's Cl, Ruis. HA4 ... **84** D2
St. Peter's Ct, NW4 ... **71** J5
St. Peters Ct, SE3 *off Eltham Rd* ... **155** F5
SE4 *off Wickham Rd* ... **153** J2
West Molesey KT8 ... **179** G4
St. Peter's Gdns, SE27 ... **169** G3
St. Peter's Gro, W6 ... **127** G4
St. Peters Ms, N4 *off Warham Rd* ... **75** H5
St. Peter's Pl, W9 ... **6** A6
St. Peters Rd, N9 ... **61** F1
St. Peter's Rd, W6 ... **127** G5
Croydon CR0 ... **202** A4
St. Peters Rd, Kings.T. KT1 ... **182** A2
Southall UB1 ... **103** G5
Twickenham TW1 ... **145** E5
St. Peter's Rd, W.Mol. KT8 ... **179** G4
St. Peter's Sq, E2 ... **13** J2
W6 ... **127** G5
St. Peters St, N1 ... **111** H1
St. Peter's St, S.Croy. CR2 ... **202** A5
St. Peter's St Ms, N1 ... **11** H1
St. Peters Ter, SW6 ... **128** B7
St. Peter's Vil, W6 ... **127** F4
St. Peter's Way, N1 ... **94** B7
St. Peters Way, W5 ... **105** G5
Hayes (Harling.) UB3 ... **121** G5
St. Philip's Av, Wor.Pk. KT4 ... **197** H2
St. Philips Gate, Wor.Pk. KT4 ... **197** H2
St. Philip Sq, SW8 ... **150** B2
St. Philip's Rd, E8 ... **94** D6
St. Philips Rd, Surb. KT6 ... **181** G6
St. Philip St, SW8 ... **150** B2
St. Philip's Way, N1 *off Linton St* ... **111** J1
St. Quentin Ho, SW18 *off Fitzhugh Gro* ... **149** G6
St. Quentin Rd, Well. DA16 ... **157** J3
St. Quintin Av, W10 ... **107** J5
St. Quintin Gdns, W10 ... **107** J5
St. Quintin Rd, E13 ... **115** H2
St. Raphael's Way, NW10 ... **88** C5
St. Regis Cl, N10 ... **74** B2
St. Ronans Cres, Wdf.Grn. IG8 ... **63** G7
St. Rule St, SW8 ... **150** C2
St. Saviour's Est, SE1 ... **29** F5
St. Saviour's Rd, SW2 ... **151** F5
St. Saviours Rd, Croy. CR0 ... **187** J6
Saints Cl, SE27 *off Wolfington Rd* ... **169** H4
Saints Dr, E7 ... **98** A5
St. Silas Pl, NW5 ... **92** A6
St. Silas St Est, NW5 ... **92** A6
St. Simon's Av, SW15 ... **147** J5
St. Stephens Av, E17 ... **78** C5
W12 ... **127** H2
W13 ... **104** E6
St. Stephens Cl, E17 ... **78** B5
NW8 *off Avenue Cl* ... **109** H1
Southall UB1 ... **103** G5
St. Stephens Cres, W2 ... **108** D6
Thornton Heath CR7 ... **187** G3
St. Stephens Gdn Est, W2 *off Shrewsbury Rd* ... **108** D6
St. Stephens Gdns, SW15 *off Manfred Rd* ... **148** C5
W2 ... **108** D6
Twickenham TW1 ... **145** F6
St. Stephens Gro, SE13 ... **154** C3
St. Stephens Ms, W2 *off Chepstow Rd* ... **108** D5
St. Stephen's Par, E7 *off Green St* ... **97** J7
St. Stephen's Pas, Twick. TW1 *off Richmond Rd* ... **145** F6
St. Stephen's Rd, E3 ... **113** J2
St. Stephens Rd, E6 ... **97** J7
St. Stephen's Rd, E17 *off Grove Rd* ... **78** B5
St. Stephens Rd, W13 ... **105** E6
St. Stephen's Rd, Barn. EN5 ... **40** A5
St. Stephens Rd, Houns. TW3 ... **143** G6
St. Stephen's Rd, West Dr. UB7 ... **120** A1
St. Stephens Row, EC4 ... **20** B4
St. Stephens Ter, SW8 ... **131** F7
St. Stephen's Wk, SW7 ... **30** C1
St. Swithin's La, EC4 ... **20** B5
St. Swithun's Rd, SE13 ... **154** D5
St. Theresa's Rd, Felt. TW14 ... **141** J4
St. Thomas' Cl, Surb. KT6 ... **195** J1
St. Thomas Ct, Bex. DA5 ... **159** G7
St. Thomas Dr, Orp. BR5 ... **207** F1
St. Thomas' Dr, Pnr. HA5 ... **67** E1
St. Thomas Gdns, Ilf. IG1 ... **99** F6
St. Thomas Rd, E16 ... **115** G6
N14 ... **42** D7
St. Thomas' Rd, W4 ... **126** C6
St. Thomas Rd, Belv. DA17 ... **139** J2
St. Thomas's Gdns, NW5 *off Queen's Cres* ... **92** A6
St. Thomas's Ms, SW18 *off West Hill* ... **148** D5
St. Thomas's Pl, E9 ... **95** F7
St. Thomas's Rd, N4 ... **93** G2
NW10 ... **107** E1
St. Thomas's Sq, E9 ... **95** E7
St. Thomas St, SE1 ... **28** B2
St. Thomas's Way, SW6 ... **128** C7
St. Timothy's Ms, Brom. BR1 *off Wharton Rd* ... **191** H1
St. Ursula Gro, Pnr. HA5 ... **66** D5
St. Ursula Rd, Sthl. UB1 ... **103** G6
St. Vincent Cl, SE27 ... **169** H5
St. Vincent Rd, Twick. TW2 ... **143** J6
St. Vincents La, NW7 ... **55** J5
St. Vincent St, W1 ... **16** C2
St. Wilfrids Cl, Barn. EN4 ... **41** H5
St. Wilfrids Rd, Barn. EN4 ... **41** G5
St. Winefride's Av, E12 ... **98** C5
St. Winifreds Cl, Chig. IG7 ... **65** F5
St. Winifred's Rd, Tedd. TW11 ... **163** E6
Sakura Dr, N22 ... **74** D1
Sala Ho, SE3 *off Pinto Way* ... **155** H4
Salamanca Pl, SE1 ... **34** C2
Salamanca St, SE1 ... **34** B2
Salamander Cl, Kings.T. KT2 ... **163** F5
Salcombe Dr, Mord. SM4 ... **198** A1
Romford RM6 ... **83** F6
Salcombe Gdns, NW7 ... **55** J6
Salcombe Pk, Loug. IG10 ... **48** A5
Salcombe Rd, E17 ... **77** J7
N16 ... **94** B5
Salcombe Vil, Rich. TW10 *off The Vineyard* ... **145** H5
Salcombe Way, Ruis. HA4 ... **84** A2
Salcott Rd, SW11 ... **149** H5
Croydon CR0 ... **201** E3
Salehurst Cl, Har. HA3 ... **69** H5
Salehurst Rd, SE4 ... **153** J6
Salem Pl, Croy. CR0 ... **201** J3
Salem Rd, W2 ... **14** B5
Salento Cl, N3 ... **56** D7
Sale Pl, W2 ... **15** G2
Sale St, E2 ... **13** H5
Salford Rd, SW2 ... **168** D1
Salhouse Cl, SE28 *off Rollesby Way* ... **118** C6
Salisbury Av, N3 ... **72** C3
Barking IG11 ... **99** G7
Sutton SM1 ... **198** C6
Salisbury Cl, SE17 ... **36** B1
Worcester Park KT4 ... **197** F3
Salisbury Ct, EC4 ... **19** G4
Edgware HA8 ... **53** J4
Salisbury Gdns, SW19 ... **166** B7
Buckhurst Hill IG9 ... **64** A2
Salisbury Hall Gdns, E4 ... **62** A6

Salisbury Ho, E14 *off Hobday St* **114** B6
Salisbury Ms, SW6 *off Dawes Rd* **128** C7
Bromley BR2 **192** B5
Salisbury Pl, SW9 **131** H7
W1 **15** J1
Salisbury Rd, E4 **62** A3
E7 **97** G6
E10 **96** C2
E12 **98** A5
E17 **78** C5
N4 **75** H5
N22 **75** H1
SE25 **188** D6
SW19 **166** B7
W13 **124** D2
Barnet EN5 **40** B3
Bexley DA5 **177** G1
Bromley BR2 **192** B5
Carshalton SM5 **199** J6
Dagenham RM10 **101** H6
Feltham TW13 **160** C1
Harrow HA1 **68** A5
Hounslow TW4 **142** C3
Hounslow (Lon.Hthrw Air.) TW6 **141** F5
Ilford IG3 **99** H2
New Malden KT3 **182** D3
Pinner HA5 **66** A4
Richmond TW9 **145** H4
Southall UB2 **123** E4
Worcester Park KT4 **197** F3
Salisbury Sq, EC4 **19** F4
Salisbury St, NW8 **7** F6
W3 **126** C2
Salisbury Ter, SE15 **153** F3
Salisbury Wk, N19 **92** C2
Salix Cl, Sun. TW16 *off Oak Gro* **160** B7
Salliesfield, Twick. TW2 **144** A6
Sally Murray Cl, E12 **98** D4
Salmen Rd, E13 **115** F2
Salmond Cl, Stan. HA7 **52** D6
Salmon La, E14 **113** H6
Salmon Rd, Belv. DA17 **139** G5
Salmons Rd, N9 **60** D1
Chessington KT9 **195** G6
Salmon St, E14 *off Salmon La* **113** J6
NW9 **88** B1
Salomons Rd, E13 *off Chalk Rd* **115** J5
Salop Rd, E17 **77** G6
Saltash Cl, Sutt. SM1 **198** C4
Saltash Rd, Ilf. IG6 **65** G7
Welling DA16 **158** C1
Saltcoats Rd, W4 **126** E2
Saltcroft Cl, Wem. HA9 **88** B1
Salter Cl, Har. HA2 **85** F3
Salterford Rd, SW17 **168** A6
Saltern Ct, Bark. IG11 *off Puffin Cl* **118** B3
Salter Rd, SE16 **133** G1
Salters Hall Ct, EC4 **20** B5
Salters Hill, SE19 **170** A5
Salters Rd, E17 **78** D4
W10 **108** A4
Salter St, E14 **114** A7
NW10 **107** G3
Salter St Alleyway, NW10 *off Hythe Rd* **107** G4
Salterton Rd, N7 **93** E3
Saltley Cl, E6 *off Dunnock Rd* **116** B6
Saltoun Rd, SW2 **151** G4
Saltram Cl, N15 **76** C4
Saltram Cres, W9 **108** C3
Saltwell St, E14 **114** A7
Saltwood Gro, SE17 **36** B4
Salusbury Rd, NW6 **108** B1
Salutation Rd, SE10 **135** E4
Salvia Gdns, Grnf. (Perivale) UB6 *off Selborne Gdns* **104** D2
Salvin Rd, SW15 **148** A3
Salway Cl, Wdf.Grn. IG8 **63** F7
Salway Pl, E15 *off Broadway* **96** E6
Salway Rd, E15 *off Great Eastern Rd* **96** D6
Samantha Cl, E17 **77** J7
Sam Bartram Cl, SE7 **135** J5
Sambruck Ms, SE6 **172** B1
Samels Ct, W6 *off South Black Lion La* **127** G5
Samford Ho, N1 *off Barnsbury Rd* **111** G1
Samford St, NW8 **7** F6
Samira Cl, E17 *off Colchester Rd* **77** J6
Samos Rd, SE20 **189** E2
Sampson Av, Barn. EN5 **40** A5
Sampson Cl, Belv. DA17 *off Carrill Way* **138** D3
Sampson St, E1 **29** J2
Samson St, E13 **115** J2
Samuel Cl, E8 *off Pownall Rd* **112** C1
SE14 **133** G6
SE18 **136** B4
Stanmore HA7 **52** D2
Samuel Gray Gdns, Kings.T. KT2 **181** G1
Samuel Johnson Cl, SW16 **169** F4
Samuel Lewis Trust Dws, N1 *off Liverpool Rd* **93** G6
SW3 **31** G2
SW6 **128** D7
W14 *off Lisgar Ter* **128** C4
Samuel Lewis Trust Est, SE5 *off Warner Rd* **151** J1
Samuels Cl, W6 *off South Black Lion La* **127** G5
Samuel St, SE15 **37** F7
SE18 **136** C4
Sancroft Cl, NW2 **89** H3
Sancroft Rd, Har. HA3 **68** C2
Sancroft St, SE11 **34** D3
Sanctuary, The, SW1 **25** J4
Bexley DA5 **158** D6
Morden SM4 **184** D6
Sanctuary Ms, E8 *off Queensbridge Rd* **94** C6
Sanctuary Rd, Houns. (Lon.Hthrw Air.) TW6 **140** D6
Sanctuary St, SE1 **28** A4
Sandale Cl, N16 *off Stoke Newington Ch St* **94** A3
Sandall Cl, W5 **105** H4
Sandall Ho, E3 *off Daling Way* **113** H2
Sandall Rd, NW5 **92** C6
W5 **105** H4
Sandal Rd, N18 **60** D5
New Malden KT3 **182** D5
Sandal St, E15 **114** E1
Sandalwood Cl, E1 *off Solebay St* **113** H4
Barn. EN5 **39** F5
Sandalwood Rd, Felt. TW13 **160** B3
Sandbach Pl, SE18 **137** F4
Sandbourne Av, SW19 **184** E3
Sandbourne Rd, SE4 **153** H2
Sandbrook Cl, NW7 **54** D6
Sandbrook Rd, N16 **94** B3
Sandby Grn, SE9 **156** B3
Sandcroft Cl, N13 **59** H6
Sandell St, SE1 **27** E3
Sanders Cl, Hmptn. (Hmptn H.) TW12 **161** J5
Sanders La, NW7 **56** A7
Sanderson Cl, NW5 **92** B4
Sanderson Sq, Brom. BR1 **192** D3
Sanderstead Av, NW2 **90** B2
Sanderstead Cl, SW12 **150** C7
Sanderstead Rd, E10 **95** H1
South Croydon CR2 **202** A7
Sanders Way, N19 *off Sussex Way* **92** D1
Sandfield Gdns, Th.Hth. CR7 **187** H3
Sandfield Pas, Th.Hth. CR7 **187** J3
Sandfield Rd, Th.Hth. CR7 **187** H3
Sandford Av, N22 **59** J7
Loughton IG10 **49** F3
Sandford Cl, E6 **116** C4
Sandford Ct, N16 **94** B1
Sandford Rd, E6 **116** B4
Bexleyheath DA7 **159** E4
Bromley BR2 **191** G4
Sandford St, SW6 *off King's Rd* **129** E7
Sandgate Ho, E5 *off Downs Pk Rd* **95** E4
W5 *off Queens Wk* **105** F5
Sandgate La, SW18 **167** H1
Sandgate Rd, Well. DA16 **138** C7
Sandgate St, SE15 **132** E6
Sandham Pt, SE18 *off Vincent Rd* **137** E4
Sandhills, Wall. SM6 **200** D4
Sandhills, The, SW10 *off Limerston St* **30** D5
Sandhurst Av, Har. HA2 **67** H6
Surbiton KT5 **182** B7
Sandhurst Cl, NW9 **70** A3
Sandhurst Dr, Ilf. IG3 **99** J4
Sandhurst Rd, N9 **45** F6
NW9 **70** A3
SE6 **172** D1
Bexley DA5 **158** D5
Sidcup DA15 **175** J3
Sandhurst Way, S.Croy. CR2 **202** B7
Sandifer Dr, NW2 **90** A3
Sandiford Rd, Sutt. SM3 **198** C2
Sandiland Cres, Brom. BR2 **205** F2
Sandilands, Croy. CR0 **202** D2
Sandilands Rd, SW6 **148** E1
Sandison St, SE15 **152** C3
Sandland St, WC1 **18** D2
Sandling Ri, SE9 **174** D3
Sandlings, The, N22 **75** G2
Sandlings Cl, SE15 *off Pilkington Rd* **152** E2
Sandmartin Way, Wall. SM6 **186** A7
Sandmere Rd, SW4 **150** E4
Sandon Cl, Esher KT10 **180** A7
Sandow Cres, Hayes UB3 **121** J3
Sandown Av, Dag. RM10 **101** J6
Sandown Cl, Houns. TW5 **142** A1
Sandown Ct, Sutt. SM2 *off Grange Rd* **198** E7
Sandown Rd, SE25 **188** E5
Sandown Way, Nthlt. UB5 **85** E6
Sandpiper Cl, E17 **77** G1
SE16 **133** J2
Sandpiper Rd, Sutt. SM1 **198** C5
Sandpit Pl, SE7 **136** B5
Sandpit Rd, Brom. BR1 **172** E5
Sandpits Rd, Croy. CR0 **203** G4
Richmond TW10 **163** G2
Sandra Cl, N22 **75** J1
Hounslow TW3 **143** H5
Sandridge Cl, Har. HA1 **68** B4
Sandridge St, N19 **92** C2
Sandringham Av, SW20 **184** B1
Sandringham Cl, SW19 **166** A1
Enfield EN1 **44** B2
Ilford IG6 **81** F3
Sandringham Ct, W9 **6** D4
Kingston upon Thames KT2 *off Skerne Wk* **181** G1
Sandringham Cres, Har. HA2 **85** G2
Sandringham Dr, Well. DA16 **157** H2
Sandringham Flats, WC2 *off Charing Cross Rd* **17** J5
Sandringham Gdns, N8 **75** E6
N12 **57** F6
Hounslow TW5 **142** A1
Ilford IG6 **81** F3
West Molesey KT8 *off Rosemary Av* **179** G4
Sandringham Ms, W5 *off High St* **105** G7
Hampton TW12 *off Oldfield Rd* **179** F1
Sandringham Rd, E7 **97** J5
E8 **94** C5
E10 **78** D6
N22 **75** J3
NW2 **89** H6
NW11 **72** B7
Barking IG11 **99** J6
Bromley BR1 **173** G5
Hounslow (Lon.Hthrw Air.) TW6 **140** B5
Northolt UB5 **85** G7
Thornton Heath CR7 **187** J5
Worcester Park KT4 **197** G3
Sandrock Pl, Croy. CR0 **203** G4
Sandrock Rd, SE13 **154** A3
SANDS END, SW6 **149** F1
Sand's End La, SW6 **149** E1
Sandstone La, E16 **115** H7
Sandstone Pl, N19 **92** B2
Sandstone Rd, SE12 **173** H2
Sands Way, Wdf.Grn. IG8 **64** B6
Sandtoft Rd, SE7 **135** H6
Sandwell Cres, NW6 **90** D6
Sandwich St, WC1 **10** A4
Sandwick Cl, NW7 **55** G7
Sandy Bury, Orp. BR6 **207** G3
Sandycombe Rd, Felt. TW14 **160** A1
Richmond TW9 **146** A3
Sandycoombe Rd, Twick. TW1 **145** F6
Sandycroft, SE2 **138** A6
Sandy Hill Av, SE18 **136** E5
Sandy Hill Rd, SE18 **136** E5
Sandyhill Rd, Ilf. IG1 **98** E4
Sandy La, Har. HA3 **69** J6
Kingston upon Thames KT1 **162** D7
Mitcham CR4 **186** A1
Northwood HA6 **50** A5
Richmond TW10 **163** F2
Sidcup DA14 **176** D7
Sutton SM2 **198** B7
Teddington TW11 **162** D7
Walton-on-Thames KT12 **178** B6
Sandy La Est, Richmond TW10 **163** G2
Sandy La N, Wall. SM6 **200** D6
Sandy La S, Wall. SM6 **200** D6
Sandymount Av, Stan. HA7 **53** F5
Sandy Ridge, Chis. BR7 **174** D6
Sandy Rd, NW3 **90** E3
Sandy's Row, E1 **21** E2
Sandy Way, Croy. CR0 **203** J3
Sanford La, N16 *off Lawrence Bldgs* **94** C2
Sanford St, SE14 **133** H6
Sanford Ter, N16 **94** C3
Sanford Wk, N16 *off Sanford Ter* **94** C2
SE14 *off Cold Blow La* **133** H6
Sangam Cl, Sthl. UB2 *off Dudley Rd* **122** E3
Sanger Av, Chess. KT9 **195** H5
Sangley Rd, SE6 **154** B7
SE25 **188** B4
Sangora Rd, SW11 **149** G4
San Ho, E9 *off Bradstock Rd* **95** G6
Sansom Rd, E11 **97** E2
Sansom St, SE5 **132** A7
Sans Wk, EC1 **11** F5
Santley St, SW4 **151** F4
Santos Rd, SW18 **148** D5
Santway, The, Stan. HA7 **52** B5
Sapcote Trd Cen, NW10 **89** F5
Saperton Wk, SE11 **34** D1
Saphora Cl, Orp. BR6 **207** G5
Sapperton Ct, EC1 **11** J5
Sapphire Cl, E6 **116** D6
Dagenham RM8 **100** C1
Sapphire Rd, NW10 **88** C7
SE8 **133** H4
Saracen Cl, Croy. CR0 **188** A6
Saracen's Head Yd, EC3 **21** E4
Saracen St, E14 **114** A6
Sara Ct, Beck. BR3 **190** B1
Sarah Ho, SW15 **147** F4
Saratoga Rd, E5 **95** F4
Sardinia St, WC2 **18** C4
Sarita Cl, Har. HA3 **68** A2
Sarjant Path, SW19 *off Queensmere Rd* **166** A2
Sark Cl, Houns. TW5 **123** G7
Sark Ho, N1 *off Clifton Rd* **93** J6
Sark Twr, SE28 **137** F2
Sark Wk, E16 **115** H6
Sarnesfield Ho, SE15 *off Pencraig Way* **132** E6
Sarnesfield Rd, Enf. EN2 *off Church St* **44** A3
Sarre Rd, NW2 **90** C5
Sarsen Av, Houns. TW3 **143** F2
Sarsfeld Rd, SW12 **167** J1
Sarsfield Rd, Grnf. (Perivale) UB6 **105** E2
Sartor Rd, SE15 **153** G4
Sarum Ter, E3 *off Bow Common La* **113** J4
Satanita Cl, E16 *off High Meads Rd* **116** A6
Satchell Mead, NW9 **71** F1
Satchwell Rd, E2 **13** H4
Sattar Ms, N16 *off Clissold Rd* **94** A3
Saturn Ho, E3 *off Garrison Rd* **114** A1
Sauls Grn, E11 *off Napier Rd* **97** E3
Saunders Cl, E14 *off Limehouse Causeway* **113** J7
Ilford IG1 **99** G1
Saunders Ness Rd, E14 **134** C5
Saunders Rd, SE18 **137** J5
Saunders St, SE11 **34** E2
Saunders Way, SE28 *off Oriole Way* **118** B7
Saunderton Rd, Wem. HA0 **86** E5
Saunton Av, Hayes UB3 **121** J7
Savage Gdns, E6 **116** C6
EC3 **21** E5
Savannah Cl, SE15 *off Chandler Way* **132** C7
Savera Cl, Sthl. UB2 *off Scotts Rd* **122** C3
Savernake Rd, N9 **44** D6
NW3 **91** J4
Savery Dr, Surb. (Long Dit.) KT6 **181** F7
Savile Cl, N.Mal. KT3 **183** E5
Thames Ditton KT7 **194** C1
Savile Gdns, Croy. CR0 **202** C2
Savile Row, W1 **17** F5
Saville Rd, E16 **136** B1
W4 **126** D3
Romford RM6 **83** F6
Twickenham TW1 **162** C1
Saville Row, Brom. BR2 **205** F1
Enfield EN3 **45** G2

Savill Gdns, SW20 *off Bodnant Gdns* **183** G3
Savill Row, Wdf.Grn. IG8 **63** F6
Savona Cl, SW19 **166** B7
Savona Est, SW8 **130** C7
Savona St, SW8 **130** C7
Savoy Av, Hayes UB3 **121** H5
Savoy Bldgs, WC2 **18** C6
Savoy Circ, W3 **107** F7
Savoy Cl, E15 *off Arthingworth St* **114** E1
Edgware HA8 **54** A5
Savoy Ct, WC2 **18** B6
Savoy Hill, WC2 **18** C6
Savoy Ms, SW9 **150** E3
Savoy Pl, WC2 **18** B6
Savoy Row, WC2 **18** C5
Savoy Steps, WC2 *off Savoy Row* **18** C6
Savoy St, WC2 **18** C5
Savoy Way, WC2 **18** C6
Sawbill Cl, Hayes UB4 **102** D5
Sawkins Cl, SW19 **166** B2
Sawley Rd, W12 **127** G1
Sawmill Yd, E3 **113** H1
Sawtry Cl, Cars. SM5 **185** G7
Sawyer Cl, N9 **60** D2
Sawyers Cl, Dag. RM10 **101** J6
Sawyer's Hill, Rich. TW10 **146** B7
Sawyers Lawn, W13 **104** C6
Sawyer St, SE1 **27** J3
Saxby Rd, SW2 **150** E7
Saxham Rd, Bark. IG11 **117** H2
Saxlingham Rd, E4 **62** D3
Saxon Av, Felt. TW13 **161** F2
Saxonbury Av, Sun. TW16 **178** B3
Saxonbury Cl, Mitch. CR4 **185** G3
Saxonbury Gdns, Surb. (Long Dit.) KT6 **195** F1
Saxon Cl, E17 **78** A7
Surbiton KT6 **181** G6
Saxon Dr, W3 **106** B6
Saxonfield Cl, SW2 **151** F7
Saxon Gdns, Sthl. UB1 *off Saxon Rd* **103** E7
Saxon Rd, E3 **113** J2
E6 **116** C4
N22 **75** H1
SE25 **188** A5
Bromley BR1 **173** F7
Ilford IG1 **99** E6
Kingston upon Thames KT2 **181** H1
Southall UB1 **123** E1
Wembley HA9 **88** C3
Saxon Ter, SE6 *off Neuchatel Rd* **171** J2
Saxon Wk, Sid. DA14 **176** C6
Saxon Way, N14 **42** D6
Saxton Cl, SE13 **154** D3
Sayers Wk, Rich. TW10 *off Stafford Pl* **145** J7
Sayesbury La, N18 **60** D5
Sayes Ct, SE8 *off Sayes Ct St* **133** J6
Sayes Ct St, SE8 **133** J6
Scadbury Pk, Chis. BR7 **175** J6
Scads Hill Cl, Orp. BR6 **193** J6
Scala St, W1 **17** G1
Scales Rd, N17 **76** C3
Scampston Ms, W10 **108** A6
Scampton Rd, Houns. (Lon.Hthrw Air.) TW6 *off Southampton Rd E* **140** C6
Scandrett St, E1 **132** E1
Scarba Wk, N1 *off Marquess Rd* **94** A6
Scarborough Rd, E11 **96** D1
N4 **75** G7
N9 **45** F7
Hounslow (Lon.Hthrw Air.) TW6 *off Southern Perimeter Rd* **141** F6
Scarborough St, E1 **21** G4
Scarbrook Rd, Croy. CR0 **201** J3
Scarle Rd, Wem. HA0 **87** G6
Scarlet Rd, SE6 **172** E3
Scarlette Manor Way, SW2 *off Papworth Way* **151** G7
Scarsbrook Rd, SE3 **156** A3
Scarsdale Pl, W8 **22** A5
Scarsdale Rd, Har. HA2 **85** J3
Scarsdale Vil, W8 **128** D3
Scarth Rd, SW13 **147** F3
Scawen Cl, Cars. SM5 **200** A4
Scawen Rd, SE8 **133** H5
Scawfell St, E2 **13** G2
Scaynes Link, N12 **56** D5
Sceaux Gdns, SE5 **152** B1
Sceptre Rd, E2 **113** F3
Schofield Wk, SE3 *off Dornberg Cl* **135** H7
Scholars Cl, Barn. EN5 **40** B4
Scholars Pl, N16 *off Oldfield Rd* **94** B3
Scholars Rd, E4 **62** C1
SW12 **168** C1
Scholefield Rd, N19 **92** D1
Schomberg Ho, SW1 *off Page St* **33** J1
Schonfeld Sq, N16 **94** A2
Schoolbank Rd, SE10 **135** F4
Schoolbell Ms, E3 *off Arbery Rd* **113** H2
Schoolhouse Gdns, Loug. IG10 **48** E4
Schoolhouse La, E1 **113** G7
School Ho La, Tedd. TW11 **163** E7
Schoolhouse Yd, SE18 *off Bloomfield Rd* **137** E5
School La, Chig. IG7 **65** J4
Kingston upon Thames KT1 *off School Rd* **181** F1
Pinner HA5 **66** E4
Surbiton KT6 **196** A1
Welling DA16 **158** B3
School Pas, Kings.T. KT1 **181** J2
Southall UB1 **123** F1
School Rd, E12 *off Sixth Av* **98** C4
NW10 **106** D4
Chislehurst BR7 **193** F1
Dagenham RM10 **119** G1
East Molesey KT8 **180** A4
Hampton (Hmptn H.) TW12 **161** J6
Hounslow TW3 **143** J3
Kingston upon Thames KT1 **181** F1
West Drayton (Harm.) UB7 **120** A6
School Rd Av, Hmptn. (Hmptn H.) TW12 **161** J6
School Sq, SE10 *off Greenroof Way* **135** F3
School Way, N12 **57** F4
Schoolway, N12 (Woodhouse Rd) **57** G6
School Way, Dag. RM8 **100** C3
Schooner Cl, E14 **134** D3
SE16 *off Kinburn St* **133** G2
Barking IG11 **118** B3
Schubert Rd, SW15 **148** C5
★ **Science Mus**, SW7 **23** F6
Scilly Isles, Esher KT10 **194** B2
Sclater St, E1 **13** F5
Scoble Pl, N16 *off Shacklewell La* **94** C4
Scoles Cres, SW2 **169** G1
Scope Way, Kings.T. KT1 **181** H4
Scoresby St, SE1 **27** G2
Scorton Av, Grnf. (Perivale) UB6 **104** D2
Scotch Common, W13 **104** D5
Scoter Cl, Wdf.Grn. IG8 **63** H7
Scot Gro, Pnr. HA5 **50** D7
Scotia Rd, SW2 **151** G7
Scotland Grn, N17 **76** C2
Scotland Grn Rd, Enf. EN3 **45** G5
Scotland Grn Rd N, Enf. EN3 **45** G4
Scotland Pl, SW1 **26** A1
Scotland Rd, Buck.H. IG9 **63** J1
Scotney Cl, Orp. BR6 **206** D4
Scotsdale Cl, Orp. BR5 **193** H4
Sutton SM3 **198** B7
Scotsdale Rd, SE12 **155** H5
Scotswood St, EC1 **11** F5
Scotswood Wk, N17 **60** D7
Scott Av, SW15 **148** B6
Scott Cl, SW16 **187** F1
Epsom KT19 **196** C5
West Drayton UB7 **120** C4
Scott Ct, SW8 *off Silverthorne Rd* **150** B2
W3 *off Petersfield Rd* **126** D2
Scott Cres, Har. HA2 **85** H1
Scott Ellis Gdns, NW8 **6** E4
Scottes La, Dag. RM8 *off Valence Av* **100** D1
Scott Fm Cl, T.Ditt. KT7 **194** E1
Scott Gdns, Houns. TW5 **122** D7
Scott Ho, E13 *off Queens Rd W* **115** G2
N18 **60** D5
Scott Lidgett Cres, SE16 **29** H4
Scott Rd, Edg. HA8 **70** B2
Scott Russell Pl, E14 *off Westferry Rd* **134** B5
Scotts Av, Brom. BR2 **190** D2
Scotts Dr, Hmptn. TW12 **161** H7
Scotts Fm Rd, Epsom KT19 **196** C6
Scotts La, Brom. BR2 **190** D3
Scotts Pas, SE18 *off Spray St* **137** E4
Scotts Rd, E10 **96** C1
W12 **127** H2
Bromley BR1 **173** G7
Southall UB2 **122** C3
Scott St, E1 **112** E4
Scott Trimmer Way, Houns. TW3 **143** E2
Scottwell Dr, NW9 **71** F5
Scoulding Rd, E16 **115** F6
Scouler St, E14 *off Quixley St* **114** D7
Scout App, NW10 **88** E4
Scout La, SW4 *off Old Town* **150** C3
Scout Way, NW7 **54** D4
Scovell Cres, SE1 **27** J4
Scovell Rd, SE1 **27** J4
Scrattons Ter, Bark. IG11 **118** D2
Scriven St, E8 **112** C1
Scrooby St, SE6 **154** B6
Scrubs La, NW10 **107** G3
W10 **107** G3
Scrutton Cl, SW12 **150** D7
Scrutton St, EC2 **12** D6
Scudamore La, NW9 **70** C3
Scutari Rd, SE22 **153** F5
Scylla Cres, Houns. (Lon.Hthrw Air.) TW6 **141** E7
Scylla Rd, SE15 **152** E3
Hounslow (Lon.Hthrw Air.) TW6 **141** E6
Seabright St, E2 *off Bethnal Grn Rd* **112** E3
Seabrook Dr, W.Wick. BR4 **204** E2
Seabrook Gdns, Rom. RM7 **83** G7
Seabrook Rd, Dag. RM8 **100** D3
Seacole Cl, W3 **106** D5
Seacon Twr, E14 **133** J2
Seacourt Rd, SE2 **138** D2
Seacroft Gdns, Wat. WD19 **50** D3
Seafield Rd, N11 **58** D4
Seaford Rd, E17 **78** B3
N15 **76** A5
W13 **124** E1
Enfield EN1 **44** B4
Hounslow (Lon.Hthrw Air.) TW6 **140** A5
Seaford St, WC1 **10** B4
Seaforth Av, N.Mal. KT3 **183** H5
Seaforth Cres, N5 **93** J5
Seaforth Gdns, N21 **43** F7
Epsom KT19 **197** F4
Woodford Green IG8 **63** J5
Seaforth Pl, SW1 *off Buckingham Gate* **25** G5
Seagrave Cl, E1 *off Wellesley St* **113** G5
Seagrave Rd, SW6 **128** D6
Seagry Rd, E11 **79** G6
Seagull Cl, Bark. IG11 **118** A3
Seagull La, E16 **115** G7
Sealand Rd, Houns. (Lon.Hthrw Air.) TW6 **140** D6
Sealand Wk, Nthlt. UB5 *off Wayfarer Rd* **102** E3
Seal St, E8 **94** C4
Searle Pl, N4 **93** F1
Searles Cl, SW11 **129** H7
Searles Dr, E6 **116** E5
Searles Rd, SE1 **36** C1
Sears St, SE5 **36** B7
Seasons Cl, W7 **124** B1
Seasprite Cl, Nthlt. UB5 **102** D3
Seaton Av, Ilf. IG3 **99** H5
Seaton Cl, E13 *off New Barn St* **115** H4
SE11 **35** F3
SW15 **165** H1
Twickenham TW2 **144** A6
Seaton Gdns, Ruis. HA4 **84** A3
Seaton Pt, E5 **94** D4
Seaton Rd, Hayes UB3 **121** G4
Mitcham CR4 **185** H2
Twickenham TW2 **143** J6
Welling DA16 **138** C7
Wembley HA0 **105** H2
Seaton Sq, NW7 *off Tavistock Av* **56** A7
Seaton St, N18 **60** D5
Sebastian Ct, Bark. IG11 *off Meadow Rd* **99** J7
Sebastian St, EC1 **11** H4
Sebastopol Rd, N9 **60** D4
Sebbon St, N1 **93** H7
Sebergham Gro, NW7 **55** G7
Sebert Rd, E7 **97** H5
Sebright Pas, E2 **13** J2
Sebright Rd, Barn. EN5 **40** A2
Secker Cres, Har. HA3 **67** J1
Secker St, SE1 **27** E2
Second Av, E12 **98** B4
E13 **115** G3
E17 **78** A5
N18 **61** F4
NW4 **72** A4
SW14 **146** E3
W3 **127** F1
W10 **108** B4
Second Av, Dag. RM10 **119** H1
Enfield EN1 **44** C5
Hayes UB3 **121** J1
Romford RM6 **82** C5
Walton-on-Thames KT12 **178** B6
Wembley HA9 **87** G2
Second Cl, W.Mol. KT8 **179** J4
Second Cross Rd, Twick. TW2 **162** B2
Second Way, Wem. HA9 **88** B4
Sedan Way, SE17 **36** D3
Sedcombe Cl, Sid. DA14 *off Knoll Rd* **176** B4
Sedcote Rd, Enf. EN3 **45** F5
Sedding St, SW1 **32** B1
Seddon Highwalk, EC2 *off The Barbican* **19** J1
Seddon Ho, EC2 *off The Barbican* **19** J1
Seddon Rd, Mord. SM4 **185** G5
Seddon St, WC1 **10** D4
Sedgebrook Rd, SE3 **156** A2
Sedgecombe Av, Har. HA3 **69** F5
Sedgeford Rd, W12 **127** F1
Sedgehill Rd, SE6 **172** B5
Sedgemere Av, N2 **73** F3
Sedgemere Rd, SE2 **138** C3
Sedgemoor Dr, Dag. RM10 **101** G4
Sedge Rd, N17 **61** F7
Sedgeway, SE6 **173** F1
Sedgewood Cl, Brom. BR2 **191** F7
Sedgmoor Pl, SE5 **132** B7
Sedgwick Rd, E10 **96** C2
Sedgwick St, E9 **95** G5
Sedleigh Rd, SW18 **148** C6
Sedlescombe Rd, SW6 **128** C6
Sedley Pl, W1 **16** D4
Sedley Ri, Loug. IG10 **48** C2
Sedum Cl, NW9 **70** B5
Seeley Dr, SE21 **170** B4
Seelig Av, NW9 **71** G7
Seely Rd, SW17 **168** A6
Seething La, EC3 **21** E6
Seething Wells La, Surb. KT6 **181** F6
Sefton Av, NW7 **54** D5
Harrow HA3 **68** A1
Sefton Cl, Orp. BR5 **193** J4
Sefton Rd, Croy. CR0 **202** D1
Orpington BR5 **193** J4
Sefton St, SW15 **147** J2
Segal Cl, SE23 **153** H7
Sekforde St, EC1 **11** G6
Sekhon Ter, Felt. TW13 **161** G3
Selan Gdns, Hayes UB4 **102** B5
Selbie Av, NW10 **89** F5
Selborne Av, E12 *off Walton Rd* **98** D4
Bexley DA5 **176** E1
Selborne Gdns, NW4 **71** G4
Greenford (Perivale) UB6 **104** D1
Selborne Rd, E17 **77** J5
N14 **58** E3
N22 **75** F1
SE5 *off Denmark Hill* **152** A2
Croydon CR0 **202** B3
Ilford IG1 **98** D2
New Malden KT3 **182** E2
Sidcup DA14 **176** B4
Selborne Wk, E17 *off The Mall Walthamstow* **77** J4
Selbourne Av, E17 **77** J4
Surbiton KT6 **195** J2
Selby Chase, Ruis. HA4 **84** B2
Selby Cl, E6 *off Linton Gdns* **116** B5
Chessington KT9 **195** H7
Chislehurst BR7 **174** D6
Selby Gdns, Sthl. UB1 **103** G4
Selby Grn, Cars. SM5 **185** H7
Selby Rd, E11 **96** E3
E13 **115** H5
N17 **60** B6
SE20 **188** D2
W5 **105** E4
Carshalton SM5 **185** H7
Selby Sq, W10 **108** B3
Selby St, E1 **13** J6
Selden Rd, SE15 **153** F2
Selden Wk, N7 *off Durham Rd* **93** F2
★ **Selfridges**, W1 **16** C4
SELHURST, SE25 **188** B6
Selhurst Cl, SW19 **166** A1
Selhurst New Rd, SE25 **188** B6
Selhurst Pl, SE25 **188** B6
Selhurst Rd, N9 **60** A3
SE25 **188** B5
Selinas La, Dag. RM8 **83** E7
Selkirk Rd, SW17 **167** H4
Twickenham TW2 **161** J2

Sellers Cl, Borwd. WD6 . . . . **38** C1
Sellers Hall Cl, N3 . . . . **56** D7
Sellincourt Rd, SW17 . . . . **167** H5
Sellindge Cl, Beck. BR3 . . . **171** J7
Sellons Av, NW10 . . . . **107** F1
Sellwood Dr, Barn. EN5 . . . **40** A5
Sellwood St, SW2
off Brockwell Pk Row . **151** G7
Selsdon Av, S.Croy. CR2 . . **202** A6
Selsdon Cl, Rom. RM5 . . . . **83** J1
Surbiton KT6 . . . . **181** H5
Selsdon Rd, E11 . . . . **79** G7
E13 . . . . **115** J1
NW2 . . . . **89** F2
SE27 . . . . **169** H3
South Croydon CR2 . . . **202** A5
Selsdon Rd Ind Est,
S.Croy. CR2
off Selsdon Rd **202** A7
Selsdon Way, E14 . . . . **134** B3
Selsea Pl, N16
off Crossway **94** B5
Selsey Cres, Well. DA16 . . . **158** D1
Selsey St, E14 . . . . **114** A5
Selvage La, NW7 . . . . **54** D5
Selway Cl, Pnr. HA5 . . . . **66** B4
Selway Ho, SW8
off South Lambeth Rd . . **151** E1
Selwood Pl, SW7 . . . . **30** E3
Selwood Rd, Chess. KT9 . . **195** G4
Croydon CR0 . . . . **202** E2
Sutton SM3 . . . . **198** C1
Selwood Ter, SW7 . . . . **31** E3
Selworthy Cl, E11 . . . . **79** G5
Selworthy Ho, SW11 . . . . . **149** G1
Selworthy Rd, SE6 . . . . **171** J3
Selwyn Av, E4 . . . . **62** C6
Ilford IG3 . . . . **81** H6
Richmond TW9 . . . . **145** H3
Selwyn Cl, Houns. TW4 . . . . **143** E4
Selwyn Ct, SE3 . . . . **155** E3
Edgware HA8 . . . . **54** B7
Selwyn Cres, Well. DA16 . . **158** B4
Selwyn Rd, E3 . . . . **113** J2
E13 . . . . **115** H1
NW10 . . . . **88** D7
New Malden KT3 . . . . . . **182** D5
Semley Pl, SW1 . . . . **32** C2
Semley Rd, SW16 . . . . **187** E2
Senate St, SE15 . . . . **153** F2
Senator Wk, SE28
off Broadwater Rd **137** G3
Sendall Ct, SW11 . . . . **149** G3
Seneca Rd, Th.Hth. CR7 . . . **187** J4
Senga Rd, Wall. SM6 . . . . . **200** A1
Senhouse Rd, Sutt. SM3 . . **198** A3
Senior St, W2 . . . . **14** A1
Senlac Rd, SE12 . . . . **173** H1
Sennen Rd, Enf. EN1 . . . . . **44** C7
Sennen Wk, SE9 . . . . **174** B3
Senrab St, E1 . . . . **113** G6
Sentamu Cl, SE24 . . . . **169** H1
Sentinel Cl, Nthlt. UB5 . . . **103** E4
Sentinel Pt, SW8
off St. George Wf **34** A5
Sentinel Sq, NW4 . . . . **71** J4
September Way, Stan.
HA7 . . . . **53** E6
Sequoia Cl, Bushey
(Bushey Hth) WD23
off Giant Tree Hill **52** A1
Sequoia Gdns, Orp. BR6 . . **193** J7
Sequoia Pk, Pnr. HA5 . . . . . **51** H6
Serbin Cl, E10 . . . . **78** C7
Serenaders Rd, SW9 . . . . . . **151** G2
Serjeants Inn, EC4 . . . . **19** F4
Serle St, WC2 . . . . **18** D3
Sermon La, EC4 . . . . **19** J4
★ **Serpentine, The**, W2 . . . **23** G2
★ **Serpentine Gall**, W2 . . . **23** F2
Serpentine Rd, W2 . . . . **23** J2
Serviden Dr, Brom. BR1 . . **192** A1
Setchell Rd, SE1 . . . . **37** F1
Setchell Way, SE1 . . . . **37** F1
Seth St, SE16
off Swan Rd **133** F2
Seton Gdns, Dag. RM9 . . . **100** C7
Settle Pt, E13
off London Rd **115** G2
Settle Rd, E13
off London Rd **115** G2
Settlers Ct, E14
off Newport Av **114** D7
Settles St, E1 . . . . **21** J2
Settrington Rd, SW6 . . . . . **148** E2
Seven Acres, Cars. SM5 . . **199** H2
Northwood HA6 . . . . **50** A6
SEVEN KINGS, Ilf. IG3 . . . . **81** H7
Seven Kings Rd, Ilf. IG3 . . . . **99** J2
Seven Kings Way, Kings.T.
KT2 . . . . **181** H1
Sevenoaks Cl, Bexh. DA7 . **159** J4
Sevenoaks Ho, SE25 . . . . . **188** D3
Sevenoaks Rd, SE4 . . . . . . **153** H6
Orpington BR6 . . . . **207** J5
Orpington (Pr.Bot.)
BR6 . . . . **207** J7
Sevenoaks Way, Orp.
BR5 . . . . **176** C7
Sidcup DA14 . . . . **176** C7
Sevenseas Rd, Houns.
TW6 *off Stratford Rd* . . . **141** F6
Seven Sisters Rd, N4 . . . . . . **93** F3
N7 . . . . **93** F3
N15 . . . . **75** J7
Seven Stars Cor, W12
off Goldhawk Rd **127** G3
Seven Stars Yd, E1 . . . . **21** G1
Seventh Av, E12 . . . . **98** C4
Hayes UB3 . . . . **122** A1
Severnake Cl, E14 . . . . **134** A4
Severn Av, W10
off Selby Sq **108** B3
Severn Dr, Esher KT10 . . . . **194** D2
Severn Way, NW10 . . . . **89** F5
Severus Rd, SW11 . . . . **149** H4
Seville Ms, N1 . . . . **94** B7
Seville St, SW1 . . . . **24** A4
Sevington Rd, NW4 . . . . **71** H6
Sevington St, W9 . . . . **6** A6
Seward Rd, W7 . . . . **124** D2
Beckenham BR3 . . . . **189** G2
SEWARDSTONE, E4 . . . . **46** C1
SEWARDSTONEBURY, E4 . . **46** E4
Sewardstone Gdns, E4 . . . . **46** B5
Sewardstone Grn, E4 . . . . . **46** E4
Sewardstone Rd, E2 . . . . . **113** F2
E4 . . . . **46** B7
Seward St, EC1 . . . . **11** H5
Sewdley St, E5 . . . . **95** G3
Sewell Rd, SE2 . . . . **138** A3
Sewell St, E13 . . . . **115** G3
Sextant Av, E14 . . . . **134** D4
Sexton Ct, E14
off Newport Av **114** D7
Seymour Av, N17 . . . . **76** D2
Morden SM4 . . . . **184** A7
Seymour Cl, E.Mol.
KT8 . . . . **179** J5
Loughton IG10 . . . . **48** B6
Pinner HA5 . . . . **67** F1
Seymour Ct, E4 . . . . **63** F2
N10 . . . . **74** A2
Seymour Dr, Brom.
BR2 . . . . **206** C1
Seymour Gdns, SE4 . . . . . **153** H3
Feltham TW13 . . . . **160** C4
Ilford IG1 . . . . **98** C1
Ruislip HA4 . . . . **84** D1
Surbiton KT5 . . . . **181** J5
Twickenham TW1 . . . . . . **144** E7
Seymour Ms, W1 . . . . **16** B3
Seymour Pl, SE25 . . . . **188** E4
W1 . . . . **15** J2
Seymour Rd, E4 . . . . **62** B1
E6 . . . . **116** A2
E10 . . . . **95** J1
N3 . . . . **57** E7
N8 . . . . **75** G5
N9 . . . . **61** E2
SW18 . . . . **148** C7
SW19 . . . . **166** A2
W4 . . . . **126** C4
Carshalton SM5 . . . . **200** A5
East Molesey KT8 . . . . . **179** J5
Hampton (Hmptn H.)
TW12 . . . . **161** J5
Kingston upon Thames
KT1 . . . . **181** G1
Mitcham CR4 . . . . **186** A7
Seymours, The, Loug.
IG10 . . . . **48** D1
Seymour St, SE18 . . . . **137** F3
W1 . . . . **15** J4
W2 . . . . **15** J4
Seymour Ter, SE20 . . . . **188** E1
Seymour Vil, SE20 . . . . **188** E1
Seymour Wk, SW10 . . . . **30** C5
Seyssel St, E14 . . . . **134** C4
Shaa Rd, W3 . . . . **106** D7
Shacklegate La, Tedd.
TW11 . . . . **162** B4
Shackleton Cl, SE23
off Featherstone Av . . . **171** E2
Shackleton Ct, E14
off Maritime Quay **134** A5
W12 . . . . **127** H2
Shackleton Rd, Sthl.
UB1 . . . . **103** F7
SHACKLEWELL, N16 . . . . . . **94** C4
Shacklewell Grn, E8 . . . . . . **94** C4
Shacklewell La, E8 . . . . **94** C5
Shacklewell Rd, N16 . . . . . . **94** C4
Shacklewell Row, E8 . . . . . . **94** C4
Shacklewell St, E2 . . . . **13** G5
Shadbolt Av, E4 . . . . **61** H5
Shadbolt Cl, Wor.Pk.
KT4 . . . . **197** F2
Shad Thames, SE1 . . . . **29** F2
SHADWELL, E1 . . . . **113** F7
Shadwell Ct, Nthlt. UB5
off Shadwell Dr **103** F2
Shadwell Dr, Northolt
UB5 . . . . **103** F3
Shadwell Gdns Est, E1
off Martha St **113** F7
Shadwell Pierhead, E1
off Glamis Rd **113** F7
Shadwell Pl, E1
off Sutton St **113** F7
Shaef Way, Tedd. TW11 . . . **162** D7
Shafter Rd, Dag. RM10 . . . **101** J6
Shaftesbury, Loug. IG10 . . . **48** A3
Shaftesbury Av, W1 . . . . **17** H5
WC2 . . . . **17** H5
Barnet (New Barn.)
EN5 . . . . **41** F4
Enfield EN3 . . . . **45** G2
Feltham TW14 . . . . **142** A6
Harrow (Kenton) HA3 . . . **69** G6
Harrow (S.Har.) HA2 . . . . **85** H1
Southall UB2 . . . . **123** G4
Shaftesbury Circle, Har.
(S.Har.) HA2
off Shaftesbury Av **85** J1
Shaftesbury Ct, N1 . . . . **12** B2
SE1 *off Alderney Ms* **28** B5
Shaftesbury Gdns, NW10 . **107** E4
Shaftesbury Ms, SW4
off Clapham
Common S Side **150** C5
W8 *off Stratford Rd* **128** D3
Shaftesbury Pl, W14
off Warwick Rd **128** C4
Shaftesbury Pt, E13
off High St **115** H2
Shaftesbury Rd, E4 . . . . **62** D1
E7 . . . . **97** J7
E10 . . . . **96** A1
E17 . . . . **78** B6
N18 . . . . **60** B6
N19 . . . . **92** E1
Beckenham BR3 . . . . **189** J2
Carshalton SM5 . . . . **185** G7
Richmond TW9 . . . . **145** H3
Shaftesburys, The, Bark.
IG11 . . . . **117** F1
Shaftesbury St, N1 . . . . **12** A2
Shaftesbury Way, Twick.
TW2 . . . . **162** A3
Shaftesbury Waye, Hayes
UB4 . . . . **102** B5
Shafto Ms, SW1 . . . . **23** J6
Shafton Rd, E9 . . . . **113** G1
Shakespeare Av, N11 . . . . . **58** C5
NW10 . . . . **106** D1
Feltham TW14 . . . . **142** A6
Hayes UB4 . . . . **102** B4
Shakespeare Cres, E12 . . . . **98** C6
Shakespeare Dr, Har. HA3 . . **69** J6
Shakespeare Gdns, N2 . . . . **73** J4
Shakespeare Rd, E17 . . . . . . **77** G2
N3 *off Popes Dr* **72** D1
NW7 . . . . **55** F4
NW10 . . . . **106** D1
SE24 . . . . **151** H5
W3 . . . . **126** C1
W7 . . . . **104** C7
Bexleyheath DA7 . . . . . . **158** E1
★ **Shakespeare's Globe**
Thea, SE1 . . . . **19** J6
Shakespeare Sq, Ilf. IG6 . . . **65** F6
Shakespeare Twr, EC2 . . . . . **20** A1
Shakespeare Way, Felt.
TW13 . . . . **160** C4
Shakspeare Ms, N16
off Shakspeare Wk **94** B4
Shakspeare Wk, N16 . . . . . . **94** B4
Shalbourne Sq, E9 . . . . **95** J5
Shalcomb St, SW10 . . . . **30** D6
Shalden Ho, SW15
off Tunworth Cres **147** F6
Shaldon Dr, Mord. SM4 . . . **184** B5
Ruislip HA4 . . . . **84** C3
Shaldon Rd, Edg. HA8 . . . . . **69** J1
Shalfleet Dr, W10 . . . . **108** A7
Shalford Cl, Orp. BR6 . . . . **207** F4
Shalimar Gdns, W3 . . . . . . **106** C7
Shalimar Rd, W3 . . . . **106** C7
Shallons Rd, SE9 . . . . **174** E4
Shalstone Rd, SW14 . . . . . **146** B3
Shalston Vil, Surb. KT6 . . . **181** J6
Shamrock Ho, SE26
off Talisman Sq **170** D4
Shamrock Rd, Croy. CR0 . . **187** F6
Shamrock St, SW4 . . . . **150** D3
Shamrock Way, N14 . . . . **58** B1
Shandon Rd, SW4 . . . . **150** C6
Shand St, SE1 . . . . **28** D3
Shandy St, E1 . . . . **113** G5
Shanklin Gdns, Wat.
WD19 . . . . **50** C4
Shanklin Ho, E17
off Sherwood Cl **77** J2
Shanklin Rd, N8 . . . . **74** D5
N15 . . . . **76** D4
Shannon Cl, NW2 . . . . **90** A3
Southall UB2 . . . . **122** D5
Shannon Commercial Cen,
N.Mal. KT3
off Beverley Way **183** G4
Shannon Cor, N.Mal.
KT3 . . . . **183** G4
Shannon Cor Retail Pk,
N.Mal. KT3 . . . . **183** G4
Shannon Gro, SW9 . . . . . . **151** F4
Shannon Pl, NW8 . . . . **7** H1
Shannon Way, Beck. BR3 . . **172** B6
Shap Cres, Cars. SM5 . . . . **199** J1
Shapland Way, N13 . . . . **59** F5
Shapwick Cl, N11 . . . . **57** J5
Shardcroft Av, SE24 . . . . . . **151** H5
Shardeloes Rd, SE4 . . . . . . **153** J3
SE14 . . . . **153** J3
Sharland Cl, Th.Hth. CR7
off Dunheved Rd N . . . **187** G6
Sharman Ct, Sid. DA14 . . . **176** A4
Sharnbrooke Cl, Well.
DA16 . . . . **158** C3
Sharnbrook Ho, W14
off Marchbank Rd **128** D6
Sharon Cl, Surb.
(Long Dit.) KT6 . . . . **195** F1
Sharon Gdns, E9 . . . . **113** F1
Sharon Rd, W4 . . . . **126** D5
Enfield EN3 . . . . **45** H2
Sharpe Cl, W7
off Templeman Rd **104** C5
Sharpleshall St, NW1 . . . . . **91** J7
Sharpness Cl, Hayes
UB4 . . . . **102** E5
Sharratt St, SE15 . . . . **133** F6
Sharsted St, SE17 . . . . **35** G4
Sharvel La, Nthlt. UB5 . . . . **102** A1
Shavers Pl, SW1 . . . . **17** H6
Shaw Av, Bark. IG11 . . . . . . **118** E2
Shawbrooke Rd, SE9 . . . . . **155** J5
Shawbury Cl, NW9 . . . . **71** E2
Shawbury Rd, SE22 . . . . . . **152** C5
Shaw Cl, SE28 . . . . **138** B1
Bushey (Bushey Hth)
WD23 . . . . **52** B2
Shaw Ct, SW11 . . . . **149** G3
Morden SM4 . . . . **185** F7
Shaw Cres, E14 . . . . **113** H5
Shaw Dr, Walt. KT12 . . . . . **178** C7
Shawfield Ct, West Dr.
UB7 . . . . **120** B3
Shawfield Pk, Brom.
BR1 . . . . **192** A2
Shawfield St, SW3 . . . . **31** H4
Shawford Ct, SW15 . . . . . . **147** G7
Shawford Rd, Epsom
KT19 . . . . **196** D6
Shaw Gdns, Bark. IG11 . . . **118** E2
Shaw Ho, N17
off Queen St **60** B6
Shaw Path, Brom. BR1
off Shroffold Rd **173** F3
Shaw Rd, SE22 . . . . **152** B4
Bromley BR1 . . . . **173** F3
Enfield EN3 . . . . **45** G1
Shaws Cotts, SE23 . . . . . . **171** H3
Shaw Sq, E17 . . . . **77** H1
Shaw Way, Wall. SM6 . . . . **200** E7
Shearing Dr, Cars. SM5
off Stavordale Rd **185** F7
Shearling Way, N7 . . . . **93** E6
Shearman Rd, SE3 . . . . **155** F4
Shearsmith Ho, E1 . . . . **21** J5
Shearwater Cl, Bark.
IG11 . . . . **118** A3
Shearwater Rd, Sutt.
SM1 . . . . **198** C5
Shearwater Way, Hayes
UB4 . . . . **102** D6
Sheaveshill Av, NW9 . . . . . . **71** E4
Sheba Pl, E1 . . . . **13** G6
Sheen Common, SW14 . . . . **146** B5
Sheen Common Dr, Rich.
TW10 . . . . **146** A4
Sheen Ct, Rich. TW10 . . . . . **146** A4
Sheen Ct Rd, Rich. TW10 . . **146** A4
Sheendale Rd, Rich. TW9 . **145** J4
Sheenewood, SE26 . . . . . . **171** E5
Sheen Gate Gdns, SW14 . . **146** C4
Sheen Gate Mans Pas,
SW14
off East Sheen Av **146** D4
Sheen Gro, N1
off Richmond Av **111** G1
Sheen La, SW14 . . . . **146** C3
Sheen Pk, Rich. TW9 . . . . . **145** J4
Sheen Rd, Orp. BR5 . . . . . . **193** J4
Richmond TW9, TW10 . . **145** H5
Sheen Way, Wall. SM6 . . . . **201** F5
Sheen Wd, SW14 . . . . **146** C5
Sheepcote Cl, Houns.
TW5 . . . . **122** A7
Sheepcote La, SW11 . . . . . **149** J2
Sheepcote Rd, Har. HA1 . . . **68** C6
Sheepcotes Rd, Rom.
RM6 . . . . **82** D4
Sheephouse Way, N.Mal.
KT3 . . . . **182** E7
Sheep La, E8 . . . . **112** E1
Sheep Wk Ms, SW19 . . . . . **166** A6
Sheerness Ms, E16 . . . . . . **137** E2

Sheerwater Rd, E16 ...... **116** A5
Sheffield Rd, Houns. (Lon.Hthrw Air.) TW6 *off Southern Perimeter Rd* **141** G5
Sheffield Sq, E3 *off Malmesbury Rd* ... **113** J3
Sheffield St, WC2 .... **18** C4
Sheffield Ter, W8 .... **128** D1
Shefton Ri, Nthwd. HA6 ... **50** A7
Shelbourne Cl, Pnr. HA5 ... **67** F3
Shelbourne Pl, Beck. BR3 . **171** J7
Shelbourne Rd, N17 ...... **76** E2
Shelburne Dr, Houns. TW4 *off Hanworth Rd* **143** G6
Shelburne Rd, N7 .... **93** F4
Shelbury Cl, Sid. DA14 ... **176** A3
Shelbury Rd, SE22 .... **153** E5
Sheldon Av, N6 .... **73** H7
Ilford IG5 .... **80** E2
Sheldon Cl, SE12 .... **155** H5
SE20 .... **189** E1
Sheldon Ct, SW8 *off Thorncroft St* **130** E7
Sheldon Pl, E2 .... **13** J2
Sheldon Rd, N18 .... **60** B4
NW2 .... **90** A4
Bexleyheath DA7 ...... **159** F1
Dagenham RM9 .... **100** E7
Sheldon Sq, W2 .... **14** D2
Sheldon St, Croy. CR0 .... **201** J3
Sheldrake Cl, E16 .... **136** C1
Sheldrake Pl, W8 .... **128** C2
Sheldrick Cl, SW19 .... **185** G2
Shelduck Cl, E15 .... **97** F5
Sheldwich Ter, Brom. BR2 .... **192** B6
Shelford Pl, N16 *off Stoke Newington Ch St* **94** A3
Shelford Ri, SE19 .... **170** C7
Shelford Rd, Barn. EN5 .... **39** J6
Shelgate Rd, SW11 ...... **149** H5
★ **Shell Cen**, SE1 .... **26** D2
Shell Cl, Brom. BR2 ...... **192** C6
Shellduck Cl, NW9 *off Swan Dr* **70** E2
Shelley Av, E12 .... **98** B6
Greenford UB6 .... **104** A3
Shelley Cl, SE15 .... **153** E2
Borehamwood WD6 .... **38** A4
Edgware HA8 .... **54** A4
Greenford UB6 .... **104** A3
Hayes UB4 .... **102** A5
Orpington BR6 .... **207** H3
Shelley Ct, N4 .... **93** F1
Shelley Cres, Houns. TW5 .... **142** D2
Southall UB1 .... **103** F6
Shelley Dr, Well. DA16 .... **157** H1
Shelley Gdns, Wem. HA0 .. **87** F2
Shelley Gro, Loug. IG10 ... **48** C4
Shelley Ho, SW1 .... **33** G5
Shelley Rd, NW10 .... **106** D1
Shelley Way, SW19 ...... **167** G6
Shellgrove Est, N16 .... **94** B5
Shellness Rd, E5 .... **95** E5
Shell Rd, SE13 .... **154** B3
Shellwood Rd, SW11 ..... **149** J2
Shelmerdine Cl, E3 ...... **114** A5
Shelton Rd, SW19 .... **184** D1
Shelton St, WC2 .... **18** A4
Shenfield Ho, SE18 *off Shooters Hill Rd* .. **136** A7
Shenfield Rd, Wdf.Grn. IG8 .... **63** H7
Shenfield St, N1 .... **12** E2
Shenley Rd, SE5 .... **152** B1
Borehamwood WD6 .... **38** A4
Hounslow TW5 .... **142** E1
Shepcot Ho, N14 .... **42** C6
Shepherd Cl, Felt. (Han.) TW13 .... **161** E4
Shepherdess Pl, N1 .... **12** A3
Shepherdess Wk, N1 ...... **12** A1
Shepherd Mkt, W1 .... **24** D1
SHEPHERD'S BUSH, W12 .... **127** J1
Shepherds Bush Grn, W12 .... **127** J2
Shepherds Bush Mkt, W12 .... **127** J2
Shepherds Bush Pl, W12 .. **128** A2
Shepherds Bush Rd, W6 .... **127** J4
Shepherds Cl, N6 .... **74** B6
W1 *off Lees Pl* **16** B5
Orpington BR6 *off Stapleton Rd* **207** J3
Romford RM6 .... **82** D5
Stanmore HA7 .... **52** D5
Shepherds Ct, W12 *off Shepherds Bush Grn* **128** A2
Shepherds Grn, Chis. BR7 .... **175** G7
Shepherds Hill, N6 .... **74** B6
Shepherds Ho, N7 *off York Way* **92** E6
Shepherds La, E9 .... **95** G5
SE28 .... **137** H1
Shepherds Path, Nthlt. UB5 *off Cowings Mead* .. **85** E6
Shepherd's Pl, W1 .... **16** B5
Shepherd St, W1 .... **24** D2
Shepherds Wk, NW2 ...... **89** G2
NW3 .... **91** G5
Bushey (Bushey Hth) WD23 .... **52** A2
Shepherds Way, S.Croy. CR2 .... **203** G7
Shepiston La, Hayes UB3 .... **121** G4
West Drayton UB7 ..... **121** F4
Shepley Cl, Cars. SM5 .... **200** A3
Sheppard Cl, Kings.T. KT1 *off Beaufort Rd* **181** H4
Sheppard Dr, SE16 .... **132** E5
Sheppard St, E16 .... **115** F4
Shepperton Cl, Borwd. WD6 .... **38** D1
Shepperton Rd, N1 .... **111** J1
Orpington BR5 .... **193** F6
Sheppey Gdns, Dag. RM9 *off Sheppey Rd* **100** C7
Sheppey Rd, Dag. RM9 ... **100** B7
Sheppey Wk, N1 *off Ashby Gro* **93** J7
Shepton Hos, E2 *off Globe Rd* **113** F3
Sherard Ct, N7 *off Manor Gdns* **92** E3
Sherard Rd, SE9 .... **156** B5
Sheraton Business Cen, Grnf. (Perivale) UB6 .... **105** E2
Sheraton St, W1 .... **17** H4
Sherborne Av, Enf. EN3 .... **45** F2
Southall UB2 .... **123** G4
Sherborne Cl, Hayes UB4 . **102** C6
Sherborne Cres, Cars. SM5 .... **185** H7
Sherborne Gdns, NW9 .... **70** A3
W13 .... **105** E6
Sherborne Ho, SW8 *off Bolney St* **131** F7
Sherborne La, EC4 .... **20** B5
Sherborne Rd, Chess. KT9 .... **195** H5
Feltham TW14 .... **141** G7
Orpington BR5 .... **193** J4
Sutton SM3 .... **198** D2
Sherborne St, N1 .... **112** A1
Sherboro Rd, N15 *off Ermine Rd* **76** C6
Sherbourne Pl, Stan. HA7 .. **52** D6
Sherbrooke Cl, Bexh. DA6 .... **159** G4
Sherbrooke Rd, SW6 ..... **128** C7
Sherbrooke Way, Wor.Pk. KT4 .... **183** H7
Sherbrook Gdns, N21 ..... **43** H7
Shere Cl, Chess. KT9 ..... **195** G5
Sheredan Rd, E4 .... **62** D5
Shere Rd, Ilf. IG2 .... **80** D5
Sherfield Cl, N.Mal. KT3 .. **182** B4
Sherfield Gdns, SW15 .... **147** F6
Sheridan Ct, Houns. TW4 *off Vickers Way* **143** E5
Northolt UB5 .... **85** H5
Sheridan Cres, Chis. BR7 . **192** E2
Sheridan Gdns, Har. HA3 .. **69** G6
Sheridan Ms, E11 *off Woodbine Pl* **79** H6
Sheridan Pl, SW13 *off Brookwood Av* **147** F2
Bromley BR1 .... **192** A2
Hampton TW12 .... **179** H1
Sheridan Rd, E7 .... **97** F3
E12 .... **98** B5
SW19 .... **184** C1
Belvedere DA17 ...... **139** G4
Bexleyheath DA7 ...... **158** E3
Richmond TW10 ...... **163** F3
Sheridan Ter, Nthlt. UB5 *off Whitton Av W* **85** H5
Sheridan Wk, NW11 .... **72** D6
Carshalton SM5 *off Carshalton Pk Rd* .. **199** J5
Sheridan Way, Beck. BR3 *off Turners Meadow Way* **189** J1
Sheringham Av, E12 ...... **98** C4
N14 .... **42** D5
Feltham TW13 .... **160** A3
Romford RM7 .... **83** J6
Twickenham TW2 ...... **161** F1
Sheringham Ct, Hayes UB3 *off Clayton Rd* **121** J2
Sheringham Dr, Bark. IG11 .... **99** J5
Sheringham Rd, N7 .... **93** F6
SE20 .... **189** E3
Sheringham Twr, Sthl. UB1 .... **103** H7
Sherington Av, Pnr. HA5 ... **51** G7
Sherington Rd, SE7 ...... **135** H6
Sherland Rd, Twick. TW1 .. **162** C1
Sherlies Av, Orp. BR6 .... **207** H2
★ **Sherlock Holmes Mus**, NW1 .... **8** A6
Sherlock Ms, W1 .... **16** B1
Sherman Gdns, Rom. (Chad.Hth) RM6 .... **82** C6
Sherman Rd, Brom. BR1 .. **191** G1
Shernhall St, E17 .... **78** C5
Sherrard Rd, E7 .... **97** J6
E12 .... **98** A6
Sherrards Way, Barn. EN5 .. **40** D5
Sherrick Grn Rd, NW10 .... **89** H5
Sherriff Rd, NW6 .... **90** D6
Sherringham Av, N17 ..... **76** D2
Sherrin Rd, E10 .... **96** A4
Sherrock Gdns, NW4 ...... **71** G4
Sherry Ms, Bark. IG11 ..... **99** G7
Sherwin Rd, SE14 .... **153** G1
Sherwood Av, E18 .... **79** H3
SW16 .... **168** D7
Greenford UB6 .... **86** B6
Hayes UB4 .... **102** B4
Sherwood Cl, E17 .... **77** J2
SW13 *off Lower Common S* .. **147** H3
W13 .... **124** E1
Bexley DA5 .... **158** C6
Sherwood Gdns, E14 ..... **134** A4
SE16 .... **37** J4
Barking IG11 .... **99** G7
Sherwood Pk Av, Sid. DA15 .... **158** A7
Sherwood Pk Rd, Mitch. CR4 .... **186** C4
Sutton SM1 .... **198** D5
Sherwood Rd, NW4 .... **71** J3
SW19 .... **166** C7
Croydon CR0 .... **188** E7
Hampton (Hmptn H.) TW12 .... **161** J5
Harrow HA2 .... **85** J2
Ilford IG6 .... **81** G4
Welling DA16 .... **157** H2
Sherwood St, N20 .... **57** G3
W1 .... **17** G5
Sherwood Ter, N20 .... **57** G3
Sherwood Way, W.Wick. BR4 .... **204** B2
Shetland Cl, Borwd. WD6 .. **38** D6
Shetland Rd, E3 .... **113** J2
Shield Dr, Brent. TW8 .... **124** D6
Shieldhall St, SE2 .... **138** C4
Shifford Path, SE23 ...... **171** G3
Shillibeer Pl, W1 .... **15** H1
Shillibeer Wk, Chig. IG7 ... **65** J3
Shillingford Cl, NW7 ...... **56** A7
Shillingford St, N1 *off Hawes St* **93** H7
Shinfield St, W12 .... **107** J6
Shinglewell Rd, Erith DA8 .... **139** G7
Shinners Cl, SE25 .... **188** D5
Ship All, W4 *off Thames Rd* **126** A6
Ship & Half Moon Pas, SE18 *off Warren La* **136** E3
Ship & Mermaid Row, SE1 .... **28** C3
Shipka Rd, SW12 .... **168** B1
Ship La, SW14 .... **146** C2
Shipman Rd, E16 .... **115** H6
SE23 .... **171** G2
Ship St, SE8 .... **154** A1
Ship Tavern Pas, EC3 ...... **20** D5
Shipton Cl, Dag. RM8 .... **100** D3
Shipton St, E2 .... **13** G3
Shipwright Rd, SE16 ..... **133** H2
Shipwright Yd, SE1 .... **28** D2
Ship Yd, E14 *off Napier Av* **134** B5
Shirburn Cl, SE23 *off Tyson Rd* **153** F7
Shirbutt St, E14 .... **114** B7
Shirebrook Rd, SE3 ...... **156** A2
Shire Ct, Epsom KT17 .... **197** F7
Erith DA18 *off St. John Fisher Rd* **138** D3
Shirehall Cl, NW4 .... **72** A6
Shirehall Gdns, NW4 ...... **72** A6
Shirehall La, NW4 .... **72** A6
Shirehall Pk, NW4 .... **72** A6
Shire Horse Way, Islw. TW7 .... **144** C3
Shire La, Kes. BR2 .... **206** C7
Orpington BR6 .... **207** G6
Shire Ms, Twick. TW2 *off Prospect Cres* **143** J6
Shire Pl, SW18 *off Swaffield Rd* **149** E7
Shires, The, Rich. (Ham) TW10 .... **163** H4
Shirland Ms, W9 .... **108** C3
Shirland Rd, W9 .... **108** D3
SHIRLEY, Croy. CR0 ...... **203** G3
Shirley Av, Bex. DA5 ..... **158** D7
Croydon CR0 .... **203** F1
Sutton SM1 .... **199** H4
Shirley Ch Rd, Croy. CR0 .. **203** G3
Shirley Cl, E17 *off Addison Rd* **78** B5
Hounslow TW3 .... **143** J5
Shirley Ct, Croy. CR0 ..... **203** G3
Shirley Cres, Beck. BR3 ... **189** H4
Shirley Dr, Houns. TW3 ... **143** J5
Shirley Gdns, W7 .... **124** C1
Barking IG11 .... **99** H6
Shirley Gro, N9 .... **45** F7
SW11 .... **150** A3
Shirley Hills Rd, Croy. CR0 .... **203** G5
Shirley Ho Dr, SE7 ...... **135** J7
Shirley Oaks Rd, Croy. CR0 .... **203** G1
Shirley Pk Rd, Croy. CR0 .... **203** E1
Shirley Rd, E15 .... **97** E7
W4 .... **126** D2
Croydon CR0 .... **189** E7
Enfield EN2 .... **43** J3
Sidcup DA15 .... **175** H3
Shirley St, E16 .... **115** F6
Shirley Way, Croy. CR0 ... **203** H3
Shirlock Rd, NW3 .... **91** J4
Shirwell Cl, NW7 .... **56** A7
Shobden Rd, N17 .... **76** A1
Shobroke Cl, NW2 .... **89** J3
Shoebury Rd, E6 .... **98** C7
Shoe La, EC4 .... **19** F3
Sholto Rd, Houns. (Lon.Hthrw Air.) TW6 ... **140** C5
Shona Ho, E13 *off Prince Regent La* .. **115** J5
Shooters Av, Har. HA3 ..... **69** F4
SHOOTER'S HILL, SE18 .. **157** F1
Shooters Hill, SE18 ...... **156** D1
Welling DA16 .... **156** D1
Shooters Hill Rd, SE3 .... **155** F1
SE10 .... **154** D1
SE18 .... **135** H7
Shooters Rd, Enf. EN2 ..... **43** H1
Shoot Up Hill, NW2 .... **90** B5
Shore Cl, Felt. TW14 ...... **142** A7
Hampton TW12 *off Stewart Cl* **161** E5
SHOREDITCH, E1 .... **13** F6
Shoreditch High St, E1 .... **13** E6
Shoreditch Ho, N1 .... **12** C4
Shore Gro, Felt. TW13 .... **161** G2
Shoreham Cl, SW18 *off Ram St* **148** E5
Bexley DA5 .... **176** D1
Croydon CR0 .... **189** F6
Shoreham Rd E, Houns. (Lon.Hthrw Air.) TW6 ... **140** B5
Shoreham Rd W, Houns. (Lon.Hthrw Air.) TW6 ... **140** B5
Shoreham Way, Brom. BR2 .... **191** G6
Shore Pl, E9 .... **95** F7
Shore Pt, Buck.H. IG9 ..... **63** H2
Shore Rd, E9 .... **95** F7
Shore Way, SW9 .... **151** G2
Shorncliffe Rd, SE1 .... **37** F3
Shorndean St, SE6 ...... **172** C1
Shorne Cl, Sid. DA15 ..... **158** B6
Shornefield Cl, Brom. BR1 .... **192** D3
Shornells Way, SE2 *off Willrose Cres* **138** C5
Shorrolds Rd, SW6 .... **128** C7
Shortcroft Rd, Epsom KT17 .... **197** F7
Shortcrofts Rd, Dag. RM9 .... **101** F6
Shorter St, E1 .... **21** G5
Shortgate, N12 .... **56** C4
Short Hedges, Houns. TW3, TW5 .... **143** H1
Short Hill, Har. HA1 *off High St* **86** B1
SHORTLANDS, Brom. BR1 .... **190** E3
Shortlands, W6 .... **128** A4
Hayes (Harling.) UB3 ... **121** G6
Shortlands Cl, N18 .... **60** A3
Belvedere DA17 .... **139** F3
Shortlands Gdns, Brom. BR2 .... **191** E2
Shortlands Gro, Brom. BR2 .... **190** D3
Shortlands Rd, E10 .... **78** B7
Bromley BR2 .... **190** D3
Kingston upon Thames KT2 .... **163** J7
Short Path, SE18 *off Long Wk* **136** E6
Short Rd, E11 .... **96** E2
W4 .... **126** E6
Hounslow (Lon.Hthrw Air.) TW6 .. **140** B6
Shorts Cft, NW9 .... **70** B4

Shorts Gdns, WC2 . . . . .18 A4
Shorts Rd, Cars. SM5 . . . .199 H4
Short St, NW4
off New Brent St 71 J4
SE1 . . . . .27 F3
Short Wall, E15 . . . . .114 C3
Shortway, N12 . . . . .57 H6
Short Way, SE9 . . . . .156 B3
Twickenham TW2 . . . . . .143 J7
Shotfield, Wall. SM6 . . . . .200 B6
Shott Cl, Sutt. SM1
off Turnpike La 199 F5
Shottendane Rd, SW6 . . . .148 D1
Shottery Cl, SE9 . . . . .174 B3
Shottfield Av, SW14 . . . . .146 E4
Shoulder of Mutton All,
E14 off Narrow St 113 H7
Shouldham St, W1 . . . . .15 H2
Showers Way, Hayes
UB3 . . . . .122 A1
Shrapnel Cl, SE18 . . . . . . .136 B7
Shrapnel Rd, SE9 . . . . .156 C3
Shrewsbury Av, SW14 . . . .146 C4
Harrow HA3 . . . . .69 H4
Shrewsbury Cl, Surb.
KT6 . . . . .195 H2
Shrewsbury Ct, EC1
off Whitecross St 12 A6
Shrewsbury La, SE18 . . . .156 E1
Shrewsbury Ms, W2
off Chepstow Rd 108 D5
Shrewsbury Rd, E7 . . . . . . .98 A5
N11 . . . . .58 C6
NW10
off Shakespeare Rd . . .106 D1
W2 . . . . .108 D6
Beckenham BR3 . . . . . . .189 H3
Carshalton SM5 . . . . . . .185 H6
Hounslow
(Lon.Hthrw Air.) TW6 . .141 F6
Shrewsbury St, W10 . . . . . .107 J4
Shrewsbury Wk, Islw. TW7
off South St 144 D3
Shrewton Rd, SW17 . . . . .167 J7
Shroffold Rd, Brom. BR1 . .173 E4
Shropshire Cl, Mitch.
CR4 . . . . .187 E4
Shropshire Ho, N18 . . . . . . .61 E5
Shropshire Pl, WC1 . . . . .9 G6
Shropshire Rd, N22 . . . . . . .59 F7
Shroton St, NW1 . . . . .15 G1
Shrubberies, The, E18 . . . . .79 G2
Chigwell IG7 . . . . .65 F5
Shrubbery, The, E11 . . . . . . .79 H5
Shrubbery Cl, N1
off St. Paul St 111 J1
Shrubbery Gdns, N21 . . . . .43 H7
Shrubbery Rd, N9 . . . . .60 D3
SW16 . . . . .168 E4
Southall UB1 . . . . .123 F1
Shrubland Gro, Wor.Pk.
KT4 . . . . .197 J3
Shrubland Rd, E8 . . . . .112 D1
E10 . . . . .78 A7
E17 . . . . .78 A5
Shrublands Av, Croy.
CR0 . . . . .204 A4
Shrublands Cl, N20 . . . . . . .57 G1
SE26 . . . . .171 F3
Chigwell IG7 . . . . .65 F6
Shrubsall Cl, SE9 . . . . .174 B1
Shuna Wk, N1
off St. Paul's Rd 94 A6
Shurland Av, Barn. EN4 . . . .41 G6
Shurland Gdns, SE15 . . . . .37 G7
Shurlock Dr, Orp. BR6 . . . .207 F4
Shuters Sq, W14
off Sun Rd 128 C5
Shuttle Cl, Sid. DA15 . . . . .157 J7
Shuttlemead, Bex. DA5 . . .159 F7
Shuttle St, E1 . . . . .13 H6
Shuttleworth Rd, SW11 . . .149 H2
Siamese Ms, N3
off Station Rd 72 D1
Siani Ms, N8 . . . . .75 H4
Sibella Rd, SW4 . . . . .150 D2
Sibford Ct, Mitch. CR4
off Lower Grn W 185 J3
Sibley Cl, Bexh. DA6 . . . . .158 E5
Bromley BR1 . . . . .192 B5
Sibley Gro, E12 . . . . .98 B7
Sibthorpe Rd, SE12 . . . . . .155 H6
Sibthorp Rd, Mitch. CR4
off Holborn Way 185 J2
Sibton Rd, Cars. SM5 . . . .185 H7
Sicilian Av, WC1 . . . . .18 B2
Sidbury St, SW6 . . . . .148 B1
SIDCUP, DA14 & DA15 . . .175 J4
Sidcup Bypass, Chis.
BR7 . . . . .175 H4
Orpington BR5 . . . . .176 D7
Sidcup DA14 . . . . .175 H4
Sidcup High St, Sid.
DA14 . . . . .176 A4
Sidcup Hill, Sid. DA14 . . . .176 B4
Sidcup Hill Gdns, Sid.
DA14 off Sidcup Hill . . .176 C5
Sidcup Pl, Sid. DA14 . . . . .176 A5
Sidcup Rd, SE9 . . . . .156 A7
SE12 . . . . .155 H5
Sidcup Tech Cen, Sid.
DA14 . . . . .176 D5
Siddeley Dr, Houns.
TW4 . . . . .142 E3
Siddons La, NW1 . . . . .8 A6
Siddons Rd, N17 . . . . .76 D1
SE23 . . . . .171 H2
Croydon CR0 . . . . .201 G3
Side Rd, E17 . . . . .77 J5
Sidewood Rd, SE9 . . . . . . .175 G1
Sidford Ho, SE1
off Briant Est 26 D6
Sidford Pl, SE1 . . . . .26 D6
Sidi Ct, N15 . . . . .75 H3
Sidings, The, E11 . . . . .96 C1
Loughton IG10 . . . . .48 B6
Sidings Ms, N7 . . . . .93 G3
Sidmouth Av, Islw. TW7 . . .144 B2
Sidmouth Cl, Wat. WD19 . . .50 B2
Sidmouth Dr, Ruis. HA4 . . .84 A3
Sidmouth Par, NW2
off Sidmouth Rd 89 J7
Sidmouth Rd, E10 . . . . .96 C3
NW2 . . . . .89 J7
Welling DA16 . . . . .138 C7
Sidmouth St, WC1 . . . . .10 B4
Sidney Av, N13 . . . . .59 F5
Sidney Elson Way, E6
off Edwin Av 116 D2
Sidney Gdns, Brent. TW8 . .125 F6
Sidney Gro, EC1 . . . . .11 G2
Sidney Rd, E7 . . . . .97 G3
N22 . . . . .59 F7
SE25 . . . . .188 D5
SW9 . . . . .151 F2
Beckenham BR3 . . . . . . .189 H2
Harrow HA2 . . . . .67 J3
Twickenham TW1 . . . . . .144 D6
Walton-on-Thames
KT12 . . . . .178 A7
Sidney Sq, E1 . . . . .113 F6
Sidney St, E1 . . . . .113 E5
Sidney Webb Ho, SE1 . . . . .28 C5
Sidworth St, E8 . . . . .95 E7
Siebert Rd, SE3 . . . . .135 G6
Siemens Rd, SE18 . . . . . . .136 A3
Sienna Cl, Chess. KT9 . . . .195 G6
Sigdon Pas, E8
off Sigdon Rd 94 D5
Sigdon Rd, E8 . . . . .94 D5
Sigers, The, Pnr. HA5 . . . . . .66 B6
Signmakers Yd, NW1
off Delancey St 110 B1
Sigrist Sq, Kings.T. KT2 . . .181 H1
Silbury Av, Mitch. CR4 . . . .185 H1
Silbury Ho, SE26
off Sydenham Hill Est . .170 D3
Silbury St, N1 . . . . .12 B3
Silchester Rd, W10 . . . . . . .108 A6
Silecroft Rd, Bexh. DA7 . . .159 G1
Silesia Bldgs, E8
off London La 95 E7
Silex St, SE1 . . . . .27 H4
Silk Br Retail Pk, NW9 . . . . .71 F6
Silk Cl, SE12 . . . . .155 G5
Silkfield Rd, NW9 . . . . .71 E5
Silkin Ms, SE15
off Fenham Rd 132 D7
Silk Ms, SE11 . . . . .35 F4
Silk Mills Pas, SE13
off Egeremont Rd 154 B2
Silk Mills Path, SE13
off Lewisham Rd 154 C3
Silk Mills Sq, E9 . . . . .95 J6
Silkstream Rd, Edg. HA8 . . .70 C1
Silk St, EC2 . . . . .20 A1
Silsoe Ho, NW1
off Park Village E 8 E2
Silsoe Rd, N22 . . . . .75 F2
Silver Birch Av, E4 . . . . . . .61 J6
Silver Birch Cl, N11 . . . . . . .58 A6
SE6 . . . . .171 J3
SE28 . . . . .138 A1
Silver Birch Gdns, E6 . . . . .116 C4
Silver Birch Ms, Ilf. IG6
off Fencepiece Rd 65 F6
Silvercliffe Gdns, Barn.
EN4 . . . . .41 H4
Silver Cl, SE14
off Southerngate Way . .133 H7
Harrow HA3 . . . . .52 A7
Silver Cres, W4 . . . . .126 B4
Silverdale, NW1 . . . . .9 F3
SE26 . . . . .171 F4
Enfield EN2 . . . . .43 E4
Silverdale Av, Ilf. IG3 . . . . . .81 H5
Silverdale Cl, W7 . . . . .124 B1
Northolt UB5 . . . . .85 F5
Sutton SM1 . . . . .198 C4
Silverdale Dr, SE9 . . . . . . .174 B2
Sunbury-on-Thames
TW16 . . . . .178 B2
Silverdale Gdns, Hayes
UB3 . . . . .122 A2
Silverdale Rd, E4 . . . . .62 D6
Bexleyheath DA7 . . . . . .159 H2
Hayes UB3 . . . . .122 A2
Orpington (Petts Wd)
BR5 . . . . .193 F4
Silvergate, Epsom KT19 . . .196 C5
Silverhall St, Islw. TW7 . . .144 D3
Silverholme Cl, Har. HA3 . . .69 G7
Silver Jubilee Way, Houns.
TW4 . . . . .142 B2
Silverland St, E16 . . . . . . .136 C1
Silver La, W.Wick. BR4 . . . .204 D2
Silverleigh Rd, Th.Hth.
CR7 . . . . .187 F4
Silvermead, E18
off Churchfields 79 G1
Silvermere Dr, N18 . . . . . . .61 G6
Silvermere Rd, SE6 . . . . . .154 B6
Silver Pl, W1 . . . . .17 G5
Silver Rd, SE13 . . . . .154 B3
W12 . . . . .108 A7
Silver Spring Cl, Erith
DA8 . . . . .139 H6
Silverston Way, Stan.
HA7 . . . . .53 F6
Silver St, N18 . . . . .60 B4
Enfield EN1 . . . . .44 A3
Silverthorne Rd, SW8 . . . .150 B2
Silverthorn Gdns, E4 . . . . . .62 A2
Silverton Rd, W6 . . . . .128 A6
SILVERTOWN, E16 . . . . . . .135 J2
Silvertown Way, E16 . . . . .115 F6
Silvertree La, Grnf. UB6
off Cowgate Rd 104 A3
Silver Wk, SE16 . . . . .133 J1
Silver Way, Rom. RM7 . . . . .83 H3
Silverwing Ind Est, Croy.
CR0 . . . . .201 F5
Silverwood Cl, Beck.
BR3 . . . . .172 A7
Silvester Rd, SE22 . . . . . . .152 C5
Silvester St, SE1 . . . . .28 A4
Silvocea Way, E14 . . . . . . .114 D6
Silwood Est, SE16
off Concorde Way 133 G4
Silwood St, SE16 . . . . .133 F4
Simla Ho, SE1 . . . . .28 C4
Simmil Rd, Esher (Clay.)
KT10 . . . . .194 B5
Simmons Cl, N20 . . . . .57 H1
Chessington KT9 . . . . . .195 F6
Simmons Dr, Dag. RM8 . . .101 E3
Simmons La, E4 . . . . .62 D2
Simmons Rd, SE18 . . . . . .136 E5
Simmons Way, N20 . . . . . . .57 H2
Simms Cl, Cars. SM5 . . . . .199 H2
Simms Gdns, N2 . . . . .73 F2
Simms Rd, SE1 . . . . .37 H2
Simnel Rd, SE12 . . . . .155 H7
Simon Cl, W11
off Portobello Rd 108 C7
Simon Ct, N11
off Ringway 58 C6
Simonds Rd, E10 . . . . .96 A2
Simone Cl, Brom. BR1 . . . .192 A1
Simons Wk, E15
off Waddington Rd 96 D5
Simpson Cl, N21
off Macleod Rd 43 E5
Croydon CRO 187 J6
Simpson Dr, W3 . . . . .106 D6
Simpson Rd, Houns.
TW4 . . . . .143 F6
Richmond TW10 . . . . . . .163 F4
Simpsons Rd, E14 . . . . . . .114 B7
Bromley BR2 . . . . .191 G3
Simpson St, SW11 . . . . . . .149 H2
Simpson Way, Surb. KT6
off Portsmouth Rd 181 F6
Simrose Ct, SW18
off Wandsworth
High St 148 D5
Sims Wk, SE3 . . . . .155 F4
Sinclair Ct, Beck. BR3 . . . . .172 A7
Sinclair Gdns, W14 . . . . . . .128 A2
Sinclair Gro, NW11 . . . . . . .72 A6
Sinclair Pl, SE4 . . . . .154 A6
Sinclair Rd, E4 . . . . .61 J5
W14 . . . . .128 A2
Sinclare Cl, Enf. EN1 . . . . . .44 C1
Singapore Rd, W13 . . . . . .124 D1
Singer St, EC2 . . . . .12 C4
Singleton Cl, SW17 . . . . . .167 J7
Croydon CR0
off St. Saviours Rd . . .187 J7
Singleton Rd, Dag. RM9 . .101 F5
Singleton Scarp, N12 . . . . .56 D5
Sinnott Rd, E17 . . . . .77 G1
Sion Rd, Twick. TW1 . . . . . .162 E1
SIPSON, West Dr. UB7 . . . .120 D6
Sipson Cl, West Dr.
(Sipson) UB7 . . . . .120 D6
Sipson La, Hayes
(Harling.) UB3 . . . . .120 D6
West Drayton
(Sipson) UB7 . . . . .120 D6
Sipson Rd, West Dr. UB7 . .120 D5
Sipson Way, West Dr.
(Sipson) UB7 . . . . .120 D7
Sir Alexander Cl, W3 . . . . .127 F1
Sir Alexander Rd, W3 . . . . .127 F1
Sir Cyril Black Way,
SW19 . . . . .166 D7
Sirdar Rd, N22 . . . . .75 H3
W11 . . . . .108 A7
Mitcham CR4
off Grenfell Rd 168 A6
Sir Giles Gilbert Scott
Bldg, The, SW15 . . . . . .148 B6
Sirinham Pt, SW8 . . . . .34 C6
Sirius Rd, Nthwd. HA6 . . . .50 A5
Sir James Black Ho, SE5
off Coldharbour La . . .152 A2
Sir John Kirk Cl, SE5 . . . . . .35 J7
★ Sir John Soane's Mus,
WC2 off Lincoln's
Inn Flds 18 C3
Sir Martin Bowles Ho, SE18
off Calderwood St . . .136 D4
Sir Thomas More Est,
SW3 . . . . .31 F6
Sise La, EC4 . . . . .20 B4
Siskin Cl, Borwd. WD6 . . . .38 A4
Sisley Rd, Bark. IG11 . . . . .117 H1
Sispara Gdns, SW18 . . . . .148 C6
Sissinghurst Cl, Brom.
BR1 . . . . .173 E5
Sissinghurst Rd, Croy.
CR0 . . . . .188 D7
Sissulu Ct, E6 . . . . .115 J1
Sister Mabel's Way, SE15 . .37 H7
Sisters Av, SW11 . . . . .149 J4
Sistova Rd, SW12 . . . . . . .168 B1
Sisulu Pl, SW9 . . . . .151 G3
Sittingbourne Av, Enf.
EN1 . . . . .44 A6
Sitwell Gro, Stan. HA7 . . . .52 C5
Siverst Cl, Nthlt. UB5 . . . . .85 H6
Sivill Ho, E2 . . . . .13 G3
Siviter Way, Dag. RM10 . . .101 H7
Siward Rd, N17 . . . . .76 A1
SW17 . . . . .167 F3
Bromley BR2 . . . . .191 H3
Six Acres Est, N4 . . . . .93 G2
Six Bridges Trd Est, SE1 . . .37 J4
Sixth Av, E12 . . . . .98 C4
W10 . . . . .108 B3
Hayes UB3 . . . . .121 J1
Sixth Cross Rd, Twick.
TW2 . . . . .161 J3
Skardu Rd, NW2 . . . . .90 B5
Skeena Hill, SW18 . . . . . . .148 B7
Skeffington Rd, E6 . . . . . . .116 B1
Skeffington St, SE18 . . . . .137 F3
Skelbrook St, SW18 . . . . .167 E2
Skelgill Rd, SW15 . . . . . . .148 C4
Skelley Rd, E15 . . . . .97 F7
Skelton Cl, E8
off Buttermere Wk 94 C6
Skelton Rd, E7 . . . . .97 G6
Skeltons La, E10 . . . . .78 B7
Skelwith Rd, W6 . . . . .127 J6
Skenfrith Ho, SE15
off Commercial Way . .132 E6
Skerne Rd, Kings.T. KT2 . .181 G1
Skerne Wk, Kings.T. KT2 . .181 G1
Sketchley Gdns, SE16 . . . .133 G5
Sketty Rd, Enf. EN1 . . . . . .44 B3
Skiers St, E15 . . . . .114 E1
Skiffington Cl, SW2 . . . . . .169 G1
Skinner Ct, E2
off Parmiter St 113 E2
Skinner Pl, SW1 . . . . .32 B2
★ Skinners' Hall, EC4
off Dowgate Hill 20 B5
Skinners La, EC4 . . . . .20 A5
Hounslow TW5 . . . . .143 H1
Skinner St, EC1 . . . . .11 F4
Skipsea Ho, SW18
off Fitzhugh Gro 149 G6
Skipsey Av, E6 . . . . .116 C3
Skipton Cl, N11 . . . . .58 A6
Skipton Dr, Hayes UB3 . . .121 F3
Skipworth Rd, E9 . . . . .113 F1
Skomer Wk, N1
off Ashby Gro 93 J7
Skylines Village, E14 . . . . .134 C2
Sky Peals Rd, Wdf.Grn.
IG8 . . . . .78 D1
Skyport Dr, West Dr.
(Harm.) UB7 . . . . .120 A7
Skyvan Cl, Houns. TW6
off Southern
Perimeter Rd 141 F5
Slade, The, SE18 . . . . .137 H6
Sladebrook Rd, SE3 . . . . . .156 A3
Sladedale Rd, SE18 . . . . . .137 H5
Slade Ho, Houns. TW4 . . . .143 F6
Slades Cl, Enf. EN2 . . . . . . .43 G3
Slades Dr, Chis. BR7 . . . . .175 F3
Slades Gdns, Enf. EN2 . . . .43 G2
Slades Hill, Enf. EN2 . . . . . .43 G3
Slades Ri, Enf. EN2 . . . . . . .43 G3
Slade Twr, E10 . . . . .96 A2

Slade Wk, SE17 . . . **35** H6
Slade Way, Mitch. CR4 . . . **186** A1
Slagrove Pl, SE13 . . . **154** A5
Slaidburn St, SW10 . . . **30** D6
Slaithwaite Rd, SE13 . . . **154** C4
Slaney Pl, N7
off Hornsey Rd . . . **93** G5
Slater Cl, SE18
off Woolwich New Rd . **136** D5
Slater Ms, SW4
off Old Town . . . **150** C3
Slattery Rd, Felt. TW13 . . . **160** C1
Sleaford Grn, Wat.
WD19 . . . **50** D3
Sleaford Ho, E3 . . . **114** A4
Sleaford St, SW8 . . . **33** F7
Slievemore Cl, SW4
off Voltaire Rd . . . **150** D3
Slingsby Pl, WC2 . . . **18** A5
Slippers Pl, SE16 . . . **133** E3
Slippers Pl Est, SE16
off Slippers Pl . . . **133** E3
Sloane Av, SW3 . . . **31** H2
Sloane Ct E, SW3 . . . **32** B3
Sloane Ct W, SW3 . . . **32** B3
Sloane Gdns, SW1 . . . **32** B2
Orpington BR6 . . . **207** F3
Sloane Ms, N8 . . . **75** E5
Sloane Sq, SW1 . . . **32** B2
Sloane St, SW1 . . . **24** A5
Sloane Ter, SW1 . . . **32** A1
Sloane Wk, Croy. CR0 . . . **189** J6
Slocum Cl, SE28 . . . **118** C7
Slough La, NW9 . . . **70** C6
Sly St, E1
off Cannon St Rd . . . **112** E6
Smaldon Cl, West Dr. UB7
off Walnut Av . . . **120** D3
Smallberry Av, Islw. TW7 . . **144** C2
Smallbrook Ms, W2 . . . **14** E4
Smalley Cl, N16 . . . **94** C3
Smalley Rd Est, N16
off Smalley Cl . . . **94** C2
Smallwood Rd, SW17 . . . **167** G4
Smardale Rd, SW18
off Alma Rd . . . **149** F5
Smarden Cl, Belv. DA17
off Essenden Rd . . . **139** G5
Smarden Gro, SE9 . . . **174** C4
Smarts La, Loug. IG10 . . . **48** A4
Smarts Pl, N18 . . . **60** D5
Smart's Pl, WC2 . . . **18** B3
Smart St, E2 . . . **113** G3
Smead Way, SE13 . . . **154** B3
Smeaton Cl, Chess. KT9 . . **195** G6
Smeaton Ct, SE1 . . . **27** J6
Smeaton Rd, SW18 . . . **148** D7
Woodford Green IG8 . . . **64** C5
Smeaton St, E1 . . . **132** E1
Smedley St, SW4 . . . **150** D2
SW8 . . . **150** D2
Smeed Rd, E3 . . . **96** A7
Smiles Pl, SE13 . . . **154** C2
Smith Cl, SE16 . . . **133** G1
Smithfield St, EC1 . . . **19** G2
Smithies Rd, SE2 . . . **138** B4
Smith's Ct, W1 . . . **17** G5
Smiths Fm Est, Nthlt.
UB5 . . . **103** G2
Smithson Rd, N17 . . . **76** A1
Smiths Pt, E13 . . . **115** G1
Smith Sq, SW1 . . . **26** A6
Smith St, SW3 . . . **31** J3
Surbiton KT5 . . . **181** J6
Smiths Yd, SW18
off Summerley St . . . **167** F2
Smith's Yd, Croy. CR0
off St. Georges Wk . . . **201** J3
Smith Ter, SW3 . . . **31** J4
Smithwood Cl, SW19 . . . **166** B1
Smithy St, E1 . . . **113** F5
Smock Wk, Croy. CR0 . . . **187** J6
Smokehouse Yd, EC1 . . . **19** H1
Smugglers Way, SW18 . . . **149** E4
Smyrks Rd, SE17 . . . **36** E4
Smyrna Rd, NW6 . . . **90** D7
Smythe Cl, N9 . . . **60** D3
Smythe St, E14 . . . **114** B7
Snakes La, Barn. EN4 . . . **42** B3
Snakes La E, Wdf.Grn.
IG8 . . . **63** J6
Snakes La W, Wdf.Grn.
IG8 . . . **63** G6
Snakey La, Felt. TW13 . . . **160** A4
SNARESBROOK, E11 . . . **79** E5
Snaresbrook Dr, Stan.
HA7 . . . **53** G4
Snaresbrook Rd, E11 . . . **78** E4
Snarsgate St, W10 . . . **107** J5
Sneath Av, NW11 . . . **72** C7
Snells Pk, N18 . . . **60** C6
Sneyd Rd, NW2 . . . **89** J4
Snowberry Cl, E15 . . . **96** D4
Snowbury Rd, SW6 . . . **149** E2
Snowden St, EC2 . . . **12** D6
Snowdon Cres, Hayes
UB3 . . . **121** F3
Snowdon Dr, NW9 . . . **70** E6
Snowdon Rd, Houns.
(Lon.Hthrw Air.) TW6
off Southern
Perimeter Rd . . . **141** F5
Snowdown Cl, SE20 . . . **189** G1
Snowdrop Cl, Hmptn.
TW12 *off Gresham Rd* . **161** G6
Snow Hill, EC1 . . . **19** G2
Snow Hill Ct, EC1 . . . **19** H3
Snowman Ho, NW6 . . . **109** E1
Snowsfields, SE1 . . . **28** C3
Snowshill Rd, E12 . . . **98** B5
Snowy Fielder Waye, Islw.
TW7 . . . **144** E2
Soames Pl, Barn. EN4 . . . **41** E2
Soames St, SE15 . . . **152** C3
Soames Wk, N.Mal. KT3 . . **182** E1
Soane Cl, W5 . . . **125** G2
Soap Ho La, Brent. TW8
off Ferry La . . . **125** H6
Socket La, Brom. BR2 . . . **191** H6
SOHO, W1 . . . **17** H5
Soho Sq, W1 . . . **17** H3
Soho St, W1 . . . **17** H3
Sojourner Truth Cl, E8
off Richmond Rd . . . **95** E6
Solander Gdns, E1
off Dellow St . . . **113** E7
Solebay St, E1 . . . **113** H4
Solent Ri, E13 . . . **115** G3
Solent Rd, NW6 . . . **90** D5
Soley Ms, WC1 . . . **10** E3
Solna Av, SW15 . . . **147** J5
Solna Rd, N21 . . . **60** A1
Solomon Av, N9 . . . **60** D4
Solomon's Pas, SE15 . . . **152** E4
Solon New Rd, SW4 . . . **150** E4
Solon Rd, SW2 . . . **151** E4
Solway Cl, E8
off Buttermere Wk . . . **94** C6
Hounslow TW4 . . . **143** E3
Solway Rd, N22 . . . **75** H1
SE22 . . . **152** D4
Somaford Gro, Barn. EN4 . . **41** G6
Somali Rd, NW2 . . . **90** C4
Somborne Ho, SW15
off Fontley Way . . . **147** G7
Somerby Rd, Bark. IG11 . . . **99** G7
Somercoates Cl, Barn.
EN4 . . . **41** H3
Somerfield Rd, N4 . . . **93** H2
Somerfield St, SE16 . . . **133** G5
Somerford Cl, Pnr.
(Eastcote) HA5 . . . **66** A4
Somerford Gro, N16 . . . **94** C4
N17 . . . **60** D7
Somerford Gro Est, N16
off Somerford Gro . . . **94** C4
Somerford St, E1 . . . **112** E4
Somerford Way, SE16 . . . **133** H2
Somerhill Av, Sid. DA15 . . **158** B7
Somerhill Rd, Welling
DA16 . . . **158** B2
Somerleyton Pas, SW9 . . . **151** H4
Somerleyton Rd, SW9 . . . **151** G4
Somersby Gdns, Ilf. IG4 . . . **80** C5
Somers Cl, NW1 . . . **9** H1
Somers Cres, W2 . . . **15** G4
Somerset Av, SW20 . . . **183** H2
Chessington KT9 . . . **195** G4
Welling DA16 . . . **157** J5
Somerset Cl, N17 . . . **76** A2
New Malden KT3 . . . **183** E6
Sutton SM3 . . . **197** J3
Woodford Green IG8 . . . **79** G1
Somerset Est, SW11 . . . **149** G1
Somerset Gdns, N6 . . . **74** A7
N17 . . . **60** B7
SE13 . . . **154** B2
SW16 . . . **187** F3
Teddington TW11 . . . **162** B5
Somerset Hall, N17 . . . **60** B7
★ **Somerset Ho**, WC2 . . . **18** C5
Somerset Ho, SW19 . . . **166** A3
Somerset Rd, E17 . . . **78** A5
N17 . . . **76** C3
N18 . . . **60** C5
NW4 . . . **71** J4
SW19 . . . **166** B4
W4 . . . **126** D3
W13 . . . **125** E1
Barnet (New Barn.)
EN5 . . . **41** E5
Brentford TW8 . . . **125** F6
Harrow HA1 . . . **67** J6
Kingston upon Thames
KT1 . . . **181** J2
Southall UB1 . . . **103** F5
Teddington TW11 . . . **162** B5
Somerset Sq, W14 . . . **128** B2
Somerset Waye, Houns.
TW5 . . . **122** E6
Somersham Rd, Bexh.
DA7 . . . **159** E2
Somers Ms, W2 . . . **15** G4
Somers Pl, SW2 . . . **151** F7
Somers Rd, E17 . . . **77** J4
SW2 . . . **151** F6
SOMERS TOWN, NW1 . . . **9** J3
Somerton Av, Rich. TW9 . . **146** B3
Somerton Rd, NW2 . . . **90** B3
SE15 . . . **153** E4
Somertrees Av, SE12 . . . **173** H2
Somervell Rd, Har. HA2 . . . **85** F5
Somerville Av, SW13 . . . **127** H6
Somerville Cl, SW9
off Stockwell Pk Cres . **151** F2
Somerville Rd, SE20 . . . **171** G7
Romford RM6 . . . **82** C6
Sonderburg Rd, N7 . . . **93** F2
Sondes St, SE17 . . . **36** B5
Songhurst Cl, Croy. CR0 . . **187** F6
Sonia Ct, Har. HA1 . . . **68** C6
Sonia Gdns, N12 . . . **57** F4
NW10 . . . **89** F4
Hounslow TW5 . . . **123** G7
Sonning Gdns, Hmptn.
TW12 . . . **161** E6
Sonning Rd, SE25 . . . **188** D6
Soper Cl, E4 . . . **61** J5
SE23 . . . **171** G1
Sophia Cl, N7
off Mackenzie Rd . . . **93** F6
Sophia Rd, E10 . . . **96** B1
E16 . . . **115** H6
Sophia Sq, SE16
off Rotherhithe St . . . **113** H7
Sopwith Av, Chess. KT9 . . **195** H5
Sopwith Cl, Kings.T. KT2 . **163** J5
Sopwith Rd, Houns. TW5 . **122** C7
Sopwith Way, SW8 . . . **32** D7
Kingston upon Thames
KT2 . . . **181** H1
Sorrel Cl, SE28 . . . **138** A1
Sorrel Gdns, E6 . . . **116** B5
Sorrel La, E14 . . . **114** D6
Sorrell Cl, SE14
off Southerngate Way . . **133** H7
Sorrento Rd, Sutt. SM1 . . . **198** E3
Sotheby Rd, N5 . . . **93** H3
Sotheran Cl, E8 . . . **112** D1
Sotheron Rd, SW6 . . . **129** E7
Soudan Rd, SW11 . . . **149** J1
Souldern Rd, W14 . . . **128** A3
South Access Rd, E17 . . . **77** H7
Southacre Way, Pnr. HA5 . . **66** C1
SOUTH ACTON, W3 . . . **126** A3
South Acton Est, W3 . . . **126** B2
South Africa Rd, W12 . . . **127** H1
SOUTHALL, UB1 & UB2 . . **122** D1
Southall La, Houns. TW5 . . **122** B6
Southall UB2 . . . **122** B6
Southall Pl, SE1 . . . **28** B4
Southampton Bldgs, WC2 . . **18** E3
Southampton Gdns, Mitch.
CR4 . . . **186** E5
Southampton Ms, E16
off Wesley Av . . . **135** H1
Southampton Pl, WC1 . . . **18** B2
Southampton Rd, NW5 . . . **91** J5
Southampton Rd E, Houns.
(Lon.Hthrw Air.) TW6 . . **140** D6
Southampton Rd W, Houns.
(Lon.Hthrw Air.) TW6 . . **140** B6
Southampton Row, WC1 . . **18** B1
Southampton St, WC2 . . . **18** B5
Southampton Way, SE5 . . . **36** C7
Southam St, W10 . . . **108** B4
South Audley St, W1 . . . **16** C6
South Av, E4 . . . **46** B7
Carshalton SM5 . . . **200** A7
Richmond TW9
off Sandycombe Rd . . **146** A2
Southall UB1 . . . **103** F7
South Av Gdns, Sthl.
UB1 . . . **103** F7
South Bk, Chis. BR7 . . . **175** F3
Surbiton KT6 . . . **181** H6
Southbank, T.Ditt. KT7 . . . **180** E7
Southbank Business Cen,
SW8 . . . **33** J6
South Bk Ter, Surb. KT6 . . **181** H6
SOUTH BEDDINGTON,
Wall. SM6 . . . **200** D6
South Birkbeck Rd, E11 . . . **96** D3
South Black Lion La, W6 . . **127** G5
South Bolton Gdns, SW5 . . **30** B3
SOUTHBOROUGH, Brom.
BR2 . . . **192** C6
Southborough Cl, Surb.
KT6 . . . **195** G1
Southborough La, Brom.
BR2 . . . **192** B5
Southborough Rd, E9 . . . **113** F1
Bromley BR1 . . . **192** B3
Surbiton KT6 . . . **195** H1
Southbourne, Bromley
BR2 . . . **191** G7
Southbourne Av, NW9 . . . **70** C2
Southbourne Cl, Pinner
HA5 . . . **67** E7
Southbourne Cres,
NW4 . . . **72** B4
Southbourne Gdns,
SE12 . . . **155** H5
Ilford IG1 . . . **99** F5
Ruislip HA4 . . . **84** B1
Southbridge Pl, Croy.
CR0 . . . **201** J4
Southbridge Rd, Croy.
CR0 . . . **201** J4
Southbridge Way, Sthl.
UB2 . . . **123** E2
Southbrook Ms, SE12 . . . **155** F6
Southbrook Rd, SE12 . . . **155** F6
SW16 . . . **187** E1
Southbury Av, Enf. EN1 . . . **44** D5
Southbury Rd, Enf.
EN1, EN3 . . . **44** A3
South Carriage Dr, SW1 . . . **23** J3
SW7 . . . **23** F4
SOUTH CHINGFORD, E4 . . . **61** J5
Southchurch Rd, E6 . . . **116** C2
South Circular Rd,
SE6 (A205) . . . **154** D7
SE9 (A205) . . . **156** C3
SE12 (A205) . . . **155** H6
SE18 (A205) . . . **136** D6
SE21 (A205) . . . **170** B1
SE22 (A205) . . . **171** E1
SE23 (A205) . . . **171** J1
SW2 (A205) . . . **169** G1
SW4 (A205) . . . **150** A5
SW11 (A3) . . . **149** H5
SW12 (A205) . . . **169** G1
SW14 (A205) . . . **147** E4
SW15 (A205) . . . **147** J4
SW18 (A3) . . . **149** H5
W4 (A205) . . . **126** A5
Brentford (A205) TW8 . . **126** A5
Richmond (A205) TW9 . . **146** B2
South City Ct, SE15 . . . **36** E7
South Cl, N6 . . . **74** B6
Barnet EN5 . . . **40** C3
Bexleyheath DA6 . . . **158** D4
Dagenham RM10 . . . **119** G1
Morden SM4 . . . **184** D6
Pinner HA5 . . . **67** F7
Twickenham TW2 . . . **161** G3
West Drayton UB7 . . . **120** C3
South Colonnade, The,
E14 . . . **134** A1
Southcombe St, W14 . . . **128** B4
Southcote Av, Surbiton
KT5 . . . **182** B7
Southcote Rd, E17 . . . **77** G5
N19 . . . **92** C4
SE25 . . . **189** E6
Southcott Ms, NW8 . . . **7** G2
South Countess Rd, E17 . . . **77** J3
South Cres, E16 . . . **114** D4
WC1 . . . **17** H2
Southcroft Av, Well.
DA16 . . . **157** H3
West Wickham BR4 . . . **204** C2
Southcroft Rd, SW16 . . . **168** A6
SW17 . . . **168** A6
Orpington BR6 . . . **207** H3
South Cross Rd, Ilf. IG6 . . . **81** F5
South Croxted Rd, SE21 . . **170** A3
SOUTH CROYDON, CR2 . . **201** J6
Southdale, Chig. IG7 . . . **65** G6
Southdean Gdns, SW19 . . . **166** C2
South Dene, NW7 . . . **54** D3
Southdown Av, W7 . . . **124** D3
Southdown Cres, Har.
HA2 . . . **85** H1
Ilford IG2 . . . **81** H5
Southdown Dr, SW20 . . . **166** A7
Southdown Rd, SW20 . . . **184** A1
South Dr, Orp. BR6 . . . **207** H5
South Ealing Rd, W5 . . . **125** G2
South Eastern Av, N9 . . . **60** C3
South Eaton Pl, SW1 . . . **32** C1
South Eden Pk Rd, Beck.
BR3 . . . **190** B6
South Edwardes Sq, W8 . . **128** C3
SOUTHEND, SE6 . . . **172** B4
South End, W8 . . . **22** B5
Croydon CR0 . . . **201** J4
South End Cl, NW3 . . . **91** H4
Southend Cl, SE9 . . . **156** E6
Southend Cres, SE9 . . . **156** D6
South End Grn, NW3
off South End Rd . . . **91** H4
Southend La, SE6 . . . **171** J4
SE26 . . . **171** J4
Southend Rd, E4 . . . **61** H5
E6 . . . **98** C7
E17 . . . **78** B1
E18 . . . **79** G1
South End Rd, NW3 . . . **91** H4
Southend Rd, Beck. BR3 . . **172** A7
Woodford Green IG8 . . . **79** J2
South End Row, W8 . . . **22** B5
Southern Av, SE25 . . . **188** C3
Feltham TW14 . . . **160** A1
Southern Dr, Loug. IG10 . . . **48** C6
Southerngate Way, SE14 . . **133** H7
Southern Gro, E3 . . . **113** J3

Southernhay, Loug. IG10 48 A5
Southern Perimeter Rd, Houns. (Lon.Hthrw Air.) TW6 141 G5
Southern Pl, Har. HA1 86 C4
Southern Rd, E13 115 H2
N2 73 J4
Southern Row, W10 108 B4
Southern St, N1 10 C1
Southern Way, SE10 135 F4
Romford RM7 83 G6
Southerton Rd, W6 127 J3
South Esk Rd, E7 97 J6
Southey Ms, E16
off Wesley Av 135 G1
Southey Rd, N15 76 B5
SW9 151 G1
SW19 166 D7
Southey St, SE20 171 G7
Southfield, Barn. EN5 40 A6
Southfield Cotts, W7
off Oaklands Rd 124 C2
Southfield Gdns, Twick. TW1 162 C4
Southfield Pk, Har. HA2 67 H4
Southfield Rd, N17
off The Avenue 76 B2
W4 126 E3
Chislehurst BR7 193 J3
Enfield EN3 45 E6
SOUTHFIELDS, SW18 166 D1
Southfields, NW4 71 G3
East Molesey KT8 180 B6
Southfields Ct, SW19 166 B1
Sutton SM1 *off Sutton Common Rd* 198 D2
Southfields Ms, SW18
off Southfields Rd 148 D6
Southfields Pas, SW18 148 D6
Southfields Rd, SW18 148 D6
Southfleet Rd, Orp. BR6 207 H3
South Gdns, SW19 167 G7
Wembley HA9
off The Avenue 87 J2
SOUTHGATE, N14 58 C2
Southgate Circ, N14
off The Bourne 58 D1
Southgate Gro, N1 94 A7
Southgate Rd, N1 112 A1
South Gipsy Rd, Well. DA16 158 D3
South Glade, The, Bex. DA5 177 F1
South Grn, NW9
off Clayton Fld 71 E1
South Gro, E17 77 J5
N6 92 A1
N15 76 A5
South Gro Ho, N6 92 A1
SOUTH HACKNEY, E9 95 F7
SOUTH HAMPSTEAD, NW6 91 E7
SOUTH HARROW, Har. HA2 85 H3
South Hill, Chis. BR7 174 C6
South Hill Av, Har. HA1, HA2 85 J3
South Hill Gro, Har. HA1 86 B4
South Hill Pk, NW3 91 H4
South Hill Pk Gdns, NW3 91 H4
South Hill Rd, Brom. BR2 190 E3
Southholme Cl, SE19 188 B1
South Huxley, N18 60 A5
Southill La, Pnr. HA5 66 A4
Southill Rd, Chis. BR7 174 B7
Southill St, E14
off Chrisp St 114 B6
South Island Pl, SW9 131 F7
SOUTH KENSINGTON, SW7 30 C2
South Kensington Sta Arc, SW7 *off Pelham St* 31 F1
South Kensington Underground Sta, SW7 31 F1
SOUTH LAMBETH, SW8 151 E1
South Lambeth Est, SW8
off Dorset Rd 131 F7
South Lambeth Pl, SW8 34 B5
South Lambeth Rd, SW8 34 B6
Southland Rd, SE18 137 J7
Southlands Av, Orp. BR6 207 G4
Southlands Dr, SW19 166 A2
Southlands Gro, Brom. BR1 192 B3
Southlands Rd, Brom. BR1, BR2 191 J5
Southland Way, Houns. TW3 144 A5
South La, Kings.T. KT1 181 G3
New Malden KT3 182 D4
South La W, N.Mal. KT3 182 D4
South Lo, NW8 6 E3
SW7
off Knightsbridge 23 H4
South Lo Av, Mitch. CR4 186 E4
South Lo Cres, Enf. EN2 42 D4
South Lo Dr, N14 42 E5
★ **South London Art Gall**, SE5 152 B1
Southly Cl, Sutt. SM1 198 D3
South Mall, N9
off Edmonton Grn Shop Cen 60 D3
South Mead, NW9 71 F1
Epsom KT19 197 E7
Southmead Gdns, Tedd. TW11
off Cromwell Rd 162 D6
South Meadows, Wem. HA9 87 H5
Southmead Rd, SW19 166 B1
South Molton La, W1 16 D4
South Molton Rd, E16 115 G6
South Molton St, W1 16 D4
Southmont Rd, Esher KT10 194 B2
Southmoor Way, E9 95 J6
SOUTH NORWOOD, SE25 188 C3
South Norwood Hill, SE25 188 B2
South Oak Rd, SW16 169 F4
Southold Ri, SE9 174 C3
Southolm St, SW11 150 B1
Southover, N12 56 D4
Bromley BR1 173 G5
SOUTH OXHEY, Wat. WD19 50 C3
South Par, SW3 31 F3
W4 126 D4
Edgware HA8
off Mollison Way 70 A2
South Pk, SW6 148 D2
South Pk Cres, SE6 173 F1
Ilford IG1 99 G3
South Pk Dr, Bark. IG11 99 H4
Ilford IG3 99 H4
South Pk Gro, N.Mal. KT3 182 C4
South Pk Hill Rd, S.Croy. CR2 202 A5
South Pk Ms, SW6 148 E3
South Pk Rd, SW19 166 D6
Ilford IG1 99 G3
South Pk Ter, Ilf. IG1 99 G3
South Pk Way, Ruis. HA4 84 C6
South Penge Pk Est, SE20 188 E2
South Pl, EC2 20 C1
Enfield EN3 45 F5
Surbiton KT5 181 J7
South Pl Ms, EC2 20 C2
South Pt, Sutt. SM1 199 F6
Southport Rd, SE18 137 G4
South Quay Plaza, E14 134 B2
South Quay Sq, E14
off Marsh Wall 134 B2
Southridge Pl, SW20 166 A7
South Ri Way, SE18 137 G5
South Rd, N9 60 D1
SE23 171 G2
SW19 167 F6
W5 125 G4
Edgware HA8 70 B1
Feltham TW13 160 D5
Hampton TW12 161 E6
Romford (Chad.Hth) RM6 82 E6
Romford (Lt.Hth) RM6 82 C5
Southall UB1 123 F2
Twickenham TW2 162 A3
West Drayton UB7 120 C3
South Row, SE3 155 F2
SOUTH RUISLIP, Ruis. HA4 84 C4
Southsea Rd, Kings.T. KT1 181 H4
South Sea St, SE16 133 J3
South Side, W6 127 F3
Southside Common, SW19 165 J6
Southside Shop Cen, SW18 148 E6
Southspring, Sid. DA15 157 G7
South Sq, NW11 72 E6
WC1 18 E2
South St, W1 24 C1
Bromley BR1 191 G2
Enfield EN3 45 G5
Isleworth TW7 144 D3
Rainham RM13 119 J2
South Tenter St, E1 21 G5
South Ter, SW7 31 G1
Surbiton KT6 181 H6
SOUTH TOTTENHAM, N15 76 B5
South Vale, SE19 170 B6
Harrow HA1 86 B4
Southvale Rd, SE3 155 E2
South Vw, Brom. BR1 191 H2
Southview Av, NW10 89 F5
Southview Cl, SW17 168 A5
Bexley DA5 159 F6
Southview Cres, Ilf. IG2 80 E6
South Vw Dr, E18 79 H3
Southview Gdns, Wall. SM6 200 C7
South Vw Rd, N8 74 D3
Southview Rd, Brom. BR1 172 D4
South Vw Rd, Loug. IG10 48 C6
Pinner HA5 50 B6
South Vil, NW1 92 D6
Southville, SW8 150 D1
Southville Rd, T.Ditt. KT7 180 E7
South Wk, W.Wick. BR4 204 E3
SOUTHWARK, SE1 27 H2
Southwark Br, EC4 28 A1
SE1 28 A1
Southwark Br Rd, SE1 27 H5
★ **Southwark Cath**, SE1 28 B1
Southwark Pk, SE16 133 F4
Southwark Pk Est, SE16 133 E4
Southwark Pk Rd, SE16 37 G1
Southwark Pl, Brom. BR1 192 C3
Southwark St, SE1 27 H1
Southwater Cl, E14 113 J6
Beckenham BR3 172 B7
South Way, N9 61 F2
N11 *off Ringway* 58 C6
Southway, N20 56 D2
NW11 72 E6
SW20 183 J4
South Way, Brom. (Hayes) BR2 191 G7
Croydon CR0 203 H3
Harrow HA2 67 G4
Southway, Wall. SM6 200 C4
South Way, Wem. HA9 88 A5
Southway Cl, W12 127 H2
Southwell Av, Nthlt. UB5 85 G6
Southwell Gdns, SW7 30 C1
Southwell Gro Rd, E11 96 E2
Southwell Rd, SE5 151 J3
Croydon CR0 187 G6
Harrow HA3 69 G6
South Western Rd, Twick. TW1 144 D6
Southwest Rd, E11 96 D1
South Wf Rd, W2 15 E3
Southwick Ms, W2 15 F3
Southwick Pl, W2 15 G4
Southwick St, W2 15 G3
SOUTH WIMBLEDON, SW19 166 E7
Southwold Dr, Bark. IG11 100 A5
Southwold Rd, E5 95 E2
Bexley DA5 159 H6
Southwood Av, N6 74 B7
Kingston upon Thames KT2 182 C1
Southwood Cl, Brom. BR1 192 C4
Worcester Park KT4 198 A1
Southwood Dr, Surb. KT5 182 C7
SOUTH WOODFORD, E18 79 F2
Southwood Gdns, Esher KT10 194 D3
Ilford IG2 80 E4
Southwood La, N6 74 A7
Southwood Lawn Rd, N6 74 A7
Southwood Pk, N6 74 A7
Southwood Rd, SE9 174 E2
SE28 138 B1
Southwood Smith St, N1
off Old Royal Free Sq 111 G1
South Worple Av, SW14 146 E3
South Worple Way, SW14 146 D3
Sovereign Business Cen, Enf. EN3 45 J2
Sovereign Cl, E1 113 E7
W5 105 F5
Sovereign Ct, W.Mol. KT8 179 F4
Sovereign Cres, SE16
off Rotherhithe St 133 H1
Sovereign Gro, Wem. HA0 87 G3
Sovereign Ms, E2 13 F1
Barnet EN4 41 J3
Sovereign Pk, NW10 106 B4
Sovereign Pl, Har. HA1 68 C5
Sovereign Rd, Bark. IG11 118 C3
Sowerby Cl, SE9 156 B5
Space Waye, Felt. TW14 142 A5
Spa Cl, SE25 188 B1
Spafield St, EC1 11 E5
Spa Grn Est, EC1 11 F3
Spa Hill, SE19 188 A1
Spalding Cl, Edg. HA8 55 E7
Spalding Rd, NW4 71 J6
SW17 168 B5
Spanby Rd, E3 114 A4
Spaniards Cl, NW11 91 G1
Spaniards End, NW3 91 F1
Spaniards Rd, NW3 91 F2
Spanish Pl, W1 16 C3
Spanish Rd, SW18 149 F5
Spareleaze Hill, Loug. IG10 48 C5
Sparkbridge Rd, Har. HA1 68 B4
Sparkes Cl, Brom. BR2 191 H4
Sparke Ter, E16
off Clarkson Rd 115 F6
Sparkford Gdns, N11 58 A5
Sparkford Ho, SW11 149 G1
Sparks Cl, W3 106 D6
Dagenham RM8 100 D2
Hampton TW12
off Victors Dr 161 E6
Spa Rd, SE16 29 F6
Sparrow Cl, Hmptn. TW12 160 E6
Sparrow Dr, Orp. BR5 207 F1
Sparrow Fm Dr, Felt. TW14 142 D7
Sparrow Fm Rd, Epsom KT17 197 G4
Sparrow Grn, Dag. RM10 101 H3
Sparrows La, SE9 157 F7
Sparsholt Rd, N19 93 E1
Barking IG11 117 H1
Spartan Cl, Wall. SM6 200 E7
Sparta St, SE10 154 B1
★ **Speaker's Cor**, W2 16 A5
Speaker's Ct, Croy. CR0
off St. James's Rd 202 A1
Spearman St, SE18 136 D6
Spear Ms, SW5 128 D4
Spearpoint Gdns, Ilf. IG2 81 J4
Spears Rd, N19 92 E1
Speart La, Houns. TW5 122 E7
Spedan Cl, NW3 91 E3
Speechly Ms, E8
off Alvington Cres 94 C5
Speed Highwalk, EC2
off Silk St 20 A1
Speed Ho, EC2 20 B1
Speedway Ind Est, Hayes UB3 121 G2
Speedwell St, SE8
off Comet St 134 A7
Speedy Pl, WC1 10 A4
Speer Rd, T.Ditt. KT7 180 C5
Speirs Cl, N.Mal. KT3 183 F6
Spekehill, SE9 174 C3
Speke Rd, Th.Hth. CR7 188 A2
Speldhurst Cl, Brom. BR2 191 F5
Speldhurst Rd, E9 95 G7
W4 126 D3
Spellbrook Wk, N1
off Basire St 111 J1
Spelman St, E1 21 H1
Spence Cl, SE16
off Vaughan St 133 J2
Spencer Av, N13 59 F6
Hayes UB4 102 A5
Spencer Cl, N3 72 C2
NW10 105 J3
Orpington BR6 207 H2
Woodford Green IG8 63 J5
Spencer Ctyd, N3
off Regents Pk Rd 72 C2
Spencer Dr, N2 73 F6
Spencer Gdns, SE9 156 C5
SW14 146 C5
Spencer Hill, SW19 166 B6
Spencer Hill Rd, SW19 166 B7
★ **Spencer Ho**, SW1 25 F2
Spencer Ms, SW8
off Lansdowne Way 151 F1
W6 *off Greyhound Rd* 128 B6
Spencer Pk, SW18 149 G5
Spencer Pl, N1
off Canonbury La 93 H7
Croydon CR0 188 A7
Spencer Ri, NW5 92 B4
Spencer Rd, E6 116 A1
E17 78 C2
N8 75 F5
N11 58 B4
N17 76 D1
SW18 149 G4
SW20 183 H1
W3 126 C1
W4 126 C7
Bromley BR1 173 E7
East Molesey KT8 179 J5
Harrow HA3 68 B2
Ilford IG3 99 J1
Isleworth TW7 144 A1
Mitcham CR4 186 A3
Mitcham (Bedd.Cor.) CR4 186 A7
South Croydon CR2 202 B5
Twickenham TW2 162 B3
Wembley HA0 87 F2
Spencer St, EC1 11 G4
Southall UB2 122 D2
Spencer Wk, NW3 91 G4
SW15 148 A4

Spencer Yd, SE3
off Blackheath Village 155 F2
Spenser Gro, N16 94 B4
Spenser Ms, SE21 170 A1
Spenser Rd, SE24 151 G5
Spenser St, SW1 25 G5
Spensley Wk, N16
off Clissold Rd 94 A3
Speranza St, SE18 137 J5
Sperling Rd, N17 76 B2
Spert St, E14 113 H7
Speyside, N14 42 C6
Spey St, E14 114 C5
Spezia Rd, NW10 107 G2
Sphere, The, E16
off Hallsville Rd 115 F6
Spice Quay Hts, SE1 29 G2
Spicer Cl, SW9 151 H2
Walton-on-Thames KT12 178 C6
Spice's Yd, Croy. CR0 201 J4
Spigurnell Rd, N17 76 A1
Spikes Br Moorings, Hayes UB4 102 E7
Spikes Br Rd, Sthl. UB1 103 E6
Spindle Cl, SE18 136 B3
Spindlewood Gdns, Croy. CR0 202 B4
Spindrift Av, E14 134 B4
Spinel Cl, SE18 137 J5
Spinnaker Cl, Bark. IG11 118 B3
Spinnells Rd, Har. HA2 85 F1
Spinney, The, N21 43 G7
SW16 168 D3
Barnet EN5 41 E2
Loughton IG10 48 E4
Sidcup DA14 176 E5
Stanmore HA7 53 H4
Sunbury-on-Thames TW16 178 A1
Sutton SM3 197 J4
Wembley HA0 86 D3
Spinney Cl, Beck. BR3 190 B4
New Malden KT3 182 E5
Worcester Park KT4 197 F3
Spinney Dr, Felt. TW14 141 F7
Spinney Gdns, SE19 170 C5
Dagenham RM9 101 E5
Spinney Oak, Brom. BR1 192 B2
Spinneys, The, Brom. BR1 192 C2
Spire Ho, W2 14 D5
Spires Shop Cen, The, Barn. EN5 40 B3
Spirit Quay, E1 29 J1
★ **Spitalfields City Fm**, E1 13 H6
Spital Sq, E1 21 E1
Spital St, E1 21 H1
Spital Yd, E1 21 E1
Spitfire Business Pk, Croy. CR0 201 G6
Spitfire Est, Houns. TW5 122 C5
Spitfire Rd, Wall. SM6 201 E7
Spitfire Way, Houns. TW5 122 C5
Spode Ho, SE11
off Lambeth Wk 26 E6
Spode Wk, NW6
off Dresden Cl 91 E5
Spondon Rd, N15 76 D4
Spoonbill Way, Hayes UB4
off Cygnet Way 102 D5
Spooners Ms, W3
off Churchfield Rd 126 D1
Spooner Wk, Wall. SM6 200 D5
Sporle Ct, SW11 149 G3
Sportsbank St, SE6 154 C7
Sportsman Ms, E2
off Whiston Rd 112 D1
Spotted Dog Path, E7
off Upton La 97 G6
Spottons Gro, N17 75 J1
Spout Hill, Croy. CR0 204 A5
Spratt Hall Rd, E11 79 G6
Spray La, Twick. TW2 144 B6
Spray St, SE18 137 E4
Spreighton Rd, W.Mol. KT8 179 H4
Sprimont Pl, SW3 31 J3
Springall St, SE15 133 E7
Springbank, N21 43 F6
Springbank Rd, SE13 154 D6
Springbank Wk, NW1
off St. Paul's Cres 92 D7
Springbourne Ct, Beck. BR3 190 C1
Spring Br Ms, W5
off Spring Br Rd 105 G7
Spring Br Rd, W5 105 G7
Spring Cl, Barn. EN5 40 A5
Borehamwood WD6 38 A1
Dagenham RM8 100 D1
Springclose La, Sutt. SM3 198 B6
Spring Cotts, Surb. KT6 181 G5
Spring Ct, Sid. DA15
off Station Rd 176 A3
Springcroft Av, N2 73 J4
Springdale Ms, N16
off Springdale Rd 94 A4
Springdale Rd, N16 94 A4
Spring Dr, Pnr. HA5 66 A6
Springfield, E5 94 E1
Bushey (Bushey Hth) WD23 52 A1
Springfield Av, N10 74 C3
SW20 184 C3
Hampton TW12 161 H6
Springfield Cl, N12 56 E5
Stanmore HA7 52 D3
Springfield Ct, Wall. SM6
off Springfield Rd 200 B5
Springfield Dr, Ilf. IG2 81 F6
Springfield Gdns, E5 95 E1
NW9 70 D5
Bromley BR1 192 C4
Ruislip HA4 84 B1
West Wickham BR4 204 B2
Woodford Green IG8 63 J7
Springfield Gro, SE7 135 J6
Springfield Gro Est, SE7 135 J6
Springfield La, NW6 108 E1
Springfield Mt, NW9 70 E5
Springfield Pl, N.Mal. KT3 182 C4
Springfield Ri, SE26 170 E3
Springfield Rd, E4 62 E1
E6 98 C7
E15 115 E3
E17 77 J6
N11 58 B5
N15 76 D4
NW8 109 F1
SE26 171 E5
SW19 166 C5
W7 124 B1
Bexleyheath DA7 159 H3
Bromley BR1 192 C4
Harrow HA1 68 B6
Hayes UB4 122 C1
Kingston upon Thames KT1 181 H3
Teddington TW11 162 D5
Thornton Heath CR7 187 J1
Twickenham TW2 161 G1
Wallington SM6 200 B5
Welling DA16 158 B3
Springfield Wk, NW6 108 E1
Orpington BR6
off Place Fm Av 207 G1
Spring Gdns, N5
off Grosvenor Av 93 J5
SW1 25 J1
Romford RM7 83 J5
Wallington SM6 200 C5
West Molesey KT8 179 J5
Woodford Green IG8 63 J7
Spring Gdns Business Pk, Rom. RM7 83 J5
SPRING GROVE, Islw. TW7 144 C1
Spring Gro, SE19
off Alma Pl 170 C7
W4 126 A5
Hampton TW12
off Plevna Rd 179 H1
Loughton IG10 48 A6
Mitcham CR4 186 A1
Spring Gro Cres, Houns. TW3 143 J1
Spring Gro Rd, Houns. TW3 143 H1
Isleworth TW7 143 H1
Richmond TW10 145 J5
Spring Hill, E5 76 D7
SE26 171 F4
Springhill Cl, SE5 152 A3
Springhurst Cl, Croy. CR0 203 J4
Spring Lake, Stan. HA7 52 E4
Spring La, E5 95 E1
N10 74 A3
SE25 188 E6
Spring Ms, W1 16 A1
Richmond TW9
off Rosedale Rd 145 H4
Spring Pk Av, Croy. CR0 203 G2
Spring Pk Dr, N4 93 J1
Springpark Dr, Beck. BR3 190 C3
Spring Pk Rd, Croy. CR0 203 G2
Spring Pas, SW15
off Embankment 148 A3
Spring Path, NW3 91 G5
Spring Pl, N3
off Windermere Av 72 D2
NW5 92 B5
Springpond Rd, Dag. RM9 101 E5
Springrice Rd, SE13 154 C6
Spring St, W2 15 E4
Spring Ter, Rich. TW9 145 H5
Spring Tide Cl, SE15
off Staffordshire St 152 D1
Spring Vale, Bexh. DA7 159 H4
Springvale Av, Brent. TW8 125 G5
Springvale Est, W14
off Blythe Rd 128 B3
Springvale Ter, W14 128 A3
Spring Vil Rd, Edg. HA8 54 A7
Spring Wk, E1 21 J1
Springwater Cl, SE18 156 D1
Springway, Har. HA1 68 A7
Springwell Av, NW10 107 F1
Springwell Cl, SW16
off Etherstone Rd 169 G4
Springwell Ct, Houns. TW4 142 D2
Springwell Rd, SW16 169 G4
Hounslow TW4, TW5 142 D1
Springwood Cl, E3 114 A2
Springwood Cres, Edg. HA8 54 B2
Sprowston Ms, E7 97 G6
Sprowston Rd, E7 97 G5
Spruce Ct, W5
off Elderberry Rd 125 H3
Sprucedale Gdns, Croy. CR0 203 G4
Spruce Hills Rd, E17 78 C2
Spruce Pk, Brom. BR2
off Cumberland Rd 191 F4
Sprules Rd, SE4 153 H2
Spurfield, W.Mol. KT8 179 H3
Spurgeon Av, SE19 188 A1
Spurgeon Rd, SE19 188 A1
Spurgeon St, SE1 28 B6
Spurling Rd, SE22 152 C4
Dagenham RM9 101 F6
Spur Rd, N15
off Philip La 76 A4
SE1 26 E3
SW1 25 F4
Barking IG11 117 F2
Edgware HA8 53 H4
Feltham TW14 142 B5
Isleworth TW7 124 E7
Spur Rd Est, Edg. HA8
off Green La 53 J4
Spurstowe Rd, E8
off Marcon Pl 94 E5
Spurstowe Ter, E8 94 E5
Square, The, E10 96 C3
W6 127 J5
Carshalton SM5 200 A5
Ilford IG1 80 D7
Richmond TW9 145 G5
Uxbridge UB11 121 G1
Woodford Green IG8 63 G5
Square Rigger Row, SW11
off York Pl 149 F3
Squarey St, SW17 167 F3
Squire Gdns, NW8 7 E4
Squires, The, Rom. RM7 83 J6
Squires Ct, SW19 166 D4
Squires La, N3 73 E2
Squires Mt, NW3
off East Heath Rd 91 G3
Squires Wd Dr, Chis. BR7 174 B7
Squirrel Cl, Houns. TW4 142 C2
Squirrel Ms, W13 104 D7
Squirrels, The, SE13 154 D3
Pinner HA5 67 F3
Squirrels Cl, N12 57 F4
Orpington BR6 207 H1
Squirrels Grn, Wor.Pk. KT4 197 F1
Squirrels La, Buck.H. IG9 64 A3
Squirrels Trd Est, The, Hayes UB3 121 J3
Squirries St, E2 13 J3
Stable Cl, Kings.T. KT2 163 J6
Northolt UB5 103 G2
Stable Ms, NW5
off Grafton Rd 92 B6
Twickenham TW1 162 C1
Stables, The, Buck.H. IG9 47 J7
Stables End, Orp. BR6 207 F3
Stables Ms, SE27 169 J5
Stables Way, SE11 35 E3
Stable Wk, N1
off Wharfdale Rd 111 E2
N2 *off Old Fm Rd* 73 G1
Stable Way, W10
off Latimer Rd 107 J6
Stable Yd, SW1 25 F3
SW9
off Broomgrove Rd 151 F2
SW15 *off Danemere St* 147 J3
Stable Yd Rd, SW1 25 F2
Stacey Av, N18 61 F4
Stacey Cl, E10
off Halford Rd 78 D5
Stacey St, N7 93 G3
WC2 17 J4
Stackhouse St, SW3 23 J5
Stacy Path, SE5
off Harris St 132 B7
Staddon Cl, Beck. BR3 189 H4
Stadium Business Cen, Wem. HA9 88 B3
Stadium Retail Pk, Wem. HA9
off Wembley Pk Dr 88 A3
Stadium Rd, NW2 71 H7
SE18 136 B7
Stadium Rd E, NW2 71 J7
Stadium St, SW10 129 F7
Stadium Way, Wem. HA9 87 J4
Staffa Rd, E10 95 H1
Stafford Cl, E17 77 J6
N14 42 C5
NW6 108 D3
Sutton SM3 198 B6
Stafford Ct, SW8
off Allen Edwards Dr 130 E7
W8 128 D3
Stafford Cripps Ho, E2
off Globe Rd 113 F3
SW6
off Clem Attlee Ct 128 C6
Stafford Cross Business Pk, Croy. CR0 201 F5
Stafford Gdns, Croy. CR0 201 F5
Stafford Pl, SW1 25 F5
Richmond TW10 145 J7
Stafford Rd, E3 113 J2
E7 97 J7
NW6 108 D3
Croydon CR0 201 G4
Harrow HA3 51 J7
New Malden KT3 182 C3
Sidcup DA14 175 H4
Wallington SM6 200 C6
Staffordshire St, SE15 152 D1
Stafford St, W1 25 F1
Stafford Ter, W8 128 D3
Staff St, EC1 12 C4
Stag Cl, Edg. HA8 70 B2
Staggart Grn, Chig. IG7 65 J6
Stag La, NW9 70 C3
SW15 165 F2
Buckhurst Hill IG9 63 H2
Edgware HA8 70 B2
Stag Ride, SW19 165 F3
Stagshaw Ho, SE22
off Pytchley Rd 152 B3
Stags Way, Islw. TW7 124 C6
Stainbank Rd, Mitch. CR4 186 B3
Stainby Cl, West Dr. UB7 120 B3
Stainby Rd, N15 76 C4
Stainer Ho, SE3
off Ryan Cl 155 J4
Stainer St, SE1 28 C2
Staines Av, Sutt. SM3 198 A2
Staines Rd, Felt. TW14 141 G7
Hounslow TW3, TW4 143 H3
Ilford IG1 99 F4
Twickenham TW2 161 G3
Staines Rd E, Sun. TW16 160 A7
Staines Wk, Sid. DA14
off Evry Rd 176 C6
Stainforth Rd, E17 78 A4
Ilford IG2 81 G7
Staining La, EC2 20 A3
Stainmore Cl, Chis. BR7 193 G1
Stainsbury St, E2
off Royston St 113 F2
Stainsby Rd, E14 114 A6
Stainton Rd, SE6 154 D6
Enfield EN3 45 F1
Stalbridge St, NW1 15 H1
Stalham St, SE16 133 E3
Stalham Way, Ilf. IG6 81 E1
Stambourne Way, SE19 170 B7
West Wickham BR4 204 C3
Stamford Brook Av, W6 127 F3
Stamford Brook Gdns, W6 *off Stamford Brook Rd* 127 F3
Stamford Brook Rd, W6 127 F3
Stamford Cl, N15 76 D4
W6 *off Cromwell Gro* 127 J3
Harrow HA3 52 B7
Southall UB1 103 G7
Stamford Cotts, SW10 30 B7
Stamford Ct, W6 127 F4
Edgware HA8 53 J4
Stamford Dr, Brom. BR2 191 F4
Stamford Gdns, Dag. RM9 100 C7
Stamford Gro E, N16
off Oldhill St 94 D1
Stamford Gro W, N16
off Oldhill St 94 D1
STAMFORD HILL, N16 94 B1
Stamford Hill, N16 94 C2
Stamford Hill Est, N16 94 C1
Stamford Rd, E6 116 B1
N1 94 B7
N15 76 D5
Dagenham RM9 118 B1
Stamford St, SE1 27 E2
Stamp Pl, E2 13 F3
Stanard Cl, N16 76 B7

Stanborough Cl, Hmptn. TW12 **161** F6
Stanborough Pas, E8
off Kingsland Rd **94** C6
Stanborough Rd, Houns. TW3 **144** A3
Stanbridge Pl, N21 **59** H2
Stanbridge Rd, SW15 **147** J3
Stanbrook Rd, SE2 **138** B2
Stanbury Rd, SE15 **153** E1
Stancroft, NW9 **70** E4
Standard Ind Est, E16 **136** C2
Standard Pl, EC2 **12** E4
Standard Rd, NW10 **106** C4
Belvedere DA17 **139** G5
Bexleyheath DA6 **159** E4
Hounslow TW4 **143** E3
Standen Rd, SW18 **148** C7
Standfield Gdns, Dag. RM10
off Standfield Rd **101** G6
Standfield Rd, Dag. RM10 **101** G5
Standish Ho, SE3
off Elford Cl **155** J4
Standish Rd, W6 **127** G4
Standlake Pt, SE23 **171** G3
Stane Cl, SW19 **167** E7
Stane Gro, SW9 **150** E2
Stane Way, SE18 **136** A7
Stanfield Ho, NW8
off Frampton St **7** F5
Stanfield Rd, E3 **113** H2
Stanford Cl, Hmptn. TW12 **161** F6
Romford RM7 **83** H6
Woodford Green IG8 **64** B5
Stanford Ct, SW6
off Bagley's La **149** E1
Stanford Ho, Bark. IG11 **118** B2
Stanford Ms, E8
off Dalston La **94** D5
Stanford Pl, SE17 **36** D2
Stanford Rd, N11 **57** J5
SW16 **186** D2
W8 **22** B5
Stanford St, SW1 **33** H2
Stanford Way, SW16 **186** D2
Stangate, SE1 **26** C5
Stangate Cres, Borwd. WD6 **38** E5
Stangate Gdns, Stan. HA7 **53** E4
Stanger Rd, SE25 **188** D4
Stanhope Av, N3 **72** C3
Bromley BR2 **205** F1
Harrow HA3 **68** A1
Stanhope Cl, SE16
off Middleton Dr **133** G2
Stanhope Gdns, N4 **75** H6
N6 **74** B6
NW7 **55** F5
SW7 **30** D1
Dagenham RM8 **101** F3
Ilford IG1 **98** C1
Stanhope Gate, W1 **24** C1
Stanhope Gro, Beck. BR3 **189** J5
Stanhope Ms E, SW7 **30** D1
Stanhope Ms S, SW7 **30** D2
Stanhope Ms W, SW7 **30** D1
Stanhope Par, NW1
off Stanhope St **9** F3
Stanhope Pk Rd, Grnf. UB6 **103** J4
Stanhope Pl, W2 **15** J4
Stanhope Rd, E17 **78** B5
N6 **74** C6
N12 **57** F5
Barnet EN5 **39** J6
Bexleyheath DA7 **159** E2
Carshalton SM5 **200** A7
Croydon CR0 **202** B3
Dagenham RM8 **101** F2
Greenford UB6 **103** J5
Sidcup DA15 **176** A4
Stanhope Row, W1 **24** D2
Stanhope St, NW1 **9** F4
Stanhope Ter, W2 **15** F5
Stanier Cl, W14
off Aisgill Av **128** C5
Stanlake Ms, W12 **127** J1
Stanlake Rd, W12 **127** H1
Stanlake Vil, W12 **127** H1
Stanley Av, Bark. IG11 **117** J2
Beckenham BR3 **190** C2
Dagenham RM8 **101** F1
Greenford UB6 **103** J1
New Malden KT3 **183** G5
Wembley HA0 **87** H7
Stanley Cl, SE9 **175** F1
SW8 **34** C6
Wembley HA0 **87** H7
Stanley Ct, Cars. SM5
off Stanley Pk Rd **200** A7
Stanley Cres, W11 **108** C7
Stanleycroft Cl, Islw. TW7 **144** B1
Stanley Gdns, NW2 **89** J5
W3 **126** E1
W11 **108** C7
Mitcham CR4
off Ashbourne Rd **168** A6
Wallington SM6 **200** C6
Stanley Gdns Ms, W11
off Kensington Pk Rd **108** C7
Stanley Gdns Rd, Tedd. TW11 **162** B5
Stanley Gro, SW8 **150** A2
Croydon CR0 **187** G6
Stanley Pk Dr, Wem. HA0 **87** J7
Stanley Pk Rd, Cars. SM5 **199** J7
Wallington SM6 **200** B6
Stanley Rd, E4 **62** D1
E10 **78** B6
E12 **98** B5
E15 **114** D1
E18 **79** F1
N2 **73** G3
N9 **60** C1
N10 **58** B7
N11 **58** D6
N15 **75** H4
NW9
off West Hendon Bdy **71** G7
SW14 **146** B4
SW19 **166** D7
W3 **126** C3
Bromley BR2 **191** H4
Carshalton SM5 **200** A7
Croydon CR0 **187** G7
Enfield EN1 **44** B3
Harrow HA2 **85** J2
Hounslow TW3 **143** J4
Ilford IG1 **99** G2
Mitcham CR4 **168** A7
Morden SM4 **184** D4
Northwood HA6 **66** A1
Sidcup DA14 **176** A3
Southall UB1 **102** E7
Sutton SM2 **198** E6
Teddington TW11 **162** B4
Twickenham TW2 **162** A3
Wembley HA9 **87** J6
Stanley St, SE8 **133** J7
Stanley Ter, N19 **92** E2
Stanliff Ho, E14
off Lightermans Rd **134** A3
Stanmer St, SW11 **149** H1
STANMORE, HA7 **52** D5
Stanmore Gdns, Rich. TW9 **145** J3
Sutton SM1 **199** F3
Stanmore Hall, Stan. HA7 **52** E3
Stanmore Hill, Stan. HA7 **52** D3
Stanmore Rd, E11 **97** F1
N15 **75** H4
Belvedere DA17 **139** J4
Richmond TW9 **145** J3
Stanmore St, N1
off Caledonian Rd **111** F1
Stanmore Ter, Beck. BR3 **190** A2
Stanmore Way, Loug. IG10 **48** D1
Stannard Ms, E8 **94** D6
Stannard Rd, E8 **94** D6
Stannary St, SE11 **35** F5
Stannet Way, Wall. SM6 **200** C4
Stannington Path, Borwd. WD6 **38** A1
Stansbury Sq, W10
off Beethoven St **108** B3
Stansfeld Rd, E6 **116** A5
E16 **116** A5
Stansfield Ho, SE1 **37** G2
Stansfield Rd, SW9 **151** F3
Hounslow TW4 **142** B2
Stansgate Rd, Dag. RM10 **101** G2
Stanstead Cl, Brom. BR2 **191** F5
Stanstead Gro, SE6
off Stanstead Rd **171** J1
Stanstead Manor, Sutt. SM1 **198** D6
Stanstead Rd, E11 **79** H5
SE6 **171** G1
SE23 **171** G1
Hounslow (Lon.Hthrw Air.) TW6 **140** C6
Stansted Cres, Bex. DA5 **176** D1
Stanswood Gdns, SE5 **132** B7
Stanthorpe Cl, SW16 **168** E5
Stanthorpe Rd, SW16 **168** E5
Stanton Av, Tedd. TW11 **162** B5
Stanton Cl, Epsom KT19 **196** B5
Worcester Park KT4 **198** A1
Stanton Ho, SE16
off Rotherhithe St **133** J2
Stanton Rd, SE26
off Stanton Way **171** J4
SW13 **147** F2
SW20 **184** A2
Croydon CR0 **187** J7
Stanton Sq, SE26
off Stanton Way **171** J4
Stanton Way, SE26 **171** J4
Stanway Cl, Chig. IG7 **65** H5
Stanway Ct, N1 **13** E2
Stanway Gdns, W3 **126** A1
Edgware HA8 **54** C5
Stanway St, N1 **12** E1
STANWELL, Stai. TW19 **140** B7
Stanwell Cl, Stai. (Stanw.) TW19 **140** A6
Stanwell Gdns, Stai. (Stanw.) TW19 **140** A6
Stanwell Rd, Felt. TW14 **141** F7
Stanwick Rd, W14 **128** C4
Stanworth St, SE1 **29** F4
Stanwyck Dr, Chig. IG7 **65** F5
Stapenhill Rd, Wem. HA0 **86** E3
Staplefield Cl, SW2 **169** E1
Pinner HA5 **50** E7
Stapleford Av, Ilf. IG2 **81** H5
Stapleford Cl, E4 **62** C3
SW19 **148** B7
Kingston upon Thames KT1 **182** A3
Stapleford Rd, Wem. HA0 **87** G7
Stapleford Way, Bark. IG11 **118** B3
Staplehurst Rd, SE13 **154** E5
Carshalton SM5 **199** H7
Staple Inn, WC1 **19** E2
Staple Inn Bldgs, WC1 **18** E2
Staples Cl, SE16 **133** H1
Staples Cor, NW2 **89** H1
Staples Cor Retail Pk, NW2
off Geron Way **89** H2
Staples Rd, Loug. IG10 **48** B3
Staple St, SE1 **28** C4
Stapleton Gdns, Croy. CR0 **201** G5
Stapleton Hall Rd, N4 **75** F7
Stapleton Rd, SW17 **168** A3
Bexleyheath DA7 **139** F7
Orpington BR6 **207** J3
Stapley Rd, Belv. DA17 **139** G5
Stapylton Rd, Barn. EN5 **40** B3
Star All, EC3 **20** E5
Star & Garter Hill, Rich. TW10 **163** H1
Starboard Way, E14 **134** A3
Starbuck Cl, SE9 **156** D7
Starch Ho La, Ilf. IG6 **81** G2
Star Cl, Enf. EN3 **45** F6
Starcross St, NW1 **9** G4
Starfield Rd, W12 **127** G2
Star La, E16 **115** E4
Starlight Way, Houns. TW6 *off Southern Perimeter Rd* **141** F5
Starling Cl, Buck.H. IG9 **63** G1
Croydon CR0 **189** H6
Pinner HA5 **66** C3
Starling Wk, Hmptn. TW12
off Oak Av **161** E5
Starmans Cl, Dag. RM9 **119** E1
Star Path, Nthlt. UB5
off Brabazon Rd **103** G2
Star Pl, E1 **21** G6
Star Rd, W14 **128** C6
Isleworth TW7 **144** A2
Star St, E16 **115** F5
W2 **15** F3
Starts Cl, Orp. BR6 **206** D3
Starts Hill Av, Orp. (Farnboro.) BR6 **207** E5
Starts Hill Rd, Orp. BR6 **206** D3
Starveall Cl, West Dr. UB7 **120** C3
Star Yd, WC2 **18** E3
State Fm Av, Orp. BR6 **207** E4
Staten Bldg, E3
off Fairfield Rd **114** A2
Staten Gdns, Twick. TW1 **162** C1
Statham Ct, N7 **92** E3
Statham Gro, N16
off Green Las **94** A4
N18 **60** B5
Station App, E4 (Chingford)
off Station Rd **46** E7
E4 (Highams Pk)
off The Avenue **62** D6
E7 *off Woodford Rd* **97** H4
E11 (Snaresbrook)
off High St **79** G5
N11
off Friern Barnet Rd **58** B5
N12 (Woodside Pk) **56** E4
N16 (Stoke Newington)
off Stamford Hill **94** C2
NW10 *off Station Rd* **107** F3
SE1 **26** D2
SE3
off Kidbrooke Pk Rd **155** H3
SE9 (Mottingham) **174** C1
Station App,
SE26 (Lwr Sydenham)
off Worsley Br Rd **171** J5
SE26 (Sydenham)
off Sydenham Rd **171** F4
SW6 **148** B3
SW16 **168** D5
SW20 **183** J2
W7 **124** B1
Barnet (High Barn.) EN5
off Barnet Hill **40** D4
Barnet (New Barn.) EN5 **41** F4
Beckenham BR3
off Rectory Rd **190** A1
Bexley DA5
off Bexley High St **159** G7
Bexleyheath DA7
off Avenue Rd **159** E2
Bexleyheath (Barne.) DA7 **159** J2
Bromley (Hayes) BR2 **205** G1
Buckhurst Hill IG9
off Cherry Tree Ri **64** A4
Chislehurst BR7 **192** D1
Chislehurst (Elm.Wds) BR7 **174** B6
Epsom (Stoneleigh) KT19 **197** G5
Esher (Hinch.Wd) KT10 **194** C3
Greenford UB6 **86** A7
Hampton TW12
off Milton Rd **179** G1
Harrow HA1 **68** B7
Hayes UB3 **121** J2
Kingston upon Thames KT1 **182** A1
Loughton IG10 **48** B5
Loughton (Debden) IG10 **49** F4
Orpington BR6 **207** J2
Pinner HA5 **66** E3
Pinner (Hatch End) HA5
off Uxbridge Rd **51** G7
Richmond TW9 **146** A1
Ruislip (S.Ruis.) HA4 **84** B5
Sunbury-on-Thames TW16 **178** A1
Sutton (Cheam) SM2 **198** B7
Watford (Carp.Pk) WD19
off Prestwick Rd **50** D3
Wembley HA0 **87** E6
West Drayton UB7 **120** B1
West Wickham BR4 **204** C1
Woodford Green IG8
off The Broadway **63** H6
Worcester Park KT4 **197** G1
Station App N, Sid. DA15 **176** A2
Station App Path, SE9
off Glenlea Rd **156** C5
Station App Rd, W4 **126** C7
Station Av, SW9
off Coldharbour La **151** H3
New Malden KT3 **183** E3
Richmond (Kew) TW9 **146** A1
Station Cl, N3 **72** D1
N12 (Woodside Pk) **56** E4
Hampton TW12 **179** H1
Station Ct, SW6 **149** F1
Station Cres, N15 **76** A4
SE3 **135** G5
Wembley HA0 **87** E6
Stationers Hall Ct, EC4
off Ludgate Hill **19** H4
Station Est, Beck. BR3
off Elmers End Rd **189** G4
Station Est Rd, Felt. TW14 **160** B1
Station Gar Ms, SW16
off Estreham Rd **168** D6
Station Gdns, W4 **126** C7
Station Gro, Wem. HA0 **87** H6
Station Hill, Brom. BR2 **205** G2
Station Ho Ms, N9
off Fore St **60** D4
Station Ms Ter, SE3
off Halstow Rd **135** G5
Station Par, E11 **79** G5
N14 *off High St* **58** D1
NW2 **89** J6
SW12
off Balham High Rd **168** A1
W3 **106** A6
W5 *off Uxbridge Rd* **125** J1
Barking IG11 **99** F7
Barnet EN4
off Cockfosters Rd **42** A4
Edgware HA8 **53** H7
Feltham TW14 **142** B7
Harrow HA2 **85** H4
Richmond TW9 **146** A1
Station Pas, E18
off Maybank Rd **79** H2
SE15 **153** F1
Station Path, E8
off Amhurst Rd **95** E6

Station Pl, N4
off Seven Sisters Rd ...93 G2
Station Ri, SE27
off Norwood Rd 169 H2
Station Rd,
E4 (Chingford) 62 D1
E7 ....97 G4
E12 ....98 A4
E17 ....77 H6
N3 ....72 D1
N11 ....58 B5
N17 ....76 D3
N19 ....92 C3
N21 ....59 H1
N22 ....75 F2
NW4 ....71 G6
NW7 ....55 E5
NW10 ....107 F2
SE13 ....154 C3
SE20 ....171 F6
SE25 (Norwood Junct.) ..188 C4
SW13 ....147 G3
SW19 ....185 F1
W5 ....105 J6
W7 (Hanwell) 124 B1
Barnet (New Barn.)
EN5 ....40 E5
Belvedere DA17 ....139 G3
Bexleyheath DA7 ......159 E3
Borehamwood WD6 ....38 A4
Brentford TW8 ....125 F6
Bromley BR1 ....191 G1
Bromley (Short.) BR2 ..191 E2
Carshalton SM5 ....199 J4
Chessington KT9 ......195 H5
Chigwell IG7 ....64 E3
Croydon CR0 ....201 J1
Edgware HA8 ....54 A6
Esher KT10 ....194 A2
Esher (Clay.) KT10 .....194 A5
Hampton TW12 ....179 G1
Harrow HA1 ....68 C7
Harrow (N.Har.) HA2 ....67 H5
Hayes UB3 ....121 J3
Hounslow TW3 ....143 H4
Ilford IG1 ....98 E3
Ilford (Barkingside) IG6 ..81 G3
Kingston upon Thames
KT2 ....182 A1
Kingston upon Thames
(Hmptn W.) KT1 ......181 F1
Loughton IG10 ....48 B4
New Malden (Mots.Pk)
KT3 ....183 H5
Orpington BR6 ....207 J2
Romford (Chad.Hth)
RM6 ....82 D7
Sidcup DA15 ....176 A4
Sunbury-on-Thames
TW16 ....160 A7
Teddington TW11 ......162 C5
Thames Ditton KT7 ....180 C7
Twickenham TW1 ......162 C1
West Drayton UB7 .....120 A1
West Wickham BR4 ....204 C1
Station Rd N, Belv. DA17 .139 H3
Station Sq, Orp.
(Petts Wd) BR5 ....193 F5
Station St, E15 ....96 D7
E16 ....136 E1
Station Ter, NW10 ....108 A2
SE5 ....151 J1
Station Vw, Grnf.
UB6 ....104 A1
Station Way, Buck.H.
(Rod.Val.) IG9 ....63 J4
Esher (Clay.) KT10 .....194 B6
Sutton (Cheam) SM3 ...198 B6
Station Yd, Twick. TW1 ....144 D7
Staunton Rd, Kings.T.
KT2 ....163 H6
Staunton St, SE8 ....133 J6
★ **Stave Hill Ecological Pk**,
SE16 ....133 H2
Staveley Cl, E9
off Churchill Wk 95 F5
N7 ....93 E4
SE15 off Asylum Rd ...153 E1
Staveley Gdns, W4 ....146 D1
Staveley Rd, W4 ....126 D7
Staverton Rd, NW2 ....89 J7
Stave Yd Rd, SE16 ....133 H1
Stavordale Rd, N5 ....93 H4
Carshalton SM5 ....185 F7
Stayner's Rd, E1 ....113 G4
Stayton Rd, Sutt. SM1 ....198 D3
Steadfast Rd, Kings.T.
KT1 ....181 G1
Stead St, SE17 ....36 B2
Steam Fm La, Felt. TW14 ..141 J4
Stean St, E8 ....112 C1
Stebbing Ho, W11 ....128 A1
Stebbing Way, Bark. IG11 .118 A2
Stebondale St, E14 ......134 C5
Stedham Pl, WC1 ....18 A3
Steedman St, SE17 ....35 J2
Steeds Rd, N10 ....73 J1
Steeds Way, Loug. IG10 ....48 B3
Steele Rd, E11 ....96 E4
N17 ....76 B3
NW10 ....106 C2
W4 ....126 C3
Isleworth TW7 ....144 D4
Steeles Ms N, NW3
off Steeles Rd 91 J6
Steeles Ms S, NW3
off Steeles Rd 91 J6
Steeles Rd, NW3 ....91 J6
Steele Wk, Erith DA8 .....139 H6
Steel's La, E1
off Devonport St 113 F6
Steelyard Pas, EC4 ....20 B6
Steen Way, SE22
off East Dulwich Gro ..152 B5
Steep Cl, Orp. BR6 ....207 J6
Steep Hill, SW16 ....168 D3
Croydon CR0 ....202 B4
Steeple Cl, SW6 ....148 B2
SW19 ....166 B5
Steeple Ct, E1
off Coventry Rd 113 E4
Steeplestone Cl, N18 ......59 J5
Steeple Wk, N1
off Basire St 111 J1
Steerforth St, SW18 .....167 E2
Steering Cl, N9 ....61 F1
Steers Mead, Mitch. CR4 ..185 J1
Steers Way, SE16 ....133 H2
Stellar Ho, N17 ....60 C6
Stella Rd, SW17 ....167 J6
Stellman Cl, E5 ....94 D3
Stembridge Rd, SE20 ....188 E2
Stephan Cl, E8 ....112 D1
Stephen Cl, Orp. BR6 ....207 J3
Stephendale Rd, SW6 ....149 E2
Stephen Ms, W1 ....17 H2
Stephen Pl, SW4
off Rectory Gro 150 C3
Stephen Rd, Bexh. DA7 ...159 J3
Stephenson Cl, Well.
DA16 ....158 A2
Stephenson Ho, SE1
off Bath Ter 27 J5
Stephenson Rd, E17 ......77 H5
W7 ....104 C6
Twickenham TW2 ......143 G7
Stephenson St, E16 ......114 E4
NW10 ....107 E3
Stephenson Way, NW1 .....9 G5
Stephen's Rd, E15 ....115 E1
Stephen St, W1 ....17 H2
STEPNEY, E1 ....113 F5
Stepney Causeway, E1 ...113 G6
Stepney Cl, Mitch. CR4 ...186 A1
Stepney Grn, E1 ....113 F5
Stepney High St, E1 ......113 G5
Stepney Way, E1 ....112 E5
Sterling Av, Edg. HA8 .....53 J4
Sterling Cl, NW10 ....89 G6
Sterling Gdns, SE14 ......133 H6
Sterling Ho, SE3
off Cambert Way 155 H4
Sterling Ind Est, Dag.
RM10 ....101 H4
Sterling Pl, W5 ....125 H4
Sterling Rd, Enf. EN2 ......44 A1
Sterling St, SW7 ....23 H5
Sterling Way, N18 ....60 A5
★ **Sternberg Cen**, N3 ....72 E2
Stern Cl, Bark. IG11 ......118 C2
Sterndale Rd, W14 ....128 A3
Sterne St, W12 ....128 A2
Sternhall La, SE15 ....152 D3
Sternhold Av, SW2 ....168 D2
Sterry Cres, Dag. RM10
off Alibon Rd 101 G5
Sterry Dr, Epsom KT19 ...196 E4
Thames Ditton KT7 ....180 B6
Sterry Gdns, Dag. RM10 ..101 G6
Sterry Rd, Bark. IG11 .....117 J1
Dagenham RM10 ......101 G4
Sterry St, SE1 ....28 B4
Steucers La, SE23 ....153 H7
Steve Biko La, SE6 ....172 A4
Steve Biko Rd, N7 ....93 G3
Steve Biko Way, Houns.
TW3 ....143 G3
Stevedale Rd, Well. DA16 .158 C2
Stevedore St, E1
off Waterman Way 132 E1
Stevenage Rd, E6 ....98 D6
SW6 ....128 A7
Stevens Av, E9 ....95 F6
Stevens Cl, Beck. BR3 ....172 A6
Hampton TW12 ....161 E6
Pinner HA5 ....66 C5
Stevens Grn, Bushey
(Bushey Hth) WD23 .....51 J1
Stevens La, Esher (Clay.)
KT10 ....194 D7
Stevenson Cl, Barn. EN5 ...41 G6
Stevenson Cres, SE16 .....37 J3
Stevens Rd, Dag. RM8 ....100 B3
Stevens St, SE1 ....29 E5
Stevens Way, Chig. IG7 ....65 H4
Steventon Rd, W12 ......107 F7
Stewards Holte Wk, N11
off Coppies Gro 58 B4
Steward St, E1 ....21 E2
Stewart Cl, NW9 ....70 C6
Chislehurst BR7 ....175 E5
Hampton TW12 ....161 E5
Stewart Rainbird Ho, E12 ..98 D5
Stewart Rd, E15 ....96 C4
Stewartsby Cl, N18 ....59 J5
Stewart's Gro, SW3 ....31 F3
Stewart's Rd, SW8 ....130 C7
Stewart St, E14 ....134 C2
Stew La, EC4 ....19 J5
Steyne Rd, W3 ....126 C1
Steyning Gro, SE9 ....174 C4
Steynings Way, N12 ....56 D5
Steyning Way, Houns.
TW4 ....142 C4
Steynton Av, Bex. DA5 ...176 D2
Stickland Rd, Belv. DA17
off Picardy Rd 139 G4
Stickleton Cl, Grnf. UB6 ..103 H3
Stilecroft Gdns, Wem.
HA0 ....86 E3
Stile Hall Gdns, W4 ......126 A5
Stile Hall Par, W4
off Chiswick High Rd ..126 A5
Stile Path, Sun. TW16 ....178 A4
Stiles Cl, Brom. BR2 .....192 C6
Erith DA8
off Riverdale Rd 139 H5
Stillingfleet Rd, SW13 ....127 G6
Stillington St, SW1 ....33 G1
Stillness Rd, SE23 ....153 H6
Stipularis Dr, Hayes UB4 ..102 D4
Stirling Av, Pnr. HA5 ......66 E7
Wallington SM6 ....201 E7
Stirling Cl, SW16 ....186 C1
Sidcup DA14 ....175 H4
Stirling Cor, Barn. EN5 ....38 D6
Borehamwood WD6 ....38 D6
Stirling Gro, Houns. TW3 .143 J2
Stirling Ind Cen, Borwd.
WD6 ....38 D5
Stirling Retail Pk, Borwd.
WD6 ....38 D6
Stirling Rd, E13 ....115 H2
E17 ....77 H3
N17 ....76 D1
N22 ....75 H1
SW9 ....150 E2
W3 ....126 B3
Harrow HA3 ....68 C3
Hayes UB3 ....102 B7
Hounslow
(Lon.Hthrw Air.) TW6 ..140 C6
Twickenham TW2 ......143 G7
Stirling Rd Path, E17 ......77 H3
Stirling Wk, N.Mal. KT3 ..182 C5
Surbiton KT5 ....182 B6
Stirling Way, Borwd. WD6 ..38 D6
Croydon CR0 ....186 E7
Stiven Cres, Har. HA2 .....85 F3
Stockbury Rd, Croy. CR0 ..189 F6
Stockdale Rd, Dag. RM8 ..101 F2
Stockdove Way, Grnf.
(Perivale) UB6 ....104 C3
Stocker Gdns, Dag. RM9 ..100 C7
★ **Stock Exchange**, EC4 ...19 H3
Stockfield Rd, SW16 .....169 F3
Esher (Clay.) KT10 .....194 B5
Stockford Av, NW7 ....56 A7
Stockholm Ho, E1 ....112 D7
Stockholm Rd, SE16 .....133 F5
Stockholm Way, E1 ....29 H1
Stockhurst Cl, SW15 .....147 J2
Stockingswater La, Enf.
EN3 ....45 H3
Stockleigh Hall, NW8
off Prince Albert Rd 7 J1
Stockley Cl, West Dr.
UB7 ....120 E2
Stockley Fm Rd, West Dr.
UB7 off Stockley Rd ...120 E3
Stockley Pk, Uxb. UB11 ...121 E1
Stockley Pk Rbt, Uxb.
UB11 ....120 E1
Stockley Rd, West Dr.
UB7 ....120 E4
Stock Orchard Cres, N7 ....93 F5
Stock Orchard St, N7 ......93 F5
Stockport Rd, SW16 .....186 D1
Stocksfield Rd, E17 ....78 C3
Stocks Pl, E14
off Grenade St 113 J7
Stock St, E13 ....115 G2
Stockton Cl, Barn.
(New Barn.) EN5 ....41 F4
Stockton Gdns, N17 ......59 J7
NW7 ....54 D3
Stockton Ho, E2
off Ellsworth St 112 E3
Stockton Rd, N17 ....59 J7
N18 ....60 D6
STOCKWELL, SW9 ....151 F1
Stockwell Av, SW9 ....151 F3
Stockwell Cl, Brom. BR1 ..191 H2
Edgware HA8 ....70 C2
Stockwell Gdns, SW9 ....151 F2
Stockwell Gdns Est,
SW9 ....151 E2
Stockwell Grn, SW9 .....151 F2
Stockwell La, SW9 ....151 F2
Stockwell Ms, SW9
off Stockwell Rd 151 F2
Stockwell Pk Cres, SW9 ..151 F2
Stockwell Pk Est, SW9 ...151 F2
Stockwell Pk Rd, SW9 ....151 F1
Stockwell Pk Wk, SW9 ...151 F3
Stockwell Rd, SW9 ....151 F2
Stockwell St, SE10 ......134 C6
Stockwell Ter, SW9 ......151 F1
Stodart Rd, SE20 ....189 F1
Stofield Gdns, SE9
off Aldersgrove Av 174 A3
Stoford Cl, SW19 ....148 B7
Stokenchurch St, SW6 ...148 E1
STOKE NEWINGTON,
N16 ....94 B2
Stoke Newington Ch St,
N16 ....94 A3
Stoke Newington Common,
N16 ....94 C3
Stoke Newington High St,
N16 ....94 C3
Stoke Newington Rd,
N16 ....94 C5
Stoke Pl, NW10 ....107 F3
Stoke Rd, Kings.T. KT2 ...164 C7
Stokesby Rd, Chess. KT9 .195 J6
Stokesley St, W12 ....107 F6
Stokes Rd, E6 ....116 B4
Croydon CR0 ....189 G6
Stoll Cl, NW2 ....89 J3
Stonard Rd, N13 ....59 G3
Dagenham RM8 ....100 B5
Stonards Hill, Loug. IG10 ..48 C6
Stondon Pk, SE23 ....153 H7
Stondon Wk, E6 ....116 A2
Stonebanks, Walt. KT12 ..178 A7
STONEBRIDGE, NW10 ....106 B1
Stonebridge Common, E8
off Mayfield Rd 94 C7
Stonebridge Pk, NW10 ....88 D7
Stonebridge Rd, N15 ......76 B5
Stonebridge Way, Wem.
HA9 ....88 B6
Stone Bldgs, WC2 ....18 D2
Stonechat Sq, E6
off Peridot St 116 B5
Stone Cl, SW4
off Larkhall Ri 150 C2
Dagenham RM8 ....101 F2
West Drayton UB7 .....120 C1
Stonecot Cl, Sutt. SM3 ...198 B1
Stonecot Hill, Sutt. SM3 ..198 B1
Stone Cres, Felt. TW14 ....141 J7
Stonecroft Cl, Barn. EN5 ...39 H4
Stonecroft Rd, Erith DA8 ..139 J7
Stonecroft Way, Croy.
CR0 ....187 E7
Stonecrop Cl, NW9 ....70 D3
Stonecutter St, EC4 ....19 G3
Stonefield, N4 ....93 F2
Stonefield Cl, Bexh. DA7 ..159 G3
Ruislip HA4 ....84 E5
Stonefield St, N1 ....111 G1
Stonefield Way, SE7
off Greenbay Rd 136 A7
Ruislip HA4 ....84 E4
Stonegrove, Edg. HA8 .....53 H4
Stonegrove Est, Edg. HA8
off Lacey Dr 53 J4
Stonegrove Gdns, Edg.
HA8 ....53 J5
Stonehall Av, Ilf. IG1 ......80 B6
Stone Hall Gdns, W8 ......22 A6
Stone Hall Pl, W8 ....22 A6
Stone Hall Rd, N21 ....43 F7
Stoneham Rd, N11 ....58 C6
Stonehill Business Pk, N18
off Silvermere Dr 61 G6
Stonehill Cl, SW14 ....146 D5
Stonehill Grn, Dart. DA2 ..177 J7
Stonehill Rd, SW14 ......146 C5
W4 off Wellesley Rd ...126 A5
Stonehills Ct, SE21 ......170 B3
Stonehill Wds Pk, Sid.
DA14 ....177 H6
Stonehorse Rd, Enf. EN3 ...45 F5
Stone Ho Ct, EC3 ....20 D3
Stone Lake Retail Pk,
SE7 ....135 H4
Stone Lake Rbt, SE7 .....135 J4
STONELEIGH, Epsom
KT17 ....197 G5
Stoneleigh Av, Enf. EN1 ...45 E1
Worcester Park KT4 ...197 G4
Stoneleigh Bdy, Epsom
KT17 ....197 G5
Stoneleigh Cres, Epsom
KT19 ....197 F5

Stoneleigh Ms, E3
off Stanfield Rd **113** H2
Stoneleigh Pk Av, Croy. CR0 **189** G6
Stoneleigh Pk Rd, Epsom KT19 **197** F6
Stoneleigh Pl, W11 **108** A7
Stoneleigh Rd, N17 **76** C3
Bromley BR1 **192** E3
Carshalton SM5 **185** H7
Ilford IG5 **80** B3
Stoneleigh St, W11 **108** A7
Stoneleigh Ter, N19 **92** B2
Stonells Rd, SW11
off Chatham Rd **149** J5
Stonemasons Cl, N15 **76** A4
Stonenest St, N4 **93** F1
Stone Pk Av, Beck. BR3 **190** A4
Stone Pl, Wor.Pk. KT4 **197** G2
Stone Rd, Brom. BR2 **191** F5
Stones End St, SE1 **27** J4
Stonewall, E6 **116** D5
Stoney All, SE18 **156** D2
Stoneyard La, E14
off Poplar High St **114** B7
Stoneycroft Cl, SE12 **155** F7
Stoneycroft Rd, Wdf.Grn. IG8 **64** B6
Stoneydeep, Tedd. TW11
off Twickenham Rd **162** D4
Stoneydown, E17 **77** H4
Stoneydown Av, E17 **77** H4
Stoneyfields Gdns, Edg. HA8 **54** C4
Stoneyfields La, Edg. HA8 **54** C5
Stoney La, E1 **21** E3
SE19 *off Church Rd* **170** C6
Stoney St, SE1 **28** B1
Stonhouse St, SW4 **150** D3
Stonor Rd, W14 **128** C4
Stonycroft Cl, Enf. EN3
off Brimsdown Av **45** H2
Stony Path, Loug. IG10 **48** C2
Stopes St, SE15 **132** C7
Stopford Rd, E13 **115** G1
SE17 **35** H4
Store Rd, E16 **136** D2
Storers Quay, E14 **134** D4
Store St, E15 **96** D5
WC1 **17** H2
Storey Ct, NW8
off St. John's Wd Rd **7** E4
Storey Rd, E17 **77** J4
N6 **73** J6
Storey's Gate, SW1 **25** J4
Storey St, E16 **136** D1
Stories Ms, SE5 **152** B2
Stories Rd, SE5 **152** B3
Stork Rd, E7 **97** F6
Storksmead Rd, Edg. HA8 **54** E7
Storks Rd, SE16 **29** J6
Stormont Rd, N6 **73** J7
SW11 **150** A3
Stormont Way, Chess. KT9 **195** F5
Stormount Dr, Hayes UB3 **121** F2
Storrington Rd, Croy. CR0 **202** C1
Story St, N1
off Carnoustie Dr **93** F7
Stothard Pl, E1
off Bishopsgate **21** E1
Stothard St, E1
off Colebert Av **113** F4
Stott Cl, SW18 **149** G6
Stoughton Av, Sutt. SM3 **198** A5
Stoughton Cl, SE11 **34** D2
SW15
off Bessborough Rd **165** G1
Stour Av, Sthl. UB2 **123** G3
Stourcliffe St, W1 **15** J4
Stour Cl, Kes. BR2 **205** J4
Stourhead Cl, SW19
off Castlecombe Dr **148** A7
Stourhead Gdns, SW20 **183** G3
Stourhead Ho, SW1
off Tachbrook St **33** H3
Stour Rd, E3 **96** A7
Dagenham RM10 **101** G2
Stourton Av, Felt. TW13 **161** F4
Stowage, SE8 **134** A6
Stow Cres, E17 **61** H7
Stowe Gdns, N9 **60** C1
Stowe Pl, N15 **76** B3
Stowe Rd, W12 **127** H2
Stowting Rd, Orp. BR6 **207** H4
Stox Mead, Har. HA3 **68** A1
Stracey Rd, E7 **97** G4
NW10 **106** D1
Strachan Pl, SW19 **165** J6
Stradbroke Dr, Chig. IG7 **64** D6
Stradbroke Gro, Buck.H. IG9 **64** A1
Ilford IG5 **80** B3
Stradbroke Pk, Chig. IG7 **64** E6
Stradbroke Rd, N5 **93** J4
Stradbrook Cl, Har. HA2
off Stiven Cres **85** F3
Stradella Rd, SE24 **151** J6
Strafford Av, Ilf. IG5 **80** D2
Strafford Rd, W3 **126** C2
Barnet EN5 **40** B3
Hounslow TW3 **143** F3
Twickenham TW1 **144** D7
Strafford St, E14 **134** A2
Strahan Rd, E3 **113** H3
Straight, The, Sthl. UB1 **122** D2
Straightsmouth, SE10 **134** C7
Strait Rd, E6 **116** B7
Straker's Rd, SE15 **152** E4
STRAND, WC2 **18** A5
Strand, WC2 **18** A6
Strand Ct, SE18
off Strandfield Cl **137** H5
Strand Dr, Rich. TW9 **126** B7
Strandfield Cl, SE18 **137** H5
Strand Ho, SE28
off Merbury Cl **137** G1
Strand La, WC2 **18** D5
Strand on the Grn, W4 **126** A6
Strand Pl, N18 **60** A4
Strand Sch App, W4
off Thames Rd **126** A6
Strangways Ter, W14
off Holland Pk Rd **128** C3
Stranraer Rd, Houns. (Lon.Hthrw Air.) TW6 **140** B6
Stranraer Way, N1 **93** E7
Strasburg Rd, SW11 **150** B1
Stratfield Pk Cl, N21 **43** H7
Stratfield Rd, Borwd. WD6 **38** A3
STRATFORD, E15 **96** C6
Stratford Av, W8
off Stratford Rd **128** E3
Stratford Cen, The, E15 **96** D7
Stratford Cl, Bark. IG11 **100** A7
Dagenham RM10 **101** J7
Stratford Ct, N.Mal. KT3 **182** D4
Stratford Gro, SW15 **148** A4
Stratford Ho Av, Brom. BR1 **192** B3
Stratford Pl, W1 **16** D4
Stratford Rd, E13 **115** F1
NW4 **72** A4
W8 **128** D3
Hayes UB4 **102** B4
Hounslow (Lon.Hthrw Air.) TW6 **141** E6
Southall UB2 **122** E4
Thornton Heath CR7 **187** G4
Stratford Vil, NW1 **92** C7
Strathan Cl, SW18 **148** B6
Strathaven Rd, SE12 **155** H6
Strathblaine Rd, SW11 **149** G4
Strathbrook Rd, SW16 **169** F7
Strathcona Rd, Wem. HA9 **87** G2
Strathdale, SW16 **169** F5
Strathdon Dr, SW17 **167** G3
Strathearn Av, Hayes UB3 **121** J7
Twickenham TW2 **161** H1
Strathearn Pl, W2 **15** F5
Strathearn Rd, SW19 **166** D5
Sutton SM1 **198** D5
Stratheden Par, SE3
off Stratheden Rd **135** G7
Stratheden Rd, SE3 **155** G1
Strathfield Gdns, Bark. IG11 **99** G6
Strathleven Rd, SW2 **151** E5
Strathmore Gdns, N3 **72** E1
W8
off Palace Gdns Ter **128** D1
Edgware HA8 **70** B2
Strathmore Rd, SW19 **166** D3
Croydon CR0 **187** J7
Teddington TW11 **162** B4
Strathnairn St, SE1 **37** J2
Strathray Gdns, NW3 **91** H6
Strath Ter, SW11 **149** H4
Strathville Rd, SW18 **166** E2
Strathyre Av, SW16 **187** G3
Stratton Cl, SW19 **184** D2
Bexleyheath DA7 **159** E3
Edgware HA8 **53** J7
Hounslow TW3 **143** F1
Stratton Ct, Surb. KT6
off Adelaide Rd **181** H5
Strattondale St, E14 **134** C3
Stratton Dr, Bark. IG11 **99** J5
Stratton Gdns, Southall UB1 **103** F6
Stratton Rd, SW19 **184** D2
Bexleyheath DA7 **159** E3
Stratton St, W1 **25** E1
Strauss Rd, W4 **126** D2
Strawberry Flds, Orp. (Farnboro.) BR6 **207** E5
STRAWBERRY HILL, Twick. TW1 **162** B3
Strawberry Hill, Twick. TW1 **162** C3
Strawberry Hill Cl, Twick. TW1 **162** C3
Strawberry Hill Rd, Twick. TW1 **162** C3
Strawberry La, Cars. SM5 **199** J3
Strawberry Vale, N2 **73** G1
Twickenham TW1 **162** D3
Streakes Fld Rd, NW2 **89** G2
Streamdale, SE2 **138** A6
Stream La, Edg. HA8 **54** B5
Streamline Ms, SE22 **170** D1
Streamside Cl, N9 **60** C1
Bromley BR2 **191** G4
Streamway, Belv. DA17 **139** G6
Streatfeild Av, E6 **116** C1
Streatfield Rd, Har. HA3 **69** G3
STREATHAM, SW16 **169** E4
Streatham Cl, SW16 **169** E2
Streatham Common N, SW16 **168** E5
Streatham Common S, SW16 **169** E6
Streatham Ct, SW16 **168** E3
Streatham High Rd, SW16 **168** E5
STREATHAM HILL, SW2 **151** F7
Streatham Hill, SW2 **169** E2
STREATHAM PARK, SW16 **168** C4
Streatham Pl, SW2 **150** E7
Streatham Rd, SW16 **186** A1
Mitcham CR4 **186** A1
Streatham St, WC1 **17** J3
STREATHAM VALE, SW16 **168** D7
Streatham Vale, SW16 **168** C7
Streathbourne Rd, SW17 **168** A2
Streatley Pl, NW3
off New End **91** F4
Streatley Rd, NW6 **90** C7
Streeters La, Wall. SM6 **200** D3
Streetfield Ms, SE3 **155** G3
Streimer Rd, E15 **114** C2
Strelley Way, W3 **106** E7
Stretton Mans, SE8
off Glaisher St **134** A6
Stretton Rd, Croy. CR0 **188** B7
Richmond TW10 **163** F2
Strickland Row, SW18 **149** G7
Strickland St, SE8 **154** A2
Strickland Way, Orp. BR6 **207** J4
Stride Rd, E13 **115** F2
Strimon Cl, N9 **61** F2
Strode Cl, N10 **58** A7
Strode Rd, E7 **97** G4
N17 **76** B2
NW10 **89** G6
SW6 **128** A7
Strone Rd, E7 **97** J6
E12 **98** A6
Strone Way, Hayes UB4 **102** E4
Strongbow Cres, SE9 **156** C5
Strongbow Rd, SE9 **156** C5
Strongbridge Cl, Har. HA2 **85** G1
Stronsa Rd, W12 **127** F2
Stroud Cres, SW15 **165** G3
Stroudes Cl, Wor.Pk. KT4 **183** E7
Stroud Fld, Nthlt. UB5 **84** E6
Stroud Gate, Har. HA2 **85** H4
STROUD GREEN, N4 **75** F6
Stroud Grn Gdns, Croy. CR0 **189** F7
Stroud Grn Rd, N4 **93** F1
Stroud Grn Way, Croy. CR0 **189** E7
Stroudley Wk, E3 **114** B3
Stroud Rd, SE25 **188** D6
SW19 **166** D3
Strouds Cl, Rom. (Chad.Hth) RM6 **82** B5
Strouts Pl, E2 **13** F3
Strutton Grd, SW1 **25** H5
Strype St, E1 **21** F2
Stuart Av, NW9 **71** G7
W5 **125** J1
Bromley BR2 **205** G1
Harrow HA2 **85** F3
Stuart Cres, N22 **75** F1
Croydon CR0 **203** J3
Stuart Evans Cl, Well. DA16 **158** C3
Stuart Gro, Tedd. TW11 **162** B5
Stuart Pl, Mitch. CR4 **185** J1
Stuart Rd, NW6 **108** D3
SE15 **153** F4
SW19 **166** D3
W3 **126** C1
Barking IG11 **99** J7
Barnet (E.Barn.) EN4 **41** H7
Harrow HA3 **68** C2
Richmond TW10 **163** E2
Thornton Heath CR7 **187** J4
Welling DA16 **158** B1
Stuart Twr, W9 **6** D4
Stubbs Cl, NW9 **70** C5
Stubbs Dr, SE16 **132** E5
Stubbs Ms, Dag. RM8
off Marlborough Rd **100** B4
Stubbs Pt, E13 **115** H4
Stubbs Way, SW19
off Ruskin Way **185** G1
Stucley Pl, NW1
off Hawley Cres **92** B7
Stucley Rd, Houns. TW5 **123** J7
Studdridge St, SW6 **148** D2
Studd St, N1 **111** H1
Studholme Ct, NW3 **90** D4
Studholme St, SE15 **132** E7
Studio Ms, NW4
off Glebe Cres **71** J4
Studio Pl, SW1 **24** A4
Studio Way, Borwd. WD6 **38** C2
Studland, SE17 **36** B3
Studland Cl, Sid. DA15 **175** J3
Studland Ho, E14
off Aston St **113** H6
Studland Rd, SE26 **171** G5
W7 **104** A6
Kingston upon Thames KT2 **163** H6
Studland St, W6 **127** H4
Studley Av, E4 **62** D7
Studley Cl, E5 **95** H5
Studley Ct, E14
off Jamestown Way **114** D7
Sidcup DA14 **176** B5
Studley Dr, Ilf. IG4 **80** A6
Studley Est, SW4 **150** E1
Studley Gra Rd, W7 **124** B2
Studley Rd, E7 **97** H6
SW4 **150** E1
Dagenham RM9 **100** D7
Stukeley Rd, E7 **97** H7
Stukeley St, WC1 **18** B3
WC2 **18** B3
Stumps Hill La, Beck. BR3 **172** A6
Sturdy Rd, SE15 **152** E2
Sturge Av, E17 **78** B2
Sturgeon Rd, SE17 **35** J4
Sturges Fld, Chis. BR7 **175** G6
Sturgess Av, NW4 **71** H7
Sturge St, SE1 **27** J3
Sturmer Way, N7 **93** F5
Sturminster Cl, Hayes UB4 **102** C6
Sturrock Cl, N15 **76** A4
Sturry St, E14 **114** B6
Sturt St, N1 **12** A2
Stutfield St, E1 **21** J4
Styles Gdns, SW9 **151** H3
Styles Way, Beck. BR3 **190** C4
Stylus Ho, E1
off Devonport St **113** F6
Sudbourne Rd, SW2 **151** E5
Sudbrooke Rd, SW12 **149** J6
Sudbrook Gdns, Rich. TW10 **163** G3
Sudbrook La, Rich. TW10 **163** H1
SUDBURY, Wem. HA0 **86** D5
Sudbury, E6
off Newark Knok **116** D6
Sudbury Av, Wem. HA0 **87** G3
Sudbury Ct, SW8
off Allen Edwards Dr **150** E1
Sudbury Ct Dr, Har. HA1 **86** C3
Sudbury Ct Rd, Har. HA1 **86** C3
Sudbury Cres, Brom. BR1 **173** G6
Wembley HA0 **87** E5
Sudbury Cft, Wem. HA0 **86** C4
Sudbury Gdns, Croy. CR0 **202** B4
Sudbury Hts Av, Grnf. UB6 **86** C5
Sudbury Hill, Har. HA1 **86** B2
Sudbury Hill Cl, Wem. HA0 **86** C4
Sudbury Ho, SW18
off Wandsworth High St **148** E5
Sudbury Rd, Bark. IG11 **99** J5
Sudeley St, N1 **11** H2
Sudlow Rd, SW18 **148** D4
Sudrey St, SE1 **27** J4
Suez Av, Grnf. UB6 **104** C2
Suez Rd, Enf. EN3 **45** H4
Suffield Rd, E4 **62** B3
N15 **76** C5
SE20 **189** F2
Suffolk Cl, Borwd. WD6 **38** D5
Suffolk Ct, E10 **78** A7
Ilford IG3 **81** H6
Suffolk La, EC4 **20** B5
Suffolk Pk Rd, E17 **77** H4
Suffolk Pl, SW1 **25** J1
Suffolk Rd, E13 **115** F3
N15 **76** A6
NW10 **89** E7
SE25 **188** C4

Suffolk Rd, SW13 ....**127** F7
Barking IG11 ....**99** G7
Dagenham RM10 ....**101** J5
Enfield EN3 ....**45** E5
Harrow HA2 ....**67** F6
Ilford IG3 ....**81** H6
Sidcup DA14 ....**176** C6
Worcester Park KT4 ....**197** F2
Suffolk St, E7 ....**97** G5
SW1 ....**25** J1
Sugar Bakers Ct, EC3
off Creechurch La **21** E4
Sugar Ho La, E15 ....**114** C2
Sugar Loaf Wk, E2
off Victoria Pk Sq **113** F3
Sugar Quay Wk, EC3 ....**20** E6
Sugden Rd, SW11 ....**150** A3
Thames Ditton KT7 ....**194** E1
Sugden Way, Bark. IG11 ....**117** J2
Sulgrave Gdns, W6
off Sulgrave Rd **127** J2
Sulgrave Rd, W6 ....**127** J2
Sulina Rd, SW2 ....**150** E7
Sulivan Ct, SW6 ....**148** D3
Sulivan Rd, SW6 ....**148** D3
Sulkin Ho, E2
off Knottisford St **113** G3
Sullivan Av, E16 ....**116** A5
Sullivan Cl, SW11 ....**149** H3
Hayes UB4 ....**102** C5
West Molesey KT8
off Victoria Av **179** G3
Sullivan Ho, SW1
off Churchill Gdns **33** E4
Sullivan Rd, SE11 ....**35** F1
Sultan Rd, E11 ....**79** H4
Sultan St, SE5 ....**35** J7
Beckenham BR3 ....**189** G2
Sultan Ter, N22
off Vincent Rd **75** G2
Sumatra Rd, NW6 ....**90** D5
Sumburgh Rd, SW12 ....**150** A6
Summer Av, E.Mol. KT8 ....**180** B5
Summercourt Rd, E1 ....**113** F6
Summer Crossing, T.Ditt.
KT7 ....**180** B4
Summerene Cl, SW16 ....**168** C7
Summerfield Av, NW6 ....**108** B2
Summerfield La, Surb.
(Long Dit.) KT6 ....**195** G2
Summerfield Rd, W5 ....**105** E4
Loughton IG10 ....**48** A6
Summerfields Av, N12 ....**57** H6
Summerfield St, SE12 ....**155** F7
Summer Gdns, E.Mol.
KT8 ....**180** B5
Summer Gro, W.Wick.
BR4 ....**205** E2
Summer Hill, Borwd.
(Els.) WD6 ....**38** A5
Chislehurst BR7 ....**192** D2
Summerhill Cl, Orp. BR6 ....**207** H3
Summerhill Gro, Enf. EN1 ....**44** B6
Summerhill Rd, N15 ....**76** A4
Summer Hill Vil, Chis.
BR7 ....**192** D1
Summerhill Way, Mitch.
CR4 ....**186** A1
Summerhouse Av, Houns.
TW5 ....**142** E1
Summerhouse La, West Dr.
(Harm.) UB7 ....**120** A6
Summerhouse Rd, N16 ....**94** B2
Summerland Gdns, N10 ....**74** B3
Summerlands Av, W3 ....**106** C7
Summerlee Av, N2 ....**73** J4
Summerlee Gdns, N2 ....**73** J4
Summerley St, SW18 ....**167** E2
Summer Rd, E.Mol. KT8 ....**180** B5
Thames Ditton KT7 ....**180** C5
Summersby Rd, N6 ....**74** B6
Summers Cl, Sutt. SM2
off Overton Rd **198** D7
Wembley HA9 ....**88** B1
Summerskill Cl, SE15
off Philip Wk **152** E3
Summerskille Cl, N9 ....**60** E2
Summers La, N12 ....**57** G7
Summers Row, N12 ....**57** H6
Summers St, EC1 ....**11** E6
SUMMERSTOWN, SW17 ....**166** E3
Summerstown, SW17 ....**167** F3
Summerton Way, SE28 ....**118** D6
Summer Trees, Sun. TW16
off The Avenue **178** B1
Summerville Gdns, Sutt.
SM1 ....**198** C6
Summerwood Rd, Islw.
TW7 ....**144** C5
Summit, The, Loug. IG10 ....**48** C1
Summit Av, NW9 ....**70** D5
Summit Cl, N14 ....**58** C2
NW9 ....**70** D4
Edgware HA8 ....**54** A7
Summit Ct, NW2 ....**90** B5
Summit Dr, Wdf.Grn. IG8 ....**80** A2
Summit Est, N16 ....**76** D7
Summit Rd, E17 ....**78** B4
Northolt UB5 ....**85** G7
Summit Way, N14 ....**58** B2
SE19 ....**170** B7
Sumner Av, SE15
off Peckham Rd **152** C1
Sumner Cl, Orp. BR6 ....**207** F4
Sumner Ct, SW8
off Darsley Dr **150** E1
Sumner Gdns, Croy. CR0 ....**201** G1
Sumner Pl, SW7 ....**31** F2
Sumner Pl Ms, SW7 ....**31** F2
Sumner Rd, SE15 ....**37** G6
Croydon CR0 ....**201** G1
Harrow HA1 ....**67** J7
Sumner Rd S, Croy. CR0 ....**201** G1
Sumner St, SE1 ....**27** H1
Sumpter Cl, NW3 ....**91** F6
Sun All, Rich. TW9
off Kew Rd **145** H4
Sunbeam Cres, W10 ....**107** J4
Sunbeam Rd, NW10 ....**106** C4
SUNBURY, Sun. TW16 ....**178** B3
Sunbury Av, NW7 ....**54** D5
SW14 ....**146** D4
Sunbury Cl, Walt. KT12 ....**178** A6
Sunbury Ct, Sun. TW16 ....**178** D2
Sunbury Ct Island, Sun.
TW16 ....**178** D3
Sunbury Ct Ms, Sun.
TW16 *off Lower Hampton Rd* **178** D2
Sunbury Ct Rd, Sun.
TW16 ....**178** C2
Sunbury Cross, Sun. TW16
off Staines Rd E **160** A7
Sunbury Gdns, NW7 ....**54** D5
Sunbury La, SW11 ....**149** G1
Walton-on-Thames
KT12 ....**178** A6
Sunbury Lock Ait, Walt.
KT12 ....**178** B4
Sunbury Rd, Sutt. SM3 ....**198** A3
Sunbury St, SE18 ....**136** C3
Sunbury Way, Felt. (Han.)
TW13 ....**160** C5
Sunbury Workshops, E2
off Swanfield St **13** F4
Sun Ct, EC3 ....**20** C4
Suncroft Pl, SE26 ....**171** F3
Sunderland Ct, SE22 ....**152** D7
Sunderland Mt, SE23 ....**171** G2
Sunderland Rd, SE23 ....**171** G1
W5 ....**125** G3
Sunderland Ter, W2 ....**14** A3
Sunderland Way, E12 ....**98** A2
Sundew Av, W12 ....**107** G7
Sundew Cl, W12 ....**107** G7
Sundial Av, SE25 ....**188** C3
Sundorne Rd, SE7 ....**135** H5
Sundra Wk, E1
off Beaumont Gro **113** G4
SUNDRIDGE, Brom. BR1 ....**173** J6
Sundridge Av, Brom. BR1 ....**192** A1
Chislehurst BR7 ....**174** A7
Welling DA16 ....**157** G2
Sundridge Ho, Brom. BR1
off Burnt Ash La **173** H5
Sundridge Pl, Croy. CR0
off Inglis Rd **202** D1
Sundridge Rd, Croy. CR0 ....**188** C7
Sunfields Pl, SE3 ....**135** H7
Sun-In-The-Sands, SE3 ....**135** H7
Sunken Rd, Croy. CR0 ....**203** F5
Sunland Av, Bexh. DA6 ....**159** E4
Sun La, SE3 ....**135** H7
Sunleigh Rd, Wem. HA0 ....**105** H1
Sunley Gdns, Grnf.
(Perivale) UB6 ....**104** D1
Sunlight Cl, SW19 ....**167** F6
Sunlight Sq, E2 ....**113** E3
Sunmead Rd, Sun. TW16 ....**178** A3
Sunna Gdns, Sun. TW16 ....**178** B2
Sunningdale, N14 ....**58** D5
Sunningdale Av, W3 ....**107** E7
Barking IG11 ....**117** G1
Feltham TW13 ....**160** E2
Ruislip HA4 ....**84** C1
Sunningdale Cl, E6 ....**116** C3
SE16 *off Ryder Dr* **132** E5
SE28 ....**118** E6
Stanmore HA7 ....**52** D7
Surbiton KT6
off Culsac Rd **195** H2
Sunningdale Gdns, NW9 ....**70** C5
W8 *off Lexham Ms* **128** D3
Sunningdale Rd, Brom.
BR1 ....**192** B4
Sutton SM1 ....**198** C4
Sunningfields Cres,
NW4 ....**71** H2
Sunningfields Rd, NW4 ....**71** H2
Sunninghill Ct, W3
off Bollo Br Rd **126** C2
Sunninghill Rd, SE13 ....**154** B2
Sunny Bk, SE25 ....**188** D3
Sunny Cres, NW10 ....**88** C7
Sunnycroft Rd, SE25 ....**188** D3
Hounslow TW3 ....**143** H2
Southall UB1 ....**103** G5
Sunnydale, Orp. BR6 ....**206** D2
Sunnydale Gdns, NW7 ....**54** D6
Sunnydale Rd, SE12 ....**155** H5
Sunnydene Av, E4 ....**62** D5
Ruislip HA4 ....**84** A1
Sunnydene Gdns, Wem.
HA0 ....**87** F6
Sunnydene St, SE26 ....**171** H4
Sunnyfield, NW7 ....**55** F4
Sunny Gdns Par, NW4
off Great N Way **71** J2
Sunny Gdns Rd, NW4 ....**71** H2
Sunny Hill, NW4 ....**71** H3
Sunnyhill Cl, E5 ....**95** H4
Sunnyhill Rd, SW16 ....**168** E4
Sunnyhurst Cl, Sutt.
SM1 ....**198** D3
Sunnymead Av, Mitch.
CR4 ....**186** C3
Sunnymead Rd, NW9 ....**70** D7
SW15 ....**147** H5
Sunnymede Dr, Ilf. IG6 ....**80** E4
Sunny Nook Gdns, S.Croy.
CR2 ....**202** A6
Sunny Pl, NW4
off Sunny Gdns Rd **71** J4
Sunny Rd, The, Enf. EN3 ....**45** G1
Sunnyside, NW2 ....**90** C3
SW19 ....**166** B6
Walton-on-Thames
KT12 ....**178** C5
Sunnyside Dr, E4 ....**46** C7
Sunnyside Pas, SW19 ....**166** B6
Sunnyside Pl, SW19
off Sunnyside **166** B6
Sunnyside Rd, E10 ....**96** A1
N19 ....**74** D7
W5 ....**125** G1
Ilford IG1 ....**99** F3
Teddington TW11 ....**162** A4
Sunnyside Rd E, N9 ....**60** D3
Sunnyside Rd N, N9 ....**60** C3
Sunnyside Rd S, N9 ....**60** C3
Sunnyside Ter, NW9
off Edgware Rd **70** D3
Sunny Vw, NW9 ....**70** D4
Sunny Way, N12 ....**57** H7
Sun Pas, SE16 ....**29** H5
Sunray Av, SE24 ....**152** A4
Bromley BR2 ....**192** B6
Surbiton KT5 ....**196** B2
West Drayton UB7 ....**120** A2
Sunrise Cl, Felt. TW13
off Exeter Rd **161** F3
Sun Rd, W14 ....**128** C5
Sunset Av, E4 ....**62** B1
Woodford Green IG8 ....**63** F4
Sunset Ct, Wdf.Grn. IG8
off Navestock Cres **63** J7
Sunset Gdns, SE25 ....**188** C2
Sunset Rd, SE5 ....**151** J4
SE28 ....**138** A2
Sunset Vw, Barn. EN5 ....**40** B2
Sunshine Way, Mitch.
CR4 ....**185** J2
Sun St, EC2 ....**20** D2
Sun Wk, E1 ....**21** H6
Sunwell Cl, SE15
off Cossall Wk **152** E2
Superior Dr, Orp.
(Grn St Grn) BR6 ....**207** J6
SURBITON, KT5 & KT6 ....**181** J7
Surbiton Ct, Surb. KT6 ....**181** F6
Surbiton Cres, Kings.T.
KT1 ....**181** H4
Surbiton Hall Cl, Kings.T.
KT1 ....**181** H4
Surbiton Hill Pk, Surb.
KT5 ....**182** A5
Surbiton Hill Rd, Surb.
KT6 ....**181** H4
Surbiton Par, Surb. KT6
off St. Mark's Hill **181** H6
Surbiton Rd, Kings.T.
KT1 ....**181** H4
Surlingham Cl, SE28 ....**118** D7
Surma Cl, E1 ....**112** E4
Surmans Cl, Dag. RM9 ....**118** C1
Surrendale Pl, W9 ....**108** D4
Surrey Canal Rd, SE14 ....**133** F6
SE15 ....**133** F6
Surrey Cl, N3 ....**72** B3
Surrey Cres, W4 ....**126** A5
★ **Surrey Docks Fm**,
SE16 ....**133** J2
Surrey Gdns, N4 ....**75** J6
Surrey Gro, SE17 ....**36** D4
Sutton SM1 ....**199** G3
Surrey La, SW11 ....**149** H1
Surrey La Est, SW11 ....**149** H1
Surrey Ms, SE27
off Hamilton Rd **170** B4
Surrey Mt, SE23 ....**171** E1
Surrey Quays Rd, SE16 ....**133** F3
Surrey Quays Shop Cen,
SE16 ....**133** G3
Surrey Rd, SE15 ....**153** G5
Barking IG11 ....**117** H1
Dagenham RM10 ....**101** H5
Harrow HA1 ....**67** J5
West Wickham BR4 ....**204** B1
Surrey Row, SE1 ....**27** G3
Surrey Sq, SE17 ....**36** D3
Surrey St, E13 ....**115** H3
WC2 ....**18** D5
Croydon CR0 ....**201** J3
Surrey Ter, SE17 ....**36** E2
Surrey Water Rd, SE16 ....**133** G1
Surridge Gdns, SE19
off Hancock Rd **170** A6
Surr St, N7 ....**92** E5
Sury Basin, Kings.T. KT2 ....**181** H1
Susan Cl, Rom. RM7 ....**83** J3
Susan Constant Ct, E14
off Newport Av **114** D7
Susan Lawrence Ho, E12
off Walton Rd **98** D4
Susannah St, E14 ....**114** B6
Susan Rd, SE3 ....**155** H2
Susan Wd, Chis. BR7 ....**192** D1
Sussex Av, Islw. TW7 ....**144** B3
Sussex Cl, N19 ....**92** E2
Ilford IG4 ....**80** C6
New Malden KT3 ....**183** E4
Twickenham TW1
off Westmorland Cl **145** E6
Sussex Cres, Nthlt. UB5 ....**85** G6
Sussex Gdns, N4 ....**75** J5
N6 ....**73** J5
W2 ....**15** E5
Chessington KT9 ....**195** G6
Sussex Ms, SE6
off Ravensbourne Pk **154** A7
Sussex Ms E, W2 ....**15** F4
Sussex Ms W, W2 ....**15** F5
Sussex Pl, NW1 ....**7** J4
W2 ....**15** F4
W6 ....**127** J5
Erith DA8 ....**139** H7
New Malden KT3 ....**183** E4
Sussex Ring, N12 ....**56** D5
Sussex Rd, E6 ....**116** D1
Carshalton SM5 ....**199** J6
Erith DA8 ....**139** H7
Harrow HA1 ....**67** J5
Mitcham CR4
off Lincoln Rd **186** E5
New Malden KT3 ....**183** E4
Sidcup DA14 ....**176** B5
South Croydon CR2 ....**202** A6
Southall UB2 ....**122** D3
West Wickham BR4 ....**204** B1
Sussex Sq, W2 ....**15** F5
Sussex St, E13 ....**115** H3
SW1 ....**32** E4
Sussex Way, N7 ....**93** E2
N19 ....**92** E1
Barnet (Cockfos.) EN4 ....**42** A5
Sutcliffe Cl, NW11 ....**73** E5
Sutcliffe Ho, Hayes UB3 ....**102** A6
Sutcliffe Rd, SE18 ....**137** H6
Welling DA16 ....**158** C2
Sutherland Av, W9 ....**6** C4
W13 ....**104** E6
Hayes UB3 ....**122** A4
Orpington BR5 ....**193** J6
Welling DA16 ....**157** H4
Sutherland Cl, Barnet
EN5 ....**40** B4
Sutherland Ct, NW9 ....**70** B5
Sutherland Dr, SW19 ....**185** G1
Sutherland Gdns, SW14 ....**147** E3
Worcester Park KT4 ....**197** H1
Sutherland Gro, SW18 ....**148** B6
Teddington TW11 ....**162** B5
Sutherland Pl, W2 ....**108** D6
Sutherland Rd, E17 ....**77** G2
N9 ....**60** D1
N17 ....**60** D7
W4 ....**126** E6
W13 ....**104** D6
Belvedere DA17 ....**139** G3
Croydon CR0 ....**187** G7
Enfield EN3 ....**45** G5
Southall UB1 ....**103** F6
Sutherland Rd Path,
E17 ....**77** G3
Sutherland Row, SW1 ....**32** E3
Sutherland Sq, SE17 ....**35** J4
Sutherland St, SW1 ....**32** D3
Sutherland Wk, SE17 ....**36** A4
Sutlej Rd, SE7 ....**135** J7
Sutterton St, N7 ....**93** F6
SUTTON, SM1 - SM3 ....**198** E6
Sutton Cl, Beck. BR3 ....**190** B1
Loughton IG10 ....**48** B7
Pinner HA5 ....**66** A5
Sutton Common Rd, Sutt.
SM1, SM3 ....**184** C7
Sutton Ct, W4 ....**126** C6
Sutton SM2 ....**199** F6

Sutton Ct Rd, E13 **115** J3
W4 **126** C7
Sutton SM1 **199** F6
Sutton Cres, Barn. EN5 **40** A5
Sutton Dene, Houns.
TW3 **143** H1
Sutton Est, SW3 **31** H3
W10 **107** J5
Sutton Est, The, N1 **93** H7
Sutton Gdns, Bark. IG11
off Sutton Rd **117** H1
Croydon CR0 **188** C5
Sutton Grn, Bark. IG11
off Sutton Rd **117** H1
Sutton Gro, Sutt. SM1 **199** G4
Sutton Hall Rd, Houns.
TW5 **123** G7
Sutton Hts, Sutt. SM2 **199** G7
★ **Sutton Ho**, E9 **95** F5
Sutton La, EC1 **11** H6
Hounslow TW3 **143** F3
Sutton La N, W4 **126** C5
Sutton La S, W4 **126** C6
Sutton Par, NW4
off Church Rd **71** J4
Sutton Pk Rd, Sutt. SM1 **198** E6
Sutton Path, Borehamwood
WD6 **38** A3
Sutton Pl, E9 **95** F5
Sutton Rd, E13 **115** F4
E17 **77** G1
N10 **74** A2
Barking IG11 **117** H2
Hounslow TW5 **143** G1
Sutton Row, W1 **17** J3
Sutton Sq, E9
off Urswick Rd **95** F5
Hounslow TW5 **143** F1
Sutton St, E1 **113** F6
Sutton's Way, EC1 **12** A6
Sutton Wk, SE1 **26** D2
Sutton Way, W10 **107** J5
Hounslow TW5 **143** F1
Swaby Rd, SW18 **167** F1
Swaffham Way, N22 **59** H7
Swaffield Rd, SW18 **149** E7
Swain Cl, SW16 **168** B6
Swain Rd, Th.Hth. CR7 **187** J5
Swains Cl, West Dr. UB7 **120** B2
Swains La, N6 **92** A3
Swainson Rd, W3 **127** F2
Swains Rd, SW17 **167** J7
Swain St, NW8 **7** G5
Swaledale Cl, N11
off Ribblesdale Av **58** A6
Swallands Rd, SE6 **172** A3
Swallow Cl, SE14 **153** F1
Bushey WD23 **51** J1
Swallow Dr, NW10
off Kingfisher Way **88** D6
Northolt UB5 **103** G2
Swallowfield, NW1
off Munster Sq **9** E4
Swallowfield Rd, SE7 **135** H5
Swallowfield Way, Hayes
UB3 **121** G2
Swallow Gdns, SW16 **168** D5
Swallow Ho, NW8
off Allitsen Rd **7** G1
Swallow Pas, W1
off Swallow Pl **17** E4
Swallow Pl, W1 **17** E4
Swallow St, E6 **116** B5
W1 **17** G6
Swanage Ho, SW8
off Dorset Rd **131** F7
Swanage Rd, E4 **62** C7
SW18 **149** F6
Swanage Waye, Hayes
UB4 **102** C6
Swan App, E6 **116** B5
Swanbourne, SE17 **35** J2
Swanbridge Rd, Bexh.
DA7 **159** G1
Swan Cen, The, SW17
off Rosemary Rd **167** F3
Swan Cl, E17 **77** H1
Croydon CR0 **188** B7
Feltham TW13 **161** E4
Swan Ct, SW3 **31** H4
Swandon Way, SW18 **149** E5
Swan Dr, NW9 **70** E2
Swanfield St, E2 **13** F4
Swan Junct, The, W.Wick.
BR4 **204** C2
Swan La, EC4 **20** B6
N20 **57** F3
Loughton IG10 **47** J7
Swanley Rd, Well. DA16 **158** C1
Swan Mead, SE1 **28** D6
Swan Ms, SW6
off Purser's Cross Rd **148** D1
Romford RM7 **83** H4
Swan Pas, E1
off Cartwright St **21** G6
Swan Path, E10
off Jesse Rd **96** C1
Swan Pl, SW13 **147** F2
Swan Rd, SE16 **133** F2
SE18 **136** A3
Feltham TW13 **160** E5
Southall UB1 **103** H6
West Drayton UB7 **120** A2
Swanscombe Ho, W11
off St. Anns Rd **128** A1
Swanscombe Rd, W4 **127** E5
W11 **128** A1
Swansea Ct, E16
off Fishguard Way **137** E1
Swansea Rd, Enf. EN3 **45** F4
Hounslow
(Lon.Hthrw Air.) TW6
off Southern
Perimeter Rd **141** F6
Swanshope, Loug. IG10 **49** E2
Swansland Gdns, E17
off McEntee Av **77** H1
Swanston Path, Wat.
WD19 **50** C3
Swan St, SE1 **28** A5
Isleworth TW7 **144** E3
Swanton Gdns, SW19 **166** A1
Swanton Rd, Erith
DA8 **139** H7
Swan Wk, SW3 **31** J5
Swan Way, Enf. EN3 **45** G2
Swanwick Cl, SW15 **147** F7
Swan Yd, N1
off Highbury Sta Rd **93** H6
Swaton Rd, E3 **114** A4
Swaylands Rd, Belv.
DA17 **139** G6
Swaythling Cl, N18 **61** E4
Swaythling Ho, SW15
off Tunworth Cres **147** F6
Swedenborg Gdns, E1 **21** J5
Sweden Gate, SE16 **133** H3
Sweeney Cres, SE1 **29** G4
Sweet Briar Grn, N9 **60** C3
Sweet Briar Gro, N9 **60** C3
Sweet Briar Wk, N18 **60** C4
Sweetmans Av, Pnr.
HA5 **66** D3
Sweets Way, N20 **57** G2
Swetenham Wk, SE18
off Sandbach Pl **137** F5
Swete St, E13 **115** G2
Sweyn Pl, SE3 **155** G2
Swift Cl, E17 **61** H7
SE28
off Greenhaven Dr **118** B6
Harrow HA2 **85** H2
Swift Rd, Felt. TW13 **161** E3
Southall UB2 **123** F3
Swiftsden Way, Brom.
BR1 **173** E6
Swift St, SW6 **148** C1
Swinbrook Rd, W10 **108** B5
Swinburne Ct, SE5
off Basingdon Way **152** A4
Swinburne Cres, Croy.
CR0 **189** F6
Swinburne Rd, SW15 **147** G4
Swinderby Rd, Wem. HA0 **87** H6
Swindon Cl, Ilf. IG3
off Salisbury Rd **99** H2
Swindon Rd, Houns.
(Lon.Hthrw Air.) TW6 **141** F5
Swindon St, W12 **127** H1
Swinfield Cl, Felt. TW13 **160** E4
Swinford Gdns, SW9 **151** H3
Swingate La, SE18 **137** H6
Swinnerton St, E9 **95** H5
Swinton Cl, Wem. HA9 **88** B1
Swinton Pl, WC1 **10** C3
Swinton St, WC1 **10** C3
Swires Shaw, Kes. BR2 **206** A4
Swiss Ct, W1 **17** J6
Swiss Ter, NW6 **91** G7
Switch Ho, E14
off Blackwall Way **114** D7
Swithland Gdns, SE9 **174** D4
Swyncombe Av, W5 **125** E4
Swynford Gdns, NW4 **71** G4
Sybil Ms, N4
off Lothair Rd N **75** H6
Sybil Phoenix Cl, SE8 **133** G5
Sybourn St, E17 **77** J7
Sycamore Av, E3 **113** J1
W5 **125** G3
Sidcup DA15 **157** J6
Sycamore Cl, E16
off Clarence Rd **115** E4
N9 **60** D4
SE9 **174** B2
W3 *off Bromyard Av* **126** E1
Barnet EN4 **41** G6
Carshalton SM5 **199** J4
Edgware HA8
off Ash Cl **54** C4
Feltham TW13 **160** A3
Loughton IG10 **49** E2
Northolt UB5 **103** E1
South Croydon CR2 **202** B5
Sycamore Ct, Surb. KT6
off Penners Gdns **181** H7
Sycamore Gdns, W6 **127** H2
Mitcham CR4 **185** G2
Sycamore Gro, NW9 **70** C7
SE6 **154** C6
SE20 **170** D7
New Malden KT3 **182** D3
Sycamore Hill, N11 **58** A6
Sycamore Ho, NW3
off Maitland Pk Vil **91** J6
Sycamore Ms, SW4 **150** C3
Sycamore Pl, Brom. BR1 **192** D3
Sycamore Rd, SW19 **165** J6
Sycamore St, EC1 **11** J6
Sycamore Wk, W10
off Fifth Av **108** B4
Ilford IG6
off Civic Way **81** F4
Sycamore Way, Tedd.
TW11 **163** F6
Thornton Heath CR7 **187** G5
SYDENHAM, SE26 **171** F5
Sydenham Av, N21
off Fleming Dr **43** F5
SE26 **171** E5
Sydenham Cotts, SE12 **173** J2
Sydenham Hill, SE23 **170** E1
SE26 **170** D3
Sydenham Hill Est, SE26 **170** D3
Sydenham Pk, SE26 **171** F3
Sydenham Pk Rd, SE26 **171** F3
Sydenham Pl, SE27
off Lansdowne Hill **169** H3
Sydenham Ri, SE23 **170** E2
Sydenham Rd, SE26 **171** F4
Croydon CR0 **188** A7
Sydmons Ct, SE23 **153** F7
Sydner Ms, N16
off Sydner Rd **94** C4
Sydner Rd, N16 **94** C4
Sydney Chapman Way,
Barn. EN5 **40** C2
Sydney Cl, SW3 **31** F2
Sydney Gro, NW4 **71** J5
Sydney Ms, SW3 **31** F2
Sydney Pl, SW7 **31** F2
Sydney Rd, E11
off Mansfield Rd **79** H6
N8 **75** G4
N10 **74** A1
SE2 **138** C3
SW20 **184** A2
W13 **124** D1
Bexleyheath DA6 **158** D4
Enfield EN2 **44** A4
Feltham TW14 **160** A1
Ilford IG6 **81** F2
Richmond TW9 **145** H4
Sidcup DA14 **175** H4
Sutton SM1 **198** D4
Teddington TW11 **162** C5
Woodford Green IG8 **63** G4
Sydney St, SW3 **31** G3
Sylvan Av, N3 **72** D2
N22 **59** F7
NW7 **55** F6
Romford RM6 **83** F6
Sylvan Ct, N12 **56** E4
Sylvan Est, SE19 **188** C1
Sylvan Gdns, Surb. KT6 **181** G7
Sylvan Gro, NW2 **90** A4
SE15 **133** E7
Sylvan Hill, SE19 **188** B1
Sylvan Rd, E7 **97** G6
E11 **79** G5
E17 **78** A5
SE19 **188** C1
Ilford IG1 **99** F2
Sylvan Wk, Brom. BR1 **192** C3
Sylvan Way, Dag. RM8 **100** B3
West Wickham BR4 **204** E4
Sylverdale Rd, Croy. CR0 **201** H3
Sylvester Av, Chis. BR7 **174** C6
Sylvester Path, E8
off Sylvester Rd **95** E6
Sylvester Rd, E8 **95** E6
E17 **77** J7
N2 **73** F2
Wembley HA0 **87** F5
Sylvestrus Cl, Kings.T.
KT1 **182** A1
Sylvia Av, Pnr. HA5 **51** F6
Sylvia Ct, Wem. HA9
off Harrow Rd **88** B7
Sylvia Gdns, Wem. HA9 **88** B7
Symes Ms, NW1 **9** F1
Symington Ho, SE1 **28** B6
Symington Ms, E9
off Coopersale Rd **95** G5
Symister Ms, N1 **12** D4
Symons Cl, SE15 **153** F2
Symons St, SW3 **32** A2
Symphony Cl, Edgware
HA8 **54** B7
Symphony Ms, W10
off Third Av **108** B3
Syon Gate Way, Brent.
TW8 **124** D7
★ **Syon Ho & Pk**, Brent.
TW8 **145** F1
Syon La, Islw. TW7 **124** E7
Syon Pk Gdns, Islw. TW7 **124** C7
Syon Vista, Rich. TW9 **145** G1

T

Tabard Cen, SE1
off Prioress St **28** C6
Tabard Gdns Est, SE1 **28** C4
Tabard St, SE1 **28** B4
Tabernacle Av, E13
off Barking Rd **115** G4
Tabernacle St, EC2 **12** C6
Tableer Av, SW4 **150** C5
Tabley Rd, N7 **92** E4
Tabor Gdns, Sutt. SM3 **198** C6
Tabor Gro, SW19 **166** B7
Tabor Rd, W6 **127** H3
Tachbrook Est, SW1 **33** J4
Tachbrook Ms, SW1 **33** F1
Tachbrook Rd, Felt. TW14 **141** J7
Southall UB2 **122** D4
Tachbrook St, SW1 **33** G2
Tack Ms, SE4 **154** A3
Tadema Ho, NW8 **7** F6
Tadema Rd, SW10 **30** D7
Tadmor St, W12 **128** A1
Tadworth Av, N.Mal. KT3 **183** F5
Tadworth Rd, NW2 **89** G2
Taeping St, E14 **134** B4
Taffy's How, Mitch. CR4 **185** H3
Taft Way, E3
off Franklin St **114** B3
Tagg's Island, Hmptn.
TW12 **180** A2
Tailworth St, E1 **21** H2
Tait Ct, SW8
off Darsley Dr **150** D1
Tait Rd, Croy. CR0 **188** B7
Tait Rd Ind Est, Croy.
CR0 **188** B7
Tait St, E1 **112** E6
Takhar Ms, SW11
off Cabul Rd **149** H2
Talacre Rd, NW5 **92** A6
Talbot Av, N2 **73** G3
Talbot Cl, N15 **76** C4
Talbot Ct, EC3 **20** C5
Talbot Cres, NW4 **71** G5
Talbot Gdns, Ilf. IG3 **100** A2
Talbot Ho, E14
off Giraud St **114** B6
N7 *off Harvist Est* **93** G3
Talbot Pl, SE3 **154** E2
Talbot Rd, E6 **116** D2
E7 **97** G4
N6 **74** A6
N15 **76** C4
N22 **74** C2
SE22 **152** B4
W2 **108** D6
W11 **108** C6
W13 **104** D7
Carshalton SM5 **200** A5
Dagenham RM9 **101** F6
Harrow HA3 **68** C2
Isleworth TW7 **144** D4
Southall UB2 **123** E4
Thornton Heath CR7 **188** A4
Twickenham TW2 **162** B1
Wembley HA0 **87** G5
Talbot Sq, W2 **15** F4
Talbot Wk, NW10
off Garnet Rd **89** E6
W11 **108** B6
Talbot Yd, SE1 **28** B2
Talehangers Cl, Bexh.
DA6 **158** D4
Talfourd Pl, SE15 **152** C1
Talfourd Rd, SE15 **152** C1
Talgarth Rd, W6 **128** B5
W14 **128** B5
Talgarth Wk, NW9 **70** E5
Talisman Cl, Ilf. IG3 **100** B1
Talisman Sq, SE26 **170** D4
Talisman Way, Wem. HA9 **87** J3
Tallack Cl, Har. HA3 **52** B7
Tallack Rd, E10 **95** J1
Tall Elms Cl, Brom. BR2 **191** F5
Tallis Cl, E16 **115** H6
Tallis Gro, SE7 **135** H6
Tallis St, EC4 **19** F5
Tallis Vw, NW10 **88** D6
Tallow Cl, Dag. RM9
off Hedgemans Rd **100** D7
Tallow Rd, Brent. TW8 **125** F6
Tall Trees, SW16 **187** F3
Tally Ho Cor, N12 **57** F5
Talma Gdns, Twick. TW2 **144** B6
Talmage Cl, SE23
off Tyson Rd **153** F7
Talman Gro, Stan. HA7 **53** G6

Talma Rd, SW2 . . . . **151** G4
Talwin St, E3 . . . . **114** B3
Tamar Cl, E3
off Legion Ter **113** J1
Tamarind Yd, E1 . . . . **29** J1
Tamarisk Sq, W12 . . . . **107** F7
Tamar Sq, Wdf.Grn. IG8 . . . . **63** H6
Tamar St, SE7
off Woolwich Rd **136** B4
Tamar Way, N17 . . . . **76** D3
Tamesis Gdns, Wor.Pk. KT4 . . . . **196** E1
Tamian Way, Houns. TW4 . **142** C4
Tamworth Av, Wdf.Grn. IG8 . . . . **63** E6
Tamworth La, Mitch. CR4 . **186** B2
Tamworth Pk, Mitch. CR4 . **186** B4
Tamworth Pl, Croy. CR0 . . **201** J2
Tamworth Rd, Croy. CR0 . . **201** H2
Tamworth St, SW6 . . . . . . **128** D6
Tancred Rd, N4 . . . . **75** H6
Tandem Cen, SW19 . . . . . . **185** G1
Tandem Way, SW19 . . . . . . **185** G1
Tandridge Dr, Orp. BR6 . . . **207** G1
Tandridge Pl, Orp. BR6 . . . **207** G1
Tanfield Av, NW2 . . . . **89** F4
Tanfield Rd, Croy. CR0 . . . . **201** J4
Tangier Rd, Rich. TW10 . . . **146** B3
Tangleberry Cl, Brom. BR1 . . . . **192** B4
Tangle Tree Cl, N3 . . . . **73** E2
Tanglewood Cl, Croy. CR0 . . . . **203** F3
Stanmore HA7 . . . . **52** B2
Tanglewood Way, Felt. TW13 . . . . **160** B3
Tangley Gro, SW15 . . . . . . **147** F7
Tangley Pk Rd, Hmptn. TW12 . . . . **161** F6
Tangmere Gdns, Nthlt. UB5 . . . . **102** C2
Tangmere Gro, Kings.T. KT2 . . . . **163** G5
Tangmere Way, NW9 . . . . . . **71** E2
Tanhurst Wk, SE2
off Alsike Rd **138** D3
Tankerton Rd, Surb. KT6 . . . . **195** J2
Tankerton St, WC1 . . . . **10** B4
Tankerton Ter, Croy. CR0
off Mitcham Rd **187** F7
Tankerville Rd, SW16 . . . . . **168** D6
Tankridge Rd, NW2 . . . . **89** H2
Tanner Pt, E13 . . . . **115** G1
Tanners Cl, Walt. KT12 . . . . **178** B6
Tanners End La, N18 . . . . . . **60** B4
Tanners Hill, SE8 . . . . **153** J1
Tanners La, Ilf. IG6 . . . . **81** F3
Tanners Ms, SE8
off Tanners Hill **153** J1
Tanner St, SE1 . . . . **28** E4
Barking IG11 . . . . **99** F6
Tanners Yd, E2
off Treadway St **112** E2
Tannery Cl, Beck. BR3 . . . . **189** G5
Dagenham RM10 . . . . . . **101** H3
Tannington Ter, N5 . . . . **93** G3
Tannsfeld Rd, SE26 . . . . . . **171** G5
Tansley Cl, N7
off Hilldrop La **92** D5
Tanswell Est, SE1 . . . . **27** E4
Tanswell St, SE1 . . . . **27** E4
Tansy Cl, E6 . . . . **116** D6
Tantallon Rd, SW12 . . . . . . **168** A1
Tant Av, E16 . . . . **115** F6
Tantony Gro, Rom. RM6 . . . **82** D3
Tanworth Gdns, Pnr. HA5 . . . . **66** B2
Tanyard Ho, Brent. TW8
off High St **125** F7
Tanyard La, Bex. DA5 . . . . . **177** G1
Tanza Rd, NW3 . . . . **91** J4
Tapestry Cl, Sutton SM2 . . . . **198** E7
Taplow, NW3 . . . . **91** G7
SE17 . . . . **36** C3
Taplow Rd, N13 . . . . **59** J4
Taplow St, N1 . . . . **12** A2
Tappesfield Rd, SE15 . . . . . **153** F3
Tapp St, E1 . . . . **113** E4
Tapster St, Barn. EN5 . . . . . **40** C4
Tara Ms, N8
off Edison Rd **74** D6
Taransay Wk, N1
off Essex Rd **94** A6
Tarbert Ms, N15
off Roslyn Rd **76** B5
Tarbert Rd, SE22 . . . . **152** B5
Tarbert Wk, E1
off Juniper St **113** F7
Target Cl, Felt. TW14 . . . . . **141** H6
Target Rbt, Nthlt. UB5
off Western Av **103** F1
Tariff Cres, SE8 . . . . **133** J4
Tariff Rd, N17 . . . . **60** D6
Tarleton Gdns, SE23 . . . . . **171** E1
Tarling Cl, Sid. DA14 . . . . . **176** B3
Tarling Rd, E16 . . . . **115** F6
N2 . . . . **73** F2
Tarling St, E1 . . . . **113** E6
Tarling St Est, E1 . . . . **113** F6
Tarnbank, Enf. EN2 . . . . **43** E5
Tarn St, SE1 . . . . **27** J6
Tarnwood Pk, SE9 . . . . **174** C1
Tarquin Ho, SE26 . . . . **170** D4
Tarragon Cl, SE14 . . . . **133** H7
Tarragon Gro, SE26 . . . . . . **171** G6
Tarrant Pl, W1 . . . . **15** J2
Tarrington Cl, SW16 . . . . . . **168** D3
Tarver Rd, SE17 . . . . **35** H4
Tarves Way, SE10 . . . . **134** B7
Tash Pl, N11 . . . . **58** B5
Tasker Cl, Hayes (Harling.) UB3 . . . . **121** F7
Tasker Ho, Bark. IG11
off Dovehouse Mead . . **117** G2
Tasker Rd, NW3 . . . . **91** J5
Tasman Ct, E14
off Westferry Rd **134** B4
Tasmania Ter, N18 . . . . **59** J6
Tasman Rd, SW9 . . . . **151** E3
Tasman Wk, E16
off Royal Rd **116** A6
Tasso Rd, W6 . . . . **128** B6
Tatam Rd, NW10 . . . . **88** C7
Tatchbury Ho, SW15
off Tunworth Cres **147** F6
Tate & Lyle Jetty, E16 . . . . **136** B2
★ **Tate Britain**, SW1 . . . . . . **34** A2
★ **Tate Modern**, SE1 . . . . . **27** H1
Tate Rd, E16
off Newland St **136** C1
Sutton SM1 . . . . **198** D5
Tatham Pl, NW8 . . . . **7** F1
Tatnell Rd, SE23 . . . . **153** H6
Tattersall Cl, SE9 . . . . **156** B5
Tatton Cl, Cars. SM5 . . . . . **200** A1
Tatton Cres, N16
off Clapton Common . . **76** C7
Tatum St, SE17 . . . . **36** C2
Tauheed Cl, N4 . . . . **93** J2
Taunton Av, SW20 . . . . **183** H2
Hounslow TW3 . . . . **143** J2
Taunton Cl, Ilf. IG6 . . . . **65** J6
Sutton SM3 . . . . **198** D1
Taunton Dr, N2 . . . . **73** F2
Enfield EN2 . . . . **43** G3
Taunton Ms, NW1 . . . . **7** J6
Taunton Pl, NW1 . . . . **7** J5
Taunton Rd, SE12 . . . . **155** E5
Greenford UB6 . . . . **103** H1
Taunton Way, Stan. HA7 . . . **69** H3
Tavern Cl, Cars. SM5 . . . . . **185** H7
Taverners Cl, W11
off Addison Av **128** B1
Taverner Sq, N5
off Highbury Gra **93** J4
Taverners Way, E4 . . . . **62** E1
Tavern La, SW9 . . . . **151** G2
Tavistock Av, E17 . . . . **77** H3
NW7 . . . . **56** A7
Greenford (Perivale) UB6 . . . . **104** D2
Tavistock Cl, N16
off Crossway **94** B5
Tavistock Ct, WC2
off Tavistock St **18** B5
Tavistock Cres, W11 . . . . . . **108** C5
Mitcham CR4 . . . . **186** E4
Tavistock Gdns, Ilford IG3 . . . . **99** H4
Tavistock Gate, Croy. CR0 . . . . **202** A1
Tavistock Gro, Croydon CR0 . . . . **188** A7
Tavistock Ms, E18
off Avon Way **79** G4
N19 . . . . **92** E3
Tavistock Pl, E18
off Avon Way **79** G3
N14 . . . . **42** B6
WC1 . . . . **9** J5
Tavistock Rd, E7 . . . . **97** F4
E15 . . . . **97** F6
E18 . . . . **79** G3
N4 . . . . **76** A6
NW10 . . . . **107** F2
W11 . . . . **108** C6
Bromley BR2 . . . . **191** F4
Carshalton SM5 . . . . **199** G1
Croydon CR0 . . . . **202** A1
Edgware HA8 . . . . **70** A1
Welling DA16 . . . . **158** C1
West Drayton UB7 . . . . . **120** A1
Tavistock Sq, WC1 . . . . **9** J5
Tavistock St, WC2 . . . . **18** B5
Tavistock Ter, N19 . . . . **92** D3
Tavistock Twr, SE16
off Finland St **133** H3
Tavistock Wk, Cars. SM5
off Tavistock Rd **199** G1
Taviton St, WC1 . . . . **9** H5
Tavy Cl, SE11 . . . . **35** F3
Tawney Rd, SE28 . . . . **118** B7
Tawny Cl, W13 . . . . **124** E1
Feltham TW13
off Chervil Cl **160** A3
Tawny Way, SE16 . . . . **133** G4
Tayben Av, Twick. TW2 . . . . **144** B6
Taybridge Rd, SW11 . . . . . **150** A3
Tayburn Cl, E14 . . . . **114** C6
Taylor Av, Rich. TW9 . . . . . . **146** B2
Taylor Cl, N17 . . . . **60** D7
SE8 . . . . **133** J6
Hampton (Hmptn H.) TW12 . . . . **161** J5
Hounslow TW3 . . . . **143** J1
Orpington BR6 . . . . **207** J4
Taylor Pl, E3
off Payne Rd **114** B2
Taylor Rd, Mitch. CR4 . . . . **167** H7
Wallington SM6 . . . . **200** B5
Taylors Bldgs, SE18
off Spray St **137** E4
Taylors Cl, Sid. DA14 . . . . . **175** J4
Taylors Ct, Felt. TW13 . . . . **160** A2
Taylors Grn, W3 . . . . **107** E6
Taylors La, SE26 . . . . **170** E4
Barnet EN5 . . . . **40** C1
Taymount Ri, SE23 . . . . **171** F2
Tayport Cl, N1 . . . . **93** E7
Tayside Dr, Edg. HA8 . . . . . . **54** B3
Taywood Rd, Nthlt. UB5 . . **103** F3
Teak Cl, SE16 . . . . **133** H1
Teal Cl, E16
off Fulmer Rd **116** A5
Teal Ct, Wall. SM6
off Carew Rd **200** C6
Teale St, E2 . . . . **13** J1
Tealing Dr, Epsom KT19 . . **196** D4
Teal Pl, Sutt. SM1
off Sandpiper Rd **198** C5
Teal St, SE10 . . . . **135** F3
Teasel Cl, Croy. CR0 . . . . . **203** G1
Teasel Cres, SE28 . . . . **137** H1
Teasel Way, E15 . . . . **114** E3
Tebworth Rd, N17 . . . . **60** C7
Teck Cl, Islw. TW7 . . . . **144** D2
Tedder Cl, Chess. KT9 . . . . **195** F6
Ruislip HA4
off West End Rd **84** B5
Tedder Rd, S.Croydon CR2 . . . . **203** F7
TEDDINGTON, TW11 . . . . . **162** D6
Teddington Lock, Tedd. TW11 . . . . **162** E4
Teddington Pk, Tedd. TW11 . . . . **162** C5
Teddington Pk Rd, Tedd. TW11 . . . . **162** C4
Tedworth Gdns, SW3 . . . . . **31** J4
Tedworth Sq, SW3 . . . . **31** J4
Tee, The, W3 . . . . **106** E6
Tees Av, Grnf. (Perivale) UB6 . . . . **104** B2
Teesdale Av, Islw. TW7 . . . . **144** D1
Teesdale Cl, E2 . . . . **13** J2
Teesdale Gdns, SE25 . . . . . **188** B2
Isleworth TW7 . . . . **144** D1
Teesdale Rd, E11 . . . . **79** F6
Teesdale St, E2 . . . . **112** E2
Teesdale Yd, E2 . . . . **13** J1
Teeswater Ct, Erith DA18
off Middle Way **138** D3
Teevan Cl, Croy. CR0 . . . . . **188** D7
Teevan Rd, Croy. CR0 . . . . **188** D7
Tegan Cl, Sutt. SM2 . . . . . . **198** D7
Teign Ms, SE9 . . . . **174** B2
Teignmouth Cl, SW4 . . . . . **150** D4
Edgware HA8 . . . . **69** J2
Teignmouth Gdns, Grnf. (Perivale) UB6 . . . . **104** C2
Teignmouth Par, Grnf. UB6
off Teignmouth Gdns . . **104** E2
Teignmouth Rd, NW2 . . . . . **90** A5
Welling DA16 . . . . **158** C2
Telcote Way, Ruis. HA4
off Woodlands Av **66** C7
★ **Telecom Twr**, W1 . . . . . . **17** F1
Telegraph Hill, NW3 . . . . **90** E3
Telegraph La, Esher (Clay.) KT10 . . . . **194** C6
Telegraph Ms, Ilf. IG3 . . . . . **100** A1
Telegraph Path, Chis. BR7 . . . . **174** E5
Telegraph Pl, E14 . . . . **134** B4
Telegraph Rd, SW15 . . . . . **147** H7
Telegraph St, EC2 . . . . **20** B3
Telemann Sq, SE3 . . . . **155** H3
Telephone Pl, SW6
off Lillie Rd **128** C6
Telfer Cl, W3
off Church Rd **126** C2
Telferscot Rd, SW12 . . . . . . **168** D1
Telford Av, SW2 . . . . **168** E1
Telford Cl, E17 . . . . **77** H7
SE19
off St. Aubyn's Rd **170** C6
Telford Dr, Walt. KT12 . . . . **178** C7
Telford Ho, SE1 . . . . **27** J6
Telford Rd, N11 . . . . **58** C6
NW9
off West Hendon Bdy . . **71** G6
SE9 . . . . **175** G2
W10 . . . . **108** B5
Southall UB1 . . . . **103** H7
Twickenham TW2 . . . . . . **143** G7
Telfords Yd, E1 . . . . **21** J6
Telford Ter, SW1 . . . . **33** F5
Telford Way, W3 . . . . **106** E5
Hayes UB4 . . . . **102** E5
Telham Rd, E6 . . . . **116** D2
Tell Gro, SE22 . . . . **152** C4
Tellson Av, SE18 . . . . **156** B1
Telscombe Cl, Orp. BR6 . . . **207** H2
Temair Ho, SE10
off Tarves Way **134** B7
Temeraire Pl, Brent. TW8 . . **125** J5
Temeraire St, SE16
off Albion St **133** F2
Temperley Rd, SW12 . . . . . **150** A7
Templar Ct, NW8
off St. John's Wd Rd **7** E4
Templar Dr, SE28 . . . . **118** D6
Templar Ho, NW2
off Shoot Up Hill **90** C6
Harrow HA2
off Northolt Rd **86** A2
Templar Pl, Hmptn. TW12 . **161** G7
Templars Av, NW11 . . . . **72** C6
Templars Cres, N3 . . . . **72** D2
Templars Dr, Har. HA3 . . . . . **52** A6
Templar St, SE5 . . . . **151** H2
★ **Temple, The**, EC4 . . . . . . **19** E5
Temple Av, EC4 . . . . **19** F5
N20 . . . . **41** G7
Croydon CR0 . . . . **203** J2
Dagenham RM8 . . . . **101** G1
★ **Temple Bar**, EC4 . . . . . . **19** H4
★ **Temple Bar Mem**, EC4 . **18** E4
Temple Cl, E11 . . . . **78** E7
N3 *off Cyprus Rd* **72** C2
SE28 . . . . **137** F3
Templecombe Rd, E9 . . . . . **113** F1
Templecombe Way, Mord. SM4 . . . . **184** B5
Temple Ct, E1
off Rectory Sq **113** G5
SW8
off Thorncroft St **130** E7
Temple Dws, E2
off Temple St **112** E2
Temple Fortune Hill, NW11 . . . . **72** D5
Temple Fortune La, NW11 . . . . **72** D6
Temple Fortune Par, NW11
off Finchley Rd **72** C5
Temple Gdns, N21
off Barrowell Grn **59** H2
NW11 . . . . **72** C6
Dagenham RM8 . . . . **100** D3
Temple Gro, NW11 . . . . **72** D6
Enfield EN2 . . . . **43** H3
Templehof Av, NW2 . . . . **71** J7
Temple La, EC4 . . . . **19** F4
Templeman Rd, W7 . . . . . . **104** C5
Templemead Cl, W3 . . . . . . **106** E6
Temple Mead Cl, Stan. HA7 . . . . **52** E6
Templemead Ho, E9
off Kingsmead Way **95** H4
Temple Mill La, E15 . . . . **96** B4
★ **Temple of Mithras**, EC4
off Queen Victoria St . . . **20** B4
Temple Pl, WC2 . . . . **18** D5
Temple Rd, E6 . . . . **116** B1
N8 . . . . **75** F4
NW2 . . . . **89** J4
W4 . . . . **126** C3
W5 . . . . **125** G3
Croydon CR0 . . . . **202** A4
Hounslow TW3 . . . . **143** H4
Richmond TW9 . . . . **145** J3
Temple Sheen, SW14 . . . . **146** C5
Temple Sheen Rd, SW14 . . **146** B4
Temple St, E2 . . . . **112** E2
Templeton Av, E4 . . . . **62** A4
Templeton Cl, N16
off Boleyn Rd **94** B5
SE19 . . . . **188** A1
Templeton Ct, NW7
off Kingsbridge Dr **56** A7
Templeton Pl, SW5 . . . . **128** D4
Templeton Rd, N15 . . . . **76** A6
Temple Way, Sutt. SM1 . . . **199** G3
Temple W Ms, SE11 . . . . **27** G6
Templewood, W13 . . . . **105** E5
Templewood Av, NW3 . . . . . . **90** E3
Templewood Gdns, NW3 . . . **91** E3
Templewood Pt, NW2 . . . . . **90** C2
Temple Yd, E2
off Temple St **112** E2
Tempsford Av, Borwd. WD6 . . . . **38** D4
Tempsford Cl, Enf. EN2
off Gladbeck Way **43** J3

Tempus, Har. HA2 ... 85 J2
Tempus Ct, E18 ... 79 G1
Temsford Cl, Har. HA2 ... 67 J2
Tenbury Cl, E7
off Romford Rd ... 98 A5
Tenbury Ct, SW2 ... 168 D1
Tenby Av, Har. HA3 ... 68 E2
Tenby Cl, N15 ... 76 C4
Romford RM6 ... 82 E6
Tenby Gdns, Nthlt. UB5 ... 85 G6
Tenby Rd, E17 ... 77 H5
Edgware HA8 ... 69 J1
Enfield EN3 ... 45 F3
Romford RM6 ... 83 E6
Welling DA16 ... 158 D1
Tench St, E1 ... 132 E1
Tenda Rd, SE16
off Roseberry St ... 132 E4
Tendring Way, Rom. RM6 ... 82 C5
Tenham Av, SW2 ... 168 D1
Tenison Ct, W1 ... 17 F5
Tenison Way, SE1 ... 26 E2
Tenniel Cl, W2 ... 14 C4
Tennis Ct La, E.Mol. KT8
off Hampton Ct Way ... 180 B3
Tennison Av, Borwd. WD6 ... 38 B5
Tennison Rd, SE25 ... 188 C4
Tennis St, SE1 ... 28 B3
Tenniswood Rd, Enf.
EN1 ... 44 C1
Tennyson Av, E11 ... 79 G7
E12 ... 98 B7
NW9 ... 70 C3
New Malden KT3 ... 183 H5
Twickenham TW1 ... 162 C1
Tennyson Cl, Enf. EN3 ... 45 G5
Feltham TW14 ... 141 J6
Welling DA16 ... 157 H1
Tennyson Rd, E10 ... 96 B2
E15 ... 96 E7
E17 ... 77 J6
NW6 ... 108 C1
NW7 ... 55 G5
SE20 ... 171 G7
SW19 ... 167 F6
W7 ... 104 C7
Hounslow TW3 ... 143 J2
Tennyson St, SW8 ... 150 B2
Tensing Rd, Sthl. UB2 ... 123 G3
Tentelow La, Sthl. UB2 ... 123 G5
Tenterden Cl, NW4 ... 72 A3
SE9 ... 174 C4
Tenterden Dr, NW4 ... 72 A3
Tenterden Gdns, NW4 ... 72 A3
Croydon CR0 ... 188 D7
Tenterden Gro, NW4 ... 71 J4
Tenterden Rd, N17 ... 60 C7
Croydon CR0 ... 188 D7
Dagenham RM8 ... 101 F2
Tenterden St, W1 ... 16 E4
Tenter Grd, E1 ... 21 F2
Tenter Pas, E1 ... 21 G4
Tent Peg La, Orp. BR5 ... 193 F5
Tent St, E1 ... 112 E4
Tequila Wf, E14
off Commercial Rd ... 113 H6
Terborch Way, SE22
off East Dulwich Gro ... 152 B5
Teredo St, SE16 ... 133 G3
Terence Ct, Belv. DA17
off Nuxley Rd ... 139 F6
Teresa Ms, E17 ... 78 A4
Teresa Wk, N10
off Connaught Gdns ... 74 B5
Terling Cl, E11 ... 97 F3
Terling Rd, Dag. RM8 ... 101 G2
Terling Wk, N1
off Britannia Row ... 111 J1
Terminal Four Rbt,
Houns. TW6
off Shrewsbury Rd ... 141 F6
Terminus Pl, SW1 ... 25 E6
Terrace, The, E4
off Chingdale Rd ... 62 E3
N3 *off Hendon La* ... 72 C2
NW6 ... 108 D1
SW13 ... 147 E2
Woodford Green IG8
off Broadmead Rd ... 63 G6
Terrace Apts, N5
off Drayton Pk ... 93 G5
Terrace Gdns, SW13 ... 147 F2
Terrace La, Rich. TW10 ... 145 H6
Terrace Rd, E9 ... 95 F7
E13 ... 115 G1
Walton-on-Thames
KT12 ... 178 A7
Terrace Wk, Dag. RM9 ... 101 E5
Terrapin Rd, SW17 ... 168 B3
Terretts Pl, N1 ... 93 H7
Terrick Rd, N22 ... 75 E1
Terrick St, W12 ... 107 H6
Terrilands, Pnr. HA5 ... 67 F3
Terront Rd, N15 ... 75 J5
Tersha St, Rich. TW9 ... 145 J4
Tessa Sanderson Pl,
SW8 ... 150 B3
Tessa Sanderson Way,
Grnf. UB6
off Lilian Board Way ... 86 A5
Testerton Wk, W11 ... 108 A7
Tetbury Pl, N1
off Upper St ... 111 H1
Tetcott Rd, SW10 ... 30 C7
Tetherdown, N10 ... 74 A3
Tetty Way, Brom. BR2 ... 191 G2
Teversham La, SW8 ... 151 E1
Teviot Cl, Well. DA16 ... 158 B1
Teviot St, E14 ... 114 C5
Tewkesbury Av, SE23 ... 171 E1
Pinner HA5 ... 67 E5
Tewkesbury Cl, N15
off Tewkesbury Rd ... 76 A6
Barnet EN4
off Approach Rd ... 41 G4
Loughton IG10 ... 48 B6
Tewkesbury Gdns, NW9 ... 70 B3
Tewkesbury Rd, N15 ... 76 A6
W13 ... 104 D7
Carshalton SM5 ... 199 G1
Tewkesbury Ter, N11 ... 58 C6
Tewson Rd, SE18 ... 137 H5
Teynham Av, Enf. EN1 ... 44 A6
Teynham Grn, Brom.
BR2 ... 191 G5
Teynton Ter, N17 ... 75 J1
Thackeray Av, N17 ... 76 D2
Thackeray Cl, SW19 ... 166 A7
Isleworth TW7 ... 144 D2
Thackeray Dr, Rom. RM6 ... 82 A7
Thackeray Rd, E6 ... 116 A2
SW8 ... 150 B2
Thackeray St, W8 ... 22 B4
Thakeham Cl, SE26 ... 170 E5
Thalia Cl, SE10 ... 134 D6
Thame Rd, SE16 ... 133 G2
Thames Av, SW10 ... 149 F1
Dagenham RM9 ... 119 H4
Greenford (Perivale)
UB6 ... 104 C2
Wor.Pk. KT4 ... 197 J1
Thames Bk, SW14 ... 146 C2
Thamesbank Pl, SE28 ... 118 C6
★ **Thames Barrier Information & Learning Cen**, SE18 ... 136 A3
Thames Circle, E14
off Westferry Rd ... 134 A4
Thames Cl, Hmptn. TW12 ... 179 H2
Thames Ct, W.Mol. KT8 ... 179 H2
Thames Cres, W4 ... 127 E7
THAMES DITTON, KT7 ... 180 C6
Thames Ditton Island,
T.Ditt. KT7 ... 180 D5
Thamesgate Cl, Rich. TW10
off Locksmeade Rd ... 163 F4
Thames Gateway, Dag.
RM9 ... 119 F2
Thames Gateway Pk, Dag.
RM9 ... 119 F3
Thameshill Av, Rom. RM5 ... 83 J2
Thameside, Tedd. TW11 ... 163 G7
Thameside Ind Est, E16 ... 136 B2
Thameside Wk, SE28 ... 117 J6
Thames Link, SE16
off Salter Rd ... 133 G1
THAMESMEAD, SE28 ... 137 J1
Thamesmead, Walt.
KT12 ... 178 A7
THAMESMEAD NORTH,
SE28 ... 118 D6
Thames Meadow, W.Mol.
KT8 ... 179 G2
Thamesmead Spine Rd,
Belv. DA17 ... 139 H2
THAMESMEAD WEST,
SE18 ... 136 E3
Thamesmere Dr, SE28 ... 118 A7
Thames Pl, SW15 ... 148 A3
Thames Pt, SW6
off The Boulevard ... 149 F2
Thamespoint, Tedd. TW11 ... 163 G7
Thames Quay, SW10
off Harbour Av ... 149 F1
Thames Rd, E16 ... 136 A1
W4 ... 126 A6
Barking IG11 ... 117 J3
Thames Side, Kings.T.
KT1 ... 181 G1
Thames St, SE10 ... 134 B6
Hampton TW12 ... 179 H1
Kingston upon Thames
KT1 ... 181 G2
Sunbury-on-Thames
TW16 ... 178 B4
Thames Tunnel Mills,
SE16
off Rotherhithe St ... 133 F2
Thamesvale Cl, Houns.
TW3 ... 143 G3
Thames Vw, Ilf. IG1
off Axon Pl ... 99 F2
Thames Village, W4 ... 146 C1
Thames Wf, E16 ... 135 F1
Thanescroft Gdns, Croy.
CR0 ... 202 B3
Thanet Dr, Kes. BR2
off Phoenix Dr ... 206 A3
Thanet Pl, Croy. CR0 ... 201 J4
Thanet Rd, Bex. DA5 ... 159 G7
Thanet St, WC1 ... 10 A4
Thane Vil, N7 ... 93 F3
Thane Wks, N7 ... 93 F3
Thanington Ct, SE9 ... 157 H6
Thant Cl, E10 ... 96 B3
Tharp Rd, Wall. SM6 ... 200 D5
Thatcham Gdns, N20 ... 41 F7
Thatcher Cl, West Dr. UB7
off Classon Cl ... 120 B2
Thatchers Cl, Loug. IG10 ... 49 F2
Thatchers Way, Islw. TW7 ... 144 A5
Thatches Gro, Rom. RM6 ... 82 E4
Thavies Inn, EC1 ... 19 F3
Thaxted Ct, N1 ... 12 B2
Thaxted Ho, Dag. RM10 ... 101 H7
Thaxted Pl, SW20 ... 166 A7
Thaxted Rd, SE9 ... 175 F2
Buckhurst Hill IG9 ... 48 B7
Thaxton Rd, W14 ... 128 C6
Thayers Fm Rd, Beck.
BR3 ... 189 H1
Thayer St, W1 ... 16 C2
★ **Theatre Royal**, WC2 ... 18 B4
Theatre Sq, E15
off Great Eastern Rd ... 96 D6
Theatre St, SW11 ... 149 J3
Theberton St, N1 ... 111 G1
Theed St, SE1 ... 27 E2
Thelma Gdns, SE3 ... 156 A1
Feltham TW13 ... 161 E3
Thelma Gro, Tedd. TW11 ... 162 D6
Theobald Cres, Har. HA3 ... 67 H1
Theobald Rd, E17 ... 77 J7
Croydon CR0 ... 201 H2
Theobalds Av, N12 ... 57 F4
Theobalds Ct, N4
off Queens Dr ... 93 J3
Theobald's Rd, WC1 ... 18 C1
Theobald St, SE1 ... 28 B6
Theodore Rd, SE13 ... 154 C6
Therapia La, Croy. CR0 ... 187 E6
Therapia Rd, SE22 ... 153 F6
Theresa Rd, W6 ... 127 G4
Therfield Ct, N4
off Brownswood Rd ... 93 J2
Thermopylae Gate, E14 ... 134 B4
Theseus Wk, N1 ... 11 H2
Thesiger Rd, SE20 ... 171 G7
Thessaly Rd, SW8 ... 130 C7
Thetford Cl, N13 ... 59 H7
Thetford Gdns, Dag.
RM9 ... 100 D7
Thetford Rd, Dag. RM9 ... 118 D1
New Malden KT3 ... 182 D6
Thetis Ter, Rich. TW9
off Kew Grn ... 126 A6
Theydon Gro, Wdf.Grn.
IG8 ... 63 J6
Theydon Pk Rd, Epp.
(They.B.) CM16 ... 49 H1
Theydon Rd, E5 ... 95 F2
Theydon St, E17 ... 77 J7
Thicket Cres, Sutt. SM1 ... 199 F4
Thicket Gro, SE20
off Anerley Rd ... 170 D7
Dagenham RM9 ... 100 C6
Thicket Rd, SE20 ... 170 D7
Sutton SM1 ... 199 F4
Third Av, E12 ... 98 B4
E13 ... 115 G3
E17 ... 78 A5
W3 ... 127 F1
W10 ... 108 B3
Dagenham RM10 ... 119 H1
Enfield EN1 ... 44 C5
Hayes UB3 ... 121 J1
Romford RM6 ... 82 C5
Wembley HA9 ... 87 G2
Third Cl, W.Mol. KT8 ... 179 H4
Third Cross Rd, Twick.
TW2 ... 162 A2
Third Way, Wem. HA9 ... 88 B4
Thirleby Rd, NW7 ... 56 B5
SW1 ... 25 G6
Edgware HA8 ... 70 D1
Thirlmere Av, Grnf.
(Perivale) UB6 ... 105 F3
Thirlmere Gdns, Wem.
HA9 ... 87 F1
Thirlmere Ho, Islw. TW7
off Summerwood Rd ... 144 C5
Thirlmere Ri, Brom. BR1 ... 173 F6
Thirlmere Rd, N10 ... 74 B1
SW16 ... 168 D4
Bexleyheath DA7 ... 159 J2
Thirsk Cl, Nthlt. UB5 ... 85 G6
Thirsk Rd, SE25 ... 188 A4
SW11 ... 150 A3
Mitcham CR4 ... 168 A7
Thirston Path, Borwd.
WD6 ... 38 A2
Thistlebrook, SE2 ... 138 C3
Thistlebrook Ind Est, SE2 ... 138 C2
Thistlecroft Gdns, Stan.
HA7 ... 69 G1
Thistledene, T.Ditt. KT7 ... 180 B6
Thistledene Av, Har. HA2 ... 85 E3
Thistlefield Cl, Bex. DA5 ... 176 D1
Thistle Gro, SW10 ... 30 D3
Thistlemead, Chis. BR7 ... 192 E2
Thistle Mead, Loug. IG10 ... 48 D3
Thistlewaite Rd, E5 ... 95 E3
Thistlewood Cl, N7 ... 93 F2
Thistleworth Cl, Islw.
TW7 ... 124 A7
Thistley Cl, N12 ... 57 H6
Thistley Ct, SE8
off Glaisher St ... 134 B6
Thomas a'Beckett Cl, Wem.
HA0 ... 86 C4
Thomas Baines Rd, SW11 ... 149 G3
Thomas Cribb Ms, E6 ... 116 C6
Thomas Darby Ct, W11 ... 108 B6
Thomas Dean Rd, SE26 ... 171 J4
Thomas Dinwiddy Rd,
SE12 ... 173 H2
Thomas Doyle St, SE1 ... 27 G5
Thomas Hardy Ho, N22 ... 59 F7
Thomas Hollywood Ho, E2
off Approach Rd ... 113 F2
Thomas Jacomb Pl, E17 ... 77 J4
Thomas La, SE6 ... 154 A7
Thomas More Ho, EC2
off The Barbican ... 19 J2
Thomas More Sq, E1 ... 21 H6
Thomas More St, E1 ... 21 H6
Thomas More Way, N2 ... 73 F3
Thomas N Ter, E16
off Barking Rd ... 115 F5
Thomas Pl, W8 ... 22 A6
Thomas Rd, E14 ... 113 J6
Thomas St, SE18 ... 136 D4
Thomas Wall Cl, Sutt. SM1
off Clarence Rd ... 198 E5
Thompson Av, Rich. TW9 ... 146 A3
Thompson Cl, Ilf. IG1
off High Rd ... 99 F2
Sutton SM3
off Barrington Rd ... 198 D1
Thompson Rd, SE22 ... 152 C6
Dagenham RM9 ... 101 F3
Hounslow TW3 ... 143 H4
Thompsons Av, SE5 ... 35 J7
Thompson's La, Loug.
(High Beach) IG10 ... 47 F1
Thomson Cres, Croy.
CR0 ... 201 G1
Thomson Rd, Har. HA3 ... 68 B3
Thorburn Sq, SE1 ... 37 H2
Thorburn Way, SW19 ... 185 F1
Thoresby St, N1 ... 12 A3
Thorkhill Gdns, T.Ditt.
KT7 ... 194 D1
Thorkhill Rd, T.Ditt. KT7 ... 180 E7
Thornaby Gdns, N18 ... 60 D6
Thorn Av, Bushey
(Bushey Hth) WD23 ... 51 J1
Thornbury Av, Islw. TW7 ... 124 A7
Thornbury Cl, N16
off Boleyn Rd ... 94 B5
NW7
off Kingsbridge Dr ... 56 A7
Thornbury Gdns, Borwd.
WD6 ... 38 C4
Thornbury Rd, SW2 ... 150 E6
Isleworth TW7 ... 144 A1
Thornbury Sq, N6 ... 92 C1
Thornby Rd, E5 ... 95 F3
Thorncliffe Rd, SW2 ... 150 E6
Southall UB2 ... 123 F5
Thorn Cl, Brom. BR2 ... 192 D6
Northolt UB5 ... 103 F3
Thorncombe Rd, SE22 ... 152 B5
Thorncroft Rd, Sutt. SM1 ... 198 E4
Thorncroft St, SW8 ... 130 E7
Thorndean St, SW18 ... 167 F2
Thorndene Av, N11 ... 58 A1
Thorndike Av, Nthlt. UB5 ... 102 D1
Thorndike Cl, SW10 ... 30 C7
Thorndike Ho, SW1
off Vauxhall Br Rd ... 33 H3
Thorndike Rd, N1 ... 93 J6
Thorndike St, SW1 ... 33 H2
Thorndon Cl, Orp. BR5 ... 193 J2
Thorndon Gdns, Epsom
KT19 ... 196 E4
Thorndon Rd, Orp. BR5 ... 193 J2
Thorndyke Ct, Pnr. HA5
off Westfield Pk ... 51 F7
Thorne Cl, E11 ... 96 E4
E16 ... 115 G6
Erith DA8 ... 139 J6
Esher (Clay.) KT10 ... 194 D7
Thorneloe Gdns, Croy.
CR0 ... 201 G5
Thorne Pas, SW13 ... 147 E2
Thorne Rd, SW8 ... 130 E7
Thornes Cl, Beck. BR3 ... 190 C3

Thorne St, E16 ... 115 F6
 SW13 ... 147 E3
Thornet Wd Rd, Brom. BR1 ... 192 D3
Thorney Cres, SW11 ... 129 G7
Thorneycroft Cl, Walt. KT12 ... 178 C6
Thorney Hedge Rd, W4 ... 126 B4
Thorney St, SW1 ... 34 A1
Thornfield Av, NW7 ... 72 B1
Thornfield Rd, W12 ... 127 H2
Thornford Rd, SE13 ... 154 C5
Thorngate Rd, W9 ... 108 D4
Thorngrove Rd, E13 ... 115 H1
Thornham Gro, E15 ... 96 D5
Thornham St, SE10 ... 134 B6
Thornhaugh Ms, WC1 ... 9 J6
Thornhaugh St, WC1 ... 17 J1
Thornhill Av, SE18 ... 137 H7
 Surbiton KT6 ... 195 H2
Thornhill Br Wf, N1 off Caledonian Rd ... 111 F1
Thornhill Cres, N1 ... 93 F7
Thornhill Gdns, E10 ... 96 B2
 Barking IG11 ... 99 H7
Thornhill Gro, N1 off Lofting Rd ... 93 F7
Thornhill Rd, E10 ... 96 B2
 N1 ... 93 G7
 Croydon CR0 ... 187 J7
 Surbiton KT6 ... 195 H2
Thornhill Sq, N1 ... 93 F7
Thorn Ho, Beck. BR3 ... 189 H1
Thornlaw Rd, SE27 ... 169 G4
Thornley Cl, N17 ... 60 D7
Thornley Dr, Har. HA2 ... 85 H2
Thornley Pl, SE10 off Caradoc St ... 134 E5
Thornsbeach Rd, SE6 ... 172 C1
Thornsett Pl, SE20 ... 188 E2
Thornsett Rd, SE20 ... 188 E2
 SW18 ... 167 E2
Thornside, Edg. HA8 ... 54 A6
Thorn Ter, SE15 off Nunhead Gro ... 153 F3
Thornton Av, SW2 ... 168 D1
 W4 ... 127 E4
 Croydon CR0 ... 187 F6
 West Drayton UB7 ... 120 C3
Thornton Cl, West Dr. UB7 ... 120 C3
Thornton Ct, SW20 ... 184 A5
Thornton Dene, Beck. BR3 ... 190 A2
Thornton Gdns, SW12 ... 168 D1
Thornton Gro, Pnr. HA5 ... 51 G6
THORNTON HEATH, CR7 ... 187 H4
Thornton Heath Pond, Th.Hth. CR7 ... 187 G5
Thornton Hill, SW19 ... 166 B7
Thornton Ho, SE17 ... 36 C2
Thornton Pl, W1 ... 16 A1
Thornton Rd, E11 ... 96 D2
 N18 ... 61 F3
 SW12 ... 150 D7
 SW14 ... 146 D3
 SW19 ... 166 A6
 Barnet EN5 ... 40 B3
 Belvedere DA17 ... 139 H4
 Bromley BR1 ... 173 G5
 Carshalton SM5 ... 199 G1
 Croydon CR0 ... 187 F7
 Ilford IG1 ... 98 E4
 Thornton Heath CR7 ... 187 F7
Thornton Rd E, SW19 off Thornton Rd ... 166 A6
Thornton Rd Ind Est, Croy. CR0 ... 187 E6
Thornton Row, Th.Hth. CR7 off London Rd ... 187 G5
Thornton St, SW9 ... 151 G2
Thornton Way, NW11 ... 73 E5
Thorntree Rd, SE7 ... 136 A5
Thornville Gro, Mitch. CR4 ... 185 F2
Thornville St, SE8 ... 154 A1
Thornwood Cl, E18 ... 79 H2
Thornwood Gdns, W8 off Campden Hill ... 128 D2
Thornwood Rd, SE13 ... 154 E5
Thorogood Gdns, E15 ... 97 E5
Thorold Rd, N22 ... 59 E7
 Ilford IG1 ... 98 E2
Thorparch Rd, SW8 ... 150 D1
Thorpebank Rd, W12 ... 127 G1
Thorpe Cl, W10 off Cambridge Gdns ... 108 B6
 Orpington BR6 ... 207 H2
Thorpe Cres, E17 ... 77 J2
Thorpedale Gdns, Ilf. IG2, IG6 ... 80 D4
Thorpedale Rd, N4 ... 93 E1
Thorpe Hall Rd, E17 ... 78 C1
Thorpe Rd, E6 ... 116 C1
 E7 ... 97 F4
 E17 ... 78 C2
Thorpe Rd, N15 ... 76 B6
 Barking IG11 ... 99 G7
 Kingston upon Thames KT2 ... 163 H7
Thorpe Wk, Grnf. UB6 ... 104 B2
Thorpewood Av, SE26 ... 171 E2
Thorsden Way, SE19 off Oaks Av ... 170 B5
Thorverton Rd, NW2 ... 90 B3
Thoydon Rd, E3 ... 113 H2
Thrale Rd, SW16 ... 168 C5
Thrale St, SE1 ... 28 A2
Thrasher Cl, E8 off Dunston Rd ... 112 C1
Thrawl St, E1 ... 21 G2
Threadneedle St, EC2 ... 20 C4
Three Barrels Wk, EC4 ... 20 A6
Three Colts Cor, E2 ... 13 H5
Three Colts La, E2 ... 113 E4
Three Colt St, E14 ... 113 J7
Three Cors, Bexh. DA7 ... 159 H2
Three Cranes Wk, EC4 off Bell Wf La ... 20 A6
Three Cups Yd, WC1 ... 18 D2
Three Kings Rd, Mitch. CR4 ... 186 A3
Three Kings Yd, W1 ... 16 D5
Three Meadows Ms, Har. HA3 ... 68 C1
Three Mill La, E3 ... 114 C3
Three Oak La, SE1 ... 29 F3
Three Quays Wk, EC3 ... 20 E6
Threshers Pl, W11 ... 108 B7
Thriffwood, SE26 ... 171 F3
Thrift Fm La, Borwd. WD6 ... 38 B2
Thrigby Rd, Chess. KT9 ... 195 J6
Throckmorton Rd, E16 ... 115 H6
Throgmorton Av, EC2 ... 20 C3
Throgmorton St, EC2 ... 20 C3
Throwley Cl, SE2 ... 138 C3
Throwley Rd, Sutt. SM1 ... 199 E5
Throwley Way, Sutt. SM1 ... 199 E4
Thrupp Cl, Mitch. CR4 ... 186 B2
Thrush Grn, Har. HA2 ... 67 G4
Thrush St, SE17 ... 35 J3
Thunderer Rd, Dag. RM9 ... 118 E4
Thurbarn Rd, SE6 ... 172 B5
Thurland Ho, SE16 off Manor Est ... 132 E4
Thurland Rd, SE16 ... 29 H5
Thurlby Cl, Har. HA1 off Gayton Rd ... 68 D6
 Woodford Green IG8 ... 64 C5
Thurlby Rd, SE27 ... 169 G4
 Wembley HA0 ... 87 G6
Thurleigh Av, SW12 ... 150 A6
Thurleigh Rd, SW12 ... 150 A6
Thurleston Av, Mord. SM4 ... 184 B5
Thurlestone Av, N12 ... 57 J6
 Ilford IG3 ... 99 J4
Thurlestone Rd, SE27 ... 169 G3
Thurloe Cl, SW7 ... 31 G1
Thurloe Pl, SW7 ... 31 F1
Thurloe Pl Ms, SW7 ... 31 F1
Thurloe Sq, SW7 ... 31 G1
Thurloe St, SW7 ... 31 F1
Thurlow Cl, E4 off Higham Sta Av ... 62 B6
Thurlow Gdns, Ilf. IG6 ... 65 G6
 Wembley HA0 ... 87 G5
Thurlow Hill, SE21 ... 169 J1
Thurlow Pk Rd, SE21 ... 169 H1
Thurlow Rd, NW3 ... 91 G5
 W7 ... 124 D2
Thurlow St, SE17 ... 36 C3
Thurlow Ter, NW5 ... 92 A5
Thurlstone Rd, Ruis. HA4 ... 84 A3
Thurnby Ct, Twick. TW2 ... 162 B3
Thursland Rd, Sid. DA14 ... 176 E5
Thursley Cres, Croy. (New Adgtn) CR0 ... 204 D7
Thursley Gdns, SW19 ... 166 A2
Thursley Rd, SE9 ... 174 C3
Thurso Ho, NW6 ... 6 A2
Thurso St, SW17 ... 167 G4
Thurstan Rd, SW20 ... 165 H7
Thurston Rd, SE13 ... 154 B2
 Southall UB1 ... 103 F6
Thurston Rd Ind Est, SE13 off Jerrard St ... 154 B3
Thurtle Rd, E2 ... 112 C1
Thwaite Cl, Erith DA8 ... 139 J6
Thyer Cl, Orp. BR6 off Isabella Dr ... 207 F4
Thyme Cl, SE3 ... 155 J3
Thyra Gro, N12 ... 57 E6
Tibbatts Rd, E3 ... 114 B4
Tibbenham Pl, SE6 ... 172 A2
Tibbenham Wk, E13 ... 115 F2
Tibberton Sq, N1 off Popham Rd ... 93 J7
Tibbets Cl, SW19 ... 166 A1
Tibbet's Cor, SW15 ... 148 A7
Tibbet's Cor Underpass, SW15 off West Hill ... 148 A7
Tibbet's Ride, SW15 ... 148 A7
Tiber Cl, E3 off Garrison Rd ... 114 A1
Tiber Gdns, N1 off Copenhagen St ... 111 E1
Ticehurst Cl, Orp. BR5 ... 176 A7
Ticehurst Rd, SE23 ... 171 H2
Tickford Cl, SE2 off Ampleforth Rd ... 138 C2
Tidal Basin Rd, E16 ... 115 F7
Tide Cl, Mitch. CR4 ... 186 A1
Tideham Ho, SE28 off Merbury Cl ... 137 G1
Tidenham Gdns, Croy. CR0 ... 202 B3
Tideslea Path, SE28 ... 137 G1
Tideslea Twr, SE28 ... 137 G2
Tideswell Rd, SW15 ... 147 J5
 Croydon CR0 ... 204 A3
Tideway Cl, Rich. TW10 off Locksmeade Rd ... 163 F4
Tideway Ind Est, SW8 ... 33 G6
Tideway Wk, SW8 ... 33 F6
Tidey St, E3 ... 114 A5
Tidford Rd, Well. DA16 ... 157 J2
Tidlock Ho, SE28 ... 137 G2
Tidworth Ho, SE22 off Albrighton Rd ... 152 B3
Tidworth Rd, E3 ... 114 A4
Tiepigs La, Brom. BR2 ... 205 E2
 West Wickham BR4 ... 205 E2
Tierney Rd, SW2 ... 168 E1
Tiger Way, E5 ... 94 E4
Tigris Cl, N9 ... 61 F2
Tilbrook Rd, SE3 ... 155 J3
Tilbury Cl, SE15 ... 37 G7
 Pinner HA5 ... 51 F7
Tilbury Rd, E6 ... 116 C2
 E10 ... 78 C7
Tildesley Rd, SW15 ... 147 J6
Tile Fm Rd, Orp. BR6 ... 207 G3
Tilehurst Pt, SE2 off Yarnton Way ... 138 C2
Tilehurst Rd, SW18 ... 167 G1
 Sutton SM3 ... 198 B5
Tile Kiln La, N6 ... 92 C1
 N13 ... 59 J5
 Bexley DA5 ... 177 J2
Tile Yd, E14 off Commercial Rd ... 113 J6
Tileyard Rd, N7 ... 92 E7
Tilford Gdns, SW19 ... 166 A2
Tilia Cl, Sutt. SM1 ... 198 C5
Tilia Rd, E5 off Clarence Rd ... 95 E4
Tilia Wk, SW9 ... 151 H4
Tiller Rd, E14 ... 134 A3
Tillett Cl, NW10 ... 88 C6
Tillett Sq, SE16 off Howland Way ... 133 H2
Tillett Way, E2 ... 13 H3
Tilley Rd, Felt. TW13 ... 160 A1
Tillingbourne Gdns, N3 ... 72 C3
Tillingbourne Way, N3 off Tillingbourne Gdns ... 72 C4
Tillingham Way, N12 ... 56 D4
Tilling Rd, NW2 ... 89 J1
Tillings Cl, SE5 ... 151 J1
Tilling Way, Wem. HA9 ... 87 G2
Tillman St, E1 off Bigland St ... 113 E6
Tilloch St, N1 off Carnoustie Dr ... 93 F7
Tillotson Ct, SW8 off Wandsworth Rd ... 130 E7
Tillotson Rd, N9 ... 60 C2
 Harrow HA3 ... 51 H7
 Ilford IG1 ... 80 D7
Tilney Ct, EC1 ... 12 A5
Tilney Dr, Buck.H. IG9 ... 63 G2
Tilney Gdns, N1 ... 94 A6
Tilney Rd, Dag. RM9 ... 101 F6
 Southall UB2 ... 122 C4
Tilney St, W1 ... 24 C1
Tilson Cl, SE5 ... 36 D7
Tilson Gdns, SW2 ... 150 E7
Tilson Ho, SW2 ... 150 E7
Tilson Rd, N17 ... 76 D1
Tilston Cl, E11 off Matcham Rd ... 97 F3
Tiltman Pl, N7 ... 93 F3
Tilton St, SW6 ... 128 B6
Tiltwood, The, W3 ... 106 C7
Tilt Yd App, SE9 ... 156 C6
Timber Cl, Chis. BR7 ... 192 D2
Timbercroft, Epsom KT19 ... 196 E4
Timbercroft La, SE18 ... 137 H6
Timberdene, NW4 ... 72 A2
Timberdene Av, Ilford IG6 ... 81 E1
Timberland Cl, SE15 off Peckham Hill St ... 132 D7
Timberland Rd, E1 ... 113 E6
Timber Mill Way, SW4 ... 150 D3
Timber Pond Rd, SE16 ... 133 G2
Timber St, EC1 ... 11 J5
Timber Wf, E2 off Kingsland Rd ... 112 C1
Timberwharf Rd, N16 ... 76 D6
Timbrell Pl, SE16 off Silver Wk ... 133 J1
Time Sq, E8 ... 94 C5
Times Sq, Sutt. SM1 ... 199 E5
Times Sq Shop Cen, Sutt. SM1 off High St ... 199 E5
Timms Cl, Brom. BR1 ... 192 C4
Timothy Cl, SW4 ... 150 C5
 Bexleyheath DA6 ... 158 E5
Timothy Ho, Erith DA18 off Kale Rd ... 138 E2
Timsbury Wk, SW15 ... 165 G1
Tindal St, SW9 ... 151 H1
Tinderbox All, SW14 ... 146 D3
Tine Rd, Chig. IG7 ... 65 H5
Tinniswood Cl, N5 off Drayton Pk ... 93 G5
Tinsley Cl, SE25 ... 188 E3
Tinsley Rd, E1 ... 113 F5
Tintagel Cres, SE22 ... 152 C4
Tintagel Dr, Stan. HA7 ... 53 G4
Tintagel Gdns, SE22 off Oxonian St ... 152 C4
Tintern Av, NW9 ... 70 B3
Tintern Cl, SW15 ... 148 B5
 SW19 ... 167 F7
Tintern Ct, W13 off Green Man La ... 104 D7
Tintern Gdns, N14 ... 43 E7
Tintern Path, NW9 off Ruthin Cl ... 71 E6
Tintern Rd, N22 ... 75 J1
 Carshalton SM5 ... 199 G1
Tintern St, SW4 ... 151 E4
Tintern Way, Har. HA2 ... 85 H1
Tinto Rd, E16 ... 115 G4
Tinwell Ms, Borwd. WD6 ... 38 C5
Tinworth St, SE11 ... 34 B3
Tippetts Cl, Enf. EN2 ... 43 J1
Tipthorpe Rd, SW11 ... 150 A3
Tipton Dr, Croy. CR0 ... 202 B4
Tiptree Cl, E4 off Mapleton Rd ... 62 C3
Tiptree Cres, Ilf. IG5 ... 80 D3
Tiptree Dr, Enf. EN2 ... 44 A4
Tiptree Est, Ilf. IG5 ... 80 D3
Tiptree Rd, Ruis. HA4 ... 84 B4
Tirlemont Rd, S.Croy. CR2 ... 201 J7
Tirrell Rd, Croy. CR0 ... 187 J6
Tisbury Ct, W1 off Rupert St ... 17 H5
Tisbury Rd, SW16 ... 186 E2
Tisdall Pl, SE17 ... 36 C2
Tissington Ct, SE16 off Rotherhithe New Rd ... 133 G4
Titchborne Row, W2 ... 15 H4
Titchfield Rd, NW8 ... 109 J1
 Carshalton SM5 ... 199 G1
Titchfield Wk, Cars. SM5 off Titchfield Rd ... 185 G7
Titchwell Rd, SW18 ... 149 G7
Tite St, SW3 ... 31 J4
Tithe Barn Cl, Kings.T. KT2 ... 181 J1
Tithe Barn Way, Nthlt. UB5 ... 102 B3
Tithe Cl, NW7 ... 71 G1
 Walton-on-Thames KT12 ... 178 B6
Tithe Fm Av, Har. HA2 ... 85 G3
Tithe Fm Cl, Har. HA2 ... 85 G3
Tithe Wk, NW7 ... 71 G1
Titley Cl, E4 ... 62 A5
Titmuss Av, SE28 ... 118 B7
Titmuss St, W12 off Goldhawk Rd ... 127 J2
Tiverton Av, Ilf. IG5 ... 80 D3
Tiverton Cl, Croy. CR0 off Exeter Rd ... 188 C7
Tiverton Dr, SE9 ... 175 F1
Tiverton Ho, Enf. EN3 ... 45 G3
Tiverton Rd, N15 ... 76 A6
 N18 ... 60 B5
 NW10 ... 108 A1
 Edgware HA8 ... 69 J2
 Hounslow TW3 ... 143 J2
 Ruislip HA4 ... 84 A3
 Thornton Heath CR7 off Willett Rd ... 187 G5
 Wembley HA0 ... 105 H2
Tiverton St, SE1 ... 27 J6
Tiverton Way, NW7 ... 56 A7
 Chessington KT9 ... 195 F5
Tivoli Ct, SE16 ... 133 J2
Tivoli Gdns, SE18 ... 136 B4
Tivoli Rd, N8 ... 74 D5
 SE27 ... 169 J5
 Hounslow TW4 ... 142 E4
Toad La, Houns. TW4 ... 143 F4
Tobacco Dock, E1 ... 112 E7
Tobacco Quay, E1 off Wapping La ... 113 E7

Tobago St, E14 *off Manilla St* 134 A2
Tobin Cl, NW3 91 H7
Toby La, E1 113 H4
Toby Way, Surb. KT5 196 B2
Todds Wk, N7 *off Andover Rd* 93 F2
Todhunter Ter, Barn. EN5 *off Prospect Rd* 40 D4
Tokenhouse Yd, EC2 20 B3
Token Yd, SW15 *off Montserrat Rd* 148 B4
TOKYNGTON, Wem. HA9 88 B6
Tokyngton Av, Wem. HA9 88 A6
Toland Sq, SW15 147 G5
Tolcarne Dr, Pnr. HA5 66 B3
Toley Av, Wem. HA9 69 H7
Tolhurst Dr, W10 *off Beethoven St* 108 B3
Tollbridge Cl, W10 *off Kensal Rd* 108 B4
Tollesbury Gdns, Ilf. IG6 81 G3
Tollet St, E1 113 G4
Tollgate Dr, SE21 170 B2
Hayes UB4 102 D7
Tollgate Gdns, NW6 6 A1
Tollgate Ho, NW6 6 A1
Tollgate Rd, E6 116 A5
E16 115 J5
Tollhouse Way, N19 92 C2
Tollington Pk, N4 93 F2
Tollington Pl, N4 93 F2
Tollington Rd, N7 93 F4
Tollington Way, N7 92 E3
Tolmers Sq, NW1 9 G5
Tolpuddle Av, E13 *off Rochester Av* 115 J1
Tolpuddle St, N1 10 E1
Tolsford Rd, E5 95 E5
Tolson Rd, Islw. TW7 144 D3
Tolverne Rd, SW20 183 J1
TOLWORTH, Surb. KT6 196 A2
Tolworth Bdy, Surb. KT6 196 B1
Tolworth Cl, Surb. KT6 196 B1
Tolworth Gdns, Rom. RM6 82 D5
Tolworth Junct, Surb. KT5 196 B2
Tolworth Pk Rd, Surb. KT6 195 J2
Tolworth Ri N, Surb. KT5 *off Elmbridge Av* 182 C7
Tolworth Ri S, Surb. KT5 *off Warren Dr S* 196 C1
Tolworth Rd, Surb. KT6 195 H2
Tolworth Twr, Surb. KT6 196 B2
Tomahawk Gdns, Nthlt. UB5 *off Javelin Way* 102 D3
Tom Coombs Cl, SE9 156 B4
Tom Cribb Business Cen, SE28 *off Tom Cribb Rd* 137 G3
Tom Cribb Rd, SE28 137 F3
Tom Gros Cl, E15 *off Maryland St* 96 D5
Tom Hood Cl, E15 *off Maryland St* 96 D5
Tom Jenkinson Rd, E16 135 G1
Tomlins Gro, E3 114 A3
Tomlinson Cl, E2 13 G4
W4 126 B5
Tomlins Orchard, Bark. IG11 117 F1
Tomlins Ter, E14 *off Rhodeswell Rd* 113 J5
Tomlins Wk, N7 *off Briset Way* 93 F2
Tom Mann Cl, Bark. IG11 117 H1
Tom Nolan Cl, E15 114 E2
Tompion Ho, EC1 *off Percival St* 11 H5
Tompion St, EC1 11 G4
Tom Smith Cl, SE10 *off Maze Hill* 134 E6
Tomswood Ct, Ilf. IG6 81 F1
Tomswood Hill, Ilf. IG6 65 E7
Tomswood Rd, Chig. IG7 64 D6
Tom Thumbs Arch, E3 *off Malmesbury Rd* 114 A2
Tom Williams Ho, SW6 *off Clem Attlee Ct* 128 C6
Tonbridge Cres, Har. HA3 69 H4
Tonbridge Ho, SE25 188 D3
Tonbridge Rd, W.Mol. KT8 179 E4
Tonbridge St, WC1 10 A3
Tonbridge Wk, WC1 *off Bidborough St* 10 A3
Tonfield Rd, Sutt. SM3 198 C1
Tonge Cl, Beck. BR3 190 A5
Tonsley Hill, SW18 149 E5
Tonsley Pl, SW18 149 E5
Tonsley Rd, SW18 149 E5
Tonsley St, SW18 149 E5
Tonstall Rd, Mitch. CR4 186 A2
Tony Cannell Ms, E3 *off Maplin St* 113 J3
Tooke Cl, Pnr. HA5 66 E1
Tookey Cl, Har. HA3 69 J7
Took's Ct, EC4 19 E3
Tooley St, SE1 28 C1
Toorack Rd, Har. HA3 68 A2
Tooting Bec, SW17 167 J3
Tooting Bec Gdns, SW16 168 D4
Tooting Bec Rd, SW16 168 A3
SW17 168 A3
Tooting Bdy, SW17 167 H4
TOOTING GRAVENEY, SW17 167 H6
Tooting Gro, SW17 167 H5
Tooting High St, SW17 167 H6
Tooting Mkt, SW17 *off Tooting High St* 167 J4
Tootswood Rd, Brom. BR2 190 E5
Topaz Ct, E11 *off High Rd Leytonstone* 97 E1
Topaz Ho, E15 *off Romford Rd* 97 F6
Topaz Wk, NW2 *off Marble Dr* 72 A7
Topcliffe Dr, Orp. BR6 207 G4
Topham Sq, N17 75 J1
Topham St, EC1 11 E5
Top Ho Ri, E4 *off Parkhill Rd* 46 C7
Topiary Sq, Rich. TW9 145 J3
Topley St, SE9 156 A4
Topmast Pt, E14 134 A2
Top Pk, Beck. BR3 190 E5
Topp Wk, NW2 89 J2
Topsfield Cl, N8 *off Wolseley Rd* 74 D5
Topsfield Par, N8 *off Tottenham La* 75 E5
Topsfield Rd, N8 74 E5
Topsham Rd, SW17 167 J3
Torbay Rd, NW6 90 C7
Harrow HA2 84 E2
Torbay St, NW1 *off Hawley Rd* 92 B7
Torbitt Way, Ilf. IG2 81 J5
Torbridge Cl, Edg. HA8 53 H7
Torbrook Cl, Bex. DA5 159 E6
Torcross Dr, SE23 171 F2
Torcross Rd, Ruis. HA4 84 B3
Tor Gdns, W8 128 D2
Tor Gro, SE28 137 H1
Tormead Cl, Sutt. SM1 198 D6
Tormount Rd, SE18 137 H6
Tornay Ho, N1 *off Priory Grn Est* 10 C1
Toronto Av, E12 98 C4
Toronto Rd, Ilf. IG1 99 E1
Torquay Gdns, Ilf. IG4 80 A4
Torquay St, W2 14 A2
Torrance Cl, SE7 136 A6
Torrens Rd, E15 97 F6
SW2 151 F5
Torrens Sq, E15 97 E6
Torrens St, EC1 11 F2
Torres Sq, E14 *off Maritime Quay* 134 A5
Torre Wk, Cars. SM5 199 H1
Torrey Dr, SW9 *off Overton Rd* 151 G2
Torriano Av, NW5 92 D5
Torriano Cotts, NW5 *off Torriano Av* 92 D5
Torriano Ms, NW5 92 C5
Torridge Gdns, SE15 153 F4
Torridge Rd, Th.Hth. CR7 187 H5
Torridon Ho, NW6 6 A2
Torridon Rd, SE6 172 D1
SE13 154 D7
Torrington Av, N12 57 G5
Torrington Cl, N12 57 G4
Esher (Clay.) KT10 194 B6
Torrington Dr, Har. HA2 85 H4
Loughton IG10 49 F4
Torrington Gdns, N11 58 C6
Greenford (Perivale) UB6 87 F7
Loughton IG10 49 F4
Torrington Gro, N12 57 H5
Torrington Pk, N12 57 F5
Torrington Pl, E1 29 J1
WC1 17 G1
Torrington Rd, E18 79 G3
Dagenham RM8 101 F1
Esher (Clay.) KT10 194 B6
Greenford (Perivale) UB6 105 F1
Torrington Sq, WC1 9 J6
Croydon CR0 *off Tavistock Gro* 188 A7
Torrington Way, Mord. SM4 184 D6
Tor Rd, Well. DA16 158 C1
Torr Rd, SE20 171 G7
Torver Rd, Har. HA1 68 B4
Torver Way, Orp. BR6 207 G3
Torwood Rd, SW15 147 G5
Tothill Ho, SW1 *off Page St* 33 J1
Tothill St, SW1 25 H4
Totnes Rd, Well. DA16 138 B7
Totnes Wk, N2 73 G4
Tottan Ter, E1 113 G6
Tottenhall Rd, N13 59 G6
TOTTENHAM, N17 76 B1
Tottenham Ct Rd, W1 9 G6
Tottenham Grn E, N15 76 C4
TOTTENHAM HALE, N17 76 E3
Tottenham Hale, N17 76 C4
Tottenham Hale Retail Pk, N15 76 D4
★ **Tottenham Hotspur FC**, N17 60 C7
Tottenham La, N8 74 E5
Tottenham Ms, W1 17 G1
Tottenham Rd, N1 94 B6
Tottenham St, W1 17 G2
Totterdown St, SW17 167 J4
TOTTERIDGE, N20 56 B1
Totteridge Common, N20 55 G2
Totteridge Grn, N20 56 D2
Totteridge Ho, SW11 149 G2
Totteridge La, N20 56 D2
Totteridge Village, N20 56 B1
Totternhoe Cl, Har. HA3 69 F5
Totton Rd, Th.Hth. CR7 187 G3
Toucan Cl, NW10 106 A3
Toulmin St, SE1 27 J4
Toulon St, SE5 35 J7
Tournay Rd, SW6 128 C7
Tours Pas, SW11 149 G4
Toussaint Wk, SE16 29 J5
Tovil Cl, SE20 188 D2
Tovy Ho, SE1 37 H4
Towcester Rd, E3 114 B4
Tower 42, EC2 20 D3
Tower Br, E1 29 F2
SE1 29 F2
Tower Br App, E1 29 F1
★ **Tower Br Exhib**, SE1 29 F2
Tower Br Ms, Har. HA1 *off Greenford Rd* 86 C4
Tower Br Piazza, SE1 29 F2
Tower Br Rd, SE1 28 D6
Tower Br Wf, E1 29 H2
Tower Bldgs, E1 *off Brewhouse La* 133 E1
Tower Cl, NW3 *off Lyndhurst Rd* 91 G5
SE20 170 E7
Ilford IG6 65 E6
Orpington BR6 207 J2
Tower Ct, WC2 18 A4
Tower Gdns, Esher (Clay.) KT10 194 D7
Tower Gdns Rd, N17 75 J1
Tower Hamlets Rd, E7 97 F4
E17 78 A3
Tower Hill, EC3 21 F6
Tower Hill Ter, EC3 *off Byward St* 21 E6
Tower La, Wem. HA9 *off Main Dr* 87 G3
Tower Ms, E17 78 A4
★ **Tower Millennium Pier**, EC3 29 E1
Tower Mill Rd, SE15 36 D6
★ **Tower of London**, EC3 21 F6
Tower Pl E, EC3 20 E6
Tower Pl W, EC3 20 E6
Tower Pt, Enf. EN2 44 A4
Tower Ri, Rich. TW9 *off Jocelyn Rd* 145 H3
Tower Rd, NW10 89 G7
Belvedere DA17 139 J4
Bexleyheath DA7 159 H4
Orpington BR6 207 J2
Twickenham TW1 162 C3
Tower Royal, EC4 20 A5
Towers Pl, Rich. TW9 145 H5
Towers Rd, Pnr. HA5 66 E1
Southall UB1 103 G4
Tower St, WC2 17 J4
Tower Ter, N22 *off Mayes Rd* 75 F2
SE4 *off Foxberry Rd* 153 H4
Tower Vw, Croy. CR0 189 G7
Towfield Rd, Felt. TW13 161 F2
Towing Path Wk, N1 10 A1
Town, The, Enf. EN2 44 A3
Towncourt Cres, Orp. BR5 193 F5
Towncourt La, Orpington BR5 193 G6
Town Ct Path, N4 93 J1
Towney Mead, Nthlt. UB5 103 F2
Towney Mead Ct, Nthlt. UB5 *off Towney Mead* 103 F2
Town Fm Way, Stai. (Stanw.) TW19 *off Town La* 140 A7
Townfield Rd, Hayes UB3 121 J1
Townfield Sq, Hayes UB3 121 J1
Townfield Way, Islw. TW7 144 D2
Town Hall App, N16 *off Milton Gro* 94 B4
Town Hall App Rd, N15 76 C4
Town Hall Av, W4 126 D5
Town Hall Rd, SW11 149 J3
Townholm Cres, W7 124 C3
Town La, Stai. (Stanw.) TW19 140 A6
Townley Ct, E15 97 F6
Townley Rd, SE22 152 B5
Bexleyheath DA6 159 F5
Townley St, SE17 36 B3
Townmead Business Cen, SW6 *off William Morris Way* 149 F3
Town Meadow, Brent. TW8 125 G6
Townmead Rd, SW6 149 F2
Richmond TW9 146 B2
Town Quay, Bark. IG11 117 E1
Town Rd, N9 60 E2
Townsend Av, N14 58 D4
Townsend Ind Est, NW10 106 D2
Townsend La, NW9 70 D7
Townsend Ms, SW18 *off Waynflete St* 167 F2
Townsend Rd, N15 76 C5
Southall UB1 122 E1
Townsend St, SE17 36 C2
Townsend Yd, N6 92 B1
Townshend Cl, Sid. DA14 176 B6
Townshend Est, NW8 7 G1
Townshend Rd, NW8 109 H1
Chislehurst BR7 174 E5
Richmond TW9 145 J4
Townshend Ter, Rich. TW9 145 J4
Townson Av, Nthlt. UB5 102 A3
Townson Way, Nthlt. UB5 *off Townson Av* 102 A2
Town Sq, Bark. IG11 *off Clockhouse Av* 117 F1
Towpath Rd, N18 61 G6
Towpath Wk, E9 95 J5
Towpath Way, Croy. CR0 188 C6
Towton Rd, SE27 169 J2
Toynbec Cl, Chis. BR7 *off Beechwood Ri* 175 E4
Toynbee Rd, SW20 184 B1
Toynbee St, E1 21 F2
Toyne Way, N6 *off Gaskell Rd* 73 J6
Tracey Av, NW2 89 J5
Tracy Ct, Stan. HA7 53 F7
Trade Cl, N13 59 G4
Trader Rd, E6 116 E6
Tradescant Rd, SW8 131 E7
Trading Est Rd, NW10 106 C4
Trafalgar Av, N17 60 B6
SE15 37 G4
Worcester Park KT4 198 A1
Trafalgar Business Cen, Bark. IG11 117 J4
Trafalgar Cl, SE16 *off Greenland Quay* 133 H4
Trafalgar Ct, E1 *off Glamis Rd* 113 F7
Trafalgar Gdns, E1 113 G5
W8 22 A5
Trafalgar Gro, SE10 134 D6
Trafalgar Ms, E9 95 J6
Trafalgar Pl, E11 79 G4
N18 60 D5
Trafalgar Rd, SE10 134 D6
SW19 167 E7
Twickenham TW2 162 A2
Trafalgar Sq, SW1 25 J1
WC2 25 J1
Trafalgar St, SE17 36 B3
Trafalgar Ter, Har. HA1 *off Nelson Rd* 86 B1
Trafalgar Trd Est, Enf. EN3 45 H4
Trafalgar Way, E14 134 C1
Croydon CR0 201 F2
Trafalgar Way Retail Park, Croydon CRO 201 G2
Trafford Cl, Ilf. IG6 65 J6
Trafford Rd, Th.Hth. CR7 187 F5
Trahorn Cl, E1 112 D4
Tralee Ct, SE16 *off Masters Dr* 133 E5
Tram Cl, SE24 *off Hinton Rd* 151 H3
Tramsheds Ind Est, Croy. CR0 186 D7
Tramway Av, E15 96 E7
N9 45 E7
Tramway Cl, SE20 189 F1
Tramway Path, Mitch. CR4 185 J5

Tranby Pl, E9
off Homerton High St 95 G5
Tranley Ms, NW3
off Fleet Rd 91 H5
Tranmere Rd, N9 44 C7
SW18 167 F2
Twickenham TW2 143 H7
Tranquil Pas, SE3
off Tranquil Vale 155 F2
Tranquil Vale, SE3 155 E2
Transept St, NW1 15 G2
Transmere Cl, Orp. BR5 193 F6
Transmere Rd, Orp. BR5 193 F6
Transom Cl, SE16
off Plough Way 133 H4
Transom Sq, E14 134 B4
Transport Av, Brent. TW8 124 D5
Tranton Rd, SE16 29 J5
Trappes Ho, SE16
off Manor Est 132 E4
Traps Hill, Loug. IG10 48 C3
Traps La, N.Mal. KT3 182 E1
Travellers Way, Houns.
TW4 142 C2
Travers Cl, E17 77 G1
Travers Rd, N7 93 G3
Treacy Cl, Bushey
(Bushey Hth) WD23 51 J2
Treadgold St, W11 108 A7
Treadway St, E2 112 E2
Treasury Cl, Wall. SM6 200 D5
Treaty Cen, Houns. TW3 143 H3
Treaty Rd, Houns. TW3
off Hanworth Rd 143 H3
Treaty St, N1 111 F1
Trebeck St, W1 24 D1
Trebovir Rd, SW5 128 D5
Treby St, E3 113 J4
Trecastle Way, N7
off Carleton Rd 92 D4
Tredegar Ms, E3
off Tredegar Ter 113 J3
Tredegar Rd, E3 113 J2
N11 58 D7
Tredegar Sq, E3 113 J3
Tredegar Ter, E3 113 J3
Trederwen Rd, E8 112 D1
Tredown Rd, SE26 171 F5
Tredwell Cl, SW2
off Hillside Rd 169 F2
Bromley BR2 192 B4
Tredwell Rd, SE27 169 H4
Tree Cl, Rich. TW10 163 G1
Treen Av, SW13 147 F3
Tree Rd, E16 115 J6
Treeside Cl, West Dr. UB7 120 A4
Treetops Cl, SE2 139 E5
Treetops Vw, Loug. IG10 48 A7
Treeview Cl, SE19 188 B1
Treewall Gdns, Brom.
BR1 173 H4
Trefgarne Rd, Dag. RM10 101 G2
Trefil Wk, N7 93 E4
Trefoil Ho, Erith DA18
off Kale Rd 138 E2
Trefoil Rd, SW18 149 F5
Tregaron Av, N8 74 E6
Tregaron Gdns, N.Mal.
KT3 183 E4
Tregarvon Rd, SW11 150 A4
Tregenna Av, Har. HA2 85 F4
Tregenna Cl, N14 42 C5
Tregenna Ct, Har. HA2 85 G4
Tregony Rd, Orp. BR6 207 J4
Trego Rd, E9 96 A7
Tregothnan Rd, SW9 151 E3
Tregunter Rd, SW10 30 C5
Trehearn Rd, Ilf. IG6 65 G7
Treherne Ct, SW9
off Eythorne Rd 151 H1
SW17 168 A4
Trehern Rd, SW14 146 D3
Trehurst St, E5 95 H5
Trelawney Cl, E17
off Orford Rd 78 B4
Trelawney Est, E9 95 F6
Trelawney Rd, Ilf. IG6 65 G7
Trelawn Rd, E10 96 C3
SW2 151 G5
Trellick Twr, W10 108 C4
Trellis Sq, E3
off Malmesbury Rd 113 J3
Treloar Gdns, SE19
off Hancock Rd 170 A6
Tremadoc Rd, SW4 150 D4
Tremaine Cl, SE4 154 A2
Tremaine Rd, SE20 189 E2
Trematon Pl, Tedd. TW11 163 F7
Tremlett Gro, N19 92 C3
Tremlett Ms, N19 92 C3
Trenance Gdns, Ilf. IG3 100 A3
Trenchard Av, Ruis. HA4 84 B4
Trenchard Cl, NW9
off Fulbeck Dr 70 E1
Stanmore HA7 52 D6
Trenchard Ct, Mord. SM4
off Green La 184 D6
Trenchard St, SE10 134 D5
Trenchold St, SW8 34 A6
Trenholme Cl, SE20 171 E7
Trenholme Rd, SE20 170 E7
Trenholme Ter, SE20 170 E7
Trenmar Gdns, NW10 107 H3
Trent Av, W5 125 F3
Trentbridge Cl, Ilf. IG6 65 J6
Trent Gdns, N14 42 B6
Trentham St, SW18 166 D1
★ **Trent Park Country Pk**,
Barn. EN4 42 A2
Trent Rd, SW2 151 F5
Buckhurst Hill IG9 63 H1
Trent Way, Wor.Pk. KT4 197 J3
Trentwood Side, Enf. EN2 43 F3
Treport St, SW18 149 E7
Tresco Cl, Brom. BR1 172 E6
Trescoe Gdns, Har. HA2 67 E7
Tresco Gdns, Ilf. IG3 100 A2
Tresco Rd, SE15 153 E4
Tresham Cres, NW8 7 G5
Tresham Rd, Bark. IG11 99 J7
Tresham Wk, E9
off Churchill Wk 95 F5
Tresilian Av, N21 43 F5
Tressell Cl, N1
off Sebbon St 93 H7
Tressillian Cres, SE4 154 A3
Tressillian Rd, SE4 153 J4
Trestis Cl, Hayes UB4
off Jollys La 102 E5
Treswell Rd, Dag. RM9 119 E1
Tretawn Gdns, NW7 55 E4
Tretawn Pk, NW7 55 E4
Trevanion Rd, W14 128 B5
Treve Av, Har. HA1 67 J7
Trevelyan Av, E12 98 C4
Trevelyan Cres, Har. HA3 69 G7
Trevelyan Gdns, NW10 107 J1
Trevelyan Ho, E2
off Morpeth St 113 G3
Trevelyan Rd, E15 97 E4
SW17 167 H5
Treveris St, SE1 27 G2
Treverton St, W10 108 A4
Treves Cl, N21 43 F5
Treville St, SW15 147 H7
Treviso Rd, SE23
off Farren Rd 171 H2
Trevithick Ho, SE16 133 E4
Trevithick St, SE8 134 A5
Trevone Gdns, Pnr. HA5 67 E6
Trevor Cl, Barn. (E.Barn.)
EN4 41 G5
Bromley BR2 191 F7
Harrow HA3
off Kenton La 52 C7
Isleworth TW7 144 C5
Northolt UB5 102 C2
Trevor Gdns, Edg. HA8 70 D1
Northolt UB5 102 C2
Trevor Pl, SW7 23 H4
Trevor Rd, SW19 166 B7
Edgware HA8 70 D1
Hayes UB3 121 H2
Woodford Green IG8 63 G7
Trevor Sq, SW7 23 J4
Trevor St, SW7 23 H4
Trevor Wk, SW7
off Trevor Sq 23 J4
Trevose Rd, E17 78 D1
Trevose Way, Wat. WD19 50 C3
Trewenna Dr, Chess. KT9 195 G5
Trewince Rd, SW20 183 J1
Trewint St, SW18 167 F2
Trewsbury Ho, SE2
off Hartslock Dr 138 D2
Trewsbury Rd, SE26 171 G5
Triandra Way, Hayes UB4 102 D5
Triangle, The, EC1 11 H5
N13 *off Green Las* 59 F4
Barking IG11
off Tanner St 99 F6
Hampton TW12
off High St 179 J1
Kingston upon Thames
KT1 *off Kenley Rd* 182 C2
Triangle Business Cen,
NW10
off Enterprise Way 107 G3
Triangle Ct, E16
off Tollgate Rd 116 A5
Triangle Est, SE11 35 E4
Triangle Ms, West Dr. UB7 120 C1
Triangle Pas, Barn. EN4
off Station App 41 F4
Triangle Pl, SW4 150 D4
Triangle Rd, E8 112 E1
Triangle Wks, N9
off Centre Way 61 F2
Tricorn Ho, SE28
off Miles Dr 137 G1
Trident Gdns, Nthlt. UB5
off Jetstar Way 102 D3
Trident Ho, SE28
off Merbury Rd 137 G1
Trident St, SE16 133 G4
Trident Way, Sthl. UB2 122 B3
Trig La, EC4 19 J5
Trigon Rd, SW8 34 D7
Trilby Rd, SE23 171 G2
Trimmer Wk, Brent. TW8 125 H6
Trim St, SE14 133 J6
Trinder Gdns, N19 93 E1
Trinder Ms, Tedd. TW11 162 D5
Trinder Rd, N19 93 E1
Barnet EN5 39 J5
Tring Av, W5 125 J1
Southall UB1 103 F6
Wembley HA9 88 A6
Tring Cl, Ilf. IG2 81 F5
Trinidad St, E14 113 J7
Trinity Av, N2 73 G3
Enfield EN1 44 C6
Trinity Buoy Wf, E14 115 F7
Trinity Business Pk, E4
off Trinity Way 61 J6
Trinity Ch Pas, SW13 127 H6
Trinity Ch Rd, SW13 127 H6
Trinity Ch Sq, SE1 28 A5
Trinity Cl, E8 94 C6
E11 97 E2
NW3
off Willoughby Rd 91 G4
SE13 154 D4
SW4 *off The Pavement* 150 C4
Bromley BR2 206 B1
Hounslow TW4 143 E4
Trinity Cotts, Rich. TW9
off Trinity Rd 145 J3
Trinity Ct, N1
off Downham Rd 94 B7
N18 60 C6
NW2 *off Anson Rd* 89 J5
SE7 *off Charlton La* 136 A4
Trinity Cres, SW17 167 J2
Trinity Gdns, E16
off Cliff Wk 115 F5
SW9 151 F4
Trinity Gro, SE10 154 C1
★ **Trinity Ho**, EC3 21 E5
Trinity Ho, SE1
off Bath Ter 28 A5
Trinity Ms, SE20 189 E1
W10
off Cambridge Gdns 108 A6
Trinity Path, SE26 171 F3
Trinity Pl, EC3 21 F6
Bexleyheath DA6 159 F4
Trinity Ri, SW2 169 G1
Trinity Rd, N2 73 G3
N22 75 E1
SW17 167 J2
SW18 149 G5
SW19 166 D6
Ilford IG6 81 F3
Richmond TW9 145 J3
Southall UB1 122 E1
Trinity Sq, EC3 21 E6
Trinity St, E16
off Vincent St 115 G5
SE1 28 A4
Enfield EN2 43 J2
Trinity Wk, NW3 91 F6
Trinity Way, E4 61 J6
W3 107 E7
Trio Pl, SE1 28 A4
Tristan Sq, SE3 155 E3
Tristram Cl, E17 78 D3
Tristram Dr, N9 60 D3
Tristram Rd, Brom. BR1 173 F4
Triton Sq, NW1 9 F5
Tritton Av, Croy. CR0 200 E4
Tritton Rd, SE21 170 A3
Triumph Cl, Hayes
(Harling.) UB3 121 F7
Triumph Ho, Bark. IG11 118 A3
Triumph Rd, E6 116 C6
Triumph Trd Est, N17 60 D6
Trojan Way, Croy. CR0 201 F3
Troon Cl, SE16
off Masters Dr 133 E5
SE28 *off Fairway Dr* 118 D6
Troon St, E1
off White Horse Rd 113 H6
Trosley Rd, Belv. DA17 139 G6
Trossachs Rd, SE22 152 B5
Trothy Rd, SE1 37 J1
Trott Rd, N10 57 J7
Trott St, SW11 149 H1
Trotwood, Chig. IG7 65 G6
Troughton Rd, SE7 135 H5
Troutbeck Rd, SE14 153 H1
Trout Rd, West Dr. UB7 120 A1
Trouville Rd, SW4 150 C6
Trowbridge Est, E9
off Osborne Rd 95 J6
Trowbridge Rd, E9 95 J6
Trowlock Av, Tedd. TW11 163 F6
Trowlock Island, Tedd.
TW11 163 G5
Trowlock Way, Tedd.
TW11 163 G6
Troy Ct, SE18
off Wilmount St 137 E4
W8 *off Kensington
High St* 128 D3
Troy Rd, SE19 170 A6
Troy Town, SE15 152 D3
Trubshaw Rd, Sthl. UB2
off Havelock Rd 123 H3
Trueman Cl, Edg. HA8 54 C7
Truesdale Rd, E6 116 C6
Trulock Ct, N17 60 D7
Trulock Rd, N17 60 D7
Truman's Rd, N16 94 B5
Trumpers Way, W7 124 B3
Trumpington Rd, E7 97 F4
Trump St, EC2 20 A4
Trundlers Way, Bushey
(Bushey Hth) WD23 52 B1
Trundle St, SE1 27 J3
Trundleys Rd, SE8 133 G5
Trundleys Ter, SE8 133 G4
Truro Gdns, Ilf. IG1 80 B7
Truro Rd, E17 77 J4
N22 59 E7
Truro St, NW5 92 A6
Truslove Rd, SE27 169 G5
Trussley Rd, W6 127 J3
Trust Wk, SE21
off Peabody Hill 169 H1
Tryfan Cl, Ilf. IG4 80 A5
Tryon Cres, E9 113 F1
Tryon St, SW3 31 J3
Trystings Cl, Esher (Clay.)
KT10 194 D6
Tuam Rd, SE18 137 G6
Tubbenden Cl, Orp. BR6 207 H2
Tubbenden Dr, Orp. BR6 207 G4
Tubbenden La, Orp. BR6 207 H3
Tubbenden La S, Orp.
BR6 207 G5
Tubbs Rd, NW10 107 F2
Tudor Av, Hmptn. TW12 161 G6
Worcester Park KT4 197 H3
Tudor Cl, N6 74 C7
NW3 91 H5
NW7 55 G6
NW9 88 C2
SW2 151 F6
Chessington KT9 195 H5
Chigwell IG7 64 D4
Chislehurst BR7 192 C1
Pinner HA5 66 A5
Sutton SM3 198 A5
Wallington SM6 200 C7
Woodford Green IG8 63 H5
Tudor Ct, E17 77 H7
Feltham TW13 160 C4
Tudor Ct N, Wem. HA9 88 A5
Tudor Ct S, Wem. HA9 88 A5
Tudor Cres, Enf. EN2 43 H1
Ilford IG6 65 E6
Tudor Dr, Kings.T. KT2 163 H5
Morden SM4 184 A6
Tudor Est, NW10 106 B2
Tudor Gdns, NW9 88 C2
SW13 *off Treen Av* 147 E3
W3 106 A6
Harrow HA3
off Tudor Rd 68 A2
Twickenham TW1 162 C1
West Wickham BR4 204 C3
Tudor Gro, E9 95 F7
N20 57 H3
Tudor Ho, Surb. KT6
off Lenelby Rd 196 A1
Tudor Pl, Mitch. CR4 167 H7
Tudor Rd, E4 62 B6
E6 115 J1
E9 113 E1
N9 45 E7
SE19 170 C7
SE25 189 E5
Barking IG11 117 J1
Barnet EN5 40 D3
Tudor Rd, Beckenham
BR3 190 B3
Hampton TW12 161 G7
Harrow HA3 68 A2
Hounslow TW3 144 A4
Kingston upon Thames
KT2 164 A7
Pinner HA5 66 C2
Southall UB1 102 E7
Tudor St, EC4 19 F5
Tudor Wk, Bex. DA5 159 E6
Tudor Way, N14 58 D1
W3 126 A2
Orpington BR5 193 G6
Tudor Well Cl, Stan. HA7 53 E5
Tudway Rd, SE3 155 H3
TUFNELL PARK, N7 92 D4
Tufnell Pk Rd, N7 92 C4
N19 92 C4
Tufter Rd, Chig. IG7 65 J5
Tufton Gdns, W.Mol.
KT8 179 H2
Tufton Rd, E4 62 A4

Tufton St, SW1 25 J5
Tugboat St, SE28 137 H2
Tugela Rd, Croy. CR0 188 A6
Tugela St, SE6 171 J2
Tugmutton Cl, Orp. BR6 207 E4
Tuilerie St, E2 13 H1
Tulip Cl, E6
off Bradley Stone Rd 116 C5
Croydon CR0 203 G1
Hampton TW12
off Partridge Rd 161 F6
Southall UB2
off Chevy Rd 123 J2
Tulip Ct, Pnr. HA5 66 C3
Tulip Gdns, Ilf. IG1 98 E6
Tulip Way, West Dr. UB7 120 A4
Tull St, Mitch. CR4 185 J7
Tulse Cl, Beck. BR3 190 C3
TULSE HILL, SE21 169 J1
Tulse Hill, SW2 151 G6
Tulse Hill Est, SW2 151 G6
Tulsemere Rd, SE27 169 J2
Tumbling Bay, Walt. KT12 178 A6
Tummons Gdns, SE25 188 B2
Tump Ho, SE28 137 H1
Tuncombe Rd, N18 60 B4
Tunis Rd, W12 127 H1
Tunley Grn, E14
off Burdett Rd 113 J5
Tunley Rd, NW10 106 E1
SW17 168 A1
Tunmarsh La, E13 115 J3
Tunnan Leys, E6 116 D6
Tunnel Av, SE10 134 D2
Tunnel Gdns, N11 58 C7
Tunnel Rd, SE16
off St. Marychurch St 133 F2
Tunstall Cl, Orp. BR5 207 H4
Tunstall Rd, SW9 151 F4
Croydon CR0 202 B1
Tunstall Wk, Brent. TW8 125 H6
Tunstock Way, Belv. DA17 139 E3
Tunworth Cl, NW9 70 C6
Tunworth Cres, SW15 147 F6
Tun Yd, SW8
off Peardon St 150 B2
Tupelo Rd, E10 96 B2
Tuppy St, SE28 137 F3
Turenne Cl, SW18 149 F4
Turin Rd, N9 45 F7
Turin St, E2 13 H4
Turkey Oak Cl, SE19 188 B1
Turk's Head Yd, EC1 19 G1
Turks Row, SW3 32 A3
Turle Rd, N4 93 F1
SW16 186 E2
Turlewray Cl, N4 93 F1
Turley Cl, E15 115 E1
Turnagain La, EC4 19 G3
Turnage Rd, Dag. RM8 100 E1
Turnberry Cl, NW4 72 A2
SE16 *off Ryder Dr* 133 E5
Turnberry Ct, Wat. WD19 50 C3
Turnberry Quay, E14
off Pepper St 134 B3
Turnberry Way, Orp. BR6 207 G1
Turnbury Cl, SE28 118 D6
Turnchapel Ms, SW4
off Cedars Rd 150 B3
Turner Av, N15 76 B4
Mitcham CR4 185 J1
Twickenham TW2 161 J3
Turner Cl, NW11 72 E6
SW9 151 H1
Wembley HA0 87 G5
Turner Ct, N15
off St. Ann's Rd 76 A5
Turner Cres, Croy. CRO 187 J6
Turner Dr, NW11 72 E6
Turner Ho, E14
off Cassilis Rd 134 A2
Turner Ms, Sutt. SM2 198 E7
Turner Pl, SW11
off Cairns Rd 149 H5
Turner Rd, E17 78 C3
Edgware HA8 69 J3
New Malden KT3 182 D7
Turners Cl, N20 57 J3
Turners Meadow Way, Beck. BR3 189 J1
Turners Rd, E3 113 J5
Turner St, E1 112 E5
E16 115 F6
Turners Way, Croy. CR0 201 G2
Turners Wd, NW11 91 F1
Turneville Rd, W14 128 C6
Turney Rd, SE21 152 A7
Turnham Grn Ter, W4 126 E4
Turnham Grn Ter Ms, W4
off Turnham Grn Ter 126 E4
Turnham Rd, SE4 153 H5
Turnmill St, EC1 11 F6
Turnpike Cl, SE8
off Amersham Vale 133 J7
Turnpike Ho, EC1 11 H4
Turnpike La, N8 75 F4
Sutton SM1 199 F5
Turnpike Link, Croy. CR0 202 B2
Turnpike Ms, N8 75 G4
Turnpike Way, Islw. TW7 144 D1
Turnpin La, SE10 134 C6
Turnstone Cl, E13 115 G3
NW9 *off Kestrel Cl* 71 E2
Turpentine La, SW1 32 E3
Turpington Cl, Brom. BR2 192 B6
Turpington La, Brom. BR2 192 B7
Turpin Ho, SW11
off Strasburg Rd 150 B1
Turpin Rd, Felt. TW14
off Staines Rd 141 J6
Turpins La, Wdf.Grn. IG8 64 C5
Turpin Way, N19 92 D2
Wallington SM6 200 B7
Turquand St, SE17 36 A2
Turret Gro, SW4 150 C3
Turton Rd, Wem. HA0 87 H5
Turville St, E2 13 F5
Tuscan Ho, E2 113 F3
Tuscan Rd, SE18 137 G5
Tuscany Ho, E17
off Sherwood Cl 77 J2
Tuskar St, SE10 134 E5
Tustin Est, SE15 133 F6
Tuttlebee La, Buck.H. IG9 63 G2
Tweeddale Rd, Cars. SM5 199 G1
Tweedmouth Rd, E13 115 H2
Tweedy Cl, Enf. EN1 44 C5
Tweedy Rd, Brom. BR1 191 F1
Tweezer's All, WC2 18 E5
Twelve Acre Ho, E12
off Grantham Rd 98 D3
Twelvetrees Business Pk, E3
off Twelvetrees Cres 114 D4
Twelvetrees Cres, E3 114 C4
Twentyman Cl, Wdf.Grn. IG8 63 G5
TWICKENHAM, TW1 & TW2 162 D2
Twickenham Br, Rich. TW9 145 F5
Twickenham TW1 145 F5
Twickenham Cl, Croy. CR0 201 F3
Twickenham Gdns, Grnf. UB6 86 D5
Harrow HA3 52 B7
Twickenham Rd, E11 96 D2
Feltham TW13 161 F3
Isleworth TW7 144 D3
Richmond TW9 145 F4
Teddington TW11 162 D5
Twickenham Trd Est, Twick. TW1 144 C6
Twig Folly Cl, E2
off Roman Rd 113 G2
Twilley St, SW18 148 E7
Twine Cl, Bark. IG11
off Thames Rd 118 B3
Twine Ct, E1 113 F7
Twineham Grn, N12 56 D4
Twine Ter, E3
off Ropery St 113 J4
Twining Av, Twick. TW2 161 J3
Twinn Rd, NW7 56 B6
Twin Tumps Way, SE28 118 A7
Twisden Rd, NW5 92 B4
Twitten Gro, Brom. BR1 192 C3
Two River's Ct, Felt. TW14 141 G6
Twybridge Way, NW10 88 C7
Twycross Ms, SE10
off Blackwall La 135 E4
Twyford Abbey Rd, NW10 105 J3
Twyford Av, N2 73 J3
W3 106 A7
Twyford Cres, W3 126 A1
Twyford Ho, N15 76 B6
Twyford Pl, WC2 18 C3
Twyford Rd, Cars. SM5 199 G1
Harrow HA2 85 H1
Ilford IG1 99 F5
Twyford St, N1 111 F1
Tyas Rd, E16 115 F4
Tybenham Rd, SW19 184 D3
Tyberry Rd, Enf. EN3 45 E3
Tyburn La, Har. HA1 68 B7
Tyburn Way, W1 16 A5
Tycehurst Hill, Loug. IG10 48 C4
Tye La, Orp. BR6 207 F5
Tyers Est, SE1 28 D3
Tyers Gate, SE1 28 D3
Tyers St, SE11 34 C3
Tyers Ter, SE11 34 C4
Tyeshurst Cl, SE2 139 E5
Tylecroft Rd, SW16 186 E2
Tylehurst Gdns, Ilford IG1 99 F5
Tyler Cl, E2 13 F1
Erith DA8 139 H7
Tyler Rd, Sthl. UB2
off McNair Rd 123 H3
Tylers Cl, Loug. IG10 48 B7
Tyler's Ct, W1 17 H4
Tylers Gate, Har. HA3 69 H6
Tylers Path, Cars. SM5
off Rochester Rd 199 J4
Tyler St, SE10 135 E5
Tylney Av, SE19 170 C5
Tylney Cl, Chig. IG7 65 J4
Tylney Rd, E7 97 J4
Bromley BR1 192 A2
Tymperley Ct, SW19
off Windlesham Gro 166 B1
Tynan Cl, Felt. TW14
off Sandycombe Rd 160 A1
Tyndale Ct, E14 134 B5
Tyndale La, N1
off Upper St 93 H7
Tyndale Ter, N1
off Canonbury La 93 H7
Tyndall Rd, E10 96 C2
Welling DA16 157 J3
Tyneham Cl, SW11
off Shirley Gro 150 A3
Tyneham Rd, SW11 150 A2
Tynemouth Cl, E6
off Covelees Wall 116 E6
Tynemouth Rd, N15 76 C4
SE18 137 J5
Mitcham CR4 168 A7
Tynemouth St, SW6 149 F2
Tyne St, E1
off Old Castle St 21 G3
Tynsdale Rd, NW10 88 E7
Tynwald Ho, SE26
off Sydenham Hill Est 170 D3
Type St, E2 113 G2
Typhoon Way, Wall. SM6 200 E7
Tyrawley Rd, SW6 148 E1
Tyre La, NW9 70 E4
Tyrell Cl, Har. HA1 86 B4
Tyrell Ct, Cars. SM5 199 J4
Tyrols Rd, SE23
off Wastdale Rd 171 G1
Tyrone Rd, E6 116 C2
Tyron Way, Sid. DA14 175 H4
Tyrrell Av, Well. DA16 158 A5
Tyrrell Rd, SE22 152 D4
Tyrrell Sq, Mitch. CR4 185 H1
Tyrrel Way, NW9 71 F7
Tyrwhitt Rd, SE4 154 A3
Tysoe St, EC1 11 E4
Tyson Rd, SE23 153 F7
Tyssen Pas, E8 94 C6
Tyssen Rd, N16 94 C3
Tyssen St, E8 94 C6
N1 12 E1
Tytherton Rd, N19 92 D3

U

Uamvar St, E14 114 B5
Uckfield Gro, Mitch. CR4 186 A1
Udall St, SW1 33 G2
Udney Pk Rd, Tedd. TW11 162 D5
Uffington Rd, NW10 107 G1
SE27 169 G4
Ufford Cl, Har. HA3 51 H7
Ufford Rd, Har. HA3 51 H7
Ufford St, SE1 27 F3
Ufton Gro, N1 94 A7
Ufton Rd, N1 94 A7
Uhura Sq, N16 94 B3
Ujima Ct, SW16 169 E4
Ullathorne Rd, SW16 168 C4
Ulleswater Rd, N14 59 E4
Ullin St, E14
off St. Leonards Rd 114 C5
Ullswater Cl, SW15 164 D4
Bromley BR1 173 E6
Ullswater Ct, Har. HA2 67 G7
Ullswater Cres, SW15 164 D4
Ullswater Rd, SE27 169 H2
SW13 127 G7
Ulster Gdns, N13 59 J4
Ulster Pl, NW1 8 D6
Ulster Ter, NW1 8 D6
Ulundi Rd, SE3 135 E6
Ulva Rd, SW15 148 A5
Ulverscroft Rd, SE22 152 C5
Ulverstone Rd, SE27 169 H2
Ulverston Rd, E17 78 D2
Ulysses Rd, NW6 90 C5
Umberston St, E1
off Hessel St 112 E6
Umbria St, SW15 147 G6
Umfreville Rd, N4 75 H6
Undercliff Rd, SE13 154 A3
UNDERHILL, Barn. EN5 40 D5
Underhill, Barn. EN5 40 D5
Underhill Pas, NW1
off Camden High St 110 B1
Underhill Rd, SE22 152 E6
Underhill St, NW1
off Arlington Rd 110 B1
Underne Av, N14 58 B2
Undershaft, EC3 20 D4
Undershaw Rd, Brom. BR1 173 E3
Underwood, Croy. (New Adgtn) CR0 204 C5
Underwood, The, SE9 174 C2
Underwood Rd, E1 13 H6
E4 62 B5
Woodford Green IG8 64 A7
Underwood Row, N1 12 A3
Underwood St, N1 12 A3
Undine Rd, E14 134 B4
Undine St, SW17 167 J5
Uneeda Dr, Grnf. UB6 104 A1
Unicorn Pas, SE1
off Tooley St 28 E2
Union Cl, E11 96 D4
Union Cotts, E15
off Welfare Rd 97 E7
Union Ct, EC2 20 D3
Richmond TW9
off Eton St 145 H5
Union Dr, E1
off Canal Cl 113 H4
Union Gro, SW8 150 D2
Union Jack Club, SE1 27 E3
Union Pk, SE10 135 F5
Union Rd, N11 58 D6
SW4 150 D2
SW8 150 D2
Bromley BR2 192 A5
Croydon CR0 187 J7
Northolt UB5 103 G2
Wembley HA0 87 H6
Union Sq, N1 111 J1
Union St, E15 114 C1
SE1 27 H2
Barnet EN5 40 B4
Kingston upon Thames KT1 181 G2
Union Wk, E2 13 E3
Union Wf, N1 11 J2
West Drayton UB7
off Bentinck Rd 120 B1
Unity Cl, NW10 89 G6
SE19 *off Crown Dale* 169 J5
Unity Ct, SE1
off Mawbey Pl 37 G3
Unity Ter, Har. HA2
off Scott Cres 85 H1
Unity Trd Est, Wdf.Grn. IG8 80 A3
Unity Way, SE18 136 A3
Unity Wf, SE1 29 G3
University Cl, NW7 55 F7
★ **University Coll London**, WC1 9 H5
University Gdns, Bex. DA5 159 F7
★ **University of London**, WC1 17 J1
University Pl, Erith DA8
off Belmont Rd 139 J7
University Rd, SW19 167 G6
University St, WC1 9 G6
University Way, E16 116 D7
Unwin Av, Felt. TW14 141 H5
Unwin Cl, SE15 37 H6
Unwin Rd, SW7 23 F5
Isleworth TW7 144 B3
Upbrook Ms, W2 14 D4
Upcerne Rd, SW10 129 F7
Upchurch Cl, SE20 171 E7
Upcroft Av, Edg. HA8 54 C5
Updale Rd, Sid. DA14 175 J4
Upfield, Croy. CR0 203 E2
Upfield Rd, W7 104 C4
Upgrove Manor Way, SW2
off Trinity Ri 151 G7
Uphall Rd, Ilf. IG1 99 E5
Upham Pk Rd, W4 127 E4
Uphill Dr, NW7 55 E5
NW9 70 C5
Uphill Gro, NW7 55 E4
Uphill Rd, NW7 54 E4
Upland Ms, SE22
off Upland Rd 152 D5
Upland Rd, E13
off Sutton Rd 115 F4
SE22 152 D5
Bexleyheath DA7 159 F3
South Croydon CR2 202 A5
Sutton SM2 199 G7
Uplands, Beck. BR3 190 A2
Uplands, The, Loug. IG10 48 C3
Ruislip HA4 84 A1
Uplands Av, E17
off Blackhorse La 77 G2
Uplands Business Pk, E17 77 G2
Uplands Cl, SW14
off Monroe Dr 146 B5
Uplands End, Wdf.Grn. IG8 64 B7
Uplands Pk Rd, Enf. EN2 43 G3

Uplands Rd, N8 75 F5
Barnet (E.Barn.) EN4 58 A1
Romford RM6 82 D3
Woodford Green IG8 64 B7
Uplands Way, N21 43 G5
Upney La, Bark. IG11 99 H6
Upnor Way, SE17 37 E3
Uppark Dr, Ilf. IG2 81 F6
Upper Abbey Rd, Belv. DA17 139 F4
Upper Addison Gdns, W14 128 B2
Upper Bk St, E14 134 B1
Upper Bardsey Wk, N1 *off Clephane Rd* 93 J6
Upper Belgrave St, SW1 24 C5
Upper Berenger Wk, SW10 *off Blantyre St* 30 E7
Upper Berkeley St, W1 15 J4
Upper Beulah Hill, SE19 188 B1
Upper Blantyre Wk, SW10 *off Blantyre St* 30 E7
Upper Brighton Rd, Surb. KT6 181 G6
Upper Brockley Rd, SE4 153 J2
Upper Brook St, W1 16 B6
Upper Butts, Brent. TW8 125 F6
Upper Caldy Wk, N1 *off Clifton Rd* 93 J6
Upper Camelford Wk, W11 *off St. Marks Rd* 108 B6
Upper Cavendish Av, N3 72 D3
Upper Cheyne Row, SW3 31 G6
UPPER CLAPTON, E5 94 E1
Upper Clapton Rd, E5 94 E1
Upper Clarendon Wk, W11 *off Clarendon Wk* 108 B6
Upper Dartrey Wk, SW10 *off Blantyre St* 30 E7
Upper Dengie Wk, N1 *off Popham Rd* 111 J1
UPPER EDMONTON, N18 60 D6
UPPER ELMERS END, Beck. BR3 189 J6
Upper Elmers End Rd, Beck. BR3 189 H4
Upper Fm Rd, W.Mol. KT8 179 F4
Upper Fosters, NW4 *off New Brent St* 71 J5
Upper Grn E, Mitch. CR4 185 J3
Upper Grn W, Mitch. CR4 *off London Rd* 185 J3
Upper Grosvenor St, W1 16 B6
Upper Grotto Rd, Twick. TW1 162 C2
Upper Grd, SE1 26 E1
Upper Gro, SE25 188 B4
Upper Gro Rd, Belv. DA17 139 F6
Upper Gulland Wk, N1 *off Nightingale Rd* 93 J6
Upper Hampstead Wk, NW3 *off New End* 91 F4
Upper Ham Rd, Kings.T. KT2 163 G4
Richmond TW10 163 G4
Upper Handa Wk, N1 *off Clephane Rd* 93 J6
Upper Hawkwell Wk, N1 *off Popham Rd* 111 J1
Upper Hitch, Wat. WD19 51 E1
UPPER HOLLOWAY, N19 92 C3
Upper Holly Hill Rd, Belv. DA17 139 H5
Upper James St, W1 17 G5
Upper John St, W1 17 G5
Upper Lismore Wk, N1 *off Clephane Rd* 93 J6
Upper Mall, W6 127 G5
Upper Marsh, SE1 26 D5
Upper Montagu St, W1 15 J1
Upper Mulgrave Rd, Sutt. SM2 198 B7
Upper N St, E14 114 A5
UPPER NORWOOD, SE19 170 A7
Upper Palace Rd, E.Mol. KT8 179 J3
Upper Pk, Loug. IG10 48 A4
Upper Pk Rd, N11 58 B5
NW3 91 J5
Belvedere DA17 139 H4
Bromley BR1 191 H1
Kingston upon Thames KT2 164 A6
Upper Phillimore Gdns, W8 128 D2
Upper Ramsey Wk, N1 *off Ramsey Wk* 94 A6
Upper Rawreth Wk, N1 *off Popham Rd* 111 J1
Upper Richmond Rd, SW15 148 B4
Upper Richmond Rd W, SW14 146 B4
Richmond TW10 146 A4
Upper Rd, E13 115 G3
Wallington SM6 200 D5
Upper St. Martin's La, WC2 18 A5
Upper Selsdon Rd, S.Croy. CR2 202 C7
Upper Sheridan Rd, Belv. DA17 *off Coleman Rd* 139 G4
Upper Shirley Rd, Croy. CR0 203 F2
Upper Sq, Islw. TW7 144 D3
Upper St, N1 11 F1
Upper Sunbury Rd, Hmptn. TW12 179 E1
Upper Sutton La, Houns. TW5 123 G7
UPPER SYDENHAM, SE26 170 D4
Upper Tachbrook St, SW1 33 F1
Upper Tail, Wat. WD19 51 E3
Upper Talbot Wk, W11 *off Talbot Wk* 108 B6
Upper Teddington Rd, Kings.T. KT1 181 F1
Upper Ter, NW3 91 F3
Upper Thames St, EC4 19 H5
Upper Tollington Pk, N4 93 G1
Upperton Rd, Sid. DA14 175 J5
Upperton Rd E, E13 *off Inniskilling Rd* 115 J3
Upperton Rd W, E13 115 J3
UPPER TOOTING, SW17 167 H3
Upper Tooting Pk, SW17 167 J2
Upper Tooting Rd, SW17 167 J4
Upper Town Rd, Grnf. UB6 103 H4
Upper Tulse Hill, SW2 151 F7
Upper Vernon Rd, Sutt. SM1 199 G5
UPPER WALTHAMSTOW, E17 78 B4
Upper Walthamstow Rd, E17 78 D4
Upper Whistler Wk, SW10 *off Blantyre St* 30 D7
Upper Wickham La, Well. DA16 138 B7
Upper Wimpole St, W1 16 D1
Upper Woburn Pl, WC1 9 J4
Uppingham Av, Stan. HA7 69 E1
Upsdell Av, N13 59 G6
Upstall St, SE5 151 H1
UPTON, E7 97 H7
Upton Av, E7 97 G7
Upton Cl, NW2 *off Somerton Rd* 90 B3
Bexley DA5 159 F6
Upton Ct, SE20 *off Blean Gro* 171 F7
Upton Dene, Sutt. SM2 198 E7
Upton Gdns, Har. HA3 69 E5
Upton La, E7 97 G7
UPTON PARK, E6 115 J1
Upton Pk Rd, E7 97 H7
Upton Rd, N18 60 D5
SE18 137 F6
Bexley DA5 159 F6
Bexleyheath DA6 158 E4
Hounslow TW3 143 G3
Thornton Heath CR7 188 A2
Upton Rd S, Bex. DA5 159 F6
Upway, N12 57 H7
Upwood Rd, SE12 155 F6
SW16 187 E1
Urban Ms, N4 75 H7
Urlwin St, SE5 35 J6
Urlwin Wk, SW9 151 G2
Urmston Dr, SW19 166 B1
Ursula Ms, N4 93 H1
Ursula St, SW11 149 H1
Urswick Gdns, Dag. RM9 *off Urswick Rd* 100 E7
Urswick Rd, E9 95 F5
Dagenham RM9 100 D7
Usborne Ms, SW8 34 C7
Usher Rd, E3 113 J2
Usk Rd, SW11 149 F4
Usk St, E2 113 G3
Utah Bldg, SE13 *off Deals Gateway* 154 B1
Utopia Village, NW1 *off Chalcot Rd* 110 A1
Uvedale Rd, Dag. RM10 101 G3
Enfield EN2 44 A5
Uverdale Rd, SW10 129 F7
Uxbridge Gdns, Felt. TW13 *off Marlborough Rd* 160 D2
Uxbridge Rd, W3 105 H7
W5 105 F7
W5 (Ealing Com.) 105 H7
W7 124 B1
W12 127 G1
W13 124 E1
Feltham TW13 160 C2
Hampton TW12 161 G4
Uxbridge Rd, Harrow HA3 51 J7
Hayes UB4 102 C7
Kingston upon Thames KT1 181 G4
Pinner HA5 51 H7
Southall UB1 123 G1
Stanmore HA7 52 C6
Uxbridge St, W8 128 D1
Uxendon Cres, Wem. HA9 87 H1
Uxendon Hill, Wem. HA9 87 J1

V

Valance Av, E4 63 F1
Valan Leas, Brom. BR2 191 E3
Vale, The, N10 74 A1
N14 42 D7
NW11 90 A3
SW3 31 E5
W3 126 D1
Croydon CR0 203 G2
Feltham TW14 142 B6
Hounslow TW5 122 E6
Ruislip HA4 84 C4
Sunbury-on-Thames TW16 *off Ashridge Way* 160 A6
Woodford Green IG8 63 G7
Vale Av, Borwd. WD6 38 B5
Vale Cl, N2 73 J3
W9 6 C4
Orpington BR6 206 D4
Vale Cotts, SW15 164 E3
Vale Ct, W3 *off The Vale* 127 F1
W9 6 C4
Vale Cres, SW15 165 E3
Vale Cft, Pnr. HA5 66 E5
Vale Dr, Barn. EN5 40 C4
Vale End, SE22 *off Grove Vale* 152 B4
Vale Gro, N4 75 J7
W3 *off The Vale* 126 D1
Vale Industrial Park, SW16 186 C2
Vale La, W3 106 A5
Valence Av, Dag. RM8 100 D3
Valence Circ, Dag. RM8 100 D3
★ **Valence Ho Mus**, Dag. RM8 100 D3
Valence Wd Rd, Dag. RM8 100 D3
Valencia Rd, Stan. HA7 53 F4
Valentia Pl, SW9 *off Brixton Sta Rd* 151 G4
Valentine Av, Bex. DA5 176 E2
Valentine Ct, SE23 171 G2
Valentine Ho, E3 *off Garrison Rd* 113 J1
Valentine Pl, SE1 27 G3
Valentine Rd, E9 95 G6
Harrow HA2 85 J3
Valentine Row, SE1 27 G4
Valentines Rd, Ilf. IG1 98 E1
Vale of Health, NW3 *off East Heath Rd* 91 G3
Vale Par, SW15 *off Kingston Vale* 164 E3
Valerian Wk, N11 *off Nurserymans Rd* 58 A2
Valerian Way, E15 115 E3
Valerie Ct, Sutt. SM2 *off Stanley Rd* 198 E7
Vale Ri, NW11 90 C1
Vale Rd, E7 97 H6
N4 75 J7
Bromley BR1 192 D2
Epsom KT19 197 F4
Mitcham CR4 186 D3
Sutton SM1 198 E4
Worcester Park KT4 197 F4
Vale Rd N, Surb. KT6 195 H2
Vale Rd S, Surb. KT6 195 H2
Vale Row, N5 *off Gillespie Rd* 93 H3
Vale Royal, N7 92 E7
Valery Pl, Hmptn. TW12 161 G7
Vale St, SE27 170 A3
Valeswood Rd, Brom. BR1 173 F5
Vale Ter, N4 75 J6
Valetta Gro, E13 115 G2
Valetta Rd, W3 126 E2
Valette St, E9 95 E6
Valiant Cl, Nthlt. UB5 *off Ruislip Rd* 102 D3
Romford RM7 83 G2
Valiant Ho, SE7 135 J5
Valiant Path, NW9 71 E1
Valiant Way, E6 116 C5
Vallance Rd, E1 13 J4
E2 13 J4
N22 74 C2
Vallentin Rd, E17 78 C4
Valley Av, N12 57 G4
Valley Cl, Loug. IG10 48 C6
Pinner HA5 66 B2
Valley Dr, NW9 70 A6
Valleyfield Rd, SW16 169 F5
Valley Flds Cres, Enf. EN2 43 G2
Valley Gdns, SW19 167 G7
Wembley HA0 87 J7
Valley Gro, SE7 135 J5
Valley Hill, Loug. IG10 48 B7
Valleylink Est, Enf. EN3 *off Meridian Way* 45 H6
Valley Ms, Twick. TW1 *off Cross Deep* 162 D2
Valley Pt Ind Est, Croy. CR0 186 E7
Valley Rd, SW16 169 F4
Belvedere DA17 139 H4
Bromley BR2 191 E2
Valley Side, E4 62 A2
Valley Side Par, E4 *off Valley Side* 62 A2
Valley Vw, Barn. EN5 40 B6
Valley Wk, Croy. CR0 203 F2
Valliere Rd, NW10 107 H3
Valliers Wd Rd, Sid. DA15 175 G1
Vallis Way, W13 104 D5
Chessington KT9 195 G4
Valmar Rd, SE5 151 J1
Val McKenzie Av, N7 *off Parkside Cres* 93 G3
Valnay St, SW17 167 J5
Valognes Av, E17 77 H1
Valonia Gdns, SW18 148 C6
Vambery Rd, SE18 137 F6
Vanbrough Cres, Nthlt. UB5 102 C1
Vanbrugh Cl, E16 *off Fulmer Rd* 116 A5
Vanbrugh Dr, Walt. KT12 178 C7
Vanbrugh Flds, SE3 135 F7
Vanbrugh Hill, SE3 135 F5
SE10 135 F5
Vanbrugh Pk, SE3 135 F7
Vanbrugh Pk Rd, SE3 135 F7
Vanbrugh Pk Rd W, SE3 135 F7
Vanbrugh Rd, W4 126 D3
Vanbrugh Ter, SE3 155 F1
Vanburgh Cl, Orp. BR6 207 H1
Vancouver Rd, SE23 171 H2
Edgware HA8 70 B1
Hayes UB4 102 B4
Richmond TW10 163 F4
Vanderbilt Rd, SW18 167 E1
Vanderville Gdns, N2 73 F2
Vandome Cl, E16 115 H6
Vandon Pas, SW1 25 G5
Vandon St, SW1 25 G5
Van Dyck Av, N.Mal. KT3 182 D7
Vandyke Cl, SW15 148 A7
Vandyke Cross, SE9 156 B5
Vandy St, EC2 12 D6
Vane Cl, NW3 91 G4
Harrow HA3 69 J6
Vanessa Cl, Belv. DA17 139 G5
Vane St, SW1 33 G1
Van Gogh Cl, Islw. TW7 *off Twickenham Rd* 144 D3
Vanguard Cl, E16 115 G5
Croydon CR0 201 H1
Romford RM7 83 H2
Vanguard Ho, E8 *off Martello St* 95 E7
Vanguard St, SE8 154 A1
Vanguard Way, Wall. SM6 200 E7
Vanneck Sq, SW15 147 G5
Vanner Pt, E9 *off Wick Rd* 95 G6
Vanoc Gdns, Brom. BR1 173 G4
Vansittart Rd, E7 97 F4
Vansittart St, SE14 133 H7
Vanston Pl, SW6 128 D7
Vantage Business Park, Enf. EN3 45 H6
Vantage Ms, E14 *off Prestons Rd* 134 C1
Vantage Pl, W8 *off Abingdon Rd* 128 D3
Feltham TW14 *off Staines Rd* 142 A6
Vant Rd, SW17 167 J5
Varcoe Rd, SE16 133 E5
Vardens Rd, SW11 149 G4
Varden St, E1 112 E6
Vardon Cl, W3 106 D6
Varley Par, NW9 70 E4
Varley Rd, E16 115 H6
Varley Way, Mitch. CR4 185 G2
Varna Rd, SW6 128 B7
Hampton TW12 179 H1
Varndell St, NW1 9 F3
Varnishers Yd, N1 *off Caledonian Rd* 111 E2
Varsity Dr, Twick. TW1 144 B5
Varsity Row, SW14 146 C2
Vartry Rd, N15 76 A6
Vassall Rd, SW9 131 G7

Vauban Est, SE16 **29** G6
Vauban St, SE16 **29** G6
Vaughan Av, NW4 **71** G5
W6 **127** F4
Vaughan Cl, Hmptn. TW12
off Oak Av **161** E6
Vaughan Gdns, Ilf. IG1 **80** C7
Vaughan Rd, E15 **97** F6
SE5 **151** J2
Harrow HA1 **67** J7
Thames Ditton KT7 **180** E7
Welling DA16 **157** J2
Vaughan St, SE16 **133** J2
Vaughan Way, E1 **21** H6
Vaughan Williams Cl, SE8
off Watson's St **134** A7
VAUXHALL, SE11 **34** B4
Vauxhall Br, SE1 **34** A4
SW1 **34** A4
Vauxhall Br Rd, SW1 **33** G1
Vauxhall Gdns, S.Croy.
CR2 **201** J6
Vauxhall Gdns Est, SE11 **34** C4
Vauxhall Gro, SW8 **34** C5
Vauxhall St, SE11 **34** D3
Vauxhall Wk, SE11 **34** C3
Vawdrey Cl, E1 **113** F4
Veals Mead, Mitch. CR4 **185** H1
Vectis Gdns, SW17
off Vectis Rd **168** B6
Vectis Rd, SW17 **168** B6
Veda Rd, SE13 **154** A4
Veldene Way, Har. HA2 **85** F3
Velde Way, SE22
off East Dulwich Gro **152** B5
Velletri Ho, E2 **113** G2
Vellum Dr, Cars. SM5 **200** A3
Venables Cl, Dag. RM10 **101** H4
Venables St, NW8 **7** F6
Vencourt Pl, W6 **127** G5
Venetian Rd, SE5 **151** J2
Venetia Rd, N4 **75** H6
W5 **125** G2
Venner Rd, SE26 **171** F6
Venn St, SW4 **150** C4
Ventnor Av, Stan. HA7 **69** E1
Ventnor Dr, N20 **56** E3
Ventnor Gdns, Bark. IG11 **99** H6
Ventnor Rd, SE14 **133** G7
Sutton SM2 **199** E7
Venture Cl, Bex. DA5 **158** E7
Venue St, E14 **114** C5
Venus Ho, E3
off Garrison Rd **114** A1
E14 *off Crews St* **134** A4
Venus Ms, Mitch. CR4 **185** H3
Venus Rd, SE18 **136** C3
Vera Av, N21 **43** G5
Vera Lynn Cl, E7
off Dames Rd **97** G4
Vera Rd, SW6 **148** B1
Verbena Cl, E16
off Pretoria Rd **115** F4
West Drayton UB7
off Magnolia St **120** A5
Verbena Gdns, W6 **127** G5
Verdant La, SE6 **173** E1
Verdayne Av, Croy. CR0 **203** G1
Verdi Cres, W10
off Herries St **108** B2
Verdun Rd, SE18 **138** A6
SW13 **127** G6
Vereker Dr, Sun. TW16 **178** A3
Vereker Rd, W14 **128** B5
Vere Rd, Loug. IG10 **49** F4
Vere St, W1 **16** D4
Veridion Way, Erith DA18
off Waldrist Way **139** F2
Verity Cl, W11 **108** B6
Vermeer Gdns, SE15
off Elland Rd **153** F4
Vermont Cl, Enf. EN2 **43** H4
Vermont Rd, SE19 **170** A6
SW18 **149** E6
Sutton SM1 **198** E3
Verney Gdns, Dagenham
RM9 **100** E4
Verney Rd, SE16 **37** J5
Dagenham RM9 **100** E5
Verney St, NW10 **88** D3
Verney Way, SE16 **132** E5
Vernham Rd, SE18 **137** F6
Vernon Av, E12 **98** C4
SW20 **184** A2
Woodford Green IG8 **63** H7
Vernon Cl, Epsom KT19 **196** C6
Vernon Ct, Stan. HA7
off Vernon Dr **68** E1
Vernon Cres, Barnet
EN4 **42** A6
Vernon Dr, Stan. HA7 **68** D1
Vernon Ms, E17
off Vernon Rd **77** J4
W14 *off Vernon St* **128** B4
Vernon Pl, WC1 **18** B2
Vernon Ri, WC1 **10** D3
Greenford UB6 **86** A5
Vernon Rd, E3 **113** J2
E11 **97** E1
E15 **97** E7
E17 **77** J5
N8 **75** G3
SW14 **146** D3
Ilford IG3 **99** J1
Sutton SM1 **199** F5
Vernon Sq, WC1 **10** D3
Vernon St, W14 **128** B4
Vernon Yd, W11
off Portobello Rd **108** C7
Veroan Rd, Bexh. DA7 **158** E2
Verona Ct, W4
off Chiswick La **127** E5
Verona Dr, Surb. KT6 **195** H2
Verona Rd, E7
off Upton La **97** G7
Veronica Gdns, SW16 **186** C1
Veronica Rd, SW17 **168** B3
Veronique Gdns, Ilf. IG6 **81** E5
Verran Rd, SW12 **150** B7
Versailles Rd, SE20 **170** D7
Verulam Av, E17 **77** J6
Verulam Bldgs, WC1 **18** D1
Verulam Ct, NW9 **71** G7
Verulam Ho, W6
off Hammersmith Gro **127** J2
Verulam Rd, Grnf. UB6 **103** G4
Verulam St, WC1 **18** E1
Verwood Dr, Barn. EN4 **41** J3
Verwood Rd, Har. HA2 **67** J2
Vesage Ct, EC1 **19** F2
Vesey Path, E14
off East India Dock Rd **114** B6
Vespan Rd, W12 **127** G2
Vesta Ct, SE1
off Morocco St **28** D4
Vesta Ho, E3
off Garrison Rd **114** A1
Vesta Rd, SE4 **153** H2
Vestris Rd, SE23 **171** G2
Vestry Ms, SE5 **152** B1
Vestry Rd, E17 **78** B4
SE5 **152** B1
Vestry St, N1 **12** B3
Vevey St, SE6 **171** J2
Veysey Gdns, Dag. RM10 **101** G3
Viaduct Pl, E2
off Viaduct St **112** E3
Viaduct St, E2 **112** E3
Vian St, SE13 **154** B3
Vibart Gdns, SW2 **151** F7
Vibart Wk, N1
off Outram Pl **111** E1
Vibia Cl, Stai. TW19
off Hadrian Way **140** A7
Vicarage Av, SE3 **155** G1
Vicarage Cl, Erith DA8 **139** J6
Northolt UB5 **85** F7
Worcester Park KT4 **196** E1
Vicarage Ct, W8
off Vicarage Gate **22** A3
Feltham TW14 **141** F7
Vicarage Cres, SW11 **149** G1
Vicarage Dr, SW14 **146** D5
Barking IG11 **99** F7
Beckenham BR3 **190** A1
Vicarage Fm Rd, Houns.
TW3, TW5 **142** E2
Vicarage Flds, Walt.
KT12 **178** C6
Vicarage Fld Shop Cen,
Bark. IG11 **99** F7
Vicarage Gdns, SW14
off Vicarage Rd **146** C5
W8 **128** D1
Mitcham CR4 **185** H3
Vicarage Gate, W8 **22** A3
Vicarage Gro, SE5 **152** A1
Vicarage La, E6 **116** C3
E15 **97** E7
Chigwell IG7 **65** F2
Ilford IG1 **99** G1
Vicarage Par, N15
off West Grn Rd **75** J4
Vicarage Pk, SE18 **137** F5
Vicarage Path, N8 **74** E7
Vicarage Rd, E10 **96** B1
E15 **97** F7
N17 **60** D7
NW4 **71** G6
SE18 **137** F5
SW14 **146** C5
Bexley DA5 **177** H1
Croydon CR0 **201** G3
Dagenham RM10 **101** H6
Kingston upon Thames
KT1 **181** G2
Kingston upon Thames
(Hmptn W.) KT1 **181** F1
Sutton SM1 **198** E4
Teddington TW11 **162** D5
Twickenham TW2 **162** B2
Twickenham (Whitton)
TW2 **143** J6
Woodford Green IG8 **64** B7
Vicarage Wk, SW11
off Battersea Ch Rd **149** G1
Vicarage Way, NW10 **88** D3
Harrow HA2 **67** G7
Vicars Br Cl, Wem. HA0 **105** H2
Vicars Cl, E9
off Northiam St **113** F1
E15 **115** G1
Enfield EN1 **44** B2
Vicars Hill, SE13 **154** B4
Vicars Moor La, N21 **43** G7
Vicars Oak Rd, SE19 **170** B6
Vicars Rd, NW5 **92** A5
Vicars Wk, Dag. RM8 **100** B3
Viceroy Cl, N2
off Market Pl **73** H4
Viceroy Ct, NW8 **7** H1
Viceroy Par, N2
off High Rd **73** H4
Viceroy Rd, SW8 **150** E1
Vickers Cl, Wall. SM6 **201** F7
Vickers Way, Houns.
TW4 **143** E5
Victor Gro, Wem. HA0 **87** H7
★ **Victoria & Albert Mus**,
SW7 **23** F6
Victoria Arc, SW1
off Terminus Pl **25** E6
Victoria Av, E6 **116** A1
EC2 **20** E2
N3 **72** C1
Barnet EN4 **41** G4
Hounslow TW3 **143** F5
Surbiton KT6 **181** G7
Wallington SM6 **200** A3
Wembley HA9 **88** B6
West Molesey KT8 **179** G3
Victoria Cl, SE22
off Underhill Rd **152** D5
Barnet EN4 **41** G4
West Molesey KT8
off Victoria Av **179** G3
★ **Victoria Coach Sta**,
SW1 **32** D2
Victoria Cotts, Rich.
TW9 **145** J1
Victoria Ct, Wem. HA9 **88** A6
Victoria Cres, N15 **76** B5
SE19 **170** B6
SW19 **166** C7
Victoria Dock Rd, E16 **115** F6
Victoria Dr, SW19 **148** A7
Victoria Embk, EC4 **18** C6
SW1 **26** B3
WC2 **18** C6
★ **Victoria Embankment
Gdns**, WC2 **18** B6
Victoria Gdns, W11 **128** D1
Hounslow TW5 **142** E1
Victoria Gro, N12 **57** F5
W8 **22** C5
Victoria Gro Ms, W2
off Ossington St **108** E7
Victoria Ho, SW8
off South Lambeth Rd **34** B7
Victoria Ind Est, NW10 **106** E3
Victoria La, Barn. EN5 **40** C4
Hayes (Harling.) UB3 **121** F5
Victoria Mans, SW8
off South Lambeth Rd **34** B7
Victoria Ms, E8
off Dalston La **94** D6
NW6 **108** D1
SW4 *off Victoria Ri* **150** B4
SW18 **167** F1
Victoria Mills Studios, E15
off Burford Rd **114** D1
Victorian Gro, N16 **94** B3
Victorian Hts, SW8
off Thackeray Rd **150** B2
Victorian Rd, N16 **94** B3
★ **Victoria Park**, E9 **95** H7
Victoria Pk Rd, E9 **113** F1
Victoria Pk Sq, E2 **113** F3
Victoria Pas, NW8 **7** E5
Victoria Pl, SW1 **32** E1
Richmond TW9 **145** G5
Victoria Pt, E13
off Victoria Rd **115** G2
Victoria Retail Pk, Ruis.
HA4 **84** D5
Victoria Ri, SW4 **150** B3
Victoria Rd, E4 **63** E1
E11 **96** E4
E13 **115** G2
E17 **78** C2
E18 **79** H2
N4 **75** F7
N9 **60** C4
N15 **76** D4
N18 **60** C4
N22 **74** C1
NW4 **71** J4
NW6 **108** C1
NW7 **55** F5
NW10 **106** D5
SW14 **146** D3
Victoria Rd, W3 **106** D5
W5 **105** E5
W8 **22** C6
Barking IG11 **99** E6
Barnet EN4 **41** G4
Bexleyheath DA6 **159** G4
Bromley BR2 **192** A5
Buckhurst Hill IG9 **64** A2
Bushey WD23 **51** H1
Chislehurst BR7 **174** D5
Dagenham RM10 **101** H5
Feltham TW13 **160** B1
Kingston upon Thames
KT1 **181** J2
Mitcham CR4 **167** H7
Ruislip HA4 **84** C5
Sidcup DA15 **175** J3
Southall UB2 **123** F3
Surbiton KT6 **181** G6
Sutton SM1 **199** G5
Teddington TW11 **162** D6
Twickenham TW1 **144** D7
Victoria Sq, SW1 **24** E5
Victoria Sta, SW1 **32** E1
Victoria Steps, Brent. TW8
off Kew Br Rd **125** J6
Victoria St, E15 **96** E7
SW1 **25** F6
Belvedere DA17 **139** F5
Victoria Ter, N4 **93** G1
NW10 *off Old Oak La* **107** E4
Harrow HA1 **86** B1
Victoria Vil, Rich. TW9 **145** J3
Victoria Way, SE7 **135** H5
Ruislip HA4
off Civic Way **84** D5
Victoria Wf, E14 **113** H7
Victoria Yd, E1 **21** J4
Victor Rd, NW10 **107** H3
SE20 **171** G7
Harrow HA2 **67** J3
Teddington TW11 **162** B4
Victors Dr, Hmptn.
TW12 **161** E6
Victors Way, Barn. EN5 **40** C3
Victor Vil, N9 **60** A3
Victor Wk, NW9 **71** E2
Victory Av, Mord. SM4 **185** F5
Victory Business Cen, Islw.
TW7 **144** C3
Victory Ms, Sthl. UB2 **123** E3
Victory Pl, E14
off Northey St **113** H7
SE17 **36** B1
SE19 *off Westow St* **170** B6
Victory Rd, E11 **79** H4
SW19 **167** F7
Victory Rd Ms, SW19
off Victory Rd **167** F7
Victory Wk, SE8
off Ship St **154** A1
Victory Way, SE16 **133** H2
Hounslow TW5 **122** C5
Romford RM7 **83** H2
Vidler Cl, Chess. KT9
off Merritt Gdns **195** F6
Vienna Cl, Ilf. IG5 **80** A3
View, The, SE2 **139** E5
View Cl, N6 **73** J7
Chigwell IG7 **65** G5
Harrow HA1 **68** A4
Viewfield Cl, Har. HA3 **69** H7
Viewfield Rd, SW18 **148** C6
Bexley DA5 **176** C1
Viewland Rd, SE18 **137** J5
View Rd, N6 **73** J7
Viga Rd, N21 **43** G6
Vigilant Cl, SE26 **170** D4
Vignoles Rd, Rom. RM7 **83** G7
Vigo St, W1 **17** F6
Viking Cl, E3
off Selwyn Rd **113** J2
Viking Ct, SW6 **128** D6
Viking Gdns, E6
off Jack Dash Way **116** B4
Viking Pl, E10 **95** J1
Viking Rd, Sthl. UB1 **103** E7
Viking Way, Erith DA8 **139** J3
Villacourt Rd, SE18 **138** A7
Village, The, SE7 **135** J6
Village Arc, E4
off Station Rd **62** D1
Village Cl, E4 **62** C5
NW3 *off Belsize La* **91** G5
Village Ct, E17
off Eden Rd **78** B5
Village Hts, Wdf.Grn.
IG8 **63** F5
Village Ms, NW9 **88** D2
Village Pk Cl, Enf. EN1 **44** B6
Village Rd, N3 **72** B1
Enfield EN1 **44** B6
Village Row, Sutt. SM2 **198** D7
Village Way, NW10 **88** D4
SE21 **152** A6
Beckenham BR3 **190** A2
Ilford IG6 **81** F3

Village Way, Pinner HA5 ...67 E7
Village Way E, Har. HA2 ...67 F7
Villa Rd, SW9 ...151 G3
Villas Rd, SE18 ...137 F4
Villa St, SE17 ...36 C4
Villiers Av, Surb. KT5 ...181 J5
Twickenham TW2 ...161 F1
Villiers Cl, E10 ...96 A2
Surbiton KT5 ...181 J4
Villiers Ct, N20
off Buckingham Av ...41 F7
Villiers Path, Surb. KT5 ...181 H5
Villiers Rd, NW2 ...89 G6
Beckenham BR3 ...189 G2
Isleworth TW7 ...144 B2
Kingston upon Thames
KT1 ...181 J3
Southall UB1 ...123 F1
Villiers St, WC2 ...18 A6
Vimy Cl, Houns. TW4
off Vickers Way ...143 F5
Vincam Cl, Twick. TW2 ...143 G7
Vince Ct, N1
off Charles Sq ...12 C4
Vincent Av, Surb. KT5 ...196 B1
Vincent Cl, SE16 ...133 H2
Barnet EN5 ...40 D3
Bromley BR2 ...191 H4
Ilford IG6 ...65 F6
Sidcup DA15 ...175 H1
West Drayton (Sipson)
UB7 ...120 D6
Vincent Gdns, NW2 ...89 F3
Vincent Ms, E3
off Fairfield Rd ...114 A2
Vincent Rd, E4 ...62 D6
N15 ...75 J4
N22 ...75 G2
SE18 ...137 E4
W3 ...126 C3
Croydon CR0 ...188 B7
Dagenham RM9 ...100 E7
Hounslow TW4 ...142 D2
Isleworth TW7 ...144 A1
Vincent Rd, Kingston upon
Thames KT1 ...182 A3
Wembley HA0 ...87 J7
Vincent Row, Hmptn.
(Hmptn H.) TW12 ...161 J6
Vincents Path, Nthlt. UB5
off Arnold Rd ...84 E6
Vincent Sq, N22 ...75 G2
SW1 ...33 G1
Vincent St, E16 ...115 F5
SW1 ...33 H1
Vincent Ter, N1 ...11 G1
Vince St, EC1 ...12 C4
Vine Cl, Surb. KT5 ...181 J6
Sutton SM1 ...199 F3
West Drayton UB7 ...120 D4
Vine Ct, E1 ...21 J2
Harrow HA3 ...69 H6
Vinegar All, E17 ...78 B4
Vine Gdns, Ilf. IG1 ...99 F5
Vinegar St, E1
off Reardon St ...132 E1
Vinegar Yd, SE1 ...28 D3
Vine Hill, EC1 ...10 E6
Vine La, SE1 ...28 E2
Vine Pl, W5
off St. Mark's Rd ...125 H1
Hounslow TW3 ...143 H4
Viner Cl, Walt. KT12 ...178 C6
Vineries, The, N14 ...42 C6
SE6 ...172 A1
Enfield EN1 ...44 B3
Vineries Bk, NW7 ...55 H5
Vineries Cl, Dag. RM9 ...101 G6
West Drayton (Sipson)
UB7 ...120 D6
Vine Rd, E15 ...97 F7
SW13 ...147 F3
East Molesey KT8 ...179 J4
Orpington BR6 ...207 J6
Vines Av, N3 ...72 E1
Vine Sq, W14 ...128 C5
Vine St, EC3 ...21 F5
W1 ...17 G6
Romford RM7 ...83 J5
Vine St Br, EC1 ...11 F6
Vine Yd, SE1 ...28 A3
Vineyard, The, Rich.
TW10 ...145 H5
Vineyard Av, NW7 ...56 B7
Vineyard Cl, SE6 ...172 A1
Kingston upon Thames
KT1 ...181 J3
Vineyard Gro, N3 ...73 E1
Vineyard Hill Rd, SW19 ...166 D4
Vineyard Pas, Rich. TW9
off Paradise Rd ...145 H5
Vineyard Path, SW14 ...146 D3
Vineyard Rd, Felt. TW13 ...160 A3
Vineyard Row, Kings.T.
(Hmptn W.) KT1 ...181 F1
Vineyard Wk, EC1 ...11 E5
Viney Rd, SE13 ...154 B3
Vining St, SW9 ...151 G4
★ **Vinopolis**, SE1 ...28 A1
Vintage Ms, E4 ...62 A4
Vintners Ct, EC4 ...20 A5
Vintners Pl, EC4
off Vintners Ct ...20 A5
Vintry Ms, E17
off Cleveland Pk Cres ...78 A4
Viola Av, SE2 ...138 B4
Feltham TW14 ...142 C6
Viola Sq, W12 ...107 F7
Violet Cl, E16 ...115 E4
SE8 *off Dorking Cl* ...133 J6
Sutton SM3 ...198 B1
Wallington SM6 ...200 A1
Violet Gdns, Croy. CR0 ...201 H5
Violet Hill, NW8 ...6 C2
Violet La, Croy. CR0 ...201 H5
Violet Rd, E3 ...114 B4
E17 ...78 A6
E18 ...79 H2
Violet St, E2
off Three Colts La ...113 E4
Virgil Pl, W1 ...15 J2
Virgil St, SE1 ...26 D5
Virginia Cl, Kes. BR2 ...190 E3
N.Mal. KT3
off Willow Rd ...182 C4
Virginia Gdns, Ilf. IG6 ...81 F2
Virginia Rd, E2 ...13 F4
Thornton Heath CR7 ...187 H1
Virginia St, E1 ...21 J6
Virginia Wk, SW2 ...151 F6
Visage Apts, NW3
off Winchester Rd ...91 G7
Viscount Cl, N11 ...58 B5
Viscount Dr, E6 ...116 C5
Viscount Gro, Nthlt.
UB5 ...102 D3
Viscount St, EC1 ...11 J6
Viscount Way, Houns.
(Lon.Hthrw Air.) TW6 ...141 H4
Vista, The, E4 ...46 D7
SE9 ...156 A6
Sidcup DA14 ...175 J5
Vista Av, Enf. EN3 ...45 G2
Vista Bldg, The, SE18
off Calderwood St ...136 D4
Vista Dr, Ilf. IG4 ...80 A5
Vista Ho, SW19
off Chapter Way ...185 G1
Vista Way, Har. HA3 ...69 H6
Viveash Cl, Hayes UB3 ...121 J3
Vivian Av, NW4 ...71 H5
Wembley HA9 ...88 A5
Vivian Cl, Wat. WD19 ...50 A1
Vivian Comma Cl, N4
off Blackstock Rd ...93 H3
Vivian Ct, W9 ...6 A1
Vivian Gdns, Wat. WD19 ...50 A1
Wembley HA9 ...88 A5
Vivian Rd, E3 ...113 H2
Vivian Sq, SE15
off Scylla Rd ...152 E3
Vivian Way, N2 ...73 G5
Vivien Cl, Chess. KT9 ...195 H7
Vivien Ct, N9
off Galahad Rd ...60 D2
Vivienne Cl, Twick. TW1 ...145 F6
Voce Rd, SE18 ...137 G7
Voewood Cl, N.Mal. KT3 ...183 F6
Vogans Mill, SE1 ...29 G3
Volta Cl, N9
off Hudson Way ...61 F3
Voltaire Bldgs, SW18
off Garratt La ...167 E1
Voltaire Rd, SW4 ...150 D3
Volt Av, NW10 ...106 D3
Volta Way, Croy. CR0 ...201 F1
Voluntary Pl, E11 ...79 G6
Vorley Rd, N19 ...92 C2
Voss Ct, SW16 ...169 E6
Voss St, E2 ...13 J4
Voyagers Cl, SE28 ...118 C6
Voysey Cl, N3 ...72 B3
Vulcan Cl, E6 ...116 D6
Vulcan Gate, Enf. EN2 ...43 G2
Vulcan Rd, SE4 ...153 J2
Vulcan Sq, E14
off Britannia Rd ...134 A4
Vulcan Ter, SE4 ...153 J2
Vulcan Way, N7 ...93 F6
Vyne, The, Bexh. DA7 ...159 H3
Vyner Rd, W3 ...106 D7
Vyner St, E2 ...113 E1
Vyse Cl, Barn. EN5 ...39 J4

W

Wadbrook St, Kings.T.
KT1 ...181 G2
Wadding St, SE17 ...36 B2
Waddington Cl, Enf.
EN1 ...44 B4
Waddington Rd, E15 ...96 D5
Waddington St, E15 ...96 D6
Waddington Way, SE19 ...169 J7
WADDON, Croy. CR0 ...201 G2
Waddon Cl, Croy. CR0 ...201 G3
Waddon Ct Rd, Croy.
CR0 ...201 G4
Waddon Marsh Way, Croy.
CR0 ...201 F1
Waddon New Rd, Croy.
CR0 ...201 H3
Waddon Pk Av, Croy.
CR0 ...201 G4
Waddon Rd, Croy. CR0 ...201 G3
Waddon Way, Croy. CR0 ...201 H6
Wades Gro, N21 ...43 G7
Wades Hill, N21 ...43 G6
Wades La, Tedd. TW11
off High St ...162 D5
Wadeson St, E2 ...113 E2
Wades Pl, E14 ...114 B7
Wadeville Av, Rom. RM6 ...83 F7
Wadeville Cl, Belv.
DA17 ...139 G6
Wadham Av, E17 ...62 B7
Wadham Gdns, NW3 ...109 H1
Greenford UB6 ...86 A6
Wadham Rd, E17 ...78 B1
SW15 ...148 B4
Wadhurst Cl, SE20 ...188 E2
Wadhurst Rd, SW8 ...150 C1
W4 ...126 D3
Wadley Rd, E11 ...78 E7
Wadsworth Business Cen,
Grnf. UB6 ...105 F2
Wadsworth Cl, Enf. EN3 ...45 G5
Greenford (Perivale)
UB6 ...105 F2
Wadsworth Rd, Grnf.
(Perivale) UB6 ...105 E2
Wager St, E3 ...113 J4
Waggoners Rbt, Houns.
TW5 *off Bath Rd* ...142 B1
Waggon Ms, N14
off Chase Side ...58 C1
Waghorn Rd, E13 ...115 J1
Harrow HA3 ...69 G3
Waghorn St, SE15 ...152 D3
Wagner St, SE15 ...133 F7
Wagstaff Gdns, Dag.
RM9 ...100 C7
Wagtail Cl, NW9 ...70 E2
Enfield EN1 ...45 E1
Wagtail Wk, Beck. BR3 ...190 C5
Waights Ct, Kings.T. KT2 ...181 H1
Wainfleet Av, Rom. RM5 ...83 J2
Wainford Cl, SW19
off Windlesham Gro ...166 A1
Wainwright Gro, Islw.
TW7 ...144 A4
Waite Davies Rd, SE12 ...155 F7
Waite St, SE15 ...37 F5
Waithman St, EC4 ...19 G4
Wakefield Gdns, SE19 ...170 B7
Ilford IG1 ...80 B6
Wakefield Ms, WC1 ...10 B4
Wakefield Rd, N11 ...58 D5
N15 ...76 C5
Richmond TW10 ...145 G5
Wakefield St, E6 ...116 A1
N18 ...60 D5
WC1 ...10 B5
Wakeford Cl, SW4 ...150 C5
Wakehams Hill, Pnr. HA5 ...67 F3
Wakeham St, N1 ...94 A6
Wakehurst Rd, SW11 ...149 H5
Wakeling La, Wem. HA0 ...86 E3
Wakeling Rd, W7 ...104 C5
Wakeling St, E14 ...113 H6
Wakelin Rd, E15 ...114 E2
Wakeman Rd, NW10 ...107 J3
Wakemans Hill Av,
NW9 ...70 D5
Wakering Rd, Bark. IG11 ...99 F7
Wakerley Cl, E6
off Truesdale Rd ...116 C6
Wakley St, EC1 ...11 G3
Walberswick St, SW8 ...131 E7
Walbrook, EC4 ...20 B5
Walbrook Ho, N9 ...61 F2
Walbrook Wf, EC4
off Bell Wf La ...20 A6
Walburgh St, E1
off Bigland St ...112 E6
Walcorde Av, SE17 ...36 A2
Walcot Ho, SE22
off Albrighton Rd ...152 B3
Walcot Rd, Enf. EN3 ...45 J2
Walcot Sq, SE11 ...35 F1
Walcott St, SW1 ...33 G1
Waldair Ct, E16
off Barge Ho Rd ...137 E2
Waldair Wf, E16 ...136 E2
Waldeck Gro, SE27 ...169 H3
Waldeck Rd, N15 ...75 H4
SW14 *off Lower*
Richmond Rd ...146 C3
W4 ...126 A6
W13 ...104 E6
Waldeck Ter, SW14
off Lower
Richmond Rd ...146 C3
Waldegrave Av, Tedd. TW11
off Waldegrave Rd ...162 C5
Waldegrave Gdns, Twick.
TW1 ...162 C2
Waldegrave Pk, Twick.
TW1 ...162 C4
Waldegrave Rd, N8 ...75 G3
SE19 ...170 C7
W5 ...105 J6
Bromley BR1 ...192 B4
Dagenham RM8 ...100 C2
Teddington TW11 ...162 C4
Twickenham TW1 ...162 C4
Waldegrove, Croy. CR0 ...202 C3
Waldemar Av, SW6 ...148 B1
W13 ...125 F1
Waldemar Rd, SW19 ...166 D5
Walden Av, N13 ...59 J4
Chislehurst BR7 ...174 C4
Walden Cl, Belv. DA17 ...139 F5
Walden Ct, SW8
off Wandsworth Rd ...150 D1
Walden Gdns, Th.Hth.
CR7 ...187 F3
Walden Par, Chis. BR7
off Walden Rd ...174 C6
Walden Rd, N17 ...76 A1
Chislehurst BR7 ...174 C6
Waldenshaw Rd, SE23 ...171 F1
Walden St, E1 ...112 E6
Walden Way, NW7 ...56 A6
Ilford IG6 ...65 H7
Waldo Cl, SW4 ...150 C5
Waldo Pl, Mitch. CR4 ...167 H7
Waldo Rd, NW10 ...107 G3
Bromley BR1 ...192 A3
Waldram Cres, SE23 ...171 F1
Waldram Pk Rd, SE23 ...171 G1
Waldram Pl, SE23
off Waldram Cres ...171 F1
Waldrist Way, Erith DA18 ...139 F2
Waldron Gdns, Brom.
BR2 ...190 D3
Waldronhyrst, S.Croy.
CR2 ...201 H4
Waldron Ms, SW3 ...31 F5
Waldron Rd, SW18 ...167 F3
Harrow HA1, HA2 ...86 B1
Waldrons, The, Croy. CR0 ...201 H4
Waldrons Path, S.Croy.
CR2 ...201 J4
Waldrons Yd, Har. HA2
off Northolt Rd ...86 A2
Waldstock Rd, SE28 ...118 A7
Waleran Cl, Stan. HA7 ...52 C6
Walerand Rd, SE13 ...154 C2
Waleran Flats, SE1 ...36 D1
Wales Av, Cars. SM5 ...199 J5
Wales Cl, SE15 ...132 E7
Wales Fm Rd, W3 ...106 D5
Waleton Acres, Wall.
SM6 ...200 C6
Waley St, E1 ...113 G5
Walfield Av, N20 ...41 E7
Walford Rd, N16 ...94 B4
Walfrey Gdns, Dag. RM9 ...101 E7
WALHAM GREEN, SW6 ...128 E7
Walham Grn Ct, SW6
off Waterford Rd ...128 E7
Walham Gro, SW6 ...128 D7
Walham Ri, SW19 ...166 B6
Walham Yd, SW6
off Eustace Rd ...128 D7
Walkden Rd, Chis. BR7 ...174 D5
Walker Cl, N11 ...58 C4
SE18 ...137 F4
W7 ...124 B1
Feltham TW14 ...141 J7
Hampton TW12
off Fearnley Cres ...161 F6
Walker Ms, SW2
off Effra Rd ...151 G5
Walkers Ct, E8
off Wilton Way ...94 D6
W1 ...17 H5
Walkerscroft Mead, SE21 ...169 J1
Walkers Pl, SW15
off Felsham Rd ...148 B4
Walks, The, N2 ...73 G3
Walkynscroft, SE15
off Firbank Rd ...153 E2
Wallace Cl, SE28
off Haldane Rd ...118 D7
★ **Wallace Collection**,
W1 ...16 B3
Wallace Cres, Cars. SM5 ...199 J5
Wallace Rd, N1 ...93 J6
Wallace Way, N19
off Giesbach Rd ...92 D2
Wallbutton Rd, SE4 ...153 H2
Wallcote Av, NW2 ...90 A1
Walled Gdn Cl, Beck.
BR3 ...190 B4
Wall End Rd, E6 ...98 C7

Waller Dr, Nthwd. HA6 . . . .66 A2
Waller Rd, SE14 . . . . .153 G1
Wallers Cl, Dag. RM9 . . . . .119 E1
Woodford Green IG8 . . . .64 C6
Waller's Hoppet, Loug. IG10 . . . . .48 B2
Waller Way, SE10 off Greenwich High Rd 134 B7
Wallflower St, W12 . . . . . . .107 F7
Wallgrave Rd, SW5 . . . . . . .30 A1
Wallingford Av, W10 . . . . . .108 A5
WALLINGTON, SM6 . . . . .200 C5
Wallington Cor, Wall. SM6 off Manor Rd N 200 B4
Wallington Grn, Wall. SM6 off Croydon Rd 200 B4
Wallington Rd, Ilf. IG3 . . . . .81 J7
Wallington Sq, Wall. SM6 off Woodcote Rd 200 B6
Wallis All, SE1 . . . . .28 A3
Wallis Cl, SW11 . . . . .149 G3
Wallis Ms, N8 off Courcy Rd 75 G3
Wallis Rd, E9 . . . . .95 J6
Southall UB1 . . . . .103 H6
Wallis's Cotts, SW2 . . . . . .150 E7
Wallman Pl, N22 off Bounds Grn Rd 75 F1
Wallorton Gdns, SW14 . . .146 D4
Wallside, EC2 . . . . .20 A2
Wall St, N1 . . . . .94 A6
Wallwood Rd, E11 . . . . .96 D1
Wallwood St, E14 . . . . .113 J5
Walmar Cl, Barn. EN4 . . . . .41 G1
Walmer Cl, E4 . . . . .62 B2
Orpington (Farnboro.) BR6 off Tubbenden La S 207 G4
Romford RM7 . . . . .83 H2
Walmer Gdns, W13 . . . . . .124 D2
Walmer Ho, N9 . . . . .44 C7
Walmer Pl, W1 . . . . .15 J1
Walmer Rd, W10 off Latimer Rd 107 J6
W11 . . . . .108 B7
Walmer St, W1 . . . . .15 J1
Walmer Ter, SE18 . . . . .137 F4
Walmgate Rd, Grnf. (Perivale) UB6 . . . . .104 E1
Walmington Fold, N12 . . . .56 D6
Walm La, NW2 . . . . .90 A5
Walmsley Ho, SW16 off Colson Way 168 C4
Walney Wk, N1 off St. Paul's Rd 93 J6
Walnut Av, West Dr. UB7 . .120 D3
Walnut Cl, SE8 off Clyde St 133 J6
Carshalton SM5 . . . . . . .199 J5
Ilford IG6 off Civic Way 81 F4
Walnut Ct, W5 . . . . .125 H2
Walnut Gdns, E15 off Burgess Rd 96 E5
Walnut Gro, Enf. EN1 . . . . .44 A5
Walnut Ms, Sutt. SM2 . . . .199 F7
Walnut Rd, E10 . . . . .96 A2
Walnut Tree Av, Mitch. CR4 off De'Arn Gdns 185 H3
Walnut Tree Cl, SW13 . . . .147 F1
Chislehurst BR7 . . . . . . .193 F1
Walnut Tree Cotts, SW19 off Church Rd 166 B5
Walnut Tree Rd, SE10 . . . . .135 E5
Brentford TW8 . . . . .125 H6
Dagenham RM8 . . . . . . .100 D2
Hounslow TW5 . . . . .123 F6
Walnut Tree Wk, SE11 . . . . .34 E1
Walnut Way, Buck.H. IG9 . . .64 A3
Ruislip HA4 . . . . .84 C6
Walpole Av, Rich. TW9 . . . .145 J2
Walpole Cl, W13 . . . . .125 F2
Pinner HA5 . . . . .51 G6
Walpole Cres, Tedd. TW11 .162 C5
Walpole Gdns, W4 . . . . . . .126 C5
Twickenham TW2 . . . . . .162 B2
Walpole Ms, NW8 off Queen's Gro 109 G1
SW19 off Walpole Rd . . .167 G6
Walpole Pk, W5 . . . . .125 F1
Walpole Pl, SE18 off Brookhill Rd 136 E4
Teddington TW11 . . . . . .162 C5
Walpole Rd, E6 . . . . .97 J7
E17 . . . . .77 H4
E18 . . . . .79 F1
N17 (Downhills Way) 75 J3
N17 (Lordship La) 75 J2
SW19 . . . . .167 G6
Bromley BR2 . . . . .192 A5
Croydon CR0 . . . . .202 A2
Surbiton KT6 . . . . .181 H7
Teddington TW11 . . . . . . .162 C5
Twickenham TW2 . . . . . .162 B2
Walpole St, SW3 . . . . .31 J3
Walrond Av, Wem. HA9 . . . .87 H5
Walsham Cl, N16 off Clarke Path 94 D1
SE28 . . . . .118 D7
Walsham Rd, SE14 . . . . . . .153 G2
Feltham TW14 . . . . .142 B7
Walsingham Gdns, Epsom KT19 . . . . .197 E4
Walsingham Pk, Chis. BR7 . . . . .193 G2
Walsingham Pl, SW4 off Clapham Common W Side 149 J4
SW11 . . . . .150 A6
Walsingham Rd, E5 . . . . . . .94 D3
W13 . . . . .124 D1
Enfield EN2 . . . . .44 A4
Mitcham CR4 . . . . .185 J5
Walsingham Wk, Belv. DA17 . . . . .139 G6
Walter Hurford Par, E12 off Walton Rd 98 D4
Walter Rodney Cl, E6 off Stevenage Rd 98 C6
Walters Cl, SE17 . . . . .36 A2
Hayes UB3 . . . . .121 J2
Walters Ho, SE17 . . . . .35 G6
Walters Rd, SE25 . . . . .188 B4
Enfield EN3 . . . . .45 F5
Walter St, E2 . . . . .113 G3
Kingston upon Thames KT2 off Sopwith Way .181 H1
Walters Way, SE23 . . . . . . .153 G6
Walters Yd, Brom. BR1 . . . .191 G2
Walter Ter, E1 . . . . .113 G6
Walterton Rd, W9 . . . . .108 C4
Walter Wk, Edg. HA8 . . . . . .54 C6
Waltham Av, NW9 . . . . .70 A6
Hayes UB3 . . . . .121 F3
Waltham Dr, Edg. HA8 . . . .70 A2
Waltham Pk Way, E17 . . . . .78 A1
Waltham Rd, Cars. SM5 . . .185 G7
Southall UB2 . . . . .122 E3
Woodford Green IG8 . . . .64 B6
WALTHAMSTOW, E17 . . . . .78 B2
Walthamstow Av, E4 . . . . . .61 J7
Walthamstow Business Cen, E17 . . . . .78 C2
Waltham Way, E4 . . . . .61 J4
Waltheof Av, N17 . . . . .76 A1
Waltheof Gdns, N17 . . . . . . .76 A1
Walton Av, Har. HA2 . . . . . .85 F5
New Malden KT3 . . . . . .183 F4
Sutton SM3 . . . . .198 C3
Wembley HA9 . . . . .88 B3
Walton Cl, E5 off Orient Way 95 G3
NW2 . . . . .89 H2
SW8 . . . . .34 B7
Harrow HA1 . . . . .68 A4
Walton Cres, Har. HA2 . . . . .85 F4
Walton Dr, NW10 . . . . .88 D6
Harrow HA1 . . . . .68 A4
Walton Gdns, W3 . . . . .106 B5
Wembley HA9 . . . . .87 H2
Walton Grn, Croy. (New Adgtn) CR0 . . . . . .204 C7
Walton Pl, SW3 . . . . .23 J5
Walton Rd, E12 . . . . .98 D4
E13 . . . . .115 J2
Walton Rd, N15 . . . . .76 C4
East Molesey KT8 . . . . .179 G4
Harrow HA1 . . . . .68 A4
Sidcup DA14 . . . . .176 C2
Walton-on-Thames KT12 . . . . .178 C5
West Molesey KT8 . . . . .179 E5
Walton St, SW3 . . . . .31 H1
Enfield EN2 . . . . .44 A1
Walton Way, W3 . . . . .106 B5
Mitcham CR4 . . . . .186 C4
Walt Whitman Cl, SE24 off Shakespeare Rd . . .151 H4
WALWORTH, SE17 . . . . .35 J3
★ Walworth Garden Fm - Horticultural Training Cen, SE17 . . . . .35 H4
Walworth Pl, SE17 . . . . .36 A4
Walworth Rd, SE1 . . . . .35 J1
SE17 . . . . .35 J1
Walwyn Av, Brom. BR1 . . .192 A3
Wanborough Dr, SW15 . . . .165 H1
Wanderer Dr, Bark. IG11 . .118 B3
Wandle Bk, SW19 . . . . . . .167 G6
Croydon CR0 . . . . .200 E3
Wandle Ct, Epsom KT19 . . . . .196 C4
Wandle Ct Gdns, Croy. CR0 . . . . .200 E3
Wandle Rd, SW17 . . . . . . .167 H2
Croydon CR0 . . . . .201 J3
Croydon (Bedd.) CR0 . . .201 E3
Morden SM4 . . . . .185 F4
Wallington SM6 . . . . . . .200 B2
Wandle Side, Croy. CR0 . . .201 F3
Wallington SM6 . . . . . . .200 B3
Wandle Tech Pk, Mitch. CR4 . . . . .185 J7
Wandle Trd Est, Mitch. CR4 off Budge La 185 J7
Wandle Way, SW18 . . . . . .166 E1
Mitcham CR4 . . . . .185 J5
Wandon Rd, SW6 . . . . .129 E7
WANDSWORTH, SW18 . . .148 C5
Wandsworth Br, SW6 . . . .149 E3
SW18 . . . . .149 E3
Wandsworth Br Rd, SW6 .148 E1
Wandsworth Common, SW12 . . . . .149 H6
Wandsworth Common W Side, SW18 . . . . .149 F5
Wandsworth High St, SW18 . . . . .148 D5
★ Wandsworth Mus, SW18 off Garratt La 148 E5
Wandsworth Plain, SW18 . . . . .148 E5
Wandsworth Rd, SW8 . . . . .34 A5
Wandsworth Town, SW18 . . . . .148 D5
Wangey Rd, Rom. RM6 . . . .82 D7
Wanless Rd, SE24 . . . . . . .151 J3
Wanley Rd, SE5 . . . . .152 A4
Wanlip Rd, E13 . . . . .115 H4
Wannock Gdns, Ilf. IG6 . . . .65 E7
Wansbeck Rd, E3 . . . . .95 J7
E9 . . . . .95 J7
Wansdown Pl, SW6 . . . . . . .30 A7
Wansey St, SE17 . . . . .36 A2
Wansford Pk, Borwd. WD6 .38 E4
Wansford Rd, Wdf.Grn. IG8 . . . . .79 J1
WANSTEAD, E11 . . . . .79 H7
Wanstead Cl, Brom. BR1 . .191 J2
Wanstead La, Ilf. IG1 . . . . . .80 A6
Wanstead Pk, E11 . . . . .80 A7
Wanstead Pk Av, E12 . . . . . .98 A2
Wanstead Pk Rd, Ilf. IG1 . . .98 C1
Wanstead Pl, E11 . . . . .79 G6
Wanstead Rd, Brom. BR1 . . . . .191 J2
Wansunt Rd, Bex. DA5 . . .177 J1
Wantage Rd, SE12 . . . . . . .155 F5
Wantz Rd, Dag. RM10 . . . .101 H4
WAPPING, E1 . . . . .29 J1
Wapping Dock St, E1 off Cinnamon St 133 E1
Wapping High St, E1 . . . . . .29 H2
Wapping La, E1 . . . . .113 E7
Wapping Wall, E1 . . . . .133 F1
Warbank La, Kings.T. KT2 . . . . .165 F7
Warbeck Rd, W12 . . . . .127 H1
Warberry Rd, N22 . . . . .75 F2
Warboys App, Kings.T. KT2 . . . . .164 B6
Warboys Cres, E4 . . . . .62 C5
Warboys Rd, Kings.T. KT2 . . . . .164 B6
Warburton Cl, N1 off Culford Rd 94 B6
Harrow HA3 . . . . .52 A6
Warburton Ho, E8 off Warburton Rd 112 E1
Warburton Rd, E8 . . . . .113 E1
Twickenham TW2 . . . . . .161 H1
Warburton St, E8 off Warburton Rd 112 E1
Warburton Ter, E17 . . . . . . .78 B2
Wardalls Gro, SE14 . . . . . .133 F7
Ward Cl, S.Croy. CR2 . . . . .202 B5
Wardell Cl, NW7 . . . . .55 E7
Wardell Fld, NW9 . . . . .71 E1
Warden Av, Har. HA2 . . . . . .85 F1
Warden Rd, NW5 . . . . .92 A6
Wardens Fld Cl, Orp. (Grn St Grn) BR6 . . . . . .207 H6
Wardens Gro, SE1 . . . . .27 J2
Wardle St, E9 . . . . .95 G5
Wardley St, SW18 off Garratt La 149 E7
Wardo Av, SW6 . . . . .148 B1
Wardour Ms, W1 . . . . .17 G4
Wardour St, W1 . . . . .17 H5
Ward Pt, SE11 . . . . .35 E2
Ward Rd, E15 . . . . .114 D1
N19 . . . . .92 C3
Wardrobe Pl, EC4 off St. Andrew's Hill . . .19 H4
Wardrobe Ter, EC4 . . . . .19 H4
Wards Rd, Ilf. IG2 . . . . .81 G7
Wards Wf App, E16 . . . . . .136 A2
Wareham Cl, Houns. TW3 . . . . .143 H4
Wareham Ho, SW8 . . . . . . .34 C7
Waremead Rd, Ilf. IG2 . . . . .80 E5
Warenford Way, Borwd. WD6 . . . . .38 A1
Ware Pt Dr, SE28 . . . . .137 G2
Warfield Rd, NW10 . . . . . . .108 A3
Feltham TW14 . . . . .141 H7
Hampton TW12 . . . . . . .179 H1
Warfield Yd, NW10 off Warfield Rd 108 A3
Wargrave Av, N15 . . . . .76 C6
Wargrave Rd, Har. HA2 . . . .85 J3
Warham Rd, N4 . . . . .75 G5
Harrow HA3 . . . . .68 C2
South Croydon CR2 . . . .201 H5
Warham St, SE5 . . . . .35 H7
Waring Cl, Orp. BR6 . . . . . .207 J6
Waring Dr, Orp. BR6 . . . . .207 J6
Waring Rd, Sid. DA14 . . . .176 C6
Waring St, SE27 . . . . .169 J4
Warkworth Gdns, Islw. TW7 . . . . .124 D7
Warkworth Rd, N17 . . . . . . .60 A7
Warland Rd, SE18 . . . . . . .137 G7
Warley Av, Dag. RM8 . . . . . .83 F7
Hayes UB4 . . . . .102 A5
Warley Cl, E10 off Millicent Rd 95 J1
Warley Rd, N9 . . . . .61 F2
Hayes UB4 . . . . .102 A6
Ilford IG5 . . . . .80 D1
Woodford Green IG8 . . . .63 H7
Warley St, E2 . . . . .113 G3
Warlingham Rd, Th.Hth. CR7 . . . . .187 H4
Warlock Rd, W9 . . . . .108 D4
Warlters Cl, N7 off Warlters Rd 93 E4
Warlters Rd, N7 . . . . .93 E4
Warltersville Rd, N19 . . . . . .74 E7
Warmington Cl, E5 off Denton Way 95 G3
Warmington Rd, SE24 . . . .151 J6
Warmington St, E13 off Barking Rd 115 G4
Warminster Gdns, SE25 . .188 D2
Warminster Rd, SE25 . . . . .188 C2
Warminster Sq, SE25 . . . . .188 D2
Warminster Way, Mitch. CR4 . . . . .186 B1
Warmwell Av, NW9 . . . . . . .70 E1
Warndon St, SE16 . . . . . . .133 G4
Warneford Rd, Har. HA3 . . .69 G3
Warneford St, E9 . . . . .113 E1
Warne Pl, Sid. DA15 off Westerham Dr 158 B6
Warner Av, Sutt. SM3 . . . .198 B2
Warner Cl, E15 . . . . .97 E5
NW9 . . . . .71 F7
Hampton TW12 off Tangley Pk Rd 161 F5
Hayes (Harling.) UB3 . . .121 G7
Warner Ho, SE13 off Conington Rd 154 B2
Warner Par, Hayes UB3 . . .121 G7
Warner Pl, E2 . . . . .13 J2
Warner Rd, E17 . . . . .77 H4
N8 . . . . .74 D4
SE5 . . . . .151 J1
Bromley BR1 . . . . .173 F7
Warners Cl, Wdf.Grn. IG8 . . . . .63 G5
Warners La, Kings.T. KT2 . . . . .163 G4
Warners Path, Wdf.Grn. IG8 . . . . .63 G5
Warner St, EC1 . . . . .11 E6
Warner Ter, E14 off Broomfield St 114 A5
Warner Yd, EC1 . . . . .10 E6
Warnford Ho, SW15 off Tunworth Cres 147 F6
Warnford Ind Est, Hayes UB3 . . . . .121 H2
Warnford Rd, Orp. BR6 . . .207 J5
Warnham Ct Rd, Cars. SM5 . . . . .199 J7
Warnham Rd, N12 . . . . .57 H5
Warple Ms, W3 off Warple Way 126 E2
Warple Way, W3 . . . . .126 E1
Warren, The, E12 . . . . .98 B4
Hayes UB4 . . . . .102 A6
Hounslow TW5 . . . . .123 F7
Worcester Park KT4 . . . .196 D4
Warren Av, E10 . . . . .96 C3
Bromley BR1 . . . . .172 E7
Orpington BR6 . . . . .207 J5
Richmond TW10 . . . . . . .146 B4
South Croydon CR2 . . . .203 G7
Warren Cl, N9 . . . . .45 G7
SE21 . . . . .151 J7
Bexleyheath DA6 . . . . . .159 G5
Hayes UB4 . . . . .102 C5
Wembley HA9 . . . . .87 G2
Warren Ct, N17 off High Cross Rd 76 D3
SE7 . . . . .135 J5
Chigwell IG7 . . . . .65 G4
Warren Cres, N9 . . . . .44 C7
Warren Cutting, Kings.T. KT2 . . . . .164 D7
Warrender Rd, N19 . . . . .92 C3
Warrender Way, Ruis. HA4 .66 A7
Warren Dr, Grnf. UB6 . . . . .103 H4
Ruislip HA4 . . . . .66 D7
Warren Dr, The, E11 . . . . . . .79 J7
Warren Dr N, Surb. KT5 . . .196 B1

Warren Dr S, Surb. KT5 ... **196** C1
Warren Flds, Stan. HA7
off Valencia Rd ... **53** F4
Warren Footpath, Twick. TW1 ... **145** G7
Warren Gdns, E15
off Ashton Rd ... **96** D5
Warren Gro, Borwd. WD6 ... **38** D4
Warren Hts, Loug. IG10 ... **47** J5
Warren Hill, Loug. IG10 ... **47** J6
Warren Ho, E3
off Bromley High St ... **114** B3
Warren La, SE18 ... **136** E3
Stanmore HA7 ... **52** C3
Warren La Gate, SE18 ... **136** E3
Warren Ms, W1 ... **9** F6
Warren Pk, Kings.T. KT2 ... **164** C6
Warren Pk Rd, Sutt. SM1 ... **199** G6
Warren Pond Rd, E4 ... **63** F1
Warren Ri, N.Mal. KT3 ... **182** D1
Warren Rd, E4 ... **62** C2
E10 ... **96** C3
E11 ... **97** J1
NW2 ... **89** F2
SW19 ... **167** H6
Bexleyheath DA6 ... **159** G5
Bromley BR2 ... **205** G2
Bushey (Bushey Hth) WD23 ... **51** J1
Croydon CR0 ... **202** B1
Ilford IG6 ... **81** G5
Kingston upon Thames KT2 ... **164** C6
Orpington BR6 ... **207** J5
Sidcup DA14 ... **176** C3
Twickenham TW2 ... **143** J6
Warrens Shawe La, Edg. HA8 ... **54** B1
Warren St, W1 ... **9** E6
Warren Ter, Rom. RM6 ... **82** D4
Warren Wk, SE7 ... **135** J6
Warren Way, Edg. HA8 ... **70** B2
Warren Wd Cl, Brom. BR2 ... **205** F2
Warriner Dr, N9 ... **60** D3
Warriner Gdns, SW11 ... **149** J1
Warrington Cres, W9 ... **6** C6
Warrington Gdns, W9 ... **6** C6
Warrington Rd, Croy. CR0 ... **201** H3
Dagenham RM8 ... **100** D2
Harrow HA1 ... **68** B5
Richmond TW10 ... **145** G5
Warrington Sq, Dag. RM8 ... **100** D2
Warrior Cl, SE28 ... **137** G1
Warrior Sq, E12 ... **98** D4
Warsaw Cl, Ruis. HA4
off Glebe Av ... **84** B6
Warsdale Dr, NW9
off Mardale Dr ... **70** D5
Warspite Rd, SE18 ... **136** B3
Warton Rd, E15 ... **96** C7
Warwall, E6 ... **116** E6
Warwick Av, W2 ... **6** C6
W9 ... **6** C6
Edgware HA8 ... **54** B3
Harrow HA2 ... **85** F4
Warwick Bldg, SW8 ... **32** D7
Warwick Chambers, W8
off Pater St ... **128** D3
Warwick Cl, Barn. EN4 ... **41** G5
Bexley DA5 ... **159** F7
Hampton TW12 ... **161** J7
Warwick Ct, SE15 ... **152** D2
WC1 ... **18** D2
Surbiton KT6 ... **195** H2
Warwick Cres, W2 ... **14** C1
Warwick Dene, W5 ... **125** H1
Warwick Dr, SW15 ... **147** H3
Warwick Est, W2 ... **14** A2
Warwick Gdns, N4 ... **75** J5
W14 ... **128** C3
Ilford IG1 ... **99** E1
Warwick Gdns, Thames Ditton KT7 ... **180** C5
Thornton Heath CR7
off London Rd ... **187** G3
Warwick Gro, E5 ... **94** E1
Surbiton KT5 ... **181** J7
Warwick Ho St, SW1 ... **25** J1
Warwick La, EC4 ... **19** H4
Warwick Pas, EC4 ... **19** H3
Warwick Pl, W5
off Warwick Rd ... **125** G2
W9 ... **14** C1
Warwick Pl N, SW1 ... **33** F2
Warwick Rd, E4 ... **62** A5
E11 ... **79** H5
E12 ... **98** B5
E15 ... **97** F6
E17 ... **77** J1
N11 ... **58** D6
N18 ... **60** B4
SE20 ... **189** E3
SW5 ... **128** C4
W5 ... **125** G2
Warwick Rd, W14 ... **128** C4
Barnet EN5 ... **40** E4
Borehamwood WD6 ... **38** D3
Hounslow TW4 ... **142** B3
Kingston upon Thames KT1 ... **181** F1
New Malden KT3 ... **182** C3
Sidcup DA14 ... **176** B5
Southall UB2 ... **123** F3
Sutton SM1 ... **199** F4
Thames Ditton KT7 ... **180** C5
Thornton Heath CR7 ... **187** G3
Twickenham TW2 ... **162** B1
Welling DA16 ... **158** C3
West Drayton UB7 ... **120** B2
Warwick Row, SW1 ... **25** E5
Warwickshire Path, SE8 ... **133** J7
Warwick Sq, EC4 ... **19** H3
SW1 ... **33** F3
Warwick Sq Ms, SW1 ... **33** F2
Warwick St, W1 ... **17** G5
Warwick Ter, SE18 ... **137** G6
Warwick Way, SW1 ... **33** F2
Warwick Yd, EC1 ... **12** A6
Washington Av, E12 ... **98** B4
Washington Bldg, SE13
off Deals Gateway ... **154** B1
Washington Cl, E3 ... **114** B3
Washington Rd, E6
off St. Stephens Rd ... **97** J7
E18 ... **79** F2
SW13 ... **127** G7
Kingston upon Thames KT1 ... **182** A2
Worcester Park KT4 ... **197** H2
Wastdale Rd, SE23 ... **171** G1
Watchfield Ct, W4 ... **126** C5
Watcombe Cotts, Rich. TW9 ... **126** A6
Watcombe Pl, SE25
off Albert Rd ... **189** E4
Watcombe Rd, SE25 ... **188** E5
Waterbank Rd, SE6 ... **172** C4
Waterbeach Rd, Dag. RM9 ... **100** C6
Water Brook La, NW4 ... **71** J5
Watercress Pl, N1
off Hertford Rd ... **94** B7
Waterdale Rd, SE2 ... **138** A6
Waterden Cres, E15 ... **96** A5
Waterden Rd, E15 ... **96** A5
Waterer Ri, Wall. SM6 ... **200** D6
Waterfall Cl, N14 ... **58** C3
Waterfall Cotts, SW19 ... **167** G6
Waterfall Rd, N11 ... **58** B4
N14 ... **58** C3
SW19 ... **167** G6
Waterfall Ter, SW17 ... **167** H6
Waterfield Cl, SE28 ... **138** B1
Belvedere DA17 ... **139** G3
Waterfield Gdns, SE25 ... **188** A4
Waterford Rd, SW6 ... **149** E1
Waterford Way, NW10 ... **89** H5
Waterfront Studios Business Cen, E16
off Silvertown Way ... **135** G1
Water Gdns, Stan. HA7 ... **53** E6
Water Gdns, The, W2 ... **15** H3
Watergardens, The, Kings.T. KT2 ... **164** C6
Watergate, EC4 ... **19** G5
Watergate, The, Wat. WD19 ... **50** D2
Watergate St, SE8 ... **134** A6
Watergate Wk, WC2 ... **26** B1
Waterhall Av, E4 ... **62** E4
Waterhall Cl, E17 ... **77** G1
Waterhouse Cl, E16 ... **116** A5
NW3 *off Lyndhurst Rd* ... **91** G5
W6 *off Great Ch La* ... **128** A5
Waterhouse Sq, EC1 ... **19** E2
Wateridge Cl, E14
off Westferry Rd ... **134** A3
Water La, E15 ... **97** E6
EC3 ... **20** D6
N9 ... **60** E1
NW1
off Kentish Town Rd ... **92** B7
Water La, SE14 ... **133** F7
Ilford IG3 ... **99** H3
Kingston upon Thames KT1 ... **181** G1
Richmond TW9 ... **145** G5
Sidcup DA14 ... **177** F2
Twickenham TW1
off The Embankment ... **162** D1
Water Lily Cl, Sthl. UB2
off Navigator Dr ... **123** J2
Waterloo Br, SE1 ... **18** C6
WC2 ... **18** C6
Waterloo Cl, E9
off Churchill Wk ... **95** F5
Waterloo Est, E2 ... **113** F2
Waterloo Gdns, E2 ... **113** F2
N1 *off Barnsbury St* ... **93** G7
Waterloo Pas, NW6 ... **90** C7
Waterloo Pl, SW1 ... **25** H1
Richmond TW9
off The Quadrant ... **145** H4
Richmond (Kew) TW9 ... **126** A6
Waterloo Rd, E6 ... **97** J7
E7 *off Wellington Rd* ... **97** F5
E10 ... **78** A7
NW2 ... **89** G1
SE1 ... **27** E3
Ilford IG6 ... **81** F2
Sutton SM1 ... **199** G5
Waterloo Sta, SE1 ... **26** E3
Waterloo Ter, N1 ... **93** H7
Waterlow Ct, NW11
off Heath Cl ... **72** E7
Waterlow Rd, N19 ... **92** C1
★ **Watermans Art Cen**, Brent. TW8 ... **125** H6
Waterman's Cl, Kings.T. KT2 *off Woodside Rd* ... **163** H7
Waterman St, SW15 ... **148** A3
Waterman's Wk, EC4
off Allhallows La ... **20** B6
Watermans Wk, SE16 ... **133** H3
Waterman Way, E1 ... **132** E1
Watermead Ho, E9
off Kingsmead Way ... **95** H5
Watermead La, Cars. SM5
off Middleton Rd ... **185** J7
Watermeadow La, SW6 ... **149** F2
Watermead Rd, SE6 ... **172** C4
Watermead Way, N17 ... **76** E3
Watermen's Sq, SE20 ... **171** F7
Water Ms, SE15 ... **153** F4
Watermill Business Cen, Enf. EN3 ... **45** J2
Watermill Cl, Rich. TW10 ... **163** F3
Watermill La, N18 ... **60** B5
Watermill Way, SW19 ... **185** F1
Feltham TW13 ... **161** F2
Watermint Quay, N16 ... **76** D7
Water Rd, Wem. HA0 ... **105** J1
Watersedge, Epsom KT19 ... **196** C4
Watersfield Way, Edg. HA8 ... **53** G7
Waters Gdns, Dag. RM10 ... **101** G5
Waterside, Beck. BR3 ... **189** J1
Waterside Av, Beck. BR3
off Brockwell Av ... **190** B5
Waterside Cl, E3 ... **113** J1
SE16 ... **29** J4
SE28 ... **137** J1
Barking IG11 ... **100** A4
Northolt UB5 ... **103** F3
Surbiton KT6
off Culsac Rd ... **195** H2
Waterside Ct, SE13
off Weardale Rd ... **154** D4
Waterside Dr, Walt. KT12 ... **178** A5
Waterside Path, SW18
off Smugglers Way ... **149** E4
Waterside Pl, NW1
off Princess Rd ... **110** A1
Waterside Pt, SW11 ... **31** H7
Waterside Rd, Sthl. UB2 ... **123** G3
Waterside Twr, SW6 ... **149** F1
Waterside Trd Cen, W7 ... **124** B3
Waterside Way, SW17 ... **167** F4
Watersmeet Way, SE28 ... **118** C6
Waterson St, E2 ... **13** E3
Waters Pl, SW15
off Danemere St ... **147** J2
Watersplash Cl, Kings.T. KT1 ... **181** H3
Watersplash La, Hayes UB3 ... **122** A4
Hounslow TW5 ... **122** B5
Waters Rd, SE6 ... **172** E3
Kingston upon Thames KT1 ... **182** B2
Waters Sq, Kings.T. KT1 ... **182** B3
Water St, WC2 ... **18** D5
Water Twr Hill, Croy. CR0 ... **202** A4
Water Twr Pl, N1
off Old Royal Free Sq ... **111** G1
Waterview Cl, Bexh. DA6
off Danson Rd ... **158** D5
Waterview Ho, E14 ... **113** H5
Waterway Av, SE13 ... **154** B3
Waterway Business Pk, Hayes UB3 ... **121** G2
Waterworks Cor, E18 ... **79** E2
Waterworks La, E5 ... **95** G2
Waterworks Rd, SW2 ... **151** E6
Waterworks Yd, Croy. CR0
off Surrey St ... **201** J3
Watery La, SW20 ... **184** C2
Northolt UB5 ... **102** C2
Sidcup DA14 ... **176** B6
Wates Way, Mitch. CR4 ... **185** J6
Wates Way Ind Est, Mitch. CR4 ... **185** J6
Wateville Rd, N17 ... **75** J1
Watford Cl, SW11
off Petworth St ... **149** H1
WATFORD HEATH, Wat. WD19 ... **50** E1
Watford Rd, E16 ... **115** G5
Harrow HA1 ... **86** D2
Wembley HA0 ... **86** D2
Watford Way, NW4 ... **71** G4
NW7 ... **55** F6
Watkin Rd, Wem. HA9 ... **88** B3
Watkinson Rd, N7 ... **93** F6
Watling Av, Edg. HA8 ... **54** D7
Watling Ct, EC4 ... **20** A4
Watling Fm Cl, Stan. HA7 ... **53** F1
Watling Gdns, NW2 ... **90** B6
Watlings Cl, Croy. CR0 ... **189** H6
Watling St, EC4 ... **19** J4
SE15 ... **36** E6
Bexleyheath DA6 ... **159** H4
Watlington Gro, SE26 ... **171** H5
Watney Cotts, SW14
off Lower Richmond Rd ... **146** C3
Watney Mkt, E1
off Commercial Rd ... **113** E6
Watney Rd, SW14 ... **146** C3
Watneys Rd, Mitch. CR4 ... **186** D5
Watney St, E1 ... **113** E6
Watson Av, E6 ... **98** D7
Sutton SM3 ... **198** B2
Watson Cl, N16
off Matthias Rd ... **94** A5
SW19 ... **167** H6
Watsons Ms, W1 ... **15** H2
Watsons Rd, N22 ... **75** F1
Watson's St, SE8 ... **134** A7
Watson St, E13 ... **115** H2
Watsons Yd, NW2
off North Circular Rd ... **89** F2
Wattisfield Rd, E5 ... **95** F3
Watts Cl, N15 ... **76** B5
Wattsdown Cl, E13 ... **115** G1
Watts Gro, E3 ... **114** B5
Watts La, Chis. BR7 ... **193** E1
Teddington TW11 ... **162** D5
Watts Rd, T.Ditt. KT7 ... **180** D7
Watts St, E1 ... **133** E1
SE15 ... **152** C1
Watts Way, SW7 ... **23** F5
Wat Tyler Rd, SE3 ... **154** C2
SE10 ... **154** C2
Wauthier Cl, N13 ... **59** H5
Wavell Dr, Sid. DA15 ... **157** H6
Wavel Ms, N8 ... **74** D4
NW6 *off Acol Rd* ... **90** E7
Wavel Pl, SE26
off Sydenham Hill ... **170** C4
Wavendon Av, W4 ... **126** D5
Waveney Av, SE15 ... **153** E4
Waveney Cl, E1 ... **29** J1
Waverley Av, E4 ... **61** J4
E17 ... **78** D3
Surbiton KT5 ... **182** B6
Sutton SM1 ... **199** E2
Twickenham TW2 ... **161** F1
Wembley HA9 ... **87** J5
Waverley Cl, E18 ... **79** J1
Bromley BR2 ... **192** A5
Hayes UB3 ... **121** G4
West Molesey KT8 ... **179** G5
Waverley Cres, SE18 ... **137** G5
Waverley Gdns, E6
off Oliver Gdns ... **116** B5
NW10 ... **105** J3
Barking IG11 ... **117** H2
Ilford IG6 ... **81** F2
Northwood HA6 ... **66** A1
Waverley Gro, N3 ... **72** A3
Waverley Ind Est, Har. HA1 ... **68** A3
Waverley Pl, N4 ... **93** H1
NW8 ... **6** E1
Waverley Rd, E17 ... **78** C3
E18 ... **79** J1
N8 ... **74** D6
N17 ... **60** E7
SE18 ... **137** F5
SE25 ... **188** E4
Enfield EN2 ... **43** H4
Epsom KT17 ... **197** H5
Harrow HA2 ... **85** F1
Southall UB1 ... **103** G7
Waverley Vil, N17 ... **76** C2
Waverley Wk, W2 ... **108** D5
Waverley Way, Cars. SM5 ... **199** H6
Waverton Ho, E3 ... **113** J1
Waverton Rd, SW18 ... **149** F7
Waverton St, W1 ... **24** C1
Wavertree Ct, SW2
off Streatham Hill ... **169** E1
Wavertree Rd, E18 ... **79** G2
SW2 ... **169** E1
Waxham, NW3 ... **91** J5
Waxlow Cres, Sthl. UB1 ... **103** G6
Waxlow Rd, NW10 ... **106** C2
Waxlow Way, Nthlt. UB5 ... **103** F4
Waxwell Cl, Pnr. HA5 ... **66** D2
Waxwell La, Pnr. HA5 ... **66** D2

Waye Av, Houns. TW5 **142** A1
Wayfarer Rd, Nthlt. UB5 **102** D4
Wayfield Link, SE9 **157** G6
Wayford St, SW11 **149** H2
Wayland Av, E8 **94** D5
Wayland Ho, SW9 **151** G2
Waylands Mead, Beck. BR3 **190** B1
Wayleave, The, SE28 **118** B7
Waylett Ho, SE11 **34** E4
Waylett Pl, SE27 **169** H3
Wembley HA0 **87** G4
Wayman Ct, E8 **94** E6
Wayne Cl, Orp. BR6 **207** J3
Waynflete Av, Croy. CR0 **201** H3
Waynflete Sq, W10 **108** A7
Waynflete St, SW18 **167** F2
Wayside, NW11 **90** B1
SW14 **146** C5
Croydon (New Adgtn) CR0 **204** B6
Wayside Cl, N14 **42** C6
Wayside Commercial Est, Bark. IG11 **118** A1
Wayside Ct, Twick. TW1 **145** F6
Wembley HA9 *off Oakington Av* **88** A3
Wayside Gdns, SE9 *off Wayside Gro* **174** C4
Dagenham RM10 **101** G5
Wayside Gro, SE9 **174** C4
Wayside Ms, Ilf. IG2 *off Gaysham Av* **80** D5
Weald, The, Chis. BR7 **174** C6
Weald Cl, SE16 *off Stevenson Cres* **132** E5
Bromley BR2 **206** B2
Weald La, Har. HA3 **68** A2
Weald Ri, Har. HA3 **52** C7
Weald Sq, E5 **94** D2
WEALDSTONE, Har. HA3 **68** C3
Wealdstone Rd, Sutt. SM3 **198** C2
Weald Way, Rom. RM7 **83** H6
Wealdwood Gdns, Pnr. HA5 *off Highbanks Rd* **51** H6
Weale Rd, E4 **62** D3
Weardale Gdns, Enf. EN2 **44** A1
Weardale Rd, SE13 **154** D4
Wear Pl, E2 **112** E3
Wearside Rd, SE13 **154** B4
Weatherley Cl, E3 **113** J5
Weaver Cl, E6 *off Trader Rd* **116** E7
Croydon CR0 **202** C4
Weavers Almshouses, E11 *off New Wanstead* **79** G6
Weavers Cl, Islw. TW7 **144** B4
Weavers Ter, SW6 **128** D6
Weaver St, E1 **13** H6
Weavers Way, NW1 **110** D1
Weaver Wk, SE27 **169** H4
Webb Cl, W10 **107** J4
Webber Row, SE1 **27** F5
Webber St, SE1 **27** F3
Webb Est, E5 **76** D7
Webb Gdns, E13 *off Kelland Rd* **115** G4
Webb Pl, NW10 **107** F3
Webb Rd, SE3 **135** F6
Webbscroft Rd, Dag. RM10 **101** H4
Webbs Rd, SW11 **149** J5
Hayes UB4 **102** B3
Webb St, SE1 **28** D6
Webheath Est, NW6 **90** C7
Webster Gdns, W5 **125** G1
Webster Rd, E11 **96** C3
SE16 **29** J6
Wedderburn Rd, NW3 **91** G5
Barking IG11 **117** G1
Wedgwood Ho, SE11 **27** E6
Wedgwood Ms, W1 **17** J4
Wedgwood Wk, NW6 *off Dresden Cl* **91** E5
Wedgwood Way, SE19 **169** J7
Wedlake St, W10 *off Kensal Rd* **108** B4
Wedmore Av, Ilf. IG5 **80** D1
Wedmore Gdns, N19 **92** D2
Wedmore Ms, N19 **92** D3
Wedmore Rd, Grnf. UB6 **104** A3
Wedmore St, N19 **92** D3
Weech Rd, NW6 **90** D4
Weedington Rd, NW5 **92** A5
Weekley Sq, SW11 *off Thomas Baines Rd* **149** G3
Weigall Rd, SE12 **155** G4
Weighhouse St, W1 **16** C4
Weighton Rd, SE20 **188** E2
Harrow HA3 **68** A1
Weihurst Gdns, Sutt. SM1 **199** G5
Weimar St, SW15 **148** B3
Weirdale Av, N20 **57** J2
Weir Est, SW12 **150** C7
Weir Hall Av, N18 **60** A6
Weir Hall Gdns, N18 **60** A5
Weir Hall Rd, N17 **60** A5
N18 **60** A5
Weir Rd, SW12 **150** C7
SW19 **167** E3
Bexley DA5 **159** H7
Walton-on-Thames KT12 **178** A6
Weirside Gdns, West Dr. UB7 **120** A1
Weir's Pas, NW1 **9** J3
Weiss Rd, SW15 **148** A3
Welbeck Av, Brom. BR1 **173** G4
Hayes UB4 **102** B4
Sidcup DA15 **176** A1
Welbeck Cl, N12 **57** G5
Borehamwood WD6 **38** A3
Epsom KT17 **197** G7
New Malden KT3 **183** F5
Welbeck Rd, E6 **116** A3
Barnet EN4 **41** G6
Carshalton SM5 **199** H1
Harrow HA2 **85** H1
Sutton SM1 **199** G2
Welbeck St, W1 **16** D3
Welbeck Wk, Cars. SM5 *off Welbeck Rd* **199** H1
Welbeck Way, W1 **16** D3
Welby St, SE5 **151** H1
Welch Pl, Pnr. HA5 **66** C1
Weldon Cl, Ruis. HA4 **84** B6
Weldon Dr, W.Mol. KT8 **179** F4
Weld Pl, N11 **58** B5
Welfare Rd, E15 **97** E7
Welford Cl, E5 *off Denton Way* **95** G3
Welford Pl, SW19 **166** B4
Welham Rd, SW16 **168** A5
SW17 **168** A5
Welhouse Rd, Cars. SM5 **199** H1
Wellacre Rd, Har. HA3 **69** E6
Wellan Cl, Sid. DA15 **158** B5
Welland Gdns, Grnf. (Perivale) UB6 **104** C2
Welland Ms, E1 **29** J1
Wellands Cl, Brom. BR1 **192** C2
Welland St, SE10 **134** C6
Well App, Barn. EN5 **39** J5
Wellbrook Rd, Orp. BR6 **206** D4
Wellby Cl, N9 **60** D1
Well Cl, SW16 **169** F4
Ruislip HA4 *off Parkfield Cres* **84** E3
Wellclose Sq, E1 **21** J5
Wellclose St, E1 **21** J6
★ **Wellcome Trust**, NW1 **9** G5
Well Cottage Cl, E11 **79** J7
Well Ct, EC4 **20** A4
SW16 **169** F4
Welldon Cres, Har. HA1 **68** B6
Weller Ms, Brom. BR2 **191** H4
Enf. EN2 **43** G1
Weller St, SE1 **27** J3
Wellesley Av, W6 **127** H3
Wellesley Cl, SE7 *off Wellington Gdns* **135** J5
Wellesley Ct, W9 **6** C3
Sutton SM3 *off Stonecot Hill* **198** B1
Wellesley Ct Rd, Croy. CR0 **202** A2
Wellesley Cres, Twick. TW2 **162** B2
Wellesley Gro, Croy. CR0 **202** A2
Wellesley Pk Ms, Enf. EN2 **43** H2
Wellesley Pas, Croy. CR0 *off Wellesley Rd* **201** J2
Wellesley Pl, NW1 **9** H4
Wellesley Rd, E11 **79** G5
E17 **78** A6
N22 **75** G2
NW5 **92** A5
W4 **126** A5
Croydon CR0 **201** J1
Harrow HA1 **68** B5
Ilford IG1 **98** E2
Sutton SM2 **199** F6
Twickenham TW2 **162** A3
Wellesley St, E1 **113** G5
Wellesley Ter, N1 **12** A3
Wellfield Av, N10 **74** B3
Wellfield Rd, SW16 **169** E4
Wellfields, Loug. IG10 **48** D3
Wellfield Wk, SW16 **169** F5
Wellfit St, SE24 *off Hinton Rd* **151** H3
Wellgarth, Grnf. UB6 **86** E6
Wellgarth Rd, NW11 **91** E1
Well Gro, N20 **41** F7
Well Hall Par, SE9 *off Well Hall Rd* **156** C4
Well Hall Rd, SE9 **156** C3
Well Hall Rbt, SE9 **156** B3
Wellhouse La, Barn. EN5 **39** J4
Wellhouse Rd, Beck. BR3 **189** J4
Wellhurst Cl, Orp. BR6 **207** J7
WELLING, DA16 **158** A3
Welling High St, Well. DA16 **158** B3
Wellings Ho, Hayes UB3 **122** B1
★ **Wellington Arch**, W1 **24** C3
Wellington Av, E4 **62** A2
N9 **61** E3
N15 **76** C6
Hounslow TW3 **143** G5
Pinner HA5 **67** F1
Sidcup DA15 **158** A6
Worcester Park KT4 **197** J3
Wellington Bldgs, SW1 **32** C4
Wellington Cl, SE14 *off Rutts Ter* **153** G1
W11 *off Ledbury Rd* **108** D6
Dagenham RM10 **101** J7
Watford WD19 **51** F3
Wellington Ct, NW8 **7** E2
Staines TW19 *off Clare Rd* **140** B7
Wellington Cres, N.Mal. KT3 **182** C3
Wellington Dr, Dag. RM10 **101** J7
Wellington Gdns, SE7 **135** J6
Twickenham TW2 **162** A4
Wellington Gro, SE10 *off Crooms Hill* **134** D7
Wellington Ms, SE7 **135** J6
SE22 *off Peckham Rye* **152** D4
SW16 *off Woodbourne Av* **168** D3
Wellington Par, Sid. DA15 **158** A5
Wellington Pk Est, NW2 **89** G2
Wellington Pas, E11 *off Wellington Rd* **79** G5
Wellington Pl, N2 *off Great N Rd* **73** H5
NW8 **7** F3
Wellington Rd, E6 **116** C2
E7 **97** F4
E10 **95** H1
E11 **79** G5
E17 **77** H3
NW8 **7** E1
NW10 **108** A3
SW19 **166** D2
W5 **125** F3
Belvedere DA17 **139** F5
Bexley DA5 **158** D6
Bromley BR2 **191** J4
Croydon CR0 **187** H7
Enfield EN1 **44** B4
Feltham TW14 **141** H5
Hampton TW12 **162** A5
Harrow HA3 **68** B3
Pinner HA5 **67** F1
Twickenham TW2 **162** A5
Wellington Rd N, Houns. TW4 **143** F3
Wellington Rd S, Houns. TW4 **143** F4
Wellington Row, E2 **13** G3
Wellington Sq, N1 *off Pembroke Av* **111** F1
SW3 **31** J3
Wellington St, SE18 **136** D4
WC2 **18** B5
Barking IG11 *off Axe St* **117** F1
Wellington Ter, E1 **132** E1
W2 *off Notting Hill Gate* **14** A6
Harrow HA1 *off West St* **86** A1
Wellington Way, E3 **114** A3
Welling Way, SE9 **157** G3
Welling DA16 **157** G3
Well La, SW14 **146** C5
Wellmeadow Rd, SE6 **155** E7
SE13 **154** E6
W7 **124** D4
Wellow Wk, Cars. SM5 **199** G1
Well Pas, NW3 **91** G3
Well Rd, NW3 **91** G3
Barnet EN5 **39** J5
Wells, The, N14 **42** D7
Wells Cl, Nthlt. UB5 *off Yeading La* **102** C3
South Croydon CR2 **202** B5
Wells Dr, NW9 **88** D1
Wells Gdns, Dag. RM10 **101** H5
Ilford IG1 **80** B7
Wells Ho Rd, NW10 **106** E5
Wellside Cl, Barnet EN5 **39** J4
Wellside Gdns, SW14 *off Well La* **146** C5
Wells Ms, W1 **17** G2
Wellsmoor Gdns, Brom. BR1 **192** D3
Wells Pk Rd, SE26 **170** D3
Wells Pl, SW18 **149** F7
Wellspring Cres, Wem. HA9 **88** B3
Wellspring Ms, SE26 **171** E3
Wells Ri, NW8 **109** J1
Wells Rd, W12 **127** J2
Bromley BR1 **192** C2
Wells Sq, WC1 **10** C4
Wells St, W1 **17** F2
Wellstead Av, N9 **45** F7
Wellstead Rd, E6 **116** D2
Wells Ter, N4 **93** G2
Well St, E9 **95** E7
E15 **96** E6
Wells Way, SE5 **36** C5
SW7 **22** E5
Wells Yd S, N7 *off George's Rd* **93** G5
Well Wk, NW3 **91** G4
Wellwood Rd, Ilf. IG3 **100** A1
Welmar Ms, SW4 **150** D4
Welsford St, SE1 **37** H3
Welsh Cl, E13 **115** G3
Welshpool Ho, E8 *off Benjamin Cl* **112** D1
Welshpool St, E8 *off Broadway Mkt* **112** E1
Welshside Wk, NW9 *off Fryent Gro* **71** E6
Welstead Way, W4 **127** F4
Weltje Rd, W6 **127** G5
Welton Rd, SE18 **137** H7
Welwyn Av, Felt. TW14 **141** J6
Welwyn St, E2 *off Globe Rd* **113** F3
WEMBLEY, HA0 & HA9 **87** H5
Wembley Commercial Cen, Wem. HA9 **87** G2
Wembley Hill Rd, Wem. HA9 **87** J5
WEMBLEY PARK, Wem. HA9 **87** J2
Wembley Pk Business Cen, Wem. HA9 **88** B3
Wembley Pk Dr, Wem. HA9 **87** J3
Wembley Pt, Wem. HA9 **88** B7
Wembley Rd, Hmptn. TW12 **161** G7
★ **Wembley Stadium**, Wem. HA9 **88** A4
Wembley Way, Wem. HA9 **88** B6
Wemborough Rd, Stan. HA7 **53** F7
Wembury Ms, N6 *off Wembury Rd* **74** B7
Wembury Rd, N6 **74** B7
Wemyss Rd, SE3 **155** F2
Wendela Ct, Har. HA1 **86** B3
Wendell Rd, W12 **127** F2
Wendle Ct, SW8 **34** A6
Wendle Sq, SW11 *off Petworth St* **149** H1
Wendling, NW5 **91** J5
Wendling Rd, Sutt. SM1 **199** G1
Wendon St, E3 **113** J1
Wendover, SE17 **36** D3
Wendover Cl, Hayes UB4 **102** D4
Wendover Ct, W3 **106** B4
Wendover Dr, N.Mal. KT3 **183** F6
Wendover Rd, NW10 **107** F2
SE9 **156** A3
Bromley BR2 **191** H3
Wendover Way, Well. DA16 **158** A5
Wendy Cl, Enf. EN1 **44** C6
Wendy Way, Wem. HA0 **105** H1
Wenlock Ct, N1 **12** C2
Wenlock Gdns, NW4 **71** G4
Wenlock Rd, N1 **11** J1
Edgware HA8 **54** B7
Wenlock St, N1 **12** A2
Wennington Rd, E3 **113** G2
Wensley Av, Wdf.Grn. IG8 **63** F7
Wensley Cl, N11 **58** A6
SE9 **156** C6
Wensleydale Av, Ilf. IG5 **80** B2
Wensleydale Gdns, Hmptn. TW12 **161** H7
Wensleydale Pas, Hmptn. TW12 **179** G1
Wensleydale Rd, Hmptn. TW12 **161** G6
Wensley Rd, N18 **60** E6
Wentland Cl, SE6 **172** D2
Wentland Rd, SE6 **172** D2
Wentworth Av, N3 **56** D7
Wentworth Cl, N3 **56** E7
SE28 **118** D6
Bromley (Hayes) BR2 *off Hillside La* **205** G2
Morden SM4 **184** D7
Orpington BR6 **207** H5
Surbiton (Long Dit.) KT6 **195** G2
Wentworth Ct, Surb. KT6 *off Culsac Rd* **195** H2
Wentworth Cres, SE15 **132** D7
Hayes UB3 **121** G3

Wentworth Dr, Pnr. HA5 ...66 A5
Watford WD19 ...50 D5
Wentworth Gdns, N13 ...59 H4
Wentworth Hill, Wem. HA9 ...87 J1
Wentworth Ms, E3
off Eric St ...113 J4
W3 ...107 E6
Wentworth Pk, N3 ...56 D7
Wentworth Pl, Stan. HA7
off Greenacres Dr ...52 E6
Wentworth Rd, E12 ...98 A4
NW11 ...72 C6
Barnet EN5 ...40 A3
Croydon CR0 ...187 G7
Southall UB2 ...122 C4
Wentworth St, E1 ...21 F3
Wentworth Way, Pnr. HA5 .66 D4
Wenvoe Av, Bexh. DA7 ...159 H2
Wepham Cl, Hayes UB4 ..102 D5
Wernbrook St, SE18 ...137 F6
Werndee Rd, SE25 ...188 D4
Werneth Hall Rd, Ilf. IG5 ...80 C3
Werrington St, NW1 ...9 G2
Werter Rd, SW15 ...148 B4
Wesleyan Pl, NW5
off Gordon Ho Rd ...92 B4
Wesley Av, E16 ...135 G1
NW10 ...106 D3
Hounslow TW3 ...143 E2
Wesley Cl, N7 ...93 F2
SE17 ...35 H2
Harrow HA2 ...85 J2
Wesley Ct, SW19 ...166 E7
Wesley Rd, E10 ...78 C7
NW10 ...106 C1
Hayes UB3 ...102 A7
★ Wesley's Ho, EC1 ...12 B6
Wesley Sq, W11
off Bartle Rd ...108 B6
Wesley St, W1 ...16 C2
Wessex Av, SW19 ...184 D2
Wessex Cl, Ilf. IG3 ...81 H6
Kingston upon Thames KT1 ...182 B1
Thames Ditton KT7 ...194 C2
Wessex Ct, Wem. HA9 ...87 J2
Wessex Dr, Pnr. HA5 ...51 E7
Wessex Gdns, NW11 ...90 B1
Wessex Ho, SE1 ...37 G3
Wessex La, Grnf. UB6 ...104 A2
Wessex St, E2 ...113 F3
Wessex Way, NW11 ...72 B7
Wessonmead, SE5
off Camberwell Rd ...131 J7
West 12 Shop Cen, W12 ...128 A2
Westacott Cl, N19 ...92 D1
WEST ACTON, W3 ...106 A6
Westall Rd, Loug. IG10 ...49 E3
West App, Orp. BR5 ...193 F5
West Arbour St, E1 ...113 G6
West Av, E17 ...78 B4
N3 ...56 D6
NW4 ...72 A5
Pinner HA5 ...67 F6
Southall UB1 ...103 F7
Wallington SM6 ...201 E5
West Av Rd, E17 ...78 A4
West Bk, N16 ...76 B7
Barking IG11
off Highbridge Rd ...117 E1
Enfield EN2 ...43 J2
Westbank Rd, Hmptn. (Hmptn H.) TW12 ...161 J6
WEST BARNES, N.Mal. KT3 ...183 G5
West Barnes La, SW20 ...183 H2
New Malden KT3 ...183 H3
Westbeech Rd, N22 ...75 G3
Westbere Dr, Stan. HA7 ...53 G4
Westbere Rd, NW2 ...90 B4
Westbourne Av, W3 ...106 D6
Sutton SM3 ...198 B2
Westbourne Br, W2 ...14 C2
Westbourne Cl, Hayes UB4 ...102 B4
Westbourne Cres, W2 ...14 E5
Westbourne Cres Ms, W2 ...14 E5
Westbourne Dr, SE23 ...171 G2
Westbourne Gdns, W2 ...14 A3
WESTBOURNE GREEN, W2 ...108 D5
Westbourne Gro, W2 ...108 D6
W11 ...108 D6
Westbourne Gro Ms, W11
off Westbourne Gro ...108 D6
Westbourne Gro Ter, W2 ...14 A3
Westbourne Ho, Houns. TW5 off Wheatlands ...123 G6
Westbourne Pk Ms, W2 ...14 A3
Westbourne Pk Pas, W2
off Westbourne Pk Vil .108 D5
Westbourne Pk Rd, W2 ...108 D5
W11 ...108 B6
Westbourne Pk Vil, W2 ...108 D5
Westbourne Pl, N9 ...61 E3
Westbourne Rd, N7 ...93 G6
SE26 ...171 G6
Bexleyheath DA7 ...138 E7
Croydon CR0 ...188 C6
Westbourne St, W2 ...15 E5
Westbourne Ter, SE23
off Westbourne Dr ...171 G2
W2 ...14 D3
Westbourne Ter Ms, W2 ...14 C3
Westbourne Ter Rd, W2 ...14 C2
West Br Cl, W12
off Percy Rd ...127 G1
Westbridge Rd, SW11 ...149 G1
WEST BROMPTON, SW10 .30 A5
Westbrook Av, Hmptn. TW12 ...161 F7
Westbrook Cl, Barn. EN4 ..41 G3
Westbrook Cres, Barn. (Cockfos.) EN4 ...41 G3
Westbrooke Cres, Well. DA16 ...158 C3
Westbrooke Rd, Sid. DA15 ...175 G2
Welling DA16 ...158 B3
Westbrook Rd, SE3 ...155 H1
Hounslow TW5 ...123 F7
Thornton Heath CR7 ...188 A1
Westbrook Sq, Barn. EN4
off Westbrook Cres ...41 G3
Westbury Av, N22 ...75 H3
Esher (Clay.) KT10 ...194 C6
Southall UB1 ...103 G4
Wembley HA0 ...87 H7
Westbury Cl, Ruis. HA4 ...66 A7
Westbury Gro, N12 ...56 D6
Westbury La, Buck.H. IG9 ..63 J2
Westbury Lo Cl, Pnr. HA5 ..66 D3
Westbury Par, SW12
off Balham Hill ...150 B6
Westbury Pl, Brent. TW8 ..125 G6
Westbury Rd, E7 ...97 H5
E17 ...78 A4
N11 ...58 E6
N12 ...56 D6
SE20 ...189 G1
W5 ...105 H6
Barking IG11 ...117 G1
Beckenham BR3 ...189 H3
Bromley BR1 ...192 A1
Buckhurst Hill IG9 ...63 J2
Croydon CR0 ...188 A6
Feltham TW13 ...160 D1
Ilford IG1 ...98 C2
New Malden KT3 ...182 D4
Wembley HA0 ...87 H7
Westbury St, SW8 ...150 C2
Westbury Ter, E7 ...97 H6
West Carriage Dr, W2 ...23 F2
West Cen St, WC1 ...18 A3
West Cen Av, W10
off Harrow Rd ...107 H3
West Chantry, Har. HA3
off Chantry Rd ...67 H1
Westchester Dr, NW4 ...72 A3
Westcliffe Apts, W2 ...15 F2
West Cl, N9 ...60 C3
Barnet EN5 ...39 H5
Barnet (Cockfos.) EN4 ...42 A4
Greenford UB6 ...103 J2
Hampton TW12
off Oak Av ...161 E6
Wembley HA9 ...87 J1
Westcombe Av, Croy. CR0 ...187 E6
Westcombe Ct, SE3
off Westcombe Pk Rd .135 F7
Westcombe Dr, Barn. EN5 .40 D5
Westcombe Hill, SE3 ...135 G5
SE10 ...135 G5
Westcombe Pk Rd, SE3 ...135 E6
West Common Rd, Brom. BR2 ...205 G2
Keston BR2 ...205 H4
Westcoombe Av, SW20 ...183 F1
Westcote Rd, SW16 ...168 C5
West Cotts, NW6 ...90 D5
Westcott Cl, N15
off Ermine Rd ...76 C6
Bromley BR1 ...192 B5
Westcott Cres, W7 ...104 B6
Westcott Ho, E14
off East India Dock Rd .114 A7
Westcott Rd, SE17 ...35 G5
West Ct, SE18
off Prince Imperial Rd ...156 C1
Houns. TW3 ...123 J7
Westcourt, Sun. TW16 ...178 B2
West Ct, Wem. HA0 ...87 F2
Westcroft Cl, NW2 ...90 B4
Westcroft Gdns, Mord. SM4 ...184 C3
Westcroft Rd,
Carshalton SM5 ...200 A4
Wallington SM6 ...200 A4
Westcroft Sq, W6 ...127 G4
Westcroft Way, NW2 ...90 B4
West Cromwell Rd, SW5 ...128 C4
W14 ...128 C4
West Cross Cen, Brent. TW8 ...124 D6
West Cross Route, W10 ...108 A7
W11 ...108 A7
West Cross Way, Brent. TW8 ...124 E6
Westdale Pas, SE18 ...136 E6
Westdale Rd, SE18 ...137 E6
Westdean Av, SE12 ...173 H1
Westdean Cl, SW18 ...149 E5
West Dene, Sutt. SM3
off Park La ...198 B6
Westdown Rd, E15 ...96 C4
SE6 ...154 A7
WEST DRAYTON, UB7 ...120 A3
West Drayton Pk Av, West Dr. UB7 ...120 B3
West Dr, SW16 ...168 C4
Harrow HA3 ...52 A6
West Dr Gdns, Har. HA3 ...52 A6
WEST DULWICH, SE21 ...170 A3
West Eaton Pl, SW1 ...32 B1
West Eaton Pl Ms, SW1 ...32 B1
West Ella Rd, NW10 ...88 E7
West End Av, E10 ...78 C5
Pinner HA5 ...66 D4
West End Cl, NW10 ...88 C7
West End Ct, Pnr. HA5 ...66 D4
West End Gdns, Nthlt. UB5
off Edward Cl ...102 C2
West End La, NW6 ...90 D7
Barnet EN5 ...40 A4
Hayes (Harling.) UB3 ...121 F7
Pinner HA5 ...66 D3
West End Rd, Nthlt. UB5 ...84 C7
Ruislip HA4 ...84 B5
Southall UB1 ...122 E1
Westerdale Rd, SE10 ...135 G5
Westerfield Rd, N15 ...76 C5
Westergate Rd, SE2 ...138 E6
Westerham Av, N9 ...60 A3
Westerham Dr, Sid. DA15 ...158 B6
Westerham Rd, E10 ...78 B6
Keston BR2 ...206 A6
Westerley Cres, SE26 ...171 J5
Westerley Ware, Rich. TW9
off Kew Grn ...126 A6
Western Av, NW11 ...72 A6
W3 ...106 D5
W5 ...105 J3
Dagenham RM10 ...101 J6
Greenford UB6 ...104 C3
Northolt UB5 ...103 F1
Western Av Business Pk, W3 off Mansfield Rd ...106 B4
Western Av Underpass, W5
off Western Av ...105 J3
Western Beach Apts, E16
off Hanover Av ...135 G1
Western Ct, N3
off Huntly Dr ...56 D6
Western Gdns, W5 ...106 A7
Western Gateway, E16 ...115 G7
Western Int Mkt, Sthl. UB2 ...122 B4
Western La, SW12 ...150 A7
Western Ms, W9
off Great Western Rd ..108 C4
Western Par, Barn. (New Barn.) EN5
off Great N Rd ...40 D5
Western Pl, SE16
off Canon Beck Rd ...133 F2
Western Rd, E13 ...115 J1
E17 ...78 C5
N2 ...73 J4
N22 ...75 F2
NW10 ...106 C4
SW9 ...151 G3
SW19 ...185 G1
W5 ...105 G7
Mitcham CR4 ...185 G1
Southall UB2 ...122 D3
Sutton SM1 ...198 D5
Western Ter, W6
off Chiswick Mall ...127 G5
Western Trd Est, NW10 ...106 C4
Western Vw, Hayes UB3 ...121 J2
Westernville Gdns, Ilf. IG2 .81 F7
Western Way, SE28 ...137 G3
Barnet EN5 ...40 D6
WEST EWELL, Epsom KT19 ...196 E7
Westferry Circ, E14 ...133 J1
Westferry Rd, E14 ...134 A1
Westfield, Loug. IG10 ...47 J5
Westfield Cl, NW9 ...70 C3
SW10 ...129 F7
Enfield EN3 ...45 H3
Sutton SM1 ...198 C4
Westfield Dr, Har. HA3 ...69 G5
Westfield Gdns, Har. HA3 ..69 G4
Romford RM6 ...82 C6
Westfield La, Har. HA3 ...69 G4
Westfield London, W12 ...127 J1
Westfield Pk, Pnr. HA5 ...51 F7
Westfield Pk Dr, Wdf.Grn. IG8 ...64 B6
Westfield Rd, NW7 ...54 D3
W13 ...124 D1
Beckenham BR3 ...189 J2
Bexleyheath DA7 ...159 J2
Croydon CR0 ...201 H2
Dagenham RM9 ...101 E4
Mitcham CR4 ...185 J2
Surbiton KT6 ...181 G5
Sutton SM1 ...198 C4
Walton-on-Thames KT12 ...179 E7
Westfields, SW13 ...147 F3
Westfields Av, SW13 ...147 E3
Westfields Rd, W3 ...106 B5
Westfield St, SE18 ...136 A3
Westfield Way, E1 ...113 H3
W12 ...128 A1
West Gdn Pl, W2 ...15 H4
West Gdns, E1 ...113 E7
SW17 ...167 H6
West Gate, W5 ...105 H3
Westgate Ct, SW9
off Canterbury Cres ...151 G3
Westgate Rd, SE25 ...188 E4
Beckenham BR3 ...190 B2
Westgate St, E8 ...112 E1
Westgate Ter, SW10 ...30 B4
Westglade Ct, Har. HA3 ...69 G5
WEST GREEN, N15 ...75 J3
West Grn Pl, Grnf. UB6
off Uneeda Dr ...104 A1
West Grn Rd, N15 ...75 H4
West Gro, SE10 ...154 C1
Woodford Green IG8 ...63 J6
Westgrove La, SE10 ...154 C1
West Halkin St, SW1 ...24 B5
West Hallowes, SE9 ...174 A1
West Hall Rd, Rich. TW9 ..146 B1
WEST HAM, E15 ...97 F7
West Ham La, E15 ...96 E7
West Ham Pk, E7 ...97 F7
WEST HAMPSTEAD, NW6 .90 E5
West Hampstead Ms, NW6 ...90 E6
★ West Ham United FC, E13 ...115 J2
West Harding St, EC4 ...19 F3
WEST HARROW, Har. HA1 .67 J7
Westhay Gdns, SW14 ...146 B5
WEST HEATH, SE2 ...138 D6
West Heath Av, NW11 ...90 D1
West Heath Cl, NW3 ...90 D3
West Heath Dr, NW11 ...90 D1
West Heath Gdns, NW3 ...90 D2
West Heath Rd, NW3 ...90 D2
SE2 ...138 C6
WEST HENDON, NW9 ...71 E7
West Hendon Bdy, NW9 ...71 F6
West Herts Business Cen, Borwd. WD6
off Brook Rd ...38 B3
West Hill, SW15 ...148 A7
SW18 ...148 D5
Harrow HA2 ...86 B2
Wembley HA9 ...87 J1
West Hill Ct, N6 ...92 A3
West Hill Pk, N6
off Merton La ...91 J2
West Hill Rd, SW18 ...148 D6
West Hill Way, N20 ...56 E1
Westholm, NW11 ...72 E4
West Holme, Erith DA8 ...159 J1
Westholme, Orp. BR6 ...193 H7
Westholme Gdns, Ruis. HA4 ...84 A1
Westhorne Av, SE9 ...155 J6
SE12 ...155 G7
Westhorpe Gdns, NW4 ...71 J3
Westhorpe Rd, SW15 ...147 J3
West Ho Cl, SW19 ...166 B1
Westhurst Dr, Chis. BR7 ..175 E5
West India Av, E14 ...134 A1
West India Dock Rd, E14 ..113 J6
West Kensington Ct, W14
off Edith Vil ...128 C5
WEST KILBURN, W9 ...108 C3
Westlake Cl, N13 ...59 G3
Hayes UB4 ...102 E4
Westlake Rd, Wem. HA9 ...87 G2
Westland Cl, Stai. (Stanw.) TW19 ...140 B6
Westland Dr, Brom. BR2 ..205 F2
Westland Ho, E16
off Rymill St ...136 D1
Westland Pl, N1 ...12 B3
Westlands Cl, Hayes UB3
off Granville Rd ...122 A4
Westlands Ter, SW12
off Gaskarth Rd ...150 C6
West La, SE16 ...132 E2
Westlea Rd, W7 ...124 D3
Westleigh Av, SW15 ...147 H5

Westleigh Dr, Bromley BR1 192 B1
Westleigh Gdns, Edgware HA8 70 A1
Westlinks, Wem. HA0 *off Alperton La* 105 G2
Westlinton Cl, NW7 56 B6
West Lo Av, W3 126 A1
West Mall, W8 *off Palace Gdns Ter* 128 D1
Westmark Pt, SW15 *off Norley Vale* 165 H1
Westmead, SW15 147 H6
West Mead, Epsom KT19 197 E6
Ruislip HA4 84 C4
Westmead Cor, Cars. SM5 *off Colston Av* 199 H4
Westmead Rd, Sutt. SM1 199 G4
Westmede, Chig. IG7 65 F6
Westmere Dr, NW7 54 D3
West Mersea Cl, E16 *off Hanameel St* 135 H1
West Ms, N17 60 E6
SW1 33 E2
WESTMINSTER, SW1 25 F5
★ **Westminster Abbey**, SW1 26 A5
★ **Westminster Abbey Mus**, SW1 26 A5
Westminster Av, Th.Hth. CR7 187 H2
Westminster Br, SE1 26 B4
SW1 26 B4
Westminster Br Rd, SE1 26 D4
Westminster Business Sq, SE11 *off Durham St* 34 C4
★ **Westminster Cath**, SW1 25 F6
★ **Westminster City Hall**, SW1 25 G5
Westminster Cl, Felt. TW14 160 A1
Ilford IG6 81 G2
Teddington TW11 162 D5
Westminster Dr, N13 58 E5
Westminster Gdns, E4 63 E1
SW1 34 A1
Barking IG11 117 H2
Ilford IG6 81 F2
★ **Westminster Millennium Pier**, SW1 26 B3
Westminster Palace Gdns, SW1 *off Artillery Row* 25 H6
Westminster Rd, N9 61 E1
W7 124 B1
Sutton SM1 199 G2
Westmoat Cl, Beck. BR3 172 C7
WEST MOLESEY, KT8 179 F5
Westmont Rd, Esher KT10 194 B2
Westmoor Gdns, Enf. EN3 45 G2
Westmoor Rd, Enf. EN3 45 G2
Westmoor St, SE7 135 J3
Westmoreland Av, Well. DA16 157 H3
Westmoreland Pl, SW1 33 E4
W5 105 G5
Bromley BR1 191 G3
Westmoreland Rd, NW9 70 A4
SE17 36 A5
SW13 147 F1
Bromley BR1, BR2 191 E5
Westmoreland St, W1 16 C2
Westmoreland Ter, SE20 171 E7
SW1 32 E4
Westmoreland Wk, SE17 36 C5
Westmorland Cl, E12 98 A2
Twickenham TW1 144 E6
Westmorland Rd, E17 78 A6
Harrow HA1 67 H5
Westmorland Sq, Mitch. CR4 *off Westmorland Way* 186 E5
Westmorland Way, Mitch. CR4 186 D4
Westmount Rd, SE9 156 C2
WEST NORWOOD, SE27 169 J3
West Oak, Beck. BR3 190 D1
Westoe Rd, N9 61 E2
Weston Av, T.Ditt. KT7 180 B7
West Molesey KT8 179 E3
Weston Ct, N4 *off Queens Dr* 93 J3
N20 *off Farnham Cl* 41 F7
Weston Dr, Stan. HA7 68 E1
West One Shop Cen, W1 16 C4
Weston Gdns, Islw. TW7 144 A1
WESTON GREEN, T.Ditt. KT7 194 C1
Weston Grn, Dag. RM9 101 F4
Thames Ditton KT7 194 B1
Weston Grn Rd, Esher KT10 194 A1
Thames Ditton KT7 194 B1
Weston Gro, Bromley BR1 191 F1
Weston Pk, N8 75 E6
Kingston upon Thames KT1 *off Clarence St* 181 H2
Thames Ditton KT7 194 B1
Weston Pk Cl, T.Ditt. KT7 *off Weston Pk* 194 B1
Weston Ri, WC1 10 D2
Weston Rd, W4 126 C3
Bromley BR1 173 F7
Dagenham RM9 101 E4
Enfield EN2 44 A1
Thames Ditton KT7 194 B1
Weston St, SE1 28 C4
Weston Wk, E8 *off Mare St* 95 E7
Westover Hill, NW3 90 D2
Westover Rd, SW18 149 F6
Westow Hill, SE19 170 B6
Westow St, SE19 170 B6
West Pk, SE9 174 B2
West Pk Av, Rich. TW9 146 A1
West Pk Cl, Houns. TW5 *off Heston Gra La* 123 F6
Romford RM6 82 D5
West Pk Rd, Rich. TW9 146 A1
Southall UB2 123 J1
West Parkside, SE10 135 E2
West Pier, E1 *off Wapping High St* 132 E1
West Pl, SW19 165 J5
West Pt, SE1 37 H3
Westpoint Apts, N8 *off Turnpike La* 75 F4
West Pt Cl, Houns. TW4 *off Ede Cl* 143 F3
Westpoint Trd Est, W3 106 B5
Westpole Av, Barn. (Cockfos.) EN4 42 A4
Westport Rd, E13 115 H4
Westport St, E1 113 G6
West Poultry Av, EC1 19 G2
West Quarters, W12 107 G6
West Quay Dr, Hayes UB4 102 E5
West Ramp, Houns. (Lon.Hthrw Air.) TW6 140 D1
West Ridge Gdns, Grnf. UB6 103 J2
West Rd, E15 115 F1
N17 60 E6
SW3 32 A4
SW4 150 D5
W5 105 H5
Barnet EN4 58 A1
Feltham TW14 141 G6
Kingston upon Thames KT2 182 C1
Romford (Chad.Hth) RM6 82 D6
West Drayton UB7 120 C3
Westrow, SW15 147 J5
West Row, W10 108 B4
Westrow Dr, Bark. IG11 99 J6
Westrow Gdns, Ilf. IG3 99 J2
West Sheen Vale, Rich. TW9 145 J4
Westside, NW4 71 H2
Westside Apts, Ilf. IG1 *off Roden St* 98 D3
West Side Common, SW19 165 J5
West Smithfield, EC1 19 G2
West Sq, SE11 27 G6
West St, E2 113 E2
E11 96 E3
E17 *off Grove Rd* 78 B5
WC2 17 J4
Bexleyheath DA7 159 F4
Brentford TW8 125 F6
Bromley BR1 191 G1
Carshalton SM5 199 J3
Croydon CR0 201 J4
Harrow HA1 86 A1
Sutton SM1 198 E5
West St La, Carshalton SM5 199 J4
West Temple Sheen, SW14 146 B4
West Tenter St, E1 21 G4
West Thamesmead Business Pk, SE28 137 J3
West Twrs, Pnr. HA5 66 D6
Westvale Ms, W3 127 E1
West Vw, NW4 71 J4
Feltham TW14 141 F7
Loughton IG10 48 C3
Westview Cl, NW10 89 F5
W7 104 B6
W10 107 J6
Westview Cres, N9 44 B7
Westview Dr, Wdf.Grn. IG8 80 A2
Westville Rd, W12 127 G2
Thames Ditton KT7 194 D1
West Wk, W5 105 H5
Barnet (E.Barn.) EN4 42 A7
Hayes UB3 122 A1
West Walkway, The, Sutt. SM1 *off Cheam Rd* 198 E5
Westward Rd, E4 61 J5
Westward Way, Harrow HA3 69 H6
West Warwick Pl, SW1 33 F2
West Way, N18 60 A4
NW10 88 D3
Westway, SW20 183 H3
W2 108 D5
W9 108 D5
W10 108 B6
W12 107 G7
West Way, Croy. CR0 203 H2
Edgware HA8 54 B6
Hounslow TW5 143 F1
Orpington (Petts Wd) BR5 193 G5
Pinner HA5 66 D4
West Wickham BR4 190 D6
Westway Cl, SW20 183 H3
Westway Cross Shop Pk, Grnf. UB6 104 B1
West Way Gdns, Croy. CR0 203 G2
Westways, Epsom KT19 197 F4
Westwell Rd, SW16 168 E6
Westwell Rd App, SW16 *off Westwell Rd* 168 E6
Westwick Gdns, W14 128 A2
Hounslow TW4 142 B2
WEST WICKHAM, BR4 204 C2
Westwood Av, SE19 187 J1
Harrow HA2 85 H4
Westwood Cl, Brom. BR1 192 A3
Westwood Gdns, SW13 147 F3
Westwood Hill, SE26 170 D5
Westwood La, Sid. DA15 158 A5
Welling DA16 157 J3
Westwood Pk, SE23 153 E7
Westwood Pl, SE26 170 D4
Westwood Rd, E16 135 H1
SW13 147 F3
Ilford IG3 99 J1
West Woodside, Bex. DA5 159 E7
West World, W5 105 H3
Wetheral Dr, Stan. HA7 69 E1
Wetherby Cl, Nthlt. UB5 85 H6
Wetherby Gdns, SW5 30 C2
Wetherby Ms, SW5 30 A3
Wetherby Pl, SW7 30 C2
Wetherby Rd, Enf. EN2 43 J1
Wetherby Way, Chess. KT9 195 H7
Wetherden St, E17 77 J7
Wetherell Rd, E9 113 G1
Wetherill Rd, N10 74 A1
★ **Wetland Cen, The**, SW13 127 H7
Wexford Rd, SW12 149 J7
Weybourne St, SW18 167 F2
Weybridge Ct, SE16 37 J4
Weybridge Pt, SW11 150 A2
Weybridge Rd, Th.Hth. CR7 187 G4
Wey Ct, Epsom KT19 196 C4
Weydown Cl, SW19 166 B1
Weyhill Rd, E1 21 J3
Weylond Rd, Dag. RM8 101 F3
Weyman Rd, SE3 155 J1
Weymouth Av, NW7 54 E5
W5 125 F3
Weymouth Cl, E6 *off Covelees Wall* 116 E6
Weymouth Ct, Sutt. SM2 198 D7
Weymouth Ho, SW8 *off Bolney St* 131 F7
Weymouth Ms, W1 16 D1
Weymouth St, W1 16 C2
Weymouth Ter, E2 13 G1
Weymouth Wk, Stan. HA7 52 D6
Whadcote St, N4 93 G2
Whaddon Ho, SE22 *off Albrighton Rd* 152 B3
Whalebone Av, Rom. RM6 83 F6
Whalebone Ct, EC2 20 C3
Whalebone Gro, Rom. RM6 83 F6
Whalebone La, E15 *off West Ham La* 96 E7
Whalebone La N, Rom. RM6 83 E5
Whalebone La S, Dag. RM8 83 F7
Romford RM6 83 F7
Whales Yd, E15 *off West Ham La* 96 E7
Wharfdale Cl, N11 58 A6
Wharfdale Ct, E5 *off Pedro St* 95 G4
Wharfdale Rd, N1 10 B1
Wharfedale Gdns, Th.Hth. CR7 187 F4
Wharfedale St, SW10 30 A4
Wharf La, E14 *off Commercial Rd* 113 J6
Twickenham TW1 162 D1
Wharf Pl, E2 112 D1
Wharf Rd, N1 11 J1
N1 (King's Cross) 10 A1
Enfield EN3 45 H6
Wharfside Rd, E16 114 E5
Wharf St, E16 114 E5
Wharncliffe Dr, Sthl. UB1 124 A1
Wharncliffe Gdns, SE25 188 B2
Wharncliffe Rd, SE25 188 B2
Wharton Cl, NW10 89 E6
Wharton Cotts, WC1 *off Wharton St* 10 D4
Wharton Rd, Brom. BR1 191 H1
Wharton St, WC1 10 D4
Whateley Rd, SE20 171 G7
SE22 152 C5
Whatley Av, SW20 184 B3
Whatman Rd, SE23 153 G7
Wheatcroft Ct, Sutt. SM1 *off Cleeve Way* 199 E1
Wheatfields, E6 *off Oxleas* 116 E6
Enfield EN3 45 H2
Wheatfield Way, Kings.T. KT1 181 H2
Wheathill Rd, SE20 188 E3
Wheatland Ho, SE22 *off Albrighton Rd* 152 B3
Wheatlands, Houns. TW5 123 G6
Wheatlands Rd, SW17 *off Stapleton Rd* 168 A3
Wheatley Cl, NW4 71 G2
Wheatley Cres, Hayes UB3 102 A7
Wheatley Gdns, N9 60 B2
Wheatley Ho, SW15 *off Tangley Gro* 147 G7
Wheatley Rd, Islw. TW7 144 C3
Wheatley's Ait, Sun. TW16 178 A5
Wheatley St, W1 16 C2
Wheat Sheaf Cl, E14 134 B4
Wheatsheaf Cl, Nthlt. UB5 84 E5
Wheatsheaf La, SW6 127 J7
SW8 34 B7
Wheatsheaf Ter, SW6 128 C7
Wheatstone Cl, Mitch. CR4 185 H1
Wheatstone Rd, W10 108 B5
Wheeler Cl, Wdf.Grn. IG8 *off Chigwell Rd* 64 C5
Wheeler Gdns, N1 *off Outram Pl* 111 E1
Wheeler Pl, Brom. BR2 191 H4
Wheelers Cross, Bark. IG11 117 G2
Wheel Fm Dr, Dag. RM10 101 J3
Wheelock Cl, Erith DA8 139 H7
Wheelwright St, N7 93 F7
Whelan Way, Wall. SM6 200 D3
Wheler St, E1 13 F6
Whellock Rd, W4 126 E3
Whenman Av, Bex. DA5 177 J2
Whernside Cl, SE28 118 C7
WHETSTONE, N20 57 E2
Whetstone Cl, N20 57 G2
Whetstone Pk, WC2 18 C3
Whetstone Rd, SE3 155 J2
Whewell Rd, N19 93 E2
Whichcote St, SE1 26 E2
Whidborne Cl, SE8 *off Cliff Ter* 154 A2
Whidborne St, WC1 10 B4
Whimbrel Cl, SE28 118 C7
Whimbrel Way, Hayes UB4 102 D6
Whinchat Rd, SE28 137 G3
Whinfell Cl, SW16 168 D5
Whinyates Rd, SE9 156 B3
Whipps Cross, E17 78 D5
Whipps Cross Rd, E11 78 D5
Whiskin St, EC1 11 G4
Whisperwood Cl, Har. HA3 52 B7
Whistler Gdns, Edg. HA8 69 J2
Whistler Ms, SE15 *off Kelly Av* 132 C7
Dagenham RM8 *off Fitzstephen Rd* 100 B5
Whistlers Av, SW11 129 G7
Whistler St, N5 93 H4
Whistler Twr, SW10 30 D7
Whistler Wk, SW10 *off Blantyre St* 30 D7
Whiston Rd, E2 13 F1
Whitacre Ms, SE11 35 F4
Whitakers Way, Loug. IG10 48 C1
Whitbread Cl, N17 76 D1
Whitbread Rd, SE4 153 H4
Whitburn Rd, SE13 154 B4
Whitby Av, NW10 106 B3

Whitby Ct, N7 *off Camden Rd* 93 E4
Whitby Gdns, NW9 70 A3
Sutton SM1 199 G2
Whitby Rd, SE18 136 C4
Harrow HA2 85 J3
Ruislip HA4 84 B3
Sutton SM1 199 G2
Whitby St, E1 13 F5
Whitcher Cl, SE14 133 H6
Whitcher Pl, NW1 *off Rochester Rd* 92 C7
Whitchurch Av, Edg. HA8 53 J7
Whitchurch Cl, Edg. HA8 53 J6
Whitchurch Gdns, Edg. HA8 53 J6
Whitchurch La, Edg. HA8 53 G7
Whitchurch Rd, W11 108 A7
Whitcomb Ct, WC2 *off Whitcomb St* 17 J6
Whitcomb St, WC2 17 J6
Whitcome Ms, Rich. TW9 146 B1
Whiteadder Way, E14 134 B4
Whitear Wk, E15 96 D6
Whitebarn La, Dag. RM10 119 G1
Whitebeam Av, Brom. BR2 192 D6
Whitebeam Cl, SW9 *off Clapham Rd* 131 F7
Whitebeam Ho, NW3 *off Maitland Pk Rd* 91 J6
White Bear Pl, NW3 *off New End Sq* 91 G4
White Br Av, Mitch. CR4 185 G4
Whitebridge Cl, Felt. TW14 141 J6
White Butts Rd, Ruis. HA4 84 D3
WHITECHAPEL, E1 21 H4
★ **Whitechapel Art Gall**, E1 21 G3
Whitechapel High St, E1 21 G3
Whitechapel Rd, E1 21 H3
White Ch La, E1 21 H3
White Ch Pas, E1 21 H3
White City Cl, W12 107 J7
White City Est, W12 107 H7
White City Rd, W12 107 H7
White Conduit St, N1 11 F1
Whitecote Rd, Sthl. UB1 103 H6
White Craig Cl, Pnr. HA5 51 G5
Whitecroft Cl, Beck. BR3 190 D4
Whitecroft Way, Beck. BR3 190 C5
Whitecross Pl, EC2 20 C1
Whitecross St, EC1 12 A5
★ **White Cube**, N1 *off Hoxton Sq* 12 D4
★ **White Cube**, SW1 25 G1
Whitefield Av, NW2 71 J7
Whitefield Cl, SW15 148 B6
Whitefoot La, Brom. BR1 172 C4
Whitefoot Ter, Brom. BR1 173 E3
Whitefriars Av, Har. HA3 68 B2
Whitefriars Dr, Har. HA3 68 A2
Whitefriars St, EC4 19 F4
White Gdns, Dag. RM10 101 G6
Whitegate Gdns, Har. HA3 52 C7
Whitehall, SW1 26 A1
Whitehall Cl, Borwd. WD6 38 A4
Whitehall Ct, SW1 26 A2
Whitehall Cres, Chess. KT9 195 G5
Whitehall Gdns, E4 62 E1
SW1 26 A2
W3 126 A1
W4 126 B6
Whitehall La, Buck.H. IG9 63 G2
Whitehall Pk, N19 92 C1
Whitehall Pk Rd, W4 126 B6
Whitehall Pl, E7 *off Brooking Rd* 97 G5
SW1 26 A2
Wallington SM6 *off Bernard Rd* 200 B4
Whitehall Rd, E4 62 E2
W7 124 D2
Bromley BR2 192 A5
Harrow HA1 68 B7
Thornton Heath CR7 187 G5
Woodford Green IG8 62 E2
Whitehall St, N17 60 C7
White Hart Av, SE18 137 J3
SE28 137 J3
White Hart Ct, EC2 20 D2
White Hart La, N17 60 A7
N22 75 G1
NW10 *off Church Rd* 89 F6
SW13 147 E3
Romford RM7 83 G1
White Hart Rd, SE18 137 H4
White Hart Rbt, Nthlt. UB5 *off The Parkway* 102 D2
White Hart Slip, Brom. BR1 *off Market Sq* 191 G2
White Hart St, EC4 19 H3
SE11 35 F3
White Hart Yd, SE1 28 B2
Whitehaven Cl, Brom. BR2 191 G4
Whitehaven St, NW8 7 G6
Whitehead Cl, N18 60 A5
SW18 149 F7
Whitehead's Gro, SW3 31 H3
White Heron Ms, Tedd. TW11 162 C6
Whitehills Rd, Loughton IG10 48 D3
White Horse All, EC1 19 G1
White Horse Hill, Chis. BR7 174 D4
White Horse La, E1 113 G4
Whitehorse La, SE25 188 A4
White Horse Ms, SE1 27 F5
White Horse Rd, E1 113 H6
E6 116 C3
Whitehorse Rd, Croy. CR0 188 A6
Thornton Heath CR7 188 A6
White Horse St, W1 24 D2
White Horse Yd, EC2 20 B3
Whitehouse Apts, SE1 *off Belvedere Rd* 26 D2
Whitehouse Av, Borwd. WD6 38 B3
White Ho Dr, Stan. HA7 53 F4
Whitehouse Way, N14 58 B2
Whitehurst Dr, N18 61 G6
White Kennett St, E1 21 E3
Whitelands Cres, SW18 148 B7
Whiteledges, W13 105 F6
Whitelegg Rd, E13 115 F2
Whiteley Rd, SE19 170 A5
Whiteleys Shop Cen, W2 14 A4
Whiteleys Way, Felt. (Han.) TW13 161 G3
White Lion Ct, EC3 20 D4
White Lion Hill, EC4 19 H5
White Lion St, N1 11 E2
White Lo, SE19 169 H7
White Lo Cl, N2 73 G6
Isleworth TW7 144 D2
Sutton SM2 199 F7
White Lyon Ct, EC2 19 J1
White Oak Dr, Beck. BR3 190 C2
White Oak Gdns, Sid. DA15 157 J7
Whiteoaks La, Grnf. UB6 104 A2
White Orchards, N20 40 C7
Stanmore HA7 52 D5
White Post La, E9 96 A6
SE13 154 A3
White Post St, SE15 133 F7
White Rd, E15 97 E7
Whites Av, Ilf. IG2 81 H6
Whites Grds, SE1 28 E4
Whites Grds Est, SE1 *off Whites Grds* 28 E3
Whites Meadow, Brom. BR1 *off Blackbrook La* 192 D4
White's Row, E1 21 F2
White's Sq, SW4 *off Nelson's Row* 150 D4
Whitestile Rd, Brent. TW8 125 F5
Whitestone La, NW3 *off Heath St* 91 F3
Whitestone Wk, NW3 *off North End Way* 91 F3
White St, Sthl. UB1 122 D2
White Swan Ms, W4 *off Bennett St* 126 E6
Whitethorn Gdns, Croy. CR0 203 E2
Enfield EN2 44 A5
Whitethorn St, E3 114 A4
Whitewebbs Way, Orp. BR5 193 J1
Whitfield Pl, W1 9 F6
Whitfield Rd, E6 97 J7
SE3 154 D1
Bexleyheath DA7 139 F7
Whitfield St, W1 17 H2
Whitford Gdns, Mitch. CR4 185 J3
Whitgift Av, S.Croy. CR2 201 H5
Whitgift Cen, Croy. CR0 201 J2
Whitgift Ho, SW11 *off Westbridge Rd* 149 H1
Whitgift St, SE11 34 C1
Croydon CR0 201 J3
Whiting Av, Bark. IG11 99 E7
Whitings, Ilf. IG2 81 G5
Whitings Rd, Barn. EN5 39 J5
Whitings Way, E6 116 D5
Whitland Rd, Cars. SM5 199 G1
Whitley Cl, Stai. (Stanw.) TW19 140 B6
Whitley Ho, SW1 33 G4
Whitley Rd, N17 76 B2
Whitlock Dr, SW19 148 B7
Whitman Rd, E3 *off Mile End Rd* 113 H4
Whitmead Cl, S.Croy. CR2 202 B6
Whitmore Cl, N11 58 B5
Whitmore Est, N1 112 B1
Whitmore Gdns, NW10 107 J2
Whitmore Rd, N1 112 B1
Beckenham BR3 189 J3
Harrow HA1 67 J7
Whitnell Way, SW15 148 A5
Whitney Av, Ilf. IG4 80 A4
Whitney Ho, SE22 *off Albrighton Rd* 152 B3
Whitney Rd, E10 78 B7
Whitney Wk, Sid. DA14 176 E6
Whitstable Cl, Beck. BR3 189 J1
Whitstable Ho, W10 108 A6
Whitstable Pl, Croy. CR0 201 J4
Whitstone La, Beck. BR3 190 B5
Whittaker Av, Rich. TW9 *off Hill St* 145 G5
Whittaker Rd, E6 97 J7
Sutton SM3 198 C3
Whittaker St, SW1 32 B2
Whittaker Way, SE1 37 J2
Whitta Rd, E12 98 A4
Whittell Gdns, SE26 171 F3
Whittingstall Rd, SW6 148 C1
Whittington Av, EC3 20 D4
Whittington Ct, N2 73 J5
Whittington Ms, N12 57 F4
Whittington Rd, N22 58 E7
Whittington Way, Pnr. HA5 67 E5
Whittlebury Cl, Cars. SM5 199 J7
Whittle Cl, E17 77 H6
Southall UB1 103 H6
Whittle Rd, Houns. TW5 122 C7
Southall UB2 *off Post Rd* 123 H2
Whittlesea Cl, Har. HA3 51 J7
Whittlesea Path, Har. HA3 67 J1
Whittlesea Rd, Har. HA3 67 J1
Whittlesey St, SE1 27 E2
WHITTON, Twick. TW2 143 H7
Whitton Av E, Grnf. UB6 86 B5
Whitton Av W, Grnf. UB6 85 J5
Northolt UB5 85 J5
Whitton Cl, Grnf. UB6 87 E6
Whitton Dene, Houns. TW3 143 H5
Isleworth TW7 144 A5
Whitton Dr, Grnf. UB6 86 D6
Whitton Manor Rd, Islw. TW7 143 J5
Whitton Rd, Houns. TW3 143 H4
Twickenham TW1, TW2 144 C6
Whitton Rd Rbt, Twick. TW1 *off Chertsey Rd* 144 C6
Whitton Wk, E3 114 A2
Whitton Waye, Houns. TW3 143 G6
Whitwell Rd, E13 115 G3
Whitworth Ho, SE1 28 A6
Whitworth Rd, SE18 136 D7
SE25 188 B3
Whitworth St, SE10 135 E5
Whorlton Rd, SE15 152 E3
Whychcote Pt, NW2 *off Claremont Rd* 71 J7
Whymark Av, N22 75 G3
Whytecroft, Houns. TW5 122 D7
Whyte Ms, Sutt. SM3 198 B7
Whyteville Rd, E7 97 H6
Wickersley Rd, SW11 150 A2
Wickers Oake, SE19 170 C4
Wicker St, E1 *off Burslem St* 112 E6
Wicket, The, Croy. CR0 204 A5
Wicket Rd, Grnf. (Perivale) UB6 104 D3
Wickets Way, Ilf. IG6 65 J6
Wickford St, E1 113 F4
Wickford Way, E17 77 G4
Wickham Av, Croy. CR0 203 H2
Sutton SM3 197 J5
Wickham Chase, W.Wick. BR4 190 D7
Wickham Cl, E1 113 F5
Enfield EN3 45 E3
New Malden KT3 183 F5
Wickham Ct Rd, W.Wick. BR4 204 C2
Wickham Cres, W.Wick. BR4 204 C2
Wickham Gdns, SE4 153 J3
Wickham La, SE2 138 A5
Welling DA16 138 A5
Wickham Ms, SE4 153 J2
Wickham Rd, E4 62 C7
SE4 153 J4
Beckenham BR3 190 B2
Croydon CR0 203 G2
Harrow HA3 68 A2
Wickham St, SE11 34 C3
Welling DA16 157 H2
Wickham Way, Beck. BR3 190 C4
Wick La, E3 114 A2
Wickliffe Av, N3 72 B2
Wickliffe Gdns, Wem. HA9 88 B2
Wicklow St, WC1 10 C3
Wick Rd, E9 95 G6
Teddington TW11 163 E7
Wicks Cl, SE9 174 A4
Wicksteed Ho, SE1 28 A6
Brentford TW8 *off Green Dragon La* 125 J5
Wickway Ct, SE15 37 F6
Wickwood St, SE5 151 H2
Widdecombe Av, Har. HA2 84 E2
Widdenham Rd, N7 93 F4
Widdin St, E15 96 D7
Widecombe Gdns, Ilf. IG4 80 B4
Widecombe Rd, SE9 174 B3
Widecombe Way, N2 73 G5
Widegate St, E1 21 E2
Widenham Cl, Pnr. HA5 66 C5
Wide Way, Mitch. CR4 186 D3
Widewing Cl, Tedd. TW11 163 E7
Widgeon Cl, E16 *off Maplin Rd* 115 H6
Widley Rd, W9 108 D3
WIDMORE, Brom. BR1 191 H3
WIDMORE GREEN, Brom. BR1 191 J1
Widmore Lo Rd, Brom. BR1 192 A2
Widmore Rd, Brom. BR1 191 G2
Wieland Rd, Nthwd. HA6 50 A7
Wigan Ho, E5 94 E1
Wigeon Path, SE28 137 G3
Wigeon Way, Hayes UB4 102 D6
Wiggins La, Rich. TW10 163 F2
Wiggins Mead, NW9 55 F7
Wigginton Av, Wem. HA9 88 B6
Wigham Ho, Bark. IG11 99 F7
Wightman Rd, N4 75 G5
N8 75 G4
Wighton Ms, Islw. TW7 *off London Rd* 144 B2
Wigley Rd, Felt. TW13 160 D1
Wigmore Ct, W13 *off Singapore Rd* 124 D1
Wigmore Pl, W1 16 D3
Wigmore Rd, Cars. SM5 199 G2
Wigmore St, W1 16 B4
Wigmore Wk, Cars. SM5 199 G2
Wigram Rd, E11 79 J6
Wigram Sq, E17 78 C2
Wigston Cl, N18 60 B5
Wigston Rd, E13 115 H4
Wigton Gdns, Stan. HA7 69 H1
Wigton Pl, SE11 35 F4
Wigton Rd, E17 77 J1
Wilberforce Ct, Edg. HA8 53 J4
Keston BR2 206 A6
Wilberforce Ms, SW4 150 D4
Wilberforce Rd, N4 93 H2
NW9 71 G6
Wilberforce Way, SW19 166 A6
Wilbraham Pl, SW1 32 A1
Wilbury Way, N18 60 A5
Wilby Ms, W11 128 C1
Wilcox Cl, SW8 34 B7
Borehamwood WD6 38 C1
Wilcox Pl, SW1 25 G6
Wilcox Rd, SW8 34 A7
Sutton SM1 198 E4
Teddington TW11 162 A4
Wild Ct, WC2 18 C3
Wildcroft Gdns, Edg. HA8 53 G6
Wildcroft Rd, SW15 147 J7
Wilde Cl, E8 112 D1
Wilde Pl, N13 59 H6
SW18 149 G7
Wilder Cl, Ruis. HA4 84 B1
Wilderness, The, E.Mol. KT8 179 J5
Hampton (Hmptn H.) TW12 *off Park Rd* 161 H4
Wilderness Ms, SW4 *off The Chase* 150 B4
Wilderness Rd, Chis. BR7 175 E7
Wilde Rd, Erith DA8 139 H7
Wilderton Rd, N16 76 B7
Wildfell Rd, SE6 154 B7
Wild Goose Dr, SE14 153 F1
Wild Hatch, NW11 72 D6
Wild's Rents, SE1 28 D5
Wild St, WC2 18 B4
Wildwood Cl, SE12 155 F7
Wildwood Gro, NW3 *off North End Way* 91 F1
Wildwood Ri, NW11 91 F1
Wildwood Rd, NW11 73 F7
Wildwood Ter, NW3 91 F1
Wilford Cl, Enf. EN2 44 A3
Wilfred Owen Cl, SW19 167 F6
Wilfred St, SW1 25 F5
Wilfred Turney Est, W6 *off Hammersmith Gro* 127 J2
Wilfrid Gdns, W3 106 C5

Wilkes Rd, Brent.TW8 125 H6
Wilkes St, E1 21 G1
Wilkins Cl, Hayes UB3 121 J5
Mitcham CR4 185 H1
Wilkins Ho, SW1 *off Churchill Gdns* 33 F5
Wilkinson Gdns, SE25 188 B1
Wilkinson Rd, E16 115 J6
Wilkinson St, SW8 131 F7
Wilkinson Way, W4 126 D2
Wilkin St, NW5 92 B6
Wilkin St Ms, NW5 *off Wilkin St* 92 B6
Wilks Gdns, Croy. CR0 203 H1
Wilks Pl, N1 12 E2
Willan Rd, N17 76 A2
Willan Wall, E16 *off Victoria Dock Rd* 115 F7
Willard St, SW8 150 B3
Willcocks Cl, Chess. KT9 195 H3
Willcott Rd, W3 126 B1
Will Crooks Gdns, SE9 155 J4
Willen Fld Rd, NW10 106 C2
Willenhall Av, Barn. (New Barn.) EN5 41 F6
Willenhall Rd, SE18 136 E5
Willersley Av, Orp. BR6 207 G3
Sidcup DA15 175 J1
Willersley Cl, Sid. DA15 175 J1
WILLESDEN, NW10 89 F6
WILLESDEN GREEN, NW10 89 H7
Willesden La, NW2 90 A6
NW6 90 A6
Willes Rd, NW5 92 B6
Willett Cl, Nthlt. UB5 *off Broomcroft Av* 102 C3
Orpington BR5 193 H6
Willett Ho, E13 *off Queens Rd W* 115 G2
Willett Pl, Th.Hth. CR7 *off Willett Rd* 187 G5
Willett Rd, Th.Hth. CR7 187 G5
Willett Way, Orp. BR5 193 G5
William Ash Cl, Dag. RM9 *off Rugby Rd* 100 B6
William Barefoot Dr, SE9 174 D4
William Bonney Est, SW4 150 D4
William Booth Rd, SE20 188 D1
William Carey Way, Har. HA1 68 B7
William Cl, N2 73 G2
SE13 154 C2
SW6 *off Pellant Rd* 128 B7
Romford RM5 83 J1
Southall UB2 *off Windmill Av* 123 J2
William Dr, Stan. HA7 52 D6
William Dunbar Ho, NW6 108 C2
William Dyce Ms, SW16 *off Babington Rd* 168 D4
William Ellis Way, SE16 29 J6
William Foster La, Well. DA16 158 A2
William IV St, WC2 18 A6
William Gdns, SW15 147 H5
William Guy Gdns, E3 *off Talwin St* 114 B3
William Harvey Ho, SW19 *off Whitlock Dr* 166 B1
William Henry Wk, SW8 33 H6
William Margrie Cl, SE15 *off Moncrieff St* 152 D2
William Ms, SW1 24 A4
William Morley Cl, E6 116 A1
William Morris Cl, E17 77 J3
★ **William Morris Gall**, E17 *off Lloyd Pk* 78 A3
William Morris Way, SW6 149 F3
William Perkin Ct, Grnf. UB6 *off Greenford Rd* 86 B6
William Pl, E3 *off Roman Rd* 113 J2
William Rd, NW1 9 F4
SW19 166 B7
Sutton SM1 199 F5
William Rushbrooke Ho, SE16 *off Eveline Lowe Est* 37 H1
Williams Av, E17 77 J1
William Saville Ho, NW6 108 C2
Williams Bldgs, E2 113 F4
Williams Cl, N8 *off Coolhurst Rd* 74 D6
Williams Dr, Houns. TW3 143 G4
Williams Gro, N22 75 G1
Surbiton (Long Dit.) KT6 181 F6
William's La, SW14 146 C3
Williams La, Mord. SM4 185 F5
Williamson Cl, SE10 *off Lenthorp Rd* 135 F4
Williamson St, N7 93 E4
William Sq, SE16 *off Rotherhithe St* 113 H7
Williams Rd, W13 104 D7
Southall UB2 122 E4
Williams Ter, Croy. CR0 201 G6
William St, E10 78 B6
N17 60 C7
SW1 24 A4
Barking IG11 99 F7
Carshalton SM5 199 H3
Willifield Way, NW11 72 C4
Willingale Cl, Loug. IG10 *off Willingale Rd* 49 F2
Woodford Green IG8 63 J6
Willingale Rd, Loug. IG10 49 F3
Willingdon Rd, N22 75 H2
Willingham Cl, NW5 92 C5
Willingham Ter, NW5 92 C5
Willingham Way, Kings.T. KT1 182 A3
Willington Ct, E5 *off Mandeville St* 95 H3
Willington Rd, SW9 150 E3
Willis Av, Sutt. SM2 199 H6
Willis Ho, E12 *off Grantham Rd* 98 D3
Willis Rd, E15 115 F1
Croydon CR0 187 J7
Erith DA8 139 J4
Willis St, E14 114 B6
Willmore End, SW19 184 E1
Willoughby Av, Croy. CR0 201 F4
Willoughby Gro, N17 60 E7
Willoughby Ho, EC2 *off The Barbican* 20 B2
Willoughby La, N17 61 E7
Willoughby Ms, SW4 *off Wixs La* 150 B4
Willoughby Pk Rd, N17 60 E7
Willoughby Pas, E14 134 A1
Willoughby Rd, N8 75 G3
NW3 91 G4
Kingston upon Thames KT2 181 J1
Twickenham TW1 145 G6
Willoughbys, The, SW14 *off Upper Richmond Rd W* 147 E3
Willoughby St, WC1 18 A2
Willoughby Way, SE7 135 H4
Willow Av, SW13 147 F2
Sidcup DA15 158 A6
Willow Bk, SW6 148 B3
Richmond TW10 163 E3
Willowbay Cl, Barn. EN5 40 A6
Willow Br Rd, N1 93 J6
Willowbrook Est, SE15 *off Shurland Gdns* 37 G7
Willowbrook Rd, SE15 37 G6
Southall UB2 123 G3
Willow Cen, Mitch. CR4 185 J5
Willow Cl, SE6 *off Verdant La* 173 F1
Bexley DA5 159 F6
Brentford TW8 125 F6
Bromley BR2 192 C5
Buckhurst Hill IG9 64 A3
Thornton Heath CR7 187 H6
Willow Cotts, Mitch. CR4 186 C3
Richmond TW9 *off Kew Grn* 126 A6
Willow Ct, EC2 12 D5
Edgware HA8 53 H4
Willowcourt Av, Har. HA3 69 E5
Willowdene, N6 *off Denewood Rd* 73 J7
Willow Dene, Pnr. HA5 66 D2
Willowdene Cl, Twick. TW2 143 J7
Willow Dr, Barn. EN5 40 B4
Willow End, N20 56 D2
Northwood HA6 50 A6
Surbiton KT6 195 H1
Willow Fm La, SW15 *off Queens Ride* 147 H3
Willowfields Cl, SE18 137 H5
Willow Gdns, Houns. TW3 143 G1
Willow Grn, NW9 *off Clayton Fld* 71 E1
Borehamwood WD6 38 D5
Willow Gro, E13 *off Libra Rd* 115 G2
Chislehurst BR7 174 D6
Willowhayne Dr, Walt. KT12 178 B7
Willowhayne Gdns, Wor.Pk. KT4 197 J3
Willow Ho, NW3 *off Maitland Pk Vil* 91 J6
Willow La, SE18 136 C4
Mitcham CR4 185 J5
Willow La Ind Est, Mitch. CR4 185 J5
Willowmead Cl, W5 105 G5
Willow Mt, Croy. CR0 *off Langton Way* 202 B3
Willow Pl, SW1 33 G1
Willow Rd, NW3 91 G4
W5 125 H2
Enfield EN1 44 B3
New Malden KT3 182 C4
Romford RM6 83 E6
Wallington SM6 200 B7
Willows, The, Buck.H. IG9 64 A3
Esher (Clay.) KT10 194 B6
Willows Av, Mord. SM4 185 E5
Willows Cl, Pnr. HA5 66 C2
Willow St, E4 46 D7
EC2 12 D5
Romford RM7 83 J4
Willow Tree Cl, E3 *off Birdsfield La* 113 J1
SW18 *off Cargill Rd* 167 E1
Hayes UB4 102 C4
Willowtree Cl, Nthlt. UB5 85 E6
Willow Tree La, Hayes UB4 102 C4
Willowtree Marina, Hayes UB4 103 E6
Willow Tree Rbt, Hayes UB4 *off The Parkway* 102 D5
Willow Tree Wk, Brom. BR1 191 H1
Willowtree Way, Th.Hth. CR7 *off Kensington Av* 187 G1
Willow Vale, W12 127 G1
Chislehurst BR7 174 E6
Willow Vw, SW19 185 G1
Willow Wk, E17 77 J5
N2 73 G2
N15 75 H4
N21 43 F6
SE1 37 E1
Orpington BR6 206 E3
Sutton SM3 198 C3
Willow Way, N3 56 E7
SE26 171 E3
W11 *off Freston Rd* 108 A7
Epsom KT19 196 D6
Sunbury-on-Thames TW16 178 A4
Twickenham TW2 161 H2
Wembley HA0 86 D3
Willow Wd Cres, SE25 188 B6
Willrose Cres, SE2 138 C5
Wills Cres, Houns. TW3 143 H6
Wills Gro, NW7 55 G5
Wilman Gro, E8 94 D7
Wilmar Gdns, W.Wick. BR4 204 B1
Wilmcote Ho, W2 108 D5
Wilmer Cl, Kings.T. KT2 163 J5
Wilmer Cres, Kings.T. KT2 163 J5
Wilmer Gdns, N1 112 B1
Wilmer Ho, E3 *off Daling Way* 113 H2
Wilmer Lea Cl, E15 96 C7
Wilmer Pl, N16 *off Stoke Newington Ch St* 94 C2
Wilmer Way, N14 58 D5
Wilmington Av, W4 126 D7
Wilmington Gdns, Bark. IG11 99 G6
Wilmington Sq, WC1 11 E4
Wilmington St, WC1 11 E4
Wilmot Cl, N2 73 F2
SE15 132 D7
Wilmot Pl, NW1 92 C7
W7 124 B1
Wilmot Rd, E10 96 B2
N17 76 A3
Carshalton SM5 199 J5
Wilmot St, E2 112 E4
Wilmount St, SE18 136 E4
Wilna Rd, SW18 149 F7
Wilsham St, W11 128 A1
Wilshaw Cl, NW4 71 G3
Wilshaw St, SE14 154 A1
Wilsmere Dr, Har. (Har.Wld) HA3 52 B7
Northolt UB5 85 E6
Wilson Av, Mitch. CR4 167 H7
Wilson Cl, S.Croy. CR2 *off Bartlett St* 202 A5
Wembley HA9 69 J7
Wilson Dr, Wem. HA9 69 J7
Wilson Gdns, Harrow HA1 67 J7
Wilson Gro, SE16 132 E2
Wilson Ho, SE7 *off Springfield Gro* 135 J6
Wilson Rd, E6 116 A3
SE5 152 B1
Chessington KT9 195 J6
Ilford IG1 80 C7
Wilsons Pl, E14 *off Salmon La* 113 J6
Wilsons Rd, W6 128 A5
Wilson St, E17 78 C5
EC2 20 C1
N21 43 G7
Wilstone Cl, Hayes UB4 102 E4
Wilthorne Gdns, Dag. RM10 *off Acre Rd* 101 H7
Wilton Av, W4 127 E5
Wilton Cl, West Dr. (Harm.) UB7 120 A6
Wilton Cres, SW1 24 B4
SW19 184 C1
Wilton Est, E8 *off Greenwood Rd* 94 D6
Wilton Gdns, W.Mol. KT8 179 G3
Wilton Gro, SW19 166 C7
New Malden KT3 183 F6
Wilton Ho, SE22 *off Albrighton Rd* 152 B3
Wilton Ms, SW1 24 C5
Wilton Par, Felt. TW13 *off High St* 160 A2
Wilton Pk Ct, SE18 *off Prince Imperial Rd* 156 D1
Wilton Pl, SW1 24 B4
Wilton Rd, N10 74 A2
SE2 138 C3
SW1 25 E6
SW19 167 H7
Barnet (Cockfos.) EN4 41 J4
Hounslow TW4 142 D3
Ilford IG1 98 E4
Wilton Row, SW1 24 B4
Wilton Sq, N1 112 A1
Wilton St, SW1 24 D5
Wilton Ter, SW1 24 B5
Wilton Vil, N1 112 A1
Wilton Way, E8 94 D6
Wiltshire Cl, NW7 55 F5
SW3 31 J1
Wiltshire Gdns, N4 75 J6
Twickenham TW2 161 J1
Wiltshire Rd, SW9 151 G3
Thornton Heath CR7 187 G3
Wiltshire Row, N1 112 A1
Wilverley Cres, N.Mal. KT3 183 E6
Wimbart Rd, SW2 151 F7
WIMBLEDON, SW19 166 B6
★ **Wimbledon (All England Tenn & Croquet Club)**, SW19 166 B4
Wimbledon Br, SW19 166 C6
★ **Wimbledon Common**, SW19 165 F4
Wimbledon Hill Rd, SW19 166 B6
WIMBLEDON PARK, SW19 166 C3
Wimbledon Pk, SW19 166 C2
Wimbledon Pk Est, SW19 166 B1
Wimbledon Pk Rd, SW18 148 C7
SW19 166 C1
Wimbledon Pk Side, SW19 166 A2
Wimbledon Rd, SW17 167 F4
Wimbledon Stadium Business Cen, SW17 167 E3
Wimbledon Sta, SW19 166 C6
★ **Wimbledon Windmill Mus**, SW19 165 H2
Wimbolt St, E2 13 H3
Wimborne Av, Chis. BR7 193 J4
Hayes UB4 102 B6
Orpington BR5 193 J4
Southall UB2 123 G4
Wimborne Cl, SE12 155 F5
Buckhurst Hill IG9 63 H2
Worcester Park KT4 197 J1
Wimborne Dr, NW9 70 A3
Pinner HA5 66 D7
Wimborne Gdns, W13 105 E6
Wimborne Ho, SW8 *off Dorset Rd* 131 F7
Wimborne Rd, N9 60 D2
N17 76 B2
Wimborne Way, Beck. BR3 189 G3
Wimbourne Ct, N1 12 B1
Wimbourne St, N1 12 B1
Wimpole Cl, Brom. BR2 191 J4
Kingston upon Thames KT1 181 J2
Wimpole Ms, W1 16 D1
Wimpole Rd, West Dr. UB7 120 A1
Wimpole St, W1 16 D3
Wimshurst Cl, Croy. CR0 201 E1
Winans Wk, SW9 151 G2
Wincanton Cres, Nthlt. UB5 85 G5
Wincanton Gdns, Ilf. IG6 80 E3
Wincanton Rd, SW18 148 C7
Winchcombe Rd, Cars. SM5 185 G7
Winchcomb Gdns, SE9 156 A3
Winchelsea Av, Bexh. DA7 139 F7
Winchelsea Cl, SW15 148 A5

Winchelsea Rd, E7 . . . . .97 G3
N17 . . . . .76 B3
NW10 . . . . .106 D1
Winchelsey Ri, S.Croy.
CR2 . . . . .202 C6
Winchendon Rd, SW6 . . . .128 C7
Teddington TW11 . . . . . .162 A4
Winchester Av, NW6 . . . . .108 B1
NW9 . . . . .70 A3
Hounslow TW5 . . . . .123 F6
Winchester Cl, E6
off Boultwood Rd 116 C6
SE17 . . . . .35 H2
Bromley BR2 . . . . .191 F3
Enfield EN1 . . . . .44 B5
Kingston upon Thames
KT2 . . . . .164 B7
Winchester Ct, E17
off Billet Rd 77 H1
Winchester Dr, Pnr. HA5 . . .66 D5
Winchester Ho, SE18
off Shooters Hill Rd . .136 A7
Winchester Ms, NW3
off Winchester Rd 91 G7
Worcester Park KT4 . . . .198 A2
Winchester Pk, Brom.
BR2 . . . . .191 F3
Winchester Pl, E8
off Kingsland High St . .94 C5
N6 . . . . .92 B1
Winchester Rd, E4 . . . . .62 C7
N6 . . . . .92 B1
N9 . . . . .60 D1
NW3 . . . . .91 G7
Bexleyheath DA7 . . . . . .158 D2
Bromley BR2 . . . . .191 F3
Feltham TW13 . . . . .161 F3
Harrow HA3 . . . . .69 H4
Hayes UB3 . . . . .121 H7
Ilford IG1 . . . . .99 G3
Twickenham TW1 . . . . . .144 E6
Winchester Sq, SE1 . . . . . . .28 B1
Winchester St, SW1 . . . . . .32 E3
W3 . . . . .126 C1
Winchester Wk, SE1 . . . . . . .28 B1
Winchet Wk, Croy. CR0 . . .189 F6
Winchfield Cl, Har. HA3 . . . .69 F6
Winchfield Ho, SW15
off Highcliffe Dr 147 F6
Winchfield Rd, SE26 . . . . .171 H5
Winchilsea Cres, W.Mol.
KT8 . . . . .179 J2
WINCHMORE HILL, N21 . . .43 F7
Winchmore Hill Rd, N14 . . .58 D1
N21 . . . . .58 D1
Winckley Cl, Har. HA3 . . . . .69 J5
Wincott St, SE11 . . . . .35 F1
Wincrofts Dr, SE9 . . . . . . .157 G4
Windall Cl, SE19 . . . . .188 D1
Windborough Rd, Cars.
SM5 . . . . .200 A7
Windermere Av, N3 . . . . . . .72 D3
NW6 . . . . .108 B1
SW19 . . . . .184 E3
Harrow HA3 . . . . .69 F7
Ruislip HA4 . . . . .66 C7
Wembley HA9 . . . . .69 F7
Windermere Cl, Orp.
BR6 . . . . .206 E3
Windermere Ct, SW13 . . . .127 F6
Wembley HA9
off Windermere Av 69 F7
Windermere Gdns, Ilf.
IG4 . . . . .80 B5
Windermere Gro,
Wem. HA9
off Windermere Av 87 F1
Windermere Ho, Islw. TW7
off Summerwood Rd .144 C5
Windermere Pt, SE15
off Ilderton Rd 133 F7
Windermere Rd, N10 . . . . . .74 B1
N19 . . . . .92 C2
SW15 . . . . .164 E4
SW16 . . . . .186 C1
W5 . . . . .125 F3
Bexleyheath DA7 . . . . . .159 J2
Croydon CR0 . . . . .202 C1
Southall UB1 . . . . .103 F5
West Wickham BR4 . . . .204 E2
Windermere Way,
West Dr. UB7
off Providence Rd 120 B1
Winders Rd, SW11 . . . . . . .149 H2
Windfield Cl, SE26 . . . . . . .171 G4
Windham Rd, Rich. TW9 . .145 J3
Winding Way, Dag.
RM8 . . . . .100 C3
Harrow HA1 . . . . .86 B4
Windlass Pl, SE8 . . . . .133 H4
Windlesham Gro, SW19 . .166 A1
Windley Cl, SE23 . . . . .171 F2
Windmill All, W4
off Windmill Rd 127 E4
Windmill Av, Sthl. UB2 . . .123 J2
Windmill Br Ho, Croy.
CR0 . . . . .202 A1
Windmill Cen, Sthl. UB2 . .123 J1
Windmill Cl, SE1 . . . . .37 J1
SE13 . . . . .154 C2
Surbiton (Long Dit.)
KT6 . . . . .195 E1
Windmill Ct, NW2 . . . . .90 B6
Windmill Dr, NW2 . . . . .90 B3
SW4 . . . . .150 C5
Keston BR2 . . . . .205 J4
Windmill Gdns, Enf. EN2 . .43 G3
Windmill Gro, Croy. CR0 . .187 J7
Windmill Hill, NW3 . . . . . . .91 F3
Enfield EN2 . . . . .43 H3
Windmill Ho, E14
off Westferry Rd 134 A4
Windmill La, E15 . . . . .96 D6
Barnet EN5 . . . . .39 F6
Bushey (Bushey Hth)
WD23 . . . . .52 B1
Greenford UB6 . . . . .103 J5
Isleworth TW7 . . . . .124 B4
Southall UB2 . . . . .123 J3
Surbiton (Long Dit.)
KT6 . . . . .181 E6
Windmill Ms, W4
off Windmill Rd 126 E4
Windmill Pas, W4 . . . . .126 E4
Windmill Ri, Kings.T. KT2 .164 B7
Windmill Rd, N18 . . . . .60 A4
SW18 . . . . .149 G6
SW19 . . . . .165 H1
W4 . . . . .126 E4
W5 . . . . .125 F4
Brentford TW8 . . . . .125 G5
Croydon CR0 . . . . .187 J7
Hampton (Hmptn H.)
TW12 . . . . .161 H5
Mitcham CR4 . . . . .186 C5
Windmill Row, SE11 . . . . . .35 E4
Windmill St, W1 . . . . .17 H2
Bushey (Bushey Hth)
WD23 . . . . .52 B1
Windmill Trd Est, Mitch.
CR4 . . . . .186 C4
Windmill Wk, SE1 . . . . .27 F2
Windmore Cl, Wem. HA0 . .86 D5
Windover Av, NW9 . . . . . . .70 D4
Windrose Cl, SE16 . . . . . . .133 G2
Windrush, N.Mal. KT3 . . . .182 B4
Windrush Cl, N17 . . . . .76 B1
SW11 *off Maysoule Rd* .149 G4
W4 . . . . .146 C1
Windrush La, SE23 . . . . . .171 G3
Windrush Rd, NW10 . . . . .106 D1
Windrush Sq, SW2
off Rushcroft Rd 151 G4
Windsock Cl, SE16 . . . . . . .133 J4
Windsor Av, E17 . . . . .77 H2
SW19 . . . . .185 F1
Edgware HA8 . . . . .54 B4
New Malden KT3 . . . . . .182 C5
Sutton SM3 . . . . .198 B3
West Molesey KT8 . . . . .179 G3
Windsor Cen, The,
SE27 . . . . .169 J4
Windsor Cl, N3 . . . . .72 B2
SE27 . . . . .169 J4
Borehamwood WD6 . . . .38 A1
Brentford TW8 . . . . .124 E6
Chislehurst BR7 . . . . . . .175 E5
Harrow HA2 . . . . .85 G3
Northwood HA6 . . . . .66 A2
Windsor Ct, N14 . . . . .42 C7
Sunbury-on-Thames
TW16
off Windsor Rd 160 A6
Windsor Cres, Har. HA2 . . .85 G4
Wembley HA9 . . . . .88 B3
Windsor Dr, Barn. EN4 . . . .41 J6
Windsor Gdns, W9 . . . . . . .108 D5
Croydon CR0
off Richmond Rd 201 E3
Hayes UB3 . . . . .121 G3
Windsor Gro, SE27 . . . . . . .169 J4
Windsor Ho, N1 . . . . .11 J1
Windsor Ms, SE6 . . . . .172 C1
SE23 . . . . .171 H1
Windsor Pk Rd, Hayes
UB3 . . . . .121 J7
Windsor Pl, SW1 . . . . .25 G6
Windsor Rd, E4
off Chivers Rd 62 B4
E7 . . . . .97 H5
E10 . . . . .96 B2
E11 . . . . .97 G1
N3 . . . . .72 B2
N7 . . . . .93 E3
N13 . . . . .59 G3
N17 . . . . .76 D2
NW2 . . . . .89 H6
W5 . . . . .105 H7
Barnet EN5 . . . . .40 A6
Bexleyheath DA6 . . . . . .158 E4
Dagenham RM8 . . . . . . .101 E3
Harrow HA3 . . . . .68 A1
Hounslow TW4 . . . . .142 B2
Ilford IG1 . . . . .99 E4
Windsor Rd, Kings.T. KT2 .163 H7
Richmond TW9 . . . . .145 J2
Southall UB2 . . . . .123 F3
Sunbury-on-Thames
TW16 . . . . .160 A6
Teddington TW11 . . . . . .162 A5
Thornton Heath CR7 . . .187 H2
Worcester Park KT4 . . . .197 G2
Windsors, The, Buck.H.
IG9 . . . . .64 B2
Windsor St, N1 . . . . .111 H1
Windsor Ter, N1 . . . . .12 A3
Windsor Wk, SE5 . . . . .152 A2
Windsor Way, W14 . . . . . . .128 A4
Windsor Wf, E9 . . . . .95 J5
Windspoint Dr, SE15
off Ethnard Rd 132 E6
Windus Rd, N16 . . . . .94 C1
Windus Wk, N16 . . . . .94 C1
Windy Ridge, Brom. BR1 .192 B1
Windy Ridge Cl, SW19 . . .166 A5
Wine Cl, E1 . . . . .113 F7
Wine Office Ct, EC4 . . . . . . .19 F3
Winery La, Kings.T. KT1 . .181 J3
Winey Cl, Chess. KT9
off Nigel Fisher Way . .195 F7
Winford Ho, E3 . . . . .95 J7
Winford Par, Sthl. UB1
off Telford Rd 103 H6
Winforton St, SE10 . . . . . .154 C1
Winfrith Rd, SW18 . . . . . . .149 F7
Wingate Cres, Croy. CR0 . .186 D6
Wingate Rd, W6 . . . . .127 H3
Ilford IG1 . . . . .99 E5
Sidcup DA14 . . . . .176 C5
Wingfield Ct, E14
off Newport Av 114 D7
Wingfield Ho, NW6
off Tollgate Gdns 6 A1
Wingfield Ms, SE15
off Wingfield St 152 D3
Wingfield Rd, E15 . . . . .96 E5
E17 . . . . .78 B5
Kingston upon Thames
KT2 . . . . .164 A6
Wingfield St, SE15 . . . . . . .152 D3
Wingfield Way, Ruis. HA4 . .84 B6
Wingford Rd, SW2 . . . . . . .150 E6
Wingmore Rd, SE24 . . . . . .151 J3
Wingrave Rd, W6 . . . . .127 J6
Wingrove Rd, SE6 . . . . . . .173 E2
Wings Cl, Sutt. SM1 . . . . .198 D4
Winifred Cl, Barn. EN5 . . . .39 F6
Winifred Gro, SW11 . . . . . .149 J4
Winifred Pl, N12
off High Rd 57 F5
Winifred Rd, SW19 . . . . . . .184 D1
Dagenham RM8 . . . . . . .101 E2
Hampton (Hmptn H.)
TW12 . . . . .161 G4
Winifred St, E16 . . . . .136 C1
Winifred Ter, E13
off Victoria Rd 115 G2
Enfield EN1 . . . . .44 C7
Winkfield Rd, E13 . . . . .115 H2
N22 . . . . .75 G1
Winkley St, E2 . . . . .112 E2
Winlaton Rd, Brom. BR1 . .172 D4
Winmill Rd, Dag. RM8 . . . .101 F3
Winn Common Rd, SE18 . .137 H6
Winnett St, W1 . . . . .17 H5
Winningales Ct, Ilf. IG5
off Vienna Cl 80 B3
Winnings Wk, Nthlt. UB5
off Arnold Rd 85 E6
Winnington Cl, N2 . . . . .73 G6
Winnington Rd, N2 . . . . . . .73 G7
Winnipeg Dr, Orp.
(Grn St Grn) BR6 . . . . . .207 J6
Winnock Rd, West Dr.
UB7 . . . . .120 A1
Winn Rd, SE12 . . . . .173 G1
Winns Av, E17 . . . . .77 H3
Winns Ms, N15 . . . . .76 B4
Winns Ter, E17 . . . . .78 A2
Winsbeach, E17 . . . . .78 D3
Winscombe Cres, W5 . . . . .105 G4
Winscombe St, N19 . . . . . . .92 B2
Winscombe Way, Stan.
HA7 . . . . .52 D5
Winsford Rd, SE6 . . . . .171 J3
Winsford Ter, N18 . . . . .60 A5
Winsham Gro, SW11 . . . . .150 A5
Winslade Rd, SW2 . . . . . . .151 E5
Winslade Way, SE6
off Rushey Grn 154 B7
Winsland Ms, W2 . . . . .15 E3
Winsland St, W2 . . . . .15 E3
Winsley St, W1 . . . . .17 F3
Winslow, SE17 . . . . .36 D4
Winslow Cl, NW10
off Neasden La N 88 E3
Pinner HA5 . . . . .66 B6
Winslow Gro, E4 . . . . .62 E2
Winslow Rd, W6 . . . . .127 J6
Winslow Way, Felt. TW13 .160 D3
Winsor Ter, E6 . . . . .116 D5
Winstanley Est, SW11 . . . .149 G3
Winstanley Rd, SW11 . . . .149 G3
Winstead Gdns, Dag.
RM10 . . . . .101 J5
Winston Av, NW9 . . . . .70 E7
Winston Cl, Har. HA3 . . . . . .52 C6
Romford RM7 . . . . .83 H4
Winston Ct, Har. HA3 . . . . .51 H7
Winston Rd, N16 . . . . .94 A4
Winston Wk, W4
off Beaconsfield Rd . . .126 D4
Winston Way, Ilf. IG1 . . . . . .99 E3
Winstre Rd, Borwd. WD6 . . .38 A1
Winter Av, E6 . . . . .116 B1
Winterborne Av, Orp.
BR6 . . . . .207 G3
Winterbourne Rd, SE6 . . . .171 J1
Dagenham RM8 . . . . . . .100 C2
Thornton Heath CR7 . . .187 G4
Winter Box Wk, Rich.
TW10 . . . . .145 J4
Winterbrook Rd, SE24 . . . .151 J6
Winterburn Cl, N11 . . . . . . .58 A6
Winterfold Cl, SW19 . . . . .166 B2
Winter Gdn Ho, WC2
off Macklin St 18 B3
Wintergreen Cl, E6
off Yarrow Cres 116 B5
Winters Rd, T.Ditt. KT7 . . . .180 E7
Winterstoke Gdns, NW7 . . .55 G5
Winterstoke Rd, SE6 . . . . .171 J1
Winterton Ho, E1 . . . . .113 F6
Winterton Pl, SW10 . . . . . . .30 D5
Winterwell Rd, SW2 . . . . .151 E5
Winthorpe Rd, SW15 . . . . .148 B4
Winthrop St, E1 . . . . .112 E5
Winthrop Wk, Wem. HA9
off Everard Way 87 H3
Winton Av, N11 . . . . .58 C7
Winton Cl, N9 . . . . .45 G7
Winton Gdns, Edg. HA8 . . .53 J7
Winton Rd, Orp. BR6 . . . . .206 E4
Winton Way, SW16 . . . . . .169 G5
Wirrall Ho, SE26
off Sydenham Hill Est . .170 D3
Wirral Wd Cl, Chis. BR7 . . .174 D6
Wisbeach Rd, Croy. CR0 . .188 A5
Wisdons Cl, Dag. RM10 . . .101 H1
Wise La, NW7 . . . . .55 H6
West Drayton UB7 . . . . .120 A4
Wiseman Ct, SE19 . . . . . . .170 B5
Wiseman Rd, E10 . . . . .96 A2
Wise Rd, E15 . . . . .114 D1
Wiseton Rd, SW17 . . . . . . .167 H1
Wishart Rd, SE3 . . . . .156 A1
Wishaw Wk, N13
off Elvendon Rd 59 E6
Wisley Rd, SW11 . . . . .150 A5
Orpington BR5 . . . . .176 A7
Wistaria Cl, Orp. BR6 . . . .207 E2
Wisteria Cl, NW7 . . . . .55 F6
Ilford IG1 . . . . .98 E5
Wisteria Rd, SE13 . . . . . . .154 D4
Witanhurst La, N6 . . . . .92 A1
Witan St, E2 . . . . .113 E3
Witcombe Pt, SE15 . . . . . .152 D1
Witham Cl, Loug. IG10 . . . . .48 B6
Witham Rd, SE20 . . . . .189 F3
W13 . . . . .124 D1
Dagenham RM10 . . . . . .101 G5
Isleworth TW7 . . . . .144 A1
Witherby Cl, Croy. CR0 . . .202 B5
Witherington Rd, N5 . . . . . .93 G5
Withers Cl, Chess. KT9
off Coppard Gdns 195 F6
Withers Mead, NW9 . . . . . .71 F1
Witherston Way, SE9 . . . . .174 D2
Withycombe Rd, SW19 . . . .148 A7
Withy Mead, E4 . . . . .62 D3
Witley Cres, Croy.
(New Adgtn) CR0 . . . . . .204 C6
Witley Gdns, Sthl. UB2 . . .123 F4
Witley Pt, SW15
off Wanborough Dr . . .165 H1
Witley Rd, N19
off Holloway Rd 92 C2
Witney Cl, Pnr. HA5 . . . . . . .51 F6
Witney Path, SE23 . . . . . . .171 G3
Wittenham Way, E4 . . . . . . .62 D3
Wittering Cl, Kings.T.
KT2 . . . . .163 G5
Wittersham Rd, Brom.
BR1 . . . . .173 F5
Wivenhoe Cl, SE15 . . . . . .152 E3
Wivenhoe Ct, Houns.
TW3 . . . . .143 F4
Wivenhoe Rd, Bark. IG11 . .118 A2
Wiverton Rd, SE26 . . . . . . .171 F6
Wixom Ho, SE3
off Romero Sq 155 J4
Wix Rd, Dag. RM9 . . . . . . .118 D1
Wixs La, SW4 . . . . .150 B4
Woburn Cl, SE28
off Summerton Way . .118 D6
SW19 . . . . .167 F6
Woburn Ct, SE16
off Masters Dr 133 E5

Woburn Pl, WC1 **9** J5
Woburn Rd, Cars. SM5 **199** H1
Croydon CR0 **201** J1
Woburn Sq, WC1 **9** J6
Woburn Wk, WC1 **9** J4
Wodeham Gdns, E1 **21** J1
Wodehouse Av, SE5 **152** C1
Woffington Cl, Kings.T. KT1 **181** F1
Woking Cl, SW15 **147** F4
Woldham Pl, Brom. BR2 **191** J4
Woldham Rd, Brom. BR2 **191** J4
Wolds Dr, Orp. BR6 **206** D4
Wolfe Cl, Brom. BR2 **191** G6
Hayes UB4
off Ayles Rd **102** B3
Wolfe Cres, SE7 **136** A5
SE16 **133** G2
Wolferton Rd, E12 **98** C4
Wolffe Gdns, E15 **97** F6
Wolffram Cl, SE13 **154** E5
Wolfington Rd, SE27 **169** H4
Wolftencroft Cl, SW11 **149** G3
Wollaston Cl, SE1 **35** J1
Wolmer Cl, Edg. HA8 **54** B4
Wolmer Gdns, Edg. HA8 **54** A3
Wolseley Av, SW19 **166** D2
Wolseley Gdns, W4 **126** B6
Wolseley Rd, E7 **97** H7
N8 **74** D6
N22 **75** F1
W4 **126** C4
Harrow HA3 **68** B3
Mitcham CR4 **186** A7
Wolseley St, SE1 **29** G4
Wolsey Av, E6 **116** D3
E17 **77** J3
Thames Ditton KT7 **180** C5
Wolsey Cl, SW20 **165** H7
Hounslow TW3 **143** J4
Kingston upon Thames KT2 **182** B1
Southall UB2 **123** J3
Worcester Park KT4 **197** G4
Wolsey Cres, Mord. SM4 **184** B7
Wolsey Dr, Kings.T. KT2 **163** H5
Wolsey Gdns, Ilf. IG6 **65** F6
Wolsey Gro, Edg. HA8 **54** D7
Wolsey Ms, NW5 **92** C6
Orpington BR6 **207** J5
Wolsey Rd, N1 **94** A5
East Molesey KT8 **180** A4
Enfield EN1 **45** E2
Hampton (Hmptn H.) TW12 **161** H6
Wolsey St, E1
off Sidney St **113** F5
Wolsey Way, Chess. KT9 **196** A5
Wolstonbury, N12 **56** D5
Wolvercote Rd, SE2 **138** D2
Wolverley St, E2
off Bethnal Grn Rd **112** E3
Wolverton, SE17 **36** C3
Wolverton Av, Kings.T. KT2 **182** A1
Wolverton Gdns, W5 **105** J7
W6 **128** A4
Wolverton Rd, Stan. HA7 **53** E6
Wolverton Way, N14 **42** C5
Wolves La, N13 **59** G7
N22 **59** G7
Womersley Rd, N8 **75** F6
Wonford Cl, Kings.T. KT2 **183** E1
Wontner Cl, N1
off Greenman St **93** J7
Wontner Rd, SW17 **167** J2
Woodall Cl, E14
off Lawless St **114** B7
Chessington KT9 **195** G7
Woodall Rd, Enf. EN3 **45** G6
Woodbank Rd, Brom. BR1 **173** F3
Woodbastwick Rd, SE26 **171** G5
Woodberry Av, N21 **59** G2
Harrow HA2 **67** H4
Woodberry Cl, NW7 **56** A7
Sunbury-on-Thames TW16
off Ashridge Way **160** A6
Woodberry Cres, N10 **74** B3
Woodberry Down, N4 **75** J7
Woodberry Down Est, N4 **75** J7
Woodberry Gdns, N12 **57** F6
Woodberry Gro, N4 **75** J7
N12 **57** F6
Woodberry Way, E4 **62** C1
N12 **57** F6
Woodbine Cl, Twick. TW2 **162** A2
Woodbine Gro, SE20 **171** E7
Woodbine La, Wor.Pk. KT4 **197** H3
Woodbine Pl, E11 **79** G6
Woodbine Rd, Sid. DA15 **175** H1
Woodbines Av, Kings.T. KT1 **181** G3
Woodbine Ter, E9
off Morning La **95** F6
Woodborough Rd, SW15 **147** H4
Woodbourne Av, SW16 **168** D3
Woodbourne Cl, SW16
off Woodbourne Av **168** E3
Woodbourne Dr, Esher (Clay.) KT10 **194** C6
Woodbourne Gdns, Wall. SM6 **200** B7
Woodbridge Cl, N7 **93** F2
NW2 **89** G3
Woodbridge Ct, Wdf.Grn. IG8 **64** B7
Woodbridge Rd, Bark. IG11 **99** J5
Woodbridge St, EC1 **11** G5
Woodbrook Rd, SE2 **138** A6
Woodburn Cl, NW4 **72** A5
Woodbury Cl, E11 **79** H4
Croydon CR0 **202** C2
Woodbury Gdns, SE12 **173** H3
Woodbury Hill, Loug. IG10 **48** B3
Woodbury Hollow, Loug. IG10 **48** B2
Woodbury Pk Rd, W13 **104** E4
Woodbury Rd, E17 **78** B4
Woodbury St, SW17 **167** H5
Woodchester Sq, W2 **14** A1
Woodchurch Cl, Sid. DA14 **175** G3
Woodchurch Dr, Brom. BR1 **174** A7
Woodchurch Rd, NW6 **90** D7
Wood Cl, E2 **13** H5
NW9 **70** D7
Harrow HA1 **68** A7
Woodclyffe Dr, Chis. BR7 **192** D2
Woodcock Ct, Har. HA3 **69** H7
Woodcock Dell Av, Har. HA3 **69** G7
Woodcock Hill, Har. HA3 **69** G7
Woodcocks, E16 **115** J5
Woodcombe Cres, SE23 **171** F1
Woodcote Av, NW7 **55** J6
Thornton Heath CR7 **187** H4
Wallington SM6 **200** B7
Woodcote Cl, Enf. EN3 **45** F6
Kingston upon Thames KT2 **163** J5
Woodcote Dr, Orp. BR6 **207** G1
Woodcote Ms, Loug. IG10 **48** A7
Wallington SM6 **200** B6
Woodcote Pl, SE27 **169** H5
Woodcote Rd, E11 **79** G7
Wallington SM6 **200** B6
Woodcott Ho, SW15
off Ellisfield Dr **147** G7
Wood Ct, W12
off Heathstan Rd **107** G6
Woodcroft, N21 **59** F1
SE9 **174** C3
Greenford UB6 **86** D6
Woodcroft Av, NW7 **55** E7
Stanmore HA7 **68** C1
Woodcroft Ms, SE8
off Croft St **133** H4
Woodcroft Rd, Th.Hth. CR7 **187** H5
Wood Dr, Chis. BR7 **174** B6
Woodedge Cl, E4 **63** F1
Woodend, SE19 **169** J6
Sutton SM1 **199** F2
Wood End Av, Har. HA2 **85** H4
Wood End Cl, Nthlt. UB5 **86** A5
Woodend Gdns, Enf. EN2 **42** E4
Wood End Gdns, Nthlt. UB5 **85** J5
Wood End La, Nthlt. UB5 **85** H6
Woodend Rd, E17 **78** C2
Wood End Rd, Har. HA1 **86** A4
Wood End Way, Nthlt. UB5 **85** J5
Wooder Gdns, E7 **97** F4
Wooderson Cl, SE25 **188** B4
Woodfall Av, Barn. EN5 **40** C5
Woodfall Rd, N4 **93** G1
Woodfall St, SW3 **31** J4
Woodfarrs, SE5 **152** A4
Wood Fld, NW3
off Parkhill Rd **91** J5
Woodfield Av, NW9 **71** E4
SW16 **168** D3
W5 **105** F4
Carshalton SM5 **200** A6
Wembley HA0 **87** F3
Woodfield Cl, SE19 **169** J7
Enfield EN1 **44** B4
Woodfield Cres, W5 **105** F4
Woodfield Dr, Barn. (E.Barn.) EN4 **58** A1
Woodfield Gdns, W9
off Woodfield Rd **108** C5
New Malden KT3 **183** F5
Woodfield Gro, SW16 **168** D3
Woodfield La, SW16 **168** D3
Woodfield Pl, W9 **108** C4
Woodfield Rd, W5 **105** F4
W9 **108** C5
Hounslow TW4 **142** B2
Thames Ditton KT7 **194** C2
Woodfield Way, N11 **58** D7
WOODFORD, Wdf.Grn. IG8 **63** H6
Woodford Av, Ilf. IG2, IG4 **80** C5
Woodford Green IG8 **80** A3
WOODFORD BRIDGE, Wdf.Grn. IG8 **64** C7
Woodford Br Rd, Ilf. IG4 **80** A3
Woodford Ct, W12
off Shepherds Bush Grn **128** A2
Woodford Cres, Pnr. HA5 **66** B2
WOODFORD GREEN, IG8 **63** F4
Woodford New Rd, E17 **78** E4
E18 **79** E1
Woodford Green IG8 **79** E1
Woodford Pl, Wem. HA9 **87** H1
Woodford Rd, E7 **97** H4
E18 **79** G4
WOODFORD WELLS, Wdf.Grn. IG8 **63** H4
Woodgate Av, Chess. KT9 **195** G5
Woodgate Cres, Nthwd. HA6 **50** A6
Woodgate Dr, SW16 **168** D7
Woodger Rd, W12
off Goldhawk Rd **127** J2
Woodget Cl, E6
off Remington Rd **116** B6
Woodgrange Av, N12 **57** G6
W5 **126** A1
Enfield EN1 **44** D6
Harrow HA3 **69** F5
Woodgrange Cl, Har. HA3 **69** G5
Woodgrange Gdns, Enf. EN1 **44** D6
Woodgrange Rd, E7 **97** H4
Woodgrange Ter, Enf. EN1 **44** D6
WOOD GREEN, N22 **74** E1
Wood Grn Shop City, N22 **75** G2
Woodhall, NW1 **9** F4
Woodhall Av, SE21 **170** C3
Pinner HA5 **66** E2
Woodhall Dr, SE21 **170** C3
Pinner HA5 **66** D1
Woodhall Gate, Pnr. HA5 **50** D7
Woodhall Ho, SW18
off Fitzhugh Gro **149** G6
Woodhall La, Wat. WD19 **50** D4
Woodhall Rd, Pnr. HA5 **50** D7
Woodham Ct, E18 **79** F4
Woodham Rd, SE6 **172** C3
Woodhatch Cl, E6
off Remington Rd **116** B6
Woodhaven Gdns, Ilf. IG6
off Brandville Gdns **81** F4
Woodhayes Rd, SW19 **165** J7
Woodhead Dr, Orp. BR6
off Sherlies Av **207** H2
Woodheyes Rd, NW10 **88** D5
Woodhill, SE18 **136** B4
Woodhill Cres, Har. HA3 **69** G6
Wood Ho, SW17
off Laurel Cl **167** H5
Woodhouse Av, Grnf. (Perivale) UB6 **104** C2
Woodhouse Cl, SE22 **152** D4
Greenford (Perivale) UB6 **104** C2
Hayes UB3 **121** H3
Woodhouse Eaves, Nthwd. HA6 **50** A5
Woodhouse Gro, E12 **98** B6
Woodhouse Rd, E11 **97** F3
N12 **57** G6
Woodhurst Av, Orp. BR5 **193** F6
Woodhurst Rd, SE2 **138** A5
W3 **106** C7
Woodington Cl, SE9 **156** D6
Woodknoll Dr, Chis. BR7 **192** C1
Woodland App, Grnf. UB6 **86** D6
Woodland Cl, NW9 **70** C6
SE19 **170** B6
Epsom KT19 **197** E6
Woodford Green IG8 **63** H3
Woodland Cres, SE10 **134** E6
SE16 **133** G2
Woodland Gdns, N10 **74** B5
Isleworth TW7 **144** B2
Woodland Gro, SE10 **134** E5
Woodland Hts, SE3
off Vanbrugh Hill **135** F6
Woodland Hill, SE19 **170** B6
Woodland Ms, SW16 **169** E2
Woodland Ri, N10 **74** B4
Greenford UB6 **86** D6
Woodland Rd, E4 **62** C1
N11 **58** B5
SE19 **170** B5
Loughton IG10 **48** B3
Woodland Rd, Th.Hth. CR7 **187** G4
WOODLANDS, Islw. TW7 **144** B2
Woodlands, NW11 **72** B6
SW20 **183** J4
Harrow HA2 **67** G4
Woodlands, The, N14 **58** B1
SE13 **154** D7
SE19 **169** J7
Beckenham BR3 **190** C1
Isleworth TW7 **144** C2
Woodlands Av, E11 **97** H1
N3 **57** F7
W3 **126** B1
New Malden KT3 **182** C1
Romford RM6 **82** E6
Ruislip HA4 **84** C1
Sidcup DA15 **175** H1
Worcester Park KT4 **197** F2
Woodlands Cl, NW11 **72** B5
Borehamwood WD6 **38** B4
Bromley BR1 **192** C2
Esher (Clay.) KT10 **194** C7
Woodlands Dr, Stan. HA7 **52** C6
Sunbury-on-Thames TW16 **178** C2
Woodlands Gro, Islw. TW7 **144** B2
Woodlands Pk, Bex. DA5 **177** J4
Woodlands Pk Rd, N15 **75** H5
SE10 **134** E6
Woodlands Rd, E11 **96** E2
E17 **78** C3
N9 **61** F1
SW13 **147** F3
Bexleyheath DA7 **159** E3
Bromley BR1 **192** B2
Enfield EN2 **44** A1
Harrow HA1 **68** C5
Ilford IG1 **99** F3
Isleworth TW7 **144** B2
Southall UB1 **122** D1
Surbiton KT6 **181** G7
Woodlands St, SE13 **154** D7
Woodland St, E8
off Dalston La **94** C6
Woodlands Way, SW15 **148** C5
Woodland Ter, SE7 **136** B4
Woodland Wk, NW3 **91** H5
SE10
off Woodland Gro **135** E5
Bromley BR1 **172** E4
Epsom KT19 **196** A6
Woodland Way, N21 **59** G2
NW7 **55** E6
SE2 **138** D4
Croydon CR0 **203** H1
Mitcham CR4 **168** A7
Morden SM4 **184** C4
Orpington BR5 **193** F4
Surbiton KT5 **196** B2
West Wickham BR4 **204** B4
Woodford Green IG8 **63** H3
Wood La, N6 **74** B6
NW9 **70** E7
W12 **107** J6
Dagenham RM8, RM9, RM10 **100** C4
Isleworth TW7 **124** C7
Stanmore HA7 **52** D3
Woodford Green IG8 **63** F5
Woodlawn Cl, SW15 **148** C5
Woodlawn Cres, Twick. TW2 **161** H2
Woodlawn Dr, Felt. TW13 **160** D2
Woodlawn Rd, SW6 **128** A7
Woodlea Dr, Brom. BR2 **191** E5
Woodlea Rd, N16 **94** B3
Woodleigh, E18
off Churchfields **79** G1
Woodleigh Av, N12 **57** H6
Woodleigh Gdns, SW16 **169** E3
Woodley Cl, SW17
off Arnold Rd **167** J7
Woodley La, Cars. SM5 **199** G3
Wood Lo Gdns, Brom. BR1 **174** B7
Wood Lo La, W.Wick. BR4 **204** C3
Woodman La, E4 **46** E5
Woodman Ms, Rich. TW9 **146** B1
Woodman Path, Ilf. IG6 **65** H6
Woodmans Gro, NW10 **89** F5
Woodmans Ms, W12 **107** H5
Woodmansterne Rd, SW16 **186** D1
Woodman St, E16 **136** D1
Woodmere, SE9 **174** C1
Woodmere Av, Croy. CR0 **189** G7
Woodmere Cl, SW11
off Lavender Hill **150** A3
Croydon CR0 **189** G7
Woodmere Gdns, Croy. CR0 **189** G7
Woodmere Way, Beck. BR3 **190** D5

Woodmill Rd, E5 *off Mount Pleasant Hill* **95** F2
Woodnook Rd, SW16 **168** B5
Woodpecker Cl, N9 **44** E6
Bushey WD23 **51** J1
Harrow HA3 **68** C1
Woodpecker Ms, SE13 *off Mercator Rd* **154** D4
Woodpecker Rd, SE14 **133** H6
SE28 **118** C7
Woodquest Av, SE24 **151** J5
Wood Retreat, SE18 **137** G7
Wood Ride, Barn. EN4 **41** G1
Orpington BR5 **193** G4
Woodridge Cl, Enf. EN2 **43** G1
Woodridings Av, Pnr. HA5 **67** F1
Woodridings Cl, Pnr. HA5 **51** E7
Woodriffe Rd, E11 **78** D7
Wood Ri, Pnr. HA5 **66** A5
Wood Rd, NW10 **88** C7
Woodrow, SE18 **136** C4
Woodrow Cl, Grnf. (Perivale) UB6 **87** E7
Woodrow Ct, N17 **61** E7
Woodrush Cl, SE14 *off Southerngate Way* **133** H7
Woodrush Way, Rom. RM6 **82** D4
Woods, The, Nthwd. HA6 **50** A5
Wood's Bldgs, E1 *off Whitechapel Rd* **112** E5
Woodseer St, E1 **21** G1
Woodsford, SE17 **36** B4
Woodsford Sq, W14 **128** B2
Woodshire Rd, Dag. RM10 **101** H3
WOODSIDE, SE25 **188** D6
Woodside, NW11 **72** D5
SW19 **166** C6
Buckhurst Hill IG9 **63** J2
Woodside Av, N6 **73** J5
N10 **73** J5
N12 **57** F4
SE25 **188** E6
Chislehurst BR7 **175** F5
Esher KT10 **180** B7
Wembley HA0 **105** H1
Woodside Cl, Stan. HA7 **52** E5
Surbiton KT5 **182** C7
Wembley HA0 **105** H1
Woodside Ct, N12 **57** E4
Woodside Ct Rd, Croy. CR0 **188** D7
Woodside Cres, Sid. DA15 **175** H3
Woodside End, Wem. HA0 **105** H1
Woodside Gdns, E4 **62** B5
N17 **76** B2
Woodside Gra Rd, N12 **57** E4
Woodside Grn, SE25 **188** E6
Woodside Gro, N12 **57** F3
Woodside La, N12 **57** E3
Bexley DA5 **158** D6
Woodside Ms, SE22 *off Heber Rd* **152** C6
Woodside Pk, SE25 **188** D5
Woodside Pk Av, E17 **78** D4
Woodside Pk Rd, N12 **57** E4
Woodside Pl, Wem. HA0 **105** H1
Woodside Rd, E13 **115** J4
N22 **59** F7
SE25 **188** E6
Bromley BR1 **192** B5
Kingston upon Thames KT2 **163** H7
New Malden KT3 **182** D2
Sidcup DA15 **175** H3
Sutton SM1 **199** F3
Woodford Green IG8 **63** G4
Woodside Way, Croy. CR0 **189** E6
Mitcham CR4 **186** B1
Woods Ms, W1 **16** A5
Woodsome Rd, NW5 **92** A3
Woods Pl, SE1 **28** E6
Woodspring Rd, SW19 **166** B2
Woods Rd, SE15 **152** E1
Woodstead Gro, Edg. HA8 **53** H6
Woodstock, The, Sutt. SM3 **184** B7
Woodstock Av, NW11 **72** B7
W13 **124** D3
Isleworth TW7 **144** D5
Southall UB1 **103** F3
Sutton SM3 **184** C7
Woodstock Cl, Bex. DA5 **177** F1
Stanmore HA7 **69** H2
Woodstock Ct, SE12 **155** G6
Woodstock Cres, N9 **44** E6
Woodstock Gdns, Beck. BR3 **190** B1
Ilford IG3 **100** A2
Woodstock Gro, W12 **128** A2
Woodstock La N, Surb. (Long Dit.) KT6 **195** F2
Woodstock La S, Chess. KT9 **195** F4
Esher (Clay.) KT10 **194** E5
Woodstock Ms, W1 **16** C2
Woodstock Ri, Sutt. SM3 **184** C7
Woodstock Rd, E7 **97** J7
E17 **78** D2
N4 **93** G1
NW11 **72** C7
W4 **127** E3
Woodstock Rd, Carshalton SM5 **200** A5
Croydon CR0 **202** A3
Wembley HA0 **87** J7
Woodstock St, W1 **16** D4
Woodstock Ter, E14 **114** B7
Woodstock Way, Mitch. CR4 **186** B2
Woodstone Av, Epsom KT17 **197** G5
Wood St, E17 **78** C3
EC2 **20** A4
W4 **126** E5
Barnet EN5 **39** J4
Kingston upon Thames KT1 **181** G1
Mitcham CR4 **186** A7
Woodsyre, SE26 **170** C4
Woodthorpe Rd, SW15 **147** H4
Woodtree Cl, NW4 **71** J2
Wood Vale, N10 **74** C5
SE23 **170** E1
Woodvale Av, SE25 **188** C3
Wood Vale Est, SE23 **153** F6
Woodvale Est, SE27 **169** J5
Woodvale Wk, SE27 **169** J5
Woodvale Way, NW11 *off The Vale* **90** A3
Woodview Av, E4 **62** C4
Woodview Cl, N4 **75** H7
SW15 **164** D4
Orpington BR6 **207** F2
Woodville, SE3 **155** H1
Woodville Cl, SE12 **155** G5
Teddington TW11 **162** D4
Woodville Gdns, NW11 **72** A7
W5 **105** H6
Ilford IG6 **80** E3
Woodville Gro, Well. DA16 **158** A3
Woodville Rd, E11 **97** F1
E17 **77** H4
E18 **79** H2
N16 **94** B5
NW6 **108** C2
NW11 **72** A7
W5 **105** G6
Barnet EN5 **40** E3
Morden SM4 **184** D4
Richmond TW10 **163** E3
Thornton Heath CR7 **187** J4
Woodville St, SE18 **136** B4
Woodward Av, NW4 **71** G5
Woodward Cl, Esher (Clay.) KT10 **194** C6
Woodwarde Rd, SE22 **152** B6
Woodward Gdns, Dag. RM9 *off Woodward Rd* **100** C7
Stanmore HA7 **52** C7
Woodward Rd, Dag. RM9 **100** B7
Wood Way, Orp. BR6 **206** D2
Woodway Cres, Har. HA1 **68** D6
Woodwell St, SW18 *off Huguenot Pl* **149** F5
Wood Wf, SE10 **134** B6
Wood Wf Apts, SE10 *off Horseferry Pl* **134** C6
Woodyard Cl, NW5 *off Gillies St* **92** A5
Woodyard La, SE21 **152** B7
Woodyates Rd, SE12 **155** G6
Woolacombe Rd, SE3 **155** J1
Woolacombe Way, Hayes UB3 **121** H4
Wooler St, SE17 **36** B4
Woolf Cl, SE28 **138** B1
Woolf Ms, WC1 **9** J5
Woollaston Rd, N4 **75** H6
Woolmead Av, NW9 **71** G7
Woolmer Gdns, N18 **60** D6
Woolmer Rd, N18 **60** D5
Woolmore St, E14 **114** C7
Woolneigh St, SW6 **148** E3
Woolridge Way, E9 *off Loddiges Rd* **95** F7
Wool Rd, SW20 **165** H6
Woolstaplers Way, SE16 **29** H6
Woolston Cl, E17 *off Riverhead Cl* **77** G2
Woolstone Rd, SE23 **171** H2
WOOLWICH, SE18 **136** D5
Woolwich Ch St, SE18 **136** B3
★ **Woolwich Common**, SE18 **136** C7
Woolwich Common, SE18 **136** D6
Woolwich Dockyard Ind Est, SE18 *off Woolwich Ch St* **136** B3
Woolwich Ferry Pier, E16 **136** D2
Woolwich Foot Tunnel, E16 **136** D2
SE18 **136** D2
Woolwich Garrison, SE18 **136** B6
Woolwich High St, SE18 **136** D3
Woolwich Manor Way, E6 **116** C4
E16 **117** E7
Woolwich Mkt, SE18 **136** E4
Woolwich New Rd, SE18 **136** D5
Woolwich Rd, SE2 **138** D6
SE7 **135** G5
SE10 **135** F5
Belvedere DA17 **138** D6
Bexleyheath DA6, DA7 **159** G4
Woolwich Trade Pk, SE28 **137** G3
Wooster Gdns, E14 **114** D6
Wooster Ms, Har. HA2 *off Fairfield Dr* **67** J3
Wooster Pl, SE1 **36** C1
Wootton Gro, N3 **72** D1
Wootton St, SE1 **27** F3
Worbeck Rd, SE20 **189** E2
Worcester Av, N17 **60** D7
Worcester Cl, NW2 *off Newfield Ri* **89** H3
Croydon CR0 **203** J2
Mitcham CR4 **186** A2
Worcester Cres, NW7 **54** E3
Woodford Green IG8 **63** H5
Worcester Dr, W4 **127** E2
Worcester Gdns, SW11 *off Grandison Rd* **149** J5
Greenford UB6 **85** J6
Ilford IG1 **80** B7
Worcester Park KT4 **197** E3
Worcester Ho, SE11 *off Kennington Rd* **27** E6
Worcester Ms, NW6 *off Dresden Cl* **91** E6
WORCESTER PARK, KT4 **197** F2
Worcester Pk Rd, Wor.Pk. KT4 **196** C3
Worcester Rd, E12 **98** C4
E17 **77** G2
SW19 **166** C5
Sutton SM2 **199** E6
Wordsworth Av, E12 **98** B7
E18 **79** F3
Greenford UB6 **104** A2
Wordsworth Dr, Sutt. SM3 **197** J4
Wordsworth Gdns, Borwd. WD6 **38** A5
Wordsworth Pl, NW5 *off Southampton Rd* **91** J5
Wordsworth Rd, N16 **94** B4
SE1 **37** F2
SE20 **171** G7
Hampton TW12 **161** F4
Wallington SM6 **200** C6
Welling DA16 **157** H1
Wordsworth Wk, NW11 **72** C4
Wordsworth Way, West Dr. UB7 **120** B4
Worfield St, SW11 **129** H7
Worgan St, SE11 **34** C3
SE16 **133** G3
Worland Rd, E15 **97** E7
WORLD'S END, Enf. EN2 **43** G3
Worlds End La, N21 **43** F5
Enfield EN2 **43** F5
Orpington BR6 **207** J6
World's End Pas, SW10 **30** E7
World's End Pl, SW10 *off King's Rd* **30** D7
Worleys Dr, Orp. BR6 **207** G4
Worlidge St, W6 **127** J5
Worlingham Rd, SE22 **152** C4
Wormholt Rd, W12 **107** G7
Wormwood St, EC2 **20** D3
Wornington Rd, W10 **108** B5
Woronzow Rd, NW8 **109** G1
Worple Av, SW19 **166** A7
Isleworth TW7 **144** D5
Worple Cl, Har. HA2 **85** F1
Worple Rd, SW19 **166** B7
SW20 **183** J2
Isleworth TW7 **144** D4
Worple Rd Ms, SW19 **166** C6
Worple St, SW14 **146** D3
Worple Way, Har. HA2 **85** F1
Richmond TW10 **145** H5
Worship St, EC2 **12** C6
Worslade Rd, SW17 **167** G4
Worsley Br Rd, SE26 **171** J4
Beckenham BR3 **171** J5
Worsley Gra, Chis. BR7 **175** F6
Worsley Gro, E5 **94** D4
Worsley Rd, E11 **96** E4
Worsopp Dr, SW4 **150** C5
Worth Cl, Orp. BR6 **207** H4
Worthfield Cl, Epsom KT19 **196** D7
Worth Gro, SE17 **36** B4
Worthing Cl, E15 *off Mitre Rd* **115** E1
Worthing Rd, Houns. TW5 **123** F6
Worthington Cl, Mitch. CR4 **186** B3
Worthington Rd, Surb. KT6 **195** J1
Worthy Down Ct, SE18 *off Prince Imperial Rd* **156** D1
Wortley Rd, E6 **98** A7
Croydon CR0 **187** G7
Worton Gdns, Islw. TW7 **144** A2
Worton Hall Ind Est, Islw. TW7 **144** B4
Worton Rd, Islw. TW7 **144** B3
Worton Way, Houns. TW3 **144** A2
Isleworth TW7 **143** J1
Wotton Rd, NW2 **89** J4
SE8 **133** J6
Wouldham Rd, E16 **115** F6
Wragby Rd, E11 **97** E3
Wrampling Pl, N9 **60** D1
Wrangthorn Wk, Croy. CR0 *off Fernleigh Cl* **201** G4
Wray Av, Ilf. IG5 **80** D3
Wray Cres, N4 **93** E2
Wrayfield Rd, Sutt. SM3 **198** A3
Wraysbury Cl, Houns. TW4 **143** E5
Wrekin Rd, SE18 **137** F7
Wren Av, NW2 **89** J5
Southall UB2 **123** F4
Wren Cl, E16 *off Ibbotson Av* **115** F6
N9 *off Chaffinch Cl* **61** G1
Wren Cres, Bushey WD23 **51** J1
Wren Dr, West Dr. UB7 **120** A3
Wren Gdns, Dag. RM9 **100** D5
Wren Landing, E14 *off Cabot Sq* **134** A1
Wren Ms, SE13 *off Lee High Rd* **154** E4
Wren Path, SE28 **137** G3
Wren Rd, SE5 **152** A1
Dagenham RM9 **100** D5
Sidcup DA14 **176** C4
Wren St, WC1 **10** D5
Wren Ter, Ilf. IG5 *off Tiptree Cres* **80** D3
Wrentham Av, NW10 **108** A2
Wrenthorpe Rd, Brom. BR1 **172** E4
Wrenwood Way, Pnr. HA5 **66** B4
Wrestlers Ct, EC3 *off Camomile St* **20** D3
Wrexham Rd, E3 **114** A2
Wricklemarsh Rd, SE3 **155** H1
Wrigglesworth St, SE14 **133** G7
Wright Rd, N1 *off Burder Cl* **94** B6
Hounslow TW5 **122** C7
Wrights All, SW19 **165** J6
Wrights Cl, SE13 **154** D4
Dagenham RM10 **101** H3
Wrights Grn, SW4 *off Nelson's Row* **150** D4
Wrights La, W8 **22** A5
Wrights Pl, NW10 *off Mitchell Way* **88** C6
Wrights Rd, E3 **113** J2
SE25 **188** B3
Wrights Row, Wall. SM6 **200** B4
Wrights Wk, SW14 **146** D3
Wrigley Cl, E4 **62** D5
Wrotham Rd, NW1 *off Agar Pl* **92** C7
W13 *off Mattock La* **125** F1
Barnet EN5 **40** B2
Welling DA16 **158** C1
Wroths Path, Loug. IG10 **48** C1
Wrottesley Rd, NW10 **107** G2
SE18 **137** F6
Wroughton Rd, SW11 **149** J6
Wroughton Ter, NW4 **71** J4
Wroxall Rd, Dag. RM9 **100** C6
Wroxham Gdns, N11 **58** C7
Wroxham Rd, SE28 **118** D7
Wroxham Way, Ilf. IG6 **81** E1
Wroxton Rd, SE15 **153** E2
WRYTHE, THE, Cars. SM5 **199** J2
Wrythe Grn, Cars. SM5 *off Wrythe Grn Rd* **199** J3
Wrythe Grn Rd, Cars. SM5 **199** J3

Wrythe La, Cars. SM5 .... **199** F1
Wulfstan St, W12 .... **107** F6
Wyatt Cl, SE16 .... **133** J2
Feltham TW13 .... **160** C1
Hayes UB4 .... **102** A5
Wyatt Dr, SW13 .... **127** J7
Wyatt Pk Rd, SW2 .... **169** E2
Wyatt Pt, SE28
off Erebus Dr **137** F2
Wyatt Rd, E7 .... **97** G6
N5 .... **93** J3
Wyatts La, E17 .... **78** C3
Wybert St, NW1 .... **9** E5
Wyborne Way, NW10 .... **88** C7
Wyburn Av, Barn. EN5 .... **40** C3
Wyche Gro, S.Croy.
CR2 .... **201** J7
Wych Elm Pas, Kings.T.
KT2 .... **163** J7
Wycherley Cl, SE3 .... **135** F7
Wycherley Cres, Barn.
(New Barn.) EN5 .... **40** E6
Wychwood Av, Edg.
HA8 .... **53** G6
Thornton Heath CR7 .... **187** J3
Wychwood Cl, Edg. HA8 .... **53** G6
Sunbury-on-Thames
TW16 .... **160** A6
Wychwood End, N6 .... **74** C7
Wychwood Gdns, Ilf. IG5 .... **80** C4
Wychwood Way, SE19
off Roman Ri **170** A6
Wyclif Ct, EC1
off Wyclif St **11** G4
Wycliffe Cl, Well. DA16 .... **157** J1
Wycliffe Rd, SW11 .... **150** A2
SW19 .... **167** E6
Wyclif St, EC1 .... **11** G4
Wycombe Gdns, NW11 .... **90** D2
Wycombe Pl, SW18 .... **149** F6
Wycombe Rd, N17 .... **76** D1
Ilford IG2 .... **80** C5
Wembley HA0 .... **106** A1
Wycombe Sq, W8 .... **128** C1
Wydehurst Rd, Croy.
CR0 .... **188** D7
Wydell Cl, Mord. SM4 .... **183** J6
Wydeville Manor Rd,
SE12 .... **173** H4
Wye Cl, Orp. BR6 .... **193** J7
Wyemead Cres, E4 .... **62** E2
Wye St, SW11 .... **149** G2
Wyevale Cl, Pnr. HA5 .... **66** A3
Wyfields, Ilf. IG5
off Ravensbourne Gdns **81** E1
Wyfold Ho, SE2
off Wolvercote Rd **138** D2
Wyfold Rd, SW6 .... **128** B7
Wyhill Wk, Dag. RM10 .... **101** J6
Wyke Cl, Islw. TW7 .... **124** C6
Wyke Gdns, W7 .... **124** D3
Wykeham Av, Dag. RM9 .... **100** C6
Wykeham Cl, West Dr.
(Sipson) UB7 .... **120** D5
Wykeham Grn, Dag.
RM9 .... **100** C6
Wykeham Hill, Wem.
HA9 .... **87** J1
Wykeham Ri, N20 .... **56** B1
Wykeham Rd, NW4 .... **71** J5
Harrow HA3 .... **68** E4
Wyke Rd, E3 .... **96** A7
SW20 .... **183** J2
Wyldes Cl, NW11
off Hampstead Way **91** F1
Wyldfield Gdns, N9 .... **60** C2
Wyld Way, Wem. HA9 .... **88** B6
Wyleu St, SE23 .... **153** H7
Wylie Rd, Sthl. UB2 .... **123** G3
Wyllen Cl, E1 .... **113** F4
Wylo Dr, Barn. EN5 .... **39** G6
Wymering Rd, W9 .... **108** D3
Wymond St, SW15 .... **147** J3
Wynan Rd, E14 .... **134** B5
Wynash Gdns, Cars.
SM5 .... **199** H5
Wynaud Ct, N22 .... **59** F6
Wyncham Av, Sid. DA15 .... **175** H1
Wynchgate, N14 .... **58** D1
N21 .... **58** E1
Harrow HA3 .... **52** B7
Wyncroft Cl, Brom. BR1 .... **192** C3
Wyndale Av, NW9 .... **70** A6
Wyndcliff Rd, SE7 .... **135** H6
Wyndcroft Cl, Enf. EN2 .... **43** H3
Wyndham Cl,
Orp. BR6 .... **207** F1
Sutton SM2 .... **198** D7
Wyndham Cres, N19 .... **92** C3
Hounslow TW4 .... **143** G6
Wyndham Est, SE5 .... **35** J7
Wyndham Ms, W1 .... **15** J2
Wyndham Pl, W1 .... **15** J2
Wyndham Rd, E6 .... **98** A7
SE5 .... **131** H7
W13 .... **124** E3
Wyndham Rd, Barnet EN4 .... **57** J1
Kingston upon Thames
KT2 .... **163** J7
Wyndham St, W1 .... **15** J1
Wyndham Yd, W1 .... **15** J2
Wyndhurst Cl, S.Croy.
CR2 .... **201** H7
Wyneham Rd, SE24 .... **152** A5
Wynell Rd, SE23 .... **171** G3
Wynford Pl, Belv. DA17 .... **139** G6
Wynford Rd, N1 .... **10** C1
Wynford Way, SE9 .... **174** C3
Wynlie Gdns, Pnr. HA5 .... **66** B2
Wynn Br Cl, Wdf.Grn. IG8
off Chigwell Rd **79** J1
Wynndale Rd, E18 .... **79** H1
Wynne Rd, SW9 .... **151** G2
Wynns Av, Sid. DA15 .... **158** A5
Wynnstay Gdns, W8 .... **128** D3
Wynter St, SW11 .... **149** F4
Wynton Gdns, SE25 .... **188** C5
Wynton Pl, W3 .... **106** B6
Wynyard Ter, SE11 .... **34** D3
Wynyatt St, EC1 .... **11** G4
Wyre Gro, Edg. HA8 .... **54** B3
Hayes UB3 .... **122** A4
Wyresdale Cres, Grnf.
(Perivale) UB6 .... **104** C3
Wythburn Pl, W1 .... **15** J4
Wythenshawe Rd, Dag.
RM10 .... **101** G3
Wythens Wk, SE9 .... **156** E6
Wythes Cl, Brom. BR1 .... **192** C2
Wythes Rd, E16 .... **136** B1
Wythfield Rd, SE9 .... **156** C6
Wyvenhoe Rd, Har. HA2 .... **85** J3
Wyvern Est, N.Mal. KT3 .... **183** G4
Wyvern Gro, Hayes UB3 .... **121** E7
Wyvil Est, SW8 .... **34** A7
Wyvil Rd, SW8 .... **34** A6
Wyvis St, E14 .... **114** B5

X

Xstrata Treetop Walkway,
Richmond TW9 .... **145** H1

Y

Yabsley St, E14 .... **134** C1
Yalding Rd, SE16 .... **29** H6
Yale Cl, Houns. TW4 .... **143** F5
Yarborough Rd, SW19 .... **185** G1
Yardley Cl, E4 .... **46** B5
Yardley Ct, Sutt. SM3
off Hemingford Rd **197** J4
Yardley La, E4 .... **46** B5
Yardley St, WC1 .... **10** E4
Yarmouth Cres, N17 .... **76** E5
Yarmouth Pl, W1 .... **24** D2
Yarnfield Sq, SE15
off Clayton Rd **152** D1
Yarnton Way, SE2 .... **138** D2
Erith DA18 .... **139** F3
Yarrow Cres, E6 .... **116** B5
Yateley St, SE18 .... **136** A3
Yates Ct, NW2 .... **90** A6
Yates Ho, E2
off Roberta St **13** J3
YEADING, Hayes UB4 .... **102** B3
Yeading Av, Har. HA2 .... **84** E2
Yeading Fork, Hayes UB4 .... **102** C5
Yeading Gdns, Hayes
UB4 .... **102** B5
Yeading La, Hayes UB4 .... **102** B6
Northolt UB5 .... **102** C3
Yeames Cl, W13 .... **104** D6
Yeate St, N1 .... **94** A7
Yeatman Rd, N6 .... **73** J6
Yeats Cl, NW10 .... **88** E6
W7 .... **104** C7
Yeats Ct, N15
off Tynemouth Rd **76** C4
Yeend Cl, W.Mol. KT8 .... **179** G4
Yeldham Rd, W6 .... **128** A5
Yellow Hammer Ct, NW9
off Eagle Dr **71** E2
Yelverton Rd, SW11 .... **149** G2
Yenston Cl, Mord. SM4 .... **184** D6
Yeoman Cl, E6
off Ferndale St **116** E7
SE27 .... **169** H3
Yeoman Rd, Nthlt. UB5 .... **85** E7
Yeomans Acre, Ruis. HA4 .... **66** A6
Yeoman's Ms, Islw. TW7 .... **144** B5
Yeoman's Row, SW3 .... **23** H6
Yeoman St, SE8 .... **133** H4
Yeomans Way, Enf. EN3 .... **45** F2
Yeomans Yd, E1 .... **21** G5
Yeomen Way, Ilf. IG6 .... **65** F6
Yeo St, E3 .... **114** B5
Yeovil Cl, Orp. BR6 .... **207** H2
Yeovilton Pl, Kings.T.
KT2 .... **163** F5
Yerbury Rd, N19 .... **92** D3
Yester Dr, Chis. BR7 .... **174** B7
Yester Pk, Chis. BR7 .... **174** C7
Yester Rd, Chis. BR7 .... **174** C7
Yew Cl, Buck.H. IG9 .... **64** A2
Yewdale Cl, Bromley
BR1 .... **173** E6
Yewfield Rd, NW10 .... **89** F7
Yew Gro, NW2 .... **90** A4
Yew Tree Cl, N21 .... **43** G7
Yewtree Cl, N22 .... **74** C1
Yew Tree Cl, SE13
off Bankside Av **154** C3
Yewtree Cl, Har. HA2 .... **67** H4
Yew Tree Cl, Well. DA16 .... **158** A1
Worcester Park KT4 .... **197** E1
Yew Tree Gdns, Rom.
(Chad.Hth) RM6 .... **83** E5
Yew Tree Lo, SW16 .... **168** C4
Yew Tree Rd, W12 .... **107** F7
Beckenham BR3 .... **189** J3
Yew Tree Wk, Houns.
TW4 .... **143** F5
Yew Wk, Har. HA1 .... **86** B1
YIEWSLEY, West Dr.
UB7 .... **120** B1
Yoakley Rd, N16 .... **94** B2
Yoga Way, Wor.Pk. KT4 .... **197** G2
Yoke Cl, N7 *off Ewe Cl* **93** E6
Yolande Gdns, SE9 .... **156** B5
Yonge Pk, N4 .... **93** G3
York Av, SW14 .... **146** C5
W7 .... **124** B1
Sidcup DA15 .... **175** H2
Stanmore HA7 .... **68** E1
York Br, NW1 .... **8** B5
York Bldgs, WC2 .... **18** B6
York Cl, E6
off Boultwood Rd **116** C6
W7 *off York Av* **124** B1
Morden SM4 .... **184** E4
York Cres, Borwd. WD6 .... **38** D2
Loughton IG10 .... **48** B3
York Gate, N14 .... **42** E7
NW1 .... **8** B6
York Gro, SE15 .... **153** F1
York Hill, SE27 .... **169** H3
Loughton IG10 .... **48** B3
York Hill Est, SE27 .... **169** H3
York Ho, Wem. HA9 .... **87** J4
York Ho Pl, W8 .... **22** A3
Yorkland Av, Welling
DA16 .... **157** J3
York Ms, NW5
off Kentish Town Rd **92** B5
Ilford IG1 .... **98** D3
York Par, Brentford
TW8 .... **125** G5
York Pl, SW11 .... **149** G3
WC2 .... **18** B6
Dagenham RM10 .... **101** J6
Ilford IG1
off York Rd **98** D2
York Ri, NW5 .... **92** B3
Orpington BR6 .... **207** H1
York Rd, E4 .... **62** A5
E7 .... **97** G6
E10 .... **96** C3
E17 .... **77** G5
N11 .... **58** D6
N18 .... **60** E6
N21 .... **44** A7
SE1 .... **26** D3
SW11 .... **149** F4
SW18 .... **149** F4
SW19 .... **167** F6
W3 .... **106** C6
W5 .... **125** F3
Barnet (New Barn.)
EN5 .... **41** G5
Brentford TW8 .... **125** G5
Croydon CR0 .... **187** G7
Hounslow TW3 .... **143** H3
Ilford IG1 .... **98** D3
Kingston upon Thames
KT2 .... **163** J7
Northwood HA6 .... **66** A2
Richmond TW10
off Albert Rd **145** J5
Sutton SM2 .... **198** D6
Teddington TW11 .... **162** B4
Yorkshire Cl, N16 .... **94** B3
Yorkshire Gdns, N18 .... **60** E5
Yorkshire Grey, SE9 .... **156** A5
Yorkshire Grey Pl, NW3
off Heath St **91** F4
Yorkshire Grey Yd, WC1 .... **18** C2
Yorkshire Rd, E14 .... **113** H6
Mitcham CR4 .... **186** E5
York Sq, E14 .... **113** H6
York St, W1 .... **16** A1
Mitcham CR4 .... **186** A7
Twickenham TW1 .... **162** D1
York Ter, Erith DA8 .... **159** J1
York Ter E, NW1 .... **8** C6
York Ter W, NW1 .... **8** B6
Yorkton St, E2 .... **13** H2
York Way, N1 .... **111** E1
York Way, N7 .... **92** D6
N20 .... **57** J3
Borehamwood WD6 .... **38** D2
Chessington KT9 .... **195** H7
Feltham TW13 .... **161** F3
York Way Ct, N1 .... **111** E1
York Way Est, N7
off York Way **92** E6
Youngmans Cl, Enf. EN2 .... **43** J1
Young Rd, E16 .... **115** J6
Young's Bldgs, EC1 .... **12** A5
Youngs Ct, SW11
off Charlotte Despard Av **150** A1
Youngs Rd, Ilf. IG2 .... **81** G5
Young St, W8 .... **22** A4
Yoxley App, Ilf. IG2 .... **81** F6
Yoxley Dr, Ilf. IG2 .... **81** F6
Yukon Rd, SW12 .... **150** B7
Yunus Khan Cl, E17 .... **78** A5

Z

Zambezie Dr, N9 .... **61** F3
Zampa Rd, SE16 .... **133** F5
Zander Ct, E2 .... **13** J2
Zangwill Rd, SE3 .... **156** A1
Zealand Av, West Dr.
(Harm.) UB7 .... **120** A7
Zealand Rd, E3 .... **113** H2
Zennor Rd, SW12 .... **168** C1
Zennor Rd Ind Est, SW12
off Zennor Rd **168** C1
Zenoria St, SE22 .... **152** C4
Zermatt Rd, Th.Hth. CR7 .... **187** J4
Zetland St, E14 .... **114** B5
Zion Ho, E1
off Jubilee St **113** F6
Zion Pl, Th.Hth. CR7 .... **188** A4
Zion Rd, Th.Hth. CR7 .... **188** A4
ZK Park, Croy. CR0 .... **201** F3
Zoar St, SE1 .... **27** J1
Zodiac Ct, Croy. CR0
off London Rd **201** H1
Zoffany St, N19 .... **92** D2